AF539205

BANSAL'S NEW ILLUSTRATED MEDICAL DICTIONARY

English–English

BANSAL'S

NEW ILLUSTRATED MEDICAL DICTIONARY

English–English

Edited by

Dr. Shrinandan Bansal

(An author of Various Medical Books)

AITBS Publishers, India

MEDICAL PUBLISHERS

J-5/6, Krishan Nagar, Delhi-110051 (INDIA)

Phone: 011-40167052, 49067602

E-mail: aitbsindia@gmail.com & aitbsindia@hotmail.com

Website: www.aitbspublishersindia.com

First Edition : 2005
Second Edition : 2010
Third Edition : 2026

ISBN: 978-81-7473-288-0

Published by:
Virender Kumar Arya for
AITBS Publishers, India
Medical Publishers
J-5/6, Krishan Nagar, Delhi - 110051 (INDIA)
Phone: 011-40167052, 49067602
E-mail: aitbsindia@gmail.com & aitbsindia@hotmail.com

Printed by AITBS, Delhi

Preface

Though various medical dictionaries in English to English are available in the market but such a medical dictionary as I am presenting to you with the name of "Bansal's New Illustrated Medical Dictionary (Eng-Eng)" is hardly traceable. In this medical dictionary the meaning of each and every medical term is written in English in short, to the point, in simple and easily understandable language which the readers, especially the medical students can see and grasp at a glance.

Wherever possible, the synonymous words of the medical terms have also been given. The book contains 946 pages in which 37839 words and 630 figures are incorporated. Subheads in appropriate number of many of the medical terms have also been given, In the end of the book 7 pages of Weights and Measurements, Symbols and their meanings, and Abbreviations and their meanings have also been added.

I hope that this medical dictionary will be very useful for the students of Medical, Ayurvedic, Homoeopathic and Dental Colleges, Nurses and Compounders, Pharmacists and Medical practitioners etc., and will be appreciated by them.

I am very much indebted to Mr. Virender kumar Arya who encouraged me by publishing this dictionary.

Suggestions from the readers will be considered carefully

Editor
Dr. Shrinandan Bansal

CONTENTS

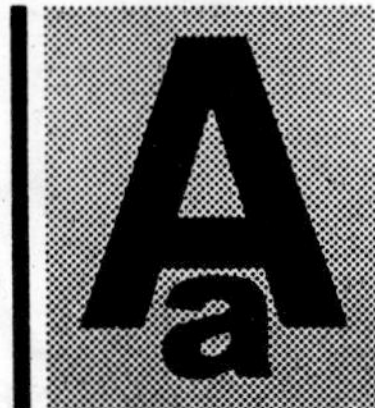

Ab—From, away from
Abacterial—Without bacteria
Abaissement—Depression, falling
Abalienation—Mental derangement
Abandon—To give up to another's control, to forsake
Abandonment —Renunciation of a claim
Abapical —Opposite the apex.
Abaptiston—Instrument for perforation of the skull.
Abarognosis—Loss of sense of weight.
Abarthrosis—Abarticulation, freely movable joint.
Abarticular—At a distance from a joint.
Abarticulation—Dislocation of a joint.
Abasia—Inability to walk.

1. **Abasia astasia** — Inability to stand or walk due to lack of motor coordination.
2. **Abasia atactica** — Uncertain movements in walking.
3. **Abasia choreic** — Abasia due to Chorea of the legs.
4. **Abasia paralytic** — Abasia due to paralysis of the leg muscles.
5. **Abasia spastic** — Abasia due to stiffening or rigidity of the legs.
6. **Abasia trembling** — Abasia due to trembling of the legs.

Abasic —The person unable to walk.
Abate —To lessen or to decrease.
Abatement —Decrease in severity of a pain or symptom.
Abater —The person who decreases, relieving agent.
Abatic — Abasic.
Abattoir —Slaughter house.
Abaxial, Abaxile —Not situated in line of axis of the body or part.
Abdomen —The whole part of the trunk below the thorax containing stomach, intestines, liver, spleen, kidneys and urinary bladder etc. There are nine regions of the abdomen.

1. Right hypochondriac region
2. Epigastric region
3. Left hypochondriac region
4. Right lumbar region
5. Umbilical region

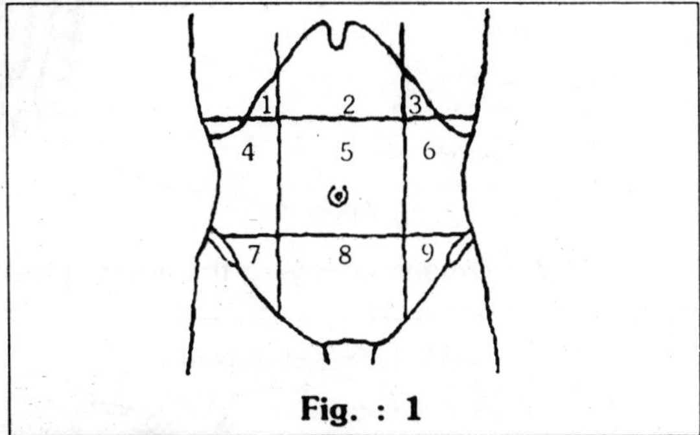

Fig. : 1

6. Left lumbar region
7. Right iliac region
8. Hypogastric region
9. Left iliac region

Abdomen proper—The part of the trunk below the thorax and above the pelvis is known as abdomen proper. The part below it is known as pelvis which contains urinary bladder etc.

Acute abdomen —Any intra-abdominal condition that gives rise to severe pain for which an immediate operation may be required.

Carinate abdomen — A sloping of the sides with prominence of the central line of the abdomen.

Pendulous abdomen — The abdomen hanging down over the pubis, due to excessively relaxed anterior abdominal wall.

Scaphoid, boat-shaped or navicular abdomen —Sunken or boat-shaped abdomen as occurs in emaciation.

Tumid abdomen — Swollen abdomen.

Abdominal —Pertaining to abdomen.
Abdominal cavity —The cavity within the abdomen.
Abdominal crisis —Severe pain in the abdomen.
Abdominal gestation — Extrauterine pregnancy in the abdominal cavity.
Abdominalgia —Pain in the abdomen.
Abdominal paracentesis —To puncture the peritoneal cavity to drain out fluid of ascites.
Abdominal reflexes — Contraction of the muscles of the abdominal wall upon stimulation of the overlying skin.

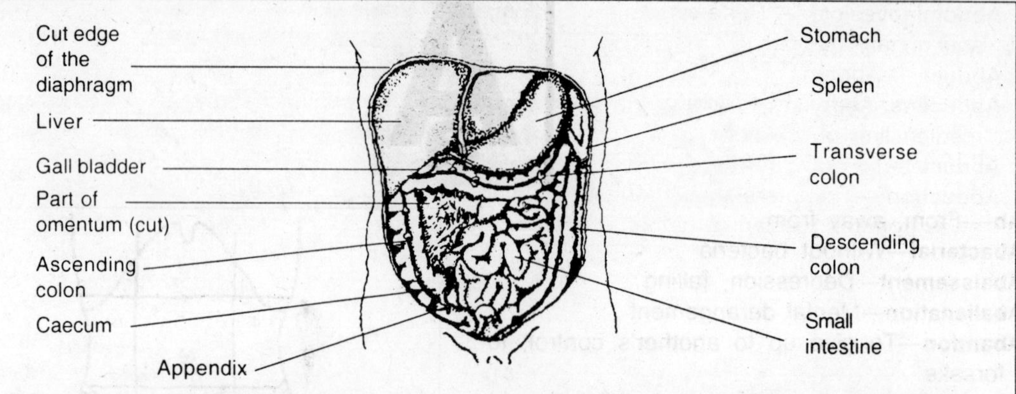

Fig. 2 A : Organs ocupying the anterior part of the abdominal cavity, and cut diaphragm.

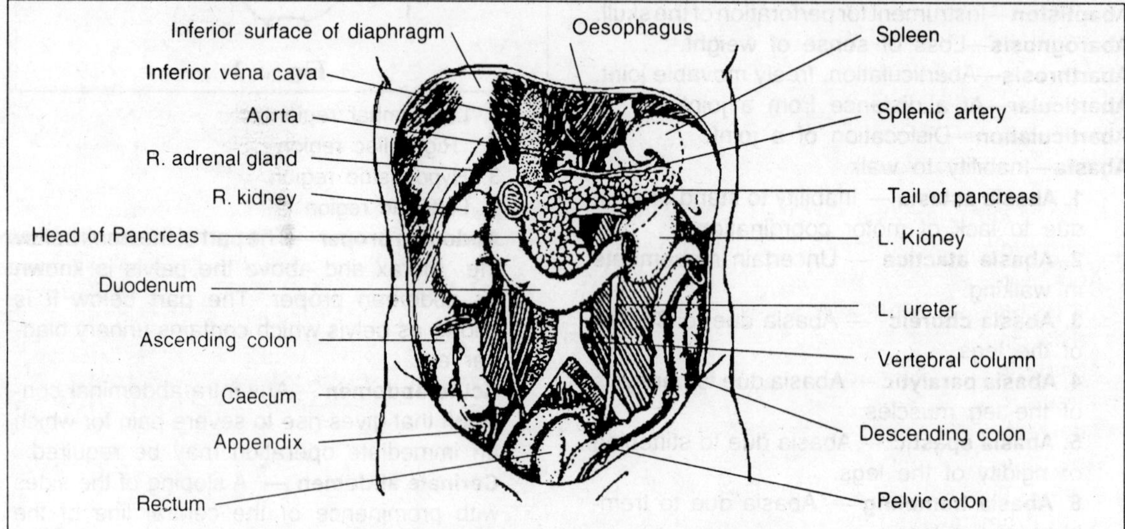

Fig. 2 B : Organs occupying the posterior part of the abdominal cavity, and inferior surface of the diaphragm. Intersected line shows the postition of the stomach.

Abdominal section — Laparotomy, abdominal incision for any operation on abdominal organs.

Abdominocardiac reflex —Changes in the heart rate usually a slowing, resulting from mechanical stimulation of abdominal viscera.

Abdominocentesis —Puncture of the abdomen with an instrument to withdraw fluid from the abdominal cavity.

Abdominocyesis —Abdominal pregnancy.

Abdominocystic —Pertaining to the abdomen and the gallbladder.

Abdominogenital —Pertaining to the abdomen and the genital organs.

Abdominohysterectomy — Removal of the uterus through abdominal incision.

Abdominohysterotomy — Incision of the uterus through an abdominal incision.

Abdominopelvic —Pertaining to the abdomen and the pelvis.

Abdominoperineal— Pertaining to the abdomen and the perineum.

Abdominoplasty —Plastic surgery performed on the abdominal wall for cosmetic purposes.

Abdominoscopy— Examination of the abdominal cavity by endoscope.

Abdominoscrotal —Pertaining to the abdomen and scrotum.

Abdominothoracic — Pertaining to the abdomen and thorax.

Abdominous —Having a large belly.

Abdominovaginal — Pertaining to the abdomen and vagina.

Abdominovesical — Pertaining to the abdomen and urinary bladder.
Abduce —Abduct.
Abducens, Abducent — Drawing away from the median line of the body.
Abduct —To draw from the median plane.
Abduction —The lateral movements of the limbs away from the median plane of the body or the

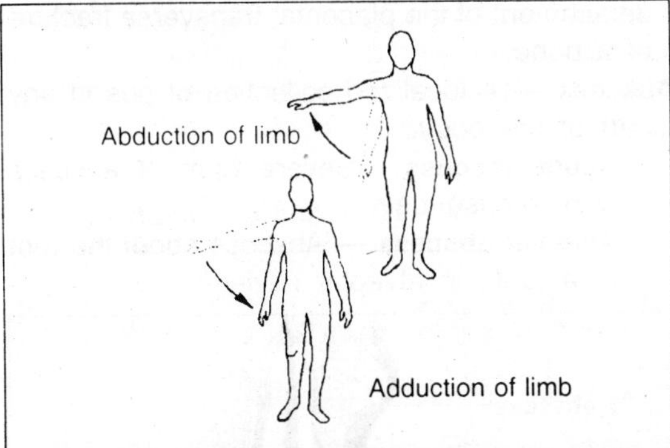

Fig. 3 : Abduction and adduction of a limb.

lateral bending of the head or trunk. Movement of the digits away from the axial line of a limb.
Abductor —A muscle which on contraction draws a part away from median plane of the body or axial line of an extremity.
Abenteric —Organs situated outside the intestines.
Aberrant —Abnormal.
Aberratio, Aberration — Deviation from the normal. Imperfect refraction of light rays.

Chromatic aberration—Unequal refraction of light rays of different wavelength through a lens producing a blurred and coloured image.

Chromosomal aberration — Abnormalities in chromosomes as regard to the number or chromosomal material.

Distantial aberration — Blurring of vision for a distant object.

Mental aberration —Any deviation from normal mental functions.

Spherical aberration — Inability of a spherical lens to bring all rays of light to a single focus.

Aberrometer — An instrument for measuring optic aberrations.
Abevacuation —Abnormal evacuation, either excessive or deficient.
Abeyance —Temporary suspension of activity, sensation or pain.
Abiogenesis —The production of livings from non-living matters.
Abiology —Study of non-living things.
Abiosis —Absence of life, death.
Abiotic —Incompatible with life.
Abiotrophy, Abiotrophia — Premature loss of vitality of certain tissues or organs leading to loss of function.
Abirritant —Relieving irritation, soothing.
Abirritate —To relieve irritation, to sooth.
Abirritation —Diminution or abolition of irritability.
Ablactation —Cessation of milk secretion; weaning of a child.
Ablate —To remove by cutting.
Ablation, Ablatio —Removal by cutting.
Ablepharia —Congenital absence or reduction in size of the eyelids.
Ablepharous —Without eyelids.
Ablepsia —Blindness.
Abluent —Cleansing agent.
Ablution —A cleansing or washing.
Ablutomania —Mania for cleansing or washing.
Abnerval —Away from a nerve.
Abneural —Situated at a distance from the central nervous system.
Abnormal —Not normal.
Abnormality —The state of being abnormal.
Abocclusion —Dentition in which the teeth of the mandible and the maxilla are not in contact.
Abolition —Complete suspension.
Aborad —Away from the mouth.
Aboral —Opposite to, or away from the mouth.
Abort —To expel fetus before it is viable; to arrest the development of a disease.
Aborticide —Abortifacient.
Abortient —Abortifacient.
Abortifacient —Anything that induces abortion.
Abortigenic —Abortifacient.
Abortion —Termination of pregnancy before six months.

1. Accidental abortion —Abortion caused by an accident.

2. Artificial abortion, Abactio —Abortion induced purposely, as by a surgeon.

3. Complete abortion — Abortion in which complete products of conception have been expelled.

4. Criminal abortion — Illegal abortion.

5. Habitual abortion — Termination of 3 or more successive pregnancies before 20 weeks of gestation. Recurrent abortion.

6. Incomplete abortion —Abortion in which part of the product of conception has been retained in the uterus.

7. **Inevitable abortion** —An abortion that cannot be prevented.

8. **Menstrual extraction abortion** — To expel out the products of conception from the uterus, a few days after the first missed menstrual period.

9. **Missed abortion** — Retention of a dead fetus in the uterus for at least 4 months after its death.

10. **Septic abortion** — Abortion due to infection of the fetus and the internal uterine wall.

11. **Spontaneous abortion** —Abortion that occurs spontaneously without apparent cause.

12. **Therapeutic abortion**—Abortion performed to save the life of the mother when her mental or physical health is endangered by continuation of pregnancy, or to prevent birth of a deformed child or a child resulting from rape or illegal sexual contact.

13. **Threatened abortion** — A condition in which there is slight vaginal bleeding with or without intermittent pain, that may or may not be followed by expulsion of the fetus, during the first 20 weeks of pregnancy. If the fetus is alive and not detached from the uterine wall, pregnancy may continue.

14. **Tubal abortion** — Rupture of that fallopian tube in which ectopic pregnancy was established, and expulsion of the embryo through the fimbriated end of the fallopian tube.

Abortionist —One who performs an abortion.

Abortive — 1. Abortifacient, that which prevents the normal continuation of pregnancy. 2. Not-reaching the completion, e.g. a disease subsiding before it has fully developed.

Abortiveness — Untimely birth.

Abortus — An aborted fetus.

Aboulia — Abulia.

Aboulomania — Abulomania.

Abrachia —Congenital absence of the arms.

Abrachiocephalia, Abrachiocephaly—Congenital absence of the arms and head.

Abrachius —An armless fetus.

Abrade —To scrape off.

Abrasion —A scraping away of a portion of skin or of a mucous membrane. In dentistry, grinding or wearing away of tooth substance (enamel) by incorrect tooth-brushing or foreign objects.

Abrasive —An agent which produces abrasion. In dentistry, a substance used for abrading, grinding or polishing.

Abrasiveness —1. The property of a substance to cause wear away of a surface by friction. 2. The quality of being able to scratch or wear away another material.

Abreact —To become strongly emotional on recalling of past painful experiences.

Abreast — Side by side.

Abrosia — Fasting, a wasting away.

Abruptio, Abruption — Separation as premature detachment of the placenta; transverse fracture of a bone.

Abscess — A localized collection of pus in any part of the body.

Acute abscess —Severe form of abscess with intense pain.

Alveolar abscess — Abscess about the root of a tooth in alveolar cavity.

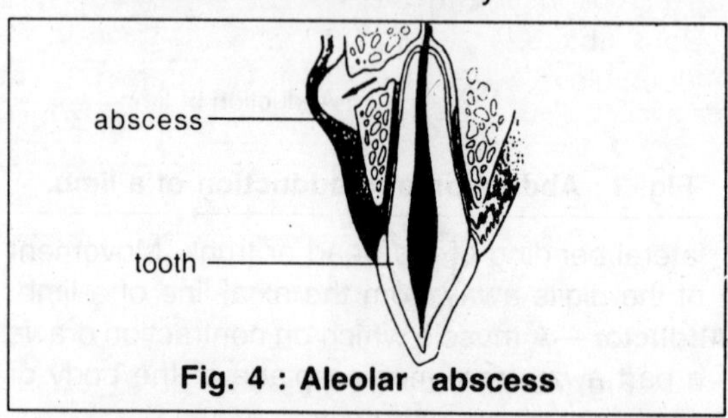

Fig. 4 : Aleolar abscess

Amebic abscess —An abscess of the liver as a complication of amebic dysentery containing amebae.

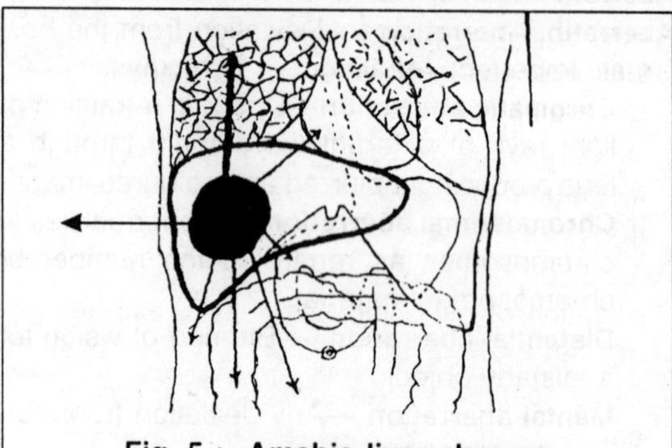

Fig. 5 : Amebic liver abscess
Arrows showing directions in which the abscess may burst.

Anorectal abscess — Abscess surrounding the anus and rectum.

Appendicular abscess —An abscess of the vermiform appendix.

Axillary abscess — Abscess in the axilla.

Bone abscess —Pus formation within the medullary cavity (osteomyelitis), cortex or periosteum of the bone.

Brain abscess — Intracranial abscess.
Breast abscess — Mammary abscess.

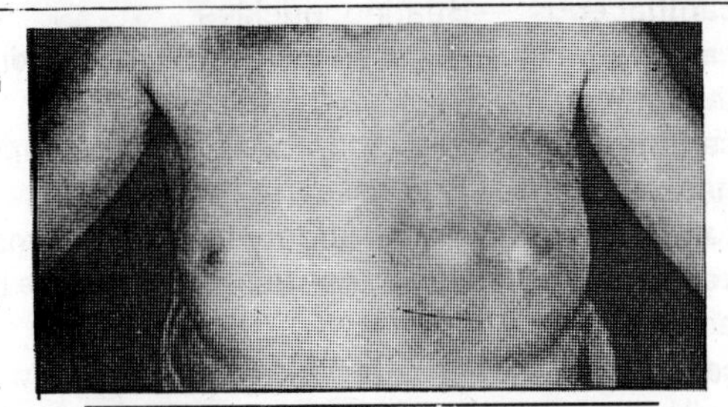

Fig. 6 : Breast abscess

Chronic abscess —An abscess of slow development with pus formation but without signs of inflammation.

Cold abscess —Chronic abscess usually tuberculous which feels cold to touch.

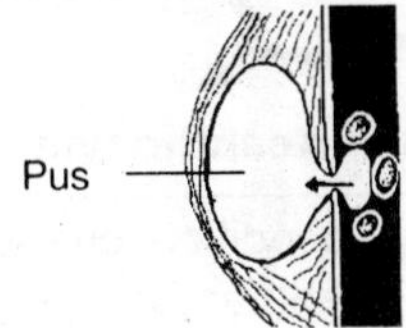

Fig. 7 : Cervical cold abscess.

Dental abscess — Abscess beside a tooth, usually near the root.

Dry abscess —The remains of an abscess after the pus is absorbed.

Gas abscess —An abscess containing gas.

Glandular abscess — Abscess around a lymph gland.

Metastatic abscess — Secondary abscess that is formed at a distance from the primary focus of infection, as a result of the transportation of pyogenic bacteria by the lymph or blood stream

Otitic abscess — An abscess of the middle ear.

Pelvic abscess — Abscess of the pelvic peritoneum.

Perforating abscess —An abscess that is perforated.

Periapical abscess — An alveolar abscess localized around the apex of a tooth. Apical abscess.

Periarticular abscess—An abscess surrounding a joint.

Periodontal abscess —An alveolar abscess.

Perivesical abscess — Abscess around the urinary bladder.

Pott's abscess — Tuberculous abscess of the vertebral column.

Prostatic abscess — Abscess within the prostate gland.

Psoas abscess — Tuberculous abscess originating in tuberculous spondylitis and extending through the iliopsoas muscle to the inguinal region.

Pulmonary abscess — Abscess in the lung.

Pulp abscess —An abscess involving the soft tissue within the pulp chamber of a tooth, usually resulting from dental caries or less frequently from trauma.

Pyemic abscess— An abscess resulting from pyemia, septicemia or bacteremia.

Radicular abscess — An abscess around a tooth root. Alveolar abscess.

Renal abscess — Abscess of the renal cortex.

Residual abscess — An abscess recurring at the site of a former abscess resulting from persistance of micro-organisms and pus.

Stercoral abscess — An abscess formed as a result of collection of pus and feces. Fecal abscess.

Sterile abscess — An abscess which is not caused by pyogenic bacteria.

Stich abscess —Syn. Suture abscess.

Subungual abscess —Abscess formed beneath a fingernail or toenail.

Suture abscess — Abscess formed at the site of stiching.

Tonsillar abscess — Abscess of the tonsil.

Traumatic abscess— Abscess caused by injury.

Abscission —Removal by excision.

Absconsio —A cavity or fossa.

Absence seizure —Seizure in which there is a sudden lapse of consciousness for several seconds.

Absent-minded —Who does not pay attention to.

Absent-mindedness —The condition of being inattentive.

Absolute alcohol —Ethyl alcohol with not more than 1% of water.

Absorb —To suck in.

Absorbefacient —Which causes absorption.

Absorbency —The ability of being absorbed.

Absorbent —The substance which absorbs.

Absorptiometer —An instrument for measuring the absorption of gas by a liquid.

Absorption —1. The passage of a substance through some surface of the body into the tissues and body fluids. 2. In radiology, the uptake of energy from radiation by the tissue or medium through which it passes.

Cutaneous absorption —Syn. Percutaneous absorption.

Parenteral absorption — Absorption by any route other than the alimentary canal.

Pathologic absorption —Parenteral absorption of any excremental or pathologic material into the blood stream, e.g., pus, urine or bile etc.

Percutaneous absorption —The absorption of drugs and other substances through unbroken skin.

Absorptive —Absorbent.

Absorptivity —Ability to absorb.

Abstain —To keep oneself away; to refrain from.

Abstainer — One who does not drink.

Abstemious —Sparing in diet.

Abstergent —Cleansing agent.

Abstersion —The cleansing.

Abstinence —Refraining from indulgence in food, alochol, stimulants, or sexual intercourse.

Abstinence syndrome — Withdrawal syndrome, a group of symptoms arising from withdrawal of alcohol, etc.

Abstract —A preparation containing the soluble principles of a drug concentrated or dried to powder by evaporating the preparation and mixed with lactose. (Sugar of milk).

Abstraction — 1. Separation of a constituent from a mixture or compound. 2. The making of an abstract from the crude drug.

Abterminal —Away from the end and toward the centre.

Abulia, Aboulia —Loss or deficiency of will power.

Abulomania — Mental disorder with loss of will power.

Abuse —Misuse as that of a drug or alcohol etc.

Abutment — In dentistry, substitute of a natural or implanted tooth, used for the support of a fixed or movable prosthesis.

A.C. — Before meals.

Acalcicosis —A condition due to deficiency of calcium in the diet.

Acalculia —Inability to solve mathematical problems.

Acampsia —Rigidity of a part or limb.

Acantha — Spinous process as that of a vertebra.

Acanthaceous —Bearing prickles.

Acanthesthesia —A sensation as of a pin pricking the body.

Acanthion — A point at the base of the anterior nasal spine.

Acanthocephala — The thorny-headed worms.

Acanthocephaliasis —The disease caused by acanthocephala.

Acanthocyte —Thorny red blood cell. Red blood cell with protoplasmic projections giving it thorny appearance.

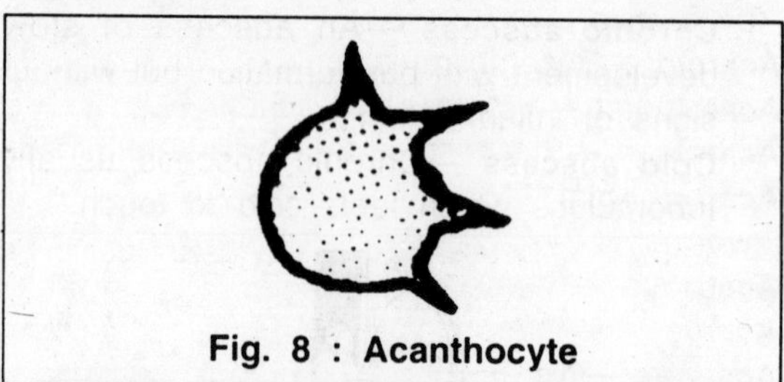

Fig. 8 : Acanthocyte

Acanthocytosis —A condition characterised by the presence of acanthocytes in the blood.

Acanthoid —Spine-shaped

Acanthokeratodermia — Hypertrophy of the horny portion of the skin of the palms of hands and soles of feet, and thickening of the nails.

Acantholysis —Degeneration of the intercellular substance of the cells of the outer or horny layer of the skin.

Acanthoma —Benign tumor of the skin.

Acanthopodia —Toothlike pseudopodia observed in some amebae.

Acanthosis —Increased thickness of the prickle cell layer of the skin.

Acanthotic —The skin with increased thickness of the prickle cell layer.

Acanthulus — An instrument for removing the thorns from wounds.

Acapnia — The presence of carbon dioxide in the blood and tissues below normal.

Acarbia —Diminution of bicarbonate in the blood.

Acardia —Congenital absence of the heart.

Acardiac — Having no heart since birth.

Acardiohemia —Lack of blood in the heart.

Acardiotrophia —Atrophy of the heart.

Acardius —A twin without a heart that remains viable by using placental blood circulation of its mate.

Acariasis —Any disease caused by a mite.

Acaricide —An agent that destroys the mites.

Acarid, Acaridan —Tick or mite.

Fig. 9 : Acarid (Mite)

Acaridiasis, Acarinosis — Disease caused by a mite.

Acarodermatitis — Inflammation of the skin caused by a mite.

Acaroid —Resembling a mite.

Acarologist —Specialist in acarology.

Acarology —Scientific study of mites and ticks.

Acarophobia —Morbid fear of mites, ticks or worms.

Acarpous —Sterile.

Acarus —A mite or tick.

Acaryote —Non-nucleated, without nucleus.

Acatalepsia —Uncertainty or doubt. Mental deficiency.

Acataleptic—Uncertain or doubtful. Mentally deficient.

Acatamathesia —Inability to understand the spoken words.

Acataphasia —Inability to express the thoughts in connected manner due to cerebral lesion.

Acatastasia —Irregularity, deviation from the normal.

Acatharsia —Failure to obtain desired purgation.

Acathetic —Unable to retain.

Acathexia —Inability to retain the secretions of the body.

Acathexis —A mental disorder in which there is lack of emotional response toward a thing or idea which is normally very important to the individual.

Acathisia —Feeling of discomfort on sitting.

Acaudal, Acaudate —Having no tail.

Acceleration —An increase in the speed.

Accelerator —Any thing which increases the speed of a function.

Accelerometer — An instrument for measuring the rate of change of velocity per unit of time.

Accentuation —Emphasis.

Accentuator — A substance, such as aniline which allows combination between a tissue or histologic element and a stain that might otherwise not be possible.

Acceptor —A substance which unites with another substance.

Access — A way or means of approach or admittance. In dentistry—1. The space required for visualization and for manipulation of instruments to remove decay and prepare a tooth for restoration. 2. The opening in the crown of a tooth required to allow adequate admittance to the pulp space to clean, shape and seal the root canal.

Accessory —Supplementary or assisting.

Accessory sign —A sign which is not indicative of a disease.

Accident —An unexpected event, mishap.

Accidental —Pertaining to or due to an accident.

Accident-prone —The person specially susceptible to the accidents due to psychological factors.

Accipiter —A facial bandage with the tails resembling the claws of a hawk.

Acclimation, Acclimatization —The process of becoming accustomed to a new environment.

Accommodation —Adjustment or adaptation. Adjustment of the eye for seeing objects at various distances. It may be of the following types.

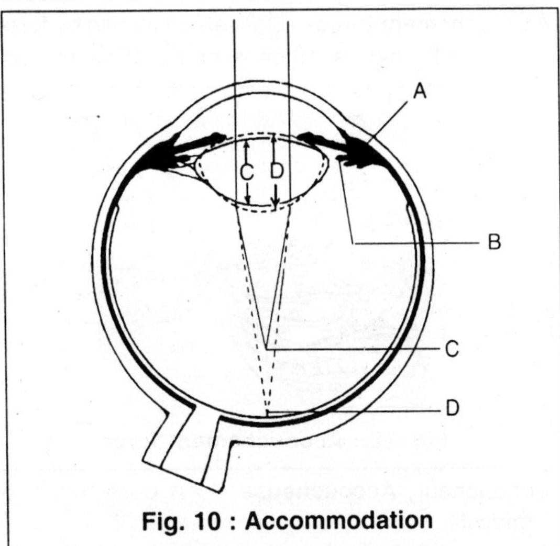

Fig. 10 : Accommodation

A- Ciliary muscle B-Suspensory ligaments C-Lens focuses image in front of the retina; image is blurred. D- Lens accommodates to focus on retina; image is sharp.

Absolute accommodation — Accommodation of either eye separately.

Binocular accommodation —Accommodation of both the eyes jointly.

Negative accommodation — Adjustment of eye for seeing the objects of long distances by relaxation of the ciliary muscles.

Positive accommodation — Adjustment of eye for seeing the objects of short distances by contraction of the ciliary muscles.

Accommodometer —As instrument for measuring the accommodative power of the eye.

Accouchee — The woman who delivered a child.

Accouchement —Delivery of a child.

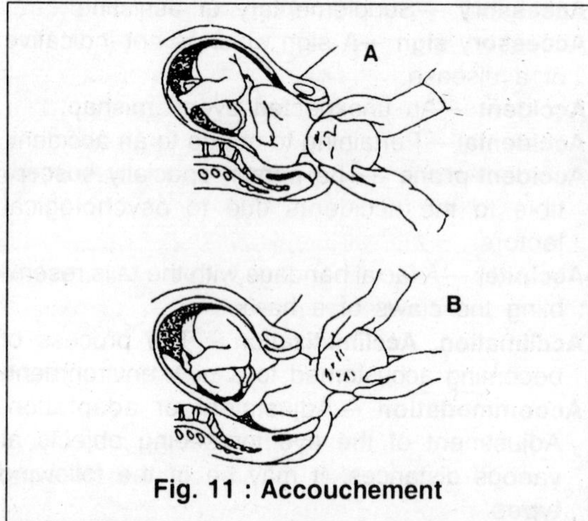

Fig. 11 : Accouchement

Accouchement force —Delivery of a child by force applied by hands, forceps or by other means.

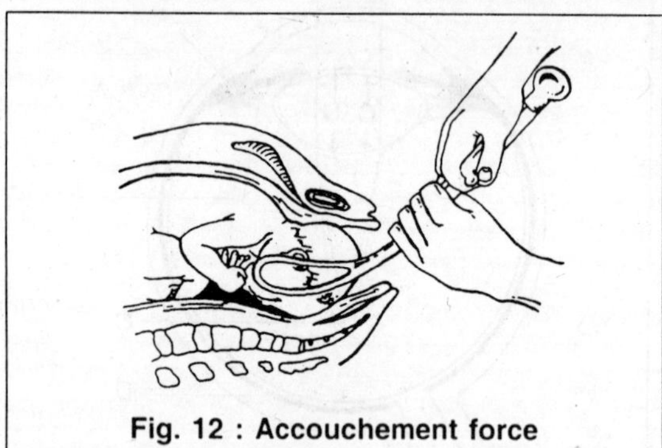
Fig. 12 : Accouchement force

Accoucheur, Accoucheuse —An obstetrician or midwife.

Accrementition —Growth of tissues by the addition of similar tissue.

Accretio cordis —Adhesion of the pericardium to adjacent extracardiac structures.

Accretion —1. Growth by addition of material. 2. Accumulation. 3. Coherence of the parts naturally separated. 4. In dentistry, foreign material such as plaque or calculus collecting on the surface of a tooth or in a cavity.

Accumulation —Collection.

Accustomed —Customary, familiar.

ACD —Absolute cardiac dullness.

Acecia —Recovery, cure.

Acedia —Apathy, insensibility, lack of emotion.

Acelious —Without a belly.

Acellular —A structure made up of without cells.

Acenesthesia —Loss of feeling of well-being.

Acentric —Not situated in the center, peripheral.

Acephalia, Acephalism — Congenital absence of the head.

Acephalo- —Combining form meaning without a head.

Acephalobrachia —Congenital absence of the head and arms.

Acephalocardia—Congenital absence of the head and heart.

Acephalocardius —A fetus without a head and heart.

Acephalochiria —Congenital absence of the head and the hands.

Acephalogaster —A fetus without a head and stomach.

Acephalogastria—Congenital absence of the head, chest and the upper part of the abdomen.

Acephalopodia —Congenital absence of the head and feet.

Acephalopodius —A fetus without a head and feet.

Acephalorrhachia —Congenital absence of the head and spinal column.

Acephalostomia —Congenital absence of the head, only an aperture representing the mouth is present on the upper part of the body.

Acephalothoracia —Congenital absence of the head and thorax.

Acephalous, Acephalus —A fetus without head.

Acephaly —Acephalia.

Acerate —Sharp, pointed.

Acerb —Acrid, acidic.

Acerbity —Astringency combined with acidity.

Acervuline —Aggregated, occurring in clusters as certain glands.

Acervulus —Brain sand. The laminar particles consisting mainly of phosphates and carbonates of calcium and magnesium found in the pineal gland of the cerebrum.

Acescence —1. Slight acidity. 2. Process of souring.

Acescent —Slightly acid.

Acesodyne —Anodyne. An agent which relieves the pain.

Aceta —Plural of acetum.

Acetabular —Pertaining to the acetabulum.

Acetabulectomy —Excision of the acetabulum.

Acetabuloplasty —Repair of the acetabulum by plastic surgery.

Acetabulum—The cup-shaped cavity on the lateral surface of the hip bone, in which the head of the femur is fitted.

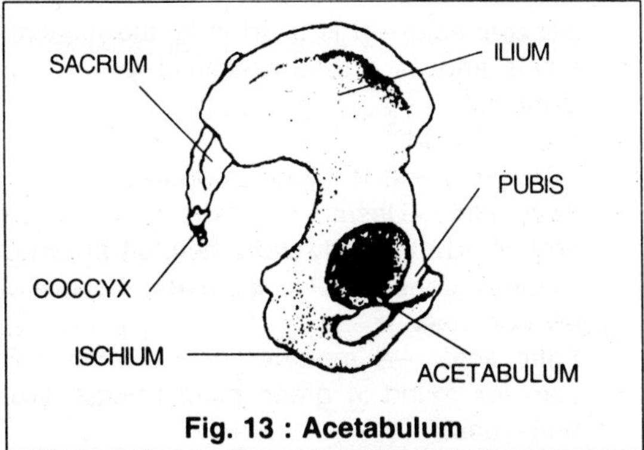

Fig. 13 : Acetabulum

Acetic —Pertaining to vinegar, sour.

Acetimeter —The instrument which determines the amount of acetic acid in fluid.

Acetone—Ketone. A colorless, volatile substance with sweet fruity odor found in the blood and urine in diabetes and after lengthy fasting.

Acetonemia —Presence of large amounts of acetone in the blood.

Acetonemic —Relating to or caused by acetonemia.

Acetonitrile —Methyl cyanide, a substance found in an increased amount in the urine of persons smoking three or more cigarettes a day.

Acetonuria—Ketonuria. Presence of ketone bodies in the urine as in diabetes or starvation.

Acetous —1. Pertaining to, producing or resembling acetic acid. 2. Sour in taste.

Acetum —Vinegar.

Acetyl —The univalent radical, CH_3CO. The combining form of acetic acid.

Acetylation —Introduction of an acetyl radical into an organic molecule.

Acetylator —The organism that is capable of metabolic acetylation.

Acetylbetamethylcholine — A derivative of acetylcholine which is a strong stimulus to the parasympathetic nervous system and lowers the blood pressure.

Acetylcholine —A substance essential for transmitting the nerve impulses at the myoneural junction, produced at the endings of the nerve fibres as a result of stimulation and is quickly destroyed by the enzyme cholinesterase.

Acetylcholinesterase —An enzyme present in muscles, nerve cells and red blood cells which stops the action of acetylcholine.

Acetylene —A colorless, volatile, explosive gas with a garlic-like odor.

Achalasia —Failure to relax, *e.g.,* achalasia cardia in which the food passes with difficulty into the stomach due to failure of relaxation of the cardiac sphincter.

Ache —A dull or severe continuous pain distinguished from a sudden or spasmodic pain.

Acheilia —Congenital absence of one or both lips.

Acheilous, Achilous —Characterized by or relating to acheilia.

Acheiria —1. Congenital absence of one or both hands. 2. Sense of loss of one or both hands. 3. Inability to determine that which side of the body has been stimulated.

Acheiropodia—Congenital absence of both hands and feet.

Acheiropody, Achiropody — Acheiropodia.

Acheirous, Acheirus — A fetus without hands.

Achilloburstitis —Inflammation of the bursa lying over the Achilles tendon.

Achillodynia —Pain in the Achilles tendon or its bursa.

Achillorrhaphy —Suturing of the Achilles tendon.

Achillotenotomy, Achillotomy —Surgical division of the Achilles tendon.

Achiria —Acheiria.

Achlorhydria —Absence of hydrochloric acid in gastric secretion.

Achloride —A salt other than a chloride.

Achlorophyllous—Without chlorophyll, as in fungi.

Achloropsia —Color blindness in which there is inability to distinguish green colors.

Acholia —Absence or lack of bile secretion, or a condition which prevents bile from entering the duodenum.

Acholic —Pertaining to acholia.

Acholuria —Absence of bile pigments in the urine.

Acholuric —Without bile in the urine.

Achondrogenesis —Failure of the growth of the bones of the extremites so that they become shortened while the head and trunk remain normal.

Achondroplasia —Chondrodystrophy. Defect in the cartilage formation at the epiphyses of long bones producing a type of dwarfism.

Achondroplastic —Pertaining to or characterized by achondroplasia.

Achoresis —Permanent contraction of a hollow organ such as the stomach or urinary bladder, whereby its capacity is reduced.

Achroacyte —A colorless cell.

Achroma —Absence of color or pigmentation in the skin as in leukoderma.

Achromacyte —Achromocyte.

Achromasia — 1. Lack of normal skin pigmentation. 2. Inability of tissues or cells to be stained.

Achromat —A color blind person.

Achromatic —1. Colorless 2. Staining with difficulty, especially the tissues and cells.

Achromatin —The weakly staining substance of a cell nucleus.

Achromatinic —Relating to or containing achromatin.

Achromatism —Colorlessness.

Achromatocyte —Achromocyte. A decolorized red blood cell.

Achromatolysis —Dissolution of cell achromatin.

Achromatophil —Achromophil. A cell or tissue not stainable in the usual manner.

Achromatophilia —A condition of being not responsive to staining processes.

Achromophilic, Achromophilous— Achromatophil.

Achromatopsia —Complete color blindness.

Achromatosis, Achroma — Condition of being without natural pigmentation.

Achromatous —Colorless.

Achromaturia —Colorless urine.

Achromia —The lack or absence of normal color or pigmentation, as of the skin.

Achromic —Lacking color.

Achromocyte — Pale crescent-shaped red blood cell.

Achromodermia —Colorlessness of the skin.

Achromophil — Achromatophil.

Achromotrichia —Canities. Colorlessness or greying of the hair. Greyness of the hair may be due to nutritional deficiency.

Achylia, Achylosis — Absence of chyle or other digestive juices, *e.g.* the absence or deficiency of the gastric or the pancreatic juice.

Achylous —1. Deficient in any kind of digestive secretion. 2. The person without chyle.

Achymia, Achymosis — Deficiency or total absence of chyme.

Acicular —Needle-shaped.

Acid —The substance which forms a salt reacting with a metal and turns blue litmus paper to red. Sour.

Acetic acid —Acid of vinegar.

Acetylsalicylic acid —Aspirin.

Amino acid —The end product of protein digestion essential for growth of the body and repair of the tissues.

Ascorbic acid —Vitamin C.

Benzoic acid —It is used in keratolytic ointments and as a food preservative.

Boric acid

Carbolic acid

Citric acid —It is found in lemon.

Fatty acid —Unsaturated fatty acid which is not formed in the body and is therefore provided by diet. It does not allow the blood cholesterol level to rise.

Folic acid —A member of the vitamin B complex found in green plant tissues, liver and yeast.

Hydrochloric acid

Lactic acid —Occurring in sour milk from fermentation of lactose and in the muscles during exercise.

Nicotinic acid —A member of the vitamin B complex.

Nitric acid

Organic acid —An acid containing the carbon atom.

Oxalic acid — It is the strongest organic acid and is poisonous and its solution is effective in removing the ink and rust stains from cloth.

Pantothenic acid —A member of the vitamin B complex.

Para-aminobenzoic acid — A member of the vitamin B complex.

Para-aminosalicylic acid, PAS —A drug used in tuberculosis.

Phosphoric acid

Salicylic acid

Saturated fatty acid

Stearic acid —Used in manufacture of soaps and glycerine suppositories.

Sulphuric acid

Tannic acid

Tartaric acid

Taurocholic acid —A bile acid.

Unsaturated fatty acid

Uric acid

Acidaminuria —Excess of amino acids in the urine.

Acid-base balance —The mechanisms by which the acidity and alkalinity of the body fluids are kept in equilibrium.

Acidemia —Excess of acid in the blood.

Acid-fast—Not decolorized by staining with acids, usually used for examination of bacteria, as that of Mycobacterium tuberculosis, the tuberculosis producing bacillus, which is acid-fast bacillus.

Acidic —Sour.

Acidifiable —Capable of being made an acid.

Acidification—Becoming sour, conversion into an acid.

Acidifier, Acidulant—A substance which increases the acidity of that to which it is added; a substance to increase the gastric acidity.

Acidify —To make sour, to convert into an acid.

Acidimeter —An instrument for determining the amount of free acid in a solution.

Acidimetry —Determination of the acidity of a fluid.

Acidism, Acidismus — Poisoning caused by the acids introduced from outside the body.

Aciditoxicity —Poisoning due to acids.

Acidity —The quality of being acidic, sourness.

Acidocyte —Eosinophil cell of the leukocytes.

Acidocytopenia —Abnormal decrease in number of eosinophil cells in the blood.

Acidocytosis —Abnormal increase in number of eosinophil cells in the blood.

Acidogenic —Causing acidity.

Acidophil, Acidophilic, Acidophilous—1. The cell or the tissue capable of being stained with acid dyes. 2. The acid-staining or the alpha cell of the anterior pituitary gland. 3. The organism growing well in an acid medium.

Acidophilus milk —The milk fermented by the culture of Lactobacillus acidophilus.

Acidosis —Excessive acidity of the blood due to accumulation of acids or excessive loss of alkali as bicarbonate from the body.

Carbon dioxide or respiratory acidosis — Acidosis resulting from retention of CO_2 in the body as in drowning or due to respiratory insufficiency.

Diabetic acidosis —Acidosis occurring in advanced uncontrolled diabetes mellitus due to accumulation of ketone bodies.

Hyperchloremic acidosis —Acidosis due to an abnormally high level of chloride in the blood serum.

Metabolic acidosis — Acidosis due to an increase in acids other than the carbonic acid, which may be due to excessive ingestion of acids, ketosis, impairment of liver function, vomiting, diarrhea, dehydration, starvation and renal disease, etc.

Renal acidosis — Acidosis due to impairment of the renal function or chronic renal disease due to excessive loss of bicarbonate or inability to excrete acids.

Acidotic —Pertaining to acidosis.

Acid-proof —Acid-fast.

Acidulate —To make somewhat acid or sour.

Acidulous —Slightly acid or sour.

Acidum —Acid.

Aciduria —Presence of acid in the urine.

Aciduric —Capable of growing in acid medium as some bacteria.

Acinar —Acinic. Pertaining to the acinus.

Acinesia —Akinesia.

Acinesic, Acinetic — Akinetic.

Acini —Plural of acinus.

Acinic —Acinar.

Aciniform —Shaped like grapes.

Acinitis —Inflammation of the acini of a gland.

Acinose —Formed of acini. Acinous.

Acinous—Pertaining to glands resembling a bunch of grapes. Aciniform.

Acinus —The smallest portion of a gland.

Acladiosis —Formation of ulcer on the skin due to fungus Acladium.

Aclasis, Aclasia—An abnormal tissue which arises from a normal structure and continuous with it, as in chondrodysplasia.

Aclastic —1. Pertaining to or characterized by aclasia. 2. Not refracting light rays.

Acme —Climex of a disease.

Acne —An inflammatory disease of the sebaceous glands and hair follicles of the skin, characterized by papules or pustules; comedone.

Acne artificialis — Acne venenata. Artificial acne which are produced by scratching the skin, by external irritants or drugs administered internally, such as iodides or bromides etc.

Acne atrophica —Acne after which pits and signs of scars are formed on the skin.

Acne ciliaris —Acne affecting the edges of the eyelids.

Acne indurata —Solid comedones in which the skin is discolored and becomes solid.

Acne keloid —An infection of the hair follicles at the back of the neck forming the scars and the skin becomes thickened.

Acne neonatorum — Acne in the newborn child.

Acne rosacea —Pink color acne appearing on the face.

Acne steroid —Acne caused by the use of corticosteroid drugs systemically or locally.

Acne tropical —A severe form of acne occurring in hot humid climate in which the skin of the entire trunk, shoulders, upper arms, buttocks and legs is most commonly affected.

Acne vulgaris —Most common form of acne. Comedones occur predominently on the face, upper back and chest and most commonly during puberty and adolescence.

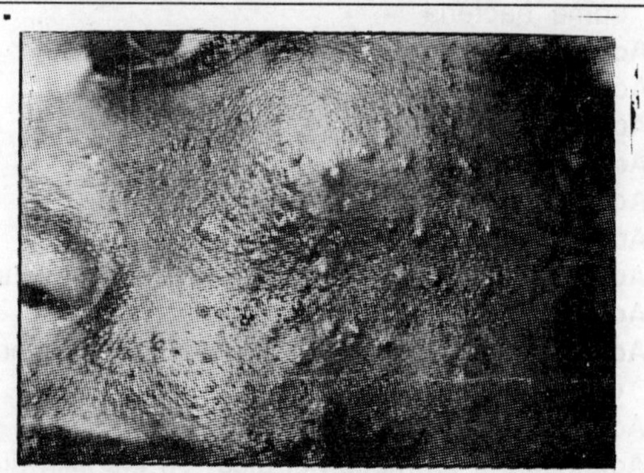

Fig. 14 : Acne vulgaris (Comedones)

Acnegenic —Producing acne.

Acneiform —Acneform, resembling acne.

Acnemia —Wasting of the calves of the legs.

Acnitis —A papular eruption which becomes pustular, leaving slight scars.

Acognosia —A knowledge of drugs.

Acology —Science of remedies.

Acomia, Alopecia — Baldness.

Aconite —A poisonous drug derived from the dried roots of Aconitum napellus.

Aconitine —Active principle of aconite.

Aconuresis, Enuresis — Involuntary urination.

Acopic —Allaying the tiredness.

Acorea —Absence of the pupil.

Acoria —Taking of excessive food not due to hunger but due to lack of satisfaction after eating food.

Acormus —A fetus having a head and the extremities without a trunk.

Acostate —Having no ribs.

Acouesthesia —Acoustic sensibility.

Aculation—An apparatus used in teaching speech to deaf-mutes.

Acoumeter —An instrument for measuring the acuteness of hearing.

Acousma —Nonverbal auditory hallucination.

Acousmatagnosia —Inability to understand what is said, due to mental disorder.

Acousmatamnesia — Forgetfulness for sounds.

Acoustic —Pertaining to sound or hearing.

Acoustic center —The hearing center situated in the temporal lobe.

Acoustic meatus —External or internal auditory canal.

Acoustic nerve —Auditory nerve, eighth cranial nerve.

Acousticophobia —Abnormal fear of loud sounds.

Acoustics —The science of sound or of hearing.

Acquired —Not inherited.

Acquired immune deficiency syndrome- AIDS — An infectious sexually transmitted disease caused by a virus (Human immunodeficiency virus –HIV), occurring usually in homosexual men due to immune deficiency and characterized by pyrexia, generalised enlargement of the lymph glands and weight loss.

Acquisitus —Acquired.

Acral —Pertaining to or affecting the extremities.

Acrania —Partial or complete absence of the cranium congenitally.

Acranial —Having no cranium since birth. Pertaining to acrania.

Acranius —The fetus with partial or complete absence of the cranium.

Acrasia —Lack of self control.

Acratia —Weakness.

Acraturesis —Difficulty in urination due to atony or weakness of the urinary bladder.

Acribometer —An instrument for measuring very minute objects.

Acrid —Sharp to taste, bitter.

Acridity —Sharpness, bitterness.

Acrimony —The quality of being intensively irritant, acrid or pungent.

Acrinia —Decreased or absent secretion.

Acritical —Without crisis.

Acritochromacy —Colorblindness.

Acro- —Combining form meaning extremity.

Acroagnosis —Absence of the feeling of the presence of a limb.

Acroanesthesia —Absence of sensation in one or more of the extremities.

Acroarthritis —Inflammation of the joints of the upper or lower extremity.

Acroasphyxia —Impairment of digital circulation causing a mild form of Raynaud's disease, marked by a purplish or waxy white color of the fingers, with subnormal local temperature and paresthesia.

Acroataxia —Incoordination of the muscles of the fingers and toes.

Acrobiology —Scientific study of the airborne organisms.

Acrobrachycephaly —The condition of the head being short in anteroposterior dimension.

Acrobystitis —Inflammation of the prepuce.

Acrocentric —Pertaining to a chromosome in which the centromere is located near one end.

Acrocephalia, Acrocephaly —The condition of having a pointed head.

Acrocephalic —Having a pointed head.

Acrocephalosyndactylia, Acrocephalosyndactyly — The congenital condition of having a peaked head and webbed fingers and toes.

Acrocephalous —Acrocephalic.

Acrochordon —Loose skin in the form of bag with a peduncle hanging from the neck, eyelids, upper part of the chest and axillae in the women in middle or older age.

Acrocinesia, Acrocinesis —Acrokinesia. Excessive movements of the extremities.

Acrocinetic —Showing excessive movements of the extremities.

Acrocontracture —Contracture of the muscles of the hand or foot.

Acrocyanosis —Cyanosis of the extremities.

Acrocyanotic —Characterized by acrocyanosis.

Acrodermatitis —Inflammation of the skin of the extremities.

Chronic atrophic acrodermatitis —Chronic inflammation of unknown etiology of the skin of the extremities leading to atrophy of the skin.

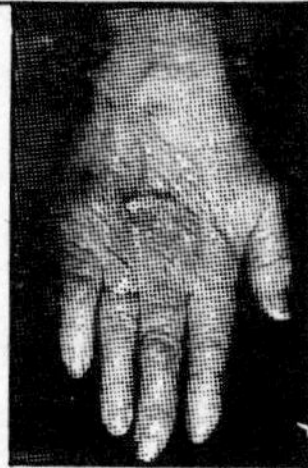

Fig 15 : Chronic atrophic acrodermatitis

Continuous acrodermatitis —Chronic inflammation of the skin of the extremities which spreads in the whole of the body.

Enteropathica acrodermatitis —A hereditary disease of insidious onset in which there are vesiculopustulous lesions of the skin on head, elbow, knees, hands and feet associated with diarrhea and loss of hair due to malabsorption of zinc, occurring at the age between 3 weeks and 18 months.

Hiemalis acrodermatitis — Inflammation of the skin of the extremities occurring in winter season and disappearing spontaneously.

Acrodermatosis —Any disease of the skin of the hands and feet.

Acrodolichomelia —The condition in which the hands and feet are abnormally long.

Acrodynia —A disease of infancy and early childhood marked by pain and swelling of the extremities, lesions of the skin of the hands and feet with itching. The hands & feet along with the cheeks and tip of the nose become pink.

Acrodysesthesia —Occurrence of abnormal and unpleasant sensations in the outer parts of the limbs.

Acrodysostosis —A disorder in which the hands and feet are short with stubly fingers and toes.

Acrodysplasia —Acrocephalosyndactyly.

Acroesthesia —1. Exaggerated sensitiveness of the limbs. 2. Pain in the limbs.

Acrogeria —The condition in which the skin of the hands and feet shows sings of premature aging.

Acrognosis —Sensory recognition of the limbs.

Acrohyperhidrosis — Excessive sweating of the hands and feet.

Acrohypothermy —Abnormal coldness of the limbs.

Acrokeratosis —A hereditary disease involving the skin of the extremities mainly of the backs of the hands and the feet with the appearance of the horny growths.

Acrokinesia —Abnormal movements of the extremities.

Acromacria —Abnormal length of the fingers.

Acromania —Mania in which the patient is too much excited.

Acromastitis —Inflammation of the nipple.

Acromegalia —Acromegaly.

Acromegalic —Pertaining to or characterized by acromegaly.

Acromegaly —Undue enlargement of the face, extremities, hands and feet of middle-aged persons, due to hypersecretion of the pituitary growth hormone. Diabetes mellitus may develop.

Acromelalgia —The condition in which the skin

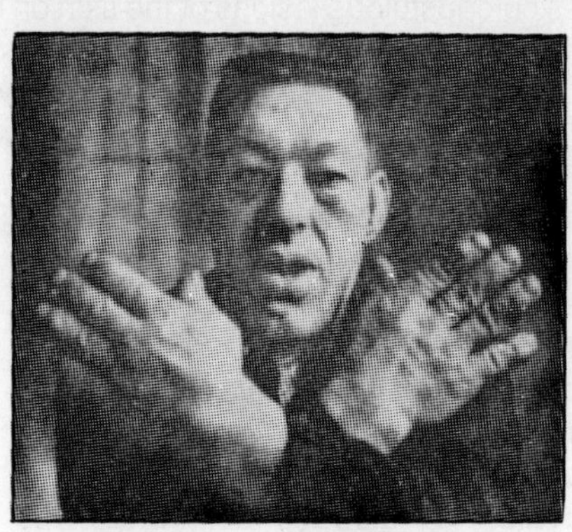
Fig. 16 : Acromegaly

of the hands and feet becomes reddened, warm and painful due to vasodilation.

Acromelic —Pertaining to the end of the extremities.

Acrometagenesis —Undue growth of the limbs.

Acromial —Pertaining to acromion.

Acromicria —Congenital shortness of the limbs.

Acromioclavicular — Pertaining to the acromion and the clavicle.

Acromiocoracoid — Pertaining to the acromion and coracoid process.

Acromiohumeral —Pertaining to the acromion and the humerus bone.

Acromion —The lateral triangular projection of the spine of the scapula bone forming the highest

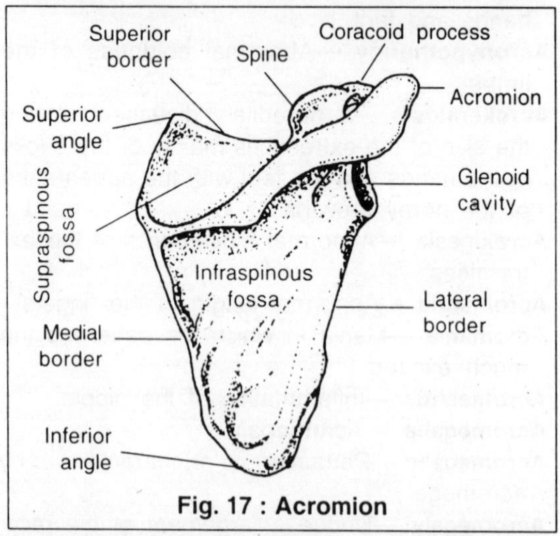

Fig. 17 : Acromion

point of the shoulder where it articulates with the calvicle bone.

Acromionectomy —Excision of the acromion.

Acromioscapular —Pertaining to the acromion and scapula.

Acromiothoracic —Pertaining to the acromion and thorax.

Acromphalus —Center of the umbilicus, or its bulging as occurs prior to umbilical hernia.

Acromyotonia, Acromyotonus —Myotonia of the extremities.

Acroneurosis —Any nervous disease of the extremities.

Acronyx —A nail growing into the flesh.

Acro-osteolysis —A familial disease in which there is softening and destruction of the bones of the distal phalanges of the fingers and toes in young children.

Acropachy —Clubbing of the fingers and toes.

Acropachyderma —Thickening of the skin of the scalp, face and extremities; clubbing of the fingers and deformities of the long bones.

Acroparalysis —Paralysis of one or more limbs.

Acroparesthesia —Sensation of prickling, tingling or numbness, and stiffness in the extremities, mainly in the fingers, hands and forearms.

Acropathology —Pathology of the diseases of the extremities.

Acropathy —Any disease of the extremities.

Acropetal —Developing from below upward.

Acrophobia —Morbid fear of high places.

Acropigmentation —Punctate and reticulate hyperpigmentation of the dorsal surfaces of the fingers and toes beginning in early childhood and usually increasing with the age.

Acroposthia —The prepuce.

Acroposthitis —Inflammation of the prepuce of the penis.

Acropurpura —Purpura affecting the extremities, especially the digits.

Acropustulosis —Pustular eruption occurring on the hands and feet.

Acroscleroderma —Hardening and thickening of the skin of the fingers and toes.

Acrosclerosis —Scleroderma of the upper extremities extending to the neck and face particularly the nose, usually following Raynaud's disease.

Acrosome —The caplike, membranous structure covering the anterior portion of the head of a spermatozoon, which contains the enzymes for penetration of the ovum.

Acrosphacelus —Gangrene of the digits which may be due to Raynaud's disease.

Acroteric —Pertaining to the tips of the digits.

Acrotic —1. Pertaining to the weakness or absence of the pulse. 2. Pertaining to the surface of the skin.

Acrotism —Absence or imperceptibility of the pulse.

ACTH —Adrenocorticotropic hormone of the pituitary gland which stimulates the cortex of the adrenal glands.

Acrotrophoneurosis — Trophoneurosis of the extremities with trophic, neuritic and vascular changes, usually caused by prolonged immersion in water.

Actin —One of the two proteins of the muscle, the other being the myosin, along with which it is responsible for contraction and relaxation of the muscle.

Actinic —Pertaining to the capability of radiant energy such as X-rays, ultraviolet light and sunlight to produce chemical changes.

Actinic burns —Burns caused by ultraviolet or sun rays.

Actinic dermatitis — Inflammation of the skin caused by X-rays, ultraviolet or sun rays.

Actinism — The property of the radiant energy which produces chemical changes, as in photography.

Actinium —A radioactive element.

Actino- —The word combining with the other word indicates rays or radiation.

Actinodermatitis — Inflammation of the skin caused by exposure to radiation.

Actinoform —Like an X-ray.

Actinogen —Any radioactive element.

Actinogenesis —Production of radiation.

Actinogenic —1. Producing radiation. 2. Caused by radiation.

Actinology —Science of radiation.

Actinomycoma —A tumor produced by actinomycosis.

Actinomycosis —A bacterial disease in man caused by the bacteria Actinomyces israelii, present in the mouth. In this disease a growth is formed in the cervicofacial, thoracic or abdominal region, which later on breaks down and discharges pus containing minute yellowish sulphur granules.

Actinomycotic —Pertaining to actinomycosis.

Actinoneuritis — Inflammation of a nerve or nerves due to exposure to radium or X-rays.

Actinophytosis —Infection caused by the bacterium Actinomyces.

Actinopraxis —Application of light or radioactive rays in the diagnosis and treatment.

Actinoscopy —Examination of the tissues & structures of the body by means of X-ray.

Actinotherapy —Treatment of disease by sun rays, ultraviolet rays, X-rays or radium.

Actinotoxemia —A toxic reaction produced by an excessive dose of radiation.

Action —Performance of a function, or process as of a drug, or the attainment of an effect.

Antagonistic action —The action of a drug or muscle opposite to that of the other drug or muscle.

Astringent action —The action in which the cells shrink.

Bacteriocidal action —The action that kills bacteria.

Bacteriostatic action —The action which stops or prevents the growth of bacteria without killing them.

Cumulative action —A sudden increased action of a drug after administration of its several doses.

Reflex action — Involuntary movements produced by the stimulation of the sensory nerves, as the constriction of the pupils in bright light and immediate drawing of the hand on touching the fire, etc.

Specific action —The particular action of a drug on a substance or upon an organism.

Specific dynamic action —Increased metabolic rate produced by the ingestion and assimilation of certain foods, especially the proteins.

Synergistic action — The action of a drug or muscle to enhance the action of another drug or muscle.

Thermogenic action — The action by which the body temperature rises.

Trigger action —The inhibition of an activity.

Activate —To make active or radioactive.

Activation —1. To render active. 2. Stimulation of the brain by light, sound, electricity or chemical substances, in order to elicit abnormal activity in the electroencephalogram.

Activator —A substance which converts an inactive substance into an active substance.

Active principle —The chemical substance present in a medicine, mainly responsible for its effects.

Activity —1. The production of energy or motion. 2. The condition of being active.

Actometer —An apparatus for measuring the activity.

Actomyosin —The combination of two types of proteins, actin and myosin present in a muscle.

Actuator — A component of a mechanical or electronic device that initiates a given action.

Acu —Needle.
Acufilopressure —Combination of acupressure and ligation.
Acuity —Severity, clearness or sharpness as of vision.
Aculeate —Pointed, covered with sharp spines.
Acuminate, Acuminated — Conical or pointed.
Acuminatous —Having a pointed apex.
Acuminous —Possessing sharp wit.
Acuology —The study of the use of needles for therapeutic purposes, as in acupuncture.
Acupressure —Compression of a bleeding blood vessel by needles inserting into the surrounding tissues.
Acupressure forceps —Spring-handled forceps for compressing the blood vessels.
Acupuncture —The piercing of a specific area of the body through the skin along with the peripheral nerves with fine and long needles to relieve pain, to anesthesize the body area and to treat some disease as asthma.
Acus —Surgical needle.
Acusis —Normal hearing.
Acusticus —The auditory nerve.
Acute —1. Sharp 2. The disease having rapid onset with severe symptoms and a short course.
Acutenaculum —A needle holder.
Acuteness —Sharpness, severity.
Acutorsion —Twisting of a blood vessel with a needle to control bleeding.
Acyanoblepsia —Acyanopsia. Inability to distinguish the blue colours.
Acyanosis —Absence of cyanosis.
Acyanotic —Having no cyanosis.
Acyclia —Failure of circulation.
Acyesis —1. Sterility in woman. 2. Nonpregnancy.
Acystia —Congenital absence of the urinary bladder.
Acystinervia, Acysteneuria —Defective nerve supply to bladder or paralysis of the bladder.
ad —Add. In prescription it indicates that a substance should be added to the other medicines up to a specific volume.
ad- —Prefix indicating adherence, increase or toward as in adduct.
-ad —Suffix indicating toward or in direction of as in cephalad.
Adacrya —Absence of tears, tearlessness.
Adactylia, Adactylism, Adactyly —Congenital absence of fingers or toes.
Adactylous —Having no digits.
Adamantine —1. Pertaining to the enamel of teeth. 2. Very hard like the enamel of teeth.
Adamantinoma —A tumor of the jaw, especially of the lower jaw, that arises from the enamel forming cells.
Adamantoblast —Ameloblast.
Adamantoblastoma, Adamantoma —Ameloblastoma.
Adam's apple —Laryngeal prominence in front of the neck especially in adult male.
Adams-Stokes syndrome —Unconsciousness with convulsions due to decreased blood flow of the brain.
Adaptability —Ability to adjust according to the circumstance.
Adaptable —Capable of being adapted.
Adaptation —1. Adjustment of an organism to a changed environment 2. Adjustment of the eyes to variations in the intensity of light by changing the size of their pupils. 3. Immunization. 4. In dentistry, proper fitting of a denture.
Adapter —A device for connecting one part of an apparatus to another.
Adaptometer —An instrument used to measure the time required for regeneration of the visual purple.
Adaxial —Toward the medial plane.
Addict —The person physically or psychologically or both dependent on a substance, especially on alcohol or durgs with the use of increasing amounts.
Addiction —Physical or psychological or both dependence on a substance, especially alcohol or drugs with the use of increasing amounts.
Addisonism —The symptoms resembling to that of Addison's disease but actually they are not caused by the disease of adrenal glands, as hyperpigmentation of the skin with general debility and loss of weight may be seen in pulmonary tuberculosis.
Addison's disease —A disease caused by the deficiency of adrenocortical hormones characterized by hyperpigmentation of the skin with debility and loss of weight.
Addison's planes —Imaginary planes dividing the abdomen into nine regions to aid in the location of internal structures.
Additive —A substance added to another substance to improve its qualities as substance added to food to increase its taste, color, flavor, and other qualities.
Additivity —The quality or state of being additive.

Adducent —Drawing toward the middle line of the body.

Adduct —To draw toward the midline of the body.

Adduction —Movement of an organ toward the middle line of the body or in case of digits towards the axial line of a limb.

Adductor —Which draws toward the middle line of the body or toward a center, said of a muscle.

Adelomorphous —Of indefinite form.

Adenalgia —Pain in a gland.

Adenasthenia —Deficient glandular activity.

Adendric, Adendritic — Nerve cells without dendrites.

Adenectomy —Excision of a gland.

Adenectopia —The presence of a gland in an abnormal position.

Adenemphraxis —An obstruction to the discharge of a glandular secretion.

Adenia —Chronic enlargement of a lymph gland due to inflammation.

Adeniform —Like a gland in shape.

Adenitis —Inflammation of a gland.

Adenization —Abnormal change into a gland like structure.

Adeno- —Prefix denoting a gland.

Adenoblasts —Embryonic cells producing glandular tissue.

Adenocanthoma — Adenocarcinoma.

Adenocarcinoma, Adenocanthoma —Carcinoma arising from a glandular tissue.

Adenocele —A cystic tumor arising from a gland.

Adenocellulitis — Inflammation of a gland with its surrounding tissues.

Adenochondroma —A tumor containing both glandular and cartilaginous elements.

Adenocyst, Adenocystoma —A cystic tumor arising from a gland.

Adenocystoma —Adenocyst.

Adenocyte —A mature secretary cell of a gland.

Adenodynia —Pain in a gland.

Adenoepithelioma —Tumor consisting of glandular and epithelial elements.

Adenofibroma —Tumor composed of glandular and fibrous tissue.

Adenofibrosis —Degeneration of a tumor by fibrous tissues.

Adenogenous —Originating from a glandular tissue.

Adenography —X-ray of the glands.

Adenohypophysectomy — Excision of the glandular portion (anterior lobe) of the pituitary gland.

Adenohypophysial — Pertaining to adenohypophysis.

Adenohypophysis — Anterior lobe of the pituitary gland.

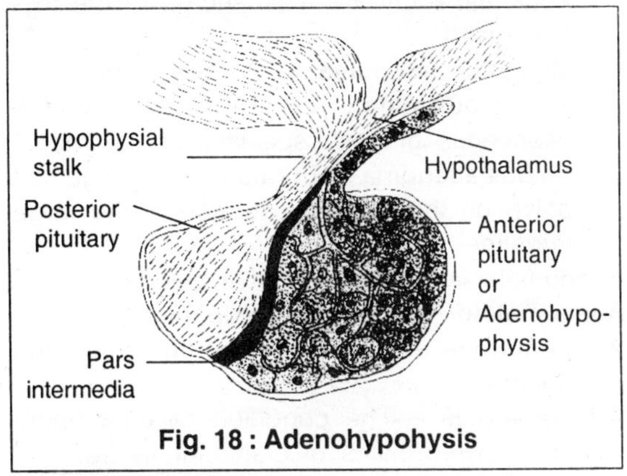

Fig. 18 : Adenohypohysis

Adenohypophysitis — Inflammation of the anterior pituitary gland.

Adenoid —1. Resembling a gland. 2. Hypertrophy of the pharyngeal tonsil.

Adenoidectomy —Excision of adenoids.

Adenoid hypertrophy — Enlargement of the pharyngeal tonsil occuring commonly in children.

Adenoids —1. Pharyngeal tonsils 2. The term usually used for enlarged pharyngeal tonsils due to infection, of the children.

Adenoiditis —Inflammation of the adenoid.

Adenolipoma —A tumor composed of both glandular and fatty tissues.

Adenolipomatosis — Formation of a large number of adenolipomas in the neck, axilla and groin.

Adenology —Study of the glands.

Adenolymphitis —Lymphadenitis. Inflammation of a lymph gland.

Adenolymphocele — Lymphadenocele. Dilatation of a lymph gland by the formation of a cyst due to obstruction.

Adenolymphoma —Adenoma of a lymph gland.

Adenoma —A benign tumor of the epithelial cells of a gland.

Acidophilic adenoma —A tumor of the alpha cells of the anterior lobe of the pituitary gland, which secretes the growth hormone in excess causing acromegaly or gigantism.

Basophilic adenoma — A tumor of the beta cells of the anterior lobe of the pituitary gland, which secretes adrenocorticotropic hormone (ACTH) in excess causing Cushing's syndrome.

Chromophobic adenoma —A tumor of the anterior lobe of the pituitary gland composed of cells which do not stain readily with either acid or basic dyes and may cause diabetes insipidus.

Follicular adenoma — Adenoma of the thyroid gland.

Malignant adenoma — Adenocarcinoma.

Sebaceous adenoma — Hypertrophy of the sebaceous glands especially of the face.

Villous adenoma — Formation of a large soft polyp on the mucosal surface of the large intestine.

Adenomalacia —Softening of a gland.

Adenomatoid —Resembling adenoma.

Adenomatone —An instrument for removing adenoids.

Adenomatosis —The condition of developing multiple overgrowths of glandular tissue.

Adenomatous —Pertaining to adenoma or adenoid.

Adenomegaly —Enlargement of a gland.

Adenomere —The functional part of a gland.

Adenomyofibroma —A fibroma containing both glandular and muscular elements.

Adenomyoma — A benign tumor containing both glandular and smooth muscular tissues.

Adenomyomatosis —The formation of multiple adenomyomatous nodules in the tissues or in the uterus.

Adenomyomatous —Pertaining to or resembling adenomyoma.

Adenomyometritis — Hyperplasia of the uterus due to pelvic inflammation which resembles adenomyoma.

Adenomyosarcoma — Adenosarcoma which includes muscle tissues.

Adenomyosis—Benign growth of the endometrium invading into the myometrium of the uterus.

Adenoncus —Enlargement of a gland.

Adenopathy —Any disease of a gland.

Adenopharyngitis—Inflammation of the adenoids and the pharynx.

Adenophlegmon —Acute inflammation of a gland and the adjacent connective tissue.

Adenophthalmia—Inflammation of the meibomian glands situated in the eyelids.

Adenosarcoma —A malignant tumor composed of both glandular and sarcomatous elements.

Adenosclerosis —Hardening of a gland.

Adenose —Gland like.

Adenosis —1. Any disease of a gland, especially the lyrnph gland 2. Abnormal development of a gland.

Adenotome —An instrument for excising the adenoids.

Adenotomy —Incision of a gland or of adenoids.

Adenotonsillectomy—Removal of the tonsils and adenoids by surgery.

Adenous —Like a gland.

Adenovirus —Any of a large group of viruses causing infection of the upper respiratory tract.

Adeps —Lard.

Adermia —Congenital defect or absence of the skin.

Adermogenesis —Imperfect development of the skin.

A.D.H. —Antidiuretic hormone.

Adherence —The act or quality of sticking to something.

Adherence, bacterial —The attachment of bacteria to any surface.

Adherent —Attached to or sticking, as of two surfaces.

Adhesion —Attachment of two surfaces together as in wound healing.

Adhesiotomy —Surgical division of adhesions.

Adhesive —Sticky or that which causes adhesion.

Adhesive tape —A cloth with its one side coated with an adhesive substance so that the cloth remain in contact with the skin after its application.

Adiabatic —Referring to a thermodynamic process in which there is no gain or loss of heat between system and its surroundings.

Adiadochokinesia, Adiadochokinesis —Inability to perform fine, rapidly repeated movements.

Adiaphoresis —Deficiency or absence of sweat.

Adiaphoretic —Preventing or reducing perspiration.

Adiaphoria —Non-response to stimuli as a result to previous exposure to the similar stimuli.

Adiapneustia —Anhidrosis. Diminished or complete absence of sweat.

Adiastole —Absence of diastole.

Adiathermancy —Impermeability to heat.

Adiemorrhysis —Arrest of capillary circulation.

Adient —Tending to move toward a stimulus.

Adipectomy —Excision of fatty tissues.

Adipic —Pertaining to fat.

Adipo-,Adip- — Combining with other word which means pertaining to fat.

Adipocele —A hernia containing fatty tissue.

Adipocelluar —Composed of fat and connective tissue.

Adipoceratous —Lipoceratous. Pertaining to adipocere.

Adipocere —A waxy substance produced during decomposition of dead animal bodies.

Adipocerous —Relating to adipocere.

Adipocyte —Fat cell.

Adipofibroma —A lipoma with fibrous tissues.

Adipogenesis —Lipogenesis. Occurrence of production of fat.

Adipogenous, Adipogenic —Producing fat or fatness.

Adipoid —Lipoid, fat-like.

Adipokinesis —Mobilization and metabolism of fat in the body.

Adipokinetic —A substance or factor causing mobilization of fat in the body.

Adipokinin —A hormone of the anterior pituitary gland which quickens the mobilization of the fat stored in the body.

Adipolysis —Digestion of fat.

Adipoma —Lipoma.

Adipometer —An instrument for measuring the thickness of the skin.

Adiponecrosis —Necrosis of the fatty tissue.

Adipopexis —Storing of fat.

Adiposalgia —Development of painful areas in subcutaneous fat.

Adipose —Pertaining to fat, fatty.

Adiposis —1. Obesity or excessive accumulation of fat in the body. 2. Fatty change in an organ or tissue.

Adiposis cerebralis —Obesity due to cerebral disease, especially of the pituitary gland.

Adiposis dolorosa — Scattered painful cutaneous nodules of fat occurring in women of menopausal age.

Adiposis hepatica — Fatty degeneration or infiltration of the liver.

Adipositis —Inflammation of the fatty tissues.

Adiposity —Obesity.

Adiposogenital dystrophy —Frohlich's syndrome.

Adiposuria —Presence of fat in the urine.

Adipsia, Adipsy —Absence of thirst.

Aditus —Entrance into an organ or part.

Adjunct —An addition to the treatment.

Adjuster —A device for holding together the ends of the wire forming a suture.

Adjustment —Adaptation. In dentistry, any modification made upon artificial denture for its proper insertion and function.

Adjuvant —1. Assisting. 2. A substance which on adding to a medicine enhances its property.

Ad lib, Ad-libitun —As much as desired.

Admedial, Admedian — Toward or near the median plane.

Adminicula —Plural of adminiculum.

Adminiculum —That which gives support to a part of the body.

Adnerval —Toward a nerve.

Adneural —Adnerval.

Adnexa —Accessory structures of an organ as the eyelids and lacrimal glands of the eye or ovaries and fallopian tubes of the uterus.

Adnexal —Adjacent.

Adnexectomy —1. Excision of any adnexa. 2. In gynecology, excision of the fallopian tube and ovary.

Adnexitis —Inflammation of the adnexa of the uterus.

Adnexogenesis —Development of the adnexae in embryo.

Adnexopexy —To fix the ovary and the fallopian tube to the abdominal wall.

Adolescence —The period from starting of the puberty to the maturity which is roughly from 11 to 19 years of age.

Adolescent —1. Pertaining to adolescence. 2. Young man or woman.

Adoral —Toward or near the mouth.

Adren (O)- —Prefix indicating adrenal gland.

Adrenal — 1. The word used in reference to the adrenal gland or its secretions. 2. Near or upon the kidney.

Adrenal crisis —A condition of shock caused by the deficiency of adrenocortical hormones. Death may result if the condition is not properly treated.

Adrenalectomy — Excision of one or both adrenal glands.

Adrenal gland —A triangular endocrine gland situated on the superior surface of each kidney.

Adrenaline —Epinephrine.

Adrenalinemia —Presence of epinephrine in the blood.

Adrenalinuria —Presence of epinephrine in the urine.

Adrenalism —Illness due to adrenal dysfunction.

Adrenalitis—Adrenitis. Inflammation of the adrenal glands.

Adrenalopathy —Any disease of the adrenal gland.

Adrenal virilism —A condition of development of male characteristics in a woman, as development of moustache and beard, masculine voice

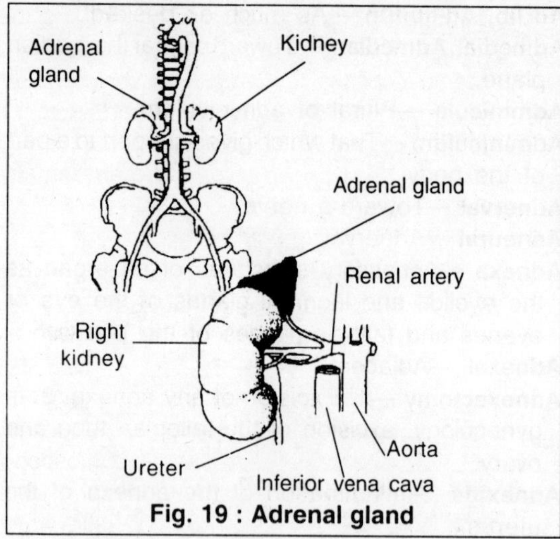

Fig. 19 : Adrenal gland

and excessive growth of hair over the body called hirsutism, as a result of excessive production of male sex hormone by the adrenal glands.

Adrenarche —Changes occurring at puberty due to increased secretion of the adrenocortical hormone, such as axillary and pubic hair growth etc.

Adrenergic –Nerve fibres which on stimulation release epinephrine at their endings.

Adrenic —Pertaining to the adrenal glands.

Adrenitis –Adrenalitis. Inflammation of the adrenal glands.

Adrenoceptive—Concerning the sites in the organs or tissues which are acted upon by the adrenergic transmitters.

Adrenocortical —Pertaining to or arising from adrenal cortex.

Adrenocortical hormones — The hormones produced by the adrenal cortex, collectively known as corticosteroids and are classified according to their chemical structure and biological activity into 3 main groups— Glucocorticoids (Cortisol, Corticosterone) which act mainly on carbohydrate metabolism; mineralocorticoids (aldosterone, dehydroepiandrosterone) which affect the metabolism of the electrolytes sodium and potassium; and sex hormones (androgens, estrogens and progesterone) which are concerned with the reproduction and sexual development.

Adrenocorticoid — Corticosteroid.

Adrenocorticomimetic — Having the actions similar to those of adrenocortical hormones.

Adrenocorticotropic— Having a stimulating effect on the adrenal cortex.

Adrenocorticotropic hormone, Adrenocorticotropin — A hormone secreted by the anterior lobe of the pituitary gland which is necessary for the development and continued function of the adrenal cortex.

Adrenogenic —Adrenogenous.

Adrenogenous —Arising from the adrenal gland.

Adrenoleukodystrophy —A disease of the young males characterized by chronic adrenocortical insufficiency, hyperpigmentation of the skin, progressive dementia, spastic paralysis and other intellectual and neurological disturbances, due to myelin degeneration in the white matter of the brain.

Adrenolytic —Preventing or inhibiting the action of the adrenergic nerves or interfering with the response of epinephrine.

Adrenomegaly —Enlargement of one or both adrenal glands.

Adrenomimetic — Sympathicomimetic. Having the actions similar to those resulting from stimulation of the sympathetic nervous system such as effects following the injection of epinephrine or adrenaline.

Adrenomyeloneuropathy — A disorder of adult males characterized by chronic adrenal insufficiency, hypogonadism, progressive myelopathy, peripheral neuropathy and dysfunction of the sphinctures.

Adrenopathy —Any disease of the adrenal gland.

Adrenopause —The age at which the activity of the adrenal glands cease.

Adrenoreceptor —Adrenergic receptor.

Adrenotoxin —Any substance toxic to the adrenal glands.

Adrenotropic —Stimulating the adrenal glands.

Adsorb —To adhere other material on its surface.

Adsorbate —Anything which is adsorbed.

Adsorbent —A substance which adheres the particles of other materials on its surface.

Adsorption —Adherence of a substance to the surface of another substance.

Adsternal —Near or toward the sternum.

Adterminal —Toward the extremity of any structure, as end of a nerve or muscle.

Adtorsion —Inward rotation of both the eyes, convergent squint.

Adult —Fully developed and mature person or organism.

Adultery —Violation of the marriage-bed.

Adulterant —An impure and cheap substance used to add to a product for adulteration.

Adulteration —Addition of an impure and cheap substance to a product to cheat, admixture.

Adulterer —A person, especially a man, who commits adultery.

Adultomorphism —To consider the children's behavior as that of the adults.

Advance —1. To move or bring forward. 2. To detach a muscle or a tendon by surgery and to reattach it to a place away from the point of detachment.

Advancement —To detach a muscle or a tendon by surgery and to reattach it to a place away from the point of detachment.

Adventitia —The outermost coat of an organ or structure, such as the tunica adventitia or outer coat of an artery.

Adventitious —1. Situated at an abnormal place. 2. Acquired or accidental, not hereditary or natural.

Adynamia —Debility.

Adynamic —Pertaining to adynamia. Debilitated person.

Adynamic ileus —Intestinal obstruction resulting from lack of intestinal motility.

Adynatus —Sicky.

Aeluropsis —Slanting and narrowing of the eye and the palpebral fissure.

Aer- —Combining with another word indicates the relationship to air or a gas.

Aerate —1. To supply oxygen. 2. To exchange carbon dioxide for oxygen by the blood in the lungs, i.e. to expose the blood circulation for purification in the lungs. 3. To charge a fluid with a gas.

Aerated —Containing air or a gas.

Aeration —1. The act of airing. 2. The exchange of carbon dioxide for oxygen by the blood in the lungs. 3. Charging of a fluid with a gas.

Aerendocardia —Presence of air bubble in the blood within the heart.

Aerenterectasia —Distension of the intestine with gas.

Aerial —Belonging to air.

Aeriferous —Carrying air.

Aeriform —Gaseous, like air.

Aero- —Combining with another word indicates the relationship to air or a gas.

Aerobe, Aerobion —The micro-organism which lives and grows in the presence of oxygen.

Aerobic —Pertaining to a micro-organism which lives and grows in the presence of oxygen.

Aerobiology —The study of the living and non-living things of biological significance of the environment, pathogenic bacteria, pollutants and allergenic substances etc.

Aerobioscope —An apparatus for determining the bacterial content of the air.

Aerobiosis —The living in an environment containing oxygen.

Aerobiotic —Pertaining to aerobiosis.

Aerocele —A tumor formed by air filling a pouch, or distention of a cavity with gas.

Aerocolpos — Distention of the vagina with air or a gas.

Aerocoly —Distention of the colon with gas.

Aerocystoscopy —Examination of the urinary bladder distended by the air, with a cystoscope.

Aerodermectasia —Subcutaneous emphysema, i.e., accumulation of air under the skin which may be spontaneous, traumatic or surgical.

Aerodontalgia —Pain in the teeth due to lowered atmospheric pressure at high altitudes.

Aerodontia —A branch of dentistry concerned with the effects of changes in the atmospheric pressure on the teeth.

Aerodynamics —The science of air or gases in motion.

Aeroembolism —Presence of a air bubble in a blood vessel.

Aerogastria —Distention of the stomach with gas.

Aerogen —A gas-forming bacterium.

Aerogenesis —Formation of gas.

Aerogenic, Aerogenous — Gas forming.

Aerogram —X-ray of a hollow organ after it has been filled with air or gas.

Aerohydrotherapy —Treatment by air and water.

Aerometer —An apparatus for measuring the density of gases.

Aeroneurosis —A functional nervous disorder occurring in aviators.

Aero-odontodynia — Aerodontalgia.

Aero-otitis —Barotitis.

Aeropathy —Any disease caused by the change in atmospheric pressure, *e.g.,* decompression sickness.

Aeroperitoneum, Aeroperitonia —Distention of the peritoneal cavity with gas.

Aerophagia, Aerophagy — Swallowing of the air.

Aerophilic, Aerophilous — Aerobic. Requiring air for development.

Aerophobia —Morbid fear of air.

Aerophore —An apparatus for inflating the lungs of the new born child.

Aerophyte —Plant organism which lives upon the air.

Aeropiesotherapy —Treatment by air at increased or decreased pressure.

Aeroplethysmograph —An apparatus for measuring the respiratory volume.

Aeroscope —An apparatus for examining the visible particles in the air.

Aerosialophagy —Sialoaerophagy. The swallowing of saliva and air.

Aerosinusitis —Inflammation of the nasal sinuses due to changes in the atmospheric pressure.

Aerosis —Accumulation of gas in the tissues.

Aerosol —The suspension of the particles of a solid or liquid drug or other substance in a gas to be dispensed in the form of a fine spray.

Aerosolization —Dispersion of a liquid in the air in the form of fine spray.

Aerotaxis —Movement of the organisms away from or towards the air.

Aerotherapy —Treatment by air.

Aerothermotherapy —Treatment of diseases by hot air.

Aerotitis —Barotitis.

Aerotonometer —An instrument for measuring the tension of oxygen in blood.

Aerotropism —Tendency of bacteria and protozoa, to move toward air (positive aerotropism) or away from the air (negative aerotropsim).

Aerourethroscope —An apparatus for visual examination of the urethra after dilatation by air.

Aerourethroscopy —Visual examination of the urethra after distending it with the air.

Aesthetics —Science of beauty and arts.

Aestival —Pertaining to summer.

Afebrile —Without fever.

Affect —1. To exert influence upon. 2. Emotional reactions such as happiness or unhappiness caused by a stimulus.

Affection —1. Love 2. The condition of physical or mental disease.

Affective —Pertaining to an emotion or mental state.

Afferent, Afferentia — Carrying toward a center, e.g., a sensory nerve which carries impulses or message toward the brain, or certain veins which carry blood toward the heart.

Affiliation —Adoption, to take to oneself as a son.

Affinity —Attraction.

Afflict —To give physical or mental trouble.

Afflux —Rush of blood to a part of the body.

Affusion —To pour upon, to sprinkle.

Afibrinogenemia —Deficiency or absence of fibrinogen in the blood.

Afteraction —The continuance of a reaction for some time after the stimulus ceases.

Afterbirth —The placenta and the membranes which are expelled from the uterus after child birth.

Aftercare —To look after a convalescent person.

Aftercataract —Development of the opacity of the lens after removal of a cataract.

Aftercontraction —A muscular contraction persisting for a little time after the stimulus has ceased.

Aftercurrent —An electrical current induced in a muscle upon the termination of a constant current that has been passed through it.

Afterdischarge —Persistence of response of a muscle or nerve after cessation of stimulation.

Aftereffect —A physical, physiologic, psychologic or emotional effect that continues after removal of the stimulus.

Afterglow —Stage of physical and mental relaxation exhibiting satisfaction with happiness in both the partners following the successful completion of sexual intercourse.

Afterhearing —Perception of sound after the stimulus causing the sound has ceased to act.

Afterimage —Image that persists after cessation of the stimulus causing it.

Afterimpression —Aftersensation.

Afterload —Stress or tension developing in the ventricular wall during systole.

Afterpains —Cramp-like pains due to contractions of the uterus occurring during first few days after child birth.

Afterperception —Perception of a sensation after cessation of its stimulus.

Afterplay —Sexual play after completion of sexual intercourse causing the partners to reach the climax of the sexual excitement.

Aftersensation —Sensation persisting after cessation of the stimulus causing it.

Aftersound —Sensation of a sound persisting after the stimulus causing it has ceased.

Aftertaste —A taste continuing after removal of the substance causing it.

Aftervision —Afterimage.

Afunction —Dysfunction.

Ag —Chemical symbol for silver.

Agalactia —Absence of milk secretion after child birth.

Agalactorrhea —Absence of flow of breast milk.

Agalactosis —Agalactia. Absence of milk secretion by the breasts after child birth.

Agalactous —Checking the secretion of milk.

Agalactus —Pertaining to agalactia or to the diminution or absence of breast milk.

Agalorrhea —Arrest of flow of milk.

Agamic —1. Reproducing asexually 2. Asexual.

Agammaglobulinemia — Deficiency of gamma globulins in the blood.

Agamogenesis —Asexual reproduction.

Agamogenetic —Indicating asexual reproduction.

Agamogony —Asexual reproduction.

Agamous —Without sex organs.

Aganglionic —Without ganglion cells.

Aganglionosis —Congenital absence of parasympathetic ganglion cells.

Agape —With mouth open in wonder.

Agastria —Absence of the stomach.

Agastric —Having no stomach.

Agastroneuria —Lessened nervous control of the stomach.

Age —1. The time from the birth of a living individual or from the existance of non-living thing to the present, which is measured in units of time. 2. A particular period of life, as middle age or old age. 3. To undergo changes as a result of passage of time.

Achievement age —The age of a person with regard to the level of learning acquired.

Anatomical age —The age estimated on the basis of body structure.

Bone age —The age estimated on the basis of X-ray examination of the stages of development of ossification centers of the long bones of the extremities.

Childbearing age — The period in a woman's life between puberty and menopause.

Chronological age — The actual measure of time elapsed since birth of a person.

Developmental age — Age determined by the physical, mental and social development of an individual.

Gestational age —Age of a fetus which is determined from the date of onset of the last menstrual period.

Menarcheal age —The time elapsed from menarche, expressed in years.

Mental age —The age determined on the basis of mental ability of a person which is measured by standard intelligence tests.

Physiological age — The age determined by the function of the body.

Age critique —Critical age; age of about 50 years, menopausal or climacteric period.

Aged —Old person.

Ageless —Never seen to grow old.

Agenesia, Agenesis —1. Imperfect development of an organ or part of the body. 2. Sterility or impotence.

Agenitalism —Absence of genital organs or their secretions.

Agenosomia —Congenital absence of the genital organs or their poor development and the protrusion of the intestine from an incompletely developed abdominal wall.

Agent —1. Something producing an effect 2. A factor such as a micro-organism or chemical substance which causes a disease.

Agerasia —Appearance of an old man as a young man.

Ageusia, Ageustia —Absence or partial loss of the sense of taste.

Agger —A small eminence or elevation, e.g., agger nasi, the ridge of the nose.

Agglomerate —To form a mass.

Agglomeration —Aggregation.

Agglutinable —Capable of agglutination.

Agglutinant —Agglutinin. Substance causing union by adhesion as in healing of a wound, or an antibody produced in the body in response to stimulation by an antigen.

Agglutination —1. Aggregation into clumps, as of blood corpuscles when incompatible bloods are mixed. 2. The process of union of the surfaces by adhesion in wound healing.

Agglutinative, Agglutinator — Causing or capable of causing agglutination.

Agglutinin —An antibody or a substance present in the serum of the blood which combining with its antigen causes the antigen elements to adhere to one another in clumps.

Anti-Rh agglutinin —An agglutinin not normally present in the plasma of the human blood, which is sometimes produced in Rh-negative mothers carrying a Rh-positive fetus or after transfusion of Rh-positive blood into Rh-negative patient.

Cold agglutinin —An agglutinin which acts only in low temperatures (O°—20°C).

Group agglutinin —An agglutinin which has a specific action on a particular group of micro-organisms.

Immune agglutinin —A specific agglutinin causing immunity, found in the blood because of either recovery from the disease or having been inoculated with the micro-organisms causing disease.

Major agglutinin, Chief agglutinin —An immune agglutinin of which the largest concentration is present in the blood.

Minor agglutinin, Partial agglutinin —An immune agglutinin present in the blood in lesser concentration than the major agglutinin.

Specific agglutinin — Normal agglutinin. An agglutinin found in the blood which is not produced by a disease or by the injection of disease producing organisms.

Agglutinogen —Any substance which stimulates the production of agglutinin, thereby acting as an antigen, e.g., agglutinogen Rh. Rh is a specific substance called the Rh factor present in red blood cells of a large number of people. The person in whom it is present is called Rh^+ (Rh positive), in whom it is absent, is called Rh^- (Rh negative). When the blood of a Rh^+ (Rh positive) person is transfused to a Rh^- (Rh negative) person, it produces an antibody anti-Rh, which on subsequent transfusion of Rh^+ blood, agglutinates the red blood cells of the transfused blood.

Agglutinogenic —Pertaining to the production of agglutinin; producing agglutinin.

Agglutinophilic —Readily agglutinating.

Aggravate —To make more severe.

Aggregate —To cluster or to come together.

Aggregated —Collected together, thereby forming a cluster or clump.

Aggregation —A clustering or coming together of the substances as clustering of the blood cells, especially the platelets or red blood cells.

Aggregometer —An instrument for measuring the platelet aggregation.

Aggression —Destructive and attacking behavior.

Aggressive —Having destructive and attacking behavior.

Aging —The gradual structural changes occurring in the body with the passage of time. The process of growing old.

Agitation —Excessive physical activity.

Agitographia —Writing very rapidly.

Agitolalia —Agitophasia.

Agitophasia —Abnormally rapid speech in which words are spoken imperfectly.

Aglaucopsia, Aglaukopsia — Green blindness.

Aglossia —Congenital absence of the tongue.

Aglossostomia —Congenital absence of the tongue and mouth opening.

Aglutition —Inability to swallow.

Aglycemia —Absence of sugar in the blood.

Aglycosuria —The condition of absence of sugar in the urine.

Aglycosuric —Free from glycosuria.

Agminated or agminate —Grouped in clusters.

Agnathia —Congenital absence of the lower jaw.

Agnathus —A fetus without lower jaw.

Agnea —Inability to recognize the things.

$AgNO_3$ —Chemical symbol of silver nitrate.

Agnogenic —Of unknown origin or etiology.

Agnosia —Inability to recognize.

Auditory agnosia — Inability to recognize sound, words or music.

Color agnosia —Inability to recognize colour.

Gustatory agnosia — Inability to identify the taste.

Tactile agnosia — Inability to recognize the objects by touch.

Visual agnosia — Inability to recognize the things by sight.

-agogue —Suffix meaning a producer.

Agomphiasis —Absence of the teeth.

Agomphious —Having no teeth.

Agonad, Agonadal —Having no sex glands.

Agonadism —The condition of being without sex glands.

Agonal —Pertaining to death or occurring just before death.

Agonise —To torture or to suffer agony.

Agonist —Agonist is a type of muscle which contracts a part and is opposed by another muscle (antagonist) as in bending the elbow, the biceps brachii muscle is the agonist, *i.e.*, it contracts the elbow joint while the triceps is the antagonist muscle which relaxes the joint.

Agony —1. Death struggle. 2. Extreme physical or mental suffering.

Agoraphobia —Morbid fear of crowds.

Agoraphobic —Pertaining to agoraphobia.

-agra —Suffix indicating sudden severe pain.

Agraffe —An instrument for clumping together the edges of a wound.

Agrammatica —Agrammatism.

Agrammatism — Inability to speak grammatical or intelligible sentences due to cerebral disease affecting the speech centre.

Agrammatologia —Agrammatism.

Agranulocyte —A white blood cell without granules.

Agranulocytic —Pertaining to agranulocytosis.

Agranulocytosis —A condition occurring due to decrease in the number of granulocytes in the blood characterized by high fever, ulceration of the mouth and other mucous membranes.

Agranuloplastic —Not forming granular cells but forming only nongranular cells.

Agranulosis —Agranulocytosis.

Agraphia —Inability to write.

Absolute agraphia — Complete inability to write.

Acoustic agraphia — Inability to write the words which are heard.

Amnemonic agraphia — Inability to write the sentences, although the letters or words can be written.

Cerebral agraphia — Inability to express the thoughts in writing due to a lesion of the cerebral cortex.

Motor agraphia — Inability to write due to muscular incoordination.

Optic agraphia — Inability to copy the words.

Verbal agraphia — Inability to write the words although the letters can be written.

Agraphic —Relating to or characterized by agraphia.

Agria —Severe pustular eruption.

Agromania —Keen desire to live in a lonely place.

Agrypnia —Insomnia.

Agrypnotic—1. Suffering from insomnia. 2. Causing wakefulness.

Ague —Malarial fever or chill.

Agyiophobia —A form of agoraphobia characterized by a morbid fear of being in the street.

Agyria—Incompletely developed gyri of the cerebral cortex and the brain is usually small.

Ahypnia —Agrypnia or insomnia (Sleeplessness).

A.I. —Aortic insufficiency; artificial insemination.

Aichmophobia —Morbid fear of being touched by pointed objects or fingers.

A.I.D. —Artificial insemination by donor.

Aid —Help to a sick or injured person such as hearing aid with a device to amplify the sound, is provided to a hearing-impaired person to hear, or first aid treatment given to an injured or ill person before regular surgical or medical treatment.

Aidolites —Inflammation of the vulva due to infection.

Aidolomania —Abnormally keen desire for sexual intercourse.

AIDS —Acquired immune deficiency syndrome.

A.I.H. —Artificial insemination by husband's semen.

Ailment —A minor disease.

Ailurophobia —Morbid fear of cats.

Ainhum —Constriction of a digit of unknown etiology causing its amputation.

Air —The mixture of invisible, tasteless and odorless gases surrounding the earth which comprises of approximately 78% nitrogen, 21% oxygen and .03% carbon dioxide by volume. The remaining .97% of the air contains water vapour, and traces of other gases such as ammonia, helium, neon and argon etc.

Alveolar air —Air in the alveoli of the lungs that is involved in the exchange of gases between air and the blood in the lungs.

Complemental air —Inspiratory reserve volume. The volume of the air that can be inspired over the volume of air which flows in and out of the lungs with each normal respiration (tidal air).

Dead space air —The volume of air that fills the respiratory passages and is not available for exchange of gases with the blood.

Functional residual air —The volume of air in the lungs at the end of a normal expiration.

Liquid air —Air that has been liquified by means of intense cold and pressure.

Minimal air —The small volume of air trapped in the alveoli of the lungs which cannot be expelled out even after the lungs have been removed from the body.

Reserve air —Supplemental air.

Residual air —Air remaining in the lungs after the full expiration which is about 1500 cc in the adult.

Supplemental air —The volume of air that can be expired after a full normal expiration which is about 1600 cc in an adult.

Tidal air —Tidal volume. The volume of air that flows in and out of the lungs with each normal respiration which is about 500 cc. for a man.

Vitiated air —Air in which percentage of oxygen is lessened .

Air cell —An air vesicle.

Air cushion —A cushion filled with air.

Air embolism —An air bubble obstructing a blood vessel.

Air hunger —Dyspnea.

Air passages —The nares, mouth, pharynx, larynx, trachea, bronchi and bronchioles, etc.

Air pollution — Contamination of air by harmful substances, as from smoke coming out of the automobiles or emitted by burning coal.

Air sac —Air vesicle.

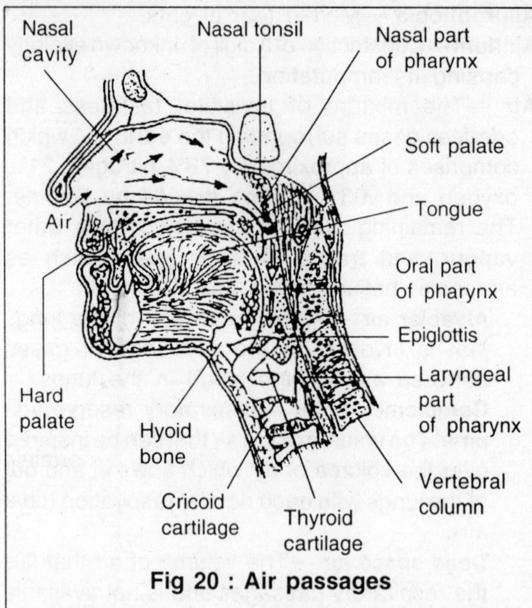

Fig 20 : Air passages

Air sickness —The condition of headache, nausea, vomiting and giddiness occurring during air flight.

Airway —1. The passage from the nares or mouth to the terminal bronchioles in the lungs by which the air enters and leaves the lungs. 2. An apparatus used to prevent the obstruction of respiratory passage, especially during anesthesia.

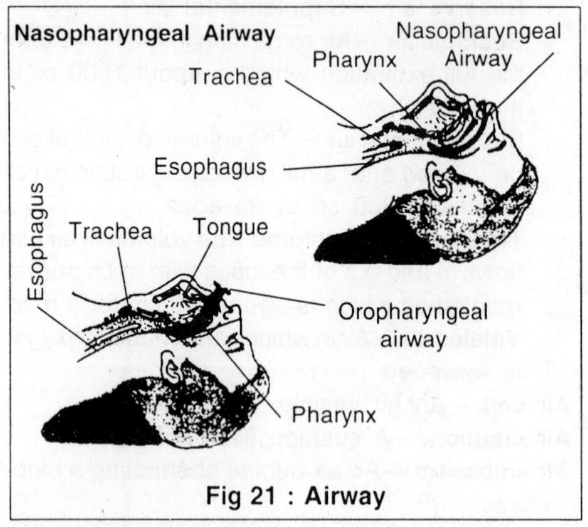

Fig 21 : Airway

A.K. —Above knee.

Akaryocyte —A non-nucleated cell, *e.g.*, an erythrocyte.

Akaryote —Non-nucleated.

Akatamathesia —Inability to understand.

Akathisia —Acathisia. A condition marked by anxiety, restlessness and inability to sit down or lie as seen in toxic reactions of phenothiazines.

Akinesia, Akinesis —Acinesia. Complete or partial loss of movements.

Akinesthesia —Absence of movement sense.

Akinetic —Pertaining to akinesia.

Al —Chemical symbol for aluminium.

-al —Suffix indicating connection with.

Ala —An expanded or wing-like process, as auricle or pinna of the external ear.

Alacrima —Deficiency or absence of tears.

Alalia —Aphasia.Inability to speak due to defect or paralysis of the vocal organs.

Alalic —Unable to speak.

Ala-nasi —Cartilaginous lateral wall of each nostril.

Alar —Pertaining to an ala, or wing, or like a wing.

Alarming — Exciting fear.

Alate —Winged.

Alba —White or white substance of the brain.

Albation —To make white.

Albedo —Whiteness.

Albicans, Albidum, Albidus —White.

Albiduria —Albinuria. Passing of white or colorless urine.

Albinism —Congenital total or partial absence of pigmentaion in the skin, hair and eyes due to defect in melanin formation.

Albini's nodules — Minute nodules present on the margins of mitral and tricuspid valves of the heart.

Albino —A person suffering from albinism.

Albinoidism —Deficiency of pigment in the skin, hair and eyes, but not to such an extent as seen in albinism.

Albinuria —Albiduria.

Albocinereous —Pertaining to both, white and gray matter of the brain and spinal cord.

Albuginea —A layer of firm, white fibrous tissue investing a part or an organ as of the eye, testis, ovary or spleen.

Albugineotomy —Incision of tunica albuginea, especially of the testis.

Albugineous —Pertaining to or resembling tunica albuginea.

Albuginitis —Inflammation of tunica albuginea.

Albugo —White corneal opacity.

Albumen, Albumin —A kind of protein found in plant and animal tissues, which is soluble in cold water and coagulable by heat. It is found in blood serum as serum albumin.

Albuminate —A compound formed when albumin combines with an acid or alkali.

Albuminaturia —Presence of albumin in the urine.

Albuminemia —Excess of albumin in the blood.

Albuminiferous —Producing albumin.

Albuminiparous —Producing albumin.

Albuminocholia —Presence of albumin in the bile.

Albuminogenous —Producing albumin.

Albuminoid —1. Resembling albumin. 2. A protein.

Albuminolysin — Lysin (an antibody) which splits the albumin.

Albuminolysis — Decomposition or splitting of albumin.

Albuminometer —An instrument for measuring the amount of albumin in the urine.

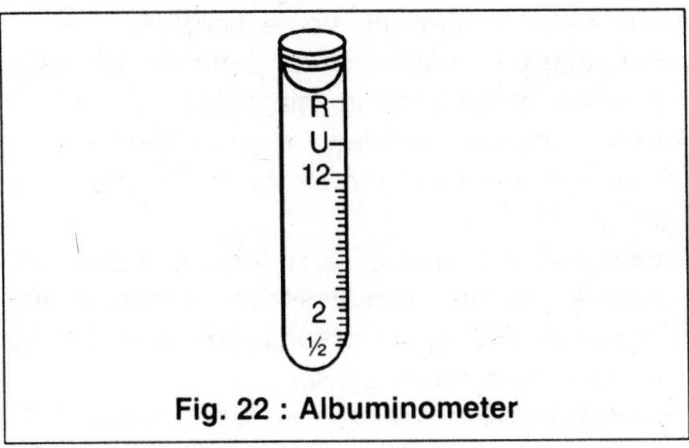

Fig. 22 : Albuminometer

Albuminoptysis —Presence of albumin in the sputum.

Albuminorrhea —Albuminuria. Presence of albumin in the urine.

Albuminose, Albuminous — Pertaining to, resembling or containing albumin.

Albuminosis—Excess of albumin in blood plasma.

Albuminuretic —Pertaining to or causing albuminuria.

Albuminuria —Presence of serum albumin in the urine.

Adolescent albuminuria — Presence of small amounts of albumin in the urine of adolescents.

Albuminuria of athletes —Albuminuria occurring following excessive muscular exertion in athelets.

Cardiac albuminuria — Albuminuria caused by congestive heart failure.

Dietetic albuminuria — Albuminuria occurring following ingestion of certain foods.

Extrarenal albuminuria, Accidental albuminuria — Albuminuria occurring due to contamination of urine with pus or blood etc.

Febrile albuminuria — Albuminuria associated with fever.

Neuropathic albuminuria — Albuminuria associated with epilepsy or other convulsive disorders.

Orthostatic albuminuria — Postural albuminuria.

Patholoigcal albuminuria —Albuminuria caused by a disease.

Physiological or functional albuminuria — Temporary albuminuria not associated with any disease, a trace of albumin is present in normal urine.

Postural albuminuria —The presence of albumin in the urine when the individual has been erect for a long period.

Albumoscope —An instrument for determining the presence of albumin in the urine.

Albumose —The intermediate product of protein digestion which is converted by further digestion into peptone.

Albumosemia —Presence of albumose in the blood.

Albumosuria—Presence of albumose in the urine.

Albus —White.

Alcohol —Alcohol is a colourless, volatile and flammable liquid obtained by the fermentation and distillation of sugar containing food materials such as grapes, vinegar and grains, etc.

Common alcohol —A mixture of ethyl alcohol 95% and water 5% by weight which is commonly used.

Denatured alcohol — Alcohol which is made unfit for drinking by adding toxic substances.

Diluted aicohol — Alcohol containing 41-42% of ethyl alcohol and 58-59% of water by weight. It is used as a solvent.

Ethyl, absolute, dehydrated or grain alcohol —That contains 99% alcohol and not more than 1% of water by weight, having the chemical formula C_2H_5OH.

Methyl alcohol or Wood alcohol —Alcohol obtained from the distillation of wood and having the chemical formula CH_3OH. It is used as a solvent, for fuel and as an additive for denaturing ethyl alcohol. It is not fit for human consumption.

Alcoholemia —Presence of alcohol in the blood.

Alcoholic —1. Pertaining to or containing alcohol or produced by alcohol. 2. A person suffering from alcoholism. 3. One who abuses or is dependent upon alcohol.

Alcoholic blackout —To forget all or part of what occurred during or following a period of alcohol intake.

Alcoholic disinfectant — Ethyl alcohol is the best disinfectant against both gram positive and gram negative bacteria and also Mycobacterium tuberculosis.

Alcoholic fermentation — The conversion of carbohydrates to alcohol through action of yeast.

Alcoholic psychosis — Mental disorder caused by alcoholism.

Alcoholism —Alcohol intoxication.

Acute alcoholism —A condition occurring due to excessive use of alcohol characterized by temporary mental disorders, staggering in walking, blurred or double vision, dilated pupils, flushing of the face, increased pulse rate, low blood pressure, drowsiness or coma. Death may also occur.

Chronic alcoholism —A chronic progressive condition occurring in a person taking alcohol since a long time characterized by occurrence of withdrawal symptoms from decreasing or ceasing the consumption of alcohol, changes in behavior and personality, mental deterioration, peripheral neuropathy, tremulousness, seizures, delirium tremens, anorexia, gastritis, cirrhosis of the liver and vitamin deficiency.

Alcoholization —Saturation with alcohol.

Alcoholomania —Excessive craving for alcohol.

Alcoholometer —An instrument for measuring the quantity of alcohol in a fluid.

Alcoholophilia —Morbid craving for alcohol.

Alcoholophobia —Morbid fear of alcohol, or of becoming an alcoholic.

Alcoholuria — Presence of alcohol in the urine.

Alcohol withdrawal syndrome —Signs and symptoms developed following sudden withdrawal of alcohol from a chronic alcoholic which include tremor or shaking of the hands; increased pulse rate, respiratory rate and temperature; flushing of the face and sweating with dilated pupils, anxiety, panic, hallucinations and confusion etc.

Alcoholysis —Decomposition of a compound by mixing alcohol.

Aldolase — An enzyme present in the skeletal and cardiac muscle and the liver, which converts glycogen into lactic acid.

Aldosterone —A mineralocorticoid hormone secreted by the adrenal cortex which regulates the metabolism of sodium, chloride and potassium.

Aldosteronism —A condition in which the blood contains a large amount of aldosterone hormone.

Aldosteronogenesis — Formation of aldosterone hormone.

Aleppo boil, Delhi boil, Oriental sore —Cutaneous leishmaniasis, caused by infection with the parasite Leishmania tropica and characterized by one or more ulcer formations.

Aleukemia —Absence or deficiency of whie blood cells in the blood.

Aleukemic —Characterized by aleukemia.

Aleukia —Decrease or absence of leukocytes (W.B.C.) in the blood.

Aleukocytic —Showing no leukocytes.

Aleukocytosis —Absence or extreme decrease of white blood cells in the blood.

Alexia —Inability to read, or word blindness.

Alexic —1. Pertaining to alexia. 2. Defensive as an alexin.

Alexin —Complement. A defensive substance present in the normal serum, which in the presence of a specific sensitizer destroys the bacteria and other cells.

Alexipyretic, Antipyretic —Reducing fever.

Alexithymia —Inability to recognize and describe one's feelings, and defining them in terms of physical symptoms, that commonly occurs after an injury.

Algae —The very small plants without roots, stems or leaves containing chlorophyll living generally in moist places.

Algefacient —Refrigerant or cooling.

Algesia, Algesthesia — Hypersensitiveness to pain.

Algesic —Painful.

Algesichronometer —An instrument for measuring the time taken to feel pain.

Algesimeter, Algometer —An instrument for measuring the degree of sensitivity to pain as produced by pricking with a sharp pointed object.

Algesimetry —Measurement of sensitivity to pain.

Algesiogenic —Pain producing.

Algesthesia, Algesia —1. Perception of pain. 2. Hypersensitiveness to pain.

Algetic —Algesic. Painful.

-algia —Suffix indicating pain.

Algicide —Destroying algae.

Algid —Cold or chilly.

Algiomotor, Algiomuscular —Causing painful muscular contractions..

Algiomuscular —Algiomotor.
Algo- —Prefix indicating pain.
Algodystrophy —Pain with dystrophic changes in a bone.
Algogenesis —Production of pain.
Algogenic —1. Producing pain. 2. Lowering temperature of the body below normal.
Algolagnia —Sexual satisfaction occurring by feeling pain.
Algology, Phycology — Scientific study of pain.
Algometer —Algesimeter.
Algometry —Algesimetry.
Algophilia —Increasement in pleasure of sexual intercourse by experiencing pain.
Algophobia —Morbid fear of pain.
Algor —Chill or rigor.
Algor mortis —The lowering of body temperature gradually after death.
Algos —Pain.
Algospasm —Painful spasm or cramp.
Algovascular —Pertaining to the changes in the lumen of the blood vessels occurring under the influence of pain.
Alible —Nutritive.
Alien —Foreigner.
Alienate —To isolate oneself.
Alienation —Isolation especially from the society.
Alienia —Absence of the spleen.
Alienist —Specialist in mental diseases.
Aliform —Wing-shaped.
Aliform process —Wing of the sphenoid bone.
Alignment—To arrange in a straight line or to bring in normal position as in orthopedics, placing the portions of a fractured bone into normal position or in dentistry, bringing teeth in correct position.
Aliment —Food, nutritive material.
Alimentary —Pertaining to food or nutritive material or to the digestive organs.
Alimentary canal —The digestive tube extending from the mouth to the anus.
Alimentation —The process of nourishing the body, which includes mastication, swallowing, digestion, absorption and assimilation.
  Artificial alimentation —Nourishment of the body by feeding by intravenous route or by a nasal tube passed into the stomach of the patient unable to take nourishment orally.
  Rectal alimentation — Feeding by enemas of nutrient materials.
Alimentotherapy, Dietotherapy — Treatment of diseases by food.
Alinement —Alignment.
Aliphatic —Fatty or oily.
Alipotropic —Having no effect upon fat metabolism.
Alkalemia —Increased alkalinity of the blood.
Alkalescence —Process of becoming alkaline.
Alkalescent —Alkaline or becoming alkaline.
Alkali —An alkali is a strong base, especially the metallic hydroxide which neutralizes acid and combining with it forms salt. It turns red litmus paper blue.
Alkalimeter —An apparatus for measuring the degree of alkalinity of a mixture.
Alkalimetry —Measurement of degree of alkalinity of a mixture.
Alkaline —Having the reaction of an alkali.
Alkaline reserve —The amount of base mainly the bicarbonates present in the blood. When it decreases, the condition is known as acidosis, when it increases, the condition is known as alkalosis.
Alkaline tide —The increase in alkaline reserve and occurrence of alkaline urine after taking food during gastric digestion.
Alkalinity —The condition of being alkaline.
Alkalinize —Alkalize. To make alkaline.
Alkalinuria —Alkaluria. Alkaline urine.
Alkalipenia —Low alkaline reserve of the body.
Alkali reserve —Alkaline reserve.
Alkalitherapy —Treatment of diseases with alkalies.
Alkalization —Process of making alkaline.
Alkalize —Alkalinize. To make alkaline.
Alkalizer —That which causes alkalization.
Alkaloid —One of a group of organic alkaline substances obtained from the plants. Alkaloids react with the acids to form salts which are used in medicine.
Alkalometery —Determination of the alkali content of a substance.
Alkalosis —A condition caused by a rise of alkali reserve in the blood.
  Altitude alkalosis — Increased alkalinity in the blood due to exposure to high altitudes. This causes respiratory alkalosis.
  Compensated alkalosis—A condition in which the compensatory mechanisms have returned the pH of blood to normal.
  Hypochloremic alkalosis —Metabolic alkalosis due to loss of chloride, which is produced by severe vomiting.
  Hypokalemic alkalosis —Metabolic alkalosis due to excess of potassium loss, which may be caused by diuretic therapy.

Metabolic alkalosis —Alkalosis caused by loss of acid by excessive vomiting, loss of potassium from the body and ingestion of sodium bicarbonate in excess.

Respiratory alkalosis —A condition due to excessive loss of carbon dioxide from the body.

Alkalotherapy —Alkalitherapy. Treatment of diseases by alkalies.

Alkalotic —Pertaining to alkalosis.

Alkaluria —Alkalinuria. Alkalinity of urine.

Alkaptonuria —Presence of alkapton bodies in the urine.

All-, Allo- —Prefix meaning other, different or divergence from the normal.

Allachesthesia — Allesthesia Feeling of pain at the place remote from the point of actual pricking by a pointed object.

Allantiasis —Sausage poisoning.

Allantochorion —Fusion of allantois and chorion into one structure.

Allantogenesis —Formation and development of allantois.

Allantoic —Pertaining to allantois.

Allantoid —Resembling allantois.

Allantoin —A white crystalline substance occurring in allantoic and amniotic fluids in mammals as the end product of purine metabolism.

Allantoinuria —Presence of allantoin in the urine.

Allantois —A fetal appendage arising from the ventral surface of the fetus and its blood vessels give rise to those of the umbilical cord.

Allay —To put down, to calm, to lighten, to repress.

Allele —One of two or more different genes occupying the corresponding sites on homologous paired chromosomes, due to which the hereditary characters are altered.

Allelic —Pertaining to alleles.

Allelic gene —Allele.

Allelocatalysis —Stimulation of a bacterial culture by the addition of cells of the same type.

Allelocatalytic —Mutually catalytic. Denoting two substances each of which is decomposed in the presence of other.

Allelomorph —Allele.

Allelotaxis —Development of an organ from several embryonic structures.

Allenthesis —Introduction of a foreign substance into the body.

Allergen, Allergenic —Any substance causing allergy.

Allergenic — Allergen.

Allergic —Pertaining to, sensitive to, or caused by allergen.

Allergid —A papular or nodular allergic skin reaction.

Allergist —Physician specialist in allergy.

Allergization —To cause allergy by introducing a foreign substance into the body.

Allergology —The science of study of allergy.

Allergosis —Any abnormal condition characterized by allergy.

Allergy —Occurrence of a hypersensitive reaction to a substance (allergen) which does not normally causes any reaction. It is due to the release of histamine or histamine-like substances from the damaged cells. Allergic condition include urticaria, shock, bronchial asthma, allergic rhinitis or coryza and eczema etc.

Causes :—Inhalants—dust, pollen grains, fur, hair, smoke, perfumes, foul smells etc. Foods— milk, egg, potatoes etc. Drugs—antibiotics such as penicillin, serums etc. Infectious agents—bacteria, viruses, fungi and parasites etc. Contactants—Chemicals, insect or animal bites, plants and metals etc. Physical agents—Heat, cold, light, radiation, pressure etc.

Allesthesia —Perception of a sensation, *e.g.*, pain or touch at a place remote from the point of stimulation.

Alleviate —To relieve.

Alliaceous —Tasting like garlic or onions.

Allochesthesia —Allestheisa.

Allochezia, Allochetia—Excretion of feces through an abnormal opening.

Allochiria, Allocheiria — Allesthesia.

Allochroism —Change in color.

Allochromasia —Change in color of the hair or skin.

Allocinesia —Movement on the side of the body opposite to the one the patient has been directed to move.

Allodynia—Pain resulting from non-noxious stimulus.

Alloerotism —Sexual attraction toward another person.

Allograft —Transplant tissue obtained from the same species.

Allokinesis —Involuntary movements.

Alokinetic —Pertaining to or characterized by involuntary movements.

Allolalia —Speech defect due to brain lesion.

Allomerism —Change in chemical constitution without a change in form.

Allomorphism —Change in form without a change in chemical constitution.

Allongement —Lengthening of a structure by surgery.

Allopath —The person who practices in allopathy.

Allopathic —Pertaining to allopathy.

Allopathy —A system of treatment of a disease by producing a pathological reaction which is antagonistic to the disease.

Allophasis —To speak incoherent words.

Alloplasia, Heteroplasia —Development of a tissue at a place where it should not occur normally.

Alloplast —A harmless foreign body used for implantation into the tissue.

Alloplastic —Pertaining to an alloplast.

Alloplasty —1. Direction of sexual desire away from self to other people. 2. Plastic surgery using inert material.

Alloploid —Relating to a hybrid individual with two or more sets of chromosomes derived from two different ancestral species.

Alloploidy —The condition of being alloploid.

Allopolyploid —An alloploid having three or more haploid sets of chromosomes.

Allopolyploidy —The condition of being allopolyploid.

Allopsychic —Pertaining to the mental processes in relation to the external world.

Allopsychosis —Derangement of perceptive powers.

Allorhythmia —Irregularity of the regular heart beat or pulse.

Allorhythmic —Relating to or characterized by allorhythmia.

All-or-none law —In response to a stimulus, the heart will either contract to its full extent or not at all.

Allosome —A foreign constituent of the cytoplasm of a cell which has entered from out side.

Allotherm —An animal whose body temperature varies according to the temperature of the environment.

Allotoxin —A substance present in the body which neutralizes a specific toxin.

Allotransplantation — Transplantation of tissue from one individual into another of the same species.

Allotriodontia —1. Growth of a tooth in some abnormal location. 2. Transplantation of teeth.

Allotriogeustia —Perverted sense of taste.

Allotriophagy —Perversion of appetite with ingestion of material unfit for food as clay, ash or plaster, etc.

Allotriosmia —Incorrect identification of odor.

Allotriuria —Abnormal urine.

Allotropic —1. Showing or pertaining to allotropism. 2. A person interested in others.

Allotropism, Allotropy — Existence of an element in two or more distinct forms with different physical properties.

Alloy —A metallic substance, *e.g.,* brass made by fusion of two or more metals.

Alochia — Absence of vaginal discharge after child-birth.

Aloe —Dry extract of the plant aloe which is used in preparing medicines.

Alogia —Inability to speak due to lesion of the central nervous system.

Alopecia — Baldness, loss of hair from the skin especially of the head.

Alopecia adnata — Congenital baldness.

Alopecia areata — Loss of hair appearing in well defined patches usually involving the scalp or beard.

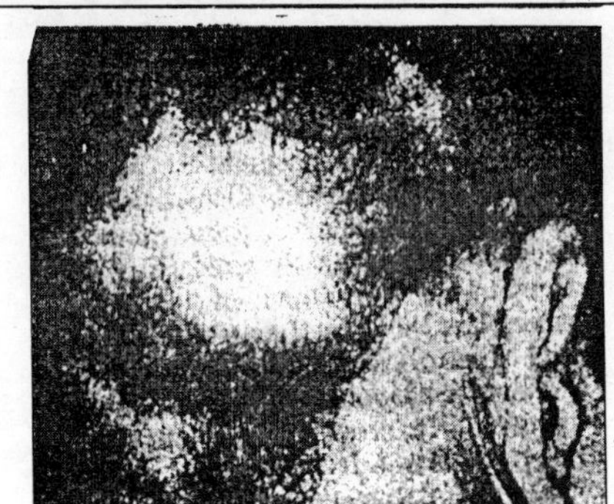

Fig. 23 A : Alopecia areata

Alopecia capitis totalis —Complete absence of hair of the scalp.

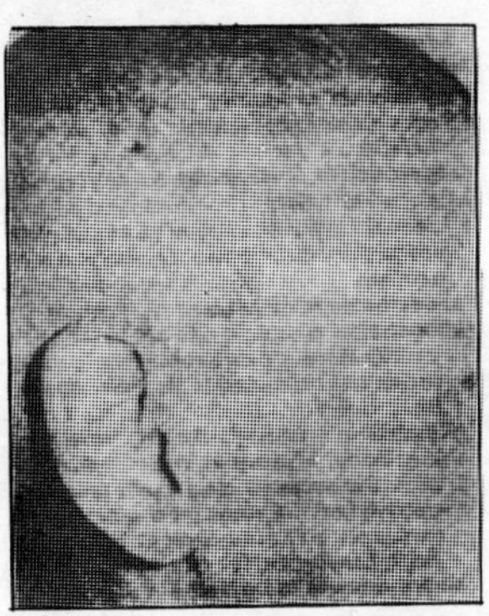

Fig. 23 B : Alopecia capitis totalis

Alopecia cicatricial —Loss of hair due to scar tissue formation.

Alopecia follicularis —Baldness due to inflammation of the hair follicles on the scalp.

Alopecia generalisata —Loss of hair from the whole of body.

Alopecia leprotica — Lack of lateral third of the eyebrows, eyelashes and body hairs in leprosy.

Alopecia medicamentosa — Loss of hair produced by some medicines, especially by those containing cytotoxic substances.

Alopecia neurotica — Loss of hair due to psychological causes, mental stress, after a nervous disease or injury to the nervous system.

Alopecia senilis — Baldness occurring in old age.

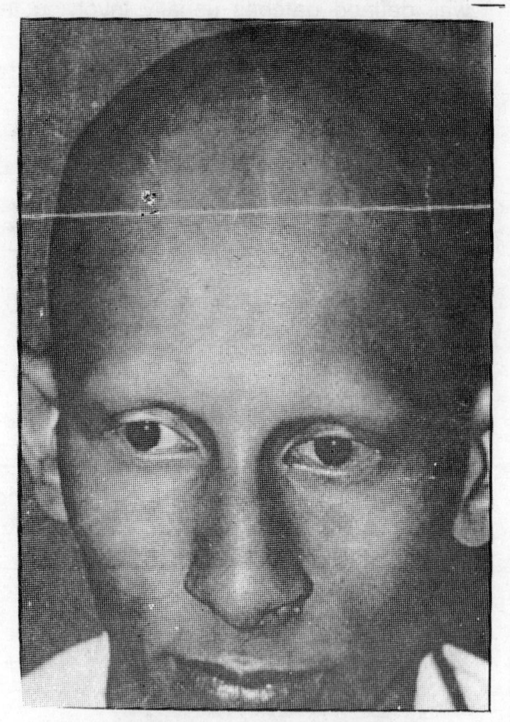

Fig 23 C : Alopecia universalis

Alopecia symptomatica —Alopecia occurring after a prolonged fever as typhoid fever or during the course of a disease.

Alopecia syphilitica —Alopecia occurring in the form of patches at the back of neck in secondary syphilis, which appears as moth-eaten.

Alopecia totalis — Complete absence of the hair from the scalp.

Alopecia toxica — Loss of hair due to toxins of the infectious disease.

Alopecia universalis — Complete absence of hair from whole of the body.

Alopecic —Pertaining to or suffering from alopecia.

Alpha —1. First letter of the Greek alphabet. 2. In chemistry, a letter used to indicate the first in a series of isomeric compounds or to indicate the position of substituting atoms or groups.

Alpha-adrenergic blocking agents —These are the exciters of the effects of sympathomimetic drugs such as adrenaline and noradrenaline, and raise the blood pressure.

Alpha-adrenergic receptor — A site in the pathways of the autonomic nervous system wherein excitatory responses occur when adrenergic substances such as adrenaline and noradrenaline are released.

Alpha-tocopherol —Vitamin E.

Alter —To castrate, to change.

Alteration —Change.

Alternans —Alternation as alternans pulsus in which strong pulses alternate with the weak ones.

Altherm, Altherm pad —An apparatus containing heat-producing chemicals for applying heat to the eye or a sinus.

alt. hor. —Every other hour.

Altitude sickness —A disease caused by decreased atmospheric oxygen as on flying or climbing on mountain and characterized by headache, dyspnea, malaise, fainting and even death if severe.

Altricious —Slowly developing, requiring long nursing.

Al-trigenderism —Natural tendency of mixing up with the person of opposite sex by playing games, lengthy conversation etc.

Alum — A kind of mineral salt used usually locally to check the bleeding.

Aluminosis —Chronic inflammation of the lungs due to inhalation of the alum particles in alum workers.

Alvei —Plural of alveus.

Alveoalgia —Alveolalgia.

Alveobronchiolitis, Alveobronchitis — Inflammation of the bronchioles and pulmonary alveoli.

Alveo-labial —Pertaining to the alveolus and the lips.

Alveolalgia —Pain in the alveolus of a tooth.

Alveolar —Pertaining to an alveolus.

Alveolar duct —A branch of a bronchiole which passes into the alveoli of the lung.

Alveolar periosteum — Periodontium. The connective tissue between a tooth and the alveolar bone.

Alveolar process —The part of the mandible and maxilla containing the tooth sockets.

Alveolate —Honeycombed; pitted.

Alveolectomy —Removal of the whole or part of the alveolar process by surgery.

Alveoli —Plural of alveolus

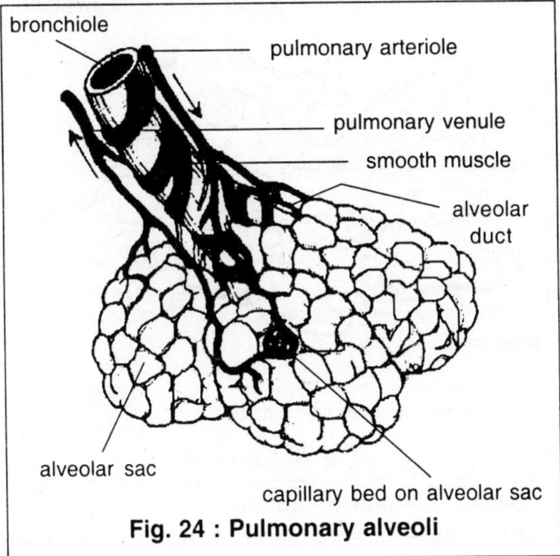

Fig. 24 : Pulmonary alveoli

Alveolitis —Inflammation of an alveolus.

Alveoloclasia —Destruction of a tooth socket or alveolus.

Alveolodental —Pertaining to the alveolus of the tooth and to the tooth itself.

Alveololingual — Pertaining to the alveolar process and the tongue.

Alveoloplasty —Repair of the alveolar process by plastic surgery.

Alveolotomy —To make an incision into the alveolus of a tooth.

Alveolus —1. Tooth socket. 2. Air cell of the lungs.

Alveus —A canal or groove.

Alvine —Pertaining to the abdomen or intestines.

Alvus —Abdomen and viscera.

Alymphia —Complete or partial deficiency of lymph.

Alymphocytosis — Lymphopenia; deficiency or absence of lymphocytes in the blood.

Alymphoplasia — Failure of lymph tissue to develop.

a.m.a. —Against medical advice.

Amaas —A mild form of smallpox.

Amacrine —Without long processes.

Amacrine cell —A modified nerve cell in retina with short branches (dendrites) but without long process (axon).

Amalgam —An alloy containing mercury which is used in dentistry to restore teeth.

Amalgamate —To make an amalgam.

Amalgamation —The process of mixing metals with mercury to produce amalgam.

Amalgamator —An apparatus for mixing the metal with the mercury.

Amarthritis —Polyarthritis. Inflammation of more than one joint at a time.

Amasesis —Inability to masticate the food.

Amastia —Congenital absence of one or both breasts.

Amathophobia —Morbid fear of dust or dirt.

Amativeness —1. Sexual desire. 2. Desire to love.

Amaurosis —Blindness, especially that which is not due to any lesion of the eye.

- **Albuminuric amaurosis** —Amaurosis caused by kidney disease.
- **Congenital amaurosis** —Blindness since birth.
- **Diabetic amaurosis** — Blindness associated with diabetes mellitus.
- **Epileptoid amaurosis** —Sudden blindness occurring after an attack of epilepsy.
- **Fugax amaurosis** — Temporary blindness occurring due to insufficient blood flow to the retina, which may last upto 10 minutes.
- **Reflex amaurosis** — Blindness due to reflex action caused by irritation of a remote part.
- **Saburral amaurosis** — Blindness occurring with acute gastritis.
- **Toxic amaurosis** — Blindness due to optic neuritis caused by toxins which may be endogenous, such as in diabetes, or exogenous, as in alcohol or tobacco.
- **Uremic amaurosis** — Blindness occurring in uremia.

Amaurotic —Pertaining to amaurosis or suffering from it.

Amaxophobia —Morbid fear of vehicles.

Amazia —Amastia.

Ambageusia — Loss of taste from both sides of the tongue.

Ambi- —Prefix indicating both, both sides, around or about.

Ambidexterity —The ability to use both the hands with equal ease.

Ambidextrism —Syn. Ambidexterity.

Ambidextrous — Capable of working effectively with either hand.

Ambient —Surrounding.

Ambiguous —To have several meanings or interpretations.

Ambilateral — Pertaining to both sides.

Ambilevous —Unable to use both hands with equal strength.

Ambiopia —Diplopia. Double vision.

Ambisexual —Pertaining to both sexes.

Ambitendency —Ambivalence of the will.

Ambivalence—Coexistence of contradictory ideas about a person or an object.

Ambivalent —Pertaining to or characterized by ambivalence.

Amblyacousia —Dullness of hearing.

Amblyaphia —Dullness of the sense of touch.

Amblychromasia —The condition in which the cell nucleus stains faintly.

Amblychromatic —Staining faintly.

Amblygeustia —Defective taste.

Amblyogenic —Inducing amblyopia.

Amblyope —Suffering from amblyopia.

Amblyopia —Dimness of vision without apparent cause of the eye.

Color amblyopia — Dimness of color vision.

Crossed amblyopia — Amblyopia of one eye with hemianesthesia of the opposite side of the face.

Deprivation amblyopia — Amblyopia resulting from nonuse of the eye as usually occurs in cataract.

Ex anopsia amblyopia — Amblyopia occurring usually in one eye due to disuse since a long time.

Nutritional amblyopia — Amblyopia resulting from lack of vit. B complex.

Reflex amblyopia — Amblyopia due to irritation of the peripheral area.

Toxic amblyopia — Amblyopia due to tobacco, alcohol, drugs or any other toxic substances.

Uremic amblyopia — Dimness of vision occurring in uremia.

Amblyopiatrics —Treatment of amblyopia.

Amblyopic —Pertaining to, or suffering from amblyopia.

Amblyoscope —An instrument for increasing the vision in an amblyopic eye.

Ambon —The elevated ring of fibrocartilage around the edge of a bone socket.

Ambos —Incus or anvil bone of the middle ear.

Ambulance —A vehicle for carrying the patient and injured person to the hospital.

Ambulant, Ambulatory —Able to walk, not confined to bed.

Ameba —A unicellular animal found in soil and water and inhabitates as parasite in man having fingerlike processes of protoplasm known as pseudopodia, by which it moves about and gets its food. It causes amebic dysentery.

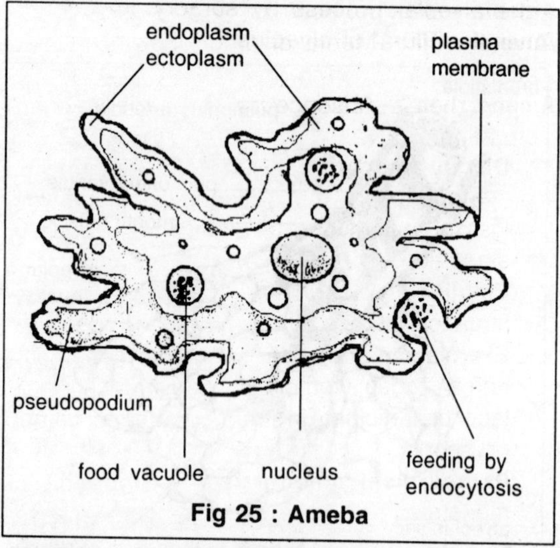

Fig 25 : Ameba

Amebae —Plural of ameba.

Amebiasis —Inflammation of the mucous membrane of the colon caused by Entameba histolytica associated with dysentery with the passage of mucus, and amebic hepatitis (inflammation of the liver) may occur as a complication with abscess formation.

Amebic —Pertaining to or caused by ameba.

Amebicidal —Amebicide.

Amebicide, Amebacide — Destroying amebae.

Amebiform —Ameba-shaped.

Amebocyte —Any cell showing ameboid movements.

Ameboid —Amebiform. Resembling an ameba.

Ameboidism —Ameba-like movements.

Ameboma —A tumor-like mass in the intestine caused by amebiasis.

Ameburia —Presence of amebae in the urine.

Amelanotic —Lacking melanin pigments. Unpigmented.

Amelia —Congenital absence of one or more limbs.

Amelification —Formation of dental enamel by ameloblasts.

Amelioration—Improvement.

Ameloblast —Enamel forming cell.

Ameloblastoma —A tumor of the jaw especially of the lower jaw, which is characteristic of the enamel.

Amelodentinal —Pertaining to both, enamel and dentin.

Amelogenesis —Formation of dental enamel.

Amelogenic —Forming enamel.

Amelus —A fetus without arms and legs.

Amenia —Amenorrhea.

Amenomania —Mental disorder of pleasing character.

Amenorrhea —Absence or stoppage of menstruation.

Dietary amenorrhea, Nutritional amenorrhea —Stoppage of menstruation accompanying loss of weight due to dietary restrictions or starvation.

Emotional amenorrhea — Stoppage of menstruation due to shock, fright or hysteria.

Exercise amenorrhea — Amenorrhea occurring in those women who do hard physical labor or participate in strenuous outdoor games or sports.

Pathological amenorrhea —Stoppage of menstruation due to some organic disease.

Physiological amenorrhea —Absence of menstruation before puberty and its stoppage during pregnancy, lactation and after menopause, not related to any organic disease.

Postpartum amenorrhea — Amenorrhea following childbirth that lasts for only a month or two.

Primary amenorrhea —Absence of menstruation after puberty, *i.e.,* after the age of 18 yrs.

Secondary amenorrhea —Stoppage of menstruation after it has once been started at puberty.

Amenorrheal, Amenorrheic —Pertaining to, accompanied by, or due to amenorrhea.

Amenorrheic —Pertaining to amenorrhea.

Amensalism —Symbiosis in which one is harmed and the other is benefitted.

Ament —Idiot.

Amentia —1. Congenital mental deficiency 2. Mental disorder characterized by confusion and disorientation.

Amentia agitata — Amentia characterized by excitement.

Amentia attonita — Amentia characterized by lazyness.

Amential —Pertaining to amentia.

Amerism —The quality of not dividing into parts.

Ameristic —Not divided into parts.

Ametria —Congenital absence of the uterus.

Ametrohemia —Less blood supply to the uterus.

Ametrometer —Instrument for measuring the degree of ametropia.

Ametropia —A condition of the eye in which an image of an object does not come to a proper focus on the retina, which causes hyperopia (farsightedness), myopia (nearsightedness) or astigmatism.

Ametropic —The person suffering from ametropia.

Amianthinopsy —Voilet blindness.

Amicrobic —1. Lacking microbes. 2. Not produced by microbes.

Amicroscopic —Too small to be visible by the microscope.

Amimia —Loss of power of expression of the ideas by signs or gestures.

Amimia amnesic — Amimia in which signs and gestures can be made but their meaning is not remembered.

Amimia ataxic — Amimia in which signs and gestures cannot be made.

Amino acids —These are the end products of protein digestion and are body builders.

Aminoacidemia —Presence of an excess of amino acids in the blood.

Aminoacidopathies —Various diseases of amino acid metabolism.

Aminoaciduria —An excess of amino acids in the urine.

Aminuria —Presence of amines in the urine.

Amitosis —Direct cell division, *i.e.,* the cell divides by simple cleavage of the nucleus without any change in it.

Ammoaciduria —Abnormal amount of ammonia and amino acids in the urine.

Ammonemia, Ammoniemia —Excess of ammonia in the blood.

Ammonia —An alkaline gas formed by the decomposition of proteins and amino acids. (NH_3).

Ammoniacal —Having the characteristic of or pertaining to ammonia.

Ammoniated —Containing ammonia.

Ammoniuria —Excess of ammonia in the urine.

Amnesia —Loss of memory.

Anterograde amnesia — Loss of memory for the events occurring after receiving an injury.

Emotional amnesia — Loss of memory due to some psychological cause.

Retrograde amnesia — Loss of memory for the events occurring before receiving an injury.

Transient global amnesia —Transient loss of memory occurring in healthy persons, which may last for a few hours. There is loss of memory for recent events though remote memory is retained.

Traumatic amnesia — Loss of memory caused by sudden physical injury.

Visual amnesia — Inability to remember the appearance of the objects or to have a knowledge of the printed words.

Amnesiac —Amnesic.

Amnesic —Pertaining to or suffering from amnesia.

Amnesic aphasia —Loss of memory for words.

Amnestic —Pertaining to or causing amnesia.

Amniocentesis —Transabodominal puncture of the amniotic sac using a needle and syringe in order to aspirate the amniotic fluid.

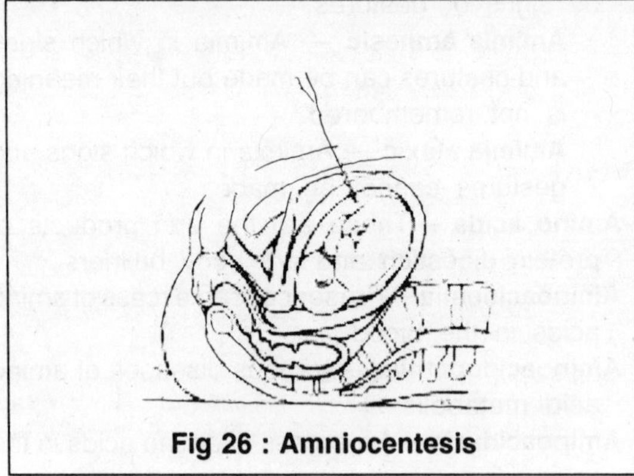

Fig 26 : Amniocentesis

Amniochorial, Amniochorionic—Pertaining to both amnion and chorion.

Amniogenesis —Formation of the amnion.

Amniography —X-ray examination of the amniotic sac after injection of a radiopaque substance into the amniotic fluid to diagnose the fetal abnormalities.

Amniohook —An instrument for making a hole in the amniotic sac without injuring the fetus.

Amnioinfusion —Injection of solutions into the amniotic fluid, usually done to induce abortion.

Amnion —Amniotic sac. A bag of thin transparent membrane which is commonly called as bag of waters and which holds the fetus floating in a fluid known as amniotic fluid.

Amnionic —Amniotic. Pertaining to amnion.

Amnionitis —Inflammation of the amnion.

Amniorrhea —Escape of the amniotic fluid.

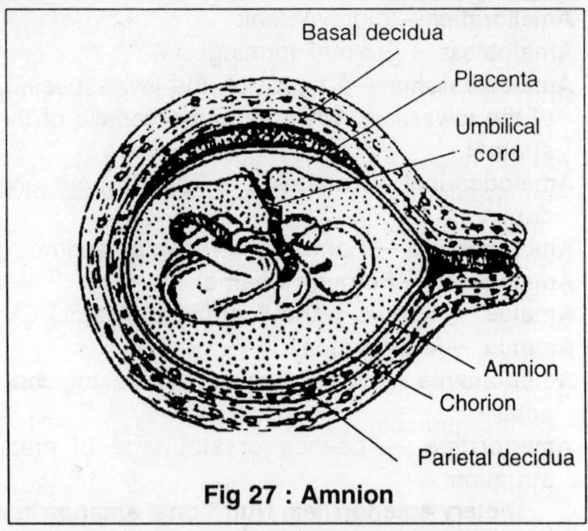

Fig 27 : Amnion

Amniorrhexis —Rupture of the amnion.

Amnioscope —An endoscope which is used to visualize the fetus and the amniotic fluid by passing it through the abdominal wall into the amniotic cavity of the mother.

Amnioscopy —Examination of the fetus and the amniotic fluid by using endoscope.

Amniotic —Pertaining to amnion.

Amniotic cavity —The cavity of the amnion filled with fluid.

Amniotic fluid —A colorless and transparent liquid contained in the amniotic sac.

Amniotic sac —Amnion.

Amniotitis —Inflammation of the amnion.

Amniotome —An instrument for cutting the fetal membranes.

Amniotomy —Surgical rupture of the fetal membranes to induce labor.

Amnitis — Inflammation of the amnion.

Amoeba —Ameba.

Amor —Love, especially sexual love.

Amorous —Inclined to love.

Amorphagnosia —Inability to recognize the size and shape of the objects.

Amorphia, Amorphism —The condition of being without definite form.

Amorphous, Amorphic — Without definite structure.

Amorphus —A malformed fetus with undeveloped head, limbs and heart.

Amotio —A removing or detachment, e.g., detachment of retina.

Amphi- —Prefix indicating on both sides, on all sides, double.

Amphiarthrosis —A joint in which the opposite bony surfaces are connected by cartilages so that the joint move slightly, as the joints of the vertebrae.

Amphiblestritis —Retinitis. Inflammation of the retina.

Amphibolia —Vacillating period of disease.

Amphibolic —1. Uncertain 2. Having both, an anabolic and a catabolic function.

Amphicelous —Concave at both ends, as a vertebra.

Amphicentric—Beginning and ending in the same vessel.

Amphichroic, Amphichromatic —1. Turning red litmus paper blue, and blue red. 2. Reacting both as an acid and an alkali. 3. Showing double colors.

Amphicrania —Pain on both sides of the head.

Amphigonadism —Possession of both ovarian and testicular tissue.

Amphigony —Sexual reproduction.

Amphimicrobe —A microorganism that is either aerobic or anaerobic according to the environment.

Amphimixis —Mixing of maternal and paternal germ cells in reproduction, thus giving rise to the hereditary characteristics from both parents.

Ampho- —Prefix indicating both.

Amphocyte —A cell staining with either acid or basic stains.

Amphodiplopia —Double vision in each eye.

Ampholyte —An organic or inorganic substance acting as an acid or alkali.

Amphophil, Amphophilous —Staining with either acid or basic dyes.

Amphoric —Similar to the sound produced by blowing into a hollow jar.

Amphoric voice —The sound heard in percussion and auscultation resembling the noise made by blowing across the mouth of a bottle.

Amphoteric, Amphoterous — Capable of reacting both as an acid and a base.

Amphotericity —The quality of being amphoteric.

Amphoterism —The possession of both acid and basic properties.

Amphoterodiplopia — Amphodiplopia.

Amphotonia, Amphotony —Hyperexcitability of both, the sympathetic and parasympathetic nervous systems.

Amplification —Increasement.

Amplifier —That which increases.

Amplitude —Extent, largeness, abundance or fullness.

Ampule —A small perfectly sealed glass container containing sterilized medicine for use by injection.

Ampulla —The dilated portion of a tubular structure.

Ampulla ductus deferens—The enlarged and twisted distal end of the vas deferens.

Ampulla hepatopancreatica —The dilatation formed by junction of the common bile duct and the pancreatic duct before their opening into the duodenum.

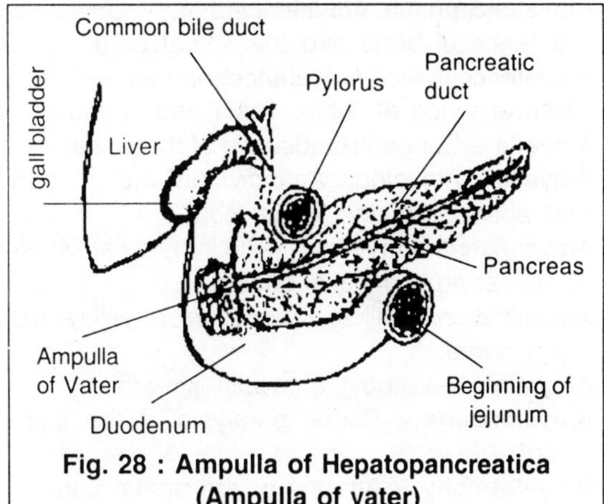

Fig. 28 : Ampulla of Hepatopancreatica (Ampulla of vater)

Ampulla of rectum — Slight dilatation of the rectum just before beginning of the anal canal.

Ampulla of semicircular ducts —The dilatation at one end of each of the three semicircular ducts.

Ampulla of uterine tube —The dilated distal end of the uterine tube.

Ampulla phrenic —Lower dilated end of the esophagus.

Ampullar —Pertaining to an ampulla.

Ampullitis —Inflammation of an ampulla.

Ampullula —A small dilatation, especially of a lymph or blood vessel.

Amputation —Removal, usually by surgery of a limb, part or organ, from the body.

Amputation congenital —Amputation of the fetal parts in uterus.

Amputation in contiguity —Amputation at a joint.

Amputation in continuity —Amputation elsewhere than at a joint.

Amputation primary—Amputation performed before the inflammation sets in.

Amputation secondary — Amputation performed during the period of suppuration.

Amputation spontaneous —Separation of an extremity or digit from the body without surgery.

Amputation tertiary — Amputation performed after the subsidence of the inflammation.

Amputee —The person who has been amputated.

Amuck —Madly.

Amusia —Inability to produce or recognize music.

Amychophobia—1. Morbid fear of being scratched. 2. Fear of the claws of any animal.

Amyelencephalia, Amyelencephaly —Congenital absence of brain and the spinal cord.

Amyelencephalic, Amyelencephalous —A fetus with absence of both brain and spinal cord.

Amyelia —Congenital absence of the spinal cord.

Amyelic —Amyelous. An individual with congenital absence of the spinal cord.

Amyelinated, Amyelinic — Unmyelinated. Not possessing a myelin sheath.

Amyelination—Failure of formation of myelin sheath of a nerve.

Amyelinic —Without a myelin sheath.

Amyeloneuria —Partial paralysis of the spinal cord.

Amyelotrophy —Atrophy of the spinal cord.

Amyelus —A fetus without spinal cord.

Amygdala —Almond. Tonsil.

Amygdaline —1. Almond-shaped. 2. Pertaining to a tonsil, tonsillar.

Amygdaloid —Resembling a tonsil or an almond.

Amygdalolith —Stone in a tonsil.

Amygdalopathy —Any disease of a tonsil.

Amygdalotome —An instrument for excising a tonsil.

Amygdalotomy —To incise the tonsil.

Amylaceous —Starchy.

Amylasuria —Excretion of amylase in the urine.

Amylemia —Presence of starch in the blood.

Amylodyspepsia —Inability to digest the starchy foods.

Amylogen —Soluble starch.

Amylogenesis —The formation of starch.

Amylogenic —Forming starch.

Amyloid —A homogenous, waxy, translucent material, probably a glycoprotein resembling starch and deposited in intercelluar spaces in various diseases.

Amyloid nephrosis —A nephrotic syndrome from myeloid degeneration of the kidney.

Amyloidoma —A tumor within which amyloid is produced.

Amyloidosis —It is a disease in which amyloid is deposited extracellularly in tissues and organs. The disease may be primary without any cause, secondary to chronic diseases such as tuberculosis, syphilis, Hodgkin's disease and rheumatoid arthritis etc. and hereditary.

Amylolysis —Hydrolysis of starch into sugar in the process of digestion.

Amylolytic —Pertaining to or characterized by amylolysis.

Amylolytic enzyme, Amylase —An enzyme that hydrolysis starch.

Amylopectin, Amylin — The insoluble constituent of starch, the soluble constituent is amylose.

Amylophagia —Excessive desire for starch.

Amylorrhea —Presence of excessive starch in the stools.

Amylorrhexis —Enzymatic splitting of starch.

Amylose —1. Any carbohydrate other than glucose or saccharose. 2. The soluble constituent of starch.

Amylosis —Amyloidosis.

Amylosuria —Presence of amylose in the urine.

Amylum —Starch.

Amyluria —An excess of starch in the urine.

Amyocardia —Weakness of the heart muscle.

Amyoesthesia, Amyoesthesis —Absence of muscle sensation.

Amyoplasia —Absence of muscle formation.

Amyoplasia congenita — Congenital rigidity and deformity of most of the joints due to lack of muscle formation or development.

Amyostasia —Difficulty in standing due to muscular tremors.

Amyostatic —Showing muscular tremors.

Amyosthenia —Weakness of the muscles.

Amyosthenic —Pertaining to or causing muscular weakness.

Amyotaxia —Amyotaxy

Amyotaxy —Muscular ataxia.

Amyotonia —Lack of muscular tone.

Amyotrophia, Amyotrophy —Atrophy of the muscles.

Amyotrophic —Pertaining to atrophy of the muscles.

Amyous —1. Deficient in muscular power. 2. Without muscle.

Amyxia —Absence of mucus.

Amyxorrhea —Absence of mucous secretion.

An- —Prefix indicating without or not.

Anabasis —Period of increased severity of a disease.

Anabiosis —Resuscitation. Bringing back to consciousness.
Anabiotic —Restorative.
Anabolergy —The energy spent in anabolism.
Anabolic —Promoting or pertaining to anabolism.
Anabolin, Anabolite —A product of anabolism.
Anabolism —The constructive process in which a cell takes from the blood the substance required for building up the body and converts this non-living substance into the living cytoplasm of the cell.
Anabolite —Anabolin.
Anabrosis —Superficial ulceration of the soft tissue.
Anabrotic —A substance that produces anabrosis.
Anacamptics—Study of reflexion of light or sound.
Anacamptometer —An apparatus for measuring the intensity of deep reflexes.
Anacatharsis —Severe prolonged vomiting.
Anacathartic —Emetic. The substance which causes vomiting.
Anacidity —Deficiency of acidity especially of hydrochloric acid in the gastric juice.
Anaclasis — Reflection of light or sound.
Anaclisis —The state of leaning against or depending on something.
Anaclitic —Leaning or depending upon.
Anacousia —Anakusis. Total deafness.
Anacrotic pulse —A pulse in which two small waves occur on ascending limb of tracing of a pulse wave, as in aortic stenosis.
Anacrotism —Existence of two small waves on the ascending limb of tracing of a pulse wave.
Anacusis —Anacusia, anakusis. Total deafness.
Anadenia —1. Absence of glands. 2. Reduced glandular function.
Anadicrotic —Anacrotic.
Anadicrotism —Anacrotism.
Anadidymus —The condition in which the lower extremities of two fetuses are joined together.
Anadipsia —Intense thirst.
Anadrenalism —Failure of the adrenal function.
Anaerobe —An organism that can live and grow in the absence of oxygen.
Anaerobic —Pertaining to anaerobe.
Anaerobiosis —1. Life only in the absence of oxygen. 2. Functioning of an organ or tissue in the absence of free oxygen.
Anaerogenic —Producing little or no gas.
Anaeroplasty—The method of dressing the wounds in which the air is excluded.
Anaerosis —Interruption of respiratory function.
Anagen —Growing stage of hair development.
Anagenesis —1. Repair of the tissue 2. Regeneration of the lost organs.
Anagenetic —Pertaining to anagenesis.
Anakatadidymus —A congenital anomaly in which twins are separated above and below but are joined in the middle.
Anal —Pertaining to the anus.
Analbuminemia —Deficiency or absence of serum albumins.
Anal coitus —Sodomy.
Analepsis —Gaining of strength after an illness.
Analeptic —The drug used to stimulate the central nervous system.
Anal erotism —Concentration of libido in the anal region.
Anal fetishism —Sexual attraction only in anal intercourse, the person is interested either in performing anal coitus or to get sodomised by other person.
Analgesia —Absence of sensation of pain.
Analgesic —Relieving pain.
Analgetic —Analgesic.
Analgia —Painlessness.
Analgic —Without pain.
Anal incontinence — Involuntary expulsion of feces and gas from the lower intestine through anus.
Anallergic —Not allergic. Causing no anaphylaxis.
Analog —Analogue.
Analogous—Similar in function or appearance but different in origin or structure.
Analogue —1. Two organs similar in function but different in structure. 2. In chemistry, a compound which is structurally similar to another.
Analogy —The quality of being analogue.
Anal stage —Anal erotism.
Analysand —In psychoanalysis, the person being analyzed.
Analysis —1. Separation of a thing into its component parts. 2. In chemistry, determination of or separation into constituent parts of a substance or compound. 3. Psychoanalysis.

Blood gas analysis — The determination of oxygen and carbon dioxide concentration of the blood.

Densimetric analysis —Analysis by determining the density of a solution and then estimating the amounts of solids.

Gastric analysis — Analysis of the gastric juice to determine the concentration of free acid and the total acid.

Qualitative analysis —Determination of the qualities of the elements in a substance.
Quantitative analysis —Determination of the quantity of each element in a substance.
Volumetric analysis —Quantitative analysis by measuring the volume of the liquids.

Analyst —Psychoanalyst. 1. The person who analyzes. 2. The licensed practitioner of psychoanalysis.

Analyte —A substance determined by a chemical analysis.

Analytic —Pertaining to analysis.

Analytical balance —A very sensitive scale used in chemical analysis.

Analyze —To separate into parts.

Analyzer —An apparatus used to determine the optical rotation produced when polarized light passes through a solution. An apparatus used for analyzing a voice; the breath for presence of certain chemicals such as alcohol; images; cells in a solution; and chemicals.

Anamnesis —The past medical history of a patient:

Anamnestic —Pertaining to past medical history of a patient.

Anamniotic —Without an amnion.

Ananabasia —Loss of will to ascend heights.

Ananaphylaxis — Desensitization. Prevention of anaphylaxis.

Ananastasia —Loss of will to rise from a sitting position.

Anancastia —An obsession in which a person is forced to act against his or her will.

Anandria —Absence of masculinity.

Anandrous —The man having no semen, infertile, impotent man.

Angioplasia —Imperfect vascularization of a part.

Anangioplastic —Pertaining to imperfect vascularization of a part.

Anaphalantiasis — Loss of hair of the eye.

Anaphase —The third stage of division of the nucleus in either meiosis or mitosis.

Anaphia —Lack or loss of sense of touch.

Anaphoresis —Insufficient respiration.

Anaphoretic —An agent checking respiration.

Anaphoria —Anatropia. Tendency of eyeballs to turn upward.

Anaphrodisia —Absence or loss of sexual desire.

Anaphrodisiac —An agent repressing sexual desire.

Anaphrodite —Person with diminished or absence of sexual desire.

Anaphylactia —Anaphylaxis.

Anaphylactic —Pertaining to or characterised by anaphylaxis.

Anaphylactic shock — Severe allergic (hypersensitivity) reaction occurring after an injection of a substance to which a person is sensitive.

Anaphylactogen —Allergen. Any substance which produces anaphylaxis.

Anaphylactogenesis —The process of producing anaphylaxis.

Anaphylactogenic —Any thing producing anaphylactic reactions.

Anaphylactoid —Pertaining to or resembling anaphylaxis.

Anaphylaxis — Allergic or hypersensitivity reaction of the body to a foreign protein or drug due to release of histamine, serotonin and other vasodilator substances, characterized by redness of the skin, itching and urticaria, dyspnea, cyanosis, rapid and thready pulse, low blood pressure, unconsciousness and even death.

Anaplasia —Dedifferentiation. Loss of differentiation of cells, characteristic of most malignancies.

Anaplastic —Pertaining to anaplasia.

Anapnea —1. Respiration. 2. Regaining the breathing.

Anapneic —Relieving dyspnea.

Anapophysis —An accessory spinal process of a vertebra.

Anaptic —Pertaining to or characterized by anaphia.

Anarithmia —Inability to count due to cerebral lesion.

Anarthria —Inability to speak distinctly.

Anasarca —Dropsy. Generalized heavy edema.

Anasarcous —Edematous.

Anaspadias —Congenital opening of the urethra on the dorsum of the penis.

Anastalsis —Perversion of peristalsis.

Anastaltic —Astringent or styptic.

Anastate —Any product of anabolism.

Anastigmatic —Not astigmatic.

Anastigmats —Lenses in which astigmatism is corrected.

Anastole —Retraction, as of the edges of a wound.

Anastomose —To connect two parts together, especially the nerves or the blood vessels.

Anastomosis —The union of two parts, especially of the nerves or the blood vessels.

Anastomotic —Pertaining to or marked by anastomosis.

Anatomic, Anatomical — Pertaining to the structure of an organism.

Anatomical position — Position in which a person is standing erect with the feet facing forward, arms hanging to the sides, and the palms of the hands facing forward.

Anatomist —A specialist in anatomy.

Anatomy —The science of the structure of the organisms.

Applied anatomy — Anatomy applied to the diagnosis and treatment, especially surgical treatment.

Comparative anatomy — Anatomy in which homologous structures of different animals are compared.

Descriptive anatomy, Systematic anatomy — Anatomy in which the individual parts of the body are described.

Developmental anatomy —Study of the structural developments from the time of fertilization upto the adulthood.

Gross anatomy, Macroscopic anatomy — Study of the structures which can be seen with the naked eyes.

Microscopic anatomy —Histology. Study of the structures by using a microscope, which cannot be seen with the naked eyes.

Morbid anatomy, Pathological anatomy — Study of the abnormal, diseased or injured structures.

Radiological anatomy, X-ray anatomy—Study of the structures of tissues based on their appearance in the X-ray films.

Special anatomy —The study of the structures of particular organs or parts.

Surface anatomy —Study of form and markings of the surface of the body.

Anatripsis —The use of rubbing or massage in the treatment.

Anatriptic —An agent applied by rubbing.

Anatropia —Anaphoria.

Anaxon, Anaxone —A nerve cell without axon, as of the retina.

Anazoturia —Deficiency of nitrogenous substances especially urea, in the urine.

Anchor —A metal implant placed in the dental alveolus for the retention of a tooth.

Anchorage —Surgical fixation of a displaced organ.

Ancillary —Auxillary.

Ancipital —Two edged or two headed.

Ancon —Elbow.

Anconad —Toward the elbow.

Anconagra —Gout of the elbow.

Anconal, Anconeal — Pertaining to the elbow.

Anconitis —Inflammation of the elbow joint.

Anconoid —Resembling the elbow.

Ancylostoma duodenale —Hookworm.

Ancylostomiasis —The disease caused by hookworm.

Ancyroid —Shaped like the fluke of an anchor.

Andriatrics —Andrology. Study of male diseases, especially of male genital organs.

Andro- —Prefix indicating man, male or masculine.

Androblastoma —Benign tumor of the testis.

Androgalactozemia —Oozing of milk from a man's breast.

Androgen —Any substance which produces or stimulates the development of male characteristics (masculinization), such as the hormones testosterone and androsterone.

Androgenic —Causing masculinization.

Androgenicity —The quality of exerting a masculinizing effect.

Androgenous —Giving birth to males.

Androgynism — The condition of possessing both female and male characteristics of a woman.

Androgynoid —A male resembling a female or possessing female characteristics.

Androgynous —A woman possessing both female and male characteristics.

Android —Resembling a man.

Andrology —Andriatrics.

Andromania —Nymphomania.

Andromimetic —Androgenic.

Andromorphous —In physical structure and appearance resembling a male.

Andropathy —Any disease peculiar to the male.

Andropause —The decrease in function of male genital organs with increasing age, analogous to menopause.

Androphilic, Anthropophilic —Preferring man to animals, as certain parasites.

Androphobia —Morbid fear of the male sex.

Anechoic —An object with the property of being non-echoic.

Anechoic room —The room without echoes.

Anel's probe —A probe for the lacrimal and nasal ducts.

Anemia —Reduced oxygen carrying capacity of the blood which may be due to reduction in the number of red blood cells or quantity of hemoglobin in the blood, below normal. It is a symptom of various diseases characterized by pallor of the skin and the mucous membrane, weakness, headache, vertigo, dyspnea, palpitation, amenorrhea, slight fever and ankle edema in severe cases.

Achlorhydric anemia —A hypochromic microcytic anemia in achlorhydria.

Aplastic anemia — Anemia caused by destruction of the bone marrow by some medicines or X-ray etc. with the impairment of regeneration of red blood cells.

Deficiency or nutritional anemia —Anemia caused by the deficiency of nutritious elements in the diet, or the inability of the intestine to absorb them, such as iron or vitamins etc.

Folic acid deficiency anemia —Anemia resulting from deficiency of folic acid.

Hemolytic anemia —Anemia resulting from breaking down or destruction of red blood cells, which may be hereditary or acquired, as that resulting from infection or by the toxic effects of certain drugs.

Hyperchromic anemia —Anemia in which mean corpuscular hemoglobin concentration (MCHC) is greater than normal, so the red blood cells are stained darker than normal.

Hypochromic anemia—Anemia in which there is hemoglobin deficiency which is much greater than the decrease in number of red blood cells, so the mean corpuscular hemoglobin concentration is lesser than normal.

Iron-deficiency anemia—Anemia due to iron deficiency in the blood serum, low or absent iron stores, which may be due to inadequate intake of iron, its malabsorption, chronic blood loss, pregnancy and lactation period.

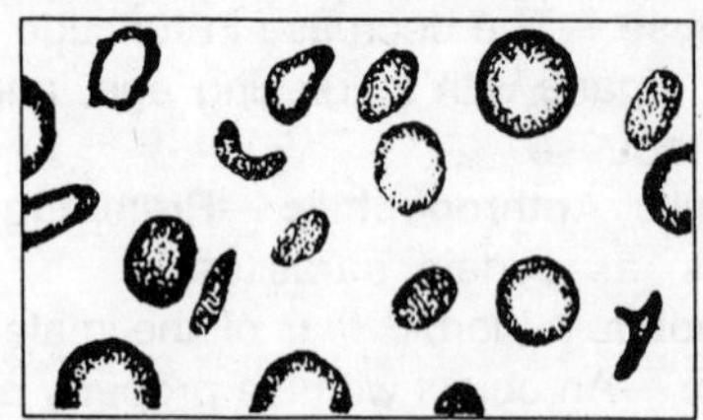

Fig. 29 A Iron deficiency anemia

Macrocytic anemia —Anemia in which the red blood cells are abnormally enlarged.

Megaloblastic anemia —Anemia in which megaloblasts are found in the blood.

Microcytic anemia—Anemia in which the red blood cells become abnormally small.

Pernicious anemia — A chronic macrocytic anemia occurring in 50-80 years old people due to failure of the stomach to secrete enough intrinsic factor for the intestinal absorption of Vit. B_{12}, the extrinsic factor, in the absence of hydrochloric acid, which is characterized by weakness, sore tongue, lemon yellow colored skin, tingling and numbness of the extremities, dyspnea on exertion, palpitation and at times angina pectoris due to anoxia of the heart muscle and in some cases swelling of the feet and ankles.

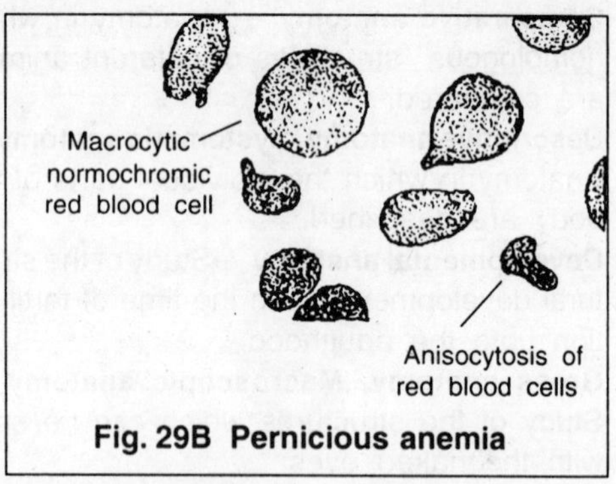

Fig. 29B Pernicious anemia

Physiologic anemia —Anemia caused by increased plasma volume of the blood as occurs in pseudoanemia of pregnancy.

Posthemorrhagic anemia —Anemia occurring suddenly following hemorrhage (bleeding from the body) caused by some injury.

Septic anemia —Anemia caused by severe infections.

Sickle cell anemia — Anemia due to the presence of large numbers of crescent or sickle-shaped red blood cells in the blood.

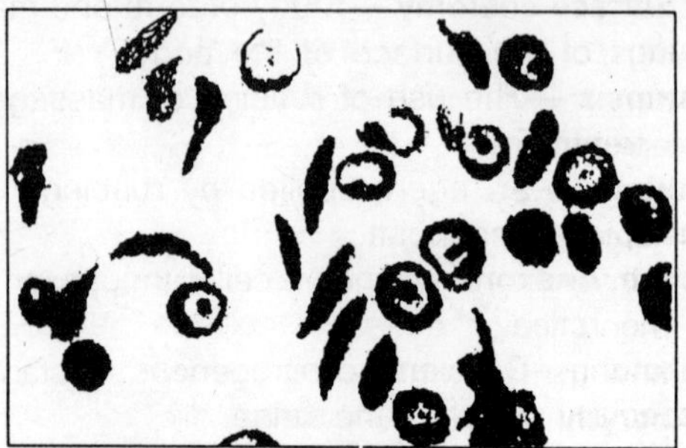

Fig. 29 C Sickle cell anemia

Splenic anemia— Enlargement of spleen due to portal or splenic hypertension accompanied by anemia.

Anemic —Pertaining to anemia. The person suffering from anemia.

Anemic hypoxia — Inadequate oxygen supply due to reduction in amount of hemoglobin to transport oxygen.

Anemometer —An apparatus for measuring the speed of wind.

Anemophobia — Morbid fear of wind or draught.

Anemotrophy —Lack of substances essential for the formation of blood, thereby resulting in hypoplastic anemia.

Anencephalic, Anencephalous—Having no brain.

Anencephaly, Anencephalia—Congenital absence of the cranial vault with the cerebral hemispheres completely missing or reduced to small masses.

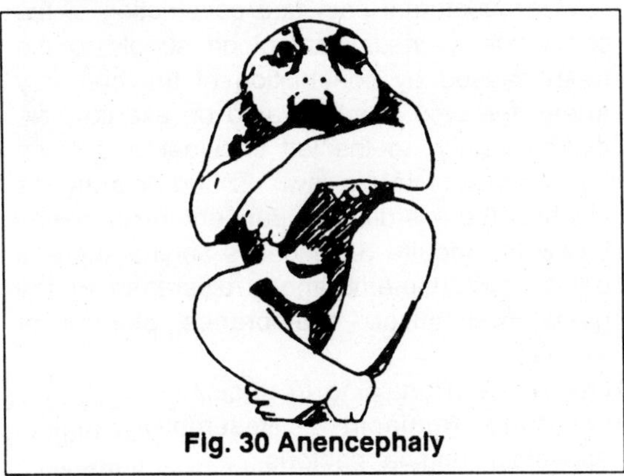

Fig. 30 Anencephaly

Anenterous —Having no intestine.

Anenzymia —Congenital absence of an enzyme.

Anephric — Without kidneys.

Anephrogenesis —Congenital absence of kidneys.

Anergasia —Anergia. Lack of functional activity resulting from a structural lesion of the central nervous system.

Anergia —Anergasia.

Anergic —Deficient in energy.

Anergy —Diminished ability to react to specific antigens.

Anergy stupor —Acute phase of dementia.

Aneroid — Operating without fluid as aneroid sphygmomanometer (Blood pressure instrument) which does not contain mercury (fluid) and used to measure the B.P.

Anerythroplasia —Absence of red blood cells formation.

Anerythroplastic — Pertaining to or characterized by anerythroplasia.

Anerythropoiesis —Deficient production of red blood cells.

Anerythropsia —Inability to recognize the red color.

Anerythroregenerative — Pertaining to or characterized by lack of regeneration of red blood cells.

Anesthecinesia, Anesthekinesia —Combined sensory and motor paralysis.

Anesthesia — Partial or complete loss of sensation with or without loss of consciousness as a result of some disease, injury or administration of an anesthetic agent usually by injection or inhalation for the performance of surgery.

General anesthesia — General anesthesia in which the whole body is affected with loss of consciousness. It may be produced by intravenous injection of an anesthetic or by inhalation of gas anesthetic such as ether, chloroform or nitrous oxide etc., by injection of an anesthetic into the subarachnoid space of the spinal cord or by introducing an anesthetic agent into the rectum, usually done for surgical performances.

Local anesthesia — Local anesthesia may be produced by blocking a nerve by an injection of alcohol or other substance into or very near a nerve trunk, by cooling the part of the body with ice or by applying a volatile liquid such as ethyl chloride, by injecting a local anesthetic solution such as procaine hydrochloride directly into the tissues as into the gums for extraction of a tooth or by application of an anesthetic directly to the surface to be anesthetized as by applying an anesthetic ointment.

Anesthesimeter —1. An apparatus for measuring the degree of loss of sensation. 2. An apparatus for regulating the amount of anesthetic given.

Anesthesiologist —Specialist in anesthesiology.

Anesthesiology —Science of anesthesia.

Anesthetic —1. Pertaining to or producing anesthesia. 2. An agent that produces anesthesia, subdivided into general or local according to their action.

Anesthetist —The person trained in administering anesthetics, especially for general anesthesia.

Anesthetization —Production of anesthesia.

Anesthetize —To produce anesthesia.

Anetoderma —Atrophy of the skin with large loose masses.

Aneurysm —Formation of a sac by localized dilatation of a blood vessel due to congenital defect or weakness of the wall of the blood vessel, *e.g.*, aneurysm of the aorta.

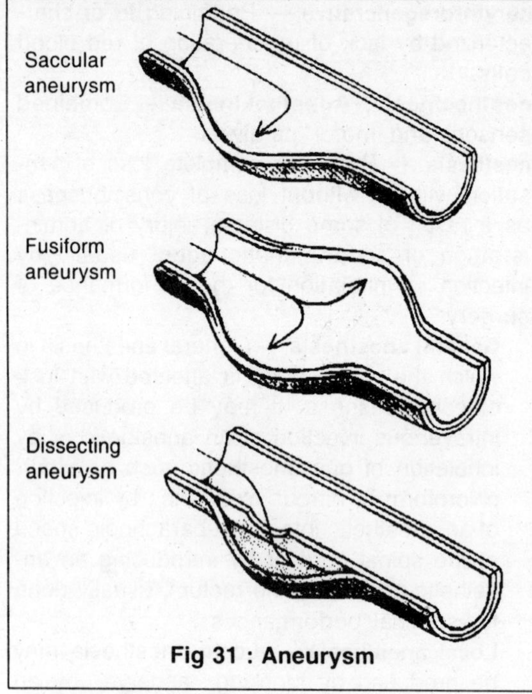

Fig 31 : Aneurysm

Saccular aneurysm—Saclike bulging on one side of an artery.
Fusiform aneurysm—Spindle-shaped dilataion of an artery.
Dissecting aneurysm—The condition resulting from passing of blood from the true lumen of an artery into a false lumen within the arterial wall.

Aneurysmal, Aneurysmatic —Pertaining to aneurysm.

Aneurysmectomy —Removal of an aneurysm by surgery.

Aneurysmoplasty —Repair of an aneurysm by plastic surgery.

Aneurysmorrhaphy —To close the sac of aneurysm by suturing.

Aneurysmotomy —To make an incision in an aneurysm.

Anfractuosity —A cerebral sulcus or fissure.

Anfractuous —Twisted.

Angi(o)- —Prefix meaning a blood or lymph vessel.

Angiasthenia —Loss of tone of the blood or lymph vessels.

Angiectasia, Angiectasis —Dilatation of a blood or lymph vessel.

Angiectatic —Characterized by dilated blood vessels.

Angiectomy —Excision of a blood vessel.

Angiectopia —Displacement of a vessel.

Angiemphraxis —Obstruction of a vessel.

Angiitis, Vasculitis — Inflammation of a blood or lymph vessel.

Angina —1. Sudden severe pain in the muscles which is a form of crying of the muscles for want of oxygen in anoxia caused by less blood supply, due to constriction of the arteries supplying those muscles, *e.g.*, angina abdominis, in which there is severe abdominal pain resulting from sclerosis of the abdominal arteries; angina cruris in which there is pain and cyanosis of the leg due to obstruction of an artery; angina pectoris in which there is sudden severe substernal pain and constriction of the chest due to insufficient blood supply to the heart caused by constriction of the coronary artery, the pain is aggravated on exertion, radiating usually to the left shoulder and down the left arm or to the jaw. 2. Ludwig's angina in which there is diffused purulent inflammation below the mouth. 3. Vincent's angina–there is painful pseudomembranous ulceration of the gums, oral mucous membranes, pharynx or tonsils.

Anginal — Pertaining to angina.

Anginiform, Anginoid — Resembling angina, especially angina pectoris.

Anginophobia —Morbid fear of angina pectoris.

Anginose —Pertaining to or resembling angina.

Angioarchitecture —The arrangement and distribution of the blood vessels of an organ or tissue.

Angioataxia —Variations in the arterial tonicity.

Angioblast —A cell which takes part in vessel formation.

Angioblastoma —A tumor of a particular blood vessel of the brain, or of the meninges of the brain or the spinal cord.

Angiocardiogram —X-ray film of the heart and the great blood vessels taken after intravenous injection of a radiopaque dye.

Angiocardiography — Radiography of the heart and the great blood vessels after intravenous injection of a radiopaque dye.

Angiocardiokinetic — Causing the movements (contraction and dilatation) of the heart and the blood vessels.

Angiocardiopathy —Disease of the heart and the blood vessels.

Angiocarditis —Inflammation of the heart and the large blood vessels.

Angiocholecystitis — Inflammation of the gallbladder and the bile vessels.

Angiocholitis —Cholangitis. Inflammation of the biliary vessels.

Angiochondroma —A cartilaginous tumor with excessive development of the blood vessels.

Angiodysplasia — Abnormalities of the small blood vessels, especially of the intestine.

Angiodystrophia —Defective nutrition of the blood vessels.

Angioedema —Angioneurotic edema.

Angioelephantiasis — Occurrence of elephantiasis due to excessive thickening of the skin caused by increased vascularity of the subcutaneous tissues.

Angiofibrolipoma —A tumor consisting of fibroblasts, blood capillaries and adipose tissue.

Angiofibroma —An angioma containing fibrous tissue.

Angiofibrosis — Fibrosis of the walls of the blood vessels.

Angiofollicular —Pertaining to a lymphoid follicle and its blood vessels.

Angiogenesis —Development of the blood vessels in the embryo.

Angiogenic —1. Pertaining to angiogenesis. 2. Of vascular origin.

Angioglioma —A mixed tumor of angioma and glioma.

Angiogliomatosis, Angiogliosis —Occurrence of multiple angiogliomas.

Angiogram —X-ray film of a blood vessel taken after injection of a radiopaque substance into the vessel.

Angiograph —An instrument used in angiography to obtain an angiogram of a blood vessel.

Angiographic —Pertaining to, or using angiography.

Angiography —Radiography of a blood vessel after injection of a radiopaque substance into the blood vessel.

Angiohyalinosis —Hyaline degeneration of the walls of the blood vessels.

Angiohypertonia — Angiospasm, vasospasm. Spasm of the blood vessels, especially of the arteries.

Angiohypotonia — Angioparalysis, angioparesis or vascular dilatation.

Angioid —Resembling blood vessels.

Angioinvasive —Entering the blood vessels.

Angiokeratoma —A skin disease occurring chiefly on the legs and feet, characterized by the formation of telangiectases or warty growths, together with epidermal thickening.

Angiokeratosis —The occurrence of multiple angiokeratomas.

Angiokinetic —Vasomotor. Pertaining to the constriction and dilatation of the blood vessels.

Angioleukitis —Inflammation of the lymphatics.

Angiolipoma —A tumor composed of angioma and lipoma.

Angiolith —A calcareous deposit in the wall of a blood vessel usually a venous wall.

Angiolithic —Pertaining to angiolith.

Angiology —The science of the blood and lymph vessels.

Angiolupoid —A tuberculous lesion of the skin occurring chiefly on the side of the nose, consisting of small red, oval plaques with telangiectases over the surface.

Angiolymphitis —Lymphangitis. Inflammation of the lymph vessels.

Angiolysis —Obliteration of the blood vessels, as in the umbilical cord when it is tied after birth.

Angioma —A benign tumor composed of blood vessels (hemangioma) or lymph vessels (lymphangioma).

Angiomalacia —Softening of the walls of the blood vessels.

Angiomatoid —Resembling angioma.

Angiomatosis —A disease in which multiple angiomas are formed.

Angiomatous —Resembling an angioma.

Angiomegaly —Enlargement of the blood vessels, especially in the eyelids.

Angiometer —Instrument for measuring tension and diameter of the blood vessels.

Angiomyocardiac — Pertaining to the blood vessels and the cardiac muscle.

Angiomyofibroma —A benign tumor composed of vessels, muscular tissue and fibrous connective tissue.

Angiomyolipoma —A benign tumor containing vascular, fatty and muscular tissues.

Angiomyoma —A tumor composed of blood vessels and muscular tissue.

Angiomyoneuroma —A painful, benign tumor of the arteriovenous anastomoses of the skin.

Angiomyopathy —Any disease of the blood vessels involving the muscle layer.

Angiomyosarcoma —A tumor composed of elements of angioma, myoma and sarcoma.

Angiomyxoma — A myxoma in which there is a large number of vessels.

Angioneurectomy —Excision of vessels and nerves.

Angioneuromyoma — Angiomyoneuroma.

Angioneuropathy —A vasculonervous disease.

Angioneurosis —Spasm or paralysis of the blood vessels due to a disturbance of vasomotor system.

Angioneurotic —Pertaining to angioneurosis.

Angioneurotic edema —Angioedema. A benign allergic swelling of the skin, mucous membranes or the viscera, caused usually by food allergy.

Angioneurotomy —To incise the vessels and the nerves.

Angionoma —Ulceration of a vessel.

Angioparalysis —Vasomotor paralysis of a blood vessel.

Angioparesis —Vasomotor weakness of a blood vessel.

Angiopathic —Pertaining to angiopathy.

Angiopathology —Pathological changes in diseases of the blood vessels.

Angiopathy —Any disease of a blood or lymph vessel.

Angioplany —Wandering of a blood vessel from its normal place.

Angioplasty —Repair of the blood vessels by plastic surgery.

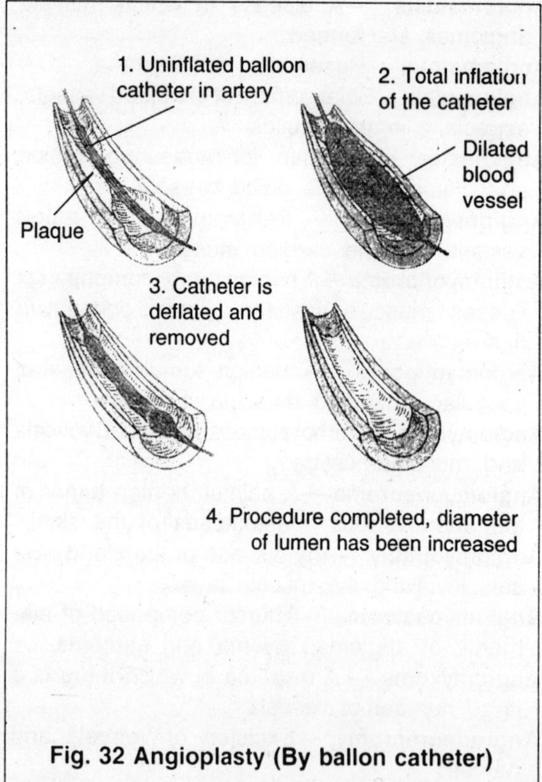

Fig. 32 Angioplasty (By ballon catheter)

Angiopoiesis —The formation of blood vessels.

Angiopoietic —Pertaining to or causing the formation of blood vessels.

Angiopressure —The pressure applied to a blood vessel to check the hemorrhage.

Angiorhigosis —Rigidity of the blood vessels.

Angiorrhaphy —Suture of a vessel.

Angiorrhexis —Rupture of a vessel.

Angiosarcoma —Hemangiosarcoma. Malignant tumor of the blood vessels.

Angiosclerosis —Hardening of the walls of the blood vessels.

Angioscope —A microscope for observing the capillaries.

Angioscopy —Visualization of the interior of the blood vessels.

Angioscotoma—The defect produced in the visual field by the shadows of the blood vessels of the retina.

Angiosialitis —Inflammation of a salivary duct.

Angiosis —Angiopathy.

Angiospasm —Spasmodic contraction of a blood vessel.

Angiospastic —Pertaining to angiospasm.

Angiostaxis —Hemorrhagic tendency.

Angiostenosis —Narrowing of the lumen of a vessel, especially the blood vessel.

Angiosteosis —Calcification of a vessel.

Angiostomy —To make an opening into a blood vessel by operation.

Angiostrophe, Angiostrophy —The twisting of the cut end of a blood vessel to arrest bleeding.

Angiosynizesis —The condition in which the walls of a vessel are weakened and later on they adhere together.

Angiotelectasis —Dilatation of the blood capillaries.

Angiotensin —It is produced by the action of an enzyme renin released from the kidney, on angiotensinogen. It raises the blood pressure by causing vasoconstriction.

Angiotensinogen —It is the precursor of angiotensin. It is formed in the liver, released into the blood serum and converted to angiotensin by the action of renin released from the kidney.

Angiotensinogenase — Renin.

Angiotitis — Inflammation of blood vessels of the ear.

Angiotomy —Incision of a blood or lymph vessel.

Angiotonic —Increasing arterial tension.

Angiotribe —An instrument for crushing the end of an artery and the surrounding tissue to arrest the bleeding.

Angiotripsy —To arrest the bleeding by using an angiotribe.
Angiotrophic —Pertaining to nutrition of blood or lymph vessels.
Angitis —Inflammation of the blood or lymph vessels.
Angor —Severe pain, as in angina pectoris.
Angor animi —The feeling that one is dying, as in angina pectoris.
Angstrom unit —An international unit of wave length. equal to 10^{-10} meter or '1 nanometer.
Anguish —Extreme mental or physical pain.
Angular —Having corners or angles.
Angular artery —The artery at the inner canthus of the eye; facial artery.
Angular cheilitis — Inflammation of the lips at the mouth corners which is characterized by fissuring, burning and dryness of the angles of the mouth and cracking of the lips.
Angulation —Formation of an angle by tubular structures, such as the intestine, a blood vessel, or ureter.
Angulus —Angle.
Anhaphia —Anaphia. Loss of sense of touch.
Anhedonia —Feeling no pleasure in the acts which are normally pleasurable.
Anhematosis —Defective blood formation.
Anhemolytic —Not destructive to the blood cells.
Anhepatica —Failure or deficiency of liver function.
Anhepatogenic —Not produced by the liver.
Anhidrosis —Absent or deficient sweat secretion, which may be localized or generalized, temporary or permanent.
Anhidrotic —Inhibiting or preventing the flow of sweat.
Anhistic, Anhistous — Without apparent structure.
Anhydrase —An enzyme which promotes the removal of water from a chemical compound.
Anhydration —Dehydration.
Anhydremia —Deficiency of plasma in the blood.
Anhydride —Compound formed by removal of water from a substance.
Anhydrochloric —Deficient in hydrochloric acid.
Anhydromyelia —Deficiency of fluid in the spinal cord.
Anhydrous —Containing no water.
Anianthinopsy —Inability to recognize the violet color.
Anicteric —Without jaundice.
Anidean —Shapeless.
Anidous —Anidean.
Anidrosis —Anhidrosis.
Anidrotic —Anhidrotic.
Anile —Senile.
Anilingus —Sexual stimulation by licking or kissing the anus.
Anility —Senility, old age.
Anima —The soul or spirit.
Animalcule —An animal or organism which is seen only by microscope.
Animate —Living.
Animatism —The belief that everything in nature, living and non living, contains a spirit or soul.
Animation suspended — Temporary cessation of the vital functions with loss of consciousness.
Animi agitatio --Mental agitation.
Anion —A negatively charged ion, which is attracted to the positive electrode (anode) in an electrolytic cell.
Anionic —Pertaining to anion.
Aniridia —Iridleremia. Congenital absence of the iris.
Aniseikonia —A condition in which retinal images of two eyes differ in size and shape.
Anismus —Excessive contraction of the external sphincter of the rectum.
Aniso- —Prefix meaning unequal or asymmetrical.
Anisoaccommodation — Difference in the ability to accommodate, of the two eyes.
Anisochromasia —Unequal distribution of hemoglobin in the red blood cells, such that the periphery is pigmented due to deposition of hemoglobin, and the central region remains colorless as is observed in iron deficiency anemia.
Anisochromatic —Not of the same color throughout.
Anisochromia — The state of being of different color of an object.
Anisocoria —Inequality of the size of the pupils of the eyes.
Anisocytosis —Condition in which the cells, especially the red blood cells are excessively unequal in size.
Anisodactylous —Pertaining to anisodactyly.
Anisodactyly —Unequal length of the corresponding fingers of both the hands.
Anisognathous —Having the upper jaw wider than the lower one.
Anisohypercytosis —A condition in which the white blood cells are increased in number with the changed proportion of the different varieties.

Anisohypocytosis —A condition in which the white blood cells are decreased in number with the changed proportion of the different varieties.

Anisokaryosis —Unequal size of the cell nuclei.

Anisomastia —Condition in which the breasts are markedly unequal.

Anisomelia —Condition in which the paired limbs are unequal in length.

Anisometrope —The person afflicted with anisometropia.

Anisometropia —The condition in which the refractive power of the two eyes is unequal.

Anisometropic —Pertaining to or characterized by anisometropia.

Anisonormocytosis — Condition in which the total number of white blood cells is normal but the ratio of the different types of cells is abnormal.

Anisophoria —Condition in which the horizontal visual plane of one eye is different from that of the other.

Anisopia —Condition in which the visual power of the eyes is unequal.

Anisopiesis —Inequality of blood pressure taken of the different parts of the body.

Anisopoikilocytosis — The condition in which the white blood cells of different sizes and abnormal shapes are present in the blood.

Anisorrhythmia —Irregular action of the heart.

Anisosphygmia —Difference in volume, force or time of the pulse in the radial arteries of the two hands.

Anisosthenic — Of unequal strength, as of paired muscles.

Anisotonic —1. Not isotonic. 2. Varying in tension.

Anisotropal, Anisotropous — 1. Not equal in every direction. 2. Unequal in refractive power.

Anisotropic — Having different optical properties in different directions.

Anisotropous — Anisotropal

Anisotropy —The quality of being anisotropic.

Anisuria —Alternating oliguria and polyuria.

Ankle —The joint between the leg and foot, which is formed by the union of tibia, fibula and talus bones.

Ankle clonus —Repetitive extension and flexion of the ankle.

Ankle jerk —Contraction of the calf muscles resulting in extension of the foot, following a blow upon the Achilles tendon.

Ankylo- —Prefix meaning twisted, bent or fusion of parts of the body.

Ankyloblepharon —Adhesion of the edges of the upper and lower eyelids to each other.

Ankylocheilia —Adhesion of the upper and lower lips to each other.

Ankylocolpos —Imperforation or closure of the vagina.

Ankylodactylia, Ankylodactyly — Adhesion of two or more fingers or toes.

Ankyloglossia —Tongue-tie. Congenital shortening of the frenulum of the tongue.

Ankylomele —A curved or bent probe.

Ankylopoietic —Producing ankylosis.

Ankyloproctia —Stricture or imperforation of the anus.

Ankylosed —Immobile and fixed joint, stiff joint.

Ankylosis —Immobility and fixation of a joint, stiffness.

Ankylotia—Closure of the external auditory meatus of the ear.

Ankylotic —Characterized by or pertaining to ankylosis.

Ankylotome —An instrument for cutting the frenulum of the tongue in tongue-tie.

Ankylurethria —Stricture or imperforation of the urethra.

Ankyroid —Hook-shaped.

Anlage —The original form.

Annectant —Linked, connected, joined.

Annexa —Adnexa. Accessary parts of a structure.

Annexitis — Adnexitis. Inflammation of the adnexa of the uterus.

Annexopexy —Adnexopexy. Fixation of the fallopian tube and the ovary to the abdominal wall.

Annoy —To irritate, to harass.

Annoyance —Vexation.

Annular —Ring-shaped.

Annuloplasty —Repair of a cardiac valve by plastic surgery.

Annulorrhaphy —Closure of a hernial ring by suture.

Annulus —A small ring or ring-shaped structure.

Anochromasia —Anisochromasia.

Anococcygeal —Pertaining to both, the anus and the coccyx.

Anodal —Pertaining to the anode.

Anode —The positive pole of an electrical source to which the negative ions are attracted.

Anodmia —Anosmia. Absence of the sense of smell.

Anodontia —Edentia. Congenital absence of some or all of the teeth.

Anodontism —Congenital absence of tooth germ development.
Anodyne —Analgesic. Pain relieving drug.
Anodynia —Cessation of pain.
Anogenital —Pertaining to the anal and genital areas.
Anoia —Idiocy.
Anomaloscope —An apparatus used to detect the color blindness.
Anomalous —Deviating from the normal.
Anomaly —Deviation from the normal, especially as a result of congenital or hereditary defects.
Anomia —Inability to remember the names of the objects.
Anonychia, Anonychosis — Absence of a nail or nails.
Anonymous —Without name.
Anoperineal —Pertaining to both, the anus and the perineum.
Anophelicide —An agent destroying the Anopheles mosquitoes.
Anophelifuge —An agent that drives away or prevents the bite of Anopheles mosquitoes.
Anophoria —Anopsia.
Anophthalmia —Congenital absence of one or both eyes.
Anophthalmos —Anophthalmia.
Anophthalmose —The person born without eyes.
Anopia —1. Anophthalmia. 2. Anophoria.
Anoplasty —Plastic surgery of the anus.
Anopsia —1. Non-use of vision in one eye. 2. Hypertropia.
Anorchia —Anorchism.
Anorchid —A person having no testes, or with undescended testes.
Anorchidism, Anorchism — Congenital absence of one or both testes.
Anorchism — Anorchidism
Anorectal —Pertaining to both, the anus and the rectum.
Anorectic, Anorectous —1. Having no appetite. 2. An agent which diminishes the appetite. 1-
Anorectocolonic —Pertaining to the anus, rectum and the colon.
Anorexia —Loss of appetite.
Anorexia nervosa —Loss of appetite caused by mental disturbances.
Anorexiant —Causing loss of appetite.
Anorexic —Anorectic.
Anorexigenic —Causing loss of appetite.
Anorgasmic —One who does not experience orgasm during sexual intercourse.
Anorgasmy —Inability to achieve orgasm during sexual intercourse or masterbation.
Anorthography —Agraphia. Inability to write.
Anorthopia —Distorted vision, in which straight lines do not appear straight.
Anorthosis — Failure to achieve penile erection.
Anoscope —A speculum for examining the anus and the lower rectum.
Anoscopy —Examination of the anal canal with an anoscope.
Anosigmoidoscopy —Direct visual examination of the anus, rectum and sigmoid colon by using endoscope.
Anosmatic — Having no sense of smell.
Anosmia —Anodmia. Loss of sense of smell.
Anosmic, Anosmous —1. Having no sense of smell. 2. Odorless.
Anosodiaphoria —Indifference regarding the presence of a disease, especially of paralysis.
Anosognosia —Ignorance of the presence of a disease in the body.
Anosognosic —Pertaining to anosognosia.
Anosphrasia —Absence of or imperfect sense of smell.
Anospinal —Pertaining to the anus and the spinal cord.
Anosteoplasia —Failure of bone formation.
Anostosis —Defective formation of bone.
Anotia —Congenital absence of the ears.
Anotropia —Tendency of the eyes to turn upward.
Anotus —A fetus without ears.
Anovaginal —Pertaining to the anus and the vagina.
Anovarism —Absence of ovaries.
Anovesical —Pertaining to the anus and the urinary bladder.
Anovular, Anovulatory — Not associated with the production and discharge of an ovum.
Anovulation —Cessation of ovulation.
Anoxemia —Reduction of oxygen in the blood below normal level.
Anoxia —Absence of oxygen supply to the tissues, the term is often used to indicate hypoxia which means reduced oxygen supply.

Altitude anoxia — Anoxia due to reduced oxygen in the atmosphere at the high altitudes.

Anemic anoxia — Anoxia due to decrease in the amount of hemoglobin or the number of red blood cells in the blood.

Anoxic anoxia — Anoxia due to interference in the oxygen supply which may be in pulmonary diseases.

Histotoxic anoxia —Anoxia resulting from diminished ability of the cells to utilize available oxygen.

Stagnant anoxia — Anoxia due to interference with the peripheral blood circulation as occurs in cardiac failure.

Ansa, Ansiform —Loop-shaped.

Ansate —Ansiform.

Ansotomy —To divide a loop, usually a constricting loop by surgery.

Ant- —Prefix denoting against.

Antacid —An agent neutralizing the acidity, especially in the stomach.

Antagonism —Opposition or contrary action between similar things as between muscles, medicines or organisms.

Antagonist — 1. A drug neutralizing the effects of another. 2. A muscle counteracting the action of another muscle.

Antalgic —Analgesic.

Antalkaline —A substance which neutralizes the alkalinity.

Antaphrodisiac —Anaphrodisiac. An agent which depresses the sexual desire.

Antaphroditic —Anaphrodisiac.

Antarthritic —Alleviating arthritis and gout.

Antasthenic —Relieving weakness.

Antasthmatic —Relieving or preventing asthma.

Antatrophic —Preventing or curing atrophy.

Ante- — Prefix meaning before.

Antebrachial —Pertaining to forearm.

Antebrachium —The forearm, the part of the arm between the elbow and the wrist.

Antecardium—Precordium. The area of the anterior surface of the body overlying the heart.

Antecedent —Precursor.

Ante cibum—A.C. —It is used in prescription-writing to indicate before meals.

Antecubital — In front of the elbow.

Antecurvature —Anteflexion. Bending forward.

Antefebrile —Before fever.

Anteflect —To bend anteriorly (forward).

Anteflex —Anteflect.

Anteflexion —Abnormal forward bending of an organ or part of the body as uterus.

Antegrade —In the direction of normal movement, as in blood flow or peristalsis.

Antelocation —Forward displacement of an organ.

Antemeridian—Time between midnight and noon.

Antemortem —Before death.

Antemortem statement — Statement given by an individual just before death.

Antenatal —Prenatal. Occurring before child birth.

Antepartal, Antepartum — Occurring before the onset of labor, used with reference to the mother.

Anteposition —Forward position.

Anteprandial —Before dinner.

Antepyretic —Antefebrile.

Anterior —Situated before or infront of, opposite of posterior.

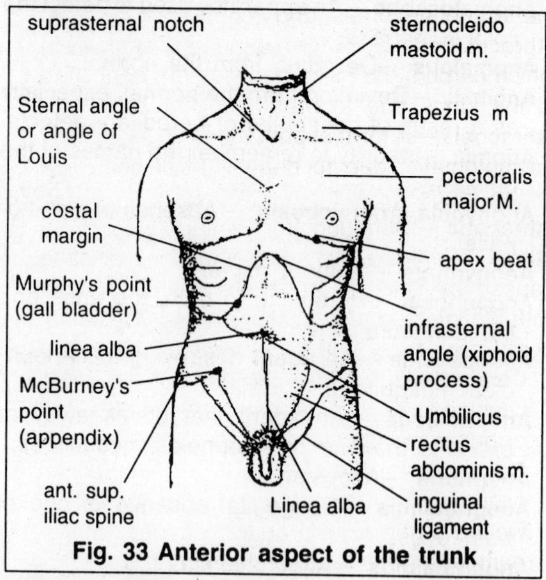

Fig. 33 Anterior aspect of the trunk

Antero- —Prefix denoting anterior, front or before.

Anteroexternal —Situated in front and laterally.

Anterograde —Moving forward.

Anteroinferior —Situated in front and below.

Anterointernal —Located in front and to the inner side.

Anterolateral —Situated in front and to one side.

Anteromedial —Anteromedian.

Anteromedian —Situated in front and toward the median plane.

Anteroposterior —Passing from the front to the back.

Anterosuperior —Situated in front and above.

Anterotic —Pertaining to the effort of avoiding erotic feelings.

Anteversion —A turning forward of an organ as a whole, without bending.

Anteverted —Turned forward.

Anthelix —Antihelix. The semicircular ridge of the external ear, infront and below to the helix.

Anthelminthic —Anthelmintic.

Anthelmintic —Destroying worms.

Anthemorrhagic —Antihemorrhagic. Preventing or arresting hemorrhage.

Anthoma —Fatty growth of the skin.

Anthophobia —Morbid fear of flowers.

Anthracia —Presence of carbuncles.
Anthracic —Pertaining to anthrax.
Anthracoid —Resembling or pertaining to anthrax.
Anthracometer —An instrument for measuring the amount of carbon dioxide in the air.
Anthraconecrosis —Gangrene of a tissue in which the tissue becomes dry and black.
Anthracosilicosis —A form of pneumoconiosis in which carbon and silica particles are deposited in the lungs due to breathing coal dust.
Anthracosis —A form of pneumoconiosis, usually asymptomatic, due to deposition of coal dust in the lungs.
Anthracotic —Suffering from anthrax.
Anthrax ¼—A specific acute infectious disease caused by Bacillus anthracis due to contact with the infected animals such as sheep, cattle, goats and horses, etc.

Cerebral anthrax — Anthrax of the brain causing violent delirium and frequently hemorrhagic meningitis.
Cutaneous anthrax — That due to infection occurring through an abrasion or superficial wound of the skin, producing a black malignant pustule on an edematous area.
Intestinal anthrax —It is a rare form of anthrax characterized by pain in abdomen, vomiting, diarrhea, enlargement of the spleen and the presence of bacilli anthrax in the feces. It is usually fatal.
Pulmonary anthrax —Anthrax of the lungs due to inhalation of dust or animal hair containing anthrax producing organisms, characterized by shivering followed by pain in the chest, cough, expectoration with frothy and blood-stained sputum containing bacilli anthrax, pyrexia and marked weakness, usually fatal within a few days.

Anthropo- —Prefix denoting relationship to man or human life.
Anthropobiology —The study of biologic relationships of humans.
Anthropogenesis — Anthropogeny.
Anthropogenic, Anthropogenetic —Pertaining to anthropogeny.
Anthropogeny —Origin and development of man.
Anthropoid —Resembling man.
Anthropologist —Specialist of anthropology.
Anthropology —The science of man, which includes his origin and development.
Anthropometer —An apparatus for measuring the human body and its parts.
Anthropometric —Pertaining to anthropometry.
Anthropometry —Science of measuring the human body and its parts.
Anthropophagy —The eating of human flesh.
Anthropophilic —Androphilic. Preferring man to animals, said of some parasites.
Anthropophobia —Fear of society.
Anthroposomatology —The part of the anthropology concerning with the human body, *e.g.*, anatomy, physiology or pathology.
Anthropozoonosis —An infectious disease acquired by humans from infected vertebrate animals, *e.g.*, rabies from dog.
Anthysteric —Antihysteric. Preventing or relieving hysteria.
Anti- —Prefix meaning against.
Antiabortifacient — Preventing abortion.
Antiadrenergic —Preventing or counteracting the adrenergic action.
Antiagglutinin —An antibody opposing the action of an agglutinin.
Antiaggregant, platelet —A medicine, such as aspirin, that interferes with the aggregaton of platelets.
Antiallergic —Preventing allergy.
Antiamebic —The medicine used to prevent or treat the infection of ameba, especially Entamoeba histolytica.
Antianabolic —Preventing synthesis of body protein.
Antianaphylactin —An antibody counteracting the anaphylactin.
Antianaphylaxis — Desensitization. Prevention of anaphylaxis by giving too small doses of a sensitizing substance repeatedly, which cannot cause anaphylaxis.
Antiandrogen —Any substance inhibiting or preventing the action of androgen.
Antianemic —Preventing or curing anemia.
Antiantibody —An antibody produced in the body following administration of another anitbody.
Antiantitoxin —An antibody, produced in the body in response to the administration of an antitoxin, which counteracts the effect of the antitoxin.
Antiapoplectic —Preventing or relieving apoplexy.
Antiarrhythmic —A drug or exercise controlling or preventing the cardiac arrhythmias.
Antiarthritic —Antarthritic. Relieving arthritis.
Antiasthmatic —Relieving or preventing asthma.

Antibacterial —Destroying or stopping the production of bacteria.

Antibechic —Relieving cough.

Antibiosis —The association of two organisms in which one is harmful to the other.

Antibiotic —A chemical substance produced by a microorganism, which is capable of inhibiting the growth or to destroy the other micro-organisms. The antibiotics non-toxic to the host are used in the treatment of infectious diseases.

Antibody —A protein substance present in the blood serum, produced in response to a reaction with a specific antigen. Antibodies may be present due to previous infection, vaccination, transfer from the mother to the fetus in the uterus or may occur accidentally without any antigenic stimulation. In addition there may be natural antibodies without any cause. According to the mode of action, the antibodies are classified as agglutinin, bacteriolysin, hemolysin, opsonin or precipitin.

Antibrachial —Antebrachial.

Antibrachium —Antebrachium; forearm.

Antibromic —A deodorant.

Anticalculous —Suppressing the formation of calculi.

Anticardium —Antecardium, precordium.

Anticariogenic, Anticarious —Preventing dental-caries production.

Anticarious — Anticariogenic.

Anticatarrhal —Relieving catarrh.

Anticephalalgic —Relieving or preventing headache.

Anticheirotonous —Spasmodic bending inward of a thumb.

Anticholagogue —The drug which decreases the secretion of bile.

Anticholelithogenic — Preventing the formation of gallstones.

Anticholesteremic —Reducing blood cholesterol level, *e.g.,* clofibrate.

Anticholinergic —Parasympatholytic; blocking the passage of impulses through the parasympathetic nerves.

Anticipate —The occurrence of a disease or symptom before its usual time of onset.

Anticlinal —Inclined in opposite directions.

Anticoagulant — An agent which prevents or delays clotting of blood, *e.g.,* sodium citrate and heparin, etc.

Anticomplement —A substance which counteracts a complement.

Anticomplementary — Denoting a substance possessing the power of diminishing or abolishing the action of a complement.

Anticontagious —Preventing contagion.

Anticonvulsant —Preventing or relieving convulsions.

Anticonvulsive — Anticonvulsant.

Anticus —Anterior.

Antidepressant —Preventing or relieving depression.

Antidiabetic —Preventing or relieving diabetes.

Antidiarrheal —The substance or a drug used to prevent or treat diarrhea.

Antidinic —Preventing or relieving vertigo.

Antidiuresis —The suppression of secretion of urine by the kidneys.

Antidiuretic —Decreasing urine secretion.

Antidotal —Acting as or pertaining to an antidote.

Antidote —A substance which neutralizes the effect of a poison.

Chemical antidote — Antidote which reacts with the poison forming a harmless chemical compound.

Mechanical antidote — Antidote which prevents absorption of the poison.

Physiologic antidote —Antidote which counteracts the effects of the poison by producing the opposing physiologic effects.

Antidromic —Conducting the nerve impulses in the opposite direction from the normal.

Antidysenteric —Preventing, relieving or curing the dysentery.

Antidysuric —Preventing or relieving dysuria.

Antieczematic —An agent effective against eczema.

Antiemetic —Preventing or relieving nausea and vomiting.

Antienergic —Acting against or in opposition.

Antienzyme —The substance which acts against an enzyme.

Antiepileptic —A medicine, procedure or diet combating epilepsy.

Antiestrogen —The substance which blocks the action of estrogen.

Antiexpectorant —Preventing expectoration.

Antifebrile —Antipyretic. Reducing fever.

Antifermentative —Preventing or inhibiting fermentation.

Antifibrillatory — Preventing fibrillation.

Antifibrinolysin —An inhibitor of fibrinolysin.

Antifibrinolytic —The substance counteracting the fibrinolysis.

Antiflatulent —Relieving or preventing flatulence.

Antifungal —Destroying or inhibiting the growth of fungi.

Antigalactagogue, Antigalactic —Preventing or diminishing the secretion of milk.

Antigen —A substance introduced into or formed within the body, induces the formation of antibody that specifically reacts with it. The antigen-antibody reaction is the basis of the immunity. Examples of antigens are bacteria, toxins and foreign blood, etc.

Antigenemia —Presence of antigen in the blood.

Antigenic —Capable of causing the production of an antibody.

Antigenicity —The capacity to stimulate the production of antibodies or the capacity to react with an antibody.

Antiglobulin —The substance counteracting the action of globulin.

Antigoitrogenic —Preventing the formation of a goitre.

Antigonorrheic —Curing gonorrhea.

Antihelix —Anthelix.

Antihelminthic —Anthelmintic.

Antihemagglutinin —A substance including antibody that inhibits the clumpsing of red blood cells.

Antihemolysin —A substance including antibody that inhibits the effects of hemolysin.

Antihemolytic —Preventing hemolysis.

Antihemophilic factor — Blood coagulation factor VIII.

Antihemorrhagic —Preventing or arresting hemorrhage.

Antihidrotic —Anhidrotic.

Antihistamine —A drug which counteracts the effect of histamine.

Antihistaminic —Counteracting the effects of histamine.

Antihormone —The substances opposing the action of a hormone.

Antihydropic —Relieving generalized edema.

Antihypercholesterolemic — An agent preventing or controlling hypercholesterolemia.

Antihypertensive —Preventing or controlling high blood pressure.

Antihypnotic —Preventing or inhibiting sleep.

Antihypotensive — Counteracting the low blood pressure.

Antihysteric —Preventing or relieving hysteria.

Anti-icteric —Preventing or relieving jaundice.

Anti-immune —Preventing immunity.

Anti-infective —Counteracting the infection.

Anti-inflammatory —An agent diminishing the inflammation.

Antiketogenesis —Prevention or inhibition of formation of ketone bodies.

Antiketogenic —Inhibiting the formation of ketone bodies.

Antilethargic —Counteracting lethargy.

Antileukocytic —Destructive to the white blood cells.

Antilipemic —Preventing or counteracting the accumulation of fatty substances in the blood.

Antilithic —Preventing calculus formation.

Antiluetic —Antisyphilitic. An agent curing or relieving syphilis.

Antiluteogenic —Inhibiting the growth of corpus luteum.

Antilysin —Antibody that opposes the action of lysin.

Antilysis —Inhibition of lysis due to action of antilysin.

Antilyssic —Antirabic. Preventing or curing rabies.

Antilytic —Preventing or inhibiting the lysis.

Antimalarial —Preventing or relieving malaria.

Antimetabolite —Against a metabolite.

Antimetropia —An ocular disorder in which there may be hyperopia in one eye and the myopia in the other.

Antimicrobial, Antimicrobic —Destructive or preventing the growth of microorganisms.

Antimitotic —Any agent preventing the reproduction of a cell by mitosis.

Antimongoloid —A condition in which lateral portion of the palpebral fissure is lower than the medial portion.

Antimycotic —Antifungal. Inhibiting or preventing the growth of fungi.

Antinarcotic —Counteracting the action of a narcotic.

Antinatriuresis —The decrease in the excretion of sodium in the urine.

Antinauseant —Preventing or relieving nausea.

Antineoplastic —Inhibiting or preventing the development of tumors.

Antinephritic —Preventing or inhibiting the inflammation of the kidneys.

Antineuralgic —Relieving neuralgia.

Antineuritic —Preventing or inhibiting inflammation of a nerve.

Antinuclear —Reacting with the nucleus of a cell.

Antiodontalgic —Relieving toothache.

Antiovulatory —Suppressing ovulation.

Antioxidant —An agent preventing or inhibiting oxidation.

Antioxidation —Prevention or inhibition of oxidation.

Antipaludian —Antimalarial. Preventing or curing malaria.

Antiparalytic —Relieving paralysis.

Antiparasitic —Destroying parasites.

Antipathic —Antagonistic.

Antipathy —Antagonism.

Antipedicular, Antipediculotic —A drug or a procedure effective against lice.

Antiperistalsis —Reversed peristalsis, *i.e.*, running of the peristaltic movements from the intestine towards the stomach.

Antiperistaltic —Pertaining to antiperistalsis.

Antiperspirant —Anhidrotic, antihydrotic.

Antiphagocytic —Preventing the action of the phagocytes.

Antiphlogistic —Preventing or reducing inflammation.

Antiphobic —Controlling phobias.

Antipilus —Hair destroyer.

Antiplastic —Preventing or inhibiting wound healing.

Antiplatelet —Destructive to platelets.

Antipolycythemic —Effective against polycythemia.

Antiprostaglandin —Drug interfering with the prostaglandin activity, which is used to treat arthritis and dysmenorrhea.

Antiprostate —Cowper's gland.

Antiprostatitis —Inflammation of the Cowper's gland.

Antiprothrombin — An anticoagulant that retards the conversion of prothrombin into thrombin.

Antiprotozoal —Destructive to protozoa.

Antipruritic —Preventing or relieving itching.

Antipsoriatic —Preventing or relieving psoriasis.

Antipsychotic —Effective against mental disorder.

Antiputrefactive —Preventing putrefaction.

Antipyic, Antipyogenic — Preventing or inhibiting pus formation.

Antipyresis —Symptomatic treatment of fever and not of the underlying disease, by the use of antipyretics.

Antipyretic — Reducing fever.

Antipyrotic — Effective in the treatment of burns.

Antirabic —Antilysic. Preventing or curing rabies.

Antirachitic —Curing rickets.

Antirheumatic —Preventing or relieving rheumatism.

Antiscabietic —Effective in the prevention or relief of scabies.

Antiscorbutic —Effective in the prevention or relief of scurvy.

Antiseborrheic —Effective in the treatment of seborrhea.

Antisecretory —Inhibiting or diminishing the secretion of a gland or organ.

Antisepsis —The prevention of sepsis by the prevention or destruction of the causative microorganisms.

Antiseptic —1. Preventing sepsis. 2. The substance which inhibits the growth and development of the causative microorganisms but does not necessarily kill them.

Antiserum —The serum containing antibodies for a specific antigen, obtained from an animal or human being.

Monovalent antiserum —Antiserum containing antibodies specific for one antigen.

Polyvalent antiserum —Antiserum containing antibodies specific for more than one antigen.

Antisialagogue —An agent, as atropine preventing or diminishing the flow of saliva.

Antisialic —Checking the secretion of saliva.

Antisocial —Against society.

Antispasmodic —Preventing or relieving spasm.

Antisudoral, Antisudorific —Inhibiting perspiration.

Antisyphilitic —An agent curing or relieving syphilis.

Antitetanic —Preventing or alleviating muscular contraction.

Antithenar —The eminence on the ulnar side of the palm.

Antithrombin —An agent that prevents the action of thrombin.

Antithrombotic —Preventing thrombosis or blood coagulation.

Antithyroid —Counteracting the function of the thyroid gland, especially the formation of thyroid hormones.

Antitonic —Diminishing tonicity.

Antitoxic —Neutralizing a poison, especially a bacterial toxin.

Antitoxic serum —Serum that contains antitoxin.

Antitoxigen —Antitoxinogen.

Antitoxin —An antibody produced in the body in response to a toxin, which neutralizes the effect of that toxin, *e.g.*, the antitoxins of diphtheria, gas gangrene and tetanus, etc., which counteract the toxins produced by them.

Antitoxinogen —Antitoxigen. An antigen stimulating the production of antitoxin.

Antitragicus —A small muscle in the pinna of the ear.

Antitrichomonal — Counteracting Trichomonas.

Antitrismus —A condition in which the mouth remains open due to tonic muscular spasm.

Antitryptic —Inhibiting the action of trypsin.

Antituberculotic —Effective in the treatment of tuberculosis.

Antitumorigenesis — Inhibition of the development of a tumor.

Antitussive —Preventing or relieving cough.

Antityphoid —Preventive or curative of typhoid fever.

Antivenene, Antivenin —A serum that contains antitoxin specific for an animal or insect venom, which is prepared from the serum of the immunized animals and is used in the treatment of poisoning by animal or insect venom, e.g., an antisnake bite serum obtained from the serum of horses immunized against venom of specific snakes, which is used in the treatment of those snake bites.

Antivenereal —Preventing or curing venereal diseases.

Antivenin —Antivenene. An antitoxin specific for an animal or insect venom.

Antivenom —Antivenin.

Antivenomous —Opposing the action of venom.

Antiviral —Destroying the viruses.

Antivitamin —Opposing the action of a vitamin.

Antivivisection —Opposition to the use of living animals in experiments.

Antixerophthalmic — Counteracting xerophthalmia.

Antixerotic —Preventing dryness of the skin.

Antizymotic —An agent which prevents or arrests fermentation.

Antra —Plural of antrum.

Antral —Pertaining to an antrum.

Antrectomy —Excision of an antrum.

Antritis —Inflammation of an antrum.

Antro- —Prefix denoting relationship to an antrum.

Antrobuccal—Concerning with the maxillary sinus and the cheek.

Antrocele —Accumulation of fluid in a cyst in the maxillary sinus.

Antroduodenectomy — Removal of the pyloric antrum and the upper portion of the duodenum by operation.

Antronasal —Pertaining to the maxillary sinus and the nasal fossa.

Antrophore —A medicated bougie for local treatment of any approachable antrum.

Antrophose —Sensation of light or color produced in the visual centres of the brain by mechanical or electrical stimulation.

Antropyloric —Pertaining to or affecting the pyloric antrum.

Antroscope —An instrument for visual examination of the maxillary sinus or antrum.

Antroscopy —Visual examination of the maxillary sinus or antrum by using an antroscope.

Antrostomy —To make a permanent opening in an antrum for drainage.

Antrotome —An instrument to perform antrotomy.

Antrotomy —To make an incision into an antrum.

Antrotympanic —Pertaining to the mastoid antrum and the tympanic cavity.

Antrotympanitis — Inflammation of the mastoid antrum and the tympanic cavity.

Antrum —A cavity or chamber, *e.g.,* external auditory canal, dilatation of the duodenum near the pylorus (duodenal cap) seen during digestion, air space in the mastoid portion of the temporal bone, maxillary sinus, dilated part of the pyloric portion of the stomach between the body of the stomach and the pyloric canal.

Anuclear —Without nucleus, as red blood cells.

Anular —Annular. Ring-shaped.

Anulus —Ring-shaped or encircling structure of the body.

Anuresis —Absence of urination.

Anuria —Absence of urine formation by the kidneys.

Anuric —Pertaining to anuria.

Anus —The opening of the rectum on the body surface, situated between the buttocks, may be closed congenitally completely or partially, called imperforate anus.

Anvil —Incus. The second of the three bones in the middle ear.

Anxietas, Anxiety —A feeling of apprehension, uneasiness of mind, uncertainty and fear for the future associated with physiological changes as tachycardia, sweating and tremor etc.

Anxiety neurosis —A mental disorder characterized by excessive anxiety associated with physical symptoms such as palpitation, cardiac pain, dyspepsia, constriction of the throat, headache, cold sweating with tremulousness of the extremities.

Anxiety presenilis —Anxiety occurring before old age.

Anxiolytic —Counteracting or diminishing anxiety which may be done by the medicinal or psychological treatment.

Aorta —The main trunk of the arterial system of the body arising from the left ventricle.

Aortal —Pertaining to the aorta.

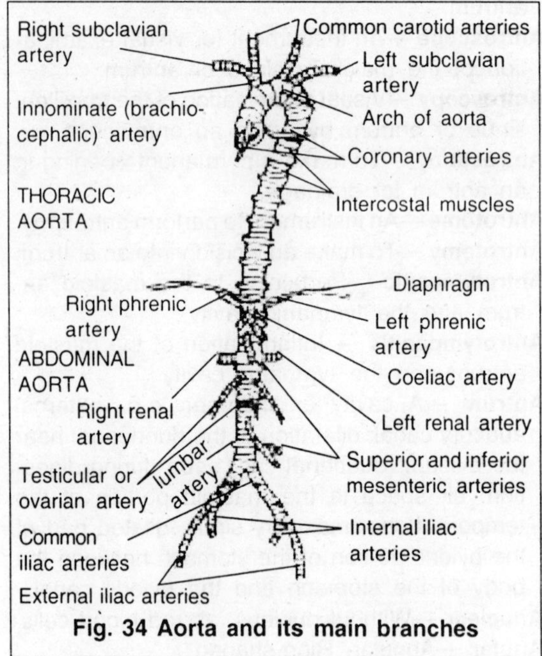

Fig. 34 Aorta and its main branches

Aortalgia —Pain in the region of the aorta.

Aortarctia —Narrowing of the aorta.

Aortartia —Aortostenosis.

Aortectasia —Dilatation of the aorta.

Aortectomy —Excision of a part of the aorta.

Aortic —Pertaining to the aorta or its opening in the left ventricle of the heart.

Aortic incompetence —Back flow of blood into the left ventricle through the aortic valve.

Aorticopulmonary — Pertaining to or lying between the aorta and the pulmonary artery.

Aortitis —Inflammation of the aorta.

Aortoclasia —Rupture of the aorta.

Aortocoronary —Pertaining to or communicating with the aorta and coronary arteries.

Aortocoronary bypass — Coronary bypass.

Aortogram —X-ray film produced by aortography.

Aortography —Radiography of the aorta after introduction of a radiopaque substance into it by injection.

Aortolith —Deposition of the calculi in the wall of the aorta.

Aortomalacia —Softening of the walls of the aorta.

Aortopathy —Any disease of the aorta.

Aortoplasty —Repair of the aorta by plastic surgery.

Aortoptosia, Aortoptosis — Downward displacement of the abdominal aorta.

Aortorrhaphy —Suture of the aorta.

Aortosclerosis —Sclerosis of the aorta.

Aortostenosis —Aortic stenosis. Narrowing of the aorta and its orifice.

Aortotomy —To make an incision into the aorta.

Aosmic —Odourless.

Apallesthesia —Loss of sense of vibrations on the skin.

Apancrea —Absence of the pancreas.

Apancreatic —Caused by the absence of the pancreas.

Aparalytic —Without paralysis.

Aparathyreosis —Hypoparathyroidism.

Aparathyroidism —Congenital absence or surgical removal of the parathyroid glands.

Aparathyrosis —Parathyroid deficiency.

Apareunia —Inability to accomplish sexual intercourse.

Aparthrosis —Diarthrosis. Dislocation of a joint.

Apastia —To refuse to eat.

Apathetic, Apathic — Indifferent. Having no interest.

Apathism —Slowness of response to the stimuli.

Apathy —Indifference, lack of feeling or emotion.

Apellous —1. Not covered with the skin, as a wound. 2. Having no prepuce, as is done in circumcision.

Apenteric —Abenteric. Outside the intestine.

Apepsia —Cessation of digestion.

Apepsinia —Lack of pepsin in the gastric juice.

Aperient —A mild laxative.

Aperiodic —Not occurring periodically.

Aperistalsis —Absence of peristaltic movements.

Aperitif —Wine.

Aperitive —Increasing the appetite.

Apert's syndrome —A congenital condition in which the head is peaked and the fingers and toes are webbed.

Apertura, Aperture —An opening or orifice.

Apex —The pointed end of a conical structure.

Apex beat —The heart sound produced on striking of the apex of the left ventricle against the chest wall in systole, which is felt in the left 5th intercostal space approximately 3½ inches from the middle of the sternum and about an inch within a line drawn down from the middle of the clavicle parallel to the sternum.

Apexigraph —An apparatus for determining the size and position of the apex of a tooth root.

Aphacia —Aphakia.

Aphacic —Aphakic.

Aphagia —Inability to swallow.

Aphakia —Absence of the lens of the eye.

Aphakic —Pertaining to aphakia, the person without eye lens.

Aphalangia —Absence of fingers or toes.

Aphanisis —Fear that the sexual potency will be lost.

Aphasia —Inability to express the thoughts by speech, writing and signs, due to injury or disease of the brain centers.

Amnesic aphasia — Loss of memory for words.

Anomic aphasia — Inability to name the objects and their qualities.

Auditory aphasia — Inabiiity to understand the spoken words.

Fluent aphasia —The words are easily spoken but they are not correct and may be incoherent to the other words spoken.

Gibberish aphasia — Speaking of the meaningless phrases.

Global aphasia —Total aphasia involving the failure of all means of communication, the patient cannot speak, understand, read and write.

Motor aphasia, Expressive aphasia —Aphasia in which the patient understands the written and spoken words and knows what he wants to say, but he cannot utter the words.

Nominal aphasia — Inability to name the objects.

Nonfluent aphasia —Aphasia in which the words are spoken slowly and with great effort.

Optic aphasia — Inability to name some object seen with the eyes without the help of sound, taste or touch etc.

Semantic aphasia — Inability to understand the meaning of words.

Sensory aphasia — Inability to understand spoken or written words.

Traumatic aphasia — Aphasia caused by head injury.

Visual aphasia —Word blindness. Inability to understand the written words.

Aphasic, Aphasiac — Pertaining to aphasia.

Aphasiologist —A neurologist or psychologist who is specialist in aphasiology.

Aphasiology —The scientific study of aphasia.

Aphemesthesia —Sensory aphasia. Inability to understand the words.

Aphemia —Loss of power to speak due to a lesion in the central nervous system.

Aphephobia —Morbid fear of being touched.

Apheresis —A procedure in which the components of blood, as white blood cells, red blood cells and platelets etc. are separated from the blood.

Aphilopony —Lack of desire in performing a work.

Aphonia —Inability to produce speech sounds from the larynx as may occur in chronic laryngitis. It is not caused by a brain lesion.

Aphonic — 1. Pertaining to aphonia. 2. The person suffering from aphonia.

Aphonogelia —Inability to laugh loudly.

Aphonous —Aphonic.

Aphose —Visual perception of darkness or of a shadow.

Aphotesthesia — Decreased sensitivity of the retina to light caused by excessive exposure to sunlight.

Aphrasia —Inability to speak or understand the spoken words.

Aphrenia —Dementia.

Aphrenic, Aphrenous — Pertaining to dementia or the person suffering from dementia.

Aphrodisia —Excessive sexual passion.

Aphrodisiac —An agent that arouses sexual desire.

Aphrodisiomania —Mania or madness for gaining excessive sexual pleasures.

Aphthae —Small white or red ulcers found on the mucous membrane of the mouth or beneath the tongue, which are the characteristics of aphthous stomatitis.

Aphthoid —Resembling aphthae.

Aphthongia —Inability to speak due to spasm of the muscles controlling the speech.

Apthosis —A condition characterized by the presence of aphthae.

Aphthous —Pertaining to or characterized by aphthae.

Aphylactic —Deficient in immunity.

Aphylaxis —Absence of immunity.

Apical —Pertaining to the apex of a structure.

Apicectomy —Excision of the apex of the petrous portion of the temporal bone.

Apiceotomy —Apicotomy.

Apices —Plural of the apex.

Apicitis —Inflammation of an apex as of a lung or root of a tooth.

Apicoectomy —Excision of the apex of a tooth root.

Apicolocator —An apparatus for locating the root apex of a tooth.

Apicolysis —Collapse of the apex of a lung by surgery, by making an opening through the anterior chest wall, to obliterate the cavity of the apex.

Apicostome —The trocar and cannula used in apicostomy.

Apicostomy —An operation in which the alveolar plate is perforated with a trocar and cannula to reach the root apex of a tooth.

Apicotomy —To make an incision in the apex of a structure.

Apiculate —Terminated abruptly in a small point.

Apinealism —Absence of the pineal gland.

Apiphobia —Melissophobia. Morbid fear of bees.

Apituitarism —Loss of pituitary function or the absence of pituitary gland.

Aplacental —Having no placenta.

Aplanatic lens —A lens correcting the spherical aberration.

Aplanatism —The condition of a lens of being free from spherical aberration.

Aplasia —Lack of normal development of an organ or tissue e.g., aplasia cutis congenita in which there is defective development of the localized area of the skin congenitally, most commonly of the scalp, the area is covered by the translucent membrane, and aplasia gonadal in which there is congenital absence of gonadal tissue.

Aplastic —Pertaining to aplasia; having deficient or arrested development.

Aplastic anemia —Anemia caused by deficient production of red blood cells due to some disorder or destruction of the bone marrow.

Apleuria —Congenital absence of one or more ribs.

Apnea —Cessation of respiration for some time.

Apneic —Pertaining to or suffering from apnea.

Apneic oxygenation —The supplying of oxygen to the upper respiratory tract of patients who are suffering from apnea.

Apneumatic —Free of air, as in a collapsed lung.

Apneumia —Congenital absence of the lungs.

Apneusis —Sustained inspiratory effort not relieved by expiration.

Apo- —Prefix denoting separation or originating from.

Apobiosis —Death, especially death of a part.

Apocamnosis —Tiredness.

Apochromatic —Free from chromatic and spherical aberrations.

Apochromatic lens —A lens that corrects both spherical and chromatic aberrations.

Apocope —Amputation.

Apocoptic —Pertaining to or resulting from amputation.

Apocrine —It is a type of sweat gland located in the axilla, pubic region, mammary gland and labia majora, which opens into the hair follicle instead of opening directly onto the surface of the skin like accrine sweat gland.

Apocrustic —Astringent and repellent.

Apodal —Having not feet.

Apodemialgia —Abnormal desire to leave the home.

Apodia —Congenital absence of one or both feet.

Apodous —Apodal.

Apody —Apodia.

Apoenzyme —The protein portion of an enzyme.

Apoferritin —A protein which combines with the iron to form ferritin.

Apogamia, Apogamy — Parthenogenesis.

Apogee —The state of greatest severity of a disease.

Apolar —Having no poles or processes.

Apolepsis —1. Cessation of a function. 2. Retention of an excretion or secretion.

Aponeurectomy —Excision of an aponeurosis.

Aponeurology —The branch of anatomy which deals with the study of aponeurosis.

Aponeurorrhaphy —Suture of an aponeurosis.

Aponeurosis —A sheet of fibrous membrane connecting a muscle with the parts it moves.

Aponeurositis —Inflammation of an aponeurosis.

Aponeurotic —Pertaining to an aponeurosis.

Aponeurotome —An instrument for cutting an aponeurosis.

Aponeurotomy —To make an incision in the aponeurosis.

Aponia —1. To keep onself away from exertion. 2. Absence of pain.

Aponic —1. Pertaining to aponia. 2. Relieving pains.

Apophyseal, Apophysial — Pertaining to an apophysis.

Apophysis —An outgrowth, especially of a bone which forms a part of the bone and is never entirely separated from it, such as a process, tubercle or tuberosity *e.g.,* mastoid process of the temporal bone.

Apophysitis —Inflammation of an apophysis.

Apoplasmia —Decrease in the amount of blood plasma.

Apoplectic —Pertaining to apoplexy.

Apoplectiform, Apoplectoid —Resembling apoplexy.

Apoplexy, Apoplexia — 1. Copious extravasation of blood into an organ, as abdominal, pulmonary or uterine apoplexy. 2. Sudden loss of consciousness followed by paralysis caused by hemorrhage into the brain, formation of an embolus or thrombus which obstructs an artery.

Aposia —Adipsia. Absence of thirst.

Aposiopesis —Sudden cessation of speech in the middle of a sentence as if one is unable or not willing to speak.

Apositia —A great dislike to food.

Apostasis —1. An abscess. 2. The crisis or end of a disease.

Apostaxis —Slight haemorrhage or bleeding in drops.

Apostem, Apostema —An abscess.

Aposthia —Congenital absence of the prepuce.

Apothanasia —Prolongation of life.

Apothecary —Pharmacist.

Apotripsis —Removal of a corneal opacity.

Apparatus —1. An arrangement for a number of parts acting together to perform a special function, *e.g.,* a device for performing artificial respiration. 2. A group of structures or organs of the body working together to perform a common function, *e.g.,* biliary apparatus comprising of liver, gallbladder, hepatic, cystic and common bile ducts, which is concerned with the secretion and excretion of bile; lacrimal apparatus which consists of the lacrimal (tear-secreting) gland, lacrimal duct, lacrimal sac and other associated structures concerned with the secretion and passage of tears from the eye to the nasal cavity.

Appearance —Outlook.

Appendage —Any structure attached to, or an outgrowth of a major part, *e.g.,* a limb of the trunk, eyelids and eyelashes of the eye, hair and the nails of the skin and fallopian tubes of the uterus.

Appendalgia —Pain in the abdomen in the region of vermiform appendix.

Appendectomy —Excision of the vermiform appendix.

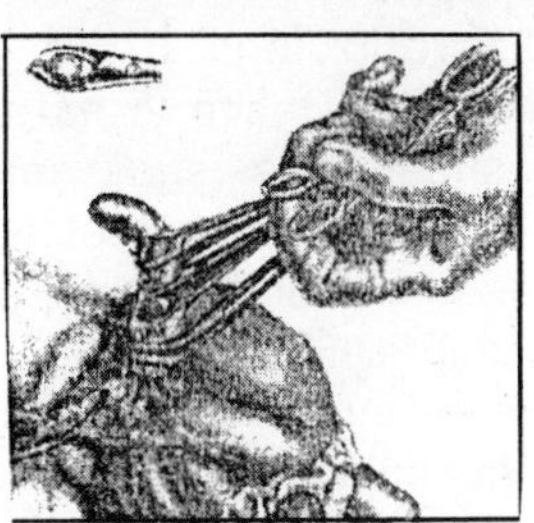

Fig. 35 : Appendectomy

Appendical, Appendiceal — Pertaining to an appendix.

Appendicectasis —Dilatation of the vermiform appendix.

Appendicectomy — Appendectomy.

Appendices —Plural of appendix.

Appendicitis —Inflammation of the vermiform appendix.

Appendicocele —The vermiform appendix in a hernial sac.

Appendicoenterostomy — Appendicostomy.

Appendicolithiasis — Formation of calculi in the vermiform appendix.

Appendicolysis —To separate the vermiform appendix from the adhesions by surgery.

Appendicopathy —Any disease of the vermiform appendix.

Appendicostomy —To make an opening into the vermiform appendix by surgery to irrigate or drain the large intestine.

Appendicula —A small appendage.

Appendicular—1. Pertaining to an appendix. 2. Pertaining to the limbs or an appendage.

Appendicular skeleton —The bony structure forming the shoulder girdle, upper extremities, pelvic girdle and lower extremities.

Appendix —A supplementary or accessary part attached to a main structure, e.g., vermiform appendix, which is a wormlike projection about 9 cms. long from the blind end of the cecum; and xiphoid process etc.

Apperception —The process of receiving and interpreting the sensory stimuli.

Apperceptive —Pertaining to apperception.

Appersonation, Appersonification —The delusion in which a person assumes the characteristics of another person.

Appestat —The area of the brain (probably in the hypothalamus) concerned in controlling the appetite.

Appetence, Appetency —Strong appetite.
Appetite —Desire for food.
Appetite perverted —Desire to eat unnatural or indigestible substances, such as paint, etc.
Appetizer —Promoting the appetite.
Applanation —Abnormal flattening, especially of the corneal surface.
Applanometer —Tonometer. An apparatus for measuring the intraocular pressure.
Applanometry —Use of tonometer for measuring the intraocular pressure.
Appliance —A device used to facilitate a particular function, such as artificial denture in dentistry.
Applicator —A wooden or metallic stick, at one end of which is attached a pledget of cotton or other substance, used to apply medicine to a part of the body.
Apposition —The condition of being fitted together or addition of one substance to another one as one layer of tissue upon another.
Apprehension —Anticipatory fear or anxiety.
Apprehensive —Fearful for future or anxious.
Approach —Surgical procedures by which an organ or part is exposed.
Approximal —Close together.
Approximate —To bring close together.
Approximation —The process of bringing close together.
Apraxia —1. Inability to perform purposeful movements in the absence of sensory or motor impairment. 2. Inability to use objects properly.
Apraxic —Pertaining to or characterized by apraxia.
Aproctia —Imperforation of the anus.
Aprofen, Aprofene, Aprophen — Analgesic and antispasmodic.
Apron —A type of coat which is put on during anatomy dissection, surgery, certain nursing procedures, while plastering etc. for protecting the clothes.
Aprosexia —Inability to fix attention.
Aprosody —Absence of normal variations of pitch, rhythm and stress in the speech.
Aprosopia —Partial or complete congenital absence of face.
Aprosopus —A fetus with partial or complete absence of the face.
Apselaphesia —Absence of tactile sense.
Apsithyria —Loss of voice in hysteria.
Apsychia —Unconsciousness.
Aptitude —Inherent ability or skill in learning or performing physical or mental works.
Aptyalia, Aptyalism — Xerostomia; deficiency or absence of saliva.
Apulmonism —Congenital partial or complete absence of a lung.
Apus —The person having no feet.
Apyetous —Non-suppurative.
Apyogenous —Not due to pus.
Apyous —Apyetous.
Apyretic —Afebrile. Without fever.
Apyrexia —Absence of fever.
Apyrexial —Afebrile.
Apyrogenetic, Apyrogenic —Not producing fever.
Aqua —Water, *e.g.* distilled water, hot water, lime water, lukewarm water, medicated water, pure water, sterilized water.
Aquanaut —The person working under water.
Aquaphobia —Hydrophobia. Morbid fear of water.
Aquapuncture —Subcutaneous injection of water.
Aquatic —1. Pertaining to water. 2. Inhabiting water.
Aqueduct —Canal or channel.
Aqueductus —Aqueduct.
Aqueous —Watery. Prepared by water.
Aqueous chambers —Anterior and posterior chambers of the eye, which contain the aqueous humor.
Aqueous humor —Transparent liquid contained in the anterior and posterior chambers of the eye.
Aquiparous —Producing water.
Aquosity —1. The state of being watery 2. Moisture.
Arachnephobia —Arachnophobia. Morbid fear of spiders.
Arachnidism —Arachnoidism. A systemic condition produced from spider bite.
Arachnitis —Arachnoiditis. Inflammation of the arachnoid.
Arachnodactyly —The condition in which the fingers and toes are abnormally long and curved.
Arachnoid —1. The membranous structure lying between the dura mater and the pia mater. 2. Resembling a spider's web.
Arachnoidal —Pertaining to the arachnoid mater.
Arachnoidism —Arachnidism.
Arachnoiditis —Arachnitis.
Arachnophobia —Morbid fear of spiders.
Arborescent —Branching, treelike.
Arborization —Terminal branching of nerve fibers and capillaries.
Arborize —To spread in branches like tree.
Arbor vitae —Branching like a tree.
Arc —A curved line or the portion of a circle.

Arcade —Arch.
Arcanum —Secret remedy.
Arcate —Bow-shaped.
Arch-, Arche-, Archi- —Prefixes meaning first, chief and beginning.
Arch —A curved or bow-like structure.
Alveolar arch, Dental arch —The arch formed by the alveolar process and the teeth in each jaw.
Aortic arch —Arch of the aorta at about the level of the fourth thoracic vertebra.
Costal arch —Arch formed by the ribs.
Nasal arch —Arch formed by the nasal bones and by the nasal processes of the maxilla.
Palmar arch —Arch formed in the palm.
Plantar arch —Arch formed in the sole of the foot.
Supraorbital arch — The bony arch formed by the upper margin of the orbit.
Archencephalon —The primitive brain from which the midbrain and forebrain develop.
Archenteron —The primitive intestinal tract.
Archigaster —The primitive embryonic alimentary canal.
Archinephron —Primordial kidney.
Architis —Inflammation of the anus, proctitis.
Archo- —Prefix denoting relationship to the rectum or anus.
Archocele —Hernia of the rectum.
Archocystocolposyrinx — Fistula of rectum, vagina and bladder.
Archoptosis —Prolapse of the rectum.
Archostenosis —Stenosis of the rectum.
Archosyrin —Fistula in ano.
Arciform —Arcuate. Shaped like an arc.
Arctation —Narrowing of any opening or canal.
Arcuate —Arciform.
Arcuation —A bending.
Arcus —Arch.
Arcus aortae —Aortic arch.
Arcus dentalis —Dental arch.
Arcus plantaris — Plantar arch.
Arcus senilis —An opaque white ring seen at the periphery of the cornea in aged persons.
Ardanesthesia — Thermanesthesia. Inability to feel heat.
Ardent —Feverish. Burning.
Ardor —Burning, as burning sensation during micturition.
Areata, Areatus — Occurring in circumscribed areas or patches.
Arefaction —The act of drying.
Areflexia —Absence of the reflex actions.
Arenaceous, Arenoid — Resembling sand or gravel.
Arenation —Application of hot sand on the body.
Areola —A circular area of different pigmentation surrounding a central part as around the nipple of the breast, pigmented area around the umbilicus, or the part of the iris around the pupil.
Areolar —Pertaining to an areola.
Areolitis —Inflammation of the areola of the breast.
Areometer —Hydrometer. An instrument for measuring the specific gravity of fluids.
Argamblyopia —Reduction in vision due to not using the eye.
Argema —White corneal ulcer.
Argentaffin, Argentaffine —Denoting cells staining readily with silver salts, giving rise to a brown or black color.
Argentaffinoma —A tumor formed of the argentaffin cells, which may develop in the gastrointestinal tract, bile ducts, pancreas, bronchus or ovary and may produce carcinoid syndrome.
Argentation —Impregnation with a silver salt.
Argentine —Pertaining to, resembling or containing silver.
Argentum —Silver.
Argyll Robertson pupil — A condition of the pupils of the eyes occurring in syphilis of the brain, discovered by the scientist Douglas Argyll Robertson, in which the pupils become smaller and unequal in size with irregular outline, which may be pentagonal instead of circular, do not react to light but their power of contraction during accommodation is not changed.
Argyria —A condition caused by prolonged administration of silver salts in which the skin and the mucous membranes become blue.
Argyric —Pertaining to the silver.
Argyrism —Argyria.
Argyrophil —The cell capable to bind with the silver salts.
Argyrosis —Argyira.
Arhinia —Arrhinia. Congenital absence of the nose.
Ariboflavinosis —The condition arising from a deficiency of riboflavin in the diet characterized by cheilosis.
Arithmomania —Mania for counting or solving arithmatical problems.
Arm —Brachium. The part of the upper extremity from shoulder to the elbow.

Armamentarium —The total equipment of a practitioner or a hospital including medicines, diagnostic and surgical instruments, and books etc.
Armpit —Axilla.
Aroma —Agreeable odor.
Aromatic —Having agreeable odor.
Aromatization —To convert a non-aromatic substance into an aromatic substance.
Arousal —1. The state of being prepared to act 2. Sexual excitement.
Arrector —Erector. Raising as an arrector muscle.
Arrest —Stoppage, as of a function or a disease process.
  Cardiac arrest —Sudden cessation of the heart beat.
  Epiphyseal arrest —Stoppage of growth of long bones.
  Pelvic arrest —The condition in whch the presenting part of the fetus becomes fixed in the pelvis of the mother.
  Sinus arrest —The condition in which the sinus node of the heart does not produce impulses for the heart beat.
Arrhenoblastoma —A tumor of the ovary which secretes male sex hormone producing secondary male sex characteristics (virilization) in the female.
Arrhinia —Congenital absence of the nose.
Arrhythmia —Irregularity of the heart beat.
Arrhythmic —Pertaining to or marked by arrhythmia.
Arrhythmogenic —Capable of inducing cardiac arrhythmias.
Arseniasis, Arsenicism —Chronic arsenic poisoning.
Arsenical —Pertaining to or containing arsenic.
Arsenicalism —Arseniasis. Chronic arsenic poisoning.
Arsenicophagy —Habitual eating of arsenic.
Arsenifast —Resistant to the poisonous action of arsenic.
Arsenium —Arsenic.
Arsenotherapy —Treatment of the diseases by arsenic.
Arsine —A very poisonous gas used in chemical warfare.
Artefact —A structure in a cell or tissue produced by death or use of reagents.
Arteralgia —Pain in the artery.
Arterectomy —Excision of an artery or arteries.
Arteri- —Arterio-.
Arteria —Artery.
Arteriagra —Pain in an artery.
Arterial —Pertaining to one or more arteries.
Arterialization —1. Becoming arterial. 2. Oxygenation of blood whereby it is changed from venous to arterial. 3. Conversion of a venous structure to function as an artery.
Arterial varix —An enlarged and twisted artery.
Arteriasis —Degeneration of an artery.
Arteriectasis, Arteriectasia —Dilatation of an artery.
Arteriectomy —Excision of a portion of an artery.
Arterio- —Prefix denoting relationship to an artery.
Arterioatony —Lack of tone in the walls of an artery.
Arteriocapillary —Pertaining to both, arteries and the capillaries.
Arteriogram —X-ray film of an artery after injection of a radiopaque substance.
Arteriographic —-Pertaining to or utilizing arteriography.
Arteriogarphy —Radiography of an artery after injection of a radiopaque substance.
Arteriola —Arteriole. Small artery.
Arteriolar —Pertaining to an arteriole.
Arteriole —Arteriola. A minute artery which leads to a capillary.
Arteriolith —A calculus in an artery.
Arteriolitis —Inflammation of the arterioles.
Arteriology —Scientific study of the arteries.
Arteriolonecrosis —Necrosis or destruction of the arterioles.
Arteriolosclerosis — Thickening and hardening of the walls of the arterioles with the loss of elasticity and contractility.
Arteriolosclerotic — Pertaining to or characterized by arteriolosclerosis.
Arteriolovenous — Arteriolovenular. Pertaining to both, the arterioles and the veins.
Arteriolovenular — Arteriolovenous.
Arteriomalacia —Abnormal softening of the arteries.
Arteriometer —An instrument for measuring the diameter of an artery, or its change in size during pulsation.
Arteriomotor —Causing dilatation and constriction and thus changing the internal diameter of the arteries.
Arteriomyomatosis — Thickening of the walls of an artery due to overgrowth of muscle fibres.
Arterionecrosis —Necrosis of arteries.
Arteriopalmus —Throbbing sensation of an artery.

Arteriopathy —Any disease of an artery.
Arterioplasty —Repair of an artery by plastic surgery.
Arteriopressor —Increasing the arterial blood pressure.
Arteriorrhaphy —Suture of an artery.
Arteriorrhexis —Rupture of an artery.
Arteriosclerosis —Thickening and hardening of the walls of the arteries with loss of elasticity and contractility.
Arteriosclerotic —Pertaining to or characterized by arteriosclerosis.
Arteriospasm —Spasm of an artery.
Arteriostenosis —Narrowing of an artery.
Arteriostosis —Calcification of an artery.
Arteriostrepsis —Twisting of the cut end of an artery to arrest hemorrhage.
Arteriotome —A knife for opening an artery.
Arteriotomy —To divide or open an artery by surgery.
Arteriotony — Tonicity of an artery.
Arteriovenous —Pertaining to both, the arteries and the veins.
Arterioversion —To evert the wall of an artery to check the hemorrhage from the cut end.
Arterioverter —An instrument used to evert the cut end of an artery to arrest the hemorrhage.
Arteritis —Inflammation of an artery.
Artery —One of the blood vessels carrying oxygenated blood from the heart to all the parts of the body.

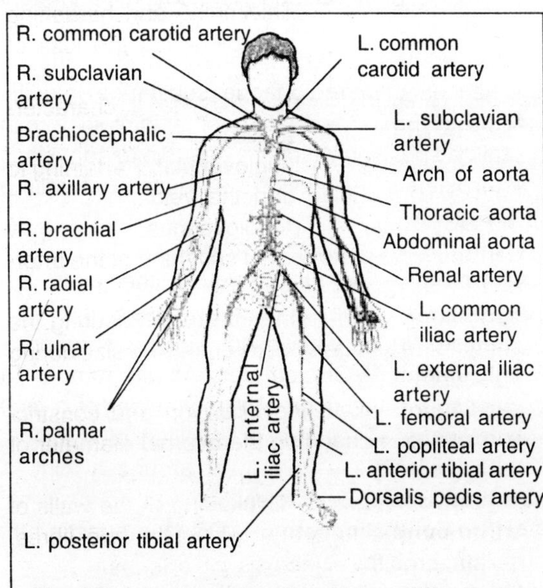

Fig. 36A : Aorta and main arteries of the limbs.

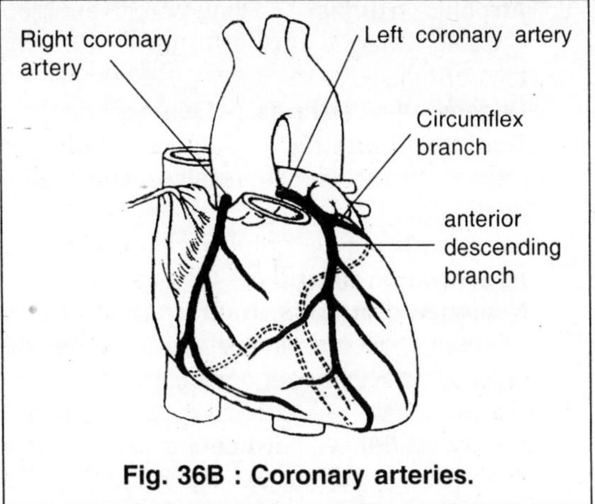

Fig. 36B : Coronary arteries.

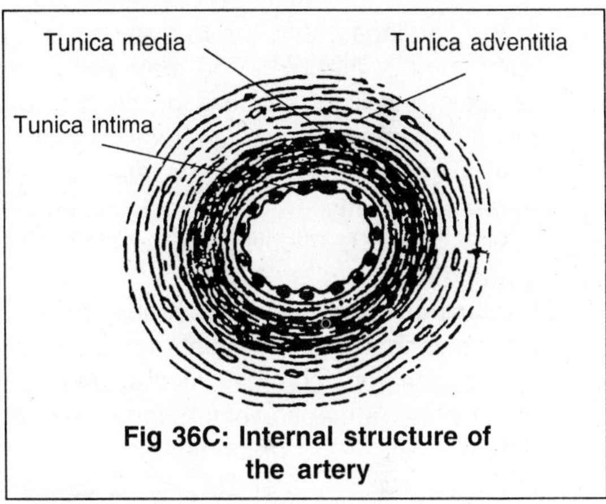

Fig 36C: Internal structure of the artery

Arthral —Pertaining to a joint.
Arthralgia —Pain in a joint.
Arthralgic —Pertaining to or suffering from arthralgia.
Arthrectomy —Excision of a joint.
Arthredema —Edema of a joint.
Arthrempyesis —Suppuration in a joint.
Arthresthesia —The perception of joint movements.
Arthritic —1. Pertaining to arthritis. 2. The person suffering from arthritis.
Arthritide —A skin eruption caused by gout or arthritis.
Arthritides —Plural of arthritis.
Arthritis —Inflammation of a joint.
Acute arthritis — Severe form of arthritis in which there is pain, swelling, heat and redness of the joint.
Allergic arthritis — Arthritis occurring as a result of food allergy or due to hypersensitivity reaction following the administration of some drug.

Atrophic arthritis — Rheumatoid arthritis.

Chronic inflammatory arthritis — Rheumatoid arthritis.

Degenerative arthritis —Osteoarthritis.

Gonorrheal arthritis — Arthritis due to gonorrheal infection which usually occurs in knee joint.

Gouty arthritis — Arthritis caused by gout.

Hypertrophic arthritis —Osteoarthritis.

Neurogenic arthritis, Neurotrophic arthritis —Arthritis occurring due to some nervous disease, as in syringomyelia.

Osteoarthritis —A chronic disease involving especially the weight bearing joint such as knee joint, occurring usually in man over 50 years of age, characterized by degeneration of the cartilages, and the outgrowths of the bony ends of the joint. The main symptoms are pain, swelling, stiffness of the joint and restricted movements. On examination, a click sound is felt on moving the affected joint.

Psoriatic arthritis — Arthritis associated with severe psoriasis affecting the terminal interphalangeal joints.

Rheumatoid arthritis —A chronic systemic disease primarily of the joints characterized by inflammatory changes in the joints and atrophy and rarefaction of the bones, with the development of the deformity and ankylosis of the joint in the later stages. Its cause is unknown but antigen-antibody reaction and viral infection are considered to be the cause.

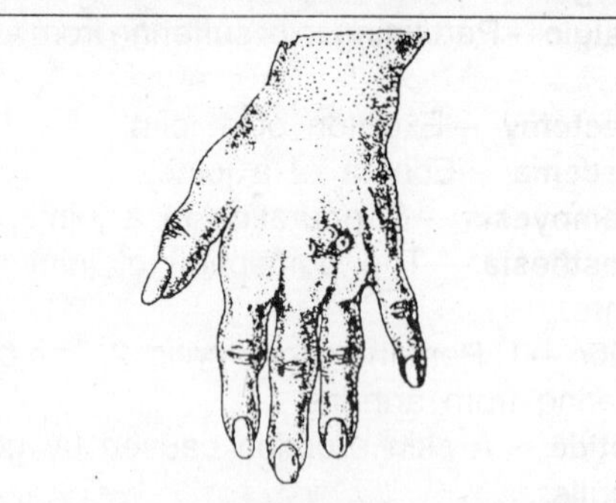

Fig. 37 Rheumatoid arthritis of the joints of hand.

Suppurative arthritis —Inflammation of the synovial membrane of a joint with pus formation in the joint capsule which is usually due to bacterial infection.

Syphilitic arthritis —Inflammation of a joint occurring in secondary and tertiary stages of syphilis, characterized by tenderness, swelling and difficulty in movements.

Tuberculous arthritis —A chronic inflammation of a joint due to tuberculous infection.

Arthro- —Prefix pertaining to joints.

Arthrocace —Infected cavity of a joint.

Arthrocele —1. Hernia of the synovial membrane of a joint. 2. A joint swelling.

Arthrocentesis —Puncture of a joint space by a needle to aspirate the fluid accumulated therein.

Arthrochalasis —Abnormal relaxation of a joint.

Arthrochondritis — Inflammation of the cartilage of a joint.

Arthroclasia —Surgical breaking down of the ankylosis of a joint to provide movement.

Arthrodesis —To immobilize a joint by surgical procedure. Artificial ankylosis.

Arthrodia —A joint with a gliding movement.

Arthrodial —Pertaining to arthrodia.

Arthrodynia —Arthralgia. Pain in a joint.

Arthrodynic —Arthralgic. Pertaining to or suffering from pain in the joint.

Arthrodysplasia —Hereditary deformity of various joints.

Arthroempyesis —Suppuration within a joint.

Arthroendoscopy —Inspection of the interior of a joint by using an endoscope.

Arthrogenous —Originating from or forming a joint.

Arthrogram —X-ray film of a joint taken after an injection of a radiopaque substance into the joint.

Arthrography —Radiography of a joint after an injection of a radiopaque substance into it.

Arthrogryposis —Fixation of a joint in a contracted position which may be due to adhesions.

Arthrokleisis —Ankylosis produced naturally or surgically.

Arthrolith —Calculus in a joint.

Arthrology —Scientific study of the joints.

Arthrolysis —The process of loosening the adhesions in an ankylosed joint by surgery.

Arthrometer —Goniometer. An instrument for measuring the degree of movement of a joint.

Arthroncus —A tumor or swelling of a joint.

Arthroneuralgia —Pain in or around a joint.

Arthronosos —Joint disease.

Arthro-ophthalmopathy — Disease affecting the joints and the eyes.

Arthropathology —The pathology of a joint disease.

Arthropathy —Any disease of a joint.
Arthrophyma —A joint swelling.
Arthrophyte —Abnormal growth in a joint cavity.
Arthroplasty —Repair of a joint by plastic surgery.
Arthropneumoradiography — Radiography of a synovial joint after it has been injected with a radiolucent medium such as air or helium.
Arthropyosis —Pus formation in a joint cavity.
Arthrorisis —An operation performed on a joint for limiting its undue mobility caused by paralysis.
Arthrorrhagia —Hemorrhage into a joint.
Arthrosclerosis —Stiffening or hardening of the joints.
Arthroscope —An endoscope for examination of the interior of a joint.
Arthroscopy —Examination of the interior of a joint with an endoscope.
Arthrosis —1. A joint. 2. A disease of a joint.
Arthrosteitis —Inflammation of the bony portion of a joint.
Arthrostenosis—Pathological narrowing of a joint.
Arthrostomy --Surgical formation of an opening into a joint for drainage.
Arthrosynovitis — Inflammation of the synovial membrane of a joint.
Arthrotome —A knife for making incisions into a joint.
Arthrotomy —To make an incision into a joint.
Arthrotropic —Tending to affect the joints.
Arthrous —Jointed or pertaining to a joint.
Arthroxesis —Scraping of the diseased portion of a joint.
Articular —Pertaining to a joint.
Articularis —A small joint.
Articulate —1. To join together as a joint. 2. In dentistry, to fit the teeth on a denture.
Articulatio —The site of union of two bones.
Articulation —The place of junction of two or more bones of the skeleton, joint.
  Amphiarthrosis — Slightly movable joint.
  Diarthrosis —Freely movable joint.
  Synarthrosis —Immovable joint.
Articulator —An instrument used in dentistry to maintain the casts of the teeth in the correct position.
Articulatory —Pertaining to an articulation.
Articulo mortis —At the moment of death.
Articulus —A knuckle or a joint.
Artifact, Artefact —Anything produced artificially.
Artisan's cramp —The cramps occurring in the muscles used in doing the same work for a long time as writing, piano playing, sewing the cloths, etc.
Aryepiglottic —Pertaining to the arytenoid cartilage and the epiglottis.
Arytenoid —Denoting arytenoid cartilage and muscles.
Arytenoidectomy —Excision of arytenoid cartilage.
Arytenoideus —Arytenoid muscles.
Arytenoiditis —Inflammation of arytenoid cartilage or muscle.
Arytenoidopexy—Surgical fixation of the arytenoid muscle or cartilage.
Asaphia —Inability to speak distinctly.
Asbestiform —Fibrous in structure like asbestos.
Asbestos —A fibrous incombustible form of magnesium and calcium silicate.
Asbestosis —A pneumoconiosis due to inhalation of asbestos particles.
Ascariasis —The condition occurring from the infection of the roundworms, Ascaris lumbricoides.
Ascaricide —An agent which kills the roundworms.
Ascaris —Roundworm.

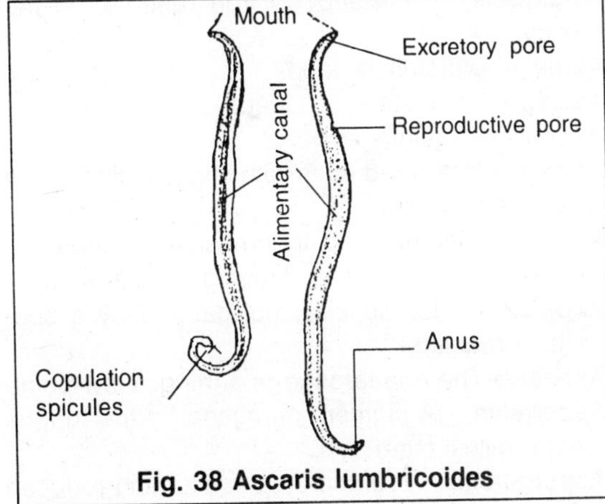

Fig. 38 Ascaris lumbricoides

Ascendens —Going upward.
Ascending —Proceeding towards the superior part of the body.
Ascensus —To go upward.
Aschheim-Zondek test —A test for pregnancy previously used in which the patient's urine is injected subcutaneously into immature female mice.
Aschner's phenomenon, Reflex sign — Oculocardiac reflex. Slowing of the pulse following pressure applied to the eyeball or the carotid sinus.

Aschoff's nodes —Nodes in the myocardium in rheumatism.

Ascites —The accumulation of serous fluid in the abdominal cavity.

Ascites chylous —Presence of chyle in the ascitic fluid usually resulting from the injury or obstruction of the thoracic duct.

Ascitic —Pertaining to ascites.

Ascitogenous —Producing ascites.

Asecretory —Without secretion.

Asemasia —A type of aphasia in which there is loss of ability to communicate by words or by signals.

Asemia —The aphasia in which there is loss of ability to understand the spoken words or signs.

Asepsis —Sterile. A condition of freedom from infection.

Aseptic —Pertaining to or marked by asepsis.

Asexual —Without sex.

Asexualizaiton —Sterilization by removing the ovaries or the testes.

Ash —Residue of combustion.

Asialia —Aptyalism. Deficient secretion or absence of saliva.

Asialism —Absence of saliva.

Asiderosis —Deficiency of iron reserve in the body.

Asitia —Aversion to food.

Asleep —In a state of sleep.

Asocial —Against society.

Asoma —Deformed fetus with imperfectly formed trunk and head.

Asonia —Deafness to the musical sounds.

Aspastic —Non-spastic. Having no spasms.

Aspecific —Non-specific; not caused by a specific organism.

Aspect —The appearance of a thing. View-point.

Aspergillin —A pigment produced by the fungus Aspergillus niger.

Aspergilloma —A granulomatous tumor produced by the fungus Aspergillus in a bronchus or pulmonary cavity.

Aspergillosis —A disease caused by the infection of the fungus Aspergillus characterized by inflammatory granulomatous lesions in the skin, ear, orbit, nasal sinuses, lungs and sometimes in the bones and meninges.

Aspergillus —A kind of fungus.

Aspermatic —Pertaining to aspermatism.

Aspermatism, Aspermia — Lack of formation or non-ejaculation, of semen.

Aspermatogenesis —Lack of production of the sperms by the sperm producing system of the testicles.

Aspermatogenic —Not producing spermatozoa.

Aspermia —Lack of ejaculation of the semen from the male urethra.

Aspermous —Aspermatic.

Asperous —Uneven or having small elevations.

Aspersion —The hydrotherapy in which water of a given temperature is sprinkled on the body.

Asphalgesia —A burning sensation felt on touching certain articles during hypnosis.

Asphyctic, Asphyctous — Pertaining to or affected with asphyxia.

Asphygmia —Temporary absence of pulse.

Asphyxia —The condition caused by insufficient intake of oxygen. Suffocation.

Asphyxia carbonica —Suffocation caused by inhalation of coal gas, water gas or carbon monoxide.

Asphyxia fetal — Asphyxia occurring in a fetus in the uterus due to interference in blood circulation of the placenta or injudicious use of anesthetics.

Asphyxia livida or asphyxia cyanotic —Asphyxia in which the skin becomes blue due to deficiency of oxygen in the blood.

Asphyxia local — Suffocation in which a limited portion of the body is affected, such as the fingers, hands, toes or feet due to stagnation in blood circulation as seen in Raynaud's disease.

Asphyxia neonatorum —Asphyxia occurring in the newborn.

Asphyxia traumatica —Asphyxia due to severe compression of the thorax or upper abdomen or both.

Asphyxial —Pertaining to asphyxia.

Asphyxiant —Causing asphyxia.

Asphyxiate —To cause asphyxia.

Asphyxiation —The act of producing asphyxia.

Aspirate —To draw in or out by suction.

Aspiration —Drawing out or in by suction as withdrawing a fluid from a cavity by suction with an instrument called the aspirator, or drawing in some foreign body into the nose, throat or lungs on inspiration.

Aspirator —An apparatus for removing the fluids or gases from a cavity by suction.

Asplenia —Absence of the spleen.

Asplenic —Having no spleen.

Asporogenic —Not reproducing by spores.

Asporogenous —Not producing spores.

Asporous —Having no spores.
Assault —To make a violent attack.
Assay —The analysis of a substance or mixture to determine its constituents and their amounts.
Assimilable —Capable of undergoing assimilation.
Assimilation —Oxidation of the absorbed food in the cells of the body, and its conversion into protoplasm.
Association neuron —A neuron transmitting the impulses from the afferent to efferent neurons.
Astasia —Inability to stand or sit erect due to motor incoordination.
Astasia-abasia —The inability to either stand or walk in a normal manner.
Astatic —Unable to stand in normal manner.
Asteatosis —Any disease characterized by permanent scaling of the skin indicating deficiency or absence of sebaceous secretion.
Aster —Star.
Astereognosis —Inability to recognize the objects by touch.
Asterixis —Abnormal muscle tremor consisting of involuntary jerky movements, especially in the hands.
Asternal —1. Not joined with the sternum. 2. Having no sternum.
Asternia —Congenital absence of the sternum.
Asteroid —Star-shaped.
Asthenia —Weakness.
Asthenic —Weak person.
Asthenocoria —Sluggishness of the pupillary light reflex.
Asthenometer —An instrument for determining the muscular strength.
Asthenope —The person affected with asthenopia.
Asthenopia —Weakness or tiredness of the eyes with the pain in the eyes, headache and diminess of vision.
Asthenopic —Pertaining to asthenopia.
Asthenospermia —Reduction of motility of spermatozoa in semen.
Asthenoxia —Deficient oxygenation of the waste products.
Asthenozoospermia — Weakness of the spermatozoa in the semen.
Asthma —Difficulty in breathing accompanied by wheezing sound due to bronchial spasm. Dyspnea.

Bronchial asthma — Asthma due to chronic infections of the respiratory tract; allergy due to inhalation of the pollen grains or dust, etc., food like eggs or drugs such as aspirin, etc; exposure to smoke; mental stress and physical fatigue. Time taken in inspiration is reduced to 1/3 of the expiration which should be equal normally.

Cardiac asthma — Dyspnea associated with heart disease such as congestive heart failure. The breathing is less labored, but more rapid.

Renal asthma —Dyspnea in chronic nephritis.

Asthmatic —Pertaining to or suffering from asthma.
Asthmogenic —Causing asthma.
Astigmatic —The person afflicted with astigmatism.
Astigmatism —Defective vision in which the refracted light rays are spread over a diffused area and not focused sharply on the retina due to the differences in the curvature in different meridians of the refractive surfaces, *i.e.,* the surface of the cornea and the lens of the eye.

Compound astigmatism —Defective vision in which there is hypermetropia or myopia in all meridians.

Corneal astigmatism —Astigmatism due to irregularity in the curvature or refractive power of the cornea.

Hyperopic astigmatism —Astigmatism in which the light rays are focused behind the retina.

Lenticular astigmatism —Astigmatism due to defect of the lens.

Mixed astigmatism — Astigmatism in which one meridian is myopic and the other hyperopic.

Myopic astigmatism —That in which the light rays are focused in front of the retina.

Simple astigmatism — Astigmatism in one meridian only.

Astigmatometer —An instrument used for measuring astigmatism.
Astigmatometry, Astigmometry —Determination of the form and measurement of the degree of astigmatism.
Astigmatoscope —An instrument for detecting astigmatism.
Astigmatoscopy —To detect the astigmatism by using astigmatoscope.
Astigmia —Astigmatism.
Astigmometer —Astigmatometer.
Astigmoscope —Astigmatoscope.

Astomatous, Astomous — Without mouth or oral aperture.

Astomia —Congenital absence or atresia of the mouth.

Astomous —Astomatous.

Astragalar —Pertaining to the astragalus or talus bone.

Astragalectomy —Surgical excision of the astragalus or the talus bone.

Astragalocalcaneum — Pertaining to both, the astragalus (talus) and the calcaneus bone.

Astragalofibular —Pertaining to both, the astragalus (talus) and the fibula bone.

Astragaloscaphoid—Talonavicular. Pertaining to both, the astragalus (talus) and the scaphoid (navicular) bone.

Astragalotibial —Pertaining to both, the astragalus (talus) and the tibia bone.

Astragalus —Talus bone of the ankle.

Astraphobia —Fear of thunder and lightening.

Astrapophobia —Astraphobia.

Astrict —To compress as to an artery to arrest bleeding.

Astriction —1. Astringent action. 2. Compression of an artery to check bleeding.

Astringent —An agent checking the hemorrhage by constricting the blood vessels, or the secretion by coagulating its protein, *e.g.*, ferric chloride, zinc oxide and tannic acid, etc.

Astroblast —A cell which develops into an astrocyte.

Astroblastoma —An astrocytoma of Grade II. composed of cells with abundant cytoplasm and two or three nuclei.

Astrocyte —A star-shaped neuroglial cell.

Astrocytoma —A malignant tumor composed of astrocyte cells, which is divided into four grades according to the increasing malignancy.

Astroglia — Astrocytes making up the neuroglial tissue.

Astrophobia—Morbid fear of stars and the heaven.

Asyllabia — A form of word blindness in which the patient recognizes the letters but cannot form the words.

Asylum—A place for the care of incapable persons.

Asymbolia —Asemia. Inability to understand the symbols, as words, gestures, figures and signs, etc.

Asymmetrical —Having no symmetry.

Asymmetry —Lack of symmetry.

Asymphytous —Separate.

Asymptomatic —Having no symptoms.

Asynchronism —Incoordination.

Asynclitism —Oblique presentation of the fetal head in labor.

Asyndesis —A mental disorder in which the related elements of a sentence can not be assembled together as a whole.

Asynechia —Absence of continuity of a structure.

Asynergia, Asynergy — Incoordination of parts or organs of the body, normally acting in hormony.

Asynergic —Characterized by asynergy.

Asynesia, Asynesis — Lack of easy comprehension and common sense.

Asynodia —Impotence for sexual intercourse.

Asynovia —Deficiency of secretion of synovial fluid of a joint.

Asyntaxia —Lack of proper development of the embryo.

Asystematic —That which is not in a proper arrangement.

Asystole, Asystolia — Absence of cardiac contraction or heart-beat.

Asystolic —Pertaining to asystole or not systolic.

Atactic —Ataxic. Incoordinate or irregular.

Atactiform —Similar to ataxia.

Atactilia —Loss of the sense of touch.

Ataractic —Pertaining to or producing ataraxia, a tranquilizer.

Ataraxia, Ataraxy —A state of mental calmness without depression or unconsciousness.

Ataraxic —Ataractic.

Atavism —The appearance of a character from remote ancestor rather than the immediate ones.

Atavistic —Pertaining to atavism.

Atavus —An ancestor.

Ataxaphasia —Inability to arrange words into sentences.

Ataxia —Defective muscular coordination or irregularity of muscular action.

Alcoholic ataxia — Ataxia due to loss of sense of the position and movements in chronic alcoholism.

Bulbar ataxia —Ataxia due to a lesion in the medulla oblongata or pons.

Cerebellar ataxia — Ataxia due to cerebellar disease.

Choreic ataxia —Ataxia found in the persons suffering from chorea.

Friedreich's ataxia — Hereditary sclerosis of the dorsal and lateral columns of the spinal cord, usually beginning in childhood or youth, accompanied by ataxia, impairment of speech, lateral curvature of the spinal column and peculiar irregular movements with paralysis of the muscles, especially of the lower extremities.

Hysterical ataxia — Ataxia of the muscles of the leg due to hysteria.

Locomotor ataxia — Tabes dorsalis. Ataxia due to infection of the central nervous system with Treponema pallidum, the causative organism of syphilis.

Spinal ataxia —Ataxia due to spinal cord disease.

Ataxiadynamia —Muscular weakness with incoordination.

Ataxiagram —A record or tracing produced by an ataxiagraph.

Ataxiagraph —An instrument for measuring the degree and direction of swaying of the body in ataxia.

Ataxiameter—An apparatus for measuring ataxia.

Ataxiamnesia —Ataxia with amnesia.

Ataxiaphasia —Inability to arrange the words into sentences.

Ataxic, Ataxial—Pertaining to or marked by ataxia.

Ataxophemia—Incoordination of speech muscles.

Ataxophobia—Morbid fear of disorder or dirtiness.

Ataxy —Ataxia.

Atel- —Prefix indicating incomplete or imperfectly developed.

Atelectasis —1. Total or partial absence of expansion of the lungs of a fetus at birth. 2. The condition of collapsed or airless lung of an adult.

Atelencephalia —Congenital imperfect development of the brain.

Atelia —Imperfect or incomplete development.

Ateliosis —Incomplete development of the body or any of its parts, as in infantilism and dwarfism.

Ateliotic—Pertaining to or characterized by atelia.

Atelo- —Prefix denoting incomplete ateliosis.

Atelocardia—Congenital incomplete development of the heart.

Atelocephalous —Having an incomplete head.

Atelocephaly —Incomplete development of the head.

Atelocheilia —Incomplete development of the lip.

Atelocheiria—Incomplete development of the hand.

Ateloglossia —Incomplete development of the tongue.

Atelognathia —Incomplete development of jaw.

Atelomyelia—Incomplete development of the spinal cord.

Atelopodia —Incomplete development of the foot.

Ateloprosopia —Incomplete development of the face.

Atelorhachidia —Imperfect development of the vertebral column.

Atelostomia —Incomplete development of the mouth.

Athelia —Congenital absence of the nipples.

Atherectomy —Removal of an atheroma from the coronary or any other artery by surgery or specialized catheterization.

Athermancy —No effect of heat.

Athermic, Athermous —The person having no fever.

Athermosystaltic —Not contracting under the action of cold or heat, said of skeletal muscle.

Atherogenesis —Formation of atheroma in the walls of the arteries.

Atherogenic —Capable of producing atheroma.

Atheroma —A mass formed on the intima of the arterial walls due to fatty degeneration occurring in atherosclerosis.

Atheromatosis —Generalized atheromatous disease of the arteries.

Atheromatous —Pertaining to atheroma.

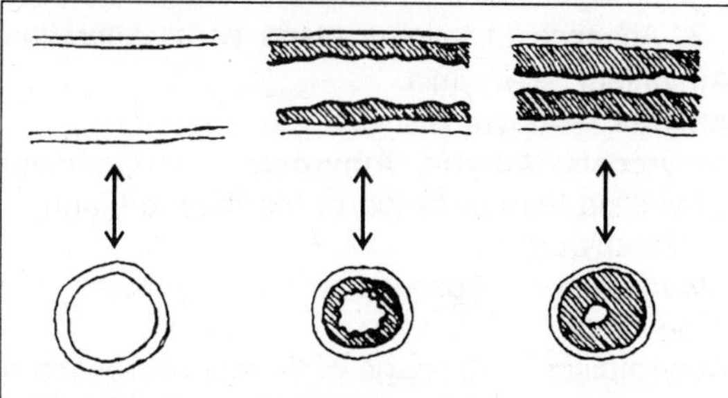

Fig. 39 Progress in atheroma formation in the arteries : In longitudinal and transverse sections.

Atherosclerosis —Thickening and hardening of the arterial walls due to the formation of atheromas in their intimas resulting in narrowing of their lumen.

Atherosclerotic —Pertaining to or characterized by atherosclerosis.

Atherosis —Atheroma.

Atherothrombosis —Thrombus formation in an atheromatous blood vessel.

Atherothrombotic —An atheromatous blood vessel in which an thrombus has been formed.

Athetoid —Resembling or affected with athetosis.

Athetosis —Repetitive involuntary, slow, irregular, twisting, snakelike movements of the upper extremities, especially of the hands and the fingers due to encephalitis and tabes dorsalis.

Athlete —A robust person.

Athlete's foot —Tinea pedis. Fungus infection of the foot.

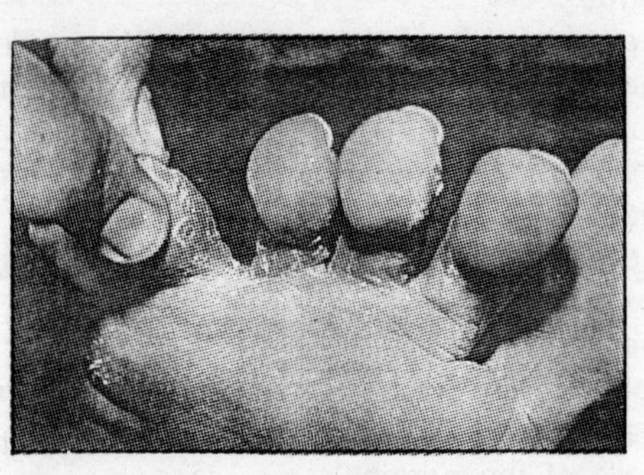

Fig. 40 Athlete's foot

Athrepsia, Athrepsy — Marasmus.

Athreptic —Marasmic.

Athrombia —Defective blood clotting due to deficiency of thrombin.

Athymia —1. Condition of being without feeling or emotion, seen in certain mental disorders. 2. Absence of thymus gland or its secretion.

Athymism —Athymia.

Athyrea —Athyreosis.

Athyreosis, Athyria, Athyrosis —1. Condition resulting from absence of the thyroid gland. 2. Hypothyroidism.

Athyroidemia —Absence of thyroid hormone from the blood.

Athyroidism —Stoppage of thyroid secretions or absence of the thyroid gland; hypothyroidism.

Athyrotic —Pertaining to athyroidism.

Atlantad —Toward the atlas bone.

Atlantal —Pertaining to the atlas.

Atlantoaxial —Pertaining to the atlas, and the axis.

Atlantodidymus —A malformed fetus with one body and two heads.

Atlanto-occipital — Pertaining to the atlas and the occipital bone.

Atlas —The first cervical vertebra.

Atloaxoid —Atlantoaxial.

Atlodidymus —Atlantodidymus.

Atloid —Atlantal.

Atlo-occipital —Atlanto-occipital.

Atmiatrics, Atmiatry — Treatment of respiratory diseases by medicated vapors.

Atmolysis —Separation of mixed gases by passing them through a porous medium, the light gases pass through the medium at a rapid speed.

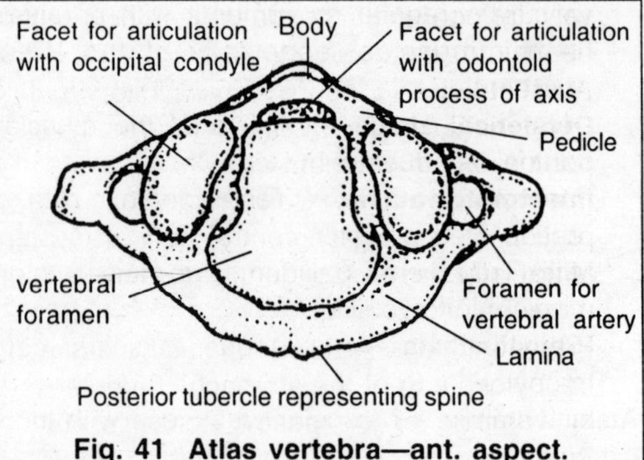

Fig. 41 Atlas vertebra—ant. aspect.

Atmometer —An instrument for measuring the rate of evaporation.

Atmosphere —1. The entire gaseous envelope surrounding the earth and extending upto the height of about 16 kilometers. 2. Climatic condition of a locality.

Atmospheric —Pertaining to the atmosphere.

Atmospherization —Conversion of venous blood into arterial blood.

Atocia —Sterility in the female.

Atom —The smallest part of an element which has all the properties of that element.

Atomic —Pertaining to an atom or atoms.

Atomization —The process of converting a liquid into a spray or vapor.

Atomize —To convert a liquid into a spray or vapor.

Atomizer —An apparatus for changing the stream of a liquid into a spray.

Atonia —Atony.

Atonic —Without normal tension or tone.

Atonicity —The state of being without tone.

Atony —Lack of normal tone, tension or strength, debility.

Atopen —An allergen causing atopy.

Atopic —1. Pertaining to atopy; allergic. 2. Displaced.

Atopognosia, Atopognosis — Inability to locate correctly the sensation of touch.

Atopomenorrhea —Vicarious menstruation.

Atopy —Hereditary tendency to develop allergy.

Atoxic —Non-poisonous, not due to a poison.

Atraumatic —Not causing injury.

Atremia —1. Absence of tremor. 2. Inability to walk due to hysteria.

Atresia —Congenital absence or closure of a normal body opening or tubular structure.

Anal atresia —Imperforate anus.

Aortic atresia — Congenital absence of the

valvular opening from the left ventricle of the heart into the aorta.

Aural atresia —Closure of the auditory canal.

Duodenal atresia — Congenital closure of a portion of the duodenum.

Intestinal atresia — Congenital closure of a portion of the intestine.

Mitral atresia — Congenital closure of the mitral valve opening.

Prepyloric atresia — Congenital closure of the pyloric end of the stomach characterized by vomiting of the gastric contents only.

Pulmonary atresia — Congenital closure of the pulmonary valve opening between the right ventricle and the pulmonary artery.

Tricuspid atresia — Congenital closure of the tricuspid valve opening between the right atrium and the ventricle.

Urethral atresia —Closure of the urethral opening.

Vaginal atresia — Congenital absence or closure of the vagina.

Atresic —Pertaining to atresia.

Atretic —Atresic.

Atreto- — Prefix denoting the absence of an opening.

Atretocystia —Absence of an opening of a bladder.

Atretogastria —Congenital absence of an opening of the stomach.

Atria —Plural of atrium.

Atrial —Pertaining to the atrium.

Atrial fibrillation —In atrial fibrillation the impulses arise in the atrium at the rate of 350-600 per minute instead of the sinoatrial node from which they are normally conducted along the bundles of His to the ventricles, so the atria only contract rapidly and irregularly and not the ventricles.

Atrial flutter —It is a condition characterized by rapid and regular atrial contractions and the heart rate becomes 200 to 350, usually 300 per minute, resulting from rapid and regular stimulation of the atria. Heart block is generally present causing the ratio of the number of the impulses of the atria and the ventricles to be 2:1, i.e. pulse rate becomes 100 to 175, usually 150.

Atrial natriuretic factor — Atrial natriuretic hormone. A substance produced by the atrial tissue of the heart when the blood pressure is increased. It acts to lower the blood pressure by increasing the excretion of sodium and water in the urine.

Atrial septal defect —A congenital heart defect in which there is an opening in the septum situated in between the atria.

Atrichia —1. Alopecia or absence of hair. 2. Absence of cilia or flagella.

Atricosis —Congenital absence of hair.

Atrichous —1. Having no hair. 2. Having no flagella.

Atriomegaly —Abnormal enlargement of an atrium of the heart.

Atrionector —Sinoatrial node.

Atriopeptin —Atrial natriuretic factor.

Atrioseptopexy, Atrioseptoplasty —Repair of a defect in the interatrial septum by plastic surgery.

Atriotome —A surgical instrument used in opening the cardiac atrium.

Atriotomy —Surgical opening of an atrium.

Atrioventricular —Pertaining to both, the atrium and the ventricle of the heart.

Atrioventricular bundle — Bundle of His. A bundle of cardiac muscle fibres extending from the atrioventricular (A-V) node upto a short distance in the interventricular septum and then dividing into two branches which supply fibres to both the ventricles. It conducts the impulses from the atrioventricular node to the ventricles of the heart through its branches, the Purkinje fibers.

Atrioventricular node — Atrioventricular node is a small collection of specialized cardiac muscle fibres located in the septal wall of the right atrium immediately posterior to the tricuspid valve. It delays the transmission of the cardiac impulse from the atria into the ventricles, which is necessary for the atria to empty their contents into the ventricles before ventricular contraction begins.

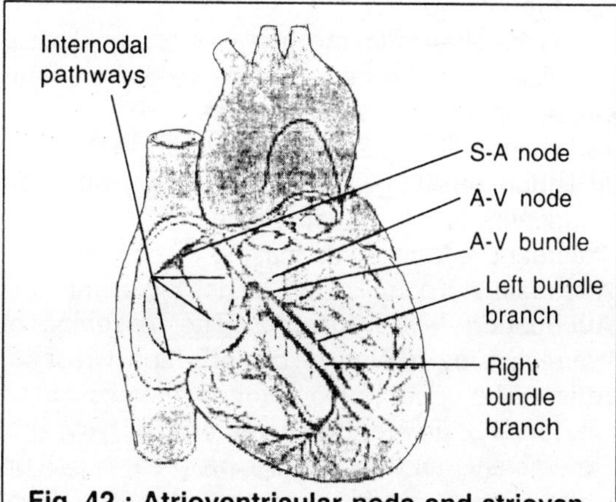

Fig. 42 : Atrioventricular node and atrioventricular bundle (Bundle of His).

Atrium —A chamber or cavity communicating with another structure, organ or chamber, *e.g.*, upper smaller chamber on each side of the heart.

Atrophia —Atrophy.

Atrophic —Pertaining to or characterized by atrophy.

Atrophied —Afflicted with atrophy.

Atrophoderma —Atrophy of the skin.

Atrophodermatosis —A disease of the skin in which its atrophy is a prominent symptom.

Atrophy —1. A decrease in size of a tissue, organ or part of the body. 2. To undergo or cause atrophy.

Acute yellow atrophy — Shrunken yellow liver with jaundice, as a complication of hepatitis.

Atrophy of disuse —Atrophy of the muscles due to lack of the normal exercise of a part.

Compression atrophy — Atrophy of a part of the body due to constant pressure on it.

Duchenne-Aran atrophy —Spinal muscular atrophy.

Eccentric atrophy—Atrophy of a hollow organ with increase in size of the cavity.

Muscular atrophy — Atrophy of the muscles.

Myelopathic atrophy — Muscular atrophy due to a lesion of the spinal cord.

Optic atrophy —Atrophy of the optic disk due to degeneration of the optic nerve.

Pathologic atrophy — Atrophy resulting from the effects of disease processes.

Physiologic atrophy — Atrophy occurring in the body due to old age.

Senile atrophy —Wasting of tissues and organs with advancing age.

Sudeck's atrophy — Atrophy of a bone at the site of injury.

Trophoneurotic atrophy —Atrophy due to disease of the nerves or nerve centers supplying the affected muscles.

Attendant—The person who looks after the patient.

Attention reflex —Change in size of pupil on suddenly fixing the attention.

Attenuant —Diluting or making the blood thin.

Attenuate —To make thin or less virulent.

Attenuation —1. Dilution 2. The lessening of virulence by freeing of bacteria and viruses.

Attic —The upper portion of the tympanic cavity, extending above the level of the tympanic membrane and containing the greater portion of the incus and the head of the malleus bone.

Atticitis —Inflammation of the attic of the ear.

Atticoantrotomy —Surgical opening of the attic and the mastoid antrum.

Atticomastoid —Pertaining to the attic and the mastoid antrum of the ear.

Atticotomy —To make an incision into the attic.

Attitude —1. A posture or position of the body; in obstetrics, the relation of the various parts of the body of the fetus to one another. 2. Behavior toward a person or thing or the views formed about them on the basis of previous experience.

Attitudinal —Pertaining to a posture of the body.

Attolens —Raising or lifting up.

Attrachens —To bring or draw toward.

Attrition —The wearing away of the skin by friction or rubbing.

Atypia —Deviation from the normal.

Atypical —Deviating from the normal.

Audible —Capable of being heard.

Audile —1. Pertaining to hearing 2. The person retaining more of what is heard than the informations received by other means.

Audio- —Prefix denoting the sense of hearing.

Audioanalgesia, Audioanesthesia —To alloy pain by sound, as done by a dentist to kill pain.

Audiogenic —Produced by sound.

Audiogram —A graphic record of the findings obtained by audiometry.

Audiologist —The person specialist in audiology.

Audiology —Science of hearing.

Audiometer —An instrument for testing hearing.

Audiometric —Related to the measurement of the levels of hearing or an audiometer.

Audiometrician, Audiometrist —The person specialist in audiometry.

Audiometry —Testing of the hearing sense.

Audiosurgery —Surgery of the ear.

Audiovisual —Pertaining or stimulating to both, the senses of hearing and sight.

Audiphone —An instrument for conveying sound to the auditory nerve through the teeth or a bone.

Audition —Hearing.

Audition chromatic —The condition in which a sense of color is produced by sound.

Audition gustatory —The condition in which the sense of taste is produced by sound.

Auditive —The person depending upon hearing for learning.

Audito-oculogyric reflex —Sudden turning of the head and the eyes in the direction of an alarming sound.

Auditory —Pertaining to the sense of hearing.

Auditory epilepsy —The epilepsy that is triggered off by certain sounds.

Audiotry meatus —External auditory tube from the tympanic membrane to the external ear.

Auditory nerve —The 8th cranial nerve.

Auditory ossicles —The bones of the middle ear.

Auditory reflex —Blinking of the eyes upon sudden production of a sound.

Auditory tube —Eustachian tube.

Augment —To add or to increase.

Augmentation —The process of adding or increasing.

Augnathus —A fetus with a double lower jaw.

Aula —Red swollen area formed around vaccination vesicle.

Aura —A subjective sensation before an attack of a disease as occurs in epilepsy.

Auditory aura —The aura that is characterized by illusions or hallucinations of sounds as occurs in epilepsy.

Visual aura —The aura that is characterized by visual illusions or hallucinations as occurs in epilepsy.

Aurae —Plural of aura.

Aural —Pertaining to the ear or to an aura.

Aural syringe —A long metallic syringe used to wash and remove the foreign body and wax from the ear.

Aurantiasis cutis — Carotenemia. Yellow pigmentation of the skin due to ingestion of excessive amount of foods containing carotene such as carrots, oranges, etc.

Auriasis —1. Occurrence of gray patches on the skin after administration of gold. 2. Deposition of gold in the tissues.

Auric —Pertaining to the gold.

Auricle, Auricula —1. The portion of the external ear remaining outside the head, the flap or the pinna. 2. A small conical appendage projecting from the upper anterior portion of each atrium. 3. A term formely used for the entire atrium of the heart.

Auriculae —Plural of auricula.

Auricular —Pertaining to the auricle of the ear.

Auriculare —A point at the top of the opening of the external auditory meatus.

Auriculocranial —Concerning with the ear and cranium.

Auriculotemporal —Pertaining to the ear and the region of the temporal bone.

Auriculoventricular — Pertaining to both, the auricle and the ventrcile.

Auriform —Ear-shaped.

Aurilave —An apparatus for cleansing the external auditory canal.

Auripuncture —Surgical puncture of the tympanic membrane.

Auris —The ear.

Auriscalp, Auriscalpium — 1. An instrument used to remove the foreign matter from the ear by scraping. 2. Ear-pick.

Auriscope —Otoscope. An instrument used for visual examination of the ear.

Auriscopy —Examination of the ear with auriscope.

Aurist —Otologist. Ear specialist.

Aurium —The ear.

Aurotherapy —Treatment of diseases like rheumatoid arthritis by administration of gold salts.

Aurum —Gold.

Auscult, Auscultate —To examine by auscultation.

Auscultation —The process of listening for the sounds within the body, usually the sounds of thoracic or abdominal viscera, to detect some abnormal conditions or the pregnancy. It may be performed with the unaided ear (direct or immediate auscultation) or with the aid of an instrument such as stethoscope (mediate auscultation).

Auscultatory —Pertaining to auscultation.

Auscultatory percussion — Auscultation at the same time when the percussion is made.

Auscultoplectrum —An instrument used for both, auscultation and percussion.

Autarcesis —Resistance to infection through natural immunity.

Autechoscope —An instrument used for self-auscultation.

Authenticity —The quality of being authentic.

Autism —The self-centered mental state.

Autism infantile —Autism occurring in childhood at the age of about 3 years, characterized by loneliness, shameness, and day dreaming.

Autistic —The person who is self centered, day dreaming and unaware of the outer world.

Auto- —Prefix meaning self.

Autoactivation —The activation of a gland by its own secretion.

Autoagglutination —Clumpsing of blood cells by the person's own serum.

Autoagglutinin —The substance present in a person's blood which agglutinates that person's own red blood cells.

Autoallergic —Pertaining to autoallergy.

Autoallergization —To induce autoallergy.

Autoallergy —A reaction in which antibodies (autoantibodies) are produced against an individual's own tissues, which are destructive rather than protective.

Autoamputation —Spontaneous amputation of a part of the body.

Autoanalysis —Self-analysis. A patient's own analysis of the mental state causing his or her mental disorder.

Autoanalyzer —An instrument conducting analysis automatically, commonly used in chemical analysis.

Autoantibody —An anitbody formed in response to an antigen of the person's own tissues and reacting against it.

Autoantigen —A substance stimulating the production of antibodies in the person from whom it was obtained.

Autoantitoxin —Antitoxin produced by the body itself.

Autoaudible —That which can be heard by one's self.

Autocatalysis —A chemical reaction in which the products formed increase the rate of reaction and so act as catalysts.

Autocatheterization, Autocatheterism —Catheterization by oneself, especially urethral catheterization.

Autochthonous —1. Found at the same place where it has developed, as in the case of a blood clot or a calculus. 2. Denoting a tissue graft to a new site on the same person.

Autochthonous infection — Infection caused by the organisms normally present in the patient's body.

Autocinesia, Autocinesis —Autokinesis. Voluntary movement.

Autoclasis —Destruction of a part of the body from some internal cause.

Autoclave —An apparatus for the sterilization of materials by steam under pressure.

Autoclaving —Sterilizing by steam.

Autocrine factor —A growth factor produced by the cell, probably in response to a virus which is important in the development of cancer.

Autocystoplasty —Repair of the urinary bladder by plastic surgery taking the grafts from the patient's own body.

Autocytolysin —Autolysin. Antibody found within the patient's own blood plasma capable of destroying cells or tissues.

Autocytolysis —Self-digestion or self-destruction of cells.

Autocytotoxin —A cytotoxic autoantibody.

Autodermic —Pertaining to one's own skin.

Autodigestion —Digestion of tissues by thier own secretion as of the stomach wall by gastric juice in gastric ulcer.

Autodiploid —Having two sets of chromosomes.

Autodrainage —Drainage of the fluid of a cavity by a channel into one's own contiguous tissues.

Autoecholalia —Repetition of one's own words.

Autoerotic —Pertaining to autoerotism.

Autoeroticism —Autoerotism.

Autoerotism —Sexual excitement by seeing one's own body, as in masturbation.

Autoexamination —Self-examination as is performed for the breast.

Autogenesis —Self-generation; origination within the organism.

Autogenetic, Autogenic — Pertaining to the self-generation.

Autogenous —Self generating within the body.

Autograft —A tissue graft taken from a part of the patient's body and transferred to the other part.

Autografting — Autotransplantation. To take a tissue graft from a part of the patient's body and transfer it to his/her other part.

Autogram —A wheal-like lesion on the skin following pressure by a blunt instrument or by stroking.

Autohemagglutination — Clumpsing of the red blood cells by a factor produced in the patient's own body.

Autohemagglutinin —A substance produced in the body of a person causing clumpsing of his own red blood cells.

Autohemolysin —An antibody that causes lysis of the red blood cells of the same individual in whose blood it is formed.

Autohemolysis —Hemolysis of a person's red blood cells by that person's own serum.

Autohemotherapy —Treatment by withdrawing the blood from patient's body and injecting it into the muscle of the patient.

Autohypnosis —Self-produced artificial sleep.

Autohypnotic —Pertaining to autohypnosis.

Autohypnotism —Autohypnosis.

Autoimmune —The antibodies produced against one's own tissues, as in autoimmune diseases.

Autoimmune disease —When the body's immune

mechanism becomes defective, it produces antibodies against normal parts of the body as to cause the disease such as rheumatoid arthritis, etc., known as autoimmune disease.

Autoimmunity —The condition in which the antibodies are produced against the body's own tissues which may result in hypersensitivity reactions or autoimmune diseases.

Autoimmunization — Immunization produced by the process remaining in the body.

Autoinfection —Infection produced by an agent already present in the body.

Autoinfusion —Forcing of blood from the extremities to the vital organs by applying bandage or pressure device to raise the blood pressure, which is usually done after excessive loss of blood or other fluid from the body.

Autoinoculation —Inoculation with organisms obtained from one's own body.

Autointoxicant —Autotoxin.

Autointoxication —Toxicosis. Poisoning caused by a poisonous substance produced within the body.

Autoisolysin —An antibody that causes lysis of the cells, *e.g.,* the blood cells of the individual in whom it is formed as well as those of other members of the same species.

Autokeratoplasty —Grafting of the cornea by the tissue obtained from the other eye of the same person.

Autokinesia, Autokinesis —Voluntary movement.

Autokinesis —Autocinesia. Voluntary movement.

Autokinetic —Capable of moving voluntarily.

Autolesion —A self-inflicted injury.

Autologous —Related to the same organism.

Autolysate —A specific substance produced by autolysis.

Autolysin —An antibody produced in an organism and capable of destroying the cells and tissues of the same organism.

Autolysis —1. Spontaneous disintegration of the cells or tissues by the enzymes present in the cells themselves, as occurs after death or in some pathological condition. 2. Destruction of the cells of the body by its own serum.

Autolytic —Pertaining to autolysis.

Automatic —Involuntary.

Automaticity —The property of cardiac muscle to contract without nervous stimulation.

Automatism —Occurrence of spontaneous activities in the body without the knowledge to the person as a the movements of the cilia.

Automatograph —An instrument for recording automatic movements.

Automysophobia —Morbid fear of personal uncleanliness.

Autonomic —1. Not controlled by another one but functioning independently. 2. Pertaining to the autonomic nervous system.

Autonomic nervous system —The part of the nervous system which is concerned with the control of the involuntary functions of the body, such as the function of the heart, and is divided into two parts– sympathetic and parasympathetic nervous system.

Autonomotropic —Acting on the autonomic nervous system.

Autonomous —Independent of the external influences.

Autonomy —Independence.

Auto-oxidation —The direct combination of a substance with the oxygen.

Auto-oxidizable —Denoting substances that react directly with the oxygen.

Autopathy —The disease originating without apparent external cause.

Autophagia, Autophagy — 1. The act of eating one's own flesh. 2. Nutrition of the body by consumption of one's own body tissues.

Autophagic —Pertaining to or characterized by autophagia.

Autophagocytosis —The digestion of the injured or atrophied mitochondria etc., by the cell itself.

Autophilia —Narcissism. Self-love.

Autophill —A person who has a sensitive autonomic nervous system.

Autophobia —A morbid fear of being alone.

Autophony —Increased hearing of one's own voice, breath sounds and murmurs; usually due to diseases of the middle ear.

Autoplasmotherapy — Treatment by injecting patient's own blood plasma.

Autoplastic —Pertaining to autoplasty.

Autoplasty —Replacement or reconstruction of a diseased or injured part of the body by grafts taken from the patient's own body.

Autopodium, plural. **-autopodia** —A hand or foot.

Autopoisonous —Autotoxic.

Autopolyploidy —The condition of having more than two complete sets of chromosomes.

Autopsy —Postmortem examination of the organs and tissues of the body to determine the cause of death or the pathological condition.

Autopsychic —Aware of one's own personality.

Autopsychosis —A mental disease in which the patients' ideas about themselves are disordered.

Autopyotherapy —Treatment of disease by the administration of patients' own pathological excretions as pus, etc.

Autoradiogram, Autoradiograph —The X-ray film produced by radioactive materials present in the tissue or individual.

Autoradiography — Radioautography. Making of an X-ray film of the tissue or the individual by recording on the photographic plate the radiation emitted by radioactive materials present in them.

Autoreactive —Pertaining to an immune response which is against the body's own tissue.

Autoregulation —The act of self-controlling, *e.g.*, the flow of blood through the tissues of the body remains constant (does not increase or decrease) by the self-controlling pumping action of the cardiac muscle.

Autoreinfusion —To inject the blood to the patient intravenously collected from the bleeding sites such as abdominal or pleural cavity of the same patient.

Autorrhaphy —To close the wound by strands of tissue taken from the edges of the wound.

Autoscopy —Self examination.

Autosensitization — Autoimmunization.

Autosensitize —Isosensitize. To sensitize against one's own body cells.

Autosepticemia —Septicemia occurring from poisons existing within the body.

Autoserodiagnosis — Diagnosis through the serum from patient's blood.

Autoserotherapy —Treatment by injection of the patient's own blood serum.

Autoserous —Pertaining to autoserum.

Autoserum —Serum obtained from `the patient's own blood to be reinjected into the patient.

Autosite —The larger than normal member of the asymmetrical conjoined twin fetuses, the other twin depending on the autosite for its nutrition.

Autosmia —Awareness of the odor of one's own body.

Autosomal —Pertaining to an autosome.

Autosomatognosis —The feeling that a part of the body that has been removed, is still present.

Autosomatognostic —Pertaining to autosomatognosis.

Autosome —Any of the chromosomes other than the sex (x and y) chromosomes, in man there are 22 pairs of autosomes.

Autosplenectomy —Almost complete disappearance of the spleen due to fibrosis and shrinkage.

Autostimulation — Stimulation or motivation of oneself.

Autosuggestibility —A mental state in which any suggestion originating in one's own mind is readily accepted.

Autosuggestion —The acceptance of an idea arising from within one's own mind, bringing about some physical or mental action or change.

Autosynnoia —Self-centered.

Autosynthesis —Self-reproduction.

Autotemnous —Pertaining to cells propagating by spontaneous division.

Autotherapy —Treatment of some diseases by administering the patient's own secretions, usually an autogenous vaccine.

Autotopagnosia —Inability to orient correctly the different parts of the body.

Autotoxemia, Autotoxicosis —To become poisonous due to absorption of a toxic substance produced within the body.

Autotoxic —Autopoisonous. Becoming poisonous by a poisonous substance produced within the body.

Autotoxin —A poison produced in the same body upon which it acts.

Autotransfusion —Reinfusion of a patient's own blood.

Autotransplant —Autograft.

Autotransplantation — Transfer of a piece of tissue from one part of the body to another part by surgery.

Autotroph —An autotrophic organism.

Autotrophic —Self-nourishing as the green plants and the bacteria which prepare their food *i.e.* protein and carbohydrate themselves from inorganic salts and carbon dioxide.

Autotrophy —The condition of being self-nourishing.

Autotuberculin —Tuberculin prepared from cultures of patients' own sputum.

Autovaccination —Treatment with autovaccine.

Autovaccine —Vaccine prepared from the viruses isolated from the patient's own body.

Autoxidation —Spontaneous oxidation of a substance that is in direct contact with the oxygen.

Auxanogram —A plate culture of bacteria in which variable conditions are provided to determine their effect on the growth of the bacteria.

Auxanographic —Pertaining to auxanogram or auxanography.

Auxanography—A method used to determine the most suitable medium for cultivation of the microorganisms.
Auxanology —The study of growth.
Auxesis —Increase in size of an organism due to growth of its individual cells instead of increase in their number.
Auxiliary —Helping or asissting.
Auxiliomotor —Increasing motility.
Auxilytic —Increasing the destructive power of a lysin.
Auxocardia —Enlargement of the heart by hypertrophy or dilatation.
Avalvular —Without valves.
Avascular —Lacking of blood vessels or bloodless as cartilage.
Avascularization —Expulsion of blood from the tissues as by ligation of the blood vessels or tight bandaging.
A–V Block —A heart block in which the impulses are impeded at the atrioventricular node.
A–V Bundle —A bundle of fibres arising from A–V node, enters the interventricular septum, where it divides into two branches whose fibres pass to the right and left ventricles, the fibres of each branch become continuous with the Purkinje fibres of the ventricles.
Avenolith —Stone in the feces.
Aversion —Great dislike, hatred.
Aversive —Avoiding.
Avian —Of or pertaining to birds.
Aviation —Traveiling in aeroplane.
Avidity —1. A strong attraction for something. 2. Concerning the ability of antibodies to bind to antigens.
Avirulent —Without virulence.
Avitaminosis —Disease caused by the vitamin deficiency in the diet.
Avitaminotic —Pertaining to or affected with avitaminosis.
Avivement —The trimming of the wound edges by surgery, before suturing them.
Avulsion —The tearing away of a part or structure of the body.
Axanthopsia —Yellow blindness.
Axenic —Germ-free or sterile.
Axial —Situated in or pertaining to an axis.
Axial line —A line running through the main axis of the body or part of it, *e.g.*, axial line of the hand runs through the middle digit and of the foot through the second digit.
Axial skeleton —Head and trunk.
Axiation —To establish an axis.
Axifugal —Centrifugal. Away from the axis.
Axil —Axilla.
Axile —Axial.
Axilemma —Axolemma.
Axilla —Armpit.
Axillary —Pertaining to the axilla.
Axion —Cerebrospinal axis.
Axioplasm —Neuroplasm of an axon.
Axiopodium, plural **-axiopodia** —Axopodium.
Axipetal —Centripetal. Axopetal.
Axiramificate —Denoting a nerve cell whose axon is usually short which breaks up into many branches.
Axis —1. A line which runs through the center of a body or about which a structure revolves. 2. Second cervical vertebra.

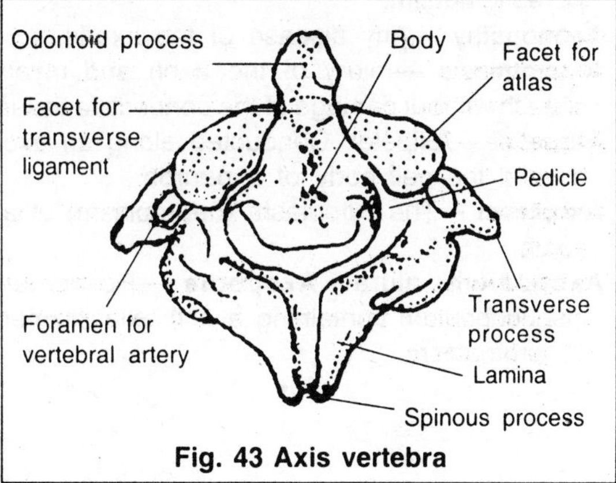

Fig. 43 Axis vertebra

Axis cylinder —Axon.
Axis traction —To draw the fetus in the direction of the long axis of the birth canal.
Axo- —Prefix pertaining to axis or axon.
Axodendrite —Process arising from an axon.
Axofugal —Axifugal.
Axolemma —Axilemma. The outer sheath of an axon.
Axolysis —Destruction of an axon.
Axometer —A measuring device for adjusting eye-glasses so that the lenses become suitable for the optic axes of the eyes.
Axon, Axone —Axis cylinder. A process of a neuron (nerve cell) which conducts the impulses away from the cell body.
Axonal —Pertaining to an axon.
Axoneme —Axial thread of a chromosome.
Axoneuron —A nerve cell of the cerebrospinal system.
Axonography—The recording of electrical changes occurring in axons. Electroaxonography.

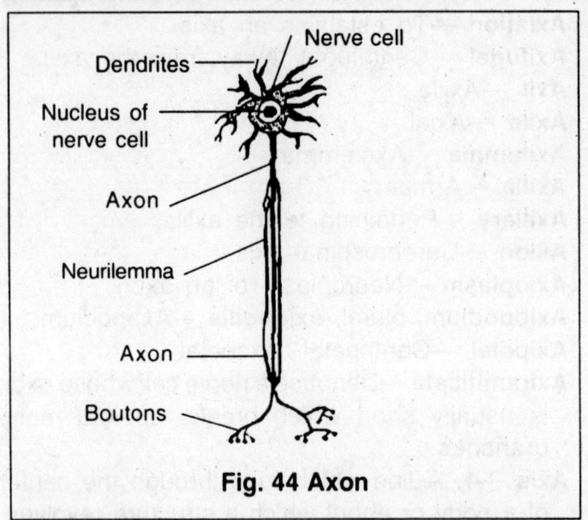

Fig. 44 Axon

Axonometer —A device for determining the axis of astigmatism.

Axonopathy —Any disease of the axons.

Axonotmesis —Injury of the axon and myelin sheath without damage of the connective tissue.

Axopetal —Axipetal. Conducted along an axon toward the cell body of a neuron.

Axoplasm —The cytoplasm (neuroplasm) of an axon.

Axopodium, plural- **Axopodia** —Permanent pseudopodium containing a stiff axial filament of protoplasm.

Axosomatic —Pertaining to the synaptic relationship of an axon with a nerve cell body.

Axospongium —The fine fibrillar network of the axon substance of a nerve cell.

Axotomy —To incise an axon.

Axungia —Lard. The internal fat of the body.

Azoic —Containing no living organisms.

Azoospermia —Absence of spermatozoa in the semen.

Azotation —Absorption of nitrogen from the air.

Azote —Nitrogen.

Azotemia —An excess of nitrogenous compounds, especially the urea in the blood.

Azotemic —Pertaining to azotemia.

Azotenesis —Disease due to excess of nitrogen in the system.

Azothermia —Fever resulting from uremia.

Azotification —Fixation of the nitrogen of the atmosphere.

Azotized —Containing nitrogen.

Azotobacter —Nitrogen fixing bacteria.

Azoturia —An excess of urea in the urine.

Azygos —Occurring singly, not in pairs.

Azygous —Single, not paired.

Azymia —The condition of being without a ferment or enzyme.

Azymic, Azymous —1. Unfermented. 2. Denoting the absence of an enzyme.

B—Beta, second letter of the Greek Alphabet.

Ba —Symbol of barium.

Babcocks's operation— Extirpation of the saphenous vein which is a treatment of varicose veins.

Babinski's sign —Bending upward of the big toe on scratching the outer edge of the sole of foot which is a sign of the disease of brain or spinal cord.

Baby —Infant (who is unable to walk).

Baby battered—Baby whose body suffered from bruises, wounds, scars, fractures or abdominal visceral injuries in the past.

Baby blue —New-born infant who became blue due to lack of oxygen.

Baby collodion—New-born infant completely covered by parchment-like membrane of desquamated skin.

BAC—Blood alcohol concentration.

Bacca —A berry.

Bacciform—Berry-shaped.

Bacillar, Bacillary—Pertaining to or caused by bacilli. Rodlike.

Bacille calmette-Guerin—BCG (Vaccine)

Bacillemia—The presence of bacilli in the blood.

Bacilli—Plural of bacillus.

Bacilliform—Resembling a bacillus in shape.

Bacilliparous—Producing bacilli.

Bacillogenous—Due to or producing bacilli.

Bacillophobia—A morbid fear of bacilli.

Bacillosis —Infection by bacilli.

Bacillotherapy—Treatment by bacilli.

Bacilluria —Presence of bacilli in the urine.

Bacillus—Any rod-shaped bacterium.

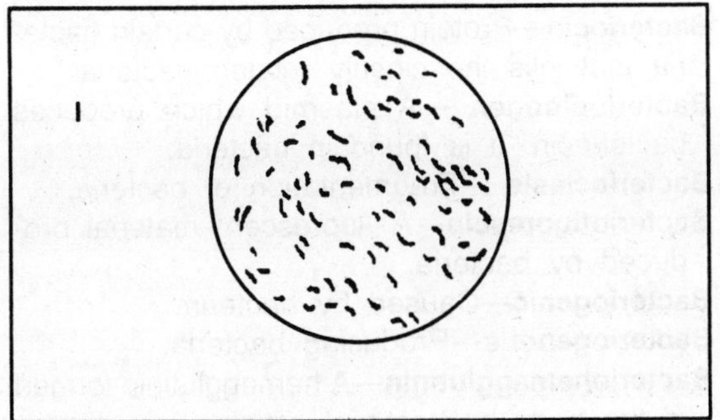

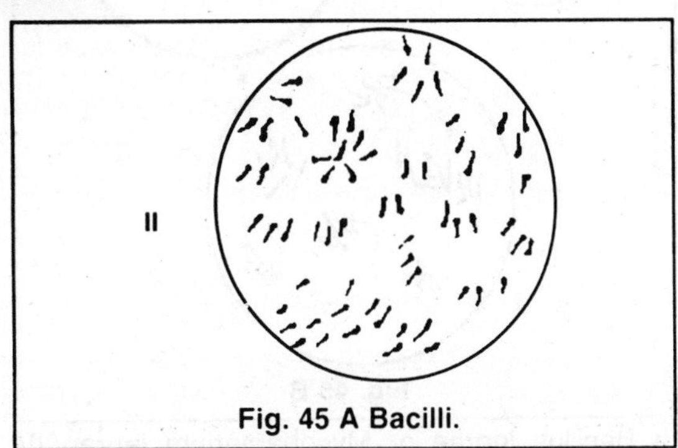

Fig. 45 A Bacilli.

I. Bacillus cholerae or vibrio cholerae.

II. Bacillus diphtheriae or Corynebacterium diphtheriae.

Bacillus acid fast— Bacillus which is not decolorized by staining with acid.

Bacillus cholerae, Vibrio cholerae —Causative organism of cholera.

Bacillus diphtheriae corynebacterium diphtheriae —The causative bacillus of diphtheria.

Bacillus doderlein —It is present in the vagina and maintains its normal acidity by converting the glycogen of the epithelial cells of the vaginal walls into lactic acid.

Bacillus lactobacillus acidophilus—A bacillus that produces lactic acid by fermenting the sugars in the milk, so that milk become sour.

Bacillus leprae, Mycobacterium leprae — The bacillus causing leprosy.

Bacillus streptococcus pneumoniae —It causes pneumonia.

Bacillus tetani, Clostridium tetani—The bacillus causing tetanus.

Bacillus tubercle, Mycobacterium tuberculosis —The bacterium causing tuberculosis.

III. Bacillus leprae or Mycobacterium leprae.

IV. Bacillus tetani or Clostridium tetani.

V. Bacillus tubercle or Mycobacterium tuberculosis.

Bacillus typhoid, Salmonella typhi—It causes typhoid.

Back—The posterior region of the trunk from neck to pelvis.

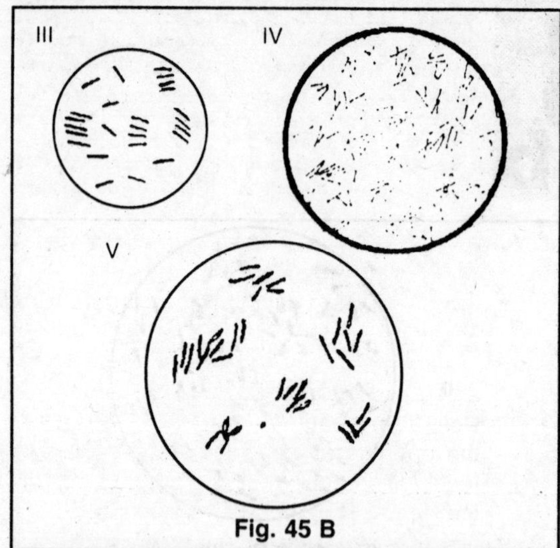

Fig. 45 B

III Bacillus leprae or Mycobacterium leprae IV Bacillus Tetani or Clostridium tetani V Bacillus tubercle or Mycobacterium tuberculosis

Backache —Pain in the back.

Back board A stiff, board placed on a stretcher so that the patient's back is kept flat in cases of injury of the vertebral column.

Back bone —Vertebral column.

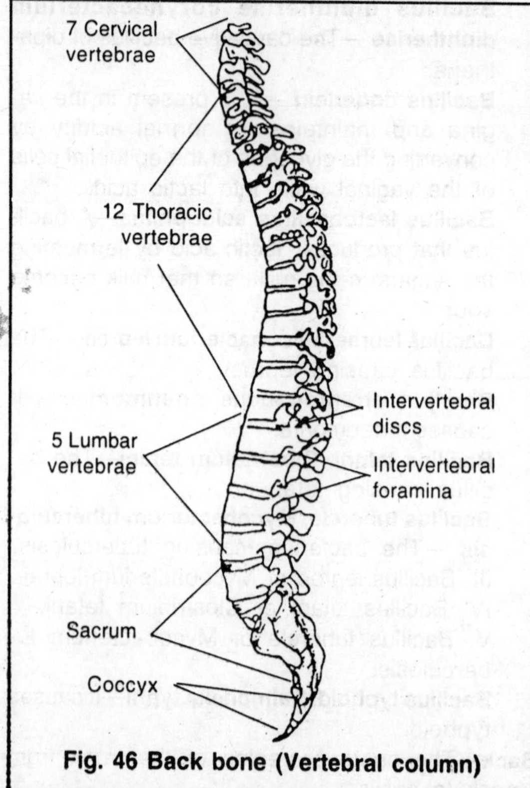

Fig. 46 Back bone (Vertebral column)

Backflow —Abnormal backward flow of fluids.

Backrest—An adjustable device that supports the back in bed.

Bacteremia—Presence of bacteria in the blood.

Bacteria—A group of micro-organisms, plural of bacterium.

Bacterial—Pertaining to or caused by bacteria.

Bacterial antagonism — The action of certain bacteria to prevent the growth of other micro-organisms.

Bacterial meningitis— Inflammation of the meninges caused by bacteria.

Bacterial resistance— Development of resistance to a drug in a bacterium previously susceptible to it, as the resistance is developed in the bacterium Mycobacterium tuberculosis, the causative organism of tuberculosis, to streptomycin after treatment for some days, so that the drug has no more effect on the pateint.

Bactericholia —Bacteria in bile.

Bactericidal—Destructive to or destroying the bacteria.

Bactericide —An agent which destroys the bacteria.

Bactericidin —Bactericidal antibody, antibody which kills bacteria.

Bacterid—Any skin rash caused by bacterial toxins or bacteria. The bacterial infection is remote from the rash.

Bacteriemia—Bacteremia.

Bacterin—Vaccine prepared from a specific bacterium.

Bacterioagglutinin—An antibody in the blood-serum that causes agglutination or clumpsing of bacteria.

Bacteriochlorophyll —A form of chlorophyll produced by certain bacteria and capable of carrying out photosynthesis.

Bacteriocidal—Bactericidal.

Bacteriocide—Bactericide.

Bacteriocidin—Any substance in the blood which kills bacteria.

Bacteriocin—Protein produced by certain bacteria that kills the closely related bacteria.

Bacteriocinogen —A plasmid which produces bacteriocin. It is found in bacteria.

Bacterioclasis —Fragmentation of bacteria.

Bacteriofluorescin—A fluorescent material produced by bacteria.

Bacteriogenic—Caused by bacteria.

Bacteriogenous—Producing bacteria.

Bacteriohemagglutinin—A hemagglutinin formed in the body by bacterial action.

Bacteriohemolysin—A hemolysin formed in the body by the action of bacteria.

Bacterioid—Resembling bacteria.

Bacteriologic, Bacteriological —Pertaining to bacteriology.

Bacteriologist—Specialist in bacteriology.

Bacteriology—Scientific study of bacteria.

Bacteriolysin—An antibacterial antibody that lysis the bacterial cells.

Bacteriolysis —Destruction of bacteria.

Bacteriolytic—Pertaining to bacteriolysis.

Bacteriolyze—To cause the digestion of bacterial cells.

Bacteriopexy—Fixation of bacteria by histiocytes.

Bacteriophage—A virus that destroys bacteria.

Bacteriophagia —Destruction of bacteria by some substance or agent.

Bacteriophagology—The study of bacteriophages. Protobiology.

Bacteriophobia—Morbid fear of bacteria.

Bacteriophytoma—A tumorlike growth caused by bacteria.

Bacterioprecipitin— Precipitin produced in the body by bacterial action.

Bacterioprotein—Any of the proteins within the cells of the bacteria.

Bacteriopsonin—An antibody which acts on bacteria.

Bacteriosis —Any disease which is caused by bacteria.

Bacteriospermia—The presence of bacteria in the semen.

Bacteriostasis—Inhibition of growth or multiplication of bacteria.

Bacteriostat —Bacteriostatic.

Bacteriostatic—An agent which inhibits the growth or multiplication of bacteria.

Bacteriotherapy—Treatment by bacteria.

Bacteriotoxic—1. Toxic to bacteria. 2. Due to bacterial toxins.

Bacteriotoxin—Toxin specifically produced by or destructive to bacteria.

Bacteriotropic —Turning, moving or attracted toward the bacteria.

Bacteriotropin —Any substance which enhances the ability of phagocytes to engulf the bacteria.

Bacteriotrypsin —A trypsin-like enzyme produced by the bacteria particularly vibrio cholerae.

Bacteristatic — Inhibiting the growth of bacteria.

Bacterium—Unicellular micro-organism, singular of bacteria.

Bacteriuria—Presence of bacteria in the urine.

Bacteroid —Resembling a bacterium.

Baculiform—Rod-shaped.

Baffle —A component of a nebulizer used to remove large air borne particles.

Bag—A sac or pouch.

Bag of waters—The membrane enclosing the liquor amnii and the fetus in uterus, amnion.

Barnes' bag—A water-filled rubber bag for dilating the cervix of the uterus.

Breathing bag—A collapsible bag from which gases are inhaled and into which gases may be exhaled during general anesthesia or artificial respiration.

Colostomy bag—A receptacle placed over the opening at the abdomen to receive the fecal discharge after colostomy operation.

Ice bag—

Micturition bag—A receptacle used for collecting the urine by ambulatory patients with urinary incontinence.

Politjer's bag—A soft bag of rubber for inflating the auditory tube.

Bagassosis—A lung disease occurring due to inhalation of the dust from the residue of cane after extraction of sugar (bagasse).

Baker leg—Knock-knee, genu valgum.

Baker's cyst—A synovial cyst arising from the synovial membrane lining the knee joint which occurs in the popliteal fossa.

BAL—British anti-lewisite. Trade name of dimercaprol.

Balan- —Prefix indicating glans penis or glans clitoridis.

Balance—1. An apparatus for measuring weight. 2. A state in which the intake and output of substances are approximately equal. 3. Harmonious adjustment and functioning of the different parts of the body.

Acid-base balance—A normal balance between production and excretion of acid and base by the body.

Analytical balance— A very sensitive laboratory balance which can measure the weight upto .05 mg.

Electrolyte balance— The condition in which electrolytes, especially sodium and potassium are maintained in suitable concentration for cellular and metabolic processes.

Fluid balance—Balance between intake and excretion of fluids especially water in the body.

Nitrogen balance —The state of the body in regard to ingestion and excretion of nitrogen in the urine and feces.

Balanic—Pertaining to the glans penis or glans clitoridis (clitoris).

Balanitis—Inflammation of the glans penis.

Balano-—Balan.

Balanoblennorrhea— Inflammation of the external glans penis by gonorrhoea.

Balanocele—Protrusion of the glans penis through a rupture of the prepuce.

Balanochlamyditis— Inflammation of the sheath of glans clitoridis.

Balanoplasty—Repairing of the glans penis by plastic surgery.

Balanoposthitis—Inflammation of the glans penis and the prepuce.

Balanopreputial—Pertaining to the glans penis and the prepuce.

Balanorrhagia—Haemorrhage from the glans penis.

Balanorrhea—Balanitis with pus discharge.

Balantidiasis—Infection caused by the protozoa Balantidium coli.

Balantidium coli—B.coli — Largest protozoon that lives in the intestine of man and may cause dysentery.

Balantidosis—Balantidiasis.

Balanus—Glans penis or glans clitoridis.

Balbuties—Stammering.

Bald—Having no hair or a decreased number of hair on the scalp.

Baldness—Alopecia. Absence of hair from the head.

Ball-and-socket joint —A synovial joint in which rounded head of one bone moves within a concavity or cavity of another bone, as hip joint.

Ballism, Ballismus—A condition characterized by jerky, twisting movements as seen in Chorea.

Ballistics—The science of the motion and trajectory of bullets, bombs, rockets and guided missiles.

Ballistocardiogram—A record of the impact of the body caused by contraction of the heart, the ejection of blood into the aorta and the forces applied in filling of the ventricles with the blood.

Ballistocardiograph BCG — The instrument for taking a ballistocardiogram.

Ballistocardiography—The recording of the impact, i.e., the movement of the body imparted by forces, as contraction of the heart, ejection of blood into the aorta and forces applied in filling of the ventricles.

Ballistophobia—Morbid fear of a projectile or missile.

Balloon—To expand, dilate or distend.

Balloon catheter—A type of catheter with one or more balloons which when inserted in a narrow artery and inflated, expand the narrow artery.

Ballooning—The distention of a cavity, as the vagina by air, etc., for examination.

Ballottable—Capable of showing the ballottement.

Ballottement—By this method of examination a floating object in the body such as an organ or fetus is detected. It is especially used for detecting pregnancy by inserting two fingers into the vagina and pushing the fetus, causing it to leave and quickly return to the examining fingers.

Ball-valve action —Action of a mass such as a pedunculated cyst or a thrombus moving to open and close the passage of a tube or chamber causing intermittent obstruction.

Balm—A soothing or healing ointment.

Balneology —The science of baths.

Balneotherapy, Balneotherapeutics —The treatment of disease by baths, hydrotherapy.

Balneum—Bath.

Balsam—A semi-solid, fragrant, resinous, oily juice from various trees and plants.

Balsamic—Pertaining to balsam.

Bamboo spine—X-ray of the vertebral column in ankylosing spondylitis shows it as the stalk of the bamboo plant.

Bancroftiasis, Bancroftosis —Bancroft's filariasis.

Bancroft's filariasis —A filarial infection caused by Wuchereria bancrofti.

Band—A strip. A tape that connects the structures together.

Bandage—A long piece of gauze or other material for wrapping or binding a body part. It is used for binding wounds, fractures and dislocations.

Adhesive bandage —A bandage made of adhesive tape.

Barton's bandage —A double figure-of-8 bandage for fracture of the lower jaw.

Butterfly bandage — An adhesive bandage used to be applied on the sutures to hold the wound edges together.

Capeline bandage —A bandage applied to the head, shoulder or to an amputation stump like a cap or hood.

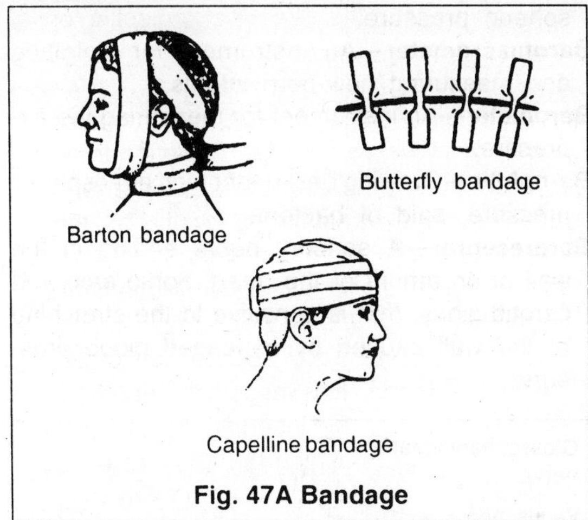

Fig. 47A Bandage

Circular bandage —A bandage applied in circular turns about a part.

Compression bandage —It is used to give support without constriction of the vessels.

Cravat-bandage—It is made by bringing the point of a triangular bandage to the middle of its base and then folding lengthwise to the desired width.

Crucial bandage—A bandage in the shape of a cross.

Demigauntlet bandage —A bandage that covers the hand but leaves the fingers exposed.

Desault's bandage—A bandage binding the elbow to the side, with a pad in the axilla, for fractured clavicle.

Elastic bandage— Bandage which has the property of stretching and specially used for varicose veins.

Esmarch's bandage— Rubber bandage applied upward around a part in order to expel the blood from it.

Figure-of-8 bandage — A bandage in which the turns cross each other like the figure 8.

Four-tailed bandage—A strip of cloth split into two at each end, thus becoming a four-tailed bandage, the central portion of which is placed to cover a prominence such as chin, nose, elbow or knee etc. and 4 tails are tied over the neighbouring main part of the body as over the head in case of mandible, to limit the motion of the prominent part.

Fricke's bandage —A special bandage for supporting and immobilizing the scrotum.

Gauntlet bandage—A bandage which covers the hand and fingers like a glove.

Immovable bandage — A bandage used for immobilization of a part of the body.

Plaster bandage—A bandage stiffened with a paste of plaster of Paris, which sets and becomes very hard.

Pressure bandage—A bandage for applying pressure, usually used to stop haemorrhage.

Protective bandage—A bandage for covering the underlying injured tissues or for keeping the dressings in place.

Quadrangular bandage —A towel or handkerchief, folded in many ways and applied as a bandage of head, chest, breast or abdomen.

Spiral bandage —A bandage in which each turn covers one half of the preceding one.

Suspensory bandage—A bandage which supports a part of the body but especially the breast or the scrotum.

T.bandage—A bandage shaped like the letter T, used for the perineum.

Triangular bandage—A triangle of cloth used as a sling of arm.

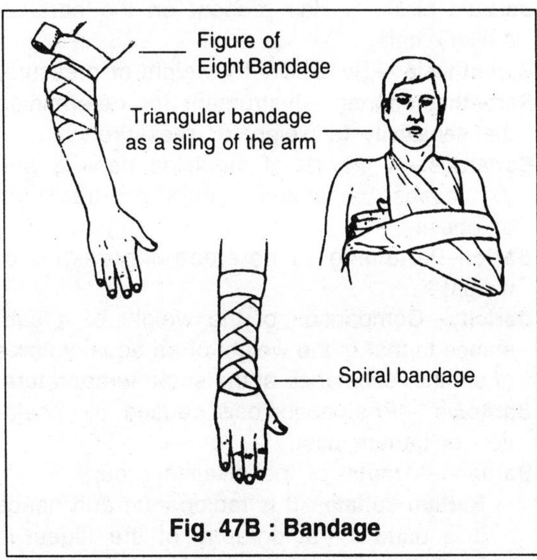

Fig. 47B : Bandage

Velpeau's bandage—A bandage used in immobilization of certain fractures about the upper end of the humerus and shoulder joint, binding the arm and shoulder to the chest.

Bandl's ring—Ringlike thickening and indentation at the junction of the upper and lower segment of the uterus that causes obstruction in delivery of the child.

Bandy leg—A leg in which the bones are curved outward or inward, bow leg.

Bane—A poison or blight.

Bank—A stored supply of human material or tissues for future use by other individuals *e.g.,* blood bank, eye bank, kidney bank, bone bank, sperm bank, etc.

Banti's syndrome—A syndrome combining anemia, splenic enlargement, haemorrhages and ultimately cirrhosis of the liver.

Bar —1. A rod. 2. Obstruction 3. Unit for measuring the pressure.

Bar median—Fibrosis of the prostate gland producing obstruction of the urethra.

Baragnosis—Loss of sense of weight or pressure.

Barba—Beard.

Barber's itch—Ringworm of the beard.

Barbiturate—A salt or derivative of barbituric acid and is used for its hypnotic and sedative effects.

Barbiturism—Chronic poisoning of barbiturate.

Barbotage—Repeated alternate injection and withdrawal of fluid with a syringe, as in gastric lavage.

Barbula hirci—1. Hair present on the ears. 2. Axillary hair.

Baresthesia —Sensibility for weight or pressure.

Baresthesiometer —Instrument for determining the sensitivity to weight or pressure.

Bariatrics—A branch of medicine dealing with the causes, prevention, control and treatment of obesity.

Baric—Pertaining to barometric pressure or weight.

Baricity—Comparison of the weight of a substance to that of the weight of an equal volume of another substance at the same temperature.

Baritosis —Pneumoconiosis caused by inhalation of barium dust.

Barium—A metal of the alkaline group.

Barium sulfate—It is radiopaque and hence it is used in radiography of the digestive tract.

Barlow's disease —A disease of infants which occurs in both breast-fed and bottle-fed babies between 6 and 12 months of age due to Vitamin C (ascorbic acid) deficiency.

Baro- —Prefix indicating weight or heaviness.

Barognosis—The ability to estimate weights.

Barograph—Barometrograph. An apparatus used to measure and record changes in the atmospheric pressure.

Baromacrometer—An instrument for weighing and measuring new-born infants.

Barometer—An instrument for measuring the air-pressre.

Barophilic—Growing best under high atmospheric pressure, said of bacteria.

Baroreceptor—A sensory nerve ending in the wall of an atrium of the heart, aortic arch and carotid sinus, that is sensitive to the stretching of the wall caused by increased blood pressure.

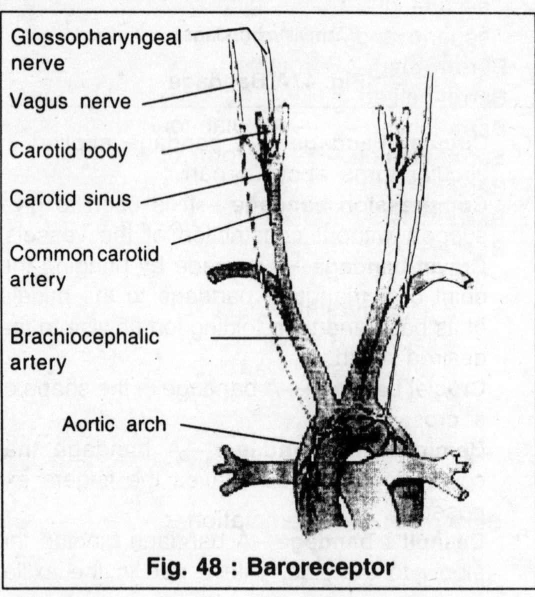

Fig. 48 : Baroreceptor

Baroreceptor reflex— Process in which baroreceptors detect changes in blood pressure and produce changes in the heart rate, force of cardiac contraction and the diameter of blood vessel that cause the blood pressure to return to normal.

Baroreflexes—The sensitivity response of the nerves located in the various blood vessels in the thorax and cervical region, and in the heart and its great vessels, to mechanical changes produced by the pressure of blood in them, is called baroreflexes.

Baroscope—An instrument which registers the changes in the density of air.

Barosinusitis—Inflammation of the nasal sinuses due to changes of the atmospheric pressure. This usually occurs when flying at a time at different altitudes.

Barospirator—An apparatus producing artificial respiration by changing the air pressure in a closed chamber.

Barostat—A receptor that is sensitive to changes in blood pressure and provides feedback stimuli to counteract it as is present in the carotid sinus that is sensitive to changes in blood pressure.

Barotaxis—Stimulation of living matter by change of the atmospheric pressure.

Barotitis— Inflammation of the ear due to sudden changes in the atmospheric pressure such as occurs while flying.

Barotrauma—Injury due to pressure, as to the structures of the ear while flying at a very high altitude due to the difference between atmospheric and intratympanic pressure.

Barotropism—Barotaxis.

Barrel-bellied —Having a large belly.

Barrel-chest—The globular form of the chest.

Barrel-shaped—Of the form of a barrel.

Barren—Sterile.

Barrenness—Sterility.

Barrier—An obstruction, boundary, or separation.

Barrier nursing—A method of preventing the spread of infection from an infectious patient to the others in an open ward.

Barrier placental—The tissue layers of the placenta which regulate the exchange of the substances between the fetal and maternal blood.

Bartholinitis—Inflammation of the Bartholin's gland.

Bartholin's abscess—Abscess of the Bartholin's gland.

Bartholin's cyst—A cyst formed in the Bartholin's gland.

Bartholin's gland—One of two small glands situated in each lateral wall of the vagina, near the vaginal opening at the base of the labia majora.

Baruch's law—Theory that water at the skin temperature has a sedative effect while below or above the skin temperature, it has a stimulating effect.

Baruria—High specific gravity of the urine.

Bary- —Prefix indicating heavy or hard.

Baryecoia —Deafness.

Baryglossia—To speak slow and with thick voice.

Barylalia—Indistinct and husky speech due to lesion of the central nervous system.

Baryophobia—Morbid fear that one's child will become obese.

Baryphonia—Deepness and hoarseness of the voice.

Basad—Toward a base.

Basal—Pertaining to or situated near a base.

Basal cell carcinoma— Carcinoma (cancer) occurring in the basal cells of the skin, generally of the face and neck, and is usually caused by skin damage from ultraviolet rays. It starts as a small, flat nodule which grows slowly breaking down at the centre forming an ulcer.

Basal ganglia—These are also known as basal nuclei. These are four large masses of grey matter located in the white matter of each cerebral hemisphere called caudate, lentiform, amygdaloid body and claustrum which control motor functions.

Basalis—Basal.

Basal metabolic rate —BMR. The metabolic rate which is measured under the basal conditions as 12 hrs. after eating and restful sleep with no exercise before the test, elimination of emotional excitement and in a suitable temperature. It is expressed in terms of calories per square meter of the body surface per hour.

Basal metabolism—The amount of energy required for maintenance of life when the person is at complete bed rest.

Basal ration—Minimal diet containing only essential components.

Basal temperature chart—A daily chart of temperature obtained upon awakening.

Basculation—The replacement of a displaced uterus by hands.

Base—1. The lowest part of anything. 2. The main substance of a mixture. 3. A substance that combines with acid to form salt.

Baseball finger—Hammer finger.

Basedow's disease—Grave's disease, exophthalmic goitre.

Baseline—A known value or quantity used to measure or assess an unknown, as a baseline temperature or blood pressure.

Basement—A space partially or completely separated from a larger space above it.

Basement lamina—Basement membrane.

Basement membrane—A thin, delicate, noncellular membrane, composed of collagen, underlying the epithelium.

Base plate—Sheet of plastic material used in making trial plates for artificial dentures.

Basi-, Basio—Prefix indicating base or basis.

Basial or basialis— Pertaining to a basis or the basion.

Basiarachnoiditis— Inflammation of the arachnoid membrane at the base of brain.

Basic—1. Pertaining to or having the properties of a base. 2. Capable of neutralizing the acids. 3. Fundamental.

Basicity —1. The quality of being a base or basic. 2. The combining power of an acid.

Basicranial—Pertaining to the base of the skull.

Basicranium —Base of the skull or cranium.

Basifacial—Pertaining to the lower portion of the face.

Basihyal—Body of the hyoid bone.

Basilad—Toward the base.

Basilar—Pertaining to a base or basal part.

Basilaris—Basilar.

Basilateral—Both basilar and lateral.

Basilemma—Basement membrane.

Basilic

Basilicus—Denoting a prominent or important part or structure.

Basiloma—Basal cell carcinoma.

Basin—A bowl-like receptacle for holding fluids.

Basinasal—Pertaining to the basion and the nasion.

Basioccipital —Pertaining to the basilar process of the occipital bone.

Basiocciput —Basilar part of the occipital bone.

Basion—The middle point on the anterior border of the foramen magnum.

Basipetal—Descending towards the base or developing in the direction of the base.

Basiphobia—Fear of walking.

Basirhinal—Pertaining to base of brain and nose.

Basis —The lowest or the fundamental part of an object.

Basisphenoid—Pertaining to the base of the sphenoid bone.

Basitemporal—Pertaining to the lower part of the temporal region.

Basivertebral —Pertaining to the body of a vertebrum.

Basoerythrocyte—A red blood cell containing basophil granules.

Basoerythrocytosis—An increase of red blood cells with changes of degeneration of basophils.

Basophil, Basophile—1. Cells or any structure that are readily stained with basic dyes. 2. A type of cell found in the anterior lobe of the pituitary gland. 3. A type of white blood cells containing coarse granules that stain readily and intensely with basic dyes.

Basophilia—Abnormal increase in number of the basophilic white blood cells in the blood.

Basophilic—Staining readily with basic dyes.

Basophilism—Abnormal increase of basophilic cells.

Basophobia—1. Abnormal fear of walking. 2. Emotional inability to stand or walk.

Basophobiac—That person who suffered from basophobia.

Basoplasm—The part of the cytoplasm that stains readily with basic dyes.

Bastard —Illegitimate child.

Bath —1. The medium for example water, vapour, light, air, sand or mud in which the body is wholly or partially immersed for cleansing or for therapeutic purposes or the application of such medium to the body. 2. The apparatus in which the body is immersed.

Acid bath—This consists of 5 ounce of hydrochloric acid or 1 gallon of vinegar added to 30 gallons of water.

Air bath—Warmed or cooled air is applied to the naked body.

Alkaline bath—8 ounce of sodium bicarbonate is added to 30 gallons of water.

Antipyretic bath— Cold bath.

Cold bath—Bath in cold water at a temperature below 65°F (18.3°C). It is used for hyperpyrexia.

Contrast bath—Alternate immersion of a body part in hot and cold water.

Douche bath—Application of water locally in the form of stream.

Foot bath—Immersion of legs in cold water.

Full bath—A bath in which the whole body except the head is immersed in water.

Hip bath—A bath of the hips and lower part of the body.

Hot bath —Immersion of the body in water at a temperature gradually raised from 98° to 120°F.

Mud bath—To apply wet mud to the body.

Mustard bath—It is a stimulating bath for feet consisting of a mixture of about 1 tablespoonful of dry mustard in a liter of water which is poured into a large basin filled with water of 100° to 104°F temperature in which feet ar immersed.

Needle bath —A bath in which water is forcibly sprayed on the body in many very fine jets.

Salt bath—Immersion of body in a mixture of 3.5 kgs. of sodium chloride and 230 gms of magnesium sulfate in 120 liters of water.

Sitz bath—Immersion of only the hips and buttocks.

Sponge bath—In this type of bath the patient is not immersed in water but is washed with a wet cloth or sponge.

Steam bath—The patient lies in a box with the head out side and steam from a chamber under low pressure is passed over him.

Sun bath—Exposure of the naked body or its part to the sunlight.

Therapeutic bath—A bath in which a part or whole of the body is immersed in water containing some medicine.

Bathophobia—Morbid fear of great heights or of looking downwards from a high place.

Bathy —Deep.

Bathyanesthesia —Loss of deep sensibility.

Bathycardia—Low position of the heart in the thorax due to anatomical condition and not due to any disease.

Bathyesthesia—Deep sensibility.

Bathygastry—Gastroptosis.

Bathyhyperesthesia— Excessive sensitiveness of muscular tissues and the deep body structures.

Bathyhypesthesia— Impairment of the sensitiveness in the muscular tissues and the deep body structures.

Bathypnea —Deep respiration.

Batten disease—A disease caused by hereditary disturbance of metabolism, characterized by blindness and mental retardation.

Battered child syndrome—Physical injuries such as bruises, scratches, hematomas, wounds, burns with fire or cigarette etc. or breaking of bones, inflicted in a child by her some parent or guardian in the form of punishing the child to show anger.

Battle sign—Bogginess of the temporal or postauricular region of the head, which indicates fracture of the basilar area of the skull.

Baudelocque's method —To convert the face presentation of a fetus into vertex presentation by hands.

Baume scales—A hydrometer scale for determinig the specific gravity of the liquids.

Bay —Depression in the body filled with liquid.

Bayonet leg—Backward dislocation of tibia and fibula at the knee joint.

BCG vaccine—A vaccine prepared from Bacille Calmette-Guerin strain of Mycobacterium tuberculosis for immunization against tuberculosis.

B.D.—Twice a day.

B.E. —Below elbow, barium enema.

Beaded—Marked by numerous small rounded projections.

Beading—Appearance of numerous small rounded projections.

Beads rachitic—Visible swellings in rickets seen at the junction of the ribs with their cartilages.

Beaker —A widemouthed, thin glass vessel with a lip or beak for pouring the liquid, used for mixing or holding the liquids.

Beard —Hair that grow on the cheeks and chin.

Bearing down —To apply force by the pregnant woman in the second stage of labour to expel the fetus outside.

Beast-fetishism—Sexual love for domestic animals.

Beat —Pulsation or throb as of the heart or of a blood vessel.

Apex beat —The beat felt by the hand over apex of the heart which is situated in the 5th intercostal space in the mid clavicular line on the left side.

Artificially paced beat —A heart beat stimulated by an artificial pacemaker.

Dropped beat—The absence of a ventricular contraction of the heart.

Ectopic beat —A heart beat originating from a point other than the sino-atrial node or sinus node.

Escaped beat —Heart beat that occurs after an abnormally long pause.

Forced beat—Extrasystole brought on by cardiac stimulation artificially.

Premature beat—An extrasystole.

Beau's lines—White lines across the finger nails which are usually produced due to injury, coronary occlusion, hypercalcemia, or skin disease.

Bechic—Pertaining to cough.

Bechterew's reflex—1. Contraction of the facial muscles due to irritation of the nasal mucosa. 2. Dilatation of the pupil on exposure to light.

Bed—1. A supporting structure. 2. A couch or support for the body during rest.

Air bed—Bed inflated with air which is used in burn cases and to prevent bedsores.

Capillary bed—A network of capillaries.

Fracture bed —The bed used by the patients with broken bones.

Metabolic bed—Bed arranged to facilitate collecting the feces and urine of the patient.

Nail bed—The skin lying beneath a nail at the tip of a digit.

Recovery bed—Portable bed or stretcher which is used to receive the patient just after an operation.

Surgical bed—Bed equipped with mechanism by which its head or foot can be raised or lowered independently of each other.

Water bed—A rubber mattress filled with water used to prevent the bedsore.

Bed blocking—Placing of blocks under the bed to raise it at head or foot.

Bedbug—An insect that remains in bed.

Bedfast—Unable or unwilling to leave the bed, bedridden.

Bedpan—The vessel used for defecation and urination by the patients confined to bed.

Bedrest—Complete rest.

Bedridden—One who is unable or not willing to leave the bed.

Bedsore—A sore caused in the back by lying in bed constantly for many days; decubitus ulcer.

Bedwetting—Enuresis, nocturnal involuntary urination, involuntary discharge of urine during sleep.

Beef—The flesh of cow.

Bee sting—Injury resulting from bee's venom.

Beeswax—Yellow wax obtained from honeycomb of bees which is used in ointments.

Beet—A kind of vegetable.

Beeturia—Pink to deep red color of the urine due to eating of beets in excess.

Behavior—Conduct, manners.

Behavioral—Pertaining to behavior.

Behaviorism—The psychologic theory based upon objectively observable and measurable data rather than subjective phenomena, such as ideas and emotions.

Behaviorist—One who is specialist in behavioral science.

Behcets' syndrome—A chronic, recurrent disease marked by ulceration of the mouth and genital organs and iritis, uveitis, arthritis and thrombophlebitis.

Bel—A unit for measuring the intensity of sound.

Belch—To expel the gas from the stomach through the mouth, to eructate.

Belching—Raising of gas from the stomach and expelling it through the mouth and nose.

Belemnoid —1. Dart shaped. 2. Styloid process.

Bellini's tubule —The straight connecting tubule of the kidney.

Bell's mania—Acute delirium.

Bell's palsy—Unilateral facial paralysis of sudden onset.

Bellocq's cannula—An instrument for drawing a plug of blood and mucus through the nose and the mouth to control epistaxis.

Belly —1. Abdomen. 2. Fleshy central part of muscle.

Bellyache —Pain in the abdomen.

Belly button —Umbilicus.

Belonephobia—Morbid fear of sharp pointed things.

Belonoid—Needle-shaped.

Bends—Pain in the limbs and abdomen caused by the bubbles of nitrogen in the blood and tissues due to rapid reduction of air pressure.

Benediction hand—The hand extended at the wrist with some fingers flexed, caused by paralysis of the ulnar and median nerves.

Benedict's solution—A solution used to detect the presence of sugar in the urine.

Benedict's test—A test to detect the presence of sugar in the urine.

Benign—Not malignant, not recurrent and favourable for recovery.

Bent-knee —Knock-knee.

Benzidine—A compound which is used to determine the traces of blood in feces.

Berard's aneurysm—An arteriovenous aneurysm in the tissues surrounding the injured vein.

Berdache —An individual who is either a male or female but acts like that of the opposite sex.

Bereavement —The reaction of grief and sadness and suffering, following the death of a loved one or some heavy financial loss.

Beri-Beri —A disease characterized by numbness or tingling in the legs, weakness, dyspnea on exertion, palpitation and swelling of the legs due to deficiency of vit. B_1 (thiamine hydrochloride).

Berkefeld filter—The filter that is designed to allow the virus-size particles to pass through.

Bernard's duct —Accessory duct of the pancreas.

Bernard's glandular layer— Inner layer of cells lining the acini of the pancreas.

Bertin's ligament—Iliofemoral ligament.

Berylliosis—Poisoning by berylium, usually of the lungs.

Bestial form—Resembling an animal.

Bestiality—Sexual intercourse with animal.

Beta—1. Second letter of the Greek alphabet

which is written as β. 2. Used in names of chemical compounds to distinguish one of two or more isomers.

Beta-adrenergic blocking drugs or beta blockers—These are the inhibitors (antagonists) of the effects of sympathomimetic drugs such as adrenaline and noradrenaline and lower the blood pressure, *e.g.*, propranolol.

Beta-adrenergic receptor —A site in the pathways of the autonomic nervous system wherein inhibitory responses occur when adrenergic substances such as adrenaline and noradrenaline are released.

Beta blocker—Beta-adrenergic blocking drugs.

Beta cells—1. Basophilic cells found in the anterior pituitary gland. 2. Cells of the islets of Langerhans in the pancreas which secrete insulin.

Betacism—Speech defect in which there is excessive use of b sound.

Beta-lactamase resistance —The ability of micro-organisms that produce the enyzme beta-lactamase, to resist the action of certain types of antibiotics including penicillin. The enyzme is also known as penicillinase.

Betatron —An apparatus producing high-energy electrons or X-rays.

Bevel —Slanting surface as that of the edge of a cutting instrument.

Beverage —A drink.

Bezoar — A hard mass in the form of a ball of hair and vegetables found in the stomach and intestine.

Bhang—A name of cannabis indica.

Bi—Chemical symbol of bismuth.

Bi-—Prefix indicating two, double, twice.

Biarticular—Pertaining to two joints.

Biarticulate—Having two joints.

Bias—Partiality.

Biauricular—Pertaining to both the external ears.

Biaxial —Having two axes.

Bibasic—Pertaining to an acid with two hydrogen atoms which can be replaced by bases to form salts.

Bibliomania —Mania for collecting the books.

Bibliotherapy—Treatment of some mental diseases by teaching the books only.

Bibulous—Having the property of absorbing the moisture.

Bicameral—Having two cavities or chambers.

Bicapitate—Having two heads.

Bicapsular—Having two capsules.

Bicaudal, Bicaudate — Having two tails.

Bicellular—1. Made of two cells. 2. Having two chambers.

Bicentric—Having two centres.

Bicephalic, Bicephalous —Having two heads.

Biceps—A muscle with two heads as biceps brachii muscle in the upper arm.

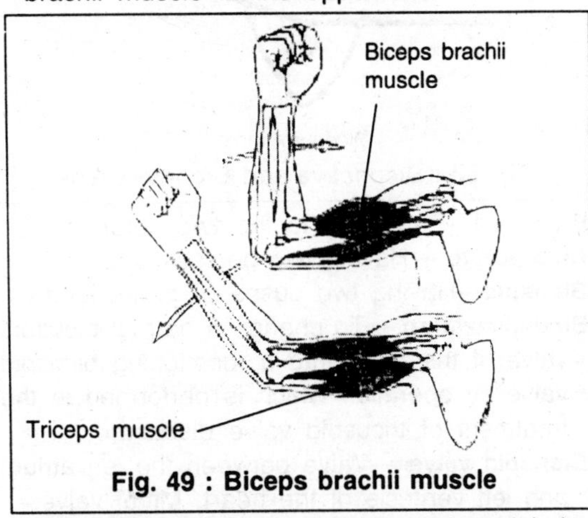

Fig. 49 : Biceps brachii muscle

During flexion (above) biceps muscle and during extension (below) triceps muscle.

Biceps reflex—Normal contraction of biceps muscle on percussion of its tendon.

Bichat's fissure—Horseshoe shaped fissure between the cerebrum and the cerebellum.

Bichat's tunic—The tunica intima (innermost layer) of the blood vessels.

Biciliate—Having two cilia.

Bicipital—Pertaining to a muscle having two heads.

Bicollis —Having two necks.

Biconcave—Hollow on both sides, especially as a type of lens.

Biconvex—Convex on both sides, especially as a type of lens.

Bicornous, Bicornuate, Bicornate —Having two horns or processes.

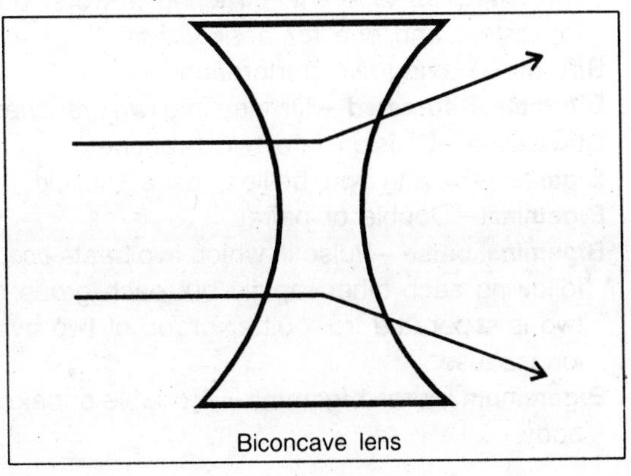

Biconcave lens

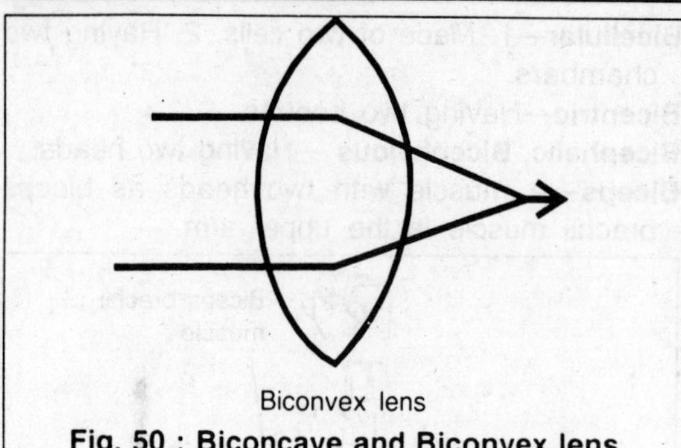

Fig. 50 : Biconcave and Biconvex lens

Bicoronal—Pertaining to the two coronas.

Bicorporate —Having two bodies.

Bicuspid—Having two cusps or projections.

Bicuspidization —To change a normal tricuspid valve of the heart into a functioning bicuspid valve by operation which is performed in the treatment of tricuspid valve disease.

Bicuspid valve —Valve between the left atrium and left ventricle of the heart. Mitral valve.

B.I.D. —Twice a day.

Bidactyly, Bidigital — Having two fingers.

Bidet—A basin in which one may sit with the legs apart and a stream of water from an attachment is flown over the genital and the perineal areas to clean them excellently.

Bidiscoidal—Resembling or consisting of two disks.

Biduous—Continuing for two days.

Bifacial—Having similar opposite surfaces.

Bifid—Split into two parts or there is a cleft.

Bifid spine—Congenital fissure of the vertebral column.

Bifid tongue—Cleft tongue.

Bifocal—Having two foci, as bifocal lens of the spectacles.

Bifocal glasses—Eye glasses each containing two lenses of different refracting powers, one for distant and one for near vision.

Biforate—Having two perforations.

Bifurcate, Bifurcated— Divided into two branches.

Bifurcation—Division into two branches.

Bigaster—Having two bellies, as a muscle.

Bigeminal—Double or paired.

Bigeminal pulse—Pulse in which two beats occur following each other rapidly but each group of two is separated from other group of two by a long pause.

Bigeminum Plural–**bigemina**—A double or paired body.

Bigeminy—The condition of occurring in pairs, especially bigeminal pulse.

Bigerminal—Pertaining to two germs or ova.

Bi-ischial—Pertaining to both the ischial tuberosities.

Bilabe—An instrument which is introduced into the bladder through the urethra for the removal of small calculi from the bladder.

Bilateral —Pertaining to both sides; having two sides.

Bilateralism—A condition in which the two sides are symmetrical.

Bile —A thick, viscous fluid of bitter taste secreted by the liver, collected in the gallbladder and poured into the duodenum via the common bile duct for the digestion of fats, when needed.

Bile acids—Cholic acid, glycocholic acid and taurocholic acids are the main complex acids of bile which are present in bile in the form of salts.

Bile ducts—The small ducts situated in the liver and carry the bile from there to hepatic duct which unites with the cystic duct comming from the gallbladder to form common bile duct which enters the duodenum.

Bile pigments—Two bile pigments bilirubin and biliverdin derived from haemoglobin of the blood & giving the brown colour to the feces.

Bile salts—Sodium glycocholate and sodium taurocholate, the alkali salts of bile.

Bilharziasis or Schistosomiasis—Disease produced by the parasite Schistosoma.

Bilharziosis—Schistosomiasis.

Bili- —Prefix pertaining to bile.

Biliary—Pertaining to the bile.

Biliary calculus—A gallbladder stone.

Biliary colic—Pain caused by pressure or passing of the gallstone.

Biliary tract—The organs and ducts connected with the storage and the drainage of bile into the duodenum.

Bilicyanin—A blue or purple pigment derived from biliverdin by oxidation.

Biliflavin—Yellow pigment derived from biliverdin.

Bilifulvin—Bilirubin mixed with other substances.

Bilifuscin—A dark brown pigment from bile and gallstone.

Biligenesis—Production of bile.

Biligenetic, Biligenic— Producing bile.

Bilious—1. Pertaining to bile. 2. Characterized by biliousness.

Bilious fever—Fever with vomiting of bile.

Biliousness—A condition characterized by the

symptoms of constipation, headache, loss of appetite, nausea, vomiting of bile and abdominal discomfort due to excess of bile.

Biliprasin —Green pigment similar to biliverdin found in the bile.

Bilirachia—Presence of bile pigments in the spinal fluid.

Bilirubin—An orange or yellow colored pigment derived from the substances present in haemoglobin, which are liberated on the break-down of the red blood cells. Excess of bilirubin in blood causes jaundice in which there is a yellow discoloration of the skin and conjunctiva.

Bilirubinate—A salt of bilirubin.

Bilirubinemia—Presence of bilirubin in the blood.

Bilirubinuria —Presence of bilirubin in the urine.

Bilitherapy—Treatment with bile or bile salts.

Biliuria—The presence of bile or bile salts in the urine.

Biliverdin —A green pigment of the bile formed by the oxidation of bilirubin.

Bilobate—Having two lobes.

Bilobectomy —Removal of the two lobes of the right lung, either right upper and middle or right middle and lower by surgery.

Bilobular—Having two lobules.

Bilocular—Having two cells or compartments.

Biloma—An encapsulated collection of bile in the peritoneal cavity.

Bimanous—Having two hands.

Bimanual—With both the hands.

Bimastoid—Pertaining to both the mastoid processes.

Binary—Made up of two elements or separating into two branches.

Binary gas—A toxic gas having two ingredients neither of which is toxic by itself.

Binaural—Pertaining to both ears.

Binauricular—Pertaining to both auricles of the ears.

Binder—A broad bandage used to support the abdomen or the breast.

Binder's syndrome—A syndrome in which face is flattened, nose is elongated and there is smaller maxillary arch with crowding of the teeth and malocclusions.

Binge eating—Rapid consumption of large amounts of food in a short period.

Binocular —Pertaining to both eyes.

Binocular vision—Normal vision with both the eyes.

Binotic, Binaural— Pertaining to or having two ears.

Binovular—Pertaining to or derived from two ova.

Binuclear, Binucleate— Having two nuclei.

Binucleation—Formation of two nuclei within a cell through division of the nucleus without division of the cytoplasm.

Binucleolate—Having two nucleoli.

Bio- —Prefix indicating the relationship to life.

Bioacoustics—The science dealing with the effects of sound on the living beings.

Bioactive —Having an effect on the living matter.

Bioassay —The determination of the strength of a drug or substance in pharmacology by comparing its effect on living matter to the effect of a standard preparation.

Bioastronautics—The study of the effects of travelling and living in the space on the living beings.

Bioavailability—The degree to which a drug or substance becomes available to the site of action.

Bioburden —The number of micro-organisms contaminating an object.

Biocatalyst—A substance produced by a living thing that can catalyze a reaction, *e.g.*, an enzyme.

Biochemical —Pertaining to biochemistry.

Biochemist—Specialist in biochemistry.

Biochemistry —The chemistry of living things and of vital processes.

Biochemorphic —Denoting the relationship between biologic action and chemical structure, as in foods and drugs.

Biochemorphology —Science of the relationship between chemical structure and biological action.

Biocidal, Biocide —A substance destroying the living organisms, *e.g.*, antibiotics.

Bioclimatology—Study of the relationship of climate to life.

Biocompatibility—The quality of not having any toxic effect on the living body.

Biodegradable —Susceptible to degradation by biological processes as by bacterial or enzymatic action.

Biodegradation —The breakdown of organic materials into simple chemicals by biochemical process.

Biodynamic —Pertaining to biodynamics.

Biodynamics—Science of the force or energy of living matter.

Bioenergetics—Study of the transference of energy and relationship between all living systems.

Bioequivalence —The relationship between two preparations of the drug in the same dosage form which have a similar bioavailability.

Biofeedback —To train someone to control one's autonomic nervous system, after which the individual becomes able to control heart rate, blood pressure and skin temperature etc.

Biogenesis—The theory that living things can originate only from living things and never from nonliving material.

Biogenetic—Pertaining to biogenesis.

Biogenic—Produced by some living being.

Biogenic amines—Chemical substances that change the cerebral and vascular functions, *e.g.*, adrenaline, noradrenaline, dopamine and serotonin.

Biohazard—Anything that is harmful to human being or the environment.

Bioinstrument—An instrument attached to or placed in the human body to record and to transmit the data of body functions from the individual to a receiving and monitoring station.

Biokinetics—The study of growth changes and movements of the living organisms.

Biologic, Biological— 1. Pertaining to biology. 2. A medicinal preparation made from living organisms and their products such as serums and vaccines etc.

Biological— Biologic

Biological warfare— Warfare in which the disease-producing microorganisms are used to destroy the human life *e.g.*, anthrax, etc.

Biologic half-life—The time required to reduce the concentration of a drug in the blood, plasma, or serum by 50%, which is a measure of the rate of drug distribution and elimination.

Biologist—Specialist in biology.

Biology—The science of life and living things.

Bioluminescence—Emission of light from living organisms.

Biolysis—Destruction of life.

Biolytic—Capable of destroying life.

Biomarker—An indicator of the state of the body as body temperature.

Biomas—The collection of many living organisms in a specified area.

Biome—The totality of living organisms occupying and characterizing a particular geographical area.

Biomechanics—The science of the action of internal or external force, on the living body.

Biomedical —Pertaining to the use of natural sciences to the study of medicine.

Biomedical engineering— The use of engineering science in medicine, *e.g.*, development of devices such as cardiac pacemakers, hearing aids, artificial limbs etc.

Biomedicine—Clinical medicine based on the principles of the natural sciences (biology, biochemistry, etc.)

Biomembrane—Any membrane of an organism *e.g.*, cell membrane.

Biometeorology—Study of the effects of meteorology on all forms of life.

Biometer—An apparatus used to measure carbon dioxide given off by organisms and hence, to determine the quantity of living matter present.

Biometrician—Specialist in biometry.

Biometrics, Biometry—1. The application of statistics to biological facts. 2. The measurement of life-time.

Biometry — Biometrics.

Biomicroscope—A microscope for examining the living tissues in the body.

Biomicroscopy—Microscopic examination of living tissues in the body.

Biomolecule —A molecule produced by the living cells, *e.g.*, protein, carbohydrate etc.

Bion—A living organism.

Bionergy—Vital force or life energy.

Bionics—The scientific study of the functions and characteristics of the living things and to apply the knowledge gained there from to the nonliving things.

Bionomics—Ecology.

Bionomy—The science pertaining to life processes.

Bionosis—Any disease caused by pathogenic organisms.

Biophage—Obtaining nourishment from living things for its existence.

Biophagism, Biophagy— The obtaining of nourishment from the living matter.

Biophagous—Biophage.

Biophagy — Biophagism

Biophotometer—An instrument used to determine the presence or absence of vitamin A deficiency.

Biophylactic —Pertaining to biophylaxis.

Biophylaxis—Defence reactions of the body. *e.g.*, phagocytosis and inflammation etc.

Biophysics—Application of physical theories and methods to biological problems.

Bioplasm—Protoplasm.

Bioplasmic—Pertaining to the protoplasm.

Biopsy—Removal and microscopic examination of a small piece of tissue from a living body to establish a diagnosis.

Biopsychosocial—Biological, psychological and social.

Bioptone—A cutting instrument for taking biopsy specimens.

Biorbital—Pertaining to both the orbits.

Bioremediation—The conversion of hazardous waste products and pollutants into harmless materials by the action of microorganisms.

Biorhythmic—A cyclic phenomenon as menstrual cycle which occurs regularly.

Bios—Life.

Bioscience—Life science.

Biosis—Way of living.

Biospectrometry—Use of a spectroscope to determine the amounts and kinds of substances in the tissues.

Biospectroscopy—Examination of tissues by spectroscope.

Biosphere—All the regions of the land and water on the earth, and atmosphere in which living organisms are found.

Biostatics—Science of the relationship of the structure to function.

Biostatistics—Vital statistics.

Biosynthesis—Formation of chemical compounds by a living organism.

Biosynthetic—Pertaining to or produced by biosynthesis.

Biota—All the living organisms including the animals and plants in a particular area.

Biotaxis, Biotaxy—The classification of living beings according to their anatomic characteristics.

Biotechnology—The application of biological system and organisms to technical and industrial processes as yeast is used in preparing bread.

Biotelemetery—By electronic devices the measuring of temperature, heart rate and the taking of E.C.G. and E.E.G., etc. at a distance from the patient.

Biotest—Biologic assay. Test for detecting the effects of a chemical compound or technique on an organism.

Biotic—Pertaining to the life or living organism.

Biotics—The science of vital functions.

Biotoxication—Toxicity due to living organisms.

Biotoxicology—Scientific study of poisons produced by the living organisms and treatment of the conditions produced by them.

Biotoxin—A poisonous substance produced by or found in living organisms.

Biotransformation—The chemical alterations of a substance, *e.g.*, of a drug, occurring in the body.

Biot's breathing—Breathing marked by several short breaths followed by long period of apnea.

Biotype—Individuals with similar body constitution.

Biovular—Derived from or pertaining to two ova.

Biovular twins—Twins from two separate ova.

Bipara—A woman who has delivered second time a child, alive or dead, weighing more than 500 gms.

Biparasitic—Pertaining to a parasite living upon another parasite.

Biparasitism—Hyperparasitism.

Biparental—Derived from two parents, male and female.

Biparietal—Pertaining to both the parietal bones.

Biparous—Producing two ova or offspring at a time.

Bipartite—Consisting of two portions.

Biped—Having two feet.

Bipedal—Walking on two feet.

Bipennate, Bipenniform— Pertaining to a muscle in which fibers come from each side of a tendon as the barbs come from the central shaft of a feather

Biperforate—Having two openings or perforations.

Biphasic—Having two phases.

Bipolar—1. Having two poles. 2. Pertaining to both poles.

Bipotentiality—Ability to develop or act in either of two possible ways.

Biramous—Having two branches.

Birefractive —Splitting a ray of light into two, doubly refractive.

Birefringence—Double refraction. The splitting of a ray of light into two.

Birefringent—Birefractive.

Birth—The process of being born.

Complete birth—Complete separation of the body of the infant from the mother.

Cross birth—Labor with the fetus lying transversely across the uterus.

Live birth—Birth of an infant showing one of the three evidences of life, i.e. breathing, heart beating and movements of the limbs.

Multiple birth—Birth of two or more infants produced in the same pregnancy.

Premature birth—Delivery of a premature child.

Birth canal—The canal composed of cervix,

vagina and vulva through which the fetus passes in birth.

Birth certificate—A legal written record of the birth of a child.

Birth control—Prevention of conception by any means.

Birth defect—A congenital abnormality.

Birthing—Parturition. To give birth to a child.

Birth injury—Injury sustained by the neonate during labor.

Birth mark—Presence of a mole since birth.

Birth palsy—Paraplegia or hemiplegia of the new-born child due to birth injury.

Birth rate—The number of live births per 1000 of population per year in a country.

Bis- —Prefix indicating two or twice.

Bisaxillary—Pertaining to both the axillae.

Bisection—Division into two parts by cutting.

Bisexual—Having the characteristics of both sexes.

Bisexuality—The condition of being bisexual.

Bisferious—Having two beats.

Bis in die—B.D. Twice in a day.

Bismuthosis—Chronic bismuth poisoning.

Bistoury—A small, narrow, straight or curved surgical knife.

Bistratal—Having two strata or layers.

Bite—1. To cut with the teeth. 2. A wound made by an animal bite. 3. Sting-bite as by scorpion. 4. In dentistry, an impression made by the closure of the teeth upon some plastic material e.g., wax.

Bite-block—Occlusion rim.

Bitelock—A dental device for retaining occlusion rims in the same position outside the mouth as they were inside the mouth.

Bitemporal—Pertaining to both temporal bones.

Bite plate—Dental device used to correct or diagnose the malocclusion.

Bitot's spots—Shiny grey colored spots on the conjunctiva, due to vitamin A deficiency.

Bitropic—Affecting two.

Bitter—Having disagreeable taste.

Bituminosis—A form of pneumoconiosis due to dust of soft coal.

Biuret—A derivative of urea obtained by heating.

Biuret test—A method for measuring protein in the serum.

Bivalence, Bivalency—A combining power (valence) of 2.

Bivalent—Having a valence of two.

Biventer, Biventral —Having two bellies, e.g., a muscle with two bellies.

Biventricular—Pertaining to or affecting both ventricles of the heart.

Bizygomatic—Pertaining to the most prominent point of each of the two zygomatic arches.

B.K.—Below knee.

Black—1. Absence of color or reflecting no light. 2. Marked dark pigmentation.

Black death—Black plague.

Black eye—Blackness of eyelids and the tissues around the eye due to trauma.

Black head—Comedo.

Black lung—Pneumoconiosis found in coal miners.

Black measles—The measles in which the eruption is dark colored.

Black out—Sudden loss of vision and a temporary loss of consciousness due to less blood supply to the retina and the brain.

Black vomit—Vomit which appears black due to the presence of blood from the stomach.

Blackwater fever—Malerial fever with excretion of black urine.

Bladder—The membranous sac for a secretion as the gallbladder and the urinary bladder. The term is commonly used for urinary bladder.

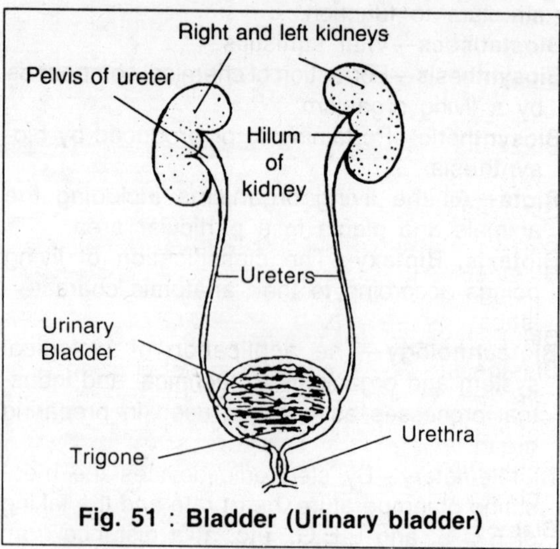

Fig. 51 : Bladder (Urinary bladder)

Atony of bladder— Inability to urinate due to lack of muscular tone.

Extrophy of bladder— Congenital eversion of urinary bladder. The abdominal wall does not close since birth and the bladder protrudes through it.

Hypertonic bladder— Bladder with increased muscular tone. Increased muscular activity of the bladder.

Irritable bladder—There is increased frequency of contraction of the urinary bladder with desire to urinate.

Nervous bladder—A constant desire to urinate without the power to do so completely.

Neurogenic bladder— Any dysfunction of the urinary bladder from the lesions of the central nervous system or nerves supplying the bladder.

Bladder worm—Cysticercus. A larval form of a tapeworm.

Bladder sound—It is a metallic rod, 10 inches long that is gradually curved at the distal end and is not graduated. It is used to determine the limits of the urinary bladder during operation and to diagnose a calculus in the bladder.

Blain—Boil or blister.

Blanch—To become pale suddenly.

Bland—Soothing, mild.

Bland diet—It means a diet without spices, pickles and excess of ghee or oil and not to cause irritation to the gastric mucosa. Bland diet includes milk, curd, cream, cheese, bread, pulses, rice, eggs, fish, fruits and vegetables etc.

Blast—A violent sound as produced on explosion of bomb.

-blast—A suffix indicating a cell that produces something, *e.g.,* osteoblast and fibroblast etc.

Blastema—The primitive substances or cells from which cells and tissues are formed.

Blastemic—Pertaining to blastema.

Blasto- —Prefix indicating germ or bud.

Blastocele —The cavity in the blastula filled with fluid.

Blastochyle —Fluid contained in the blastocele.

Blastocyst—The embryo of a mammalian after the morula stage, consisting of the outer layer of the trophoblast to which is attached the inner cell mass and the enclosed cavity is the blastocele.

Blastocyte—An undifferentiated blastomere of the morula or blastula stage of an embryo.

Blastocytoma—Blastoma.

Blastoderm—The single layer of cells forming the wall of the blastula.

Blastodermal, Blastodermic —Pertaining to the blastoderm.

Blastogenesis—Reproduction of protozoa by budding. *i.e.,* asexual reproduction.

Blastogenetic, Blastogenic— Pertaining to blastogenesis.

Blastolysis—Destruction of a blastocyst.

Blastolytic—Pertaining to blastolysis.

Blastoma—A neoplasm composed of embryonic cells derived from the blastema of an organ or tissue.

Blastomatosis—Formation of blastoma or tumor formation.

Blastomere —One of the cells produced by the segmentation of a fertilized ovum.

Blastomerotomy —Destruction of the blastomeres.

Blastomogenic—Producing blastoma.

Blastoneuropore—A temporary opening formed in some embryos by the union of the blastopore and neuropore.

Blastopore—The opening of the archenteron outside the embryo, at the gastrula stage.

Blastula—The hollow spherical body produced by cleavage of a fertilized ovum, consisting of a single layer of cells (blastoderm) surrounding a cavity, the blastocele which is filled with a fluid.

Blastular—Pertaining to the blastula.

Blastulation—Conversion of morula to the blastula by the development of a blastocele.

Bleaching powder—Calcium hypochloride.

Bleb—Blister.

Bleed —To lose blood on rupture or severance of blood vessels.

Bleeder—The person whose ability to coagulate the blood is either absent or deficient, thus a small injury leads to profuse bleeding.

Bleeding—Escape of blood, as from an injured blood vessel.

Arterial bleeding — Blood of bright red color coming out of the injured arteries in spurts.

Break through bleeding—Intermenstrual bleeding.

Dysfunctional uterine bleeding—Bleeding occurring from the uterus without any general, or local cause such as fibroid or cancer or inflammation of the uterus or pregnancy, is called dysfunctional uterine bleeding.

Internal bleeding— Hemorrhage from the internal organs or site, especially gastrointestinal tract.

Menstrual bleeding—Monthly normal uterine bleeding.

Occult bleeding— Escape of blood in such small quantity, especially that which occurs into the intestine, which can be detected only by chemical tests or microscopic examination of the feces.

Placentation bleeding—Uterine bleeding during the early weeks of pregnancy.

Venous bleeding — Bleeding of blood of dark red color.

Bleeding time —Time taken for bleeding to stop, which is usually 3 minutes.

Blending —Mixture of various things.

Blenn-, Blenno- —Prefixes indicating mucus.

Blennadenitis—Inflammation of the mucous glands.

Blennelytria—Leucorrhoea.

Blennemesis—Vomiting of mucus.

Blennogenic, Blennogenous—Producing mucus.

Blennoid—Like mucus.

Blennometritis—Inflammation of the uterus.

Blennophthalmia—Conjunctivitis.

Blennoptysis—Expectoration of mucus.

Blennorrhagia, Blennorrhea—1. Any excessive discharge from the mucous membranes. 2. Gonorrhea.

Blennorrhagic—Blennorrheal.

Blennorrhea—Blennorrhagia.

Blennorrheal—Blennorrhagic. Pertaining to any excessive discharge from the mucous membrane.

Blennorrhoeria—Flow of mucus from the intestines.

Blennostasis—Diminution or suppression of mucus discharge.

Blennostatic—Diminishing mucous secretion.

Blennothorax—Accumulation of mucus in the chest.

Blennuria—Presence of mucus in the urine.

Blephara—Plural of blepharon.

Blepharadenitis—Inflammation of the meibomian glands.

Blepharal—Pertaining to eyelid.

Blepharectomy —Surgical partial or complete excision of an eyelid.

Blepharedema—Edema of the eyelids due to which the eyelids appear like the bags.

Blepharism—Blinking of the eyelids.

Blepharitis—Inflammation of the eyelids at the edges.

Blepharitis angularis— Inflammation involving the angle of the eyelids due to which the openings of the lacrimal ducts are blocked.

Blepharitis ciliaris— Inflammation of the ciliary margins of the eyelids.

Blepharitis parasitica—Inflammation of the eyelids caused by parasites such as mites or lice.

Blepharitis squamosa—Chronic blepharitis in which the edge of the eyelid is covered with small, white or grey scales.

Blepharitis ulcerative—There are many ulcers along the margin of the eyelid and loss of lashes.

Blepharo-—Prefix pertaining to the eyelid.

Blepharoadenitis— Inflammation of the meibomian glands.

Blepharoadenoma —Glandular tumor of the eyelid.

Blepharoatheroma—Sebaceous cyst of an eyelid.

Blepharochalasis—Hypertrophy due to loss of elasticity of the skin of the upper eyelid.

Blepharochromhidrosis— Colored sweat, usually of blue color from the eyelids.

Blepharoclonus—Chronic spasm of the muscles orbicularis oculi that close the eyelids.

Blepharocoloboma— Ankyloblepharon.

Blepharoconjunctivitis— Inflammation of the eyelid and conjunctiva.

Blepharodiastasis—Excessive separation of eyelids, causing the eye to open wide.

Blepharokeratoconjunctivitis—Inflammation of the eyelids, cornea and conjunctiva.

Blepharon—Eyelid.

Blepharoncus—Tumor of the eyelid.

Blepharopachynsis—Abnormal thickening of the eyelid.

Blepharophimosis—Narrowing of the palpebral fissures abnormally.

Blepharoplast—A minute mass of chromatin found in a cell, forming the base of a flagellum.

Blepharoplastic—Pertaining to blepharoplasty.

Blepharoplasty—Plastic surgery of the eyelids.

Blepharoplegia—Paralysis of an eyelid.

Blepharoptosis—Dropping of an upper eyelid.

Blepharopyorrhea—Purulent discharge from an eyelid.

Blepharorrhaphy—Stitching of the margins of the eyelids to reduce the length of the palpebral fissure.

Blepharorrhea—Discharge from the eyelid.

Blepharospasm—Spasm of the muscles of the eyelids.

Blepharostat—An instrument for holding the eyelids apart during an operation.

Blepharostenosis—Narrowing of the palpebral fissure.

Blepharosynechia—Adhesion of the margins of the upper and lower eyelids.

Blepharotomy —Surgical incision of an eyelid.

Blind—Without the sense of sight.

Blindness—Lack or loss of ability to see.

Amnesic color blindness—Inability to remember the names of the colors seen.

Color blindness— Inability to recognize the colors.

Cortical blindness— Blindness due to the lesion of the visual area of the cerebral cortex.

Day blindness—Inability to see in day light.

Eclipse blindness— Blindness due to burning of the macula while viewing an eclipse without using the glasses.

Hysterical blindness—Blindness which occurs at the attack of hysteria.

Letter blindness— Inability to understand the meaning of letters.

Night or nocturnal blindness—Inability to see at night.

Object blindness—Inability to recognize the things even though the eyes are functioning normally, it may be due to some mental disorder.

Psychic blindness— Sight without recognition due to brain lesion.

Snow blindness— Blindness, usually temporary due to glare of sunlight upon snow.

Transient blindness —Temporary blindness of sudden onset due to the interference of blood supply to the retina.

Word blindness— Inability to understand written or spoken words.

Blind spot or Optic disk—Area in retina for the entrance of optic nerve which is devoid of rods and cones.

Blink —To open and close the eyes quickly, may be voluntary or involuntary.

Blink reflex—Automatic closing of the eyes in response to a sudden movement of an object towards the eyes.

Blister—A collection of fluid below or within the epidermis of the skin.

Blister blood—Presence of blood in a blister produced by the rupture of blood vessels.

Blister fever—Herpes simplex of the lip.

Blister water—Blister with clear watery contents.

Blistering—Vesiculation. The formation of vesicles.

Bloat—Flatulence of the stomach.

Bloated—A hollow organ distended by gas, water or serum beyond its normal size.

Bloating—Distention of the abdomen caused by swallowed air or intestinal gas produced by fermentation.

Block—1. An obstruction or stoppage. 2. Local anaesthesia to stop the passage of sensory impulses in a nerve. 3. To obstruct a passage or opening.

Air block—Leakage of air from the airways to accumulate in the connective tissues of the lungs and thus forming an obstruction to the normal flow of air.

Ear block—Blockage of the auditory canal by infection or accumulation of wax.

Field block—Local anesthesia produced by injecting an anesthetic agent, by blocking the impulses in the nerves for minor operations.

Heart block—The impulses arising from the sino-atrial node are stopped at the atrioventricular node or somewhere in the bundle of His.

Neuromuscular block—The blockage of impulses from motor endplate to a muscle which may be caused by the deficiency of acetylcholine.

Spinal block—Blockage in the flow of cerebrospinal fluid within the spinal canal.

Blockade—Prevention of the action of something, such as the effect of a drug or of a body function.

Blocker—Something that blocks the passage or activity etc.

Blood —The fluid circulating through the heart, arteries, capillaries and veins, carrying the nourishment, hormones, antibodies, heat and oxygen to the cells of the body and removing the waste products and carbon dioxide from there. It consists of a fluid plasma and the three types of cells – red blood cells, white blood cells and platelets.

Aerated or arterial blood—Blood which carries oxygen to the tissues.

Central blood—Blood obtained from the heart or from the bone marrow.

Citrated blood—Blood treated with sodium citrate to prevent its coagulation.

Clotted blood—The blood changed into jelly-like nonfluid mass by the process of coagulation.

Cord blood—Blood contained in the umbilical blood vessels of the infant at the time of delivery.

Defibrinated blood— Whole blood from which fibrin was separated during the clotting process.

Menstrual blood—Blood of menstruation.

Occult blood —The presence of blood in such small quantities that it is not visible to the naked eye but it can be detected only by chemical tests or microscopic examination.

Peripheral blood—The blood obtained from the circulation remote from the heart.

Sludged blood —Blood in which red blood cells have massed together in the smaller blood vessels and block or slow the blood flowing through them.

Splanchnic blood—The blood circulating in the thoracic, abdominal and pelvic viscera, *e.g.*, pulmonary, hepatic and splenic blood.

Unit of blood— Approximately 1 pint (about 20 ounces or 473 mls.) of blood, the amount usually available for transfusion.

Venous blood—Blood which has given up its oxygen to the tissues, mixed with carbon dioxide and becomes dark red.

Whole blood —Blood drawn from a donor containing an anticoagulant such as sodium citrate or heparin.

Blood bank—A place where the blood is kept after withdrawal from donors, until required for transfusion.

Blood-brain barrier—A membrane between the circulating blood and the brain which prevents the damaging substances from reaching the brain tissues and the cerebrospinal fluid.

Blood casts—Masses of red blood cells molded by the renal tubules and found in the urine.

Blood clot—Coagulated mass of blood.

Blood component—One of the components forming the blood. Blood may be transfused in its whole state or one of its components may be administered.

Blood component therapy —Treatment of a disease by transfusing one or more of the components of the whole blood, as packed red blood cells etc.

Blood corpuscles—The blood cells—red blood cells, white blood cells and platelets.

Blood count—Determination of the number of white blood cells and red blood cells per cu. m.m. of whole blood.

Complete blood count—A combination of red blood cell count, hematocrit—Packed cell volume (PCV), erythrocytic indices—Mean cell volume (MCV), Mean cell hemoglobin (MCH) and Mean cell hemoglobin concentration (MCHC), total white blood cell count, differential W.B.C. count and platelet count.

Differential W.B.C. count— Determination of the number of each type of white blood cell in 100 white blood cells.

Blood crossmatching—The process of mixing the donor's red blood cells with the recipient's serum (major cross matching) and mixing of the recipient's blood with the serum of the donor (minor cross matching).

Blood culture —Withdrawal of blood from a vein with sterile precautions and placing it on a suitable culture media and at an optimum temperature for the multiplication of any organisms contained in the blood and so be isolated and identified under the microscope.

Blood donor—The person who gives his blood to be used for transfusion.

Blood doping—Infusion of blood into the same person who donated it which is usually done to enhance his/her athletic performance.

Blood gas analysis— Chemical analysis of the blood to know the concentration of oxygen and carbon dioxide.

Blood groups—Human blood is divided into four groups—A, B, AB and O. There are antigens located at the surface of the red blood cells and the antibody present in the plasma of blood. Antigens and antibodies are of two types – A and B. The blood of group A contains antigen-A and antibody-B, the blood of group B contains antigen-B and the antibody-A, blood of group AB contains both antigens but no antibodies, blood of group O contains no antigen but both antibodies. When a patient is needed of blood transfusion, it is done only after detecting the blood groups of the patient and the blood donor. The patient of blood group A is given the blood of the donor of blood group A and O, the patient of blood group B is given the blood of group B and O, to the patient of blood group AB (universal recipient) the blood of any group may be given and the blood of the donor of O group (universal donor) can be given to the patient of any blood group. So before blood transfusion the detection of blood group of the patient and the donor is necessary.

Blood incompatibility— The reaction occurring in a patient due to transfusion of mismatched blood. The immediate symptoms of the reaction include shivering of the body, rise in body temperature, pain in the lumbar region, nausea and vomiting. Late symptoms are jaundice and oliguria.

Blood letting—Removal of blood from the body as a treatment.

Blood plasma—The fluid portion of the blood in which white blood cells, red blood cells and the platelets are suspended.

Blood platelets—Small, colorless cells in the blood measuring about 3 microns in diameter which play an important role in clotting of the blood. .

Blood poisoning, Septicemia, Toxemia—Presence of large numbers of bacteria or their toxins in the blood.

Blood pressure—The pressure exerted by the blood on the blood vessel walls. It varies with the age, sex, altitude, physical development and according to the mental states, lower in women than in men, low in childhood and higher in elderly persons. When blood pressure is low it is known as hypotension, when it is high it is known as hypertension.

Diastolic blood pressure—Blood pressure during the dilatation phase of the heart, between the heart beats which is normally 80 m.m. of Hg.

Normal blood pressure—In healthy young person 100 to 140 m.m. Hg is systolic and 60 to 90 m.m. Hg is diastolic blood pressure.

Systolic blood pressure—The greatest force exerted on the vessel walls by the contraction of the heart which is normally 100 to 140 m.m. Hg.

Blood pressure monitor—An apparatus which automatically obtains and records the blood pressure at certain intervals, an alarm or a light signal being attached to it is activated when the blood pressure rises up or falls down below the normal.

Blood serum—A clear fluid which separates from the blood when it is allowed to clot completely, and thus it is the plasma from which the fibrinogen is being removed during clotting of blood. That is why the serum does not clot while the plasma clots.

Bloodshot—Local congestion of the small blood vessels of a part, as when the blood vessels of the conjunctiva are congested and visible (red eyes).

Blood shunting—A condition in which the blood flows through an abnormal pathway, not through its normal route.

Blood smear—A drop of blood which is spread thin on a slide for the purpose of examination.

Blood sugar—The amount of sugar in the form of glucose in the circulating blood.

Blood thinner—An anticoagulant.

Blood transfusion—Transfer of blood of one person to another through the intravenous route. In direct or immediate transfusion the blood is transferred through a tube directly from the donor to the recipient. In indirect transfusion the blood is collected in a receptacle from the donor before transfusion.

Blood urea—The urea present in the blood. Normally it is 15 to 38.5 mg. per 100 ml. of blood. An increase in the blood urea indicates the deficiency of renal function.

Blood vessels—The arteries, capillaries and veins.

Blood warmer—An apparatus for warming the blood of blood bank to body temperature before transfusion.

Bloody —Of the nature of or accompanied by blood.

Bloody sweat, Hemathidrosis—Excretion of blood or blood pigments in sweat through the sweat glands.

Bloody weeping—Hemorrhage from the conjunctiva.

Blotch—A spot of discoloration on the skin.

Blow —A hard stroke.

Blowing—A whistling sound.

Blowpipe—A tube through which a current of air or a gas is passed under pressure upon a flame to concentrate and intensify the heat of the flame.

Blue —Cyanotic due to lack of oxygen.

Blue balls—Testicular pain which is relieved by discharge of the semen.

Blue nevus—Blue birthmark or mole.

Blues—State of depression or sadness.

Blumberg's sign —The occurrence of severe pain when the doctor presses his hand over the McBurney's point and then suddenly he removes his hand. The sign indicates the peritoneal inflammation. Syn. Rebound tenderness.

Blurring—Unclear vision.

Blush—Redness of the face and neck due to

dilatation of the blood vessels caused by emotion or heat.

B.M.R.—Basal metabolic rate.

Boas' point—A tender spot present on the left of the 12th dorsal vertebra in patients with gastric ulcer.

Boat-belly—The sunken appearance of the belly.

Bobbing—An up-and-down movement.

Bodily—Pertaining to the body.

Body—1. The human physical part distinguished from mind and spirit. 2. The principal part of any structure. 3. The largest and most important part of any organ. 4. Any mass or collection of material.

Acetone or ketone bodies—The substances which increase in the blood of the person suffering from diabetes mellitus, due to faulty fat metabolism.

Amygdaloid body— An almond-shaped mass of gray matter in the lateral wall and roof of the third ventricle of the brain.

Aortic bodies—Small structures located on either side of the aorta in the region of the aortic arch and contain the endings of the aortic nerve. They respond to the oxygen concentration in the blood and to changes in blood pressure.

Aschoff bodies— Microscopic nodules found in the cardiac muscle in rheumatic myocarditis.

Body of penis—The free pendulous portion of the penis, consisting of the shaft and glans penis.

Body of stomach—The greatest portion of the stomach between the fundus and the pylorus.

Carotid body—A small flat structure lying at the bifurcation of the common carotid artery which contains cells that respond to changes in the concentration of oxygen in the blood and to changes in blood pressure, thus help in regulating the circulation.

Ciliary body—It is the thickened portion of the middle layer of the eye ball, the uveal tract, which is continuous anteriorly with the iris and posteriorly with the choroid.

Foreign body—An object present at the place where it should not be normally present.

Immune body—Antibody.

Leishman-Donovan body— Intracellular, non-flagellate form of the unicellular parasite Leishmania donovani causing Kala-azar.

Malpighian body— Renal corpuscle consisting of a glomerulus enclosed in Bowman's capsule.

Mammary body—Body of the breast.

Negri bodies —Small, round or oval structures seen in the brain cells after death of the animal infected with rabies.

Perineal body—A mass of tissue which separates the anus from the vestibule and the lower part of the vagina.

Pineal body —A small conical structure in the brain attached by a stalk to the posterior wall of the third ventricle.

Pituitary body—The pituitary gland.

Suprarenal body— Adrenal gland.

Vitreous body—A transparent, thick, jelly-like substance within the eye that fills the space between the lens and the retina.

Body mass index—An index for estimating obesity, obtained by dividing weight of body in kilograms by height of the body in meters squared.

Body surface area—The surface area of the body expressed in square meters, which can be calculated by using a standard formula, when the height and weight of a person is known. It is important in calculating the dosage for the children, in the treatment of burn patients and in determining the radiation doses.

Boerhaave syndrome— Complete, spontaneous rupture of the esophagus usually associated with violent retching or vomiting.

Boil—Inflammation of the hair follicle. Furuncle.

Boiling—Process of vaporization of a liquid.

Boiling point—The degree of heat required to vaporize a liquid, which varies according to the chemicals present in it.

Bolometer—1. An instrument for measuring the force of the heart beat. 2. An instrument for measuring minute degrees of radiant heat.

Bolus —A rounded mass of masticated food or of medicine ready to be swallowed.

Bonding—1. Development of strong emotional attachment between two individuals, e.g., mother and child, lovers or husband and wife after frequent or prolonged close contact. 2. In dentistry, the correction of badly stained, malformed, two widely separated or broken teeth by using plastic material, porcelein or acrylic etc.

Bone —The hard and rigid connective tissue constituting the skeleton and composed chiefly

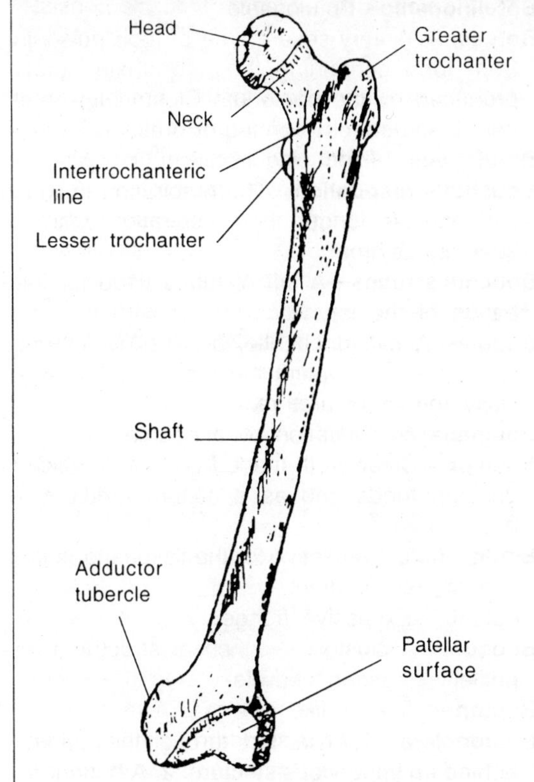

Fig. 52A : Anterior aspect of left femur bone.

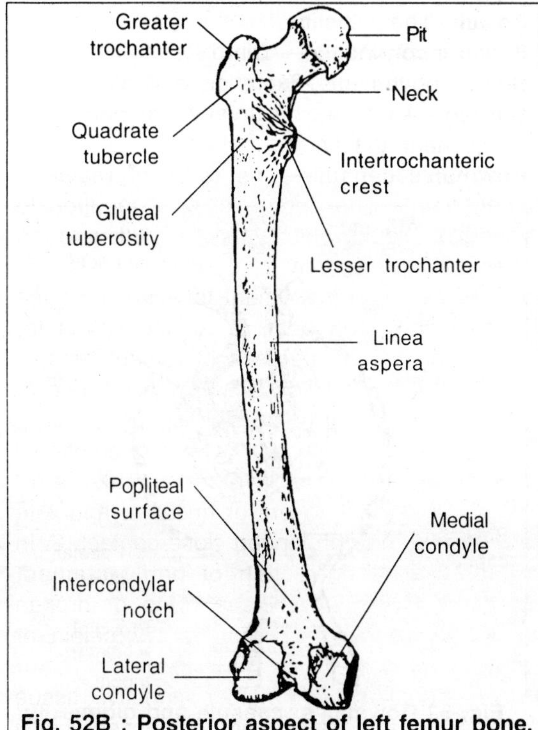

Fig. 52B : Posterior aspect of left femur bone.

of calcium salts. The bones provide the shape and support for the body.

Alveolar bone—Bony structure supporting the teeth.

Ankle bone—The astragalus or talus bone.

Breast bone—The sternum.

Brittle bone—Abnormal fragile bone.

Cancellous bone—Spongy bone.

Cartilage bone—Bone which develops within the cartilage.

Cheek bone—Zygomatic bone.

Collar bone—The clavicle bone.

Compact bone—Dense and hard bone.

Cranial bone—A bone of the cranium or brain case.

Exercise bone—A bone developed in a muscle, tendon or fascia, due to excessive exercise.

Flat bone—The bone which has very slight thickness.

Heel bone—Calcaneus bone.

Innominate bone—Hip bone, composed of three bones—ilium, ischium and pubis.

Ivory or marble bone—Abnormally calcified bone.

Jaw bone—The mandible or maxilla bone, especially the mandible.

Long bone—The bone of which the length exceeds its breadth and thickness.

Pelvic bone—Hip bone.

Perichondrial bone— Bone formed beneath the perichondrium.

Periosteal bone—Bone formed by the osteoblast cells of the periosteum.

Pisiform bone—A small bone resembling a pea in size and shape found in the proximal row of the carpus.

Pneumatic bone—The bone which contains air-filled spaces.

Replacement bone—Any bone developing within cartilage.

Semilunar bone— Lunate bone. A bone of the proximal row in the carpus between the scaphoid and triquetral bone.

Sesamoid bone—A bone developing in a tendon and passing over a joint, as patella.

Short bone—The bone of approximately equal length, width and thickness.

Spongy bone—Cancellous bone.

Sutural bone or Wormian bone —Irregularly shaped bones as found in the sutures of the cranium.

Tail bone—Coccyx.

Thigh bone — The femur.

Bone age —The age determined by X-ray examination of the stage of development of ossification centers of the long bones of the extremities.

Bone cells—Bone forming cells— the osteoblasts, osteocytes and osteoclasts.

Bone cyst—Cystic tumor of the bone.

Bone graft—A piece of bone is taken from an animal or from a bone of the patient which is used to take the place of a removed bone or bony defect.

Bonelet—A small bone.

Bone marrow—A soft organic substance filling the bone cavities.

Bone marrow transplant— Transplantation of bone marrow from one person to another, usually used in treating aplastic anaemia.

Bony—Resembling or of the nature of bone.

Booster—An additional dose of an immunizing medicine to increase the effect of the previous injections, which is given some months or years after the initial immunization.

Boot—A special shoe or bandage for covering the foot, ankle and lower part of the leg.

Borborygmus—A gurgling sound heard over the large intestine caused by the propulsion of gas through the intestine.

Border—The edge or boundary.

Border brush—The presence of cilia arranged in a brush like manner on the free surface of the epithelial cells as found in the cells lining the mucous membrane of the respiratory tract.

Bordetella pertussis—The bacterium causing whooping cough.

Boredom—Feeling of tiredness or depression due to lack of activity.

Borism—Symptoms of borax poisoning when used internally which include dry skin, eruptions, and gastric disturbances.

Borreliosis—Disease caused by the bacteria of the genus Borrelia.

Boss—A rounded eminence.

Bosselated—Covered with bosses.

Bosselation—A condition in which one or more rounded protuberances are present.

Bossing—Prominence of the forehead.

Botryoid—Resembling a bunch of grapes.

Botulin—A neurotoxin produced by the bacterium Clostridium botulinum, responsible for botulism and is not destroyed by the action of gastric or intestinal secretions.

Botulinogenic—Botulogenic.

Botulism—A very severe type of food poisoning from food containing the neurotoxin botulin, produced by the bacterium Clostridium botulinum in imperfectly canned or preserved foods.

Botulogenic—Producing botulism.

Bouchut's respiration—The respiration in which expiration is longer than inspiration which is seen in asthma.

Bouchut's tubes—A set of tubes used for intubation of the larynx.

Bougie—A cylindrical, flexible, hollow or solid instrument for dilating the tubal organs, especially the male urethra.

Bougienage—Dilatation by a bougie.

Bouillon—Clear broth made from meat, which is used in foods and as a culture medium for bacteria.

Bouin's fluid—A fixative for the tissues for microscopic examination.

Boulimia—Excessive hunger.

Bouquet—A cluster or bunch of structures, especially of blood vessels.

Bouton— A knob-like swelling.

Boutonniere—1. An incision through the perineum behind an impervious stricture. 2. A buttonhole-like opening in a membrane produced by injury.

Bovine—Pertaining to or derived from the cattle.

Bowel—The intestine.

Bowel incontinence— Diarrhea.

Bowel movement—Excretion of feces.

Bowleg—An outward curvature of one or both legs near the knee.

Bowman's capsule—The renal or malpighian

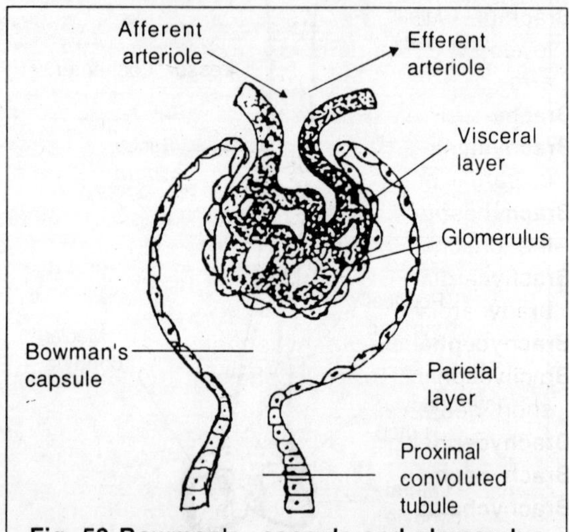

Fig. 53 Bowman's capsule and glomerulus

corpuscle which acts as a filter in the formation of urine.

Bowman's glands—The olfactory glands which produce mucus and keeps the olfactory surface moist.

Bowman's membrane—The membrane which separates the corneal epithelium from corneal substance.

Box-note—In emphysema, a hollow sound heard on percussion over the chest.

Boyle's law—A law that at a constant temperature, the volume of a gas varies inversely with the pressure.

B.P.—Blood pressure, British pharmacopoeia.

b.p.—Boiling point.

Brace—Any apparatus used in orthopedics for holding the joints or limbs in place.

Brachia—Plural of brachium.

Brachial—Pertaining to the arm.

Brachialgia—Pain in the arm.

Brachialis—A muscle of the arm lying immediately under the biceps brachii muscle.

Brachial plexus—A collection of the last four cervical and the first thoracic spinal nerves supplying the upper arm, forearm and hand.

Brachial veins—Veins accompanying the brachial artery.

Brachiocephalic—Pertaining to the arm and head.

Brachiocrural—Pertaining to the arm and thigh.

Brachiocubital—Pertaining to the arm and forearm.

Brachiocyllosis—Abnormal curvature of the arm.

Brachioradialis—A muscle lying on the lateral side of the forearm.

Brachium—1. The part of the arm from shoulder to elbow. 2. The structure which resembles an arm.

Brachy- —Prefix for short.

Brachybasia—A slow gait with shuffling of feet in partial paraplegia.

Brachybasophalangia— Abnormal shortness of the proximal phalanges.

Brachycardia—Slowness of the heart rate. Syn. bradycardia.

Brachycephalia—Brachycephaly.

Brachycephalic, Brachycephalous —One who has short head.

Brachycephalism— Brachycephaly.

Brachycephaly—Shortness of the head.

Brachycheilia—Condition of having abnormally short lip or lips.

Brachycnemic—Having short legs.

Brachydactylia—Abnormal shortness of the fingers and toes.

Brachydactyly—Brachydactylia.

Brachyesophagus—Abnormally short esophagus.

Brachyglossal—Denoting an abnormally short tongue.

Brachygnathia—Abnormal shortness of the lower jaw.

Brachygnathous—Having an abnormally short lower jaw.

Brachymelia—Disproportionate shortness of the limbs.

Brachymesophalangia—Abnormal shortness of the middle phalanges.

Brachymetacarpalia, Brachymetacarpalism — Brachymetacarpia.

Brachymetacarpia—Abnormal shortness of the metacarpal bones.

Brachymetatarsia—Abnormal shortness of the metatarsal bones.

Brachymetropia—Myopia, near sightedness.

Brachymorphic—Shorter and broader than usual.

Brachyodont—Having abnormally short teeth.

Brachyonychia—Shorter nails.

Brachyphalangia—Abnormal shortness of a bone or bones of a finger or toe.

Brachypodous—Having abnormally short feet.

Brachyprosopic—Having a disproportionately short face.

Brachyrhinia—Abnormal shortness of the nose.

Brachyrhynchus—Abnormal shortness of the nose and maxilla.

Brachyskelic—Pertaining to abnormally short legs.

Brachystasis—Condition in which a muscle does not relax on contraction but maintains its shortened state.

Brachysyndactyly —Abnormal shortness of the fingers or toes with a webbing between the adjacent digits.

Brachytelephalangia— Abnormal shortness of the distal phalanges.

Brachytherapy—Implantation of radioactive materials in the body such as radium, etc. in radiation therapy.

Brady-—Prefix indicating slow.

Bradyacusia—Dullness of hearing.

Bradyarrhythmia—Bradycardia with irregular heart beats.

Bradyarthria—Bradylalia or bradyglossia.

Bradycardia—Slowness of the heart beat with the pulse rate, below 60 per minute.

Bradycardiac—Bradycardic. Pertaining to or characterized by bradycardia.

Bradycardic—Bradycardiac.

Bradycinesia—Bradykinesia.

Bradycrotic—Pertaining to slowness of the pulse.

Bradydiastole—Prolongation of the diastole of the heart.

Bradyecoia—Partial deafness.

Bradyesthesia—Slowness of perception.

Bradyglossia—Abnormal slowness of speech.

Bradykinesia—Abnormal slowness of movement.

Bradykinetic—Pertaining to or characterized by slow movement.

Bradylalia or Bradyglossia—Abnormal slowness of speech.

Bradylexia—Abnormal slowness in reading which is not due to lack of intelligence or defect of vision.

Bradylogia—Abnormal slow speech due to mental impairment.

Bradypepsia—Abnormally slow digestion.

Bradyphagia—Slowness in eating.

Bradyphemia, Bradyphrasia—To speak very slowly as seen in some mental diseases.

Bradyphrasia — Bradyphemia.

Bradypnea—Abnormally slow breathing.

Bradypsychia—Occurrence of mental reactions slowly.

Bradyrhythmia—Slowness of the heart or pulse rate.

Bradyspermatism—Very slow ejaculation of semen.

Bradysphygmia—Abnormally slow pulse.

Bradystalsis—Very slow peristaltic movement.

Bradytachycardia—Increased heart rate alternating with slow heart rate.

Bradytocia—Abnormally slow delivery.

Bradyuria—Passing of urine very slowly.

Braille—A device which has raised words which can be identified only by touching with the fingers and thus it is used by the blind persons to read.

Brain —A large soft mass, the part of the central nervous system contained within the cranium, comprising the fore-brain, mid-brain and the hind-brain.

Brain death—Cessation of brain function.

Brain edema—The increase in volume of the brain due to an increase of its water content.

Brain fever—Meningitis.

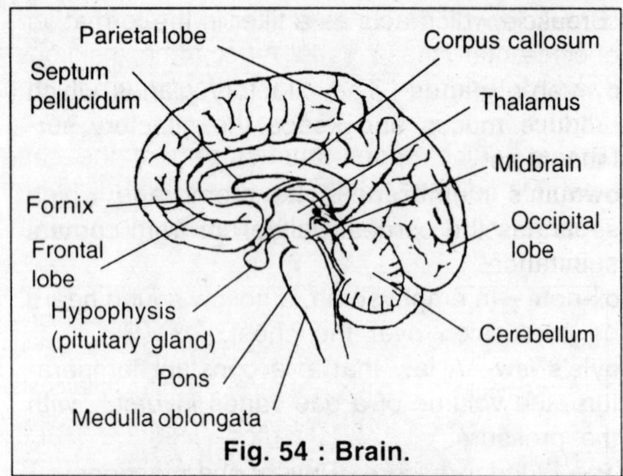

Fig. 54 : Brain.

Brain scan—To inject intravenously the radioactive isotopes and to detect the abnormalities in the structure and function of the brain.

Brain stem —The stem-like portion of the brain connecting the cerebral hemispheres with the spinal cord and comprising the medulla oblongata, pons and the mid-brain.

Brain washing—To displace the previous thoughts by the new ones in the brain of a person by psychological treatment, as is sometimes done in politics.

Bran—Husk of the cereal grains as that of wheat.

Brandt-Andrews maneuver—A technique used to expel the placenta from the uterus during the IIIrd stage of labor by putting gentle traction on the umbilical cord by one hand and pressing the anterior surface of the uterus backward by the other hand.

Brandy—An alcoholic liquid obtained by the distillation of fermented grapes which contains 50% ethyl alcohol by volume.

Brash—Burning sensation behind the sternum bone (in the chest) with regurgitation of sour fluid or tasteless saliva into the mouth.

Brawny induration—Abnormal hardening and thickening of the tissues.

Braxton Hicks sign—There are painless uterine contractions occurring at the interval of 10 to 20 minutes. They start to occur after the 3rd month of pregnancy. At this time the uterus becomes hard and its boundaries can be felt by palpation. This is a sign which confirms the occurrence of pregnancy. These are the uterine contractions only which further change into labor contractions.

Breakbone fever, Dengue—A disease characterized by sudden onset with headache, fever and pain in the muscles and joints especially in the back.

Breakdown —Nervous breakdown. An emotional or mental illness usually occurring insidiously and interferring with the normal mental functions.

Breast —The upper anterior part of the chest which contains milk secreting glands which secrete the milk for the nourishment of the infant.

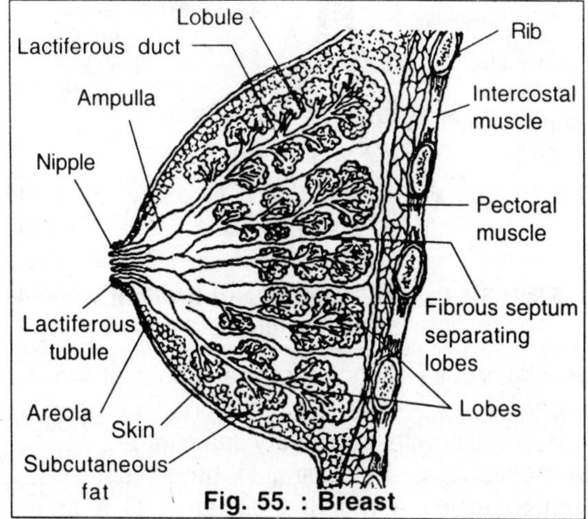

Fig. 55. : Breast

Breast bone—The sternum.

Breast fed—Being brought up on mother's milk.

Breast feeding —Nursery of an infant on mother's milk.

Breast pump—An instrument for drawing milk from the female breast.

Breath—The alternate inhalation and exhalation of air into and out of the lungs.

Breath holding—Cessation of breathing as is usually seen in young children.

Breathing—The act of inhaling and exhaling the air.

Asthmatic breathing— Breathing in which the expiration is prolonged than the inspiration found in bronchial asthma.

Biot's breathing— Irregularly alternating cessation of breathing with deeper breathing which generally occurs in meningitis and disorders of the brain that cause increased intracranial pressure.

Cheyne-stokes breathing—A period of apnea (without breathing at all) lasting for 10 to 60 seconds followed by gradually increasing and then decreasing respirations.

Intermittent positive-pressure breathing — It is a mechanical method for assisting pulmonary ventilation. For this an apparatus fills the air or oxygen into the lungs under pressure. It is used in severe respiratory failure.

Kussmaul's breathing— Deep, gasping breathing characteristic of air hunger or diabetic coma.

Mouth breathing— Respiration through the mouth instead of the nose, usually due to obstruction of the nasal airways.

Shallow breathing— Breathing is not deep so the breathing rate is increased. It occurs in acute pulmonary disease.

Breatholyzer —An apparatus used to analyze the specific contents of the expired air, which is generally used to detect the presence of alcohol in the expired air in order to determine whether a person is legally intoxicated or not.

Breech —Buttocks.

Breech presentation—An abnormal delivery in

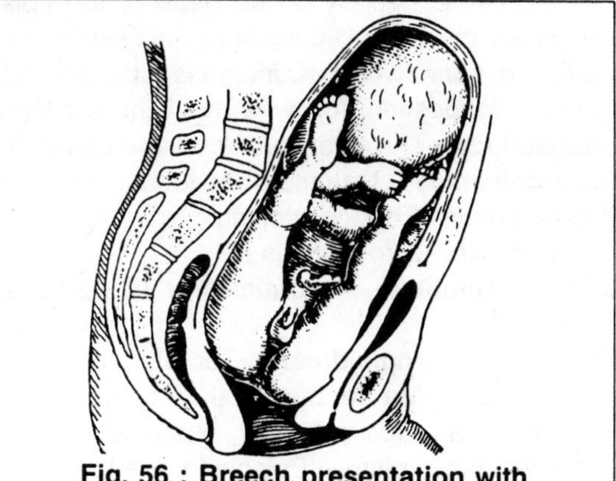

Fig. 56 : Breech presentation with extended legs.

which the child takes birth presenting her buttocks instead presenting head.

Bregma—The point on the surface of the skull at the junction of the coronal and sagittal sutures.

Bregmatic—Pertaining to the bregma.

Bregmocardiac reflex— The reduction of heart rate on applying pressure on the posterior fontanelle.

Brenner's tumor—A benign fibroepithelioma of the ovary.

Brevicollis—Shortness of the neck.

Brevilineal—Shorter and broader body than usual.

Brevis—Short.

Bridge—A narrow band of the tissues which connects two organs.

Bridge of the nose—The upper portion of the external nose formed by the union of the nasal bones.

Bridle—The frenum.

Bright's disease—Nonsuppurative inflammatory or degenerative kidney disease with specific symptoms of edema, hypertension, proteinuria and hematuria.

Brim—An edge or margin.

Brine—Sea or salty water.

Brisement— The breaking up of any thing by force as of an ankylosis.

Brittle—Apt to break.

Broach—A dental instrument used for enlarging the tooth canal or for extracting the pulp.

Broca's area—Motor speech area at the posterior end of the inferior frontal gyrus on the left cerebral hemisphere which controls movements of the tongue, lips and vocal cords. Hemorrhage in this area may cause loss of speech.

Brodie's abscess—An abscess of the head of a long bone, especially of the head of the tibia in which the patient complains of pain in the affected bone which is increased by warmth due to congestion, followed by slight swelling.

Bromatology—The science of food and dietetics.

Bromatotherapy—Treatment by food.

Bromatoxism—Food poisoning.

Bromhidrosis—Bromidrosis.

Bromidrosiphobia—Abnormal fear of personal odors.

Bromidrosis, Bromhidrosis—Secretion of offensive sweat due to bacterial decomposition which occurs mostly on feet, groins and axilla.

Bromism, Brominism— Poisoning due to excessive or prolonged use of bromides.

Bromoderma—Skin eruption due to allergic sensitivity to bromides.

Bromohyperhidrosis, Bromohyperidrosis— Excessive secretion of sweat with foul smell.

Bromomania—Mental disorder induced by chronic misuse of bromides.

Bromomenorrhea—Menstruation with foul smell.

Bromopnea—Offensive breath.

Bronchadenitis—Inflammation of the bronchial glands.

Bronchi —The two main branches leading from the trachea to the lungs.

Bronchial—Pertaining to the bronchi or bronchioles.

Bronchial glands—Mucous or mixed glands in the bronchi or bronchioles.

Bronchial tree—Bronchi and bronchial tubes.

Bronchial tubes—Smaller divisions of the bronchi.

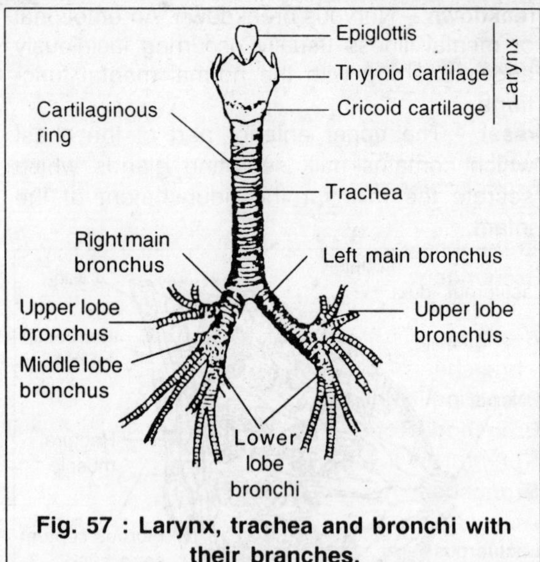

Fig. 57 : Larynx, trachea and bronchi with their branches.

Bronchiarctia—Stenosis of the bronchial tubes.

Bronchiectasis—Chronic dilatation of a bronchus or bronchi with secondary infection.

Bronchiectatic—Pertaining to bronchiectasis.

Bronchiocele—A rounded dilatation of a bronchus.

Bronchiogenic—Having origin in the bronchi.

Bronchiole—One of the smaller subdivisions of the bronchial tubes.

Bronchiolectasia— Bronchiolectasis.

Bronchiolectasis—Dilatation of the bronchioles.

Bronchioli—Plural of bronchiolus.

Bronchiolitis—Inflammation of the bronchioles.

Bronchiolus—Bronchiole.

Bronchiospasm—Spasms of the bronchi and the bronchioles.

Bronchiostenosis—Narrowing of the bronchial tubes.

Bronchitic—One who is suffering from bronchitis.

Bronchitis—Inflammation of the mucous membrane of the bronchi.

Acute or catarrhal bronchitis— Bronchitis with a short, severe course with profuse mucopurulent discharge.

Asthmatic bronchitis— The bronchitis that causes, or aggravates the existing asthma.

Chronic bronchitis— The bronchitis of long duration for at least three months with increased mucus secretion.

Plastic bronchitis— Bronchitis in which there is violent cough with paroxysmal dyspnea in which casts of the bronchial tubes are expectorated.

Bronchium—Bronchus.

Broncho- —Prefix relating to the bronchi.

Bronchoadenitis— Inflammation of the bronchial glands.

Bronchoalveolar—Pertaining to the bronchi and the alveoli.

Bronchoblennorrhea—Chronic bronchitis with copious and thin sputum.

Bronchocele—Localized dilatation of a bronchus.

Bronchoconstriction— Constriction of the bronchial tubes.

Bronchoconstrictor—Causing constriction of a bronchus or bronchial tube.

Bronchodilatation—Dilatation of a bronchus.

Bronchodilator—Causing dilatation of a bronchus or bronchial tube.

Bronchoedema—Edematous swelling of the bronchial mucosa reducing the size of air paths and thus causing dyspnea.

Bronchoesophageal— Pertaining to the bronchus and the esophagus.

Bronchoesophagoscopy— Instrumental examination of the bronchi and esophagus.

Bronchogenic—Originating in a bronchus.

Bronchogram—X-ray film of the lungs and bronchi.

Bronchography— Radiography of the bronchi after injecting a radiopaque substance into them.

Broncholith—A calculus in the bronchus.

Broncholithiasis— Inflammation or obstruction of the bronchi caused by the calculi.

Bronchology—The study and treatment of diseases of the trachea and the bronchi.

Bronchomalacia—Softening of a bronchus.

Bronchomotor—Causing dilatation or constriction of the bronchi.

Bronchomycosis—A disease of the lungs resembling tuberculosis, caused by fungus candida.

Bronchopathy—Any disease of the bronchi or bronchioles.

Bronchophony—A sound heard over a normal bronchus through the stethoscope.

Bronchoplasty—Repairing of a bronchial defect by surgery.

Bronchoplegia—Paralysis of the muscles of the walls of the bronchial tubes.

Bronchopleural—Pertaining to the bronchi and the pleural cavity.

Bronchopleural fistula— Occurrence of a connection between the pleural cavity and a bronchus.

Bronchopneumonia— Inflammation of the lungs usually beginning in the terminal bronchioles.

Bronchopneumopathy —Disease of the bronchi and the lung tissue.

Bronchopulmonary—Pertaining to the bronchi and the lungs.

Bronchopulmonary lavage —Washing out of the bronchi and bronchioles to remove the tenacious secretions.

Bronchorrhagia—Hemorrhage in the bronchi.

Bronchorrhaphy—Suture of a wound of the bronchus.

Bronchorrhea—Excessive discharge of mucus from the bronchi sometimes very offensive.

Bronchoscope—An instrument for visual inspection of the trachea and the bronchi.

Bronchoscopy—Visual examination of trachea and the bronchi by using a bronchoscope.

Bronchosinusitis—Infection of bronchi and the sinus at a time.

Bronchospasm—Spasm of the bronchi as occurs in asthma.

Bronchospasmolytic— Relieving a bronchospasm.

Bronchospirochetosis—Hemorrhagic bronchitis. Chronic bronchitis due to infection with spirochetes.

Bronchospirometer—An instrument for measuring the volume of air inspired by one lung and for collecting the air for analysis.

Bronchospirometry—The measuring of the volume of air inspired by one lung and to collect the air for analysis by a bronchospirometer.

Bronchostaxis—Bleeding from a bronchial wall.

Bronchostenosis—Stenosis of a bronchus.

Bronchostomy—The formation of an opening through the chest wall into a bronchus by surgery.

Bronchotomy—Surgical incision of a bronchus.

Bronchotracheal—Pertaining to the bronchi and trachea both.

Bronchovesicular—Pertaining to the bronchi and alveoli.

Bronchus—One of the two larger branches of the trachea.

Brontophobia—Abnormal fear of thunder.

Broth—1. Liquid extract of meat used for food. 2. Used in making the culture medium of bacteria.

Brow—1. The eyebrow. 2. The forehead.

Brow presentation—Delivery of an infant on forehead or face presentation.

Brucellosis—An infectious disease caused by the bacterium of the genus brucella.

Bruise—An injury in which the skin is not broken but is discolored due to hemorrhage from the ruptured blood vessels into the subcutaneous tissues.

Bruissement—A purring sound heard upon auscultation.

Bruit—An adventitious sound heard on auscultation *e.g.*, placental bruit in which a blowing sound from the pregnant uterus due to fetal blood circulation is heard.

Bruxism—Grinding of the teeth, especially during sleep.

Bryants' traction—A vertical traction applied to the lower leg in case of the fracture of femur bone.

Bubo—An enlarged and inflamed lymph node, particularly in the groin or axilla due to infections such as syphilis, gonorrhea and tuberculosis.

Bubonadenitis—Inflammation of an inguinal gland.

Bubonalgia—Pain in the bubo.

Bubonic—Characterized by or pertaining to bubo.

Bubonic plague—The plague in which lymph nodes, especially in the groin or axilla are enlarged.

Bubonocele —Inguinal or femoral hernia forming a swelling in the groin.

Bubonulus—An abscess occurring along the course of a lymphatic vessel.

Bucardia—Severe hypertrophy of the heart.

Bucca—The cheek.

Buccal—Pertaining to the cheek or mouth.

Buccal cavity—The mouth.

Buccal glands—Salivary glands situated in the mucous membrane of the mouth.

Buccinator—The muscle of the cheek.

Bucco- —A prefix indicating cheek.

Buccoaxial—Denoting the angle formed by the buccal and axial walls of a cavity.

Buccoaxiocervical— Denoting the angle formed by the junction of the buccal, axial and cervical (gingival) walls of a cavity.

Buccocervical —Pertaining to the cheek and the neck.

Buccodistal—Pertaining to the buccal and distal surfaces of a tooth.

Buccogingival —Pertaining to the buccal and the gingival surfaces of a tooth.

Buccolabial—Concerning the buccal and labial surfaces of a tooth.

Buccolingual—Concerning the buccal and lingual surfaces of a tooth.

Buccomesial—Pertaining to the buccal and mesial surfaces of a tooth.

Bucconasal —Pertaining to both, the mouth and the nose.

Buccopharyngeal —Pertaining to both, the mouth and pharynx.

Buccoversion—The turning of a posterior tooth toward the cheek.

Buccula—A fold of fatty tissue under the chin known as double chin.

Buck's extension—An apparatus consisting of a weight and pulley for extending a limb, by attaching it to the limb to apply the force in the long axis of the limb.

Buck's traction—Traction of a leg applied in line with its long axis. The force is applied to adhesive tape attached to the skin.

Bucnemia—Tense inflammatory swelling of a leg.

Bud —Any small structure in the body resembling a bud of a plant.

Buerger's disease —The disease in which there is arterial occlusion of the leg in which the patient complains of pain in the leg on walking, which is due to diminution of blood supply.

Buffalo hump —Deposition of fat at the back below the cervical region.

Buffer—A substance of which the acidity or alkalinity is not changed upon adding a small amount of acid or alkali, *e.g.*, hemoglobin in the blood.

Bugger—A man who practices anal intercourse.

Buggery —Sodomy. Anal intercourse.

Bulb—Any rounded or globular structure as bulb of the eye.

Bulbar—Pertaining to or shaped like a bulb.

Bulbi—Plural of bulbus.

Bulbiform—Shaped like a bulb.

Bulbitis—Inflammation of the urethra in its bulbous portion.

Bulbocavernosus—The portion of the two lateral muscles of the penis, *i.e.*, corpora cavernosa, covering the bulb of the penis.

Bulbocavernosus reflex —Contraction of the bulbocavernosus muscle on percussing the dorsum of the penis.

Bulboid—Bulb-shaped.

Bulbomimic reflex— Contraction of the facial muscles following pressure on the eyeball.

Bulbonuclear—Pertaining to the nuclei in the medulla oblongata.

Bulbospinal—Pertaining to the medulla oblongata and spinal cord.

Bulbospongiosus—One of the three muscles of the penis.

Bulbourethral glands— Cowper's glands– two small glands, one on each side of the prostate gland.

Bulbous—Terminating in an enlarged bulb-shaped structure.

Bulbus—Bulb.

Bulesis—The will or an act of the will.

Bulimarexia, Bulimia— Excessive hunger.

Bulimia—Excessive hunger.

Bulimic—Pertaining to bulimia.

Bulkage—Anything such as sugar that increases the bulk of material in the intestine, thereby stimulating peristalsis.

Bulla, Bleb—A large blister on the skin filled with fluid.

Bullous—Having the nature of a bulla.

Bundle—A collection of fibers as the bundle of His in the heart.

Bundle branch block—Failure of the impulses originating from atrioventricular node to pass down the branches of the bundle of His.

Bunion—Inflammation and thickening of the bursa of the joint of the great toe with enlargement of the joint.

Bunionectomy—Excision of a bunion.

Bunodont—With curved teeth.

Buphthalmia, Buphthalmos— Infantile glaucoma with enlargement of the eye.

Bur, Burr —An instrument that rotates at a high speed and used to cut a tooth or bone by grinding.

Buret, Burette—A graduated glass tube, with a stop-cock at its lower end used to deliver a measured amount of liquid..

Burn—Injury to the tissues caused by thermal (contact with fire, hot objects or fluids), chemicals (acids or alkalies), electricity or radiant energy as from X-rays or sunlight etc. Burns are of three degrees. Ist degree—superficial burns, damage is only of outer layer of the epidermis. There is redness and tenderness. No vesicles are formed. IInd degree—damage extends through the epidermis into the dermis. Vesicles are formed. IIIrd degree—Both epidermis and dermis are destroyed with damage of the underlying tissues.

Burner—An apparatus from which the flame issues to burn or warm an object.

Burners—Burning pain occurring in the upper extremity frequently.

Burning foot syndrome— Feeling of burning on the sole of the foot which occurs in certain vitamin deficiences and in patients with chronic renal failure.

Burnish—To make smooth and polish the surface or edge of a dental repairing instrument.

Burnisher—An instrument for smoothing and polishing the surface or edge of a dental repairing instrument.

Burnout—1. Rendering a thing useless by excessive heat. 2. A state of physical and mental tiredness which is a reaction to inability to face the difficulties arising in, or to meet the demands of one's occupation characterized by insomnia, impaired work performance and frustration and the person becomes more vulnerable to physical illness.

Burp—To belch.

Burr—Bur.

Burrow—A small hole formed in the skin by itch mite, the parasite Sarcoptes scabiei.

Burrowing—The formation of a small hole in the skin by itch mite, the parasite Sarcoptes scabiei.

Bursa—A sac or cavity filled with synovial fluid which reduces the friction between the structures, especially of the joints where the friction is likely to occur.

Bursa Achilles—A bursa located between the tendon of Achilles and the calcaneus.

Bursa adventitious—Bursa not usually present but it develops in response to a friction or pressure.

Bursal—Pertaining to bursa.

Bursa patellar—One of the several bursae found in the region of the patellar bone.

Bursa pharyngeal—A small blind sac found in the lower part of the pharyngeal tonsil.

Bursae—Plural of bursa.

Bursalogy—Anatomy, physiology and pathology of the bursae.

Bursectomy—Excision of a bursa.

Bursitis—Inflammation of a bursa, especially those of the shoulder and knee joint.

Bursolith—A calculus formed in a bursa.

Bursopathy—Any disease of a bursa.

Bursotomy—Incision of a bursa.

Bursula—A small bursa.

Burton's line—A blue line seen along the margin of the gums in chronic lead poisoning.

Butt—To join the ends of two objects together.

Butterfly rash—Skin rash on the face which seems like a butterfly.

Buttocks—The external prominences posterior to the hips.

Button—An anatomical or pathological structure in the body resembling a button.

Buttonhole—A straight cut through a cavity wall.

Butyraceous—Containing or resembling butter.

Butyrin—A soft, yellow semi-liquid fat that is present in butter.

Butyroid—Like butter in appearance or consistency.

Butyrometer—An apparatus for measuring the amount of butter-fat in milk.

Butyrous—Of butter like consistency.

Bypass—After the obstruction of an artery as coronary artery or the abdominal aorta, an alternate route to be formed by a surgeon for blood circulation.

Double bypass surgery of the heart using internal mammary artery graft, and saphenous vein graft from the leg, to be transplanted on the coronary arteries, below the level of their blockages.

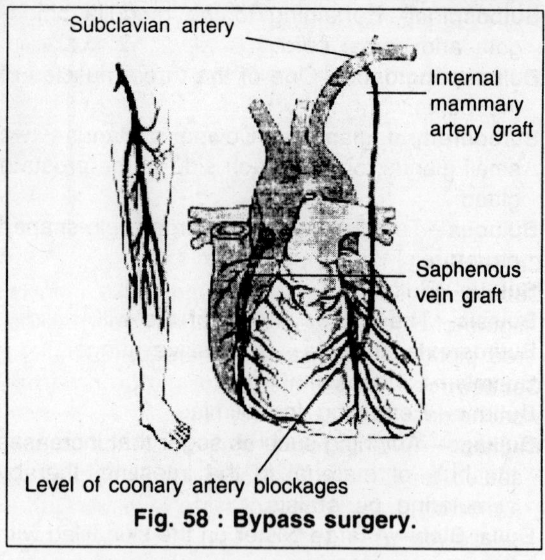

Fig. 58 : Bypass surgery.

Bysma—A plug or tampon.

Byssinosis—Pneumonoconiosis due to inhalation of cotton dust characterized by wheezing and tightness in the chest.

Ca — Symbol for calcium.

Cabots' rings —Blue stained threadlike, ring or figure-of-eight shaped structures, found in the red blood cells in severe anemia.

Cachectic —Pertaining to or suffering from cachexia.

Cachet —Two concave pieces of rice paper, sealed together at the margin between which a medicine of unpleasant taste is placed to be swallowed as a whole.

Cachexia —Wasting and weakness.

Cancerous cachexia — Cachexia caused by cancer disease.

Lymphatic cachexia —Cachexia caused by Hodgkin's disease of the lymph nodes.

Malarial cachexia — Cachexia due to chronic malaria.

Pituitary cachexia — Cachexia due to atrophy of the pituitary gland.

Strumipriva cachexia —Cachexia due to removal of the thyroid gland.

Tuberculous cachexia —Cachexia caused by tuberculosis.

Cachinnation —Excessive hysterical laughter.

Cacochylia —Indigestion.

Cacoethes —Any bad habit.

Cacogenesis —Any abnormal development or growth.

Cacogeusia —Bad taste in the mouth.

Cacomelia —Congenital deformity of a limb.

Cacoplastic —1. Pertaining to or causing abnormal growth. 2. Incapable of normal or perfect formation.

Cacosmia —Bad odor, or a hallucination of an unpleasant odor.

Cocospermia —A bad condition of the sperms.

Cacotrophy —Malnutrition.

Cadaver —A human dead body preserved for dissection.

Cadaveric —Pertaining to human dead body.

Cadaveric spasm —The continuation of muscular contraction even after death.

Cadaverous —Having the pallor and appearance resembling a dead body.

Caduca —Thickened membrane of the uterus.

Caecal —Pertaining to caecum.

Caecum —The distended beginning portion of the large intestine, at the end of the small intestine.

Caelotherpay —Treatment by religion.

Caesarian section —The taking out of the fetus from the uterus through an abdominal incision.

Caffeine —An alkaloid present in coffee and tea which is central nervous system stimulant and a diuretic.

Caffeinism —Toxic effects of chronic excessive use of caffeine.

Cage —A box.

Cage thoracic —The body structure consisting of the ribs, vertebral column and sternum, enclosing the thorax.

Cainotophobia — Fear of a novelty.

Caisson disease —A disease due to sudden reduction of the atmospheric pressure, which generally occurs in divers and the people flying at a height of 30,000 feet or over. In water at high atmospheric pressure, more and more nitrogen is absorbed by the tissues of the bdoy which is liberated from the tissues in the from of bubbles on reduction of the atmospheric pressure, as the diver comes out of the water suddenly on the surface of the earth, causing headache, pain in the joints, itching or burning of the skin, in severe cases giddiness, abdominal pain, nausea, vomiting, shortness of breath and even paraplegia.

Caked breast —Accumulation of the milk in the breast after delivery.

Calcaneal, Calcanean — Pertaining to the calcaneus or heel bone.

Calcaneoapophysitis — Pain and swelling of the posterior part of the calcaneus bone where the insertion of Achilles tendon takes place.

Calcaneoastragaloid — Pertaining to the calcaneus and the astragalus bone.

Calcaneocuboid —Pertaining to the calcaneus and the cuboid bone.

Calcaneodynia —Pain in the heel.

Calcaneofibular —Pertaining to the calcaneus and the fibula bone.

Calcaneonavicular — Pertaining to the calcaneus and the navicular bone.

Calcaneoscaphoid — Pertaining to the calcaneus and the scaphoid bone.

Calcaneotibial —Pertaining to the calcaneus and tibia bone.

Calcaneum, Calcaneus — The heel bone which articulates with the astragalus and the cuboid bone.

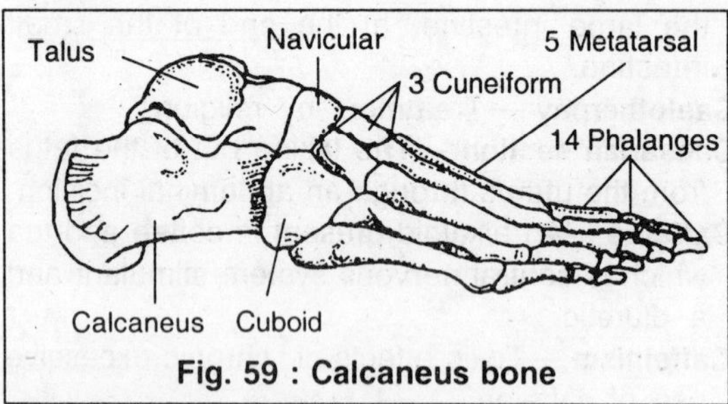

Fig. 59 : Calcaneus bone

Calcanodynia —Calcaneodynia.

Calcar —A spur.

Calcarea —Lime.

Calcareous —Of the nature of lime, chalky.

Calcarine —1. Spur-shaped. 2. Pertaining to the calcar.

Calcariuria —Presence of lime (calcium) salts in the urine.

Calcaroid —Deposit of a substance in the brain tissue which resembles calcification.

Calcemia —Increased calcium in he blood.

Calces —Plural of calx.

Calcibilia —Presence of calcium in the bile.

Calcic —Pertaining to calcium or lime.

Calcicosis —Lung disease caused by inhalation of lime stone (marble) dust.

Calciferol —Vitamin D_2, Ergocalciferol.

Calciferous —Containing calcium or lime.

Calcific —Forming or composed of lime.

Calcification —The process of deposition of the calcium salts in a tissue.

Calcific tendinitis — Deposition of calcium in chronically inflamed tendon, especially the tendons of the shoulder.

Calcify —To deposit calcium as in the formation of bone.

Calcigerous —Producing or containing calcium.

Calcination —Drying by roasting to produce a powder.

Calcine —To expel water and volatile matter by heating to a high temperature.

Calcinosis—Abnormal deposition of calcium salts in the tissues.

Calciokinesis —Mobilization of stored calcium.

Calciokinetic —Pertaining to or causing calciokinesis.

Calciol —Cholecalciferol.

Calciorrhachia —Presence of calcium in the cerebrospinal fluid.

Calcipectic —Pertaining to calcipexis.

Calcipenia —Deficiency of calcium in the body.

Calcipenic —Pertaining to deficiency of calcium in the body.

Calcipexic —Calcipectic.

Calcipexis, Calcipexy — Fixation of calcium in the tissues.

Calciphilia —A tendency to calcification.

Calciprivia —Loss of calcium.

Calciprivic —Deprived of calcium.

Calcitonin —A hormone from the thyroid gland in man which is important in calcium metabolism.

Calcitriol —A metabolite of vitamin D that promotes the absorption of calcium and phosphate from the intestines and their deposition in the bone tissue.

Calcium —It is a silver white metallic element of which Ca is the symbol and which is necessary for the formation and hardness of bones and teeth and is of great importance in blood coagulation. It is found mostly in milk. The following are its salts.

Calcium carbonate —A fine, white, tasteless and odorless powder found in the chalk and is used as an antacid.

Calcium chloride — Having a saline taste and is used to raise the calcium content of the blood in the case of hypocalcemic condition and as an antidote for magnesium poisoning.

Calcium gluconate —A granular white powder without odor and taste, of which the actions are the same as that of calcium chloride.

Calcium lactate —White odorless and tasteless powder used orally or parenterally as an alternative to calcium gluconate. It is used in chronic plumbism.

Calcium oxalate —It is present in the urine in crystalline form and is a constituent of some renal calculi.

Calcium pantothenate —One of the factors of vitamin B complex which is generally used for burning feet syndrome.

Calcium phosphate —It is a white powder

which is used as antacid in the treatment of hyperacidity.

Calcium sulfate —A white powder that absorbs water and used in making plaster of paris.

Calcium antagonists — Calcium channel blockers.

Calcium channel blockers —The drugs which act by slowing the influx of calcium ions into the muscle cells.

Calciuria —Presence of calcium in the urine.

Calcophorous —Containing or producing calcium salts or lime.

Calcularly —Pertaining to a calculus.

Calculi —Plural of calculus.

Calculifragus —The breaking up of the calculi.

Calculogenesis —Formation of calculi.

Calculosis —A condition produced by the formation of calculi.

Calculous —Like a stone.

Calculus —An abnormal collection of mineral salts in the kidney, ureter, bladder or urethra; stone.

Biliary calculus —A stone in the gallbladder which is composed of bile or cholesterol and bile pigments with calcium deposits, gallstone.

Pancreatic calculus — Calculus formed in the pancreatic duct as a result of obstruction or infection and which is composed of calcium carbonate and other salts.

Pulmonary calculus — Stone formed in a bronchus of the lung.

Renal calculus —A calculus present in the kidney.

Salivary calculus — Calculus present in a salivary duct, usually of the submandibular gland.

Urinary calculus — Calculus in any part of the urinary system.

Vesical calculus — Calculus in the urinary bladder.

Calefacient —Causing a sensation of warmth when applied to a part of the body.

Calf, plural Calves — The fleshy back part of the leg below the knee.

Calf-bone —Fibula bone.

Caliber —The diameter of any orifice or of the opening of a canal.

Calibrate —To measure the internal diameter of a tubular structure.

Calibration —Measurement of the internal diameter of an orifice or the opening of a canal.

Calibrator —An instrument for dilating the tubes, or measuring the internal diameter of tubes or orifices.

Caliceal —Calyceal. Pertaining to the calix.

Calicectasis —Dilatation of the renal calyx.

Calicectomy —Excision of a renal calyx.

Calices —Plural of calyx.

Caliciform —Calyciform. Shaped like a cup.

Calicine —Calycine. Of the nature of, or resembling a calix.

Calicoplasty —Calioplasty.

Calicotomy —Calicectomy, Caliotomy. To make an incision into a calix, usually for removal of a calculus.

Caliculus —A cup-shaped structure.

Caliectasis —Calicectasis. Dilatation of the renal calyx.

Caligo —Dimness of vision.

Calioplasty —Repair of a calyx by plastic surgery.

Caliorrhaphy —Suturing of a calyx.

Caliotomy —Calicotomy.

Caliper (s) —Instrument for measuring the diameters of solid organs, such as those of the chest or the pelvis.

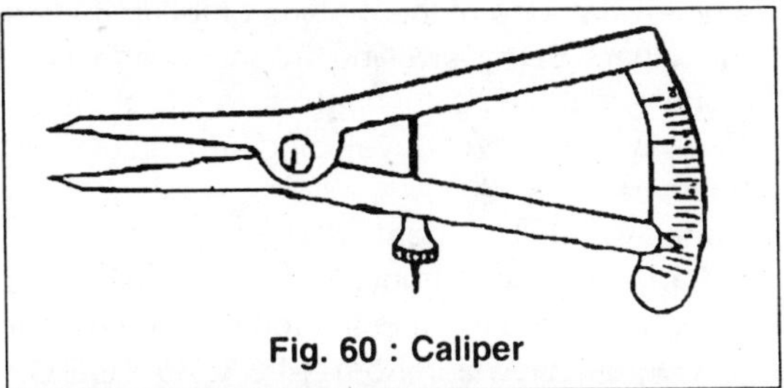

Fig. 60 : Caliper

Calix —Cup-shaped organ or cavity, calyx.

Callomania —To consider herself the most beautiful.

Callosal —Pertaining to the corpus callosum.

Callosity, Callositas —The oval or elongated areas of hard and thickened skin caused by friction, pressure or other irritants, appearing on the hands and feet.

Callosomarginal —Pertaining to the corpus callosum and the marginal gyrus.

Callous —Hard; like a callus.

Callus —1. Callosity. 2. The osseous material formed between the ends of a fractured bone which is ultimately replaced by bone in the healing process.

Callus formation in the bone fracture healing process.

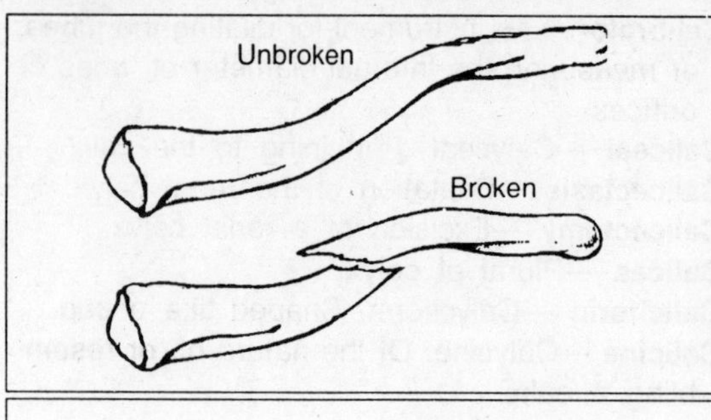

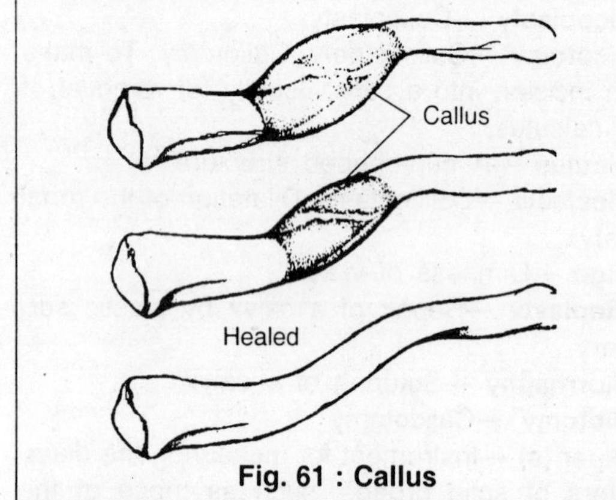

Fig. 61 : Callus

Calmative —Sedative. Soothing.

Calor —Heat, one of the 4 signs of inflammation, the others being swelling, redness and pain.

Caloric —Pertaining to heat or to a calorie.

Caloricity—Power of developing and maintaining body heat.

Calorie —A unit of heat. It is of two types.

Large calorie —Kilocalorie. The amount of heat required to raise the temperature of one kilogram of water from 14.5°C to 15.5°C.

Small calorie — Microcalorie. The amount of heat required to raise the temperature of one gram of water by one degree centigrade.

Calorifacient —Producing heat.

Calorific —Producing heat.

Calorigenic —Pertaining to the produciton of heat or energy.

Calorimeter —An instrument for measuring the amount of heat produced in a chemical reaction.

Calorimetric —Pertaining to calorimetry.

Calorimetry —Measurement of heat loss or gain.

Caloritropic —Pertaining to thermotropism.

Calvaria —The dom-like superior portion of the cranium, composed of the superior portions of the frontal, parietal and occipital bones.

Calvarial —Pertaining to the calvaria (Cap of the skull).

Calvities —Baldness, alopecia.

Calx —1. Lime 2. The heel.

Calyceal —Caliceal. Pertaining to the calyx.

Calyces —Plural of calyx.

Calyciform —Cup-shaped.

Calycine —Calicine. Of the nature of, or resembling a calyx.

Calyx —Calix.

Camera —A cavity or chamber.

Anterior chamber of the eye ball —The closed space between the cornea and the iris.

Posterior chamber of the eye ball —The closed space between the iris and the lens.

Camphor —Kapur.

Camphoraceus—Resembling camphor in appearance, consistency, or odor.

Camphorated —Containing camphor.

Campimeter —An apparatus for measuring the field of vision.

Campimetry—Measurement of the field of vision.

Camplodactyly —Camptodactyly.

Campospasm —Camptocormia.

Camptocormia —Deformity in which there is flexion of the trunk forward when the person is erect.

Camptodactylia —Permanent flexion of one or more fingers or toes.

Camptodactyly — Camptodactylia.

Camptomelia —Bending of the limbs, producing permanent bowing or curvature of the affected part.

Camptomelic —Bending the limbs, resulting in a permanent bowing or curvature of the affected part.

Camptospasm —Camptocormia.

Canal —A narrow tube or passage.

Alimentary canal —The digestive tract extending from the mouth to the anus.

Anal canal —Terminal portion of the rectum opening at the anus.

Auditory canal — External acoustic meatus.

Birth canal —The canal through which the child passes in birth, which consists of cervix, vagina and vulva.

Cervical canal —Canal in the cervix of the uterus extending from the internal os to the external os.

Inguinal canals —An oblique passage from the internal to the external abdominal ring.

Semicircular canals — The three canals of the labyrinth of the ear.

Spinal, vertebral canal —The canal formed by the series of the foramina of the vertebrae which contains the spinal cord and its meninges.

Canales —Plural of canalis.

Canalicular —Pertaining to a canalicuius.

Canaliculi —Plural of canaliculus.

Canaliculitis —Inflammation of the lacrimal canaliculus.

Canaliculization —The formation of canaliculi in any tissue.

Canaliculus —A small canal.

Canalis —Canal.

Canalization —Formation of a canal in tissue.

Canaloplasty —Repairing by plastic surgery of a passage, as of the external auditory meatus.

Cancellated —Cancellous.

Cancelli —Plural of cancellus.

Cancellous —A spongy structure, the word is especially used for spongy bone.

Cancellus —A lattice-like structure, as in spongy bone.

Cancer —A malignant tumour which spreads very rapidly. Cancers are divided into two main categories —carcinoma which develops from epithelial tissues and sarcoma which develops from connective tissues.

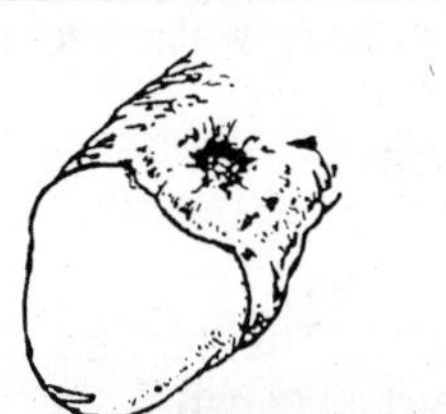

Fig. 62 : Cancer of the penis

Canceremia —The presence of cancer cells in the blood.

Cancericidal —Destructive to cancer cells.

Cancerigenic, Cancerogenic —Causing cancer.

Cancerophobia —Morbid fear of cancer.

Cancerous —Pertaining to a malignant growth.

Cancra — Plural of cancrum.

Cancriform —Resembling a cancer.

Cancroid —Cancriform. 1. Like a cancer. 2. Epithelioma (a type of skin cancer).

Cancrum —A rapidly spreading ulcer.

Candida —A type of yeast-like fungus which normally lives in the mouth, skin, intestinal tract and vagina but can cause many diseases such as vaginitis.

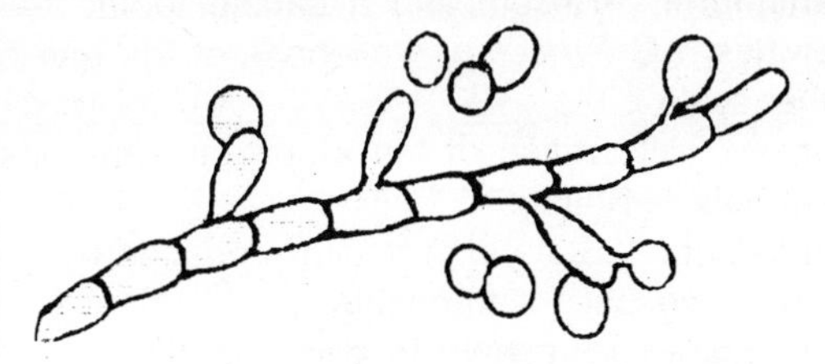

Fig. 63 : Fungus candida albicans

Candida albicans —It is a small, oval fungus growing by budding like yeast and is found normally on the moist skin, in the mouth, intestinal tract, lungs and vagina which becomes pathogenic and causes candidiasis (fungal infection) in which white patches (thrush) are formed on the mucous membrane of the mouth and vagina, when there is immunodeficiency as in old age, following a disease and prolonged treatment with antibiotics and corticoids.

Candidal —Pertaining to or caused by candida.

Candidemia —Presence of the fungus candida in the blood.

Candidiasis —Infection by the fungus candida albicans of the skin, mucous membrane of the mouth (thrush), lungs and vagina.

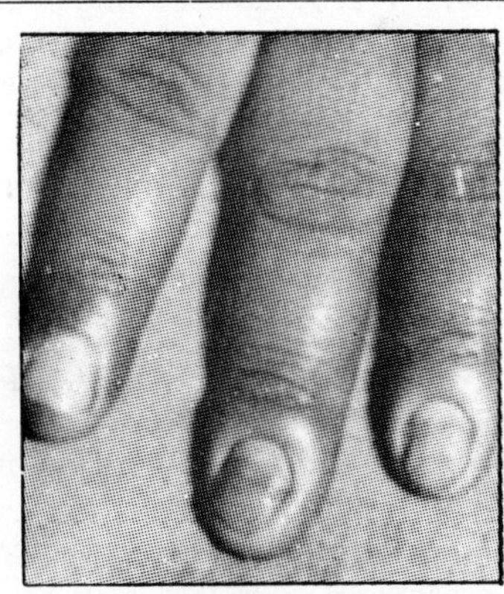

Fig. 64 : Candidiasis

Inflammation of the nail folds surrounding the nails caused by the infection of candida albicans.

Candidosis —Candidiasis.

Candiduria —Presence of candida in the urine.

Canine —1. Pertaining to, or characteristic of a dog. 2. A type of tooth, the four teeth (two upper and two lower) between the incisors and molars.

Caniniform —Resembling a canine tooth.
Canities —Greyness or whiteness of the hair of the scalp.
Canker —Ulceration of the mouth and the lips.
Cannabis —Bhang.
Cannabism —State of ill-health produced by the excessive use of cannabis.
Canning —To preserve food in tins.
Cannula —A tube with a trocar in it for insertion into a duct or cavity, the fluid escapes after withdrawal of the trocar from the body.
Cannulation —Cannulization. Introduction of a cannula into a tube-like organ or a cavity in the body.
Canthal —Pertaining to a canthus.
Canthectomy —Excision of a canthus.
Canthi —Plural of canthus.
Canthitis —Inflammation of a canthus.
Cantholysis —Incision of a canthus of an eye to widen the palpebral fissure.
Canthoplasty —Plastic surgery of a canthus.
Canthorrhaphy —Suturing of a canthus.
Canthotomy —Division of a canthus by surgery.
Canthus —The angle at either end of the fissure between the eyelids.
Cap —1. A covering. 2. The first part of the duodenum.
Capacitation —A process occurring in the female reproductive tract that enables a spermatozoon to fertilize an ovum.
Capacity —1. Ability to do something. 2. Measurement of a vessel to contain something.
Capeline —A bandage used for the head or the stump of an amputated limb.
Capiat —To take.
Capillarectasia —Dilatation of the capillaries.
Capillaries —Plural of capillary.
Capillariography —X-ray examination of the capillaries after injecting a radiopaque substance.
Capillariomotor —Causing dilatation or contraction of the blood capillaries.
Capillarioscopy — Capillaroscopy. Microangioscopy. Microscopic examination through low power of the cutaneous blood capillaries at the base of the fingernail.
Capillaritis —Inflammation of the capillaries.
Capillarity, Capillary attraction —The action by which the surface of a liquid where it is in contact with a solid, as in a capillary tube, is elevated or depressed.
Capillaropathy —A disease of the capillaries.
Capillaroscopy —Examination of the capillaries for diagnostic purposes.
Capillary —1. One of the minute blood vessels measuring about .008 mm. in diameter which connect the smallest arteries (arterioles) with the smallest veins (venules). 2. Pertaining to or resembling a hair.

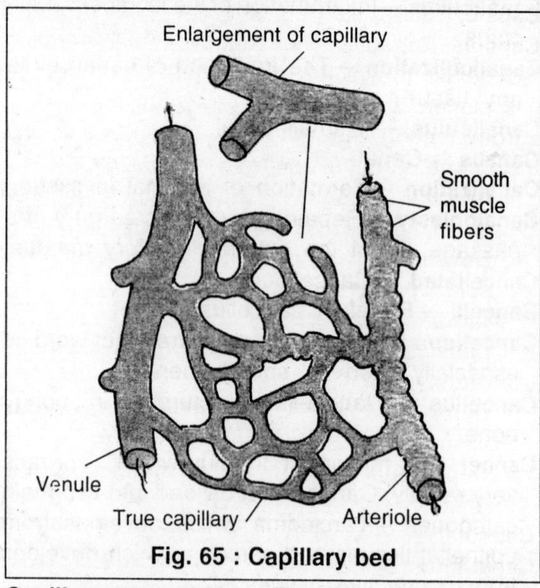

Fig. 65 : Capillary bed

Capillary permeability —The ability of substances to diffuse through the capillary walls into the tissue spaces.
Capillus —Hair of the scalp.
Capita —Plural of caput.
Capital —Pertaining to the head.
Capitate —1. Head-shaped. 2. The third bone in the distal row of the carpus (wrist).
Capitellum —Capitulum.
Capitopedal —Pertaining to the head and feet.
Capitula —Plural of capitulum.
Capitular —Pertaining to a capitulum.
Capitulum —A small rounded articular end of a bone.
Capitulum fibulae — Head of the fibula which articulates with the tibia.
Capitulum humeri — Rounded distal end of the humerus which articulates with the radius.
Capnogram —A continuous record of carbon dioxide content of the expired air.
Capnograph —An instrument by which CO_2 content in the expired air is measured.
Capnography —To record the level of carbon dioxide continuously in the expired air in the patients kept on artificial respiration.

Capnophilic —Pertaining to the bacteria that grow best in an atmosphere containing carbon dioxide.

Capping —1. To place a protective substance over the exposed pulp of a tooth. 2. To place an artificial crown over a tooth so that it may look nice.

Capsid fructus — Red chilly.

Capsula, Capsule —1. A soluble container made of gelatin in which a single dose of a medicine is placed, the enclosure prevents the patient from tasting the medicine. 2. An enclosing structure, around an organ or a structure.

Articular capsule — Capsule of a joint made up of fibrous tissue.

Bowman's capsule —The glomerular capsule of the kidneys.

Cardiac capsule — Pericardium.

Lens capsule —The outer transparent membrane enclosing the lens of the eye.

Renal capsule — Fat-containing connective tissue surrounding the kidney.

Suprarenal capsule — Connective tissue enclosing the suprarenal gland.

Capsular —Pertaining to a capsule.

Capsulation —Enclosure in a capsule.

Capsulectomy —To remove a capsule by operation, especially a joint capsule or lens capsule.

Capsulitis —Inflammation of a capsule.

Capsulociliary —Pertaining to the lens capsule and the ciliary structures of the eye.

Capsulolenticular —Pertaining to the lens of the eye and its capsule.

Capsuloma —A capsular or subcapsular tumour of the kidney.

Capsuloplasty —Repair of a capsule, especially one of a joint, by plastic surgery.

Capsulorrhaphy —Suturing of a capsule, especially of a joint capsule or of a tear in a capsule.

Capsulotome —An instrument for incising the capsule of the lens of the eye.

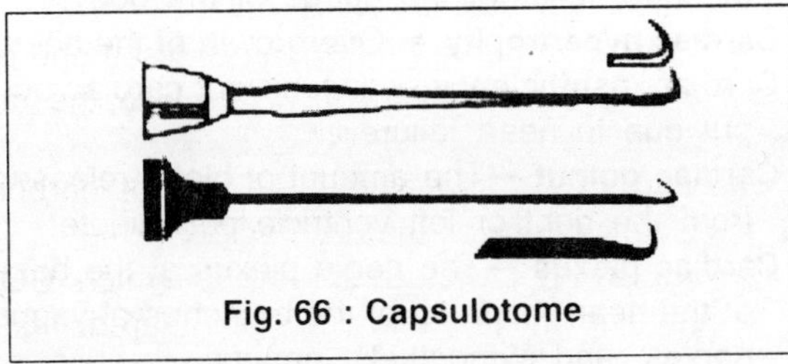

Fig. 66 : Capsulotome

Capsulotomy —Incision of a capsule, as that of the lens of the eye or of a joint.

Caput — 1. The head, 2. Chief extremity of an organ or part.

Caput medusae —A plexus of dilated cutaneous veins around the umbilicus as seen in case of cirrhosis of the liver and in the newborn child.

Caput succedaneum — Swelling produced in and under the scalp of the fetus during labor.

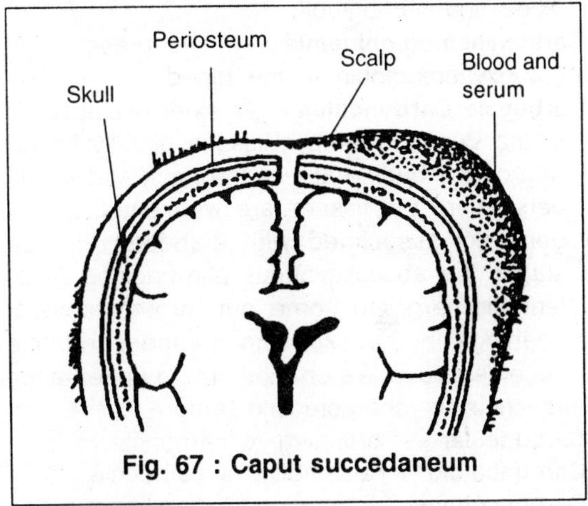

Fig. 67 : Caput succedaneum

Carbamide —Urea in an anhydrous, sterile powder form.

Carbaminohemoglobin — Combination of carbon dioxide and hemoglobin.

Carbohydrase —An enzyme that hydrolyzes carbohydrate.

Carbohydrate —A compound of carbon, hydrogen and oxygen in which hydrogen and oxygen are in the ratio of 2:1. Carbohydrates are sugars, glycogen, starches, dextrines and celluloses.

Carbohydraturia —Excretion of one or more carbohydrates in the urine.

Carbolic acid —Phenol.

Carbolism —Poisoning due to carbolic acid.

Carbolize —To touch a wound with carbolic acid.

Carboluria —Presence of carbolic acid in the urine.

Carbon —It is a non-metallic element and its compounds are constituents of all the living tissues.

Carbon dioxide —It is a colorless gas that is produced in the combustion of carbon or its compounds. It is the final metabolic product of carbon compounds present in the food and is generally eliminated through the lungs. Normally inspired air contains 0.03 percent while expired air contains 4% of CO_2.

Carbonemia —Excess of carbonic acid in the blood.

Carbonic —Pertaining to carbon.

Carbonic acid —Acid resulting from mixture of carbon dioxide and water.

Carbonize —To convert into charcoal.

Carbonuria —Excretion of carbon dioxide or other carbon compounds in the urine.

Carboxyhemoglobin — Combined carbon monoxide and hemoglobin.

Carboxyhemoglobinemia — The presence of carboxyhemoglobin in the blood.

Carbuncle, Carbunculus — An extensive abscess of the skin and deeper tissues usually occurring on the back, nape of the neck and shoulders where the tissues are weakened, and is generally associated with diabetes. In later stages the abscess bursts allowing the purulent discharge to come out through several openings in the skin and so the carbuncle becomes sieve like or cribriform in appearance which is its characteristic feature.

Carbuncular —Pertaining to carbuncle.

Carbunculoid —Resembling a carbuncle.

Carbunculosis —Formation of many carbuncles in succession.

Carcass —The body of a dead animal.

Carcinectomy —Excision of a carcinoma.

Carcinelcosis —An ulcer of a cancerous nature.

Carcinogen —Any substance which causes cancer.

Carcinogenesis —The production of cancer.

Carcinogenic —Producing cancer.

Carcinogenicity —The ability or tendency to produce cancer.

Carcinoid syndrome —A condition produced by metastatic carcinoid tumors that secrete excessive amounts of serotonin. It is characterized by episodic flushing of the face, palpitation of the heart, low blood pressure, intermittent abdominal pain with diarrhea and loss of weight.

Carcinoid tumor —A tumor derived from argentaffin cells in the intestinal tract, bile ducts, pancreas, bronchus or ovary which secretes a vasoconstrictor, the serotonin.

Carcinolysis —Destruction of the cancer cells.

Carcinolytic —Destructive to the cancer cells.

Carcinoma or Cancer —A malignant tumor occurring in the epithelial tissue and spreading rapidly by direct extension, through the blood circulation or the lymphatic channels and giving rise to secondary metastasis. It may affect any organ or part of the body.

Carcinomata —Plural of carcinoma.

Carcinomatophobia, Carcinophobia —Morbid fear of carcinoma.

Carcinomatosis, Carcinosis —The condition of having wide-spread dissemination of cancer throughout the body.

Carcinomatous —Pertaining to or of the nature of cancer, malignant.

Carcinophilia —Attraction for cancer cells.

Carcinophobia — Carcinomatophobia.

Carcinosarcoma —A malignant tumour composed of both carcinomatous and sarcomatous tissues.

Carcinosis —Carcinomatosis.

Carcinostatic —1. Pertaining to an inhibitory effect on the development of a cancer. 2. An agent which has such effect.

Cardamom, Cardamon —Dried ripe fruit of an herb Elettaria cardamomum.

Cardia —Upper part of the stomach connected with the esophagus.

Cardiac —1. Pertaining to the heart. 2. Pertaining to the cardia of the stomach.

Cardiac arrest —Sudden stoppage of the cardiac function.

Cardiac atrophy — Atrophy of the heart.

Cardiac or cardio catheterization —To pass a tiny plastic tube into the heart through a blood vessel.

Cardiac compensation —The ability of the heart to compensate for any deficiency in the functions of its valves through its reserved power.

Cardiac cycle —The period from the beginning of one beat of the heart to the beginning of the second one in which there is a systolic phase—the contraction of the atria and the ventricles propelling the blood onwards and the diastolic phase—dilatation of the atria and the ventricles, during which they are refilled with blood.

Cardiac failure —The condition caused by the inability of the heart to pump sufficient amount of blood to meet the needs of the body.

Cardiac hypertrophy — Overgrowth of the heart.

Cardiac insufficiency — Insufficient cardiac output due to heart failure.

Cardiac output —The amount of blood released from the right or left ventricle per minute.

Cardiac plexus —The nerve plexus at the base of the heart made up of the branches of vagus nerves, and sympathetic nerves.

Cardiac reflex —The change in the heart rate in response to some stimulation, *e.g.* stimulation of sensory nerve endings in the wall of the carotid sinus by increased arterial blood pressure reflexly slows the heart rate.

Cardiac reserve —The capacity of the heart to increase output and to raise the blood pressure to meet the body requirement.

Cardialgia —Pain in the heart region.

Cardiaortic —Pertaining to the heart and aorta.

Cardiasthenia —Neurasthenia with predominance of cardiac symptoms.

Cardiasthma —Dyspnea due to heart disease.

Cardiataxia — Extreme irregularity in the heart's action.

Cardiatelia —Incomplete development of the heart.

Cardiectasia, Cardiectasis —Dilatation of the heart.

Cardiectomy —Excision of the cardiac portion of the stomach.

Cardiectopia —Placement of the heart at an abnormal place.

Cardinal —Very important.

Cardio- —Prefix pertaining to the heart.

Cardioaccelerator —That which increases the heart rate.

Cardioactive —Acting upon the heart.

Cardioangiography —Angiocardiography.

Cardioangiology —The science of the heart and the blood vessels.

Cardioaortic —Cardiaortic.

Cardioarterial —Pertaining to the heart and the arteries.

Cardiocele —Herniation of the heart through an opening in the diaphragm or through a wound.

Cardiocentesis —Surgical puncture of the heart.

Cardiochalasia —Relaxation of the muscles of the cardiac opening of the stomach.

Cardiocirrhosis —Cirrhosis of the liver and the heart disease.

Cardiodiaphragmatic — Pertaining to the heart and the diaphragm.

Cardiodilator —An instrument for dilating the cardia of the stomach at the gastroesophageal junction.

Cardiodiosis —Dilatation of the cardiac opening of the stomach.

Cardiodynamics —The science of the forces involved in the heart's action.

Cardiodynia —Pain in the heart.

Cardioesophageal — Pertaining to the junction of the esophagus and the stomach.

Cardiogenesis —Development of the heart in embryo.

Cardiogenic—Originating from the heart.

Cardiogram, Electrocardiogram —A tracing of the cardiac electrical activity on a special paper by electrocardiographic machine.

Cardiograph —A machine for recording the electrical activity of the heart.

Cardiography —The recording and study of the cardiac electrical activity.

Cardiohepatic —Pertaining to heart and the liver.

Cardiohepatomegaly — Enlargement of the heart and liver.

Cardioid —Resembling the heart.

Cardioinhibitory —Inhibiting the cardiac activity.

Cardiokinetic —Cardiac stimulant.

Cardiolith —A calculus in the heart.

Cardiologist —A physician who is specialist in the diagnosis and treatment of heart diseases.

Cardiology —The study of the heart and its functions and diseases.

Cardiolysin —An antibody which is destructive to the heart muscle.

Cardiolysis —An operation for separating the adhesions from the heart in adhesive mediastinopericarditis.

Cardiomalacia —Softening of the heart muscle.

Cardiomegaly —Enlargement of the heart.

Cardiometry —Measurement of the dimensions of the heart or the force of its action.

Cardiomotility —Movements of the heart.

Cardiomuscular —Pertaining to the cardiac muscle.

Cardiomyoliposis —Fatty degeneration of the heart muscle.

Cardiomyopathy —Any disease of the cardiac muscle.

Cardiomyopathy alcoholic —Disease of the cardiac muscle due to alcohol consumption.

Cardiomyopexy —An operation performed for fixation of a muscle such as pectoral muscle to the heart to improve its blood supply.

Cardiomyoplasty —An operation performed for the implantation of a skeletal muscle to either supplement or replace the myocardial muscle.

Cardiomyotomy — Esophagomyotomy. An operation performed for achalasia cardia in which muscles surrounding the cardioesophageal junction are cut, while the underlying mucous membrane is left intact.

Cardionecrosis —Necrosis of the heart muscle.

Cardionector —Regulator of heart beat. The sinoatrial node.

Cardionephric —Pertaining to heart and kidney.

Cardioneural —Pertaining to the heart and the nervous system.

Cardioneurosis —Functional neurosis with cardiac symptoms.

Cardioomentopexy —An operation for the attachment of omentum to the heart to improve its blood supply.

Cardiopaludism —Heart disease due to malaria.

Cardiopath —An individual suffering from heart disease.

Cardiopathy —Any disease of the heart.

Cardiopericarditis — Inflammation of the myocardium and the pericardium.

Cardiophobia —Morbid fear of heart disease.

Cardiophone —An instrument for listening to the heart sound, especially the stethoscope.

Cardioplasty —An operation on the cardiac opening of the stomach for relieving the cardiospasm.

Cardioplegia —Arrest of myocardial contractions, paralysis of the heart.

Cardioplegic —Pertaining to cardioplegia.

Cardiopneumatic —Pertaining to the heart and the lungs.

Cardiopneumograph —An apparatus for recording the motion of the heart and lungs.

Cardioptosis —Downward displacement of the heart.

Cardiopulmonary —Pertaining to the heart and lungs.

Cardiopuncture —Surgical puncture of the heart. Cardiocentesis.

Cardiopyloric —Pertaining to the cardia and the pylorus of the stomach.

Cardiorenal —Pertaining to both, the heart and kidneys.

Cardiorrhaphy —Suturing of the cardiac muscle.

Cardiorrhexis —Rupture of the heart.

Cardiosclerosis —Hardening of the cardiac muscle.

Cardioscope —An instrument for examining the interior of the heart.

Cardioscopy —Examination of the interior of the heart by cardioscope.

Cardiospasm —Spasm of the cardiac part of the stomach due to which the cardiac opening is constricted.

Cardiosphygmograph —An instrument for recording graphically the movements of the heart, and pulse.

Cardiostenosis —Constriction of the heart.

Cardiotachometer —An instrument for measuring the heart rate for a long time.

Cardiotachometry —The measuring of the heart rate continuously for a long time by cardiotachometer.

Cardiotherapy —Treatment of the heart diseases.

Cardiothrombus —Cardiohemothrombus. A blood clot present in one of the cardiac chambers.

Cardiothyrotoxicosis — Heart disease due to hyperthyroidism.

Cardiotomy —Incision of the heart.

Cardiotonic —The drugs increasing the tonicity of the heart.

Cardiotopometry — Measurement of the area of cardiac dullness.

Cardiotoxic —Exerting a toxic effect upon the heart.

Cardiovalvulitis — Inflammation of the cardiac valves.

Cardiovalvulotome —An instrument for incising a heart valve.

Cardiovascular —Pertaining to the heart and the blood vessels.

Cardiovasculorenal — Pertaining to the heart, arteries and the kidneys.

Cardiovasology —Science of the heart and blood vessels.

Cardioversion —Conversion of a cardiac arrhythmia into normal sinus rhythm.

Cardiovert —The act of cardioversion by administring the electric shock to the heart.

Cardioverter —An electrical apparatus which by administring the electric shock to the heart convert the cardiac arrhythmia into normal sinus rhythm.

Carditis —Inflammation of the cardiac muscle.

Caries —Decay of bone or teeth, *e.g.* a dental caries—in which there is decalcification of the

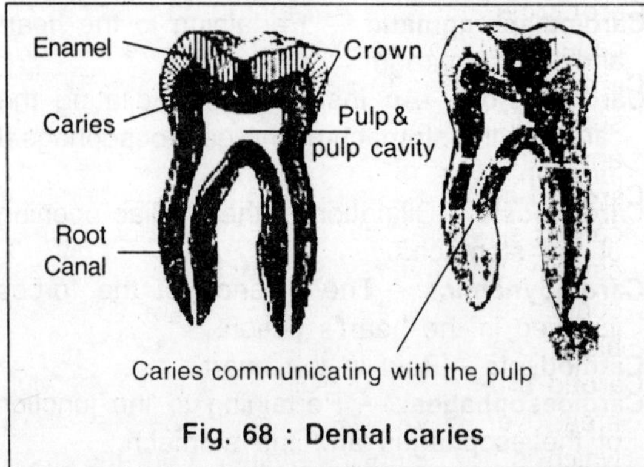

Fig. 68 : Dental caries

enamel and dentin of a tooth, and spinal caries—caries of the vertebrae usually due to tuberculosis or Pott's disease.

Carina —A structure with ridges, *e.g.* trachea, a ridge at the lower end of the trachea separating the openings of the right and left principal bronchi.

Carinate —Having a conspicuous ridge.

Cariogenesis —The formation of caries.

Cariogenic —Producing caries.

Cariostatic —Inhibiting the progress of dental caries.

Carious —1. Affected with caries. 2. Having pits or perforations.

Carminative —An agent that relieves gases from the gastrointestinal tract.

Carnal —Pertaining to the appetite of flesh.

Carneous —Fleshy.

Carnivorous —Flesh-eating.

Carnophobia —Abnormal aversion to meat.

Carnose —Flesh like.

Carnosity —A fleshy growth.

Caro, Carnis —The fleshy part of the body.

Carotenase —An enzyme that converts carotene into vitamin A.

Carotene —A yellow pigment present in yellow vegetables like carrot and in some animals and is converted into vitamin A in the liver.

Carotenemia, Carotinemia or Carotenosis — Presence of carotene in the blood causing the skin yellow.

Carotenodermia —Yellowness of the skin due to carotenemia.

Carotenoid —1. Resembling carotene. 2. One of a group of pigments ranging in color from light yellow to red.

Carotenosis cutis —Yellow coloration of the skin caused by increased carotene.

Carotic —Stuporous.

Caroticotympanic —Pertaining to the carotid canal and the tympanic cavity (the middle ear).

Carotid —1. Pertaining to the carotid arteries supplying the head and neck. 2. Pertaining to any carotid part as carotid sinus.

Carotid body —A small flat structure near the carotid sinus on both sides of the body, which contains cells that respond to changes in oxygen concentration in the blood and to changes in blood pressure.

Carotid bruit —A murmur heard in the cervical area, over the bifurcation of the carotid artery, which is not being transmitted from the heart.

Carotid sinus —The dilated portion of the common carotid artery at its bifurcation containing the sensory nerve endings of the vagus nerve.

Carotidynia, Carotodynia —Pain on pressure along the course of the common carotid artery.

Carpal —Pertaining to the carpus or wrist.

Carpale —Any bone of the wrist.

Carpal spasm —Involuntary contraction of the muscels of the hand.

Carpal tunnel —A cannal in the wrist.

Carpal tunnel syndrome — Pain, tenderness, weakness and sore formation of the thumb.

Carpectomy —Removal of a carpal bone by the surgery.

Carphologia, Carphology — Involuntary picking at the bedclothes as is often seen in hyperpyrexia.

Carpocarpal —Midcarpal.

Carpometacarpal —Pertaining to both, the carpus and the metacarpus.

Carpopedal —Pertaining to the wrist and foot.

Carpoptosis —Wrist drop.

Carpus —A joint between the arm and the hand made up of eight carpal bones, the wrist.

Carrier —1. The person who harbors the disease-causing organisms in his body in the absence of any signs and symptoms of the disease, but who is able to spread the organisms to others, thus acting as a carrier or distributor of the infection. 2. The animal that carries infective organisms to man. 3. The mother may be a carrier to spread the infection to the fetus during pregnancy through her blood. 4. A heterozygote, one who carries a recessive gene, autosomal or sex-linked, together with its normal allele.

Cartilage —A specialized type of fibrous connective tissue of bluish-white or grey color, translucent with no nerve and blood vessels, forming a part of the skeleton. They are of three types :— I. Hyaline cartilage —It is bluish-white, glassy translucent cartilage found in the articular surfaces of the bone, costal cartilages, nasal septum, larynx and trachea. II. Elastic cartilage—It is yellowish and elastic in nature found in the epiglottis, external ear and the auditory canal. III. Fibrocartilage—cartilage consisting of the fibrous tissues, found in the intervertebral disks.

Cartilaginification — Formation of cartilage.

Cartilaginoid —Resembling cartilage.

Cartilaginous —Pertaining to or consisting of cartilage.

Cartilago, Plural cartilagines — Cartilage.

Caruncle —A small fleshy growth.

Caruncula, Plural caruncuIae —Caruncle.

Carver —An implement used in correcting the anatomical positions of the teeth in artificial denture.

Case —1. Spoken for the patient. 2. Any surrounding structure.

Caseate —To undergo cheesy degeneration, as occurs in certain necroses.

Caseation —1. The process of conversion of the necrotic tissue into cheesy material. 2. Precipitation of the protein casein during coagulation of milk.

Case history —By asking the patient taking his individual, family, environmental, social, medical, occupational and psychiatric history completely at the time of admission in the hospital for the present illness.

Casein —The principal protein of milk, the basis of curd and cheese.

Caseinogen —The principal protein, from which casein is derived in milk. The conversion of caseinogen into casein is necessary in the curdling of milk.

Caseous —1. Cheese-like. 2. Pertaining to the transformation of tissue into a cheesy mass.

Cassette —A light proof box for keeping the X-ray film, or a case for film, or tape.

Cast —1. A positive copy of an object *e.g.,* a mold of a hollow organ as that of the renal tubule formed of effused plastic matter and excreted from the body as urinary cast named according to the constituents as epithelial, blood, waxy and fatty casts. 2. A solid mold of a bony part made up of plaster of Paris which is applied for immobilization in fracture of bones, dislocations, etc. 3. In dentistry, a positive copy of the tissues of the jaw over which the bases of the denture may be made.

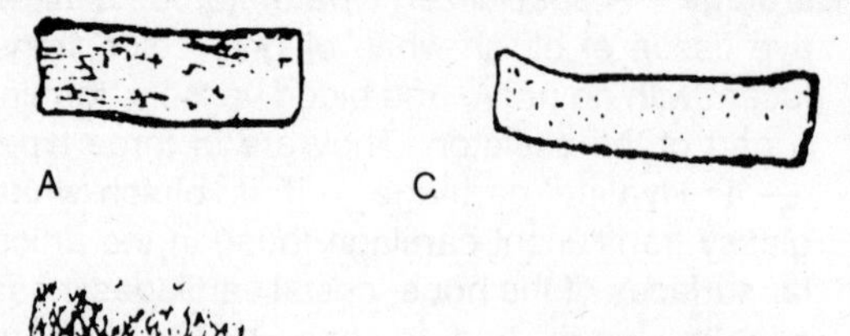

A C B1 D B2

Fig. 69 : Urinary casts

Casting —To mold.

Castle's intrinsic factor —A substance secreted by the stomach which is essential for the absorption of cyanocobalamin (Vitamin B_{12}— The extrinsic factor).

Castrate —To remove the testicles or ovaries due to which the individual becomes incapable of reproduction.

Castrated —A male whose testicles or a female whose ovaries have been removed and rendered incapable of reproduction.

Castration —Removal of the testicles or ovaries, or their destruction or inactivation.

Castration complex —Morbid fear of castration.

Casualty —1. An accident causing injury or death. 2. Person injured or killed in an accident. 3. In the army, the soldier missing from his unit as a result of death, injury, illness or captured by the enemy, because his whereabouts are unknown.

Catabasis —The stage of decline of a disease.

Catabatic —Pertaining to catabasis.

Catabolic —Pertaining to catabolism.

Catabolism —The destructive phase of metabolism, opposite to anabolism.

Catabolite, Catabolin —Anything produced in catabolism.

Catacrotic —Indicating a pulse tracing in which one or more small upward waves appear in the descending limb of the pulse tracing.

Catacrotism —An anomaly of the pulse in which one small additional wave or notch appear in the descending limb of the pulse tracing.

Catadicrotic —Indicating an anomally of the pulse in which two small additional waves or notches appear in the descending limb of the pulse tracing.

Catadicrotism —A condition of the pulse marked by two minor expansions of the artery following the main beat, producing two secondary upward waves on the descending limb of the tracing.

Catagenesis —Involution or retrogression.

Catalepsy —A condition of diminished responsiveness which occurs in psychological illness in which the patient remains in a state of trance, he does not want to be disturbed and tends to remain in the same position in which he is placed.

Cataleptic —Pertaining to or suffering from catalepsy.

Cataleptiform, Cataleptoid —Like catalepsy.

Cataleptoid —Resembling catalepsy.

Catalysis —Increase in the rate of a chemical reaction produced by a catalyst.

Catalyst, Catalyzer —A substance which increases the rate of a chemical reaction without itself being affected in the reaction.

Catalytic —Pertaining to or affecting catalysis.

Catalyze —To cause catalysis.

Catalyzer —Catalyst.

Catamenia —Monthly discharge of blood from the uterus, menstruation.

Catamnesis —The medical history of a patient after illness.

Catamnestic —Pertaining to catamnesis.

Cataphasia—A speech disorder with constant repetition of a word or sentence.

Cataphoresis —Movement of positively charged particles (cations) in a solution toward the cathode of electric current in electrophoresis.

Cataphoretic —Pertaining to cataphoresis.

Cataphoria —An inclination of the visual axis below the horizontal plane.

Cataphrenia —A type of dementia which occur in recovery.

Cataphylaxis —The movement of leukocytes and antibodies to the site of an infection.

Cataplasia, Cataplasis — Atrophic change in the tissues or cells.

Cataplasm —A poultic.

Cataplectic —Pertaining to cataplexy.

Cataplexy, Cataplexia —A sudden emotional shock without loss of consciousness and muscular weakness, causing the patient to fall on the floor.

Cataract —An opacity of the lens of the eye or its capsule or both.

Atopic cataract —It usually occurs in adults between the age of 20 and 30 years.

Black cataract —Brown cataract.

Blue cataract —The cataract with small blue dots.

Brown cataract, Brunescent cataract — Cataract occurring in old age with brown opacity.

Capsular cataract — Cataract of the capsule of the lens.

Complicated cataract — Cataract occurring due to some intraocular disease.

Congenital cataract — Cataract present since birth, usually in both the eyes.

Coronary cataract —Ring like opacity around the lens, the middle portion remaining clear.

Cortical cataract — Opacity in the cortex (outer layers) of he lens.

Diabetic cataract — Cataract occurring in insulin-dependent diabetes mellitus.

Immature cataract — Incomplete opacity of the lens.

Lenticular cataract — Opacity of the lens not affecting the capsule.

Mature cataract, Ripe cataract —Complete opacity of the lens.

Secondary cataract — Complicated cataract. Cataract accompanying or following some other eye disease such as uveitis.

Senile cataract —Cataract of the old persons.

Toxic cataract —Cataract due to toxicity of a drug, e.g., naphthalene.

Traumatic cataract —Lens opacity due to injury to the eye.

Cataractogenesis —The process of cataract formation.

Cataractogenic —Forming the cataract.

Cataractous —Having the nature of a cataract.

Catarrh —Inflammation of the mucous membrane especially of the head and throat.

Catarrhal —Pertaining to or affected with catarrh.

Catatonia —Catatonic schizophrenia, a type of schizophrenia in which the patient tends to remain in a fixed position and unable to move or to talk.

Catatonic —Pertaining to or characterized by catatonia.

Catatricrotic —Denoting a pulse-tracing with 3 minor elevations on its descending limb.

Catatricrotism —A condition in which a pulse tracing shows 3 minor elevations on its descending limb.

Catatropia —The condition in which both eyes are turned downward.

Catenating —1. Occurring in a chain or series 2. Pertaining to a disease that is linked with another.

Catenoid —Chainlike.

Catgut —An absorbable ligature made up of sheep's intestine, used in surgery for ligation of the internal organs.

Catharsis —Purgation.

Cathartic —Purgative.

Catheresis —Weakness caused by medication.

Catheter —A tube made of rubber, metal, glass or plastic to be passed into the body for withdrawal of fluids, *e.g.* urine from the body, or introduction of fluids into a body cavity.

Catheter fever —Fever caused by urinary tract infection after catheterization.

Catheterization —Passage of a catheter into a body canal or a cavity.

Cardiac catheterization — Passage of a long, fine catheter through a vein in an arm or leg or the neck into the heart to obtain cardiac blood samples, for detecting cardiac abnormalities and determining the intracardiac pressure.

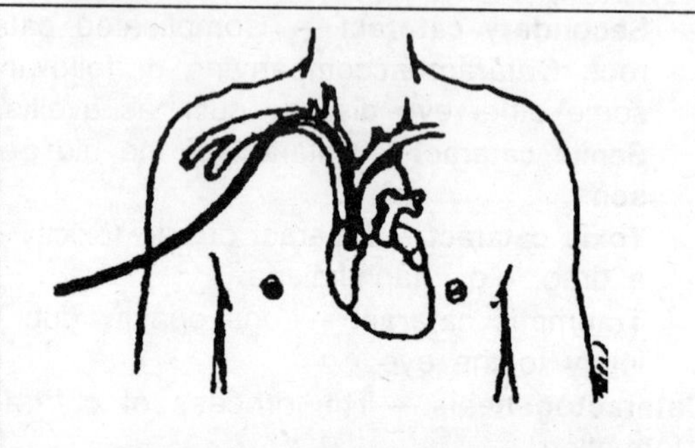

Fig. 70 : Cardiac catheterization

Urinary bladder catheterization —Introduction of a catheter through the urethra into the bladder for withdrawal of urine.

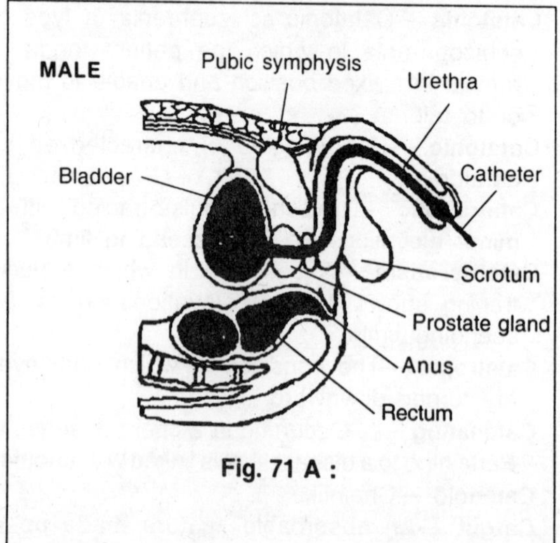

Fig. 71 A :

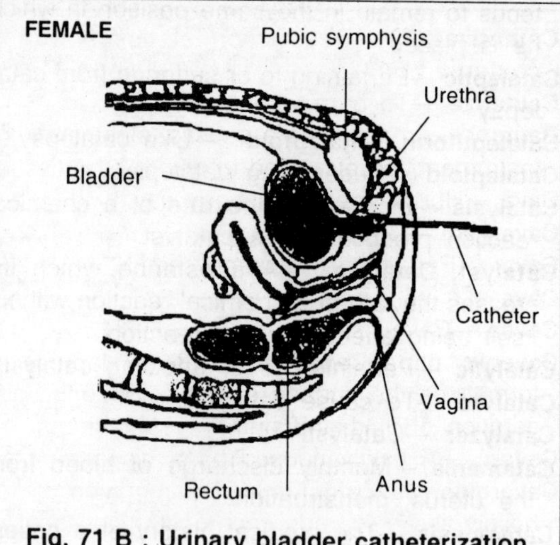

Fig. 71 B : Urinary bladder catheterization

Catheterize—To introduce a catheter into a part of the body, this term is usually used for catheterization of urinary bladder.

Cathexis —To concentrate the mental or emotional energy on an object or idea.

Cathode —The negative electrode, opposite of the anode or positive pole from which electrons are emitted.

Cathodic —Pertaining to a cathode.

Cation —An ion with a positive electric charge, opposite of an anion.

Catlin —A surgical knife with double edges.

Catoptrophobia —Morbid fear of mirrors or of breaking them.

Cauda —A tail or tail-like structure.

Caudad —Toward the tail or distal end, opposite to the head.

Cauda equina —The terminal portion of the spinal cord.

Caudal —1. Pertaining to a tail-like structure. 2. Inferior in position.

Caudate — Having a tail.

Caudocephalad —Moving from the tail end toward the head.

Caudotomy —Incision of the cauda equina.

Caumesthesia —Feeling of warmth when the surrounding temperature is normal.

Causalgia —Severe burning pain often with tropic skin changes, due to injury of the peripheral nerves.

Caustic —The substance which destroys the living tissues by burning, as an alkali.

Cauterant —An agent performing cauterization.

Cauterization —Destruction of tissue with a cautery.

Cauterize —To burn with a cautery.

Cautery —An agent as a caustic, electricity, hot instrument, ice etc. used to destroy the tissue.

Cava —Hollow area or a body cavity.

Cavagram —Cavogram.

Caval —Pertaining to a vena cava.

Cave —A hollow space or cavity.

Cavea —Cave.

Caveola, plural Caveolae —A small depression formed on the surface of the cells during absorption of fluid and nutritive substances.

Cavern —A cavity caused by a disease.

Cavernitis, Cavernositis — Inflammation of the hollow tissue (corpus cavernosum) of the penis.

Cavernoma —A cavernous angioma.

Cavernositis —Cavernitis.

Cavernostomy —The drainage of a lung abscess cavity by surgery.

Cavernous —Containing hollow spaces.

Cavitary —Pertaining to a cavity or having a cavity or cavities.

Cavitation —Formation of a cavity.

Cavitis —Inflammation of a vena cava.

Cavity —A hollow space in the body or in one of its organs or a hole produced by caries in a tooth.

Abdominal cavity — The cavity of the body between the diaphragm and the pelvis, containing all the abdominal organs.

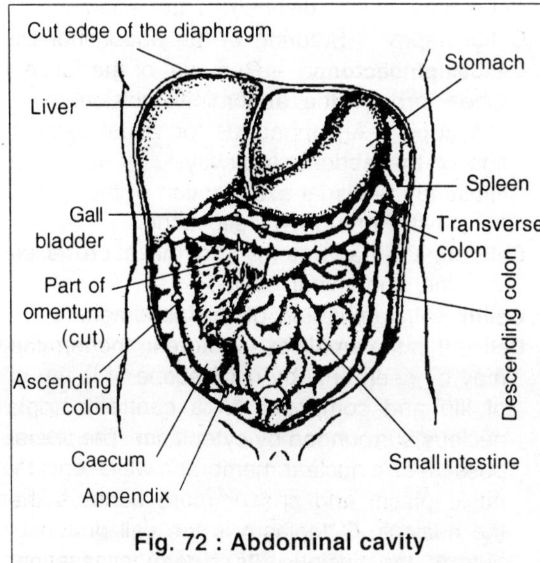

Fig. 72 : Abdominal cavity

Amniotic cavity —A closed sac between the embryo and the amnion, containing the amniotic fluid.

Articular cavity —The cavity in a joint surrounded by the synovial membrane.

Buccal cavity —Cavity of the mouth.

Cavity of the middle ear —Tympanic cavity.

Cranial cavity —The space enclosed by the cranial bones which contains the brain.

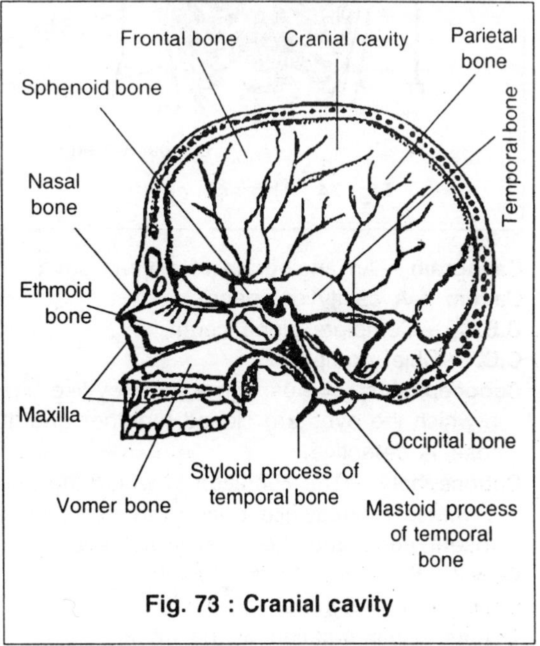

Fig. 73 : Cranial cavity

Dental cavity —A hole in a tooth caused by dental caries.

Nasal cavity —The cavity on either side of the nasal septum.

Oral cavity —Mouth.

Pelvic cavity —The space within the walls of the pelvis.

Pericardial cavity — The space between the epicardium and pericardium.

Peritoneal cavity — The space between the parietal and visceral layers of the peritoneum containing serous fluid.

Pleural cavity —The space between the parietal and the visceral pleura.

Pulp cavity —Cavity in a tooth containing dental pulp and the nerve fibers.

Thoracic cavity —The space within the thoracic walls bounded below by the diaphragm and above by the neck.

Tympanic cavity — Cavity of the middle ear.

Uterine cavity —Hollow space in the body of the uterus.

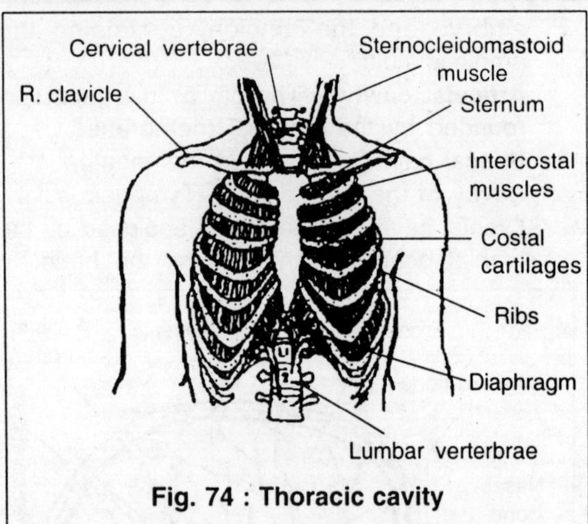

Fig. 74 : Thoracic cavity

Cavogram —An angiogram of a vena cava.

Cavum —A cavity or space.

C.B.C. —Complete blood count.

C.C. —Chief complaint.

Cebocephalus —Fetus with a monkey-like head in which the eyes are closed together and the nose is defective.

Cabocephaly —The condition in which the fetus is with a monkey-like head with defective or absent nose and the closely set eyes.

Cecal —Pertaining to the cecum.

Cecectomy —Excision of the cecum.

Cecitis —Inflammation of the cecum.

Cecocolopexy —Fixation of the colon and the rectum by surgery.

Cecocolostomy —An operation of joining the cecum to the colon.

Cecofixation —Cecopexy.

Cecoileostomy —An operation for joining the cecum and the ileum together.

Cecopexy —Surgical fixation of the cecum to the abdominal wall.

Cecoplication —Reduction of a dilated cecum by making a fold in its wall.

Cecoptosis —Falling down of the cecum.

Cecorrhaphy —Suture of the cecum.

Cecosigmoidostomy —To make a connection between the cecum and the sigmoid colon by an operation.

Cecostomy —Surgical formation of an artificial opening into the cecum.

Cecotomy —Incision of the cecum.

Cecum —The dilated first part of the large intestine located at the distal end of the ileum, and from which the vermiform appendix arises.

Cel–, Celo- —Prefixes indicating tumor, swelling or hernia.

-cele —Suffix indicating a tumor, swelling or henia.

Celiac —Pertaining to the abdominal cavity.

Celiectomy —1. Excision of an abdominal organ. 2. Excision of the celiac branches of the vagus nerve.

Celiocentesis —Puncture in the abdomen.

Celiocolpotomy —An incision of the vagina through the abdominal wall.

Celioenterotomy —Incision through the abdominal wall into the intestine.

Celiogastrostomy —Incision in the abdominal wall for making a gastric fistula.

Celiogastrotomy — Incision through the abdominal wall into the stomach.

Celiohysterectomy —Excision of the uterus through the abdomen.

Celiohysterotomy —To open the uterus through an abdominal incision.

Celioma —A tumour of the abdomen.

Celiomyalgia —Pain in the muscles of the abdomen.

Celiomyomectomy —To cut the muscular tissue through an abdominal incision.

Celiomyomotomy —Incision of the muscles of the abdomen.

Celiomyositis —Inflammation of abdominal muscles.

Celioparacentesis — Puncture of the abdomen for drainage purpose.

Celiopathy —Any disease of the abdomen.

Celiorrhaphy —Suturing of the abdominal wall.

Celiosalpingectomy — Removal of the fallopian tubes through the abdominal incision.

Celioscope —An apparatus for visual examination of the abdominal cavity.

Celioscopy —Visual examination of the abdominal cavity through a celioscope.

Celiotomy —Laparotomy. To make an incision into the abdominal cavity.

Celitis —Inflammation of the abdomen.

Cell —It is the smallest structure in the body that may be seen only by microscope. It is the unit of life and composed of a centrally located nucleus surrounded by cytoplasm. The nucleus possesses a nuclear membrane which encloses nucleoplasm and one or more dense bodies, the nucleoli. Cytoplasm is the cell protoplasm outside the nucleus. Its outermost layer constitutes the cell membrane.

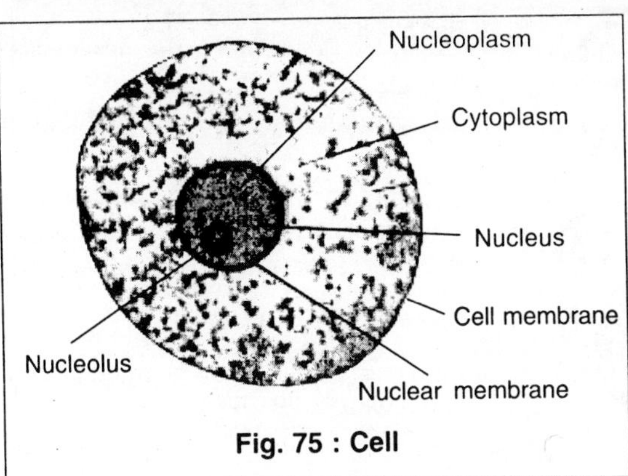

Fig. 75 : Cell

Acidophil cells —Cells staining with acid dyes.
Adipose cell —A fat cell.
Air cell —A cell containing air as in an alveolus of the lung or auditory tube.
Alpha cells —Cells found in the islets of Langerhans of the pancreas which secrete glucagon and they are the cells of the anterior lobe of the pituitary gland.
Basal cell —A type of cell found in the basal layer of the epidermis.
Basophil cells —Cells staining with basic dyes.
Beta cells —Cells of the islets of Langerhans of the pancreas which secrete insulin, and the basophil cells of the anterior lobe of the pituitary gland.
Blood cells —White blood cells, red blood cells and platelets found in the blood.
Columnar cell —An epithelial cell of which the height is greater than width.
Cuboid cell —A cell of which the height, width and depth are all about equal.
Daughter cell —Any cell formed from the division of a mother cell.
Endothelial cell —A flat cell making up the lining of the vessels and the endocardium.
Epithelial cells —Cells forming the epithelial surfaces of the skin and mucous membranes.
Ganglion cell —Any neuron whose cell body is located in a ganglion.
Germ cell —A cell whose function is to reproduce the organism as a spermatozoon or an ovum.
Giant cell —1. A large cell with many nuclei, found in bone marrow which produces blood platelets. 2. A very large cell whether it contains one or multiple nuclei.
Mucous cell —Mucus secreting cell found in the mucus-secreting glands.
Nerve cell —A cell of the nerve which consists of a cell body and a long process, the axon which transmits nerve impulses and the others, the dendrites which receive impulses and transmit them to the cell body.
Pigment cell —A cell containing pigment.
Plasma cell —The spherical cell of plasma, the fluid portion of blood, which is important in antibody production.
Pus cells —They are formed of white blood cells.
Red blood cells —The erythrocytes of the blood which carry oxygen to the cells of the body.
Stellate cells —Star-shaped cells.
Taste cells —Cells of a taste bud.
Visual cell —A rod or cone cell of the retina.
White blood cells —Leucocytes of the blood.

Cellicolous —Living within cells.

Cell kinetics —The study of cells, their growth and division.

Cell mass —In embryology, the mass of cells which develops into an organ or structure.

Cell membrane, Cell wall —The membrane which encloses a cell and made up of proteins, lipids and carbohydrates.

Cell organelle —Any structure in the cytoplasm of a cell as mitochondria, Golgi bodies etc.

Cellucidal —Destructive to cells.

Cellula —A very small cell.

Cellular —Pertaining to or composed of cells.

Cellular immunity —Immunity developed by the antibodies produced by T-lymphocytes.

Cellularity —The degree, quality or condition of cells present.

Cellulase —An enzyme which converts cellulose to cellobiose, secreted by bacteria and fungi, which destroy wood.

Cellulicidal —Destroying the cells.

Cellulifugal —Moving away from a cell.

Cellulipetal —Moving toward a cell.

Cellulitis —A diffuse inflammation of the connective tissue due to infection.

Cellulofibrous —Both cellular and fibrous.

Celluloneuritis —Inflammation of the neurons or nerve cells.

Cellulose —A fibrous form of carbohydrate forming the skeleton of the plants. On eating the cellulose it stimulates the peristaltic movement of the intestine and helps in evacuation so the

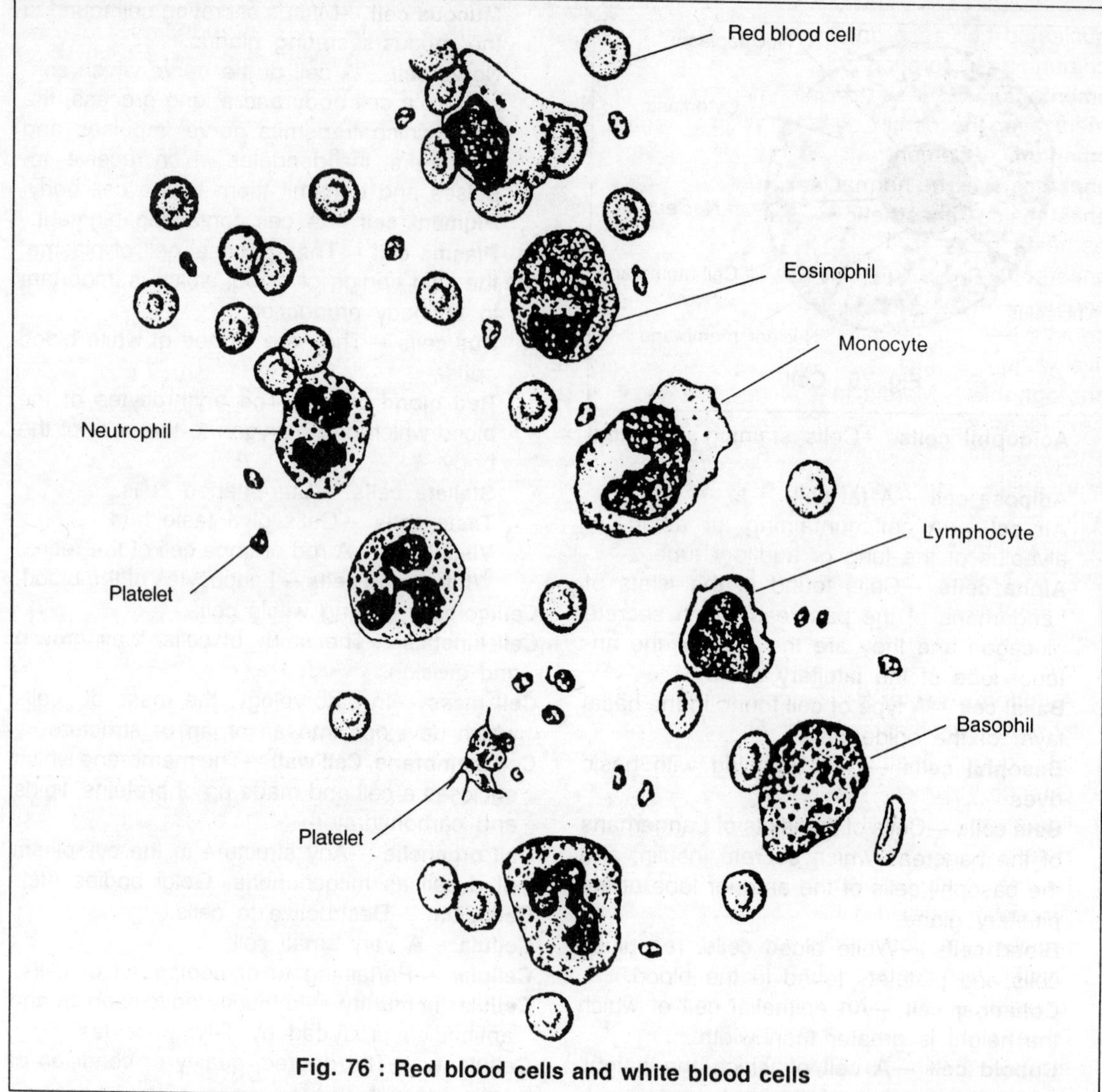

Fig. 76 : Red blood cells and white blood cells

food containing cellulose as turnip etc. can be used in case of constipation.

Cellulotoxic —1. Poisonous to cells. 2. Caused by cell toxins.

Celom, Celoma —Body cavity.

Celomic —Pertaining to the body cavity.

Celophlebitis —Inflammation of a vena cava.

Celoschisis —Congenital fissure of the abdominal wall.

Celoscope —An apparatus for visual examination of a body cavity.

Celoscopy —Examination of a body cavity with an optical instrument.

Celosomia —Congenital fissure of the sternum with herniation of the viscera.

Celsius scale —Centigrade thermometer, a thermometer on which the boiling point of water is 100°and freezing point of water is 0°.

Cement, Cementum —A thin layer of calcified tissue formed by cementoblasts which covers the dentin of the root and neck of a tooth.

Cementation —The process of attaching the teeth by means of a cement.

Cementitis —Inflammation of the dental cement.

Cementoblast — A cell that is concerned with the formation of the layer of cement on the roots of teeth.

Cementoclasia —Destruction of cement by cementoclasts.

Cementoclast —Odontoclast. A very large multinucleated cell associated with the removal of cement by resorption.

Cementogenesis —The development of the cement over the dentin of the root of a tooth.

Cementum —Cement.

Cenesthesia —The normal feeling of being alive.

Cenesthesic, Cenesthetic — Pertaining to cenesthesia.

Cenesthopathia —Not feeling well.

Cenosis —Morbid discharge.

Cenosite —A parasitic microorganism that can live without a host.

Cenotophobia —Morbid fear of new things and new ideas.

Census —Official counting of the population.

Centenarian —The person over the age of 100.

Center —1. The middle point of a body. 2. The group of nerve cells within the central nervous system to control a specific function.

Auditory center —The center for hearing in the anterior part of the transverse temporal gyri.

Autonomic center — The center in the brain or spinal cord that regulates the activity under the control of autonomic nervous system.

Gustatory center —Taste center. A center in the brain that controls taste.

Heat-regulating center —Two centers, one for the heat loss and other for the heat production located in the hypothalamus which regulate the body temperature.

Ossification center — The spot in the bones where ossification begins.

Respiratory center —The center situated in the medulla oblongata which controls the respiratory movements.

Speech center — Broca's area. The center located in the left (or right) inferior frontal gyrus which controls the speaking.

Thermoregulatory center — Temperature center. Temperature-regulating center present in the hypothalamus.

Vasoconstrictor center — A center located in the medulla which brings about the constriction of the blood vessels.

Vasodilator center —A center located in the medulla which brings about the dilatation of the blood vessels.

Vasomotor center —The center present in the medulla oblongata that controls constriction and dilation of blood vessels.

Visual center —A center located in the occipital lobe which controls the sight.

Centesis —Puncture of a cavity and aspiration of fluid from it.

Centigrade —A thermometer divided into 100° of which the boiling point of water is 100° and the freezing point is 0°.

Centigram —Hundredth part of a gram.

Centiliter —Hundredth part of a liter.

Centimeter —Hundredth part of meter.

Centinormal —One hundredth of the normal, as the concentration of a solution.

Centrad —Toward the center.

Central —Situated at or pertaining to a center.

Centralis —Central. In the center.

Central nervous system —A part of the nervous system which includes brain, spinal cord and their nerves.

Centraphose —Subjective sensation of darkness or light originating in the visual centers of the brain.

Centric —Pertaining to a center.

Centriciput —The central part of the upper surface of the skull, between the occiput and sinciput.

Centrifugal —Moving away from the center.

Centrifugation —The process of separating the lighter portion of a solution, mixture or suspension from the heavier portion by causing sedimentation of the heay portion

Centrifuge —A machine which rotates the test tubes placed in it at a very high speed by which

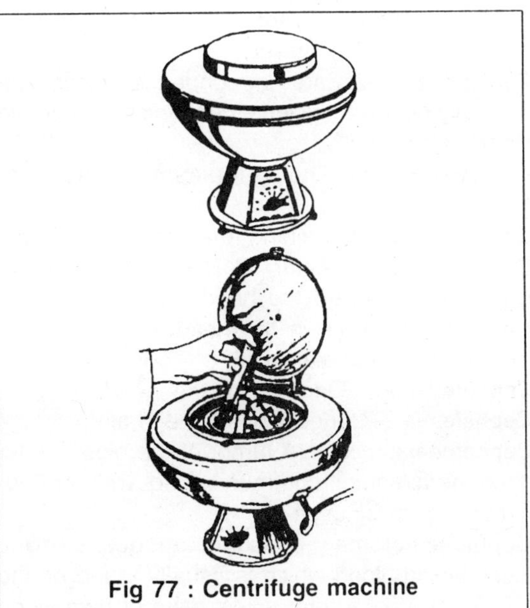

Fig 77 : Centrifuge machine

the heavy substance in the liquid in the tubes settles down and the lighter substance goes to the top.

Centrifuge tube —It has a tappered bottom and is used in centrifugation. It is of two types—–non graduated and graduated.

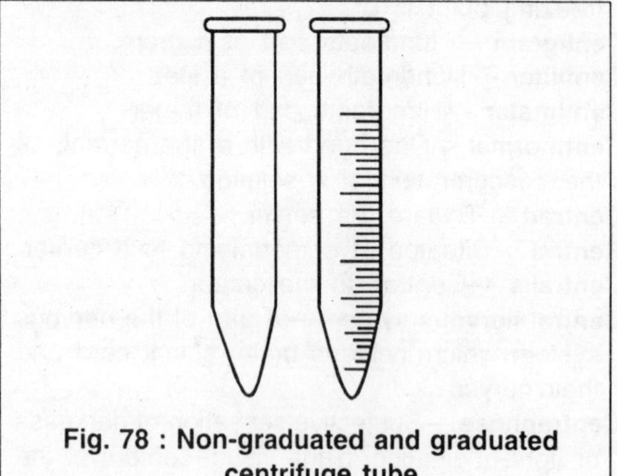

Fig. 78 : Non-graduated and graduated centrifuge tube

Centrilobular —Pertaining to the center of a lobule.

Centriole —A minute organelle found in the centrosome of the cell.

Centripetal —Moving toward a center.

Centrocyte —A cell with single or double granules of varying size stainable with hematoxylin, in its protoplasm.

Centromere —A clear constricted portion of a chromosome which divides the chromosome into two parts.

Centrosclerosis —Filling of the bone marrow space with bone tissue.

Centrosome —An area of condensed cytoplasm usually near the nucleus, containing one or two centrioles.

Centrosphere —The cytoplasm of the centrosome.

Centrostaltic —Pertaining to a center of motion.

Centrum —1. A center. 2. Body of a vertebra.

Cephalad —Toward the head.

Cephalalgia —Pain in the head.

Cephalea —Cephalalgia.

Cephaledema —Oedema of the head.

Cephalemia —Congestion of the brain.

Cephalhematocele —A tumor of the blood under the pericranium communicating with one or more dural sinuses.

Cephalhematoma —A subcutaneous swelling containing blood which is usually found on the head of a baby after a few days of birth when the delivery was performed with the forceps. The swelling disappears within two to three months.

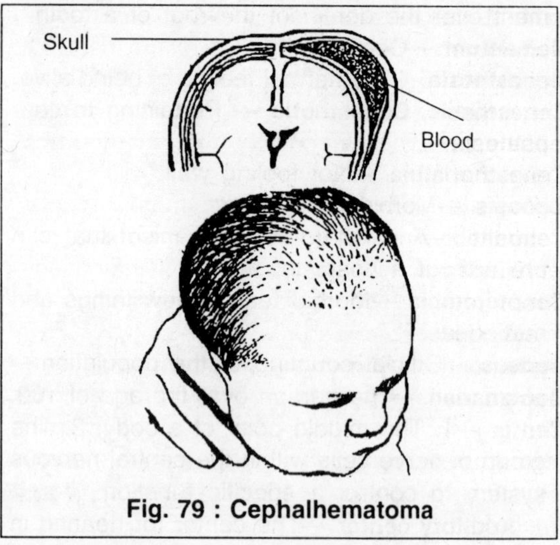

Fig. 79 : Cephalhematoma

Cephalhydrocele — Accumulation of watery fluid under the periosteum of the skull.

Cephalic —1. Pertaining to the head. 2. Superior.

Cephalic index —Length-breadth index. The ratio of the maximal breadth to the maximal length of the head, obtained by dividing the value of the maximal breadth multiplied by 100, with the maximal length of the head, (breadth x 100)/ length.

Cephalitis —Encephalitis, inflammation of the brain.

Cephalocele —Protrusion of a part of the brain from the cranial cavity.

Cephalocentesis —Surgical puncture of the head.

Cephalodynia, Cephalalgia —Pain in the head.

Chephalogenesis —Formation of the head in the embryonic stage.

Cephalogram —X-ray picture of the head.

Cephalogyric —Pertaining to the rotation of the head.

Cephalohematocele —Cephalhematocele.

Cephalohematoma —Cephalhematoma.

Cephalohemometer —An instrument for determining changes in intracranial pressure.

Cephaloid —Resembling the head.

Cephalomegaly —Enlargement of the head.

Cephalomelus —A monster having a limb growing from the head.

Cephalomenia —Vicarious menstruation from the head or nose.

Cephalomeningitis — Inflammation of the cerebrum and its meninges.

Cephalometer —An apparatus for measuring the head.

Cephalometrics —Scientific study of the measurements of the head.

Cephalometry —Measurement of the head.

Cephalomotor —Pertaining to the movement of the head.

Cephalone —The person mentally retarded and having a large head.

Cephalonia —A condition in which there is mental retardation and enlargement of the head.

Cephalopagus —Conjoined twins with their heads fused together but the rest of the bodies remaining separate.

Cephalopathy —Any disease of the head.

Cephalopelvic —Pertaining to the relationship of the fetal head to the pelvis of the mother.

Cephalopelvimetry —Pelvicephalography. Pelvocephalography. Measurement of the dimensions of the pelvis of the mother and the head of the fetus.

Cephaloplegia —Paralysis of the muscles of the head or of the face.

Cephalorrhachidian — Pertaining to the head and spine.

Cephalothoracic —Pertaining to the head and the thorax.

Cephalothoracopagus —A double fetus joined together at the head and thorax.

Cephalotome —An instrument for cutting the head of the fetus to facilitate the delivery.

Cephalotomy —The cutting of the head of the fetus to facilitate delivery.

Cephalotractor —The forceps for extracting the head of the fetus during delivery.

Cephalotribe —An instrument for crushing the fetal head.

Cephalotrophic —Inclining toward the brain tissue.

Cephalotrypesis —To remove a portion of the skull bone.

Cera —Wax.

Cera alba —White wax.

Cera flava —Yellow wax.

Ceraceous —Waxen.

Ceramics dental —The use of porcelain or porcelain type materials in dental work.

Ceramodontia —Dental ceremics.

Ceratotome — A knife for dividing the cornea.

Ceratonosus —Any disease of the cornea.

Cerclage —Encircling of tissues or of an organ with a ligature, wire or loop.

Cercus —A hair-like structure.

Cerea flexibilitas —A state in which the limbs remain in the same position in which they were being placed.

Cereals —Grains.

Cerebellar —Pertaining to the cerebellum.

Cerebellifugal —Going away from the cerebellum.

Cerebellipetal —Extending toward the cerebellum.

Cerebellitis —Inflammation of the cerebellum.

Cerebellomedullary —Pertaining to the cerebellum and the medulla oblongata.

Cerebellopontine —Pertaining to the cerebellum and the pons varolii.

Cerebellospinal —Pertaining to the cerebellum and the spinal cord.

Cerebellum —The portion of the brain lying on the back of the pons and medulla oblongata to which it is attached, and consists of a middle portion, the vermis and two lateral lobes (hemispheres).

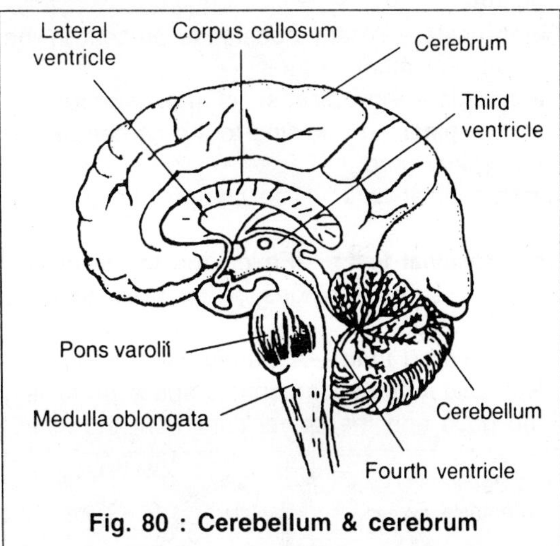

Fig. 80 : Cerebellum & cerebrum

Cerebral —Pertaining to the cerebrum.

Cerebral anoxia —Lack of oxygen in the brain.

Cerebral hemorrhage — Hemorrhage in the cerebrum due to rupture of the blood vessels.

Cerebrasthenia —Weakness of the mind.

Cerebration —Mental activity; thinking.

Cerebriform —Resembling the external fissures and convolutions of the brain.

Cerebrifugal —Proceeding away from the cerebrum.

Cerebripetal —Proceeding toward the cerebrum.

Cerebritis —Inflammation of the cerebrum.

Cerebroid —Resembling the cerebrum.

Cerebroma —Any abnormal mass of brain tissue.

Cerebromalacia —Abnormal softening of the cerebrum.

Cerebromedullary — Cerebrospinal. Pertaining to the cerebrum and the spinal cord.

Cerebromeningitis — Inflammation of the cerebrum and its meninges.

Cerebropathia —Encephalopathy.

Cerebropathy —Any disease of the brain.

Cerebrophysiology —The physiology of the brain.

Cerebropontile —Pertaining to the cerebrum and pons varolii.

Cerebropsychosis —Any mental disease due to cerebral lesion.

Cerebrosclerosis —Hardening of the substance of the cerebrum.

Cerebroscope —An ophthalmoscope used for diagnosing the diseases of the brain.

Cerebroscopy —The use of ophthalmoscope in diagnosing the cerebral diseases.

Cerebrose —Brain sugar derived from the brain tissue.

Cerebroside —A fatty substance present in the nerve and other tissues.

Cerebrosis —Any disease of the cerebrum.

Cerebrospinal —Pertaining to the cerebrum and the spinal cord.

Cerebrospinal axis —The central nervous system.

Cerebrospinal fever —Fever due to the inflammation of the meninges of the brain and the spinal cord.

Cerebrospinal fluid —A watery, clear and colorless fluid in the subarachnoid space protecting the brain and the spinal cord from the injury.

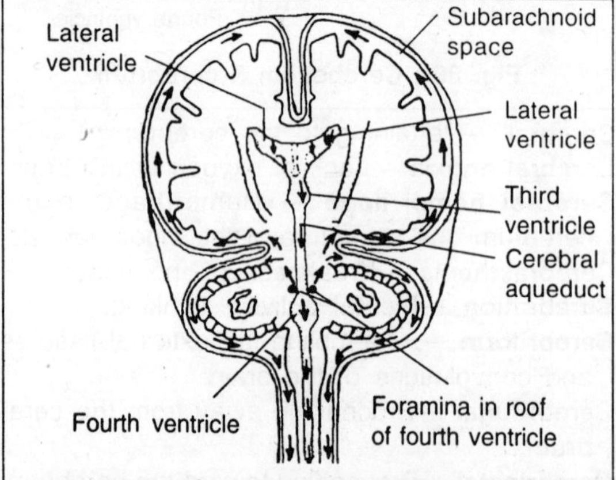

Fig 81 : Arrows showing the flow of cerebrospinal fluid (CSF)

Cerebrospinal puncture —A puncture to collect the cerebrospinal fluid which is usually done in the spinal cord at the lumbar region.

Cerebrotomy —To make an incision in the brain.

Cerebrovascular —Pertaining to the blood vessels of the brain.

Cerebrum —The largest part of the brain consisting of two hemispheres separated by a longitudinal fissure.

Ceroplasty —The making of anatomical models in wax.

Certifiable —1. Concerning with the infectious diseases which must be reported to the health authorities. 2. A mentally dull person who requires care of a guardian or institution.

Cerumen —Earwax, waxlike substance found within the external auditory canal.

Ceruminal —Pertaining to the cerumen.

Ceruminolysis —The dissolution of the wax in the external auditory canal.

Ceruminolytic —A substance instilled into the ear to soften the wax.

Ceruminoma —A benign tumor of the ceruminous glands situated in the external auditory canal.

Ceruminosis —Excessive secretion of cerumen.

Ceruminous —Pertaining to cerumen.

Ceruminous glands —Sweat glands situated in the external auditory canal which secrete cerumen.

Cervical —Pertaining to the neck or to the cervix.

Cervical cap —A device of an elastic material for covering the cervix of the uterus, used to prevent the conception.

Cervical ripening —The process of softening and dilatation of the cervix of the uterus in preparation for child birth.

Cervical spondylosis — Degenerative arthritis of the cervical vertebrae and their related tissues.

Cervicectomy —Excision of the cervix of the uterus.

Cervices —Plural of cervix.

Cervicitis —Inflammation of the cervix of the uterus.

Cervico- —Prefix pert. to the neck or to the neck of an organ.

Cervicobrachial —Pertaining to the neck and the arm.

Cervicobrachialgia —Pain in the neck radiating to the arm.

Cervicocolpitis — Inflammation of the cervix and the vagina.

Cervicodynia —Pain in the neck.

Cervicofacial —Pertaining to the neck and face.

Cervicography —Study of the uterine cervix by obtaining its photograph.

Cervico-occipital — Pertaining to the neck and the occiput.

Cervicoplasty —Plastic surgery of the uterine cervix.

Cervicoscopy —Visual examination of the uterine cervix.

Cervicothoracic —Pertaining to the neck and thorax.

Cervicotomy —To incise the uterine cervix.

Cervicovaginitis — Inflammation of the cervix of the uterus and the vagina.

Cervicovesical —Pertaining to the cervix of the uterus and urinary bladder.

Cervix —The neck or a constricted portion of an organ.

Cervix uteri —Lower narrow part of the uterus, between the isthmus and the opening of the uterus into the vagina.

Cervix vesicae —Lower constricted part of the urinary bladder.

Cesarean section —Removal of the fetus by means of an incision in the uterus through the incision of the abdominal wall, which is usually done when the fetus is too large to be delivered through the pelvis or the pelvis is abnormally small or both the conditions are present there.

Cesticidal —Destructive to cestodes.

Cestode —A type of tapeworm.

Cestodiasis —Infestation with tapeworm.

Cestoid —Like a tapeworm.

Chadwick's sign —A sign of pregnancy which becomes evident at about the 4th week of gestation in which uterus and cervix would have become deep blue-violet colored due to increased vascularity at that time.

Chafe —To injure the skin by rubbing or friction.

Chafing —Superficial inflammation with maceration and sometimes fissuring of the skin by friction from clothes or adjacent skin which generally occur at the axilla, groin, anal region or between digits of hands and feet.

Chalasia —Relaxation of the sphincters.

Chalaza —Chalazion.

Chalazion —A small hard tumor in the eyelid formed by distension of a meibomian gland with secretion.

Chalcosis —Deposition of copper in the lungs and tissues.

Chalicosis —Pneumoconiosis due to inhalation of fine particles produced by stone cutting.

Chalinoplasty —Plastic surgery of the mouth and lips.

Chalkitis —Chalcosis.

Chalybeate —1. Pertaining to or composed of iron. 2. Anything containing iron.

Chamber —Any closed space.

Aqueous chamber —The part of the eyeball filled with a fluid—the aqueous humour, which is divided into anterior and posterior chambers. The space between the cornea and the iris is the anterior chamber and the space behind it, between the iris and the anterior surface of the lens is the posterior chamber.

Vitreous chamber —The rest whole space behind the lens within the eyeball is the vitreous chamber containing a fluid vitreous humor.

Chamecephalic —Having a flat head.

Chamecephalous —Chamecephalic.

Chameprosopic —Having a broad face.

Chancre —A hard, painless primary ulcer of syphilis occurring at the site of entry of infection.

Chancriform —Resembling a chancre.

Chancroid —An infectious nonsyphilitic venereal ulcer caused by the bacillus Hemophilus ducreyi, which begins as a painless macule in the genital organs, which enlarges and becomes pustular, then it bursts and an ulcer with rough floor and yellowish discharge is formed.

Chancroidal —Pertaining to or of the nature of chancroid.

Chancrous —Having a chancre.

Change of life —Menopause; climacteric.

Channel —Canal. A tube or groove like passageway.

Chapped —The inflammed, roughened, and fissured skin as from exposure to cold.

Character —Qualities of a person, especially those of personality, thoughts and morality as evidenced by the individual's speech, writings and actions which differentiate one person from another.

Characteristic —The typical character of a person.

Charcoal —The carbon prepared by charring the wood.

Charcot-Leyden crystals — They are long, colorless, hexagonal, double-pointed, needle-shaped crystals found in the sputum of the patient of bronchial asthma and bronchitis.

Charcot's joint —A type of diseased joint with slight pain and abnormal mobility following marked destruction of the bones, associated with tabes dorsalis, syringomyelia and peripheral neuritis.

Charlatan —The person who pretends to have a special knowledge or ability as are quacks in medical line.

Charlatanism —Quackery. To treat the patients without medical knowledge or authority to practice medicine.

Charlatanry —Charlatanism.

Charles law —At constant pressure the volume of a gas varies in direct proportion to the temperature.

Charleyhorse —Pain and tenderness in the muscles of the thigh due to muscular strain or tear which suddenly starts and aggravated on movement.

Chart —1. A paper sheet for recording the course of the patient's illness, his temperature, pulse, blood pressure, respiratory rate, urinary and fecal output and doctor's and nurse's notes. 2. Reading chart—A chart of the letters of the types of gradually increasing sizes for reading in testing the acuity of near vision.

Charting —Clinical recording. To make a record of the progress of a patient's condition.

Chartula —A small piece of paper folded to form a receptacle containing a dose of some medicine.

Chasma —An opening or a cleft.

Chastisement —Penalty.

Chaude-pisse —Burning sensation during micturition.

Chebulic myrobalans —

Check bite —A sheet of hard wax placed between the teeth used to check occlusion of the teeth.

Check-up —Physical examination.

Cheek —Fleshy sides of the face forming the lateral walls of the mouth, below the eyes.

Cheek-bone —Zygomatic bone.

Cheek retractor —An apparatus for drawing aside the cheeks at the angle of the mouth so that the operating area may be exposed properly.

Cheese —The coagulum of milk compressed into a solid mass.

Cheesy —Resembling the cheese.

Cheilalgia, Chilalgia —Pain in a lip.

Cheilectomy —1. Removal of a lip by an operation. 2. Removal of an abnormal bone by surgery around a joint to facilitate joint mobility.

Cheilectropion —Eversion of the lip.

Cheilitis —Inflammation of the lip.

Cheilo-, Cheil- —Prefixes pertaining to the lips.

Cheilognathopalatoschisis —A congenital defect in which there is cleft in the hard and soft palates, upper jaw and lip.

Cheilophagia —Habit of biting one's own lip.

Cheiloplasty —Plastic surgery upon the lips.

Cheilorrhaphy —Repair of the cleft lip by surgery.

Cheiloschisis —Cleft-lip.

Cheilosis —Fissures at the corners of the mouth with redness, seen in riboflavin deficiency.

Cheilostomatoplasty — Restoration of the lips and mouth by plastic surgery.

Cheilotomy, Chilotomy — Incision into the lip.

Cheiralgia —Pain in the hand.

Cheirarthritis —Inflammation of the joints of the hands and fingers.

Cheiro-, Cheir- —Prefixes pertaining to the hand.

Cheirognostic, Chirognostic — Able to distinguish between right and left side of the body; able to perceive which side of the body is being touched.

Cheirokinesthesia —The subjective sensation of movement of the hands. Chirokinesthesia.

Cheirology —Dactylology.

Cheiromegaly —Abnormal enlargement of the hands and fingers.

Cheiroplasty —Plastic surgery on the hand.

Cheiropodalgia —Pain in the hands and feet.

Cheirospasm —Spasm of the muscles of the hand as in writer's cramp.

Cheloid —Keloid.

Chemabrasion —Use of a chemical to destroy the superficial layers of the skin which is usually done to treat the scars and hyperpigmentation etc.

Chemical —Pertaining to chemistry.

Chemical compound —A substance consisting of two or more chemical elements, in definite proportions and in chemical combination, for which chemical formula can be written, as H_2O for water and NaCl for salt.

Chemical warfare —Warfare in which toxic chemical substances and the disease-producing organisms are introduced into the general public.

Chemiluminescence —Cold light, light produced by chemical reaction without production of heat, *e.g.* light produced by certain bacteria, fungi, fireflies and fishes etc.

Chemist —The person trained in chemistry.

Chemistry —The branch of science which deals with the molecular and atomic structure of matters, the elements and the various compounds of the elements.

Analytical chemistry — Chemistry concerned with the detection or the determination of the amounts of chemical substances in a compound.

Biological chemistry —The chemistry of living things which includes all the chemical processes which take place within an organism such as the digestion, respiration, excretion etc.

Clinical chemistry —1. Chemistry of the human health and disease. 2. Chemistry applied in medical laboratory for testing the materials obtained from the patients.

Inorganic chemistry — Chemistry of compounds not containing carbon.

Organic chemistry — Chemistry of the compounds containing carbon.

Pathological chemistry —The study of chemical changes produced by the diseases in the tissues, organs and blood etc., of the body.

Pharmaceutical chemistry —The chemistry of preparing the medicines, their actions and uses etc.

Chemocautery —Cauterization by chemical agents.

Chemocoagulation —To coagulate by some chemical agent.

Chemohormonal —Pertaining to the drugs having hormonal activity.

Chemokinesis —Increased activity of an organism by a chemical substance.

Chemokinetic —Pertaining to chemokinesis.

Chemoluminescence —A chemical reaction which produces light.

Chemolysis —Destruction by chemical action.

Chemoprophylaxis —Prevention of a disease by use of a drug or a chemical agent such as the prevention of malaria by taking the suitable medicine.

Chemopsychiatry —Treatment of mental diseases by use of drugs.

Chemoreceptor —A sense organ or a sensory nerve ending sensitive to stimulation by chemical substances.

Chemoreflex —Reflex resulting from a chemical stimulus.

Chemoresistance —The resistance of bacteria or some body cells to the inhibitory effect of a chemical substance or drug.

Chemoresponse —A reaction to the stimulation of a chemical substance.

Chemosensitive —Reacting to a chemical change.

Chemoserotherapy —Treatment of a disease by the combined use of a drug and serum.

Chemosis —Edema of the conjunctiva around the cornea.

Chemosterilant —1. A chemical substance which kills the micro-organisms. 2. A chemical substance whcih produces sterility, usually in man.

Chemosurgery —Destruction of tissues by the use of a chemical compound.

Chemosynthesis —The formation of a chemical compound from other chemical substances.

Chemotactic —Pertaining to chemotaxis.

Chemotaxin —A substance released by the bacteria, injured tissue and white blood cells that stimulates the movement of W.B.C. to the injured area.

Chemotaxis, Chemotropism — Attraction and repulsion of the living protoplasm to a stimulation of a chemical substance.

Chemothalamectomy — Chemical destruction of a part of the thalamus.

Chemotherapeutic —Pertaining to chemotherapy.

Chemotherapeutics —The branch of therapeutics concerned with chemotherapy.

Chemotherapy —Treatment of a disease by a chemical agent which is toxic to the disease-producing organisms.

Chemotic —Pertaining to chemosis.

Chemotropism —Chemotaxis.

Chest —Thorax.

Emphysematous chest — In the patient of emphysema the chest becomes round, its anteroposterior diameter becomes equal to the transverse diameter, the ribs become horizontal. It is also known as barrel-shaped chest.

Flat chest —The chest becomes flat, its anteroposterior diameter is short than that of the transverse diameter, ribs are oblique, the scapula bone is prominent and the spaces above and below the calvicles are depressed.

Funnel-shaped chest —The sternum is depressed so that the chest becomes funnel-shaped since birth.

Pigeon-shaped chest — Chest in which the sides are flattened and the sternum is elevated so that the chest looks like a pigeon. It is found in rickets.

Chest thump —A sharp blow to the chest in the precordial area in an attempt to restore the normal heart-beat in patients with cardiac arrest.

Cheyne-stokes respiration — See cheyne-stokes breathing.

Chiari-Frommel syndrome — Persistent lactation and amenorrhea after child birth which is due to the continued secretion of prolactin and the decreased gonadotrophic hormones.

Chiasm, Chiasma —A crossing or decussation, *e.g.* optic chiasma in which there is the point of crossing of the fibers of the optic nerves.

Chiasma— Chiasm.

Chiasmapexy —Fixation of the optic chiasma by surgery.

Chiasmatic —Pertaining to a chiasma.

Chickenpox —An acute viral disease which is highly infectious and characterized by headache, high fever and followed by eruptions on the body.

Chilblain —A recurrent localized itching and swelling of the feet, toes or fingers caused by mild frost bite.

Child —The human of the age between the infancy and the puberty.

Child abuse —Emotional, physical or sexual injury to a child.

Childbed, Puerperium — Puerperal period.

Childbed fever —Puerperal sepsis.

Child birth —The process of giving birth to a child.

Childhood —The period of life between infancy and puberty.

Childproof —Harmless to the children, used especially for medicine containers that children cannot open.

Chilectropion —Cheilectropion. Eversion of the lip.

Chilits —Inflammation of the lips.

Chill —Shivering accompanied by the sensation of coldness.

Chimney sweeps' cancer — Epithelioma of the scrotum.

Chin —The portion of the lower jaw below the lip.

Chin jerk —Reflex contraction of the muscles of mastication on depressing the jaw suddenly.

Chin reflex —Clonic movement resulting from stroking the lower jaw.

Chip —Small piece of a thing.

Chiragra —Pain in the hand.

Chiralgia —Nontraumatic or neuralgic pain in the hand.

Chirarthritis —Cheirarthritis.

Chirismus —Spasm of the muscles of the hand.

Chirognostic —Cheirognostic. Able to distinguish the right from the left or the side of the body which is stimulated.

Chirokinesthesia — Cheirokinesthesia.

Chiromegaly —Enlargement of the hands and feet.

Chiroplasty —Plastic surgery of the hand.

Chiropodalgia —Cheiropodalgia.

Chiropodist —The person who practices in chiropody.

Chiropody —Treatment of the diseases of the feet.

Chiropractic —Medical practice in chiropody.

Chiropractor —A person certified and licensed in practice of chiropody.

Chirospasm —Spasm of the muscles of the hand, writer's cramp.

Chirurgery, Chirurgia — Surgery.

Chirurgia— Chirurgery

Chisel —A bevelled end steel cutting instrument used in dentistry and orthopedics.

Chlamydial —Pertaining to or caused by chlamydia.

Chloasma —Yellowish-brown or black pigmentation of the skin in patches.

Chloasma gravidarum — Brownish pigmentation of the face which occurs in pregnancy and disappear after delivery.

Chloasma hepaticum — Discoloration of the skin due to liver diseases.

Chloasma idiopathic — Chloasma caused by external agents such as sun, heat, mechanical means and X-ray etc.

Chloasma symptomatic — Chloasma caused by some diseases such as syphilis and cancer etc.

Chloasma traumaticum —Skin discoloration due to trauma.

Chloasma uterinum — Chloasma of pregnancy and due to other conditions of the uterus.

Chloracne —Acneiform eruption which occurs in persons exposed to chlorine compounds.

Chloremia —Excess of chlorides in the blood.

Chlorhydria —Excess of hydrochloric acid in the stomach.

Chloridemia —Presence of chlorides in the blood.

Chloridimetry —The process of determining the amount of chlorides in the body fluids.

Chloridometer —An apparatus for determining the amount of chlorides in the body fluids.

Chloridorrhea —Diarrhea with an excess of chlorides in the stool.

Chloriduria —Excess of chlorides in the urine.

Chlorinated —Charged with chlorine.

Chlorination —Mixing of chlorine in water in concentration of .5 to 1 part of chlorine per million parts of water for killing the bacteria.

Chlorine— A very irritating and poisonous gas which is destructive to the mucous membrane of the respiratory passages and may cause death on inhalation excessively. It is an active germicide and so widely used to disinfect the water supplies in the concentration of .5 to 1 part per million parts.

Chlorite —A salt of chlorous acid which is used as a disinfectant and bleaching agent.

Chloroform —A colorless, clear, heavy liquid with strong ether-like odor and sweet taste used as a solvent. At one time it was widely used by inhalation to produce anesthesia.

Chloroformism —Formation of habit to inhale the chloroform as a narcotic.

Chloroleukemia —Leukemia with green color of the body organs and fluids.

Chloroma —A greenish sarcoma of the periosteum of the cranial bones; green cancer.

Chloropenia, Hypochloremia —Deficiency of chloride in the blood.

Chloropenic —Deficient in chloride.

Chlorophane —A greenish yellow pigment in the retina.

Chlorophenothane —The insecticide D.D.T. powder.

Chlorophyll —A green pigment in the plants, which is essential for the process of photosynthesis by which the plants prepare food for them.

Chloropia, Chloropsia —Defect of vision in which all things appear green.

Chloroprivic —Lacking in chlorides or due to loss of chlorides.

Chlorosis —A form of iron-deficiency anemia which usually occurs in the adolescent females and characterized by greenish yellow discoloration of the skin.

Chlorotic —Pertaining to or suffering from chlorosis.

Chlorous —Pertaining to chlorine.

Chloruresis —Excretion of chlorides in the urine.

Chloruretic —Increasing the excretion of chloride in the urine.

Chloruria —Excess of chlorides in the urine.

Choana —Any funnel-shaped opening, especially the paired openings between the nasal cavity and the nasopharynx.

Choanal —Pertaining to choana.

Choanate —Having a funnel-shaped opening.

Choanoid —Funnel-shaped.

Choke —To prevent the respiration by compression or obstruction of the larynx or trachea or the condition resulting from such prevention.

Choked disk —Edema of the optic disk.

Chokes —Respiratory symptoms such as dyspnea, cough and asphyxia occurring in decompression or altitude sickness resulting from exposure to pressure lower than atmospheric pressure.

Choking —Obstruction within the respiratory passage by which the breathing and the blood circulation of the brain is interferred.

Cholagogue —An agent which stimulates the gallbladder to contract and thus to increase the flow of bile into the intestine.

Cholangeitis —Cholangitis.

Cholangiectasis —Dilatation of a bile duct.

Cholangioadenoma —A tumor of the glandular epithelium of a bile duct.

Cholangiocarcinoma — Cancer of the bile ducts.

Cholangioenterostomy — To form a connection between the bile duct and the intestine by surgery.

Cholangiofibrosis —Fibrosis of the bile ducts.

Cholangiogastrostomy —To form a passage between a bile duct and the stomach by surgery.

Cholangiogram —X-ray film of the bile ducts.

Cholangiography — X-ray examination of the bile ducts.

Cholangiole —The small terminal portion of the bile duct.

Cholangiolitis —Inflammation of the cholangiole.

Cholangioma —A tumor of the biliary ducts.

Cholangioscopy —Visual examination of the bile ducts by an endoscope.

Cholangiostomy —To form a fistula into the gallbladder by an operation.

Cholangiotomy —Incision into a bile duct for removal of gall stones.

Cholangitis —Inflammation of a bile duct.

Cholanopoiesis —Synthesis of cholic acid in the liver.

Cholecalciferol —Vitamin D_3, a fat-soluble antirachitic vitamin.

Cholechromopoiesis — Formation of bile pigments by the liver.
Cholecyst —The gallbladder.
Cholecystagogue —An agent which stimulates the emptying of the gall-bladder.
Cholecystalgia —Biliary colic.
Cholecystangiography—X-ray examination of the gallbladder and the biliary ducts after an injection of a radiopaque substance.
Cholecystectasia —Dilatation of the gallbladder.
Cholecystectomy —Removal of the gallbladder by an operation.
Cholecystenterorrhaphy — Suture of the gallbladder to the intestinal wall.
Cholecystenterostomy —To establish a connection between the gallbladder and the small intestine by surgery.
Cholecystenterotomy—To incise both, intestine and the gallbladder.
Cholecystic —Pertaining to the gallbladder.
Cholecystitis —Inflammation of the gallbladder which may be acute or chronic.
Cholecystnephrostomy — Surgical formation of a passage between the gallbladder and the renal pelvis.
Cholecystocolostomy—To make a passage from the gallbladder to the colon by surgery.
Cholecystocolotomy—To make an incision into the gallbladder and the colon.
Cholecystoduodenostomy — To form a passage from the gallbladder to the duodenum by an operation.
Cholecystogastrostomy — Formation of a passage from the gallbladder to the stomach by surgery.
Cholecystogram —An X-ray film of the gallbladder.
Cholecystography —X-ray examination of the gallbladder.
Cholecystoileostomy —To form a passage between the gallbladder and the ileum.
Cholecystojejunostomy — To make a passage between the gallbladder and the jejunum.
Cholecystokinetic — Stimulating contraction of the gallbladder.
Cholecystokinin —A hormone secreted by the upper part of the small intestine into the blood, which stimulates the gallbladder contraction and the pancreatic enzyme secretion.
Cholecystolithiasis —Stone in the gallbladder.
Cholecystolithotripsy — Crushing of a gallstone without opening the gallbladder.
Cholecystomy, Cholecystotomy —To make an incision in the gallbladder.
Cholecystopathy —An disease of the gallbladder.
Cholecystopexy —Suturing of the gallbladder to the abdominal wall.
Cholecystoptosis —Downward displacement of the gallbladder.
Cholecystorrhaphy—Suturing of the gallbladder.
Cholecystosonography — Ultrasonic examination of the gallbladder.
Cholecystostomy —To form an opening into the gallbladder through the abdominal wall.
Cholecystotomy —To incise the gallbladder through the abdominal wall to remove the gallstones.
Choledoch —Bile duct.
Choledochal —Pertaining to the common bile duct.
Choledochectasia —Dilatation of the common bile duct.
Choledochectomy —Excision of a part of the common bile duct.
Choledochiarctia —Stenosis of the bile duct.
Choledochitis—Inflammation of the common bile duct.
Choledochoduodenostomy —To make a passage between the common bile duct and the duodenum.
Choledochoenterostomy — To form a passage between the common bile duct and the intestine.
Choledochogastrostomy — To form a passage between the common bile duct and the stomach.
Choledochography —X-ray examination of the bile duct after giving radiopaque substance.
Choledochojejunostomy — To join the common bile duct to the jejunum of the small intestine by surgery.
Choledocholith —Stone in the common bile duct.
Choledocholithiasis — Presence of stones in the common bile duct.
Choledocholithotomy — Removal of a gallstone through an incision of the bile duct.
Choledocholithotripsy —To crush a gallstone in the common bile duct.
Choledochoplasty —Surgical repair of the common bile duct.
Choledochorrhapy —Suturing of the severed ends of the common bile duct.

Choledochostomy —To make an opening into the common bile duct through the abdominal wall.

Choledochotomy —To incise the common bile duct.

Choledochous —Containing or conveying bile.

Choledochus —The common bile duct.

Cholehemia —Cholemia.

Choleic —Pertaining to the bile.

Cholelith —Gallstone formed by the stagnation of bile.

Cholelithiasis —Presence or formation of gallstones in the gallbladder or the common bile duct.

Cholelithic —Pertaining to or caused by biliary calculus.

Cholelithotomy —Removal of the gallstones through an incision into the the gallbladder or the common bile duct.

Cholelithotripsy, Cholelithotrity —Crushing of a gallstone.

Cholemesis —Vomiting of bile.

Cholemia —Presence of bile or bile pigments in the blood.

Cholemic —Pertaining to cholemia.

Cholepathia —Disease of the bile duct.

Choleperitoneum —Presence of bile in the peritoneum.

Cholepoiesis —Formation of bile.

Cholepoietic —Pertaining to the formation of bile.

Cholera —An acute infectious disease caused by the bacillus Cholerae vibrio characterized by severe diarrhea of rice water type, vomiting, dehydration, oliguria, muscle cramps and marked weakness.

Choleragen —The toxin produced by the bacillus Cholerae vibrio which acts on the mucosa of the small intestine to cause increased secretion of water, chlorides and carbonates into the intestine.

Choleraic —Pertaining to, or of the nature of cholera.

Chloleresis —Secretion of bile by the liver.

Choleretic —An agent which stimulates excretion of bile by the liver.

Cholerheic —Denoting diarrhea produced secondary to unabsorbed bile salts.

Choleric —To become irritable without any apparent cause.

Choleriform —Resembling cholera.

Cholerigenic, Cholerigenous —Which produces cholera.

Choleroid —Resembling cholera.

Choleromania —Occasional madness in cholera.

Cholerophobia —Morbid fear of suffering from cholera.

Cholerrhagia —Excessive flow of bile.

Cholerrhagic —Pertaining to the flow of bile.

Cholestasia —Stoppage of bile excretion.

Cholestasis —Cholestasia.

Cholestatic —Diminishing or stopping the flow of bile.

Cholesteatoma —A cyst filled with epithelial cells and cholesterol, most commonly found in the middle ear, usually resulting from the chronic otitis media.

Cholesteatomatous —Of or pertaining to cholesteatoma.

Cholesteremia, Cholesterolemia or hypercholesterolemia —Excess of cholestrol in the blood.

Cholesterin —Cholesterol.

Cholesterinemia — Cholesteremia.

Cholesterinosis — Cholesterolosis.

Cholesterinuria —Presence of cholesterol in the urine.

Cholesterohydrothorax — Presence of fluid containing cholesterol in the pleural cavity.

Cholesterol —A fat-like substance (lipid) which is present in animal fats, various oils, milk, egg yolk, blood, nervous tissue, liver, bile, kidneys and the adrenal glands and is a principal constituent of most gallstones and occurs in atheroma of the arteries.

Cholesterologenesis — Production of cholesterol.

Cholesterolosis —Cholesterol deposition in abnormal amounts in the tissues.

Cholesteroluria —Presence of cholesterol in the urine.

Choletherapy —Treatment by bile salts.

Choleuria or **Choluria** — Presence of bile in the urine.

Choleverdin —Green pigment of the gallstones occurring in the urine in the jaundice.

Cholic —Choleic.

Cholicele —Enlargement of the gallbladder due to retained fluid.

Cholinergic —1. Nerve endings which liberate acetylcholine. 2. Anything which produces the effect of acetylcholine.

Cholinoceptive —Pertaining to the sites on the effector organs which are acted upon by the cholinergic transmitters.

Cholinolytic —Blocking the action of acetylcholine or of cholinergic agents.

Cholinomimetic —Having an action similar to that of acetylcholine, parasympathomimetic.
Cholochrome —Any bile pigment.
Cholognic —Producing bile.
Cholohemothorax —Presence of bile and blood in the thorax.
Chololith —A gallstone.
Chololithiasis —Cholelithiasis.
Choloplania —The presence of bile salts in the blood or tissues.
Cholopoiesis —Cholepoiesis.
Cholorrhea —Formation of bile in excess.
Cholothorax —Presence of bile in the pleural cavity.
Choluria —Presence of the bile salts in the urine, discoloration of the urine with bile pigments.
Chondral —Pertaining to the cartilage.
Chondralgia —Pain in a cartilage.
Chondralloplasia —Presence of cartilage in abnormal places.
Chondrectomy —To remove a cartilage by surgery.
Chondric —Pertaining to a cartilage.
Chondrification —To be changed into cartilage.
Chondrin —Gelatin like substance obtained by boiling cartilage.
Chondritis —Inflammation of a cartilage.
Chondro- —Prefix pertaining to the cartilage.
Chondroblast —Cartilage forming cell.
Chondroblastoma —A benign tumor arising from chondroblasts in the epiphysis of a bone.
Chondrocalcinosis — Calcification of the cartilage.
Chondroclast —A giant cell involved in the absorption of cartilage.
Chondrocostal —Pertaining to the ribs and the costal cartilages.
Chondrocranium —The cartilaginous parts of the developing skull.
Chondrocyte —A mature cartilage cell.
Chondrodermatitis nodularis chronica helicis — An inflammatory condition of the cartilage and the skin, especially a painful nodule on the helix of the ear.
Chondrodynia —Pain in or about a cartilage.
Chondrodysplasia — Achondroplasia.
Chondrodystrophy — Achondroplasia.
Chondroendothelioma —An endothelioma containing cartilage tissue.
Chondrofibroma —A mixed tumor with elements of chondroma and fibroma.
Chondrogenesis —Formation of cartilage.
Chondrogenic —Forming cartilage.
Chondroid —Resembling cartilage.
Chondrolipoma —A benign tumor containing cartilaginous and fatty tissue.
Chondrology —Science of the cartilages.
Chondrolysis —The breaking down and absorption of cartilage.
Chondroma —A tumor of the cartilage which causes no pain.
Chondromalacia —Abnormal softening of the cartilage.
Chondromatosis —Formation of multiple chondromas of the hands and feet.
Chondromatous —Pertaining to chondroma or tumor of a cartilage.
Chondromere —A cartilaginous vertebra of, the fetal vertebral column.
Chondromucoprotein —A fluid or solid substance occupying the space between the cells and fibers of the cartilage.
Chondromyoma —A benign tumor which contains the elements of both, myoma and chondroma.
Chondromyxoma —A tumor composed of mucous connective tissue tumor (myxoma) and the tumor of the cartilage (chondroma).
Chondromyxosarcoma —A sarcoma containing cartilaginous and mucous tissue.
Chondronecrosis —Necrosis of a cartilage.
Chondro-osseus —Composed of cartilage and bone.
Chondro-osteodystrophy — Congenital deformity of the epiphyses due to which dwarfism, kyphosis and pigeon breast is produced.
Chondropathology —Pathology of the diseases of the cartilages.
Chondropathy —Any disease of cartilage.
Chondrophyte —An abnormal cartilaginous mass developing at the articular surface of a bone.
Chondroplasia —Formation of cartilage.
Chondroplast, Chondroblast —Cartilage forming cell.
Chondroplasty —Plastic surgery of cartilage.
Chondroporosis —The formation of sinuses or spaces in the cartilage.
Chondrosarcoma —A malignant tumor of the cartilage.
Chondrosis —The formation of cartilage.
Chondrosternal —Pertaining to the sternal cartilage.
Chondrosternoplasty — Surgical correction of a deformed sternum.
Chondrotome —An instrument for cutting the cartilage.

Chondrotomy —To divide a cartilage by surgery.

Chondrotrophic —Affecting the development and growth of the cartilage.

Chondroxiphoid —Pertaining to the sternum and the xiphoid process.

Chondrus —Cartilage.

Chorda plural **-Chordae**—A cord.

Spermatic Cord	Spinal Cord
Umbilical Cord	Vocal Cord

Chordal —Pertaining to a chorda or cord.

Chordee —Downward deviation of the penis on erection due to congenital anomaly or to urethral infection.

Chorditis —Inflammation of the vocal or the spermatic cords.

Chordotomy —Division of any cord to relieve pain.

Chorea —Occurrence of rapid, jerky, involuntary movements in the body usually associated with acute rheumatic infection.

Huntington's chorea —A hereditary disease of the central nervous system which usually occurs between the age of 30 to 50 years, with chronic progressive chorea and mental deterioration.

Sydenham's chorea — A disease usually of the childhood commonly occurring between 5 and 15 years of age and during pregnancy, usually in those women who have had chorea before, especially in the 1st pregnancy. It is usually associated with rheumatic fever characterized by involuntary purposeless movements which gradually become severe. There may be impairment of memory and sometimes of speech.

Choreal, Choreic —Pertaining to chorea.

Choreiform —Of the nature of chorea. Resembling chorea.

Choreoathetoid —Pertaining to or characterized by choreoathetosis.

Choreoathetosis —Combination of jerky involuntary movements of the body (of the chroeic type) and involuntary slow, irregular, twisting, snakelike movements of the hands and fingers (of the athetoid type), seen frequently in cerebral palsy.

Choreoid —Choreiform.

Choreomania —Dancing mania.

Choreophrasia —Repetition of meaningless words or phrases.

Chorial —Pertaining to the chorion.

Chorioadenoma —Adenoma of the chorion.

Chorioallantoic —Pertaining to the chorioallantois.

Chorioallantois —The structure formed by the union of the chorion and the allantois which develops into placenta.

Chorioamnionitis — Inflammation of the membranes covering the fetus.

Chorioangioma —A tumor of the blood vessels of the chorion.

Chorioangiomatosis — Chorioangiosis.

Chorioangiosis —Abnormal increasement in the number of blood vessels in the placental villi.

Choriocapillaris—Capillary layer of the choroid.

Choriocarcinoma —Carcinoma (cancer) of the chorion.

Choriocele —Protrusion of the choroid coat of the eye through an aperture of the sclera.

Chorioepithelioma — Choriocarcinoma.

Choriogenesis —Formation of the chorion.

Choriomammotropin —Human placental lactogen.

Chorion —The outermost membrane of the fetus.

Chorionic —Pertaining to the chorion.

Chorionic plate —The portion of the chorion attached to the uterus through the placenta.

Chorionic villi —Vascular projections arising from the chorion.

Chorionitis —Inflammation of the chorion.

Chorioretinal —Pertaining to the choroid and the retina of the eye.

Chorioretinitis —Inflammation of the choroid and the retina.

Chorioretinopathy —An non inflammatory disease of both, the choroid and the retina.

Chorista —Defective development in which the tissues have grown in a displaced position.

Choristoma —A tumor of the overdeveloping embryonic rudiments.

Choroid —The middle vascular coat of the eye between the sclera and the retina.

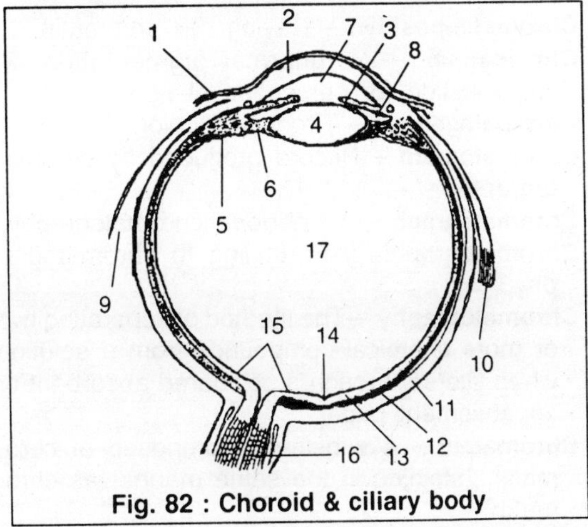

Fig. 82 : Choroid & ciliary body

1. Conjunctiva 2. Cornea. 3. Iris. 4. Lens. 5. Ciliary body. 6. Suspensory ligament. 7. Anterior chamber. 8. Posterior chamber 9. & 10. Muscles of the eyeball 11. Sclera. 12. Choroid. 13. Retina. 14. Macula lutea. 15. Optic disc. 16. Optic nerve. 17. Vitreous body.

Choroidal —Pertaining to the choroid.

Choroidea —Choroid.

Choroideremia —Hereditary primary degeneration of the choroid, which causes blindness in male but females are not affected and so the vision is usually normal in them.

Choroiditis —Inflammation of the choroid.

Choroidocyclitis — Inflammation of the choroid and the ciliary processes.

Choroidoiritis — Inflammation of the choroid and the iris.

Choroidopathy —Any disease of the choroid.

Choroidoretinitis — Inflammation of the choroid and the retina.

Choroidosis —Choroidopathy.

Choromania —A form of chorea. Dance mania.

Chromaffin —Staining strongly with chromium salts, as certain cells of the adrenal glands.

Chromaffinoma —1. Tumor containing chromaffin cells. 2. Pheochromocytoma.

Chromaffinopathy —Any disease of the chromaffin tissue.

Chromatic —Pertaining to color.

Chromatid —One of the two halves into which a chromosome is divided.

Chromatin —A deeply staining substance present in the nucleus of a cell which contains the genetic material.

Chromatin-negative —Lacking sex chromatin.

Chromatinolysis —Destruction of chromatin.

Chromatinorrhexis — Fragmentation of the chromatin.

Chromatin-positive —Having sex chromatin.

Chromatism —1. Abnormal pigmentation. 2. Hallucination for perception of color.

Chromatogenous —Producing color.

Chromatogram —Record produced by chromatography.

Chromatograph —To perform chromatography.

Chromatographic —Pertaining to chromatography.

Chromatography —The method of separating two or more chemical compounds from a solution when filtered through a powdered absorbent or an absorbent paper.

Chromatoid —A substance composed of chromatin ; staining in the same manner as chromatin.

Chromatokinesis —The movement of chromatin during a cell division.

Chromatolysis —1. Disintegration of the chromatin of cell nuclei. 2. Disintegration of Nissl's bodies in neurons as a result of injury or in some pathological conditions.

Chromatolytic —Pertaining to chromatolysis.

Chromatometer —Colorimeter. An instrument for measuring color perception.

Chromatopectic —Chromopectic. Pertaining to or causing chromatopexis.

Chromatopexis —Chromopexis. The fixation of color or staining fluid.

Chromatophil, Chromatophilic —A cell or structure staining easily.

Chromatophilia —Chromophilia.

Chromatophobia—Chromophobia.

Chromatophore—A pigment-containing cell.

Chromatoplasm—The part of the cytoplasm containing pigment.

Chromatopsia —A defective vision in which the colorless things appear to be colored and colored things seem colorless.

Chromatoptometry—Measurement of color perception.

Chromatosis —Pigmentation.

Chromatotropism —A change of color.

Chromaturia —Abnormal color of the urine.

Chromesthesia —Association of color sensations with words, taste, smell or sounds.

Chromhidrosis —Chromidrosis.

Chromidiosis —Movement of chromatin and nuclear substance from the nucleus to the cytoplasm of the cell.

Chromidrosis, Chromhidrosis —Excretion of colored sweat.

Chromoblast —An embryonic cell which develops into a pigment cell.

Chromocenter —Karyosome.

Chromocrinia —Secretion or excretion of pigmented matter.

Chromocystoscopy —Cystoscopic examination of the ureteral orifices after giving a dye substance orally to the patient.

Chromocyte—Any colored or pigmented cell.

Chromocytometer—Instrument for determining the hemoglobin in red blood cells.

Chromodacryorrhea—The flow of bloody tears.

Chromogen —Any substance which gives rise to a coloring matter.

Chromogenesis —Formation of pigment.

Chromogenic —Producing the color or pigment.

Chromolysis —Chromatolysis.

Chromometer —Colorimeter. An apparatus for determining the pigment in a substance.

Chromometry —Colorimetry. Measuring of coloring matter in a substance.

Chromomycosis —A chronic fungal infection of the skin which is characterized by itching and wart like nodules or papillomas which may ulcerate.

Chromonychia —Abnormality in the color of the nails.

Chromoparic —Chromogenic.

Chromopectic —Chromatopectic.

Chromopexis —Chromatopexis.

Chromophane —Pigment of retina.

Chromophil —Easily stainable cell or tissue.

Chromophilia —Chromatophilia. The property of most of the cells of staining readily with appropriate dyes.

Chromophilic, Chromophilous —Chromatophilic. Chromatophilous. Staining readily with appropriate dyes.

Chromophobe —Any cell, tissue or structure which does not stain easily or stains poorly or not at all—as the chromophobe cells of the anterior pituitary gland.

Chromophobia —Condition of staining poorly with dyes.

Chromophobic —Resistant to staining.

Chromophore —A chemical present in a compound which gives a definite color to the compound.

Chromophoric —1. Pertaining to a chromophore. 2. Bearing color.

Chromophose —Subjective sensation of a color spot in the eye.

Chromophototherapy — Chromotherapy.

Chromopsia —Chromatopsia.

Chromoptometer —An instrument for measuring the acuity of vision.

Chromoradiometer —An instrument for measuring the penetrative power of X-rays.

Chromoscope —An instrument for determining the color perception.

Chromoscopy —Examination of color vision.

Chromosomal —Pertaining to the chromosomes.

Chromosome —A thread-like structure in the nucleus of a cell which transmits the hereditary characters to the offspring.

Chromotherapy —Treatment of diseases by colored light.

Chromotoxic —A condition caused by toxic action of a substance on the hemoglobin.

Chromotrichia —Coloration of the hair.

Chromotrichial —Pertaining to the coloring of the hair.

Chromotropic —1. Being attracted towards a color. 2. Attracting color.

Chromoureteroscopy — Inspection of the ureteral orifices by cystoscope after giving a dye substance orally, which makes the urine colored.

Chronaxie, Chronaxy —The minimum time taken by an electric current to flow at double voltage to cause a muscle to contract.

Chronaximeter —An apparatus for measuring chronaxie.

Chronaximetry —The measurement of chronaxie.

Chronic —Of long duration, old.

Chronicity —State of being chronic.

Chronognosis —Realization of the lapse of time.

Chronograph —An apparatus for recording short intervals of time.

Chronometry —Measurement of intervals of time.

Chronological —Occurring in natural sequence according to time.

Chronophobia —Morbid fear of the duration of time especially in prisoners.

Chronoscope —An apparatus for measuring extremely short intervals of time.

Chronotaraxis —Inability to perceive the sense of time.

Chronotropic —Affecting the rate of occurrence of a periodical movement such as the heart beat.

Chronotropism —Interference with the regularity of a periodical movement, such as the heart beat.

Chronotropism negative —It decreases the rate of the heart beat.

Chronotropism positive —It increases the rate of the heart beat.

Chrysiasis —Deposition of gold in the living tissues as in gold therapy.

Chrysocyanosis —Bluish coloration of the skin as a reaction occurring as a result of the treatment of a disease with gold salts.

Chrysoderma —Pigmentation of the skin due to deposition of gold.

Chrysotherapy —Treatment with gold.

Chylangioma —A tumor of the intestinal lymph vessels filled with chyle.

Chylaqueous —Pertaining to watery chycle.

Chyle —A milky fluid consisting of the products of digestion and mainly of absorbed fat, present in the lacteals of the villi of the small intestine, which is carried by the lymphatic vessels to the cisterna chyli (dilatation of the thoracic duct in the abdomen) and then through the thoracic duct to the left subclavian vein, where it enters the blood stream.

Chylectasia —Dilatation of a lacteal.

Chylemia —Presence of chyle in the blood.

Chylidrosis —Sweating of a milky fluid resembling the chyle.

Chylifacient —Forming chyle.

Chylifaction, Chylification —The formation of chyle.

Chylifactive —Chylopoietic.

Chyliferous —1. Forming chyle. 2. Carrying chyle.

Chyliform —Resembling chyle.

Chylocele —Elephantiasis of the scrotum or the enlargement of the scrotum due to distension of the tunica vaginalis, the covering layers of the testes, with chyle.

Chylocyst —Cisterna chyli, dilated portion of the thoracic duct in the abdomen.

Chyloderma —Accumulation of lymph in the enlarged lymphatic vessels and the thickened skin of the scrotum, due to filaria; scrotal elephantiasis.

Chylology —The study of chyle.

Chylomediastinum — Presence of chyle in the mediastinum.

Chylomicron —Small particle of chyle in the blood after digestion and absorption of fat of the food.

Chylomicronemia —The presence of increased number of chylomicrons in the blood.

Chylopericardium —Chyle in the pericardium.

Chyloperitoneum —Chyle in the peritoneal cavity.

Chylophoric —Carrying chycle, chyliferous.

Chylopleura —Chylothorax.

Chylopneumothorax —Presence of chyle and air in the pleural cavity.

Chylopoiesis —Formation of chyle and its absorption by lacteals in the intestines.

Chylopoietic —Chylofactive. Pertaining to the formation of chyle.

Chylorrhea —Escape of chyle due to rupture of the thoracic duct.

Chylosis —The formation of chyle from the ingested food in the intestine, its digestion, and absorption by the intestinal walls into the blood and conveyance to the tissues.

Chylothorax —Presence of the chyle in the pleural cavities.

Chylous —Pertaining to or of the nature of chyle.

Chyluria —Presence of chyle in the urine due to which the urine becomes white.

Chymase —An enzyme in the gastric juice that accelerates the action of the pancreatic juice.

Chyme —The partly digested semifluid food mixed with the digestive secretions found in the stomach and the small intestine during digestion of food.

Chymification —Conversion of food into chyme.

Chymopoiesis —Chymification.

Chymorrhea —The flow of chyme.

Chymotrypsin —A digestive enzyme produced by the pancreas.

Chymous —Pertaining to chyme.

Chymus —Chyme.

Chytide —A skin wrinkle.

Cibisotome —An instrument for incision of capsule of a lens of the eye.

Cibophobia —Morbid fear of food.

Cicatrectomy —Excision of a scar.

Cicatrices —Plural of cicatrix.

Cicatricial —Pertaining to a scar.

Cicatricotomy —To incise a scar.

Cicatrix —A scar, fibrous tissue left by the healed wound.

Cicatrizant —Helping in or causing cicatrization.

Cicatrization —Healing of a wound by the formation of a scar.

Cicatrize —To heal by scar formation.

-cide —A suffix denoting an agent that kills.

Cilia —1. The eyelashes. 2. Minute hairlike processes projecting from a cell surface as from the epithelial cells in the bronchi that propel the mucus, pus and dust particles.

Ciliariscope —An instrument for examination of the ciliary portion of the eye.

Ciliarotomy —Surgical division of the ciliary zone as done in glaucoma.

Ciliary —Pertaining to or resembling the cilia, used particularly for eyelashes or the ciliary body or muscle of the eye.

Ciliary apparatus, Ciliary body —The thickened middle part of the tunica vasculosa oculi, the middle membrane of the eyeball.

Ciliary glands —A form of the sweat glands of the eyelid.

Ciliary muscle —Smooth muscle forming a part of the ciliary body of the eye.

Ciliate, Ciliated —Possessing cilia.

Cilliectomy —Excision of a portion of the ciliary body or of the eyelid containing the roots of the lashes.

Ciliocytophthoria —The presence of detached motile ciliary tufts in various body fluids, especially respiratory secretion.

Ciliogenesis —Formation of cilia.
Cilioretinal —Pertaining to the ciliary body and the retina.
Cilioscleral —Pertaining to the ciliary body and the sclera.
Ciliospinal —Pertaining to the ciliary body and the spinal cord.
Ciliostatic —Preventing the movements of the cilia.
Ciliotomy —Surgical cutting of the ciliary nerve.
Ciliotoxicity —The action of a drug or substance that interferes the ciliary activity.
Cilium —Singular of cilia.
Cillosis —Spasmodic twitching of an eyelid.
Cimex —Bedbug.
Cimicosis —Itching produced by biting of a bedbug.
Cinanesthesia —Kinanesthesia.
Cinchona —The dried bark of the tree cinchona, which is the source of quinine.
Cinchonism or quininism — Poisoning by cinchona or its alkaloid quinine.
Cinclisis —Speedy spasmodic movement of any part of the body.
Cincture sensation —Feeling of a tight girdle around the waist (the part of body below the ribs and above the hips).
Cinder —Ash.
Cine- —Prefix indicating a relationship to the movement.
Cineangiocardiography — Photographic recording of heart and the blood vessels by using fluoroscope after an injection of a radiopaque substance.
Cinecystourethrogram —A radiograph of the moving urinary bladder and urethra when they have been filled with and are eliminating a radiopaque substance.
Cinefluorography — Cineradiography.
Cinematics —Science of motion.
Cinematoradiography —X-ray of an organ in motion.
Cinemicrography —To record a motion picture of an object seen through microscope.
Cineraceous —Like ashes.
Cineradiography — Cinefluorography, Cinefluoroscopy. The making of a motion picture record of images produced during fluoroscopic examination.
Cinerea —Gray matter of the brain or the spinal cord.
Cinereal —Pertaining to the cinerea.
Cineritious —Ashen-grey color.
Cineurography —Radiography of the urinary tract in motion.
Cion —The uvula.
Cionitis —Inflammation of the uvula.
Circadian —Occurring at about 24 hrs. intervals.
Circhoral —Occurring once in an hour.
Circinate —Circular.
Circle —Any ring-shaped structure.
Circoid —Snake like.
Circuit —1. Circular path of an electric current. 2. Path of a fluid circulating in tubes. 3. The path of nerve impulses in a reflex arc from sensory receptor to the effector organ.
Circular —1. Circle-shaped. 2. Recurrent.
Circulation —Movement in a regular or circular course as blood moves through the heart and blood vessels.

Blood circulation —The circulation in which the blood leaving the heart flowing through the arteries, capillaries and veins, returns back to the heart.

Circulation of bile salts —Bile salts sodium glycocholate and taurocholate with other substances excreted by the liver, are absorbed by the intestinal mucosa and returned back to the liver via the portal circulation.

Collateral circulation — Circulation taking place through the secondary channels after obstruction of the principal channel supplying the part.

Coronary circulation — Circulation of blood in the myocardium of the heart through the coronary vessels.

Extracorporeal circulation —Circulation of blood outside the body as through an artificial kidney or heart-lung apparatus.

Fetal circulation —Flow of impure blood from the fetus to the placenta through the umbilical artery and the returning of oxygenated or pure blood from the placenta to the fetus through the umbilical vein.

Lymph circulation — Lymph formed from the tissue fluid filling the tissue spaces of the body, is collected into the lymphatic capillaries and carried to the larger lymph vessels, which unite together to form right lymphatic duct, and the thoracic duct which drain the whole body and empty in the larger veins.

Portal circulation —In general, circulation of blood from the capillaries of one organ, through larger vessels to those of another; applied especially to the flow of blood from the gastrointestinal tract and spleen through the portal vein to the liver.

Pulmonary circulation — Flow of blood from the right ventricle through pulmonary artery to the lungs, where the blood is purified *i.e.*, oxygenated and returned back through the pulmonary vein to the left atrium.

Systemic circulation —General circulation of blood through the whole body except the lungs.

Venous circulation — Circulation of blood via the veins.

Circulation rate —The amount of blood escaped from the heart per minute which in adult of average size with the pulse rate of 70, is about 3 litres per square meter of body surface each minute.

Circulation time —The time taken by the blood to flow through both, the systemic and pulmonary circulatory systems, to complete the circuit which is measured by injecting a substance into a vein and determining the time of its appearance in the arteries at the point of injection.

Circulatory —Pertaining to circulation.

Circulatory collapse —Shock.

Circulatory failure — Failure of the cardiovascular system to provide the body tissues with enough blood for proper functioning.

Circulatory system —The system consisting of the heart and the blood vessels. (arteries, arterioles, capillaries, venules, veins and sinuses) and lymphatic system.

Circulus —Circle or ring.

Circum- —Prefix meaning around.

Circumanal —Surrounding the anus.

Circumarticular —Around a joint.

Circumcise —To remove the end of the prepuce or foreskin of the penis by operation.

Circumcision —Surgical removal of the end of the foreskin or prepuce of the penis.

Circumcorneal —Surrounding the cornea.

Circumduction —Circular movement of a limb or eye.

Circumference —Circumferentia. The outer boundary of a circular area.

Circumferentia —Circumference.

Circumferential —Encircling or concerning the periphery or circumference of the body.

Circumflex —Winding around, as a vessel.

Circumintestinal —Perienteric. Around the intestine.

Circumlental —Situated or occurring around the lens of the eye.

Circummandibular —Around the mandible.

Circumnuclear —Surrounding or occurring around the nucleus.

Circumocular —Surrounding or occurring around the eye.

Circumoral —Perioral. Around the mouth.

Circumorbital —Surrounding the orbit.

Circumrenal —Around the kidney.

Circumscribed —Confined to a limited space.

Circumstantiality —A symptom of the mental disease in which there is disturbance in the flow of thought and the patient begins to make irrelevant talks.

Circumvallate —Surrounded by a wall, ridge or raised structure.

Circumvascular —Perivascular, around a blood vessel.

Cirrhosis —Hardening of the liver due to the formation of fibrous tissue.

Alcoholic cirrhosis — Cirrhosis of the liver occurs in about 20% of chronic alcoholics.

Atrophic cirrhosis — Cirrhosis in which the liver is atrophied *i.e.,* decreased in size.

Biliary cirrhosis — Cirrhosis of the liver due to chronic retention of the bile, inflammation of the bile ducts or obstruction of the common bile duct by a stone or tumor, etc.

Cardiac cirrhosis —Cirrhosis occurring in congestion of the liver due to congestive heart failure.

Fatty cirrhosis — Cirrhosis of the liver in which the liver cells become infiltrated with fat.

Hypertrophic cirrhosis — Cirrhosis in which the liver is enlarged due to hypertrophy.

Infantile cirrhosis — Cirrhosis of the liver occurring in childhood due to protein deficiency.

Metabolic cirrhosis — Cirrhosis of the liver due to metabolic diseases such as hemochromatosis, glycogen storage disease, galactosemia and wilson's disease etc.

Posthepatitic cirrhosis —Cirrhosis of the liver following hepatitis.

Syphilitic cirrhosis —Cirrhosis of the liver occurring in the tertiary stage of syphilis in which gummas are formed in the liver.

Toxic cirrhosis — Cirrhosis resulting from

toxic substances as in poisoning by carbon tetrachloride or phosphorus.

Cirrhotic —Pertaining to or suffering from cirrhosis.

Cirsectomy —Excision of a portion of a varicose vein.

Cirsoid —Resembling a varix. Varicose.

Cirsomphalos —Varicose veins around the umbilicus, caput medusae.

Cirsophthalmia —Varicosity of the blood vessels of the conjunctiva.

Cirsotome —An instrument for cutting the varicose veins.

Cirsotomy —Treatment of varicosity by making multiple incisions in the varicose vein.

Cissa —Abnormal craving to eat not eatable materials.

Cistern —A receptacle for storage of fluid.

Cisterna —A sac or cavity.

Cisterna chyli —The dilated portion of the thoracic duct at its origin in the abdominal cavity.

Cisterna subarachnoidalis —The wide space between the arachnoid and the pia mater of the brain, which contains cerebrospinal fluid.

Cisternal —Pertaining to a closed space filled with fluid.

Cisternal puncture —A puncture with a hollow needle between the cervical vertebrae, into the space between the dura mater and the arachnoid mater of the spinal cord.

Cisternography —X-ray examination of the basal cistern of the brain after giving an injection of a radiopaque substance into the subarachnoid space.

Citrated —Containing a citrate as blood containing sodium citrate to prevent its clotting.

Citrate solution —A solution which is used to prevent clotting of the blood.

Citrulline —An amino acid formed from ornithine. It is present in watermelons.

Citrullinemia —Presence of increased amount of citrulline in the blood.

Citrullinuria —Presence of increased amount of citrulline in the urine.

Clairvoyance —Ability to be aware of a distant event without using the senses.

Clammy —Adhesive, sticky.

Clamp —A surgical instrument used to grasp, join, compress or support an organ, structure or vessel.

Clang —Loud metallic sound.

Clap —Gonorrhea.

Clapotage, Clapotement — A splashing sound heard in succussion of a dilated stomach.

Clapping —Percussion of the chest to loosen secretions, also called tapping.

Clapton's lines —Green lines on dental margin of gums in copper poisoning.

Clarificant —The substance which clears the turbidity of a liquid.

Clarification —The process of making a solution free of turbidity.

Clark's rule —A method of calculating the pediatric drug dosages. For this the weight of the child in pounds is multiplied by the adult dose and the result is divided by 150.

Clasmatocyte —Macrophage.

Clasmatosis —Fragmentation, as of the cells.

Clasp —An apparatus by which something is held.

Clastic —That divides into parts.

Clastogen —An agent that causes breaks in chromosomes.

Clastogenic —Which breaks.

Clastothrix —Splitting of the hair.

Claudication —Lameness.

Intermittent claudication —A severe pain in the calf muscles which occurs during walking but subsides with rest and results from inadequate supply of blood which may be due to occlusive arterial diseases.

Venous claudication — Claudication due to venous stasis.

Claudicatory —Pertaining to claudication, especially intermittent claudication.

Claustra —Plural of claustrum.

Claustral —Pertaining to claustrum.

Claustrophilia —A morbid fear of being in an open place and an abnormal desire to be in a closed room or space.

Claustrophobia —Morbid fear of being in a locked room or closed places.

Claustrum —1. A barrier. 2. A thin layer of gray matter lateral to the external capsule, separating it from the white matter of the insula, in the cerebral hemisphere.

Clausura —Atresia .

Clava —An elevation on the dorsal surface of the medulla oblongata.

Claval —Pertaining to the clava.

Clavate —Club-shaped.

Clavicle —Collar bone, the bone curved like the

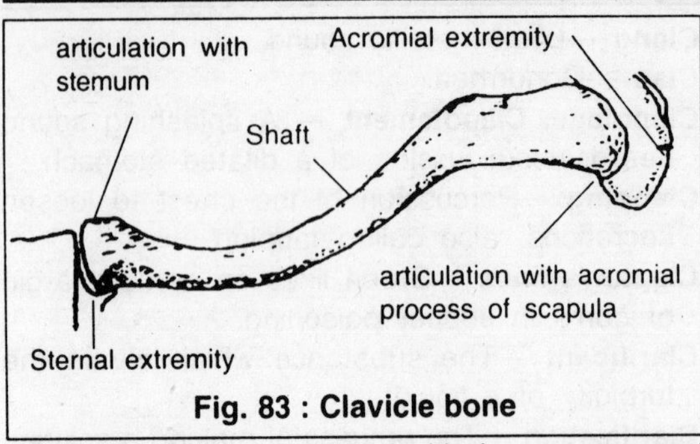

Fig. 83 : Clavicle bone

letter `f ' which articulates with the sternum and the scapula.

Clavicotomy —Surgical division of the clavicle bone.

Clavicular —Pertaining to the clavicle bone.

Clavipectoral —Pertaining to the clavicle and the chest.

Clavus —1. A corn or callosity. 2. A sharp pain in the head which is felt like a nail being driven into it.

Clawfoot —A deformity of the foot in which the sole of the foot is higly arched and the toes hyperextended at the metatarsophalangeal joints and flexed at the distal joints.

Clawhand —A deformity of the hand in which there is hyperextension of the proximal phalanges of the fingers and extreme flexion of the middle and distal phalanges, which is usualy due to injury to the ulnar and median nerves.

Claw toe, Hammer toe —A toe in which there is dorsal flexion of the first phalanx and plantar flexion of the second and third phalanges so that the toe looks like a hammer.

Clearance —Complete elimination of a substance by the kidneys from the blood.

Clearing agent —The substance which causes elimination.

Cleavage —Division, especially the cell division of a fertilized ovum.

Cleavage cell —Blastomere.

Cleaver —A heavy knife for cutting or chopping.

Cleft —A fissure or an elongated opening.

Cleft anal —Anal fissure.

Cleft lip —Hare lip. A congenital cleft of the upper lip which may be associated with cleft palate.

Fig. 84 : Cleft lip

Cleft palate —A congenital fissure in the roof of the mouth by which the mouth and the nasal cavities are connected.

Cleidagra, Clidagra —Sudden severe pain in the clavicle, resembling gout.

Cleidal —Clidal. Pertaining to the clavicle.

Cleido- —Prefix pertaining to the clavicle.

Cleidocostal —Pertaining to the clavicle and the ribs.

Cleidocranial —Pertaining to the clavicle and the head.

Cleidomastoid —Pertaining to the clavicle and the mastoid.

Cleidorrhexis —Fracture or bending of the clavicles of the fetus for delivery.

Cleidotomy —Surgical division of a clavicle bone of the fetus in difficult labour to facilitate the delivery.

Clenching —Grinding the teeth.

Cleoid —A dental instrument with a pointed elliptical cutting end used in evacuating the dental cavities.

Cleptomania —Mania for stealing the things in which there is no relation with the intrinsic value of the stolen article and there is often deep regret following the act.

Click —A sharp short sound heard during a joint movement.

Climacophobia —Morbid fear of climbing up.

Climacteric —The end of the reproductive period in female (female climacteric or menopause), a diminution of sexual activity in the male (male climacteric).

Climatology, medical —A branch of meteorolgy which includes the study of climate (rainfall, temperature etc.) and its relationship to the disease.

Climatotherapy —Treatment of a disease by changing the climate.

Climax —1. The period of greatest intensity, as in the course of a disease. 2. The sexual orgasm.

Climograph —A diagram showing the effect of climate on health.

Clinic —A place where the diagnosis is made and the treatment is given to a patient.

Clinical —Pertaining to a clinic or to actual observation and treatment of patients.

Clinical analysis —The chemical analysis and study of body fluids, excreta and tissues, etc., in the diagnosis and treatment of a disease.

Clinical thermometer —A mercury or electronic instrument that measures the body temperature.

Clinical trial —Observation of the effects of a drug given to a patient for curing a certain disease.

Clinician —A physician or dentist expert in clinical practice.

Clinicopathologic — Pertaining to both, the symptoms and pathology of a disease.

Clinocephalic, Clinocephalous —Pertaining to clinocephaly.

Clinocephaly —Congenital flatness or concavity of the top of the head.

Clinodactyly —Permanent deviation of one or more fingers.

Clinography —To prepare a graphic record of the signs and symptoms of a disease.

Clinoid —Resembling a bed in shape.

Clinometer —Clinoscope.

Clinoscope —An instrument for measuring the weakness of the ocular muscles.

Clinostatism —The recumbent position.

Clip —A metallic instrument for holding the edges of a wound, or other material together, or for preventing the bleeding from small blood vessels.

Cliseometer —An instrument for measuring the angles between the axis of the body and that of the pelvis.

Clithrophobia —Morbid fear of being locked in.

Clitoridean —Pertaining to the clitoris.

Clitoridectomy —Excision of the clitoris.

Clitoriditis —Inflammation of the clitoris.

Clitoridotomy —To incise the clitoris.

Clitoris —A small, elongated, erectile structure in the female genital organs, homologous to the penis in the male.

Clitoris crisis —Sudden sexual excitement in woman with tabes dorsalis.

Clitorism —1. Persistent painful erection of the clitoris homologous to priapism in man. 2. Enlargement of the clitoris due to hypertrophy.

Clitoritis, Clitoriditis —Inflammation of the clitoris.

Clitoromegaly, Clitorimegaly —Enlargement of the clitoris.

Clitoroplasty —Plastic surgery of the clitoris.

Clival —Pertaining to the clivus.

Clivus —Slopping surface, as the sphenoid bone.

Clonal —Pertaining to a clone.

Clone —A group of organisms or cells derived from a single organism or cell by asexual reproduction.

Clonic —Pertaining to clonus; alternately contracting and relaxing the muscles.

Clonicity —Condition of being clonic.

Clonicotonic —Both clonic and tonic as some forms of muscular spasm.

Clonic spasm —Spasm in which there is muscular rigidity and then relaxation.

Clonism —A long continued state of clonic spasm.

Clonogenic —Arising from or consisting of a clone.

Clonograph —An apparatus for recording spasmodic movements of the parts.

Clonospasm, Clonic spasm —Rapid alternate contraction and relaxation of the muscles.

Clonus —Rapid involuntary alternate muscular contraction and relaxation.

Clostridia —Plural of clostridium.

Clostridial —Pertaining to any bacterium of the genus Clostridium.

Clostridium —A type of bacteria which is found in the soil, intestinal tract of man and domestic animals, and in the wound infections. There are about 250 species of it, some of them are as follows.

Clostridium bifermentans —It is found in the soil and feces and causes gas gangrene.

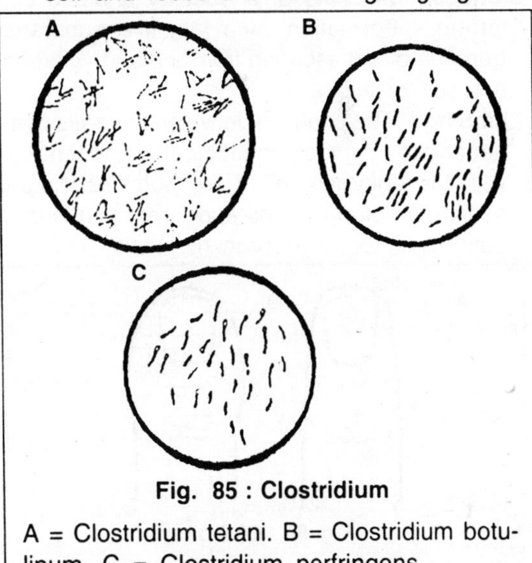

Fig. 85 : Clostridium

A = Clostridium tetani. B = Clostridium botulinum. C = Clostridium perfringens

Clostridium botulinum —It grows in improperly preserved foods and produces a powerful toxin which causes botulism.

Clostridium difficile —Species of bacteria whose toxin causes enterocolitis.

Clostridium novyi —It is an important cause of gas gangrene.

Clostridium perfringens —It commonly causes gas gangrene.

Clostridium tetani — The bacterium which causes tetanus or lockjaw.

Clostridium welchii — Bacterium producing gas gangrene.

Clot —1. A thrombus or a coagulum, as of blood or lymph. 2. To coagulate.

Clot agony —Clot formed in the heart during death agony.

Clot antemortem —Clot formed in the heart before death.

Clot of blood —A coagulum formed of blood.

Clot external —Clot formed outside the blood vessel.

Clot internal —Clot of blood formed inside the blood vessel.

Clot muscle —Clot formed in a muscle.

Clot passive —Clot formed in the sac of an aneurysm causing cessation or slowing of blood circulation through the aneurysm.

Clot plastic —Clot formed from the intima of an artery at the point of ligation.

Clot postmortem —Clot formed in the heart or a large blood vessel after death.

Clottage —Blocking of a duct by a blood clot.

Clotting —Formation of a jelly-like substance from the blood escaped from a blood vessel as a result of injury.

Clubbing —The condition in which the nails of the hands are curved longitudinally and laterally with the enlargement of the soft tissues presenting a bulbous shiny appearance. It is most commonly found in bronchiectasis.

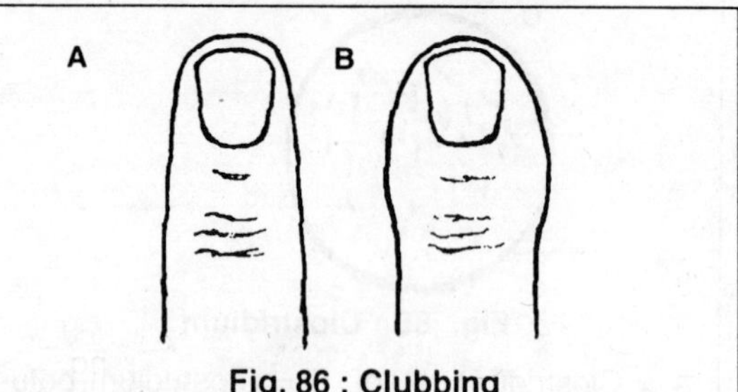

Fig. 86 : Clubbing

A = Normal finger
B = Clubbed finger

Clubfoot —Talipes equinovarus. Congenitally deformed foot.

Clubhand —Talipomanus. Deformity of the hand resembling clubfoot.

Clump —1. A mass of bacteria in solution. 2. To bring together.

Clumping —The aggregation of particles, such as bacteria, into masses.

Cluneal —Pertaining to the buttocks.

Clunes —The buttocks.

Cluttering —A speech defect characterized by omission of letters or syllables.

Clysis —Administration of a fluid into the body other than orally to replace the lost body fluid, supply nutrients or to raise the blood pressure.

Clysma, Clyster —An enema.

Cm —Centimeter.

Cm2 —Square centimeter.

Cm3 —Cubic centimeter.

C/min —Counts per minute.

C.mm —Cubic millimeter.

Cnemial —Pertaining to the leg, especially the shin.

Cnemis —Shin, lower leg, tibia bone.

Cnemitis —Inflammation of the shin.

Cnemoscoliosis —Bending of the leg laterally.

C.N.S. —Central nervous system.

Co —Chemical symbol for cobalt.

CO —Symbol for carbon monoxide.

CO_2 —Formula for carbon dioxide.

Coadaptation —Mutual correlated, adaptive changes in two interdependent organs.

Coadunation —Union of two dissimilar substances in one mass.

Coagglutination —The aggregation of the corpuscles of another organism by an antigen and the homologous antibody.

Coagula —Plural of coagulum.

Coagulability —The condtion of being capable of forming clots, especially the blood clots.

Coagulable —Capable of being clotted.

Coagulant —Which causes coagulation of a fluid.

Coagulase —Any enzyme such as thrombin which causes coagulation.

Coagulate —1. To clot. 2. To become clotted.

Coagulated —Clotted.

Coagulation —The process of clotting or the formation of a clot as in the coagulation of blood. In clotting of the blood the substances–prothrombin, thrombin, thromboplastin, calcium in ionic form and fibrinogen play an important role. Prothrombin is converted into thrombin by the action of thromboplastin in the presence of calcium ions. Thrombin then acts on the soluble fibrinogen of the plasma converting it into insoluble fibrin which forms a network of fibers in which the blood corpuscles are entangled, thus forming a clot.

Coagulative —That causes coagulation.
Coagulometer —An apparatus for measuring the blood's coagulation time.
Coagulopathy —Any defect in blood clotting.
Coagulum —1. A blood clot. 2. Curd.
Coalesce —To fuse.
Coalescence —The fusion together of two or more parts of the body.
Coal worker's pneumoconiosis —A form of pneumoconiosis in which carbon and silica are accumulated in the lungs due to breathing of the coal dust.
Coapt —To bring together as in suturing the edges of a wound.
Coaptation —The process of bringing together as the edges of a wound in suturing.
Coarct —Coarctate.
Coarctate —To press together.
Coarctation —Stricture or narrowing.
Coarctotomy —Cutting or division of a stricture.
Coarse — Rough
Coat —A covering or a layer lining an organ as the mucous membrane lining the inner walls of the stomach.
Coca —Dried leaves of a plant from which cocaine is obtained.
Cocaine baby —During pregnancy an infant exposed to cocaine in the uterus through maternal use of cocaine which may cause premature delivery, low birth weight and birth defects.
Cocainism —The habitual use of cocaine.
Cocainization —Production of analgesia by cocaine.
Cocainomania —Intense desire for cocaine.
Cocarcinogen —Any substance or environmental factor which increases the effect of a carcinogen so that a cancer is developed.
Cocarcinogenesis — Development of cancer only in preconditioned cells as a result of favourable conditions to its growth.
Coccal —Pertaining to or caused by cocci.
Cocci —Plural of coccus.

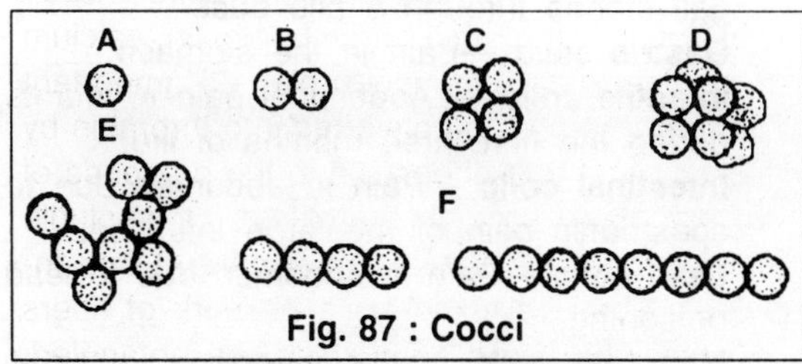

Fig. 87 : Cocci

A = Monococcus. B = Diplococcus. C = Tetrad. D = Cuboid cocci as Sarcina. E = Staphylococci. F = Streptococci

Coccidioidin —An antigenic substance prepared from the fungus Coccidioides immitis, which is used as a skin test in diagnosing coccidioidomycosis.
Coccidioidomycosis, Coccidioidosis —An infection caused by inhalation of the spores of the fungus Coccidioides immitis characterized by respiratory infection with the symptoms of common cold or influenza or the formation of granuloma which may involve any part of the body.
Coccigenic —Produced by cocci.
Coccobacillary —Pertaining to or of a coccobacillus.
Coccobacilli —Plural of coccobacillus.
Coccobacillus —Oval, short and thick bacterium.
Coccobacteria —Spheroid bacteria or any kind of cocci.
Coccogenous —Produced by cocci.
Coccoid —Resembling a coccus.
Coccus—Spherical bacterium slightly less than 1 μ in diameter.
Coccyalgia , Coccydynia —Pain in the coccyx.
Coccycephalus —A monster with beak-shaped head.
Coccycephaly —A malformation in which the head is beak-shaped.
Coccygeal —Pertaining to or in the region of the coccyx.
Coccygectomy —Excision of the coccyx.
Coccygeus, Coccygeal — Pertaining to the coccyx.
Coccygodynia —Pain in the coccyx and the neighbouring region.
Coccygotomy —Incision of the coccyx.
Coccyodynia —Coccydynia. Pain in the coccygeal region.
Coccyx —The lowest bone of the vertebral column formed by the fusion of 3 to 5 vertebrae which articulates above with the sacrum bone.
Cochlea —A spiral tube forming a portion of the inner ear, which is essential for hearing.

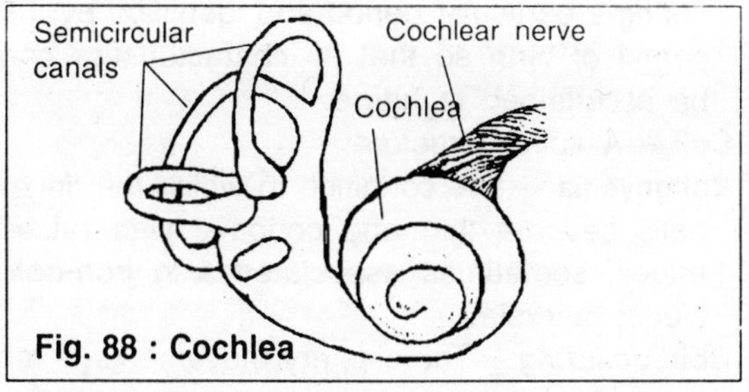

Fig. 88 : Cochlea

Cochlear —Pertaining to the cochlea.

Cochleare —Latin word which indicates a spoon or spoonful, used in writing the prescriptions.

Cochleariform —Spoon-shaped.

Cochleitis, Cochlitis — Inflammation of the cochlea.

Cochleovestibular —Pertaining to the chochlea and vestibule of the ear.

Cock-up toe —A toe deformity with dorsiflexion of the metatarsophalangeal joint and flexion of the interphalangeal joints.

Coctolabile —Capable of being altered or destroyed by heating.

Coctostabile —Incapable of being altered or destroyed by heating.

Codependency —Individual's dependency upon others, alcohol, gambling or sexual activity.

Coefficient —1. A number put before a chemical formula to indicate how many times the formula is to be multiplied. 2. An expression of ratio between two different quantities or the effect produced by variation in certain factors.

Coenesthesia —Cenesthesia.

Coenzyme —An enzyme activator.

Coetaneous —Having the same age or date of birth.

Coeur —Heart.

Coexcitation —Excitement of two parts of the body simultaneously.

Cofactor —A factor with which another factor must unite to function.

Cogan's syndrome —Interstitial keratitis associated with tinnitus, vertigo and deafness.

Cognition —Perception.

Cognitive —Pertaining to perception.

Cogwheel respiration —Repeated sudden brief interruptions of inspiration and expiration.

Coherent —Sticking together as parts of the body.

Cohesion —The property of sticking together.

Cohesive —Adhesive or sticky.

Cohort —A component of the population born during a particular period and identified by the period of birth so that its characteristics can be ascertained in future.

Coil —A spiral structure.

Coilonychia —The condition in which the finger nails become thin and concave with raised edges, sometimes associated with iron-deficiency anemia.

Coin counting —The slippery movements of the tip of thumb and index finger over each other, which seem as the counting of the coins, in paralysis agitans.

Coinfection —The simultaneous infection of an individual by two different micro-organisms.

Coital —Pertaining to the sexual intercourse.

Coition, Coitus —Sexual intercourse.

Coitophobia —Morbid fear of sexual intercourse.

Coitus —Coition.

Colalgia —Pain in the colon.

Colation —The process of filtering.

Colauxe —Distention of the colon.

Cold —1. Lacking heat or having low temperature. 2. Coryza or common cold in which there is the inflammation of the upper respiratory tract and marked by chilliness, slight rise in temperature with sneezing.

Cold blooded —Changing in temperature according to the temperature of the environment as frog.

Cold pack —Wrapping of a part or the whole body of the patient in wet cloths.

Cold sore —Herpes simplex of the lips and face.

Cold stress —Hypothermia. The falling down of body temperature to below normal.

Colectasia —Distention of the colon.

Colectomy —Excision of the colon or of a portion of it.

Coleocystitis —Inflammation of the vagina and urinary bladder.

Coleoptosis —Prolapse of the vaginal wall.

Coleotomy —Colpotomy. Incision into the vagina.

Colibacillemia —The presence of Escherichia coli in the blood.

Colibacillosis —Infection with Escherichia coli.

Colibacilluria —Presence of Escherichia coli in the urine.

Colic, Colica —1. Spasm of a hollow organ accompanied by pain. 2. Pertaining to the colon.

Appendicular colic — Severe pain in abdomen due to acute appendicitis.

Biliary colic —Colic due to the passage of gall stones through a bile duct.

Gastric colic —Pain in the stomach.

Infantile colic — Abdominal pain in infants during the first three months of life.

Intestinal colic —Pain in abdomen due to spasmodic pain of the large intestine.

Lead colic —Pain in abdomen due to lead poisoning.

Menstrual colic or **dysmenorrhea** —Pain in abdomen at the time of menstruation.

Renal colic —Pain in the kidney region radiating into the thigh, which is usually due to a calculus.

Colicky —Pertaining to or affected by colic.

Colicolitis —Inflammation of the large intestine due to Escherichia coli.

Colicoplegia —Colic and paralysis, both due to lead poisoning.

Colicystitis —Inflammation of the urinary bladder due to Escherichia coli infection.

Colicystopyelitis — Inflammation of the urinary bladder and pelvis of the kidney due to Escherichia coli.

Coliform —1. Sieve like. 2. Pertaining to the bacteria causing fermentation in the intestine, especially to Escherichia coli.

Colinephritis —Inflammation of the kidney caused by Escherichia coli.

Coliplication —Operation for correcting a dilated colon.

Colipuncture, Colocentesis —Surgical puncture of the colon to relieve distention.

Colipyelitis —Inflammation of the renal pelvis and the calices due to Escherichia coli.

Colipyuria —Presence of pus in the urine due to Escherichia coli.

Colisepsis —Infection with Escherichia coli.

Colitis —Inflammation of the colon.

Amebic colitis —Colitis due to the parasite Entameba histolytica.

Mucous colitis —A chronic disease characterized by the colic with diarrhea with the passage of mucus.

Ulcerative colitis — Chronic ulcerations in the colon, manifested by cramping abdominal pain, rectal bleeding, pus and mucus with scanty fecal matter.

Colitoxemia —Toxemia caused by the colon bacillus, Escherichia coli.

Colitoxicosis —Systemic poisoning caused by Escherichia coli.

Colitoxin —A toxin produced by the colon bacillus, Escherichia coli.

Coliuria —Presence of Escherichia coli in the urine.

Colla —Plural of collum.

Collagen —An insoluble protein of white fibers found in the skin, tendon, bone, cartilage, ligament and all other connective tissues.

Collagenation —The appearance of collagen in developing cartilage.

Collagenic, Collagenous — 1. Pertaining to collagen. 2. Producing or containing collagen.

Collagenitis —Inflammation of collagen fibers characterized by pain, swelling and low grade pyrexia.

Collagenization —Production of collagen by fibroblasts.

Collagenogenic —Pertaining to collagen production or forming collagen or collagen fibers.

Collagenolysis —Dissolution or destruction of collagen.

Collagenolytic —Causing lysis or dissolution of the collagen.

Collagenosis —A collagen disease.

Collagenous —Producing or containing collagen.

Collapse —1. A state of sudden extreme depression and weakness due to decreased blood circulation. 2. Abnormal retraction of the walls of an organ.

Collapsing —The person suddenly falling into extreme prostration like shock.

Collar bone —Calvicle bone.

Collateral —1. Accessory or secondary. 2. An accompanying small side branch as of a blood vessel or a nerve.

Collateral circulation — Circulation through collateral vessels when the main artery is obstructed.

Collecting tubules —Small ducts which receive urine from renal tubules.

Colles' fracture —The transverse fracture of the distal end of the radius just above the wrist with the displacement of hand backwards and outwards.

Colliculectomy —Excision of the colliculus seminalis, *i.e.*, an elevation in the floor of the prostatic portion of the urethra.

Colliculitis —Inflammation of the colliculus seminalis.

Colliculus —A small eminence.

Colligation —A combination in which the components are distinguishable from one another.

Collimation —The process of making the light rays parallel. Thus, the X-ray machines are fitted with a collimator to ensure that the rays are parallel and not diffuse.

Colliotomy —Adhesiotomy.

Colliquation —1. Abnormal discharge of a body fluid. 2. Softening of tissues to liquefaction by degeneration.

Colliquative —Pertaining to excessive liquid discharge or to softening of tissues to liquefaction by degeneration.

Collodiaphyseal —Pertaining to the neck and shaft of a long bone, especially of the femur.

Collodion —A liquid preparation containing pyroxylin (gun powder), ether and alcohol which dries to form a strong, thin, transparent film and so it is applied to the skin to close the small wounds.

Collodium —Collodion.

Colloid —A homogenous solution, a solution in which the fine particles of a substance, when dispersed in a solvent, are uniformly distributed and do not settle down on standing silently.

Colloidal—Pertaining to or characteristic of a colloid.

Colloid cyst —A sac containing a jelly-like liquid.

Colloidin —Colloid.

Colloidoclasia —A disturbance in the equilibrium of colloid in the body causing anaphylactic shock.

Colloidogen —A substance that is capable to give rise to a colloidal solution or suspension.

Colloma —A colloid degeneration of a cancer.

Collonema —A tumor, especially a lipoma which has undergone mucoid degeneration.

Collopexia —Fixation of the cervix of the uterus.

Collum —The neck, or the neck-like part of an organ.

Collunarium —A nose-wash.

Collutorium or Collutory —A mouth-wash, gargle.

Collyrium —A lotion for the eyes, an eye wash.

Coloboma —A congenital, pathological or surgical defect of the eye usually a fissure or cleft of the optic nerve, choroid, retina, ciliary body, lens, iris or eye lid.

Colocecostomy —Surgical joining of the colon to the cecum.

Colocentesis—Colipuncture; Colopuncture. Puncture of the colon by surgery to relieve distention.

Colocholecystostomy —To make a connection between colon and the gall bladder.

Coloclysis, Coloclyster — An enema of the colon, a fluid injected into the colon for washing it through the rectum.

Colocolic —From colon to colon.

Colocolostomy —Surgical formation of a connection between two portions of the colon.

Colocutaneous —1. Pertaining to the colon and the skin. 2. A pathological or surgical connection between the colon and the skin.

Colocystoplasty —Enlargement of the urinary bladder by attaching a segment of colon to it.

Coloenteritis —Inflammation of the mucous membranes of the small and large intestines.

Colofixation —The fixation or suspension of the colon in the treatment of ptosis.

Colohepatopexy —Attachment of the colon to the liver by adhesions.

Colomysis —The process of freeing the colon from adhesions.

Colon —The part of the large intestine extending from the cecum to the rectum which is divided into 4 parts—ascending, transverse, descending and sigmoid or pelvic colon. Ascending colon passes upwards from the cecum to the hepatic flexure, where it turns as the transverse colon and passing beneath the liver and stomach reaches the spleen, where at splenic flexure it turns downward and continues as the descending colon to the brim of the pelvis, where it is continous with the sigmoid colon which is situtated in the pelvis and extends to the rectum.

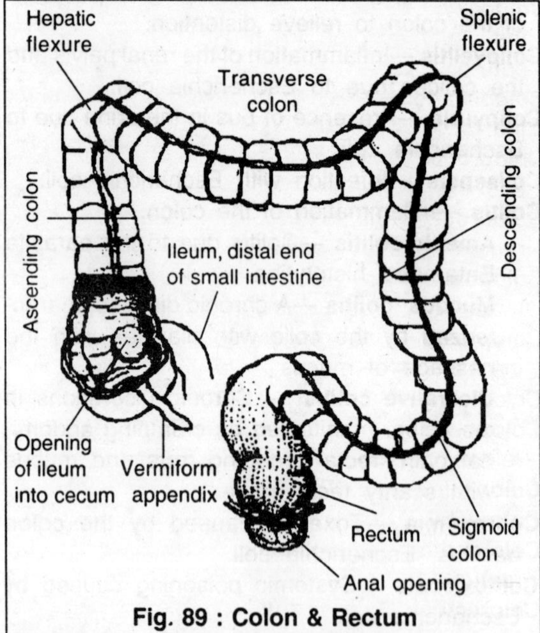

Fig. 89 : Colon & Rectum

Colonalgia —Pain in the colon.

Colonic —Pertaining to the colon.

Colonic irrigation —Injection of a large amount of fluid into the colon in order to fill and flush it.

Colonitis —Colitis. Inflammation of the colon.

Colonization —The process of living together by forming the colonies, as by the bacteria.

Colonogram —Graphic record of movements of the colon.

Colonometer —An apparatus for counting bacterial colonies.

Colonopathy —Any disease of the colon.

Colonopexy —Surgical attachment of a part of the colon to the abdominal wall.

Colonorrhagia —Hemorrhage from the colon.

Colonorrhea —Watery discharge from the colon.

Colonoscope —An instrument for the visual examination of the entire colon.

Colonoscopy —Visual examination of the colon by colonoscope.

Colony —A group of micro-organisms, usually considered to have grown from a single micro-organism as a collection of bacteria in a culture.

Colony counter —An apparatus for counting the bacterial colonies in a culture plate.

Colopexostomy —To cut down a part of the colon and fixing it to the abdominal wall to establish an artificial anus.

Colopexotomy —Incision and fixation of the colon.

Colopexy, Colopexia — Fixation of the cecum or the sigmoid colon to the abdominal wall by suture.

Coloplication —Making of folds in the walls of the colon to reduce its lumen.

Coloproctectomy —Surgical removal of the colon and the rectum.

Coloproctitis —Inflammation of the colon and the rectum.

Coloproctostomy —To make a connection between a segment of the colon and the rectum.

Coloptosia —Prolapse of the colon, especially of the transverse colon.

Coloptosis —Downward displacement of the colon.

Colopuncture —Surgical puncture of the colon to relieve distention.

Color blindness —Defect in color-perception.

Colorectal —Pertaining to the colon and rectum.

Colorectitis —Inflammation of the colon and the rectum.

Colorectostomy —Formation of a passage between the colon and the rectum.

Colorectum —The colon and the rectum.

Color gustation —The sense of color of a thing caused by tasting it.

Color hearing —The sense of color of a thing caused by hearing its sound.

Colorimeter —An instrument for measuring the intensity of color in a substance, especially for measuring the intensity of color of blood to determine the percentage of hemoglobin in the blood.

Colorimetric —Pertaining to colorimetry.

Colorimetry —The process of measurement of the intensity of the blood to determine the percentage of hemoglobin in the blood.

Color Index —The old method of expressing the amount of hemoglobin present in each red blood cell.

Colorrhagia —Colonorrhagia.

Colorrhaphy —Suture of the colon.

Colorrhea —Colonorrhea.

Coloscopy —Colonoscopy. Visual examination of the colon by use of sigmoidoscope.

Colosigmoidostomy — Surgical joining of the descending colon to the sigmoid colon.

Colostomy —Surgical formation of an opening between the colon and the surface of the abdomen.

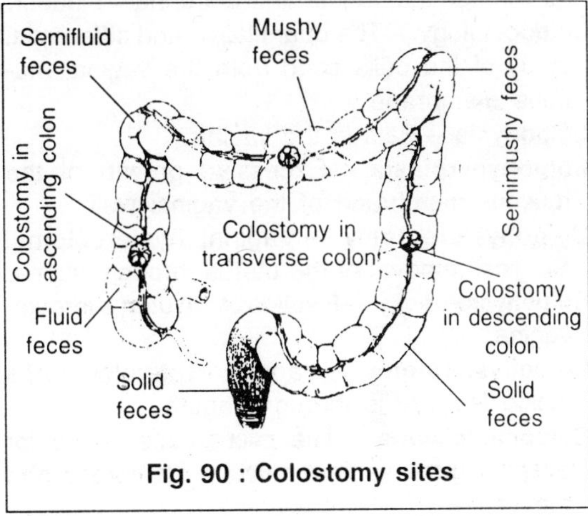

Fig. 90 : Colostomy sites

Colostrorrhea —Abnormal discharge of colostrum.

Collostrous —Containing colostrum.

Colostrum —A thin, yellow fluid secreted by the breasts a few days before, or in the first 2 to 3 days after, birth of the child and before the onset of true lactation.

Colotomy —Incision of the colon.

Colovaginal —Pertaining to the colon and vagina.

Colovesical —Pertaining to the colon and the bladder.

Colpalgia —Pain in the vagina.

Colpatresia —Closure of the vagina.

Colpectasia —Dilatation of the vagina.

Colpectasis —Colpectasia

Colpectomy —Excision of the vagina.

Colpeurynter —Vaginal dilator.

Colpeurysis —Dilatation of the vagina by surgery.

Colpitis —Inflammation of the vagina.
Colpo-, Colp- — A prefix pertaining to the vagina.
Colpocele —Hernia into the vagina.
Colpoceliotomy —To enter the abdomen through the vagina by surgery.
Colpocleisis —To close the vagina by surgery.
Colpocystitis —Inflammation of the vagina and the urinary bladder.
Colpocystocele —Prolapse of the urinary bladder into the vagina.
Colpocystoplasty —Surgical treatment of vesicovaginal fistula.
Colpocystosyrinx —Fistula between urinary bladder and the vagina.
Colpocystotomy —To make an incision into the urinary bladder through the vagina.
Colpocystoureterotomy — Incision into the ureter through the vagina and the urinary bladder.
Colpocytology —The quantitative and differential study of the cells shed from the vaginal mucous membrane.
Colpodynia —Pain in the vagina.
Colpohyperplasia —Excessive growth of the mucous membrane of the vaginal wall.
Colpohysterectomy —Vaginal hysterectomy. Surgical removal of the uterus through vagina.
Colpohysteropexy —Fixation of the uterus through vagina.
Colpohysterotomy —Vaginal hysterotomy. To incise the uterus through vagina.
Colpomicroscope —The microscope used for examining the vaginal mucous membrane and the cervix.
Colpomicroscopy — Examination of the vaginal mucous membrane and the cervix by colpomicroscope.
Colpomycosis — Vaginomycosis.
Colpomyomectomy —Surgical removal of a fibroid tumor of the uterus through the vagina.
Colpomyomotomy —To make an incision into the uterus through the vagina.
Colpoperineoplasty —Repair of the vagina and perineum by plastic surgery.
Colpoperineorrhaphy — Suture of the ruptured perineum and the vagina.
Colpopexy —To fix the relaxed and prolapsed vagina to the abdominal wall by suturing.
Colpoplasty —Plastic surgery of the vagina.
Colpopoiesis —Surgical construction of a vagina.
Colpoptosis —Prolapse of the vagina.
Colporectopexy —Repair of a prolapsed rectum by fixing it to the wall of the vagina.
Colporrhagia —Excessive discharge from the vagina or vaginal hemorrhage.
Colporrhaphy —Suturing of the vaginal wall to narrow the vagina.
Colporrhexis —Laceration of the vaginal walls.
Colposcope —A speculum for examining the vagina and the cervix by means of a magnifying lens.
Colposcopy —Examination of the vagina and cervix by using a colposcope.
Colpospasm, Colpospasmus —Spasm of the vagina.
Colpostat—A device for use in vagina for holding an instrument, such as radium applicator, for the treatment of cancer of the cervix.
Colpostenosis —Narrowing of the vagina.
Colpostenotomy —In vaginal stricture an operation for cutting the stricture to dilate the lumen of the vagina.
Colpotherm —An electrical heating apparatus which is introduced into the vagina.
Colpotomy —Incision into the vagina.
Colpoureterotomy —Incision of the ureter through the vagina.
Colpoxerosis —Abnormal dryness of the vagina.
Columella —A little column, as the anterior fleshy part of the nasal septum.
Column, Columna —A pillar-like supporting structure, as vertebral column which consists of 26 vertebrae (7 cervical, 12 thoracic, 5 lumbar, a sacrum and a coccyx) joined together by the intervertebral disks, forming the main supporting structure of the body, enclosing and protecting the spinal cord.
Columna —Column.
Columnar —Column-shaped.
Columnella —Columella.
Columning, Columnization —The introduction of a tampon into the vagina to support the prolapsed uterus.
Colypeptic —Retarding digestion.
Coma —A state of deep unconsciousness from which the patient cannot be aroused, even by powerful external stimuli.
- **Alcoholic coma** —Coma due to severe alcoholic intoxication.
- **Apoplectic coma** — Coma caused by cerebral stroke.
- **Diabetic coma** —Coma occurring in diabetes due to lack of insulin, and excess production of acetone bodies, causing acidosis.
- **Hepatic coma** —Coma due to liver failure.

Hypoglycemic coma —Coma due to decreased blood sugar level.

Irreversible coma — Brain death, coma from which the patient cannot recover.

Uremic coma —Coma in uremia.

Vigil coma —Coma in which the patient's eyes are widely opened and look as they are staring. Face is expressionless and it may occur in typhoid.

Comatose —Pertaining to or affected with coma.

Combustible —Capable of burning.

Combustion —Burning, or the oxidation of food with production of heat.

Comedo —Black head.

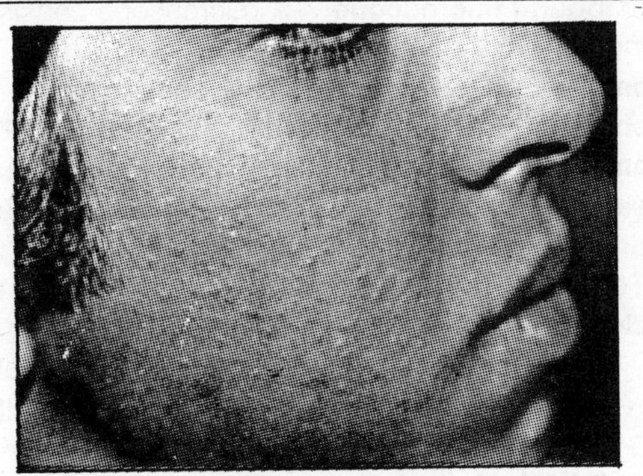

Fig. 91 : Comedones (black heads)

Comedogenic —Producing comedones.

Comes plural **Comites** —A blood vessel which accompanies a nerve or another blood vessel.

Commensal —Living on or within another organism in non-parasitic relationship *i.e.,* deriving benefit without harming or benefiting the host.

Commensalism —Symbiosis in which one is benefitted but the other (host) is neither benefitted, nor-harmed.

Comminute —To break into pieces.

Comminuted fracture —A fracture in which the bone is crushed.

Comminution —Breaking of a solid thing into small pieces.

Commissural —Pertaining to a commissure.

Commissure —The site of junction of two corresponding parts as that of the lips or eyelids etc., or the structure connecting the two similar structures as a transverse band of nerve fibers connecting the two cerebral hemispheres.

Commissurorrhaphy —The Joining of the parts of a commissure together by suture to decrease the size of the opening.

Commissurotomy —Surgical incision into a commissure to increase the size of the opening as is done in mitral stenosis.

Commode —A receptacle for feces and urine.

Common bile duct —The duct which carries the bile to the duodenum from the cystic duct of the gallbladder, and the hepatic ducts.

Commotio —Concussion.

Communicable —Capable of being transmitted from one person to another.

Communicans —Communicating nerves or arteries.

Communication —An opening or connecting passage between two structures.

Communis —Common, not specific.

Comorbidity —A concomitant but unrelated disease process.

Comose —Having much hair.

Compact —Closely and tightly packed together. Dense.

Compact bone —Hard or dense bone which is the superficial layer of all the bones and the shafts of long bones.

Compaction —A complication of labor in which there is simultaneous engagement of the presenting parts of the twins in the pelvis so that the labor is obstructed.

Compatibility —The condition of suitability of mixing together without bad results, as drugs.

Compatible —Capable of being mixed with another substance without unfavourable results.

Compensating —Making up for a deficiency.

Compensation —The making up for a defect of a structure or function.

Compensatory —Providing compensations; making up for a deficiency or loss.

Complaint —Symptom.

Complement —Accessory.

Complemental, Complementary —Supplying the thing which is lacking.

Complement fixation test — The test also known as wassermann reaction, is used for the diagnosis of syphilis in which an antigen which is usually an alcoholic extract of the normal animal tissues with the addition of cholesterol as a sensitizer, is added to the serum of the individual, the complement of which is inactivated by heating the serum at 56°C for 30 minutes and the complement from the serum of guinea-pig is added to it. In the presence of the reagin (a type of antibody produced by syphilis) in the serum, the complement is destroyed, so the test is positive *i.e.,* the individual is suffering from syphilis, if the complement is free, the test is negative, i.e., the individual is not suffering from syphilis.

Complementoid —A complement of which the lysis causing power has been destroyed.

Complementophil —Capable of combining with a complement.

Complex —1. Combination of various like or unlike things. 2. Intricate or complicated. 3. A group of wholly or partially associated repressed ideas of which the patient is usually unaware and which can make the patient emotional and his behavior may be changed. 4. The portion of an electrocardiogram representing the systole of an atrium or ventricle.

Antigen-antibody complex —Complex formed by the binding of antigen to antibody.

Castration complex — Morbid fear of damage or loss of sexual organs in castration.

Clerambault Kandinsky complex —A mental state in which the patient thinks that his mind is controlled by some other person.

Ghon complex —Primary complex in pulmonary tuberculosis usually in children, consisting of the affected area of the lung and a corresponding lymph node, which heals and becomes calcified.

Inferiority complex —A state of mind in which one feels inferior to others and as a compensation exaggerated aggressiveness and expression of superiority occurs.

Superiority complex —A mental state in which one feels superior to others or pretends to be superior, to compensate for a supposed inferiority.

Complexion —The color and appearance of the skin of the face.

Complexity —The state of consisting of many interrelated parts.

Compliance —The quality of being altered in size and shape in response to application of force, weight or pressure without disruption *e.g.,* lung or urinary bladder. It is measured in terms of volume change per unit of pressure change.

Complicated —Made complex; a disease upon which the process of morbidity has been superimposed, altering symptoms and modifying its course for the worse.

Complication —Disease concurrent with another disease as pneumonia is a complication of measles.

Component —A constituent part.

Component blood therapy —Treatment by the blood constituents as plasma or red blood cells instead of using the whole blood.

Compos mentis —Of healthy mind.

Compound —A substance made of two or more materials combined in definite proportion by weight and having specific properties of its own.

Compound astigmatism — Myopia of both vertical and horizontal meridians.

Compounder —A dispenser of medicine.

Compound fracture —Fracture of a bone where its broken end has passed through the skin.

Compounding —Mixing of medicines.

Compound microscope —A microscope consisting of two or more lenses.

Comprehend —To understand something.

Comprehension —Faculty of understanding.

Compress —1. Folded cloth applied with pressure on a part of the body, which may be wet, dry, hot or cold and sometimes medicated. 2. To press the two structures together as to close a wound by squeezing its edges.

Cold compress —Folded cloth dipped in cold water applied to a given part of the body to maintain a constant temperature.

Cribriform compress —Cloth perforated with holes.

Fenestrated compress — Compress with an opening for discharge of secretions.

Forehead compress —A soft towel moist with water applied to the forehead and changed every two minutes.

Hot compress —Folded cloth dipped in hot water applied to the place of the body to be treated, and changed frequently to maintain a constant temperature.

Compressible —Capable of being compressed.

Compression —The act of pressing together or the state of being pressed together.

Compression gloves —The gloves made of stretch material to maintain the pressure against the fingers and the palm, which help to reduce the edema.

Compressor —An instrument or anything making pressure on a part of the body.

Compressorium —Compressor.

Compulsion neurosis — Psychoneurosis which compels one to perform an absurd act.

Conarium —The pineal body of the brain.

Conation —The desire to do something arising from inside.

Conative —Pertaining to the desire to do something arising from inside as demonstrated by the behavior and actions of the person.

Conatus —Performing work for self-protection and of self-interest.

Concameration —A system of interconnecting cavities.

Concatenate —Indicating the arrangement of a number of structures, e.g., enlarged lymph glands in a row like the links of a chain.

Concave —Having a depressed or hollowed surface.

Concavity —The condition of being depressed or hollow.

Concavoconcave —Concave on each of the two opposite surfaces.

Concavoconvex —Having one surface concave and the other convex.

Conceive —1. To become pregnant. 2. To form an idea.

Concentration —1. Increase in strength of a fluid by evaporation. 2. Fixation of mind on one subject excluding all other thoughts from the mind.

Concentric —Having a common center.

Concept —An idea formed of a thing in the mind.

Concepti —Plural of conceptus.

Conception —1. Fertilization 2. The mental process of forming an idea.

Conceptual —Pertaining to the formation of ideas in the mind.

Conceptus —The product of conception.

Concha —1. The outer ear or the pinna. 2. One of the three nasal chonchae.

Chonchitis —Inflammation of the choncha.

Conchoidal —Having the shape of a shell.

Conchoscope —An instrument for examination of the nasal cavity.

Conchotome —An instrument for excising the middle turbinate bone.

Conchotomy —Incision of a nasal concha.

Concoction —Mixing of two medicines by heat.

Concomitance —Co-existence.

Concomitant —Occurring at the same time.

Concordance —In twins, the equal representation of genetic trait in each.

Concrement —A deposit of calcareous material in a part of the body.

Concrescence —Coalescence. The union of separate parts.

Concrete —Condensed, hardened or solidified.

Concretio cordis —Obliteration of the pericardial cavity caused by extensive adhesion between parietal and visceral layers of the pericardium.

Concretion —A stone or calculus.

Concretization —Inability to abstract some details.

Concubitus —Sexual intercourse.

Concussion —1. An injury from impact with an object. 2. Loss of function of an organ resulting from a blow or fall.

Concussion of the brain, Cerebral concussion — Loss of consciousness either temporary or prolonged due to a blow to the head, or fall.

Concussion of the labyrinth —Deafness due to a blow to the head, or ear.

Condensation —1. Making more dense. 2. Changing of liquid into solid or gas into liquid. 3. In dentistry, the packing of filling material into a tooth cavity. 4. The union of ideas or concepts to form a new and similar concept. 5. In chemistry, a type of reaction in which two or more molecules of the same substance react with each other and form a new and heavier substance with different chemical properties.

Condense —To make more dense.

Condenser —1. An apparatus for solidifying the gases and liquids. 2. An apparatus for storing the electricity. 3. A device for illuminating microscopic objects. 4. A dental instrument for packing the filling material into the tooth cavity.

Condiment —Substance which makes the food tasty.

Condition —State.

Conditioned reflex —Reflex acquired as a result of training and repetition.

Conditioning —To improve the physical capability of a person by exercise.

Condom —A thin rubber sheath worn over the penis during sexual intercourse to prevent sperms from entering the vagina and to check the infection.

Conductance —The ability to conduct or transmit the energy as electricity.

Conducting —The act of transmitting energies through suitable media.

Conduction —The transmission of energy as of heat, sound or electricity.

Conductivity —Capacity for conduction.

Conductor —Medium through which sound, heat or electricity is transmitted.

Conduit —A channel, especially an artificial one surgically constructed for the passage of fluid.

Conduplicate —Folded upon itself lengthwise.

Conduplicatocorpore —The condition in which the fetus is doubled upon itself in shoulder presentation.

Condylar —Pertaining to a condyle.

Condylarthrosis —A joint as that of the knee that is formed by condylar surfaces.

Condyle —A rounded protuberance at the end of a bone forming an articulation.

Condylectomy —Excision of a condyle.

Condylion —A point on the lateral outer or medial inner surface of the mandibular condyle.

Condyloid —Pertaining to or resembling a condyle.

Condyloma —A soft fleshy growth of the skin usually seen on the external genital organs or at the anus. There are two types of condyloma.

(a) Condyloma acuminatum —A small pointed growth on the external genital organs or in the perianal region caused by a virus.

(b) Condyloma latum —Flat growth with grey exudate occurring on the folds of moist skin, especially about the genital organs and the anus in syphilis.

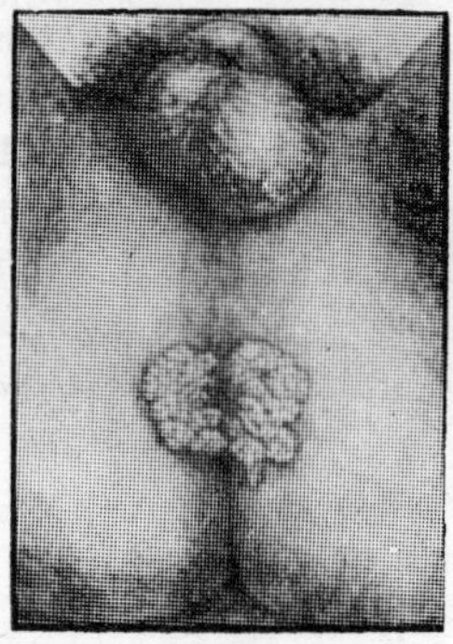

Fig. 92 : Condyloma ani

Condylomatous —Pertaining to a condyloma.

Condylotomy —Incision of a condyle.

Condylus —Condyle.

Cones —The flask-shaped cells in the outer layer of the retina of the eye, along with the rods, are light-sensitive and receive color stimuli.

Conexus —A connecting structure.

Confabulation —Familiar talk.

Confectio, Confection — Sugar-like sweat substance in which a medicine of bitter taste is incorporated to be swallowed.

Confertus —Arranged closely together.

Configuration —1. Shape and appearance of a thing. 2. Position of atoms in a molecule.

Confinement —The period of child-birth.

Conflict —The arising of two opposite desires or emotions in the mind. Struggle.

Confluence —Union, as the union of the sagittal sinus with the transverse sinuses.

Confluent —Joining as certain skin lesions which join together to form a patch.

Conformation —The shape of a part, body or material.

Conformer —A mold, usually made up of plastic material, used in surgical repair to maintain space in a cavity or to prevent closing by healing of an artificial or natural opening.

Confrontation —The act of interpreting a patient's resistances, attitudes, feelings or effects upon others.

Confusion —A mental state in which an individual is out of touch with the reality of a place, time or a person but associated with cloudy awareness.

Confusional —Pertaining to or characterized by confusion.

Congelation —The freezing or a frostbite.

Congener —Something similar to another as a muscle having the same function as another.

Congenerous —Possessing the same function, as synergistic muscles.

Congenital —Existing from birth.

Congenitus —Congenital.

Congested —Containing an abnormal amount of blood.

Congestion —Presence of an excessive amount of blood in a part of the body.

Active congestion — Congestion due to increased blood flow to a part of the body or dilataion of blood vessels.

Hypostatic congestion —Congestion of a dependent part of the body or an organ due to gravitational forces, as in venous insufficiency.

Passive congestion — Congestion due to interference with flow of blood from the capillaries into venules, may result from myocardial insufficiency.

Pulmonary congestion — Engorgement of the pulmonary vessels due to heart-disease, infections or injury.

Congestive —Pertaining to congestion.

Congius —A gallon.

Conglobate —Aggregated in one mass, as lymph glands.

Conglobation —Aggregation into a rounded mass.

Conglomerate —1. Aggregation in one mass. 2. Clustered.

Conglutin —A kind of protein resembling casein found in peas, beans and almonds.

Conglutinant —Promoting adhesion, as of the edges of a wound.

Conglutinate —Having the property of adhesiveness.

Conglutination —1. Coalescence or adhesion of tissues with each other. 2. Agglutination of erythrocytes.

Coni —Plural of conus.

Coniasis —Dust like calculi in the gallbladder and bile ducts.

Conical —Cone shaped.

Conidia —Plural of conidium.

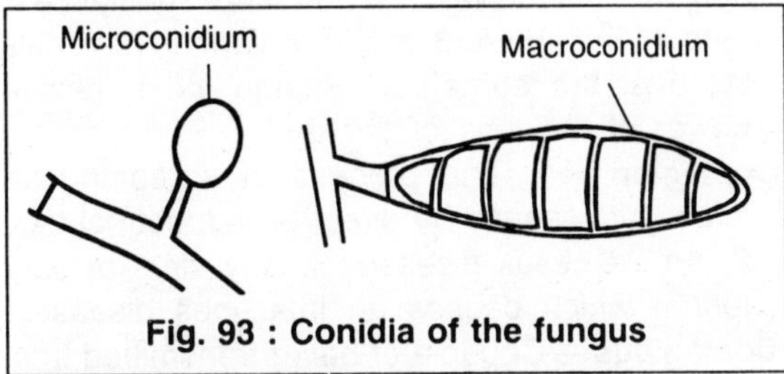

Fig. 93 : Conidia of the fungus

Conidiogenous —Producing conidium.

Conidiophore —A specialized hypha which bears conidia, in fungi.

Conidium, plural **conidia** —Conidium is an asexual spore of the fungi.

Coniofibrosis — Pneumoconiosis caused by the dust of asbestos or silica which causes fibrosis in the lung.

Coniology —Study of dust.

Coniometer —An apparatus for estimating the amount of dust in the air.

Coniosis —The condition produced by inhalation of dust.

Coniosporosis— Hypersensitivity reaction characterized by asthma and acute pneumonitis caused by inhalation of the spores of the fungus Coniosporium corticale, growing under the bark of certain trees; found in workers who strip the bark from these trees.

Conization —Removal of a cone of tissue, as of the mucous membrane of the cervix.

Conjugata, Conjugate —1. Paired or joined. 2. Diameter of the pelvis measured from the center of the promontory of the sacrum to the back of the pubic symphysis.

Conjugation —1. A coupling or joining together. 2. The union of two unicellular organisms accompanied by interchange of nuclear materials as in paramecium. 3. The union of a toxic substance with some natural substance of the body to form a detoxified substance which is eliminated from the body.

Conjunctiva —The mucous membrane covering the eyeballs and lining the eyelids.

Conjunctival —Pertaining to the conjunctiva.

Conjunctival reflex —Closure of the eyelids on touching the conjunctiva or only on threatening to touch.

Conjunctiviplasty — Conjunctivoplasty.

Conjunctivitis —Inflammation of the conjunctiva.

Allergic conjunctivitis — Conjunctivitis caused by allergens such as pollen grains, spores, dust and animal hair etc.

Catarrhal conjunctivitis —Conjunctivitis caused by foreign bodies, various bacteria; irritation from heat, cold or chemicals.

Gonorrheal conjunctivitis —Severe purulent conjunctivitis due to gonococci.

Granular conjunctivitis —Conjunctivitis with granulations on the inner sides of the eyelids, which may ulcerate and cicatrize. Trachoma.

Membranous conjunctivitis —Acute conjunctivitis with the formation of false membrane.

Phlyctenular conjunctivitis — Characterized by nodules which may ulcerate usually seen in children.

Spring conjunctivitis —Conjunctivitis occurring in the spring season.

Conjunctivoma —A tumor of the conjunctiva.

Conjunctivoplasty —Repair of the conjunctiva by plastic surgery.

Conjunctivorhinostomy — To form a passage through the conjunctiva into the nasal cavity.

Connective —Pertaining to that which connects or binds together two separate parts.

Connective tissue —Tissue which connects and supports other tissues, *e.g.*, fibrous tissue, fatty tissue, cartilage and bone etc.

Connector —Which joins or binds together two separate parts.

Conoid —Resembling a cone, cone-shaped (conical).

Consanguineous —Denoting blood relationship.

Consanguinity —Blood relationship.

Conscience —The intense sense of feeling.

Conscious —Being aware, awake, capable of responding to sensory stimuli.

Consciousness —The state of being conscious or of awareness, responsiveness of the mind to the sensory stimuli.

Consensual —Reflex stimulation of one part or side due to excitement of another part or opposite side.

Consensual light index — On exposing one eye to more intense light than that of the other, the pupils of both the eyes constrict.

Consensual reflex —Any reflex action occurring on opposite side of the body from the point of stimulation.

Consenting adult —An adult who consents to take part in homosexuality.

Conservation —Preservation from loss, injury, or decay.

Conservative —Old methods of the treatment of diseases and for the restoration of health.

Conserve —Confection.

Consistency —The density or hardness.

Consolidant —A substance that promotes healing or union.

Consolidation —Solidification, the process of becoming solid, especially used for the solidification of the lungs as occurs in pneumonia.

Conspecific —Of the same species.

Constancy —The state of being constant.

Constant —Unchanging.

Constellation —In psychiatry, all the factors that determine a particular action.

Constipate —To cause constipation.

Constipated —Suffering from constipation.

Constipation —Difficult defecation, infrequent defecation with passage of hard and dry feces.

Constituent —Forming part of a whole as that of a medicine.

Constitution —Make-up of the body and its functional habits.

Constitutional —Affecting the whole constitution of the body.

Constitutional disease — Disease which affects the whole body instead of a specific part.

Constriction —Narrowing of a vessel or opening, as constriction of the blood vessels or the pupil of the eye.

Constrictor —That which causes constriction.

Consultant —The doctor who gives some advice.

Consultation —Advice.

Consummation —The first act of intercourse after marriage.

Consumption —1. The process of being used. 2. Wasting of the body as in tuberculosis.

Consumptive —Pertaining to or afflicted with tuberculosis.

Contact —1. Mutual touching or apposition of two bodies. 2. An individual who has been recently exposed to an infectious disease.

Contact complete — Contact of the entire adjoining surfaces of two teeth.

Contact direct —The contact of a healthy person with a person who is the carrier of or suffering from an infectious disease.

Contact indirect — The spread of an infectious disease by some medium, other than directly touching the infected person, as through the air or by means of fomites.

Contactant —A substance which causes allergy when it is in direct contact with the skin.

Contact dermatitis — Inflammation of the skin due to contact with an irritating substance.

Contact lens —A lens made of various materials fits over the cornea to change the refractive power of the lens of the eye.

Contagion —1. The process of spreading an infectious disease by direct or indirect contact. 2. An infectious disease. 3. Any virus or bacterium which causes an infectious disease.

Contagious —Capable of being transmitted from one person to another directly or indirectly, as an organism which causes a disease.

Contagiousness —The quality of being contagious.

Contagium, Contagion — The agent causing infection.

Containment —The conception of regional or global eradication of a communicable disease.

Contaminant —The substance or the organism that causes contamination.

Contaminate —To cause contamination.

Contamination —The process of contaminating or polluting, especially the introduction of the disease-producing organisms or infectious material into the sterile things.

Content —That which is contained within something.

Contiguity —Contact.

Contiguous —Adjacent or in close contact.

Continence —1. Self-restraint. 2. The ability to control urination and defecation.

Continent —1. Having no sexual desire. 2. Capable of controlling urination and defecation.

Contortion —A twisting into an unusual shape.

Contour —Outline of a part.

Contoured —Having an irregular, undulating surface.

Contra- —Prefix indicating opposite or against, as contraindication.

Contra-aperture —A second opening made in an abscess to facilitate the discharge of its contents.

Contraception —Prevention of conception.

Contraceptive —Any medicine, process, apparatus or method that prevents conception.

Contract —1. To draw, reduce in size or shorten 2. To acquire a disease through infection.

Contractile —Capable of being contracted or shortened.

Contractility —Capability of being contracted or shortened.

Contraction —Shortening or tightening or shrinking as that of a muscle.

Carpopedal contraction —A condition resulting from shrinkage of the flexor muscles of the hands and feet in tetany.

Cicatricial contraction —Shrinkage and spontaneous closing of the open wounds of the skin.

Clonic contraction — Muscular contraction alternating with relaxation.

Hicks' contraction — Painless uterine contractions during pregnancy.

Idiomuscular contraction —Contraction produced by direct electrical stimulation of a wasted muscle.

Isometric contraction —Muscular contraction in which the muscle does not change its length.

Isotonic contraction —Muscular contraction in which the muscle maintains constant force of contraction by changing its length during action.

Postural contraction — The contraction of the muscles that maintain the posture of the body.

Tetanic contraction, Tonic contraction — Continuous muscular contraction without intervals of relaxation.

Contracture —1. Permanent shortening of muscle due to spasm or paralysis. 2. A state of permanent muscular rigidity.

Dupuytren's contracture —Contracture of the palmar fascia causing the ring and the little fingers of the hand to be flexed permanently.

Fixed contracture —Organic contracture.

Functional contracture — Muscular shortening that ceases during sleep or general anesthesia, caused by prolonged active muscle contraction.

Ischemic contracture — Contraction of a muscle with fibrous degeneration due to interference in the blood supply from pressure, injury or cold.

Organic contracture —Fixed contracture. It occurs due to fibrosis within the muscle that persists in consciousness and unconsciousness, both.

Physiological contracture —Contracture of a muscle induced by heat, action of drugs or acids.

Volkmann's contracture —Flexion of the hand with atrophy of the muscles of the forearm resulting from interference in the blood circulation due to pressure from a cast, constricting dressing or injury to the radial artery.

Contrafissura —A fracture of the skull at the point opposite to the site of the blow.

Contraincision —Counterincision to promote drainage.

Contraindicant —Indicating the contrary.

Contraindication —Any symptom or circumstance which suggest avoidance of certain medical or surgical treatment, which is otherwise advisable.

Contralateral —Situated on or affecting the opposite side.

Contralateral reflexes — Passive flexion of one leg causes the flexion of the opposite leg.

Contrast —Difference, in radiography the difference between the densities of the part of the body radiographed and of the radiographic film.

Contrast medium —In radiology, a radiopaque substance used in the study of a contrast in the densities of the organ being x-rayed and the medium (radiopaque substance), as the barium sulphate when swallowed helps to show the outline of the intestinal tract, when it is x-rayed during its passage.

Contrast sprays —Let the patient be seated at one side of the bath tub and spray his feet and legs with warm water for one minute, and then with cold water for one minute, alternatively for 10 minutes twice daily to stimulate the blood circulation.

Contravolitional —Against the will, involuntary.

Contrecoup —Occurring on the opposite side.

Contrecoup injury —An injury of the brain occurring at the site opposite to that of the blow.

Control —1. To regulate or maintain. 2. Governing or limitation of certain events as limitation of child-bearing (birth control) by means of the methods to prevent conception. 3. A standard against which observations or conclusions of the experiments may be checked to establish their validity.

Contrude —To aggregate together, as the teeth.

Contrusion —Having the teeth crowded.

Contuse —To bruise.

Contusion —Bruise. Any injury in which the skin is not broken and there is pain, swelling and discoloration.

Conus, plural **coni** —A cone or cone-shaped structure as the conical portion of the lower spinal cord.

Convalescence —The period of recovery after the termination of an illness or an operation.

Convalescent —The person recovering from an illness or operation.

Convection —The act of conveying heat in liquids or gases by movement of the heated particles.

Convergence —1. Moving of two or more things toward the same point. 2. The direction of the visual lines to a near point.

Convergent —Tending toward a common point.

Conversion —1. The change from one state to another. 2. In obstetrics, the manipulative change of malposition of a fetus in the uterus, to facilitate the delivery.

Convertase —An enzyme that converts a substance to its active state.

Convex —Having the curved surface on one side and the plain on the other side, resembling the segment of a sphere.

Convexity —The state of being convex.

Convexobasia —Forward bending of the occipital bone.

Convexoconcave —Having one side convex and the other concave.

Convexoconvex —Convex on both sides.

Convolute, Convoluted — Rolled.

Convoluted —Convolute. Rolled together with one part over the other.

Convoluted tubule —In the kidney, the proximal convoluted tubule lying between the Henle's loop and the bowman's capsule, the distal convoluted tubule lying between Henle's loop and the collecting tubule.

Convolution —1. A fold, twist or coil of an organ which is convoluted. 2. A gyrus on the surface of the cerebral hemisphere which is separated from the other by a sulcus.

Convulsant —The drugs or toxic substances that cause convulsions, *e.g.,* strychnine.

Convulsion —Involuntary muscle contractions and relaxations.

Clonic convulsions — Convulsions in which the muscles contract and relax alternately.

Epileptiform convulsions —Convulsion in which there is unconsciousness, as in epilepsy and eclampsia.

Febrile convulsion — Convulsion associated with high fever, occurring especially in children.

Hysterical convulsion —Convulsion caused by hysteria.

Mimetic or mimic convulsion —Facial convulsion or tic.

Puerperal convulsion — Convulsion in a woman occurring just before, during or just after childbirth.

Salaam convulsion — Nodding spasm.

Tonic convulsion — Convulsion in which the contractions are made for a time, as in tetany.

Toxic convulsion — Convulsion caused by the action of a toxin on the nervous system.

Uremic convulsion — Convulsion caused by uremia.

Convulsive —Pertaining to convulsion.

Coordinate —To perform the work in coordination.

Coordination —The working together of interrelated organs of the body.

Coossification —State of being joined by bone formation.

Coossify —To unite into one bone.

Cope —The ability to deal with the difficulty, a person has to face.

Cophosis —Deafness, loss of hearing.

Coping —To encounter the stresses of daily life.

Copiopia —Eye strain.

Copious —Profuse, excessive.

Copodyskinesia —Fatigue or difficulty in moving a group of muscles used in a work.

Coppears —Bluish-green crystals of ferrous sulphate used as a disinfectant and deodorizer.

Copremesis —The vomiting of fecal matter.

Copro- —A prefix pertaining to feces.

Coproantibody —An antibody of a IgA type present in the intestine, associated with immunity to enteric bacteria.

Coprolagnia —A sexual stimulation of seeing or smelling the feces.

Coprolalia —The speaking of obscene words, especially related to feces as seen in some mental diseases.

Coprolith —Hard fecal concretion in the intestine.

Coprology —Study of the feces.

Coproma —Fecaloma.

Coprophagia —Coprophagy.

Coprophagous —The individual who eats feces.

Coprophagy —Eating of the feces or dung.

Coprophile —An organism that eats fecal material excreted by other organisms.

Coprophilia —Abnormal interest in feces.

Coprophilic —The bacteria that normally live in the feces or dung.

Coprophobia —Abnormal dislike to defecation and to feces.

Coprophrasia —Coprolalia.

Coproplanesia —Passage of feces through a fistula or artificial anus.

Coproporphyria —A hereditary disease in which there is excessive excretion of coproporphyrin in the feces.

Coproporphyrin —One of the two porphyrin compounds as a decomposition product of bilirubin normally found in feces in minute quantity but its amount is increased in certain diseases such as poliomyelitis, infectious hepatitis etc.

Coproporphyrinuria —The presence of coproporphyrin in the urine.

Coprostanol —A derivative of cholesterol present in the feces.

Coprostasis —Fecal impaction.

Coprozoa —Protozoa found in the feces outside of the intestine.

Coprozoic —Pertaining to coprozoa, found in the feces.

Copula —Any connecting structure.

Copulation —Sexual intercourse.

Cor —The heart.

Coracoacromial —Pertaining to the acromial and the coracoid process.

Coracobrachialis —Pertaining to the coracoid process of the scapula, and the arm.

Coracoclavicular —Scapuloclavicular. Pertaining to the coracoid process and the clavicle.

Coracohumeral —Pertaining to the coracoid process and the humerus bone.

Coracoid —Like a crow's beak.

Cord —A long, cylindrical, flexible structure.

Spermatic cord —A cord connecting the abdominal inguinal ring to the testis and consisting of vas deferens, blood vessels, lymphatics and nerves, supplying the testis and epididymis.

Spinal cord —The portion of the central nervous system situated in the vertebral canal, extending from the foramen magnum to the upper part of the lumbar region.

Umbilical cord —The cord which connects the fetus with the placenta and contains the blood vessels through which fetal blood passes to and from the placenta.

Vocal cord —The cords producing sound situated in the larynx.

Cordal —Pertaining to a cord.

Cordate —Heart-shaped.

Cord bladder —Distended urinary bladder without discomfort.

Cordectomy —-Surgical removal of a cord as of a vocal cord.

Cordial —Stimulating the heart.

Cordiform —Heart shaped.

Cordis —Of the heart.

Corditis, Funiculitis — Inflammation of the spermatic cord.

Cordocentesis —A technique for obtaining a blood sample from the umbilical cord of the intrauterine infant.

Cordopexy —Surgical fixation of a cord, especially of the vocal cord.

Cordotomy —Chordotomy.

Core —Center of a structure.

Coreclisis —Closure of the pupil.

Corectasia, Corectasis — Dilatation of the pupil due to some disease.

Corectome, Iridectome —An instrument for cutting the iris.

Corectomy —Iridectomy. Surgical removal of the iris.

Corectopia —Location of the pupil of the eye to one side of the center of the iris.

Coredialysis —Separation of the outer border of the iris from the ciliary body.

Corediastasis —Dilatation of the pupil.

Corelysis —To remove the adhesions between lens capsule and the iris.

Coremorphosis —To form an artificial pupil by surgery.

Corenclisis —Coreclisis.

Coreometer —An instrument for measuring the pupil.

Coreometry —Measurement of the pupil of the eye.

Corepexy —To suture the iris to change shape or size of the pupil.

Coreoplastly —Plastic surgery of the pupil.

Corepraxy —The procedure of widening a small pupil.

Corestenoma —Narrowing of the pupil.

Core temperature —Temperature of the deeply situated structures such as the liver or heart.

Coretomedialysis —Making of an artificial pupii through the iris.

Coretomy —An incision of the iris.

Coria —Plural of corium.

Corium —Dermis, the layer of the skin just beneath the epidermis containing blood capillaries, lymph vessels, nerve endings, hair follicles, sebaceous and sweat glands with their ducts.

Corn —A horny hard and thickening of the skin caused by friction or pressure.

Cornea —The clear transparent anterior portion comprising about one sixth of the eye ball and continuous with the sclera at the periphery.

Corneal reflex —Closure of the eyelids resulting from direct irritation of the cornea.

Corneitis —Inflammation of the cornea.

Corneoblepharon —Adhesion of the eyelid to the cornea.

Corneocyte —Horny cell.

Corneoiritis —Inflammation of the cornea and the iris.

Corneosclera —The cornea and the sclera considered as one organ.

Corneoscleral —Pertaining to the cornea and sclera.

Corneous —Hornlike.

Corneous layer, Stratum corneum —Outer horny layer of the epidermis.

Corneum —Stratum corneum epidermidis, the outermost layer of the epidermis.

Corniculate —Containing small horn-shaped projections.

Corniculum —A small hornlike process.

Cornification —Conversion into hard horny material as that of the skin.

Cornified —Converted into horny tissue, keratinized.

Cornu —Any projection like a horn.

Cornua —Plural of cornu.

Cornual —Pertaining to a cornu.

Corona, plural **coronae** — Crown as that of a tooth.

Coronad —Toward the corona or the crown of the head.

Coronale —Frontal bone.

Coronalis —Coronal. Pertaining to a corona.

Coronal plane —Plane dividing the body into front and back portions.

Coronal suture —Suture joining the parietal and frontal bones of the cranium.

Coronaria —A coronary artery of the heart.

Coronarism —1. Coronary insufficiency 2. Angina pectoris.

Coronaritis —Coronary arteritis or the inflammation of the coronary artery.

Coronary —Encircling as the blood vessels supplying directly to the heart.

Coronary arteries —A pair of arteries which supply blood to the myocardium of the heart.

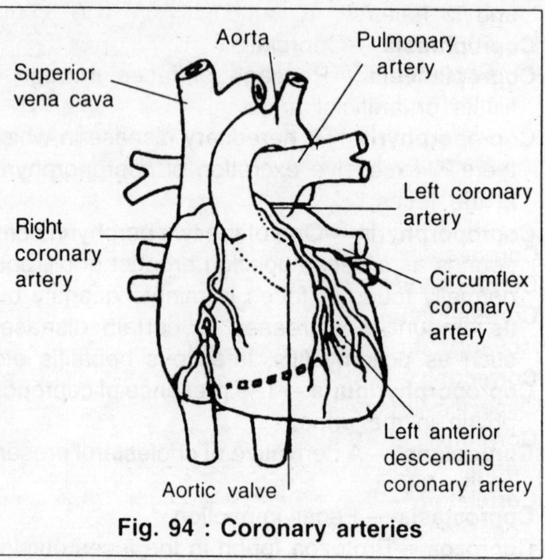

Fig. 94 : Coronary arteries

Coronary bypass surgery — A shunt established by surgery, due to which the blood flows from the aorta to a branch of the coronary artery at a point past an obstruction.

Coronary care unit —A department of the hospital, especially equipped with modern devices to provide intensive nursing and medical care for patients suffering from severe coronary thrombosis.

Coronary occlusion —Closing off of a coronary artery.

Coronary thrombosis — Clotting of blood in one or more of the coronary arteries of the heart.

Coronoid —Crown-shaped.

Coronoidectomy —Surgical remvoal of the coronoid process of the mandible.

Coroparelcysis —To bring the pupil to one side by surgery in case of central corneal opacity so that it lies under a transparent area of the cornea.

Coroscopy —Retinoscopy.

Corotomy — Iridotomy To make an incision into the iris.
Corpora —Plural of corpus.
Corporeal —Consisting of a physical body.
Corpse —Dead human body.
Corpulence —Obesity. Fatness.
Corpulent —Obese. Fatty person.
Cor pulmonale —Enlargement of the right ventricle of the heart due to rise in pulmonary arterial pressure.
Corpus —Body. Main part of an organ.
Corpuscle — A small rounded mass.
Blood corpuscle —An erythrocyte or red blood corpuscle and a leucocyte or white blood corpuscle.
Chromophil —Tiny body found in the cytoplasm of a nerve cell, also known as Nissl body.
Malpighian corpuscle, Renal corpuscle — A glomerulus and a capsule (Bowman's capsule) enclosing it in the kidney.
Corpuscular —Pertaining to the corpuscle.
Corpusculum —Corpuscle.
Corpus luteum —The yellow mass formed in the ovary after rupture of a graafian follicle.
Correction —To set right, *e.g.,* the provision of specific lenses for improvement of vision.
Corrective —Pertaining to a drug which sets right.
Correlation —The processes by which the various activities of the body, especially nervous impulses, occur in proper relation to each other.
Corrigent —Corrective.
Corrode —To cause or to be affected, by corrosion.
Corrosion —Wearing away slowly of a thing by a destructive agent.
Corrosive —Causing corrosion.
Corrugation —Wrinkle.
Corrugator —A muscle drawing the skin causing it to wrinkle.
Cortex —An outer layer of an organ which is distinguished from the inner portion medulla, as is found in adrenal gland, kidney, cerebrum and the cerebellum of the brain.
Cortiadrenal —Pertaining to adrenal cortex.
Cortical —Pertaining to a cortex.
Corticate —Possessing a cortex or bark.
Corticectomy —Surgical removal of an area of the cerebral cortex in the treatment of epilepsy.
Cortices —Plural of cortex.
Corticifugal —Moving or conducting away from the cortex.
Corticipetal —Proceeding or moving toward the outer surface or cortex.
Corticoadrenal —Pertaining to the adrenal cortex.
Corticoafferent —Corticipetal.
Corticobulbar —Pertaining to the cerebral cortex and upper portion of the brain stem.
Corticocerebellum —Pertaining to the cortex and cerebellum.
Corticoefferent —Corticofugal.
Corticofugal —Passing away from the outer surface.
Corticoid —Corticosteroid. A steroid hormone of the adrenal cortex.
Corticopeduncular —Pertaining to the cerebral cortex and cerebral peduncles.
Corticopleuritis — Inflammation of the outer parts of pleura.
Corticopontine —Pertaining to or connecting the cerebral cortex and the pons of the brain.
Corticospinal —Pertaining to cerebral cortex and spinal cord.
Corticosteroid —Any of the steroids, produced by the adrenal cortex, excluding the sex hormones.
Corticosterone —A hormone of the adrenal cortex which affects carbohydrate, potassium and sodium metabolism.
Corticothalamic —Pertaining to or connecting the cerebral cortex and the thalamus of the brain.
Corticotroph —A cell of the anterior pituitary gland that produces adrenocorticotropic hormone.
Corticotrophic, Corticotropic —Pertaining to corticotrophin.
Corticotrophin, Corticotropin —A hormone secreted by the anterior lobe of the pituitary gland, which stimulates the adrenal cortex to secrete steroid hormones.
Cortin —An extract of the cortex of the adrenal gland.
Cortisol —A corticosteroid hormone produced by the adrenal cortex. Hydrocortisone.
Cortisone —A hormone isolated from the cortex of the adrenal gland which is related to hydrocortisone, used as an anti-inflammatory agent and for adrenal replacement therapy.
Coruscation —Sensation of a flash of light before the eyes.
Corynebacterium diphtheriae —Rod-shaped and non-motile bacteria causing diphtheria in children.

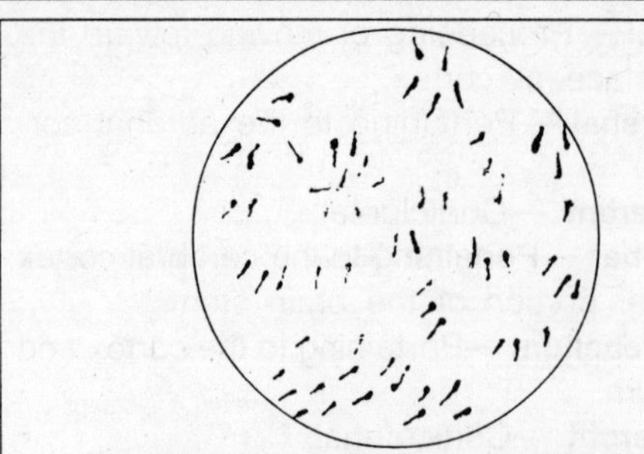

Fig. 95 : Corynebacterium diphtheriae

Coryza —Acute inflammation of the nasal mucous membrane with profuse discharge from the nose.

Cosmesis —An operation performed for the improvement of appearance of the patient.

Cosmetic —1. A beautifying substance or preparation such as cream or powder etc. 2. Preserving the attractiveness.

Cosmetic surgery —Plastic surgery for the preservance of beauty or correcting the ugly scars or burns.

Costa —Rib.

Costa fluctuans —A floating rib.

Costa spuria —A false rib.

Costa vera —True rib.

Costal —Pertaining to a rib.

Costal cartilage —A cartilage which connects the end of a true rib with the sternum.

Costalgia —Pain in the rib.

Costalis —Costal.

Costectomy —Excision of a rib.

Costiform —Rib-shaped.

Costive —Producing constipation.

Costiveness —Constipation.

Costocervical —Pertaining to the ribs and the neck.

Costochondral —Pertaining to a rib and its cartilage.

Costochondritis —Costal chondritis. Inflammation of one or more costal cartilages.

Costoclavicular —Pertaining to the ribs and clavicle.

Costocoracoid —Pertaining to the ribs and the coracoid process of scapula.

Costogenic —Arising from a rib.

Costoinferior —Pertaining to the lower ribs.

Costophrenic —Pertaining to the ribs and diaphragm.

Costopneumopexy —To fix a lung to a rib.

Costoscapular —Pertaining to the ribs and the scapula.

Costosternal —Pertaining to a rib and the sternum.

Costosternoplasty —Surgical repair of a funnel-shaped chest, a portion of a rib is used to support the sternum.

Costosuperior —Pertaining to the upper ribs.

Costotome —A knife for cutting through a rib or cartilage.

Costotomy —Incision or division of a rib or of a costal cartilage.

Costotransverse —Lying between the ribs and the transverse processes of the vertebrae.

Costotransversectomy — Excision of a part of a rib along with the transverse process of a vertebrum.

Costovertebral —Pertaining to a rib and a vertebrum.

Costoxiphoid —Pertaining to or connecting the ribs and the xiphoid process of the sternum.

Cotinine —The principal metabolite of nicotine excreted in the urine which indicates that the individual has recently smoked cigarettes.

Cotton —A soft, white, fibrous material obtained from the seeds of Gossypium.

Absorbent cotton, Purified cotton —Cotton fibers from which the oil and the impurities are completely removed, and is sterilized, to be used in surgery.

Styptic cotton —Cotton mixed with an astringent, which helps to check haemorrhage.

Co-twin —Either one of twins.

Cotyle —Acetabulum. Any cup-shaped structure.

Cotyloid —Cup-shaped.

Couching —An old treatment of cataract in which the lens is displaced downward.

Cough —A sudden, noisy expulsion of the air from the lungs through the glottis.

Asthmatic cough — Cough associated with an attack of dyspnea.

Bronchial cough —1. Cough heard in patients with bronchiectasis, may be stimulated by change in posture, as by getting up in the morning. 2. Cough heard in bronchitis which in earlier stages is hacking, frequent and irritating, in the later stages looser or easier with thin sputum.

Dry cough —Cough without expectoration.

Hacking cough —The cough which is short, frequent and shallow (not deep) as occurs in the early stages of pulmonary tuberculosis.

Moist cough, Wet cough, Productive cough —Cough with expectoration.

Reflex cough —Cough due to irritation of some remote organ such as stomach, middle ear, pharynx or intestine.

Whooping cough —Cough occurring in whooping cough.

Counter —An apparatus for counting anything as coulter counter for automatically counting the blood cells.

Counteract —To do against something.

Counteraction —The action of a drug against that of another drug.

Countercurrent —A current flowing in a direction opposite to another current.

Counter-drainage — Drainage in a direction opposite to another drainage.

Counter extension — Countertraction.

Counterimmunoelectrophoresis —The process in which antigens and antibodies move in opposite directions, when they are placed in separate wells, i.e., antigens toward the anode and antibodies toward the cathode and they precipitate and form a precipitin line upon meeting in the diffusion medium, when an electric current is passed through the diffusion medium.

Counterincision — A second incision made to promote drainage or to relieve the stress on the edges of a wound when they are sutured.

Counterirritant —Producing counterirritation.

Counterirritation —Superficial irritation to relieve some other irritation of the deeper structures.

Counteropening —Counterpuncture.

Counter poison —A poison given to underact the another poison.

Counterpuncture —A second puncture made at the dependent part of an abscess, which is not draining satisfactorily through a previous puncture.

Countershock —The application of an electric shock to the heart to terminate a disturbance of its rhythm.

Counterstain —Application of a second stain of different color, to the tissues that have already been stained for microscopic examination, to help to contrast the tissues originally stained.

Countertraction —Traction applied in opposition to another traction, used in reduction of fractures.

Coup —A blow, stroke.

Coup de soleil —Sunstroke.

Couple —1. To join together 2. To perform sexual intercourse.

Coupling —In cardiology, the occurrence of a premature systole, just after a normal systolic heart beat, regularly.

Cover glass, Cover slip —A thin glass plate to cover a tissue to be examined under the microscope.

Cowperitis —Inflammation of the cowper's glands.

Cowper's glands —In male, two yellow, small, rounded bodies about the size of a pea, one on each side of the urethra before the prostate gland and emptying its mucous secretion into the urethra through its duct.

Coxa —Hip or hip joint.

Coxalgia, Coxodynia — Pain in the hip.

Coxarthropathy —Any disease of the hip joint.

Coxarthrosis —Osteoarthritis of the hip joint.

Coxitis —Inflammation of the hip joint.

Coxodynia —Coxalgia.

Coxofemoral —Pertaining to the hip and femur.

Coxotomy —An operation of opening the hip joint.

Coxotuberculosis — Tuberculosis of the hip joint.

Cracked pot sound —Percussion sound of the lungs resembles that heard on striking a cracked pot, which indicates the presence of a pulmonary cavity.

Crackle —Rale.

Cradle —An arched frame to keep the bed clothes away from pressing on a wound or fractured part.

Cradle cap —Seborrheic dermatitis of the newborn.

Cramp —A painful spasmodic muscular contraction.

Crania —Plural of cranium.

Craniad —In the direction of a cranium or toward the superior end of the body.

Cranial —Pertaining to the cranium.

Cranialis —Cranial.

Craniectomy —An operation of opening the skull and removing a portion of it.

Cranio- —Prefix pertaining to the skull or cranium.

Cranioacromial —Pertaining to the cranium and the acromion.

Cranioaural —Pertaining to the cranium and the ear.

Craniocele —Herniation of the brain through the skull.

Craniocerebral —Pertaining to the skull and the brain.

Cranioclasis —Crushing of the fetal head to facilitate delivery.

Cranioclast —An instrument for crushing the fetal head to facilitate delivery.

Cranioclasty —Crushing of the fetal head in difficult labor produced either by the fetus or the small size of the pelvic outlet.

Craniocleidodysostosis —A congenital condition in which there is defective ossification of the bones of the head, face, and clavicles.

Craniodidymus —Conjoined twins with fused bodies but with two heads.

Craniofacial —Pertaining to the head and face.

Craniofenestria —Defective development of the fetal skull with areas in which there is no bone formation.

Craniograph —An apparatus to make the graphs of the skull.

Craniography —Study of the graphs of the skull.

Craniolacunia —Defective development of the fetal skull in which there are depressed areas on the inner side.

Craniology —The study of the skull.

Craniomalacia —Abnormal softening of the skull bones.

Craniomeningocele — Protrusion of the meninges through a defect in the skull.

Craniometer —An instrument for measuring the skull.

Craniometric —Pertaining to craniometry.

Craniometric points —Any prominence or marks on the skull defining the shape of the cranium.

Craniometry —Measurement of the skull.

Craniopagus —Twins joined at the head.

Craniopathy —Any disease of the skull.

Craniopharyngeal —Pertaining to the skull and to the pharynx.

Craniopharyngioma — Pituitary adamantinoma or pituitary ameloblastoma.

Craniophore —An apparatus for holding a skull while taking its measurements.

Cranioplasty —To correct a cranial defect by plastic surgery.

Craniopuncture —Puncture of the cranium for exploratory purposes.

Craniorrhachidian — Craniospinal.

Craniorrhachischisis — Congenital fissure of the skull and the vertebral column.

Craniosacral —Pertaining to the cranium and the sacrum.

Cranioschisis —Congenital fissure of the cranium.

Craniosclerosis —Abnormal thickening of the bones of the skull.

Cranioscopy —Examination of the intracranial structures by endoscopy.

Craniospinal —Pertaining to the skull and the spinal column.

Craniostenosis —Contraction of the skull due to premature closure of the cranial sutures.

Craniostosis —Congenital ossification of the cranial sutures.

Craniosynostosis — Premature closure of the sutures of the skull.

Craniotabes —Abnormal softening of the bones of the skull in infancy.

Craniotome —An instrument for perforating and dividing the fetal skull.

Craniotomy —1. Any operation on the cranium. 2. Perforation of the skull to remove its contents and to decrease the size of the head of the fetus to facilitate the delivery.

Craniotrypesis —Trephining of the skull.

Craniotympanic —Pertaining to the skull and the middle ear.

Cranium —The portion of the skull which encloses the brain.

Crapulent, Crapulous —Pertaining to the effects of excessive drinking and eating; pertaining to intoxication.

Crater —A circular depression surrounded by an elevated margin.

Crateriform —Crater-shaped as the colonies of some bacteria.

Craterization —Saucerization.

Cravat bandage —Triangular bandage.

Craving —Longing, earnest desire.

Crazing —In dentistry, the appearance of minute cracks on the surface of the filling material.

Cream —The oily or fatty part of milk from which butter is prepared.

Crease —A line or slight linear depression which is made by a fold of the skin.

Creatine —A nitrogenous constituent of the muscles.

Creatinemia —Excess of creatine in the blood.

Creatinine —The end product of creatine metabolism, found in the muscle and blood and excreted in the urine.

Creatinuria —Increased amount of creatinine in the urine.

Creatorrhea —The presence of undigested

muscle fibers in the feces as seen in some cases of pancreatice disease.

Cremaster —One of the muscles suspending and enveloping the testicles and spermatic cord.

Cremasteric —Pertaining to the cremaster muscle.

Cremasteric reflex — Retraction of the testis on striking the skin.

Cremate —Burning of a dead body.

Crematorium —A place for burning the dead body.

Cremnocele —A protrusion of the intestine into the labium majus.

Cremnophobia —Morbid fear of precipices or steep places.

Crena, plural **crenae** —A V-shaped space or a notch into which the opposing projections fit in the cranial sutures.

Crenate —Notched as crenated condition of red blood cells.

Crenation —The conversion of normally round red blood cells into notched forms on mixing the blood with salt solution of 5% strength.

Crenocyte —Crenated red blood cell.

Crenocytosis —The presence of crenocytes in the blood.

Creophagy, Creophagism — The eating of flesh.

Crepitant —Having a dry and crackling sound.

Crepitation —1. A crackling sound heard by stethoscope in certain lung diseases as the rales heard in pneumonia . 2. A dry crackling sound produced by grating of the ends of a fractured bone.

Crepitus —1. The noise of the gas discharged from the intestine. 2. Crepitation.

Crescent , Crescentic —Shaped like a new moon.

Crescograph —An apparatus for recording the degree and rate of growth.

Cresol —A yellow-brown substance obtained from coal tar and containing not more than 5% of phenol, used as disinfectant.

Cresomania, croesomania — Delusion of being a great wealthy.

Crest —A ridge, projection or an elongated prominence, especially on a bone.

Cretin —The person suffering from cretinism.

Cretinism —Arrested physical and mental development with dystrophy of bones and soft tissues and lowered basal metabolism, due to lack of thyroid secretion since birth.

Cretinistic —Cretinous

Cretinoid —Resembling a cretin or having the symptoms of cretinism.

Cretinous —Pertaining to a cretin or to cretinism; affected with cretinism.

Crevice —A small fissure or crack.

Crevicular —Pertaining to a crevice, especially the gingival crevice.

Crib —1. A supporting structure around a tooth or a denture. 2. A small bed with long legs and high sides for an infant or young child.

Cribbing —Aerophagia,swallowing of the air.

Cribra —Plural of cribrum.

Cribrate —Perforated like a sieve.

Cribration —The state of being perforated.

Cribriform —Sieve like.

Cribrum —Cribriform plate of the ethmoid bone.

Crick —A muscle spasm, especially in the neck.

Cricoarytenoid —Pertaining to the cricoid and arytenoid cartilages.

Cricoid —1. Ring-shaped. 2. Cricoid cartilage.

Cricoidectomy —Excision of the cricoid cartilage.

Cricoidynia —Pain in the cricoid cartilage.

Cricopharyngeal —Pertaining to the cricoid cartilage and the pharynx.

Cricothyroid —Pertaining to the cricoid cartilage and the thyroid gland.

Cricothyroidotomy — Cricothyrotomy.

Cricothyrotomy —Division of the cricoid and the thyroid cartilage.

Cricotomy —Incision into the cricoid cartilage.

Cricotracheotomy —Incision of the trachea through the cricoid cartilage.

Cri du chat syndrome —A hereditary congenital disease in which the infant's cry resembles that of the cat.

Criminal —Guilty, the person who has committed a crime.

Criminology —Study of the crimes.

Crinogenic —Causing secretion in a gland.

Cripple —A lame person.

Crisis —The turning point of a disease for betterment as sudden decrease of high temperature to normal or below normal within 24 hours, or for worse as the occurrence of sharp pain during the course of a disease.

Abdominal crisis — Severe abdominal pain due to many causes.

Addisonian crisis, Adrenal crisis — Acute failure of the adrenal gland due to Addison's disease.

Celiac crisis —Rapid onset of malnutrition in

celiac disease in which there is severe watery diarrhea, vomiting and dehydration.

Dietl's crisis —Sudden severe pain in the kidney region, chills, fever, nausea, vomiting and general collapse due to partial turning of the kidney upon its pedicle.

Salt-depletion crisis —Severe vomiting, dehydration, hypotension and sudden death due to severe loss of sodium chloride from the body.

Tabetic crisis —Severe pain in abdomen due to syphilis.

Thyroid crisis, Thyrotoxic crisis — Sudden increase in the severity of the symptoms of thyrotoxicosis.

Crista —A crest or ridge.

Critical —Pertaining to a crisis, or dangerous.

Crocated —Containing saffron.

Crocus sativus —Saffron.

Cross —1. Structure in the shape of a cross. 2. An organism produced by cross breeding.

Cross birth —Transverse presentation of the fetus which requires version.

Cross bite —Dental malocclusion in which the mandibular teeth are in the buccal direction so that the maxillary teeth remain outside the mandibular teeth.

Crossbreed —Hybrid. An organism born as a result of copulation of male and female of different species.

Crossbreeding —The production of an organism as a result of copulation of male and female of different species.

Cross-eye —Inward deviation of the visual axis of one eye toward that of the other eye while looking at an object.

Cross-fertilization —The fusion of the male and female gametes from the individuals of different species.

Cross-matching —Test to establish the blood compatibility before transfusion.

Cross-section —A transverse section through a structure.

Crossway —The crossing of two nerve paths.

Croup —The condition seen chiefly in childhood due to acute obstruction of the larynx caused by inflammation, allergy, spasm, foreign body, new growth or sometimes by the formation of a membrane as in diphtheria, marked by a resonant barking cough, hoarseness of the voice and suffocative and difficult respiration.

Croupous —Pertaining to croup.

Croupy —Characterized by croup.

Crowing —A noisy, harsh sound heard on inspiration.

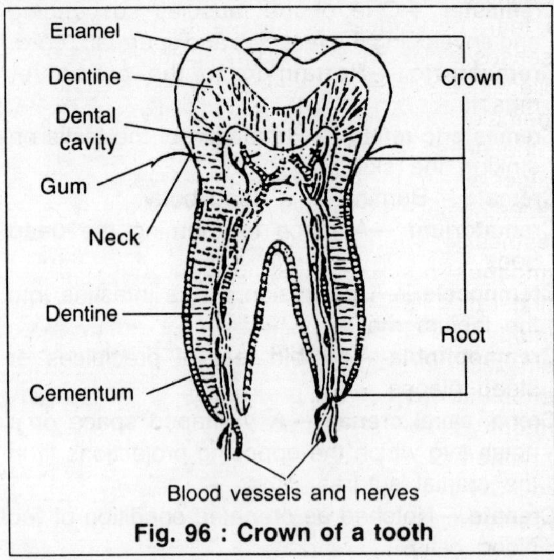

Fig. 96 : Crown of a tooth

Crown —The top most part of an organ or a structure as the top of a tooth or the head.

Crowning —The stage of delivery in which the largest portion of the scalp of the fetus appear at the vulva.

Crown-rump —The axis for measurement of a fetus.

Crownwork —Artificial crown for a tooth.

Crucial —1. Cross-shaped. 2. Critical.

Cruciate —Shaped like a cross.

Crucible —A vessel in which the substances are melted, burnt or dehydrated exposing them to high temperature.

Cruciform —Cross-shaped.

Crude —Raw, in a natural state or unrefined.

Crunch —The sound heard on auscultation of the chest synchronous with cardiac contraction.

Cruor —Coagulated blood.

Crura —Elongated masses resembling the legs.

Crural —Pertaining to the leg or thigh.

Crural hernia —Femoral hernia.

Crural nerve —Femoral nerve.

Crus —1. The leg extending from knee to the foot. 2. Any structure resembling the leg.

Crush —To make into small fragments.

Crust, Crusta —An outer layer on the skin formed by drying of a body secretion.

Crutch —An apparatus for helping a lame, weak or injured person in walking.

Crutch paralysis —Paralysis of the muscles of one or both arms due to pressure of the crutch on the nerves of the brachial plexus.

Crux, plural **cruces** — A junction or crossing.

Cry —Sudden production of dumb sounds with or without weeping in response to such stimuli as fear, pain, grief or joy, or due to some diseases as sudden loudy cry at the onset of epileptic seizure, night cry in children with acute tuberculous meningitis or the cry at night due to the onset of acute joint pain.

Cryalgesia —Pain from the application of cold.

Cryanesthesia —Loss of sense of cold.

Cryesthesia —Sensitiveness to the cold.

Crymoanesthesia —Anesthesia produced by refrigeration.

Crymodynia —Pain due to cold as rheumatic pain occurring in cold or damp weather.

Crymophilic —Showing preference for cold.

Crymophylactic —Resistant to cold.

Crymotherapy —Treatment of diseases by cold.

Cryo-, Cry- —A prefix concerning cold.

Cryoaerotherapy —Treatment of diseases by cold air.

Cryoanalgesia —Relief of pain by applying cold.

Cryoanesthesia —Local anesthesia produced by the application of cold.

Cryobank —Storage and preservation of living tissues as the semen at very low temperatures for future use.

Cryobiology —The study of effects of cold on body systems.

Cryocautery —A device for application of cold enough to kill the tissues.

Cryofibrinogen —An abnormal fibrinogen which precipitates on cooling, and dissolves on heating at body temperature.

Cryofibrinogenemia — The presence of cryofibrinogen in the blood.

Cryogen —Substance which produces low temperature.

Cryogenic —Producing or pertaining to low temperatures.

Cryogenics —The science dealing with the production and effects of cold or very low temperatures.

Cryoglobulin —An abnormal protein—globulin which precipitates at low temperatures and redissolves at body temperature.

Cryoglobulinemia — Presence of cryoglobulin in the blood which forms gel on exposure to cold.

Cryohypophysectomy — Destruction of the pituitary gland by the use of cold.

Cryolesion —An injury inflicted by exposure to cold for therapeutic purposes.

Cryolysis —Destruction by cold.

Cryometer —A thermometer for measuring very low temperature.

Cryopathy —Any disease caused by cold.

Cryophilic —Crymophilic, showing preference for cold.

Cryophylactic —Resistant to very low temperatures as are some bacteria.

Cryoprecipitate —Precipitate formed when soluble material is cooled.

Cryoprecipitation —The process of forming a cryoprecipitate from sobule material.

Cryopreservation — Preservation of the tisssues, organs, fluids, blood or semen etc., removed from the body, at very low temperatures for use in future in another person.

Cryoprobe —An instrument for applying cold to a tissue.

Cryoprostatectomy — Destruction of the prostate gland by freezing with a special cryoprobe.

Cryoprotective —Capable of protecting from the effect of cold.

Cryoprotein —Any protein of the blood as cryofibrinogen or cryoglobulin which precipitates on cooling.

Cryoscope —An instrument for measuring the freezing point.

Cryoscopy —The determination of the freezing point of a fluid, usually blood or urine, compared with that of distilled water.

Cryospasm —Spasm produced by cold.

Cryospray —Spraying of liquid nitrogen on the tissues to destroy them.

Cryostat —A device for maintaining very low temperatures.

Cryosurgery —Destruction of a tissue by application of extreme cold.

Cryotherapy —Treatment of disease by cold.

Cryotolerant —Able to tolerate very low temperatures.

Crypt —1. A small sac or a cavity 2. A tubular gland especially of the intestine.

Cryptanamnesia, Cryptomnesia —Subconscious memory.

Cryptectomy —Excision of a crypt.

Cryptitis —Inflammation of a crypt.

Crypto-, Crypt- —Prefixes indicating hidden, occult, without apparent cause.

Cryptocephalus —A fetus having an inapparent head.

Cryptococcoma —An infectious granuloma caused by the fungus Cryptococcus neoformans which is usually found in the brain, but also found in the lungs and elsewhere.

Cryptococcosis —Torulosis. Fungus infection caused by Cryptococcus neoformans which may involve lungs, skin, brain and its meninges.

Cryptocrystalline —Having very minute crystals.

Cryptodidymus —A congenital anomaly in which one fetus is being concealed within the body of the other.

Cryptogenic —Of unknown or indeterminate etiology.

Cryptolith —A stone in a crypt.

Cryptomenorrhea —The occurrence of menstrual symptoms without flow of blood as in imperforate hymen.

Cryptophthalmia —Congenital absence of the palpebral fissure, the skin extending from the forehead to the cheek leaving a small hole for the rudimentary eye.

Cryptophthalmus —Complete adhesion of the eye lids to the eyeball since birth.

Cryptopodia —Swelling of the lower part of the leg and the foot.

Cryptopyic —Having concealed suppuration.

Cryptorchid, Cryptorchis — The person having undescended testes which do not reach the scrotum.

Cryptorchidectomy —An operation for correction of an undescended testis.

Cryptorchidism, Cryptorchism —Failure of one or both testes to descend into the scrotum.

Cryptorrhea —Excessive secretion of an endocrine gland.

Cryptorrhetic, Cryptorrheic —Pertaining to the internal secretions.

Cryptoscope —Simple x-ray fluoroscope.

Cryptoxanthin —A substance present in various foods, *e.g.,* eggs and corn which can be converted into vitamin A in the body.

Crystal —A regular, angular solid substance in which the faces lying at definite angles to each other.

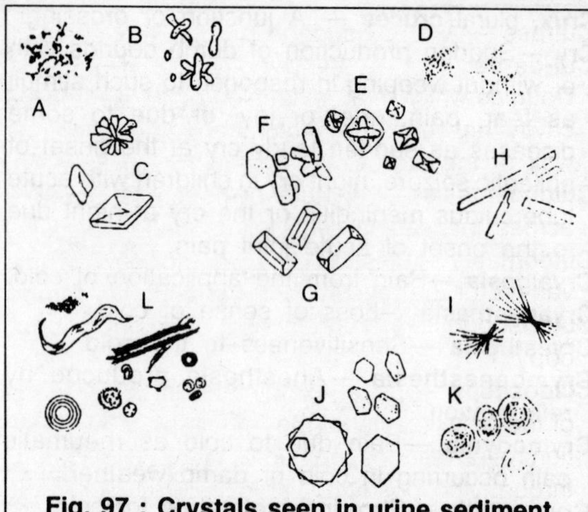

Fig. 97 : Crystals seen in urine sediment

A - Amorphous phosphate
B - Calcium carbonate
C - Uric acid
D - Amorphous urate
E - Calcium oxalate
F - Uric acid (in acidic urine)
G - Triple phosphate
H - Crystals of cholesterol
I - Crystals of tyrosine
J - Crystals of cystine
K - Crystals of leucine
L - Various other materials such as hair, cotton fibres, minute drops of the oil, air bubbles and various unicellular organisms

Crystalline —Resembling a crystal.

Crystalline lens —Lens of the eye in the capsule.

Crystallization —Formation of the crystals.

Crystallography —Study of crystals which is useful in investigating renal calculi.

Crystalloid —1. Like a crystal. 2. Capable of crystallization.

Crystalloiditis —Inflammation of the crystalline lens of the eye.

Crystallophobia —A morbid fear of glass or the things made of glass.

Crystalluria —Presence of crystals in the urine.

Crystal violet —A compound that has been used in the external treatment of burns, wounds, and fungal infections of the skin and mucous membranes.

C.S. —Cesarean section.

C.S.F. —Cerebrospinal fluid.

Cubital —Pertaining to the ulna or to the forearm.

Cubital fossa —Antecubital fossa.

Cubitus —Elbow, forearm, hand.

Cubitus valgus —A deformity of the arm in which the forearm deviates laterally.

Cubitus varus —A deformity of the arm in which the forearm deviates medially.

Cuboid —Like a cube.

Cu cm —Cubic centimeter.

Cuff —A band-like structure encircling a part or an object.

Cuffing —The collection of white blood cells in the shape of a ring around a blood vessel seen in certain infections.

Cuirass —A firm bandage around the chest.
Cul-de-sac —1. A blind pouch. 2. Pouch of Douglas which is an extension of the peritoneal cavity between the rectum and the posterior wall of the uterus.
Culdocentesis —Puncture of pouch of Douglas across the vaginal wall for aspiration of fluid.
Culdoplasty —Plastic surgery performed on the vagina for the relaxation of the posterior fornix.
Culdoscope —An endoscope used in culdoscopy.
Culdoscopy —Visual examination of the viscera of the pelvic cavity of the female after introduction of an endoscope into the pelvic cavity, through the posterior vaginal fornix.
Culdotomy —To incise the posterior vaginal wall into the pouch of Douglas.
Culex — A type of mosquito that carries disease-producing organisms.
Culicidal —Destructive to the mosquitoes.
Culicide —An agent that destroys the mosquitoes.
Culicifuge —An agent to drive away the mosquitoes.
Cullen's sign —Bluish discoloration of the skin around the umbilicus due to intraperitoneal hemorrhage, caused by ruptured ectopic pregnancy or acute pancreatitis.
Culling —The process of removal of abnormal or damaged blood cells from the circulation by the spleen.
Culmen, plural **culmina** — The top or summit of a thing.
Cultivation —The growing of living microorganisms in an artificial medium.
Cultural —Pertaining to the culture.
Culture —1. To induce the propagation of microorganisms or of living tissue cells in special media which are promoting their growth. 2. Civilization.
Cu mm —Cubic millimeter.
Cumulation —Accumulation.
Cumulative —Accumulative.
Cumulus —A small elevation.
Cuneate, Cuneiform —Wedge-shaped.
Cuneiform —Cuneate.
Cuneocuboid —Pertaining to the lateral cuneiform and the cuboid bones.
Cuneohysterectomy —The excision of a wedge-shaped piece of tissue from the posterior surface of the cervix uteri.
Cuneonavicular —Cuneoscaphoid. Pertaining to the cuneiform and the navicular bones.
Cuneoscaphoid —Cuneonavicular.
Cuneus —A wedge-shaped lobule on the medial aspect of the occipital lobe of the cerebrum.
Cuniculus —A burrow in the skin made by the itch mite.
Cunnilingus —Stimulation of the female genital organs by using the mouth and the tongue.
Cunnus —The vulva.
Cup —1. A depression or hollow. 2. A cupping glass.
Cupola —Cupula.
Cupped —Hollowed ; made cup-shaped.
Cupping —The application of a glass vessel to the skin from which the air has been drawn out by heat, to draw the blood to the surface.
Cuprum —Copper.
Cupruresis —Excretion of copper in the urine.
Cupruretic —Pertaining to or promoting the excretion of copper in the urine.
Cupula —A small, inverted cup or dome-shaped cap over a structure.
Cupular —1. Pertaining to cupula. 2. Dome-shaped.
Cupulate —Cupular.
Cupuliform —Cupular.
Curage —Curettage by means of the finger only.
Curare —1. A poisonous extract of some plants. 2. An extract of a plant used as a muscle relaxant.
Curariform —Denoting a drug having an action like curare.
Curarimimetic —Having a curarelike action.
Curarization —Administration of curare (tubocurarine) for the relaxation of the muscle.
Curative —To be cured.
Curd —The coagulum of milk.
Cure —Restoration to health.
Curet, Curette —A spoon-shaped scraping instrument used for removing the foreign matter from a cavity, or for cleansing a diseased surface.
Curettage —Scarping of a cavity as of the uterine cavity, or the cleansing of a diseased surface, with a curette.
Curettement —Curettage.
Curietherapy —Radium therapy.
Curing —The process of making someone well.
Curling's ulcer —An acute peptic ulcer that usually follows an acute stress, e.g., a severe burn.
Current —A stream or flow of fluid, air or electricity.

Curschmann's spirals —Coiled fibres of mucus surrounding the eosinophils found occasionally in the sputum of asthmatic persons.

Curse —1. To use foul, offensive language or to abuse. 2. To attempt to inflict injury.

Curvature —Bending or sloping.

Curve —A bend.

Curvilinear —Pertaining to a curved line.

Cushingoid —Resembling cushing's syndrome.

Cushion —A mass of fatty tissues which prevents undue pressure upon underlying structures.

Cusp —A projection on the grinding surface of a tooth, or a segment of a cardiac valve.

Cuspad —Toward the cusp of a tooth.

Cuspal —Pertaining to cusp.

Cuspid, Cuspidate —1. Having one cusp. 2. A canine tooth.

Cuspis —Cusp.

Cutaneous —Pertaining to the skin.

Cutdown —To create a small opening by incision over a vein to facilitate the vene puncture and allow the passage of a needle or cannula for withdrawal of blood or administration of fluids.

Cuticle —Epidermis or the outer horny layer of the skin.

Cuticula —Cuticle.

Cuticularization —Growth of the skin over a wound.

Cutin —A specially prepared, thin, animal membrane used as a protective covering for wounds.

Cutireaction —Inflammatory or irritative reaction of the skin.

Cutis —The skin.

Cutization —The changing of mucous membrane into the skin at the mucocutaneous junction.

Cuvet, Cuvette —A small, transparent glass or plastic container or cup in which solutions are placed for photometric examinations.

C V S —Cardiovascular system.

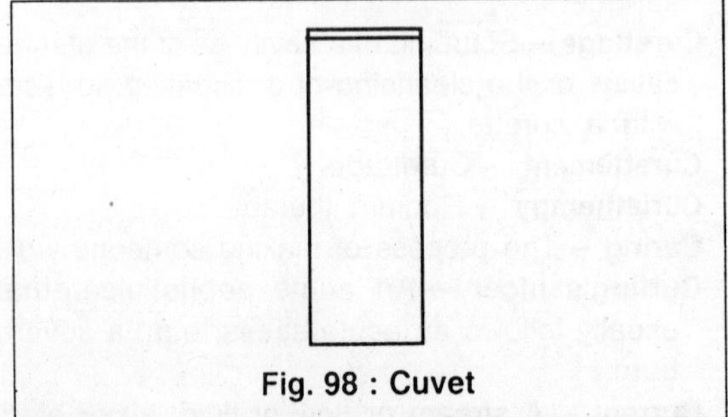

Fig. 98 : Cuvet

Cyanemia —Blueness of the blood.

Cyanephidrosis, Cyanhidrosis —Exudation of bluish sweat.

Cyano-, Cyan- — Prefixes meaning blue.

Cyanochroic, Cyanochrous —Cyanotic.

Cyanoderma —Blue discoloration of the skin.

Cyanogen —A poisonous gas.

Cyanomycosis —Development of blue pus due to Micrococcus pyocyaneus.

Cyanopathy —Blue discoloration of the skin.

Cyanophil, Cyanophile —A cell or tissue that is differentially colored blue by a staining procedure.

Cyanophilous —Having attraction for the blue color.

Cyanopia, Cyanopsia — Defective vision in which all the things appear to be blue.

Cyanosed —Affected wtih cyanosis.

Cyanosis —The bluish discoloration of the skin due to deficiency of oxygen and hemoglobin and excess of carbon dioxide in the blood.

Cyanotic —Affected with or pertaining to cyanosis.

Cyanuria —The excretion of blue urine.

Cybernetics —Comparative study of the computers and the human nervous system.

Cyberphilia —Attraction toward the use of machines, especially the computers.

Cyberphobia —Morbid fear of using the computer.

Cyclarthrodial —Pertaining to cyclarthrosis.

Cyclarthrosis —A joint capable of rotation.

Cycle —A series of movements or events occurring at regular intervals.

Cardiac cycle —The process of systole (contraction), diastole (relaxation) and short rest pause, comprises a cardiac cycle which corresponds to one pulse beat.

Menstrual cycle —A series of periodically recurring changes in the endometrium and of the hormonal changes in women, culminating in menstruation.

Cyclectomy —1. Excision of a portion of the ciliary body or muscle. 2. Excision of the ciliary borders of the eyelids.

Cyclencephalus —A monster with the cerebral hemispheres blended into one.

Cyclencephaly, Cyclencephalia —Poor development and fusion of the two cerebral hemispheres in a malformed fetus.

Cyclic —Periodic, occurring in cycles.

Cyclicotomy —Incision of the ciliary muscle.

Cyclic vomiting —Periodic and recurrent vomiting occurring in a person of nervous temperament.

Cyclitis —Inflammation of a ciliary body.

Cyclo-, Cycl- — Prefixes meaning circular or pertaining to the ciliary body of the eye.

Cyclocephaly, Cyclocephalia —Cyclencephaly, Cyclencephalia.

Cycloceratitis —Inflammation of the ciliary body and the cornea.

Cyclochoroiditis — Inflammation of the ciliary body and the choroid of the eye.

Cyclocryotherapy — Treatment of glaucoma by freezing the ciliary body.

Cyclodestructive —Pertaining to destruction of the ciliary body to diminish the production of aqueous fluid in case of glaucoma.

Cyclodialysis —To create a communication between the anterior chamber of the eye and the suprachoroidal space, in glaucoma.

Cyclodiathermy —Destruction of a part of the ciliary body by diathermy.

Cycloduction —Circumduction.

Cycloid —Resembling a circle.

Cyclokeratitis —Cycloceratitis. Inflammation of the cornea and ciliary body.

Cyclopea —Cyclopia.

Cyclopean —Cyclopian.

Cyclophoria —Rotation of the eyeball due to weakness of the muscles.

Cyclophotocoagulation — Photocoagulation of the ciliary processes to reduce the secretion of aqueous humor in glaucoma.

Cyclopia —The condition of the congenital absence of one eye.

Cyclopian —Cyclopean. Denoting or pertaining to cyclopia.

Cycloplegia —Paralysis of the ciliary muscle.

Cycloplegic —Producing cycloplegia.

Cyclops —An individual with one eye only since birth.

Cyclothymia —A tendency to change the mood from depression to hypothymia.

Cyclothymiac, Cyclothymic —Pertaining to cyclothymia.

Cyclotomy —To make an incision into the ciliary muscle of the eye.

Cyclotorsion —Cycloduction.

Cyclotropia —Permanent cyclophoria, rotation of the eyeball due to weakness of the muscles, permanently.

Cyema —The product of conception.

Cyemology —Embryology.

Cyesis —Pregnancy.

Cyetic —Pertaining to pregnancy.

Cylicotomy —To make an incision into the ciliary muscle.

Cylinder —A hollow tube like structure.

Cylindrical —Having a shape of a cylinder.

Cylindroadenoma — Cylindroma.

Cylindroid —1. Shaped like a cylinder. 2. A long, thin, tubular urinary cast which is twisted upon itself.

Cylindroma —Malignant tumor of the skin occurring on the face and the scalp containing cylindrical masses of the epithelial cells surrounded by hyaline material.

Cylindruria —Presence of cylindroids in the urine.

Cyllosis —Clubfoot.

Cymbocephalic —Having a boat-shaped head.

Cymbocephaly —The condition of having a boat-shaped head.

Cynanche —Severe sore throat with threatened suffocation.

Cynanthropy —A mental disease in which the patient behaves like a dog.

Cynic —Pertaining to a dog.

Cynic spasm —Spasm of the facial muscles causing a grin.

Cynobex —Dry barking cough.

Cynocephaly —The condition in which the skull slopes backward from the orbits resembling to the head of a dog.

Cynodont —A canine tooth.

Cynophobia —Morbid fear of dogs.

Cyotrophy —Nutrition of the fetus.

Cypridophobia —1. Morbid fear of the sexual intercourse and of the venereal disease. 2. False belief of having a venereal disease.

Cypriphobia —A great dislike for and fear of coitus.

Cyrtometer —An apparatus for measuring the circumference of the chest and other curved surfaces of the body.

Cyrtosis —A condition of an abnormal curvature of the spine.

Cyst —1. A closed cavity or sac, normal or abnormal, usually containing liquid or semisolid material. 2. A structure enclosing certain organisms, in which they become inactive and are known as encysted, as the cyst of certain protozoa.

Adventitious cyst — Cyst formed around a foreign body.

Alveolar cyst — Dilatation and rupture of the pulmonary alveoli forming air cysts.

Baker's cyst —The swelling formed behind

the knee due to escape of synovial fluid from the knee joint, enclosed in a membranous sac.

Blood cyst —Bloody tumor, hematoma.

Chocolate cyst —Ovarian cyst containing chocolate colored gelatinous substance.

Daughter cyst —Cyst growing from the walls of another cyst.

Dentigerous cyst —Cyst containing teeth.

Dermoid cyst —Cyst containing hair, sebum or skin.

Exudative cyst —Cyst formed by an exudate in a closed cavity.

Hydatid cyst —Cyst formed by the growth of the larvae of the tapeworm Echinococcus granulosus in the liver.

Meibomian cyst — Chalazion, cyst of the meibomian gland of the eyelid.

Mucoid cyst —Cyst containing mucus.

Ovarian cyst —Cyst formed in the ovary.

Sebaceous cyst —Cyst of a sebaceous gland.

Vaginal cyst —Cyst formed in the vagina.

Cystadenocarcinoma —The cancer of the gland which forms cysts as it grows.

Cystadenoma —An adenoma containing cysts.

Cystalgia —Pain in the bladder.

Cystauxe —Enlargement or thickening of the urinary bladder.

Cystectasia —Dilatation of the urinary bladder.

Cystectomy —1. Removal of a cyst. 2. Removal of the cystic duct and the gallbladder both, or of cystic duct alone. 3. Excision of the urinary bladder or a part of it.

Cystelcosis —Formation of ulcers in the urinary bladder.

Cystencephalus —The fetus having a membranous sac in place of a brain.

Cystic —1. Pertaining to or containing cysts. 2. Pertaining to the urinary bladder or to the gallbladder.

Cystic duct —The duct of the gallbladder which unites with the hepatic duct from the liver to form the common bile duct.

Cysticercoid —The larval encysted form of a tapeworm.

Cysticercosis —Infection with the larval forms of tapeworm (Taenia solium).

Cysticercus —A larval form of a tapeworm.

Cysticotomy —Choledochotomy.

Cystiform —Resembling a cyst.

Cystigerous —Containing cysts.

Cystine —A sulfur-containing amino acid, produced by the digestion of protein.

Cystinemia —Presence of cystine in the blood.

Cystinosis —A hereditary disease of childhood in which there is deposition of cystine throughout the tissues of the body.

Cystinuria —1. The presence of cystine in the urine. 2. A hereditary disease in which there is excretion of large amounts of cystine, and other amino acids as lysine, ornithine and arginine in the urine.

Cystirrhagia —Hemorrhage from the urinary bladder.

Cystistaxia, Cystistaxis —Oozing of blood from the mucous membrane into the urinary bladder.

Cystitis —Inflammation of the urinary bladder.

Cystitome —An instrument for incision into the lens capsule of the eye.

Cystitomy —To make an incision into the capsule of the lens of the eye or into the gallbladder.

Cystoadenoma —Cystadenoma.

Cystocarcinoma —Carcinoma associated with cysts.

Cystocele —Herniation of the urinary bladder into the vagina.

Cystochromoscopy — Examination of the interior of the urinary bladder after administration of a colored dye to identify the ureteral orifices.

Cystocolostomy —To form a communication between the gallbladder and the colon.

Cystoduodenostomy — Duodenocholecystostomy.

Cystodynia —Pain in the urinary bladder.

Cystoelytroplasty —Repair of vesicovaginal injuries by plastic surgery.

Cystoenterocele —Herniation of the urinary bladder and the intestine usually into the vagina.

Cystoepiplocele —Protrusion of the portions of the urinary bladder and of the omentum.

Cystofibroma —Fibrous tumor containing cysts.

Cystogastrostomy —Joining of an adjacent cyst as of pancreas to the stomach for drainage.

Cystogram —X-ray of the urinary bladder.

Cystography —The taking an X-ray of the urinary bladder after injecting a radiopaque substance into it.

Cystoid —Resembling a cyst.

Cystojejunostomy —Joining of an adjacent cyst to the jejunum.

Cystolith —Vesical calculus.

Cystolithectomy —Removal of a vesical calculus by surgery.

Cystolithiasis —Formation of stones in the urinary bladder.

Cystolithic —Pertaining to vesical calculus.

Cystolitholapaxy —Removal of the calculi from the urinary bladder by crushing, and then irrigating to remove the fragments.

Cystolithotomy — Cystolithectomy.

Cystoma —A cystic tumor.

Cystometer —An instrument for measuring the capacity of the urinary bladder and its changes due to pressures.

Cystometrography — Cystometry.

Cystometry —Measurement of the pressure/volume relationship of the urinary bladder.

Cystomorphous —Cystoid, cystlike.

Cystomyoma —A myoma containing cysts.

Cystomyxoadenoma —An adenoma containing cysts with myxoma.

Cystomyxoma —A myxoma containing cysts.

Cystoparalysis —Cystoplegia.

Cystopexy —Fixation of the urinary bladder to the abdominal wall by surgery.

Cystophotography —The photographing of the interior of the urinary bladder.

Cystoplasty —Repair of the urinary bladder by plastic surgery.

Cystoplegia —Paralysis of the urinary bladder.

Cystoproctostomy —Surgical formation of a connection between the urinary bladder and the rectum.

Cystoptosia, Cystoptosis —Prolapse of the mucous membrane of the urinary bladder into the urethra.

Cystopyelitis —Inflammation of the urinary bladder and the renal pelvis.

Cystopyelonephritis — Inflammation of the urinary bladder, and the kidney with its pelvis combined.

Cystoradiography —X-ray examination of the gallbladder or urinary bladder.

Cystorectostomy —Formation of a surgical connection between the urinary bladder and the rectum.

Cystorrhagia —Hemorrhage from the urinary bladder.

Cystorrhaphy —Suture of the urinary bladder.

Cystorrhea —Mucus discharge from the urinary bladder.

Cystorrhexis —Rupture of the urinary bladder.

Cystosarcoma — Sarcoma containing cysts.

Cystoscope —An instrument for visual examination of the interior of the urinary bladder and the ureter.

Cystoscopy —Visual examination of the urinary bladder and the ureter with a cystoscope.

Cystospasm —Spasmodic contractions of the urinary bladder.

Cystostomy —Surgical formation of an opening into the urinary bladder.

Cystotome —Instrument for incision of the urinary bladder. or gallbladder.

Cystotomy —Incision of the urinary bladder or gallbladder.

Cystotrachelotomy —To make an incision into the neck of the urinary bladder.

Cystoureteritis —Inflammation of both, the urinary bladder and the ureter.

Cystoureterogram —X-ray of the urinary bladder and the ureter.

Cystoureterography —X-ray examination of the urinary bladder and the ureters.

Cystourethritis —Inflammation of the urinary bladder and the urethra.

Cystourethrocele —Prolapse of the urinary bladder and the urethra in female.

Cystourethrogram —X-ray of the urinary bladder and the urethra.

Cystourethrography —X-ray examination of the urinary bladder and the urethra by using a radiopaque substance.

Cystourethropexy —Surgical fixaton of the urinary bladder and the urethra.

Cystourethroscope —An instrument for examining the posterior part of the urethra, and urinary bladder.

Cystovesiculography —X-ray examination of the urinary bladder and seminal vesicles after administration of a radiopaque substance.

Cytapheresis —The process of separating various cells from the withdrawn blood, with the plasma reinfused into the donor.

-cyte —A suffix meaning cell.

-cyto — -cyte

Cytoanalyzer —An apparatus for detecting the malignant cells in a microscopic smear or a fluid.

Cytoarchitectonic — Pertaining to the structure and the arrangement of cells in tissues.

Cytoarchitectonics — Cytoarchitecture.

Cytoarchitectural — Pertaining to cytoarchitecture.

Cytoarchitecture —The arrangement of cells in a tissue.

Cytobiology —Biology of the cells.
Cytobiotaxis —The influence of cells upon other living cells.
Cytochemistry —Chemistry of the living cell.
Cytochrome —An iron-containing protein found in the mitochondria of eukaryotic cells, and cytochromes are classified into 4 groups — a, b, c and d.
Cytochylema —Hyaloplasm.
Cytocidal —Causing the death of the cells.
Cytocide —An agent which destroys cells.
Cytoclasis —Destruction of cells.
Cytoclastic —Destructive to cells.
Cytoclesis, Cytobiotaxis —The influence of living cells upon other living cells.
Cytodendrite —A dendrite given off from the body of a nerve cell.
Cytodiagnosis —Diagnosis made by examination of the cells present in the exudates, fluids, etc.
Cytodieresis —Cell division.
Cytogenesis —Origin and development of the cell.
Cytogenetics —A branch of genetics concerned with the study of cells, especially of the chromosomes.
Cytogenic, Cytogenous — Producing cells.
Cytogenous —Cytogenic.
Cytogeny —Formation and development of the cells.
Cytoglycopenia —Deficiency of glucose in the blood cells.
Cytohistogenesis —The development of the structure of the cells.
Cytoid —Resembling a cell.
Cytokalipenia —Potassium deficiency in the body or blood cells.
Cytokeratin —Keratin.
Cytokinesis —The separation of cytoplasm in two parts in cell division.
Cytolemma —Cell membrane.
Cytologic —Pertaining to the cytology.
Cytologist —Specialist in cytology.
Cytology —The study of the formation, structure and functions of the cells.
Cytolysin —An antibody that causes destruction of the cells.
Cytolysis — Destruction of living cells.
Cytolytic —Pertaining to cytolysis.
Cytomegalic —Characterized by markedly enlarged cells.
Cytometaplasia —Change in the form or function of cells.
Cytometer —An instrument for counting and measuring the cells.
Cytometry —The counting and measuring of cells.
Cytomicrosome —A minute granule in the cytoplasm of the cell.
Cytomorphology —The morphology of body cells.
Cytomorphosis —The changes which occur in the development of the cells.
Cyton —1. A cell. 2. The body of a nerve cell.
Cytopathic —1. Pertaining to the pathological changes in the cells. 2. Concerning the ability to destroy a cell.
Cytopathogenesis —Production of pathological changes in cells.
Cytopathogenic —Capable of producing pathological changes in the cells.
Cytopathogenicity —The ability to produce pathological changes in the cells.
Cytopathologic, Cytopathological —Indicating the changes in cells in a disease.
Cytopathologist —A specialist in cytopathology.
Cytopathology —Study of cellular changes in disease.
Cytopathy —Any disease of a cell or any of its constituents.
Cytopenia —Deficiency of cells in the blood.
Cytophagocytosis — Destruction of other cells by phagocytes.
Cytophagus —Destroying cells.
Cytophagy —Destruction of other cells by phagocytes.
Cytophilic —Having an attraction for cells, e.g. antibodies.
Cytophotometry —Cytometry.
Cytophylactic —Pertaining to cytophylaxis.
Cytophylaxis —Protection of cells against lysis.
Cytophysiology —Physiology of the cell.
Cytopipette —A pipette for taking specimens of cells, especially from body fluids or cavities.
Cytoplasm —The protoplasm of a cell outside the nucleus.
Cytoplasmic —Pertaining to the cytoplasm.
Cytopoiesis —Formation of cells.
Cytopreparation —Preparation of a cellular specimen for cytologic examination.
Cytoreticulum —The network of fibres supporting fluid of protoplasm.
Cytorrhyctes —Inclusion bodies in the cells.
Cytoscopy —Microscopic examination of cells for diagnosis purpose.

Cytosis —The condition in which the number of cells is increased than normal.

Cytoskeleton —The internal structural framework of a cell.

Cytosol —Hyaloplasm Liquid porton of the cytoplasm of a cell which contains no solid materials.

Cytosolic —Pertaining to or contained in the cytosol.

Cytosome —The portion of a cell except its nucleus.

Cytospasm —Spasm of the urinary bladder.

Cytost —A specific toxin released by an injured or destroyed cell.

Cytostasis —Stoppage of the circulation of white blood cells as occurs in earlier stages of inflammation.

Cytostatic —Preventing the growth and multiplication of cells.

Cytostome —The mouth opening of a unicellular organism.

Cytotactic —Pertaining to cytotaxia.

Cytotaxia, Cytotaxis —The movement and arrangement of cells in response to a stimulation.

Cytotechnologist —A medical laboratory technologist who is specially trained in cytopathology.

Cytotechnology —Microscopic examination of the cells to detect abnormalities.

Cytothesis —Repair of the injured cells.

Cytotoxic —Destructive to cells.

Cytotoxicity —The state of being cytotoxic.

Cytotoxin —A toxin or antibody which is toxic to the cells of particular organs.

Cytotrophoblast —The thin inner layer of the trophoblast composed of cuboid cells.

Cytotropic —Having attraction for cells.

Cytotropism —1. Movement of cells in response to external stimulation. 2. The tendency of certain chemicals, drugs, bacteria, viruses and heat or cold etc. to exert their effect upon certain cells of the body.

Cytozoic —Living within or attached to a cell, as certain protozoa.

Cytozoon —A protozoon that lives as intracellular parasite.

Cytula —The impregnated ovum.

Cyturia —Presence of cells of any kind in the urine.

Dacnomania—Mania for killing.

Dacry-, Dacryo- —Prefixes indicating lacrimal gland or lacrimal apparatus or tears.

Dacryadenalgia, Dacryoadenalgia —Pain in a lacrimal gland.

Dacryadenitis—Inflammation of a lacrimal gland.

Dacryadenoscirrhus— Hardening of a lacrimal gland.

Dacryagogatresia—Occlusion of a tear duct.

Dacryagogue, Dacryagogic—Stimulating the secretion of tears.

Dacrycystalgia—Pain in a lacrimal sac.

Dacryelcosis—Ulceration of the lacrimal apparatus.

Dacryoadenalgia—Pain in a lacrimal gland.

Dacryoadenectomy —Removal of the lacrimal gland by surgery.

Dacryoadenitis— Inflammation of a lacrimal gland.

Dacryoblennorrhea—1. Mucous discharge from a lacrimal sac. 2. Chronic inflammation of the lacrimal sac.

Dacryocele —Herniation of a lacrimal sac.

Dacryocyst—The lacrimal sac.

Dacryocystalgia—Pain in the lacrimal sac.

Dacryocystectomy—Excision of the membranes of the lacrimal sac.

Dacryocystitis—Inflammation of a lacrimal sac.

Dacryocystoblennorrhea—Chronic inflammation of the lacrimal sac with discharge.

Dacryocystocele —Herniation of a lacrimal sac.

Dacryocystogram—An x–ray film of the lacrimal apparatus.

Dacryocystography—X-ray examination of a nasolacrimal duct after introduction of a contrast medium in it.

Dacryocystoptosis—Prolapse of the lacrimal sac.

Dacryocystorhinostenosis—Narrowing of the canal connecting the lacrimal sac with the nasal cavity.

Dacryocystorhinostomy—To make a surgical connection between lacrimal sac and the nasal cavity.

Dacryocystorhinotomy —To make the passage of a probe through the lacrimal sac into the nasal cavity.

Dacryocystotome—An instrument for incision of lacrimal sac.

Dacryocystotomy—Incision of the lacrimal sac.

Dacryogenic—Stimulating the flow of tears.

Dacryohelcosis—Ulceration of the lacrimal sac or duct.

Dacryohemorrhea—Discharge of tears mixed with the blood.

Dacryolith, — Lacrimal calculus.

Dacryolithiasis—Presence of calculi in the lacrimal apparatus.

Dacryoma—A tumor-like swelling of the lacrimal duct due to obstruction.

Dacryon—The point where the lacrimal, frontal and upper maxillary bones meet.

Dacryops—Dacryorrhea, the flow of tears constantly.

Dacryopyorrhea—Discharge of pus from the lacrimal duct.

Dacryopyosis—Formation of pus in the lacrimal apparatus.

Dacryorrhea—Excessive flow of tears.

Dacryosolenitis— Inflammation of the lacrimal or nasal duct.

Dacryostenosis—Narrowing of a lacrimal duct.

Dacryosyrinx—1. A lacrimal fistula. 2. A syringe for irrigating the lacrimal ducts.

Dactyl—Digit.

Dactylalgia—Dactylodynia. Pain in the fingers.

Dactylate, Dactylic, Dactylose—Like a finger or toe.

Dactyledema—Edema of the fingers or toes.

Dactylion—Adhesions between the fingers or toes.

Dactylitis —Inflammation of a finger or toe.

Dactylocampsis—Permanent flexion of the fingers.

Dactylocampsodynia— Painful contraction of one or more fingers

Dactylodynia—Dactylalgia.

Dactylogram—A finger print.

Dactylography—The study of fingers print.

Dactylogryposis —Permanent contraction of the fingers.

Dactylology—Communication between the persons by signs made by the fingers.

Dactylolysis—Destruction of a digit as in leprosy.
Dactylomegally—Abnormally large fingers or toes.
Dactyloscope —An instrument for performing dactyloscopy.
Dactyloscopy —Examination of the finger prints for the purpose of identification.
Dactylospasm—Cramp of a finger or toe.
Dactylus—A finger or a toe.
Daft—Insane, foolish.
Daltonism—Red-green color blindness.
Dalton's law—The law of Dalton stating that in a mixture of gases, the total pressure is equal to the sum of the partial pressure of each gas.
Dam—A thin rubber sheet used in dentistry and surgery to isolate a part from the surrounding tissues and fluids.
Damp—Moist.
Damping—The diminution of the amplitude of successive vibrations uniformly, as of an electric current.
Damp-proof—Resistant to damp.
D & C—Dilatation of the cervix and curettage of the uterus.
D & E—Dilation and evacuation of the uterus.
Danders—Small scales from the skin of the animals causing allergy when breathed.
Dandruff—1. White, dry, scaly material shed from the epidermis of the scalp normally or in excess associated with a disease. 2. Seborrheic dermatitis of the scalp.
Dartoid—Resembling the tunica dartos.
Dartos—The muscular, contractile tissue under the skin of the scrotum.
Dartos muscle reflex— Wormlike contraction of the dartos muscle of the scrotum following the application of ice to the perineum.
Dartrous—Herpetic.
Dasymeter—An apparatus for estimating density of gases.
Data— Figures.
Daughter—1. A decay product 2. Arising from a cell division, as a daughter cell or nucleus. 3. One's female child.
Dazzle—Occurrence of dimness of vision in very bright light.
dB, db—Decibel.
D.D.S.—Doctor of dental surgery.
D.D.T.—Dichlorodiphenyltrichloroethane, a powerful insecticide used in dilution as a powder or in an oily solution as a spray to destroy the mosquitos etc.
De- —Prefix indicating down or from.
Deacidification — Neutralization of acidity.
Deactivation—The process of making or becoming inactive.
Dead—Without life.
Deaf—Partially or completely lacking the power of hearing.
Deafferentation—Cutting of the afferent nerve supply.
Deaf-mute —A person unable to hear & to speak.
Deaf-mutism—Inability to hear & to speak.
Deafness—Partial or complete loss of hearing.

Central deafness— Deafness caused by brain lesion.

Ceruminous deafness—Deafness produced by the plugs of ear wax.

Conductive deafness—Deafness due to inability of the sound waves to be transmitted to the auditory receptors which may result from wax obstructing the external auditory canal or the inflammation of the middle ear etc.

Hysterical deafness— Deafness which may appear or disappear in a hysterical patient without any cause.

Nerve deafness—Deafness due to lesion of the auditory nerve or central pathways.

Occupational deafness—Deafness caused due to working in places where there is very loud noise.

Tone deafness— Inability to distinguish the musical sounds.

Word deafness—Deafness in which the sounds are heard but the interpretation of the words is impossible.

Dealbation—The act of whitening or bleaching.
Dealcoholization—Removal of alcohol from an object.
Deallergize—Desensitize.
Deaquation—Dehydration, removal of water from anything.
Dearterialization — Changing of arterial blood into venous blood, removal of oxygen from the blood.
Dearticulation—Dislocation of a joint.
Death—Cessation of the heart's action or of all vital bodily functions.

Brain death—Irreversible coma or brain damage.

Cell death—Complete degeneration or necrosis of the cells.

Cerebral death —Brain death.

Fetal death— Death of a fetus in uterus.
Local death—Gangrene or necrosis of a part.

Deathbed statement—Dying declaration.

Death certificate— The certificate of death of a person issued by a registered medical practitioner or the health authority of municipality or nagar nigam that includes — Name of the person, sex, age, date of birth, birth place, place of residence, occupation, date of death, place of death, cause of death and descendent's name etc.

Death rate—The number of deaths occurring per 1000 of the population in a given area within a specified time.

Death rattle—A sound heard in the throat of the dying person caused by the accumulation of mucus.

Debilitant—1. Remedy for reducing the excitement. 2. That which causes weakness.

Debilitate —To produce weakness.

Debilitating—Causing weakness.

Debility—Weakness.

Debond—To separate a dental appliance from the tooth to which it has been attached.

Debouch—To open or empty into another part.

Debouchment—The opening or emptying into another part.

Debride—To remove by debridement.

Debridement—The removal of foreign material and damaged or dead tissue from a wound until the surrounding healthy tissue is exposed.

Debris—The remains of damaged tissues.

Debt—Deficit or deficiency.

Debulking—Removal of a portion of a tumor by surgery, when it is not possible to excise it completely.

Deca- —Prefix indicating ten.

Decagram—10 grams.

Decalcification—1. Loss of calcium from a bone or tooth. 2. The process of removing calcareous matter.

Decalcify—To remove the calcium or its salts from the bone by acids.

Decalcifying—An agent or process that causes decalcification.

Decaliter—10 Liters.

Decalvant—Destroying hair or making bald.

Decameter—10 meters.

Decannulation—Removal of a canula.

Decanormal—Pertaining to a solution 10 times stronger than normal solution.

Decant—To pour off gently the upper clear portion of a fluid leaving the sediment in the bottom of the container.

Decantation—The pouring off the clear fluid floating on the surface of the sediment remaining in the bottom of the container.

Decapitate—To cut off the head, especially of a fetus to facilitate delivery in case of difficult labor.

Decapitation—1. The removal of the head from the body 2. Separation of the head from the shaft of a bone.

Decapsulation—Removal of a capsule of an organ, especially the renal capsule.

Decay—1. Gradual decomposition of dead organic matter by the action of microorganisms. 2. Gradual loss of physical and mental energy as occurs in aging.

Deceleration—Decrease in rapidity.

Decentration—Removal from a center.

Decerebrate—To eliminate cerebral function by transecting the brain stem or by ligating the common carotid arteries and basilar artery at the center of the pons.

Decerebration —Removal of the brain or cutting of the spinal cord at the level of the brain stem.

Decerebrize— To remove the brain.

Dechlorination, Dechloridation—To reduce the amount of chlorides in the body by reducing the amount of salt in the diet.

Decholesterolization— Reduction of cholesterol in the blood.

Deci- —Prefix indicating one tenth.

Decibel—Unit of intensity of sound.

Decidophobia—Fear of taking a decision.

Decidua—The endometrium or the lining of the pregnant uterus which is shed off at the time of delivery.

Decidual—Pertaining to or resembling decidua.

Deciduation—The shedding of the decidua during menstruation.

Deciduitis—Inflammation of the decidua.

Deciduoma—A tumor of the uterus containing decidual cells.

Deciduomatosis—Formation of excessive and irregular decidual tissue in the non-pregnant uterus.

Deciduosarcoma—Choriocarcinoma. Chorioepithelioma. A tumor of the chorion.

Deciduous—Falling off, subject to being shed.

Deciduous teeth—The milk teeth or temporary teeth, 10 in each jaw, which appear at the age of 6 months and fall off by the end of 6 years.

Decigram—One tenth of a gram.

Deciliter—One tenth of a liter, one hundred milliliters.

Decimeter—One tenth of a meter.

Decinormal—Having one tenth of the strength of a normal solution.

Decipara—A woman who has given birth for the tenth living or dead baby weighing 500 grams or more.

Declination—Rotation of the eye-ball due to weakness of the oblique muscles.

Declinator—Retractor. An instrument for holding apart certain structures of the body during an operation.

Decline—Decrease.

Decoction—The liquid medicine prepared by boiling the vegetable substances with water.

Decollation—Decapitation, especially of the fetus during labor.

Decollement—To separate two adherent structures.

Decoloration—Removal of color, bleaching.

Decompensation—Inability of the heart to maintain adequate blood circulation, which is indicated by dyspnea, venous engorgement and edema.

Decompose—1. To decay or putrefy. 2. To disintegrate a compound into its constituents.

Decomposition—1. Decay. 2. Disintegration of a compound substance into its constituents.

Decompress—To relieve by reducing the pressure of air or gas.

Decompression—1. The removal of pressure as from the expulsion of gas from the intestines. 2. The slow reduction of pressure on deep-sea divers as they come out of the sea on the earth or on the persons who ascend to great heights, to prevent the development of nitrogen bubbles in the blood and tissues which cause pain in the limbs and abdomen.

Decompression chamber —A chamber in which the patient suffering from decompression illness is placed after which the pressure inside the chamber is increased to the level which relieves the symptoms of the patient, and then it is very slowly decreased until the pressure is equal to outside pressure.

Decompression illness—An illness characterized by pain in the limbs and abdomen due to the presence of nitrogen bubbles in the blood and tissues in the persons subjected to rapid reduction of air pressures as in the sea-divers or aviators.

Decongestant, Decongestive—Reducing congestion or swelling.

Decongestion—Reduction in congestion.

Decontamination—Freeing of a person, object or place from contaminating substances such as bacteria, poisonous gas or a radioactive substance etc.

Decortication—Removal of the outer covering layer of a structure or organ as the removal of a portion of the cerebral cortex from the underlying white portion.

Decrepitate—To cause decrepitation.

Decrepitation—A crackling sound.

Decrudescence—Decrease in the severity of the symptoms of a disease.

Decubation—The act of lying down.

Decubital—Pertaining to a decubitus ulcer.

Decubitus—Position assumed in lying down.

Decubitus ulcer—Bed-sore. An ulcer resulting from constant pressure to an area of the body as the ulcer formed on the back on lying on the bed for a long time, in some disease.

Decurrent—Extending downward.

Decussate—To cross or crossed in the form of the letter X.

Decussation —Crossing of two structures in the form of X.

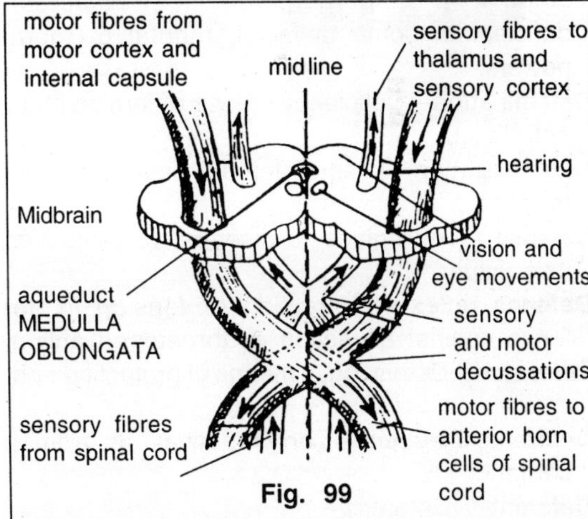

Fig. 99

Decussations of sensory and motor nerves are shown in the medulla oblongata below midbrain,

Dedentition—Loss of teeth.

Dedifferentiation—The return of parts to a homogenous state.

Dedolation—A slicing wound made by a sharp instrument grazing the surface.

De-efferentation—A loss of the motor nerve fibers to an area of the body.

D E F—An expression in which D representing the number of teeth indicated for filling, E for the number indicated for extraction and F the number of filled teeth.

Defatigation—Extreme tiredness.

Defatted—Deprived of fat.

Defecalgesiophobia—Fear of defecating because of pain.

Defecate—To excrete the feces.

Defecation—Excretion of feces through the anus.

Defecography—X-ray examination of the act of defecation following application of a radiopaque substance into the rectum.

Defect—Imperfection,failure or absence from a place.

Congenital defect—A defect present since birth.

Filling defect—The breakage in the continuity of the inner surface of the stomach and the intestinal canal seen in the X-ray after barium meal.

Retention defect—Memory defect.

Septal defect—A defect in one or more of the septa between the cardiac chambers resulting in an abnormal connection between the opposite chambers of the heart.

Defective—1. Imperfect, faulty, 2. A person deficient in some physical, mental or moral powers.

Defemination—Deficiency or loss of femine characteristics.

Defeminization—Loss of female sexual characteristics.

Defense —Resistance to disease, or protection from injury.

Defence reflex —Retraction or tension in defense against an action or threatened action.

Defensive—Defending, a means of protecting from injury.

Deferens, Deferent—Carrying away as from a center.

Deferent —Deferens

Deferentectomy—Excision of a ductus deferens-

Deferential—Pertaining to or accompanying the ductus deferens.

Deferentitis—Inflammation of the ductus deferens.

Deferred shock —Delayed onset of the symptoms of shock.

Defervescence—The period of abatement of fever.

Defibrillation—Stopping of fibrillation of the heart by using drugs or by physical means such as electric shock.

Defibrillator—An electric apparatus which produces defibrillation of the heart.

Defibrination, Defibrinization—The process of removing the fibrin from the blood.

Defibrinization — Defibrination

Deficiency—Shortage, less than the normal amount.

Deficiency disease—The disease produced by the deficiency of some essential substance in the body as night blindness due to deficiency of vitamin A.

Deficit —A lack or deficiency as oxygen, muscular or mental deficit.

Deflection—To turn away from the previous course.

Deflexion—The descending of the fetal head in the maternal pelvis in a nonflexed or extended position before delivery.

Defloration—Rupture of the hymen during sexual intercourse, by accident, surgically or through vaginal examination.

Deflorescence—Disappearance of a skin eruption.

Defluoridation—To remove the extra fluoride from the community water supply.

Defluvium—A falling out as of the hair.

Defluxion, Defluxio—1. A copious discharge. 2. A falling out, as of the hair.

Deformability—Capability of being deformed as the red blood cells change their shape as they pass through narrow spaces.

Deformation—The process of alterating the shape of a previously normally formed part.

Deforming—Causing a deviation from the normal form.

Deformity —Alteration in the shape of previously normally formed part.

Defunction—Inactivity.

Defundation—Excision of the fundus of the uterus.

Defurfuration—Shedding of epidermis in the form of scales.

Deganglionate—To deprive of ganglia.

Degenerate—To deteriorate.

Degeneration—Deterioration in a tissue or organ.

Amyloid degeneration— Degeneration resulting from the deposition of amyloid in the tissues and organs.

Atheromatous degeneration—Deposition of lipid material in the intima of the arteries, causing narrowing of them.

Calcareous degeneration— Degeneration due

to deposition of calcium salts into the tissues.

Cystic degeneration— Degeneration due to cyst formation.

Fatty degeneration— Degeneration due to deposition of fat in the tissues.

Fibroid degeneration—Change of membranous tissue into the fibrous tissue.

Hyaline degeneration— Degeneration due to deposition of hyaline in the tissues with glassy appearance.

Macular degeneration— Degeneration of the macula of the eye.

Mucoid degeneration— Degeneration due to deposition of mucus in the connective tissues.

Pigmentary degeneration—Degeneration due to development of abnormal color in the affected cells.

Senile degeneration— Physical and mental changes occurring in old age.

Subacute combined degeneration of the spinal cord —A disease characterized by degeneration of the posterior and lateral columns of the spinal cord due to Vitamin B_{12} deficiency and usually associated with pernicious anemia producing many symptoms of the nervous system.

Degenerative—Pertaining to or accompanied by degeneration.

Deglutible—Capable of being swallowed.

Deglutition—The act of swallowing.

Deglutitive—Pertaining to deglutition.

Degradation—Conversion of a chemical compound into a less complex form, as the conversion of protein into amino acids and the carbohydrate into sugars during the process of digestion.

Degranulation —Disappearance or loss of granules, especially in a phagocyte.

Degree—1. A unit of measure of the temperature. 2. A stage of severity of a disease. 3. Academic rank. 4. A unit of measure of arcs and angles, one degree means 1/360th part of a circle.

Degustation—The sense of taste, the act or function of tasting.

Dehiscence—A splitting open, as of a surgical wound.

Dehumanization—Loss of human qualities.

Dehumidifier —An apparatus for reducing the moisture of the air.

Dehydrate—To lose water from the body or tissues; to become dry.

Dehydration—1. Removal of water from a substance. 2. Condition resulting from excessive loss of body fluid as occurs in severe diarrhea or cholera.

Dehydrogenate—To remove hydrogen from a chemical compound.

Dehypnotize—To bring out of the hypnotic state.

Deionization—Removal of ions from a substance producing a mineral-free substance.

Dejavu—Feeling of having been in a place before.

Dejecta—Feces.

Dejection—1. Mental depression. 2. Defecation.

Delacrimation—Excessive flow of tears.

Delactation—Weaning or cessation of lactation.

Delamination—Division into separate layers.

Delead—To remove lead from the body or tissues.

Deleterious—Harmful, injurious.

Deletion—Omission; loss of genetic material from a chromosome.

Delicate—A tender and fragile thing.

Deligation—The application of a bandage or ligature.

Delimitation—Determination of limits of an area or organ in diagnosis.

Delinquency—The antisocial, illegal or criminal acts especially of a minor person.

Delinquent—A person especially a minor whose behaviour is antisocial, illegal or criminal.

Deliquesce—To cause liquefaction or moistening.

Deliquescence—The condition of becoming moist or liquefied as a result of absorption of water from the air.

Deliquescent—Pertaining to a substance which absorbs water from the atmosphere.

Delire de toucher—An abnormal desire to touch the things.

Deliria—Plural of delirium.

Deliriant, Delirifacient—The thing which produces delirium, e.g., atropine.

Delirious—In a state of delirium.

Delirium—A mental disturbance of short duration occurring in some diseases as fever etc., marked by the symptoms of illusions (inaccurate perceptions), hallucinations (false perceptions), delusions (false believes), excitement as tearing of the clothes and running away from the bed, restlessness and speaking of incoherent words etc.

Acute delirium— Delirium occurring suddenly and speedly following which the patient recovers or dies.

Delirium epilepticum— Delirium following an attack of epilepsy or appearing instead of an attack.

Delirium tremens— Delirium occurring in habitual heavy drinkers either after overdrinking of, or withdrawal from alcohol, with trembling and great excitement.

Febrile delirium— Delirium occurring with fever.

Hysterical delirium— Delirium of hysteria.

Toxic delirium— Delirium produced by the presence of toxins in the body.

Traumatic delirium — Delirium produced after injury.

Delitescence —1. Sudden subsidence of symptoms. 2. Disappearance of a tumor or cutaneous lesions.

Deliver—To help in the child birth.

Delivery—Expulsion of the child with placenta and membranes from the mother at birth

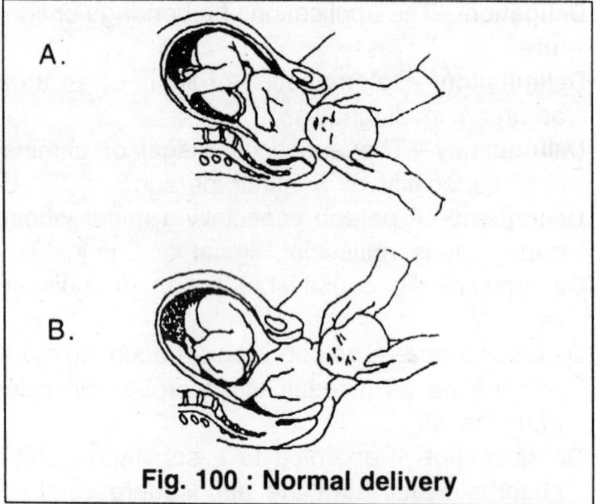

Fig. 100 : Normal delivery

A. Down traction releases the anterior shoulder.
B. An upward curve allows the posterior shoulder to escape over the perineum.

Abdominal delivery— Removal of the fetus by making an incision into the uterus through the abdominal wall.

Breech delivery—The delivery in which the 1st part for expulsion of the fetus are buttocks instead of the head.

Forceps delivery— Delivery of the child by using the instruments.

Postmortem delivery— Delivery of a child either by abdominal or vaginal route after death of the mother.

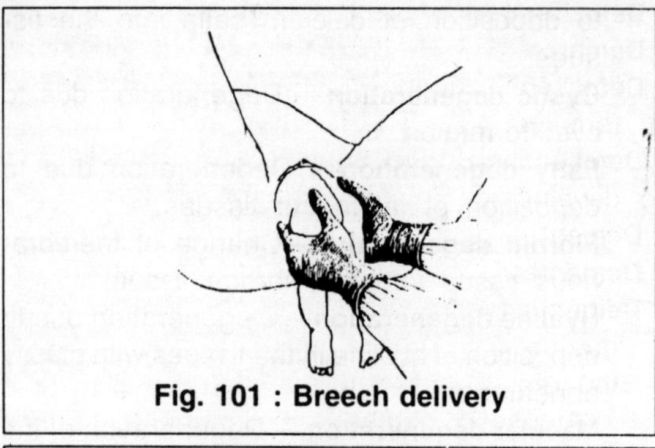

Fig. 101 : Breech delivery

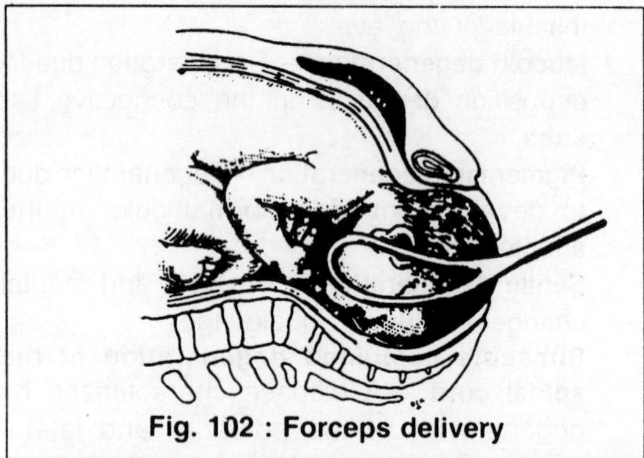

Fig. 102 : Forceps delivery

Premature delivery— Delivery of a fetus before full term.

Spontaneous delivery— Delivery of a child without any help from the attendant.

Vaginal delivery— Delivery of a child through the birth canal.

Delle—The clear area in the center of a stained erythrocyte.

Dellen—A depression in the corneal surface of the eye.

Delomorphous—Having a definite form and shape as a cell or tissue.

Delouse—To remove the lice from the body.

Delousing—Removing the lice from the body.

Delta—1. δ, the fourth letter of the Greek alphabet. 2. A triangular space.

Deltoid—1. Shaped like the Greek letter δ. 2. Triangular.

Delusion—False belief brought about without external stimulation.

Delusion of grandeur—A false belief of having great wealth or power.

Delusion of persecution—Delusion in which a patient feels that everybody around him is against him.

Depressive delusion—A delusion of unworthiness.

Delusional—Pertaining to delusion.

Demarcation—The marking of boundaries.

Demasculinization—Loss of male sexual characteristics.

Demasculinizing—Depriving of, or inhibiting the development of male sexual characteristics.

Dement—The person afflicted with dementia.

Demented—The person of unsound mind.

Dementia—Deterioration of the mental faculties due to some organic disease of the brain with the reduction in intellectual function.

Alcoholic dementia — Dementia in chronic alcoholics.

Apoplectic dementia— Dementia following cerebral hemorrhage or tumors.

Epileptic dementia— Dementia seen in some cases of long-continued epilepsy.

Organic dementia— Dementia produced by the lesion of nerve centers.

Paralytic dementia— Dementia with general paralysis as found in neurosyphilis.

Postfebrile dementia— Dementia following severe infectious diseases associated with fever.

Posttraumatic dementia— Dementia occurring following physical injury to the brain.

Presenile dementia— Dementia occurring in middle age due to cerebral arteriosclerosis.

Primary dementia— Dementia occurring by itself, not in association with another form of psychosis.

Secondary dementia— Dementia occurring after a primary mental disease such as mania.

Senile dementia— Dementia occurring in old age characterized by progressive mental deterioration with loss of memory, especially for recent events with occasional intercurrent attacks of excitement.

Toxic dementia— Dementia due to excessive use of a drug.

Demi—-Prefix indicating half.

Demibain—Half bath, sitz bath.

Demigaunlet—A glovelike bandage for the fingers and hand.

Demilune —A crescent-shaped structure or cell.

Demineralization—Loss of mineral salts especially from the bones.

Demise—Destruction or death.

Demography—Statistical study of the human populations as regard their health, disease, births and deaths.

Demonomania—A madness in which a person thinks himself a devil.

Demonstration—Show.

Demonstrator—The person who takes part in demonstration.

Demorphinization —Gradual decrease in the dose of morphine being used by an addicted person to the morphine.

Demotivate—To cause loss of motivation.

Demucosation—Removal of the mucous membrane from a part of the body.

Demulcent—Soothing the part of the body (from pain etc.) or softening the skin to which it is applied.

Demyelinate—To destroy or remove the myelin sheath of a nerve.

Demyelinating—Destructive to the healthy myelin shealth.

Demyelination—Destruction or removal of the myelin sheath of a nerve.

Denarcotize—To remove narcotism from a narcotized person.

Denaturant—A denaturing agent.

Denaturation—A change in the usual nature of a substance as by the addition of acetone to alcohol to make it unfit for drinking.

Denatured—Changed by denaturation.

Dendric—Pertaining to or possessing a dendron.

Dendriform—Branching or like a tree in shape.

Dendrite—One of the thread-like extensions of the cytoplasm of a neuron which branch into the tree-like processes which form synaptic connections with other neurons.

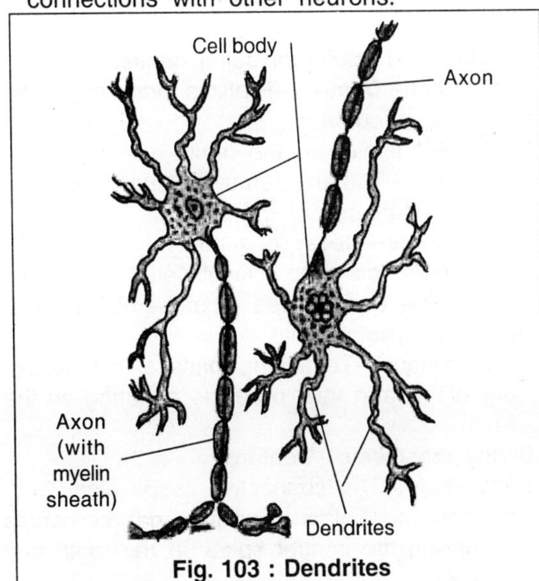

Fig. 103 : Dendrites

Dendritic—Tree-like in shape or pertaining to dendrite.
Dendritic calculus—A renal stone molded in the form of the pelvis and the calyx.
Dendroid—Branching like a tree or pertaining to dendrites.
Dendron—Dendrite.
Denervate—To cause denervation.
Denervated —Affected with loss of nerve supply.
Denervation—Loss of nerve supply.
Dengue—Breakbone fever; an acute viral disease characterized by severe headache, fever, joint and muscle pain and sometimes a skin eruption.
Denial—Refusal, contraindication.
Denidation—Expulsion of the necrosed superficial surface of the mucous membrane lining the uterus, during menstruation.
Denitration—Denitrification.
Denitrification—Removal of nitrogen from any material or chemical compound.
Denitrify —To remove nitrogen from any material or chemical compound.
Denitrogenation—Expulsion of nitrogen from the lungs and body tissues of a person preparing to fly in the low atmospheric pressure.
Denominator—The lower portion of a fraction used to calculate a rate or ratio.
Dens—A tooth or toothlike structure.
Densimeter, **Densitometer**—An instrument for measuring densities.
Densitometer — Densimeter
Densitometry—Determination of the density of a substance.
Density—The quality of being dense.
Dent-, Denti-, Dento- —Prefixes indicating teeth.
Dentagra —Toothache.
Dental—Pertaining to the teeth.
Dental arch—The arch formed by the cutting and chewing surfaces of the teeth.
Dental caries—Decay of teeth.
Dental geriatrics—The scientific study and treatment of the dental diseases of the old persons.
Dentalgia—Toothache.
Dental plaque—Tenacious mass of oral microorganisms and their products adhering on the teeth.
Dental prosthesis—Denture.
Dental pulp—The connective tissue along with the network of blood capillaries and the nerves occupying the central space in the tooth and its roots.
Dentaphone—An instrument placed on the teeth aids hearing.
Dentate—Notched, tooth-shaped.
Dentes—Plural of dens, teeth.
Dentia —The process of eruption of teeth.
Dentia praecox — Premature eruption of the teeth as the presence of teeth in the mouth at birth.
Dentia tarda—Delayed eruption of the teeth.
Dentibuccal—Pertaining to both, the cheek and the teeth.
Denticle—1. A small toothlike process. 2. A small tooth.
Denticulate—Finely toothed or serrated.
Dentification—Formation of the tooth substance.
Dentiform—Toothlike.
Dentifrice—The substance for cleansing the teeth.
Dentigerous—Bearing teeth.
Dentilabial—Pertaining to both, the teeth and the lips.
Dentilingual —Pertaining to both, the teeth and the tongue.
Dentimeter—An instrument for measuring the teeth.
Dentin—The chief substance of a tooth surrounding the pulp cavity and covered by enamel on the crown and by cementum (thin layer of modified bone) on the roots.
Dentinal—Pertaining to dentin.
Dentinalgia—Dentalgia.
Dentine—Dentin.
Dentinification—Formation of dentin.
Dentinitis—Inflammation of the dentin.
Dentinocemental—Pertaining to the dentin and cementum of teeth.
Dentinoenamel—Pertaining to the dentin and enamel.
Dentinogenesis—Formation of dentin in the development of a tooth.
Dentinogenesis imperfecta—A hereditary condition in which there is imperfect formation of the dentin of a tooth.
Dentinogenic—Producing dentin.
Dentinoid—Resembling dentin.
Dentinoma—A tumor of the dentin.
Dentinosteoid—A tumor of both, the dentin and the bone.
Dentinum—Dentin.
Dentiparous—Pertaining to the development and formation of teeth. Tooth-bearing.
Dentist—The person who is authorized to practice dentistry.

Dentistry—A branch of medicine concerned with the prevention, diagnosis and treatment of the diseases of the teeth, gums and other associated structures of the oral cavity.

Dentition—The type, number and arrangement of teeth in their alveoli in the dental arch.

Dentolegal—Pertaining to the dentistry and the law.

Dentulous—Having natural teeth.

Denture—A complete set of artificial teeth set in a plastic material to be substituted for the natural teeth and related tissues.

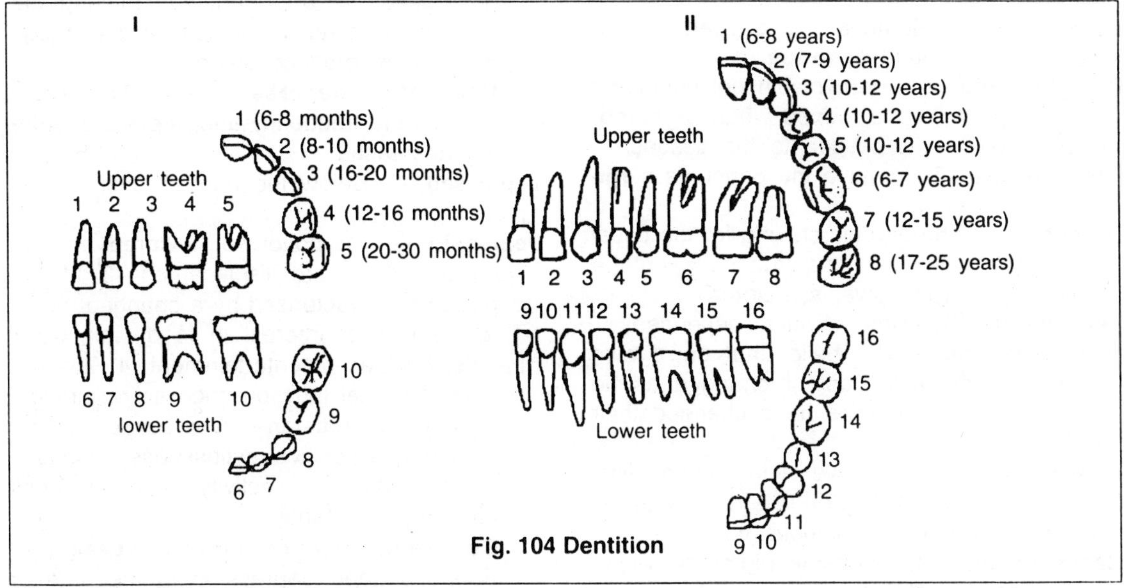

Fig. 104 Dentition

I. Dentition primary or deciduous dentition

1,6- Central incisor teeth; 2, 7-lateral incisor teeth; 3,8 - canine teeth; 4,9 - first molar teeth; 5,10 - second molar teeth

II Dentition permanent

1,9 - Central incisor teeth; 2,10 - lateral incisor teeth; 3,11 - canine teeth; 4,12 - first bicuspid teeth; 5,13 -second bicuspid teeth; 6,14 - first molar teeth; 7,15 - second molar teeth; 8,16 - third molar teeth

Dentition permanent—The eruption of 32 permanent teeth at the age of about 6 years and completed by 15th year with the exception of wisdom teeth, which appear between the age of 17 and 25 years.

Dentition primary—The eruption of 20 deciduous or milk teeth which start at about the age of 6 months and completed by two and a half years.

Dentoalveolar—Pertaining to a tooth and its alveolus.

Dentoalveolitis—Pyorrhea alveolaris.

Dentofacial—Pertaining to the teeth and the face.

Dentoid—Dentiform, tooth-shaped.

Dentoidin—Dentinoid. The organic ground substance of dentin.

Full denture—A denture which replaces all the teeth in both the jaws.

Immediate denture—A complete set of artificial teeth to be inserted immediately after extraction of the natural teeth.

Partial denture—A denture which replaces less than the full number of teeth in either jaw.

Denturist—A dental technician who fabricates and fits the dentures without supervision of a dentist.

Denucleated—Deprived of the nucleus.

Denudation—Removal of a protecting or covering layer or laying bare of any part.

Denude—To remove a protecting or covering layer or laying bare any part.

Denutrition—Malnutrition.

Deodorant—The substance which absorbs foul smells.

Deodorize —To remove or to absorb foul smell.

Deodorizer—A deodorizing agent.

Deontology—Study of medical ethics.

Deorsum—Downward or the turning downward.

Deorsumduction—The bending downward.

Deorsumversion—The downward movements of the eyes.

Deossification—Loss or removal of the mineral elements of bone.

Deoxidate—To remove oxygen from a chemical.

Deoxidation—The process of removing the oxygen from a chemical.

Deoxidizer—The substance which removes oxygen.

Deoxygenation—Removal of oxygen from a chemical compound or tissue.

Deoxyhemoglobin— Hemoglobin not combined with oxygen which is formed when oxyhemoglobin releases its oxygen to the tissues.

Depancreatize—To remove the pancreas surgically.

Dependence—The psychic craving for the usual or the increasing doses of a drug to prevent the onset of the withdrawal symptoms.

Dependency—The state of being dependent.

Depersonalization—The belief that one's own reality is temporarily lost or changed as he feels that his extremities have changed their sizes.

Depersonalize —To deprive of the personality.

De Pezzer's catheter—Self-retaining urethral catheter which has a bulbous tip.

Depigmentation—Loss of the pigments, especially from the skin.

Depilate—To remove the hair.

Depilation—The process of removing the hair. removal of hair.

Depilatory—1. Having the quality of removing the hair. 2. An agent for removing or destroying the hair.

Depilous—Without hair.

Deplete—To empty or to produce depletion.

Depletion—Removal of the substances such as blood, fluids etc. from the body.

Deplumation—Loss of eyelashes due to some diseases.

Depolarization—Reduction in or destruction of polarity.

Depolarize—To deprive of polarity.

Depolymerization—The breakdown of polymers into their monomers as the breakdown of polymer glycogen into monomer glucose.

Deposit—1. Sediment 2. Matter collected in any part of the body.

Depot—A place of storage in the body as for a drug from which it can be distributed or an area in the body in which a large quantity of fat is stored, as in adipose tissue.

Depravation—Pathological deterioration of a function or secretion.

Depravity—Depravation.

Depressant—An agent diminishing a body function.

Cardiac depressant—A depressant which decreases the heart rate and contractility.

Cerebral depressant— Depressant which decreases the brain activity, making the patient dull minded and less active. Large doses may produce sleep.

Respiratory depressant— A depressant causing the frequency and depth of breathing decreased.

Depressed—1. Below the normal level. 2. Dejected.

Depression—1. A hollow or lowered part. 2. Downward or inward displacement. 3. Mental depression characterized by a changed mood. There is lack of interest in food, sex, work, friends, hobbies or entertainment. 4. The decrease of a vital function such as respiration.

Agitated depression— Depression accompanied by excessive restlessness, increased mental and physical activity, the person does his work constantly.

Congenital chondrosternal depression — Funnel-shaped depression in the anterior chest wall since birth.

Endogenous depression —Mental depression without any apparent cause.

Exogenous depression— Depression caused by external factors as social or environmental factors etc.

Situated or reactive depression —Depression due to some external situation such as a death in the family, loss of job or financial loss.

Depressive—Pertaining to or causing depression.

Depressomotor—A drug diminishing the muscular movements by lessening the impulses for movements sent from the brain or spinal cord to the muscle.

Depressor—An instrument for depressing a part as a tongue depressor which depresses the tongue to facilitate visual examination of the throat.

Depressor muscle—The muscle which depresses or draws down a part.

Depressor nerve—A nerve on stimulation decreases the activity of an organ or tissue.

Deprivation—Loss or absence of necessary parts, organs, powers or functions.

Depulization—Destruction of fleas that convey the plague bacillus from animals to humans.

Depurant—A medicine which helps to purify by removing the waste material from the body.

Depuration—The process of purifying by removing the impurities.

Depurative—Having the property of cleansing.

Depurator—An agent which purifies.

Deradelphus—Twins fused above the thorax, having one head and separated below the chest as two separate bodies.

Deradenitis—Inflammation of a lymph gland of the neck.

Deradenoncus—Swelling or tumor of a neck gland.

Deranencephaly, Deranencephalia—The condition of being rudimentary head congenitally.

Derangement—1. Disorder of the mental functions affecting the intellect. 2. Disarrangement of a part or organ of the body.

Derbyshire neck—Goitre.

Derealisation—Feeling of unreality.

Dereism—The condition of living in fantasy or imagination and ignoring reality, as seen in daydreams.

Dereistic—Living in fantasy or imagination and ignoring the reality.

Derencephalia—Derencephaly.

Derencephalocele—Herniation of the rudimentary brain through a hole in the upper cervical spinal canal.

Derencephalus—Congenitally deformed fetus with a rudimentary skull and bifid cervical vertebrae, the brain resting in the bifurcation.

Derencephaly—Congenital fissure of the cervical vertebral column with absent or rudimentary brain.

Derivation —The source or origin of a substance.

Derivative—A chemical substance which is not original but derived from another substance.

Derma—Corium or true skin.

Dermabrader—An apparatus used to abrade the skin.

Dermabrasion—Abrasion of the disfigured skin caused by acne scars, nevi, tattos or fine wrinkles etc., by mechanical means such as sand paper, wire brushes etc.

Dermad—Toward the skin or externally.

Dermadrome—Complication in the skin of a systemic disease.

Dermal—Pertaining to the skin.

Dermalaxia—Excessive relaxation or softness of the skin.

Dermalgia—Localized pain in the skin.

Dermat-, Dermato—Prefixes indicating relationship to the skin.

Dermatalgia—Paresthesia with localized skin pain.

Dermatatrophia—Atrophy of the skin.

Dermatauxe—Hypertrophy of the skin.

Dermatitides—Plural of dermatitis.

Dermatitis—Inflammation of the skin.

Actinic dermatitis—Dermatitis due to exposure to actinic radiation such as that from the sun light, ultraviolet light or X-ray etc.

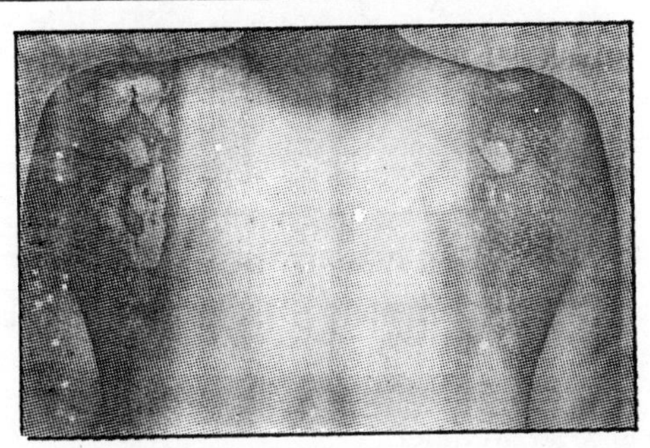

Fig. 105 Actinic dermatitis

Aestivalis dermatitis—Dermatitis produced in hot weather.

Allergic dermatitis— Inflammation of the skin due to allergy.

Atopic dermatitis— Dermatitis of unknown etiology characterized by itching and scratching with eruption. Allergy, hereditary and psychological factors may be involved.

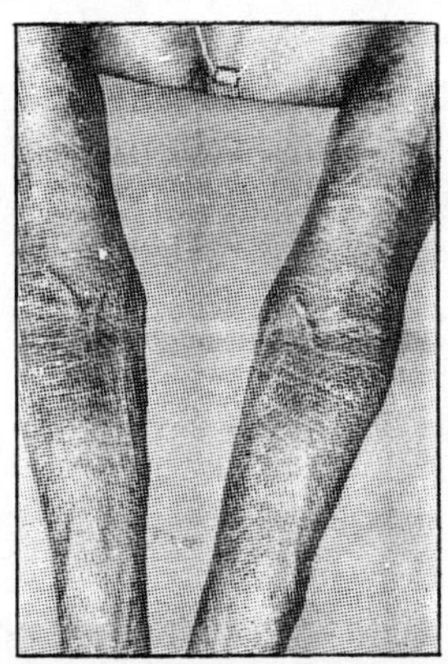

Fig. 106 Atopic dermatitis

Chemical dermatitis— Dermatitis caused by the application of a chemical characterized by redness, edema and vesicle formation on the contacted site of the skin.

Contact dermatitis—Inflammation of the skin due to contact with a substance to which the person is sensitive.

Fig. 107 Contact dermatitis : due to application of a medicine locally

Cosmetic dermatitis— Cutaneous eruption caused by the application of a cosmetic.

Dermatitis hiemalis— Dermatitis occurring in cold weather.

Dermatitis medicamentosa—Drug eruption.

Dermatitis verrucosa— Chronic fungal infection of the skin characterized by the formation of wart like nodules.

Exfoliative dermatitis—Chronic inflammation of the skin commonly involving the whole body and characterized by redness, desquamation and itching of the skin and loss of hair.

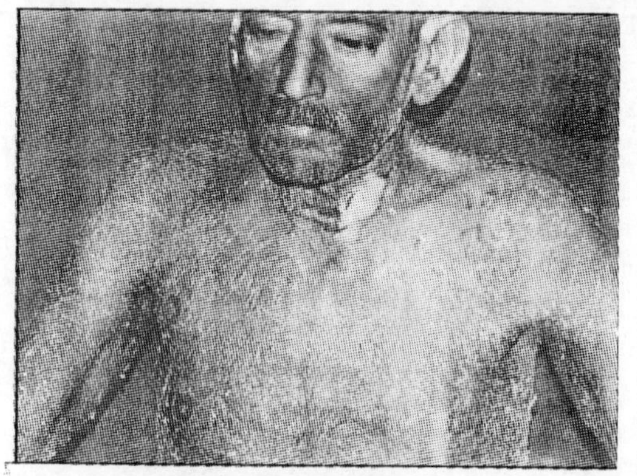

Fig. 108 Exfoliative dermatitis

Infectious eczematoid dermatitis— Pustular eczematoid eruption occurring during or following a pus-forming disease.

Seborrheic dermatitis—Chronic inflammation of the skin of unknown etiology, beginning on the scalp characterized by rounded or irregular lesions covered with yellowish gray dry, moist or greasy scales with itching and exfoliation of the excessive amount of dry scales (dandruff).

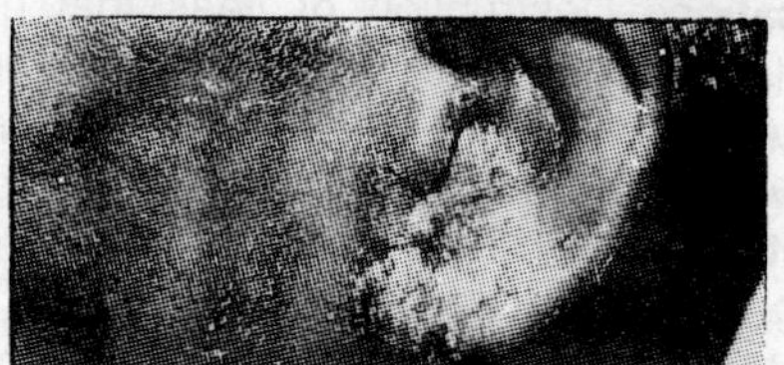

Fig. 109 Infectious eczematoid dermatitis : Purulent discharge from the ear causing eczematous reaction.

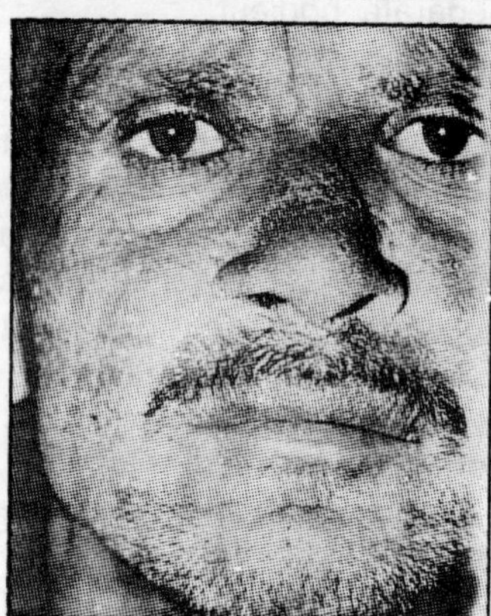

Fig. 110 Seborrheic dermatitis

Stasis dermatitis— Eczematous dermatitis involving the inner side of the lower leg just above the internal malleolus, which later on may involve the whole of the lower leg, marked by ulceration, edema and pigmentation due to venous insufficiency.

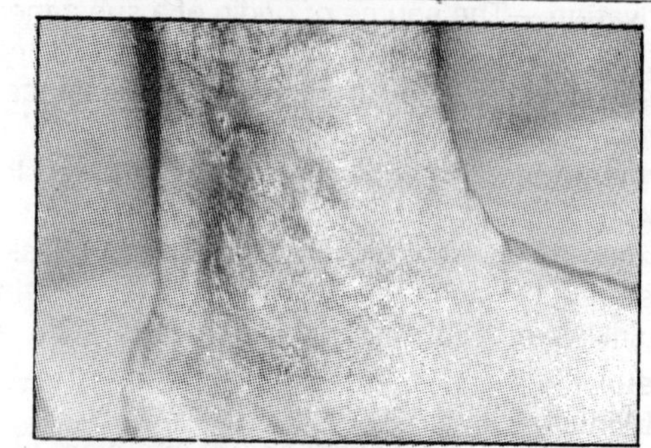

Fig. 111 : Stasis dermatitis

X-ray dermatitis— Inflammation of the skin due to the effect of X-rays on the skin.

Dermato-, Dermat-, Derm- —Prefixes meaning skin.

Dermatoarthritis—Skin disease associated with arthritis.
Dermatoautoplasty—Skin grafting done by the skin taken from some part of the patient's own body.
Dermatocele—Cutis laxa. Loose skin.
Dermatocellulitis— Inflammation of the skin and subcutaneous connective tissue.
Dermatochalasis—Deficiency of elastic fibers in the skin causing it to hang in folds.
Dermatoconiosis—Dermatitis caused by irritation from dust, especially in industrial places.
Dermatocyst—A cyst of the skin.
Dermatodynia—Pain in the skin.
Dermatofibroma—A fibrous tumor-like nodule of the skin.
Dermatofibrosarcoma— Fibrosarcoma of the skin.
Dermatogen—An antigen from a skin disease.
Dermatogenous—Producing skin or a disease of the skin.
Dermatoglyphics—Study of the markings of the hands and feet on the skin.
Dermatograph—A pale raised wheal, writing or figure made by the finger on pressing the skin.
Dermatographia, Dermatographism, Dermatography—The writing or making a figure on the skin by pressing it with the fingers, due to liberation of histamine in some persons.
Dermatographism —A form of allergy in which a pale raised wheal is produced on pressing the skin with the finger or on friction or scratching it.
Dermatoheliosis—Sun-induced skin degeneration characterized by wrinkling and atrophy.
Dermatoheteroplasty—Skin grafting done by the skin taken from an individual of different species.
Dermatoid—Dermoid. Dermal. Resembling skin.
Dermatologic, Dermatological—Pertaining to dermatology or affecting the skin.
Dermatological — Dermatologic.
Dermatologist—Skin specialist.
Dermatology—Scientific study of the skin and its diseases.
Dermatolysis—Cutis laxa. Loosening of the skin.
Dermatoma—Thickening of the skin in a limited area.
Dermatome —An instrument for incising the skin or for cutting thin skin slices for grafting.
Dermatomegaly—Loose skin.
Dermatomucosomyositis—Inflammation of the mucous membrane and the muscles.
Dermatomycosis—Fungal infection of the skin.
Dermatomyoma—Myoma of the skin.
Dermatomyositis— Inflammation of the skin and the muscles.
Dermatopathia—Dermatopathy.
Dermatopathic—Pertaining to a skin disease.
Dermatopathology—Pathology of the skin diseases.
Dermatopathy—Any disease of the skin.
Dermatophobia—Abnormal fear of having a skin disease.
Dermatophylaxis—Protection of the skin against harmful agents such as infection and excessive sunlight etc.
Dermatophyte—A fungus parasite which grows on the skin.
Dermatophytid—A secondary skin eruption due to hypersensitivity to the fungus occurring at the place remote from the site of infection.
Dermatophytosis—Athlete's foot. A fungus infection of the skin of the hands and feet, especially between the toes.
Dermatoplastic —Pertaining to the skin grafting.
Dermatoplasty —Skin grafting; replacement of the skin lost by injury, operation or disease by graft of the living skin.
Dermatopolyneuritis— Acrodynia.
Dermatorrhagia—Hemorrhage from the skin.
Dermatorrhea—Excessive secretion of the sebaceous glands.
Dermatorrhexis—Rupture of the skin and blood capillaries in the skin.
Dermatosclerosis—Hardening of the skin.
Dermatoscopy—Examination of the skin with the lens or microscope.
Dermatosis—Any skin disease in which inflammation is not necessarily a feature.
Dermatotherapy—Treatment of skin diseases.
Dermatothlasia—Intense desire to pinch and bruise the skin.
Dermatotome—1. One of the skin segments of the fetus. 2. An instrument for incising the skin.
Dermatotropic—Acting especially on the skin.
Dermatoxerasia—Roughening of the skin.
Dermatozoon—Any animal parasite on the skin.
Dermatozoonosis—Any skin disease caused by animal parasite.
Dermatrophia—Atrophy of the skin.
Dermatrophy — Dermatrophia.
Dermic—Pertaining to the skin.
Dermis—The true skin or corium.
Dermoblast—The part of the mesoblast which develops into the true skin.

Dermographia, Dermography— Dermatographia.

Dermoid—Like the skin.

Dermoid cyst —A benign cystic tumor occurring in the ovary or lungs or on the skull etc. in which hair, teeth or the skin are found.

Fig. 112 Dermoid cyst

Dermoidectomy—Removal of a dermoid cyst.

Dermolipoma—Lipoma of the skin.

Dermolysis—Dermatolysis. Cutis laxa.

Dermomycosis— Dermatomycosis.

Dermonarcotic—Pertaining to any application or illness causing necrosis of the skin.

Dermonosology—The science of classification of skin diseases.

Dermopathy—Any skin disease.

Dermophlebitis—Inflammation of the superficial veins and the skin surrounding them.

Dermorrhagia—Hemorrhage from the skin.

Dermoskeleton—External covering of the body; hair, nails and teeth etc.

Dermostenosis—Pathologic contraction of the skin.

Dermosynovitis— Inflammation of the skin overlying an inflammed bursa or tendon.

Dermotoxin—An exotoxin produced by the bacteria etc. causing pathological changes in the skin, e.g., erythema, degeneration or necrosis.

Dermotropic—Acting especially on the skin.

Dermovascular—Pertaining to the skin and its blood vessels.

Derodidymus—Dicephalus, a deformed fetus with two heads.

Derotation—A turning back.

Desalination—Partial or complete removal of salts from a substance as from sea-water.

Desaturate—To cause desaturation.

Desaturation—The process by which a saturated organic compound is converted into an unsaturated one.

Desault's apparatus—Bandage used for fracture of the clavicle.

Descemetitis—Cyclitis; inflammation of Descemet's membrane on the posterior surface of the cornea.

Descemetocele—Herniation of the Descemet's membrane.

Descemet's membrane—A fine membrane situated between the endothelial layer of the cornea and the substantia propia.

Descendens—Descending.

Descending—Descendens. Running downward.

Descensus—Process of descending down or prolapse.

Descensus testis— Normal descend of the testes from the abdominal cavity into the scrotum which occurs during the last few months of pregnancy.

Descensus uteri— Prolapse of the uterus through vagina due to defective pelvic floor.

Descent—Descensus. The appearance of the presenting part of the fetus outside, through the birth canal.

Desensitization—The prevention or reduction of immediate hypersensitivity reaction by the administration of repeated graded doses of the sensitizing substance, i.e., allergen too small to cause the hypersensitivity reaction.

Desensitize—1. To deprive of the sensation by blocking or cutting the nerve. 2. To prevent the hypersensitivity reaction by administration of the specific antigen in low dosage.

Desexualize—To castrate.

Deshydremia—Deficiency of water in the blood.

Desiccant—Causing dryness.

Desiccate—To dry.

Desiccation—The process of drying up.

Desiccative—Desiccant.

Desiccator—1. Desiccant. 2. An apparatus containing some drying substance, such as calcium chloride or sulfuric acid etc., in which a material is placed for drying.

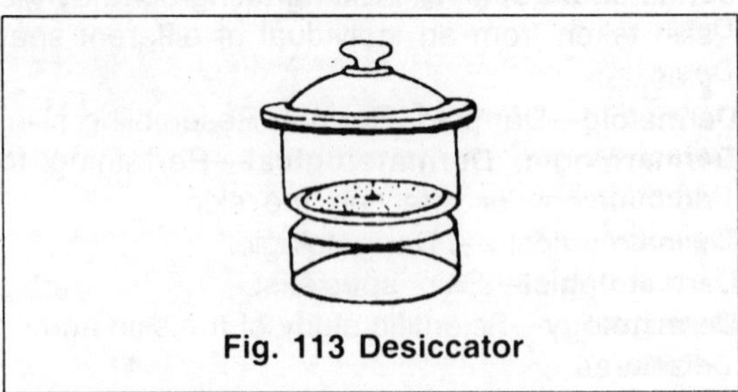

Fig. 113 Desiccator

Desmalgia—Pain in the ligament.

Desmectasia, Desmectasis—Stretching of a ligament.

Desmepithelium—Epithelial lining of vessels and the synovial cavities.

Desmitis—Inflammation of a ligament.

Desmo- —Prefix indicating a band or a ligament.

Desmocranium—The earliest form of the skull of the fetus.

Desmocyte—Fibroblast. Fibrocyte. A supporting tissue cell.

Desmocytoma—A tumor formed of desmocytes.

Desmodynia—Pain in a ligament.

Desmogenous—Produced from a ligament.

Desmography—To describe the ligaments or to write about them.

Desmoid—1. Tendonlike 2. Fibrous tumor or fibroid.

Desmology—Science of ligaments and tendons.

Desmopathy—Any disease of the ligaments.

Desmoplasia—Excessive formation and development of fibrous tissues.

Desmoplastic—Forming the fibrous tissues.

Desmorrhexis—Rupture of a ligament.

Desmosis—Any disease of the connective tissue.

Desmotomy —Incision or division of a ligament.

Desnoma—Tumor of the connective tissue.

Desorb—To remove a substance from the state of absorption or adsorption.

Despondency—Dejection.

Despumation—Separation of froth or scum from a liquid.

Desquamate—To shed off or peel the epidermis or the outer layer of any surface, in the form of scales.

Desquamation—Shedding of the epidermis in the form of scales or sheets.

Desquamative—Of the nature of desquamation, pertaining to or causing desquamation.

Destructive—Causing destruction.

Desudation—Excessive sweating followed by pustular eruption.

Detachment—The condition of being separated.

Detection—Discovery.

Detector—An apparatus for determining the presence of something *e.g.,* lie-detector.

Detergent—A cleansing agent.

Deterioration—Retrogression ; slow impairment of the physical and mental function.

Determinant—An agent which determines the quality of anything.

Determination—The establishment of the exact nature of a substance, organisms or an event, such as sex determination.

Determinism—The theory that all human actions are the result of antecedent conditions and nothing occurs by chance and do not depend on the will of the individual.

Detersive—Detergent.

Detonation—Explosion.

Detortion, Detorsion—1. Surgical treatment of twisting of a testicle, ureter or the bowel. 2. Correction of a deformity of the body.

Detoxicate—Detoxify, to remove the toxic quality of a substance.

Detoxication—Detoxification.

Detoxification—Removal of the toxic property of a poisonous substance.

Detoxify—1. To remove the toxic quality of a substance. 2. Treatment of a toxic overdose of any medicine.

Detrition—The wearing away of a part of the body as of the teeth by friction.

Detritus—The matter remaining after wearing away of a part of the body or disintegration of a substance or tissue.

Detruncation, Decollation—Decapitation, especially of a fetus.

Detrusor—The part of the body which pushes down, *e.g.* a muscle.

Detumescence—1. Subsidence of a swelling. 2. Subsidence of erectile tissue of genital organs (penis and clitoris) following erection.

Deuteranomalopia—Partial color blindness with imperfect perception of green color.

Deuteranopia, Deuteranopsia—Color blindness in which green color is not perceived.

Deuteroplasm, Deutoplasm—A store of nutrient material in the ovum, from which the embryo draws nutrition for its growth.

Devasation—Destruction of the blood vessels.

Devascularization— Interruption of blood circulation to a part of the body due to obstruction or destruction of the blood vessels supplying it.

Development—Growth towards the maturity, as of an egg to an adult state.

Developmental—Pertaining to development.

Deviance—Deviation.

Deviant—One who turns aside from the normal.

Deviate—1. To move away from the normal 2. The person whose behavior, especially sexual behavior is abnormal socially, morally or legally.

Deviation—The turning aside from the normal, going out of the way, departing from the normal.

Device—An apparatus or a machine to perform a specific function.

Intrauterine contraceptive device or Intrauterine device—I.U.C.D. or I.U.D —Device made up of various shapes as loops, coils, rings etc. from several different materials such as plastic or copper, placed in the uterus to prevent implantation of the fertilized ovum.

Deviometer—Instrument for measuring the deviation in strabismus.

Devisceration—Removal of an organ.

Devitalization —Destruction of vitality or life.

Devitalize—To deprive of vitality or life.

Devitalized —Devoid of life; dead.

Devolution—1. The reverse of evolution. 2. Degradation.

Dew cure—A form of hydrotherapy in which there is walking with bare feet on the grass wet with dew.

Dew point—The temperature at which the dew forms.

Dexter—On the right side.

Dextrad —1. Toward the right side. 2. A right handed person.

Dextral—Pertaining to the right side.

Dextrality—Right handedness.

Dextraural—Hearing better with the right ear.

Dextrinuria —Presence of dextrin in the urine.

Dextro- —Prefix indicating to the right.

Dextrocardia—Location of the heart on the right side of the body.

Dextrocardiogram—That part of the electrocardiogram that is derived from the right ventricle.

Dextrocerebral—Having a dominant right cerebral hemisphere.

Dextrocular—Having a stronger (greater visual power) right eye than the left.

Dextrocularity—The condition of having the right eye stronger (of greater visual power) than the left, so using it more than the left.

Dextroduction—The movement of the visual axis to the right.

Dextrogastria—Displacement of the stomach to the right.

Dextrogyration—A turning to the right side.

Dextrogyre—A substance turning to the right side.

Dextromanual—Right-handed.

Dextropedal—Right-footed.

Dextrophobia—Morbid fear of, or aversion to the objects on the right side of the body.

Dextroposition—Displacement to the right.

Dextrorotation—A turning to the right side.

Dextrorotatory—Turning light rays to the right side.

Dextrosinistral—Extending from right to left.

Dextrosuria—Presence of dextrose in the urine.

Dextrotorsion—A twisting to the right side.

Dextrotropic—Turning to the right.

Dextroversion—1. The turning towards the right, especially the movement of the eyes to the right. 2. Location of the heart in the right side of the chest.

Dezymotize—To free of ferments or germs.

Dhobie itch—Ringworm infection of the skin caused by the fungus Tinea cruris common in males localised to groins, scrotum, thighs and buttocks.

Di- —Prefix indicating twice.

Dia- —Prefix meaning through out or completely.

Diabetes—A disease characterized by excessive excretion of urine.

Diabetes insipidus — Diabetes occurring in the young person characterized by polyuria (excessive excretion of urine) and polydipsia (excessive thirst).

Diabetes mellitus— A disease of carbohydrate metabolism due to inadequate production or utilization of insulin, characterized by hyperglycemia (sugar in the blood above normal), glycosuria (presence of sugar in the urine), polyuria (excessive urination) and polyphagia (excessive hunger).

Diabetes mellitus includes mainly the following types of diabetes —

(1) Juvenile onset diabetes – JOD, or insulin dependent diabetes mellitus –IDDM, or type I diabetes. This type of diabetes mellitus develops abruptly before the age of 25 years, mostly at the age of 5 years and in early adolescence in which insulin is required to be injected to survive, i.e., this type of diabetes is dependent on insulin.

(2) Maturity onset diabetes —MOD, or Non-insulin dependent diabetes mellitus -NIDDM or type II diabetes. This type of diabetes mellitus develops after the age of 40 years in which insulin is not required to survive, i.e. it is not dependent on insulin and it may be controlled by oral hypoglycemic medicines. This type of diabetes mellitus is of the following two types according to the obesity.

1. Obese Non-insulin dependent diabetes mellitus (obese NIDDM)

2. Non-obese Non-insulin dependent diabetes mellitus (Non-obese NIDDM)

(3) Malnutrition related diabetes.

(4) Secondary diabetes. Diabetes developing as a secondary to some diseases.
(5) Gestational diabetes mellitus- GDM—Diabetes mellitus developing during pregnancy.

Diabetic—Pertaining to diabetes.

Diabetic—A patient suffering from diabetes.

Diabetic coma—See coma, Diabetic coma.

Diabetid—Diabetic dermopathy.

Diabetogenic—Causing diabetes.

Diabetogenous—Caused by diabetes.

Deiabetology—Study of diabetes.

Diabrosis—A corrosion causing perforation of a vessel or organ.

Diabrotic—A corrosive or ulcerative substance causing perforation of a vessel or organ.

Diacele—The third ventricle of the brain.

Diacetemia—Acidosis due to the presence of acetoacetic acid in the blood.

Diacetonuria—Diaceturia.

Diaceturia—Excretion of acetoacetic acid in the urine.

Diachorema—Excrement, feces.

Diachoresis—Defecation.

Diaclasia—A bone fracture, especially breaking of a bone before surgery.

Diaclasis—Diaclasia.

Diaclast —An instrument for perforating the fetal skull.

Diacrinous cells—Exocrine cells. The cells secreting outwardly rather than into the blood circulation.

Diacrisis—1. A change in the character of a secretion. 2. A disease in which a secretion is altered.

Diacritic, Diacritical— Diagnostic.

Diadochocinesia— Diadochokinesia.

Diadochokinesia—Ability to make antagonistic movements such as the pronation (palm facing downwards) and supination (palm facing upwards) movements of the hands.

Diagnose—To recognize a disease.

Diagnosis—1. The term denoting the name of a disease from which a person is suffering. 2. To establish the nature of a disease by taking the history of the patient, signs and symptoms present, laboratory findings and special tests such as X-ray and electrocardiogram etc.

Clinical diagnosis—To determine the diagnosis of a disease on the basis of signs and symptoms.

Diagnosis by exclusion—To establish a diagnosis by excluding other possibilities.

Differential diagnosis—To establsih a diagnosis by comparing the symptoms of the two similar diseases.

Pathological diagnosis—The diagnosis of a disease made on the basis of pathological investigations.

Diagnostic—Pertaining to a diagnosis.

Diagnostician—Expert in diagnosis.

Diagnostics—The science and practice of diagnosis of diseases.

Diagram—A figure made by outlines.

Dialy- —Prefix meaning to separate.

Dialysance—The rate of net exchange of solute molecules per minute passing through a membrane in dialysis.

Dialysate—The liquid that passes through the membrane in dialysis.

Dialysis—The process of separating the crystalloids and colloids in a solution by the difference in their rates of diffusion through a semipermeable membrane as the crystalloids pass through more rapidly than the colloids.

Renal dialysis—The dialysis of blood to remove the liquids and the chemicals which the kidneys would normally remove if they were present and functioning normally.

Dialysis dementia— Dementia seen in patients who have been on dialysis for several years.

Dialytic—Pertaining to dialysis or resembling the process of dialysis.

Dialyzable—Capable of dialysis.

Dialyze—To perform dialysis.

Dialyzer—An apparatus for performing the dialysis.

Diamagnetic—Repelled by the magnet.

Diamelia—Absence of two limbs.

Diameter—The length of a straight line passing through the center of a circle connecting the opposite points on its circumference.

Diamniotic—The twins, each developing within a separate amniotic cavity.

Diapason—An instrument, the tuning fork for measuring the degree of deafness.

Diapause—A period of life in which metabolism is decreased and development is arrested.

Diapedesis—Outward passage of blood cells, especially the white blood cells by ameboid movements through the unruptured blood vessel wall.

Diaper—Underwear of the infant.

Diaphane—A very small electric light used in transillumination.

Diaphanography—Examination of a body part by transillumination, especially of the breast for the detection of cancer.

Diaphanometer—An apparatus for estimating the amount of solids in a fluid by its transparency.

Diaphanometry—Determination of the translucency of a fluid.

Diaphanoscope—An instrument for transillumination of a body cavity.

Diaphanoscopy—Examination by the use of a diaphanoscope; transillumination.

Diaphemetric—Pertaining to the degree of tactile sensibility.

Diaphoresis—Profuse sweating.

Diaphoretic—1. Pertaining to profuse sweating or the person who sweats profusely. 2. The thing which causes profuse sweating.

Diaphragm—1. The musculomembranous partition separating the thoracic cavity from the abdominal cavity. 2. Any separating membrane or structure. 3. A rubber or plastic cup-shaped sheet which fits over the cervix of the uterus as a contraceptive method.

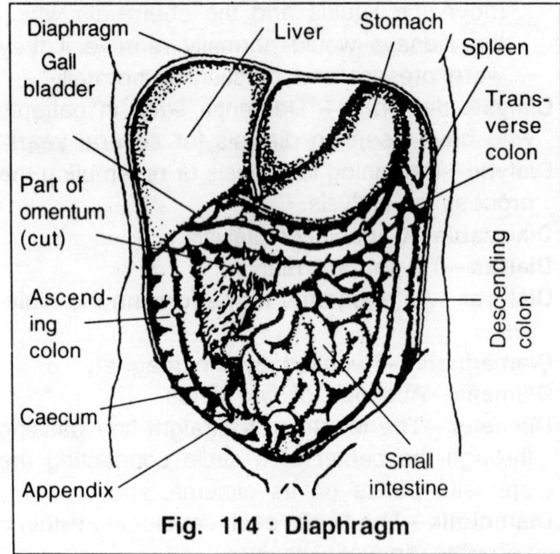

Fig. 114 : Diaphragm

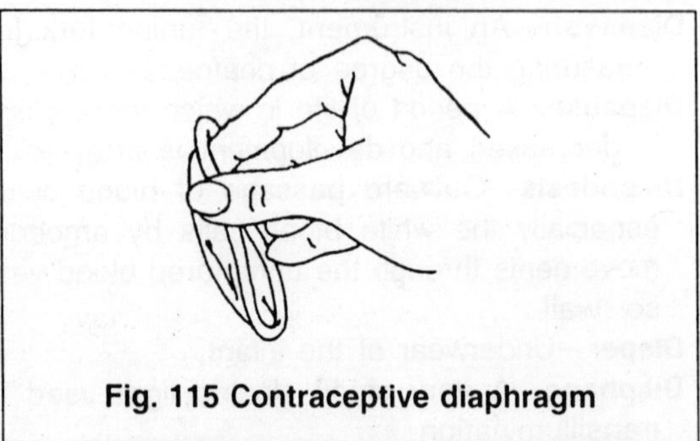

Fig. 115 Contraceptive diaphragm

Diaphragmalgia—Pain in the diaphragm.

Diaphragmatic—Pertaining to the diaphragm.

Diaphragmatocele—Hernia of the diaphragm.

Diaphragmodynia—Pain in the diaphragm.

Diaphyseal—Pertaining to or affecting the shaft of a long bone (diaphysis).

Diaphysectomy—Excision of part of the shaft of a long bone.

Diaphysial—Diaphyseal.

Diaphysis—The shaft of a long bone.

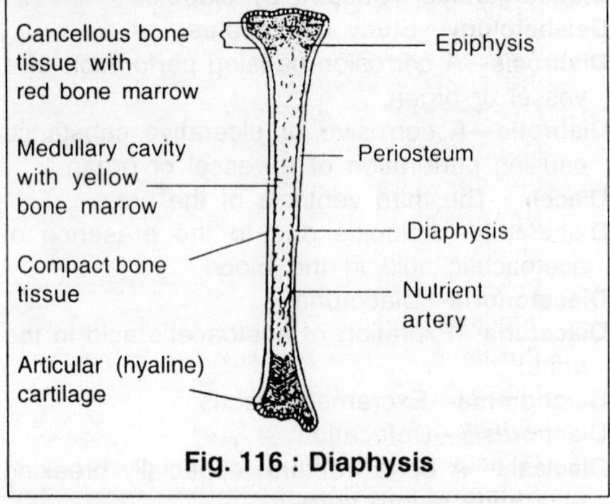

Fig. 116 : Diaphysis

Diaphysitis—Inflammation of the shaft of a long bone.

Diapiresis—Outward passage of the minute particles or the blood cells through the unruptured walls of the blood vessels.

Diaplacental —Passing through the placenta.

Diaplasis—The setting of a fracture or reduction of a dislocation.

Diapne—Perspiration.

Diapnoic, Diapnotic— Pertaining to or causing perspiration.

Diapophysis—An upper transverse process of a vertebra.

Diapyesis—Suppuration.

Diapyetic—Promoting suppuration.

Diarrhea—Frequent passage of loose or watery motions.

Acute diarrhea— Diarrhea which occurs suddenly.

Cachectic diarrhea— Diarrhea occurring in patients with severe wasting.

Choleraic diarrhea— Diarrhea occurring in cholera in which the stools are of a 'rice-water' character.

Dysenteric diarrhea— Diarrhea due to dysentery characterized by mucous or bloody stools.

Emotional diarrhea— Diarrhea caused by the emotional stress.

Fatty diarrhea— Diarrhea in which the stools contain undigested fat particles.

Fermentative diarrhea—Diarrhea caused by fermentation due to micro-organisms.

Infantile diarrhea— Diarrhea occurring in the children under two years of age.

Lienteric diarrhea— Diarrhea characterized by watery stools containing undigested food particles.

Membranous diarrhea— Diarrhea in which the stools contain the pieces of intestinal mucosa.

Mucous diarrhea— Diarrhea with mucus in the stools.

Nocturnal diarrhea— Diarrhea occurring chiefly at night.

Parenteral diarrhea— Diarrhea due to the infection outside the gastrointestinal tract.

Purulent diarrhea— Diarrhea in which the stools contain pus.

Simple diarrhea— Diarrhea in which stools contain only normal excreta.

Summer diarrhea— Diarrhea occurring in children during summer season due to intense heat.

Diarrheal, Diarrheic— Diarrhetic. Pertaining to diarrhea.

Diarrheogenic—Giving rise to diarrhea.

Diarrhetic—Diarrheal.

Diarthric—Pertaining to two or affecting two different joints.

Diarthrodial—Of the nature of a diarthrosis.

Diarthrosis—An articulation in which the opposite bones move freely.

Diarticular—Diarthric, pertaining to two joints.

Diaschisis—A condition in which there is a change in the function of some distant part of the body due to injury of a part of the central nervous system.

Diascope—A glass or clear plastic plate pressed against the skin for examining the superfical lesions.

Diascopy—Examination of the superficial lesions of the skin by using a diascope.

Diastalsis—The type of peristalsis as that of intestinal tract in which a wave of inhibition precedes the wave of contraction.

Diastaltic—Pertaining to diastalsis.

Diastasis—1. Separation of two normally united bones without a joint between them. 2. A rest phase of the cardiac cycle at the end of diastole and occurring just before systole.

Diastatic—Pertaining to diastasis.

Diastema—1. Fissure or cleft. 2. A space between two adjacent teeth.

Diastematocrania—Congenital longitudinal fissure of the cranium.

Diastematomyelia— Congenital fissure of the spinal cord.

Diastematopyelia— Congenital median fissure of the pelvis.

Diastole—The period of relaxation or dilatation of the heart following systole or contraction.

Diastolic—Pertaining to diastole.

Diastolic pressure—It is the minimum pressure exerted by the blood laterally on the vessel walls during diastole.

Diastology—Study of cardiac diastole.

Diastrephia—Insanity towards cruelty.

Diastrophic—Bent or curved structure.

Diastrophism—Distortion that occurs in objects as a result of bending.

Diataxia—Ataxia affecting both the sides of the body.

Diathermal—Able to absorb heat.

Diathermanous—Diathermal.

Diathermia, Diathermy— The use of a high-frequency electric current to generate heat within some part of the body to increase the blood flow and warm it in medical treatment, and to destroy the tissues by electrocoagulation and cauterization in surgical treatment.

Diathermic—Of the nature of diathermy.

Diathermy—Diathermia.

Diathesis—An unusual constitutional predisposition to a particular disease as allergy.

Diathetic—Pertaining to diathesis.

Diatomic—Denoting a compound with a molecule with two atoms.

Diaxon, Diaxone—A neuron with two axons.

Dibasic—A molecule containing two atoms of hydrogen replaceable by a base.

Diblastula—A blastula containing the ectoderm and entoderm.

Dicalcic, Dicalcium— One molecule containing two atoms of calcium.

Dicelous—Having two cavities on opposite surfaces.

Dicentric—1. Developing from or having two centers. 2. Having two centromeres.

Dicephalous—Having two heads.

Dicephalus—A fetus having two heads.

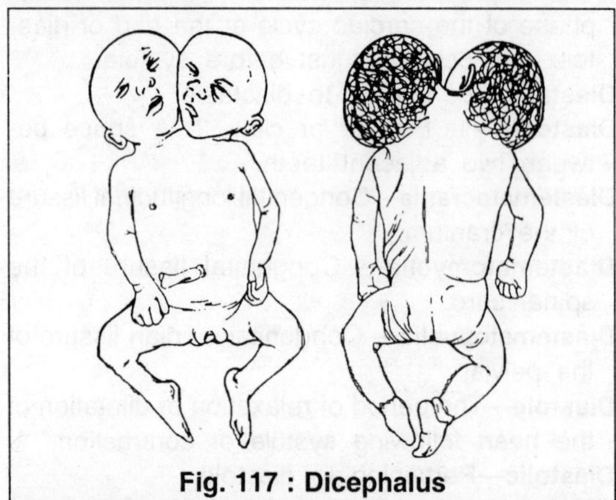

Fig. 117 : Dicephalus

Dicheilia, Dichilia—A lip appearing to be doubled.

Dicheiria, Dichiria —The condition of having double hands.

Dichirus—Having the hands divided into two branches.

Dichotomous—Divided into two.

Dichotomy, Dichotomization—1. Bifurcation of a vein. 2. Dividing into two parts.

Dichroic—Pertaining to dichroism.

Dichroism—The property of appearing to be one color by direct light and another by transmitted light.

Dichromat—Dichromatic.

Dichromatic —Capable of seeing only two colors.

Dichromatism, Dichromatopsia—The ability to perceive only two colors.

Dichromic—1. Containing two atoms of chromium. 2. Seeing only two colors.

Dichromophil—A cell or tissue staining with both, acid and basic dyes.

Dichromophilic—Staining with both, the acids and the bases.

Dichromophilism—The capacity for double staining.

Dicoelus—1. Concave or hollowed on each of the two sides. 2. Having two cavities.

Dicoria—Presence of double pupil in each eye.

Dicrotic—Pertaining to a double pulse or having a double beat.

Dicrotic notch —In a pulse tracing, a notch on the descending limb.

Dicrotism—The condition of being dicrotic.

Dictyoma, Diktyoma—A tumor of the ciliary epithelium.

Dicyclic—Having two cycles.

Didactylism—Presence of only two digits on a hand or foot congenitally.

Didactylous—Having only two digits in one hand or foot congenitally.

Didelphia—The condition of having a double uterus.

Didelphic—Having double uterus.

Didymalgia, Didymodynia—Pain in a testis.

Didymitis—Inflammation of a testis.

Didymous—Occurring in pairs.

Didymus—1. A testis. 2. Conjoined symmetrical twins.

Die—1. To cease living. 2. In dentistry, an artificial duplicate tooth made from an impression of a tooth.

Dieb. alt.—Every other day.

Diembryony—The development of two embryos from a single egg.

Diencephalohypophysial—Pertaining to the diencephalon and hypophysis.

Diencephalon—It is a midline structure of brain which is largely embedded in the cerebrum, so not visible from outside and consists of epithalamus, thalamus, metathalamus and hypothalamus.

Dieresis—1. Separation of the normally joined parts. 2. Separation of the parts by surgery.

Dieretic—Pertaining to dieresis, separable.

Diet—Solid and liquid food substances taken by a person daily regularly in the normal living, or a food prescribed for a particular disease such as diabetes and peptic ulcer etc.

Balanced diet—The diet containing carbohydrates, fats, proteins, minerals, water and vitamins in proper proportion for adequate nutrition.

Diabetic diet—Sugar free diet prescribed for the patients of diabetes.

High-calorie diet —A diet containing above 4000 calories per day.

High-fat diet—A diet containing large amounts of fat.

High-fiber diet—A diet containing large amounts of fibers, which are generally found in vegetables and fruits etc.

High-protein diet—The diet containing large amounts of protein such as milk, fish, meat, pulses and nuts, etc.

Liquid diet—Milk, fruit juice, etc.

Low-calorie diet —The diet containing fewer calories than needed to maintain weight, as a diet of less than 1200 calories per day for an adult.

Low-fat diet—The diet which contains a little

amount of fat which is usually used in diseases of the liver.

Roughage diet—It includes vegetables and fruits, etc. which due to their fibers promote the peristaltic movements of the intestine and hence they are used in case of constipation.

Salt free diet—The diet devoid of sodium chloride used in case of hypertension and edematous states.

Dietary—1. Pertaining to diet. 2. A system of dieting.

Dietetic—Pertaining to diet or its regulation.

Dietitian, Dietician—An individual expert in nutrition and able to regulate the diet in the healthy and sick persons.

Dietl's crisis—In case of movable kidney when the kidney moves, renal colic occurs radiating to the inner side of the thigh, due to kinking or partial obstruction of the ureter accompanied by blood stained scanty urine.

Dietotherapy—Treatment of diseases by the regulation of diet.

Differential—Pertaining to a difference or differences.

Differential diagnosis— Diagnosis made on the basis of comparison of symptoms of two or more similar diseases to determine, which the patient is suffering from.

Differential white blood cells –W.B.C. count —Determination of the number of each type of W.B.C. in one cubic millimeter of blood.

Differentiated—Having a different character or function from the surrounding structures or from the original type, that is usually used for tissues, cells or a portion of the cytoplasm.

Differentiation—The distinguishing of one thing from another.

Diffluence—The process of becoming fluid.

Diffraction—Bending or breaking up of a ray of light into its component parts.

Diffusate—The material diffused through a membrane.

Diffuse—To spread.

Diffusible—Capable of being diffused.

Diffusion—1. Osmosis. 2. The process by which various gases interpenetrate and mixed, or the solutions of different substances if stand in contact, mix together on standing even if they are separated by a thin membrane. 3. The tendency of molecules of a substance to move from the region of high concentration to one of lower concentration.

Digametic—Heterogametic.

Digastric—1. Having two bellies. 2. Digastric muscle.

Digastricus—Digastric.

Digenesis—Reproduction in which alternate generations are asexual.

Digenetic—Having two stages of multiplication, one sexual and the other asexual.

Digerant—A digestant.

Digest—To undergo digestion.

Digestant—The agent which digests food or helps in digestion such as pepsin or pancreatin.

Digestible—Capable of being digested.

Digestion—The process by which the solid foods in the gastrointestinal tract are mechanically and chemically converted into liquids, the absorbable forms.

Digestive—Pertaining to digestion.

Digestive juice—One of the several secretions which aid in the process of digestion.

Digestive system—All the organs and glands associated with ingestion and digestion of food; the tract from the mouth to the anus.

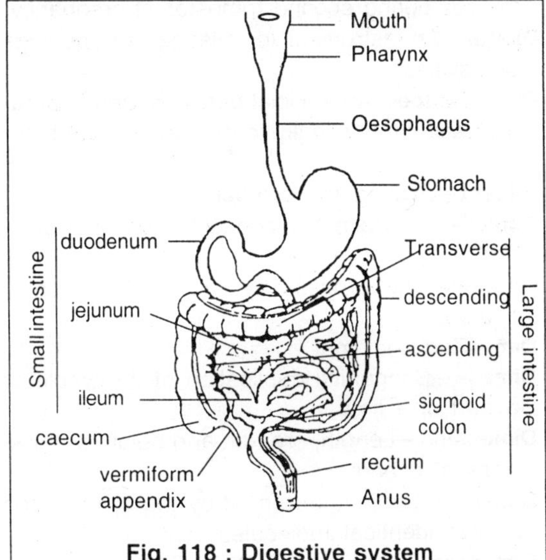

Fig. 118 : Digestive system

Digit—A finger or toe.

Digital—Pertaining to or resembling a digit.

Digitalism—Digitalis poisoning. The symptoms caused by the overdose of the drug digitalis.

Digitalization—Administration of the drug digitalis until desired therapeutic effects are produced.

Digitate—Having digit-like processes.

Digitation—A digit-like process.

Digiti—Plural of digitus or digit.

Digitiform—Finger-like.
Digitigrade—Walking on the toes.
Digitus—A digit.
Diglossia—Bifid tongue.
Dignathus—A fetus having two lower jaws.
Dihysteria—The condition of having two uteri.
Diktyoma—Dictyoma.
Dilaceration—A tearing apart, as of a cataract.
Dilatant—Any thing that causes dilatation or dilation.
Dilatation, Dilation—1. Expansion of an organ, vessel or orifice. 2. Expansion of an orifice with a dilator.
Dilatator—Dilator.
Dilate—To perform or undergo dilation.
Dilation—Dilatation.
Dilation and curettage—D & C — To expand the cervix of the uterus with the dilator (dilation) and scrap the inner wall of the uterus with the curette (curettage).
Dilation and evacuation —D&E—To dilate the cervix of the uterus and to remove the products of conception by curetting the uterus and using forceps during second trimester of pregnancy.
Dilator—An instrument for dilating the openings or cavities.
Dildo, Dildoe—An artificial penis-shaped apparatus used intravaginally to produce sexual pleasure.
Diluent—Diluting the solution.
Dilute—To reduce the concentration of a solution.
Dilution—The process by which a solution is diluted.
Dim—Reduced light.
Dimelia—Congenital duplication of the whole or a part of a limb.
Dimension—Length, breadth and height or thickness of a body.
Dimer—A compound formed by the combination of two identical molecules.
Dimerous—Consisting of two parts.
Dimetria—A condition of having double uterus.
Dimorphic—Dimorphous.
Dimorphism—The quality of existing in two forms.
Dimorphous—Occurring in two different forms.
Dimple—Slight depression.
Dimpling—The formation of slight depressions in the flesh due to retraction of the subcutaneous tissue as occurs in cancer of the breast.
Dineuric—Having two axis cylinder processes.
Dinical—Pertaining to giddiness or vertigo.
Dinomania—Dancing mania.
Dinus—Vertigo.
Diobus alternis—Alternate day.
Diopter, Dioptre—A unit for the measurement of refractive power of a lens per meter of focal length.
Dioptometer—An apparatus for measuring the ocular refraction.
Dioptometry—Determination of the refraction and accomodation of the eye.
Dioptral—Pertaining to a diopter.
Dioptric—Pertaining to refraction of light.
Dioptrics—The science of refraction of light.
Diotic—Simultaneous presentation of the same sound to each ear.
Diovular—Having two ova.
Diovulatory—Production of two ova in one ovarian cycle.
Dioxide—A compound having two atoms of oxygen per molecule.
Dip—1. Downward inclination or slope. 2. To immerse into a liquid.
Diphallus—Complete or incomplete double penis or clitoris.
Diphasic—Occurring in or having two phases.
Diphonia—Simultaneous production of two different voice tones in speaking.
Diphtheria—An acute infectitious disease of the children caused by the bacterium Corynebacterium diphtheriae affecting the mucous membranes of the throat, larynx or nose and marked by the formation of a gray-white membrane with fever, pain, obstruction in swallowing, aphonia and respiratory distress.
Diphtheria antitoxin— The antitoxin used in the treatment of diphtheria.
Diphtherial—Pertaining to diphtheria.
Diphtheriaphor—A diphtheria carrier or vector.
Diphtheria toxoid— Immunizing agent for diphtheria.
Diphtheric, Diphtheritic— Pertaining to diphtheria.
Diphtherin—The toxin of Corynebacterium diphtheriae.
Diphtheritic—Diphtherial. Diphtheric.
Diphtheroid—1. Resembling diphtheria or its causative organism bacillus Corynebacterium diphtheriae. 2. The formation of a false membrane not due to bacillus Corynebacterium diphtheriae.
Diphtherotoxin—The specific toxin of the bacillus Corynebacterium diphtheriae.

Diphthongia—The production of double vocal sounds due to defect in the larynx.

Diphyodont—Having two sets of teeth, a deciduous and a permanent as in man.

Diplacusis—The perception of a single auditory stimulus as two separate sounds.

Diplegia—Paralysis of the similar parts on both sides of the body.

Diplegic—Pertaining to diplegia.

Diplo- —A prefix meaning double or twofold.

Diploalbuminuria—The coexistence of physiological and pathological abuminuria.

Diplobacillus—A short, rod-shaped bacterium found in pairs.

Diplobacterium— Diplobacillus.

Diploblastic—Having ectoderm and endoderm, two germ layers.

Diplocardia—Partial separation of the two halves of the heart by a groove.

Diplocephalus—Dicephalus.

Diplocephaly—The condition of having two heads.

Diplococcemia—Presence of diplococci in the blood.

Diplococci—Plural of diplococcus.

Diplococcus—A type of spherical bacteria appearing in pairs.

Diplocoria—Double pupil in an eye.

Diploe—A layer of spongy tissue between the outer and inner layers of compact bone of the skull.

Diplogenesis—Production of a double fetus or the doubling of some fetal parts.

Diploic—Pertaining to diploe.

Diploid—Having two sets of chromosomes.

Diploidy—The state of being diploid.

Diplokaryon—Tetraploid nucleus. A nucleus having four sets of chromosomes.

Diplomelituria—The occurrence of diabetic and nondiabetic glycosuria in the same individual.

Diplomyelia—Lengthwise fissuring of the spinal cord so that it apears to be doubled.

Diploneural—Having two nerves from different sources, said of certain muscles.

Diplopagus—Conjoined twins, see under twin.

Diplophonia—Diphonia.

Diplopia—Double vision. The perception of two images of a single object.

Binocular diplopia—Perception of a separate image of a single object by each of the two eyes.

Crossed diplopia, Heteronymous diplopia—Double vision in which right-hand image appears on the left-side and left-hand image on the right-side.

Direct diplopia, Homonymous diplopia —Double vision in which right-hand image appears on the right side and left-hand image on the left-side.

Monocular diplopia, Unocular diplopia —Double vision with one eye.

Vertical diplopia— Diplopia in which one image appears above the other in the same vertical plane.

Diplopiometer—An apparatus for estimating the diplopia.

Diplopodia—The doubling of the toes.

Diploscope—An apparatus for studying the binocular diplopia.

Diplosomatia, Diplosomia—The condition in which the twins are joined together at some of their body parts.

Dipodia—Complete or incomplete duplicaton of a foot.

Dipping —1. Palpation of the liver by pressing the fingers of the right hand in the right hypochondriac region, while the hand is held flat on the abdomen. 2. Immersion of an object in a fluid.

Diprosopus—A fetus having double face.

Dipsesis—Dipsosis.

Dipsogen—An agent which induces thirst.

Dipsomania—Mania for alcohol, desire for alcohol every time.

Dipsopathy—Diseases associated with the thirst.

Dipsophobia—Morbid fear of drinking.

Dipsosis—Excessive thirst.

Dipsotherapy—Limitation of water and fluid intake in the treatment of certain diseases.

Dipygus—A fetus with a double pelvis.

Dipylidiasis—Infestation with the tapeworm, Dipylidium caninum.

Direct light reflex — Immediate constriction of the pupil on throwing light over it.

Director—A grooved instrument for guiding a knife in surgery.

Direct reflex—Reflex in which response occurs on the same side on which is the stimulus.

Dirigomotor—Controlling or directing muscular activity.

Dirofilariasis—Infection with the organisms of the genus Dirofilaria.

Dis- —1. Prefix indicating to ruin, reverse or separate. 2. Prefix means double or twice.

Disability —Lack of ability to perform physical and mental functions that one can normally do in capacity.

Disabled—Handicapped, crippled.
Disaggregation—The breaking of an object into its component parts.
Disarticulation—Amputation at a joint.
Disassimilation—Failure or loss of assimilative power.
Disc—Disk. A flat, round, platelike structure.
Discectomy—Discotomy. Excision of an intervertebral disk, in part or as a whole.
Discharge—1. The escape of the accumulated energy or material. 2. The flowing away of a secretion or excretion of pus, feces and urine etc. 3. The material thus ejected.
Disci.—Plural of discus.
Disciform—Disk-shaped.
Discission—Incision or cutting into as of the capsule of the lens of the eye in the operation of cataract.
Discitis—Inflammation of the disc.
Disclination—Outward rotation of both the eyes.
Discogenic—Caused by an intervertebral disk.
Discoid—Like a disc.
Discoloration—The act of staining.
Disconjugate—That which is not joined to other.
Discopathy—Any disease of an intervertebral disk.
Discoplacenta—A disklike placenta.
Discordance—In genetics, the presence of a given trait in only one of the twins.
Discotomy—Discectomy.
Discrete—Separate.
Discrimination—The process of differentiating.
Discus—A disk.
Discutient—Scattering or causing a disappearance.
Disease—Any interruption of the normal structure or function of any body part, organ or system manifested by some signs and symptoms whose causes, pathology and prognosis may be known or unknown.

Acute disease—Disease marked by rapid onset and of relatively short duration.
Anticipated disease— The disease which can be predicted to occur.
Autoimmune disease— The disease in which the system of body's immune mechanisms becomes defective and produces antibodies against the normal parts of the body to such an extent as to cause tissue injury. Rheumatoid arthritis is considered as autoimmune disease.
Chronic disease—A disease marked by slow onset and lasting for a long time.
Communicable disease—A disease, the causative organism of which is transmissible from person to person either directly or indirectly through a carrier.
Complicating disease — A disease which occurs during the course or as a complication of another disease.
Congenital disease— The disease which is present since birth.
Constitutional disease—The disease affecting the whole body.
Contagious disease— An infectious disease transmitted from one person to another.
Deficiency disease— Disease caused by inadequate intake or absorption of some nutritive elements such as vitamins and minerals.
Degenerative disease— Disease resulting from degenerative changes occurring in tissues and organs, characteristic of old age.
Endemic disease—The disease which is present continuously or recurs frequently in a community.
Epidemic disease—A disease affecting a large number of people in a community at the same time.
Familial disease—The disease which occurs in several members of the same family.
Focal disease—The disease located at a specific and distinct area such as tonsils, adenoids etc.
Functional disease— The disease in which the symptoms are present without any anatomical change in the body.
Hemorrhagic disease of the newborn — Bleeding disease in the newborn such as melena and purpura etc.
Hereditary disease— Disease caused by hereditary factors transmitted from parent to offspring.
Idiopathic disease— Disease occurring without any cause.
Infectious disease — Disease produced by the presence of the disease producing organisms in the body.
Intercurrent disease — The disease occurring during the course of another unrelated disease.
Malignant disease— Cancer or a disease progressing extremely rapidly and generally threatening or resulting in death in a short time.

Metabolic disease— Disease produced due to disturbance in the metabolism such as diabetes due to deficiency of insulin.

Occupational disease— The disease caused by the factors associated with the occupation of the patient.

Organic disease— Disease resulting from the anatomical changes in an organ or a tissue of the body.

Pandemic disease—An epidemic disease spreading in the whole world.

Parasitic disease—The disease caused by the plant or animal parasites.

Psychosomatic disease—Physical illness caused by some psychological factors as urticaria sometimes occurs in emotional state or excessive angerness.

Secondary disease—A disease occurring as a result of another disease, *e.g.* a secondary joint disease of the lower extremity may be caused by obesity.

Self-limited disease — The disease even without treatment goes away.

Sporadic disease—The disease which occurs only occasionally.

Subacute disease— The disease in which the symptoms are less severe than that of an acute disease but it is more prolonged. It is the intermediate between an acute and a chronic disease.

Systemic disease—The disease affecting the whole body.

Venereal disease— Disease caused by sexual contacts as syphilis and gonorrhea etc.

Disengagement—The emergence of the head of the fetus from within the pelvis of the mother.

Disfluency—Inability to speak smoothly, the flow of speech is interrupted and repetitions of sentences may occur.

Disfluent—Pertaining to disfluency.

Disgerminoma—Dysgerminoma.

Disharmony—Lack of harmony, discord.

Disimpaction—Removal of impaction as removal of feces manually in fecal impaction.

Disinfect—To free from disease-producing organisms.

Disinfectant—The chemical substance which prevents infections by killing bacteria.

Disinfection—Destruction of disease-producing micro-organisms or their toxins or vectors by chemical or physical means.

Disinfector—That which disinfects.

Disinfestant—That which kills the parasites and insects causing diseases.

Disinfestation—The process of killing the parasites and insects causing diseases.

Disinhibition—Removal of an inhibition.

Disinsected—Freed of insects.

Disinsection, Disinsectization—Freeing an area from the insects.

Disinsertion—Detachment of the retina at the periphery.

Disintegrant—An agent which separates the constituents of a substance as the presence of a substance in a tablet causing it to disintegrate and release its medicinal substances on contact with moisture.

Disintegrater—That which breaks down a substance into its constituents.

Disintegration—The breaking down of a substance into its constituents.

Disinvagination—Relieving an invagination.

Disjoint—To disarticulate or separate the bones from their natural position in a joint.

Disjunction—State of being separated.

Disk, Disc—A flat, circular, plate-like structure, e.g. the intervertebral disk—the fibrocartilaginous tissue between the vertebral bodies, and optic disk which is the area on the retina of the eye where the optic nerve enters it, or blind spot.

Diskectomy—Removal of a herniated intervertebral disk by surgery.

Diskiform—Disk shaped.

Diskitis—Inflammation of a disk, especially of an intervertebral disk.

Diskogram—X-ray film produced by diskography.

Diskography—X-ray examination of the vertebral column after giving an injection of a radiopaque substance into an intervertebral disk.

Dislocate—To displace a part of the body, especially a bone from its normal position in a joint.

Dislocation —Displacement of a part of the body,

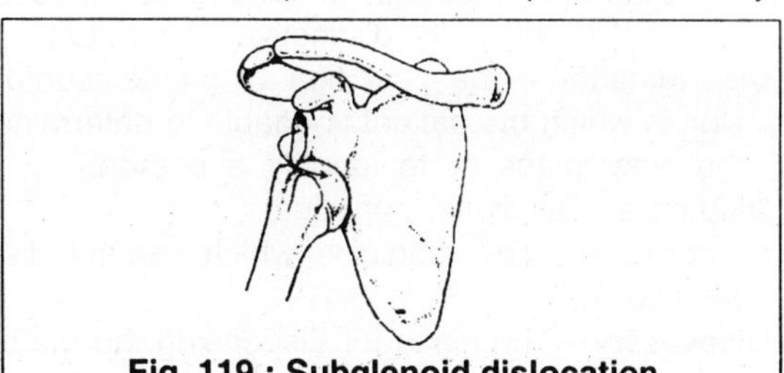

Fig. 119 : Subglenoid dislocation

especially the displacement of a bone from its normal position in a joint.

Complete dislocation — A dislocation which separates the surfaces of a joint completely.

Complicated dislocation—The dislocation associated with other injuries.

Compound dislocation—The dislocation in which the joint communicates with the air through a wound.

Congenital dislocation—Dislocation present at birth.

Incomplete dislocation—A partial dislocation.

Metacarpophalangeal joint dislocation — Dislocation of a finger.

Old dislocation—The dislocation in which no reduction has been done even after many days.

Pathological dislocation—Dislocation resulting from paralysis, or a disease of joint or supporting tissues.

Recent dislocation— Dislocation seen soon after it has occurred.

Simple dislocation — The dislocation which does not communicate with the external air through a wound.

Traumatic dislocation— Dislocation caused by trauma.

Dismember—To amputate an extremity or a portion of it.

Dismemberment—Amputation of an extremity or a portion of it.

Disobliteration—Opening of a pathologically closed channel.

Disocclusion—Loss of contact between the opposing teeth.

Disomic—Pertaining to disomy.

Disomus—A fetus with two trunks.

Disomy—The presence of two members of a pair of homologous chromosomes in one's cells, which is a normal state in humans.

Disorder—Abnormality of a function; physical or mental illness.

Disorganization—Any change in the tissues of an organ or a structure, which causes the loss of most or all of its distinctive characters.

Disorientation—The condition of mental confusion in which the patient is unable to determine the time, place or to identify a person.

Disparate—Dissimilar, unequal.

Dispensable—The medicine which can be dispensed.

Dispensary—The place for dispensing the medicines and treatment.

Dispensatory—A book which describes the medicines, their preparation and their uses.

Dispense—To prepare a prescription and to hand over it to the patient.

Dispermy, Dispermia— Entrance of two spermatozoa into one ovum.

Dispersal—Dispersion.

Dispersate—Suspension of very fine particles in a liquid.

Disperse—To scatter, as of the fine particles in a liquid.

Dispersion—The process of scattering.

Dispersoid—A colloid solution with very fine particles.

Dispersonalization—A mental disease in which the patient denies the existence of his or her personality or body parts.

Displaceability—The capability of being displaced.

Displacement—Removal from the normal position or place to an abnormal position or place.

Disposal—Termination.

Disposition—A natural tendency which may be manifested towards acquiring a certain disease.

Disproportion—The size of an object different from that considered to be normal as cephalopelvic disproportion, *i.e.* a condition in which the fetal head is larger than the mother's pelvis.

Disruption—The process of separating by force or a condition of being abnormally separated.

Disruptive—Bursting, rending.

Dissect—To cut apart or separate the tissues and the parts of a cadaver for anatomical study.

Dissection—The cutting apart of body parts for study.

Dissector—1. An instrument used for dissecting. 2. A book for guiding dissection. 3. One who performs dissection.

Dissemble—To mislead, to give a false impression, or to conceal the truth.

Disseminated—Scattered or distributed over a considerable area, especially applied to disease–producing organisms.

Dissemination—Diffusion.

Dissepiment—A separating tissue or septum.

Dissimilation—Disassimilation.

Dissimulation—Concealment of the truth, especially about the state of the health, as by a malingerer.

Dissipation—Dispersion of a matter.

Dissociation—Separation as the separation of a complex compound into simpler molecules by heat.

Dissolution—1. The process in which a substance is dissolved into another. 2. The separation of a compound into its components by chemical action. 3. Breaking up of the tissues of the body. 4. Liquefaction. 5. Death.

Dissolve—To mix a solid substance into a liquid.

Dissolvent—1. Having the power to dissolve. 2. Capable of being dissolved.

Dissolving—Making a solution.

Dissonance—1. Discord or disagreement. 2. Unpleasant sounds, especially of music.

Dissymmetry—Asymmetry.

Distad—Away from the center.

Distal—Further from the medial line. Opposite to proximal.

Distalis—Distal.

Distance—Space between two objects.

Distend—To stretch out or to inflate.

Distensibility—Property of being distensible.

Distension—The state of being distended.

Distichiasis—The presence of two rows of eyelashes, one or both of which are turned inward toward the eyeball.

Distill—To extract a substance by distillation.

Distillate—A product of distillation.

Distillation—Vaporization by heat and condensation of the vapor to purify a substance or to separate a volatile substance from less volatile substances. It is generally used to purify the water.

Distinct—Clearly visible.

Distobuccal—Pertaining to or formed by the distal and buccal walls of a tooth, or by the distal and buccal walls of a tooth cavity.

Distobucco-occlusal— Pertaining to the distal, buccal and occlusal surfaces of a molar or bicuspid tooth.

Distocervical—Pertaining to the distal surface of the neck of a tooth.

Distoclusion—The condition in which the lower teeth meet the upper teeth behind the normal position.

Distogingival—Pertaining to or formed by the distal and gingival walls of a tooth cavity.

Distolabial—Pertaining to the distal and labial surfaces of a tooth.

Distolingual—Pertaining to the distal and lingual surfaces of a tooth.

Distolinguo-occlusal— Pertaining to the distal, lingual and occlusal surfaces of a molar or bicuspid tooth.

Distomia—A fetus with two mouths.

Disto-occlusal—Pertaining to the distal and occlusal surfaces of a tooth.

Disto-occlusion—Distal occlusion.

Distoplacement—Distoversion.

Distortion—1. The state of being twisted out of the normal shape or position. 2. Twisting movements as of the muscles of the face. 3. A deformity in which a structure or a part of the body is changed in shape. 4. The difference in the size and shape of a X-ray film in comparison to the actual part examined.

Distoversion—Distoplacement. Malposition of a tooth distal and posteriorly to normal.

Distractibility—The wandering of the mind.

Distraction—1. Diversion of attention. 2. Separation of the surfaces of a joint without rupture of their ligaments and displacement.

Distress—Physical or mental suffering.

Districhiasis—Growing of two hairs from the same hair follicle.

Distrix—The splitting of the hairs at their ends.

Disturbance—Interruption of the normal sequence or divergence from the normal.

Emotional disturbance—Mental disorder.

Ditch—Fossa.

Diurese—To cause diuresis.

Diuresis—Increased excretion of the urine.

Diuretic—An agent increasing the excretion of urine.

Diurnal—Occurring during the day time or pertaining to it.

Divagation—Disconnected and incoherent speech.

Divarication—Diastasis.

Divergence—The moving away from a common point.

Divergent—Moving away in different directions.

Diver's paralysis—Paralysis occurring in divers due to returning too suddenly to normal atmospheric pressure after living in the water at high air pressure.

Diverticula—Plural of diverticulum.

Diverticular—Pertaining to or resembling a diverticulum.

Diverticulectomy—Removal of a diverticulum by surgery.

Diverticulitis—Inflammation of a diverticulum or of deverticula which may be acute or chronic.

Diverticulogram—X-ray of a diverticulum.

Diverticuloma—A tumor in the wall of the colon.

Diverticulopexy—An operation to obliterate a

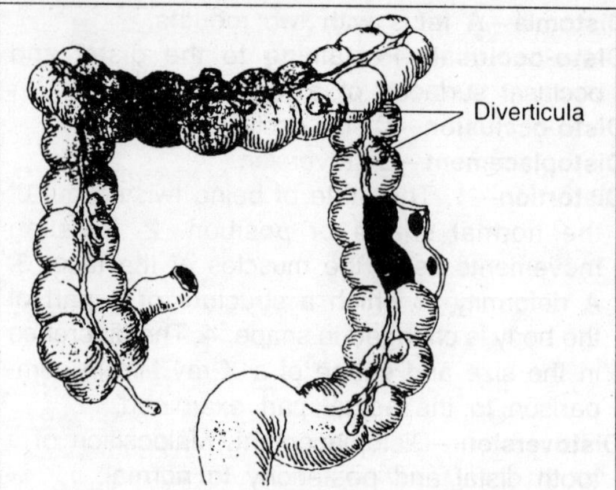

Fig. 120 : Multiple diverticula in the walls of the colon

diverticulum by securing its tip to a nearby structure so that it no longer fills.

Diverticulosis—The presence of diverticula in the colon without inflammation.

Diverticulum—A pouch or sac protruding from the walls of a canal or hollow organ *e.g.*, the diverticula found in the walls of the colon.

Divulse—To tear away or pull apart by force.

Divulsion—A pulling apart by force.

Divulsor—An instrument for dilating a part, especially the urethra.

Dizygotic, Dizygous— Pertaining to or produced by two separate zygotes (fertilized ova).

Dizziness—Vertigo.

D.M.D.—Abbreviation for Doctor of Dental Medicine.

D.M.F.—Decayed, missing, filled teeth.

DNA—Abbreviation for deoxyribonucleic acid.

DOA—Abbreviation for dead on arrival.

Doctor—1. The recipient of an advanced degree such as doctor of medicine (M.D.), doctor of philosophy (Ph. D.), doctor of science (D.Sc.), doctor of dental medicine (D.M.D.). 2. The person licensed by a state government to practice of medicine, veterinary medicine or dentistry.

Doctrine—The system of the principles taught.

Dohle bodies—These are minute (1 to 5 μm) discrete round or oval bodies which stain sky blue and found in the neutrophils of the patients with severe infections, burns, trauma, pregnancy or cancer.

Dol—Symbol for the degree of intensity of pain registered on the dolorimeter.

Dolicho—Long.

Dolichocephalic—Long headed.

Dolichocephalous—Dolichocephalic.

Dolichocephaly, Dolichocephalism—The condition of being long headed.

Dolichocolon—Abnormally long colon.

Dolichocranial— Dolichocephalic.

Dolichoderus—Having a long neck.

Dolichofacial—Pertaining to or having a long face.

Dolichohieric—Having a long, slender sacrum.

Dolichomorphic—Pertaining to or having a long thin body.

Dolichopellic, Dolichopelvic—Having a long pelvis.

Dolichoprosopic— Dolichofacial.

Dolichoprosopous—Dolichofacial.

Dolichosigmoid—Having a long sigmoid colon.

Dolichuranic—Pertaining to a long alveolar arch of the maxilla.

Dolor—Pain, one of the chief signs of inflammation.

Dolorific—Producing pain.

Dolorimeter—An instrument for measuring the degree of pain in dols.

Dolorimetry—Measurement of pain.

Dolorogenic—Causing pain.

Dolorology—The study and treatment of pain.

Dolorous—Painful, distressing.

Domatophobia—Morbid fear of living in a house.

Dome—Rounded roof.

Domestic—Belonging to household.

Domiciliary—Pertaining to a dwelling place.

Dominance—Supermacy or ascendancy.

Dominant, Dominator— Supreme.

Donee—One who receives something, such as blood from a donor.

Donor—An organism that supplies living tissues to be used in another body, as a person who supplies blood for transfusion, or an organ for transplantation.

Donovan bodies—These are blue or black staining bodies found in clusters in the large mononuclear cells in the granulation tissue of the patients infected with Calymmatobacterium granulomatis which causes granuloma inguinale or granuloma venereum.

Doozing—Sleeping slightly.

Dopa —Chemical substance produced by the oxidation of tyrosine to tyrosinase and which is a precursor of catecholamines and melanin.

Dopamine—A catecholamine synthesized by the adrenal gland and is the intermediate product in the synthesis of norepinephrine. It acts to increase the blood pressure, especially the systolic blood pressure and acts as a neurotransmitter in the central nervous system.

Dopaminergic—1. Caused by dopamine. 2. Pertaining to the tissues or organs affected by dopamine.

Dopa-oxidase—An enzyme which oxidises dopa to melanin in the skin, producing pigmentation.

Dope —1. Any drug administered for its temporary effect, or taken habitually. 2. To administer or to take such a drug.

Doping—The administration of a drug or other substance to an individual, especially to an athlete to improve performance.

Doppler effect—The frequency of waves such as that of sound varies with the change in distance between the source of the sound and its receiver. It decreases as the distance increases and increases as the distance decreases.

Doraphobia—Aversion to touching the hair or fur of the animals.

Dormancy—Sleeping stage.

Dormant—Sleeping.

Doromania—Mania for giving gifts.

Dorsa—Plural of dorsum.

Dorsabdominal—Pertaining to the back and abdomen.

Dorsad—Toward the back.

Dorsal—1. Pertaining to the back. 2. Situated on the back surface. 3. Opposed to ventral surface

Dorsalgia—Pain in the back.

Dorsalis—Dorsal, *i.e.* pertaining to the back.

Dorsal vertebrae—Twelve bones of the spinal column between the cervical and lumbar vertebrae.

Dorsi-, Dorso-, Dors-—Prefixes indicating back.

Dorsiduct—To draw toward the back side.

Dorsiduction—Drawing toward the back.

Dorsiflect—To bend backward.

Dorsiflexion —Movement of a part of the body as of the hand or foot at its joint as to bend toward the posterior surface of the body.

Dorsimesad—Toward the dorsimeson.

Dorsimeson—Median plane of the back.

Dorsiscapular—Pertaining to the dorsal surface of the scapula.

Dorsispinal—Pertaining to the back and the vertebral column.

Dorsocentral—Pertaining to the center of the back.

Dorsocephalad—Toward the back of the head.

Dorsodynia—Pain in the muscles of upper part of the back.

Dorsolateral—Pertaining to the back and the side.

Dorsolumbar—Pertaining to the back and the lumbar region.

Dorsoplantar—Pertaining to the dorsal and the plantar surface of the foot.

Dorsosacral position, Lithotomy position — Position in which the patient lies upon her back with thighs flexed upon abdomen and legs upon thighs, which are abducted, used for gynaecological examinations and treatments.

Dorsoventral—1. Pertaining to the back and frontal surfaces of the body. 2. Passing from the back to the front.

Dorsum—The back, posterior or superior surface of a body or body part.

Dosage—Determination and regulation of the amount, frequency and number of doses of a medicine or radiation for a patient.

Dose—The amount of a medicine or of radiation to be administered at one time.

Booster dose—An additional dose of an immunizing agent as a vaccine or toxoid etc., usually smaller than the original amount, injected to sustain the effect of the primary immunization, at an appropriate interval.

Curative dose—The dose which is sufficient to cure a disease.

Divided dose—A fraction of the total quantity of a medicine to be given at intervals in a day.

Effective dose—The quantity of a medicine which produces the effects for which it is given.

Fatal or lethal dose— The dose which kills.

Infective dose—The amount of infectious organisms, especially the bacteria and the viruses, that causes a disease in human being.

Maintenance dose—Dose of a medicine to maintain the desired effect.

Maximum dose—The largest dose which is safe to give.

Median curative dose—The dose which cures a disease in 50% of the persons treated.

Minimum dose—Smallest dose which produces the desired effect.

Single dose—Not more than one dose in a day.

Therapeutic dose— Dose required to produce the desired effect.

Toxic dose—The dose which causes toxicity.

Dosimeter—An instrument for measuring the X-ray output.

Dosimetric—Pertaining to dosimeter.

Dosimetry—The measurement of amount of radiation.

Dot—A small spot.

Dotage—Senility.

Double consciousness— Expression of two phases of personality.

Double personality—Dual personality. The condition in which a person shows two personalities as seen in hysteria and schizophrenia.

Doublet—A combination of two lenses designed to correct the chromatic and spherical aberration.

Double touch—To investigate with a finger in one cavity and the thumb into another.

Double uterus—Presence of two uteri.

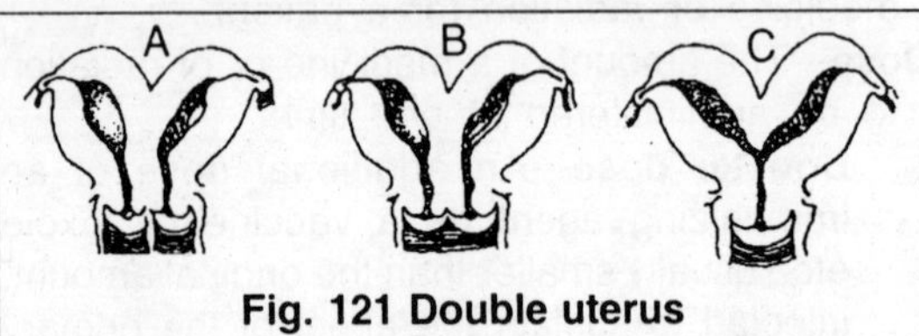

Fig. 121 Double uterus

A. Double uterus in which uterine body, cervix and vagina all are double.

B. Double uterus in which uterine body and cervix are double but the vagina is single.

C. Double uterus in which uterine body is double but cervix and vagina are single.

Double vision, Diplopia— Seeing of two images of a thing at the same time.

Douche—A stream of plain or medicated cold or hot water or a current of air or vapor directed against a part of the body or into a cavity.

Air douche—A current of air blown into a cavity, especially into the tympanum for opening the eustachian tube.

Astringent douche— Douche containing the astringent substances such as alum or zinc sulfate for shrinking the mucous membrane.

Cleansing douche—An external douche containing a mild antiseptic or disinfectant substance for cleansing the perineal area including the genital organs after defecation or an operation.

Scotch douche—Douche of alternating hot and cold water jets against a local area of the skin.

Vaginal douche—Douche of a vagina done to disinfect it when it is infected.

Dough—Kneaded flour.

Doughy feeling—Feeling of kneaded flour.

Douglas' cul-de-sac, Pouch — The sac of the peritoneum lying behind the uterus and in front of rectum.

Douglasitis—Inflammation of the Douglas' cul-de-sac.

Dowel—A metal pin for fastening an artificial crown to a natural tooth root.

Down regulate—To inhibit or suppress the normal response of an organ or system.

Down's syndrome—Mongolism. It is a congenital disease caused by the presence of an extra 21th chromosome or trisomy (normally there are 23 pairs of chromosomes in the nucleus of each human cell, 22 pairs are autosomes and 1 pair of sex chromosomes) in the nucleus of the human cell, characterized by severe mental retardation, retarted growth, sloping forehead, short flat nose, small low-set ears, constant protrusions of a thickened and fissured tongue, broad hands and feet and little fingers curved inwards. Congenital heart disease may be present.

Doyeres eminence—An elevation where a nerve filament enters a muscle.

D.P.H.—Department of public health, diploma in public health.

D.P.T.—Vaccine for diphtheria, pertussis and tetanus used for immunizing the infants and children.

D.R.—Reaction of degeneration.

Dr.—Doctor.

dr.—Drachm; dram.

Drachm, Dram—A unit of weight which is equal to 60 grains or 1/8th part of an ounce.

Draft, Draught—An amount of a liquid medicine to be taken in a single dose.

Dragee—A sugar-coated pill.

Drain—1. Exit or a tube for discharge of a waste material. 2. To draw off a liquid.

Drainage—Discharge or withdrawal of fluids from the body.

Discharge of pus—Free discharge of pus from a wound or cavity.

Drainage by glass funnels—Drainage with glass funnels.

Drainage by rubber tube— Drainage of a wound or cavity such as abdominal cavity by rubber tube.

Postural drainage—Drainage of the nose,

sinuses and lungs by keeping the patient in the position in which gravity allows drainage.

Suction drainage—Drainage by creating a negative pressure in a tube.

Drainage tube—An apparatus usually of rubber used to allow the escape of pus, serum, blood or other fluids from wound or abscess.

Dram—Drachm.

Dramatism—Dramatic behavior and high speech seen in psychological disturbances.

Drape—1. To cover the parts of the body other than those to be examined or operated upon. 2. The cloth or other material used for covering.

Drapetomania—Insanity in which a person runs away from the home.

Drastic—Acting strongly.

Draught—1. A drink. 2. A dose of a liquid medicine to be taken all at once. 3. Current of air in a room.

Draw-sheet—A sheet stretched across the bed under the patient, which is easier to change for both the patient and nurse, than the entire bed and it is used to protect the bed from soilage and drainage.

Dream—Experience of ideas, emotions, scenes and events during sleep, as they are real.

Drepanocyte—Sickle or crescent cell.

Drepanocytemia—Sickle cell anemia.

Drepanocytic—Pertaining to or resembling a sickle cell.

Drepanocytosis—Presence of sickle cells in the blood.

Dresser—The person who dresses the wounds.

Dressing—Covering, protecting or supporting the diseased part or wound by any of the various materials.

Absorbent dressing— Dressing with sterilized gauze or absorbent cotton.

Antiseptic dressing— Dressing with gauze impregnated with an antiseptic solution.

Dry dressing—Dressing by dry gauze, cotton or other dry material.

Fixed dressing—Dressing with plaster of paris which is usually done in fracture and some diseases of the bone. When this dressing dries up, it fixes the part so treated.

Occlusive dressing— Dressing which seals a wound completely to prevent infection and air from outside and the moisture escaping from the wound.

Pressure dressing— Dressing which is used to apply pressure on the wound to prevent the collection of fluids.

Dribble—To fall in drops, as the urine from the distended urinary bladder.

Drift —Movement due to an external force which is often aimless.

Drill —1. To bore in a bone or other hard substance. 2. A boring tool.

Drill-out —The scooping out.

Drinker —The person who takes alcohol.

Drip —The administration of a liquid medicine slowly drop by drop.

Intravenous drip — Intravenous injection of a suitable solution with a drop at a time.

Murphy drip — Slow administration of a liquid drop by drop per rectum.

Drive —The force to act.

Drivelling —An involuntary flow of saliva.

Dromomania —Insanity in which someone wanders.

Dromotropic —Affecting the conductivity of a nerve fiber.

Drop —1. A minute spherical mass of a liquid which hangs or falls. 2. Failure of a part of the body to maintain its normal position, usually due to paralysis or injury as foot drop in which the foot hangs due to paralysis of the anterior tibial muscles, and the wrist drop in which the hand hangs down from the forearm due to paralysis of the extensor muscles.

Dropfoot —Footdrop.

Droplet —Very small drop.

Droplet infection —Spreading of infection by fine infected particles as by sneezing from the nose or by spitting from the mouth.

Dropper —A tube narrowed at one end for dispensing liquids in drops.

Dropsical —Affected with or pertaining to dropsy.

Dropsy —Accumulation of fluid in the tissues causing edema.

Abdominal dropsy — Ascites.

Cardiac dropsy —Edema occurring as a result of cardiac failure.

Nutritional dropsy — Edema occurring due to hypoproteinemia secondary to malnutrition.

Drowning —Suffocation and death resulting from filling of the lungs with fluid due to immersion in it.

Drowsiness —The state of being sleepy.

Dr. P.H. —Doctor of public health.

Drug —Any substance when enters a living

organism, may alter one or more of its functions.

Addictive drug —A drug that makes somebody addictive to itself.

Crude drug —An unrefined drug usually obtained from the plants.

Psychotropic drug —Any drug that affects the mind.

Drug abuse —Overuse or misuse of a drug by self-administration.

Drug addiction —A condition caused by excessive or continued use of a drug, characterized by loss of appetite and weight, dulmindedness, incoordination of movements and having the appearance of intoxication, blood shot eyes and sometimes a discharge of watery fluid from the nose.

Drug-fast —Resistance, as of the bacteria to action of a drug.

Druggist —Pharmacist, one who prepares medicines.

Drug interaction —Synergistic, antagonistic or in some cases lethal effects of the drugs, when two or more drugs are taken concurrently.

Drug receptors —The part or parts of a cell which interact with a drug or drugs.

Drum —1. The cavity of the middle ear. 2. The tympanic membrane.

Drumhead —The tympanic membrane.

Drunkard —An alcoholic person.

Drunkenness —Alcoholic intoxication.

Druse —Rupture of the tissues.

Drusen —Small bright structures seen in the retina and the optic disk.

Dry Ice —Solid carbon dioxide in the form of a pencil used for the treatment of certain skin disorders, such as warts, etc., by freezing.

Dry measure —The measure of the volume of a dry substance.

Dualism —1. The condition of being double. 2. The theory that various blood cells arise from two types of stem cells, myeloid cells arise from myeloblasts and the lymphatic cells from lymphoblasts. 3. The theory that an individual consists of two independent units, body and mind.

Duchenne -Erb paralysis —Paralysis of the muscles supplied by nerves from the upper brachial plexus as may occur in the fetus during difficult labor or in the case of adults by falling of weights on the shoulder.

Ducrey's bacillus —Small, rod-shaped bacteria found in pairs, which cause chancroid or soft chancre.

Duct —A tubular structure for the passage of secretions or excretions or a narrow enclosed channel containing a fluid.

Common bile duct —The duct formed by the union of the cystic and hepatic ducts which carries bile to the duodenum.

Cystic duct —Excretory duct of the gallbladder.

Efferent duct —Any duct which carries secretion from a gland.

Ejaculatory duct —The duct which conveys semen into the urethra.

Excretory duct —A duct that carries a waste product from an organ.

Hepatic ducts —Ducts which receive bile from the right and left lobes of the liver and carry it to the common bile duct.

Lacrimal duct —The duct of tears.

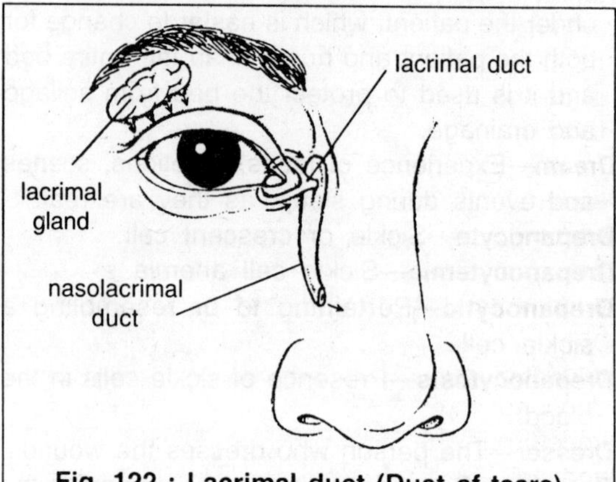

Fig. 122 : Lacrimal duct (Duct of tears)

Lactiferous ducts —15 to 20 ducts which convey the milk secreted by the lobes of the mammary gland to the nipple.

Lymphatic duct —One of two main ducts conveying lymph to the blood stream, the left lymphatic duct (Thoracic duct) and the right lymphatic duct.

Pancreatic duct — The duct which conveys pancreatic juice to the duodenum.

Parotid duct —The duct through which the secretion from the parotid gland enters into the mouth.

Semicircular ducts —Three long ducts of the membranous labyrinth of the inner ear.

Seminal or spermatic duct —Any one of the ducts that coneys semen or spermatozoa from the epididymis to the urethra.

Ductal —Pertaining to a duct.

Ductile —Capable of being elongated without breaking.

Duction —1. The act of conducting. 2. The rotation of an eye about an axis.

Ductless —Without duct.

Ductless glands —Glands without ducts.

Ductular —Pertaining to a ductule.

Ductule, Ductulus —A very small duct.

Ductulus— Ductule.

Duipara —A woman who becomes pregnant for the second time.

Dull —1. Not resonant on percussion. 2. Mentally inactive.

Dullard —A stupid person.

Dullness, Dulness —1. State of lack of normal resonance on percussion. 2. State of being mentally inactive.

Dumb —Mute, unable to speak.

Dumbness —Muteness.

Dummy —Pontic.

Dumping syndrome —A syndrome characterized by sweating and weakness after eating, which is due to rapid emptying of the stomach contents into the small intestine resulting from the gastric resections.

Duodenal —Pertaining to the duodenum.

Duodenal bulb —Area of duodenum just beyond the pylorus.

Duodenectasis —Chronic dilatation of the duodenum.

Duodenectomy —Partial or total excision of the duodenum.

Duodenitis —Inflammation of the duodenum.

Duodeno- —A prefix pertaining to duodenum.

Duodenocholangitis — Inflammation of the duodenum and common bile duct.

Duodenocholecystostomy —Formation of a connection between the duodenum and the gallbladder.

Duodenocholedochotomy —To make an incision into the duodenum to reach the gallbladder.

Duodenocystostomy—Duodenocholecystostomy.

Duodenoenterostomy — Formation of passage between the duodenum and intestine.

Duodenogram — X-ray of the duodenum.

Duodenography —Radiography of the duodenum.

Duodenohepatic —Pertaining to duodenum and liver.

Duodenoileostomy — Formation of a connection between the duodenum and ileum.

Duodenojejunal —Pertaining to duodenum and jejunum.

Duodenojejunostomy — Formation of a passage between the duodenum and jejunum.

Duodenolysis — Incision of the adhesions to the duodenum.

Duodenopancreasectomy —Excision of the duodenum and part of the pancreas.

Duodenoplasty —Repair of the duodenum by plastic surgery.

Duodenorrhaphy —Suturing of the duodenum.

Duodenoscope —An endoscope for examining the duodenum.

Duodenoscopy —Inspection of the duodenum with an endoscope.

Duodenostomy —Surgical formation of a permanent opening into the duodenum through the abdominal wall.

Duodenotomy —An incision into the duodenum.

Duodenum —The first part of the small intestine extending from the pylorus to the jejunum.

Duplex —Providing two functions.

Duplication —A doubling or folding.

Duplicitas —Cephalic or the pelvic end of a fetus is doubled.

Dupp —The second heart sound which is shorter and of higher pitch than lubb, the first heart sound, heard on auscultation over the apex.

Dupuytren's contracture — Bending of the little and ring fingers into the palm permanently due to the contracture of the palmar fascia.

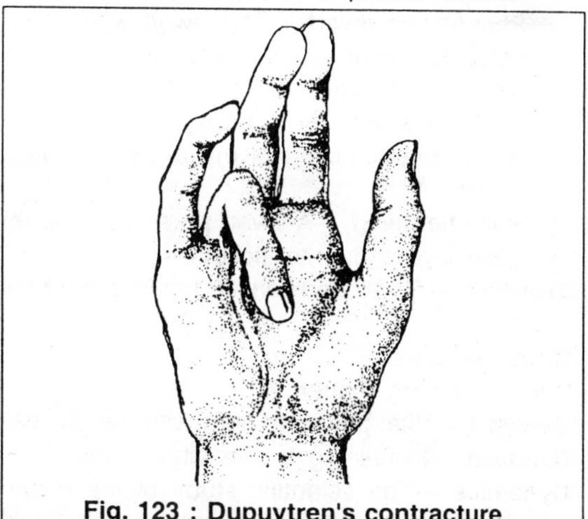

Fig. 123 : Dupuytren's contracture

Dura —Dura mater.

Dural —Pertaining to the dura mater.

Dura mater —The outermost membranous layer covering the brain and the spinal cord.

Duramatral —Dural.

Duraplasty —Repair of the dura mater by plastic surgery.

Duration —Continuance of time.
Durematoma —Accumulation of blood between arachnoid mater and dura mater.
Duritis —Inflammation of the dura mater.
Duroarachnitis —Inflammation of the dura mater and arachnoid mater.
Dust —Fine powder of a substance.
Dust cell —A macrophage found in the walls of the alveoli of the lungs that ingest the disease-producing micro-organisms and particles of air pollution.
Dusting powder --Any fine powder for dusting on the skin.
Dusty —Filled with dust. Dust-like.
Dwarf —An abnormally short or undersized person.

Achondroplastic dwarf — A dwarf person with normal trunk but shortened extremities, large head and prominent buttocks.
Asexual dwarf — An adult dwarf with deficient sexual development.
Ateliotic dwarf —A dwarf with infantile skeleton.
Infantile dwarf —Dwarf with marked physical, mental and sexual underdevelopment.
Micromelic dwarf — Dwarf with very small limbs.
Ovarian dwarf —A female dwarf due to absence or underdevelopment of the ovaries.
Phocomelic dwarf —The dwarf with abnormally short diaphyses of long bones of eiher pair of extremities or of all four.
Pituitary dwarf —A dwarf whose condition is due to hypofunction of the anterior pituitary gland.
Rachitic dwarf —A dwarf person whose this condition is due to rickets.

Dwarfism —The condition of being abnormally small.
Dyad —A pair.
Dye —Coloring matter.
Dynamia —Vital power to fight with the disease.
Dynamic —Pertaining to the vital power.
Dynamics —The scientific study of the moving bodies and their forces.
Dynamo- — A prefix denoting force or energy.
Dynamogenesis —Development of energy.
Dynamogenic —Pertaining to or caused by an increase of energy.
Dynamogeny —Dynamogenesis.
Dynamograph —An apparatus for recording the muscular strength.
Dynamometer —1. An apparatus for measuring the muscular strength. 2 An apparatus for determining the magnifying power of a lens.
Dynamoscope —An instrument for auscultation of the muscles.
Dynamoscopy —Auscultation of a contracting muscle.
Dynatherm —An apparatus for inducing diathermy.
Dyne —Metric unit of force, that amount of force which is required to accelerate a weight of one gram to one centimeter in one sec.
Dys- —Prefix indicating bad, difficult and painful.
Dysacousia, Dysacusis, Dysacousma —1. Difficulty in hearing. 2. Discomfort caused by loud sounds.
Dysadaptation —Inability of the iris and retina to accomodate well to varying intensities of light.
Dysadrenalism —Functional disorder or a disease of the adrenal gland.
Dysantigraphia —Inability to copy written or printed letters.
Dysaphia —Impairment of the sense of touch.
Dysaphic —Pertaining to impaired tactile sensibility.
Dysarteriotony —Abnormal blood pressure, either too high or too low.
Dysarthria —Difficult and defective speech.
Dysartheric —Pertaining to dysarthria.
Dysarthrosis —Deformity of a joint.
Dysautonomia —Abnormal functioning of the autonomic nervous system.
Dysbarism —A group of symptoms arising following exposure of the body to a less atmospheric pressure as in air flight. In severe cases it is called decompression sickness or bends.
Dysbasia —Difficulty in walking especially due to the disease of the central nervous system.
Dysbolism —Disordered metabolism.
Dysbulia —1. Weak and uncertain will power. 2. Inability to fix the attention.
Dysbulic —Pertaining to or characterized by dysbulia.
Dyscalculia —Inability to solve the mathematical problems due to brain disease or injury.
Dyscephalia —Dyscephaly. Malformation of the head and the face.
Dyscephaly —Malformation of the cranium and the facial bones.
Dyscheiral, Dyschiral —Pertaining to dyscheiria.
Dyscheiria —Dyschiria.
Dyschezia —Painful or difficult defecation.

Dyschiria —Inability to tell which the side of the body has been touched.

Dyscholia —Any pathological condition of the bile.

Dyschondrogenesis — Maldevelopment of the cartilages.

Dyschondroplasia — Maldevelopment of the cartilages.

Dyschondrosteosis —A skeletal dysplasia, more severe in females.

Dyschroa, Dyschroia — Discoloration of the skin.

Dyschromatopsia —Disorder of color vision.

Dyschromia —Discoloration of the skin or any disorder of the pigmentation of the skin or hair.

Dyscinesia, Dyskinesia —Inability to perform voluntary movement.

Dyscoria —Abnormality in the form or shape of the pupil or in the light reflex actions in the two pupils.

Dyscrasia —Morbid condition or any pathological condition as that of blood.

Dyscrasic, Dyscratic — Pertaining to or affected with dyscrasia.

Dyscrinism —Any disorder of the secretions, especially of endocrine glands.

Dysdiadochokinesia, Dysdiadochocinesia — Inability to perform rapidly alternating movements.

Dysdiadochokinesis — Adiadochokinesis.

Dysembryoma —Teratoma, congenital tumor containing hair and teeth.

Dysembryoplasia — Malformation of the fetus in the uterus.

Dysemia —Any blood disease.

Dysenteric —Pertaining to dysentery.

Dysentery —A condition characterized by the inflammation of the intestine, especially of the colon with abdominal pain, tenesmus and passing of stools frequently containing mucus and blood.

Amebic dysentery — Dysentery caused by Entamoeba histolytica in which mucus passes in the stools in large quantity.

Bacillary dysentery — Dysentery caused by the bacteria of the genus Shigella in which blood passes in the stool.

Dyserethesia —Impaired response to the stimuli or insensibility.

Dyserethism —The slow response to stimuli.

Dysergasia —Inability to function properly.

Dysergastic reaction — Hallucinations, fears, disorientation, dream states and other mental disorders due to deficient blood circulation and metabolism of the brain.

Dysergia —Incoordination in muscular voluntary movements due to defect of efferent nerve impulse.

Dysesthesia —1. Feeling of sensations of pricks of pins and needles or of crawling on the skin. 2. Impairment of any sense, especially of touch. 3. Feeling pain of any sensation which normally does not produce pain.

Auditory dysesthesia — Dysacusia. Discomfort from loud noises.

Pedis dysesthesia — Severe itching and burning sensation on the plantar surface of the feet and toes.

Dysfibrinogenemia — Presence of abnormal fibrinogens of various types in the blood.

Dysfunction —Abnormal, inadequate or impaired function of an organ or part of the body.

Dysgalactia —Defective secretion of the milk.

Dysgammaglobulinemia — Disproportion in the concentration of immunoglobulins in the blood which may be congenital or acquired.

Dysgenesis —Maldevelopment, especially in the embryo.

Gonadal dysgenesis —In female there is amenorrhoea, sexual immaturity and dwarfism due to failure of the ovaries to respond to the pituitary hormone (gonadotropin) stimulation.

Dysgenic —Pertaining to dysgenesis.

Dysgenitalism —Condition caused by abnormal genital development.

Dysgerminoma —A malignant tumor of the ovary.

Dysgeusia —Impairment of the sense of taste.

Dysglandular —Abnormal functioning of glands, especially those of internal secretion.

Dysglobulinemia —Presence of globulins in the blood of abnormal quantity or quality.

Dysglycemia —Any disorder of the metabolism of blood sugar.

Dysgnathia —Abnormality of the mandible and maxilla.

Dysgnathic —Pertaining to or characterized by abnormality of the maxilla and mandible.

Dysgnosia —Any abnormality of the intellect.

Dysgonesis —1. Functional disorder of the genital organs. 2. Poor growth of bacteria in culture.

Dysgonic —Pertaining to the slow growth of bacteria in culture.

Dysgraphia —1. Inability to write properly usually due to brain lesion. 2. Writer's cramp.

Dyshematopoiesia — Defective blood formation.

Dyshematopoiesis — Dyshemopoiesis. Defective formation of blood.

Dyshematopoietic — Pertaining to or characterized by defective formation of blood.

Dyshemopoiesis — Dyshematopoiesis.

Dyshemopoietic — Dyshematopoietic.

Dyshesion —Disorder of cell adherence.

Dyshidria, Dyshidrosis, Dysidrosis —Any disorder of the sweat glands, present in the skin.

Dyshidrosis —Dyshidria.

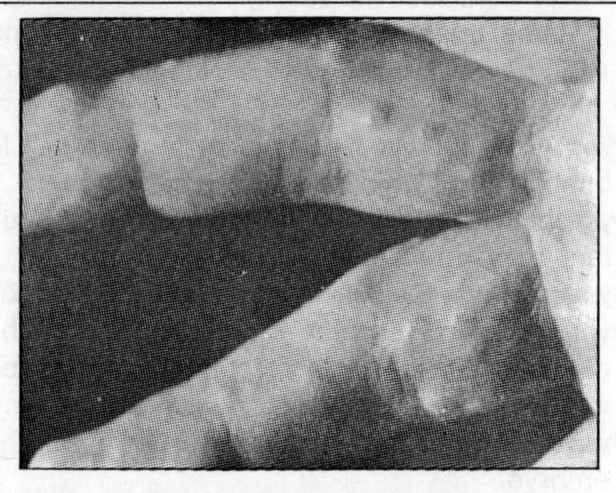

Fig. 124 : Dyshidrosis

Dysjunction —Cleavage. A separation of normally joined structures or parts.

Dyskaryosis —Abnormality of the nucleus of a cell.

Dyskaryotic —Pertaining to or characterized by dyskaryosis.

Dyskeratoma —A kind of skin tumor in which there is solitary brownish red nodule occurring on the face, neck, head or axilla.

Dyskeratosis — Any change in the keratinization of the epithelial cells of the epidermis which is a symptom of many skin diseases.

Dyskinesia —Impairment of the power of voluntary movement.

Dyskinesia algera — Condition in which the movement is painful if done quickly but not painful if done slowly, the condition is found in hysteria.

Dyskinesia intermittens —The disability of the limbs occurring intermittently due to impaired blood circulation.

Dyskinesia orofacial —Dyskinesia affecting primarily the mouth and the face.

Dyskinesia tarda, dyskinesia tardive — Repeated involuntary movements of the facial, oral and cervical muscles, affecting chiefly the elder persons.

Dyskinesia uterine — Pain in the uterus on movement.

Diskinesis —Dyskinesia.

Dyskinetic —Pertaining to dyskinesia.

Dyslalia —Impairment of ability to speak due to defect of the external speech organs.

Dyslexia —Inability to interpret the written language due to a defect in the central nervous system.

Dyslexic —Pertaining to dyslexia.

Dyslochia —Disordered lochial discharge.

Dyslogia —Difficulty in expressing the ideas due to mental disorders.

Dysmasesis —Difficulty in masticating.

Dysmature —Defective development or ripening.

Dysmaturity —The condition of the fetus of being small or immature for its gestational age.

Dysmegalopsia —Inability to see the actual size of the objects, they appear larger than they actually are.

Dysmelia —Congenital deformity of a limb or limbs.

Dysmenorrhea —Pain during menstruation.

Congestive dysmenorrhea —Dysmenorrhea caused by the congestion of the uterus.

Essential dysmenorrhea —Dysmenorrhea without apparent cause.

Inflammatory dysmenorrhea —Dysmenorrhea caused by pelvic inflammation.

Mechanical dysmenorrhea— Dysmenorrhea occurring due to obstruction in menstrual bleeding.

Membranous dysmenorrhea —Dysmenorrhea associated with the passage of the membranous casts from the uterus.

Neurotic dysmenorrhea —Dysmenorrhea caused by neurosis.

Obstructive dysmenorrhea —That which is caused by mechanical obstruction.

Ovarian dysmenorrhea — A form of secondary dysmenorrhea occurring due to a disease of an ovary.

Primary dysmenorrhea —Pain during menstruation which starts at the first menstrual period.

Secondary dysmenorrhea —The pain during menstruation which starts some years after the first menstrual period.

Spasmodic dysmenorrhea —Dysmenorrhea caused by the spasmodic contractions of the uterus.

Tubal dysmenorrhea — A form of secondary dysmenorrhea caused by stenosis or other abnormal condition of the fallopian tubes.

Uterine dysmenorrhea —A form of secondary dysmenorrhea resulting from the disease of the uterus.

Vaginal dysmenorrhea —A form of secondary dysmenorrhea due to obstruction or other abnormal conditon in the vagina.

Dysmetabolism —Defective metabolism.

Dysmetria —Inability to control the speed of muscular movement or of an act.

Dysmetropsia —Inability to see the correct size and shape of the things.

Dysmimia —Inability to express the thoughts by signs or gestures.

Dysmnesia —Impairment of memory.

Dysmorphia —Dysmorphism.

Dysmorphism —Dysmorphia. Abnormality of shape.

Dysmorphogenesis —The process of abnormal tissue formation.

Dysmorphology —Study of the abnormal formation of tissues.

Dysmorphophobia —Morbid fear of being deformed.

Dysmorphosis —Abnormal in form.

Dysmyelination —Breakdown of a myelin sheath of a nerve fiber.

Dysmyotonia —Abnormal tonicity of the muscle.

Dysnystaxis —Light sleep. A condition of half sleep.

Dysodontiasis —Painful or difficult eruption of teeth.

Dysontogenesis —Defective development of an embryo.

Dysontogenetic —Pertaining to dysontogenesis.

Dysopia, Dysopsia — Defective vision.

Dysorexia —Disordered appetite.

Dysosmia —Impairment of the sense of smell.

Dysosteogenesis, Dysostosis —Defective ossification, or the bone formation.

Dysostosis —Defective ossification.

Dysoxidizable —Not easy to be oxidized.

Dyspancreatism —Impairment of the pancreatic function.

Dyspareunia —Occurrence of pain during sexual intercourse.

Dyspepsia —Impairment of the process of digestion, which is characterized by discomfort in the epigastric region after meals.

Acid dyspepsia — Dyspepsia due to excessive acidity of the stomach.

Alcoholic dyspepsia —Dyspepsia caused by excessive use of alcohol.

Biliary dyspepsia — Dyspepsia which is due to insufficient secretion of bile.

Cardiac dyspepsia — Dyspepsia occurring during heart disease.

Fermentative dyspepsia — Dyspepsia occurring with fermentation of the gastric contents as usually occurs in gastric dilatation.

Gastrointestinal dyspepsia —Dyspepsia due to faulty functions of the stomach and intestines.

Hepatic dyspepsia — Dyspepsia due to liver disease.

Hysterical dyspepsia — Dyspepsia which occurs during hysterical attacks.

Nervous dyspepsia — Dyspepsia due to nervous disorder.

Dyspeptic —Pertaining to or affected with dyspepsia.

Dyspermasia, dyspermatism, dyspermia —Pain in the emission of sperms during sexual intercourse.

Dysphagia, Dysphagy — Difficulty in swallowing.

Dysphasia —Impairment of speech due to lesion in the brain.

Dysphemia —Stammering or other disorder of speech due to psychological causes.

Dysphonia —Difficulty in speaking, hoarseness.

Dysphoria —Depression and restlessness without any cause.

Dysphrasia —Dysphasia, impairment of speech due to a lesion in the brain.

Dysphylaxia —Waking too early from sleep.

Dyspigmentation —A disorder of the pigmentation of the skin or hair.

Dyspinealism —The condition resulting from the deficiency of pineal gland secretion.

Dyspituitarism —A condition due to disordered function of the pituitary gland.

Dysplasia —Abnormality in the development of tissues.

Anhydrotic dysplasia —Absence or deficiency of sweat glands, and abnormal development of teeth and nails congenitally.

Chondroectodermal dysplasia —A condition marked by defective development of the skin, hair, bones, teeth, nails, and congenital septal defect of the heart.

Congenital ectodermal dysplasia — Congenital incomplete development of the ectodermal structures such as of the skin which is smooth and hairless, and teeth and nails may be affected.

Cretinoid dysplasia —A condition characterized by cretinism, *i.e.,* lack of physical and mental development.

Monostotic fibrous dysplasia — Replacement of bone by fibrous tissue, marked by pain in tibia or femur bone.

Polyostotic fibrous dysplasia — Replacement of bone by bloodless firbous tissue, marked by difficulty in walking and bone deformities and even fractures.

Dysplastic —Pertaining to or affected with dysplasia.

Dyspnea —Labored or difficult breathing.

Cardiac dyspnea — Dyspnea due to cardiac insufficiency, as in acute myocardial infarction.

Exertional dyspnea — Dyspnea occurring after exercise or exertion.

Functional dyspnea — Dyspnea due to anxiety.

Paroxysmal nocturnal dyspnea —Dyspnea occurring usually at night due to posture as in congestive heart failure with pulmonary edema.

Respiratory dyspnea — Dyspnea occurring in bronchial asthma.

Dyspneic —Affected with or due to dyspnea.

Dyspragia, Dyspraxia — Pain or difficulty in performing any function.

Dysproteinemia —Disorder of the protein of the blood.

Dysraphia, Dysraphism — Incomplete closure of a raphe.

Dysrhythmia —Disordered rhythm.

Dyssebacea —A condition seen in riboflavin deficiency marked by greasy, excessive secretion of the sebaceous glands on the middle portion of the face.

Dyssomnia —Disturbance in sleep.

Dysspermia —Impairment of the spermatozoa or of the semen.

Dysspondylism —An abnormality of development of the vertebral column.

Dysstasia —Difficulty in standing.

Dysstatic —The person with difficulty in standing.

Dyssyllabia —A form of stuttering in which halting occurs at certain words which are difficult to be pronounced for the speaker.

Dyssynergia —Ataxia, muscular incoordination or failure of muscular coordination.

Dystaxia —Difficulty in controlling the voluntary movements.

Dystectia —In the embryo, failure of closure of the neural tube which may cause spina bifida or meningocele.

Dysthymia —1. Any condition caused by the defective function of the thymus gland. 2. Mental depression.

Dysthymic —Pertaining to dysthymia.

Dysthyreosis —Disordered or defective functioning of the thyroid gland.

Dysthyroidism —Imperfect development and function of the thyroid gland.

Dystocia —Difficult labor or childbirth.

Fetal dystocia — Dystocia due to the shape, size or position of the fetus.

Maternal dystocia — Dystocia due to some condition present in the mother such as contracted pelvis or the presence of a tumor in the uterus.

Placental dystocia — Delivery of the placenta with difficulty.

Dystonia —Disordered muscular tone.

Dystonic —Pertaining to dystonia.

Dystopia —Malposition, displacement of any organ.

Dystopic —Not in place.

Dystopy —Dystopia.

Dystrophia, Dystrophy — Any disorder caused by defective nutrition or metabolism.

Adiposogenital dystrophy, Frohlich's syndrome —The condition characterized by the obesity and under development of the genital organs due to a disturbance in the hypothalamus, which controls the food intake, and of the pituitary gland which controls gonadal development.

Progressive muscular dystrophy —A familial disease characterized by progressive atrophy and wasting of the muscles. It occurs usually at an early age and is more frequently in males than females.

Pseudohypertrophic muscular dystrophy — A hereditary disease beginning in childhood marked by muscular dystrophy affecting the shoulder and pelvic girdles with increasing weakness, pseudohypertrophy of the muscles, followed by atrophy.

Dystrophic —Pertaining to dystrophia or dystrophy.

Dystrophoneurosis —1. Any nervous disorder caused by faulty nutrition. 2. Defective nutrition due to a nervous disease.

Dystrophy —Dystrophia

Dystrypsia —Impairment of pancreatic secretion.

Dysuria —Painful or difficult micturition.

Dysuriac —The person affected with dysuria.

Dysversion — A turning in any direction but not inversely.

Dyszoospermia —Imperfect formation of spermatozoa.

Ear —Organ of hearing.

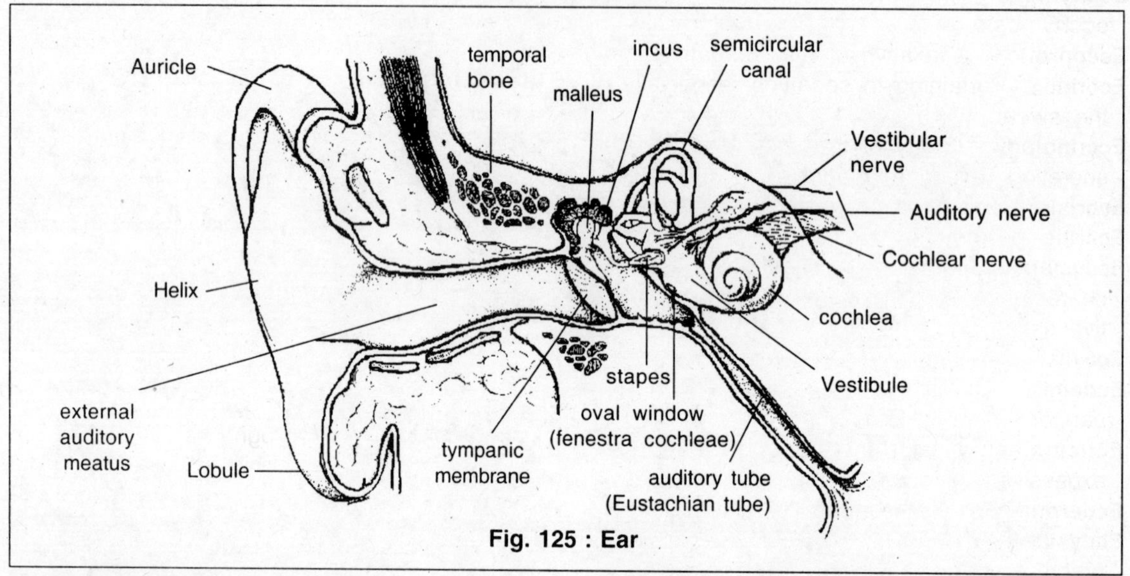

Fig. 125 : Ear

External ear —Auris externa. Pinna and external auditory canal.

Internal ear —Auris interna. Labyrinth.

Middle ear —Auris media. Tympanic cavity.

Earache —Otalgia. Pain in the ear.

Eardrum —Tympanum. The cavity of the middle ear.

Ear-lobe —The lower fleshy part of the auricle.

Ear-plug —A device for preventing the sound from entering the ear by causing obstruction in the external auditroy canal.

Earth —1. The ground. 2. Clay or soil.

Earwax —Cerumen.

Ebonation —Removal of the pieces of bones from a wound.

Ebranlement — Twisting a polyp on its stalk to cause atrophy.

Ebriecation —Mental derangement due to excessive use of alcohol.

Ebrietas —Drunkenness.

Ebullism —Formation of water vapor in the body tissues.

Ebur —A tissue resembling ivory in outward appearance.

Eburnation —Conversion of bone into a dense and hard, ivory-like mass.

Eburneous —Like ivory.

Eburnitis —Increased density and hardness of the dentin.

Ecarteur —A type of retractor.

Ecaudate —Without a tail.

Ecbolic —Oxytocic. Producing or hastening labor or abortion by causing uterine muscular contractions.

Eccentric —1. Situated, occurring or proceeding away from a center. 2. Peripheral.

Eccentrochondroplasia — Abnormal development of the epiphysis from eccentric centers of ossification.

Eccentro-osteochondrodysplasia —A disease of bones caused by ossification occurring in several different centers instead of in one common center.

Eccentropiesis —The pressure exerted from within outwards.

Ecchondroma —A hyperplastic growth or tumor of a cartilage.

Ecchondrosis —Ecchondroma.

Ecchondrotome —A knife for excision of cartilage.

Ecchymoma —A swelling due to accumulation of blood in the subcutaneous tissues.

Ecchymosis —A spot in the skin or mucous membrane produced by hemorrhage, which is not elevated and is round or irregular and blue or purple in color.

Ecchymotic —Pertaining or resembling to an ecchymosis.

Eccoprotic —A laxative or mild purgative.

Eccrine —Pertaining to secretion, especially of the sweat.

Eccrinology —Study of the secretions and the secreting (exocrine) glands.

Eccrisis —Excretion of waste products.

Eccritic —Promoting excretion.

Eccyclomastopathy —A disease of the breast characterized by a mass made up of connective tissue and epithelial cells.

Eccyesis —Extrauterine or ectopic pregnancy.

Ecdemic —Denoting a disease brought into a part of the body from without.

Ecdemomania —Dromomania. Wander lust, excessive desire for wandering.

Ecderon —Epidermis or outer portion of the skin.

Ecdysiasm —A tendency to become naked before others to produce sexual desire in them.

Ecdysis —Desquamation. Shedding off of the epidermis.

Ecdysist — The person who becomes naked before others to produce sexual desire in them.

E.C.G. —Electrocardiogram.

Echeosis —Mental disturbance caused by the noise.

Echinate —Echinulate. Prickly or spinous.

Echinococcosis —Infection with the tapeworm Echinococcus

Echinococcus —A type of tapeworm which causes disease in man.

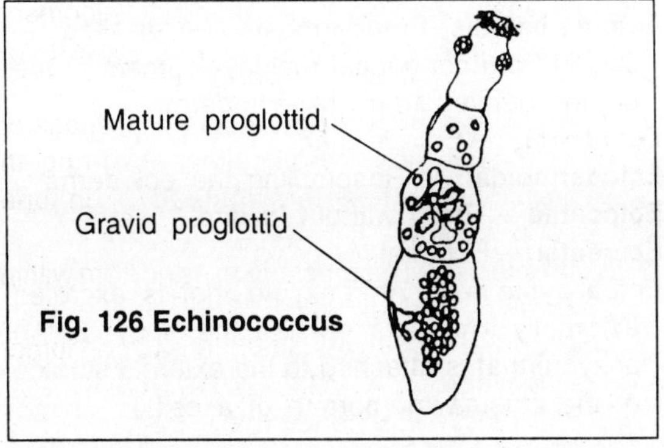

Fig. 126 Echinococcus

Echinosis — A condition in which the outlines of the red blood cells become serrated instead of being smooth.

Echinulate —Echinate. A growth of the bacteria having pointed process or spine.

Echo —Repetition of sound caused by reflection of sound waves.

Echoacousia —To have a sensation of hearing echos after normally heard sounds.

Echocardiogram —The graphic record produced by echocardiography.

Echocardiography —To visualize the internal cardiac structures by the use of ultrasound.

Echoencephalogram —The record produced by echoencephalography.

Echoencephalography —It is a method of diagnosis in which the ultrasonic sound waves are beamed through the head from both sides and echos from the structures of the midline of the brain are recorded graphically.

Echogenic —In ultrasonography, producing echos of ultrasound waves.

Echogram —The record made by echography.

Echographer —Ultrasonographer.

Echographia —The agraphia in which one cannot write spontaneously, but can write from dictation or copy.

Ecography —Ultrasonography. The use of ultrasound to produce an image or photograph of an organ or tissue as a diagnostic aid, which is produced when the sound waves are reflected from an organ or tissues of different density.

Echokinesia —Involuntary repetition of the gestures of another person.

Echolalia —Automatic parrot-like repetition of the words spoken to him by others.

Echomimia —Echopraxia.

Echomotism —Echopraxia.

Echopathy —A neurosis in which there is automatic repetition by a patient, of words or actions of others.

Echophonia, Echophony — Double voice sound heard during auscultation of the chest.

Echophrasia —Echolalia.

Echopraxia —To copy the actions of others.

Echoscope —An instrument for displaying the echoes by means of ultrasonic pulses on an oscilloscope, to demonstrate the structures lying at depth within the body.

Echo sign —Repetition of the last word of a sentence which is a sign of epilepsy or other brain conditions.

Eclabium —Eversion of a lip.

Eclampsia —Coma and convulsions occurring in between the 20th week of pregnancy and the end of the 1st week after delivery associated with hypertension, edema and albuminuria.

Eclampsism —Pre-eclampsia.

Eclamptic —Pertaining to or of the nature of eclampsia.

Eclamptogenic —Causing eclampsia.

Eclamptogenous — Eclamptogenic.

Eclectic —Selecting from various sources what appears to be the best.

Eclecticism —An ancient method of treatment of the individual signs or symptoms rather than for the diseases, mainly by the botanical remedies.

Ecmnesia —Forgetfullness of the recent events but the remembrance of the past events.

Ecocide —To destroy some portion of the environment willingly.

Ecoendocrinology —The study of the interactions of endocrine systems with the environment.

Ecological —Pertaining to ecology.

Ecologist —A specialist in ecology.

Ecology —Study of the life history of the organisms and their relations to the environment.

Ecomania —A mental attitude to dominate on own family but humbleness toward the authorities.

Ecorche —An animal or human form without skin so that the muscles are clearly seen.

Ecosphere —The portion of the universe habitable by living organisms and the plants.

Ecostate —Without ribs.

Ecosystem —The fundamental unit of ecology comprising of the living organisms, plants, and nonliving things interacting in a certain defined area.

Ecouvillon —A brush used for cleansing a cavity and to apply a medicine in it.

Ecouvillonage —The cleansing of a cavity and to apply a medicine in it by a brush or swab.

Ecphylaxis —A condition in which the antibodies in the blood become impotent.

Ecphyma —A warty growth or protuberance.

Ecrasement —Excision by means of an ecraseur.

Ecraseur —A wire loop used for excision.

Ecstasy —The condition of much happiness.

Ecstatic —An individual with much happiness.

Ecstrophe —Exstrophy. Turning of an organ from inside out ward congenitally.

E.C.T. —Electroconvulsive therapy.

Ectad —Outward, externally.

Ectal —Outer, external.

Ectasia, Ectasis —Dilatation, expansion or distension.

Ectasia iridis —Smallness of the pupil of the eye due to displacement of the iris.

Ectatic —Capable of being stretched.

Ectental —Pertaining to the ectoderm and endoderm and their line of junction.

Ecthyma —An infection of the skin characterized by superficial lesions with crust formation and may be followed by pigmentation and scarring.

Ectiris —The external portion of the iris.

Ecto- —Prefix meaning outside.

Ectoantigen —An antigen that is loosely attached to the outside of the bacterium and may be separated from the bacterial cell, or it is formed in the cell membrane of the bacterium.

Ectoblast —The ectoderm.

Ectocardia —Congenital displacement of the heart.

Ectocervical —Pertaining to the vaginal part of the cervix of the uterus.

Ectocervix —Portio vaginalis, or intravaginal portion of the uterine cervix.

Ectocineria —The outer gray matter of the brain.

Ectocolostomy —To form an opening into the colon through the abdominal wall.

Ectocondyle —The outer condyle of a bone.

Ectocornea —External layer of the cornea.

Ectocuneiform —External cuneiform bone.

Ectocytic —Outside of the cell.

Ectodactylism —Absence of a digit or digits.

Ectoderm —Epiblast. The outermost of the three cellular layers of the developing embryo from which the epidermis, glands of the skin, nails, hair, teeth, nervous system, ear and eye etc., develop.

Ectodermal —Pertaining to the ectoderm.

Ectodermatosis, Ectodermosis —A disease resulting from congenital maldevelopment of the organs derived from the ectoderm.

Ectodermic —Ectodermal.

Ectodermoidal —Resembling the ectoderm.

Ectoentad —From without inward.

Ectoental —Ectental.

Ectoenzyme —1. An enzyme that is excreted externally and acts outside the body. 2. An enzyme that is attached to the external surface of the plasma membrane of a cell.

Ectogenous —1. Entering the body from without as an infection. 2. Growing outside of the body as a parasite.

Ectoglobular —Formed outside the blood cells.

Ectogony —Influence of the embryo on the mother.

Ectomere —One of the blastomeres taking part in the formation of ectoderm.

Ectomorph —The person exhibiting ectomorphy. Emaciated.

Ectomorphic —Pertaining to the ectomorph.

Ectomorphy —A type of body build in which the tissues derived from the ectoderm predominate, the viscera being slightly developed and the body becomes linear with less muscular development.

-ectomy —Suffix meaning surgical removal of an organ or growth.

Ectonuclear —Occurring outside the nucleus of a cell.

Ectopagus —Two fetuses joined together at the thorax.

Ectoparasite—A parasite living on the outside of the body, e.g., lice or ticks etc.

Ectoparasiticide —An agent that is applied directly to the host to kill the ectoparasites.

Ectoparasitism —Infestation.

Ectophyte —A vegetable parasite growing on the skin.

Ectopia —Malposition or displacement, especially congenital, of an organ or a structure e.g., congenital displacement of the heart outside the thoracic cavity.

Ectopic —1. Located in an abnormal position. 2. Arising from an abnormal place.

Ectopic beat —Premature systole or extrasystole. An impulse for cardiac contraction arising from the atria, atrioventricular node, bundle of His or ventricles instead from the sinoatrial node, which causes premature contraction of the heart.

Ectopic pregnancy — Implantation of the fertilized ovum outside the uterus, generally in the fallopian tubes.

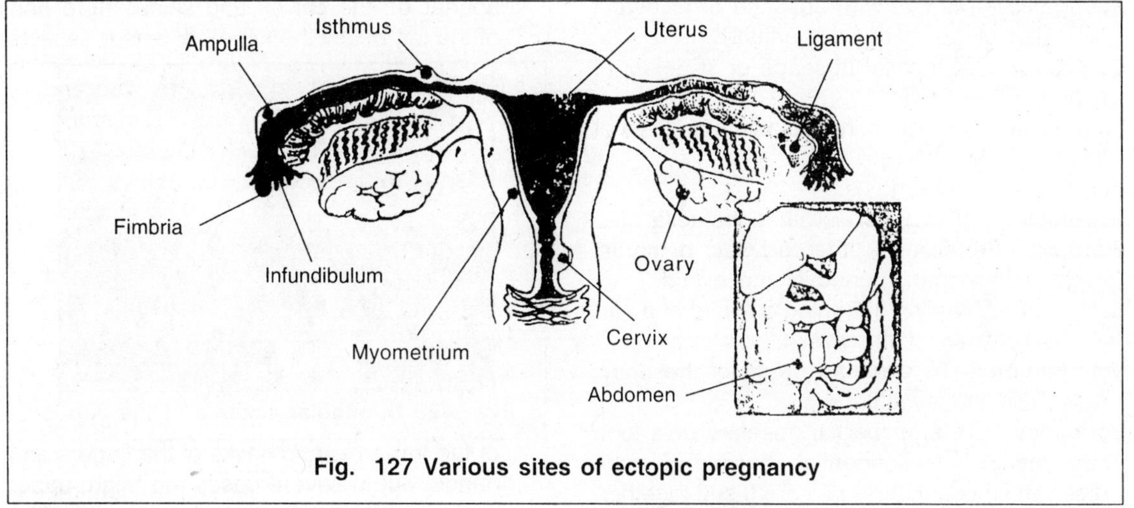

Fig. 127 Various sites of ectopic pregnancy

Ectopic rhythm —Any abnormal or irregular cardiac rhythm.

Ectopic secretion —The secretion of the hormones by the tumors arising from the tissues that do not normally secrete the hormones.

Ectoplacental —Outside or surrounding the placenta.

Ectoplasm —The outermost layer of cell protoplasm.

Ectoplasmic—Ectoplastic. Pertaining to the ectoplasm.

Ectoplast —Cell membrane.

Ectoplastic —Ectoplasmic. Formed at the periphery.

Ectopotomy —Removal of the fetus in ectopic pregnancy.

Ectopy —Ectopia. Displacement of an organ or structure.

Ectoretina—Outer layer of the retina.

Ectosarc —The outer membrane, or ectoplasm of a protozoon.

Ectoscopy —External examination of an organ.

Ectosteal —Situated outside a bone.

Ectostosis —Formation of bone beneath the periosteum.

Ectothrix —A fungus as microsporum that produces arthrospores on the hair shafts.

Ectotoxin —Exotoxin

Ectozoon —Ectoparasite.

Ectro- —A prefix meaning congenital absence of a part of the body.

Ectrodactylism, Ectrodactyly —Congenital absence of all or part of a digit.

Ectrogenic —Marked with absence of or defect of a part of the body congenitally.

Ectrogeny —Congenital absence of or defect of a part of the body.

Ectromelia —Congenital hypoplasia or aplasia of the long bones of the limbs.

Ectormelic —Ectromelus.

Ectromelus —The person with ectromelia.

Ectropic —Pertaining to the complete or partial eversion of a part, generally the eyelid.

Ectropion —Eversion or turning outward of a part of the body as of the eyelid.

Ectropionize —To evert an organ of the body, especially the eyelid.

Ectropody —Total or partial absence of a foot.

Ectrosyndactyly —Congenital absence of some digits and those that remain are fused together.

Eczema —An acute or chronic inflammatory condition of the superficial skin marked early by redness and itching with the formation of minute papules and vesicles which soon rupture through which the serum exudates on to the surface of the skin, which afterwards dries up and forms crust. It is called as the dry eczema. When the swelling of the epidermis resolves before the vesication and oozing occurs, it is known as the weeping eczema.

Atopic eczema —In this type of eczema the skin is not raised. It becomes red and rough with great itching, and minute cracks cause to ooze serum which dries up and forms crust. It is classified into three, according to the age. 1. Infantile atopic eczema. 2. Atopic eczema of the childhood. 3. Adolescent and adult atopic eczema.

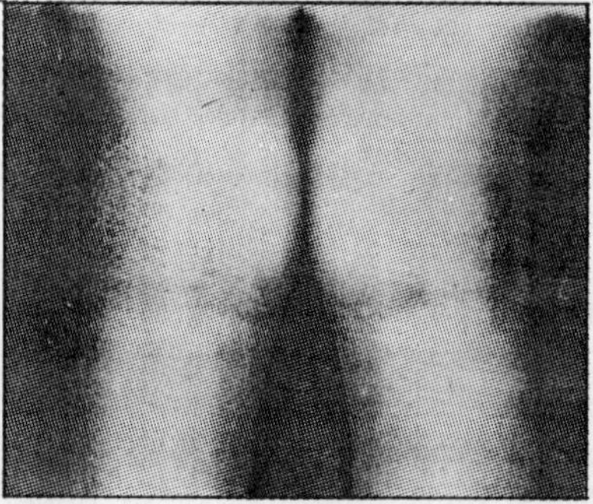

Fig. 128 : Atopic eczema in childhood

Eczema caused by ringworm.

Eczema marginatum — Tinea cruris.

Nummular eczema — The eczema in which the lesions are oval or coin shaped which appear on the calves and shines (fore part of the leg below the knee), extensor aspects of the forearms and backs of the fingers and hands, but in severe cases the thigh, upper arms and trunk may also be involved. The condition usually remains in the oozing or crusted stage.

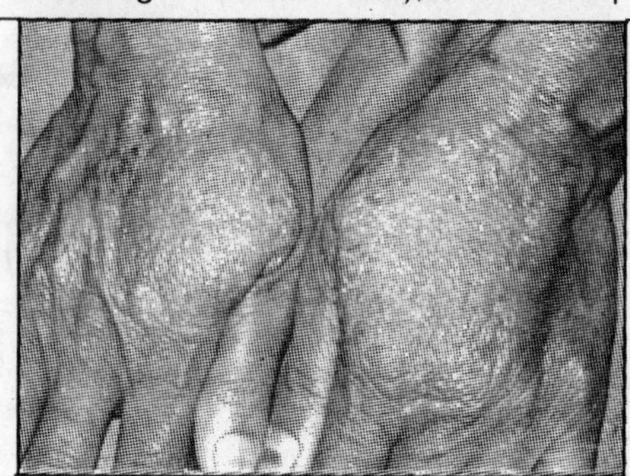

Fig. 129 Nummular eczema of the hands

Pompholyx eczema — Eczema of the hands and feet - In this type of eczema the vesicles are formed on the sides and front of the fingers and palms and in the similar positions on the toes and feet, which do not rupture readily but remain for some days like grains of boiled sago in the skin.

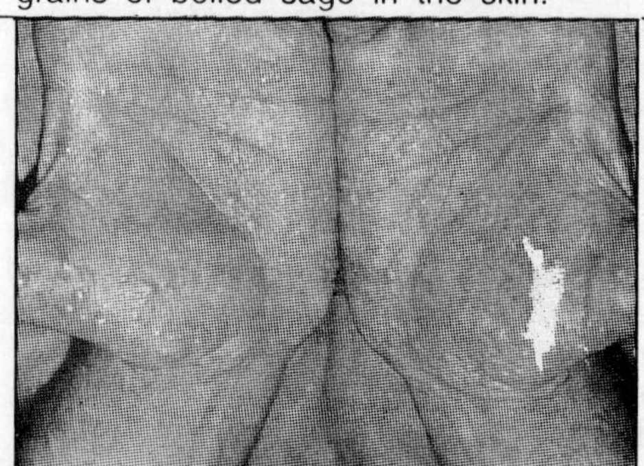

Fig. 130 : Pompholyx eczema on the palms

Seborrheic eczema — It is a form of eczema marked by excessive secretion from the sebaceous glands beginning on the scalp, may spread to the forehead, temples and down the neck behind the ears.

Varicose eczema — Eczema occurring on the inner or outer side of the lower one third or half of one or both legs, depending on which side the veins are varicose, in the person suffering from varicose veins.

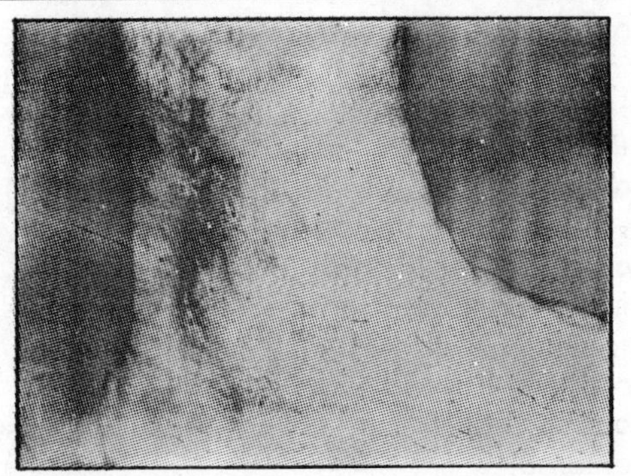

Fig. 131 : Varicose eczema

Weeping eczema —Moist oozing eczema.

Eczematization —1. Formation of an eruption resembling eczema. 2. Occurrence of eczema secondary to a preexisting skin disease.

Eczematoid —Resembling eczema.

Eczematous —Marked by or resembling eczema.

EDC —Expected date of confinement.

EDD —Expected date of delivery.

Edea —The external genital organs.

Edema —A localized or generalized swelling in which there is excessive accumulation of fluid in the intercellular spaces of the body. Generalized edema is also known as dropsy or anasarca.

Angioneurotic edema — Recurring attacks of sudden appearance of the swelling of the skin, subcutaneous tissues or mucous membranes which may be due to allergy to drugs, food or physical agents as cold or wind but the exact cause is not known.

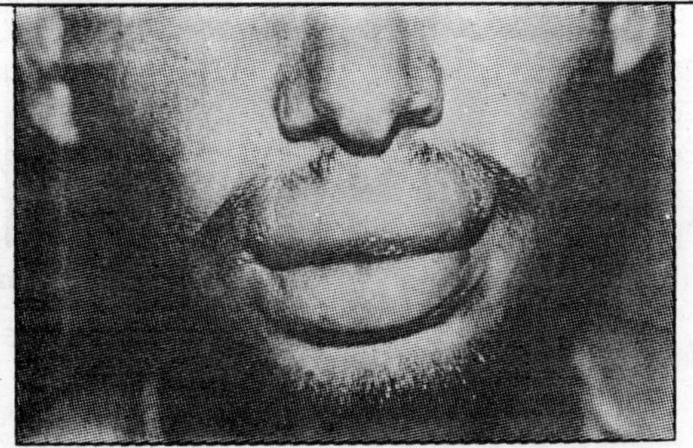

Fig. 132 : Angioneurotic edema of the lips

Brain edema —Swelling of the brain tissue due to accumulation of fluid, which may be caused by a tumor, toxic chemicals or infections.

Cardiac edema — Accumulation of fluid in the body tissues due to congestive heart failure, which is most apparent in the dependent part of the body.

Cerebral edema —Brain edema.

Dependent edema — Edema occurring in the most dependent part of the body as the feet in heart disease.

Edema neonatorum — Transitory edema in the newborn, especially the premature infants affecting the hands, face, feet and genitalia.

Nutritional edema —Edema caused by insufficient intake of protein resulting in hypoproteinemia.

Pitting edema —Edema in which the firm pressure with a finger leaves a depression.

Pulmonary edema — Accumulation of fluid in the lungs due to left sided cardiac failure.

Salt edema —Edema due to increased salt in the diet.

Edemagen —An irritant producing edema by causing capillary damage but not the cellular response of true inflammation.

Edematization —The act of making edematous.

Edematogenic—Causing edema.

Edematous —Pertaining to or affected with edema.

Edentate —Edentulous.

Edentia —Absence of teeth.

Edentulate, Edentulous — Having no teeth.

Edentulous —Toothless.

Edge — Margin

Edible —Fit to be eaten.

Educable —Capable of being educated.

Educt —An extract.

Eduction —The coming out of a particular condition, e.g., coming out of the effects of general anesthesia.

Edulcorant —Sweetening.

Edulcorate —1. To sweeten. 2. To wash out salts or acids.

EEG —Electroencephalogram.

EENT —Eye, ear, nose and throat.

Effacement —The dilatation of the cervix during labor to permit the passage of the fetus.

Effect —Result of an action, e.g., additive effect—the therapeutic effect of a combination of two or more drugs that is greater than the sum of the individual drug effects, and cumulative effect—the effect of a drug which is apparent only after a number of doses have been given.

Effective —Powerful in effect.

Effectiveness —The ability to produce a specific result.

Effector —A muscle which contracts or a gland which secretes, in direct response to nerve impulses.

Effeminate —Pertaining to the condition of a male having the physical characteristics of a female.

Effemination —Feminization. Production of female physical characteristics in a male.

Efferent —Carrying away from a central organ as efferent nerves which conduct the impulses from the brain or spinal cord to the periphery.

Effervesce —To boil or form bubbles on the surface of a liquid.

Effervescence —Formation of gas bubbles on the surface of a liquid.

Effervescent —Boiling or bubbling.

Efficacy —The ability to produce a desired effect.

Efficiency —Capability.

Effleurage —The stroking in massage.

Effloresce —To become powdery from the loss of water in crystallization.

Efflorescence —Exanthem. Redness of the skin.

Efflorescent —Becoming powdery or dry from the loss of water in crystallization.

Effluent —Flowing out.

Effluvium —1. An outflowing, or shedding as of the hair. 2. A malodorous exhalation, especially that of the toxic nature.

Effuse —Thin, widely spreading.

Effusion —Escape of a fluid into a part of the body as the escape of pus into the pleural cavity causing pyothorax.

Egersis —Extreme wakefullness.

Egesta —Waste matter, especially the excrement thrown out from the body.

Egestion —The throwing out of the waste matter from the body, especially the excrement.

Egg —Fertilized female reproductive cell, which is passed from the body and develops outside.

Eglandulous —Without glands.

Ego —The conscious sense of the self.

Egocentric —Withdrawan from the outer world and concentrated in one's self.

Egocentricity —The condition of being egocentric.

Ego-dystonic —Pertaining to something that is against an individual.

Egoism —The seeking one's own advantage at the expense of others; overvaluation of the self.

Egomania —Mania for self-esteem and self-interest.

Egophony —An abnormal sound, like the bleating of a goat, heard in auscultation of the chest about the upper level of fluid in pleurisy with effusion, when the subject speaks normally.

Ego-syntonic —Pertaining to something which is in favour of an individual.

Egotism —The tendency to think one's self overvalued and to boast, of one's abilities or achievements.

Egotistical —Proudy.

Egotropic —Interested chiefly in one's self; self-centered.

Eidetic —Pertaining to or having the ability to see exactly in imagination of events or objects seen previously.

Eidoptometry —Measurement of the acuity of vision.

Eikonometer —An instrument for measuring the degree of aniseikonia.

Eikonometry —1. Measurement of aniseikonia. 2. Determination of distance of an object by measuring its image produced by a lens of known focus.

Eiloid —Having a coil-like structure.

Eisodic —Centripetal or afferent.

Ejaculate —1. To expel suddenly 2. Semen expelled in ejaculation.

Ejaculatio —Ejaculation.

Ejaculatio praecox — Premature ejaculation.

Ejaculation —Forcible, sudden expulsion, especially of the semen from the male urethra.

Ejaculation retrograde —Ejaculation in which the semen is discharged into the urinary bladder instead of the outside through the urethra as usually occurs following prostatectomy.

Ejaculator —Muscle that ejects semen.

Ejaculatory —Pertaining to ejaculation.

Ejecta —Waste material excreted by the body.

Ejection —Sudden removal of something.

Ejection fraction —The percentage of blood ejected from the ventricle during systole, which is 60% to 70%.

Ejector —An apparatus for expelling forcibly a material from the body, e.g. Saliva ejector which is used for removal of the saliva and water from the mouth during operation on the teeth.

Elaborate —To produce complex substances out of simpler materials.

Elaboration —1. The process of producing complex substances out of simpler materials. 2. Metabolization of food for its utilization by the body.

Elaiopathia —Eleopathy.

Elaiopathy —Eleopathy. Swelling of the joints caused by contusion and followed by fatty degeneration.

Elastance —The tendency of a structure to return to its original form after removal of the force causing deformity in the structure.

Elastic —Having the quality of being stretched and to return to its original size.

Elastica —Elastic.

Elastic cartilage —Yellow cartilage such as found in the pharynx and the external ears etc.

Elasticity —The quality of returning to its original size after stretching.

Elastin —A yellow extracellular connective tissue protein of elastic structures, e.g., large blood vessels, tendons and ligaments etc.

Elastofibroma — A tumor consisting of both, elastic and fibrous elements.

Elastoid —Pertaining to a substance formed by hyaline degeneration.

Elastoidin —A complex collagen.

Elastoidosis, nodular — Appearance of comedones and yellowish, circumscribed, thickened plaques around the orbits or the nose.

Elastolysis —Digestion of the elastic tissue.

Elastoma —Pseudoxanthoma. A tumor of the skin containing elastic tissue fibers.

Elastometer —A device for measuring the elasticity.

Elastometry —The measurement of elasticity of the tissues.

Elastorrhexis —Rupture of the elastic tissue.

Elastosis —Any disease of elastic tissues.

Elation —Joyful emotion.

Elbow —The joint between the upper arm and the forearm.

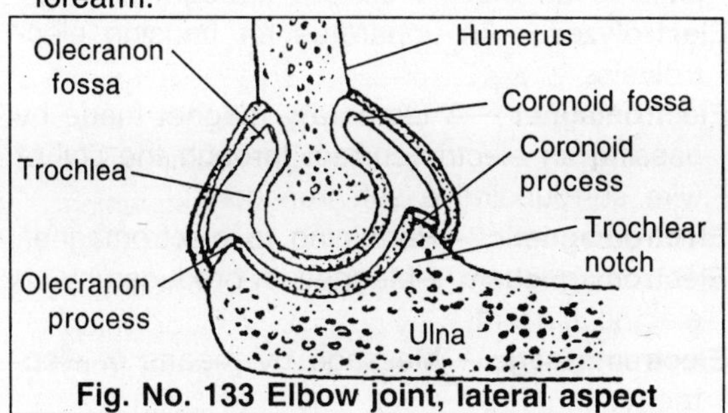

Fig. No. 133 Elbow joint, lateral aspect

Elcosis —Fetid ulceration.

Electe —Alongwith the milk.

Elective therapy —A medical or surgical treatment which is not necessary immediately but can be done according to the patient's convenience.

Electric, Electrical— Pertaining to, or caused by electricity.

Electrical alternans — Beat-to-beat changes in one or more portions of the electrocardiogram.

Electric light baker —A device for warming a part of the body, as is used in arthritis.

Electric shock —Unconsciousness due to contact with electricity.

Electro-, Electr- —Prefixes indicating relationship to electricity.

Electroacupuncture — Acupuncture in which the needles are stimulated electrically.

Electroanalgesia —To cause relief from pain by using electricity.

Electroanalysis —To make a chemical analysis by the use of electricity.

Electroanesthesia —Local or general anesthesia induced by electricity.

Electroaxonography — Axonography.

Electrobiology —Study of the electric phenomena in the living body.

Electrobioscopy —Electric test to determine the presence of life.

Electrocardiogram —A tracing of the cardiac impulses by an electrical instrument.

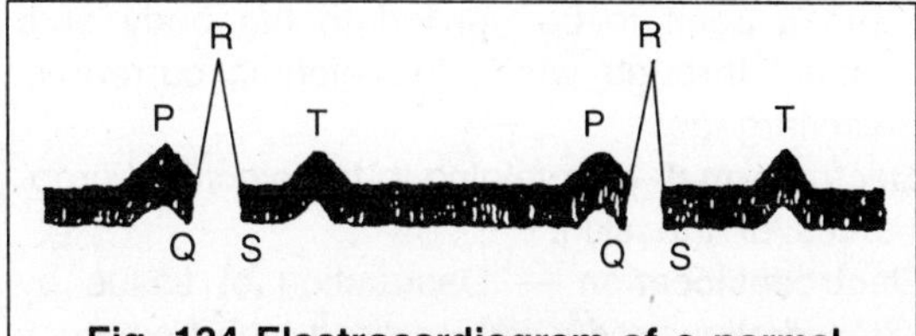

Fig. 134 Electrocardiogram of a normal healthy person

Electrocardiograph —An apparatus for recording the electrical variations in the action of cardiac muscle.

Electrocardiography — The making of a tracing of the cardiac impulses by an electrical instrument.

Electrocardiophonogram —The record of heart sounds obtained by electrocardiophonography.

Electrocardiophonograph — An apparatus for recording the heart sounds.

Electrocardiophonography —The recording of the heart sounds by electrical method.

Electrocatalysis —Chemical decomposition produced by electricity.

Electrocauterization —The cauterization by electricity or by a metal wire heated by electricity.

Electrocautery —Cauterization of the tissues by a platinum wire fitted in a holder, heated by electric current.

Electrochemical —Pertaining to electrochemistry.

Electrochemistry —Study of chemical changes produced by electricity.

Electrocision —Excision by electric current.

Electrocoagulation — Coagulation of tissue by means of an electric current.

Electrocontractility — Contraction of a muscle by electrical stimulation.

Electroconvulsive therapy — Treatment of some specific mental disease by inducing convulsions by means of electricity.

Electrocorticogram —The record produced by electrocorticography.

Electrocorticography —To record the electrical impulses from the brain by placing electrodes directly on the cerebral cortex.

Electrocryptectomy — Destruction of the crypt of the tonsil by diathermy.

Electrocute —To destroy the life by means of an electric current.

Electrocution —The destruction of life by means of electric current.

Electrode —The part of an electric apparatus with a point to be applied to the body of a patient through which the electric current is discharged.

Electrodermal —Pertaining to the electrical properties of the skin.

Electrodesiccation — Destruction of tissue by dehydration produced by a short-high-frequency electric current.

Electrodiagnosis —Diagnosis especially of the disease of the heart, nerves and muscles by means of electric devices.

Electrodiagnostics —The science and practice of electrodiagnosis.

Electrodialysis —A method of separating the electrolytes from the colloids by passing an electric current through a solution containing both.

Electrodynamometer —An instrument to measure the strength of an electric current.

Electroencephalogram —A tracing of an electroencephalograph.

Electroencephalograph — An instrument used in electroencephalography.

Electroencephalography — The taking of a tracing of an electroencephalograph.

Electroendosmosis — Endosmosis caused by electricity.

Electrogenesis —Production by electricity.

Electrogoniometer —An electrical apparatus for measuring angles of joints and their range of movements.

Electrogram —Any record made by an electric event on a paper or film.

Electrograph —A graphic record of the electrical activity produced by the living tissues.

Electrohemostasis —Arrest of bleeding by means of a high-frequency electric current.

Electrohysterograph —An instrument for recording uterine electrical activity.

Electrohysterography — Recording of the electrical activity of the myometrium.

Electrokymogram —The record produced by electrokymography.

Electrokymograph —The instrument used in electrokymography.

Electrokymography —The taking of photograph on X-ray film of the motion of the heart or of other structure which can be visualized radiographically.

Electrology —The branch of science dealing with the electricity.

Electrolysis —The decomposition of a substance by passing an electric current through it. Excessive hairs may be removed from the body by this method.

Electrolyte —A substance which in solution is capable of conducting the electricity and is decomposed into ions by the passage of an electric current, e.g. acids, bases and salts.

Electrolytic —Pertaining to or caused by electrolysis.

Electrolyze —To decompose a substance by passing an electric current through it.

Electrolyzer —An apparatus for causing electrolysis.

Electromagnet —A temporary magnet made by passing an electric current through the coil of wire surrounding a soft iron core.

Electromagnetic —Pertaining to electromagnet.

Electromagnetism —Magnetism produced by an electric current.

Electromassage —Massage by means of electricity.

Electrometer —An instrument for measuring the differences in electric potential.

Electromicturition —Electrical stimulation of the urinary bladder for micturition in patients with paraplegia.

Electromotive —Pertaining to the passage of electricity in a current or motion produced by it.

Electromotive force —EMF —The energy causing a flow of electricity from one place to another, producing an electric current. It is measured in volt.

Electromyogram —The graphic record of contraction of a muscle obtained by electrical stimulation of the muscle.

Electromyograph —An instrument used in electromyography.

Electromyography —The taking of an electromyogram of a skeletal muscle and its study.

Electron —Any of the negatively charged particles arranged in orbits around the nucleus of an atom.

Electronarcosis — Unconsciousness by applying the electricity to the brain.

Electronegative —Charged with negative electricity, which attracts the positively charged bodies and repels the negatively charged bodies.

Electroneurography —The measurement of the conduction velocity and latency of the peripheral nerves.

Electroneurolysis — Destruction of a nerve by an electric needle.

Electroneuromyography — Electromyography in which the nerve of the muscle to be studied is stimulated by applying an electric current.

Electronic —Pertaining to the electrons.

Electronics —The science of the electrical equipments.

Electronystagmogram —The record obtained by electronystagmography.

Electronystagmography —A method of recording the movements of the eyeball by detecting the electrical activity of the extraocular muscles.

Electro-oculogram — Record of the electrical currents produced by eye movements.

Electro-osmosis —The diffusion of a substance through a membrane in an electric field.

Electroparacentesis — Removal of a fluid, as from the eye, with an electric instrument.

Electropathology —To determine the electrical reaction of muscles and nerves as a means of diagnosis.

Electrophobia —A morbid fear of electricity.

Electrophoresis —The movement of charged particles suspended in a liquid, on a medium such as filter paper, in an electric field, toward an electric pole (anode or cathode); used to separate and purify a substance.

Electrophoretic —Pertaining to electrophoresis.

Electrophrenic —Pertaining to the stimulation of the phrenic nerve by electricity.

Electrophysiology —A branch of physiology in which the electrical changes in the living tissues are studied.

Electroplexy —Convulsion by electricity.

Electropositive —Charged with positive electricity.

Electropuncture —Puncture of the tissues by an electric needle.

Electroresection —Removal of the tissue by an electrical apparatus such as a cautery.

Electroretinogram —A record of the electrical activity of the retina produced by light stimulation.

Electroretinograph —An instrument for measuring the electrical activity of the retina produced by light stimulation.

Electroscission —Cutting of tissue by means of electrocautery.

Electroscope —An instrument for detecting the intensity of radiation.

Electroshock —Shock produced by an electric current.

Electroshock therapy — Treatment of some diseases as of acute depression by causing electric shock.

Electrospinogram —The record obtained by electrospinography.

Electrospinography —The recording of spontaneous electrical activity of the spinal cord.

Electrostatic —Pertaining to the static electricity.

Electrostethograph —Electrical instrument that records the respiratory and cardiac sounds of the chest.

Electrostimulation —To stimulate a tissue such as a muscle or bone by an electric current.

Electrosurgery —Surgery performed by electrical methods.

Electrosynthesis —To synthesize the chemical compounds by the use of electricity.

Electrotaxis —The movement of a cell or an

organism toward or away from an electrical stimulus.

Electrothanasia —Death due to electric shock.

Electrothanatosis —Death by electricity.

Electrotherapeutics — Treatment of the diseases by electricity.

Electrotherapist —The person expert in electrical treatment.

Electrotherapy — Electrotherapeutics.

Electrothermotherapy —The treatment of diseases by the production of heat within the body by an electric current.

Electrotome —An electrocautery device used in surgery.

Electrotomy —Electrosurgery.

Electrotonic —Of or pertaining to electrotonus.

Electrotonus —The change in the irritability of a nerve or muscle during the passage of an electric current.

Electrotropism —Reaction of cells to an electric current.

Electroversion —The act of terminating a cardiac dysrhythmia by electricity.

Electrovert —To apply the electricity to the heart or precordium to terminate a cardiac dysrhythmia.

Electuary —A medicinal substance mixed with honey or sugar to form a paste suitable to be taken orally.

Element —1. Any of the primary constituents of a thing. 2. In Chemistry, a substance which cannot be decomposed into the substances different from itself, by ordinary chemical processes.

Eleoma —A swelling caused by injection of oil into the tissues.

Eleopathy —Swelling of the joints due to deposition of fat in them.

Eleoptene —The most volatile constituent of a volatile oil.

Eleosaccharum —A mixture of powdered sugar with a volatile oil.

Eleotherapy —Treatment of diseases by the use of oils.

Elephantiasis —A chronic condition characterized by hypertrophy of the skin and subcutaneous tissues, chiefly of the lower extremities and the scrotum, resulting from the obstruction of the lymphatic vessels mostly due to filaria infection.

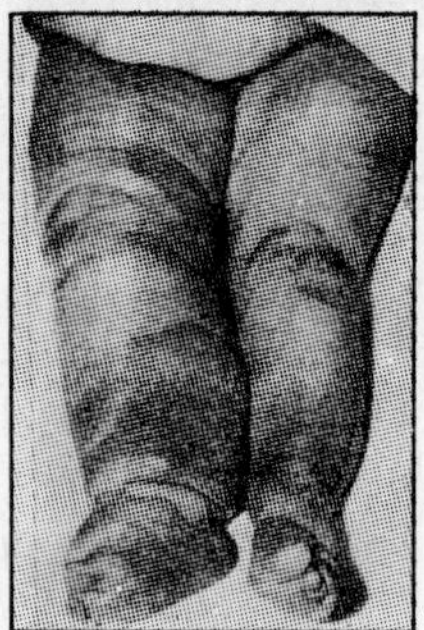

Fig. 135 Elephantiasis

Elevation —Raised area.

Elevator —An instrument for raising the tissues as the depressed bone or the roots of the teeth.

Eliminant —Aiding in expulsion or evacuation.

Eliminate —To expel.

Elimination —The act of expulsion.

Elinguation —The operation of removing the tongue from the oral cavity.

ELISA —Abbreviation for enzyme-linked immunosorbent assay.

Elixir —A sweetened, aromatic liquid containing some alcohol, used in compounding of oral medicines.

Ellipsis —During the treatment of mental illness, the omission of important words by the patient.

Ellipsoid —Spindle-shaped, fusiform, tapering at both ends.

Elliptical —Oval in shape.

Elliptocyte —Oval-shaped red blood cell.

Elliptocytosis —Condition of increased number of oval-shaped red blood cells in the blood.

Elongation —The act of extending.

Elope —Pertaining to the patient who is ready to go away from the hospital without permission.

Eluant —The material that has been eluted.

Eluate —The substance separated by elution.

Eluent —The solvent used in elution as water.

Elutant —Eluent.

Elute —To perform elution.

Elution —In Chemistry, separation of one substance from another by washing. In this process the material is powdered and mixed with water, the heavier constituent of the material settles down on the bottom while the lighter one remains upwards, whcih can be separated easily.

Elutriate —Elute.

Elutriation —Purification of a substance by dissolving it in a solvent and pouring off the solution. It's undissolved foreign materials (impurities) being left in the vessel and thus the substance become purified.

Elytritis —Inflammation of the vagina.

Elytroptosis —Prolapse of the vagina.

Emaciate —To cause to become extremely lean.

Emaciated —Extremely lean.

Emaciation —The condition of being extremely lean.

Emaculation —Removal of spots from the skin.

Emailloid —A tumor arising from a tooth enamel.

Emanation —The act of coming out of any thing from the body, emission, radiation.

Emansio Mensium —Delayed menstruation.

Emarginate —With broken margin or notched.

Emargination —Notch.

Emasculation —1. Castration. 2. Surgical removal of the male genital organs.

Embalm —To treat a dead body with chemicals to preserve it from decay.

Embalming —The use of antiseptics and preservatives in and on the dead body to protect from decomposition.

Embarrass —To obstruct.

Embarrassment —Obstruction.

Embedding —To place a tissue in a firm medium such as paraffin in order to keep it intact during cutting of thin sections.

Embolalia, Embololalia, Embolophrasia — Meaningless language of the insane.

Embole —1. Reduction of a dislocation. 2. Emboly. Formation of the gastrula by invagination of the blastula.

Embolectomy —Surgical removal of an embolus from the blood vessel.

Embolemia —The presence of emboli in the blood.

Emboli —Plural of embolus.

Embolia —Embole.

Embolic —Pertaining to or caused by embolism.

Emboliform —Of the form of an embolus.

Embolism —Obstruction of a blood vessel by a blood clot or a foreign substance.

Air embolism — Embolism caused by air bubble which enters the blood vessel after trauma or surgical procedures.

Atheromatous embolism — Embolism caused by the formation of an atheroma in a vessel.

Cerebral embolism — Embolism of a cerebral artery.

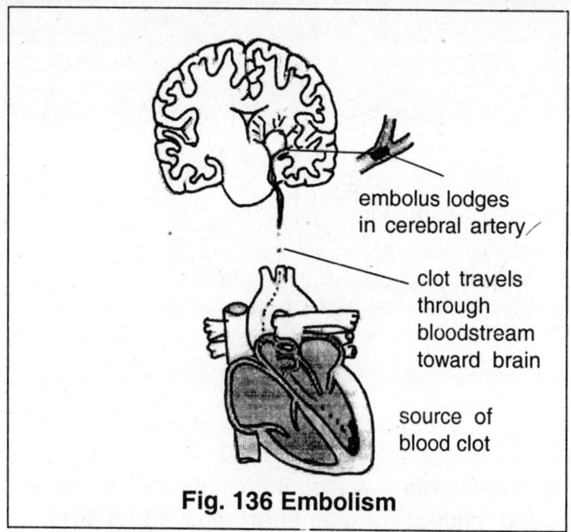

Fig. 136 Embolism

Coronary embolism — Embolism of a coronary artery.

Fat embolism — Obstruction of a blood vessel by a fat embolus, occurring especially after fractures of long bones.

Infective embolism — Obstruction of a blood vessel by an embolus containing bacteria or septic poison.

Pulmonary embolism — Obstruction of the pulmonary artery or one of its branches by an embolus.

Embolization —The process of becoming an embolus.

Embololalia —Embolalia.

Embolomycotic —Pertaining to or caused by an infective embolus.

Embolophrasia —Embolalia.

Embolotherapy —The treatment of a disease by causing embolism, as to control bleeding by inserting a substance into the bleeding vessel, which acts as an embolus.

Embolus —A mass of undissolved matter present in the blood vessel or lymphatic vessel causing obstruction, which is brought there by the blood or lymph and it may be solid, liquid or gaseous.

Emboly —Embole.

Embolysis —The dissolution of an embolus, especially of a blood clot.

Embouchment —The opening of one blood vessel into another.

Embrocation —1. Application of a liniment to the skin. 2. A drug which is rubbed into the skin.

Embryectomy —Surgical removal of an extrauterine embryo or fetus.

Embryo —The developing fertilized ovum from the second week to 8th week of pregnancy.

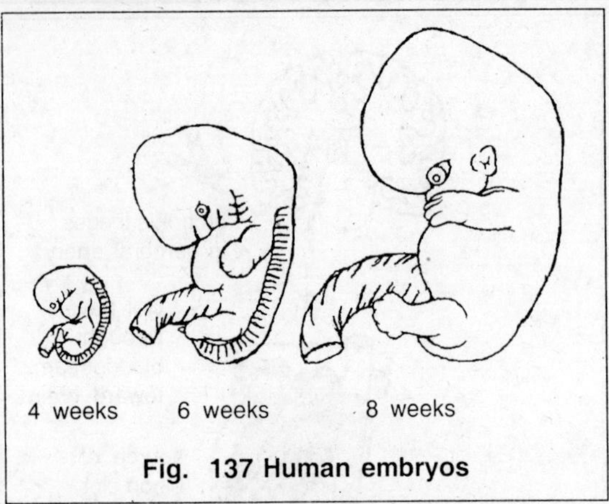

Fig. 137 Human embryos

Embryocardia —A symptom in which the 1st and 2nd sounds of the heart are equal and resemble those of the fetus.

Embryocidal —Anything that kills an embryo.

Embryoctony —To destroy the living embryo or fetus in the uterus.

Embryogenesis —Production of an embryo.

Embryogenetic, Embryogenic —Pertaining to or giving rise to an embryo.

Embryogeny —The growth and development of an embryo.

Embryography —To write something about an embryo.

Embryoid —Embryonoid.

Embryologist —Specialist in embryology.

Embryology —The science of the development of the individual during the embryonic stage.

Embryoma —A tumor of the embryonic cells or tissues.

Embryomorphous —Pertaining to the formation and structure of the embryo.

Embryonal —Pertaining to or resembling an embryo.

Embryonic —Pertaining to or in condition of an embryo.

Embryoniform —Embryonoid.

Embryonization —Reversion of a cell or tissue to the embryonic structure.

Embryonoid —Looking like an embryo.

Embryony —The formation of an embryo.

Embryopathy —Any disease existing in the embryo.

Embryoplastic —Taking part in the formation of an embryo, said of cells.

Embryoscopy —Direct visualization of the embryo or fetus in the uterus by fetoscope.

Embryotocia —Abortion.

Embryotome —An instrument used to dissect the fetus in uterus.

Embryotomy —The dissection of a fetus in utero to facilitate delivery.

Embryotoxicity —Poisonous state of an embryo, which may result in abnormal development of a part of the body, growth retardation or even death.

Embryotoxon —Arcus juvenilis. Congenital ring-like opacity at the margin of the cornea.

Embryotroph —A nutritive material supplied to the embryo during its development in the uterus.

Embryotrophic —Pertaining to any process or nutritive substances involved in the nourishment of the embryo.

Embryotrophy —Nutrition of the fetus.

Embryulcia —To remove the fetus by instruments forcibly.

Embryulcus —An instrument for extracting a dead fetus from the uterus.

Emedullate —To remove the marrow from a bone.

Emeiocytosis —Exocytosis.

Emergence —Restoration of health following a period of unconsciousness.

Emergency —A patient's condition requiring immediate medical or surgical treatment.

Emergent —1. Coming out from a cavity or other part. 2. Coming on suddenly.

Emery —An abrasive substance containing aluminium oxide and iron.

Emesis —Vomiting.

Emetic —Causing vomiting.

Emetocathartic —Producing emesis and purgation both.

Emetogenecity —The property of being emetogenic.

Emetogenic —Causing vomiting.

Emetology —Study of the anatomy of the organs and physiology of vomiting.

-emia —A suffix denoting blood.

Emiction —Discharge of urine.

Emictory —A medicine promoting the flow of urine.

Emigration —The passage of white blood cells through the walls of the minute blood vessels in the process of inflammation.

Eminence —A prominence, projection or boss, especially of a bone.

Eminentia —Eminence.

Emiocytosis —Exocytosis.

Emissary —Outlet.

Emissio —A discharge, emission.

Emission —Discharge, e.g., nocturnal emission or the night dream in which there is involuntary discharge of semen during sleep.

Emmenagogue —A substance which increases the menstrual flow.

Emmenia —The menstrual flow.

Emmenic —Pertaining to the menses.

Emmeniopathy —Any disorder of the menstruation.

Emmenology —The study of the menstruation and its disorders.

Emmetrope —The person having no refractive error or vision.

Emmetropia —Normal eye condition in refraction in which, when the eye is at rest, the parallel rays are focused exactly on the retina.

Emmetropic —Pertaining to norml vision.

Emollient —An agent that softens the skin and soothes the irritation in the skin or mucous membrane.

Emotion —A mental state or feeling such as fear, hate, love, anger, grief or joy characterized by the physiological changes such as alteration in the heart rate and respiratory activity and changes in the muscle tone, and the behavior is changed.

Emotional —Relating to any of the emotions.

Emotiovascular —Pertaining to the vascular changes, such as pallor and blushing, caused by emotions of various kinds.

Emotivity —The capability of a person for emotional response.

Empasm, Empasma — A perfumed powder for external application to remove the foul smell of the body.

Empathic —The person who recognizes and enters into another's feelings.

Empathy —To recognize and enter into another's feelings.

Emperipolesis —Penetration of, and movement within another cell by lymphocyte.

Emphractic —Obstructive.

Emphraxis —Stoppage or obstruction, an infarction.

Emphysatherapy —Treatment by injecting gas into a cavity.

Emhysema —A pathological distention of the tissues by gas or air, e.g., pulmonary emphysema in which there is distention of the pulmonary alveoli due to accumulaton of air, and surgical emphysema in which there is subcutaneous accumulation of the air after an operation.

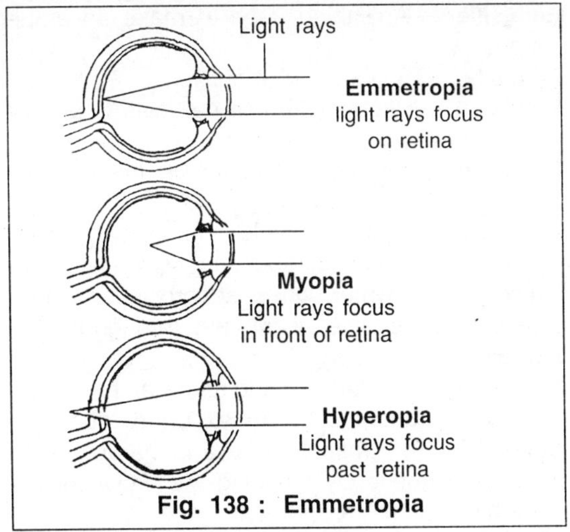

Fig. 138 : Emmetropia

I Emmetropia : Light rays focus on retina.
II Myopia : Light rays focus in front of retina
III Hyperopia : Light rays focus past retina.

Emphysematous —Affected with or pertaining to emphysema.

Empiric, Empirical —Based on experience. Quack.

Empirical— Empiric.

Empiricism —Experience, the basis of medical science. Quackery.

Emplastic —1. A medicine causing constipation 2. Adhesive or able to be used as plaster

Emplastrum —A plaster.

Emprosthotonos —The spasm in which the body is bent forward.

Emptysis —Hemoptysis. The spitting of the blood.

Empyectomy —Excision of an empyema.

Empyema —Accumulation of pus in a body cavity, especially in the pleural cavity (pyothorax).

Empyemic —Pertaining to empyema.

Empyesis —1. A pustular eruption. 2. Hypopyon, accumulation of pus in the anterior chamber of the eye.

Empyocele —Formation of pus in a hydrocele.

EMS —Abbreviation for emergency medical service.

EMT —Abbreviation for emergency medical technician.

Emulgent —1. Affecting a straining or purifying process. 2. A renal artery or vein. 3. A medicine that stimulates bile or urine flow.

Emulsification — The process of making an emulsion, i.e. the breaking down of the large fat globules into smaller, uniformly distributed particles.

Emulsifier —Any thing used to make an emulsion.

Emulsify —To make an emulsion.

Emulsion —A liquid with fine particles of an oily substance suspended in it.

Emulsive —Denoting a substance that can be emulsified.

Emulsoid —A colloid in which the highly complex organic substances, such as starch etc. are dispersed in water, which absorb much water, swell and become distributed throughout the whole water.

Emunctory —1. Pertaining to an organ having an excretory function. 2. An excretory duct.

Enamel —The white, dense and hardest substance in the body covering the crown of the teeth.

Enamelum —Enamel.

Enanthem, Enanthema — Eruption on the mucous membrane.

Enanthema — Enanthem

Enanthematous —Of the nature of an enanthema.

Enanthesis —A skin eruption caused by a systemic disease such as typhoid fever or syphilis.

Enanthrope —Any disease originating in the body.

Enantiobiosis —The condition in which the associated organisms are antagonistic to each other.

Enantiomorph —One of a pair of isomeric substances, each of which is a mirror image of the other.

Enantiomorphic —Pertaining to two organs which are similar in form and actions, no one is superior to other as two hands.

Enantiomorphism —The relation of two organs which are similar in form and actions, as the two hands.

Enantiomorphous — Enantiomorphic.

Enantiopathy —Treatment of one disease by producing another disease.

Enarthritis —Inflammation of a ball-and-socket joint.

Enarthrodial —Pertaining to enarthrosis.

Enarthrosis —A ball-and-socket joint (the joint in which the rounded head of one bone is fitted into the socket of another bone) such as hip joint. It is a form of diarthrosis.

En bloc —A whole or a lump.

Encanthis —A new growth at the inner angle of the eye.

Encapsulated —Enclosed in a capsule.

Encapsulation —1. The process of the formation of a capsule or a sheath surrounding a structure. 2. Enclosure within a capsule or sheath which is abnormal to the part.

Encapsuled —Encapsulated.

Encarditis —Endocarditis.

Encatarrhaphy —Insertion of an organ or tissue into a part of the body where it is not found normally.

Enceinte —Pregnant.

Encelitis, Enceliitis — Inflammation of any of the abdominal organs.

Encephalalgia —Cephalalgia. Deep-seated pain in the head.

Encephalatrophy —Atrophy of the brain.

Encephalemia —Congestion in the brain.

Encephalic —Pertaining to the brain or its cavity.

Encephalitic —Pertaining to encephalitis.

Encephalitis —Inflammation of the brain.

Encephalitogen —Any agent that causes encephalitis.

Encephalitogenic —Causing encephalitis.

Encephalocele —Hydrencephalocele. Protrusion of the brain substance through a cranial fissure.

Encephalocystocele — Hernia of the brain in which the sac of hernia is filled with the cerebrospinal fluid.

Encephalodynia — Headache.

Encephalodysplasia --Any congenital abnormality of the brain.

Encephalogram —X-ray film of the brain.

Encephalography —X-ray examination of the brain after withdrawal of the cerebrospinal fluid and introduction of air or other gas into the ventricles through a lumbar or cisternal puncture, as a contrast medium.

Encephaloid —1. Resembling the brain substance. 2. Denoting a carcinoma of soft, brain-like structure.

Encephalolith —A calculus of the brain.

Encephalology —Study of the structure, functions and the diseases of the brain.

Encephaloma —Tumor of the brain.

Encephalomalacia —Softening of the brain.

Encephalomeningitis — Inflammation of the brain and its membranes (meninges).

Encephalomeningocele — Protrusion of the meninges and the brain substance through a fissure in the cranium.

Encephalomeningopathy — Meningoencephalopathy.

Encephalomere —One of the segments of the embryonic brain.

Encephalometer —An instrument for measuring the cranium and locating the brain regions.

Encephalomyelitis — Inflammation of the brain and the spinal cord.

Encephalomyeloneuropathy —Any disease of the brain, spinal cord and the nerves.

Encephalomyelopathy —Any disease of the brain and spinal cord.

Encephalomyeloradiculitis —Inflammation of the brain, spinal cord and the spinal nerve roots.

Encephalomyocarditis —Inflammation of the brain and the cardiac muscle.

Encephalon —The brain, including the cerebrum, cerebellum, medulla oblongata, pons, diencephalon and mid-brain.

Encephalopathia — Encephalopathy.

Encephalopathy —Any disease of the brain.

Encephalopuncture —Surgical puncture of the brain.

Encephalopyosis —Brain abscess.

Encephalorrhagia —Cerebral hemorrhage.

Encephalosclerosis — Hardening of the brain.

Encephaloscope —An instrument used for inspection of a brain abscess or a cavity in the brain through an opening in the skull.

Encephaloscopy —Inspection of a brain abscess or a cavity in the brain by encephaloscope.

Encephalosis —Any degenerative disease of the brain.

Encephalospinal —Pertaining to brain and the spinal cord.

Encephalotome —An instrument for incising the brain.

Encephalotomy —1. Dissection of the brain. 2. Surgical destruction of the brain of a fetus to facilitate delivery.

Enchondral —Intracartilaginous.

Enchondroma —Enchondrosis. A benign cartilaginous tumor occurring in the metaphysis of a bone or at the place where the cartilage is absent.

Enchondromatosis —The formation of enchondromas.

Enchondromatous —Pertaining to or having the elements of enchondroma.

Enchondrosarcoma —A sarcoma of the cartilage.

Enchondrosis —Enchondroma.

Enclave —A tissue which becomes enclosed within the tissue of another kind.

Enclitic —Having the fetal head whose planes are inclined to those of the maternal pelvis.

Encolpitis —Endocolpitis. Inflammation of the vaginal mucous membrane.

Encopresis —Condition of constipation in which the watery colonic contents bypass the hard fecal masses and pass through the rectum, which is often confused with diarrhoea.

Encranial —Situated in the cranium.

Encranius —In conjoined twins, the smaller child lying partly or wholly within the cranial cavity of the larger child.

Encrustation —Incrustation.

Encrusted —Incrusted.

Encyesis —Normal uterine pregnancy.

Encysted —Surrounded by membrane. Encapsulated.

Encystment —The condition of being encysted or encapsulated.

End —A termination.

Endadelphos —Two fetuses, one of which is enclosed in the body or in a cyst of the other congenitally.

Endamoeba —Entamoeba.

Endangeitis, Endangiitis — Inflammation of inner coat of a blood vessel.

Endangium —Tunica intima, the innermost coat of a blood vessel.

Endaortitis —Inflammation of the inner coat of the aorta.

Endarterectomy —Surgical removal of the innermost coat of an artery.

Endarterial —1. Pertaining to the inner portion of a an artery. 2. Within an artery.

Endarteritis —Inflammation of the inner most coat (tunica intima) of an artery.

Endartery —An artery which does not communicate with the other arteries.

Endaural —Within an ear.

Endbrain —Telencephalon.

End-brush —Telodendron. Teledendrite. The terminal processes of an axon.

End-bud, End-bulb —The terminal portion of a sensory nerve fiber.

End-diastolic —Occurring at the end of diastole, immediately before the next systole.

Endectocide —A drug destroying both, endoparasites and ectoparasites.

Endemic —A disease occurring in a particular population but has low mortality rate, as measles.

Endemiology —The study of all the factors relating to the occurrence of endemic disease.

Endemoepidemic —Endemic, but occasionally becoming epidemic.

Endergonic —Pertaining to chemical reactions requiring energy for their occurrence.

Endermatic, Endermic —Introduced by absorption through the abraded surface of the skin.

Endermosis —1. Administration of medicine through the skin. 2. Herpes disease of any mucous membrane.

End-feet —Button or knoblike terminal enlarged portion of a naked nerve fiber, which at the end is related to the dendrite of another nerve cell.

Endgut —Hindgut.

Ending —A termination, especially the peripheral termination of a nerve or nerve fiber.

Endoaneurysmoplasty — Aneurysmoplasty.

Endoaneurysmorrhaphy — Opening of an aneurysmal sac and suturing of its orifice.

Endoangiitis —Endangiitis, Endoarteritis. Inflammation of the inner coat of the blood vessels.

Endoantitoxin —An antitoxin within a cell.

Endoaortitis —Inflammation of the inner coat (intima) of the aorta.

Endoappendicitis — Inflammation of the mucous membrane of the vermiform appendix.

Endoarteritis —Endarteritis.

Endoauscultation — Auscultation by a tube passed into the stomach or the heart.

Endobag —Endosac.

Endobiotic —Pertaining to an organism living as a parasite in the host.

Endoblast —Endoderm. 1. The nucleus of a cell. 2. Inner layer of the blastoderm.

Endobronchial —Intrabronchial.

Endobronchitis —Inflammation of the epithelial lining of the bronchi.

Endocardiac, Endocardial —1 Situated or occurring within the heart. 2. Arising from or pertaining to the endocardium.

Endocarditic —Pertaining to endocarditis.

Endocarditis —Inflammation of the endocardium which occurs most commonly in a valve of the heart, but the endocardium of the cardiac chambers may also be affected.

Acute bacterial endocarditis — Inflammation of the endocardium occurring suddenly and progressing rapidly, usually due to the bacteria named staphylococci, pneumococci, gonococci, streptococci etc.

Atypical verrucous endocarditis —Nonbacterial inflammation of the endocardium associated with various wasting diseases.

Infective endocarditis —Endocarditis caused by the infection of the microorganisms and fungi.

Malignant endocarditis —Endocarditis usually secondary to the suppurative inflammation elsewhere in the body, which is fatal.

Mural endocarditis — Inflammation of the walls of the cardiac chambers but not of the valves.

Nonbacterial endocarditis —Endocarditis occurring as a result of accumulation of debris on the endocardium and not due to infection.

Rheumatic endocarditis —Endocarditis occurring following rheumatic fever.

Subacute bacterial endocarditis —A condition usually caused by infection of the bacteria of the group Streptococcus viridans, which tends to run a prolonged course in an abnormal heart or in the valves damaged previously by rheumatic fever.

Syphilitic endocarditis — Endocarditis as a complication of syphilis.

Tuberculous endocarditis —Endocarditis caused by Mycobacterium tuberculosis, in which the valves are affected.

Ulcerative endocarditis —It is a form of a rapidly destructive acute bacterial endocarditis characterized by the ulceration of the valves.

Valvular endocarditis —Inflammation of the endocardium of the valves only and not that of the cardiac chambers.

Vegetative endocarditis —In this type of endocarditis small fibrinous nodules are formed on the ulcerated surfaces of the valves.

Endocardium — Innermost membranous coat of the cavities of the heart covering the valves and continuous with the intima (innermost coat) of the arteries.

Endoceliac —Within one of the body cavities.

Endocervical —Pertaining to the endocervix.

Endocervicitis —Inflammation of the endocervix.

Endocervix —The inner coat of the cervical canal.

Endochondral —Situated, formed or occurring within a cartilage.

Endocoagulation — Thermocoagulation.

Endocolitis —Inflammation of the mucous membrane of the colon.

Endocolpitis —Encolpitis. Inflammation of the mucous membrane of the vagina.

Endocorpuscular —Within a corpuscle.

Endocranial —Situated within the cranium.

Endocranitis —Inflammation of the endocranium.

Endocranium —The dura mater of the brain or the

lining membrane of the cranium.

Endocrinasthenia — Neurasthenia due to dysfunction of the endocrine glands.

Endocrine —1. Pertaining to a gland which has no duct and discharges its secretion directly into the blood or lymph. 2. An internal secretion.

Endocrine gland —A ductless gland producing an internal secretion as hormone, discharging it into the blood or lymph. The endocrine glands are pituitary gland, thyroid gland, parathyroid glands, adrenal glands, islets of Langerhans of the pancreas and the gonads (ovaries and testes).

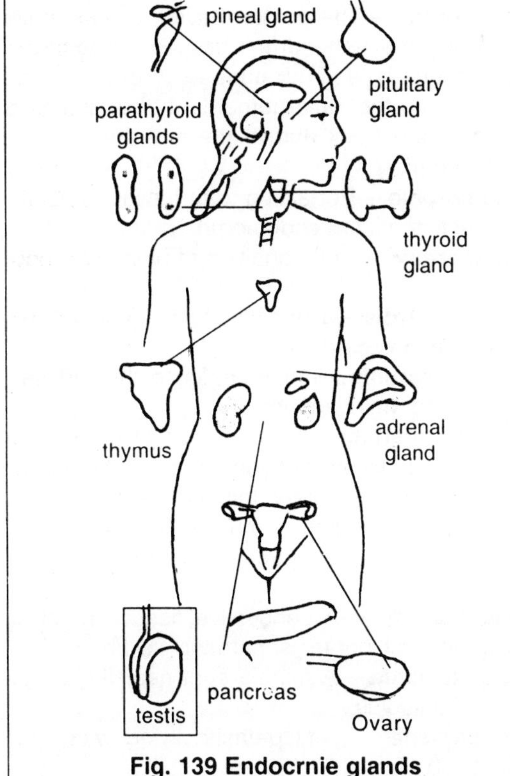

Fig. 139 Endocrnie glands

Endocrinologist —Specialist in endocrinology.

Endocrinology —The science of the endocrine glands which deals with their functions and diseases, with their diagnosis and treatment.

Endocrinopathic —Suffering from a disease resulting from disorder of an endocrine gland.

Endocrinopathy —Any disease resulting from disorder of an endocrine gland or glands.

Endocrinosis —Dysfunction of an endocrine gland.

Endocrinotherapy — Treatment of the diseases with the endocrine preparations.

Endocrinous —Pertaining to the endocrine.

Endocystitis —Inflammation of the mucous membrane of the urinary bladder.

Endocytosis —The method of ingestion of a foreign substance by a cell by invagination of its wall.

Endoderm —Entoderm. Inner layer of cells of an embryo.

Endodermal —Entodermal. Pertaining to the entoderm.

Endodiascope —X-ray tube which is placed in a body cavity for X-ray examination and radiation therapy.

Endodiascopy —X-ray examination of a body cavity by an endodiascope.

Endodontia —Endodontics.

Endodontics —A branch of dentistry concerning with the etiology, diagnosis, prevention and treatment of the diseases of the dental pulp, root and the surrounding tissues.

Endodontist —Specialist in endodontics, a branch of dentistry.

Endodontitis —Pulpitis. Inflammation of the dental pulp.

Endodontium —Dental pulp.

Endodontologist — Endodontist.

Endodontology —Endodontics.

Endodyocyte —Merozoite.

Endoectothrix —Any fungus growth on and in the hair.

Endoenteritis —Inflammation of the mucous membrane of the intestine.

Endoenzyme —An intracellular enzyme.

Endoesophagitis — Inflammation of the internal lining of the esophagus.

Endogastric —Pertaining to the interior of the stomach.

Endogastritis —Inflammation of the inner coat of the stomach.

Endogenic —Endogenous. Produced within the organism.

Endogenous —Endogenic.

Endogeny —Formation of growth within the cell.

Endoglobar, Endoglobular —Situated in a blood corpuscle.

Endointoxication —Poisoning by an endogenous toxin.

Endolabyrinthitis — Inflammation of the membranous labyrinth.

Endolaryngeal —Situated or occurring within the larynx.

Endolith —A stone found in the pulp cavity of a tooth.

Endolumbar —In the lumbar region of the spinal cord.

Endolymph —Pale transparent fluid within the labyrinth of the ear.

Endolymphatic —Pertaining to the endolymph.

Endolymphic —Pertaining to the endolymph.

Endolysin —A bactericidal substance within a white blood cell, which destroys the bacteria.

Endolysis —Disintegration of the cytoplasm of cells.

Endomastoiditis — Inflammation of the mucous lining of the mastoid cavity.

Endomerogony —Production of merozoites in the asexual reproduction of sporozoan protozoa by a process originating in the interior of schizont.

Endometer —An electronic device for the determination of the length of a tooth's root canal.

Endometrectomy —Excision of the uterine mucosa.

Endometria —Plural of endometrium.

Endometrial —Pertaining to the endometrium.

Endometrioid —Resembling endometrial tissue microscopically.

Endometrioma —A solitary tumor containing endometrial tissue found mostly in the ovary.

Endometriosis —Proliferation of endometrial tissue outside the cavity of the uterus. Common affected areas may be myometrium of the uterus, ovary, urinary bladder, rectum, peritoneum, umbilicus and laparotomy scar etc.

Fig.140 : Endometriosis

Endometritis —Inflammation of the endometrium.

Decidual endometritis — Inflammation of the mucous membrane of the gravid uterus.

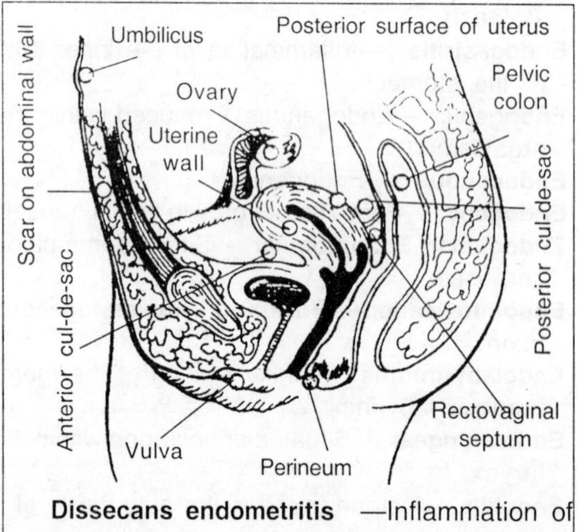

Dissecans endometritis —Inflammation of the endometrium accompanied by the development of ulcers and shedding of the mucous membrane.

Puerperal endometritis —Acute endometritis occurring after childbirth.

Tuberculous endometritis —Chronic inflammation of the endometrium due to infection of Mycobacterium tuberculosis.

Endometrium —The mucous membrane lining the inner surface of the uterus.

Endometropic —Denoting an external stimulus capable of producing a response of the uterus, especially the endometrium.

Endometry —Measurement of the interior of a cavity or organ.

Endomorph —The person having a body build in which the endodermal tissues predominate and there is soft roundness throughout the body with the enlargement of the digestive organs, the trunk and thighs and the extremities tapering.

Endomorphic —Pertaining to or having the characteristics of an endomorph.

Endomorphy —The condition of being an endomorph.

Endomyocardial —Pertaining to the endocardium and the myocardium.

Endomyocarditis — Inflammation of the endocardium and myocardium.

Endomyometritis — Inflammation of the interior of the muscular wall (myometrium) of the uterus.

Endomysium —A very thin connective tissue sheath surrounding a muscle fiber.

Endoneuritis —Inflammation of the endoneurium.

Endoneurium —A connective tissue sheath in a peripheral nerve, separating its fibers.

Endonucleolus —A minute spot near the center of a nucleolus.

Endoparasite —Any parasite living within the host's body.

Endopathy —Any disease produced within the body.

Endopelvic —Situated within the pelvis.

Endoperiarteritis — Panarteritis.

Endopericardiac — Intrapericardiac. Within the pericardial cavity.

Endopericarditis — Inflammation of the endocardium with that of the pericardium.

Endoperimyocarditis — Inflammation of the pericardium, myocardium and endocardium.

Endoperitonitis — Inflammation of the inner surface of the peritoneum.

Endophasia —Formation of the words by the lips without producing sound.

Endophlebitis —Inflammation of the intima (inner coat) of a vein.

Endophthalmitis — Inflammation of the interior of the eye.

Endophyte —A plant parasite living within its host's body.

Endophytic —Pertaining to an endophyte.

Endoplasm —The middle portion of the cytoplasm of a cell.

Endoplasmic —Pertaining to endoplasm.

End-organ —The terminal expanded portion of a sensory nerve fiber.

Endorhinitis —Coryza. Inflammation of the mucous membranes of the nose.

Endorphin —A chemical substance polypeptide produced in the brain, which produces analgesia by increasing the pain threshold.

Endorrhachis —Membrane lining the spinal canal.

Endosac —A sac or bag used in laparoscopic surgery in which tissue is placed to facilitate removal.

Endosalpingitis — Inflammation of the mucous membrane lining the fallopian tubes.

Endosalpingoma — Adenomyoma of the uterine tube.

Endosalpinx —The mucous membrane lining the uterine tube.

Endosarc —Entosarc. The endoplasm of a protozoon.

Endoscope —An instrument used for observing the inside of a hollow organ or cavity through a natural opening in the body or through a small incision.

Endoscopist —A specialist trained in the use of an endoscope.

Endoscopy —Inspection of the inside of the hollow organs or the cavities of the body by using an endoscope.

Endosepsis —Septicemia originated from within the body.

Endoskeleton —The internal bony framework of the body.

Endosmometer —A device for estimating the passage of a liquid through a membrane by osmosis.

Endosmosis —Inward passage of a liquid through a membrane of a cell or cavity.

Endospore —Spore formed within the bacterial cell.

Endosteal —Pertaining to the endosteum.

Endosteitis —Endostitis. Inflammation of the endosteum.

Endosteoma —A tumor in the medullary cavity of a bone.

Endosteum —The membrane lining the medullary cavity of a bone.

Endostitis —Endosteitis.

Endostoma —Endosteoma.

Endostosis —Formation of the tumors in the medullary cavity of a bone.

Endotendineum —The delicate connective tissue in the tendon between the bundles of fibers.

Endothelial —Pertaining to or made up of the endothelium.

Endotheliocyte —Endothelial cell.

Endotheliocytosis —An abnormal increase in the endothelial cells.

Endothelioid —Resembling endothelium.

Endotheliolytic —Capable of destroying the endothelial tissue.

Endothelioma —Malignant tumor of the endothelium lining the blood vessels.

Endotheliomatosis — Formation of multiple diffuse endotheliomas.

Endotheliomyoma — Muscular tumor with the elements of the endothelium.

Endotheliomyxoma —A tumor composed of mucous connective tissue mixed with the endothelial cells.

Endotheliosis —Proliferation of endothelial cells.

Endotheliotoxin —A specific toxin which acts on the endothelial cells of the capillaries and causes hemorrhage.

Endothelium —The layer of the epithelium consisting of flat cells lining the blood and lymph vessels, the cavities of the heart and the various other cavities of the body.

Endothermal, Endothermic — Absorbing heat.

Endothermy —Diathermy. To generate heat within some part of the body by using high-frequency electric current.

Endothrix —Any fungus growing within the hair shaft.

Endothyropexy —To displace the thyroid gland and fix it to the side of the neck.

Endotoscope —Otoscope. Ear speculum. An instrument for examining the ear.

Endotoxemia —Toxemia caused by the presence of endotoxins in the blood.

Endotoxic —Pertaining to endotoxin.

Endotoxicosis —Poisoning caused by the endotoxin.

Endotoxin —Bacterial toxin confined to the body

of the bacterium and freed only when the bacterium is broken down.

Endotracheal —Situated within the trachea.

Endotracheitis —Inflammation of the mucous membrane lining the trachea.

Endotrachelitis — Endocervicitis.

Endourology —Diagnostic and therapeutic surgical procedures performed on the genitourinary system through the instruments.

Endovaccination —Oral administration of vaccines.

Endovasculitis —Endangiitis.

Endovenous —Intravenous. Within a vein.

End-piece —The terminal part of the tail of a spermatozoon.

Endplate —The terminal flattened and circular expanded portion of a nerve fiber ending on a muscle cell.

End product —The final substance left at the end of a series of reactions.

End-stage —The final phase of a disease process.

End-tidal —At the end of a normal expiration.

Endurance —The ability to withstand unusual mental or physical stress for a prolonged period.

Endyma —Ependyma.

Enema —Introduction of a fluid into the rectum.

Analeptic enema — Enema used to stimulate the central nervous system in which a pint of water containing 1/2 teaspoonful of salt is injected into the rectum.

Barium enema —Contrast enema. It is used as the diagnostic aid in X-ray examination of the colon in which barium sulphate solution as a contrast medium is injected into the rectum and retained in the intestines during X-ray examination, intestinal deformities are demonstrated by filling defects displayed by the column of radiopaque barium.

Carminative enema — Enema given to relieve the distension of the abdomen caused by air, and to stimulate peristalsis.

Cleansing enema — Enema used to empty the lower intestine or the colon.

Double-contrast enema —Injection and evacuation of barium sulphate solution or other radiopaque material followed by injection of air, and then the X-ray film of the lower intestine is taken.

Emollient enema — Enema given to allay the local pain and irritation by protecting the intestinal mucous membrane by making a coating over it, and to act as the vehicle for the medicines to be administered in the rectum.

Glycerine enema — Glycerine is mixed with equal quantity of warm water and injected into the rectum by an enema syringe in case of constipation, which is usually given to the children.

Lubricating enema — The enema given after an operation for the piles, to soften the feces and lubricate the anal canal. On impaction of feces, a lubricating enema may be given followed in two hours by cleansing enema.

Medicinal enema —An enema to which some medicine is added. It is given in some diseases of the rectum or colon or for the absorption of a medicine for its systemic effects.

Nutrient enema — Nutritive enema. Enema containing nutrients given to the patient unable to take food in any other way.

Retention enema —It is of the small volume and is retained in the rectum to provide nourishment, or medication.

Saline enema Enema of normal saline solution or of magnesium sulphate in warm water.

Soap and water enema —Enema given of soap dissolved in warm water.

Enemator —An apparatus used to give an enema.

Enemiasis —The use of enemas.

Energetics —Scientific study of the energy.

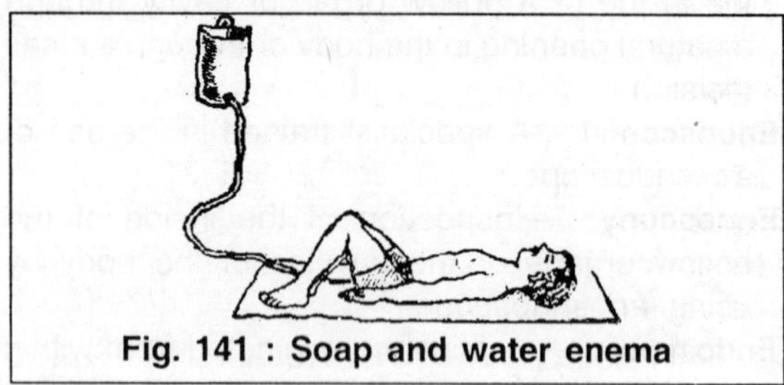

Fig. 141 : Soap and water enema

Energizer —Giving energy.

Energy —Power. The ability to do work.

Kinetic energy —Energy of motion.

Latent energy —Dormant or concealed energy.

Nuclear energy — Energy given off during nuclear reaction.

Nutritional energy — Energy produced by nutrition.

Potential energy —Energy existing in a body which is not utilized at the time.

Radiant energy —Energy contained in light rays or any other form of radiation.

Solar energy —Energy derived from sunlight.

Enervation —1. Lack of nervous strength. 2. Removal or a section of a nerve.

Enflagellation —Production and development of flagella.

Enflurane —A nonflammable and nonexplosive potent volatile inhalation anesthetic.

Engagement —The entrance of the fetal head or the part being presented, into the superior pelvic narrow passage.

Fig. 142 : Engagement of the fetus

Engastrium —A double monster in which one fetus is contained within the abdomen of the other.

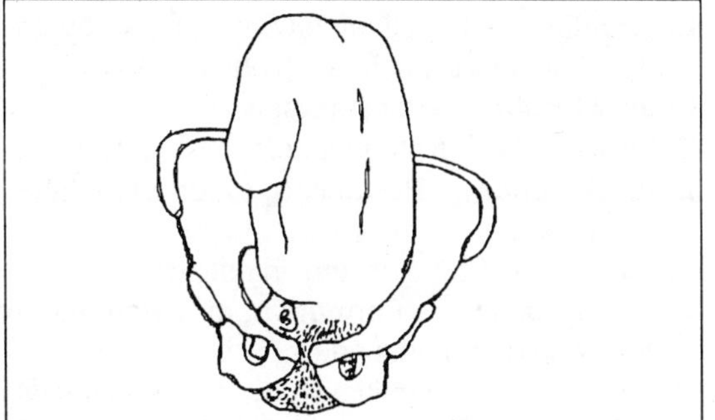

Englobe —To take in by a spherical body, as the ingestion of bacteria by the phagocytes.

Engorged —Distended with a fluid as with the blood.

Engorgement —Hyperemia. Congestion of blood vessels. Distention with fluids.

Engram —A trace in the protoplasm of the cells of the nervous system left by a stimulus or experience.

Engraphia —The theory that stimuli leave traces (engrams) in the protoplasm of the cells of the nervous system, which, with repetition, induce a habit which persists after the stimuli have ceased.

Enissophobia —Fear of criticism.

Enkatarrhaphy —An operation of burying a structure by suturing the adjacent tissues over it.

Enkephalin —Endorphin.

Enlargement —Increase in size.

Enology, Oenology —Scientific study of the wine.

Enomania —Mania for alcoholic beverages.

Enophthalmia —Enophthalmos.

Enophthalmos —Recession of the eyeball into the orbit.

Enosimania —A mental condition in which the patient is terrified excessively.

Enostosis —A tumor present in the cavity of a bone.

Enriched —The addition of something extra as the addition of vitamins or minerals to a food.

Ensiform —Sword-shaped structure, xiphoid.

Ensisternum —Xiphoid process. The lowest portion of the sternum.

Ensomphalus —Two fetuses whose bodies are blended together but each of them having its own umbilicus and umbilical cord.

Enstrophe —Inversion or a turning inward, especially of the eyelids.

E.N.T. —Ear, Nose, Throat.

Entad —Toward the inside or a center, inwardly.

Ental —Pertaining to the inside. Central.

Entamebiasis —The condition caused by the infection of Entamoeba.

Entamoeba —A genus of the amoebas parasitic in the human intestine. The most common species found in the intestine of man is Entamoeba histolytica.

Entasia —A constrictive spasm.

Enteradenitis —Inflammation of the intestinal glands.

Enteral —1. Pertaining to the small intestine. 2. Situated within the small intestine.

Enteralgia —Pain in the intestine.

Enteramphalos —Umbilical hernia.

Enterdynia —Enteralgia.

Enterectasia —Dilatation of the intestine.

Enterectasis — Enterectasia.

Enterectomy —Excision of a portion of the intestine.

Enterelcosis —Ulceration of the intestine.

Enteric —Pertaining to the small intestine.

Enteric-coated —A tablet or capsule coated with a special compound which is not dissolved until the tablet or capsule reaches the small intestine and is exposed to the fluids in it.

Enteric fever —Typhoid fever.

Enteritis —Inflammation of the intestines, especially the small intestine.

Entero-, Enter- —Prefix denoting some relationship to the intestines.

Enteroanastomosis — Intestinal anastomosis.

Enteroantigen —An antigen derived from the intestine.

Enterobacteriotherapy — Treatment of diseases by the vaccines containing intestinal bacteria.

Enterobiasis —Oxyuriasis. The infection with threadworms (Enterobius vermicularis)

Enterobiliary —Pertaining to the intestines and the bile ducts.

Enterocele —Hernia of the intestine through the vagina.

Enterocentesis —Surgical puncture of the intestine.

Enterocholecystostomy — Cholecystenterostomy. To make a connection between the gallbladder and the small intestine by making an opening.

Enterocholecystotomy — To make an incision in both, the intestine and the gallbladder.

Enterocidal —Killing the parasites living in the intestines.

Enterocinesia —Peristalsis. Movements of the intestine.

Enterocinetic —Pertaining to or promoting peristalsis.

Enteroclysis —Injection of a liquid into the intestine.

Enterococcus —Any Streptococcus of the human intestine.

Enterocoele —The abdominal cavity.

Enterocolectomy —Excision of the ileum, cecum and ascending colon.

Enterocolitis —Inflammation of the small intestine and the colon.

Enterocolostomy —To join the small intestine to the colon by surgery.

Enterocutaneous —Pertaining to or communication between the skin and the intestine.

Enterocyst —A benign cyst of the intestinal wall.

Enterocystocele —Hernia of the bladder wall and the intestine.

Enterocystoma —Cystic tumor of the intestinal wall.

Enterocystoplasty — Enlargement of the urinary bladder by plastic surgery using a portion of the intestine.

Enterocyte —An epithelial cell of the intestine.

Enterodynia —Enteralgia. Pain in the intestine.

Enteroenterostomy —To make a communication between two segments of the intestine, which are not continuous, by surgery.

Enteroepiplocele —Hernia of the small intestine and the omentum.

Enterogastric —Pertaining to the intestine and the stomach.

Enterogastritis — Inflammation of the intestine and the stomach.

Enterogastrone —A hormone of the duodenum which depresses the gastric motility and reduces the gastric secretion thus controls the release of food from the stomach into the duodenum.

Enterogenous —Arising from the small intestine.

Enterogram —Tracing of the intestinal movements.

Enterograph —An instrument used in enterography.

Enterography —To make an enterogram of the intestinal movements.

Enterohepatic —Pertaining to the intestine and the liver.

Enterohepatitis —Inflammation of the intestine and the liver.

Enterohepatocele —An umbilical hernia containing intestine and the liver.

Enterohydrocele —Hydrocele with a loop of intestine in its sac.

Enteroidea —Intestinal fevers caused by the intestinal bacilli such as typhoid fever.

Enterokinesia —Peristalsis.

Enterokinesis —Enterokinesia.

Enterokinetic —Pertaining to or stimulating peristalsis.

Enterolith —Stone in the intestine.

Enterolithiasis —Formation or existence of stones in the intestine.

Enterology —Scientific study of the intestine.

Enterolysis —To separate the adhesions of the intestine by surgery.

Enteromegalia, Enteromegaly —Megacolon. Enlargement of the intestines.

Enteromenia —Vicarious menstruation in which bleeding occurs from the intestine at the time of menstruation.

Enteromerocele —Femoral hernia.

Enterometer —An instrument used for measuring the diameter of the intestine.

Enteromycosis —Fungal disease of the intestine.

Enteromyiasis —Disease caused by the presence of the maggots (larvae of the flies) in the intestines.

Enteron —The alimentary canal.

Enteroneuritis —Inflammation of the nerves of the intestine.

Enteroparesis —Depressed peristaltic movements of the intestines followed by dilatation of their walls.

Enteropathogen —Any microorganism producing intestinal disease.

Enteropathogenesis — Production of any intestinal disease.

Enteropathy —Any disease of the intestines.

Enteropexy —Fixation of the intestine to the abdominal wall by surgery.

Enteroplasty —Repair of the intestine by plastic surgery.

Enteroplegia —Paralysis of the intestines.

Enteroplex —An instrument for joining the cut ends of the intestines.

Enteroplexy —Union of the divided parts of the intestine.

Enteroproctia —The condition of having an artificial anus.

Enteroptosis —Abnormal downward displacement of the intestine.

Enteroptotic —Pertaining to or suffering from enteroptosis.

Enterorenal —Pertaining to both, the intestines and the kidneys.

Enterorrhagia —Bleeding from the intestine.

Enterorrhaphy —To stitch the intestinal wound, or the intestine to some other structure.

Enterorrhexis —Rupture of the intestine.

Enteroscope —A device used for visual examination of the inside of the intestines.

Enterosepsis —Enterotoxism. Sepsis developed from the intestinal contents.

Enterospasm —Intestinal spasm.

Enterostasis —Intestinal stasis due to which there is delay in the passage of food through the intestine.

Enterostaxis —Slow bleeding through the mucous membrane of the intestine.

Enterostenosis —Narrowing of the intestine.

Enterostomy —Surgical formation of a permanent opening into the intestine through the abdominal wall.

Enterotome —An instrument for incision of the intestines.

Enterotomy —To make an incision into the intestine.

Enterotoxemia —A condition characterized by the presence of toxins in the blood which are produced in the intestine.

Enterotoxication —A disease resulting from the absorption of waste infected material from the intestine.

Enterotoxigenic —Producing, produced by or pertaining to the production of the enterotoxin.

Enterotoxin —1. A toxin produced in the intestinal contents. 2. A toxin specific for the cells of the intestinal mucosa. 3. An exotoxin produced by the bacteria Staphylococci which produce the symptoms of food poisoning.

Enterotoxism —Absorption of toxins from the intestinal contents.

Enterotropic —Affecting, or attracted by, the intestines.

Enterovaginal —Pertaining to the intestine and the vagina.

Enterovenous —Communicating between the lumen of intestine and that of a vein.

Enterovesical —Pertaining to, or communicating between the intestine and urinary bladder.

Enterovirus —The viruses affecting the intestine and are excreted in the feces.

Enterozoic —Pertaining to the parasites living in the intestines.

Enterozoon —An animal parasite in the intestine.

Enthelmintha —Intestinal worm.

Entheomania —Religious insanity.

Enthesis —1. The use of metallic or other inert substance in the repair of a defect or deformity of the body. 2. The site of attachment of a muscle or ligament to bone.

Enthesitis —Inflammation of the site of insertion of a muscle on a bone which tends to be fibrotic and calcified.

Enthesopathic —Denoting or characteristic of enthesopathy.

Enthesopathy —A disease occurring at the stie of insertion of muscle tendons and ligaments into bones or joint capsule.

Enthetic —Exogenous. 1. Pertaining to enthesis. 2. Introduced from outside.

Enthetobiosis —Dependency on a mechanical implant, as on artificial cardiac pacemaker.

Enthlasis —Comminuted fracture of the skull containing bone fragments.

Entire —Having a smoothly continuous border without indentations or projections.

Entity —The real existence of a thing.

Ento- —Prefix indicating within or inside.

Entoblast —1. The entoderm. 2. The nucleolus of a cell.

Entocele —1. Internal hernia. 2. Displacement of a part inwardly.

Entochondrostosis —The development of bone in the cartilage.

Entochoroidea —Inner layer of the choroid.

Entocornea —Descemet's membrane. Inner layer of the cornea.

Entocranial —Endocranial.

Entocranium —Endocranium.

Entocyte —Endoplasm. Interior part of a cell within the ectoplasm.

Entoderm —Innermost of the three primary germ layers of an embryo from which the epithelium of the pharynx, respiratory tract, digestive tract, urinary bladder, vagina and urethra develops.

Entoected —Comming from within outward.

Entome —A knife to divide the stricture of the urethra.

Entomion —The tip of the mastoid angle of the parietal bone.

Entomology —That branch of biology which is concerned with the study of insects.

Entomophobia —Morbid fear of insects.

Entophthalmia —Inflammation of the inner part of the eye-ball.

Entophyte —Any vegetable parasite living in the human body.

Entopic —Occurring or situated at the normal place.

Entoplasm —Endoplasm.

Entoptic —Pertaining to the interior of the eye.

Entoptoscopy —To inspect the interior of the eye.

Entoretina —Inner layer of the retina.

Entosarc —Endosarc.

Entotic —1. Pertaining to the interior of the ear. 2. Situated or occurring within the ear.

Entozoal —Pertaining to entozoa.

Entozoon, plural **entozoa** —An animal parasite living in the internal organs of the body.

Entrainment —Control of heart rhythm by external stimulus or with a cardiac pacemaker.

Entropion —The rolling in or the turning inward, as of the margin of an eyelid.

Entropionize —To correct by turning in.

Entropy —That part of the energy within a system which cannot be utilized to perform work.

Enucleate —To take out as a whole as the eyeball from its orbit.

Enucleation —Removal of an organ from its supporting structures as of the eyeball from its orbit.

Enucleator —An instrument for removing a tumor.

Enuresis —Involuntary urination or incontinence of urine.

Diurnal enuresis — Incontinence of urine occurring during the day.

Nocturnal enuresis — Incontinence of urine during the night.

Envelope —A structure that encloses or covers a structure.

Envenomation —Entrance of the poison into the body through a bite or sting.

Environment —The external conditions and influences affecting the life, health and development of an organism.

Envy —Jealousy.

Enzootic —Endemic.

Enzygotic —Developed from the same ovum.

Enzygotic twins —Monozygotic twins. Twins developed from one ovum.

Enzymatic —Pertaining to, caused by, or of the nature of an enzyme.

Enzyme —A complex protein produced in a cell, which is capable of greatly speeding up the chemical reaction of a substance by its catalytic action for which it often works specifically. The substance acted upon by an enzyme is called substrate.

Amylolytic enzyme —Enzyme that catalyzes the conversion of starch into sugar.

Autolytic enzyme — An enzyme producing autolysis or cell digestion.

Bacterial enzyme — Enzyme developed by bacteria.

Coagulating enzyme — Coagulase. An enzyme which speeds up the conversion of soluble proteins into insoluble proteins.

Deamidizing enzyme —An enzyme dividing amino acids into ammonia compounds.

Decarboxylating enzyme —Enzyme that separates CO_2 from organic acids, such as carboxylase.

Digestive enzyme —An enzyme that takes part in the digestive processes in the digestive canal.

Extracellular enzyme —The enzyme producing its effects outside the cell that produces it.

Fermenting enzyme — Enzyme produced by bacteria or yeasts which causes the fermentation of the substances, especially the carbohydrates.

Glycolytic enzyme —The enzyme which catalyzes the oxidation of sugar.

Heat-stable enzyme — Thermostable enzyme. An enzyme which is not affected by heat.

Hydrolytic enzyme — Hydrolase. Enzyme that speeds up the process of hydrolysis.

Hydrolyzing enzyme — Hydrolase.

Inhibitory enzyme — The enzyme which blocks a chemical reaction.

Intracellular enzyme —An enzyme acting within the cell which produces it.

Lipolytic enzyme — Lipase. Enzyme that catalyzes the hydrolysis of fats.

Oxidizing enzyme — Oxidase. Enzyme catalyzing the oxidative reactions.

Proteolytic enzyme —An enzyme that catalyzes conversion of proteins into peptides.

Reducing enzyme — Reductase. The enzyme removing oxygen.

Respiratory enzyme — The enzyme acting within the cells catalyzing the oxidative reactions by which the energy is released, such as cytochromes and flavoproteins.

Splitting enzyme — Any enzyme that acts to facilitate removal of the part of a molecule.

Steatolytic enzyme —Lipolytic enzyme.

Transferring enzyme — Transferase. Any enzyme which facilitates the moving of one molecule to another compound.

Uricolytic enzyme —An enzyme which catalyzes the conversion of uric acid into urea.

Enzymic —Enzymatic.

Enzymologist —A specialist in enzymology.

Enzymology —Study of the enzymes and their actions.

Enzymolysis —Chemical change or disintegration caused by an enzyme.

Enzymopathy —Any disease caused by the defectiveness or deficiency of an enzyme.

Enzymopenia —Deficiency of an enzyme.

Enzymuria —Presence of enzymes in the urine.

Eosinoblast —Myeloblast. A bone marrow cell developing into a myelocyte.

Eosinocyte —Eosinophil.

Eosinopenia —Deficiency or abnormally small number of eosinophils in the blood.

Eosinophil —A granular leucocyte (white blood cell) containing a nucleus with two lobes connected by a thread of chromatin.

Eosinophilia —Presence of a large number of eosinophils in the blood.

Eosinophilic —1. Pertaining to eosinophila or the eosinophils. 2. Staining readily with the eosin.

Eosinophilous —1. Easily staining with eosin. 2. Having eosinophilia.

Eosinophiluria —Presence of eosinophils in the urine.

Eosinotactic —Attraction or repulsion of eosinophil cells.

Eosinotaxis —Movement of eosinophils in response to a stimulus.

Eosophobia —Morbid fear of dawn.

Epactal —Exceeding usual numbers.

Epamniotic —Above the amnion.

Eparterial —Situated above an artery.

Epaxial —Situated above or behind any axis.

Epencephalon —Metencephalon.

Ependyma —Membrane lining the cerebral ventricles and central canal of the spinal cord.

Ependymal —Pertaining to the ependyma.

Ependymitis —Inflammation of the ependyma.

Ependymoblast —An embryonic ependymal cell.

Ependymoblastoma —A glial neoplasm of the central nervous system.

Ependymocyte —An ependymal cell.

Ependymoma —A tumor arising from ependymal cells.

Ephebiatrics —A branch of medicine dealing with the study of the diseases of adolescents.

Ephebic —Pertaining to the adolescence.

Ephebogenesis —The changes occurring in the body at puberty.

Ephebology —The study of puberty.

Ephelis —Freckle.

Ephemeral —Of short duration.

Ephialtes —Nightmare.

Ephidrosis —Abnormal or excessive sweating.

Ephidrosis cruenta — Sweat containing blood.

Ephidrosis tincta — Chromidrosis. Colored sweat.

Epi-, Ep- —Prefixes meaning over or above, in addition to, after.

Epiandrosterone —An androgenic hormone excreted in small amounts in normal urine.

Epiaxial —Above the axis.

Epiblast —Ectoderm. Outer layer of cells of the blastoderm.

Epiblastic —Pertaining to the epiblast.

Epiblepharon —A horizontal fold of skin which passes across the border of the upper or lower eyelid, so that the eye lashes are pressed inward against the eye.

Epibulbar —Situated upon the eye-ball.

Epicanthus —A vertical fold of skin on either side of the nose covering the inner canthus and caruncle.

Epicardia —The portion of the esophagus extending from below the diaphragm to the stomach, which is about 2 cms. in length.

Epicardial —Pertaining to the epicardium.

Epicardium —Inner layer of the pericardium.

Epichordal —Situated toward the back of the notochord.

Epichorion —The portion of decidua of the placenta covering the ovum.

Epicolic —The surface of the abdomen above the colon.

Epicomus —A fetus with a parasitic twin attached to its head.

Epicondylalgia —Pain in the elbow joint in the region of the epicondyle of the humerus.

Epicondyle —An eminence upon a bone, at its articular end above a condyle.

Epicondyli —Plural of epicondyle.

Epicondylic —Epicondylian. Pertaining to an epicondyle.

Epicondylitis —Inflammation of an epicondyle.

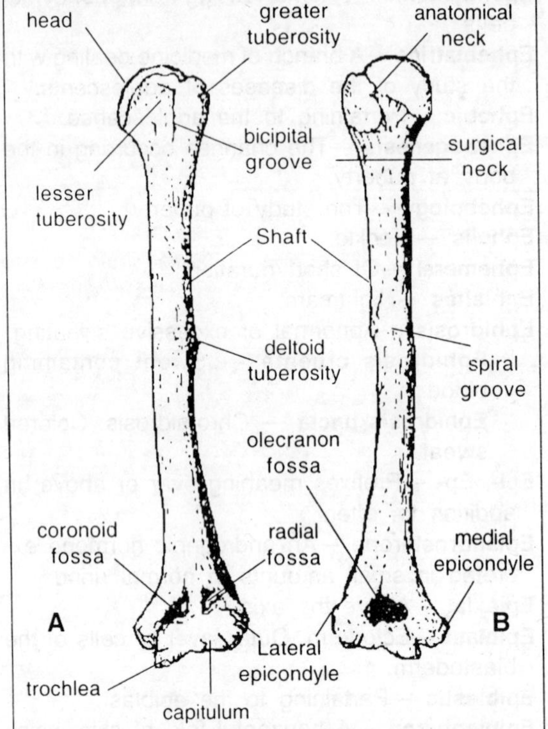

Fig. 143 Epicondyle on left humerus bone

Epicondylus —Epicondyle.

Epicoracoid —Above the coracoid process.

Epicranial —Situated above the cranium.

Epicranium —The soft structures covering the cranium are collectively known as epicranium.

Epicrisis —A secondary crisis after an initial critical stage of a disease.

Epicritic —1. Pertaining to an epicrisis. 2. Pertaining to the extreme sensibility such as that of the skin which is sensitive to fine variations of touch or temperature.

Epicystitis —Inflammation of the tissues above the urinary bladder.

Epicystotomy —To incise the urinary bladder above the pubic symphysis.

Epicyte —Cell membrane.

Epidemic —A disease spreading rapidly and attacking a large number of people in a region at the same time.

Epidemicity —The prevailing of a disease in epidemic form.

Epidemiography —Graphic description of epidemic diseases.

Epidemiologic —Pertaining to the study of epidemics.

Epidemiologist —Specialist in epidemiology.

Epidemiology —Scientific study of the epidemic diseases.

Epiderm, Epiderma — Epidermis.

Epidermal, Epidermic — Pertaining to the epidermis.

Epidermalization —Squamous metaplasia.

Epidermatoplasty —Grafting with the pieces of epidermis including the underlying corium.

Epidermic —Pertaining to the epidermis.

Epidermidalization — Development of the epidermal cells from the mucous cells.

Epidermidosis —Any disease of the epidermis.

Epidermis —Cuticle. Outer nonvascular layer of the skin.

Epidermitis — Inflammation of the epidermis.

Epidermization —Skin grafting.

Epidermodysplasia verruciformis —The development of warts throughout the body due to a virus.

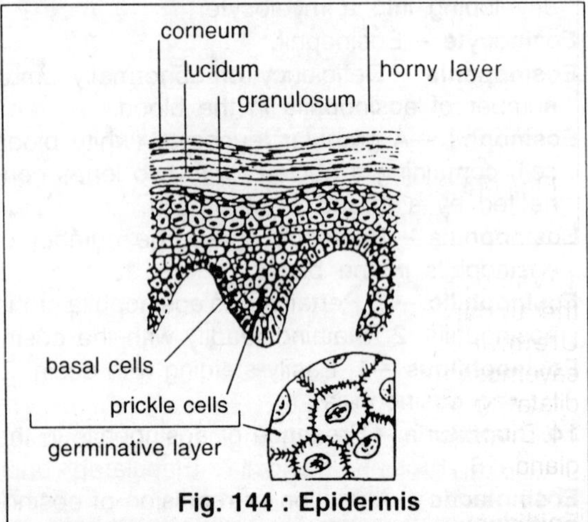

Fig. 144 : Epidermis

Epidermoid —1. Resembling the epidermis. 2. A tumor arising from the epidermis.

Epidermolysis —Loosening of the epidermis with

the formation of blisters spontaneously or after rubbing of a part.

Epidermoma —An outgrowth of the epidermis.

Epidermomycosis —Skin disease caused by a fungus.

Epidermophyton —A genus of fungi which attacks the skin and the nails but not the hair.

Epidermophytosis —The condition caused by the infection of a species of the genus Epidermophyton of fungi.

Epidermosis —Any disease of the epidermis.

Epidermotropism —Movement towards the epidermis.

Epididymal —Pertaining to the epididymis.

Epididymectomy —Excision of the epididymis.

Epididymis —An elongated, cord like structure attached to the posterior border of each testis.

Epididymitis —Inflammation of the epididymis.

Epididymodeferentectomy —Excision of the epididymis and the vas deferens.

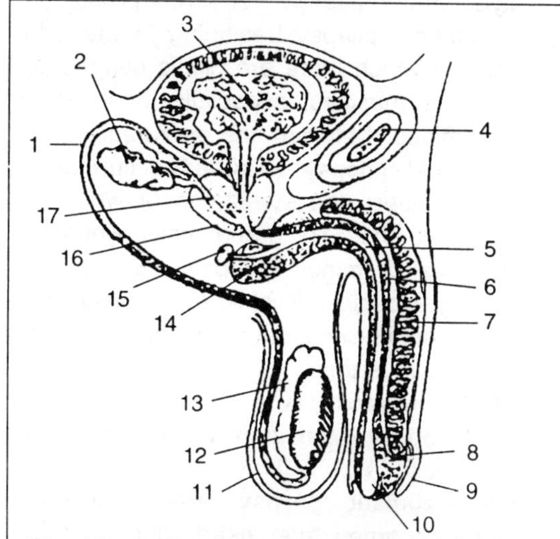

Fig. 145 A Epididymis associated with other male internal genital organs

1. Vas deferens 2. Seminal vesicles 3. Cavity of the urinary bladder, 4. Symphysis pubis 5. Urethra 6. Corpus spongiosum 7. Corpus cavernosum 8. Glans penis 9. Prepuce 10. Urethral dilatation 11. Scrotum 12. Testis 13. Epididymis 14. Dilatation of corpus spongiosum 15. Cowper's gland 16. Prostate gland 17. Ejaculatory duct

Epididymodeferential — Pertaining to both, the epididymis and the vas deferens.

Epididymography —X-ray examination of the epididymis after introduction of a contrast medium.

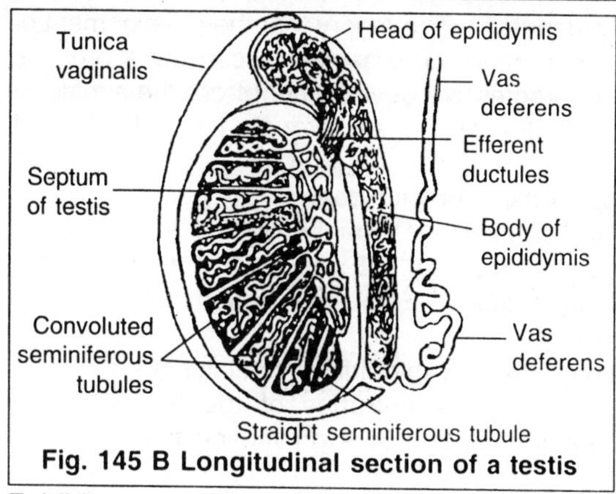

Fig. 145 B Longitudinal section of a testis

Epididymo-orchitis — Inflammation of both, the epididymis and the testis.

Epididymoplasty —Surgical repair of the epididymis.

Epididymotomy —To make an incision into the epididymis.

Epididymovasectomy — Surgical removal of the epididymis and the vas deferens.

Epididymovasostomy — Surgical anastomosis between the epididymis and the vas deferens.

Epididymovesiculography —X-ray examination of the epididymis and the seminal vesicle after introduction of a contrast medium.

Epidosis —Abnormal growth of any part of the body.

Epidural —Situated upon the dura mater.

Epidural space —Space outside of the dura mater of the brain and the spinal cord.

Epidurography —X-ray examination of the spinal column after injecting a radiopaque substance into the epidural space.

Epifascial —Upon a fascia.

Epifolliculitis —Inflammation of the hair follicles of the scalp.

Epigaster —Hindgut. An embryonic structure developing into the large intestine.

Epigastralgia —Pain in the epigastrium.

Epigastric —Pertaining to the epigastrium.

Epigastric reflex — Contraction of the upper portion of the rectus abdominis muscle on scratching the skin of the epigastric region.

Epigastrium —The upper and middle part of the abdomen about the xiphisternum.

Epigastrius —Unequal conjoined twins, the smaller child being attached to the larger one in the epigastric region.

Epigastrocele —Hernia in the epigastrium.

Epigastrorrhaphy —Suture of an abdominal wound in the epigastric region.

Epigenesis —The theory that the development of the parts of an organism occurs by a process of progressive development from the simple to complex structures through the utilization of cells.

Epiglottic —Epiglottidean.

Epiglottidean —Pertaining to the epiglottis.

Epiglottidectomy —Excision of the epiglottis.

Epiglottiditis —Epiglottitis. Inflammation of the epiglottis.

Epiglottis —A thin lidlike cartilaginous structure covering the entrance of the larynx during swallowing and thus preventing the food from entering the air passage.

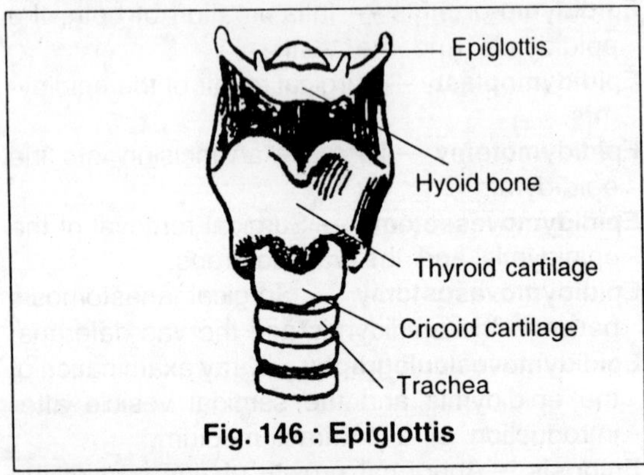

Fig. 146 : Epiglottis

Epiglottitis —Inflammation of epiglottis.

Epignathus —Unequal conjoined twins, the smaller child being attached to the larger one at the lower jaw.

Epihyal —Above the hyoid arch.

Epihyoid —Upon the hyoid bone.

Epikeratoprosthesis —A contact lens attached to the corneal stroma to replace the epithelium.

Epilamellar —Upon or above a basement membrane.

Epilate —To remove the hair by the roots.

Epilating —Removing the hair.

Epilation —Removal of the hair by the roots.

Epilatory —Depilatory. Pertaining to the removal of the hair, or that which removes the hair.

Epilemma —Endoneurium.

Epilepsia partialis continua —Continuous seizures involving a limited part of the body and lasting for a few hours to some days.

Epilepsy —A recurrent paroxysmal disorder of the brain function characterized by sudden attacks of unconsciousness of short duration with or without convulsions, without known causes in the majority of cases.

Cursive epilepsy — Epilepsy characterized by running.

Focal epilepsy —Epilepsy in which the seizures are local or one sided.

Generalized epilepsy —Epilepsy in which the seizures are generalized, they may be generalized from the beginning or may become generalized after a local onset.

Grand mal or major epilepsy —Epilepsy which is preceded by an aura and characterized by sudden loss of consciousness immediately followed by generalized convulsions.

Idopathic epilepsy — Epilepsy of unknown cause.

Jacksonian epilepsy — Epilepsy in which the convulsions start in certain group of muscles of one side of the body and then spread throughout the whole body.

Myoclonic epilepsy — A slowly progressive hereditary epilepsy beginning in the childhood in which there are clonic contractions of some muscles, especially those of the extremities, between the seizures.

Nocturnal epilepsy — Epilepsy occurring only during sleep, the symptoms of which are similar to those of grand mal epilepsy.

Petit mal or minor epilepsy —Epilepsy occurring especially in children in which there are no convulsions but a sudden momentary unconsciousness.

Photogenic epilepsy — Epileptic convulsions produced by intermittent flash of lights into the eyes.

Post-traumatic epilepsy —Recurrent convulsions occurring after head injury.

Reflex epilepsy — Epileptic convulsions occurring in response to sensory stimuli.

Sensory epilepsy —The epilepsy manifested by the hallucinations of sight, smell or taste.

Temporal lobe epilepsy — Epilepsy occurring due to disease of the temporal lobe of the brain in which there is impaired consciousness associated with behavioral changes and antisocial acts.

Tonic epilepsy —Epileptic convulsions characterized by generalized rigidity.

Epileptic —1. Pertaining to epilepsy. 2. The person suffering from epilepsy.

Epileptiform —Like epilepsy.

Epileptogenic, Epileptogenous —Causing epileptoid convulsions.

Epileptoid —Epileptiform. Resembling epilepsy.

Epileptology —Study of epilepsy.

Epilesional —Occurring on or introduced on the surface of a lesion.

Epiloia —Tuberous sclerosis.

Epilose —Bald. Hairless.

Epimandibular —Situated upon the lower jaw.

Epimastical —Increasing continuously until eruption occurs, as a fever.

Epimenorrhagia —Menstruation occurring too frequently and excessively.

Epimenorrhea —Menstruation occurring frequently abnormally.

Epimorphosis —The regeneration of a part of an organism by growth at the cut surface.

Epimysiotomy —To incise the sheath of a muscle.

Epimysium —Outermost connective tissue sheath surrounding a skeletal muscle.

Epinephrine —Adrenaline. A hormone secreted by the adrenal medulla, which is a potent stimulator of the sympathetic nervous system, powerful vasopressor, vasoconstrictor, increasing the blood pressure, stimulating cardiac muscle, accelerating the heart rate, increasing the cardiac output and bronchiodilator.

Epinephrinemia —Presence of epinephrine in the blood.

Epinephritis —Inflammation of the adrenal gland.

Epinephroma —Hypernephroma. A lipomatoid tumor of the kidney.

Epinephros —Suprarenal or adrenal gland.

Epineural —Situated upon a neural arch.

Epineurial —Pertaining to the epineurium.

Epineurium —The connective tissue sheath of a nerve.

Epiotic —Situated above the ear.

Epipastic —Usable as a dusting powder.

Epipericardial —Upon the pericardium.

Epipharynx —Rhinopharynx. Nasal portion of the pharynx.

Epiphenomenon —The occurrence of an exceptional or accidental symptom in the course of a disease, which is not related to the disease.

Epiphora —Overflow of tears due to excess secretion of tears or to obstruction of the lacrimal duct.

Epiphrenic, Epiphrenal — Upon or above the diaphragm.

Epiphylaxis —The increase of defensive powers of the body.

Epiphyseal —Epiphysial. Pertaining to or of the nature of an epiphysis.

Epiphyseolysis — Epiphysiolysis. Separation of an epiphysis.

Epiphyseopathy —Any disease of an epiphysis.

Epiphysial —Epiphyseal.

Epiphysiodesis —1. Premature union of the epiphysis with the diaphysis, resulting in cessation of bony growth. 2. To destroy an epiphysis partially or totally by an operation.

Epiphysis —1. The end of a long bone which is wider than the shaft and separated from it by a cartilaginous disk. 2. Part of a bone formed from a secondary center of ossification, commonly found at the ends of long bones or at the margins of flat bones. see fig 116.

Epiphysitis —Inflammation of an epiphysis, or of the cartilage joining the epiphysis to the shaft of a long bone.

Epipial —Situated above or upon the pia mater.

Epiplocele —Hernia containing omentum.

Epiploenterocele —Hernia containing omentum and intestine.

Epiploic —Pertaining to the omentum.

Epiploic foramen —The opening between the greater and lesser cavities of the peritoneum.

Epiploitis —Inflammation of the omentum.

Epiplomerocele —Femoral hernia containing omentum.

Epiplomphalocele —Umbilical hernia containing omentum.

Epiploon —The omentum.

Epiplopexy —Suturing of the omentum to the anterior abdominal wall.

Epiplorrhaphy —Omentorrhapy. Suturing of the omentum.

Epiplosarcomphalocele — Epiplomphalocele.

Epiploscheocele —A scrotal hernia containing omentum.

Epipygus —An extra limb attached to the buttocks.

Episclera —Outermost layer of the sclera of the eye.

Episcleral —1. Pertaining to the episclera. 2. Overlying the sclera of the eye.

Episcleritis —Inflammation of the episclera.

Episioelytrorrhaphy —To narrow the vagina and the vulva by suturing.

Episioperineoplasty — Repair of the vulva and the perineum by plastic surgery.

Episioperineorrhaphy — Suturing of the vulva and the perineum.

Episioplasty —Plastic surgery of the vulva.

Episiorrhaphy —1. To sew the labia majora. 2. Suture of a lacerated perineum.

Episiostenosis —Narrowing of the opening of the vulva.

Episiotomy —To make an incision into the perineum and vagina at the end of the second stage of labor to facilitate the delivery and to avoid the laceration of the perineum.

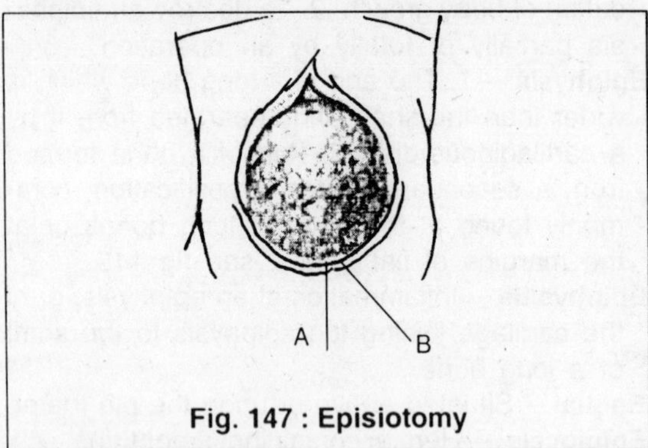

Fig. 147 : Episiotomy

(A) Median incision

(B) Mediolateral incision

Episode —An event or happening or a topic.

Epispadias —Anaspadias. Congenital opening of the urethra anywhere on the dorsum of the penis.

Epispastic —A blistering agent.

Epispinal —Upon the vertebral column or spinal cord.

Episplenitis —Inflammation of the capsule of the spleen.

Epistasis —Suppression of any discharge.

Epistasy —Epistasis.

Epistatic —Pertaining to epistasis.

Epistaxis —Nosebleed. Hemorrhage from the nose.

Epistemophilia —Interest in gaining knowledge.

Episternal —Situated above the sternum.

Episternum —Manubrium sterni. Upper portion of the sternum.

Epistropheus —Axis.

Epitendineum —The fibrous sheath covering a tendon.

Epitenon —Epitendineum.

Epithalamus —The uppermost part of the diencephalon of the brain just superior and posterior to the thalamus including the pineal body, trigonum habenulae, habenula, and the habenular commissure.

Epithalaxia —Desquamation of the epithelium, especially that of the intestine.

Epithelia —Plural of epithelium.

Epithelial —Pertaining to or composed of epithelium.

Epithelial casts — Aggregation of the desquamated renal epithelial cells and assuming the shape of the renal tubules.

Epithelial cells —The cells situated on a membrane, called basement membrane, packed together, irregular in shape, having a single nucleus and may be with cilia or without cilia.

Epithelialization —Healing of a wound by the growth of epithelium over it.

Epithelialize —To cover with epithelium.

Epitheliitis —Inflammation of the epithelium.

Epithelioblastoma —A tumor of the epithelial cell.

Epitheliofibril —Tonofibril.

Epitheliogenic, Epitheliogenetic —Caused by the growth of epithelium.

Epithelioglandular — Concerning with the epithelial cells of a gland.

Epithelioid —Resembling epithelium.

Epitheliolysis —The destruction of epithelial cells by epitheliolysin.

Epitheliolytic —Destructive to epithelium.

Epithelioma —A malignant tumor of the epithelium.

Epitheliomatous —Pertaining to an epithelioma.

Epitheliopathy —Any disease of the epithelium.

Epitheliosis —The growth of the conjunctival epithelium into trachomas.

Epitheliotropic —Having affinity for epithelium.

Epithelium —The layer of cells covering the internal and external surface of the body, including the lining of the vessels, ducts, canals and small cavities and making up the glands. It consists of cells of different shapes packed together with a little intercellular substance. The cells rest on a membrane. The functions of epithelium are of protection, absorption, secretion, excretion, transport, sensory reception and lubrication etc. It is classified according to the number of layers and shape of the cells as follows.

Ciliated epithelium — The epithelium bearing vibrating hairlike protuberances at its free border.

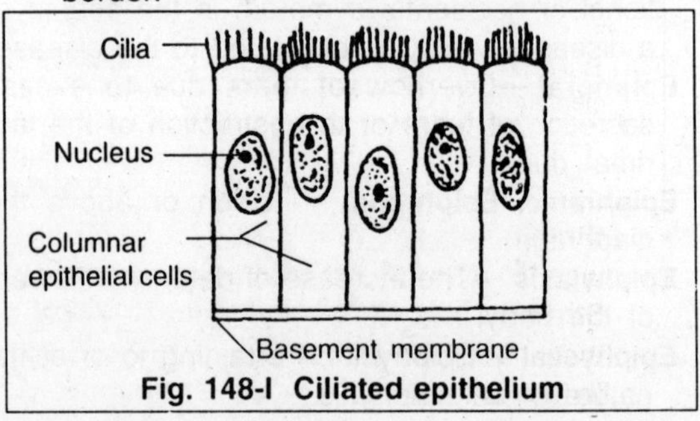

Fig. 148-I Ciliated epithelium

Columnar epithelium — Epithelium consisting of the cells shaped like pillars.

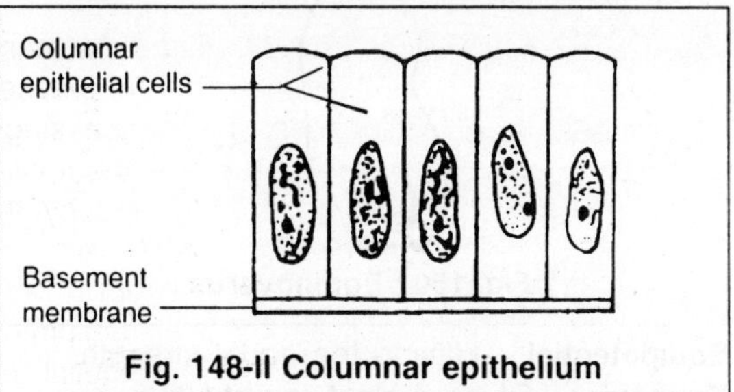

Fig. 148-II Columnar epithelium

Cuboidal epithelium —Epithelium consisting of the cube-shaped cells.

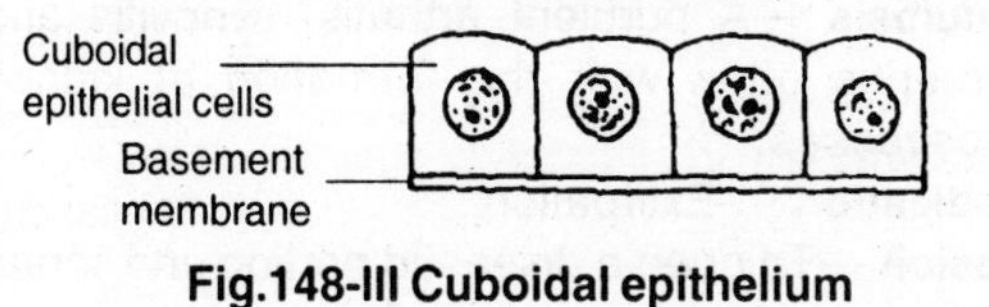

Fig.148-III Cuboidal epithelium

Germinal epithelium —Thickened peritoneal epithelium of the embryo giving rise to the seminiferous tubules of the testes and surface layer of the ovary.

Glandular epithelium —Epithelium consisting of the secreting cells.

Pigmented epithelium —Epithelium containing pigment granules.

Pseudostratified epithelium — Epithelium in which the bases of the cells rest on the basement membrane but the distal ends of some of the cells do not reach the surface. The nuclei of the cells lie at different levels so the epithelium looks as stratified, i.e., multilayered.

Simple epithelium — The epithelium composed of a single layer of cells.

Squamous epithelium — Epithelium consisting of the flattened plate like cells.

Fig. 148-IV Squamous epithelium

Stratified epithelium —Epithelium consisting of more than one layer of cells.

Stratified squamous epithelium —The epithelium composed of more than one layer of flattened cells.

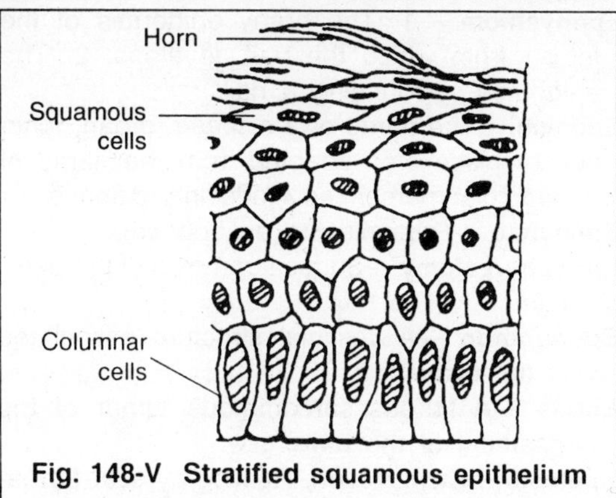

Fig. 148-V Stratified squamous epithelium

Transitional epithelium —A form of stratified epithelium lining the hollow organs, the cells of which are adjustable to the mechanical changes occurring in the organs such as stretching and contracting.

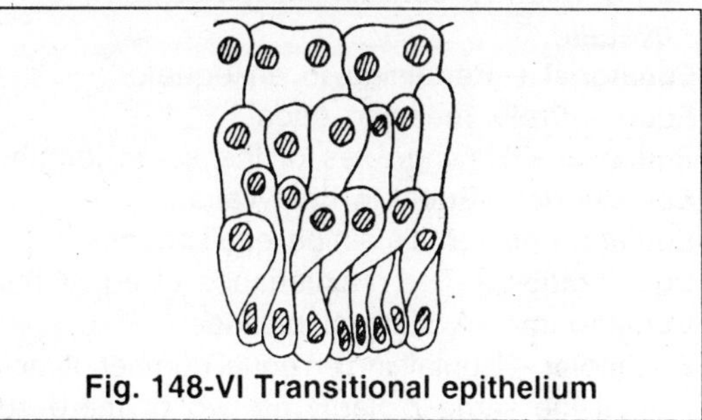

Fig. 148-VI Transitional epithelium

Epithelization — Epithelialization.

Epithem —An agent used externally such as a poultice, but not a plaster or ointment.

Epithesis —Surgical correction of a deformity.

Epithet —Characterizing name.

Epitrichial —Pertaining to the epitrichium.

Epitrichium —Periderm. Superficial layers of the epidermis of the fetus.

Epitrochlea —The inner condyle of the humerus bone.

Epitrochlear —Pertaining to the inner condyle of the humerus bone.

Epitympanic —Above or in the upper part of the tympanic cavity.

Epitympanum —The area above the tympanic membrane.

Epityphlitis —Inflammation of the tissues around the cecum.

Epizoic —Living as a parasite on the skin.

Epizoon, plural **Epizoa** —An animal parasite living on the body surface.

Eponychia —Infection of the proximal nail fold.

Eponychium —1. The horny epidermis of the fetus from which the nail develops. 2. The epidermis surrounding a nail.

Eponym —The name of a disease, organ, function or place etc., adapted from the name of a particular person as Hodgkin's disease.

Eponymic —Pertaining to an eponym.

Epoophorectomy —Surgical removal of the parovarium.

Epoophoron —A vestigial structure associated with the ovary.

Epulis —A fibrous sarcomatous tumor of the periosteum of the lower jaw.

Epulosis —Cicatrization. Healing by scar formation.

Epulotic —Promoting cicatrization.

Equation —An expression of equality between two parts.

Equator —An imaginary line encircling a globular body midway between its poles e.g., of the eyeball.

Equatorial —Pertaining to an equator.

Equi- —Prefix meaning equal.

Equiaxial —Having axes of the same length.

Equicaloric —Equal in heat value.

Equilibrating —Maintaining equilibrium.

Equilibration —The maintenance of equilibrium.

Equilibrium —A state of balance.

Equimolar —Containing an equal number of moles or of the same molarity as two or more substances.

Equimolecular —Containing an equal number of molecules.

Equine —Pertaining to or derived from the horse.

Equinovalgus —Talipes equinovalgus. A deformity of the foot in which the heel and the foot are everted, i.e. turned outward so that the patient walks on the inner side of the foot.

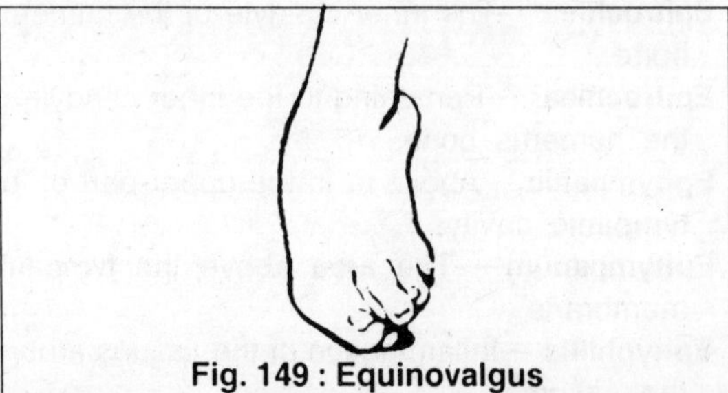

Fig. 149 : Equinovalgus

Equinovarus —Talipes equinovarus. A deformity of the foot in which the heel and the foot are inverted, i.e. turned inward so that the patient walks on the outer side of the foot.

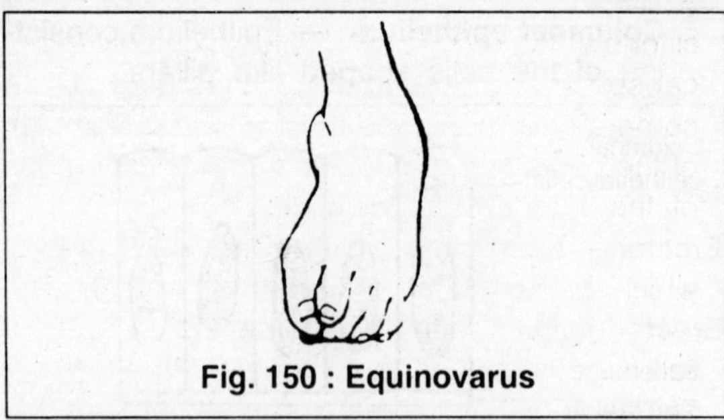

Fig. 150 : Equinovarus

Equipotential —Having the equal strength.

Equitoxic —Of equivalent toxicity.

Equivalence —The quality of being equivalent.

Equivalent —Equal in power or value.

Equulosis —A purulent arthritis, synovitis and enteritis often with the formation of kidney abscesses.

Eradication —Extirpation.

Erasion —To open a diseased portion and scraping away the diseased tissue.

Erben's reflex —Slowing of the pulse rate on bending the head and the trunk forward forcibly.

Erb's paralysis —Paralysis of the muscles of the shoulder and upper arm due to involvement of the cervical roots of the 5th and 6th spinal nerves. The arm hangs loosely, the hand rotates inward and the movements are lost.

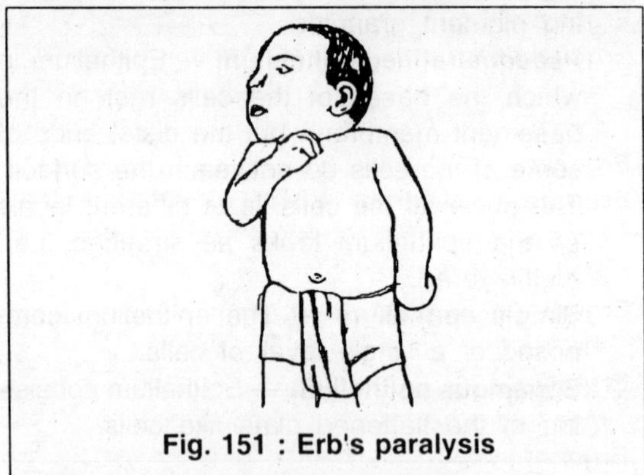

Fig. 151 : Erb's paralysis

Erb's point —The point at the side of the neck 2 to 3 cm. above the clavicle and infront of the transverse process of the sixth cervical vertebra, which on electrical stimulation causes the various muscles to contract.

Erectile —Capable of being erect.

Erectile tissue —Vascular tissue which when filled with blood, becomes erect or rigid as the clitoris, penis or nipples.

Erection —The condition of rigidity and elevation as observed in the penis of the male and in the clitoris of the female, due to sexual excitement caused by engorgement with blood of the corpora cavernosa and the corpus spongiosum of the penis of the male, and corpus cavernosa of the clitoris of the female.

Erector —A structure which erects as a muscle which raises a part.

Erector spinae reflex — Dorsal reflex, lumbar reflex. Irritation of the skin over the erector spinae muscles causing contractions of the muscles of the neck.

Eremophobia —Dread of being alone.

Erethism —Excessive sensibility to stimuli.

Erethismic —Erethitic. Pertaining to or causing erethism.

Erethisophrenia —Exaggerated mental excitability.

Erethistic —Erethismic. Exciting.

Erethitic —Erethismic.

Ereuthophobia —Morbid fear of blushing.

Ergasia —A mentality towards the activity.

Ergasiomania —An abnormal desire to be busy at work.

Ergasiophobia —Abnormal dislike for any work or for taking responsibility.

Ergasthenia —Weakness caused by over work.

Ergastic —Having latent energy.

Ergocalciferol —Vitamin D_2.

Ergodynamograph —An instrument for recording both, the degree of muscular force and the amount of work done by muscular contraction.

Ergogenic —Tending to increase the work.

Ergograph —An apparatus for recording the contractions of the muscles and measuring the work done in muscular action.

Ergographia —Pertaining to the ergograph and the record made by it.

Ergometer —Dynamometer. An apparatus for measuring the amount of work done by a person.

Ergonomics —The science dealing with how to fit a job according to man's anatomical, physiological and psychological conditions, in such a way that the job can be performed and human energy may be utilized efficiently.

Ergophobia —Morbid fear of working.

Ergostat —A machine used for measuring the work done by a contracting muscle.

Ergosterol —Precursor of vitamin D_2.

Ergotherapy —Treatment of diseases by physical works.

Ergotism —Chronic poisoning produced by ingestion of ergot.

Erode —To wear away.

Erodent —A caustic drug.

Erogenous —Erotogenic. Causing sexual excitement.

Erogenous zone —Any part of the body causing sexual excitement on touching or stroking it.

Erose —Denoting an irregularly notched or indented margin used especially in reference to bacterial colonies.

Erosion —An eating away or the destruction gradually of the tissue e.g. dental erosion in which there is loss of substance of a tooth by chemical process, or cervical erosion in which there is destruction of the squamous epithelium of the vaginal portion of the cervix of the uterus as a result of irritation by infection.

Erosive —Causing erosion.

Erotic —Pertaining to sexual passion.

Eroticism —Sexual desire.

Anal eroticism —Sexual desire arising during defecation.

Auto eroticism —Sexual desire derived from masturbation.

Oral eroticism — Sexual pleasure derived from the use of the mouth.

Erotism —Eroticism.

Erotization —A process of rendering an object or action sexually exciting.

Erotogenesis —The production of sexual excitement.

Erotogenic —Producing sexual excitement.

Erotology —The study of love and its manifestations.

Erotomania —Exaggerated sexual behavior.

Erotomonomania — Erotomania.

Erotopathia —Any abnormal sex impulse.

Erotopathic —Pertaining to erotopathy.

Erotopathy —Any abnormality of the sexual impulse.

Erotophobia —Morbid fear of sexual love.

Erratic —Eccentric. Wandering.

Errhine —Causing increased nasal discharge.

Error —A defect.

Erubescence —A reddening of the skin.

Eructation —Ejection of wind from the stomach through the mouth, usually with a characteristic sound; belching.

Eruption —1. Skin rash accompanying some diseases such as measles, resulting from ingestion of certain drugs such as iodides or occurring after an injection of a serum. 2. The breaking of a tooth through the gum.

Eruptive —Pertaining to breaking out.

Erysipelas —A contagious disease of the skin and subcutaneous tissues due to infection with Streptococcus pyogenes characterized by redness and swelling of the skin with fever and other systemic symptoms.

Erysipelatous —Pertaining to or of the nature of erysipelas.

Erysipeloid —Resembling erysipelas.

Erysipelotoxin —The toxin produced by the bacteria Streptococcus pyogenes, which causes erysipelas.

Erysiphake —A small spoon-shaped instrument used to remove the lens in cataract surgery.

Erythema —Abnormal redness of the skin due to congestion of the blood capillaries.

Erythema ab igne — Erythema due to exposure to radiant heat.

Erythema annulare — Erythema that is ring shaped.

Fig.152 Erythema annulare

Erythema diffuse — Erythema occurring throughout the body.

Erythema hyperaemicum —Erythema caused by cold or artificial heat as by hot water bottle or electrical pad.

Erythema induratum — Chronic vasculitis of the skin occurring on the calves of young women.

Erythema infectiosum —A mildly contagious form of erythema occurring in children between the ages of 4 and 12 years marked by rose-colored eruption.

Erythema intertrigo — Erythema occurring due to rubbing of the opposite sides of the skin.

Erythema marginatum —Erythema with the central faded area and the elevated margins.

Erythema multiforme —Erythema having many shapes.

Erythema nodosum —An inflammatory skin disease marked by tender red nodules on the legs associated usually with rheumatism but may also be caused by drugs or food poisoning.

Erythema nodosum leprosum —A form of lepra reaction occurring in lepromatous persons as tender inflammed subcutaneous nodules.

Erythema punctate — Erythema occurring in minute points.

Erythema toxic or venenatum —Generalized erythema caused by the administration of a drug, or due to bacterial toxins or other toxic substances, or localized erythema by contact with a toxic substance.

Erythematic, Erythematous —Pertaining to or characterized by erythema.

Erythemogenic —Causing erythema.

Erythralgia —Erythromelalgia. Painful redness of the skin.

Erythrasma —Reddish-brown patches in the major folds of the skin such as axilla and the groin caused by the infection of Corynebacterium minutissimum.

Erythredema —Acrodynia.

Erythremia —Polycythemia vera. An excess of red blood cells with increased hemoglobin concentration.

Erythrism —Redness of the hair and beard with ruddy complexion.

Erythristic —Rufous. Having red hair and beard with ruddy complexion.

Erythro- —Prefix meaning red.

Erythroblast —Any form of nucleated red blood cell.

Erythroblastemia —Presence of of erythroblasts in the blood in excessive number.

Erythroblastic —Pertaining to the erythroblasts.

Erythroblastoma —A tumor composed of the nucleated red blood cells.

Erythroblastopenia — Abnormal deficiency of erythroblasts in the blood.

Erythroblastosis —The condition caused by the presence of erythroblasts in the blood.

Erythroblastosis fetalis — Hemolytic anemia of the new born due to transmission of the antibody formed in the mother, through placenta against the fetus' red blood cells, associated with jaundice, enlargement of the liver and spleen, and generalized edema (hydrops fetalis).

Erythroblastotic —Pertaining to erythroblastosis, especially erythroblastosis fetalis.

Erythrocatalysis — Phagocytosis of the red blood cells.

Erythrochloropia —Ability to recognize the red and green color but not the blue or yellow color.

Erythrochromia —A red coloration or staining.

Erythroclasis —The breaking up of the red blood cells into pieces.

Erythroclastic —Destructive to the red blood cells.

Erythrocyanosis —Bluish discoloration of the skin occurring especially in females due to cold.

Erythrocytapheresis — Withdrawal of the blood, separation and retention of red blood cells and to retransfuse the remainder into the donor.

Erythrocyte —A mature i.e. non-nucleated red blood cell or corpuscle containing hemoglobin.

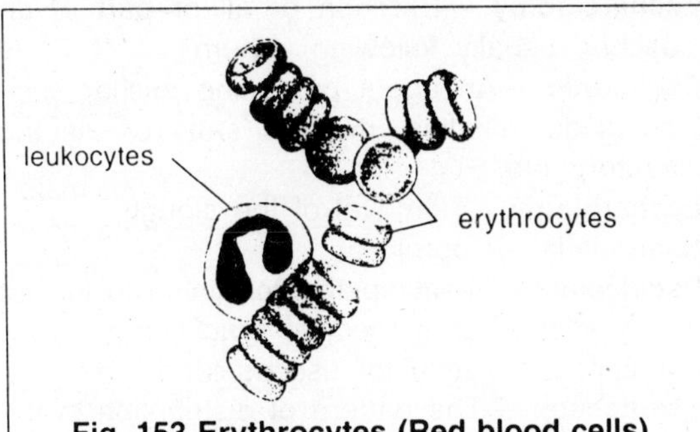

Fig. 153 Erythrocytes (Red blood cells)

Achromatic erythrocyte —Colorless erythrocyte due to dissolution of the hemoglobin.

Basophilic erythrocyte —Erythrocyte which stains blue indicating the presence of basophilic material.

Crenated erythrocyte — Serrated erythrocyte.

Hypochromic erythrocyte —Erythrocyte containing less than normal concentration of hemoglobin so appearing palor than normal.

Immature erythrocyte —Any erythroblast.

Normochromic erythrocyte —The erythrocyte of normal color with a normal concentration of hemoglobin.

Orthochromatic erythrocyte —Erythrocyte that stains with acid stains only and the cytoplasm appearing pink.

Polychromatic erythrocyte —Erythrocyte that stains with blue combined with pink stains.

Erythrocyte sedimentation rate —It is a test to determine the speed at which the erythrocytes settle down. In this test an anticoagulant is added to the blood to be tested and the blood is then placed in a long narrow tube and the distance the erythrocytes fall in one hour is noted which is the erythrocyte sedimentation rate (E.S.R.).

Erythrocythemia —An increase in the number of red blood cells in the blood.

Erythrocytic —Pertaining to or of the nature of erythrocytes.

Erythrocytoblast — Erythroblast.

Erythrocytolysin —Anything breaking up the red blood cells.

Erythrocytolysis — Dissolution of the red blood cells and escape of the hemoglobin.

Erythrocytometer —An instrument for counting the red blood cells.

Erythrocytopenia — Erythropenia. Decreased number of red blood cells in the blood.

Erythrocytopoiesis — Erythropoiesis. Formation of red blood cells.

Erythrocytorrhexis —The breaking up of the red blood cells with the escape of round shiny granules and the small pieces of the cells into the plasma.

Erythrocytoschisis —The breaking up of red blood cells into small platelet-like bodies.

Erythrocytosis —Abnormal increase in the number of red blood cells in the blood due to some systemic disease.

Erythrocyturia —Presence of red blood cells in the urine.

Erythrodegenerative — Pertaining to or characterized by degeneration of the red blood cells.

Erythroderma —Abnormal redness of the skin over widespread areas of the body.

Erythrodermatitis — Erythroderma.

Erythrodermia —Erythroderma.

Erythrodontia —Reddish-brown pigmentation of the teeth.

Erythrogenesis —The production of red blood cells.

Erythrogenic —1. Producing red blood cells. 2. Causing erythema.

Erythroid —1. Of a red color or reddish. 2.Pertaining to the erythrocytes.

Erythrokeratodermia —A reddening and hardening of the skin.

Erythrokinetics —Study of the rate of production of red blood cells in number and their life span.

Erythroleukemia —A malignant tumor of both, the red and white blood cells forming tissues.

Erythroleukosis —Abnormal increase of the red blood cells and the granular white blood cells in the blood.

Erythrolysin —Hemolysin. Erythrocytolysin. An agent causing erythrolysis or dissolution of red blood cells.

Erythrolysis —Erythrocytolysis. Dissolution of red blood cells.

Erythromania —Redness of the face and neck which is not controllable.

Erythromelalgia —Redness with increased skin temperature and burning pain affecting the exremities, especially the feet due to vasodilation.

Erythromelia —Painless erythema of the extensor surfaces of the extremities.

Erythron —The total mass of the circulating red blood cells and the tissue from which they are derived.

Erythroneocytosis — Presence of immature red blood cells in the peripheral blood.

Erythroparasite —A red blood cell parasite.

Erythropathy —Any disease of the red blood cells.

Erythropenia —Deficiency in the number of red blood cells.

Erythrophage —A phagocyte that ingests the red blood cells.

Erythrophagia —Destruction of red blood cells by phagocytes.

Erythrophil —Erythrophilic. Staining readily with red dyes.

Erythrophile —An agent that readily stains red.

Erythrophilic —Erythrophil.

Erythrophilous —Erythrophile.

Erythrophobia —1. Morbid fear of becoming red. 2. Aversion to red color.

Erythrophose —A pigment-bearing cell containing granules of a red pigment.

Erythropia, Erythropsia — The condition in which the things appear to be red.

Erythroplakia —A red, velvety, plaquelike lesion of the mucous membrane which is often converted into malignant growth, i.e. cancer.

Erythroplasia —A condition of the mucous membranes characterized by the appearance of the erythematous lesions.

Erythropoiesis —The formation of red blood cells.

Erythropoietic —Pertaining to the formation of the red blood cells.

Erythropoietin —A hormone secreted by the kidney which stimulates the formation of red blood cells.

Erythroprosopalgia —A nervous disorder characterized by redness and pain in the face.

Erythropsia —A visual defect in which all the things look red.

Erythropsin —Rhodopsin. Pigment in the outer part of the rods of the retina.

Erythrorrhexis — Erythrocytorrhexis.

Erythrosis —A reddish-purple discoloration of the skin and mucous membrane as seen in polycythemia vera.

Erythrostasis —Accumulation of red blood cells in the blood vessels due to obstruction in the blood flowing.

Erythrotoxin —An exotoxin attacking the red blood cells.

Erythruria —Excretion of red urine.

Escape – To get free.

Eschar —A slough produced by burn, cauterization or by application of a corrosive substance.

Escharectomy —Excision of all or part of an eschar, usually following a burn.

Escharotic —An agent producing eschar such as acids, alkalies, metallic salts or electric cautery etc.

Escharotomy —Removal of the slough.

Eschrolalia —Coprolalia.

Esculapian —Aesculapian. Pertaining to the art of medicine, or a medical practitioner.

Esculent —Suitable for use as food.

Escutcheon —The pattern of distribution of the pubic hair which is different in the male and female.

-esis — -Suffix indicating a condition, action or process.

Esmarch's bandage —1. A triangular bandage. 2. A rubber bandage used to control bleeding.

Eso- —Prefix indicating within.

Esodeviation —1. Esophoria. 2. Esotropia.

Esodic —Afferent, centripetal.

Esogastritis —Inflammation of the mucous membrane of the stomach.

Esophagalgia —Pain in the esophagus.

Esophageal —Pertaining to the esophagus.

Esophageal apoplexy —A hematoma formed within the walls of the esophagus.

Esophagectasia, Esophagectasis —Dilatation of the esophagus.

Esophagectomy —Excision of a part of the esophagus.

Esophagi —Plural of esophagus.

Esophagism —Spasm of the esophagus causing dysphagia.

Esophagismus —Spasm of the esophagus.

Esophagitis —Inflammation of the esophagus.

Esophagobronchial —Pertaining to the esophagus and the bronchus.

Esophagocardioplasty — Repair of the esophagus and the cardiac end of the stomach by plastic surgery.

Esophagocele —Hernia of the esophagus.

Esophagocoloplasty — Excision of a portion of the esophagus and to replace it by a segment of the colon.

Esophagoduodenostomy — To join the esophagus with the duodenum.

Esophagodynia —Pain in the esophagus.

Esophagoenterostomy —To make a connection between the esophagus and the intestine, after excision of the stomach.

Esophagoesophagostomy — Formation of communication between two remote parts of the esophagus.

Esophagogastrectomy — Excision of all or part of the stomach, and the esophagus.

Esophagogastric —Pertaining to the esophagus and the stomach.

Esophagogastroanastomosis —The joining of the esophagus with the stomach.

Esophagogastroduodenoscopy EGD —Examination of the esophagus, stomach and duodenum by an endoscope.

Esophagogastromyotomy — Esophagomyotomy.

Esophagogastroplasty — Repair of the esophagus and the stomach by plastic surgery.

Esophagogastroscopy — Inspection of the esophagus and the stomach by using an endoscope.

Esophagogastrostomy —To make a connection between the esophagus and the stomach.

Esophagogram —Esophagram.

Esophagography —X-ray examination of the esophagus.

Esophagojejunostomy — Anastomosis of the esophagus to the jejunum.

Esophagology —Study of the structure, functions and diseases of the esophagus.

Esophagomalacia —Softening of the walls of the esophagus.

Esophagomycosis —Fungus infection of the esophagus.

Esophagomyotomy —To make a surgical incision into the muscular coat of the esophagus.

Esophagoplasty —Repair of the esophagus by plastic surgery.

Esophagoplication —Reduction of esophageal dilatation by infolding its walls.

Esophagoptosia, Esophagoptosis —Prolapse of the esophagus.

Esophagorespiratory — Pertaining to or communication of the esophagus with the respiratory tract.

Esophagoscope —A type of endoscope for examination of the esophagus.

Esophagoscopy —Examination of the esophagus by using an endoscope.

Esophagospasm —Spasm of the esophagus.

Esophagostenosis —Narrowing of the esophagus.

Esophagostomy —To make an opening into the esophagus.

Esophagotome —An instrument for forming a fistula of the esophagus.

Esophagotomy —To make an incision into the esophagus by surgery.

Esophagotracheal —Pertaining to the esophagus and the trachea or a communication between the two.

Esophagram —An x-ray film of the esophagus taken after swallowing radiopaque substance such as barium sulfate.

Esophagus —A musculomembranous canal about 9 inches long extending from the pharynx to the stomach, which carries the swallowed food from the mouth to the stomach.

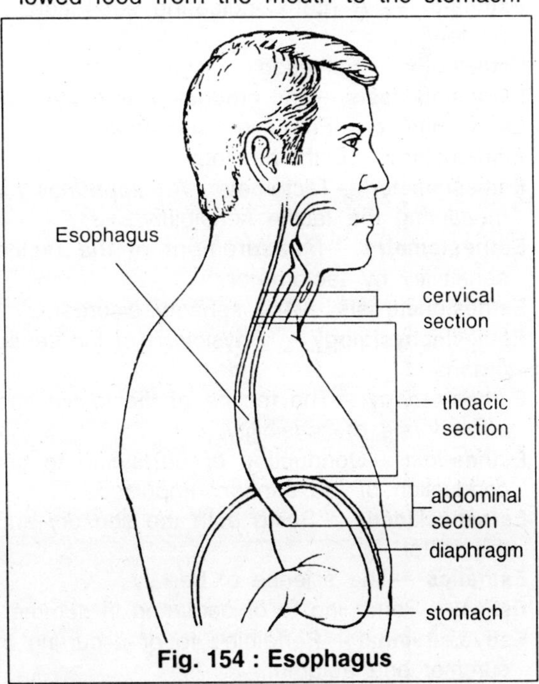

Fig. 154 : Esophagus

Esophoria —Deviation of the visual axis inward or turning of an eye inward.

Esophoric —Pertaining to esophoria.
Esotropia —Esophoria.
Esotropic —Pertaining to or marked by esotropia.
Esquinancea —Feeling of suffocation caused by an inflammatory swelling as tonsillitis in the throat.
ESR —Erythrocyte sedimentation rate.
-ess —Suffix denoting female sex.
Essence —The extracted qualities of a drug.
Essential —1. Pertaining to an essence. 2. Having no obvious external cause, idiopathic. 3. Indispensible but supplied in the diet as essential fatty acids.
Ester —A compound formed by the combination of an organic acid with an alcohol with the elimination of water.
Esterification —Combination of an organic acid with an alcohol to form an ester.
Esterify —To combine with an alcohol with the elimination of water, forming an ester.
Esterize —To convert into an ester.
Estervation —Sexual excitement.
Esthematology —Science of the sense organs and their functions.
Esthesia —Sensation, feeling or a disease affecting sensation.
Esthesic —Pertaining to esthesia.
Esthesio- — A prefix indicating sensation or perception.
Esthesiodic —Esthesodic.
Esthesiogenesis —The production of sensation.
Esthesiogenic —Producing sensation.
Esthesiology —Esthematology.
Esthesiometer —Tactometer. An apparatus for measuring the tactile sensibility.
Esthesiometry —Measurement of the tactile sensibility by tactometer.
Esthesioneurosis —Any sensory disorder.
Esthesiophysiology — Physiology of the sense organs.
Esthesioscopy —The testing of the tactile and other forms of sensibility.
Esthesodic —Conducting or pertaining to the conduction of the sensory impulses.
Estheticokinetic —Being both the sensory and the motor.
Esthetics —The science of beauty.
Estival —Pertaining to or occurring in summer.
Estivoautumnal —Pertaining to or occurring in summer and autumn.
Estradiol —A steroid produced by the ovary and having the qualities of estrogen.
Estrin —Estrogen.
Estrinization —Production of the cellular changes in the epithelium of the vagina characteristic of estrogen stimulation.
Estrogen —A female sex hormone produced by the ovary which is responsible for the development of the secondary sexual characteristics.
Estrogenic —Producing or pertaining to estrogen.
Estrone —An estrogenic hormone found in the urine of pregnant woman.
Estuarium —Vapor bath.
Etat —A condition or state.
Etat crible —Perforations of the Peyer's patches of the intestines in typhoid fever.
Ethanol —Ethyl alcohol.
Ether asphyxia —Suffocation occurring during ether anesthetization.
Ethereal —Pertaining to or made with ether.
Etherification —Conversion of alcohol into ether.
Etherization —To induce anesthesia by using ether.
Etherize —To anesthetize by means of ether.
Etheromania —Addiction to use of ether.
Ethical —Pertaining to ethics.
Ethics —A system of morals.
Ethmo- —A prefix denoting ethmoid bone.
Ethmocarditis —Inflammation of the connective tissue of the heart.
Ethmocephalus —A fetus with imperfect head, eyes united and a rudimentary nose.
Ethmocranial —Pertaining to the ethmoid bone and the cranium.
Ethmofrontal —Pertaining to the ethmoid and frontal bones.
Ethmoid —Sieve-like, cribriform.
Ethmoidal —Pertaining to the ethmoid bone.
Ethmoidectomy —Excision of ethmoidal cells or of a portion of the ethmoid bone.
Ethmoiditis —Inflammation of the ethmoid bone or ethmoid sinuses.
Ethmoidotomy —To make an incision into the ethmoid sinus.
Ethmolacrimal —Pertaining to the ethmoid and lacrimal bones.
Ethmomaxillary —Pertaining to the ethmoid and the maxillary bones.
Ethmonasal —Pertaining to the ethmoid and the nasal bones.
Ethmopalatal —Pertaining to the ethmoid and the palate bones.
Ethmosphenoid —Pertaining to the ethmoid and sphenoid bones.

Ethmoturbinals —The three— superior, middle and inferior conchae of the ethmoid bone.

Ethmovomerine —Pertaining to the ethmoid and vomer bone.

Ethnic —Pertaining to race.

Ethnobiology —Study of the biological characteristics of various races.

Ethnocentrism —To give more importance to the caretaker rather than considering the patient's condition.

Ethnogerontology —The study of population groups in reference to the age, race, nationality and culture.

Ethnography —The study of the culture of a single society.

Ethnology —The science dealing with different races of men.

Ethologist —Specialist in ethology.

Ethology —The scientific study of animal behavior.

Ethopharmacology —The study of drug effects on behaviour.

Etiolated —Suffering from etiolation.

Etiolation —To process by which the skin becomes pale due to lack of sunlight.

Etiologic, Etiological — Pertaining to the cause or causes of a disease.

Etiological — Etiologic.

Etiology —The study of the causes of diseases.

Etiopathology —Consideration of the cause of an abnormal state or finding.

Etiotropic —The drug or treatment removing the cause of a disease.

Etymology —The science of the origin and development of words.

Eu- —Prefix meaning normal, good, well, healthy.

Eubiotics —The science of healthy and hygienic living.

Eubolism —Normal metabolism.

Eucapnia —Presence of normal amount of carbon dioxide in the blood.

Euchlorhydria —Presence of the normal amount of free hydrochloric acid in the gastric juice.

Eucholia —Normal condition of the bile.

Euchromatic —Orthochromatic.

Euchromatin —Uncoiled portions of the chromosomes during the interval between two successive cell divisions.

Euchromatopsy —Normal color vision.

Euchylia —Normal condition of the chyle.

Euchymy —A healthy state of the fluids of the body.

Eucorticalism —Normal functioning of the adrenal cortex.

Eucrasia —Condition of normal health.

Eudiaphoresis —Normal secretion of perspiration.

Eudiemorrhysis —Normal flow of blood through the blood capillaries.

Eudiometer —An instrument for testing the purity of air and making analysis of the gases.

Eudipsia —Normal thirst.

Euesthesia —Normal condition of the senses.

Eugenic —Pertaining to eugenics.

Eugenics —The science that deals with the genetic and prenatal effects on the characteristics in the offspring.

Euglycemia —Presence of glucose in the blood in normal amount.

Euglycemic —Normoglycemic.

Eugnosia —Normal ability to produce sensory stimuli.

Eugonic —Pertaining to a luxuriant growth of bacteria.

Eugony —Luxuriant growth.

Euhydration —The state of normal amount of water in the body.

Eukaryon —A complicated nucleus surrounded by a nuclear membrane, a characteristic of the cells of the higher organisms.

Eukaryote —An organism whose cells have a nucleus surrounded by a nuclear membrane.

Eukeratin —Hard keratin present in the hair and nails etc.

Eukinesia —Normal motor function.

Eumelanin —Melanin present in normal amount in the skin.

Eumetria —A normal condition of the nerve impulse so that there is a proper voluntary movement.

Eumorphism —Preservation of the natural form of a cell.

Eunoia —Soundness of the mind.

Eunuch —A castrated male whose testes have been removed, especially before puberty so that male secondary sex characteristics do not develop.

Eunuchism —Condition resulting from complete absence of male sex hormones which may be due to atrophy or removal of the testicles.

Eunuchism pituitary —A condition produced by failure of the anterior lobe of the pituitary gland to secrete gonadotrophic hormones.

Eunuchoid —Having the characteristics of an eunuch.

Eunuchoidism —Deficiency of the testes or of the production of male hormones.

Euosmia —Normal smell.
Eupancreatism —Normal condition of the pancreas.
Eupepsia —Normal digestion.
Eupeptic —Pertaining to normal digestion.
Euphonia —The condition of having a normal clear voice.
Euphoretic —Pertaining to, characterized by or producing euphoria.
Euphoria —A condition of physical and mental good health.
Euphoriant —Euphoretic.
Euplasia —Normal state of cells or tissues.
Euplastic —Readily becoming organized or healing quickly.
Euploid —Having balanced sets of chromosomes.
Euploidy —The condition of having complete sets of chromosomes.
Eupnea —Normal respiration.
Eupraxia —Normal capability of inducing the coordinated movements.
Eupraxic —Having the normal capability of inducing the coordinated movements.
Eurhythmia —Regularity of the pulse.
Eury- —A prefix indicating broad.
Euryblepharon —Sagging of the lateral aspect of the lower eyelid congenitally.
Eurycephalic —Having a broad head.
Eurycephalous —Eurycephalic.
Eurygnathic —Eurygnathous. Having a wide jaw.
Eurygnathism —The condition of having a wide jaw.
Eurygnathous —Eurygnathic.
Euryopic —Wide-eyed.
Euscope —An instrument for showing an enlarged image from a microscope on the screen.
Eusitia —Normal appetite.
Eustachian —Pertaining to the auditory canal.
Eustachianography —X-ray examination of the eustachian tube and middle ear after introduction of a contrast medium.
Eustachian tube —The auditory canal, 3 to 4 cm. long extending from the middle ear to the pharynx.
Eustachitis —Inflammation of the eustachian tube.
Eusthenia —Normal strength.
Eusystole —The normal systole in time and force.
Eusystolic —Pertaining to eusystole.
Eutectic —Easily melted.
Euthanasia —An easy or painless death.
Euthenics —The science dealing with the improvement of a population by regulation of environment.
Eutherapeutic —Having curative properties.
Euthermic —Characterized by proper temperature or promoting warmth.
Euthymia —Mental piece.
Euthymic —Pertaining to or characterized by euthymia.
Euthyroid —Thyroid gland with normal function.
Euthyroidism —A condition in which the thyroid gland is functioning normally.
Eutocia —Normal labor or childbirth.
Eutonia —Feeling healthy.
Eutonic —Normotonic.
Eutrichosis —A normal growth of the healthy hair.
Eutrophia —A state of normal (good) nutrition.
Eutrophic —Pertaining to or characterized by eutrophia.
Eutrophy —Eutrophia.
Evacuant —Purgative.
Evacuate —To empty or to purgate.
Evacuation —1. The act of emptying, especially of the intestines. 2. The material discharged from the intestines, i.e., the stool.
Evacuator —An apparatus for emptying as the intestines, or for irrigating the urinary bladder and removing the calculi.
Evaginate —Pertaining to the protrusion of a part or organ of the body from its normal place.
Evagination —Protrusion of a part or an organ of the body.
Evaluation —1. Investigation 2. Assessment of physical and mental health of a person considered to be healthy.
Evanescent —Of short duration, not permanent, passing away quickly, unfixed.
Evaporate —Volatilize.
Evaporating —Changing from liquid into vapor.
Evaporation —Change from liquid form to vapor.
Evasion—The act of escaping or avoiding.
Evenomation —Removal of venom from the victim of a snake or insect bite.
Eventration —1. Protrusion of the intestines through an opening in the abdominal wall. 2. Removal of the abdominal organs.
Eversion —The turning outward.
Evert —To turn outward.
Evidement —Scraping away of the diseased tissue.
Evil —Disease.
Eviration —1. Castration. 2. The thought of a man that he has become a woman.
Evisceration —Pushing out of the internal organs.

Evisceroneurotomy —Pushing out of the eye with division of the optic nerve.
Evocation —To create a new thing on the basis of memory or by imagination.
Evocator —A factor that controls the morphogenesis in the embryo.
Evolution —The development from a simple to a complex, perfect form.
Evulsion —1. A tearing away of a part or new growth. 2. Extraction by force as of a tooth.
Ex- —Prefix indicating away from, without, outside, completely.
Exacerbation —Increase in the severity of a disease.
Exaggerated —Aggravated, intensified.
Exaltation —1. Feeling of excessive joy. 2. Abnormal feeling of personal well being or self importance.
Examination —Physical testing and investigations made for the diagnosis of a disease.
Exangia —Any dilatation of a blood vessel.
Exanthem —Any eruption of the skin accompanied by inflammation with pyrexia e.g., measles.
Exanthema —Exanthem.
Exanthematous —Pertaining to an eruption or rash.
Exanthesis —The coming out of rash or eruption on the skin.
Exanthrope —A cause of a disease originating outside of the body.
Exanthropic —Originating outside of the body.
Exarteritis —Periarteritis.
Exarticulation —1. Amputation of a limb through a joint. 2. Partial removal of a joint.
Excalation —Absence of one member of a normal series, such as a vertebra.
Excavatio —Excavation.
Excavation —1. A hollow-out space, depression or pouch-like cavity. 2. Formation of a cavity.
Excavator —A spoon-shaped instrument for removing the tissue or bone.
Excementosis —A nodular growth of cementum on the root surface of a tooth.
Excentric —Eccentric.
Excerebration —Removal of the brain, especially that of the fetus to facilitate the delivery.
Excernent —Causing an evacuation.
Exchanger —An apparatus by which something may be exchanged.
Exchange transfusion —The whole blood is withdrawn in small amounts repeatedly and the new blood is transfused in place of that, which is usually done in infants born with hemolytic disease and in patients with uremia.
Excipient —Any inert substance added to a medicine to give suitable consistency and form to the medicine.
Excise —To cut out or remove surgically.
Excision —Removal by cutting.
Excitability —Irritability. Readiness to respond to a stimulus.
Excitable —Capable of being excited in response to a stimulus.
Excitant —An agent exciting a special function of the body.
Excitation —The act of stimulation.
Excitatory —Stimulatory.
Excitement —The state of being stimulated.
Exciting —Causing stimulation.
Excitoglandular —Increasing the functions of the glands.
Excitometabolic —Inducing metabolic changes.
Excitomotor —Producing movement or motor function.
Excitomuscular —Causing muscular activity.
Excitor —Stimulant. That which stimulates a part to greater activity.
Excitosecretory —Stimulating to increased secretion.
Excitotoxic —Exciting and then poisoning the cells or tissues.
Excitovascular —Causing vascular changes.
Exclave —1. A detached part of an organ. 2. An accessory gland such as spleen or pancreas.
Exclusion —Elimination, isolation or to remove.
Excochleation —The scraping or curetting a cavity.
Excoriate —To abrade.
Excoriated —Abraded skin.
Excoriating —Abrading the skin.
Excoriation—Abrasion of the skin.
Excrement —Waste material passed out of the body, especially the fecal matter.
Excrementitious —Of the nature of or pertaining to excrement.
Excrescence —Any outgrowth of a part.
Excreta —Waste matter as feces, urine and perspiration etc. excreted from the body.
Excrete —To eliminate the waste matter from the body.
Excretion —The elimination of the waste matter from the body.
Excretory —Pertaining to or bringing about excretion.

Excruciating —Extremely painful.
Excursion —A range of a movement regularly repeated to perform a function e.g., excursion of the jaws in mastication.
Excurvation —A curvature outward.
Excyclotorsion —Extorsion.
Excystation —To get free from a cyst or an envelope.
Exduction —Lateroduction.
Exemia —Loss of fluid from the blood vessels leaving the red blood cells behind.
Exencephalia —Exencephaly. The condition in which the brain is located outside the skull.
Exencephalic —Exencephalous. Pertaining to exencephaly.
Exencephalocele —Herniation of the brain.
Exencephalous —Exencephalic.
Exencephaly —Exencephalia.
Exenteration —Evisceration.
Exenterative —Pertaining to or requiring exenteration.
Exenteritis —Inflammation of the peritoneum covering the intestine.
Exercise —Bodily exertion or performance of the muscular activity for the improvement of health or correction of physical deformity.
Exercise bone —Development of bony growth in a muscle due to over exercise.
Exeresis —Excision or surgical removal.
Exergonic —Pertaining to the chemical reactions producing energy.
Exertion —Labor.
Exfetation —Ectopic or extrauterine pregnancy.
Exflagellation —The formation of flagelliform microgametes from a microgametocyte, occurring in the malarial parasite plasmodium in the stomach of a mosquito.
Exfoliation —The falling off in layers of the dead tissue.
Exfoliative —The dead tissue falling off in the form of layers.
Exhale —1. To breathe out or expire. 2. To emit a gas or odor.
Exhalation —1. The process of breathing out. 2. The substance breathed out. 3. Opposite to inhalation.
Exhaustion —1. The state of being extremely tired. 2. The act of drawing off the air. 3. The process of emptying a vessel.
Exhibit —1. To show. 2. Collection of the things for public inspection.
Exhibitionism —Tendency to attract attention to oneself by any means usually by exposing the genital organs to the person of the opposite sex.
Exhibitionist —The person having abnormal desire to attract attention of others, especially by exposing the genitals.
Exhilarant —Exciting gladness.
Exhilaration —Cheerfulness.
Exhumation —Removal of a dead body from the grave after it has been buried.
Exit —A passage to go out.
Exitus —Death.
Exo- —Prefix indicating outside.
Exoantigen —Ectoantigen.
Exobiology —Biology of the universe excluding the earth.
Exocardia —Ectocardia.
Exocardial —Situated or occurring outside the heart.
Exocataphoria —Downward and outward deviation of the visual axis.
Exocolitis —Inflammation of the peritoneal coat of the colon.
Exocrine —The gland secreting externally through a duct.
Exocytosis —1. The discharge from a cell of the particles which are too large to pass through the cell membrane by diffusion or osmosis. 2. The aggregation of the moving white blood cells in the epidermis as inflammatory response.
Exodeviation —A turning outward.
Exodic —Efferent; Centrifugal.
Exodontia —1. Extraction of a tooth. 2. Protrusion of teeth forward.
Exodontics —The branch of dentistry which is concerned with the extraction of teeth.
Exodontist —The dentist practicing in exodontics.
Exodontology —Exodontics.
Exoenzyme —An enzyme which acts outside of the cell which secretes it.
Exoerythrocytic —Occurring outside the red blood cell.
Exogamy —1. Fertilization of the protozoa by union of the gametes derived from different cells. 2. Marriage outside a particular group of people.
Exogastritis—Inflammation of the peritoneal coat of the stomach.
Exogenetic —Exogenous.
Exogenous —Occurring outside an organ or part.
Exohysteropexy —Fixation of the uterus to the abdominal wall.

Exolever —A modified elevator for the extraction of tooth roots.

Exometritis —Inflammation of the peritoneal coat of the uterus.

Exomphalos —Umbilical hernia.

Exopathic —Pertaining to a disease occurring outside of the body.

Exophoria —Deviation of the visual axis outward.

Exophoric —Pertaining to exophoria.

Exophthalmia —Exophthalmos. Protrusion of the eyeball from its orbit.

Exophthalmic —Pertaining to, or marked by the protrusion of the eyeball or exophthalmia.

Exophthalmic goiter — Thyrotoxicosis. Enlargement of the thyroid gland associated with the exophthalmia.

Exophthalmometer —An instrument for measuring the degree of protrusion of the eyeballs.

Exophthalmometry —To measure the degree of protrusion of eyeball in exophthalmia.

Exophthalmos, Exophthalmus —Exophthalmia.

Exophytic —Growing outward.

Exoplasm —Ectoplasm. Outer portion of the protoplasm of a cell.

Exorcism —Expulsion of evil spirits.

Exoserosis —An oozing of serum or exudate.

Exoskeleton —The structures produced by the epidermis as hair, teeth and nails etc.

Exosmosis —The diffusion of a fluid from within outward through a membrane.

Exosplenopexy —Suturing of the spleen to an opening in the abdominal wall.

Exospore —A spore present outside an organ or part of the body.

Exosporium —The outer covering of a spore.

Exostectomy —Exostosectomy. Surgical removal of an exostosis.

Exostosectomy —Exostectomy.

Exostosis —Osteoma. A benign tumor of the bone.

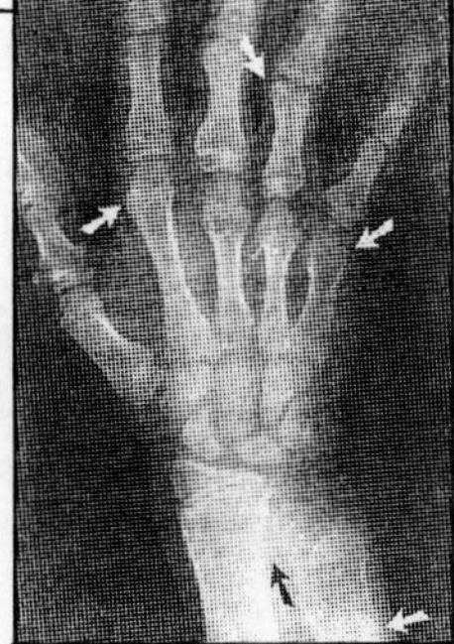

Fig. 155 : Exotosis

Exoteric —Exopathic.

Exothermal, Exothermic —A chemical reaction producing heat or energy.

Exothymopexy —Suturing of an enlarged thymus gland to the sternum.

Exotic —Originating in the foreign countries.

Exotoxic —Pertaining to an exotoxin.

Exotoxin —A toxin produced by a bacterium and excreted into its surrounding medium, which is sensitive to the effects of chemicals, light and heat.

Exotropia —Strabismus with deviation of the visual axis of one eye away from that of the other, resulting in diplopia.

Expander —That which increases the size or volume of something, e.g., plasma volume expander.

Expansion —Increase in size or volume; the spreading out of any structure

Expansive delusion —To think oneself more powerful and wealthy.

Expectant —Waiting.

Expectation —Hope.

Expectorant —A substance or medicine stimulating the expectoration.

Expectorate —To spit or to eject sputum from the mouth.

Expectoration —1. Expulsion of the mucous, mucopurulent, serous or frothy material from the throat or lungs. 2. Sputum.

Expel —To drive out.

Experiment —A test or trial.

Experimental —Concerning with the experiments.

Expert —Skilful, specialist.

Expirate —The exhaled air or gas.

Expiration —1. The act of expelling the air from the lungs. 2. Termination or death.

Expiratory —Pertaining to the expiration or death.

Expire —1. To breathe out. 2. To die.

Expired —1. Breathed out or exhaled. 2. Died.

Explant —1. To remove a piece of living tissue from the body and to place it in an artificial culture medium for growth. 2. The piece of living tissue taken from the body and grown in an artificial culture medium.

Explode —1. To burst out. 2. To have rapid onset or starting rapidly such as an epidemic disease.

Exploration —Examination or investigation for diagnostic purposes.

Exploratory —Pertaining to an exploration.

Explorer —An instrument used in exploration.

Explosion —Sudden and violent outburst.

Expose —1. To make somebody naked. 2. Opening up as of the abdominal cavity in surgical procedures. 3. To be in contact with an infected person or infectious agent, extreme cold, heat or radiation. 4. To show one's genital organs publicly.

Exposure —1. The act of making somebody naked. 2. The act of opening up as of the abdominal cavity in surgical procedures. 3. The condition of being in contact with an infected person or infectious agent, extreme cold or heat or radiation. 4. The act of showing one's genital organs publicly. 5. The measure of the amount of ionizing radiation at the surface of the body.

Express —1. To squeeze out. 2. To state one's opinion.

Expressate —The material forced out by expression.

Expression —Facies. 1. The act of squeezing out or expelling anything by pressure. 2. The act of stating one's opinion. 3. Appearance of the face being formed as a result of feeling something or some physical discomfort.

Expulsion —The act of expelling.

Expulsive —Tending to expel.

Exquisite —Extremely intense or sharp, usually said of the pain.

Exsanguinate —1. To withdraw the circulating blood 2. Anemic or bloodless.

Exsanguination —Heavy loss of blood due to internal or external hemorrhage.

Exsanguine —Anemic, bloodless.

Exsanguinity —Anemia, bloodlessness.

Exsection —Excision.

Exsiccant —1. Drying up or absorbing moisture. 2. A dusting or drying powder.

Exsiccate —Desiccate.

Exsiccation —Desiccation . The process of drying up.

Exsiccative —Desiccative. Causing to dry up or that which dries.

Exsomatize —To remove from the body.

Exsorption —The movement of the substances as of the cells and electrolytes from the blood into the lumen of the intestine.

Exstrophy —Eversion. The turning inside out of an organ.

Exsufflation —To expel the air forcibly from a cavity by means of an instrument, the exsufflator.

Ext. —Extract.

Extemporaneous —Not prepared according to the formula but prepared especially for the occasion.

Extend —1. To straighten a limb. 2. To increase the angle formed by flexion as in a limb. 3. To enlarge 4. To spread out. 5. To dilate 6. To prolong.

Extender —That which enlarges or prolongs.

Extension —1. Enlargement. 2. The movement by which the two ends of any united part are drawn away from each other. 3. The movement by which the parts of a limb become straight, i.e. opposite to flexion. 4. The application of a pull (traction) to a fractured or dislocated limb.

Extensor —A muscle extending a part.

Exterior —External. Situated or occurring on the outside.

Exteriorize —1. To expose an internal organ temporarily in surgery. 2. To turn one's interest outward.

Extern (e) —A medical student or a graduate who assists in the medical and surgical care of the patients in the hospital but living outside of the hospital.

External —Exterior. Opposite to internal.

Externalia —External genital organs.

Externalize —1. In surgery, to expose some part of the body to the outside. 2. In psychiatry, to direct outwards one's inner conflicts instead of keeping them hidden.

Externus —External. The structure situated away from the center of a part or cavity of body.

Exteroceptive —Pertaining to the end organs receiving stimuli from outside.

Exteroceptor —A sensory organ as the eye adapted to receive the stimuli from outside of the body.

Exterofective —Responding to the external stimuli.

Extima —Outermost coat as the outermost coat of a blood vessel.

Extinction —1. The process of putting out or abolishing. 2. The complete disappearance of a conditioned reflex as a result of non-reinforcement.

Extinguish —To abolish.

Extirpation —Complete removal of an organ or tissue; taking out by the roots.

Extorsion —Rotation of an organ or limb outward.

Extortor —An outward rotator.

Extra- —A prefix meaning outside, beyond and in addition to.

Extra-articular —Situated or occurring outside a joint.

Extra-axial —Off the axis.

Extra beat —Extrasystole.

Extrabuccal —Outside of the cheek.

Extracapsular —Situated or occurring outside a capsule, e.g. capsule of a joint or lens of the eye.

Extracarpal —Outside of the carpus.

Extracellular —Outside the cell.

Extrachromosomal —Outside or separated from a chromosome.

Extracorporeal —Situated or occurring outside of the body.

Extracranial —Situated or occurring outside of the skull.

Extract —1. To pull out or remove forcibly, as to extract a tooth. 2. Active principle of a drug obtained by distillation or chemical processes, which may be liquid, of soft consistency, in powder form or solid.

Extractant —An agent used to extract a substance from a mixture of substances, from the tissue, or from a crude drug.

Extraction —1. The pulling out or removing forcibly as a tooth. 2. The removing of the active principle of a drug by distillation.

Extractive —The substance removed in the process of extraction.

Extractives —Substances present in vegetable or animal tissues that can be separated by dissolving the tissues in solvents and then recovering by evaporating the solution.

Extractor —An instrument for removing the foreign bodies.

Extractum —Extract.

Extracystic —Situated or occurring outside of a cyst or the urinary bladder.

Extradural —On outer side of the dura mater.

Extraembryonic —External to an embryo.

Extraepiphysial —Not connected with an epiphysis.

Extragenic —Occurring outside of a gene.

Extragenital —Outside of, or unrelated to the genital organs.

Extrahepatic —Outside of, or unrelated to the liver.

Extraligamentous —Occurring outside of, or unrelated to a ligament.

Extramalleolus —The external or lateral malleolus of the ankle.

Extramedullary —Situated or occurring outside of a medulla, especially the medulla oblongata.

Extramitochondrial — Outside of the mitochondria.

Extramural —Situated or occurring outside of the wall of an organ.

Extraneous —Situated outside of, or unrelated to an organism.

Extranuclear —Outside of a nucleus.

Extraocular —Situated or occurring outside of an eyeball.

Extraoral —Outside of the oral cavity.

Extraosseous —Occurring outside of a bone.

Extraperineal —Not connected with the perineum.

Extraperiosteal —Unrelated to the periosteum.

Extraperitoneal —Outside of the peritoneal cavity.

Extraplacental —Unrelated to placenta.

Extrapulmonary —Occurring outside of, or unrelated to the lungs.

Extrapyramidal —Situated outside the pyramidal tract of the central nervous system.

Extrarenal —Outside of the kidney.

Extrasensory —Perception not depending on the five senses, such as transference of thoughts.

Extraserous —Outside of the serous cavity.

Extrasomatic —Outside of the body.

Extrasystole —A premature contraction of the heart, in addition to the normal contraction, occurring in response to an impulse originating outside the sinoatrial node.

Atrial extrasystole — Extrasystole in which the impulse arises in the atrium at some place other than the sinoatrial node.

Atrioventricular extrasystole —The extrasystole in which the impulse arises in the atrioventricular node or in the bundle of His.

Ventricular extrasystole —Premature contraction of the heart occurring as a result of an impulse arising in the ventricle.

Extrathoracic —Outside of the thorax.

Extratracheal —Outside of the trachea.

Extratubal —Outside of a tube, especially the fallopian tube.

Extrauterine —Outside of the uterus.

Extravaginal —Outside of the vagina.

Extravasate —1. To escape from a vessel into the tissues as the serum, blood or lymph. 2. Fluid escaping from the vessels.

Extravasation —Suffusion. Escaping of blood or other substance from a vessel into the surrounding tissues.

Extravascular —Outside of a vessel.

Extraventricular —Situated or occurring outside of a ventricle.

Extraversion —Extroversion.

Extravert —Extrovert.

Extravisual —Outside the field of vision.

Extremital —Distal. Pertaining to an extremity.

Extremitas —Extremity.

Extremity —1. The distal or terminal portion of anything. 2. The arm or leg.

Extrinsic —Situated or occurring externally.

Extrinsic factor —Vitamin B_{12}.

Extrinsic muscle —The muscles outside an organ that control its position, such as that of the eye or tongue.

Extrospection —To see his or her skin continuously for evidence of dirt.

Extroversion —1. A turning inside out. 2. The direction of one's attention and energy outward from the self.

Extrovert —The person who is interested in external things and actions.

Extrude —1. To force out or to occupy an abnormal external position. 2. In dentistry, for a tooth to occupy a position external to the line of occlusion.

Extrudoclusion —Extrusion.

Extrusion —1. The forcing out or occupying an abnormal external position. 2. In dentistry, the condition of a tooth being pushed forward too far from the line of occlusion.

Extubate —To remove a tube.

Extubation —Removal of a tube.

Exuberant —1. Excessive in production 2. Happy.

Exudate —The fluid escaped from the blood vessels and deposited in the tissues as a result of inflammation, containing protein, cellular debris and other solid materials.

Exudation —The escape of fluid from the blood vessels and deposition in tissues.

Exudative —Pertaining to or having the quality of exudation.

Exude —To pass off slowly through the tissues.

Exulcerans —Ulcerating.

Exumbilication —Exomphalos Umbilical hernia.

Exuviae —Material shed. Cast.

Ex vivo —Outside the living body.

Eye —The organ of vision.

Aphakic eye —The eye from which the lens has been removed.

Black eye —Bruise of the tissues surrounding the eyes marked by discoloration, swelling and pain.

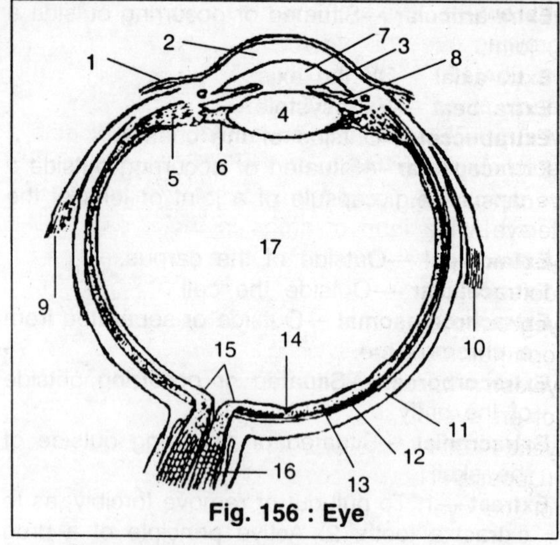

Fig. 156 : Eye

1. Conjunctiva 2. Cornea 3. Iris 4. Lens 5. Ciliary body 6. Suspensory ligament 7. Anterior chamber 8. Posterior chamber 9 and 10. Muscles of the eyeball 11. Sclera 12. Choroid 13. Retina 14. Macula lutea 15. Optic disc 16. Optic nerve 17. Vitreous body

Crossed eye —Strabismus with the deviation of the visual axis of one eye toward that of the other eye.

Dark-adapted eye —The eye which has become adjusted to see the things in dim light.

Dominant eye —One of the two eyes to which a person gives more preference for using as in sighting a gun or in using a monocular microscope.

Exciting eye —The injured eye which involves the other eye also in sympathetic ophthalmia.

Klieg eye —Conjunctivitis, swelling of the eyelids, lacrimation and photophobia due to exposure to intense light.

Light-adapted eye —The eye which has become adjusted to see the objects in bright light.

Pink eye —Acute contagious conjunctivitis.

Squinting eye — Deviating eye from the object of fixation in strabismus.

Sympathizing eye —In sympathetic ophthalmia, the uninjured eye which is influenced from the injured eye.

Eyeball —The globe of the eye.

Eye bank —A place where corneas of the eyes removed after death are preserved for subsequent keratoplasty.

Eyebrow —1. The arch over the eye. 2. The hairs growing over this arch.

Eye contact —The gazing of two persons, at each other.

Eyecup —A small cup containing a medicated solution which fits over the eye to wash it.

Eye drops —A liquid medicine of eyes administered in the form of drops in the eyes.

Eyeglass —A glass lens used to correct the defective vision.

Eyeground —Fundus of the eye as seen with the ophthalmoscope.

Eyelash —Cilium. A hair growing on the margin of an eyelid.

Eyelid —One of the two movable protective folds (Upper and Lower) covering the anterior surface of the eyeball.

Eyepiece —The portion of a microscope or telescope consisting of one or more than one lens, nearest the user's eye.

Eye-sight —Vision.

Eye specialist —Expert in eye diseases.

Eye spot —A colored spot in an unicellular organism.

Eyestrain —Tiredness of the eye due to overuse or from defective vision.

Eye-tooth —Canine tooth.

Eye-wash —A suitable liquid material used for washing the eyes, eye lotion.

Eye-witness —The person who has seen something being done.

Fabella—A sesamoid bone that sometimes develops in the tendon of the head of the gastrocnemius muscle.

Fabism—Favism.

Fabrication—To tell a lie in such a way as it seems true.

Face—Anterior or ventral part of the head from the forehead to the chin, extending laterally upto but excluding the ears.

Face-lift—Rhytidectomy. Rhytidoplasty.

Facet, Facette —A small plane area on a bone or some other hard surface of the body.

Facetectomy—Excision of the articular facet of a vertebra.

Facial—Pertaining to the face.

Facial center—A center situated in the brain causing facial movements.

Facialis—Facial.

Facial reflex—Contraction of the facial muscles following pressure on the eyeball.

Facial spasm—Spasms of the facial muscles supplied by the facial nerve, on one side of the face or the area around the eye.

-facient—A suffix denoting that which causes something.

Facies—1. The face 2. The specific surface of any body structure. 3. The expression or appearance of the face.

Facies abdominalis—Anxious, shrunken and pinched face seen in the abdominal diseases.

Facies adenoid—Dull expression, with open mouth usually seen in children with the enlargement of the adenoids.

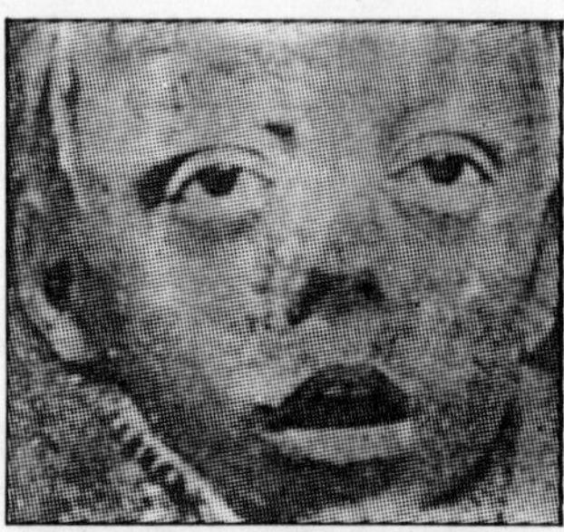

Fig. 157 : Facies adenoid

Facies hepatica—A thin face with sunken eyes, yellow conjunctivae and the sallow skin seen in certain chronic liver diseases.

Facies hippocratica—Face with pale skin, hollow cheeks and temples, sunken eyes and with the lips relaxed, seen in those dying from a long continued disease or from cholera.

Facies leontina— Lion-like appearance of the face seen in certain forms of leprosy.

Facies mitralis—Face with the cheeks cyanotic and the blood capillaries visible on them, seen in mitral insufficiency.

Facies parkinsonian—Masklike and expressionless face with blinking of the eyes, seen in a person suffering from parkinson's disease.

Hound-dog facies—A facial appearance in which the loose facial skin hangs in the form of bags as that of the hound-dog, which occurs in cutis laxa.

Moon facies—Round face as seen in Cushing's disease.

Facilitation—Hastening or assistance of a process.

Facing—A piece of porcelain cut to represent the outer surface of a tooth.

Facio- —A prefix indicating face.

Faciobrachial—Pertaining to the face and the arm.

Faciocephalalgia—Pain in the face and the head.

Faciocervical —Pertaining to the face and the neck.

Faciolingual—Pertaining to the face and the tongue.

Facioplasty—Plastic surgery of the face.

Facioplegia—Prosopoplegia. Facial paralysis.

Facioscapulohumeral— Pertaining to the face, scapula and the upper arm.

Factitial—Artificially produced.

Factitious—Artificial, not natural.

Factitious disorders—The diseases which are not real but produced artificially just to stay in a hospital.

Factor—1. An agent which is contributory to

bring about a result. 2. In genetics, a gene. 3. An essential element such as a vitamin in the food.

Accessory food factor—A substance present in the food which does not produce energy for the user but is essential for the normal growth and development or metabolism, as a vitamin.

Antianemic factor—A substance formed in the stomach and the intestine by the interaction of an extrinsic factor vitamin B_{12}, and an intrinsic factor present in the gastric juice, and stored in the liver, which is essential for the normal development of the red blood cells in the bone marrow.

Antihemorrhagic factor—Vitamin K.

Antiinfective factor—The substance which acts against some infection.

Antisterility factor—Vitamin E.

Coagulation factors— The substances present in the blood essential for the normal blood clotting.

Extrinsic factor— Vit. B_{12} or cyanocobalamin which is mostly found in milk and pernicious anemia occurs in its deficiency.

Intrinsic factor—A glycoprotein secreted by the gastric glands, necessary for the absorption of Vit. B_{12}, lack of which causes vit. B_{12} deficiency, which results in pernicious anemia.

Platelet factors—The factors important to arrest the bleeding which are contained in or attached to the platelets.

Predisposing factor —Showing a tendency or susceptibility to a disease.

Rh factor—An antigen present on the surface of red blood cells, the incompatibility between the antigen of the mother and that of the child produces the disease erythroblastosis fetalis in child.

Factorial—Pertaining to a factor.

Facultative—Pertaining to or characterized by the ability to live in certain particular circumstances.

Faculty—1. A normal power or function especially of the mind. 2. A department of an educational institution.

Faget's sign—Slowness of the pulse rate than would be expected with the elevated temperature, as seen in typhoid fever.

Fahrenheit thermometer— A temperature scale marked with the freezing point of water at 32° and the boiling point at 212° indicated by F.

Failure—Inability to function properly, *e.g.* heart failure in which the heart becomes unable to pump the blood properly, renal failure in which the kidneys become unable to excrete the excretory products properly resulting in uremia and respiratory failure in which the lungs become unable to perform properly their function of inhaling the air and expelling the carbon dioxide.

Faint—Syncope. Unconsciousness due to insufficient blood supply to the brain.

Falcate—Sickle-shaped.

Falces—Plural of falx.

Falcial—Pertaining to any sickle-shaped structure.

Falciform —Sickle-shaped.

Falcine—Falcial.

Falcula—Falx cerebelli.

Falcular—1. Sickle-shaped. 2. Pertaining to the falx cerebelli.

Fallectomy—To cut away a part of a fallopian tube.

Falling drop—A ringing sound heard over the stomach and intestine when filled with air; and large cavities containing fluid and air, as in hydropneumothorax.

Falling of womb—Prolapse of uterus.

Falling sickness—Epilepsy.

Fallopian ligament—Round ligament of the uterus.

Fallopian tube—A tube extending laterally from each side of the upper portion of the uterus and terminating in the peritoneal cavity near the ovary, through which the ovum passes from the ovary to the uterus and the spermatozoa from the uterus toward the ovary.

Fallotomy—Salpingotomy. To make an incision into the fallopian tube.

Fallot's tetralogy—A congenital disease characterized by the combination of pulmonary artery stenosis, interventricular septal defect, arrival of the aorta into the right ventricle passing through the interventricular septum, which receives blood from both the ventricles, and the hypertrophy of the right ventricle.

Fallout—The settling on the surface of earth of radioactive fission products from the atmosphere after release of such materials into the air after an atomic explosion.

False—Spurious. Untrue, incorrect.

False-negative—A test which indicates that a disease being investigated is not present when in fact it is present.

False pains—Pains resembling labor pains.

False-positive—A test which indicates that a disease being investigated is present when in fact it is not present.

False ribs—The lower five pairs of the ribs which do not unite directly with the sternum.

Falsification—The act of writing or stating the false things, so as to deceive.

Falsification retrospective—Occurrence of change in the memory for the past events unconsciously.

Falsifying—Pretending to feel something which is actually not present or showing no feeling even when excited.

Falx—Any sickle-shaped structure.

Falx cerebelli—A fold of the dura mater separating the cerebellar hemispheres vertically.

Fames—Hunger.

Familial—Pertaining to a family or occurring in the same family, as a disease.

Family—1. A group of persons descended from a common ancester. 2. In biological classification, the division between an order and a genus.

Family planning—Birth control.

Famine—Extreme scarcity of food causing hunger.

Fang—1. The root of a tooth. 2. A sharp-pointed tooth.

Fannia —A genus of small house flies.

Fantast—A day dreamer.

Fantasy—Day dreaming, imagination.

Farad—A unit of electric capacity.

Faradic—Pertaining to induced electricity.

Faradism—The use of an interrupted electric current to stimulate the nerves and muscles in the treatment of their diseases.

Faradization—Treatment of the nerves or muscles by faradic current.

Faradocontractility— Contractility of the muscles under the stimulus of faradic current.

Faradotherapy—Treatment of the diseases by faradic current.

Farcy—A chronic form of glanders disease.

Farina —Finely ground meal of wheat or other grain.

Farinaceous—1. Starchy or containing starch. 2. Pertaining to or of the nature of flour.

Farmer's lung—It is allergic alveolitis seen in farmers, caused by inhalation of dust from mouldy hay, straw or grain containing the causative micro-organisms actinomycetes, and characterized by dry cough, tightness of the chest and breathlessness on exertion.

Farpoint—The farthest point at which the objects can be seen distinctly with the eyes.

Farre's tubercles—Malignant masses on the surface of the liver.

Farsighted—Pertaining to farsightedness.

Farsightedness—Hyperopia or hypermetropia. Ability to see the distant objects clearly but not the near objects.

Fascia—A sheet of fibrous tissue lying deep to the skin, uniting it with the underlying tissues, or covering, supporting and separating the muscles and the various organs of the body.

Fasciae—Plural of fascia.

Fascial—Pertaining to or of the nature of fascia.

Fascial reflex—Contraction of the muscles resulting from percussing the facial fascia.

Fasciaplasty—Plastic surgery of the fascia.

Fascicle—Fasciculus. A small bundle or cluster, especially of nerve or muscle fibres.

Fascicular—Pertaining to a fascicle.

Fasciculated—Occurring in bundles or clusters.

Fasciculation—1. Formation of fascicles. 2. A small local involuntary contraction or twitching of the muscles visible under the skin.

Fasciculi—Plural of fasciculus.

Fasciculus—Fascicle.

Fasciectomy—Excision of a piece of fascia.

Fasciitis—Inflammation of a fascia.

Fascio- —A prefix indicating fascia.

Fasciodesis—The attachment of a fascia to a tendon, bone or another fascia by surgery.

Fasciola, plural **fasciolae**—A small bundle of nerve or muscle fibers.

Fascioplasty —Repair of the fascia by plastic surgery.

Fasciorrhaphy—To suture a fascia.

Fasciotomy—To make an incision into the fascia to divide it.

Fascitis—Inflammation of the fascia.

Fast—1. Quick. 2. To go without food. 3. Resistant to the effects of a chemical substance, *e.g.,* the bacteria Mycobacterium tuberculosis that are not decolorized after staining with acid dyes.

Fastidious—In microbiology, an organism requiring appropriate nutrition and environment for its growth and survival.

Fastidium—Aversion to food or to eating.

Fastigium—The highest point.

Fastness—The ability of bacteria to resist stains, a drug or other destructive agent.

Fat—1. Adipose tissue of the body which is a

store of energy. 2. Grease, oil. 3. An ester of glycerol with fatty acids usually palmitic, oleic or stearic acid.

Fatal—Lethal. Causing death.

Fatality—The ending of a disease in death.

Fate—Ultimate outcome.

Fatigability—The condition of becoming easily tired.

Fatigable—Tiring on very slight exertion.

Fatigue—Tiredness due to excessive activity or exertions, loss of power or capacity to respond to stimulation.

Fatty—Pertaining to or of the nature of fats or fatty substances, adipose.

Fatty acids—Fatty acids and glycerol are formed in the small intestine as a result of fat digestion, which are absorbed through the lacteals or lymphatic vessels present in the intestinal walls, into the lymph and then ultimately are carried into the blood stream. The most important fatty acids are linoleic, linolenic, arachidonic, stearic, palmitic and oleic acid etc.

Essential fatty acids—The fatty acids essential for maintaining health. They include the three fatty acids named linoleic, linolenic and arachidonic acid.

Saturated fatty acids—These fatty acids are saturated with hydrogen and so are incapable of absorbing more hydrogen. Stearic acid and palmitic acid, etc. are saturated fatty acids.

Unsaturated fatty acids—These fatty acids are not saturated with hydrogen, so are capable of absorbing extra hydrogen. Oleic acid, linoleic acid and linolenic acid etc. are unsaturated fatty acids.

Fatty degeneration —Fat deposition in the cytoplasm of the cells.

Fauces—The constricted passage between the throat and the pharynx.

Faucial—Pertaining to the fauces.

Faucial reflex—Gagging or vomiting resulting from irritation of the fauces.

Faucitis—Inflammation of the fauces.

Fauna—All the animals including the microorganisms in a given locality.

Faveolate—Alveolate. Honey-combed.

Faveoli—Plural of faveolus.

Faveolus—Foveola. A small depression or a pit.

Favus—A fungus disease of the skin characterized by honeycomb-like masses accompanied by itching.

F.D.—Fatal dose, focal distance.

F.D.A. —Food and drug administration.

Fe—Chemical symbol for iron.

Features —Various parts of the face, as forehead, eyes, nose, mouth, chin, cheeks and ears that give to someone's individuality.

Febricant—Febrifacient.

Febricide—Antipyretic. Destructive to fever.

Febricula—A mild fever of short duration.

Febrifacient—Producing fever.

Febrific—Producing or conveying fever.

Febrifugal—Reducing fever.

Febrifuge —Antipyretic. Reducing fever.

Febrile—Feverish. Pertaining to a fever.

Febriphobia—Anxiety or fear of a rise in body temperature.

Febris—Pyrexia or fever.

Febris enterica—Typhoid fever.

Febris nervosa—Nervous fever.

Fecal—Pertaining to or of the nature of feces.

Fecalith—Coprolith. A stone formed around the fecal matter in the intestine.

Fecaloid—Resembling feces.

Fecaloma—Scatoma. Stercoroma. A large mass of the accumulated feces in the rectum resembling a tumor.

Fecaluria—Presence of fecal matter in the urine.

Fecal vomit—Presence of feces in the vomitus which occurs generally in strangulated hernia and the intestinal obstruction.

Feces—Stool, excreta, dejecta or excrement discharged from the intestines by way of the anus.

Fecula—1. Sediment. 2. Starch.

Feculent—1. Having sediment. 2. Foul.

Fecund—Fertile.

Fecundate—To fertilize or impregnate.

Fecundation—Fertilization or impregnation.

Fecundation artificial—Impregnation by injecting the seminal fluid into the uterus by mechanical means. Artificial insemination.

Fecundity—Ability to produce offspring, fertility.

Feeble—Weak.

Feeble minded—Dull minded.

Feeble mindedness—Dullness of the mind, mental retardation.

Feed—To put food into the mouth. To nourish.

Feedback—The return of some of the output of a system as input so as to control the process to some extent. Feedback may be positive or negative. It is positive when the return exerts a stimulatory effect and negative when the return exerts an inhibitory control, e.g., the blood sugar is regulated by the feedback mechanism in which a positive feedback signal indicates that more blood sugar is required when the blood sugar level falls, *i.e.,* the additional blood sugar exerts a stimulatory effect. Conversely, negative feedback signal indicates that the production of the blood sugar should be reduced or stopped when the blood sugar level rises to normal. i.e. the additional blood sugar exerts an inhibitory control.

Feeder—One who feeds or gives food.

Feeding—Taking or giving a food.

Artificial feeding— Feeding of a baby with food other than mother's milk.

Breast feeding —Feeding of an infant at the breast.

Forcible feeding—To feed a person by force who cannot or will not receive it.

Intravenous feeding— Administration of fluids and nutrients through a vein.

Rectal feeding—Nutritive enema. The introduction of nutritive fluid, such as 5% to 10% glucose with normal saline solution through the rectum.

Tube feeding—Feeding with liquid food through a tube which passes through the nose into the stomach in case where the patient is unable to swallow or masticate food.

Feeling—Physical and mental sensation.

Feet —Plural of foot. The lower parts of the legs.

Fehling's solution—An alkaline, copper containing solution used for detecting the presence and determining the percentage of sugar in the urine.

Fel—Bile.

Feline —Concerning cats.

Fellatio—Oral stimulation of the penis.

Fellatrix, Fellatrice—A woman who performs fellatio.

Felon—Whitlow. Infection or abscess of the pulp of the distal phalanx of a finger.

Feltwork—A network of nerve fibrils.

Female—An individual of the sex that produces ova or gives birth to a child.

Feminine—Pertaining to the female sex or having the characteristics of the female.

Feminism—Gynecomastia. The development of female secondary sexual characteristics in the male.

Feminization—The normal or the pathologic development of female secondary sexual characteristics in the male.

Femoral—Pertaining to the femur or thigh bone.

Femoral reflex—Extension of the knee and flexion of the foot occurring due to irritation of the skin over the upper one third of the thigh.

Femorocele—Femoral hernia.

Femorotibial—Pertaining to the femur and the tibia bone.

Femto- —In the metric system, a prefix indicating that the basic unit following it is to be multiplied by 10^{-15}, i.e. divided by 1000,000,000,000,000. Thus a femtogram is 10^{-15}g or 1000,000,000,000,000th part of a gram.

Femur—The long bone of thigh articulating with the hip bone above, and the tibia and patella below.

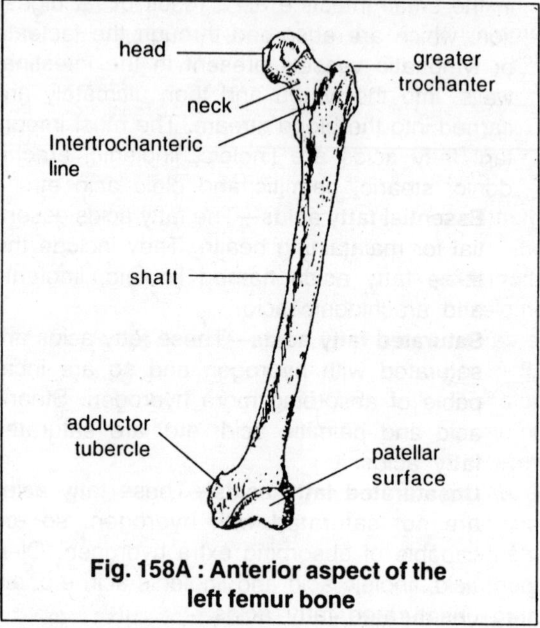

Fig. 158A : Anterior aspect of the left femur bone

Fenestra—An aperture or opening usually closed by a membrane, *e.g.* fenestra cochleae in which there is round opening in the inner wall of the middle ear or the tympanic membrane which is covered by a secondary tympanic membrane.

Fenestrate—To make one or more openings.

Fenestrated–Having openings.

Fenestration—1. The act of perforating or the condition of being perforated. 2. To make an artificial opening in the labyrinth of the ear by an operation in case of otosclerosis to treat deafness.

Feral—Denoting an animal that is wild and untamed.

Ferment—Any substance causing fermentation.

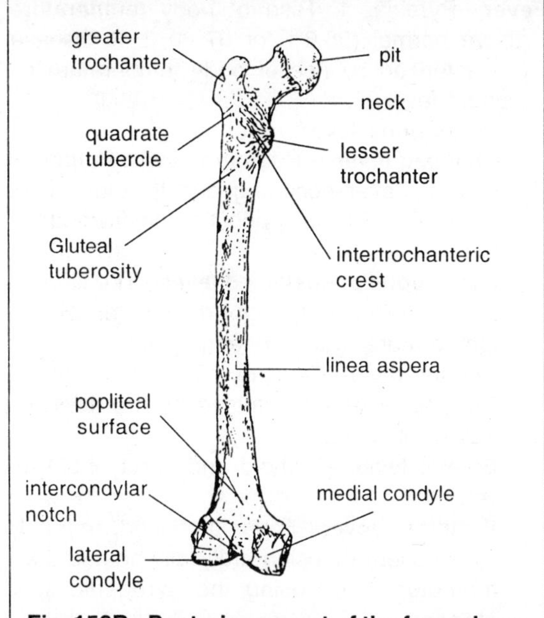

Fig. 158B : Posterior aspect of the femur bone

Fermentable—Capable of undergoing fermentation.

Fermentation—The oxidative decomposition of complex substances into simpler ones, as of the carbohydrate into ethyl alcohol through the action of enzymes or ferments, produced by bacteria, molds or yeasts etc., with the production of energy. The economic importance of the fermentation is in the production of alcohol and the baking of bread etc.

Fermentative—Causing fermentation.

Fermenter—Fermentative.

Fermentum—A ferment, yeast.

Ferning—Fern-like appearance of the dried cervical mucus which indicates the presence of estrogen.

-ferous—Suffix meaning producing.

Ferrated—Containing iron.

Ferri-, Ferro- —Prefixes indicating the presence of iron.

Ferric—Pertaining to the iron.

Ferritin—The form of iron in which it is deposited in the body tissues.

Ferro- —A prefix indicating the presence of iron.

Ferrokinetics—Study of the absorption, utilization, storage and excretion of iron.

Ferrometer—An instrument for determining the amount of iron present in the blood.

Ferropexia—Iron fixation.

Ferrotherapy—Treatment of anemia with the iron.

Ferrous—Ferruginous. Pertaining to or containing iron.

Ferrugination—Deposition of iron with other minerals in the walls of small blood vessels.

Ferruginous—1. Pertaining to or containing iron. 2. Of the color of iron rust.

Ferrule—A ring of metal applied to the end of the root or crown of a tooth to give it strength.

Ferrum—Iron.

Fertile—Capable of conception or reproduction.

Fertility—The capability to conceive or reproduce.

Fertilization—The union of an ovum of the female with the spermatozoon of the male.

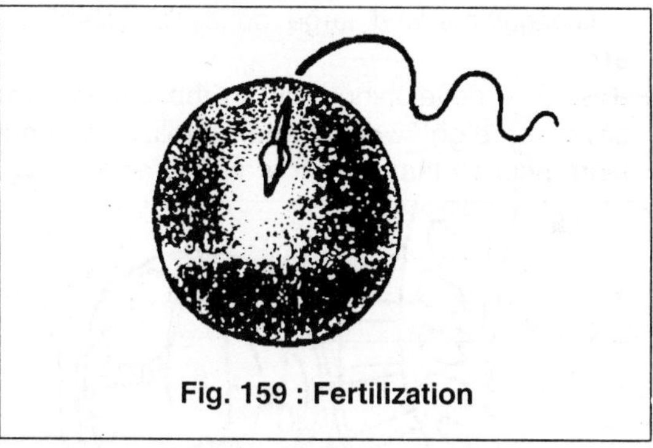

Fig. 159 : Fertilization

Fervescence—Increase of fever or body temperature.

Fester—To become inflammed and suppurate.

Festinant—Accelerating.

Festination—Involuntary tendency to increase the speed of walking.

Festoon—A carving in the base material of a denture that stimulates the natural indentinations of the gums.

Fetal—Pertaining to a fetus.

Fetalism—Retention of a fetal structure in the uterus after birth.

Fetation—Pregnancy.

Feticide—The destruction of the fetus.

Fetid—Having an offensive smell.

Fetish—An object or body part charged with special sexual interest.

Fetishism—The condition in which a particular object, *e.g.* a cloth etc. becomes the source of sexual attraction.

Fetochorionic—Pertaining to the fetus and the chorion or chorionic membrane.

Fetography—X-ray examination of the fetus in uterus.

Fetology—Study of the fetus.

Fetometry—Measurement of the fetus, especially of its head before delivery.

Fetopathy—Embryopathy.

Fetoplacental—Pertaining to the fetus and its placenta.

Fetoprotein—An antigen present in the fetus.

Fetor—Foul smell.

Fetoscope—1. A special form of stethoscope for listening to the fetal heart sound. 2. An endoscope used for direct visualization of the fetus in the uterus.

Fetoscopy—Direct visualization of the fetus in the uterus by using a fetoscope.

Fetotoxic—Anything that is toxic to the fetus, *e.g.* morphine, sedatives, tobacco smoking, anticoagulants and large doses of vitamin K etc.

Fetus—The developing child in the uterus from seven or eight weeks after fertilization until birth, prior to that time it is called an embryo.

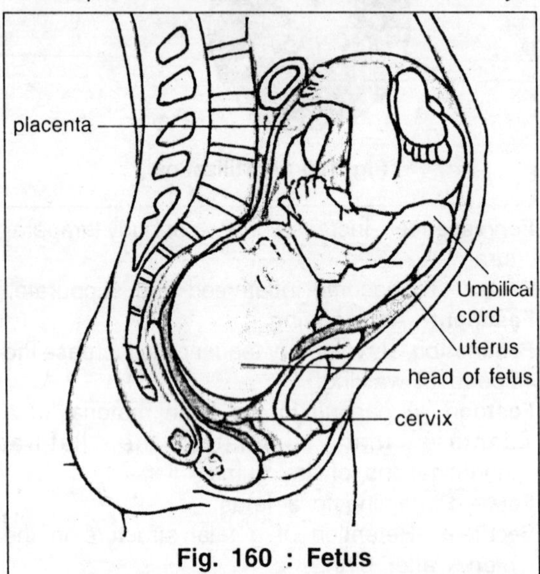

Fig. 160 : Fetus

Amorphus fetus—The fetus without a definite form so it is not recognizable as a fetus.

Calcified fetus— Lithopedion. The fetus that has died in the uterus and become calcified.

Fetus in fetu—The condition in which a small and imperfectly developed fetus is contained in a large and perfectly developed fetus.

Mummified fetus—The dead, dried and shriveled fetus.

Papyraceus fetus—A dead fetus pressed flat by the development of the living twin.

Parasitic fetus, Fetus in fetu —A small imperfect fetus that cannot live independently but contained within the body of another fetus as a parasite.

Fever—Pyrexia. 1. Rise of body temperature above normal (98.6°F or 37°C) 2. A disease characterized by rise of body temperature as typhoid fever.

Break bone fever— Dengue.

Childbed fever— Puerperal fever. Puerperal sepsis. Fever occurring due to infection of the birth canal following trauma from childbirth.

Continuous or sustained fever—The fever in which there is only slight diurnal variation in temperature as in pneumonia.

Dengue fever—Dengue.

Drug fever—Fever caused by the administration of a drug.

Enteric fever—Typhoid and paratyphoid fever.

Factitious fever—Fever produced artificially by a patient by using artificially heated thermometer or by using the pyrogenic substances.

Fever of unknown etiology—A continuous fever of at least 3 weeks duration of which the diagnosis has not been established after one week of hospital investigation.

Fever therapy—The use of artificially produced fever in the treatment of some diseases.

Induced fever—Fever artificially produced.

Intermittent fever— The fever in which the temperature becomes normal during the day but rises to its maximum in the evening.

Malaria fever—See malaria.

Puerperal fever—Childbed fever. Puerperal sepsis.

Relapsing fever—The condition marked by alternating periods of fever and normal temperature, each lasting from 5 to 7 days.

Remittent fever—Fever which never falls to normal temperature but slightly fluctuates.

Septic fever—Fever occurring due to presence of disease-producing bacteria in the blood.

Feverish—Suffering from fever.

Fiat—A term used in writing the prescriptions which means let there be made.

Fiber—1. An elongated thread-like structure as a nerve fiber or muscle fiber. 2. The components of the food which are not digested by the gastrointestinal enzymes, made up of cellulose, hemicellulose, pectin etc., which increase the volume of the diet by absorbing large amounts of water and therefore are used in the diet to cause evacuation. Foods rich in fibers are fruits, leafy and root vegetables etc.

Fibercolonoscope—A fiberoptic endoscope used for examining the colon.

Fibergastroscope—A fiberoptic endoscope used for examining the stomach.

Fiber-illumination— Transmission of light to an object by means of bundles of glass or plastic fibers.

Fiberoptic—A flexible material made of bundles of glass or plastic fibers having the property of transmitting the light and used usually in making the endoscope.

Fiberoptics—The transmission of an image along the flexible bundles of glass or plastic fibers.

Fiberscope —A flexible endoscope whose lumen is coated with glass or plastic fibers having the property of transmitting the light.

Fibra, plural **fibrae**— Fiber.

Fibre—Fiber.

Fibremia—Inosemia. Presence of fibrin in the blood causing embolism or thrombosis.

Fibril—A small fiber or filament.

Fibrilla—Fibril.

Fibrillae—Plural of fibrilla.

Fibrillar, Fibrillary—Pertaining to or consisting of fibrils.

Fibrillate—Fibrillated.

Fibrillated—Fibrillar. Fibrous. Made of minute fibers, or fibrils.

Fibrillation—1. The formation of fibrils. 2. A small, local, involuntary muscular contraction due to spontaneous activation of the individual muscle fibers.

Atrial fibrillation— Extremely rapid and incomplete contraction of the atrial myocardium resulting in fine, rapid, irregular and uncoordinated movements.

Ventricular fibrillation — Extremely rapid, totally incoordinate contraction of the ventricular myocardial fibers resulting in the very rapid, irregular and uncoordinated movements of the ventricle.

Fibrillogenesis—Formation of fibrils.

Fibrillolysis—Dissolution of the fibrils.

Fibrillolytic—Dissolving the fibrils.

Fibrin—A whitish, filamentous, insoluble protein formed from fibrinogen by the action of thrombin on it, which is essential for clotting the blood.

Fibrino- —A prefix denoting fibrin.

Fibrinocellular—Made up of fibrin and cells.

Fibrinogen—A protein present in the blood plasma which through the action of thrombin in the presence of calcium ions is converted into fibrin which is essential for clotting of the blood.

Fibrinogenemia—Excess of fibrinogen in the blood.

Fibrinogenesis—Production of fibrin.

Fibrinogenic, Fibrinogenous—Producing fibrin.

Fibrinogenolysis— Decomposition or dissolution of fibrinogen in the blood.

Fibrinogenopenia— Deficiency of fibrinogen in the blood usually due to liver disorder.

Fibrinoid—Resembling fibrin.

Fibrinolysin—Plasmin, a substance formed from plasminogen, which dissolves the fibrin.

Fibrinolysis—Dissolution of fibrin by fibrinolysin.

Fibrinolytic—Pertaining to the substance dissolving the fibrin.

Fibrinopenia—Deficiency of fibrin in the blood.

Fibrinopeptide—The substance removed from fibrinogen during coagulation of blood by the action of thrombin.

Fibrinoplastic—Pertaining to fibroplastin.

Fibrinoplatelet—Composed of fibrin and platelets, as a blood clot.

Fibrinopurulent—Consisting of fibrin and pus.

Fibrinoscopy—Inoscopy. To make the diagnosis of a disease by examining the fibrin of blood clots.

Fibrinosis—Presence of fibrin in the blood in excess.

Fibrinous—Pertaining to or of the nature of, or containing fibrin.

Fibrinuria—Presence of fibrin in the urine.

Fibro- —A prefix indicating relationship to the fibers or fibrous tissues.

Fibroadenia—Fibrous degeneration of the glands.

Fibroadenoma—Adenoma containing firbous tissues.

Fibroadipose—Both fibrous and fatty.

Fibroangioma—An angioma containing much fibrous tissue.

Fibroareolar—Containing both, fibrous and areolar tissues.

Fibroblast—Fibrocyte. Any cell producing fibers of the connective tissue.

Fibroblastic—Pertaining to fibroblasts.

Fibroblastoma—A tumor arising from the fibroblasts or connective tissue.

Fibrobronchitis—Croupous bronchitis.

Fibrocalcific—Pertaining to or characterized by partially calcified fibrous material.

Fibrocarcinoma—Carcinoma of the fibrous tissue.

Fibrocartilage—A form of cartilage in which the matrix contains thick bundles of white or collagenous fibers as seen in the intervertebral disk.

Fibrocartilaginous— Pertaining to or composed of fibrocartilage.

Fibrocaseous—A soft, cheesy material formed by the fibroblasts, and infiltrated in the fibrous tissue.

Fibrocellular—Fibroareolar. Both fibrous and cellular.

Fibrochondritis— Inflammation of fibrocartilage.

Fibrochondroma—Tumor of the fibrous tissue and cartilage.

Fibrocyst—A fibrous tumor that has undergone cystic degeneration.

Fibrocystic—Pertaining to or consisting of fibrocysts.

Fibrocystoma—Fibroma combined with cystoma.

Fibrocyte—A fibroblast.

Fibrodysplasia—Abnormal development of fibrous connective tissue.

Fibroelastic—Containing both fibrous and elastic tissues.

Fibroelastosis—Overgrowth of the fibroelastic tissue, *e.g.*, fibroelastosis endocardial in which there is fibroelastosis of the endocardium, causing cardiac failure.

Fibroenchondroma—An enchondroma containing fibrous elements.

Fibroepithelial—Pertaining to the fibrous tissue and the epithelium.

Fibroepithelioma—A tumor containing both, fibrous and epithelial elements.

Fibrofatty—Fibroadipose.

Fibrogenesis—The production or development of fibers.

Fibroglioma—A fibroma combined with glioma.

Fibroid—A tumor containing fibrous tissue or a growth resembling fibrous structure or a fibroma, *e.g.,* fibroid uterus.

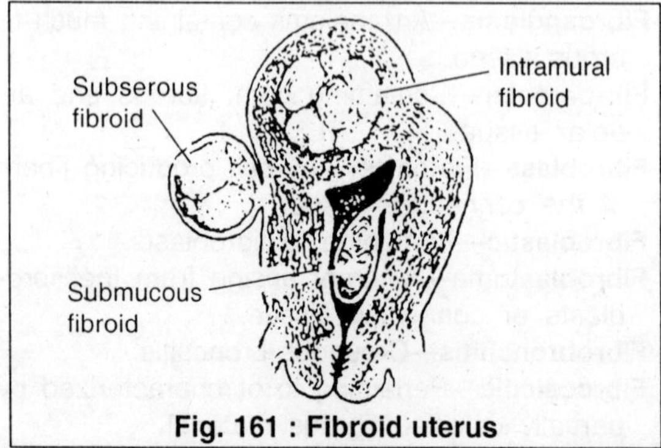

Fig. 161 : Fibroid uterus

Fibroidectomy—Excision of a fibroid tumor.

Fibroleiomyoma—Fibroid.

Fibrolipoma—A lipoma containing fibrous tissue in excess.

Fibroma—A tumor composed of fibrous or connective tissue, e.g., fibroid uterus and fibroma breast.

Fibromatogenic—Producing fibroma.

Fibromatoid—Resembling fibroma, fibroma-like.

Fibromatosis—Fibrosis —Occurrence of many fibromas at a time.

Fibromatous—Pertaining to or of the nature of fibroma.

Fibromectomy—Excision of a fibroid tumor.

Fibromembranous—Having both, the fibrous and the membranous tissue.

Fibrometer—An instrument for measuring the blood clot formation.

Fibromuscular—Consisting of both, the fibrous tissue and the muscle.

Fibromyalgia—Chronic pain in the muscles and soft tissues surrounding the joints.

Fibromyitis—Inflammation of the muscle followed by fibrous degeneration of the muscle.

Fibromyoma—A myoma (tumor containing muscle tissue) containing fibrous tissue.

Fibromyomectomy—Removal of a fibromyoma, especially from the uterus.

Fibromyositis—Inflammation of the fibromuscular tissue.

Fibromyotomy—To make an incision into a fibroid tumor.

Fibromyxoma—A fibroma which has undergone myxomatous degeneration partially.

Fibromyxosarcoma—A sarcoma containing fibrous and mucoid elements.

Fibroneuroma—Neurofibroma. A fibroma combined with neuroma.

Fibro-osteoma—Osteofibroma. A tumor of bony and fibrous tissue.

Fibropapilloma—A mixed tumor containing fibroma and papilloma sometimes occurring in the bladder.

Fibroplasia—Formation of fibrous tissue as in wound healing.

Fibroplastic—Forming fibrous tissue.

Fibroplastin—Paraglobulin. A globulin present in the blood serum and other body fluids.

Fibroplate—Articular disk; a plate composed of fibrocartilage attached to the joint capsule, separating the articular surfaces of the bones.

Fibropolypus—A polyp composed chiefly of fibrous tissue.

Fibropurulent —Containing both, fibers and pus.

Fibroreticulate—Pertaining to or consisting of a network of fibrous tissue.

Fibrosarcoma—A sarcoma containing fibrous tissue.

Fibrose—To form fibrous tissue.

Fibroserous—Consisting of both, the fibrous tissue and the serous elements.

Fibrosis—An abnormal formation of fibrous tissue, e.g., fibrosis of the lungs following pneumonia or pulmonary tuberculosis.

Fibrositis—Inflammation of the white fibrous connective tissue, especially of the locomotor system.

Fibrothorax —Fibrosis causing the two pleural layers of the lung to adhere to each other.

Fibrotic—Pertaining to or characterized by fibrosis.

Fibrous—Composed of or containing fibers.

Fibrovascular—Both, fibrous and vascular.

Fibula—The outer and thinner bone of the leg from the knee to the ankle, articulating above with the tibia and below with the tibia and talus.

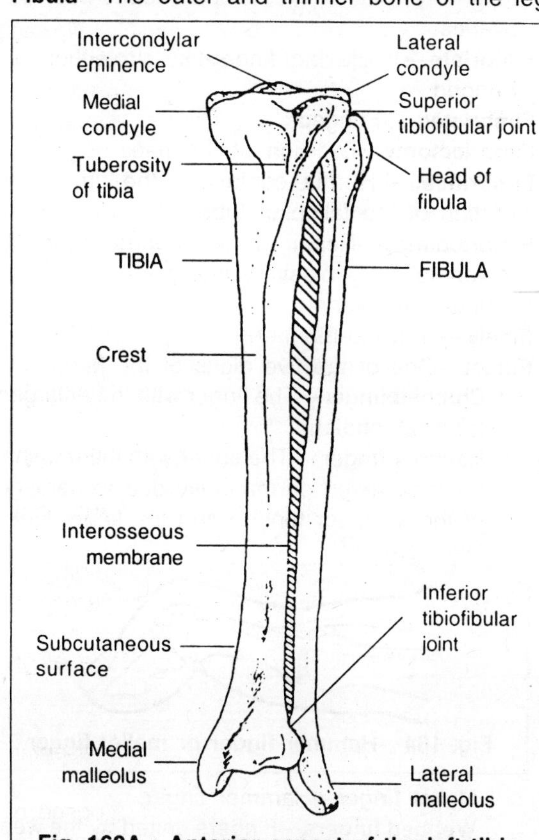

Fig. 162A : Anterior aspect of the left tibia and fibula bone

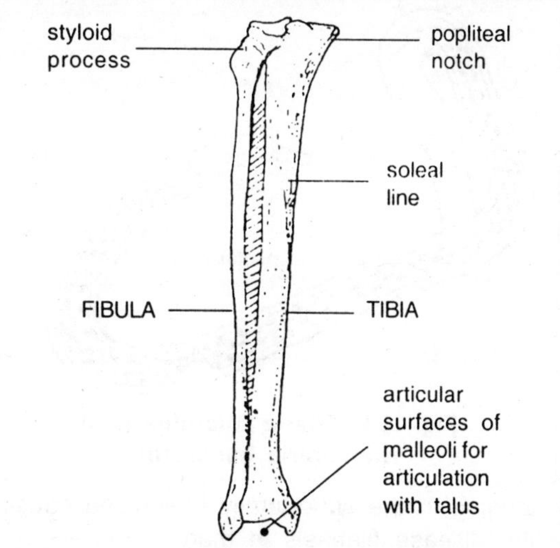

Fig. 162B : Posterior aspect of the left tibia and fibula bone

Fibular—Pertaining to the fibula.

Fibularis— Fibular.

Fibulocalcaneal —Pertaining to the fibula and the calcaneus bones.

F.I.C.D—Fellow of the International College of Dentists.

F.I.C.S.—Fellow of the International College of Surgeons.

Ficus—A fig-wart.

Fidgety—Uneasy, restless.

Field—A specific area in relation to an object, *e.g.*, auditory field—the maximum distance from which one can hear the sound or field of vision—the maximum area upto which an eye can see.

Figurate —Skin lesions that have a certain form such as geographic, rectangular, cuboid, circular etc.

Figure—1. The shape, form or outline of the body. 2. A number.

Fig-wart—Fig looking wart.

Fila—Plural of filum.

Filaceous—Composed of filaments.

Filament —A fine thread-like structure.

Filamentary—Of the nature of a filament.

Filamentous—Composed of fine thread-like structures.

Filamentum, plural **filamenta**—Filament.

Filar—Filamentous.

Filaria—A long thread-like nematode worm be-

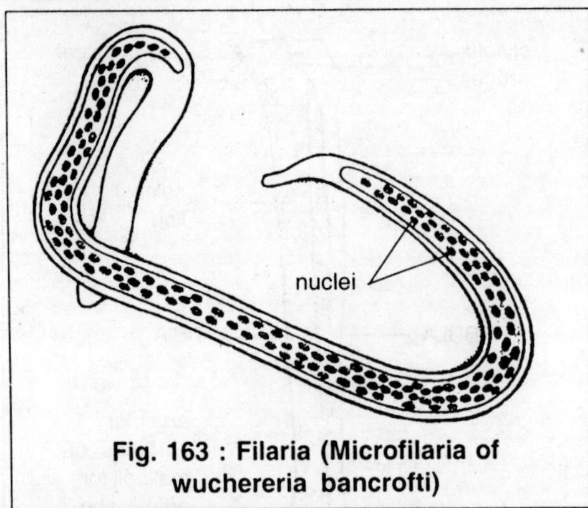

Fig. 163 : Filaria (Microfilaria of wuchereria bancrofti)

longing to the superfamily Filarioidea causing the disease filariasis in man.

Filariae—Plural of filaria. Filaria

Filarial—Pertaining to or caused by filariae.

Filariasis—A chronic disease caused by filaria.

Filaricidal—Pertaining to that which destroys filariae.

Filaricide—An agent destroying filariae.

Filariform—Resembling filaria.

File—A metal instrument with roughened surface used for rasping and smoothing.

Filial—Pertaining to a son or daughter.

Filiform—Long thread-like, filamentous.

Filioparental—Pertaining to a child-parent relationship.

Fillet—1. A loop of thread, cord or tape for making traction or to suspend the tissues during surgery. 2. In the nervous system, bundle of nerve fibers in the medulla, pons, and brain.

Filling—1. The material to be inserted in a prepared tooth cavity, usually the amalgam. 2. The operation of filling the tooth cavities.

Film—1. A thin layer. 2. A thin sheet of material usually of gelatin or cellulose coated with a light-sensitive emulsion, used in radiography. 3. A thin layer of blood or other material spread on a slide or coverslip.

Filopressure—Compression of a blood vessel by a ligature.

Filovaricosis—Dilatation or thickening of the axon of a nerve fiber.

Filter—1. To pass a liquid through any porous substance which prevents particles larger than a certain size to pass through. 2. An apparatus for filtering liquids, light rays or radiations.

Berkefeld filter—This type of filter is made of a special type of earth that removes bacteria from the solutions filtered through it and so it is also known as bacterial filter, but viruses are passed through it into the filtrate.

Seitz filter—It consists of a disc of asbestos that is inserted into metal holders which ensure a tight joint. The solution to be sterilized is filtered through it, bacteria are stayed above it and the filtrate below it contains bacteria free solution. This disc is used only once.

Filterable—Capable of being passed through the pores of a filter.

Filter paper—A coarse paper used for filtration.

Filth—Dirt.

Filtrate—The liquid that has passed through a filter.

Filtration—The process of removing particles from a liquid by passing it through a filter.

Filum—A thread-like structure, e.g., filum terminale—a long thread-like end of the spinal cord.

Fimbria—Any structure resembling fringe, e.g., fringe-like ends of the fallopian tubes near the ovaries.

Fimbriate—1. Having finger-like projection. 2. Fringed.

Fimbriated —Fringed.

Fimbriectomy—Excision of fimbriae.

Fimbriocele—Hernia containing the fimbriated portion of the fallopian tube.

Fimbrioplasty—Repair of the fimbriae of the fallopian tube by plastic surgery.

Finding—Discovery.

Finely—In a fine manner.

Finger—One of the five digits of the hand.

Clubbed finger—The finger with the enlarged terminal phalanx.

Hammer finger— The finger with the terminal phalanx flexed permanently due to damage of the extensor tendon and the finger looks like hammer.

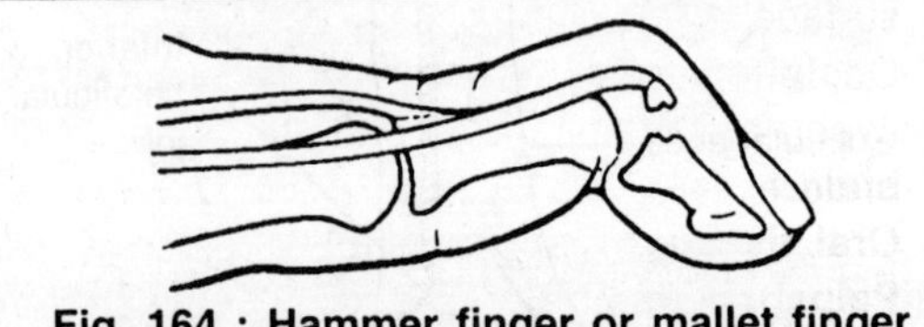

Fig. 164 : Hammer finger or mallet finger

Mallet finger—Hammer finger.

Webbed fingers—Fingers united by the web.

Finger cot—Finger-stall. A covering made up of plastic, rubber, leather or metal to protect the injured finger from trauma during the healing process.

Finger print—The impression made by cutaneous ridges of the fleshy distal portion of a finger.

Finger spelling—The method of communication used for deaf persons in which the words are spelled out letter by letter by different positions of the fingers.

Finger-stall—Finger cot.

Finite—Having boundaries.

Fire—In dentistry, the mixing of water and a powder containing substances to produce porcelain used in restoration and artificial teeth.

Fireplace—Hearth.

First aid—An emergency help and treatment given to an injured or ill person before the arrival of a doctor, reaching a hospital or doctor's clinic.

Fishskin disease—Ichthyosis. Dry, scaly and horny skin like that of the fish.

Fission—1. The process of splitting into two or more parts. 2. A method of asexual reproduction seen in bacteria, protozoa or lower animals in which the cell or body divides into two or more parts, each of which develops into a new complete organism. 3. Nuclear fission—the splitting of the atomic nucleus, with the release of energy.

Fissiparous—Reproducing by fission.

Fissula—A small cleft.

Fissura—Cleft, sulcus. A fissure.

Fissurae—Plural of fissura.

Fissural—Pertaining to a fissure.

Fissuration—The condition of being fissured.

Fissure—1. A cleft, groove or deep furrow in the brain, spinal cord, liver and other organs. 2. Cracklike ulcer. 3. A break in the enamel surface of a tooth.

Anal fissure—A painful linear ulcer at the margin of the anus.

Longitudinal fissure—A fissure on the lower surface of the liver.

Occipitoparietal fissure —The fissure between the occipital and parietal lobes of the brain.

Oral fissure—Oral opening.

Palpebral fissure —The gap between the upper and lower eye lids.

Transverse fissure—The fissure between the cerebellum and cerebrum of the brain.

Fistula—An abnormal passage between two internal organs or from an internal organ to the outside of the body, which may be congenital or may result from abscesses or injuries.

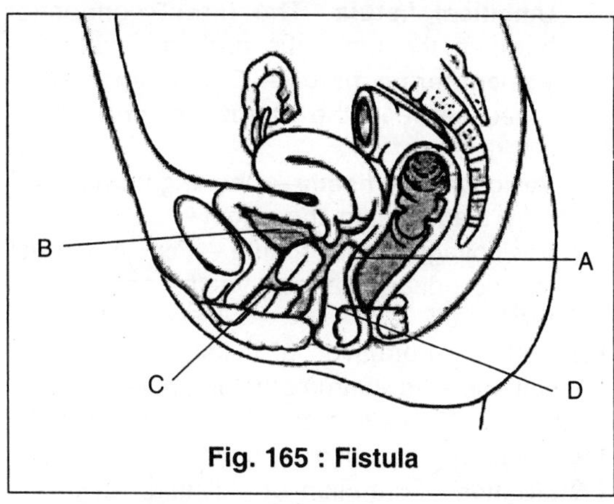

Fig. 165 : Fistula

A. Rectovaginal fistula
B. Vesicovaginal fistula
C. Urethrovaginal fistula
D. Vaginoperineal fistula

Anal fistula—Fistula situated near the anus which may or may not communicate with the rectum.

Arteriovenous fistula —A passage between an artery and a vein.

Blind fistula —A fistula that opens at one end only or the fistula opening on the skin.

Cervical fistula—1. An abnormal opening into the cervix of the uterus. 2. An opening in the neck leading to the pharynx.

Colovesical fistula—Vesicocolic fistula. Fistula between the colon and the urinary bladder.

Complete fistua—Fistula which is opened at both ends, externally and internally.

Enterovaginal fistula—A passage between the intestine and the vagina.

Enterovesical fistula— Fistula between the intestine and the urinary bladder.

Fecal fistula—A passage between an opening of the large intestine (colon) and that situated on the external surface of the body, through which the feces discharges.

Gastric fistula—A passage made between the stomach and the skin.

Incomplete fistula— Blind fistula.

Parotid fistula—A passage made between the parotid gland and the skin surface.

Rectovaginal fistula—A communication established between the rectum and the vagina.

Rectovesical fistula— Fistula between the rectum and the urinary bladder.

Umbilical fistula—The direct connection between the umbilicus and the intestine.

Vesicouterine fistula—Connection established between the uterus and the urinary bladder.

Vesicovaginal fistula—Opening from the urinary bladder into the vagina.

Vesicovaginorectal fistula —Fistula connecting the urinary bladder, vagina and the rectum.

Fistulation —Formation of a fistula.

Fistulatome—An instrument for operating a fistula.

Fistulectomy—Excision of a fistula.

Fistulization—Formation of a fistula.

Fistuloenterostomy—To close a biliary fistula and form a new passage of bile into the intestine, by surgery.

Fistulotomy—To make an incision into a fistula.

Fistulous—Pertaining to, containing or of the nature of a fistula.

Fit—1. Convulsion, a sudden attack of a disease or paroxysm. 2. Modification of one structure to that of another. 3. Suitable.

Fitness—The state of being fit.

Clinical fitness— Total absence of disease from which someone was suffering.

Fix —To treat a tissue chemically so that the components and products of its cells are preserved for staining and microscopic examination.

Fixation—1. The act of making immovable or the state of being immovable 2. Immobility. 3. The cessation of development of personality. 4. For microscopic examination, the preservation of tissue for the examination of its structure in detail without changing its normal state.

Fixation complement—See behind complement fixation test.

Fixative—1. A substance which fixes or makes rigid. 2. A substance used to harden and preserve the pathological specimens so as to maintain their normal structures.

Fixing—Destroying the tissue elements rapidly so that their normal living form is preserved for microscopic examination.

FL—Fluid.

Flaccid—Relaxed, flebby, having deficient muscular tone, weak or soft.

Flaccidity—Relaxation, flebbiness, deficiency in muscular tone, weakness or softness.

Flaccid paralysis—Paralysis associated with loss of muscle tone.

Flagella—Plural of flagellum.

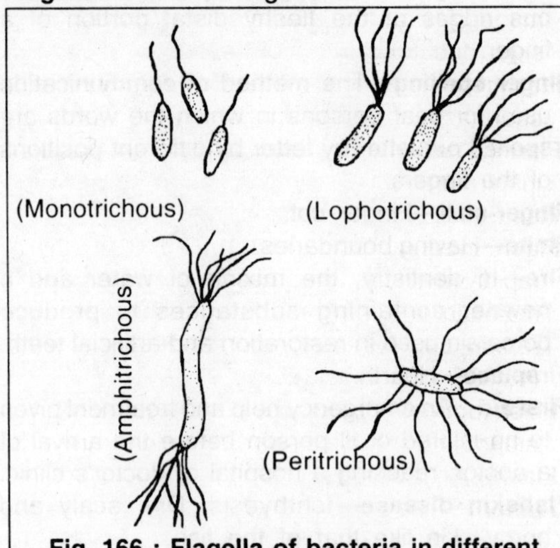

Fig. 166 : Flagella of bacteria in different arrangement

Flagellant—1. Pertaining to flagellum. 2. Pertaining to stroking in massage. 3. The person who practices in massage by strokes.

Flagellar—Of or pertaining to a flagellum.

Flagellate—A group of protozoa possessing one or more flegella, belonging to the class mastigophora.

Flagellated—Possessing one or more flagella.

Flagellation—1. Production of flagella. 2. Massage by strokes. 3. Sexual stimulation by whipping or by being whipped.

Flagelliform—Shaped like a flagellum.

Flagellosis—Disease produced by flagellate protozoa.

Flagellum—A long hairlike moving appendage arising from the external surface of a bacterium or a protozoon.

Flail—Exhibiting abnormal or pathologic mobility, as flail chest due to multiple fractures of the ribs or flail joint due to paralysis of the muscles controlling it.

Flake—Layer, crust.

Flaking—Crusting or desquamation.

Flammable—Likely to burn.

Flange—A projecting edge or rim.

Flank—The side of the body between the ribs and the upper border of the ilium.

Flannelmouth—A person who speaks with thick voice.

Flap—1. A piece of tissue usually the skin removed from some part of the body, for gráfting in plastic surgery. 2. An uncontrolled movement seen in some diseases.

Flare—A diffuse area of redness around a line made by drawing a pointed instrument on the skin, due to vasomotor reaction.

Flarimeter—An apparatus for measuring the shortness of breath.

Flaring, nasal —Dilatation of the nostrils during inspiration.

Flash—1. Sudden blaze. 2. Hot flash.

Flash method—The pasteurization of milk by rapidly raising its temperature to 178°F (80.1°C), maintain it there for a few minutes and then rapidly cooling it until the temperature is 40°F (4.4°C).

Flash point—The temperature at which a substance bursts into flame spontaneously.

Flask—A glass vessel with a constricted neck.

Flatfoot—The condition in which the arch of the foot becomes flattened.

Flatness—The state of being flat.

Flattened—Made flat.

Flatulence—Formation of gas in excess in the stomach and intestine.

Flatulent—The person affected with the gas formation in the stomach and intestines due to imperfect digestion and other causes.

Flatus—1. Gas in the digestive tract. 2. Gas passed through the anus.

Flatus tube—A rubber rectal tube used to facilitate the expulsion of gases in severe cases of distension, or before a saline enema.

Flavedo—Yellowness or sallowness as of the skin.

Flavescent—Yellowish.

Flavin—Any of a group of water soluble yellow pigments occurring in milk, yeasts, bacteria and some plants.

Flavism—The condition of having a yellow tinge.

Flavo- —A prefix indicating yellow.

Flavoprotein—A form of protein that constitutes the yellow enzymes essential in cellular respiration.

Flavor—1. Pleasing smell. 2. A material added to food or medicine for improving its taste.

Flavoring—A substance used to give a flavor.

Flavus—Yellow.

fl. dr. —Fluidram.

Flea— A small, wingless, bloodsucking, jumping insect. Fleas of the genus Xenopsylla transmit the bacteria of the plague (yersinia pestis) from rats to humans.

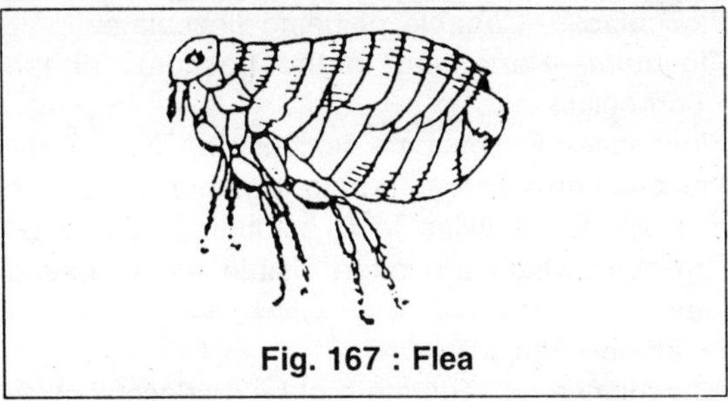

Fig. 167 : Flea

Flea infestation—The trouble caused by flea bites.

Flesh—The soft tissues, especially the muscle of the body.

Fletcherism—The taking of small amounts of food at a time with mastication excessively.

Flex—To bend.

Flexibilitas cerea—The condition in which the limbs remain in the same position in which they are placed.

Flexibility—Pliability. Capability of bending without breaking.

Flexible—Capable of being bent without breaking.

Flexile—Pliant, flexible.

Fleximeter—Goniometer.

Flexion—The act of bending.

Flexor—A muscle that bends a joint.

Flexura—Flexure.

Flexurae —Plural of flexura.

Flexure—Flexura. A bend as in an organ or structure.

Flicker—To quiver, to flutter.

Flint disease—Chalicosis. Pneumoconiosis caused by the inhalation of dust produced by cutting the stones.

Floaters—Spots of various sizes and shapes appearing before the eyes, which are due to small bits of protein or cells floating in the vitreous humor.

Floating—Swimming, moving about.

Floating kidney—Kidney movable from its normal site.

Floating ribs—11th and 12th ribs which do not articulate with the sternum.

Floccillation, Floccitation—Carphologia. Carphology. Picking at bedclothes in semiconscious state in fever, and stupor and delirium.

Flocci volitantes—Specks floating before the eyes.

Floccose—Woolly. Pertaining to a growth composed of short and densely but irregularly interwoven filaments.

Flocculable—Capable of being flocculated.

Floccular—Pertaining to the flocculus of the cerebellum.

Flocculate—To become flocculent.

Flocculation—The gathering together of the fine dispersed particles in a solution into larger masses which are often visible to the naked eye.

Floccule—Flocculus.

Flocculence—1. The state of being flocculent. 2. Flakiness.

Flocculent—1. Woolly 2. Containing whitish flaky fragments of mucus.

Flocculi—Plural of flocculus.

Flocculoreaction— Flocculation of a serum reaction.

Flocculus—1. A small bunch of a fibrous material. 2. A small lobe situated below each cerebral hemisphere, behind the middle peduncle, on each side of the median fissure.

Flood—Excessive bleeding from the uterus, as occurs after childbirth or in menorrhagia.

Flooding—1. Excessive blood flow as often occurs during menstruation 2. In behavior therapy, the treatment of phobias by repeated exposures to the aversive stimuli until they no longer produce anxiety.

Flora—The collective plant organisms of a particular region.

Intestinal flora—The bacteria living in the intestines.

Vaginal flora—The bacteria living in the vagina.

Florid—Flushed. The skin of bright red color.

Floss—A waxed thread made of silk, used to clean the spaces between the teeth.

Flotation—The process for separating solids by their tendency to float on, or sink into a liquid.

Flour—Finely ground meal obtained from wheat or other grains.

Flow—1. Menstrual discharge. 2. Movement of a liquid as blood, or gas.

Flowmeter—An apparatus for measuring the rate of flow of liquids or gases.

fl-oz—Fluid ounce, 29.57 milliliters.

Flu—Influenza.

Fluctuance—Fluctuation.

Fluctuant—Varying. Unstable, Changeable.

Fluctuate—To move in waves or to vary from time to time as blood pressure, or concentration of a substance such as sugar in the blood.

Fluctuation—Variation. Unstability, change.

Fluency—To speak smoothly without interruptions or repetitions.

Fluent—Flowing.

Fluid—Any liquid of the body.

Amniotic fluid—A clear yellowish fluid found within the fetal membranes in pregnancy, which protects the fetus from injury.

Cerebrospinal fluid—The fluid found within the ventricles of the brain, the subarachnoid space about the brain and in the central canal of the spinal cord.

Extracellular fluid —Fluid present outside the tissue cells, and blood plasma, constituting about 20% of body weight.

Extravascular fluid—All the body fluids outside the blood vessels.

Intracellular fluid— Fluid present within the tissue cells, constituting about 30-40% of the body weight.

Intraocular fluid— The fluid present within the anterior and posterior chambers of the eye.

Pleural fluid —The fluid present in the pleural cavity.

Seminal fluid —Semen.

Serous fluid—Fluid secreted by serous membranes that reduces friction in the serous cavities, as in peritoneal cavity.

Synovial fluid—Fluid contained within the synovial cavities.

Fluidextract, Fluidextractum—Solution of the soluble portion of a vegetable drug containing alcohol as a solvent or preservative, of such strength that each milliliter contains 1 gm. of the drug.

Fluidity—The state of being fluid, liquidity.

Fluidram—Fluid drachm. A measure of fluid volume which is equal to 3.697 mls.

Fluke—A broad, flat parasitic worm belonging to the phylum platyhelminthes infesting blood, intestine or liver in man.

Flumen—A flow or stream.

Flumina pilorum—The curved lines along which the hairs of the body are arranged.

Fluor albus—Leukorrhea, white discharge from the vagina.

Fluoresce—To produce or exhibit fluorescence.

Fluorescence—The property of a substance to emit light when exposed to certain types of light radiation as ultraviolet rays.

Fluorescent—Emitting light or shining when exposed to other light rays.

Fluoridation—The addition of fluoride to a water supply in order to prevent the dental caries.

Fluoride—A compound of fluorine.

Fluoridization—Fluoridation. Application of fluoride solution to the teeth.

Fluorine—A gaseous chemical element found in the soil in combination with the calcium, which is necessary for the development of the plants. It is also found in cow's milk, egg yolk and brain and helps to form the bones and teeth in man.

Fluorography —Photofluorography.

Fluorometer—An apparatus for measuring the amount of radiation produced by X-rays.

Fluorometry—To measure the amount of radiation produced by X-rays, by means of a fluorometer.

Fluoronephelometer—An instrument for analysing a solution by measuring the light scattered or emitted by it.

Fluorophotometry—To measure light emitted by a fluorescent substance.

Fluororoentgenography — Photofluorography.

Fluoroscope—An apparatus consisting of a fluoroscent screen and an X-ray tube, used for observing the deep structures of the body by means of X-ray shadows projected on the fluoroscent screen.

Fluoroscopic—Pertaining to or affected by fluoroscopy.

Fluoroscopy—Photoscopy. To observe the deep structures of the body by using a fluoroscope.

Fluorosis—Chronic fluorine poisoning due to much fluoride in the drinking water or to chronic inhalation of industrial dusts or gases containing fluorides, characterized by osteosclerosis and osteomalacia combined, and mottling of the enamel of the teeth.

Fluorouracil—An antimetabolite used in the treatment of certain forms of cancer.

Flush—1. Redness of the face and neck, *e.g.*, hectic flush in which there is redness of the cheeks in chronic debilitating diseases such as pulmonary tuberculosis (chronic flush) or in pyrexia (acute flush), and hot flush in which the flush is accompanied with the sensation of heat, common in psychoneurosis and during menopause. 2. Irrigation of a cavity with water.

Flutter—Rapid movement, especially of the heart as atrial flutter in which the contractions of the atrium become 200 to 400 per minute and ventricular flutter in which the contractions of the ventricles become 250 or more per minute.

Flutter-fibrillation—Impure atrial flutter resembling to flutter and fibrillation.

Flux—1. An excessive flow or discharge from an organ or cavity of the body. 2. Discharge from the intestines.

Fluxion—The act of flowing or passing away.

Fly—An insect possessing sucking mouth parts, two wings and is the carrier of the disease-producing organisms as house fly.

Flying blister—A blister rapidly changing its place.

f.m.—Let a mixture be made. It is used in prescription writing.

Foam—Collection of small bubbles on the surface of a liquid.

Foaming—Producing foams.

Foamy—Full of foam.

Focal—Pertaining to a focus.

Focal infection—Infection occurring near a focus, such as the cavity of a tooth.

Focal lesion—A lesion occurring in a limited central area.

Foci—Plural of focus.

Focimeter—Lensometer.

Focus—1. Center. 2. The point at which the light rays or the sound waves meet. 3. The starting point of a disease process.

Focussing—The act of meeting at a point.

Fog—Mist.

Fogging—A method of determining the refractive error in astigmatism.

Foil —Very thin and flexible sheet of a metal.

Fold—Plica. A thin recurved margin or doubling back.

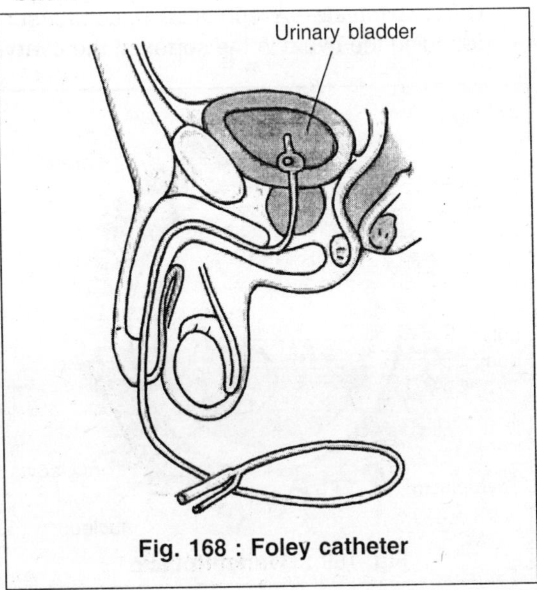

Fig. 168 : Foley catheter

Foley catheter—A type of urinary tract catheter with a balloon attached at one end which is filled with sterile water after the catheter is inserted into the urinary bladder, to prevent the catheter from leaving the bladder until the balloon is emptied.

Folia—Plural of folium.

Foliaceous—Foliate. Pertaining to or resembling a leaf.

Foliar—Foliate. Pertaining to or resembling a leaf.

Foliate —Foliar. Foliaceous.

Folie—Psychosis. Mania.

Folie a deux—Occurrence of similar psychosis at the same time in two closely associated persons.

Folie circulaire—Mania for making rounds.

Folie du doute —Abnormal doubts about ordinary things.

Folie du pourquoi—Mania for putting up the unreasonable and unrelating questions constantly.

Foliose—Foliate.

Folium—Thin, broad, leaf-like structure.

Follicle—A small secretory sac, cavity or gland.

Gastric follicle— Lymph glands present in the mucosa of the stomach.

Hair follicle—A tubular invagination of the epidermis enclosing the hair and from which the hair grows.

Nabothian follicle— Cystic dilatation of the glands in the mucosa of the cervix of the uterus.

Ovarian follicle—A spherical structure surrounding the ovum in the cortex of the ovary.

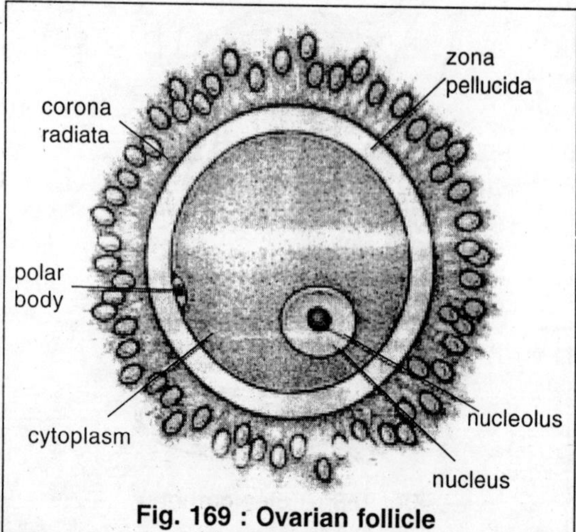

Fig. 169 : Ovarian follicle

Sebaceous follicle—An oil gland of the skin.

Follicle-stimulating hormone—FSH. A hormone produced by the anterior pituitary gland, which stimulates the growth of the follicle in the ovary and spermatogenesis in the testis.

Follicle-stimulating hormone-releasing hormone—FSH-RH. A hormone of the hypothalamus which stimulates the release of follicle-stimulating hormone from the anterior pituitary gland.

Follicular—Pertaining to a follicle or follicles.

Follicular tonsillitis— Inflammation of the follicles on the surface of the tonsil, which become filled with pus.

Folliculi—Plural of folliculus or follicle.

Folliculitis—Inflammation of a follicle or follicles *e.g.,* ringworm of the beard (barber's itch).

Folliculogenesis— Development of follicles.

Folliculogenesis, induction of—Stimulation of follicle development in the ovary by using drugs or hormones.

Folliculoma—A tumor of the graafian follicle of the ovary.

Folliculose—Made up of follicles.

Folliculosis—Excessive development of the lymph follicles.

Folliculus—A follicle.

Follow up—To strive after.

Foment—To apply hot, moist flannel etc., externally for the relief of pain or inflammation.

Fomentation—External application of hot, moist flannel, etc., for the relief of pain or inflammation.

Fomes—Anything as clothes, towel and utensils etc. that harbor and transmit a disease–producing organism.

Fomit —Fomes.

Fomites—Plural of fomes.

Fontanel, Fontanelle—One of the spaces situated between the cranial bones of a fetus or infants covered by a membrane.

Anterior fontanel— Fontanel at the junction of the coronal, frontal and sagittal sutures.

Posterior fontanel— Fontanel at the junction of the sagittal and lambdoid sutures.

Fonticuli—Plural of fonticulus.

Fonticulus—Fontanel.

Food—Anything which when taken into the body supply heat, produce energy and maintains growth by building up the tissues.

Food additives—Substances added to food to increase its flavor, taste and other qualities.

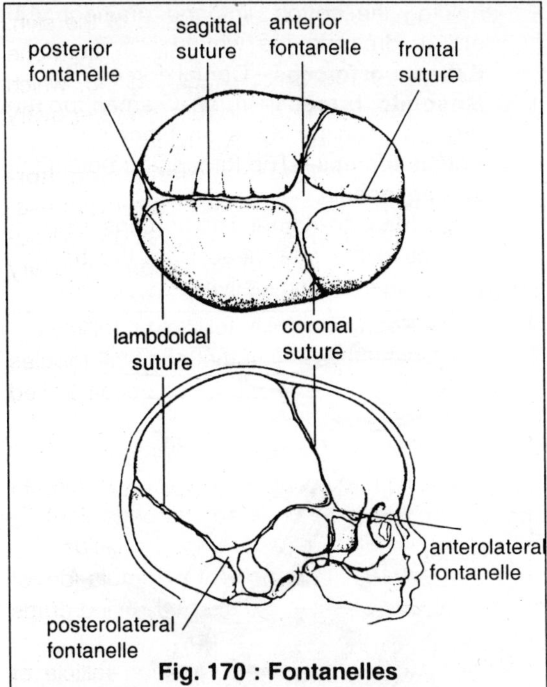

Fig. 170 : Fontanelles

Food adulterant—A substance added to food which makes the food impure and cheap.

Food ball—A spherical mass formed in the stomach of the ingested food.

Food poisoning—A condition resulting from ingestion of food containing poisonous substances.

Foot—1. The terminal portion of the leg upon which a person stands and walks. 2. A unit of length containing 12 inches (30.48 Cms.)

Athlete's foot—Tinea pedis.

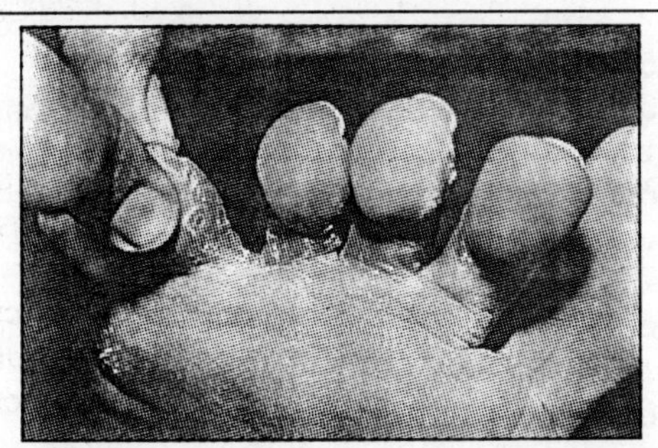
Fig. 171 : Athlete's foot=Tinea pedis

Foot board —A board placed vertically at the end of the patient's bed to prevent foot drop.

Foot candle—An amount of light equivalent to 1 lumen per square foot.

Foot drop—Plantar flexion of the foot from weakness or paralysis of the anterior muscles of the lower leg, which may occur in a patient lying on bed continuously for a long time, especially if comatose.

Footling presentation—The coming out of the feet at first in childbirth.

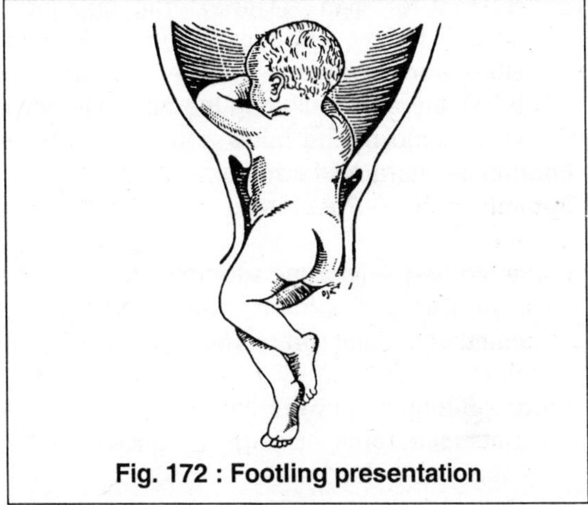
Fig. 172 : Footling presentation

Foot plate—The flat portion of the stapes bone in the middle ear, which is set on the oval opening on the medial wall of the middle ear.

Foot-pound—The amount of energy necessary to lift one pound weight to a vertical distance of one foot.

Foot-poundal—The amount of energy exerted, when a force of one poundal displaces a body 1 foot in the direction of the force; energy equal to about 0.01 calorie.

Foot print—An impression of the foot, especially an ink impression used for identification of the infants.

Forage—1. To create a channel through an enlarged prostate gland by means of an electric cautery. 2. Food for horses and cattles.

Foramen—An opening, orifice or hole, especially in a bone for passage of blood vessels or nerves; a communication between two cavities of an organ.

External auditory foramen —External auditory meatus through which the sound waves reach the tympanic membrane.

Foramen magnum—An opening in the occipital bone through which passes the spinal cord from the brain.

Foramen ovale —1. A large, oval opening in the base of the greater wing of the sphenoid bone, transmitting the mandibular branch of the trigeminal nerve and a small meningeal artery. 2. The opening between the two atria of the fetal heart which usually closes after birth.

Intervertebral foramen—Opening between the articulated vertebrae for the passage of the spinal nerves and vessels.

Nutrient foramen— The external opening in a bone for the entrance of blood vessels.

Obturator foramen— A large, oval foramen below the acetabulum in the hip bone which is bounded by the pubis and ischium bone.

Foramina—Plural of foramen

Foraminiferous—Possessing foramina or openings.

Foraminotomy—To dilate a foramen by an operation as that of the intervertebral foramen.

Foraminulum, plural **foraminula** —A very minute foramen.

Force—Strength, power, energy.

Catabolic force—Energy produced by metabolism of food.

Dynamic force—Energy.

Electromotive force -EMF— Energy that causes the flow of electricity from one point to another.

Gravitational force—Force produced by gravity.

Reserve force—The energy available above that required for normal functioning of the heart.

Forced expiratory volume —FEV — The volume of air that can be expired after a full inspiration.

Forced feeding—Feeding by force as of the insane.

Forceps—A two bladed instrument with a handle used for compressing or grasping tissues, holding the sewing needle during operation or for handling the sterile dressings.

Artery forceps—The forceps used for compressing and grasping an artery.

Bone forceps—Forceps used for cutting bone and for removal of small bone pieces.

Capsule forceps—The forceps for removing the lens capsule in cataract.

Clamp forceps—The forceps with an automatic lock.

Clip forceps—A small forceps used to compress the end of a bleeding vessel, to check bleeding.

Dental forceps—The forceps used for extraction of teeth.

Dressing forceps—The forceps used for holding the cotton, lint and drainage tube etc. in dressing the wound.

Extracting forceps—Dental forceps.

Mosquito forceps—A very small pointed forceps used for arresting bleeding.

Needle forceps—The forceps for holding the sewing needle.

Obstetrical forceps—The forceps used for extracting the fetal head from the pelvis of the mother during delivery.

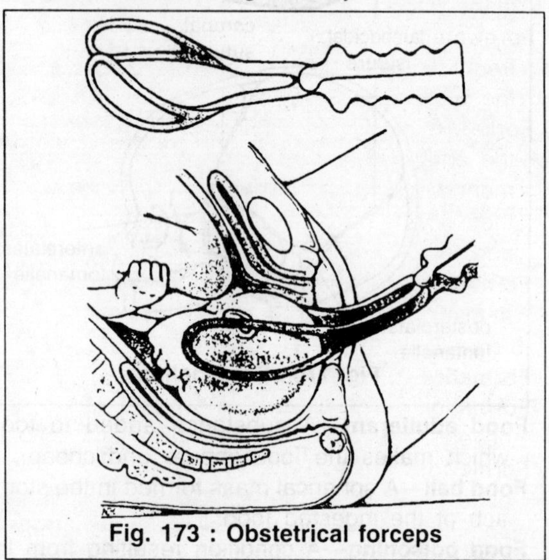

Fig. 173 : Obstetrical forceps

Rongeur forceps— Forceps used for cutting the bone.

Tissue forceps—Forceps with tiny teeth for grasping the delicate tissues.

Towel forceps—Forceps for clipping the towels at the site of the wound to be operated.

Forcipate—Shaped like a forceps.

Forcipressure—The arresting of hemorrhage by applying pressure on an artery with forceps.

Fore- —A prefix meaning before or in front of.

Forearm —The part of the arm between the elbow and the wrist.

Forebrain—Prosencephalon. Anterior portion of the brain of the embryo.

Forefinger—The first or the index finger.

Forefoot—The fore part of the foot.

Foregut—The first part of the digestive tract of an embryo from which pharynx, esophagus, stomach and duodenum are formed.

Forehead—Frons. The part of the face above the eyes and below the hairline.

Forelock—A tuft of hair growing just above the forehead.

Foremilk—Colostrum.

Forensic—Pertaining to or applied in legal proceedings.

Forensic medicine—Medicine in relation to the law, as in autopsy proceedings, the medicine used for the determination of healthy mind.

Foreplay—Mutual sexual stimulation and pleasurable acts before the intercourse.

Forepleasure—Sexual pleasure before orgasm.

Foreskin—The prepuce. A fold of skin over the glans penis.

Forewaters—A thin mucus secretion discharged from the vagina during pregnancy, produced by the uterine glands.

Fork—An instrument with two or more prongs at the end, e.g. tunning fork which is an instrument with two prongs which when are struck, they vibrate and their vibrations can be heard and felt. It is used in testing the hearing.

Form—Size, shape and external appearance of a thing.

-form—Suffix meaning having the form of.

Formatio—Formation.

Formation —The process of giving shape or the development of a structure.

Forme fruste, plural **formes frustes** —An incomplete disease which is being arrested before completion its course.

Formic—Pertaining to ants or formic acid.

Formication—A sensation as of small insects creeping upon the body.

Formiciasis—Irritation caused by ant bites.

Formula—An expression, using numbers or symbols of the composition of, or of directions for preparing a medicine or of a procedure to follow to obtain a desired result.

Chemical formula—The expression of the structure of a molecule by symbols which are letters, each letter denoting one atom of one element and the number with the letter denoting the number of atoms present, as in H_2O (water).

Empirical formula — In chemistry, the formula of a compound that shows the atoms and their numbers in a molecule.

Structural formula— Formula in which the connections of the atoms and groups of atoms, as well as their kinds and numbers are indicated.

Formulae—Plural of formula.

Formulary—A collection of formulae.

Formulate—1. To state in the form of a formula. 2. To prepare according to a prescribed formula.

Formulation—The process of preparing according to a prescribed formula.

Fornicate—1. Arched or vault-like 2. To have sexual intercourse with the person to whom one is not married.

Fornication—Sexual intercourse between two unmarried partners.

Fornices—Plural of fornix.

Fornix—An arch shaped structure or vault-like space formed by such a structure.

Fornix cerebri—A fibrous vault-like band connecting the cerebral hemispheres.

Fornix conjunctivae—Loose fold of mucous membrane connecting the palpebral and bulbar conjunctivae.

Fornix uteri —Anterior and posterior spaces made by the protrusion of the cervix of the uterus into the vagina.

Fornix vaginae—Vaginal fornix.

Fortification—Strengthening.

Fortification spectrum— Teichopsia. Appearance of dark patch with zigzag outlines before the eyes causing temporary blindness in that portion of the eye.

Fortify—To strengthen.

Fortis—Strengthy.

Fossa—A hollow or slightly depressed area.

Axillary fossa—Armpit or axilla.

Cerebral fossa—Any of the depressions situated on the inside of the cranium.

Fossa cubitalis— Cubital fossa.

Glenoid fossa—A depression situated on the scapula in which the head of the humerus bone is fitted.

Hypophyseal fossa—Sella turcica. A depression present in the sphenoid bone in which the pituitary gland is situated.

Iliac fossa—One of the depressions of the iliac bones of the pelvis.

Infraspinous fossa — The hollow space on the dorsal surface of the scapula bone below the spine to which infraspinous muscle is attached.

Popliteal fossa—A diamond-shaped hollow space in the posterior region of the knee joint.

Supratonsillar fossa—Space between the anterior and posterior pillars of the fauces above the tonsil.

Temporal fossa—The depression situated

on the side of the skull below the temporal lines.

Fossae—Plural of fossa.

Fossette—1. A small depression. 2. A small, deep corneal ulcer.

Fossula—A small fossa.

Fossulate—Containing a small fossa.

Foudroyant—Occurring suddenly and with violence.

Foulage—Kneading and pressing in massage of the muscles.

Foulbrood—A contagious disease of honeybees due to Bacillus alvei.

Fourchette —A fold of mucous membrane at the posterior junction of the labia minora.

Fovea—A small pit or cuplike depression *e.g.* fovea centralis retinae, a small pit in the center of the macula lutea of the retina.

Foveae—Plural of fovea.

Foveate, Foveated—Pitted. Having depressions.

Foveation—Formation of pits on the skin as in smallpox.

Foveola—A minute pit or depression.

Foveolae—Plural of foveola.

Foveolar—Pertaining to foveola.

Foveolate—Foveate or foveated.

Fowler's position—Semisitting position.

Fraction—A part or fragment.

Fractional—Pertaining to a fraction.

Fractionation—The separation of components of a substance or mixture.

Fracture —The breaking of a bone.

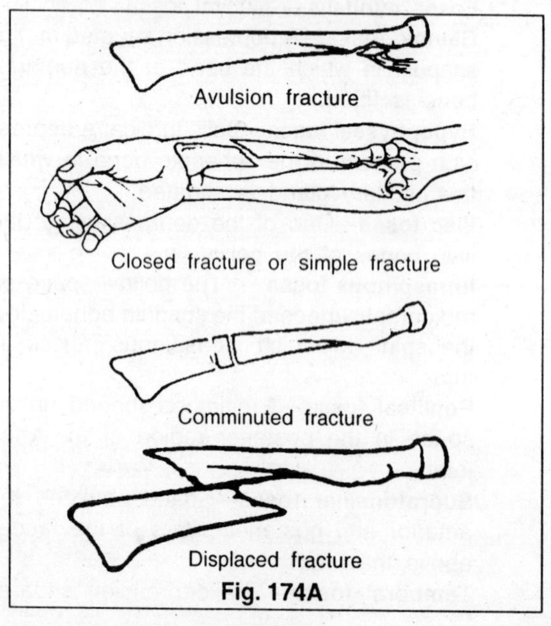

Fig. 174A

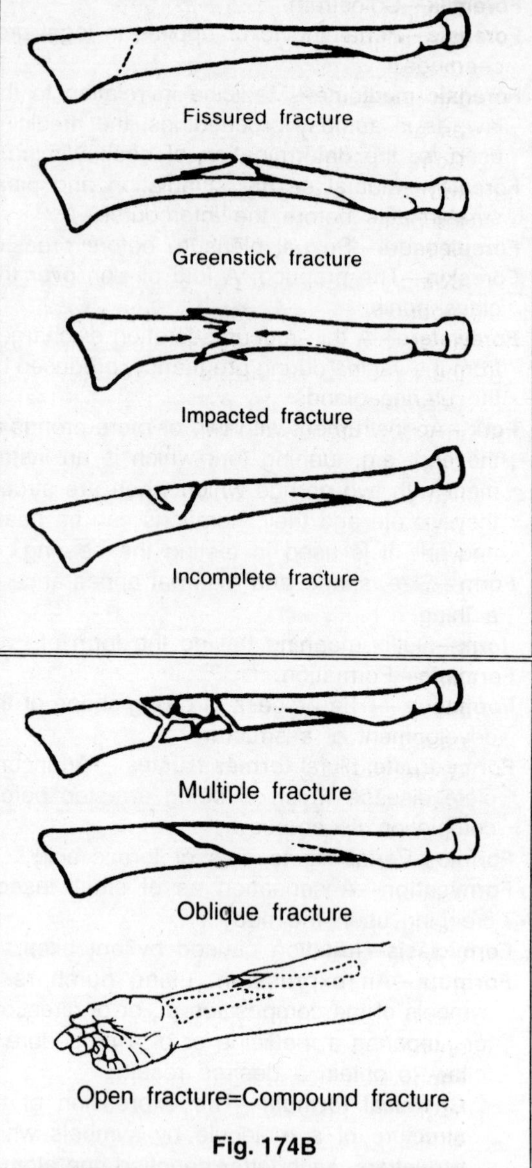

Fig. 174B

Avulsion fracture—Separation of a small piece of bone at the site of attachment of a ligament or tendon, by the force of muscular contractions.

Birth fracture—Fracture occurring in infants during delivery.

Blow-out fracture— Fracture of the orbital wall due to a blow on the eye.

Closed fracture—A fracture in which an open wound on the skin is not formed.

Comminuted fracture—A fracture in which the bone is broken into pieces.

Complete fracture— A fracture in which the bone is completely broken.

Complex fracture—A fracture with soft tissue injury.

Complicated fracture—A fracture in which the broken bone injures some internal organ as a broken rib pierces a lung.

Compound fracture— The breaking of a bone with the formation of an external wound or the protrusion of bone fragments through the skin.

Compression fracture— Fracture of a bone produced by compression, e.g., fracture of a vertebra caused by pressure exerted along the long axis of the vertebral column.

Depressed fracture— Fracture of the skull in which a piece is driven inwards.

Direct fracture— Fracture produced at the site of injury.

Dislocation fracture—Fracture near a joint which is dislocated.

Displaced fracture—A fracture in which the broken bones are displaced.

Double fracture—Fracture of a bone at two places.

Fissured fracture—A crack which does not pass through to the other side of the bone.

Greenstick fracture— The fracture in which the bone is partially broken and partially bent so that it looks like a broken greenstick. This type of fracture usually occurs in children, especially in those suffering from rickets.

Hairline fracture —A minor fracture seen only on X-ray examination, in which there is a very thin hairline between the two segments of the bone, which does not extend entirely through the bone.

Impacted fracture—The fracture in which one fragment of the bone is firmly driven into the other.

Incomplete fracture —The fracture in which the line of fracture does not cross the entire bone.

Indirect fracture—The fracture occurring at the place distant from the site of injury.

Intrauterine fracture—Fracture of a bone of the fetus in uterus.

Linear fracture— Longitudinal fracture.

Longitudinal fracture— Fracture in a bone occurring longitudinally.

Multiple fracture— Fracture occurring at two or more places in a bone.

Oblique fracture—Fracture in a bone occurring obliquely.

Open fracture— Compound fracture.

Pathologic fracture— Fracture occurring due to weakness of the bone produced by some diseases such as cancer of the bone, secondary metastasis from primary cancer, osteomalacia or osteomyelitis, etc.

Ping-pong fracture—A depressed fracture of the skull resembling the indentation that can be produced with the fingers pressing firmly in a ping-pong ball.

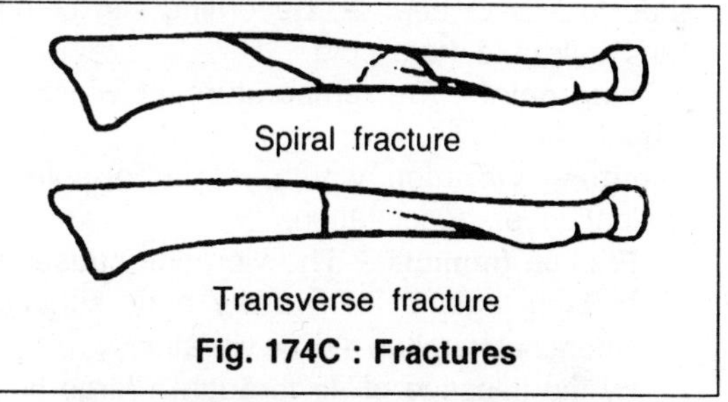

Fig. 174C : Fractures

Simple fracture—Closed fracture.

Spiral fracture—Coiled fracture.

Spontaneous fracture—A fracture occurring without external injury.

Transverse fracture— Fracture in which the fracture line is at right angles to the long axis of the bone.

Fracture dislocation—A fracture occurring near a joint which is dislocated.

Fragilitas—Fragility, brittleness.

Fragilitas capillary—Tendency of the blood capillaries to break down causing hemorrhage.

Fragilitas crinium—Brittleness of the hair.

Fragilitas ossium— Brittleness of the bones.

Fragilitas unguium—Brittleness of the nails.

Fragility—Fragilitas. Brittleness. Readiness to be broken.

Fragilocyte—A fragile red blood cell.

Fragilocytosis—Presence of abnormally fragile red blood cells in the blood.

Fragment—A detached portion, a broken part or a small piece.

Fragmentation—Division into small pieces.

Frambesia tropica—Yaws.

Frambesiform—Resembling yaws.

Frame—A hard structure for supporting or immobilizing a part of the body or an object, e.g., an eyeglass frame for holding the lenses.

Framework—That which supports a structure, as skeleton of the body.

Frank—Obvious.

Fraternal twins—Dizygotic twins.

Fratricide—Murder of one's brother or sister.

F.R.C.P. —Fellow of the Royal College of Physicians.

F.R.C.S.—Fellow of the Royal College of Surgeons.

Freckle—A brownish or yellowish spot on the skin due to accumulation of melanin resulting from exposure to sunlight.

Freezing—1. Passing from liquid to solid state due to loss of heat. 2. Becoming stiff or rigid and inflexible from cold.

Freezing point—The temperature at which the liquids freeze.

Fremitus—Vibration which is perceptible by palpation or auscultation.

Friction fremitus —The vibration caused by rubbing together of two dry body surfaces.

Rhonchal fremitus — The vibrations produced by the passage of air through a large bronchial tube filled with mucus, and felt by palpation.

Tactile fremitus—The vibration or thrill felt by the hand kept on the chest while the patient is speaking.

Tussive fremitus — Vibrations felt by the hand kept on the chest when the patient coughs.

Vocal fremitus — Vibrations of the voice felt by the ears on auscultation of the chest of the patient, while speaking.

Frena—Plural of frenum.

Frenal —Pertaining to the frenum.

Frenectomy—Excision of a frenum.

Frenoplasty—Correction of an abnormally attached frenum by plastic surgery.

Frenotomy—To divide any frenum, especially the tongue–tie.

Frenuloplasty—Frenoplasty.

Frenulum plural **frenula**—A small frenum e.g., frenulum of the tongue—a frenulum attaching the lower side of the tongue to the floor of the buccal cavity, and frenulum preputti—the frenulum uniting the prepuce to the glans penis.

Frenum—A fold of mucous membrane that connects two parts, one is movable and the other is fixed, and limits the movements of the movable part.

Frenzy—Violent mental agitation.

Frequency—The number of occurrences of a periodic process in a unit of time, *e.g.*, frequency of the heart beat or of micturition etc.

Fret —To irritate.

Fretting—Irritating.

Fretum—A constriction.

Friable —Easily broken or pulverized.

Friction—The act of rubbing.

Friction rub—The sound heard when two dry surfaces are rubbed together.

Fright—Extreme sudden fear.

Frigid—1. Cold. 2. The female in whom sexual desire does not arise even on stimulation.

Frigidity —1. Coldness. 2. Non arousal of the sexual desire in a female even on stimulation.

Frigolabile—Easily destroyed by cold.

Frigorific —Producing coldness.

Frigorism—A condition caused by exposure to cold for a long time.

Frigostabile—Incapable to be destroyed by cold.

Frigotherapy—Cryotherapy. Treatment of diseases by cold.

Fringe—Fimbria.

Frit—1. The material used in making the glass. 2. A similar material used for making the glaze of artificial teeth.

Frog belly—The hanging abdomen in children suffering from rickets.

Frog face—Flattened face due to intranasal disease.

Frohlich's syndrome—A disease occurring in children characterized by dwarfism, obsesity and sexual undevelopment, caused by the damage of hypothalamus or pituitary gland, which usually occurs due to a tumor.

Frolement—1. A very light friction with the hand in massage. 2. A rustling sound heard on auscultation in pericardial disease.

Frons—The forehead.

Frontad—Toward the front.

Frontal—1. Anterior 2. Pertaining to the bone of the forehead.

Frontal bone—Bone of the forehead.

Frontalis—Frontal.

Fronto- —A prefix indicating anterior position or relationship with the forehead.

Frontomalar—Pertaining to the frontal and malar bones.

Frontomaxillary—Pertaining to the frontal bone and the maxillary bones.

Frontonasal —Pertaining to the frontal sinus and the nose.

Fronto-occipital —Pertaining to the forehead and the occiput.

Frontoparietal —Pertaining to the frontal and the parietal bones.

Fronto-pontine —Pertaining to the forehead and the pons.

Frontotemporal—Pertaining to the frontal and temporal bones.

Frontozygomatic— Frontomalar. Pertaining to the frontal and the zygomatic bones.

Frost—Frozen dew or vapor.

Frostbite—Injury due to excessive cold to the exposed parts such as ears, cheeks, nose, fingers and toes etc.

Frost-itch—Itching caused by cold.

Froth—Foam.

Frothing—Foaming.

Frottage—1. Arousal of sexual desire by pressing or rubbing against someone of the opposite sex. 2. Massage by rubbing.

Frotteur—The person who practices frottage.

Frotteurism—Intense sexual desire causing someone to touch and rub against the body of a person of opposite sex, which is usually performed in crowded places.

Frozen—Past perfect tense of freeze.

Frozen section —The cutting of a thin piece of tissue from a frozen specimen.

Fructivorous—Living on eating fruits.

Fructose—The fruit-sugar.

Fructosemia—Presence of fructose in the blood.

Fructoside—A carbohydrate that yields fructose upon hydrolysis.

Fructosuria—The presence of fruit-sugar in urine.

Fruit —The matured ovary of a plant.

Fruitarian—The person who takes only fruits in the diet.

Frumentaceous—Resembling or belonging to grain.

Frustration—Increased emotional tension due to failure to achieve the desired thing or being sexually unsatisfied.

Frying—Cooking in fat.

FSH—Follicle-stimulating hormone secreted by the anterior lobe of the pituitary gland.

FSH-RH—Follicle-stimulating hormone-releasing hormone.

ft. haust —Make a single dose of a medicine.

Fuchsin—A red dye used for staining in histology and bacteriology.

Fuchsinophil —Staining readily with fuchsin dye.

Fuchsinophilia—The property of being stained readily with fuchsin.

Fuchsinophilic—Fuchsinophil.

Fugacity—The wandering from one place to another.

-fugal—A suffix meaning fleeting.

-fuge—A suffix meaning to expel or drive away.

Fugitive—1. Temporary or transient 2. Wandering.

Fugue —A dissociative reaction in hysterical neurosis in which the person acts normally but does not remember the happenings of the past when recovery occurs.

Fugue psychogenic—In this form of fugue someone suddenly and unexpectedly runs away from one's home or place of work and return back after some days with inability to remember of the past. It may follow quarrels in the family. Recovery usually occurs without recurrences.

Fulcrum—The object or point on whcih a lever moves.

Fulgurant—Coming and going suddenly like a flash of light, as a severe pain.

Fulgurate—1. To come and go like a flash of light. 2. To destroy by contact with electric sparks.

Fulgurating—Pertaining to fulguration.

Fulguration—Destruction of tissues by electricity.

Fulling—In massage, kneading with the limb held between the hands and rolling it backward and forward.

Full term—Mature, an infant born after the completion of 38 weeks of pregnancy.

Fulminant—Fulgurant.

Fulminate—To occur suddenly with great intensity.

Fulminating—Fulgurant.

Fulmination—Explosion of certain preparations by heat or friction.

Fume—Vapor, smoke, fit of anger.

Fumigant—The substance used for disinfecting a room by producing fume which is lethal to the insects and rats etc.

Fumigate —To apply smoke or fumes of any kind for disinfection or to destroy the insects and rats etc.

Fumigation—To destroy the insects and rats etc. of the house by means of poisonous gases or fumes.

Fuming—Emitting a visible vapor.

Functio—Function.

Function—The action performed by any organ or structure of the body.

Functional—1. Pertaining to a function. 2. Affecting the functions but not the structure of an organ or part of the body.

Functional disease—A disease caused by the functional disturbances of an organ or part of the body without its structural changes, *e.g.*, atrial flutter and atrial fibrillation are the functional diseases of the heart.

Funda—A four-tailed bandage.

Fundal—Pertaining to a fundus.

Fundament —1. A base or foundation 2. The anus.

Fundectomy—Removal of the fundus of any organ.

Fundic—Pertaining to a fundus.

Fundiform—Shaped like a loop.

Fundoplication—Surgical reduction of the size of the opening into the fundus of the stomach, and suturing of the previously removed end of the esophagus to the opening, which is usually done in treating the reflux of the gastric contents into the esophagus.

Fundus—1. The bottom or base of any organ. 2. Major portion or body of a hollow organ. 3. The part of a hollow organ farthest from its mouth.

Fundus of the eye— Black inner portion of the eyeball seen through the pupil by using ophthalmoscope.

Fundus of the gallbladder—Lower dilated part of the gallbladder.

Fudus of the stomach— The uppermost part of the stomach, to the left and above the level of the opening of the esophagus.

Fundus of the urinary bladder—The base of the urinary bladder closest to the rectum.

Fundus of the uterus—The body of the uterus above the openings of the fallopian tubes.

Funduscope—An ophthalmoscope for examining the fundus of the eye.

Funduscopy—Ophthalmoscopy. Examination of the fundus of the eye with ophthalmoscope.

Fundusectomy—Cardiectomy. Excision of the fundus of the stomach.

Fungal—Pertaining to or caused by a fungus.

Fungal septicemia—Presence of disease–producing fungi in the blood.

Fungate—To produce fungus like growths.

Fungating—Growing rapidly like a fungus, as do some tumors.

Fungemia—Fungal septicemia.

Fungi—Plural of fungus.

Fungicidal —Fungicide.

Fungicide—An agent destroying the fungi.

Fungiform—Shaped like a fungus.

Fungiliform —Fungiform.

Fungistasis —Inhibition of the growth of fungi.

Fungistat —An agent that inhibits the growth of fungi.

Fungistatic—Fungistat.

Fungitoxic—Exerting a toxic effect upon fungi.

Fungitoxicity —The property of being fungitoxic.

Fungoid—Having the appearance of a fungus.

Fungosity —A soft, spongy fungus like growth.

Fungous—Of the nature of, caused by or resembling a fungus.

Fungus—A vegetable cellular organism living on organic matter, marked by the absence of chlorophyll and the presence of a rigid cell wall, *e.g.*, molds, yeasts and mushrooms, etc.

Funic—Pertaining to the umbilical cord.

Funic souffle—A sound heard over the pregnant uterus due to flowing of the blood through the blood vessels in the umbilical cord, having the same rate as the heart rate of the fetus.

Funicle—Funiculus. A small thread-like structure.

Funicular—Pertaining to the spermatic cord or the umbilical cord.

Funicular process—The part of the tunica vaginalis which covers the spermatic cord.

Funiculitis—Inflammation of the spermatic cord.

Funiculoepididymitis— Inflammation of the spermatic cord and the epididymis.

Funiculopexy—Suturing of the spermatic cord with the tissues in case of undescended testes.

Funiculus A cord or cordlike structure.

Funiform—Cordlike.

Funipuncture—Puncture of the umbilical vein of the fetus in utero to obtain a blood sample.

Funis—A cordlike structure, especially the spermatic cord or the umbilical cord.

Funisitis—Inflammation of the umbilical cord.

Funnel—A conical device with a wide open mouth at one end, for pouring liquid through its open tube at another end, into another vessel.

Funny bone—Internal condyle of the humerus bone called funny bone because pressure applied over it stimulates the ulnar nerve and causes a pleasant sensation.

F.U.O.—Fever of unknown origin.

Fur—Short, soft, fine hair of certain animals.

Furcal—Forked.

Furcation—The anatomical area of a multirooted tooth where the root divides.

Furfur—Dandruf scales.

Furfuraceous—Scaly or resembling scales of dandruff.

Furor—An attack of extremely violent anger.

Furred—Coated with dust like material as said of the tongue.

Furrow—A groove or crease, *e.g.*, furrow digital—a transverse line on the palmar aspect of a finger across the joint, and furrow gluteal—the vertical groove on the skin between the buttocks.

Furuncle—Furunculus. A boil.

Furuncular—Pertaining to a boil.

Furunculi—Plural of furunculus.

Furunculoid—Furunculous. Resembling a furuncle or boil.

Furunculosis —1. A condition resulting from boils. 2. Occurrence of many boils at a time.

Furunculous —Pertaining to or of the nature of a boil.

Furunculus—Furuncle, boil.

Fuscin—A brown pigment present in the retinal epithelium.

Fusible—Capable of being melted.

Fusiform—Spindle-shaped, tapering at both ends.

Fusion—1. The process of fusing or uniting. 2. The process of melting.

Fusional—Pertaining to or marked by fusion.

Fusocellular—Having spindle-shaped cells.

Fusospirillosis—Necrotizing ulcerative gingivitis.

Fusospirochetal—Pertaining to or caused by fusiform bacilli and spirochetes.

Fusospirochetosis— Infection with the fusiform bacilli and spirochetes.

Fusostreptococcosis— Infection with fusiform bacteria and streptococcus.

Fustigation—Beating with light rods in massage.

Futile—Useless.

g —Abbreviation for gram.

Gag —1. An apparatus for keeping the mouth open during an operation. 2. To make an effort for vomiting.

Gage —Gauge.

Gag reflex —Gogging and vomiting due to irritation of fauces.

Gain —Improvement, increasement or profit.

Gait —Manner or style of walking.

Antalgic gait —To walk in a limping manner to avoid the pain in the affected leg.

Ataxic gait —To walk in a staggering manner and tending to fall down as usually seen in the person who has taken alcohol in excess.

Calcaneal gait —A gait characterized by walking on heels due to paralysis of the calf muscles caused by poliomyelitis or some other diseases of the nervous system.

Cerebellar gait — Staggering walk seen in cerebellar disease.

Double step gait —The walking in which each alternate step is of different length or at a different rate.

Equine gait —Walking characterized by high steps.

Festinating gait —The gait in which the patient starts walking slowly and then rapidly only on toes with short steps and may continue until the patient grasp something to stop.

Helicopod gait —The gait in which the foot describes a half circle with each step as is sometimes seen in hysteria.

Hemiplegic gait —This form of gait is seen in the patient suffering from hemiplegia. The patient draws the paralyzed leg away from the median plane of the body and swinging it round brings the foot on the ground infront of the foot of the normal leg.

Hysterical gait —The walking in which foot is dragged or pushed ahead, instead of lifting it up, seen in hysteria.

Parkinson's gait —A gait marked by short-steps in shuffling manner as seen in patients with Parkinson's disease.

Scissor gait —Gait in which the legs cross each other in walking.

Spastic gait —Gait in which the hips and the knee joints are slightly flexed, legs are held together and move in a stiff manner.

Steppage gait —This form of gait is seen in case of foot drop, in which the leg is lifted high so that the toes can clear the ground, heal is brought down first and then the toes.

Tabetic gait —The high-stepping ataxic gait in which the feet slap the ground. It is seen in tabes dorsalis.

Waddling gait —Gait in which the feet are wide apart, and walk resembles that of a duck.

Galact-, Galacto- — Prefixes which mean pertaining to milk.

Galactacrasia —An abnormal composition of the breast milk.

Galactagogue —An agent which increases the flow of milk.

Galactan —A complex carbohydrate which upon hydrolysis forms galactose.

Galactemia —The presence of milk in the blood.

Galactia —Defective or abnormal secretion of milk.

Galactic —Pertaining to flow of milk.

Galactidrosis —A milk-like sweat.

Galactischia —Suppression of the milk secretion.

Galactoblast —A colostrum corpuscle in the acini of the mammary gland.

Galactocele —1. A tumor of a milk duct of the mammary gland formed by the accumulation of the milk due to obstruction. 2. A hydrocele filled with a milky fluid.

Galactography —X-ray examination of the milk ducts after an injection of a radiopaque substance into them.

Galactoid —Resembling milk.

Galactoma —Galactocele. Cystic tumor of a female breast.

Galactometer —Lactometer. An apparatus for measuring the specific gravity of the milk.

Galactopexy —The fixation of galactose by the liver.

Galactophagous —Depending upon milk food.

Galactophlysis —Formation of vesicles containing milk-like substance.

Galactophore —A milk duct.

Galactophoritis —Inflammation of a milk duct.

Galactophorous —Giving milk.

Galactophthisis —Debility and emaciation due to excessive secretion of milk.

Galactophygous —Arresting the flow of milk.

Galactoplania —Secretion of milk from some part of the body other than the mammary gland.

Galactopoiesis —Production of milk by the mammary glands.

Galactopoietic —1. Pertaining to milk production or capable of producing milk. 2. A substance which promotes the secretion of milk.

Galactoposia —Treatment by milk.

Galactopyra —Milk fever.

Galactorrhea —Excessive or continuous flow of milk after cessation of nursing.

Galactoscope —Lactoscope.

Galactose —It is an isomer of glucose and is formed, along with glucose, in the hydrolysis of lactose.

Galactosemia —Presence of galactose in the blood of a newly born child as an inborn error of metabolism due to congenital absence of the enzyme galactose-1- phosphate uridyl transferase which converts galactose into glucose.

Galactoside —A carbohydrate which contain galactose.

Galactosis —Secretion of milk.

Galactostasis —Cessation of milk secretion.

Galactosuria —Presence of galactose in the urine.

Galactotherapy —Lactotherapy. 1. Treatment of the diseases of the nursing infant by giving the drugs to the mother. 2. Treatment of diseases by milk diet.

Galactotoxin —A toxic substance produced by the bacteria in the milk.

Galactotoxism —Milk poisoning.

Galactotrophy —Living on only milk.

Galactoxism —Galactotoxism.

Galacturia —Chyluria. Passing of milky urine.

Galea —1. A helmet-shaped structure 2. A type of head bandage.

Galeanthropy —A delusion that one has become a cat.

Galenicals —1. Crude drugs or the drugs obtained from the vegetable kingdom. 2. Medicines prepared according to an official formula.

Galeophilia —Fondness for cats.

Galeophobia —Morbid fear of cats.

Galeropia, Galeropsia — Unusual clearness of vision.

Gall —Bile.

Gallbladder —A pear-shaped sac situated on the undersurface of the right lobe of the liver holding bile receiving from the liver until it passes to the duodenum through the cystic duct.

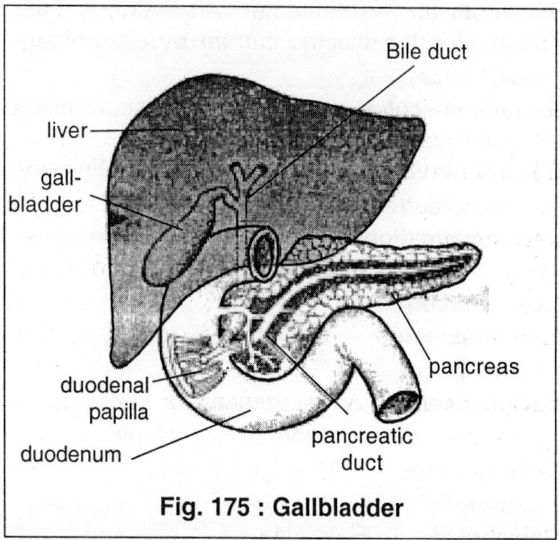

Fig. 175 : Gallbladder

Gall duct —Bile duct. A tube carrying bile from the liver and gallbladder.

Gallon —A unit of liquid measure which is equal to 4 quarts, 3.785 liters or 3785 mls.

Gallop —The swifest pace of a horse.

Gallop rhythm —An abnormal third or fourth sound found in the tachycardia of 100 or more beats per minute, which resembles that produced by a galloping horse, which indicates a serious heart disease.

Gallstone —A calculus formed in the gallbladder or bile duct.

Galton's whistle —A whistle used for testing the hearing.

Galvanic —Pertaining to galvanism.

Galvanism —1. Direct electric current produced

by chemical action, as by a battery. 2. In dentistry, occurrence of direct electric current in the mouth when two metals of dissimilar electric potential such as silver and gold used to restore teeth come in contact, characterized by pain and the development of leukoplakic areas.

Galvanization —The use of direct current of electricity in the treatment of diseases.

Galvano- —Prefix denoting direct electric current.

Galvanocautery —Electrocautery.

Galvanocontractility — Capability of contracting under galvanic stimulation.

Galvanofaradization — Combined use of continuous and interrupted electrical current in the treatment of a nerve or a muscle disease.

Galvanometer —Rheometer. An instrument for measuring the electric current by electromagnetic action.

Galvanomuscular —Denoting the effect of direct electric current to a muscle.

Galvanonervous —Produced by applying the galvanic current to a nerve.

Galvanopalpation —Testing of the tectile sensibility of nerves of the skin by means of direct electric current.

Galvanopuncture —To pierce the skin by electric needles.

Galvanoscope —An instrument for showing the presence and direction of a galvanic current.

Galvanosurgery —Use of galvanic current in surgery.

Galvanotaxis —Electrotaxis.

Galvanotherapeutics Galvanotherapy —Electrotherapy. Treatment of diseases by means of galvanic current.

Galvanothermy —Treatment of diseases by the heat from a galvanic battery.

Galvanotonus —Tonic contractions caused by galvanic current.

Galvanotropism —Tendency of an organism to grow or move according to the intensity of electricity.

Gametangium —A structure in which gametes are produced.

Gamete —1. A mature male or female reproductive cell, i.e., a spermatozoon or an ovum. 2. The malarial parasite in its sexual form in a mosquito's stomach, either male (microgamete) or female (macrogamete).

Gametic —Pertaining to gametes.

Gametocide —An agent which destroys the gametes or gametocytes, particularly those of malaria.

Gametocyte —An oocyte or spermatocyte producing gametes, or a stage in the development of malarial parasite in the blood of Anopheles mosquito.

Gametogenesis —The development of the male and female reproductive cells (gametes).

Gametogonia —Gametogony.

Gametogony —1. Reproduction by means of gametes. 2. The phase in the life cycle of the malarial parasite plasmodium in which the male and female gametocytes, which infect the mosquito, are formed.

Gametoid —Resembling gamete.

Gametokinetic —Promoting the conjugation of male and female gametes.

Gametophagia —Disappearance of the male or female gamete during the formation of zygote.

Gamic —Sexual.

Gamma —1. The third letter `γ' of the Greek alphabet. 2. In chemistry, used to name the chemical compounds to distinguish one of three or more isomers, or to indicate the position of substituting atoms. 3. One microgram or one thousandth of a milligram or one millionth of a gram.

Gammacism —Inability to pronounce correctly the sounds of the letter `g' and `k'.

Gamma globulin —A protein formed in the blood.

Gammaglobulinopathy — Gammopathy.

Gamma rays —Electromagnetic waves of very short wavelength emitted by radioactive substances, which have greater penetrating power than alpha or beta rays.

Gammopathy —A disease in which there is an increase of immunoglobulin in the serum of blood as in myeloma.

Gamo- —A prefix indicating relationship to marriage or sexual union.

Gamogenesis —Sexual reproduction.

Gamogony —Gametogony.

Gamont —Gametocyte.

Gamophagia —Gametophagia.

Gamophobia —Morbid fear of marriage.

Gampsodactylia —Claw foot.

Ganglia —Plural of ganglion.

Ganglial —Ganglionic. Pertaining to a ganglion.
Gangliated —Having ganglia.
Gangliectomy —Excision of a ganglion.
Gangliform —Ganglion-shaped.
Gangliitis —Inflammation of a ganglion.
Ganglioblast —An embryonic ganglion cell.
Gangliocyte —A ganglion cell.
Gangliocytoma —Ganglioneuroma.
Ganglioform —Gangliform.
Ganglioglioma —Glioma of a ganglion cell.
Ganglioglioneuroma —A nerve tumor containing ganglion cells, glia cells and nerve fibers.
Gangliolysis —The breaking up of a ganglion.
Ganglioma —Tumor of a lymphoid tissue.
Ganglion —1. A mass of nervous tissue principally of nerve-cell bodies and lying outside the central nervous system, e.g., spinal ganglia which are the enlargement of the spinal nerves dorsal roots. 2. A form of cystic tumor on an aponeurosis or a tendon as sometimes occurs on the back of the wrist.

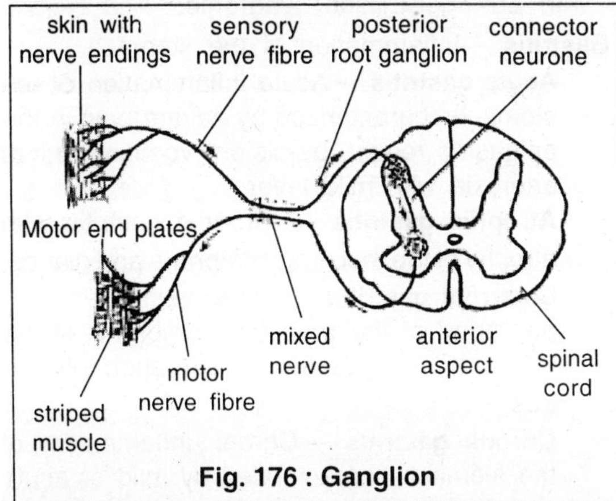

Fig. 176 : Ganglion

Ganglionated —Having or consisted of ganglia.
Ganglionectomy —Excision of a ganglion.
Ganglioneuroma —A benign tumor consisted of the nerve fibres and mature ganglion cells.
Ganglioneuromatosis —The condition of having many widespread ganglioneuromas.
Ganglionic —Pertaining to or of the nature of a ganglion.
Ganglionic blockade —The drug blocking the transmission of stimuli in the ganglia of the autonomic nervous system.
Ganglionitis —Inflammation of a ganglion.
Ganglionostomy —To make an incision into a simple ganglion.
Ganglioplegia —Blockage of transmission of nervous stimuli through a ganglion.
Ganglioplegic —Blocking transmission of nervous stimuli through a ganglion.
Gangosa —Ulceration of the nose and hard palate, seen in leprosy or leishmaniasis.
Gangrene —Necrosis or death of the tissue usually due to partial or complete absence of blood supply.

Diabetic gangrene — Moist gangrene associated with diabetes.
Dry gangrene —The gangrene in which the dead part has little blood and remains aseptic. The tissues become dry and shrivelled.
Embolic gangrene — Gangrene caused due to an obstruction in the blood supply by an embolism.
Gas gangrene —The gangrene in which the muscles and the subcutaneous tissues become filled with gas due to infection of a wound by a gas bacillus, the most common of which is Clostridium perfringens.
Hospital gangrene — Decubitus ulcer.
Hot gangrene —Gangrene occurring following an inflammation.
Idiopathic gangrene —Gangrene of which the cause is unknown.
Inflammatory gangrene —Gangrene associated with acute infections and inflammation.
Moist gangrene —Wet gangrene as a result of necrosis of the tissues and bacterial infection.
Presenile spontaneous gangrene —Gangrene occurring in middle age as a result of thromboangitis obliterans.
Pressure gangrene — Decubitus ulcer.
Primary gangrene — Gangrene developing in a part of the body without previous inflammation.
Secondary gangrene — Gangrene developing following a local inflammation.
Senile gangrene — Gangrene occurring in old age following occlusion of an artery, especially of a limb.
Symmetrical gangrene — Gangrene occurring on opposite sides of the body in corresponding parts, due to vasomotor disturbances, e.g., gangrene occurring in Raynaud's disease and Buerger's disease.
Traumatic gangrene — Gangrene resulting from extensive injuries.

Gangrenosis —The development of gangrene.

Gangrenous —Of the nature of gangrene or having gangrene.

Ganoblast —Ameloblast. The cell which forms the enamel of a tooth.

Gap —An opening or a break in the continuity.

Gape —Yawning, to open mouth wide.

Garbage —Refuse.

Gargarism —A gargle or throat wash.

Gargle —1. A wash for the throat. 2. To wash out the mouth and throat.

Gargoylism —A congenital disease characterized by dwarfism, kyphosis and other skeletal abnormalities, disturbance in lipoid metabolism and usually mental deficiency.

Garlic —The bulb of Allium sativum with a strong smell and pungent taste.

Gas —A substance in the form of vapor.

Gas bacillus —Clostridium perfringens.

Gaseous —Of the nature of gas.

Gasometer —A calibrated instrument or vessel for measuring the volume of a gas.

Gasometric —Pertaining to measurement of gases.

Gasometry —To measure the amount of gas present in a mixture.

Gasp —To catch the breath. To inhale and exhale quickly and with difficulty.

Gas pain —Abdominal pain caused by gas distention of the intestines.

Gaster-, Gastero-, Gastro- —Prefixes indicating stomach or the area of the stomach.

Gasteralgia —Gastralgia. Pain in the stomach.

Gastorrhagia —Gastrorrhagia. Hemorrhage from the stomach.

Gastradenitis —Inflammation of the gastric glands.

Gastral —Pertaining to the stomach.

Gastralgia —Pain in the stomach from any cause.

Gastralgokenosis —Hunger pain. Pain in the stomach due to its emptiness.

Gastratrophia —Atrophy of the stomach.

Gastrectasia, Gastrectasis —Dilatation of the stomach.

Gastrectomy —Excision of a part or the whole of the stomach.

Gastrelcosis —Ulceration of the stomach.

Gastric —Pertaining to the stomach.

Gastricism —Any disease of the stomach.

Gastric juice —The secretion of the gastric glands of the stomach, which is a thin, colorless, liquid containing pepsin (the chief enzyme of gastric juice), hydrochloric acid, mucin (a glycoprotein), inorganic salts in small quantities and the intrinsic factor of the antianemic principle.

Gastric lavage —To wash out the stomach.

Gastricsin —A proteolytic (hastening the hydrolysis of protein) enzyme of the gastric secretion.

Gastric ulcer —Peptic ulcer. An ulcer present in the stomach.

Gastricus —Gastric.

Gastrins —A group of hormones secreted by certain cells of the mucous membrane of the pyloric area of the stomach, which stimulate the secretion of gastric acid and pepsin and the secretion of pancreatic enzymes and causes the contraction of the gallbladder.

Gastrinoma —A tumor of the non-beta islet cell of the pancreas secreting gastrin, associated with Zollinger-Ellison syndrome.

Gastritis —Inflammation of the stomach.

- **Acute gastritis** —Acute inflammation of the stomach characterized by severe pain in the epigastric region, persistent vomiting, thirst, anorexia with mild fever.
- **Atrophic gastritis** — Chronic gastritis with atrophy of the mucous membrane and glands.
- **Catarrhal gastritis** — Inflammation and hypertrophy of the mucous membrane of the stomach, with excessive secretion of mucus.
- **Chronic gastritis** —Chronic inflammation of the stomach characterized by mild or acute pain in the epigastric region, fullness of the abdomen after taking a little food, mild nausea, bad taste in the mouth and anorexia.
- **Erosive gastritis or exfoliative gastritis** — Gastritis in which the surface epithelium of the stomach is eroded.
- **Giant hypertrophic gastritis** —Gastritis with excessive proliferation of the gastric mucous membrane, producing diffuse thickening of the wall of the stomach.
- **Hypertrophic gastritis** —Gastritis with the infiltration and hypertrophy of the glands.
- **Phlegmonous gastritis** —Gastritis in which the abscesses are formed in the stomach wall.

Toxic gastritis — Inflammation of the gastric mucosa caused by the action of a poison or corrosive substance.

Gastro- —A prefix denoting stomach.

Gastroacephalus —A twin monster, the autosite bearing a headless parasite on its abdomen.

Gastroamorphus —The smaller, amorphus twin contained in the abdomen of the larger and normal twin, as a parasite.

Gastroanastomosis —The formation of passage between the pyloric and cardiac ends of the stomach.

Gastroatonia —Loss of tone of the gastric muscles.

Gastroblennorrhea —Excessive mucus discharge from the stomach.

Gastrobrosis —Perforation of the stomach.

Gastrocamera —A small camera to be swallowed to take the photographs of the inside of the stomach.

Gastrocardiac —Pertaining to the stomach and the heart.

Gastrocele —Hernia of the stomach.

Gastrochronorrhea —Excessive gastric secretion continuously.

Gastrocoele —Archenteron.

Gastrocolic —Pertaining to the stomach and the colon.

Gastrocolic reflex — Occurrence of the peristaltic movements in the colon induced by the entrance of food into the empty stomach.

Gastrocolitis —Inflammation of the stomach and the colon.

Gastrocoloptosis —Prolapse of the stomach and the colon downwards.

Gastrocolostomy —To make a passage between the stomach and the colon.

Gastrocolotomy —To make an incision into the stomach and the colon.

Gastrocolpotomy —To make an incision into the upper part of the vagina through the abdominal wall.

Gastrocutaneous —Pertaining to stomach and the skin, or communicating with the stomach and the surface of the skin of the body as a gastrocutaneous fistula.

Gastrodialysis —1. Stomach wash. 2. Sloughing of the mucosa of the stomach.

Gastrodiaphane —A small electric lamp used for transilluminating the interior of the stomach and making its outlines visible through the abdomen.

Gastrodiaphanoscopy — Examination of the interior of the stomach by transillumination of its walls by means of a gastrodiaphane introduced through the esophagus into the stomach.

Gastrodiaphany — Transillumination of the stomach.

Gastrodidymus —Symmetrical twins united at the abdominal region.

Gastroduodenal —Pertaining to stomach and the duodenum.

Gastroduodenitis — Inflammation of the stomach and the duodenum.

Gastroduodenoscopy — Visual examination of the stomach and duodenum by using an endoscope.

Gastroduodenostomy — Excision of the pylorus of the stomach, and anastomosis of the upper portion of the stomach to the duodenum.

Gastrodynia —Gastralgia. Pain in the stomach.

Gastroenteralgia —Pain in the stomach and intestine.

Gastroenteric —Pertaining to the stomach and intestine or a disease affecting both.

Gastroenteritis —Inflammation of the stomach and intestine.

Gastroenteroanastomosis — Gastroenterostomy.

Gastroenterocolitis — Inflammation of the stomach, small intestine and colon.

Gastroenterocolostomy — To make a passage between the stomach, small intestine and the colon.

Gastroenterologist —Specialist in gastroenterology.

Gastroenterology —The study of the stomach and intestine and their diseases.

Gastroenteropathy —Any disease of the stomach and intestine.

Gastroenteroplasty —Repair of the defects of the stomach and intestine by plastic surgery.

Gastroenteroptosis —Prolapse of the stomach and intestine.

Gastroenterostomy —To make a passage between the stomach and intestine by surgery.

Gastroenterotomy —To make an incision into the stomach and intestine through the abdominal wall.

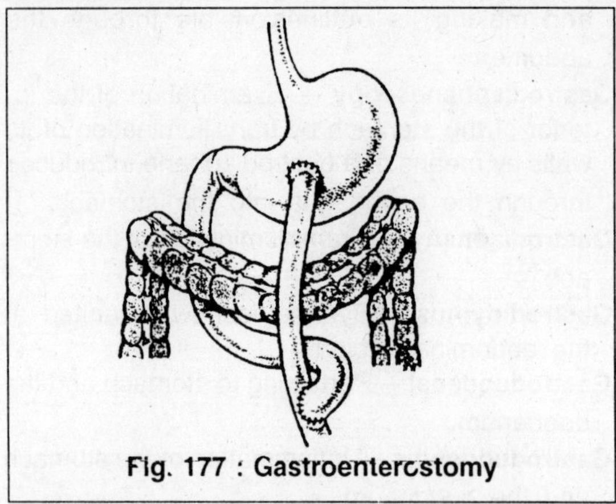
Fig. 177 : Gastroenterostomy

Gastroepiploic —Pertaining to the stomach and the greater omentum.

Gastroesophageal —Pertaining to the stomach and the esophagus.

Gastroesophagitis — Inflammation of the stomach and esophagus.

Gastroesophagostomy —To make a passage from the esophagus into the stomach.

Gastrofiberscope —A fiberscope for visual examination of the stomach.

Gastrogastrostomy — Gastroanastomosis. To make a passage between two previously remote portions of the stomach.

Gastrogavage —Artificial feeding through a tube passed into the stomach.

Gastrogenic —Originating from the stomach.

Gastrograph —An instrument for noting the motions of the stomach.

Gastrohelcosis —Ulceration of the stomach.

Gastrohepatic —Pertaining to the stomach and liver.

Gastrohepatitis —Inflammation of the stomach and the liver.

Gastroileac —Pertaining to the stomach and ileum.

Gastroileac reflex — Opening of the ileocecal valve on arrival of the food into the stomach.

Gastroileitis —Inflammation of the stomach and the ileum.

Gastroileostomy —Anastomosis between the stomach and the ileum by surgery.

Gastrointestinal —Pertaining to the stomach and the intestine.

Gastrojejunocolic —Pertaining to the stomach, jejunum and the colon.

Gastrojejunostomy —To make a passage between the stomach and jejunum.

Gastrokinesograph — Gastrograph.

Gastrolavage —The washing out of the stomach.

Gastrolienal —Gastrosplenic. Pertaining to the stomach and the spleen.

Gastrolith —A calculus in the stomach.

Gastrolithiasis —Presence or formation of calculi in the stomach.

Gastrologist —A specialist in gastrology.

Gastrology —Study of the stomach, its functions and diseases.

Gastrolysis —Breaking of the adhesions between stomach and the adjoining structures by surgery to mobilize the stomach.

Gastromalacia —Softening of the stomach walls.

Gastromegaly —Enlargement of the stomach.

Gastromelus —A fetus with a supernumerary leg on the abdomen.

Gastromycosis —Fungal disease of the stomach.

Gastromyotomy —Incision into the muscular coats of the stomach.

Gastromyxorrhea —Excessive secretion of the mucus by the stomach.

Gastronephritis —Inflammation of the stomach and the kidney.

Gastronesteostomy — Gastrojejunostomy.

Gastropagus —Conjoined twins united at the abdomen.

Gastropancreatic — Pertaining to the stomach and the pancreas.

Gastropancreatitis — Inflammation of the stomach and the pancreas.

Gastroparalysis —Paralysis of the stomach.

Gastroparasitus —Conjoined twins of unequal size, the smaller twin is attached to, or within, the abdomen of the larger twin, as a parasite.

Gastroparesis — Gastroparalysis.

Gastropathic —Pertaining to gastropathy.

Gastropathy —Any disease of the stomach.

Gastropexy, Gastropexis —Fixation of the stomach to the abdominal wall.

Gastrophrenic —Pertaining to the stomach and the diaphragm.

Gastroplasty —Repair of the stomach by plastic surgery.

Gastroplegia —Paralysis of the stomach.

Gastroplication —The stitching a fold in the stomach wall to reduce dilatation.

Gastropneumonic — Pneumogastric.

Gastroptosia —Gastroptosis.

Gastroptosis —Downward displacement of the stomach.

Gastroptyxis —Gastroplication.

Gastropulmonary —Pertaining to the stomach and the lungs.

Gastropylorectomy —Excision of the pyloric part of the stomach.

Gastropyloric —Pertaining to the stomach and pylorus.

Gastroradiculitis — Inflammation of the posterior spinal nerve roots, the sensory fibers of which supply the stomach.

Gastrorrhagia —Hemorrhage from the stomach.

Gastrorrhaphy —Suture of the stomach.

Gastrorrhea —Excessive secretion of the gastric juice.

Gastrorrhexis —A rupture or tearing of the stomach.

Gastroschisis —A congenital fissure in the abdominal wall.

Gastroscope —An endoscope for inspecting the interior of the stomach.

Gastroscopic —Pertaining to gastroscopy.

Gastroscopy —Inspection of the interior of the stomach by using gastroscope.

Gastrosis —Any disease of the stomach.

Gastrospasm —Spasm of the stomach.

Gastrosplenic —Of or pertaining to stomach and the spleen.

Gastrostaxis —Oozing of blood from the mucous membrane of the stomach.

Gastrostenosis —Narrowing of the stomach.

Gastrostenosis cardiaca — Stenosis of cardiac orifice of the stomach.

Gastrostenosis pylorica —Stenosis of the pylorus of the stomach.

Gastrostogavage —Feeding by a tube passed into the stomach through a gastric fistula.

Gastrostolavage —Irrigation of the stomach through a gastric fistula.

Gastrostoma —A fistula of the stomach.

Gastrostomy —To make an artificial opening into the stomach.

Gastrosuccorrhea — Hypersecretion. Excessive secretion of gastric juice with increased acidity.

Gastrotherapy —Treatment of the gastric diseases.

Gastrothoracopagus — Congenitally deformed twins joined at the thorax and abdomen.

Gastrotome —An instrument for incising the stomach or the abdomen.

Gastrotomy —To make an incision into the stomach or the abdomen.

Gastrotonometer —An instrument for measuring the intragastric pressure.

Gastrotonometry —The measurement of intragastric pressure.

Gastrotoxic —Poisonous to the stomach.

Gastrotoxin —A cytotoxin specific for the cells of the mucous membrane of the stomach.

Gastrotropic —Attracted to or affecting the stomach.

Gastrotympanites —Distention of the stomach by gas or air.

Gastrula —Stage of the development of embryo following blastula in which embryo becomes double layered. The outer layer is the ectoderm or epiblast, the inner one, the endoderm or hypoblast. Both these layers invaginate at some place in the gastrula forming a cavity which is gastrocoele or archenteron and the opening formed by the invagination of the layers is known as blastopore.

Gastrulation —The process by which a blastula becomes a gastrula.

Gatch bed —The bed in which patient can be raised and held in a half-sitting position.

Gatism —Incontinence of urine or feces.

Gauge —1. An apparatus for measuring size, capacity, amount or power of an object or a substance. 2. A standard of measurement.

Gaunlet—A bandage covering the hand and fingers like a glove.

Gauss —A unit of magnetic field intensity.

Gauze —A thin, loosely woven cloth for dressing purpose.

Gavage —Gastrostogavage. Feeding of liquid food with a tube passed into the stomach through the nares, pharynx and esophagus.

Gay —Homosexual, especially male.

Gaze —To look in one direction for a long time or the state of staring.

Gegenhalten —An involuntary resistance to passive movement as may occur in the disease of the cerebral cortex.

Gel —Semisolid or jellylike colloid.

Gelasmus —Laughter of the insane.

Gelastic —Pertaining to the laughter.

Gelate —To cause formation of a gel.

Gelatin —A protein which is obtained by the hydrolysis of the collagen present in the connective tissues of the skin and bones etc. of the animals, used in the manufacture of capsules etc.

Gelatinase —An enzyme present in the bacteria, molds and yeast which liquefies gelatin.

Gelatiniferous —Producing gelatin.

Gelatinization —Conversion into gelatin.

Gelatinize — To convert into, or become converted into gelatin.

Gelatinoid —Resembling gelatin.

Gelatinolytic —Dissolving or splitting up gelatin.

Gelatinous —Containing gelatin, or jellylike.

Gelation —Conversion of a solution into jellylike substance.

Gelosis —A hard lump occurring especially in the muscle tissue.

Gelotherapy —Treatment of some mental diseases by inducing laughter.

Gelotripsy —Rubbing of the hardened swelling.

Gemellipara —The woman who has borne twins.

Gemellology —Study of the twins.

Geminate —Occurring in pairs.

Gemination —The development in pairs.

Geminous —Geminate.

Gemistocyte —In the central nervous system, a round or oval astrocyte with abundant cytoplasm containing an eccentric nucleus, seen near an edema or infarct.

Gemistocytoma —Astrocytoma.

Gemma —Any small, budlike or bulblike structure, such as a taste bud or end bulb.

Gemmation —Cell division by budding. A portion of the cell in projected like a bud which is separated afterwards from the mother cell forming a new cell.

Gemmule —1. A reproductive bud. 2. One of the many little processes present on the dendrites of a neuron.

Gen- —A prefix meaning being born, producing, coming to be.

-gen —Suffix denoting "precursor of."

Gena —Side of the face. Cheek.

Genal —Pertaining to the cheeks.

Gender —The sex of an individual.

Gene —The basic unit of heredity. Each gene is self-reproducing, ultramicroscopic and located at a definite position on a chromosome giving rise to a new character. Hereditary characters are controlled by pairs of genes located on the same site on a pair of chromosomes.

Allelic genes —Genes in paires located at the same site on the pairs of chromosomes.

Autosomal gene —A gene located on any chromosome other than the sex chromosomes.

Complementary genes —Two independent pairs of non-allelic genes, neither of which will produce its effect in the absence of the other.

Dominant gene —A gene which produces its effect without the aid from its allele.

Holandric genes —Genes located on the Y chromosomes and appearing only in the male offspring.

Inhibiting gene —A gene which prevents the effects of another gene.

Lethal gene —A gene whose presence causes death of the individual, usually in utero.

Modifying gene —A gene which influences or alters the effect of another gene.

Mutant gene —A changed gene which permanently works in a different way.

Operator gene —A gene controlling the actions of other genes.

Pleiotropic gene —A gene having multiple effects.

Recessive gene —A gene producing its effect only when it is present in both chromosomes, or a gene which produces an effect in the offspring only when it is transmitted by both the parents.

Regulator gene —A gene which controls some specific activity of another gene.

Sex-linked gene —A gene located on a sex chromosome, especially on X chromosome.

Genealogy —Study of the ancestry of the patient for diagnosing a hereditary disease.

Genera —Plural of genus.

General —1. Relating to a whole body. 2. Usual.

Generalization —1. The becoming or rendering general or widespread 2. The becoming systemic, as a local disease.

Generalize —1. To become or to make general 2. To become systemic as a local disease.

Generalized —Involving the whole of an organ or a part of the body.

Generate —To produce.

Generation (जेनेरेशन)—1. The process of reproduction. 2. The men born about the same time. 3. The production of electric current.

Generational —Pertaining to generations.

Generative —Pertaining to the reproduction.

Generator —An apparatus which produces heat, electricity or impulses.

Generic —1. Pertaining to a genus. 2. General. 3. Distinctive. 4. Denoting a drug name not protected by a trade mark.

Genesial —Pertaining to generation.

Genesiology —The study of reproduction.

Genesis —1. The act of reproducing 2. The origin of any thing e.g., carcinogenesis.

Genetic —Pertaining to reproduction.

Geneticist —Specialist of genetics.

Genetics —Study of heredity.

Behavioral genetics — Study of heritable factors in the investigation of behavior.

Biochemical genetics —The study of the biochemistry of genes and chemical inluences on genes.

Clinical genetics — Application of genetics in the diagnosis, prevention and treatment of genetic diseases.

Human genetics —The study of the genetic aspects of human being.

Genetopathy —Any disease which affects the reproductive system.

Genetotrophic —Pertaining to the genetics and the nutrition.

Genetous —Congenital.

Genial —Pertaining to the chin.

Genic —Pertaining to or caused by genes.

-genic —Suffix denoting producing, forming; produced or, formed by.

Genicula —Plural of geniculum.

Genicular —Pertaining to the knee.

Geniculate —1. Bent like a knee. 2. Pertaining to the ganglion of the facial nerve.

Geniculated —Geniculate.

Geniculate otalgia — Referred pain from the facial nerve to the ear.

Geniculum —1. A knot-like structure. 2. Knee.

Genion —The tip of the mental spine.

Genioplasty —Repair of the chin or the cheek by plastic surgery.

Genital —Pertaining to the sex organs.

Genitalia, Genitals — Reproductive organs.

Female genitalia — External female genital organs, which are collectively known as vulva. It includes mons pubis, labia majora, labia minora, clitoris, vestibule of the vagina, Bartholin's glands, hymen, openings of the vagina and the external urethral orifice. Internal genital organs are two ovaries, two fallopian tubes, a uterus and a vagina.

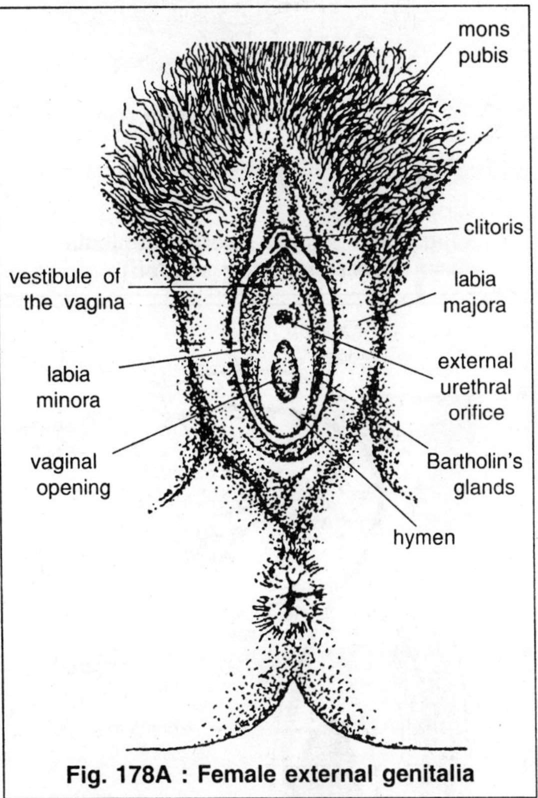

Fig. 178A : Female external genitalia

Male genitalia — External male genital organs which include scrotum containing two testes with their epididymises which produce spermatozoa, and the penis with urethra. Internal genital organs are two testes with epididymises, two spermatic cords with vas deferences or the seminal ducts, two seminal vesicles, two ejaculatory ducts, a prostate gland and two cowper's glands.

Genito- —A prefix indicating the reproductive organs.

Genitocrural —Pertaining to the genital organs and the leg.

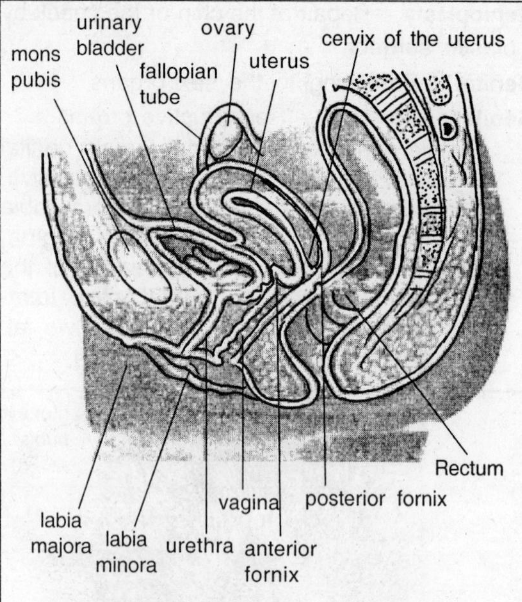

Fig.178B : Female internal genitalia (anteroposterior section)

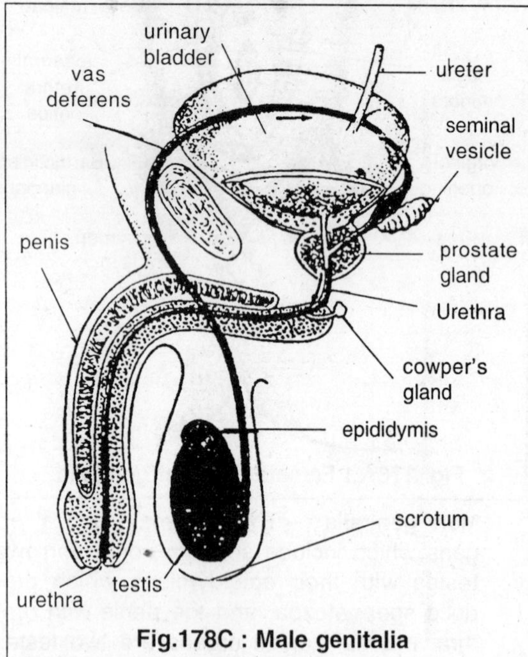

Fig.178C : Male genitalia

Genitofemoral —Genitocrural.

Genitography —X-ray examination of the urogenital sinus and internal ducts after giving an injection of a contrast medium through the sinus opening.

Genitoplasty —Repair of the genital organs by plastic surgery.

Genitourinary —Pertaining to the genital and the urinary organs.

Genitourinary system — The system consisting of the organs concerning with the formation and excretion of the urine, and the genital organs.

Genius —The person having special intellectual power.

Genoblast —The nucleus of the fertilized ovum.

Genocide —To kill the people of a particular ethnic or social group willingly and with planning.

Genodermatology —Study of the hereditary aspects of the skin diseases.

Genodermatosis —Any genetic disease of the skin.

Genogram —A family record of three or more generations, which includes relationships, occupations, health, history of diseases and death.

Genome —The complete set of hereditary factors contained in the haploid set of chromosomes.

Genomic —Pertaining to the genome.

Genomics —Study of the structure of the genome of particular organisms.

Genotoxic —Toxic to the genetic material in the cells.

Genotype —A group of individuals who resemble each other in genetic constitution.

Genotypic —Genotypical.

Genotypical —Genotypic. Pertaining to the genotype.

-genous —A suffix which denotes originating or produced by.

Genu —1. The knee. 2. Any structure resembling a bent knee.

Genu extrorsum —Genu varum.

Genu introrsum —Genu valgum.

Genu recurvatum — Hyperextension at the knee joint.

Genu valgum —Knock-knee. In this condition the knees are vary close to each other and the ankles are apart.

Genu varum —Bowleg. In this condition the legs are bent outwards.

Genua —Plural of genu.

Genual —Pertaining to the knee.

Genuclast —An instrument for breaking the adhesions of the knee-joint.

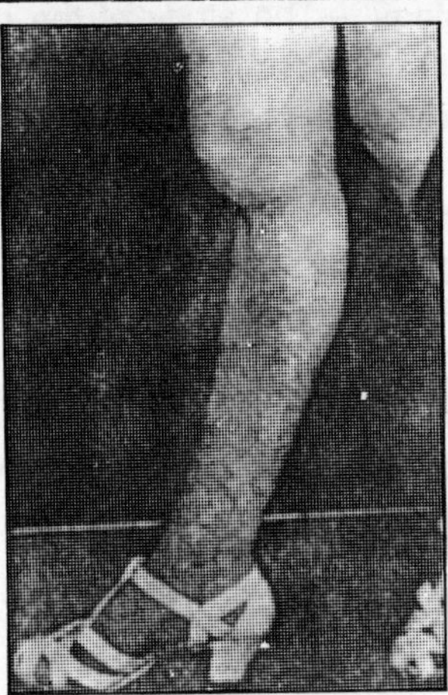
Fig. 179 : Genu recurvatum

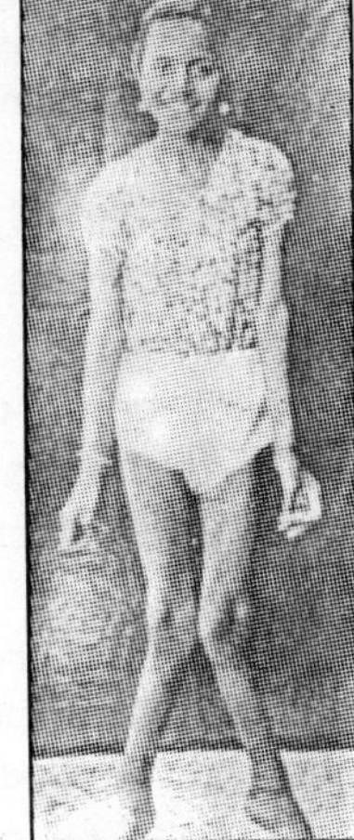
Fig. 180 : Genu valgum

Genucubital —Pertaining to the knee and the elbow.

Genucubital position — Position in which the patient sits on the knees, the thighs remain upright, body resting on the elbows and the head down on the hands.

Genuflex —Bent at the knee.

Genupectoral —Pertaining to the knees and the chest.

Genupectoral position — Knee-chest position.

Genus, plural **genera** —In biology, the division between the species and the family.

Genyantralgia —Pain in the frontal nasal sinuses.

Genyantritis —Inflammation of the frontal nasal sinuses.

Genyplasty —Any plastic operation on the jaw.

Geo- —A prefix indicating earth or the soil.

Geode —A dilated lymph space.

Geographical tongue — Formation of denuded patches on the tongue resembling maps.

Geomedicine —Study of the climatic and environmental effects on health.

Geopathology —The study of the diseases in relation to regions and climate.

Geophagia, Geophagism, Geophagy —The eating of inedible substances such as chalk or clay etc.

Geophilic —Living on the earth or in the soil.

Geotaxis —Geotropism.

Geotragia —Geophagia.

Geotrichosis —Fungus infection of the lungs, mouth or intestine due to Geotrichum candidum.

Geotropism —The influence of gravity on living organisms.

Gephyrophobia —Morbid fear of water, of crossing on the bridges over water, or of traveling on the boats.

Ger-, Gero-, Geronto- —Prefixes meaning old age, the aged.

Geratic —Pertaining to old age.

Geratology —The scientific study of the old age.

Gereology —Geratology.

Geriatric —Pertaining to old age or geriatrics.

Geriatrician —Specialist in geriatrics.

Geriatrics —The branch of medical science which deals with the health problems and diseases of the old age.

Geriodontics —Gerodontics.

Germ —1. A microorganism producing disease. 2. A living substance capable of developing into a part or organism as a whole.

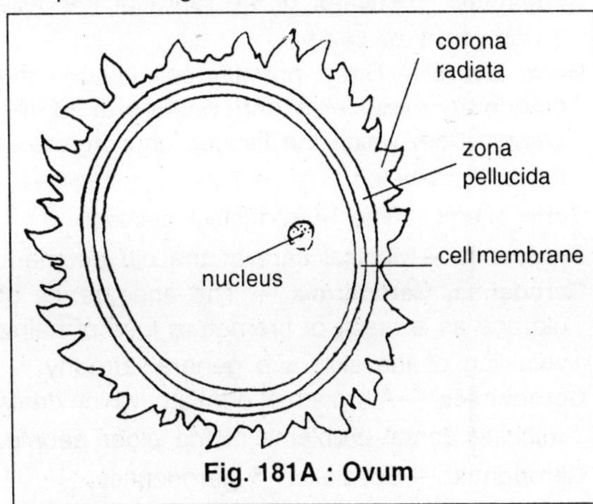

Fig. 181A : Ovum

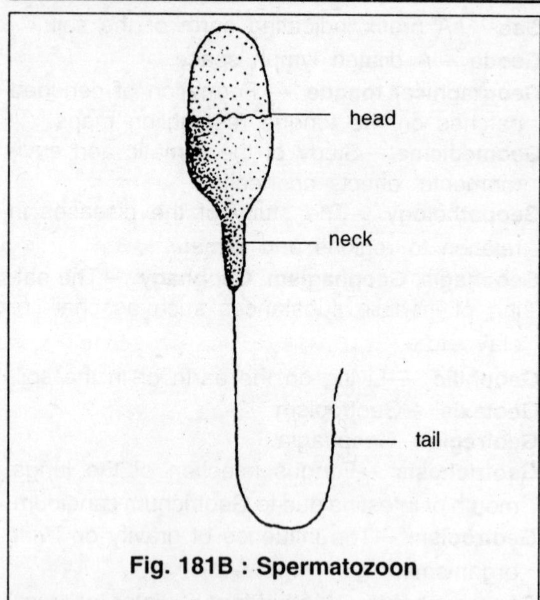

Fig. 181B : Spermatozoon

German measles —Rubella.

Germ cell —An ovum or spermatozoon.

Germicidal —Destroying the disease-producing microorganisms.

Germicide —Germicidal.

Germinal —Pertaining to a germ or reproductive cell or to germination, or of the nature of a germ cell.

Germinal disk —Blastoderm.

Germinal epithelium —The epithelium covering the surface of the genital ridge of an embryo.

Germination —1. Development of a fertilized ovum into an embryo. 2. The sprouting of the seeds of a plant.

Germinative —Pertaining to germination or to a reproductive cell.

Germinoma —A tumor of the reproductive cells in the testis or ovary.

Germ layers —Three primary cell layers—the ectoderm, mesoderm and endoderm of the embryo from which the tissues and organs of the body develop.

Germ plasm —The reproductive tissues.

Gerocomia —Medical care of the old people.

Geroderma, Gerodermia — The appearance of old age as a result of premature loss of hairs, wrinkling of the skin and general atrophy.

Gerodontics —A branch of dentistry which deals with the dental problems of the older people.

Gerodontist —Specialist in gerodontics.

Gerodontology —The study of the dental problems of the old age.

Geromarasmus —Emaciation accompanying the extreme old age.

Geromorphism —Premature senility. Appearance of old age in youth.

Gerontal —Senile. Pertaining to old man or old age.

Gerontologist —Specialist in gerontology.

Gerontology —Geriatrics. The scientific study of aging.

Gerontophilia —Love for old people.

Gerontophobia —Morbid fear of old persons.

Gerontopia —Senopia. Improvement of the near vision in old people due to the formation of a nuclear cataract.

Gerontotherapeutics — Treatment of a person to prevent the development of many aspects of the old age.

Gerontotherapy —Treatment of diseases of old persons.

Gerontoxon —Arcus senilis.

Geropsychiatry —The diagnosis and treatment of mental disorders in old persons.

Gestagen —Producing the effects of progesterone.

Gestaltism —The concept that the objects are of complete forms or configurations which can not be split into parts, e.g., a square is perceived as such rather than as four separate lines.

Gestation —Pregnancy. The period from the time of fertilization of the ovum until birth of the child.

Ectopic gestation — Gestation in which the fetus develops outside the uterus, e.g., in the fallopian tube, ovary or abdominal cavity etc.

Plural gestation — Gestation in which there is more than one embryo.

Prolonged gestation — Gestation which is prolonged beyond the usual period.

Secondary gestation — Gestation in which the ovum becomes dislodged from its original place of implantation and continues to develop in a new situation.

Gestational age —The age of the fetus which is calculated from the 1st day of the last menstrual period expressed in weeks.

Gestation sac —Amniotic sac.

Gestation time —The duration of a normal pregnancy.

Gestoses —Plural of gestosis.

Gestosis —Any disorder of pregnancy.

Gesture —Any movement expressing an idea, opinion or emotion.

Geumaphobia —Morbid fear of taste.

GFR —Glomerular filtration rate.

GH —Growth hormone.

Ghon's primary lesion, tubercle —A small spot seen in the X-ray film of the lung of the children suffering from primary pulmonary tuberculosis.

Ghost —Spectre, spirit, shadowy outline.

Ghost corpuscle —Red blood corpuscle without pigmentation.

GH-RH —Growth hormone-releasing hormone.

Giant —Much larger than normal.

Giant cell —A large cell with several nuclei appearing to be made up of many cells but not clearly outlined.

Giantism —Gigantism. Excessive growth in the size of cells, tissues, organs, parts or whole of the body.

Giardia —A genus of pear-shaped unicellular animals possessing flagella, living in the small intestine of man and attaching themselves to its mucous membrane from which they absorb their nourishment.

Giardia lamblia —A species of Giardia found in man causing diseases.

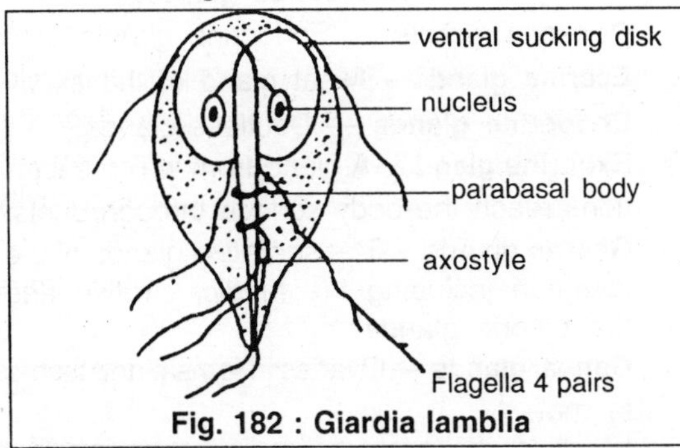

Fig. 182 : Giardia lamblia

Giardiasis —Lambliasis. Disease caused by the infection of Giardia lamblia characterized by diarrhea with fatty stools and abdominal distention.

Gibbon's hydrocele —A hydrocele and a large hernia combined.

Gibbosity —The condition of having humpback or kyphosis.

Gibbous —The person having humpback.

Gibbus —Hump.

Giddiness —Dizziness. The state of being inconstant or unstable.

Gigantism —Giantism. Excessive overgrowth of the body or of a part.

Fig. 183 : Gigantism

Gigantoblast —A very large nucleated red blood cell.

Gigantocyte —1. A giant cell. 2. A very large red blood cell.

Gigantomastia —Extreme enlargement of the breast.

Gigantosoma —Giantism. Gigantism. Abnormal size of the body.

Gingiva —Gum.

Gingival —Pertaining to the gum.

Gingivalgia —Pain in the gums.

Gingivally —Toward the gums.

Gingivectomy —Excision of the diseased portion of gum.

Gingivitis —Inflammation of the gums.

Gingivo- —A prefix meaning gingivae.

Gingivoglossitis — Stomatitis. Inflammation of the gums and the tongue.

Gingivolabial —Pertaining to the gums and the lips.

Gingivoplasty —To correct the margins of the gums by plastic surgery.

Gingivosis —Chronic diffuse inflammation of the

gums characterized by degeneration and atrophy of the gum tissue.

Gingivostomatitis — Inflammation of the gums and the mucous membrane of the mouth.

Herpetic gingivostomatitis —Inflammation of the gums and the oral mucosa due to infection with herpes simplex virus characterized by redness inside the mouth, formation of multiple vesicles and painful ulcers and pyrexia.

Necrotizing ulcerative gingivostomatitis — Severe stomatitis with the formation of ulcers and necrosis of the oral mucosa and the gums.

Ginglyform —Ginglymoid. Resembling a hinged joint.

Ginglymoarthrodial — Pertaining to a joint which is partly hinged and partly arthrodial.

Ginglymoid —Pertaining to or resembling a hinged joint.

Ginglymus —A hinge joint, diarthrosis. A joint which allows movement only in one plane, forward and backward.

Girdle —Anything encircling the body.

Pectoral or shoulder girdle —Encircling bony structure, composed of clavicle and scapula bones to which the upper limbs are attached.

Pelvic girdle —Encircling bony structure composed of two hip bones to which the lower limbs are attached.

Girdle pain —Zonesthesia.

Girdle symptom —A feeling of constriction about the chest as seen in Pott's disease owing to the constriction of the spinal cord resulting from collapse of the vertebrae.

Girth —Circumference.

Gitter cell —A macrophage present at the sites of brain injury.

Glabella —The smooth area on the frontal bone above the nose and between eyebrows.

Glabellad —Toward the glabella.

Glabrate —1. Bald. 2. Smooth.

Glabrous —Glabrate.

Glacial —Like ice.

Gladiate —Ensiform, xiphoid. Sword-shaped.

Gladiolus —Corpus sterni. The middle and the main part of the sternum.

Glaire —The white of egg.

Glairy —Resembling the white of egg.

Gland —Unicellular or multicellular soft mass or an organ secreting a fluid which is discharged and is used in some other parts of the body.

Accessory gland —A small gland functioning as accessory and situated near or at some distance from a gland of similar structure.

Adrenal gland, Suprarenal gland —An endocrine gland situated above each kidney.

Apocrine gland —A gland whose discharged secretion contains some parts of the secreting cells.

Areolar glands — Sebaceous glands present in the areola surrounding the nipple in the breast of the female.

Axillary glands — Axillary lymph nodes.

Brachial glands — Lymph glands present in the upper arm and forearm.

Ceruminous glands — Glands present in the external auditory canal, which excrete cerumen.

Cervical glands — Lymph glands situated in the neck.

Cowper's gland —One of the two small glands of yellow color, about the size of a pea situated beneath the bulb of the urethra in the male with a duct carrying the mucous secretion of the gland into the urethra. This secretion forms a part of the semen.

Cutaneous glands — Glands of the skin, especially the sebaceous glands.

Ductless glands — Endocrine glands.

Eccrine gland —Sweat gland of the skin.

Endocrine glands — Ductless glands.

Exocrine gland —A gland from which secretions reach the body surface through ducts.

Gastric glands —The secreting glands of the stomach including the fundic, cardiac and the pyloric glands.

Genital glands — Ovaries in female and testes in male.

Inguinal glands — Lymph nodes in the inguinal region.

Lacrimal glands —Tear–secreting glands.

Lactiferous gland —Mammary gland.

Lymph gland, Lymphatic gland — Nodule of the lymphatic tissue which is found in the way of a lymphatic vessel.

Mammary glands —Two milk secreting

glands found in the female. Each gland contains 15 to 20 lactiferous ducts in it, each of which discharges milk through a separate opening on the surface of the nipple.

Meibomian glands —Tarsal glands.

Mixed gland —A gland which has both, endocrine and exocrine function, e.g., pancreas.

Muciparous glands — Glands which secrete mucus.

Mucous glands —Mucus–secreting glands.

Oxyntic glands —Gastric glands found in the mucous membrane of the fundus and body of the stomach.

Parathyroid glands —Four small glands situated on the posterior surface of the thyroid gland, secreting parathyroid hormone—the parathormone which regulates calcium and phosphorus metabolism.

Parotid glands —Two largest salivary glands, each one of which is situated in front of the ear.

Pineal gland —Pineal body.

Pituitary gland — Hypophysis. A small gray, oval gland attached to the base of the brain, connected with the hypothalamus and divided into anterior and posterior lobes.

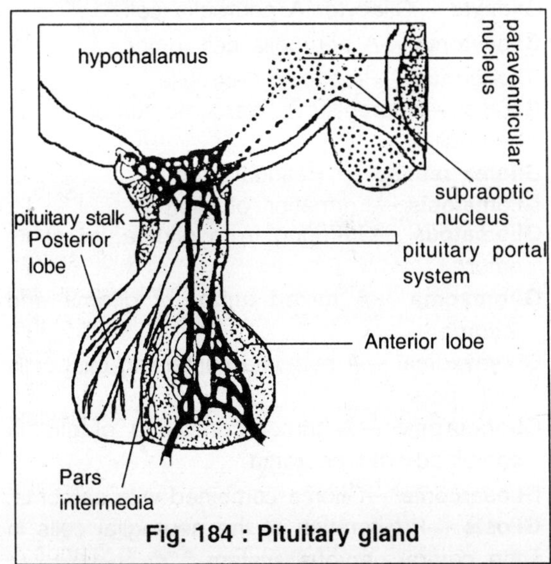

Fig. 184 : Pituitary gland

Prostate gland —A gland consisting of three lobes, surrounds the neck of the urinary bladder and the urethra in the male, with ducts opening into the prostatic portion of the urethra and discharging the secretion of the gland into it, which forms a portion of the semen.

Pyloric glands — Gastric glands situated near the pylorus that secrete gastric juice.

Salivary glands —The three—parotid, sublingual and submandibular salivary glands.

Sebaceous glands — The glands of the skin secreting sebum.

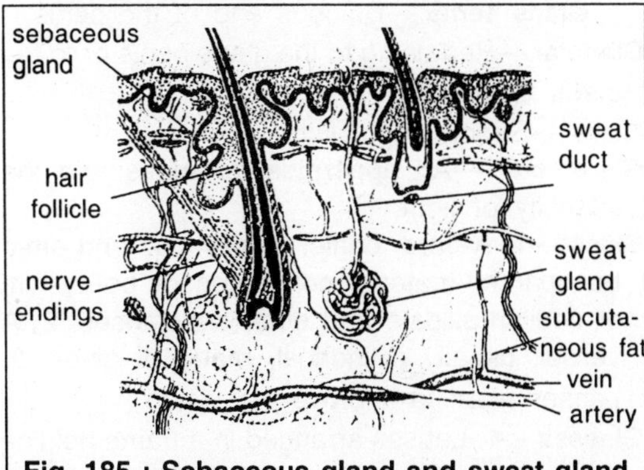

Fig. 185 : Sebaceous gland and sweat gland

Seromucous gland —A mixed serous and mucous gland.

Sex glands —Ovaries in the female and testes in the male.

Submandibular glands — Two salivary glands, one lying on each side below the mandible.

Sudoriferous glands — Sweat glands.

Sweat glands —The glands which secrete sweat situated under the skin, opening by a duct on the surface of the skin.

Tarsal glands — Meibomian glands. Glands located in the eyelid that secrete an oily substance which keep the lids from adhering to each other.

Thyroid gland —A ductless gland consisting of two lobes, one on each side of the upper part of the trachea connected by isthmus, producing hormones thyroxine and triiodothyronine which are concerned in regulating the metabolic rate.

Glanders —A contagious disease of horses transmitted to man by Pseudomonas mallei, marked by fever, inflammation of the skin and the mucous membrane with the formation of abscesses and ulcers.

Glandes —Plural of glans.

Glandilemma —The outer covering of a gland.

Glandula —Glandule. A small gland.

Glandular —1. Pertaining to, or of the nature of a gland. 2. Pertaining to the glans penis.

Glandular therapy —Treatment of diseases by the endocrine glands or their extracts.

Glandule —Glandula.

Glans —A rounded mass or glandlike structure.

Glans clitoridis — The head of the clitoris.

Glans penis —Bulbous end of the penis.

Glanular —Pertaining to the glans penis or to the glans clitoridis.

Glare —Strong bright light.

Glarometer —An apparatus for measuring the intensity of light.

Glass —1. A hard, brittle, amorphous and often transparent material composed of potassium or sodium silicate and other substances. 2. A vessel, usually cylindrical, made of glass. 3. Lenses worn to improve the vision.

Glasses —1. Lenses arranged in a frame holding them in the proper position before the eyes of the patient to correct the refractive errors. The glasses may be bifocal *i.e.* the lenses have two different refracting powers, in which the lower portion is used for seeing the near objects or reading while the upper portion is used for seeing the distant objects. 2. Spectacles for protecting the eyes from glare and particles in the air.

Glassy tissue —Hyaline. A tissue which looks like glass.

Glaucoma —A disease of the eye characterized by an increase of the intraocular pressure resulting in the atrophy of the optic nerve and diminution of vision.

Glaucomatocyclitic — Denoting increased intraocular pressure associated with cyclitis.

Glaucomatous —Pertaining to glaucoma or of the nature of glaucoma.

Glaze —To make shiny like the glass.

Glazy —Shiny.

Gleet —A mucous or purulent discharge from the urethra in chronic urethritis.

Gleety —Pertaining to gleet.

Glenard's disease — Splanchnoptosia. Prolapse of one or more of the internal organs.

Glenohumeral —Pertaining to the humerus bone and the glenoid cavity.

Glenoid —Like a socket in appearance.

Glenoid cavity —The socket in the scapula bone in which head of the humerous bone is fitted.

Glenoid fossa —The fossa of the temporal bone in which condyle of the mandible is fitted.

Glenoid labrum —The ring of fibrocartilaginous tissue around the glenoid cavity on the scapula bone.

Glenoid lip —A rim of fibrous tissue around the margin of the glenoid socket.

Glia —Neuroglia.

Gliacyte —A neuroglia cell.

Gliadin —A protein present in wheat, which contains the toxic factor causing celiac disease. The sticky mass resulting from mixing the wheat flour with water is due to gliadin.

Glial —Of or pertaining to the neuroglia .

Glide —To slide.

Glidewire —A lubricated guidewire, generally used in the urinary tract.

Gliding —Sliding.

Glioblast —An early neural cell developing from the early ependymal cell of the neural tube.

Glioblastoma —A neuroglia cell malignant tumor.

Glioblastoma multiforme —A rapidly growing malignant tumor of the central nervous system, especially of the cerebrum, consisting of the spongioblasts, astroblasts and astrocytes cells.

Gliocyte —Gliacyte. A neuroglia cell.

Gliocytoma —A neuroglia cell tumor.

Gliogenous —Producing neuroglia.

Glioma —Neuroglioma. Sarcoma tumor of the neuroglia.

Glioma retinae — Retinoblastoma.

Gliomatosis —Formation of glioma.

Gliomatous —Suffering from glioma, or of its nature.

Gliomyoma —A mixed tumor of glioma and myoma.

Gliomyxomal —A myxoma containing glial cells and fibers.

Glioneuroma —A tumor consisting of glioma combined with neuroma.

Gliosarcoma —Glioma combined with sarcoma.

Gliosis —Proliferation of the neuroglial cells in the central nervous system.

Gliosome —One of the rounded masses seen in neuroglia cells.

Glissade —A gliding involuntary movement occurring in the eye while changing the point of fixation.

Glissonian cirrhosis — Perihepatitis. Inflammation of the peritoneal coat of the liver.

Glissonitis —Inflammation of the Glisson's capsule.

Glisson's capsule —Outer covering of the liver made up of the fibrous tissue.

Glisson's disease —Rickets.

Globe — A ball as the eye-ball.

Globi —Plural of globus.

Globin —1. The protein constituent of hemoglobin 2 Any member of a particular group of proteins.

Globinometer —An instrument for measuring the globin.

Globoid —Of the form of a globe, spheroid.

Globular —Spherical

Globule —A small spherical mass.

Globuliferous —Containing globules or corpuscles, especially red blood cells.

Globulin —A group of simple proteins which are insoluble in water but soluble in saline solution (euglobulins) or water soluble proteins (pseudoglobulins).

Accelerator globulin —A globulin present in the serum of blood, which increases the speed of conversion of prothrombin to thrombin in the presence of thromboplastin and calcium ions.

Alpha globulins — Globulins present in the plasma of blood, which in neutral or alkaline solutions move excessively by electrophoresis so resemble the albumins.

Antihemophilic globulin —It is a coagulation factor i.e., the protein present in the plasma of blood, which is necessary for the normal coagulation of blood. It is deficient in the patient suffering from hemophilia.

Beta globulins — Globulins present in the plasma of blood, which in neutral or alkaline solutions, by electrophoresis move with the speed between that of the alpha and gamma globulins.

Gamma globulins —A group of globulins present in the plasma of blood, which in neutral or alkaline solutions, by electrophoresis move with the lowest speed than that of the alpha or beta globulins, and to which most of the immune antibodies are associated.

Immune globulins —A sterile solution of globulins with antibodies, normally present in the adult human blood, derived from donor plasma or serum, used for passive immunization of a nonimmune person against infectious hepatitis, poliomyelitis, mumps etc., and in the treatment of gamma globulin deficiency.

Pertussis immune globulin —A sterile solution of globulins derived from the donor's blood plasma, immunized with the pertussis vaccine, used for the prophylaxis and treatment of pertussis.

Rabies immune globulin — A sterile solution of globulins derived from the donor's blood plasma who has been immunized with rabies vaccine, used as a passive immunizing agent for the prophylaxis of rabies.

Rh0 (D) immune globulin —A sterile solution of globulins derived from the human blood plasma containing antibodies to the erythrocyte factor Rh_0 (D). It is used in the prevention of the formation of Rh_0 (D) antibodies in Rh_0(D)-negative mothers, after a miscarriage, therapeutic abortion or delivery of a Rh_0 (D)-positive fetus or child and thus it is beneficial in preventing the development of erythroblastosis fetalis in the next pregnancy if the child is Rh_0-positive.

Serum globulin — Globulins, a fraction of blood serum present in the blood serum or plasma with which the antibodies are associated. By electrophoresis they are divided into alpha, beta and gamma globulins, which differ from each other by the difference of speed of the mobility by electrophoresis.

Tetanus immune globulin —A sterile solution of the gamma globulins derived from blood plasma of the human donors who have been immunized with tetanus toxoid, used in the prophylaxis and treatment of tetanus.

Globulinuria —Presence of globulin in the urine.

Globulose —Albumose or protein produced by the digestion of globulins.

Globulus —Globule.

Globus —A spherical structure.

Globus hystericus —To feel a lump in the throat in hysteria.

Glomal —Pertaining to or involving a glomus.

Glomangioma —A benign tumor arising from the arteriovenous glomus, usually occurring at the tip of the fingers or toes or in the skin.

Glomangiosis —The occurrence of multiple complexes of small blood vessels, each resembling a glomus.

Glome —Glomus.

Glomectomy —Removal of a glomus by surgery.

Glomera —Plural of glomus.

Glomerate —Clustered or grouped.

Glomerular —Pertaining to, or of the nature of a glomerulus.

Glomerule —Glomerulus.

Glomeruli —Plural of glomerulus.

Glomerulitis —Inflammation of the renal glomeruli.

Glomerulonephritis — Nephritis with inflammation and degeneration of the renal glomeruli and the renal tubules.

Glomerulonephropathy —Any noninflammatory disease of the renal glomeruli.

Glomerulopathy—Any disease of the glomerulus of the kidney.

Glomerulosclerosis — Fibrosis of the renal glomeruli.

Glomerulose —Glomerular.

Glomerulus —A cluster of blood capillaries in the Bowman's or glomerular capsule of the kidney, which together with the capsule constitutes the renal corpuscle.

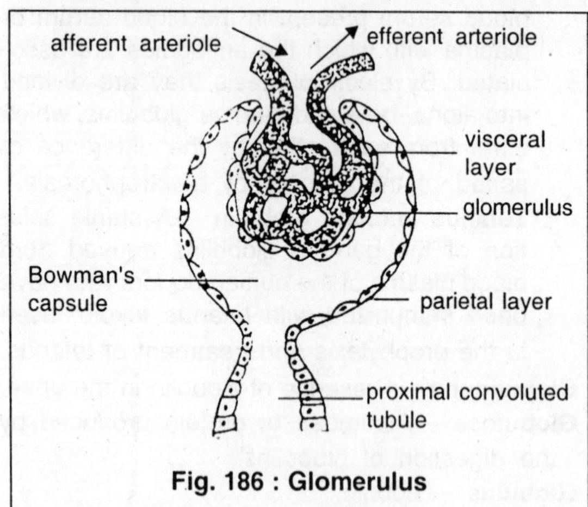

Fig. 186 : Glomerulus

Glomoid —Resembling a glomus.

Glomus —A small round mass, composed of fine arterioles connecting directly with the veins, containing many nerve fibers, e.g., glomus caroticum which is a flat structure at the bifurcation of the common carotid body, containing the cells which respond to changes in the concentration of oxygen in the blood and to changes in blood pressure.

Glossa —The tongue.

Glossagra —Glossalgia. Glossodynia. Pain in the tongue.

Glossal —Pertaining to the tongue.

Glossalgia —Glossodynia. Pain in the tongue.

Glossectomy —Elinguation. Partial or complete excision of the tongue.

Glossitis —Inflammation of the tongue.

Acute glossitis — Inflammation of the tongue usually associated with the stomatitis, in which the tongue is covered with the ulcers and it is painful and tender.

Glossitis areata exfoliativa — Geographical tongue.

Glossitis parasitica —Black or hairy tongue.

Median rhomboidal glossitis —A diamond–shaped inflammatory area found on the tongue.

Moeller's glossitis — Glossodynia exfoliativa. A chronic superficial glossitis characterized by burning or pain and increased sensitivity to heat and spicy foods.

Glosso- —Prefix pertaining to tongue.

Glossocele —Swelling and protrusion of the tongue.

Glossodynamometer —An apparatus for measuring the contractile power of the muscles of the tongue.

Glossodynia —Glossalgia. Pain in the tongue.

Glossoepiglottic —Pertaining to the tongue and the epiglottis.

Glossoepiglottidean — Glossoepiglottic.

Glossograph —An instrument for recording the movements of the tongue in speaking.

Glossohyal —Hyoglossal. Pertaining to the tongue and the hyoid bone.

Glossoid —Resembling the tongue.

Glossokinesthetic —Pertaining to the movements of the tongue.

Glossolabial —Pertaining to the tongue and the lips.

Glossolalia —Senseless and unrelated talkings.

Glossology —Glottology. The study of the tongue and its diseases.

Glossolysis —Glossoplegia. Paralysis of the tongue.

Glossoncus —Swelling of any type of the tongue.

Glossopalatine —Pertaining to the tongue and the palatine.

Glossopalatinus —Palatoglossus, a muscle of the saft palate and the tongue.

Glossopathy —Any disease of the tongue.

Glossopharyngeal —Pertaining to the tongue and the pharynx.

Glossophytia —Black or hairy tongue.

Glossoplasty —Repair of the tongue by plastic surgery.

Glossoplegia —Paralysis of the tongue.

Glossoptosis, Glossoptosia —Downward displacement of the tongue toward the pharynx.

Glossopyrosis —Burning sensation of the tongue.

Glossorrhaphy —Suturing of a wound on the tongue.

Glossoscopy —Inspection of the tongue.

Glossospasm —Spasm of the tongue.

Glossosteresis —Glossectomy.

Glossotomy —To make an incision into the tongue.

Glossotrichia —Hairy tongue.

Glossy —Smooth and shining.

Glottal —Pertaining to the glottis.

Glottic —Of or pertaining to the tongue, or the glottis.

Glottides—Plural of glottis.

Glottidospasm — Laryngospasm.

Glottis —The sound–producing apparatus of the larynx consisting of two vocal cords and the open space between them.

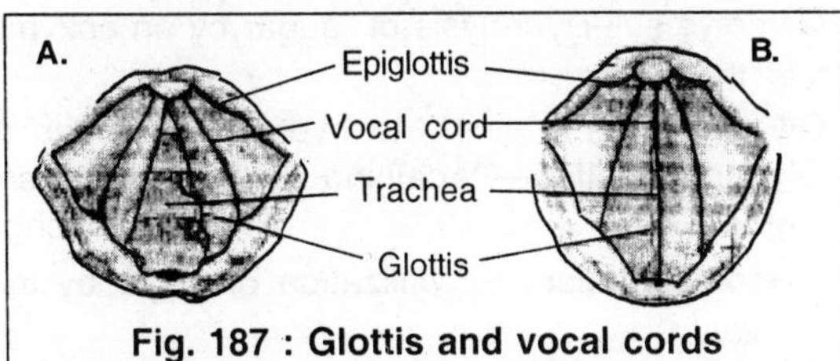

Fig. 187 : Glottis and vocal cords

Glottitis —Inflammation of the glottis.

Glottology —Glossology. The study of the tongue and its diseases.

Glove —A protective covering for the hand made of rubber, used generally in surgical procedures.

Glucagon —A polypeptide hormone which increases the concentration of glucose in the blood, secreted by the alpha cells of the islets of Langerhans of the pancreas in response to hypoglycemia.

Glucagonoma —A malignant tumor of the alpha cells of the islets of Langerhans.

Glucocorticoid —One of the groups of the corticosteroid hormones secreted by the cortex of the adrenal gland, which is concerned with the carbohydrate and protein metabolism and many other activities such as inhibition of the inflammation and the allergic reactions. There are two main glucocorticoids—hydrocortisone and cortisone.

Glucocorticotrophic —A factor of the anterior pituitary gland that stimulates the production of glucocorticoid hormones of the adrenal cortex.

Glucogenesis —Formation of glucose from glycogen.

Glucogenic —Producing glucose.

Glucokinetic —Maintaining the blood glucose level.

Glucolysis —Glycolysis.

Glucometer —An apparatus for measuring the blood sugar in a few drops of blood obtained from the finger.

Gluconeogenesis — Glyconeogenesis. The formation of glycogen by the liver from the noncarbohydrate sources, such as amino or fatty acids.

Glucopenia —Hypoglycemia.

Glucoplastic —Glucogenic.

Glucoregulation —Regulation of glucose metabolism.

Glucose —It is the end product of carbohydrate metabolism and is the chief source of energy for the body. Excess of glucose is converted into glycogen which is stored in the liver and muscles for the use when needed, and when it is much more, it is converted into fat which is stored as adipose tissue. Normal blood sugar (glucose) level is 80 to 120 mg. per 100 ml. of blood, which is maintained by insulin. In the deficiency of insulin less glucose is converted into glycogen so it rises above this level in the blood, the condition is known a hyperglycemia. When the glucose becomes above renal threshold, it appears in the urine, the condition is known as glycosuria which is a symptom of diabetes mellitus. In excess of insulin the more glucose is converted into glycogen so the blood glucose level falls below normal, the condition is known as hypoglycemia.

Glucose tolerance test —A test by which the ability of the patient to metabolize sugar (glucose) is determined. It is done by giving a certain amount of glucose to the patient orally or intravenously and the blood samples at hourly intervals for six times are taken and the glucose in the blood of each sample is determined. In case of excess of insulin in the blood, glucose continues to fall below normal level after three hours, i.e. from the 3rd sample, conversely, when the insulin is less, the sugar does not continue to fall below normal level after three hours.

Glucoside —A glycoside containing sugar as glucose.

Glucosuria —Glycosuria. Presence of glucose in the urine.

Glutathionuria —Presence of excessive amount of glutathione in the urine.

Gluteal —Pertaining to the buttocks.

Gluteal fold —Rump. The crease between the thigh and the buttocks.

Gluteal reflex —Contraction of the gluteal muscles from stimulation of their skin.

Glutelin —A simple protein found in the grain seeds which is soluble in alkalies and dilute acids but not in the neutral solutions.

Gluten —A protein of wheat and other grains.

Gluten enteropathy —Celiac disease ; a disease associated with the malabsorption of food from the intestinal tract characterized by diarrhea and malnutrition.

Gluteofemoral —Pertaining to the buttock and the thigh.

Gluteoinguinal —Pertaining to the buttock and the groin.

Glutin —Gliadin.

Glutinous —Adhesive ; sticky.

Glutitis —Inflammation of the muscles (glutei) of the buttocks.

Glycemia —Glycosemia. Presence of sugar or glucose in the blood.

Glycerin —Glycerol. A clear, colorless, syrupy liquid, soluble in water and alcohol, used as a solvent for drug, as a preservative and as an emollient in various skin diseases.

Glycerite —A medicine mixed in a glycerin solution.

Glycerol —Glycerin.

Glycerolize —To mix with glycerin or to preserve in glycerin.

Glycinuria —The excretion of glycine in the urine.

Glyco- —A prefix meaning sugar.

Glycocholate —A salt of glycocholic acid.

Glycoclastic —Pertaining to the hydrolysis and digestion of sugars.

Glycogen —Glycogen is the form in which the carbohydrate after digestion and absorption is stored in the liver or muscles for conversion into sugar, and for use in performing muscular work or for liberating heat in future.

Glycogenase —An enzyme which hydrolyzes the glycogen by which dextrose is formed.

Glycogenesis —The formation of glycogen from glucose.

Glycogenetic —Pertaining to the formation of glycogen.

Glycogenic —Pertaining to or producing glycogen.

Glycogenolysis —Conversion of glycogen into glucose in the tissues of the body.

Glycogenolytic —Pertaining to the hydrolysis of glycogen.

Glycogenosis —Glycogen storage disease.

Glycogenous —Glycogenic. Producing glycogen.

Glycogen storage disease —Any disease characterized by abnormal storage of glycogen in the liver.

Glycogeusia —A sweet taste in the mouth.

Glycohemia —Glycosemia. Abnormal amount of sugar in the blood.

Glycolysis —Hydrolysis of sugar by an enzyme in the body.

Glycolytic —Pertaining to hydrolyzing sugar.

Glycometabolic —Pertaining to the metabolism of sugar.

Glycometabolism — Utilization of sugar by the body.

Glyconeogenesis — Gluconeogenesis.

Glycopenia —Hypoglycemia. Blood glucose level below normal.

Glycopexic —Pertaining to the fixing or storing of sugar.

Glycopexis —The storing of glycogen in the liver.

Glycophilia —The condition in which a small amount of glucose produces hyperglycemia.

Glycophorin —A protein projecting through the

thickness of the cell membrane of red blood cells.

Glycopolyuria —Diabetes mellitus in which the sugar in the urine is increased moderately but the uric acid is much more increased.

Glycoprival, Glycoprivous —Without carbohydrates.

Glycoprotein —A compound consisting of carbohydrate and protein.

Glycoptyalism —Glycosialia. Presence of glucose in the saliva.

Glycorrhachia —Presence of sugar in the cerebrospinal fluid.

Glycorrhea —Discharge of sugar from the body.

Glycosecretory —Concerning with the formation of glycogen.

Glycosemia —Glycemia.

Glycosialia —Glycoptyalism.

Glycosialorrhea —Excessive secretion of saliva containing glucose.

Glycoside —A substance produced by the plants which on hydrolysis yields sugar and other products.

Glycostatic —Acting to maintain a constant sugar level in the body.

Glycosuria —Presence of glucose in the urine.

Alimentary glycosuria —Glycosuria may occur after taking large amounts of carbohydrates or sugars.

Diabetic glycosuria —Glycosuria occurring in diabetes mellitus due to insulin deficiency.

Emotional glycosuria —Glycosuria occurring in emotional states as may occur in anxiety.

Pituitary glycosuria —Glycosuria resulting from dysfunction of the anterior pituitary gland.

Renal glycosuria — Glycosuria occurring in the condition where the renal threshold for reabsorption of glucose by the renal tubules is decreased.

Glycotrophic —Glycotropic.

Glycotropic —Acting against insulin, or increasing blood sugar level.

Glycuresis —Glycosuria.

Glycuretic —That which increases the sugar in the urine.

Glycuronuria —Presence of glycuronic acid in the urine.

gm —Gram.

Gnashing —The grinding of the teeth together.

Gnat —The insects smaller than mosquitoes.

Gnathalgia —Pain in the jaw.

Gnathic —Pertaining to the jaw or cheeks.

Gnathion —The middle and the lowest point on the chin.

Gnathitis —Inflammation of the jaw.

Gnatho- —Prefix pertaining to jaw or cheek.

Gnathocephalus —The fetus without head, having jaws only.

Gnathodynamometer —An apparatus for measuring the force exerted in closing the upper and lower jaws.

Gnathodynia —Gnathalgia. Pain in the jaw.

Gnathological —Pertaining to the study of the anatomy, physiology, pathology and the diseases of the jaws.

Gnathology —The study of the anatomy, physiology, pathology and the diseases of the jaws.

Gnathometer —An instrument for measuring the jaw.

Gnathoplasty —Repair of the jaws or cheeks by plastic surgery.

Gnathoschisis —Congenital cleft of the jaws.

Gnosia —Mental ability to recognize the things and their forms.

GnRH —Gonadotropin-releasing hormone.

Goblet —Cup-shaped.

Goblet cells —A type of secretory cells present in the epithelium of the intestine and the respiratory tracts.

Goggle-eyed —Having abnormally protruding eyes. Exophthalmic.

Goiter —Enlargement of the thyroid gland causing swelling in front of the neck, which may be due to deficiency of iodine in the diet, inflammation of the thyroid gland, tumor, or hyper or hypo function of the thyroid gland.

Cystic goiter —Enlarged thyroid gland in which one or more than one cysts are formed.

Diffuse goiter —Goiter in which the tissue of the thyroid gland is diffused to all sides in comparison to its nodular form.

Diving or wandering goiter —A movable goiter which is usually situated sometimes below and at other times above the sternal notch.

Endemic goiter — Goiter occurring in a certain geographical locality, especially in which iodine is deficient in food and water.

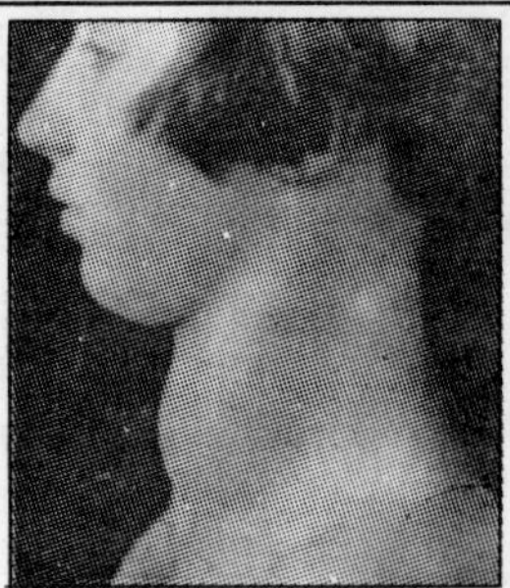

Fig. 188 : Diffuse goiter

Fig. 189 : Exophthalmic goiter

Exophthalmic goiter —Thyrotoxicosis. Graves' disease. Goiter characterized by protrusion of the eyes.

Lingual goiter — Enlargement of the upper end of the thyroglossal duct, forming a tumor at the posterior part of the dorsum of the tongue.

Nodular goiter — Enlarged thyroid gland containing nodules.

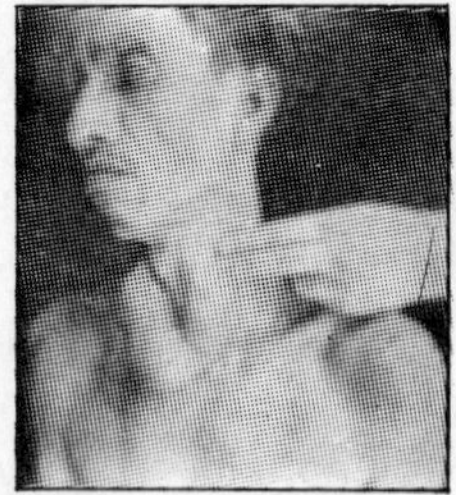

Fig. 190 : Nodular goiter

Parenchymatous goiter —Diffuse goiter.

Simple goiter —A goiter without causing general symptoms.

Suffocative goiter — Goiter causing shortness of breath due to pressure.

Toxic goiter — Exophthalmic goiter.

Goitrin —A goitrogenic substance isolated from cabbage and turnips etc.

Goitrogen —An agent producing goiter.

Goitrogenic —Goitrogen.

Goitrogenicity —The tendency to produce goiter.

Goitrous —Denoting or characteristic of a goiter.

Golgi apparatus —A minute tubular membranous structure found near the nucleus of almost all the cells, containing very minute saccules, best seen by electron microscope. The secretory product of the cell is collected in these saccules so these are mostly found in secretory cells.

Golgiokinesis —In mitosis, the process of division of the Golgi apparatus and its distribution to the two daugther cells.

Gomphiasis —Looseness of the teeth.

Gomphosis —A type of fibrous joint in which a conical process fits into a bony socket in an immovable joint, as the root of a tooth into the socket in the alveolus.

Gon- —A prefix which means. 1. Seed or semen 2. Knee.

Gonad —Female sex glands or ovaries producing ova and the male sex glands or testes producing spermatozoa, the cells for the reproduction.

Gonadal —Gonadial. Pertaining to a gonad.

Gonadal dysgenesis — Turner's syndrome.

Gonadectomy —Removal of a gonad by surgery.

Gonadial —Gonadal.

Gonadoblastoma —A benign tumor of a sex gland.

Gonadoliberin — Gonadotropin-releasing hormone. A hypothalamic substance causing the release of gonadotropin.

Gonadopathy —Any disease of the gonads.

Gonadorelin —Gonadotropin-releasing hormone.

Gonadotherapy —Treatment of the diseases by administration of the extracts of the testes or ovaries containing their hormones.

Gonadotrope —A basophilic cell of the anterior pituitary gland secreting follicle-stimulating or luteinizing hormones.

Gonadotroph —Gonadotrope.

Gonadotrophic—1. Stimulating the gonads. 2. Applied to the hormones of the anterior pituitary gland which influence the gonads.

Gonadotrophic hormone —Gonadotropin.

Gonadotrophin —Gonadotropin.

Gonadotropic —Gonadotrophic.

Gonadotropin —A gonad stimulating hormone.

Anterior pituitary gonadotropins —Two hormones—follicle-stimulating hormone and luteinizing hormone produced by the anterior pituitary gland.

Chorionic gonadotropins — Gonadotropins produced by the chorionic villi of the placenta, present in the blood and urine of the pregnant woman. Their presence in the urine is the basis of Aschheim-Zondeck test for pregnancy.

Gonadotropin-releasing hormone —A hormone produced by the hypothalamus, which acts on the pituitary gland to cause release of the gonadotropic hormones.

Gonaduct —The seminal duct or the oviduct.

Gonagra —Gout in the knee.

Gonalgia —Pain in the knee.

Gonangiectomy —Vasectomy. To cut and remove a portion or as a whole of the vas deferens.

Gonarthritis —Inflammation of the knee joint.

Gonarthrocace —Tuberculous arthritis of the knee.

Gonarthromeningitis — Synovitis of the knee joint.

Gonarthrotomy —To make an incision into the knee joint.

Gonatocele —White swelling or tumor of the knee.

Gonecyst, Gonecystis —A seminal vesicle.

Gonecystitis —Inflammation of the seminal vesicle.

Gonecystolith —A calculus in a seminal vesicle.

Gonecystopyosis —Formation of pus in a seminal vesicle.

Gonia —Plural of gonion.

Goniocraniometry — Measurement of the angles of the cranium.

Goniometer —An apparatus for measuring the movements and angles of a joint.

Goniometer finger —An apparatus for measuring the range of movement of a finger.

Gonion —The point of angle of the mandible or lower jaw.

Goniopuncture —To make an incision into the cornea for allowing drainage of the aqueous humour from the anterior chamber of the eye which is usually done in the treatment of glaucoma.

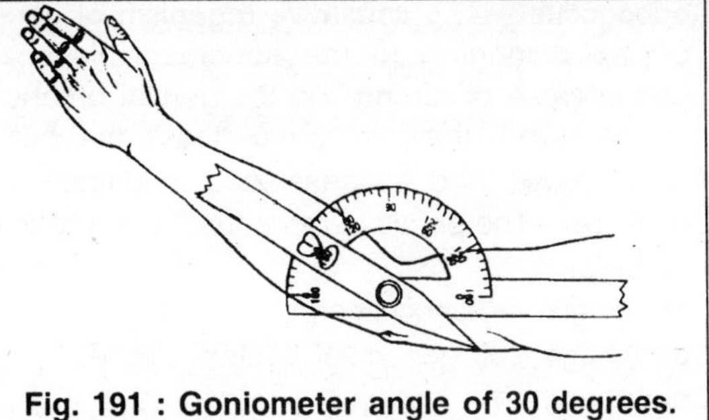

Fig. 191 : Goniometer angle of 30 degrees.

Gonioscope —An instrument used for inspecting the angle of the anterior chamber of the eye and determining the ocular motility and rotation.

Gonioscopy —Examination of the angle of the anterior chamber of the eye with a gonioscope.

Goniosynechia —Adhesion of the iris to the cornea of the eye.

Goniotomy —To remove the obstruction to allow free flow of the aqueous humour into the canal of Schlemm of the eye, by surgery.

Gono-, Gon- —A prefix which means genital organs, semen, generation or offspring.

Gonochorism, Gonochorismus —Normal differentiation of the gonads appropriate to the sex.

Gonocide —Destructive to the gonococci.

Gonococcal —Pertaining to or caused by gonococci.

Gonococcal conjunctivitis —Gonorrheal conjunctivitis. Severe purulent conjunctivitis caused by gonococcus, the causative organism of gonorrhea.

Gonococcemia —Gonohemia. Presence of gonococci in the blood.

Gonococci —Plural of gonococcus.

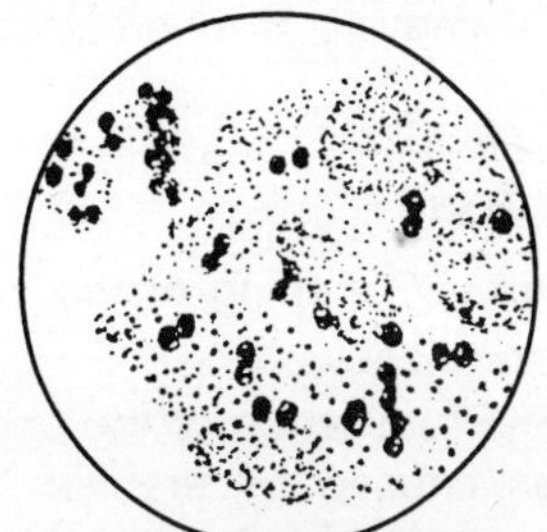

Fig. 192 : Gonococci

Gonococcic —Pertaining to gonococcus.

Gonococcide —An agent killing the gonococci.

Gonococcocide —Gonococcide.

Gonococcus —The causative organism of gonorrhea belonging to the species Neisseria gonorrhoeae occurring on the genital organs, in the blood, the joints, the heart, the eye, urine, feces, and abscess etc., in pairs.

Gonocyte —The primitive reproductive cell of the embryo.

Gonohemia —Gonococcemia.

Gonophage —A gonocidal bacteriophage.

Gonophore —An accessory reproductive organ such as spermatic duct, seminal vesicle or oviduct etc.

Gonorrhea —Infection with the bacteria gonococci transmitted from one person to another through sexual contacts characterized in the male by urethritis with pain and purulent discharge from the urethra associated with burning sensation during micturition. In the female, gonorrhea is generally asymptomatic but there may be urethral or vaginal discharge, painful and frequent micturition and pain in the lower abdomen.

Gonorrheal —Pertaining to gonorrhea.

Gonorrheal arthritis — Inflammation of a joint due to gonorrhea.

Gonoscheocele —Swelling of a testis with semen.

Gonotoxemia —The toxic condition caused by the absorption of endotoxin into the blood produced by gonococci.

Gonotoxin —The toxin produced by the gonococcus.

Gonyalgia —Pain in the knee joint.

Gonycampsis —Abnormal curvature of the knee.

Gonycrotesis —Genu valgum. Knock-knee.

Gonyectyposis —Genu varum. Bowleg.

Gonyocele —Synovitis or tuberculous arthritis of the knee.

Gonyoncus —Tumor of the knee.

Gonzo —Wild behavior.

Goodells' sign —Softening of the cervix of the uterus in pregnancy.

Goose skin —Prominence of the skin about the hair follicles caused by erection of the skin papillae due to cold, shock or fear.

Gordon's reflex —Extension of the great toe on applying pressure on deep flexor muscles of calf of the leg.

Gorget —An instrument widely grooved used to protect the soft tissues from injury on point of the knife.

Gouge —A hollow instrument for cutting and removing the hard tissue of bone.

Gout —Inflammation of the joints usually of the metatarso-phalangeal joint of the big toe, due to the presence of excess of uric acid in the blood and deposition of sodium urate in the tissues and joints accompanied by severe pain which begins usually during night, and this disease mostly occurs in chronic alcoholics.

Gout-tophaceous —Gout marked by the development of sodium urate deposits i.e., the tophi in the joints, the external ear and about the fingernails.

Gouty —Of the nature of, or pertaining to gout.

Gouty diathesis — Predisposition to gout.

G.P. —General practitioner.

Gr. —Grain.

Graafian follicle —A mature vesicular follicle of the ovary developing at approximately monthly intervals, since puberty until the menopause, except during pregnancy.

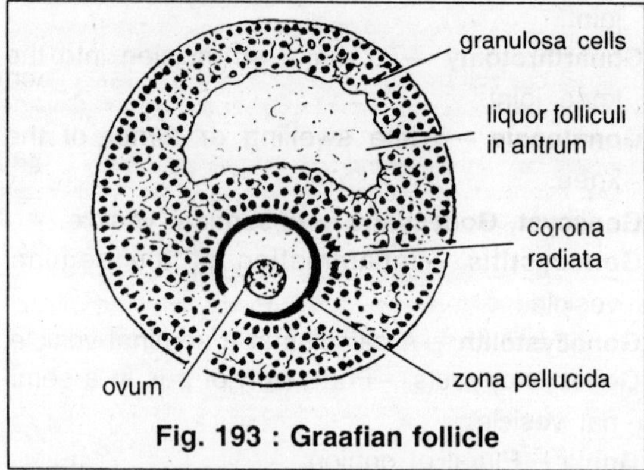

Fig. 193 : Graafian follicle

Gracile —Slender, thin, delicate.

Gradatim —Gradually.

Grade —Order, degree.

Graded milk —Milk kept in degrees.

Gradient —A proportional rise and fall.

Grading —To arrange in order.

Graduate —1. A vessel marked by lines for measuring liquids. 2. The person who has been awarded an academic degree from a college or university.

Graduated —Marked by the lines of the degrees of measurement, weight or volume.

Graduated tenotomy —Partial surgical division of a tendon of an eye muscle.

Graefe's sign —Failure of the upper eye lid to move on downward movement of the eyeball when the patient looks from up to downward, which is seen in exophthalmos or Grave's disease.

Graft —1. Any tissue or organ to be implanted or transplanted. 2. The process of implantation or transplantation.

Animal graft —Zooplastic graft.

Autogenous graft — Graft taken from the patient's own body.

Bone graft —A piece of bone generally taken from the tibia bone used to take place of a removed bone or a bony defect.

Cable graft —A nerve graft made up of bundles of segments in the form of a cable from an unimportant nerve.

Cadaver graft —Grafting tissue such as skin, bone and cornea etc. taken from the dead body immediately after death.

Composite graft —A graft composed of several tissues, such as skin and cartilage.

Corneal graft — Keratoplasty. To remove a portion of the cornea containing an opacity and replace it by a graft of cornea taken from elsewhere.

Dermal graft, Dermic graft —The skin graft from which epidermis and subcutaneous fat have been removed.

Epidermic graft —A piece of epidermis transplanted on a raw surface.

Fascia graft —A graft taken from the fascia lata used for repairing defects of other tissues.

Free graft —The graft that is completely freed from its site (instead of taking a piece) and then transferred.

Full-thickness graft —The graft consisting of the full thickness of the skin without subcutaneous fat.

Heterodermic graft —A skin graft taken from a donor of another species.

Heterologous graft, Heteroplastic graft —A graft taken from another person.

Homologous graft, Homoplastic graft — Graft of which the donor is of the same species as the recipient.

Lamellar graft —Very thin corneal layer taken from a donor of clear cornea, to replace the superficial layers of an opaque cornea.

Nerve graft —A piece of a healthy nerve taken for transplantation to replace an area of a defective nerve.

Ovarian graft —The implantation of a section of an ovary into the muscles of the abdominal wall.

Post-mortem graft — The tissue taken from a body after death and preserved for use in future on a patient requiring a graft of such tissue.

Skin graft —A piece of skin transplanted to replace a lost portion of the skin as is done in large superficial burn.

Split-skin graft — Graft of only a portion of the skin thickness.

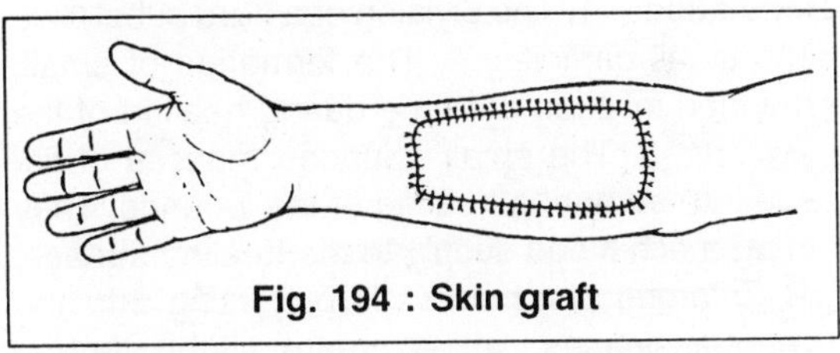

Fig. 194 : Skin graft

Sponge graft —A small piece of sponge placed over a wound to stimulate the formation of granulations.

Zooplastic graft —Graft taken from an animal.

Grafting —The implanting or transplanting of a tissue or an organ.

Graham's law —A law stating that the rate of diffusion of a gas is inversely proportional to the square root of its density.

Grain —1. A seed especially of a cereal plant. 2. A weight of ·065 gm.

Gram —A unit of weight of the metric system which is equal to approximately to the weight of a cubic centimeter or a milliliter of water. It is equal to 15·432 grains or ·03527 ounce. One thousand grams are equal to one kilogram.

Gram-centimeter —The energy exerted or work done when a weight of 1 gram is raised to a height of 1 centimeter.

Graminivorous —Eating or depending on cereal grains.

Gram-meter —A unit of work energy which is equal to that required to raise a weight of one gram vertically to a height of one meter.

Gram molecule —The weight of a substance in grams equal to its molecular weight.

Gram-negative —Losing the stain or decolorized by alcohol in Gram's method of staining.

Gram-positive —Becoming stained with gentian violet in Gram's method of staining.

Gram's method —A method for staining the bacteria for their identification.

Grandiose —In psychiatry, pertaining to one's exaggerated concept of being more wealthy, important and capable.

Grandiosity —An exaggerated concept of being more wealthy, important and capable.

Grand mal —Major form of epilepsy.

Granular —Made up of or characterized by the presence of granules or grains.

Granulatio —A granule.

Granulation —1. The division of a hard substance into small particles. 2. The formation of small, rounded masses of tissue during healing of the wounds. 3. The small, rounded masses of tissue formed during healing of the wounds. They bring a rich blood supply to the healing surface. 4. Enlarged arachnoid villi projecting into the venous sinuses, which create slight depressions on the inner surface of the cranium.

Granule —1. A small, grainlike body. 2. A minute structure in a cell without any definite shape as found in neutrophil leukocytes.

Granuloadipose —Showing fatty degeneration containing fatty granules.

Granuloblast —1. Mother cell of a granulocyte. 2. Myeloblast found in bone marrow.

Granulocyte —A granular white blood cell such as eosinophil or basophil etc.

Granulocytopathy —Any disorder of the granulocytes.

Granulocytopenia — Reduction of granulocytes in the blood abnormally.

Granulocytopoiesis —The formation of granulo cytes.

Granulocytopoietic — Pertaining to the formation of granulocytes.

Granulocytosis —Excess of granulocytes in the blood.

Granuloma —A tumor or growth formed of the granulation tissues.

Annulare granuloma — The development of reddish nodules arranged in the form of a circle.

Apical granuloma — Dental granuloma.

Benign granuloma of the thyroid —Chronic inflammation of the thyroid gland converting into a tumor which later on becomes very hard.

Dental granuloma —A granuloma developing at the root of a tooth.

Eosinophilic granuloma —A form of Xanthomatosis with eosinophilia and the formation of cysts on the bone.

Foreign body granuloma —Chronic inflammation around a foreign body such as a suture, etc.

Granuloma fissuratum —A circumscribed, firm, reddish, fissured, fibrotic tumor formed by chronic irritation.

Granuloma inguinale —A granulomatous ulcerative lesion in the inguinal region secondary to a painless nodule appearing on the external genital organs.

Granuloma iridis — A granuloma developing in the iris of the eye.

Infectious granuloma —Granuloma formed in some specific infectious diseases such as tuberculosis, syphilis and fungus infection, etc.

Lipoid granuloma — Granuloma containing fatty tissue or cholesterol.

Malignant granuloma —Hodgkin's disease.

Pyogenic granuloma —Septic granuloma. A granuloma containing pyogenic organisms occurring at the site of trauma or elsewhere on the body, which bleed easily and is usually tender.

Swimming pool granuloma —A granuloma complicating injuries sustained in swimming pool, caused by Mycobacterium balnei, tending to heal within a few months or years spontaneously.

Granulomatosis —The formation of multiple granulomas.

Granulomatous —Consisted of granulomas.

Granulopenia —Granulocytopenia. Decrease of granulocytes in the blood abnormally.

Granuloplasm —Granular cytoplasm.

Granuloplastic —Developing granules.

Granulopoiesis —The formation of granulocytes.

Granulopoietic —Granulocytopoietic. Pertaining to the formation of granulocytes.

Granulopotent —Capable of forming granules.

Granulosa —A layer of cells in the theca of the graafian follicle of the ovary.

Granulose —The soluble portion of starch which is converted into sugar by hydrolysis.

Granulosis —The formation of granules, or a mass of minute granules.

Granum —Grain.

Grape sugar —Dextrose.

Graph —The diagram representing the varying relationships between the various data.

-graph —Suffix indicating the instrument used in recording the data.

Graphanesthesia —Inability to recognize figures or letters written on the skin by touching, which may be due to spinal cord or brain disease.

Graphesthesia —Ability to recognize the lines, symbols, numbers or words traced or written on the skin by touching.

Grapho- —Prefix meaning to write.

Graphology —Study of the handwriting in the diseases of the nerves, or for determining the personality.

Graphomania —Mania for writing.

Graphomotor —Pertaining to the movements involved in writing.

Graphopathology —Interpretation of personality disorders from the study of handwriting.

Graphophobia —Morbid fear of writing.

Graphorrhea —The writing of meaningless words.

Graphospasm —Writer's cramp.

-graphy —Suffix meaning writing or recording.

Grasp —1. To hold firmly 2. Power of intellect.

Grating —Harsh.

Grating sound —Harsh sound produced by the friction of rough surfaces.

Grattage —Removal of a disease-producing outgrowth by rubbing with a brush or by scraping.

Grave —Serious, dangerous.

Gravedo —Coryza or nasal catarrh.

Gravel —Very small calculi occurring in the form of particles.

Grave's disease —Exophthalmic goiter.

Gravid —Pregnant.

Gravida —Pregnant woman.

Gravida macromastia —Rapid enlargement of the breasts during pregnancy.

Gravidic —Occurring in pregnancy.

Gravidism —The state of being pregnant.

Graviditas —Pregnancy.

Gravidity —The total number of pregnancies of a woman.

Gravidocardiac —Pertaining to the heart diseases resulting from pregnancy.

Gravimeter —Hydrometer.

Gravimetric —1. Pertaining to the measurement by weight. 2. Determined by weight.

Gravireceptors —Receptor organs and nerve endings that give the information to the brain about body position.

Gravistatic —Resulting from gravitation, as the basal congestion of the lungs results from gravitation.

Gravitation —The attraction of the earth for the objects which are at a distance from it.

Gravity —1. Property of having weight. 2. The force of attraction of the earth on the objects which are at a distance from it.

Gray matter —The term applied to the outer gray portion of the brain and the inner gray portion of the spinal cord.

Graze —Slight abrasion.

Green blindness —Inability to distinguish the green color.

Greenstick fracture —See fracture. Fracture in which only a part of the thickness of a bone is involved.

Gression —Displacement of a tooth backward.

GRH —Gonadotropin-releasing hormone.

Grid —1. In radiology, an apparatus consisting of a series of parallel narrow strips of lead with a low density material between them, used to reduce the amount of scattered radiation reaching the X-ray film. 2. A chart with the horizontal and perpendicular lines to plot the graphs.

Grief —A normal emotional response to an external loss, deep sorrow, regret.

Griffe des orteils —Clawfoot. Muscular atrophy with contraction of the foot.

Grill-like —Like a grating of iron.

Grimace —An affected expression of the face. To make grimaces.

Grinder —That which grinds; chewing.

Grinder's disease — Pneumoconiosis. Chronic lung disease due to inhalation of the dust.

Grinder teeth —Molar teeth.

Grinding —Forceful rubbing together as in chewing, or pulverizing.

Grinding pains —Pains occurring in the first stage of labor.

Grip, Grippe —1. Influenza. 2. Grasping.

Gripes —Colic. Intermittent severe pains in the intestines.

Griping —Occurrence of severe cramplike pains, especially in the abdomen intermittently.

Grippe —Influenza.

Griseus —Grey.

Gristle —Cartilage.

Grit —Small particles of mud, dust or sand.

Grittiness —The quality of being gritty.

Groan —To make the sound expressing grief or pain.

Grocer's itch —Eczema of the hands occurring due to irritation from handling flour and sugar.

Grog —A drink of alcohol and water.

Grogginess —The state of being groggy.

Groggy —Tipsy, drunk.

Groin —Inguinal region. The depressed part between the abdomen and the thigh.

Groove —A narrow, long hollow space or depression, e.g., Harrison's groove (sulcus) in which a horizontal groove extends from the xiphoid process of the sternum, along the lower border of the chest, and which marks the attachment of the diaphragm to the costal margin. It is seen in advanced rickets in children.

Grooved —Having groove.

Gross —Large enough or visible to the naked eye.

Ground —1. Basic substance 2. Reduced to a powder or pulverized.

Ground bundle —A bundle of nerve fibers surrounding immediately the gray matter of the spinal cord.

Ground itch —Itching on the sole of the foot caused by entrance of a larva of Ankylostoma duodenale, a type of hookworm, into the sole, when the person walks on bare feet.

Group —A number of similar objects or structures considered together, e.g., bacteria of similar metabolic characteristics are considered together as a group.

Grover's disease —Occurrence of pruritus suddenly which is aggravated by heat and accompanied by warty papules, vesicles and eczematous palques.

Growth —An increase in the size of an organism, which may be normal as in the growth of a child, or pathological as in a tumor.

Gruel —Any cereal boiled in water.

Grumose, Grumous —In the form of a lump or clotted.

Grumpy —Ill-tempered.

Gryposis —Abnormal curvature of any part of the body, especially the nails.

gt. —gutta, a drop.

gtt. —guttae, drops.

G.U. —Genitourinary.

Guard —An apparatus used to protect something, as a mouth guard.

Guarded prognosis —A prognosis given by a doctor when the result of a patient's disease is in doubt.

Guardian ad litem —A guardian for the child appointed by the court in case of mental or physical injury to a child.

Gubernaculum —A guiding structure. A cord like structure uniting two structures.

Gubler's tumor —A fusiform swelling on the wrist in lead palsy.

Guidance —Direction.

Guide —An apparatus directing the motion of one's hand or of an instrument one holds.

Guidewire —A wire or spring used as a guide for placemennt of a catheter or other instrument.

Guillotine —An instrument for excising a tonsil or the uvula.

Guilt —Crime. An emotion resulting from doing wrong work, which needs punishment.

Guinea pig —A small rodent used in the laboratory for experimental purposes.

Gullet —The esophagus.

Gull's disease —Atrophy of the thyroid gland causing myxedema.

Gum —1. A substance obtained from certain plants, which is sticky when moist but becomes hard upon drying. 2. A fleshy substance that surrounds the necks of the teeth and covers the alveolar processes of the maxilla and mandible. Gingiva.

Gumboil —Gingival abscess.

Gumma —A granulomatous tumor of the tissues most frequently occurring in the liver but may occur in other organs such as the brain, heart, testis, bone and skin—a characteristic of the tertiary stage of syphilis.

Gummatous —Having the character of a gumma.

Gummy —Resembling gum or gumma.

Gunn's dots —White spots on the retina of the eye, close to the macula.

Gunshot wound —Perforating or penetrating wound which may contain a foreign body, as a bullet etc.

Gurgling sound —The sound produced by air passing through the fluid in a cavity.

Gurney —A wheeled cot used in hospitals for transporting the patients.

Gusher —Overflow of a fluid.

Gustation —Sense of taste.

Gustatory —Pertaining to sense of taste.

Gustometry —Measurement of the acuteness of the sense of taste.

Gut —The intestine or the bowel.

Gutta —A drop.

Guttae —Plural of gutta.

Gutta-percha —A kind of greyish flexible substance obtained by drying or coagulating the milk of certain trees, used as a dental cement in dentistry and in splints in orthopedics.

Guttat —Drop by drop.

Guttate —Resembling a drop, said of certain lesions of the skin.

Guttatim —Drop by drop.

Gutter —A groove.

Guttering —Cutting a groove in a bone.

Guttur —The throat.

Guttural —Pertaining to the throat.

Gutturotetany —Spasm of the larynx with temporary stutter.

Guyon's sign —Ballottement of the kidney.

Gymnastics —Systematic exercise of the body with or without special apparatus.

Gymnophobia —Morbid fear of seeing a naked body.

Gyn-, Gyne-, Gyneco-, Gyno- —Prefixes which mean female or women.

Gynander—Pseudohermaphrodite. The individual having both, male and female characteristics.

Gynandrism —1. Hermaphroditism. 2. Female pseudohermaphroditism.

Gynandrobastoma —A tumor of the ovary containing the elements of both, arrhenoblastoma and granulosa cell tumor.

Gynandroid —A hermaphrodite or a female pseudohermaphrodite.

Gynandromorph —The individual showing gynandromorphism.

Gynandromorphism —The condition of having both, male and female sexual characters produced by the chromosomes of both the sexes present in the different tissues of the body.

Gynandromorphous —Having both male and female characteristics.

Gynatresia —Closure of the vagina.

Gynecic —Pertaining to the woman.

Gyneco-, Gyno- —Prefixes meaning woman.

Gynecogenic —Producing female characteristics.

Gynecogram —X-ray film of the female reproductive organs.

Gynecography —X-ray examination of the female reproductive organs.

Gynecoid —Woman-like.

Gynecologic, Gynecological —Pertaining to the study of woman diseases.

Gynecologist —Specialist in gynecology.

Gynecology —The study of the diseases of the female genital organs including the breasts.

Gynecomania —Satyriasis. Excessive sexual desire in man.

Gynecomastia —Abnormally enlarged mammary glands in the male, sometimes secreting milk.

Gynecopathy —Any disease peculiar to women.

Gynecophonus —Having a female voice.

Gynephobia —Abnormal aversion to women or morbid fear of women.

Gynesic —Pertaining to the woman diseases.

Gyniatrics —Treatment of the women diseases.

Gyniatry —Gyniatrics.

Gynopathic —Pertaining to the diseases of women.

Gynopathy —Any disease peculiar to women.

Gynoplastics, Gynoplasty —Repair of the female genital organs by plastic surgery.

Gypsum —1. A natural form of hydrated calcium sulfate which on heating to 130°C loses its water content and becomes plaster of paris. 2. Semihydrated gypsum used as a dental stone in preparing investments for dental casting.

Gyrate —1. Ring-shaped or convoluted 2. To rotate.

Gyration —Rotatory movement.

Gyre —Gyrus. Convolution.

Gyrectomy —To remove a cerebral gyrus by surgery.

Gyrencephala —Having a brain marked by numerous gyri.

Gyrencephalic —Gyrencephala.

Gyri —Plural of gyrus.

Gyro- —Prefix meaning a circle, spiral or a ring.

Gyrochrome —Denoting a nerve cell in which chromophil substance is arranged in rings.

Gyroma —An ovarian tumor consisting of a convoluted mass.

Gyrometer —A device for measuring the cerebral gyri.

Gyrosa —Vertigo.

Gyrose —Arranged in wavy lines or circles, as the bacterial colonies.

Gyrospasm —Rotatory spasm of the head.

Gyrous —Gyrose.

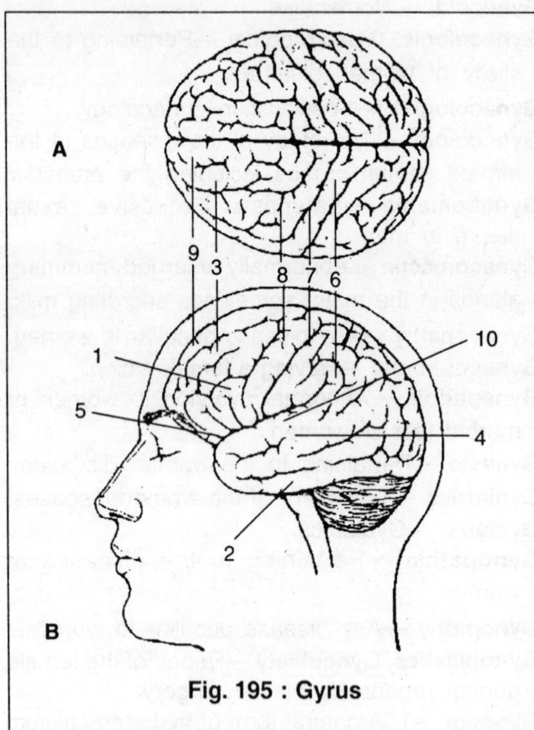

Fig. 195 : Gyrus

Gyrus —One of the many convolutions of the cerebral cortex separated by shallow grooves (sulci) and the deeper grooves (fissures). (A) Superior and (B) Lateral views of the brain. 1.Inferior frontal gyrus, 2.Inferior temporal gyrus, 3.Middle frontal gyrus, 4.Middle temporal gyrus, 5. Orbital gyrus, 6. Postcentral gyrus, 7. Central sulcus, 8. Precentral gyrus, 9. Superior frontal gyrus, 10. Superior temporal gyrus

Inferior frontal gyrus — Broca's gyrus. A gyrus on the external surface of the frontal lobe of the cerbrum, between the inferior frontal sulcus and the sylvian fissure.

Inferior temporal gyrus —A gyrus on the inferolateral surface of the temporal lobe of the cerebrum, separated from the middle temporal gyrus by the inferior temporal sulcus.

Middle frontal gyrus —A gyrus on each frontal lobe of th cerebrum between the superior and inferior frontal sulci.

Middle temporal gyrus —A longitudinal gyrus on the lateral surface of the temporal lobe, between the superior and inferior temporal sulci.

Orbital gyrus —One of the four gyri (anterior, posterior, lateral and medial) forming the inferior surface of the frontal lobe.

Postcentral gyrus —A gyrus situated posterior to the central sulcus.

Precentral gyrus —A gyrus situated in front of the central sulcus.

Superior frontal gyrus — A broad gyrus of the cerebral frontal lobe situated above the superfrontal fissure.

Superior temporal gyrus —A longitudinal gyrus on the lateral surface of each temporal lobe between the sylvian fissure and the superior temporal sulcus.

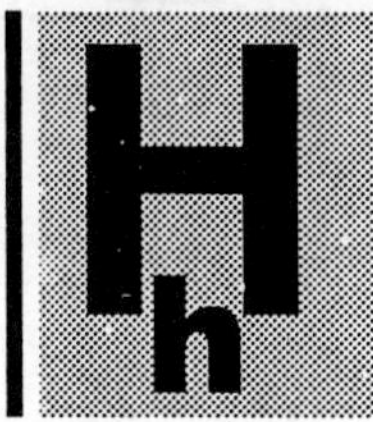

H —Chemical symbol for hydrogen.

h—Symbol for hecto-; height; hour.

Habb's reflex —Contraction of the pupils on gazing at a bright object without alteration of accomodation.

Habena—Habenula.

Habenula—1. A frenum or whiplike structure. 2. A peduncle or stalk attached to the pineal gland of the brain. 3. Bandage for a wound.

Habenular—Pertaining to the stalk of the pineal gland.

Habit—1. The action which is characterized by repetition 2. Nature 3. Bodily constitution, especially in relation to a disease. 4. Addiction to the use of drugs or the beverage.

Habitat—Natural dwelling place of an animal or plant.

Habit spasm—Tic. Spasmodic muscular contraction of the face.

Habituated—Accustomed.

Habituation—The state of being accustomed.

Habitus—The body built of a person that indicates a tendency to develop a specific disease.

Hachement —Chopping stroke with the edge of the hand in massage.

Hacking—Short and interrupted.

Hacking cough—The interrupted cough.

Haem- —Hem-.

Hagedorn needle —A surgical curved needle with flattened sides.

Hagiotherapy—Treatment of a disease by performing worship of God, visiting temple or mosque, or by other religious observances.

Hahnemannian—Pertaining to Hahnemann, the founder of Homeopathy.

Hair—A threadlike structure composed of keratin developing from the papilla embedded in the dermis.

Hairball —Trichobezoar. A mass of hairs in the stomach.

Hair bulb—The lower expanded portion of a hair root.

Hair follicle—It is a cylindrical invagination of the epidermis penetrating the dermis into the connective tissue, which holds the hair root. Sebaceous glands, secreting the oily fluid and the muscle arrector pili which causes the hair to stand are attached to this follicle.

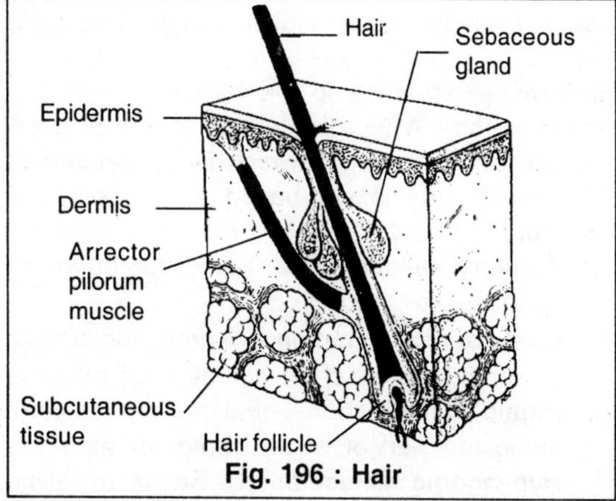

Fig. 196 : Hair

Hair papilla—A projection of the dermis extending into the hair bulb at the bottom of a hair follicle, which contains blood capillaries through which the hair receives its nourishment.

Hairy—1. Of or resembling hair 2. Covered with hair.

Halation —Blurring of vision due to intense light coming from wrong direction.

Half-life—1. Time taken for half the nuclei of a radioactive substance to lose their activity through radioactive decay. 2. The time taken by the living body, tissue or organ to metabolize or inactivate half the amount of a substance taken in.

Half-value layer, Half-value thickness—The layer or thickness of a given substance, which when placed in the path of a given beam of rays, will reduce its intensity to one half of the initial value.

Half way house—A residence for the patients of mental diseases, drug addicts, alcoholics etc. who do not require hospitalization but require an intermediate degree of care until they can return to the community.

Halide—A compound of one of the halogens.

Haliphagia—Ingestion of a salt, especially of sodium chloride in excessive quantity.

Halisteresis—Deficiency of calcium in the bones. Osteomalacia.

Halisteretic—Pertaining to or affected with halisteresis.

Halitosis—Offensive breath.

Halitus—1. The expired breath. 2. Expiration of vapor.

Hallex, plu.al **hallices**— Hallux, hallus. The great toe.

Hallucal —Pertaining to the hallux.

Hallucination—A false perception of sound, taste, touch, smell and sight which is not related to the reality and is not based on the external stimuli.

Auditory hallucination—False perception of sounds.

Gustatory hallucination — Perception of taste of something which is actually not present.

Haptic hallucination— False perception of being touched or of the temp. or pain.

Hypnagogic hallucination—Sense of falling and sinking etc. occurring in the awakening stage before sleep, which are actually to be perceived in dreams during sleep.

Kinetic hallucination — Sensation of flying or of moving the body or a part of it.

Microptic hallucination— Hallucination in which the things are seen reduced in size.

Motor hallucination— Imaginary perception of movement.

Olfactory hallucination —False perception of smell.

Tactile hallucination —False perception of touching something.

Visual hallucination— Sense of seeing the things which are not existed in reality.

Hallucinogen—An agent (drugs, alcohol etc.) producing hallucinations.

Hallucinogenesis—The process of producing hallucination.

Hallucinogenic—Causing hallucination.

Hallucinosis—The state of being affected with hallucination, *e.g.* acute alcoholic hallucination marked by fear or anxiety and auditory hallucinations.

Hallus—Hallux.

Hallux—The great toe.

Hallux valgus —The great toe displaced toward the other toes.

Hallux varus—The great toe displaced from other toes.

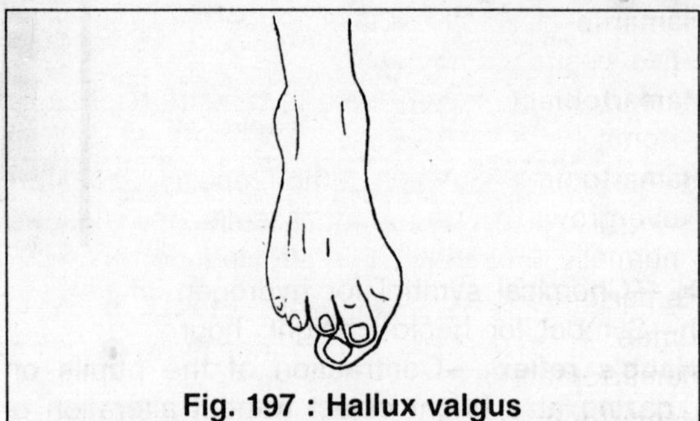

Fig. 197 : Hallux valgus

Halmatogenesis—Sudden alteration of type from one generation to the other.

Halo—1. Areola, especially of the nipple. 2. A ring seen surrounding the macula lutea in ophthalmoscopic examination. 3. A circle of light or color surrounding a shinning body or light.

Halodermia—Appearance of the skin eruption due to exposure to a halogen.

Haloduric—Capable of living in a salt solution of high concentration.

Halogen—A nonmetallic element which combines with the hydrogen to form acids, and with the metal to form salts, e.g. chlorine, bromine, iodine, and fluorine etc., having similar properties.

Halogenation—Production of halogens.

Halogenoderma—A skin disease caused by ingestion or injection of a halogen such as bromide or iodide.

Haloid—Resembling salt or a halogen.

Halometer—1. An instrument for measuring ocular halos. 2. An instrument for estimating the size of the erythrocytes by measuring the diffraction halos produced by them.

Halophil—The organism which grows in concentrated salt solution.

Halophilic—Pertaining to halophil.

Halosteresis—Halisteresis. Deficiency of calcium salts in the bones.

Halo symptom—Colored single or more than one circle appearing around the lights, which are seen by the patients of glaucoma or with punctate opacities of the lens.

Halsted's operation—1. Operation for inguinal hernia. 2. Removal of the breast completely by surgery in case of cancer breast.

Halsted's suture—The interrupted suture for the intestinal wounds.

Ham—1. The popliteal region behind the knee. 2. The collective name for the thigh, hip and buttock.

Hamartia—Defective development due to defective tissue combination.

Hamartoblastoma—A tumor arising from a hamartoma.

Hamartoma—A benign tumor resulting from an overgrowth of the mature cells and tissues normally present in the affected part.

Hamartomatosis—Presence of many hamartomas.

Hamartomatous—Having hamartoma.

Hamartophobia—Morbid fear of error or sin.

Hamate—Hooked.

Hamatum—Hamate bone.

Hamaxophobia—Morbid fear of riding in a vehicle.

Hamilton's ruler test— Normally, a straight ruler cannot be made to touch the acromion of the scapula and the lateral epicondyle of the humerus simultaneously. This becomes possible in a dislocation of the shoulder or a fracture of the scapular neck as the head of the humerus is displaced medially.

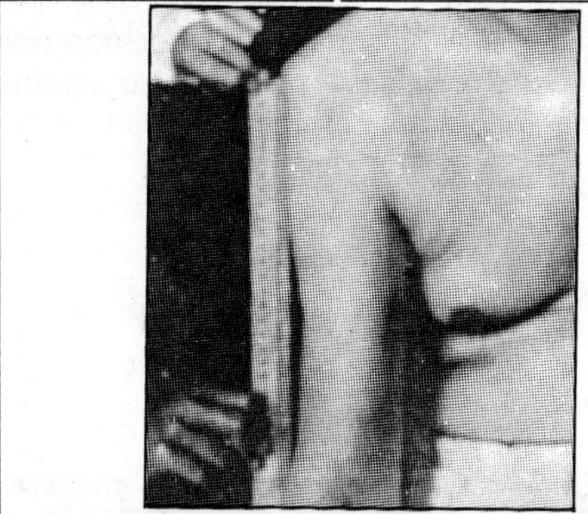

Fig 198 : Hamilton's ruler test

Hammer—1. An instrument with the head attached to a handle for striking blows. 2. Common name for the malleus—the hammer-shaped bone of the middle ear.

Hammer finger—Mallet finger. A deformity of the distal joint of a finger in which it is flexed so that it looks like a hammer.

Hammer for reflex responses —A hammer with a rubber head used for tapping the body parts such as muscles, tendons or nerves to initiate certain reflex responses.

Hammer toe—Claw toe. A toe in which the 1st phalanx is flexed dorsally and the 2nd and 3rd phalanges are flexed toward the plantar side so the toe looks like a hammer.

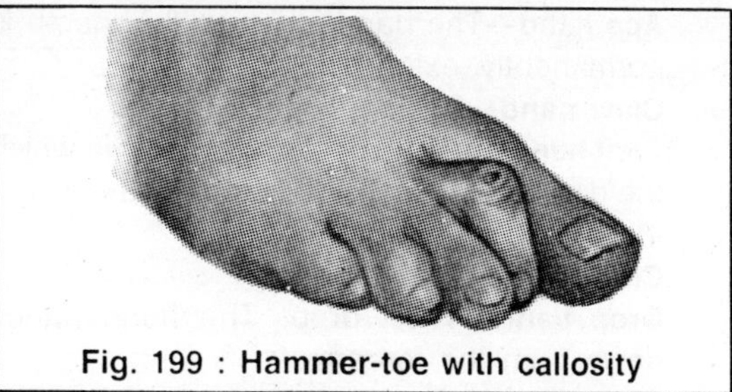

Fig. 199 : Hammer-toe with callosity

Hamster—A small rodent, used in the laboratories for experiments.

Hamstring—One of the tendons making the boundaries of the popliteal space medially and laterally.

Hamular—Hook-shaped.

Hamulus—Any hook-shaped structure or hook like process on the hamate bone.

Hand—Manus. The part of the upper limb attached to the forearm at the wrist, which includes the wrist (carpus) with its 8 short carpal bones, metacarpus (palm) or the body of the hand with its 5 long bones and the fingers with their 14 phalanges.

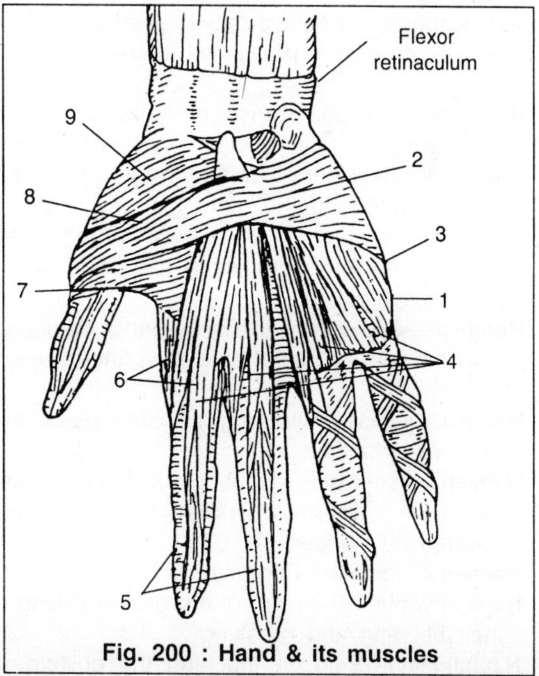

Fig. 200 : Hand & its muscles

1. Abductor digiti quinti 2. Transverse carpal ligament 3. Flexor digiti quinti brevis 4. Tendon of flexor digitorum sublimis 5. Tendon of flexor digitorum profundus 6. Vermiculate muscles 7. Adductor pollicis 8. Flexor pollicis brevis 9. Abductor pollicis brevis

Ape hand—The hand in which the thumb is permanently extended.

Claw hand—See clawhand.

Cleft hand—A deformity of the hand in which the division between the fingers extends into the metacarpus or palm.

Club hand—See clubhand.

Drop hand—Wrist drop. The hand hangs down from the forearm.

Obstetrician's hand—A deformity of the hand in which the hand in tetany is extended at the metacarpophalangeal and interphalangeal joints and the thumb is moved toward the median plane of the body.

Writing hand—The position of the hand in which the tips of the thumb and the first finger are touching and other fingers are flexed as if someone holding a pen in writing as seen in paralysis agitans.

Handedness—The tendency to use the hand of one side in preference to the other.

Handicap—Congenital or acquired any physical or mental defect preventing a person from leading. a normal life.

Handicapped—The physically or mentally defective person who is prevented to lead a normal life.

Handpiece —A dental instrument which is held in the surgeon's hand, which contains a chuck for holding the tool which may rotate or vibrate, used in preparing the teeth for restoration.

Handsocks—A type of gloves without individual spaces for the fingers, so it makes to grasp the objects difficult.

Hangnail—A piece of the skin partly detached from the root or lateral side of a finger or toe nail.

Hanot's disease—Hypertrophic cirrhosis of the liver with jaundice.

Hansen's bacillus— Mycobacterium leprae, the causative organism of leprosy, which was discovered by Hansen in 1871.

Hansen's disease—Leprosy.

Hapalonychia—Thinning of the nails resulting in their bending and breaking.

Haphalgesia—Pain on touching the objects.

Haphazard —Out of order.

Haphephobia—Morbid fear of being touched by another person.

Haplodont—Having teeth without ridges or tubercles on the crown.

Haploid—Having half the normal (diploid) number of chromosomes found in somatic or body cells, as the germ cells—ova or spermatozoa in which the number of chromosomes is 2 3, half of the diploid number 46.

Haploidy—The condition of being haploid.

Haplology—The omission of some letters because of speaking speedly.

Haplopia—The condition in which an object seen by two eyes appears as a single object in comparison to diplopia in which it appears as two objects.

Haploscope—A stereoscope for examining the visual axis.

Haploscopic—Pertaining to haploscope.

Haplotype—The group of alleles of linked genes contributed by either parent.

Haptic—Tactile. Pertaining to touch.

Haptics—The science of the sense of touch.

Haptodysphoria—An unpleasant sensation caused by touching certain objects.

Haptometer—An apparatus for measuring the acuteness of sense of touch.

Hard—Firm, rigid.

Hard chancre—A hard painless ulcer occurring on the genital organs in the first stage of syphilis, appearing about two or three weeks after infection.

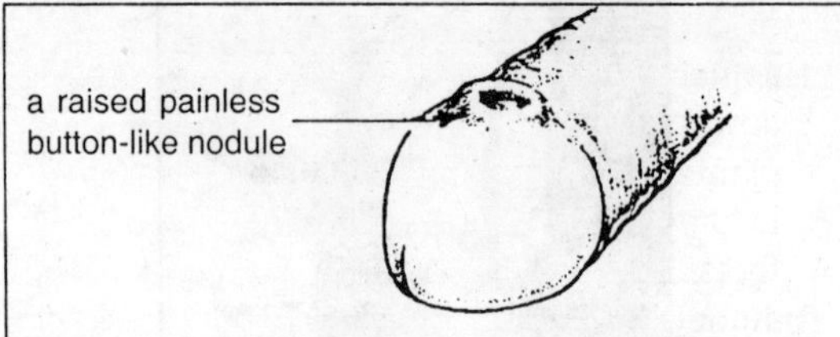

Fig. 201 : Primary chancre or Hard chancre

Hardening—Making firm or hard.

Hardiness—Boldness.

Hardness—1. Firmness, rigidity. 2. The quality of water containing mineral substances, especially the calcium and magnesium salts.

Hard palate—Anterior hard portion of the roof of the mouth (palate) which is supported by the maxillary and palatine bones.

Harelip—A congenital vertical cleft or clefts, of the upper lip.

Fig. 202 : Harelip

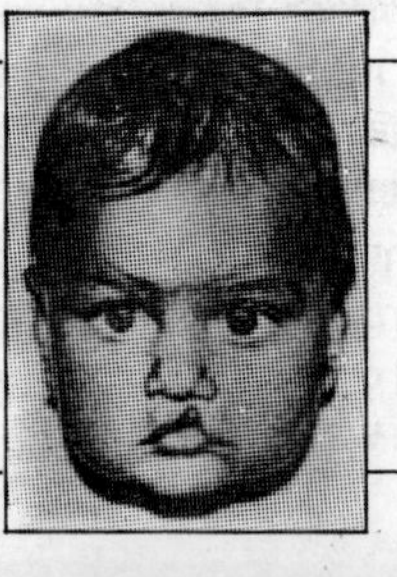

Harlequin fetus—A newborn infant with a thick horny skin which is divided into areas by deep red fissures and such infants die within a few days.

Harlequin sign—A transient color change in neonates in which one half of the body becomes pale while the other half red, with a clear line of demarcation between them.

Harmonic—Pertaining to harmony.

Harmony—The condition of working or living together smoothly, coordination.

Harpaxophobia—Morbid fear of robbers.

Harpoon—An instrument with a hook at its end used for obtaining a small piece of tissue such as muscle for examination.

Harrison's groove—A shallow depression extending laterally from the xiphoid process of the sternum, seen in children suffering from rickets.

Hartmann's solution— Lactated Ringer's injection. A sterile solution of 0.6 gm. of sodium choride, 0.03 gm. of potassium chloride, 0.02 gm. of calcium chloride and 0.31 gm. of sodium lactate diluted with water to make upto 100 mls. for injection, used for the treatment of dehydration.

Harvest—To obtain samples or remove bacteria or other microorganisms from a culture.

Hashish—A purified extract prepared from the flowers, stalks and leaves of the female hemp plants—cannabis sativa. The gummy substance is smoked or chewed for its intoxicating effects. It is more powerful than marijuana.

Hatchet—A dental instrument with a cutting blade at the end at an angle to the axis of the handle.

Haunch—The hips and the buttocks.

Haustorium, pl. **haustoria**—An organ for the absorption of nutritious substances.

Haustra—The sacculated pouches of the colon.

Haustral—Pertaining to the colonic haustra.

Haustration—The process of formation of a haustrum.

Haustrum—Singular of haustra.

Haustus —A draught of medicine.

Haversian canal—Minute vascular canals found in the osseous tissue.

Hawk—To clear the throat with a noise.

Hay fever—An allergic disease of the mucous membrane of the nose and upper respiratory passages caused by inhalation of the pollen grains and characterized by coryza, sneezing, watery discharge from the eyes and headache.

Haygarth's deformities—Tumors of the bones of the joints in rheumatoid arthritis.

Hazardous—Injurious or damaging.

HB—Hemoglobin.

HCG—Human chorionic gonadotrophin.

HCl—Hydrochloric acid.

H.D.—Hearing distance.

h.d.—The hour of going to bed.

HDL—High-density lipoprotein.

Head—1. Caput. 2. The part of the body containing brain and the organs of special sense. 3. The upper, anterior or proximal end of a bone or other structure.

Headache—Pain in the head which may be acute or chronic, may be diffuse, frontal, temporal, occipital, may occur in one side of the head or in the upper portion of the head.

Coital headache—Headache occurring suddenly during sexual intercourse or just after orgasm.

Exertional headache —An acute headache of short duration occurring after doing strenuous physical work.

Headache associated with high blood pressure —Pain occurring in occipital region on awakening in the morning in the person suffering from high blood pressure.

Headache due to brain diseases— Headache occurring in the diseases of the brain such as cerebral arteriosclerosis, cerebral atherosclerosis, cerebral thrombosis, cerebral hemorrhage, meningitis, encephalitis, subdural hematoma, cerebral aneurysm, brain abscess and brain tumor etc.

Headache due to diseases of the throat —Headache occurring in the diseases of the throat such as pharyngitis, tonsillitis and adenoids etc.

Headache due to fever —Headache occurring in fever as in malaria and typhoid fever.

Headache due to general disease— Headache usually occurs in some general diseases such as dyspepsia, constipation, anemia, diabetes, nephritis with uremia, rheumatism and syphilis etc.

Headache due to menal diseases — Headache occurring in hysteria etc.

Headache due to middle ear disease —Headache occurring in middle ear disease as in otitis media.

Headache due to toxic factors —1. Exogenous toxic factors —Foul air in a poorly ventilated room; poisonous gases; drugs like quinine, morphine, atropine and histamine etc; tobacco and alcohol etc. containing high concentration of histamine. 2. Endogenous toxic factors —Headache occurring due to absorption of toxins of the bacterial infection from the nose, sinuses, teeth, pharynx, tonsils, middle ear, gallbladder and appendix, and influenza etc.

Headache occurring specifically in women —Headache occurring specifically in women in menstruation, dysmenorrhea, premenstrual tension, menopause and pregnancy.

Histamine headache—A throbbing pain due to dilatation and stretching of the pial and dural arteries caused by histamine in allergy.

Idiopathic stabbing headache—Brief repetitive sharp pain of unknown cause occurring in the temporoparietal region of the head.

Migraine—The pain occurring in one half of the head, which starts on awakening in the morning, *i.e.* on rising of the sun, reaches its maximum till noon and then gradually subsides and stops completely in the evening at sunset.

Miscellaneous causes —Headache may be due to external pressure and constriction of the head, injury to the head, sunstroke, travelling to a high altitude, physical or mental fatigue.

Nasal and paranasal infections— Headache occurs in nasal catarrh (coryza), rhinitis or in sinusitis.

Ocular headache— Headache occurring due to errors of refraction, glaucoma or inflammation of the different parts of the eye.

Post-traumatic headache—Headache ocurring following head injury.

Tension headache— Headache occurring in mental tension caused by anxieties, excitement and anger, felt in the occipital region accompanied by tender spots in the occipital muscles and there may be contraction of the head and neck muscles.

Headgear—A protective covering for the head, such as a helmet.

Head-louse—Pediculus capitis.

Head-nodding—Tremors of head.

Heal—To cure or make healthy.

Healer—The person who or a substance which heals or cures.

Healing—The restoration to the normal physical or mental condition, especially of an inflammation or a wound which may be of two types—healing by First intention in which the edges of a wound unite directly without formation of granulation tissue between them, and healing by Second intention in which a wound is closed by the formation of granulation tissue filling the gap between the edges of the wound.

Health—The condition of physical, mental and social well-being.

Healthful—Conducive to good health.

Health screening—Public health examination.

Healthy—Pertaining to or being in a state of health.

Hear—To perceive sounds by the ears or to listen.

Hearing—The act of perceiving sound or the capacity to perceive sound.

Hearing after—Perception of sound after the stimulus producing it has ceased to produce it.

Hearing aid—An apparatus for amplifying the sound, used for hearing by the deaf persons.

Hearing hallucinations— Sensation of hearing a sound which is actually not present.

Hearing loss—Partial or complete deafness.

Heart—A conical, hollow, muscular, four chambered, contractile organ situated in the middle mediastinum enclosed within a fibrous sac—the pericardium, which pumps the blood through the vascular system to the various parts of the body for their nutrition.

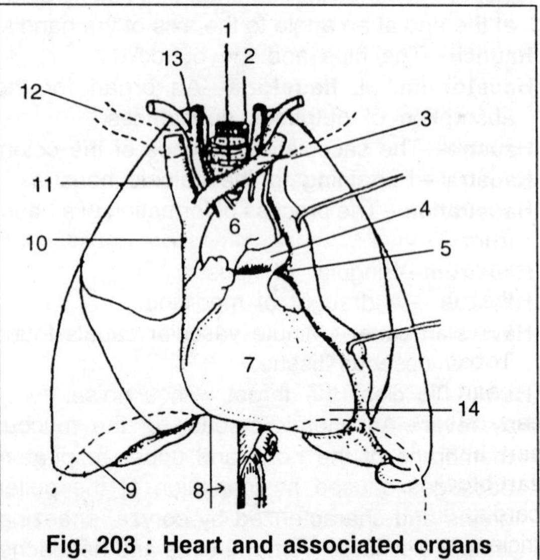

Fig. 203 : Heart and associated organs

1. Trachea 2. Oesophagus 3. L.brachiocephalic vein 4. Pulmonary artery 5. A left pulmonary vein 6. Aorta 7. Heart 8. Inferior vena cava 9. Diaphragm 10. Superior vena cava 11. R. brachiocephalic vein 12. Clavicle 13. Apex of lung 14. Cardiac apex

Abdominal heart —A heart which is displaced into the abdominal cavity.

Athlete's heart—Enlarged heart of the athlete's as a result of prolonged exercise.

Beri beri heart—Enlarged heart in the disease beri beri caused by the deficiency of vitamin B_1 (thiamine hydrochloride).

Boat-shaped heart—Heart in which one ventricle is dilated with hypertrophy due to aortic regurgitation.

Bony heart—The heart in which calcareous matter is deposited.

Cervical heart —A heart which is displaced into the neck region.

Dilated heart—Enlarged heart due to stretching of its walls.

Drop heart—Cardioptosis or cardioptosia

Fatty heart—1. The heart that has undergone fatty degeneration 2. The heart upon which abnormal amount of fat is deposited.

Fibroid heart—The heart affected with chronic myocarditis in which a portion of the myocardium is replaced by the fibrous tissue.

Hypertrophied heart— Enlarged heart due to increased size of the myocardium and not due to the dilatation of the heart.

Irritable heart— Neurocirculatory asthenia characterized by breathlessness, palpitation, weakness and tiredness.

Movoble heart—A heart that moves unduly on change of position of the body.

Pendulous heart—A type of movable heart which apears to be suspended by the great vessels.

Three-chambered heart— Congenital absence of the atrial or ventricular septum so that the heart has a single atrium with two ventricles or a single ventricle with two atria.

Tobacco heart—The heart showing irregular heart beats due to excessive use of tobacco.

Heart attack—Myocardial infarction.

Heart beat—Apex beat.

Heart block—Failure of conduction of the normal cardiac impulses from the atrium to the ventricle through the conductive tissue of the heart—the sinoatrial (S-A) and atrioventricular (A-V) nodes, bundle of His and Purkinje fibers and this causes the rhythm of the heart beat changed, which is known as cardiac arrhythmia.

Atrioventricular heart block —A form of heart block in which the impulses are obstructed at the atrioventricular node. It is of first degree when A-V conduction time is prolonged, of second degree (partial heart block) when some but not all impulses from the atrium reach the ventricle, of third degree (complete heart block) when no impulses from the atrium reach the ventricle, and the atria and ventricles act independently of each other.

Bundle-branch heart block—A form of heart block in which the impulses are blocked in one of the branches of the bundle of His so that one ventricle is stimulated to beat slightly before the other.

Congenital heart block—Heart block present since birth due to defective development of the impulse conducting system.

Interventricular heart block— Bundle-branch heart block.

Sinoatrial heart block—Heart block in which there is partial or complete blockage of impulses from sinoatrial node to the atria, resulting in delay or absence of an atrial beat.

Heart burn—Brash. Pyrosis. Burning sensation occurring in the esophagus below the sternum in hyperacidity.

Heart failure—1. Cessation of the heart beat. 2. Inability of the heart to maintain the blood circulation sufficient to meet the body's requirement, may result from failure of the right or left ventricle or both.

Backward heart failure—Heart failure due mainly to failure of the right ventricle in which the return of blood to the heart through the veins is reduced, resulting in venous stasis and congestion.

Congestive heart failure—Heart failure resulting from venous stasis and congestion and reduced output of blood from the heart, characterized by weakness, breathlessness, abdominal discomfort and edema of the lower parts of the body.

Forward heart failure—Heart failure in which the forward flow of blood from the heart to the tissues is insufficient because of the inability of the left ventricle to pump out sufficient blood, or due to insufficient blood reaching the ventricle.

High output heart failure—Heart failure in which the cardiac output remains high as occurs in hyperthyroidism, anemia and emphysema etc.

Left-sided heart failure—Left ventricular heart failure. Heart failure to maintain the left ventricular output, marked by pulmonary congestion and edema.

Left ventricular heart failure— Left sided heart failure.

Low output heart failure—The condition in which the cardiac output is diminished and the heart is failed to maintain blood output.

Right-sided heart failure —Right ventricular heart failure. Failure to maintain sufficient output by the right ventricle, marked by venous congestion, enlargement of the liver and pitting edema.

Right ventricular heart failure —Right sided heart failure.

Heart-lung machine—A device for maintaining the functions of the heart and lungs while either or both fail to function properly.

Heart murmur—An abnormal or adventitious sound heard on auscultation of the heart.

Heart rate—The number of the beats of the heart per minute.

Heart sounds—Two separate sounds are heard on auscultation of the heart. The first sound (systolic) is prolonged and dull, which results from the contraction of the ventricle and striking of the heart at the chest wall. It is heard like the word "lubb". The second sound (diastolic) is short and high pitched occurring after a short pause from the first sound, which results from the closure of the aortic and pulmonary valves. It is heard like the word "dupp". After the second sound a longer pause follows before the first sound is heard again.

Heart transplantation— Transplantation of the heart by surgery from the body of the patient died of some accident or some other disease that left the heart intact and capable of functioning properly in the recipient.

Heat—1. The sensation of an increase in temperature. 2. The energy which increases the temperature. 3. A form of energy transferred as a result of variation in temperature. 4. Condition of being hot, opposite to cold. 5. High temperature, fever or a localized heat due to inflammation.

Conductive heat—The heat transferred by conduction from the source of heat to a cold object when both of them are in contact with each other, as with a hot water bottle.

Convective heat—The heat flown from the source of heat to an object or part of the body by passage of heated solid, liquid or gaseous materials.

Conversive heat—Heat produced in the tissues by a current of electricity or by some form of radiant energy.

Diathermy heat— Electrical energy converted into heat by diathermy.

Dry heat—Heat that has no moisture. It may be applied in the form of hot, dry pack as with blankets, hot water bottle, hot bricks, by electric bath or by hot air bath etc.

Heat of combustion—Heat produced on burning of an object.

Heat of compression— Heat produced when a gas is compressed.

Heat of evaporation— Heat absorbed in the evaporation of a liquid.

Latent heat—Heat required to convert a solid into a liquid or a liquid into a gas at a given temperature.

Luminous heat—Heat produced by light.

Moist heat—Heat that has moisture, which may be applied in the form of hot or cold water bath, hot or cold fomentation, poultice or vapor bath etc.

Radiant heat—Heat given off from a heated body, which passes through the air in the forms of waves.

Specific heat—The heat required to raise the temperature of one gram of a substance 1°C.

Heat cramps—Acute painful spasms in the body occurring after doing hard work in the hot environment or in the sun without taking fluid or salt.

Heat exhaustion—Acute reaction to the exposure of heat marked by the symptoms of headache, dizziness, nausea and weakness. The skin becomes cold and the pupils are dilated, body temperature is usually normal but the blood pressure may be decreased.

Heat labile—Thermolabile. Destroyed or changed easily by heat.

Heat stable—Resistant to heat.

Heatstroke—Sunstroke. Acute and serious reaction to heat exposure due to failure of the heat regulating mechanisms of the body, characterized by headache, high body temperature usually above 106°C and unconsciousness. Skin becomes hot and dry, the face is flushed and the pupils are dilated which are constricted before death, pulse and respirations are rapid and convulsions may occur.

Heave—To sigh.

Hebephrenia—A form of chronic schizophrenia characterized by senseless actions, delusions and hallucinations. Patient may be excited at once and may be depressed and may cry at the next moment. The patient may laugh without any cause and talk incoherently and excessively.

Hebephrenic—Pertaining to hebephrenia.

Heberden's disease—Arthritis deformans. Rheumatoid arthritis.

Heberden's nodes—Enlarged tubercles of the last phalanges of the fingers seen in osteoarthritis.

Hebetic—Pertaining to or occurring at the time of puberty.

Hebetude—Dullness or apathy.

Hebiatrics—Ephebiatrics. The branch of medicine which deals with the diagnosis and treatment of the diseases of the youth especially.

Hebosteotomy—Hebotomy.

Hebotomy—Pubiotomy. To make an incision across the pubis to enlarge the pelvic passage, facilitating the delivery of the fetus.

Hecateromeric. Hecatomeric—Denoting a spinal neuron whose axon possesses two processes, one supplying each side of the spinal cord.

Hecatomeral—Hecateromeric.

Hectic—1. Habitual 2. Denoting the evening rise of temperature as seen in tuberculosis.

Hecto- —In metric system, a prefix indicating 100 times (10^2) in naming the unit. Thus hectoliter (10^2 liters) is 100 liters.

Hectogram—One hundred grams.

Hectoliter—One hundred liters.

Hectometer—One hundred meters.

Hedonic—Pertaining to the pleasure.

Hedonism—The way of thinking in which the main aim of life is the pleasure.

Hedonophobia—Morbid fear of pleasure.

Hedrocele—Proctocele. Hernia or prolapse through the anus.

Heel—Calx. Rounded posterior most portion of the foot.

Heel bone—Calcaneous bone.

Hegar's sign—Marked softening of the uterine cervix in early pregnancy.

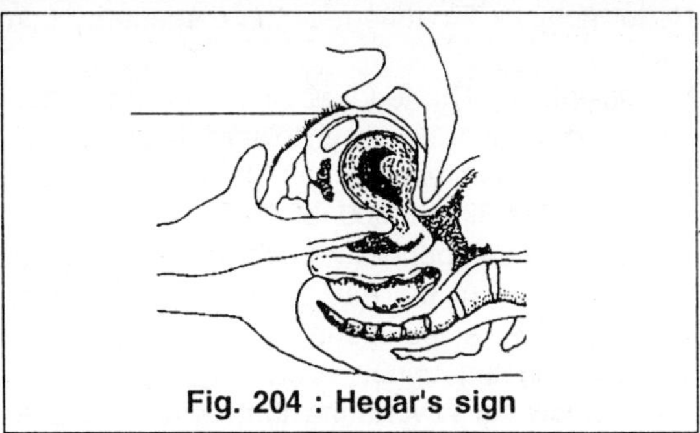

Fig. 204 : Hegar's sign

Height—Vertical measurement from the bottom to the top of an object, structure, organ or body.

Heimlich maneuver—A technique for removing a foreign body from the trachea or pharynx.

Heimlich sign—Grasping one's throat with the thumb and index finger to signal choking.

Heinz bodies—Granules present in the red blood cells due to damage of the hemoglobin particles seen in premature infants and the hemolytic anemia.

Helcoid—Like an ulcer.

Helcology—The study of ulcers.

Helcoma—Ulcer of the cornea.

Helcomenia—Occurrence of ulcers at the time of menstruation.

Helcoplasty—Dermatoplasty. Repairing of a wound by plastic surgery.

Helcosis—Ulceration. Formation of an ulcer.

Heli (O)- —A prefix indicating sun.

Helical—1. Pertaining to a helix. 2. Shaped like a helix.

Helices—Plural of helix.

Helicine—1. Spiral 2. Pertaining to a helix or coil.

Helicoid—Resembling a helix or spiral.

Helicopodia—Helicopod gait. A gait in which the foot describes half circles as seen in somes cases of hysteria.

Helicotrema—A semilunar opening at the tip of the cochlear canal where the scala of tympanum and the vestibule unite.

Heliencephalitis— Inflammation of the brain from exposure to the sun (sunstroke).

Heliopathy—A disease caused from exposure to sunlight.

Heliophobia—Morbid fear of the sun rays, especially by one who has suffered from a sunstroke.

Heliosis—Sunstroke.

Heliotaxis—A tendency to grow or move toward (positive taxis) or away from (negative taxis) the sunlight.

Heliotherapy—Treatment of the disease by sunlight.

Heliotropism—The tendency of the living organisms to turn or to grow toward the sun.

Helium—A gas present in the atmosphere in very minute quantity (0.000 524%)

Helix—1. The superior and posterior free margin of the pinna of the ear. 2. A coiled structure.

Heller's test—A test done for the presence of albumin in the urine.

Hellin's law—A law stating that twins take birth once in 80 pregnancies, triplets once in 6400 pregnancies, quadruplets in 512,000 pregnancies.

Helmet—Defensive covering for the head.

Helminth—Worm-like animal.

Helminthagogue—Vermifuge. The medicine expelling the parasitic worms from the intestines.

Helminthemesis—Vomiting of worms.

Helminthiasis—The condition of having intestinal worns.

Helminthic—Anthelmintic, vermifugal. 1. Pertaining to helminth or wormlike animal. 2. Caused by helminths. 3. Pertaining to that which expels the worms from the intestines.

Helminthicide—Vermicide. A medicine which kills the worms.

Helminthism—Helminthiasis.

Helminthoid—Resembling a worm.

Helminthology—The scientific study of parasitic worms.

Helminthoma—A tumor formed by parasitic worms.

Helminthophobia—Morbid fear of the worms or delusion of being infested by the worms.

Helminthous—Infested with worms.

Helmintic—Pertaining to or diseased from parasitic worms.

Heloma—Clavus. Callosity or corn. (see behind)

Helosis—Eversion of the eye-lids.

Helotomy—Excision of a heloma.

Helper T cells—T cells.

Helplessness—The dependency of some body on others for his or her life support

Hema- —A prefix indicating blood.

Hemachrome—The coloring matter of the blood—hemoglobin or hematin.

Hemachrosis—Excessive redness of the blood.

Hemacytometer—An apparatus used in counting blood cells.

Hemacytozoon—A unicellular parasite which infest the red blood cells.

Hemad—Hemal. 1. Pertaining to the blood or blood vessels. 2. Pertaining to the ventral side of the body in which the heart is situated.

Hemadostenosis—Contraction of the blood vessels.

Hemadsorption—The adherence of red blood cells to other cells, particles or surfaces.

Hemadynamometer—An apparatus for measuring the blood pressure.

Hemadynamometry— Measurement of the blood pressure.

Hemafacient—Hemopoietic.

Hemafecia—Feces containing blood.

Hemagglutination—Clustering of red blood cells.

Hemagglutination-inhibition—Prevention of clustering of red blood cells by blocking of the antibody or virus causing clustering of the red blood cells.

Hemagglutinative—Causing agglutination of the red blood cells.

Hemagglutinin—An antibody causing clustering of the red blood cells.

Hemagogic—Promoting blood flow.

Hemagogue—An agent increasing the blood flow, especially the menstrual flow.

Hemal—Hemad.

Hemal gland—A blood–containing or blood and lymph containing gland.

Hemal node—Hemal gland. A structure resembling a lymph node but associated with blood vessels instead of lymph vessels.

Hemanalysis—Any type of blood analysis.

Hemangiectasia— Hemangiectasis.

Hemangiectasis—Dilatation of the blood vessels.

Hemangioameloblastoma —A highly vascular ameloblastoma tumor.

Hemangioblast—A mesodermal cell from which vascular endothelial cells or hemocytoblasts are formed.

Hemangioblastoma—A capillary hemangioma of the brain usually located in the cerebellum.

Hemangioendothelioblastoma—A tumor of the endothelial cells lining the blood vessels.

Hemangioendothelioma —A hemangioma of the capillaries commonly seen in the cerebral meninges, of which the major portion is consisted of the endothelium.

Hemangioendotheliosarcoma— Hemangiosarcoma.

Hemangiofibroma—A hemangioma containing fibrous tissue.

Hemangioma—A benign tumor made up of dilated blood vessels.

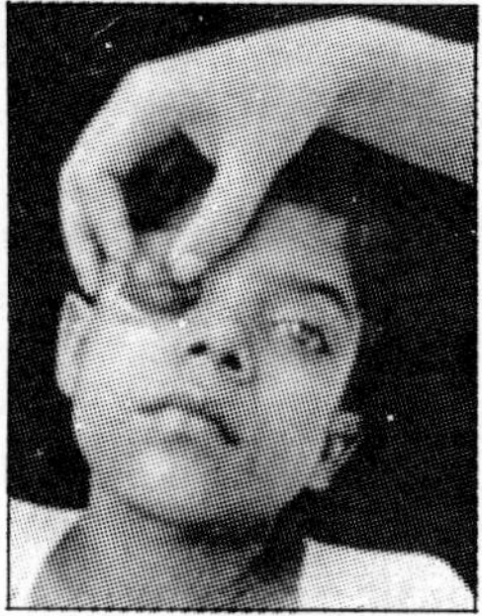

Fig. 205 : Hemangioma of the upper eyelid

Hemangiomatosis—Formation of multiple hemangiomas.

Hemangiopericytoma—A tumor arising in the capillaries. It is composed of pericytes, which are the connective tissue cells around the capillary walls.

Hemangiosarcoma— Angiosarcoma. A malignant tumor of the blood vessels formed of the endothelial and fibroblastic tissue.

Hemaphein—Brown coloring material in the blood and urine derived from hemoglobin.

Hemapheism—The presence of hemaphein in the blood plasma and urine.

Hemapheresis—The procedure by which blood is withdrawn and a portion of it containing plasma, white blood cells and platelets etc., is separated and retained and the remainder is retransfused into the donor.

Hemaphobia—Morbid fear of the sight of blood.

Hemapoiesis—Hematopoiesis. Formation of blood.

Hemapoietic—Hematopoietic. Pertaining to hemapoiesis.

Hemarthros, Hemarthrosis —Effusion of blood into a joint.

Hemat- —A prefix meaning blood.

Hematachometer— Hemotachometer.

Hematapostema—An abscess containing blood.

Hematemesis—Vomiting of blood.

Hematencephalon—Cerebral or brain hemorrhage.

Hematherapy—Treatment of diseases by administering the fresh blood.

Hematherm—Homeotherm.

Hemathermal—Hematothermal. Warm blooded animal whose blood remains at a constant temperature.

Hemathermous—Hemathermal, hematothermal.

Hemathidrosis, Hematidrosis —Excretion of sweat containing blood.

Hemathorax—Hemothorax.

Hematic—Hematinic. 1. Pertaining to or containing blood. 2. The medicine used for the treatment of anemia.

Hematimeter—Hematometer. Hemocytometer. An apparatus for counting the blood cells in a cubic millimeter of blood.

Hematin—The non-protein portion of the hemoglobin molecule.

Hematinemia—The presence of hematin in the circulating blood.

Hematinic—1. Pertaining to the blood. 2. An agent increasing the hemoglobin level and the number of red blood cells in the blood.

Hematinuria—Hemoglobinuria. Presence of hematin in the urine.

Hemato- —A prefix indicating blood.

Hematobilia—Presence of blood in the bile or bile ducts.

Hematobium—A parasite living in the blood.

Hematoblast—Hemocytoblast.

Hematocele—A cavity filled with blood e.g., swelling of the scrotum due to presence of blood in the tunica vaginalis of the testis.

Hematocelia—Hemorrhage into the peritoneal cavity.

Hematocephalus—A fetus born with the effusion of blood in its head.

Hematocephaly—The effusion of blood in the cranium in a fetus.

Hematochezia—Excretion of the stools containing blood.

Hematochlorin—A green coloring matter derived from hemoglobin obtained from the placenta.

Hematochromatosis— Hemochromatosis. Staining of the tissues of the body with blood pigment due to excessive deposition of iron from hemoglobin or excessive ingestion of iron.

Hematochyluria—Presence of blood and chyle in the urine.

Hematocoelia—Hematocelia.

Hematocolpometra— Accumulation of menstrual blood in the vagina and uterus.

Hematocolpos—Retention of menstrual blood in the vagina due to imperforate hymen.

Hematocrit—1. The volume percentage of the red blood cells in the given blood. 2. An apparatus or procedure used in determining the volume percentage of the red blood cells in the given blood.

Hematocryal—Poikilothermic.

Hematocyst—1. A cyst containing blood. 2. Hemorrhage into the urinary bladder.

Hematocystis—Presence of blood in the urinary bladder.

Hematocyte—Any blood cell.

Hematocytoblast— Hemocytoblast.

Hematocytolysis— Hemolysis. Dissolution of the red blood cells.

Hematocytometer—An apparatus for counting the red blood cells in a given sample.

Hematocytozoon—A parasite living in the red blood cells.

Hematocyturia—Presence of red blood cells in the urine.

Hematodyscrasia— Hemodyscrasia.

Hematodystrophy— Hemodystrophy.

Hematogenesis—Hematopoiesis. Formation of blood cells.

Hematogenic, Hematogenous—1. Hematopoietic. Pertaining to the formation of blood. 2. Pertaining to or originating in the blood.

Hematohidrosis— Hemathidrosis. Excretion of sweat containing blood.

Hematohistioblast— Hemohistioblast.

Hematohiston —Globin.

Hematoid—Resembling blood.

Hematoidin—A yellow crystalline substance—biliverdin, formed from hemoglobin and remains in the tissues when the red blood cells are destroyed.

Hematologist—Specialist in hematology.

Hematology—The science of the blood and blood forming tissues and their diseases.

Hematolymphangioma—A tumor consisting of the dilated blood vessels and lymph vessels.

Hematolysis—Hemolysis.

Hematolytic—Hemolytic.

Hematoma—A mass of blood (usually clotted) in an organ, tissue or space, caused by rupture of a blood vessel e.g., subdural hematoma in which there is a mass of clotted blood beneath the dura mater, usually the result of head injury.

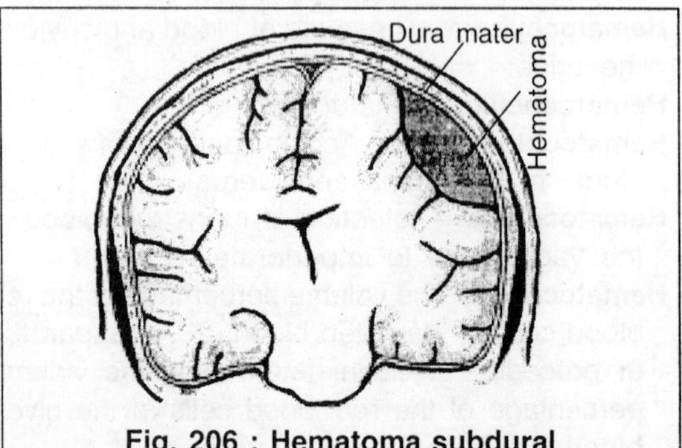

Fig. 206 : Hematoma subdural

Hematomediastinum— Effusion of blood in the mediastinum.

Hematometer— Hemoglobinometer.

Hematometra—Accumulation of menstrual blood in the uterus.

Hematometry—Measurement of the amount of hemoglobin, and determination of the percentage of various cells, in the blood.

Hematomphalocele—An umbilical hernia containing blood.

Hematomyelia—Hemorrhage in the spinal cord.

Hematomyelitis— Inflammation of the spinal cord with effusion of blood.

Hematomyelopore—Formation of cavities and canals in the spinal cord due to hemorrhage.

Hematonephrosis— Accumulation of blood in the pelvis of the kidney.

Hematonic—Hematinic.

Hematopathology—The study of the diseases of blood.

Hematopathy—Hemopathy.

Hematopenia—Deficiency of blood.

Hematopericardium— Accumulation of blood in the pericardial sac.

Hematoperitoneum— Accumulation of blood in the peritoneal cavity.

Hematopexin—Hemopexin. Any substance which causes blood to coagulate.

Hematopexis—Coagulation of blood.

Hematophage —The phagocytic cell destroying the red blood cells.

Hematophagia—1. Drinking of blood. 2. Dependency on blood. 3. Destruction of red blood cells by phagocytes.

Hematophagous—Living on blood, blood drinker.

Hematophilia—Hemophilia.

Hematophobia—Hemophobia.

Hematophyte—Plant organism or bacteria in the blood.

Hematoplastic—Hematopoietic.

Hematopoiesis—Formation and development of blood cells normally in the bone marrow or outside the bone marrow as in the spleen, liver, etc.

Hematopoietic—Hematogenic. Hematoplastic. 1. Pertaining to the formation and development of blood cells. 2. An agent that stimulates the formation of blood cells.

Hematopoietic system— The organs forming the blood such as bone marrow, etc.

Hematopoietin—Erythropoietin.

Hematoporphyrin—Iron free heme, a product of the decomposition of hemoglobin.

Hematoporphyrinemia— Presence of hematoporphyrin in the blood.

Hematoporphyrinuria— Hematoporphyrin in the urine.

Hematopsia—Hemophthalmia.

Hematorrhachis —Hemorrhage into the spinal cord.

Hematorrhea —Excessive bleeding.

Hematosalpinx—Accumulation of blood in the fallopian tubes.

Hematoscheocele— Accumulation of blood in the scrotum.

Hematoscope—An apparatus for opitcal examination of blood.

Hematoscopy—Optical examination of the blood by hematoscope.

Hematose—Full of blood.

Hematosepsis—Septicemia. Presence of disease-producing micro-organisms in the blood.

Hematosin—Hematin.

Hematosis—1. Hemopoiesis. Formation and development of blood cells. 2. Oxygenation of the venous blood in the lungs.

Hematospectroscope—A spectroscope for examining and analyzing the blood.

Hematospectroscopy— Examination of blood by hematospectroscope.

Hematospermatocele—A spermatocele filled with blood.

Hematospermia —Hemospermia. Semen containing blood.

Hematostatic—Hemostatic. Checking hemorrhage.

Hematostaxis—Occurrence of bleeding spontaneously due to a blood disease.

Hematosteon —Hemorrhage into the medullary cavity of bone.

Hematothermal —Hemathermal.. Hemathermous.

Hematothorax—Hemothorax. Thorax containing blood.

Hematotoxic—1. Pertaining to the blood poisoning. 2. Toxic to the blood cells.

Hematotoxin—Hemotoxin.

Hematotrachelos—Distension of the cervix of the uterus due to accumulation of menstrual blood.

Hematotropic—Having special affinity for, or exerting special effect on, the red blood cells.

Hematotympanum —Presence of blood in the middle ear.

Hematoxin—Hemotoxin.

Hematoxylin—A type of stain which is widely used in histology, especially for staining cell nuclei and chromosomes.

Hematozoic—Hemozoic.

Hematozoon—The organism living in the blood.

Hematozymosis—Fermentation of the blood.

Hematuria—Presence of blood in the urine, which may come from the kidney (renal hematuria), from the urethra (urethral hematuria) or from the urinary bladder (vesical hematuria).

Hemaxis—Blood-letting.

Heme—An iron-containing protein-free portion of the hemoglobin molecule, responsible for its oxygen-carrying properties.

Hemeralope—The person affected with day-blindness.

Hemeralopia—Day-blindness.

Hemeranopia—Hemeralopia.

Hemi- —A prefix meaning half.

Hemiacardius—One of the twin fetuses, in which about half of the blood is circulated by its own heart, the rest by the heart of the other twin.

Hemiacephalus—Anencephalus. A fetus without half portion of the brain.

Hemiachromatopsia—Color blindness in one half of the visual field.

Hemiageusia—Loss of sense of taste on one side of the tongue.

Hemiageustia—Hemiageusia.

Hemialbumin—A product resulting from the digestion of albumin.

Hemialgia—Pain in one half of the body.

Hemiamaurosis— Hemiamblyopia. Hemianopia. Blindness in one half of the visual field.

Hemiamblyopia— Hemiamaurosis. Hemianopia.

Hemiamyosthenia— Hemiparesis. Absence of normal muscular power in one half of the body.

Hemianacusia—Deafness in one ear.

Hemianalgesia —Analgesia on one side of the body.

Hemianencephaly—Congenital absence of the half of the brain.

Hemianesthesia—Anesthesia i.e., loss of sensation on one side of the body.

Hemianopia, Hemianopsia— Hemiamaurosis. Hemiamblyopia. Blindness in one half of the visual field.

Hemianopic—Affected with hemianopia.

Hemianopsia—Hemianopia.

Hemianosmia—Absence of the smell in one nostril.

Hemiaplasia—Absence of one lobe of a bilobed organ, especially of the thyroid gland.

Hemiapraxia—Inability to perform movements according to one's own will on one side of the body.

Hemiarthroplasty--Plastic surgery of a joint in which one joint surface is replaced with an artificial material, usually metal.

Hemiarthrosis—Synchondrosis. False articulation between two bones.

Hemiasynergia—Lack of coordination of parts affecting one side of the body.

Hemiataxia—Occurrence of awkward movements on one side of the body.

Hemiathetosis—Slow, irregular, twisting, snakelike, involuntary movements occurring in the upper extremity, especially in the hands and fingers on one side of the body.

Hemiatrophy—Atrophy of one side of the body, one half of an organ or part.

Hemiaxial—At an oblique angle to the long axial line of the body or a part.

Hemiballism—Hemichorea. Jerking and twitching movements of one side of the body.

Hemiballismus—Hemiballism.

Hemibladder—The urinary bladder formed of two separate parts each with its own ureter.

Hemiblock—Failure in the conduction of the cardiac impulses in either the anterior (superior) or posterior (inferior) division of the left branch of bundle of His.

Hemic—Hemal. Pertaining to the blood.

Hemicanities—Grayness of the hair on one side of the body.

Hemicardia—Half of a four-chambered heart.

Hemicastration—The removal of one testicle or ovary.

Hemicentrum—Either lateral half of a vertebral centrum.

Hemicephalgia—Hemicrania. Pain occurring in one lateral half of the head, as occurs in migrane.

Hemicephalia —Congenital absence of one half of the cerebrum.

Hemicephalus—Having only one cerebral hemisphere since birth.

Hemicephaly—Hemicephalia.

Hemicerebrum—Half portion of the cerebral hemisphere.

Hemichorea—Hemiballism. Chorea affecting only one side of the body.

Hemichromatopsia—Hemiachromatopsia. Color blindness in half of the visual field.

Hemicolectomy—Excision of half of the colon.

Hemicorporectomy—Surgical removal of the lower half of the body.

Hemicrania—Unilateral headache, usually migraine. 2. Congenital development of only one half of the skull.

Hemicraniectomy —To incise the cranial vault from front backward, separate and reflect one half of it, as usually done prior to an operation upon the brain.

Hemicraniosis—Enlargement of one half of the cranium or face.

Hemicraniotomy— Hemicraniectomy.

Hemidiaphoresis—Hemidrosis. Sweating on one side of the body.

Hemidiaphragm—Half of the diaphragm.

Hemidrosis—1. Hemidiaphoresis. Hemihidrosis. Sweating on one side of the body. 2. Hemathidrosis. Secretion of sweat containing blood.

Hemidysergia —Non-coordination of the muscles on one side of the body.

Hemidysesthesia—Disordered sensation on one half of the body.

Hemidystrophy—Inequality in the development of the two sides of the body.

Hemiectromelia—Deformed extremities on one side of the body.

Hemiepilepsy—Epilepsy affecting one lateral half of the body.

Hemifacial—Pertaining to or affecting one half of the face.

Hemigastrectomy—Excision of one half of the stomach.

Hemigeusia—Loss of sense of taste on one side of the tongue.

Hemiglossal—Pertaining to one side of the tongue.

Hemiglossectomy —Excision of one side of the tongue.

Hemiglossitis—Inflammation of one half of the tongue.

Hemignathia—Congenital absence of one half of the lower jaw.

Hemihepatectomy—Excision of one half of the liver.

Hemihidrosis—Hemidiaphoresis. Hemidrosis. Sweating on only one side of the body.

Hemihydranencephaly— Absence of one cerebral hemisphere with excess of cerebrospinal fluid (CSF) occupying its place.

Hemihypalgesia—Diminished sensitivity to pain on one side of the body.

Hemihyperesthesia— Increased sensitiveness of one side of the body.

Hemihyperhidrosis— Hemihyperidrosis.

Hemihyperidrosis— Hemihyperhidrosis. Excessive sweating on one side of the body.

Hemihyperplasia—Excessive development of one half of the body or of an organ.

Hemihypertonia—Increased muscle tone on one side of the body.

Hemihypertrophy—Overgrowth of half of the body, of a part or of an organ.

Hemihypesthesia, Hemihypoesthesia —Diminished sensitiveness of one side of the body.

Hemihypoplasia—Decreased development of one half of the body or of an organ.

Hemihypotonia—Decreased muscle tone on one side of the body.

Hemikaryon—A nucleus of a cell with half the diploid number of chromosomes.

Hemilaminectomy—Removal of vertebral lamina on one side only by surgery.

Hemilaryngectomy—Excision of the lateral half of the larynx.

Hemilateral —Pertaining to or affecting one lateral half of the body.

Hemilesion—A lesion on one side of the body.

Hemilingual—Pertaining to or affecting the lateral half of the tongue.

Hemimacroglossia— Enlargement of one lateral half of the tongue.

Hemimandibulectomy— Surgical removal of half of the mandible.

Hemimelia—Congenital absence of all or a part of the distal half of a limb.

Hemimelus —A fetus with absence of all or a part of the distal half of a limb.

Heminephrectomy—Excision of a portion of a kidney.

Hemineurasthenia— Neurasthenia affecting only one side of the body.

Hemiopalgia—Pain in one side of the head and the eye of that side.

Hemiopia—Hemianopia. Blindness in one half of the visual field.

Hemiopic—Pertaining to hemiopia.

Hemipagus—Two fetuses joined at the thorax and umbilicus.

Hemipancreatectomy— Removal of half of the pancreas by surgery.

Hemiparalysis—Hemiplegia. Paralysis of one side of the body.

Hemiparanesthesia— Anesthesia of the lower half of one side of the body.

Hemiparaplegia—Paralysis of the lower half of one side of the body or of one leg.

Hemiparesis—Paresis affecting only one side of the body.

Hemiparesthesia—Numbness of one side of the body.

Hemiparetic—1. Pertaining to numbness of one side of the body. 2. The person suffering from numbness of one side of the body.

Hemipelvectomy—Surgical removal of half of the pelvis and the leg.

Hemiplegia—Paralysis of one side of the body.

Alternate hemiplegia— Paralysis of one side of the face and of the rest of the body of the opposite side.

Cerebral hemiplegia— Hemiplegia caused by brain lesion.

Crossed hemiplegia— Alternate hemiplegia.

Facial hemiplegia— Paralysis of one side of the face.

Spastic hemiplegia— Hemiplegia with spasticity of the affected muscles.

Spinal hemiplegia— Hemiplegia occurring due to lesion in the spinal cord.

Hemiplegic—Pertaining to or affected with hemiplegia.

Hemisacralization—Abnormal development of one half of the fifth lumbar vertebra so that it is fused with the sacrum.

Hemisection—Bisection. To divide an organ or tissue into two equal parts.

Hemisensory—Loss of sensation on one side of the body.

Hemiseptum—A lateral half of any septum.

Hemisomus—A fetus with the lateral half of the body either missing or malformed.

Hemispasm—Spasm of only one side of the body or face.

Hemisphere—Half portion of a spherical structure, e.g., cerebral or cerebellar hemispheres.

Hemispherectomy—Removal of one cerebral hemisphere by surgery.

Hemisphericum—Hemisphere of cerebellum.

Hemispherium—Either cerebral hemisphere.

Hemistrumectomy—Surgical removal of half portion of the goiter.

Hemisyndrome—1. A condition in which one-half of the body is atrophied or hypertrophied 2. Unilateral lesion of the spinal cord.

Hemiterata—The person having congenital malformations but not to such a great extent as to cause disability or disfigurement.

Hemiteric, Hemiteratic— The congenitally deformed person but not to a great extent.

Hemithermoanesthesia — Absence of sensations of heat and cold on one side of the body.

Hemithorax—One half of the chest.

Hemithyroidectomy—Excision of one lobe of the thyroid gland.

Hemitomias—The person having one testicle only.

Hemitremor—Tremor present in one lateral half of the body.

Hemivertebra—Congenital absence or incomplete development of one lateral half of a vertebra.

Hemizygosity—The condition of having only one of a pair of alleles (genes) determining a specific character.

Hemizygotic—Hemizygous.

Hemizygous—Possessing only one of a pair of alleles (genes) that determines a specific character.

Hemo- —A prefix meaning blood.

Hemoagglutination—The clustering of red blood cells.

Hemoagglutinin—An agglutinin clustering the red blood cells.

Hemobilia—Presence of blood in the bile or bile ducts.

Hemobilinuria—Presence of urobilin in the blood and urine.

Hemoblast—Hemocytoblast. A large bone marrow cell producing red blood cells, white blood cells and platelets.

Hemoblastosis—Excessive production of the blood-forming cells from the bone marrow.

Hemocatharsis—A cleansing of the blood.

Hemocatheresis—The destruction of red blood cells.

Hemocatheretic—Pertaining to hemocatheresis or destruction of red blood cells.

Hemocele—Hematocele.

Hemocholecystitis— Hemorrhagic cholecystitis.

Hemochorial—Denoting a type of placenta in which the blood of mother comes in direct contact with the chorion.

Hemochromatosis—A disorder of iron metabolism in which the iron is deposited in the tissues in excess with the enlargement of the liver and the bronze skin pigmentation and diabetes mellitus.

Hemocrhome—Hemoglobin.

Hemochromometer—A colorimeter for estimating the amount of hemoglobin in the blood.

Hemochromoprotein—Any protein combined with the hemoglobin.

Hemoclasia—Hemolytic crisis.

Hemoclasis—Hemolysis. Destruction of red blood cells.

Hemoclastic—Hemolytic. Destructive to the red blood cells.

Hemoclip —A metal clip used to ligate blood vessels.

Hemoconcentration— Anhydremia. A relative increase in the number of red blood cells as a result of decrease in the fluid portion of the blood.

Hemoconia—Hemokonia. Blood dust. Small colorless bodies in the blood produced by the breaking down of the red blood cells.

Hemoconiosis—Presence in the blood of blood dust in excess.

Hemocryoscopy—Determination of the freezing point of the blood.

Hemocrystallin—Hemoglobin.

Hemocuprein—A blue copper-containing compound present in the red blood cells.

Hemocyte—Red blood cell.

Hemocytoblast—The embryonic cell found in the bone marrow from which all the blood cells are thought to be formed.

Hemocytoblastoma—The tumor containing hemocytoblasts.

Hemocytocatheresis— Hemolysis.

Hemocytogenesis— Hematopoiesis. Formation of blood cells.

Hemocytology—The study of the structure and functions of the blood cells.

Hemocytolysis—Hemolysis.

Hemocytometer—An apparatus used for counting the blood cells.

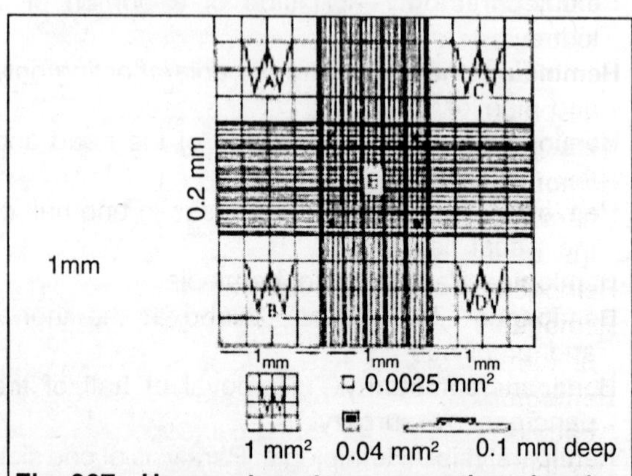

Fig. 207 : Hemocytometer or counting chamber

Hemocytometry—The counting of red blood cells.

Hemocytophagia—The phagocytic ingestion of the red blood cells.

Hemocytopoiesis—The development of blood cells.

Hemocytotripsis—Destruction of red blood cells by extreme pressure.

Hemocytozoon—Hematobium. A unicellular parasitic animal living in the blood.

Hemodiagnosis—Diagnosis of a disease made by examination of the blood.

Hemodialysis—Removal of certain chemical substances from the blood by passing it through the tubes made of semipermeable membrane, due to difference in rates of their diffusion through the semipermeable membrane. It is used to cleanse the blood in case where one or both kidneys are defective or absent.

Hemodialyzer—An apparatus used for performing hemodialysis.

Hemodilution —An increase in the fluid portion of the blood so that the concentration of red blood cells is reduced.

Hemodynamic—Pertaining to the physical aspects of the blood circulation.

Hemodynamics—The study of the movements of blood and of the forces involved in circulating the blood through the body.

Hemodynamometer—An apparatus for measuring the movement of the blood.

Hemodyscrasia—Any disorder of the blood and hemopoietic tissue.

Hemodystrophy—Any disease of the blood and hemopoietic tissues.

Hemofiltration—A technique of ultrafiltration for removing excess of normal metabolic products from the blood, in which the blood flows from the body to the hemofilter and is then returned to the body.

Hemoflagellate—Any flagellate protozoon living as parasite in the blood. They are usually of the genera Leishmania and Trypanosoma.

Hemofuscin—Brown pigment produced by the hemoglobin, which produces a reddish color in the urine.

Hemogenesis—Hemopoiesis. Formation of blood.

Hemogenic—Pertaining to the formation of blood, or forming blood.

Hemoglobin—The iron containing and oxygen carrying pigment of the red blood cell formed in the bone marrow, which gives red color to the blood. It is 12—16 gms. per 100 mls. of blood in adult females and 14—18 gms. per 100 mls. of blood in adult males and somewhat less in children.

Hemoglobinemia—Presence of hemoglobin in the blood plasma.

Hemoglobinocholia— Presence of hemoglobin in the bile.

Hemoglobinolysis— Disintegration of hemoglobin.

Hemoglobinometer—An instrument for determining the amount of hemoglobin in the blood.

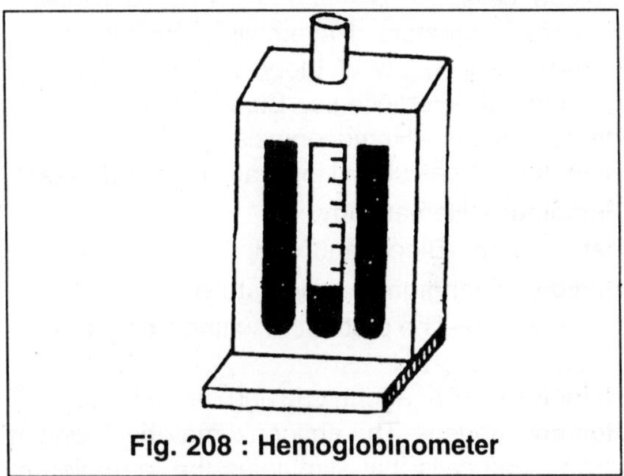

Fig. 208 : Hemoglobinometer

Hemoglobinometry— Measurement of hemoglobin in the blood.

Hemoglobinopathy—Any disease caused by the presence of defective or abnormal hemoglobin in the blood.

Hemoglobinopepsia— Hemoglobinolysis. Destruction of hemoglobin.

Hemoglobinophilia—The quality of growing better in the presence of hemoglobin.

Hemoglobinophilic—Pertaining to the organisms growing better in the presence of hemoglobin.

Hemoglobinous—Pertaining to or containing hemoglobin.

Hemoglobinuria —Presence of hemoglobin in the urine, free from red blood cells.

Cold hemoglobinuria—Hemoglobinuria occurring after local or general exposure to cold.

Epidemic hemoglobinuria —Winckel's disease. Hemoglobinuria occurring in the new born infants characterized by jaundice, cyanosis and fatty degeneration of the heart and liver.

Intermittent hemoglobinuria—Hemoglobinuria occurring at night intermittently.

Malarial hemoglobinuria—Black water fever. Hemoglobinuria following chronic falciparum malaria infection.

March hemoglobinuria —Hemoglobinuria occurring after prolonged exercise.

Toxic hemoglobinuria—Hemoglobinuria may occur after ingestion of various poisons.

Hemoglobinuric—Pertaining to or the person suffering from hemoglobinuria.

Hemogram—A written record or graph of the differential blood count.

Hemohistioblast—A primitive mesenchymal cell which is capable of developing into all types of blood cells.

Hemoid—Hematoid. Resembling the blood.

Hemokinesis—Flow of blood in the body.

Hemokonia—Hemoconia. Blood dust.

Hemokoniosis—Hemoconiosis.

Hemolith—A calculus in the wall of a blood vessel.

Hemology—Hematology.

Hemolymph—Blood and lymph.

Hemolymphangioma— Hematolymphangioma.

Hemolysate—The product resulting from hemolysis.

Hemolysin—An agent causing hemolysis.

Hemolysinogen—The antigenic material found in red blood cells that stimulates the formation of hemolysin.

Hemolysis—The breaking down of the red blood cells with the liberation of hemoglobin into the plasma.

Hemolytic—Pertaining to the hemolysis or an agent causing hemolysis.

Hemolytopoietic—Pertaining to the production and destruction of blood cells.

Hemolyzation—The occurrence of hemolysis.

Hemolyze—To produce hemolysis.

Hemomediastinum— Hematomediastinum.

Hemometra—Hematometra.

Hemometry—Hematometry.

Hemonephrosis— Hematonephrosis.

Hemopathic—Pertaining to or due to disease of the blood.

Hemopathology—The study of the blood diseases.

Hemopathy—Any disease of the blood.

Hemoperfusion—To pass the blood through adsorptive material, such as activated charcoal to remove toxic substances from the blood.

Hemopericardium— Hematopericardium.

Hemoperitoneum—Hematoperitoneum.

Hemopexis—Coagulation of blood.

Hemophage—A cell which destroys the red blood cells by phagocytosis.

Hemophagia—Hematophagia.

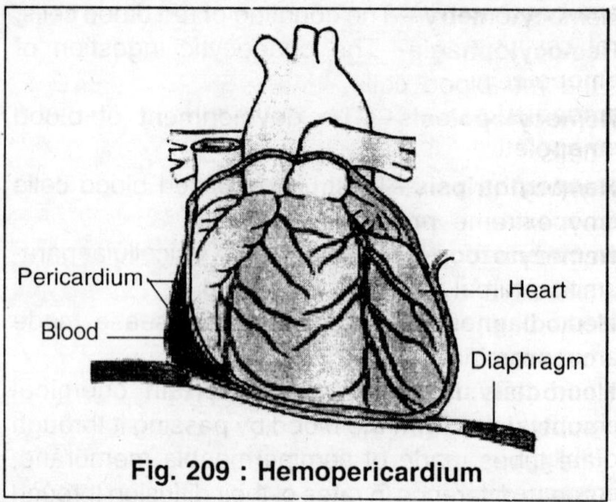

Fig. 209 : Hemopericardium

Hemophagocyte—A phagocyte that ingests red blood cells.

Hemophagocytosis— Ingestion of red blood cells by phagocytes.

Hemophil—Bacteria growing best in the media containing hemoglobin.

Hemophile—Hemophil.

Hemophilia—A hereditary hemorrhagic disease in which blood fails to clot due to deficiency of a blood coagulation factor and abnormal bleeding occurs with swelling of the joints.

Hemophiliac—The person affected with hemophilia.

Hemophilic—1. Growing well in media containing blood, said of bacteria 2. Pertaining to hemophilia, or hemophiliac.

Hemophilioid—1. Resembling hemophilia according to the symptoms. 2. Applied to a number of hereditary or acquired hemorrhagic diseases which are not due solely to coagulation factor deficiency.

Hemophilosis—Any disease caused by the bacteria of the genus Hemophilus.

Hemophilus—A genus of hemophilic gram-negative bacteria.

Hemophobia —Morbid fear of seeing bleeding.

Hemophoresis—Blood irrigation of the tissues.

Hemophoric—Carrying blood.

Hemophthalmia—Effusion of blood within the eye.

Hemophthalmus— Hemophthalmia.

Hemoplastic —Hematopoietic.

Hemoplasty—Formation of blood by the hemopoietic tissues.

Hemopleura—Presence of blood in the pleural cavity.

Hemopneumopericardium —Presence of blood and air in the pericardial cavity.

Hemopneumothorax—Blood and air in the pleural cavity.

Hemopoiesis—Hematopoiesis.

Hemopoietic—Hematopoietic.

Hemopoietin—Erythropoietin.

Hemoporphyrin—Hematoporphyrin.

Hemoposia—The drinking of blood.

Hemoprecipitin—A precipitin in the blood.

Hemoprotein—Any protein combined with the blood pigment heme.

Hemopsonin—An antibody that makes the red blood cells more susceptible to phagocytosis.

Hemoptysis—Spitting of blood or expectoration of blood–mixed sputum.

Hemorepellant—Opposing blood.

Hemorheology—Study of the flow of the blood.

Hemorrhage—Escape of blood from the blood vessels, bleeding, which may be internal or concealed when it is not visible and external when it is visible. It may be arterial in which the blood is bright red and comes in spurts, capillary in which the bleeding occurs from minute blood vessels and may be checked by applying pressure only, venous bleeding in which the blood is profuse, of dark red color and the blood flow is continuous.

Antepartum hemorrhage—Bleeding occurring before the onset of labor.

Cerebral hemorrhage — Hemorrhage occurring into the cerebrum.

Concealed hemorrhage— Internal hemorrhage.

Consecutive hemorrhage—Hemorrhage occurring some time after an injury.

Extradural hemorrhage— Bleeding between the skull and the dura mater.

Fibrinolytic hemorrhage —Hemorrhage occurring due to a defect in the fibrin component in blood coagulation.

Hemorrhage from the lung—Bleeding occurring from the lung in which the blood is bright red and frothy.

Hemorrhage from the stomach—Bleeding occurring from the stomach in which the blood is dark and may be clotted.

Internal hemorrhage— Bleeding into the organs or cavities of the body.

Intracranial hemorrhage— Bleeding into the cranium.

Intrapartum hemorrhage— Bleeding occurring during delivery of the child.

Nasal hemorrhage— Epistaxis.

Petechial hemorrhage — Subcutaneous hemorrhage occurring in the form of small rounded spots.

Postmenopausal hemorrhage —Bleeding from the vagina after menopause which may be a sign of malignancy of the reproductive tract.

Postpartum hemorrhage —Bleeding from the uterus occurring after childbirth.

Primary hemorrhage— Hemorrhage occurring immediately after injury.

Secondary hemorrhage— Hemorrhage occurring sometime after an injury.

Subdural hemorrhage— Bleeding occurring between dura mater and arachnoid mater.

Unavoidable hemorrhage— Continuous, painless bleeding caused by the detachment of a placenta previa.

Uterine hemorrhage— Bleeding occurring in the uterine cavity.

Hemorrhagenic—Causing hemorrhage.

Hemorrhagic—Pertaining to or marked by hemorrhage.

Hemorrhagiparous— Hemorrhagenic. Producing hemorrhage.

Hemorrhea—Hematorrhea.

Hemorrhoid—Pile. A mass of the dilated and tortuous hemorrhoidal veins in the anorectal region.

External hemorrhoid — A hemorrhoid present at the junction of the anal mucous membrane with the anal skin.

Internal hemorrhoid —A hemorrhoid present at the anorectal junction.

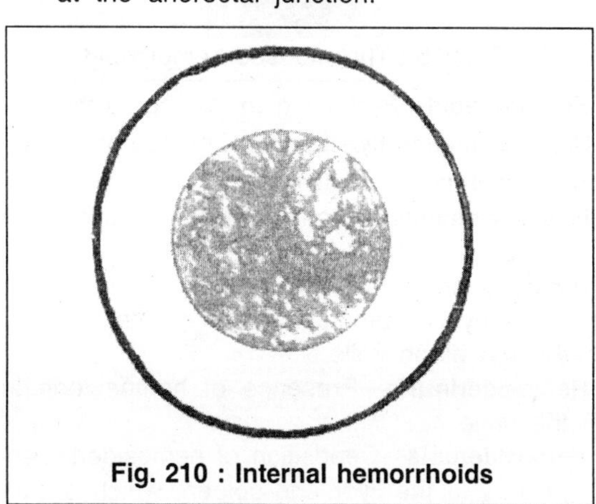

Fig. 210 : Internal hemorrhoids

Prolapsed hemorrhoid —An internal hemorrhoid protruded through the anus outside.

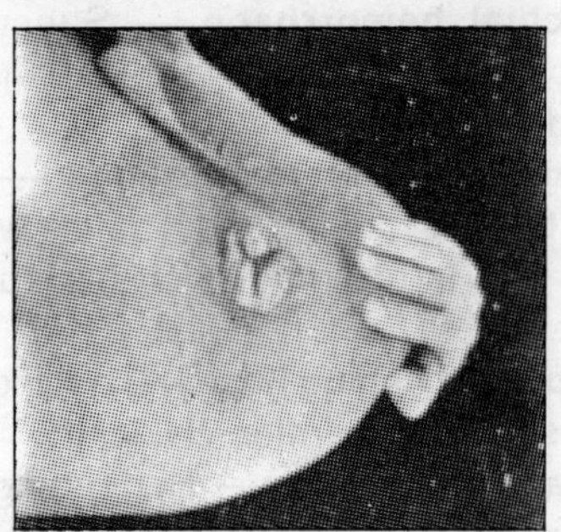

Fig. 211 : Prolapsed internal hemorrhoids

Strangulated hemorrhoid—A prolapsed internal hemorrhoid, of which the blood supply is obstructed by constriction of the anal sphincture.

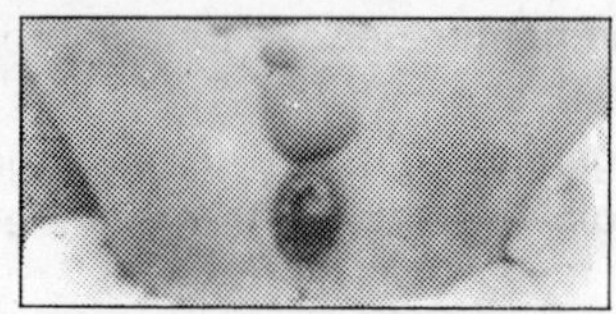

Fig. 212 : Strangulated internal hemorrhoids

Thrombosed hemorrhoid—The hemorrhoid containing clotted blood.

Fig. 213 : Thrombosed hemorrhoid

Hemorrhoidal—Pertaining to the hemorrhoid.

Hemorrhoidectomy—Excision of hemorrhoids.

Hemosalpinx—Hematosalpinx.

Hemosialemesis—Vomiting of blood mixed with saliva.

Hemosiderin—An iron-containing pigment produced by the hemoglobin from disintegration of the red blood cells.

Hemosiderinuria—Presence of hemosiderin in the urine.

Hemosiderosis—Deposition of hemosiderin, especially in the liver and spleen, which occurs in the diseases marked by red cell destruction such as hemolytic anemias, pernicious anemia and chronic infection etc.

Hemospasia—Withdrawal of blood by cupping or leeching.

Hemospermia—Hematospermia.

Hemostasia—Hemostasis.

Hemostasis, Hemostasia—1. Arrest of bleeding or of blood circulation. 2. Stagnation of blood.

Hemostat—1. A medicine or an instrument such as small clamp for constricting the blood vessels, for checking the blood flow. 2. A compressor for controlling the hemorrhage of the tonsils.

Hemostatic—Checking hemorrhage.

Hemostyptic—Hemostatic.

Hemosuccuspancreaticus—Bleeding into the pancreatic duct usually as a result of injury, tumor or inflammation etc.

Hemotachogram—The record produced by hemotachometer.

Hemotachometer— Hematachometer. An instrument for measuring the rapidity of blood flow in the arteries.

Hemotherapeutics—The use of blood in the treatment of diseases.

Hemotherapy—Treatment of diseases by the use of blood or its products.

Hemothorax—Accumulation of blood in the pleural cavity.

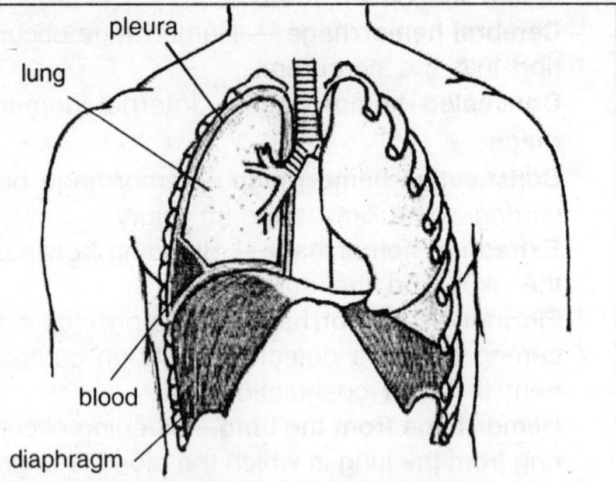

Fig. 214 : Hemothorax in the right pleural cavity

Hemothymia—Excessive excitement to murder.

Hemotoxic—Hematotoxic.

Hemotoxin—Hemolysin. A toxin which destroys the red blood cells.

Hemotrophe—Nutritive substances supplied to the developing embryo from the mother via the maternal blood.

Hemotrophic—Pertaining to the nutritive substances supplied to the developing embryo by the mother.

Hemotropic—Attracted towards the blood or blood cells.

Hemotympanum—Hemorrhage into the middle ear.

Hemozoic—Hematozoic. Parasitic protozoa in the blood.

Hemozoon—Hematozoon.

Hemp—Cannabis indica, the Indian hemp.

Henry—The unit of electrical inductance.

Henry's law—A law stating that the weight of a gas dissolved by a given volume of a liquid at a constant temperature is directly proportional to the pressure.

Hepar—The liver.

Heparin—It is an anticoagulant principle found in various tissues, especially the liver and lungs, and mast cells.

Heparinemia—The presence of heparin in excess in the circulating blood.

Heparinize —To inhibit the coagulation of blood by heparin.

Hepat-, Hepato-—Prefixes meaning liver.

Hepatalgia—Hepatodynia. Pain in the liver.

Hepatalgic—Pertaining to pain in the liver.

Hepatatrophia—Atrophy of the liver.

Hepatatrophy —Atrophy of the liver.

Hepatectomize—To remove the liver surgically.

Hepatectomized—Surgically removed liver.

Hepatectomy—Excision of a part or all of the liver.

Hepatic—Pertaining to the liver.

Hepatic amebiasis—Infection of the liver by Entamoeba histolytica as a complication of amebic dysentery, resulting in inflammation and abscess formation.

Hpatic coma—Coma due to liver failure.

Hepatic duct—The duct which receives bile from the liver and uniting with the cystic duct form the common bile duct.

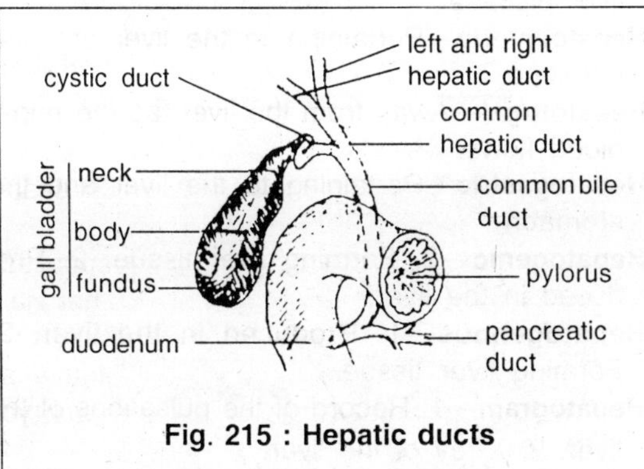

Fig. 215 : Hepatic ducts

Hepatic flexure—The right bend of the colon under the liver, or the junction of the ascending and transverse colon.

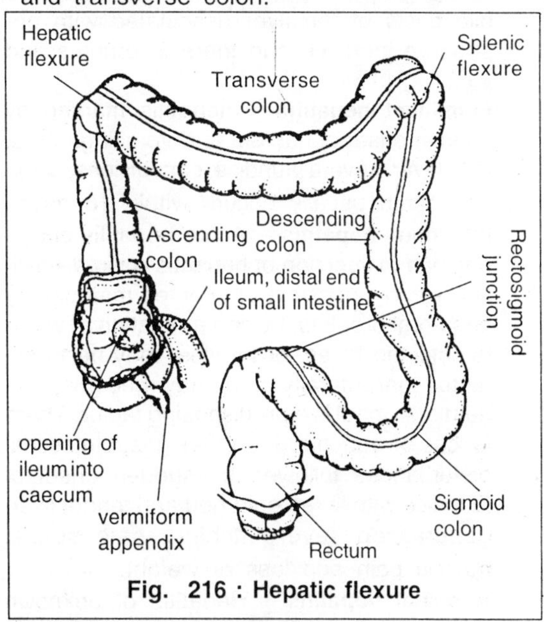

Fig. 216 : Hepatic flexure

Hepatic lobes—The divisions of the liver.

Hepaticodochotomy—To incise the hepatic duct and the common bile duct concurrently.

Hepaticoduodenostomy— To make an opening between hepatic duct and the duodenum.

Hepaticoenterostomy—To make an opening between the hepatic duct and the intestine.

Hepaticogastrostomy—To make a passage between the hepatic duct and the stomach.

Hepaticojejunostomy—To make a passage between the hepatic duct and the jejunum.

Hepaticolithotomy—To make an incision into the hepatic duct and remove the calculi present in it.

Hepaticolithotripsy—To crush a biliary calculus in the hepatic duct.

Hepaticopulmonary— Hepatopneumonic. Pertaining to the liver and the lungs.

Hepaticostomy—To make a permanent fistula into the hepatic duct.

Hepaticotomy—To make an incision into the hepatic duct.

Hepatis—Liver.

Hepatitic—Pertaining to hepatitis.

Hepatitis—Inflammation of the liver.

Acute anicteric hepatitis—Inflammation of the liver marked by slight fever, loss of appetite, gastrointestinal upset without jaundice.

Amebic hepatitis— Inflammation of the liver

caused by infection of Entamoeba histolytica as a complication of amebic dysentery.

Cholangiolitic hepatitis—Inflammation of the bile ducts of the liver associated with obstructive jaundice and there is pruritus and vomiting of bile.

Fulminant hepatitis— Hepatitis marked by sudden onset of nausea and vomiting, chills, high fever, severe jaundice, convulsions, coma and death usually occurs within 10 days.

Infectious hepatitis— Acute hepatitis occurring due to infection of hepatitis A virus which spreads by ingestion of infected material, by naso-oral droplets, by contamination of water by infected feces, or by files, may be transmitted parenterally and may become epidemic. Alcohol is a predisposing factor. There is loss of appetite and other gastrointestinal disturbances followed by sudden onset of jaundice with fever, enlarged and tender liver, generalized severe itching, pale stools, muscle pain and loss of weight.

Neonatal hepatitis— Hepatitis of unknown etiology occurring in an infant soon after birth marked by jaundice from the beginning, which may progress to cirrhosis of the liver.

Non-A, non-B hepatitis—Viral hepatitis caused neither by hepatitis A virus nor by hepatitis B virus but closely resembling viral hepatitis type B as may occur after blood or plasma transfusion marked by sudden onset of headache, chills, fever, general weakness, nausea, vomiting, abdominal pain, jaundice, pruritus, enlarged and tender liver.

Toxic hepatitis— Hepatitis caused by some poisons such as carbon tetrachloride or drugs as sulphonamides etc.

Transfusion hepatitis —Viral hepatitis type B. Hepatitis occurring after blood or plasma transfusion caused by hepatitis B virus transmitted from the donor's blood which was not harmful in the donor but becomes very dangerous in the recipient who may die within a short time.

Viral hepatitis—General inflammation of the liver caused by one of several viruses including two known as hepatitis A virus and hepatitis B virus.

Hepatization—Transformation into a liver-like mass *e.g.,* in the consolidation stage in lobar pneumonia the lung surface has the appearance of the liver tissue.

Hepato- —Prefix indicating the liver.

Hepatobiliary —Pertaining to the liver and bile.

Hepatoblastoma —A malignant teratoma of the liver occurring in infants and young children.

Hepatocarcinogen—Any thing that causes cancer of the liver.

Hepatocarcinoma—Carcinoma of the liver.

Hepatocele —Hernia of the liver.

Hepatocellular—Pertaining to or affecting the cells of the liver.

Hepatocholangiocystoduodenostomy—To establish the drainage of bile ducts into the duodenum through the gallbladder.

Hepatocholangioduodenostomy —To establish the drainage of the bile ducts into the duodenum.

Hepatocholangioenterostomy—To make a passage between the liver and the intestine.

Hepatocholangiogastrostomy—To open the bile ducts into the stomach.

Hepatocholangiojejunostomy —Union of the hepatic duct to the jejunum.

Hepatocholangiostomy— To make an opening into the common bile duct to establish drainage.

Hepatocholangitis— Inflammation of the liver and the bile ducts.

Hepatocirrhosis—Cirrhosis of the liver.

Hepatocolic—Pertaining to both, the liver and the colon.

Hepatocuprein—A copper-containing protein in the liver.

Hepatocystic—Pertaining to both, the liver and the gallbladder.

Hepatocyte—A hepatic cell.

Hepatoduodenostomy — Hepaticoduodenostomy. To make an opening from the liver into the duodenum.

Hepatodynia—Pain in the liver.

Hepatodysentery—Dysentery associated with liver disease.

Hepatoenteric—Pertaining to the liver and the intestine.

Hepatofugal—Away from the liver, as the portal blood flows.

Hepatogastric—Pertaining to the liver and the stomach.

Hepatogenic—1. Forming liver tissue. 2. Produced in the liver.

Hepatogenous—1. Produced in the liver. 2. Forming liver tissue.

Hepatogram—1. Record of the pulsations of the liver. 2. X-ray of the liver.

Hepatography—1. Recording of the pulsations of liver. 2. X-ray examination of the liver.
Hepatohemia —Congestion of the liver.
Hepatoid—Liver-shaped.
Hepatojugular—Pertaining to the liver and jugular vein.
Hepatojugular reflex— Pressure on the liver increases the cervical venous pressure in the person affected with right-sided heart failure.
Hepatolienography—X-ray examination of the liver and spleen after an intravenous injection of a radiopaque substance.
Hepatolienomegaly— Enlargement of the liver and spleen.
Hepatolith —A biliary calculus in the liver.
Hepatolithectomy—To remove a calculus from the liver by surgery.
Hepatolithiasis—The presence of the calculi in the liver.
Hepatologist—Specialist in the liver diseases.
Hepatology —The scientific study of the liver and its diseases.
Hepatolysin—A cytolysin destructive to the liver cells.
Hepatolysis—Destruction of the liver cells.
Hepatolytic—Destructive to the liver cells.
Hepatoma—A tumor of the liver.
Hepatomalacia—Softening of the liver.
Hepatomegalia—Hepatomegaly.
Hepatomegaly—Enlargement of the liver.
Hepatomelanosis—Melanosis or the deposition of the black pigments in the liver.
Hepatomphalocele—Herniation of the liver through the umbilicus.
Hepatomphalos — Hepatomphalocele.
Hepatonecrosis—Necrosis of liver.
Hepatonephric—Pertaining to the liver and kidney.
Hepatonephritis—Inflammation of both, the liver and kidneys.
Hepatonephromegaly— Enlargement of both, the liver and the kidneys.
Hepatopathic—Causing liver disease.
Hepatopathy—Any disease of the liver.
Hepatoperitonitis— Perihepatitis. Inflammation of the peritoneal covering of the liver.
Hepatopetal —Toward the liver.
Hepatopexy—To fix the displaced or movable liver to the abdominal wall by surgery.
Hepatophage—A phagocyte which attacks the liver cells.
Hepatophyma—Rounded or nodular tumor of the liver.
Hepatopleural—Pertaining to the liver and the pleura.
Hepatopneumonic—Pertaining to, affecting or communicating with the liver and the lungs.
Hepatoportal—Pertaining to the portal system of the liver.
Hepatoportogram—X-ray film of the portal vein and its branches in the liver.
Hepatoptosia—Downward displacement of the liver.
Hepatoptosis—Hepatoptosia.
Hepatopulmonary—Pertaining to both, the liver and the lungs.
Hepatorenal—Pertaining to the liver and the kidneys.
Hepatorrhagia—Hemorrhage into or from the liver.
Hepatorrhaphy—The suturing of a wound of the liver.
Hepatorrhexis—Rupture of the liver.
Hepatoscan—Autoradiograph of the liver.
Hepatoscopy—Inspection of the liver.
Hepatosis—Any disease of the liver not associated with the inflammation.
Hepatosplenitis— Inflammation of the liver and the spleen.
Hepatosplenography—X-ray examination of the liver and spleen.
Hepatosplenomegaly— Enlargement of the liver and spleen.
Hepatosplenopathy—Any disease affecting both, the liver and spleen.
Hepatostomy—Establishment of a fissure into the liver.
Hepatotherapy—1. Treatment of diseases by using the liver or liver extract. 2. Treatment of the liver diseases.
Hepatotomy—To make an incision into the liver.
Hepatotoxemia—Poisoning of blood by the toxins produced in the liver.
Hepatotoxic—Having toxic effect on the liver cells, as alcohol.
Hepatotoxicity—The state of the liver of being poisonous.
Hepatotoxin—A toxin which destroys the liver cells.
Hepta- —A prefix meaning seven.
Heptachromic—Able to distinguish all the seven colors.
Heptaploidy—Having seven sets of chromosomes.
Heptose—Any sugar whose molecule contains seven carbon atoms.

Heptosuria—Presence of heptose in the urine.

Herb—A small plant with soft stem containing no wood, used as a household remedy or as a flavor.

Herbal — Pertaining to herbs.

Herbalist—The person who promotes healing or health through the use of herbs.

Herbicide—A substance seems to be a chemical that destroys the herbs.

Herbivorous—Vegetarian. Subsisting on plants.

Herd—Aggregation of a large number of people or animals.

Hereditary—Transmitted from one generation to another.

Heredity—The transmission of qualities from parents to the offsprings.

Heredo- —A prefix meaning heredity.

Heredoataxia—Friedreich's ataxia. Hereditary spinal ataxia.

Heredofamilial—Occurring (disease) in certain families due to the inherited defect.

Heredoimmunity—Inherited immunity.

Heritability—The quality of being heritable.

Heritable —Capable of being inherited.

Heritage—Total characters transmitted to the offspring.

Hermaphrodism— Hermaphroditism.

Hermaphrodite—An individual possessing genital and sexual characteristics of both sexes (male and female).

Hermaphroditism— Hermaphrodism. The condition in which both, testicular and ovarian tissues are present in the same individual which occurs rarely in humans.

Bilateral hermaphroditism—The condition in which an ovary and a testicle are present on both sides.

Complex hermaphroditism—A condition in which an individual possesses internal and external organs of both sexes.

False hermaphroditism — Pseudohermaphroditism. To have the internal genital organs of one sex (testis or ovary) but accompanied by the external genital organs and secondary sexual characteristics of the opposite sex.

Lateral hermaphroditism—Having a testis on one side and an ovary on the other side.

Transverse hermaphroditism—The condition in which the external genital organs are of one sex and the internal genital organs are of the other sex.

True hermaphroditism — The condition in which an individual possesses both, testicular and ovarian gonads.

Unilateral hermaphroditism— Hermaphroditism in which a testis or an ovary is present on one side of the body and either a testis or an ovary present on the other side.

Hermetic—Air tight. Impenetrable to air.

Hernia—The protrusion of an organ or a part of an organ through the wall of the cavity normally containing it, e.g., inguinal hernia in which the intestine is protruded at the inguinal ring, femoral hernia in which the intestines are descended through the femoral ring into the femoral canal, umbilical hernia in which the intestine is protruded at the umbilicus through the defect in the abdominal wall and epigatric hernia in which the intestine is protruded through an opening in the abdominal wall in the midline above the umbilicus.

Abdominal hernia— Hernia occurring through the abdominal wall.

Cerebral hernia—Protrusion of a part of the brain through a defect in the skull.

Complete hernia—Hernia in which the sac and its contents have passed through the hernial opening completely.

Concealed hernia—Hernia which is not perceptible on palpation.

Congenital hernia— Hernia existing since birth.

Diaphragmatic hernia— Protrusion of the abdominal contents into the thoracic cavity through an opening in the diaphragm.

Epigastric hernia— Protrusion of abdominal contents through linea alba above the umbilicus.

Femoral hernia—A descending of the intestines through the femoral ring.

Incarcerated hernia— Hernia completely obstructing the intestines.

Incisional hernia—Hernia occurring through an old surgical scar.

Incomplete hernia—Hernia in which only a part of an organ passes through an opening.

Inguinal hernia—The protrusion of the hernial sac containing intestine, at the inguinal opening. In an indirect (oblique) inguinal hernia, the sac passes through the internal inguinal ring into the inguinal canal, often descending into the scrotum which becomes

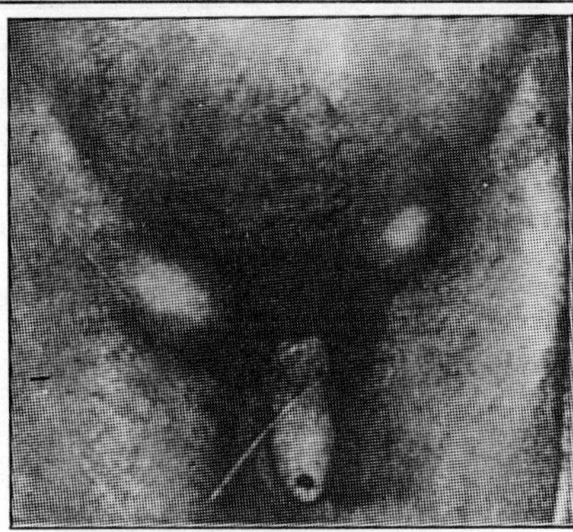

Fig. 217 : The patient with left inguinal and right femoral hernia

apparent when the patient coughs. In a direct inguinal hernia the hernial sac protrudes through the abdominal wall in the region of Hesselbach's triangle which is bounded medially by the lateral border of the rectus abdominis muscle, laterally by the deep epigastric artery and below by the inguinal ligament, which becomes prominent as soon as the patient stands and disappears immediately after he lies down before any pressure is applied.

Internal hernia—Hernia occurring within the abdominal cavity.

Irreducible hernia— Hernia which cannot be returned to its original position by manipulation.

Reducible hernia— Hernia which can be returned to its original position by manipulation.

Strangulated hernia— Hernia which is so tightly constricted that its blood supply is obstructed and hence gangrene occurs which is cured only by surgery.

Umbilical hernia— Protrusion of the intestine or omentum through the abdominal wall under the skin at the umbilicus.

Hernial—Pertaining to the hernia.

Hernial sac—A pouch of peritoneum into which a hernia descends.

Herniated—Having a hernia or protruding like a hernia.

Herniation—The development of hernia.

Hernio- —A prefix denoting hernia.

Hernioenterotomy—To make an incision in the intestine following the reduction of a hernia.

Herniography—X-ray examination of a hernia after introducing a contrast medium.

Hernioid—Resembling a hernia.

Herniology—Scientific study of the hernia.

Hernioplasty—Plastic surgery for hernia.

Herniopuncture—Punture of the hernia with a hollow needle for withdrawal fluid or gas from the hernia.

Herniorrhaphy—Surgical repair of hernia, with suturing.

Herniotome—The knife for the operation of hernia.

Herniotomy—A cutting operation done for the correction of a hernia.

Heroic measure—In medical practice, a daring procedure or therapy applied in a seriously ill patient which may in itself endanger the patient's life but may be successful and the patient's life may be saved.

Heroin—A narcotic substance derived from morphine.

Heroinism—Addiction to use of heroin.

Herpangina—An infectious disease characterized by the formation of vesicles in the throat and the posterior part of the mouth, which rupture and form the ulcers.

Herpes—1. An inflammatory disease of the skin marked by the formation of small vesicles in clusters. 2. Diseases caused by herpes viruses. Four types of herpes viruses are found in man. (1) Herpes simplex, which is of two types : I Type 1 & II Type 2, which grow differently. (2) Herpes varicella-zoster virus (3) Epstein-Barr virus (4) Cytomegalovirus. Only two, Herpes simplex and Herpes varicella-zoster virus mainly cause diseases in man.

Herpes menstrualis — Herpes occurring at the time of menstrual period.

Herpes simplex —Herpes simplex, an acute infectious disease caused by herpes simplex virus type 1 characterized by the formation of thin walled vesicles at the junction of the mucous membrane with the skin such as on the borders of the lips or on the nasal mucous membrane, which usually tend to recur in the same area. Herpes genitalis, the infection with the herpes simplex virus type 2, of the skin of the genital organs and of the anorectal skin and mucous membrane, which is sexually transmitted.

Herpes zoster —Herpes zoster is an acute infectious disease caused by the herpes varicella-zoster virus, characterized by in-

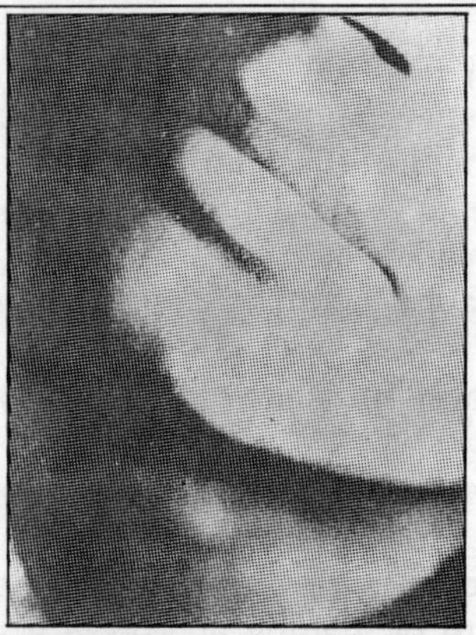

Fig. 218 : Herpes simplex on the lips

flammation of the cerebral ganglia, ganglia of the posterior nerve roots and peripheral nerves in a segmented distribution. Small painful vesicles are formed on the skin of the chest or back unilaterally along the course of the affected nerves. The virus is the same which causes chicken pox. Herpes zoster ophthalmicus— Herpes zoster affecting the ophthalmic nerve, the first division of the 5th cranial nerve with the formation of vesicular and erythematous rash on the forehead, eyelid and cornea supplied by the ophthalmic nerve.

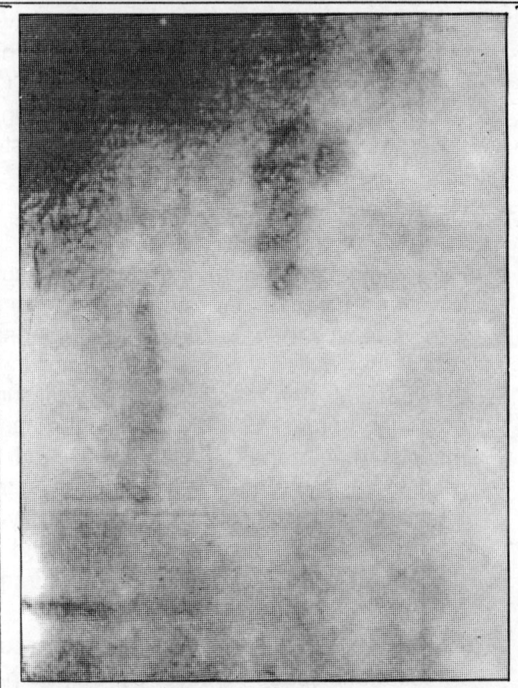

Fig. 219 : Herpes zoster on the back

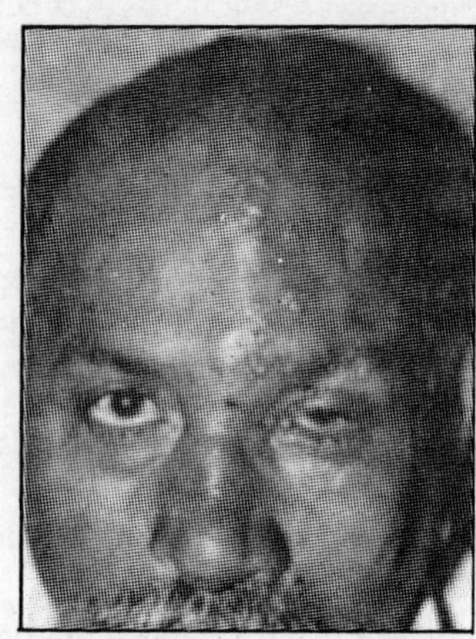

Fig. 220 : Herpes zoster ophthalmicus

Herpetic —Pertaining to herpes.

Herpetic neuralgia —Neural pain in the herpes.

Herpetiform —Resembling herpes.

Herpetism —Predisposition to herpetic eruption.

Herpetologist —Specialist in herpetology.

Herpetology —The branch of zoology concerned with the study of reptiles and amphibians.

Hersage —Splitting of a peripheral nerve into separate fibers.

Hertz —A unit of frequency equal to one cycle per second. Symbol is Hz.

Hesitancy —An involuntary delay or inability in starting urinary stream.

Hesperidin —A chemical present in the bark of orange and lemon, which reduces the permeability or increases the strength of the capillaries.

Heteradelphus —Two joined fetuses, one fetus much more developed than the other.

Heteradenia —Presence of glandular tissue in an abnormal place.

Heteradenic —Pertaining to heteradenia.

Heteradenoma —A glandular tumor which arises from an area that does not usually contain glands.

Heterauxesis —Disproportionate growth of the body parts.

Heteraxial —Having axes of unequal length which are perpendicular to each other.

Heterecious —Parasitic on different hosts at different stages of its development.

Heterecism —Development of different life cycles of a parasite on different hosts.

Heterergic —Having different effects.

Heteresthesia —Variation of the sensibility to the cutaneous stimuli.

Hetero-, Heter- —Prefixes indicating different, or relationship to another.

Heteroagglutination — Agglutination of the red blood cells of an animal by the serum of an animal of another species.

Heteroagglutinin —1. An agglutinin that agglutinates the red blood cells of the animal of other species. 2. Agglutinin formed as a result of an injection of an antigen from an animal of a different species.

Heteroalbumose —Hemialbumose. Albumose insoluble in water but soluble in saline solutions or acidic or alkaline solutions.

Heteroantibody —An antibody combining with antigens originating from other species.

Heteroantigen —An antigen produced from the species other than that from which the antibody is produced.

Heteroantiserum —Antiserum developed in the animal of one species against antigen or cells of the animal of another species.

Heteroautoplasty —Grafting of the skin taken from another person.

Heteroblastic —Originating in a different kind of tissue. Opposite to homoblastic.

Heterocellular —Composed of the cells of different kinds.

Heterocentric —Having different centres.

Heterocephalus —A fetus having two heads of unequal size.

Heterocheiral, Heterochiral —Pertaining to or referred to the other hand.

Heterochromatic —Characteristic of heterochromatin.

Heterochromatin —Highly condensed or coiled portion of the chromosome found during interphase that stains differently from the remaining portion of the chromosome.

Heterochromatosis — Heterochromia. 1. Pigmentation of the skin from foreign substance. 2. Difference in color.

Heterochromia —A difference in color, *e.g.*, heterochromia irides in which the iris in two eyes are of different colors.

Heterochromic —Having different colors.

Heterochromosome —1. The X and Y or sex chromosomes. 2. A chromosome containing heterochromatin, which stains differently from the remainder of the chromatin material.

Heterochromous —Of abnormal different color.

Heterochronia —Irregularity in time for the occurrence of a phenomenon or production of a structure.

Heterochronic —Occurring at different times.

Heterochthonous —Originated from a different place where it was found.

Heterocinesia —To make different movements from those the patient is instructed to make.

Heterocladic —Pertaining to the anastomosis between branches of two different arteries.

Heterocrine —Secreting more than one kind of matter.

Heterocrisis —Irregular crisis with abnormal symptoms.

Heterocytotropic —Having an affinity for the cells of a different species.

Heterodermic — Dermatoheteroplasty. Pertaining to the method of skin grafting in which the skin graft is taken from another person.

Heterodisperse —An aerosol whose particles are of different sizes.

Heterodont —Having teeth of different shapes.

Heterodromus —Moving or arranged in opposite direction.

Heterodymus —A fetus with second head, neck, and thorax attached to its thorax.

Heteroeroticism —Sexual excitement brought about by a person of the opposite sex.

Heterogametic —The man producing two types of sperms, one containing X chromosome and the other containing Y chromosome.

Heterogamous —Pertaining to heterogamy.

Heterogamy —The union of the gametes of the different size and structure.

Heterogeneity —The condition of being heterogeneous.

Heterogeneous —1. Of different nature. 2. Made up of different substances.

Heterogenesis —Metagenesis. Production of offspring with different characteristics in alternate generations.

Heterogenetic —Pertaining to heterogenesis.

Heterogenic, Heterogeneic —Having different gene constitutions.

Heterogenous —Of foreign origin.

Heterogeusia —Perception of abnormal taste

when food is placed in the mouth or when it is chewed.

Heterogony —Heterogenesis.

Heterograft —Xenograft. A graft transferred from an animal of one species to one of another species.

Heterography —To write different words from those one likes to get written.

Heterohemagglutination — Agglutination of red blood cells by the hemagglutinins derived from an animal of another species.

Heterohemagglutinin —A hemagglutinin which agglutinates red blood cells of the animal of another species.

Heteroimmunity —Immunity to an antigen from another species.

Heteroinfection —Infection by a microorganism from outside of the body.

Heteroinoculation —Inoculation of a microorganism from outside of the body.

Heterokeratoplasty —Plastic surgery of the cornea by the corneal tissue taken from the individual of another species.

Heterokinesia —The making of movements in the reverse direction.

Heterokinesis —Heterokinesia.

Heterolalia —Heterophasia. Heterophemia. Speaking of meaningless words instead of those intended.

Heterolateral —Contralateral. Situated or occurring on the other side.

Heteroliteral —In speaking, pertaining to an incorrect letter being put in place of another correct one.

Heterologous —1. Made up of tissue which is not normal to that part. 2. Cells, tissue or blood obtained from a different individual or species.

Heterology —A departure from the normal in structure and development etc.

Heterolysin —A lysin that is formed in one species of the animal and causes lysis of the cells of different species of animal.

Heterolysis —Dissolution of the cells of one species of the animal by a lytic agent from different species of the animal.

Heterolytic —Pertaining to heterolysis.

Heteromastigote —A flagellate having two flagella, one anterior and one posterior.

Heteromeral —Heteromeric. Having a different chemical composition.

Heteromeric —Heteromeral.

Heteromerous —Heteromeric.

Heterometaplasia —Formation of the tissue foreign to the part where it is formed.

Heterometric —Depending upon a change in size.

Heterometropia —The condition in which the refraction in two eyes is different.

Heteromorphism —In cytogenetics, a difference of shape or size between the two homologous chromosomes in metaphase of cell division.

Heteromorphosis — 1. The regeneration of an organ different from the one that it replaced. 2. Abnormal position of an organ.

Heteromorphous —Of abnormal structure.

Heteronomous —Abnormal.

Heteronomy —The state of being heteronomous.

Heteronymous —Having opposite relations.

Hetero-osteoplasty —Bone grafting with a graft taken from an animal.

Heteropagus —Two joined fetuses having unequally developed parts.

Heteropathy —1. Morbid sensibility to the stimuli. 2. Creation of a disease to neutralize another disease.

Heterophagy —The taking into a cell of an exogenous material, by phagocytosis.

Heterophasia —Heterolalia. Heterophemia.

Heterophemia, Heterophemy —Heterolalia. Heterophasia.

Heterophil (e) —1. A Granular white blood cell. 2. Pertaining to a tissue or microorganism staining with a type of stain other than the usual one. 3. Pertaining to an antibody reacting with other than the specific antigen.

Heterophilic —1. Attracted toward abnormal. 2. Having antibody response to an antigen other than the specific one. 3. Staining with a type of stain other than the usual one.

Heterophonia —Change of voice.

Heterophoralgia —Deviation of one eye accompanied by pain.

Heterophoria —The tendency of the eyes to deviate from their normal position.

Heterophthalmia —Difference in the direction of the visual axes, or in the color, of the two eyes.

Heterophthalmus —Difference in appearance of the eyes due to the irides of the different color.

Heterophthongia — Heterophonia.

Heteroplasia —Alloplasia. Development of a tissue at the place where it would not normally occur.

Heteroplastic —Pertaining to heteroplasia.

Heteroplastid —The graft in heteroplasty.

Heteroplasty —Grafting with the tissue taken from other person or an animal.

Heteroploid —Possessing an abnormal number of chromosomes.

Heteroploidy —The condition of possessing an abnormal number of chromosomes.

Heteroprosopus —A fetus having one head and two faces.

Heteropsia —Unequal vision in the two eyes.

Heteroptics —Perversion of vision such as seeing those things which do not exist.

Heteropyknosis —The quality of the various parts of a chromosome to be stained with varying degrees of intensity.

Heteropyknotic —Pertaining to heteropyknosis.

Heteroscopy —Heteropsia.

Heteroserotherapy —Treatment of the diseases by serum obtained from another person.

Heterosexual —1. Pertaining to the opposite sex. 2. The person sexually attracted to the person of the opposite sex.

Heterosexuality —Sexual attraction to the persons of the opposite sex.

Heterosis —More growth and strength seen in the first hybrid generation.

Heterosmia —Alltriosmia. Incorrect perception of an odor.

Heterosome —In genetics, a pair of chromosomes that is different in persons of both the sexes.

Heterosuggestion —Suggestion received from another person, not of one's self.

Heterotaxia —Abnormal position of organs or parts of the body.

Heterotaxic —Abnormally placed or arranged.

Heterotaxis —Heterotaxia.

Heterotaxy —Heterotaxia.

Heterotherm —An animal whose temperature varies considerably in different situations.

Heterothermic —Having partial regulation of body temperature.

Heterothermy —The condition in which temperature of an animal varies considerably in different situations.

Heterotic —Pertaining to heterosis.

Heterotonia —Occurrence of variations in the tension or tone.

Heterotopia —1. Presence of a tissue in an abnormal place. 2. Displacement of an organ or part from its normal place.

Heterotopic —1. Pertaining to heterotopia. 2. Misplaced.

Heterotopous —Heterotopic.

Heterotopy —Displacement of an organ or a part of the body.

Heterotoxin —A toxin introduced from outside the patient's body.

Heterotransplantation — Transplantation of a heterograft (xenograft).

Heterotrichosis —Growth of hairs of different colors on the body.

Heterotroph —The organism as man requiring complex organic food for growth and development.

Heterotrophic —Not self-sustaining.

Heterotropia —Deviation of the eyes from the normal position.

Heterotropy —Heterotropia.

Heterotypic —Pertaining to the different type than that which is discussed or examined.

Heterovaccine —A vaccine prepared from a source other than that of the disease in which it is to be administered.

Heteroxenous —Requiring two hosts to complete the life cycle, said of some parasites.

Heterozoic —Pertaining to another animal or another species of animal.

Heterozygosis —Heterozygosity.

Heterozygosity —The state of having different alleles in regard to a given character.

Heterozygote —An individual having different alleles for a given characteristic.

Heterozygous —Possessing different alleles at a given locus.

Hettocyrtosis —A slight curvature.

Heuristic —Encouraging investigation.

Hex-, Hexa- —Prefixes indicating six.

Hexabasic —An acid containing six hydrogen (H) atoms which can be replaced by six hydroxyl (OH) radicals.

Hexachromic —1. Pertaining to six colors. 2. Able to distinguish only six of the seven colors of the spectrum.

Hexad —1. A group of six similar things. 2. An element with six valency.

Hexadactylism —The condition of having six fingers or toes in one limb.

Hexadactylous —Having six fingers or toes.

Hexadactyly —The occurrence of six digits on one limb.

Hexagonal —Having six angles.

Hexaploid —Having six sets of chromosomes.

Hexaploidy —Condition of having six sets of chromosomes.

Hexavaccine —A vaccine made from six different microorganisms.

Hexavalent —Having six chemical valencies.

Hg —Symbol for mercury.

Hiatus —An opening, an aperture, a foramen or gap, *e.g.,* hiatus aorticus—an opening in the diaphragm through which pass the aorta and the thoracic duct, and hiatus esophageus—an opening in the diaphragm through which esophagus passes.

Hibernation —Sleeping state in which some animals, e.g., frogs pass the winter season.

Hiccough, **Hiccup** —Short, sharp inspiratory sound with spasm of the glottis and spasmodic lowering of the diaphragm, caused generally by the irritation of diaphragm, and in indigestion.

Hiccup —Hiccough.

Hick's sign —Braxton Hick's sign. A sign of pregnancy in which painless contractions of the uterus occur after the third month of pregnancy at every 10 to 20 minutes, and these only are converted into labor contractions before delivery.

Hidebound disease — Scleroderma. Hardening and thickening of the skin with loss of elasticity.

Hidradenitis —Inflammation of the sweat gland.

Hidradenoma —Adenoma of the sweat gland.

Hidrocystoma —A cystic tumor of a sweat gland.

Hidromeiosis —A decrease in sweating during exposure to heat.

Hidropoiesis —Formation of sweat.

Hidropoietic —Sudorific. Pertaining to hidropoiesis, or forming sweat.

Hidrorrhea —Hyperhidrosis. Excessive sweating.

Hidrosadenitis —Hidradenitis. Inflammation of the sweat glands.

Hidroschesis —Anhidrosis. Suppression of perspiration.

Hidrose —Full of sweat.

Hidrosis —Excessive sweating.

Hidrotic —Pertaining to or causing sweating.

Hieralgia —Pain in the region of the sacrum.

Hierarchy —The classification of persons or things with reference to their importance or value.

Hierolisthesis —Displacement of the sacrum.

Hierophobia —Abnormal fear of the sacred things or the religious persons.

Hierotherapy —Treatment of diseases by religious acts.

High-residue diet —Diet containing roughage, i.e. the indigestible fibers of fruits, vegetables and cereals, which act as a stimulant for the intestinal peristalsis and causes evacuation, hence this type of diet is used in constipation.

Hila —Plural of hilum. Hilum

Hilar —Pertaining to the hilum or hilus.

Hilitis —Inflammation of a hilum, especially of the hilum of the lung.

Hillock —A small eminence or elevation.

Hill's sign —A sign used to determine aortic regurgitation. When the blood pressure in the leg is 20 to 40 mm. Hg. higher than in the arm, this sign is positive and indicates aortic regurgitation.

Hilton's law —A law stating that the trunk of a nerve sends branches not only to a particular muscle but also to the joint moved by that muscle and to the skin overlying the insertion of the muscle.

Hilton's line —A white line at the junction of the skin of perineum and the mucous membrane of the anus.

Hilum —Hilus.

Hilus or hilum —1. A depression on an organ at the entrance or exit of a duct, blood vessels and nerves. 2. The root of the lungs at the level of the 4th and 5th dorsal vertebrae. 3. A depression on the medial border of the kidney through which pass the renal artery & vein and renal nerves, and where the apex of the renal pelvis is situated.

Himantosis —Abnormal lengthening of the uvula.

Hindbrain —Rhombencephalon. The part of the brain developed from the posterior most of the three divisions of the embryonic brain comprising the metencephalon, which gives rise to cerebellum and the pons, and the myelencephalon, which gives rise to the medulla oblongata.

Hindfoot —Posterior portion of the foot consisting of the region of the talus and calcaneous bone.

Hindgut —The embryonic structure from which the alimentary canal from ileum to the rectum develops.

Hind water —Amniotic fluid in the uterus behind the presenting part of the fetus.

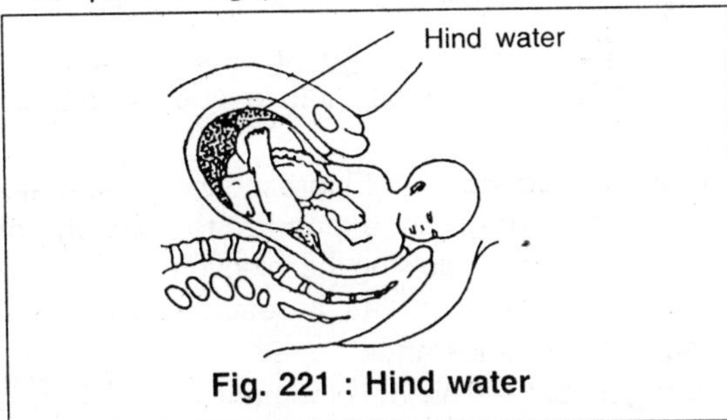

Fig. 221 : Hind water

Hinge joint —See under joint.

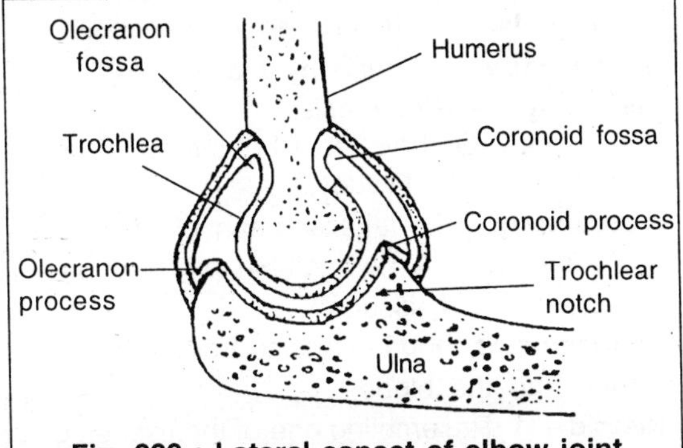

Fig. 222 : Lateral aspect of elbow joint

An example of hinge joint

Hip —Upper part of the thigh formed by pelvic and the femur bones on each side of the body.

Hip joint —A ball and socket joint formed by the head of the femur bone fitting into the acetabulum cavity of the pelvic bone.

Hippocampal —Pertaining to hippocampus.

Hippocampus —An elevation of the floor of the inferior horn of the lateral ventricle of the brain.

Hippocrates —The famous Greek physician 500 years B.C., known as the "Father of medicine" as he discovered medical science.

Hippocratic facies — Appearance of the face in the person dying from long-continued disease or from cholera, in which the cheeks and temples become hollow, eyes sunken and the lips are relaxed.

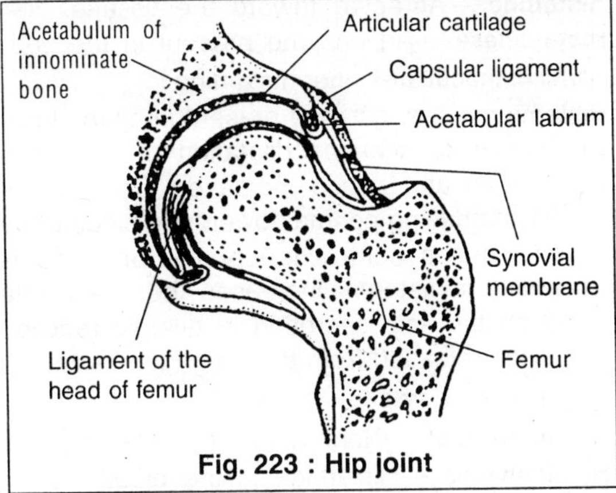

Fig. 223 : Hip joint

Hippocratism —A method of treatment of diseases based on the natural processes, attributed to Hippocrates.

Hippurate —A salt of hippuric acid.

Hippuria —Presence of large amounts of hippuric acid in the urine.

Hippus —Exaggerated rhythmic contraction and dilatation of the pupil or the tremors of the iris.

Hirci —Axillary hair.

Hircismus —Foul smell in the axilla due to bacterial action on the sweat.

Hircus —Singular of hirci.

Hirschberg's reflex — Adduction of foot on irritation of the sole below the great toe.

Hirschsprung's disease — Extremely dilated colon which is usually congenital but may occur in infancy or childhood.

Hirsute —Hairy.

Hirsuties —Hirsutism.

Hirsutism —Excessive growth of hair or the presence of hair in abnormal places, especially in women.

Hirtelous —Having or resembling fine hairs.

Hirudicide —An agent destructive to the leeches.

Hirudin —The active principle secreted by the mucous membrane of the mouth of the leeches, which prevents blood to coagulate.

Hirudiniasis —Condition caused by leeches.

Hirudinization —To render the blood non-coagulable by giving an injection of hirudin or by applying leeches.

Hirudo —A genus of leeches.

Hissing —Hissing noise as made by a snake.

Histaffine —Attracted toward the tissues.

Histaminase —An enzyme present in the body which inactivates the histamine.

Histamine —A substance present in all the body tissues which causes dilatation of the blood capillaries and hence increases their permeability producing edema, lowers the blood pressure, causes contraction of the bronchioles resulting in asthma, increases the heart-rate and gastric acid secretion in allergic reaction or when released from the damaged tissues in injuries or burns.

Histamine fast —Nonreactive to histamine.

Histaminemia —Histamine in the blood.

Histaminia —Shock occurring due to histamine in the body.

Histase —An enzyme which digests the tissue.

Histidine —An amino acid obtained by the hydrolysis of the tissue proteins, which is necessary for the repair and growth of the tissues.

Histidinemia —A hereditary metabolic disease marked by the presence of excessive histidine in the blood and urine due to deficiency of the activity of enzyme histidase.

Histidinuria —Presence of histidine in the urine.

Histio- —A prefix denoting a tissue.

Histioblast —A tissue histiocyte.

Histiocyte —Macrophage. A large phagocytic cell of the reticuloendothelial system.

Histiocytoma —A tumor containing histiocytes.

Histiocytosis —Presence of histiocytes in the blood in large numbers.

Histiogenic —Histogenous. Formed by the tissues.

Histioid —Histoid. Resembling or developed from one of the tissues of the body.

Histioirritative —Irritative to the connective tissue.

Histioma —Histoma. A tumor of the tissue.

Histionic —Developing from a tissue.

Histo- —A prefix indicating pertaining to a tissue.

Histoangic —Histangic. Pertaining to the structure of blood vessels.

Histoblast —A tissue cell.

Histochemistry —Chemistry of the cells and tissues.

Histochromatosis —Any disease of the reticuloendothelial system.

Histoclastic —Decomposing the tissues.

Histocompatibility —The quality of the cells of the donor of being accepted by the blood of the recipient in blood transfusion and transplantation, *i.e.*, the cells of the donor remain alive and are not destroyed by the blood of the recipient.

Histocyte —Histiocyte. A tissue cell.

Histocytosis —The occurrence of histocytes in the blood.

Histodiagnosis —Diagnosis made by microscopic examination of the tissue.

Histodialysis —Histolysis. Disintegration of the tissue.

Histodifferentiation —The process by which a primitive cell develops into a specific mature cell.

Histofluorescence — Fluorescence of the tissues occurring on exposure to sunlight or ultraviolet rays following the injection of a fluorescent substance, or as a result of a natural fluorescing substance.

Histogenesis —The development of the tissues from the undifferentiated cells of the germ layer of the embryo.

Histogenetic —Pertaining to histogenesis.

Histogenous —Formed by the tissues.

Histogeny —Histogenesis.

Histogram —Graphic record of the structure and function of the tissues.

Histography —To take a graph of the tissues.

Histohematin —A hemoglobin pigment present in the various tissues.

Histohematogenous —Arising from both, the tissues and the blood.

Histoid —1. Resembling one of the tissues of the body. 2. Developed from one type of tissue, as fibroma.

Histoincompatibility —The quality of the cells of the donor of being not accepted by the blood of the recipient in blood transfusion and transplantation, *i.e.* the cells of the donor are destroyed by the blood of the recipient.

Histoincompatible —Referring to the tissues that are not suitable for transplantation.

Histokinesis —Movement in the tissues of the body.

Histologic —Histological.

Histological —Pertaining to histology.

Histologist —Specialist in histology.

Histology —Microscopic study of the minute structures of the tissues.

Normal histology —Study of the healthy tissue.

Pathologic histology — Study of the diseased tissue.

Histolysis —Histodialysis. Disintegration of the tissues.

Histolytic —Pertaining to histolysis.

Histoma —Histioma. Any tumor of the tissues.

Histometaplastic —Stimulating metaplasia of the tissue.

Histone —A simple protein derived from the cell nuclei which interferes with blood coagulation.

Histoneurology —Neurohistology.

Histonomy —A law of the development and structure of the tissues of the body.

Histonuria —Presence of histone in the urine.

Histopathogenesis —Abnormal development of the embryo or growth of the tissues.

Histopathological — Pertaining to the histology and pathology.

Histopathology —Histology of the diseased tissues.

Histophysiology —Study of the functions of the cells and tissues.

Histoplasma —A genus of parasitic fungi causing histoplasmosis.

Histoplasmin —An antigen prepared from cultures of the fungus histoplasma capsulatum and used as a skin test for the diagnosis of histoplasmosis.

Histoplasmoma —An infectious granuloma caused by the fungus Histoplasma capsulatum.

Histoplasmosis —The disease caused by the infection of the fungus Histolplasma capsulatum characterized by pneumonia, fever, anemia and enlargement of the liver and spleen.

Historadiography —X-ray examination of the tissues.

Historetention —Retention of the substances in the tissues.

Historrhexis —The breaking up of the tissue.

Histotherapy —Organotherapy. Treatment of diseases by the administration of animal tissues.

Histothrombin —A thrombin derived from the connective tissue.

Histotome —Microtome. An instrument for cutting the tissue in very thin slices for its microscopic examination.

Histotomy —Microtomy. To cut a tissue into very thin slices for its microscopic examination, by histotome.

Histotoxic —Poisonous to a tissue.

Histotribe —An instrument for cutting the tissues to stop bleeding.

Histotroph —The total nutritive substances supplied to the developing embryo in early stages, other than the mother's blood.

Histotrophic —1. Pertaining to histotroph. 2. Stimulating tissue formation.

Histotropic —Having attraction for the tissue cells, as certain parasites, stains or chemical substances.

Histozoic —Living within or on the tissues, *e.g.* certain unicellular parasites.

Histrionic —Dramatic. Appearing suddenly.

HIV —Human immunodeficiency virus. A virus causing AIDS.

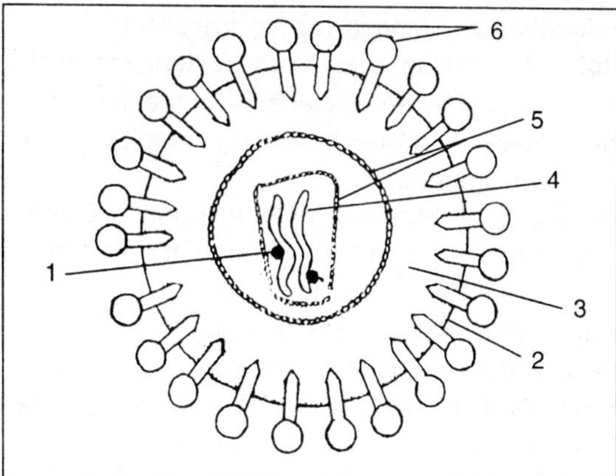

Fig. 224 : HIV Human Immunodeficiency virus causing AIDS

1. Enzyme reverse transcriptase, 2. Outer envelope, 3. Outer shell, 4. Inner shell, 5. Core proteins, 6. Envelope proteins.

Hives —Urticaria.

Hoarse —A rough or harsh voice.

Hoarseness —A roughness or harshness of voice.

Hobnail liver —A liver with irregular or nodular surface.

Hodgkin's disease —A disease of the lymphoid tissue characterized by painless generalized enlargement of the lymph nodes beginning in the cervical region with the enlargement of the liver and spleen.

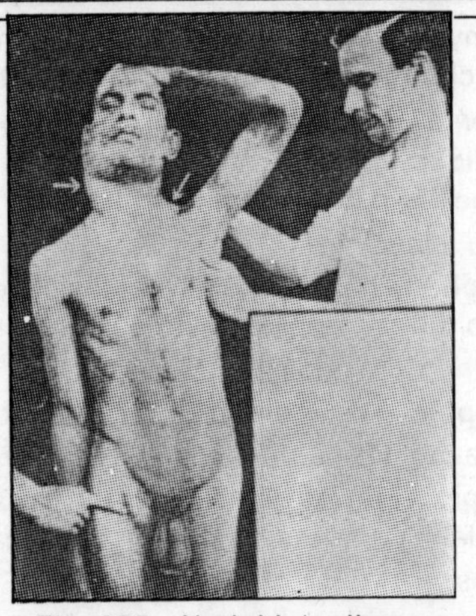

Fig. 225 : Hodgkin's disease

A patient of Hodgkin's disease with enlarged cervical, axillary and inguinal lymph nodes.

Hodgson's disease —Dilatation of the aorta due to formation of the aneurysm.

Hodophobia —Morbid fear of travelling.

Hof —The hollow area in the cytoplasm of the cell in which the nucleus is embedded.

Hol-, Holo- —Prefixes indicating complete, entire or homogenous.

Holandric —Inherited only through the male descent or transmitted through the genes located on the y chromosome.

Holarthritic —Pertaining to holarthritis.

Holarthritis —Inflammation of all the joints.

Holden's line —A wrinkle or furrow at the junction of the thigh and abdomen..

Holding area —An Emergency Department in which patients are kept temporarily before being transferred to an intensive care unit.

Holergasia —A mental disorder affecting the entire personality.

Holergastic —Pertaining to the mental disorder affecting the entire personality.

Holism —The conception that a person works as a whole, *i.e.* the individual parts, as brain and heart etc. do not work independently.

Holistic—Pertaining to holism.

Hollow —Depressed area.

Hollow-back —Lordosis. Anterior posterior curvature of the vertebral column.

Holo- —Prefix meaning whole, complete, entire.

Holoacardius —Two unequal conjoined fetuses, in smaller of which the heart is absent so in it the blood is circulated through the heart of the larger fetus.

Holoblastic —Dividing completely.

Holocephalic —The fetus with the complete head but having deficiencies in other body parts.

Holocord —Pertaining to the entire spinal cord.

Holocrania —Congenital absence of the bones of the vault of the skull.

Holocrine —Having glandular secretion in which the entire secretory cell with its secretory products is cast off.

Holodiastolic —Pertaining to the entire diastole as a murmur occurring during the entire diastole.

Holoencephaly —Complete absence of the cranium and the brain.

Holoendemic —A disease affecting all the population of a particular region.

Holoenzyme —A complete enzyme, i.e., apoenzyme with coenzyme.

Hologastroschisis —A congenital malformation in which there is a cleft in the entire length of the abdomen.

Hologram —An image made by holography in all the three dimensions—length, breadth and height.

Holography —To produce a three dimensional image of an object on the film.

Hologynic —Inherited only through the female descent or transmitted through the genes located on the X chromosome.

Holomastigote —Having flagella over the entire surface.

Holomiantic infection —An infection affecting all the persons of a group when they are exposed to it.

Holophrase —A single word, usually a verb, used to express different meanings.

Holophytic —Obtaining food like the plants, *i.e.* by photosynthesis as do some protozoa.

Holoprosencephaly — Congenital absence of one forebrain lobe caused by an extra chromosome (Trisomy).

Holorachischisis —Fissure of the entire vertebral column with the protrusion of the spinal cord completely.

Holosystolic —Pertaining to the entire systole.

Holotetanus, Holotonia —Muscular spasm of the whole body.

Holotonia— Holotetanus.

Holotonic —Pertaining to or affected by holotonia.

Holotrichous —Covered entirely with cilia, as occurs in certain protozoa and bacteria.

Holozoic —Like an animal in mode of obtaining nourishment.

Homalocephalus — Homalocephalous. The person with a flat skull.

Homaluria —Production and excretion of the urine at the normal and even rate.

Homan's sign —Pain occurring in the calf on dorsiflexion of the toe passively which is an early sign of thrombosis in deep veins of the calf.

Homaxial —Having all axes of the same length, as a sphere.

Homeo- —A prefix indicating resemblance.

Homeometric —Without change in size.

Homeomorphous —Resembling in shape but different in composition.

Homeo-osteoplasty — Grafting of a piece of bone that is like the bone one onto which it is grafted.

Homeopathic —Pertaining to homeopathy.

Homeopathist —The person who practices in homeopathy.

Homeopathy —A system of treatment based on the theory that large dose of a drug which produces symptoms of a disease in healthy person, cures the same symptoms when administered in small amounts.

Homeoplasia —Formation of new tissue similar to that present already in that part of the body.

Homeoplastic —Pertaining to or resembling the structure of the adjacent parts.

Homeostasis —Stability in the normal physiological state.

Homeostatic —Pertaining to homeostasis.

Homeotherapeutic —1. Homeopathic. 2. Pertaining to homeotherapy.

Homeotherapy —Prevention or treatment of a disease with a substance similar to the causative agent of the disease.

Homeotherm —Hematherm. Warm-blooded. An animal that maintains a constant body temperature.

Homeothermal —Pertaining to a warm-blooded organism.

Homeothermic —Pertaining to, or having the characteristic of homeotherm.

Homeotransplant —A tissue taken from one individual to be transplanted into another of the same species.

Homeotransplantation — Transplantation of a tissue from one individual to another of the same species.

Homeotypical —Like normal or usual.

Homergic —Having the same effect as said of two drugs.

Homicidal —Having a tendency of killing.

Homicide —1. Murder. 2. Murderer.

Homo- —Prefix meaning the same.

Homoblastic —Developing from a single type of tissue.

Homocentric —Having the same center.

Homochronous —Occurring at the same time or at the same age in each generation.

Homocladic —Pertaining to an anastomosis between the branches of the same artery.

Homocytotropic —Attracted toward the cells of the same species.

Homodont —Having all the teeth alike in form.

Homodromous —Moving in the same direction.

Homoerotic —Homosexual.

Homoerotism, **Homoeroticism** —Homosexuality.

Homogametic —Producing only one kind of gamete as concerned with the sex chromosomes, as is the X X human female from whom produced all the ova contain X chromosomes.

Homogamy —Similarity of husband and wife in a specific trait.

Homogenate —Material obtained by homogenization.

Homogeneity —The state of being homogenous.

Homogeneous —Of uniform composition.

Homogenesis —Reproduction by the same process in each generation.

Homogenic —Homozygous.

Homogenization —The process of making homogeneous.

Homogenize —To make homogeneous or to form a uniform solution of two immiscible substances.

Homogenized —Made homogeneous.

Homogenizer —Making homogeneous.

Homogentisuria — Alkaptonuria.

Homogeny —Homogenesis.

Homoglandular —Pertaining to the same gland.

Homograft —Allograft. The tissue for transplantation obtained from the individual of the same species.

Homoioplasia —Homeoplasia.

Homoiopodal —Having only one kind of process, as nerve cells.

Homoiotherm —Warm-blooded organism.

Homoiothermal —Homeothermic.

Homoiothermic —Homoiothermal. Pertaining to or characterized by homoiothermy.

Homoiothermy —Maintenance of a constant body temperature in spite of the variation in the environmental temperature, as in birds.

Homokaryon —Indentical multiple nuclei in a common cytoplasm.

Homokaryotic —Having homokaryon.

Homokeratoplasty — Transplantation of a corneal tissue taken from the individual of the same species.

Homolateral —Ipsilateral. Pertaining to, or on the same side.

Homolog —Homologue.

Homologous —Similar in structure and in origin.

Homologue —1. Any homologous organ or part of the body. 2. In chemistry, any member of a series that resembles the other members in action and general structure but is different in composition.

Homology —The state of being homologous.

Homolysin —Isolysin. An agent in the serum destructive to the red blood cells.

Homolysis —Lysis of the red blood cells by hemolysin or Isolysin.

Homomorphic —Denoting two or more structures of similar size and shape.

Homonomous —Pertaining to the homologous serial organs as the fingers and toes.

Homonomy —The condition of being homonomous.

Homonymous —Having the same name.

Homonymous diplopia —A type of diplopia in which the image seen by the right eye is on the right side and the image seen by the left eye is on the left side.

Homophenes —Words in which the visible organs of speech behave the same, e.g., tug, tongue and tuck etc.

Homophil —Pertaining to an antibody which reacts only with a specific antigen.

Homophile —Homosexual.

Homophobe —One who dislikes or fears of homosexuals.

Homophobia —Morbid fear of homosexual.

Homoplastic —1. Pertaining to homoplasty. 2. Having similar organs or parts which resemble one another in structure and function.

Homoplasty —By using the similar tissue, repair by plastic surgery of the damaged tissue.

Homorganic —Produced by the same or homologous organs.

Homosexual —Homophile. Sexually attracted to another person of the same sex.

Homosexuality —Sexual attraction toward the persons of the same sex.

Homostimulant —Stimulating the organ from which an extract is obtained.

Homotherm —Homoiotherm. Warmblooded.

Homothermal —Homoiothermic.

Homotonic — Having a uniform tension.

Homotopic —Occurring at the same place on the body.

Homotransplantation — Allotransplantation.

Homotype —One organ or part similar to another in form and function as one of the two paired organs or parts as the hand.

Homotypic, Homotypical — Of the same type or form as one of the paired organs or parts.

Homozoic —Pertaining to the same animal or the same species of animal.

Homozygosis —The formation of a zygote by the union of gametes having one or more identical alleles.

Homozygosity —The condition of having the identical alleles for producing a specific character.

Homozygote —The person exhibiting homozygosity.

Homozygous —Produced by similar alleles.

Homunculus —A dwarf in whom the parts of the body develop in their normal proportions.

Honey —A sweet, thick, liquid substance produced by the honeybees from the nectar of flowers and is deposited in the honeycomb. It is used as excipient in Ayurvedic therapy, or as a food.

Hook—A curved instrument for holding or traction.

Hooklets —Small hook-like structures encircling the rostellum of the scolex of certain types of tapeworms as Taenia solium, for the attachment to the intestinal wall of the man.

Hookworm —Ancylostoma duodenale, a parasite living in the human intestine causing ancylostomiasis.

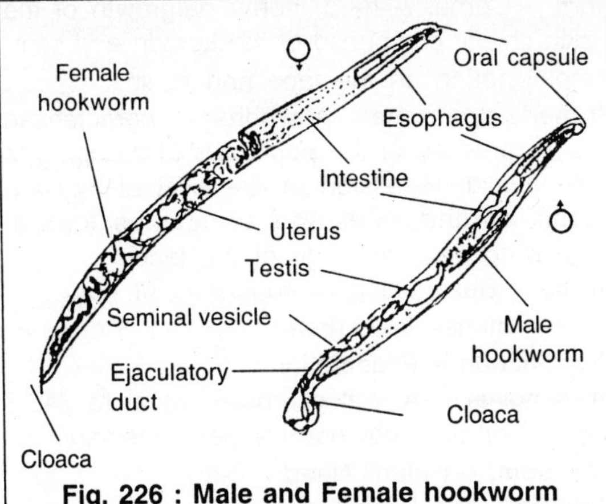

Fig. 226 : Male and Female hookworm

Hoover sign —A sign of unilateral hysterical paralysis. To elicit this sign the patient is made to lie supine and the examiner places a hand under the heel of the paralyzed leg and asks the patient to raise the normal leg against resistance. In hysterical paralysis the examiner will feel pressure against the hand under the paralyzed leg. In true paralysis no pressure will be felt.

Hor. decub —At bed time.

Hordeolum —Style. Inflammation of a sebaceous gland (meibomian or Zeisian) of the eye lid.

Horizon —One of the 23 stages of the development of an embryo beginning from fertilization upto the fetal stage.

Horizontal —A transverse plane of the body that is at right angles to the vertical axis of the body.

Hormesis —The stimulating effect of a small amount of a substance that is toxic in large amount.

Hormion —The junction of the posterior border of the vomer with the sphenoid bone.

Hormonagogue —Increasing the production of a hormone.

Hormonal —Pertaining to or acting as a hormone.

Hormone —A chemical substance produced in a gland, organ or part of the body, which is carried through the blood to another part of the body, stimulating it by chemical action to increase its activity or to increase secretion of another hormone.

Adrenocortical hormone —Hormone produced by the cortex of the adrenal gland.

Adrenocorticotropic hormone —Corticotropin. A hormone secreted by the anterior lobe of the pituitary gland which stimulates the cortex of the adrenal gland.

Adrenomedullary hormones —Two hormones -epinephrine and norepinephrine produced by the medulla of the adrenal gland.

Androgenic hormones — Developing male secondary sexual characteristics, or the masculinizing hormones—the androsterone and testosterone.

Antidiuretic hormone — Vasopressin. A hormone secreted by the posterior lobe of the pituitary gland which decreases the urine secretion and raises the blood pressure by vasopressor effect.

Estrogen hormone —A hormone secreted by the ovarian follicles which stimulates the development and maintenance of female sexual characteristics.

Follicle-stimulating hormone —FSH. A hormone secreted by the anterior lobe of the pituitary gland, which stimulates the growth and maturation of the ovarian follicles in the female and maintains spermatogenesis in the male.

Gonadotropic hormone —A hormone produced by the anterior pituitary gland which affects the gonads.

Growth hormone —A hormone secreted by the anterior lobe of the pituitary gland which stimulates the growth of the body.

Insulin hormone —A hormone secreted by the beta cells of the islets of Langerhans of the pancreas, which is essential for the metabolism of the carbohydrate. Its deficiency causes diabetes mellitus.

Lactogenic hormone — Prolactin.

Luteal hormone — Progesterone.

Luteinizing hormone —A hormone produced by the anterior lobe of the pituitary gland, which working with follicle-stimulating hormone causes maturation and ovulation (rupture) of the ovarian follicle and its transformation into corpus luteum in the female, and in the male it stimulates the development of interstitial cells of the testes and their secretion of testosterone.

Luteotropic hormone — A hormone produced by the anterior lobe of the pituitary gland, which stimulates the secretion of progesterone by the corpus luteum and secretion of milk by the mammary gland.

Melanocyte-stimulating hormone —A hormone produced by the anterior pituitary gland, which causes pigmentation of the skin.

Oxytocin hormone —A hormone produced by the posterior pituitary gland, which causes contraction of the uterus.

Parathyroid hormone — Parathormone. A hormone produced by the parathyroid glands, which regulates the calcium and phosphorus metabolism.

Progesterone hormone —A hormone produced by the corpus luteum, adrenal glands, or placenta, which causes changes in the endometrium of the uterus in the second half of the menstrual cycle in the preparation for the implantation of the fertilized ovum, development of the placenta and mammary glands.

Prolactin hormone —A hormone of the anterior pituitary gland, which stimulates lactation.

Thyrotropic hormone —A hormone produced by the anterior pituitary gland, which controls the development and activity of the thyroid gland.

Thyroxine hormone —An iodine-containing hromone of the thyroid gland, which increases the rate of cell metabolism. Its deficiency causes hypothyroidism.

Vasopressor hormone —A hormone produced by the posterior lobe of the pituitary gland, which causes constriction of the blood vessels and raises the blood pressure.

Hormonic —Hormonal. Pertaining to or acting as a hormone.

Hormonogenesis — Hormonopoiesis. Production of hormones.

Hormonogenic —Hormonopoietic. Producing hormones.

Hormonology —The study of hormones.

Hormonopoiesis — Hormonogenesis.

Hormonopoietic — Hormonogenic.

Hormonoprivia —Partial or total deprivation of the hormones.

Hormonotherapy —Treatment of diseases by hormones.

Hormonotropic —Increasing the production of a hormone.

Horn —Cornu. A hard, horny outgrowth of the skin chiefly composed of the keratin and commonly found on the face and scalp.

Horner's syndrome —A syndrome characterized by contraction of the pupil, partial dropping of the eyelid, recession of the eyeball into the orbit, of one side, and sometimes loss of sweating over one side of the face.

Horny —Resembling or consisting of horn.

Horr —Intense fear; dread.

Horripilation —Piloerection.

Horsepower —A unit of power equal to 745.7 watts, or 550 foot pounds per second.

Hor. som. —Before sleep.

Hospice —An institution where physical, psychological, social and spiritual service is provided to the dying persons and their families by professionals and volunteers.

Hospital —An institution for the treatment of the sick and injured person.

Hospitalism —A tendency to be admitted in a hospital even for a minor ailment, and once admitted, to resist being discharged.

Hospitalist —Hospital based doctor. A doctor who performs duty chiefly within a hospital, e.g., anesthetist, pathologist and radiologist etc.

Hospitalization —The placing of a patient in a hospital for the treatment.

Host —1. The organism from which a parasite obtains its nourishment. 2. The larger and the normal one of the two joined fetuses. 3. The person who receives the graft in transplantation of tissue.

Hostility —Angerness or enemity.

Hot flashes —Hot flushes. The passing of the waves of heat toward the head with the face becoming red followed by sweating, which generally occurs at the menopause.

Hottentotism —Abnormal form of stuttering.

Hourglass contraction — Excessive and irregular contraction of an organ at its center.

Hourglass stomach —The stomach divided by the muscular constriction at its center, which often occurs in gastric ulcer.

House fly —Musca domestica, which transmits

Fig. 227 : House fly

the organisms of many infectious diseases.

Housemaids' knee —A knee with the swelling infront of the patella bone due to trauma resulting from bending the knees and falling on them in prayer.

House officer —A person who passed a medical course and employed by a hospital to provide service to the patients while receiving training in medical practice.

House physician —A physician who treats the patients and takes care of them in a hospital under the direction of a senior physician.

House surgeon —A surgeon who treats the patients by surgical procedures and takes care of them in hospital under the direction of a senior surgeon.

Howell-jolly bodies —They are spherical granules seen in the red blood cells in the slides of stained blood, which are thought to be nuclear particles. They are found in congenital absence of the spleen or following splenectomy; in hemolytic anemia, pernicious anemia, thalassemia and leukemia.

Howship lacunae —Tiny pits, depressions or grooves found in a bone where it is reabsorbed by osteoclasts.

H.S. —House Surgeon.

h.s. —At bedtime.

Hue —Color, tint.

Huhner test —A test for the sterility in male in which an aspiration of the vagina is done within an hour after intercourse without using any contraceptive device, to investigate the motility of the sperms.

Hum —A soft continuous sound, *e.g.* venous hum in which a sound from large veins is heard in certain anemia.

Human —Pertaining to man or mankind.

Human Immunodeficiency virus —HIV — A virus that causes Acquired Immunodeficiency syndrome, i.e. AIDS.

Humectant —A moistening agent.

Humectation —1. Application of moisture in the treatment of diseases. 2. Soaking of a crude drug in water for making an extract.

Humeral —Pertaining to the humerus bone.

Humeroradial —Pertaining to the humerus and the radius bone.

Humeroscapular —Pertaining to the humerus and the scapula bone.

Humeroulnar —Pertaining to the humerus and the ulna bone.

Humerus —The upper bone of the arm extending from the shoulder joint where it articulates with the scapula, to the elbow joint where it articulates with the radius and ulna bones.

Humid —Moist or damp, especially the air.

Humid gangrene —Moist gangrene.

Humidification —To render moist.

Humidifier —An apparatus to increase the humidity of the air in a room.

Humidity —Moisture in the atmosphere.

Humor —Any fluid or semifluid substance present in the body, *e.g.* aqueous humor which is clear, watery fluid in the anterior and posterior chambers of the eye, and vitreous humor which is the semifluid, transparent substance present in the space between lens and the retina.

Humoral—Pertaining to the fluid of the body.

Humoralism, Humorism —An ancient theory that the various types of body fluids determined health and the disease.

Humpback —Kyphosis. Curvature of the vertebral column to such an extent in the front that there appears a protuberance on the back.

Hunchback —A person with the kyphosis that there is a prominent rounded deformity of the back.

Hunger —A strong desire for food or for air (air hunger—dyspnea or breathlessness).

Hunterian chancre —Hard syphilitic chancre. See chancre.

Huntington's chorea —See chorea.

Hutchinson's pupil —Widely dilated pupil in syphilis of the central nervous system.

Hutchinson's teeth —The central permanent upper incisors notched at the cutting edge, found in congenital syphilis.

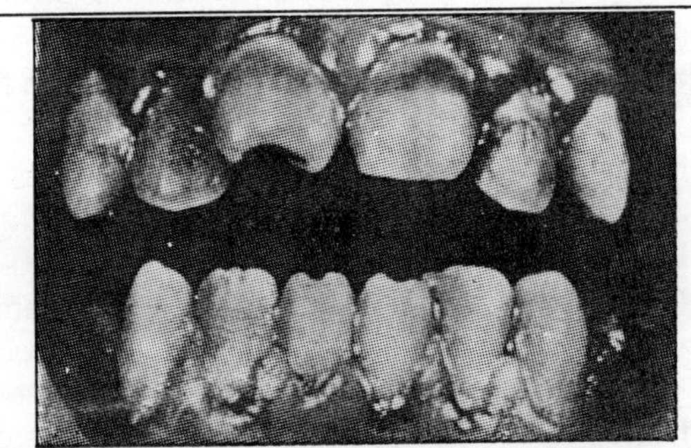

Fig. 228 : Hutchinson's teeth

Hyalin —A clear substance present in the tissues that have undergone amyloid degeneration.

Hyaline —Glassy and translucent.

Hyaline cartilage —The glassy, smooth and translucent cartilage which is true cartilage, covering the articular surfaces of the bones.

Hyaline casts —Pale, glassy and transparent casts found in the urine.

Hyalinization —The conversion of a tissue into a glasslike substance.

Hyalinosis —Hyaline degeneration.

Hyalinuria —Presence of hyaline in the urine.

Hyalitis —Hyaloiditis. Inflammation of the vitreous humor.

Hyalo- —Prefix indicating resemblance to glass.

Hyalocyte —A cell occurring in the peripheral part of the vitreous body.

Hyaloenchondroma — Chondroma of hyaline cartilage.

Hyalogen —A protein substance found in the cartilage and vitreous humor etc. which is convertable into hyaline.

Hyaloid —Glassy.

Hyaloiditis —Hyalitis. Inflammation of the hyaloid membrane of the vitreous humor.

Hyaloid membrane —The membrane enveloping the vitreous humor.

Hyalomere —Pale, homogeneous part of a blood platelet.

Hyalomucoid —The mucoid of the vitreous body.

Hyalonyxis —Puncturing of the vitreous body.

Hyalophagia, **Hyalophagy** —The eating of glass.

Hyalophobia —Morbid fear of touching the glass.

Hyaloplasm —The fluid portion of the cytoplasm of a cell.

Hyaloserositis —Inflammation of a serous membrane with the hyalinization of the serous exudate.

Hyalosis —Pathological changes occurring in the vitreous humor of the eye.

Hyalosome —A round or oval structure resembling the nucleolus of a cell but it stains slightly.

Hyalotome —Hyaloplasm.

Hybaroxia —Oxygen therapy in which oxygen is applied to the entire body in a chamber or room with the pressure greater than 1 atmosphere.

Hybrid —An offspring of the parents of different species.

Hybridism —1. The state of being hybrid. 2. The production of hybrids.

Hybridization —The production of hybrids.

Hybridoma —The cell produced by the fusion of an antigen-producing cell and a multiple myeloma cell.

Hydatid —1. Hydatid cyst formed by the growth of larvae of the tapeworm Echinococcus granulosus, usually in the liver. 2. A small cyst like structure as a remnant of an embryonic structure, e.g, hydatid sessile—the hydatid of Morgagni connected to a testis without stalk, and hydatid stalked—the hydatid of Morgagni connected to a fallopian tube by a stalk.

Hydatid fremitus —A tremulous sensation felt on palpating a hydatid tumor.

Hydatidiform —Resembling a hydatid.

Hydatid mole —A mass of multiple cysts due to cystic degeneration occurring in chorionic villi, resulting in rapid growth of the uterus with hemorrhage.

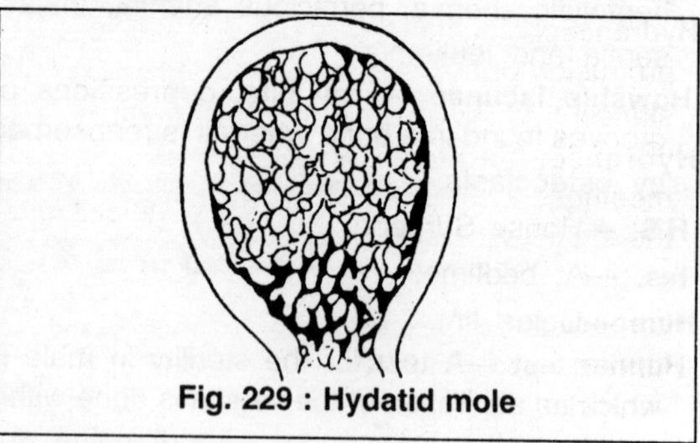

Fig. 229 : Hydatid mole

Hydatidocele —Hydatid cyst of the scrotum or testicle.

Hydatidoma —A tumor consisting of hydatids.

Hydatidosis —A disease of a hydatid.

Hydatidostomy —Incision and drainage of a hydatid cyst by surgery.

Hydatiform —Hydatidiform.

Hydatism —The sound produced by fluid in a cavity.

Hydatoid —1. Watery or resembling water. 2. Pertaining to the aqueous humor.

Hydradenitis —Inflammation of a sweat gland.

Hydradenoma —A tumor of a sweat gland.

Hydraeroperitoneum — Accumulation of fluid and gas in the peritoneal cavity.

Hydragogue —A purgative which causes evacuation of the bowels by producing watery stools, *e.g.* magnesium sulphate.

Hydramnion, Hydramnios —Excess of amniotic fluid in the amniotic cavity causing overdistention of the uterus.

Hydranencephaly —Congenital absence of the cerebral hemispheres, and the cerebrospinal fluid in excess occupies their place. Internal hydrocephalus.

Hydrargyria —Mercury poisoning.

Hydrargyrism —Mercury poisoning.

Hydrargyrum —Mercury.

Hydrarthrodial —Pertaining to hydrarthrosis.

Hydrarthrosis —Accumulation of the effused watery fluid in a joint cavity.

Hydrate —A crystalline substance formed by water combining with various compounds.

Hydrated —Combined with water forming a hydrate.

Hydration —Combination with water.

Hydraulics —The science of fluids.

Hydremia —Excess of water in the blood.

Hydrencephalocele — Hydroencephalocele. The protrusion of the meninges and the brain substance through a defect in the cranium.

Hydrencephalomeningocele—Hernia of the meninges containing cerebrospinal fluid and the brain substance through a defect in the skull.

Hydrencephalus — Hydrocephalus. Accumulation of cerebrospina! fluid in excess in the ventricles of the brain or outside of the brain.

Hydriatic —Hydriatric.

Hydriatric —Pertaining to the treatment of diseases by water as hydriatric institution.

Hydriatrics — Hydrotherapeutics. Application of water in the treatment of diseases.

Hydriatrist —The person who practices in hydrotherapy.

Hydric —Pertaining to hydrogen in chemical combination.

Hydro- —A prefix pertaining to water or hydrogen.

Hydroa —Formation of vesicles with intense itching and burning on the skin surfaces exposed to sunlight.

Hydroadipsia —Absence of thirst of water.

Hydroappendix —Vermiform appendix distended with the watery fluid in it.

Hydrobilirubin — A dark brown-red pigment derived from bilirubin.

Hydrocalycosis —Cystic dilatation of a major renal calix due to obstruction in the infundibulum.

Hydrocarbon —An organic compound made up only of hydrogen and carbon.

Hydrocele —Accumulation of fluid in a saclike cavity especially in the tunica vaginalis of the testis.

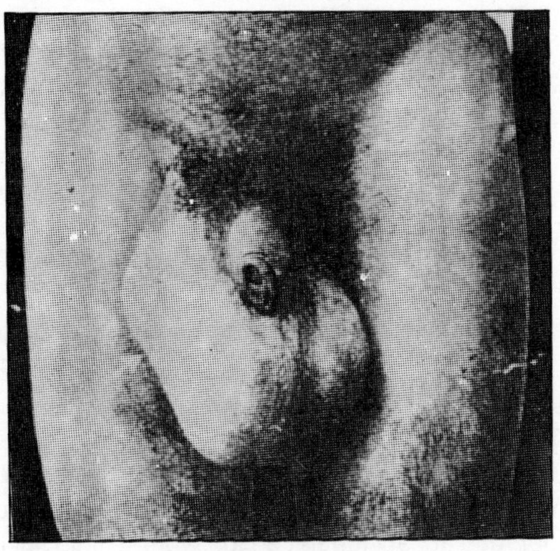

Fig. 230 : Hydrocele

Hydrocelectomy —Excision of a hydrocele.

Hydrocephalic —Pertaining to, or affected with hydrocephalus.

Hydrocephalocele — Hydrencephalocele. Watery hernia of the brain.

Hydrocephaloid —Resembling hydrocephalus.

Hydrocephalus — Dilatation of the cerebral ventricles resulting from obstruction in the pathways of cerebrospinal fluid, accompanied by accumulation of fluid within the skull, characterized by enlargement of the head.

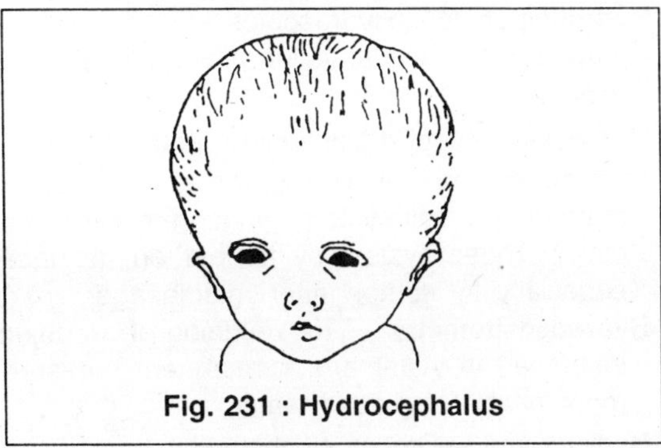

Fig. 231 : Hydrocephalus

Communicating hydrocephalus —Hydrocephalus in which the normal communication between the 4th cerebral ventricle and the subarachnoid space is maintained.

Congenital hydrocephalus —Chronic hydrocephalus occurring in infancy.

External hydrocephalus —Accumulation of fluid in subdural spaces.

Internal hydrocephalus —Accumulation of fluid within the ventricles of the brain.

Noncommunicating hydrocephalus —Hydrocephalus due to obstruction in the flow of the cerebrospinal fluid within the ventricles of the brain.

Normal pressure hydrocephalus — Hydrocephalus with enlarged cerebral ventricles due to inadequacy of the subarachnoid spaces but the pressure of the cerebrospinal fluid remains normal.

Secondary hydrocephalus —Hydrocephalus occurring after an injury or infections such as meningitis, otitis media or syphilis.

Hydrocephaly —Hydrocephalus.

Hydrochlorate —Any salt of hydrochloric acid.

Hydrocholecystitis — Distention of the gallbladder due to accumulation of watery fluid in it.

Hydrocholeresis —Secretion of bile by the liver with increased amount of water resulting in low specific gravity, viscosity and total solid content.

Hydrocholeretic —Pertaining to or stimulating hydrocholeresis.

Hydrocirsocele —Hydrocele combined with varicocele.

Hydrocollidine —A toxic substance from putrefying fish or animal flesh.

Hydrocolloid —A colloidal suspension in which water is the dispersion medium.

Hydrocolpocele —Hydrocolpos.

Hydrocolpos —Accumulation of water fluid in the vagina.

Hydrocyst —A cyst containing watery fluid.

Hydrocystoma —Hidrocystoma. A disease marked by small cysts originating in the sweat gland. These cysts may appear on the face, especially in women after middle age.

Hydrodensitometry —The weighing of an object immersed in water and subsequent measurement of the displaced water.

Hydroderma —Dropsy of the skin.

Hydrodiascope —An apparatus used to treat astigmatism.

Hydrodictiotomy —To correct the displacement of the retina by surgery.

Hydrodipsia —Thirst for water.

Hydrodipsomania —Thirst for water occurring frequently as occasionally found in epilepsy.

Hydrodiuresis —Diuresis affected by water.

Hydrodynamics —The branch of physics concerned with the study of the flow of fluids.

Hydroencephalocele — Hydrencephalocele.

Hydrogel —A gell containing water.

Hydrogen —A colorless, odorless and tasteless gas possessing atomic No. 1.; atomic weight 1.00794 and specific gravity 0.069.

Hydrogenate —To bring about a combination with hydrogen.

Hydrogenated —Combined with hydrogen.

Hydrogenation —The process of changing an unsaturated fat to a solid saturated fat by adding hydrogen.

Hydroglossa —Ranula. A cystic tumor beneath the tongue.

Hydrogymnasium —A tank made for exercise.

Hydrogymnastics —Under water exercises. Exercises performed in the water.

Hydrohematonephrosis — Urine mixed with blood distending the pelvis of the kidney.

Hydrokinetic —Pertaining to the motion of fluids and the forces giving rise to such motion.

Hydrokinetics —Science of fluids in motion.

Hydrolabile —Loosing weight because of loss of fluids, decreased intake of salt, fat or carbohydrate.

Hydrolability —The state in which the fluid in the tissues readily changes in amount.

Hydrolase —An enzyme which causes hydrolysis.

Hydrology —The science of water.

Hydrolysate —The compound produced by hydrolysis, e.g, amino acids which are obtained by hydrolysis of the proteins.

Hydrolysis —A chemical decomposition in which a substance is split into its components by the addition of water.

Hydrolytic —Pertaining to hydrolysis.

Hydrolyze —To perform hydrolysis by adding water to a substance.

Hydromassage —Massage caused by streams of water.

Hydroma —1. Hygroma. 2. Any cyst containing a watery substance.

Hydromeningitis — Inflammation of the meninges with serous effusion.

Hydromeningocele — Protrusion of the meninges of the brain or of the spinal cord in the form of a sac containing fluid, through a defect in the skull or vertebral column.

Hydrometer —Areometer An instrument for measuring the specific gravity or density of a fluid.

Hydrometra —A collection of watery fluid in the uterus.

Hydrometric —Concerning with the measurement of the specific gravity of a fluid with hydrometer.

Hydrometrocolpos —A collection of watery fluid in the uterus and vagina.

Hydrometry —Measurement of the specific gravity of a fluid with hydrometer.

Hydromicrocephaly —The condition in which the head is very small and it contains an increased amount of cerebrospinal fluid.

Hydromphalus —A cystic tumor containing watery fluid at the umbilicus.

Hydromyelia —Hydrorrhachis. Dilatation of the central canal of the spinal cord and accumulation of increased amount of fluid in it.

Hydromyelocele —Protrusion of a sac containing cerebrospinal fluid through a spina bifida (a congenital defect in the walls of the spinal canal caused by lack of union between the vertebrae).

Hydromyelomeningocele —A defect in the vertebral column through which a fluid-filled sac containing spinal cord tissue and the meninges protrudes.

Hydromyoma —Cystic fibroid of the uterus filled with fluid.

Hydroncus —A watery tumor.

Hydronephrosis — Nephrohydrosis. Distension of the renal pelvis and calices with the collection of urine due to obstruction in the ureter and the atrophy of the kidney.

Hydronephrotic —Pertaining to hydronephrosis.

Hydroparasalpinx — Accumulation of serous fluid in the accessory tubes of the fallopian tube.

Hydroparotitis —Inflammation of the parotid gland with the accumulation of fluid in it.

Hydropathic —Pertaining to hydropathy.

Hydropathy —Hydrotherapy. Treatment of diseases by the use of water.

Hydropenia —Deficiency in body water.

Hydropenic —Pertaining to or characterized by hydropenia.

Hydropericarditis — Inflammation of the pericardium with serous effusion.

Hydropericardium — Accumulation of watery fluid in the pericardial cavity without inflammation.

Hydroperinephrosis — Accumulation of the serum in the connective tissue surrounding the kidney.

Hydroperitoneum —Ascites. Accumulation of fluid in the peritoneal cavity.

Hydroperoxide —Hydrogen peroxide.

Hydropexis —The retaining or fixing of water.

Hydrophil —Hydrophile. A substance that absorbs the water of moisture.

Hydrophilia —Hydrophilism. The quality of absorbing water.

Hydrophilic —Hygroscopic. Absorbing readily the water or moisture.

Hydrophilism —Hydrophilia.

Hydrophilous —Hydrophilic. Hygroscopic.

Hydrophobia —Lyssa. 1. Morbid fear of water. 2. Rabies, an infectious disease resulting from the bite of a rabid dog or another animal.

Hydrophobic —Pertaining to hydrophobia or rabies.

Hydrophobophobia —Morbid fear of contracting hydrophobia (rabies).

Hydrophthalmia — Hydrophthalmos.

Hydrophthalmos —Glaucoma. Distention of the eyeball due to accumulation of fluid within it.

Hydrophthalmus — Hydrophthalmos.

Hydrophysometra —Presence of water and gas in the uterus.

Hydropic —Pertaining to or affected with dropsy.

Hydropneumatosis —Presence of fluid and gas in the tissues producing combined edema and emphysema.

Hydropneumogony —To inject air into a joint for the detection of effusion in it.

Hydropneumopericardium —Presence of fluid and gas in the pericardium.

Hydropneumoperitoneum —Presence of fluid and gas in the peritoneal cavity.

Hydropneumothorax—Pneumohydrothorax. Presence of fluid and gas in the pleural cavity.

Hydroposia —Water-drinking.

Hydrops, Hydropsy—Dropsy or edema. Accumulation of excessive amount of serous fluid in the tissues or in a body cavity, *e.g.* edema in the lower part of the body in congestive heart failure, and ascites, *i.e.* the accumulation of serous fluid in the abdominal cavity.

Hydropyonephrosis — Presence of pus and urine in the renal pelvis.

Hydrorchis —Hydrocele.

Hydrorheostat —A rheostat in which resistance to the flow of electric current is provided by water.

Hydrorrhachis —Hydromyelia.

Hydrorrhachitis —Inflammation of the spinal cord with serous effusion.

Hydrorrhea —Copious watery discharge from any part of the body as from the nose.

Hydrorrhea gravidarum — Watery discharge from the vagina during pregnancy.

Hydrosalpinx —Accumulation of watery fluid in the fallopian tube.

Hydrosarca —Anasarca.

Hydrosarcocele —Hydrocele and sarcocele combined.

Hydroscheocele —Scrotal hernia containing fluid.

Hydrosis —Hidrosis.

Hydrosol —A solution in which the dispersion medium is water.

Hydrosphygmograph —A sphygmograph in which the pulse beat is transmitted to the recorder through a column of water.

Hydrostat —An apparatus used for maintaining the water level in a container at a predetermined level.

Hydrostatic —Pertaining to the pressure of liquids in equilibrium.

Hydrostatics —Study of the properties of fluids in equilibrium.

Hydrostomia —Salivation. An excessive secretion of fluids into the mouth.

Hydrosudotherapy —Treatment of the diseases by sweating and by use of water.

Hydrosyringomyelia — Dilatation of the central canal of the spinal cord and an abnormal accumulation of fluid in it with the formation of fluid-filled cavities in the substance of the spinal cord.

Hydrotaxis —The moving toward or away from water, or moisture.

Hydrotherapeutic — Hydriatric.

Hydrotherapeutics — Hydrotherapy.

Hydrotherapist —The person practicing in hydrotherapy.

Hydrotherapy —Treatment of the diseases by use of water.

Hydrothermal —Pertaining to hot water.

Hydrothermic —Pertaining to the effect of heated water.

Hydrothionemia —Presence of hydrogen sulfide in the blood.

Hydrothionuria —Presence of hydrogen sulfide in the urine.

Hydrothorax —The collection of serous fluid in the pleural cavity.

Hydrotis —Serous effusion in the internal ear or middle ear.

Hydrotomy —In histology, the tearing of the tissues by injecting the water.

Hydrotropism —Growth of plants in moisture (positive hydrotropism) or in the absence of moisture (negative hydrotropism).

Hydrotubation —Injection of a liquid medicine or saline solution through the cervix into the uterus and fallopian tubes to dilate or treat the fallopian tubes.

Hydrotympanum —Collection of serous fluid in the middle ear.

Hydroureter —Distention of the ureter with the urine or watery fluid due to obstruction.

Hydroureteronephrosis — Ureterohydronephrosis.

Hydrous —Containing water.

Hydrovarium —Collection of fluid in the ovary.

Hydruria —Excessive secretion and excretion of urine of low specific gravity.

Hygieiology —The science of hygiene and sanitation.

Hygieist —Hygienist.

Hygiene —Study of health and the methods of preserving it.

Hygienic —Pertaining to hygiene. In healthy condition.

Hygienist —A specialist in hygiene.

Hygienization —To establish sanitation and rules of hygiene.

Hygric —Pertaining to moisture.

Hygro- —Prefix indicating relationship to moisture.

Hygroblepharic —Any structure such as the lacrimal gland or agent which moistens the eye.

Hygroma —A sac, cyst or bursa containing fluid.

Hygrometer —An instrument for measuring the amount of moisture in the air.

Hygrometry —Measurement of moisture in the air.

Hygrophobia —Morbid fear of dampness or moisture.

Hygroscopic —Hydrophilous. Absorbing moisture readily.

Hygroscopy —Hygrometry.

Hygrostomia —Salivation. Ptyalism. Excessive flow of saliva.

Hyl-, Hylo- —Prefixes denoting wood or matter.

Hyla —A lateral extension of the cerebral aqueduct.

Hylephobia —Morbid fear of the forests.

Hymen —A fold of mucous membrane which partially or wholly covers the vaginal opening.

- **Annular hymen** —Hymen with a ring-shaped opening in the center.
- **Biforis hymen** —Hymen in which there are two parallel openings with a thick septum between them.
- **Cribriform hymen** — Fenestrated hymen. Hymen with many small perforations.
- **Imperforate hymen, Unruptured hymen** — The hymen without any opening in it.
- **Lunar hymen** —Moon-shaped hymen.
- **Ruptured or perforated hymen** —The hymen which has been torn by coitus, injury or surgery.

Hymenal —Pertaining to the hymen.

Hymenectomy —Excision of the hymen.

Hymenitis —Inflammation of the hymen.

Hymenoid —1. Resembling the hymen. 2. Membranous.

Hymenolepiasis —Infection with the tapeworm of the genus Hymenolepis.

Hymenolepis —The largest genus of tapeworms.

Hymenology —The science of the membranes and their diseases.

Hymenorrhaphy —The suturing of the ruptured hymen to close the vagina partially or completely.

Hymenotome —A knife used to divide the membranes.

Hymenotomy —To incise the hymen.

Hyo- (हॉय-)—Prefix indicating connection with the hyoid bone.

Hyobasioglossus —The part of the hyoglossal muscle attached to the hyoid bone.

Hyoepiglottic, **Hyoepiglottidean** —Pertaining to the hyoid bone and epiglottis.

Hyoepiglottidean — Hyoepiglottic.

Hyoglossal —Pertaining to the hyoid bone and the tongue, or to the hyoglossus muscle.

Hyoglossus —A muscle of the tongue which originates from the body and greater horn of the hyoid bone and inserted into the dorsum of the tongue. It retracts and pulls down the side of the tongue.

Hyoid —U-shaped or horse shoe-shaped.

Hyoid bone —Horse shoe-shaped bone lying at the base of the tongue.

Hyomandibular —Pertaining to both, the hyoid bone and the mandible.

Hyopharyngeus —Middle constrictor muscle of the pharynx.

Hypacousia, Hypacusia, Hypacusis —Impaired hearing.

Hypalbuminemia — Hypoalbuminemia.

Hypalbuminosis —Deficiency of the albumin in the body.

Hypalgesia —Diminished sensitivity to pain.

Hypalgesic, Hypalgetic —Pertaining to hypalgesia or having diminished sensitiveness to pain.

Hypalgia —Hypalgesia.

Hypamnios —Deficiency of amniotic fluid.

Hypanakinesia — Hypanakinesis.

Hypanakinesis —Hypokinesia.

Hypaphrodisia —Decreased sexual desire.

Hyparterial —Beneath an artery.

Hypaxial —Situated below the long axis of the body.

Hypazoturia —Hypoazoturia.

Hypencephalon —The midbrain, pons and medulla oblongata.

Hypengyophobia —Morbid fear of responsibility.

Hyper- —A prefix meaning above, excessive or increased.

Hyperabduction — Superabduction.

Hyperabsorption —Increased absorption of a substance from the intestine.

Hyperacid —Containing acid in excess.

Hyperacidaminuria — Acidaminuria. Presence of amino acids in the urine in excess.

Hyperacidity —Presence of an excess of acid in the stomach.

Hyperactive —Hyperkinetic. Pertaining to or characterized by hyperactivity.

Hyperactivity —Hyperkinesia. Increased or excessive activity.

Hyperacuity —Increased acuity of the special senses such as hearing or sight.

Hyperacusia —Hyperacusis.

Hyperacusis —Oxyacusis. Excessive sensitivity to sound.

Hyperacute —Very acute.

Hyperadenosis — Enlargement of the glands.

Hyperadiposis, Hyperadiposity —Excessive fatness.

Hyperadiposity — Hyperadiposis.

Hyperadrenalcorticalism —Hypercorticoidism.

Hyperadrenalism —Increased secretion from the adrenal gland.

Hyperadrenia — Hyperadrenalism.

Hyperadrenocorticalism — Hyperadrenocorticism. Increased secretion from the cortex of the adrenal gland.

Hyperalbuminemia — Presence of increased amount of albumin in the blood.

Hyperalbuminosis — Hyperalbuminemia.

Hyperaldosteronism — Increased production of aldosterone by the adrenal gland.

Hyperalgesia —Hyperalgia.

Hyperalgesic —Pertaining to hyperalgesia.

Hyperalgia —Hyperalgesia. Increased sensitivity to pain.

Hyperalimentation —1. Ingestion or administration of a greater than the optimal amount of nutritive substances. 2. Administration of all the nutritive substances through intravenous route in very sick patients or in the persons suffering from gastrointestinal disease.

Hyperalkalinity —Excess of alkalinity.

Hyperaminoacidemia — Presence of amino acids in excess in the blood.

Hyperaminoaciduria — Aminoaciduria.

Hyperammonemia —An excess of ammonia in the blood.

Hyperamylasemia —Presence of increased amylase in the blood serum.

Hyperanacinesia, Hyperanacinesis —Hyperanakinesia.

Hyperanakinesia — Hyperanakinesis.

Hyperanakinesis —Excessive function or movement activity of an organ.

Hyperaphia —Tactile hyperesthesia. Excessive sensitiveness to touch.

Hyperaphic —The person having excessive sensitivity to touch.

Hyperarousal —A state of psychological and physiological tension marked by insomnia, fatigue and reduced pain tolerance and the change of personality.

Hyperasthenia —Extreme weakness.

Hyperazotemia —Excess of nitrogenous substances such as urea, in the blood.

Hyperazoturia —Excess of nitrogenous substances in the urine.

Hyperbaric —At a greater weight, pressure or specific gravity than normal.

Hyperbarism —The condition of being exposed to greater pressure or having pressure greater than atmospheric pressure.

Hyperbilirubinemia — Excess of bilirubin in the blood.

Hyperbrachycephaly — Extremely disproportionate shortness of the head, with the cephalic index of over 85.

Hyperbradykininemia — An excess of bradykinin in the blood.

Hyperbradykininism — Bradykininemia associated with the fall in systolic blood pressure on standing, increased diastolic pressure and the heart rate, the skin becomes purple and there are ecchymoses over the legs.

Hyperbulia —Excessive will power.

Hypercalcemia —An excess of calcium in the blood.

Hypercalcinuria — Hypercalciuria.

Hypercalciuria —An excess of calcium in the urine.

Hypercalcuria — Hypercalciuria.

Hypercapnia —An excess of carbon dioxide in the blood.

Hypercarbia —Hypercapnia.

Hypercardia —Hypertrophy of the heart.

Hypercatabolic —Pertaining to hypercatabolism.

Hypercatabolism —Excessive breakdown of a substance or body tissue in metabolism, leading to weight loss and wasting.

Hypercatharsis —Excessive loose motions in response to the administration of cathartics.

Hypercathexis —One's excessive interest in an object, person or planning.

Hypercellularity —Increase in the number of cells present, especially in the bone marrow.

Hypercementosis —Overgrowth of the cement of the tooth roots.

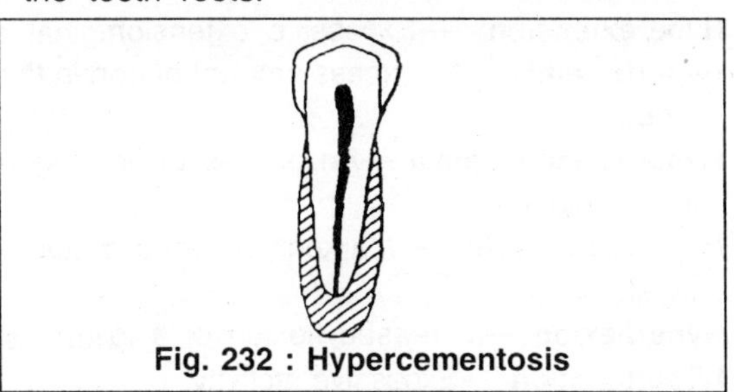

Fig. 232 : Hypercementosis

Hyperchloremia —Excessive amount of chlorides in the blood.

Hyperchlorhydria —An excess of hydrochloric acid in the gastric juice.

Hyperchloridation — Excessive sodium chloride (common salt) intake.

Hyperchloruria —Increased excretion of chlorides in the urine.

Hypercholesteremia — Excess of cholesterol in the blood.

Hypercholesterinemia — Hypercholesteremia.

Hypercholesterolemia — Hypercholesteremia.

Hypercholesterolemic — Marked with hypercholesterolemia.

Hypercholesterolia —An excess of cholesterol in the bile.

Hypercholia —Excessive secretion of bile.

Hyperchromasia —Hyperchromatism.

Hyperchromatic —Marked with excessive pigmentation.

Hyperchromatic cell —A cell staining more densely.

Hyperchromatism — Hyperchromatosis. 1. Excessive pigmentation. 2. Increased staining capacity of any structure.

Hyperchromatopsia — Defective vision in which all the objects appear colored.

Hyperchromatosis — Hyperchromatism.

Hyperchromia — Hyperchromatism.

Hyperchromic —1. Pertaining to excessive pigmentation. 2. Stained densely.

Hyperchylia —Excessive secretion of the gastric juice.

Hyperchylomicronemia — Presence of fat particles (chylomicrons) in the blood in excess.

Hypercinesia —Hyperkinesis.

Hypercinesis —Hyperkinesis.

Hypercoagulability — Increased ability of the blood to coagulate.

Hypercoagulable — Characterized by abnormally increased coagulation of blood.

Hypercorticism —Hyperadrenocorticism. Excessive production of adrenal cortical hormones.

Hypercorticoidism — Hypercorticism.

Hypercortisolism — Hyperadrenocorticalism.

Hypercrinism —The condition produced by excessive activity of any endocrine gland.

Hypercryalgesia — Hypercryesthesia. Excessive sensitivity to cold.

Hypercryesthesia — Hypercryalgesia.

Hypercupremia —An excess of copper in the blood.

Hypercupriuria —An excess of copper in the urine.

Hypercyanosis —Extreme cyanosis.

Hypercyanotic —Marked by extreme cyanosis.

Hypercyesis —Superfetation. Presence of more than one fetus in a uterus.

Hypercythemia —Excessive number of red blood cells in the blood.

Hypercytochromia — Increased intensity of staining of blood cells.

Hypercytosis —Leukocytosis. Abnormal increase in the number of white blood cells in the blood.

Hyperdactylia —State of having supernumerary fingers or toes.

Hyperdactyly —Hyperdactylia.

Hyperdefecation —Excretion of feces occurring frequently but the total weight of stool is not increased above normal. It is not considered as diarrhea.

Hyperdicrotic —Abnormally dicrotic.

Hyperdicrotism —Extreme dicrotism.

Hyperdiploid —Having chromosomes in large number than diploid number.

Hyperdipsia —Intense thirst.

Hyperdistention —Excessive distention.

Hyperdiuresis —Excessive excretion of urine.

Hyperdontial —Presence of more than the normal number of teeth.

Hyperdynamia —Excessive activity of the muscles.

Hypereccrisia, Hypereccrisis —Excretion in an abnormal amount.

Hyperechema —Exaggeration of auditory sensations.

Hyperechoic —1. In ultrasonography, pertaining to the material producing echoes of higher amplitude. 2. Denoting a region in an ultrasound image in which echoes are more stronger than normal.

Hyperekplexia —A hereditary disorder in which protective reactions as shouting, jerking, jumping and falling occur, to unanticipated and threatening stimuli, particularly auditory.

Hyperelastosis —Excessive elasticity.

Hyperemesis —Excessive vomiting.

Hyperemesis gravidarum — Excessive vomiting during pregnancy.

Hyperemetic —Marked by excessive vomiting.

Hyperemia —Congestion or an excess of blood in a part of the body shown by redness of the skin.

Hyperemic —Pertaining to hyperemia.

Hyperemization —To produce hyperemia artificially for treatment purposes.

Hyperemotivity —Excessive response to stimuli.

Hyperencephalus —A fetus with the cranial vault absent and the brain exposed.

Hyperencephaly —A defect in the development of the cranial vault in the fetus causing exposure of the poorly developed brain.

Hypereosinophilia — Marked increase in the number of eosinophils in the blood.

Hyperepinephrinemia — Presence of large amounts of epinephrine in the blood.

Hyperequilibrium — Excessive tendency to vertigo even on turning slightly.

Hypererethism —Excessive irritability.

Hyperergasia —Excessive functional activity.

Hyperergia —1. Hyperergasia. 2. Hyperergy.

Hyperergic —Hypergic. Pertaining to hyperergia.

Hyperergy —Hypersensitivity to allergens, or extreme allergy.

Hypererythrocythemia — Hypercythemia.

Hyperesophoria —Upward and inward deviation of the visual axis.

Hyperesthesia —Algesia. Increased sensitivity to stimulation such as pain or touch, e.g. acoustic or auditory hyperesthesia—increased sensitivity to sound, gustatory hyperesthesia—increased sensitivity to taste, optic hyperesthesia—increased sensitivity to light, tactile hyperesthesia—increased sensitivity to touch.

Hyperesthetic —Pertaining to hyperesthesia.

Hypereuryprosopic — Pertaining to or characterized by a very low and wide face.

Hyperexcitability — Increased excitability.

Hyperexophoria —Upward and outward deviation of the visual axis.

Hyperextension —Excessive extension.

Hyperferremia —An excess amount of iron in the blood.

Hyperfibrinogenemia —An excess of fibrinogen in the blood.

Hyperfibrinolysis — Markedly increased fibrinolysis.

Hyperflexion —Increased flexion of a joint.

Hyperfunction —Excessive activity.

Hypergalactia —Excessive secretion of milk.

Hypergalactosis —Hypergalactia.

Hypergammaglobulinemia — An excess of gamma globulins in the blood.

Hyperganglionosis — Hyperplasia of the neuron.

Hypergenesis —Hyperplasia. Over-production.

Hypergenetic —Pertaining to hypergenesis.

Hypergenitalism —Excessive development of the genital organs.

Hypergeusesthesia, Hypergeusia —Excessive acuteness of the sense of taste.

Hypergia —Diminished sensitivity to allergens.

Hypergic —Hyperergic.

Hyperglandular —Having excessive glandular secretions.

Hyperglobulia —Polycythemia. Excess of red blood cells in the blood.

Hyperglobulinemia — Excessive globulins in the blood.

Hyperglobulism — Hyperglobulia.

Hyperglucagonemia —Excess of glucagon in the blood.

Hyperglycemia —Increase of sugar in the blood as in diabetes.

Hyperglycemic —1. Pertaining to or affected by hyperglycemia. 2. An agent increasing the blood sugar level.

Hyperglyceridemia —An excess of glycerides, especially triglycerides in the blood.

Hyperglycinemia —A congenital metabolic disease with excessive glycine in the blood.

Hyperglycinuria —An excess of glycine in the urine.

Hyperglycogenolysis — Excessive conversion of glycogen into glucose by hydrolysis resulting in excessive glucose in the body.

Hyperglycoplasmia — Excessive sugar in the plasma of blood.

Hyperglycorrhachia — Excess of sugar in the cerebrospinal fluid.

Hyperglycosemia — Hyperglycemia.

Hyperglycosuria —Extreme glycosuria.

Hypergnosia —An exaggerated perception of a thought.

Hypergonadism —Increased functional activity of the sex glands with precocious sexual development.

Hypergonadotropic — Denoting an increased production or excretion of gonadotropic hormones.

Hypergranulosis —Increased thickness of the granular layer of the epidermis in hyperkeratosis.

Hypergynecosmia — Overdevelopment of secondary sexual characters of the mature woman, or their precocious development in the young girl.

Hyperhedonia, Hyperhedonism —1. Excessive pleasure in anything. 2. Abnormal sexual excitement.

Hyperhemoglobinemia — An excess of hemoglobin in the blood.

Hyperheparinemia — Increased amount of heparin in the blood.

Hyperhidrosis —Excessive sweating.

Hyperhydration —Excess of water in the body.

Hyperhydrochloria — Hyperchlorhydria.

Hyperhydrochloridia — Hyperchlorhydria.

Hyperhydropexy, Hyperhydropexis —Increased fixation of water in the tissues.

Hyperimmune —Having a large quantity of specific antibodies in the serum.

Hyperimmunity —A state of high immunity.

Hyperimmunization —To produce a high degree of immunity by giving injections of an antigen repeatedly.

Hyperimmunoglobulinemia —Presence of excessive immunoglobulins in the serum.

Hyperinfection —Infection caused by a very large numbers of micro-organisms.

Hyperinflation —Excess of air in any organ, especially the lungs.

Hyperinosemia —1. Increased coagulability of the blood. 2. Excess of fibrinogen in the blood.

Hyperinosis —Hyperinosemia. Excess of fibrinogen in the blood.

Hyperinsulinemia — Hyperinsulinism.

Hyperinsulinism —Presence of an excess amount of insulin in the blood.

Hyperinvolution — Superinvolution. Reduction in size below normal of uterus after childbirth.

Hyperirritability —Increased irritability to a stimulus.

Hyperisotonic —Hypertonic. One of the two solutions possessing greater osmotic pressure.

Hyperkalemia, Hyperkaliemia —Hyperpotassemia An excess of potassium in the blood.

Hyperkaluresis —Excretion of potassium in the urine in excess.

Hyperkeratinization — Excessive thickening of the epidermis, especially of the palms and soles due to development of keratin.

Hyperkeratomycosis — Hypertrophy of the horny layer of the epidermis due to fungal infection.

Hyperkeratosis—Keratodermia. Overgrowth of the horny layer of the epidermis or of the cornea of the eye.

Hyperketonemia —An excess of ketone bodies in the blood.

Hyperketonuria —An excess of ketone bodies in the urine.

Hyperketosis —Excessive production of ketone bodies in the body.

Hyperkinemia —Abnormally increased cardiac output.

Hyperkinesia, Hyperkinesis —Highly increased physical activity.

Hyperkinetic —Pertaining to or characterized by hyperkinesia.

Hyperlactation —Superlactation. Excessive secretion of milk.

Hyperleukocytosis — Highly increased number of white blood cells in the blood.

Hyperlexia —In mentally retarded children, the presence of relatively advanced reading ability.

Hyperlipemia —Excessive quantity of fat in the blood.

Hyperlipemic —Pertaining to or affected with hyperlipemia.

Hyperlipidemia —A general term used for high concentration of any one or all of the lipids in the plasma.

Hyperlipoidemia — Hyperlipemia.

Hyperlipoproteinemia — An excess or lipoprotein in the blood.

Hyperliposis —Excess of fat in the blood or tissues.

Hyperlithuria —Presence of an excess of lithic (uric) acid in the urine.

Hyperlogia —Excessive talkativeness.

Hyperlordosis —Extreme lordosis.

Hyperlucent —Over translucent.

Hyperlysinemia —Increased amount of lysine in the blood.

Hypermagnesemia —Presence of magnesium in the blood serum in high concentration.

Hypermastia —Excessively enlarged mammary glands or the presence of one or more extra mammary glands.

Hypermature —Overripe.

Hypermegasoma —Giantism. Excessive growth of the body.

Hypermelanosis —Excessive deposition of melanin pigment in the skin, which is generally caused in pregnancy,in chronic renal failure, in chronic pruritus and by ACTH producing tumors, etc.

Hypermenorrhea —Excessive menstrual bleeding.

Hypermetabolism —Increased metabolism.

Hypermetamorphosis — Excessive structural or functional change.

Hypermetaplasia —Excessive transformation from one type of tissue to another as cartilage to bone.

Hypermetria —Excessive muscular activity.

Hypermetrope —Hyperope. Farsighted person.

Hypermetropia —Hyperopia. Farsightedness.

Hypermetropic —Pertaining to farsightedness.

Hypermimia —Speaking accompanied by a great number of gestures.

Hypermnesia —Exaggeration of memory.

Hypermobility —Increased mobility.

Hypermorph —The person whose height in standing is high in proportion to sitting height.

Hypermotility —Abnormally increased motility as peristaltic movements of the intestine.

Hypermyatrophy —Abnormal wasting of a muscle.

Hypermyesthesia —Muscular hyperesthesia.

Hypermyotonia —Excessive muscular tonicity.

Hypermyotrophy —Excessive development of a muscle.

Hypernatremia —Excess of sodium in the blood.

Hyperneocytosis —Excess of number of white blood cells with their immature forms in the blood.

Hypernephroid—Resembling or of the type of the adrenal gland.

Hypernephroma —A tumor of the kidney whose structure resembles to that of adrenal cortex.

Hyperneurotization — Grafting of a motor nerve into a muscle to increase its energy.

Hypernitremia —Excess of nitrogen in the blood.

Hypernoia —Excessive mental activity.

Hypernutrition —Overfeeding.

Hyperonychia —Hypertrophy of the nails.

Hyperope —Hypermetrope. The farsighted person.

Hyperopia —Farsightedness; a visual defect in which the parallel light rays reaching the eye come to a focus behind the retina, resulting in farsightedness.

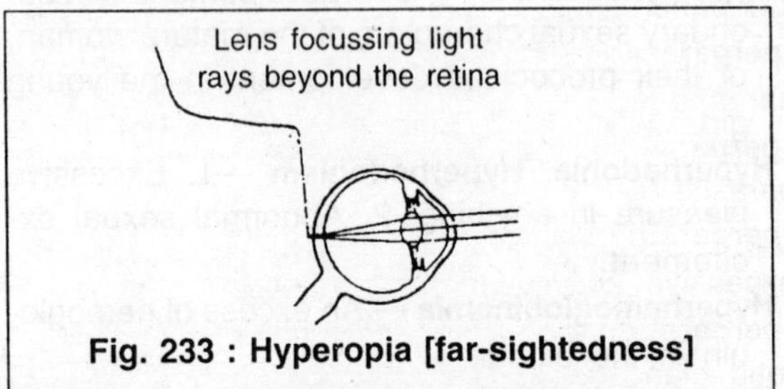

Fig. 233 : Hyperopia [far-sightedness]

Hyperopic —Pertaining to hyperopia.

Hyperorality —A condition in which inappropriate things are placed in the mouth.

Hyperorchidism —Excessive functional activity of the testes.

Hyperorexia —Excessive hunger.

Hyperorthocytosis — Increased white blood cells with normal proportion of their various forms and without immature white blood cells in the blood.

Hyperosmia —Excessive sensitivity to the foul smell.

Hyperosmolality —Increased osmotic concentration of the body fluids.

Hyperosmolarity — Abnormally increased concentration of the osmotically active particles in solution, e.g., in blood.

Hyperosmotic —1. Pertaining to increased osmosis. 2. Having greater osmolality than that of another fluid.

Hyperostosis —Exotosis. Overgrowth of a bone.

Hyperostotic —Pertaining to overgrowth of a bone.

Hyperovaria —Premature sexual development in young girls due to excessive secretion of the sex hormones from the ovaries as a result of their premature development.

Hyperovarianism —Precocious sexual development in young girls owing to excessive secretion of ovarian hormones.

Hyperovulation —The production of a large number of ova, usually in response to the administration of hormones.

Hyperoxaluria —An excess of oxalates in the urine.

Hyperoxemia —Excessive acidity of the blood.

Hyperoxia —Increased oxygen in the blood.

Hyperoxidation —Excessive oxidation.

Hyperoxygenation —The administration of excess of oxygen to a patient of hypoxemia.

Hyperpancreatism — Excessive secretion from the pancreas.

Hyperparasite —A parasite living upon another parasite.

Hyperparasitism —The condition in which a parasite lives in or upon another parasite.

Hyperparathyroidism — The condition due to excessive activity of the parathyroid glands.

Hyperparotidism —Increased activity of the parotid glands.

Hyperpathia —Increased sensitivity to sensory stimuli.

Hyperpepsia —Indigestion due to hyperchlorhydria.

Hyperpepsinia —Excess of pepsin in the gastric secretion.

Hyperperistalsis —Excessive peristaltic movements of the intestine.

Hyperphagia —Excessive eating.

Hyperphalangism —The presence of an extra phalanx on a finger or toe.

Hyperphasia —Intense desire for talking.

Hyperphenylalaninemia —Excess of phenylalanine in the blood.

Hyperphonesis —Intensification of sound on auscultation or percussion.

Hyperphonia —Stuttering or stammering due to irritability of the vocal cords.

Hyperphoria —Anoopsia, anophoria. Turning of one eye upward.

Hyperphosphatasemia — Increased alkaline phosphatase in the blood.

Hyperphosphatasia —A hereditary disorder in which there is increased amount of alkaline phosphatase in the blood serum characterized by excessively large skull, short neck and thorax, lateral bowing of the femurs, and anterior bowing of the tibias, and occasionally mental retardation.

Hyperphosphatemia —An excess of phosphorus in the blood.

Hyperphosphaturia — Presence of phosphates in the urine in excess.

Hyperphospheremia — Hyperphosphatemia. Increased amount of phosphorus compounds in the blood.

Hyperphrenia —Accelerated mental activity.

Hyperpiesia, Hyperpiesis —Extremely high blood pressure.

Hyperpietic —Pertaining to extremely high blood pressure.

Hyperpigmentation — Increased pigmentation.

Hyperpigmented —Marked by hyperpigmentation.

Hyperpituitarism —The condition resulting from increased activity of the anterior lobe of the pituitary gland.

Hyperplasia —Hypergenesis. Overgrowth of an organ or a part of the body due to marked increase in the number of its cells.

Hyperplasmia —1. Excess of plasma in comparism to the blood cells 2. Increase in size of the red blood cells due to absorption of plasma.

Hyperplastic —Pertaining to hyperplaisa.

Hyperploid —The person or cell having an extra chromosome and thus not having the balanced sets of chromosomes.

Hyperploidy —The condition of having one extra chromosome and thus not balanced sets of chromosomes.

Hyperpnea —Abnormal increase in rate and depth of respiration.

Hyperpolarization —An increase in the polarization of membranes of nerves or muscle cells.

Hyperporosis —Excessive formation of callous after a bone fracture.

Hyperposia —Excessive drinking of fluids within a short time.

Hyperpotassemia — Hyperkalemia. An excess of potassium in the blood.

Hyperpragic —Marked with excessive mental activity.

Hyperpraxia —Excessive mental activity and restlessness.

Hyperproinsulinemia — High level of proinsulin or proinsulin-like substance in the blood.

Hyperprolactinemia —An increase of prolactin hormone in the blood.

Hyperproteinemia —An excess of protein in the blood.

Hyperproteinuria —Excess of protein in the urine.

Hyperproteosis —A condition caused by an excess of protein in the diet.

Hyperpselaphesia — Hyperaphia.

Hyperpsychosis —Exaggerated mental activity.

Hyperptyalism —Salivation. Excessive secretion of saliva.

Hyperpyretic —Pertaining to high fever.

Hyperpyrexia —Very high temperature of the body.

Hyperpyrexial —Denoting high body temperature.

Hyperreactive —Denoting increased response to stimuli.

Hyperreflexia —Exaggerated reflex actions.

Hyperreninemia —Excess of renin in the blood.

Hyperresonance —An increased resonance produced on percussion of an area of the body.

Hyperresonant —Over-resonant on percussion.

Hypersalemia —Excess of salt in the blood.

Hypersaline —A saline solution containing salt (sodium chloride) in excess.

Hypersalivation —Plyalism. Excessive secretion of saliva.

Hypersecretion —Excessive secretion.

Hypersegmentation —Excessive division into segments of a tissue or part of the body.

Hypersensibility — Anaphylaxis. Hypersensitivity of the body to a foreign body or drug.

Hypersensitive —Oversensitive.

Hypersensitiveness — Excessive susceptibility or sensitivity to a stimulus.

Hypersensitivity — Hypersensitiveness.

Hypersensitization —To produce increased sensitivity to something.

Hyperserotonemia — Presence of serotonin in the circulating blood in excess.

Hypersexuality —Excessive sexual desire.

Hypersialosis —Ptyalism.

Hyperskeocytosis — Hyperneocytosis.

Hypersomatotropism —The condition characterized by excessive secretion of growth hormone(somatotropin) from the anterior pituitary gland.

Hypersomnia —Excessive sleeping or drowsiness.

Hypersonic —Any speed above the speed of sound.

Hypersphyxia —A condition of high blood pressure and increased circulatory activity.

Hypersplenism—Increased activity of the spleen.

Hypersteatosis —Excessive sebaceous secretion.

Hypersthenia —Great strength or tonicity of the whole body or part of it.

Hypersthenic —Having great strength or tonicity.

Hypersthenuria —Excretion of the urine of high concentration, usually due to dehydration or excess loss of fluids in the sweat.

Hypersusceptibility —The state of being affected greatly.

Hypersystole —Abnormal force or duration of systole.

Hypersystolic —Pertaining to or marked by hypersystole.

Hypertelorism —Increased distance between the two paired organs or parts of the body, *e.g.* the eyes.

Hypertensinogen—A precursor of angiotensin.

Hypertension —High blood pressure in which systolic is above 140 mm. of mercury and diastolic is above 90 mm. of mercury.

Benign hypertension — Chronic mild hypertension.

Essential hypertension, Primary hypertension —Idiopathic hypertension. Hypertension without apparent cause.

Malignant hypertension —Severe hypertension accompanied by the vascular damage with left ventricular hypertrophy, and cerebral hemorrhage may occur which may result in death.

Portal hypertension —High blood pressure caused by obstruction in the portal vein as seen in the cirrhosis of liver.

Postpartum hypertension —High blood pressure occurring immediately following the completion of labor.

Pregnancy-induced hypertension —Increased blood pressure during pregnancy.

Renal hypertension — Hypertension due to a kidney disease produced by the constriction of the renal arteries, which is caused by a substance renin produced in an ischemic kidney.

Hypertensive —Marked by high blood pressure.

Hypertensor —An agent raising the blood pressure.

Hypertestoidism — Hypergonadism in the male, characterized by excessive production of male hormone, testosterone.

Hyperthecosis —Hyperplasia of the theca cells of the graafian follicles in the ovary.

Hyperthelia —The presence of more than two nipples.

Hyperthermalgesia —Extreme sensitiveness to heat.

Hyperthermia —1. Hyperpyrexia or very high fever 2. Treatment of the disease by raising body temperature.

Hyperthermoesthesia — Hyperthermalgesia.

Hyperthrombinemia —An excess of thrombin in the blood.

Hyperthymia —To become very emotional.

Hyperthymic —Pertaining to hyperthymia or hyperthymism.

Hyperthymism —Increased activity of the thymus gland.

Hyperthymization — Hyperthymism.

Hyperthyrea —Hyperthyroidism.

Hyperthyroidism — Hyperactivity of the thyroid gland marked by exophthalmic goiter in which the eyeballs are protruded with the enlargement of thyroid gland.

Fig. 234 : Hyperthyroidism

A case of hyperthyroidism with four cardinal signs—1. Swelling of the thyroid gland, 2. Protrusion of the eyes. 3. Increased pulse rate. 4. Tremor.

Hyperthyrosis — Hyperthyroidism.

Hyperthyroxinemia —An excess of thyroxine in the blood.

Hypertonia —Increased tone of the arteries or muscles.

Hypertonic —1. Having increased tone. 2. The solution having greater osmotic pressure than the solution with which it is compared.

Hypertonicity —The condition of being hypertonic; excessive tonicity.

Hypertonous —Increased tension, as muscular tension in spasm.

Hypertoxicity —The condition of being excessively poisonous.

Hypertrichiasis — Hypertrichosis.

Hypertrichophobia—Fear of hair on the body.

Hypertrichophrydia — Increased thickness of the eyebrows.

Hypertrichosis—Growth of hair in excess.

Hypertriglyceridemia — Excess of triglycerides in the blood.

Hypertroph —A microorganism that requires living cells for supplying enzymes necessary for growth and reproduction.

Hypertrophia —Hypertrophy. Overgrowth of an organ or part of the body due to increase of its cells in size.

Hypertrophic —Pertaining to hypertrophy.

Hypertrophy —Hypertrophia.

Hypertropia —Strabismus in which the visual axis of one eye deviates upwards permanently.

Hyperuricemia —Excess of uric acid in the blood.

Hyperuricemic —Pertaining to or characterized by hyperuricemia.

Hyperuricuria —Excess of uric acid in the urine.

Hypervaccination —Repeated vaccination in an individual already immunized.

Hypervascular —Extremely vascular.

Hyperventilation —Abnormally increased pulmonary ventilation.

Hyperviscosity —Excessive viscosity or adhering property, as of the blood.

Hypervitaminosis —The condition caused by ingestion of one or more vitamins in excess.

Hypervolemia —Increase in the circulating blood volume.

Hypervolemic —Pertaining to or characterized by hypervolemia.

Hypervolia —Increase in water content or volume of a compartment as that of a cell.

Hypesthesia —Hypoesthesia.

Hypha —One of the filaments composing the mycelium of a fungus.

Hyphedonia —Diminution of pleasure in the acts from which one should normally gain pleasure.

Hyphema —Hemorrhage in the anterior chamber of the eye.

Hyphemia —Hypovoiemia. Oligemia or deficiency of blood.

Hyphidrosis —Diminished secretion of sweat.

Hypnagogic —1. Hypnotic. Producing sleep. 2. Pertaining to the dreams occurring just before sleep.

Hypnagogic state —A state between sleeping and awaking.

Hypnagogue —Hypnotic. Pertaining to sleep or drowsiness.

Hypnalgia —Pain experienced during sleep.

Hypnic —Hypnotic.

Hypno - —A prefix meaning sleep or hypnosis.

Hypnoanalysis —A method of psychotherapy in which combined psychoanalysis and hypnosis is applied.

Hypnoanalytic —Pertaining to hypnoanalysis.

Hypnoanesthesia —To produce anesthesia by hypnosis.

Hypnodontics —The treatment of a dental disease by hypnosis.

Hypnogenesis —The induction of sleep or to hypnotize.

Hypnogenetic —Hypnotic.

Hypnogenic —Hypnotic.

Hypnogenous —Pertaining to hypnogenesis or an agent that induces hypnosis.

Hypnoid —Resembling hypnosis.

Hypnoidal —Pertaining to a condition between sleep and waking, resembling sleep.

Hypnoidization —To induce hypnosis.

Hypnolepsy —Narcolepsy. Recurrent attacks of drowsiness and sleep.

Hypnology —Scientific study of sleep.

Hypnonarcosis —Combination of hypnosis and hypoacusia narcosis.

Hypnophobia —Morbid fear of sleep.

Hypnopompic —Pertaining to the dreams or visual images persisting after sleep before complete awakening.

Hypnosis —Artificial sleep, a subconscious condition.

Hypnosophy —The study of sleep.

Hypnotherapy —Treatment of diseases by inducing sleep.

Hypnotic —1. Inducing sleep. 2. Pertaining to sleep.

Hypnotics —The drugs causing unconsciousness induce sleep. They include sedatives, analgesics, anesthetics and intoxicants.

Hypnotism —The act of inducing hypnosis.

Hypnotist —The person who practices hypnotism.

Hypnotize —To put into a condition of hypnosis or to induce sleep artificially.

Hypo-, Hyp- — Prefixes indicating less than, below or under.

Hypoacidity —Deficiency of hydrochloric acid in the stomach.

Hypoacusis, Hypoacusia —Slightly diminished sensitivity to sound stimuli.

Hypoadenia —Decreased activity of the glands.

Hypoadrenalism —Deficiency of the adrenal gland activity.

Hypoadrenocorticism — Decreased activity of the adrenal cortex.

Hypoaffectivity —Abnormally decreased sensitivity to emotional stimuli.

Hypoalbuminemia — Decreased albumin in the blood.

Hypoaldosteronism — Deficiency of aldosterone in the body associated with low blood pressure and increased salt excretion.

Hypoalgesia —Hypalgesia.

Hypoalimentation — Insufficient nourishment.

Hypoallergenic —Diminished potential for causing an allergic reaction.

Hypoazoturia —Diminished urea in the urine.

Hypobaric —Characterized by less than normal atmospheric pressure or weight.

Hypobarism —Hypobaria. The condition produced when the atmospheric pressure becomes lower than that of the pressure within the body tissues.

Hypobaropathy —The diseases caused by diminished air pressure at high altitudes as mountain sickness or aviator's sickness, etc.

Hypoblast —Entoderm.

Hypoblastic —Pertaining to the entoderm.

Hypobulia —Impairment of the will power.

Hypocalcemia —Decrease of calcium in the blood below normal.

Hypocalcification —Deficient calcification of the bones or teeth.

Hypocalciuria —Diminished calcium in the urine.

Hypocapnia —Deficiency of carbon dioxide in the blood.

Hypocarbia —Hypocapnia.

Hypocellularity —Decreased cells in a tissue.

Hypochloremia —Deficiency of chloride in the blood.

Hypochloremic —Pertaining to or characterized by hypochloremia.

Hypochlorhydria —Deficiency of hydrochloric acid in the gastric juice.

Hypochlorization —Reduction of sodium chloride in the diet in treating hypertension and certain renal diseases.

Hypochloruria —Diminished chlorides in the urine.

Hypocholesteremia — Decreased blood cholesterol.

Hypocholesterinemia — Hypocholesterolemia.

Hypocholesterolemia — Hypocholesteremia.

Hypochondria — Hypochondriasis.

Hypochondriac —1. Pertaining to the region of the hypochondrium or to hypochondriasis. 2. The person affected with hypochondriasis.

Hypochondriacal —Pertaining to or suffering from hypochondriasis.

Hypochondriac region — Hypochondrium.

Hypochondriasis —Excessive anxiety about one's health and fear of disease and having false belief of suffering from some disease.

Hypochondrium —Upper part of the abdomen on both sides of the epigastrium below the lower ribs.

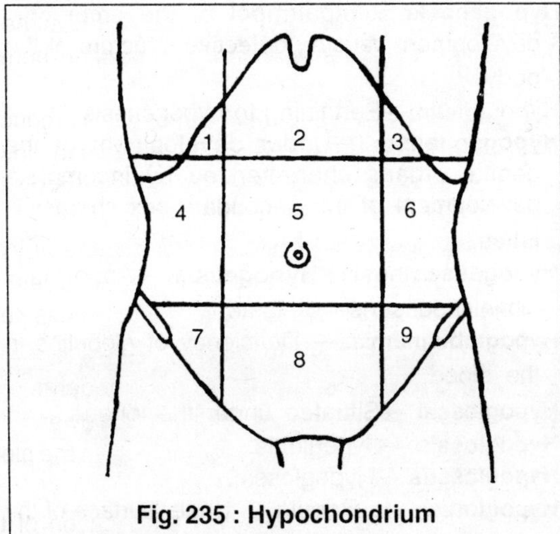

Fig. 235 : Hypochondrium

The abdomen is divided into nine regions by two horizontal and two vertical lines. Hypochondrium consists of two regions—right and left hypochondriac regions, in the upper part of the abdomen, below the ribs.

Hypochondroplasia — Deficient development of the cartilages.

Hypochordal —On the ventral side of the spinal cord.

Hypochromasia —Deficiency of hemoglobin in the red blood cells.

Hypochromatic —Hypochromic.

Hypochromatism —1. Abnormally decreased pigmentation. 2. Deficiency of chromatin in a cell nucleus.

Hypochromatosis — Chromatolysis. Gradual disappearance of the chromatin or nucleus in a cell.

Hypochromia —Hypochromasia.

Hypochromic —Pertaining to or characterized by the deficiency of hemoglobin in the red blood cells.

Hypochrosis —Hypochromia.

Hypochylia —Deficiency of chyle.

Hypocinesia —Hypocinesis. Hypokinesia. Diminished power of movement.

Hypocomplementemia — Diminution of complement in the blood.

Hypocondylar —Below a condyle.

Hypocorticism — Hypoadrenocorticism. Deficiency of the hormone of cortex of the adrenal gland.

Hypocorticoidism — Hypocorticism.

Hypocrinism —The condition produced by the deficient secretion of a gland, especially an endocrine gland.

Hypocupremia —Deficiency of copper in the blood.

Hypocyclosis —Insufficient accommodation in the eye which may be due to weakness of the ciliary muscle or due to lack of elasticity in the crystalline lens.

Hypocystotomy —To open the urinary bladder through the perineum.

Hypocythemia —Deficiency in the number of red blood cells in the blood.

Hypocytosis —A decrease in the number of blood cells.

Hypodactylia —Having decreased number of fingers or toes.

Hypodactyly —The presence of less than the normal number of fingers or toes.

Hypoderm —Subcutaneous tissue.
Hypodermatic —Hypodermic.
Hypodermatoclysis — Hypodermoclysis.
Hypodermatomy —To incise a subcutaneous structure,as a muscle or tendon.
Hypodermiasis —Skin eruption caused by the infection with hypoderma fly.
Hypodermic —Inserted under the skin as a hypodermic injection.
Hypodermis —Subcutaneous tissue.
Hypodermoclysis —The injection of fluids, *e.g.*, saline solution into the subcutaneous tissues.
Hypodiploid—Having a chromosome number less than the diploid number.
Hypodipsia —Diminished thirst abnormally.
Hypodontia—Diminished development or absence of teeth.

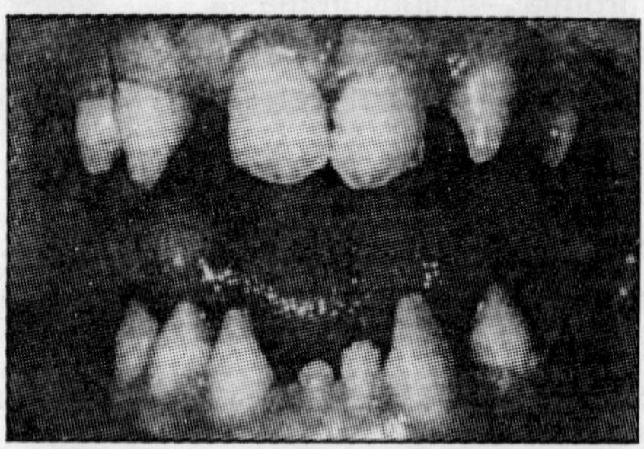

Fig. 236 : Hypodontia

Hypodynamia —Abnormally diminished muscular power.
Hypodynamic —Having diminished energy.
Hypoeccrisia—Diminished excretion of the waste materials.
Hypoeccrisis —Hypoeccrisia.
Hypoeccritic —1. Diminishing the normal excretion. 2. Pertaining to insufficient or defective excretion.
Hypoechoic —A region in an ultrasound image in which the echoes are weaker than normal.
Hypoendocrinism — Insufficiency of the activity of one or more endocrine glands.
Hypoendocrisia — Hypoendocrinism. Diminished secretion of an endocrine gland.
Hypoeosinophilia — Decreased number of eosinophil cells in the blood.
Hypoepinephria —Diminished secretion of epinephrine.
Hypoergasia —Diminution of functional activity.
Hypoergia —Diminished sensitivity to any stimulus.
Hypoergic —Pertaining to the diminished sensitivity to any stimulus.
Hypoergy —Hypoergia.
Hypoesophoria —Downward and inward deviation of the eye.
Hypoesthesia —Diminished sensitivity to touch.
Hypoexophoria —Downward and outward deviation of the eye.
Hypoferremia —Deficiency of iron in the blood.
Hypofertility —Diminished fertility.
Hypofibrinogenemia — Diminished fibrinogen in the blood.
Hypofunction —,Diminished function.
Hypogalactia —Deficiency in milk production.
Hypogalactous —Producing or secreting the milk in less amount than normal.
Hypogammaglobulinemia —Deficiency of gamma globulins in the blood which may be acquired or congenital.
Hypoganglionosis —The reduction occurring in the number of ganglionic nerve cells.
Hypogastric —Pertaining to the hypogastrium.
Hypogastrium —Lower middle part of the abdomen or the part of the abdomen below the umbilicus and between the right and left iliac regions. See. Fig. 235 (8)
Hypogastrocele —Hernia present in the hypogastrium.
Hypogastropagus —Two fetuses joined at the hypogastrium.
Hypogastroschisis — Congenital fissure of the hypogastrium.
Hypogenesis —Impairment of the embryonic development causing defective structure of the body.
Hypogenetic —Pertaining to hypogenesis.
Hypogenitalism —Under development of the genital organs characterized by incomplete development of the secondary sex characteristics.
Hypogeusesthesia, Hypogeusia —Abnormally diminished sense of taste.
Hypoglobulinemia — Deficiency of globulins in the blood.
Hypoglossal —Situated under the tongue.
Hypoglossis —Hypoglottis.
Hypoglossus —Hypoglossal.
Hypoglottis —1. Ranula. 2. Under surface of the tongue.

Hypoglucagonemia — Deficiency of glucagon in the blood.

Hypoglycemia —Deficiency of glucose or sugar in the blood.

Hypoglycemic —Pertaining to, affected by or causing hypoglycemia.

Hypoglycogenolysis — Diminished conversion of glycogen into glucose by hydrolysis in the body.

Hypoglycorrhachia — Deficiency of glucose in the cerebrospinal fluid as usually occurs in meningitis.

Hypognathous —Having the lower jaw smaller than the upper one.

Hypognathus—Conjoined twins of unequal size in which smaller twin is attached to the mandible of the larger one.

Hypogonadism —Decreased functional activity of the sex glands resulting in impairment of the sexual development.

Hypogonadotropic — Pertaining to or caused by the deficiency of gonadotropin.

Hypogranulocytosis — Granulocytopenia.

Hypohepatica —Deficient liver function.

Hypohidrosis —Hyphidrosis. Excessively diminished secretion of the sweat.

Hypohydremia —Deficiency in fluid in the blood.

Hypohydrochloria — Hypochlorhydria.

Hypoinsulinism —Diabetes mellitus. Deficient secretion of insulin.

Hypoisotonic —Hypotonic.

Hypokalemia —Hypopotassemia. Deficiency of potassium in the blood.

Hypokalemic —Pertaining to the deficiency of potassium in the blood.

Hypokinemia —Decrease in circulatory rate and cardiac output below normal.

Hypokinesia —Abnormally diminished motor reaction to a stimulus.

Hypokinesis —Hypokinesia. Hypomotility or slow movement.

Hypokinetic —Pertaining to hypokinesia.

Hypolemmal —Situated below a membrane.

Hypoleydigism —Excessively diminished secretion of androgens by the interstitial cells of the testes.

Hypolipidemic —Decreasing the lipid concentration of the blood.

Hypolipoproteinemia— Decrease in the amount of lipoprotein in the blood serum.

Hypoliposis —Deficiency of fat in the tissues.

Hypologia —Inability to speak adequately.

Hypolymphemia —Decreased number of lymphocytes in the blood without change in number of white blood cells.

Hypomagnesemia —Deficiency of magnesium in the blood.

Hypomania —Mild mania with slight change in behavior.

Hypomastia —Hypomazia. Abnormally smallness of the mammary glands.

Hypomazia —Hypomastia.

Hypomelancholia —Mild mental depression.

Hypomelanosis —Leukoderma.

Hypomenorrhea — Oligomenorrhea. Diminished menstrual flow.

Hypometabolism —Decreased metabolism.

Hypometria —Shortness of movements on reaching the destination.

Hypometropia —Myopia or shortsightedness.

Hypomnesia, Hypomnesis —Diminution of memory.

Hypomorph—The person possessing short legs in proportion to the length of trunk.

Hypomotility —Hypokinesia.

Hypomyelination, **Hypomyelinogenesis** —Defective formation of myelin in the spinal cord and brain.

Hypomyotonia —Deficiency in muscular tone.

Hypomyxia —Diminished secretion of mucus.

Hyponanosoma —Extreme dwarfism.

Hyponatremia —Deficiency of sodium in the blood; salt depletion.

Hyponeocytosis —Decreased number of white blood cells with the presence of immature white blood cells in the blood.

Hyponeuria —Nervous weakness.

Hyponoia —Sluggish mental activity.

Hyponychial —Pertaining to hyponychium or nail-bed.

Hyponychium —The nail-bed. The portion of a finger or toe covered by the nail.

Hyponychon —Hemorrhage beneath the nail.

Hypo-orthocytosis — Leukopenia with the normal proportion of various types of white blood cells.

Hypo-osmolality —Decrease in the osmotic concentration of the body fluids.

Hypo-ovarianism — Inadequate ovarian function

resulting in decreased secretion of ovarian hormones.

Hypopancreatism — Diminished activity of the pancreas.

Hypopancreorrhea — Diminution in discharge of pancreatic digestive enzyme secretions.

Hypoparathyreosis — Hypoparathyroidism.

Hypoparathyroidism —The condition produced by excessivley diminished functional activity due to diminished secretion of parathyroid hormones of the parathyroid glands.

Hypopepsia —Impaired digestion due to deficiency of the enzyme pepsin.

Hypopepsinia —Deficiency of the enzyme pepsin in the gastric juice.

Hypoperfusion —Decreased flow of blood through an organ.

Hypoperistalsis —Diminished peristaltic movements.

Hypophalangism —Absence of a phalanx on a finger or toe.

Hypopharynx —Laryngopharynx. The lower most portion of the pharynx which is continuous with the larynx.

Hypophonesis —A diminished sound in auscultation or percussion.

Hypophonia —Abnormally weak voice due to incoordination of the vocal muscles.

Hypophoria —Downward deviation of the visual axis of one eye.

Hypophosphatasemia — Hypophosphatasia.

Hypophosphatasia —A congenital metabolic disease in which there is deficiency of alkaline phosphatase in the serum of blood and excretion of phosphoethanolamine in the urine, manifested by rickets, defective tooth development and osteomalacia.

Hypophosphatemia — Deficiency of phosphates in the blood.

Hypophosphaturia — Decreased excretion of phosphate in the urine.

Hypophrasia —Slowness or lack of speech associated with a psychosis or brain injury.

Hypophrenia —Mental deficiency.

Hypophrenic —1. The person affected with mental deficiency. 2. Below the diaphragm.

Hypophyseal —Hypophysial Pertaining to the pituitary gland.

Hypophysectomize —To remove the pituitary gland by surgery.

Hypophysectomy —Excision of the pituitary gland.

Hypophyseoportal — Pertaining to the portal system of the pituitary gland.

Hypophysial —Hypophyseal.

Hypophysin — An aqueous extract of the posterior pituitary gland.

Hypophyseoprivic — Hypophysioprivic. The pituitary gland deficient in hormonal secretion.

Hypophysiotropic — Hypophyseotropic. Denoting a hormone that stimulates the pituitary gland.

Hypophysis —Hypophysis cerebri. The pituitary gland, an endocrine gland situated in the sella turcica of the sphenoid bone consisting of two portions—anterior and posterior lobe, attached to the hypothalamus of the brain by hypophyseal stalk.

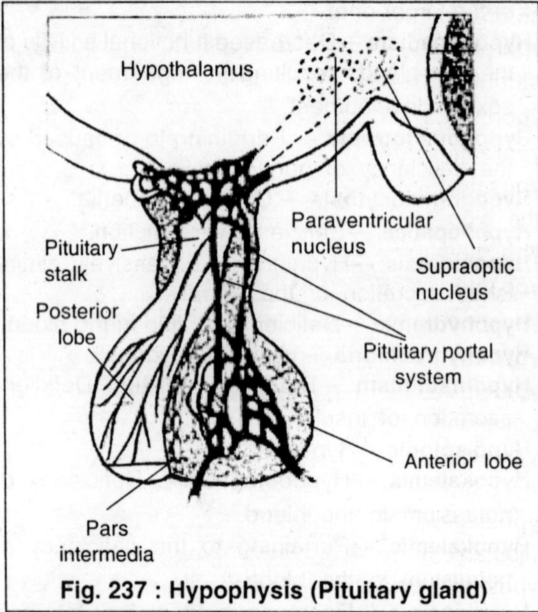

Fig. 237 : Hypophysis (Pituitary gland)

Hypophysitis —Inflammation of the pituitary gland.

Hypopiesis —Abnormally low blood pressure.

Hypopigmentation — Diminished pigmentation.

Hypopinealism —Diminished activity of the pineal gland.

Hypopituitarism —The condition resulting from diminution in the secretion of hormones from the pituitary gland, especially from the anterior lobe.

Hypoplasia —Underdevelopment of the tissue.

Hypoplastic —Pertaining to or characterized by hypoplasia.

Hypopnea —Abnormally decrease in rate and depth of respiration.

Hypoporosis —Deficient callus formation at the site of a bone fracture.

Hypoposia —Diminished intake of fluids.

Hypopotassemia — Hypokalemia.

Hypopraxia —Abnormally diminished activity.

Hypoproteinemia —Deficiency of protein in the blood.

Hypoproteinosis —Condition of deficiency of proteins in the body or diet.

Hypoprothrombinemia — Deficiency of prothrombin in the blood.

Hypopselaphesia —Diminished sensibility to touch.

Hypoptyalism —Hyposalivation. Diminished secretion of saliva.

Hypopyon —Accumulation of pus in the anterior chamber of the eye.

Hyporeactive —Showing diminished response to stimuli.

Hyporeflexia —Diminution of reflex actions.

Hyporeninemia — Deficiency of renin in the blood.

Hyposalemia —Deficiency of sodium chloride in the blood.

Hyposalivation — Hypoptyalism.

Hyposcleral —Beneath the sclera of the eye.

Hyposecretion —Diminished secretion.

Hyposensitive —Having diminished sensitivity.

Hyposensitivity —The condition of being hyposensitive.

Hyposensitization — Production of hyposensitiveness.

Hyposialadenitis — Inflammation of the submandibular salivary gland.

Hyposkeocytosis — Hyponeocytosis.

Hyposmia —Diminished sensibility of smell.

Hyposmolarity —Abnormally decreased osmolar concentration, especially of the blood or urine.

Hyposmosis —A reduction in the rapidity of osmosis.

Hyposmotic — Having an osmolality less than that of another fluid.

Hyposomatotropism —The condition characterized by deficient secretion of growth hormone (somatotropin) from the anterior pituitary gland.

Hyposomia—Inadequate development of the body.

Hyposomnia —Insomnia.

Hyposomniac —The person suffering from insomnia.

Hypospadia, Hypospadias —Opening of the urethra upon the under surface of the penis in male and into the vagina in female congenitally.

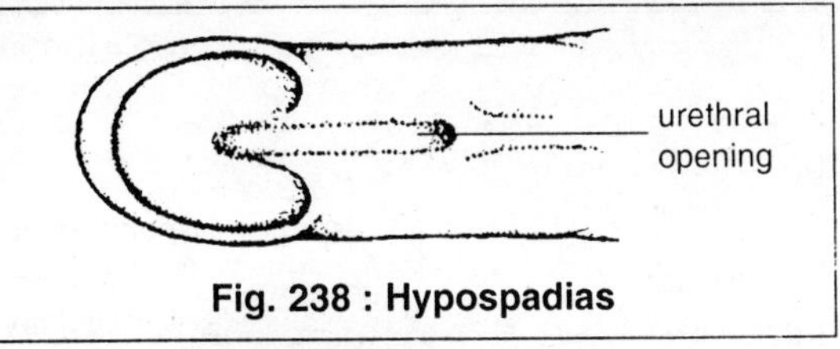

Fig. 238 : Hypospadias

Hypospadiac —Pertaining to or affected with hypospadia or hypospadias.

Hyposphresia —Hyposmia.

Hyposplenism —Diminished functioning of the spleen.

Hypostasis —Diminished blood circulation in a dependent part of the body or an organ.

Hypostatic —Pertaining to hypostasis.

Hyposthenia —Weakness.

Hyposthenic —Enfeebled or weakened person.

Hyposthenuria —Excretion of urine of low specific gravity.

Hypostomia —Congenital defect in which the mouth is a small vertical slit.

Hypostosis —Diminished development of bone.

Hypostypsis —Slight astringency.

Hypostyptic —Slight astringent.

Hyposynergia —Poor coordination.

Hyposystole —A weak or incomplete cardiac systole.

Hypotelorism —Abnormally decreased distance between two organs such as eyes.

Hypotension —1. Decreased systolic and diastolic blood pressure to below normal. 2. Diminished tone or tension.

Hypotension orthostatic —Hypotension occurring upon suddenly standing or when standing in a fixed position.

Hypotensive —Suffering from low blood pressure or an agent lowering the blood pressure.

Hypotensor —A hypotensive agent.

Hypothalamic —Pertaining to hypothalamus.

Hypothalamohypophysial — Pertaining to both, the hypothalamus and the hypophysis (pituitary gland).

Hypothalamus —A part of the diencephalon below the thalamus forming the floor and lateral wall of the third ventricle including optic chiasma, tuber cinereum, infundibulum, mamillary bodies and pituitary gland.

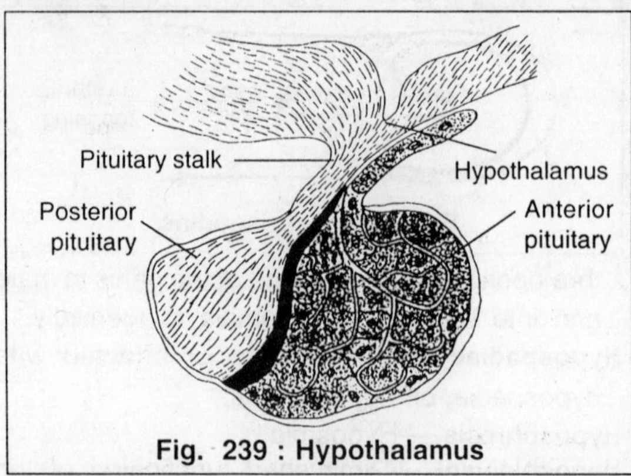

Fig. 239 : Hypothalamus

Hypothenar —A fleshy eminence on the palm on the side of ulna bone, below the little finger.

Hypothermal —Below normal temperature.

Hypothermia —Body temperature below normal due to exposure to cold or induced artificially to alleviate hyperpyrexia, to reduce blood pressure or to reduce oxygen need during surgery.

Hypothesis —Supposition or assumption.

Hypothrombinemia — Deficiency of thrombin in the blood.

Hypothromboplastinemia — Deficiency of thromboplastin in the blood.

Hypothymia —Diminution of emotional reaction to the stimuli.

Hypothymic —Pertaining to or characterized by hypothymia.

Hypothymism —Diminished activity of the thymus gland.

Hypothyroid —The thyroid gland marked by deficient activity.

Hypothyroidism —Myxedema. Deficiency of the activity of thyroid gland resulting in decreased basal metabolic rate, depressed all functions and characterized by obesity owing to weight gain, dry skin and hair, puffiness of the face, low blood pressure and pulse rate, tiredness and lethargy, intolerance of cold and goitre.

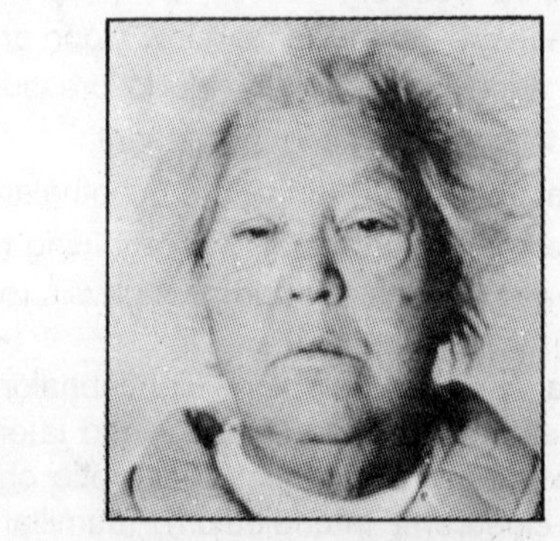
Fig. 240 : Hypothyroidism

Hypothyroxinemia — Presence of thyroxine hormone in the blood in less than normal concentration.

Hypotonia —Diminished tone of the muscles.

Hypotonic —1. Pertaining to diminished tone of the muscles. 2. A solution of lower osmotic pressure than another.

Hypotonicity —The condition of being hypotonic.

Hypotonus —Hypotonic.

Hypotony —Hypotonic.

Hypotoxicity —Abnormally reduced toxic quality.

Hypotransferrinemia — Deficiency of transferrin in the blood.

Hypotrichiasis —Hypotrichosis.

Hypotrichosis —Deficiency of hair.

Hypotrophy —Abiotrophy. Atrophy. Progressive degeneration and loss of functions of the cells and the tissues.

Hypotropia —Strabismus in which the visual axis of one eye deviates downwards permanently.

Hypotympanotomy —To make an incision in the tympanic membrane.

Hypotympanum —The part of the cavity of the middle ear beneath the level of the tympanic membrane.

Hypouresis —Reduction in flow of the urine.

Hypouricemia —Deficiency of uric acid in the blood.

Hypouricuria —Deficiency of uric acid in the urine.

Hypovaria —Decreased activity of the ovaries resulting in underdevelopment in girls.

Hypovarianism — Hypo-ovarianism.

Hypovenosity —Incomplete development of the venous system in an area of the body resulting in atrophy or degeneration.

Hypoventilation —Reduction in the amount of air entering the pulmonary alveoli.

Hypovitaminosis —The condition produced by the deficiency of a vitamin in the diet.

Hypovolemia —Oligemia. Oligohemia. Diminution of the volume of blood.

Hypovolemic —Pertaining to or characterized by hypovolemia.

Hypovolia —Diminished water content.

Hypoxemia —Hypoxia. Insufficient oxygenation of the blood.

Hypoxia —Deficiency of oxygen in the body tissues.

Altitude hypoxia — Hypoxia due to insufficient oxygen in the inspired air at high altitude.

Hypoxic —Pertaining to or characterized by hypoxia.

Hypsibrachycephalic — Having a broad and high skull.

Hypsicephalic —Oxycephalic.

Hypsicephaly —Oxycephaly.

Hypsiconchous —Having a high orbit.

Hypsiloid —U or Y shaped.

Hypsistaphylia —A condition in which the palate is high and narrow.

Hypsistenocephalic—Having a high, narrow head.

Hypsocephalous —Hypsicephalic or oxycephalic.

Hypsocephaly —Oxycephaly.

Hypsodont —Having long teeth.

Hypsokinesis —To fall backward when standing, seen in paralysis agitans.

Hypsophobia —Acrophobia. Morbid fear of being at a great height.

Hypurgia —The factor changing the course of a disease for betterment.

Hyster- —A prefix indicating uterus.

Hysteralgia —Hysterodynia. Pain in the uterus.

Hysteratresia —Atresia of the uterus.

Hysterectomy —Surgical removal of the uterus.

Abdominal hysterectomy —Surgical removal of the uterus through an incision in the abdominal wall.

Cesarean hysterectomy —Excision of the uterus at the time of cesarean section.

Radical hysterectomy — Surgical removal of the uterus along with the fallopian tubes, ovaries, adjacent lymph nodes and the upper portion of the vagina.

Subtotal, partial or supracervical hysterectomy —Excision of the uterus leaving the cervix in place.

Total or complete hysterectomy —Hysterectomy in which the uterus and the cervix both are completely removed.

Vaginal hysterectomy — Removal of the uterus through the vagina.

Hysteresis —1. Failure of related phenomenon to keep pace with each other.2. A time lag in the occurrence of two associated phenomena, as between cause and effect.3. The difference between inflation and deflation of the lung.

Hystereurynter —An instrument for dilating the mouth of the uterus.

Hystereurysis —Dilatation of the mouth of the uterus.

Hysteria —A condition resulting from mental dissociation without organic disease of the nervous system, presenting physical symptoms and signs, sensory disturbances and personality changes. It usually occurs in adult women characterized by lack of control over acts and emotions.

Anxiety hysteria — Hysteria occurring with an attack of anxiety.

Fixation hysteria — Hysteria occurring with the symptoms of an organic disease.

Major hysteria —Very severe form of hysteria accompanied by convulsions.

Minor hysteria —Mild form of hysteria in which consciousness is not lost.

Hysteriac —The person affected with hysteria.

Hysteric, Hysterical — Pertaining to hysteria.

Hysteric ataxia —Ataxia of the leg muscles in hysteria.

Hystericoneuralgic —Pertaining to the pain of hysterical origin, but resembling neuralgia.

Hystericus —An expression of emotion accompanied often by crying, laughing and screaming.

Hysteritis —Inflammation of the uterus.

Hystero-, Hyster- —Prefixes indicating uterus or hysteria.

Hysterobubonocele —Inguinal hernia surrounding the uterus.

Hysterocatalepsy —Major hysteria with cataleptic symptoms.

Hysterocele —Hernia of the uterus.

Hysterocleisis —To close the mouth of the uterus by surgery.

Hysterocolposcope —An instrument for inspection of the uterine cavity and vagina.

Hysterocystocleisis —The fastening of the cervix of the uterus to the wall of the urinary bladder.

Hysterocystopexy —Attachment of both, uterus and the urinary bladder to the abdominal wall.

Hysterodynia —Hysteralgia. Pain in the uterus.

Hysteroepilepsy —Severe hysteria with epileptiform convulsions.

Hysterogastrorrhaphy — Hysteropexy. Fixation of the uterus to the wall of the stomach.

Hysterogenic —Causing hysteria.

Hysterogenous —Hysterogenic.

Hysterogram —X-ray film of the uterus.

Hysterograph —An apparatus for recording the strength of uterine contractions.

Hysterography —1. Radiography of the uterus after introducing a radiopaque substance into the uterus. 2. Graphic recording of the frequency and intensity of the uterine contractions during labor.

Hysteroid —Resembling hysteria.

Hysterolaparotomy —To make an incision in the uterus through the abdominal wall.

Hysterolith —A calculus in the uterus.

Hysterology —Scientific study of the uterus.

Hysterolysis —To make the uterus free from its adhesions.

Hysteromania —Excessive sexual desire in female.

Hysterometer —An instrument for measuring the uterus.

Hysterometry —To measure the size of the uterus.

Hysteromyoma —Myoma or fibromyoma tumor of the uterus.

Hysteromyomectomy — Excision of a fibroid tumor of the uterus.

Hysteromyotomy —To incise the uterus to remove a solid tumor.

Hysteroneurosis —A neurosis related to the disease of the uterus.

Hystero-oophorectomy — Removal of the uterus with one or both ovaries.

Hysteroparalysis —Paralysis of the uterine walls.

Hysteropathy —Any disease of the uterus.

Hysteropexy —Surgical fixation of a displaced uterus.

Hysteropia —A hysterical defect of vision.

Hysteroplasty —Plastic surgery of the uterus.

Hysteropsychosis —Mental disorder due to uterine disease.

Hysteroptosia, Hysteroptosis —Procidentia. Prolapse of the uterus.

Hystcrorrhaphy —Suturing of the uterus.

Hysterorrhexis —Rupture of the uterus, especially in pregnancy.

Hysterosalpingectomy —To remove the uterus with the fallopian tubes by surgery.

Hysterosalpingogram —X-ray film of the uterus and fallopian tubes.

Hysterosalpingography — Radiography of the uterus and fallopian tubes after introducing a radiopaque substance into these organs.

Hysterosalpingo-oophorectomy —Surgical remvoal of the uterus, fallopian tubes and the ovaries.

Hysterosalpingostomy — Anastomosis of a fallopian tube with the uterus.

Hysteroscope —An instrument for visual examination of the uterine cavity.

Hysteroscopy —Visual examination of the uterine cavity by the use of hysteroscope.

Hysterospasm —Spasm of the uterus.

Hysterostomatomy —To enlarge the mouth of the uterus by an operation.

Hysterosystole —A delayed contraction of the heart.

Hysterothermometry —To measure temperature of the uterus.

Hysterotome —An instrument for incision of the uterus.

Hysterotomy —To make an incision into the uterus.

Hysterotrachelectomy — Excision of the cervix of the uterus.

Hysterotracheloplasty — Repair of the cervix of the uterus by plastic surgery.

Hysterotrachelorrhaphy — Suture of the uterine cervix.

Hysterotrachelotomy —To make an incision into the uterine cervix.

Hysterotraumatic —Pertaining to traumatic hysteria.

Hysterotraumatism — Occurrence of hysteria after an injury.

Hysterotubography — Hysterosalpingography

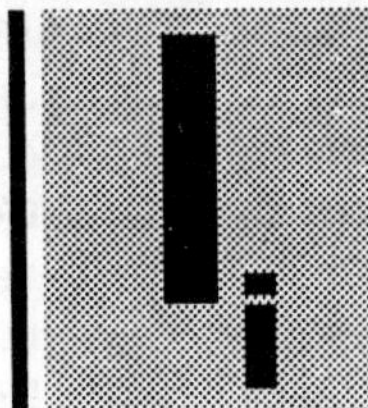

I—Chemical symbol for iodine.
Iamatology—Science of medicines.
I and O—Intake and output.
Ianthinopsia—Defective vision in which all the things are seen violet.
-iasis—Suffix denoting condition or state.
Iateria—Therapeutics.
Iatraliptics—Treatment of the diseases by massage.
Iatric—Pertaining to medicine or to a physician.
Iatro- —Prefix indicating relationship to medicine or a physician.
Iatrochemistry—An old theory that all the phenomena of life and the disease are based on chemical action.
Iatrogenesis—Induction of a mental or physical disease in a patient through the effects of treatment applied by a physician or surgeon.
Iatrogenic—Denoting medical or surgical treatment that itself induces some mental or physical disease, as a remedy for the present disease.
Iatrogenic disorder—An adverse mental or physical condition in a patient, resulting from the treatment by a physician or surgeon.
Iatrogeny—An adverse condition of a patient produced by a doctor.
Iatrology—Medical science.
Iatrophysics—1. Treatment of diseases by physical or mechanical means. 2. Medical physics.
Iatros—A physician.
Iatrotechnics, Iatrotechniques— The techniques of medical and surgical practice.
I.C.D.—Intrauterine contraceptive device.
Ice bag—A water-tight rubber bag containing ice used for applying cold locally.
Ichnogram—A foot-print taken while standing.
Ichor—Thin, fetid, watery discharge from a wound.
Ichoremia—Ichorrhemia. Septicemia or blood poisoning.
Ichoroid, Ichorous— Resembling watery fetid discharge.
Ichorous—Ichoroid.
Ichorrhea—Excessive fetid watery discharge from a wound.
Ichorrhemia—Sepsis resulting from infection accompanied by watery pus discharge.
Ichthyism, Ichthyismus— Ichthyotoxism. Poisoning from eating decomposed or toxic fish.
Ichthyo- —Combining form meaning fish.
Ichthyoacanthotoxin—A poison present in the sting, spines, or teeth of certain poisonous fishes.
Ichthyoacanthotoxism— Poisoning from biting of poisonous fishes.
Ichthyohemotoxin—A toxin present in the blood of certain poisonous fishes.
Ichthyohemotoxism— Poisoning resulting from the ingestion of fish containing the toxin ichthyohemotoxin.
Ichthyoid—Like a fish.
Ichthyology—The study of fishes.
Ichthyophagous—Eating or subsisting on fishes.
Ichthyophobia—Morbid fear of fish.
Ichthyosarcotoxin—A toxin found in the flesh of poisonous fishes.
Ichthyosarcotoxism— Ichthyism.
Ichthyosis—Fish-like dry, rough and scaly skin.

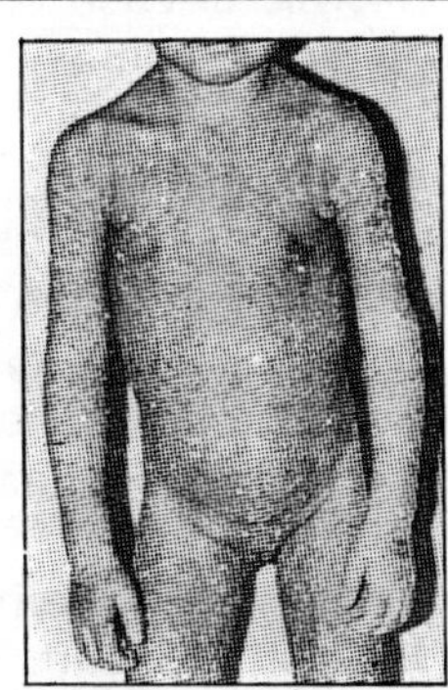

Fig. 241 Ichthyosis

Ichthyotic—Pertaining to ichthyosis.
Ichthyotoxicology—The study of the poisons of fishes.
Ichthyotoxicon—Fish poison.
Ichthyotoxin—Any toxic substance present in the fish.
Ichthyotoxism—Poisoning due to an ichthyotoxin.

Icing—Application of ice to a recently traumatized area to reduce pain and swelling.

ICN—International Council of Nurses.

Iconolagny—Sexual stimulation produced by seeing the pictures or objects.

ICP—Intracranial pressure.

ICRP—International Commission on Radiological protection.

-ics—A suffix meaning science or knowledge.

I.C.S.—International college of surgeons.

ICSH—Interstitial cell-stimulating hormone. The hormone in male which stimulates the secretion of testosterone hormone from the interstitial cells of the testes.

Ictal—Pertaining to, marked by or caused by a sudden attack or stroke such as acute epilepsy.

Icteric—Pertaining to jaundice.

Icteritious—Yellowish, like jaundice.

Ictero- —A prefix denoting icterus, i.e. jaundice.

Icteroanemia—Jaundice associated with hemolytic anemia and enlargement of the spleen.

Icterogenic, Icterogenous— Causing jaundice.

Icterohematuric—Pertaining to icterus and hematuria.

Icterohemoglobinuria— Pertaining to icterus and hemoglobinuria.

Icterohepatitis—Inflammation of the liver with jaundice.

Icteroid—Resembling jaundice.

Icterus—Jaundice.

Icterus gravis neonatorum—Physiologic icterus. Hemolytic disease of the newborn.

Infectious icterus—Icterus caused by an infection of the liver, i.e. occurring in infective hepatitis.

Obstructive icterus—Icterus or jaundice caused by obstruction to the flow of bile in the common bile duct or hepatic duct which may result from the gall stones, parasites in the ducts, pressure by tumors, cysts or cirrhosis of the liver etc.

Ictometer—An apparatus for determining the force of the apex beat of the heart.

Ictus—Sudden attack, blow or stroke.

I.C.U.—Intensive care unit.

Id— A skin rash appearing remote from the main lesion of the disease which is usually due to an allergic reaction to the causative agent of the disease.

–id—Suffix indicating a skin rash appearing remote from the main lesion of the disease.

Idea—A mental image or conception.

Autochthonous idea—A strainge idea coming unexpectedly into the mind which has no connection with the others.

Compulsive idea—An idea which persists against the will and stimulates to perform an inappropriate work.

Dominant idea—An idea that controls one's all actions and thoughts.

Fixed idea—A persistent morbid idea or belief which completely dominates the mind and cannot be changed inspite of the contrary evidence.

Flight of idea—An idea occurring in certain mental diseases in which the patient speaks rapidly which is often disconnected and incoherent.

Idea of reference—A wrong idea formed in the mind with the reference of the conversation or actions of others.

Ideal—Perfect type.

Idealization—A mental process in which a person consciously or unconsciously overestimates an admitted fact or the characteristic quality of a person.

Ideation—The process of thinking or formation of ideas.

Ideational—Pertaining to ideation.

Idee fixe—Fixed idea.

Identical—Exactly similar.

Identification—Recognition.

Identity—The total physical and mental characteristics by which a person is recognized and differentiated from others.

Ideo- —A prefix denoting the words pertaining to ideas.

Ideogenetic—Ideogenous.

Ideogenous—Stimulated by an idea.

Ideoglandular—Increased glandular secretion or glandular activity by mental image.

Ideokinetic—Ideomotor.

Ideology—The science of ideas.

Ideomotion—Muscular movement induced by a dominant idea.

Ideomotor—Pertaining to ideomotion.

Ideomuscular—Pertaining to both, the idea and the muscular activity.

Ideophobia—Morbid fear of new or different ideas.

Ideophrenia—Insanity with marked perversion of ideas.

Ideophrenic—Insane marked by abnormally perverted ideas.

Ideovascular—Pertaining to the vascular changes as the elevation of blood pressure by ideas, memories or emotions.

Idio- —Prefix indicating individual or distinct.

Idioagglutinin—An agglutinin occurring naturally in the blood, without injection of a stimulating antigen.

Idiocy—A condition of severe mental deficiency.

Complete idiocy—Idiocy in which there is congenital absence of primitive instincts.

Cretinoid idiocy—Idiocy associated with cretinism.

Epileptic idiocy—Idiocy accompanied by epilepsy.

Hemiplegic idiocy—Hemiplegia accompanied by idiocy in infants.

Hydrocephalic idiocy—Idiocy combined with chronic hydrocephalus.

Microcephalic idiocy—Idiocy accompanied by microcephalia.

Paralytic idiocy—Idiocy combined with paralysis.

Sensorial idiocy—Idiocy caused by loss of one of the special senses.

Traumatic idiocy—Idiocy caused by an injury received at birth, in infancy or in early childhood.

Idiogamist—The person sexually potent with only one or a few partners.

Idiogenesis—Origin without known cause, as said of a disease.

Idioglossia—Defective articulation with the emittance of meaningless vocal sounds.

Idioglottic—Pertaining to idioglossia.

Idiogram—Photograph of the chromosomes of a cell.

Idiohypnotism—Autohypnosis.

Idiolalia—To speak in one's own invented language.

Idiolysin—A lysin normally present in the blood.

Idiometritis—Inflammation of the uterine parenchyma.

Idiomuscular—Pertaining to the muscles alone.

Idioneurosis—Any functional neurosis arising without any stimulation.

Idionodal—Arising from the AV node itself.

Idiopathic—Occurring without any known cause.

Idiopathy—A disease without known cause.

Idiophrenic—Pertaining to or originating in the mind alone.

Idiopsychologic—Concerning the ideas produced in one's own mind.

Idiospasm—Spasm occurring only in one area.

Idiosyncrasy—1. A habit or physical or mental peculiarity by which a person differs from the others. 2. An abnormal susceptibility to an action, to a drug, a food or other substance peculiar to a person.

Idiosyncratic—Pertaining to an idiosyncrasy.

Idiot—The person with severe mental deficiency or a perfect fool.

Idiotic—Pertaining to or like an idiot.

Idiotism—The state of idiocy.

Idiotrophic—Capable of securing its own nourishment.

Idiotropic—Egocentric. Introspective. Withdrawing from the external world and concentrating upon inner self.

Idiot-savant—The person severely mentally deficient in some respects, but very intelligent for high intellectual works, as for mathematics or music etc.

Idiovariation—A mutation occurring without known cause.

Idioventricular—Pertaining to the cardiac ventricle alone.

Igneous—Pertaining to or containing fire.

Igniextirpation—Excision by cauterization.

Ignioperation—An operation done by cauterization.

Ignipedities—Burning pain in the soles of the feet, in multiple neuritis.

Ignipuncture—To puncture with heated needles.

Ignis—Fire.

Ignition—The act of firing.

IHS—Indian Health Service.

I.L.A.—International Leprosy Association.

Ilea—Plural of ileum.

Ileac—1. Pertaining to the ileum. 2. Pertaining to or of the nature of ileus.

Ileal—Pertaining to the ileum.

Ileectomy—Excision of the ileum.

Ileitis—Inflammation of the ileum.

Ileo- —A prefix denoting ileum.

Ileocecal—Pertaining to both, the ileum and the cecum.

Ileocecocystoplasty—Reconstruction of the urinary bladder with a segment of ileocecum.

Ileocecostomy—Surgical formation of an opening between the ileum and the cecum.

Ileocecum—Ileum and cecum combined.

Ileocolic—Pertaining to the ileum and the colon.

Ileocolitis—Inflammation of the ileum and colon.

Ileocolonic—Ileocolic.

Ileocolostomy—Surgical anastomosis between the ileum and the colon.

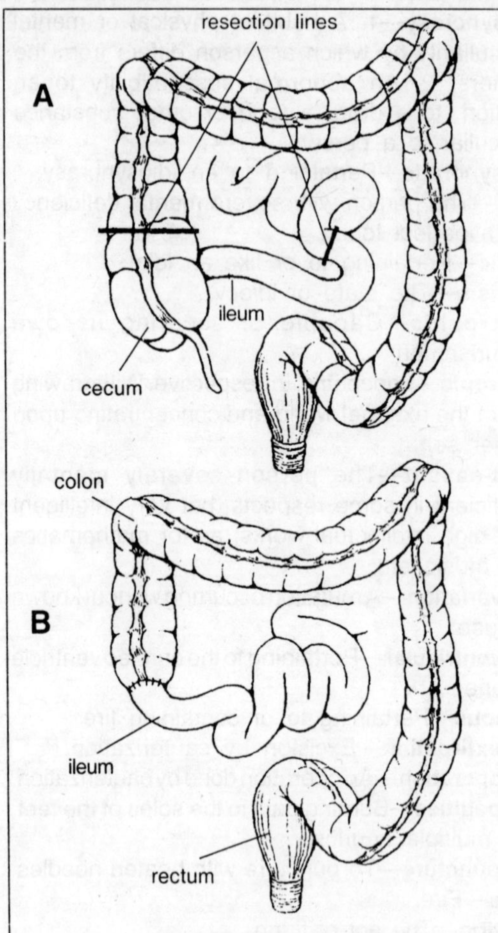

Fig. 242 Ileocolostomy

A = Resection of the diseased portions of the ileum. B = Anastomosis of the cut ends.

Ileocolotomy—To make an incision into the ileum and the colon.

Ileocystoplasty—Repair of the wall of the urinary bladder with a separated segment of the wall of the ileum.

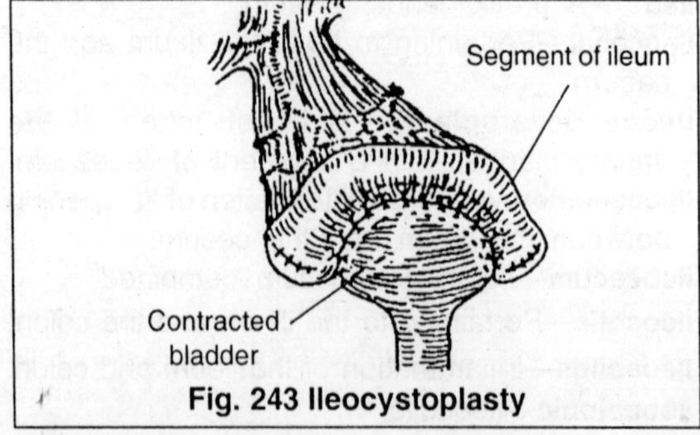

Fig. 243 Ileocystoplasty

Repair of the urinary bladder by using a 6-inch segment of ileum.

Ileocystostomy—To make an opening between the ileum and the urinary bladder by surgery.

Ileoileostomy—Anastomosis between one part of the ileum and the other part.

Ileojejunitis—Inflammation of the jejunum and ileum.

Ileopexy—Surgical fixation of the ileum.

Ileoproctostomy—Ileorectostomy. To make an opening between ileum and the rectum.

Ileorectal—Pertaining to the ileum and the rectum.

Ileorectostomy— Ileoproctostomy.

Ileorrhaphy—Suture of the ileum.

Ileosigmoidostomy—Surgical anastomosis between the ileum and the sigmoid colon.

Ileostomy—Surgical formation of a passage through the abdominal wall into the ileum.

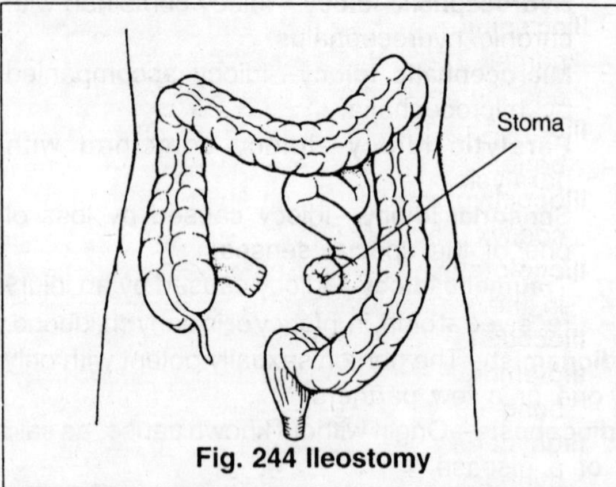

Fig. 244 Ileostomy

Ileostomy urinary—Surgical formation of a passage between ileum and the urinary bladder.

Ileotomy—To make an incision into the ileum.

Ileotransversostomy—Anastomosis of the ileum to the transverse colon.

Ileum—Lower portion of the small intestine extending from the jejunum to the cecum.

Ileum duplex—Congenital doubling of the ileum.

Ileus—Intestinal obstruction.

Adynamic ileus—Paralyticus ileus. Intestinal obstruction caused by the paralysis of the intestinal muscles.

Dynamic ileus—Intestinal obstruction caused by the contraction of the intestinal muscles.

Mechanical ileus—Intestinal obstruction produced by mechanical causes such as hernia, adhesions and volvulus etc.

Meconium ileus—Intestinal obstruction in the newborn due to blocking of the intestine with thick meconium.

Paralytic ileus—Adynamic ileus.

Postoperative ileus—Intestinal obstruction produced after an abdominal operation due to handling the intestine during surgery or by anesthesia.

Spastic ileus—Intestinal obstruction due to spasm of a segment of the intestine.

Subparta ileus—Intestinal obstruction caused by the pressure of the pregnant uterus on the colon.

Ilia—Plural of ilium.

Iliac—Pertaining to the ilium.

Iliac crest—Hip. Upper free margin of the iliac bone.

Iliac fossa—One of the depressions of the iliac bones of the pelvis.

Iliac region—Inguinal region on either side of the hypogastrium.

Iliac spine—Anyone of the four spines of the ilium, namely the anterior and posterior inferior spines, and the anterior and posterior superior spines.

Ilio- —A prefix indicating relationship to the iliac bone.

Iliococcygeal—Pertaining to the ilium and the coccyx bones.

Iliocolotomy—To make an opening into the colon in the inguinal region.

Iliocostal—Pertaining to the ilium and the ribs.

Iliofemoral--Pertaining to the iliac and the femur bone.

Iliohypogastric—Pertaining to the ilium and the hypogastrium.

Ilioinguinal—Pertaining to the groin and inguinal region.

Iliolumbar—Pertaining to the iliac and lumbar regions.

Iliopagus—Two fetuses joined at the iliac region.

Iliopectineal—Pertaining to the ilium and the pubic bones.

Iliopelvic—Pertaining to the iliac region and the pelvis.

Iliosacral—Pertaining to the ilium and sacrum.

Iliosciatic—Pertaining to the ilium and the ischium.

Iliospinal—Pertaining to the ilium and the spinal column.

Iliothoracopagus—Two fetuses joined from the pelvis to the thorax.

Iliotibial—Pertaining to the ilium and the tibia bone.

Iliotrochanteric—Pertaining to the ilium and the greater trochanter of the femur bone.

Ilioxiphopagus—Two fetuses joined from the pelvis to the xiphoid process.

Ilium—The upper and the widest part of the innominate or hip bone in each half of the pelvis.

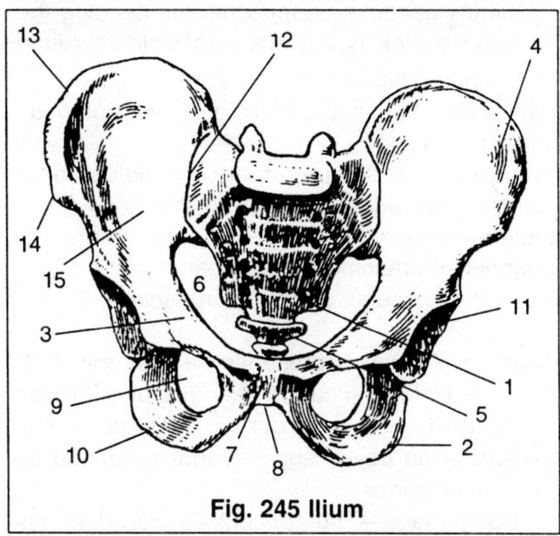

Fig. 245 Ilium

1. Sacrum 2. Ischium 3. Pubis 4. Ilium 5. Coccyx 6. Inlet of true pelvis 7. Pubic symphysis 8. Angle under symphysis (pubic angle) 9. Obturator foramen 10. Ischial tuberosity 11. Acetabulum 12. Sacroiliac joint 13. Iliac crest 14. Anterior superior Iliac spine 15. Iliac fossa

Ill—Sick or unhealthy.

Illegitimacy —Unlawfulness.

Illegitimate—Illegal, against the law.

Illinition—The friction of a surface to facilitate the absorption of an ointment.

Illiterate—Being unable to read and write.

Illness—Sickness, unhealthyness.

Mental illness—An illness of the mind characterized by abnormal behavior as schizophrenia etc.

See other types of illnesses under `Disease'.

Illumination—1. The lighting up of a part or an organ of the body or an object for inspection.

2. The amount of light thrown upon an object.

Dark-field illumination—In this type of illumination a special type of condenser is used in the microscope, which contains a black area in its centre which stops the central light rays from entering the microorganisms on the slide. The light rays pass through the sides of the black area and form a ring of light around the micro-organisms. This causes the microorganisms to appear bright against the dark background and the visible light appears to emit from the microorganisms and not from the light source. This method is applied in investigating very minute bacteria as spirochaetes causing the disease syphilis, which are not visible through ordinary microscope.

Illuminator—The source of light for seeing an object.

Illuminism—The state of having delusion of communion with supernatural beings.

Illusion—False perception.

Illusional—Pertaining to an illusion.

I.m.—Intramuscular. Within a muscle.

Ima—Lowest.

Image—1. An idea representing a real object. 2. A more or less accurate likeness of a person or thing with the other person or thing. 3. The picture of an object such as that produced by a lens or mirror.

Body image—The concept an individual has about his or her body, e.g. an obese person has the body image of a much less obese person.

Double image—False image. Double vision, diplopia.

False image—The image in the deviating eye in strabismus.

Inverted image—Image which is turned upside down.

Mental image—A picture of an object not present, produced in the mind by memory or imagination.

Mirror image—The image of an object reflected in a mirror in which right and left are reversed.

Real image—Image formed by the collection of the emanating rays of light from an object, which is inverted.

Virtual image—Direct image. The image produced by the imaginary focus of the rays.

Imagery—Imagination.

Imaginary—Unreal.

Imagination—The formation of ideas about the things, persons or places which are not known previously.

Imaging—The production of a picture or an image for diagnostic purposes, e.g., an X-ray picture or the image produced by ultrasonography.

Imago—1. An image or shadow. 2. A memory of childhood of a loved person which persists in adult life.

Imbalance—Out of balance.

Autonomic imbalance— Defective coordination between the sympathetic and the parasympathetic divisions of the autonomic nervous system, especially with respect to the vasomotor reactions.

Occlusal imbalance—Absence of occlusion between the teeth of the upper jaw (maxilla) and lower jaw (mandible) during closing of the mouth.

Sympathetic imbalance— Vagotonia. Increased excitability of the vagus nerve.

Vasomotor imbalance— Excessive constriction or dilatation of the blood vessels resulting from impulses to them.

Imbecile—Mentally deficient.

Imbecility —Mental deficiency.

Imbed—To place a piece of a tissue in a firm medium such as paraffin to keep it intact during subsequent cutting into thin sections for microscopic examinations.

Imbedding—The process by which a piece of a tissue is placed in a firm medium such as paraffin to keep it intact during subsequent cutting into thin sections for microscopic examinations.

Imbibition—Absorption of fluid by a solid.

Imbricate, Imbricated—Overlapping like the scales of the fishes.

Imbrication—To overlap the aponeurotic layers in abdominal operation.

Iminoglycinuria—Presence of excessive amount of glycine and amino acids (proline and hydroxyproline) in the urine.

Immature—Not fully developed, unripe.

Immediate—Direct; without intervening steps; proximate or nearest.

Immedicable—Incurable; the wound which cannot be healed.

Immersion—1. The dipping of the body under water or other fluid. 2. In microscopy, filling of the space between the objective lens and the top of the cover glass with a fluid such as water or oil.

Immigration—To go to another country to be settled.

Immiscible—Which is not able to be mixed as oil and water.

Immobility—The state of being fixed.

Immobilization—The process of making a part unable to move.

Immobilize—To make unable to move.

Immovable—Not moving.

Immune—1. Protected from, or resistant to a disease due to the formation of humoral antibodies or the development of cellular immunity or both.

2. Characterized by the formation of the humoral antibodies or cellular immunity or both.

Immunifacient—Producing immunity.

Immunity—1. The condition of being immune to, or protected from a disease, especially an infectious disease. 2. The response of the body and its tissues to various antigens.

Acquired immunity—The immunity occurring as a result of prior experience to an infectious agent or its antigens.

Active immunity—Acquired immunity.

Antiviral immunity—Immunity resulting from the viral infection, either naturally acquired or produced artificially by vaccination.

Artificial immunity— Immunity produced artificially as by vaccination.

Cellular immunity—Acquired immunity in which the role of the T-lymphocytes predominates.

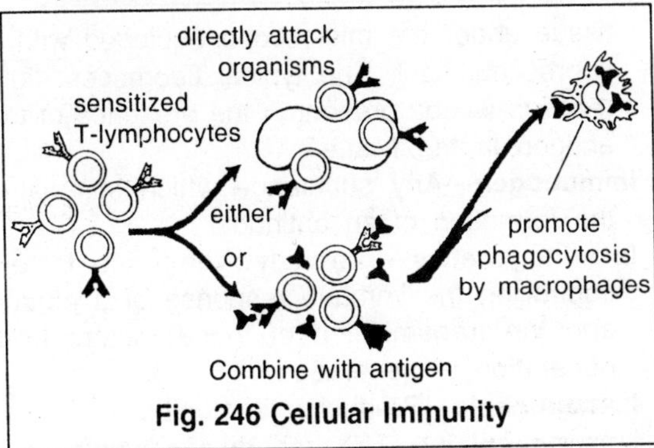

Fig. 246 Cellular Immunity

Sensitized T-lymphocytes either directly attack organisms or combine with antigen that promote phagocytosis by macrophages.

Concomitant immunity —Infection immunity.

Congenital immunity—Immunity present since birth.

General immunity—Immunity associated with the mechanisms protecting the whole body.

Herd immunity—Immunity to a certain disease present in a group of people or population.

Humoral immunity—Acquired immunity produced by circulating antibodies present in the body fluids as blood serum and milk etc.

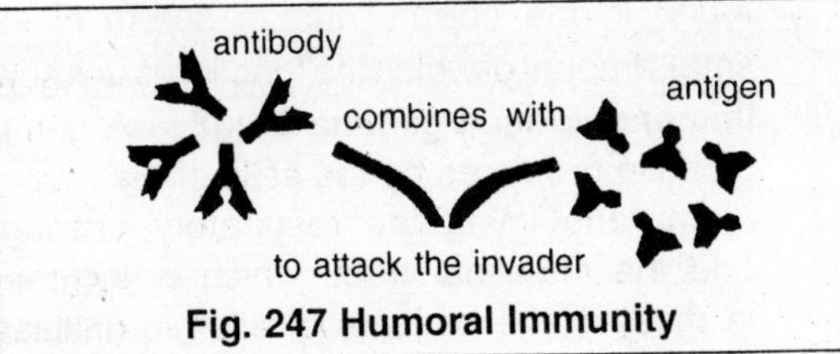

Fig. 247 Humoral Immunity

Antibody present in the body fluids combines with antigen to attack the invader.

Infection immunity—Immunity developing following an infection so the body resists the reinfection of the original type and then that infection never occurs.

Local immunity—Immunity that is limited to a given area or tissue of the body.

Maternal immunity—Humoral immunity which is passively transferred across the placenta from the mother to the fetus.

Natural immunity—Permanent immunity to a disease since birth due to the presence of some natural inherent factors.

Passive immunity—Immunity acquired in a fetus in the uterus from the antibodies passing from the mother to it through the placenta, or the immunity acquired by the newborn by drinking mother's milk. This type of immunity can also be produced by an injection of antibodies in the person to be protected from a disease.

Specific immunity—Immunity against a particular disease or antigen.

Immunization—The process of rendering a patient immune or of becoming immune.

Deliberate immunization — The introduction of the immunogens, usually by injections to protect the individual from developing the specific diseases.

Natural immunization —The development of immunity to the antigens of the bacteria normally present in the intestine and on the skin.

Immunize—To render immune.

Immuno- —A prefix indicating immune, immunity.

Immunoabsorbent— Immunosorbent.

Immunoadjuvant—A nonspecific stimulator of the immune response e.g., B.C.G. Vaccine.

Immunoadsorbent—An antigen in an insoluble form which adsorbs homologous antibodies from a mixture of immunoglobulins.

Immunoagglutination—Specific agglutination affected by antibody.

Immunoassay—To measure the amount of proteins in the body fluids concerned with the reaction of an antigen with its specific antibody.

Immunobiology—The branch of biology dealing with the study of immune response to the infectious diseases, transplantation of organs, allergy, autoimmunity and cancer, etc.

Immunochemistry—Chemistry of immunization.

Immunochemotherapy—The treatment of the diseases by combination of immunotherapy and chemotherapy.

Immunocompetence—Capability of developing an immune response to stimulation by an antigen.

Immunocompetent—Having the ability of a normal immune response.

Immunocomplex—Complex of an antigen and antibody.

Immunocompromised—Having the immune response attenuated by use of immunosuppressive drugs, by irradiation, by malnutrition or by the development of certain diseases such as a cancer.

Immunoconglutinin—Antibody formed against certain fixed complement components of an antigen-antibody complex.

Immunocyte—Any lymphoid cell reacting with the antigen to produce antibody.

Immunocytoadherence—The collection of red blood cells around the lymphocytes with surface immunoglobulins, forming rosettes.

Immunodeficiency—A deficiency of the immune response to antigenic stimuli due to hypoactivity or the decreased number of lymphocytes.

Immunodeficient—Deficient in immune response to antigenic stimuli.

Immunodepressant—Immunosuppressant.

Immunodepressor—Immunosuppressant.

Immunodiagnosis—To make diagnosis of the diseases by using specific immune responses.

Immunodiffusion—A method of studying the antigen-antibody reactions by placing an antigen and antibody in a gel and observing the precipitate formed by their diffusion to each other.

Immunoelectrophoresis—A method of investigating the amount and character of proteins and antibodies in the body fluids by electrophoresis. A method of distinguishing proteins and other materials on the basis of their electrophoretic mobility.

Immunoenhancement—The increasement in immune response.

Immunoenhancer—Any substance that increases the degree of immune response.

Immunofluorescence—A method of determining the location of antigen in the tissues by fluorescence. For this, the tissue is stained with fluorescein. The antibodies in the tissue combine with their specific antigens. The presence of antigen is determined by examining the stained tissue under the microscope equipped with a fluorescent light. The typical fluorescent light reaction will be present in the presence of the antigen in the tissue.

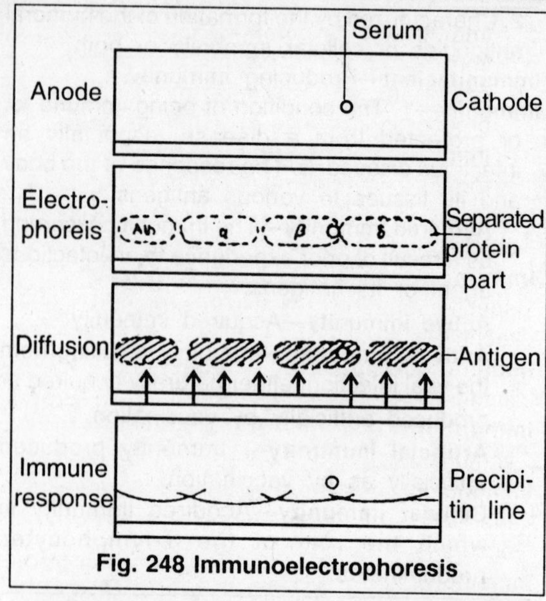

Fig. 248 Immunoelectrophoresis

Immunogen—Any substance which stimulates the formation of an antibody.

Immunogenetics—The study of the genetic factors controlling the immune response of a person and the transmission of these factors from generation to generation.

Immunogenic—Producing immunity.

Immunogenicity—The property of a substance to produce immunity.

Immunoglobulin—A type of the protein acting as an antibody, formed by the lymphocytes and plasma cells, found in the serum and in another body fluids and tissues, written in short as Ig.

Immunoglobulin gamma A, IgA—The principal immunoglobulin found in the secretions of the exocrine glands such as milk, in the mucus of the respiratory passages and the intestinal tract and tears, etc., which protects the surface of the mucous membrane from bacterial and viral infection.

Immunoglobulin gamma D, IgD—A protein found in the normal human serum in very small amount of which the function is unknown.

Immunoglobulin gamma E, IgE—A gamma globulin produced by the cells of the mucous membrane lining the respiratory passages and the intestinal tract, which is increased in most of the patients of allergic diseases.

Immunoglobulin gamma G, IgG—The principal immunoglobulin in the human serum which passes through the placenta to the infant producing immunity in it before birth.

Immunoglobulin gamma M,IgM —A globulin formed in immune response at an early stage.

Immunohematology —The study of the autoimmune and blood diseases.

Immunohistochemistry—Demonstration of specific antigens in the tissues by special technique.

Immunoincompetency—Inability to produce immune response.

Immunoincompetent—Unable to develop an immune response to an antigenic stimulus.

Immunologic diseases—The diseases caused by the action of antibodies to the antigens as occurs in allergy or hypersensitivity.

Immunologist—Specialist in immunology.

Immunology—The study of all the aspects of immunity.

Immunomodulation—The ability to change immune responses.

Immunomodulatory—Capable of changing or modifying the immune responses.

Immunoparesis—Inadequate immune response to an infectious agent.

Immunopathogenesis—The process of development of a disease involving an immune response.

Immunopathology —The study of the changes in the tissues resulting from immune response to diseases or allergic reactions.

Immunopathy—An immunity disorder.

Immunophysiology—Physiology of the immunological process.

Immunopotency —The power of an individual to produce antibody against some antigen.

Immunopotentiation—To make the immune response powerful by the administration of another substance.

Immunopotentiator—Any substance which on inoculation enhances the immune response.

Immunoprecipitation—The formation of a precipitate when an antigen and antibody interact.

Immunoproliferative— Characterized by the proliferation of the lymphocytes producing immunoglobulins.

Immunoprotein—Any protein which confers immunity.

Immunoreactant —Any substance involved in immunologic reactions.

Immunoreaction—The reaction of an antibody to an antigen.

Immunoreactive—Exhibiting immunoreaction.

Immunoregulation—The control of specific immune response and interactions between B- and T-lymphocytes and macrophages.

Immunoresponsiveness—The capacity to react in the production of immune response.

Immunoselection—Survival of certain cells depending on their surface antigenicity.

Immunosenescence—The effect of age on the immune system and host defence mechanisms.

Immunosorbent—An antibody or antigen used to remove specific antigen or antibody from solution or suspension.

Immunostimulant—A substance stimulating the formation of antibody.

Immunostimulation—Stimulation of an immune response.

Immunostimulator—That which stimulates the immune system.

Immunosuppressant—Suppressing immune response.

Immunosuppression—Prevention or diminution of the immune response as by use of radiation.

Immunosuppressive— Immunosuppressant.

Immunosurgery—To use a specific antigenic substance in surgical treatment.

Immunotherapy—Immunization of a person by the administration of the preformed antibodies (serum or gamma globulin).

Immunotoxin—An antitoxin.

Immunotransfusion— Transfusion of blood from a donor containing the antibodies of the disease from which the patient is suffering.

Immunotropic—Enhancing the immune response.

Impact—1. Collision. 2. To press firmly together.

Impacted—Pressed firmly together so that neither of which is movable, e.g. a fracture in which the ends of the bones are wedged together, a

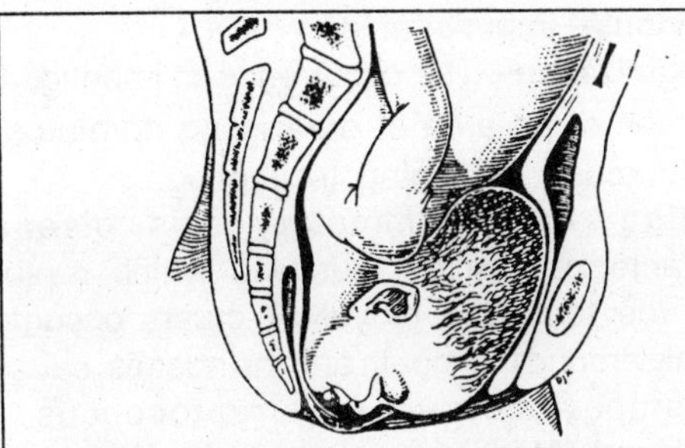

Fig. 249 Impaction of the fetus in the pelvis. Head being moulded.

fetus wedged in birth canal, a calculus wedged in the ureter or accumulation of feces in the rectum.

Impaction—The condition of being tightly wedged.

Dental impaction—Confinement of a tooth in the alveolus and prevention of its eruption into normal position.

Fecal impaction—Accumulation of hardened feces in the colon or rectum.

Impairment—Any loss or abnormality of physical or mental health, structure or function of the body organs or parts.

Impaled object—A foreign body that penetrates the skin and remains imbedded in the body tissue.

Impalpable—Not detectable by touch.

Impar—Azygous.

Imparidigitate—Having an uneven number of fingers or toes.

Impassable—That cannot be traversed, impenetrable.

Impatent—Closed, not open.

Impatience—Lack of patience, restlessness.

Impedance—Obstruction in the flow as of an electric current or other form of energy, e.g., obstruction in the transmission of sound waves.

Impenetrable—That cannot be penetrated into, impervious.

Imperative—Involuntary, not controlled by the will.

Imperception—Inability to form an idea.

Imperfect—Incomplete.

Imperforate—Without an opening.

Imperforation—The state of being without opening or being closed.

Imperious acts—Tics and motions not controlled by the will.

Impermeable—Impenetrable.

Imperment—Unable to pass through a particular semipermeable membrane.

Impersistence—Occurrence only for a short time.

Impervious—Impenetrable.

Impetiginization—The occurrence of impetigo by infection of an area of preexisting dermatosis.

Impetiginous—Pertaining to impetigo.

Impetigo—An inflammatory skin disease characterized by the pustules which rupture with the formation of yellow crusts occurring mainly around the mouth and the nostrils, caused by staphylococcus or streptococcus or combined infection.

Impetigo contagiosa—A contagious form of impetigo occurring mainly in children characterized by the formation of vesicles and bullae which become pustular. They dry up and the yellow crusts are formed.

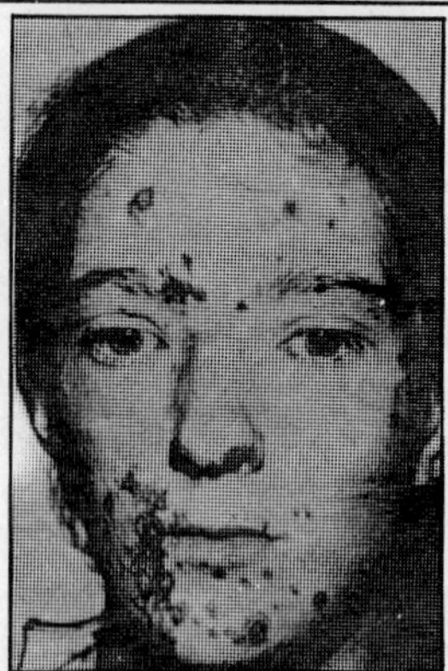

Fig. 250 Impetigo contagiosa

Impetigo herpetiformis—Rare pustular lesions of unknown cause occurring chiefly in pregnancy and hypocalcemia.

Impetus—Impulse.

Implant—1. To graft or insert. 2. Any material grafted or inserted.

Implantation—1. Embedding of the fertilized ovum into the endometrium of the uterus six or seven days after fertilization. 2. Grafting of a tissue or insertion of an organ. 3. To place a substance into a new location.

Implantology—The science dealing with the implants.

Implosion—1. The treatment of phobias by presenting repeatedly the most fearful and anxiety- producing objects before the patient until the phobia and anxiety do not occur. 2. A sudden collapse.

Imponderable—Unable to be weighed or measured, as heat, light etc.

Imposters—Quacks.

Impotence, Impotency— Lack of sexual power in the male to achieve penile erection.

Anatomic impotency—Organic impotency. Impotency caused by a defect in the genital organs.

Atonic impotency—Impotency caused by paralysis of the nerves conveying impulses to bring about erection of the penis.

Functional impotency— Impotency due to psychological causes.

Pharmacological impotency—Impotency caused by the side effects of certain medicines, or narcotics such as alcohol, Bhang and opium etc.

Psychic impotency—Impotency due to mental disorder.

Symptomatic impotency— Impotency due to ill health, drugs or the presence of a disease.

Vasculogenic impotency—Impotency due to inadequate supply of arterial blood to the corpora cavernosa of the penis.

Impotent—Sexually weak man to achieve penile erection.

Impotentia—Impotence.

Impregnate—1. To establish pregnancy or to fertilize ovum. 2. To saturate.

Impregnated—1. Rendered pregnant 2. Saturated.

Impregnation—1. Fertilization of an ovum. 2. Saturation.

Impressio—Impression.

Impression—1. A mark made by pressure as thumb impression. 2. A slight depression made on the surface of an organ by pressure exerted by another. 3. The imprint of an object or the teeth on plastic material, which later on solidifies. 4. Effect produced upon the mind by external stimuli. 5. An idea.

Impulse—1. The act of driving onward with sudden force. 2. A sudden uncontrollable determination to act. 3. A change transmitted through certain tissues, especially the nerve fibers and muscles resulting in their hyper or hypoactivity, e.g. cardiac beat or apex. beat.

Impulsion—Sudden arousal of an idea in the mind to do something wrong or to commit crime.

Impulsive—Pertaining to or caused by an impulse.

Impure—Dirty, defiled.

Impurity—Dirtyness, defilement.

Imus—Lowest.

In-—A prefix indicating inside, within and negative.

-in—A suffix used to form the names of biochemical substances, as globulin, insulin, digoxin, aspirin and streptomycin etc.

Inaction—Total absence of or decreased response to a stimulus.

Inactivate—To make inactive.

Inactivation—The process of making inactive or inert as the destruction of disease-producing bacteria by heat or by other means.

Inactivator—Making inactive or inert.

Inactive—Not active, inert.

Inactivity—The condition of being not active.

Inadequacy—Insufficiency.

Inanimate—Lifeless, dead.

Inanition—A debilitated condition due to prolonged starvation or under nutrition.

Inapparent—Not apparent.

Inappetence—Lack of desire for food or loss of appetite.

Inarticulate—1. Having no joints. 2. Unable to pronounce the words clearly and intelligibly.

In articulo mortis—At the very moment of death.

Inassimilable—Not assimilable or which is unable to be utilized by the body.

Inattention—Lack of attention.

Inborn—Inherent or congenital.

Inbred—Denoting the persons descended over several generations.

Inbreeding—The mating of closely related individuals.

Incandescent—Growing in light.

Incapacitate—Being made incapable physically or mentally or both, of performing some function.

Incarcerated—Confined or constricted or imprisoned.

Incarceration—Confinement, constriction or imprisonment.

Incarnant—Incarnative. Accelerating the granulation of a wound.

Incarnatio, incarnation—1. To grow in, e.g. ingrowing of a fingernail or toenail. 2. The process of becoming flesh.

Incarnative—Incarnant.

Incasement—To become surrounded by a structure or wall.

Incendiarism—Pyromania.

Incentive—Provocative.

Inception—1. The beginning of anything. 2. Ingestion. 3. Intussusception.

Incertaesedis—Of doubtful position.

Incest—Intercourse between closely related persons in whom the marriage is legally not possible.

Incestuous—1. Pertaining to incest. 2. Guilty of incest.

Incidence—The rate of occurrence of an event or a disease.

Incident—An event or happening.

Incineration—Destruction by fire.

Incinerator—Destroying by fire.

Incisal—Cutting; pertaining to the cutting edges of the incisor and cuspid teeth.

Incipient—Beginning to exist.

Incise—To cut with a sharp instrument.

Incised—Cut with a sharp instrument or with a knife.

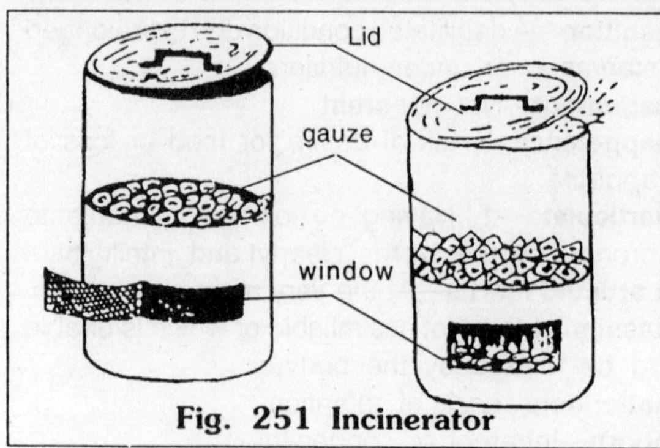

Fig. 251 Incinerator

Incision—1. A cut or a wound made by cutting with a sharp instrument or with a knife. 2. The process of cutting.

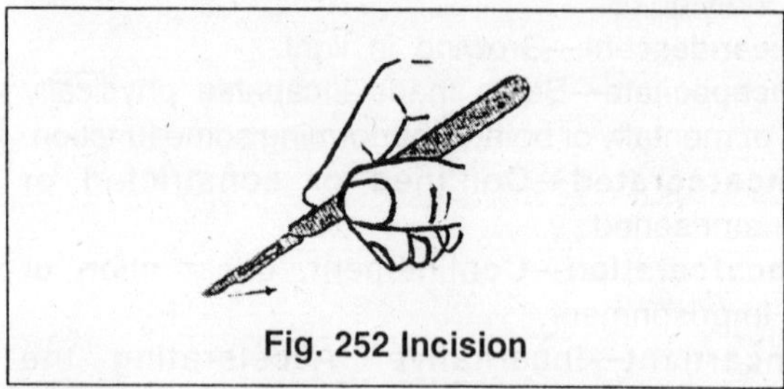
Fig. 252 Incision

Incisive—1. Having the power of cutting, or sharp. 2. Pertaining to the incisor teeth.

Incisor—1. That which cuts. 2. One of the four front cutting teeth in each jaw of an adult.

Incisura—Incisure.

Incisure—1. An incision. 2. Notch.

Inclinatio—Inclination.

Inclination—Leaning from the normal or from the vertical as of a tooth.

Inclinometer—Device for measuring the ocular diameter from vertical and horizontal lines.

Inclusion—1. The act of including. 2. Anything that is enclosed.

Inclusion bodies—The bodies present in the nucleus of cytoplasm of certain cells in the infection of filterable viruses.

Incoagulability—Inability to be coagulated.

Incoherence—The condition of being not connected.

Incoherent—Not adherent; disjointed.

Incombustible—That which cannot be burnt.

Incompatibility—1. The quality of not being suitable for combination. 2. Condition of not being in harmony with one's situation, environment or associates, especially a spouse or friend.

Incompatible—1. Unable to combine. 2. Antagonistic in action, said of some drugs. 3. Not being in harmony with one's situation, environment or associates, especially a spouse or friend.

Incompetence, incompetency—1. Inability of an organ or a part of the body to perform normal function properly, e.g., incompetency of one or more cardiac valves resulting in regurgitation of blood at the time when the valves might have been closed completely. 2. Inability of a person declared legally to perform his/her duties properly.

Aortic incompetence—Defective closure of the aortic valve allowing the back flow of blood into the left ventricle during diastole.

Cardiac incompetence—Inability of the ventricles to pump out blood.

Mitral incompetence—Defective closure of the mitral valve allowing the back flow of blood into the left atrium during systole.

Pulmonary incompetence—Defective closure of the pulmonary valve allowing the back flow of blood into the right ventricle during diastole.

Incompetent—1. An organ or a part of the body or a person unable to perform normal function properly. 2. Legally unable person to perform his/her duties, who may be mentally retarded or insane.

Incompressible—Not compressible or which cannot be squeezed.

Incongruity—Inappropriateness.

Inconstant—Not fixed; changing; irregular.

Incontinence—Inability to retain the excretory products such as urine, feces, semen or milk etc. due to loss of sphincter control or because of some damage in the brain or in the spinal cord.

Fecal incontinence— Involuntary passage of feces and flatus.

Incontinence of milk — Excessive milk flow.

Overflow incontinence—A form of incontinence in which the bladder is full of urine, which does not empty normally but the urine passes off drop by drop involuntarily.

Stress incontinence—The occurrence of involuntary passage of urine due to strain on the orifice of the bladder as in coughing, laughing, sneezing, lifting or sudden movement.

Urinary incontinence— Inability to control the passage of urine.

Incontinent—Denoting incontinence.

Incontinentia—Incontinence.

Incoordinate—1. Unable to make coordinated muscular movements. 2. Unable to adjust one's work harmoniously with the others.

Incoordination—Non functioning harmoniously of the interrelated organs and parts of the body.

Incorporation—Combination of two or more substances to form a homogenous mass.

Incrassate—Thickened.

Incrassation—Thickness.

Increment—1. Increase or addition in number, size or extent. 2. The amount added to increase the quality of an object.

Incretion—The functional activity of an endocrine gland.

Incrustation—Formation of crusts, scabs or scales.

Incubate—To place a premature infant in an incubator to maintain an artificial environment for her.

Incubation—1. The period between entrance of the disease-producing organisms into the body and the appearance of symptoms of the disease. 2. The period of culture development of bacteria or tissues. 3. The maintenance of an artificial environment for a premature infant by placing her in an incubator.

Incubator—An apparatus used for maintaining the optimum temperature and humidity, etc., for caring of premature infants or one used for providing the suitable environment for culturing bacteria or for maintaining the eggs until they hatch.

Fig. 253 Incubator

Incubus—1. Nightmare. 2. Heavy mental stress.

Incudal—Pertaining to the incus bone.

Incudectomy—Surgical removal of the incus bone.

Incudes—Plural of incus.

Incudiform—Incus-shaped.

Incudomalleal—Pertaining to incus and the malleus bones.

Incudostapedial—Pertaining to incus and the stapes bones.

Incurable—The disease which cannot be cured.

Incurvate—Curved inward.

Incurvation—To be curved inward.

Incus—Anvil. The middle of the three small bones in the middle ear.

Incyclophoria—Rotation of the affected eye inward about its anteroposterior axis, when covered.

Incyclotropia—Rotation of the affected eye inward toward the nose, even when both the eyes are open.

In d.—In dies daily.

Indagation—A careful examination, especially of the genital organs at the termination of puerperium.

Indecision—Inability to decide.

Indenization—Innidiation.

Indentation—A notch or depression.

Index—1. The first or forefinger. 2. The ratio of the measurement of a part of the body or a given substance with that of a fixed standard.

Cephalic index—The number obtained by multiplying the breadth of the skull by 100 and dividing it by its length.

Cerebral index—Ratio of the greatest transverse to the greatest anteroposterior diameter of the cranial cavity, multiplied by 100.

Refractive index—The ratio of the angle made by falling rays of light on the lens (angle of incidence) to that made by emergent rays (angle of refraction).

Thoracic index—Ratio of the thoracic anteroposterior diameter to its transverse diameter.

Vital index—The ratio of the number of births to the number of deaths in a population in a specific period.

Indian hemp—Cannabis indica.

Indicanemia—Presence of indican in the blood.

Indicanidrosis—Excretion of indican in the sweat.

Indicant—Something which indicates the presence of a disease, or an absence of a symptom or sign which indicates the treatment is proper and effective.

Indicanuria—Presence of an excess of indican in the urine.

Indication—A sign or circumstance which indicates the proper treatment of a disease.

Causal indication—Indication of the treatment of a disease on the basis of its causes.

Symptomatic indication— Indication of treatment of a disease according to its symptoms.

Indicator—1. The index finger. 2. In chemical analysis, a substance which indicates the appearance or disappearance of a chemical by color change or attainment of a certain pH.

Indices—Plural of index.

Indifferent—1. Neutral 2. Not responsive to normal stimuli.

Indiffusible—Unable to be diffused.

In dies—Daily.

Indigenous—Native to country.

Indigestible—Not digestible.

Indigestion—Dyspepsia. Failure of digestion characterized by one or more of the symptoms, as abdominal discomfort after taking food, nausea, vomiting, heart burn, hyperacidity with acid regurgitation, accumulation of gas and belching.

Indigitation—Invagination.

Indignant—Angry.

Indignation—Anger caused by injustice or wickedness.

Indigouria—Presence of indigo in the urine.

Indispensable—Which cannot be dispensed.

Indisposition—Disorder or slight illness.

Indistinct—Which is not clear.

Individual—Single, particular.

Individuation—During development the emergence of individual characteristics.

Indole—A solid, crystalline substance, the product of bacterial decomposition of tryptophan in the intestine, found in the feces by which a peculiar odor arises from the feces.

Indolence—Laziness, inactivity.

Indolent—Lazy, inactive.

Indolent ulcer—The ulcer that heals slowly but it is not painful.

Indologenous—Producing indole.

Indoluria—Excretion of indole in the urine.

Indoxylemia—Presence of indoxyl in the blood.

Indoxyluria—Presence of indoxyl in the urine.

Induce —To prompt or to cause.

Induced—Caused or produced.

Inducer—That which causes or produces.

Induction—1. The process of causing something as induction of labor by the use of oxytocic drugs. 2. The process of producing as the generation of electric current in a body by electricity in an object near it.

Inductor—Any substance which causes the cells exposed to it to differentiate into an organized tissue.

Inductotherm—An apparatus for producing fever by electricity.

Inductothermy—Treatment of a disease by producing artificial fever by electromagnetic process.

Indulin—Any one of a group of dyes used in histology.

Indulinophil, Indulinophile—Readily staining with indulin.

Indurate—To make harden. Hardened.

Indurated—Hardened.

Induration—1. Process of hardening 2. The property of being hard. 3. An abnormally hard tissue or organ in the body, e.g. hardening of the liver in cirrhosis.

Indurative—Pertaining to induration.

Indusium—1. A membranous covering. 2. The amnion.

Indwelling—Remaining inside the body, as a catheter, drainage tube or other device for a long period.

-ine—A suffix used to form the names of chemical substances, as chlorine, caffeine etc.

Inebriant—1. Any intoxicant 2. Causing drunkenness.

Inebriate—Drunken or to make drunk.

Inebriation—Drunkenness.

Inebriety—The drinking of alcohol in excessive amounts habitually.

Inelastic—Not elastic.

Inert—1. Inactive 2. In chemistry, not reacting with other chemicals.

Inertia—Inactivity or inability to move spontaneously, e.g. uterine inertia in which there is absence or weakness of uterine contraction during labor.

In extremis—At the point of death.

Infancy—The period of first one year of life.

Infant—The child from the time of birth to one year of age.

Fig. 254 Infant. Age—10 months

Immature infant—The infant weighing between 500 and 999 gms. at birth with little chance of survival.

Mature infant—The infant weighing 2500 gms. (two and half kgs.) or more at birth, with maximum chance of survival.

Newborn infant—The infant during the 1st two to four weeks after birth.

Postmature infant, Post-term infant—The infant born at any time after beginning of the 42nd week (288 days) of pregnancy.

Premature infant—The infant weighing between 1000 and 2499 gms. at birth with fair chance of survival.

Preterm infant—The infant born before the completion of 37th week (259 days) of pregnancy.

Stillborn infant—The infant born after the completion of 20th week of pregnancy but showing no signs of life after birth; dead newborn infant.

Term infant—The infant born at any time from the beginning of 38th week (260 days) to the end of 41st week (287 days) of pregnancy.

Infanticide—The killer of an infant.

Infantile—Pertaining to infancy or an infant.

Infantilism—A condition in which the childhood characters persist in adult life. The affected person suffers from mental retardation, stunted growth often with dwarfism and underdevelopment of the sex organs.

Angioplastic infantilism—Infantilism caused by defective development of the vascular system.

Cachectic infantilism— Infantilism due to chronic infection or poisoning.

Dysthyroidal infantilism—Infantilism caused by a defect in the thyroid gland.

Hepatic infantilism—Infantilism caused by cirrhosis or some other disease of the liver.

Pituitary infantilism— Dwarfism and the sexual immaturity resulting from hyposecretion of the growth and gonadotrophic hormones of the anterior lobe of pituitary gland.

Renal infantilism—Infantilism caused by a defect in the renal function.

Sexual infantilism— Continuation of the childish sexual characteristics and behavior beyond the age of puberty.

Symptomatic infantilism—Infantilism caused by the poor development of the tissues.

Universal infantilism— General dwarfism with absence of secondary sexual characteristics.

Infarct—An area of a tissue of the body which becomes necrosed by occlusion of the arterial blood supply or more rarely from occlusion of the vein which drains that tissue.

Anemia infarct—Necrosis of the tissues occurring as a result of lack of blood supply in anemia, in which the tissue becomes pale or white.

Embolic infarct—An infarct caused by an embolus.

Hemorrhagic infarct—Red infarct. An infarct that is swollen and red due to hemorrhage.

Infected infarct—Septic infarct. An infarct caused by pathogenic bacteria or infected material.

Pale infarct—Anemic infarct.

Red infarct—Hemorrhagic infarct.

Septic infarct—Infected infarct.

Thrombotic infarct—Infarct caused by a thrombus.

Uric acid infarct—An infarct in the kidney caused by obstruction of the renal tubules by uric acid crystals.

White infarct—Anemic infarct.

Infarctectomy—Surgical removal of an infarct.

Infarction—1. The formation of an infarct. 2. An infarct.

Cerebral infarction—An infarct formed in the cerebrum due to failure of blood supply.

Myocardial infarction— Necrosis of an area of the cardiac muscle usually due to the formation of a thrombus in the coronary artery.

Pulmonary infarction—A necrosed area in the lung tissue due to obstruction of the arterial blood supply resulting from pulmonary embolism.

Infect—To introduce the disease-producing organisms into the body or upon a wound.

Infected— Affected with infection.

Infection — The invasion and multiplication of disease-producing agents as bacteria, viruses, fungi and animal parasites producing harmful effects.

Acute infection— The infection occurring suddenly of short duration.

Air-borne infection— Infectious organisms transported through the air.

Apical infection— An infection of the apex of a tooth root.

Blood-borne infection—An infection transmitted through contact with the blood of an infected individual, such as hepatitis or AIDS etc.

Chronic infection— Infection of long duration.

Cross infection—Infection spreading from person to person, animal to person, or from other source to a person.

Cryptogenic infection —Any bacterial, viral or other infection, the source of which is not known.

Droplet infection— Infection due to inhalation of the micro-organisms suspended on liquid particles, which come out in the atmosphere from a person already infected, by exhalation, coughing or sneezing.

Endogenous infection—Infection caused by bacteria, which are normally nonpathogenic and living in the intestine as occurs in tuberculosis etc.

Exogenous infection— Infection caused by the bacteria present outside the body.

Food-borne infection— Infection caused by taking the infected food.

Fungus infection— Infection caused by a fungus.

Latent infection—Asymptomatic or hidden infection which is manifested under particular circumstances.

Local infection—Infection occurring at a point in a tissue and remaining there by the pathogenic organisms, lodging and multiplying there, as a boil.

Low-grade infection—Mild infection with slight inflammation and without pus formation.

Mixed infection— Infection caused by two or more organisms.

Nosocomial infection—An infection that is acquired during hospitalization.

Protozoal infection— Infection caused by a protozoon, e.g. malaria.

Pyogenic infection— Infection caused by pus-forming organisms.

Secondary infection— Infection caused by a different organism than one causing the primary infection.

Subacute infection— An infection intermediate between acute and chronic.

Subclinical infection — An infection that is confirmed by pathological examination but does not show any symptom.

Systemic infection— Infection remaining throughout the body and not localized.

Water-borne infection— Infection caused by the organisms present in water.

Infectiosity—Infectiousness.

Infectious— 1. Causing infection. 2. Pertaining to a disease due to pathoorganisms. 3. Capable of being transmitted by infection.

Infectiousness—Infectiosity. The sate of being infectious.

Infective—1. Capable of producing infection. 2. Pertaining to or characterized by the presence of disease producing organisms.

Infectivity—The capability of a disease-producing organism to transmit the infection.

Infecundity— Barrenness; sterility in women.

Inference—Presumption.

Inferior— 1. Situated below or lower. 2. In anatomy, used in reference to the under surface of an organ or indicating a structure below another structure.

Inferiority complex— Feeling of oneself inferior to others.

Infertile— Unable to produce offspring.

Infertility— Inability or diminished ability to produce offsprings.

Infest—To cause trouble.

Infestation—1. Trouble. 2. The attack of animal parasites as insects and ticks etc., on the skin and of helminths in the intestine of the human body.

Infibulation—The process of fastening, as in joining the edges of a wound by clasps.

Infiltrate—To pass through a tissue or a substance, or the material so passed and deposited.

Infiltration—The process of passing of a substance through a tissue or a substance and being deposited in a cell, tissue or an organ; also the material so deposited.

Adipose infiltration— Fatty infiltration. Deposition of fat in the tissues.

Anesthesia infiltration— Injection of an anesthetic solution directly into the tissue.

Calcareous infiltration— Deposits of calcium or magnesium salts in the tissues.

Cellular infiltration— Infiltration of cells, especially of blood cells into the tissues.

Fatty infiltration—Amyloid infiltration, adipose infiltration.

Infinite— Unlimited.

Infinite distance— A distance without limit.

Infinity— 1. Condition of being infinite. 2. Space, time or quantity without limits.

Infirm— Weak, especially from old age or disease.

Infirmary — A hospital or a place for the care of weak person or for the treatment of the sick persons.

Infirmity— 1. Weakness 2. Illness.

Inflame— To undergo inflammation.

Inflammable—Flammable.

Inflammation— A tissue reaction as a protective response to an injury characterized by pain, heat, redness and swelling and loss of function of that part of the tissue. Most words denoting inflammation end with the suffix 'itis'

Acute inflammation— Inflammation of sudden onset and of short duration.

Adhesive inflammation—Inflammation characterized by the adherence of the adjacent tissues.

Allergic inflammation—Inflammation occurring in allergic reaction.

Bacterial inflammation— Inflammation produced by the growth of bacteria.

Catarrhal inflammation— Inflammation of a mucous membrane characterized by the excessive secretion of mucus.

Chronic inflammation—Inflammation which is not so severe and progresses slowly or as a continuation of an acute form, and of long duration, which persists for several weeks, months or years, characterized by low-grade fever and pain.

Exudative inflammation—Inflammation in which there is an exudate which may be chiefly serous, serofibrinous, fibrinous or mucous.

Fibrinous inflammation— Inflammation marked by exudate containing a great amount of fibrin.

Granulomatous inflammation—Chronic inflammation marked by the formation of granulomas as seen in tuberculosis, syphilis and some fungal infections.

Hyperplastic inflammation— Inflammation characterized by excessive production of fibrous tissues.

Necrotic inflammation, Necrotizing inflammation—An acute inflammation in which necrosis occurs in the affected tissue.

Proliferative inflammation—Hyperplastic inflammation.

Pseudomembranous inflammation — Inflammation in which a pseudomembrane is formed in the mouth, nasal cavity and respiratory tract in diphtheria, due to a toxin which necrotizes the tissues.

Purulent inflammation— Suppurative inflammation.

Reactive inflammation— Inflammation produced around a foreign body or dead tissue.

Serous inflammation— The inflammation in which the exudate is chiefly composed of serum or inflammation of a serous membrane.

Specific inflammation—Inflammation caused by a specific organism.

Subacute inflammation—Inflammation of the intermediate type between acute and chronic.

Suppurative inflammation— The inflammation in which pus is formed.

Traumatic inflammation— Inflammation caused by an injury.

Ulcerative inflammation—The inflammation over which an ulcer is formed.

Inflammatory— Pertaining to or having an inflammation.

Inflation— Distention or the act of distending an organ or part of the body with air, gas or fluid.

Inflator— An apparatus for distending an organ with air.

Inflection— Inflexion . The act of bending inward, or the state of being bent inward.

Influenza— An acute contagious viral infection of the respiratory tract lasting 2-7 days occurring in isolated persons, epidemically or pandemically, with the inflammation of the nasal mucosa, pharynx and conjunctiva with the injected eyes, characterized by the symptoms of sudden onset of chills, fever, the temp. being101^{0}F to 103^{0}F, headache and backache, coryza, sneezing, cough and sore throat with hoarseness of the voice.

Influenzal— Pertaining to influenza.

Influx— The act of flowing in.

Infold—To enclose within a fold, as is done in the operation of a stomach ulcer, which is closed by suturing the walls together of either side of the lesion.

Infolding — The process of enclosing in a fold.

Informatics—The study of information technology.

Infra- — A prefix meaning below, under, beneath or inferior to or after.

Infra-axillary— Below the axilla.

Infracardiac— Below the heart.

Infracerebral—Below the cerebrum.

Infraclavicular— Below the clavicle bone.

Infraclusion— The condition in which a tooth of a jaw remains out of contact with the opposing tooth of the other jaw, when the jaws are closed.

Infracolic— Below the colon.
Infracortical— Below the cortex of an organ.
Infracostal— Below a rib.
Infracotyloid —Below the acetabulum of the hip bone.
Infraction— An incomplete fracture. A fracture of a bone in which the parts of the bone are not displaced.
Infradentale—A bony point between the mandibular central incisor teeth.
Infradian— Pertaining to a period longer than 24 hours.
Infradiaphragmatic— Sub-diaphragmatic. Below the diaphragm.
Infraglenoid—Subglenoid. Below the glenoid cavity of the scapula bone.
Infraglottic— Below the glottis.
Infrahepatic—Subhepatic. Below the liver.
Infrahyoid— Below the hyoid bone.
Inframamillary—Situated below the nipple of a mammary gland.
Inframammary— Below the mammary gland.
Inframandibular— Below the mandible.
Inframarginal— Below a margin or edge.
Inframaxillary— Below the maxilla (upper jaw).
Infranatant—The lower portion of the contents of a vessel after settling out of an insoluble liquid or solid by gravitation or centrifugal force.
Infraocclusion— Infraclusion.
Infraorbital— Below the orbit.
Infrapateller— Below the patella bone.
Infrapsychic— Below the level of consciousness, automatic.
Infrapubic— Below the pubis.
Infrared —The portion of the electromagnetic spectrum with wavelengths between 730 and 1000 nm.
Infrared rays— Invisible heat rays of wavelength greater than that of the red end of the spectrum, having wavelength of .75—1000μ or 7500 Angstrom units to 1mm, used usually as fomentation in the treatment of some diseases.
Infrascapular— Below the scapula bone.
Infrasonic— Sound wave frequency lower than those normally heard.
Infraspinous— Below the spine of the scapula bone.
Infrasplenic—Beneath or below the spleen.
Infrasternal— Below the sternum.
Infratemporal—Below the temporal fossa.
Infratentorial— Beneath the tentorium of the cerebellum.
Infrathoracic—Below the thorax.
Infratonsillar— In the pharynx below the tonsils.
Infratrochlear— Below the trochlea.
Infraumbilical— Below the umbilicus.
Infraversion— Downward deviation of the eye.
Infriction— Inunction. Rubbing of an ointment into the skin.
Infundibula—Plural of infundibulum.
Infundibular— Pertaining to the infundibulum.
Infundibulectomy— Excision of the infundibulum of an organ.
Infundibuliform— Funnel-shaped.
Infundibuloma—A tumor of the stalk of the pituitary gland.
Infundibulo-ovarian—Pertaining to the fimbriated extremity of a fallopian tube and the ovary.
Infundibulopelvic—Pertaining to the infundibulum and the pelvis of an organ, especially the kidney.
Infundibulum— 1. A funnel-shaped structure or passage. 2. The stalk of pituitary gland. 3. A division of renal pelvis. 4. Distal, funnel-shaped portion of the fallopian tube.
Infused— Steeped.
Infusible— Capable of being steeped or made into an infusion.
Infusion— 1. The steeping of a substance into hot or cold water to obtain its soluble active principles. 2. The product obtained by this process. 3. A liquid substance introduced into the body through intravenous route for the treatment of some diseases.
Infusodecoction— Steeping of a substance in cold water followed by decoction.
Infusor— An instrument for slow injection of a liquid into a vein.
Infusum— Infusion. Product obtained from steeping a substance in hot or cold water.
Ingesta— Material received into the body through the mouth.
Ingestant— Any food substance or drink which is taken by mouth.
Ingestion— The process of taking food material or drink into the gastrointestinal tract or the process by which a cell takes in the foreign particles.
Ingestive—Pertaining to ingestion.
Ingravescent—Gradually becoming more severe.
Ingredient—Any part of a compound or a mixture.
Ingression—Entrance.
Ingrowing—Growing inwards.
Ingrown nail—The nail with the edge grown into the soft tissue causing inflammation and pain.
Inguen— The groin.

Inguinal—Pertaining to groin.

Inguinal canal— An oblique passage of about 4 cm (1.5 inches) long in the lower part of the anterior abdominal wall extending from the deep inguinal ring to the superficial inguinal ring, running downwards, forwards and medially, carrying spermatic cord in the male and the round ligament in the female. It may be a site of a hernia or undescended testis.

Inguinal glands— Lymph nodes in the groin region.

Inguinal region—Groin.

Inguinal ring— Deep inguinal ring–the opening of the inguinal canal in the interior of the abdomen and the superficial inguinal ring– the end of the inguinal canal situated just above and lateral to the pubic crest.

Inguinocrural—Pertaining to the groin and the thigh.

Inguinodynia—Pain in the groin or inguinal region.

Inguinolabial—Pertaining to the groin and the labium.

Inguinoperitoneal—Pertaining to inguinal region and peritoneum.

Inguinoscrotal— Pertaining to the groin and the scrotum.

Inhalant— The substance which can be taken into the body by inhalation.

Inhalation— 1. Inspiration. 2. Drawing of air, vapor or gas into the lungs. 3. Introduction of a gas or vapor into the lungs through the nasal route for the treatment of some diseases, such as spirit ammonia aromatica for fainting or solution of durgs by neubilizer for the treatment of the diseases of the nose and the upper respiratory tract.

Inhale—To draw in the air or to inspire.

Inhaler—1. An apparatus for administering the medicines by inhalation into the lungs. 2. The person who inhales.

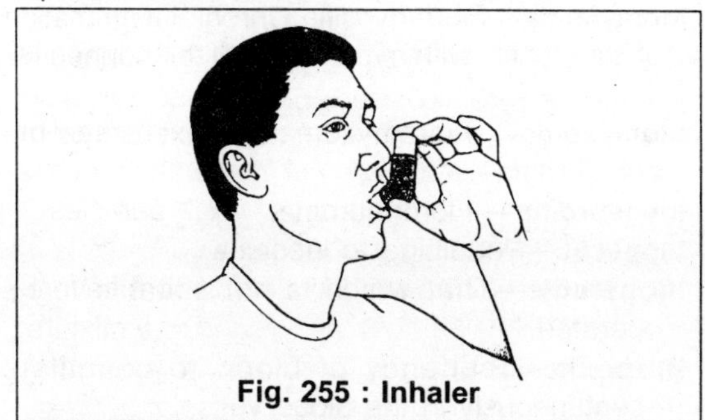

Fig. 255 : Inhaler

Inherent— Intrinsic. Natural, not as a result of circumstances.

Inherent cauterization— Deep cauterization.

Inheritance— 1. The acquisition of the parenteral characters or qualities to the offspring by transmission. 2. That which is transmitted from the parent to the offspring.

Inherited—Transmitted from one's parents, not acquired.

Inhibin—A hormone secreted by Serotoli cells in the testis and granulosa cells in the ovary, that inhibits the secretion of follicle-stimulating hormone by the anterior pituitary gland.

Inhibition— Stopping of a function of an organ, or arrest or suppression of a mental impulse, thought, action or speech.

Inhibitor— That which inhibits.

Inhibitory—Preventing.

Inhibitrope— The person in whom certain stimuli cause partial arrest of function.

Inhomogeneity— Absence of uniform quality or consistency.

Iniac—Inial. Pertaining to the inion.

Iniad—In a direction toward the inion.

Inial—Iniac.

Iniencephalus—A congenitally deformed fetus in which the brain substance protrudes through a fissure in the occiput.

Iniencephaly—A congenital malformation in an infant in which the brain substance protrudes through a fissure in the occiput.

Inion— External occipital protuberance.

Iniopagus— Two fetuses fused at the occiput.

Iniops— A fetus with two faces, the posterior face being incomplete.

Initial— Incipient. Original or occurring at the beginning.

Initiation—Start of a chemical or an enzymatic reaction.

Initis— 1. Inflammation of the substance of muscle. 2. Inflammation of fibrous tissue. 3. Inflammation of a tendon.

Inject— To introduce fluid into the body or a part of the body by injection.

Injectable—1. Capable of being injected. 2. Capable of receiving an injection.

Injected— 1. Introduced by injection 2. Congested.

Injection— 1. The forcing of a fluid into an organ or a part of the body by intramuscular, subcutaneous or intravenous route. 2. The substance introduced in this manner. 3. Congestion.

Epidural injection— Injection of an anesthetic solution or of other medicine into the epidural space of the spinal cord.

Fractional injection—Injection of small amount at a time until the total amount of medicine is injected.

Hypodermic injection— Injection into the subcutaneous tissues.

Intra-alveolar injection—An infiltration of an anesthetic solution into the soft tissues adjacent to the tooth.

Intracardial injection—Injection into the heart.

Intracutaneous injection— Injection into the skin.

Intradermal injection— Intracutaneous injection.

Intramuscular injection—Injection made into the substance of a muscle e.g in the deltoid muscle or in the muscle of one of the buttocks.

Intrathecal injection—An injection given by means of lumbar puncture to introduce the medicine in the subarachnoid space.

Intravenous Injection— Injection made into a vein.

Rectal injection—An enema.

Sclerosing injection—Injection of a substance into a blood vessel or into a tissue which causes obliteration of the blood vessel or hardening of the tissue.

Spinal injection—Injection made into the spinal canal.

Subcutaneous injection— Hypodermic injection.

Vaginal injection—Vaginal douche.

Injector—An instrument for making injections.

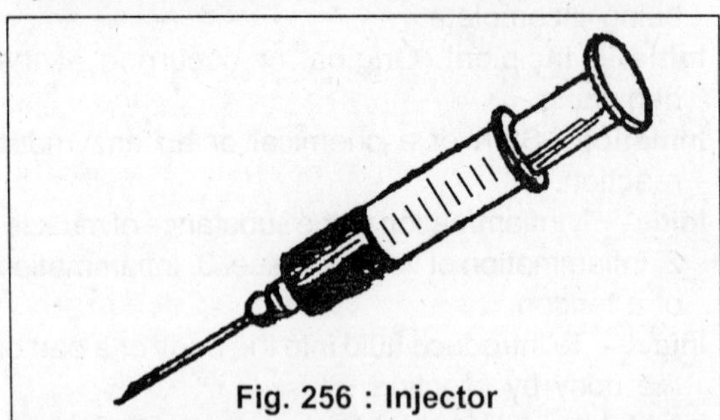

Fig. 256 : Injector

Injure—To damage; to hurt; to do harm.

Injury— A trauma or damage to some part of the body producing inflammation or causing the formation of wound and there may be disability of that part.

Inlay— A solid material filled into a tissue defect or a filling corresponding the shape of a tooth cavity, made outside the tooth and then cemented it into the tooth.

Inlet—The passage of entrance into a cavity, e.g. inlet of pelvis i.e. the upper limit of the pelvic cavity.

Innate— Inherent.

Innervate—To stimulate the nerve supply of an organ.

Innervation—The nerve supply or the nerve stimulation of a part of the body.

Innidiation— Multiplication of cells in a part of the body to which they have been carried by metastasis.

Innocent—Harmless or benign.

Innocuous— Innocent.

Innominatal—Pertaining to the hip bone.

Innominate— Nameless.

Innoxious— Innocent, innocuous.

Innutrition— Lack of nutrition.

Inochondritis— Inflammation of a fibrocartilage.

Inochondroma— Fibrochondroma. A tumor or chondroma with much fibrous tissues.

Inoculability— The quality of being inoculable.

Inoculable— 1. Transmissible by inoculation. 2. Susceptible or capable of being inoculated.

Inoculate— To inject a microorganism, serum or toxic materials into the body.

Inoculation— The process of injecting a microorganism, serum or toxic materials into the body.

Inoculum— The substance introduced by inoculation.

Inocyst— A fibrous capsule.

Inocyte— Fibroblast.

Inodorous— Having no smell.

Inogenesis— Formation of fibrous tissue.

Inogenous— Forming tissue or produced by it.

Inohymenitis— Inflammation of a fibrous membrane or of an aponeurosis.

Inolith— A calculus formed from fibrous tissue.

Inoma—Fibroma.

Inomyositis—Fibromyositis. Chronic inflammation of the muscle with hyperplasia of the connective tissue.

Inomyxoma— Fibromyxoma. A mixed myxoma and fibroma.

Inoneuroma— Fibroneuroma.

Inopectic—Pertaining to inopexia.

Inoperable—That which is not suitable to be operated.

Inopexia—Tendency of blood to coagulate spontaneously in the blood vessels.

Inorganic— 1. Chemical compounds having no carbon 2. Not pertaining to the living organism.

Inorganic acid— Mineral acid. An acid composed of inorganic constituents.

Inorganic chemistry— Chemistry in which only inorganic compounds are studied.

Inorganic compound— A compound without carbon.

Inosclerosis— Increased hardness of the fibrous tissue.

Inoscopy— Diagnosis of disease by examining the fibrinous matter in the body fluids such as in blood and sputum etc.

Inosculating— Anastomosing. Directly communicating .

Inosculation—Anastomosis. Union of two vessels.

Inose — Inositol.

Inosemia— 1. The presence of inositol in the blood 2. An excess of fibrin in the blood.

Inositis— Inflammation of fibrous tissue.

Inosituria— Presence of inositol in the urine.

Inosuria— Inosituria.

Inotropic— Affecting the force of muscular contractility.

Inquest— A legal inquiry made before a medical examiner into the manner of sudden and unexpected death.

Insalivation— The process of mixing saliva with food in chewing.

Insalubrious— 1. Unhealthy. 2. Injurious to health.

Insane— Mentally deranged.

Insanitary— Unhealthfull.

Insanity— A legal term for any mental illness, characterized by inability to distinguish between right and wrong.

Insatiable— Unable to be satisfied.

Inscriptio— Inscription.

Inscription— 1. The main part of a prescription containing the names and doses of the medicines. 2. A mark or line.

Insect— Any organism belonging to the class insecta of the phylum Arthropoda, as flies, mosquitoes, lice, ticks, spiders, scorpions and bees, etc.

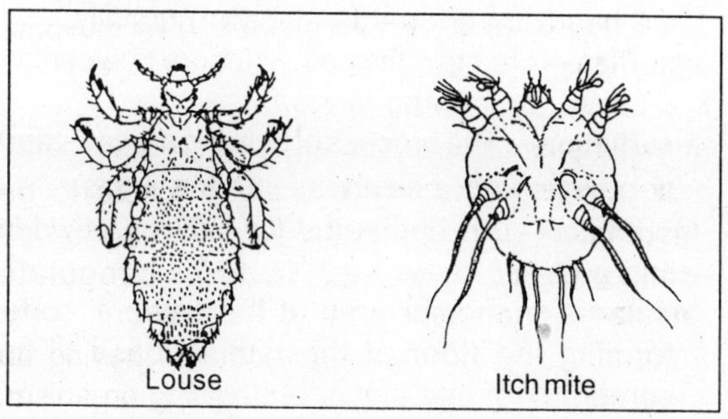

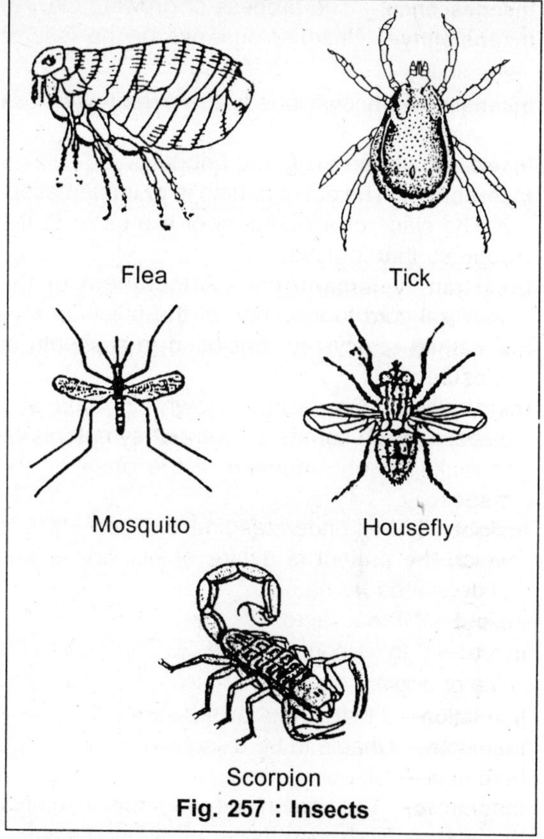

Fig. 257 : Insects

Insecta—A class of the phylum Arthropoda whose organisms are characterized by three distinct body divisions as head, thorax and abdomen, three pairs of jointed legs and usually two pairs of wings.

Insectarium—Place for keeping insects for scientific purposes.

Insect-born—Caused or transmitted by insects.

Insecticide— An agent which kills the insects.

Insectifuge—Insect-repellent.

Insectivorous—Insect–eating.

Insectology—The science of insects.

Insect-repellent— Insectifuge. Driving back the insects.

Insecurity—Unprotectedness.

Insemination— Deposit of semen from the penis into vagina or the cervix during intercourse. It may be artificial when the semen is introduced into the vagina, cervix or the uterus by artificial means. When the semen is obtained from a person other than the husband, it is known as heterologous artificial insemination and when the semen is obtained from the husband, it is known as homologous artificial insemination.

Insenescence— The process of growing old.

Insensibility— Unconsciousness or the loss of sensibility.

Insensible—Unconscious or the person with loss of sensibility.

Insert—To fit one thing into another.

Insertion—1. The act of putting in or implantation. 2. The place of attachment of a muscle to the bone so that it moves.

Insertion velamentous— Attachment of the umbilical cord to the edge of the placenta.

Insheathed—Encysted. Enclosed in a sheath or capsule.

Insidious—1. Developing slowly. 2. Said of a disease which comes on without symptoms as to make patient unaware of the onset of the disease.

Insight—1. Self-understanding 2. The extent to which the patient is aware of his illness and understands its nature.

Insipid—Without taste.

In situ—1. In its normal place. 2. Confined to the site of origin.

Insolation— Heat stroke or sunstroke.

Insoluble— Unable to be dissolved.

Insomnia— Sleeplessness.

Insomniac— The person suffering from insomnia.

Insonate— To expose to the ultrasound ways.

Insorption—The entrance of a substance into the blood, especially from the digestive tract into the circulating blood.

Inspect—To examine visually.

Inspection—Visual examination.

Inspersion—Sprinkling, as of the powder.

Inspirate— The air inhaled at a single inspiration.

Inspiration—Inhalation; drawing of air into the lungs.

Inspirator— A type of respirator or inhaler.

Inspiratory— Pertaining to the inspiration.

Inspire—Inhale. To draw in the breath.

Inspired— Inhaled.

Inspirometer— An apparatus for determining the amount of inspired air.

Inspissate— To thicken by evaporation or absorption of fluid.

Inspissated— Being thickened or dried by evaporation or absorption of fluid.

Inspissation— Thickening by evaporation or absorption of fluid.

Inspissator—An apparatus for evaporating fluids.

Instability— Lack of stability, or firmness, unsteadiness , fickleness.

Instable— Fickle

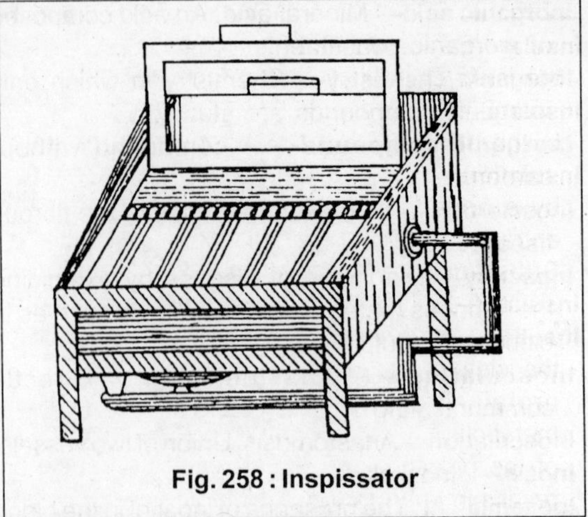

Fig. 258 : Inspissator

Instep— Archlike medial portion of the foot.

Instillation— Pouring a liquid drop by drop.

Instillator—An apparatus for introducing liquids drop by drop.

Instinct— The inherited tendency to react to certain environmental conditions and stimuli in a particular way.

Instinctive—Determined by instinct.

Instrument—A special tool for performing some specific work, e.g. a surgical knife, stethoscope, microscope etc.

Instrumental— Pertaining to an instrument.

Instrumentarium—A collection of instruments for an operation or for a medical procedure.

Instrumentation—1. The use of instruments. 2. Performance of a work with instruments.

Insucation—Maceration or soaking, especially of a crude drug.

Insudation— 1. The accumulation of a substance derived from the blood , as in the kidney. 2. The substance so accumulated.

Insufficiency— 1. Inadequacy, e.g. diminished secretion of the adrenal cortical hormones in Addison's disease. 2. Inability of an organ or part of the body to perform its function normally, e.g. cardiac insufficiency in which there is inability of the heart to perform its function normally.

Insufflate— To blow air, gas , vapor or powder into a cavity, as into the lungs.

Insufflation—The process of blowing air, gas, vapor or powder into a cavity as into the lungs.

Insufflator— An apparatus for blowing powders into a cavity.

Insula—A triangular area of the cerebral cortex forming the floor of the lateral fossa of the cerebrum.

Insular—Pertaining to the insula or to an islet, as the islets of Langerhans in the pancreas.

Insulate—To prevent the flow of an electric current by the interposition of a non-conducting material.

Insulation— 1. Protection of a body or substance by a nonconducting material to prevent the entrance or escape of radiation or electricity. 2. Substance or material used in insulation.

Insulator— A nonconducting material.

Insulin— A hormone secreted by the beta cells of the isiets of Langerhans of the pancreas. It is a protein which is essential for the proper metabolism of carbohydrate and for maintenance of the proper blood sugar level. Its deficiency results in improper metabolism of carbohydrate and causes diabetes mellitus characterized by hyperglycemia and glycosuria.

Insulin preparations are divided into three categories according to how quickly their actions start and the duration of actions after an intracutaneous injection. The three categories of insulin are—fast, intermediate and long acting insulin.

Crystalline or soluble insulin — It is a fast-acting insulin. It starts to act within half an hour to one hour after intracutaneous injection and the duration of its action is about 6 hours, so it is given twice a day.

Globin Zinc insulin—Intermediate-acting insulin. It consists of insulin modified by the addition of Zinc chloride and Globin and starts to act within one to two hours and the duration of action is 24 hours.

Isophane insulin or NPH insulin— A neutral crystalline intermediate acting insulin which starts its action in 1/2 to 1 hour and the duration of its action is 24 hours.

Lente insulin—Insulin zinc suspension. It is long-acting insulin, the action starts in 5 to 8 hours, and the duration of action is over 36 hours.

Protamine Zinc insulin— It is long-acting insulin prepared by the addition of a protein protamine and zinc to insulin hydrochloride. Its action starts within 6-8 hours and lasts 20 to 28 hrs.

Regular insulin—A rapidly acting insulin which is a clear solution and may be administered intravenously as well as subcutaneously and may be mixed with long-acting insulin.

Semilente insulin— Insulin zinc suspension (amorphous) - It is effective for about 10 to 15 hours.

Ultralente insulin— Insulin zinc suspension (crystalline)–Its action persists for 24 to 36 hours.

Insulinase— An enzyme that inactivates insulin.

Insulinemia— Excess of insulin in the blood.

Insulin lipodystrophy— Atrophy or hypertrophy of the subcutaneous fat at the site where insulin injection administered repeatedly.

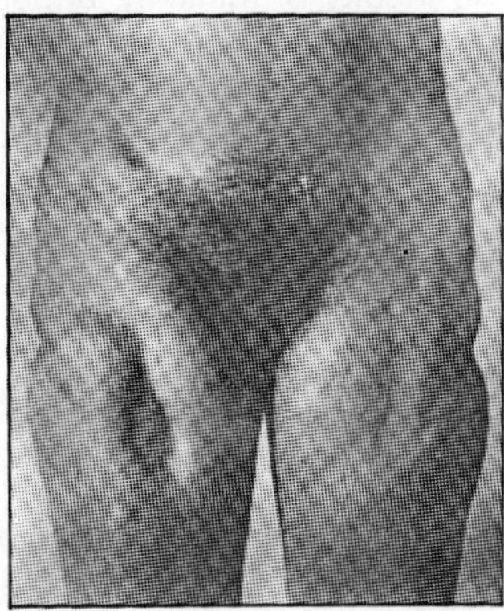

Fig. 259 : Insulin lipodystrophy

Insulinogenesis—The production and release of insulin by the islets of Langerhans of the pancreas.

Insulinogenic—1. Pertaining to the production of insulin. 2. Caused by insulin.

Insulinoid—Resembling insulin or having the properties of insulin.

Insulinoma—Insuloma.

Insulin shock—The condition of shock caused by over reduction of blood sugar (hypoglycemia) resulting from an overdose of insulin.

Insulitis—Inflammation of the islets of Langerhans of the pancreas.

Insuloma—A benign tumor of the beta cells of the islets of Langerhans which causes hypoglycemia.

Insulopathic—Pertaining to or caused by abnormal secretion of the insulin.

Insulopenic—Diminishing or pertaining to diminution, level of insulin in the circulating blood.

Insult—Insultus. An injury, trauma or attack.

Insultus—An attack.

Insusceptibility—Immunity or the state of being unaffected by a disease.

Intake— All the substances taken in and utilized by the body.

Int. cib.—Between meals.

Integral—Complete, whole.

Integration—The joining or bringing together.

Integrator— An apparatus for measuring the body surfaces.

Integrity—Wholesomeness, soundness, honesty, purity.

Integument— A covering or skin.

Integumentary—Cutaneous or dermal. Pertaining to the integument.

Integumentum—Integument.

Intellect—The faculty of thinking, understanding.

Intellectual— 1. Pertaining to the mind . 2. Possessing intellect.

Intellectualization— The analysis of the personal and social problems on an intellectual basis.

Intelligence— Ability to understand and to solve the problems.

Intelligence quotient— The index of intelligence of a person determined by his/her answers to the selected questions.

Intemperance— Excessive use of a thing.

Intensifying— Making intense or magnifying.

Intensity— The extent of activity, strength and electric current etc.

Intensive—Pertaining to or marked by intensity.

Intensive care unit—See under unit.

Intention—1. Purpose. 2. Manner of healing—see under healing.

Inter- — A prefix meaning in the middle or in between.

Interacinar—Interacinous. Between the acini of a gland.

Interacinous—Interacinar.

Interaction—The process of two or more things acting on each other.

Interalveolar— Between the alveoli, especially of the lungs.

Interarticular—Situated between articulating surfaces.

Interarytenoid—Between the arytenoid cartilages.

Interatrial—Between the atria of the heart.

Interauricular— Situated between the auricles, or pinnae of the ears.

Interbody—Between the bodies of the adjacent vertebrae.

Interbrain—1. Thalamencephalon 2. Diencephalon.

Intercadence—The occurrence of an extra beat between the two regular pulse beats.

Intercadent—An individual in whom an extra beat occurs between the two regular pulse beats.

Intercalary— Inserted or interposed between.

Intercalated— Inserted between.

Intercanalicular— Between the canaliculi of a tissue.

Intercapillary—Between the capillaries.

Intercarotic— Between the internal and external carotid arteries.

Intercarpal—Between the carpal bones.

Intercartilaginous— Between or connecting the cartilages.

Intercavernous—Between the cavernous sinuses.

Intercellular—Between the cells.

Intercentral—Between two or more centers.

Interception— Obstruction , hindrance.

Intercerebral— Between the two cerebral hemispheres.

Interchange—To exchange with each other, to alternate.

Interchondral—Intercartilaginous. Between cartilages.

Intercilium—Glabella. The space between the eyebrows .

Interclavicular—Between the clavicle bones.

Intercoccygeal—Situated between the segments of the coccyx.

Intercolumnar—Between the two columns.

Intercondylar, Intercondylous—Between two condyles.

Interconversion—A mutual alteration of the physical or chemical properties of a substance.

Intercostal—Between the ribs.

Intercostobrachial—Pertaining to the intercostal space and the arm.

Intercostohumeral— Pertaining to or connecting an intercostal space and the humerus bone.

Intercourse—Mutual exchange, communication.
 Sexual intercourse—Coitus.

Intercricothyrotomy— Surgical incision of the larynx through the cricothyroid membrane.

Intercristal— Between two crests of a bone or organ.

Intercritical—Denoting the period between attacks as of gout.

Intercrural— Between two legs.

Intercurrent— Occurring during and modifying the course of another disease.

Intercuspation—Intercusping.

Intercusping—The fitting together of the occlusive surfaces of the opposite teeth naturally.

Intercutaneomucous—Between the skin and mucous membrane as at the mucocutaneous border of the lips or anus.

Interdeferential—Between the deferent ducts.

Interdental— Between the teeth.

Interdentium—The space between two adjacent teeth.

Interdigit—The part of the hand or foot lying between two fingers or toes.
Interdigital— Between two digits (fingers or toes).
Interdigitation—1. Interlocking of the parts of the body by fingerlike processes. 2. One of a finger-like processes so interlocked.
Interface—A surface forming a common boundary of two bodies.
Interfacial—Pertaining to interface.
Interfascicular—Between the fasciculi.
Interfemoral— Between the thighs.
Interference— Interposition.
Interfibrillar, Interfibrillary— Between the fibrils.
Interfibrous—Between the fibers.
Interfilamentous— Between the filaments.
Interfilar mass—The fluid portion of the protoplasm.
Interganglionic— Between the ganglia.
Intergemmal— Between the taste buds.
Intergenal—Between different genes.
Interglobular— Between globules.
Intergluteal— Between the buttocks.
Intergonial—Between the two gonia.
Intergyral— Between the cerebral gyri.
Interhemicerebral—Situated between the cerebral hemispheres.
Interictal—Occurring between the attacks or the seizures.
Interior— The internal portion of a thing.
Interischiadic—Between the ischia of the pelvis.
Interkinesis—The period between the Ist and second meiotic division of the cells.
Interlabial—Between the lips or any two labia.
Interlamellar— Between the lamellae.
Interlobar— Between the lobes.
Interlobitis—The inflammation of the pleura separating the pulmonary lobes.
Interlobular— Between the lobules of an organ.
Interlobular emphysema—Air between the pulmonary lobules.
Intermalleolar— Between the malleoli.
Intermammary— Between the breasts.
Intermammillary— Between the nipples of the breasts.
Intermarriage—Marriage in relationship.
Intermaxilla—Incisive bone.
Intermaxillary— Between the maxillae or upper jaw bones.
Intermediary—1. Situated between the two bodies. 2. Occurring between the two periods of time.
Intermediate— Lying between; occurring after the beginning and before the end.
Intermedin— A melanocyte-stimulating hormone secreted by the middle portion of the pituitary gland.
Intermediolateral—Intermediate but not central.
Intermedius—The middle of the three structures.
Intermembranous—Between the membranes.
Intermeningeal— Between the meninges.
Intermenstrual— Between the menstrual periods.
Interment— Burial.
Intermetacarpal—Between the metacarpal bones.
Intermetameric—Between two metameres.
Intermetatarsal—Between the metatarsal bones.
Intermission—1. Temporary cessation. 2. Interval.
Intermit—To cease for a time.
Intermittence—1. Temporary cessation of the symptoms of a disease. 2. A loss of one or more pulse beats.
Intermittent—Becoming inactive periodically.
Intermural—Between the walls of an organ.
Intermuscular—Between the muscles.
Intern—A medical graduate working in a hospital as an apprentice prior to be eligible to be licensed to practice.
Internal—Situated or occurring on the inside, enclosed, inward.
Internalization—A mental process in which the values, attitudes and standards of others are unconsciously taken as one's own.
Internarial—Between the nares.
Internasal—Between the nasal bones.
Internatal—Between the buttocks.
Interne—Intern.
Interneuromeric—Between the neuromeres.
Interneuron—The neuron whose processes are entirely confined within a specific area, as within the olfactory lobe.
Interneuronal—Lying between neurones.
Internist—Specialist in internal medicine.
Internoctem—During night.
Internodal—1. Between two nodes. 2. Pertaining to an internode.
Internode—The space between two adjacent nodes.
Internship—The period of a medical graduate which he/she spends in a hospital as an intern.
Internuclear— Situated between the nuclei.
Internuncial—Acting as a connecting medium.
Internus—Internal.
Interocclusal— Situated between the occlusal surfaces of the opposing teeth.
Interoceptive—Pertaining to the sensations arising within the body.
Interoceptor— A sensory nerve ending located

within the body and transmits impulses from the internal organs.

Interofective—Affecting the interior of the organism.

Interoinferior—Pertaining to an inward and downward position.

Interolivary—Between the olivary bodies.

Interorbital—Between the orbits.

Interosseal—Interosseous.

Interossei—Plural of interosseus.

Interosseous—Between the bones.

Interpalpebral— Between the eyelids.

Interpandemic—Denoting the occurrence of a disease between its pandemic attacks, e.g, influenza .

Interparietal—1. Intermural. 2. Between the parietal bones. 3. Between the parietal lobes of the cerebrum.

Interparoxysmal— Between the paroxysms.

Interpediculate—Between vertebral pedicles.

Interpeduncular—Between the peduncles.

Interpersonal—Pertaining to the relations and interactions between persons.

Interphalangeal—Between two adjacent phalanges.

Interphase—The interval between two successive cell divisions.

Interpolar—Between two poles.

Interpolation—1. In surgery, the transplantation of a tissue. 2. Determination of an intermediate value in a series on the basis of known values.

Interposed — Inserted between the parts of the body.

Interposition— Insertion between the parts of the body.

Interpretation— In psychotherapy, the meaning and significance of what he says or does.

Interproximal—Between two adjoining surfaces.

Interpubic—Between the pubic bones.

Interpupillary— Between the pupils.

Interpupillary distance—The distance between the centers of the pupils of the eyes.

Interradial—Between the rays.

Interradicular—Between the roots of the teeth.

Interrenal—Between the kidneys.

Interrupted—Intermitted, broken.

Interscapilium— Area between the shoulders.

Interscapular—Between the scapula bones.

Interscapulum—Interscapilium.

Intersciatic—Interischiadic.

Intersection—A site where one structure crosses another.

Intersegmental—Between the segments.

Interseptal—Between two septa.

Interseptum—Diaphragm.

Intersex—An individual having both male and female characteristics.

Intersexual—Pertaining to or characterized by intersexuality.

Intersexuality—The mixing of both, the male and female physical and sexual characteristics in the same individual in varying degrees.

Interspace—A space between similar structures.

Interspinal—Between two spinous processes of the spine.

Interspinous—Interspinal.

Interstice—A small space or gap in a tissue or structure.

Interstitial—Lying or placed between parts or in the interspaces of a tissue.

Interstitial cells—The cells interspersed between the seminiferous tubules of the testes that secrete the male hormone testosterone.

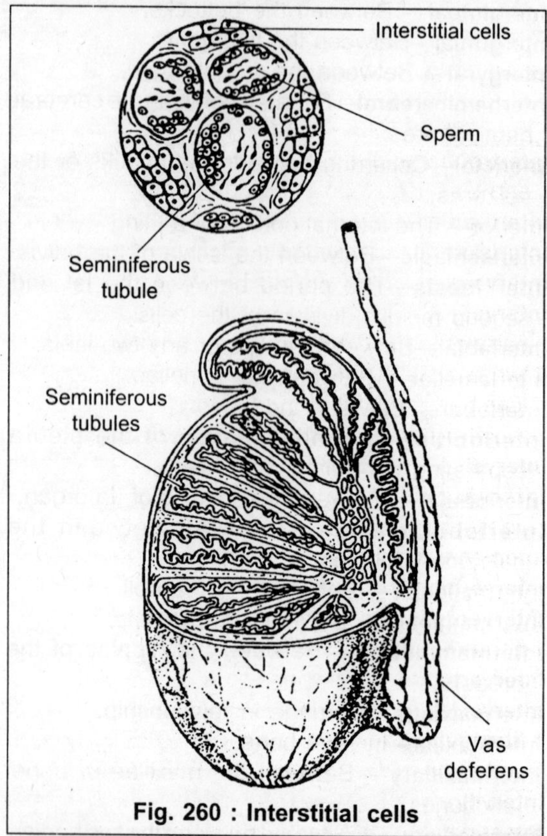

Fig. 260 : Interstitial cells

Interstitial fluid—The fluid surrounding the interstitial cells.

Interstitial tissue—The connective tissue between the cells.

Interstitium—Very small place between the body parts, tissues or cells.

Intersystole—The period between the end of the atrial systole and the beginning of the ventricular systole.

Intertarsal— Between the tarsal bones of the foot.

Intertendinous—Between the tendons.

Interthalamic—Between the thalami.

Intertransverse—Between the vertebrae or joining the transverse processes of a vertebra.

Intertriginous— Affected by intertrigo.

Intertrigo— An erythematous eruption occurring on the opposite surfaces of the skin from friction or rubbing.

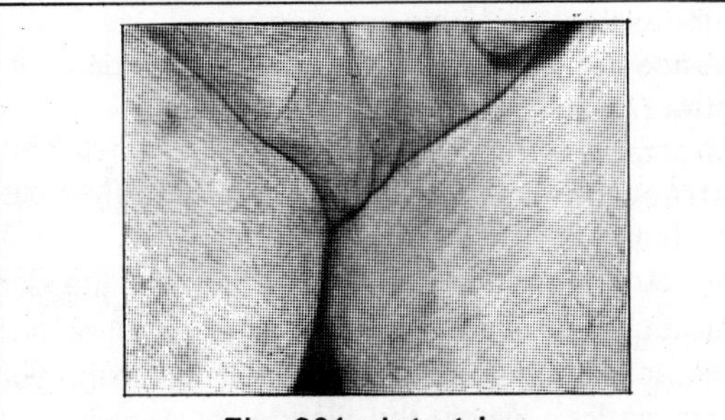

Fig. 261 : Intertrigo

Intertrochanteric—Situated between the greater and lesser trochanters of the femur.

Intertubular—Between the tubules.

Interureteral, Interureteric—Between the ureters.

Intervaginal—Between the sheaths.

Interval—1. The space between two objects or parts of the body. 2. The lapse of time between two events, e.g. cardioarterial interval, i.e., the time between the apex beat and pulsation of the radial artery. 3. Break in the progress of a disease.

Intervalvular— Between the valves.

Intervascular— Situated between the blood vessels.

Intervenous— Between the veins.

Intervention—An interposition, mediation.

Interventricular—Between the ventricles of the heart.

Intervertebral— Between two adjacent vertebrae.

Intervertebral disk— A broad and flattened disk of fibrocartilage lying between the bodies of vertebrae.

Intervillous— Between the villi.

Intestinal—Pertaining to the intestine.

Intestinal flora—The nonpathogenic bacteria normally present in the intestine which are favorable and protect the body from the invasion of pathogenic bacteria.

Intestinal obstruction—Blockage of the lumen of the intestine.

Intestinal perforation—Formation of a hole in the intestine.

Intestinal putrefaction— Pus formation in the intestine.

Intestinal reflex—Intestinal contraction and relaxation above the portion of the intestine where it is stimulated.

Intestine—The part of the alimentary canal

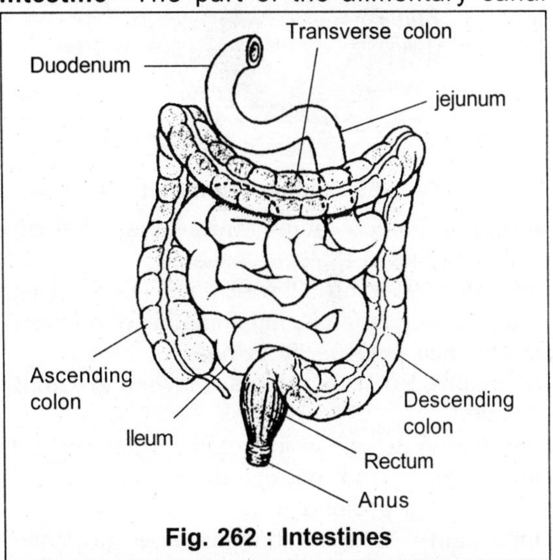

Fig. 262 : Intestines

extending from the pyloric opening of the stomach to the anus and divided into two parts.

(1) Large intestine—The distal portion of the intestine , about 5 feet long, extending from its junction with the small intestine to the anus and consisting of the cecum with vermiform appendix, colon (ascending, transverse, descending and sigmoid colon), rectum and anal canal.

(2) Small intestine—It is smaller in caliber than the large intestine. It extends from the pyloric opening of the stomach to the end of ileum which is attached to the large intestine by the ileocecal valve, consisting of duodenum which is about 8-10 inches long and connects with the jejunum which is about 9 feet long. The jejunum, in turn joins the ileum, the twisted portion of the small intestine which is about 13.7 feet long and attached to the large intestine.

Intestinum— Intestine.

Intestinum crassum— Large intestine.

Intestinum rectum— Rectum.

Intestinum tenue— Small intestine.

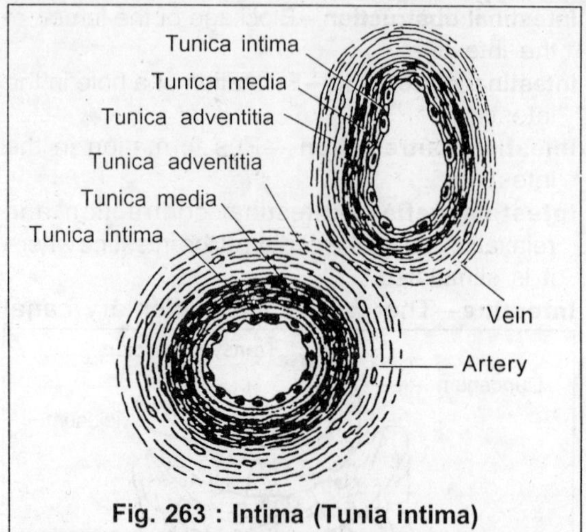

Fig. 263 : Intima (Tunia intima)

Intima— Tunica intima. Innermost coat of a structure as of a blood vessel.

Intimal—Pertaining to the intima of a blood vessel.

Intimitis—Endarteritis. Inflammation of an intima.

Intolerance—Incapacity to bear.

Intorsion—Rotation of the eye inward toward the nose.

Intortor—A muscle which rotates a part medially.

Intoxation—Poisoning, especially by the toxin of bacteria or poisonous animals.

Intoxicant— An agent that produces intoxication.

Intoxication—1. The state of being intoxicated or poisoned. 2. The condition produced by excessive use of alcohol.

Intra- — A prefix meaning within.

Intra-abdominal— Within the abdomen.

Intra-acinous—Within an acinus.

Intra-adenoidal—Within the adenoids.

Intra-alveolar—Inside the alveoli.

Intra-amniotic—Within the amniotic fluid.

Intra-arterial— Within the artery or arteries.

Intra-articular— Within a joint.

Intra-atrial— Within the atrium or atria of the heart.

Intra-aural—Within the ear.

Intra -auricular— Within an auricle.

Intrabronchial— Within a bronchus.

Intrabuccal— Within the tissue of the cheek or within the mouth.

Intracanalicular—Within a canaliculus.

Intracapsular—Within the capsule.

Intracardiac— Within the heart.

Intracarpal— Within the wrist.

Intracartilaginous— Within a cartilage.

Intracatheter—A plastic tube used to be inserted into a blood vessel.

Intracavitary—Within an organ or body cavity.

Intracelial—Intracavitary.

Intracellular— Within the cells.

Intracerebellar— Within the cerebellum of the brain.

Intracerebral— Within the cerebrum.

Intracervical— Within the canal of the cervix uteri.

Intracisternal— Within a cistern of the brain.

Intracolic—Within the colon.

Intracordal—Intracardiac.

Intracoronal—Within the crown portion of a tooth.

Intracorporeal—Within the body.

Intracorpuscular—Within a corpuscle, especially a red blood corpuscle.

Intracortical— Within the cortex.

Intracostal— On the inner surface of a rib.

Intracranial— Within the cranium.

Intractable— Incurable.

Intracutaneous— Intradermal. Within the substance of the skin.

Intracutaneous injection— Injection into the skin.

Intracutaneous reaction — Intradermoreaction. Reaction occurring after an injection into the skin.

Intracystic— Within the bladder or a cyst.

Intrad— Inwardly.

Intradermal—Within the dermis.

Intradermic—Intradermal.

Intradermoreaction— Intracutaneous reaction.

Intraduct—Within a duct.

Intraductal—Inside a duct.

Intraduodenal—Within the duodenum.

Intradural— Within or enclosed by the dura mater.

Intraembryonic—Within the embryonic body.

Intraepidermal—Within the epidermis.

Intraepiphysial—Within the epiphysis of a long bone.

Intraepithelial—Within the epithelium.

Intrafaradization—Application of faradic cauterizing current to the inner surface of a cavity or hollow organ.

Intrafascicular—Within the fasciculi of a strucutre.

Intrafat—Situated in or introduced into the fatty tissue.

Intrafebrile—Intrapyretic. During the febrile stage.

Intrafilar—Within a network or reticulum.

Intragalvanization—Application of a galvanic cauterizing current to the inner surface of a cavity or hollow organ.

Intragastric—Within the stomach.

Intragemmal—Within a budlike or bulblike structure as a nerve ending.

Intragenal—Within a gene.
Intraglandular—Within a gland.
Intraglobular—Within a globule.
Intragyral— Within a gyrus of the brain.
Intrahepatic—Within the liver.
Intraintestinal—Within the intestine.
Intralaryngeal—Within the larynx.
Intralesional—Within a lesion.
Intraligamentous—Within a ligament.
Intralobar— Within a lobe.
Intralobular— Within a lobule.
Intralocular— Within the cavity of any structure.
Intralumbar — Within the lumbar region of the spinal cord.
Intraluminal— Intratubal. Within any tubular structure.
Intramedullary— 1. Within the medulla oblongata of the brain. 2. Within the spinal cord. 3. Within a bone marrow cavity.
Intramembranous—Within a membrane.
Intramitochondrial—Within the mitochondria.
Intramolecular—Within a molecule.
Intramural—Within the walls of an organ.
Intramuscular— Within a muscle.
Intramyocardial—Within the myocardium.
Intramyometrial—Within the myometrium, i.e., muscular coat of the uterus.
Intranasal—Within a nasal cavity.
Intranatal—At the time of birth.
Intraneural—Within a nerve.
Intranuclear—Within the nucleus of a cell.
Intraocular—Within the eye ball.
Intraoperative—Occurring during an operation.
Intraoral— Within the mouth.
Intraorbital— Within the orbit.
Intraosseous— Within the bone substance.
Intraosteal—Intraosseous.
Intraovarian— Within the ovary.
Intraovular— Within the ovum.
Intraparietal— 1. Within the parietal lobe of the brain. 2. Intramural.
Intrapartum— Occurring during delivery.
Intrapelvic— Within the pelvis.
Intrapericardiac, Intrapericardial—Within the pericardial cavity.
Intraperitoneal— Within the peritoneal cavity.
Intrapersonal—Intrapsychic.
Intrapial—Within the pia mater.
Intraplacental— Within the placenta.
Intrapleural— Within the pleural cavity.
Intrapontine—Within the pons of the brain-stem.
Intraprostatic—Within the prostate gland.
Intraprotoplasmic—Within the protoplasm of a cell.
Intrapsychic— Originating in the mind such as conflicts.
Intrapulmonary— Within the substance of the lung.
Intrapyretic— Intrafebrile. During the period of fever.
Intrarectal—Within the rectum.
Intrarenal—Within the kidney.
Intraretinal—Within the retina of the eye.
Intrascrotal—Within the scrotum.
Intrasegmental—Within the segments.
Intraspinal— Within the spinal column.
Intrasplenic—Within the spleen.
Intrasynovial—Within the synovial sac of a joint.
Intratarsal—Within the tarsus; among the tarsal bones.
Intrathecal— 1. Within a sheath. 2. Within the spinal canal.
Intrathoracic— Within the thorax.
Intratonsillar—Within the substance of a tonsil.
Intratracheal— Within the trachea.
Intratubal— Intraluminal. Within a tube, especially the fallopian tube.
Intratubular—Within a tubule.
Intratympanic— Within the tympanic cavity.
Intrauterine— Within the uterus.
Intrauterine contraceptive device, I U C D— An apparatus made up of plastic and copper etc., placed in the uterus for a long time to prevent conception.
Intravasation— The entrance of foreign substances into the blood vessels.
Intravascular—Within the blood vessels.
Intravenous—Within a vein.

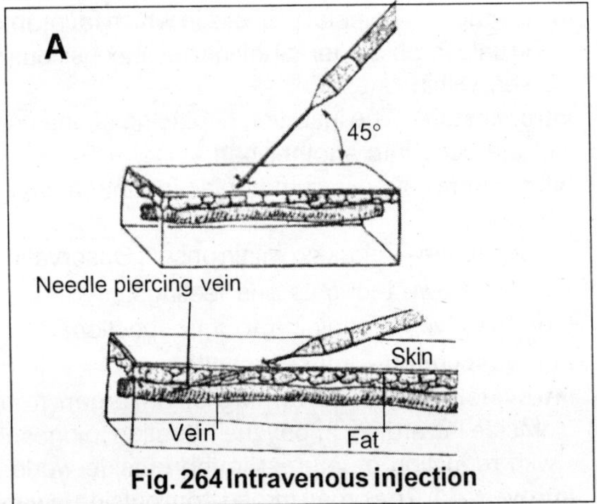

Fig. 264 Intravenous injection

A - To pierce the skin with the needle at an angle of 45°.

B- Decrease the angle to 15° to puncture the vein.

Intravenous feeding—To provide all the nutritive elements intravenously.

Intravenous infusion— Injection of a solution into a vein to gain the immediate effect as in hemorrhage, shock etc.

Intravenous medication— Intravenous injection or infusion of a sterile solution of a drug.

Intraventricular— Within a ventricle.

Intravesical— Within the urinary bladder.

Intravital—Occurring during life.

Intra vitam— During life.

Intravitelline— Within the vitelline or yolk.

Intravitreous— Within the vitreous humor of the eye.

Intrinsic— Inherent. Situated entirely within a part or belongs exclusively to a part, which is essential and natural.

Intrinsic factor— A substance normally present in the gastric juice which makes absorption of vit.B_{12}. Its absence causes deficiency of vitamin B_{12} resulting in pernicious anemia.

Intrinsic muscles— The muscles having their origin and insertion entirely within a structure, e.g. the muscles of the tongue, larynx or eye.

Intro- —A prefix meaning in.

Introducer—An apparatus which introduces some instrument as catheter etc.

Introflexion—A bending inward.

Introgastric—Leading to or passed into the stomach.

Introitus—An opening or entrance into a canal or cavity, e.g. upper opening of the larynx or the exterior orifice of the vagina.

Introject—Taking in within self.

Introjection—A mental process in which favorable and unfavorable external things are unconsciously taken within oneself.

Intromission—The insertion or placing of one part of the body into another part.

Intromittent—Conveying or injecting into a cavity or body.

Introspection —Looking within onself. Observation of one's own thoughts and feelings.

Introspective—Pertaining to introspection.

Introsusception—Intussusception.

Introversion—1. The turning of an organ from outside inward. 2. To pay the attention to oneself with reduction of interest in the outside world.

Introvert— 1. The organ turned from outside inward 2. The person who takes interest in himself/ herself only and does not take interest in the outside world.

Intubate— To insert a tube into a body part, especially into the larynx.

Intubation— Insertion of a tube into a body part, especially into the larynx for entrance of air.

Intubator—Introducer.

Intuition— Instinct.

Intumesce— To enlarge or swell.

Intumescence—Tumefaction 1. A swelling 2. The process of swelling or enlarging.

Intumescent— Swelling.

Intumescentia— Intumescence.

Intussusception— Introsusception, invagination. The prolapse of one part of the intestine into the lumen of another part situated just below the intestine.

Intussusceptive—Pertaining to or afflicted with intussusception.

Intussusceptum— The portion of the intestine prolapsed in intussusception.

Intussuscipiens—The portion of the intestine in the intussusception, which receives the other portion.

Inunction— 1. The process of applying ointment or a medicated substance by rubbing into the skin. 2. The ointment or a medicated substance so rubbed into the skin.

Inustion— To cauterize deeply.

In utero— Within the uterus.

In vacuo— Within a cavity or space from which air has been expelled.

Invaginate— 1. To ensheath 2. To insert one part of a structure within a part of the same structure.

Invaginated—Ensheathed or enclosed in a sheath.

Invagination—The process of becoming enclosed in a sheath.

Invaginator —An instrument for pushing a tissue inward.

Invalid—Declared disabled by disease.

Invalidate—To render invalid or to weaken.

Invalidism—The condition of being invalid.

Invalidity— Disability or weakness due to some disease.

Invasion— 1. The period between the entrance of the infective organisms of a disease into the body and the appearance of its symptoms. 2. The entrance of infective organisms into the body and their distribution into the tissues.

Invasive— 1. Having the property to enter the body and to spread in the tissues, as are some microorganisms. 2. Having the ability to infiltrate and destroy the surrounding tissue as of a malignant growth.

Invasiveness— 1. The ability of micro-organisms to enter the body and to spread in the tissues. 2. The ability to infiltrate and destroy the surrounding tissue as occurs by a malignant tumor.

Inventory—A list of items.

Invermination—Infestation by intestinal worms.

Inversion— 1. Reversal of the normal relationship of an organ or a part, or turning inside out of an organ or a part. e.g. the uterus 2. Homosexuality.

Invert— 1. To turn inside out or upside down 2. Homosexual.

Invertebrate—The animals having no vertebral column.

Invertor—A muscle which rotates a part inward.

Investigation—Examination, research.

Investing—Encircling with a sheath or covering, as tissue.

Investment—A covering or sheath.

Inveterate—Confirmed and chronic disease which is difficult to cure.

Inviscation— The mixing of saliva with the food during chewing.

In vitro— Within a glass test tube.

In vivo— Within the living body.

Involucre, Involucrum— A covering or sheath as of the sequestrum in the infection of a bone.

Involuntary— Independent of the will.

Involution—1. A rolling or turning inward. 2. Reduction in size of the uterus following delivery. 3. Diminution of an organ of the body in its power or in size. 4. Progressive degeneration occurring naturally with advancing age, resulting in shrivelling of organs or tissues. 5. Change in the body occurring after menopause.

Involutional—Pertaining to the involution.

Inward—Directed towards inside.

Iodinate—To treat or combine with iodine.

Iodination— To mix up with iodine.

Iodinophil, Iodinophile—Iodinophilous.

Iodinophilous—Easily stained with iodine.

Iodism—The condition produced by prolonged and excessive use of iodine or its compounds.

Iodize—To administer or impregnate with iodine.

Iodized—Impregnated with iodine.

Iodized salt—Salt containing iodine.

Iododerma—Any skin disease due to iodine.

Iodoform—A preparation of iodine in yellow crystalline form, used locally as an antiseptic.

Iodoformism—Poisoning caused by iodoform.

Iodophilia— The condition in which certain cells as polymorphonuclear white blood cells, in certain pathological conditions, as toxemia and severe anemia show diffuse brownish-red coloration on staining with iodine or iodides.

Iodotherapy—Treatment of diseases by the use of Iodine.

Iodum—Iodine.

Ioduria—Excretion of iodine in the urine.

Iometer—An apparatus for measuring ionization.

Ion— The particle carrying an electric charge.

Ionic—Pertaining to the ion.

Ionization—Dissociation of a substance in solution into ions.

Ionize—To separate into ions.

Ionogen—Any thing that can be ionized.

Ionophore—Any particle, as of a drug, which increases the permeability of a cell membrane to a specific action.

Ionophoresis—The process of travelling of the ions.

Ionophoretic—Pertaining to ionophoresis.

Ionophose— Production of a violet color.

Ionotherapy—Iontophoresis. Treatment of diseases by introducing ions of soluble salts in the body.

Iontophoresis 1. The process of travelling of electric current through a salt solution. 2. Introduction of ions of soluble salts into the body tissues through the skin by means of electric current.

Iontoquantimeter— Ionometer. An apparatus for measuring the amount of radiation used by, and the intensity of X-rays.

Iontoradiometer— Iontoquantimeter. Ionometer.

Iontotherapy— Treatment of diseases by introducing ions into the body by electric current.

Iophobia—1. Morbid fear of being poisoned .2. Fear of touching rusty things.

Iotacism—A speech defect marked by the frequent substitution of a long `e' sound for other vowels.

Ipsation— Masturbation.

Ipsefact—The environment chemically or physically modified by the behavior of an individual, colony, population or animals.

Ipsi - —A prefix indicating the same.

Ipsilateral— Homolateral. Situated or affecting the same side of the body.

IQ— Intelligence quotient.

Iralgia— Iridalgia. Pain in the iris.

Irascible— To become suddenly angry.

Irid - — A prefix indicating relationship to the iris of the eye.

Iridadenosis—Formation of glands in the iris of the eye.

Iridal —Iridic, iritic. Pertaining to the iris.

Iridalgia— Iralgia.
Iridauxesis— Thickening of the iris.
Iridectome— An instrument for cutting the iris in iridectomy.
Iridectomesodialysis — Excision and separation of adhesions on the inner margin of the iris.
Iridectomize— To excise a portion of the iris.
Iridectomy— Surgical removal of a portion of the iris.
Iridectomy optical— Iridectomy done to make an artificial pupil.
Iridectropium— Eversion of the iris.
Iridemia— Hemorrhage from the iris.
Iridencleisis— An operation for excision of the iris and a portion of the limbus, done to relieve the increased intraocular pressure in glaucoma, by allowing the increased volume of aqueous humor under the conjunctiva.
Iridentropium— Inversion of the iris.
Irideremia— Aniridia. Congenital total or partial absence of the iris.
Irides— Plural or iris.
Iridescence— Capability to disperse the light into the colors of spectrum.
Iridescent— Capable to disperse the light into the colors of spectrum.
Iridesis— Iridodesis. Artificial formation of a pupil by ligation of the iris.
Iridic—Iritic. Pertaining to the iris.
Irido - —A prefix meaning pertaining to the iris.
Iridoavulsion—A tearing away of the iris.
Iridocapsulitis—Inflammation of the iris and the capsule of the lens.
Iridocele—Protrusion of a portion of the iris through the cornea.
Iridochorioiditis, Iridochoroiditis—Inflammation of both, iris and the choroid.
Iridocoloboma— Congenital fissure of the iris.
Iridoconstrictor— A muscle or a drug which acts to constrict the pupil of the eye.
Iridocorneal— Pertaining to the iris and cornea.
Iridocyclectomy— Surgical removal of a part of the iris and the ciliary body.
Iridocyclitis—Inflammation of the iris and the ciliary body.
Iridocyclitis heterochromic— Inflammation with depigmentation of the iris of the eye.
Iridocyclochoroiditis — Inflammation of the iris, ciliary body and choroid of the eye.
Iridocystectomy— Excision of a cyst from the iris.
Iridodesis— Iridesis.
Iridodiagnosis— Diagnosis of a disease made by examination of the iris.
Iridodialysis—The separation of the iris from its attachments.
Iridodilator — A muscle or a substance which acts to dilate the pupil of the eye.
Iridodonesis—Hippus. Tremulousness of the iris on movement of the eye as seen in aphakic eye or in subluxation of the lens.
Iridokeratitis—Inflammation of iris and the cornea.
Iridokinesia, Iridokinesis— Contraction and expansion of the iris.
Iridokinetic—Pertaining to the movements of the iris.
Iridoleptynsis— Thinning or atrophy of the iris.
Iridology— The study of the iris during the course of a disease in which it is affected.
Iridomalacia— Softening of the iris.
Iridomedialysis— Iridomesodialysis. Separation of the adhesions at the inner margin of the iris.
Iridomesodialysis— Iridomedialysis.
Iridomotor—Pertaining to the movements of the iris.
Iridoncus—Tumor or swelling of the iris.
Iridoparalysis— Iridoplegia. Paralysis of the iris.
Iridoparelkysis— To induce prolapse of the iris surgically in order to displace the pupil artificially.
Iridopathy—Any disease of the iris of the eye.
Iridoperiphacitis, Iridoperiphakitis—Inflammation of the iris and anterior portion of the capsule of the lens.
Iridoplegia—Iridoparalysis. Paralysis of the sphincter of the iris.
Iridoptosis— Prolapse of the iris.
Iridopupillary— Pertaining to the iris and the pupil of the eye.
Iridorrhexis— Rupture or the tearing away of the iris from its attachment.
Iridoschisis—Separation of the stroma of the iris into two layers with disintegration of the anterior layer.
Iridosclerotomy— To make an incision into the sclera and the margin of the iris as done in glaucoma.
Iridosteresis— Removal of all or a portion of the iris.
Iridotasis— To stretch the iris by surgery in the treatment of glaucoma.
Iridotomy— To make an incision into the iris.
Iris—The circular pigmented contractile membrane between the lens and cornea of the eye, separating the anterior and posterior chamber of the eye ball, and perforated in the center by pupil.

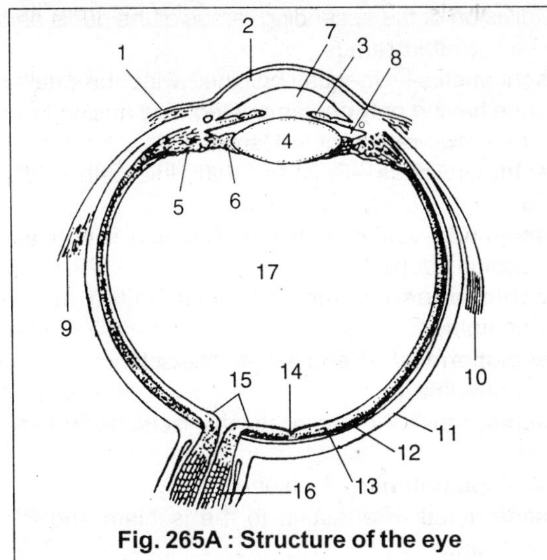

Fig. 265A : Structure of the eye

1. Conjunctiva 2. Cornea 3. Iris 4. Lens 5. Ciliary body 6. Suspensory ligament 7. Anterior chamber 8. Posterior chamber 9 and 10. Muscles of the eyeball 11. Sclera 12. Choroid 13. Retina 14. Macula lutea 15. Optic disc 16. Optic nerve 17. Vitreous body

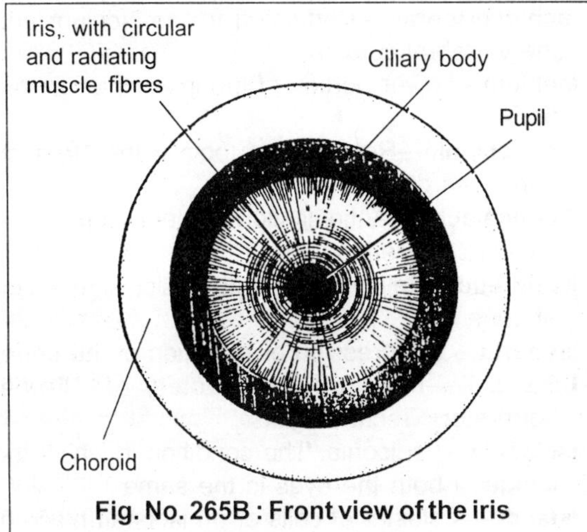

Fig. No. 265B : Front view of the iris

Irisopsia—Visual defect in which colored circles are seen around lights.

Iritic— Iridic. Pertaining to the iris.

Iritis— Inflammation of the iris.

Plastic iritis—Iritis in which the fibrinous exudate forms the new tissue.

Purulent iritis—Iritis with a purulent exudate.

Quiet iritis—Iritis without inflammatory signs such as redness or edema of the cornea.

Secondary iritis—Iritis in which the inflammation has spread from the neighboring parts, as from the cornea and sclera.

Serous iritis—Inflammation of the iris with a serous exudate in the anterior chamber.

Sympathetic iritis—Iritis occurring as a consecutive to the iritis in the other eye.

Iritoectomy— In the treatment of cataract, excision of the inflammed portion of the iris which is occluding the pupil.

Iritomy— Iridotomy. Irotomy.

Iron lung— An apparatus for providing artificial respiration.

Iron storage disease—Hemochromatosis.

Irotomy—Iridotomy. Iritomy. Formation of an artificial pupil.

Irradiate—To expose to X-rays or other forms of radiation.

Irradiated—Exposed to a radiation.

Irradiating—Spreading out from a common center.

Irradiation—Exposure to radiant energy as X-rays, ultraviolet rays, light and heat etc., in the treatment and diagnosis of the diseases.

Irrational—Not reasonable.

Irreducible—Unable to be reduced or to become smaller , as a fracture, dislocation or hernia, etc.

Irregular— Not regular, disorderly, asystematic, recurring not uniformly.

Irregularity— Not regularity.

Irrelevance— Inapplicability.

Irrelevant— Not to the point.

Irrespirable—Incapable of being inspired as a poisonous gas, air with foul smell or air containing insufficient oxygen.

Irresuscitable—Incapable of being revived.

Irreversible—Which cannot be reversed.

Irrigate— To wash out with water or other fluid.

Irrigation—The washing by a stream of water or other fluid as of the stomach, colon and the urinary bladder, etc.

Irrigator— An apparatus used in washing a part or cavity of the body with water or some other fluid.

Irritability— 1. Abnormal sensitiveness to stimuli 2. Capability of reacting to a stimulus as muscular or nervous irritability in which there is normal response of a muscle or a nerve to a stimulus.

Irritable—1. Abnormally sensitive to stimuli 2. Capable of reacting to a stimulus.

Irritant—Any thing which on local application causes local inflammatory reaction or irritation.

Irritating—Irritant.

Irritation—1. The act of stimulating 2. The condition

of being over excited and sensitive to an irritant. 3. Normal response to stimulus of a nerve or a muscle.

Irritative—Causing irritation.

Irrumation—Fellatio. Oral stimulation of the penis.

Irruption—The process of breaking through to a surface, a bursting.

Irruptive—Pertaining to or characterized by irruption.

Isauxesis—Growth of the parts at the same rate as growth of the whole.

Ischemia—Temporary deficiency of blood supply in a part due to constriction or obstruction of a blood vessel, e.g. myocardial ischemia, i.e. insufficient blood supply to the heart muscle.

Ischemic—Pertaining to ischemia.

Ischesis —Suppression of a normal discharge.

Ischi-, Ischio- — Prefixes meaning ischium.

Ischia— Plural of ischium.

Ischiac—Sciatic.

Ischiadic—Sciatic.

Ischiadicus—Sciatic.

Ischial—Ischiatic. Ischiadic. Pertaining to the ischium.

Ischialgia—Pain in the ischium.

Ischiatic— Ischiac. Ischiadic. Pertaining to the ischium.

Ischiatitis—Inflammation of the ischium.

Ischidrosis—Anhidrosis.

Ischio- —A prefix pertaining to the ischium.

Ischioanal—Pertaining to the ischium and the anus.

Ischiobulbar—Pertaining to the ischium and the bulb of the urethra.

Ischiocapsular—Pertaining to the ischium and the capsule of the hip joint.

Ischiocavernosus—A muscle extending from the ischium to the penis or clitoris which assists in their erection.

Ischiocavernous—Pertaining to the ischium and the corpus cavernosum.

Ischiocele—Sciatic hernia. A hernia through the sciatic notch.

Ischiococcygeal— Pertaining to the ischium and the coccyx.

Ischiodidymus—Conjoined twins united at the pelvis.

Ischiodynia—Pain in the ischium.

Ischiofemoral—Pertaining to the ischium and the femur bone.

Ischiofibular—Pertaining to the ischium and the fibula bone.

Ischiohebotomy—Ischiopubiotomy. Surgical division of the ascending ramus of the pubis and ischiopubic ramus.

Ischiomelus—Unequal conjoined twins, the smaller one having only one arm or leg, and arising from the pelvic region of the larger one.

Ischioneuralgia—Sciatica. Neuralgic pain in the hip.

Ischionitis—Inflammation of the tuberosity of the ischium bone.

Ischiopagus—Conjoined twins united at the ischium.

Ischioperineal—Pertaining to the ischium and the perineum.

Ischiopubic—Pertaining to the ischium and the pubis.

Ischiopubiotomy— Ischiohebotomy.

Ischiorectal—Pertaining to the ischium and the rectum.

Ischiosacral—Pertaining to the ischium and the sacrum.

Ischiothoracopagus—Iliothoracopagus.

Ischiotibial—Pertaining to, or connecting the ischium and the tibia.

Ischiovaginal—Pertaining to the ischium and the vagina.

Ischiovertebral —Pertaining to the ischium and the vertebral column.

Ischium—Lower portion of the innominate or hip bone.

Ischochymia—Retention of food in the stomach due to its dilation.

Ischogalactic—Antigalactic. An agent suppressing the milk secretion.

Ischuretic—Relieving the suppression or retention of urine.

Ischuria— Suppression or retention of the urine.

I.S.C.L.T.—International Society of Clinical Laboratory Technologists.

Iseikonia— Isoiconia. The condition in which the image in both the eyes is the same.

Island— A cluster of cells or an isolated piece of tissue, e.g. islets of Langerhans which are the collection of cells in the pancreas.

Islet— Island.

-ism— Suffix meaning theory of.

-ismus—A suffix used to form words meaning spasm or contraction.

Iso- — A prefix meaning equal.

I.S.O.—International standards organization.

Isoagglutination— Agglutination of the red blood cells by agglutinins from the blood of another member of the same species.

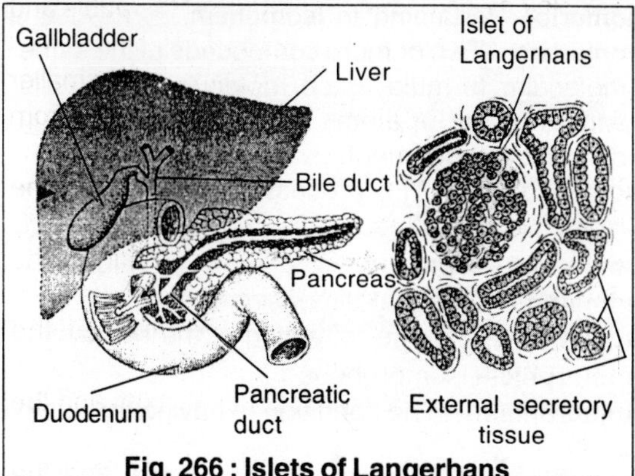

Fig. 266 : Islets of Langerhans

Isoagglutinin—An antibody in a serum which agglutinates the red blood cells of the individual of the same species from which it is derived.

Isoagglutinogen—One of the two substances A and B attached on the surface of red blood cells by which the cells become agglutinated when mixed with the serum containing the corresponding isoagglutinins (anti—A or anti—B).

Isoallele—Identical allele (gene).

Isoanaphylaxis—Anaphylaxis produced by the serum from an individual of the same species.

Isoantibody—An antibody produced by an isoantigen.

Isoantigen—Alloantigen. A substance present in certain individuals which produce antibodies in other individuals of the same species, but not in the donor.

Isobar—In chemistry, one of two or more chemical bodies having the same atomic weight but different atomic number.

Isobaric—Of the same specific gravity with which it is compared.

Isocaloric— Having the same number of calories as the food with which it is being compared.

Isocapnia—The condition in which the arterial carbon dioxide pressure remains constant or unchanged.

Isocellular— Made up of the equal and similar cells.

Isochromatic— 1. Having the same color 2. Of uniform color.

Isochromatophil(e)— Having the same affinity for a dye.

Isochronal— Isochronous. Acting or occurring at regular intervals.

Isochronia— The correspondence of events with respect to time, rate or frequency.

Isochronic—Isochronal.

Isochronous—Isochronal.

Isochroous—Isochromatic.

Isocoria—The condition of the pupils of both the eyes of being equal in size.

Isocortex—Neocortex. Neopallium.

Isocytosis—The condition of the cells of being equal in size, especially of red blood cells.

Isocytotoxin—Cytotoxin destructive to homologous cells of the same species.

Isodactylism—The condition of having fingers or toes of equal length.

Isodense—The tissue having the same radiodensity as another or adjacent tissue.

Isodiametric—With equal diameters.

Isodontic—Having teeth of equal size.

Isodose—Equal radiation dose to different parts of the body.

Isodynamic—With equal strength.

Isodynamogenic—Isoenergetic.

Isoelectric—Having equal electric potentials.

Isoenergetic—Showing equal energy.

Isoenzyme—One of a group of enzymes that catalyze the same reaction but may be separated from each other by special chemical tests.

Isoerythrolysis—Destruction of erythrocytes (red blood cells-RBC) by isoantibodies.

Isogamete—1. A cell that through fusion with a similar cell reproduces. 2. A gamete of the same size as the gamete with which it unites.

Isogamy—Reproduction resulting from union of isogametes or identical cells.

Isogeneic—Syngeneic.

Isogeneric—Of the same kind or belonging to the same species.

Isogenesis—Similarity in the developmental processes.

Isogenic—Isologous.

Isogenous—Of the same origin, as in the development of a tissue or cell.

Isognathous—Having the jaws of approximately the same width.

Isograft—A graft taken from a genetically identical individual.

Isohemagglutination— Isoagglutination. Agglutination of red blood cells caused by an isohemagglutinin.

Isohemagglutinin—A substance normally present in the serum of human blood, which when mixed with an incompatible blood, agglutinates the red blood cells of the blood of the recipient.

Isohemolysin— Isolysin. The substance which causes hemolysis of the red blood cells of the individuals of the same species from which it is obtained.

Isohemolysis—Isolysis. Hemolysis produced by isohemolysin.

Isohydric—Denoting two substances possessing the same pH.

Isohypercytosis— Increase in the number of white blood cells with the normal proportions of the polymorphonuclear white blood cells.

Isohypocytosis— Decrease in the number of white blood cells with the normal proportions of the polymorphonuclear white blood cells.

Isoiconia—Equality of the image of an object in both eyes.

Isoiconic—The person having equal images in both the eyes.

Isoimmunization— Development of antibodies in an individual in response to isoantigens.

Isolate— 1. To separate a person from others as in an infectious disease. 2. In chemistry, to obtain a substance in pure form from the mixture or solution.

Isolated—Separated from others.

Isolation—The act of isolating or state of being isolated, e.g. (a) separation of a body part (b) separation of a patient suffering from infectious disease, from others (c) the process of obtaining a substance in pure form from a mixture or solution (d) successive propagation of a growth of microorganisms until a pure culture is obtained.

Isolecithal—The ovum in which there is moderate amount of yolk distributed uniformly.

Isoleucine— An amino acid formed by the hydrolysis of fibrin and other proteins.

Isoleukoagglutinin—An abnormal antibody in the blood of some persons, which is capable of agglutinating white blood cells.

Isologous— Isogenic. Genetically identical.

Isolophobia— Fear of being alone.

Isolysin— Isohemolysin. A substance that dissolves the red blood cells of animals of the same species from which it is derived.

Isolysis— Isohemolysis. Dissolution of red blood cells by isolysin.

Isolytic— Pertaining to the isolysis.

Isomastigote—A protozoon having two or four flagella of equal length at one extremity.

Isomer— One of two or more chemical substances that have the same molecular formula but different physical and chemical properties due to different arrangement of the atoms in the molecule.

Isomeric—Pertaining to isomerism.

Isomerism—Two or more compounds of the same molecular formula, each molecule having the same number of atoms of each element but in different arrangement.

Isomerization— The process of converting one isomer into another.

Isomerous—Isomeric.

Isometric— Of equal dimensions.

Isometropia— Same refraction of the two eyes.

Isomorphic—Isomorphous.

Isomorphism— The condition of having the same form.

Isomorphous— Having the same shape.

Isonormocytosis— The condition of having the normal total and differential W.B.C. count.

Iso-osmotic—Isosmotic.

Isopathy— Isotherapy. Treatment of a disease by the causative organisms of the same disease or by the material obtained from the affected organ.

Isophagy—Autolysis.

Isophoria— Tendency of the eyeballs not to turn upward or downward.

Isopia— Equal vision in both the eyes.

Isoplastic— The term used for a graft taken from one individual and transplanted it to the another of the same species.

Isopotential—Isoelectric.

Isoprecipitin—An antibody that combines with and precipitates soluble antigen in the plasma or serum.

Isopters— Lines on a chart of field of vision connecting points of equal visual acuity.

Isopyknic—Having the same density.

Isopyknosis—The condition of having uniform density.

Isorrhea— The equilibrium between the intake and output of water and solutes by the body.

Isosensitization— Sensitization to isoantigens as to Rh antigens during pregnancy.

Isosensitize—Autosensitize.

Isoserotherapy—Treatment of the disease with the serum of the person suffering from the same disease as the patient.

Isoserum— A serum from the person suffering from the same disease for which the patient is to be treated.

Isosexual— Pertaining to or characteristic of the same sex.

Isosmotic— Having the same osmotic pressure.

Isosthenuria— Maintenance of the constant specific gravity and osmotic pressure of the urine in spite of the variations in fluid intake.

Isotherapy— Isopathy.
Isothermal— Having the equal temperature.
Isothermic— Isothermal.
Isothermognosis— Stimulations by pain, heat and cold, are all felt as heat.
Isotonia— 1. The condition of equal tone, tension or activity. 2. The condition of equal osmotic pressure of two or more substances or solutions.
Isotonic—1. Of the equal tone or tension 2. Having the same osmotic pressure.
Isotonicity— The condition of being isotonic.
Isotope—One of a series of chemical elements which have the same chemical properties but differ in their atomic weights and electric charge.
Isotopic—Having the same chemical composition but differing in some physical property.
Isotransplantation—Transplantation of an isograft.
Isotropic—1. Having the same properties in every direction. 2. Having the equal refraction.
Isotropy— Condition of being isotropic.
Isotype—In immunology, an antigenic determinant on the immunoglobulin molecule that distinguishes among the main classes of antibodies of a given species.
Isotypic—Pertaining to isotype.
Isotypical— Belonging to the same category.
Isovolume—Equal volume.
Isovolumetric—Isovolumic.
Isovolumic—Occurring without causing change in volume.
Issue— 1. Offspring. 2. A discharge of pus, blood or other matter.
Isthmectomy— Surgical removal of an isthmus, especially the isthmus of the thyroid gland.
Isthmian— Pertaining to an isthmus.
Isthmitis— Inflammation of the isthmus.
Isthmoparalysis— Isthmoplegia. Paralysis of the isthmus of the fauces.
Isthmoplegia— Isthmoparalysis.
Isthmospasm— Spasm of the isthmus as of the fauces or of the fallopian tubes.
Isthmus— A narrow passage connecting the two larger bodies or parts, e.g. isthmus of the thyroid gland which connects the right and left lobes of the thyroid gland.

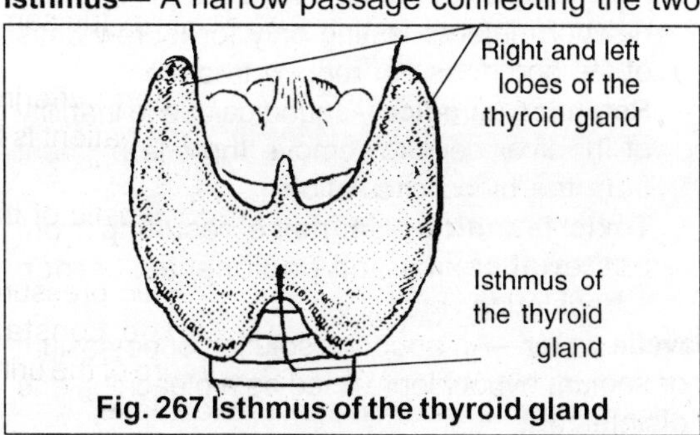

Fig. 267 Isthmus of the thyroid gland

Isuria— Excretion of urine at the uniform rate.
Itch— Pruritus. Irritation of the skin inducing a desire to scratch.
Barber's itch —Fungus infection of the beard.
Dhobie itch—Fungus infection of the groin and perineum.
Ground itch—The skin lesion in the foot produced by penetration by larvae of the hookworm, due to walking on bare feet on the ground.
Scabies— A contagious skin disease caused by itch mite characterized by intense itching, usually between fingers of the hand which increases at night.
Itching— Pruritus; irritation of the skin causing desire to rub or scratch the part of the body.
Itch mite— Sarcoptes scabiei. A small parasite causing scabies.
-ite—A suffix meaning 'of the nature of'.
Iter— A tubular passage between the two parts of the body.
Iteral— Pertaining to an iter.
Iteroparity—Condition of reproducing more than once in a life-time.
Ithycyphosis, Ithyokyphosis—Kyphosis with backward projection of the vertebral column.
Ithylordosis— Lordosis without lateral curvature of the vertebral column.
-itis— A suffix meaning 'inflammation of'.
I . U .— Immunizing unit; international unit.
I . U . C . D—Intrauterine contraceptive device.
I . U. D—Intrauterine device.
I . V.—Intravenous.
I-V—Abbreviation for intraventricular.
I.V.B.—Abbreviation for intraventricular block.
I . V . P— Intravenous pyelography. To make X-ray picture of the renal pelvis and the ureter after an intravenous injection of a contrast medium.
I . V . T— Intravenous transfusion.
I . V . U— Intravenous urography. To make X-ray picture of any part of the urinary tract after an intravenous injection of a radiopaque substance.
Ixodiasis— Any disease or skin lesion caused by tick bites.
Ixodic— Pertaining to or caused by ticks.
Ixodides— Ticks.
Ixomyelitis— Inflammation of the spinal cord in the lumbar region.

J—Symbol for joule.

Jab—Stabbing with something pointed material.

Jaboulay's amputation— Amputation of the thigh and removal of the hip bone.

Jack—1. A. knave person. 2. A stupid or foolish man. 3. A machine for lifting heavy weights.

Jacket—A bandage of plaster of paris applied to the trunk to immobilize the spinal column or to correct deformities.

Jack-knife position— The position in which the patient lies on the back and the shoulders are raised, the lower legs are flexed on the thighs and the thighs are at right angles to the trunk.

Jackscrew—A device operated by means of a screw used to expand the dental arch or for correcting the position of the bone fragments after fracture.

Jacksonian epilepsy—A localized form of epilepsy in which the seizures occur only in a limited portion of the body such as at the angle of mouth, index finger and the thumb or at the big toe.

Jacquemier's sign—Blue or purplish coloration of the vaginal mucous membrane in pregnancy.

Jactatio— Restless tossing of the head and body in acute illness.

Jactitation—Restless, to-and-fro movement of the body in acute illness.

Jadelots's lines—Lines on the face of the children which indicate some disease.

Jaeger's test types—Lines of types of various sizes, printed on card for testing the near vision.

Jagged—Notched.

Jaimais vu—Feeling of being in a completely strange environment while the individual being in a familiar environment.

Janeway lesion—A small, painless, red-blue spot found on the palms and soles in bacterial endocarditis.

Janiceps—A double monster with one head and two opposite faces.

Jar—1. A big vessel made up of glass, stone, earth or plastic, may be cylindrical or in other shapes. 2. To jolt.

Jargon—1. Senseless speech. 2. Speech or writing of unfamiliar words which are peculiar to the persons in a special field of science

Jarvis's snare—An instrument for removing the growths in the nasal cavities.

Jaundice—Condition characterized by yellow discoloration of the skin, the sclerae and the conjunctivae of the eyes, mucous membranes and urine due to deposition of the bile pigment resulting from excess bilirubin in the blood (hyperbilirubinemia).

Acholuric jaundice— Jaundice without bile pigment in the urine.

Cholestatic jaundice—Jaundice due to failure of bile to reach the duodenum due to an obstruction or to changes in the liver cells.

Congenital jaundice— Jaundice occurring since birth.

Hematogenous jaundice, Hemolytic jaundice— Jaundice caused by hemolysis of the red blood cells.

Hepatocellular jaundice—Jaundice due to injury to or disease of the liver cells.

Hepatogenous Jaundice—Jaundice due to disease of the liver.

Infectious jaundice—Jaundice occuring in infectious hepatitis.

Jaundice of the newborn—Icterus neonatorum. Jaundice occurring in the new born infants.

Malignant jaundice—Acute yellow atrophy of the liver.

Obstructive jaundice—Jaundice resulting from some mechanical obstruction in the flow of bile from the liver to the duodenum.

Physiologic jaundice— Mild jaundice in the newborn infants lasting only for Ist few days of life and does not require treatment.

Retention jaundice—Jaundice due to inability of the liver cells to remove the bile pigment from the blood circulation.

Toxic jaundice—Jaundice resulting from bacterial toxins, or poisons as carbon tetrachloride, etc.

Javelle water—An aqueous solution of potassium or sodium hypochlorite used as a bleaching and disinfectant.

Jaw—Either or both of the maxillary and mandibular bones, containing teeth and forming the frame of mouth.

Crackling jaw—A jaw in which a sound is heard in the normal or diseased temporomandibular joint during movement of the jaw.

Lock-jaw—Tonic spasm of the jaw muscles as seen in tetanus.

Lower jaw—Mandible.

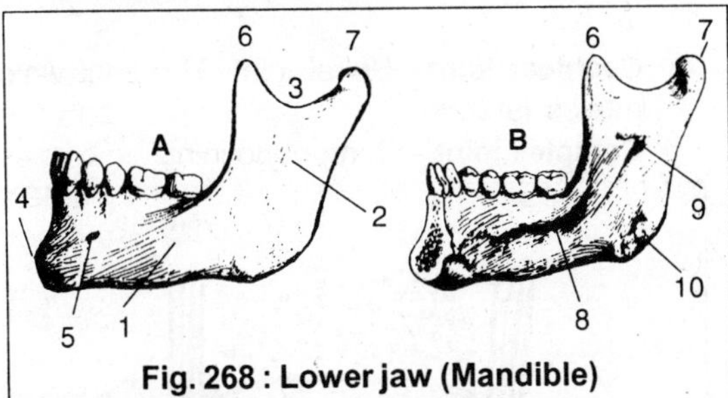

Fig. 268 : Lower jaw (Mandible)

A. Left half, external aspect
B. Right half, internal aspect
1. Body 2. Branch 3. Notch 4. Mental protuberance 5. Mental foramen 6. Coronoid process 7. Articular process 8. Mylohyoid line 9. Mandibular foramen 10. Mandibular angle

Lumpy jaw—Actinomycosis.

Parrot jaw —A condition caused by protrusion of the incisor teeth.

Upper jaw—Maxilla.

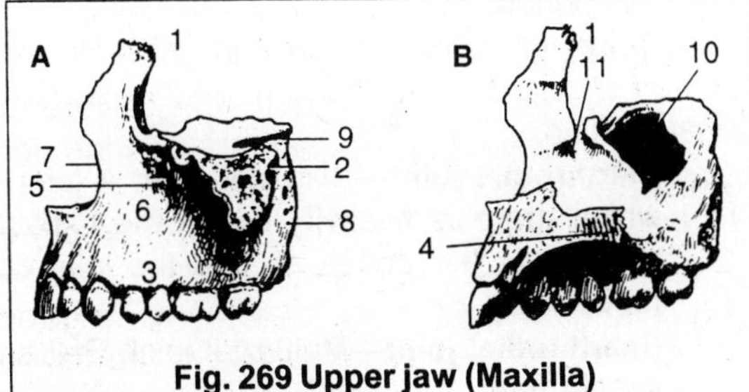

Fig. 269 Upper jaw (Maxilla)

A. Left, external aspect
B. Right, internal aspect
1. Frontal process 2. Zygomatic process 3. Alveolar process 4. Palatine process 5. Infraorbital foramen 6. Canine fossa 7. Nasal notch 8. Maxillary tuberosity 9. Infraorbital sulcus 10. Maxillary sinus 11. Lacrimal groove

Jejunal—Pertaining to the jejunum.

Jejunectomy—Excision of part or all of the jejunum.

Jejunitis—Inflammation of the jejunum.

Jejuno- —A prefix indicating pertaining to jejunum.

Jejunocecostomy—Surgical joining of the cecum and the jejunum.

Jejunocolostomy—Formation of a passage by surgery between the jejunum and the colon.

Jejunoileal—Pertaining to the jejunum and the ileum.

Jejunoileitis—Inflammation of the jejunum and ileum.

Jejunoileostomy—Formation of a passage between the jejunum and ileum.

Jejunojejunostomy—Formation of a passage between two parts of the jejunum.

Jejunoplasty—Repairing of the jejunum by plastic surgery.

Jejunorrhaphy—Surgical repair of the jejunum.

Jejunostomy—To create a permanent opening between the jejunum and the surface of the abdominal wall.

Jejunotomy—To make an incision into the jejunum.

Jejunum—The second part of the small intestine extending from the duodenum to the ileum, which is about 8 feet long and is about 2/5th of the small intestine.

Jelly—A soft, thick, sticky, semisolid mass, e.g. contraceptive jelly—a jelly introduced into the vagina for the prevention of the conception and Wharton's jelly—a soft jelly like connective substance of the umbilical cord.

Jerk—1. A sudden muscular movement. 2. Reflex action occurring from striking a muscle or tendon.

Achilles jerk, Ankle jerk —Contraction of the calf muscles occurring on striking Achilles tendon.

Elbow jerk—Extension of the forearm by stimulation of the tendon of the stretched triceps muscle.

Knee jerk—The forward jerking of the lower leg upon striking the patellar tendon when the knee is flexed at right angle.

Jerking—Making sudden movements.

Jet—Escape of blood from the cut end of a blood vessel at very high velocity.

Jitters—Shakes.

Joffroy's reflex—Twitching of the gluteal muscles on applying pressure on the buttock.

Joffroy's sign—1. Inability to solve very simple arithmetical problems in the early stages of organic brain disease. 2. The absence of facial muscle contraction when the eyes turn up in exophthalmos.

Jog—To shake with a jerk, to move up and down.

Jogger—The person who moves slowly.

Jogging—Running for enjoyment or to maintain physical fitness.

Joint—An articulation. The site of junction or union between two or more bones, made up of fibrous connective tissue and cartilage. It is broadly divided into three categories as follows :—1. Synarthrosis—Immovable joint. 2. Amphiarthrosis—Slightly movable joint. 3. Diarthrosis—Freely movable joint.

Amphidiarthrodial joint—A joint which is both, ginglymoid and arthrodial.

Arthrodial joint—Gliding joint.

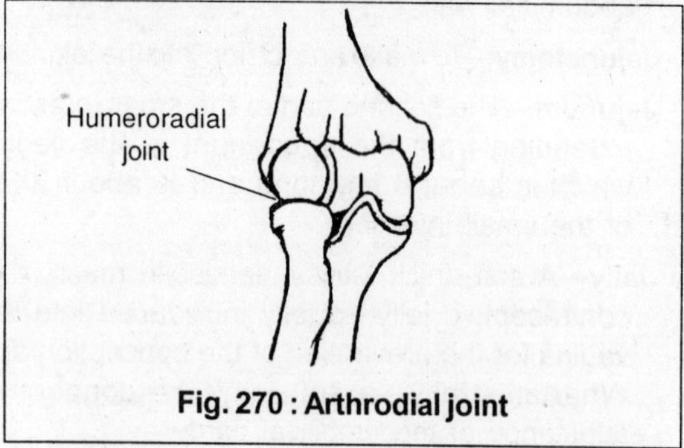

Fig. 270 : Arthrodial joint

Ball and socket joint—Enarthrosis; Multiaxial. The joint in which the round end of a bone fits into the cavity of another bone, *e.g.* hip joint.

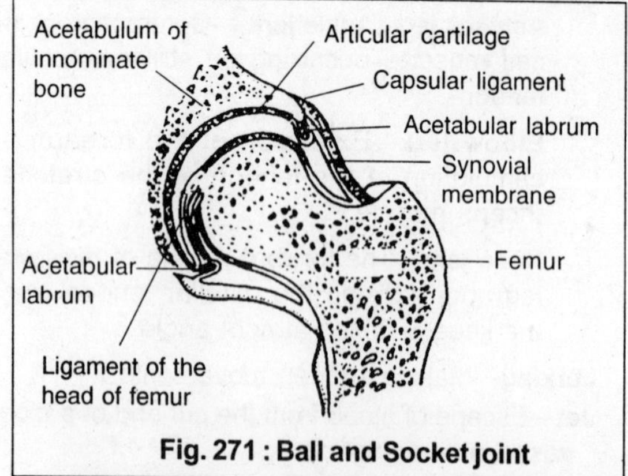

Fig. 271 : Ball and Socket joint

Biaxial joint—A joint in which there are two chief axes of movement at right angles to each other.

Bicondylar joint—A synovial joint in which two rounded surfaces of one bone articulate with shallow depressions on another bone.

Bilocular joint—A joint separated into two sections by interarticular cartilage.

Bleeder's joint—Hemophilic joint. Joint of hemophiliac patient in which bleeding occurs.

Cartilaginous joint—A joint in which the bones are connected by the cartilage.

Charcot's joint—See in the section of letter 'c'.

Cochlear joint—Spiral joint. The joint which moves laterally.

Complex joint—Compound joint.

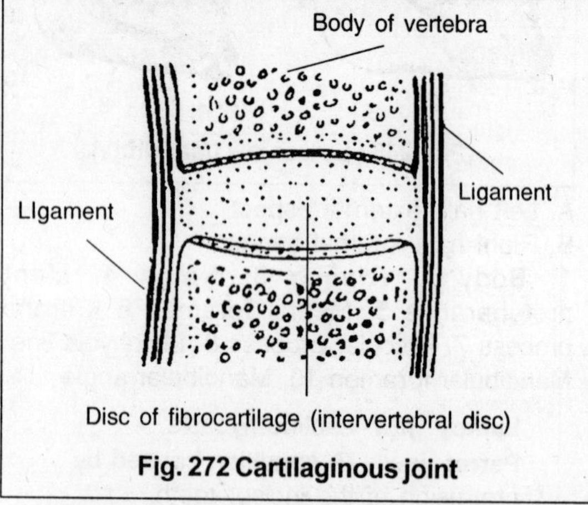

Fig. 272 Cartilaginous joint

Compound joint—Joint made up of more than two bones.

Condyloid joint—The joint in which all forms of angular movements can occur except axial rotation.

Diarthrodial joint—Synovial joint. A joint in which there is a cavity within the capsule separating the bones so that the joint can move freely.

Enarthrodial joint—Multiaxial joint. Ball and socket joint.

False joint—The joint formed after a fracture.

Fibrous joint—A joint in which the bones are connected by the fibrous tissue.

Flail joint—Extremely movable joint.

Ginglymoid joint—Ginglymus. Hinge joint. A synovial joint having only forward and backward movement.

Gliding joint—Arthrodial joint. The joint in which the bony ends glide or slip over each other.

Hemophilic joint—Bleeder's joint.

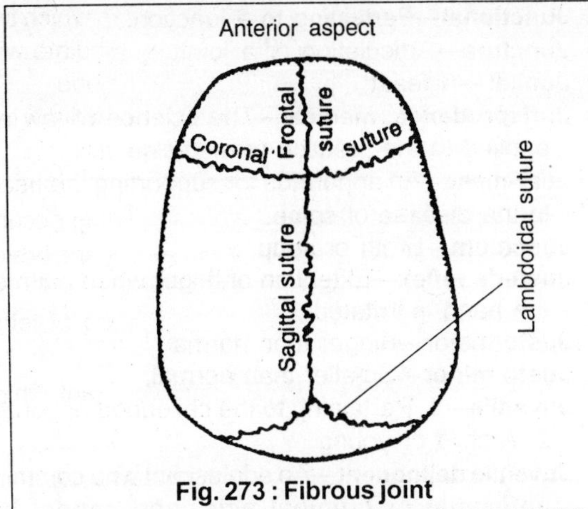

Fig. 273 : Fibrous joint

Anterior aspect of the skull showing the main sutures.

Hinge joint—Ginglymoid joint. A joint which moves forward and backward only as elbow joint.

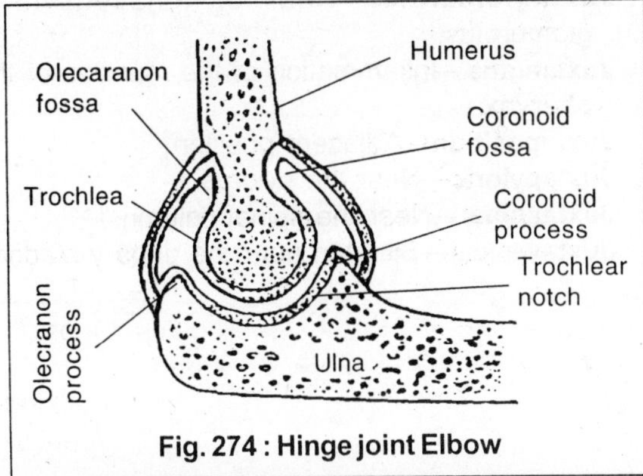

Fig. 274 : Hinge joint Elbow

Immovable joint—Synarthrosis. A joint which does not move at all as a joint between two vertebrae in the spinal column.

Mixed joint—A joint in which the features of different types of joints are combined.

Movable joint—The joint which moves.

Pivot joint—Rotatory joint. A synovial joint in which a section of a cylinder of one bone fits into a corresponding cavity on the other bone, as is seen in the proximal radioulnar joint.

Plane joint—A synovial joint in which the opposed bony surfaces are flat or slightly curved so that only gliding movements can occur.

Saddle joint—Receptive joint. The joint in which the surface of one bony end is convex while that of its opposite side is concave.

Simple joint—A joint composed of two bones.

Synarthrodial joint—Immovable joint.

Synovial joint—A joint in which capsule encloses a cavity lined by synovial membrane which contains the synovial fluid.

Uniaxial joint—Joint moving on a single axis.

Unilocular joint—A joint containing a single cavity.

Joint capsule—A saclike structure enclosing the bony ends in a movable joint, consisting of an outer fibrous layer and an inner layer of the synovial membrane. It contains synovial fluid.

Joint cavity—The space within the joint capsule lined by synovial membrane and filled with synovial fluid.

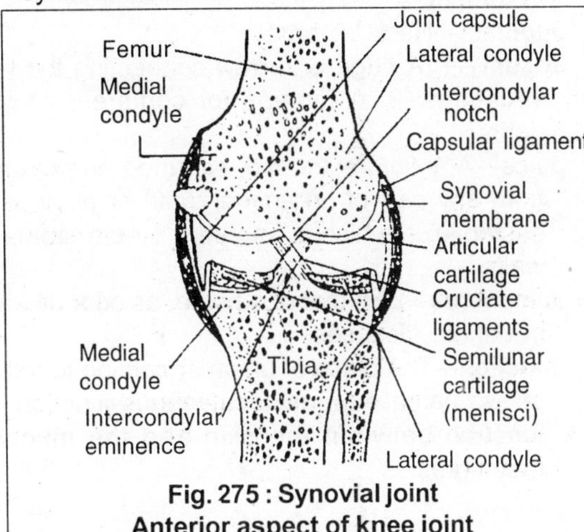

Fig. 275 : Synovial joint
Anterior aspect of knee joint

Joint mice—Free small pieces of bone or cartilage present in the joint space, especially the knee joint, which may be due to a previous injury.

Joule—Work done in one second by an electric current of 1 amp. against a resistance of one ohm.

JRA—Juvenile rheumatoid arthritis.

Juga—Plural of jugum.

Jugal—United or pertaining to the malar or zygomatic bone or the cheek.

Jugal bone—Malar or zygomatic bone.

Jugale—The point at the margin of the zygomatic process.

Jugal process—Zygomatic process.

Jugate—1. Coupled 2. Having ridges.

Jugomaxillary—Pertaining to the maxilla and the zygomatic bone.

Jugular—1. Pertaining to the neck. 2. Jugular vein.

Jugular foramen—An opening formed by the jugular notches of the occipital and temporal bones.

Jugular fossa—A depression in the petrosal part of the temporal bone for the jugular vein.

Jugular process—A projection from the occipital bone towad the temporal bone.

Jugular veins—Veins of the neck region. They are divided into two :—1. External jugular vein—it receives the blood from the exterior of the cranium and the deeper parts of the face. 2. Internal jugular vein —it receives the blood from the brain and the superficial parts of the face and neck.

Jugulate—To arrest quickly the progress of a disease by treatment.

Jugulation—Sudden arrest of a disease by the treatment.

Jugulum—Neck or throat.

Jugum—1. A ridge or furrow connecting the two structures. 2. A forceps for compressing the penis.

Juice—Any fluid extracted, secreted or excreted from any part of an animal, man or plant, e.g. gastric juice which is secreted by the stomach walls.

Jumentous—Like that of a horse, as odor of urine in certain diseases.

Junction—The place of union or coming together of two parts, e.g., mucocutaneous junction—a junction between the skin and the mucous membrane.

Junctional—Pertaining to a junction.

Junctura—Articulation or a joint.

Junket—A feast.

Jurisprudence, medical—The science of law as applied to the practice of medicine.

Jury-mast—An apparatus for supporting the head in the disease of spine.

Jusculum—Broth or soup.

Juster's reflex—Extention of finger when palm of the hand is irritated.

Justo major—Bigger than normal.

Justo minor—Smaller than normal.

Juvenile—1. Pertaining to the childhood or youth. 2. A child or young.

Juvenile delinquent—An adolescent who commits antisocial or criminal acts, and cannot be controlled by his parents.

Juxta- —A prefix meaning situated near.

Juxta-articular—Situated near a joint.

Juxtaepiphysial—Close to or adjoining an epiphysis.

Juxtaglomerular—Near or adjacent to a glomerulus.

Juxtangina—Inflammation of the muscles of the pharynx.

Juxtaposition—Adjacent position.

Juxtapyloric—Near the pylorus.

Juxtaspinal—Near the spinal column.

Juxtavesical—Situated near the urinary bladder.

K —Chemical symbol for potassium.

Kaes's feltwork—Nerve fiber network in the cerebral cortex.

Kahler's disease—Multiple myeloma.

Kaif—Dreamy tranquility produced by the use of drugs.

Kainophobia—Neophobia. Abnormal fear of the new situations and things.

Kakidrosis—Bromidrosis. Foul smelling sweat.

Kakke—Beriberi. Endemic form of polyneuritis.

Kakosmia—Cacosmia. Perception of foul smell which actually does not exist.

Kakotrophy—Cacotrophy. Malnutrition.

Kala-azar—A fatal infectious disease spreading in the tropic and subtropic areas of the world caused by a flagellated protozoon Leishmania donovani, transmitted by the bite of infected sandflies, which is characterized by fever, anemia, wasting, enlargement of the spleen and liver.

Kali—Potash or potassium.

Kaliemia—Presence of potassium in the blood.

Kaligenous—Forming potash.

Kalimeter—Alkalimeter. An apparatus for measuring the degree of alkalinity of a substance.

Kaliopenia—Hypokalemia. The deficiency of potassium in the blood.

Kaliopenic—Pertaining to kaliopenia.

Kalium—Potassium.

Kaliuresis—Excretion of potassium in the urine.

Kaliuretic—Pertaining to or causing kaliuresis.

Kanner syndrome—Infantile autism. A mental condition in which the child from the childhood pays attention toward herself only and likes to live alone, cut off from the outer world.

Kaolin—Hydrated aluminium silicate which is used internally as absorbent, and externally as a soothing and protective by absorbing moisture.

Kaolinosis—Pneumonoconiosis caused by the inhalation of kaolin particles.

Karman cannula—A flexible plastic cannula used in performing early abortion.

Karyo- —A prefix meaning nucleus of a cell.

Karyochromatophil—Having a nucleus that stains.

Karyochrome—A nerve cell with an easily staining nucleus.

Karyoclasis—Karyorrhexis. The fragmentation of a cell nucleus.

Karyocyte—A nucleated red blood cell.

Karyogamic—Pertaining to karyogamy.

Karyogamy—The union of nuclei in cell conjugation.

Karyogenesis—The formation of a cell nucleus.

Karyogenic—1. Pertaining to karyogenesis. 2. Forming the nucleus.

Karyogonad—Micronucleus.

Karyokinesis—The equal division of the nucleus in the process of cell division.

Karyokinetic—Pertaining to karyokinesis.

Karyoklasis—Disintegration of the cell nucleus.

Karyolobic—Having a lobed nucleus.

Karyolobism—The condition of a cell of having a lobed nucleus as in polymorphonuclear white blood cells.

Karyology—The branch of cytology that deals with the study of the cell nucleus.

Karyolymph—The fluid portion of a cell nucleus.

Karyolysis—Chromatolysis. The destruction of a cell nucleus.

Karyolytic—Pertaining to or causing karyolysis.

Karyomegaly—Abnormal enlargement of a cell nucleus.

Karyomere—A vesicle containing only a small portion of the nucleus.

Karyomicrosome—Any small particle in the karyoplasm.

Karyomitome—The nuclear chromatin network.

Karyomitosis—Karyokinesis. Nuclear changes in ceil division.

Karyomorphism—The form of a cell nuceus.

Karyon—The nucleus of a cell.

Karyophage—A unicellular parasite within the cell destroying its nucleus.

Karyoplasm—Nucleoplasm.

Karyoplasmolysis—Achromatolysis.

Karyoplast—A cell nucleus surrounded by a thin band of cytoplasm and a plasma membrane.

Karyopyknosis—Shrinkage of a cell nucleus with condensation of the chromatin.

Karyorrhexis—Karyoclasis. The disintegration of the chromatin into small granules on rupture of the cell nucleus.

Karyosome—Chromocenter. Prochromosome. Any of the condensed irregular clumps of chromatin material in the nuclei of the cells which are not dividing.

Karyostasis—Resting stage of a cell nucleus.

Karyotheca—The membrane surrounding a cell nucleus.

Karyotype—The chromosomal constitution of the cell nucleus.

Karyozoic—Living within the cell nucleus as an intracellular unicellular parasite.

Kata- —A prefix meaning down, back, against or reversing process.

Katabolism—Catabolism.

Kataplasia—Cataplasia.

Katatonia—Catatonia.

Kathisophobia—Fear of sitting down.

Kation—An ion positively charged of electricity.

Katophoria—Katotropia.

Katotropia—Katophoria. Tendency of the eyeball to drop too far downward.

Katzenjammer—The symptoms of mental depression, headache, thirst, nausea, irritability and fatigue occurring after awakening following an excess intake of alcohol.

KBr—Potassium bromide.

Kcal—Kilocalorie.

KCl—Potassium chloride.

Kegel exercises—Exercises for strengthening the perineal muscles of the female which help in childbirth process and in sexual enjoyment.

Keith-Flack node —Sinoatrial node of the heart.

Keith's bundle —Sinoatrial node of the heart.

Kelectome—An instrument for removing a piece of a tumor substance for examination.

Kelis—Keloid.

Kelly's pad—A drainage pad for operation table or bed.

Keloid—Raised, red, thickened and firm scar in the skin following an injury, operation or after an acne.

Keloidosis—Formation of keloids.

Kelosomia—Celosomia.

Kelosomus—A fetus with the congenital fissure of the sternum with the protrusion of the fetal viscera.

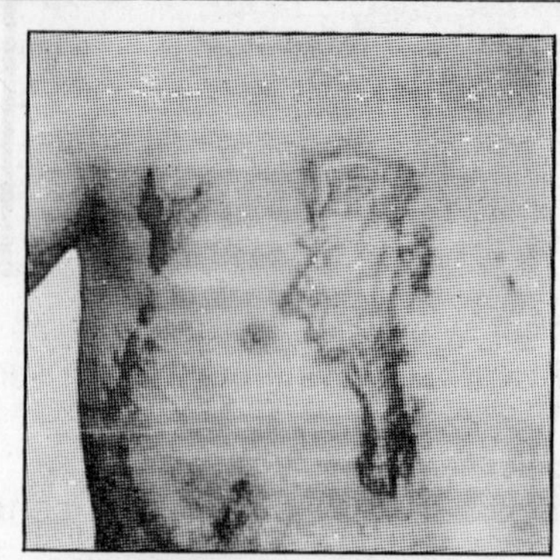

Fig. 276 : Keloid

Kelotomy—Operation for strangulated hernia through the tissues of the constricting neck.

Kelvin scale—A temperature scale in which zero is equal to minus 273° on the celsius scale. On the Kelvin scale the freezing point of water is 273°K, and the boiling point 373°K.

Kenny treatment—Physical therapy used in treating poliomyelitis.

Kenophobia—Morbid fear of empty spaces.

Kerasin—A cerebroside isolated from the brain tissue.

Keratalgia—Pain in the cornea.

Keratectasia—Protrusion of the cornea.

Keratectomy—Excision of a portion of the cornea.

Keratiasis—Formation of the horny warts on the skin.

Keratic—1. Horny. 2. Pertaining to the keratin. 3. Pertaining to the cornea.

Keratin—A hard protein substance found in the epidermis, hair and nails.

Keratinase—An enzyme which hydrolyzes the keratin.

Keratinisation—The process of becoming hard or horny.

Keratinize—To become hard or horny.

Keratinized—Cornified.

Keratinocyte—Any cell of the skin which synthesize the keratin.

Keratinophilic—Denoting fungi that live on keratin, e.g. dermatophytes.

Keratinous—Composed of or of the nature of keratin.

Keratitis—Inflammation of the cornea.

Actinic keratitis—Keratitis occurring as a reaction of the cornea to ultraviolet light.

Deep punctate keratitis—Keratitis with opacities in a clear cornea, occurring in syphilitic iritis.

Herpetic keratitis—1. Branching ulceration of the cornea due to infection with herpes simplex virus. 2. Vesicular keratitis in herpes zoster ophthalmicus.

Interstitial keratitis—Chronic, deep, nonsuppurative keratitis with haziness of the cornea commonly found in children between the age of 5 and 15 years, in syphilis or tuberculosis.

Keratitis bullosa—The formation of blebs upon the cornea.

Keratitis disciformis—Gray disk-shaped opacity in the middle of the cornea.

Keratitis hypopyon—A serpent-like ulcer with pus in the anterior chamber of the eye.

Mycotic keratitis—Inflammation of the cornea caused by fungus infection.

Necrotizing keratitis—Severe inflammation and necrosis of the cornea that is usually seen in herpes infection.

Neuroparalytic keratitis—Neurotrophic keratitis.

Neurotrophic keratitis—Inflammation of the cornea after corneal anesthesia.

Phlyctenular keratitis—An allergic form of conjunctivitis with keratitis seen in children, characterized by the formation of small nodules known as phlyctenules which ulcerate.

Purulent keratitis—Inflammation of the cornea with the formation of pus.

Sclerosing keratitis—Keratitis with inflammation of the sclera.

Superficial punctate keratitis—Small gray spots in the superficial layers of the cornea under Bowman's membrane, occurring in young persons.

Trachomatous keratitis—Keratitis occurring in trachoma.

Traumatic keratitis—Keratitis produced in injury of the cornea.

Xerotic keratitis—Keratitis occurring in dryness of the conjunctiva.

Kerato-, Kerat-— Prefixes indicating the relation of horny substances or to the cornea.

Keratoacanthoma—A benign papular lesion filled with a keratin plug.

Keratoangioma—Angiokeratoma.

Keratocele—Protrusion of Descemet's membrane through the cornea as a result of injury or ulcer.

Keratocentesis—Puncture of the cornea.

Keratoconjunctivitis—Inflammation of the cornea and the conjunctiva.

Epidemic keratoconjunctivitis—An acute highly infectious viral keratoconjunctivitis spreading epidemically with enlargement of the regional lymph nodes.

Flash keratoconjunctivitis—Painful keratoconjunctivitis due to exposure of the eyes to intense ultraviolet irradiation.

Keratoconjunctivitis sicca—Hyperemia of the conjunctiva with thickness and dryness of the corneal epithelium, itching and burning of the eyes and reduced visual acuity.

Phlyctenular keratoconjunctivitis—Keratoconjunctivitis marked by the formation of phlyctenules.

Ultraviolet keratoconjunctivitis—Actinic conjunctivitis. Acute keratoconjunctivitis resulting from exposure to intense ultraviolet irradiation.

Virus Keratoconjunctivitis—Epidemic keratoconjunctivitis.

Keratoconus—Conical protrusion of the central portion of the cornea.

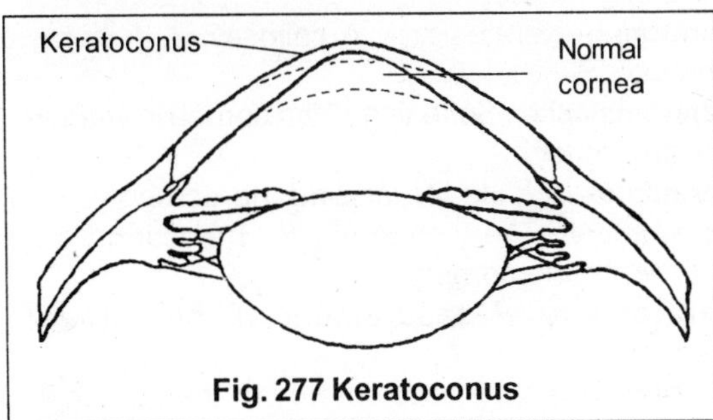

Fig. 277 Keratoconus

Keratocyte—A deformed red blood cell with two or more horn-shaped structures.

Keratoderma—Hypertrophy of the horny layer of the skin.

Keratodermatitis—Inflammation of the horny layer of the skin.

Keratodermia—Keratoderma.

Keratoectasia—Keratectasia. Corneal ectasia.

Keratoelastoidosis—Hyperkeratosis and degeneration of the elastic tissue of the skin.

Keratoepithelioplasty—Repair of the defects of the corneal epithelium by plastic surgery.

Keratogenesis—Production of horny cells.

Keratogenetic—Pertaining to keratogenesis.

Keratogenous—Causing horny growth.

Keratoglobus—Globular and enlarged cornea in congenital glaucoma.

Keratohelcosis—Ulceration of the cornea.

Keratohemia—Presence of blood in the cornea.

Keratohyalin—A substance present in the form of granules in the cytoplasm of the cells of epidermis which is involved in keratinization.

Keratohyaline—1. Keratohyalin. 2. Both horny and hyaline. 3. Pertaining to keratohyalin.

Keratoid—Horny or resembling corneal tissue.

Keratoiditis—Inflammation of the cornea.

Keratoiritis—Inflammation of the cornea and the iris.

Keratoleptynsis—An operation performed on the sightless eye for cosmetic reasons in which corneal surface is removed and replaced by bulbar conjunctiva.

Keratoleukoma—White opacity of the cornea.

Keratolysis—Loosening or shedding of the horny layer of the skin.

Keratolysis pitted, Keratolysis plantare sulcatum—A disease occurring in tropical areas during rainy season in barefooted adults, marked by thickening and deep fissuring of the skin of the soles.

Keratolytic—Desquamative. Pertaining to or causing keratolysis.

Keratoma—Keratosis. 1. A callosity. 2. A horny growth.

Keratomalacia—Softening of the cornea in vitamin A deficiency.

Keratome—A knife for incising the cornea.

Keratometer—An instrument for measuring the curves of the cornea.

Keratometry—Measurement of the corneal curves.

Keratomileusis—Plastic surgery of the cornea in which a portion of the cornea is removed, shaped to the desired curvature and then reattached to the cornea.

Keratomycosis —Fungal infection of the cornea.

Keratonosis—Any noninflammatory disease or deformity of the horny layer of the skin.

Keratonyxis—Keratocentesis.

Keratopachyderma—A syndrome of the congenital deafness with development of hyperkeratosis of the skin of the palms, soles of the feet, elbows and knees in childhood.

Keratopathia—Keratopathy.

Keratopathy—Any noninflammatory disease of the cornea.

Keratophakia—Implantation of a donor's cornea to remove refractive error.

Keratoplasia—The formation or renewal of a horny layer.

Keratoplasty—Plastic surgery on the cornea or cornea grafting.

Allopathic keratoplasty—Corneal transplantation with glass, plastic or other inert material.

Autogenous keratoplasty—Corneal transplantation with the material taken from the same individual.

Heterogenous keratoplasty—Corneal transplantation with the material taken from other living being.

Homogenous keratoplasty—Corneal transplantation with the material taken from other human being.

Keratoplasty optic—To remove the corneal scar and replace it with corneal tissue.

Keratoplasty tectonic—Transplantation of the corneal tissue to replace the lost due to trauma or disease.

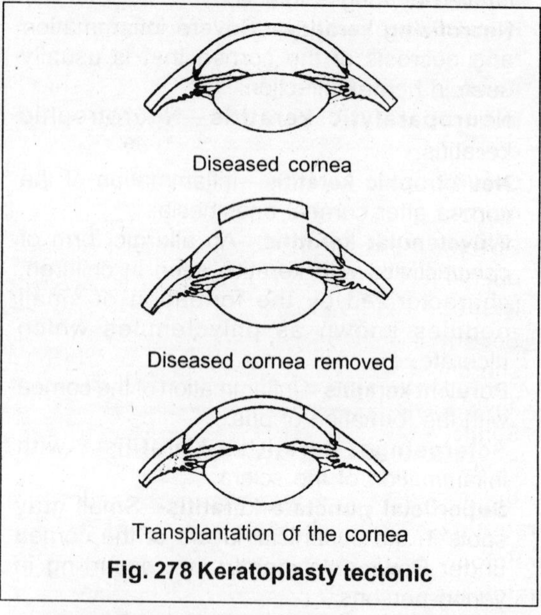

Fig. 278 Keratoplasty tectonic

Nonpenetrating keratoplasty —Keratoplasty in which only the anterior layer of the cornea is used.

Penetrating keratoplasty—Perforating keratoplasty. Corneal transplantation in which all the layers of the cornea are replaced, but the peripheral cornea is retained.

Refractive keratoplasty—Keratoplasty in which shape of the cornea is modified to remove the refractive error of the eye; as if the cornea is flattened, the eye becomes less myopic.

Total keratoplasty—Corneal transplantation in which the entire cornea is removed and replaced.

Keratoprotein—The protein of the hair, nails and epidermis.

Keratorrhexis—Rupture of the cornea.

Keratoscleritis—Inflammation of both, the cornea and the sclera.

Keratoscope—An instrument for visual examination of the cornea.

Keratoscopy—Visual examination of the cornea.

Keratose—Horny.

Keratosis—Keratoma. Any horny growth.

Actinic keratosis—The horny growth of the skin caused by excessive exposure to sunlight, which may also become malignant.

Climactericum keratosis—Circumscribed overgrowth of the horny layer of the epidermis of the palms and soles occurring in women during menopause.

Keratosis linguae—Leukoplakia of the tongue.

Keratosis palmaris et plantaris—Congenital thickness of the skin of the palms and soles sometimes with painful fissuring.

Oral keratosis—Horny growth of the oral mucosa.

Pharyngeal keratosis—Horny growth of the pharyngeal tonsils and the adjacent lymphoid tissue.

Seborrheic keratosis—Numerous pigmented, sharply defined, oval, raised lesions of the skin composed of the epithelial cells.

Senile keratosis—Dry, harsh skin of the old people.

Solar keratosis—Actinic keratosis.

Keratotome—Keratome.

Keratotomy—To make an incision into the cornea.

Keratotorus—A vaultlike protrusion of the cornea.

Keraunoneurosis—A neurosis caused by fear of thunder and lightning.

Keraunophobia—Morbid fear of thunder and lightning.

Kerectomy—Keratectomy.

Kerion—Fungal infection of the scalp caused by Trichophyton tonsurans, marked by inflammatory, boggy mass containing broken hairs with oozing purulent material.

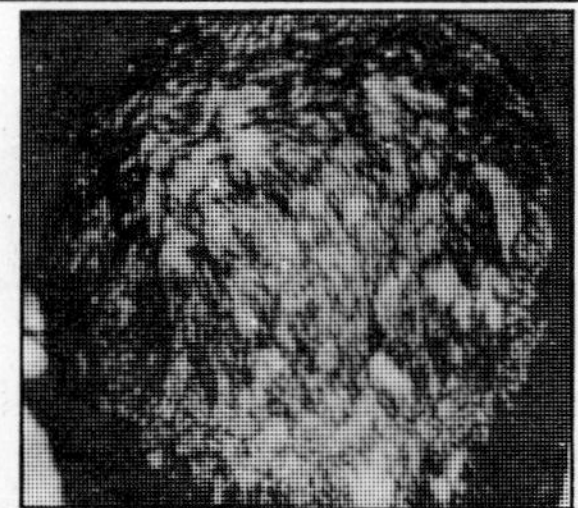

Fig. 279 Kerion (Tinea capitis)

Kernel—The body of a seed.

Kernicterus—A form of icterus neonatorum occurring in infants during the second to eighth day of life due to increased amount of bilirubin in the blood.

Kernig's sign—A sign of meningitis in which pain occurs in the back of the thigh on extending the leg after flexing the thigh upon the body.

Ketoacidosis—Acidosis due to an excess of ketone bodies.

Ketoaciduria—Presence of ketoacids in the urine.

Ketogenesis—Production of ketone bodies.

Ketogenic—Forming or capable of being converted into ketone bodies.

Ketolysis—The dissolution of ketone bodies.

Ketolytic—Pertaining to ketolysis.

Ketone—A substance containing carbonyl group (C= 0) which is formed in the liver by the partial oxidation of fatty acids, the end products of fat metabolism, in the deficiency of glycogen in the liver in case of diabetes mellitus and starvation.

Ketone bodies—A group of three compounds formed during the oxidation of fatty acids, the end products of fat metabolism, in the liver, which includes acetoacetic acid, β-hydroxybutric acid and acetone, resulting in ketonemia and ketonuria.

Ketonemia—An excess of ketone bodies in the blood.

Ketone threshold—The level of ketone in the blood above which the ketone bodies appear in the urine.

Ketonic—Pertaining to or possessing the characteristics of a ketone.

Ketonization—Conversion into a ketone.

Ketonuria—Presence of ketone bodies in the urine.

Ketoplasia—Formation of ketones.

Ketoplastic—Pertaining to the formation of ketones.

Ketose—Any carbohydrate containing the ketones.

Ketosis—Accumulation of ketone bodies in the body.

Ketosuria—Ketonuria.

Ketotic—Pertaining to the ketosis.

Kg.—Abbreviation for kilogram.

Kibe—Chilblain. An inflammed patch on the hands or feet caused by exposure to cold.

Kidney—One of the two excretory organs, purplish brown in color situated in the lumbar region on each side of the vertebral column on the posterior abdominal wall behind the peritoneum. It filtrates the blood and excretes the urine and maintains the water and electrolyte balance of the body.

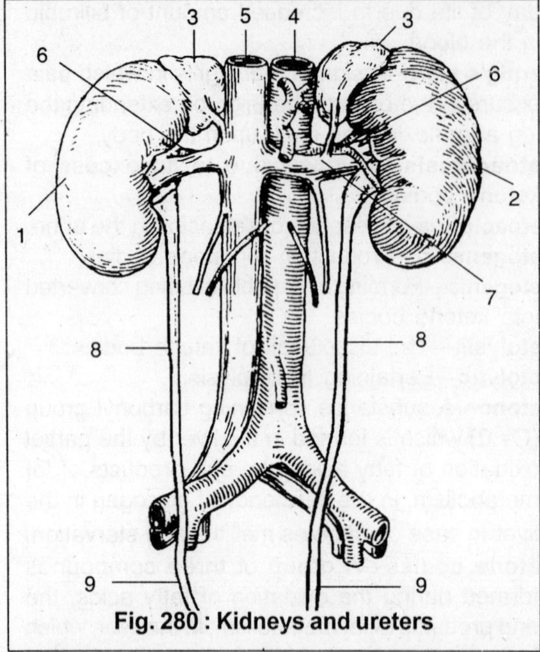

Fig. 280 : Kidneys and ureters

1. Right kidney 2. Left Kidney 3. Adrenal glands 4. Aorta 5. Inferior vena cava 6. Renal artery 7. Renal vein 8 & 9. Ureters

Amyloid kidney—Waxy kidney. The kidney in which amyloid is deposited.

Artificial kidney—An apparatus used in treating the patients of renal failure or absent kidneys, which receives blood from the patient, dialyses it to remove its waste products, which are normally excreted in the urine by the kidney, and then returns the blood to the patient.

Atrophic kidney—A kidney that is reduced in size because of inadequate blood circulation and/or loss of nephrons.

Contracted kidney—Small kidney in chronic interstitial nephritis.

Cystic kidney—Kidney in which cysts are formed.

Ectopic kidney—Kidney at abnormal site.

Fatty kidney—Kidney with fatty degeneration.

Floating kidney—Movable kidney.

Formad kidney—An enlarged and deformed kidney that is sometimes seen in chronic alcoholism.

Fused kidney—The two kidneys are fused.

Goldblatt kidney—The kidney with obstruction of its blood supply resulting in hypertension.

Horseshoe kidney—Congenital malformation in which the kidney is horse shoe-shaped.

Pelvic kidney—A kidney lying in the pelvis congenitally.

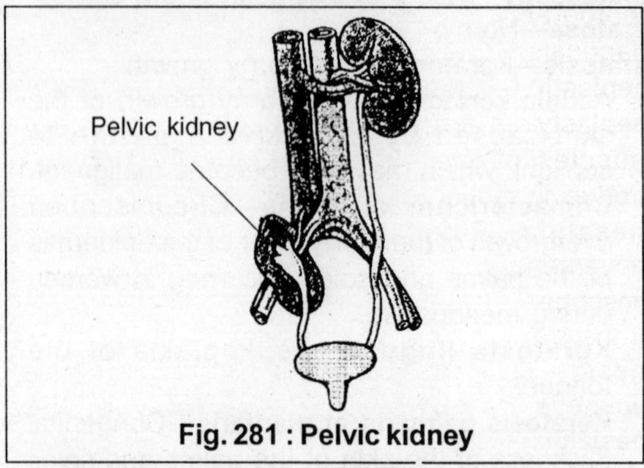

Fig. 281 : Pelvic kidney

Pyelonephritic kidney—A deformed kidney caused by chronic pyelonephritis.

Sacculated kidney—The condition in which the kidney has been absorbed and only the distended capsule remains.

Sponge kidney—Cystic kidney.

Kilian's pelvis—Pelvis spinosa. Pelvis affected with osteomalacia.

Kilo - —A prefix indicating one thousand.

Kilocalorie —1. A unit of heat equal to 1000 calories. 2. In nutrition, a kilocalorie is known as large calorie which is written with capital C.

Kilocycle—One thousand cycles per second.

Kilogram—A weight of 1000 gms.

Kilogram-meter—The work done to raise one kilogram weight one meter.

Kilohertz—In electricity a unit of one thousand cycles.

Kilojoule—One thousand joule.

Kiloliter—One thousand liters.

Kilometer—1000 meters or 3280.83 feet or 0.62 of a mile.

Kilounit—1000 units.

Kilovolt—1000 Volts.

Kilovoltage—The highest voltage of the X-ray tube occurring during an exposure.

Kilowatt—A unit of electrical energy equal to one thousand watts.

Kimmelstiel-wilson syndrome—A syndrome that may develop in patient of diabetes mellitus of ten or more years' standing characterized by hypertension, generalized edema and albuminuria associated with hypoalbuminemia and rise of blood urea.

Kinanesthesia—Inability to perceive the sensation of movement.

Kine- —A prefix meaning movement.

Kinematics—Science of motion.

Kinematograph—An apparatus for taking photographs of the moving objects, used in diagnosis.

Kineplastic—Pertaining to kineplasty.

Kineplasty—A form of amputation in which the muscles of the stump can be utilized for producing motion of the artificial limb.

Kinesalgia—Pain occurring on muscular movement.

Kinescope—An apparatus for testing the refraction of the eye.

Kinesia—Sickness caused by motion as car sickness.

Kinesialgia—Kinesalgia.

Kinesiatrics—Kinesitherapy.

Kinesics—The study of the body movements.

Kinesimeter—An apparatus for measuring the extent of movement of a part of the body.

Kinesiology—Scientific study of the muscular movements of the body.

Kinesiometer—Kinesimeter.

Kinesioneurosis—Functional nervous disorder marked by tics and spasms.

Kinesiotherapy—Kinesitherapy. Kinetotherapy. Treatment of diseases by exercises.

Kinesipathist—A non-medical person who treats the diseases by exercises.

Kinesis—Motion.

Kinesitherapy—Kinesiatrics. Kinesiotherapy.

Kinesophobia—Morbid fear of movement.

Kinesthesia—The sense by which the position, weight and movement are perceived.

Kinesthesiometer—An instrument for testing kinesthesia.

Kinesthesis—Kinesthesia.

Kinesthetic—Pertaining to kinesthesia.

Kinetic—Pertaining to, producing or consisting of motion.

Kinetics—Science of motion.

Kinetocardiogram—The graphic record produced by kinetocardiography.

Kinetocardiograph—An instrument for recording precordial impulses due to cardiac movement.

Kinetocardiography—The graphic recording of slow precordial vibrations which are not audible.

Kinetochore—Centromere.

Kinetocyte—A wandering cell.

Kinetogenic—Causing movement.

Kinetoscope—An apparatus for taking serial photographs to record the movement.

Kinetosis—Kinesia.

Kinetotherapy—Kinesiotherapy. Kinesitherapy.

Kingdom—A category of the living beings, as animal kingdom that includes all animals and the plant kingdom that includes all plants.

Kinin—Any of a group of endogenous peptides that induce smooth muscle contraction, increase permeability of the blood capillaries and increase the blood flow and cause hypotension.

Kininogen—The substance producing a kinin.

Kink—Unnatural bend in a tube as in the intestine or ureter etc.

Kinking—Twisting.

Kino- — A prefix meaning movement.

Kinomometer—An apparatus for measuring the degree of movement in a joint.

Kinship—The descendants from a common ancestor.

Kiotome—An instrument for amputating the uvula.

Kiotomy—Amputation of the uvula by using kiotome.

Klebs-Loeffler bacillus—Corynebacterium diphtheriae. The bacillus of diphtheria.

Kleptolagnia—Feeling of sexual pleasure from stealing.

Kleptomania—Mania for stealing in which a person steals the objects with compulsion.

Kleptomaniac—1. Pertaining to kleptomania. 2. The person exhibiting kleptomania.

Kleptophobia—Morbid fear of stealing.

Klieg eye—The eye in which there is conjunctivitis, lacrimation and photophobia from exposure to the intense lights used in making motion pictures or television films.

Klippel-Feil syndrome—A congenital anomaly characterized by a short, wide neck, low hairline, reduction in the number of cervical vertebrae, and their fusion and abnormalities of the brain-stem and the cerebellum.

Klismaphilia—The derivation of sexual pleasure by receiving enemas.

Klumpke's paralysis—Paralysis with atrophy of the forearm.

Knapp's forceps—A forceps for expressing the granulations of trachoma, having the two cylindrical blades.

Kneading—The act of working into a dough.

Knee—Genu. 1. The articulation of the femur with

the tibia covered by patella bone or knee cap anteriorly. 2. Any kneelike structure.

Housemaid's knee—Inflammation of the bursa anterior to the patella bone with the accumulation of fluid within it. It occurs in persons who have to kneel frequently or work continuously while kneeling.

Knock knee—See below knock-knee.

Locked knee—The condition in which the leg cannot be extended which is usually due to displacement of the semilunar cartilage.

Knee cap—Patella bone.

Knee joint—The articulation of the femur and the tibia bones.

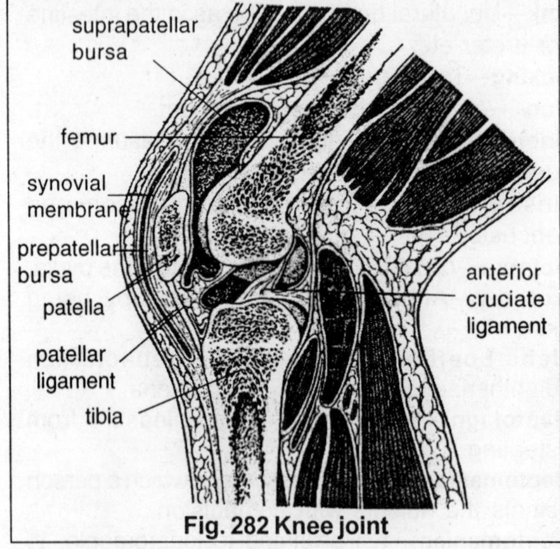

Fig. 282 Knee joint

Kneipp cure—Hydrotherapy.

Kneippism—Walking bare-foot on dewy grass or taking bath in cold water as a form of hydrotherapy.

Knife—A cutting instrument used in surgery and dissection.

Knismogenic—Producing tickling sensation.

Knitting—The process of union of the fragments of a broken bone or of the edges of a wound.

Knob—A protuberance or nodule.

Knock—To strike with a blow.

Knock-knee—Genu valgum. The condition in which the knees are abnormally close together while the ankles are far apart.

Knot—1. Twisting and binding of the ends or parts of one or more threads, sutures, ligatures or bandage, etc. 2. In anatomy, enlargement of a structure forming a knoblike structure.

False knot—An external bulging of the umbilical cord resulting from coiling of the umbilical blood vessels.

Granny knot—A double knot in which the free ends of second cord are not in the same plane as the free ends of the first cord, but alternate being over and under each other.

Fig. 283 A Granny knot

Square knot—A double knot in which the free ends of the second cord are in the same plane as the ends of the first cord.

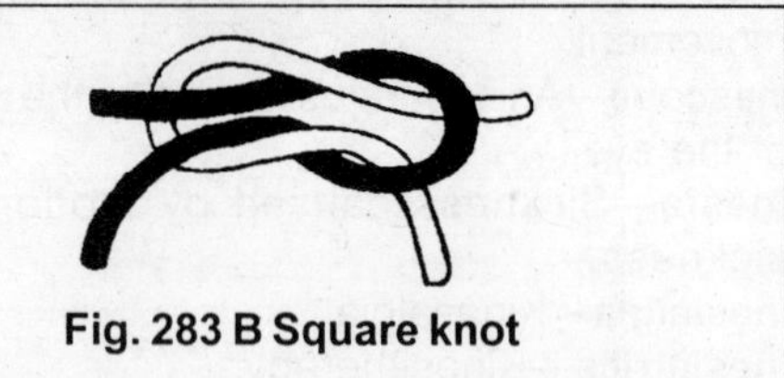

Fig. 283 B Square knot

Surgical knot—A double knot in which the thread or a suture is passed twice through the 1st loop.

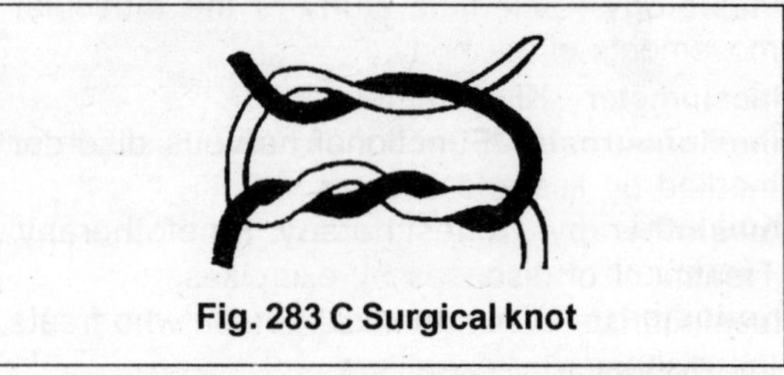

Fig. 283 C Surgical knot

True knot—A knot formed by the fetus slipping through a loop of the umbilical cord.

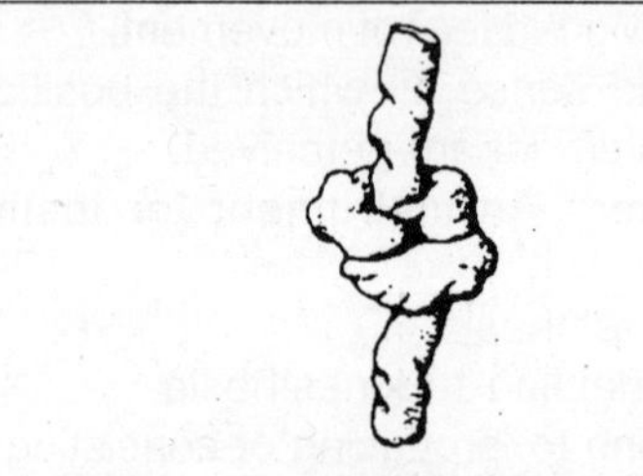

Fig. 283 D True knot
A true knot appeared in an umbilical cord.

Knotting—Formation of knots.

Knotty—Having knots.

Knuckle—Prominence of the dorsal aspect of any phalangeal joint.

Kocher's reflex—Contraction of the abdominal muscles on pressing the testicle.

Koch's bacillus—Mycobacterium tuberculosis. The bacillus causing tuberculosis.

Koch's phenomenon—Inflammation of the skin at the site of injection of tuberculin in a person suffering from tuberculosis.

Kohnstamm's phenomenon —After movement.

Koilocyte—An abnormal cell of the squamous epithelium of the cervix uteri.

Koilonychia—Dystrophy of the finger nails in which they become thinned and concave with raised margins.

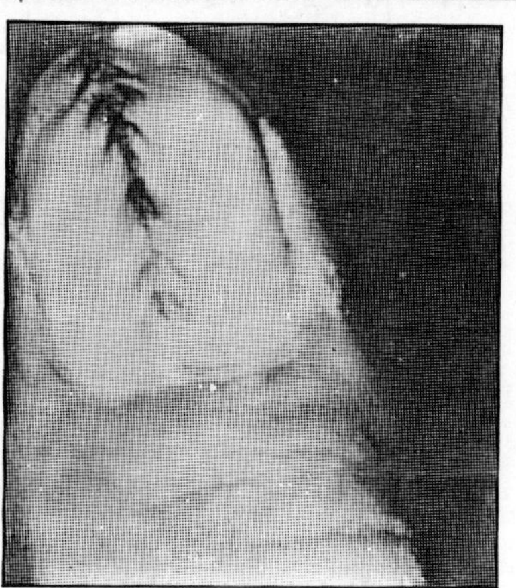

Fig. 284 : Koilonychia

Koilorrhachic—Having an excessively concave vertebral column anteriorly.

Koilosternia—The condition of having funnel-shaped chest.

Kolp- —A prefix indicating vagina.

Kolpitis—Vaginitis. Inflammation of the vagina.

Kolypeptic—Checking digestion.

Kolyseptic—Preventing putrefaction.

Kolytic—Denoting an inhibitory action.

Kondoleon's operation—An operation for removing the subcutaneous tissue to relieve elephantiasis.

Koniology—Coniology. Scientific study of dust and its effects.

Koniometer—An apparatus for estimating the amount of dust in the air.

Koniosis—Coniosis. Any disease caused by dust.

Kophemia—Word deafness.

Koplik's spots—Small red spots with bluish white centers on the mucous membrane of the mouth before the rash appears in measles.

Kopophobia—Abnormal fear of tiredness.

Koranyi's sign—A sign of pleural effusion in which there is increased resonance on percussion of the dorsal spine.

Koro—A phobia that the penis will retract into the abdomen and the belief that when the penis will disappear completely, the individual will die.

Korotkoff's sounds—Sounds heard in auscultation of blood pressure.

Koumiss—Kumiss. Kumyss. Fermented cow's milk or a substance used for fermenting cow's milk.

Kraurosis—Dried and shrivelled condition of the skin and mucous membrane resulting from atrophy, especially of the vulva.

Kraurosis vulvae—Atrophic condition of the female external genital organs seen mostly in old women, characterized by drying and shriveling of the external genital organs with severe itching and a white marble-like patch on the skin. If the condition is not treated, malignancy of the skin may develop, i.e. the cancer may be caused.

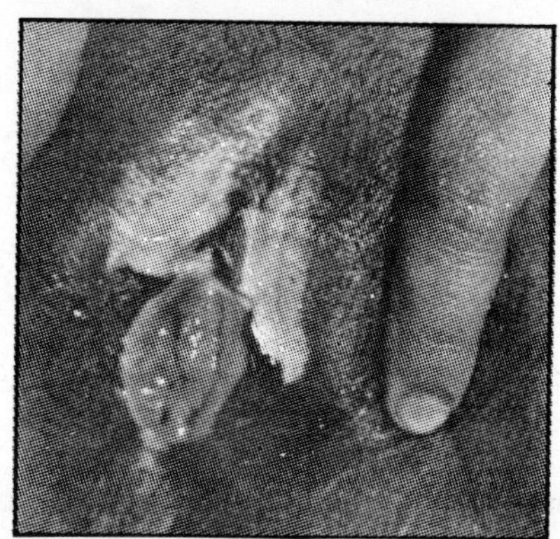

Fig. 285 : Kraurosis vulvae

Kreatin—A nitrogenous constituent of the muscles.

Krukenberg's tumor—A secondary malignant tumor of the ovary which is usually bilateral.

Krypton—A gaseous element present in the atmosphere in small amount.

K.U.B.—Kidney, ureter and bladder, used in reference to X-ray study of the abdomen.

Kubisagari, Kubisagaru—Vestibular neuronitis.

Kufs' disease—The adult form of cerebral sphingolipidosis.

Kumiss, Kumyss—Koumiss.

Kummell's disease or spondylitis—Spondylitis following compression fracture of the vertebrae.

Kussmaul's breathing—Very deep gasping respiration in severe diabetic acidosis and coma.

Kussmaul's disease—Periarteritis nodosa.

K.V.—Kilovolt.

Kwashiorkor—A condition due to severe protein deficiency in children characterized by the symptoms of lethargy, retarded growth, mental deficiency, increased susceptibility to infections, edema, dermatitis with changes in the skin and hair pigment and enlargement of the liver.

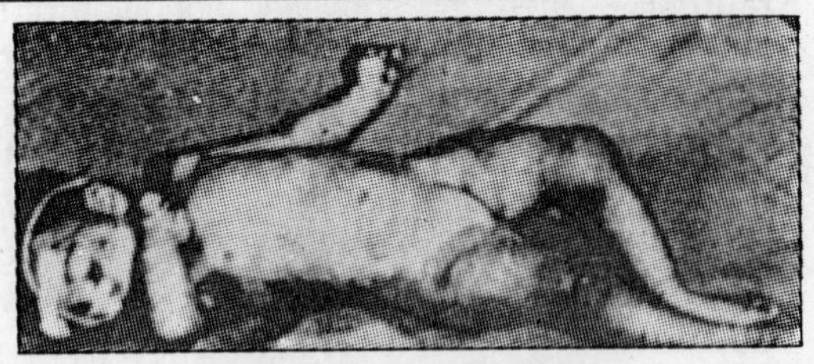

Fig. 286 Kwashiorkor

Kyestein, Kiestein—A thin layer of bacteria or impurities floating on the surface of the stale urine.

Kyllosis—Clubfoot.

Kymatism—Myokymia. Twitching of fibers of a muscle.

Kymogram—A tracing or recording made by a kymograph.

Kymograph—1. An apparatus used to record the changes of blood pressure, pulsations, muscular contractions, respiratory movements, etc. 2. A radiographic apparatus for recording the range of movements of the heart or diaphragm.

Kymography—The use of kymograph.

Kymoscope—An apparatus for measuring the blood flow and pressure.

Kynocephalus—A fetus with the head which resembles that of a dog.

Kynurenine—An intermediate compound in the metabolism of tryptophan.

Kyogenic—Inducing pregnancy.

Kypho-—A prefix indicating humped.

Kyphorachitis—Deformity of the thorax and spinal column in rickets resulting in the development of a hump at the back.

Kyphos—The hump in the spinal column in kyphosis.

Kyphoscoliosis—Backward and lateral curvature of the spinal column.

Kyphosis—Humback. Increased curvature of the spinal column in the thoracic region with convexity backward.

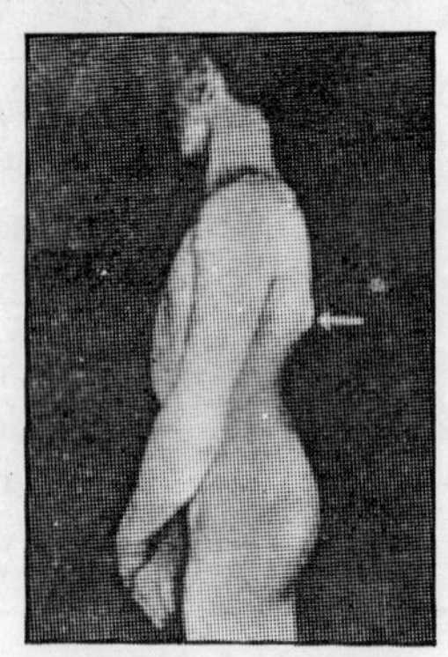

Fig. 287 : Kyphosis

Kyphotic—Affected by or pertaining to kyphosis.

Kyrtorrhachic—Curvature of the spinal column with backward concavity.

Kysthitis—Vaginitis, colpitis. Inflammation of the vagina.

Kysthoptosis—Prolapse of the vagina.

Kyto-—Cyto—A prefix denoting a cell.

L—Left, length.

L A —Left atrium.

Labia—Plural of labium.

Labial—Pertaining to the lips,

Labialism—Defective speech produced by lip sounds.

Labialy —Toward the lips.

Labile—Not fixed, unstable, gliding from one place to another.

Lability—The state of being not fixed, or unstable or changeable.

Labio- —A prefix denoting lip.

Labioalveolar—Pertaining to the lips and sockets of the tooth.

Labiocervical—Pertaining to the buccal surface of the lips, and the neck of the tooth.

Labiochorea—Spasm of the lips in chorea causing stammering in the patient.

Labioclination—Deviation of a tooth from the normal vertical to the side of the lip.

Labiodental—Pertaining to the lips and tooth.

Labiogingival—Pertaining to the lips and the gums or the labial and gingival surfaces of a tooth.

Labioglossolaryngeal—Pertaining to the lips, tongue and larynx.

Labioglossopharyngeal—Pertaining to the lips, tongue and pharynx.

Labiograph—An apparatus for registering lip movements in speaking.

Labiomental—Pertaining to the lower lip and the chin.

Labiomycosis—Fungus disease of the lips.

Labionasal—Pertaining to the lips and the nose.

Labiopalatine—Pertaining to the lips and the palate.

Labioplacement—Displacement of a tooth toward the lip.

Labioplasty—Cheiloplasty. Plastic surgery of the lips.

Labiotenaculum—An instrument for holding the lips during an operation.

Labioversion—Displacement of a tooth toward the lips from the line of occlusion.

Labitome —Cutting forceps.

Labium—A fleshy border or a lip.

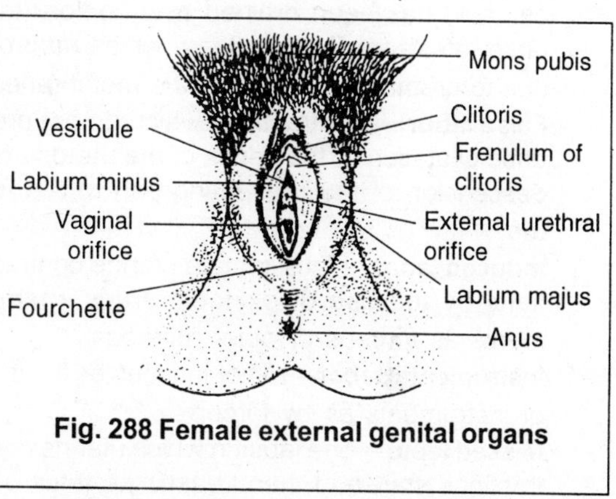

Fig. 288 Female external genital organs

Labium majus—Labia majora (plural). A fold of skin on either side of the vaginal opening forming the lateral border of the vulva.

Labium minus—Labia minora (plural). A small fold of skin on either side between the labia majus and the vaginal opening.

Labium oris—Lips of the mouth.

Labor—The function of the female by which the fetus is expelled from the uterus through vagina to the outside of the body. It is divided into three stages :—

First stage (Stage of dilatation)—It starts with the onset of regular uterine contractions and ends at the complete dilatation of the cervix.

Second stage (Stage of expulsion)—The period from the complete dilatation of cervix until the fetus is expelled completely.

Third stage (Placental stage)—The period from the complete expulsion of the fetus until the placenta and the membranes are completely expelled.

Active labor —Normal labor.

Arrested labor—Failure of the normal labor due to uterine inertia, obstruction of the pelvis or systematic disease.

Artificial labor—Induction of labor by artificial means, as by the use of oxytocic drugs or other methods to stimulate the uterine contractions before the time they would normally occur.

Back labor —Labor with the malposition of the fetal head in which the occiput lies opposite the mother's sacrum. Mother experiences severe back pain.

Complicated labor—Labor occurring with a complication such as hemorrhage or uterine inertia.

Dry labor—Labor in which most of the amniotic fluid has been drained away before the onset of uterine contractions, which may be due to premature rupture of the membranes.

False labor —Contractions which do not produce dilatation of the cervix of the uterus and descension of the presenting part of the fetus.

Induced labor —To stimulate uterine contractions by the use of oxytocic drugs, instruments as forceps or other methods.

Instrumental labor—Labor induced by the use of instruments as by forceps.

Missed labor—The labor in which uterine contractions start and then cease, the fetus being retained in the uterus for weeks or months.

Normal labor—Regular uterine contractions with progressive dilatation of the cervix and descent of the presenting part of the fetus.

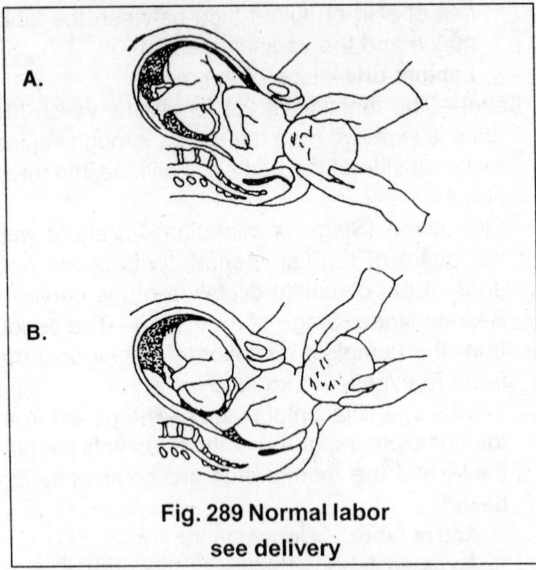

Fig. 289 Normal labor
see delivery

Obstructed labor —Obstruction occurring in the passage of fetus through the birth canal due to fetal malposition, malpresentation or disproportion between the head of the fetus and the pelvis of the mother.

Precipitate labor—Labor occurring very rapidly i.e., within two to three hours.

Premature labor—Labor which begins before the completion of 37 weeks of pregnancy.

Postmature labor—That occurring two weeks or more after expected date of confinement.

Spontaneous labor—Labor which is completed without mechanical means or operation.

Laboratorian —The person working in a laboratory.

Laboratory —A room equipped for performing scientific experiments, tests or for clinical studies of the materials such as blood, sputum, urine and stool etc. obtained from the patient.

Labra —Plural of labrum.

Labrocyte—A mast cell.

Labrum—Lip or liplike structure.

Labyrinth—The internal ear consisting of osseous or bony and membranous labyrinths.

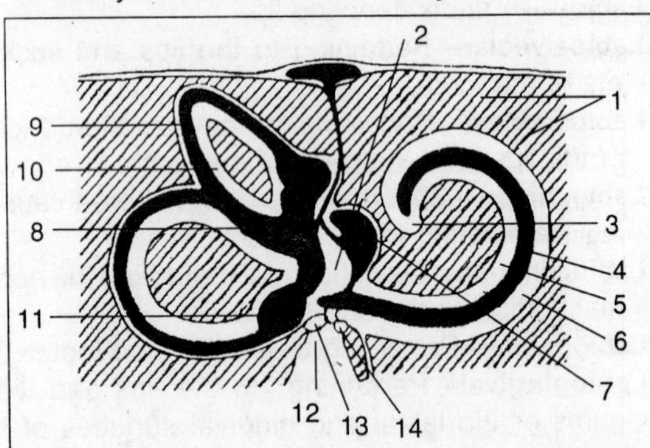

Fig. 290 Structure of the osseous and membranous labyrinths.

1. Petrous pyramid 2. Vestibule 3. Communication between scala vestibuli and scala tympani 4. Membranous cochlear canal 5. Scala vestibuli 6. Scala tympani 7. Saccule 8. Utricle 9. Membranous semicircular canal 10. Osseous semicircular canal 11. Membranous ampulla 12. Tympanic cavity 13. Fenestra ovalis 14. Fenestra rotunda

Membranous labyrinth—It is the structure in the osseous or bony labyrinth consisting of utricle and saccule of the vestibule, three semicircular canals and the cochlear duct.

Osseous or bony labyrinth—It consists of vestibule, three semicircular canals and cochlea.

Labyrinthectomy—Excision of the labyrinth.

Labyrinthine—Pertaining to a labyrinth.

Labyrinthitis—Inflammation of the labyrinth.

Labyrinthotomy—To make an incision into the labyrinth.

Labyrinthus—Labyrinth.

Lac—1. Milk. 2. Any milklike medicinal substance.

Lacerable—Capable of being lacerated.

Lacerate—To tear.

Lacerated—Torn; broken.

Laceration—1. The act of tearing. 2. Wound or irregular tear of the flesh.

Lacertus—1. Muscular part of the arm. 2. Muscular or fibrous band.

Lachrymal —Lacrimal.

Laciniae tubae —Fimbriae of the fallopian tube.

Laciniate—Jagged or fringed.

Lacrima—Tear.

Lacrimal—Pertaining to the tears.

Lacrimal apparatus —An apparatus concerned with the secretion and flow of tears, which includes the lacrimal gland and its ducts, lacrimal superior and inferior canaliculi, lacrimal sac, and nasolacrimal duct which causes the tears to flow into the nasal cavity.

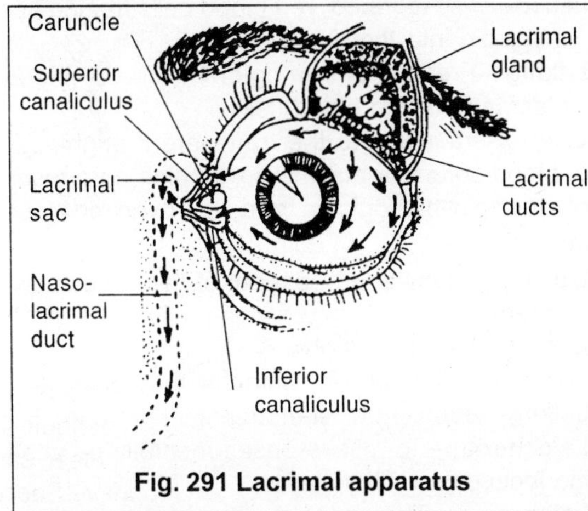

Fig. 291 Lacrimal apparatus

Lacrimal reflex —Secretion of the tears resulting from irritation of the corneal conjunctiva.

Lacrimation—Secretion and discharge of the tears.

Lacrimator—The substance, e.g. a gas which increases the flow of tears.

Lacrimatory—Causing the production of tears.

Lacrimonasal—Pertaining to the lacrimal apparatus and the nose.

Lacrimotome—An instrument for making an incision into the lacrimal sac or duct.

Lacrimotomy—To make an incision into the lacrimal sac or duct.

Lact-, Lacto- —Prefixes meaning milk.

Lactacidemia—Excess of lactic acid in the blood.

Lactacidosis —Acidosis due to increased lactic acid.

Lactaciduria—Presence of lactic acid in the urine.

Lactagogue—Galactagogue. An agent which induces secretion of milk.

Lactalbumin—Albumin, a soluble protein of the milk which coagulates and appears as a film on the surface of the milk when the milk is heated.

Lactant—Suckling.

Lactase—A sugar-splitting enzyme converting lactose into dextrose and galactose, found in the intestinal juice.

Lactate—1. Any salt of lactic acid. 2. To secrete milk.

Lactation—1. The secretion of milk .2. The period of milk secretion.

Lactational —Pertaining to lactation.

Lacteal—1. Pertaining to milk . 2. Any intestinal lymphatic which transports the chyle.

Lacteous—Milky.

Lactescence—Resemblance to milk.

Lactescent —Resembling milk, milky.

Lactic—Pertaining to the milk.

Lactic acidemia —Lactacidemia, Presence of lactic acid in the blood.

Lacticemia—Lactacidemia. Presence of lactic acid in the blood.

Lactiferous—Secreting and carrying milk.

Lactiferous ducts—Ducts of the mammary gland.

Lactiferous glands—1. Mammary glands. 2. Montgomery's glands in the areola of the nipple.

Lactification—Production of lactic acid.

Lactifugal —Lactifuge.

Lactifuge —Stopping milk secretion.

Lactigenous—Secreting or producing milk.

Lactigerous — Secreting or carrying milk.

Lactimorbus —Milk sickness.

Lactin—Lactose, milk sugar.

Lactinated—Containing or prepared with milk sugar.

Lactivorous—Living upon milk.

Lactobacilli —Plural of lactobacillus.

Lactobacillus—The bacteria which produce lactic acid by the fermentation of carbohydrates. They make the milk sour.

Lactobacillus acidophilus—The bacteria which produce lactic acid by the fermentation of sugars in milk. They are found in the milk, feces of the bottle-fed infants, carious teeth, saliva and the vagina.

Lactobutyrometer—An instrument for estimating the amount of cream in the milk.

Lactocele—Galactocele. Formation of a cyst in the breast due to occlusion of a milk duct.

Lactocrit—An apparatus for determining the amount of fat in the milk.

Lactodensimeter—Lactocrit.

Lactogen—Any substance which increases the production of milk.

Lactogenesis—Production of milk.

Lactogenic—Stimulating milk production.

Lactogenic hormone —Prolactin.

Lactoglobulin—A globulin (protein) found in the milk.

Lactoglobulin's immune —Antibodies (immunoglobulins) occurring in the colostrum.

Lactolase—Lactacidase. An enzyme forming the lactic acid.

Lactometer—An apparatus for determining the specific gravity of milk.

Lactoprotein—Any protein present in the milk.

Lactorrhea—Galactorrhea. Excessive or continued flow of milk.

Lactoscope —Galactoscope. An instrument for examining the quality and purity of milk.

Lactose—Sugar of milk which on hydrolysis yields glucose and galactose.

Lactose intolerance —Intolerance to milk due to deficiency of the enzyme lactase which is essential for the absorption of lactose from the intestine.

Lactosuria —Presence of lactose in the urine.

Lactotherapy —Galactotherapy. Treatment of diseases by milk diet.

Lactotoxin —Any toxic substance present in the decomposed milk.

Lactotrope —An acidophilic cell of the anterior pituitary gland which secretes prolactin.

Lactotroph —Lactotrope.

Lactotrophin —Prolactin.

Lactotropin —Prolactin hormone.

Lactovegetarian —1. Pertaining to the milk and vegetables. 2. The person subsisting on milk or its products and vegetables.

Lacuna—1. A small hollow space. 2. A defect or gap in the cartilage, bone or any other organ of the body.

Lacunae —Plural of lacuna.

Lacunar —Pertaining to lacuna.

Lacunes —Small, irregularly jagged cavities in the brain.

Lacunula —Small lacuna.

Lacunule —Lacunula.

Lacus—Accumulation of fluid in the small hollow space or cavity.

Lacus lacrimalis—Space at the medial canthus of the eye where the tears are collected.

Laennec's cirrhosis—Cirrhosis of the liver associated with chronic excessive intake of alcohol.

Lag—1. The time elapsed between application of a stimulus and the resulting reaction. 2. The early period after inoculation of bacteria into the culture medium, in which the growth or cell division is slow.

Lageniform—Flask- shaped.

Lagging —Diminished ventilatory movement of the affected side of chest due to pleural disease.

Lagnesis—Excessive sexual desire in men.

Lagophthalmia —Lagophthalmos.

Lagophthalmos, Lagophthalmus—Incomplete closure of the palpebral fissure on shutting the eyelids.

La grippe—Influenza.

Lake—A small cavity of fluid.

Laked—Disintegrated red blood cells freeing hemoglobin into the blood plasma.

Laking—Freeing of hemoglobin into the blood plasma from red blood cells.

Laky—Pertaining to the transparent brightness of blood serum or plasma developing as a result of release of hemoglobin from destroyed red blood cells.

Laliatry—Study and treatment of the speech disorders.

Laliophobia —Lalophobia.

Lallation—The babbling; infantile form of speech.

Lalling—Babbling or stammering.

Lalochezia —To relieve onself mentally by uttering indecent or filthy words.

Lalognosis—The understanding of speech.

Lalopathology—The branch of medical science which is concerned with the disorders of speech.

Lalopathy—Any disorder of the speech.

Lalophobia—Morbid fear to speak due to fear of stammering.

Laloplegia—Paralysis of the speech muscles.

Lalorrhea—Excessive flow of speech.

Lambda—The point of the union of lambdoid and sagittal sutures.

Lambdacism—Inability to pronounce 'L' letter properly.

Lambdoid, Lambdoidal—Shaped like Greek letter λ (lambda).

Lambert —A unit of brightness.

Lamblia—Giardia.

Lambliasis—Giardiasis. Infection with Giardia lamblia.

Lame—Crippled in a leg.

Lamella—1. A thin plate or layer as of a bone. 2. A medicated disk of gelatin to be inserted under the lower eyelid.

Lamellar—1. Pertaining to the lamella. 2. Arranged in thin plates or layers.

Lamellate, Lamellated —Lamellar.

Lameness—The state of being lame.

Lamina—1. A thin, flat layer or membrane as Bowman's membrane (A thin membrane between the epithelium and the substance of the cornea). 2. The flattened part of either side of the arch of a vertebra.

Laminae—Plural of lamina.

Laminagram —An x-ray film of a body section or tissues taken by laminagraphy.

Laminagraph —An apparatus used for laminagraphy.

Laminagraphy—X-ray examination of the body tissues.

Laminar—1. Pertaining to the lamina. 2. Made up of layers.

Laminated—Arranged in layers.

Lamination—Layer-like arrangement.

Laminectomy—The excision of the posterior arch of a vertebra.

Laminitis—Inflammation of a lamina.

Laminography —Laminagraphy.

Laminotomy—To divide a lamina of a vertebra.

Lamp—An apparatus for producing light or heat for the treatment of diseases.

Lamprophonia—Distinctness or clearness of the voice.

Lamprophonic—Having a clear voice.

Lance--1. A surgical knife with two edges or the lancet. 2. To incise with a lancet.

Lanceolate—Shaped like a spear-head.

Lancet—Lance.

Gum lancet —A lancet used for incising the gum over the crown of an erupting tooth.

Lancinate—To lacerate or tear.

Lancinating—Sharp or cutting, as pain.

L and A—The reaction of the pupils of the eyes to light and accommodation.

Landsteiner's classification — Blood group O, A, B, and AB based on the presence of antigens on the erythrocytes.

Langerhans' islands—Small isolated masses of cells throughout the pancreas, each of which is made up of three type of cells, i.e. alpha, beta and delta cells. The beta cells are predominant and produce insulin. Destruction of, or impairment of the function of the islands may result in diabetes or hyperglycemia.

Langhans' layer —Cytotrophoblast. A cellular layer present in the chorionic villi of the placenta.

Languor—Lassitude. Exhaustion or weakness.

Laniary—Capable for tearing as the canine teeth.

Lanolin—A purified, fatlike substance obtained from the wool of sheep, used as an ointment base.

Lanuginous—Covered with lanugo.

Lanugo—Fine hair on the body of the fetus.

Laparo- —A prefix which means pertaining to the flank of loin, and to the operations through the abdominal wall.

Laparocele—An abdominal hernia.

Laparocholecystotomy—To make an incision into the gallbladder through the abdominal wall.

Laparocolectomy—Colectomy. Excision of a part or all of the colon through the abdominal wall.

Laparocolostomy, Laparocolotomy —Formation of a permanent opening into the colon through the abdominal wall.

Laparocystectomy—Laparocystotomy. Removal of extrauterine fetus or a cyst through an abdominal incision.

Laparocystidotomy—To make an incision into the urinary bladder through the abdominal wall.

Laparocystotomy—Laparocystectomy. To make an incision in the abdominal wall to remove the contents of a cyst, or an extrauterine fetus.

Laparoendoscopic —Pertaining to laparoendoscopy.

Laparoenterostomy—To make an artificial opening into the intestine through the abdominal wall.

Laparoenterotomy —The formation of an opening into the intestinal cavity through an incision into the loin.

Laparogastroscopy—Visual examination of the inside of the stomach after gastrotomy.

Laparogastrostomy—Celiogastrostomy. To form a permanent gastric fistula through the abdominal wall.

Laparogastrotomy—To make an incision into the stomach through the abdominal wall.

Laparohepatotomy—To make an incision into the liver through the abdominal wall.

Laparohysterectomy— To remove the uterus through an incision in the abdominal wall.

Laparohystero-oophorectomy — To remove the

uterus and the ovaries through incision into the abdominal wall.

Laparohysteropexy—Fixation of the uterus with the abdominal wall.

Laparohysterosalpingo-oophorectomy —To remove the uterus, fallopian tubes and ovaries through incision into the abdominal wall.

Laparohysterotomy— To incise the uterus through an incision of the abdominal wall.

Laparoileotomy—To make an incision into the ileum following an incision into the abdominal wall.

Laparomyitis—Inflammation of the muscular portion of the abdominal wall.

Laparomyomectomy—Excision of a muscular tumor through the incision in the abdominal wall.

Laparomyositis —Inflammation of the lateral abdominal muscles.

Laparonephrectomy—Excision of a kidney through an incision in the loin.

Laparorrhaphy—Celiorrhaphy. Suture of a wound in the abdominal wall.

Laparosalpingectomy—Excision of a fallopian tube through an incision in the abdominal wall.

Laparosalpingo-oophorectomy —Excision of fallopian tubes and ovaries through an incision in the abdominal wall.

Laparosalpingotomy—Celiosalpingotomy. To make an incision into a fallopian tube through an incision into the abdomen.

Laparoscope—An endoscope for visual examination of the peritoneal cavity.

Laparoscopy—Visual examination of the peritoneal cavity by the use of laparoscope.

Laparosplenectomy—Excision of the spleen through the incision of abdominal wall.

Laparosplenotomy—To make an incision into the spleen through the incision into the abdominal wall.

Laparotomy—Surgical opening of the abdomen, an abdominal operation.

Laparotrachelotomy—Cesarean section with the incision into the lower segment of the uterus.

Laparotyphlotomy—To make an incision into the cecum through the incision into the lateral abdominal wall.

Lapis—Stone.

Lard—The purified internal fat of the abdomen of the hog.

Lardaceous—Resembling lard or fat, fatty.

Larva—A developing form of an insect after it has emerged from the egg and before it transforms into a pupa from which it emerges as an adult.

Larvaceous —Larvate.

Larvae —Plural of larva.

Larval—Pertaining to a larva.

Larvate—Hidden disease or a symptom of disease.

Larvicidal —Destructive to the larvae of the insects.

Larvicide—An agent that kills the insect larvae.

Larviparous —Larvae-bearing.

Larviphagic—Eating larvae as certain fishes do.

Laryngalgia—Pain in the larynx.

Laryngeal—Pertaining to the larynx.

Laryngeal reflex—Occurrence of cough as a result of irritation to the larynx or fauces.

Laryngectomee— The person whose larynx has been removed.

Laryngectomy—Surgical removal of the larynx.

Laryngemphraxis—Obstruction or closure of the larynx.

Larynges —Plural of larynx.

Laryngismal—Pertaining to the laryngeal spasm.

Laryngismus—Spasm of the larynx.

Laryngitic— 1. Pertaining to the laryngitis. 2. Resulting from laryngitis.

Laryngitis—Inflammation of the larynx.

Acute catarrhal laryngitis—Acute congestive laryngitis.

Atrophic laryngitis—Laryngitis with atrophy of the mucous membrane of the larynx and its diminished secretion.

Chronic laryngitis—Laryngitis of long duration due to recurrent irritation, following acute form, secondary to rhinitis or sinusitis, due to tumors, excessive smoking or drinking.

Croupous laryngitis —Laryngitis occurring mainly in infants and children, characterized by barky cough, hoarseness and stridor.

Diphtheritic laryngitis—Inflammation of the larynx in diphtheria with the formation of a whitish membrane.

Membranous laryngitis—Inflammation of the larynx with the formation of a false membrane which is different from that of diphtheria.

Spasmodic laryngitis —Stridulosa laryngitis.

Stridulosa laryngitis—Inflammation of the larynx in children caused by some infection characterized by whizzing sound in the throat.

Syphilitic laryngitis—A chronic form of laryngitis due to syphilis.

Tuberculous laryngitis—Inflammation of the larynx secondary to pulmonary tuberculosis.

Laryngo- —A prefix pertaining to the larynx.

Laryngocele—A congenital air sac connecting with the cavity of the larynx which may bulge outward on the neck.

Laryngocentesis—To incise or to puncture the larynx.

Laryngoedema —A swelling of the larynx caused by an allergic reaction.

Laryngofissure—To open the larynx by an incision in the median line through the thyroid cartilage.

Laryngogram—X-ray film of the larynx.

Laryngograph—An apparatus for making a record of the laryngeal movements.

Laryngography—To take an X-ray of the larynx.

Laryngologist—Specialist in laryngology.

Laryngology—The branch of medical science which deals with the throat, pharynx, larynx, nasopharynx and tracheobronchial tree.

Laryngomalacia—Softening of the larynx.

Laryngometry—To take the measurement of the larynx.

Laryngoparalysis—Paralysis of the larynx.

Laryngopathy—Any disease of the larynx.

Laryngophantom—A model of the larynx made up of plastic or other material.

Laryngopharyngeal—Pertaining to both, the larynx and pharynx.

Laryngopharyngectomy—Excision of the larynx and pharynx.

Laryngopharyngitis—Pharyngolaryngitis. Inflammation of the larynx and pharynx.

Laryngopharyngography —X-ray examination of the larynx and pharynx when filled with air.

Laryngopharynx—The portion of the pharynx below the upper edge of the epiglottis, which opens into the larynx and esophagus.

Laryngophony—Vocal sounds heard on auscultation of the pharynx.

Laryngophthisis—Tuberculosis of the larynx.

Laryngoplasty—Repair of the larynx by plastic surgery.

Laryngoplegia—Laryngoparalysis.

Laryngoptosis—Lowering of the larynx.

Laryngorhinology—The branch of medical science dealing with the larynx and nose.

Laryngorrhagia—Hemorrhage from the larynx.

Laryngorrhea—Excessive discharge of mucus from the larynx.

Laryngoscleroma—Scleroma of the larynx.

Laryngoscope—An endoscope for examining the larynx.

Laryngoscopic —Pertaining to laryngoscopy.

Laryngoscopist—The person specialist in laryngoscopy.

Laryngoscopy—Visual examination of the interior of the larynx.

Laryngospasm—Spasm of the muscles of the larynx.

Laryngostenosis—Narrowing of the larynx.

Laryngostomy—To establish a permanent opening into the larynx through the neck.

Laryngostroboscope—An instrument for inspecting the vibration of vocal cords.

Laryngotomy—To make an incision into the larynx.

Laryngotracheal—Pertaining to the larynx and trachea.

Laryngotracheitis—Inflammation of the larynx and trachea.

Laryngotracheobronchitis—Inflammation of the larynx, trachea and bronchi.

Laryngotracheoplasty —To remove subglottic stenosis by plastic surgery.

Laryngotracheotomy—To make an incision into the larynx and trachea.

Laryngoxerosis—Dryness of the larynx.

Larynx—The organ of voice, a musculocartilaginous air passage between the lower part of the pharynx and the trachea containing vocal cords.

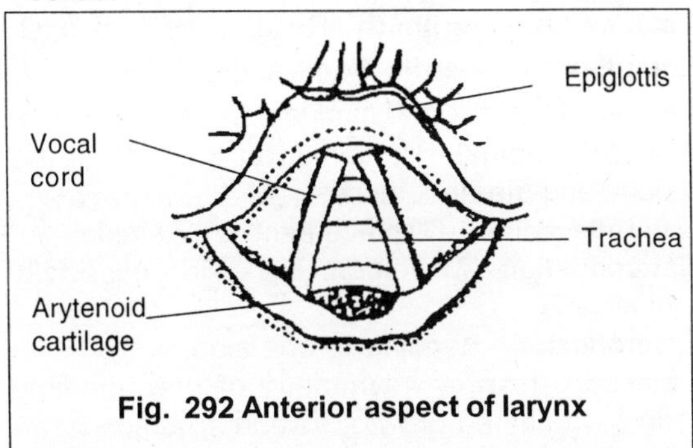

Fig. 292 Anterior aspect of larynx

Lascivia—Nymphomania, Satyriasis. Abnormally excessive sexual desire in women.

Lascivious—Lustfull.

Lasciviousness—Lustfullness.

Lase —To cut, divide or dissolve a substance, or to treat a structural defect in the body with a laser beam.

Lasegue's sign —A sign of sciatica in which discomfort and pain occurs in the back on raising gently the fully extended leg of the patient lying on bed.

Laser —An apparatus that emits laser beam used in microsurgery, ophthalmology, cauterization, dermatology and various diagnostic procedures etc.

Lasering —The use of a laser beam to cut, divide, or dissolve a substance, or to treat a defective structure in the body.

Lassitude—Weariness, exhaustion.

Latency—The state of being latent.

Latent—1. Dormant or concealed. 2. Quiet, inactive.

Latent heat—Heat consumed in changing a matter from solid to liquid or liquid to vapor without change in temperature.

Latentiation—The process of making latent.

Latent period—1. The time between the initiation of a stimulus and its response. 2. Period of incubation, i.e. the time between contracting of a disease and the appearance of its symptoms.

Laterad—Toward a side or lateral aspect.

Lateral—1. Pertaining to a side. 2. Denoting a position from the midline of the body or a structure.

Lateralis—Indicating that the structure is situated away from the midline of the body, lateral.

Laterality—The tendency to use the organs (hand, foot, ear and eyes) of the same side. In crossed laterality, to use the contralateral members of the different pairs of organs, e.g. right arm and the left leg.

Latericeous, Lateritious—Resembling brick dust.

Lateriflexion, Lateriflection —Lateroflexion.

Latero- —A prefix meaning lateral or to one side.

Lateroabdominal—Pertaining to the side of the body and the abdomen.

Laterodeviation—Displacement to one side.

Lateroduction—Movement to one side, especially of an eye.

Lateroflexion—Bending to one side.

Laterognathism —Asymmetry of the mandible due to retarded growth, fractures, tumor, or atrophy or hypertrophy of the soft tissues.

Lateroposition —Displacement to one side.

Lateropulsion—Involuntary tendency to fall down to one side.

Laterotorsion—A twisting to one side.

Lateroversion—A turning to one side.

Latissimus—Widest; in anatomy denoting a broad structure as a muscle.

Latitude —In radiology, a range of exposure to x-rays that would produce technically correct x-ray film.

Latrine—Privy, toilet.

Latus, Lata —Broad, as the broad ligament of the uterus.

Laudable—1. Praise-worthy. 2.Normal. 3. Healthy.

Laughing gas —Nitrous oxide.

Laughter reflex—Uncontrollable laughter resulting from tickling or pretense of tickling.

Lavage—Irrigation. Washing out of an organ such as stomach or the intestine or a cavity.

Lavement—Enema.

Laveur —An instrument for irrigation or lavage.

Law—A scientific statement for an occurrence which is found to be true uniformly; principle.

Avogadro's law—If the temperature and external pressure are the same, all gases contain the same number of molecules in equal volumes.

Beer law —The intensity of a color or of a light ray is inversely proportional to the depth of liquid through which it is transmitted.

Bell's law—Law of magendie. Anterior spinal nerve roots are motor, and posterior spinal nerve roots are sensory.

Boyle's law—The volume of a fixed quantity of a gas is inversely proportional and the density directly proportional to the pressure applied to the gas.

Charles' law—At constant pressure, volume of a gas varies with the variation of the temperature

Coppet law —Solutions having the same freezing point have equal concentrations of dissolved substances.

Marey's law—Heart rate is inversely proportional to the arterial blood pressure, i,e., it increases when the arterial blood pressure falls and decreases when the arterial blood pressure rises.

Law of definite proportion —Two or more elements when united to form a new substance, they do so in a constant and fixed proportion by weight.

Law of gravitation —Newton law.

Lax —1. Without tension. 2. Loose, said of intestinal movements.

Laxation —Intestinal movements.

Laxative —A food or drug used to prevent or treat constipation. Mild purgative.

Laxator —That which relaxes.

Laxity —Atony, looseness.

Layer—A stratum, a sheet-like structure of tissue of nearly uniform thickness.

Ameloblastic layer—Enamel layer of the tooth.

Enamel layer —Ameloblastic layer.

Germ layer—Any of the three primary layers of the cells of the developing embryo (ectoderm, entoderm, mesoderm) from which the various organs develop.

Germinative layer—The innermost layer of the epidermis consisting of a basal layer of cells and a layer of prickle cells (stratum spinosum)

Horny layer—Stratum corneum. The outermost layer of the skin consisting of clear, dead, scalelike desquamating cells.

Lazaretto—A hospital for treatment of contagious diseases.

lb—Pound.

LBBB —Left bundle branch block.

L.D.—Lethal dose.

L.D.L.—Low-density lipoprotein.

Leachates —The soluble constituents of a substance that are dissolved in water when water passes through the substance, and in doing so water becomes contaminated.

Leaching—Lixiviation. To remove a substance from a mixture by mixing the mixture with a solvent in which only the desired substance is soluble.

Lead—A conductor attached to an electrocardiograph, also a record made by the electrocardiograph. Usually three peripheral leads are used. Lead I Right arm to left arm. Lead II Right arm to left leg. Lead III Left arm to left leg. These are the standard leads. Other leads are as follows.

Bipolar lead —In electrocardiography, a lead consisting of two electrodes placed at different sites of the body.

Esophageal lead—The lead in which one electrode is inserted within the esophagus.

Limb lead—Any one of the three standard leads.

Precordial lead—The lead in which one electrode is placed over the precordium, the other is connected to a limb.

Unipolar lead—An array of two electrodes, only one of which transmits the potential variation.

Lead— A metallic element whose compounds are poisonous and cause lead poisoning on ingestion or absorption.

Lead colic—Colic pain occurring due to lead poisoning.

Lead line—Bluish line on the gums due to lead poisoning .

Lead pipe contraction—Catalepsy in which the limbs remain in the same position in which they are placed.

Lead poisoning — A condition caused by ingestion or absorption of a lead compound characterized by metallic taste in the mouth, pain in the abdomen (lead colic) anorexia, vomiting, diarrhea, headache, stupor, convulsions and coma. It usually occurs in painters and children who eat paint.

League of Red Cross Societies —The international federation of national Red Cross and similar societies.

Lean—Emaciated, thin.

Lean body mass—The weight of the body minus the fat content.

Leap—To jump, to spring, to cause jump.

Leber's disease —A hereditary form of atrophy of the optic nerve that affects males.

Lecat's gulf—Hollow of the bulb of the urethra.

Lecithal — Pertaining to the yolk of an egg.

Lecithin—A fatty substance of a group of phospholipids found in the blood, bile, brain, nerves, egg-yolk and other tissues of the animals.

Lecithoblast—One of the cells of entoderm which grows to form the yolk-sac.

Lectin—One of the several plant proteins which stimulate the lymphocytes to proliferate.

Lectual—Pertaining to a bed.

Lectulus—Bed.

Ledge —A structure in the body resembling a ledge.

Leech—A blood sucking water worm, which was formerly used for drawing blood.

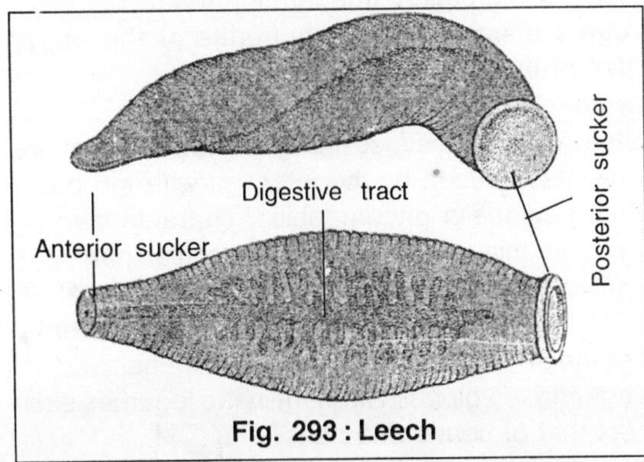

Fig. 293 : Leech

Leeching —The process of applying leeches to the body to draw blood, an ancient method of treatment.

Left—Sinistral. The opposite of right.

Left-handedness—Sinistrality, writing with the left hand.

Left lateral recumbent position—Position in which the patient lies on the left side and the right knee and thigh drawn up, used in rectal operations and sometimes in obstetrics.

Leg—Lower limb, especially the part between the knee and the ankle.

Anglesey leg—A form of jointed artificial leg.

Badger leg—The leg of inequal length.

Baker leg—Genu valgum; Knock-knee.

Bandy leg—Bowleg.

Barbados leg—The leg affected with elephantiasis.

Bayonet leg — Ankylosis of the knee after backward displacement of the tibia and fibula bones.

Bird leg—The leg reduced in size as a result of atrophy of the muscles.

Bow leg—Bandy leg, genu varum. Curving of the leg outward at the knee.

Elephant leg —Elephantiasis of the legs.

Milk leg—Phlegmasia alba dolens; white leg. Inflammed white leg due to inflammation of the femoral vein occurring occasionally after delivery or typhoid fever.

Restless leg—Restlessness of the legs at bed time, which is sometimes due to renal colic and is relieved by walking or keeping the legs moving.

Scissor leg—Deformity with crossing of the legs in walking like the blades of a scissor.

White leg—Milk leg, phlegmasia alba dolens.

Leggings—Sterile coverings used for covering the legs of the patient in operation theatre.

Legg's disease—Osteochondritis of the upper femoral epiphysis.

Legionellosis —Legionnaires' disease.

Legionnaires' disease—Legionellosis. A severe disease caused by the infection with the bacillus Legionella pneumophilia, characterized by pneumonia, dry cough and muscular pain.

Legitimacy—1. The condition of being legal. 2. The condition of being born from legal parents.

Legume—Pod as that of beans or peas.

Legumin—A globulin present in the legumes such as that of beans and peas.

Leguminivorous —Eater of legumes as beans and peas.

Leiner's disease—Exfoliative dermatitis.

Leio- — A prefix meaning smooth.

Leiodermia—Dermatitis with abnormal smoothness and glossiness of the skin.

Leiomyofibroma— A benign tumor composed of smooth muscle and fibrous connective tissue.

Leiomyoma—Myoma, a benign tumor composed of smooth muscle.

Leiomyomatosis —The state of being many leiomyomas in the body.

Leiomyomectomy —Removal of a leiomyoma by operation, usually of the uterus.

Leiomyosarcoma—Combined leiomyoma and sarcoma.

Leiotrichous—Having smooth or straight hair.

Leishmania—A genus of parasitic flagellate protozoa transmitted by the bite of phlebotomines (sandflies) causing Leishmaniasis, e.g. Leishmania donovani causing kala-azar (visceral leishmaniasis) and Leishmania tropica causing oriental sore (cutaneous leishmaniasis).

Leishmaniae —Plural of leishmania.

Leishmaniasis—Infection with a species of Leishmania, as cutaneous leishmaniasis (oriental sore) caused by infection with Leishmania tropica and visceral leishmaniasis (kala-azar) caused by infection with Leishmania donovani.

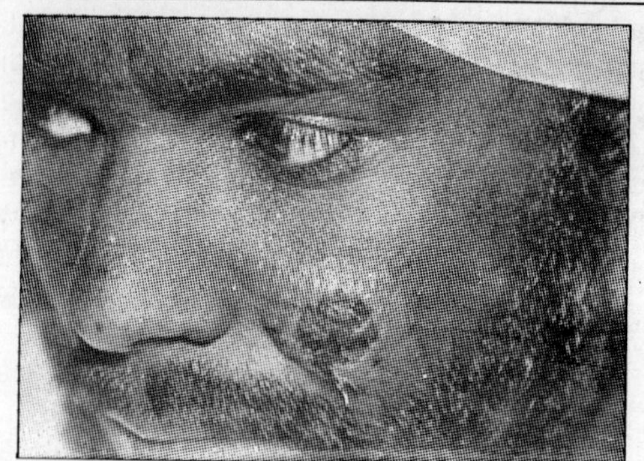

Fig. 294 : Cutaneous leishmaniasis (oriental sore)

Leishmaniosis —Leishmaniasis.

Leishmanoid —Resembling leishmaniasis.

Lema—Sebum palpebrale. The dried secretion of tarsal glands which is collected in the inner canthus of the eye.

Lemic—Pertaining to an epidemic disease.

Lemmoblastic—Forming or developing into neurilemma tissue.

Lemmocyte—A cell which becomes a neurilemma cell.

Lemnisci —Plural of lemniscus.

Lemniscus—1. A band or ribbon. 2. A band or bundle of fibers in the central nervous system.

Lemon—Fruit of the tree Citrus limon containing citrus acid and ascorbic acid (vit.C).

Lemoparalysis—Paralysis of the esophagus.

Lemostenosis—Narrowing of the esophagus.

Length—The measurement of the distance between two points.

Basialveolar length—Distance from the basion of the foramen magnum of the skull to the intermaxillary suture of the jaw.

Basinasal length—Distance from the basion of the foramen magnum of the skull to the center of the suture between the frontal and nasal bones.

Crown-heel length —In the embryo, fetus or newborn child, the distance from the crown of the head to the heel.

Crown-rump length —In the embryo, fetus or newborn child, the distance from the crown of the head to the apex of the buttocks.

Focal length —The distance between a lens and an object from which all rays of light are brought to a focus.

Greatest length —Crown heel length.

Length of stay —The number of days between the admission and discharge from a hospital.

Wave length —The distance from one point on a wave to the same point on the next wave. By the length of a wave, it is determined whether or not the wave is visible light, X-ray, gamma or radio waves.

Lenitive — Relieving.

Lens — 1. A piece of glass or other transparent material so shaped as to converge or diverge the light rays. 2. Crystalline lens of the eye.

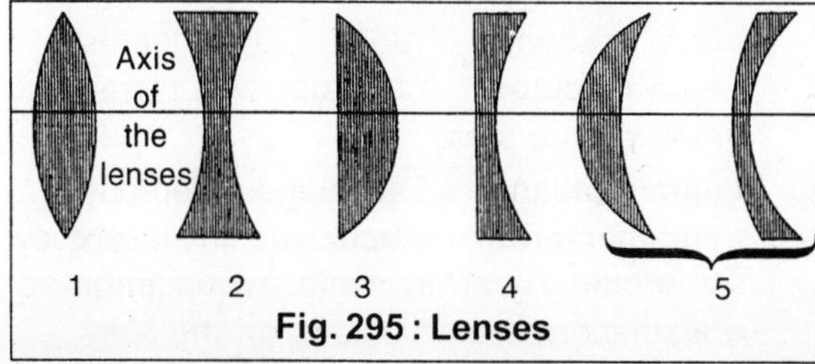

Fig. 295 : Lenses

1. Biconvex lens
2. Biconcave lens
3. Planoconvex lens
4. Planoconcave lens
5. Convexoconcave lens

Achromatic lens — Lens which corrects chromatic aberration.

Aplanatic lens — Lens which corrects spherical aberrations.

Apochromatic lens — Lens which corrects both, spherical and chromatic aberrations.

Astigmatic lens — Cylindrical lens.

Biconcave lens — The lens with concave surface on both sides.

Biconvex lens — The lens with convex surface on both sides.

Bifocal lens — The lens containing in its lower portion a lens of different power which is for seeing near objects or reading. The upper main portion is for seeing the distant objects.

Cataract lens—A lens prescribed for aphakia.

Compound lens —An optical system of two or more lenses.

Concave spherical lens —The lens which is thin at the center and thick at the margin, used in myopia.

Concavoconcave lens —Biconcave lens.

Concavoconvex lens —A lens which is concave on one side and convex on the other side.

Contact lens —A curved lens made up of glass or synthetic material, which is applied to the eye for the correction of refractive errors.

Convexconcave lens —The lens having a convex surface on one side and the concave surface on the opposite side.

Convex spherical lens —The lens which is thick at the center and thin at the margin, used in hypermetropia.

Corneal lens —Contact lens.

Crystalline lens — A biconvex, transparent, colorless structure enclosed in a capsule, just behind the pupil in the eye, held in place by suspensory ligament.

Cylindrical lens —A lens with a segment of a cylinder parallel to its axis, used in correcting astigmatism.

Implanted lens — An artificial lens implanted after the lens is removed, at cataract operation.

Oil immersion lens —It is a special lens in the microscope, which comes in contact with oil immersion placed on the object to be visualized. It produces a higher magnification than would be the case if the oil immersion were not used.

Omnifocal lens —A lens for near and distant vision.

Planoconcave lens —A lens with one side plane and the other concave.

Planoconvex lens — A lens with one side plane and the other convex.

Spherical lens —The lens in which all the surfaces are spherical.

Spherocylindrical lens —A combined spherical and cylindrical lens.

Trial lens — Any lens used in testing the vision.

Trifocal lens — The lens containing three segments, one for each—near, intermediate and distant vision.

Lensometer —An instrument for measuring the power of a lens.

Lensopathy —Any disease of a lens of the eye.

Lentectomize — To remove the lens of the eye by operation.

Lentectomy —Removal of the lens of the eye by operation.

Lenticonus — Congenital conical bulging of the anterior or posterior surface of the lens .

Lenticula —Lens shaped nucleus.

Lenticular —1. Pertaining to the lens of the eye. 2. Lentiform. Lens shaped.

Lenticulo-optic —Pertaining to the lens-shaped nucleus and the optic tract.

Lenticulopapular —Indicating an eruption with lens-shaped papules.

Lenticulostriate —Pertaining to the lenticular nucleus and corpus striatum.

Lenticulothalamic —Pertaining to the lenticular nucleus and the thalamus.

Lentiform —Lenticular. Lens-shaped.

Lentigines —Flat, brown spots appearing on the exposed skin of the older persons, usually on the back of the hands due to accumulation of melanin pigment in the tissues.

Lentiginosis — Formation of multiple lentigines.

Lentiginous —1. Affected by lentigo 2. Covered with very small dots.

Lentiglobus — Extremely curved lens of an eye producing an anterior spherical bulging.

Lentigo — Freckle. Small yellow brown pigmented areas of the skin due to accumulation of melanin caused by exposure to sun.

Lentigo maligna — Hutchinson's freckle. A noninvasive malignant melanoma.

Fig. 296 : Lentigo maligma

Lentitis —Phakitis. Inflammation of the crystalline lens of the eye.

Lentula, Lentulo —An instrument used in dentistry to fill the root canal of a tooth with paste filling material.

Leontiasis — Lionlike appearance of the face in lepromatous leprosy.

Leontiasis ossea — Facies leontina. Lionlike appearance of the face due to hypertrophy of the cranial bones.

Leper —A person suffering from leprosy.

Lepidic — Pertaining to the scales.

Lepidosis —Any scaly or desquamating eruption as pityriasis.

Lepothrix —A disease in which the shaft of the hair is encased in hard, scaly, sebaceous matter.

Lepra —A term formerly used for leprosy, but now used to indicate a reaction occurring in leprosy patients.

Lepra alba — Skin becomes anesthetic and white, followed by different forms of paralysis.

Lepra anesthetica — Leprosy with anesthetic areas on the body.

Lepra Arabum — True or nodular leprosy.

Lepra maculosa — Leprosy with pigmented areas on the skin.

Lepra mutilans — Last stage of leprosy.

Lepra nervorum —Maculoanesthetic leprosy. Tuberculoid leprosy with hypopigmented, anesthetic macular lesions on the skin.

Leprechaunism—A hereditary disease in which the infant has elfin features of the face accompanied by the retardation of physical and mental development, severe endocrine disorders, emaciation and susceptibility to infection.

Leprid —Skin lesion of tuberculoid leprosy.

Leprologist —Specialist in leprosy.

Leprology —The study of leprosy.

Leproma —A cutaneous nodule or tubercle, characteristic lesion of lepromatous leprosy.

Lepromatous — Pertaining to lepromas.

Lepromin—A substance prepared from lepromatous nodules of leprosy.

Leprosarium—A hospital for the treatment and care of lepers.

Leprosery —A leper home or colony.

Leprostatic—Inhibiting the growth of Mycobacterium leprae, the causative organism of leprosy.

Leprosy — A chronic communicable disease caused by the acid fast bacilli Mycobacterium leprae, characterized by the production of granulomatous lesions of the skin, mucous membranes and peripheral nerves. There are two principal forms of leprosy. (1) Lepromatous leprosy—It is characterized by the skin lesions with the formation of lepromas and involvement of the peripheral nerves, on both sides of the body with anesthesia, muscle weakness and paralysis. It is more contagious than the tuberculoid form. Large numbers of Mycobacterium leprae are found in the lepromas. (2) Tuberculoid leprosy—It is characterized by early damage of the nerves, so there is early occurrence of skin anesthesia. Infection is very localized and occurs only at one side of the body. Only a small number of skin lesions, usually one to three develop. The skin is dry with loss of sweating and diminished number of hairs. The digits may be amputated spontaneously, or by rat bite while the patient sleeps, because of anesthesia. Leprae bacilli are scanty in tuberculoid lesions. The skin reaction to lepromin is positive. It is not so contagious as lepromatous leprosy.

Between the above two principal forms there are three borderline leprosy in which the symptoms of the two principal forms are combined.

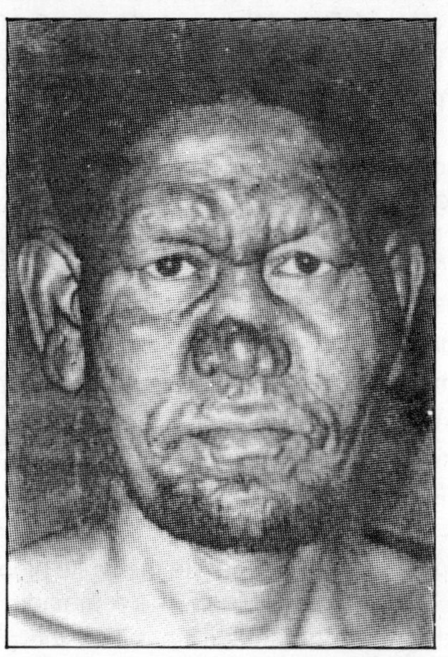

Fig No.297A : Lepromatous leprosy

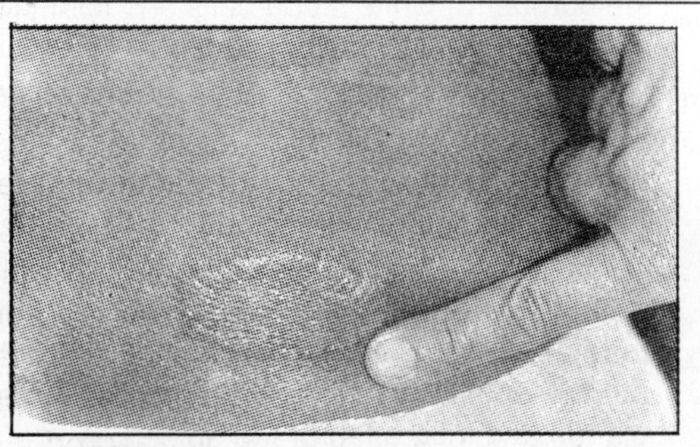

Fig. No.297B : Tubercuoid leprosy

Leprotic — 1.Pertaining to leprosy. 2. Leprous. Affected with leprosy.

Leprous —1. Pertaining to leprosy . 2. Leprotic. Affected with leprosy.

-lepsis, - lepsy —Suffixes meaning seizure or convulsion

Lepto- —A prefix meaning light, thin, fragile.

Leptocephalia — The person having an abnormally vertically elongated, narrow skull.

Leptocephalus —Leptocephalia.

Leptocephaly—The condition of being abnormally tall, narrow cranium.

Leptochromatic — Having a fine chromatin network.

Leptocyte —Target cell.

Leptocytosis — Presence of leptocytes in the blood.

Leptodactylous—Having slender digits.

Leptodactyly —Abnormal slenderness of the digits.

Leptomeningeal—Pertaining to leptomeninges.

Leptomeninges —The pia mater and the arachnoid mater to be spoken into one.

Leptomeningitis — Inflammation of the pia mater and arachnoid mater.

Leptomeningopathy —Any disease of the pia mater and arachnoid mater.

Leptomeninx —Singular of leptomeninges.

Leptonema—The early stage of prophase in meiosis in which the chromosomes contract into long, thin filaments which are separated from each other.

Leptopellic —Having an abnormally narrow pelvis.

Leptophonia —Weakness of the voice.

Leptophonic—Weak-voiced.

Leptopodia—The condition of having slender feet.

Leptoprosopia —Narrowness of the face.

Leptoprosopic —Having a long narrow face.

Leptorhine, Leptorrhine —Having a slender nose.

Leptoscope—An apparatus for measuring cell membranes.

Leptosomatic, Leptosomic—Having a thin and light body.

Leptosome —Thin and light person.

Leptospirosis—Condition resulting from infection of Leptospira interrogans.

Leresis —Talkativeness in old age.

Leriche's syndrome —Obstruction in the abdominal aorta at its bifurcation caused by a thrombus, by which intermittent ischemic pain occurs in the lower extremities and buttocks and there are diminished or absent femoral pulses.

Lesbian — Pertaining to lesbianism, or a woman who practices lesbianism.

Lesbianism —Sexual desire of a woman for one of her own sex.

Lesion —1. The breaking or discontinuity of the skin, mucous membrane or other tissues of the body due to some disease or injury. 2. Loss of function of a part of the body.

Central lesion —Any lesion of the central nervous system.

Degenerative lesion—Lesion caused by degeneration.

Diffuse lesion —Lesion spreading over a large area.

Discharging lesion — 1. A brain lesion that discharges nervous impulses. 2. A lesion that discharges an exudate.

Focal lesion —Lesion of a small definite area.

Ghon's primary lesion—Ghon focus.

Gross lesion —A lesion visible to the naked eyes. Affecting separate systems of the body.

Indiscriminate lesion—A lesion affecting the separate systems of the body.

Irritative lesion—A lesion that stimulates the activity in the part of the body where it is situated..

Local lesion —Lesion of a localized area.

Peripheral lesion —Lesion of the peripheral nerves .

Primary lesion — First lesion of a disease, especially primary or hard chancre of syphilis.

Structural lesion —A lesion causing change in the tissue.

Systemic lesion —Lesion confined to the organs of common function.

Toxic lesion —The lesion resulting from the poisons or toxins from microorganisms.

Vascular lesion —Lesion of a blood vessel.

Lethal —Fatal . Causing death.

Lethargic —1.Pertaining to lethargy. 2.Affected with lethargy, or sluggish.

Lethargy —Sluggishness or drowsiness.

Lethe —Amnesia.

Lethologica —Temporary forgetfulness for a word, name or intended action.

Leucine — It is an amino acid, a product of protein digestion present in the body tissues and is essential for mormal growth and metabolism.

Leucinosis —Excess of leucine in the body.

Leucinuria —Presence of leucine in the urine.

Leucism —A form of incomplete albinism.

Leucismus —Condition of being white.

Leucitis —Scleritis. Inflammation of the sclera.

Leuk—Leuko.

Leukapheresis —To separate the white blood cells from the withdrawn blood, the remainder of the blood is then transfused back into the patient.

Leukemia —Progressive malignant disease of the blood forming organs, marked by the increase in the number of white blood cells and their precursors in the blood; blood cancer.—(1) Acute leukemia. (2) Chloroma. (3) Chronic leukemia.

(1) Acute leukemia —The following three types of leukemia are included in acute leukemias.

1-Acute lymphatic leukemia — There is a hyperplasia of the lymphatic tissues throughout the body, with the enlargement of lymph glands and infiltration of the spleen, liver and bone marrow with lymphocytic cells.

2-Acute monocytic leukemia —The spleen, liver and bone marrow and lymph glands are infiltrated with embryonic monocytes (histiocytes).

3-Acute myeloid leukemia —The lymph glands are enlarged to a varying degree and the spleen, liver and bone marrow are infiltrated with myelocytes and premyelocytes.

In all types of acute leukemias hemorrhage may occur in such organs as the stomach, intestine, lung, brain and kidneys and into the buccal mucous membrane and under the skin.

(2) Chloroma —A variety of subacute myeloid or rarely lymphatic leukemia accompanied by the formation of tumors in the subperiosteal tissues and elsewhere.

(3) Chronic leukemia — The following two types of leukemias are included in this group.

1-Chronic lymphatic leukemia —The lymph glands are enlarged with excess of lymphoid cells and are superficial. The spleen is enlarged with lymphatic infiltration. The liver is enlarged because of the infiltration of the periportal connective tissue with lymphocytes. The bone marrow of the long bones is grey and shows lymphoid metaplasia.

2- Chronic myeloid leukemia —The lymph glands are only slightly affected, mesenteric glands may be enlarged. There is myeloid metaplasia of the spleen substance. The spleen is much more enlarged, it may weigh 18 pounds (normal weight is about 5 to 6 ounces). The liver is enlarged and areas resembling multiple abscesses consisting of myeloid metaplasia are found around the intralobular capillaries. The bone marrow is greyish red showing proliferation of myeloblasts.

Leukemic —1. Pertaining to leukemia . 2. Affected with leukemia.

Leukemid —Any nonspecific skin eruption associated with leukemia which may or may not contain leukemia cells.

Leukemogen — Any substance producing leukemia.

Leukemogenesis —Induction of leukemia.

Leukemogenic —Pertaining to the development of leukemia.

Leukemoid —Having the symptoms of leukemia, which are actually due to some other disease.

Leukemoid reaction —Occurrence of leukocytosis similar to that occurring in leukemia, as a result of some other disease.

Leukin —A thermostable bactericidal substance present in the white blood cells.

Leuko-, Leuk- —Combining form denoting white, colorless or relation to white blood cell.

Leukoagglutinin —An antibody that agglutinates the white blood cells.

Leukobilin —White bile.

Leukoblast —A general term used for an immature white blood cell.

Leukoblastosis —Presence of a large number of immature white blood cells in the blood.

Leukocidin —A substance produced by some disease-producing bacteria, which destroys the polymorphonuclear white blood cells.

Leukocoria, Leukokoria —White pupillary reflex. Reflection from a white mass within the eye giving the appearance of a white pupil.

Leukocrit —Volume percentage of white blood cells in the whole blood.

Leukocytactic—Leukocytotactic.

Leukocytal —Leukocytic. Pertaining to leukocyte or white blood cell.

Leukocytaxia, Leukocytaxis —Leukocytotaxia.

Leukocyte — White blood cell or white blood corpuscle. They are phagocytic and their main function is to protect the body from the disease-producing microorganisms. On an injury or some other stimulation, they come out of the blood vessels by penetrating their walls into the tissues and by ameboid movement engulf the disease-producing microorganisms and ingest them, thus protecting the body against them, and then return to the blood stream. When the invading microorganisms destroy the W.B.C.(white blood cells), the dead W.B.C. collect in the form of pus, forming an abscess. They increase in number (leukocytosis) in bacterial infection.

There are two main groups of leukocytes—granulocytes, those with granules in their cytoplasm and agranulocytes which are without granules. Granulocytes are juvenile neutrophils 3 to 5%; fully developed, segmented neutrophils or polymorphonuclear leukocytes (which contain several lobes) 54 to 62% ; basophils 0 to .75% and

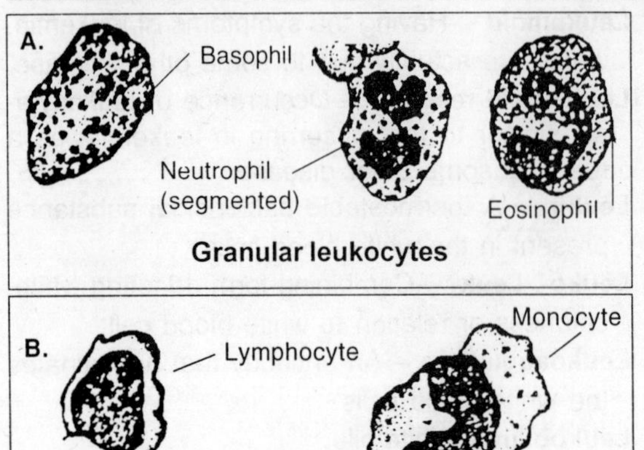

Fig 298 : Leukocytes (white blood cells) Agranular leukocytes

eosinophils 1 to 3%. Agranulocytes include lymphocytes large and small 25 to 33% and monocytes 3 to 7%.

Normally there are 5000 to 10000 of white blood cells in 1 cu.m.m. of blood. Two determinations are usually made of the leukocytes, the total number (total count) and the percentage of each type (differential count). The decrease in the total number below normal (5000) is called leukopenia and an increase in the total number above normal (10000) is called leukocytosis.

Leukocythemia —Leukemia.

Leukocytic —Pertaining to leukocytes.

Leukocytoblast —The cell from which a leukocyte arises.

Leukocytoclasis—A breaking of the nuclei of the white blood cells.

Leukocytogenesis —Leukopoiesis. Formation of white blood cells.

Leukocytoid —Resembling a leukocyte.

Leukocytolysin —A lysin destroying the leukocytes.

Leukocytolysis —Destruction of the white blood cells .

Leukocytoma —Tumorlike mass of leukocytes.

Leukocytometer—A glass slide ruled for counting white blood cells in a measured volume of accurately diluted blood.

Leukocytopenia —Leukopenia.

Leukocytoplania —Passage of white blood cells from the blood vessels into the tissues, or through the membranes.

Leukocytopoiesis —Leukocytogenesis.

Leukocytosis —A transient increase in number of white blood cells (above 10000 per cu.mm.) in the blood which occurs generally in some infection.

Leukocytotactic—Pertaining to leukocytotaxia.

Leukocytotaxia —Leukocytotaxis.

Leukocytotaxis —The movement of white blood cells toward or away from a site of infection or trauma.

Leukocytotoxicity —Lymphocytotoxicity.

Leukocytotoxin —A toxin which destroys the white blood cells.

Leukocyturia —Presence of W.B.C. in the urine.

Leukoderma —Localized absence of pigmentation of the skin.

Leukodermatous—Pertaining to or resembling leukoderma.

Leukodontia —The condition of having white teeth.

Leukodystrophia —Leukodystrophy.

Leukodystrophy —Sclerosis of the white matter of the brain in infants and children due to defective formation of myelin.

Leukoedema —Leukoplakia-like white patches on the mucous membrane of the mouth, or on the tongue.

Leukoencephalitis —Inflammation of the white matter of the brain.

Leukoencephalopathy —Any disease of the white matter of the brain

Leukoerythroblastosis —Anemia due to any disease which causes the bone marrow to be infiltrated and thus inactivated.

Leukokeratosis —Leukoplakia.

Leukokoria —Leukocoria. White reflection from the pupil of the eye due to the presence of a mass in the pupillary area.

Leukokraurosis —Kraurosis vulvae.

Leukolymphosarcoma —Lymphosarcoma cell leukemia.

Leukolysin —Leukocytolysin.

Leukolysis —Leukocytolysis.

Leukolytic —Leukocytolytic. Pertaining to the destruction of white blood cells.

Leukoma —Dense , white corneal opacity.

Leukomatous —The person suffering from dense, white corneal opacity.

Leukomyelitis —Inflammation of the white matter of the spinal cord.

Leukomyelopathy —Any disease of the white matter of the spinal cord

Leukomyoma —Lipomyoma.

Leukonecrosis —White gangrene.

Leukonychia —White spots or streaks on the nails.

Leukopathia —1. Leukoderma. 2. Disease of the leukocytes.

Leukopedesis —Passage of leukocytes through the walls of the blood vessels.

Leukopenia —Granulocytopenia, leukocytopenia. Reduction of white blood cells in the blood, below 5000 per cu.mm of blood.

Basophilic leukopenia —A decrease in the number of basophilic leukocytes in the circulating blood. Basopenia.

Eosinophilic leukopenia — A decrease in the number of eosinophilic leukocytes in the circulating blood. Eosinopenia.

Lymphocytic leukopenia—Lymphopenia.

Monocytic leukopenia —Monocytopenia.

Neutrophilic leukopenia —Neutropenia.

Leukopenic—Pertaining to leukopenia.

Leukoplakia --Formation of white, thickened and hard spots or patches on the mucous membranes of the cheeks (leukoplakia buccalis) or tongue (leukoplakia lingualis), which are irregular in size and shape. Occasionally they are fissured and become malignant.

Leukoplakia vulva —The presence of white marble-like patches with severe itching on the mucous membrane of the vulva in old women.

Leukoplakic —Pertaining to or affected with leukoplakia.

Leukoplasia—Leukoplakia.

Leukopoiesis—Leukocytogenesis.

Leukopoietic—Forming leukocytes.

Leukorrhagia—Leukorrhea. Profuse white discharge from the vagina.

Leukorrhea—A white or yellowish viscid discharge from the cervical canal or vagina.

Menstrual leukorrhea—Leukorrhea occurring at or just before each menstruation.

Leukorrheal —Pertaining to or suffering from leukorrhea.

Leukosarcoma—Sarcoma composed of leukemic cells.

Leukosarcomatosis—The development of multiple sarcomas composed of leukemic cells.

Leukosis—Proliferation of the leukocyte- forming tissues abnormally.

Leukotactic—Capable of attracting the leukocytes.

Leukotaxia—Leukocytotaxia.

Leukotaxis—The movement of leukocytes toward a site or away from it.

Leukotome—An instrument used in performing leukotomy.

Leukotomy—Lobotomy.

Leukotoxic— Destructive to the leukocytes.

Leukotoxin—Leukocytotoxin.

Leukotrichia—Canities. Whiteness of the hair.

Leukous—White, especially relating to the skin.

Levator— 1. A muscle that raises an organ or a part of the body. 2. An instrument that lifts the depressed structures.

Lever—A strong bar used to modify direction, force and motion.

Leverage —The actual elevating direction of a lever or elevator.

Levigation—The grinding of a substance into a powder form.

Levin's tube—A catheter introduced through the nose and stomach into the duodenum, used to help prevent accumulation of liquids and gas in the intestine during and after an intestinal operation.

Levis—Light.

Levitation—Feeling of rising or moving in the air without any support, which occurs in dreams and some mental disorders.

Levo- —A prefix denoting left.

Levocardia—The term used for the normal position of the heart when other viscera are inverted.

Levoclination—Rotation of the upper poles of the vertical meridians of the eyes to the left.

Levocycleduction—Levoduction.

Levocycloduction—Levoduction.

Levoduction—Movement of an eye to the left side.

Levography—X-ray examination of the left side of the heart after introduction of a contrast medium.

Levogyrate, Levogyrous—Levorotatory.

Levogyration—Levorotation.

Levogyrous —Levorotatory.

Levophobia—Morbid fear of the things on the left side of the body.

Levorotation—A turning to the left.

Levorotatory—Causing to turn toward the left.

Levotorsion, Levoversion— Levorotation.

Levulose—Fructose or fruit sugar.

Levulosemia — Presence of fructose in the blood.

Levulosuria—Presence of fructose in the urine.

Lewisite— A toxic gas used in warfare to disable and kill.

Lexical—Denoting the vocabulary of speech or language.

-lexis, -lexy—Suffixes relating to speech.

Leydig cells—Interstitial tissue cells in the testicles which secrete testosterone hormone.

LGA—Large for gestational age.

L.H.—Luteinizing hormone.

Lhermitte's sign—Occurrence of pain resembling a sudden electric shock throughout the body produced by flexing the neck.

L H R H— Luteinizing hormone releasing hormone.

Li —Chemical symbol for lithium.

Liability—Legal responsibility.

Liberator—An agent that stimulates a physiological, chemical or enzymatic action.

Liberomotor—Pertaining to voluntary movements.

Libidinization— Erotization.

Libidinous—Lustful or salacious.

Libido—Sexual desire.

Libra—1. Pound. 2. Balance .

Lice—Plural of louse.

Licensure —To grant a licence to perform medical practice.

Licentiate—The person who has been granted a licence to perform medical practice.

Lichen—Any of the papular skin diseases in which the lesions are firm papules which are very close together, e.g. lichen planus which occurs in healthy persons who are emotionally tensive, characterized by wide, flat, violaceous shiny papules in the circumscribed patches which may involve the hair follicles, nails and buccal mucosa.

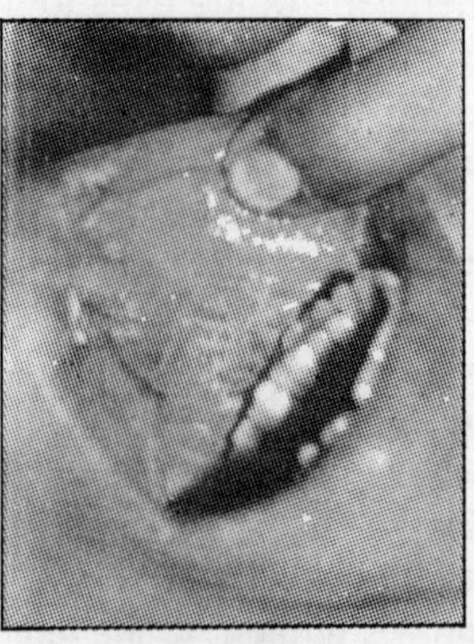

Fig 299 A : Lichen planus of the mouth

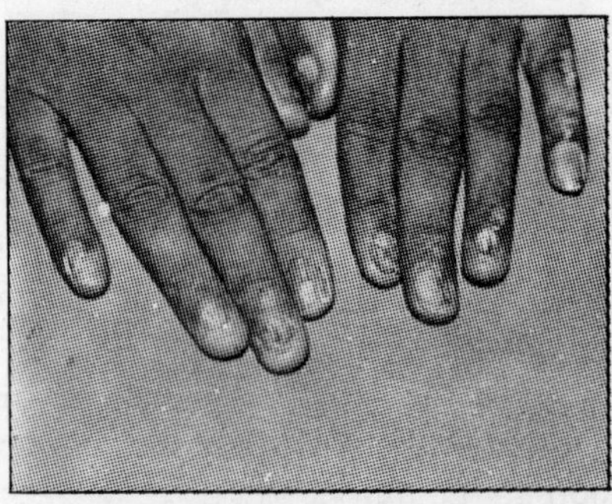

Fig 299 B : Lichen planus of the nails

Lichenification—1. Thickening and hardening of the skin from continued irritation. 2. Changing of an eruption into one resembling a lichen.

Lichenoid—Resembling lichen.

Lichtheim's syndrome—Subacute combined degeneration of the spinal cord resulting from pernicious anemia.

Lid — An eyelid.

Lid reflex — Corneal reflex. Closure of the eyelids resulting from direct stimulation of the cornea.

Lie —The position of the long axis of fetus in the uterus with respect to that of the mother, e.g., transverse lie, the position in which the long axis of the fetus in uterus crosses the long axis of the mother.

Lie detector—An instrument for detecting the lying .

Lien— The spleen.

Lien accessorius — Accessory spleen.

Lien mobilis —Floating spleen.

Lienal—Splenic. Pertaining to the spleen.

Lienculus—Accessory spleen.

Lienitis—Splenitis. Inflammation of the spleen.

Lienocele—Splenocele. Hernia of the spleen.

Lienography—X-ray examination of the spleen after introduction of a contrast medium.

Lienomalacia—Splenomalacia. Softening of the spleen.

Lienomedullary—Pertaining to both, the spleen and the bone marrow.

Lienomyelogenous—Produced from both, the spleen and the bone marrow .

Lienomyelomalacia—Softening of the spleen and the bone marrow.

Lienopancreatic—Pertaining to the spleen and pancreas.

Lienorenal—Pertaining to the spleen and the kidney.

Lienotoxin — Splenotoxin.

Lienteric—Pertaining to or marked by lientery.

Lientery—Diarrhoea in which the stool contains undigested food.

Lienunculus— Accessory spleen.

Life—1. State of being active 2. The qualities by which a living thing is distinguished from a non-living thing , such as growth and reproduction etc. 3.Time between birth and death.

Life expectancy—The period in years that a person of a given age may be expected to live.

Life span—The duration of life of an individual.

Life style —The pattern of living, habits and behavior of an individual which distinguish that individual from others.

Ligament—1.A band of strong fibrous connective tissue which connects the articular ends of the bones and forms the joint and serves to facilitate or limit the movement of the joint. 2. A thickened fold of peritoneum which supports the viscera or connects a viscus to another . 3. A band of fibrous connective tissue which connects the bones, cartilages and other structures, and serves for support or for attachment of fascia or muscles.

Accessory ligament —A ligament which assists another .

Annular ligament— Circular ligament.

Broad ligament of the uterus—Folds of peritoneum attached to the lateral borders of the uterus

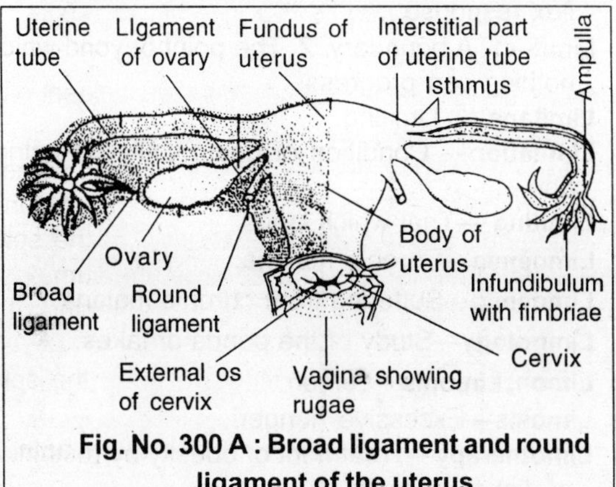

Fig. No. 300 A : Broad ligament and round ligament of the uterus

Capsular ligament—Ligaments surrounding an articulation and lined by synovial membranes.

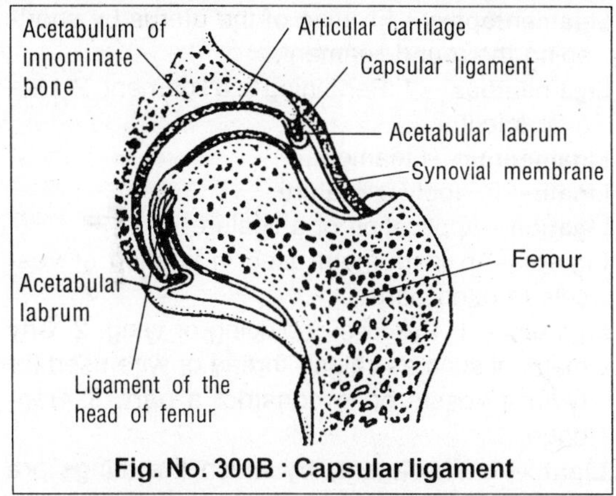

Fig. No. 300B : Capsular ligament

Inguinal ligament — The ligament running from the anterior superior spine of the ilium to the spine of the pubis.

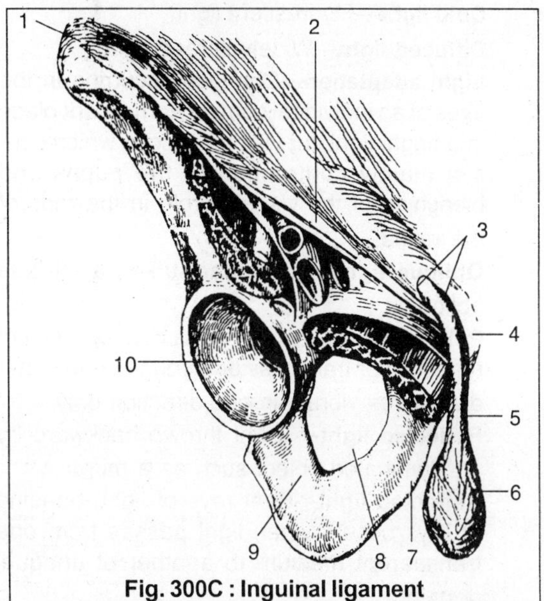

Fig. 300C : Inguinal ligament

1. Anterior superior iliac spine 2. Inguinal ligament 3. External (subcutaneous) inguinal ring 4. Public tubercle 5. Spermatic cord 6. Testis 7. Publc bone 8. Obturator foramen 9. Ischium bone 10. Acetabulum.

Round ligament of the uterus— Ligament attached to the uterus below and in front of the entrance of the fallopian tube.

Suspensory ligament—The ligament suspending an organ, e.g. suspensory ligament of the lens of the eye or the ovary.

Ligamenta—Plural of ligamentum.

Ligamentopexis—Suspension of the uterus on the round ligament.

Ligamentopexy—Fixation of the uterus by shortening the round ligament.

Ligamentous— 1. Pertaining to a ligament. 2. Like a ligament.

Ligamentum—Ligament.

Ligate—To apply a ligature.

Ligation—Application of a ligature.

Ligator—An instrument used in ligation of vessels in deep parts.

Ligature —1. Process of binding or tying. 2. Any material such as catgut, thread or wire used for tying a vessel or to constrict a part. 3. Bandage.

Light —1. The agent by which the things are rendered visible to the eye. 2. Not heavy.

Axial light —Light with rays parallel to each other and to the optic axis.

Cold light—Fluorescent light.

Diffused light—Widely spread light.

Light adaptation—Changes occurring in the eyes of an individual coming from a dark place into bright light for vision to occur, which consist mainly contraction of the pupils and bleaching of the visual purple in the rods of the retina.

Oblique light—Light that strikes a surface obliquely.

Polarized light—Light in which, as a result of reflection or transmission through certain media, waves vibrate in one direction only.

Reflected light— Light thrown backward by an illuminated object such as a mirror.

Refracted light—Bent rays of light, bending of rays occurs when light passes from one transparent medium to another of unequal density.

Transmitted light—Light that passes through an object.

Lightening—Engagement. Feeling of decreased abdominal distension produced by the descent of the presenting part of the fetus into the pelvis, two to three weeks before the beginning of labor.

Lightning pains—Sharp agonising pains occurring very quickly in attacks of sharp stabs on the outside of the knee, in the calf, heel or foot in tabes dorsalis (in secondary syphilis).

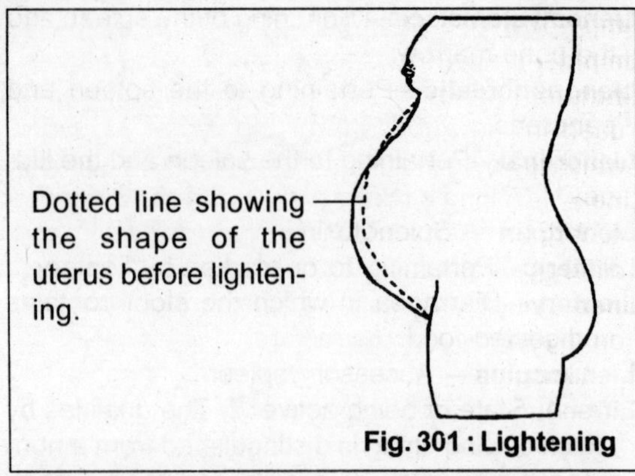

Fig. 301 : Lightening

Light reflex—Constriction of the pupil when the light is flashed into the eye.

Light therapy — Phototherapy. Treatment of diseases by light rays as by ultraviolet or infrared rays.

Ligneous—Like wood. Woody.

Lignum—Wood.

Limb—1. An arm or leg or an extremity. 2. A limblike extension of a structure.

Limbi —Plural of limbus.

Limbic—Marginal. Pertaining to a border.

Limbus—Edge or border of a part of the body.

Lime—1. Calcium oxide. 2. The acid fruit of the tree citrus aurantifolia, which contains ascorbic acid (vitamin C).

Limen—Entrance or threshold.

Limerence—Emotional excitement of being in love.

Limes—A boundary, limit or threshold.

Liminal—1. Hardly perceptible 2. Pertaining to a threshold .

Liminometer—An instrument for measuring the strength of a stimulus which can produce a reflex response.

Limit—1. A boundary. 2. The point beyond which nothing can progress.

Limitans — Limiting.

Limitation— Condition of being limited. Restriction.

Limiting —That which limits.

Limnemia—Chronic malaria.

Limnemic—Suffering from chronic malaria.

Limnology—Study of the ponds or lakes.

Limon, Limonis—Lemon.

Limosis—Excessive hunger.

Limotherapy—Treatment of obesity by restriction of diet or by fasting

Limp—To walk lamely.

Limpid—1. Pure. 2. Clear.

Lincture, Linctus—Sweet medicinal preparation used in the affections of the throat as syrup which is taken in sips, or lozenges to be sucked.

Line— 1. A long narrow mark 2. Streak 3. Stripe. 4. Wrinkle. 5. An imaginary line connecting the different anatomical landmarks.

Linea—Line ; in anatomy, a narrow ridge or streak on the surface of a structure.

Linea alba—A white line of the connective tissue in the middle of the abdomen from sternum to the pubis.

Linea albicans—Lines seen on the abdomen , buttocks and breasts due to pregnancy, obesity or prolonged treatment with the hormones of adrenal cortex.

Linea corneae —Arcus senilis.

Linea nigra— A dark line seen on the abdomen running from above the umbilicus to the pubes, of the pregnant woman during later part of pregnancy.

Lineage— Ancestry.

Linear—Pertaining to or resembling a line.

Liner—Material applied to the inside of the walls of a hollow body structure or container.

Lingua—Tongue or tonguelike structure.

Lingua frenata—Ankyloglossia. Tongue with a very short frenum, resulting in tongue tie.

Lingua geographica—Geographical tongue.

Lingua nigra—Black hairy tongue.

Lingua plicata—Fissured tongue.

Linguae —Plural of lingua.

Lingual—1. Pertaining to the tongue. 2. Tongue-shaped.

Linguiform — Tongue-shaped.

Lingula—Tongue-shaped structure.

Lingular—Pertaining to a lingula.

Lingulectomy—Excision of the lingula of the upper lobe of the left lung.

Linguo- —A prefix meaning tongue.

Linguoclasia—Displacement of a tooth toward the tongue.

Linguoclination—Axial inclination of a tooth toward the tongue.

Linguoclusion—Occlusion by the tongue.

Linguodental—Pertaining to the tongue and teeth.

Linguodistal—Pertaining to the distal part of a tooth and the tongue.

Linguogingival—Pertaining to the tongue and the gingiva.

Linguomesial—Pertaining to the lingual and mesial surfaces of a tooth.

Linguo - occlusal —Pertaining to, or bounded by lingual and occlusal surfaces of a tooth.

Linguopapillitis— Inflammation or ulceration of the papillae of the edges of the tongue.

Linguopulpal—Pertaining to the lingual and pulpal surfaces of a cavity formed.

Linguoversion—Displacement of a tooth toward the tongue.

Liniment—A medicinal preparation in oil, alcohol or water used to be rubbed on the skin or applied on a bandage to relieve the pain or to counteract the irritation.

Linimentum— Liniment.

Lining—Inner covering of anything .

Linitis— Inflammation of the lining of the stomach.

Linitis plastica— Leather-bottle stomach. Linits with thickening and fibrosis of the submucous tissue of the stomach so that the stomach is constricted, it becomes inelastic and rigid.

Linkage —1. The connection between the different atoms in a chemical compound. 2. In genetics, the association between genes that occupy closely situated loci in the same chromosomes, which results in association in the inheritance of these genes. 3. In psychology, the connection between a stimulus and its response.

Lint—Soft cloth of linen used for dressing the wounds.

Lintin— Prepared absorbent cotton.

Lip— 1. Upper or lower fleshy margin of the mouth. 2. Labia majus or labia minus. 3. Any liplike structure in the body forming the border of an opening or a groove.

Hapsburg lip — A thick, overdeveloped lower lip.

Lipacidemia—Excess of fatty acids in the blood.

Lipaciduria—Presence of fatty acids in the urine.

Liparia— Corpulency.

Liparocele—1. Scrotal hernia containing fat. 2. Fatty tumor.

Liparous— Obese, fatty.

Lipase—A fat-splitting enzyme which changes the fats into fatty acids and glycerol.

Lipasuria— Presence of lipase enzyme in the urine.

Lip cleft— Hare lip.

Lipectomy—Excision of fatty tissues.

Lipedema—An accumulation of excess of fat in the subcutaneous tissues, especially in the lower extremity.

Lipemia—Hyperlipemia. An excess of fat in the blood.

Alimentary lipemia— Lipemia occurring after eating.

Diabetic lipemia —A manifestation of uncontrolled or untreated diabetes mellitus caused by defective metabolism of dietary lipids and abolished by the administration of insulin.

Lipemia retinalis—The condition in which the retinal arteries and veins appear milky white.

Lipemic—Pertaining to lipemia.

Lipid—Anyone of a group of fats or fatlike substances which are insoluble in water and soluble in fat solvents such as alcohol, ether and chloroform. Lipids are easily stored in the body and serve as a source of fuel, are an important constituent of cell structure and serve other biological functions. Lipids are true fats (esters of fatty acids and glycerol), lipoids (phospholipids, cerebrosides and waxes) and sterols (cholesterol, ergosterol).

Lipidemia—Hyperlipidemia. An excess of lipids in the blood .

Lipidolytic—Causing lysis of lipid.

Lipidosis—Any disorder of lipid metabolism.

Lipiduria— Presence of lipids in the urine.

Lipo-, Lip- —Combining with other words form the words pertaining to fat.

Lipoarthritis—Inflammation of fatty tissue of a joint.

Lipoatrophia, Lipoatrophy—Atrophy of the subcutaneous fatty tissues of the body as may occur at the site of insulin injection.

Lipoblast—An immature fat cell.

Lipoblastoma—Lipoma. Adipoma. A benign tumor of fatty tissue.

Lipoblastomatosis—A diffused lipoblastoma that infiltrates locally but does not metastasize.

Lipocardiac— Pertaining to a fatty heart.

Lipocatabolic—Pertaining to the catabolism (breakdown) of fat.

Lipocele— Adipocele. Presence of fatty tissue in a hernia sac.

Lipoceratous—Adipoceratous. Pertaining to adipocere.

Lipocere— Adipocere. Waxy substance formed from exposure of fleshy tissue to the moisture with the exclusion of air.

Lipochondrodystrophy—Hurler syndrome. Mucopolysaccharidosis.

Lipochondroma— A tumor composed of both, fatty and cartilaginous elements.

Lipochrome— A group of fat–soluble pigments.

Lipoclasis—Lipolysis. Splitting up of fat.

Lipoclastic— Lipolytic. Pertaining to or causing lipoclasis.

Lipocyte—Fat cell.

Lipodermoid—Congenital subconjunctival yellowish-white, fatty, benign tumor.

Lipodieresis—Lipolysis.

Lipodystrophia—Lipodystrophy.

Lipodystrophy—Any defect of fat metabolism.

Congenital total lipodystrophy—Almost complete absence of subcutaneous fat congenitally.

Insulin lipodystrophy— Occurrence of atrophy or hypertrophy of the subcutaneous fat at the site of insulin injection.

Intestinal lipodystrophy— The condition is characterized by the deposits of fat in the intestinal and mesenteric lymphatic tissue, fatty diarrhea, loss of weight, weakness and arthritis.

Progressive lipodystrophy— Progressive and symmetrical loss of subcutaneous fat from the upper part of the trunk and its deposition about the thighs and buttocks.

Lipoedema—Edema of the subcutaneous fat.

Lipoferous— Producing or carrying fat.

Lipofibroma—Fibrolipoma. A lipoma containing much fibrous tissue.

Lipofuscin—One of a class of partly insoluble lipid pigments present in the cardiac and smooth muscle cells.

Lipofuscinosis—The condition caused by abnormal deposition of lipofuscin in the tissues.

Lipogenesis—Formation of fat.

Lipogenetic, Lipogenic— Lipogenous. Forming fat or caused by fat.

Lipogenous—Lipogenetic. Forming fat.

Lipogranuloma—A nodule containing lipid associated with granulomatous inflammation .

Lipogranulomatosis—The condition of fat metabolism in which necrosis occurs in the centre of a fat nodule and surrounding tissue becomes granulomatous.

Lipoid—1. Fatlike. 2. Lipid.

Lipoidemia—Lipemia. Excess of lipoids in the blood.

Lipoidosis—Lipidosis. Condition caused by the accumulation of excessive amount of lipoids in the body tissues.

Lipoiduria— Presence of lipoids in the urine.

Lipolipoidosis— Infiltration of fats and lipoids into a tissue.

Lipolysis— Lipoclasis. Decomposition of fat.

Lipolytic— Lipoclastic. Pertaining to lipolysis.

Lipolytic digestion— The conversion of neutral fats by hydrolysis into fatty acids and glycerol.

Lipolytic enzyme—Lipase. Fat-splitting enzyme.

Lipoma—Adipoma. Benign fatty tumor.

Lipoma arborescens—An abnormal treelike accumulation of fatty tissue in a joint.

Lipoma cystic—A lipoma containing cysts.

Lipoma diffuse—A lipoma which in not definitely circumscribed.

Lipoma osseous—A lipoma that has undergone calcareous degeneration.

Lipomatoid— Like lipoma.

Lipomatosis—Liposis, obesity. The condition in which there is tumor-like deposition of fat in the tissues.

Lipomatous—Of the nature of or affected with lipoma.

Lipomeningocele—A meningocele associated with an overlying lipoma.

Lipomeria—Congenital absence of a limb.

Lipometabolic—Pertaining to the metabolism of fat.

Lipometabolism— Metabolism of fat.

Lipomyoma— A myoma containing fatty tissue.

Lipomyxoma— Myxolipoma. A mixed tumor of lipoma and myxoma.

Liponucleoproteins — Complexes containing lipids, nucleic acids and proteins.

Lipopectic—Characterized by the accumulation of fat in the body.

Lipopenia— Deficiency of lipids in the body.

Lipopenic— Pertaining to the deficiency of lipids in the body.

Lipopeptid, Lipopeptide —A complex of lipids and amino acids.

Lipopexia—Accumulation of fat in the body.

Lipophage—A cell which ingests or absorbs fat.

Lipophagia—Lipophagy.

Lipophagic— Ingesting, absorbing or destroying fat.

Lipophagy—Absorption of fat.

Lipophanerosis—The change of fat in certain cells so that previously invisible fat becomes visible as droplets.

Lipophil—1. Having an affinity for fat. 2. Absorbing fat.

Lipophilia—Affinity for fat.

Lipophilic —Lipophil.

Lipoproteinemia—Presence of an excess of lipoproteins in the blood.

Lipoproteins—As the lipids (triglycerides, phospholipids and cholesterol) are unable to circulate in the blood, they are combined with the simple proteins. This combination is called lipoprotein. In the form of lipoproteins the lipids are transported in the blood. The lipoproteins are of three types (1) High-density lipoproteins (HDL)—A plasma lipoprotein containing high levels of proteins, little triglycerides, moderate levels of phospholipids and a little of cholesterol. There are less chances of coronary heart disease with high density lipoprotein. (2) Low-density lipoprotein (LDL)—A plasma lipoprotein containing a low percentage of triglycerides, high levels of cholesterol and moderate levels of phospholipids and protein . (3) Very low density lipoprotein (VLDL)—The plasma lipoprotein containing high levels of triglycerides, moderate concentrations of phospholipids and cholesterol and little protein.

Liposarcoma— A malignant tumor derived from embryonal lipoblastic cells, sometimes containing foci of normal fat cells.

Liposis—Adiposis. Abnormal accumulation of fat in the body.

Liposoluble—Soluble in fat.

Lipostomy—Congenital absence or very smallness of the mouth.

Liposuction—Method of removing extra subcutaneous fat by introducing a blunt-tipped cannula into the subcutaneous fatty tissue through a small incision and applying suction on the fat.

Liposuctioning—Removal of fat by high vacuum pressure.

Lipothymia—Faintness; syncope.

Lipotrophic—Pertaining to lipotrophy.

Lipotrophy —An increase in body fat.

Lipotropic— Acting on fat metabolism by decreasing the fat in the liver.

Lipotropic factors— The factors which help to prevent the accumulation of fat in the liver.

Lipotropin—A hormone of the pituitary gland mobilizing fat from the adipose tissue.

Lipotropism, Lipotropy—The condition of having the action for removing fat deposits in the liver.

Lipotropy—Lipotropism.

Lipovaccine— A vaccine in a vegetable oil.

Lipoxenous—Pertaining to lipoxeny.

Lipoxeny—Desertion of host by the parasite after completion its development.

Lippes loop —A type of intrauterine contraceptive device.

Lipping— The development of a bony overgrowth in degenerative joint disease.

Lippitude—Ulcerations of the margins of the eyelids..

Lippitudo —Lippitude.

Lip reading—To understand what is being said by watching the speaker's lip movements. This method is used by the deaf persons.

Lipsis— Ending or cessation.

Lipuria— Presence of fat in the urine.

Lipuric—Pertaining to lipuria.

Liquefacient—Converting a solid into liquid.

Liquefaction— Conversion of a solid into a liquid.

Liquefactive—Pertaining to liquefaction.

Liquescent— Becoming liquid.

Liqueur—Flavored and sweetened alcoholic beverage.

Liquid—1. The substance that flows easily. 2. The substance that is neither solid nor gaseous.

Liquor—1. Any liquid or fluid. 2. An alcoholic beverage. 3. Watery solution containing a medicinal substance. 4. A term applied to certain body fluids, e.g liquor amnii—the amniotic fluid, a clear watery fluid surrounding the fetus in the amniotic sac and liquor sanguinis—the blood serum or plasma.

Liquorrhea—The flow of liquid.

Lisping— To speak imperfectly; to speak with a lisp.

Lissencephalia—Lissencephaly. Agyria.

Lissencephalic—Pertaining to, or characterized by, lissencephalia.

Lissencephalous—Pertaining to the condition in which the brain is smooth due to underdeveloped gyri.

Lissencephaly— Agyria. Absence of gyri in the brain.

Lissive—Relieving muscle spasm.

Lissosphincter—Smooth muscular sphincter.

Lissotrichic, Lissotrichous—Having straight hair.

Lissotrichy—The condition of having straight hair.

Liter—A unit of volume in the metric system, equal to 1000 milliliters.

Lith- —Litho-

Lithagogue—An agent that expels the calculi.

Lithectasy—Removal of a calculus from the urinary bladder through the mechanically dilated urethra.

Lithectomy—Surgical removal of a calculus.

Lithemia— An excess of uric acid in the blood.

Lithiasis— Formation of calculi.

Lithic— Pertaining to a calculus.

Lithic acid— Uric acid.

Lithicosis—Stone cutter's silicosis; pneumoconiosis.

Litho-, Lith- — Prefixes pertaining to stone or calculus.

Lithocenosis— Removal of the crushed small pieces of calculi from the urinary bladder.

Lithoclast—Forceps for breaking up the large calculi.

Lithoclasty—Crushing of a stone into small pieces which may pass through the urethra.

Lithoclysmia— Injection of a substance into the urinary bladder which dissolves the calculi.

Lithocystotomy— Incision of the urinary bladder to remove a stone.

Lithodialysis—Litholysis. Dissolution of calculi in the urinary bladder by injection of a solvent.

Lithogenesis—Formation of calculi.

Lithogenic—Pertaining to the lithogenesis.

Lithogenous—Forming calculus.

Lithogeny—Lithogenesis.

Lithokonion—Lithomyl. An instrument for powdering the vesical calculi.

Litholabe—An apparatus for holding a calculus during its removal.

Litholapaxy—The crushing of a stone in the urinary bladder and washing out of the fragments through a catheter.

Lithology—Science of calculi.

Litholysis—Lithodialysis. Dissolution of the calculi.

Litholyte—An instrument for injecting a solvent for a calculus.

Litholytic—An agent that dissolves calculi.

Lithometer—An instrument for measuring the size of calculi.

Lithometra—Ossification of the uterine tissue.

Lithomyl—Lithokonion.

Lithonephritis— Inflammation of the kidney due to irritation of the calculi.

Lithonephrotomy—To make an incision into the kidney for removal of renal calculus.

Lithontriptic— Lithotriptic.

Lithopedion— A fetus in the uterus or outside the uterus that has died and become calcified.

Lithopedium—Lithopedion

Lithophone— An instrument for detecting the presence of calculi in the bladder by sound.

Lithoscope— An instrument for inspecting the calculi in the bladder.

Lithotome— An instrument for performing lithotomy.

Lithotomist—Specialist in lithotomy.

Lithotomy —To make an incision into a duct or an organ, especially the urinary bladder, for removal of calculi.

Lithotomy position—Dorsosacral position. Position in which the patient lies upon her back with the thighs flexed upon abdomen and legs upon the thighs, which are abducted.

Lithotresis—The drilling or making holes in a calculus to facilitate crushing.

Lithotripsy—The crushing of a calculus in the bladder or urethra.

Lithotriptic—1. Lithontriptic. Pertaining to lithotripsy. 2. An agent which dissolves calculi.

Lithotriptor— An apparatus for crushing a calculus in the bladder.

Lithotriptoscopy—The crushing of a stone in the urinary bladder under the direct vision by using a lithotriptoscope.

Lithotrite— An instrument for crushing a calculus in the bladder.

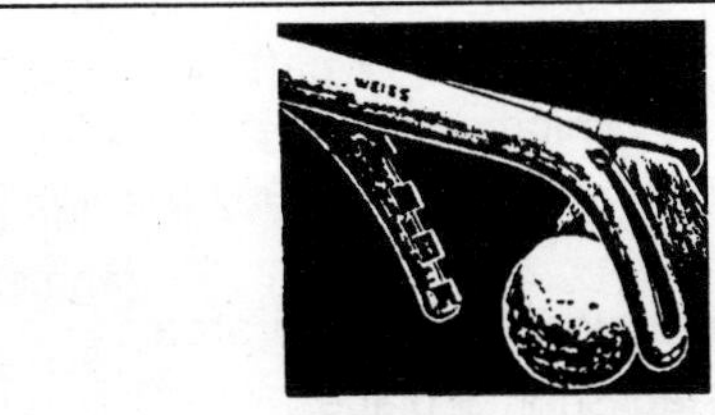

Fig. 302 : Lithotrite

Lithotrity—The crushing of a stone to small pieces in the bladder.

Lithous— Calculous. Pertaining to or of the nature of a calculus or stone.

Lithoxiduria—Presence of xanthic oxide in the urine.

Lithuresis— Passage of small stones through the urethra during urination.

Lithureteria— Disease of the ureter due to presence of calculi.

Lithuria—Excess of uric acid or of urates in the urine.

Litmus paper—A chemically prepared blue paper used as an acid-alkali indicator, which is turned red by acids and remains blue in alkali solution.

Litter—1. A stretcher for carrying the sick or wounded person. 2. The offspring produced at one birth by a multiparous mammal.

Little's disease— Congenital spastic paralysis.

Littre's glands—Urethral glands.

Littritis—Inflammation of the urethral glands.

Live birth—The birth of an infant who shows evidence of life after birth.

Livedo—Lividity. Patchy or general bluish discoloration of the skin.

Livedoid—Pertaining to or resembling livedo.

Liver—Large, four lobed, dark-red gland weighing about 1200 to 1600 gms., situated in the upper part of the abdomen on the right side just beneath the diaphragm, of which the main function is to secrete bile, conversion of glucose of the blood into glycogen and its storage and many other metabolic functions.

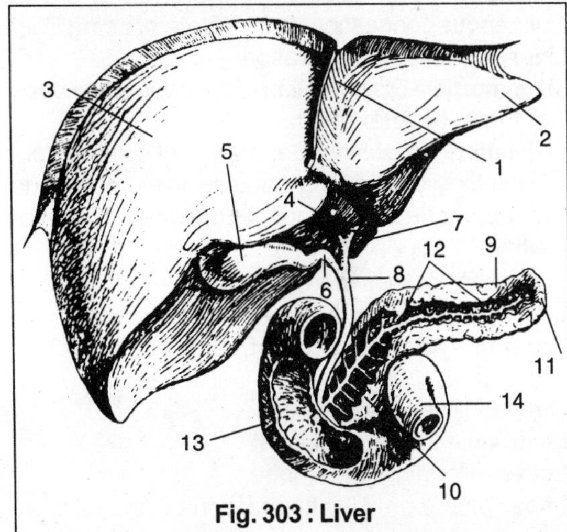

Fig. 303 : Liver

1. Falciform ligament 2. Left lobe of the liver 3. Right lobe of the liver 4. Quadrate lobe 5. Gall bladder 6. Bile duct 7. Hepatic duct 8. Common bile duct 9. Pancreas 10. Head of the pancreas 11.Tail of the pancreas 12. Pancreatic duct 13. Duodenum 14. Jejunum

Cirrhosis liver—Hardened liver due to the formation of fibrous tissue, and nodules.

Desiccated liver—A dried undefatted powder prepared from animal livers, used as human food.

Fatty liver—Enlarged liver due to deposit of fats in its cells.

Floating liver—Wandering liver. An easily displaced liver.

Foamy liver—Honeycomb-like liver caused by the presence of gas bubbles in it as a result of infection with anaerobic bacteria.

Hobnail liver— The liver whose surface is marked with nail-like projections from cirrhosis.

Lardaceous liver—Waxy liver.

Nutmeg liver —Chronic passive congestion of the liver causing a reddened central portal area and a yellowish peripheral zone.

Polycystic liver—Liver containing many cysts.

Wandering liver—Hepatoptosis.

Waxy liver—Lardaceous liver.

Liver flap — Asterixis. Liver tremor.

Liver spots— Chloasma hepaticum. Yellowish brown spots on the skin.

Livid —1. Cyanotic. 2. Having blue and black discoloration of the skin.

Lividity—1. Skin discoloration, as from a bruise or venous congestion. 2. The state of being livid.

Livor—Lividity. Discoloration.

Livor mortis—Discoloration of the dependent parts of the body after death.

Lixiviation—Leaching. Separation of soluble from insoluble substance by adding their mixture to an appropriate solvent, and drawing off the solution.

LLE—Left lower extremity.

LMP—Last menstrual period.

Loading—Administration of sufficient quantities of a substance to test an individual's ability to metabolize or absorb it.

Loathing—Extreme disgust.

Lobar—Pertaining to a lobe.

Lobar pneumonia—Inflammation of one or more lobes of the lungs.

Lobate— 1. Pertaining to a lobe. 2. Producing lobes. 3. Divided into lobes.

Lobation— 1. Formation of lobes. 2. The state of having lobes.

Lobe—A more or less well-defined portion of an organ or a gland, separated by boundaries.

Anterior lobe of the pituitary gland—Anterior portion of the pituitary gland.

Hepatic lobe —Lobe of the liver.

Lateral lobes of the thyroid gland— The two main portions of the thyroid gland, one on each side of the trachea, united below by the isthmus of the thyroid gland.

Lobes of the lungs— Large divisions of the lungs—Superior and inferior lobes of the left lung and superior, middle and inferior lobes of the right lung.

Posterior lobe of the pituitary gland —Posterior portion of the pituitary gland.

Lobectomy —Excision of a lobe of an organ or a gland.

Lobi —Plural of lobus.

Lobi cerebri —The major divisions of the cerebral hemisphere.

Lobitis —Inflammation of a lobe, as of the lung.

Lobose, Lobous —Lobate.

Lobotomy —To make an incision into a lobe.

Lobular —Lobulate. 1. Pertaining to a lobule. 2. Composed of small lobes.

Lobulate, Lobulated —Lobular. 1. Consisting of lobes or lobules. 2. Pertaining to lobes or lobules. 3. Resembling lobes.

Lobule —A small lobe or one of the smaller divisions making up a lobe.

Lobule of the epididymis —One of the conical divisions of the head of the epididymis formed by an efferent ductule of the testis.

Lobulet, Lobulette —A very small lobule.

Lobuli —Plural of lobulus.

Lobulus —A lobule or small division of a lobe.

Lobus —Lobe.

LOC —Level of consciousness.

Local —Limited to one place or part, not general.

Localization —1. Limitation to a definite area. 2. The determination of the site of any process or lesion.

Localized —Restricted to a limited area.

Locate —To establish in a place.

Locator —An apparatus for locating or discovering the site of foreign objects within the body.

Lochia —The vaginal discharge occurring during the puerperal period containing blood, serum, mucus and tissue, etc.

Lochia alba —The final vaginal discharge after childbirth in which the amount of blood is decreased and the leukocytes are increased so it is yellowish, turning to white.

Lochia cruenta, Lochia rubra —Lochia occurring immediately after childbirth for about six days, which is red due to the presence of blood almost entirely.

Lochia serosa —Thin, watery vaginal discharge occurring 4 or 5 days after childbirth which is brownish in color.

Lochial —Pertaining to lochia.

Lochiocolpos —Distention of the vagina due to retention of the lochia.

Lochiometra —Retention of lochia in the uterus.

Lochiometritis —Inflammation of the uterus during puerperal period.

Lochioperitonitis —Peritonitis occurring during puerperal period.

Lochiorrhagia —Excessive flow of lochia.

Lochiorrhea —Lochiorrhagia.

Lochioschesis —Retention or suppression of lochia.

Lochometritis—Lochiometritis.

Loci —Plural of locus.

Locked twins —Twins are locked in the birth canal during labor in the following two ways.

A- Both the twins presenting with the vertex.

B- Breech presentation of one twin and the vertex presentation of the other.

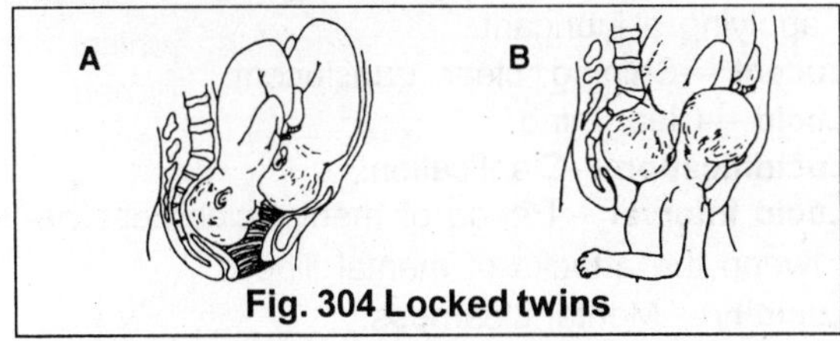

Fig. 304 Locked twins

Lockjaw —Tonic spasm of the jaw muscles as seen in tetanus.

Locomotion —Movement or power of movement from one place to another.

Locomotive —Locomotor.

Locomotor —Pertaining to locomotion.

Locomotor ataxia —See Ataxia locomotor.

Locomotorial —Pertaining to the locomotorium.

Locomotorium —The locomotor apparatus of the body.

Locomotory —Locomotor.

Locular —Divided into small cavities.

Loculate —Containing numerous loculi.

Loculated —Locular.

Loculi —Plural of loculus.

Loculus —A small space or cavity.

Locum tenant —Locum tenens. A temporary substitution of one doctor by another.

Locum tenens —The doctor who temporarily takes the place of another.

Locus —1. A spot or place. 2. The site of a gene on a chromosome.

Loeffler's bacillus —Klebs-Loeffler bacillus. The bacillus of diphtheria, Corynebacterium diphtheriae.

Loffleria —Presence of diphtheria bacillus without causing symptoms of diphtheria.

Loffler's endocarditis —Endocarditis associated with eosinophilia and fibroplastic thickening of the endocardium.

Logadectomy —Excision of a portion of the conjunctiva.

Logaditis —Scleritis. Inflammation of the sclera of the eye.

Logagnosia —A type of aphasia in which the written words are seen but their meaning is not understandable.

Logagraphia —Agraphia. Inability to express the ideas in writing.

Logamnesia —Sensory aphasia. Inability to recognize spoken or written words.

Logaphasia —Motor aphasia in which the patients know what they want to say but cannot say it.

Logasthenia —Mental impairment characterized by inability to understand the spoken words.

Logo-, Log- —Prefixes meaning speech or words.

Logoklony —Intermittent repetition of the last syllable of a word.

Logokophosis —Word deafness. Inability to understand spoken words.

Logomania —Overtalkativeness.

Logoneurosis —Any neurosis marked by speech disorders.

Logopathia —Any disorder of speech due to derangement of the central nervous system.

Logopathy —Logopathia.

Logopedia —Logopedics.

Logopedics —Study and treatment of speech defects.

Logoplegia —Paralysis of the speech organs.

Logorrhea —Logomania.

Logospasm —1. Stuttering. 2 Explosive speech.

-logy —A suffix meaning science or study of.

Loiasis —Infection with Loa loa.

Loin —Lumbus. Lower part of the back and sides, between ribs and the pelvis.

Longevity —The great length of life.

Longing —An earnest desire.

Longissimus —Longest.

Longitudinal—Lengthwise. Parallel to the long axis of the body or a part of the body.

Longitudinalis —Longitudinal.

Longitype —Ectomorph.

Longsightedness —Farsightedness. Hyperopia.

Longus —Long.

Loop —A sharp curve or bend in a cordlike structure e.g., Henle's loop, the descending and ascending loop in the renal tubule.

Lop-ear —Bat ear. Congenital abnormality of the external ear in which it is poorly developed.

Lophotrichate —Lophotrichous.

Lophotrichea —Microorganisms having flagella in tufts.

Lophotrichous —Having bunches of flagella at one end.

Loquacious —Talkative.

Loquacity —Talkativeness.

Lordoma —Lordosis.

Lordoscoliosis —Lordosis accompanied by scoliosis.

Lordosis —Forward convex curvature of the spine.

Lordotic —Pertaining to or marked by lordosis.

Lotio —Lotion.

Lotion —Liquid medicinal preparation for external use to the body, e.g. Zinc calamine lotion.

Loupe —A magnifying lens.

Louse —Pediculus.

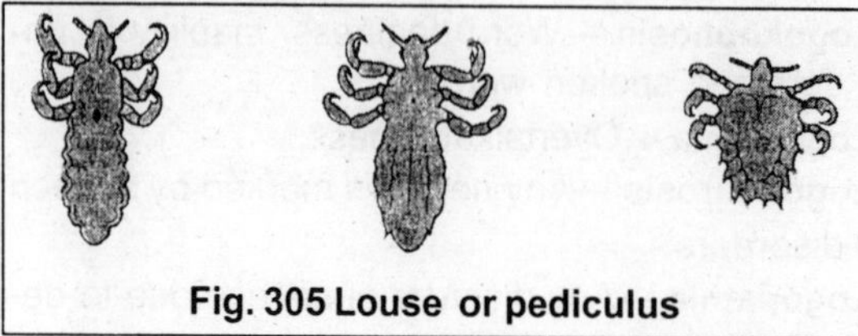

Fig. 305 Louse or pediculus

A. Pediculus humanus capitis or head louse
B. Pediculus humanus corporis or body louse
C. Phthirus pubis

Pediculus humanus capitis —Pediculus living in the hair of the head.

Pediculus humanus corporis —Pediculus living on the body and the clothes.

Phthirus pubis —That mainly lives in the hair of the pubic region, but also found in the beard, eyebrows and eyelashes.

Lousiness —Pediculosis. Condition caused by lice.

Lousy —Pediculous.

Lox —Liquid oxygen.

Loxarthron —Obliquity of a joint without dislocation.

Loxia —Wryneck; torticollis. Stiff neck caused by the spasmodic contraction of the muscles of the neck, drawing the head to one side and the chin pointing to the other side.

Loxotic —Distorted in every manner.

Loxotomy —Amputation.

Lozenge —Troche. Medicinal sucking tablet.

L.P.N. —Licensed practical nurse.

L.R.C.P. —Licentiate of the Royal college of Physicians.

L.R.C.S. —Licentiate of the Royal college of Surgeons.

L.R.F. —Luteinizing hormone releasing factor.

L.R.F.P.S. —Licentiate of the Royal Faculty of Physicians and Surgeons.

L.T.H. —Luteotropic hormone.

L.T.M. —Long-term memory.

Lubb-dupp —The two heart sounds heard on auscultation.

Lubricant —Making smooth as an oil or grease, to lessen the friction.

Lubrication —The process of making smooth by applying a lubricant.

Lucent —Shining, clear, translucent.

Lucid —Clear mind.

Lucidification —Clarification.

Lucid interval —Period of mental clearness between the attacks of mental illness.

Lucidity —Mental clearness.

Lucifugal —Repelled by bright light.

Lucipetal —Attracted to bright light.

Lucotherapy —Phototherapy. Treatment of diseases by light.

Ludwig's angina —Submaxillary cellulitis.

L.U.E. —Left upper extremity.

Lues —Syphilis.

Luetic —Syphilitic. 1. Pertaining to syphilis. 2. Affected with syphilis.

Lugol's solution —A strong iodine solution used in iodine therapy consisting of 5 gms. iodine, 10 gms. potassium iodide and water to make 100 ml.

Lumbago —Pain in the lumbar region.

Lumbar —Pertaining to the loins.

Lumbarization —The development of the first sacral vertebra as a lumbar vertebra, resulting in six lumbar vertebrae instead of five.

Lumbar puncture —Puncture into the subarachnoid space of the spinal cord done in the lumbar region at the level of 4th intervertebral space by an aspiration needle to remove the cere-

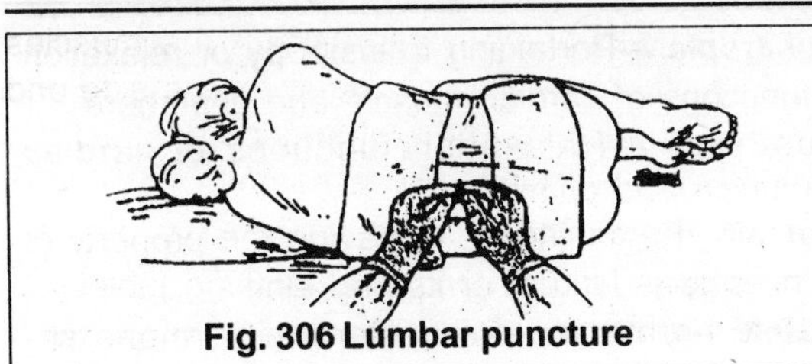
Fig. 306 Lumbar puncture

brospinal fluid for diagnostic purposes or for injection of anesthetic solution.

Insertion of the lumbar puncture needle into the subarachnoid space of the spinal cord in the lumbar region at the level of the 4th intervertebral space, while the patient lying on the bed with the head and vertebral column bent forward.

Lumbar region —Loin.

Lumbar vertebrae —Five bones of the spinal column between the sacrum and thoracic vertebrae.

Lumbi —Plural of lumbus.

Lumbo- —Combining form pertaining to the loins.

Lumboabdominal —Pertaining to the lateral and the frontal areas of the abdomen.

Lumbocolostomy —Surgical creation of an opening between the colon and the abdominal surface by incision through the lumbar region.

Lumbocolotomy —To make an incision into the colon through lumbar region.

Lumbocostal —Pertaining to the loins and ribs.

Lumbodynia —Lumbago.

Lumboiliac —Pertaining to the lumbar and inguinal regions.

Lumboinguinal —Lumboiliac.

Lumbo-ovarian —Pertaining to the lumbar region and the ovary.

Lumbosacral —Pertaining to the lumbar and sacral region or to the lumbar vertebrae and sacrum.

Lumbrical —Vermiform. Like a worm.

Lumbricidal —Destructive to the intestinal worm Ascaris lumbricoides.

Lumbricide —An agent that kills ascarides (intestinal worms).

Lumbricoid —Resembling a roundworm.

Lumbricosis —Infection with ascarides.

Lumbricus —Round worm.

Lumbus —Loin.

Lumen —The space within a tubular structure such as within an artery, vein or intestine, etc.

Lumina —Plural of lumen.

Luminal —Pertaining to a lumen as that of a blood vessel.

Luminalis —Luminal.

Luminescence —Production of light without production of heat.

Luminiferous —Producing or carrying light.

Luminophore —A chemical present in organic compounds which cause luminescence of those compounds.

Luminous —Giving off light.

Lumpectomy —Excision of a tumor from the breast.

Lunacy —Insanity.

Lunar —Pertaining to the moon, a month or silver.

Lunar caustic —Silver nitrate.

Lunare —Lunate.

Lunate —1. Moon-shaped or crescentic 2. Semilunar bone. A bone in the proximal row of the carpus.

Lunatic —Insane.

Lung —One of the two spongy organs of respiration contained within the pleural cavity, lying on either side of the heart within the chest cavity.

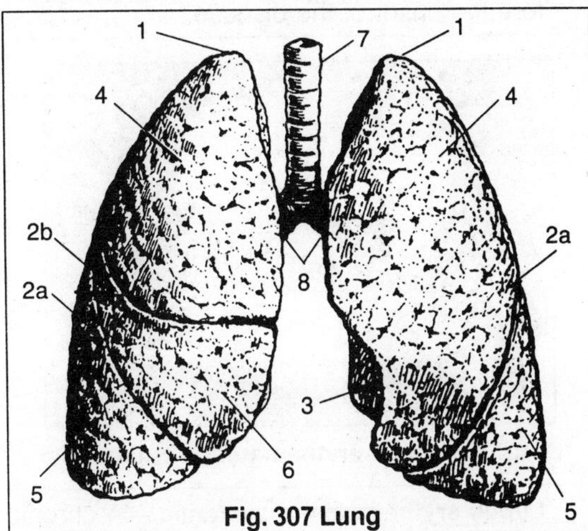

Fig. 307 Lung

1. Apex of lung 2a & 2b. Interlobar grooves 3. Cardiac notch 4. Superior lobe 5. Inferior lobe 6. Middle lobe (right lung) 7. Trachea 8. Bronchi

Black lung —Miner's lung. A form of pneumoconiosis occurring in coal miners, characterized by deposits of carbon particles in the lung.

Brown lung —Obstruction in the airway with asthma, produced by exposure to cotton dust or hemp etc., and the lungs become of brown color.

Miner's lung —Black lung.

Lung motor—An apparatus for forcing air or a mixture of air and oxygen into the lungs.

Lungworm —Any parasitic worm that infests the lungs.

Lunula—A crescentic area or structure, e.g. white area at the base of the nail of a finger or toe, or one of the segments of the semilunar valves of the heart.

Lunulae —Plural of lunula.

Lunule—Lunula.

Lupiform —Resembling lupus.

Lupoid —1. Lupiform 2. Pertaining to lupus vulgaris.

Lupous —1. Pertaining to lupus. 2. Affected with lupus.

Lupus —Any chronic, progressive, ulcerative skin disease.

Lupus erythematosus cutaneous—A chronic superficial inflammation of the skin of butterfly pattern over the nose bridge and cheeks but the other areas may be involved. There is usually a history of exposure to sunlight before the onset of the disease.

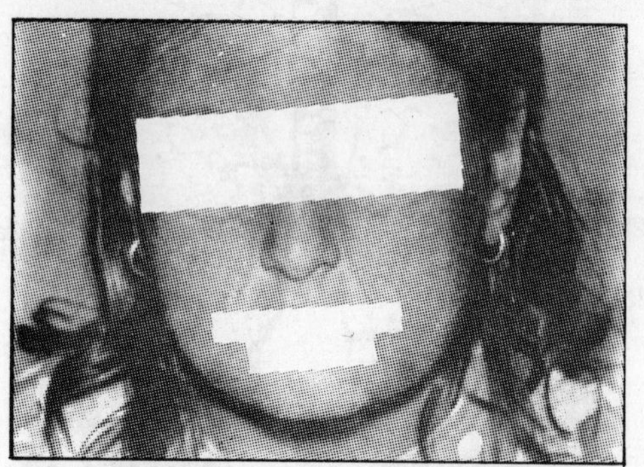

Fig. 308 Lupus erythematosus cutaneous

Lupus erythematosus systemic —A chronic inflammatory disease of unknown etiology of the body organs such as kidney, joints and nervous system etc., which usually occurs in young women. The characteristic butterfly rash or erythema may be present on the nose bridge and cheeks.

Lupus pernio —Sarcoidosis.

Lupus vulgaris —Tuberculosis of the skin most frequently affecting the face marked by the formation of reddish brown patches which break down and ulcerate leaving scars on healing.

LUQ—Abbreviation for left-upper quadrant (of abdomen).

Lusitropic —Pertaining to lusitropy or relaxation functions of cardiac muscle and chambers.

Lusitropy —Relaxation functions of cardiac muscle and chambers.

Luteal —Pertaining to, or having the property of the corpus luteum or its hormone.

Luteal hormone —Progesterone hormone secreted by the corpus luteum.

Lutein —Lipochrome or the yellow pigment derived from the corpus luteum, egg-yolk and fat cells.

Lutein cells —Cells of the ovary containing yellow pigment and form corpus luteum.

Luteinic —Pertaining to the corpus luteum of the ovary.

Luteinization —The process by which after ovulation an ovarian follicle is converted into the corpus luteum.

Luteinize —To form luteal tissue.

Luteinizing hormone —A hormone secreted by the anterior lobe of the pituitary gland which stimulates the development of the corpus luteum.

Luteinizing hormone releasing hormone—A hormone produced by the hypothalamus which controls the release and synthesis of luteinizing hormone.

Luteinoma —Luteoma.

Lutembacher's syndrome —Septal defect of the atrium of the heart with mitral stenosis.

Luteogenic —Producing corpora lutea.

Luteohormone —Progesterone.

Luteolysin —Any agent that destroys corpus luteum.

Luteolysis —Destruction of corpus luteum.

Luteolytic —Destroying corpus luteum.

Luteoma —An ovarian tumor containing lutein cells.

Luteotrophic —Luteotropic.

Luteotropic —Stimulating formation of the corpus luteum.

Luteotropin —Luteotropic hormone of the anterior pituitary gland.

Luteum —Yellow.

Luteus —Luteal.

Lux —A unit of light intensity.

Luxatio —Luxation.

Luxation —1. Displacement of an organ. 2. Dislocation of a joint.

Luxuriant —Exuberant.

Luxus —Excess of anything.

L.V. N. —Licensed vocational nurse.

Lycanthropy —Delusion in which one believes oneself a wild beast.

Lycopene —The red pigment carotene of tomatoes and other red fruits.

Lycopenemia —Excess of carotene pigment in the blood caused by eating excessive amount of carotene-containing foods.

Lycoperdonosis —A respiratory disease due to inhalation of spores from the mature mushroom, known as puffball, a fungus.

Lycorexia —Excessive hunger. Voracious.

Lying-in —The lying down on the bed of a woman in the puerperium.

Lymph —A colorless, transparent, clear, alkaline fluid within the lymphatic vessels and the cisterna chyli, of which the lymphocytes are the chief cellular component.

Lympha —Lymph.

Lymphaden —Lymph node.

Lymphadenectasis —Enlargement of a lymph node.

Lymphadenectomy —Excision of a lymph node.

Lymphadenia —Hyertrophy of the lymph nodes.

Lymphadenitis —Inflammation of the lymph nodes.

Lymphadenocele —Cyst of a lymph node.

Lymphadenogram —X-ray of a lymph gland.

Lymphadenography —Radiography of lymph glands after an injection of a radiopaque substance.

Lymphadenoid —Resembling a lymph node or lymph tissue.

Lymphadenoma —Lymphoma.

Lymphadenopathy —Disease of the lymph nodes.

Lymphadenopathy dermatopathic —Regional lymph nodes enlargement due to various skin diseases.

Lymphadenosis benigna cutis —A benign collection of lymphocytes in the skin, mainly on the face or ears in the form of nodules.

Lymphadenotomy —To make an incision into a lymph node.

Lymphadenovarix —Enlargement of the lymph nodes due to increased pressure in the lymph vessels.

Lymphagogue —Stimulating the production or flow of lymph.

Lymphangial —Pertaining to the lymphatic vessels.

Lymphangiectasia —Lymphangiectasis.

Lymphangiectasis —Lymphectasia. Dilatation of the lymphatic vessels.

Lymphangiectatic —Pertaining to or characterized by lymphangiectasis.

Lymphangiectomy —Excision of one or more lymphatic vessels.

Lymphangiitis —Inflammation of the lymphatic vessels.

Lymphangioendothelioma —Lymphendothelioma. Endothelioma arising from lymph vessels.

Lymphangiofibroma —Lymphangioma and fibroma combined.

Lymphangiogram —X-ray film of the lymph vessels.

Lymphangiography —Radiography of the lymph vessels after injecting a radiopaque substance into the lymph vessels.

Lymphangiology —The scientific study of the lymphatic system.

Lymphagioma —Tumor composed of lymphatic vessels.

Lymphangioma cavernous —Dilated lymph vessels filled with lymph.

Lymphangioma cystic —Multilocular cysts filled with lymph.

Lymphangiomatous —Pertaining to, or containing lymphangioma.

Lymphangion —A lymphatic vessel.

Lymphangiophlebitis —Inflammation of the lymphatic vessels and veins.

Lymphangioplasty —Surgical formation of lymphatic channels.

Lymphangiosarcoma —A malignant tumor arising from the endothelial lining of the lymphatics.

Lymphangiotomy —Lymphotomy. To make an incision into a lymphatic vessel.

Lymphangitis —Inflammation of a lymphatic vessel or vessels.

Lymphapheresis —Lymphocytapheresis.

Lymphatic —1. Of or pertaining to lymph. 2. A lymph vessel.

Lymphatic organ —The structure composed mainly of lymphatic tissue as lymph node, spleen and tonsil, etc.

Lymphaticostomy —To make an opening into a lymphatic duct, usually the thoracic duct.

Lymphatic system —The system including all the structures involved in the conveyance of lymph from the tissues to the blood stream. It includes the lymph capillaries, lacteals, lymph nodes, lymph vessels and thoracic and right lymphatic duct.

Lymphatic vessels —The vessels conveying lymph from the tissues.

Lymphatism — The condition due to excessive production or growth of the lymphoid tissues.

Lymphatitis —Inflammation of the lymphatic system.

Lymphatology —Study of the lymphatic system.

Lymphatolysis —Destruction of the lymphatic vessels or tissue.

Lymphatolytic —Destructive to lymphatics.

Lymph cell —Lymphocyte.

Lymphectasia —Lymphangiectasis. Dilatation of the lymphatic vessels.

Lymphedema —Edema of a part of the body due to obstruction of the lymphatic vessels.

Lymphemia —Presence of an increased number of lymphocytes in the blood.

Lymphenteritis —Serous infiltration with inflammation of the intestines.

Lymphization —Production of lymph.

Lymph node —A rounded body consisting of accumulations of lymphatic tissue, found at intervals in the course of lymphatic vessels. They act as filters for bacteria and check them from entering the blood stream and are mainly found in the neck, axilla and groin.

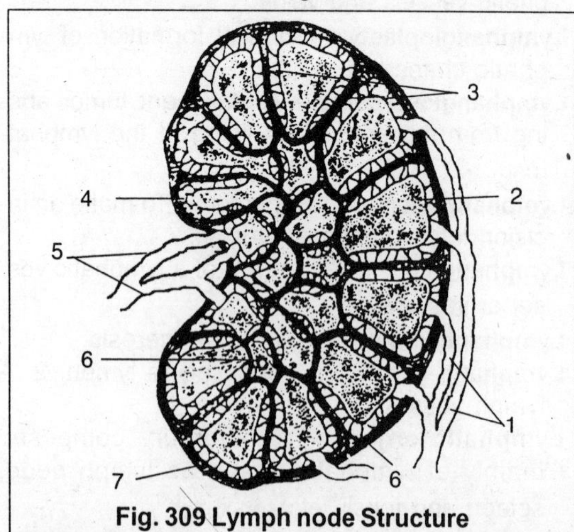

Fig. 309 Lymph node Structure

1. Afferent lymph vessels 2. and 4. Nodules in the substance of the node 3. Trabeculae 5. Efferent vessels 6. Lymph sinuses 7. Capsule of the lymph node

Lymphnoditis —Inflammation of a lymph node.

Lymphoblast —The cell which gives rise to a lymphocyte.

Lymphoblastic —Pertaining to a lymphoblast.

Lymphoblastoma —Lymphosarcoma.

Lymphoblastomatosis —The condition produced by the presence of lymphoblastomas.

Lymphoblastosis —Excessive number of lymphoblasts in the blood.

Lymphocele —Lymphocyst. A cyst containing lymph.

Lymphocinesia —Lymphokinesis.

Lymphocinesis —Lymphokinesis.

Lymphocyst —Lymphocele.

Lymphocytapheresis —To remove the selected lymhocytes from the withdrawn blood, which is then transferred into the donor.

Lymphocyte —A mononulcear, nongranular white blood cell, having a deeply staining nucleus which occupies all or most of the cell, either in the center or at one side. It is formed in the lymph node and is chiefly a product of lymphoid tissue and participates in the immunity. They are normally from 20% to 50% of the total blood cells but may increase to 90% in the lymphatic leukemia.

Lymphocythemia —Lymphocytosis. Excess of lymphocytes in the blood.

Lymphocytic —Pertaining to lymphocytes.

Lymphocytoblast —Lymphoblast.

Lymphocytoma —A malignant tumor of the lymphocytes.

Lymphocytopenia —Reduction of the number of lymphocytes in the blood.

Lymphocytopheresis —Lymphocytapharesis.

Lymphocytopoiesis —Production of lymphocytes.

Lymphocytosis —Lymphocythemia.

Lymphocytotoxicity —The quality of lysing the lymphocytes.

Lymphocytotoxin —A toxin destructive to lymphocytes.

Lymphoderma —A condition resulting from any disease of the cutaneous lymphatic vessels.

Lymphoduct —A lymphatic vessel.

Lymphoepithelioma —Squamous cell carcinoma of the lymphoid tissues of the tonsils and nasopharynx.

Lymphogenesis—Production of lymph.

Lymphogenic —Lymphogenous.

Lymphogenous —1. Producing lymph. 2. Produced from the lymph.

Lymphoglandula —Lymph gland.

Lymphogonia —Large lymphocytes with large nuclei, little chromatin, and nongranular cytoplasm.

Lymphogram —X-ray film of the lymph vessels and lymph nodes.

Lymphogranuloma inguinale, Lymphogranuloma venereum —A venereal infectious disease characterized by the formation of an ulcer on the genital organs, followed by swelling of the regional lymph nodes, later elephantiasis of the external genital organs may occur due to obstruction of the lymphatic vessels.

Lymphogranulomatosis —1. Infectious granuloma of the lymphatic system. 2. Hodgkin's disease.

Lymphography —Radiography of the lymphatic vessels and lymph nodes after an injection of a radiopaque substance into the lymphatic vessels.

Lymphohistiocytosis —Proliferation or infiltration of lymphocytes and histiocytes.

Lymphoid —Resembling lymph or lymph tissue.

Lymphoid cells —Lymphocytes.

Lymphoidectomy —Excision of a lympoid tissue.

Lymphokinesis —1. Circulation of lymph in the body. 2. Movement of endolymph in the semicircular canals of the ear.

Lympholeukocyte —Lymphocyte.

Lymphology —Science of lymphatics.

Lympholytic —Destroying the lymphocytes.

Lymphoma —Any new growth or a tumor arising from the lymphoid tissue in the body as Hodgkin's disease.

Lymphomatoid —Resembling lymphoma.

Lymphomatosis —Formation of multiple lymphomas in the body.

Lymphomatous —1. Pertaining to the lymphoma. 2. Affected with lymphoma.

Lymphomyxoma —A soft benign tumor containing lymphoid tissue.

Lymphonodus —Lymph node.

Lymphopathia —Lymphopathy.

Lymphopathy —Any disease of the lymphatic system.

Lymphopenia —Decrease in the number of lymphocytes in the blood.

Lymphoplasmapheresis —The removal of lymphocytes and plasma from the withdrawn blood and retransfusion of the remainder of the blood into the donor.

Lymphoplasmia —Absence of hemoglobin from the red blood cells.

Lymphoplasty — Lymphangioplasty.

Lymphopoiesis —Formation of lymphocytes or of lympoid tissue.

Lymphopoietic —Forming lymphocytes.

Lymphoproliferative —Pertaining to the proliferation of lymphoid tissue.

Lymphoreticular —Pertaining to the reticuloendothelial cells of the lymph nodes.

Lymphoreticulosis —Proliferation of the reticuloendothelial cells of the lymph nodes.

Lymphorrhagia —Lymphorrhea. Flow of lymph from the cut or ruptured lymph vessels.

Lymphorrhea —Lymphorrhagia.

Lymphorrhoid —Dilated lymph vessels resembling hemorrhoids.

Lymphosarcoma —A malignant neoplastic disease of the lymphoid tissue, excluding Hodgkin's disease.

Lymphosarcomatosis —The condition characterized by the presence of multiple lymphosarcomas.

Lymphostasis —Stoppage of lymph flow.

Lymphotaxis —The property of attracting or repulsing the lymphocytes.

Lymphotome —An instrument for removing the glandular growths from the tonsils and adenoids.

Lymphotomy —Lymphangiotomy.

Lymphotoxicity —Toxicity to lymphocytes.

Lymphotoxin —A lymphokine or cytokine toxin released from activated lymphocytes that affects a variety of cells.

Lymphotrophy —Nourishment of the cells by lymph in the areas devoid of blood vessels.

Lymphotropic —Attracted to lymph cells.

Lymph spaces — Spaces in the connective tissue filled with lymph.

Lymphuria —Presence of lymph in the urine.

Lyo- —Combining form meaning dissolved or loose.

Lyoenzyme —An extracellular enzyme.

Lyogel —A gel containing much water.

Lyophil —Lyophilic.

Lyophilic —Having an affinity for, or stable in solution.

Lyophilization —The process of freezing and then dehydrating in a high vacuum.

Lyophobe, Lyophobic —Not having an affinity for, or unstable in solution.

Lyosorption —Adsorption of a liquid on a solid surface.

Lyotrope —Lyotropic.

Lyotropic —Lyophilic. Readily soluble.

Lypressin —A hormone of the posterior pituitary gland obtained from the pituitary gland of the pig and used as an antidiuretic.

Lyra —A lyre-shaped structure.

Lysate —1. The products of hydrolysis. 2. That which is produced when the cells are lysed by some agent.

Lyse —To cause lysis.

Lysemia —Disintegration of red blood cells.

Lysimeter —An instrument for determining the solubilities of the substances.

Lysin —A specific antibody causing disintegration of cells, as hemolysin, bacteriolysin, etc.

Lysine —A naturally occurring amino acid, which is essential for growth and repair of tissues.

Lysinemia —Hyperlysinemia.

Lysinogen —Lysogen.

Lysinuria —The presence of lysine in the urine.

Lysis —1. Destruction or decomposition of a cell or other substance. 2. Gradual decline of a fever or disease.

Lysogen —That which produces a lysin.

Lysogenesis —Production of cell-destroying substance, the lysin.

Lysogenic —Producing lysins.

Lysogenicity —Ability of producing lysins.

Lysogenization —The process by which a bacterium becomes lysogenic.

Lysozyme —An enzyme found in neutrophils, phagocytes and macrophages, and in tears, saliva and sweat and other body secretions, that destroys bacteria by breaking down their walls.

Lysozymuria —Presence of lysozyme in the urine.

Lyssa —Rabies; hydrophobia.

Lyssoid —Resembling lyssa or rabies.

Lyssophobia —1. Hysteria resembling rabies. 2. Morbid fear of rabies.

Lyterian —Termination of a disease.

Lytic —Pertaining to lysis or a lysin.

Lyze —Lyse.

μ (mu–)—A symbol for a prefix micro-, which indicates one-millionth part of a quantity, *e.g.* microgram which is equal to one-millionth part of a gram.

μμ —Micromicro-; micromicron.

μμg —Symbol for micromicrogram.

m —1. Meter 2. Minim.

mμ —Symbol for millimicron.

M A —Abbreviation for mental age.

Macerate —To soften by soaking.

Macerated —Softened by soaking.

Maceration —Process of softening by soaking in a fluid.

Machine --Any mechanical apparatus for doing work or generating energy.

Macies —Wasting, atrophy.

Macrencephalia, Macrencephaly —Abnormal enlargement of the brain.

Macro-, Macr- —Combining forms meaning large or long.

Macrobacterium —Megabacterium. A large bacterium.

Macrobiosis —Longevity. Long life.

Macrobiota —The macroscopic living organisms of an area.

Macrobiote —A long-lived organism.

Macrobiotic —Long-lived.

Macrobiotics —The study of the prolongation of life.

Macroblast —An abnormally large, nucleated red blood cell.

Macroblepharia —Abnormal enlargement of the eyelid.

Macroblepharon —A large eyelid.

Macrobrachia —Abnormal enlargement of the arm.

Macrocardia —Cardiomegaly.

Macrocardius —A fetus with extremely large heart.

Macrocephalia —Macrocephaly. Abnormal enlargement of the head.

Macrocephalic —Megalocephalic.

Macrocephalous —Pertaining to or having, an extremely large head.

Macrocephaly —Macrocephalia.

Macrocheilia —Extremely large lips.

Macrocheiria —Extremely large hands.

Macrocnemia —The condition of extremely largeness of the legs below the knees.

Macrocolon —Megacolon.

Macrocornea —Megalocornea.

Macrocrania —Excessive largeness of the skull in comparison to the face

Macrocyst —A large cyst.

Macrocyte —Abnormally large red blood cell.

Macrocythemia, Macrocytosis —Presence of large numbers of macrocytes in the blood.

Macrocytosis —Macrocythemia.

Macrodactylia —Excessive size of one or more digits.

Macrodactyly —Macrodactylia.

Macrodont —Having large teeth.

Macrodontia —Excessive increase in size of the teeth.

Macrodontism —Macrodontia.

Macroencephalon —Megaloencephalon. An abnormally large brain.

Macroerythrocyte —Macrocyte.

Macroesthesia —The condition in which the things are seen or felt very large.

Macrofauna —In a particular area, living animal organisms visible to the naked eye.

Macroflora —In a particular area, living plant organisms visible to the naked eye.

Macrogamete —A larger, less active reproductive cell found in certain protozoa and simple plants.

Macrogametocyte —A cell producing macrogamets.

Macrogenitosomia —Excessive bodily development, with abnormal enlargement of the genital organs.

Macrogenitosomia praecox —Macrogenitosomia occurring at an early age.

Macrogingivae —Hypertrophy of the gums.

Macroglia —Astrocyte.

Macroglobulin —A globulin of high molecular weight, about 1,000,000.

Macroglobulinemia —Excess of macroglobulins in the blood.

Macroglossia —Excessive size of the tongue.

Macrognathia —Enlargement of the jaw.

Macrography —Writing with the large letters.

Macrogyria —Excessive enlargement of the cerebral gyri.

Macrolabia —Macrocheilia. Enlargement of the lips.

Macrolymphocyte —A large lymphocyte.

Macromania —The delusion in which someone thinks his or her body parts or surroundings very large.

Macromastia —Excessive largeness of the breasts.

Macromelia —Enlargement of one or more limbs.

Macromelus —The person having large limbs.

Macromere —A large blastomere.

Macromolecule —A large molecule.

Macromonocyte —A large monocyte.

Macromyeloblast —An abnormally large myeloblast.

Macronormoblast —Large nucleated red blood cell.

Macronucleus —A large nucleus occupying large portion of the cell.

Macronutrient —Any essential nutrient required in large amounts in a balanced diet, such as carbohydrates, proteins and fats.

Macronychia —Excessive increase in length of the fingernails.

Macroparasite —A parasite visible to the naked eyes, such as an intestinal worm.

Macropathology —Pathology pertaining to the gross anatomical changes in disease.

Macropenis —An abnormally large penis.

Macrophage —Large phagocyte as wandering or ameboid phagocytes found in the inflammatory area.

Macrophagocyte —Macrophage. A large phagocyte.

Macrophallus —Macropenis. Abnormally large penis.

Macrophthalmia —Abnormal enlargement of the eyeball.

Macroplasia —Abnormally large size of a part or a specific tissue.

Macropodia —Enlargement of the feet.

Macropolycyte —A large polymorphonuclear white blood cell.

Macroprosopia —Excessive largeness of the face.

Macroprosopous —Megaprosopous. Having a large face.

Macropsia —The condition in which the things appear larger than their actual size.

Macrorhinia —Extreme enlargement of the nose.

Macroscelia —Abnormal enlargement of the legs.

Macroscopic —Visible to the naked eyes.

Macroscopy —Examination of an object with the naked eyes.

Macrosigmoid —Abnormally large sigmoid colon.

Macrosis —Increase in size.

Macrosomatia, Macrosomia —Excessively large body.

Macrosmatic —Having a keen sense of smell.

Macrosomia —Macrosomatia.

Macrostereognosis —The misperception of seeing the objects larger than their size.

Macrostomia —Excessively wide mouth.

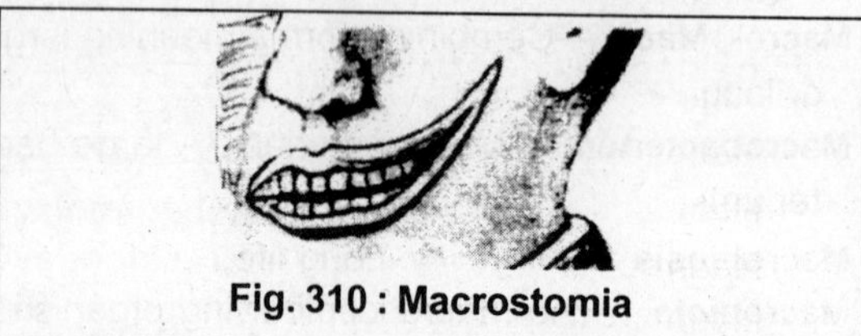

Fig. 310 : Macrostomia

Macrostructure —The gross structure of an object.

Macrothrombocyte —A large platelet.

Macrothrombocytopenia —Deficiency of macrothrombocytes in the blood.

Macrotia —Abnormal enlargement of the ears.

Macrotome —An instrument for cutting the large sections of the body.

Macrotooth —An abnormally large tooth.

Macula, plural **maculae** —Macule. A small spot or distinguishable area by color or otherwise from its surroundings, *e.g.* macula lutea retinae—macula of the retina, a discolored spot on the skin which is not raised from the surface, corneal opacity etc.

Macular —1. Pertaining to macule. 2. Having macules.

Macular degeneration —Degeneration of the macula lutea of the retina of the eye.

Maculation —Development of macules.

Macule —Macula.

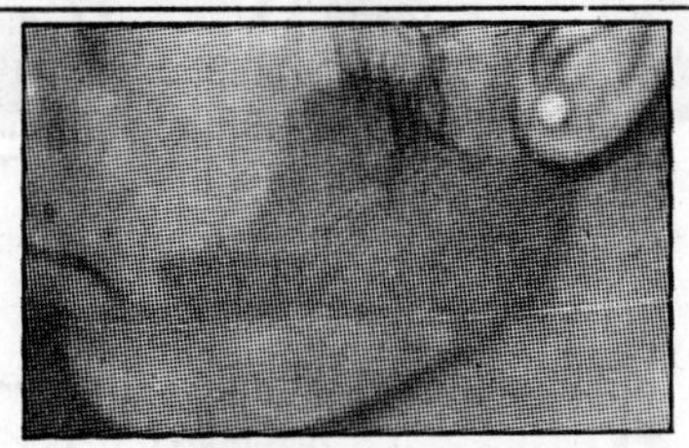

Fig. 311 : Macule

Maculocerebral—Pertaining to the macula lutea of the retina and the brain.

Maculoerythematous —Denoting the lesions that are erythematous and macular, covering a large area.

Maculopapular —Consisting of, or pertaining to both, macules and the papules.

Maculopathy —Any disease of the retina affecting its macula.

Mad —1. Insane. 2. Rabid. Suffering from rabies.

Madarosis —Loss of eyelashes or eyebrows.

Madelung's disease —Generalized symmetrical deposits of fatty tissues, on the upper part of the back, shoulders and neck.

Madescent —Slightly moist.

Madidans —From which a watery material oozes.

Madness —Insanity. The state of being mad.

Madura foot —Maduromycosis. Fungus disease of the foot.

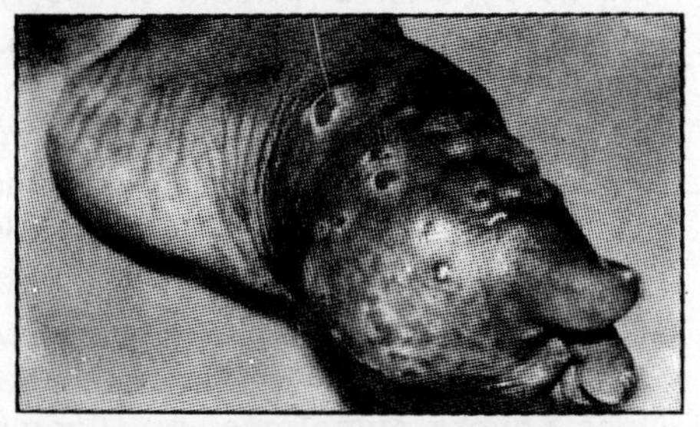

Fig. 312 : Madura foot

Maduromycosis —Chronic fungus infection of the foot, leg, hand or other parts of the body characterized by swelling, development of nodules, abscess formation and sinuses.

Maggot —Soft-bodied larva of an insect, especially of the flies living in the decaying flesh.

Magill forceps —A bent forceps used in laryngoscopy to remove a foreign body from the throat.

Magistery—1. A specially compounded remedy. 2. A precipitate.

Magistral—Concerning with the medicines prescribed by a doctor for a particular patient.

Magma—1. Suspension of finely powdered material in a small amount of water. 2. Paste. 3. The mass left after-extracting the principle.

Magnesium— A white mineral element found in soft tissus, muscles, bones and teeth etc., and obtained from milk, cheese, eggs, cereals, green vegetables and fruits mostly from bananas. The human body contains about 25 gms of magnesium that is necessary specially for the nervous system to work properly. Its deficiency causes weakness, palpitation of the heart, tremors of the limbs and convulsions.

Magnet —The substance which attracts iron.

Magnetic —1. Pertaining to a magnet. 2. Having the property of magnet.

Magnetism —The property of magnet.

Magnetoelectricity —Electricity generated by using magnet.

Magnetoencephalography —The process of recording the magnetic field of the brain.

Magnetometer —An apparatus for measuring magnetic fields.

Magneton —A unit of nuclear magnetic force.

Magnetotherapy —Treatment of the diseases by using magnet.

Magnetropism —The change in the direction of growth of a plant or an organism by the influence of a magnet.

Magnification —The process of increasing an object in size, especially while seeing by the microscope.

Magnitude —Size or extent.

Magnocellular—Composed of cells of large size.

Magnum —Large.

Magnus —Large or great.

Maidenhead —Hymen.

Maidism —Pellagra.

Maim —1. To injure seriously. 2. To deprive of the use of a part, such as arm or leg.

Main—Hand.

Main en griffe —Clawhand.

Main succulente —Edema of a hand.

Maintainer —An apparatus for holding or keeping the teeth in a given position.

Major—1. A grown-up person. 2. Chief. 3. A military officer in the rank above a captain.

Mal- —Combining form meaning ill, bad or poor.

Mal —Illness, disease or disorder.

Mala —1. The cheek. 2. The zygomatic or cheek bone.

Malabsorption syndrome—The symptoms arising from disordered or inadequate absorption of the nutrients from the intestines.

Malacia—Abnormal softening of the tissues or an organ.

Malacic —Malacotic.

Malacoma —Malacia. Softening of an organ or part of the body.

Malacoplakia—Formation of soft patches in the mucous membrane of a hollow organ.

Malacosarcosis —Malacia.

Malacosis —Malacia.

Malacosteon—Osteomalacia. Softening of the bones.

Malacotic —1. Soft. 2. Inclined to malacia. 3. Pertaining to malacia.

Malacotomy —To make an incision into the soft areas of the body, especially in the abdominal wall.

Malactic —Emollient.

Maladie —Malady.

Maladjustment —Defective adjustment to the new environment and the life problems, marked by depression, anxiety and irritability.

Malady —Disease. Illness or disorder.

Malagma —A cataplasm or emollient.

Malaise —Feeling of bodily discomfort or uneasiness.

Malalignment —Displacement out of line as of the teeth from the line of the dental arch.

Malar —Pertaining to the cheeks or the zygomatic bone (cheek bone).

Malar bone —Cheek bone. Zygomatic bone.

Malaria —An acute or chronic infectious disease due to the presence of protozoal parasites plasmodium within the red blood cells, transmitted through the bites of the infected female mosquitoes of the genus Anopheles, characterized by chill and fever (due to breaking down of the red blood cells) and sweating at intervals. In

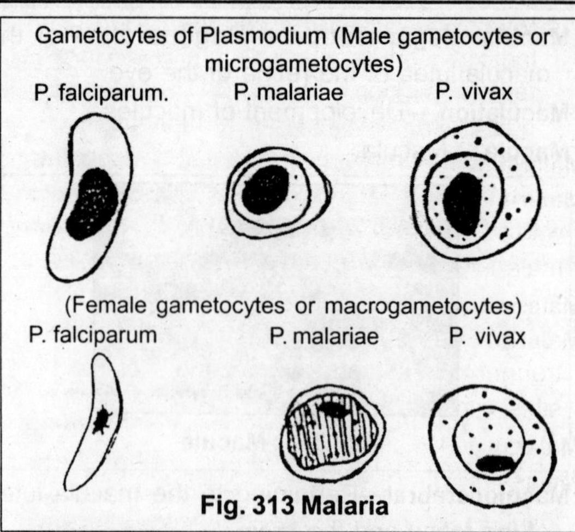

Fig. 313 Malaria

chronic cases there is usually anemia and enlargement of the spleen. Four species of genus Plasmodium, i.e. Plasmodium vivax, Plasmodium falciparum, Plasmodium malariae and Plasmodium ovale cause malaria.

Cerebral malaria —Malaria of the brain due to accumulation of malarial parasites Plasmodium falciparum in the brain, which is characterized by unconsciousness with hyperpyrexia (Temp. over 107°F) or there may be convulsions or paralysis. Death also sometimes results.

Falciparum malaria —Malaria caused by the Plasmodium falciparum which is most serious with severe symptoms, sometimes causing death.

Latent malaria —Malaria in which the parasites are present within the blood but causing no symptoms. Patient of this type of malaria is the reservoir of the disease.

Ovale malaria —A mild form of malaria caused by the malarial parasite Plasmodium ovale characterized by recurring attacks of tertian fever and tending to end in spontaneous recovery.

Quartan malaria —Malaria in which fever occurs every 72 hours or every fourth day with less severe symptoms, by Plasmodium malariae.

Quotidian malaria —Malaria due to Plasmodium vivax in which fever occurs daily with abrupt rise and fall of the temperature.

Tertian malaria —Malaria in which fever occurs on alternate day and the paroxysm is divided into chill, fever and sweating stages.

Vivax malaria—Most common form of malaria caused by Plasmodium vivax in which fever occurs on alternate day, marked by frequent recurrence.

Malariacidal —Killing malarial parasites.

Malarial —1. Pertaining to malaria. 2. Affected with malaria. 3. Causing malaria. 4. Resembling malaria.

Malariology —Scientific study of malaria.

Malariotherapy —Treatment of syphilis of the central nervous system by injecting malarial parasites into the body.

Malarious —Malarial.

Malassimilation —Defective or incomplete assimilation of the nutritive elements.

Malaxate —To knead, as in massage of a body part.

Malaxation —The act of kneading.

Maldevelopment —Abnormal development or growth.

Maldigestion—Disordered digestion.

Male —An individual of the sex, producing spermatozoa for fertilization of the ova.

Malemission —Failure of ejaculation of semen during coitus.

Maleruption —Eruption of a tooth out of its normal position.

Malformation —Deformity.

Malfunction —Defective function.

Malic —Intention to harm others or to see them suffer.

Malign —Tending to injure or harm.

Malignancy —Virulence. 1. The property of being malignant. 2. A cancerous tumor.

Malignant —Virulent. Becoming progressively worse and threatening to cause death as some cancerous growth.

Malinger —To pretend to be sick to gain sympathy, to get free from the work or to receive compensation.

Malingerer, Malingering —The person who pretends to be sick to gain sympathy, to get free from work or to receive compensation.

Malleable —Capable of being changed in shape by pressure.

Malleation —Occurrence of spasms in the hands which seem drawn to strike a near object.

Malleoincudal —Pertaining to the malleus and incus auditory ossicles.

Malleolar —Pertaining to the malleollus.

Malleolus —The protuberance on both sides of the ankle joint, of the lower end of the fibula it is known as lateral malleolus and of the lower end of the tibia as the medial malleolus.

Malleotomy —1. To divide the malleus of the inner ear. 2. To separate the malleoli of the ankle joint by operation.

Mallet —Hammer.

Mallet finger —Hammer finger.

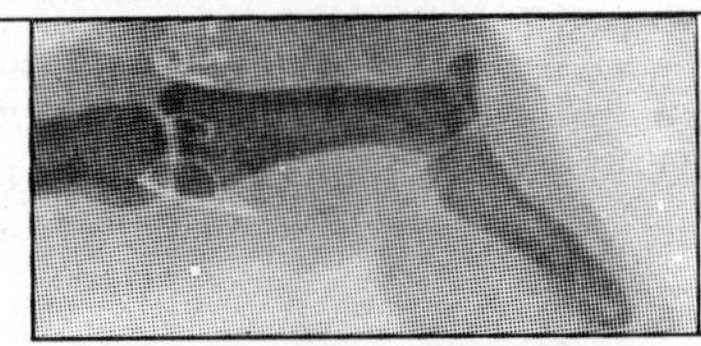

Fig. 314 : Mallet finger

Mallet toe —Hammer toe.

Mallleus —1. The largest of the three ossicles in the middle ear, attached to the eardrum. 2. Glanders.

Malnutrition —Lack of necessary substances in the body due to imbalanced diet, improper digestion or absorption of food. The person takes the full diet but his/her body does not develop.

Malocclusion —Malposition and imperfect contact of the teeth of the upper and lower jaw.

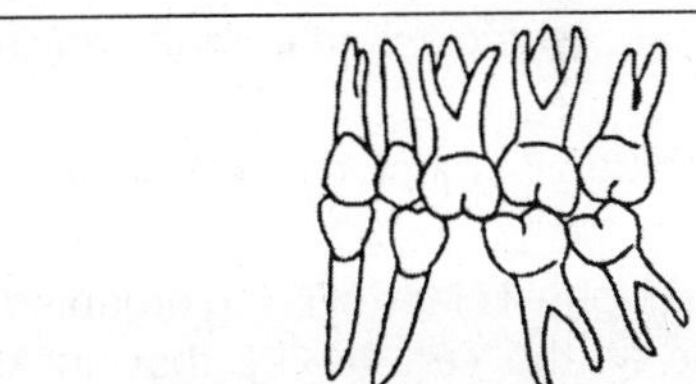

Fig. 315 : Malocclusion of the upper & lower teeth.

Malpighian body —1. Renal corpuscle consisting of a glomerulus enclosed in Bowman's capsule. 2. Lymph node found in the spleen.

Malpighian capsule —A spherical body found in the cortex of the kidney consisting of a glomerulus and Bowman's capsule.

Malpighian layer —Innermost layer of the epidermis.

Malposition —Abnormal position.

Malpractice —Incorrect or injurious treatment of a patient by the doctor.

Malpresentation —Abnormal fetal presentation.

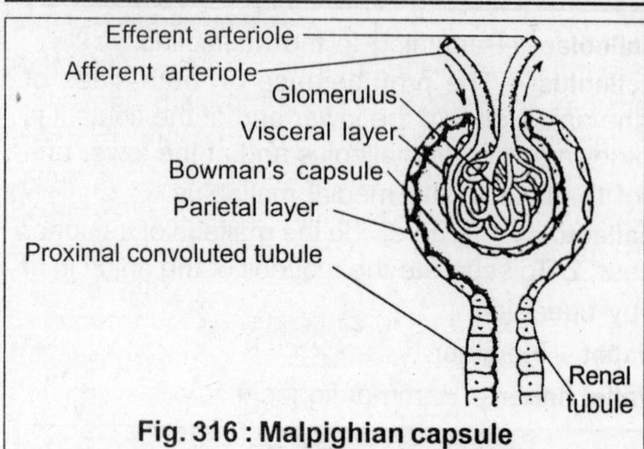

Fig. 316 : Malpighian capsule

Malrotation —Abnormal or pathological rotation, as of the vertebral column or failure of the normal rotation of an organ, as of the intestine, during embryological development.

Maltosuria —Presence of maltose in the urine.

Malturned —Abnormally turned, as a tooth.

Malum —A disease.

Malunion —Faulty union of the fragments of a fractured bone.

Mamelon —One of the three rounded protuberances present on the cutting edge of an incisor tooth when it erupts.

Mamelonated —Having nipple-like elevations.

Mamelonation —The formation of nipple-like elevations on some body structure.

Mamma —Mammary gland.

Mammal —Animal of the class mammalia having breasts.

Mammalgia —Mastalgia, mastodynia. Pain in the breast.

Mammalia —The highest class of living organisms which includes all the vertebrates that suckle their child, possess hair and give birth to a child rather than laying eggs.

Mammaplasty —Plastic surgery of the breast.

Mammary glands —Mammae. Two milk secreting glands of the female breasts. See fig. 5.

Mammectomy —Mastectomy. Excision of the breast.

Mammiform —Mammose.

Mammilla —1. The nipple of the breast. 2. Any structure resembling a nipple.

Mammillaplasty —Plastic surgery of the nipple and areola.

Mammillare —Mammillary.

Mammillary —Pertaining to or shaped like a nipple.

Mammillate —Studded with nipple-like projections.

Mammillated —Having nipple-like prominences.

Mammillation —1. The condition of having nipple-like prominences. 2. A nipple-like projection.

Mammilliform —Nipple-shaped.

Mammilliplasty —Theleplasty. Plastic surgery on a nipple.

Mammillitis —Thelitis. Inflammation of a nipple.

Mammitis —Mastitis. Inflammation of the breast.

Mammogen —Prolactin.

Mammogram —X-ray film of the breast.

Mammography —X-ray examination of the breast.

Mammoplasia —Development of the breast.

Mammoplasty —Plastic surgery of the breast.

Mammose —1. Having abnormally large breasts. 2. Shaped like a breast.

Mammotomy —Mastotomy. To incise the breast.

Mammotrophic —Having the effect of stimulating the size or function of the breast.

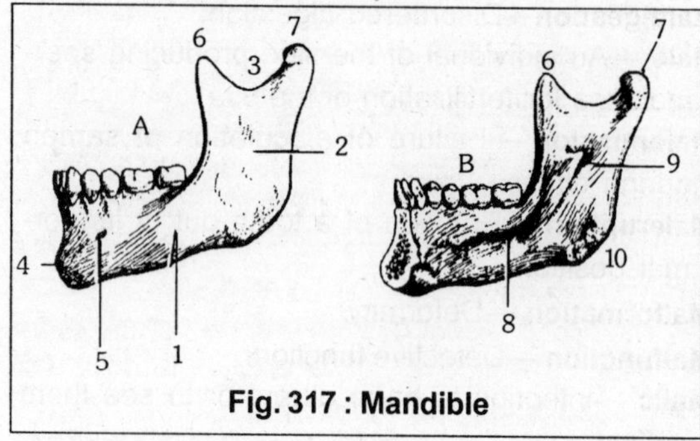

Fig. 317 : Mandible

A : Left half, external aspect B : Right half, internal aspect 1. Body 2. Ramus 3. Mandibular notch 4. Mental protuberance 5. Mental foramen 6. Coronoid process 7. Condylar process 8. Mylohyoid line 9. Mandibular foramen 10. Mandibular angle

Mancinism —Writing with the left hand.

Mandible —The horseshoe-shaped bone forming the lower jaw.

Mandibula —Mandible.

Mandibulae —Plural of mandible.

Mandibular —Pertaining to the mandible or lower jaw.

Mandibulectomy —Excision of the mandible (lower jaw).

Mandibulofacial —Pertaining to the mandible and the face.

Mandibulo-oculofacial —Pertaining to the mandible and the orbital part of the face.

Mandibulopharyngeal —Pertaining to the mandible and the pharynx.

Mandibulum —Mandible

Mandrel, Mandril —The handle for holding a dental tool so that the tool may be rotated.

Mandrin —A metal guide for a flexible catheter.

Maneuver —A skillful or dextrous procedure, *e.g.* Bracht's maneuver—a method of extracting the aftercoming head of the fetus in obstetrics in breech presentation, Brandt-Andrews maneuver—a method of expressing the placenta from the uterus during the third stage of labor, Heimlich maneuver—A technique for removing a food material or foreign body from the throat.

Mania —A mental disorder in which the patient becomes excited, restless and talkative, has delusions of grandeur and performs psychomotor overactivities. He/she has unreasonable desire for a thing.

Maniac —Affected by mania.

Maniacal —Pertaining to or suffering from mania.

Manic —Maniacal

Manic-depressive psychosis —A form of psychosis in which there are alternate attacks of mania and depression.

Manifest —Clear or evident, obvious.

Manifestation —Revelation. Disclosure of characteristic signs or symptoms of a disease.

Manikin —A model of the human body or its parts used in teaching anatomy.

Maniphalanx —A phalanx or finger of the hand.

Manipulation —Skillful or dextrous treatment by using the hands.

Mannerism —A peculiar modification of style or habit of dress, speech or action.

Mannkopf's sign —An increase in the pulse rate on pressing a painful point.

Manometer —An instrument for measuring the pressure of liquids or gases.

Manometry —To measure the pressure of the liquids or gases by manometer.

Manoscopy —Manometry.

Man. pr.—Early morning, first thing in the morning.

Mantle —A covering structure or layer such as the cerebral cortex, the brain mantle.

Mantoux reaction —Hardness and redness of the skin occurring within 24 to 72 hours after an intracutaneous injection of Old Tuberculin in case of an active or inactive tuberculous infection present in the individual.

Manual —1. Pertaining to the hands. 2. Done by the hands.

Manubrium —Any handle-shaped structure, *e.g.*, manubrium sterni.

Manudynamometer —In dentistry, a device for measuring the force exerted by the thrust of an instrument.

Manus —Hand.

Mapping —Location of genes on a chromosome.

Marantic —Marasmic. 1. Pertaining to marasmus. 2. Wasting away.

Marantology —Study, care and treatment of the weak, old persons and the persons suffering from chronic diseases, which are difficult to be cured.

Marasmic —Marantic. 1. Suffering from marasmus. 2. Wasting away.

Marasmoid —Similar to marasmus.

Marasmus —Due to inadequate food intake, malnutrition or malabsorption, there is wasting of the subcutaneous fat and muscles occurring in the infant with growth retardation and loss of weight. The eyes are sunken. The skin is dry and there are loose folds of the skin, especially on the buttocks and thighs. Abdomen is distended due to wasting, hypotonia of the muscles and gaseous distension.

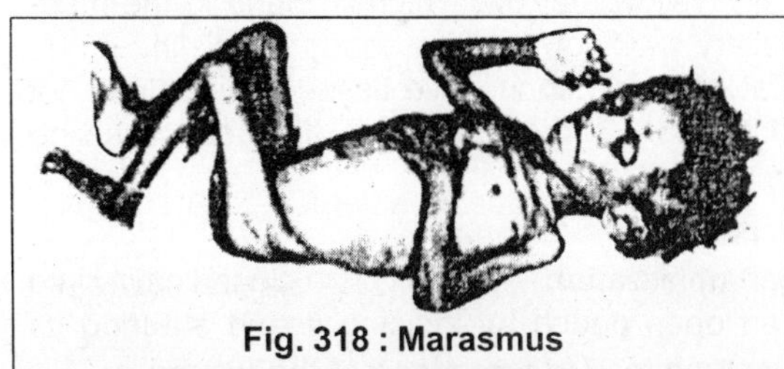

Fig. 318 : Marasmus

Marble bone disease —Osteopetrosis.

Marble bones —Abnormally calcified bones with spotted appearance, in an X-ray film.

Marc —The remaining substance after a drug has been filtered.

Marcid —1. Wasted or emaciated. 2. Exhausted.

Margarine —Artificial butter made from refined vegetable oils or a combination of vegetable oils and animal fats to which coloring material and vitamin A are added.

Margin —Edge, border or boundary.

Marginal —Limbic. Pertaining to a margin.

Margination —Accumulation and adhesion of white blood cells to the walls of the blood vessels at the site of injury in the first stage of inflammation.

Marginoplasty —Plastic surgery of a border, as of the eyelid.

Margo —Margin.

Marie's disease —Acromegaly.

Marie's sign —Tremor of the hand seen in exophthalmic goiter.

Marijuana, Marihuana —Cannabis sativa (hemp)

Mark —A spot, mole, congenital cutaneous vascular tumor (hemangioma), stain, bruise etc.

Marker —1. An apparatus or substance which marks. 2. Distinguishing between apparently similar materials or diseases.

Marmorated —The condition in which the skin becomes streaked like marble.

Marrow —The soft tissue within the long bones (bone marrow) and the vertebral column (spinal marrow or the spinal cord). The marrow is of two types—Red marrow, which is found in the cancellous tissue of the bone and is concerned with the production of blood cells and hemoglobin, Yellow marrow, which is found in the medullary cavity of the long bones consisting of the fat cells and connective tissue, which does not take part in the formation of blood cells and hemoglobin.

Marsh fever —Malaria.

Marsupialization —To convert a closed cavity into an open pouch by incising it and suturing its wall's edges to the edges of the wound.

Marsupium —Scrotum.

Maschaladenitis —Inflammation of the axillary glands.

Maschale —Axilla.

Maschaliatry —Medication by axillary inunctions.

Maschaloncus —A new growth in the axilla.

Maschalyperidrosis —Excessive sweating in the axillae.

Masculation —Development of male secondary sexual characteristics.

Masculine —1. Pertaining to male sex. 2. Having the characteristics of male.

Masculinity —The condition of having male characteristics.

Masculinization —1. The normal development of male secondary sex characteristics in the male at puberty. 2. Virilization. The abnormal development of male secondary sex characteristics in the female.

Masculinize —Virilize. To produce male secondary sex characteristics in the female.

Masculinovoblastoma —A benign tumor of the ovary producing masculinization.

Masculinus —Masculine.

Mashing —To crush into a mixture.

Mask —1. A covering made up of gauze or other material for the face of surgeon or nurse, or BLB mask for administering oxygen to the aviators and to the patient during anesthesia. 2. The appearance of the face such as appears in certain pathological conditions as erupted brown pigmentation of the cheeks, forhead and temples seen in tertiary syphilis, pigmented areas seen on the face of some pregnant women etc. 3. To cover, conceal or prevent something to enter.

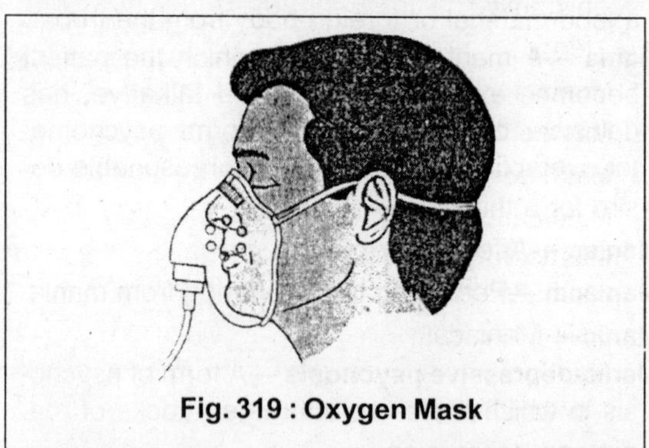

Fig. 319 : Oxygen Mask

Masked —Covered or concealed.

Masking —1. The use of noise of any kind to interfere with the hearing of another sound. 2. In audiology, the use of noise applied to one ear while testing the hearing of the other ear.

Masochism —Sexual excitement by suffering, being bound or beaten.

Masochist —The person addicted to masochism.

Mass —A lump of matter.

Massa —Mass.

Massage —Rubbing, stroking or kneading of the body for the treatment of diseases, *e.g.* cardiac massage done in case of cardiac arrest.

Masseter —The muscle that closes the mouth and is principal muscle in mastication.

Masseur —1. The man who performs massage. 2. An instrument for massage.

Masseuse —The woman who performs massage.

Massive —Bulky or heavy.

Massotherapy —Treatment of disease by massage.

Mastadenitis—Mastitis. Inflammation of a mammary gland.

Mastadenoma —A tumor of the breast.

Mastalgia —Mastodynia. Pain in the breast.

Mastatrophia —Atrophy of the breasts.

Mastatrophy —Mastatrophia.

Mastauxe —Enlargement of the breast.

Mast cells —Connective tissue cells that contain histamine in their granules, which causes allergy.

Mastectomy —Excision of the breast.

Masthelcosis —Ulceration of the breast.

Masticate —To chew.

Mastication —The process of chewing.

Masticatory —1. Pertaining to mastication. 2. Any substance to be chewed but not swallowed to stimulate the secretion of saliva.

Mastigote —A protozoon with one or more flagella.

Mastitis —Inflammation of the breast.

Fig. 320 : Mastitis

Masto-, Mast- —Prefixes meaning breast or mastoid.

Mastocarcinoma —Carcinoma of the breast.

Mastochondroma —Cartilaginous tumor of the breast.

Mastocyte —Mast cell.

Mastocytogenesis —Formation and development of mast cells.

Mastocytoma —Accumulation of mast cells resembling a tumor.

Mastocytosis —Local or systemic accumulation of mast cells.

Mastodynia —Mastalgia. Pain in the breast.

Mastography —X-ray examination of the breast.

Mastoid—1. Breast-shaped. 2. Mastoid process of the temporal bone. 3. Pertaining to the mastoid process.

Mastoidal —Pertaining to the mastoid process.

Mastoidale —The lowest point on the mostoid process.

Mastoidalgia —Pain in the mastoid process.

Mastoid antrum —A small chamber through which the mastoid cells communicate with the tympanic cavity.

Mastoid cells —Air spaces in the mastoid process of the temporal bone.

Mastoidectomy —Excision of the mastoid cells or of the mastoid process.

Mastoideocentesis —To puncture the mastoid process and then paracentesis of the mastoid cells.

Mastoiditis —Inflammation of the mostoid antrum and the cells.

Mastoidotomy —To make an incision into the mastoid process.

Mastoid process —A nipple-like projection of mastoid protion of temporal bone, extending downward and forward behind the external auditory meatus.

Mastology —Scientific study of the breasts.

Mastomenia —Vicarious menstruation from the breast.

Mastoncus —A tumor or swelling of the breast.

Masto-occipitai —Pertaining to the mastoid process and the occipital bone.

Mastoparietal —Pertaining to the mastoid process and the parietal bone.

Mastopathy —Any disease of the mammary gland.

Mastopexy —Mazopexy. To correct the pendulous breast by surgical fixation.

Mastoplasia —Masoplasia. Hyperplasia of the mammary gland tissue.

Mastoplasty—Plastic surgery of the breast.

Mastoptosis —Pendulous breasts.

Mastorrhagia —Hemorrhage from the breast.

Mastoscirrhus —Hardening of the breast.

Mastosquamous —Pertaining to the mastoid process and the squamous portion of the temporal bone.

Mastosyrinx —A fistula of the mammary gland.

Mastotomy—Mammotomy. To make an incision into the breast.

Masturbate —To practice masturbation.

Masturbation —To achieve the climax of the sexual excitement by friction of the genital organs by hands.

Matching —Comparison for selection of objects with similar characteristics, *e.g.*, matching of blood before transfusion.

Mater —Meninges. The tissue coverings of the brain and spinal cord, as arachnoid mater, dura mater and pia mater.

Materia —Substance or matter.

Materia alba —White material deposited along the margins of the gums, about the necks of the teeth and consisting of mucus, epithelial cells, food particles, white blood cells and bacteria.

Material —Matter of which a thing is made.

Materia medica —Pharmacology. The branch of medical science which deals with the drugs used in the treatment of diseases, their source, preparation, dosage and use.

Materies morbi —Any substance that is the direct cause of death.

Maternal —1. Pertaining to the mother. 2. From a mother.

Maternal deprivation syndrome —Emotional, physical and nutritional negligency of an infant or a young child, due to which the infant or the child is emotionally disturbed, withdrawn, apathetic with retarded growth and development.

Maternity —1. Motherhood. 2. The obstetrical department of a hospital.

Mating —Pairing of the individuals of the opposite sexes, especially for reproduction.

Matrass —A long-necked glass vessel used for heating dry substances.

Matrices —Plural of matrix.

Matrix —1. The intercellular substance of a tissue as bone matrix. 2. The substance from which a structure as hair or nail develops. 3. The uterus. 4. A mold for casting the amalgam in dentistry.

Matrixitis—Onychia. Inflammation of the nailbed.

Matron —The woman superintendent of a hospital.

Matter —1. Anything that occupies space. It may be solid, liquid or gaseous. 2. Pus.

Maturant —A medicine which hastens maturation.

Maturate —1. To ripen. 2. To suppurate.

Maturation —1. Ripening. 2. Suppuration.

Mature —1. Fully developed or ripened. 2. To become fully developed.

Maturity —The state of being mature.

Matutinal —Occurring in the morning, as morning sickness.

Maxilla —The bone of the upper jaw.

Maxillary —Pertaining to the upper jaw or the maxilla.

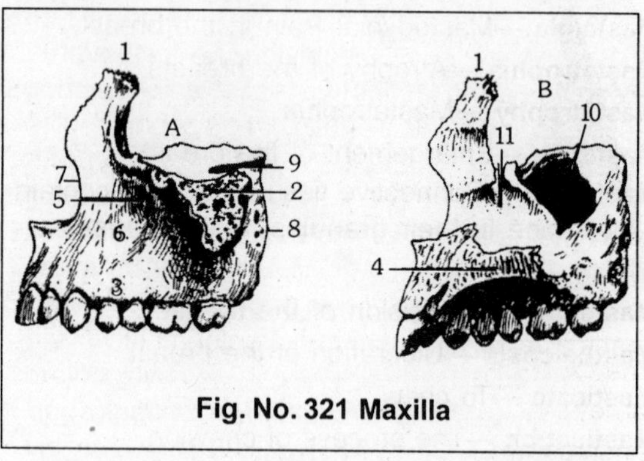

Fig. No. 321 Maxilla

A. Left half, external aspect. B. Right half, internal aspect. 1. Frontal process 2. Zygomatic process 3. Alveolar process 4. Palatine process 5. Infraorbital foramen 6. Canine fossa 7. Nasal notch 8. Maxillary tuberosity 9. Infraorbital sulcus 10. Maxillary sinus 11. Lacrimal groove

Maxillectomy —Excision of the maxilla.

Maxillitis —Inflammation of the maxilla.

Maxillodental —Pertaining to the maxilla and the teeth it contains.

Maxillofacial —Pertaining to the maxilla and face.

Maxillojugal —Pertaining to the maxilla and the zygomatic bone.

Maxillomandibular —Pertaining to the maxilla and the mandible.

Maxillopalatine —Pertaining to the maxilla and the palatine bone.

Maxillotomy —To make an incision into the maxilla.

Maxima —Plural of maximum.

Maximal —1. Greatest. 2. Highest.

Maximum —1. The greatest quantity or effect. 2. Height of a disease.

Mazodynia —Mastodynia.

Mazoitis —Mastitis.

Mazopexy —Mastopexy.

Mazoplasia —Mastoplasia.

M.B. —Bachelor of Medicine.

m.b. —A prescription sign meaning mix well.

MBD —Maximum breathing capacity.

McBurney's point —The point of tenderness in acute appendicitis at the junction of the outer and middle thirds of a line drawn from the umbilicus to the right anterior superior iliac spine.

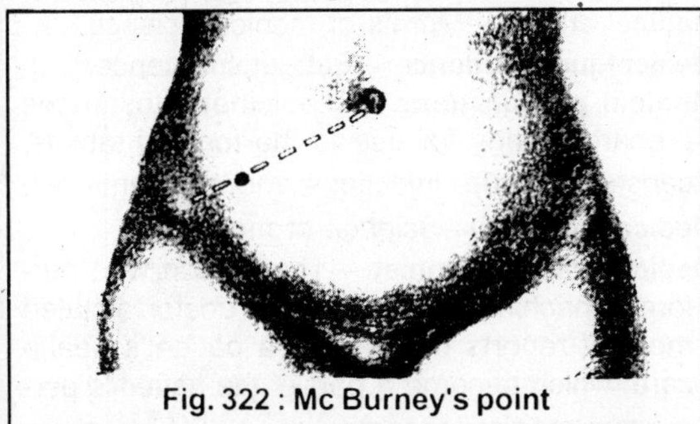

Fig. 322 : Mc Burney's point

McBurney's sign —Tenderness and rigidity at McBurney's point, a sign of acute appendicitis.

mcg —microgram.

MCH —Mean corpuscular hemoglobin.

MCHC —Mean corpuscular hemoglobin concentration.

MCV —Mean corpuscular volume.

M.D. —Doctor of medicine.

Meal —1. Portion of food taken at a particular and fixed time. 2. The eatable portion of a grain ground into powder.

Mean —Average.

Measles —Rubeola. A highly contagious disease occurring mostly in school-age children in winter and spring season caused by rubeola virus (measls virus), characterized by conjunctivitis, sneezing, nasal congestion, malaise, high fever, Koplik's spots on the buccal mucous membrane, cough, occurrence of the maculopapular rash on the whole body starting from the head.

Measles black —Measles hemorrhagic. A severe form of measles in which the rash is dark in color due to effusion of blood into the skin.

Measles German —Rubella.

Measles hemorrhagic —Measles black.

Measly —1. Affected with measles. 2. Pertaining to measles. 3. Resembling measles.

Measure —1. To determine the length, area, volume or weight of an object or a substance. 2. The apparatus used for measuring, *e.g.* a marked tape or a graduated beaker.

Measurement —The result of measuring.

Meat —Flesh.

Meatal —Pertaining to a meatus.

Meatometer —An apparatus for measuring the size of an opening or a passage.

Meatoplasty —Plastic surgery on a meatus or canal.

Meatorrhaphy —Suture of the wound made in meatotomy.

Meatoscope —An instrument for examining a meatus.

Meatoscopy —Inspection of a meatus, especially the meatus of the urethra by meatoscope.

Meatotome —A knife with probe for making an incision into a meatus and to enlarge it.

Meatotomy —To make an incision into a meatus, especially the meatus of the urethra and to enlarge it.

Meatus —An opening or passage, *e.g.* external acoustic meatus—external auditory canal from the tympanic membrane to the external ear and urinary meatus—the external opening of the urethra.

Mechanical —Pertaining to the machines.

Mechanics —The science of machinery.

Mechanism —1. The manner of combination of different parts, processes etc. which perform the same function. 2. The method of a process or the means to achieve a result as the defensive mechanism of the body—the means utilized for the protection of the body. 3. A machine or machine-like structure.

Mechanophobia —Morbid fear of machinery.

Mechanoreceptor —The receptor that is stimulated by mechanical pressure such as pressure from touch or sound.

Mechanotherapy —The use of mechanical apparatus for the exercise of the various parts of the body as a therapeutic measure.

Mecism —Abnormal lengthening of the body.

Mecometer —An instrument for measurement of newborn infants.

Meconiorrhea —Excretion of a large amount of meconium by the newborn infant.

Meconism —Poisoning by opium.

Meconium —The first feces of a newborn infant.

Meconium ileus —Intestinal obstruction in a newborn infant due to impaction of the meconium.

Meconium staining, Meconium show —Excretion of meconium by the fetus while in utero at the time of delivery that occurs with fetal distress.

Mecystasis —Process in which a muscle maintains its original tension although its length is increased.

M.E.D. —Minimal effective dose.

Medi- —A prefix indicating middle.

Media —1. Plural of medium. 2. Tunica media. Middle or muscular coat of an artery.

Mediad —Toward the median line or plane of the body.

Medial —1. Pertaining to middle. 2. Situated nearer the midline of the body or a structure.

Medialis —Medial.

Medialization —An operation to move a part toward the midline.

Median —Pertaining to or situated in the middle or centre.

Median line —An imaginary line joining the two edges of the median plane of the body.

Median plane —A vertical plane through the trunk and head dividing the body into right and left halves.

Medianus —Median.

Mediastinal —Pertaining to the mediastinum.

Mediastinitis —Inflammation of the mediastinum.

Mediastinogram —X-ray film of the mediastinum.

Mediastinography —X-ray examination of the mediastinum.

Mediastinopericarditis —Inflammation of the mediastinum and pericardium.

Mediastinoscope —An endoscope for inspection of the mediastinum through a supra sternal incision.

Mediastinoscopy —Examination of the mediastinum by a special endoscope.

Mediastinotomy —To make an incision into the mediastinum.

Mediastinum —1. A septum or cavity between two principal portions of an organ. 2. The mass of tissues and organs separating the lungs, the sternum in front and the vertebral column behind, containing the heart and its large vessels, trachea, esophagus, thymus, lymph nodes and other structures and tissues. It is divided into anterior, middle, posterior and superior regions.

Mediate —Between two parts or sides.

Mediation —The action of mediating agent.

Mediator —An agent which acts to mediate something.

Medicable —Curable.

Medical —1. Pertaining to the medicine or the study of the science of caring ill persons. 2. Requiring treatment with the medicines and not the surgical treatment.

Medical ethics —Morals of medical science.

Medical jurisprudence —See jurisprudence.

Medical preparations —Medicinal substances prepared ready for use in the form of tablets, capsules, syrup, injections and ointments etc.

Medical science —Science of medicine.

Medical transcriptionist —The person who performs machine transcription of doctor dictated medical reports concerning a patient's health care, which become a part of the patient's permanent medical record.

Medicament —A medicine or remedy.

Medicamentosus —Concerning with the drugs.

Medicate —1. To treat a disease with the drugs. 2. To impregnate with the medicine.

Medicated —Impregnated with a medicine.

Medication —1. Application of medicines externally, internally or parenterally or by other routes in the treatment of a disease. 2. Impregnation with a medicine. 3. A medicine or remedy.

Medicator —An instrument for applying medicines to the deeper parts of the body.

Medicinal —Pertaining to the medicine

Medicinal enema —An enema to which some medicine has been added, given in cases where medicines cannot be administered by mouth.

Medicine —1. A drug or remedy 2. The art and science of the diagnosis, prevention and treatment of diseases and the maintenance of health. 3. Treatment of the diseases with medicines and not by surgery.

Aerospace medicine —The branch of medicine which is concerned with the selection of aviators by studying their pathology and physiology.

Alternative medicine —Other form of therapy as Ayurveda, Homeopathy and Naturopathy etc.

Clinical medicine —1. The study of the disease and its treatment at the bedside. 2. The last two years of a medical course in a medical college.

Community medicine —Medical care of the entire population of the community with the emphasis on preventive medicine.

Dental medicine —Branch of medicine concerned with the treatment of teeth.

Emergency medicine —Branch of medicine which is specially concerned with the seriously ill or suddenly injured persons who require immediate treatment.

Environmental medicine —Branch of medicine which deals with the effects of the environment, including temperature, humidity, water and air pollution, radiation and rapid population growths, etc., on man.

Experimental medicine —Study of a disease through experimentation upon the animals in the laboratory.

Folk medicine —The use of home remedies in the treatment of diseases.

Forensic medicine —See behind. (F)

Geriatric medicine —Medicine concerned with the diseases and health problems of older people, useally those above 65 years of age.

Group medicine —Practice of medicine by a group of various specialists.

Internal medicine —That deals with treatment of the internal organs of the body by non-surgical means.

Legal medicine —Forensic medicine.

Nuclear medicine —The branch of medicine concerned with the use of radioactive substances for diagnosis and treatment of the diseases.

Occupational medicine —Environmental medicine.

Patent medicine —A medicine protected by a trademark, available in the market without doctor's prescription.

Physical medicine —Physiotherapy. Treatment of diseases by physical agents such as heat, cold, light, electricity, manipulation or the mechanical apparatus.

Preclinical medicine —1. Preventive medicine. 2. The first two years of a medical course.

Preventive medicine —The branch of medicine concerned with the prevention of the diseases.

Proprietary medicine —A medicine whose formula is owned exclusively by the manufacturer and which is sold under a registered trademark.

Socialized medicine —Practice of medicine under control of the government which bears the expenses of the treatment by levying taxes or through a national medical insurance program.

Space medicine —Branch of medicine concerned with the physiological diseases occurring due to travelling in the air.

Sports medicine —Field of medicine concerned with the injuries sustained in sports.

Tropical medicine —Medical science concerned with the diseases occurring primarily in the tropical and subtropical regions, especially of the parasites.

Veterinary medicine —Medicine concerned with diseases and health of the animals.

Medicochirurgical —Pertaining to both, medicine and surgery.

Medicolegal —Pertaining to medical jurisprudence.

Medicomechanical —Pertaining to both, medical and mechanical aspects of treating the patients.

Medicopsychology —The relationship of medicine with mental diseases.

Medicosocial —Having both medical and social aspects.

Medicus —The physician.

Medio- —Prefix meaning middle.

Mediocarpal —Pertaining to the middle part of the carpal bone.

Mediodorsal —Pertaining to the median and the dorsal plane.

Mediolateral —Pertaining to the middle and the side of a structure.

Medionecrosis —Necrosis of the tunica media of a blood vessel.

Mediopontine —Pertaining to the center of the pons varolli.

Mediotarsal —Pertaining to the middle part of the tarsal bone.

Mediotrusion —The thrusting of the mandibular condyle toward the midline during movement of the mandible.

Medisect —To cut on the median line of the body or a structure.

Meditation —Contemplating.

Medium —1. An agent or means. 2. The substance used for the cultivation of the microorganisms or cellular tissue. 3. A substance through which the impulses are transmitted.

Clearing medium —The substance which makes the histological specimens transparent.

Contrast medium —Radiopaque substance used in X-ray examination for viewing the internal structures of the body.

Medius —Situated in the middle.

Medulla —1. Inner or central part of an organ as that of the kidney (renal pyramid) or adrenal

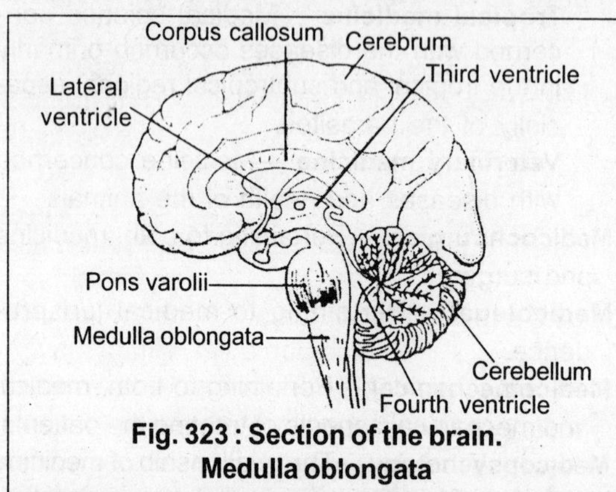

Fig. 323 : Section of the brain. Medulla oblongata

gland (the inner, reddish brown, soft part). 2. The marrow. 3. Medulla oblongata, the part of the brain stem continuous with the pons above and the spinal cord below.

Medullar —Medullary

Medullary —Pertaining to the marrow or medulla.

Medullated —Myelinated. Containing marrow or medulla.

Medullation —The process of covering by a myelin sheath.

Medullectomy —Surgical removal of a part of the medulla oblongata.

Medullitis —Myelitis. Inflammation of the marrow.

Medullization —Abnormal conversion into marrow.

Medulloadrenal —Pertaining to the adrenal medulla.

Medulloarthritis —Inflammation of the marrow of the bone ends.

Medulloblast —An immature cell of the neural tube which may develop into a neuroblast or neuroglial cell.

Medulloblastoma —A malignant tumor of the cerebellum composed of medulloblasts.

Medulloepithelioma —Glioma. Neuroepithelioma. Malignant tumor of the retinal epithelium and of neuroepithelium.

Mega- —Combining form which means great or large or it indicates one million when combined with a unit of measure.

Megabacterium —Macrobacterium.

Megabladder —Megalocystis. Permanent overdistension of the urinary bladder.

Megacalycosis —Dilatation of the renal calices without obstruction.

Megacardia —Cardiomegaly. Enlargement of the heart.

Megacephalia —Megacephaly.

Megacephalic —Macrocephalous.

Megacephalous —Megacephalic.

Megacephaly —Macrocephaly.

Megacoccus —Macrococcus. A large coccus.

Megacolon —Extremely dilated colon.

Megacycle —One million cycles per second.

Megacystis —Megalocystis

Megadactyly, Megadactylia, Megadactylism —Dactylomegaly, macrodactyly, macrodactylia, megalodactyly.

Megadolichocolon —Excessively lengthy and dilated colon.

Megadont —Having very large teeth.

Megadontia —The condition of having very large teeth.

Megadontism —Macrodontia.

Megadose —A dose of a nutrient as that of a vitamin, that is 10 times greater than its recommended daily dose.

Megaesophagus —Extremely dilated esophagus.

Megagamete —Macrogamete.

Megagnathia —Macrognathia.

Megakaryoblast —An immature megakaryocyte.

Megakaryocyte —Giant cell. Large bone marrow cell containing a greatly lobulated nucleus, from which mature blood platelets originate.

Megakaryocytopoiesis —The production of megakaryocytes.

Megakaryocytosis —1. Presence of megakaryocytes in the blood. 2. An increased number of megakaryocytes in the bone marrow.

Megakaryophthisis —Deficiency of megakaryocytes in the bone marrow.

Megalecithal —An egg having a large amount of yolk.

Megalencephaly —Abnormally large size of the brain.

Megalgia —Very severe pain.

Megalo- —A prefix meaning 'of great size.'

Megaloblast —A large, nucleated abnormal red blood cell, as found in the blood in pernicious anemia.

Megalocardia —Cardiomegaly. Hypertrophy of the heart.

Megalocephalia —Macrocephaly.

Megalocephalic —Macrocephalic. Having very large head.

Megalocephaly —Macrocephaly. Very large head.

Megalocheiria —Abnormal largeness of the hands.

Megalocornea —Macrocornea. Congenital abnormal enlargement of the cornea.

Megalocystis —Megabladder. Abnormally enlarged urinary bladder.

Megalocyte —Large red blood cell.

Megalocythemia —Macrocythemia.

Megalocytosis —Macrocythemia.

Megalodactylia —Megalodactyly.

Megalodactylism —Megalodactyly.

Megalodactylous —Having very large fingers or toes.

Megalodactyly—The condition of having very large fingers or toes.

Megalodont —Macrodont.

Megalodontia —Macrodontia.

Megaloencephalic —Having an abnormally large brain.

Megaloencephalon —Macroencephalon.

Megaloencephaly —Abnormal largeness of the brain.

Megaloenteron —Abnormally enlarged intestine.

Megaloesophagus —Enlarged esophagus.

Megalogastria —Gastromegaly. Enlargement of the stomach.

Megaloglossia —Macroglossia. Enlargement of the tongue.

Megalographia —Macrography.

Megalohepatia —Hepatomegaly.

Megalokaryoblast —Megakaryoblast.

Megalokaryocyte —Megakaryocyte.

Megalomania —A psychosis characterized by thinking for oneself as the greatman.

Megalomaniac —The person affected with the psychosis in which he thinks for himself as a greatman.

Megalomelia —Macromelia.

Megalonychosis —Hypertrophy of the nails.

Megalopenis —Macrophallus. Abnormally large penis.

Megalophthalmus —Abnormally large eyes.

Megalopodia —Abnormally large feet.

Megalopsia —Macropsia.

Megaloscope —A large magnifying lens.

Megalosplanchnic —Macrosplanchnic. Having abnormally large viscera.

Megalosplenia —Splenomegaly. Hypertrophy of the spleen.

Megalosyndactylia —Magalosyndactyly.

Megalosyndactyly —A condition of very large and webbed digits.

Megaloureter —Dilatation of the ureter.

Megalourethra —Congenital dilation of the urethra.

-megaly —A suffix which means enlargements.

Meganucleus —Macronucleus.

Megaprosopia —Macroprosopia.

Megaprosopous —Having a large face.

Megarectum —Greatly dilated rectum.

Megasigmoid —Macrosigmoid.

Megasomia —Macrosomia. Macrosomatia.

Megathrombocyte—A large platelet.

Megaureter —Megaloureter.

Megavitamin —A vitamin in excess of the normal daily requirement.

Megavolt —One million volts.

Megophthalmos —Megalophthalmus.

Megrim —Migraine.

Meibomian cyst —Chalazion.

Meibomian gland —Tarsal gland. One of the sebaceous glands situated between the tarsi and the conjunctiva of the eyelids.

Meibomianitis —Inflammation of the meibomian glands.

Meibomitis —Meibomianitis.

Meigs' syndrome —Benign tumor of the ovary associated with ascites and pleural effusion.

Meiogenic —Causing meiosis.

Meiosis —A type of cell division of the germ cells

(spermatozoa or ova) wherein, over two successive cell divisions, each daughter nucleus receives half of the number of chromosomes present in somatic cells. When the fertilization occurs, the nuclei of the sperm and the ovum fuse and produce a zygote with the full chromosome complement.

Meiotic —Pertaining to meiosis.

Mel-, Melo- —Prefixes meaning 1. Limb. 2. Cheek. 3. Honey or sugar. 4. Sheep.

Mel —Honey.

Mela —A probe.

Melagra —Muscular pain in the limbs.

Melalgia —Neuralgia in the limbs.

Melan- —A prefix which means black or melanin.

Melancholia —A mental disorder characterized by marked depression, unhappiness, sadness, brooding and abnormal inhibition of mental and physical activity.

Acute melancholia —In acute melancholia in addition to the usual symptoms there is loss of appetite, emaciation, insomnia and subnormal temperature.

Agitated melancholia —Depression with emotional excitement.

Climacteric melancholia —Melancholia occurring at the menopausal period.

Hypochondriac melancholia —State of extreme hypochondria.

Involutional melancholia —Despondency, feeling of unworthiness, anxiety, insomnia, mental agitation and suicidal tendencies occurring in the late middle age.

Panphobic melancholia —Melancholia characterized by dread of everything.

Recurrent melancholia —Melancholia occurring at more or less regular intervals.

Sexual melancholia —Melancholia associated with fear of impotence, venereal disease or unsatisfied sexual desires.

Simplex melancholia —A mild form of melancholia without delusions or great excitement.

Stuporous melancholia —A form of melancholia in which the patient lies motionless and silent with fixed eyes and indifference to the surroundings.

Suicidal melancholia —Melancholia in which suicidal tendencies arise.

Melancholic —The person affected with melancholia.

Melancholy —Melancholia.

Melanedema —Anthracosis. Melanosis of the lungs, i.e. the deposit of black pigments in the lungs.

Melanemia —Dark color of the blood.

Melanephidrosis —A form of chromhidrosis in which the sweat is black.

Melangeur —An instrument for drawing and diluting blood specimens for examination.

Melanidrosis —Melanephidrosis.

Melaniferous —Containing melanin or other black pigment.

Melanin —The dark pigment giving color to the hair, skin, substantia nigra of the brain and choroid of the eye. It is present in some tumors such as melanoma. It can be prepared chemically and is produced by the exposure to sunlight.

Melanism —Melanosis. Abnormal deposits of melanin in different parts of the body.

Melano- —A prefix meaning black.

Melanoameloblastoma —Melanotic tumor of the neuroectodermal tissue of the embryo.

Melanoblast —A cell originating from the neural crest, which develops into a melanocyte.

Melanoblastoma —A tumor containing melanin.

Melanocarcinoma —Malignant melanoma.

Melanocyte —Melanin-forming cell.

Melanocytoma —A tumor composed of melanocytes.

Melanoderma —Melanopathy. Discoloration of the skin caused by an abnormally increased amount of melanin pigment in the skin.

Melanodermatitis —Dermatitis with excess of melanin deposition in the skin.

Melanoepithelioma —A malignant epithelioma containing melanin.

Melanogen —A colorless substance that can be converted into melanin.

Melanogenemia —The presence of melanin precursors in the blood.

Melanogenesis —Formation of melanin pigment.

Melanoglossia —Glossophytia. Black tongue.

Melanoid —1. Pertaining to the melanin. 2. Resembling melanin.

Melanoleukoderma —Mottled appearance of the skin as of the skin about the neck, seen in syphilis.

Melanoma —A pigmented mole or benign or malignant tumor arising from cell forming melanin.

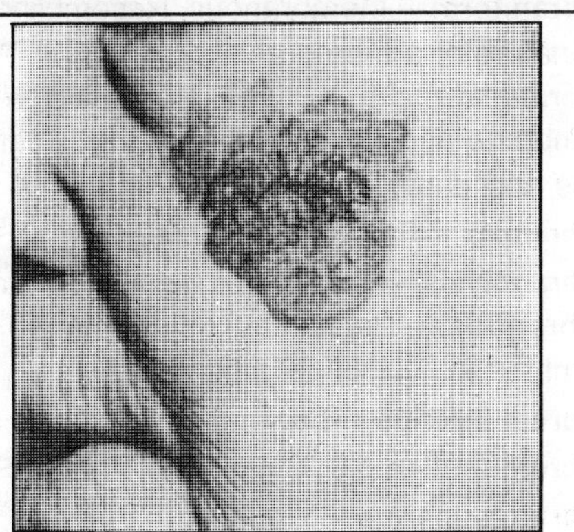

Fig. 324 : Melanoma

Melanomatosis —Formation of numerous melanomas.

Melanonychia —Black pigmentation of the nails.

Melanopathy —Any disease with dark pigmentation of the skin.

Melanophage —A phagocyte containing ingested melanin.

Melanophore —A cell containing dark pigment.

Melanoplakia —Formation of pigmented patches on the tongue and mucous membrane of the mouth.

Melanoprotein —A protein complex containing melanin.

Melanorrhagia, Melanorrhea —Melena. Black faces.

Melanorrhea —Melena.

Melanosarcoma —Sarcoma tumor containing melanin.

Melanoscirrhus—Melanocarcinoma. Cancer containing black pigments.

Melanosis —Abnormal deposition of black pigments in different parts of the body.

Melanosome —Any of the granules within the melanocytes, which produces melanin.

Melanotic —1. Pertaining to melanosis. 2. Black. 3. Characterized by the presence of melanin.

Melanotrichia —Abnormal hyperpigmentation of the hair.

Melanotrichia lingue —Black, hairy tongue.

Melanotrichous —Having black hair.

Melanotroph —A cell of the pituitary gland which produces melanocyte-stimulating hormone.

Melanuria —Excretion of dark urine due to the presence of black pigments.

Melanuric —Pertaining to or suffering from melanuria.

Melasma —Any type of the discoloration of the skin.

Melasma gravidarum —Discoloration of the skin during pregnancy.

Melena —Black feces.

Melenemesis —Vomiting of blackish material.

Melicera, Meliceris —1. Viscid or syrupy. 2. A cyst containing honey-like semifluid material.

Melissophobia —Morbid fear of bees or wasp stings.

Melitagra —Eczema in which honey-comb-like crusts are formed.

Melitemia—Abnormal amount of sugar in the blood.

Melitis —Inflammation of the cheeks.

Melitoptyalism—Glycoptyalism. Saliva containing glucose.

Melituria —Presence of sugar in the urine.

Mellitum —A medicinal preparation with honey as the vehicle for the drug.

Melo-, Mel- —Prefixes meaning extremity.

Melodidymus —An individual with an extra limb.

Melomelia —A malformation in which the fetus has one or more rudimentary limbs attached to the normal limbs.

Melomelus—A fetus with rudimentary limb attached to the normal limb.

Meloncus —A tumor of the cheek.

Melonoplasty —Plastic surgery of the cheek.

Meloplasty —Plastic surgery of the limbs.

Melorheostosis —Occurrence of longitudinal streaks in the long bones, due to hyperostosis.

Melosalgia—Pain in the lower limbs.

Meloschisis —A congenitally cleft cheek.

Melotia—Congenital displacement of the ear on the cheek.

Member—Limb.

Membra —Plural of membrum.

Membrane —A thin, soft layer of the tissue that covers an organ or structure, lines a tube or cavity, divides a space or organ or structure, or separates one part from another.

Basement membrane —A noncellular membrane underlying a layer of epithelial cells for their support.

Bowman's membrane —Anterior limiting membrane of the cornea.

Cell membrane —Plasma membrane, outer layer of the cytoplasm of a cell.

Descemet's membrane —Vitreous membrane. A thin hyaline membrane between the substantia propria and endothelial layer of the cornea.

Diphtheritic membrane —Fibrinous false membrane on the mucous surfaces in diphtheria.

Elastic membrane —The membrane made up largely of elastic connective tissue fibers.

Fetal membrane —A membrane that protects and supports the fetus, and provides it nutrition and respiration.

Interosseous membrane —1. A fibrous membrane in the forearm connecting ulna to the radius. 2. A fibrous membrane in the leg connecting tibia to the fibula.

Mucous membrane —The membrane linning the cavities and canals of the body, which secretes the mucus and keeps them moist.

Nuclear membrane—Either of the two membranes, inner and outer, surrounding the nucleus.

Oral membrane —Buccopharyngeal membrane.

Placental membrane —The membrane of the placenta separating the maternal blood from the fetal blood.

Plasma membrane —Cell membrane.

Semipermeable membrane—Selectively permeable membrane. A membrane through which only water and certain substances in solution can pass.

Serous membrane —Membrane consisting of mesothelium lying on the thin layer of the connective tissue, which lines the closed cavities as peritoneal, pleural and pericardial cavities of the body. It secretes a thin fluid which keeps the surface moist.

Synovial membrane —The inner of the two layers of the joint capsule of a synovial joint, which secretes synovial fluid which fills up the joint cavity.

Tympanic membrane —The membrane separating the tympanic cavity from the external auditory canal.

Virginal membrane —Hymen.

Membranectomy —Surgical removal of a membrane.

Membraniform —Membranous. Resembling or of the nature of a membrane.

Membranocartilaginous —1. Pertaining to both, membrane and the cartilage. 2. Partly cartilaginous and partly membranous.

Membranoid —Resembling a membrane.

Membranolysis —Rupture of a cell membrane.

Membranous —Pertaining to or resembling a membrane.

Membrum inferius —Lower limb.

Membrum muliebre —Clitoris.

Membrum superius —Upper limb.

Membrum virile —Penis.

Memory —Remembrance. Recollection. The mental registration, retention and recall of the past experience, knowledge and ideas.

Anterograde memory —Ability to remember the events occurring in the remote past but inability to remember recent events.

False memory —An inaccurate remembrance of a past event.

Long-term memory —Memory for the events occurring in the distant past.

Retrograde memory —Ability to remember the recent events but inability to remember the events occurring in the past.

Selective memory —Memory for only some of the events which are experienced.

Senile memory —A good memory for remote events but not for recent events, seen in aged persons.

Short-term memory —Memory for events occurring in the immediate past.

Menacme —The period of a woman's life during which menstruation occurs.

Menarchal, Menarcheal, Menarchial —Pertaining to menarche.

Menarche —The time of onset of the menstrual periods which is usually between 11 to 18 years.

Mendelism —The principles of heredity expressed in Mendel's laws.

Mendel's reflex —Occurrence of dorsal flexion of the second to fifth toes upon percussion of the dorsum of the foot.

Menhidrosis, Menidrosis —Vicarious menstruation through the sweat glands.

Meniere's disease —Vertigo, labyrinthine. A disease of the ear characterized by progressive deafness, ringing in the ears, dizziness and feeling of pressure in the ears.

Meningeal —Pertaining to the meninges.

Meningeocortical —Pertaining to the meninges and the cortex of the brain.

Meningeorrhaphy —Suture of the meninges.

Meninges —Plural of meninx. The three membranes covering the brain and the spinal cord, the dura mater (external), arachnoid mater (middle), and pia mater (internal).

Meningioma —A hard, vascular tumor of the dura mater causing erosion and thinning of the skull.

Meningiomatosis —Formation of multiple meningiomas.

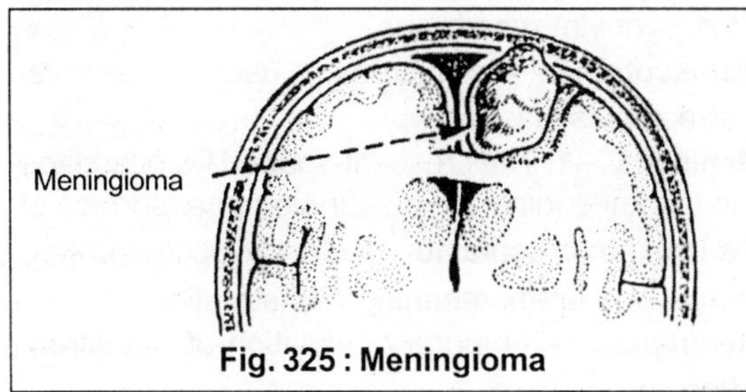

Fig. 325 : Meningioma

Meningism —Appearance of the signs and symptoms of meningitis without actual inflammation of the meninges, due to irritation of the brain and spinal cord.

Meningismus —Meningism.

Meningitic —Pertaining to meningitis.

Meningitis —Inflammation of the meninges.

Acute aseptic meningitis —Acute meningitis without pus formation, running a short course with recovery.

Acute meningitis —Acute inflammation of the meninges caused by bacteria, virus, or other organisms that reach the meninges from other sites of the body such as through trauma via blood or lymph, characterized by irregular fever, severe headache, intolerance to light and sound, contracted pupils, delirium, retraction of head, convulsions and coma.

Basilar meningitis —Inflammation of the meninges at the base of the brain.

Cerebral meningitis —Acute or chronic inflammation of the meninges of the brain.

Cerebrospinal meningitis —Inflammation of the meninges of the brain and the spinal cord.

Meningococcal meningitis —Meningitis due to meningococcus occurring in young children characterized by the onset of sudden rigor, severe headache (occipital), vomiting and convulsion.

Otitic meningitis —Meningitis following otitis media.

Pneumococcal meningitis —Meningitis occurring in young children caused by the pneumococcus characterized by headache, vomiting, fever, neck rigidity and often convulsion followed by coma.

Septicemic meningitis —Meningitis occurring due to septicemia.

Serous meningitis —Meningitis due to serous exudate in the cerebral ventricles and subarachnoid spaces.

Spinal meningitis —Inflammation of the meninges of the spinal cord.

Sterile meningitis —Meningitis occurring in the absence of the infective organisms, usually caused by the injection of contrast medium.

Traumatic meningitis—Meningitis resulting from trauma or injury.

Tuberculous meningitis —Acute meningitis occurring in children due to Mycobacterium tuberculosis, characterized by evening rise of temperature, restlessness and irritability before the onset of acute symptoms.

Meningitophobia —The condition caused by fear of meningitis, simulating meningitis.

Meningo- —A prefix denoting the relationship to the meninges.

Meningoarteritis —Inflammation of the arteries of the meninges.

Meningocele —Protrusion of the meninges through an opening in the skull or the vertebral column.

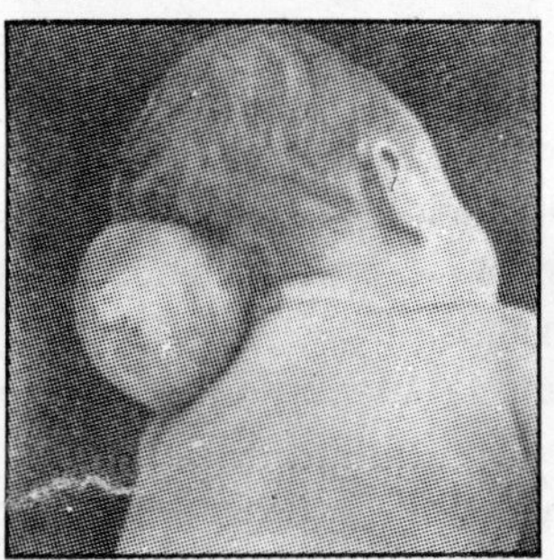

Fig. 326 : Meningocele at the occiput

Meningocerebritis —Meningoencephalitis.

Meningococcemia —Presence of meningococci in the blood.

Meningococci—Plural of meningococcus.

Meningococcidal —Lethal to meningococci.

Meningococcus —A microorganism of Neisseria meningitidis which causes cerebral meningitis.

Meningocortical —Pertaining to the meninges and the cortex of the brain.

Meningocyte —A macrophage of the meninges of the brain.

Meningoencephalitis —Inflammation of the brain and its meninges.

Meningoencephalocele —Protrusion of the brain and the meninges through an opening in the skull.

Meningoencephalomyelitis —Inflammation of the brain, spinal cord and their meninges.

Meningoencephalopathy —Any disease of the meninges and the brain.

Meningogenic —Arising from the meninges.

Meningomalacia —Softening of a membrane.

Meningomyelitis —Inflammation of the spinal cord and the meninges.

Meningomyelocele —Protrusion of the spinal cord and the meninges through an opening in the vertebral column.

Meningomyeloradiculitis —Inflammation of the meninges, spinal cord and the roots of spinal or cranial nerves.

Meningo-osteophlebitis —Periostitis and the inflammation of the veins of a bone.

Meningopathy —Any disease of the meninges.

Meningoradicular —Pertaining to the meninges and the cerebral and spinal nerve roots.

Meningoradiculitis —Inflammation of the meninges and the spinal nerve roots.

Meningorrhachidian —Pertaining to the spinal cord and the meninges.

Meningorrhagia —Hemorrhage from the cerebral or spinal meninges.

Meningorrhea —Effusion of blood between or upon the meninges.

Meningosis —Attachment of some bones by membranes.

Meningotyphoid —Typhoid ferver with symptoms of meningitis.

Meningovascular —Pertaining to the meninges and their blood vessels.

Meninx —Singular of meninges. Any one of the three membranes covering the brain or the spinal cord–the dura mater, arachnoid mater and the pia mater.

Meniscectomy —Excision of the meniscus cartilage of the knee.

Menisci —Plural of meniscus.

Meniscitis —Inflammation of the meniscus or the semilunar cartilage of the knee joint.

Meniscocyte —Sickle cell. A crescent-shaped red blood cell.

Meniscocytosis —Sickle cell anemia. Presence of large numbers of sickle or crescent-shaped red blood cells in the blood.

Meniscosynovial —Pertaining to a meniscus and the synovial membrane.

Meniscotome —An instrument used for removal of a meniscus.

Meniscus —1. The crescent-shaped fibrocartilage in the knee joint. 2. The curved upper surface of a liquid in a container. 3. Concavoconvex lens.

Meno- —A prefix meaning menstruation.

Menolipsis —Temporary cessation of menstruation.

Menometrorrhagia —Menorrhagia. Metrorrhagia. Excessive or irregular menstrual bleeding.

Menopausal —Pertaining to menopause.

Menopause —Cessation of menstruation.

- **Artificial menopause** —Menopause occurring after X-ray irradiation or radium implantation into the uterus.
- **Natural menopause** —Menopause occurring between 35 to 58 years of life.
- **Premature menopause** —Natural menopause occurring before the age of 35 years.
- **Surgical menopause** —Menopause occurring after surgical removal of the ovaries.

Menophania —First appearance of the menstruation at puberty.

Menoplania —Vicarious menstruation. Occurrence of menstruation through the abnormal outlet as through the nose.

Menorrhagia—Excessive bleeding at the time of menstruation.

Menorrhalgia —Dysmenorrhea.

Menorrhea —Menorrhagia.

Menoschesis —Retention of menstruation.

Menostasis —Amenorrhea.

Menostaxis —Prolonged menstrual period.

Menotropins —The combined follicle-stimulating hormone (FSH) and luteinizing hormone (LH) obtained from the urine of the postmenopausal women, used in the treatment of infertility.

Menouria —Menstruation occurring through the urinary bladder.

Menoxenia —Abnormal menstruation.

Menses —Monthly blood flow from the uterus.

Menstrual —Pertaining to the menstruation.

Menstrual cycle —The series of changes occurring in the uterus and ovaries associated with menstruation and the intermenstrual period. The average period of the menstrual cycle is 28 days, which is measured from the beginning of menstruation. It is divided into the following 4 phases—

Proliferative phase—This period starts from the beginning of menstruation in which the endometrium becomes thicker and more vascular. The ovarian follicle matures and secretes estrogen hormone. This phase is terminated by the rupture of follicle and liberation of ovum at about 14 days before the next menstrual period begins.

Secretary phase—During this period the endometrium becomes more thicker. The corpus luteum develops in the ovary and secretes progesterone hormone. This phase lasts for 10-14 days.

Premenstrual phase—This period is of about 2 days before the menstruation begins, during which the endometrium shrinks and the corpus luteum begins involution.

Menstrual period—It is of 4 to 5 days during which bleeding from the uterus occurs with shedding of the endometrium.

Menstruant —One who menstruates.

Menstruate —To cause menstruation.

Menstruation —Menses. Periodic blood flow from the uterus occurring on an average every 28th day in the women from the age of puberty (9 to 17 years) to menopause, lasting for 3 to 7 days. Menstruation ceases during pregnancy, lactation temporarily and after menopause permanently.

Anovulatory menstruation —Menstruation occurring without ovulation from the ovary.

Retrograde menstruation —Backward flow of the menstrual blood through the fallopian tubes into the peritoneal cavity.

Vicarious menstruation —Blood flow from the sites other than the uterus, as from the nose, at the time of menstruation.

Menstruum —A solvent or medium.

Mensual —Monthly.

Mensuration —The process of measuring.

Mental —1. Pertaining to the mind. 2. Pertaining to the chin.

Mental age —The age of a person with regard to mental ability, that is determined by a series of mental tests.

Mental deficiency —Lowered mental capacity.

Mental fog —Semiconsciousness.

Mentalis —Facial muscle of the chin.

Mentality —Mental power or activity.

Mental retardation —Below normal intellectual function.

Mentation —Mental activity.

Menton —Lowest point of the mandibular symphysis.

Mentoplasty —Plastic surgery of the chin.

Mentulagra —Priapism. Painful involuntary erection of the penis.

Mentulate —Having a large penis.

Mentulomania —Habit of masturbation.

Mentum —Genion. The chin.

Mephitic —Emitting foul smell.

Meralgia —Pain in the thigh.

Mercurial—1. Pertaining to mercury. 2. A substance containing mercury.

Mercurialisation —Saturation with the mercury.

Mercurialism —Chronic mercury poisoning characterized by soreness of the gums and loosening of the teeth, foul smell from the mouth, increased salivation, griping pains in the abdomen and diarrhea.

Mercurialized —1. Impregnated or saturated with mercury. 2. Influenced by or treated with mercury.

Mercury — A dense liquid metallic element used in thermometers, barometers, manometers and other scientific instruments. Some salts of mercury are used medicinally.

Meridian —An imaginary line on the surface of a globe or spherical structure, connecting the opposite ends of its axis.

Meridiani —Plural of meridianus.
Meridian of the eye —The circle passing through the anterior and posterior poles of the eye.
Meridional —Pertaining to a meridian.
Meridrosis—Local perspiration.
Merinthophobia —Morbid fear of being tied.
Meristic—Symmetrical at both the sides.
Mero- —A prefix which means a part.
Meroacrania —Congenital absence of a part of the cranium.
Meroblastic —Partially dividing as an ovum of which only a part divides.
Merocele —Femoral hernia.
Merocoxalgia—Pain in the thigh and the hip.
Merocrine —Denoting the secretory cells that remain intact during discharging their secretions as that of the salivary glands and pancreas, etc.
Merodiastolic —Pertaining to a part of the diastole of the heart.
Merogenesis —Multiplication or reproduction by segmentation.
Merogenetic, Merogenic —Pertaining to merogenesis.
Merogony —The development of only a part of an ovum.
Meromelia —Congenital absence of a part of a limb.
Meromicrosomia —Abnormal smallness of some part of the body.
Meronecrosis —Death of the cells.
Meropia —Partial blindness.
Merorhachischisis —Fissure of a portion of the spinal cord.
Merosmia —Inability to perceive certain odors.
Merosystolic —Pertaining to a part of the systole of the heart.
Merotomy —Division into the segments.
Merozoite —One of the organisms formed by multiple fission (schizogony) of a sporozoite within the body of the host as that of plasmodium, the malarial parasite.
Merycism —Rumination. Regurgitation with chewing of the previously swallowed food.
Mes- —A prefix which means middle.
Mesad —Toward the median point or line.
Mesal —In a middle line or plane.
Mesangium —The suspensory structure of the renal glomerulus.
Mesaortitis —Inflammation of the middle coat of the aorta.
Mesaraic, Mesareic —Mesenteric. Pertaining to the mesentery.
Mesarteritis —Inflammation of the tunica media or the middle coat of an artery.
Mesaticephalic —Mesocephalic.
Mesatipellic, Mesatipelvic —Having a pelvis of medium size.
Mesencephalic —Pertaining to the mesencephalon.
Mesencephalitis —Inflammation of the mesencephalon.
Mesencephalon —Primitive midbrain.
Mesencephalotomy—To make an incision into the midbrain.
Mesenchyma, Mesenchyme —The diffuse network of cells forming the embryonic mesoderm.
Mesenchymal —Pertaining to the mesenchyma.
Mesenchymoma —A tumor composed of mesenchymal and fibrous tissue.
Mesenterectomy —Excision of the mesentery.
Mesenteric —Mesaraic. Pertaining to the mesentery.
Mesenteriolum —A small mesentery, as one of an intestinal diverticulum.
Mesenteriopexy —To attach a torn mesentery.
Mesenteriorrhaphy—Mesorrhaphy. Suturing of the mesentery.
Mesenteriplication —Shortening of the mesentery by stitching its folds.
Mesenteritis —Inflammation of the mesentery.
Mesenterium —Mesentery.
Mesenteron —Midgut. Middle part of the embryonic digestive tract.
Mesentery —The peritoneal fold encircling and attaching the small intestine to the posterior abdominal wall.
Mesh —Network, *e.g.* of vessels or nerves.
Mesiad —Mesad.
Mesial —Median.
Mesially —Toward the median line.
Mesio- —A prefix meaning pertaining to or facing the median plane of the mouth.
Mesiobuccal —Pertaining to or formed by the medial and buccal surfaces of a tooth or the medial and buccal surfaces forming a tooth cavity.

Mesiobucco-occlusal —Pertaining to the mesial, buccal and occlusal surfaces of a tooth.

Mesiobuccopulpal—Pertaining to the mesial, buccal and pulpal sides of a tooth cavity.

Mesiocervical—Pertaining to the medial surface of the neck of a tooth.

Mesioclusion —Malocclusion of the lower teeth which come forward from the normal line of occlusion, with the upper teeth.

Mesiodens —An extra small tooth.

Mesiodistal —Pertaining to the mesial and distal surfaces of a tooth.

Mesiogingival —Pertaining to the mesial and the gingival walls of a tooth cavity.

Mesiognathic —Pertaining to the malposition of one or both jaws.

Mesioincisal —Pertaining to mesial and incisal surfaces of a tooth.

Mesiolabial —Pertaining to the mesial and labial surfaces of a tooth or a tooth cavity.

Mesiolingual —Pertaining to the mesial and lingual surfaces of a tooth or dental cavity.

Mesiolinguo-occlusal —Denoting the angle formed by the junction of the mesial, lingual and occlusal surfaces of a bicuspid or molar tooth.

Mesion —Meson. The imaginary plane dividing the body into right and left symmetrical halves.

Mesio-occlusal —Pertaining to the mesial and occlusal surfaces of a tooth or a tooth cavity.

Mesio-occlusion — Mesioclusion.

Mesioplacement —Mesioversion.

Mesiopulpal —Pertaining to the mesial and the pulpal sides of a tooth cavity.

Mesioversion —Backward displacement of a tooth in the dental arch.

Mesiris—Middle part of the iris.

Mesmeric —Pertaining to or induced by hypnotism.

Mesmerism —Hypnotism.

Meso- —A prefix which means 1. middle. 2. pertaining to a mesentery. 3. secondary or partial.

Mesoappendicitis —Inflammation of the mesoappendix.

Mesoappendix —The short mesentery of the vermiform appendix.

Mesoarium —Mesovarium.

Mesobilirubin —A compound formed by reduction of bilirubin.

Mesoblast —Mesoderm in the early stages.

Mesoblastema —The cells composing the mesoblast.

Mesoblastemic —Pertaining to or derived from mesoblastema.

Mesoblastic —Pertaining to the mesoblast.

Mesobronchitis —Inflammation of the middle coat of the bronchi.

Mesocardia —Location of the heart in the midline of the thorax.

Mesocardium —The part of the embryonic mesentery connecting the heart with the central body wall in front and the foregut behind.

Mesocarpal —Mediocarpal.

Mesocecal —Pertaining to the mesocecum.

Mesocecum —The part of the mesentery connecting the cecum to the right iliac fossa.

Mesocephalic —1. Pertaining to the midbrain. 2. Having a medium-sized head.

Mesocephalon —Mesencephalon.

Mesocephalous —Mesocephalic.

Mesocolic —Pertaining to the mesocolon.

Mesocolon —Mesentery connecting the colon with the posterior abdominal wall.

Mesocolopexy —Suspension or fixation of the mesocolon to correct the unnecessary mobility and ptosis.

Mesocoloplication —Plication of the mesocolon in order to limit its mobility.

Mesocord —The portion of the umbilical cord attached to the placenta.

Mesocuneiform —Intermediate cuneiform bone.

Mesoderm —The middle of the three primary germ layers of the embryo lying between the ectoderm and endoderm from which arise the connective tissues, muscles, bones, cartilages, blood and blood vessels, lymphatic vessels and lymphoid organs, pleura, pericardium, peritoneum, kidneys and gonads etc.

Mesodermal —Pertaining to the mesoderm.

Mesodermic —Pertaining to mesoderm.

Mesodiastolic —Pertaining to the middle of the diastole.

Mesodont —Having teeth of medium size.

Mesoduodenal —Pertaining to the mesoduodenum.

Mesoduodenum —Mesentery connecting the duodenum to the abdominal wall.

Mesoenteriolum —Mesenteriolum.

Mesoepididymis —A fold of tunica vaginalis which

sometimes connects the epididymis to the testis.

Mesogaster —Mesogastrium.

Mesogastric —Pertaining to the mesogastrium or the umbilical region.

Mesogastrium —1. The part of the mesentery of the embryo which encloses the primitive stomach. 2. The umbilical region.

Mesoglia —Microglia.

Mesognathic —1. Pertaining to mesognathion. 2. Mesognathous.

Mesognathion —A point in the lateral portion of the intermaxillary bone.

Mesognathous —Having a face with slightly projecting jaw.

Mesohyloma —Tumor of mesothelium.

Mesoileum —Mesentery of the ileum.

Mesojejunum —Mesentery of the jejunum.

Mesolymphocyte —A medium-sized lymphocyte.

Mesomelia —The condition of having abnormally short forearms and lower legs.

Mesomere —Intermediate mesoderm. The part of the mesoderm between epimere and hypomere.

Mesomeric —Pertaining to the middle segment of a limb.

Mesometritis —Myometritis.

Mesometrium —1. Uterine musculature. 2. The part of the broad ligament below the mesovarium.

Mesomorph —The individual having the type of body build in which mesodermal tissues predominate.

Mesomorphic —Pertaining to mesomorph.

Mesomorphy —The condition of being mesomorph.

Meson —Mesion.

Mesonasal —In the middle of the nose.

Mesonephric —Pertaining to the mesonephros.

Mesonephroma —A malignant tumor of the ovary.

Mesoneuritis —Inflammation of a nerve or of its connective tissue without involvement of its sheath.

Meso-ontomorph —A broad, stocky person.

Mesopexy —Mesenteriopexy.

Mesophilic —Growing best at moderate temperature (15°C to 42°C), as do some bacteria.

Mesophlebitis —Inflammation of the middle coat of a vein.

Mesophryon —Mid point of the glabella.

Mesopic —Pertaining to the vision at twilight.

Mesopneumon —Meeting point of the two pleural layers at the hilus of the lung.

Mesoprosopic —Having a face of moderate width.

Mesopulmonum —Mesentery of the !ung.

Mesorchial —Pertaining to mesorchium.

Mesorchium —The part of the primitive mesentery holding the fetal testes in place.

Mesorectum —Mesentery of the rectum.

Mesoropter —Normal position of the eyes with their muscles at rest.

Mesorhachischisis —Merorhachischisis. Fissure of a part of the spinal cord.

Mesorrhaphy —Mesenteriorrhaphy.

Mesorrhine —Having a nose of moderate width.

Mesosalpinx —The portion of the broad ligament above the mesovarium.

Mesoscope —An instrument for viewing objects that are larger than microscopic size but can not be seen distinctly with the naked eyes.

Mesosigmoid —The fold of the peritoneum which attaches the sigmoid flexure to the posterior abdominal wall.

Mesosigmoiditis —Inflammation of the mesosigmoid.

Mesosigmoidopexy —Fixation of the mesosigmoid by surgery.

Mesoskelic —Legs of normal length.

Mesosomatous —An individual of medium height.

Mesosomia —Medium height.

Mesostenium —Mesentery.

Mesosternum —Middle section of the sternum.

Mesosystolic —Midsystolic.

Mesotarsal —Mediotarsal.

Mesotendineum —The connective tissue sheath which attaches a tendon to its fibrous tissue sheath.

Mesotendon —Mesotendineum.

Mesothelia —Plural of mesothelium.

Mesothelial —Pertaining to the mesothelium.

Mesothelioma —A malignant tumor of the mesothelium.

Mesothelium —The layer of cells derived from the mesoderm lining the body cavity of the embryo. In adult, it becomes the epithelium that covers the true serous membranes (peritoneum, pericardium and pleura).

Mesotropic —Turned toward the median plane.

Mesotympanum —The part of the middle ear medial to the tympanic membrane.

Mesovarium —The portion of the peritoneal fold connecting the anterior border of the ovary to the posterior layer of the broad ligament.

Meta- —1. A prefix denoting a change or transformation. 2. A prefix indicating after, subsequent to, behind, or hindmost.

Metabasis —A change in the course of a disease.

Metabiosis —Commensalism.

Metabolic —Pertaining to metabolism.

Metabolic balance —The difference in between the intake and excretion of a specific nutrient, which may be negative when an excess of the nutrient is excreted than taken in or positive when more nutrient is taken than excreted.

Metabolic rate —The rate of utilization of energy which is measured when the individual is fasting and is at complete bed rest. Energy used is calculated from the amount of oxygen used during the test.

Metabolimeter —An apparatus for measuring the metabolic rate.

Metabolin —Metabolite.

Metabolism —The sum of all the physical and chemical processes taking place within an organism. The process by which the food materials are transformed into the body tissues, and energy for growth, repair and general functions of the body (anabolism—constructive metabolism) and the process by which the substances are broken down into the simpler substances (catabolism—destructive metabolism) which are usually excreted.

Basal metabolism —The minimum energy spent for the maintenance of vital processes such as respiration and blood circulation etc. It is measured by means of a calorimeter when the body is at complete rest, 14 to 18 hrs. after eating, and is expressed in calories per hour per square meter of body surface.

Metabolite —Any product of metabolism.

Metabolize —To change the quality of the food substance by metabolic processes.

Metacarpal —A bone of the metacarpus or pertaining to the metacarpus.

Metacarpectomy —Excision of a metacarpal bone.

Metacarpi —Plural of metacarpus.

Metacarpophalangeal —Pertaining to the metacarpus and the phalanges.

Metacarpus —The part of the hand between the wrist and the fingers containing 5 metacarpal bones.

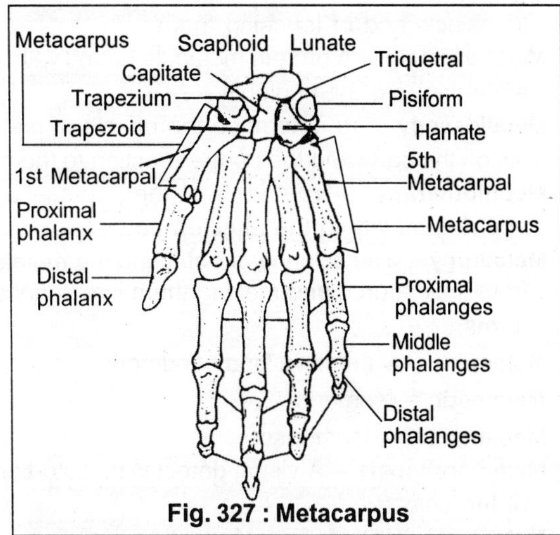

Fig. 327 : Metacarpus

Metacentric —A chromosome containing centromere in its centre.

Metachromasia, Metachromatism —The condition in which different components of the same tissue take different colors in staining. The colors are different from that of the dye solution used.

Metachromatic —Metachromophil. Components of the same tissue taking different colors in staining which are different from that of the dye solution used.

Metachromatism —Metachromasia.

Metachromophil —Not reacting normally to staining.

Metacyesis —Extrauterine pregnancy or ectopic gestation.

Metaicteric —Occurring due to jaundice.

Metainfective —Occurring after an infection.

Metakinesis, Metakinesia —The process of moving apart as that of the chromatids in a chromosome, that move to opposite poles in the anaphase of mitosis.

Metalbumin —A type of mucin present in the ovarian cysts.

Metallesthesia —To recognize the metals by touching them.

Metallic —1. Composed of the metal. 2. Pertaining to the metal. 3. Resembling a metal.

Metalloenzyme —The enzyme containing a metal ion in its structure.

Metalloid —Resembling a metal.

Metallophilia —The property of some tissues of binding certain metal salts.

Metallophobia —Morbid fear of metals and metallic objects and of touching them.

Metalloprotein —A protein molecule bound with a metal ion, *e.g.* hemoglobin.

Metalloscopy —To determine the effects of metals on the body and the body's reaction to them.

Metallotherapy —Treatment of the disease by applying metals to the affected part.

Metallurgy —The science of obtaining the metals from their source and making them into various forms.

Metamere —A primitive body-segment.

Metameric —Isomeric

Metamerism —Isomerism

Metamorphopsia —A visual defect with distortion of the objects.

Metamorphosis —1. Transformation or structural change occurring especially in the developmental stages, as from larva to adult form 2. In pathology, a degenerative change, *e.g.*, transformation of fat by degeneration.

Metamorphotic —Pertaining to metamorphosis.

Metamyelocyte —Juvenile cell.

Metaneutrophil, Metaneutrophile —Not staining normally with neutral dyes.

Metaphase —The second stage of mitotic cell division after prophase and before anaphase, in which the chromosomes, each consisting of two chromatids, are arranged in the equatorial plane of spindle prior to separation.

Metaphrenia —A mental disorder in which a person turns away from the family affairs and takes interest in his own business.

Metaphysial, Metaphyseal —Pertaining to metaphysis.

Metaphysis —The wider part of the long bone btween the shaft and epiphysis.

Metaphysitis —Inflammation of the metaphysis of a bone.

Metaplasia —Conversion of a type of tissue into a type which is abnormal for that tissue, as myeloid metaplasia in which the marrow tissue develops at the sites in which it would not normally occur.

Metaplasis —Metaplasia.

Metaplasm —Deuteroplasm. Reserve material, especially nutritive substance present in the protoplasm of a cell.

Metaplastic —Pertaining to or formed by metaplasia.

Metaplexus— Choroid plexus in the fourth ventricle of the brain.

Metapneumonic —Following pneumonia.

Metapyretic --Postfebrile. After fever.

Metarteriole —Precapillary. A small vessel connecting an arteriole to a venule.

Metarubricyte —A normally staining normoblast.

Metastases —Plural of metastasis.

Metastasis —1. Movement of bacteria or body cells (especially the cancer cells) from one part of the body to another. 2. Transfer of a disease from one organ or part of the body to another, not directly connected with it.

Metastasize —Occurrence of a disease at a distant site from the site of invasion, by metastasis.

Metastatic —Pertaining to the metastasis.

Metasternum —Xiphoid process of the sternum.

Metatarsal—1. Pertaining to the metatarsus. 2. A bone of the metatarsus.

Metatarsalgia —Pain in the metatarsus.

Metatarsectomy—Removal of the metatarsus or a metatarsal bone.

Metatarsophalangeal —Pertaining to the metatarsus and the phalanges of the toes.

Metatarsus —The part of the foot between the ankle and the toes which includes five metatarsal bones.

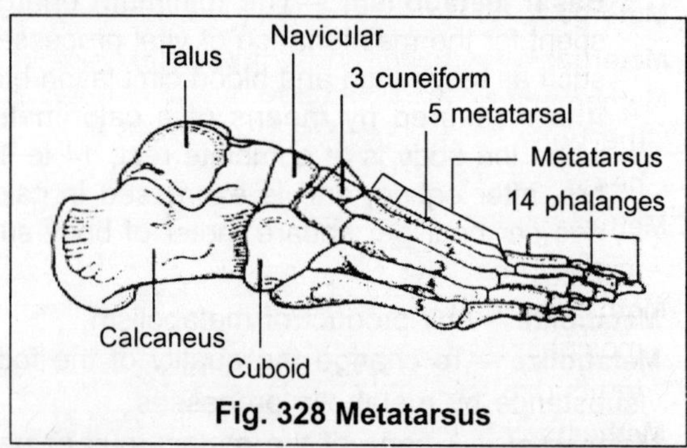

Fig. 328 Metatarsus

Metatarsus primus varus —Turning of the first metatarsal bone toward the midline of the body.

Metatarsus varus —A congenital deformity of the

foot in which the foot is adducted so when the child walks, the toes remain inside.

Metathalamus—The posterior part of the thalamus including the two geniculate bodies.

Metathesis —1. Change of place. 2. Artificial transference of a disease process from one part of the body to another, where it is more easily treated.

Metatrophia —1. Wasting due to malnutrition. 2. A change in the diet.

Metatrophic—Utilizing lifeless organic matter for food.

Metazoa —All multicellular animals.

Metazoon —Singular of metazoa. A single multicellular animal.

Metazoonosis —A zoonosis requiring both, a vertebrate and an invertebrate host for completion of its course.

Metencephalic —Pertaining to metencephalon.

Metencephalon —The anterior part of the hindbrain from which the cerebellum and the pons arise.

Meteorism —Tympanitis. Distention of abdomen by gas in the abdomen or intestines.

Meteoropathy —Disease caused by climatic changes.

Meteorotropic —Pertaining to the diseases which are affected by weather.

Meteorotropism—The effects of climatic conditions on biological events such as the occurrence of diseases, birth and death rate, etc.

Meter —An apparatus for measuring the length, breadth or height of an object in metric system which is equal to 39.371 inches.

Metergasia —Metergasis.

Metergasis —Change in the function.

Methemalbumin —A brownish pigment formed in the body by the combination of albumin with heme.

Methemalbuminemia—Presence of methemalbumin in the blood.

Methemoglobin —A compound formed from hemoglobin by the oxidation of its ferrous iron to ferric iron by injury or toxic substances.

Methemoglobinemia —The presence of methemoglobin in the blood.

Methemoglobinuria —Presence of methemoglobin in the urine.

Method —The manner, procedure or technique.

Methodology —The science of method.

Methomania —Excessive craving for the intoxicating substances.

Methylate —1. To add a methyl group to a substance. 2. A compound of methyl alcohol and base.

Methylation —The process of adding methyl groups to a compound.

Metonymy —A mental disorder in which the patient does not use the appropriate word but utters the word of similar meaning.

Metopagus—Conjoined twins united at the forehead.

Metopic —Pertaining to forehead.

Metopion —Glabella.

Metopism —Persistence of the frontal suture in adult.

Metopodynia —Frontal headache.

Metopopagus —Metopagus.

Metopoplasty —Plastic surgery of the skin or bone of the forehead.

Metoxenous —Heterecious. Living upon two different hosts to complete the life cycle, said of parasites.

Metoxeny —To live upon two different hosts to complete the life cycle.

Metr- —Metra.

Metra- —Combining form meaning the uterus.

Metralgia —Metrodynia. Pain in the uterus.

Metratome —An instrument for incising the uterus.

Metratomy —Hysterotomy.

Metratonia —Uterine atony.

Metratrophia —Atrophy of the uterus.

Metrectasia —Dilatation of the nonpregnant uterus.

Metrectopia —Displacement of the uterus.

Metrelcosis —Ulceration of the uterus.

Metreurynter —An inflatable bag to be inserted in the cervix of the uterus and distended to dilate the cervix.

Metreurysis —Dilatation of the cervix of the uterus by metreurynter.

Metria —Inflammation of the uterus during pregnancy.

Metric —1. Pertaining to the measurement. 2. Having the meter as a basis.

Metric system —A system of weights and measures based upon the meter (39.371 inches) as the unit of measurement, the gram (15.432 grains) as the unit of weight, the liter (1.057 quarts liquid or 0.908 quart dry measure) as the unit of volume.

Metriocephalic —Having a head in well proportion to height.

Metritis —Inflammation of the uterus.

Metro- —A prefix which means pertaining to the uterus.

Metrocarcinoma —Cancer of the uterus.

Metrocele —Hernia of the uterus.

Metrocolpocele —Hernia with prolapse of the uterus into the vagina.

Metrocystosis —Formation of cysts in the uterus.

Metrocyte —Mother cell.

Metrodynamometer —An instrument for measuring the force of uterine contractions.

Metrodynia —Metralgia.

Metrofibroma —Uterine fibroma.

Metroleukorrhea —Leukorrhea originating from the uterus.

Metrolymphangitis —Inflammation of the uterine lymphatic vessels.

Metromalacia —Softening of the uterus.

Metromalacosis —Softening of the uterine tissues.

Metromania —Nymphomania.

Metroparalysis —Paralysis of the uterus.

Metropathia hemorrhagica —Bleeding from the uterus associated with hypertrophy of the mucous membranes of the uterus, and the ovarian cysts.

Metropathic —Pertaining to or caused by uterine disease.

Metropathy —Any disease of the uterus.

Metroperitoneal —Pertaining to the uterus and peritoneum.

Metroperitonitis —Inflammation of the uterus and the peritoneum.

Metrophlebitis —Inflammation of the veins of the uterus.

Metroplasty —Plastic surgery of the uterus.

Metroptosis —Downward displacement or prolapse of the uterus.

Metrorrhagia —Uterine bleeding occurring at any time other than during the menstrual period.

Metrorrhea —Excessive uterine discharge.

Metrorrhexis —Rupture of the uterus.

Metrorthosis —Correction of the displacement of the uterus.

Metrosalpingitis —Inflammation of the uterus and the fallopian tubes.

Metrosalpingography —X-ray of the uterus and the fallopian tubes after an injection of air or a radiopaque substance into them.

Metroscope —Hysteroscope.

Metroscopy —Hysteroscopy.

Metrostaxis —Slight but persistent bleeding from the uterus.

Metrostenosis —Contraction or narrowing of the uterine cavity.

Metrotome —Hysterotome.

Metrotomy —Hysterotomy.

Metrourethrotome —An instrument for incising the urethra and measuring the depth to be incised.

-metry —A suffix which means to measure.

Metryperemia —Congestion of the uterus.

MFT —Minimum fatal dose.

µg. —Microgram.

mg. —Milligram.

MI —Abbreviation for myocardial infarction.

Miasma —Vapor causing disease.

Miasmal —Pertaining to miasma.

Mication —A sudden movement such as blinking of the eyes.

Micra —Plural of micron.

Micracoustic —Rendering faint sound audible.

Micracusia —An auditory illusion in which the sounds appear to be coming from far apart.

Micrencephalia —Abnormal smallness of the brain.

Micrencephalon —1. Cerebellum. 2. Small brain.

Micrencephalous —Having a small brain.

Micrencephaly —Micrencephalia.

Micro-, Micr- —Prefixes denoting small size or indicating one millionth of a unit, as a microgram is one millionth of a gram.

Microabscess —A very small abscess.

Microadenoma —A very small adenoma, as that of the anterior pituitary gland.

Microaerophil —Microaerophilic.

Microaerophile —Microaerophilic.

Microaerophilic—Growing in low concentration of oxygen, said of bacteria.

Microaggregate —Microscopic collection of particles, as of white blood cells, red blood cells and platelets, etc. in the blood.

Microalbuminuria —Excretion of albumin in the urine in minute quantities.

Microanalysis —Chemical analysis of very small quantity of a material.

Microanastomosis—Anastomosis between very small tubular structures.

Microanatomist —Histologist.

Microanatomy —Histology.

Microaneurysm —A microscopic aneurysm.

Microangiitis —Inflammation of very small blood vessels.

Microangiography —Microarteriography. X-ray examination of the finer vessels of an organ after the injection of a contrast medium.

Microangiopathy —Any disease of the small blood vessels, *e.g.*, thrombotic microangiopathy, in which thrombi are formed in the arterioles and the capillaries.

Microangioscopy —Microscopic examination of the blood capillaries.

Microarteriography —Microangiography.

Microatelectasis —A small pulmonary collapse.

Microbalance —A balance for measuring very small weight changes.

Microbe —Microorganism. Germ. Disease–producing bacterium.

Microbial —Microbic. Microbian. Pertaining to the microbes.

Microbian —Microbic. Microbial.

Microbic —Microbial. Microbian.

Microbicidal —Destroying microbe.

Microbicide —An agent which kills the microbes.

Microbiologic —Pertaining to microbiology.

Microbiologist —A specialist in microbiology.

Microbiology —Scientific study of the microorganisms.

Microbiophobia—Microphobia. Morbid fear of the microbes.

Microbiota —Microscopic living organisms of an area.

Microbiotic —Microbial.

Microbism —Infection with microbes.

Microblast —A minute nucleated red blood cell of which the diameter is 5 microns or less.

Microblepharia, Microblephary —Abnormal smallness of the eyelids.

Microblepharism —Microblepharia.

Microblepharon —Microblepharia.

Microblephary —Microblepharia.

Microbodies —Small, spherical bodies of the cytoplasm found in the liver and kidney cells.

Microbrachia —Abnormal smaliness of the arms.

Microbrachius —A fetus with very small arms.

Microburet —A small buret with a capacity of 0.1 to 10 ml.

Microcalcification —Calcification less than 1 mm. in diameter.

Microcalorie —One thousandth part of a calorie, the unit of heat.

Microcardia —Abnormal smallness of the heart.

Microcaulia —Abnormal smallness of the penis.

Microcentrum—Centrosome.

Microcephalia —Microcephaly. Abnormal smallness of the head.

Microcephalic —Having a small head.

Microcephalism—Microcephaly.

Microcephalous—Microcephalic.

Microcephaly —Microcephalia.

Microcheilia—Unusual smallness of the lips.

Microcheiria —Abnormal smallness of the hands.

Microchemistry —Chemistry in which minute quantities of chemical substances and small instruments are used.

Microchiria —Microcheiria.

Microcinematography —Photography of the moving microscopic objects.

Microcirculation —Flow of blood or lymph through very small vessels.

Micrococcus —A very small, spherical microorganism.

Microcolitis —Inflammation of a very small area of the colon that is not visible by endoscope.

Microcolon —Unusually small colon.

Microconidia —Plural of microconidium.

Microconidium —In fungi, the smaller conidium.

Microcoria —Smallness of the pupil.

Microcornea —Unusual smallness of the cornea.

Microcoulomb —One-millionth of a coulomb.

Microcrystalline —Made up of minute crystals.

Microcurie —One-millionth of a curie, the measure of radiation.

Microcyst —A very small cyst.

Microcyte —A very small red blood cell, 5 microns or less in diameter.

Microcythemia —Microcytosis.

Microcytic —Pertaining to the microcytes.

Microcytosis —Presence of excessive numbers of microcytes in the blood.

Microdactylia —Unusual smallness of the fingers or toes.

Microdactylous —Having small fingers or toes.

Microdactyly —Microdactylia.

Microdetermination—Chemical examination of very small quantities of a substance.

Microdissection —Dissection of the tissues or cells under the microscope.

Microdont —Having very small teeth.

Microdontia —Unusual smallness of a tooth or teeth.

Microdontism —Microdontia.

Microdose —Minute dose.

Microelectrophoresis —Electrophoresis of minute quantities of a solution.

Microelements —Elements present in very minute quantities in the body, *e.g.*, magnesium, zinc and manganese etc.

Microembolus —A very small embolus.

Microencephaly —Micrencephaly.

Microenvironment —The environment at the microscopic or cellular level.

Microerythrocyte —Microcyte.

Microevolution —The evolution of bacteria and other microorganisms through mutations.

Microfarad —One millionth of a farad, the microunit of electrical capacity.

Microfauna —Microscopic animal organisms of a special region.

Microfibril —Very small fibril.

Microfilament —Very fine filament in the skeletal muscle, usually 5 nm (5 nanometer) wide and 100 μm (100 micrometer) long.

Microfilaremia —Presence of microfilaria in the blood.

Microfilaria —Prelarval form of filarial worms found in the blood of man suffering from filariasis.

Microfilariae —Plural of microfilaria.

Microflora —Plant organisms of a specific area.

Microgamete —The smaller, more active male gamete which fertilizes the larger less active female gamete.

Microgametocyte —A cell that produces microgametes.

Microgastria —Unusual smallness of the stomach.

Microgenia —Abnormal smallness of the chin.

Microgenitalism —Abnormal smallness of the external genital organs.

Microglia —Non-neural cells forming a part of the adventitial structure of the central nervous system.

Microgliacyte —A precursor of a microglial cell.

Microglioma —A tumor composed of microglial cells.

Microgliosis —Presence of microglia in nervous tissue due to injury.

Microglossia —Abnormal smallness of the tongue.

Micrognathia —Unusual smallness of the jaws, especially the lower jaw.

Micrognathus —The person with small lower jaw.

Microgonioscope —An apparatus for measuring the angles of the anterior chamber of the eye.

Microgram —μg. or mcg. One thousandth of a milligram or one-millionth part of a gram.

Micrograph —1. An apparatus for magnifying minute movements and taking their photographs. 2. Photograph of an object through a microscope.

Micrography —1. Study of the minute objects by using a microscope. 2. To write very small letters.

Microgyria —Smallness of the cerebral gyri.

Microgyrus —A small, malformed gyrus of the brain.

Microhematuria —Hematuria which is detected by finding R.B.C. in the urine on microscopic examination.

Microhepatia —Unusual smallness of the liver.

Microincineration —Determination of the presence of inorganic matter in the tissues by heating a small tissue, by which organic matter is destroyed and the mineral matter is left as ash which can be examined microscopically.

Microincision —An incision made with the help of a microscope.

Microinfarct —A very small infarct due to obstruction in the circulation of blood in the minute arteries.

Microinjection —Injection of the substances into the cells or minute vessels by a micropipette.

Microinjector —An instrument for transfusion of very small amounts of fluids or drugs.

Microinvasion —Extension of malignant cells into the adjacent tissues of a malignant tumor.

Microlentia —Having a very small crystalline lens in the eye.

Microlesion —A very small lesion.

Microleukoblast —Micromyeloblast.

Microliter —One-millionth part of a liter.

Microlith —A very small calculus.

Microlithiasis —Formation of very small calculi in an organ.

Micrology —Science dealing with the microscopic examinations.

Micromanipulation —To perform surgery or dissection or to administer injections etc., under the microscope by means of micromanipulator.

Micromanipulator —An instrument for moving and dissecting etc., the minute specimens under the microscope.

Micromastia —Abnormal smallness of the breasts.

Micromazia —Micromastia.

Micromelia —Abnormal smallness of the limbs.

Micromelus —The person having small limbs.

Micromere —One of the small blastomeres formed by unequal segmentation of a fertilized ovum.

Micromerozoite —A small merozoite.

Micrometastasis —Occurrence of very small tumors as secondary metastasis, which are not detected clinically.

Micrometer —1. μm. One millionth part of a meter or one thousandth part of a millimeter. 2. An instrument for measuring small distances.

Micromethod —Any technique dealing with very small quantities of the material.

Micrometry —Measurement of the microscopic objects by means of micrometer.

Micromicrogram —μμg. One millionth part of a microgram.

Micromicron-μμ —Former name for picometer or 10^{-12} meter.

Micromillimeter —μmm. Millimicron. One-millionth part of a millimeter.

Micromolar —Of the concentration of micromole (μ mol/L) or 10^{-6} mol/L.

Micromole —One millionth of a mole or 10^{-6} mol.

Micromyelia —Abnormal smallness of the spinal cord.

Micromyeloblast —A small, immature myelocyte.

Micromyelolymphocyte —Micromyeloblast.

Micron —Micrometer.

Microneedle —Minute glass needle.

Microneurosurgery —Surgery of the microscopic vessels and structures of the central nervous system under high magnification.

Micronic —Of the size of one micron (micrometer).

Micronize —To pulverize a substance into particles only of a few micra in size.

Micronodular —Having small nodules.

Micronucleus —1. A small nucleus. 2. Nucleolus.

Micronutrient —A nutrient required only in small amounts.

Micronychia —Abnormal smallness of the nails.

Microorganism —Microscopic organism as a bacterium or protozoon. Disease-producing organisms are called as pathogenic microorganisms.

Microparasite —A parasitic microorganism.

Micropathology —Pathology of the diseases caused by microorganisms.

Micropenis —A very small penis.

Microphage, Microphagus —A small phagocyte.

Microphagocyte —A microphage.

Microphakia —Abnormal smallness of the crystalline lens of the eye.

Microphallus —Microcaulia. Micropenis.

Microphobia —Morbid fear of the small things or the germs.

Microphone —An apparatus for picking up the sound to amplify or transmit it.

Microphonia —Weakness of the voice.

Microphonoscope —A stethoscope with a diaphragm attached to it for increasing the intensity of the sound.

Microphony —Microphonia.

Microphotograph —A photograph of very small size.

Microphotography —Photography of the microscopic objects.

Microphthalmia —Abnormal smallness of one or both eyes.

Microphthalmos —Microphthalmia.

Microphthalmus —The person having unusually small eyes.

Microphyte —Any microscopic plant.

Micropia —A visual defect in which the objects are seen smaller in size.

Micropipet —Micropipette.

Micropipette —An extremely small pipette used for measuring small amounts of the fluid substances.

Microplania —Decreased horizontal diameter of red blood cells.

Microplasia —Dwarfism.

Microplethysmography —Detection of the small changes in the size of a part produced by the alteration of blood flow.

Micropodia —Abnormal smallness of the feet.

Microprobe —A very small probe used in microsurgery.

Microprojection —Projection of images of the microscopic objects upon a screen.

Microprosopia —Abnormal smallness of the face.

Micropsia —Micropia.

Micropuncture —A very small puncture of a structure as that of a single cell made with the aid of a microscope.

Micropus—The person having unusually small feet.

Micropyle —An opening in the covering membrane of certain ova for the entrance of the spermatozoon.

Microradiography —Radiography of the microscopic objects in which the X-ray films are enlarged.

Microrefractometer —Refractometer used to study the cells, especially the red blood cells.

Microrespirometer—An apparatus for measuring oxygen consumption in isolated tissues.

Microrhinia —Abnormal smallness of the nose.

Microsaccades —Minute to-and-fro movements of the eyes.

Microscelous —Having short legs.

Microscope —An optical instrument which greatly magnifies the small objects and thus used to obtain very enlarged image of the small objects, which are not visible to the naked eyes.

Binocular microscope —Microscope possessing two eyepieces.

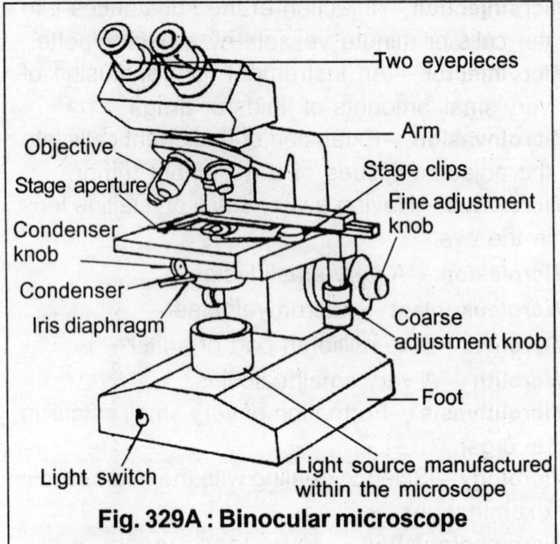

Fig. 329A : Binocular microscope

Compound microscope —Microscope consisting of two or more lenses for observing the minutest particles.

Electron microscope —The microscope in which instead of light, an electron beam forms an image for viewing on a fluorescent screen, or for photography.

Light microscope —The microscope in which the object is viewed under visible light.

Monocular or Simple microscope —The microscope consisting of a single lens; magnifying glass.

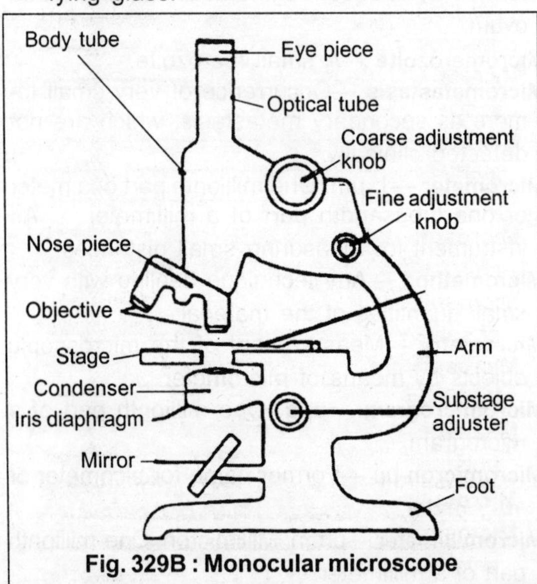

Fig. 329B : Monocular microscope

Operating microscope —A microscope used during operation upon the small vessels, etc. for viewing them.

Ultramicroscope —The microscope which diverges light rays and illuminates the object from side so that the details of the object appear against a dark black background. It is used when the objects are not visible with the ordinary microscope when direct light is used.

Ultraviolet microscope —A microscope using ultraviolet radiations as a light source and having an optical system for transmitting them.

X-ray microscope —A microscope in which X-rays are used to reveal the structure of the objects through which light cannot pass.

Microscopic, Microscopical —1. Pertaining to the microscope. 2.Visible only by using the microscope.

Microscopist —The person expert in using the microscope.

Microscopy —Examination with the microscope.

Microsecond —µs. or µsec. One millionth part of a second.

Microsmatic —Having a poorly developed sense of smell.

Microsome —Ribosome.

Microsomia —Abnormally small size of the body.

Microspectrophotometry —Histological and chemical study of the substances present in the cells such as nucleic acid, on the basis of absorption in the ultraviolet spectrum.

Microspectroscope —Microscope and spectroscope combined.

Microsphere —A minute container used for implantation or injection into the body or blood circulation.

Microspherocyte —Small, spherical red blood cell.

Microspherocytosis —Spherocytosis. Presence of small, spherical red blood cells in the blood.

Microsphygmia —A pulse difficult to palpate by the finger.

Microsphygmy —Microsphyxia. Smallness of the pulse.

Microsphyxia —Microsphygmy.

Microsplanchnia —The condition of being relatively small abdominal cavity.

Microsplanchnic —Having relatively small abdominal cavity.

Microsplenia —Abnormal smallness of the spleen.

Microsporid —A skin eruption distant from the site of infection with Microsporum, which is an expression of the hypersensitivity to that organism.

Microsporidiasis —Infection with a species of the genus microsporum of fungi.

Microsporidiosis —Microsporidiasis.

Microsporosis —Ringworm infection due to microsporum.

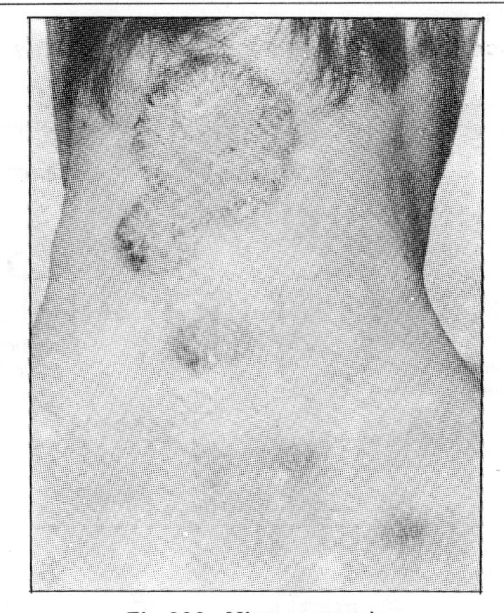

Fig 330 : Microsporosis

Microsporum —A genus of fungi that causes disease of the skin, hair or nails.

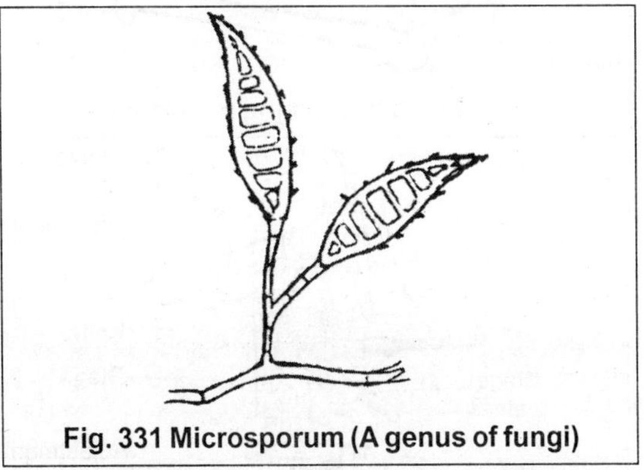

Fig. 331 Microsporum (A genus of fungi)

Microstethophone —Microstethoscope.

Microstethoscope —A very small stethoscope that magnifies the sounds heard.

Microstomia —Unusual smallness of the mouth.

Microstrabismus —Very small and quick movements of the eyes which are not visible.

Microsurgery —Dissection of the minute structures under the microscope.

Microsuture —A very fine suture used in microsurgery.

Microsyringe —A special syringe fitted with a micrometer, used for injecting very small quantities of solutions.

Microthelia —Unusual smallness of the nipples.

Microtia —Abnormal smallness of the pinna of the ear.

Microtome —An instrument for cutting thin sections of the tissues for microscopic study.

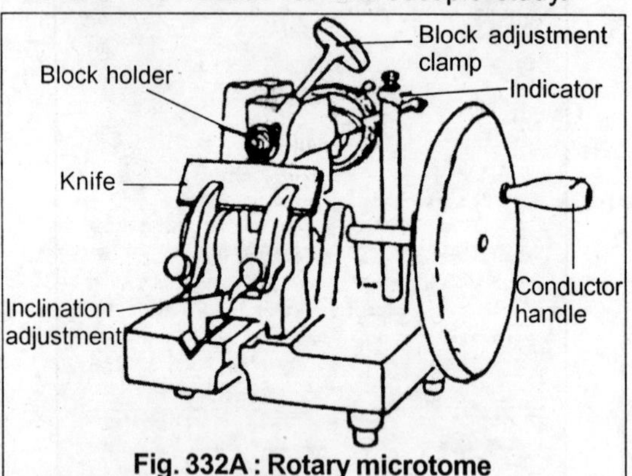

Fig. 332A : Rotary microtome

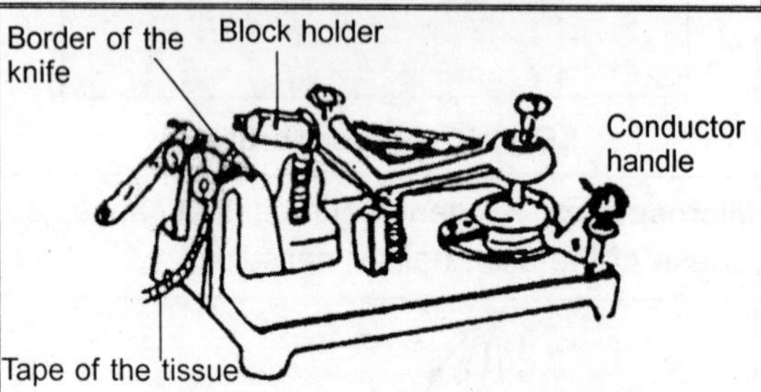

Fig. No. 332B Rocking microtome

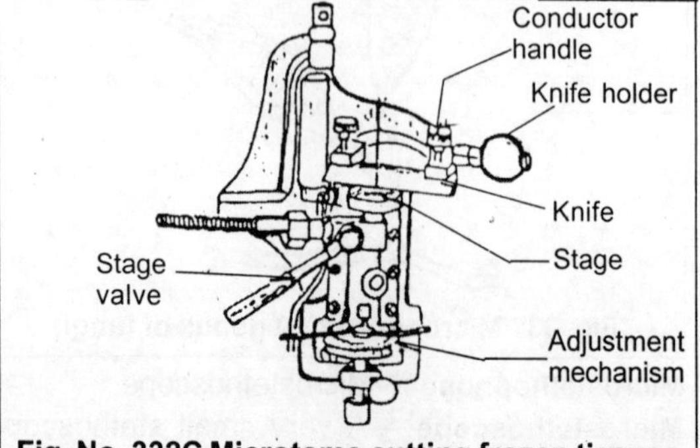

Fig. No. 332C Microtome cutting frozen tissues

Microtomy —The cutting of thin sections.

Microtonometer —An apparatus for determining the oxygen and carbon dioxide concentration in the blood.

Microtrauma —A microscopic injury.

Microtus—The person having very small ears.

Microvascular —Pertaining to very fine blood vessels of the body.

Microvasculature —The finer blood vessels of the body, as the arterioles, capillaries and venules.

Microvesicle —A very small space filled with fluid formed within the epidermis.

Microvilli —Minute projections from the free surface of the cell membranes as are found on the cells of the mucous membranes of the small intestine.

Microvillus —Singular of microvilli.

Microvolt —μv. One millionth part of a volt.

Microwave —A wave between a wavelength of 1 mm. and 30 cm.

Microxycyte —Any fine granular cell.

Microzoon —Microscopic animal.

Micrurgical —Pertaining to procedures performed on minute structures under a microscope.

Micrurgy —Microsurgery.

Miction —Urination.

Micturate —Urinate. To pass the urine.

Micturition —Urination.

MICU —Medical Intensive Care Unit.

MID —Minimum infective dose.

Mid- —A prefix meaning middle.

Midbody —In cell division, a dense stalk of microtubules formed during anaphase of mitosis and connects daughter cells during telophase.

Midbrain —Mesencephalon.

Midcarpal —1. Between the two rows of carpal bones. 2. Pertaining to the middle part of the carpal bone. Mediocarpal.

Midget —Dwarf.

Midgut —Middle portion of the embryonic intestine.

Midmenstrual —Between two menstrual periods.

Midoccipital —Pertaining to the central portion of the occiput.

Midpain —Pain occurring in between two menstruations.

Midplane —Pelvic plane.

Midriff —The diaphragm.

Midsection —Cutting through the middle of a structure.

Midsternal —Pertaining to the middle of the sternum.

Midsternum —The largest middle portion of the sternum.

Midtarsal —Pertaining to the middle of the tarsus.

Midwife —The woman who practices midwifery.

Midwifery —Obstetrics.

Migraine —Unilateral headache occurring in the day, which begins to occur at the sunrise, reaches its maximum at noon and then becoming light gradually and ceases at the evening at sunset.

Migrating —Wandering from one place to another.

Migration —To wander from one place to another.

Migratory —1. Pertaining to the migration. 2. Changing or capable of changing the positions.

Milkulicz —A folded gauz pad used for packing off the internal organs in abdominal operations, and as a sponge in general.

Mikulicz's mask —A frame containing gauze used to cover the mouth and nose during operation.

Mildew —The discoloration or superficial coating on various materials caused by the growth of fungi, occurring in damp conditions.

Milia —Plural of milium.

Miliaria —Prickly heat. Formation of vesicles caused by obstruction of ducts of the sweat glands and retention of sweat. It occurs most commonly in infants, the obese persons and those exposed to excessive heat for prolonged periods, due to excessive clothing and hyperhidrosis.

Miliaria alba —Vesicles containing a milky fluid.

Miliary —Characterized by the presence of small lesions resembling millet seed.

Miliary tubercles —Small gray nodules in the first stage of tuberculosis.

Miliary tuberculosis —Acute, generalized tuberculosis with the presence of minute tubercles in the affected organ.

Milieu —Environment.

Milium —White pinhead-size papule occurring on the face and trunk of the new born child, which disappears within a few weeks.

Milk —1. Secretion of the mammary glands which is the natural food for infants. 2. Any whitish milklike substance, *e.g.* cocconut milk.

Breast milk —Mother's milk.

Condensed milk —The milk which has been partly evaporated, thickened and sweetened with sugar.

Cow's milk —Milk obtained from the cow, which contains less amount of fat.

Evaporated milk —Condensed milk.

Fortified milk —Milk enriched by adding cream, albumin or vitamins.

Milk powder —Dry milk in the form of powder.

Modified milk —Cow's milk so made that its composition closely resembles to that of the human milk.

Mother's milk —Milk obtained from the mammary glands of a woman.

Pasteurized milk —Milk heated to a specified temperature and for a specified length of time, and then cooled rapidly. This process kills the disease-producing bacteria but the taste of the milk is not changed.

Skimmed milk —The milk from which the cream has been removed.

Sour milk —Milk with lactic acid formed by the bacteria Lactobacillus acidophilus.

Sterilized milk —Boiled milk of which the bacteria have been killed.

Milk fever —Fever occurring during puerperal period.

Milking —Removal of the contents of a tubular structure by pressing it with the fingers running along the course of the tube.

Milk leg —Phlegmasia alba dolens White leg. Swollen white leg caused by thrombosis of the iliac or femoral vein.

Milkpox —Variola minor. A mild form of smallpox.

Milk teeth —The first or deciduous teeth.

Milk tumor —The tumor formed by retention of milk in the mammary gland.

Milli- —Prefix used in metric system to denote one thousandth part *e.g.*, milligram which is one thousandth part of a gram.

Milliammeter —Ammeter registering in milliamperes.

Milliamperage —In radiography, the electric current passing in the X-ray tube during an exposure, measured in milliamperes.

Milliampere —ma. mA. One thousandth part of an ampere.

Milliampere minute —A unit of electrical quantity which is equivalent to that delivered by one milliampere in one minute.

Milliampere-seconds —mAs. A unit of radiographic exposure equal to the product of milliamperage and the exposure time in seconds.

Millicoulomb —One thousandth of a coulomb, a unit of electric current.

Milliequivalent —mEq. meq. The concentration of electrolytes in a certain volume of solution expressed as milliequivalent per liter (m Eq./L.). It is calculated by multiplying the milligrams per liter by the valency of the chemical and dividing by the molecular weight of the substance.
mEq./L. = (mg./L.) x valency /molecular weight

Milligram —mg. One thousandth part of a gram.

Milliliter —ml. One thousandth part of a liter.

Millimeter —mm. One thousandth part of a meter.

Millimicrogram —10^{-9} gram. A nanogram. One billionth part of a gram.

Millimicron —mμ. One thousandth part of a micron or one millionth part of a millimeter.

Millimole —mM. One thousandth part of a mole. Symbol is mmol.

Milling —To grind.

Milling-in —A method of adjusting the occlusion of teeth by moving them against each other and by using abrasives between the occluding surfaces.

Millinormal —mN. One thousandth part of the normal concentration of a solution.

Milliosmole —One thousandth part of an osmole (a unit of osmotic pressure).

Millipede —A worm with small body segments, each segment bearing two pairs of legs. They produce venom which causes irritation to the skin.

Millisecond —ms. One thousandth part of a second.

Millivolt —mV. One thousandth part of a volt.

Milphae —The falling out of eyelashes.

Milphosis —Loss of eyebrows or eyelashes.

Milroy's disease —Chronic hereditary edema of the legs.

Mimesis —The term applied to a disease exhibiting the symptoms of another disease.

Mimetic, Mimic —Imitative.

Mimmation —A form of stuttering in which other various letters are spoken in place of "m".

Mimosis —Mimesis.

Min. —Minim, minute.

Mind —Brain function by which one is aware of his surroundings, experiences feelings, have thoughts, desires, emotions, imagination, memory and opinion, puts reasons and make decisions.

Mineral —Inorganic, homogenous solid substance obtained from the earth.

Mineralization —Deposition of minerals in the tissues.

Mineralized —With the deposition of minerals.

Mineralocorticoid —One of the group of corticosteroid hormones of the adrenal cortex which is mainly concerned with the regulation of water and electrolyte balance through its effect on ion transport in epithelial cells of the renal tubules, resulting in retention of sodium in, and loss of potassium from, the body.

Minilaparotomy —To make a small incision in the abdomen for liver biopsy etc.

Minim —One-sixtieth part of a fluid dram or .06 milliliter; drop.

Minimal —Least; smallest.

Minimum —The least quantity.

Minimum lethal dose —Smallest quantity of a substance causing death.

Mini-stroke —Transient ischemic Heart-attack.

Minor —A person of under legal age, *i.e.* below 18 years of age.

Minute volume —The volume of air breathed in a minute.

Mio- —A prefix meaning less or smaller.

Miocardia —Systole.

Miodidymus —A fetus with two heads joined at the occiput.

Miolecithal —Pertaining to an egg with a small amount of yolk.

Mionectic —Pertaining to, or having below normal amount of oxygen, especially the blood.

Mioplasmia —Abnormal lessening of the amount of blood plasma.

Miopragia —Diminution of the functional activity.

Miopus —Conjoined twins with the heads united, with one having a rudimentary face.

Miosis —Abnormal contraction of the pupils.

Miotic —Myotic. Pertaining to, characterized by, or causing contraction of the pupil.

Mirror —Back side polished glass that reflects light rays and thus produces visible images of the objects in front of it.

Dental mirror —Mouth mirror.

Frontal mirror, Head mirror —Circular mirror strapped to the head of the examiner to reflect light into a cavity, used especially in the examination of the nasal cavity or pharynx.

Mouth mirror —A small mirror attached at an angle to a handle, used in dentistry for viewing the teeth.

Mis- —A prefix which means bad, wrong, improper or negative.

Misandry —Aversion to men.

Misanthropia —Aversion to human being.

Misanthropy —Misanthropia.

Miscarriage —Expulsion of the fetus from the uterus after 28th week (6th month) and before the completion of 9th month of pregnancy.

Miscarry —To have miscarriage.

Misce —A direction of the doctor on the prescription for the compounder to mix the ingredients.

Miscegenation —Sexual relations or marriage between the persons of different races.

Miscible —Capable of being mixed.

Misdiagnosis —A wrong or mistaken diagnosis.

Miserable —Pitiable.

Misery —Extreme emotional unhappiness.

Misinterpretation —Wrong interpretation.

Misocainia —Misoneism. Aversion to new ideas.

Misogamy —Aversion to marriage.

Misogynist —The person who hates women.

Misogyny —Aversion to women.

Misologia —Aversion to mental activity.

Misoneism —Misocainia. Aversion to new things or ideas.

Misopedia —Aversion to children.

Misopedy —Misopedia.

Misplaced —Placed in a wrong position.

Mist —Mistura.

Mistura —Mixture.

Mite —A minute animal parasitic on man and domestic animals causing various skin diseases, *e.g.*, itch mite (Sarcoptes scabiei) causing scabies in man and mange mite causing mange in domestic animals.

Mitella —A sling for the arm.

Mithridatism —Immunity to a poison acquired by taking it in gradually increasing amounts.

Miticidal —Destructive to the mites.

Miticide —The substance which kills the mites.

Mitigate —Palliate.

Mitigated —Diminished in severity.

Mitis —Mild.

Mitochondria —Oval or rod shaped cytoplasmic microscopic structures in the cells, which are the source of energy for the cells to function, and play a role in the synthesis of protein, and lipid metabolism.

Mitochondrial —Pertaining to mitochondria.

Mitochondrion —Singular of mitochondria.

Mitogen —A substance that causes cell mitosis.

Mitogenesis —To cause cell mitosis.

Mitogenetic —Pertaining to the factors promoting cell mitosis.

Mitogenic —Causing cell mitosis.

Mitoma, Mitome—A supporting fine network of protoplasm in a cell.

Mitoplasm —The chromatic substance in a cell nucleus.

Mitoplast —A mitochondrion without its outer membrane.

Mitosis —A type of cell division of somatic cells, in which the nucleus in each daughter cell contains the same number of chromosomes as the parent cell with the equal distribution of genes. It is the process by which the body grows and the somatic cells are replaced.

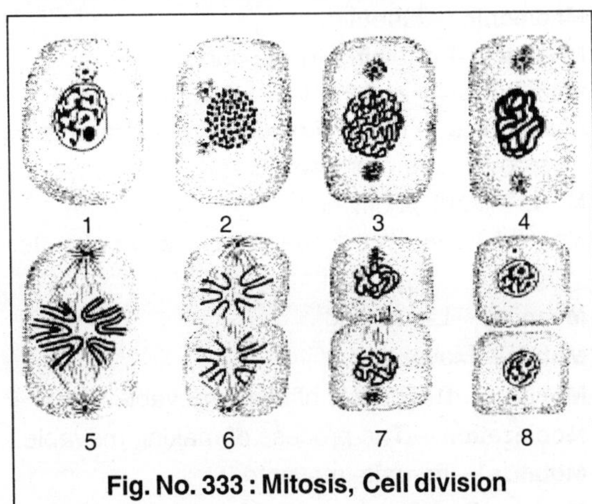

Fig. No. 333 : Mitosis, Cell division

1. Cell 2. Prophase, granular nucleus 3. Prophase, dense ball 4. Prophase, loose ball 5. Metaphase 6. Anaphase 7. Telophase 8. Two cells after division

Mitosome —Chromatin mass in a cellular nucleus.

Mitotic —Pertaining to mitosis.

Mitral—Pertaining to the mitral valve.

Mitral commissurotomy —Surgical treatment of the mitral stenosis.

Mitralization —A straightening of the left border of the heart seen in the X-ray film, due to miral stenosis.

Mitral orifice —Left atrioventricular aperture.

Mitral regurgitation —Backward flow of blood from the left ventricle into the left atrium due to failure of the mitral value to close completely.

Mitral stenosis —Narrowing of the orifice of the mitral valve.

Mitral valve —Bicuspid valve of the heart.

Mittelschmerz —Pain in abdomen occurring midway between the menstrual periods and at the time of ovulation.

Mixoscopia —Sexual satisfaction by seeing others doing sexual intercourse.

Mixture —The combination of two or more drugs.

ml —Milliliter.

M.L.A. —Medical Library Association.

M.L.D. —Minimum lethal dose.

mm. —Millimeter.

mmm. —Millimicron.

Mn. —Chemical symbol for manganese.

Mnemasthenia —Poor memory not due to organic disease.

Mneme —Memory.

Mnemenic —Mnemic.

Mnemic —Pertaining to memory.

Mnemonic —Anything which aids memory.

Mnemonics —The technique or an apparatus for improving the memory.

M. O. —Medical officer.

Moan —To produce a sound expressive of suffering.

Moaning —Lamenting.

Mobile —Movable.

Mobility —The quality of being movable.

Mobilization —The process of making movable.

Mobilize —To make movable.

Modal —Pertaining to most frequent or common.

Modality—1. The quality of occurring most frequently or commonly. 2. A method of using physical therapeutic agent. 3. Any specific sensory stimulus such as taste, touch or vision etc.

Mode —Most frequent or common.

Model —1. Pattern. 2. Perfect ideal.

Modeling —A form of behavior therapy in which the patient acquires skill by observing and imitating the behavior being performed by another individual.

Moderated —Mitigated.

Moderator—Diminishing severity.

Modification —The result of changing the form or character of an object or a structure.

Modifier —That which alters or limits.

Modioli—Plural of modiolus.

Modiolus —Axial part or columella of the chochlea.

Modulating —The person changing his facial expression to show an emotion which is not being experienced, to deceive.

Modulation —Alteration in function or position of something in response to a stimulus or due to alteration in the chemical or physical environment.

Modulator —That which regulates or adjusts.

Modus—A method or mode.

Modus operandi —Method of performing an act.

Mogiarthria —Speech defect due to muscular incoordination.

Mogilalia —Stuttering or stammering.

Mogiphonia —Difficulty in emitting vocal sounds.

Moiety —A part of something which can be divided.

Moist —Damp, slightly wet.

Moisture —Dampness, slightly wetness.

Molal —Containing one mole of solute per kilogram of solvent.

Molality —The number of moles of a solute per kilogram of solvent.

Molar —1. A grinding tooth. 2. Pertaining to a mass, not molecular. 3. Pertaining to a mole.

Molariform —Resembling a molar teeth.

Molarity —The number of moles of a solute per liter of solution.

Molar solution —The solution in which there is one mole of the solute dissolved in each liter of the solution.

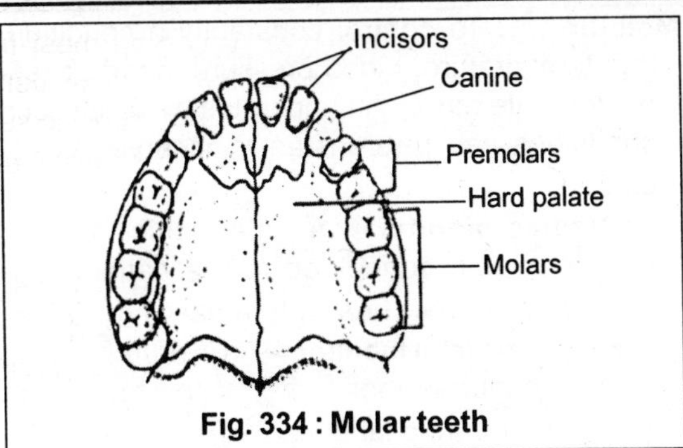

Fig. 334 : Molar teeth

Molasses —The thick syrup drained from the sugar in the process of refining.

Mold —1. Any of a group of parasitic and saprophytic fungi causing a cottony growth on the decaying vegetable matter, also the growth produced by such fungi. 2. A form in which an object is shaped, or a cast. 3. To shape a mass as a pill. 4. In dentistry, the shape of an artificial tooth.

Molding —Shaping of the fetal head and adapting it to the birth canal during labor.

Mole —1. A congenital pigmented spot elevated from the surface of the skin. 2. A quantity of a chemical compound whose weight in grams equals its molecular weight. 3. A fleshy mass formed in the uterus by degeneration or abortive development of an ovum.

Blood mole —A mass of blood, piece of placenta and membranes etc. retained in the uterus after abortion.

Carneous mole —Fleshy mole. Mole of blood which appear like flesh when retained in the uterus for some time.

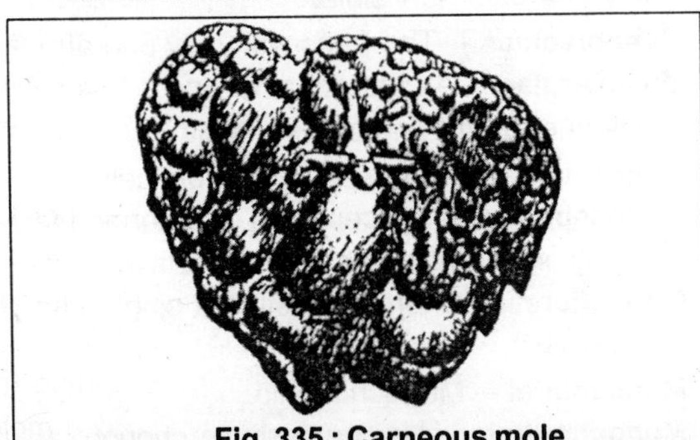
Fig. 335 : Carneous mole

Hydatid mole, Hydatidiform mole —The mole formed by cystic degeneration of the chorionic villi, in which the cysts appear like grapes.

Pigmented mole —Nevus pigmentosus.

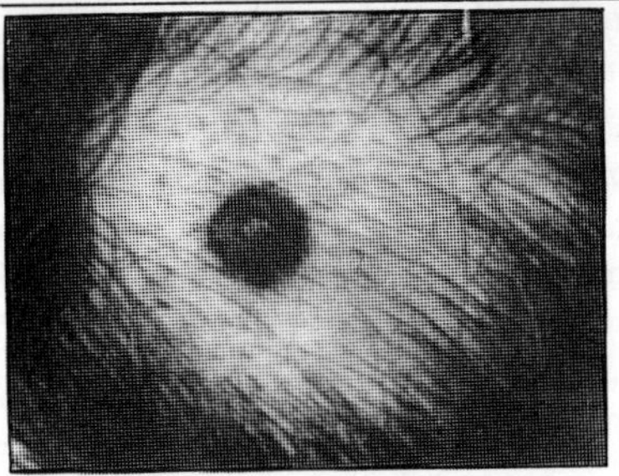
Fig. 336 : Mole on the scalp

Vascular mole —Hemangioma.

Molecular —Pertaining to a molecule.

Molecule—The smallest part of a substance which cannot be divided further.

Molilalia —Mogilalia.

Molimen —An effort to establish any normal function of the body.

Molimina —Plural of molimen.

Mollities —Abnormal softening of a part of the body.

Mollities ossium —Osteomalacia. Softening of the bones.

Moll's glands —Ciliary glands.

Mollusc—Mollusk.

Molluscum —Any skin disease characterized by the formation of soft rounded tumors on the skin.

Mollusk —Common name for the animals of the phylum mollusca.

Molt —To shed the skin, cuticle or the feathers.

Mol.wt. —Molecular weight.

Molysmophobia —Mysophobia. Morbid fear of contamination or infection.

Monad —1. A univalent element. 2. A unicellular organism. 3. In meiosis, one of the four components of a tetrad.

Monarthric—Pertaining to, or affecting a single joint.

Monarthritis —Inflammation of a single joint.

Monarticular —Monarthric.

Monaster —Single star-shaped figure formed at the end of the prophase in mitosis.

Monathetosis —Irregular, twisting, snakelike movements occurring in only one limb of the body.

Monatomic —1. Pertaining to or containing a single atom. 2. Univalent.

Monaural —Pertaining to an ear.

Monaxon—A neuron with one axon.

Monaxonic —A neuron with one axon.

Mondonesi's reflex —Bulbomimic reflex; facial reflex.

Mondor's disease —Thrombosis and sclerosis of a subcutaneous vein in the breast, characterized by long, firm, tender cordlike structure extending from the breast up into the axilla or down toward the epigastrium. The condition may occur after trauma, or spontaneously.

Monecious —Monoecious.

Monesthetic —Pertaining to or affecting a single sense.

Mongolism —Down's syndrome.

Mongoloid —1. Pertaining to Mongols. 2. Characterized by mongolism.

Monilethrix —A genetic defect which usually appears by the second month of life, in which hairs become beaded and very brittle.

Monilia —Fungus candida.

Monilial —Pertaining to or caused by fungus monilia (candida).

Moniliasis —Candidiasis. Infection with monilia (Candida).

Moniliform —Resembling a necklace or string of beads.

Moniliid —A skin eruption occurring in another part of the body, due to hypersensitivity to a monilia infection.

Moniliosis —Moniliasis.

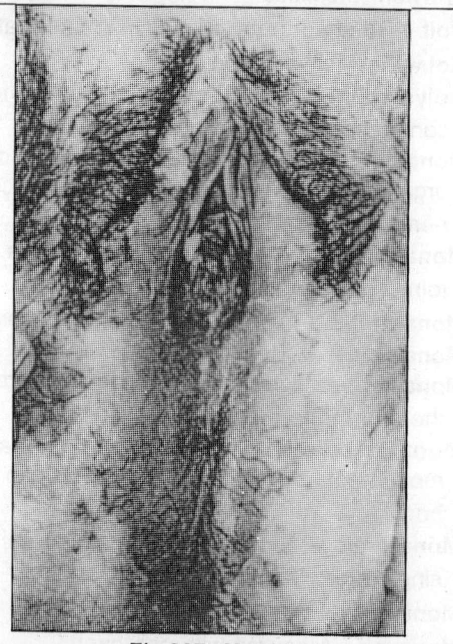

Fig 337 : Moniliasis

Monitor —1. To control constantly a condition, *e.g.* temperature, blood pressure, heart or respiratory rate etc. 2. An apparatus by which such conditions can be constantly observed or recorded.

Cardiac monitor —An electronic monitor, which when connected to the patient, signals each heart beat with a flashing light.

Electronic fetal monitor —An instrument used for continuous monitoring of the fetal heart before or during labor.

Monitoring —1. Controlling. 2. Observing or recording.

Mono-, Mon- —Prefixes denoting one or single.

Monoamelia —Absence of one limb.

Monoamine —A molecule containing one amino group, *e.g.*, serotonin, dopamine and norepinephrine.

Monoamniotic —Developing within a single amniotic cavity.

Monoanesthesia —Anesthesia of a single organ.

Monobacterial —Pertaining to a single species of bacteria.

Monobasic —Having only one replaceable hydrogen atom.

Monoblast —The cell which gives rise to a monocyte.

Monoblastoma —A tumor containing both, monoblasts and monocytes.

Monoblepsia —1. The condition in which an object is more distinctly visible when only one eye is used. 2. A type of colorblindness in which only one color is visible.

Monobrachius —The fetus with only one arm.

Monocardian —An individual having a heart with only one atrium and one ventricle.

Monocelled —Composed of a single cell.

Monocephalus —Syncephalus. A deformed fetus having one head but all the rest parts duplicated.

Monochorea —Chorea affecting a single part or extremity.

Monochorial —Monochorionic.

Monochorionic —Having a single chorion, as in the case of identical twins.

Monochroic —Monochromatic.

Monochromasia —Achromatopsia.

Monochromasy —Colorblindness in which all colors appear to be of gray color.

Monochromat —The person affected by monochromatism.

Monochromatic —1. Monochromat. 2. Having only one color.

Monochromatism —Complete color blindness.

Monochromatophil —Stainable with only one type of stain.

Monochromatophile—Monochromatophil.

Monochromic —Monochromatic.

Monochromophil —Monochromatophil.

Monochromophile —Monochromatophil.

Monoclonal —Arising from a single cell.

Monococcus —A form of coccus existing singly instead of existing in a group or chain.

Monocontaminated —Infected with a single species of organisms.

Monocranius —Syncephalus.

Monocrotic —Indicating a single pulse wave with no notches in it.

Monocrotism —The state in which the pulse is monocrotic.

Monocular —1. Pertaining to or affecting only one eye. 2. Having only one eyepiece as in a monocular microscope.

Monocyclic —Concerning with one cycle.

Monocyesis —Pregnancy with a single fetus.

Monocyte —A large mononuclear white blood cell containing an ovoid or kidney-shaped nucleus and more protoplasm.

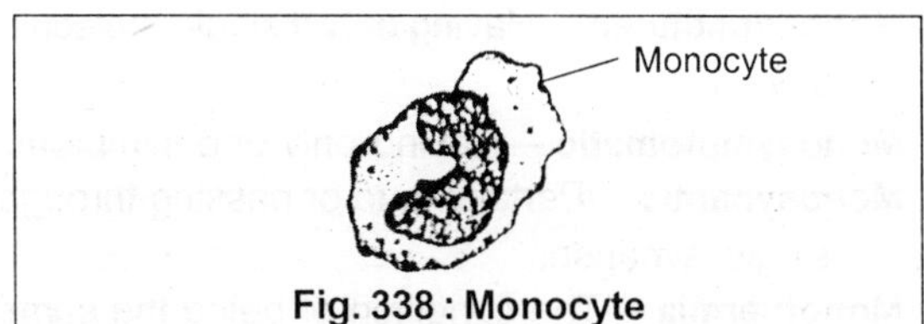

Fig. 338 : Monocyte

Monocytic —Pertaining to or resembling monocyte.

Monocytopenia —Deficiency of monocytes in the blood.

Monocytosis —Excessive number of monocytes in the blood.

Monodactylism —The condition of having only one digit on a hand or foot.

Monodactyly —The presence of only one digit on a hand or foot.

Monodermoma —A tumor developing from one germ layer only.

Monodiplopia —Double vision in one eye only.

Monodromia —Occurrence of conduction in the muscles or nerves in one direction only.

Monoecious —An individual having reproductive organs of both male and female sexes.

Monogamy —To marry to only one person at a time.

Monogenesis —Production of offspring of only one sex.

Monogenetic —Monoxenous. Pertaining to monogenesis.

Monogenic —Pertaining to a hereditary disease controlled by alleles at a single genetic locus.

Monogenous —Asexually produced.

Monogerminal —Produced from a single ovum.

Monogony —Asexual reproduction.

Monograph —A treatise on a single subject.

Monohydrated —United with only one molecule of water.

Monohydric —Having a single replaceable hydrogen atom.

Monoideism —Preoccupation with a single idea or subject, a mild form of monomania.

Monoinfection —Infection with a single species of microorganisms.

Monolayer —Having a single layer.

Monolocular —Unilocular. Having only one cell or cavity.

Monomania —Mania for a single object.

Monomaniac —An individual afflicted with monomania.

Monomastigote —Having only one flagellum.

Monomelic —Affecting a single limb.

Monomer —Any molecule that can be bound to similar molecule to form a polymer.

Monomeric —Pertaining to, consisting of or affecting a single piece of the body.

Monometallic —Containing a single atom of a metal in the formula.

Monomicrobic —Pertaining to the organisms of a single species.

Monomolecular —Pertaining to a single molecule.

Monomorphic —Maintaining the same form throughout every stage of development.

Monomphalus —Twins joined at the umbilicus.

Monomyoplegia —Paralysis of only one muscle.

Monomyositis —Inflammation of only one muscle.

Mononeural —Supplied by or pertaining to a single nerve.

Mononeuric —Mononeural.

Mononeuritis —Inflammation of a single nerve.

Mononeuropathy —Disease of a single nerve.

Mononoea —Fixation of mind on a single subject.

Mononuclear—Uninuclear. Having one nucleus.

Mononucleosis —Presence of a large number of mononuclear leukocytes in the blood.

Monoparesis —Paresis of a single part of the body.

Monoparesthesia —Paresthesia of a single part of the body.

Monopathic —Pertaining to monopathy.

Monopathy —A disease affecting a single part of the body.

Monopenia —Monocytopenia.

Monophagia —1. Eating only one meal a day. 2. Appetite for only one kind of food.

Monophagism —Monophagia.

Monophasia —Inability to speak anything except one word or phrase repeatedly.

Monophasic —Unable to speak anything except one word or phrase repeatedly.

Monophobia —Morbid fear of being alone.

Monophthalmos —Condition of having one eye only.

Monophthalmus —A cyclops. A fetus with one eye only.

Monophyletic—Descended from a common ancestor or originating from a single source.

Monophyletism —A concept that all the blood cells are derived from a single stem cell.

Monophyodont —Having a single set of teeth which are permanent.

Monoplasmatic —Made up of a single substance or tissue.

Monoplast —A unicellular organism that does not change during its life cycle.

Monoplastic —Pertaining to monoplast.

Monoplegia —Paralysis of one limb.

Monoploid —Haploid.

Monopodia —The condition of having only one foot.

Monopoiesis —The generation of monocytes.

Monopolar —Unipolar.

Monops —Cyclops.

Monopsychosis —Monomania.

Monopus —An individual having only one foot.

Monorchia —Monorchism.

Monorchid —The person having only one testis.

Monorchidism, Monorchism —The condition of having only one testis or one descended testis.

Monorhinic —1. Having a single nose as in conjoined twins. 2. Having a single nasal cavity.

Monosaccharide —A simple sugar that cannot be decomposed by hydrolysis, such as fructose, galactose or glucose.

Monoscelous —Having only one leg.

Monoscenism —Morbid concentration on some past experience.

Monosome —An accessory chromosome or unpaired sex chromosome.

Monosomia —A condition in which there are two heads and a single trunk in conjoined twins.

Monosomic —Pertaining to monosomy.

Monosomy —Missing of one member of a pair of chromosomes.

Monospasm —Spasm of a single limb or part.

Monospecific —Affecting a particular kind of cell or tissue or reacting with a single antigen.

Monospermy —Fertilization by a single spermatozoon entering an ovum.

Monostotic —Pertaining to or affecting a single bone.

Monostratal —Consisting of a single layer.

Monosubstituted —Having only a single molecule replaced.

Monosymptomatic —Having only one symptom.

Monosynaptic —Pertaining to or passing through a single synapse.

Monothermia —The condition of being the same body temperature throughout the day.

Monotocous —Producing a single offspring at a birth.

Monotricha —Bacteria having a single flagellum at one pole.

Monotrichous —Pertaining to or having a single flagellum.

Monovalence, Monovalency —Univalence.

Monovalent —Univalent. Having a single valency.

Monovular —Uniovular.

Monoxenic —Associated with a single known species of microorganisms.

Monoxenous—Requiring only one host to complete the life cycle, said of parasites.

Monoxide—An oxide having only one atom of oxygen in the molecule.

Monozygotic—Derived from a single fertilized ovum (zygote), said of identical twins.

Mons —A prominence.

Mons pubis —A rounded fleshy prominence over the pubic symphysis in female which is covered with hair after puberty.

Monster —A grossly deformed fetus or infant.

Monstriparity —To give birth to a deformed infant.

Monstrosity —1. Great congenital deformity. 2. Congenitally deformed infant or child.

Montgomery's glands —Small tubercles around the nipple of the breast that enlarge during pregnancy and lactation.

Monticuli —Plural of monticulus.

Monticulus —A small eminence.

Mood —The emotional state.

Morbid —1. Unhealthy or diseased. 2. Pertaining to a disease.

Morbidity —1. The condition of being diseased. 2. Sick rate, the ratio of sick persons to healthy persons in a community.

Morbidity rate —Number of sick persons suffering from a specific disease per year per 1000 of population.

Morbific —Pathogenic. Causing disease.

Morbigenous —Pathogenic.

Morbility —Morbidity.

Morbilli—Measles.

Morbilliform —Like measles.

Morbilous—Pertaining to measles.

Morbus —Disease.

Morcellation, Morcellement —The division of a tumor, fetus or an organ into pieces followed by their removal.

Mordant —A substance that fixes a stain or dye, as phenol.

Morgue —Mortuary.

Moria —1. Dementia. 2. Foolishness.

Moribund —A dying state.

Morioplasty —Plastic surgery to replace the lost portions of the body through accident or disease.

Morning sickness—Nausea and vomiting occurring in the morning in some women during the first few months of pregnancy.

Moron —A feebleminded person.

Moronity —Feeblemindedness.

Moro reflex —A reflex seen in infants in which they flex and extend the arms followed by an embracing motion of the arms, in response to a stimulus, such as that produced by suddenly striking the bed on which the infant rests.

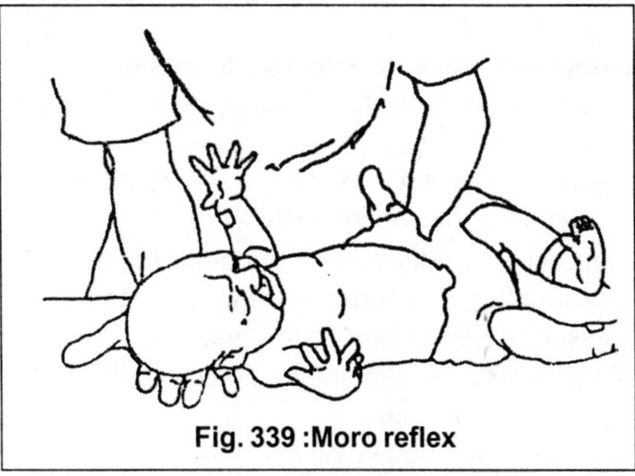

Fig. 339 :Moro reflex

Morphea —Sclerosis of the skin.

Morphia —Morphine.

Morphine —The principal alkaloid of opium.

Morphinism —Condition caused by habitual or excessive use of morphine.

Morphinomania, Morphiomania —1. Excessive desire for morphine. 2. Insanity resulting from use of morphine.

Morpho-, Morph- —A prefix meaning form, shape, structure.

Morphogenesis —Development of the shape of the body, its parts or organs.

Morphogenetic —Forming the shape of the body, its parts or organs.

Morphography —The classification of organisms on the basis of form and structure.

Morphologic —Morphological.

Morphological —Pertaining to the science of the forms and structure of organisms.

Morphology —Science of the form and structure of the organisms.

Morphometric —Pertaining to morphometry.

Morphometry —The measurement of the form of organisms or their parts.

Morphon —Any one of the structures forming an organism, such as a cell.

Morphosis —The formation of a part or organ of the body.

Mors —Death.

Morsal —Biting and chewing as the occlusal surfaces of the teeth.

Mors putativa —Apparent death.

Mors subita —Sudden death.

Morsulus —Troche, lozenge.

Morsus —The fimbriae at the ovarian end of the fallopian tube.

Mortal —1. Fatal. 2. Ending into death.

Mortality —1. Quality of being mortal. 2. Death rate.

Mortar —A vessel in which the drugs are beaten, crushed or pulverized with a pestle.

Mortician —Undertaker of the dead bodies.

Mortification —Gangrene; necrosis. Death of a tissue, organ or part of the body.

Mortinatality —Natimortality. Ratio of stillbirths to general birth rate.

Mortise joint —Ankle joint.

Mortuary —1. Morgue. The place for keeping dead bodies for identification and before burial. 2. Pertaining to dead or to death.

Morula —Solid mass of cells formed by the cleavage of a fertilized ovum.

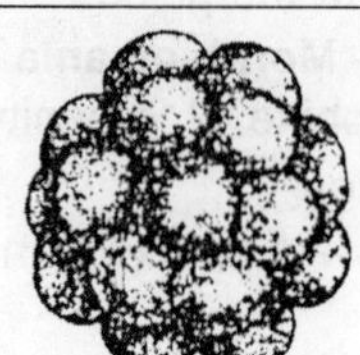

Fig. 340 : Morula

Morulation —The formation of a morula.

Moruloid —Resembling a morula.

Mosaic —A pattern made of many small pieces fitted together.

Mosaic bone —Bone appearing as small pieces fitted together, as in Paget's disease.

Mosaicism —Presence of cells of two different genetic materials in the same individual.

MOsm —Milliosmole.

Mosquito —Blood sucking and disease-transmitting insect as Anopheles mosquito that transmits malaria.

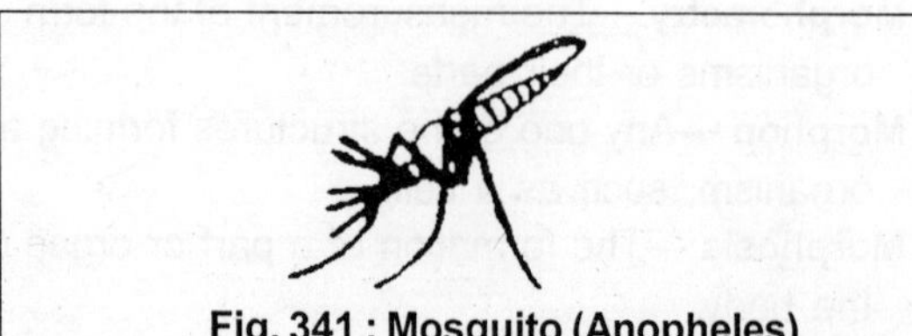

Fig. 341 : Mosquito (Anopheles)

Mosquitocide —Killing mosquitoes or their larvae.

Mosquito forceps —A very small, delicate and pointed forceps for checking the bleeding.

Mote —A small particle or spot.

Mother —1. Female parent. 2. A structure that gives rise to others.

Mother cell —A cell that by division gives rise to similar cells.

Mother's mark —A birth mark.

Motile —Able to move spontaneously.

Motilin —A hormone secreted by the mucous membrane of the small intestine, which stimulates the gastrointestinal muscles to contract, thus promoting the peristaltic movements.

Motility —Ability to move spontaneously.

Motion —1. Movement. 2. Act of emptying the bowels. 3. Stool.

Motion sickness —Nausea, vomiting and vertigo caused by travelling in the car, aeroplane and ships etc.

Motivation —1. To change the will. 2. To make movements.

Motive —1. That which changes the will. 2. Causing movements.

Motofacient —Producing motion.

Motoneuron —Motor neuron.

Motor —A nerve, muscle or part of the body causing movements.

Motor aphasia —The condition in which the patient understands but cannot express in words.

Motor area —Posterior part of the frontal lobe of the cerebrum, anterior to the central sulcus, from which impulses for voluntary movements arise.

Motor endplate —Myoneural junction. The flatly expanded end of a motor nerve fiber where it connects with a muscle fiber.

Motorial —Concerning motion or a motor center.

Motoricity —Capability of movement.

Motorium —Motor center of body or organism.

Motorius —Any motor nerve.

Motor meter —An apparatus for determining the amount, force and rapidity of movement.

Motor nerve —A nerve composed entirely of motor fibers.

Motor neuron —1. The neuron supplying a muscle tissue. 2. A neuron that carries impulses causing muscle contraction.

Motorpathy —Disease of movement.

Motor sense —The kinesthetic sense.

Motor speech area —Area in the cerebral hemisphere controlling the movements of tongue, lips and vocal cords. In right-handed person, it is situated in the left hemisphere and in the left-handed person, in the right hemisphere.

Mottled —Discolored.

Mottling —The condition of being discolored.

Moulage —1. A waxy or plastic model of some part of the body. 2. Molding of such models.

Mould —Mold

Mounding —Myoedema. Rising of a lump as in a wasting muscle following struck a firm blow.

Mount —To prepare slides of the specimens for the microscopic examination.

Mountain sickness —A condition resulting from ascents to great heights, usually over 10,000 feet as in climbing mountain or flying rapidly, due to deficient oxygen supply to the blood. It is characterized by headache, diziness, muscular weakness, palpitations, dyspnea, nausea, vomiting and fainting.

Mourn —To express grief.

Mourning —Grief.

Mouse —1. A rodent animal. 2. A small piece of tissue that has become free, especially in a body cavity or joint, *e.g.*, mouse joint in which pieces of synovial membrane or cartilage due to trauma or osteoarthritis are free in the joint space.

Mouse unit —Allen-Doisy unit. It is the quantity of estrogen hormone which is capable of producing a characteristic change in the vaginal epithelium in a mouse whose ovaries have been removed.

Mouth —1. Opening of a cavity. 2. The cavity of the cheeks containing the tongue & teeth and communicating with the pharynx.

Mouthguard —A removable plastic device used to cover the maxillary teeth to protect them from injury during contact sports.

Mouthrinse —Mouthwash.

Mouthstick —A device which is held by the teeth and utilized by handicapped persons to perform such actions as turning pages, typing and painting etc., through head movement.

Mouthwash —A solution for washing the mouth.

Movement —The passing from one place to another or changing the position of the body or of its parts.

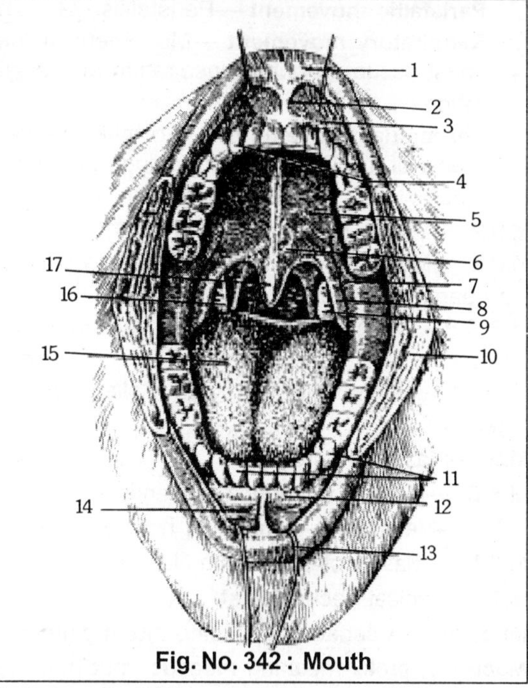

Fig. No. 342 : Mouth

1. Upper lip 2. Frenulum of upper lip 3. Gum 4. Upper teeth 5. Hard palate 6. Soft palate 7. Palatoglossal arch 8. Palatopharyngeal arch 9. Palatine tonsil 10. Section of the cheek 11. Lower teeth 12. Gum 13. Lower lip 14. Frenulum of the lower lip 15. Tongue (dorsum) 16. Fauces 17. Uvula

Active movement —Voluntary movement occurring without external stimulation.

Ameboid movement —Movement by the formation of pseudopodia like that of an ameba.

Associated movement —Movements of the parts which act together, as in the eyes.

Autonomic movement —The spontaneous and involuntary movement without external stimulation.

Brownian movement —Dancing movement of the minute particles suspended in a liquid, on boiling.

Ciliary movement —Vibratile movement. Rhythmic movement of the cilia of a ciliated cell or epithelium.

Fetal movement —Movements performed by the fetus in the uterus.

Passive movement —Movement of the body or of its part caused by external force.

Peristaltic movement —Peristalsis.

Respiratory movement —Movement of the chest occurring during inspiration and expiration.

Vermicular movement —Wormlike movements of the intestines occurring in peristalsis.

M.P.H. —Master of Public Health.

M.P.N. —Most probable number as of bacteria in a quantity of solution.

M.R.C.P. —Member of the Royal College of Physicians.

M.R.C.S. —Member of the Royal College of surgeons.

M.S. —Master of surgery.

M.S.D. —Master of Science in Dentistry.

MSH. —Melanocyte-stimulating hormone.

M.S.N. —Master of Science in Nursing.

M.T. —Medical Technologist.

Mucedin —A substance obtained from gluten.

Muci- —A prefix meaning mucous, mucin.

Mucid —Muciparous.

Muciferous —Mucigenous. Muciparous. Producing mucus.

Muciform —Resembling mucus.

Mucigen —The substance producing mucin.

Mucigenous —Muciferous.

Mucilage —The solution of a gummy substance in water, used as a vehicle.

Mucilaginous —Resembling mucilage; sticky.

Mucilloid —A mucilaginous preparation.

Mucin —A glycoprotein, the chief constituent of mucus.

Mucinase —An enzyme which acts upon mucin.

Mucinemia —Myxemia. Presence of mucin in the blood.

Mucinogen —Forming mucin.

Mucinoid —Resembling mucin.

Mucinolytic —Hydrolyzing or dissolving mucin.

Mucinosis —Abnormal deposition of the mucin in the skin.

Mucinous —Resembling or characterized by the formation of mucin.

Mucinuria —Presence of mucin in the urine.

Muciparous —Muciferous. Mucigenous.

Mucitis —Inflammation of the mucous membrane.

Muco- —Combining form indicating pertaining to mucus.

Mucocele —1. Enlargement of a cavity with mucus. 2. Mucous polyp or cyst.

Mucociliary —Pertaining to the mucus and ciliated epithelium.

Mucocolitis —Mucous colitis.

Mucocolpos —Accumulation of mucus in the vagina.

Mucocutaneous —Mucodermal. Pertaining to mucous membrane and the skin.

Mucodermal —Mucocutaneous.

Mucoenteritis —Inflammation of the mucous membrane of the intestine.

Mucoepidermoid —Composed of mucus-producing epithelial cells.

Mucoglobulin —A type of glycoprotein.

Mucoid —Resembling mucus.

Mucokinesis —A technique for removing excessive or abnormal secretions from the respiratory tract.

Mucolysis —Liquefaction, dissolution, digestion or destruction of the mucus.

Mucolytic —Destroying or dissolving mucus.

Mucomembranous —Pertaining to mucous membrane.

Mucoperichondrium —Perichondrium having a mucous surface, as that of the nasal septum.

Mucoperiosteal —Pertaining to mucoperiosteum.

Mucoperiosteum —Periosteum having a mucous surface, or mucous and periosteal surfaces combined to form a membrane.

Mucopolysaccharide —A complex substance containing protein and polysaccharide.

Mucopolysaccharidosis, Mucopolysaccharidoses —A disease caused by a disorder occurring in the metabolism of polysaccharides.

Mucopolysacchariduria —Presence of mucopolysaccharides in the urine.

Mucoprotein —A complex of protein and mucopolysaccharide.

Mucopurulent —Consisting of mucus and pus.

Mucopus —Mycopus. A mixture of mucous material and pus.

Mucor —A genus of fungi.

Mucoriferous —Covered with mold or a moldlike substance.

Mucorin —An albuminoid substance derived from molds.

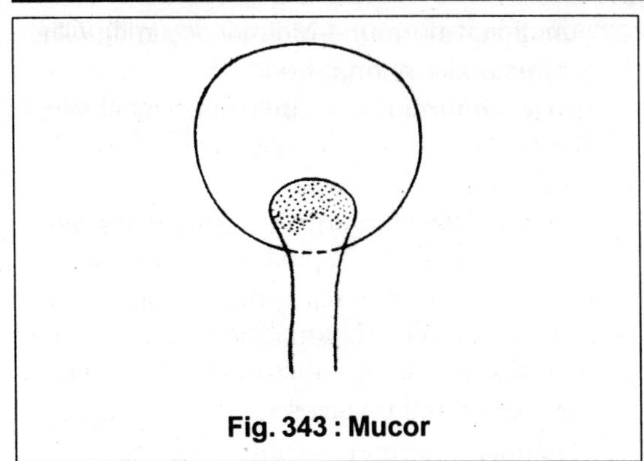

Fig. 343 : Mucor

Mucormycosis —Infection with a fungus of a species of the genus mucor.

Mucorrhea —Increased cervical discharge at the time of ovulation containing mucus.

Mucosa —Mucous membrane.

Mucosal —Pertaining to a mucous membrane.

Mucosanguineous —Containing mucus and blood.

Mucosedative —Demulcent. Soothing the mucous membranes of the body.

Mucoserous —1. Composed of mucus and serum. 2. Pertaining to mucus and serum. 3. Producing both mucus and serum.

Mucosin —Mucin found in thick sticky mucus.

Mucositis —Inflammation of a mucous membrane.

Mucosocutaneous —Pertaining to the mucous membrane and the skin.

Mucostatic —Stopping the secretion of mucus.

Mucous —Pertaining to, resembling or secreting mucus.

Mucous membrane —Membrane lining the passages and cavities communicating with the air as lining of the mouth and intestine, etc.

Mucoviscidosis —Cystic fibrosis.

Mucro —The pointed end of a structure.

Mucus —A viscid fluid secreted by the mucous glands and mucous membranes consisting of mucin, water, inorganic salts, leukocytes and epithelial cells.

Muliebria —The female genital organs.

Muliebrity —Femininity. Womanliness. To suppose by a male person that female characteristics are developing in him since puberty.

Mull —1. To grind or pulverize. 2. A type of soft muslin.

Mult-, Multi- —Prefixes indicating many or much.

Multangular —Having many angles.

Multiallelic —Pertaining to large number of genes affecting hereditary characteristics.

Multiarticular —Pertaining to or affecting many joints.

Multibacillary —Containing many bacilli.

Multicapsular —Composed of many capsules.

Multicellular —Composed of many cells.

Multicuspid, Multicuspidate —Having many cusps.

Multicystic —Polycystic.

Multifactorial —The result of many factors.

Multifamilial —Pertaining to a familial disease affecting the children in many generations.

Multifetation —A pregnancy with more than two fetuses.

Multifid —Divided into many sections.

Multifidus —Multifid.

Multifocal —Pertaining to, or arising from many foci.

Multiform —Polymorphic. Polymorphous. Having many forms or shapes.

Multiglandular —Pertaining to many glands.

Multigravida —A woman who has been pregnant for two or many times.

Multi-infection —Infection with several types of microorganisms.

Multilobar —Composed of many lobes.

Multilobular —Formed of many lobules.

Multilocular —Having many loculi.

Multimammae —Polymastia. The condition of having more than two breasts.

Multinodal —Having many nodes or knots.

Multinodular —Having many nodules or small knots.

Multinuclear, Multinucleate —Polynuclear. Having many nuclei.

Multinucleosis —Polynucleosis.

Multipara —A woman who has borne more than one viable fetus, whether alive or dead.

Multiparity —1. The condition of being a multipara. 2. Production of more than one child at one birth.

Multiparous —1. The woman having borne more than one child. 2. Producing more than one child at birth.

Multiple personality —See under personality.

Multipolar —Having more than two poles, processes.

Multisynaptic —Polysynaptic.

Multivalence, Multivalency —The state of being multivalent.

Multivalent —In chemistry, having a combining power (Valence) of more than one hydrogen atom.

Mummification —1. Drying and shriveling of a dead body 2. Dry gangrene.

Mumps —Parotitis. Inflammation of the parotid glands.

Mural —Pertaining to or occurring in the wall of an organ or cavity of the body.

Murine —Pertaining to the rats.

Murmur —An adventitious soft blowing sound during systole, diastole or both heard on auscultation of the heart or blood vessels.

Anemic murmur —A cardiac murmur heard in anemia.

Aneurysmal murmur —A murmur heard on an aneurysm.

Aortic regurgitant murmur —Blowing and hissing sound occurring after 2nd heart sound in case of aortic regurgitation.

Aortic stenotic murmur —Harsh systolic murmur heard with and after the 1st heart sound in case of aortic obstruction.

Apex murmur —A murmur heard over the apex of the heart.

Arterial murmur —A murmur occurring over an artery at the same time as the pulse.

Cardiac murmur —The murmur produced by blood flowing through the heart.

Continuous murmur —A murmur occurring continuously through systole and diastole.

Diastolic murmur —The murmur heard during diastole of the heart.

Duroziez's murmur —A systolic and diastolic murmur heard over the large peripheral arteries such as femoral artery due to aortic insufficiency.

Ejection murmur —Systolic murmur heard most intensely in mid systole at the time of maximum flow of blood from the heart, associated with pulmonary and aortic stenosis.

Friction murmur —Murmur produced by rubbing of two inflamed mucous surfaces.

Functional murmur —Murmur occurring within a structurally normal heart.

Gibson murmur —A continuous machinery-like murmur heard in patient with ductus arteriosus.

Graham Steell's murmur —An early systolic murmur occurring in pulmonary insufficiency caused by pulmonary hypertension.

Hemic murmur —Murmur heard on auscultation of the heart of anemic persons without any defect in the valves.

Machinery murmur —Gibson murmur.

Mitral murmur —Murmur produced at the orifice of mitral or bicuspid valve due to its disease.

Organic murmur —Murmur occurring due to structural changes in the heart, a vessel or the lung.

Pansystolic murmur —A heart murmur heard throughout the systole.

Pericardial murmur —A friction sound produced within the pericardium.

Prediastolic murmur —The murmur occurring just before and with the diastole.

Presystolic murmur —Murmur occurring just before the systole.

Pulmonary murmur —Murmur produced at the orifice of the pulmonary artery due to diseases of its valve.

Regurgitant murmur —Murmur occurring due to backward flow of blood through a dilated orifice of a valve.

Still's murmur —A functional cardiac murmur occurring in midsystole in children.

Systolic murmur —The murmur heard during systole, due to obstruction of flow of the blood at one or several of the heart valves or in the aorta.

Tricuspid murmur —Murmur produced at the orifice of the tricuspid valve due to its disease.

Vascular murmur —Murmur occurring within a blood vessel.

Vesicular murmur —Normal breathing sound heard over the lungs.

Murphy's sign —It is a sign for determining the inflammation of the gallbladder in which pain is produced on descending and striking of the gallbladder with the examining fingers, when it is

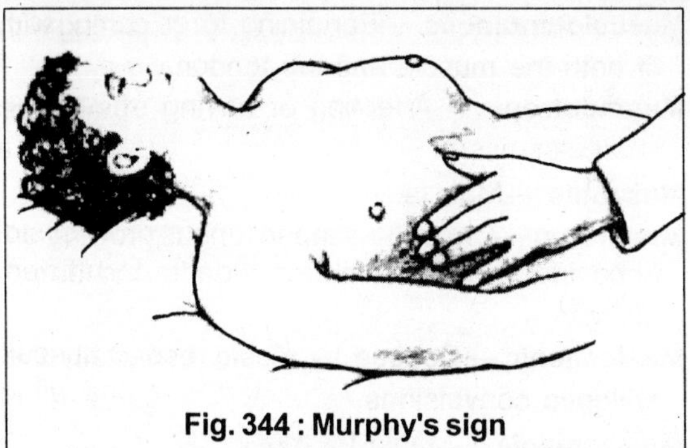
Fig. 344 : Murphy's sign

palpated by pressing the fingers under the right costal margin and the patient is asked to take deep breath.

Musca domestica —House fly.

Muscae volitantes —Black specks seen floating in vitreous humor of the eye.

Muscegenetic —Causing black specks in the vitreous humor of the eye.

Muscicide —Killing the flies.

Muscle —A type of tissue composed of the contractile cells or fibers, which by contraction causes the movement of an organ or part of the body.

Abductor muscle —The muscle which draws away an organ or part of the body from midline.

Adductor muscle —The muscle which draws an organ or part of the body toward the midline.

Agonistic muscle —A muscle the action of which is opposed by the action of another muscle.

Antagonistic muscle —A muscle which counteracts the action of another muscle.

Appendicular muscle —A muscle of a limb.

Articular muscle —A muscle attached to a joint capsule.

Axial muscle —A skeletal muscle of the head or trunk.

Cardiac muscle —Muscle of the heart.

Extensor muscle —The muscle which extends an organ or part of the body.

Extrinsic muscle —The muscle whose origin lies outside while the insertion within the organ or part of the body.

Fixation muscle —A muscle which acts to steady a part of the body.

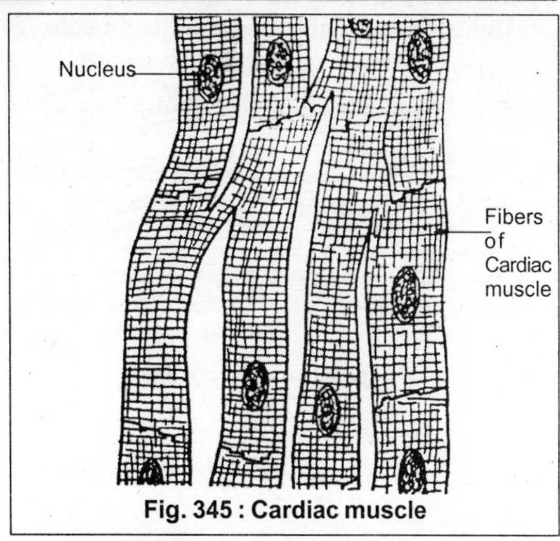

Fig. 345 : Cardiac muscle

Flexor muscle —The muscle which bends a part of the body.

Intrinsic muscle —The muscle whose origin and insertion are in the same organ or part of the body.

Involuntary muscle —The muscle which is not under control of the will.

Skeletal muscle —Muscle connected with a bone.

Smooth muscle —Nonstriated, involuntary muscle found mainly in the visceral organs.

Sphincter muscle —A muscle encircling a duct, tube or orifice thus controlling its opening.

Striated muscle, Striped muscle —A muscle that possesses alternate light and dark bands of fibers or striations. It is voluntary and skeletal muscle.

Synergistic muscles —Muscles that assist one another in action.

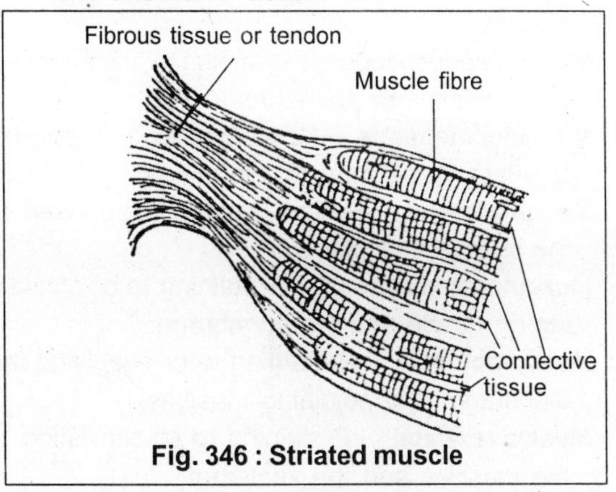

Fig. 346 : Striated muscle

Unstriated muscle —Smooth muscle. A muscle without markings or striations.

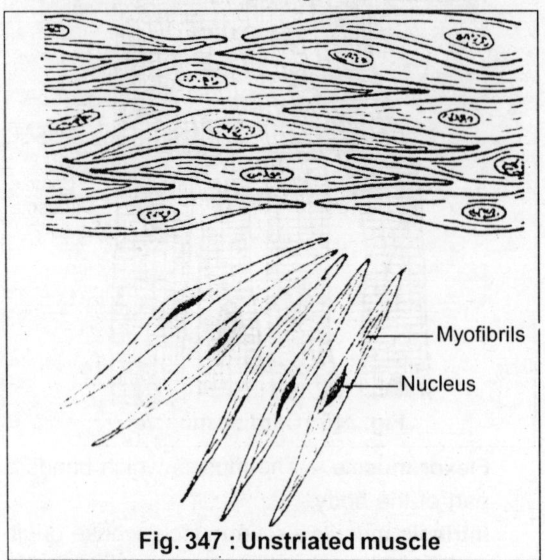

Fig. 347 : Unstriated muscle

Voluntary muscle —The muscle whose action is under control of the will.

Muscle cramps —Painful involuntary contractions of the muscles.

Muscular —Pertaining to or containing muscle.

Muscular dystrophy —Wasting away and atrophy of the muscles.

Muscularis —Muscular layer of an organ or a tubule.

Muscularity —The state or quality of being muscular.

Muscularize—To change into muscle tissue.

Musculature —The arrangement of the muscles in the body or its parts.

Musculin —A globulin in the muscle.

Musculo- —Combining form pertaining to a muscle.

Musculoaponeurotic —Pertaining to or composed of a muscle and aponeurosis.

Musculocutaneous —Pertaining to or supplying or affecting the muscle and the skin.

Musculofascial —Pertaining to or composed of the muscle and fascia.

Musculomembranous —Pertaining to or consisting of muscle and the membrane.

Musculophrenic —Pertaining to or supplying the diaphragm and adjoining muscles.

Musculoskeletal —Pertaining to or consisting of the muscles and the skeleton.

Musculotendinous —Pertaining to or composed of both the muscle and the tendon.

Musculotropic —Affecting or having affinity for muscular tissue.

Musculus —Muscle.

Mushroom —Umbrella-shaped fungus growing on decaying vegetable matter, woods and damp places.

Musicogenic —Caused by music, especially the epileptic convulsions.

Musicomania —Mania for music.

Musicotherapy —Treatment of the disease by music.

Musset's sign —Occurrence of jerking movements repeatedly of the head and neck, in synchrony with the ventricular contraction of the heart as seen in advanced aortic incompetence or aortic aneurysm.

Mussitation —The moving of the lips without sound.

Mutable —Changeable, fickle.

Mutacism —Mytacism.

Mutagen —An agent which induces genetic mutation.

Mutagenesis —The induction of genetic mutation.

Mutagenic —Mutagen.

Mutagenicity —The property of inducing genetic mutation.

Mutant —1. The organism that has undergone genetic mutation. 2. Produced by mutation.

Mutation —A permanent transmissible change in the genetic structure due to which the offspring differs from parents in a characteristic.

Induced mutation —Mutation induced by the drugs and chemicals or resulting from exposure to X-rays or radioactive substances, etc.

Natural mutation —Mutation occurring spontaneously.

Somatic mutation —Mutation occurring in somatic cells.

Mute —Dumb or unable to speak.

Mutilate —1. To deprive of a limb or part of the body. 2. To injure seriously a part of the body so that it is disfigured or becomes disable.

Mutilation —The removing or destroying an organ or a part of the body.

Mutism —Inability to speak.

Muttering —Speaking with imperfect articulation.

Mutualism —A form of symbiosis in which organisms of two different species live in close relationship and each of them is benefitted by other.

Mutualist —An organism living in close relationship with another to the mutual benefit of each.

M.W.I.A. —Medical Women's International Association.

My-, Myo- —A prefix which means pertaining to the muscle.

Myalgia —Myodynia. Pain in the muscles.

Myasis —Myiasis. Condition arising from infestation with maggots (larvae of the flies) in the body.

Myasthenia —Muscular weakness.

Myasthenia angiosclerotic —Muscular weakness occurring due to vascular changes.

Myasthenia cordis —Amyocardia. Weakness of the cardiac muscle.

Myasthenia gastrica —Weakness and atony of the muscular coats of the stomach.

Myasthenia gravis —A disease characterized by great muscular weakness without atrophy, due to lack of acetylcholine or excess of cholinesterase at the neuromuscular junction, in which the nerve impulses fail to induce normal muscular contraction.

Myasthenic —The person suffering from muscular weakness.

Myatonia —Amyotonia. Deficiency or loss of muscular tone.

Myatony —Myatonia.

Myatrophy —Atrophy of a muscle.

Myc-, Myco- —Prefixes meaning fungus.

Mycelia —Plural of mycelium.

Mycelian —Pertaining to mycelium.

Mycelium —The mass of threadlike processes (hyphae) constituting the thallus of the fungus such as that of the molds.

Mycetes —The fungi.

Mycethemia —Mycohemia. Presence of fungi in the blood.

Mycetism, Mycetismus —Fungus poisoning, especially from mushrooms.

Mycetogenetic —Caused by fungi.

Mycetogenic —Mycetogenetic.

Mycetogenous —Mycetogenetic.

Mycetoma —Madura foot. A tumorlike swelling of the fungal mycelia.

Myco- —A prefix meaning fungus.

Mycobacteria —Bacteria belonging to the genus. Mycobacterium.

Mycobacteriosis —Infection with micobacteria.

Mycobacterium —A genus of gram-positive and acid-fast bacteria belonging to the family Mycobacteriaceae which includes Mycobacterium tuberculosis (causing tuberculosis) and Mycobacterium leprae (causing leprosy), etc.

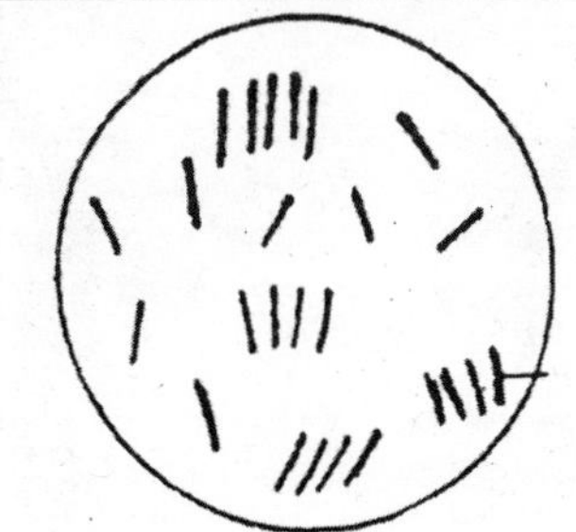

Fig. 348 : Acid-fast Mycobacterium leprae bacilli.

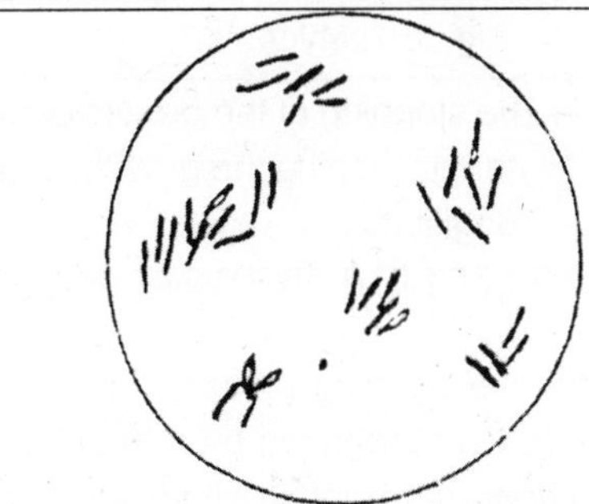

Fig. 349 : Acid-fast Mycobacterium tuberculosis bacilli.

Mycocide —Fungicide.

Mycoderma —Mucous membrane.

Mycodermatitis —Inflammation of the skin caused by fungi or yeast.

Mycodermomycosis —Candidiasis.

Mycohemia —Mycethemia.

Mycoid —Fungus-like.

Mycologist —Specialist in mycology.

Mycology —Science of fungi.

Mycomyringitis —Otomycosis. Fungus inflammation of the tympanic membrane.

Mycophage —A virus living in a fungus.

Mycophthalmia —Inflammation of the eye caused by fungus infection.

Mycoplasma —A group of bacteria that have no true cell walls but are bounded by a three-layered membrane, e.g., M. Huminis which causes genital tract infections and M. pneumoniae which causes infections of the respiratory system.

Mycopus —Mucopus

Mycosis —Any disease caused by a fungus.

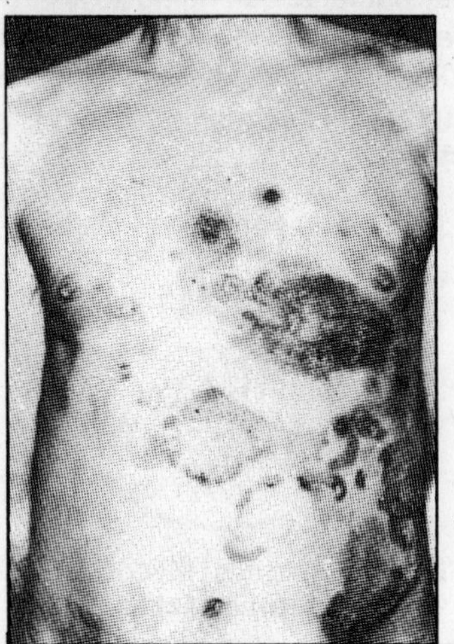

Fig. 350 : Mycosis

Mycostasis —The stopping of the growth of fungi.

Mycostat —Anything stopping the growth of fungi.

Mycostatic —Fungistatic.

Mycotic —Pertaining to a mycosis or caused by fungi.

Mycotoxicosis —Poisoning by fungal toxin.

Mycotoxin —A toxin produced by a fungus.

Mycotoxinization —Inoculation with a fungal toxin.

Mycovirus —A virus infecting the fungi.

Mydriasis —Dilation of the pupil.

Alternating mydriasis —Mydriasis affecting each eye alternately.

Paralytic mydriasis —Dilation of the pupil due to paralysis of its sphincter muscle.

Spastic mydriasis —Dilation of the pupil resulting from overactivity of the dilator muscle of the iris.

Mydriatic —1. Dilating the pupil. 2. Any drug which dilates the pupil.

Myectomy —Excision of a portion of a muscle.

Myectopia —Displacement of a muscle.

Myel- —Myelo-

Myelalgia —Pain in the spinal cord.

Myelanalosis —Wasting of the spinal cord gradually.

Myelapoplexy —Hematomyelia. Hemorrhage into the spinal cord.

Myelatelia —Defective development of the spinal cord.

Myelatrophy —Atrophy of the spinal cord.

Myelauxe —Abnormal enlargement of the spinal cord.

Myelemia —Myelocytosis.

Myelencephalon —The most posterior part of the embryonic hindbrain which gives rise to the medulla oblongata.

Myelic —Pertaining to the spinal cord.

Myelin —A substance composed of lipids and protein forming a sheath around the axons of certain nerves.

Myelinated —Having a myelin sheath.

Myelination —Myelinization. Production of a myelin sheath around an axon of a nerve.

Myelinic —Pertaining to or composed of myelin.

Myelinization —Myelination.

Myelinoclasis —Destruction of myelin.

Myelinogenesis —Myelination.

Myelinogenetic —Producing myelin or a myelin sheath.

Myelinolysis—Destruction of the myelin.

Myelinopathy —Any disease of the myelin.

Myelinosis —Fatty degeneration with the formation of myelin.

Myelinotoxic —Having a poisonous effect on the myelin.

Myelitic —Pertaining to myelitis.

Myelitis —Inflammation of the spinal cord or bone marrow.

Myelo- —Prefix denoting the spinal cord or bone marrow.

Myeloblast —Microleukoblast. An immature cell found in the bone marrow which develops into a myelocyte.

Myeloblastemia —Presence of myeloblasts in the blood.

Myeloblastoma —A malignant tumor containing myeloblasts seen in acute myelocytic leukemia.

Myeloblastosis —Excess of myeloblasts in the blood.

Myelocele —Protrusion of the spinal cord through a fissure in the vertebral column.

Myelocyst —A cyst developed from the rudimentary medullary canal of the spinal cord.

Myelocystic —Pertaining to or having a myelocyst.

Myelocystocele —Cyst of the substance of the

spinal cord through a defect in the vertebral canal.

Myelocystomeningocele —Combined myelocystocele and meningocele.

Myelocyte —1. A large cell in the red bone marrow from which granular leukocytes are produced. 2. Any cell of the gray matter of the nervous system.

Myelocythemia —An excess of myelocytes in the blood.

Myelocytic —Characterized by the presence of, or pertaining to myelocytes.

Myelocytoma —Myeloma.

Myelocytomatosis —A tumor of myelocytes.

Myelocytosis —Myelocythemia. Myelemia.

Myelodiastasis —Destruction and disintegration of the spinal cord.

Myelodysplasia —Defective formation of any part of the spinal cord.

Myeloencephalic —Pertaining to the spinal cord and brain.

Myeloencephalitis —Inflammation of the spinal cord and brain.

Myelofibrosis —Replacement of the bone marrow by fibrous tissue.

Myelogenesis —1. Development of the brain and the spinal cord. 2. Development of a myelin sheath around the axon of a nerve.

Myelogenetic —Myelogenic.

Myelogenic, Myelogenous —Producing myelin or produced in the bone marrow.

Myelogenous —Myelogenic.

Myelogeny —Maturation of the myelin sheaths during the development of the central nervous system.

Myelogram —1. X-ray film obtained by myelography. 2. Differential count of the bone marrow cells.

Myelography —X-ray examination of the spinal cord after an injection of a radiopaque substance into the subarachnoid space.

Myeloic —Pertaining to the tissue and precursor cells from which neutrophils, eosinophils and basophils are derived.

Myeloid —1. Pertaining to bone marrow or the spinal cord. 2. Resembling bone marrow or myelocytes. 3. Derived from bone marrow.

Myeloidosis —Formation of myeloid tissue.

Myelolymphangioma —Elephantiasis.

Myelolysis —Dissolution of myelin.

Myeloma —A tumor composed of the cells normally found in the bone marrow.

Multiple myeloma —Multiple malignant tumors formed by the infiltration of the bone and bone marrow with myeloma cells, which are progressive and generally fatal, manifested by pain in the bone, fracture and destruction of the bone, and anemia and increased globulin in the blood.

Myelomalacia —Abnormal softening of the spinal cord.

Myelomatosis—Multiple myeloma.

Myelomenia —Vicarious menstruation into the spinal cord.

Myelomeningitis —Inflammation of the spinal cord and its meninges.

Myelomeningocele —Protrusion of the spinal cord and its meninges through a defect in the vertebral column.

Myelomere —A segment of the embryonic spinal cord.

Myelomyces —Encephaloma.

Myeloneuritis —Inflammation of the spinal cord and the peripheral nerves.

Myelonic —Pertaining to the spinal cord.

Myeloparalysis —Paralysis of the spinal cord.

Myelopathic —Pertaining to the disease of the spinal cord.

Myelopathy —Any disease of the spinal cord.

Ascending myelopathy —A disease of the spinal cord ascending toward the head.

Descending myelopathy —A disease of the spinal cord descending toward the feet.

Focal myelopathy —A disease of a small area of the spinal cord.

Sclerosing myelopathy —A disease of the spinal cord in which it becomes hard.

Transverse myelopathy —Disease of the spinal cord extending across the spinal cord.

Traumatic myelopathy —Disease of the spinal cord resulting from trauma.

Myelopetal —Moving toward the spinal cord.

Myelophthisic —Pertaining to or suffering from myelophthisis.

Myelophthisis —1. Atrophy of the spinal cord. 2. Replacement of the bone marrow by a tumor.

Myeloplast —A leukocyte of the bone marrow.

Myeloplax —Large multinuclear cell of the bone marrow.

Myeloplaxoma —Tumor composed of myeloplaxes.

Myeloplegia —Paralysis of the spinal cord.

Myelopoiesis —Formation of bone marrow or the cells arising from it.

Myelopoietic —Pertaining to myelopoiesis.

Myelopore —An opening in the spinal cord.

Myeloproliferative —Pertaining to the unusual proliferation of myelopoietic tissue.

Myeloradiculitis —Inflammation of the spinal cord and posterior nerve roots.

Myeloradiculodysplasia —Defective development of the spinal cord and the spinal nerve roots.

Myeloradiculopathy —Any disease of the spinal cord and the spinal nerves.

Myelorrhagia —Hemorrhage into the spinal cord.

Myelorrhaphy —Suture of a wound of the spinal cord.

Myelosarcoma —Osteosarcoma. Sarcoma made up of bone marrow cells.

Myelosarcomatosis —Disseminated myelosarcomas.

Myeloschisis —Cleft spinal cord resulting from failure of the neural tube to close.

Myelosclerosis —Sclerosis of the spinal cord.

Myelosis —Formation of a tumor of the spinal cord or of a myeloma.

Myelospongium —The fibrocellular network in the spinal cord of the embryo, from which neuroglia arises.

Myelosuppressive —Inhibiting bone marrow function.

Myelosyphilis —Syphilis of the spinal cord.

Myelotome —An instrument used to dissect the spinal cord.

Myelotomy —To incise the nerves of the spinal cord.

Myelotoxic —Poisonous for bone marrow.

Myelotoxin —Toxin destroying the bone marrow cells.

Myenteric —Pertaining to the myenteron.

Myenteric reflex —Intestinal contraction above and relaxation below the point of stimulation.

Myenteron —Muscular coat of the intestine.

Myerson's sign —In Parkinson's disease, repeated blinking of the eyes in response to tapping the forehead or nasal bridge.

Myesthesia —Muscle sense.

Myiasis —The disease caused by the maggots (larvae of the flies).

Myiocephalon —Expulsion of a part of the iris through a hole in the cornea.

Myiodesopsia —The appearing of spots before the eyes.

Myiosis —Myiasis.

Myitis —Myositis. Inflammation of a muscle.

Mylodus —A molar tooth.

Mylohyoid —Pertaining to the hyoid bone and the molar tooth.

Myo- —A prefix which means pertaining to a muscle.

Myoalbumin —Albumin present in the muscular tissue.

Myoalbumose —A protein derived from the muscle.

Myoarchitectonic—Pertaining to the structural arrangement of the muscle fibers.

Myoatrophy —Muscular atrophy.

Myoblast —An embryonic cell which becomes a cell of muscle fiber.

Myoblastic —Pertaining to the myoblast or to the formation of muscle cells.

Myoblastoma —A benign tumor composed of the cells resembling myoblasts.

Myobradia —Slow reaction of a muscle to a stimulation.

Myocardia —Plural of myocardium.

Myocardial, Myocardiac —Pertaining to the myocardium.

Myocardial infarction —Heart attack. Necrosis of an area of the myocardium following occlusion of one or more of the coronary arteries, characterized by severe pain in the middle of the chest behind the sternum.

Myocardial insufficiency —Inability of the heart to perform its normal function.

Myocardiograph —An instrument for making tracings of the heart movements.

Myocardiopathy —Any disease of the myocardium.

Myocardiorrhaphy —Suture of the myocardium.

Myocarditic —Pertaining to myocardium.

Myocarditis —Inflammation of the myocardium.

Myocardium —A middle and thick layer of the wall of the heart, composed of the cardiac muscle.

Myocardosis —Any degenerative or noninflammatory disease of the myocardium.

Myocele —Protrusion of a muscle through its ruptured sheath.

Myocelialgia —Pain in the abdominal muscles.

Myocelitis —Inflammation of the abdominal muscles.

Myocellulitis —Myositis with cellulitis.

Myoceptor —The endplates of a nerve supplying a muscle.

Myocerosis —Waxy degeneration of a muscle.

Myochorditis —Inflammation of the muscles of the vocal cord.

Myochrome —Any muscle pigment.

Myochronoscope —An apparatus for determining the time for producing a muscular contraction.

Myocinesimeter —An apparatus for measuring the muscular activity.

Myoclonia —Muscular twitching.

Myoclonic —Showing muscular twitching.

Myoclonus —Myoclonia.

Myocoele —A cavity within a somite of an embryo.

Myocolpitis—Inflammation of the muscular tissue of the vagina.

Myocomma —The connective tissue septum separating the adjacent myotomes.

Myocrismus —A creaking sound sometimes heard on auscultation of contracting muscle.

Myocutaneous —Musculocutaneous.

Myocyte —A muscle cell.

Myocytolysis —Dissolution of muscle fiber.

Myocytoma —A tumor composed of muscle cells.

Myodegeneration —Muscular degeneration.

Myodemia —Fatty degeneration of a muscle.

Myodermal —Musculocutaneous.

Myodesopsia —Presence of black spots before the eyes.

Myodiastasis —Division or rupture of a muscle.

Myodynamia —Muscular strength.

Myodynamics —The science of muscular action.

Myodynamometer —An apparatus for measuring the muscular strength.

Myodynia —Myalgia. Pain in the muscle.

Myodystonia —Disorder of muscular tone.

Myodystrophia —Myodystrophy.

Myodystrophy —Muscular dystrophy.

Myoedema —Mounding. Edema of a muscle.

Myoelastic —Pertaining to muscle and the elastic tissue.

Myoelectric —Pertaining to the electric properties of muscles.

Myoendocarditis—Myocarditis combined with endocarditis.

Myoepithelial—Pertaining to the contractile epithelial cells.

Myoepithelioma —A tumor composed of myoepithelial cells from a sweat gland.

Myoepithelium —Tissue made up of contractile epithelial cells.

Myoesthesis, Myoesthesia —Kinesthesia.

Myofascial —Of or pertaining to the fascia and the muscle.

Myofascitis —Inflammation of a muscle and its fascia.

Myofibril, Myofibrilla —A very small fiber found in the muscular tissue.

Myofibrilla —Myofibril.

Myofibrillae —Plural of myofibrilla.

Myofibrillar —Pertaining to myofibril.

Myofibroblast —A cell having contractile properties, so responsible for contracture of wounds.

Myofibroma —A tumor composed of muscular and fibrous tissue.

Myofibromatosis —Tumors composed of muscle and fibrous tissue or of myofibroblasts.

Myofibrosis —Replacement of a muscle tissue by fibrous tissue.

Myofibrositis —Inflammation of the perimysium.

Myofilament —Any of the threadlike structures composing the myofibrils of striated muscle fibers, seen only by ultramicroscope, of which thick ones contain myosin and thin ones actin.

Myofunctional —Pertaining to the function of a muscle.

Myogelosis —Hardening of a part of a muscle.

Myogen —Myosinogen.

Myogenesis —Formation of the muscular tissue.

Myogenetic, Myogenic —Arising from or forming muscle tissue.

Myogenous —Originating in muscular tissue.

Myoglia —A fibrous network in muscular tissue which resembles neuroglia in appearance.

Myoglobin —Myohemoglobin.

Myoglobinuria —The presence of myoglobin in the urine.

Myoglobulin —A coagulable globulin present in the muscles.

Myognathus —Conjoined unequal twins in which the rudimentary head of the small (parasite) twin is attached to the lower jaw of the larger or normal (host or autosite) twin by muscle and skin only.

Myogram —A tracing made by myography of muscular contractions.

Myograph —An apparatus for making the tracing of muscular contractions.

Myographic —Pertaining to a myograph or the tracings made by it.

Myography —The process of making tracings of muscular contractions by a myograph.

Myohemoglobin —A respiratory pigment present in the muscle tissue, which acts as an oxygen carrier.

Myohysterectomy —Hysterectomy, subtotal.

Myoid —Resembling a muscle.

Myoidema —Myoedema.

Myoischemia —Deficiency of blood supply in a muscle.

Myokerosis —Waxy degeneration of a muscle.

Myokinesimeter —Myocinesimeter.

Myokinesis —1. Muscular activity. 2. Surgical displacement of muscular fibers.

Myokinetic —Pertaining to the muscular activity.

Myokymia —Twitching of the fibers of a muscle.

Myolemma —Sarcolemma.

Myolipoma —Muscle tumor containing fat.

Myologia —Myology.

Myologist —Specialist in myology.

Myology —Scientific study of the muscles.

Myolysis —Disintegration or fatty degeneration of a muscle.

Myoma —A tumor composed of muscular tissue.

Myomalacia —Softening of a muscle.

Myomatosis —The formation of multiple myomas.

Myomatous —Pertaining to or resembling a myoma.

Myomectomy —1. Excision of a portion of a muscle. 2. Removal of a myoma, generally of the uterus.

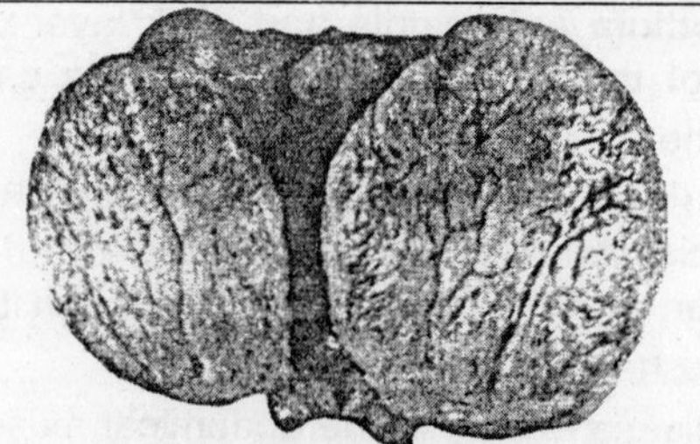

Fig. 351 : Myoma of the uterus causing narrowing of the uterine cavity

Myomelanosis —Abnormal darkening of a muscle tissue.

Myomere —Myotome. (2)

Myometer —An apparatus for measuring the muscular contractions.

Myometrial —Pertaining to the myometrium.

Myometritis —Mesometritis. Inflammation of the muscular wall of the uterus.

Myometrium —Muscular layer of the uterus.

Myomitochondria —Plural of myomitochondrion.

Myomitochondrion —A mitochondrion of a muscle fiber.

Myomotomy —To make an incision into the muscular layer of the uterus.

Myon —A single muscle unit.

Myonarcosis —Muscular numbness.

Myonecrosis —Necrosis of a muscle tissue.

Myoneme —A muscle fibril.

Myonephropexy —Fixation of a movable kidney by attaching it to a muscle.

Myoneural —Pertaining to the nerve endings in a muscle.

Myoneuralgia —Muscular pain.

Myoneurasthenia —Muscular weakness with neurasthenia.

Myoneuroma —Neuroma partially composed of muscular elements.

Myonosus —Myopathy.

Myonymy —Nomenclature of the muscles.

Myopachynsis —Abnormal thickening of a muscle tissue.

Myopalmus —Muscular twitching.

Myoparalysis —Paralysis of a muscle.

Myoparesis —Weakness or partial paralysis of a muscle.

Myopathia —Myopathy.

Myopathic —1. Pertaining to a muscular disease. 2. The person suffering from a muscular disease.

Myopathic facies —Facial expression caused by relaxation of the facial muscles in which lids drop and the lips protrude.

Myopathy —Any disease of the muscle.

Myope —The person affected with myopia or nearsightedness.

Myopericarditis —Inflammation of the myocardium with the inflammation of pericardium.

Myoperitonitis —Inflammation of the parietal peritoneum with that of the muscles of the abdominal wall.

Myophage —A macrophage destroying a muscular tissue.

Myophone —An instrument which enables an individual to hear the murmur of muscular contractions.

Myopia —Nearsightedness. A visual defect in which the parallel rays from an object are focussed in front of the retina so that the object can be seen distinctly only when it is very close to the eyes.

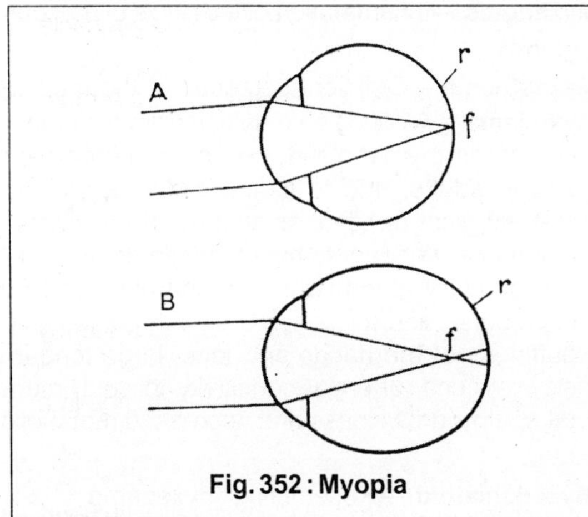

Fig. 352 : Myopia

A. Normal eye
B. Myopic eye
r. Retina
f. Focus of parallell rays

Myopic —Pertaining to or affected with myopia.

Myoplasm —The contractile part of a muscle cell.

Myoplastic —Pertaining to the plastic surgery on the muscles.

Myoplasty —Plastic surgery on the muscle.

Myopolar —Pertaining to the muscular polarity.

Myoporthosis —Correction of myopia or nearsightedness.

Myoprotein —A protein found in the muscle tissue.

Myopsis —Myodesopsia.

Myopsychopathy —Any muscular disease associated with mental disease.

Myorrhaphy —Suture of a muscle.

Myorrhexis —Rupture of a muscle.

Myosalgia —Myalgia. Pain in a muscle.

Myosalpingitis —Inflammation of the muscular tissue of a fallopian tube.

Myosalpinx —The muscular tissue of the fallopian tube.

Myosarcoma —A malignant tumor composed of myogenic cells.

Myosclerosis —Hardening of a muscle.

Myoseptum —Myocomma.

Myosin —A protein present in the myofibril.

Myosinogen —The precursor of myosin.

Myosinuria —Myosuria. The presence of myosin in the urine.

Myositic —Pertaining to myositis.

Myositis —Myitis. Inflammation of a voluntary muscle which may be due to infection, trauma or infestation by parasites.

Myositis ossificans —Myositis marked by ossification of the muscles.

Myospasm —Spasm of a muscle.

Myosteoma —A bony growth found in a muscle.

Myosthenometer —An apparatus for measuring the muscle power.

Myostroma —The supporting connective tissue of muscular tissue.

Myostromin —A protein found in muscle stroma.

Myosuria —Myosinuria.

Myosuture —Stitching of a muscle.

Myotactic —Pertaining to a muscle or kinesthetic sense.

Myotasis —Stretching of a muscle.

Myotatic —Pertaining to the stretching of muscles.

Myotenontoplasty—Tenomyoplasty. Plastic surgery of the muscles and tendons.

Myotenositis —Inflammation of a muscle and its tendon.

Myotenotomy—Surgical division of the tendon of a muscle.

Myotherapy —A method for relaxing muscle spasm, improving blood circulation and alleviating pain.

Myothermic —Pertaining to the rise in temperature of a muscle.

Myotome —1. A knife for cutting the muscles. 2. Myomere. The portion of the embryonic somite, from which the voluntary muscles develop.

Myotomy —To make an incision into a muscle.

Myotone —Myotony or myotonia.

Myotonia —Tonic spasm of a muscle.

Myotonia dystrophica —Myotonia atrophica. A hereditary disease characterized by muscular wasting, myotonia and cataract.

Myotonic —Pertaining to myotonia.

Myotonoid —Like myotonia.

Myotonometer—An instrument for measuring muscular tone.

Myotonus —Muscular tone.

Myotony —Myotonia.

Myotrophic —1. Pertaining to the myotrophy. 2. Increasing the weight of a muscle.

Myotrophy —Nutrition of the muscle.

Myotropic—Attracted to a muscle.

Myotube —A skeletal muscle fiber formed in the developing stage, which contains a nucleus in the centre occupying most of the cell.

Myovascular —Pertaining to the muscles and the blood vessels supplying to them.

Myringa—Tympanic membrane or eardrum.

Myringectomy —Myringodectomy.

Myringitis —Inflammation of the tympanic membrane or eardrum.

Myringo-, Myring- —Prefixes meaning tympanic membrane.

Myringodectomy —Myringectomy. Excision of a part or whole of the tympanic membrane.

Myringodermatitis —Inflammation of the tympanic membrance and the adjoining skin.

Myringomycosis —Inflammation of the tympanic membrane due to fungi.

Myringoplasty —Plastic surgery of the tympanic membrane.

Myringosclerosis —Formation of dense connective tissue in the tympanic membrane.

Myringoscope —An instrument used for examination of the tympanic membrane.

Myringotome —A knife for incising the tympanic membrane.

Myringotomy —To make an incision into the tympanic membrane.

Myrinx —Tympanic membrane.

Myristica —Nutmeg.

Myrmecia —A dome-shaped wart.

Myrmesia —An anthill-shaped wart.

Mysophilia —Sexual excitement by seeing the body excretions.

Mysophobia —Molysmophobia.

Mytacism —Excessive use of the letter m in speaking.

Mythomania —A tendency to lie and exaggerate.

Mythophobia —Abnormal fear of telling a lie.

Mytilotoxin —A neurotoxin present in certain muscles.

Myurous —Gradually decreasing in thickness, as a rat's tail.

Myxadenitis —Inflammation of the mucous glands.

Myxadenoma —Myxoadenoma. An epithelial tumor with the structure of a mucous gland.

Myxangitis —Inflammation of the ducts of mucous glands.

Myxasthenia —Deficient secretion of the mucus.

Myxedema —A condition resulting from hypofunction of the thyroid gland, occurring in childhood and in adults, due to iodine deficiency in the diet, surgical removal or atrophy of the thyroid gland or secondary to hypofunction of the anterior pituitary gland, which is characterized by dry, coarse and thickened skin with loss of hair, puffiness of the hands and face, large tongue, slow speech, anemia, sensitivity to cold, mental apathy, drowsiness and decreased metabolic rate.

Myxedematoid —Resembling myxedema.

Myxedematous —Pertaining to or affected with myxedema.

Myxemia —Mucinemia.

Myxiosis —A mucous secretion.

Myxo-, Myx- —Prefixes denoting relation to the mucus.

Myxoadenoma —Myxadenoma.

Myxochondrofibrosarcoma —A malignant tumor composed of myxomatous, chondromatous, fibrous and sarcomatous elements.

Myxochondroma —A benign tumor composed of myxomatous and chondromatous elements.

Myxocystoma —A benign cystic tumor containing mucus.

Myxocyte —One of the cells of mucous tissue.

Myxoedema —Myxedema.

Myxoenchondroma —A tumor of the cartilaginous tissue that has undergone partial mucous degeneration.

Myxofibroma —Myxoinoma. A tumor composed of mucous and fibrous tissue.

Myxofibrosarcoma —A fibrosarcoma with myxoma.

Myxoglioma —A tumor composed of myxomatous and gliomatous elements.

Myxoid —Resembling mucus.

Myxoinoma —Myxofibroma.

Myxolipoma —Lipomyxoma.

Myxoma —A tumor composed of mucous connective tissue.

Myxomatosis —Formation of multiple mucous tumors. (myxomas).

Myxomatous —Pertaining to myxoma or characterized by its features, said of a muscle.

Myxomyoma —A myoma that has undergone mucous degeneration.

Myxoneuroma —A tumor composed of mucous and nerve tissue elements.

Myxopapilloma —A tumor composed of myxomatous and papillomatous elements.

Myxopoiesis —Formation of mucus.

Myxorrhea —Excessive flow of mucus.

Myxosarcoma —A mixed tumor composed of myxoma and sarcoma.

Myxosarcomatous —Pertaining to or of the nature of myxosarcoma.

Myzesis —Sucking.

N —1. Chemical symbol for nitrogen. 2. Normal.

Na —Chemical symbol for sodium.

NaCl —Sodium chloride.

Nacreous —Having a pearl-like luster.

N.A.D. —No any disease.

Naegele's rule —A method to estimate the day when the labor will begin in which 90 days exactly are counted back from the day of the last menstrual period begins and seven days are added to it, which becomes the expected day of delivery.

N.A.E.M.S.P. —National Association of Emergency Medical Service Physicians.

N.A.E.M.T. —National Association of Emergency Medical Technicians.

Nail —1. The horny plate of the skin on the dorsal surface of the distal end of the finger or toe. 2. A rod of metal, bone or solid material used to attach the ends or pieces of broken bones.

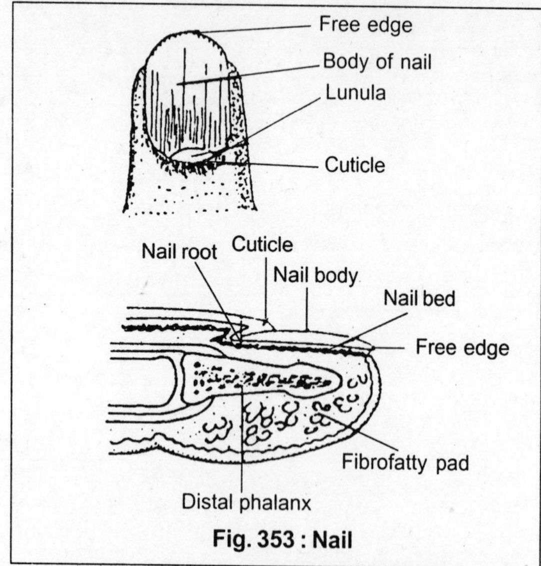

Fig. 353 : Nail

Clubbing of the nail —See clubbing.

Eggshell nail —Soft and semitransparent nail which bends easily and splits at the end, found in arthritis, peripheral neuritis, leprosy and hemiplegia.

Habit deformity nail —Disruption of the nail surface by the habit of abrading or stroking it.

Hang nail —The nail with the broken epidermis at the edge.

Ingrown nail —The nail with the margins to grow into the soft tissue causing inflammation and sometimes abscess formation.

Parrot-beak nail —A markedly curved fingernail, appearing as parrot's beak.

Reedy nail —The nail marked by longitudinal fissures.

Smith-Petersen nail —A three flanged nail used for fixing the head of femur in the fracture of femoral neck.

Splitting nail —Splitting of the nails occurring as a result of their brittleness.

Spoon nail —A nail with the concave surface.

Nailbed —Nail matrix. The portion of a finger or toe covered by the nail.

Nail fold —Groove in the skin surrounding the margins of the nail.

Nail groove —The space between the nailbed and the nail wall.

Nailing —The application of a nail for attaching the ends or pieces of the broken bones.

Nail matrix —Nailbed.

Nail-patella syndrome —Onycho-osteodysplasia.

Nail root —Proximal portion of the nail covered by the nail fold.

Nail wall —Epidermis covering the margins of the nail.

Naked —Uncovered.

Nanism —Nanosomia.

Nano- —The prefix denoting one billionth part of the unit to which it is combined, as a nanogram is one billionth part of a gram.

Nanocephalia —Microcephalia.

Nanocephalic —Nanocephalous.

Nanocephalism —Condition of having a very small head.

Nanocephalous —Having a very small head.

Nanocephaly —Microcephaly.

Nanocormia —Abnormal smallness of the trunk or body.

Nanocurie —A unit of radioactivity equal to one billionth curie.

Nanogram —One billionth part of a gram.

Nanoid —Dwarfish.

Nanomelia —Micromelia.

Nanomelus —Micromelus.

Nanometer —A unit of length equal to one billionth meter.

Nanomole —One billionth (10^{-9}) of a mole.

Nanophthalmia —Nanophthalmos.

Nanophthalmos —Microphthalmia. Abnormal smallness of one or both eyes.

Nanosecond —One billionth part of a second.

Nanosoma —Nanism. The condition of being dwarf.

Nanosomia —Nanosoma.

Nanosomus —A dwarf.

Nanous —Dwarfed.

Nanus —1. Dwarf. 2. Dwarf-like.

Nap —A short sleep.

Nape —Nucha. Scruff. Back of the neck.

Napex —Scalp beneath the occipital protuberance.

Naphthol —A petroleum substance prepared from naphthalene and used as an antiseptic and in certain dyes.

Napiform —Turnip shaped.

Narcissism —1. Self love. 2. Sexual pleasure derived from seeing one's own naked body.

Narcissistic —Pertaining to narcissism.

Narco- —A prefix which means numbness or stupor.

Narcoanalysis —A form of psychotherapy in which mild anesthesia is produced by administering the barbiturates intravenously and the patient is encouraged to talk to release his/her suppressed thoughts.

Narcoanesthesia —Anesthesia produced by a narcotic as morphine, etc.

Narcohypnia —Numbness occurring after a sleep.

Narcohypnosis —Deep sleep produced by hypnosis.

Narcolepsy —A chronic condition of recurring attacks of drowsiness and sleepness.

Narcoleptic —Pertaining to or having excessive desire to sleep.

Narcomatous —Pertaining to the deep sleep caused by narcotics.

Narcosis —Unconsciousness caused by narcotics.

Narcosynthesis—Narcoanalysis.

Narcotherapy —Treatment of diseases by producing unconsciousness by the use of narcotics.

Narcotic —1. Pertaining to or producing deep sleep or unconsciousness. 2. A drug which depresses the central nervous system in moderate doses, thus relieving pain and producing sleep, but in large doses it causes unconsciousness and even death.

Narcotism —1. Narcosis. 2. Addiction to the use of narcotics.

Narcotize —To keep somebody under the influence of a narcotic.

Nares —Nostrils. The external openings of the nasal cavity.

Naris —Singular of nares.

Naristillae —Nasal drops.

NASA —National Aeronautics and Space Administration.

Nasal —Pertaining to the nose.

Nasal flaring —Outward movement of the nostrils with each inspiration.

Nasal fossa —One of the two halves of the nasal cavity.

Nasal gavage —Feeding through a tube passing through the nose into the stomach.

Nasal height —Distance between the lower border of the nasal septum and the nasion.

Nasal polyp —A polyp with a pedicle hanging from the nasal mucosa.

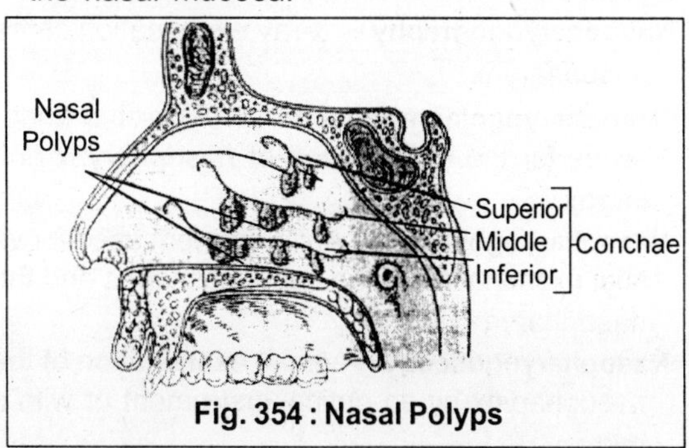

Fig. 354 : Nasal Polyps

Nasal reflex —Sneezing resulting from irritation of the mucous membrane of the nose.

Nasal septum —The wall or septum between the two nasal cavities.

Nascent —1. New born. 2. Just liberated from a chemical compound.

Nasioiniac —Pertaining to the nasion and the inion.

Nasion —The middle point of the frontonasal suture.

Nasitis —Inflammation of the nose.

Naso- —A prefix which means pertaining to the nose.

Nasoantral —Pertaining to the nose and the maxillary antrum.

Nasoantritis —Inflammation of the nose and the maxillary antrum.

Nasoantrostomy —To make a passage between the nose and the maxillary antrum.

Nasociliary —Pertaining to the nose, eyebrows and the eyes.

Nasofrontal —Pertaining to the nasal and frontal bones.

Nasogastric —Pertaining to the nose and the stomach.

Nasolabial —Pertaining to the nose and the lip.

Nasolacrimal —Pertaining to the nose and the lacrimal apparatus.

Nasology —Study of the nose and its diseases.

Nasomental —Pertaining to the nose and chin.

Naso-oral —Pertaining to the nose and oral cavity.

Nasopalatine —Pertaining to the nose and palate.

Nasopharyngeal —Pertaining to the nose and pharynx.

Nasopharyngitis —Inflammation of the nasopharynx.

Nasopharyngography —X-ray examination of the nasopharynx.

Nasopharyngolaryngoscope —A flexible endoscope for the examination of nasopharynx and larynx.

Nasopharyngoscope —An instrument used for visual examination of the nasal passages and the nasopharynx.

Nasopharyngoscopy —Visual examination of the nasopharynx by an optical instrument or with a mirror.

Nasopharynx —The part of the pharynx situated above the soft palate.

Nasorostral —Pertaining to the rostrum of the nose.

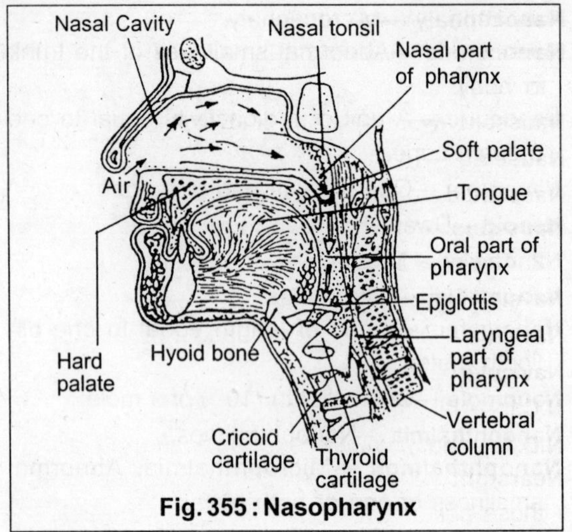

Fig. 355 : Nasopharynx

Nasoscope —Instrument for examination of the nasal cavity.

Nasoseptitis —Inflammation of the nasal septum.

Nasosinusitis —Inflammation of the accessory nasal sinuses.

Nasus —Nose.

Natal —1. Pertaining to the birth. 2. Pertaining to the buttocks.

Natality —Birth rate.

Natant —Floating or swimming.

Nates —Buttocks.

Natimortality —The portion of stillbirth's to the general birth rate.

Natis —Singular of nates.

Native —1. Indigenous. 2. Innate. 3. Inborn. 4. Original. 5. Natural. 6. Inherent.

Natremia —Presence of sodium in the blood.

Natriemia —Natremia.

Natrium —Na. Sodium.

Natriuresis —Excretion of abnormal amount of sodium in the urine.

Natriuretic —The drug or an agent which increases the excretion of sodium in the urine.

Natural —Not abnormal or artificial.

Nature —The universe, habit, qualities, kind.

Naturopath —The person who practices naturopathy.

Naturopathic —Pertaining to or by means of naturopathy.

Naturopathy —The treatment of diseases by natural sources such as light, heat, air, water and soil, etc., and not by the drugs.

Naupathia —Seasickness.

Nausea —Unpleasant sensation with a tendency to vomit.

Nauseant —Causing nausea.

Nauseate —To cause nausea.

Nauseated —Affected with nausea.

Nauseous —1. Pertaining to or causing nausea. 2. The person affected with nausea.

Navel —The umbilicus.

Navicula —A small boat-shaped structure.

Navicular —Boat-shaped.

N.C.I. —National Cancer Institute.

N.D.A. —National Dental Association.

Nearsight —Myopia. Ability to see clearly only those objects which are close to the eyes.

Nearsighted —Myopic. Able to see clearly the objects which are close to the eyes.

Nearsightedness —Myopia.

Nearthrosis —Neoarthrosis. A false or artificial joint.

Nebula —1. Slight corneal opacity. 2. Cloudiness in the urine. 3. The substance used in an atomizer.

Nebulae —Plural of nebula.

Nebulization —1. To convert a liquid into a spray. 2. Treatment of the diseases by spray.

Nebulize —To change a lquid into a fine spray or vapor.

Nebulizer —Atomizer. An apparatus for producing spray.

Neck —1. The part of the body between the head and shoulders. 2. Constricted portion of an organ. 3. The portion of a tooth between its crown and the root.

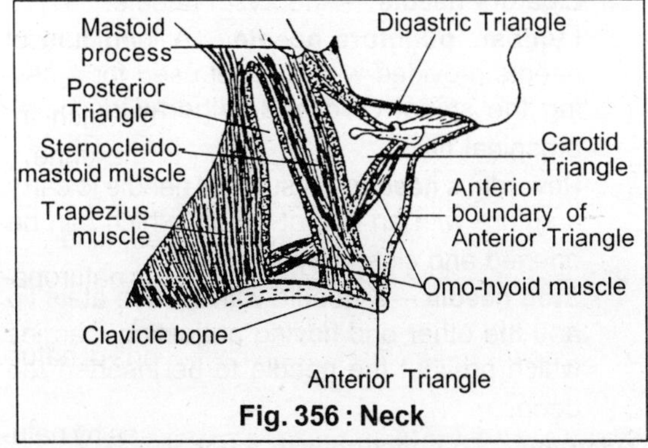

Fig. 356 : Neck

Necklace —A structure encircling the neck as the eruption in pellagra.

Necrectomy —Surgical removal of the necrotic tissue.

Necro- —A prefix which means pertaining to death, dead cells or tissue.

Necrobiosis —Degeneration and swelling of the collagen bundles in the dermis occurring gradually.

Necrobiotic —Pertaining to or affected by necrobiosis.

Necrocytosis —Death of the cells and their decomposition (decay).

Necrocytotoxin —A toxin causing death of the cells.

Necrogenic —Causing necrosis or death.

Necrogenous —Arising from dead matter.

Necrologist —Specialist of mortality statistics.

Necrology —The study of mortality statistics.

Necrolysis —Necrosis and separation of the necrotic tissue.

Necromania —Excessive desire for death or an interest in dead bodies.

Necrometer —An apparatus for measuring the organs of dead bodies.

Necromimesis —Delusion of being dead.

Necronectomy —Necrectomy.

Necroparasite —Saprophyte.

Necrophagous —Feeding upon dead bodies.,

Necrophile—The person much interested in dead bodies or having intercourse with the dead human body.

Necrophilia —1. Abnormal interest in death or dead bodies. 2. Sexual intercourse with a dead body.

Necrophilic —Necrophilous. Pertaining to necrophilia.

Necrophilism —Love with insanity for, or intercourse with the dead body.

Necrophilous —Preferring, or feeding on, dead bodies, usually said of bacteria.

Necrophobia —Thanatophobia. Morbid fear of the dead bodies.

Necropneumonia —Pulmonary gangrene.

Necropsy —Postmortem examination. Autopsy. Examination of a dead body to determine the cause of death.

Necrosadism —Sexual gratification derived from the mutilation of the dead bodies.

Necroscopy —Postmortem examination. Autopsy.

Necrose —To cause or to undergo necrosis.

Necrosectomy —Excision of the necrosed tissue.

Necrosin —A substance obtained from inflamed tissues which causes inflammatory changes in the normal tissue.

Necrosis —Death of an area of a tissue or bone, surrounded by healthy parts.

Anemic necrosis —Necrosis caused by less blood supply to the part due to anemia.

Aseptic necrosis —Necrosis occurring without infection.

Caseous necrosis —Cheesy necrosis.

Central necrosis —Necrosis occurring only in the center of a part.

Cheesy necrosis —Caseous necrosis. The necrosis in which the tissue becomes cheeselike, seen usually in tuberculosis and syphilis.

Coagulation necrosis—Necrosis with coagulation in the necrotic area.

Colliquative necrosis —Liquefactive necrosis.

Dry necrosis—Dry gangrene.

Embolic necrosis—Necrosis resulting from an embolus.

Fat necrosis —Necrosis in small scattered areas of the fatty tissue.

Fibrinous necrosis —Coagulation necrosis.

Focal necrosis —Necrosis in small scattered areas, which are usually seen in infection.

Gummatous necrosis —Necrosis occurring in syphilitic gumma.

Ischemic necrosis —Coagulation necrosis.

Liquefactive necrosis —Necrosis caused by liquefaction of the tissues.

Moist necrosis —Necrosis with softening and moistening of the dead tissue.

Postpartum pituitary necrosis —Necrosis of the pituitary gland following childbirth.

Putrefactive necrosis —Necrosis caused by bacterial decomposition.

Radiation necrosis —Necrosis caused by exposure to radiation.

Superficial necrosis —Necrosis occurring only in the outer layers of a tissue.

Thrombotic necrosis —Necrosis occurring due to thrombus formation.

Total necrosis —Necrosis occurring in the entire organ or part.

Ustilaginea necrosis —Dry necrosis occurring due to ergot poisoning.

Necrospermia —Presence of dead or immobile spermatozoa in the semen.

Necrosteon, Necrosteosis —Gangrene of the bone.

Necrotic —Pertaining to the necrosis.

Necrotizing —Causing necrosis.

Necrotomy —1. Dissection of a dead body. 2. Excision of a sequestrum or necrotic tissue.

Necrotoxin —A toxin causing necrosis.

Needle —1. A slender, solid pointed instrument used for stitching, ligaturing or puncturing, which may be straight or curved. 2. A hollow needle used for injection, aspiration etc.

Aneurysm needle —A curved needle with a handle used for ligating a blood vessel.

Aspirating needle —A long hollow needle used for removing the fluid from a cavity.

Biopsy needle —A hollow needle used to obtain the central part of a tissue for histological examination.

Cataract needle —Needle used in removing a cataract.

Cutting needle —A surgical needle with angulated surface designed to puncture the tough tissue.

Discission needle —A special cataract needle for making multiple cuts into the lens capsule.

Hagedorn needle —A curved, flattened needle for suturing.

Hypodermic needle —A short, straight, hollow needle used for injecting the drugs under the skin.

Knife needle —A slender needle-pointed knife, used in ophthalmic operations.

Ligature needle —Aneurysm needle.

Lumbar puncture needle —A long hollow needle provided with a stylet used for entering the spinal cord and withdrawing cerebrospinal fliud.

Reverdin's needle —A surgical needle to carry a suture with an eye at the tip which can be opened and closed by a lever.

Stop needle —A needle with an eye at its tip and the other end having projecting margins which prevent the needle to be inserted too deep.

Needling —To puncture with a needle.

Negation —Denial. Refusal.

Negative —Indicating absence, as in a test result.

Negativism —Not performing the suggested actions (passive negativism) or acting against them. (active negativism)

Negatron —Negative electron.

Negri bodies —Minute particles found in the nerve cells of the brain of the person affected by rabies.

Neisseria —A genus of bacteria which are gram-negative cocci and usually occur in pairs. There are two species of it causing diseases in man—Neisseria gonorrhoeae (gonococcus) which causes gonorrhea and Neisseria meningitidis (meningococcus) which causes meningitis.

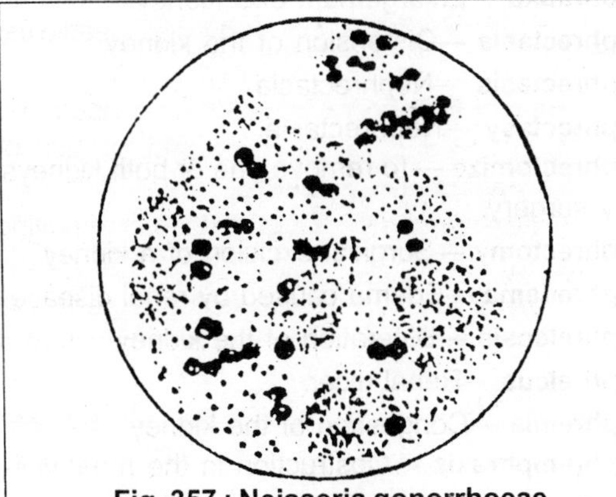

Fig. 357 : Neisseria gonorrhoeae (Gonococci)

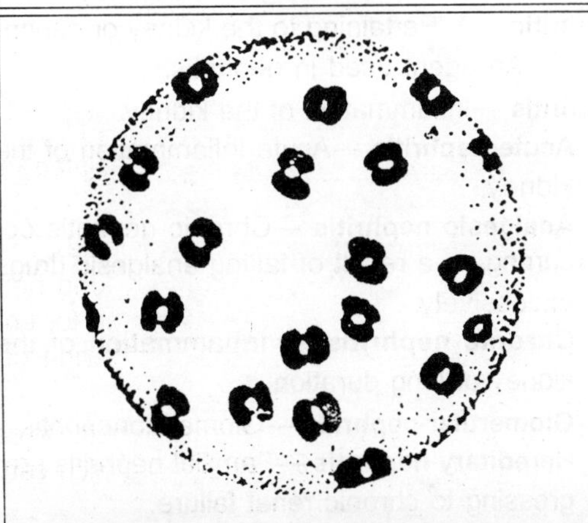

Fig. 358 : Neisseria meningitidis (Meningococci)

Nelton's line —A line drawan from the anterior superior iliac spine to the ischial tuberosity.

Nem —A unit of nutrition which is equivalent to the nutritive value of 1 gm. of breast milk.

Nema-, Nemat-, Nemato- —Prefixes meaning thread or threadlike.

Nemathelminth —A roundworm belonging to the phylum Nemathelminthes.

Nemathelminthes —The phylum of roundworms.

Nematicide —Nematocide.

Nematization —Infestation by roundworms.

Nematoblast —Spermatid. Spermatoblast.

Nematocide —An agent that kills the nematode worms.

Nematoda —A class of phylum Nemathelminthes that includes roundworms and threadworms, etc.

Nematode —Any member of the class Nematoda or roundworms.

Nematodiasis —Disease caused by a worm of the class Nematoda.

Nematoid —Like a roundworm or threadworm.

Nematologist — A specialist in nematology.

Nematology —Study of the worms of the class Nematoda.

Nematospermia —Spermatozoa with long tails.

Neo- —A prefix which means new or recent.

Neoadjuvant therapy —In the treatment of cancer, the use of medicines or radiation before operation of cancer.

Neoantigen —An intranuclear antigen present in some tumors.

Neoarthrosis —Nearthrosis. A false joint.

Neobiogenesis —A theory that life cannot arise from inorganic matter.

Neoblastic —Pertaining to, forming, originating in or of the nature of a new tissue.

Neocinetic —Neokinetic.

Neocortex —Neopallium.

Neofetal —Pertaining to an embryo of eighth or ninth week of intrauterine life.

Neofetus —Embryo during eighth or ninth week of intrauterine life.

Neoformation —1. Regeneration. 2. Neoplasm or new growth.

Neogala —The first milk coming from the breasts after childbirth.

Neogenesis —Tissue regeneration.

Neogenetic —Pertaining to the new formations or newly formed.

Neohymen —Pseudomembrane. A false or new membrane.

Neokinetic —Pertaining to the nervous motor mechanism which regulates the muscular control.

Neolalism —To speak the new words or phrases whose meanings may be known only to the patient speaking them.

Neologism —1. A new word or phrase whose meaning is known only to the patient speaking it. 2. A mental condition in which the patient speaks meaningless words or whose meanings are known only to him/her.

Neomembrane —Pseudomembrane. Neohymen.

Neomorph —New formation.

Neomorphism —Neomorph.

Neon —A gas in the air in proportion of 18 parts per million parts of the air whose chemical symbol is Ne.

Neonatal — Concerning with the newborn child.

Neonate —A newborn infant upto the age of 4 weeks.

Neonatologist —Specialist in neonatology.

Neonatology —The study of the care, diagnosis and treatment of the diseases of the newborn infants.

Neonatorum —Pertaining to the newborn infant.

Neopallium —Isocortex. The portion of the cerebral cortex with the exception of the rhinencephalon or corpus striatum (olfactory lobe).

Neopathy —A new disease or a new complication of a disease.

Neophilism —Morbid love of new persons, things or scenes.

Neophobia —Kainophobia. 1. Morbid fear of the new persons, things or scenes. 2. Aversion to all that is unknown or not understood.

Neophrenia —Mental deterioration in early youth.

Neoplasia —The formation of a neoplasm.

Neoplasm —Tumor or a new and abnormal growth which may be benign or malignant.

Neoplastic —Pertaining to or of the nature of a neoplasm.

Neoplasty —Surgical formation or restoration of parts of the body.

Neostomy —Surgical formation of an artificial opening into an organ or between two organs.

Neovascularization —Proliferation of blood vessels in a tissue in which these are not normally present or proliferation of blood vessels of a different type usually found in the tissue.

Nephelometer —An apparatus for measuring the turbidity of a fluid.

Nephelometry —To measure the turbidity of a fluid by nephelometer.

Nephelopia —Dimness of vision.

Nephr- —A prefix denoting kidney.

Nephradenoma —Renal adenoma.

Nephralgia —Pain in a kidney.

Nephralgic —Pertaining to renal pain.

Nephrapostasis —Renal abscess.

Nephratonia — Nephrotony

Nephratony —Nephratonia. Lack of normal renal tone.

Nephrauxe —Enlargement of a kidney.

Nephrectasia —Distension of the kidney.

Nephrectasis —Nephrectasia.

Nephrectasy —Nephrectasia.

Nephrectomize —To remove one or both kidneys by surgery.

Nephrectomy —Surgical excision of a kidney.

Nephredema —Edema caused by renal disease.

Nephrelcosis —Ulceration of the kidney.

Nephrelcus —Renal ulcer.

Nephremia —Congestion of the kidney.

Nephremphraxis —Obstruction in the renal vessels.

Nephric —Renal. Pertaining to the kidney.

Nephritic —1. Pertaining to the kidney or nephritis. 2. An agent used in nephritis.

Nephritis —Inflammation of the kidney.

- **Acute nephritis** —Acute inflammation of the kidney.
- **Analgesic nephritis** —Chronic nephritis occurring as a result of taking analgesic drugs excessively.
- **Chronic nephritis** — Inflammation of the kidney of long duration.
- **Glomerular nephritis** —Glomerulonephritis.
- **Hereditary nephritis** —Familial nephritis progressing to chronic renal failure.
- **Interstitial nephritis** —Inflammation of the interstitial tissue of the kidney.
- **Parenchymatous nephritis** —Inflammation affecting the parenchyma of the kidney.
- **Suppurative nephritis** —Nephritis with abscess formation.

Transfusion nephritis —Nephritis caused by transfusion of incompatible blood.

Nephritogenic —Causing nephritis.

Nephro-, Nephr- —Prefixes which mean pertaining to kidney.

Nephroabdominal —Pertaining to the kidney and the abdomen.

Nephroblastoma —Wilms' tumor.

Nephrocalcinosis —Deposition of calcium phosphate in the renal tubules.

Nephrocapsectomy —Excision of the renal capsule.

Nephrocardiac —Pertaining to the kidney and heart.

Nephrocele —Hernia of the kidney.

Nephrocolic —1. Pertaining to the kidney and colon. 2. Renal colic.

Nephrocolopexy —Surgical suspension of the kidney and colon.

Nephrocoloptosis —Downward displacement of the kidney and colon.

Nephrocystanastomosis —Formation of an artificial passage between kidney and the urinary bladder.

Nephrocystitis —Inflammation of the kidney and urinary bladder.

Nephrocystosis —Formation of renal cysts.

Nephrogenetic —Nephrogenic. Producing kidney tissue. Arising from a kidney.

Nephrogenic —Nephrogenetic.

Nephrogenous —Nephrogenetic.

Nephrogram —X-ray film of the kidney.

Nephrography —Radiography of the kidney.

Nephrohydrosis —Accumulation of urine in the renal pelvis and calyces due to obstruction.

Nephrohypertrophy —Hypertrophy of the kidney.

Nephroid —Reniform. Kidney-shaped.

Nephrolith —Stone in the kidney.

Nephrolithiasis —Presence of calculi in the kidney.

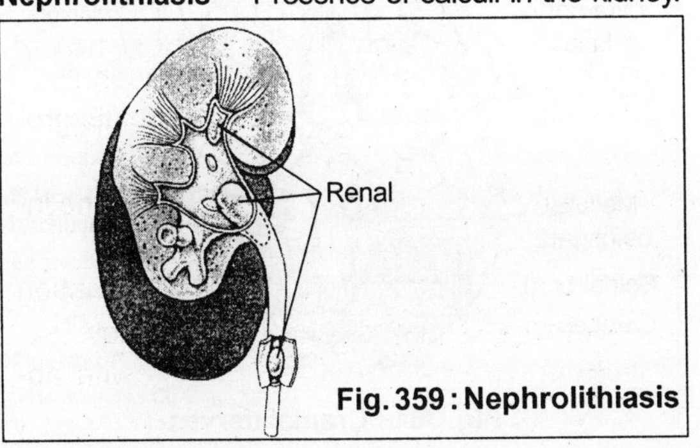

Fig. 359 : Nephrolithiasis

Nephrolithotomy —To make an incision into a kidney to remove a calculus.

Nephrology —The study of the structure and function of the kidney.

Nephrolysine —A toxic substance, especially an antigen that destroys the renal tissue.

Nephrolysis —1. Detachment of a kidney from adhesions. 2. Destruction of kidney substance.

Nephrolytic —Destructive to the kidney.

Nephroma —Renal tumor.

Nephromalacia —Softening of a kidney.

Nephromegaly —Enlargement of the kidney.

Nephromere —A segment in the embryo from which kidney develops.

Nephron —Structural and functional unit of the kidney.

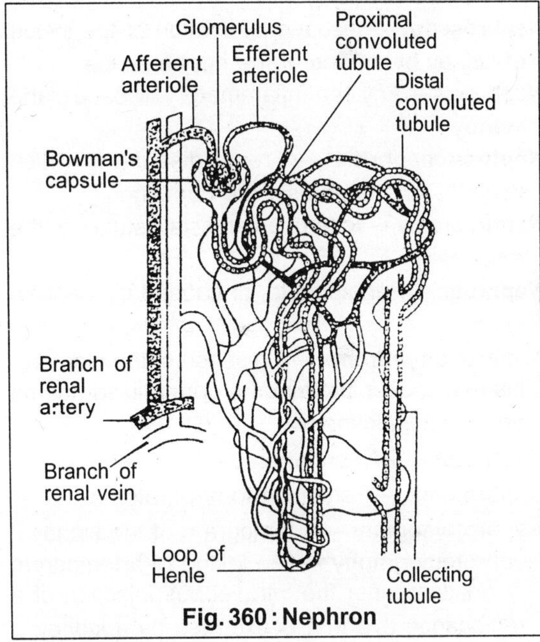

Fig. 360 : Nephron

Nephroncus —A renal tumor.

Nephronophthisis —Wasting disease of the kidney.

Nephroparalysis —Paralysis of the kidney.

Nephropathia —Nephropathy.

Nephropathic —Causing renal disease.

Nephropathy —Any disease of the kidney.

Nephropexy —To attach a floating kidney by surgery.

Nephrophthisis —Tuberculosis of the kidney.

Nephroptosia —Nephroptosis.

Nephroptosis —Prolapse or downward displacement of the kidney.

Nephropyelitis —Pyelonephritis. Inflammation of the renal pelvis and parenchyma of the kidney.

Nephropyelography —X-ray examination of the kidney and the renal pelvis.

Nephropyeloplasty —Plastic surgery on the kidney and renal pelvis.

Nephropyosis —Suppuration of a kidney.

Nephrorrhagia —Hemorrhage from the kidney.

Nephrorrhaphy —Suturing of the kidney.

Nephros —The kidney.

Nephrosclerosis —Hardening of the kidney.

Nephrosclerotic —Pertaining to or causing nephrosclerosis.

Nephroscope —An instrument for viewing the inside of the kidney.

Nephroscopy —Visual examination of the inside of kidney by means of the nephroscope.

Nephrosis —Any non-inflammatory disease of the kidney.

Nephrosonephritis —A renal disease in which nephritis and nephrosis are combined.

Nephrostomy —To form an artificial fistula into the renal pelvis.

Nephrotic —Pertaining to, or caused by, nephrosis.

Nephrotic syndrome —A disease of the glomerulus that causes proteinuria, generalized edema and hypoalbuminemia.

Nephrotome —Nephromere.

Nephrotomic —Pertaining to nephrotome.

Nephrotomogram —A tomogram of the kidney.

Nephrotomography —The taking of a tomogram of a kidney after the intravenous injection of a radiopaque dye that is excreted by a kidney.

Nephrotomy —To make an incision into a kidney.

Nephrotoxic —The substance destructive to the kidney cells.

Nephrotoxicity —The state of being toxic to the kidney.

Nephrotoxin —A toxic substance which damages kidney cells.

Nephrotresis—Formation of a permanent excretory opening in the kidney through the loin.

Nephrotrophic —Nephrotropic.

Nephrotropic —Affecting the kidneys.

Nephrotuberculosis —Tuberculosis of the kidney.

Nephrotyphoid —Renal disease complicating typhoid fever.

Nephroureterectomy —Surgical excision of the kidney with the ureter or part of it.

Nephroureterocystectomy —Excision of a kidney, ureter and part or all of the urinary bladder.

Nephrydrosis —Hydronephrosis, nephrohydrosis. Distention of the renal pelvis resulting from obstruction.

Nerve —A cord-like structure made up of nerve fibers that convey impulses between the central nervous system (brain and the spinal cord) and the various parts of the body.

Abducent nerve —VIth cranial nerve.

Accelerator nerve —A cardiac sympathetic nerve which on stimulation accelerates the heart beat.

Accessory nerve —XIth cranial nerve.

Acoustic nerve —VIIIth cranial nerve.

Adrenergic nerve —A sympathetic nerve that liberates norepinephrine at a synapse when it transmits a stimulus.

Afferent nerve —Any nerve that transmits the impulses from the periphery to the central nervous system.

Articular nerve —A nerve supplying a joint.

Autonomic nerve —A nerve of the autonomic nervous system.

Centrifugal nerve —Efferent nerve.

Centripetal nerve —Afferent nerve.

Cerebrospinal nerve —A nerve originating from the brain or the spinal cord.

Cholinergic nerve —A parasympathetic nerve which liberates acetylcholine when it transmits a stimulus.

Cranial nerve —One of the 12 pairs of nerves

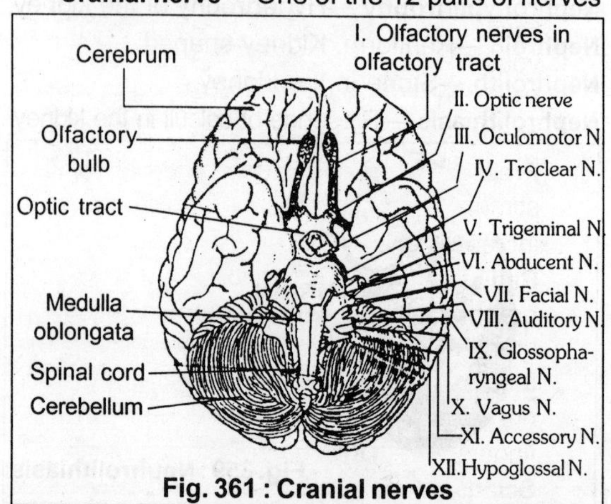

Fig. 361 : Cranial nerves

arising from the brain which pass through the foramina of the brain.

Depressor nerve —Any afferent nerve which on stimulation depresses the activity of an organ.

Efferent nerve —Motor nerve. A nerve which transmits the impulses from the central nervous system to the periphery.

Excitatory nerve —A nerve which transmits the impulses which stimulate the function of a part of the body.

Excitoreflex nerve —A visceral nerve that produces reflex action.

Facial nerve —VIIth carnial nerve.

Gangliated nerve —Any nerve of the sympathetic nervous system.

Glossopharyngeal nerve —IXth cranial nerve.

Inhibitory nerve —A nerve that upon stimulation lessens the activity of a part of the body.

Lumbar nerve —One of the five pairs of spinal nerves which correspond with the lumbar vertebrae.

Median nerve —A combined motor and sensory nerve of the arm originating from the brachial plexus.

Medullated nerve —Myelinated nerve.

Mixed nerve —A nerve composed of both afferent (sensory) and efferent (motor) fibers.

Motor nerve —Efferent nerve. A nerve containing motor fibers and conveying motor impulses, that stimulate muscle contraction.

Olfactory nerve —Ist cranial nerve.

Optic nerve —IInd cranial nerve.

Parasympathetic nerve —A nerve of the parasympathetic division of the autonomic nervous system.

Peripheral nerve —Any nerve outside the central nervous system.

Pressor nerve —An afferent nerve which on stimulation by constricting the blood vessels increases the blood pressure.

Radial nerve —It is the largest branch of the brachial plexus which supplies the triceps brachii muscle and skin of the posterior surface of the upper arm, muscles of the posterior surface and skin of the forearm, thumb, 2 fingers and lateral half of the 3rd finger.

Sciatic nerve —It is the largest nerve in the body which arises from sacral plexus and is

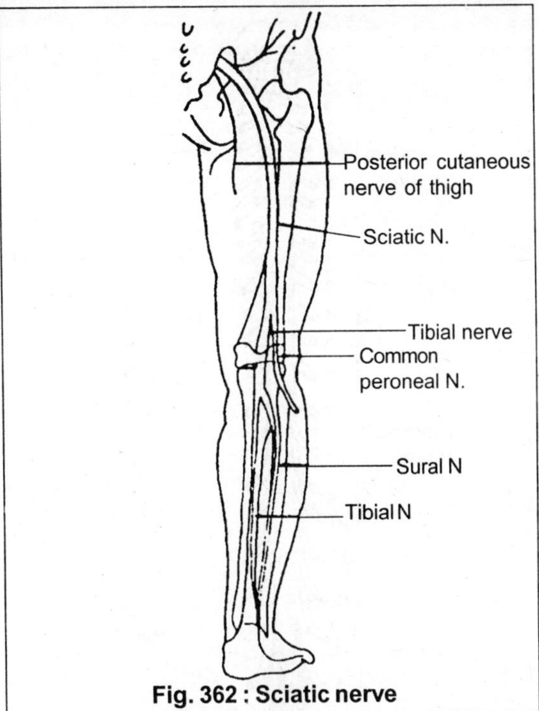

Fig. 362 : Sciatic nerve

about 2 cm. wide at its origin. It reaches the buttock from the pelvic cavity passing through the greater sciatic foramen, whence it descends into the posterior part of the thigh and supplies the hamstring muscles. It is divided into two branches in the middle of the femur bone—tibial nerve and common peroneal nerve.

Secretory nerve —An afferent nerve which on stimulation increases the glandular secretion.

Sensory nerve —A peripheral nerve that transmits the impulse from a sense organ to the spinal cord or brain.

Somatic nerves —The motor and sensory nerves supplying the skeletal muscles and the somatic tissues.

Spinal nerves — These are 31 pairs of the peripheral nerves coming out of the spinal cord, including 8 cervical, 12 thoracic, 5 lumbar, 5 sacral and 1 coccygeal.

Splanchnic nerve —A nerve which supply the visceral organs and blood vessels.

Sympathetic nerve —A nerve of the sympathetic division of the autonomic nervous system.

Trigeminal nerve —Vth cranial nerve, the chief sensory nerve of the face and motor nerve of the muscles of mastication.

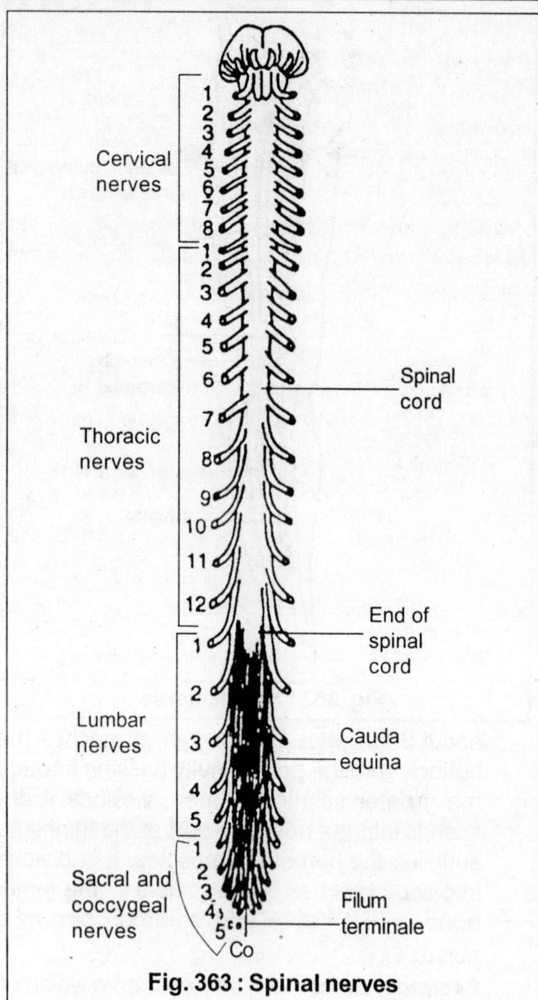

Fig. 363 : Spinal nerves

Ulnar nerve —It arises from the brachial plexus and passes down the upper arm, behind the medial epicondyle of the humerus, and down the ulnar side of the anterior compartment of the forearm to the hand and supplies the muscles of the side of the ulna bone of the forearm, and then descending downward supplies the muscles of the hypothenar and the whole little finger and the medial half part of the 3rd finger.

Vagus nerve —10th cranial nerve which on stimulation slows the heart rate.

Vasoconstrictor nerve —A nerve which on stimulation contracts the blood vessels.

Vasodilator nerve —A nerve which on stimulation dilates the blood vessels.

Vasomotor nerve —The nerve concerned with the constriction and dilatation of the vessels.

Nerve endings —The terminations of a nerve fiber (axon or dendrite) in a peripheral structure, which may be sensory or motor.

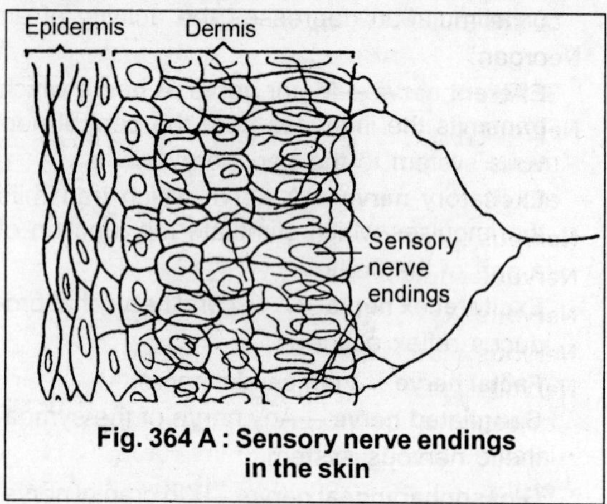

Fig. 364 A : Sensory nerve endings in the skin

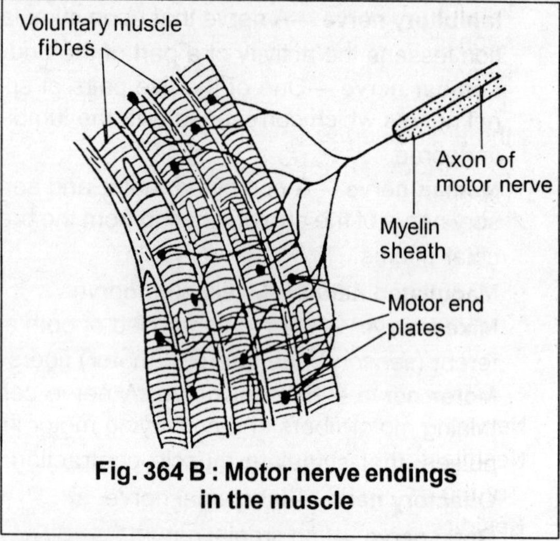

Fig. 364 B : Motor nerve endings in the muscle

Nerve fiber —Axon which is concerned with the transmission of impulses.

Nerve fibril —Neurofibrilla. A fine fiber in the cytoplasm and cell processes of a neuron.

Nerve grafting —Implantation of a piece of nerve-tissue into another nerve.

Nerve impulse —The excitatory process that travels along a nerve fiber when it is stimulated.

Nerve plexus —A network of nerves.

Nervi —Plural of nervus.

Nervimotility —Capability for movement in response to nervous stimulation.

Nervimotion —Movement in response to a nervous stimulus.

Nervimotor —Pertaining to a motor nerve.

Nervo- —A prefix which means pertaining to a nerve.

Nervomuscular —Pertaining to the nerve supply of the muscles.

Nervous —1. Anxious. 2. Pertaining to the nerves. 3. Able to be excited or irritated.

Nervous breakdown —A popular name for any mental disorder that interferes with the normal activities of the person.

Nervous debility —Neurasthenia. Nervous fatigue.

Nervous impulse —Nerve impulse.

Nervousness —State of being nervous.

Nervous prostration —Neurasthenia.

Nervous system —The system of the body which adjusts the body to the surroundings and regulates all the voluntary and involuntary activities of the body. Its sensory part collects information from the surroundings and motor part is responsible for responses of the body.
Nervous system is divided into two parts—
1. Central nervous system (CNS)—It contains the brain and the spinal cord.
2. Peripheral nervous system— It has two parts—
I. Somatic (cerebrospinal) nervous system—It is made up of 12 pairs of cranial nerves and 31 pairs of the spinal nerves.
II. Autonomic (splanchnic) nervous system—It consists of sympathetic and parasympathetic system.

Nervus —Nerve.

Nesidiectomy —Surgical excision of the islet cells of the pancreas.

Nesidioblast —One of the cells giving rise to the islet cells of the pancreas.

Nesidioblastoma —A tumor of the islet cells of the pancreas.

Nesidioblastosis —Hyperplasia of the cells of the islets of Langerhans.

Nest —A mass of cells resembling a bird nest.

Nesteostomy —Jejunostomy.

Nestiatria —Treatment of diseases by fasting.

n. et m. —Nocte et mane. Night and morning.

Ne tr. snum. —Do not deliver unless paid.

Nettle rash —Hives. Urticaria.

Network —Reticulum. The arrangement of fibers in a structure resembling a net.

Neur-, Neuri-, Neuro- —Prefixes meaning nerve, nerve tissue, the nervous system.

Neurad —Toward a nerve or its axis.

Neuragmia —Rupturing of a nerve trunk.

Neural —Pertaining to nerves or nervous system.

Neuralgia —Neurodynia. Pain occurring along the course of one or more nerves.

Neuralgic —Of or pertaining to neuralgia.

Neuralgiform —Similar to neuralgia.

Neural spine— Spinous process of vertebrae.

Neuramebimeter —An apparatus for determining the time of response of a nerve to a stimulus.

Neuranagenesis —Regeneration of a nerve.

Neurapophysis —Lamina. Either of the two sides of a vertebra which joins to form the neural arch.

Neurapraxia —Non-functioning of a peripheral nerve without structural changes, due to blunt injury, compression or ischaemia.

Neurarchy —The domination of the nervous system over the body.

Neurarthropathy —Neuroarthropathy.

Neurasthenia —Nervous debility.

Neurasthenic —1. Pertaining to neurasthenia. 2. The person suffering from neurasthenia.

Neuratrophia, Neuratrophy —1. Atrophy of the nervous tissue. 2. Deficient nutrition of the nervous system.

Neuratrophic —The person affected by atrophy of the nervous tissue or deficient nutrition of the nervous system.

Neuraxis —1. Axon. 2. Cerebrospinal axis or the central nervous system.

Neuraxitis —Encephalitis.

Neuraxon —Axon.

Neurectasia, Neurectasis, Neurectasy —Neurotension.Surgical stretching of a nerve.

Neurectomy —Partial or total excision of a nerve.

Neurectopia, Neurectopy —Displacement or abnormal position of a nerve.

Neurenteric —Pertaining to the neural canal and the intestinal tube of the embryo.

Neurepithelium —Neuroepithelium.

Neurergic —Pertaining to the activity of a nerve.

Neurexeresis —Surgical tearing out of a nerve to relieve neuralgia.

Neuriatry —Neurology.

Neurilemma —Neurolemma. A thin membranous sheath enclosing a nerve fiber.

Neurilemmitis —Inflammation of the neurilemma.

Neurilemmoma, Neurilemoma —Neurinoma, neurofibroma. A tumor of the neurilemma.

Neurilemmosarcoma —A malignant neurilemoma.

Neurility —The property of the nerves to conduct stimuli.

Neurimotility —Nervimotility.

Neurimotor —Pertaining to a motor nerve.

Neurinoma —Neurilemmoma.

Neurinomatosis —Neurofibromatosis.

Neurite —Neuraxon.

Neuritic —Pertaining to the neuritis.

Neuritis —Inflammation of a nerve or nerves.

Adventitial neuritis —Inflammation of the nerve sheath.

Ascending neuritis —Inflammation progressing upward along a nerve, away from the periphery.

Axial neuritis —Inflammation of the inner portion of a nerve.

Degenerative neuritis —Neuritis with rapid degeneration of a nerve.

Descending neuritis —Inflammation progressing downward along a nerve, toward the periphery.

Dietetic neuritis, Endemic neuritis —Beriberi.

Disseminated neuritis —Neuritis involving a large group of nerves.

Interstitial neuritis —Inflammation of the connective tissue of a nerve.

Multiple neuritis —Polyneuritis. Inflammation of more than one peripheral nerves at a time.

Nodosa neuritis—Neuritis with the formation of nodes on the nerves.

Peripheral neuritis —Inflammation of the peripheral nerves.

Rheumatic neuritis —Neuritis with the symptoms of rheumatism.

Sciatic neuritis —Sciatica. Inflammation of the sciatic nerve.

Senile neuritis —Neuritis occurring in the old persons which usually affects the extremities.

Toxic neuritis —Neuritis caused by poisons.

Traumatic neuritis —Neuritis occurring after an injury.

Neuro- —A prefix which means pertaining to a nerve, nervous tissue or nervous system.

Neuroallergy —An allergic reaction in the nervous tissue.

Neuroanastomosis —Surgical anastomosis of one nerve to another.

Neuroanatomy —Anatomy of the nervous system.

Neuroarthropathy —Any joint disease associated with a disease of central or peripheral nervous system.

Neuroastrocytoma —A tumor of the central nervous system composed of the nerve cells and glial cells.

Neuroaugmentation —To use electrical stimulation to make an addition to the activity of the nervous system.

Neuroaugmentive—Pertaining to neuroaugmentation.

Neurobiologist —A specialist in neurobiology.

Neurobiology —Biology of the nervous system.

Neurobiotaxis —Movement of the nerve cell bodies toward, or growth of their axons toward, the area from which they are stimulated.

Neuroblast —An embryonic cell from which a neuron is formed.

Neuroblastoma —A sarcoma tumor of the nervous system origin, composed chiefly of neuroblasts, occurring mostly in infants and children upto 10 years of age.

Neurocanal —The central canal of the spinal cord.

Neurocardiac —Pertaining to the nervous system and the heart.

Neurocentral —Pertaining to the centrum of a vertebra and the neural arch.

Neurocentrum —Body of a vertebra.

Neurochemistry —The branch of neurology dealing with the chemistry of the nervous system.

Neurochitin —Neurokeratin.

Neurochorioretinitis —Optic neuritis with the inflammation of the choroid and retina.

Neurochoroiditis —Inflammation of the optic nerve and the choroid.

Neurocirculatory —Pertaining to the nervous system and the circulation.

Neurocladism —The formation of new branches by the process of a neuron.

Neuroclonic —Having spasms of nervous origin.

Neurocoele —Neurocele. Formation of cavities in the cerebrospinal axis.

Neurocranium —The part of the skull enclosing the brain.

Neurocrine —1. Denoting an endocrine influence

on the nerves or the influence of the nerves on the endocrine tissues. 2. Pertaining to the secretion of the nerves.

Neurocristopathy —Any disease arising from maldevelopment of the neural crest.

Neurocutaneous —Pertaining to the nerves and the skin.

Neurocyte —Neuron. Nerve cell.

Neurocytolysis —Destruction of the neurons.

Neurocytoma —A tumor of the nerve cells.

Neurodealgia —Pain in the retina.

Neurodegenerative —Pertaining to degeneration of the tissue of the nervous system.

Neurodendrite —Dendrite.

Neurodendron —Dendrite.

Neurodermatitis —Inflammation of the skin with itching caused by emotional disturbance.

Neurodermatosis —Phacomatosis. Any skin disease of neural origin.

Neurodermatrophia —Atrophy of the skin from nervous disease.

Neurodiagnosis —Diagnosis of the nervous diseases.

Neurodynamic —Pertaining to the nervous energy.

Neurodynia —Neuralgia. Pain in a nerve or nerves.

Neuroectoderm —The embryonic tissue that gives rise to the nervous tissue.

Neuroectodermal —Pertaining to the neuroectoderm.

Neuroectomy —Neurectomy.

Neuroeffector —Of or pertaining to the junction between a neuron and the effector organ it innervates.

Neuroencephalomyelopathy —The disease of the brain, spinal cord and nerves.

Neuroendocrine —Pertaining to the nervous and the endocrine systems.

Neuroendocrinology —The study of the relationship between the nervous system and the endocrine systems.

Neuroenteric —Pertaining to the nervous system and the intestines.

Neuroepidermal —Pertaining to or giving rise to the nervous system and the epidermis.

Neuroepithelioma —Neurocytoma.

Neuroepithelium —1. Epithelium made up of specialized cells which act as sensory cells to receive the external stimuli. 2. The ectodermal epithelium from which the central nervous system develops.

Neurofibril, Neurofibrilla —One of the very small threadlike structures running in every direction in the cytoplasm of the body of the nerve cell extending into the axon and dendrites.

Neurofibrillar —Pertaining to neurofibrils.

Neurofibroma —A tumor of the connective tissue of a nerve, which may occur in the mouth, pleura or stomach.

Neurofibromatosis —Neurinomatosis. Formation of multiple tumors of various sizes on the peripheral nerves which may be neuromas or fibromas.

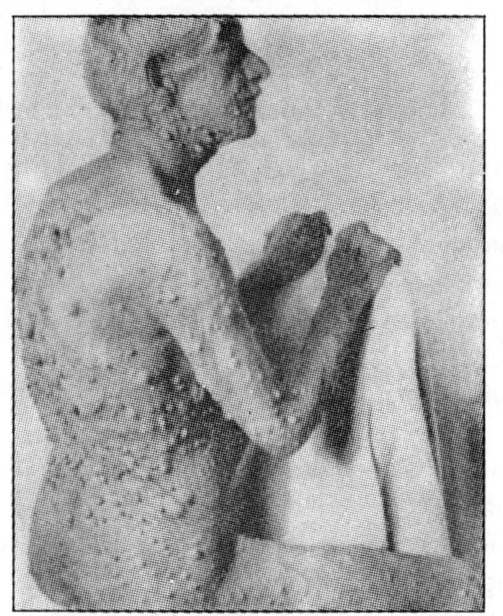

Fig. 365 : Neurofibromatosis

Neurofibrosarcoma —Neurogenic sarcoma. A malignant neurofibroma.

Neurofibrositis —Inflammation of nerve fibers.

Neurofilament —Any one of the minute threadlike structures forming a neurofibril.

Neurogangliitis —Inflammation of a neuroganglion.

Neuroganglion —A mass of nervous tissue.

Neurogastric —Pertaining to the nerves of the stomach.

Neurogenesis —Development of the nervous tissue.

Neurogenetic—1. Pertaining to the formation of a nerve. 2. Pertaining to the origin in nerves.

Neurogenic —Forming or originating from the nervous tissue.

Neurogenous —Neurogenic.

Neuroglia —The connective or supporting tissue of the nervous tissue which also plays an important role in the reaction of a nervous system to injury or to infection.

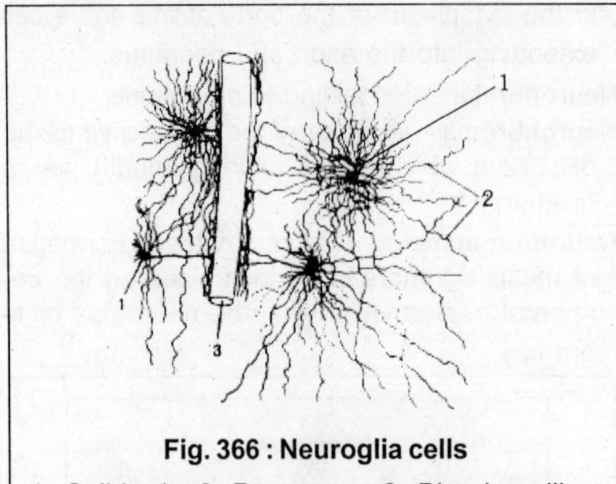

Fig. 366 : Neuroglia cells

1- Cell body, 2- Processes, 3- Blood capillary

Neurogliacyte —Glia cell. Any one of the cells composing the neuroglia.

Neuroglial —Pertaining to the neuroglia.

Neurogliar —Neuroglial.

Neuroglioma —Glioma. A tumor of the neuroglial cells.

Neurogliomatosis —Formation of multiple gliomas in the nervous system.

Neurogliosis —Formation of multiple neurogliomas.

Neuroglycopenia —Chronic hypoglycemia impairing the brain function.

Neurogram —Engram. The imprint left on the brain by the past experiences.

Neurography —The study of the nervous system.

Neurohematology —The study of the blood changes occurring in nervous diseases.

Neurohistology —Histology of the nervous system.

Neurohormone —1. A hormone affecting the function of the nervous system. 2. A hormone released due to nervous stimulation.

Neurohumor —A chemical substance such as acetylcholine, released at a nerve ending, which transmits the impulses across a myoneural junction.

Neurohypophysial —Pertaining to the neurohypophysis.

Neurohypophysis —Posterior lobe of the pituitary gland including pars intermedia.

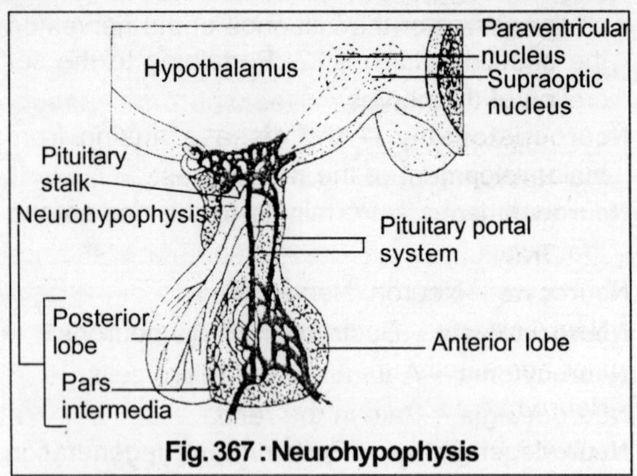

Fig. 367 : Neurohypophysis

Neuroid —Like a nerve.

Neuroinduction —Mental suggestion.

Neurokeratin —A type of keratin found in the myelin sheath of the nerve fibers.

Neurokyme —The action of a nerve.

Neurolemma —Neurilemma.

Neurolemmitis —Neurilemmitis.

Neurolemmoma —Neurilemoma.

Neuroleptanalgesia —Analgesia and amnesia produced by the administration of analgesic and neuroleptic drugs.

Neuroleptanesthesia —General anesthesia produced by intravenous injection of a neuroleptic drug, and an analgesic.

Neuroleptic —A drug acting on the nervous system.

Neurologic, Neurological —Pertaining to the study of the nervous diseases.

Neurologist —A specialist in neurology.

Neurology —The branch of medical science which deals with the nervous system and its diseases.

Neurolymphomatosis —Malignant lymphoma of the nervous system.

Neurolysin —A substance which destroys the nerve cells.

Neurolysis —1. Disintegration or destruction of the nerve tissue. 2. To stretch a nerve to relieve tension. 3. To separate the adhesions surrounding a nerve.

Neurolytic —Pertaining to neurolysis.

Neuroma —A tumor or new growth made up of nerve cells and nerve fibers.

Acoustic neuroma —A benign tumor of the eighth cranial nerve characterized by headache, tinnitis and loss of hearing.

Amputation neuroma —Neuroma occurring on the nerves of a stump after amputation.

False neuroma —Neurofibroma, pseudoneuroma.

Neuroma cutis —Neuroma occurring in the skin.

Traumatic neuroma —Neuroma occurring in a wound resulting after damage of the nerve.

Neuromalacia —Abnormal softening of the nerves or nervous tissue.

Neuromatosis —Formation of multiple neuromas in the body.

Neuromatous —Pertaining to a neuroma.

Neuromelanin —A modified melanin pigment normally found in certain neurons of the nervous system, especially in the substantia nigra.

Neuromeningeal —Pertaining to the involvement of nervous tissue and the meninges.

Neuromere —Any of a series of segmental elevations in the wall of the neural tube in the embryo and on the ventrolateral surface of the rhombencephalon.

Neuromimetic —Pertaining to the action of a drug that stimulates the response of an effector organ to nerve impulses.

Neuromuscular —Pertaining to both the nerves and the muscles.

Neuromyasthenia —Muscular weakness due to emotional disorder.

Neuromyelitis —Inflammation of the nerves and the spinal cord.

Neuromyopathic —Pertaining to the diseases of both, the nerves and the muscles.

Neuromyopathy —Any disease of both, the nerves and the muscles.

Neuromyositis —A combined neuritis and myositis.

Neuron —Nerve cell consisting of a cell body containing the nucleus and its surrounding cytoplasm and the processes—an axon and one or more dendrites. It is the structural and functional unit of the nervous system and takes part in the initiation and conduction of the impulses.

Afferent neuron —Neuron that conducts a nerve impulse from a receptor to brain or the spinal cord.

Associative neuron —A neuron that mediates impulses between a sensory and motor neuron.

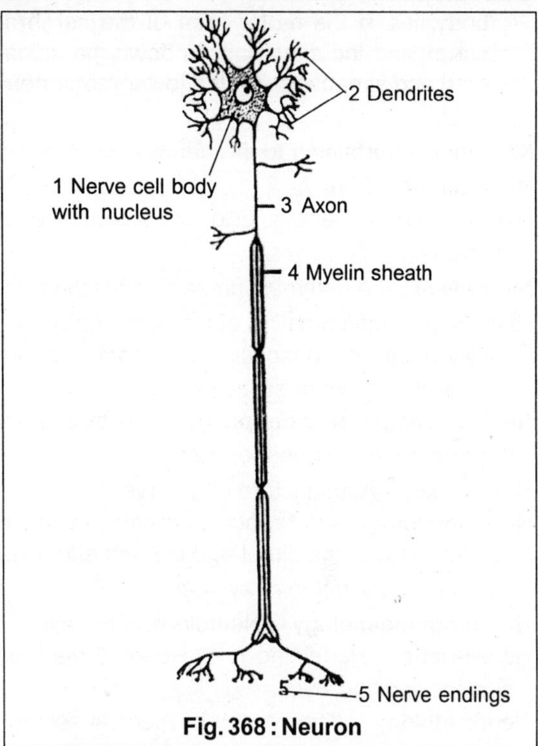

Fig. 368 : Neuron

Central neuron —Neuron which is situated only in the central nervous system.

Efferent neuron —Neuron that conducts a nerve impulse away from the brain or the spinal cord to the organ of response.

Lower motor neuron —A neuron whose cell body lies in the gray matter of the spinal cord and its axon innervates striated muscle fibers.

Motor neuron —Neuron that carries nerve impulses causing muscle contraction.

Multipolar neuron —A neuron possessing one axon and many dendrites.

Postganglionic neuron —A neuron whose cell body lies in the autonomic ganglion and the axon ends in an effector organ (smooth or cardiac muscle or glands.)

Preganglionic neuron —The neuron of the autonomic nervous system whose cell body lies in the central nervous system and the axon terminates in the peripheral ganglion.

Sensory neuron —An afferent neuron conveying sensory impulses.

Unipolar neuron —The neuron whose cell body bearing only one process.

Upper motor neuron —A neuron whose cell

body lies in the motor area of the cerebral cortex and the axon passes down the spinal cord and synapses with the lower motor neurons.

Neuronal —Pertaining to the neuron.

Neurone —Neuron.

Neuronephric —Pertaining to nervous and renal systems.

Neuronevus —A birthmark present within the skin.

Neuronitis —Inflammation of the nerve cells.

Neuronophage —A phagocyte that destroys nerve cells in the nervous system.

Neuronophagia, Neuronophagy —Destruction of the nerve cells by phagocytes.

Neuronyxis —Acupuncture of a nerve.

Neuro-oncology —A branch of medical science concerned with the direct and indirect effects of tumors on the nervous system.

Neuro-ophthalmology —Neurology of the eye.

Neuro-optic —Pertaining to the central nervous system and the eyes.

Neuro-otology —The branch of medical science concerned with the nervous system related to the auditory system.

Neuropacemaker —An apparatus to be implanted for electrical stimulation of the spinal cord.

Neuropapilitis —Optic neuritis.

Neuroparalysis —Paralysis due to disease of a nerve or nerves.

Neuroparalytic —Pertaining to or suffering from neuroparalysis.

Neuropath —The person suffering from some disease of the central nervous system.

Neuropathia —Neuropathy.

Neuropathic —Pertaining to neuropathy.

Neuropathogenesis —The origin and development of a nervous disease.

Neuropathogenicity —The ability to produce pathological changes in the nerve tissue.

Neuropathology —Pathology of the diseases of the nervous system.

Neuropathy —Any disease of the nerves.

Ascending neuropathy —A disease of the nervous system ascending upward from the lower part of the body.

Auditory neuropathy —A disease of the auditory nerves in children characterized by loss of hearing.

Descending neuropathy —A disease of the nervous system descending downward from the upper part of the body.

Diabetic neuropathy —A disease of the peripheral nervous system, autonomic nervous system and some cranial nerves occurring in diabetes mellitus.

Lead neuropathy —Disease of the various nerves seen in chronic lead poisoning usually characterized by wrist-drop.

Optic neuropathy —A disease of the optic nerves. Usually one eye is affected. In chronic stage there may be blindness in the affected eye.

Neuropharmacology —The branch of pharmacology concerned with the study of the effects of drugs on the nervous system.

Neurophilic —Attracted towards the nervous tissue.

Neurophonia —A tic or spasm of the speech muscles resulting in uncontrollable cry.

Neurophthalmology —Neuro-ophthalmology.

Neurophthisis —Wasting of nerve tissue.

Neurophysician —Physician of the nervous diseases.

Neurophysin —Any of a group of soluble proteins secreted in the hypothalamus, which takes part in the transport of oxytocin and vasopressin.

Neurophysiology —Physiology of the nervous system.

Neuropil, Neuropile —A network of unmyelinated fibrils into which the nerve processes of the central nervous system divide.

Neuroplasm —Protoplasm of a nerve cell.

Neuroplasmic —Pertaining to the protoplasm of a nerve cell.

Neuroplasty —Plastic surgery of the nerves.

Neuroplegic —Pertaining to paralysis due to a disease of the nervous system.

Neuroplexus —A network of nerve cells or fibers.

Neuropodia —Plural of neuropodium.

Neuropodium —Small bulblike terminal of an axon in one type of synapse.

Neuropore —Opening from the neural canal to the exterior in an embryo which closes as the embryo develops.

Neuropotential —Nerve energy.

Neuropraxia —The inability of a nerve to conduct the nerve impulse due to trauma without any structural change.

Neuropsychiatrist —A specialist in neuropsychiatry.

Neuropsychiatry —The neurology and psychiatry combined.

Neuropsychologic, Neuropsychological —Pertaining to neuropsychology.

Neuropsychology —Study of the nervous and psychological diseases.

Neuropsychopathic —Pertaining to neuropsychopathy.

Neuropsychopathy —Nervous and mental disease conbined.

Neuropsychopharmacology —The study of the effects of drugs on mental diseases.

Neuroradiography —Radiography of the nervous system.

Neuroradiology —X-ray examination of the nervous system.

Neuroretinitis —Inflammation of the optic nerve and retina.

Neuroretinopathy —Any disease of the optic nerve and the retina.

Neurorrhaphy —Neurosuture. Suturing of the ends of a divided nerve.

Neurosarcocleisis —An operation performed to relieve neuralgia.

Neurosarcoma —A sarcoma containing neuromatous elements.

Neuroscience —The embryology, anatomy, physiology, histopathology, biochemistry and pharmacology of the nervous system.

Neuroscientist —An expert in neuroscience.

Neurosclerosis —Hardening of a nervous tissue.

Neurosecretion —1. Secretory activities of the nerve cells. 2. The chemical substance discharged by a nerve cell

Neurosecretory —Pertaining to neurosecretion.

Neurosensory —Pertaining to a sensory nerve.

Neurosis —Psychoneurosis. An emotional disorder caused by unresolved conflicts of which anxiety is the chief symptom.

Accidental neurosis —Traumatic neurosis. A neurosis with hysterical symptoms caused by an accident or injury.

Anxiety neurosis — Neurosis in which there is excessive anxiety, which is the main symptom and interferes with the daily living.

Cardiac neurosis —Neurocirculatory asthenia. Nervous and circulatory functional disturbances with fatigue and precordial pain.

Compensation neurosis —Pension neurosis. Neurosis after an accident developing in a person who thinks that he/she can obtain compensation by being ill.

Compulsive neurosis —The neurosis in which a person has to do a work compulsorily against the will.

Fatigue neurosis —Neurasthenia.

Hypochondrial neurosis —The neurosis in which the person is abnormally aware about the health with the false belief of suffering from some disease.

Hysterical neurosis —Neurosis occurring in hysteria which is characterized by physical symptoms such as blurred vision, numbness or paralysis of the limbs and convulsions in severe cases, etc.

Obsessional neurosis —Neurosis in which uncontrollable obsessions dominate the person's behavior.

Occupational neurosis —Neurosis due to the occupation of a person.

Phobic neurosis —The neurosis in which there is great fear of avoiding an object, habit or situation which the person thinks harmless.

Sexual neurosis —Neurosis involving the sexual function.

Traumatic neurosis —Accidental neurosis.

War neurosis —Neurosis brought on by the conditions of war, seen in soldiers.

Neuroskeletal —Pertaining to the nervous and the skeletal system.

Neuroskeleton —The part of the skeleton enclosing and protecting the nervous system *i.e.*, the cranium and the vertebral column.

Neurosome —1. The body of a neuron. 2. A minute granule in the protoplasm of a neuron.

Neurospasm —Spasmodic muscular twitching occurring due to a nervous disease.

Neurosplanchnic —Pertaining to the cerebrospinal and the nervous system.

Neurospongioma —Spongioblastoma.

Neurosteroid —Steroid produced within the brain.

Neurostimulator —An apparatus used for electrical stimulation of the central or peripheral nervous system.

Neurosurgeon —Specialist in surgery of the nervous system.

Neurosurgery —Surgery of the nervous system.

Neurosuture —Neurorrhaphy.

Neurosyphilis —Syphilis of the central nervous system.

Neurotaxis —Elongation of a neuron in the direction of a target.

Neurotendinous —Pertaining to a nerve and the tendon.

Neurotension —Neurectasis.

Neurothecitis —Inflammation of a nerve sheath.

Neurothekeoma —A benign myxoma arising from the sheath of a cutaneous nerve.

Neurothele —A nerve papilla.

Neurotherapeutics —Neurotheraphy.

Neurotherapy —Treatment of the diseases of the nervous system.

Neurotic —1. Pertaining to the neurosis. 2. Suffering from neurosis. 3. Nervous person.

Neurotic disorder —Mental disorder.

Neuroticism —A neurotic condition or trait.

Neurotization —1. Regeneration of a nerve after division. 2. To introduce a nerve into a paralysed muscle.

Neurotize —To provide with nerve substance.

Neurotmesis —Nerve injury with complete loss of function of the nerve.

Neurotology —Otoneurology.

Neurotome —A needle-like fine knife used for dividing the nerves.

Neurotomography —Tomography of the central nervous system.

Neurotomy —Division or dissection of a nerve.

Neurotonic —1. Pertaining to stretching of the nerve. 2. Stimulant of the nervous system.

Neurotony —To stretch the nerve for relieving pain.

Neurotoxic —Poisonous to the nerve cells.

Neurotoxicity —Capability of exerting a poisonous effect upon the nerve tissue.

Neurotoxin —Neurolysin. A toxin which destroys the nerve cells.

Neurotransducer —A neuron which synthesizes and releases hormones which act as the functional link between the nervous system and the pituitary gland.

Neurotransmitter —On excitation a substance such as acetylcholine released at the nerve ending and takes part in the transmission of nerve impulses at synapses and myoneural junction.

Neurotrauma —Injury of a nerve.

Neurotripsy —Crushing of a nerve by surgery.

Neurotrophasthenia —Malnutrition of the nervous system.

Neurotrophic —Pertaining to neurotrophy.

Neurotrophy —The effect of nerve impulses upon the nutrition and function of an organ or structure.

Neurotropic —Neurophilic.

Neurotropism —Attraction toward the nervous tissue.

Neurotropy —Neurotropism.

Neurotrosis —Neurotrauma.

Neurotubule —One of the minute tubules seen only by electron microscope in the nerve cells, axon and dendrites.

Neurovaccine —Vaccine virus prepared by cultivating the virus in a rabbit's brain.

Neurovaricosis —Formation of multiple swellings along the course of a nerve.

Neurovascular —Pertaining to both nervous and vascular system or to the nerves controlling the caliber of blood vessels.

Neurovegetative —Pertaining to the autonomic nervous system.

Neurovirus —The virus that has been modified by its growth in the nervous tissue, which is used in preparing a vaccine.

Neurovisceral —Neurosplanchnic.

Neurula —Early stage of an embryo following gastrula, marked by the first appearance of the nervous system.

Neurulae —Plural of neurula.

Neurulation —Formation of the neural plate in the early embryo followed by its closure and the development of the neural tube.

Neutral—1. Neither alkaline nor acidic. 2. Indifferent.

Neutralization —1. The process of destroying the effect of a substance, as the neutralization of an acid by an alkali or of an alkali by the acid. 2. The process of checking the effects of an agent that produces a morbid effect.

Neutralize —1. To render neutral. 2. To counteract and make ineffective.

Neutralizing —Rendering neutral.

Neutral point —pH 7.0, a point on the pH scale at which a solution is neither acidic nor alkaline in reaction.

Neutrocyte —Neutrophil leukocyte.

Neutrocytopenia —Neutropenia.

Neutrocytosis —Neutrophilia.

Neutron —A constituent of the atomic nucleus existing along with protons in the atoms of the matter, which is electrically neutral.

Neutropenia —Diminished number of neutrophil cells in the blood.

Malignant neutropenia —Agranulocytosis.

Neutrophil —1. A granular leukocyte having a nucleus with three to five lobes connected by threads of chromatin, and cytoplasm containing very fine granules. 2. Staining easily with neutral dyes.

Fig. 369 : Neutrophil

Neutrophilia —Increase in the number of neutrophil leukocytes in the blood.

Neutrophilic —1. Pertaining to neutrophils. 2. Staining easily with the neutral dyes.

Neutrophilopenia —Neutropenia.

Neutrophilous —Neutrophilic.

Neutrotaxis —Repulsion from or attraction to something of the neutrophils.

Nevi —Plural of nevus.

Nevocarcinoma —Malignant melanoma.

Nevocyte —Nevus cell.

Nevoid —Resembling a nevus.

Nevolipoma —Lipoma containing numerous blood vessels and fatty tissues.

Nevose —The person having a mole.

Nevoxanthoendothelioma —Occurrence of yellowish brown papules or nodules on the extensor surfaces of the limbs of the infants.

Nevus —1. Birthmark. Mole. A congenital discoloration of a circumscribed area of the skin due to pigmentation. 2. A vascular tumor of a circumscribed area of the skin due to hyperplasia of the blood vessels.

Araneus nevus —Spider nevus.

Capillary nevus —A nevus of dilated capillaries elevated above the skin.

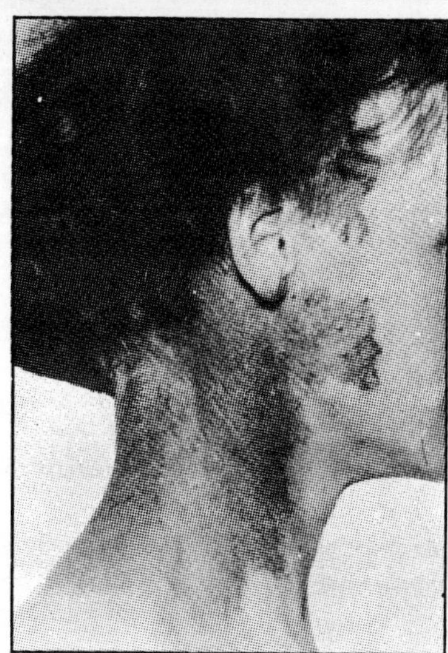

Fig. 370 : Capillary nevus

Cutaneous nevus —A nevus formation on the skin.

Hairy nevus —The nevus covered by a heavy growth of hair.

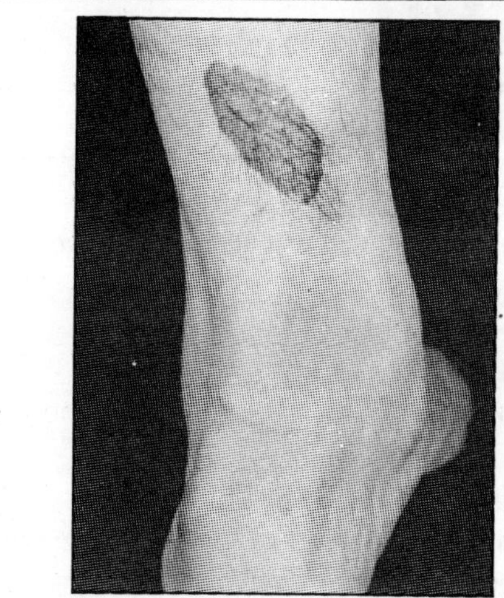

Fig. 371 : Hairy nevus

Nevocytic nevus —A common mole.

Sebaceous nevus —A nevus present in the epidermis containing sebaceous gland tissue.

Newborn —Neonate. 1. Recently born infant. 2. An infant upto one month old.

Nexus —A connection or link.

Nib —In dentistry, the smooth or serrated blade

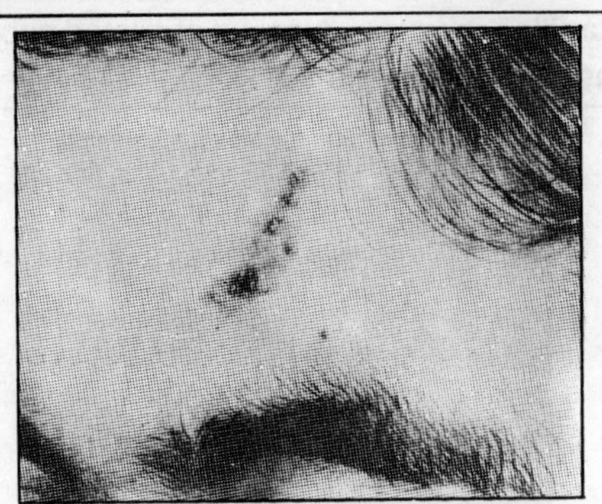

Fig. 372 : Sebaceous nevus

of a condensing instrument that comes in contact with the restorative material being condensed.

Niche —A depression on the smooth surface, especially an erosion in the wall of a hollow organ detected by X-ray examination or visible to the naked eye.

Nicking —Localized constriction of the retinal blood vessels.

Nicolas-Favre disease —Lymphogranuloma venereum.

Nicotine —A very poisonous alkaloid obtained from tobacco.

Nicotinic —Pertaining to nicotine.

Nicotinism —Poisoning from excessive use of tobacco or nicotine.

Nicotinomimetic —Producing effects similar to those of nicotine.

Nictation —Nictitation. Winking of the eyes involuntarily.

Nictitate —To wink.

Nictitating —Winking.

Nictitating spasm —Clonic spasm of the eyelid with continuous winking.

Nidal —Pertaining to a nidus.

Nidation —Implantation of the fertilized ovum in the endometrium.

Nidus —1. A nestlike structure. 2. A focus of infection. 3. A nucleus or origin of a nerve.

Nightguard —A dental apparatus worn at night to prevent traumatic grinding of the teeth during sleep.

Nightingale —A British nurse, founder of modern nursing.

Nightmare —A terrifying dream.

Nightsoil —Feces.

Night terrors —Terrifying dreams awakening a child in terror and causing her screaming.

Nigra —Substantia nigra

Nigri-, Nigro- — Prefixes which mean pertaining to blackness.

Nigricans —Blackened.

Nigrities —Blackness; black pigmentation.

Nigrities linguae —Black pigmentation of the tongue.

Nigrostriatal —Pertaining to a bundle of nerve fibers which connects the substantia nigra of the brain to the corpus striatum.

Nihilism —1. The delusion of unreality or nonexistence of everything. 2. Disbelief in the efficacy of the medical treatment.

Nikolsky's sign —A sign of pemphigus in which the external layer of the skin can be rubbed off by slight friction or injury.

Niphablepsia —Niphotyphlosis. Blindness caused by seeing snow.

Niphotyphlosis —Niphablepsia.

Nipple —1. A pigmented projection at the tip of each breast, surrounded by an areola, from which lactiferous ducts discharge milk in the female. 2. A rubber nipple of the feeding bottle which is equivalent to the female nipple.

Nipple shield —An artificial nipple used to protect the natural nipple during lactation period.

Nissl bodies —Chromophil substance in the form of granules found in the cell bodies and dendrites of the neurons, concerned with protein synthesis and metabolism. They may dissolve or disappear in fatigue and certain pathological conditions.

Nisus —Effort, exertion or force.

Nit—The egg of a louse or any other parasitic insect.

Nitremia —Azotemia.

Nitric —Pertaining to or containing nitrogen.

Nitrification —The process by which the nitrogen of ammonia or other compounds is oxidized to nitrite and nitrate as is done by the nitrifying bacteria in the soil.

Nitrifying —The process of nitrification.

Nitrite —Any salt of nitrous acid. Nitrites dilate the blood vessels and reduce the blood pressure, hence Amyl nitrite is used in the treatment of angina pectoris.

Nitritoid —Resembling a nitrite.

Nitrituria —Presence of nitrites in the urine.

Nitro-, Nitr- —Combining forms indicating the combination with nitrogen.

Nitrogen —A colorless, odorless, tasteless gas occurring in the atmosphere in about 80% of its volume. It is the constituent of all proteins and play an important role in the building of tissues.

Nitrogen dioxide —A brownish irritant gas produced by the decomposition of nitrogen peroxide or the reaction of metals on nitric acid.

Nitrogen monoxide —N_2O. Nitrous oxide. Laughing gas.

Nitrogen mustards —Mustard compounds of nitrogen which destroy the lymphoid tissue, so used in Hodgkin's disease and also in lymphosarcoma, chronic myeloid leukemia, etc. They include mechlorethamine, etc., which are administered by saline drip intravenously.

Nonprotein nitrogen —Nitrogen present in food, blood or other substance but not as a protein.

Nitrogenase —An enzyme which speeds up the reduction of nitrogen to ammonia.

Nitrogen cycle —A natural cycle in which nitrogen is discharged into the soil from the animals, it is then taken up from the soil into the plants for their nourishment and then it returns to the animals through the vegetable food.

Nitrogen equilibrium —The condition in which the amount of nitrogen excreted in the urine, feces and sweat remains equal to that taken in by the body through food.

Nitrogen fixation —Conversion of the atmospheric nitrogen into nitrates by the action of bacteria in the soil.

Nitrogen leg —The time consumed between the ingestion of a protein and the excretion of nitrogen equal to that present in the protein.

Nitrogen narcosis —The effects of high concentration of nitrogen gas on the body tissues including the brain, similar to those produced by taking an excess of alcohol, as seen in divers.

Nitrogenous —Pertaining to or containing nitrogen.

Nitroglycerin —An oily, explosive, colorless fluid formed by the action of sulfuric and nitric acids on glycerin, used as a vasodilator, especially in angina pectoris.

Nitrometer —An apparatus for measuring the amount of nitrogen produced in a chemical reaction.

Nitrous —Containing nitrogen in its lowest valency.

Nocardia —A genus of gram-positive aerobic bacteria. Species Nocardia asteroides causes the diseases of the lungs or skin in man. Abscesses in the skin are called mycetomas. Species Nocardia brasiliensis causes the formation of chronic subcutaneous abscesses.

Nocardiae —Plural of nocardia.

Nocardial —Pertaining to Nocardia.

Nocardioform —Resembling the bacteria of the genus Nocardia.

Nocardiosis —The disease caused by the infection of Nocardia.

Nocebo —An unpleasant effect caused by the administration of a placebo.

Noci- —A prefix denoting pain or injury.

Nociassociation —Unconscious discharge of the nervous energy during surgical shock or following trauma.

Nociceptive —Pertaining to, or capable of transmitting the painful stimuli to the brain.

Nociceptive impulses —Impulses producing sensations of pain.

Nociceptive reflex —A reflex occurring by painful stimuli.

Nociceptor —A nerve ending for receiving and transmitting painful stimuli.

Nocifensor —Denoting the processes or mechanisms that protect the body from injury.

Noci-influence —Injurious or traumatic influence.

Nociperception —The perception by the nerves of painful stimuli.

Noct —Night.

Noctalbuminuria —Excess of albumin excreted in the urine at night.

Noctambulation —Sleepwalking.

Noctambulism —Somnambulism. Noctambulation.

Noctiphobia —Nyctophobia. Morbid fear of night and darkness.

Noctograph —Scotograph.

Nocturia —Nycturia. Excessive urination at night.

Nocturnal —Pertaining to or occurring at night.

Nocturnal emission —Nightfall.

Nocturnal enuresis —Bedwetting. Incontinence of urine during sleep at night.

Nocuous —Harmful, injurious, poisonous.

Nodal —Pertaining to protuberance.

Nodal rhythm —Cardiac rhythm arising from the atrioventricular node.

Nodding —Nutation. Involuntary movements of the head.

Nodding spasm —Salaam convulsion. Nodding of the head due to spasm of the sternomastoid muscles, which appears as the person is performing the act of salaam.

Node —1. A small mass of tissue in the form of knot, protuberance or swelling. 2. A small rounded organ or structure.

Atrioventricular node —A collection of Purkinje fibers situated in the lower part of the interatrial septum from which the bundle of His arises.

Bouchard's node —In rheumatoid arthritis, bony swelling of the proximal interphalangeal joints.

Heberden's node —Small, hard swelling seen on the terminal interphalangeal joints of the fingers in osteoarthritis.

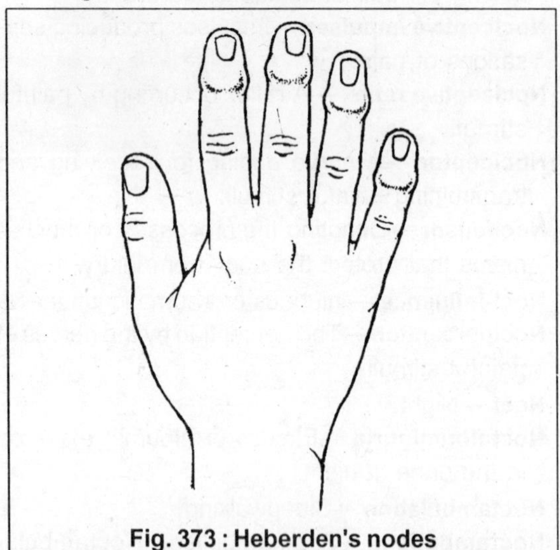

Fig. 373 : Heberden's nodes

Haygarth's nodes —Swelling of the joints seen in rheumatoid arthritis.

Lymph node —Mass of lymphoid tissue along the course of lymphatic vessels.

Rheumatoid nodules —Subcutaneous nodules of fibrous tissue occurring most commonly over bony prominences, in some patients with rheumatoid arthritis.

Sinoatrial node, Sinus node —A collection of Purkinje fibers in the wall of the right atrium near the entrance of superior vena cava, in which impulses initiating the heart beat normally originate, which is therefore called the pacemaker of the heart.

Syphilitic node —Confined swelling at the end of long bones in congenital syphilis, which is painful at night.

Virchow's node —Enlargement of one of the supraclavicular lymph nodes, usually seen in primary carcinoma of the thoracic or abdominal corgans.

Nodi —Plural of nodus.

Nodose —Having nodes or knots at intervals.

Nodosity —1. A node. 2. The condition of having nodes.

Nodular —Containing or resembling nodules.

Nodulation —Formation of nodules.

Nodule —1. A small node. 2. A small collection of cells.

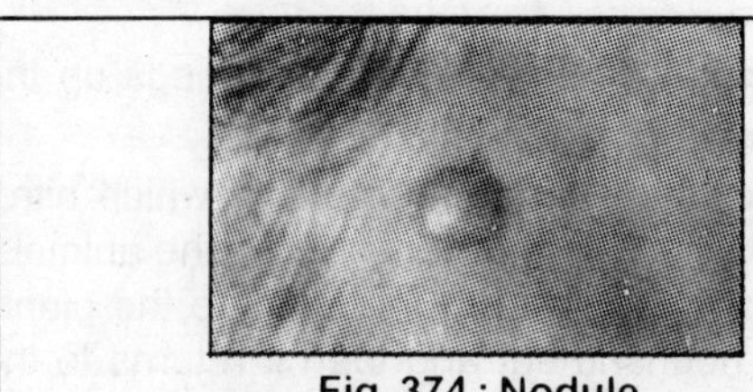

Fig. 374 : Nodule

Aggregate nodules —A group of solitary lymph nodules, such as Peyer's patches of the small intestine.

Aschoff's nodule —Nodule found in myocardium in rheumatic carditis.

Noduli —Plural of nodule.

Nodulus —Nodule.

Nodus —Node.

Noematachograph —An apparatus for recording the time taken in mental activity.

Noematachometer —An apparatus for measuring the time taken in a simple perception

Noematic —Pertaining to the mental process of thinking.

Noesis —The act of thinking.

Noetic —Pertaining to noesis.

Noise —Loud sound.

Noli me tangere —Rodent ulcer.

Noma —Cancrum oris. Gangrenous stomatitis. Gangrene spreading rapidly from the mucous membrane of the cheek or gum to the cutaneous surface, found generally in undernourished children.

Nomadism —Restlessness.

Noma pudendi —Cancrum pudendi. Noma vulvae. Ulceration of the labia majora, especially in young children.

Nomenclature —System of the technical or scientific names.

Nomina Anatomica —Anatomical terminology adopted by the International congress of Anatomists at meetings held periodically since 1955.

Nomogram —A graph on which the values of any two variables can be used to find the values of others.

Nomograph —Nomogram.

Nomography —The construction of a nomogram.

Nomotopic —Occurring at a normal place.

Non- —A prefix denoting absence or negation.

Nonabsorbable —Incapable to be absorbed.

Nonadherent —Not sticking.

Nonan —Reappearing every ninth day.

Noncariogenic—Not caries-producing.

Noncellular —Acellular.

Noncomedogenic —Not promoting the formation of comedones.

Non compos mentis —Not of sound mind.

Nonconductor —A substance which does not transmit electricity, sound or heat or which transmits it with difficulty.

Nondisjunction —Failure of two homologous chromosomes of a pair to separate at meiosis.

Nonelectrolyte —A substance which in solution does not conduct electricity.

Nonigravida —The woman who is pregnant for the ninth time.

Noninfective —Not capable of producing infection.

Non-intoxicating —Not capable of causing poisonous.

Noninvasive —Not spreading.

Nonipara —The woman who has given birth nine times.

Nonmedullated —Containing no myelin.

Non-motile —Not capable to move.

Nonmyelinated —Containing no myelin.

Non-nucleated —Without nucleus.

Nonocclusion —The condition in which the teeth are not capable to make contact.

Nonopaque —Not opaque, especially to X-rays.

Nonparous —Nulliparous.

Non-pathogenic —Causing no disease.

Nonpolar —Having no poles.

Nonprotein —Any substance not derived from protein.

Nonproteogenic —Not producing protein.

Non rep —Do not repeat.

Nonresectable —Not removable by surgery.

Nonresponder —The person who does not respond to a therapy.

Nonrestraint —Treatment of the insane without mechanical repression.

Nonrotation —Failure of normal rotation.

Nonsaponifiable —That which is not convertable into soap.

Nonsecretor —The person whose saliva does not contain the ABO blood antigens.

Nonsense —Foolish.

Nonseptate —Having no dividing walls.

Nonsexual —Asexual.

Nonspecific —Occurring not due to a particular cause, as said of a disease.

Non-suppurative —Not producing pus.

Nontoxic —Not poisonous or producing poison.

Nonunion —Failure of the ends of a fractured bone to unite.

Nonus—1. Ninth. 2. Hypoglossal nerve.

Nonuterotropic —Not causing any effect on the uterus.

Nonvalent —Having no chemical valency.

Nonvascular —Avascular.

Nonverbal —Communicable without words but by signs, symbols, facial expressions, gestures and posture etc.

Nonviable —Incapable of living.

Nookleptia —An obsession that one's thoughts are being stolen by others.

Noopsyche —Mental processes.

Noose —Loop.

Noradrenergic —Activated by or secreting norepinephrine.

Norm —1. A standard or ideal. 2. Normal.

Norm- —A prefix which means normal, usual, average.

Norma —A view or aspect, especially with reference to the skull, *e.g.*, norma anterior or norma frontalis.

Normae —Plural of norma.

Normal —1. Standard; performing proper functions; occurring naturally; regular. 2. Free from mental disorder or of average intelligence. 3. Denoting a solution containing in each 1000 ml. 1 gm. equivalent weight of the active substace.

Normalization —The rendering normal.

Normalize —To effect normalization.

Normal solution —A solution that neutralizes an equal volume of a normal solution of any base or acid.

Normative —Pertaining to the normal or usual.

Normergic —Reacting or pertaining to that which reacts, in a normal manner.

Normo- —A prefix denoting normal or usual.

Normobaric —Denoting a barometric pressure equivalent to sea level pressure.

Normoblast —A nucleated red blood cell of the same size as that of an ordinary red blood cell.

Normoblastosis —Excessive production of normoblasts.

Normocalcemia —Normal level of calcium in the blood.

Normocapnia —Presence of carbon dioxide in the blood in normal concentration.

Normocapnic —Having the normal amount of carbon dioxide in the blood.

Normocephalic —Mesocephalic.

Normocholesterolemia —Presence of normal amount of cholesterol in the blood.

Normochromasia —Normal staining capacity of a tissue.

Normochromia —Normal color of the blood.

Normochromic —Being normal in color as said of the red blood cells.

Normocyte —Normoerythrocyte. A red blood cell normal in size, shape and color.

Normocytosis —A normal state of the erythrocytes of the blood.

Normoerythrocyte —Normocyte.

Normoglycemia —Presence of sugar in the blood in normal amount.

Normoglycemic —Having a normal amount of sugar in the blood.

Normokalemia —Presence of potassium in normal amount in the blood.

Normoorthocytosis —Increase in the number of white blood cells in the blood but with the normal proportion of the different types.

Normospermic —Producing normal spermatozoa.

Normosthenuria —Excretion of urine in normal amount and of normal specific gravity.

Normotensive —The person with normal tone, tension or blood pressure.

Normothermia —Normal body temperature.

Normotonia —Normal tone or tension.

Normotonic —Having normal muscular tone.

Normotopia —Situation in the regular place.

Normotopic —1. Situated on the right place. 2. Pertaining to the normal situation.

Normovolemia —Normal blood volume.

Nos- —A prefix which means disease.

Nose —An organ of the sense of smell and as a part of the respiratory apparatus, which is a projection in the center of the face and divided into two chambers by a septum.

Hammer nose —Rhinophyma.

Saddle nose —Nose with depressed bridge seen in tertiary syphilis.

Nosebleed —Epistaxis.

Nosencephalus —A fetus with defective cranium and brain.

Nosepiece —The part of a microscope to which the objective lenses are attached.

Nosetiology —Study of the cause of a disease.

Nosh —1. Snack between meals. 2. To eat between meals.

Noso- —A prefix denoting pertaining to a disease.

Nosoacusis —Hearing loss due to a disease and not due to aging.

Nosochthonography —Nosogeography. Medical geography. Study of the geographical distribution of the diseases.

Nosocomial —Pertaining to or originating from a hospital.

Nosocomium —A hospital.

Nosode —Any disease product used as a remedy.

Nosogenesis —The development of a disease.

Nosogenic —Producing disease.

Nosogeny —Nosogenesis.

Nosogeography —Nosochthonography.

Nosographic —Pertaining to nosography.

Nosography —Written description of a disease.

Nosohemia —Disease of blood.

Nosology —The science of the classification of diseases.

Nosomania —Hypochondriasis. The delusion that one is suffering, from a disease.

Nosometry —Measurement of the morbidity rate in occupations and social conditions.

Nosomycosis —Any disease caused by a parasitic fungus.

Nosonomy —The classification of diseases.

Nosophilia —Excessive desire to be ill.

Nosophobia —Morbid fear of illness or a specific disease.

Nosophyte —A disease-producing plant microorganism.

Nosopoietic —Producing disease.

Nosotaxy —Nosology.

Nosotherapy —Treatment of a disease by producing some other disease.

Nosotoxic —Anything producing a disease-causing toxin.

Nosotoxicosis —Any disease caused by poisoning.

Nosotrophy —Nursing care and to feed the sick.

Nosotropic —Directed against the symptoms of a disease.

Nostalgia —Homesickness. Excessive desire for returning home.

Nostomania —Insanity for living at or returning home.

Nostophobia —Morbid fear of returning home.

Nostril —Naris. One of the two external apertures of the nose.

Nostrum —A quack, patent or secret remedy.

Nosus —The nose.

Notal —Dorsal. Pertaining to the back.

Notalgia —Pain in the back.

Notancephalia —Congenital absence of the back of the skull.

Notanencephalia —Absence of cerebellum.

Notch —Incisura. A deep indentation or narrow gap on the edge of a bone or other structure.

Acetabular notch —The notch in the inferior border of the acetabulum.

Anterior and posterior cerebellar notches —These are the deep notches separating the cerebellar hemispheres.

Cardiac notch —The concavity on the anterior border of the left lung into which the heart projects.

Interclavicular notch —A rounded notch at the upper surface of the manubrium of the sternum between the two clavicular notches.

Radial notch —A notch on the lateral aspect of the coronoid process of the ulna bone that articulates with the head of the raduis bone.

Sternal notch —A notch on the upper surface of the manubrium sterni.

Ulnar notch —A notch on the distal end of the radius bone for receiving the head of the ulna bone.

Vertebral notch —One of the two concavities above and below the pedicle of a vertebra.

Notched —Having a notch.

Note —1. A sound of definite pitch. 2. Brief comment.

Note blindness—Inability to recognize the musical notes.

Notencephalocele —Protrusion of the brain at the back of the head.

Notencephalus —A fetus whose brain is protruded at the back of the head.

Notifiable diseases —The diseases to be reported to the local health authorities, *e.g.*, contagious diseases such as smallpox, cholera, etc.

Noto- —A prefix indicating a relationship to the back.

Notochord —A rod-shaped cord of cells lying dorsal to the intestine and extending from anterior end to posterior end in an embryo, forming its axial skeleton.

Notochordal —Pertaining to the notochord.

Notogenesis —Development of the notochord.

Notomelus —A deformed fetus with accessory limbs attached to its back.

Noumenon —That which one knows by intelligence and not by sensory perception.

Nourishment —Nutriment. Nutritious substance. The act of nourishing.

Noxa —Anything harmful to health.

Noxious —Injurious. Harmful.

N.P.O. —Non per os, nothing by mouth

n.p.t. —Normal pressure and temperature.

NSAID —Non steroidal anti-inflammatory drugs, *e.g.*, ibuprofen etc.

Nubecula —Cloudiness of the cornea or urine.

Nubile —Pertaining to a girl who crossed the age of puberty.

Nubility —Ability for marriage.

Nucha —The nape of the neck.

Nuchal —Pertaining to the nape of the neck.

Nuclear —Pertaining to a nucleus.

Nucleate —1. To form a nucleus. 2. Having a nucleus.

Nucleated —Having a nucleus or nuclei.

Nucleation —Process of forming a nidus (Nucleus)

Nuclei —Plural of nucleus.

Nucleiform —Nucleus-shaped.

Nuclein —A chemical constituent of the cell nucleus.

Nucleo- —A prefix which means pertaining to a nucleus.

Nucleocapsid —In a virus, protein coat (capsid) and the nucleic acid in the virus.

Nucleochylema —Nuclear sap.

Nucleochyme —Nucleochylema.

Nucleofugal —Moving away from a nucleus in a cell.

Nucleoid —Resembling a nucleus.

Nucleolar —Pertaining to a nucleolus.

Nucleoli —Plural of nucleolus.

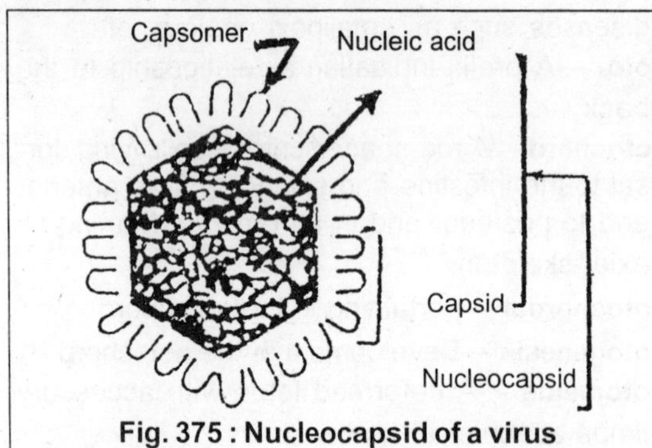

Fig. 375 : Nucleocapsid of a virus

Nucleoliform —Like a nucleolus.

Nucleoloid —Similar to nucleolus.

Nucleolonema —A network of strands of a finely granular substance in the nucleolus of a cell.

Nucleolus —A spherical structure in the nucleus of a cell.

Nucleomicrosome —Karyomicrosome.

Nucleon —One of the particles of the atomic nucleus, *i.e.*, either a proton or a neutron.

Nucleonics —Nuclear physics. The study of atomic nuclei and their reactions.

Nucleopetal —Moving toward the nucleus.

Nucleophagocytosis —The engulfing of the nuclei by phagocytes.

Nucleophilic —Attracted toward a nucleus.

Nucleoplasm —Protoplasm of a cell nucleus.

Nucleoplasmic —Pertaining to the nucleoplasm.

Nucleoprotein —A conjugated protein composed of a simple protein such as histone combined with a nucleic acid, found in the cell nuclei.

Nucleoreticulum —Any meshy framework in a nucleus.

Nucleorrhexis —Fragmentation of a nucleus.

Nucleotoxin —A toxin acting upon or produced by cell nuclei.

Nucleus —1. A spherical body within a cell, consisting of a thin nuclear membrane, nucleoplasm, chromatin, organelles (mitochondria etc.) and one or more nucleoli, which is essential for growth, metabolism, reproduction and transmission of the characteristics of a cell. 2. A group of nerve cells or mass of gray matter within the central nervous system, especially the brain, directly related to the fibers of a particular nerve. 3. A central point about which a material is deposited, as in a calculus.

Arcuate nucleus —Arch-shaped nucleus.

Atomic nucleus —The central part of an atom which contains protons and neutrons.

Auditory nucleus —A nest of nerve cells where the auditory nerves arise.

Basal nuclei —Large masses of gray matter at the base of the cerebral hemispheres.

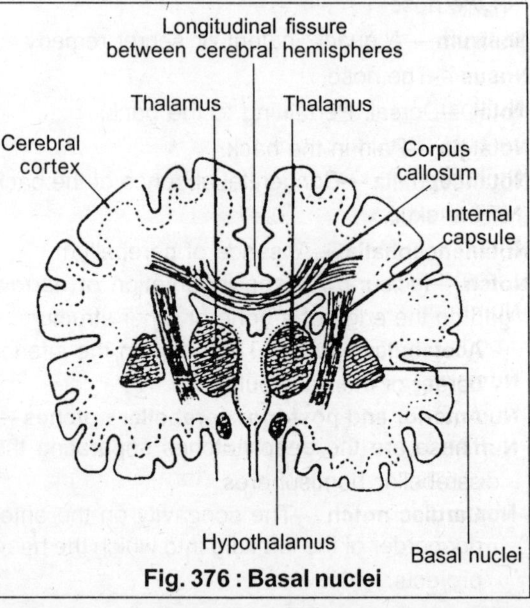

Fig. 376 : Basal nuclei

Caudate nucleus —A comma-shaped mass of gray matter related to the lateral ventricle of the brain and forming a part of the corpus striatum.

Cuneate nucleus —A nucleus in the medulla oblongata.

Fertilization nucleus —The nucleus produced by joining of the male and female nuclei in the fertilization of the ovum.

Mother nucleus —The nucleus which divides into two or more daughter nuclei.

Motor nucleus —A nucleus which gives rise to motor fibers of a nerve.

Nerve of origin —A collection of nerve cells which gives rise to fibers of a nerve or nerve tract.

Paraventricular nucleus —A collection of cells in the wall of the third ventricle in the supraoptic part of the hypothalamus.

Supraoptic nucleus —A nucleus in the hypothalamus just above the lateral part of the optic chiasma.

Nuclide—Any atomic nucleus identified by its atomic number, mass and energy.

Nude —Naked.

Nudism —1. Excessive desire for removing clothes. 2. A habit of living naked.

Nudo- —A prefix denoting naked.

Nudomania —Mania for being naked.

Nudophobia —Morbid fear of being naked.

Nulligravida —A woman who has never been pregnant.

Nullipara —Para O. A woman who has never borne a viable child.

Nulliparity —The condition of not giving birth to a viable child.

Nulliparous —Never having borne a child.

Nullisomatic —Lacking one pair of chromosomes.

Numb —Lacking in feeling or in power to move as from cold.

Numbness —Lack of sensation in a part of the body, especially from cold.

Numeral —Denoting or pertaining to a number.

Nummiform —Coin-shaped.

Nummular —1. Coin-shaped. 2. Made up of flat disks. 3. Arranged like a stack of coins.

Nummulation —The formation of a coin-shaped mass.

Nunnation —To speak the letter 'n' frequently.

Nurse —1. One who takes care of the sick. 2. To feed an infant at the breast. 3. To take care of an invalid. 4. To take care of a young child.

Nurse-midwife —A registered nurse who takes care of the pregnant woman, manages the delivery and takes care of the newborn child and its mother after delivery.

Nurse-midwifery —To take care of the pregnant woman, manage delivery and take care of the newborn child and its mother after delivery by a registered nurse.

Nursery —Department of a hospital where the newborn children are cared for.

Nurse's aide —The person who assists nurses by feeding and bathing patients and by taking temperature, etc.

Nursing —1. Feeding an infant at the breast. 2. To take care of the sick.

Nutation —Nodding, as of the head.

Nutrient —1. Nourishing. 2. Nutritious substance.

Nutrilite —Any essential nutrient required only in trace amounts.

Nutriment —1. Nourishment. 2. Nutritious substance.

Nutriology —Scientific study of nutritious substances and nutrition.

Nutrition —The sum total of the process of ingestion, digestion, absorption and assimilation and utilization of the nutritive substances.

Nutritional —Pertaining to the nutrition.

Nutritionist —Specialist of science of nutrition.

Nutritious —Nutritive.

Nutritive —1. Pertaining to the nutrition. 2. Affording nourishment.

Nutriture —The state of the body in relation to the nutrition.

Nyctalbuminuria —Noctalbuminuria.

Nyctalgia —Pain occurring at night.

Nyctalope —A person affected with nyctalopia.

Nyctalopia —Night blindness.

Nyctamblyopia —Dimness of vision at night without apparent eye changes.

Nyctanopia —Nyctalopia.

Nyctaphonia —Loss of voice during night in hysteria.

Nycterine —Occurring at night.

Nycterohemeral —Nyctohemeral.

Nycthemerus —Pertaining to both day and night.

Nycto- —A prefix denoting night or darkness.

Nyctohemeral —Nycthemerus.

Nyctophilia —Scotophilia. A more preference for the darkness or night.

Nyctophobia —Scotophobia. Morbid fear of the darkness or night.

Nyctophonia —Nyctaphonia.

Nyctotyphlosis —Nyctalopia. Night blindness.

Nycturia —Nocturia.

Nymph —A stage in the development of insect in which the wings and genital organs have not been fully developed.

Nympha —One of the labia minora.

Nymphae —Plural of nympha.

Nymphal —Pertaining to labia minora.

Nymphectomy —Surgical excision of the labia minora.

Nymphitis —Inflammation of the labia minora.

Nympho- —A prefix indicating relationship to the labia minora.

Nymphocaruncular sulcus —The depression between the caruncula of the hymen and the labium minus.

Nymphohymenal sulcus —A depression between the labium minus and hymen on both sides.

Nympholabial —Pertaining to the labia minora and labia majora.

Nympholepsy —Frenzy, especially of erotic nature.

Nymphomania —Excessive sexual desire in a female.

Nymphomaniac —The woman affected by excessive sexual desire.

Nymphomaniacal —Pertaining to, or exhibiting, nymphomania.

Nymphoncus —Swelling or tumor of the labia minora.

Nymphotomy —To make an incision into the labia minora or clitoris.

Nystagmic —Pertaining to or suffering from nystagmus.

Nystagmiform —Nystagmoid. Like nystagmus.

Nystagmogram —The tracing produced by nystagmograph.

Nystagmograph —An apparatus for recording the movements of the eyeball in nystagmus.

Nystagmography —The technique of recording nystagmus.

Nystagmoid —Similar to nystagmus.

Nystagmus —Constant, involuntary movement (horizontal, vertical, rotatory or mixed, *i.e.*, of two types) of the eyeball.

Amaurotic nystagmus —Occular nystagmus.Usually pendular nystagmus occurring in severly reduced vision.

Aural nystagmus —Nystagmus occurring due to a disease of the labyrinth of the ear.

Cheyne's nystagmus —Rhythmic nystagmus resembling the rhythm of Cheyne-Stockes respiration.

Compressive nystagmus —Jerky nystagmus.

Congenital nystagmus —Nystagmus present since birth.

Convergence nystagmus —Slow abduction of the eyes followed by rapid adduction.

Dissociated nystagmus —Nystagmus in one eye which is not similar to that of the other eye.

End-position nystagmus —Nystagmus occurring when the eyes are turned to extreme positions.

Fixation nystagmus —Nystagmus occurring only when the eyes glaze at one object.

Jerky nystagmus —Nystagmus in which the eyes move slowly in one direction and then are jerked back rapidly.

Latent nystagmus —Nystagmus that occurs only when one eye is covered.

Lateral nystagmus —Involuntary horizontal movement of the eyes.

Miner's nystagmus —Nystagmus occurring in workers in coal mines due to exposure to darkness for long periods.

Opticokinetic nystagmus —The normal nystagmus while looking at constantly moving objects such as telephone poles from moving train or car.

Positional nystagmus —Nystagmus occurs only when the head is in a particular position.

Rhythmic nystagmus —Jerk nystagmus. Nystagmus in which the eyes move slowly in one direction and then return back rapidly with jerks.

Rotatory nystagmus —Nystagmus in which the eyes rotate about the axis.

Vertical nystagmus —Up and down movements of the eyes.

Vestibular nystagmus —Nystagmus occurring due to ear diseases.

Nystaxis —Nystagmus.

Nysten's law —Law that rigor mortis starts with the muscles of mastication and progresses from the head down the body, affecting the legs and feet last.

Nyxis —Paracentesis. Puncture or piercing.

O—Chemical symbol for oxygen.

O_2—Symbol for the molecular formula of oxygen.

O_3—Symbol for ozone.

Oarialgia —Oophoralgia. Pain in the ovary.

Oario-, Oari- —Prefixes pertaining to the ovary.

Oarium —Ovary.

Oasis —Area of the health tissue surrounded by unhealthy tissue.

Oat —A grain.

Oath —A solemn, affirmation.

Oatmeal —A meal prepared from oats.

O. B. —Obstetrics.

Ob- —A prefix which means toward, against or in the way of.

Obcecation —Partial blindness.

Obdormition —Numbness in a limb produced by pressure on the nerve trunk supplying it, followed by tingling sensation. Limb is commonly said as being asleep.

Obduction —Autopsy. Postmortem examination. Examination of the dead body to determine the cause of death.

Obeliac —Pertaining to obelion.

Obeliad —Toward the obelion.

Obelion —A point on the sagittal suture on the cranium between the parietal foramina near the lambdoidal suture.

Obese —Corpulent. Fatty.

Obesity —Corpulence. Adiposity. Fatness.

Obfuscation —1. To confuse. 2. Confusion.

Obituary —Death-news.

Object —1. Anything perceptible by the sense organs. 2. Purpose.

Object blindness —The condition in which the brain does not recognize the things though they are seen correctly by the eyes.

Objective —1. Perceptible by another persons as the symptoms of a disease. 2. A result, to achieve which an effort is made. 3. The lens of a microscope that is nearest to the object, which is to be examined.

Objective sign —A sign present in the patient which can be seen, heard or felt by touch by the doctor.

Object relations —Emotional attachment for other persons or objects.

Obligate —To make necessary or to bind.

Oblique —Slanting.

Obliquimeter —An apparatus for measuring the angle between the border of the pelvis and the axis of the body.

Obliquity —The state of being slanting.

Obliquus —Oblique.

Obliterans —Obliterating.

Obliteration —Complete removal of an organ or a part of the body by disease, degeneration or surgery, etc.

Oblivion —Forgetfulness.

Oblongata —Medulla oblongata.

Obmutescence —Aphonia.

Obnubilate —To confuse.

Obnubilation —Confusion.

Obscenity —Indecency.

Obscure —1. Indistinct or hidden as the cause of a disease. 2. To make indistinct or to hide.

Observation —To see an object accurately.

Observerscope —A type of endoscope by which two persons can see a site at a time.

Obsession —A mental disorder in which there is uncontrollable desire to follow the unwanted ideas or impulses, occurring persistently in the mind.

Impulsive obsession —An obsession accompanied by action.

Inhibitory obsession —An obsession accompanied by hindrances in action.

Obsessional neurosis —Compulsion neurosis. A psychoneurosis marked by obsessions controlling the behavior of the person.

Obsessive-compulsive —Marked by compulsion to perform repeatedly certain acts or religious rites to relieve anxiety.

Obsolescence —To become useless or old.

Obstacle —Hindrance. Obstruction.

Obstetric —Pertaining to obstetrics.

Obstetrical —Pertaining to obstetrics.

Obstetrician —A doctor who treats a woman during pregnancy and after delivery, and delivers the children.

Obstetrics —The branch of medicine concerning with the pregnancy, labor and the puerperium.

Obstinacy —Stubbornness.

Obstinate —Stubborn.

Obstipation —Severe constipation.

Obstructed —Blocked.

Obstruction —Block. Obstacle.

Obstructive —Causing obstruction.

Obstruent —Causing obstruction.

Obtund —To render dull minded.

Obtundent —1. Capable of rendering dull minded or soothing pain. 2. A soothing or partially anesthetic medicine.

Obturation —Closure of a passage or an opening.

Obturator —A natural or artificial disk or plate, that closes a cavity or an opening.

Obturator foramen —A large oval foramen situated below the acetabulam cavity of the hip bone and bounded by the pubic and ischial bones.

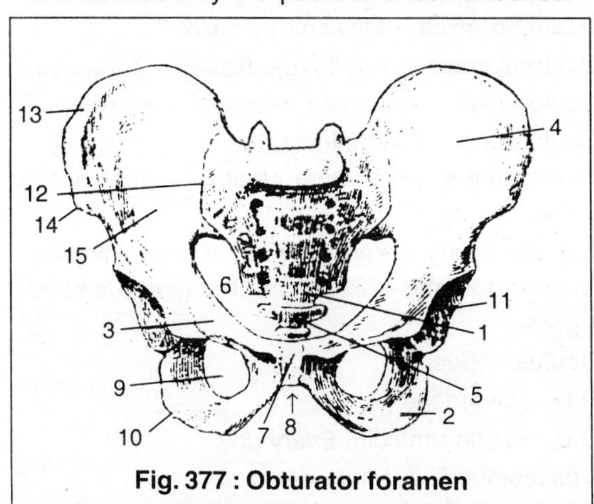

Fig. 377 : Obturator foramen

1. Sacrum 2. Ischium 3. Pubis 4. Ilium 5. Coccyx 6. Inlet of true pelvis 7. Pubic symphysis 8. Angle of pubic symphysis 9. Obturator foramen 10. Ischial tuberosity 11. Acetabulum cavity 12. Sacroiliac joint 13. Iliac crest 14. Anterior superior iliac spine 15. Iliac fossa

Obturator sign —Occurrence of pain on inward rotation of the hip, due to stretching of the obturator internus muscle, whcih is a sign of acute appendicites.

Obtuse —1. Not pointed, or blunt. 2. Dull. 3. Stupid.

Obtusion —1. Deadening or blunting of sensitiveness. 2. The act of making blunt.

O.C. —Oral contraceptive.

Occipital —Pertaining to the back of the head.

Occipitalis —Occipital.

Occipitalization —Fusion of the occipital and the atlas bones.

Occipito- —A prefix denoting the relationship between the occiput and another part.

Occipitoatloid —Pertaining to the occipital and atlas bones.

Occipitoaxial —Occipitoaxoid.

Occipitoaxoid —Pertaining to the occipital and axis bones.

Occipitobregmatic —Pertaining to the occiput and the bregma.

Occipitocervical —Pertaining to the occiput and the neck.

Occipitofacial —Pertaining to the occiput and face.

Occipitofrontal —Pertaining to the occiput and the forehead.

Occipitomastoid —Pertaining to the occiput and the mastoid process.

Occipitomental —Pertaining to the occiput and the chin.

Occipitoparietal —Pertaining to the occiput and the parietal bones or parietal lobes of the brain.

Occipitotemporal —Pertaining to the occiput and the temporal bones.

Occipitothalamic —Pertaining to the occipital lobe and the thalamus.

Occiput —The back part of the head.

Occlude —To obstruct or to close tight.

Occluder —An articulator used in dentistry.

Occlusal —Pertaining to the closure of an opening.

Occlusion —1. The closure of a passage. 2. Obstruction. 3. The relation of the teeth of both jaws when they are closed.

Occlusive —Pertaining to the occlusion.

Occlusometer — Gnathodynamometer.

Occult —Obscure or hidden.

Occult blood —Blood present in such a minute quantity that it can be detected only by microscopic examination or chemical tests.

Occupation neurosis —A mental disorder caused by certain occupations.

Ochlesis —Any disease caused by overcrowding.

Ochlophobia —Morbid fear of crowds or populated places.

Ochrodermia —Yellow discoloration of skin.

Ochrometer —An apparatus for measuring the capillary blood pressure.

Ochronosis —A condition marked by dark pigmentation of the skin, ligaments, cartilages and urine etc. caused by deposition of alkapton bodies as a result of metabolic disorder.

Ochronotic —Pertaining to or characterized by ochronosis.

Ocrylate —An adhesive tissue for surgery.

Octa-, Octo- —Prefixes which mean eight.

Octad —Octavalent.

Octagonal —Having eight sides.

Octahedron —A solid figure having eight sides.

Octan —Reappearing on every eighth day, as a fever.

Octaploid —1. Concerning octaploidy. 2. Having eight pairs of chromosomes.

Octaploidy —The condition of having 8 pairs of chromosomes.

Octarius —Pint.

Octavalent —Having a valency of eight.

Octavus —Auditory or vestibulochochlear (VIIIth cranial) nerve.

Octigravida —A woman who has been pregnant eight times.

Octipara —A woman who has given birth to eight children.

Octogenarian —The person having the age between 70 to 80 years.

Ocular —1. Pertaining to the eye or vision. 2. Eyepiece of a microscope.

Ocularist —Specialist in making and fitting the artificial eyes.

Oculenta —Plural of oculentum.

Oculentum —Eye ointment.

Oculi —Plural of oculus.

Oculist —Ophthalmologist.

Oculo- —A prefix which means relationship to the eye.

Oculoauriculovertebral — Pertaining to the eyes, ears and vertebrae.

Oculocardiac reflex —Aschner's phenomenon. Slowing of the pulse occurring after the pressure applied to the eyeball.

Oculocerebrorenal —Pertaining to the eyes, brain and kidneys.

Oculocutaneous —Pertaining to or affecting the eye and the skin.

Oculodentodigital —Pertaining to the eyes, teeth and fingers.

Oculodermal —Pertaining to the eyes and the skin.

Oculodynia —Pain in the eyeball.

Oculofacial —Pertaining to the eye and the face.

Oculoglandular —Pertaining to the eye glands.

Oculography —The recording of the position and movements of the eyes.

Oculogyration —Circular movement of the eye around its anteroposterior axis.

Oculogyria —Limits of rotation of the eyeballs.

Oculogyric —Ophthalmogyric. Oculomotor. Pertaining to, or producing movements of, the eye.

Oculomotor —Oculogyric. Pertaining to or affecting the eye movements.

Oculomotorius —Oculomotor nerve.

Oculomycosis —Any fungal disease of the eye.

Oculonasal —Pertaining to eye and the nose.

Oculopathy —Ophthalmopathy.

Oculoplastic —Denoting plastic surgery of the eye.

Oculopupillary —Pertaining to the pupil of the eye.

Oculozygomatic —Pertaining to the eye and zygoma.

Oculus —Eye.

O.D. —Overdose.

O.D. —Latin omnidie. Every day.

Odaxesmus —A biting sensation.

Odaxetic —Producing stinging sensation or itching.

Oddi's sphincter —A sphincter at the opening of the common bile duct into the duodenum at the ampulla of vater.

Odditis —Inflammation of Oddi's sphincter.

Odogenesis —Neurocladism. The outgrowth of axons from the ends of a severed nerve, which closes the gap and begins to repair the nerve.

Odont-, Odonto- —Prefixes meaning tooth or teeth.

Odontagra —Toothache.

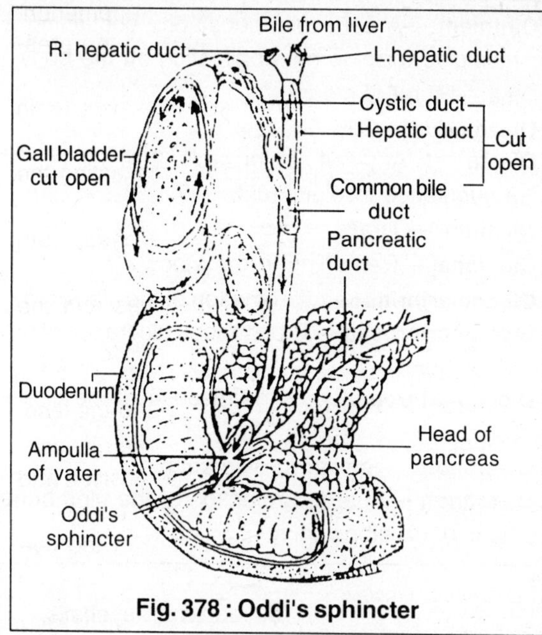

Fig. 378 : Oddi's sphincter

Odontalgia —Odontia. Toothache.

Odontalgic —Pertaining to or suffering from toothache.

Odontatrophy —Imperfect development of the teeth.

Odontectomy —Surgical removal of a tooth.

Odonterism —Chattering of the teeth.

Odontia —1. Odontalgia; odontodynia. toothache. 2. Abnormality of the teeth.

Odontiasis —Eruption of teeth.

Odontic —Pertaining to the teeth.

Odontinoid —1. Resembling dentin. 2. A small outgrowth from a tooth, most commonly from its root or neck. 3. Toothlike.

Odontitis —Inflammation of a tooth.

Odonto-, Odont- —Combining forms which mean pertaining to the tooth or teeth.

Odontoblast —One of the connective tissue cells that deposit dentin and form the outer surface of the dental pulp.

Odontoblastoma —A tumor composed of odontoblasts.

Odontobothrion —Socket of a tooth.

Odontobothritis —Inflammation of the alveolar process of the tooth.

Odontocele —An alveolodental cyst.

Odontochirurgical —Pertaining to the dental surgery.

Odontoclasis —The breaking of a tooth.

Odontoclast —An osteoclast which brings about the absorption of the roots of the deciduous teeth.

Odontodynia —Toothache.

Odontodysplasia —Abnormal development of one or of several adjacent teeth.

Odontogenesis, Odontogeny —The formation of the teeth.

Odontogenic—1. Forming teeth. 2. Arising from the tissues forming the teeth.

Odontograph —An apparatus for determining the degree of uneven surface of tooth enamel.

Odontography —To determine the degree of uneven surface of tooth enamel by odontograph.

Odontoid —Like a tooth.

Odontolith —Calcareous matter deposited upon the teeth.

Odontologist —Dentist or dental surgeon.

Odontology —Scientific study of the teeth.

Odontolysis —Loss of calcium from a tooth.

Odontoma —A tumor of the dental tissue.

Odontonecrosis —Necrosis of a tooth.

Odontoneuralgia —Facial neuralgia caused by a carious tooth.

Odontonomy —Nomenclature of the teeth.

Odontonosology —Dentistry.

Odontoparallaxis —Odontoloxia. Odontoloxy. Irregularity of the teeth.

Odontopathy —Any disease of the teeth.

Odontophobia —Morbid fear of seeing the teeth.

Odontoplasty —Plastic repair of a tooth surface.

Odontoprisis —Bruxism. Grinding of the teeth.

Odontoptosis —Downward displacement of a tooth of the upper jaw.

Odontorrhagia —Bleeding from the teeth.

Odontoschism —Fissure of a tooth.

Odontoscope —An instrument used for visual examination of the teeth and mouth.

Odontoscopy —Examination of the mouth and the teeth by an odontoscope.

Odontosis —Formation or eruption of the teeth.

Odontotherapy —Treatment of diseased teeth.

Odontotomy —To make an incision into a tooth.

Odor —Smell.

Odorant —Any substance that stimulates the sense of smell.

Odoriferous —Having some smell. Perfumed.

Odorimeter —An instrument used for measuring the ability of a substance to induce olfactory sensations.

Odorimetry —The measurement of the ability of a substance to induce olfactory sensations, by odorimeter.

Odorivection —Conveying or bearing an odor, as in the air.

Odorless —Without smell.

Odorography —Description of odors.

Odorous —Having a smell.

Odynacusis —A condition in which noises cause pain in the ear.

-odynia —A suffix which means pain.

Odynometer —An apparatus for measuring pain.

Odynophagia —Pain occurring on swallowing.

Odynophobia —Morbid fear of pain.

Odynophonia —Pain on using the voice.

Oenology —Study of wine.

Official —Authorized by Indian Pharmacopia and National formularies, said of medicines.

Officinal —Regularly kept for sale in a druggist shop.

Ohm —A unit of electrical resistance equal to that of a conductor in which a current of one ampere is produced by a potential of one volt.

Ohmammeter —Ohmmeter and ammeter combined.

Ohmmeter —An apparatus for determining the electrical resistance of a conductor.

Ohm's law —A rule that the strength of an electric current expressed in ampere, is equal to the electromotive force expressed in volts, divided by the resistance, expressed in ohm.

-oid —A suffix meaning resembling.

Oikofugic —Compelled to leave home.

Oikomania —A mental disorder created by unhappiness at home.

Oikophobia —Eversion to home.

Oil —A greasy liquid not miscible with water, obtained from the minerals such as kerosene oil, etc., vegetables such as ground-nut oil, almond oil and castor oil, etc., and animals such as cod liver oil, etc. They are divided as fixed or fatty (non volatile) oils such as castor oil, olive oil and cod liver oil, etc., and volatile oil such as peppermint oil, etc.

Ointment —A semisolid substance containing a medicine for external application on the body.

Olea —Plural of oleum.

Oleaginous —Oily. Greasy.

Oleate —1. Any salt of oleic acid. 2. A solution of a substance in oleic acid.

Oleatum —Oleate.

Olecranal —Pertaining to the elbow.

Olecranarthritis —Inflammation of the elbow joint.

Olecranarthrocae —Tuberculous ulceration of the elbow joint.

Olecranarthropathy —Any disease of the elbow joint.

Olecranoid —Similar to olecranon

Olecranon —A large projection of the ulna bone behind the elbow joint.

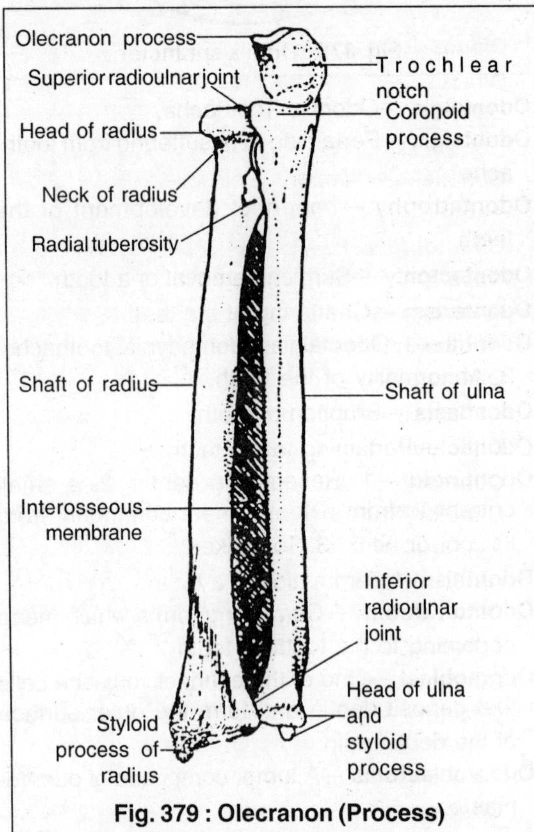

Fig. 379 : Olecranon (Process)

Oleic —Pertaining to or produced by oil.

Oleo- —A prefix which means oil.

Oleoarthrosis —To introduce oil into a joint for the treatment.

Oleogranuloma —Lipogranuloma. A granuloma caused by contact continuously with the oil, or at sites of subcutaneous injection of oily substances.

Oleoinfusion —An infusion made by mixing the drugs with the oil.

Oleoma —Oleogranuloma.

Oleometer —An apparatus for testing the purity of the oil.

Oleoresin —1. An extract of a plant containing a resinous substance and oil. 2. Balsam or balm.

Oleosus —Greasy.

Oleotherapy —Eleotherapy. Treatment of the disease by oil.

Oleothorax —Injection of oil into the pleural cavity to compress the lung in pulmonary tuberculosis.

Oleovitamin —A preparation of edible oil containing one or more fat soluble vitamins.

Oleum —Oil.

Olfactie —Unit of smell.

Olfaction —1. The act of smelling. 2. The sense of smell.

Olfactive —Olfactory. Pertaining to the sense of smell.

Olfactology —Scientific study of the sense of smell.

Olfactometer —An apparatus for testing the power of the sense of smell.

Olfactometry —To test the power of the sense of smell by olfactometer.

Olfactophobia —Morbid fear of odor.

Olfactory —Pertaining to smell.

Olfactory membrane —Mucous membrane in the upper part of the nasal cavity containing olfactory receptors.

Olfactory nasal sulcus —An anterior-posterior groove in the wall of the nasal cavity.

Olfactory organ —The nose.

Olfactory striae —Three bands of fibers (lateral, intermediate and medial) forming the roots of the olfactory tract.

Olfactory tract —Band of nerve fibers extending posteriorly from the olfactory bulb to the anterior perforated substance of the brain, where it enlarges and divides into the olfactory striae.

Olig- —oligo-

Oligamnios —Oligohydramnios.

Oligemia —Oligohemia. Deficient blood volume in the body.

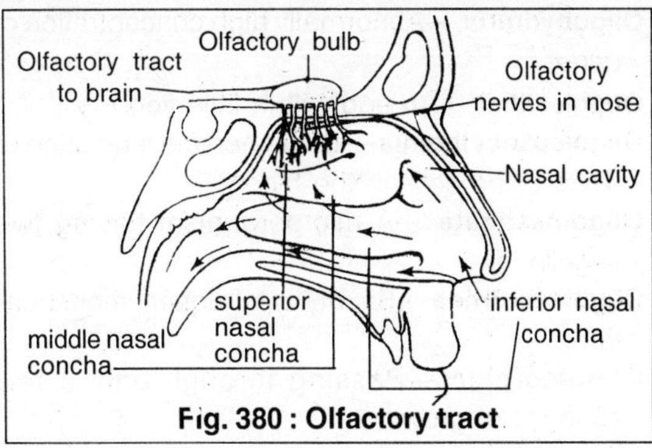

Fig. 380 : Olfactory tract

Oligemic —Having less blood volume.

Olighidria, Oligidria —Scanty perspiration.

Oligo-, Olig- —Combining forms meaning small or few.

Oligoamnios —Oligohydramnios.

Oligocardia —Bradycardia.

Oligocholia —Deficiency of bile.

Oligochromemia —Deficieny of hemoglobin in the blood.

Oligochylia —Deficiency of gastric juice.

Oligochymia —Deficiency of chyme.

Oligocystic —Having a few cysts.

Oligocythemia —Deficiency of blood cells.

Oligodactylia —Below normal number of fingers or toes.

Oligodactyly —Congenital absence of one or more fingers or toes.

Oligodendria —Oligodendroglia.

Oligodendroblast —A primitive precursor cell of the oligodendrocyte.

Oligodendroblastoma —A tumor of oligodendroblasts.

Oligodendrocyte —A cell of oligodendroglia.

Oligodendroglia —The non-neural cells forming the neuroglia of the central nervous system.

Oligodendroglioma —A malignant tumor consisting of oligodendrocytes occurring in the cerebrum.

Oligodipsia —Diminution of thirst.

Oligodontia —Presence of fewer than normal number of teeth.

Oligodynamic —Effective in small amount.

Oligogalactia —Deficient milk secretion.

Oligohemia —Oligemia. Deficiency of blood in the body.

Oligohydramnios —Abnormally small amount of amniotic fluid.

Oligohydruria —Abnormally high concentration of urine.

Oligolecithal —An egg with a little yolk

Oligoleukocythemia —Leukopenia. Diminution of white blood cells in the blood.

Oligomastigate —A microorganism having two flegella.

Oligomenorrhea —Scanty or infrequent menstruation.

Oligomorphic —Passing through only a few changes of growth.

Oligonephronic —Possessing only a few nephrons.

Oligopepsia —Hypopepsia.

Oligophosphaturia —The excretion of small amount of phosphates in the urine.

Oligophrenia —Mental retardation.

Oligoplasmia —Deficiency of plasma of the blood.

Oligoplastic —Deficient plastic repair of a tissue.

Oligopnea —Shallow respiration with reduced rate which may be 6 to 10 per minute.

Oligoposy —Insufficient intake of fluids.

Oligoptyalism —Oligosialia. Deficient secretion of saliva.

Oligoria —A form of melancholia in which there is apathy toward the things and the people.

Oligosialia —Oligoptyalism.

Oligospermatism —Oligospermia.

Oligospermia —Deficiency of spermatozoa in the semen.

Oligosymptomatic —Having a few symptoms.

Oligosynaptic —Nerve pathways involving a few synapses.

Oligotrichia —Hypotrichosis. Congenital deficiency of the hair.

Oligotrichosis —Hypotrichosis. Oligotrichia.

Oligotrophia, Oligotrophy —Insufficient nutrition.

Oligozoospermatism, Oligozoospermia —Oligospermia.

Oligozoospermia —Oligozoospermatism. Oligospermia.

Oliguresis —Scanty or infrequent urination.

Oliguria —Diminished formation of the urine.

Oliva —An oval body located at the ventrolateral surface of the medulla oblongata lateral to the pyramidal tract.

Olivae —Plural of oliva.

Olivary —Pertaining to the oliva.

Olivary body —Oliva.

Olive —Oliva.

Olivifugal —Away from the olivary nucleus of the brain.

Olivipetal —Toward the olivary nucleus of the brain.

Olivopontocerebellar —Pertaining to the olivary nucleus, the pons and the cerebellum of the brain.

-ology —A suffix which means study or science of.

Olophonia —Defective speech due to malformation of the vocal organs.

o.m. —Omni mane, every morning.

-oma —Suffix denoting a tumor.

Omagra —Gout in the shoulder.

Omalgia —Pain in the shoulder.

Omarthritis —Inflammation of the shoulder.

Ombrophobia —Morbid fear of storms, threatening clouds or rain.

Omenta —Plural of omentum.

Omental —Pertaining to the omentum.

Omentectomy —Excision of a portion or all of the omentum.

Omentitis —Inflammation of the omentum.

Omentofixation —Omentopexy.

Omentopexy —Fixation of the omentum to the abdominal wall or adjacent organ.

Omentoplasty —Plastic surgery of the omentum.

Omentorrhaphy —To suture the omentum.

Omentosplenopexy —Fixation of the spleen and the omentum.

Omentotomy —To make an incision into the omentum.

Omentovolvulus —Twisting of the omentum.

Omentum —A fold of peritoneum extending from the stomach to the adjacent organs of the abdomen. It is divided into two parts, greater omentum, which hangs down from the greater curvature of the stomach to the anterior surface of the transverse colon of the intestine, and lesser omentum which extends from the lesser curvature of the stomach and first 2 cm. of the duodenum to the liver.

Omentumectomy —Omentectomy.

Omitis—Inflammation of the shoulder.

omn. bih. —Every two hours.

omn. hor. —Every hour.

Omni- —Prefix denoting all.

Omni mane —Every morning.

Omnivorous —Eating both vegetable and animal foods.

omn. noct. —Every night.

Omno- —Combining form meaning pertaining to the shoulder.

omn. quad. hor. —Every quarter of an hour.

Omoclavicular —Pertaining to the shoulder and the clavicle.

Omodynia —Pain occurring in the shoulder.

Omohyoid —Pertaining to the shoulder and the hyoid bone.

Omophagia —The eating of raw foods, especially flesh.

Omotocia —Premature birth.

Omphal-, Omphalo- —Prefixes denoting relationship to the navel.

Omphalectomy —Excision of the umbilicus.

Omphalelcosis —Ulceration of the umbilicus.

Omphalic —Pertaining to the umbilicus.

Omphalitis —Inflammation of the umbilicus.

Omphaloangiopagus —Two conjoined fetuses, united by the vessels of the umbilical cord, one of which derives its blood from the umbilicus or placenta of the other.

Omphalocele —Congenital umbilical hernia.

Omphaloenteric —Pertaining to the umbilicus and the intestine.

Omphalomesenteric —Pertaining to the umbilicus and mesentery.

Omphaloncus —Tumor or swelling of the umbilicus.

Omphalopagus —Two fetuses joined together at the abdomen.

Omphalophlebitis —Inflammation of the umbilical veins.

Omphalorrhagia —Hemorrhage from the umbilicus.

Omphalorrhea —Discharge of lymph at the umbilicus.

Omphalorrhexis —Rupture of the umbilicus.

Omphalos —Navel. Umbilicus.

Omphalosite —The underdeveloped member of the omphaloangiopagus twins, which derives its blood supply from the umbilical vessels of the developed twins.

Omphalosotor —An apparatus used for replacing the prolapsed umbilical cord at childbirth.

Omphalospinous —Pertaining to the umbilicus and the anterior superior iliac spine.

Omphalotomy To cut the umbilical cord at birth.

Omphalotripsy —To severe the umbilical cord by crushing.

Omphalovesical —Vesicoumbilical. Pertaining to the urinary bladder and the umbilicus.

Omphalus —Umbilicus.

o.n. —Omni nocte. Every night.

Onanism —Coitus interruptus. Withdrawal of the penis from the vagina before ejaculation.

Onanist —The person who withdraws his penis from the vagina before ejaculation.

Onchogryphosis —Curveness of the nails.

Onco- —A prefix meaning tumor, swelling or mass.

Oncocyte —A large columnar cell with extremely granular and acidophilic cytoplasm containing a large number of mitochondria. It may become neoplastic.

Oncocytoma —An adenoma of the eosinophilic epithelial cells, especially of the salivary and parathyroid glands.

Oncofetal —Pertaining to the tumors in the fetus.

Oncogene —A gene in a virus that causes a cell to become malignant.

Oncogenesis —The formation of tumors.

Oncogenic —Forming tumors.

Oncogenous —Arising from a tumor.

Oncoides —Enlargement or swelling of a part of the body.

Oncologist—Specialist in oncology.

Oncology —The study of tumors.

Oncolysate —Destroying tumor cell.

Oncolysis —The absorption or dissolution of a tumor.

Oncolytic —Destructive to tumor cells.

Oncoma —A tumor.

Oncometer —An apparatus for measuring the variations in size of the internal organs.

Oncometric —Pertaining to oncometry.

Oncometry —To measure the variations in size of the internal organs.

Oncornaviruses —A group of RNA viruses that can cause cancer in human beings or animals.

Oncosis —A condition characterized by the development of tumors.

Oncotherapy —Treatment of tumors.

Oncothlipsis —Pressure caused by a tumor.
Oncotic —Pertaining to, caused by or marked by swelling.
Oncotomy —To make an incision into a tumor, abscess or boil.
Oncotropic —Having special affinity for the tumor cells.
Oncovirus —Any virus that causes cancer.
Oneir (O) - —A prefix denoting dreams.
Oneiric —Pertaining to dreams.
Oneirism —Dreams in a waking state.
Oneirodynia —Night mare. Occurrence of pains in dreams.
Oneirogmus —Night dream.
Oneirology —The scientific study of dreams.
Oneiroscopy —Analysis of the dreams for diagnosis of the mental disorder.
Oniomania —Mania for spending money.
Oniric —Oneiric.
Onlay —A graft applied on the surface of an organ.
Onomatology —Nomenclature.
Onomatomania —Mania for repeating certain words or names.
Onomatophobia —Morbid fear of hearing certain name or word.
Onomatopoiesis —Production of meaningless words and sounds.
Onset —Beginning.
Ontogenesis —Ontogeny.
Ontogenetic —Pertaining to ontogeny.
Ontogeny —Ontogenesis. The complete history of the development of an individual.
Onych-, Onycho- —Prefixes meaning pertaining to the nails.
Onychalgia —Pain in the nails.
Onychatrophia —Atrophy of the nails.
Onychatrophy —Onychatrophia
Onychauxis —Overgrowth of the nails.

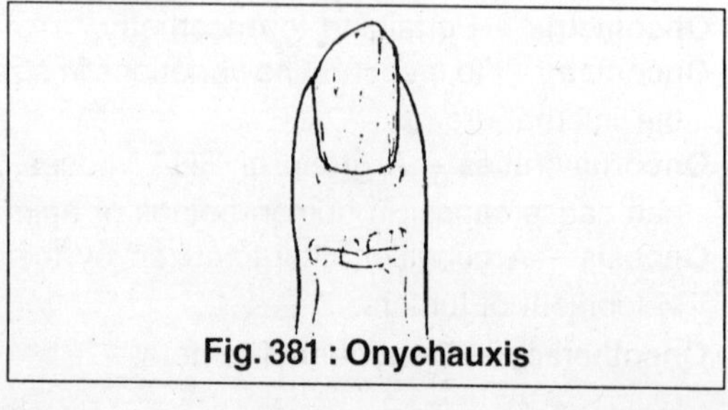
Fig. 381 : Onychauxis

Onychectomy —Surgical removal of the nail.
Onychia —Onychitis. Inflammation of the nailbed with suppuration, resulting in loss of the nail.
Onychitis —Onychia. Inflammation of the nailbed.
Onychoclasis —The breaking of the nails.
Onychocryptosis —Ingrowing of the toe-nail.
Onychodystrophy —Maldevelopment of a nail.
Onychogenic —Producing nail.
Onychograph —An apparatus for recording the capillary blood pressure under the finger nails.
Onychogryposis —Overgrowth with inward curvature of the nails.
Onychoheterotopia —Abnormal location of the nails.
Onychoid —Resembling a finger nail.
Onychology —Study of the nails.
Onycholysis —Loosening or separation of a nail from the nailbed.
Onychoma —A tumor of the nail or nailbed.
Onychomadesis —Complete loss of the nails.
Onychomalacia —Hepalonychia. Abnormal softening of the nails.
Onychomycosis —Fungus disease of the nails, in which the nails become opaque, white, thickened and friable.

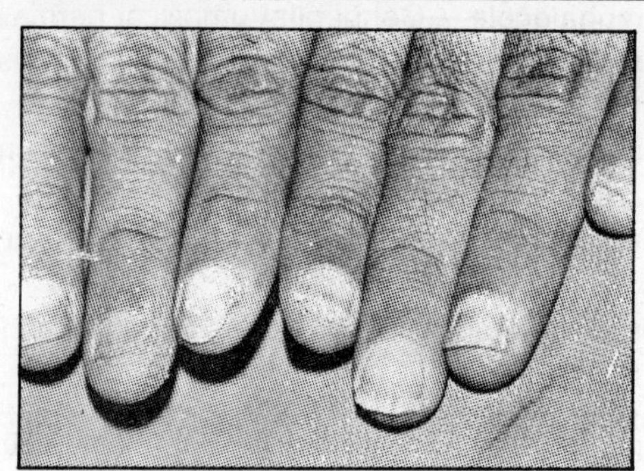
Fig. 382 : Onychomycosis

Onychopathology —Study of the diseases of the nails.
Onychopathy —Onychosis. Any disease of the nails.
Onychophagia —The habit of nail biting.
Onychophagy —Onychophagia.
Onychophosis —Deposition of the horny layers of epidermis under the toe nail.
Onychophyma —Painful degeneration of the nail with hypertrophy.

Onychoptosis —Falling off the nails.

Onychorrhexis —Spontaneous breaking of the nails.

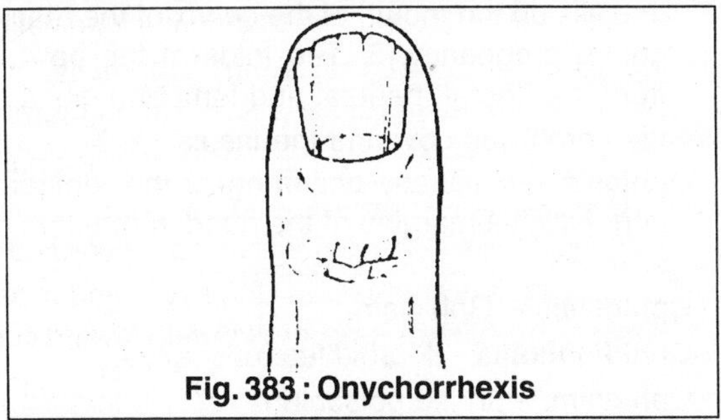

Fig. 383 : Onychorrhexis

Onychoschizia —Onycholysis.

Onychosis —Onychopathy.

Onychostroma —Nail matrix, i.e., the basic substance from which nail develops.

Onychotillomania —Mania for picking or tearing at the nails.

Onychotomy—To make an incision into a finger or toe nail.

Onychotrophy —Nourishment of the nails.

Onyx —1. A fingernail or toenail. 2. Hypopyon. Pus collection between the layers of the cornea of the eye.

Onyxis —Ingrowing of the nails.

Onyxitis —Onychia.

Oo- —A prefix meaning an egg.

Ooblast —The primitive cell from which the ovum is developed.

Oocyesis —Ectopic pregnancy in the ovary.

Oocyst —The encysted or encapsulated fertilized gamete.

Oocytase —An enzyme which destroys the ovarian cells.

Oocyte —An immature ovum.

Oogenesis—Ovigenesis. Formation and development of the ovum.

Oogenetic —Pertaining to oogenesis or producing ova.

Oogenic —Oogenetic.

Oogenous —Oogenetic.

Oogonia —Plural of oogonuim.

Oogonium —A primordial cell from which an oocyte arises.

Ookinesia —Ookinesis.

Ookinesis —Mitotic movements taking place within an ovum during maturation and fertilization.

Ookinete —An elongated motile zygote (fertilized ovum) occurring in the life cycle of malarial parasite in the mosquito's body.

Oolemma —The plasma membrane of the oocyte.

Oophagia —Oophagy.

Oophagy —Eating of eggs.

Oophor- —A prefix denoting relation to the ovary.

Oophoralgia —Ovarialgia. Pain in the ovary.

Oophorauxe —Enlargement of the ovary.

Oophorectomy —Ovariectomy. Excision of an ovary.

Oophoritis —Ovaritis, Inflammation of the ovary.

Oophorocystectomy —Surgical removal of an ovarian cyst.

Oophorocystosis —Development of an ovarian cyst.

Oophorohysterectomy —Ovariohysterectomy. Surgical removal of the uterus and the ovaries.

Oophoroma —A malignant tumor of the ovary.

Oophoromalacia —Abnormal softening of an ovary.

Oophoromania —Insanity from ovarian disease.

Oophoron —Ootheca. An ovary.

Oophoropathy —Any disease of the ovary.

Oophoropeliopexy —To suture a displaced ovary to the wall of the pelvis.

Oophoropexy —Fixation of a displaced ovary.

Oophoroplasty —Repair of the ovary by plastic surgery.

Oophororrhaphy —Suspension of the ovary by attachment to the pelvic wall.

Oophorosalpingectomy —Ovariosalpingectomy. Surgical removal of a fallopian tube and ovary.

Oophorosalpingitis —Inflammation of the ovary and fallopian tube.

Oophorostomy —To make an incision into an ovarian cyst for drainage.

Oophorotomy —To make an incision into an ovary.

Oophorrhagia —Hemorrhage from the ovary.

Oophorrhaphy —Suturing of a displaced ovary to the pelvic wall.

Ooplasm —Cytoplasm of an ovum.

Oosome —A cytoplasmic body in the ovum that passes into the germ cell.

Oosperm —A fertilized ovum.

Ootheca —Oophoron. An ovary.

Ootid —The cell produced by meiotic division of a secondary oocyte which develops into the ovum.

Ooze —To pass through pores.

Opacification —1. The process of making opaque. 2. Development of opacity.

Opacity —The state of being opaque.

Opalescent —Similar to an opal.

Opaque —1. Impervious to light rays or X-rays. 2. Which is not transparent.

O.P.D. —Outpatient department.

Open —1. Not shut. 2. Uncovered or exposed. 3. To puncture.

Opening —1. A hole or aperture. 2. Entrance to a tissue or organ. 3. The act of becoming open.

Operable —Appropriate for operation.

Operant —Any response which is not elicited by specific external stimuli but recurs at a given rate in particular circumstances.

Operate —To perform an operation.

Operation —1. Any action performed with the instruments or by the hands of a surgeon. 2. A surgical procedure.

Ablative operation —Operation in which a part is removed.

Cosmetic operation —An operation performed for improving the appearance of some part of the body.

Exploratory operation —An operation performed for the diagnosis of a disease.

Major operation —Serious or risky operation performed under general anesthesia.

Minor operation —An operation which is not serious or risky and may be performed under local anesthesia.

Plastic operation —Plastic surgery. Operation performed for repair of the surface or other structures.

Radical operation —Operation performed to remove a large amount of damaged or neoplastic tissue.

Reconstructive operation —Operation for repairing a a defective part of the body.

Subtotal operation —Operation in which only a part of an organ is removed.

Operative —Pertaining to or brought about by an operation or capable to be treated by operation.

Operative dentistry —Restorative dentistry.

Operator —The person who performs surgical operations.

Opercular —Pertaining to a covering structure.

Operculated —Having a lid.

Operculitis —Inflammation of the gingiva over the partially erupted teeth.

Operculum —1. Any covering. 2. Plug of mucus that fills up the mouth of the cervix of the uterus during pregnancy. 3. The folds of the pallium from the frontal, parietal and temporal lobes of the cerebrum, covering the insula.

Ophiasis —Baldness occurring at the temporal and occipital margins of the head in the form of a band.

Ophidiasis —Ophidism.

Ophidiophobia —Morbid fear of snakes.

Ophidism —Snake poisoning.

Ophiotoxemia —Poisoning by snake venom.

Ophritis, Ophryitis —Inflammation of the eyebrow.

Ophryogenes —Pertaining to the eyebrows.

Ophryon —A meeting point of the facial median line with a transverse line across the lowest portion of the forehead.

Ophryosis —Spasm of the eyebrows.

Ophthalmagra —Sudden pain occurring in the eye.

Ophthalmalgia —Ophthalmodynia. Pain in the eye.

Ophthalmatrophy —Atrophy of the eyeball.

Ophthalmectomy —Excision of an eye.

Ophthalmencephalon —The retina, optic nerves, optic chiasma, optic tract and visual centers of the brain.

Ophthalmia —Severe inflammation of the eye including conjunctiva.

Catarrhal ophthalmia —Severe conjunctivitis of purulent type.

Egyptian ophthalmia —Trachoma. Granular conjunctivitis.

Gonorrheal ophthalmia —Severe purulent ophthalmia due to infection with gonococcus.

Granular ophthalmia —Trachoma.

Neonatorum ophthalmia —Severe purulent conjunctivitis occurring in the new born during birth, from infected vaginal discharge of the mother.

Phlyctenular ophthalmia —Scrofulous ophthalmia. An allergenic type of conjunctivitis occurring commonly in children in which nodules are formed on the conjunctiva or cornea.

Purulent ophthalmia —Conjunctivitis with purulent discharge commonly due to infection with gonococcus.

Scrofulous ophthalmia —Phlyctenular ophthalmia.

Spring ophthalmia —Vernal conjunctivitis. Conjunctivitis occurring in the spring season of the year which is usually an allergic reaction to the pollen grains.

Ophthalmiatrics —Treatment of the eye diseases.

Ophthalmic —Pertaining to the eye.

Ophthalmitis —Inflammation of the eye.

Ophthalmo- —A prefix which means pertaining to the eye.

Ophthalmoblennorrhea —Inflammation of the eye or conjunctivitis with purulent discharge due to infection with gonococcus.

Ophthalmocele —Exophthalmos.

Ophthalmocopia —Asthenopia. Weakness or fatigue of the eyes with pain, headache and dimness of vision.

Ophthalmodesmitis—Inflammation of the tendons of the eye.

Ophthalmodiagnosis —Diagnosis of an eye disease by ophthalmo reaction.

Ophthalmodiaphanoscope —An apparatus for examining the retina by transillumination.

Ophthalmodonesis —Trembling movement of the eye.

Ophthalmodynamometer —An apparatus for measuring pressure in the ophthalmic arteries.

Ophthalmodynamometry —To measure the pressure in the ophthalmic arteries by ophthalmodynamometer.

Ophthalmodynia —Ophthalmalgia. Pain occurring in the eye.

Ophthalmoeikonometer —An apparatus for determining the refraction of the eye and measuring the relative size and shape of ocular images in the eyes.

Ophthalmofunduscope —An apparatus for examining the fundus of the eye.

Ophthalmography —Description of the eye and its diseases.

Ophthalmogyric —Oculogyric.

Ophthalmolith —A calculus in the lacrimal duct.

Ophthalmologist —Specialist in ophthalmology.

Ophthalmology —The branch of medical science dealing with the eyes.

Ophthalmomalacia —Abnormal softening of the eye.

Ophthalmomelanosis —Discoloration of the conjunctiva and its adjoining tissues caused by deposition of melanin.

Ophthalmometer —An instrument used in ophthalmometry.

Ophthalmometry —Determination of the defects and refractive powers of the eye by ophthalmometer.

Ophthalmomycosis —Any disease of the eye caused by a fungus.

Ophthalmomyiasis —Ocular myiasis. Disease of the eye caused by the invasion of the larvae of flies.

Ophthalmomyitis —Inflammation of the muscles of the eye.

Ophthalmomyositis —Ophthalmomyitis.

Ophthalmomyotomy —To make an incision into the muscles of the eye.

Ophthalmoneuritis —Inflammation of the ophthalmic nerves.

Ophthalmopathy —Any disease of the eye.

Ophthalmophacometer —An instrument for measuring the lens of the eye.

Ophthalmophlebotomy —To incise the conjunctiva of the congested eye to relieve congestion.

Ophthalmophthisis —Wasting or atrophy of the eyes.

Ophthalmoplasty —Repair of an eye by plastic surgery.

Ophthalmoplegia —Paralysis of the eye muscles.

Ophthalmoptosis —Exophthalmos.

Ophthalmoreaction —Ophthalmic reaction. Reaction of the eye following instillation of a drop of tuberculin or typhoid toxin into the eyes of persons suffering from tuberculosis or typhoid fever.

Ophthalmorrhagia —Hemorrhage from the eye.

Ophthalmorrhea —Discharge from the eye.

Ophthalmorrhexis —Rupture of an eyeball.

Ophthalmoscope —An instrument for examining the interior of the eye, especially the retina.

Ophthalmoscopic —Pertaining to ophthalmoscopy.

Ophthalmoscopy—Examination of the interior of the eye with ophthalmoscope.

Ophthalmospasm —Spasm of the ocular muscles.

Ophthalmostasis —Fixation of the eyeball with the ophthalmostat during operation.

Ophthalmostat —An instrument to fix the eyeball during an operation.

Ophthalmostatometer —An instrument used for ascertaining the position of eyes

Ophthalmosteresis —Loss of an eye.

Ophthalmosynchysis —Effusion into the eye.

Ophthalmothermometer —An instrument for measuring the temperature of the eye in its diseases.

Ophthalmotomy —To make an incision into the eyeball.

Ophthalmotonometer —An instrument for determining the tension within the eye.

Ophthalmotoxin —Any substance that is toxic to the eyes.

Ophthalmotrope —A mechanical eye to demonstrate the movements of the extraocular muscles.

Ophthalmotropometer —An instrument used for measuring the eye movements.

Ophthalmovascular —Pertaining to the blood vessels of the eye.

Ophthalmoxerosis —Xerophthalmia.

Ophthalmoxyster —An instrument used to scrape the conjunctiva.

-opia —A suffix denoting vision.

Opiate —1. Any drug derived from opium. 2. Any drug inducing sleep.

Opioid —Acting like opium but not derived from it.

Opiomania —Mania for taking opium or its derivatives.

Opiophagism —Addiction to the eating of opium.

Opisthenar —Back of the hand.

Opisthiobasial —Pertaining to both opisthion and basion.

Opisthion —A point at the middle of the lower border of the foramen magnum, opposite the basion.

Opisthionasial —Pertaining to the opisthion and the nasion.

Opistho-, Opisth- —Prefixes indicating back.

Opisthocheilia, Opisthochilia —Recession of the lips.

Opisthognathism —State of being normal size of the lower jaw.

Opisthoporeia —Uncontrollable walking backward due to loss of motor control.

Opisthotic —Situated behind or inside the ear.

Opisthotonoid —Resembling opisthotonos.

Opisthotonos —A form of spasm in which head and heels are bent backward and the rest of the body is bent forward so that the body looks like a bow, as is seen in tetanus.

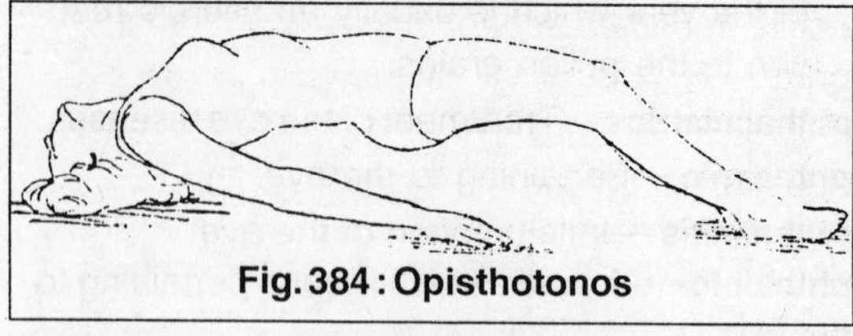

Fig. 384 : Opisthotonos

Opisthotonus —Opisthotonos.

Opium —It is an air-dried milky substance obtained by incising the unripe capsules of Papaver somniferum which contains about 20 alkaloids, most commonly the morphine.

Opiumism —1. Habit of taking opium. 2. Physical condition resulting from overuse of opium.

Opocephalus —A fetus having no nose and mouth with the ears fused together at the head. The orbit is only one or two very close together.

Opodidymus —A fetus with two fused heads and partially fused sensory organs.

Oppenheim's gait —The gait in which the head, body and the extremities move to and fro.

Oppilation —1. Obstruction. 2. Constipation.

Oppilative —1. Obstructive. 2. Constipating.

Opponens —Opposing.

Opportunistic —An organism causing disease only in that host whose resistance is lowered by other diseases or by drugs.

Oppositional —In a state of opposition.

Opposure —To bring together the tissues during suturing.

Oppression —A sense of weight about the chest, obstructing respiration.

Opsialgia —Neuralgic pain of the face.

Opsin —A protein of the retinal rods and cones forming visual pigments.

Opsinogen —An antigen causing the production of opsonins.

Opsinogenous —Capable of producing opsonins.

Opsiometer —Optometer.

Opsiuria —Excretion of urine more rapidly during fasting than after a meal.

Opsoclonia, Opsoclonus —Involuntary, non rhythmical jerking movements of the eyes.

Opsoclonus —Opsoclonia.

Opsogen —Opsinogen.

Opsomania —Craving for some special food.

Opsonic —Pertaining to opsonins or their use in the treatment.

Opsonification —Effect of opsonins in rendering the cells or bacteria phagocytized more readily.

Opsonin —A substance (antibody) in the blood serum acting upon bacteria and other cells, rendering them capable to be phagocytized.

Opsoninopathy —A condition in which the serum opsonin level is reduced, resulting in increased susceptibility to infection.

Opsonization —Opsonification.

Opsonize —To facilitate phagocytosis.

Opsonocytophagic —Pertaining to the phagocytic activity of blood in the presence of serum opsonins.

Opsonometry —To measure the amount of opsonins in blood serum.

Opsonophilia —Attraction for opsonins.

Opsonophilic —Attracted toward opsonins.

Opsonotherapy —Treatment of a disease by stimulating a specific opsonin with bacterial vaccine.

Optesthesia —Capability of perceiving visual stimuli.

Optic —Pertaining to the eye or the sight.

Optical —Pertaining to the vision.

Optic chiasma —An X-shaped crossing of the optic nerve fibers in the brain.

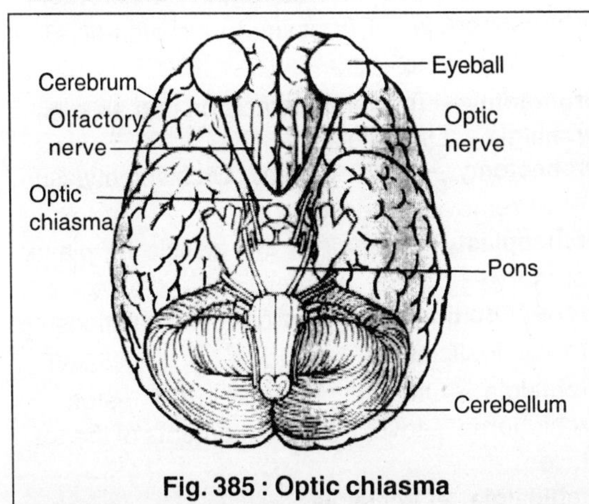

Fig. 385 : Optic chiasma

Optic disk —Blind spot. Area in the retina for the entrance of optic nerve.

Optician —Specialist in making optical apparatus.

Opticianry —The art of preparing the spectacles by fitting in them the lenses of the number given in the prescriptions.

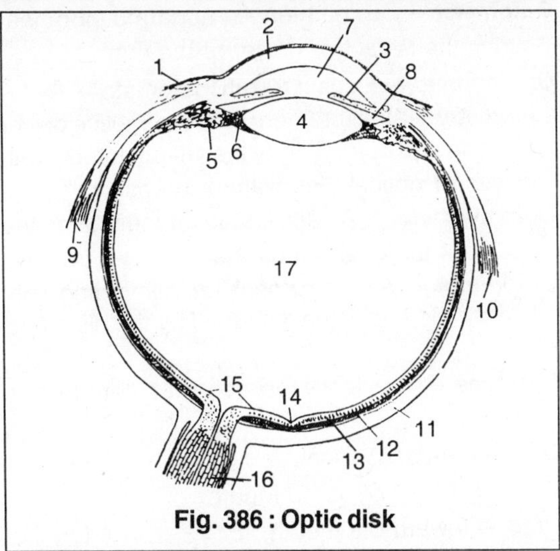

Fig. 386 : Optic disk

1. Conjunctiva 2. Cornea 3. Iris 4. Lens 5. Ciliary body 6. Suspensory ligament 7. Anterior chamber of the eye 8. Posterior chamber of the eye 9. and 10. Muscles of the eyeball 11. Sclera 12. Choroid 13. Retina 14. Macula lutea 15. Optic disc

Opticist —Specialist in optics.

Optico- —Combining form denoting relation to the eye or vision.

Opticochiasmatic —Pertaining to the optic nerves and chiasma.

Opticociliary —Pertaining to the optic and ciliary nerves.

Opticokinetic—Pertaining to the movement of the eye.

Opticopupillary —Pertaining to the optic nerve and the pupil.

Optic papilla —Optic disk.

Optics —The science of light and vision.

Optimism —A tendency to see only goodness in everything.

Optimum —The most suitable.

Opto- —A prefix meaning vision or eye.

Optochiasmic —Opticochiasmatic.

Optogram —Image of the external object formed on the retina by bleaching of the visual purple by light.

Optokinetic —Pertaining to the twitching of the eye, as in nystagmus.

Optomeninx —The retina.

Optometer —Opsiometer. An apparatus for measuring the refractive power of the eye.

Optometrist —A specialist in optometry.

Optometry —Measurement of the refractive power of vision and correction of the visual defects with lenses or optical aids without drugs.

Optomyometer —An apparatus for measuring the power of the ocular muscles.

Optophone —An instrument for converting light energy into sound waves, used by the blind person.

Optotype —The test type used for determining the acuity of vision.

O. R. —Operating room.

Ora —1. Plural of os. 2. Mouth.

Orad —Toward the mouth.

Orae —Plural of ora.

Oral —Pertaining to, taken through or applied in the mouth.

Orality —The oral stage of psychosexual development such as sucking or chewing the objects other than the food.

Oralogy —Stomatology. Study of the diseases of mouth.

Oral rehydration solution —A solution used in rehydration therapy of diarrhea and cholera etc., recommended by World Health Organization that contains 3.5 gms. sodium chloride, 2.5 gms. sodium bicarbonate, 1.5 gms. potassium chloride and 20 gms. glucose dissolved in each liter of drinking water.

Orb —A spherical body, especially the eyeball.

Orbicular —Circular.

Orbiculare —Orbicular bone. A small oval knob on the long limb of incus bone in the middle ear, articulating with the head of the stapes.

Orbicularis —A name given to the muscle that encircles an orifice.

Orbiculus —The muscle surrounding an orifice or opening, *e.g.*, ciliary muscles of the eye or circular muscle surrounding the mouth.

Orbit —The bony cavity of the skull containing the eyeball with its muscles, blood vessels and nerves.

Orbita —Orbit

Orbital —Pertaining to the orbit.

Orbitale —The lowest point in the lower margin of the bony orbit that may be felt under the skin.

Orbitalis —Orbital.

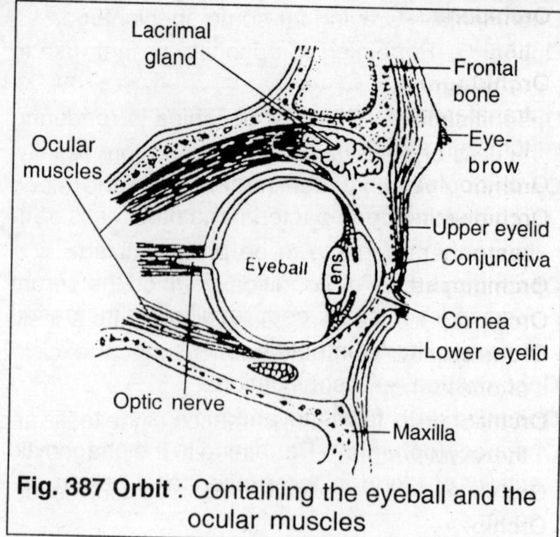

Fig. 387 Orbit : Containing the eyeball and the ocular muscles

Orbitofrontal —Pertaining to the orbit and the forehead.

Orbitonasal —Pertaining to the orbit and the nose.

Orbitonometer —An apparatus for measuring the backward displacement of the eyeball produced by a pressure on it.

Orbitonometry —To measure the backward displacement of the eyeball into the orbit produced by a pressure on it, by orbitonometer.

Orbitopagus —Unequal conjoined twins in which the smaller fetus is attached to an orbit of the larger fetus.

Orbitopathy —Any disease of the orbit.

Orbitosphenoid —Pertaining to the orbit and the sphenoid bone.

Orbitotomy —To make an incision into an orbit.

Orchalgia —Orchialgia.

Orchectomy —Orchidectomy. Orchiectomy. Surgical removal of testicle.

Orcheoplasty —Repair of the testicle by plastic surgery.

Orchi-, Orchio- —Prefixes denoting relationship to the testicles.

Orchialgia —Orchiodynia. Pain in the testes.

Orchichorea —Involuntary movements of the testicles.

Orchidalgia —Orchialgia.

Orchidectomy —Orchectomy. Orchiectomy.

Orchidic —Pertaining to the testes.

Orchiditis —Orchitis. Inflammation of the testis.

Orchido- —A prefix indicating relationship to the testes.

Orchidoncus —Orchioncus. A tumor of the testis.

Orchidopexy —Orchiopexy. Orchiorrhaphy. To transfer the undescended testis into the scrotum and suture it there.

Orchidoplasty —Orchioplasty.

Orchidoptosis —Downward displacement of the testes.

Orchidorrhaphy —Orchiopexy.

Orchidotomy —To make an incision into a testis.

Orchiectomy —Orchidectomy. Surgical excision of one or both testes.

Orchiepididymitis —Inflammation of the testis and the epididymis.

Orchilytic —Destructive to the testicular tissue.

Orchio- —Orchi.

Orchiocele —1. Herniation of a testis. 2. Tumor of a testis.

Orchiodynia —Orchialgia. Orchidalgia. Orchioneuralgia. Pain occurring in the testis.

Orchiomyeloma —Plasmacytoma of the testis.

Orchioncus —Tumor of the testicle.

Orchioneuralgia —Orchialgia. Orchidalgia. Pain occurring in the testis.

Orchiopathy —Any disease of a testis.

Orchiopexy —Orchidopexy. Orchiorrhaphy. Fixation or suturing of an undescended testis into the scrotum.

Orchioplasty —Repair of a testis by plastic surgery.

Orchiorrhaphy —Orchidopexy. Orchiopexy. Suturing of an undescended testis to the surrounding tissue in the scrotum.

Orchioscheocele —Scrotal hernia with tumor of the testis.

Orchioscirrhus —Hardening of a testis due to the formation of tumor.

Orchiotherapy —Treatment of a disease with extract of the testes.

Orchiotomy —To make an incision into a testis.

Orchis —A testicle.

Orchitic —Pertaining to or caused by orchitis.

Orchitis —Inflammation of a testis.

Orchitolytic —Orchilytic.

Orchotomy —Orchidotomy. Orchiotomy.

Order —In biologic classification, the division just below the class or subclass and above the family.

Ordure —Feces or other excretions.

Orectic—Pertaining to orexia.

Orexia —Appetite

Orexigenic —Appetizer. Increasing appetite.

Oreximania —Excessive desire for taking food because of fear of becoming thin without food.

Organ —A part of the body performing a special function, *e.g.*, excretory and reproductive organs etc.

Organelle —A specialized structure of a cell which performs a definite function as mitochondria etc.

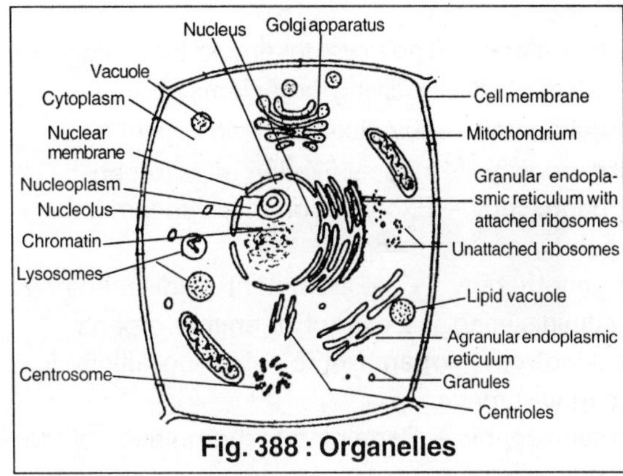

Fig. 388 : Organelles

Organic—1. Pertaining to an organ or organs. 2. Structural 3. Pertaining to or arising from an organism. 4. Denoting chemical substances containing carbon.

Organic disease —A disease associated with the detectable changes in the organs of the body.

Organicism —A theory that all diseases are due to organic disorder.

Organicist —The person who believes in organicism.

Organic psychosis —Psychoses induced by structural brain changes.

Organism —Any living thing, animal or plant.

Organismal —Pertaining to an organism.

Organization—The process of organizing or of becoming organized.

Organize —To develop from an amorphous state into a structure or organ.

Organo- —A prefix denoting a relationship to an organ.

Organoferric —Pertaining to an organic compound containing iron.

Organogenesis —The formation and development of the organs from the embryonic tissues.

Organogenetic —Pertaining to organogenesis.
Organogenic —Organogenetic.
Organogeny—Organogenesis.
Organography —Visualization of the body organs in the X-ray.
Organoid —1. Resembling an organ. 2. An organelle.
Organoleptic—Affecting an organ.
Organology —Study of the body organs.
Organoma —A tumor of an organ.
Organomegaly—Enlargement of the viscera.
Organon —Organ.
Organonomy —The laws governing the biological processes of the living organisms.
Organopathy —Any disease of an organ.
Organopexy —Surgical fixation of an organ.
Organoscopy —Examination of an abdominal organ by an endoscope.
Organotherapy —The treatment of diseases by administering the extract of animal organs.
Organotrope, Organotropic —Having affinity for certain organs.
Organotrophic —Pertaining to the nutrition of the body organs.
Organotropism —Special affinity of chemical compounds or pathogenic agents for particular tissues or body organs.
Organotropy —Organotropism.
Organ-specific—Arising from a single organ or affecting only some particular organ.
Organum —Organ.
Orgasm —The climax of sexual intercourse.
Orgasmic —Pertaining to or producing orgasm.
Oriental sore —Leishmaniasis (cutaneous)
Orientation —Ability to adjust one-self in an environment with regard to time and space.
Orifice —1. Mouth, entrance or outlet of any body cavity. 2. Any foramen, meatus, opening or aperture.
Orificia —Plural of orificium.
Orificial —Pertaining to an orifice.
Orificium —An orifice.
Origin —The source or starting point of anything, *e.g.*, the more fixed end of a muscle.
Original —Primitive.
Orinotherapy —Treatment of a disease by keeping the patient at high mountain.
Oris —Orifice
Oro- —A prefix denoting the mouth.
Orodiagnosis —Diagnosis of a disease made by using serums or serum reactions.
Orodigitofacial—Pertaining to the mouth, fingers and face.
Orofacial —Pertaining to the mouth and face.
Orogenital —Pertaining to the mouth and the genital organs.
Orolingual —Pertaining to the mouth and tongue.
Oromeningitis —Orrhomeningitis.
Oronasal —Pertaining to the mouth and nose.
Oropharyngeal —Pertaining to the mouth and pharynx.
Oropharynx —The middle part of the pharynx lying between the soft palate and upper margin of the epiglottis.
Orosomucoid —An alpha I-globulin in the blood plasma.
Orotherapy —Serotherapy. Treatment of the diseases by administering the injections of blood serum taken from immune persons or animals.
Orotracheal —Pertaining to the passage between the mouth and the trachea.
Orphan —A child whose parents have died or are unknown.
Orrhology —Serology. Study of the serums and their reactions.
Orrhomeningitis —Inflammation of serous membrane.
Orrhoreaction —Seroreaction. Serum sickness. A reaction from serum injection.
Orrhorrhea —A thin, colorless discharge from a body structure.
Orrhotherapy —Serotherapy.
O.R.S.—Oral Rehydration Solution.
O.R.T. —Oral Rehydration Therapy. To treat dehydration occurring in diarrhea or cholera, etc., by the administration of Oral Rehydration Solution by mouth.
Orthergasia —Normal mental condition.
Orthesis —Orthosis.
Orthetics —Orthotics
Orthetist —Orthotist
Ortho- —Combining form of the word which means straight, normal, correct.
Orthocephalic —Having a well-proportioned head.
Orthocephalous —Orthocephalic.
Orthochorea —A chorea which occurs in a person who is in a standing position.

Orthochromatic —Staining normally.

Orthochromophil—Staining normally with neutral dyes.

Orthochromophile —Orthochromophil.

Orthocytosis—Presence of only mature cells in the blood.

Orthodentin —Tubular dentin.

Orthodeoxia —Increment of arterial hypoxemia in the standing position.

Orthodiagraph —An instrument for accurate recording of the outlines and positions of the organs or foreign bodies as seen in X-ray.

Orthodigita —Correction of malformations of fingers or toes.

Orthodontia —Orthodontics

Orthodontics —The branch of dentistry concerning with the prevention and correction of the irregularities of the teeth.

Orthodontist —Specialist in orthodontics.

Orthodromic —Conducting nerve impulses in the normal direction, said of nerve fibers.

Orthogenesis —A biological law that evolution of an animal species is in a given direction, controlled by intrinsic factors and not by external factors.

Orthogenic —Pertaining to orthogenesis.

Orthogenics —Eugenics.

Orthognathic —Orthognathous.

Orthognathics —The science dealing with the malposition of the bones of the jaw.

Orthognathous —The person having straight jaws.

Orthograde —Walking with the body upright, as man walks.

Orthokeratology —The altering of the curvature of the cornea by pressing it with a special hard contact lens to treat the myopia.

Orthokeratosis —Formation of an anuclear layer, as in the normal epidermis.

Orthomechanical —Pertaining to the braces, prostheses and orthotic devices.

Orthomechanotherapy —Treatment of diseases with braces, prostheses and orthotic devices.

Orthomelic —Correcting deformed arms and legs.

Orthometer—An instrument for determining the degree of protrusion or retraction of the eyeballs.

Orthomolecular —Pertaining to the theory that certain diseases are associated with the biochemical changes occurring in the body which result in increased needs for certain nutrients, *e.g.*, vitamins, and can be treated by the administration of these nutrients.

Orthomyxoviruses —Viruses causing influenza.

Orthopedia —Orthopedics.

Orthopedic —1. Pertaining to orthopedics. 2. Prevention or correction of the deformities of the skeletal system.

Orthopedics —The branch of medical science dealing with the prevention and correction of the deformities of the skeletal system and its associated structures.

Orthopedist —Specialist in orthopedics.

Orthopercussion —Percussion with the distal phalanx of the percussing finger held perpendicularly to the surface percussed.

Orthophoria —The normal balance of the eye muscles.

Orthophoric—Pertaining to orthophoria.

Orthophrenia —The normal mental state in social relations.

Orthopnea —Discomfort in breathing in any except sitting or standing position.

Orthopneic —Pertaining to or suffering from orthopnea.

Orthopneic position —Sitting or half-sitting position of a patient with congestive heart failure or some pulmonary disease, which does not cause discomfort in breathing.

Orthopoxvirus —A genus of viruses that includes the virus causing smallpox, *i.e.*, variola.

Orthopraxis —Mechanical or surgical correction of the deformities.

Orthopraxy —Orthopraxis

Orthopsychiatry —The branch of psychiatry dealing with the mental and emotional development, including child psychiatry and mental hygiene.

Orthoptic—Pertaining to or producing normal vision in both the eyes.

Orthoptics —The science of correcting the visual defects in both the eyes.

Orthoptic training —Orthoptics. Exercises of the eye muscles for correcting the squint.

Orthoptist —One skilled in orthoptics.

Orthoroentgenography —Measurement of the size and position of the internal organs by radiographic procedure.

Orthoscope —An apparatus which neutralizes the corneal refraction by a layer of water.

Orthoscopic —1. Having a correct and undistorted vision. 2. Pertaining to orthoscopy.

Orthoscopy —Eye examination with the orthoscope.

Orthosis—An orthopedic apparatus to correct the deformities of the movable parts of the body.

Orthostatic —Orthotic. Pertaining to or caused by standing position.

Orthostatic hypotension —Postural hypotension.

Orthostatism —An erect standing position of the body.

Orthotast —An apparatus for straightening the curved bones.

Orthothanasia —Natural death.

Orthotic —1. Pertaining to orthosis. 2. Pertaining to or caused by standing position.

Orthotics —The science pertaining to orthoses and their uses.

Orthotist —A specialist in orthotics.

Orthotonos, Orthotonus —Tetanic spasm fixing the whole body in a rigid straight line.

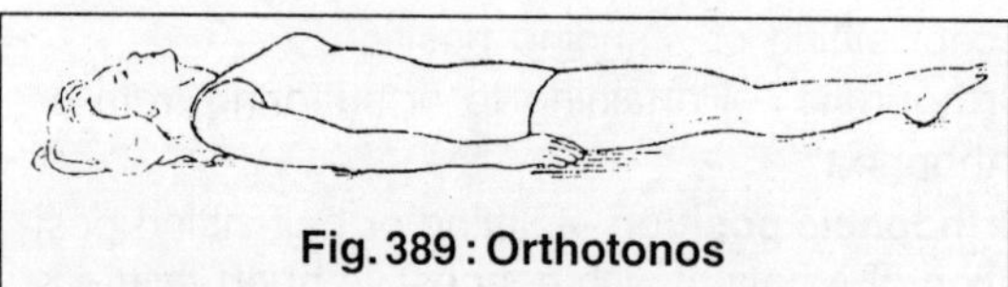

Fig. 389 : Orthotonos

Orthotopic —Occurring in a normal place.

Orthotropic —Extending or growing in a straight, especially a vertical direction.

Orthovoltage—Median voltage ranging from 140 to 400 kilovolts in X-ray therapy.

Orthropsia —Betterment of sight at dawn or dusk than in bright sunlight.

Orthuria —Normal frequency of micturition.

O.S. —Oculus sinister. Left eye.

Os —1. Mouth or opening, *e.g.*, mouth of the uterus. 2. Bone.

Oscedo —1. Yawning. 2. Aphtha. White spots on the mucous membrane of the mouth.

Oscheal —Pertaining to the scrotum.

Oscheitis —Inflammation of the scrotum.

Oschelephantiasis —Elephantiasis of the scrotum.

Oscheo- —Combining form of the word which means scrotum.

Oscheocele —Oscheoma. A swelling or tumor of the scrotum.

Oscheohydrocele —Collection of fluid in the sac of a scrotal hernia.

Oscheolith —A calculus in the sebaceous glands of the scrotum.

Oscheoma —Oscheoncus. A tumor of the scrotum.

Oscheonchus —Oscheoma.

Oscheoplasty—Repair of the scrotum by plastic surgery.

Oschitis —Oscheitis.

Oscillation —A backward and forward motion like that of a pendulum, vibration, fluctuation.

Oscillator —An apparatus for producing oscillations.

Oscillogram —A graph made by oscillograph.

Oscillograph —An apparatus for detecting and recording variations in the electrical phenomena. It is used for recording electrical activity of the brain and heart etc.

Oscillography —The study of the records made by an oscillograph.

Oscillometer —An instrument for measuring the oscillations.

Oscillometric —Pertaining to the oscillometer or the records made by its use.

Oscillometry —To take the measurement of the oscillations by oscillometer.

Oscillopsia —Visual sensation that the fixed objects are moving forward and backward.

Oscilloscope —An instrument for making visible the electrical variations on the fluorescent screen of a cathode-ray tube.

Oscitate —To yawn.

Oscitation —Yawning.

Osculation —The union of two vessels or structures by their mouth.

Osculum —A small aperture.

-osis —A suffix indicating a disease or an abnormal increase in the condition.

Osmatic —Pertaining to or having the sense of smell.

Osmazone —The flavour of cooked meat.

Osmesis —Olfaction. 1. The sense of smell. 2. The act of smelling.

Osmesthesia —Ability of perceiving and distinguishing the odors.

Osmics —The science dealing with the sense of smell.

Osmidrosis —Bromidrosis. Bromhidrosis.

Osmo- —Combining form indicating relationship to the odor or smell.

Osmodysphoria —Aversion to certain odors.

Osmolagnia —Osphresiolagnia. Sexual satisfaction from body odor.

Osmolality —The concentration of a solution in terms of osmoles of solutes per kilogram of the solvent.

Osmolar —Pertaining to the osmotic concentration of a solution.

Osmolarity —The concentration of a solution in terms of osmoles of solutes per liter of solution.

Osmole —A unit of osmotic pressure equivalent to the amount of solute substances that dissociates in the solution to form one mole of particles.

Osmology —The study of odors or osmosis.

Osmometer—An apparatus for measuring the osmotic pressure or for measuring acuity of sense of smell.

Osmometry —Measurement of osmolality by using an osmometer.

Osmonosology —A branch of medical science dealing with the diseases of the organs of smell.

Osmophil —Osmophilic.

Osmophilic —Having affinity for high osmotic pressure.

Osmophobia —Morbid fear of odors.

Osmophore—A portion of a chemical responsible for the odor of a compound.

Osmoreceptor —1. A receptor situated in the hypothalamus which is sensitive to the osmotic pressure of the serum. 2. A receptor situated in the brain which is sensitive to the olfactory stimuli.

Osmoregulation —The regulation of the internal osmotic pressure of a body cell in relation to that of the surrounding medium.

Osmoregulatory —Regulating the degree and rapidity of osmosis.

Osmose —1. To diffuse by osmosis. 2. The object which undergoes osmosis.

Osmosis —The passage of the solution of low concentration towards that of high concentration through a semipermeable membrane, separating the solutions of different concentrations.

Osmostat —The regulatory center in the hypothalamus controlling the osmolality of the extracellular fluid.

Osmotherapy —Treatment of the cerebral edema by increasing the osmolar concentration of the blood serum by introducing hypertonic solution intravenously.

Osmotic —Pertaining to the osmosis.

Osmotic pressure —The pressure that develops when two solutions of different concentrations are separated by a semipermeable membrane. It varies with the concentration of the solution and with the variation in the temperature. Solutions exerting the osmotic pressure equal to that of the inside of the blood cells are called isotonic, solutions exerting the osmotic pressure higher than that of the inside of the blood cells, cause the blood cells to shrink, are called hypertonic and the solutions exerting the osmotic pressure lower than that of the inside of the blood cells, cause the blood cells to swell, are called hypotonic solutions.

Osphresiolagnia —Osmolagnia.

Osphresiologic —Pertaining to osphresiology.

Osphresiology —Osmology. Science of odors and the sense of smell.

Osphresiometer —Osmometer.

Osphresiophilia —An abnormal interest in odors.

Osphresiophobia —Olfactophobia. Morbid fear of odors.

Osphresis —Olfaction. The sense of smell.

Osphretic —Olfactory. Pertaining to the sense of smell.

Osphus —Loin.

Osphyalgia —Pain in the loin.

Osphyitis —Inflammation of the lumbar region.

Osphyomyelitis —Inflammation of the lumbar region of the spinal cord.

Ossa —Plural of os.

Ossein, Osseine —The collagen of bone which forms the framework of bone.

Osseocartilaginous —Pertaining to the bone and cartilage.

Osseofibrous —Made up of bone and the fibrous tissue.

Osseomucin —Ground substance of bone.

Osseous —Bony. Bonelike or pertaining to a bone.

Ossi- —A prefix denoting a bone.

Ossicle —A small bone, especially one of the three—incus, malleus and stapes bones of the ear.

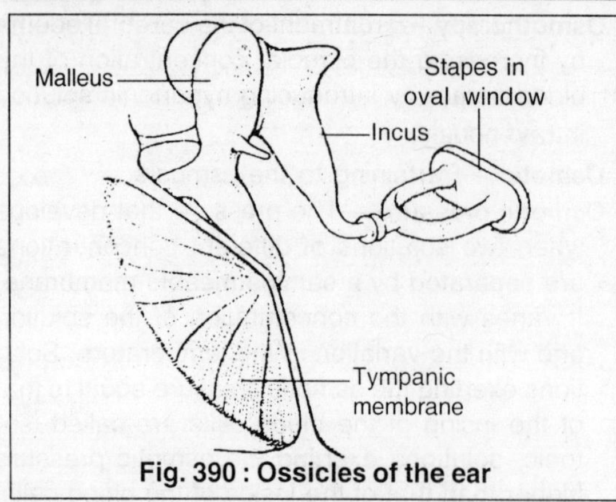

Fig. 390 : Ossicles of the ear

Ossicula —Plural of ossiculum. Little bones.

Ossicular —Pertaining to an ossicle.

Ossiculectomy —Excision of one or more ossicles of the middle ear.

Ossiculotomy —To make an incision into an ossicle of the middle ear.

Ossiculum—Ossicle.

Ossiferous —Composed of, or forming bone.

Ossific —Forming or becoming bone.

Ossification —Formation or conversion of other tissue into the bone.

Ossifluence—Softening of a bone.

Ossiform —Osteoid. Resembling bone.

Ossify—To change into bone.

Ostalgia —Osteodynia. Pain in a bone.

Osteal —Pertaining to the bone.

Ostealgia —Ostalgia.

Osteanagenesis —Reformation of bone.

Osteanaphysis —Osteoanagenesis.

Ostearthrotomy —Osteoarthrotomy. Excision of the articular end of a bone.

Ostectomy, Osteectomy —Excision of a bone or a portion of a bone.

Ostectopy —Osteectopia.

Osteectopia —Displacement of a bone.

Ostein, Osteine —Collagen.

Osteitic —Ostitic. Pertaining to or suffering from osteitis.

Osteitis —Ostitis. Inflammation of a bone.

Condensing osteitis —Sclerosing osteitis in which the bone becomes denser and heavier due to deposits of osseous tissue in the marrow cavity.

Osteitis deformans —Paget's disease. Chronic form of osteitis occurring in old people with thickening and hypertrophy of the long bones and deformity of the flat bones.

Osteitis fibrosa cystica generalisata —Hyperparathyroidism. Osteitis with rarefication and softening of the bones with fibrous degeneration and formation of cysts and fibrous nodules on the affected bones, resulting from the overactivity of the parathyroid glands.

Osteitis fragilitans —Osteogenesis imperfecta.

Osteitis gummatous —Chronic osteitis associated with syphilis with the formation of gummas on the bone.

Osteitis rarefying —Osteoporosis.

Osteitis sclerosing —Osteitis condensing.

Ostembryon —Osteopedion. An ossified fetus.

Ostemia —Congestion of blood in a bone.

Ostempyesis —Suppuration occurring within a bone.

Osteo- —A prefix which indicates relationship to a bone.

Osteoanagenesis —Regeneration of a bone.

Osteoanesthesia —Insensitivity of a bone, especially to stimuli that would normally produce pain.

Osteoaneurysm —Dilatation of a blood vessel occurring within a bone.

Osteoarthritis —Degenerative arthritis. Degenerative disease of the joints marked by destruction of the joint cartilage and overgrowth of the bones at the margin with the pain and stiffness.

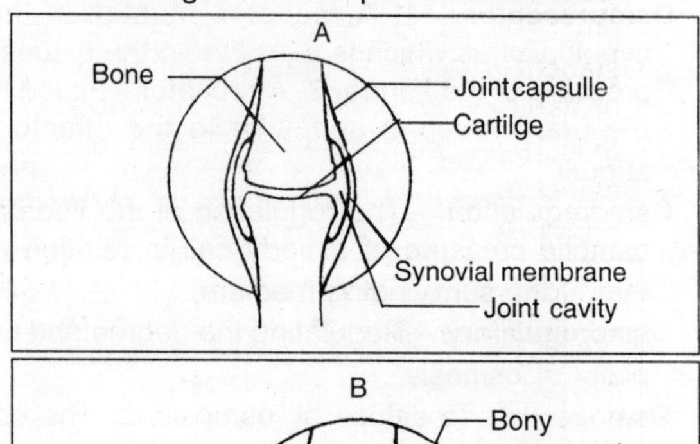

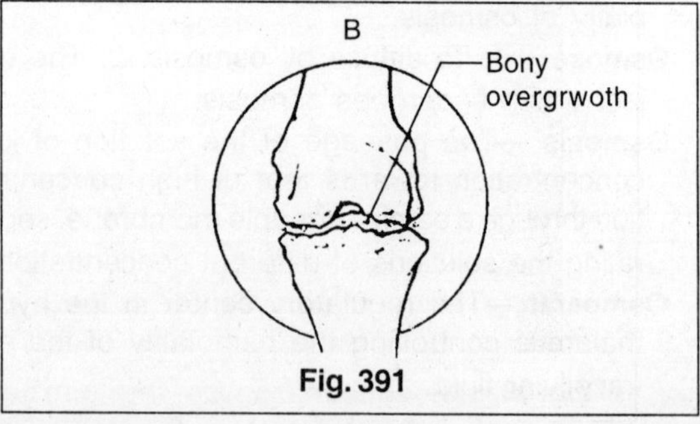

Fig. 391

Osteoarthropathy —Any disease of the joints and bones.

Osteoarthrosis —Osteoarthritis. Chronic noninflammatory disease of the bone.

Osteoarthrotomy —Ostearthrotomy.

Osteoblast —A cell arising from mesoderm that is concerned with the bone formation.

Osteoblastic —Pertaining to osteoblasts.

Osteoblastoma —A large painful benign tumor of the osteoblasts.

Osteocampsia —Curvature of a bone as occurs in osteomalacia.

Osteocarcinoma —Carcinoma of a bone.

Osteocartilaginous —Pertaining to the bone and cartilage.

Osteocele —1. A tumor of the testis or scrotum containing bony tissue. 2. A bone-containing hernia.

Osteocephaloma —A malignant brainlike tumor of a bone.

Osteochondral —Pertaining to the bone and cartilage.

Osteochondritis—Inflammation of bone and cartilage.

Osteochondrodysplasia —Any disorder of bone and cartilage growth.

Osteochondrodystrophia, Osteochondrodystrophy —Morquio's syndrome. A disorder of bone and cartilage growth producing dwarfism.

Osteochondrodystrophy —Chondro-osteodystrophy.

Osteochondrolysis —Detachment of a fragment of cartilage and its underlying bone from the articular surface.

Osteochondroma —A benign tumor composed of both bony and cartilaginous tissues.

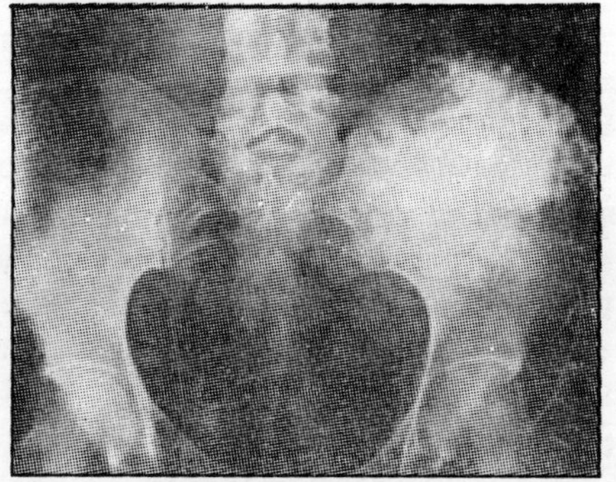

Fig. 392 : Osteochondroma of the ilium bone

Osteochondromatosis —Formation of multiple osteochondromas.

Osteochondromyxoma —Osteochondroma mixed with myxoma.

Osteochondrosarcoma —Chondrosarcoma occurring in a bone.

Osteochondrosis —Degeneration of the ossification centers followed by regeneration during the period of growth in children.

Osteochondrous —Pertaining to the bone and cartilage.

Osteoclasia, Osteoclasis —Surgical fracture of a bone to correct a deformity.

Osteoclasis— Osteoclasia.

Osteoclast —1. A large multinuclear cell formed in the bone marrow which is associated with the absorption and removal of the bone. 2. An instrument used for fracturing bones in surgery.

Osteoclastic —Pertaining to the osteoclast.

Osteoclastoma —Giant cell tumor of bone.

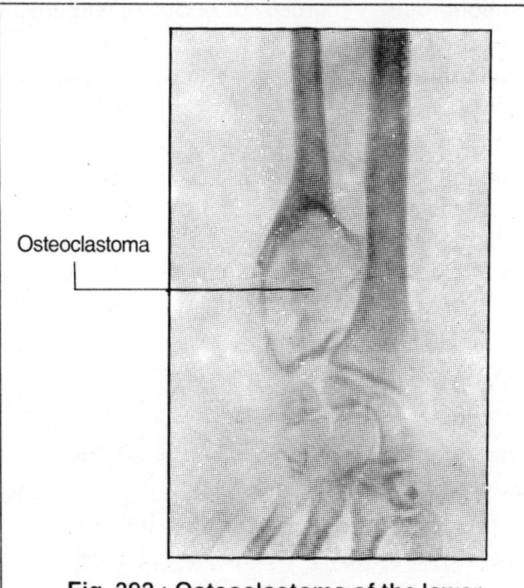

Fig. 393 : Osteoclastoma of the lower end of ulna

Osteoclasty —Osteoclasis.

Osteocope —Severe pain in a bone.

Osteocopic —Pertaining to the severe pain in the bone.

Osteocranium —The skull of a fetus during the period of ossification.

Osteocystoma —A cystic tumor of a bone.

Osteocyte —A mesodermal bone-forming cell that is embedded within the bone matrix. It occupies a bone lacuna from which branching processes come outwards through the canaliculi and make network by joining with the processes of the other osteocytes.

Osteodensitometer —An apparatus for determining the density of bones.

Osteodentin —Dentin resembling bone.

Osteodermia —Formation of bone in the skin.

Osteodesmosis —Conversion of a tendon into bone.

Osteodiastasis —Separation of two adjacent bones.

Osteodynia —Ostealgia. Pain occurring in a bone.

Osteodystrophia —Osteodystrophy. Defective bone development.

Osteodystrophy —Osteodystrophia.

Osteoectomy —Ostectomy.

Osteoepiphysis —Bony epiphysis.

Osteofibroma —Fibroosteoma. A tumor of the bony and fibrous tissues.

Osteofibrosis —Fibrosis of bone, mainly involving red bone marrow.

Osteogen —A substance composing the inner layer of the periosteum from which bone is formed.

Osteogenesis, Osteogeny —Ossification. Formation and development of bone.

Osteogeness imperfecta— An inherited disorder marked by abnormally brittle bones which are broken readily with trivial injury.

Osteogenic —Pertaining to the osteogenesis.

Osteogenous —Osteogenic.

Osteogeny —Osteogenesis.

Osteography —Description of the bones.

Osteohalisteresis —Softening of the bones due to deficiency of minerals in the bone.

Osteohypertrophy —Overgrowth of bones.

Osteoid —Resembling bone.

Osteolipochondroma —A chondroma composed of bony and fatty tissues.

Osteologia —Osteology.

Osteologist —A specialist in osteology.

Osteology —The scientific study of bones.

Osteolysis —Destruction of bone.

Osteolytic —Causing osteolysis.

Osteoma —Exostosis. A benign bony tumor or a bonelike hard structure developing on a bone or sometimes on other structures.

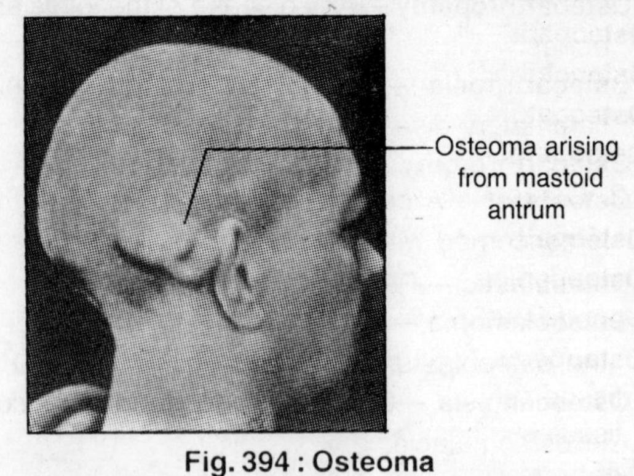

Fig. 394 : Osteoma

Osteomalacia —Softening of the bones due to vitamin D deficiency resulting in their deformities.

Osteomalacic—Pertaining to or affected by osteomalacia.

Osteomatoid —Like an osteoma.

Osteomatosis —Formation of multiple osteomas.

Osteomere —One of a series of similar bones such as the vertebrae.

Osteometry —Measurement of the bones.

Osteomyelitis —Inflammation of the bone marrow due to pathogenic organism.

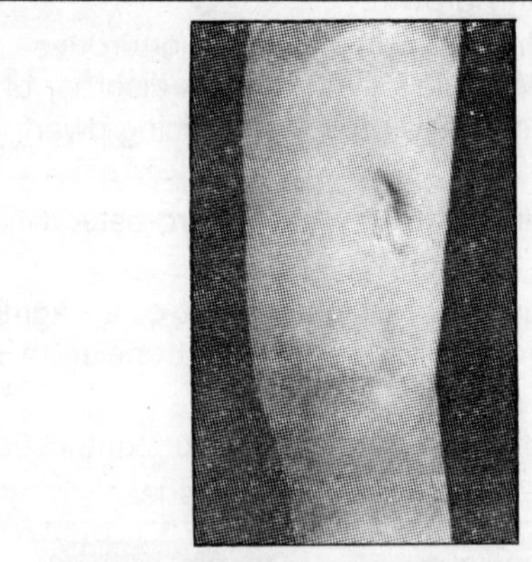

Fig. 395 : Osteomyelitis

Osteomyelodysplasia —Increment of the bone marrow cavities in size, with the thinning of bony tissue accompanied by leukopenia and fever.

Osteomyxochondroma —Osteochondromyxoma.

Osteon —The basic unit of the structure of compact bone consisting of a haversian canal and the surrounding lamellae.

Osteoncus —Osteoma. Exostosis. A bone tumor.

Osteonecrosis —Necrosis of a bone.

Osteoneuralgia —Pain occurring in a bone.

Osteopath —A practitioner of osteopathy.

Osteopathia —Osteopathy.

Osteopathic —Pertaining to the osteopathy.

Osteopathology —1. Study of the bone diseases. 2. Osteopathy.

Osteopathy —Any disease of bone.

Osteopedion —Ostembryon. A calcified or hardened fetus.

Osteopenia —Reduction in the amount of bone tissue due to decrease in the rate of osteoid tissue synthesis to keep up with the normal rate of bone lysis.

Osteoperiosteal —Pertaining to a bone and its periosteum.

Osteoperiostitis —Inflammation of a bone and its periosteum.

Osteopetrosis —A hereditary disease marked by abnormally dense bone and spontaneous fracture of the affected bone.

Osteopetrotic —Pertaining to osteopetrosis.

Osteophage —Osteoclast.

Osteophagia —Craving for eating bones caused by calcium or phosphorus deficiency.

Osteophlebitis —Inflammation of the veins of a bone

Osteophone —An apparatus used by the deaf persons for conducting the sound through the facial bones.

Osteophony—Conduction of sound through bone.

Osteophore —A bone-crushing forceps.

Osteophyma —A swelling or growth of a bone.

Osteophyte —A bony outgrowth.

Osteoplaque —A layer of the bone.

Osteoplast —Osteoblast.

Osteoplastic —1. Pertaining to the repair of a bone by plastic surgery. 2. Pertaining to the formation of bone.

Osteoplasty —Repair of a bone by plastic surgery.

Osteopoikilosis —A hereditary disease of bones in which there is excessive calcification in spots in the bones.

Osteoporosis —Increased rarefaction or porosity of bones occurring most commonly in old people, due to disuse of the bones which may occur while the patient is in bed for a prolonged period or due to loss of bone tissue following trauma or it may occur secondary to other diseases.

Osteoporotic —Pertaining to the osteoporosis.

Osteoradiologist —Specialist in radiology of the bones and joints.

Osteoradiology —Radiology of bones.

Osteoradionecrosis —Necrosis of a bone following excessive irradiation.

Osteorrhagia —Hemmorrhage from a bone.

Osteorrhaphy —Osteosuture. To fix the fragments of the bone with sutures or wires.

Osteosarcoma —Myelosarcoma. A malignant sarcoma of the bone.

Fig. 396 : Osteosarcoma of the Humerus bone

Osteosarcomatous —Pertaining to or like an osteosarcoma.

Osteosclerosis —Hardening of a bone.

Osteosclerotic —Pertaining to, due to, or marked by hardening of bone substance.

Osteoseptum —The bony area of the nasal septum.

Osteosis —Formation of bony nodules in the skin.

Osteospongioma —A spongy tumor of a bone.

Osteosteatoma —A benign fatty tumor containing bony tissues.

Osteostixis —Surgical puncture of a bone.

Osteosuture —Osteorrhaphy.

Osteosynovitis —Inflammation of a synovial membrane with that of the adjacent bones.

Osteosynthesis —Surgical fastening of the ends of a fractured bone by means of a screw or plate.

Osteotabes —Atrophy of the bone in infants due to destruction of the marrow cells.

Osteotelangiectasia—Sarcoma tumor of the bone containing dilated blood vessels.

Osteothrombosis—Formation of blood clot in the veins of a bone.

Osteotome—A knife for cutting bone.

Osteotomoclasis—Correction of bone curvature by partial division with the osteotome followed by forcible fracture.

Osteotomy—To incise or transect a bone.

Cuneiform osteotomy—Removal of a wedge-shaped portion of a bone.

Displacement osteotomy—Surgical division of a bone and shifting the divided ends to change the alignment of the bone.

Linear osteotomy—Lengthwise cutting of a bone.

Osteotribe—A file used for rubbing the bones for making their shapes.

Osteotrite—An instrument used to scrape away the diseased portion of a bone.

Osteotrophy—Nutrition of the bone.

Osteotylus—The callus formed around the fractured ends of a bone.

Osteotympanic—Otocranial.

Ostia—Plural of ostium.

Ostial—Pertaining to an orifice.

Ostitic—Osteitic. Pertaining to the inflammation of bone.

Ostitis—Osteitis.

Ostium—Mouth, opening or orifice, *e.g.*, the opening of the fallopian tube into the uterus, external opening of the urethra and external opening of the vagina etc.

Ostoid—Osseous; bony.

Ostomate—The person who has surgically formed fistula connecting the intestine to the outside, through the abdominal wall.

Ostomy—To form an artificial opening surgically as is done in colostomy etc.

Ostosis—Osteogenesis.

Otacoustic—1. Aiding or pertaining to the hearing. 2. An apparatus to aid hearing.

Otalgia—Otodynia. Earache. Pain in the ear.

Otalgic—Pertaining to otalgia or earache.

Otectomy—Excision of the tissues of the internal and middle ear.

Othelcosis—Ulceration or suppuration of the middle ear.

Othematoma—Effusion of blood between the perichondrium and cartilage of the pinna of ear

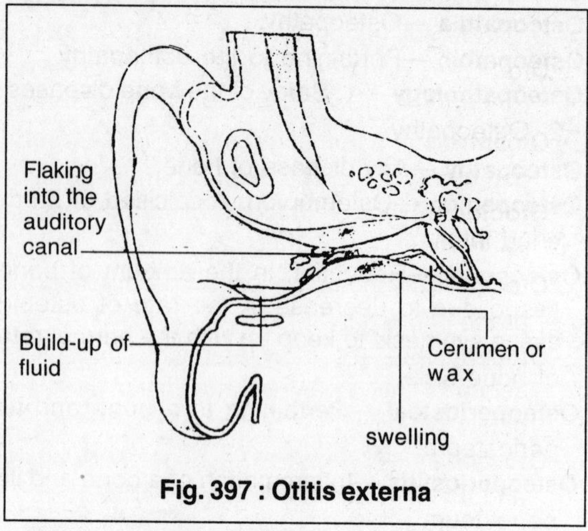

Fig. 397 : Otitis externa

causing a hard swelling.

Othemorrhea—Hemorrhage from the ear.

Othygroma—Edema of the ear lobe.

Otic—Aural. Pertaining to the ear.

Oticodinia—Meniere's disease. Vertigo occurring due to ear disease.

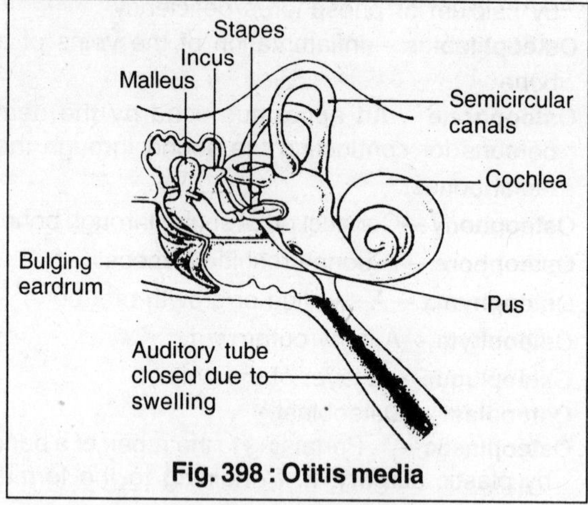

Fig. 398 : Otitis media

Otitic—Pertaining to the inflammation of the ear.

Otitis—Inflammation of the ear.

Otitis aviation—Barotitis.

Otitis externa—Inflammation of the external ear.

Otitis furuncular—Formation of the furuncles in the external auditory canal.

Otitis interna, Otitis labyrinthica—Labyrinthitis. Inflammation of the internal ear.

Otitis mastoidea—Inflammation of the mastoid spaces.

Otitis media —Inflammation of the middle ear.

Otitis mycotica —Inflammation of the ear due to fungal infection.

Oto-, Ot- —Combining forms of the word relating to the ear.

Otoantritis —The inflammation of the upper portion of the tympanic cavity and mastoid antrum.

Otoblennorrhea —Mucous discharge from the ear.

Otocatarrh —Inflammation of the mucous membrane of the ear.

Otocephalus —An individual with congenital absence of the lower jaw and fusion of the ears below the face.

Otocephaly —Congenital absence of the lower jaw and fusion of the ears below the face.

Otocerebritis —Otoencephalitis.

Otocleisis —Closure of the auditory passages.

Otoconia —Plural of otoconium.

Otoconium —Otolith.

Otocranial —Osteotympanic. Pertaining to the otocranium.

Otocranium —The auditory portion of the cranium.

Otocyst —The auditory vesicle of the embryo.

Otodynia —Otalgia. Earache. Pain in the ear.

Otoencephalitis —Inflammation of the brain due to extension of the infection from the inflamed middle ear.

Otoganglion —The ganglion of the ear.

Otogenic, Otogenous —Arising from the ear.

Otography —A description of the ear.

Otolaryngologist—A specialist in otolaryngology.

Otolaryngology —The branch of medicine dealing with the diseases of the ear and the larynx.

Otolith —Stone in the ear.

Otologic —Pertaining to otology.

Otological —Pertaining to otology.

Otologist —Specialist in otology.

Otology —A branch of medicine dealing with the structure, function and diseases of the ear.

Otomucormycosis —Mucormycosis of the ear.

Otomyasthenia —Weakness of the muscles of the ear.

Otomyces —Any fungus infection of the ear.

Otomycosis —Fungus infection of the external auditory meatus and auditory canal.

Otoncus —Tumor of the ear.

Otonecrectomy, Otonecronectomy —Excision of the necrosed portion of the ear.

Otoneuralgia —Otalgia. Otodynia. Pain in the ear.

Otoneurasthenia —Weakness due to ear disease.

Otoneurology —The branch of otology dealing with the portion of nervous system related to the ear.

Otopalatodigital —Pertaining to the ears, palate and fingers.

Otopathy —Any disease of the ear.

Otopharyngeal —Pertaining to the ear and the pharynx.

Otoplasty —Repair of the ear by plastic surgery.

Otopolypus —A polyp in the ear.

Otopyorrhea —Purulent discharge from the ear.

Otopyosis —Suppurative disease of the ear.

Otorhinolaryngology —The study of the structures, functions and diseases of the ear, nose and the larynx.

Otorhinology —Branch of medicine dealing with the ear and nose and their diseases.

Otorrhagia—Bleeding from the ear.

Otorrhea —Discharge from the ear.

Otosalpinx —Eustachian tube.

Otoscleronectomy —Surgical excision of the sclerosed and ankylosed ossicles of the ear.

Otosclerosis —The condition in which otospongiosis causes the bony ankylosis of the stapes, resulting in deafness.

Otoscope —An apparatus for examining the ear.

Otoscopy —Examination of the ear by means of otoscope.

Otosis —To misunderstand the spoken sounds.

Otospongiosis —The formation of spongy bone in the bony labyrinth of the ear.

Otosteal —Pertaining to the ossicles of the ear.

Otosteon —One of the ossicles of the ear.

Ototomy —To make an incision into the ear.

Ototoxic —Having a toxic effect on the organs of hearing.

Ototoxicity —The property of being ototoxic.

Oula —The gum.

Oulitis —Ulitis. Inflammation of the gums.

Oulorrhagia —Ulorrhagia. Bleeding from the gums.

Ounce —A measure of weight and fluid volume.

-ous —A suffix meaning possessing.

Outbreak —Sudden occurrence of a disease in a specific area.

Outcome —The result of an action.

Outflow —In neurology, the passage of impulses from the central nervous system outwards.

Outlet —An opening from which something is escaped.

Outpatient —The patient who receives treatment at a hospital or dispensary but not being admitted in the hospital.

Outpocketing —Evagination. Protrusion of an organ or part.

Outpouching —Evagination.

Output —Total of anything produced, expelled or ejected by any system of the body, *e.g.*, cardiac output which is the volume of blood pumped into the arterial system per unit of time and urinary output which is the amount of urine produced by the kidneys.

Ova—Plural of ovum.

Oval —1. Pertaining to an ovum. 2. Egg-shaped.

Ovalbumin —An albumin occurring in the white of egg.

Ovalocyte —An oval red blood cell.

Ovalocytosis —Presence of a large number of oval red blood cells in the blood.

Oval window —An oval aperture in the middle ear in which the base of the stapes fits.

Ovaralgia, Ovarialgia —Oophoralgia. Pain occurring in the ovary.

Ovarialgia —Ovaralgia.

Ovarian —Pertaining to or resembling the ovary.

Ovariectomised —The woman who has undergone the ovariectomy operation.

Ovariectomy —Oophorectomy. Excision of an ovary.

Ovario- —Combining form indicating relationship to the ovary.

Ovariocele —Hernia of an ovary.

Ovariocentesis — Puncture and drainage of an ovarian cyst.

Ovariocyesis —Pregnancy occurring in the ovary.

Ovariodysneuria —Neuralgia in an ovary.

Ovariogenic —Originating in an ovary.

Ovariohysterectomy —Oophorohysterectomy. Removal of the ovaries with uterus by surgery.

Ovariolytic —Destructive to the ovary.

Ovariopathy —Any disease of the ovary.

Ovariopexy —Surgical fixation of an ovary to the abdominal wall.

Ovariorrhexis —Rupture of an ovary.

Ovariosalpingectomy —Oophorosalpingectomy. Excision of an ovary and a fallopian tube.

Ovariosalpingitis —Oophorosalpingitis.

Ovariostomy —Oophorostomy.

Ovariotomy —1. To make an incision into, or removal of, an ovary. 2. Removal of an ovarian tumor.

Ovariotubal —Pertaining to the ovary and the fallopian tubes.

Ovarious —Ovular.

Ovariprival —Resulting from loss of the ovaries.

Ovaritis —Oophoritis

Ovarium —The ovary.

Ovary —One of the two almond-shaped female

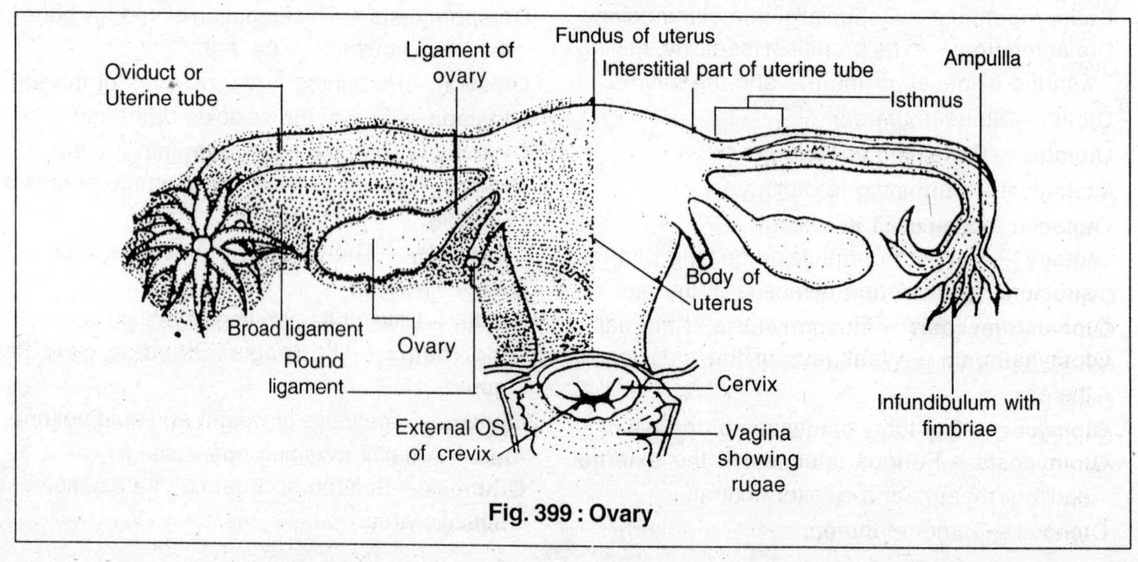

Fig. 399 : Ovary

sexual glands situated on either side of the pelvic cavity in which ova and two female hormones are formed.

Oven —Furnace.

Overbite —The extension of the upper incisor teeth over the lower ones vertically when these are in contact.

Overclosure —A dental defect in which the mandible or lower jaw closes too far before the teeth of the jaws make contact.

Overcompensation —The process by which a person makes efforts in excess of that needed to compensate for a physical or psychological defect.

Overcorrection —The use of a very powerful lens to correct a refractive error of the eye.

Overdenture —A denture supported by the soft tissue and the remaining natural teeth.

Overeruption —The projection of the occluding surface of a tooth beyond the line of occlusion.

Overgrafting —To place a second or additional grafts over a previously healed graft from which the epithelium has been removed.

Overhang —The extension of the excess of the material used, beyond the margins of a cavity.

Overhead projector —Epidiascope.

Overhydration —An excess of fluids in the body.

Overjet —Overlap of the teeth horizontally.

Overlap —To place the border of a thing on some tissue or object.

Overlay —To cover completely.

Overmedication —The taking of more medicines that are required.

Overresponse —An abnormally intense reaction to a stimulus.

Overriding —The slipping of one end of a fractured bone upon the other.

Overtoe —Displacement of the great toe toward other toes to the extent that it rests over the other toes.

Overventilation —Hyperventilation.

Ovi- —A prefix which means egg.

Ovi albumen —Ovalbumin. White of egg.

Ovicidal —Causing death of the ovum.

Ovicide —Destructive to the ova.

Oviduct —One of the two tubes extending laterally from the upper portion of the uterus, through which ova pass from the ovary to the uterus.

Oviductal —Pertaining to an oviduct or a fallopian tube.

Oviferous —Producing ova.

Ovification —The production of ova.

Oviform —Ovoid. Egg-shaped.

Ovigenesis —Oogenesis

Ovigenetic —Oogenetic.

Ovigenic —Oogenetic.

Ovigenous —Oogenetic.

Ovigerm —The cell that produces or develops into an ovum.

Ovigerous —Producing ova.

Ovine —Pertaining to sheep or sheeplike.

Oviparity —The property of being oviparous.

Oviparous —Producing eggs in which the embryo develops outside the body of the mother, as in birds.

Oviposit —To lay eggs.

Oviposition —The laying of eggs.

Ovipositor —A specialized organ in many female insects through which they lay their eggs.

Ovisac —The graafian follicle.

Ovo- —Combining form indicating relation to an egg.

Ovocenter —The centrosome of a fertilized ovum.

Ovocyte —Oocyte

Ovogenesis—Oogenesis. Production of ova.

Ovoglobulin —The globulin found in egg white.

Ovogonium —Oogonium

Ovoid —Oviform. Egg-shaped.

Ovomucoid —A mucoprotein obtained from the white of egg.

Ovoplasm —Cytoplasm of an unfertilized egg.

Ovotestis —A gonad containing both testicular and ovarian tissue.

Ovovitellin—Protein found in egg yolk.

Ovoviviparous —Reproducing by eggs which hatch within the mother.

Ovula —Plural of ovulum.

Ovular —Pertaining to an ovum.

Ovulation —The discharge of the ovum from the graafian follicle.

Ovulatory —Pertaining to the ovulation.

Ovule —1. An ovum within a graafian follicle. 2. A small egg.

Ovulogenous —1. Producing ova. 2. Arising from an ovum.

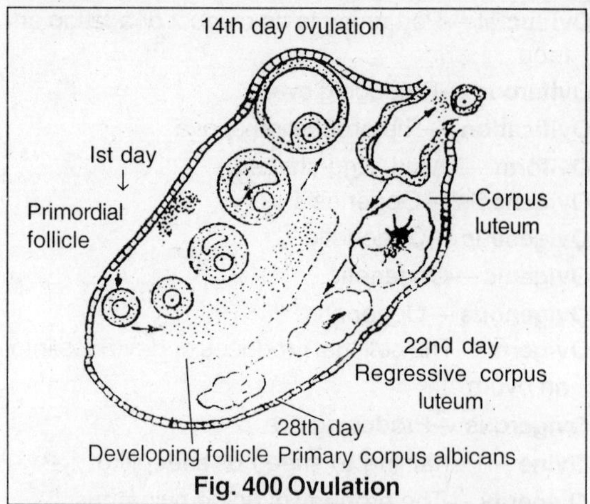

Fig. 400 Ovulation

Ovulum —1. The ovum. 2. A small egg like structure.

Ovum —The female reproductive cell, an egg.

Oxa- —A prefix indicating the presence of oxygen in place of carbon.

Oxalemia —Excess of oxalates in the blood.

Oxalism —Poisoning by oxalic acid or by an oxalate.

Oxalosis —Deposition of calcium oxalate in the body tissues, especially in the kidneys.

Oxaluria —Excretion of excess of oxalates, especially calcium oxalate in the urine.

Oxidant —In oxidation-reduction reactions, the acceptor of an electron.

Oxidasis —Oxidation by an oxidase.

Oxidation —The process of combining with oxygen.

Oxidation-reduction —The chemical reaction in which the electrons are removed from the atoms of the substance being oxidized (oxidation) and transferred to the substance being reduced (reduction).

Oxidative —Causing oxidation.

Oxidize —To combine with oxygen.

Oxidizing —Causing oxidation.

Oximeter —An apparatus for determining the amount of oxygen in the blood.

Oximetry —To determine the amount of oxygen in the blood by an oximeter.

Oxonemia —Acetonemia. Excess of acetone bodies in the blood.

Oxy- —Combining form indicating 1. The presence of oxygen in a compound. 2. Sharp, acute, quick, sour.

Oxyacoia, Oxyakoia —Increased sensitiveness to sounds, occurring in facial paralysis.

Oxyacusis —Hyperacusis.

Oxyblepsia —Abnormal acuteness of vision.

Oxybutyria —Presence of oxybutyric acid in the urine.

Oxycalcium —Of or pertaining to oxygen and calcium.

Oxycephalia —The condition of having a high and pointed skull.

Oxycephalic —Oxycephalous.

Oxycephalous —An individual having a high and pointed skull.

Oxycephaly —Oxycephalia.

Oxychromatic —Staining readily with acid dyes.

Oxychromatin —The portion of chromatin staining readily with acid dyes.

Oxycinesia —Occurrence of pain on movement.

Oxyecoia —Abnormal sensitivity to noises.

Oxyesthesia —Hyperesthesia

Oxygen —A colorless, oderless and tasteless gas occurring free in the atmosphere forming approximately 20% of its volume and essential for respiration.

Oxygenase —An enzyme that enables an organism to use atmospheric oxygen in respiration.

Oxygenate —To saturate with the oxygen.

Oxygenated —Saturated or combined with oxygen.

Oxygenation —Saturation or combination with oxygen.

Oxygenator —An apparatus for oxygenating anything but especially blood.

Oxygen concentrator —An apparatus for removing most of the nitrogen from the room air and supplying oxygen in place of that.

Oxygen debt —After strenuous physical labor, oxygen required in the recovery period, in addition to that required while resting.

Oxygenic —Pertaining to, resembling or containing oxygen.

Oxygenize —Oxidize

Oxygeusia —Extreme acuity of the sense of taste.

Oxyheme —Hematin.

Oxyhemochromogen —Hematin.

Oxyhemoglobin —The combined form of hemoglobin and oxygen which is found in arterial blood and is the oxygen carrier to the body tissues.

Oxyhemoglobinometer — An apparatus for measuring the amount of oxygen in the blood.

Oxyhydrocephalus —A type of hydrocephalus in which the head is pointed.

Oxylalia —To speak rapidly.

Oxymyoglobin —Myoglobin combined with oxygen.

Oxyntic —Secreting acid.

Oxyopia —Abnormal acuteness of vision.

Oxyopter —A unit of measuring the visual acuity.

Oxyosmia —Abnormal acuity of the sense of smell.

Oxyosphresia —Oxyosmia

Oxypathia, Oxypathy — 1. An acute condition. 2. Abnormal acuity of sensation.

Oxyperitoneum —Introduction of oxygen into the peritoneal cavity.

Oxyphil (e)- —Staining readily with acid dyes.

Oxyphilic —Oxyphil.

Oxyphilous —Oxyphil

Oxyphonia —An abnormally high pitch of the voice.

Oxypolygelatin —A modified gelatin used as plasma extender in transfusions.

Oxyrhine —Having a sharp-pointed nose or acute sense of smell.

Oxyrygmia —Eructation of acid fluid.

Oxytalan —A type of connective tissue fiber present in the periodontal tissues.

Oxytocia —Rapid labor.

Oxytocic —1. Stimulating uterine contractions. 2. Causing rapid labor by stimulating uterine contractions.

Oxytocin —A hormone of the posterior pituitary gland, which stimulates the uterine contractions and also stimulates the mammary glands to secrete the milk.

Oxyuriasis —Enterobiasis.

Oxyuricide —Destructive to oxyurids (pinworms).

Oxyurid —Pinworm or threadworm.

Oz —Ounce.

Ozena —Atrophic rhinitis marked by crusting, mucopurulent discharge and offensive odor.

Ozenous —Pertaining to ozena.

Ozochrotia —Bromidrosis

Ozonator —An apparatus for generating ozone.

Ozone —A form of oxygen in which three atoms of oxygen combine to form the molecule O_3. It is a bluish explosive gas or blue liquid which is antiseptic and disinfectant and toxic to the pulmonary system.

Ozonization —The process of converting into, or impregnating with, ozone.

Ozonize —1. To convert oxygen into ozone. 2. To impregnate with ozone.

Ozonometer —An apparatus for estimating the quantity of ozone in the atmosphere.

Ozonoscope —An apparatus for showing the presence of ozone.

Ozostomia —Halitosis. Foulness of breath.

P—1. Posterior. 2. Pressure. 3. Pulse. 4. Chemical symbol for phosphorus.

Pabular —Pertaining to the nourishment.

Pabulous —Nutritious.

Pabulum —Food. Nourishment.

Pacemaker —1. Anything which affects the rate and rhythm of a process. 2. The sinoatrial node, a group of cells in the right atrium near the entrance of superior vena cava, from which the impulses arise and spread to the other parts of the heart.

Artificial Cardiac pacemaker —An electrical apparatus substituted for a defective natural pacemaker, which by electrical impulses, causes contraction of the cardiac muscle at a certain rate.

Pacer —Pacemaker.

Pachismus —Thickening of an organ or part of the body.

Pachy-, Pach- —Prefixes which mean thick, large and heavy.

Pachyacria, Pachyakria —Enlargement of the soft parts of the extremities.

Pachyblepharon —Thickening of the margin of the eyelid.

Pachyblepharosis —Chronic thickening of the eyelid.

Pachycephalia —Pachycephaly.

Pachycephalic —Pachycephalous. Having an abnormally thick skull.

Pachycephalous —Pachycephalic.

Pachycephaly —Abnormal thickness of the skull.

Pachycheilia —Abnormal thickness of the lips.

Pachychilia —Pachycheilia.

Pachycholia —Thickening or condensation of the bile.

Pachychromatic —Possessing the chromatin in thick strands.

Pachychymia —Inspissation of the chyme.

Pachycolpismus —Pachyvaginitis. Chronic inflammation of the vagina with thickening of the vaginal walls.

Pachydactylia, Pachydactyly —Enlargement of the fingers and toes.

Pachydactylous —Pertaining to or characterized by pachydactyly.

Pachydactyly —Pachydactylia.

Pachyderma —Pachydermatosis. Abnormal thickening of the skin.

Pachydermatocele —Cutis laxa. Dermatolysis. 1. Thickened and pendulous skin looking like elephantiasis. 2. Huge neurofibroma.

Pachydermatosis —Pachyderma.

Pachydermatous —Possessing thick skin.

Pachydermodactyly —Swelling of the fingers occurring most commonly on the proximal interphalangeal joints of the index, middle and ring fingers, due to diffuse fibromatosis.

Pachydermoperiostosis —Marked thickening of the skin of the face and scalp, and the bones of the distal phalanges of the fingers and toes.

Pachyemia —Thickening of the blood.

Pachyglossia —Marked thickening of the tongue.

Pachygnathous —Possessing a large jaw.

Pachygyria —Macrogyria.

Pachyhematous —Having or pertaining to, thick blood.

Pachyhemia —Thickening of the blood.

Pachyleptomeningitis —Inflammation of the pia mater and dura mater of the brain and spinal cord.

Pachylosis —Xerosis. Abnormal thickness and dryness of the skin.

Pachymenia —Thickening of the skin or membranes.

Pachymeningitis —Inflammation of the dura mater.

Pachymeningopathy —Any noninflammatory disease of the dura mater.

Pachymeninx —The dura mater.

Pachymeter —An instrument for measuring the thickness of the body.

Pachynsis —Pathological thickening.

Pachyntic —Pertaining to pachynsis.

Pachyonychia —Abnormal thickening of the nails.

Pachyostosis —A benign thickening of the bones.

Pachyotia —Abnormal thickening of the ears.

Pachyotous —Having thick ears.

Pachyperiostitis —Thickening of the periosteum due to inflammation.

Pachyperitonitis —Inflammation and thickening of the peritoneum.

Pachypleuritis—Inflammation and thickening of the pleura.

Pachypodous —Having abnormally thick feet.

Pachyrhinic —Having thick nose.

Pachysalpingitis —Chronic inflammation of a fallopian tube with its thickening.

Pachysalpingoovaritis —Chronic inflammation of an ovary and a fallopian tube with thickening.

Pachysomia —Pathological thickening of the soft parts of the body.

Pachytic —Fatty.

Pachyvaginalitis —Inflammation and thickening of the tunica vaginalis of the testes.

Pachyvaginitis —Pachycolpismus.

Pacifier —An artificial nipple made of plastic for infants to suck for their satisfaction.

Pacing —Setting the rate of occurrence of an event, especially the heart beat.

Pack —1. To treat by wrapping a patient in dry or moist, hot or cold blanket, sheet or towel. 2. The blanket, sheet or towel used for wrapping. 3. To fill up a cavity with cotton, gauze or a similar substance.

Packed cells —Red blood cells which have been separated from the plasma.

Packer —An instrument for introducing a pack (cotton, gauze, etc.) into a cavity or a wound.

Packing —1. The filling of a cavity or wound with gauze, sponges, pads or other material. 2. The material used to fill a cavity or wound.

$PaCO_2$ —Partial pressure of carbon dioxide in the arterial blood.

Pad —A cushion-like mass of soft material, usually of cotton, used to relieve pressure or to support an organ or part of the body.

Pagetic —Pertaining to or suffering from Paget's disease.

Pagetoid —Similar to Paget's disease.

Paget's disease —Osteitis deformans. Chronic inflammation of the bones in old persons resulting in thickening and softening of bones and curving of the long bones.

Paget's disease —This is a malignant condition characterized by gradual destruction of the nipple and development of a carcinoma within the breast.

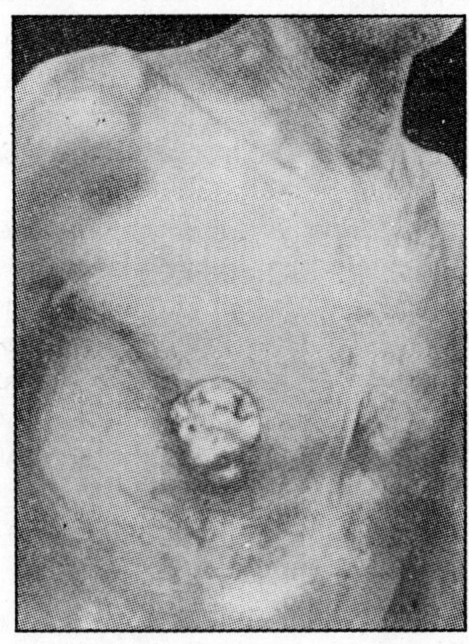

Fig. 402 : Paget's disease in a male breast

Pagophagia —The eating of ice in large quantities.

-pagus —A suffix indicating twins joined together at the site indicated in the initial part of the word.

Pain —A sensation of discomfort, distress or suffering due to stimulation of specialized nerve endings.

Aching pain —Generalized pain which may occur in infectious diseases such as influenza etc.

Acute pain —A short, sharp, cutting pain which usually occurs in acute inflammation.

After pain —Pains occurring in the abdomen after labor, caused by contraction of the uterus.

Agonizing pain —Intense, torturing pain of the body or mind.

Bearing-down pain —Pain occurring in the second stage of labor due to contraction of the uterus, which causes the woman to strain or bear down as one does to defecate.

Boring pain —Pain occurring deep in the tissues that gives the sensation as of being pierced with a boring instrument.

Burning pain —Pain experienced in burning with heat or fire.

Central pain —Pain occurring due to a lesion in the central nervous system.

Colicky pain —Abdominal pain associated with the spasm of the intestine or any other hollow organ.

Cramplike pain —Gripping pain. Pain occurring due to muscular spasm.

Dull pain —Continuous throbbing pain.

Eccentric pain —Pain occurring in the peripheral structures.

Expulsive pain —Pain occurring in the second and third stages of labor.

False pain —An ineffective pain which is mistaken for true labor pain, not accompanied by dilatation of the cervix of the uterus.

Gas pain—Pain caused by distention of the stomach or intestines with the accumulation of gas.

Growing pain —Pains occurring in the joints or limbs of growing children.

Homotopic pain —Pain felt at the site of injury.

Hunger pain —Pain occurring at the time for feeling hunger for food, which is a symptom of gastric disorder.

Imperative pain —A persistent sensation of pain occurring in psychasthenia.

Inflammatory pain —Pain occurring in the presence of inflammation, which is increased by pressure.

Intermenstrual pain —Mittelschmerz. Pain accompanying ovulation, occurring in the pelvis during the period between menses.

Intractable pain —The pain which cannot be relieved easily, as that arising from a malignant tumor.

Labor pain —Rhythmic pains of increasing severity and frequency due to contractions of the uterus, occurring during childbirth.

Lancinating pain —Acute pain.

Lightning pain —The pain occurring suddenly for a short period which may be repetitive. It occurs usually in the legs in tabes dorsalis.

Menstrual pain —Dysmenorrhea.

Mental pain —Pain occurring due to mental conditions such as grief. If persistent, it may cause true physical pain.

Middle pain —Intermenstrual pain.

Migraine pain —See migraine.

Mobile pain —Pain which moves from one place to another.

Neuralgic pain —Pain occurring along the branches of a nerve.

Night pain—Pain occurring at night in the hip or knee during muscular relaxation in sleep.

Noise pain —Odynacusis. Pain in the ear caused by noise.

Objective pain —Pain induced by some external or internal irritant, by inflammation or by injury to the nerves, organs or parts of the body.

Organic pain —Somatalgia. Pain occurring due to organic causes.

Osteocopic pain —Pain occurring in the bones.

Parenchymatous pain —Pain occurring at the peripheral end of a nerve.

Phantom limb pain —Pain felt in a limb that seems to be arising following amputation of that limb.

Postprandial pain —Pain in the abdomen occurring after eating.

Psychogenic pain —Mental pain.

Psychosomatic pain —Pain of both mental and physical origin.

Referred pain —Pain felt in a part of the body other than that in which the cause of the pain is situated.

Remittent pain —Pain with temporary abatements in severity.

Rest pain —Pain occurring in the lower leg due to ischemia which comes on when sitting or lying.

Root pain —Cutaneous pain due to disease of the sensory nerve roots.

Shifting pain —Pain that seems to arise from different sites from time to time as occurs in rheumatism.

Shooting pain —Pain which seems to travel from one place to another very quickly.

Spot pain —Pain located in a patch of the skin.

Sympathetic pain —Referred pain.

Tenesmic pain —Pain occurring during defecation or urination due to spasmodic contraction of the anal or vesical sphincter.

Thermalgesic pain —Pain caused by heat.

Thoracic pain —Pain occurring in the chest, often running down the arm to the elbow.

Throbbing pain —Pulsating pain as occurs in localized inflammation.

Wandering pain —Pain changing its site repeatedly.

Paint —1. A liquid medicine to apply to a surface as of the skin or to a tooth. 2. To apply a liquid medicine to the skin or to a tooth.

Painters' colic —Spasmodic pain occurring in abdomen due to lead poisoning in painters.

Palatable —Tasty.

Palatal —Pertaining to the palate.

Palatal reflex —Swallowing induced by stimulation of the soft palate.

Palate —Roof of the mouth. The horizontal partition separating the nasal and oral cavities.

Hard palate —Anterior hard part of the palate supported by the maxillary and palatine bones.

Soft palate —The posterior soft fleshy part of the palate.

Palatiform —Resembling palate.

Palatine —1. Pertaining to the palate. 2. The palatine bones.

Palatitis —Inflammation of the palate.

Palatoglossal —Pertaining to the palate and the tongue.

Palatognathous —Having a congenitally cleft palate.

Palatograph —An apparatus for recording the movements of the palate during speech.

Palatography —1. The recording of the movements of the palate in speech. 2. X-ray examination of the soft palate.

Palatomaxillary —Pertaining to the palate and the maxilla.

Palatomyograph —Palatograph.

Palatonasal —Pertaining to the palate and the nasal cavity.

Palatopharyngeal —Concerning the palate and the pharynx.

Palatopharyngoplasty —Plastic surgery for decreasing the size of the opening of nasopharynx to treat chronic snoring.

Palatopharyngorrhaphy —Staphylopharyngorrhaphy.

Palatoplasty —Plastic surgery of the palate.

Palatoplegia —Paralysis of the muscles of the soft palate.

Palatoplegic —The person with the paralysis of the muscles of the soft palate.

Palatorrhaphy —Suturing of the cleft palate.

Palatoschisis —Cleft palate.

Palatum —The palate.

Pale —Wan.

Paleo —A prefix which means old.

Paleogenesis —Origination in the previous generation.

Paleogenetic —Originated in the previous generation.

Paleokinetic —Old kinetic.

Paleontology —The science dealing with the study of ancient plant and animal life.

Paleopathology —Study of the diseases in the bodies preserved from ancient times.

Paleostriatal —Pertaining to paleostriatum.

Paleostriatum —Primitive portion of the corpus striatum, the globus pallidus.

Paleothalamus —The medial portion of the thalamus.

Pali-, Palin- —A prefix which means recurrence or repetition.

Palikinesia —Repetition of movements.

Palilalia —Palinphrasia. Repetition of a word or phrase with increasing rapidity.

Palinal —Moved or moving backward.

Palindromia —The recurrence of a disease or relapse.

Palindromic —Relapsing. Recurring, as a disease.

Palinesthesia —Return of sensation after recovery from coma or anesthesia.

Palingenesis —Paleogenesis.

Palingraphia —Pathological repetition of letters or words in writing.

Palinopsia —Persistence or recurrence of the visual image after the stimulus of the image is gone.

Palinphrasia —Palilalia.

Pallanesthesia —Apallesthesia. Loss or absence of sense of vibrations in the skin or bones.

Pallescence —Pallor. Paleness.

Pallesthesia —A peculiar vibrating sensation felt

in the skin or bones when a vibrating tuning fork is placed against the body.

Pallesthetic —Pertaining to pallesthesia.

Pallial — Pertaining to the pallium.

Palliate —To relieve.

Palliation—Relief in the symptoms of a disease.

Palliative —Relieving without curing a disease.

Pallid —Pale.

Pallidal —Pertaining to the pallidum.

Pallidectomy —Removal of the globus pallidus of the brain.

Pallidness —Pallidity. Paleness.

Pallidoansotomy —Production of lesions in the globus pallidus and ansa lenticularis of the brain.

Pallidotomy —Surgical destruction of the globus pallidus of the brain.

Pallidum —Globus pallidus of the brain.

Pallium —The cerebral cortex with its adjacent white substance.

Pallor —Paleness.

Palm —Anterior or flexor surface of the hand.

Palma —The palm of the hand.

Palmar —Pertaining to the palm of the hand.

Palmaris —Palmar.

Palmar reflex —A grasping reflex in infants which gradually disappears and is absent after 4 or 5 months.

Palmate —Shaped like palm.

Palmative —A union of the fingers.

Palmature —The pathological condition in which the fingers are joined.

Palmi —Pleural of palmus.

Palmic —Pertaining to the palpitation.

Palmistry —The science of fortelling events by the marks of the palm.

Palmodic —Pertaining to palmus.

Palmoplantar —Pertaining to the palms of the hands and the soles of the feet.

Palmoscopy —Examination of the cardiac pulsation.

Palmus —1. Palpitation. 2. Jerking.

Palpable —Perceptible by touch.

Palpate —To examine by touch.

Palpation —The examination by applying the hands or fingers to the external surface of the body to detect the evidence of the disease.

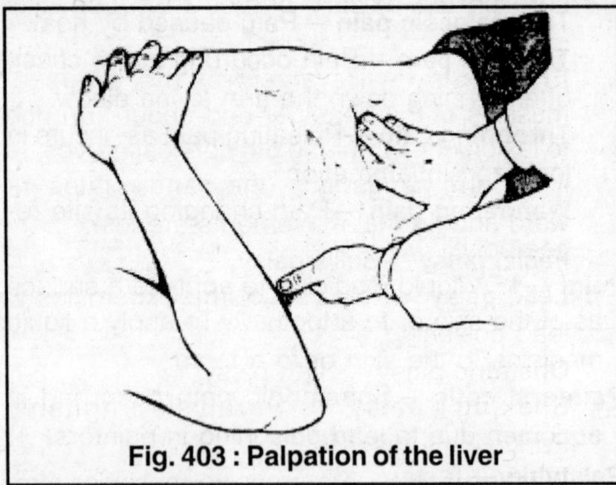

Fig. 403 : Palpation of the liver

Palpatopercussion —Palpation combined with percussion.

Palpebra —Eyelid.

Palpebrae —Plural of palpebra.

Palpebral —Pertaining to an eyelid.

Palpebral commissure —The union of the eyelids at each end of the palpebral fissure.

Palpebral fissure —The open space between the eyelids.

Palpebrate —1. To wink. 2. Having eyelids.

Palpebration —The act of winking.

Palpebritis —Blepharitis.

Palpitant —Beating or pulsating.

Palpitate —To beat or pulsate intensely or rapidly, usually said of the heart.

Palpitatio cordis —Palpitation of the heart.

Palpitation —Abnormally rapid or irregular heart beat which is felt by the patient.

Palsy —Paralysis. Temporary or permanent loss of sensation or inability to move the affected part of the body.

Bell's palsy —Unilateral facial paralysis occurring suddenly due to lesion of the facial nerve resulting in distortion of the face.

Birth palsy —Paralysis arising from an injury received at birth.

Brachial palsy —Partial or complete paralysis of one of the arms of a newborn, caused by an injury to the brachial nerve plexus resulting from traction during a difficult vaginal delivery.

Cerebral palsy —Bilateral, symmetrical, nonprogressive paralysis due to developmental defect in the brain or an injury at birth.

Crutch palsy —Paralysis resulting from pressure on the axillary nerves from use of a crutch.

Erb's palsy —Paralysis of the group of muscles of the shoulder and upper arm due to lesion of the 5th and 6th cervical nerves. In it the arm hangs limp, the hand rotates inward and normal movements are lost.

Facial palsy —Bell's palsy.

Lead palsy —Paralysis of the extremities in lead poisoning.

Obstetric palsy —Birth palsy.

Shaking palsy —Paralysis agitans, Parkinson's disease.

Wasting palsy —Progressive muscular atrophy.

Paludal —Malarial.

Paludism —Malaria.

Pampiniform —Convoluted like a tendril.

Pampiniform plexus —A network of the spermatic or ovarian veins, or the nerves supplying the testicles.

Pampinocele —Varicocele. Swollen and painful veins of the spermatic cord.

Pan- —Combining form indicating all.

Panacea —A remedy for all diseases.

Panagglutinable —Blood cells that are agglutinable by every blood group serum of the same species.

Panagglutinin —The substance capable of agglutinizing the blood cells of every blood group.

Panangiitis —Inflammation of all the coats of a blood vessel.

Panaris —Paronychia. Inflammation of the skin fold surrounding a nail.

Panarteritis —Inflammation of all the coats of an artery.

Panarthritis —Inflammation of all the joints.

Panasthenia —Neurasthenia. Generalized weakness.

Panatrophy —Diffuse atrophy.

Panautonomic —Pertaining to or affecting the entire autonomic nervous system.

Panblastic —Pertaining to all of the layers of the blastoderm.

Pancarditis —Inflammation of the entire heart.

Panchreston —Panacea.

Panchromia —The quality of staining with many dyes.

Pancolectomy —Surgical excision of the entire colon.

Pancreas —A large, elongated, racemose gland situated transversely behind the stomach, in front of the 1st and 2nd lumbar vertebrae. It is divided into three portions—head, body and tail. The head is attached to the duodenum, the tail reaches the spleen and the portion between head and tail is the body. Its external secretion—the pancreatic juice contains digestive enzymes and internal secretion—insulin produced by the beta cells of islets of Langerhans, scattered throughout its substance, plays the main role in the regulation of carbohydrate metabolism. Its deficiency causes diabetes mellitus.

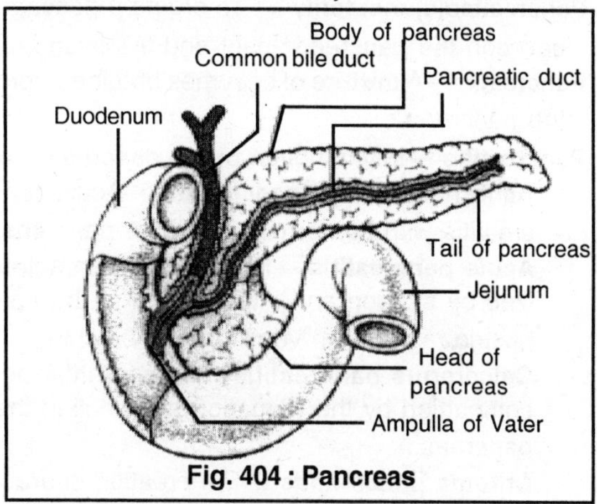

Fig. 404 : Pancreas

Pancreata —Plural of pancreas.

Pancreatalgia —Pain in the pancreas.

Pancreatectomy —Surgical excision of the pancreas.

Pancreatemphraxis —Congestion of the pancreas due to obstruction of the pancreatic duct causing swelling of the pancreas.

Pancreathelcosis —Ulceration of the pancreas.

Pancreatic —Pertaining to the pancreas.

Pancreatic duct —The duct which carries the pancreatic juice to the duodenum.

Pancreatic juice —The external secretion of the pancreas. 500 to 1200 ml pancreatic juice is secreted per day which contains sodium bicarbonate and digestive enzymes.

Pancreaticocholecystostomy —To create a passage between pancreas and the gallbladder.

Pancreaticoduodenal —Pertaining to the pancreas and the duodenum.

Pancreaticoduodenectomy —Pancreatoduodenectomy.

Pancreaticoduodenostomy —To create a passage between the pancreas and the duodenum.

Pancreaticoenterostomy —To create a passage between pancreatic duct and the intestine.

Pancreaticogastrostomy —To create a passage between pancreas and the stomach.

Pancreaticojejunostomy —To create a passage between the pancreatic duct and the jejunum.

Pancreatin —A mixture of enzymes obtained from the pancreas.

Pancreatitis —Inflammation of the pancreas.

Acute hemorrhagic pancreatitis —Acute pancreatitis with hemorrhage into the pancreas.

Acute pancreatitis —Pancreatitis characterized by sudden and intense pain in the epigastric region with vomiting and belching.

Calcareous pancreatitis —Pancreatitis accompanied by the formation of calculi in the pancreas.

Chronic pancreatitis —Pancreatitis characterized by the formation of scar tissue associated with malfunction.

Purulent pancreatitis —Pancreatitis with suppuration.

Pancreatocholecystostomy —Pancreaticocholecystostomy.

Pancreatoduodenectomy —Surgical removai of the head of pancreas along with the adjacent portion of the duodenum.

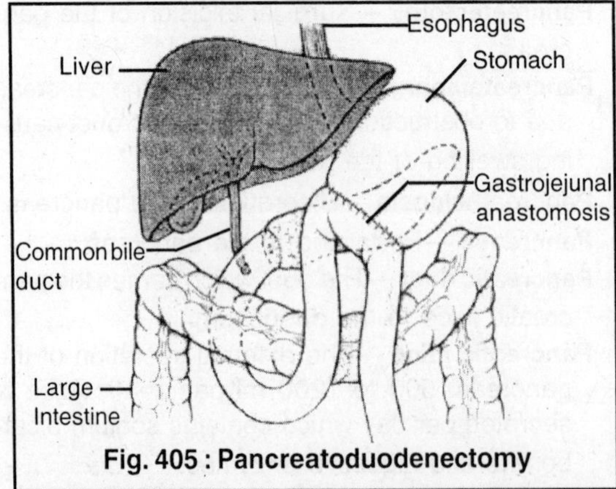

Fig. 405 : Pancreatoduodenectomy

Pancreatoduodenostomy —Surgical anastomosis of the pancreatic duct to the duodenum.

Pancreatogastrostomy —Pancreaticogastrostomy.

Pancreatogenic, Pancreatogenous —Arising from the pancreas.

Pancreatogram —X-ray film of the pancreas.

Pancreatography —To take X-ray of the pancreas after injecting a radiopaque substance into it.

Pancreatojejunostomy —Pancreaticojejunostomy.

Pancreatolith—A stone of the pancreas.

Pancreatolithectomy —Pancreatolithotomy. Removal of a calculus from the pancreas.

Pancreatolithiasis —Presence of calculi in the pancreas.

Pancreatolithotomy —Pancreatolithectomy.

Pancreatolysis —Destruction of the pancreatic tissue.

Pancreatolytic —Pancreolytic. Destructive to the pancreatic tissue.

Pancreatomegaly—Abnormal enlargement of the pancreas.

Pancreatomy —Pancreatotomy. To make an incision into the pancreas.

Pancreatoncus —A tumor of the pancreas.

Pancreatopathy —Pancreopathy.

Pancreatotomy —Pancreatomy.

Pancreatotropic —Having an affinity for the pancreas.

Pancreectomy —Partial or total excision of the pancreas.

Pancreolith —Pancreatolith.

Pancreolithotomy —Pancreatolithotomy.

Pancreolysis —Destruction of the pancreas by the enzymes.

Pancreolytic —Pancreatolytic.

Pancreopathy —Pancreatopathy. Any disease of the pancreas.

Pancreoprivic —Having no pancreas.

Pancystitis —Cystitis involving the entire thickness of the wall of the urinary bladder.

Pancytopenia —Reduction of all the blood cells.

Pandemia —Involvement of a large number of people in a large region by an epidemic disease.

Pandemic —An epidemic disease spreading throughout the world.

Pandemicity —The state of being pandemic.

Pandiculation —Stretching of the limbs and yawning, as on awakening from the normal sleep.

Panencephalitis —Inflammation of the entire brain.

Panendoscope —A cystoscope for inspection widely of the inside of the urinary bladder.

Panesthesia —The sum of the sensations experienced.

Pang —Sudden occurrence of an emotion.

Panglossia —Excessive talkativeness.

Panhidrosis —Sweating occurring over the entire surface of the body.

Panhydrometer —A hydrometer for determining the specific gravity of any liquid.

Panhygrous —Universally moist.

Panhyperemia —Hyperemia of the entire organ or part of the body.

Panhypopituitarism —Generalized hypopituitarism due to absence or damage of the pituitary gland.

Panhysterectomy —Total hysterectomy. Excision of the entire uterus including its cervix.

Panhysterocolpectomy —Total excision of the uterus and the vagina.

Panhystero-oophorectomy —Excision of the uterus, cervix of the uterus and one or both ovaries.

Panhysterosalpingectomy —Excision of the uterus, cervix and the fallopian tubes.

Panhysterosalpingo-oophorectomy —Excision of the entire uterus with its cervix, ovaries and the fallopian tubes.

Panic —Excessive terror or fright.

Panicula —A swelling or tumor.

Panidrosis —Panhidrosis.

Panimmunity —General immunity to a large number of bacterial and viral diseases.

Panis —Bread.

Panivorous —Living on bread.

Panmyeloid —Pertaining to all the elements of the bone marrow.

Panmyelophthisis —Generalized wasting of the bone marrow.

Panmyelosis —Increase in all the elements of the bone marrow.

Panneuritis —Generalized neuritis.

Panni —Plural of pannus.

Panniculectomy —Excision of the superficial layer of fat of abdomen in obese person to reduce obesity.

Panniculitis —Inflammation of the fatty connective tissue of the anterior abdominal wall.

Panniculus —A clothlike sheet of tissue.

Pannosity —Softness of the skin.

Pannus —Newly formed superficial vascular tissue over the cornea.

Panodic —Spreading in all directions, especially a nerve impulse.

Panophobia —Pantophobia. General apprehension. Morbid fear of every thing in general.

Panophthalmia, Panophthalmitis —Inflammation of all the structures of the eye.

Panoptic —Making every part visible.

Panoptosis —General prolapse of the abdominal organs.

Panosteitis —Inflammation of every part of a bone.

Panotitis —Inflammation of all the structures of the ear.

Panphobia —Pantophobia. Morbid fear of everything.

Panplegia —Total paralysis.

Pansclerosis —Hardening of the entire organ.

Pansinusitis —Inflammation of all the paranasal sinuses.

Pansphygmograph —An apparatus for recording the cardiac movements, pulse wave, and chest movements at the same time.

Pansystolic —Holosystolic. Extending from first to the second heart sound.

Pant —1. To gasp. 2. A short and shallow respiration.

Pant-, Panto- —Prefixes which mean all or the whole of something.

Pantachromatic —Entirely colorless.

Pantalgia —Pain occurring over the whole body.

Pantamorphia —Generalized malformation.

Pantamorphic —Without any shape.

Pantanencephalia —Pantanencephaly.

Pantanencephaly —Complete absence of the brain in a fetus.

Pantankyloblepharon —Generalized adhesion of the eyelids to the eyeball.

Pantatrophia, Pantatrophy —Generalized wasting and atrophy.

Panthodic —Panodic.

Panting —Rapid and shallow respiration.

Pantomography —Tomography of curved surfaces.

Pantomorphia —Capability of assuming any shape.

Pantomorphic —Capable of assuming all shapes.

Pantophobia —Panophobia.

Pantoscopic —Adjusted to see both close and distant objects.

Pantoscopic glasses —Bifocal lenses.

Pantothermia —Changing of the body temperature without any apparent cause.

Pantropic —Having affinity for many organs.

Panzootic —Any widespread disease among the animals.

PaO_2 —The partial pressure of oxygen in the arterial blood or arterial oxygen concentration.

Pap —Soft, semisolid food.

Paper —A material manufactured in thin sheets from the pulp of the fibers of wood and other substances.

Bibulous paper —Paper that absorbs water readily.

Filter paper —A porous and unglazed paper used for filtration.

Litmus paper —A paper impregnated with a solution of litmus, used to test the pH (acidity or alkalinity) of a solution, which turns red in acidic solution and blue in alkaline solution.

Papilla —A small nipple like projection, *e.g.*, filiform papillae at the tip of the tongue.

Papillae —Plural of papilla. Papilla

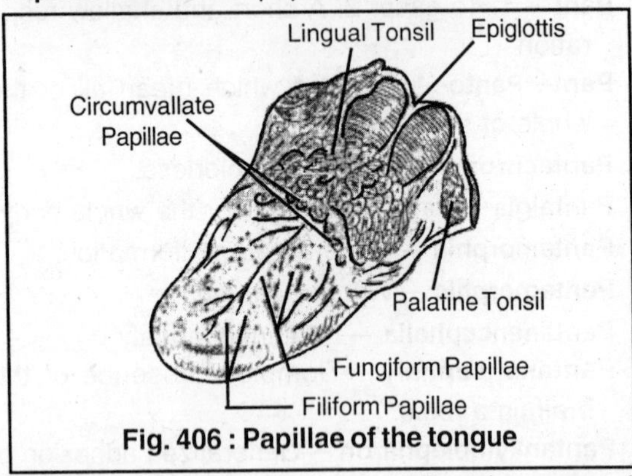

Fig. 406 : Papillae of the tongue

Papillary —Pertaining to, resembling or composed of papillae.

Papillary layer —Stratum papillare.

Papillate —Having nipple-like growth.

Papillectomy —Excision of a papilla or papillae.

Papilledema —Edema of the optic disk.

Papilliferous —Having papillae.

Papilliform —Resembling papillae.

Papillitis —Inflammation of the optic disk or a papilla.

Papilloadenocystoma —A tumor composed of papilloma, adenoma and cystoma.

Papillocarcinoma —Carcinoma of the papillae.

Papilloma —A benign tumor of the epithelium.

Papillomatosis —Formation of multiple papillomas.

Papillomatous —Pertaining to the papilloma.

Papilloretinitis —Inflammation of the papilla and the retina.

Papillotome —An instrument for incising the papilla of vater.

Papillotomy —To make an incision into a papilla.

Papillula —A small papilla.

Papillulae —Plural of papillula.

Pappataci fever —Sandfly fever.

Pappose —Covered with fine downy hair.

Pappus —The first fine, downy hair of the beard, appearing on the cheeks and chin.

Papula —Papule. Pimple.

Papular —Pertaining to the papula.

Papulation —The formation of papules or pimples.

Papule —A small, circumscribed, solid, red, elevated area on the skin.

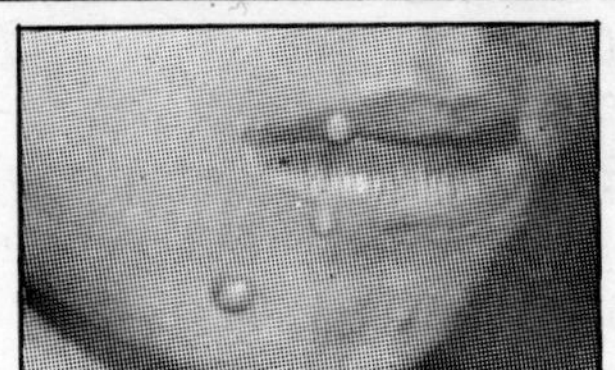

Fig. 407 : Papules

Papuliferous —Having papules or pimples.

Papuloerythematous —Occurrence of papules on erythematous surface.

Papulopustular —Marked by both papules and pustules.

Papulopustule —A papule rapidly developing into a pustule.

Papulosis —The presence of numerus papules.

Papulosquamous —Both papular and scaly.

Papulovesicle —A small skin elevation developing into a blister.

Papulovesicular —Marked by both papules and vesicles.

Papyraceous —Parchment-like.

Par —Pair.

Para —A woman who has produced one or more viable infants.

Para-, Par- —Prefixes which mean near, beside, past, beyond, the opposite, apart from, abnormal, irregular, against, etc.

Para-actinomycosis —Pseudoactinomycosis. Chronic infection, usually pulmonary resembling actinomycosis.

Para-anesthesia —Anesthesia of the lower half of the body.

Para-appendicitis —Inflammation of the connective tissue adjacent to the appendix.

Parabionts —Two individuals living in the condition of parabiosis.

Parabiosis —1. The union of two individuals congenitally, as conjoined twins, or of animals by surgery for experimentation. 2. Temporary suppression of conductivity of a nerve.

Parabiotic —Pertaining to parabiosis.

Parablepsia, Parablepsis —Abnormality of the vision.

Parabulia —Perversion of the will.

Paracanthoma —A tumor of the prickle-cell layer of the epidermis.

Paracanthosis —The development of paracanthomas.

Paracenesthesia —Decrease in the sense of well-being.

Paracentesis —Surgical puncture of a cavity for the removal of fluid, as of the abdomen in ascites or pleural cavity in pleural effusion.

Paracentetic —Pertaining to the paracentesis.

Paracentral —Situated near the center.

Paracephalus —A fetus with a small rudimentary head with imperfect sense organs.

Paracervical —Pertaining to the connective tissue adjacent to the cervix of the uterus.

Paracervix —The connective tissue adjacent to the cervix of the uterus.

Paracholera —A disease resembling cholera but not caused by vibrio cholerae.

Paracholia —Disturbance in bile secretion.

Parachordal —Lying beside the notochord in the embryo.

Parachroma —Abnormal coloration of the skin.

Parachromatism —Incorrect perception of colors, but there is no true color blindness.

Parachromatopsia —Color blindness.

Paracinesia, Paracinesis —Parakinesia. Perversion of motor powers.

Paraclinical —Pertaining to the abnormalities underlying the symptoms of a disease, *e.g.*, fever, etc.

Paracmasis —Paracme.

Paracmastic —Pertaining to the paracme.

Paracme —Denoting the stage at which the symptoms of a disease begin to subside.

Paracolitis —Inflammation of the tissue surrounding the colon.

Paracolpitis —Inflammation of the tissues surrounding the vagina.

Paracolpium —The connective tissue adjacent to the vagina.

Paracousis —Paracusis.

Paracrine —A hormone secretion from a source other than an endocrine gland.

Paracrisis —Any abnormality of the body secretions.

Paracusia —Paracusis. Any disorder of hearing.

Paracusia acris —Excessively acute hearing.

Paracusia duplicata —Diplacusis. To hear one sound as two.

Paracusia loci —Inability to point out the direction of a sound.

Paracusia willisiana —Ability to hear better in a noisy place.

Paracusis —Paracusia.

Paracyesis —Ectopic pregnancy.

Paracystic —Situated near the urinary bladder.

Paracystitis —Inflammation of the tissues surrounding the urinary bladder.

Paracystium —The connective tissue surrounding the urinary bladder.

Paracytic —Pertaining to the cells other than those normally found in a part of the body.

Paradenitis —Inflammation of the tissues around a gland.

Paradental —1. Concerning with the dentistry. 2. Situated around a tooth.

Paradentium —Periodontium.

Paradidymal —1. Pertaining to the paradidymis. 2. Adjacent to the testis.

Paradidymides —Plural of paradidymis.

Paradidymis —A body situated on the spermatic cord above the epididymis.

Paradipsia —Abnormal desire for fluids.

Paradox —Seemingly contradictory occurrence.

Paradoxic, Paradoxical —Seemingly contradictory but in demonstration it is true.

Paraequilibrium —Vertigo occurring due to a disease or malfunction of the vestibular apparatus of the ear.

Paraesthesia —An abnormality of a sensation.

Paraffin —A waxy hydrocarbon obtained from the petroleum and used as ointment base or in dressing of the wounds. It may be liquid, soft, hard and white soft or yellow soft.

Paraffinoma —A tumor produced at the site of the prolonged application of paraffin.

Paraffinum —Paraffin.

Paraflagella —Plural of paraflagellum.

Paraflagellate —Having one or more paraflegella.

Paraflagellum —A minute accessory flagellum attached to certain protozoa in addition to the ordinary flagellum.

Parafollicular —Associated with a follicle.

Parafunction —Beyond function.

Paragammacism —Inability to pronounce "G", "K" and "Ch" sounds.

Paraganglia —Plural of paraganglion.

Paraganglioma —Pheochromocytoma. A tumor of the adrenal medulla and the paraganglia, consisting of the chromaffin cells.

Paraganglion —Plural is paraganglia. A collection of chromaffin cells, associated with the sympathetic nervous system and situated in various organs and parts of the body.

Paragene —Plasmid.

Paragenital —Adjacent to the genital organs.

Parageusia, Parageusis —Disorder of the sense of taste.

Parageusic —Pertaining to parageusia.

Paraglobulin —Fibroplastin. A globulin found in the blood serum and other body fluids.

Paraglobulinuria —Excessive excretion of the paraglobulin in the urine.

Paraglossa —Enlargement of the tongue.

Paraglossia —Inflammation of the tissues underlying the tongue.

Paragnathus —1. Having an accessory jaw congenitally. 2. A parasitic fetus attached to the outer part of the jaw of the autosite.

Paragnomen —An unexpected reaction.

Paragonorrheal —Indirectly related to gonorrhea.

Paragrammatism —To use the words improperly and inability to arrange them grammatically.

Paragranuloma —A benign form of Hodgkin's disease usually limited to the lymph nodes.

Paragraphia —To write those letters or words which should not be written.

Parahemophilia —A congenital hemorrhagic tendency due to deficiency of the coagulation factor v.

Parahepatic —Adjacent to the liver.

Parahepatitis —Inflammation of the adjacent tissues of the liver.

Parahidrosis —Paridrosis.

Parahormone —A substance which is not a true hormone but exerts a hormonelike stimulating effect.

Parahypnosis —Disordered sleep.

Parahypophysis—A small piece of pituitary gland found in the dura mater lining the sella turcica.

Parainfection —Symptomatology of an infectious disease without the presence of the disease producing microorganisms.

Parakappacism —Substitution of another letter sound for that of 'K'.

Parakeratosis —Abnormal horny growth of the skin.

Parakinesia —Paracinesia.

Parakinesis —Paracinesia.

Paralalia —A speech defect in which vocal sound produced is different from that one desired or one letter is substituted for another in speech.

Paralambdacism —Inability to pronounce the letter 'L' correctly.

Paralbumin —An albumin or protein substance found in the ovarian cyst and in ascites.

Paralepsy —Psycholepsy. Occurrence of mental inertia and hopelessness suddenly and temporarily.

Paralexia —Inability to read the printed words or sentences with the substitution of the meaningless combination of words.

Paralgesia —Paralgia. An abnormal and painful sensation.

Paralgia —Paralgesia.

Paralipophobia —Morbid fear of neglecting a duty.

Parallactic —Pertaining to the parallax.

Parallagma —Displacement of a bone or of the fragments of a broken bone.

Parallax —An apparent displacement of an object caused by the change in the observer's position.

Parallelism —The condition of being parallel.

Parallergic —Pertaining to the parallergy.

Parallergy —To be allergic to other stimuli after having been sensitized to a specific allergen.

Paralogia—A disorder of thinking.

Paralogism —Paralogia.

Paralogy —Paralogia.

Paralysed —Affected with paralysis.

Paralysis —Loss of sensation or function in an organ or part of the body due to lesions of the nerves.

Acoustic paralysis —Deafness.

Alcoholic paralysis —Paralysis occurring in chronic alcoholism.

Anesthesia paralysis —Paralysis developing following administration of anesthesia.

Ascending paralysis —Paralysis which begins in the lower limb and ascends upward.

Atrophic spinal paralysis —Paralysis caused by acute poliomyelitis.

Bell's paralysis —Facial paralysis.

Birth paralysis —Paralysis caused by injury received at birth.

Brachiofacial paralysis —Paralysis of the face and the arm.

Bulbar paralysis —Paralysis caused by changes in the motor centers of the medulla oblongata.

Central paralysis —Paralysis from a lesion of the brain or the spinal cord.

Complete paralysis —Paralysis in which there is total loss of sensation and function.

Compression paralysis —Paralysis caused by prolonged pressure on a nerve.

Crossed paralysis —Paralysis affecting one side of the face, and limbs of the opposite side.

Crutch paralysis —Paralysis due to pressure on the nerves in the axilla caused by a crutch.

Decubitus paralysis —Paralysis due to pressure on a nerve from lying for a long time in one position.

Diphtheritic paralysis —Paralysis of the muscles of palate, eyes, limbs, diaphragm and intercostal muscles occurring as a complication of diphtheria.

Diver's paralysis —Bends. Caisson disease. Paralysis due to sudden decrease of the atomospheric pressure on the deep-sea diver after he comes out of the sea.

Erb-Duchenne paralysis —Paralysis of the muscles of the upper arm excluding that of the hands, due to injury of fifth and sixth cervical nerve roots.

Facial paralysis —Bell's paralysis. Paralysis of the facial nerve.

Flaccid paralysis —Paralysis associated with loss of muscular tone due to lesions of the lower motor neurons of the spinal cord.

General paralysis —Paralysis progressively affecting the whole body.

Glossolabial paralysis —Paralysis of the tongue and lips.

Hysterical paralysis —Temporary loss of movement simulating paralysis.

Incomplete paralysis —Partial paralysis of an organ or part of the body.

Infantile paralysis —Paralysis in infants occurring in poliomyelitis.

Ischemic paralysis —Volkmann's contracture. Paralysis resulting from deficiency in the blood supply.

Klumpke-Dejerine paralysis —Atrophy paralysis of the lower arms and hands resulting from birth injury.

Landry's paralysis —Flaccid paralysis beginning in the lower extremities and rapidly ascending to the trunk.

Lead paralysis —Paralysis occurring following lead poisoning.

Mimetic paralysis —Paralysis of the facial muscles.

Mixed paralysis —Combined paralysis of both the motor and sensory nerves.

Muscular paralysis —Loss of contractions of the muscles.

Musculospiral paralysis —Paralysis of the extensor muscles of the wrist and fingers due to prolonged ischemia of the musculospiral nerve, from compression of the arm against a hard edge. It results in hanging of the hand over the edge of a bed or chair.

Obstetrical paralysis —Birth paralysis.

Paralysis agitans —Parkinson's disease.

Paralysis of accommodation —Paralysis of the ciliary muscles of the eye resulting in inability of the eye to adjust itself to various distances.

Periodic paralysis —Paralysis that abates temporarily and recurs.

Phonetic paralysis —Paralysis of the vocal cords.

Pott's paralysis —Paralysis of the lower part of the body due to pott's disease.

Pressure paralysis —Paralysis occurring due to pressure on the spinal cord or a nerve, caused by a tumor or injury.

Pseudobulbar paralysis —Paralysis of the face, pharynx and tongue due to bilateral lesions of the corticospinal tract, often accompanied by uncontrolled weeping or laughing.

Pseudohypertrophic muscular paralysis —Pseudohypertrophic muscular dystrophy. See under dystrophy.

Sensory paralysis —Inability to speak or move upon awakening or just before falling asleep.

Spastic paralysis —Paralysis with excessive spasticity of a group of muscles and increased tendon reflexes due to upper motor neuron lesions.

Spinal paralysis —Paralysis due to injury or a disease of the spinal cord.

Tourniquet paralysis —Paralysis, especially of the arm resulting from tourniquet being applied for a long time.

Vasomotor paralysis —Loss of tone and dilatation of the blood vessels due to paralysis of the vasomotor centers.

Vocal paralysis —Paralysis of the vocal cords.

Volkmann's paralysis —Volkmann's contracture.

Wasting paralysis —Progressive muscular atrophy. See under atrophy.

Paralytic —1. Pertaining to paralysis. 2. The person affected with paralysis.

Paralytic ileus —Paralysis with distention of the intestines.

Paralyzant —An agent that causes paralysis.

Paralyze —To cause paralysis.

Paralyzer —Paralyzant.

Paramagnetic —Able to be attracted by the poles of a magnet.

Paramagnetism —Attraction toward the poles of a magnet.

Paramania —Mania in which one derives pleasure from complaining.

Paramastigote —Having a small extra flagellum near the larger one.

Paramastitis —Inflammation around the mammary gland.

Paramastoid —Around the mastoid.

Parameatal —Situated near or around a meatus.

Paramedian —Close to the midline.

Paramedic —A person trained and certified in the emergency care of patients who suffer from sudden illnesses or injuries.

Paramedical —Pertaining to the medical science or practice of medicine such as laboratory technicians, etc.

Paramenia —Irregular, abnormal or difficult menstruation.

Paramesial —Paramedian.

Parameter —1. In mathematics, an arbitrary constant, that can possess different values, each value determines the specific form of the equation in which it appears. 2. In statistics, a term used to define a characteristic of a population, in contrast to a sample from that population.

Parametrial —Pertaining to the parametrium.

Parametric —1. Pertaining to the tissue surrounding the uterus. 2. Situated near the uterus.

Parametritic —Concerning with the inflammation of the parametrium.

Parametritis —Inflammation of the parametrium.

Parametrium —The connective tissue around the uterus.

Paramimia —Use of inappropriate gestures while speaking.

Paramnesia —1. The use of words without meaning. 2. Unconsciously false memory.

Paramolar—A extra tooth close to a molar tooth.

Paramorphia —Abnormality in shape of a structure.

Paramucin —A glycoprotein found in the ovarian and other cysts.

Paramusia —Inability to sing songs correctly.

Paramyloidosis —Presence of atypical amyloid in the tissues.

Paramyoclonus multiplex —Sudden and frequent shock-like muscular contractions, which usually occur spontaneously but may follow fright, injury, infectious diseases and poliomyelitis.

Paramyosinogen —Protein derived from muscle plasma.

Paramyotonia —Abnormal muscular tonicity causing muscular spasms.

Paramyotonus —A condition characterized by tonic muscular spasm.

Paranalgesia —Analgesia of the lower half of the body.

Paranasal —Situated near the nasal cavities.

Paraneoplasia —Indirect effects of the malignant tumor on the health, sometimes causing death, rather than the tumor itself being the cause of death.

Paraneoplastic —Pertaining to or characterized by paraneoplasia.

Paranephric —1. Near the kidney. 2. Concerning the adrenal glands.

Paranephritis —Inflammation of the connective tissue around the kidney or of the adrenal gland.

Paranephros —An adrenal gland.

Paranesthesia —Para-anesthesia.

Paraneural —Situated beside a nerve.

Paraneurone —Aggregate of cells containing neurosecretory granules.

Paranoia —A mental disorder marked by delusion of persecution.

Paranoiac —Pertaining to or affected with paranoia.

Paranoid —1. Paranoiac. 2. Resembling paranoia.

Paranomia —Inability to remember the names of the objects shortly after seeing or using them.

Paranormal —Moderately abnormal.

Paranuclear —Situated near the nucleus of a cell.

Paranucleate —Pertaining to or having a paranucleus.

Paranucleolus —Chromosomes adjacent to the nucleolus.

Paranucleus —A small body lying near the nucleus of a cell.

Paraomphalic —Paraumbilical. Situated near the navel.

Paraoperative —Concerning all the details and accessory things of surgery and preparation of the patient for operation.

Paraoral —Adjacent to the mouth.

Paraosteoarthropathy —Paralysis of the lower part of the body with bone and joint disease.

Paraovarian —Parovarian.

Parapancreatic —Situated near the pancreas.

Paraparesis —Partial paralysis of the lower extremities.

Paraparetic —1. Pertaining to paraparesis. 2. Affected with paraparesis.

Parapedesis —Secretion or excretion through abnormal routes.

Paraperitoneal —Situated near the peritoneum.

Paraphasia —A form of aphasia in which the patient speaks wrong words, or uses words in wrong combinations.

Paraphasic —Pertaining to paraphasia.

Paraphemia —Aphasia marked by speaking of the wrong words, or mispronunciation of the words.

Paraphia —Parapsia. Perversion of the sense of touch.

Paraphilia —Expression of the sexual instinct by the acts, socially prohibited, unacceptable, or biologically undesirable.

Paraphimosis —Retraction of the tight prepuce which cannot be returned and it constricts the glans penis which becomes painful and swollen.

Paraphobia —A mild form of phobia.

Paraphonia —Abnormality of the voice.

Paraphonia puberum —Deep voice developing in the boys at puberty.

Paraphora —A mild mental disorder.

Paraphrasia —Inability to speak the words correctly and coherently.

Paraphrenitis —Inflammation of the tissues around the diaphragm.

Parapineal —Adjacent to the pineal gland.

Paraplasm —1. Any abnormal growth. 2. Hyaloplasm. The fluid portion of the protoplasm.

Paraplastic —1. Deformed. 2. Pertaining to the fluid portion of the protoplasm.

Paraplectic —Paraplegic.

Paraplegia —Paralysis of the lower portion of the body including both legs.

Alcoholic paraplegia —Paraplegia occurring due to excessive use of alcohol.

Cerebral paraplegia —Paraplegia due to a bilateral cerebral lesion.

Congenital spastic paraplegia —Spastic paralysis of the lower extremities occurring in infants, usually due to birth injury.

Paraplegia dolorosa —Paraplegia due to pressure of a tumor on the posterior spinal cord and nerve roots, which is extremely painful.

Peripheral paraplegia —Paraplegia due to pressure on, injury to, or disease of peripheral nerves.

Pott's paraplegia —Paraplegia associated with tuberculosis of the vertebral column.

Senile paraplegia —Paraplegia occurring in old age due to sclerosis of the arteries supplying the spinal cord.

Paraplegic —Paraplectic. Pertaining to or affected with paraplegia.

Paraplegiform —Similar to paraplegia.

Parapleuritis —Mild inflammation of the pleurae and the thorax.

Parapoplexy —A mild form of apoplexy with partial stupor.

Parapraxia —Parapraxis. A mental disorder in which there is inaccuracy, forgetfulness, tendency to misplace the things and to make slips of the speech or pen.

Paraproctia —Plural of paraproctium.

Paraproctitis —Inflammation of the tissues about the rectum.

Paraproctium —The connective tissue around the rectum.

Paraprostatitis—Inflammation of the tissues around the prostate gland.

Paraprotein —An abnormal plasma protein, such as a macroglobulin, cryoglobulin, or the protein present in myeloma.

Paraproteinemia —Presence of paraproteins in the blood.

Parapsia, Parapsis —Paraphia.

Parapsoriasis —Chronic scaly, red lesions of the skin.

Parapsychology —The branch of psychology dealing with the perception received without sense organs, as telepathy and clairvoyance, etc.

Pararectal —Situated near the rectum.

Parareflexia—Any abnormality of the reflexes.

Pararenal —Near the kidneys.

Pararhotacism —Constant erroneous enunciation of the letter "r".

Pararrhythmia —Parasystole. A cardiac rhythm caused by two pacemakers.

Pararthria —Difficulty in utterance of the words.

Parasacral —Situated near the sacrum.

Parasalpingitis —Inflammation of the tissues around a fallopian tube.

Parasecretion —1. An abnormality in the secretion. 2. An abnormally secreted substance.

Parasexuality —Any sexually abnormal or unacceptable act.

Parasigmatism —Faulty pronunciation of the letter "S" and "Z".

Parasinoidal —Situated near a sinus.

Parasite —1. A plant or animal that lives upon or within another living organism, known as the host from whom it obtains some advantage. 2. The smaller, incomplete member of the asymmetrical conjoined twins that is attached to and dependent upon the normal twin, known as the autosite.

Accidental parasite —Incidental parasite. Parasite living upon or within a host that is not its normal host.

External parasite —Ectoparasite. Parasite that lives on the outer surface of its host, such as lice, tick, etc.

Facultative parasite —Parasite that can live independently of its host at times.

Intermittent parasite —Occasional parasite. The parasite that reaches its host intermittently for its nourishment.

Internal parasite —Parasite that lives within the body of the host, *e.g.*, round worms etc. in the intestine of man.

Malarial parasite —Any of the four species of Plasmodium that can cause malaria.

Obligate parasite —Parasite that is entirely dependent upon its host for its survival.

Occasional parasite —Intermittent parasite.

Periodic parasite —Parasite that lives upon its host for short periods.

Permanent parasite —Parasite that lives upon its host for the whole life.

Specific parasite —A parasite requiring a specific host in order to complete its life cycle.

Temporary parasite —Parasite that lives free of its host during a part of its life cycle.

Parasitemia —The presence of parasites in the blood.

Parasitic —Pertaining to, caused by or similar to a parasite.

Parasiticidal —Parasiticide.

Parasiticide —Destructive to parasites.

Parasitism —The infection or infestation with the parasites.

Parasitize —To live upon or within a host, as a parasite.

Parasitogenesis —Development through parasites.

Parasitogenic —Caused by the parasites.

Parasitologist —A specialist in parasitology.

Parasitology —The scientific study of the parasites and parasitism.

Parasitophobia —Morbid fear of the parasites.

Parasitosis —The condition resulting from parasitism.

Parasitotropic —Having attraction for the parasites.

Parasitotropism —Special attraction of drugs or other agents for parasites.

Parasitotropy —Parasitotropism.

Paraspadia —A condition in which the urethra has an opening on one side of the penis.

Paraspadias —A congenital condition in which the urethra opens on one side of the penis.

Paraspasm —Muscular spasm of the lower extremities.

Parasteatosis —Any disorder of the sebaceous secretions.

Parasternal —Situated near the sternum.

Parastruma —Goiter-like tumor due to hypertrophy of parathyroid gland.

Parasuicide —An apparent attempt for suicide, but in which death is not desired.

Parasympathetic —Of or pertaining to the craniosacral portion of the autonomic nervous system.

Parasympathetic nervous system —The craniosacral portion of the autonomic nervous system, its preganglionic fibers originate from the nuclei in the midbrain, medulla oblongata and sacral portion of the spinal cord. They travel with the 3rd, 7th, 9th and 10th cranial nerves and 2nd, 3rd and 4th sacral nerves. It innervates the heart, smooth muscle, glands of the head and neck and internal organs of the thorax, abdomen and pelvis.

Parasympathicotonia —The condition in which the parasympathetic nervous system dominates over the sympathetic nervous system.

Parasympatholytic —Destructive to the parasympathetic nerve fibers or blocking the transmission of impulses by them.

Parasympathomimetic —Producing the effects similar to those produced by stimulation of the parasympathetic nerve of a part of the body.

Parasympathotonia —Vagotonia.

Parasynapsis —The union of chromosomes side by side during meiosis.

Parasynovitis —Inflammation of the tissues around a synovial sac.

Parasyphilis —Any condition indirectly due to syphilis.

Parasyphilitic —Denoting the diseases occurring indirectly due to syphilis.

Parasyphilosis —Parasyphilis.

Parasystole —An ectopic cardiac rhythm.

Paratarsium —The covering and the connective tissues of the tarsus of the feet.

Paratenon —Fatty or synovial tissue between a tendon and its sheath.

Paratereseomania —Mania for investigating the new scenes and subjects.

Paraterminal —Near or alongside any terminus.

Parathormone —Hormone of the parathyroid glands that regulates the calcium and phosphorus metabolism.

Parathymia —Disordered mood.

Parathyroidectomy —Surgical excision of one or more of the parathyroid glands.

Parathyroid gland —1. Situated near the thyroid gland. 2. One of the four small endocrine glands located on the back of, and at the lower border of the thyroid gland.

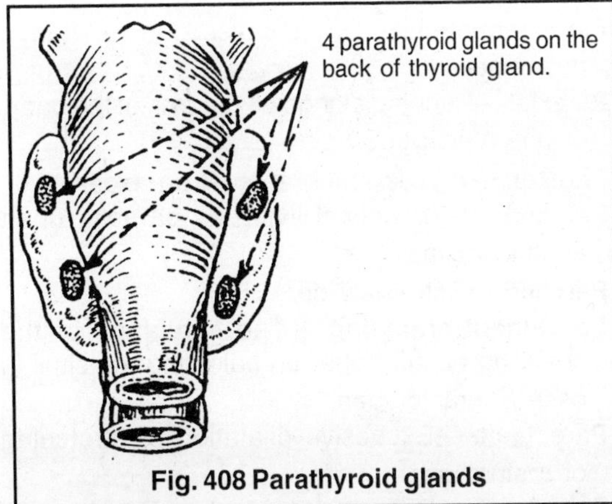

Fig. 408 Parathyroid glands

Parathyroprivia —Condition resulting from removal or nonfunctioning of the parathyroid glands.

Parathyrotropic —Attracted towards parathyroid glands.

Paratonsillar —Near or around the tonsil.

Paratope —The site on an antibody to which an antigen attaches.

Paratracheal —Near the trachea.

Paratrichosis —Abnormality of the hair.

Paratripsis —Rubbing, chafing.

Paratrophic —1. Requiring living substances for food. 2. Pertaining to the abnormal nutrition.

Paratrophy —1. The obtaining of nutrition from the host by a parasite. 2. Atrophy due to nutritional deficiency.

Paratuberculosis —A tuberculosis like disease, which is not caused by Mycobacterium tuberculosis.

Paratyphlitis—Inflammation of the connective tissue about the cecum.

Paratyphoid —Infection with Salmonella of all groups except Salmonella typhosa.

Paraumbilical —Situated near the umbilicus.

Paraurethral —Situated near the urethra.

Parauterine —Situated near or around the uterus.

Paravaginal —Located near or around the vagina.

Paravaginitis —Inflammation of the tissues around the vagina.

Paravalvular —Adjacent to a valve.

Paravenous —Situated near a vein.

Paravertebral —Near the vertebrae.

Paravertebral anesthesia —Injection of a local anesthetic at the roots of the spinal nerves.

Paravesical —Situated close to the urinary bladder.

Paravitaminosis —Any disease due to vitamin deficiency.

Paraxial —Running alongside the axis of the body, or one of its parts.

Paraxon —A collateral branch of an axon.

Parazoon —An animal living as parasite upon another animal.

Parched —Extremely dry.

Parchment crackling —The sensation of the crackling of stiff paper on palpating the skull in case of craniotabes.

Parectasia —Excessive dilatation or stretching of a structure.

Parectasis —Parectasia.

Parectropia —Apraxia.

Parelectronomic —Not stimulated by an electric stimulus.

Parencephalia —Congenital defect of the brain.

Parencephalitis —Inflammation of the cerebellum.

Parencephalocele —Protrusion of the cerebellum through a fissure in the cranium.

Parencephalous —A fetus having undeveloped cranium.

Parenchyma—The essential parts of an organ, that are concerned with its function, and which are different from its stroma or framework.

Parenchymal —Parenchymatous.

Parenchymatitis —Inflammation of the parenchyma.

Parenchymatous —Pertaining to or of the nature of parenchyma.

Parent —Father or mother.

Parental —Pertaining to the parents.

Parenteral —Not through the alimentary canal but by injection through some other route, as intramuscular, subcutaneous and intravenous, etc.

Parenteral hyperalimentation —To provide the total calories needed, by intravenous route in a patient who is unable to take food orally.

Parenting —1. Producing offspring. 2. Caring for the children.

Parepicele —The lateral cavity of the fourth ventricle of the brain.

Parepididymis —Paradidymis.

Parepithymia —Craving.

Paresis —Slight or incomplete paralysis.

Paresthesia —An abnormal sensation, as numbness, prickling, tingling, burning and insect creeping on the body, etc.

Paresthetic —Pertaining to or afflicted with paresthesia.

Paretic —Pertaining to or affected with paresis.

Pareunia —Coitus.

Paridrosis —Parahydrosis Abnormal perspiration.

Paries —A wall of an organ or a cavity.

Parietal —1. Of or pertaining to the walls of a cavity. 2. Pertaining to the parietal bone.

Parietal cells —Oxyntic cells. Large cells on the margins of the peptic glands of the stomach.

Parietal lobe —The portion of the brain on each side lying beneath each parietal bone.

Parietes —Plural of paries.

Parietofrontal —Pertaining to the parietal and frontal bones or lobes.

Parietography —X-ray examination of the walls of an organ.

Parietomastoid —Pertaining to the parietal bone and the mastoid portion of the temporal bone.

Parieto-occipital —Pertaining to the parietal and occipital bones or lobes.

Parietosphenoid —Pertaining to the parietal and the sphenoid bones.

Parietosplanchnic —Parietovisceral.

Parietosquamosal —Pertaining to the parietal bone and the squamous part of the temporal bone.

Parietotemporal —Pertaining to the parietal and temporal bones or lobes.

Parietovisceral —Pertaining to the wall of a cavity and the organs within.

Pari passu —Occurring at the same time or at the same speed.

Parity —1. Equality, similarity. 2. The ability of a woman to be pregnant upto minimum 20 weeks.

Parkinsonian —Pertaining to parkinson's disease.

Parkinsonism —Parkinson's disease.

Parkinson's disease —Paralysis agitans. A chronic disease of the nervous system characterized by tremors, muscular weakness and rigidity and a peculiar gait.

Paroccipital —Near the occipital bone.

Parodontitis —Inflammation of the tissues around a tooth.

Parodontium —Periodontium.

Parodynia —Labor pain.

Parole —The term used for the release of a patient from a mental hospital prior to formal discharge, so that the patient may be returned to the hospital if necessary without fresh legal action.

Parolfactory —Associated with the olfactory system.

Parolivary —Adjacent to the oliva.

Paromphalocele —Hernia near the umbilicus.

Paroniria —Sleepwalking.

Paronychia —Whitlow. Inflammation of the marginal tissues about a fingernail.

Paronychial —Pertaining to paronychia.

Paronychomycosis —Fungus infection about the nails.

Paronychosis —Growth of a nail in an abnormal position.

Paroophoritis —Inflammation of the tissues around an ovary.

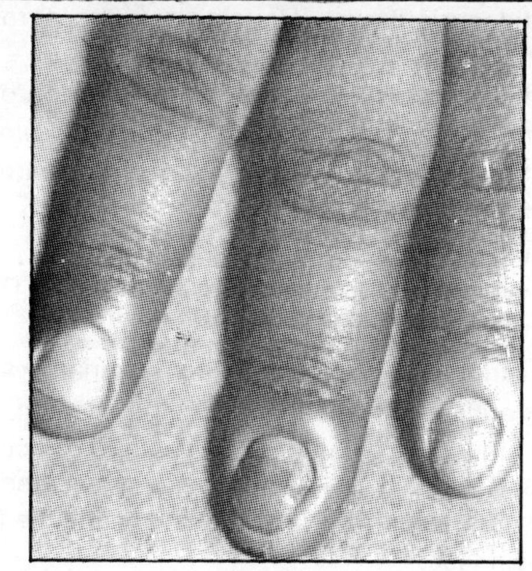

Fig. 409 Paronychia

Paroophoron —A group of minute coiled tubules present in the mesosalpinx between the uterus and ovary.

Parophthalmia —Inflammation of the tissues around the eye.

Parophthalmoncus —A tumor located near the eye.

Paropsis —Any visual defect.

Parorchidium —Ectopia testis. Displacement of a testis or testes.

Parorchis —The epididymis.

Parorexia —Excessive desire for special food or for articles inappropriate for food.

Parosmia —Perversion of the sense of the smell.

Parosphresia, Parosphresis —Parosmia.

Parosteal —Pertaining to the outermost layer of the periosteum.

Parosteitis, Parostitis —Inflammation of the tissues near the bone.

Parosteosis, Parostosis —Ossification in an abnormal location.

Parostitis —Parosteitis.

Parotic —Near the ear.

Parotid —Situated near the ear, especially the parotid gland.

Parotidectomy —Excision of a parotid gland.

Parotid gland —A pure serous largest salivary gland, situated below the external auditory meatus, between the ramus of the mandible and the sternomastoid muscle on each side.

Parotiditis —Parotitis.

Parotidoauricularis —Pertaining to the parotid gland and the external ear.

Parotidoscirrhus —1. Hardening of the parotid gland. 2. Scirrhous cancer of the parotid area.

Parotitis —Mumps. Inflammation of the parotid gland.

Parous —Having borne at least one child.

Parovarian —1. Situated near an ovary. 2. Pertaining to the parovarium.

Parovariotomy —Removal of a parovarian cyst.

Parovaritis —Inflammation of the parovarium.

Parovarium —Epoophoron. A vestigial structure associated with the ovary, which is situated in the mesosalpinx between the ovary and the fallopian tube.

Paroxysm —1. Sudden recurrence of the symptoms of a disease. 2. A sudden spasm or convulsion.

Paroxysmal —1. Pertaining to the paroxysms. 2. Occurring in paroxysms. 3. Of the nature of a paroxysm.

Parricide —Patricide. To kill one's own parent or a close relative.

Pars —The part of large structure.

Pars planitis —Inflammation of the peripheral retina.

Partes —Plural of a pars.

Parthenogenesis —Reproduction in which a female egg develops without being fertilized by a spermatozoon, as seen in certain lower animals.

Parthenophobia —Morbid fear of the virgins or the girls.

Particle —A very small piece of the material.

Particulate —Composed of particles.

Parturient —Giving birth or pertaining to childbirth.

Parturifacient —Inducing or hastening the delivery of the child.

Parturiometer —An apparatus for measuring the force of uterine contractions during labor.

Parturiphobia —Morbid fear of childbirth.

Parturition —Delivery. Childbirth. The process of giving birth to a child.

Part. vic. —Partes vicibus. In divided doses.

Parulides —Plural of parulis.

Parulis —Gumboil. Abcess of a gum.

Parumbilical —Situated near the umbilicus.

Paruresis —Obstruction in urination, especially in the presence of strangers.

Paruria —Any abnormality in the excretion of urine.

Parvocellular —Pertaining to or composed of small cells.

Parvule —A very small pill.

Parvus —Small.

Pascal —A unit of pressure equal to the force of one newton per square meter. Symbol is Pa.

Passage —1. Channel. 2. The act of passing.

Passion —Great emotion associated with sexual excitement.

Passional —Pertaining to any passion.

Passive —Inactive.

Passive congestion —Congestion due to obstruction in the return of blood through the veins.

Passive hyperemia —Increased blood in a part of the body due to decreased outflow.

Passivism —To show inactivity towards somebody.

Passivity —Dependency on others.

Paste —A semisolid preparation of medicine for external use.

Paster —The segment forming the part for near vision in two-piece bifocal lenses.

Pasteurellosis —Disease caused by infection with bacteria of the Pasteurella species.

Pasteurization—Heating of a liquid as milk to moderate temperature for a definite time, usually at 60°C for 30 minutes to destroy the pathogenic bacteria without changing its chemical composition.

Pasteurize —To treat by pasteurization.

Pasteurized —A liquid heated at the temperature of 60°C for 30 minutes, to be sterilized.

Pasteurizer —An apparatus used in pasteurization.

Pastil —Lozenge or troche.

Past-pointing — Inability to place a finger or some other part of the body accurately on a specific point.

Patagia —Plural of patagium.

Patagium —A winglike membrane.

Patch —A small circumscribed area differing from the surrounding surface as white patches on the oral mucosa in leukoplakia.

Patella —Kneecap. A small, somewhat rectangular, flattened bone situated in front of the knee in the tendon of quadriceps femoris muscle.

Patellapexy —Fixation of the patella bone to the lower end of the femur bone.

Patellar —Pertaining to the patella bone.

Patellar reflex —Knee-jerk reflex.

Patellectomy —Surgical removal of the patella bone.

Patelliform —Shaped like the patella bone.

Patellofemoral —Pertaining to the patella and the femur bones.

Patellometer —An apparatus for measuring the patellar reflex.

Patency —The condition of being quite open.

Patent —1. Open or unobstructed. 2. Evident.

Patent medicine —The medicine sold in the market without prescription of a doctor.

Paternal —Of, pertaining to or inherited from the father.

Path —Passage, route.

Path-, Patho- —Prefixes indicating disease.

Pathema —Morbid condition.

Pathergasia —Defective mental function causing functional or structural damage, marked by changed behavior.

Pathergia —Pathergy.

Pathergy —1. A condition in which the application of a stimulus causes susceptibility to other stimuli also, of different kinds. 2. A condition of being allergic to a great number of antigens.

Pathetic —1. Arousing the emotions of pity or sympathy. 2. Pertaining to the trochlear nerve.

Pathetism —Hypnotism, mesmerism.

Pathfinder —1. An instrument for locating the urethral stricture. 2. A dental instrument for tracing the course of root canals.

Pathoanatomical —Pertaining to the anatomy of diseased tissues.

Pathoanatomy —Anatomy of the diseased tissues.

Pathobiology —Pathology.

Pathoclisis —A specific sensitivity to certain toxins.

Pathocrine —Pertaining to a disorder of an endocrine gland.

Pathocrinia —Any disorder of the endocrine glands.

Pathodixia —Excessive desire of exhibiting one's illness or injury.

Pathodontia —Dental pathology.

Pathoformic —Pertaining to the earliest signs of a disease.

Pathogen —Any disease-producing microorganism or a substance.

Pathogenesis —Origination and development of a disease.

Pathogenetic, Pathogenic —Producing a disease.

Pathogenic —Pathogenetic.

Pathogenicity —The ability to produce a disease.

Pathogeny —Pathogenesis.

Pathognomonic —Denoting a sign or symptom of a disease on which the diagnosis can be made.

Pathognomy —To find out the cause of a disease by studying its signs and symptoms.

Pathognostic —Pathognomonic.

Pathography —Description of a disease.

Pathologic, Pathological —1. Pertaining to pathology. 2. Caused by a disease.

Pathologist —A specialist in patholgy.

Pathology —That branch of medical science in which the nature and cause of the disease and functional and structural changes in the tissues and organs of the body, caused by the disease, are studied.

- **Anatomic pathology** —The branch of pathology which is concerned with the study of structural changes occurring in disease.
- **Cellular pathology** —Study of the microscopical changes occurring in the body cells in disease.
- **Chemical pathology** —The study of the chemical changes occurring in the body in disease.
- **Clinical pathology** —Pathology used to aid the diagnosis of a disease by laboratory tests.
- **Comparative pathology** —Pathology which deals with the comparison of disease processes in the human body with that of the lower animals.
- **Dental pathology** —Oral pathology. Pathology of the diseases of the mouth.
- **Experimental pathology** —Study of the diseases artificially produced in animals.
- **Functional pathology** —The study of the functional changes occurring without structural changes in disease processes.
- **Geographical pathology** —Pathology related to the climate and geography.
- **Humoral pathology** —Pathology of the body fluids.
- **Medical pathology** —Pathology of the diseases not suitable for treatment by surgery.

Special pathology —Pathology of particular diseases or organs.

Surgical pathology —Pathological investigations of the tissues surgically removed, for the diagnosis of the disease.

Pathomimesis —Malingering.

Pathomimicry —Pathomimesis.

Pathomiosis —The attitude that leads a patient to minimize his or her disease.

Pathomorphism —Abnormal morphology.

Pathonomia —Study of the laws of disease processes.

Pathonomy —Pathonomia.

Pathophilia —Adjustment of the habits according to the conditions produced by a chronic disease.

Pathophobia —Morbid fear of the disease.

Pathophoric —Transmitting disease, as do certain insects.

Pathophysiology —The study of the changes in normal physiological processes produced by the disease.

Pathopoiesis —The generation of disease.

Pathopsychology —The branch of psychology dealing with the mental processes occurring during a disease.

Pathosis —A diseased condition.

Pathotropism —The attraction of drugs to the diseased tissues.

Pathway —1. A path formed by the neurons over which impulses pass from their origin to their destination. 2. A series of chemical reactions that occur in the metabolism.

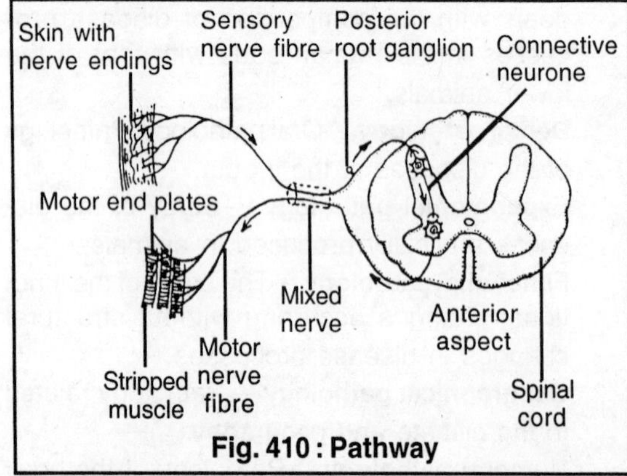

Fig. 410 : Pathway

Afferent pathway —The nerve structures through which the impulses pass from the receptor to the spinal cord and / or brain.

Central pathway —Pathway within the brain or the spinal cord.

Efferent pathway —The nerve structures through which the impulses pass from the central nervous system (brain or spinal cord) to the skeletal musculature.

Metabolic pathway —The series of chemical reactions that occurs as a substance is metabolized.

-pathy —A suffix which means disease.

Patient —A sick person.

Patricide —Parricide.

Patrilineal —Descended through paternal line.

Patten —Support applied under one shoe for the treatment of the hip disease or unequal length of the legs.

Pattern —Model, design, sample or example.

Patterning —A method of treatment for brain damage in which the patient is guided through movements such as creeping or crawling, the undamaged portion of the brain will develop the ability to perform these functions.

Patulous —Spread apart, open, distended.

Pauciarticular —The condition of juvenile rheumatoid arthritis in which one to four joints are affected at the time of onset of the disease.

Paucibacillary —Made up of or denoting the presence of few bacilli.

Paucisynaptic —Oligosynaptic.

Paulocardia —A sensation of stoppage of the heart.

Paunch —The abdominal cavity and its contents.

Pause —An interruption or a temporary cessation of an activity.

Pavement —Scaly.

Pavementing —Adherence of the white blood cells to the lining of capillaries in the condition of inflammation.

Pavor —Terror.

Pavor diurnus —Attacks of terror during the daytime, especially in children.

Pavor nocțurnus —Attacks of terror at night during sleep.

Pb —Chemical symbol of plumbum, lead.

p.c. —Post cibum. After meals.

PCV —Packed Cell Volume.

Pearl —1. A small rounded mass of tough sputum as seen in bronchial asthma. 2. A small medicated granule or glass capsule containing a single dose of some volatile medicine, which is broken in the handkerchief and the medicine is inhaled, as amyl nitrite. 3. Small mass of cells as of epithelial cells found in certain papillomas and epitheliomas.

Peau d'orange —The condition of the skin in which it becomes like orange. It becomes edematous with pitting and of orange color, as seen in carcinoma of the breast.

Peccant —Pathogenic. Morbid. Producing disease.

Peccatiphobia —Morbid fear of sinning.

Pecten —1. A comblike structure. 2. The middle part of the anal canal. 3. The pubic bone.

Pectenitis —Inflammation of the middle part of the anal canal.

Pectenosis —Narrowing of the anal canal.

Pectinate —Pectiniform. Having comb-shaped teeth.

Pectineal —Pertaining to the pubic bone or the pectineus muscle.

Pectiniform —Pectinate.

Pectora —Plural of pectus.

Pectoral —1. Of or pertaining to the chest. 2. Relieving conditions of the respiratory system, as an expectorant.

Pectoralgia —Neuralgic pain in the chest.

Pectoralis —Pertaining to the breast or chest.

Pectoriloquy —Transmission of sound of the spoken words to the ear through the chest wall in auscultation.

Pectorophony —Exaggeration of sound of the spoken words heard on auscultation of the chest.

Pectus —Breast, chest or thorax.

Pectus carinatum —Pigeon breast. The chest in which the sternum is abnormally prominent, which looks as that of the pigeon.

Pectus excavatum —Funnel shaped chest. The chest in which the sternum is abnormally depressed congenitally, which looks like a funnel.

Ped- —A prefix which means foot.

Pedal —Pertaining to the foot.

Pedal spasm —Involuntary contractions of the muscles of the feet.

Pedarthrocace —Caries of the joints in children.

Pedatrophia —Pedatrophy.

Pedatrophy —1. A wasting disease in children. 2. Marasmus.

Pederast —One who practices pederasty.

Pederasty —Sodomy. Anal intercourse between a man and a young boy.

Pedesis —To-and-fro movements of the particles of a substance in a liquid or gaseous form.

Pedi- —Ped-, Pedo-

Pedialgia —Pain in the foot.

Pediatric —Pertaining to the treatment of the children.

Pediatrician —Pediatrist. A specialist in pediatrics.

Pediatrics —Pediatry. The branch of medical science which deals with the care and treatment of diseases of the children.

Pediatrist —Pediatrician.

Pediatry —Pediatrics.

Pedicellate —Pediculate.

Pedicellation —Formation and development of a pedicle.

Pedicle —The stem attaching a new growth.

Pedicterus —Icterus neonatorum. Jaundice of the newborn infant.

Pedicular —1. Pertaining to or caused by louse. 2. Pertaining to a stalk.

Pediculate —Pedunculate. Having a pedicle.

Pediculation —1. Infestation with lice. 2. Formation and development of a pedicle.

Pediculi —Plural of pediculus.

Pediculicide —Destructive to the lice.

Pediculophobia —Morbid fear of the lice.

Pediculosis —Infestation with lice.

Pediculous —Infested with lice.

Pediculus —1. Pedicle. 2. Louse.

Pedicure —Care of the feet.

Pediform—Foot-shaped.

Pedigree —A list or chart of one's ancestors used in genetics in the analysis of mendelian inheritance.

Pediluvium —Foot bath.

Pedionalgia —Neuralgic pain in the sole of the foot.

Pediophobia —Morbid fear of the young children or dolls.

Pediphalanx —Phalanx of the foot.

Peditis —Pedalosteitis.

Fig. 411 : Pediculosis capitis

Pedobaromacrometer —An apparatus for taking measurements and weight of infants.

Pedodontia —Pedodontics.

Pedodontics —The branch of dentistry dealing with the diseases and treatment of the teeth and mouth of the children.

Pedodontist —A specialist in pedodontics.

Pedodynamometer —An apparatus for measuring the strength of the leg muscles.

Pedograph —Imprint of the foot on paper.

Pedometer —1. An instrument for indicating the number of steps taken while walking. 2. An apparatus for taking measurements of the infants.

Pedomorphism —An adult's behavior as that of the children.

Pedophilia —1. Fondness for the children. 2. A desire for making sexual relations with the children.

Pedophilic —Pertaining to or characterized by pedophilia.

Peduncle —1. Pedicle. Stalk. 2. A band of the nerve fibers connecting the different parts of the central nervous system.

Peduncular —Pertaining to a peduncle.

Pedunculate, Pedunculated —Pediculate.

Pedunculi —Plural of pedunculus.

Pedunculotomy —To make an incision into a cerebral peduncle.

Pedunculus —Peduncle.

Peel —Bark.

Peeling —Desquamation. Shedding off, of the superficial layer of the skin.

Peer —One who is equal in age or rank with another.

Peg —A projecting structure.

Peg rete —The downward projection of the epidermis into the dermis.

Pejorative —Becoming or making worse.

Pejorism —A tendency to become or make worse.

Pelade —Alopecia areata. Loss of body hair in patches.

Pelage —Hair of the whole body collectively.

Pelioma —Ecchymosis.

Peliosis —Purpura.

Pellagra —A disease due to nicotinic acid (vitamin B_7) deficiency characterized by dermatitis, diarrhea and dementia, occurring mianly in the people who live upon maize only.

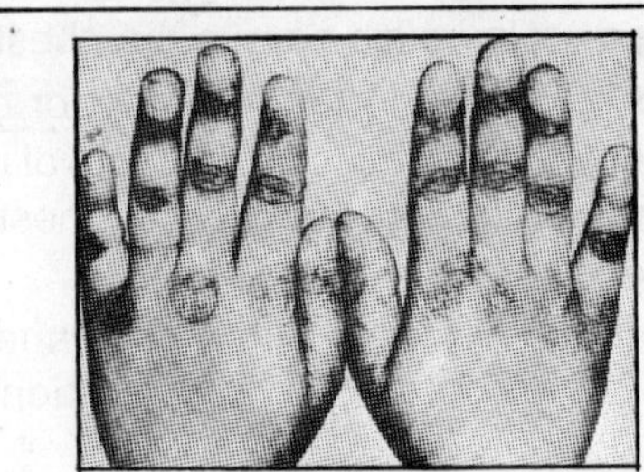

Fig. 412 : Pellagra

Pellagragenic —Producing pellagra.

Pellagrin —The person suffering from pellagra.

Pellagroid —Similar to pellagra.

Pellagrous —Pertaining to or affected with pellagra.

Pellet —A small pill or granule

Pellicle —A thin film formed on the surface of the liquids.

Pellicular, Pelliculous —Pertaining to a thin membrane formed on the surface of the liquids.

Pellucid —Translucent.

Pelma —Sole of the foot.

Pelmatic —Pertaining to the sole of the foot.

Pelmatogram —An imprint of the sole of the foot.

Pelopathy —Pelotherapy.

Pelotherapy —Treatment of the diseases by the application of mud, clay etc., on the body.

Peltation —Protection provided by inoculating an antiserum or a vaccine.

Pelvi-, Pelvio-, Pelvo- —Prefixes meaning pelvis.

Pelvic —Pertaining to a pelvis.

Pelvicaliceal, Pelvicalyceal —Pertaining to the renal pelvis and the calices.

Pelvic bone —Hip bone. It includes ilium, ischium and pubis bone.

Pelvic direction —The direction of the axis of the pelvis.

Pelvicephalography —X-ray and measurement of the fetal head and outlet of the pelvis of the mother.

Pelvicephalometry —Measurement of the diameters of the fetal head and their comparison with the diameters of the pelvis of the mother.

Pelvic girdle —Arch formed by the innominate bones.

Pelvic inlet —Upper entrance of the pelvis.

Pelvic outlet —Lower outward opening of the pelvis.

Pelvifixation —Attachment of a floating pelvic organ to the wall of the pelvic cavity by surgery.

Pelvilithotomy —Pyelolithotomy.

Pelvimeter —An instrument for measuring the pelvis.

Pelvimetry —Measurement of the capacity and diameter of the pelvis.

Pelviolithotomy —Pyelolithotomy.

Pelvioplasty —1. Pelviotomy. Enlargement of the pelvic outlet to facilitate delivery. 2. Repair of the pelvis of the kidney by plastic surgery.

Pelvioscopy —Inspection of the pelvis.

Pelviotomy —1. Enlargement of the pelvic outlet to facilitate delivery. 2. To make an incision into the renal pelvis.

Pelviperitonitis —Inflammation of the pelvic peritoneum.

Pelvirectal —Pertaining to the pelvis and the rectum.

Pelvis —1. The lower bony structure of the trunk formed anteriorly and laterally by hip bones (ilium, ischium and pubis) and posteriorly by the sacrum and coccyx. 2. Any basin-shaped structure, *e.g.*, the renal pelvis.

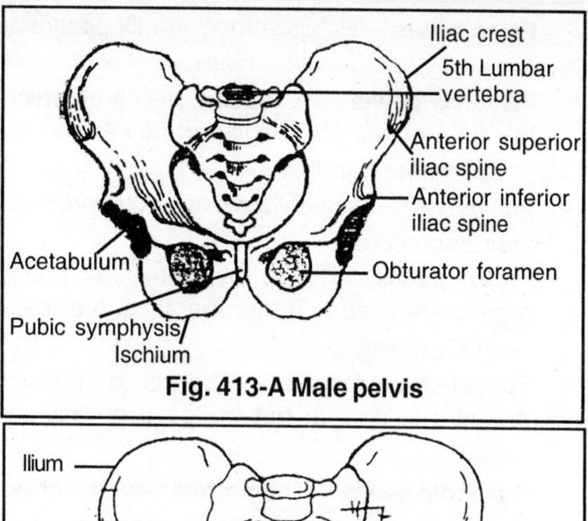

Fig. 413-A Male pelvis

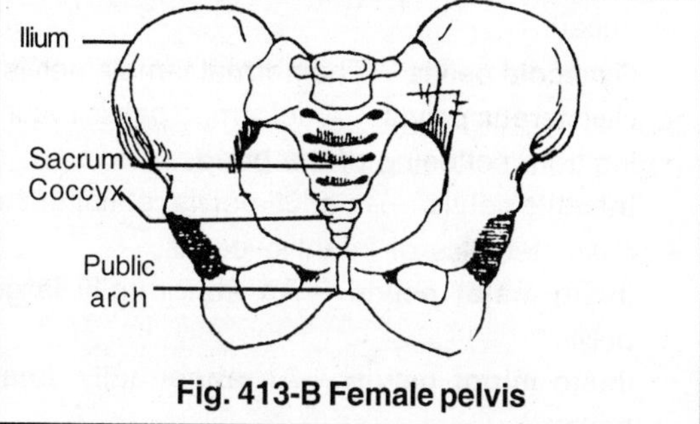

Fig. 413-B Female pelvis

Android pelvis —Masculine pelvis. A female pelvis with wedge-shaped inlet and narrow anterior segment, resembling that of a male.

Anthropoid pelvis —A female pelvis which is long and narrow.

Assimilation pelvis —The pelvis in which the iliac bones articulate with the vertebral column higher or lower, than normal.

Beaked pelvis —Rostrate pelvis. The pelvis in which pelvic bones are compressed laterally and their anterior joint is pushed forward so that the outlet becomes narrow and long.

Brachypellic pelvis —An oval pelvis in which the transverse diameter is longer than antero-posterior diameter by 1 to 3 cm.

Contracted pelvis —The pelvis which is contracted to such an extent that the delivery of a child is not possible.

Cordate pelvis —Heart-shaped pelvis.

Dolichopellic pelvis —Elongated pelvis. The pelvis in which the antero-posterior diameter is greater than the transverse diameter.

External pelvis —Renal pelvis outside the kidney.

False pelvis —Pelvis above the iliopectineal line.

Fissured pelvis —A rachitic pelvis in which the ilium bones are displaced forward so as to be almost parallel.

Flat pelvis —The pelvis which is compressed anteroposteriorly.

Frozen pelvis —The pelvis in which the pelvic organs are fixed to it due to infection or cancerous growth.

Funnel-shaped pelvis —The pelvis in which the inlet is normal but outlet is greatly reduced.

Gynecoid pelvis —The normal female pelvis.

Halisteretic pelvis —A deformed pelvis resulting from softening of the bones.

Infantile pelvis —An adult pelvis retaining the characteristics of infantile pelvis.

Justo major pelvis —An abnormally large pelvis.

Justo minor pelvis —An abnormally small pelvis.

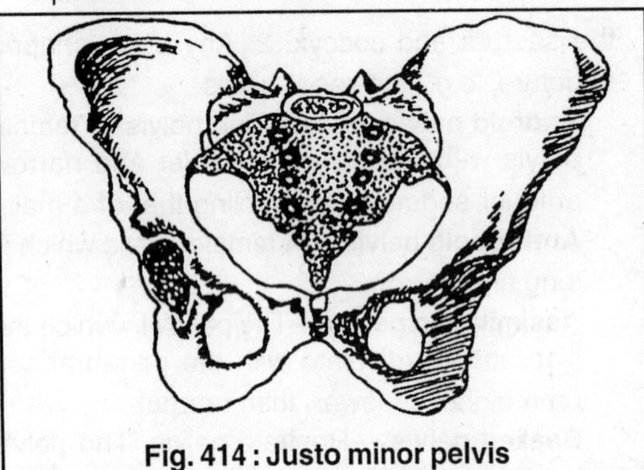

Fig. 414 : Justo minor pelvis

Lordotic pelvis —The pelvis in which vertebral column is curved anteriorly in the lumbar region.

Masculine pelvis —Android pelvis.

Mesatipellic pelvis —Round pelvis.

Osteomalacic pelvis —A pelvis deformed due to osteomalacia.

Platypellic pelvis —The pelvis in which anteroposterior diameters are shortened and the transverse diameters are widened.

Rachitic pelvis —The pelvis deformed from rickets.

Renal pelvis —The upper funnel-shaped portion of the ureter in which renal calices open.

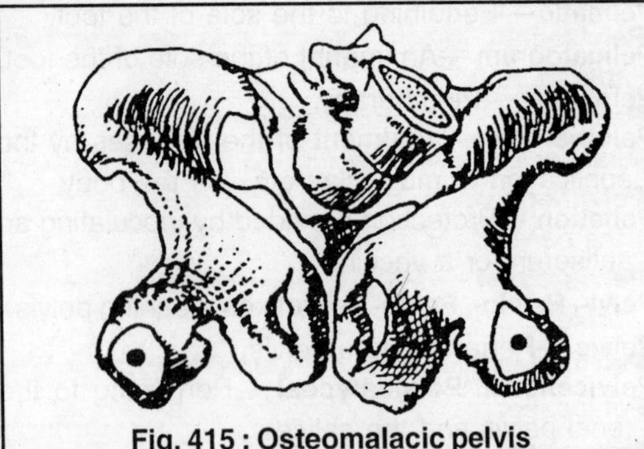

Fig. 415 : Osteomalacic pelvis

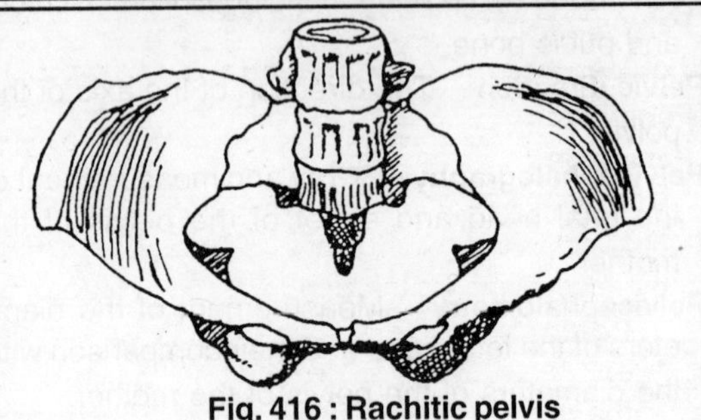

Fig. 416 : Rachitic pelvis

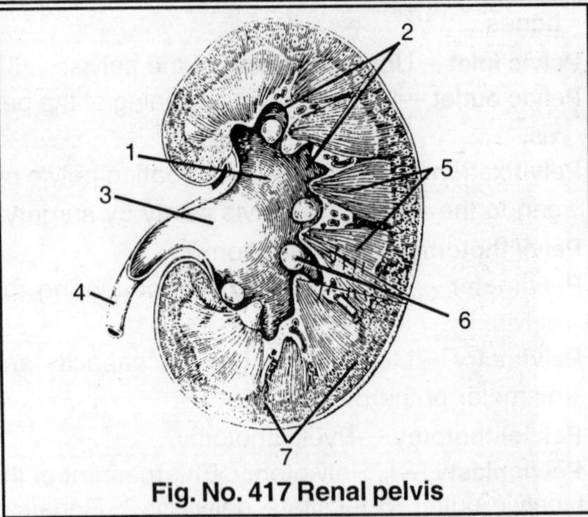

Fig. No. 417 Renal pelvis

1. Major calyx, 2. Minor calyces, 3. Renal pelvis 4. Ureter, 5. Renal pyramids, 6. Papilla, 7. Cortex

Reniform pelvis —Kidney-shaped pelvis.

Round pelvis — A pelvis with a circular inlet.

Scoliotic pelvis —Deformed pelvis due to scoliosis.

Split pelvis —Pelvis which is congenitally divided at the pubic symphysis.

Triangular pelvis —The pelvis with a triangular inlet.

True pelvis —The part of pelvis below the iliopectineal line.

Pelvisacral —Pertaining to both the pelvis and the sacrum.

Pelviscope —An endoscope for examining the interior of the pelvis.

Pelvitherm —An apparatus for applying heat to the pelvis through vagina.

Pelviureteral —Pertaining to the renal pelvis and ureter.

Pelviureterography —Pyelography.

Pelvocaliectasis —Hydronephrosis.

Pelvoscopy —Inspection of the pelvis.

Pelvospondylitis —Inflammation of pelvic portion of the vertebral column.

Pemphigoid —Resembling pemphigus.

Pemphigus —A skin disease of adults characterized by occurrence of bullae, that disappear leaving pigmented spots, and may be accompanied by itching and burning.

Pemphigus erythematous —Scaling erythematous macules and blebs, involving the sun-exposed skin, especially the face in butterfly distribution.

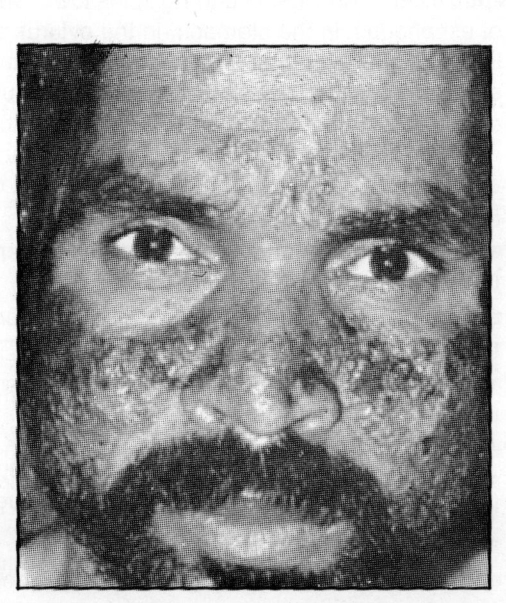

Fig. 418 : Pemphigus erythematous

Pemphigus vulgaris —The most common form of pemphigus occurring in middle age in which oval or round bullae are formed on the skin and oral mucous membrane, which bleed easily when they burst.

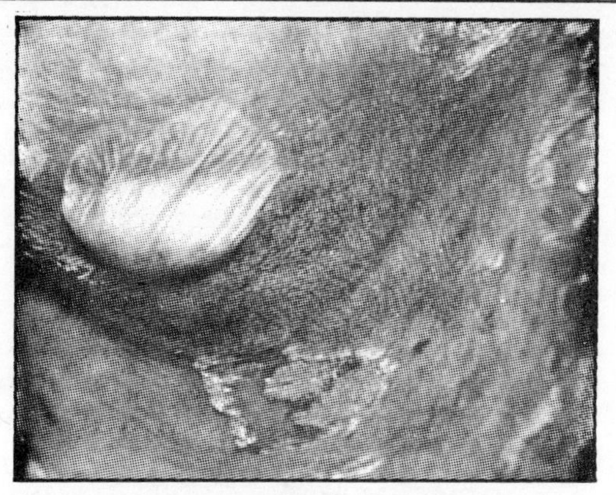

Fig. 419 : Pemphigus vulgaris

Pendular —Pendulous.

Pendulous—Swinging freely like a pendulum.

Penectomy —Phallectomy.

Penes —Plural of penis.

Penetrable —Capable to be penetrated.

Penetrance —The extent to which something enters an object.

Penetrate —To enter an object by piercing its surface.

Penetrating —Entering an object by piercing its surface.

Penetration —The process of entering into an object or part of the body by piercing its surface.

Penetrometer —An instrument for measuring the penetrating power of X-rays.

-penia —A suffix meaning deficiency.

Peniaphobia —Morbid fear of poverty.

Penicillate —Pertaining to penicillus.

Penicilliosis —The condition caused by infection with fungi of the genus Penicillium.

Penicillium —A genus of the fungi that grow on bread, fruit etc. as blue molds. From some of its species penicillin is derived.

Penicillus —A group of brushlike branches of arteries in the lobules of spleen.

Penile —Pertaining to the penis.

Penis —The male organ of copulation and urination.

Captivus penis —The penis which is held within the vagina and unable to be withdrawn

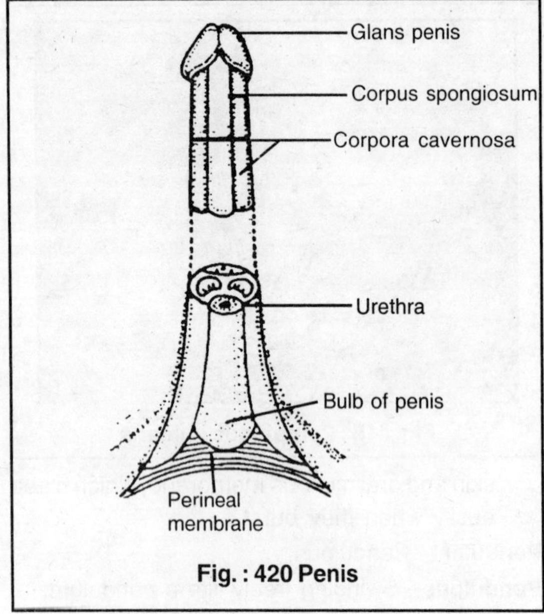

Fig. : 420 Penis

during intercourse as the result of vaginismus and contraction of the perineal muscles.

Clubbed penis —Curved penis during erection.

Double penis —A penis congenitally completely divided by the urethral groove.

Lunatus penis —Chordee. Painful curved erected penis in gonorrhea.

Palmatus penis —Penis enclosed by the scrotum.

Penischisis —Congenital opening of male urethra on the dorsum, upon under surface, at one side, or any fissuring of the penis.

Penitis —Inflammation of the penis.

Pennate —An object, the parts of which extend from a central portion like a feather.

Penniform —Feather-shaped.

Penoscrotal —Pertaining to the penis and scrotum.

Penotomy —Phallotomy. To make an incision into the penis.

Pension neurosis —See neurosis compensation.

Pent-, Penta- —Prefixes which mean five.

Pentad —1. A group of five. 2. In chemistry, an element with a valence of five.

Pentadactyle —Pentadactyl.

Pentadactyl —Possessing five digits on each hand and foot.

Pentagastrin — A synthetic gastrin used to determine the capacity of the stomach to secrete hydrochloric acid.

Pentalogy —The occurrence of five factors in combination, *e.g.*, the symptoms of a disease.

Pentaploid —Having five sets of chromosomes.

Pentatomic —1. A molecule containing five atoms. 2. An alcohol with five hydroxyl groups.

Pentavalent —Having a chemical valency of five.

Pentosemia —Presence of pentose in the blood.

Pentosuria —Presence of pentose in the urine.

Pentoxide —A chemical molecule containing five atoms of oxygen.

Peotillomania —Pseudomasterbation. Mania for pulling at the penis but without masterbation.

Peotomy —Surgical removal of penis.

Pepsic —Peptic.

Pepsin —The chief enzyme of the gastric juice, which converts protein into peptones and proteoses.

Pepsiniferous —Pepsinogenous.

Pepsinogen —Precursor of pepsin.

Pepsinogenous —Producing pepsin.

Pepsinuria —Presence of pepsin in the urine.

Peptic —Pertaining to pepsin or the digestion.

Peptic ulcer —An ulcer occurring in the lower end of esophagus, in the stomach, in the pylorus or in the duodenum, characterized by pain in the epigastric or right hypochondriac region, occurring 1/2 to 3 hrs. after meals. The pain of the ulcer of the lower end of esophagus, stomach and pylorus, is aggravated by food while that of duodenal ulcer is relieved by food.

Peptogenic, Peptogenous —1. Producing peptones and pepsin. 2. Promoting digestion.

Peptolysis —Peptonolysis. Hydrolysis of the peptones.

Peptolytic —Pertaining to the hydrolysis of peptones.

Peptone —Peptone is a nitrogenous compound, soluble in water, not coagulable by heat, formed by the action of proteolytic enzymes, acids or alkalies on certain proteins.

Peptonemia —Presence of peptones in the blood.

Peptonic —Pertaining to or containing peptone.

Peptonization —The process of conversion of protein substance into peptones by proteolytic enzyme.

Peptonize —To convert into peptones.

Peptonolysis —Peptolysis. The breakdown of peptones into peptides or amino acids.

Peptonuria —Presence of peptones in the urine.

Peptotoxin —Any toxin derived from a peptone.

Per —1. For every. 2. Through, by or by means of. 3. For each unit as milligrams per kilogram, which is usually written as mg./kg.

Per- —A prefix indicating throughout, utterly and intensity.

Per abdomen —Through the abdomen.

Peracephalous —A parasitic twin which does not contain head and arms and the thorax is deformed.

Peracidity —Abnormal acidity.

Peracute —Very acute or violent.

Per anum —Through the anus.

Perarticulation —Diarthrosis.

Peratodynia —Pain in the region of cardia of stomach.

Peraxillary —Through the axilla.

Per caput —Per head.

Perceive —To gain knowledge through the sense organs or by the mind.

Percept —The mental image of an object seen.

Perceptibility —The ability of gaining knowledge through the sense organs.

Perceptible —Capable of being perceived by the sense organs.

Perception —The process of receiving sensory impressions or of being aware of the objects.

Depth perception —The ability to recognize depth or the relative distances of different objects in a space.

Extrasensory perception —Knowledge gained not through the sense organs.

Stereognostic perception —Recognition of the objects by touch.

Perceptive —Pertaining to or having a higher than normal power of perception.

Perceptivity —Perceptibility.

Perceptorium —Sensorium.

Percolate —1. To allow a liquid to pass through a powdered substance. 2. Any filtered or percolated fluid.

Percolation —1. Filtration. 2. The extraction of the soluble portions of a drug by filtering a liquid solvent through it.

Percolator —The vessel used in percolation.

Per contiguum —By touching.

Per continuum —By continuation.

Perculsion —Inability to move.

Percussible —Detectable by percussion.

Percussion —To strike a body part with the fingertips to determine the consistency, position and size of an underlying structure and the presence of fluid or pus in a cavity. These conditions are determined by hearing the changes in the resonance and pitch of the sound emitted.

Auscultatory percussion —Auscultation of the sound produced by percussion.

Bimanual percussion —Percussion in which the finger of one hand taps the other hand.

Direct percussion, Immediate percussion —Percussion that is performed by striking the body surface directly with the fingers.

Indirect percussion, Mediate percussion —Percussion performed by placing the second hand on the body surface and then striking of a finger of it by a finger of the first hand.

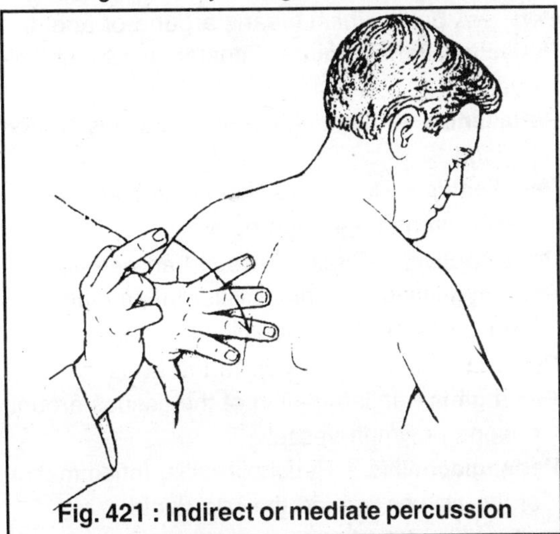

Fig. 421 : Indirect or mediate percussion

Palpatory percussion —A combination of palpation and percussion in which the finger perceives the tactile impression rather than the sounds produced.

Percussor —An instrument for performing percussion, consisting of a hammer with a rubber or metal head.

Percutaneous —Through the skin.

Perencephaly —Porencephalia.

Perfectionism —A type of neurosis in which an individual attempts to achieve impossible high standards.

Perflation —The process of blowing air into a cavity to expand its walls or to force out the secretions or other matter.

Perforans —Penetrating as a nerve or muscle.

Perforate —To make holes.

Perforated —Pierced with holes.

Perforation —The process of making holes.

Perforator —An instrument for piercing the skull and other bones.

Perfrication —Inunction. Through rubbing with an ointment.

Perfrigeration —Frostbite.

Perfusate —A liquid used to perfuse a tissue or organ.

Perfuse —To force some fluid to flow from the lumen of a hollow structure.

Perfusion —1. Passing of a fluid through the spaces, especially through the vessels. 2. Pouring of, or a fluid poured over or through an organ. 3. Supplying an organ or tissue with nutrients by injection.

Peri- —A prefix which means around or about.

Periacinal, Periacinous —Situated around an acinus.

Periadenitis —Inflammation of the tissues around a gland.

Perialienitis —Perixenitis. Non-infectious inflammation around a foreign body.

Periampullary —Situated around an ampulla.

Periamygdalitis —Peritonsillitis. Inflammation of the tissues around a tonsil.

Perianal —Around or close to the anus.

Periangiitis —Inflammation of the tissues around a blood or lymph vessel.

Periangiocholitis —Pericholangitis. Inflammation of the tissues around the bile ducts.

Periaortic —Situated around the aorta.

Periaortitis —Inflammation of the tissues around the aorta.

Periapex —The area around the apex of a tooth.

Periapical —Surrounding the apex of the root of a tooth.

Periappendicitis —Inflammation of the tissues around the vermiform appendix.

Periappendicular —Surrounding an appendix.

Periarterial —Situated around an artery.

Periarteritis —Inflammation of the outer coat of an artery and of the tissues around it.

Periarthric —Periarticular. Surrounding a joint.

Periarthritis —Inflammation of the tissues around a joint.

Periarticular —Periarthric.

Periatrial —Situated around the atria or auricles of the heart.

Periauricular —Around the external ear.

Periaxial —Situated around an axis.

Periaxillary —Situated around an axilla.

Periaxonal —Surrounding the axon of a nerve.

Peribronchial —Surrounding a bronchus or bronchi.

Peribronchiolar —Surrounding a bronchiole.

Peribronchiolitis —Inflammation of the tissues around the bronchioles.

Peribronchitis —Inflammation of the tissues around the bronchi.

Peribuccal —Surrounding the cheek.

Peribulbar —Surrounding any bulb, especially the eyeball or the bulb of the urethra.

Peribursal —Around a bursa.

Pericardia —Plural of pericardium.

Pericardiac, Pericardial —Pertaining to the pericardium.

Pericardial rub —A friction sound heard on auscultation of the precordial area when the inflamed surfaces of the pericardium rub against each other.

Pericardicentesis —Pericardiocentesis.

Pericardiectomy —Excision of a part of the pericardium.

Pericardiocentesis —Pericardicentesis. Surgical perforation of the pericardium.

Pericardiology —The study of the physiology and diseases of the pericardium.

Pericardiolysis —Separation of the adhesions between visceral and the parietal pericardium.

Pericardiomediastinitis —Inflammation of pericardium and the mediastinum.

Pericardioperitoneal —Pertaining to the pericardial and peritoneal cavities.

Pericardiopexy —To join the pericardium to an adjacent tissue to increase the blood supply to the heart, by surgery.

Pericardiophrenic —Pertaining to the pericardium and diaphragm.

Pericardiopleural —Pertaining to the pericardium and pleurae.

Pericardiorrhaphy —Suture of a wound in the pericardium.

Pericardiostomy —To make an opening into the pericardium for drainage.

Pericardiosymphysis —Adhesion between the visceral and parietal pericardium.

Pericardiotomy —To make an incision into the pericardium.

Pericarditic —Pertaining to the pericardium.

Pericarditis —Inflammation of the pericardium.

Adhesive pericarditis —Pericarditis in which the pericardium is abnormally adhered to the heart by dense fibrous tissue.

Constrictive pericarditis —Pericarditis in which the visceral and parietal layers are adhered to each other with great thickening of the whole pericardium.

Dry pericarditis —Pericarditis in which there is no effusion.

Fibrinous pericarditis —Pericarditis in which the pericardium is covered with butterlike exudate that dries up and unites the pericardial surfaces.

Hemorrhagic pericarditis —Pericarditis in which blood is found in the exudate.

Ischemic pericarditis —Pericarditis resulting from cardiac ischemia.

Neoplastic pericarditis —Pericarditis due to affection of the pericardium by malignant tumors of the adjoining structures.

Obliterative pericarditis —Pericarditis in which there is complete obliteration of the pericardial cavity.

Postraumatic pericarditis —Inflammation of the pericardium developing following an injury to the chest.

Purulent pericarditis —Pericarditis with pus in the pericardial sac.

Rheumatic pericarditis —Fibrinous pericarditis occurring in acute rheumatic fever.

Serofibrinous pericarditis —Pericarditis in which there is great amount of serous exudate but a little fibrin.

Tuberculous pericarditis —Pericarditis caused by Mycobacterium tuberculosis, the causative organism of tuberculosis.

Uremic pericarditis —Pericarditis resulting from uremia.

Viral pericarditis —Pericarditis due to a viral infection.

Pericardium —The membranous fibroserous sac enclosing the heart and roots of the great blood vessels. It is composed of an inner serous layer (visceral pericardium) and an outer fibrous layer (parietal pericardium). The space between these two layers is the pericardial cavity, which contains a small amount of serous fluid.

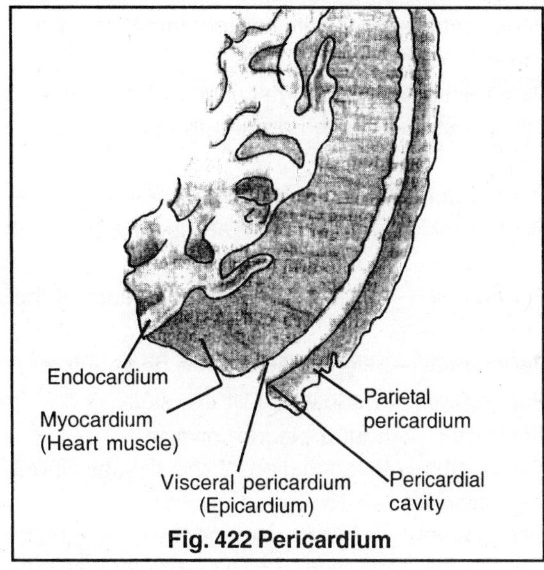

Fig. 422 Pericardium

Pericardotomy —Pericardiotomy.

Pericecal —Situated around the cecum.

Pericecitis —Inflammation of the tissues around the cecum.

Pericellular —Around a cell.

Pericemental —Periodontal.

Pericementitis —Periodontitis.

Pericementoclasia —Pyorrhea alveolaris.

Pericementum —Fibrous tissue covering the root of a tooth.

Pericentral —Around a center.

Pericholangitis —Periangiocholitis.

Pericholecystitis—Inflammation of the tissues around the gallbladder.

Perichondral, Perichondrial —Pertaining to membrane covering the cartilage.

Perichondritis —Inflammation of the perichondrium.

Perichondrium —Membrane of fibrous connective tissue around the cartilage.

Perichondroma —A tumor of the perichondrium.

Perichord —The covering of the notochord.

Perichordal —Situated around the notochord.

Perichorioidal, Perichoroidal —Situated around the choroid coat of the eye.

Perichrome —A nerve cell in which stainable material is scattered throughout the cytoplasm.

Pericolic —Surrounding the colon.

Pericolitis —Inflammation around the colon.

Pericolonitis —Pericolitis.

Pericolpitis —Perivaginitis. Inflammation of the tissues around the vagina.

Periconchal —Around the concha of the ear.

Pericorneal —Situated around the cornea of the eye.

Pericoronal—Around the crown of a tooth.

Pericoronitis —Inflammation around the crown of a tooth.

Pericranial —Pertaining to the periosteum of the skull.

Pericranitis —Inflammation of the pericranium.

Pericranium —Periosteum of the skull.

Pericystic —About a bladder or cyst.

Pericystitis —Inflammation of the tissues about the bladder.

Pericystium —1. Tissues around the urinary bladder or the gallbladder. 2. The vascular wall surrounding a cyst.

Pericyte —One of the elongated, flat, contractile, connective tissue cells around the capillary walls.

Pericytial —Located around a cell.

Peridectomy —Peritectomy.

Peridendritic —Surrounding a dendrite of a nerve cell.

Peridens —An extra tooth situated out of the dental arch.

Peridental —Periodontal.

Peridentitis —Periodontoclasia. Inflammation of the tissues around a tooth.

Peridentium —Periodontium.

Periderm —Epitrichium. The outer thin layer of flattened cells of the fetal epidermis which generally disappears before birth.

Peridermal, Peridermic —Pertaining to the periderm.

Peridesmic —Surrounding a ligament or pertaining to the peridesmium.

Peridesmitis —Inflammation of the connective tissue around a ligament.

Peridesmium —The connective tissue covering around a ligament.

Perididymis —The tunica vaginalis of the testis.

Perididymitis —Inflammation of the perididymis.

Peridiverticulitis —Inflammation around an intestinal diverticulum.

Periductal —Located around a duct.

Periduodenitis —Inflammation around the duodenum.

Peridural —Outside the dura mater of the spinal cord.

Periencephalitis —Inflammation of the surface of brain.

Periencephalomeningitis —Inflammation of the cerebral cortex and meninges.

Perienteric —Around the intestines.

Perienteritis —Inflammation of the peritoneal coat of the intestines.

Perienteron —The peritoneal cavity of the embryo.

Periependymal —Surrounding the ependyma.

Periesophageal —Surrounding the esophagus.

Periesophagitis —Inflammation of the tissues around the esophagus.

Perifistular —Situated around a fistula.

Perifocal —Surrounding a focus.

Perifollicular —Situated around a follicle.

Perifolliculitis —Inflammation around the hair follicles.

Perigangliitis —Inflammation of the tissues around a ganglion.

Periganglionic —Around a ganglion.

Perigastric —1. Around the stomach. 2. Pertaining to the peritoneal coat of the stomach.

Perigastritis —Inflammation of the peritoneal covering of the stomach.

Perigemmal —Around any bud, especially a taste bud.

Periglandular —Pertaining to the tissues around a gland.

Periglandulitis —Inflammation of the tissues around a gland.

Periglottic —Situated around the base of the tongue and epiglottis.

Periglottis —The mucous membrane of the tongue.

Perihepatic —Around the liver.

Perihepatitis —Inflammation of the peritoneal covering of liver and the surrounding tissues.

Perihernial —Around a hernia.

Peri-islet —Situated around the islets of Langerhans.

Perijejunitis —Inflammation of the tissues around the jejunum.

Perikaryon —The cell body of a neuron.

Perikeratic —Pericorneal.

Perikyma —A transverse ridge and groove on the surface of tooth enamel.

Perikymata —Plural of perikyma.

Perilabyrinthitis —Inflammation of tissues around the labyrinth.

Perilaryngeal —About the larynx.

Perilaryngitis —Inflammation of tissues about the larynx.

Perilenticular —Around the lens of the eye.

Perilesional —Located or occurring around a lesion.

Periligamentous —Around a ligament.

Perilymph, Perilympha —The fluid between the membranous and bony labyrinth of the internal ear.

Perilympha —Perilymph.

Perilymphangeal —Around a lymphatic vessel.

Perilymphangitis —Inflammation of the tissues around a lymphatic vessel.

Perilymphatic —Perilymphangeal.

Perimastitis —Inflammation of the fibrous tissue around a breast.

Perimeningitis —Pachymeningitis.

Perimenopause —A period of 3-5 years prior to the onset of menopause, during which estrogen hormones begin to decrease causing irregular menstrual cycles and incresed periods of amenorrhea.

Perimeter —1. The boundary of a structure. 2. An apparatus for determining the extent of the peripheral visual field.

Perimetric —1. Pertaining to the perimetrium. 2. Surrounding the uterus.

Perimetritic —Pertaining to the perimetritis.

Perimetritis —Inflammation of the peritoneal covering of the uterus.

Perimetrium —The serous membrane covering the uterus.

Perimetry —To measure the boundary of a body or a structure or to measure the field of vision with a perimeter.

Perimolysis —Decalcification of the teeth from gastric acid due to chronic vomiting.

Perimyelis —Enosteum. A membrane lining medullary cavity of a bone.

Perimyelitis —1. Leptomeningitis. 2. Inflammation of the membrane lining the medullary cavity of a bone.

Perimyelography —X-ray examination of the area around the spinal cord.

Perimyocarditis —Pericarditis and myocarditis occurring simultaneously, usually due to same cause.

Perimyoendocarditis —Inflammation of all the three layers—pericardium, myocardium and endocardium of the heart.

Perimyositis —Inflammation of the connective tissue around a muscle.

Perimysia —Plural of perimysium.

Perimysial —Pertaining to or of the nature of, the fibrous covering of a muscle.

Perimysiitis —Inflammation of the perimysium.

Perimysium —Connective tissue sheath enveloping each primary bundle of muscle fibers.

Perinatal —Pertaining to the period from 28th week of pregnancy to four weeks after birth.

Perinate —An infant in the perinatal period.

Perinatologist —A specialist in perinatology.

Perinatology —Study of the fetus and infant during the perinatal period.

Perineal —Pertaining to, or situated on the perineum.

Perineal body —A mass of tissue situated between the vagina and rectum in the female and penis and the rectum in the male.

Perineo- —A prefix meaning pertaining to the perineum.

Perineocele —A hernia between the rectum and vagina in the female or between rectum and the prostate in the male.

Perineocolporectomyomectomy —Excision of a myoma by incising the perineum, vagina and the rectum.

Perineometer—An instrument used to measure the strength of voluntary muscle contractions of the perineum.

Perineoplasty —Repair of the perineum by plastic surgery.

Perineorrhaphy —Suture of the perineum.

Perineoscrotal —Pertaining to the perineum and scrotum.

Perineostomy —To make a permanent opening between the urethra and skin through the perineum.

Perineotomy —To make an incision into the perineum.

Perineovaginal —Pertaining to the perineum and the vagina.

Perinephrial —Pertaining to perinephrium.

Perinephric —Located or occurring around a kidney.

Perinephritis —Paranephritis.

Perinephrium —The connective and other tissues around the kidney.

Perineum —1. The region between the vulva and anus in the female and between the scrotum and anus in the male. 2. The pelvic floor and the structures occupying the pelvic outlet, bounded anteriorly by pubic symphysis, laterally by the ischial tuberosities and posteriorly by the coccyx.

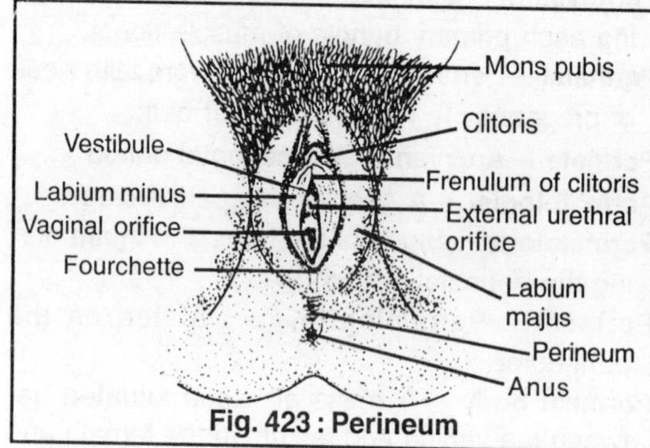

Fig. 423 : Perineum

Perineural —Around a nerve.

Perineurial —Pertaining to the perineurium.

Perineuritis —Inflammation of the perineurium.

Perineurium —A connective tissue sheath enveloping each bundle of nerve fibers.

Perinuclear —Around a nucleus.

Periocular —Around the eye.

Period —1. The interval or division of time. 2. Menses.

Childbearing period —The period from puberty to menopause in a woman during which she can give birth to the children.

Fertile period —The period in a menstrual cycle of a woman during which the ovum can be fertilized.

Gestation period —Period of pregnancy.

Incubation period —The interval of time between the exposure to an infection and the appearance of the first symptom of the disease.

Intrapartum period —The period from the onset of labor to the end of the third stage of labor.

Latent period —1. The time elapsed between a stimulation and the resulting response, e.g., contraction of a muscle. 2. Incubation period.

Menstrual period —Menses.

Missed period —Absence of menstruation at its expected time.

Neonatal period —The period of first 30 days of infant life.

Puerperal period —Interval of time from the birth of a child to 6 weeks, at which time complete involution of the uterus has occurred.

Safe period —The time during the menstrual cycle when conception is not possible.

Silent period —The time in the course of a disease when the signs and symptoms are so mild as are difficult to be detected.

Periodic —Recurring after definite intervals of time.

Periodicity —Recurrence after definite intervals of time.

Periodontal —Peridental. 1. Around a tooth. 2. Pertaining to the periodontium.

Periodontia —1. Plural of periodontium. 2. The study and treatment of diseases of the periodontal tissues.

Periodontics —Periodontia.

Periodontist —A specialist in periodontics.

Periodontitis —Inflammation of the periodontium.

Periodontium —The tissues covering and supporting the teeth, including cementum, periodontal ligament, alveolar bone and gingiva.

Periodontoclasia —Peridentitis. Inflammation accompanied by degeneration and destruction of the periodontium.

Periodontology —Branch of dentistry concerned with the study of treatment of diseases of tissues around the teeth.

Periodontolysis —Periodontoclasia.

Periodontosis —Any degenerative disease of the periodontal tissues, marked by tissue destruction.

Periodoscope —Table for calculating the expected date of delivery.

Periomphalic —Situated around or near the umbilicus.

Periontogenic —Disease caused by the environment.

Perionychia —Inflammation around a nail.

Perionychium —Epidermis surrounding a nail.

Perionyxis —Inflammation of the epidermis surrounding a nail.

Perioophoritis —Inflammation of the tissues around the ovary.

Perioophorosalpingitis —Inflammation of the tissues around an ovary and fallopian tube.

Perioothecitis —Perioophoritis.

Perioothecosalpingitis —Perioophorosalpingitis.

Perioperative —Paraoperative. Around the time of operation.

Periophthalmic —Around the eye.

Periophthalmitis —Inflammation of the tissues surrounding an eye.

Perioptometry —Perimetry.

Perioral —Circumoral. Around the mouth.

Periorbita —Connective tissue covering the eye socket.

Periorbital —Around the eye socket.

Periorbititis —Inflammation of the connective tissue covering the eye socket.

Periorchitis —Inflammation of the tissues covering a testis.

Periostea —Plural of periosteum.

Periosteal —Periosteous. Pertaining to, or of the nature of, periosteum.

Periosteitis —Periostitis. Inflammation of the periosteum.

Periosteoedema —Edema of the periosteum.

Periosteoma —A tumor of the periosteum.

Periosteomyelitis —Inflammation of the bone including periosteum and marrow.

Periosteopathy —Any disease of the periosteum.

Periosteophyte —A bony growth on the periosteum.

Periosteorrhaphy —To join the cut margins of the periosteum by suturing.

Periosteosis —Periostosis.

Periosteotome —An instrument for cutting the periosteum or removing it from the bone.

Periosteotomy —To make an incision into the periosteum.

Periosteous —Periosteal.

Periosteum —The fibrous membrane covering all the bones except at their articular surfaces.

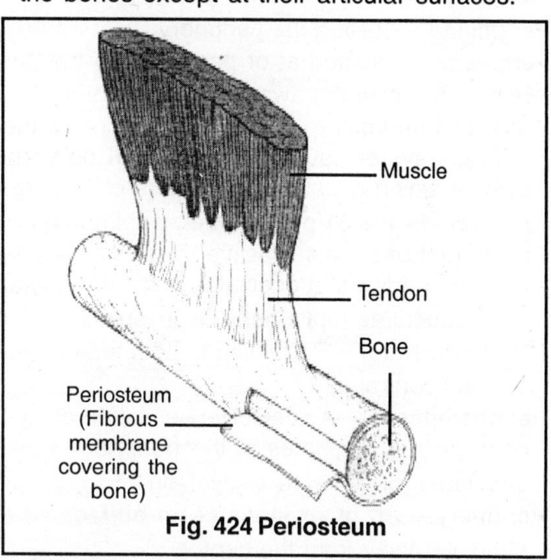

Fig. 424 Periosteum

Periostitis —Inflammation of the periosteum.

Periostoma —Periosteoma.

Periostomedullitis —Inflammation of the periosteum and bone marrow.

Periostoses —Plural of periostosis.

Periostosis —1. Deposition of the periosteum on bone. 2. Development of periosteomas.

Periostosteitis —Inflammation of the bone with its periosteum.

Periostotome —Periosteotome.

Periostotomy —Periosteotomy.

Periotic —Situated around the ear, especially the internal ear.

Periovaritis —Perioophoritis.

Periovular —Around an ovum.

Peripachymeningitis —Inflammation of the connective tissue between dura mater and bone covering it.

Peripancreatitis —Inflammation of the tissues about the pancreas.

Peripapillary —Around the papilla.

Peripartum —Occurring in the mother during the last month of pregnancy or first few months after delivery.

Peripatetic —Moving from one place to another.

Peripenial —Around the penis.

Periphacitis —Inflammation of the capsule of the lens of the eye.

Periphakus —The capsule surrounding the eye lens.

Peripharyngeal —Around the pharynx.

Peripherad —Toward the periphery.

Peripheral —Situated at or pertaining to the periphery or occurring away from the center.

Peripheral nervous system —The portion of the nervous system outside the central nervous system which consists of 12 pairs of the cranial nerves and 31 pairs of the spinal nerves.

Peripheraphose —A subjective sensation of darkness or shadow that originates in the peripheral optic structures (optic nerve or eyeball).

Catapherocentral

Peripherophose —A subjective sensation of light or color that originates in the peripheral optic structures (optic nerve or eyeball).

Periphery —An outer structure or surface or a structure away from the center.

Periphlebitic —Pertaining to periphlebitis.

Periphlebitis —Inflammation of the outer coat of a vein or of the tissues around it.

Periphoria —Cyclophoria.

Periphrenitis —Inflammation of the tissues around the diaphragm.

Periplasm —The space between the cell membrance and the cell wall, in Gram-negative bacteria, containing proteins secreted by the cell.

Periplast —Peripheral protoplasm in a cell.

Peripleural —Surrounding the pleurae.

Peripleuritis —Inflammation of the connective tissue between pleurae and chest wall.

Peripolar —Around a pole.

Peripolesis —Penetration of migrating cells between fixed tissue cells.

Periporitis —Multiple small abscesses around the sweat glands occurring most frequently on the face in children, especially as a complication of malaria.

Periportal —Around the portal vein.

Periproctic —Around the anus.

Periproctitis —Perirectitis. Inflammation of the tissues around the rectum and anus.

Periprostatic —Situated or occurring around or about the prostate gland.

Periprostatitis —Inflammation of tissues around the prostate gland.

Peripylephlebitis —Inflammation of tissues around the portal vein.

Peripylic —Periportal.

Peripyloric —Around the pylorus.

Periradicular —Around a root, especially a tooth root.

Perirectal —Around the rectum.

Perirectitis —Periproctitis.

Perirenal —Perinephric.

Perirhinal —Around or about the nose.

Perirhizoclasia —Inflammation and destruction of the tissues immediately around the roots of a tooth.

Perisalpingitis —Inflammation of the tissues around the fallopian tube.

Perisalpingoovaritis —Perioophorosalpingitis.

Perisalpinx —The peritoneum covering the upper borders of the fallopian tubes.

Periscopic —Viewing on all sides.

Perish —To disintegrate or die by unnatural means.

Perisigmoiditis —Inflammation of peritoneum about the sigmoid flexure of the colon.

Perisinuous —Surrounding a sinus.

Perisinusitis —Inflammation of the tissues about a sinus.

Perispermatitis —Inflammation of the tissues about spermatic cord.

Perisplanchnic —Around a viscus or viscera.

Perisplanchnitis —Perivisceritis. Inflammation of the tissues around the viscera.

Perisplenic —Around or about the spleen.

Perisplenitis —Inflammation of the splenic capsule.

Perispondylic —Around a vertebra.

Perispondylitis —Inflammation of the tissues around a vertebra.

Perissodactylous —Imparidigitate.

Peristalsis —A wavelike movement occurring in hollow tubular organs of the body having both longitudinal and circular muscle fibers, especially the alimentary canal, by which their contents are propelled forward.

Peristaltic —Pertaining to, or of the nature of, peristalsis.

Peristaphyline —About the uvula.

Peristasis —1. The decrease in blood flow in the affected area in the early stage of inflammation. 2. Environment.

Peristoma —The margin of a mouth.

Peristomal —Peristomatous.

Peristomatous —Around the mouth.

Peristrumitis —Perithyroiditis. Inflammation of the tissues around the goiter.

Peristrumous —Around a goiter.

Perisynovial —Around a synovial structure.

Perisystole —Presystole.

Perisystolic —Events occurring before and after ventricular systole.

Peritectomy —Excision of a ring of conjunctiva around the cornea.

Peritendinea —Plural of peritendineum.

Peritendineum —A connective tissue sheath investing fiber bundles of a tendon.

Peritendinitis —Tenosynovitis. Inflammation of the sheath of a tendon.

Peritenon —Peritendineum.

Peritenontitis —Peritendinitis.

Perithelioma —Hemangiopericytoma.

Perithelium —Fibrous connective tissue layer surrounding the smaller blood vessels and the capillaries.

Perithoracic —Around the thorax.

Perithyroiditis —Inflammation of the capsule of the thyroid gland.

Peritomist —The person who performs circumcision.

Peritomize —To perform peritomy.

Peritomy —1. To make an incision into the conjunctiva around the circumference of cornea. 2. Circumcision.

Peritonea —Plural of peritoneum.

Peritoneal —Pertaining to the peritoneum.

Peritonealgia —Pain in the peritoneum.

Peritonealize —During abdominal surgery to cover a tissue with the peritoneum.

Peritoneocentesis —To puncture the peritoneal cavity to obtain fluid.

Peritoneoclysis —To introduce the fluid into the peritoneal cavity by injection.

Peritoneopathy —Any disease of the peritoneum.

Peritoneopericardial —Pertaining to the peritoneum and pericardium.

Peritoneopexy —Fixation of the peritoneum.

Peritoneoplasty —Repair of the peritoneum by plastic surgery.

Peritoneoscope —An endoscope used to inspect the peritoneal cavity.

Peritoneoscopy —Visual examination of the peritoneal cavity by peritoneoscope.

Peritoneotomy —To make an incision into the peritoneum.

Peritoneum —The serous membrane lining the walls of the abdominal and pelvic cavities (parietal peritoneum) and investing the abdominal organs (visceral peritoneum.)

Peritonism —The condition in which there are signs of shok and peritonitis but actually there is no inflammation of the peritoneum.

Peritonitic —Pertaining to or suffering from peritonitis.

Peritonitis —Inflammation of the peritoneum.

Acute diffuse peritonitis —Serious form of peritonitis of a large area.

Adhesive peritonitis —Peritonitis in which the parietal and visceral layers of peritoneum stick together by adhesions.

Aseptic peritonitis —Non-bacterial inflammation of the peritoneum, as caused by injury, chemicals or irradiation.

Bile peritonitis —Peritonitis caused by the escape of bile into the peritoneal cavity.

Chemical peritonitis —Peritonitis caused by the presence of chemicals such as gastrointestinal juices, pancreatic juice or bile in the peritoneal cavity.

Chronic peritonitis —Peritonitis that is due to tuberculosis or cancer.

Chyle peritonitis —Peritonitis due to free chyl in the peritoneal cavity.

Gas peritonitis —Peritonitis in which gas is present in the peritoneal cavity.

Generalized peritonitis —Peritonitis affecting most of the peritoneum.

Localized peritonitis —Peritonitis in which there is inflammation of only a small area of the peritoneum.

Pelvic peritonitis —Inflammation of the peritoneum of the pelvic region.

Primary peritonitis —Peritonitis occurring due to infectious microorganisms transmitted through blood or lymph.

Puerperal peritonitis —Peritonitis developing after delivery.

Secondary peritonitis —Peritonitis resulting from extension of infection from adjoining structures.

Septic peritonitis —Peritonitis caused by pyogenic bacterial infection.

Serous peritonitis —Peritonitis with serous exudation,

Silent peritonitis —Peritonitis in which there is no sign or symptom.

Traumatic peritonitis —Acute peritonitis caused by an injury.

Tuberculous peritonitis —Peritonitis caused by tuberculosis.

Peritonize —Peritonealize.

Peritonsillar —Around a tonsil.

Peritonsillitis —Inflammation of the tissues around a tonsil.

Perltracheal —Around the trachea.

Peritrichal —Peritrichous.

Peritrichate —Peritrichous.

Peritrichic —Peritrichous.

Peritrichous —A group of unicellular organisms having flagella or cilia over the entire surface.

Peritrochanteric —Around a trochanter.

Peritubal —Around a fallopian tube.

Perityphlic —Around the cecum.

Perityphlitis —Inflammation of the tissues around the cecum and appendix.

Periumbilical —Around the umbilicus.

Periungual —Around a nail.

Periureteral —Around a ureter.

Periureteric—Periureteral.

Periureteritis —Inflammation of the tissues around a ureter.

Periurethral —Situated about the urethra.

Periurethritis —Inflammation of the tissues around the urethra.

Periuterine —Perimetric. About the uterus.

Periuvular —Around the uvula.

Perivaginal —Around the vagina.

Perivaginitis —Pericolpitis.

Perivascular —Situated around a vessel, especially a blood vessel.

Perivasculitis —Periangiitis.

Perivenous —Surrounding or occurring around a vein.

Perivertebral —Around a vertebra.

Perivesical —Around the urinary bladder.

Perivesiculitis —Inflammation of the tissues around a seminal vesicle.

Perivisceral —Perisplanchnic.

Perivisceritis —Inflammation surrounding any internal organ.

Perixenitis —Perialienitis.

Perle —A soft capsule containing some medicine.

Perleche —Fissuring and desquamation of the epidermis at the corners of mouth, especially in children.

Perlingual —Through the tongue, a method of administration of medicines.

Permanent —Enduring, lasting.

Permeability —The quality of being permeable.

Permeable —Capable of allowing the passage of fluids or substances in solution.

Permeant —Able to pass through a particular semipermeable membrane.

Permeate —1. To penetrate or pass through a filter. 2. The constituents of a solution or suspension that pass through a filter.

Permeation —The process of penetrating or passing through a filter.

Permutation —Transformation, complete change.

Pernicious —Fatal, destructive.

Pernicious anemia —A form of anemia occurring in a person, usually after 50 years of age, due to absence of Castle's intrinsic facter from the gastric juice which causes absorption of Cyanocobalamin (Vitamin B_{12}) or due to deficiency of vitamin B_{12} in the diet, characterized by a lemon-yellow color of the skin, soreness of the tongue, numbness or tingling in the legs and hands, progressive weakness, dyspnea on exertion and palpitation. The red blood cells become larger in size but greatly reduced in number.

Pernio —Chilblain. Frostbite.

Perniosis—Chilblain.

Pero- —A prefix meaning deformed.

Perobrachius—A fetus with deformed arms.

Perocephalus —A fetus with a deformed head.

Perochirus —A fetus with deformed hands.

Perocormus—An individual with a congenitally deformed trunk.

Perodactylia —The condition in which one or more fingers or toes are deformed.

Perodactylus —An individual having deformed fingers or toes congenitally.

Perodactyly —Perodactylia.

Peromelia —Congenital absence or deformity of the terminal portion of a limb or limbs.

Peromelus —An individual with congenitally absent or deformed terminal portion of a limb or limbs.

Peromely —Peromelia.

Perone —The fibula bone.

Peroneal —Fibular.

Peroneotibial —Pertaining to the fibula and tibia bones.

Peronia —Malformation.

Peropus —An individual with congenitally deformed feet.

Peroral —Administered through the mouth.

Per os—By mouth.

Perosomus —An individual having a defective body congenitally.

Perosplanchnia —Congenital malformation of the viscera.

Perosseous —Through a bone.

Perpendicular —Vertical, at right angles to a plane.

Perplication —Insertion of the cut end of an artery through an incision in its own wall to check bleeding.

Per primam, Per primam intentionem —By first intention. See healing.

Per rectum —Through the rectum.

Perseveration —Continuous repetition of the same word or phrase or continuation of an action after cessation of its stimulus.

Person —A human being.

Persona —The outer appearance a person presents to others.

Personal —Characteristic features of an individual.

Personality —The characteristics and behavior of an individual which distinguish the individual from others.

Alternating personality —Multiple personality.

Antisocial personality—A type of personality disorder characterized by performing antisocial acts such as lying, stealing, fighting, disregard of the rights of others, aggressive sexual behavior, excessive use of alcohol and gambling etc.

Asthenic personality—A type of personality disorder characterized by easy fatigability, weakness, lack of enthusiasm and over sensitivity to mental and physical stimulus.

Borderline personality —Personality in which individuals have difficulty in maintaining a consistent stable mood and characterized by rapidly changing mood, unpredictable and impulsive behavior, outburst of anger, irritability, self-mutilation or suicidal acts, job and marital instability, chronic feeling of emptiness or boredom.

Compulsive personality —Obsessive-compulsive personality.

Cyclothymic personality —The personality characterized by alternating moods of elation and sadness.

Double personality, Dual personality —Mental dissociation in which two very different personalities occur in a person in alternation.

Explosive personality —Personality in which an individual suddenly becomes explosive, abuses loudly and becomes aggressive.

Extroverted personality —A personality in which activities or libido are directed to other individuals or the environment.

Histrionic personality —A personality in which individuals are very active and dramatic, who draw attention of others toward themselves. They do not like normal routine life but like to perform some enthusiastic works and excitement.

Hysterical personality —Histrionic personality.

Inadequate personality —A personality in which a person is not affected by emotional, physical or social stresses.

Introverted personality —A personality in which activities or libido are directed to the individual himself or herself.

Multiple personality —The condition in which 3 or more personalities occur alternately in the same individual, usually with each personality unaware of others.

Neurotic personality —Personality characterized by behavior between normal and that of a neurotic individual.

Obsessive-compulsive personality —A type of personality disorder in which a person is dominated by a thought or action recognized as senseless and accompanied by a feeling that it must be resisted as he/she washes and scrubs the skin constantly to ensure cleanliness due to fear of dirt and contamination.

Paranoid personality —A personality disorder characterized by hypersensitivity, rigidity, unwarranted suspicion, jealousy, excessive self-importance and tendency to blame others. The people of this personality criticise others but do not accept their own criticism.

Psychopathic personality —Antisocial personality.

Schizoid personality —A personality disorder characterized by shyness, timidness, over sensitivity, feeling of isolation and loneliness, day dreaming and failure to form close interpersonal relationships etc.

Perspiration —1. Sweating. 2. Sweat.

Perspire —Sweat. To excrete fluid through pores of the skin.

Persuasion —To influence by advice or argument.

Per tubam —Through a tube.

Pertubation —Disturbance.

Pertussis —Whooping cough.

Pertussoid —Resembling whooping cough.

Per urethram —Through the urethra.

Per vaginam —Through the vagina.

Perversion —A turning away from the normal way.

Pervert —1. To turn from the normal way. 2. The person who has turned from the normal way, especially who has been changed sexually.

Perverted —Deviated, abnormal or disordered.

Per vias naturales —Through the natural ways.

Pervigilium —Insomnia.

Pervious —1. Permeable, capable of being penetrated. 2. Penetrating.

Pes —The foot or footlike structure.

Pes abductus —Talipes valgus. Clubfoot in which sole turns outward.

Pes adductus —Talipes varus. Clubfoot in which the sole turns inward.

Pes cavus —A foot with abnormally hollow sole.

Pes equinovalgus —Talipes equinovalgus. The foot in which the heel is elevated and turned outward.

Pes equinovarus —The foot in which heel remains downward and the sole is elevated from the earth.

Pes equinus —The foot in which heel does not touch the earth and the patient walks on toes only.

Pes gigas —Macropodia. An abnormally large foot.

Pes planus —Flatfoot.

Pes valgus —Talipes valgus.

Pes varus —Talipes varus.

Pessary —An instrument placed in the vagina to support the uterus or as a contraceptive device as diaphragm pessary, which is a cup-shaped rubber instrument which fits over the os uteri.

Pessimism —Looking at the worst side of a thing, lacking in hope.

Pest —Destructive insect.

Pesticemia —Presence of the bacterium Yersinia pestis in the blood, causing plague.

Pesticide —Any chemical used to kill the pests.

Pestiferous —Producing pestilence, carrying infection.

Pestilence —A contagious or an infectious epidemic disease.

Pestilential —Pertaining to or producing a pestilence.

Pestis —Plague.

Pestle —An instrument for pulverizing drugs in a mortar.

Petechia —Plural is petechiae. A minute red spot on the skin due to escape of a small amount of blood.

Petechiae —Plural of petechia.

Petechial —Pertaining to or having petechiae.

Petiolate —Having stem or pedicle.

Petiole —A stalk or pedicle.

Petiolus —Petiole.

Petit mal —See under epilepsy.

Petrifaction —The process of changing into hard substance or stone.

Petrified —Changed into hard substance or stone, rigid.

Petrify —Make hard.

Petrissage —Kneading and pressing of the muscles in massage.

Petro- —A prefix which means stone.

Petrolatum —Soft paraffin.

Petroleum —A natural oily inflammable liquid obtained from beneath the earth.

Petromastoid —Pertaining to the petrous portion of the temporal bone and its mastoid process.

Petro-occipital —Pertaining to petrous portion of the temporal bone and the occipital bone.

Petrosa —The petrous portion of the temporal bone.

Petrosae —Plural of petrosa.

Petrosal —Pertaining to the petrous portion of the temporal bone.

Petrositis —Inflammation of the petrous portion of the temporal bone.

Petrosomastoid —Petromastoid.

Petrosphenoid —Pertaining to petrous portion of the temporal bone, and sphenoid bone.

Petrosquamosal —Petrosquamous.

Petrosquamous —Pertaining to petrous and the squamous portions of the temporal bone.

Petrous —Petrosal. Resembling stone.

Petrousitis —Petrositis.

Pexis —Surgical fixation.

-pexy —A suffix which means fixation.

Peyer's patch —An aggregation of lymph nodules found chiefly in the ileum of the small intestine near its junction with the colon. They are circular or oval, about 1 cm. wide, and 2 to 3 cm. long. In typhoid fever they are enlarged and often ulcerated.

Peyronie's disease —Hardening of the corpora cavernosa of the penis. This condition may be painful which causes distortion and curvature of the penis, especially when erect.

pg —Symbol for picogram.

pH —A symbol for expressing the degree of acidity or alkalinity of a substance. At pH 7 a substance is neutral, i.e. it is neither acidic nor alkaline. Increasing acidity is expressed as a number less than 7 and increasing alkalinity as a number greater than 7. Maximum acidity is pH 0 and maximum alkalinity is pH 14.

Phacitis —Phakitis. Lentitis. Inflammation of the eye lens.

Phaco- —A prefix which means pertaining to the lens of the eye.

Phacoanaphylaxis —Hypersensitivity to protein of the crystalline lens of the eye.

Phacocele —Displacement of the crystalline lens into the anterior chamber of the eye.

Phacocyst —Capsule of the crystalline lens.

Phacocystectomy —Surgical excision of a part of capsule of lens of the eye for the treatment of cataract.

Phacocystitis —Inflammation of capsule of the eye lens.

Phacodonesis —Tremulousness of the lens of the eye.

Phacoemulsification —A method of treatment of cataract in which the lens is fragmented by ultrasonic vibrations, which is then aspirated and removed.

Phacoerysis —Removal of the eye lens by suction.

Phacofragmentation —Rupture and aspiration of the lens of the eye.

Phacoglaucoma —Glaucoma and changes in the lens of the eye produced by glaucoma.

Phacohymenitis —Phacocystitis.

Phacoid —Lentiform. Lens-shaped.

Phacoiditis —Phakitis.

Phacoidoscope —Phacoscope.

Phacolysis —Dissolution, disintegration or dissection of lens of the eye.

Phacolytic —Dissolving or disintegrating the lens of the eye.

Phacoma —Phakoma.

Phacomalacia —Softening of the eye lens.

Phacomatosis —Any of a group of hereditary neurocutaneous diseases spreading throughout the body tissues.

Phacometachoresis —Phacocele. Displacement of the eye lens.

Phacometer —An apparatus for determining the refractive power of a lens.

Phacoplanesis —Abnormal movement of the eye lens.

Phacosclerosis —Hardening of the eye lens.

Phacoscope —Phacoidoscope. An instrument for viewing change of curvature of the eye lens during accommodation.

Phacoscotasmus —Clouding of the eye lens.

Phacotoxic —Exerting poisonous effect upon the eye lens.

Phag-, Phago- —Prefixes which means eating, ingestion, or engulfing.

Phage —Eating bacteria.

Phagedena —A sloughing ulcer spreading rapidly.

Phagedenic —Pertaining to, or of the nature of phagedena.

-phagia, -phagy —Suffixes which mean eating or swallowing.

Phagocyte —Any cell that ingests micro-organisms or other cells and foreign particles.

Phagocytic —Pertaining to phagocytes or phagocytosis.

Phagocytize —The ingestion of bacteria and foreign particles by phagocytes.

Phagocytoblast —A cell developing into a phagocyte.

Phagocytolysis —Phagolysis. Destruction of phagocytes.

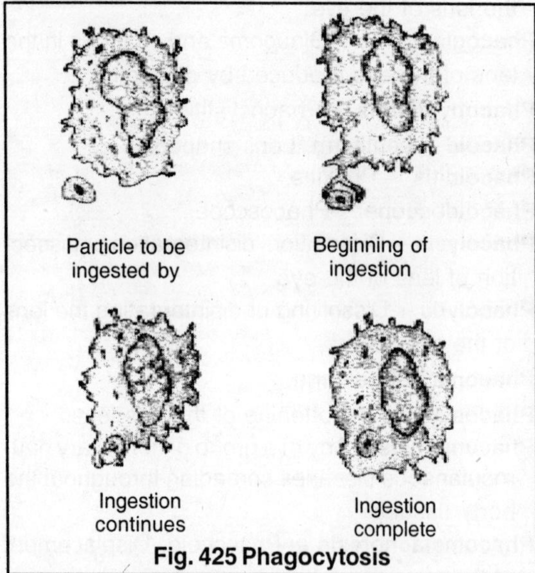

Fig. 425 Phagocytosis

Phagocytolytic —Phagolytic. Destroying phagocytes.

Phagocytose —Phagocytize.

Phagocytosis —Ingestion and digestion of bacteria and foreign particles by phagocytes.

Phagodynamometer —An apparatus for measuring the energy exerted in chewing food.

Phagokaryosis —Phagocytic action of a cell nucleus.

Phagolysis —Phagocytolysis.

Phagolytic —Phagocytolytic.

Phagomania —Excessive desire for taking food.

Phagophobia —Morbid fear of eating.

Phagopyrism —Hypersensitivity to certain foods which produce symptoms of poisoning when ingested.

Phagosome —A membrane bound vacuole in a phagocyte containing the material (bacteria or other) to be digested.

Phagotherapy —Treatment of diseases by feeding.

Phagotype —The type of bacteria which are engulfed by phagocytes.

-phagy —Phagia.

Phakic —Pertaining to the lens.

Phakitis —Phacitis.

Phakolysis —Phacolysis.

Phakoma —1. A microscopic grayish white tumor present occasionally in the retina in tuberous sclerosis. 2. A patch of myelinated nerve fibers seen very rarely in the retina in neurofibromatosis.

Phakomatosis —Phacomatosis.

Phalacrosis —Alopecia. Baldness.

Phalacrotic —Bald; bald-headed.

Phalacrous —Phalacrotic.

Phalangeal —Pertaining to a phalanx.

Phalangectomy —Excision of one or more phalanges.

Phalanges —Bones of a finger or toe.

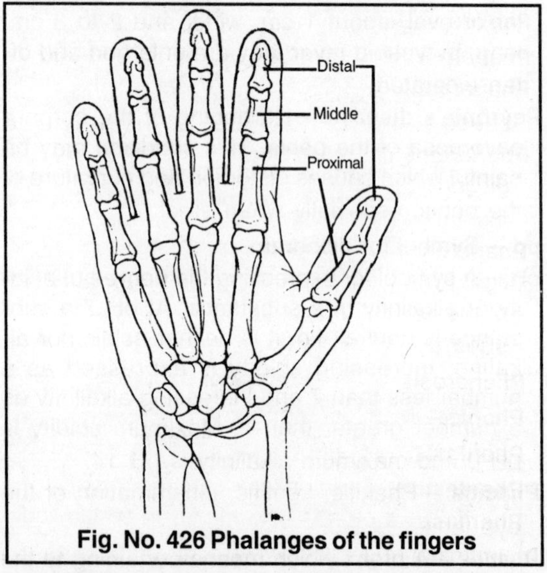

Fig. No. 426 Phalanges of the fingers

Phalangette —The distal phalanx of a digit.

Phalangitis —Inflammation of one or more phalanges.

Phalanx —Any bone of a finger or toe.

Distal phalanx —Terminal or ungual (underlying the nail bed) phalanx.

Middle phalanx —A bone in the middle of the medial four fingers and lateral four toes.

Proximal phalanx —Any phalanx that articulates with a metacarpal or metatarsal bone.

Phall-, Phalli-, Phallo- —Prefixes meaning penis.

Phallalgia— Pain in the penis.

Phallectomy —Amputation of the penis.

Phalli —Plural of phallus.

Phallic —Pertaining to the penis.

Phallicism —Phallism. Worship of the male genital organs.

Phalliform —Penis-shaped.

Phallitis —Penitis.

Phallocampsis —Downward curvature of penis during erection.

Phallocrypsis —Contraction of the penis so that it becomes invisible.

Phallodynia —Phallalgia.

Phalloid —Like a penis.

Phalloncus —Tumor or swelling on the penis.

Phalloplasty —Repair of the penis by plastic surgery.

Phallorrhagia —Hemorrhage from the penis.

Phallotomy —Penotomy. To make an incision into the penis.

Phallus —The penis.

Phanero- —A prefix meaning evident, visible.

Phanerogenic —Indicating a disease with a known cause.

Phaneromania —A tendency for biting the nails or pricking, scratching or pulling a hair, beard, mustache, a pimple or wart.

Phaneroscope —A lens used to concentrate the light from a lamp upon the skin for examination of the lesions of the skin and subcutaneous tissues.

Phanerosis —The process of becoming visible.

Phanic —Manifest, apparent.

Phantasia —An appearance that is imaginary.

Phantasm —Phantom.

Phantasmatomoria —Dementia in which foolish imaginations occur.

Phantasmology —The study of dreams and phantoms.

Phantasy —A day dream.

Phantogeusia —A taste sensation occurring in the mouth not produced by an external stimulus.

Phantom —1. An optical illusion, *i.e.* an image not formed by the external stimulus. 2. An apparition or illusion of something that does not exist. 3. A model of the body or of one of its parts.

Phantomize —In psychiatry, to create mental imagery by fantasy.

Phantom limb —The illusion that the limb still exists after amputation.

Phantom tumor —An apparent tumor due to muscular contractions or gas seen in hysteria.

Phantosmia —Intermittent or continuous perception of odor when no odor is smelt.

Pharmacal —Concerning pharmacy.

Pharmaceutical —Pertaining to the pharmacy or drugs.

Pharmaceutics —Pharmacy. Science of preparing or dispensing medicines.

Pharmaceutist —Pharmacist.

Pharmacist —A druggist. The person licensed to prepare and dispense the medicines.

Pharmaco- —A prefix which means medicine.

Pharmacochemistry —Pharmaceutical chemistry.

Pharmacodiagnosis —Use of drugs in making a diagnosis.

Pharmacodynamic —Pertaining to the drug action.

Pharmacodynamics —Study of the effects of drugs on living organisms.

Pharmacoendocrinology —The pharmacology of the function of endocrine glands.

Pharmacoepidemiology —The study of the actions and uses of the drugs in epidemic diseases in human populations.

Pharmacogenetics —Study of hereditary factors on the response of individual organisms to drugs.

Pharmacogenomics —Pharmacogenetics.

Pharmacogeriatrics —The study of the actions and uses of drugs in old persons.

Pharmacognosist —Specialist in pharmacognosy.

Pharmacognosy —The branch of pharmacology

dealing with the study of natural drugs, their constituents and properties.

Pharmacography —To write an article or a bock on the properties of drugs.

Pharmacokinetic —Pertaining to the action and metabolism of drugs in the body.

Pharmacokinetics —Study of action and metabolism of drugs in the body.

Pharmacologic, Pharmacological —Pertaining to the pharmacology.

Pharmacologist —Specialist in pharmacology.

Pharmacology —The study of the origin, nature, chemistry, properties and actions of drugs on the body, and their uses.

Pharmacomania —Uncontrollable desire for taking or giving the medicines.

Pharmacopedia —Information about drugs and their preparations.

Pharmacopeia —A book containing drugs, their preparations, formulas and dispensing of drugs.

Pharmacopeial—Pertaining to the pharmacopeia.

Pharmacophilia —Excessive fondness for medicines.

Pharmacophobia —Morbid fear of taking medicines.

Pharmacopsychosis—A mental disorder caused by alcohol, drugs or poisons.

Pharmacotherapy —Treatment of diseases by the use of medicines.

Pharmacy —1. The branch of health science that deals with the preparation and dispensing of medicines. 2. The place where drugs are prepared or dispensed.

Pharm. D. —Doctor of pharmacy.

Pharyngalgia —Pharyngodynia. Pain in the pharynx.

Pharyngeal —Pertaining to the pharynx.

Pharyngeal reflex —Try to swallow after stimulation of the pharynx.

Pharyngectomy —Excision of a part of the pharynx.

Pharyngei —Pharyngeal branches.

Pharyngemphraxis —Obstruction in the pharynx.

Pharynges —Plural of pharynx.

Pharyngeus —Pharyngeal.

Pharyngismus —Pharyngospasm. Spasm of the muscles in the pharynx.

Pharyngitic —Pertaining to pharyngitis.

Pharyngitis —Inflammation of the pharynx. —

Acute pharyngitis —Acute inflammation of the pharynx with pain in the throat.

Atrophic pharyngitis —Chronic pharyngitis accompanied by atrophy of the mucous glands and absence of their secretions.

Chronic pharyngitis —Pharyngitis associated with the diseases of the nose and sinuses, mouth breathing, excessive smoking and chronic tonsillitis.

Diphtheritic pharyngitis —Pharyngitis occurring in diphtheria in children with the formation of white membrane in the throat.

Gangrenous pharyngitis —Gangrenous inflammation of the mucous membrane of the pharynx.

Granular pharyngitis —Chronic pharyngitis with the formation of granules on the pharynx.

Ulcerative pharyngitis —Pharyngitis with fever, pain and the formation of ulcers.

Pharyngo- —Combining form pertaining to the pharynx.

Pharyngoamygdalitis —Inflammation of the pharynx and tonsil.

Pharyngocele —Herniation of the pharyngeal wall.

Pharyngoceratosis —Pharyngokeratosis.

Pharyngodynia —Pharyngalgia.

Pharyngoepiglottic —Pertaining to the pharynx and glottis.

Pharyngoepiglottidean —Pharyngoepiglottic.

Pharyngoesophageal —Pertaining to the pharynx and esophagus.

Pharyngoesophagoplasty —Plastic surgery of the pharynx and the esophagus.

Pharyngoglossal —Pertaining to the pharynx and tongue.

Pharyngography —X-ray examination of the pharynx after ingestion of a radiopaque substance.

Pharyngokeratosis —Thickening and hardening of mucous membrane of the pharynx.

Pharyngolaryngeal —Pertaining to the pharynx and larynx.

Pharyngolaryngitis —Laryngopharyngitis. Inflammation of the pharynx and larynx.

Pharyngolith —A calculus in the pharyngeal wall.

Pharyngology —Branch of medical science dealing with the study of the pharynx.

Pharyngolysis—Paralysis of the pharynx.

Pharyngomaxillary—Pertaining to the pharynx and maxilla.

Pharyngomycosis —Any fungal disease of the pharynx.

Pharyngonasal —Pertaining to the pharynx and nose.

Pharyngo-oral —Pertaining to the pharynx and the mouth.

Pharyngopalatine—Pertaining to the pharynx and the palate.

Pharyngoparalysis —Pharyngoplegia. Paralysis of the muscles of the pharynx.

Pharyngopathy —Any disease of the pharynx.

Pharyngoperistole —Narrowing of the pharynx.

Pharyngoplasty —Repair of the pharynx by plastic surgery.

Pharyngoplegia —Pharyngoparalysis.

Pharyngorhinitis —Inflammation of the nasopharynx.

Pharyngorhinoscopy —Visual examination of the nasopharynx and posterior nares.

Pharyngorrhea —Mucus discharge from the pharynx.

Pharyngoscleroma —A scleroma in the pharynx.

Pharyngoscope —An instrument for visual examination of pharynx.

Pharyngoscopy —Visual examination of the pharynx by means of a pharyngoscope.

Pharyngospasm —Pharyngismus.

Pharyngostenosis —Narrowing of the pharynx.

Pharyngotherapy —Treatment of diseases of the pharynx.

Pharyngotome —An instrument for incising the pharynx.

Pharyngotomy —To make incision into the pharynx.

Pharyngotonsillitis —Inflammation of the pharynx and tonsils.

Pharyngotympanic —Pertaining to the pharynx and middle ear.

Pharyngoxerosis —Dryness of the pharynx.

Pharynx —A musculomembranous passage for air from behind the nasal cavities to the larynx and for food from mouth to esophagus.

Phase —A stage of development, for example proliferative stage of the menstrual cycle.

Phasic —Of, or pertaining to, a phase.

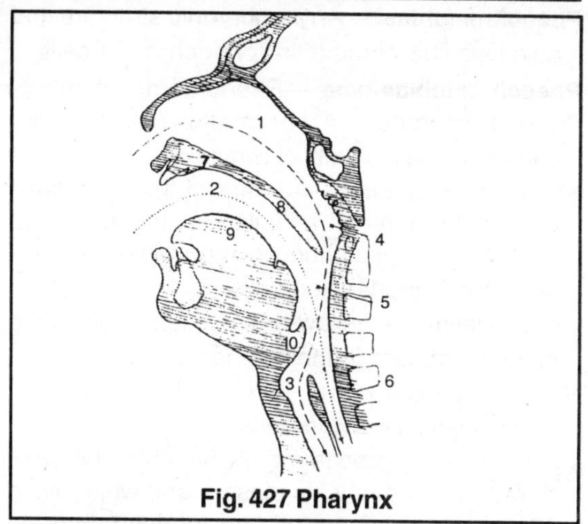

Fig. 427 Pharynx

1. Nasal cavity, 2. Oral cavity, 3. Laryngeal cavity 4. Nasal part of the pharynx, 5. Oral part of the pharynx, 6. Pharynx, 7. Hard palate, 8. Soft palate, 9. Tongue, 10. Epiglottis

Phasmophobia —Morbid fear of ghosts.

Phatnorrhagia —Hemorrhage from the socket of a tooth.

Ph. D. —Doctor of Philosophy.

Phengophobia —Photophobia. Morbid fear of light.

Phenic —Obtained frum the coal tar.

Phenic acid —Phenol.

Phenol —Carbolic acid. An extremely poisonous compound obtained from the distillation of coal tar. It is corrosive to the tissues and is used as bacteriostatic agent.

Phenolate —To sterilize with carbolic acid.

Phenolemia —Presence of phenol in the blood.

Phenologist —A specialist in phenology.

Phenology —The study of the effects of climate on living things.

Phenoluria —Presence of phenol in the urine.

Phenomenon —Any observable change occurring in an organ or vital function; an objective symptom.

Phenotype —1. The physical constitution of an individual. 2. A group of persons who resemble each other in physical characteristics.

Phenotypic —Pertaining to phenotype.

Phenozygous —Having a cranium much narrower than the face.

Phenylketonuria —Presence of phenylpyruvic acid in the urine.

Pheochrome —Chromaffin.

Pheochromoblast —Any embryonic structure that develops into chromaffin (pheochrome) cells.

Pheochromoblastoma —Pheochromocytoma.

Pheochromocyte —A chromaffin cell, that becomes yellowish with chromium.

Pheochromocytoma —A tumor of the chromaffin cells of the adrenal medulla causing increased secretion of epinephrine or norepinephrine resulting in hypertension.

Pheomelanin —A yellow-brown, sulfur-containing pigment present in the red hair.

Pheomelanogenesis —The formation of pheomelanin by living cells.

Pheresis —Any procedure in which blood is withdrawn from a donor, its plasma and white blood cells, etc. are separated and retained, and the remainder is retransfused into the donor.

Ph. G. —Graduate in pharmacy.

Phial —A small vessel containing a medicine; vial.

-philia —A suffix which means affinity toward something.

Philoneism —Excessive fondness for newness or change.

Philoprogenitive —Prolific. Producing a large number of offspring.

Philtrum —The median vertical groove on external surface of the upper lip

Phimosis —Constriction of the orifice of the prepuce, preventing it from being drawn over the glans penis.

Phlebalgia —Pain arising from a vein.

Phlebangioma —An aneurysm occurring in a vein.

Phlebarteriectasia —Dilatation of blood vessels.

Phlebarteriodialysis —Arteriovenous aneurysm.

Phlebectasia, Phlebectasis —Varicosity. Dilatation of a vein.

Phlebectomy —Surgical removal of a vein or part of a vein.

Phlebectopia —Abnormal position of a vein.

Phlebemphraxis —To make an obstruction in a vein by plug.

Phlebeurysm —Pathologic dilation of a vein.

Phlebismus —Obstruction resulting in dilatation of veins.

Phlebitic —Pertaining to the phlebitis.

Phlebitis —Inflammation of a vein.

Adhesive phlebitis —Phlebitis in which the walls of the vein adhere, causing obliteration of the vein.

Obliterative phlebitis —Phlebitis in which the lumen of a vein becomes permanently closed.

Puerperal phlebitis —Phlebitis occurring following childbirth.

Sclerosing phlebitis —Phlebitis in which veins become obstructed and hardened.

Septic phlebitis —Inflammation of a vein due to infection.

Suppurative phlebitis —Phlebitis characterized by the formation of pus.

Phlebo- —A prefix which means vein.

Phleboclysis —Injection of a medicine into a vein.

Phlebogram —1. An X-ray of a vein taken after filling it with a contrast medium. 2. A tracing of the venous pulse.

Phlebograph —An instrument for recording the venous pulse.

Phlebography —Study of the structure and function of the veins.

Phleboid —Venous. Pertaining to, resembling or of the nature of a vein.

Phlebolite —Phlebolith.

Phlebolith —A calculus in a vein.

Phlebolithiasis —Calculus formation in a vein.

Phlebology —The study of the veins and their diseases.

Phlebomanometer —An apparatus for direct measurement of the venous blood pressure.

Phlebometritis —Inflammation of the uterine veins.

Phlebomyomatosis —Thickening of the walls of a vein by an overgrowth of muscular fibers.

Phlebopexy —Transplantation of the testes outside the serous cavity for varicocele, saving the venous plexus.

Phlebophlebostomy —Surgical anastomosis of one vein to another.

Phleboplasty —Repair of an injured vein by plastic surgery.

Phleborrhagia —Bleeding from a vein.

Phleborrhaphy—Suture of a vein.

Phleborrhexis —Rupture of a vein.

Phlebosclerosis—Fibrous hardening of the walls of a vein.

Phlebostasia, Phlebostasis —1. Stoppage of blood flow in the veins. 2. Compression of veins temporarily to reduce blood flow through them.

Phlebostenosis —Constriction of a vein.

Phlebothrombosis —Formation of thrombus in a vein associated with its inflammation.

Phlebotome —An instrument for incising a vein.

Phlebotomist—The person who draws blood from the vein using a syringe and needle.

Phlebotomize—To take the blood from a vein of a person.

Phlebotomy —Venesection. To incise a vein.

Phlegm —Thick, tenacious mucus from the respiratory tract.

Phlegmasia —Inflammation.

Phlegmasia alba dolens—White leg. Milk leg. An acute inflammation of a leg occurring usually after childbirth due to venous obstruction caused by thrombosis. The leg becomes white or milky.

Phlegmatic —Apathetic. Of dull or sluggish temperament.

Phlegmon —Acute diffuse inflammation of the connective tissue.

Phlegmonous —Pertaining to inflammation of the connective tissues.

Phlogistic —Pertaining to or causing inflammation.

Phlogogenic, Phlogogenous —Producing inflammation.

Phlogosis—Inflammation.

Phlyctena—1. A small vesicle formed on the conjunctiva in certain diseases. 2. A small blister made by a first degree burn.

Phlyctenar —Pertaining to a vesicle.

Phlyctenoid —Resembling a blister or a vesicle.

Phlyctenosis —Formation of blisters or vesicles.

Phlyctenula —A tiny vesicle or pustule seen on the cornea.

Phlyctenulae —Plural of phlyctenula.

Phlyctenular —Pertaining to a phlyctenula.

Phlyctenule—A minute vesicle; an ulcerated nodule on the cornea or conjunctiva.

Phlyctenulosis —Formation of numerous phlyctenules.

Phobia—Morbid fear of, or aversion to, an object.

Phobic —Pertaining to or affected with phobia.

Phobophobia—Morbid fear of being afraid.

Phocomelia —Congenital absence of the proximal portion of a limb or limbs, the hands and feet being attached directly to the trunk by a small, irregularly shaped bone.

Phocomelus —A person with phocomelia.

Phocomely —Phocomelia.

Phon —A unit of loudness of sound.

Phonacoscope —An apparatus for increasing the voice sounds.

Phonacoscopy —Examination of the chest by means of phonacoscope.

Phonal —Pertaining to the voice.

Phonasthenia —Weakness of the voice.

Phonation —The utterance of vocal sounds.

Phonatory —Pertaining to the utterance of vocal sounds.

Phonautograph —An apparatus for registering the vibrations of the voice.

Phone—1. A sound produced in speaking a single letter. 2. Short for telephone.

Phoneme—The smallest unit of sound in speech.

Phonemic —Pertaining to or having the characteristic of a phoneme.

Phonendoscope —A stethoscope that intensifies the auscultatory sounds.

Phonendoskiascope —An apparatus for observing the cardiac movements and for hearing the heart sounds.

Phonetic —Pertaining to the voice sounds.

Phonetics —Phonology. Science of speech and pronunciation.

Phoniatrics —The study of speech defects and their treatment.

Phonic —Pertaining to the voice.

Phonism —A sensation of hearing produced by the effect of something seen, tasted, smelled or felt by touch.

Phono- —A prefix which means voice or sound.

Phonoangiography —The recording and analysis of arterial bruits.

Phonocardiogram —The record produced by phonocardiography.

Phonocardicgraph —The instrument used in phonocardiography.

Phonocardiography —To make a graphic record of the heart sounds.

Phonocatheter —A catheter with a microphone at its end.

Phonogram —A graphic record of a sound.

Phonograph —An instrument used for reproducing sounds

Phonology —Phonetics. Science of vocal sounds.

Phonomania —Mania for murdering.

Phonomassage —The treatment of ear disease by causing movements of the ossicles of the ear by an apparatus which carries musical vibrations into the ear.

Phonometer —An apparatus for measuring the intensity of sounds.

Phonomyoclonus —Invisible fibrillary muscular contractions revealed by auscultation.

Phonomyogram —A record produced by phonomyography.

Phonomyography —The recording of sounds produced by muscular contraction.

Phonopathy —Any disease of the organs of speech.

Phonophobia —Morbid fear of the sounds or noise or of speaking.

Phonophoresis —The use of ultrasound to introduce a medicine into a tissue.

Phonophotography —Photography of the vibrations produced by speech.

Phonopneumomassage —Air massage of the middle ear.

Phonopsia —Visual sensation upon hearing of certain sounds.

Phonoreceptor —A receptor for sound stimuli.

Phonorenogram —A record of the sounds produced by pulsation of the renal artery.

Phonoscope —An apparatus for recording the heart sounds.

Phonoscopy —Recording of the heart sounds by means of a phonoscope.

Phonosurgery —An operation performed for improving or changing the voice.

-phoresis —A suffix which means migration of the ions through a membrane by the action of an electric current.

-phoria —A suffix which means turning of the visual axis.

Phorology —The study of disease carriers.

Phorometer —An instrument for measuring heterophoria.

Phoropter —An apparatus containing different lenses that is used for refraction of the eye.

Phorotone —An apparatus for exercising eye muscles.

Phos- —A prefix which means light.

Phose —A subjective sensation of light.

Phosgene —Carbonyl chloride ($COCl_2$), a suffocating and highly poisonous war gas.

Phosphate —A salt of phosphoric acid.

Phosphated —Containing phosphates.

Phosphatemia —Presence of phosphates in the blood.

Phosphatic —Pertaining to or containing phosphates.

Phosphatoptosis —Precipitation of phosphates in the urine.

Phosphaturia —An excess of phosphates in the urine.

Phosphene —A sensation of light caused by a stimulus other than light, *e.g.*, by pressure upon the eyeball.

Phospholipid —A lipoid substance containing phosphorus and fatty acids, as lecithen.

Phosphonecrosis —Necrosis of the jaw bone due to effect of the phosphorus.

Phosphopenia —Deficiency of phosphorus in the body.

Phosphorated —Combined with phosphorus.

Phosphorescence —The property of shining without production of heat.

Phosphorescent —Shining without heat.

Phosphorhidrosis —Phosphoridrosis. Secretion of the shining perspiration.

Phosphoridrosis —Phosphorhidrosis.

Phosphorism —Chronic poisoning from phosphorus.

Phosphorized —Containing phosphorus.

Phosphorpenia —Phosphopenia.

Phosphoruria —Phosphaturia.

Phosphorus —A chemical element of Atomic weight 30.9738 and Atomic number 15, which is essential for the development of bones and teeth and found in them in the form of calcium phosphate. Its daily requirement is 800 mg.

Phosphorylation —The combining of a phosphate with an organic compound.

Phosphuria —Phosphaturia.

Photalgia —Photodynia. Pain produced by light, as in the eye.

Photaugiaphobia —Intolerance of bright light.

Photesthesia —Perception of light.

Photic —Pertaining to light.

Photism —Visual sensation produced by the effect of something heard, tasted, smelled or felt by touch.

Photo- —A prefix which means light.

Photoactinic —Radiation producing both luminous and chemical effects.

Photoactive —Reacting to sunlight or ultraviolet rays.

Photoaging —Damage of the skin from sun exposure for many years, particularly wrinkling of the skin.

Photoallergy —Allergy to light.

Photoautotroph —An organism solely depending on light for its energy.

Photoautotrophic—Pertaining to a photoautotroph.

Photobacteria —Plural of photobacterium.

Photobacterium —A bacterium producing light.

Photobiology —The branch of biology in which the effects of light on living organisms are studied.

Photobiotic —Living only in the light.

Photobleach —To make colorless by the action of light.

Photocatalysis —Promotion or stimulation of a chemical reaction by light.

Photocatalyst —A substance, *e.g.*, chlorophyll, that brings about a chemical reaction to light.

Photoceptor —A nerve ending receiving a light sensation.

Photochemical —Pertaining to light and chemistry.

Photochemistry —The branch of chemistry concerned with the chemical properties or effects of light rays.

Photochemotherapy —Treatment of disease by a drug, *e.g.*, methoxsalen that reacts to sunlight or ultraviolet rays.

Photochromogen —A microorganism in which pigmentation develops as a result of exposure to light.

Photocoagulation —Condensation of protein material in the tissues by ordinary light rays or an intense beam of light, used especially in the treatment of retinal detachment or retinal hemorrhage.

Photocoagulator —An apparatus used in photocoagulation.

Photoconvulsive —Convulsion due to exposure to light.

Photodermatitis —Dermatitis occurring due to sensitivity of the skin to light.

Photodermatosis —Photodermatitis.

Photodromy —The condition of particles in suspension wherein they move toward (positive photodromy), or away from (negative photodromy) light.

Photodynamic —Pertaining to the energy exerted by light on organisms.

Photodynia —Photalgia.

Photodysphoria —Photophobia. Extreme intolerance of light.

Photoelectric —Pertaining to light and the electricity.

Photoelectricity —Electricity formed by the action of light.

Photoelectron —An electron set free by the action of light.

Photoerythema —Erythema of the skin produced by light.

Photoesthetic —Sensitive to light.

Photofluorography —Photography of the images seen during fluoroscopic examination.

Photogastroscope —An apparatus for viewing and taking photographs of the inside of the stomach.

Photogen —A microorganism that produces luminescence.

Photogenesis —Production of light, as by bacteria or insects etc.

Photogenic, Photogenous —Produced by light or producing light.

Photokinesis —Alteration of movements of the motile organisms in response to light.

Photokinetic —Reacting with alteration in movements to stimulus of light.

Photokinetics —The changes in rate of a chemical reaction in response to light.

Photolabile —The characteristic of being destroyed or inactivated by light.

Photoluminescence —The quality of an object to become luminescent after exposure to light.

Photoluminescent —Able to become luminescent upon exposure to light.

Photolysis —Chemical decomposition by light.

Photolyte —The substance of decomposition by light.

Photolytic —Decomposed by light.

Photomania —Mania for light.

Photomedicine —The use of light as a medicine in the treatment of some diseases.

Photometer —An apparatus for measuring the intensity of light.

Photometry —Measurement of the intensity of light.

Photomicrograph —A photograph of an object seen under the microscope.

Photomicrography —The production of a photomicrograph.

Photomotor —Pertaining to muscular contraction induced by light.

Photomyoclonus —Clonic spasms of the muscles in response to visual stimuli.

Photon —A unit of energy of a light ray.

Photoncia —Swelling produced by light.

Photonosus —Disease produced by prolonged exposure to intense light.

Photo-onycholysis —Loosening or detachment of the nail from the nailbed, resulting from exposure to sunlight or ultraviolet rays.

Photo-ophthalmia —Inflammation of the cornea and conjunctiva due to exposure to intense light.

Photoparoxysmal —Photoconvulsive.

Photopathy —Any disease caused by light.

Photoperceptive —Able to perceive light.

Photoperiod —The time for which an organism is exposed daily to daylight.

Photoperiodism —The physiological and behavioral reactions occurring in the organisms by changes in the daylight and darkness.

Photophilic —Attracted toward light.

Photophobia —Abnormal intolerance of light.

Photophobic —Pertaining to or suffering from photophobia.

Photophone —An apparatus for production of sound by action of light.

Photophthalmia —Photo-ophthalmia.

Photopia —Adjustment of the eye to see in bright light.

Photopic —Pertaining to bright light.

Photopsia, Photopsy —Appearance of sparks or flashes of light in retinal, optic or brain diseases.

Photoptarmosis —Photic sneezing. Sneezing caused by the effect of light.

Photoptometer —An instrument for measuring the smallest amount of light that will make an object visible.

Photoptometry —To measure the light perception.

Photoradiation —Treatment of cancer by intravenous injection of a photosensitizing agent, such as hematoporphyrin, followed by exposure of tumors to light.

Photoradiometer —An apparatus for determining the ability of ionizing radiation to penetrate the substances.

Photoreaction —A chemical reaction produced by light.

Photoreactivation —Activation of something or of some previously inactive process by light.

Photoreception —Perception of light.

Photoreceptive —Sensitive to light.

Photoreceptor —A sensory nerve ending sensitive to light.

Photoretinitis —Inflammation of the retina due to exposure to intense light.

Photoretinopathy —A burn of macula of retina from excessive exposure to sunlight or other intense light.

Photoscan —A map of representation of concentration of a radioactive isotope in body tissue, printed on a photographic film.

Photoscope —Fluoroscope.

Photoscopy —Fluoroscopy.

Photosensitive —Sensitive to light.

Photosensitivity —Sensitiveness to light.

Photosensitization —The condition in which the skin reacts abnormally to light.

Photosensitizer —A substance which in combination with light, causes sensitivity reaction in the body.

Photostable —Unchanged by the effect of light.

Photostethoscope —An apparatus that converts the sound into flashes of light, used for continuous observation of the fetal heart.

Photostress —Exposure to intense illumination.

Photosynthesis —The manufacture of food (carbohydrate) by plants in sunlight, by combining carbon dioxide from the atmosphere and water from the soil in the presence of chlorophyll.

Phototaxis —Movements of cells and micro-organisms under the influence of light.

Phototherapy —Treatment of disease by exposure to light.

Photothermal —Concerning heat produced by light.

Photothermal radiation —Radiation of heat by a source of light, as that from an electric bulb.

Phototimer —An apparatus in radiography for measuring the radiation that has passed through the patient and terminates the x-ray exposure, when it is sufficient to form an image.

Phototonus —Sensitivity in an individual produced by light.

Phototopia —A subjective sensation of light.

Phototoxic —Having a toxic reaction produced by light, especially in the skin, *e.g.*, simple sunburn.

Phototoxicity —The condition resulting from overexposure to light.

Phototoxis —Disorder produced by over exposure to light or radiation.

Phototroph —Photoautotroph.

Phototrophic —Capable of deriving energy from light.

Phototropism —The tendency of an organism or a plant to turn or move towards the light.

Photuria —The excretion of the luminous urine.

Phren—1. The mind. 2. The diaphragm.

Phrenalgia —1. Pain due to psychic causes. 2. Pain in the diaphragm.

Phrenectomy —1. Surgical excision of all or a part of the diaphragm. 2. Surgical resection of a part of the phrenic nerve.

Phrenemphraxis —Crushing of the phrenic nerve.

Phrenetic —Maniacal. Afflicted with mania.

-phrenia —A suffix which means mental disorder.

Phrenic —Pertaining to the diaphragm or to the mind.

Phrenicectomy —Resection of a part of the phrenic nerve.

Phreniclasia —Phrenemphraxis.

Phrenicocolic —Phrenocolic.

Phrenicoexeresis —The taking out of a part of phrenic nerve.

Phrenicogastric —Phrenogastric.

Phrenicoglottic —Phrenoglottic.

Phrenicohepatic —Phrenohepatic.

Phreniconeurectomy —Phrenicectomy.

Phrenicosplenic —Phrenosplenic.

Phrenicotomy —Surgical division of the phrenic nerve.

Phrenicotripsy —Phrenemphraxis.

Phrenitis —1. Delirium or frenzy. 2. Encephalitis. 3. Diaphragmitis.

Phreno- —Combining form which means mind or diaphragm.

Phrenocardia —Precordial pain and dyspnea in anxiety neurosis

Phrenocolic —Pertaining to the diaphragm and colon.

Phrenocolopexy —To suture the transverse colon to the diaphragm.

Phrenodynia —Pain in the diaphragm.

Phrenogastric —Pertaining to the diaphragm and stomach.

Phrenoglottic —Pertaining to the diaphragm and glottis.

Phrenograph —An apparatus for registering the movements of the diaphragm.

Phrenohepatic —Pertaining to the diaphragm and liver.

Phrenopathy —Mental disease.

Phrenopericarditis —Inflammation of the pericardium with its attachment to the diaphragm.

Phrenoplegia —1. A sudden attack of mental disorder. 2. Paralysis of the diaphragm.

Phrenoptosia —Phrenoptosis.

Phrenoptosis —Downward displacement of the diaphragm.

Phrenospasm —Spasm of the diaphragm.

Phrenosplenic —Pertaining to the diaphragm and spleen.

Phrenotropic —Affecting the mind.

Phronosis —Soundness of the mind.

Phrynoderma —Follicular hyperkeratosis due to deficiency of vitamin A.

Phthiriasis —Pediculosis.

Phthiriophobia —Morbid fear of the lice.

Phthisic —The person affected with pulmonary tuberculosis or any wasting disease.

Phthisical —Pertaining to, or afflicted with, phthisis.

Phthisis —1. Pulmonary tuberculosis. 2. Any wasting or atrophic disease.

Phycology —The scientific study of algae.

Phycomycosis —A disease caused by the phycomycetes fungi.

Phyla —Plural of phylum.

Phylacagogic —Stimulating the production of protective antibodies.

Phylactic —Pertaining to or producing defence of the body against infection.

Phylaxis —The defence of the body against infection.

Phyletic —Phylogenetic. Pertaining to a phylum or race.

Phylogenesis —The development of a race or group of animals.

Phylogenetic —Pertaining to the development of a race or group of animals.

Phylogenic —Phylogenetic.

Phylogeny —Phylogenesis.

Phylum —A primary division of the animal or plant kingdom, next higher than a class.

Phyma —A small, rounded skin tumor or tubercle.

Phymatoid —Like a tumor.

Phymatosis —Formation of the phymata or tubercles on the skin.

Physaliferous —Physaliphorous.

Physaliform, Physalliform —Resembling a blister.

Physaliphore —A mother cell or giant cell containing a large vacuole, in a malignant growth.

Physaliphorous —Having vacuoles or bubbles.

Physalis —A vacuole in a giant cell found in certain malignant tumors.

Physiatrician —A specialist in physiatrics.

Physiatrics —The branch of medical science in which physical exercises, massage, physical agents such as light, heat, water and electricity and mechanical apparatus are used in the diagnosis, prevention and treatment of diseases.

Physiatrist —A specialist in physiatrics.

Physiatry —Physical therapy.

Physic —1. The art of treatment and curing. 2. A medicine, especially a purgative.

Physical —1. Bodily, pertaining to the body. 2. Of or pertaining to the material things. 3. Pertaining to physics.

Physical examination —Examination of the patient by inspection, palpation, percussion and auscultation.

Physical signs —Symptoms of a disease detected by physical examination.

Physical therapy —Treatment of diseases by physical means such as exercise and massage, light, heat, electricity and ultraviolet rays etc.

Physician —One who treats the diseases by medicines.

Physicist —Specialist in physics.

Physicochemical —Pertaining to both physics and chemistry.

Physics —The science which deals with the general properties of matter and energy.

Physio- —A prefix which indicates relationship to nature.

Physiochemical —Physicochemical.

Physiocogenic —Arising from physical causes.

Physiocopyrexia —Artificial fever produced by physical means.

Physiognomy —1. Determination of mental or moral character and qualities by seeing the face. 2. Face. 3. To make a diagnosis by observing the appearance and facial expression of the patient.

Physiologic —Physiological.

Physiological —Concerning body function.

Physiologicoanatomical —Pertaining to both physiology and anatomy.

Physiologist —Specialist in physiology.

Physiology —The science dealing with the functions of the lving organism and its parts and the physical and chemical processes involved.

Physiopathologic —1. Pertaining to physiology and pathology. 2. Pertaining to a change in normal function.

Physiopathology —The branch of medical science concerned with the abnormal functions of the body.

Physiopsychic —Pertaining to both mind and body.

Physiopyrexia —Fever produced by a physical agent.

Physiotherapeutic —Pertaining to physical therapy.

Physiotherapist —The person legally authorized to treat the patient by physical therapy.

Physiotherapy —Physical therapy.

Physique —Body constitution.

Physo- —A prefix which means air or gas.

Physocele —1. A hernial sac distended with gas. 2. A tumor or swelling filled with gas.

Physocephaly —Swelling of the head due to presence of excessive air under the skin of the head.

Physohematometra —Gas and blood in the uterine cavity distending the uterus.

Physohydrometra —Gas and serum in the uterine cavity distending the uterus.

Physometra —Gas in the uterine cavity.

Physopyosalpinx —Gas and pus in the fallopian tube.

Phyto-, Phyt- —Combining forms of the word indicating a plant.

Phytoagglutinin —A lectin that causes agglutination of red blood cells and white blood cells.

Phytobezoar —Food ball.

Phytochemistry —Study of plant chemistry.

Phytodermatitis —Inflammation of the skin previously exposed to the plants, by mechanical, chemical injury or allergy.

Phytogenesis —Phytogeny. The origin and development of plants.

Phytogenous —Caused by plants.

Phytohemagglutinin —A specific substance lectin, derived from the plants, which agglutinates red blood cells.

Phytohormone —Plant hormone.

Phytoid —Plant like.

Phytoparasite —A vegetable parasite.

Phytopathogenic —Producing disease in plants.

Phytopathology —Study of the plant diseases.

Phytophagous —Vegetarian.

Phytopharmacology —The study of the effects of drugs and chemicals on plants.

Phytophotodermatitis —A dermatitis caused by exposure to certain plants and then to sunlight.

Phytopneumoconiosis —A chronic lung disease with fibrous reaction, caused by inhalation of the particles of vegetable origin.

Phytosis —1. A disease caused by plant parasite. 2. Presence of plant parasites in the body.

Phytotoxic —Poisonous to the plants.

Phytotoxin —A toxin produced by a plant.

Pia —Tender, soft.

Pia-arachnitis —Leptomeningitis.

Pia-arachnoid —Leptomeninges.

Pial —Pertaining to the pia mater.

Pia mater —The thin, soft and innermost of the three meninges covering the brain and spinal cord.

Pian —Yaws.

Pianists' cramp —Spasm of muscles of fingers and forearm from piano playing.

Piarachnitis —Leptomeningitis.

Piarachnoid —Leptomeninges.

Pica —Desire for eating of unnatural things, *e.g.*, clay etc.

Piceous —Pitchlike.

Pick —1. A sharp, pointed, curved dental instrument. 2. To remove the pieces of food from the teeth.

Pico- —Combining form of the word denoting one trillionth part of the unit to which it is united.

Picometer —One-trillionth of a meter.

Picomole —One-trillionth of a mole.

Picornavirus —A virus of the family Picornaviridae.

Picro-, Picr- —Prefixes meaning bitter.

Pictograph —A set of test pictures used for testing vision in children and illiterate adults.

Piebaldism —A condition in which the skin is partly brown and partly white.

Piebaldness —Piebaldism.

Piedra —A fungus disease of the hair in which hard white or black nodules of fungi form on the shaft of the hairs.

Piesesthesia —Sensitivity to pressure.

Piesimeter, Piesometer —An instrument for measuring the skin's sensitivity to pressure.

-piesis —A suffix which means pressure.

Piezochemistry —The study of the effects of high pressure on chemical reactions.

Piezoelectricity —Electric currents generated by pressure upon certain crystals.

Piezogenic —Resulting from pressure.

Piezometer —Piesimeter.

Pigeon breast —Chicken breast. Deformity of the chest in which the sternum projects anteriorly and the sides of the chest are flattened in rickets, so that the breast looks as that of pigeon.

Pigment —Any coloring matter in the body.

Bile pigment —Any of the coloring matter of bile, *e.g.*, bilirubin and biliverdin, etc.

Blood pigment —Hemoglobin.

Endogenous pigment —Pigment produced within the body, as melanin.

Exogenous pigment —Pigment produced outside the human body.

Hematogenous pigment —Pigment derived from hemoglobin of the red blood cells.

Hepatogenous pigment —Bile pigment.

Skin pigment —Melanin.

Urinary pigment —Urochrome and some times urobilin.

Pigmentary—Pertaining to or like a pigment.

Pigmentation —Coloration due to deposition of pigments.

Pigmented —Colored by deposit of pigments.

Pigmentolysin —A substance which destroys pigment.

Pigmentophage —Any cell, especially of the hair which ingests a pigment.

Pigmentophore —Pigment-carrying cell.

Pigmentum nigrum —Melanin of the choroid coat of the eye.

Pigmy —Pygmy.

Piitis —Inflammation of the pia mater.

Pil —Pill.

Pila —A pillarlike structure in the spongy bone.

Pilae —Plural of pila.

Pilar, Pilary —Pertaining to the hair.

Pile —1. A single hemorrhoid. 2. The hair. 3. A battery for producing electricity.

Pileous —Hairy.

Piles —Hemorrhoids.

Pileum —1. A membrane or a portion of amnion that sometimes covers the head of an infant at birth. 2. Great omentum.

Pileus —1. A cerebellar hemisphere. 2. A membrane covering the head of an infant at birth.

Pili —Hair.

Piliation —Formation and development of hair.

Piliform —Like hair.

Pilimiction —Excretion of urine containing hairlike substances.

Pill —A small globular or oval mass of medicine to be swallowed or chewed.

Pillar —A supporting column.

Pillet —A small pill.

Pillion —A temporary artificial leg.

Pilo- —A prefix meaning hair.

Pilocystic —Encysted and containing hair, as a dermoid cyst.

Piloerection —Erection of hair.

Piloid —Hairlike.

Pilojection —Introduction of hairs into an aneurysm, to form a blood clot.

Pilomatrixoma —A small, firm, calcified, benign tumor of the skin, usually seen on the face, neck or arms.

Pilomotor —Causing movements of the hair.

Pilonidal —Dermoid cyst containing a nidus of hair.

Pilorum —The hair.

Pilose —Hairy; covered with hair.

Pilosebaceous —Pertaining to the hair and sebaceous glands.

Pilosis —Hirsutism. Excessive formation of hair.

Pilosity —Hairness.

Pilous —Covered with hair.

Piltz's reflex —Pupillary reflex. Change in size of the pupil on sudden fixation of attention.

Pilula —A small, spherical mass of medicine.

Pilulae —Plural of pilula.

Pilular —Pertaining to, or of the nature of, pills.

Pilule —A small pill.

Pilus —A hair.

Pimel-, Pimelo- —Prefixes meaning fat or fatty.

Pimelitis —Inflammation of the adipose tissue.

Pimeloma —Lipoma. A fatty tumor.

Pimelopterygium —A fatty outgrowth on the conjunctiva.

Pimelorrhea —Discharge of fats in the loose motions.

Pimelorthopnea —Difficulty in breathing on lying down, due to obesity.

Pimelosis —1. Conversion into fat. 2. Fatty degeneration of any tissue. 3. Fatness or obesity.

Pimeluria —Lipuria. Excretion of fat in the urine.

Pimple —A papule or pustule of the skin.

Pin —A thin, elongated piece of metal or plastic used to secure fixation of parts of the body.

Pin Steinmann —A metal rod used for the internal fixation of the fractures.

Pincement —Pinching of the flesh in massage.

Pinch—To hold the skin or an object between the thumb and index finger.

Pineal —1. Pertaining to the pineal body. 2. Shaped like a pine cone.

Pineal body —It is a small, glandlike structure in the brain, shaped like a pine cone, situated in a pocket, below the splenium of corpus callosum.

Pinealectomy —Excision of the pineal body.

Pineal gland —Pineal body.

Pinealism —The condition caused by abnormal secretion of the pineal body.

Pinealoblastoma —Pineoblastoma.

Pinealocyte —An epitheloid cell of the pineal body.

Pinealoma —A tumor of the pineal body, which is associated with precocious puberty.

Pinealopathy —Any disease of the pineal body or gland.

Pineoblastoma —A blastoma of the pineal body.

Pineocytoma —A malignant tumor of the pineal gland of the brain.

Ping-ponging —The transmission of an infectious disease, especially a sexually transmitted one, between two persons.

Pinguecula —A benign, yellowish, triangular spot on the bulbar conjunctiva, on the inner and outer margins of the cornea.

Pinguicula —Pinguecula.

Pinhole —Small hole made by a pin.

Pinhole os —A very small opening to the uterus from the vagina.

Piniform —Conical.

Pink disease —Acrodynia.

Pinkeye —Acute contagious conjunctivitis.

Pinna —The auricle or the portion of ear outside the head.

Pinnae —Plural of pinna.

Pinnal —Pertaining to the pinna.

Pinocyte —The cell exhibiting pinocytosis.

Pinocytosis —The process by which cells absorb or ingest fluid and nutritive substances.

Pinosome —A vacuole filled with fluid formed within the cell by pinocytosis.

Pint —A unit of measure of liquid which is equal to 20 ounces.

Pinus —Pineal gland.

Pinworm —Threadworm. Enterobius vermicularis.

Pionemia —Lipemia. Presence of excessive amount of fat in the blood.

Piorthopnea —Pimelorthopnea.

Pipet, Pipette —A narrow, thin and graduated tube with both ends open, for measuring and transferring liquids after sucking them, into the tube.

Piptonychia —Falling of the nails.

Piriform —Pyriform. Pear-shaped.

Piscicide —Killing the fishes.

Pisiform —1. Pea-shaped. 2. The smallest carpal bone in the proximal row on the ulnar side.

Pit —Depression.

Pitch —1. The quality of intensity of sound. 2. A black, viscous residue obtained from distillation of tar and other substances.

Pith —1. The center of a hair. 2. The spinal cord and medulla oblongata. 3. To pierce the brain of an animal being prepared for certain experiments, with a sharp instrument.

Pithecoid —Monkeylike.

Pithiatic —Curable by suggestion or persuasion.

Pithiatism —1. Hysteria or other mental disorder produced by suggestion. 2. Curing of the mental disorder by suggestion.

Pithiatric —Pithiatic.

Pithiatry —Treatment of a mental disorder by suggestion.

Pithing —Destruction of the central nervous system by the piercing of brain or spinal cord, done in the experimental animals.

Pithode —The barrel-shaped nuclear spindle formed during cell division.

Pitted —Marked by pits.

Pitting —The formation of pits as seen in smallpox.

Pitting edema —Edema that, when pressed firmly with a finger maintains the depression made by finger, after the finger is removed.

Pituicyte —The primary fusiform cell of the posterior pituitary gland related to neuroglia.

Pituita —A thick nasal secretion.

Pituitarism —Disorder of function of the pituitary gland.

Pituitarium —Pituitary gland.

Pituitary gland —See gland.

Pituitous —Pertaining to mucus.

Pityriasis—A skin disease characterized by the formation of fine branny scales.

- **Pityriasis alba** —Round or oval patches of fine adherent scales and hypopigmentation of the skin of the face, generally seen in children.
- **Pityriasis capitis** —Dandruff.
- **Pityriasis rosea** —Rose red scaly patches.
- **Pityriasis rubra pilaris** —General exfoliative dermatitis.
- **Pityriasis versicolor** —A chronic fungus infection of the skin characterized by colored scaly patches.

Pityroid —Branny, resembling bran.

Pivot —A pillar on which something revolves.

Placebo —An inactive substance given to satisfy the patients, demand for medicine.

Placenta —An oval or discoid spongy structure in the uterus during pregnancy, joining mother and fetus and through which the fetus derives its nourishment.

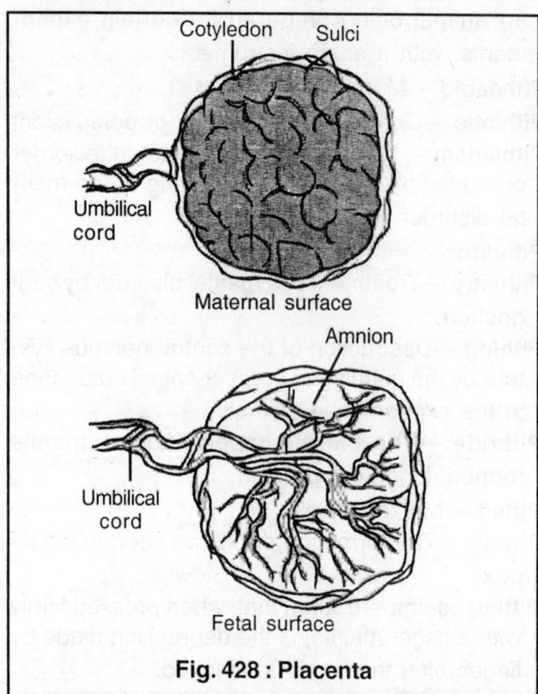

Fig. 428 : Placenta

Abruptio placenta—A placenta prematurely separated from the uterus.

Accessory placenta —An another placenta separate from the main placenta.

Accreta placenta —A placenta which is abnormally embedded into the uterine muscles, so that the separation of placenta is very difficult.

Adherent placenta —The placenta which remains attached to the uterine wall after normal period following childbirth.

Annular placenta —A round placenta like a ring.

Battledore placenta —A placenta in which the umbilical cord is inserted at its margin.

Bilobate placenta —The placenta consisting of two lobes.

Bipartite placenta —The placenta divided into two separate parts.

Central previa placenta —Placenta previa in which the placenta entirely covers the internal os of the cervix of the uterus.

Circinate placenta —Cup-shaped placenta.

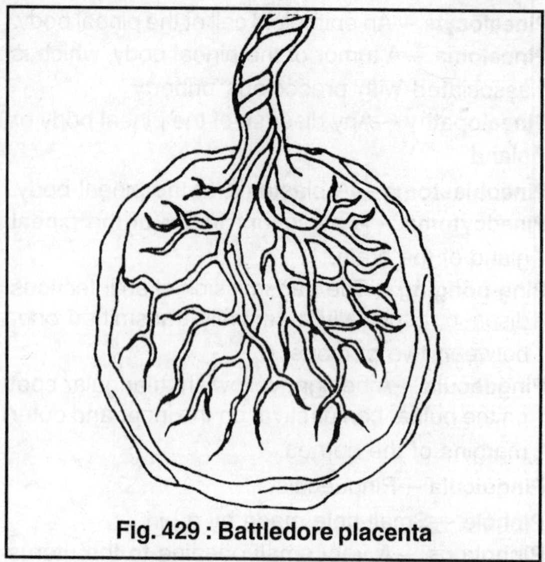

Fig. 429 : Battledore placenta

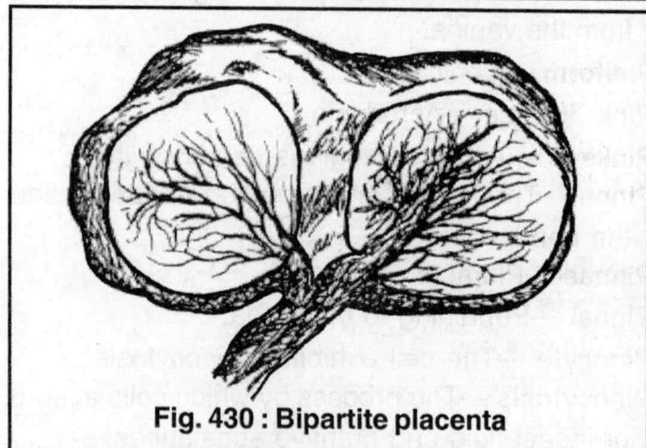

Fig. 430 : Bipartite placenta

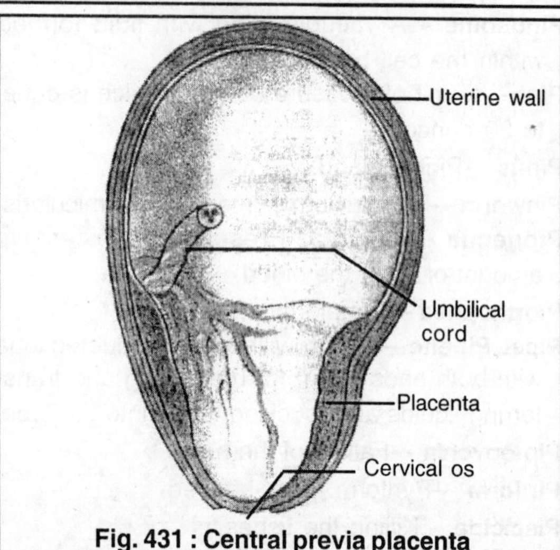

Fig. 431 : Central previa placenta

Circumvallate placenta —A cup-shaped placenta with raised margins.

Cirsoid placenta —Placenta containing varicose veins.

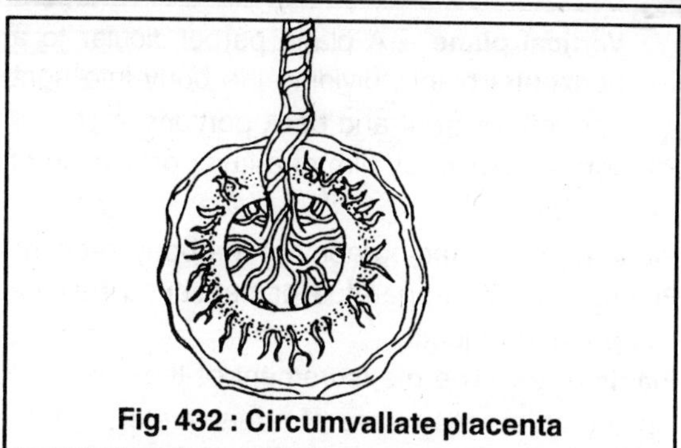

Fig. 432 : Circumvallate placenta

Cordiform placenta —Heart-shaped placenta.

Deciduate placenta —A placenta of which the maternal part escapes with delivery.

Double placenta —A mass of two placentae in a twin pregnancy.

Fenestrata placenta —The presence of only spots in the absence of placenta.

Fetal placenta —The part of placenta formed by aggregation of chorionic villi.

Fundal placenta —Placenta attached to the uterine wall within the fundal region.

Horseshoe placenta —The united placentae of twins.

Incarcerated placenta —The placenta retained in the uterus after delivery.

Increta placenta —A form of accreta placenta in which the chorionic villi penetrate the myometrium.

Lateral placenta —Placenta attached to the lateral wall of the uterus.

Maternal placenta —The portion of the placenta developing from decidua basalis of the uterus.

Membranous placenta —Thin membrane-like placenta.

Multilobate placenta —A placenta with more than three lobes.

Percreta placenta —A form of accreta placenta in which the myometrium invades its peritoneal covering sometimes causing rupture of the uterus.

Placenta previa —The placenta that is implanted in the lower segment of the uterus so that it partially or entirely covers the internal opening of the cervical canal.

Placenta reflexa —Placenta in which the margin is thickened and appears to turn back on itself.

Renifom placenta —Kidney-shaped placenta.

Retained placenta —Placenta not expelled for two hours after the second stage of labor.

Spuria placenta —An extra portion of placenta that has no blood vascular connection with the main placenta.

Succenturiate placenta —An extra portion of the placenta that has blood vascular connection with the main placenta.

Supernumerary placenta —Accessory placenta.

Trilobate placenta —A placenta with three lobes.

Velamentous placenta —A placenta with the umbilical cord attached to the membrane a short distance from the placenta, blood vessels entering the placenta at its margin.

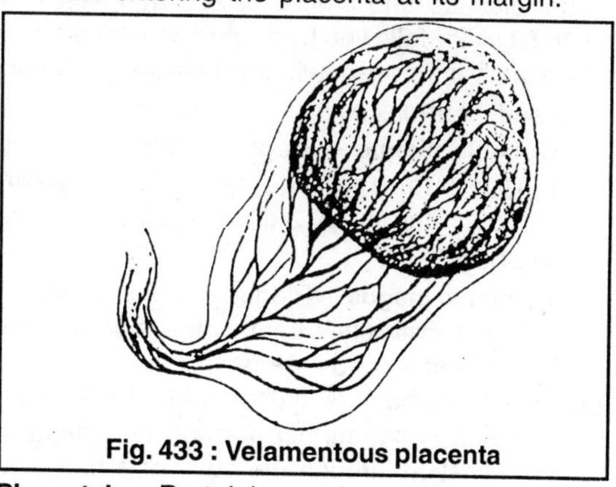

Fig. 433 : Velamentous placenta

Placental —Pertaining to the placenta.

Placental dysmature —Immaturity of the placenta so that normal function does not occur.

Placental souffle—Sound heard over the placenta in pregnancy on auscultation, due to circulation of blood.

Placentation —The process of formation and implantation of placenta in the uterus.

Placentitis —Inflammation of the placenta.

Placentography —X-ray examination of the placenta after injection of a contrast medium.

Placentoid —Like the placenta.

Placentoma —A tumor derived from retained placenta.

Placentotherapy —Treatment of the diseases by placental extract.

Placode —A platelike thickening of ectoderm in the embryo in early stage, from which a sense organ develops.

Placoid —Platelike.

Pladaroma —A soft wartlike growth on the eyelid.

Pladarosis —Pladaroma.

Plagio- —A prefix meaning oblique or slanting.

Plagiocephalic —Affected by or pertaining to plagiocephaly.

Plagiocephalism —Plagiocephaly.

Plagiocephalous —Plagiocephalic.

Plagiocephaly —An asymmetrical twisted condition of the head due to irregular closure of the cranial sutures.

Plague —It is primarily a disease of rats caused by the bacteria Yersinia pestis, from whom it is transmitted to the man through bite of fleas, or communicated from patient to patient. It is highly fatal disease and characterized by chills and fever, quickly followed by marked weakness and frequently threre is delirium, headache, vomiting and diarrhea.

Bubonic plague —Plague in which there is inflammatory enlargement of the lymph glands in the groin, axillae or other parts of the body.

Pulmonic plague —Plague in which lungs are affected, with chill, pain in the side, bloody expectoration and high fever.

Plane —1. Planum. A flat or relatively smooth surface. 2. A flat surface formed by cutting or by imagination through the body or a part of it. 3. To rub away or abrade.

Axial plane —Plane which is parallel to the long axis of the body or of its part.

Coronal or frontal plane —Vertical plane at right angle to a sagittal plane dividing the body into anterior and posterior portions.

Horizontal plane —A transverse plane at right angle to the vertical plane dividing the body into upper and lower parts.

Intraspinous plane —A transverse plane passing through the anterior superior iliac spines.

Median plane —The plane passing longitudinally through the middle of the body from front to back, dividing it into right and left halves.

Sagittal plane —A vertical plane parallel to the median plane or to the sagittal suture, dividing the body into right and left portions.

Transverse plane —A plane perpendicular to the long axis of the body or limbs.

Vertical plane —A plane perpendicular to a horizontal plane, dividing the body into right and left, or front and back portions.

Planigram—An X-ray film of a layer or section of the body.

Planigraphy —Radiography of the body section.

Planimeter —An apparatus for measuring the area of a plane object.

Planimetry —The measurement of the area of a plane object by means of a planimeter.

Planing —Dermabrasion.

Plano-, Plan- —Prefixes meaning a plane, flat, level.

Planocellular —Composed of flat cells.

Planoconcave —Plane on one side and concave on the other.

Planoconvex —Plane on one side and convex on the other.

Planography —Planigraphy.

Planomania —Excessive desire for wandering and to be free of social restraints.

Planotopokinesia —Loss of movements in a space.

Planovalgus —A condition in which the longitudinal arch of the foot is flattened and the heal is everted.

Planta —The sole of the foot.

Plantae —Plural of planta.

Plantalgia —Pain in the sole of the foot.

Plantar —Pertaining to the sole of the foot.

Plantar arch —Arcus plantaris. Vascular arch in the sole of the foot.

Plantar flexion —Flexion of the sole on extension of the foot.

Plantaris —1. Pertaining to the sole of the foot. 2. A long muscle of the calf between gastrocnemius and soleus muscles.

Plantar reflex —Contraction of the toes upon irritation of the sole.

Plantation —Insertion of a tooth in a bony socket.

Plantigrade —Walking by placing the entire sole of foot on the ground.

Planum —Plane.

Planuria —Excretion of urine from an abnormal route of the body.

Plaque —Any patch or flat area.

Fig. 434 : Plaque

Dental plaque —A patch of microorganisms adhering to the enamel surface of a tooth, which may cause dental caries and periodontal disease.

-plasia —A suffix meaning formation, growth.

Plasm- —A prefix meaning living substance.

Plasm —1. Plasma. 2. Formative substance. (protoplasm, cytoplasm etc.)

Plasma —The liquid portion of the blood or of lymph.

Plasmablast —The immature precursor of the plasma cell.

Plasmacrit—Percentage of the volume of the blood sample occupied by plasma.

Plasmacyte —Plasma cell.

Plasmacytoblast —Plasmablast.

Plasmacytoma —A plasma cell myeloma occurring in the bone marrow.

Plasmacytosis —Presence of an excess of plasma cells in the blood.

Plasmagel —The peripheral portion of the endoplasm of a cell.

Plasmalemma — Cell membrane.

Plasmapheresis —The withdrawal of blood from a person, to separate plasma from the blood and then retransfuse the packed red cells to the donor or a patient who requires red blood cells rather than the whole blood.

Plasmapheretic —Pertaining to plasmapheresis.

Plasmasome —A nucleolar substance in the cytoplasm.

Plasmatherapy —Treatment of diseases by using plasma.

Plasmatic —Pertaining to plasma.

Plasmatogamy —The union of the cytoplasm of two or more cells without joining of the nuclei.

Plasmatorrhexis —Rupture of a cell from internal pressure.

Plasmic —Pertaining to porotoplasm.

Plasmid —Any extranuclear genetic element in a cell as found in bacteria.

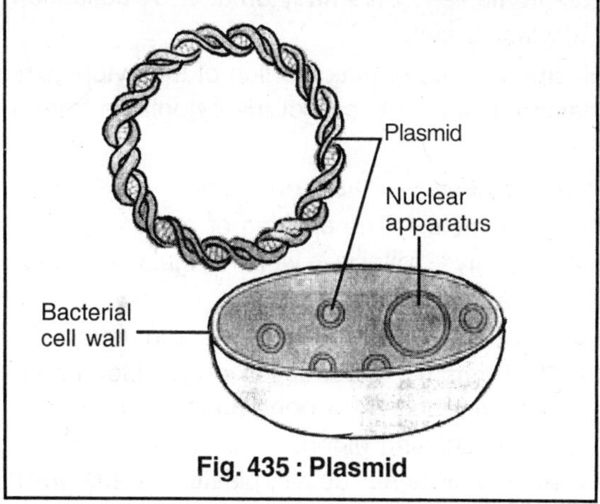

Fig. 435 : Plasmid

Plasmin —An enzyme which dissolves the formed fibrin clots.

Plasminogen —The inactive precursor of plasmin occurring in plasma.

Plasmocyte —Plasma cell. They are increased in plasma cell myeloma.

Plasmocytoma —Plasmacytoma.

Plasmodesma —The cytoplasm connecting the adjacent cells.

Plasmodia —Plural of plasmodium.

Plasmodial —Pertaining to plasmodium.

Plasmodicidal —Malariacidal. Destructive to plasmodia.

Plasmodium —The causative organism of malaria, the malarial parasite which live in red blood cells of man.

Plasmodium falciparum —It causes malignant tertian malaria.

Plasmodium malariae —It causes quartan malaria.

Plasmodium ovale —It causes benign tertian or ovale malaria.

Plasmodium vivax —It causes benign tertian or vivax malaria.

Plasmogamy —The fusion of cells.

Plasmogen —Essential portion of protoplasm.

Plasmology —Histology. The study of the cells and plasma.

Plasmolysis —The contraction of protoplasm of a cell due to loss of water by osmosis.

Plasmolytic —Pertaining to plasmolysis.

Plasmolyzable —Capable of being plasmolyzed.

Plasmolyze —To cause loss of water from the cell by osmosis.

Plasmoma —1. Plasmacytoma. 2. A collection of plasma cells.

Plasmon —The genetic portion of the cytoplasm.

Plasmoptysis —Escape of the cytoplasm from a cell.

Plasmorrhexis —Plasmatorrhexis.

Plasmoschisis —The splitting of a cell.

Plasmotomy —Mitosis in which cytoplasm divides into two or more masses.

Plasmotropic —Pertaining to plasmotropism.

Plasmotropism —Destruction of red blood cells in the liver, spleen or bone marrow rather than in the circulating blood.

Plaster —1. Material, usually plaster of Paris which is mixed with water and applied to a part of the body. On drying it becomes hard and immobilizes that part, so it is used in case of bone fractures or to support a body part in the form of casts or bandage or in dentistry for taking dental impressions. 2. A pastelike preparation of medicines which is spread direct on the skin or on a thick cloth and then on the skin to relieve pain and inflammation, *e.g.,* glycerine belladonna plaster, or for some other purposes. 3. Adhesive plaster—plaster made of a strong cloth coated on one side with an adhesive substance, such as zinc oxide etc., which is used to immobilize a body part, to exert pressure, to secure traction in fractures, to protect the wounds or to hold the dressings in place.

Plastic —1. Capable of being molded. 2. Building up new tissues.

Plasticity —The quality of being plastic.

Plastic surgery —Operation performed for repair of body structures.

Plastogamy —Plasmatogamy.

Plastron —The sternum and the attached cartilages.

-plasty —A suffix which means molding, or formation or repair by surgery.

Plate —1. Lamella or lamina. A thin, flattened structure or part of the body. 2. Dental plate, which is made up of acrylic or some other material fitted to the shape of the mouth and serves to support the artificial teeth. 3. A shallow covered dish for culturing micro-organisms. 4. To inoculate and culture bacteria in a culture plate.

Approximation plate —A dish of decalcified bone used in intestinal surgery.

Auditory plate —Bony roof of the external auditory meatus.

Bite plate —In dentistry, a plate made of some plastic material into which the patient bites with the teeth to have a record of the relationship between upper and lower jaw.

Cribriform plate —A thin, perforated, medial portion of the horizontal plate of the ethmoid bone.

End plate —The terminal mass of a nerve fiber ending on a muscle cell.

Platelet —Thrombocyte. An irregularly shaped structure in the blood, 2 to 4 μm (micrometers) in diameter and 200,000 to 300,000 per cubic m.m. of blood. They play an important role in blood coagulation.

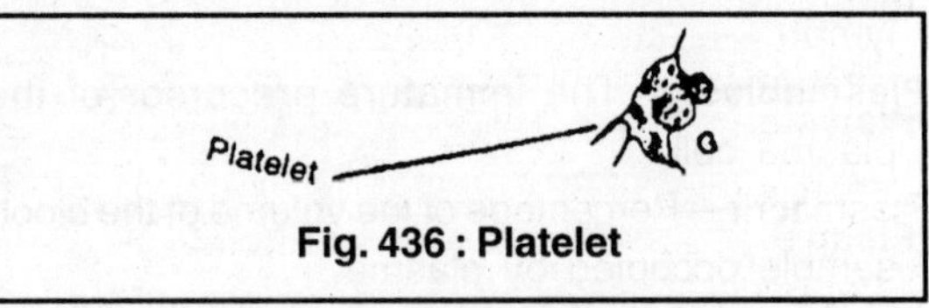

Fig. 436 : Platelet

Plateletpheresis —To receive blood form the donor, to remove its platelets and then retransfuse the remaining portion of blood to the donor.

Plating —1. In bacteriology, culture of bacteria on a solid medium in Petri dish or similar container. 2. To apply a metal bar to keep the ends of a fractured bone in apposition.

Platy- —A prefix which means broad.

Platybasia —A congenital defect of the skull in which the floor of the posterior fossa around the foramen magnum protrudes upward.

Platycelous —Having one surface concave and the other convex.

Platycephalic —Having a wide head.

Platycephalous —Platycephalic.

Platycephaly —Widening of the head.

Platycnemia —Broadening of the leg.

Platycnemic —Having broad leg.

Platycnemism —Platycnemia.

Platycoria —Mydriasis. Dilatation of the pupil.

Platycoriasis —Platycoria.

Platycrania —Platycephaly.

Platyglossal —Having a broad and flat tongue.

Platyhelminth —Any flat-worm.

Platyhelminthes —A phylum of flat worms including the class cestoidea (tapeworms).

Platyhieric —Having a broad sacrum.

Platymeric —Having an unusually broad femur.

Platymorphia —The condition of having a broad eye.

Platyopia —The condition of having very broad face.

Platyopic —Having a very broad face.

Platypellic, Platypelvic —Having a broad pelvis.

Platypelloid —Platypellic.

Platypnea —Difficulty in breathing when erect but relieved by lying down.

Platypodia —Flat-foot.

Platyrrhine —Having a very wide nose.

Platyrrhiny —Platyrrhine.

Platyspondylia —Platyspondylisis.

Platyspondylisis —Flatness of the vertebral bodies.

Platystencephaly —Having a skull wide at the occiput and narrow anteriorly.

Pledget —A small, flat piece of gauze or absorbent cotton used in bandaging, to absorb fluid, to protect or to exclude air.

-plegia —A suffix which means paralysis.

Pleio-, Pleo-, Pilo- —Combining forms which mean more.

Pleiotropia —The quality of a gene to have many effects.

Pleiotropic —A gene having many effects.

Pleiotropism —Pleiotropia.

Pleochroic —Pleochromatic.

Pleochroism —The quality of a crystal to produce different colors when light passes through it at different angles.

Pleochromatic —Pleochroic. Pertaining to pleochroism.

Pleochromatism —Pleochroism.

Pleocytosis —Presence of increased number of lymphocytes in the cerebrospinal fluid.

Pleomastia, Pleomazia —Polymastia. The condition of having more than two mammae.

Pleomorphic —Having many shapes.

Pleomorphism —1. Polymorphism. The occurrence of more than one forms in the life cycle of an organism. 2. The property of crystallizing into two or more different forms.

Pleomorphous —Having many shapes or crystallizing into many forms.

Pleonasm —1. The presence of more than the normal number of organs or parts. 2. To use more words than necessary to express an idea.

Pleonexia —Greediness.

Pleonosteosis —Abnormally increased ossification of bones.

Pleoptics —All forms of treatment, particularly eye exercises for amblyopia.

Pleoptophor —An instrument for the treatment of amblyopia.

Plesio- —A prefix which means nearness or similarity.

Plesiomorphic —Plesiomorphous.

Plesiomorphism —Similarity in form.

Plesiomorphous —Of the same shape.

Plesiopia —Increase in the convexity of eye lens.

Plessesthesia —Palpatory percussion.

Plessimeter —Pleximeter.

Plessimetric —Pertaining to a plessimeter.

Plessor —Plexor.

Plethora —Distention of blood vessels by an excess of blood.

Plethoric —Overfull.

Plethysmograph —An instrument for finding variations in size of an organ or a part of the body due to changes in amount of blood passing through it.

Plethysmography —To find out the changes in size of an organ or part of the body or extremity by means of plethysmograph.

Plethysmometry —Measurement of the fulness of a hollow organ or vessel, as of the pulse.

Pleur-, Pleuro- —Prefixes indicating relation to the pleura, rib or side.

Pleura —Plural is pleurae. Serous membrane investing the lungs (pulmonary pleura) and lining the walls of the thoracic cavity (parietal pleura). The space between the two pleurae is known as pleural cavity. The pleurae are moistened with their serous secretion that reduces friction during respiration.

Pleuracentesis —Thoracentesis.

Pleuracotomy —To make an incision into the pleura through the chest wall.

Pleurae —Plural of pleura.

Pleural —Pertaining to the pleura.

Pleural crackles —Sounds heard on auscultation of the chest as a result of inflammation of the pleura with fibrinous exudate.

Pleuralgia —Intercostal neuralgia. Pain in the pleura or in the side.

Pleurapophysis —A rib or a vertebral lateral process.

Pleurectomy —Excision of a part of the pleura.

Pleurisy —Inflammation of the pleura. It may be acute or chronic, primary or secondary, unilateral, bilateral or local.

Acute pleurisy —Acute inflammation of the pleura characterized by chilliness, pain in the affected side of the chest which is intensified by coughing or deep breathing, fever and cough.

Adhesive pleurisy —Pleurisy in which the exudate causes both the pleurae to adhere with each other so that the pleural space is obliterated.

Bilateral pleurisy —Double pleurisy. Inflammation of the pleura on both sides of the chest.

Chronic pleurisy —Chronic inflammation of the pleura.

Diaphragmatic pleurisy —Inflammation limited to the diaphragmatic pleura.

Dry pleurisy —Pleurisy in which the pleural membrane is covered with fibrinous exudate. During respiration the pleurae rub together and cause pain.

Fibrinous pleurisy —Pleurisy in which large amounts of fibrin is deposited in the pleural cavity.

Hemorrhagic pleurisy —Pleurisy with hemorrhage.

Interlobar pleurisy —Inflammation of the pleural membranes between lobes of the lung.

Plastic pleurisy —Dry pleurisy.

Purulent pleurisy —Empyema. Suppurative pleurisy. Pleurisy in which pus in formed.

Serofibrinous pleurisy —Pleurisy with fibrinous exudate and serous effusion.

Serous pleurisy —Pleurisy with serous effusion.

Suppurative pleurisy —Purulent pleurisy.

Tuberculous pleurisy —Inflammation of the pleura due to tuberculosis.

Wet pleurisy with effusion —Serous pleurisy.

Pleuritic —Pertaining to, or like, or suffering from pleurisy.

Pleuritis —Pleurisy.

Pleuritogenous —Causing pleurisy.

Pleurocele —Hernia of the lung tissue or of pleura.

Pleurocentesis —Thoracentesis. Thoracocentesis.

Pleurocentrum —The lateral half of the centrum of a vertebra.

Pleurocholecystitis —Inflammation of the pleura and gallbladder.

Pleuroclysis —Injection of fluid into the pleural cavity and its washing.

Pleurodesis —Surgical formation of adhesions between the parietal and visceral layers of pleura.

Pleurodynia —Pain occurring in the intercostal muscles.

Pleurogenic —Pleurogenous. Arising in the pleura.

Pleurogenous —Pleurogenic.

Pleurogram —An X-ray film of the lungs and pleurae.

Pleurography —X-ray examination of the lungs and pleurae.

Pleurohepatitis —Inflammation of the pleura and liver.

Pleurolith —A calculus in the pleura.

Pleurolysis —Surgical separation of pleura from its adhesions.

Pleuromelus —A congenital defect in which an accessory limb arises from the thorax or flank.

Pleuroparietopexy—Fixation of the lung to the chest wall by adhesion of the parietal and visceral pleura.

Pleuropericardial —Pertaining to the pleura and pericardium.

Pleuropericarditis —Pleuritis with pericarditis.

Pleuroperitoneal—Pertaining to the pleura and peritoneum.

Pleuroperitoneal cavity —Celom. Body cavity.

Pleuropneumonectomy —Removal of a destroyed lung with its parietal pleura in pulmonary tuberculosis, by surgery.

Pleuropneumonia —Pleurisy complicated by pneumonia.

Pleuropulmonary —Pertaining to the pleura and the lung.

Pleurorrhea —Discharge of fluid from the pleura.

Pleuroscopy —Visual examination of the pleural cavity through an incision into the thorax.

Pleurosoma —A fetus with a cleft in its thorax and abdomen through which thoracic and abdominal organs protrude.

Pleurothotonos —Tetanus-like bending of the body to one side.

Pleurotomy —To make an incision into the pleura.

Pleurotyphoid —Typhoid fever with involvement of the pleura.

Pleurovisceral —Pertaining to the pleura and viscera.

Plexal —Pertaining to, or of the nature of, a plexus.

Plexectomy —Surgical removal of a plexus.

Plexiform —Resembling a plexus.

Pleximeter —Plessimeter. A disk held over the surface of the body during percussion which bears the stroke of the percussing finger or hammer.

Plexitis —Inflammation of a nerve plexus.

Plexogenic —Producting a plexus or plexiform structure.

Plexometer —Pleximeter.

Plexopathy —Any disease of a plexus, especially of nerves.

Plexor —Plessor. Hammer or other instrument used for striking upon the pleximeter in percussion.

Plexus—A network of nerves, blood vessels or lymphatic vessels.

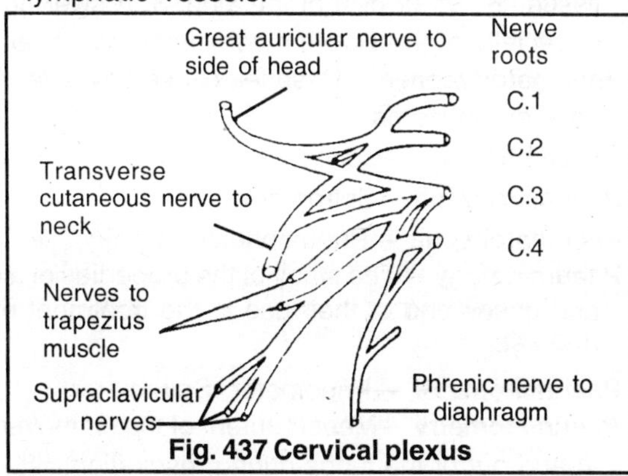

Fig. 437 Cervical plexus

Pliability —Capability of being bent or twisted easily.

Plica —A fold.

Plicate —Folded.

Plication —The stitching of folds in the walls of an organ to reduce its size.

Plicotomy —Surgical division of the posterior fold of the tympanic membrane.

Pliers —Pincers.

Plinth —The elevated plane portion of the floor where the patient sits while doing exercises.

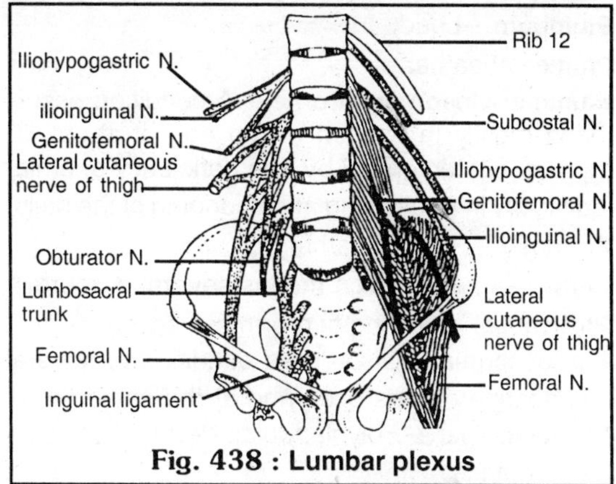

Fig. 438 : Lumbar plexus

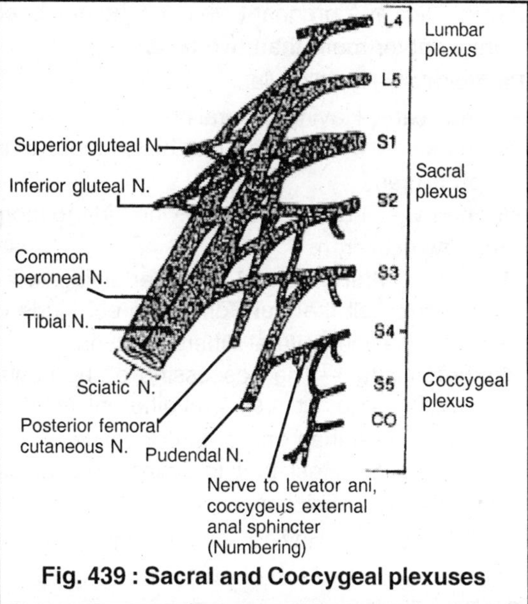

Fig. 439 : Sacral and Coccygeal plexuses

-ploid —A suffix indicating the number of chromosome pairs of the former word to which its is added.

Ploidy —The number of chromosome sets in a cell, *e.g.*, haploidy, diploidy, and triploidy for one, two and three sets respectively, of chromosomes.

Plombage —The filling of a space or cavity with an inert material.

Plug —A mass of a material that obstructs an opening, *e.g.*, a mass of mucus that closes the cervical canal during pregnancy.

Plugger —An instrument for compacting the filling material in a dental cavity.

Plumbic —Pertaining to, or containing lead.

Plumbism —Chronic lead poisoning.

Plumbum —Lead.

Plume —Feather.

Plummer-vinson syndrome —A condition occurring mostly in women at the age of about 40 years, characterized by iron deficiency anemia, difficulty in swallowing and spooning of the nails.

Plumose —Having feathery growth.

Pluri- —A prefix which means several or more.

Pluricausal —Having two or more causes.

Pluridyscrinia —Disordered condition of several endocrine organs occurring at the same time.

Pluriglandular —Polyglandular. Pertaining to several glands.

Plurigravida —A pregnant woman who has been pregnant for more than two times.

Plurilocular —Multilocular.

Plurinuclear —Having several nuclei.

Pluripara —A woman who has borne more than two children.

Pluriparity —The condition of giving birth to more than two children.

Pluripotent, Pluripotential —1. Pertaining to an embryonic cell that can form different kinds of cells. 2. Having several different actions.

Pluripotentiality —The possessing of the power to develop or to act in several different ways, or to affect more than one organ or tissue.

Pluriresistant —Resistant to several drugs, especially the antibiotics.

Plurisegmental —Having several segments.

Plutomania —Delusion of being rich.

P.M.S. —Premenstrual syndrome.

P.M.T. —Premenstrual tension syndrome.

-pnea —A suffix which means respiration or breathing.

Pneo- —A prefix which means pertaining to breath or breathing.

Pneocardiac reflex —Change occurring in cardiac rate and rhythm on smelling an irritant gas.

Pneodynamics —Pneumodynamics. The mechanism of breathing.

Pneogram —Spirogram.

Pneograph —Spirograph.

Pneometer —Spirometer.

Pneophore —An instrument to aid artificial respiration.

Pneopneic reflex —Change occurring in respiratory rate and depth on smelling an irritant gas.

Pneoscope —An apparatus for measuring movements of respiration.

Pneum-, Pneuma-, Pneumato- —Prefixes which mean pertaining to air or gas, or respiration.

Pneumarthrogram —X-ray film of a joint after an injection of air or gas into the joint as a contrast medium.

Pneumarthrography —X-ray examination of a joint after an injection of air or gas into the joint as a contrast medium.

Pneumarthrosis —Accumulation of air or gas in a joint.

Pneumascope —Pneumatoscope.

Pneumatic —Pertaining to air, gas or respiration.

Pneumatics —A branch of physics dealing with the air and gases.

Pneumatinuria —Excretion of urine containing free gas.

Pneumatization —The formation of air-filled cells or cavities in the tissue, especially in the mastoid portion of temporal bone.

Pneumatized —Filled with air.

Pneumatocardia —Presence of air or gas in the cardiac chambers.

Pneumatocele —Pneumocele. 1. Hernia of lung tissue. 2. An air cyst of the lung. 3. A swelling, especially of the scrotum containing gas or air.

Pneumatodyspnea —Dyspnea caused by pulmonary emphysema.

Pneumatogram —Spirogram.

Pneumatograph —Spirograph.

Pneumatohemia —Pneumohemia.

Pneumatology —The study of the properties of air and gases and of their use in the treatment of diseases.

Pneumatometer —Pneometer. Spirometer.

Pneumatometry —Measurement of the air moved in and out of the lungs during respiration.

Pneumatorrhachis —Presence of air or gas in the vertebral canal.

Pneumatoscope —1. An apparatus used to measure gas in the expired air. 2. Pneumascope. An instrument for measuring the movements of respiration.

Pneumatosis —Presence of air or gas in an abnormal site in the body.

Pneumatosis cystoides intestinalis —A condition characterized by the presence of thin-walled gas-filled cysts in the wall of the intestine.

Pneumatotherapy —1. Treatment of diseases by use of air. 2. Treatment of lung diseases.

Pneumatothorax —Pneumothorax.

Pneumaturia —Pneumatinuria.

Pneumatype —An apparatus used to determine the patency of the nasal fossae, by observing the deposit of moisture on a glass plate, from the breath exhaled through the nostrils with the mouth closed.

Pneumectomy —Pneumonectomy.

Pneumo-, Pneumono- —Prefixes meaning air or lung.

Pneumoangiogram —X-ray film of the vessels of the lungs obtained after introducing a contrast medium into the lungs.

Pneumoangiography —X-ray examination of the vessels of the lungs after introducing a contrast medium into the lungs.

Pneumoarthrography —Pneumarthrography.

Pneumobulbar —Pertaining to the lungs and the respiratory center situated in the medulla oblongata of the brain.

Pneumocardial —Pertaining to the lungs and the heart.

Pneumocele —Pneumatocele.

Pneumocentesis —Surgical puncture of the pleural cavity.

Pneumocephalus —Having the head with air or gas in the intracranial cavity.

Pneumocholecystitis —Inflammation of the gallbladder with gas in it.

Pneumococcal —Pertaining to or caused by pneumococci.

Pneumococcemia —Presence of pneumococci in the blood.

Pneumococci —Plural of pneumococcus.

Pneumococcidal —Destroying pneumococci.

Pneumococcolysis —Destruction or lysis of pneumococci.

Pneumococcosis —Infection with pneumococci.

Pneumococcosuria—Presence of pneumococci in the urine.

Pneumococcus —Streptococcus pneumoniae. An oval-shaped, encapsulated, gram-positive bacterium occurring usually in pairs, which causes pneumonia, bronchitis, meningitis and otitis media, etc.

Pneumocolon —Colon filled with air.

Pneumoconiosis —Any lung disease such as silicosis caused by inhalation of dust particles and their deposition in the lungs. It is an occupational disease which generally occurs in mine workers and stonecutters.

Pneumocranium —Pneumocephalus.

Pneumocystography —X-ray examination of the urinary bladder after introducing air or gas into it.

Pneumocystosis —Pneumocystis carinii pneumonia.

Pneumocyte —An alveolar cell of the lung.

Pneumoderma —Emphysema under the skin.

Pneumodynamics —Dynamics of the respiratory process.

Pneumoempyema —Pus in the pleural cavity with accumulation of gas.

Pneumoencephalitis—Inflammation of the lung and the brain.

Pneumoencephalogram —X-ray film of the brain obtained by pneumoencephalography.

Pneumoencephalography —X-ray examination of the fluid-containing structures of the brain after withdrawing cerebrospinal fluid by lumbar puncture and replacing it by air.

Pneumoenteritis —Presence of both pneumonia and enteritis.

Pneumogalactocele —A tumor of the breast, containing milk and gas.

Pneumogastric—Pertaining to the lungs and stomach.

Pneumogastrography —X-ray examination of the stomach after air has been introduced into it.

Pneumogram —1. Pneumatogram. An X-ray film of the lungs after an injection of air. 2. A record of the respiratory movements.

Pneumograph —An apparatus for recording the frequency and intensity of respiration.

Pneumography —1. Anatomical description of the lungs. 2. Recording of the respiratory movements on a graph. 3. X-ray examination of an organ or part of the body after air or a gas is injected.

Pneumohemia —Presence of air or gas in the blood vessels.

Pneumohemopericardium —Air or gas and blood in the pericardium.

Pneumohemothorax —Air or gas and blood accumulated in the pleural cavity.

Pneumohydrometra —The accumulation of gas and water in the uterus.

Pneumohydropericardium —Air and fluid accumulated in the pericardium.

Pneumohydroperitoneum—Hydropneumoperitoneum.

Pneumohydrothorax—Air or gas with fluid in the thoracic cavity.

Pneumohypoderma —Air in the tissues under the skin.

Pneumokidney —Air in the pelvis of the kidney.

Pneumolith —A calculus present in a lung.

Pneumolithiasis—Formation of calculi in the lungs.

Pneumology —The science of diseases of the lungs and air passages.

Pneumolysin —A hemolytic toxin produced by pneumococci.

Pneumolysis —Pneumonolysis. Separation of the adherent lung from the chest wall.

Pneumomalacia—Abnormal softening of the lung.

Pneumomassage —The massage of the middle ear with air.

Pneumomediastinum —Presence of air or gas in the tissues of the mediastinum, which may be due to some disease or introduced by injection for diagnostic purpose.

Pneumomelanosis —Pigmentation of the lungs seen in pneumoconiosis.

Pneumometer —Spirometer. Pneometer.

Pneumomycosis —Pneumonomycosis. A fungal disease of the lungs.

Pneumomyelography —X-ray examination of the spinal cord after withdrawal of the cerebrospinal fluid and injection of air or gas.

Pneumon —The lungs.

Pneumonectasia, Pneumonectasis —Distention of the lungs with air.

Pneumonectomy —Pneumectomy. Pulmonectomy. Surgical removal of a part or of all of a lung.

Pneumonia —Inflammation of the lungs with consolidation caused by bacteria, viruses or chemical irritants. It is characterized by chills, high fever, pain in the chest and cought.

Abortive pneumonia —Mild pneumonia of short duration.

Acute pneumonia—See lobar pneumonia.

Alba pneumonia —A fatal pneumonia of the newborn due to congenital syphilis.

Alcoholic pneumonia —Pneumonia occurring in an alcoholic, usually after taking a large amount of alcohol.

Aspiration pneumonia —Pneumonia due to inhalation of foreign material into the lungs.

Bilious pneumonia —Pneumonia occurring following aspiration of gastric contents containing bile.

Bronchopneumonia —The disease of infants and young children due to mixed bacterial infection of the terminal bronchioles, may occur as a complication of measles and whooping cough etc.

Chemical pneumonia —Pneumonia occurring after inhalation of a toxic gas, such as chlorine.

Chronic interstitial pneumonia —Chronic pneumonia with overgrowth of the fibrous tissue, characterized by chronic cough with expectoration associated with mild dyspnea.

Desquamative interstitial pneumonia —Pneumonia accompanied by fibrosis of the pulmonary interstitial tissue, characterized by cough, progressive dyspnea and clubbing of the fingers.

Double pneumonia —Pneumonia involving both the lungs.

Embolic pneumonia —Pneumonia following pulmonary embolism.

Eosinophilic pneumonia —Pneumonia occurring in eosinophilia.

Fibrous pneumonia —Pneumonia followed by the formation of scar tissue.

Friedlander's pneumonia —A form of lobar pneumonia caused by the specific organism Klebsiella pneumoniae.

Gangrenous pneumonia —Pneumonia occurring in pulmonary gangrene.

Hypostatic pneumonia —Pneumonia occurring in an elderly, or a weak person remaining constantly in the same position, due to congestion of blood in one part of the lung caused by gravity, and development of infection in the blood.

Influenzal pneumonia —A severe form of pneumonia associated with influenza, which may be fatal.

Lobar pneumonia —An acute pneumonia caused by pneumococcus and marked by inflammation of one or more lobes of the lungs, followed by consolidation.

Lobular pneumonia —Bronchopneumonia.

Primary atypical pneumonia —A mild pneumonia caused by Mycoplasma pneumoniae and characterized by pharyngitis, cough and fever.

Secondary pneumonia —Pneumonia occurring as a complication of other diseases such as typhoid, smallpox and diphtheria etc.

Septic pneumonia —Suppurative pneumonia.

Suppurative pneumonia —Pneumonia with the formation of pus in the lungs.

Traumatic pneumonia —Pneumonia occurring after an injury to the lung or the thorax.

Tuberculous pneumonia —Pneumonia caused by the bacterium Mycobacterium tuberculosis.

Pneumonic —Pertaining to the lungs or to pneumonia.

Pneumonitis —Pneumonia. Inflammation of the lung.

Pneumono- —A prefix which means pertaining to the lung.

Pneumonocele —Pneumatocele. Pneumocele.

Pneumonocentesis —Pneumocentesis.

Pneumonococcal —Pertaining to the bacteria Streptococcus pneumoniae.

Pneumonococcus —Streptococcus pneumoniae.

Pneumonoconiosis —Pneumoconiosis.

Pneumonocyte —An alveolar cell of the lungs.

Pneumonolysis —Pneumolysis.

Pneumonomelanosis—Pneumomelanosis. Dark pigmentation of the lung due to inhalation of the black dust particles such as coal dust.

Pneumonomycosis —Pneumomycosis.

Pneumonopathy —Any disease of the lung.

Pneumonoperitonitis —Inflammation of the peritoneum with gas in the peritoneal cavity.

Pneumonopexy—Pneumopexy. Surgicial attachment of a lung to the chest wall.

Pneumonopleuritis —Pneumopleuritis. Inflammation of the lungs and pleura.

Pneumonorrhaphy —Suture of the lung.

Pneumonosis —Any lung disease.

Pneumonotherapy —Pneumotherapy.

Pneumonotomy —Pneumotomy.

Pneumopathy —Pneumonopathy.

Pneumopericardium —Air or gas in the pericardial cavity.

Pneumoperitoneography —X-ray examination of the peritoneum and internal organs after introducing air into the peritoneal cavity.

Pneumoperitoneum —Presence of air or gas in the peritoneal cavity.

Pneumoperitonitis —Peritonitis with accumulation of air or gas in the peritoneal cavity.

Pneumopexy —Pneumonopexy.

Pneumophagia —Aerophagia.

Pneumopleuritis—Inflammation of the lungs and pleura.

Pneumopyelography —X-ray examination of the renal pelvis and ureters after introducing oxygen or air into the renal pelvis by injection.

Pneumopyopericardium —Air, gas and pus accumulated in the pericardial cavity.

Pneumopyothorax —Air and pus collected in the pleural cavity.

Pneumoradiography —X-ray examination of a part of the body after an injection of air or oxygen given to it.

Pneumoresection —Excision of a part of a lung.

Pneumoretroperitoneum —Accumulation of air or gas in the retroperitoneal space.

Pneumoroentgenography—Pneumography.

Pneumorrhachis —Accumulation of air or gas in the vertebral canal.

Pneumorrhagia —Hemoptysis. Hemorrhage from the lungs.

Pneumoscope —Pneumatoscope.

Pneumoserothorax —Air or gas and serum collected in the pleural cavity.

Pneumosilicosis—Silicosis.

Pneumotachograph —An instrument for recording the velocity of inspiration and expiration of air.

Pneumotachometer —An instrument for measuring the flow of the expired air.

Pneumotaxic —Regulating the respiratory rate.

Pneumotherapy —Pneumonotherapy. 1. Treatment of the lung diseases. 2. Treatment of diseases by air or gases.

Pneumothermomassage —Application of hot air to the body.

Pneumothorax —A collection of air or gas in the pleural cavity which may occur spontaneously,

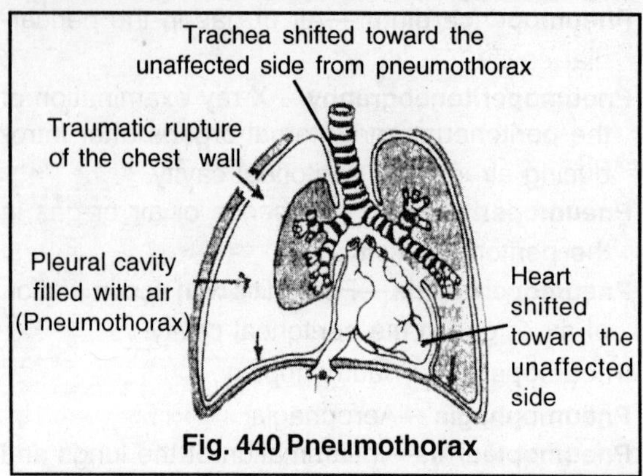

Fig. 440 Pneumothorax

or due to some disease, due to some injury or be introduced artificially as performed in the treatment of pulmonary tuberculosis.

Pneumotomy —To make an incision into the lung.

Pneumotoxin —A toxin produced by pneumococcus.

Pneumotyphus —Typhoid fever with pneumonia.

Pneumoventricle —Accumulation of air in the cerebral ventricles.

Pneumoventriculography —X-ray examination of the cerebral ventricles after removal of their fluid and giving injection of air or gas.

Pneusis —Panting. Short, shallow and rapid respiration.

Pnigophobia —Morbid fear of choking, as sometimes experienced in angina pectoris.

P.O. —Per os. By mouth; orally.

Pock —A pustule, especially of smallpox.

Pocket —A saclike cavity, *e.g.*, periodontal pocket.

Pock mark —A depressed scar left by a pustule.

Pock marked —Pitted or having depressed scars left by pustules, especially from smallpox.

Poculum —Cup.

Podagra —Gouty pain in the great toe.

Podagral, Podagric, Podagrous —Pertaining to or characterized by podagra.

Podalgia —Pain in the feet.

Podalic —Pertaining to the feet.

Podarthritis —Inflammation of the joints of the feet.

Podedema —Edema of the feet and ankles.

Podencephalus —A fetus whose brain is outside the skull and is attached by a thin pedicle.

Podiatric —Pertaining to podiatry.

Podiatrist —Chiropodist.

Podiatry — Chiropody

Podismus —Podospasm.

Poditis —Inflammation of the foot.

Podium —A footlike process.

Podo-, Pod- —Prefixes meaning foot.

Podobromidrosis —Offensive sweating from the feet.

Podocyte —A special epithelial cell of the visceral layer of a glomerulus of the kidney, having a number of footlike radiating processes (pedicles).

Pododynamometer —An apparatus for determining the strength of leg and foot muscles.

Pododynia —Neuralgic pain in the heel and sole.

Podogram —An imprint of sole of the foot.

Podograph —An apparatus for taking an imprint of sole of the foot.

Podologist —Podiatrist or chiropodist.

Podology —Podiatry.

Podomechanotherapy —Treatment of foot diseases by mechanical means, e.g., arch supports etc.

Podometer —Pedometer. An instrument for measuring the distance covered in walking.

Podospasm —Podismus.

Pogoniasis —Excessive growth of the beard or growth of a beard in a woman.

Pogonion —Anterior midpoint of the chin.

-poiesis —A suffix which means formation or production.

Poikiloblast —A nucleated red blood cell of irregular shape.

Poikilocyte —A large and irregular-shaped red blood cell.

Poikilocythemia —Poikilocytosis.

Poikilocytosis —Presence of poikilocytes in the blood.

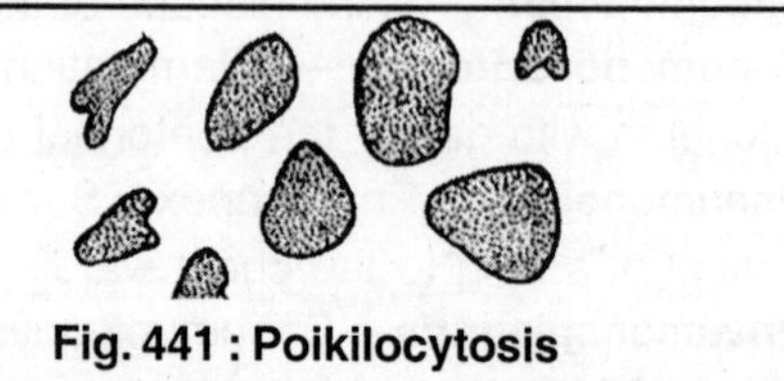

Fig. 441 : Poikilocytosis

Poikilodentosis —Mottling of the teeth, usually due to an excess of fluoride in the drinking water.

Poikiloderma —A condition of the skin characterized by pigmentation, telangiectasia, purpura, pruritus and atrophy.

Poikilotherm —Allotherm. A cold blooded animal. An animal whose body temperature changes according to the temperature of the environment.

Poikilothermal, Poikilothermic —Pertaining to poikilothermy.

Poikilothermic —Poikilothermal.

Poikilothermous —Poikilothermal.

Poikilothermy —The condition of having a body temperature which varies according to that of the environment.

Poikilothrombocyte —A platelet cell of abnormal shape.

Point —1. A minute spot. 2. The sharp end of an object. 3. To approach the surface as the pus of an abscess approaches a definite spot. 4. Position in a place, time or degree.

Boiling point —The temperature at which a liquid boils.

Contact point —The point on a tooth that touches the opposite tooth.

Craniometric point —One of the fixed points of the skull used in craniometry.

Critical point of gases —The temperature at which a gas is no longer liquefied by pressure.

Critical point of liquids —The temperature at which no pressure may retain a substance in a liquid form.

Dew point —The atmospheric temperature at which moisture begins to be condensed and deposited as dew.

Fixation point —The point at which the vision is fixed.

Focal point —The point at which a group of light rays converge.

Freezing point —The temperature at which liquid becomes solid.

Fusion point —Melting point. The temperature at which the solid liquefies.

Mc Burney's point —A point ½ to 2 inches from the right anterior superior iliac spine on the line between this spine and the umbilicus where tenderness is produced by pressing with the fingers, in acute appendicitis.

Melting point —Fusion point. The temperature at which a solid becomes a liquid.

Mental point —Pogonion.

Neutral point —That point at which a solution is neither acidic nor alkaline, *i.e.*, pH 7.

Occipital point —The most posterior point on the occipital bone.

Pointillage —Massage with finger tips.

Pointing —Reaching a point.

Poise —The unit of viscosity.

Poison —Any substance taken into the body by ingestion, inhalation, application or injection, or developed within the body, that interferes with the normal physiological functions or causes structural damage.

Poisoning —1. The morbid condition produced by introduction of a poison into the body. 2. Administration of a poison.

Blood poisoning —Septicemia.

Corrosive poisoning —Poisoning caused by ingestion of strong acids or alkalies etc.

Food poisoning —Poisoning resulting from ingestion of food containing poisonous substances.

Poisonous —Toxic. Having the properties of a poison.

Poker back —Stiff back due to spondylitis or rheumatoid arthritis.

Polar —Pertaining to a pole.

Polarimeter —An instrument for measuring the amount of polarization of light or the rotation of polarized light.

Polarimetry —The measurement of the amount of polarization of light or the rotation of polarized light.

Polariscope—An apparatus used for measuring the polarized light.

Polariscopic —Pertaining to the polariscope or polariscopy.

Polariscopy —Study of the polarized light by polariscope.

Polarity —1. The quality of having poles. 2. Exhibition of opposite effects at the two extremities in physical therapy. 3. In cell division, the relation of cell constituents to the poles of the cell.

Polarization —The condition in a ray of light in which its vibrations are parallel to each other in only one plane.

Polarize —To put into a state of polarization.

Polarizer —An apparatus for polarizing light.

Pole —1. Polus. Either extremity of any axis, as of a body organ. 2. Either one of the two points in a magnet, cell or battery which have opposite physical properties.

Polio- —A prefix indicating relation to the gray matter of the nervous system.

Polioclastic —Destroying the gray matter of the nervous system.

Poliodystrophia—Poliodystrophy.

Poliodystrophy —Atrophy of the gray matter of the cerebrum.

Polioencephalitis —Inflammatory disease of the gray matter of the brain.

Polioencephalomeningomyelitis —Inflammation of the gray matter of the brain and spinal cord and of their meninges.

Polioencephalomyelitis —Inflammation of the gray matter of the brain and spinal cord.

Polioencephalopathy —Any disease of the gray matter of the brain.

Poliomyelencephalitis —Poliomyelitis and polioencephalitis combined.

Poliomyelitis —An acute viral inflammation of the gray matter of the spinal cord, occurring in children chiefly between 2 to 5 years of age. It is characterized by fever, sore throat, headache, vomiting and stiffness of the neck and back and in severe cases by paralysis and atrophy of the muscles of the lower extremities ending in contraction and permanent deformity.

Abortive poliomyelitis —Mild poliomyelitis without involvement of the central nervous system.

Acute anterior poliomyelitis —An acute viral inflammation of anterior horns of the gray matter of the spinal cord. In minor or abortive type, which lasts only a few days, there is no paralysis of the extremities. In the major type, weakness or paralysis of the muscles of the lower extremities occurs.

Ascending poliomyelitis —Poliomyelitis in which paralysis begins in the lower extremities and progresses upwards.

Bulbar poliomyelitis —A severe form of poliomyelitis affecting the gray matter of medulla oblongata resulting in paralysis of the respiratory muscles and respiratory failure.

Chronic anterior poliomyelitis —Poliomyelitis in which there is progressive wasting of the muscles.

Nonparalytic poliomyelitis —Poliomyelitis in which there is no paralysis of the muscles.

Paralytic poliomyelitis —Poliomyelitis in which paralysis of the muscles of the lower extremities occurs.

Poliomyeloencephalitis —Poliomyelitis with encephalitis.

Poliomyelopathy —Any disease of the gray matter of the spinal cord.

Polioplasm —Granular protoplasm.

Poliosis—Canities. Premature whiteness of the hair.

Poliovirus —A virus causing poliomyelitis.

Politzer bag —A rubber bag with a rubber tip for inflating the middle ear by increasing pressure in the nasopharynx.

Politzerization —Inflation of the middle ear by means of a politzer bag.

Pollakiuria —Excretion of the urine frequently.

Pollen —The male gametophyte (gamete-producing) of the flowering plants, which develops in anther at the tip of stamen.

Pollenogenic —Caused by the pollens or producing pollens.

Pollenosis —Pollinosis.

Pollex —The thumb.

Pollex extensus —Backward deviation of the thumb.

Pollex flexus —Permanent flexion of the thumb.

Pollex valgus —Deviation of the thumb toward the ulnar side.

Pollex varus —Deviation of the thumb toward the radial side.

Pollices —Plural of pollex.

Pollicization —Surgical construction of a thumb from the adjacent tissues.

Pollinosis —Hay fever. Congestion of the nasal mucous membrance due to contact with pollen.

Pollodic —Pertaining to the nerve stimuli originating from one center.

Pollutant —An agent causing pollution.

Polluted —Defiled or dirty.

Pollution —The process of making dirty, or defiling.

Polocyte —A small cell containing a little amount of cytoplasm and a nucleus resulting from the division of the primary oocyte (first polar body) and if fertilization occurs, of the secondary oocyte (second polar body).

Poltophagy —Thorough chewing of food so that it is reduced to very small pieces.

Polus —Pole. The extremity of an organ.

Poly- —A prefix indicating many or much.

Polyadenitis —Inflammation of many glands.

Polyadenomatosis —Adenomas occurring in many glands.

Polyadenopathy —Any disease of the glands.

Polyadenosis —Disorder of many glands, especially the endocrine glands.

Polyadenous —Affecting or pertaining to many glands.

Polyalgesia —A single stimulus of a part, producing sensation in many parts.

Polyandry —The practice of having more than one husband at a time.

Polyangiitis —Inflammation of many blood or lymph vessels.

Polyarteritis —Inflammation of many arteries.

Polyarteritis nodosa —Inflammation of the medium-sized and small arteries with the formation of small aneurysms.

Polyarthralgia —Pain in several joints.

Polyarthric —Affecting or pertaining to several joints.

Polyarthritis —Inflammation of several joints.

Polyarticular —Multiarticular. Affecting several joints.

Polyatomic —Made up of several atoms.

Polyavitaminosis —Deficiency of more than one vitamin.

Polybasic —Having several replaceable hydrogen atoms.

Polyblast —Large mononuclear phagocyte.

Polyblennia —Excessive secretion of mucus.

Polycardia —Tachycardia.

Polycentric —Condition of having many centers.

Polycheiria —Having more than two hands.

Polychemotherapy —Treatment of a disease with several medicines at once.

Polycholia —Excessive secretion of bile.

Polychondritis —Inflammation of many cartilages of the body.

Polychrest —A medicine useful in many diseases.

Polychromasia —The quality of having many colors.

Polychromatic —Multicolored.

Polychromatocyte —A cell staining with various kinds of stain.

Polychromatophil —A structure staining with various kinds of stain.

Polychromatophilia —1. The quality of being stainable with various stains. 2. Excess of polychromatocytes in the blood.

Polychromatophilic —Polychromatophil.

Polychromatosis —Polychromatophilia.

Polychromemia —Increase in the coloring matter of blood.

Polychromia —Increased pigmentation of the skin.

Polychromophil —Polychromatophil.

Polychromophilia —Polychromatophilia.

Polychylia —Excessive secretion of chyle.

Polyclinic —A hospital where all kinds of diseases and injuries are treated; a general hospital.

Polyclonal —Arising from different cells.

Polyclonia —A disease characterized by many clonic spasms.

Polycoria —Presence of more than one pupil in an eye.

Polycrotic —Having several pulse waves for each heart-beat.

Polycrotism—The quality of having several pulse waves for each heart-beat.

Polycyesis —Multiple pregnancy.

Polycystic —Composed of many cysts.

Polycythemia —Erythrocytosis. An increase in the number of red blood cells in the blood.

Compensatory polycythemia —Secondary polycytemia.

Polycythemia vera —It is due to hyperplasia of the red cell-forming portion of the bone marrow, characterized by cyanosis in middle-aged person particularly in cold weather. The superficial blood vessels in the skin are dilated. The spleen and liver are enlarged. The red blood cells may increase upto 13 millions per cu. mm. of blood.

Relative polycythemia —Relative increase in the number of red blood cells as occurs in hemoconcentration (concentration of blood) due to loss of plasma.

Secondary polycythemia —Erythrocytosis. Polycythemia caused by increased erythropoiesis resulting from some physiological condition, such as lowered oxygen tension in the blood, that stimulates erythropoiesis.

Polydactylism —The presence of supernumerary fingers or toes.

Polydactylous—Pertaining to polydactyly.

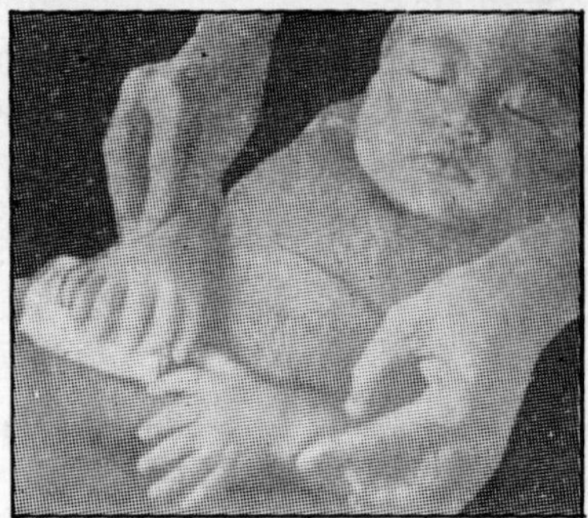

Fig. 442 : Polydactylism

Polydactyly —Presence of more than the normal number of fingers and toes.

Polydentia —Polyodontia.

Polydipsia —Excessive thirst.

Polydrosis —Excessive sweating.

Polydysplasia —Defective development of several tissues, or organs of the body.

Polydystrophic —Pertaining to or having polydystrophy.

Polydystrophy —Presence of numerous congenital abnormalities of the connective tissues.

Polyembryony —Condition of a zygote to give rise to two or more embryos.

Polyendocrine —Pertaining to several endocrine glands.

Polyendocrinopathy —A disease caused by insufficiency of multiple endocrine glands.

Polyergic —Capable to act in several different ways.

Polyesthesia —An abnormal sensation of feeling a single stimulus of touch at two or more places.

Polyesthetic —Pertaining to polyesthesia.

Polygalactia —Excessive secretion or flow of milk.

Polygamy —Practice of having several wives or husbands.

Polyganglionic —1. Pertaining to many ganglia. 2. Affecting many glands.

Polygastria —Excessive secretion or flow of gastric juice.

Polygen —1. An element having more than one valency and that can form more than one series of compounds. 2. An antigen that causes the formation of two or more specific antibodies.

Polygenic —Pertaining to or caused by several different genes.

Polyglandular —Pluriglandular.

Polygnathus —Conjoined twins of unequal size in which the smaller one is attached to the jaw of the larger.

Polygonal —Having many angles.

Polygram —A record made by a polygraph.

Polygraph —An apparatus for recording simultaneously tracing of different pulsations, as that of the arteries and veins and the apex beat of the heart.

Polygyny —Polygamy.

Polygyria —An increase in the number of convolutions in the brain.

Polyhedral —Having many surfaces.

Polyhemia —Polyemia. An increase in the amount of blood.

Polyhidrosis —Excessive sweating.

Polyhistor —A physician who has great ability and knowledge.

Polyhybrid —The offspring of parents different from each other in more than three characteristics.

Polyhydramnios —An excess of amniotic fluid in the amniotic sac.

Polyhydric —Containing more than two hydroxyl groups.

Polyhydruria —Excess of water in the urine.

Polyhypermenorrhea —Frequent and excessive menstruation.

Polyhypomenorrhea —Frequent and scanty menstruation.

Polyideic —Having several views.

Polyidrosis —Hyperhydrosis.

Polyinfection —Multi-infection. Infection with more than one microorganism.

Polyionic —Containing several different ions.

Polykaryocyte —A cell containing many nuclei.

Polyleptic —Having many remissions and exacerbations, as malaria.

Polylogia —Continuous and incoherent speech.

Polymastia —Polymazia. The presence of more than two breasts.

Polymastigote —Having many flagella.

Polymath —Polyhistor.

Polymazia —Polymastia.

Polymelia —Presence of supernumerary limbs.

Polymelus —Having supernumerary limbs.

Polymenia —Polymenorrhea.

Polymenorrhea—Polymenia. Abnormally frequent menstruation.

Polymer —A substance formed by a combination of two or more molecules of the same substance.

Polymeria —Polymerism.

Polymeric —Having the qualities of a polymer.

Polymerid —A polymer.

Polymerism —The presence of more than normal number of parts of the body.

Polymerization —The process of forming a polymer.

Polymerize —To form polymer.

Polymetacarpalia —Presence of supernumerary metacarpal bones congenitally.

Polymetacarpalism —Polymetacarpalia.

Polymetatarsalia —Presence of supernumerary metatarsal bones congenitally.

Polymetatarsalism —Polymetatarsalia.

Polymicrobial, Polymicrobic —Pertaining to or marked by the presence of several species of microorganisms.

Polymicrogyria —A brain malformation in which numerous small convolutions develop.

Polymicrolipomatosis —The occurrence of multiple nodules of lipid in the subcutaneous tissue.

Polymorph —A polymorphonuclear leukocyte.

Polymorphic —Polymorphous. Multiform. Occurring in more than one form.

Polymorphism —The quality of occurring in many forms.

Polymorphocellular—Composed of cells of many forms.

Polymorphonuclear —1. Having a nucleus consisting of several lobes. 2. Polymorphonuclear leukocyte.

Polymorphonuclear leukocyte —A white blood cell containing a nucleus composed of two or more lobes.

Polymorphous —Polymorphic. Multiform.

Polymyalgia —Pain occurring in many muscles.

Polymyoclonus —Twitching or clonic muscular spasm occurring in various parts of the body at the same time.

Polymyopathy —Disease affecting several muscles simultaneously.

Polymyositis —Inflammation of many muscles at a time.

Polynesic —Occurring in many separate places.

Polyneural —Pertaining to or supplied by many nerves.

Polyneuralgia —Neuralgia in several nerves.

Polyneuritic —Pertaining to the inflammation of many nerves.

Polyneuritis —Multiple neuritis. Inflammation of many nerves simultaneously.

Diabetic polyneuritis —Diabetic polyneuropathy.

Metabolic polyneuritis —Polyneuritis resulting from metabolic disorders such as lack of vitamin B_1 (thiamine hydrochloride).

Toxic polyneuritis —Polyneuritis resulting from poisons.

Polyneuromyositis —Polyneuritis and polymyositis combined.

Polyneuropathy —A disease affecting many nerves.

Alcoholic polyneuropathy —Polyneuropathy occurring in chronic alcoholics.

Diabetic polyneuropathy —Polyneuropathy occurring as a complication of diabetes mellitus.

Uremic polyneuropathy —Polyneuropathy occurring in uremia which results from chronic renal failure.

Polyneuroradiculitis —Inflammation of the spinal ganglia, nerve roots and peripheral nerves.

Polynuclear —Multinuclear. Possessing more than one nucleus.

Polynucleate —Having many nuclei.

Polynucleosis —The presense of many multinuclear cells in the peripheral blood.

Polyodontia —The presence of supernumerary teeth.

Polyonchosis —Formation of multiple tumors.

Polyoncosis —Polyonchosis.

Polyonychia —The presence of supernumerary nails.

Polyopia, Polyopsia —Multiple vision. Visual perception of more than one image of the same object.

Polyorchidism —Presence of more than two testes.

Polyorchis —The person having more than two testes.

Polyorchism —Polyorchidism.

Polyostotic —Pertaining to many bones.

Polyotia —The presence of more than two ears.

Polyovular —Pertaining to or derived from more than one ovum.

Polyovulatory —Releasing many ova in a single ovulatory cycle.

Polyp —A tumor with a pedicle hanging from the mucous membrane, usually found in the nose, uterus and rectum.

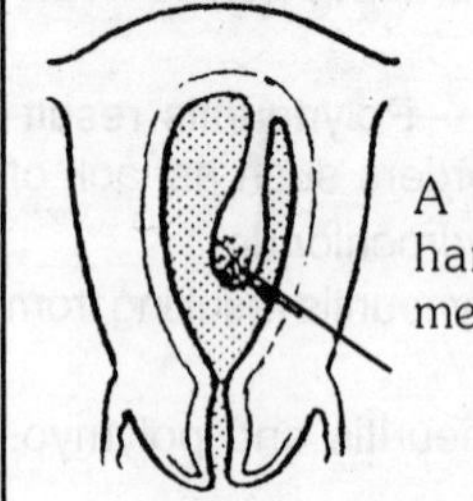

A polyp with a pedicle hanging from the mucous membrane of the uterus.

Fig. 443 : Polyp

Cardiac polyp —A pedunculated tumor attached to the inside of the heart, which many block the valve, if situated close to it.

Cervical polyp —A fibrous or mucous polyp of the cervical mucous membrane.

Colonic polyp —A polyp of the colon.

Fibrinous polyp —A polyp in the uterus made up of fibrin from the retained blood.

Juvenile polyp —A small, benign, rounded hematoma of the mucous membrane of the large intestine, usually found in children and associated with bleeding from the rectum.

Laryngeal polyp —A polyp attached to the vocal cords and extending into the air passage.

Nasal polyp —A pedunculated polyp hanging from the mucous membrane of the nose.

Polypapilloma —Yaws.

Polyparesis —Dementia paralytica.

Polypathia —Presence of many diseases at one time in the same person.

Polypectomy —Excision of a polyp.

Polypeptide —A peptide containing more than two amino acids.

Polypeptidemia —The presence of polypeptides in the blood.

Polypeptidorrhachia —Presence of polypeptides in the cerebrospinal fluid.

Polyphagia —Excessive eating of food.

Polyphalangia, Polyphalangism —Presence of extra phalanges in a finger or toe.

Polyphallic —Pertaining to the fantasy of having many penises.

Polypharmacy —1. To administer many drugs together or overdose of a drug. 2. Prescription of many drugs given at a time.

Polyphenic —Pleiotropic.

Polyphobia —Morbid fear of many things.

Polyphonic —Having many voices.

Polyphrasia —Excessive talkativeness.

Polyphyletic —Having more than one origin.

Polyphyletism —In hematology, the theory that blood cells are derived from several different stem cells.

Polyphyodont —Producing more than two sets of teeth at intervals during a lifetime.

Polypi —Plural of polypus.

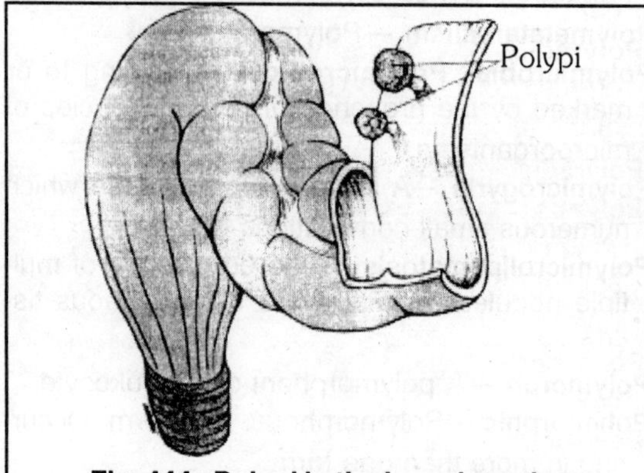

Fig. 444 : Polypi in the large intestine

Polypiform —Like a polyp.

Polyplasmia —Hydremia.

Polyplast —Composed of many cells.

Polyplastic —1. Having many substances in cellular composition. 2. Changing in many forms.

Polyplastocytosis —Increase in the formation of blood platelets.

Polyplegia —Paralysis of many muscles.

Polyploid —An individual or cell possessing more than two sets of homologous chromosomes.

Polyploidy —Possession of more than two sets of homologous chromosomes.

Polypnea —Hyperpnea. Panting.

Polypodia —The presence of more than the normal number of feet.

Polypoid —Polypiform.

Polyporous —Having many pores.

Polyposia —Ingestion of large amounts of fluid for long periods of time.

Polyposis —The formation of numerous polyps.

Polypotome —An instrument for excision of polyps.

Polypotrite —An instrument for crushing the polyps.

Polypous —Like a polyp.

Polypragmasy —To apply many different remedies at the same time.

Polypsychotropia —To use two or more psychotropic drugs together.

Polyptychial —Arranged in several layers.

Polypus —A polyp.

Polyradiculitis —Inflammation of the nerve roots.

Polyradiculoneuritis —Inflammation of the peripheral nerves, spinal nerve roots and the spinal cord.

Polyradiculoneuropathy —Guillain-Barre syndrome. Polyneuritis with progressive weakness of the extremities, which may lead to paralysis.

Polyradiculopathy —Polyradiculitis.

Polyribosome —Polysome. A cluster of ribosomes which play an important role in the transmission of genetic information and synthesis of protein.

Polyrrhea, Polyrrhoea —Excessive secretion of fluid.

Polysaccharide —A type of carbohydrate which upon hydrolysis yields more than two molecules of simple sugars.

Polysaccharose —A polysaccharide.

Polysarca —Obesity. Corpulency.

Polyscelia —The presence of more than two legs.

Polyscelus —Possessing more than two legs.

Polyscope —Diaphanoscope.

Polyserositis —General inflammation of the serous membranes, with effusion.

Polysialia —Ptyalism.

Polysinusitis —Inflammation of several sinuses simultaneously.

Polysomaty —Having reduplicated chromatin in the nucleus.

Polysome —Polyribosome.

Polysomia —The condition of being more than one body of a fetus.

Polysomic —Pertaining to or characterized by polysomy.

Polysomnogram —A record of physiologic functions obtained in polysomnography.

Polysomnography —Simultaneous and continuous measurement and recording of physiological activity during sleep.

Polysomus —A fetus having more than one body.

Polysomy —An excess of a particular chromosome.

Polyspermia —1. Excessive secretion of semen. 2. Polyspermy. Fertilization of an ovum by many spermatozoa.

Polyspermism —Polyspermia.

Polyspermy —Fertilization of an ovum by many spermatozoa.

Polystichia —Presence of two or more rows of eyelashes on a lid.

Polystomatous —Having many mouths or openings.

Polysymbrachydactyly —Malformation of the hand or foot in which the fingers or toes are short, more than the normal number and fused together.

Polysynaptic —Pertaining to two or more synapses or the nerve pathways affecting several synapses.

Polysyndactyly —Presence of more than the normal number of fingers or toes (polydactyly) and their fusion by the presence of webs between them (syndactyly).

Polytendinitis —Inflammation of many tendons.

Polytene —Composed of many strands of chromatin.

Polytenization —The process of polytene formation.

Polytenosynovitis —Inflammation of many tendon sheaths at the same time.

Polythelia —Polythelism. Presence of more than two nipples.

Polythelism —Polythelia.

Polytocous —Producing several children at one time.

Polytrichia —Hypertrichiasis. Hypertrichosis.

Polytrichosis —Hypertrichosis.

Polytrophia —Polytrophy. Excessive nutrition.

Polytrophy —Polytrophia.

Polytropic —Affecting more than one type of cell or tissue.

Polyunguia —Polyonychia.

Polyuria —Excessive excretion of urine.

Polyvacuolate —Possessing many vacuoles.

Polyvalent —Multivalent. Capable of combining with more than two atoms of hydrogen.

Polyzygotic —Polyovulatory.

Pomade —Pomatum. A medicated perfumed ointment, especially for the hair.

Pomatus —Pomade.

Pompholyx —Dyshidrosis. A recurrent vesicular eruption on the skin of the sides of digits or of the palms and soles with intense itching.

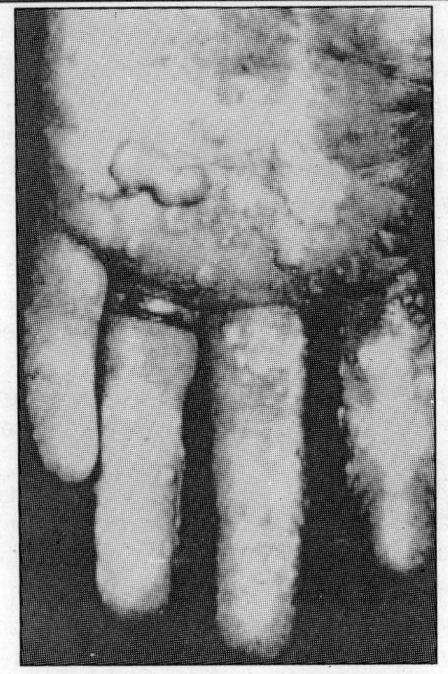

Fig. 445 : Pompholyx of the hand

Pomphus —Blister.

Ponderal —Pertaining to weight.

Pono- —A prefix which means bodily exertion, fatigue and pain.

Ponograph —An apparatus for measuring and recording the sensitivity to pain or fatigue.

Ponopalmosis —Neurocirculatory asthenia. Palpitation of the heart produced by slight exertion.

Ponophobia —1. Morbid fear of pain. 2. Aversion to exert.

Pons —1. A process or bridge of tissue connecting two or more parts of an organ, *e.g.*, pons hepatica which is a projection of the liver which crosses its longitudinal fissure. 2. Pons varolii.

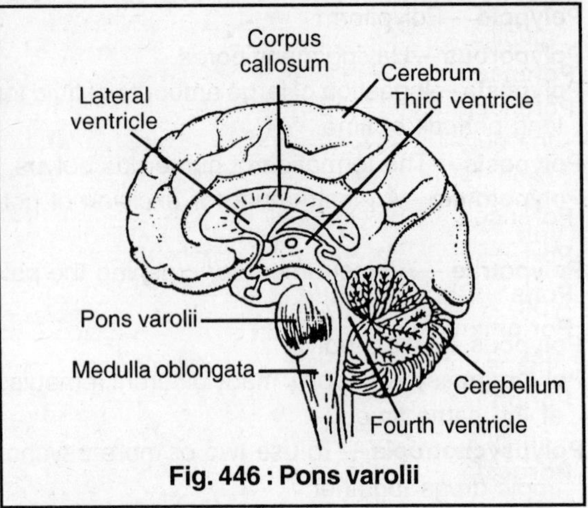

Fig. 446 : Pons varolii

A rounded middle part of the brain stem, connecting the middle brain with the medulla oblongata.

Pontes —Plural of pons.

Pontic —The portion of the dental arch which substitutes for an absent tooth.

Ponticulus —A little ridge.

Pontile —Pertaining to pons varolii.

Pontile nuclei —Gray matter in the pons.

Pontine —Pertaining to the pons varolii.

Pontobulbar —Pertaining to the pons and medulla oblongata.

Pontocerebellar —Pertaining to the pons and cerebellum.

Pontomesencephalic —Pertaining to or affecting the pons and the mesencephalon.

Pool —1. To mix the blood from several donors. 2. Accumulation of blood at a site in the body.

Poples —The popliteal or posterior region of the knee.

Popliteal —Pertaining to the posterior region of the knee.

Poppy —Any of the several plants of the genus Papaver. Opium is obtained from the juice of the unripe pods of one species P. somniferum.

Poradenitis —Inflammation of lymph nodes with formation of small abscesses.

Porcelain —A hard and translucent material made of smooth clay which is used in dentistry.

Porcelaneous, Porcelanous —Translucent or white like porcelain, as the skin.

Porcine —Like a pig.

Pore —Porus. A small opening or empty space.

Porencephalia, Porencephaly —Development of

the cysts or cavities in the brain, usually communicating with a lateral ventricle.

Porencephalic —Porencephalous.

Porencephalitis —Inflammation of the brain with the development of cysts or cavities communicating with a lateral ventricle.

Porencephalous —Pertaining to porencephalia..

Pori —Plural of porus.

Poria —Plural of porion.

Poriomania —Excessive desire for going from home.

Porion —The mid point of the upper margin of the auditory meatus.

Porocele —Scrotal hernia with hardening and thickening of the scrotum.

Poroma —1. A tumor arising in a pore. 2. A callosity.

Porosis —1. The formation of the callus in repair of a fractured bone. 2. Formation of a cavity.

Porosity —The condition of being porus.

Porotic —Porous.

Porotomy —Meatotomy.

Porous —Full of pores.

Porphyria —A disturbance of porphyrin metabolism characterized by increase in the formation and excretion of porphyrins or their precursors.

Porphyrin —Any of a group of nitrogen-containing organic compounds occurring in the protoplasm and forming the basis of respiratory pigments of animals and plants, obtained from hemoglobin and chlorophyll respectively.

Porphyrinopathy —Porphyrism. A disease resulting from abnormal metabolism of porphyrin, such as acute porphyria.

Porphyrinuria —Porphyruria. Increased excretion of porphyrin in the urine.

Porphyrism —Porphyrinopathy.

Porphyrization —The process of reducing to a powder.

Porphyruria —Porphyrinuria.

Porro's operation —Cesarean hysterectomy. Cesarean operation followed by removal of the uterus, ovaries and fallopian tubes.

Porta —The side of entrance of nerves, blood vessels and other structures into an organ, *e.g.*, porta pulmonis, the hilum of the lung for entrance and exit of the bronchi, nerves and vessels; porta hepatis, the transverse fissure on the visceral surface of the liver where the portal vein and hepatic artery enter and the hepatic duct leaves.

Portacaval —Pertaining to the portal vein and inferior vena cava.

Portacaval shunt —Surgical joining of the portal vein and inferior vena cava.

Portae —Plural of porta.

Portal —1. A way of entrance, as the way by which bacteria gain entry to the body. 2. Pertaining to the entrance to an organ, especially through which blood is carried to the liver.

Portal circulation —The circulation of blood in the liver through the branches of portal vein, that returns through hepatic veins and drain into the inferior vena cava outside the liver.

Portal system —The portal vein and its branches which collect blood from the abdominal organs and carry it to the liver, from which the blood passes through the hepatic veins to the inferior vena cava.

Portio —A part of an organ.

Porto- —A prefix meaning portal.

Portoenterostomy —Surgical anastomosis of jejunum to the portal region of the liver and to the duodenum.

Portogram —X-ray film of the portal vein.

Portography —X-ray examination of the portal vein after an injection of a radiopaque substance into it.

Portosystemic —Joining the portal and systemic venous circulation.

Portovenography —Portography.

Porus —An opening or a pore.

Posiomania —Dipsomania.

Position —1. A place at which a thing is placed. 2. Body posture or attitude. 3. The relation of some part of the body or the presenting part of fetus with the pelvis of mother.

Anatomic position —Orthograde position. The position of the human body in which a person stands erect with the arms at the side and the palms turned forward.

Batrachian position —Frog's position. A lying position of the infant which resembles the position of a frog.

Bozeman's position —The knee-elbow position wherein the patient is strapped to support.

Brickner position —The position wherein the

wrist of the patient is tied to the head of the bed to obtain traction, abduction, and external rotation of the shoulder.

Decubitus position —Position of a patient on the plane surface, which is denoted according to the side of the body touching it as dorsal decubitus (on the back), left lateral decubitus (on the left side), right lateral decubitus (on the right side) or ventral decubitus (on the abdomen).

Dorsal elevated position —The position in which the patient lies on back with the head and shoulders elevated at the angle of 30° or more. It is done to examine the genital organs by fingers or by both the hands.

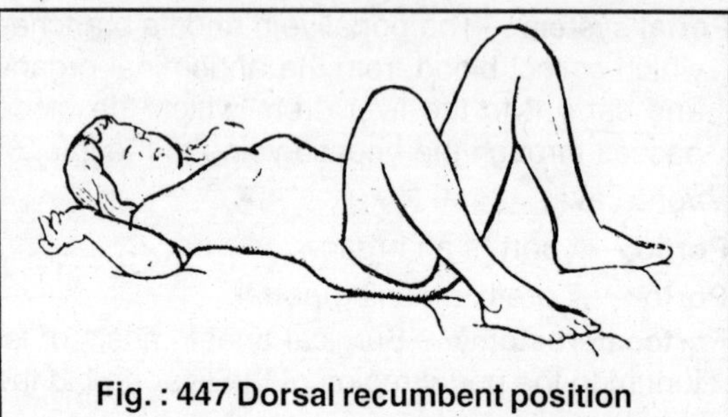

Fig. : 447 Dorsal recumbent position

Dorsal position —Supine position. The position in which the patient is lying on the back.

Dorsal recumbent position —The position in which the patient lies on back with lower limbs slightly flexed and rotated outward. It is made in the female to apply obstetrical forceps, repair of the wounds after delivery and vaginal examination etc.

Dorsosacral position —Lithotomy position.

Fowler's position —Position in which head of the patient's bed is raised 18-20 inches above the floor with the knees also elevated.

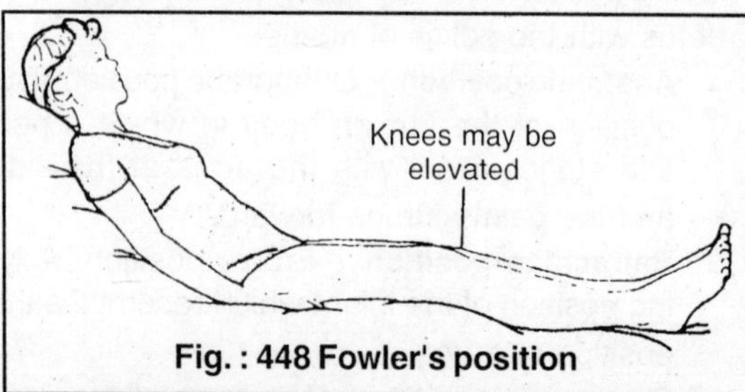

Fig. : 448 Fowler's position

Froglike position —Batrachian position.

Genucubital position —Knee-elbow position.

Genupectoral position —Knee-chest position.

Horizontal abdominal position —Position in which the patient lies on abdomen with the feet extended. It is employed in the examination of back and the vertebral column.

Horizontal position —Dorsal position with the feet extended.

Jackknife position —Reclining position. The position in which patient lies on the back with the shoulders elevated, legs flexed on thighs and thighs at right angles to the abdomen. It is employed for passing the urethral sound.

Knee-chest position —The patient resting on the knees and upper chest with the thighs upright.

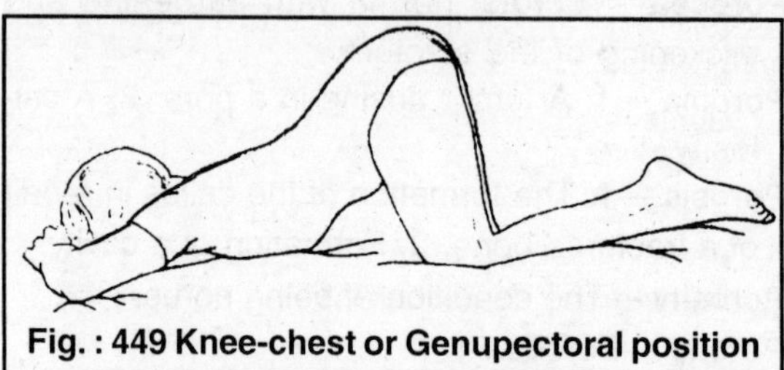

Fig. : 449 Knee-chest or Genupectoral position

Knee-elbow position —The patient resting on the knees with the thighs upright and elbows with the chest elevated, usually employed while performing proctoscopy.

Left lateral position —In this position the patient lies on the left side, right knee and thigh drawn up. It is employed in female in vaginal examination.

Lithotomy position —The position in which the patient lies on the back with the thighs flexed on the abdomen and the legs on the thighs and the thighs are abducted. It is employed usually in women in operation on genital organs.

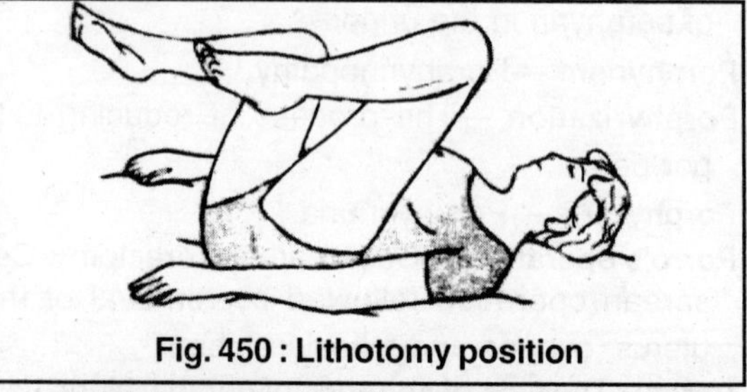

Fig. 450 : Lithotomy position

Noble's position —The position in which the patient is standing, leaning forward and supporting the upper part of the body by keeping hands on the wall or by holding a chair. It is used for the examination of kidney.

Obstetrical position —Left lateral recumbent position.

Orthograde position —Anatomic position.

Orthopneic position —Sitting erect position. It is for those who have difficulty in breathing.

Prone position —Position in which the patient lies with the face downward.

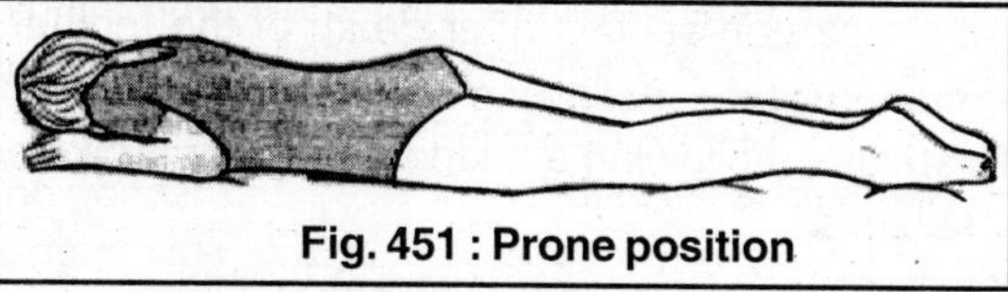

Fig. 451 : Prone position

Rose's position —Dorsal position with head fully extended and hanging over the edge of the table.

Sims' position —The position in which patient lies on the left side, the right knee and thigh are drawn up above left, and the left arm lies along the back. It is employed in rectal or intravaginal examination or in the operations of genital organs.

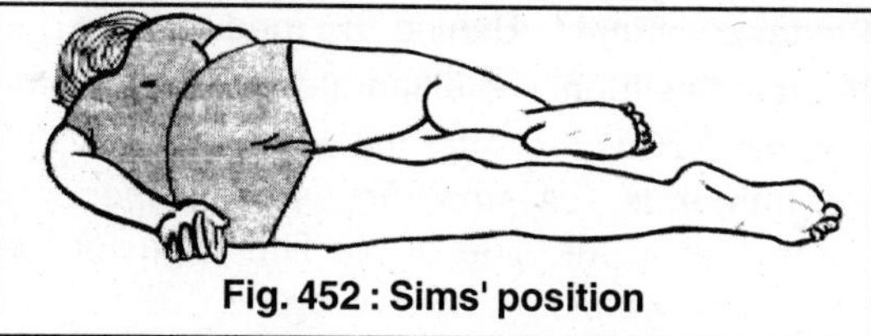

Fig. 452 : Sims' position

Supine position —Dorsal position.

Trendelenburg position —Dorsal position in which the patient lies on a bed tilted at the end at about 45° with the head low. It is employed in abdominal operations, so that the abdominal organs may remain upward by gravitation.

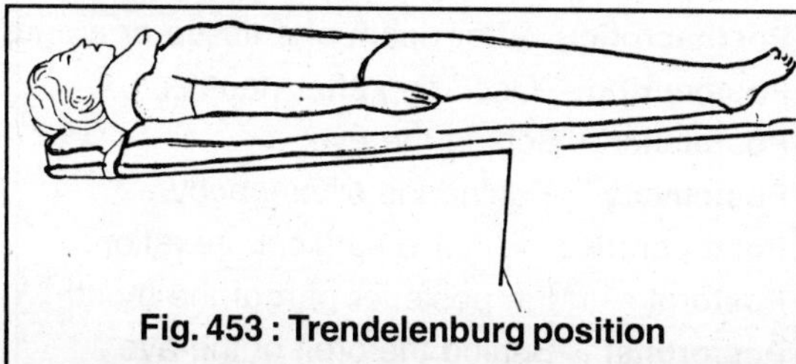

Fig. 453 : Trendelenburg position

Walcher position —Position in which the patient's hips are on the edge of table and lower limbs hanging down.

Positioner —An apparatus for holding or placing a body part, especially the head in a certain position.

Positioning —In rehabilitation, the placing of body and its extremities in position as an aid to the treatment.

Positive —1. Indicating existence or presence. 2. Definite. 3. Having the value greater than zero. 4. Indicating an abnormal condition in the examination and diagnosis.

Positron —A positively charged electron.

Posologic —Pertaining to posology.

Posological —Pertaining to the dosage of medicines.

Posology —The science dealing with the dosage of medicines.

Post- —A prefix which means after, behind or posterior.

Postabortal —Occurring or happening after an abortion.

Postacetabular —Behind the acetabulum.

Postadolescence —The period after adolescence or puberty.

Postadolescent —The person who has passed adolescence.

Postanal —Behind the anus.

Postanesthetic —Pertaining to the period following anesthesia.

Postapoplectic —Pertaining to the period immediately following a stroke or apoplexy.

Postauricular —Situated or operation performed behind the auricle of the ear.

Postaxial —Situated or occurring behind an axis.

Postbrachial —Pertaining to or situated on the posterior part of the upper arm.

Postcapillary —Venous capillary. The last capillary of a capillary network which becomes continuous with a venule.

Postcardial —Behind the heart.

Postcardiotomy —The period following open heart surgery.

Postcava —The inferior vena cava.

Postcaval —Pertaining to the inferior vena cava.

Postcentral —Situated or happening behind a center.

Postcibal —Occurring after eating.

Post-cibum —After food.

Postclavicular —Behind the clavicle bone.

Postclimacteric —Occurring after the menopause.

Postcoital —Happening after sexual intercourse.

Postcoitus —The time immediately after coitus.

Postconnubial —Occurring after marriage.

Postconvulsive —Occurring after a convulsion.

Postcordial —Posterior to the heart.

Postcornu —The posterior horn of the lateral ventricle.

Postcostal —Behind the ribs.

Postcubital —In the posterior portion of the forearm.

Postdiastolic —Occurring after a diastole.

Postdicrotic —Occurring after the dicrotic pulse wave.

Postdiphtheritic—After diphtheria.

Postencephalitic —Occurring after encephalitis.

Postepileptic —Following an epileptic convulsion.

Posterior—1. Directed toward or situated at the back or behind. 2. Coming after. 3. Opposite to anterior.

Postero- —Prefix indicating posterior or towards the back.

Posteroanterior —The word indicating from back toward the front.

Posteroexternal —Toward the back and the outer side.

Posteroinferior —Behind and below.

Posterointernal —Toward the back and inner side.

Posterolateral —Situated behind and at the side of a part of the body.

Posteromedial —Toward the back and the median plane.

Posteromedian —Situated at the back and in the median plane.

Posteroparietal —Situated at the back of the parietal bone.

Posterosuperior —Situated behind and above.

Posterotemporal —Situated behind the temporal bone.

Postesophageal —Situated behind the esophagus.

Postethmoid —Located behind the ethmoid bone.

Postfebrile —Occurring after a fever.

Postganglionic —Situated behind or distal to a ganglion.

Posthemiplegic —Occurring after hemiplegia.

Posthemorrhagic —Occurring after hemorrhage.

Posthepatic —Behind the liver.

Posthepatitic —Occurring after hepatitis.

Posthetomy —Circumcision.

Posthioplasty —Plastic surgery of the prepuce or foreskin.

Posthitis —Inflammation of the foreskin.

Postholith —A calculus occurring beneath the prepuce or foreskin.

Posthumous —1. Occurring after death. 2. Born after death of the father. 3. The child taken out by cesarean section after death of the mother.

Posthypnotic —Following hypnotic state.

Postical —Following a sudden attack or stroke or seizure.

Posticteric —Following jaundice.

Posticus —Denoting the back surface of the body.

Postinfluenzal —Occurring after influenza.

Postmalarial —Occurring after malaria.

Postmature —Pertaining to an infant born after 42 weeks of pregnancy.

Postmaturity —Over maturity, as in an infant who born after 42 weeks of pregnancy.

Postmedian —Posterior to the median plane.

Postmediastinal —Behind the mediastinum.

Postmediastinum —Behind the mediastinum.

Postmenopausal —After the menopause.

Postminimus —A small accessory appendage attached to the side of the fifth finger or toe, which resembles a normal digit.

Postmortem —Occurring or performed after death.

Postmortem examination —Autopsy.

Postnarial —Pertaining to the posterior nares or choanae.

Postnaris —Choanae.

Postnasal —Situated behind the nose.

Postnatal —Occurring after birth.

Postnecrotic —After death of a tissue or a part.

Postneuritic —Occurring after neuritis.

Postocular —Behind the eye.

Postolivary —Behind the olivary body.

Postoperative —After a surgical operation.

Postoral —In the posterior part of the mouth.

Postorbital —Behind the orbit of the eye.

Postovulatory —After ovulation.

Postpalatine —Behind the palate.

Postpaludal —After malaria fever.

Postparalytic —Following an attack of paralysis.

Post partum —After childbirth.

Postpartum —Occurring after childbirth.

Postpharyngeal —Behind the pharynx.

Postpneumonic —Occurring after pneumonia.

Postpontile —Situated behind the pons varolii.

Postprandial —After a meal.

Postpubertal —Pertaining to the period of after puberty.

Postpuberty —The period after puberty.

Postpubescent —After puberty.

Postradiation —Following exposure to radiation.

Postsacral —Below the sacrum.

Postscapular —Behind or below the scapula.

Postsphygmic —After the pulse wave.

Postsplenic —Behind the spleen.

Poststenotic —Located or occurring distal to a constricted area, especially of an artery.

Postsynaptic —Located or occurring distal to a synapse.

Post-tarsal —Behind the tarsus.

Post-term infant —An infant born after beginning of the 42nd week of pregnancy.

Post-term pregnancy —Pregnancy continuing for more than 42 weeks (294-days), counted from the first day of the last menstrual period.

Post-tibial —Behind the tibia.

Post-transcriptional —Occurring after transcription.

Post-translational —Occurring after translation.

Post-transverse —Behind a transverse process.

Post-traumatic —Following an injury.

Post-typhoid —Occurring after typhoid fever.

Postulate —A supposition or view, that is assumed without proof.

Postural —Pertaining to or affected by posture.

Postural hypotension —Decrease in blood pressure in standing position.

Posture —Attitude or position of the body.

Coiled posture —Body on one side with the legs drawn up to meet the trunk, seen in cerebral diseases, hepatic, intestinal and renal colic.

Dorsal rigid posture —In this posture the patient lies on back with both the legs drawn up, seen in peritonitis, meningitis, ascites and tympanites. In appendicitis, peritonitis of the right side and renal calculus in the right ureter, right leg is drawn up.

Kyphosis-lordosis posture —A posture in which the pelvis is tilted forward, causing hip flexion, increased lumbar lordosis, and thoracic kyphosis.

Orthopnea posture —The patient sitting upright with the hands or elbows placing on some objects for support, seen in bronchial asthma, emphysema, heart disease and dyspnea etc.

Orthotonus posture —In this posture the neck and trunk are extended rigidly in straight line, seen in tetanus, rabies or meningitis.

Prone posture —Face lying downward, seen in abdominal pain or gastric ulcer.

Postuterine —Situated behind the uterus.

Postvaccinal —Occurring after vaccination for smallpox.

Postvalvular —Posterior to a valve.

Potable—Suitable for drinking.

Potain's sign —In dilatation of the aorta, there will be dullness on percussion over the area extending from the manubrium sterni toward the second intercostal space and the third costal cartilage on the right side, and to the base of the sternum.

Potamophobia —A morbid fear of large quantities of water.

Potash —Potassium carbonate.

Potassemia —Hyperkalemia.

Potassic —Composed of or containing potash.

Potassium —A mineral element found in combination with other elements in the body and constitutes .35% of body weight.

Potbelly —Fatty abdomen.

Potency —1. Strength as of a medicine. 2. Ability as of a male to perform coitus.

Potent —1. Powerful as a medicine. 2. A male person able to perform coitus.

Potentia coeundi —Ability to perform sexual intercourse normally.

Potential —1. Existing and ready for action, but not active. 2. Electric tension or pressure.

Potentiate —To strengthen.

Potentiation —The synergistic action of two substances, in which combined effect is greater than the sum of the effects of each of the two substances.

Potentiator —A drug which in combination with other drugs makes them more powerful.

Potentiometer —A voltmeter.

Potion —A large dose of a liquid medicine.

Potted —Enclosed in a box.

Pott's disease —Tuberculosis of the vertebrae.

Pott's fracture —Fracture of the lower end of the fibula and medial malleolus of the tibia bone with the outward displacement of the foot.

Fig. 454 : Pott's disease

Pouch —Any pocket-like cavity or sac, *e.g.*, pouch of Douglas which is a peritoneal sac lying behind the uterus and in front of rectum.

Pouchitis —Acute inflammation of a surgically created pouch.

Poudrage —Application of powder to a surface, as between the visceral and parietal layers of the pleura to produce their adhesions.

Poultice —A hot, soft, moist mass of medicine spread between layers of gauze or cloth and applied to the skin to relieve pain, to subside inflammation by absorption and to act as a counterirritant.

Pound —A unit of weight which is equal to 16 ounces or 453.6 grams in avoirdupois system and 12 ounces or 373.2 grams in apothecaries' system.

Powder —1. Aggregation of the particles of one or more substances. 2. A dose of a powdered medicine, contained in paper.

Power —1. The ability to act. 2. Potency. 3. In optics, the degree of magnification of a lens or optical instrument. 4. In microscopy, the number of times the diameter of an object is magnified, which is indicated by placing an X after the number, *e.g.*, 10X indicates magnification of 10 times. 5. In mathematics, the number of times a value is to be multiplied, as 10^2=10x10=100 or 10^3=10x10x10=1000. A negative power, *e.g.*,10^{-2}=1/10^2=1/100.

Pox —A contagious eruptive disease as smallpox, chickenpox etc.

Poxvirus —A virus of the family poxviridae, that causes smallpox.

Practice —The utilization of knowledge and skill of a medical professional in the prevention, diagnosis and treatment of the diseases.

Practitioner —The person who has fulfilled the legal formalities and is engaged in the medical practice, such as a physician, physiotherapist, dentist or nurse etc.

Praecox —Early.

Praevia, Praevius —Going before.

Pragmatagnosia —Inability to recognize the familiar things.

Pragmatamnesia —Inability to remember the appearance of an object.

Pragmatic —Pertaining to pragmatism.

Pragmatism —The act of interposing.

Pragmatist —Interposing.

Prandial —Pertaining to a meal.

Praxinoscope —An apparatus for examining the larynx.

Praxiology —Study of behavior.

Praxis —An accepted practice or custom.

-praxis —A suffix which means—1. Act or activity. 2. Practice, use.

Pre- —A prefix indicating before or in front of.

Preagonal —Immediately before death agony.

Prealbuminuric —Before the appearance of albumin in the urine.

Preanal —In front of the anus.

Preanesthesia —A light anesthesia produced by medication before general anesthesia.

Preanesthetic —1. Pertaining to, or the drug used for producing preanesthesia. 2. Occurring before the administration of an anesthetic.

Preantiseptic —1. Pertaining to the time before the discovery of antisepsis. 2. Before the adoption of antisepsis in surgery.

Preaortic —Located in front of the aorta.

Preataxic —Before the onset of ataxia.

Preauricular —Located in front of the auricle of the ear.

Preaxial —Situated in front of the axis of a limb or of the body.

Precancer —A condition tending to become malignant.

Precancerous —A growth or a pathological process tending to become malignant.

Precapillary —Metarteriole. A branch of an arteriole or a venule before capillary.

Precardiac —Anterior to the heart.

Precardinal —Pertaining to the anterior cardinal veins.

Precava —Superior vena cava.

Precentral —In front of a center.

Precervical —Before the neck or the cervix uteri.

Prechordal —In front of the notochord.

Precipitable —Capable of being precipitated.

Precipitant —The substance which brings about precipitation.

Precipitate —A deposit separated from a suspension or solution by precipitation.

Precipitation —The process of settling down of a substance in a solution at the bottom of the container.

Precipitin —An antibody formed due to presence of a soluble antigen, usually a protein.

Precipitinogen —Any protein acting as an antigen, stimulates the formation of a specific precipitin.

Precipitinogenoid —A precipitinogen that is altered on heating, thereby resulting in a substance that combines with the specific precipitin, but does not lead to the formation of a precipitate.

Precipitinoid —Precipitin that can no longer cause precipitation when mixed with its antigen, but retaining its affinity to the antigen.

Precipitogen —Precipitinogen.

Precipitophore —The part of a precipitin producing precipitation.

Precipitum —The precipitate produced by the action of a precipitin.

Preclinical —Occurring before the diagnosis of a definite disease is possible.

Precocious —Earlier physical or mental development.

Precocity —Premature development of physical or mental traits.

Precocity sexual —Premature development of the genital organs.

Precognition —Prior knowledge that an event will occur through extrasensory perception.

Precoital —Before sexual intercourse.

Precoma —The mental state before coma.

Preconscious —Not present in consciousness but able to be recalled readily into it.

Preconvulsive —Before a convulsion.

Precordia —The precordium.

Precordial —Pertaining to the precordium or epigastrium.

Precordialgia —Pain in the chest or precordial area.

Precordium —Precordia. The region of anterior surface of the body overlying the heart and lower part of the thorax.

Precornu —Anterior horn of the lateral ventricle of the brain.

Precostal —In front of the ribs.

Precritical —Prior to the occurrence of a crisis.

Precuneal —Anterior to the cuneus.

Precuneate —Pertaining to the precuneus.

Precuneus — A division of the medial surface of each cerebral hemisphere between the cuneus and the paracentral lobule.

Precursor —Something that occurs before another, as a sign or symptom.

Predentin —Primary uncalcified dentin.

Prediabetes —A condition of impairment of carbohydrate metabolism before the development of actual diabetes mellitus.

Prediastole —The period immediately prior to diastole in the cardiac cycle.

Prediastolic —Occurring before the diastole.

Predicrotic —Occurring before the dicrotic wave of the sphygmogram.

Predigestion —Partial artificial digestion of food before its ingestion.

Predisposing —Showing a tendency or susceptibility to the disease.

Predisposition —A tendency or susceptibility to the disease.

Prediverticular —Indicating a condition of thickening of the muscular wall of the colon and increased intraluminal pressure.

Predormitum —State of unconsciousness immediately before actual sleep.

Pre-eclampsia —A toxemia of pregnancy, characterized by hypertension, albuminuria and edema of the legs.

Pre-epiglottic —Anterior to the epiglottis.

Pre-eruptive —Before an eruption.

Pre-excitation —Premature excitation of a portion of the ventricle of the heart.

Prefrontal —1. Situated in the anterior part of frontal lobe of the brain. 2. The central portion of the ethmoid bone.

Preganglionic —In front of a ganglion.

Preganglionic fiber —The axon of a preganglionic neuron.

Pregenital —Pertaining to the period before the development of erotic interest in the reproductive organs.

Pregnancy —The condition of having a developing embryo or fetus in the uterus.

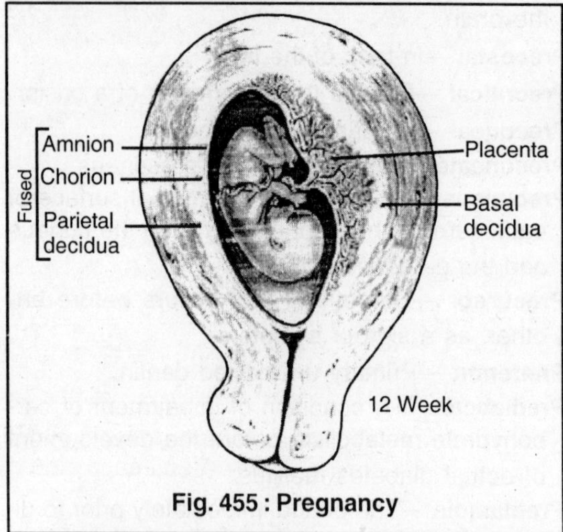

Fig. 455 : Pregnancy

Abdominal pregnancy —Extrauterine pregnancy. Ectopic pregnancy within the abdominal cavity.

Cervical pregnancy —Ectopic pregnancy within the cervical canal.

Combined pregnancy —Simultaneous intrauterine and extrauterine pregnancies.

Ectopic pregnancy —Extrauterine pregnancy. Pregnancy occurring outside the uterus.

Extrauterine pregnancy —Ectopic pregnancy.

False pregnancy —Phantom pregnancy.

Heterotopic pregnancy —Combined pregnancy.

Hydatid pregnancy —Pregnancy giving rise to a hydatidiform mole.

Interstitial pregnancy —Intramural pregnancy. Pregnancy occurring in the part of fallopian tube that lies within the uterine wall.

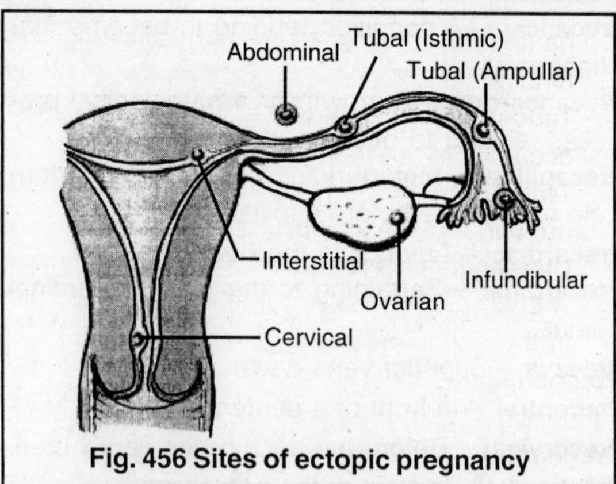

Fig. 456 Sites of ectopic pregnancy

Intraligamentary pregnancy, Intraligamentous pregnancy —Ectopic pregnancy occurring within the broad ligament.

Intramural pregnancy —Interstitial pregnancy.

Molar pregnancy —Pregnancy in which the ovum develops into a mole.

Multiple pregnancy —Pregnancy in which there is more than one fetus in the uterus.

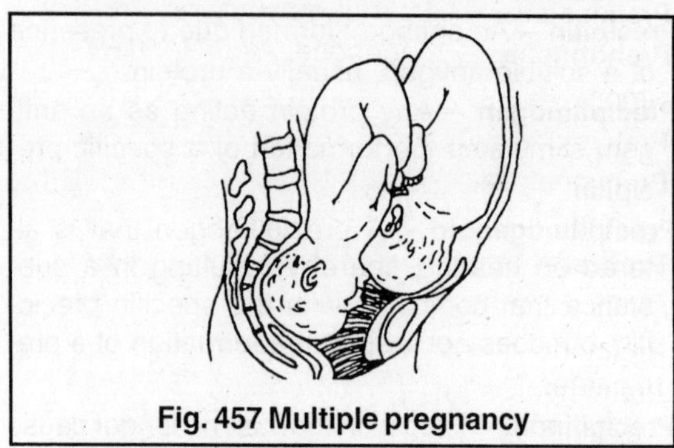
Fig. 457 Multiple pregnancy

Mural pregnancy —Interstitial pregnancy.

Ovarian pregnancy —Ectopic pregnancy occurring in an ovary.

Phantom pregnancy —False pregnancy. Enlargement of the abdomen simulating pregnancy.

Postdate pregnancy —Prolonged pregnancy. A pregnancy of more than 294 days or 42 completed weeks.

Prolonged pregnancy —Postdate pregnancy.

Tubal pregnancy —Ectopic pregnancy occurring within a fallopian tube.

Tuboabdominal pregnancy —Ectopic pregnancy occurring partly in the fallopian tube and partly in the abdominal cavity.

Tuboligamentary pregnancy —Ectopic pregnancy occurring in a fallopian tube and extending into the broad ligament.

Tubo-ovarian pregnancy —Ectopic pregnancy occurring in both the fallopian tube and ovary.

Twin pregnancy —Pregnancy in which there are two fetuses in the uterus.

Uteroabdominal pregnancy —Twin pregnancy with one embryo in the uterus and the other in the abdominal cavity.

Pregnanediol —The inactive end product of metabolism of progesterone, present in the urine.

Pregnant —Gravid. Heavy with child. Having conceived.

Pregravidic —Before pregnancy.

Prehallux —A supernumerary bone of the foot growing inwards.

Prehelicine —In front of the helix of the pinna.

Prehemiplegic —Occurring before the onset of hemiplegia.

Prehensile —Adapted for grasping or holding.

Prehension —The act of grasping.

Prehormone —Prohormone. A precursor of a hormone.

Prehyoid —In front of the hyoid bone.

Prehypophysis —The anterior lobe of the pituitary gland.

Preictal —Occurring just before a stroke or convulsion.

Preicteric —Prior to the appearance of jaundice.

Preimmunization —Immunization produced artificially in very young infants.

Preinvasive —Before the cells of a malignant tumor invade the adjacent tissues.

Prelacrimal —Anterior to the lacrimal sac.

Prelaryngeal —Anterior to the larynx.

Preleukemia —A stage of bone marrow dysfunction prior to the development of leukemia.

Prelimbic —In front of a limbus.

Preload —1. The load to which a muscle is subjected before shortening. 2. The stress or tension developing in the ventricular wall during diastole.

Prelum —Pressure or compression.

Premalignant —Precancerous.

Premaniacal —Prior to an attack of mania.

Premature —1. Not mature. 2. An infant before term or full development. 3. Occurring before the proper time.

Premature beat —Extrasystole. A cardiac contraction occurring before the normal one.

Premature infant —An infant who is not fully developed at birth and its weight is 2500 gms. or less.

Premature labor —Onset of labor before full term.

Prematurity —1. The state of being premature. 2. The state of underdevelopment of an infant at birth whose birth weight is 2500 gms. or less.

Premaxilla —Incisive bone.

Premaxillary —1. In front of the maxilla. 2. Pertaining to the incisive bone.

Premedication —Prenarcosis. Internal medication to produce unconsciousness prior to general anesthesia.

Premenarchal —Prior to the first menstrual period.

Premenstrual —Before menstruation.

Premenstrual tension syndrome —A syndrome occurring several days prior to the onset of menstruation characterized by headache, breast discomfort (swelling and tenderness), general feeling of 'bloatedness', sudden changes of mood, tension, irritability, depression or weepiness, forgetfullness and confusion.

Premenstruum —The period before the menstruation.

Premolar —1. One of the permanent teeth occurring between canine and molar on each side of the jaw. 2. In front of the molar tooth.

Premonition —Feeling of a terrible event.

Premonitory —Giving a warning, as an early symptom.

Premonocyte —Promonocyte.

Premorbid —Occurring prior to the development of disease.

Premortal —Just before death.

Premunition —Resistance to infection by the same pathogenic organisms, present in the body since a long time.

Premunitive —Pertaining to premunition.

Premyeloblast —A precursor of a mature myeloblast.

Premyelocyte —Promyelocyte.

Prenarcosis —Premedication.

Prenares —The nostrils.

Prenaris —Naris. Singular of prenares.

Prenatal —Before birth.

Preneoplastic —Before the formation of a tumor.

Preoperative —Before an operation.

Preoptic —In front of the optic chiasma.

Preoral —In front of the mouth.

Preovulatory —Occurring before ovulation.

Preoxygenation —Breathing of 100% oxygen and displacement of nitrogen from the lungs for 2 to 7 minutes prior to induction of general anesthesia.

Prep —To prepare the skin or other body surface for an operation, usually by cleaning and application of antiseptic solutions.

Prepalatal —Located in front of the teeth.

Preparalytic —Before the occurrence of paralysis.

Preparation —1. To make ready, especially a medicine for use. 2. A medicine made ready for use.

Preparturient —Pertaining to the period before birth.

Prepatellar —In front of the patella bone.

Prepatellar bursitis —Housemaid's knee. Inflammation of the bursa in front of the patella bone.

Prepatent —Before becoming evident or manifest.

Prepatent period —The period between entrance of parasites into the body and their appearance in the blood or tissues.

Preperception —The anticipation of a perception.

Preperitoneal —Located in front of the peritoneum.

Preplacental —Occurring before the formation of placenta.

Preponderance —Quality of outweighing or exceeding.

Prepotent —Pertaining to the greater power of one parent to transmit inherited characteristics to the offspring.

Preprandial —Before a meal.

Preprosthetic —Performed or occurring before insertion of a prosthesis.

Prepsychotic —Pertaining to the period prior to the onset of psychosis.

Prepuberal, Prepubertal —Before puberty.

Prepubescent —Pertaining to the period just before puberty.

Prepuce —The foreskin or fold of skin over the glans penis.

Preputia —Plural of preputium.

Preputial —Pertaining to the prepuce.

Preputiotomy —To incise the prepuce of penis to relieve phimosis.

Preputium —Prepuce.

Prepyloric —Anterior to, or before the pylorus of stomach.

Prerectal —Located in front of the rectum.

Prerenal —1. Located in front of the kidney. 2. Occurring before reaching the kidney, as changes in the blood.

Preretinal —In front of the retina of the eye.

Presacral —In front of the sacrum.

Presby-, Presbyo- —Prefixes meaning old age.

Presbyacusia, Presbyacousia —Progressive loss of hearing due to normal aging process.

Presbyatrics, Presbyatry —Geriatrics, presbytiatrics.

Presbycardia —Heart disease or decreased capacity of the cardiac function associated with aging.

Presbycusis, Presbykousis —Presbyacusia.

Presbyope —The person who is presbyopic.

Presbyophrenia —Mental disorder occurring in old age.

Presbyopia —Farsightedness in old age.

Presbyopic —Pertaining to presbyopia.

Presbytiatrics —Geriatrics. Presbyatrics.

Prescribe —To indicate the medicine to be administered.

Prescriber —The doctor who prescribes the medicines.

Prescription —A written direction for dispensing and administering medicines.

Presenile —1. Premature old age. 2. Occurring prior to old age.

Presenility —A condition occurring before the senility is established.

Presenium —Just prior to the onset of senility.

Presentation —1. Lie or the relationship of the long axis of fetus to that of the mother. 2. The position of the fetus presenting itself to the examining finger in the vagina or rectum.

Breech presentation —Presentation of buttocks or legs of the fetus in labor. Breech presentation is of three types. 1. Complete breech presentation:—In it thighs of the fetus are flexed on abdomen and the legs flexed upon the thighs. 2. Frank breech:—The legs of the fetus are extended over the trunk and the feet lying against the face. 3. Incomplete

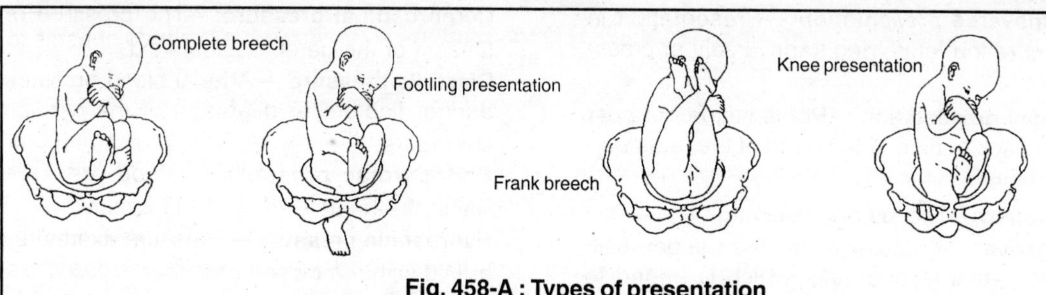

Fig. 458-A : Types of presentation

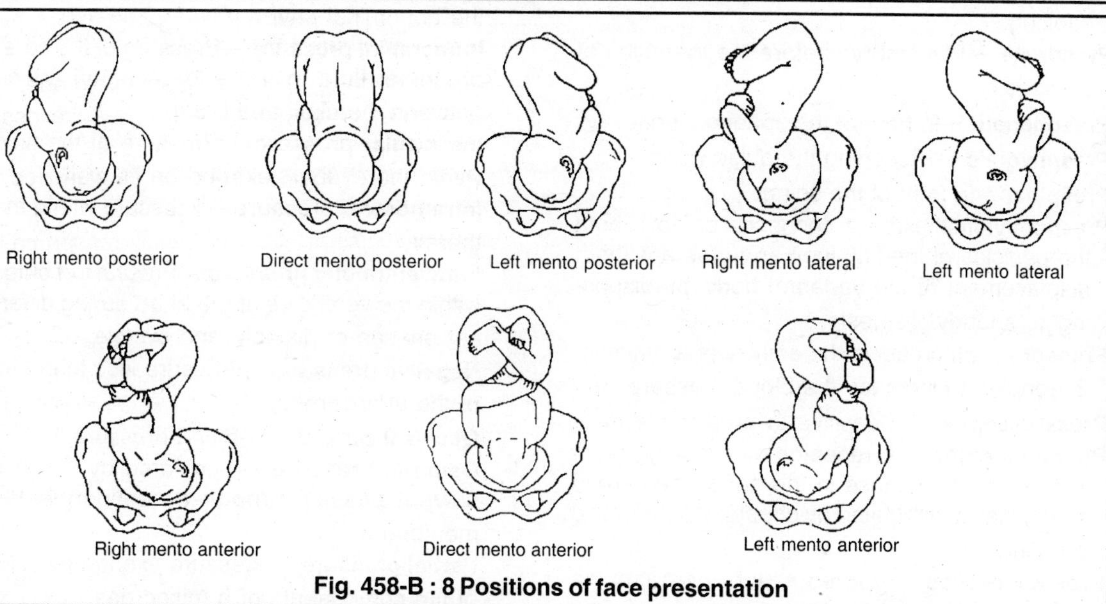

Fig. 458-B : 8 Positions of face presentation

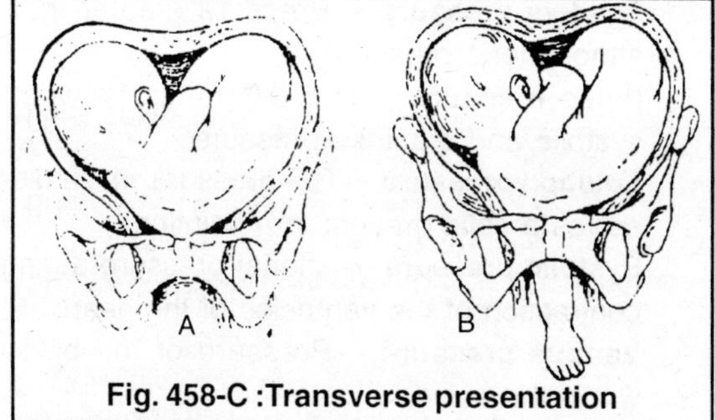

Fig. 458-C :Transverse presentation

A. Right Scapuloanterior
B. Prolapse of the arm in transverse presentation.

breech:—Prolapse of one or both feet or knees into the vagina of the mother.

Brow presentation —Presentation of brow of the fetus in labor.

Cephalic presentation —Presentation of any part of the head of the fetus.

Compound presentation —Prolapse of a limb of the fetus alongside the main presenting part.

Face presentation —Presentation of the face of the fetus in labor.

Footling presentation —Presentation of the fetus with one (single footling) or both (double footling) feet.

Funic presentation —Presentation of the umbilical cord in labor.

Longitudinal presentation —Presentation in which long axis of the fetus is parallel to that of the mother. It is normal.

Oblique presentation —Presentation in which long axis of the fetus is oblique to that of the mother.

Pelvic presentation —Breech presentation.

Placental presentation —Placenta previa. Presentation of the placenta first.

Shoulder presentation —Presentation of the shoulder of the fetus in labor.

Transverse presentation —Presentation in labor of the fetus lying transversely or crosswise.

Vertex presentation —Presentation of upper and back portion of the head of the fetus during labor.

Preservation —The act of preserving.

Preservative —A substance such as suger, salt, vinegar, ethyl alcohol, etc. which is added to medicines or food materials to prevent them from spoiling.

Presomite —The embryo before the formation of somites.

Presphenoid —In front of the sphenoid bone.

Presphygmic —Preceding the pulse wave.

Prespinal —In front of the spine.

Prespondylolisthesis —A congenital defect of both the pedicles of the fifth lumbar vertebra without displacement of the vertebral body, predisposing to spondylolisthesis.

Pressor —1. Increasing the activity of a function. 2. Tending to increase the blood pressure.

Pressoreceptive —Sensitive to pressure stimuli.

Pressoreceptor —A receptor or sensory nerve ending, such as those in the aorta and carotid sinus, that is stimulated by changes in the blood pressure.

Pressor nerves —Nerves which increase the blood pressure on stimulation.

Pressor reflex —Any reflex caused by changes in blood pressure.

Pressosensitive —Pressoreceptive.

Pressosensitivity —Ability to perceive changes in pressure.

Pressure —Stress or force exerted by compression, expansion, pulling, tension or weight.

After-pressure —The pressure remaining for a few seconds after removal of a weight or other pressure.

Arterial pressure —Pressure of blood in the arteries.

Atmospheric pressure —The pressure exerted by the atmosphere.

Biting pressure —The pressure exerted on the teeth during biting. Occlusal pressure.

Blood pressure —Pressure exerted by blood on the walls of the blood vessels.

Capillary pressure —Blood pressure in the blood capillaries.

Cerebrospinal pressure —The pressure or tension of the cerebrospinal fluid.

Diastolic pressure —Arterial blood pressure during diastole or dilatation of the cardiac chambers.

Endocardiac pressure —Blood pressure within the heart.

Hydrostatic pressure —Pressure exerted by a fluid within a closed chamber.

Intra-abdominal pressure —Pressure within the abdominal cavity.

Intracranial pressure —Pressure of the cerebrospinal fluid in the subarachnoid space between the skull and brain.

Intraocular pressure —Pressure of the fluid within the eyeball, exerted on its walls.

Intrathoracic pressure —Pressure within the thorax.

Intraventricular pressure —Pressure of blood within the ventricles of the heart during different phases of diastole and systole.

Negative pressure —Pressure less than that of the atmosphere.

Occlusal pressure —Biting pressure.

Osmotic pressure —The force by which a solvent passes through a semipermeable membrane.

Partial pressure —Pressure exerted by each of the components of a mixed gas.

Positive pressure —Pressure greater than atmospheric pressure.

Pulse pressure —The difference between systolic and diastolic pressure.

Solution pressure —The pressure which dissolves a solid present in a solution.

Systolic pressure —Arterial pressure during contraction of the ventricles of the heart.

Venous pressure —Pressure of the blood within the veins.

Pressure palsy —Temporary paralysis due to pressure on a nerve trunk.

Pressure paralysis —Paralysis due to pressure on the spinal cord.

Presternum —The manubrium or the upper part of the sternum.

Presuppurative —Before pus formation.

Presymptomatic —Before the appearance of symptoms.

Presynaptic —Located before the nerve synapse.

Presyncope —Faintness.

Presystole —Perisystole. The period just before the systole in the heart's cycle.

Presystolic —Just before the systole.

Pretarsal —In front of the tarsus.

Preterm —Occurring before 37th week of pregnancy.

Preterm birth —Delivery occurring between 20 and 38 weeks' pregnancy.

Preterm labor —Premature labor (See under labor)

Prethyroid, Prethyroideal —Anterior to the thyroid gland.

Pretibial —In front of the tibia.

Pretracheal —Anterior to the trachea.

Pretympanic —Located in front of the tympanic membrane.

Preurethritis —Inflammation around the urethral opening in female.

Prevalence —The total number of cases of a specific disease present in a given population at a certain time.

Prevention —Obstruction.

Preventive —Prophylactic. Preventing the occurrence of a disease.

Preventive medicine —The branch of medical science concerned with the prevention of physical and mental diseases.

Prevertebral —In front of a vertebra.

Prevertiginous —With the tendency to fall forward.

Prevesical —Located in front of the urinary bladder.

Previa, Praevia —Appearing before or in front of.

Previable —Pertaining to a fetus unable to survive outside the uterus.

Prezonular —Pertaining to the posterior chamber of the eye.

Prezygotic —Occurring before fertilization.

Priapism —Persistent abnormal, painful erection of the penis.

Priapitis —Inflammation of the penis.

Priapus —The penis.

Pricking —The act of piercing.

Prickle cell —A cell with rod-shaped processes.

Prickly heat —Red cutaneous eruption with itching seen in hot weather.

Priessnitz compress —A cold wet-compress.

Primacy —The state of being primary.

Primal scene —Child's observation of sexual intercourse for the first time.

Primary —Principal. First in time or order.

Primary amputation —Amputation performed before the onset of inflammation.

Primary bubo —Primarily inflamed lymph node due to a venereal disease, especially syphilis.

Primary care —General health care of the patient at his/her first contact with the doctor.

Primary lesion —1. An original lesion from which a second one arises. 2. Primary chancre of syphilis.

Primary sore —The initial sore or hard chancre of syphilis.

Primate —An individual of the order Primates.

Primates —The highest order of mammals including monkeys, men, etc.

Prime —1. Period of best health and greatest strength. 2. To give an initial treatment in preparation for either a large dose of the same medicine, or a different medicine.

Primigravida —A woman pregnant for the first time.

Primipara —A woman who has borne one alive or dead infant of 500 gms. or more (or of 20 weeks gestation).

Primiparity —The condition of giving birth to only one alive or dead infant of 500 gms. or more (or of 20 weeks of gestation).

Primiparous —Pertaining to a primipara.

Primitiae —Liquor amnii appearing just before birth of the infant.

Primitive —First in point of time; original; embryonic.

Primordia —Plural of primordium.

Primordial —1. Existing first. 2. Existing in an early or primitive form.

Primordium —The first accumulation of cells in an embryo from which a tissue, organ or part of the infant develops.

Primus —First of a series of similar structures.

Princeps —1. Original; first. 2. Chief; principal.

Principal —1. Chief. 2. Prominent.

Principes —Plural of princeps.

Principle —1. A constituent of a chemical compound representing its essential properties. 2. A substance on which certain properties of a drug depend. 3. A fundamental truth. 4. A rule of action.

Active principle —The constituent of a drug which produces therapeutic effect.

Antianemic principle —A substance formed in the stomach and intestine by the interaction of an extrinsic factor, vit. B_{12}, and Castle's intrinsic factor present in the gastric juice. It is stored in the liver and is essential for the normal development of red blood cells in bone marrow.

Hematinic principle —Vit. B_{12} or cyanocobalamin.

Priority —Precedence.

Prism —A transparent solid substance, three sides of which are parallelograms, the bases perpendicular to the three sides are triangles and the transverse section of the solid is a triangle.

Prisma —A structure resembling a prism.

Prismata —Plural of prism.

Prismatic —1. Shaped like a prism. 2. Produced by a prism.

Prismoid —Resembling a prism.

Prismoptometer —An apparatus for estimating the abnormal refraction of the eye by using prisms.

Prismosphere —A prism combined with a spherical lens.

Privacy —1. Secrecy. 2. Lonely place.

Privates —The external genitals; private parts.

Privy —Latrine.

p.r.n. —According to circumstances.

Pro- —A prefix indicating for, in front of, before and favoring.

Proaccelerin —Coagulation Factor V.

Proactivator —A precursor of an activator; a factor, which reacts with an enzyme to form an activator.

Proal —Pertaining to the forward movement.

Proantithrombin —A substance present in the blood plasma or serum, which is converted into antithrombin through the action of heparin.

Proband —Propositus.

Probang —A slim, flexible rod with a sponge or similar material attached to its one end. It is used for determining the location of stricture in the larynx or esophagus, to apply medicines or remove matter from there.

Probationary —One in a trial period for the appointment in service.

Probationer —The person working during a trial period.

Probe —A long, slender instrument for exploring the depth and direction of a wound, sinus or passage.

Proboscis —The projected portion of mouth in some animals as in elephant.

Procarcinogen —A chemical substance that becomes carcinogenic only after it is altered by metabolic processes.

Procaryotae —Plural of procaryote.

Procaryote —Prokaryote.

Procaryotic —Prokaryotic.

Procatarctic —Predisposing as the cause of a disease.

Procatarxis —The beginning of a disease through a predisposing factor.

Procedure —Method of doing work.

Procelia —A lateral ventricle of the brain.

Procelous —Concave anteriorly.

Procentriole —The immediate precursor of centrioles and ciliary basal bodies in the cell.

Procephalic —Of, or pertaining to, the anterior part of the head.

Process —1. A method of action. 2. A prominence, projection or outgrowth from a bone or tissue, *e.g.*, mastoid process which is a conical projection of the mastoid portion of the temporal bone, xiphoid process which is an elongated, thin and pointed process at the lower

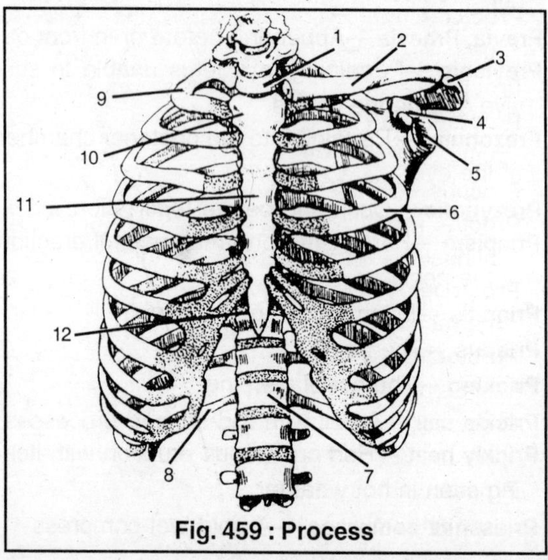

Fig. 459 : Process

1. First thoracic vertebra, 2. Clavicle 3. Acromial process of scapula, 4. Coracoid process of scapula, 5. Glenoid cavity of scapula, 6. 4th rib 7. 12th thoracic vertebra, 8. 12th rib, 9. First rib, 10. Manubrium sterni, 11. Body of the sternum, 12. Xiphoid process of sternum

end of the sternum. 3. Series of steps leading to achievement of a specific result. 4. State of progress of a disease.

Processor —A device for converting one form of energy into another form of energy or one form of material into another form of material.

Processus —Process.

Procheilon —Prominence in the center of the upper lip.

Prochilon —Procheilon.

Prochondral —Before the formation of cartilage.

Prochordal —In front of the notochord.

Procidentia —A complete prolapse, especially of the uterus.

Procoagulant —Tending to promote coagulation of blood.

Procollagen —Precursor of collagen.

Proconvertin —Coagulation factor VII.

Procreate —To generate or reproduce.

Procreation —Reproduction.

Procreative —Pertaining to reproduction.

Proctagra—Sudden pain in the rectum.

Proctalgia —Pain about the anus and in rectum.

Proctatresia —Imperforation of the anus.

Proctectasia —Dilatation of the anus or rectum.

Proctectomy —Rectectomy. Excision of the rectum.

Proctenclisis —Stricture of the anus or rectum.

Procteurynter —An instrument for dilating the anus or rectum.

Proctitis —Rectitis. Inflammation of the rectum.

Procto-, Proct- —Combining forms indicating relationship to the anus and rectum.

Proctocele —Rectocele. Protrusion of a part of the rectum into the vagina.

Proctoclysis —Introduction of a fluid into the rectum slowly drop by drop.

Proctococcypexia, Proctococcypexy —Fixation of the rectum to the coccyx.

Proctocolectomy —Surgical excision of the rectum and colon.

Proctocolitis —Inflammation of the rectum and colon.

Proctocolonoscopy —Inspection of the interior of the rectum and lower colon.

Proctocolpoplasty —Repair by plastic surgery of a rectovaginal fistula.

Proctocystocele —Herniation of the urinary bladder into the rectum.

Proctocystoplasty —Plastic surgery of the rectum and urinary bladder.

Proctocystotomy —To make an incision into urinary bladder through the rectum.

Proctodeal —Pertaining to the proctodeum.

Proctodeum —An ectodermal depression of caudal end of the embryo, which later on ruptures and the anus is formed.

Proctodynia —Proctalgia.

Proctologic —Pertaining to proctology.

Proctologist —Specialist in diseases of the colon, rectum and anus.

Proctology —The branch of medical science dealing with the treatment of diseases of the colon, rectum and anus.

Proctoparalysis —Proctoplegia. Paralysis of the anal and rectal muscles.

Proctoperineoplasty —Plastic surgery of the anus and rectum.

Proctoperineorrhaphy —Proctoperineoplasty.

Proctopexia, Proctopexy —Fixation of the rectum to some other part.

Proctophobia —Morbid fear of suffering from rectal disease.

Proctoplasty —Plastic repair of the rectum.

Proctoplegia —Proctoparalysis.

Proctopolypus —Polyp of the rectum.

Proctoptosia —Proctoptosis.

Proctoptosis —Prolapse of the rectum.

Proctorrhagia —Bleeding from the rectum.

Proctorrhaphy —Suturing of the rectum.

Proctorrhea —Mucous discharge from the anus.

Proctoscope —An instrument for inspecting the rectum.

Proctoscopy —Inspection of the rectum with a proctoscope.

Proctosigmoid —The area of the anal canal and the sigmoid colon.

Proctosigmoidectomy —Surgical removal of the anus, rectum and sigmoid colon.

Proctosigmoiditis —Inflammation of the rectum and sigmoid colon.

Proctosigmoidoscope —An instrument for inspecting the rectum and sigmoid colon.

Proctosigmoidoscopy —Visual examination of the rectum and sigmoid colon by proctosigmoidoscope.

Proctospasm —Spasm of the rectum.

Proctostasis —Constipation.

Proctostenosis —Narrowing of the rectum.

Proctostomy —To make a permanent opening from body surface into the rectum.

Proctotome —A knife for making incision into the rectum.

Proctotomy —To make an incision into the rectum or anus.

Proctotresia —Surgical correction of an imperforate anus.

Proctovalvotomy —To make an incision into the rectal valves.

Procumbent —Prone. Lying face down.

Procursive —Tending to run forward.

Procurvation —A bending forward.

Prodromal —Pertaining to the initial stage of a disease.

Prodromal rash —A rash before the appearance of true rash of an infectious disease.

Prodrome —A symptom indicating the onset of a disease.

Prodromi —Plural of prodromus.

Prodromic —Prodromal.

Prodromous —Prodromic.

Prodromus —Prodrome.

Prodrug —An inert drug which becomes active when it is converted by metabolic processes within the body.

Product—Anything produced naturally or artificially.

Production —The act of producing or forming.

Productive —Producing or forming, especially new tissue.

Proemial —Prodromal.

Proencephalon —Prosencephalon.

Proencephalus —A fetus with protrusion of the brain through a fissure in the frontal area of the skull.

Proenzyme —Zymogen. An inactive precursor of an enzyme.

Proerythroblast —Pronormoblast.

Proerythrocyte —An immature red blood cell with a nucleus. It is the precursor of the red blood cell.

Proestrogen —A substance without estrogenic activity but which is metabolized into active estrogen in the body.

Proferment —Proenzyme.

Professional —Pertaining to a profession.

Profibrinolysin —Plasminogen. The inactive precursor of the enzyme fibrinolysin.

Profile —1. An outline of the side view of an object, especially of the head or face. 2. A graph representing the characteristics determined by tests.

Profilometer —An instrument for measuring the roughness of a surface, e.g., of teeth.

Profluvium —Flux. An excessive flow or discharge.

Profluvium lactis —Excessive flow of milk.

Profunda —Deep seated.

Profundaplasty —Reconstruction of an occluded or stenosed deep femoral artery.

Profundus —Deep.

Profuse —Excessive.

Progastrin —An inactive precursor of gastrin.

Progenital —On the external surface of the genital organs.

Progenitor —An ancestor.

Progeny —Offspring.

Progeria —Premature old age occurring in childhood.

Progestational —Pertaining to the phase of the menstrual cycle just before menstruation when by the action of progesterone hormone, the endometrium is again prepared for implantation of the fertilized ovum.

Progestational agent —Progestin. Any chemical substance which has the effect of progesterone hormone which is generally used in birth control pills.

Progesterone —A steroid hormone liberated by the corpus luteum, adrenal cortex and placenta, whose function is to prepare the uterus for the implantation and development of the fertilized ovum, by causing changes in the endometrium in the second half of menstrual cycle.

Progestin —1. Progesterone. 2. A synthetic drug having the progesterone-like effect on the uterus.

Progestogen —Any hormonal substance producing the effects similar to those due to progesterone.

Proglossis —Tip of the tongue.

Proglottid —Proglottis. One of the segments of a tapewom.

Proglottis —Proglottid.

Prognathic —Prognathous.

Prognathism —Abnormal projection of one or both jaws.

Prognathous —Having projected jaws.

Prognose —To predict the course of a disease.

Prognosis —Prediction of the probable course of a disease, of the chance of recovery and even of the probability of death of the patient.

Prognosis anceps —Doubtful prognosis.

Prognosis fausta —Favorable prognosis.

Prognosis infausta —Unfavorable prognosis.

Prognostic —Pertaining to the prognosis of a disease.

Prognosticate —Prognose to give a prognosis.

Prognostician —The person skilful in prognosis.

Prograde —In the normal direction of flow.

Progranulocyte —Promyelocyte.

Progravid —Before pregnancy.

Progression —Advancement.

Progressive —Advancing as a disease.

Progressive muscular dystrophy —Gradual advancing atrophy of muscles due to degeneration of the spinal cord.

Prohibition —Forbidden.

Prohormone —A precursor of a hormone.

Proinsulin —A precursor of insulin produced in the beta cells of the pancreas.

Projectile vomiting —Vomiting in which contents of the stomach are ejected forcibly which fall down at a little distance from the patient.

Projection —1. The process of throwing forward. 2. Sharp prominence. 3. A connection between cerebral cortex and oter parts of the nervous system. 4. The act of extending. 5. The mental process by which sensations are referred to the sense organs or receptors stimulated. 6. Distortion of a perception as a result of which one hates the person without cause, who was being loved, or attracted toward them who were being hated before.

Prokaryon —1. Nuclear material scattered in the cytoplasm and not bounded by a membrane. 2. Prokaryote.

Prokaryote —Unicellular organism having a single, circular chromosome, without nucleus and nuclear membrane.

Prokaryotic —Procaryotic. Pertaining to prokaryote.

Prolabial —Denoting the prominent central portion of the upper lip.

Prolabium —The prominent central portion of the upper lip.

Prolactin —A hormone of the anterior pituitary gland which stimulates the milk formation.

Prolactinoma —A tumor of the pituitary gland which secretes prolactin.

Prolapse —Procidentia. Ptosis. A falling down or downward displacement of an organ or part of the body such as the uterus or rectum.

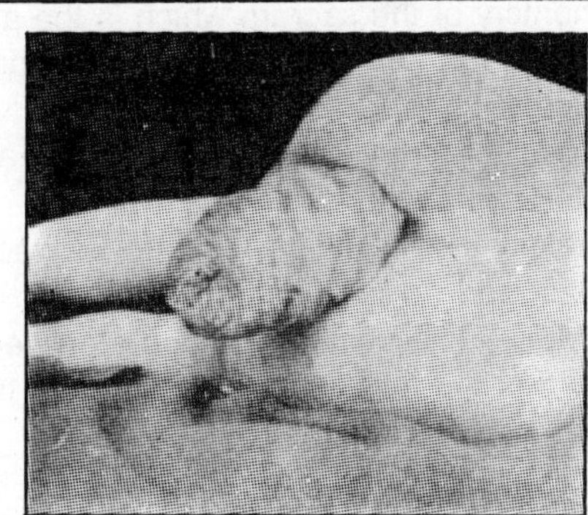

Fig. 460 : Prolapse rectum

Prolapsus —Prolapse.

Prolective —Denoting the number of deaths from a given cause in a specified period, per 100 or 1000 total deaths.

Prolepsis —Recurrence of a paroxysmal attack after short interval.

Proleptic —Recurring before the expected time.

Proleukocyte —An undeveloped leukocyte.

Proliferate —To increase by reproduction of the same forms.

Proliferation —Reproduction and multiplication of similar forms, especially of the cells.

Proliferative —Proliferous.

Proliferous —1. Multiplying, as by the formation of new tissue cells. 2. Bearing offspring.

Prolific—Fertile. Fruitful. Reproductive.

Proligerous —Producing offspring.

Prolymphocyte —A cell intermediate between the lymphoblast and lymphocyte.

Promegakaryocyte —A precursor of megakaryocyte.

Promegaloblast —A precursor of megaloblast.

Prometaphase —The stage of mitosis in which the nuclear membrane disintegrates and the centrioles reach the poles of the cell, while the chromosomes continue to contract.

Prominence —A projection or protrusion.

Prominentia —Prominence.

Prominentiae —Plural of prominentia.

Promitochondria —Premitochondria. Precursors of mitochondria.

Promonocyte —A precursor of monocyte.

Promontoria —Plural of promontorium.

Promontorium —Promontory.

Promontory —A projecting process or part, *e.g.*, promontory of the sacrum which is the anterior projecting part of the pelvic surface of the base of sacrum bone.

Promoter —A substance which assists a catalyst to act.

Promyelocyte—A cell intermediate between myeloblast and a myelocyte.

Pronasion —The point of the angle between the septum of the nose and the surface of the upper lip.

Pronate —To place or to be in a prone position.

Pronation —1. The act of lying with the face downward. 2. The act of turning the hand with the palm facing downward or backward.

Pronator —That which pronates.

Pronaus, Pronaeus —The vagina or the vestibule of vagina.

Prone —1. Lying straight with the face downward. 2. Turning the hand with the palm facing downward.

Prong —Conical such as the root of a tooth.

Pronograde —Walking on hands and feet.

Pronometer —An apparatus for showing the amount of pronation or supination of forearm.

Pronormoblast —Proerythroblast. The earliest precursor of the red blood cell.

Pronuclei —Plural of pronucleus.

Pronucleus —After fertilization of the ovum, the nucleus of the ovum or of the spermatozoon.

Prootic —In front of the ear.

Prop —An instrument used to support or hold something in place, such as mouth prop which is a metal or rubber instrument which is inserted between the jaws to maintain the mouth in an open position.

Propagate —1. To reproduce or generate. 2. To grow forward.

Propagation —Reproduction. Generation.

Propagative —Pertaining to reproduction.

Propalinal —Applied to a backward and forward movement, as of the jaws.

Propepsin —Pepsinogen.

Propeptone —Hemialbumose. An intermediate product between protein and peptone in the digestive process.

Propeptonuria —Hemialbumosuria. Excretion of propeptone in the urine.

Properitoneal —In front of the peritoneum.

Prophase —First stage of the cell division of the mitosis type.

Prophylactic —1. Any agent contributing to prevent infection and disease. 2. Pertaining to prophylaxis.

Prophylaxes—Plural of prophylaxis.

Prophylaxis—The preventive treatment.

Proplasmacyte —The precursor of plasma cell.

Proplastid —A granule in the cytoplasm from which a plastid is formed.

Proplexus —The choroid plexus in the lateral ventricle of the brain.

Proportion —Ratio.

Propositus —Proband. The original person presenting a physical or mental disorder who serves as the basis for a hereditary or a genetic investigation.

Proprietary medicine —The medicine used in the treatment of diseases, protected against free competition as to name, manufacturing process by patent, trade mark, copyright or secrecy.

Proprioception—The awareness of posture and movement of the body and the knowledge of position, weight, and resistance of objects in relation to the body.

Proprioceptive —Pertaining to proprioception.

Proprioceptor —Any of the sensory nerve endings giving information about the movements and position of the body, which occur chiefly in the muscles, tendons and the labyrinth.

Propriospinal —Pertaining to the spinal cord exclusively.

Proptometer —An instrument for measuring the degree of exophthalmos.

Proptosis —Downward displacement as of the uterus or of the upper eyelid in Myasthenia gravis.

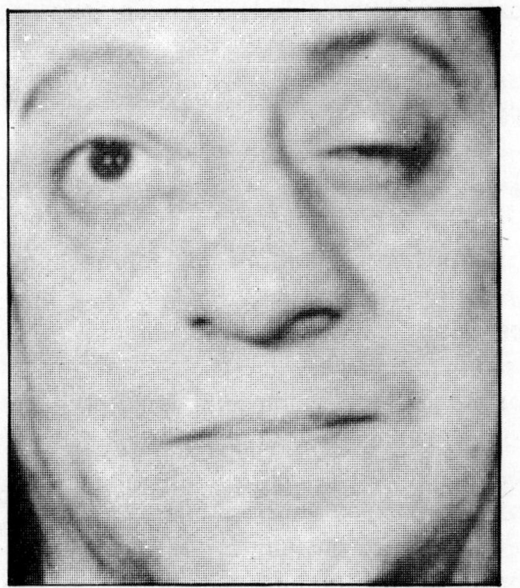

Fig. 461 : Proptosis of the upper eyelid in Myasthenia gravis

Proptotic —Pertaining to proptosis.

Propulsion —1. A tendency to fall forward in walking. 2. Festination.

Pro re nata —According to the circumstances.

Prorrhaphy—Advancement. Suturing of a muscle or tendon insertion to a place farther away, to change the action of the muscle.

Prorsad —In a forward direction.

Prorubricyte —A basophilic normoblast.

Prosecretin —A precursor of secretin.

Prosect —To dissect a cadaver or a part of it.

Prosection —Preplanned dissection for demonstrating the anatomic structure.

Prosector —The person who performs dissection.

Prosectorium —A dissecting room or a place where anatomical preparations are made for demonstration before a class.

Prosencephalon —Embryonic forebrain.

Proso- —A prefix which means forward or anterior.

Prosodemic —Spreading by contact from one person to another, said of a disease.

Prosopagnosia —Inability to recognize the faces, even one's own face.

Prosopagus —Prosopopagus.

Prosopalgia —Trigeminal neuralgia.

Prosopectasia —Enlargement of the face.

Prosopic —Pertaining to face convex anteriorly.

Prosoplasia—The transformation of cells until they develop into the cells with higher function.

Prosopoanoschisis —Oblique cleft on the face extending from the mouth to the eye.

Prosopodiplegia —Paralysis of the face and one lower limb.

Prosopodynia —Pain in the face.

Prosoponeuralgia —Prosopalgia.

Prosopopagus—Conjoined twins of unequal size in which the smaller one is attached to some part of the face other than the jaw of the larger one.

Prosopoplegia —Facial paralysis.

Prosoposchisis —Congenital fissure of the face.

Prosopospasm—Facial spasm.

Prosoposternodymia —Conjoined twins joined face to face and sternum to sternum.

Prosopothoracopagus —Two conjoined fetuses joined from the face to the thorax.

Prosopotocia —Face presentation during childbirth.

Prosopus varus —Congenital obliquity of the face due to atrophy of one side of the head.

Prostaglandins—A group of fatty acid derivatives, synthesized in the body from unsaturated fatty acids, which are found in the prostate gland, menstrual fluid, brain, lung, kidney, thymus gland, seminal fluid and pancreas. There are a great number of prostaglandins which affect many tissues and organs of the body. They stimulate the contractility of the uterus and other smooth muscle and lower the blood pressure, regulate acid secretion of the stomach, body temperature and platelet aggregation, and control inflammation. They also affect the action of certain hormones.

Prostata —Prostate.

Prostatalgia —Pain in the prostate gland.

Prostate—A three-lobed gland surrounding the neck of the urinary bladder and urethra in the male, which opens into the prostatic portion of urethra through ducts. It secretes a thin and slightly alkaline fluid that forms a portion of the semen.

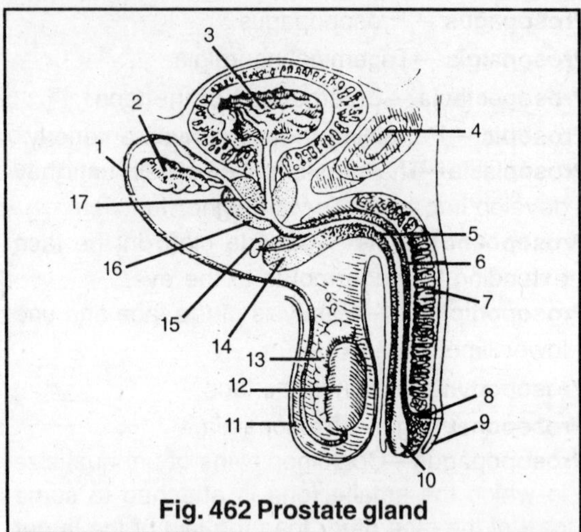

Fig. 462 Prostate gland

1. Deferent duct or vas deferens, 2. Seminal vesicle, 3. Cavity of the urinary bladder, 4. Symphysis pubis, 5. Urethra, 6. & 7. Corpus cavernosa, 8. Glans penis, 9. Prepuce, 10. Urethral dilatation, 11. Scrotum, 12. Testis, 13. Epididymis, 14. Bulb of corpus cavernosum, 15. Cowper's gland, 16. Prostate gland, 17. Ejaculatory duct

Prostatectomy —Excision of part or all of the prostate gland.

Prostathelcosis —Ulceration of the prostate gland.

Prostatic —Pertaining to the prostate gland.

Prostatic calculus —A stone in the prostate gland.

Prostatic hypertrophy —Enlargement of the prostate gland in old age, which is not due to inflammation or tumor.

Prostaticovesical —Pertaining to the prostate gland and the urinary bladder.

Prostatic plexus —1. Veins around the neck of the urinary bladder and prostate gland. 2. Nerves from the pelvic plexus to the prostate gland.

Prostatic syncope —Fainting during examination of the prostate gland.

Prostatic urethra —The portion of the urethra surrounded by the prostate gland.

Prostatism —Any condition of the prostate gland interferring with the flow of urine from the urinary bladder.

Prostatitis —Inflammation of the prostate gland.

Prostatocystitis —Inflammation of the prostatic urethra and the urinary bladder.

Prostatocystotomy —To make an incision into the prostate gland and the urinary bladder.

Prostatodynia —Prostatalgia.

Prostatography —X-ray examination of the prostate gland after introduction of a contrast medium.

Prostatolith —A stone in the prostate gland.

Prostatolithotomy —To incise the prostate gland to remove a calculus.

Prostatomegaly —Enlargement of the prostate gland.

Prostatomy —Prostatotomy.

Prostatomyomectomy —Surgical excision of a prostatic myoma.

Prostatorrhea —Abnormal discharge from the prostate gland.

Prostatoseminalvesiculectomy —Prostatovesiculectomy.

Prostatosis —Any noninflammatory and nonmalignant disease of the prostate gland.

Prostatotomy —To incise the prostate gland.

Prostatovesiculectomy —Surgical removal of the prostate gland and the seminal vesicles.

Prostatovesiculitis —Inflammation of the prostate gland and the seminal vesicles.

Prosternation —Camptocormia.

Prostheon —Prosthion.

Prostheses— Plural of prosthesis.

Prosthesis —1. Replacement of a missing part of the body by an artificial part such as an artificial limb. 2. An artificial organ or part of the body such as an eye, tooth or limb etc. 3. An apparatus for enhancing a natural function such as hearing aid.

Prosthetic —Pertaining to prostheses or prosthetics.

Prosthetics —The branch of surgery which deals with replacement of missing parts.

Prosthetist —1. Specialist in artificial dentures. 2. Maker of artificial limbs.

Prosthetosclerokeratoplasty —Replacement of diseased sclera and cornea with a transparent prosthesis by plastic surgery.

Prosthion —The lowest point on the maxillary alveolar process.

Prosthodontia —Prosthodontics.

Prosthodontics —The branch of dentistry concerned with the construction of artificial appliances for the mouth.

Prosthodontist —A dental specialist in making and fitting artificial teeth.

Prosthokeratoplasty —Replacement of a diseased or scarred cornea with a transparent prosthesis by plastic surgery.

Prostholith —A preputial calculus.

Prostitute —One who accepts money for sexual relations.

Prostitution —The act or practice of prostituting.

Prostrate —1. To deprive of energy. 2. Lying straight with the body stretched out.

Prostrated —Depleted of strength, exhausted.

Prostration —Extreme exhaustion or lack of energy.

Heat prostration —Exhaustion resulting from exposure to excessive heat.

Nervous prostration —Neurasthenia.

Protal —Congenital.

Protanomaly —Deficiency of red color perception due to deficiency of red-sensitive pigment in the cones of the retina of the eye.

Protanope —A person with red color blindness.

Protanopia —Red color blindness.

Protean —Capable to be changed into different forms as ameba.

Protease —A protein-splitting enzyme.

Protectant —Affording defence or immunity.

Protective —Protectant.

Protector —A substance in a catalyst which prolongs the rate of activity of the catalyst.

Proteid —Protein.

Proteidogenous —Producing proteins.

Protein —Any of a group of complex organic compounds containing carbon, hydrogen, oxygen, nitrogen and sulfur, which occur naturally in plants and animals. They yield amino acids on hydrolysis which are essential for growth and repair of the injured tissues and building of new tissues. Proteins are the chief constituents of plasma of cells. They are found in milk, egg, pulses, cheese, meat, fish, soyabeans etc.

Antitumor protein —A protein that inhibits the growth of tumor.

Antiviral protein —A protein that inhibits the multiplication of viruses.

Bence jones protein —An abnormal protein found in the urine in multiple myeloma, lymphosarcoma, leukemia, or Hodgkin's disease.

Blood protein —A protein present in the blood, including hemoglobin in red blood cells and serum proteins.

Carrier protein —A protein which is capable of eliciting an immune response when coupled with a hapten.

Complete protein —Protein containing all the essential amino acids.

Conjugated proteins —Protein in which the protein molecule is combined with nonprotein molecules, *e.g.*, nucleoproteins, glycoproteins, lipoproteins and metalloproteins.

C-reactive protein (CRP)—A beta-globulin found in the serum of the persons suffering from certain inflammatory, degenerative, and neoplastic diseases.

Foreign protein —A protein that differs from any protein normally found in the body.

Immune protein —Protein that protects the body against antigens.

Incomplete protein —Protein lacking one or more of the essential amino acids.

Plasma protein —Proteins present in the blood plasma such as albumin or globulin.

Serum protein —Proteins present in the blood serum, such as immunoglobulins, albumin, complement, coagulation factors and enzymes.

Proteinaceous —Pertaining to or resembling proteins.

Proteinemia —An excess of protein in the blood.

Proteinic —Pertaining to protein.

Proteinogenic —Proteogenic.

Proteinogenous —Producing protein.

Proteinophobia —Aversion to food containing protein.

Proteinosis —Accumulation of excess of protein in the tissues.

Proteinuria —Albuminuria. Presence of albumin in the urine.

Proteo-, Prot- —Prefixes meaning protein.

Proteoclastic —Splitting up protein.

Proteogenic —Proteinogenic. Capable of producing proteins.

Proteolipid —A lipid-protein complex that is insoluble in water and found chiefly in the brain.

Proteolysed —Hydrolyzed protein.

Proteolysin—A specific substance causing decomposition of proteins.

Proteolysis —The splitting of proteins by hydrolysis into simpler substances, usually by the action of enzyme.

Proteolytic —Hastening the hydrolysis of proteins.
Proteometabolic —Pertaining to the metabolism of proteins.
Proteometabolism —Digestion, absorption, and assimilation of proteins.
Proteopectic —Proteopexic.
Proteopepsis —The digestion of proteins.
Proteopeptic —Pertaining to the digestion of, or digesting protein.
Proteopexic —Pertaining to the fixation of proteins within the body.
Proteopexis —The fixation of protein in the tissues.
Proteopexy —The fixation of proteins within the body.
Proteose —An intermediate product of proteolysis between protein and peptone.
Proteosuria —Albumosuria. Presence of proteose in the urine.
Proteuria —Proteinuria.
Proteus —It is a genus of gram-negative, facultative, anaerobic, fermenting enteric bacilli, found in the intestines and fecal matter, causing protein decomposition. It causes infection of the urinary tract and septicemia. There are 4 species of Proteus—P. mirabilis. P.vulgaris. P. morganii and P. rettgeri.
Prothrombin —Coagulation Factor II. See coagulation.
Prothrombinase —Thromboplastin. An enzyme important in the coagulation of blood.
Prothrombinemia —Presence of prothrombin in the blood.
Prothrombinogen —Coagulation factor VII.
Prothrombinogenic —Enhancing the production of prothrombin.
Prothrombinopenia —Hypoprothrombinemia. Deficiency of prothrombin in the blood.
Prothrombokinase—Coagulation factor V and VIII.
Prothymocyte —A precursor of T cell in the thymus gland.
Protide —Protein.
Protist —Any member of the Protista kingdom.
Protista —A kingdom including all unicellular animals, and plants which are not easily classified as being either plants or animals.
Protistologist —One who studies the unicellular organisms.
Protistology —Microbiology. The scientific study of unicellular plants and microorganisms.
Proto-, Prot- —Prefixes meaning first in a series.
Protobiology —Bacteriophagology. The study of bacteriophages.
Protoblast —1. A naked cell. *i.e.*, cell without cell wall 2. A blastomere of the segmenting ovum from which a particular organ or part develops.
Protoblastic —Pertaining to a protoblast.
Protocol —The original notes made on examination of a patient, on an experiment or at postmortem examination.
Protodiastole —Diastole occurring immediately following the second heart sound.
Protodiastolic —Pertaining to protodiastole.
Protoduodenum —The upper half of the duodenum.
Protoerythrocyte —A primitive erythroblast.
Protogastor —Archenteron. Gastrocele. The cavity in a gastrula or developing embryo from which the digestive tract develops.
Protoleukocyte—A minute lymphoid cell in red bone marrow and in the spleen.
Proton —The positively charged part of the nucleus of an atom around which the negative electrons revolve.
Protoneuron —The first neuron in a peripheral reflex arc.
Protoplasia —The primary formation of tissue.
Protoplasm —A thick, viscous, translucent, colloid material, the essential constituent of all the living cells, including cytoplasm and nucleoplasm and which is the basis of all activities of the living organisms.
Protoplasmatic —Protoplasmic.
Protoplasmic —Pertaining to or composed of protoplasm.
Protoplasmolysis —Plasmolysis.
Protoplast —A bacterial or plant cell without cell wall but its plasma membrane intact.
Protoporphyria —Fecal excretion of protoporphyrin in excess.
Protoporphyrin —It occurs naturally and is formed from heme, *i.e.*, an iron-containing protein-free portion of the hemoglobin.
Protoporphyrinuria —Presence of protoporphyrin in the urine.
Protospasm—A spasm which begins in one area and extends to other parts.

Prototroph —An organism with the same requirements of nutrition as its ancestors.

Prototrophic —Requiring simple inorganic elements as food.

Prototrophism—Requirement of simple inorganic elements as food.

Prototype —The original form which is typical for the subsequent individuals.

Protovertebra —Primitive vertebra in the notochord.

Protovertebral —Pertaining to a protovertebra.

Protozoa —Plural of protozoon.

Protozoacide —Destructive to protozoa.

Protozoal —Pertaining to or caused by protozoa.

Protozoan —Of, or pertaining to protozoa.

Protozoiasis —Any disease caused by protozoa.

Protozoicide —Protozoacide.

Protozoologist —Specialist in protozoology.

Protozoology —Study of the protozoa.

Protozoon —Any unicellular animal.

Protozoophage —A phagocyte that ingests protozoa.

Protraction —The extension forward of a part of the body such as the mandible.

Protractor —1. An instrument for removing foreign bodies from wounds. 2. A muscle drawing a part forward.

Protrude —To project or to extend.

Protrusin —The condition of projecting or extending.

Protuberance —Prominence. A prominent part like a knob.

Protuberantia —Protuberance.

Proud —Characterized by excessive granulation tissue.

Proud flesh —A mass of excessive granulation formed when a wound does not heal.

Provertebra —Protovertebra.

Provirus —The precursor of a virus.

Provisional —Temporary.

Provitamin—The precursor of vitamin. An inactive substance which can be transformed in the body to a vitamin, *e.g.*, carotene, which is transformed in the body into vitamin A.

Provocative—An agent that excites appetite or passion.

Proxi- —Prefix which means proximal.

Proximad —Toward the proximal or central point.

Proximal —Nearest.

Proximalis —Proximal.

Proximate —Situated at the nearest point or occurring just next to.

Proximoataxia —Ataxia occurring in the proximal part of an extremity.

Proximobuccal —Pertaining to the proximal and buccal surfaces of a tooth.

Proximolabial—Pertaining to the proximal and labial surfaces of a tooth.

Proximolingual —Pertaining to the proximal and lingual surfaces of a tooth.

Prozymogen —A precursor of zymogen.

Pruriginous —Causing, or pertaining to, or of the nature of prurigo.

Prurigo —A chronic skin disease marked by the formation of dome-shaped eruptions with a small transient vesicle on the top with intense itching following by crusting.

Pruritic —Pertaining to the pruritus.

Pruritogenic —Causing pruritus or itching.

Pruritus —Itching.

- **Pruritus ani** —Itching occurring in the anal region.
- **Pruritus aquagenic** —Pruritus caused by contact with water.
- **Pruritus essential** —Itching occurring without known cause.
- **Pruritus estivalis** —Itching with prickly heat occurring in summer season.
- **Pruritus hiemalis** —Itching occurring in winter season.
- **Pruritus senilis** —Itching occurring in old age due to degeneration of the skin.
- **Pruritus symptomatic** —Itching occurring as a symptom of another disease.
- **Pruritus uremic** —Generalized itching occurring in chronic renal failure.
- **Pruritus vulvae** —Severe itching occurring at the vulva.

Psalteria —Plural of psalterium.

Psalterium —Commissure of the fornix of the brain.

Psammoma —A small tumor of the brain containing calcareous particles.

Psammoma bodies —Brain sand. Laminated bodies of calcium and magnesium phosphates, and carbonates found in the pineal body.

Psammomatous —Possessing psammoma bodies.

Psammosarcoma —A sarcoma tumor containing psammoma bodies.

Psammotherapy —Treatment of the diseases by application of sand.

Psammous —Sandy, gritty.

Pselaphesia, Pselaphesis —Carphology. Picking at bedclothes.

Psellism, Psellismus —Defective pronunciation, stuttering or stammering.

Pseud- —A prefix which means false.

Pseudacousma —Pseudacusis. False perception of sounds.

Pseudacromegaly —Enlargement of the extremities and face, not caused by acromegaly.

Pseudacusis —Pseudacousma.

Pseudagraphia —Pseudoagraphia. Inability to write independently but ability to copy the words.

Pseudalbuminuria —Pseudoalbuminuria. Albuminuria that is not associated with renal disease.

Pseudankylosis —Fibrous ankylosis.

Pseudarthritis —A disease resembling arthritis.

Pseudarthrosis —A false joint developing after a fracture that has not united.

Pseudelminth —Anything like an intestinal worm in appearance.

Pseudencephalus —A fetus with a tumor in place of brain.

Pseudesthesia —1. A false sensation, as that felt in the lost part after amputation. 2. Sensation not caused by external stimulation.

Pseudo- —Pseud.

Pseudoacephalus —Pseudencephalus.

Pseudoagglutination —Clumping together of red blood cells but differing from true agglutination in that they can be dispersed by shaking.

Pseudoagraphia —Pseudagraphia.

Pseudoalbuminuria —Pseudalbuminuria.

Pseudoallele —One of two or more genes which seem to be alleles but which have distinctive but closely linked loci.

Pseudoamenorrhea —False amenorrhea.

Pseudoanaphylaxis —A condition resembling anaphylaxis, but not due to specific antigen-antibody reaction.

Pseudoanemia —Pallor of the skin and mucous membrane without other signs of true anemia.

Pseudoaneurysm —Dilatation and tortuosity of a vessel which seems to be an aneurysm.

Pseudoangina —Symptoms arising from nervous disorder resembling angina pectoris.

Pseudoankylosis —A false ankylosis.

Pseudoanodontia —Absence of teeth due to a failure in eruption, not the true absence.

Pseudoapoplexy —Parapoplexy. A condition resembling apoplexy, but without cerebral hemorrhage.

Pseudoappendicitis —A disease resembling appendicitis but there is no inflammation of the appendix.

Pseudoapraxia —A condition in which a person is exceedingly awkward and makes wrong use of objects.

Pseudoarthrosis —Pseudarthrosis.

Pseudoataxia —A condition resembling ataxia but not due to tabes dorsalis.

Pseudobacterium —Any microscopic object resembling a form of bacteria.

Pseudoblepsia, Pseudoblepsis —False or imaginary vision.

Pseudobulbar paralysis —Paralysis resembling bulbar paralysis, but which is not due to a bulbar lesion.

Pseudocartilage —Chondroid tissue.

Pseudocartilaginous —Pertaining to, or formed of, a substance resembling cartilage.

Pseudocast —False cast.

Pseudocele —Fifth ventricle in the brain.

Pseudocephalocele —Hernia of the intracranial tissues caused by injury or a disease.

Pseudochancre —A lesion resembling the chancre of syphilis.

Pseudocholesteatoma —A hard mass of epithelial cells in the tympanic cavity in chronic inflammation of the middle ear, which resembles cholesteatoma.

Pseudochorea —The condition of general incoordination resembling chorea.

Pseudochromesthesia —False perception of color.

Pseudochromhidrosis —Pseudochromidrosis.

Pseudochromidrosis —Appearance of the sweat colored after it is excreted.

Pseudochylous —Resembling chyle.

Pseudocirrhosis —A condition with symptoms of

cirrhosis of liver but not due to cirrhosis, often due to constrictive pericarditis.

Pseudocoele —Pseudocele.

Pseudocolloid —A mucoid substance sometimes found in ovarian cysts.

Pseudocoloboma —A scar on the iris resembling a coloboma.

Pseudocoma —Locked-in syndrome.

Pseudocoxalgia —Osteochondritis of the head of femur, in children.

Pseudocrisis —Temporary fall of body temperature in fever, which may rise again.

Pseudocroup —Laryngismus stridulus. False croup.

Pseudocyesis —False pregnancy.

Pseudocylindroid —A piece of mucus in the urine resembling a cast.

Pseudocyst —A dilatation resembling a cyst

Pseudodementia —A state of indifference to the environment resembling dementia but without impairment of intelligence.

Pseudodextrocardia —Displacement of the heart to the right side, either congenitally or due to some injury, but all its chambers and vessels remain in their correct position.

Pseudodiabetes —False positive test for sugar in the urine, which indicates diabetes mellitus.

Pseudodiphtheria —The presence of a false membrane not due to Corynebacterium diphtheriae.

Pseudodipsia —False thirst in which there is no satisfaction by drinking water.

Pseudodysentery —Occurrence of symptoms resembling those of bacillary dysentery, but not due to the causative organism of bacillary dysentery.

Pseudoedema —Puffiness of the skin resembling edema.

Pseudoemphysema —A condition of the lungs resembling emphysema, but due to temporary obstruction of the bronchi.

Pseudoencephalitis —A false encephalitis due to profuse diarrhea.

Pseudoesthesia —Pseudesthesia.

Pseudofracture —A line of decalcification seen in X-ray in certain types of osteomalacia.

Pseudoganglion —A thickening of a nerve resembling a ganglion.

Pseudogeusesthesia —A false taste.

Pseudogeusia —A sensation of taste occurring in the absence of external stimulus.

Pseudoglioma —Any intraocular opacity to be mistaken for retinoblastoma.

Pseudoglottis —The aperture between the false vocal cords.

Pseudogout —Chronic arthritis marked by recurring attacks of goutlike symptoms usually affecting a single joint (particularly the knee) and not the small joints as in gout. The crystals found in the synovial fluid are calcium pyrophosphate dihydrate and not urate, like that of gout.

Pseudogynecomastia —Enlargement of the male breast due to deposition of fatty tissue but not due to increase in the glandular tissue.

Pseudohematuria —The presence of a red pigment in the urine, which makes the urine appear to have blood in it.

Pseudohemoptysis —Spitting of blood that does not arise from the lungs.

Pseudohermaphrodite —An individual with pseudohermaphroditism.

Pseudohermaphroditism —False hermaphroditism. Possession of the sex glands of one sex (ovary or testis) but secondary sex characters and external genital organs of the opposite sex.

Pseudohernia —Inflammation in the scrotal area resembling a hernia.

Pseudoheterotopia —A seeming displacement of certain tissues observed in postmortem examination.

Pseudohydronephrosis —Presence of a cyst near the kidney, resembling hydronephrosis.

Pseudohyperparathyroidism —A condition simulating hyperparathyroidism, occurring due to the formation of parathyroid-like hormone by a tumor other than the parathyroid gland.

Pseudohypertrophic —Pertaining to a false hypertrophy.

Pseudohypertrophy —Increase in size of an organ or part of the body due to overgrowth of unimportant tissue.

Pseudohypoparathyroidism —A hereditary disease resembling hypoparathyroidism, but caused by failure to response rather than the deficiency of parathyroid hormone, marked by hypocalcemia and hyperphosphatemia and commonly by short stature, obesity, moon face and mental deficiency.

Pseudoicterus —Pseudojaundice.

Pseudoinfarction —Any disease simulating myocardial infarction, *e.g.*, acute pericarditis.

Pseudoisochromatic —1. Seemingly of the same color throughout. 2. The term used for the solution for testing color blindness, containing two pigments that can be distinguished by the normal eye.

Pseudojaundice —Yellowness of the skin, which is not caused by jaundice, but by blood changes.

Pseudolipoma —Any circumscribed, soft, smooth, usually movable swelling resembling a lipoma.

Pseudologia —Falsification in writing or speech.

Pseudologia fantastica —Habitual lying about one's wealth, power and intelligence.

Pseudomalignancy —A benign tumor that appears to be a malignant tumor.

Pseudomania —1. False or pretended mental disorder. 2. Pathological lying.

Pseudomasturbation—Peotillomania.

Pseudomelanosis —Discoloration of the tissues after death, by blood pigments.

Pseudomembrane —False membrane, as in diphtheria

Pseudomembranous —Pertaining to or marked by pseudomembrane.

Pseudomeningitis —A disease resembling the symptoms of meningitis but without inflammation of the meninges.

Pseudomenorrhea —Cryptomenorrhea.

Pseudomenstruation —Bleeding from the uterus but not accompanied by the usual changes in the endometrium.

Pseudomnesia —Remembrance of that which has never occurred.

Pseudomonas —A genus of motile, gram-negative, aerobic bacilli with polar flagella. Mostly they are saprophytic, living in the soil and decaying matter. Some species cause infection in humans. The chief species is P. aeruginosa. Bacteria of this species are found in the soil, water, plants, wounds and urinary tract infections. They cause urinary tract infections, otitis externa or folliculitis and produce blue pus.

Pseudomucin —A mucin-like substance found in ovarian cysts.

Pseudomyopia —The condition in which patient holds the objects close in order to see them but there is no actual myopia.

Pseudomyxoma —A mass of mucoid matter in the peritoneal cavity resembling a myxoma.

Pseudoneoplasm —A temporary swelling simulating a tumor, which is usually inflammatory.

Pseudoneuroma —Traumatic neuroma.

Pseudonucleolus —False nucleolus.

Pseudopapilledema —Swelling of the optic nerve head that is not caused by optic neuritis.

Pseudoparalysis —Pseudoplegia.

Pseudoparaplegia —False paralysis of the lower limbs due to hysteria or malingering.

Pseudoparasite —Anything resembling a parasite.

Pseudoparesis —The condition simulating paresis which is due to hysteria.

Pseudopelade —Patchy alopecia associated with scarring, simulating alopecia areata.

Pseudoplatelet —A fragment of a neutrophil that may be mistaken for a platelet.

Pseudoplegia —Pseudoparalysis. Paralysis not due to lesion of the nervous system but due to hysteria.

Pseudopod —Pseudopodium.

Pseudopodia —Plural of pseudopodium.

Pseudopodium —A temporary protrusion of the cytoplasm of a protozoon such as an ameba, or a white blood cell, serving for locomotion and engulfing the food particles.

Pseudopolyp —A localized hypertrophy of the mucous membrane resembling a polyp.

Pseudopolyposis —Presence of a large number of pseudopolyps in the colon and rectum due to chronic inflammation.

Pseudopregnancy —False pregnancy. Phantom pregnancy. A condition in which signs and symptoms of pregnancy such as enlargement of the abdomen, weight gain, stoppage of menses and morning sickness are present but there is no pregnancy.

Pseudo-pseudohypoparathyroidism —An incomplete form of pseudohypoparathyroidism marked by the same signs and symptoms but by normal levels of calcium and phosphorus in the blood.

Pseudopsia —Pseudoblepsia. False vision. Visual hallucination.

Pseudopterygium —A scar on the conjunctiva of the eye after an injury or burn which simulates pterygium.

Pseudoptosis —Downwards projection of the upper eyelid simulating dropping.

Pseudopuberty —Puberty occurring in a young girl due to excessive secretion of estrogen hormone from the ovary, generally due to an ovarian tumor, but the ovulation and menstruation does not occur.

Pseudoreaction —A false reaction. A skin reaction in response to injection of a test substance, which is not due to that specific substance but due to an allergen present in the medium.

Pseudorickets —Renal rickets.

Pseudosclerosis —A condition with the symptoms but without the lesions, of multiple sclerosis of the nervous system.

Pseudoseizure —Psychogenic seizure.

Pseudosmallpox —A disease resembling smallpox.

Pseudosmia —The sensation of odor without stimulus.

Pseudostoma —An apparent aperture in the cell walls due to defect in staining.

Pseudostratified —Apparently composed of layers.

Pseudosyphilis —A disease resembling syphilis.

Pseudotabs —A neural disease simulating tabes dorsalis.

Pseudotetanus —Persistent muscular contractions resembling tetanus but not caused by Clostridium tetani.

Pseudotuberculosis —A group of diseases resembling tuberculosis but are due to an organism other than the Mycobacterium tuberculosis.

Pseudotumor —Phantom tumor.

Pseudovacuole —An apparent vacuole in a cell which is an artifact or an intracellular parasite.

Pseudoxanthoma —A condition resembling xanthoma.

P.S.I. —Pounds per square inch.

Psilosis —Falling out of the hair.

Psilotic —Pertaining to psilosis.

Psoas —One of two muscles of the loins.

Psoas abscess —A cold abscess in the sheath of psoas major muscle.

Psoitis —Inflammation of a psoas muscle or its sheath.

Psomophagia —The habit of swallowing food without chewing it properly.

Psomophagy —Psomophagia.

Psora —1. Scabies 2. Psoriasis.

Psorelcosis —Ulcer formation due to scabies.

Psorenteritis —Inflammation of the solitary lymphatic follicles of the intestine.

Psoriasiform —Resembling psoriasis.

Psoriasis —A chronic skin disease marked by the formation of slightly elevated bright red papules or plaques covered with fine, dry silvery scales. Psoriasis may be associated with arthritis.

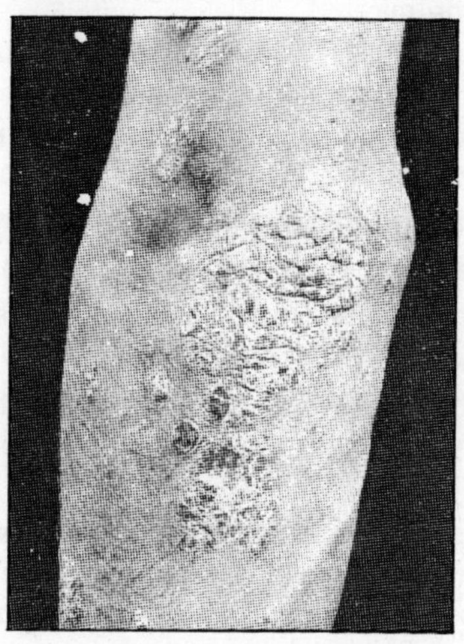

Fig. 463 : Psoriasis

Psoriatic —Pertaining to psoriasis.

Psorophthalmia —Inflammation of the margins of eyelids with ulceration.

Psorous —Pertaining to, or affected with, itch.

Psychalgia —Pain occurring due to hysteria or mental distress.

Psychanopsia —Psychic blindness.

Psychasthenia —Mental fatigue.

Psychataxia —Inability to concentrate.

Psychauditory —Pertaining to the perception and interpretation of the sounds.

Psyche —The mind.

Psychedelic —Pertaining to or causing hallucinations.

Psychiatric —Pertaining to psychiatry.

Psychiatrics —Psychiatry.

Psychiatrist —A specialist in psychiatry.

Psychiatry —The branch of medical science that deals with the study, diagnosis, prevention and treatment of mental diseases.

Psychic —Pertaining to the mind.

Psychical —Psychic.

Psychic blindness —Psychanopsia. Sight without recognition of the objects seen.

Psychic deafness —Inability to recognize the sounds heard.

Psycho-, Psych- —Prefixes which indicate relationship to the mind or mental processes.

Psychoactive —Affecting the mind or behavior, such as a drug.

Psychoanaleptic —Exerting a stimulating effect upon the mind.

Psychoanalysis —A method of determining the cause of, diagnosing the mental and emotional disorders by obtaining the details of past and present mental and emotional experience of the patients and treating them accordingly.

Psychoanalyst —Practitioner of psychoanalysis.

Psychoanalytic —Pertaining to psychoanalysis.

Psychoauditory —Psychauditory.

Psychobiology —The study of the interrelations of body and mind in the development of personality.

Psychocatharsis —The release of the emotional tension or anxiety by recalling from the patient's memory the events or traumatic experiences that were the original cause of a psychoneurosis.

Psychochrome —Color impression resulting from sensory stimulation of a part of the body other than the eyes.

Psychochromesthesia —Sensation of color produced by the stimulus of a sense organ other than that of vision.

Psychocoma —Condition of mental stupor.

Psychocortical —Pertaining to the mental process and cerebral cortex.

Psychodiagnosis —Use of psychological tests as an aid in diagnosing the diseases, especially the mental diseases.

Psychodiagnostics —Psychodiagnosis.

Psychodometry —Measurement of the rate of mental activity.

Psychodrama —Psychological treatment of a group of patients in which they convert their individual conflicting situations of daily life.

Psychodynamics —The scientific study of the human behavior and motivation.

Psychoendocrinology —Study of the interrelationships between the functions of the endocrine glands and mental states.

Psychoepilepsy —A form of hysterical neurosis accompanied by movements resembling those of epilepsy.

Psychogalvanic —Pertaining to the changes in electric properties of the skin, *e.g.*,change in the skin resistance induced by psychologic stimulus.

Psychogalvanometer —A galvanometer for determining the changes in the electrical resistance of the skin in response to emotional stimuli.

Psychogenesis —1. Mental development. 2. Origination of a disease or symptom within the mind.

Psychogenetic —Psychogenic. 1. Concerning the mental development. 2. Originating within the mind as a disease or symptom.

Psychogenic —Psychogenetic.

Psychogeriatric —Pertaining to the old persons suffering from a mental disorder.

Psychogeusic —Pertaining to the perception of taste.

Psychogram —Psychograph.

Psychograph —1. A chart for recording graphically the patient's personality traits. 2. The written description, of a person's mental functions.

Psychographic —Pertaining to psychography.

Psychography —The recording of psychoanalysis of a patient with mental disorder.

Psychokinesis —To become active or emotional caused by a thought originated in the mind.

Psycholagny —Psychic or mental masturbation. Sexual excitement by imagination only.

Psycholepsy —Paralepsy. Sudden alteration in mood or mental tension.

Psycholeptic —1. Pertaining to the sudden alteration in mood. 2. A drug affecting the mental state.

Psycholinguistics —The study of psychological factors associated with the speech.

Psychologic —Psychological.

Psychological —Pertaining to psychology.

Psychologist —A specialist in psychology.

Psychology —The science dealing with the mind and mental processes, both normal and abnormal, and their effects upon behavior.

Abnormal psychology —The study of abnormal behavior and the associated mental phenomena.

Animal psychology —The study of animal behavior.

Applied psychology —The application of the principles of psychology to special fields, such as clinical, nursing, educational and industrial etc.

Behavioral psychology —Behaviorism.

Clinical psychology —The branch of psychology concerned with the diagnosis and treatment of mental disorders.

Criminal psychology —The branch of psychology concerned with the social behavior of the criminals and their treatment.

Experimental psychology —The branch of psychology dealing with the study of mental acts, by tests and experiments.

Genetic psychology —The branch of psychology dealing with the evolution and inheritance of psychological characteristics.

Physiologic psychology —The branch of psychology dealing with the study of the structure and function of the nervous system and other organs of the body and their relationship to behavior.

Social psychology —The branch of psychology concerned with the study of the social effects on the individual's actions and mental processes.

Psychometrician —A specialist in psychometry.

Psychometrics —Psychometry.

Psychometry —The measurement of mental ability.

Psychomotor —Pertaining to, or causing physical activity associated with mental processes.

Psychoneurosis —Neurosis.

Psychoneurotic —Pertaining to or suffering from psychoneurosis.

Psychonosology —The classification of mental diseases and behavioral disorders.

Psycho-oncology —The psychologic aspects of the treatment and management of the patient with cancer.

Psychoparesis —Mental debility.

Psychopath —A person with a psychopathic personality.

Psychopathia —Psychopathy.

Psychopathic —1. Antisocial; pertaining to a psychopath. 2. Concerning the treatment of mental disorders.

Psychopathologist —Specialist in psychopathology.

Psychopathology —The branch of medical science dealing with the study of causes and nature of mental disorders or abnormal behavior.

Psychopathy —Any mental disease.

Psychopharmaceuticals —Drugs used in the treatment of mental illnesses.

Psychopharmacology —The study of the action of drugs on mental disorders.

Psychophysical —Pertaining to the relationship of mind to the body.

Psychophysics —The study of mental processes in relationship to physical processes.

Psychophysiologic —Pertaining to psychophysiology.

Psychophysiological —Psychophysiologic.

Psychophysiology —Physiology of the mind.

Psychoplegia —Mental weakness.

Psychoplegic —Causing mental weakness.

Psychoprophylaxis —A method of mental and physical preparation of the mother for natural childbirth.

Psychorelaxation —To give relief to anxiety and mental tension by causing general bodily relaxation.

Psychorhythmia —Involuntary repetition of the previous voluntary actions.

Psychosensorial —Psychosensory.

Psychosensory —1. Perceiving and understanding sensory stimuli. 2. Pertaining to the perceptions not arising in sensory organs, as hallucinations.

Psychosexual —Pertaining to the psychic or emotional aspects of sex.

Psychosis —Any major organic or emotional mental disorder characterized by personality disintegration, loss of contact with reality and usually with delusions, hallucinations or illusions.

Alcoholic psychosis —Psychosis caused by excessive use of alcohol.

Depressive psychosis—See manic-depressive psychosis.

Drug psychosis —A psychosis caused by ingestion of a drug.

Exhaustion psychosis —Psychosis occurring from extreme tiredness, chronic illness or prolonged sleeplessness.

Gestational psychosis —Psychosis occurring during pregnancy.

Hysterical psychosis —Psychosis occurring in hysterical patients, usually manifested by sudden hallucinations, delusions and odd behavior.

Manic-depressive psychosis —A major affective mental disorder characterized by alternating mood of depression and mania.

Organic psychosis —Psychosis resulting from a pathological condition of the central nervous system, such as paresis.

Postinfectious psychosis —Psychosis occurring after an infectious disease such as meningitis, pneumonia and typhoid fever etc.

Postpartum psychosis —Psychosis occurring in the puerperal period.

Puerperal psychosis —Port-partum psychosis.

Senile psychosis —Psychosis due to old age.

Situational psychosis —Psychosis occurring in an intolerable environmental situation.

Toxic psychosis —Psychosis occurring due to ingestion of toxic substances or to the presence of toxins within the body.

Traumatic psychosis —Psychosis resulting from head injury.

Psychosocial —Pertaining to both psychological and social factors.

Psychosomatic —1. Pertaining to the relationship of the mind and body. 2. Having bodily symptoms of mental or emotional origins.

Psychostimulant —Producing a temporary increase in psychomotor activity.

Psychosurgery —Brain surgery performed for some mental disorders as for the condition of excessive excitement or for antisocial acts.

Psychotechnics —Use of psychological methods in the study of economic and social problems.

Psychotherapeutic —Pertaining to psychotherapy.

Psychotherapeutics —Psychotherapy.

Psychotherapist —A doctor or a paramedical personnel engaged in psychotherapy.

Psychotherapy —Psychological treatment of the diseases, especially the mental diseases.

Psychotic —Pertaining to or affected by psychosis.

Psychotogenic —Producing a psychosis.

Psychotomimetic —Producing symptoms similar to those of a psychosis.

Psychotropic —Exerting an effect on the mind, said especially of drugs.

Psychroalgia —Painful sensation of cold.

Psychroesthesia —Sensation of cold in a warm part of the body.

Psychrometer —An apparatus for measuring the atmospheric moisture.

Psychrometry —The measurement of atmospheric moisture by psychrometer.

Psychrophil —Psychrophile.

Psychrophile —An organism growing best at low temperature.

Psychrophilic —Preferring cold, said of bacteria growing best in cold.

Psychrophobia —Aversion to, or morbid fear of cold.

Psychrophore —A double lumen catheter for applying cold.

Psychrotherapy —Treatment of diseases by use of cold.

Pt. —Pint.

Ptarmic —Causing sneezing.

Ptarmus —Spasmodic sneezing.

Pterion —A point of junction of frontal, parietal, temporal and sphenoid bones.

Pternalgia —Pain in the heel.

Pterotic —Pertaining to the pterion.

Pterygium —A triangular thickening of the bulbar conjunctiva extending from inner canthus to the cornea.

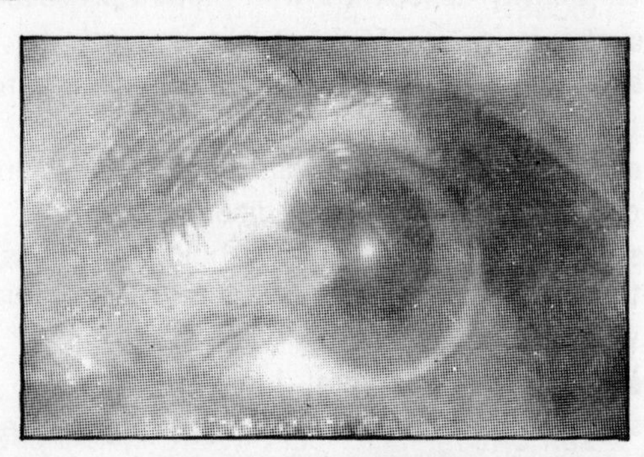

Fig. No. 464 Pterygium

Pterygoid —Alate. Wing-shaped.

Pterygomandibular —Pertaining to the pterygoid process of sphenoid bone, and the mandible.

Pterygomaxillary —Pertaining to the pterygoid process and the upper jaw.

Pterygopalatine —Pertaining to the pterygoid process and the palate bone.

Ptilosis —Loss of eye lashes.

Ptosed —Droopped.

Ptosis —Dropping of an organ, as of the upper eyelid from paralysis.

Ptotic —Pertaining to ptosis.

Ptyal-, Ptyalo- —Prefixes meaning salivary glands or saliva.

Ptyalagogue —Sialagogue.

Ptyalectasis —Condition of dilatation of, or surgical dilatation of a salivary duct.

Ptyalin —Enzyme α-amylase occurring in saliva.

Ptyalism —Excessive secretion of salvia.

Ptyalith —A calculus in a salivary gland.

Ptyalocele —Cystic tumor of the salivary gland.

Ptyalogenic —Formed from or by the action of saliva.

Ptyalogogue —Sialogogue.

Ptyalography —Sialography.

Ptyalolith —Ptyalith.

Ptyalolithiasis —Presence of a calculus in a salivary gland or duct.

Ptyalolithotomy —Surgical removal of a calculus from a salivary gland or duct.

Ptyaloreaction —A reaction occurring in saliva.

Ptyalorrhea —Excessive flow of saliva.

Ptyocrinous —A type of glandular secretion in which the contents of the cell are discharged.

Ptysis —Spitting or ejection of saliva from the mouth.

Ptysmagogue —Causing the flow of saliva.

Pubarche —1. The beginning of puberty. 2. The first appearance of the pubic hair.

Puber —At the onset of puberty.

Puberal —Pertaining to puberty.

Pubertal —Puberal.

Pubertas —Precocious puberty or puberty at an early age.

Puberty —The period of life during which the person of either sex becomes capable of reproduction. It is 13 to 15 years of age in boys and 9 to 16 in girls, when their secondary sexual characters begin to develop.

Pubes —1. The hair growing over the pubic region. 2. The pubic region.

Pubescence —1. The act of approaching puberty. 2. Lanugo. Covering of fine, soft hairs on the body.

Pubescent —1. Approaching puberty. 2. Covered with fine, soft hairs.

Pubetrotomy —To cut through the pubic bone and lower abdominal wall.

Pubic —Pertaining to the pubes.

Pubiotomy —Surgical separation of the pubic bones at the symphysis to enlarge pelvic passage facilitating delivery of the infant, when the pelvis is contracted.

Pubis —Pubic bone. Os pubis.

Pubo- —A prefix which means pubic bone or pubic region.

Pubocapsular —Pertaining to the pubic bone and the capsule of the hip joint.

Pubococcygeal —Pertaining to the pubic bone and coccyx.

Pubofemoral —Pertaining to the pubic bone and femur.

Pubomadesis —Loss of or absent pubic hair.

Puboprostatic —Pertaining to the pubic bone and prostate gland.

Puborectal —Pertaining to the pubic bone and rectum.

Pubovesical —Pertaining to the pubic bone and urinary bladder.

Pudenda —Vulva. External genital organs of the female.

Pudendagra —Pain in external genital organs of the female.

Pudendal —Pertaining to the external genital organs of the female.

Pudendum —Singular of pudenda.

Pudic —Pudendal.

Puerile —1. Pertaining to childhood or children. 2. Childlike.

Puerilism —Childishness.

Puerpera —A woman who has just borne a child.

Puerperae —Plural of puerpera.

Puerperal —Pertaining to the puerperium or a puerpera.

Puerperal eclampsia —Eclampsia occurring during puerperium.

Puerperal fever —Fever occurring after childbirth.

Puerperalism —Pathological condition occurring with childbirth.

Puerperal sepsis —Any infection of the genital

tract of the woman occurring during puerperium or as a complication of abortion. It is presumed to be present when the temperature is 100.4ºF on any two consecutive days, excluding first 24 hrs. after delivery, in the absence of other causes of fever. There is pain and tenderness of the lower abdominal area and the genital tract.

Puerperant —Puerperal.

Puerperia —Plural of puerperium.

Puerperium —The period of 42 days following childbirth and expulsion of the placenta and membrances during which the uterus returns to its normal size.

Puerperous —Puerperal.

Puff —A soft, short, blowing sound heard on auscultation.

Pulicatio —Infested with fleas.

Pulicide —Destroying fleas.

Pullulate —To bud or germinate.

Pullulation —The act of budding or germinating.

Pulmo- —Combining form meaning lung.

Pulmoaortic —Pertaining to the lungs and aorta.

Pulmolith —Pneumolith.

Pulmometer —Spirometer. An apparatus for measuring the capacity of the lung.

Pulmometry —Determination of the capacity of the lung.

Pulmonary —Pertaining to or involving the lungs.

Pulmonectomy —Pneumonectomy. Surgical removal of part or all of a lung.

Pulmonic —Pertaining to lungs or the pulmonary artery.

Pulmonitis —Pneumonia. Inflammation of the lung.

Pulmonologist —Specialist in the treatment of pulmonary diseases.

Pulmotor —An apparatus for inducing artificial respiration by forcing oxygen into the lungs.

Pulp —1. The soft part of an organ, *e.g.*, a prominence of soft tissue on the palmar or plantar surface of the last phalanx of a finger or toe. 2. Dental pulp which is richly vascularized and innervated connective tissue filling up the pulp cavity of a tooth. 3. Mass of partly digested food passed from the stomach to duodenum, known as chyme. 4. The soft part of the fruit.

Pulpa —Pulp.

Pulpal —Pertaining to pulp.

Pulpalgia —Pain in the dental pulp.

Pulp capping —Covering and protecting the dental pulp from external conditions.

Pulpectomy —Removal of dental pulp.

Pulpefaction —Conversion into pulp.

Pulp extirpation —Pulpectomy.

Pulpiform —Pulpy.

Pulpify —To make pulpy.

Pulpitis —Inflammation of a dental pulp.

Pulposus —Pulpy.

Pulpotomy —Pulp amputation.

Pulpy —Resembling pulp, flabby.

Pulsate —To throb or beat in rhythm.

Pulsatile—Throbbing or characterized by rhythmic beat.

Pulsating —Pulsatile. Throbbing.

Pulsation —The rhythmic beat, as of the heart; a throb.

Pulse —Throbbing caused by the regular contraction and expansion of an artery as the blood passes through it, which is usually felt by finger in radial artery at the wrist. Normal pulse rate of the adult in men is 70 to 72 and in women 78-82 per minute.

Accelerated pulse —Rapid pulse.

Alternating pulse —The pulse in which there is alternate weak and strong pulsation.

Anacrotic pulse —Pulse showing a secondary wave on ascending limb of the main wave, in tracing.

Anadicrotic pulse —A pulse wave in tracing with two small notches on the ascending limb.

Bigeminal pulse —An irregular pulse in which two regular beats are separated by a longer interval from other two regular beats.

Bounding pulse —Pulse that becomes very forceful than normal and then disappears quickly.

Capillary pulse —Pulsation created in the capillaries by their alternate filling and emptying with blood.

Carotid pulse —A pulse felt in a carotid artery in the neck.

Catacrotic pulse —Pulse showing a secondary wave on descending limb of the main wave, in tracing.

Catadicrotic pulse —A pulse wave with two small notches on the descending limb of the tracing.

Collapsing pulse —Weak pulse which subsides quickly and completely.

Deficit pulse —The pulse in which the number of beats per minute is less than that of the heart.

Dicrotic pulse —A pulse with double beat, one heart beat counts for two pulse beats of which one is weak.

Febrile pulse —A full, powerful pulse at the onset of fever, which becomes weak when the fever subsides.

Full pulse —Pulse fully distended with blood as observed in an artery in inflammation.

Hard pulse —Pulse which is felt hard due to changes in the arterial wall.

High-tension pulse —Pulse with forcible beat as is seen in high fever.

Intermittent pulse —Pulse in which some beats are missed occasionally.

Irregular pulse —Pulse in which the beats are changeable in force and frequency.

Jerky pulse —Pulsation created when an empty artery is suddenly filled with blood.

Jugular pulse —Pulse observed in the jugular veins in the neck.

Low-tension pulse —A less forcible pulse occurring suddenly in heart failure, collapse and debility and other conditions.

Pistol-shot pulse —Pulse in which an artery is suddenly distended and then collapsed.

Quadrigeminal pulse —Pulse with a pause after every fourth beat.

Radial pulse —Pulse felt over the radial artery.

Rapid pulse— Pulse the rate of which exceeds normal rate

Regular pulse —Pulse in which the length of beat, number of beats per minute and the strength are the same.

Riegel's pulse —Pulse which is diminished during expiration.

Slow pulse —Pulse with the rate from 40 to 60 beats per minute.

Soft pulse —Pulse which is stopped by moderate pressure of the finger.

Thready pulse —A threadlike fine, scarcely perceptible pulse.

Tricrotic pulse —Pulse in which the tracing shows three separate expansions in one beat of the artery.

Trigeminal pulse —Pulse in which there is a pause after each 3 regular beats.

Vagus pulse —Slow pulse.

Venous pulse —Pulsation over a vein, especially over the right jugular vein.

Vermicular pulse —A small, frequent pulse with a wormlike feeling.

Waterhammer pulse —Pulse in which the beat is short, powerful and jerky that suddenly collapses.

Wiry pulse —A small, tense pulse that feels like a wire.

Pulse pressure —The difference between the systolic and diastolic pressure.

Pulsimeter —An apparatus for measuring the frequency and force of the pulse.

Pulsion —A pushing forward.

Pulsometer —Pulsimeter.

Pulsus —Pulse.

Pultaceous —Pulpy. Like a poultice.

Pulv. —Powder.

Pulverisable —Capable of being converted, into powder.

Pulverization —The crushing of a substance to powder.

Pulverize —To crush a substance to powder.

Pulverulent —Powdery.

Pulvinar —The prominent medial part of the posterior end of the thalamus.

Pulvinate —Convex. Shaped like a cushion.

Pulvis —Powder.

Pump —1. An apparatus for drawing or forcing a liquid or gas. 2. To draw or force a liquid or gas.

Pump-oxygenator —An apparatus consisting of a blood pump and oxygenator, which pumps blood and oxygenates it during heart surgery.

Puna —Altitude sickness.

Punch —An instrument for making a small circular hole in the tissue, especially the skin.

Punched out —With clear cut circular edges, appearing as a hole made by a punch or boring instrument, *e.g.* punched out gummatous ulcer in the tertiary stage of syphilis.

Puncta —Points.

Punctate —Dotted. Marked with very minute holes or depressions.

Punctiform —Like a point.

Punctio —The act of puncturing or pricking.

Punctograph —An instrument for localizing foreign bodies in the tissues in X-ray examination.

Punctum —Point, *e.g.*, blind spot.

Puncture —1. The act of piercing with a sharp pointed object or instrument. 2. A hole or wound made by a sharp pointed instrument.

Cisternal puncture —Puncture of the cisterna cerebellomedullaris by introducing a needle through the suboccipital tissue to obtain a sample of cerebrospinal fluid.

Exploratory puncture —Puncture of a cavity or cyst for examining the fluid or pus removed.

Lumbar puncture —Puncture of the dura mater of the spinal cord in the lumbar region to obtain cerebrospinal fluid for examination, or to relieve cerebral dropsy.

Spinal puncture —Lumbar puncture.

Sternal puncture —Puncture of the manubrium of the sternum by a needle to remove a sample of bone marrow.

Ventricular puncture —Puncture of the ventricle of the brain for withdrawing fluid or to introduce air for ventriculography.

Pungency —The quality of sharp, strong or bitter as of an odor or taste.

Pungent —Acrid or sharp, as an odor or taste.

Pupa —The second stage in the development of an insect, between the larva and adult.

Pupae —Plural of pupa.

P.U.O. —Pyrexia of unkown origin.

Pupil —The contractile opening in the center of iris of the eye through which light enters the eye.

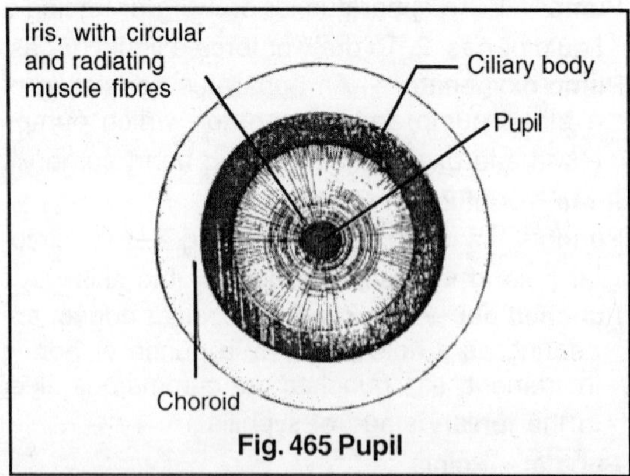

Fig. 465 Pupil

Bounding pupil —Rapidly dilated and contracted pupil.

Cats' eye pupil —A narrow and slitlike pupil.

Cornpickers pupils —Dilated pupils found in farmers who are exposed to dust.

Fixed pupil —A pupil that does not react to stimuli.

Pinhole pupil —A very minute or excessively constricted pupil.

Robertson pupil —Argyll Robertson pupil.

Pupilla —Pupil.

Pupillae —Plural of pupilla.

Pupillary —Pertaining to the pupil.

Pupillary reflex —1. Contraction of the pupil by light throwing upon it. 2. Contraction and dilatation of the pupil upon accommodation for near and far vision respectively.

Pupillography —The recording of the pupillary movements.

Pupillometer —An apparatus for measuring diameter of the pupil.

Pupillometry —Measurement of diameter of the pupil.

Pupillomotor —Pertaining to the autonomic nerve fibers supplying the smooth muscle of the iris.

Pupilloplegia —Slow reaction of the pupil.

Pupilloscopy —Examination of the pupil.

Pupillostatometer —An instrument for measuring the distance between centers of the pupils.

Pure —Uncontaminated, unadulterated.

Purgation —Evacuation of the bowels by action of a purgative medicine.

Purgative —Causing watery evacuation of the intestinal contents.

Purge —1. To evacuate the bowels by means of a purgative. 2. A purgative medicine.

Puriform —Resembling pus.

Purify —To clean.

Purine —The end product of nucleoprotein digestion which breaks to form uric acid.

Purinemia —Presence of purine in the blood.

Purity —The state of being pure, *i.e.*, free from contaminants or pollutants.

Purkinje fibers —These are very large fibers originating from the lumdle of His in the heart and enter the ventricles. They conduct the cardiac impulse from the atria to the ventricles.

Purohepatitis —Suppurative inflammation of the liver.

Puromucous —Mucopurulent. Containing both mucus and pus.

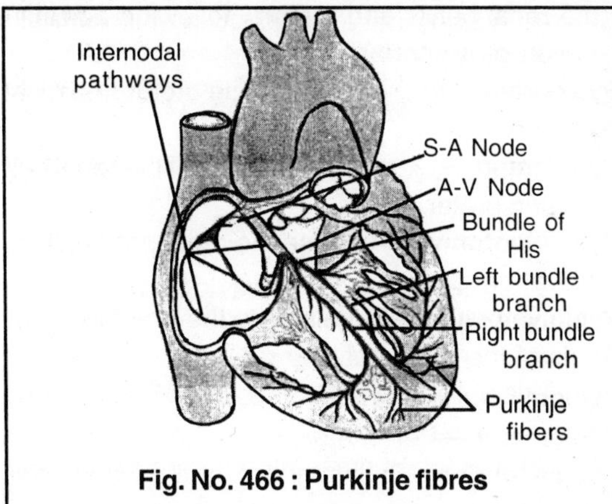

Fig. No. 466 : Purkinje fibres

Purple —Color formed by mixing red with blue.

Purpura —Purpura is hemorrhage into the skin, mucous membranes, joints, internal organs and other tissues. In hemorrhage into the skin there is at first bright red discoloration, which changes through purple to red-brown and then to yellow-brown, visible through the epidermis, which disappear within two to three weeks. The small hemorrhages are petechiae and the large irregular hemorrhages are ecchymoses. They do not disappear under pressure.

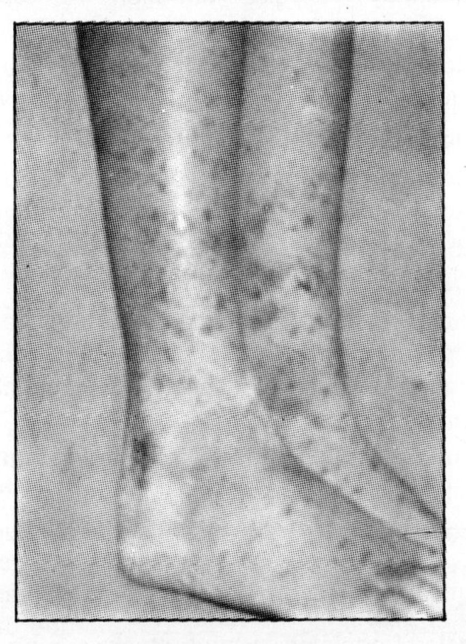

Fig. 467 : Purpura

Allergic purpura, Anaphylactoid purpura, Nonthrombocytopenic purpura —Schonlein-Henoch purpura. Purpura occurring due to allergy caused by bacteria, drugs or food in which the platelets are not decreased in the blood.

Angioneurotic purpura —Purpura marked by angioneurotic edema.

Fibrinolytic purpura —Purpura resulting from increased fibrinolytic activity of the blood.

Fulminans purpura —A rapidly progressing purpura occurring mainly in children after an infectious disease, which is usually fatal.

Hemorrhagic purpura —Idiopathic thrombocytopenic purpura.

Henoch purpura —Schonlein-Henoch purpura in which the abdominal symptoms predominate.

Idiopathic thrombocytopenic purpura —Hemorrhagic purpura due to excessive reduction of blood platelets, of which the cause is unknown.

Immune thrombocytopenic purpura —Idiopathic thrombocytopenic purpura.

Psychogenic purpura —Purpura occurring due to some mental disorder.

Rheumatica purpura —Purpura associated with joint pains.

Schonlein purpura —Schonlein-Henoch purpura in which the articular symptoms predominate.

Senile purpura —Dark purplish red ecchymoses and petechiae occurring on the forearms, back of the hands and legs of the old persons.

Simplex purpura —Purpura not associated with systemic disease.

Thrombotic thrombocytopenic purpura —Purpura characterized by embolism and thrombosis of the terminal arterioles and capillaries, marked by decrease in number of platelets.

Purpuric —Pertaining to, resembling or suffering from purpura.

Purring thrill —Thrill or vibration like a cat's purring felt to the hand kept over the precordium in mitral stenosis, aneurysm or valvular disease of the heart.

Purulence —Suppuration. The formation or presence of pus.

Purulency —Purulence.

Purulent —Suppurative. Forming or containing pus.

Puruloid —Puriform. Like pus.

Pus —Liquid product of inflammation composed of a thin fluid, protein substances, white blood cells and cellular debris, generally yellowish in color.

Pus cells —Dead leukocytes found in pus.

Pustula —Pustule.

Pustulant —Forming pustules.

Pustular —Pertaining to or consisting of pustules.

Pustulation —The formation of pustules.

Pustule —A small, elevated, pus-containing lesion of the skin.

Pustulocrustaceous —Characterized by the formation of pustules and crusts.

Pustulosis —Generalized eruption of pustules.

Putamen —The external layer of the lenticular nucleus.

Putrefaction —Decomposition of animal matter, especially proteins by bacteria or fungi with the production of foul-smelling compounds such as hydrogen sulfide, ammonia and mercaptans.

Putrefactive —Pertaining to, or causing putrefaction.

Putrefy —To undergo putrefaction.

Putrescence —Decay; rottenness.

Putrescent —Of the process of decaying.

Putrid —Decayed; decomposed; rotten; foul.

PVO_2—Partial pressure of oxygen in mixed venous blood.

Pyarthrosis —Pus in a joint cavity.

Pycnemia —Pyknemia. Thickening of the blood.

Pyecchysis —An effusion of pus.

Pyelectasia, Pyelectasis —Dilatation of the renal pelvis.

Pyelitic —Pertaining to, or affected with pyelitis.

Pyelitis —Inflammation of the renal pelvis.

Pyelo- —A prefix meaning the pelvis.

Pyelocaliceal —Pyelocalyceal. Pertaining to the renal pelvis and the calices.

Pyelocaliectasis —Dilatation of the renal pelvis and calices.

Pyelocalyceal —Pyelocaliceal.

Pyelocystitis —Inflammation of the renal pelvis and the urinary bladder.

Pyelocystostomosis —To make a communication between kidney and the urinary bladder.

Pyelofluoroscopy —Fluoroscopic examination of the renal pelvis and ureters, following administration of a contrast medium.

Pyelogram —An X-ray film of the ureter and renal pelvis.

Pyelography —X-ray examination of the renal pelvis and ureter.

Pyelolithotomy —To incise the renal pelvis for removal of calculi.

Pyelolymphatic —Pertaining to the lymphatic vessels of the renal pelvis.

Pyelometer —Pelvimeter.

Pyelometry —Pelvimetry.

Pyelonephritis —Inflammation of the kidney and its pelvis.

Pyelonephrosis—Any disease of the kidney and its pelvis.

Pyelopathy —Pyelonephrosis. Any disease of the renal pelvis.

Pyeloplasty —Repair of the renal pelvis by plastic surgery.

Pyeloplication —Reduction in the size of a dilated renal pelvis by surgical infolding of its walls.

Pyeloscopy —Examination of the renal pelvis by fluoroscope.

Pyelostomy —Surgical formation of an opening into the renal pelvis.

Pyelotomy —To make an incision into the renal pelvis.

Pyeloureterectasis —Hydronephrosis.

Pyeloureterography —Pyelography.

Pyelovenous —Pertaining to the renal pelvis and renal veins.

Pyemesis —Vomiting of pus.

Pyemia —A form of septicemia due to presence of pus forming organisms in the blood, forming multiple abscesses of secondary metastatic nature.

Pyemic —Pertaining to, or affected with pyemia or blood poisoning.

Pyencephalus —Brain abscess with suppuration.

Pyesis —Suppuration. Formation of pus.

Pyg-, Pygo- —Prefixes meaning buttocks.

Pygal —Pertaining to the buttocks.

Pygalgia —Pain in the buttocks.

Pygmalionism —A condition of loving with the things made by oneself.

Pygmy —Dwarf.

Pygoamorphus —Asymmetrical conjoined twins in which the parasite is an amorphous mass attached to the buttocks of the autosite.

Pygodidymus—A fetus with double hips and lower extremities.

Pygomelus —A fetus with supernumerary limb or limbs attached to the buttocks.

Pygopagus —Conjoined twins united at the sacral region.

Pyknemia —Pycnemia.

Pyknic —Having a short, stocky build with rounded extremities, and large chest and abdomen.

Pykno- —A prefix which means thick, compact, dense, frequent.

Pyknocardia —Tachycardia. Rapid pulse.

Pyknocyte —A small needle-shaped red blood cell.

Pyknocytosis —An excess of pyknocytes in the blood.

Pyknodysostosis —A hereditary disease that affects the bones characterized by dwarfism, osteopetrosis, open fontanels, frontal bossing and dental anomalies in children.

Pyknometer —An instrument for determining the specific gravity of liquids.

Pyknomorphous —Denoting a cell or tissue that stains deeply because the staining material is closely packed.

Pyknophrasia —Thickness of speech.

Pyknosis —A thickness, especially degeneration of a cell in which the nucleus shrinks in size and the chromatin condenses to a solid mass.

Pyknotic —Pertaining to pyknosis.

Pyla —An opening of communication between the third ventricle of the brain and the aqueduct cerebri.

Pylar —Pertaining to pyla.

Pylemphraxis —Occlusion of the portal vein.

Pylephlebectasia, Pylephlebectasis —Dilatation of the portal vein.

Pylephlebitis —Inflammation of the portal vein.

Pylethrombophlebitis —Thrombosis and inflammation of the portal vein.

Pylethrombosis —Thrombosis of the portal vein.

Pylic —Pertaining to the portal vein.

Pylon —A temporary artificial leg.

Pyloralgia —Pain in the region of the pylorus.

Pylorectomy —Surgical removal of the pylorus.

Pylori —Plural of pylorus.

Pyloric —Pertaining to the pylorus.

Pyloric antrum —The first part of the pyloric portion of the stomach.

Pyloric cap —First part of the duodenum.

Pyloristenosis —Constriction of the pylorus.

Pyloritis —Inflammation of the pylorus.

Pyloro- —A prefix meaning pylorus.

Pylorodiosis —Dilatation of the pylorus.

Pyloroduodenitis —Inflammation of the pyloric and duodenal mucosa.

Pylorogastrectomy —Excision of the pylorus and the adjacent part of the stomach.

Pyloromyotomy —To incise the longitudinal and circular muscles of the pylorus.

Pyloroplasty —Repair of the pylorus by plastic surgery.

Pyloroptosia —Downward displacement of the pylorus.

Pyloroptosis —Pyloroptosia.

Pyloroschesis —Obstruction in the pyloric orifice.

Pyloroscopy —Visual examination of the pylorus by an endoscope.

Pylorospasm —Spasm of the pylorus.

Pylorostenosis —Narrowing of the pylorus.

Pylorostomy —Surgical formation of an opening through the abdominal wall into the pylorus.

Pylorotomy —Incision of the pylorus.

Pylorus —The lower portion of the stomach opening into the duodenum.

Pyo-, Py- —Combining forms meaning pus.

Pyocele —A collection of pus, as in the scrotum.

Pyocelia —Formation of pus in the abdominal cavity.

Pyocephalus —Purulent fluid within the cranium.

Pyochezia —Pus in the feces.

Pyococcus —Any coccus forming pus.

Pyocolpocele —A vaginal tumor containing pus.

Pyocolpos —Accumulation of pus in the vagina.

Pyocyanic —Pertaining to blue pus.

Pyocyst —A cyst containing pus.

Pyocystis —Formation and retention of pus in the urinary bladder.

Pyocyte —Pus cell.

Pyoderma —Any suppurative skin disease.

Pyodermatitis —Pyogenic infection of the skin causing a dermatitis.

Pyodermatosis —Pyoderma.

Pyodermia —Pyoderma.

Pyofecia —Pyochezia.

Pyogen —An agent that causes pus formation.

Pyogenesis —Suppuration. The formation of pus.

Pyogenetic —Pyogenic.

Pyogenic —Suppurative. Forming pus.

Pyogenous —Pyogenic.

Pyohemia —Pyemia.

Pyohemothorax —Pus and blood in the pleural cavity.

Pyohydronephrosis—The accumulation of pus and urine in the kidney.

Pyoid —Like pus.

Pyolabyrinthitis —Inflammation of the labyrinth of the ear, with suppuration.

Pyometra —Accumulation of pus within the uterus.

Pyometritis —Purulent inflammation of the uterus.

Pyomyositis —Inflammation of the muscles with pus formation.

Pyonephritis —Purulent inflammation of the kidney.

Pyonephrolithiasis —Pus and stones in the kidney.

Pyonephrosis —Accumulation of pus in the renal pelvis.

Pyoovarium —Abscess of an ovary.

Pyopericarditis —Purulent inflammation of the pericardium.

Pyopericardium—Pus formation in the pericardium.

Pyoperitoneum —Pus formation in the peritoneal cavity.

Pyoperitonitis —Purulent inflammation of the peritoneum.

Pyophagia —Swallowing of pus.

Pyophthalmia —Purulent inflammation of the eye.

Pyophthalmitis —Pyophthalmia.

Pyophylactic —Protective against the formation of pus.

Pyophysometra —Accumulation of pus and gas in the uterus.

Pyopneumocholecystitis —Distention of the gallbladder with air and pus.

Pyopneumocyst —A cyst containing pus and gas.

Pyopneumohepatitis —Liver abscess with pus and gas in it.

Pyopneumopericardium —Pus and air or gas in the pericardium.

Pyopneumoperitoneum —Presence of pus and gas in the peritoneal cavity.

Pyopneumoperitonitis —Peritonitis with the presence of pus and gas.

Pyopneumothorax —Presence of pus and air or gas in the pleural cavity.

Pyopoiesis —Pyogenesis. Suppuration.

Pyopoietic —Pyogenic. Suppurative.

Pyoptysis —Spitting of pus.

Pyopyelectasis —Dilatation of the renal pelvis with pus.

Pyorrhagia —Profuse flow of pus, as occurs on rupture of an abscess.

Pyorrhea —A discharge of purulent matter.

Pyosalpingitis —Purulent inflammation of the fallopian tube.

Pyosalpingo-oophoritis —Inflammation of the fallopian tube and the ovary with suppuration.

Pyosalpingo-oothecitis —Pyosalpingo-oophoritis.

Pyosalpinx —Accumulation of pus in the fallopian tube.

Pyosemia —Pyospermia.

Pyosepticemia —Infection of the blood with pus-forming bacteria.

Pyosis —Suppuration.

Pyospermia —Pus in the semen.

Pyostatic —Preventing pus formation.

Pyostomatitis —Stomatitis with pus formation.

Pyotherapy —Treatment of diseases by pus.

Pyothorax —Empyema. Accumulation of pus in the thorax.

Pyotorrhea —Discharge of pus from the ear.

Pyourachus —Accumulation of pus in the urachus.

Pyoureter —Collection of pus in the ureter.

Pyovesiculosis —Collection of pus in the seminal vesicles.

Pyr- —A prefix meaning heat or fire.

Pyramid —A pointed or conical structure as renal pyramid.

Pyramidal —Shaped like a pyramid.

Pyramidotomy —Excision of the pyramidal tracts.

Pyramis —Pyramid.

Pyrectic —Febrile. Pertaining to the fever.

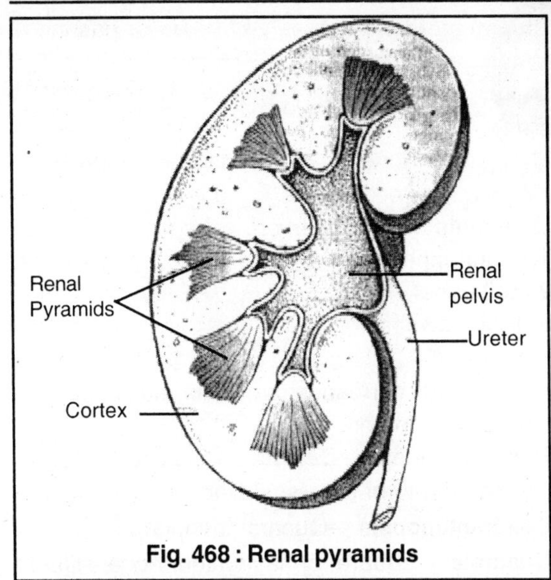

Fig. 468 : Renal pyramids

Pyrenemia —Presence of nucleated red blood cells in the blood.

Pyretherapy —Treatment of diseases by artificial fever.

Pyretic —Pyrectic.

Pyreticosis —Any condition characterized by fever.

Pyretic therapy —Pyretherapy.

Pyreto- —A prefix indicating relationship to fever.

Pyretogen —A substance producing fever.

Pyretogenesia, Pyretogenesis —Origin and production of fever.

Pyretogenetic —Pyretogenic.

Pyretogenic —Producing fever.

Pyretogenous —1. Producing fever 2. Caused by fever.

Pyretolysis —Reduction of fever.

Pyretotherapy —1. Treatment of diseases by artificial fever. 2.Treatment of fever.

Pyretotyphosis —The delirious or stuporous condition of high fever.

Pyrexia —Fever. Condition in which the body's temperature is above normal.

Pyrexial —Pertaining to fever.

Pyrexiophobia —Morbid fear of fever.

Pyriform —Piriform. Shaped like a pear.

Pyro- —A prefix which means heat or fire.

Pyrogen —Any substance producing fever.

Pyrogenic —Producing fever.

Pyroglobulinemia —Presence of an abnormal globulin in the blood of the patients of multiple myeloma and certain other diseases, which is precipitated by heat.

Pyroglobulins —Serum globulins associated with multiple myeloma and certain other diseases.

Pyrolagnia —Madness for seeing or setting fires accompanied by sexual pleasure.

Pyrolysis —Decomposition of organic matter when the temperature rises.

Pyromania —Fire madness; mania for seeing or setting fires.

Pyromaniac —The person affected with pyromania.

Pyrometer —An apparatus for measuring the temperature.

Pyronyxis —Ignipuncture. Treatment or cauterization by puncturing a part with hot needles.

Pyrophobia —Morbid fear of fire.

Pyroptothymia —A mental disorder with the imagination of flames surrounding oneself.

Pyropuncture —Treatment of disease of a part of the body by puncturing with hot needles.

Pyrosis —Heartburn. Burning sensation in the epigastric and sternal region.

Pyrotherapy —Treatment of a disease by inducing artificial fever in the patient.

Pyrotic —1. Pertaining to pyrosis. 2. Caustic; burning.

Pyrotoxin —A toxin produced during a febrile disease.

Pyruvic acid —An intermediate product in the metabolism of carbohydrates, fats and amino acids, which increases in quantity in the blood and tissues in thiamine deficiency.

Pythogenesis —The origination from decaying matter.

Pythogenic —Originating from decaying matter.

Pythogenous —Pythogenic.

Pyuria —Presence of pus in the urine.

Q —1. Quantity. 2. Symbol for coulomb.

q.d. —Every day.

q.h. —Every hour.

q.i. —As much as one pleases.

q.i.d. —Four times a day.

Q law —As temperature decreases, chemical activity decreases.

q.m. —Every morning.

q.n. —Every night.

q.q.h.—Every four hours.

QRST—Q, R, S and T are 4 waves of an electrocardiogram which are associated with the contraction of the ventricles.

q.s. —As much as necessary.

qt. —Quart.

Quack —Charlatan. The person practising in medicine, who pretends to have the medical knowledge and experience, which he does not possess.

Quackery —Charlatanry. Treatment of the patients by a quack

Quadrangular —Having four angles.

Quadrant —1. One fourth part of a circle. 2. One of the four corresponding parts, as of the surface of abdomen.

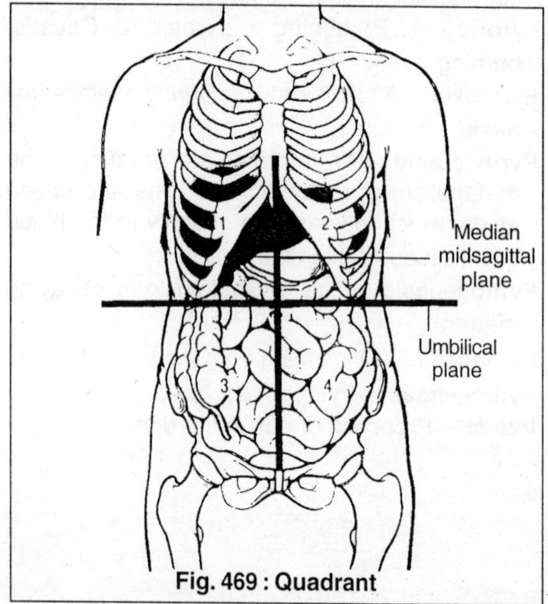

Fig. 469 : Quadrant

Quadrants of the abdomen
1. Right upper
2. Left upper
3. Right lower
4. Left lower

Quadrantanopia —Defective vision or blindness in one fourth of the visual field.

Quadrantanopsia —Quadrantanopia.

Quadrate —Square, or having four equal sides.

Quadrate lobe —A small lobe of the liver lying in contact with the pylorus and duodenum.

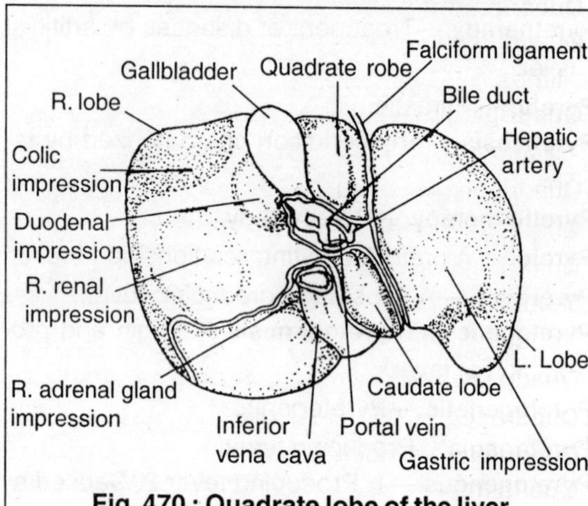

Fig. 470 : Quadrate lobe of the liver

Quadrate lobule —The square lobule of the upper surface of the cerebellum.

Quadri-, Quadr- —Prefixes which mean having four or consisting of four.

Quadriceps —Four-headed, as a quadriceps muscle.

Quadricepsplasty —Plastic surgery to remove the adhesions and scars around the quadriceps femoris muscle.

Quadriceps reflex —Extension of the leg on contraction of the quadriceps muscle resulting from a quick stroke of the patellar tendon.

Quadricuspid —Having four cusps, as a heart valve or a tooth.

Quadridigitate —Having only four fingers on a hand or four toes on a foot.

Quadrigemina —The corpora quadrigemina. The superior part of the midbrain consisting of two pairs of rounded bodies, the superior and inferior colliculi (eminences.)

Quadrigeminal —1. Fourfold. 2. Having four symmetrical parts. 3. Pertaining to the corpora quadrigemina.

Quadrigeminum —One of the four parts of corpora quadrigemina.

Quadrigeminus —Consisting of four parts.

Quadrigeminy—Quadrigeminal.

Quadrilateral —Having four sides.

Quadrilocular —Having four chambers or cavities.

Quadripara —Quartipara. A woman who has been pregnant for four times and each pregnancy continued for more than 20 weeks.

Quadriparesis —Tetraparesis.

Quadripartite —Divided into four parts.

Quadriplegia —Tetraplegia. Paralysis of all the four limbs.

Quadriplegic —Tetraplegic. Pertaining to or afflicted with quadriplegia.

Quadripolar —Pertaining to a cell having four poles.

Quadrisect —To divide into four parts.

Quadrisection —Division into four parts.

Quadritubercular —Having four tubercles or cusps.

Quadrivalent —Having a chemical valency of four.

Quadruped —An animal having four feet.

Quadruplet —One of four children born at one birth.

Qualifying —In psychology, capable of adding another facial expression to one that has just been shown, *e.g.*, a smile expression may be shown after an angry expression as a sign that the person is not as angry as he may seem.

Qualimeter —Penetrometer. An apparatus for measuring the quality of X-rays.

Qualitative —Referring to the quality of anything.

Quality —Degree of excellence.

Qualmish —Affected with nausea.

Qualmishness —Nausea.

Quanta —Plural of quantum.

Quantimeter —An apparatus for measuring quantity of X-rays to which one is exposed.

Quantitative —Pertaining to quantity.

Quantity —Amount.

Quantivalence —The number of hydrogen atoms with which an element or radical will combine.

Quantum —1. A definite amount. 2. A unit of radiant energy.

Quantum libet —As much as desired.

Quantum sufficit —As much as needed.

Quarantine —1. The period of detention from entering a country, of the persons coming from an infected area. 2. Period of isolation of the persons from public, from the onset of contagious disease.

Quart —One fourth part of a gallon (946 mls.) or two pints, written in short as qt.

Quartan —Occurring every fourth day, as malarial fever.

Quartipara —Quadripara.

Quartisect —To cut into four parts.

Quassation —Breaking up of the crude drugs into small pieces.

Quatelet index —Body mass index. It is an index for estimating the obesity. It is determined by dividing the body weight in kilograms by its height in meters squared.

Quater in die —Four times a day.

Quaternary —1. Fourth in order. 2. Composed of four elements.

Queckenstedt's sign —Rise of cerebrospinal fluid pressure upon compression of the neck veins.

Quenching —To extinguish or to cool a hot object, as a hot metal.

Querulent —1. Habitually complaining. 2. Fretful or peevish.

Questionnaire —A list of questions submitted to a patient in order to obtain information or useful data.

Quick —1. The part of the body susceptible to keen sensation as the tip of a digit. 2. Pregnant woman who feels fetal movements.

Quickening —First movement of the fetus felt in the uterus.

Quicklime —Unslaked lime.

Quiescence —Silence, calmness.

Quiescent —Silent, calm.

Quincke's disease —Angioneurotic edema or urticaria.

Quincke's pulse —Alternating redness and pallor of the capillary region as seen under the fingernails, a sign of aortic insufficiency.

Quincke's puncture —Lumbar puncture.

Quinestrol —An estrogen.

Quinine —A bitter white crystalline alkaloid derived from cinchona bark, used in malaria.

Quininism —Cinchonism. Poisoning by cinchona or its alkaloid quinine.

Quinqu —A prefix meaning five.

Quinquaud's disease —Purulent inflammation of the hair follicles of the scalp, resulting in bald patches.

Quinquetubercular —Having five cusps or tubercles.

Quinquevalent —Pentavalent.

Quinquina —Cinchona.

Quinsy —Peritonsillar abscess.

Quintan —Recurring every fifth day, as a fever.

Quinti- —A prefix which means fifth.

Quintipara —A woman who has been pregnant for five times and each pregnancy continued for more than 20 weeks.

Quintuplet —One of five children born at one birth.

Quodque —Each or every.

Quotidian —Occurring daily, as malarial fever.

Quotient —A number obtained by division, *e.g.*, respiratory quotient which is the result of dividing amount of carbon dioxide in expired air by the amount of oxygen inhaled, which is normally 0.9.

q. v. —1. Quantum vis. As much as you like. 2. Quod vide. Which see.

Q wave —A downward or negative wave of an electrocardiogram following the P wave.

R —1. Right; respiration; roentgen. 2. Chemical symbol for organic radical.

r—Abbreviation for roentgen, radius.

℞—Symbol for recipe (take in) Latin, written in the prescription.

Ra —Chemical symbol for radium.

Rabbetting —Interlocking of the jagged margins of a fractured bone.

Rbiate —Rabid. Suffering from rabies.

Rabic —Pertaining to rabies.

Rabicidal —Destructive to the virus causing rabies.

Rabid —Rabiate. Pertaining to, or affected with, rabies.

Rabies —It is an acute infectious viral, fatal disease of the central nervous system of warm-blooded mammals, especially dogs, cats, foxes, jackals, cattles and bats etc., resulting in paralysis and finally death. It is transmitted to man through bite of an animal suffering from this disease. The disease is characterized by chills, fever, headache, weakness, photophobia and myalgia, depression, irritability and convulsions after an incubation period of 6 days to one year. In the later stages, the disease is characterized by hydrophobia in which the patient runs away from water, he afraids of it, because drinking or even sight of water causes paralysis of the muscles of deglutition and laryngospasm. Death follows within a weak from the onset of disease due to paralysis of the respiratory muscles.

Rabiform —Resembling rabies.

Race —Tribe.

Racemic —Optically inactive compound.

Racemization —The production of a recemic form of an optically active compound.

Racemose —Shaped like a bunch of grapes, as a gland.

Rachi-, Rachio- —Prefixes which mean spine or vertebral column.

Rachia —Spine or vertebral column.

Rachial —Rachidial. Pertaining to the spine or vertebral column.

Rachialbuminimeter —An apparatus for determining the amount of albumin in the cerebrospinal fluid.

Rachialbuminimetry —Determination of the amount of albumin in the cerebrospinal fluid.

Rachialgia —Rachiodynia. Pain occurring in the vertebral column.

Rachianalgesia —Rachianesthesia. Anesthesia of the vertebral column.

Rachianesthesia —Rachianalgesia. Spinal anesthesia.

Rachicele —Protrusion of the contents of spinal canal in spina bifida.

Rachicentesis —Puncture of the spinal canal; lumbar puncture.

Rachidial —Pertaining to the vertebral column.

Rachidian —Rachidial.

Rachigraph —An apparatus for recording the outlines of the vertebral column and back.

Rachilysis —Correction of the lateral curvature of the vertebral column by combined traction and pressure on the convexity.

Rachio- —Rachi.

Rachiocampsis —Curvature of the vertebral column.

Rachiocentesis —Lumbar puncture.

Rachiochysis —Accumulation of fluid within the spinal canal.

Rachiodynia —Rachialgia.

Rachiometer —An instrument for measuring a curvature of the vertebral column.

Rachiomyelitis —Inflammation of the spinal cord.

Rachiopagus —Two conjoined twins joined at the vertebral column.

Rachiopathy —Any disease of the vertebral column.

Rachioplegia —Paralysis due to a lesion in the spinal cord.

Rachioscoliosis —Lateral curvature of the vertebral column.

Rachiotome —An instrument for dividing the vertebrae.

Rachiotomy —To incise a vertebra or vertebral column.

Rachipagus —Rachiopagus.

Rachis —The spinal or vertebral column.

Rachischisis —Spina bifida. Congenital fissure of the vertebral column.

Rachitic —Pertaining to or affected with rickets.

Rachitis —1. Inflammation of the vertebral column. 2. Rickets.

Rachitism —Tendency to rickets.

Rachitogenic —Causing or developing rickets.

Rachitome —Rachiotome.

Rachitomy —Rachiotomy.

Raclage —Destruction and removal of a soft growth by scraping or rubbing.

Rad —Radiation absorbed dose.

Rad —Root.

Radectomy —Surgical removal of all or a portion of the root of a tooth.

Radiability —Capability of being readily penetrated by X-rays.

Radiable —Capable of being penetrated or examined by X-rays.

Radiad —Toward the radius bone.

Radial —1. Pertaining to the radius bone or the radial (lateral) side of the arm. 2. Spreading outward from a common center.

Radialis —Pertaining to the radius bone.

Radial reflex —Flexion of forearm resulting from percussion of the lower end of the radius bone.

Radian —A SI unit of angular measurement equivalent to 57.295 degrees.

Radiant —1. Emitting light rays. 2. Diverging from a center. 3. Transmitted by radiation.

Radiate —To spread from a common center.

Radiating —Diverging from a common center.

Radiatio —A radiation or radiating structure.

Radiation —1. Process by which energy is propagated through a space or matter. 2. Emission or divergence of rays or energy in all directions from a common center. 3. A structure or group of fibers diverging from a common origin., *e.g.*, groups of fibers connecting thalamus with the cerebral hemispheres.

Radiation biology —The scientific study of the effects of radiation on living organisms.

Radiationes —Plural of radiatio.

Radiation symbol —A universal symbol used to indicate radioactive sources, containers for radioactive materials and areas where radioactive materials are stored and used.

Radiation syndrome —1. Illness resulting from exposure of body tissue to ionizing radiations from radioactive substances. 2. Illness resulting from the effects of an atomic bomb explosion.

Radiation therapy —Treatment of malignant tumors with radiation.

Radiator —An apparatus for radiating heat or light.

Radical —1. A group of atoms acting as a single unit, which passes without change in it from one compound to another but not able to exit in a free state. 2. Directed toward the root, origin or cause.

Radical cure —Complete cure from a disease.

Radical treatment —The treatment given for absolute cure, which is usually a radical surgery, *e.g.*, total hysterectomy.

Radices —Plural of radix.

Radiciform —Resembling a root.

Radicle —One of the smallest branches of a vessel or nerve, resembling a rootlet.

Radicotomy —Rhizotomy. To divide a spinal nerve root.

Radicula —Radicle

Radiculalgia —Pain occurring due to involvement of the spinal nerve roots.

Radicular —Pertaining to a root or radicle.

Radiculectomy —Excision of a spinal nerve root.

Radiculitis —Inflammation of the spinal nerve roots.

Radiculoganglionitis —Inflammation of the posterior spinal roots and their ganglia.

Radiculomedullary —Pertaining to the nerve roots and the spinal cord.

Radiculomeningomyelitis —Inflammation of the nerve roots, meninges and spinal cord.

Radiculomyelopathy —Any disease of the spinal nerve roots and spinal cord.

Radiculoneuritis —Acute polyneuritis.

Radiculoneuropathy —Any disease of the nerve roots and spinal nerves.

Radiculopathy —Any disease of the spinal nerve roots.

Radiectomy —Surgical removal of the root of a tooth.

Radiferous —Containing radium.

Radii —Plural of radius.

Radio- —1. A prefix which indicates relationship to the radiant energy, radioactive substances, radium and the radius bone of the forearm. 2. As a prefix to a chemical element indicating a radioactive isotope of that element.

Radioactive —Capable of emitting radiant energy.

Radioactive decay —The decreae in the number of radioactive atoms in a radioactive substance.

Radioactive patient —The patient treated with radioactive substances and continues to emit rays.

Radioactivity —Capability of a substance to emit rays, or particles (alpha, beta, gamma) from its nucleus.

Radioallergosorbent test —It is a blood test for allergy. Allergy is detected by measuring the quantities of antibody immunoglobulin E (IgE) in blood which is increased in the person who is allergic to foreign substances.

Radioanaphylaxis —Abnormal sensitivity to radiation.

Radioautogram —Autoradiogram.

Radioautograph —Autoradiography.

Radioautography —Autoradiograph.

Radiobicipital —Pertaining to the radius bone and biceps muscle of the arm.

Radiobiologist —Specialist in radiobiology.

Radiobiology —The branch of science dealing with the study of effects of light and of ultraviolet and ionizing radiations on the living tissues or organisms.

Radiocardiogram —The graphic record or film obtained during radiocardiography.

Radiocardiography —The graphic recording or taking a film of a radioactive substance travelling through the heart to investigate the structure and function of the heart.

Radiocarpal —Pertaining to the radius bone and carpus.

Radiochemistry —The branch of chemistry dealing with the radioactive materials.

Radiochroism —The ability of a substance to absorb radioactive rays.

Radiochrometer —An apparatus for measuring penetrating powers of X-rays.

Radiocinematograph —A moving picture camera combined with X-ray machine for taking moving pictures of the internal organs.

Radiocinematography —The taking a moving picture of internal organs by X-ray fluoroscopy.

Radiocurable —Curable by radiation therapy.

Radiocystitis —Inflammation of the urinary bladder following treatment by radium or X-rays.

Radiode —Metal container for radium, used for the treatment.

Radiodense —Radiopaque.

Radiodensity —Radiopacity.

Radiodermatitis —Dermatitis caused by exposure to X-rays or radioactive elements.

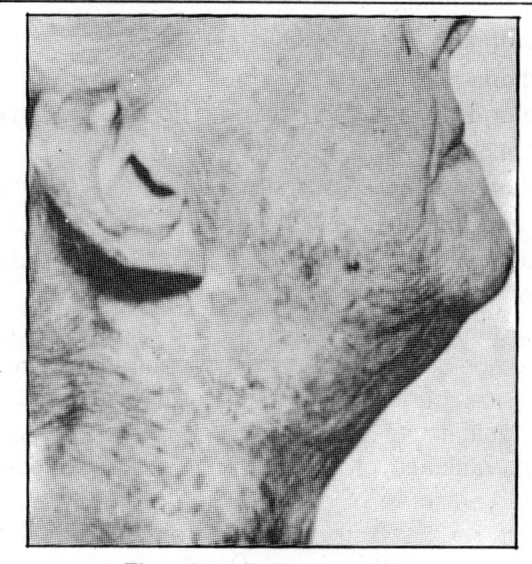

Fig. : 471 : Radiodermatitis

Radiodiagnosis —Diagnosis of disease by means of X-rays.

Radiodigital —Pertaining to the radius bone of the forearm, and fingers.

Radiodontia —Radiography of the teeth.

Radiodontics —Dental radiology.

Radiodontist —Specialist in dental radiology.

Radioecology —Study of the effect of radiation on living organisms in the environment.

Radioelectrocardiogram —The record obtained by radioelectrocardiography.

Radioelectrocardiography —Recording of the changes in heart beats by radio wave without attachment of the apparatus to the patient.

Radioelement —Any element possessing the power of radioactivity.

Radioencephalogram —Record obtained when a radioactive substance passes through the cerebral blood vessels.

Radioencephalography —The recording of radio waves transmitted from the brain of patient, without placing electrodes on the scalp.

Radioepidermitis —Inflammation of the epidermis caused by radioactive rays.

Radioepithelitis —Inflammation of the epithelium caued by exposure to radiation.

Radiogenesis —Production of radiant energy.

Radiogenic —1. Producing radiation. 2. Actinogenic. Caused by radiation.

Radiogenics —The science of radiation.

Radiogram —Roentgenogram. X-ray picture of the body organs.

Radiograph —X-ray picture or film.

Radiographer —The person who takes X-ray film.

Radiography —Roentgenography. The making of X-ray pictures.

Radiohumeral —Pertaining to the radius and humerus bones.

Radioimmunity —Diminished sensitivity to radiation.

Radioimmunoassay —It is a sensitive assay method of determining the concentration of substances particularly the antigen and antibodies. In antigen assay, known amounts of antibody and radioactively-labeled antigen are added to the specimen of antigen. The antibody binds with the radioactively-labeled antigen and with the antigen of the specimen. The portion of the mixture containing free antigen and antibody-bound antigen are separated by chromatography or other means. The concentration of the specimen antigen is inversely proportional to the radioactivity of bound fraction or directly proportional to the activity of the free fraction. In antibody assays, the roles of antigen and antibody are reversed.

Radioimmunodiffusion —Study of the antigen-antibody interaction by use of radioisotope-labeled antigens.

Radioimmunoelectrophoresis —Electrophoresis by the use of radioisotope-labeled antigen or antibody.

Radioimmunosorbent —Denoting a radioimmunoassay technique for measuring immunoglobulin gamma E (IgE) in the sample of serum.

Radioiodine —Radioactive isotope of iodine used in the diagnosis and treatment of the diseases of thyroid gland.

Radioiron —Radioactive isotope of iron.

Radioisotopes —Radioactive forms of elements.

Radiolesion —An injury caused by radiation.

Radioligand —A radioactive labeled antigen or antibody.

Radiologic, Radiological —Pertaining to radiology.

Radiologist —Specialist in radiology.

Radiology —The branch of medical science dealing with the study of use of radioactive substances and radiant energy including X-ray etc., in the diagnosis and treatment of diseases.

Radiolucency —Semitransparency to radiant energy.

Radiolucent —Semitransparent to radiant energy.

Radiolus —Probe or sound.

Radiometer —1. An instrument for estimating X-ray quantity or for measuring the penetrating power of radiant energy. 2. The instrument in which radiant heat and light may be directly converted into mechanical energy.

Radiomicrometer —An instrument for measuring small changes in radiation.

Radiomimetic —Producting the effects similar to those of radiation.

Radiomuscular —Pertaining to the radius bone or radial artery and muscles of the arm.

Radiomutation —The permanent alteration of the genetic material of a cell caused by the effects of ionizing radiation.

Radion —One of the radioactive particles given off by radioactive matter.

Radionecrosis —Destruction of the tissues by exposure to radiation.

Radioneuritis —Neuritis caused by exposure to radiant energy.

Radiopacity —The quality of obstructing the passage of radiant energy, such as X-rays.

Radiopalmar —Pertaining to the radial or lateral side of the palm.

Radiopaque —Impenetrable to the X-rays or other forms of radiation.

Radioparency —Transparency to radiant energy such as X-ray.

Radioparent —Transparent to radiant energy such as X-ray.

Radiopathology —Study of the pathological changes in the body produced by radiation.

Radiopelvimetry —Measurement of the pelvis by radiography.

Radiopharmaceutical —Radioactive drug or a chemical.

Radiophobia —Morbid fear of X-rays or radiation.

Radiopotentiation —The increasing of the power of radiation by certain drugs, and by oxygen.

Radiopraxis —Diagnosis or treatment of diseases by using some radioactive substance.

Radioprotectant —Substance that prevents or lessens the effects of radiation.

Radiopulmonography —The use of radioactive materials to measure the flow of gases through the lungs during respiration.

Radioreaction —The reaction of the body to radiation.

Radioreceptor—That which receives radiant energy such as light, heat or X-ray.

Radioresistance —Resistance of the tissues to radiation.

Radioresistant —Resistant to the action of radiation, as a tumor which cannot be destroyed by treatment with the radiation.

Radioresponsive —Radiosensitive.

Radioscopy —Fluoroscopy. Examination of the internal organs of body by X-ray.

Radiosensibility —Radiosensitivity.

Radiosensitive —Sensitive to radiant energy.

Radiosensitivity —Sensitivity, as of the skin and tumor etc., to radiant energy, such as X-rays.

Radiosensitization —To increase the sensitivity of tissue to the radiation by using chemotherapy.

Radiosensitizer —A chemical substance that increases the radiosensitivity of tissues.

Radiosurgery —The use of radioactive rays in resecting a malignant tumor etc.

Radiotelemetry —Transmission of biological data via radio waves from the patient to a remote recording apparatus for storage, analysis and interpretation.

Radiotherapeutic —Pertaining to radiotherapy or therapeutics.

Radiotherapeutics —1. Radiotherapy. 2. Study of the radiotherapeutic agents.

Radiotherapist —Specialist in radiotherapy.

Radiotherapy —Treatment of diseases by radiant energy such as by X-ray, radium, radioactive substances and ultraviolet rays etc.

Radiothermy —1. Short-wave diathermy. 2. Use of heat produced by radioactive substances in the treatment of diseases.

Radiothyroidectomy —Destruction of thyroid gland by use of radioactive iodine.

Radiothyroxin —Radioactive thyroxine hormone of the thyroid gland.

Radiotoxemia —Toxemia produced by radiant energy or radio active substances.

Radiotracer —A radioactive tracer.

Radiotransparent —Penetrable by X-rays or other forms of radiations.

Radiotropic —Affected by radiation.

Radioulnar —Pertaining to the radius and ulna bones.

Radisectomy —To rootout an organ by surgery.

Radium —A radioactive metallic element found in very small quantities, emitting alpha (α), beta (β) and gamma (γ) rays.

Radium needle —A slender container for radium which is inserted into the tissue to kill malignant cells.

Radium therapy —Radiotherapy.

Radius —1. A line from the center of a circle to a point on its circumference. 2. The outer bone of the forearm, the inner being ulna.

Radix —The root.

Radon —A radioactive gaseous element resulting from the disintegration of isotopes of radium.

Rage —Violent anger.

Rale —An abnormal respiratory sound heard on auscultation of the chest, which indicates some pathological condition.

Amphoric rale —A coarse, musical and tinkling sound heard on auscultation of the chest, wnen a fluid-containing cavity connects with a bronchus.

Atelectatic rale —Transitory rale which disappears on deep respiration or coughing.

Bronchiectatic rale —Rale heard over bronchiectatic cavities filled with secretion, which disappears with expectoration.

Bubbling rale —Rale like bubbling sound produced by passage of air through mucus in the larger respiratory tubes in inspiration and expiration.

Clicking rale —A small sticky sound heard on inspiration, by passage of air through secretions in the smaller bronchi, as in early stage of pulmonary tuberculosis.

Crackling rale —Rale as cracking sound of a

pot heard in inspiration produced by fluid in the finer bronchi.

Crepitant rale —A fine, dry, crackling sound as that made by rubbing hair between the fingers, heard at the end of inspiration, usually at the base of the lungs in hypostatic pneumonia.

Dry rale —Whistling or hissing sound heard in bronchial asthma and bronchitis produced by narrowing of the bronchioles.

Gurgling rale —Sound produced by passage of air through fluid in cavities of large bubbles, as heard in pulmonary tuberculosis after formation of cavities.

Moist rale —Sound produced by passage of air through bronchi containing fluid.

Sibilant rale —A high-pitched, whistling or hissing sound due to viscid secretions in the bronchial tubes or by thickening of their walls, heard in asthma and bronchitis.

Subcrepitant rale —Crackling rale.

Vesicular rale —Crepitant rale.

Ramal —Pertaining to a ramus.

Rami —Plural of ramus.

Ramicotomy —Ramisection.

Ramification —The process of branching.

Ramify —To spread in branches.

Ramisection —Cutting of a ramus.

Ramisectomy —Surgical excision of a ramus.

Ramitis —Inflammation of a ramus.

Ramollissement —Abnormal softening of an organ or tissue, especially of the brain.

Ramose —Branching; having many branches.

Ramous —Ramose.

Ramuli —Plural of ramulus.

Ramulus —A small branch or terminal division.

Ramus —1. A branch, as of a nerve, vein or artery. 2. A part of an irregularly shaped bone forming an angle with the main body.

Ramus communicans —A branch connecting two nerves or arteries.

Rancid —Offensive or having disagreeable taste from decomposition, especially of the fatty substance.

Rancidify —To make rancid.

Rancidity —Condition of being rancid.

Random —Occurring by chance, done suddenly.

Randomization —Allocation of individuals to groups *e.g.*, for experimental and control system, by chance.

Range —The difference between upper and lower limits.

Ranine —1. Pertaining to a ranula, to the lower surface of the tongue, or to sublingual vein. 2. Pertaining to a frog.

Ranula —A large cystic tumor on either side of the frenum, beneath the tongue.

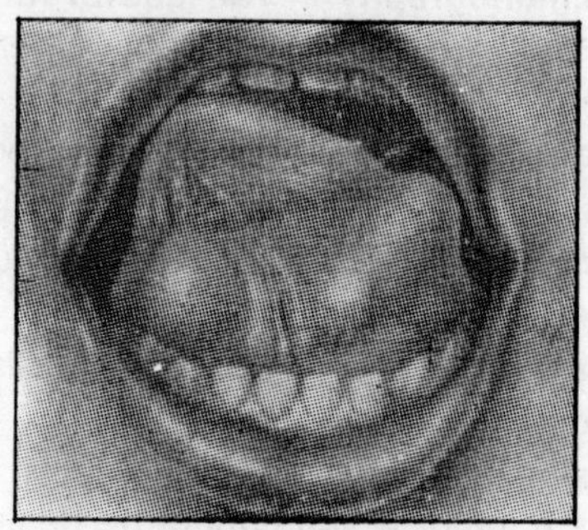

Fig. 472 : Ranula beneath the tongue

Ranular —Pertaining to a ranula.

Rape —Intercourse by force.

Raphe —A crease or ridge denoting union of two halves of a part.

Abdominal raphe —Linea alba.

Raphe of the tongue —A medium groove on the dorsum of the tongue.

Scrotal raphe —A ridge in the midline of the scrotum.

Rapport —The relationship of mutual trust between doctor and the patient.

Rapture —Extreme delight.

Raptus —A sudden attack of a disease or seizure.

Rarefaction —The condition of being less dense, as of a bone due to absorption of calcium.

Rarefy —To make less dense or to increase the porosity of.

Rasceta —The transverse wrinkling on the anterior surface of the wrist.

Rash —A temporary eruption on the skin.

Butterfly rash —Skin rash of both cheeks joined by extension across the nose bridge, as seen in lupus erythematosus and seborrheic dermatitis.

Diaper rash —Rash occurring in infants on the skin covered by the diaper.

Drug rash —Rash caused by certain medicines, such as bromide or iodine.

Heat rash —Miliaria rubra.

Hemorrhagic rash —Rash consisting of hemorrhages or ecchymoses.

Macular rash —A rash in which the lesions are flat and level with the surrounding skin.

Maculopapular rash —A rash with macular and papular lesions combined.

Nettle rash —Urticaria.

Rose rash —Roseola. Any rose-colored rash.

Serum rash —Rash occurring with serum sickness resulting from injection of a foreign serum.

Summer rash —Miliaria. Prickly heat.

Sunburn-like rash —A macular rash resembling the red skin as that of a severe sunburn.

Rasion —Grating of drugs with file.

Raspatory —File used in surgery.

RAST —Radioallergosorbent test.

Rasura —1. The process of scraping or shaving. 2. Scrapings or filing.

Rate —The speed or frequency of occurrence of an event, usually expressed in time or some other known standard.

Attack rate —The rate of occurrence of new cases of a disease.

Basal metabolic rate—See under 'B'.

Birth rate —See under 'B'.

Case fatality rate —The ratio of the number of deaths caused by a disease to the total number of people suffering from that disease.

Case rate —Morbidity rate.

Death rate —See under 'D'.

Erythrocyte sedimentation rate (ESR) —See under 'E'.

Fertility rate —The number of births per 1000 women of the age of 15 to 44 years per year in a given population.

Growth rate —The rate at which an individual, organ or tissue grows, which is usually expressed per unit of time such as hours, days, months or years.

Heart rate —See under 'H'.

Morbidity rate —See under 'M'.

Mortality rate —Death rate.

Pulse rate —The number of pulses per unit of time, caused by contraction of the heart, which are usually felt by the fingers in radial artery at the wrist. Normal pulse rate of the adult man is 70 to 72 and woman is 78-82 per minute.

Respiration rate —The number of breaths per unit of time.

Ratio —Relationship between two quantities, proportion.

Ration —Fixed amount of daily food and drink of a patient allowed for a certain period.

Rational —1. Sane. Of healthy mind. 2. Reasonable or logical.

Rationale —The fundamental reason or logical.

Rationalization —To make reasonable.

Rattle —A sound or rale heard on auscultation.

Death rattle —A gurgling sound heard on auscultation in the trachea of the dying person.

Raucous —Hoarse or harsh, as the sound of a voice.

Rave —To talk irrationally, as in delirium.

Raving —Talking irrationally.

Ray —One of the lines diverging from a common center as of radiant energy, especially light or heat.

Actinic ray —A sun ray capable of producing chemical changes.

Alpha ray —A ray of positively charged particles of helium derived from atomic disintegration of radioactive elements. They have less penetrating power than beta rays. They are completely absorbed by a thin sheet of paper and produce fluorescence.

Beta rays —Negatively charged electrons ejected from atomic disintegration of the radioactive elements, which have more penetrating power than alpha rays, but less than gamma rays.

Chemical rays —Actinic rays.

Delta rays —Highly penetrating rays emitting from radioactive substances.

Gamma rays —Electromagnetic waves of extremely short wave length emitted by radioactive substances during their atomic disintegration. They are of the same nature as X-rays. They have greater penetrating power than alpha or beta rays.

Heat ray—A visible ray from 3,900 to 7,700

A.U. or an infrared ray from 7,700 to 14,000 A.U.

Infrared rays —See under section 'I'.

Reflected ray —A ray which is thrown back from a nonpenetrable or nonabsorbing surface.

Roentgen rays —X-rays which may penetrate most of the substances, are used to take photographs of the internal organs and parts of the body. They are used for both diagnosis and treatment of the diseases.

Ultraviolet rays —See under 'U'.

X-rays —Roentgen rays.

Raynaud's disease —A peripheral vascular disease found mostly in females between the age of 18 and 30. It is characterized by abnormal constriction of blood vessels of the extremities upon exposure to cold or emotional stress, causing intermittent pallor or cyanosis of the digits usually of fingers.

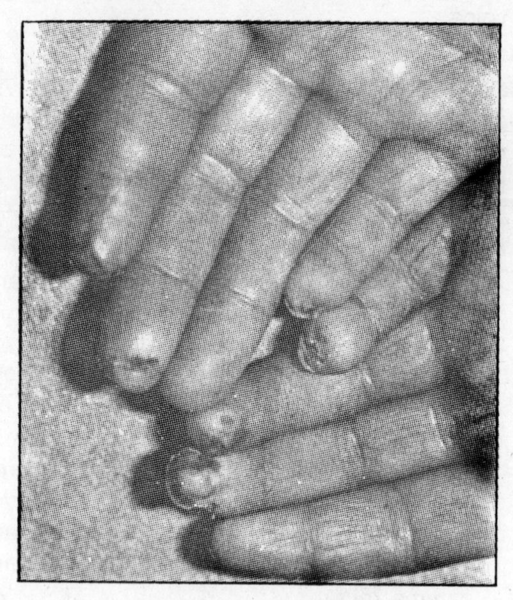

Fig. 473 : Raynaud's disease

RBC —Red blood cell.

R.C.P. —Royal College of Physicians.

R.C.S. —Royal College of Surgeons.

R.D.S. —Respiratory distress syndrome.

Re- —A prefix meaning back or again.

Reabsorb —To absorb again.

Reabsorption —The process of absorbing again.

React —1. To respond to a stimulus. 2. To take part in a chemical reaction.

Reactant —A chemical or substance taking part in a chemical reaction.

Reaction —1. Response of an organism or a part of it to a stimulus. 2. A chemical process in which a substance is transformed into another substance. 3. Opposite action or counteraction in response to a stimulus. 4. The mental and/or emotional state created by a particular situation.

Acid reaction —A reaction which is recognized by the change of blue litmus paper to red.

Adverse reaction —Any undesirable or unwanted reaction.

Alkaline reaction —A reaction which is recognized by the change of red litmus paper to blue.

Allergic reaction —A local or general reaction occurring from allergy to an antigen.

Anaphylactic reaction —Anaphylaxis. An allergic hypersensitivity reaction of the body to a foreign protein or drug.

Antigen-antibody reaction —Combination of an antigen with one or more of its specific antibody.

Complement-fixation reaction —See under section 'C'.

Defence reaction —A mental response just to protect the ego.

Delayed reaction —A reaction occurring hours or days after exposure to a stimulus such as inflammation of the skin.

Hypersensitivity reaction —Allergic reaction.

Immediate reaction —A reaction occurring within a few minutes to about an hour on exposure to an antigen.

Immune reaction —Antigen-antibody reaction.

Intracutaneous reaction —A reaction following the injection of a substance (antigen) into the skin of a sensitive person.

Intradermal reaction —Intracutaneous reaction.

Local reaction —Reaction occurring at the point of stimulation or injection.

Neutral reaction —In chemistry, a reaction which indicates absence of acid or alkaline properties, which is expressed as pH 7.0.

Serum reaction —Serum sickness.

Transfusion reaction —Reaction occurring after transfusion of incompatible blood, which causes hemolysis of red blood cells of the recipient.

Wassermann reaction —A test for syphilis based upon complement fixation.

Reactionary —Anything producing reaction.

Reactivate —To make active again.

Reactivation —The process of making active again.

Reactivative —Capable of being reactivated.

Reactivity —The process of reacting to a stimulus.

Reading —Understanding of the written or printed words.

Lip reading —To understand the speech by observing the speaker's lips movements.

Reagent —A substance used to produce a chemical reaction to detect the presence of another substance.

Reagin —1. Antibody of the class immunoglobulin gamma E (IgE) present in the serum of persons with atopy (An allergy for which there is hereditary tendency to develop) 2. A complement fixing antibody used in wassermann reaction (W. R.) test for syphilis.

Reaginic —Pertaining to reagin.

Reamer —An instrument used in dentistry for enlarging the root canal of a tooth.

Reanimate —Restore to life; to reactivate.

Reapers' keratitis —Inflammation of the cornea caused by dust from grain.

Rebase —In dentistry, to refit a denture by replacing the base material of the denture without changing the occlusal relationship of the teeth.

Rebound —Occurrence of fresh activity following sudden withdrawal of the stimulus, such as a strong contraction occurring after a moderate one.

Rebreathing —Inhalation of a gas previously exhaled.

Recalcification —Replacement of calcium salts into the tissues from which they have been withdrawn.

Recall —1. To remember or recollect. 2. To summon back.

Recanalization —Restoration of a lumen in a blood vessel following occlusion due to thrombosis.

Receptacle —A vessel into which something is placed.

Receptaculum —A vessel, receptacle or cavity in which a fluid is contained.

Receptive —Sensitive or responsive to stimulus.

Receptor —1. A sensory nerve ending which receives and transmits the stimuli. 2. A component of a cell that combines with a drug or hormone to change the function of the cell.

Recess —A small depression or cavity.

Recession —The withdrawal of a part of the body from its normal position.

Recessitivity —The state of going back.

Recessive —Tending to go back.

Recessus —Recess.

Recidivation, Recidivism —1. Recurrence of a disease. 2. Repetition of antisocial or criminal acts.

Recidivism —Recidivation.

Recidivist —1. A confirmed criminal 2. The person who repeats antisocial or criminal acts after treatment of the mental disorder or punishment.

Recidivity —Tendency to return to a former condition.

Recipe —1. The head of a prescription, indicated by the symbol R_x, which means 'thou take.' 2. A prescription or formula for the preparation of a medicine.

Recipient —The person who receives something from a donor, especially blood, tissues or organs etc.

Recipiomotor —Pertaining to the reception of motor stimuli.

Reciprocal —Interchangeable.

Reciprocate —To walk forward and backward; to interchange.

Reciprocation —Alternation, interchange.

Reciprocity —The recognition by one state of the licence to practice, granted to a doctor by another state.

Reclination —The act of lying down.

Recline —To lie down.

Reclus' disease —Multiple, benign, cystic growths in the breast.

Recombinant —1. The new cell or individual resulting from genetic recombination. 2. Pertaining to such cells or individuals.

Recombinant DNA —Deoxyribonucleic acid artificially introduced into a cell to alter the genotype and phenotype of the cell.

Recombination —Joining together again.

Recomposition —Reconstruction.

Recompression —Return to normal atmospheric pressure after exposure to greatly diminished pressure.

Recon —The smallest unit of genetic material which is capable of recombination.

Reconcentration —The process of repeated concentration.

Reconstitution —The return of a substance to its original state after it has been previously altered for preservation and storage, as is done with dried plasma.

Reconstruction —Repair of a missing organ or part.

Record —A written account of something.

Recorder —That which keeps written account of something.

Recording —Keeping of written account of something.

Recover —To regain as health after an illness.

Recovery —1. The process of becoming healthy after an illness. 2. Emergence from general anesthesia.

Recrement —Saliva or other secretion which is reabsorbed into the blood after performing its function.

Recrementitious —Of the nature of a secretion, which after performing its function is reabsorbed into the blood.

Recrudescence —Relapse. Recurrence of the symptoms of a disease after temporary abatement.

Recrudescent —Becoming active again after an illness.

Recruitment —1. Gradual increase to a maximum in a reflex action when a stimulus is prolonged, even though strength of the stimulus is not changed. 2. In audiology, excessively rapid increase in the loudness of sound caused by a slight increase in its intensity.

Rect- —Recto-

Recta —Plural of rectum.

Rectal —Pertaining to the rectum.

Rectal alimentation —Feeding through rectum.

Rectal crisis —Tenesmus and rectal pain.

Rectalgia —Pain in the rectum.

Rectal reflex —The normal desire for defecation.

Rectangle —The four-sided figure, the opposite sides of which are equal and parallel and all the four angles are right angles.

Rectangular —Having the shape of a rectangle.

Rectectomy —Proctectomy. Excision of the rectum or anus.

Rectification —1. The process of purifying a substance. 2. Act of straightening or correcting. 3. Process of changing an alternating current into a direct current.

Rectified —Made pure or straight.

Rectifier —In electricity, an apparatus for changing an alternate current into a direct one.

Rectitis —Proctitis. Inflammation of the rectum.

Recto- —A prefix which means rectum.

Rectoabdominal —Pertaining to the rectum and abdomen.

Rectocele —Herniation of a part of the rectum into vagina.

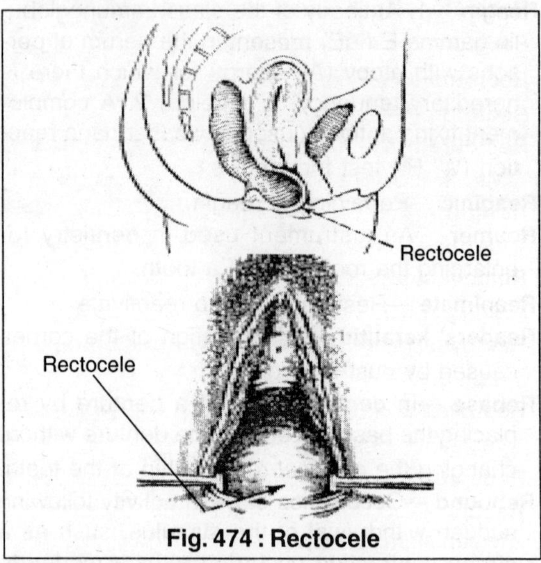

Fig. 474 : Rectocele

Rectoclysis —To introduce slowly the fluid into rectum.

Rectococcygeal —Pertaining to the rectum and coccyx.

Rectococcypexia —Fixation of rectum by suturing it to the coccyx.

Rectocolitis —Proctocolitis. Inflammation of the rectum and colon.

Rectocutaneous —Pertaining to the rectum and skin.

Rectocystotomy —To incise the urinary bladder through rectum, usually to remove a calculus.

Rectolabial —Pertaining to the rectum and a labium majus.

Rectoperineorrhaphy —Proctoperineoplasty. Surgical repair of the rectum and perineum.

Rectopexy —Proctopexy. Fixation of the rectum by suturing it to another part.

Rectophobia —Morbid fear of the possibility of having cancer with the rectal disease.

Rectoplasty —Proctoplasty. Repair of the anus and rectum by plastic surgery.

Rectorrhaphy —Proctorrhaphy. Suture of the rectum and anus.

Rectoscope —A speculum for examining the rectum.

Rectoscopy —Proctoscopy.

Rectosigmoid —Upper part of the rectum and terminal part of the sigmoid colon.

Rectosigmoidectomy —Surgical removal of the rectum and sigmoid colon.

Rectostenosis —Narrowing of the rectum.

Rectostomy —Proctostomy.

Rectotome —Proctotome.

Rectotomy —Proctotomy.

Rectourethral —Pertaining to or communicating with the rectum and urethra.

Rectouterine —Pertaining to the rectum and uterus.

Rectovaginal —Pertaining to the rectum and vagina.

Rectovesical —Pertaining to the rectum and urinary bladder.

Rectovestibular —Pertaining to the rectum and vestibule of the vagina.

Rectovulvar —Pertaining to the rectum and vulva.

Rectum —Lowest part of the large intestine, between sigmoid flexure and the anal canal, which is about 5 inches (12.7 cms.) long.

Rectus —Straight.

Recumbency —The state of lying down.

Recumbent —Lying down.

Recuperate —To return to normal health following an illness.

Recuperation —Restoration to normal health.

Recurrence —Relapse. Return of symptoms after a period of quiescence.

Recurrent —Reappearing. Returning after a period of quiescence, as the symptoms of a disease.

Recurvation —The bending backward.

Recurvatum —Bowing backward.

Recurve —To bend backward.

Red blood cell —Erythrocyte.

Red cross —A cross of red color on white background, which is an internationally recognized sign of medical person or institution.

Redifferentiation —The resuming of the characteristics of mature cells by malignant cells.

red. in pulv. —Reduced to powder.

Redintegration —1. Restitution of the lost or repair of the damaged part. 2. Restoration to health.

Redox —Combined word for oxidation and reduction.

Redressement —1. Correction of a deformity. 2. Dressing of a wound more than once.

Reduce —1. To decrease in weight or size. 2. To weaken as a solution. 3. To restore to the normal place, as the fractured bone.

Reducible —Capable of being replaced in normal position as a dislocated bone or a hernia.

Reductant —That which is reduced in oxidation-reduction reactions.

Reductase —An enzyme which accelerates the process of reduction of chemical compounds.

Reduction —1. Restoration to the normal position, as a fractured bone or a hernia. 2. The addition of hydrogen to a substance or the gain of electrons.

Redundancy —Excess.

Redundant —More than necessary.

Reduplicated —1. Doubled. 2. Bent backward, as a fold.

Reduplication —1. A doubling as of some parts of the body, or heart sounds in some diseases. 2. The bending backwards, as a fold.

Re-education —Training for regaining physical and mental health.

Reef —A fold or tuck.

Reefing —Reduction of the size of a tissue by surgery, by folding it and suturing.

Reel —Swing.

Re-entry —In cardiology, a mechanism by which a premature heart-beat can be coupled to the normal heart-beat.

Refect —To cure.

Refection —1. Recovery. 2. Refreshment.

Referral —The practice of sending a patient to another doctor or specialist for consultation or treatment.

Referred pain —Pain felt in the areas distant from its point of origin, *e.g.*, pain of angina pectoris felt in the left arm.

Refine —To purify or to render free from foreign matter.

Reflect —1. To throw back the image. 2. To bend back. 3. To think over the matter. 4. To meditate.

Reflectance —The quality of being reflected.

Reflection —1. A turning or bending back, as of the peritoneum from the wall of a body cavity to and around an organ and back to the body wall. 2. The turning of a light ray, sound or heat when it strikes against a surface that it does not penetrate.

Reflectometer —An instrument for measuring the light reflected by a surface. It is used in urine analysis.

Reflector —An apparatus or surface that reflects rays of light or waves of sound.

Reflex —A reflex action. An involuntary response to a stimulus which depends upon a neural pathway between the point of stimulation and responding organ (muscle or gland). This pathway is called reflex arc. It includes a sensory receptor, afferent or sensory neuron, reflex center in the brain or spinal cord, one or more efferent or motor neurons and an effector organ (muscle or gland).

Abdominal reflex —Contraction of the muscles of the abdominal wall upon stimulation of the skin or tapping neighboring bony structures.

Abdominocardiac reflex —Slowing of the cardiac rate resulting from stimulation of the abdominal organs.

Accommodation reflex —Adjustment of direction of visual axis, size of pupil and convexity of the lens on seeing the objects at different distances.

Achiles reflex —Achilles tendon reflex. See in the section 'A'.

Anal reflex —Contraction of the anal sphincter following irritation of the skin about the anus.

Ankle reflex —Ankle jerk. See under section 'A'.

Antagonistic reflex —Two or more reflexes occurring simultaneously but producing opposite effects.

Auditory reflex —Any reflex occurring in response to a sound.

Biceps reflex —Flexion of the forearm upon percussion of tendon of the muscle biceps brachii.

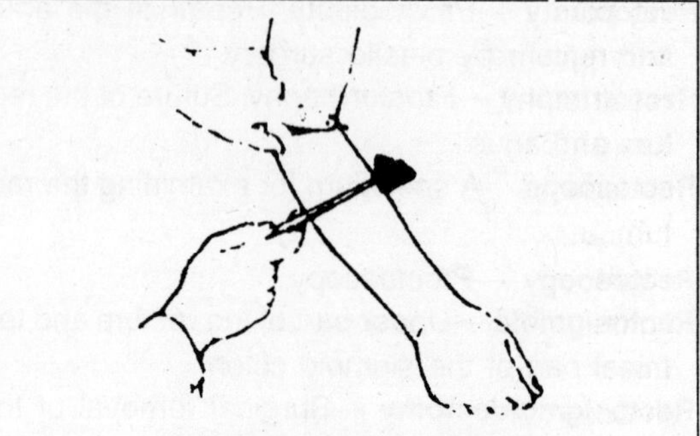

Fig. 475 : Biceps reflex

Percussion with hammer of the finger placed on the muscle brachii, causing flexion of the forearm.

Carotid sinus reflex —Slowing of the heart rate following pressure on the carotid sinus at the neck.

Ciliary reflex —Normal contraction of the pupil in accommodation of vision from distant to near.

Conditioned reflex —See under 'C'.

Conjunctival reflex —See under 'C'.

Corneal reflex —See under section 'C'.

Cough reflex —Cough occurring due to irritation from the middle ear, pharynx, stomach or intestine.

Cremasteric reflex —See under letter 'C'.

Crossed reflex —Consensual reflex. Reflex occurring on the opposite side of the body from the side of stimulation.

Cutaneous reflex —Wrinkling of the skin caused by its stimulation.

Deep reflex —Reflex caused by stimulation of the structures under the skin, such as muscles, tendons and bones etc.

Delayed reflex —A reflex that does not occur until several seconds after stimulation.

Grasp reflex —Flexion or grasping reaction

of the fingers or toes on stimulation of the palm or sole.

Heart reflex —Any reflex in which the stimulation of a sensory nerve causes the heart rate to increase or decrease.

Jaw reflex —Chin reflex.

Knee-jerk reflex —Patellar reflex. Extension of the leg resulting from percussion of patellar tendon.

Lacrimal reflex —Discharge of tears resulting from the irritation of the conjunctiva.

Laryngeal reflex —Occurrence of cough as a result of irritation of the larynx.

Laughter reflex —Continuous laughing caused by tickling.

Lid reflex —Corneal reflex.

Light reflex —Contraction of the pupil when light is fallen on the eyes.

Local reflex —Reflex which does not involve the central nervous system.

Mendel-Bechterew reflex —Plantar flexion of the toes occurring following percussion of the dorsum of foot.

Nociceptive reflex —A reflex occurring by a painful stimulus.

Palatal reflex —See under letter 'P'.

Patellar reflex —Kneejerk reflex.

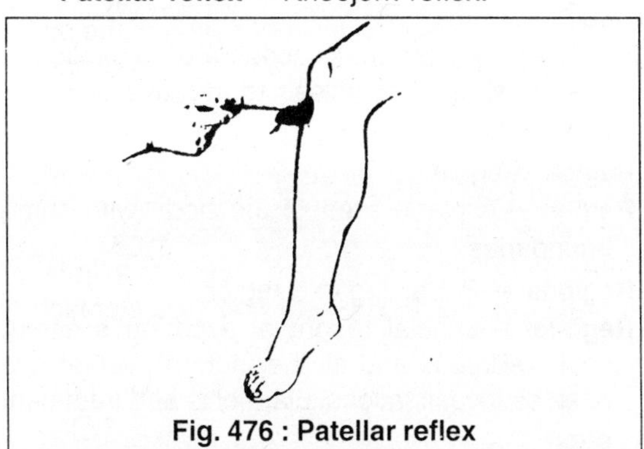

Fig. 476 : Patellar reflex

Tapping with hammer on the tendon over the patella bone causes extension of the knee joint.

Pathologic reflex —An abnormal reflex due to disease, which is one of the symptoms of the disease.

Pharyngeal reflex —See under 'P'.

Pilomotor reflex —The formation of goose skin when it is cooled, stroked or as a result of emotional reaction.

Pressor reflex —Rising of blood pressure resulting from constriction of arterioles.

Pupillary reflex —Light reflex.

Sexual reflex —Reflexes concerned with the sexual activities, especially erection and ejaculation.

Statokinetic reflex —Reflexes occurring while the body is moving.

Stretch reflex —Myotatic reflex. Contraction of a muscle on stretching the same muscle.

Sucking reflex —Sucking movements of the lips of an infant caused by touching the lips.

Superficial reflex —Reflex caused by irritation of the skin, cornea, conjunctiva and pharynx etc.

Swallowing reflex —Palatal reflex.

Tendon reflex —Contraction of a muscle caused by percussion of its tendon.

Triceps reflex —Elbow reflex. Sharp extension of the forearm resulting from tapping of the triceps tendon while the arm is held loosely in bend position.

Urinary reflex —Micturition reflex. Contraction of the walls of the urinary bladder and relaxation of the trigone and urethral sphincter in response to a rise in pressure within the bladder due to accumulation of urine, to expel urine.

Vascular reflex —Vasomotor reflex.

Vasomotor reflex —Vascular reflex. Contraction or dilatation of a blood vessel in response to a stimulus, *e.g.*, to become pale from fright.

Reflex action —A reflex.

Reflex arc —See reflex.

Reflex center —The area in the brain or spinal cord where impulses from the sensory nerve of the reflex arc initiate impulses in the motor nerves.

Reflexion —Reflection.

Reflexogenic —Causing or increasing a reflex action.

Reflexogenous —Reflexogenic.

Reflexograph —An apparatus for recording a reflex action.

Reflexology —Study of the reflex actions.

Reflexometer —An instrument for measuring the force of tap required for producing a reflex action.

Reflexophil —Characterized by exaggerated reflex actions.

Reflexophile —Reflexophil.

Reflexotherapy —Treatment of the diseases by manipulation, anesthetizing or cauterizing an area distant from the site of disease.

Reflux —A return or backward flow.

Esophageal reflux, Gastroesophageal reflux —The returning back of the stomach matter into the esophagus.

Vesicoureteral reflux —Backward flow of urine from the bladder into a ureter.

Refract —1. To turn back 2. To cause to deviate 3. To detect errors of refraction of the eyes and to correct them.

Refractable —Refrangible. Capable of being refracted.

Refracta dosi —In equal divided doses.

Refraction —1. Determination of the amount of refractive errors of the eyes and their correction with glasses. 2. The change of direction of light rays as they pass through the media of different densities.

Errors of refraction of the eyes —Ametropia. The condition of the eyes in which parallel rays of light are not focussed upon the retina because of a defect in shape of the eyeball or in the refractive media (cornea, aqueous humor, crystalline lens, vitreous body) of the eye.

Refractionist —One skilled in determining the refractive errors of the eyes and correcting them with glasses.

Refractionometer —Refractometer.

Refractive —1. Pertaining to refraction. 2. Having the power to refract.

Refractive power —The degree to which a transparent object deviates the rays of light from a straight path.

Refractivity —The quality of being refractive.

Refractometer —1. An instrument for measuring the refractive power of the eye. 2. An instrument for measuring the strength of lenses of spectacles.

Refractometry —Measurement of the refractive power of lenses.

Refractory —1. Obstinate or not being readily treated. 2. Resistant to stimulation, said of a muscle or nerve.

Refracture —To break again a bone in which the fractured parts have been united in wrong position.

Refrangible —Capable of being refractured.

Refresh —1. To restore strength or to relieve from fatigue or to renew 2. To scrape the epithelial covering from the opposite surfaces of a wound to make easy the healing of the wound and joining its surfaces together.

Refrigerant —Cooling or reducing fever.

Refrigeration —The process of cooling.

Refrigerator —Cooling apparatus or ice-chest.

Refringence —Refraction.

Refringency —Refractivity.

Refringent —Refractive.

Refusion —The removing and then returning of blood to the blood circulation.

Regainer —1. An instrument used to restore something that was lost. 2. An instrument used to regain space in the dental arch for fitting a new tooth.

Regel —Menstruation.

Regel kleine —Slight bloody discharge occurring from uterus at the time of ovulation.

Regenerate —To generate again, to reproduce.

Regeneration —Opposite to degeneration. Reproduction, repair, regrowth or restoration of the tissues.

Regimen —A systematic scheme of regulation of diet, sleep and exercises to improve or maintain health.

Regio —Region.

Region —A plane area of the body with some boundaries.

Regional —Pertaining to a region.

Register —Official record of a patient's name, caste, address and all the facts of his/her disease as investigations, diagnosis and treatment etc.

Registering —Recording.

Registrant —A nurse whose name is listed in the register as being available for the duty.

Registrar —An officer who keeps the registers.

Registration —The act of registering.

Registry —An office where the list of the nurses ready for duty is kept.

Regression —1. The act of returning back or return to a former state. 2. A return of the symptoms of a disease.

Regressive —Pertaining to, or marked by regression.

Regular —Complying a rule or custom.

Regulation —The state of being controlled, the act of regulating, law.

Regulative —Pertaining to regulation.

Regulator —An apparatus for adjusting or controlling the rate of flow of fluids, blood or oxygen.

Regurgitant —Flowing backward.

Regurgitate —1. To flow backward. 2. To expel the contents of the stomach in small amounts.

Regurgitation —A backward flowing, *e.g.*, the return of undigested food from stomach to the mouth or the backward flow of blood through a defective heart valve, named according to the valve affected-aortic, mitral, pulmonary or tricuspid regurgitation.

Rehabilitation —Restoration to the normal activities of the persons with physical or other disability.

Rehabilitee —The person rehabilitated.

Rehalation —Rebreathing.

Rehydration —Restoration of fluid orally or by injection in a person who has been dehydrated.

Reimplantation —Replacement of a part or structure at the place from which it was lost or removed, as a tooth or finger etc.

Reinfection —A second infection by the same organism.

Reinforcement —To give force again.

Reinforcer —Anything which provides force again.

Reinfusate —The fluid used for reinfusion into the body.

Reinfusion —Infusion of body fluid as blood serum into the body of the same individual from whom it has been withdrawn previously.

Reinnervation —Restoration of the nerve supply in the paralyzed part or organ of the body by anastomosis with a living nerve or by grafting of a fresh nerve.

Reinoculation —A second inoculation with the same virus or organism.

Reintegration —Resumption of normal mental functioning and behavior following a mental illness.

Reinversion —Correction of an inverted organ, as of the inverted uterus by pressure on its fundus.

Reiter's syndrome —A syndrome consisting of urethritis, arthritis and conjunctivitis.

Rejection —1. Refusal. 2. Destruction of the grafted tissue by immune reaction of cells of the host.

Rejuvenation —A return to youthfulness or to the normal.

Rejuvenescence —To become young or to return to the eralier stage of existence.

Relapse —Recurrence of a disease or symptoms after apparent cessation.

Relapsing —Recurring after apparent cessation.

Relation —The connection or the state of one thing compared to another.

Occlusal jaw relation —Relation of the mandibular teeth to the maxillary teeth when they are in contact.

Relative —1. Comparative 2. Having relation.

Relax —To loose, to decrease tension or to get rid of mental stress or anxiety.

Relaxant —1. Pertaining to or causing relaxation. 2. A drug that reduces tension. 3. A laxative.

Relaxation —The act of loosening or a lessening of tension.

Relaxin —A polypeptide hormone secreted in the corpus luteum in the ovary during pregnancy.

Relay —An instrument for reinforcing electric current.

Relief —Removal of distress.

Relieve —To provide relief.

Reline —Resurfacing the lining of a denture.

Remainder —The rest. Residue.

Remediable —Curable.

Remedial —Curative.

Remedy —Cure for a disease.

Remineralization —Replacement of a mineral into the body after it has been lost from the body by a disease or due to its deficiency in the diet.

Reminiscence —Recovery of knowledge by the effort of the mind.

Remission —1. A lessening of the symptoms of a disease. 2. The period during which lessening of the symptoms occurs.

Remit —To become less severe for a time.

Remittance —Temporary abatement of the symptoms of a disease.

Remittent —The symptoms of a disease which abate temporarily.

Remittent fever —A fever which alternately abates and returns but the temperature does not come to normal.

Remnant —Something that remains or is left over, a residue.

Remnant radiation —Ionizing radiation passing through the part being examined to make the X-ray film.

Remodeling —1. Reconstruction of a part of the body. 2. A series of changes occurring in bone formation throughout life.

Remote —Distant, far off.

Ren —The kidney.

Ren mobilis —Movable kidney.

Ren unguliformis —Horseshoe-shaped kidney.

Renal —1. Pertaining to the kidney. 2. Kidney-shaped.

Renal clearance test —A kidney function test based on the kidney's ability to eliminate a given substance in a standard time.

Renal scanning —It is a test for determining the shape and function of the kidney in which a radioactive substance which accumulates in the kidney, is given to the patient by intravenous injection. Irradiation emitted from the substance as it accumulates in the kidney is recorded on a radiographic film.

Renal tubule —A nephron.

Renes —Plural of ren.

Renicapsule —The capsule of the kidney.

Renicardiac —Cardiorenal. Pertaining to the heart and the kidney.

Reniculus —A lobule of the kidney.

Renifleur —One who is stimulated sexually by odor of urine of others.

Reniform —Nephroid. Kidney-shaped.

Renin —An enzyme produced by the kidney which plays a role in regulation of blood pressure by converting angiotensinogen into a pressor substance angiotensin I. It is produced by lowered renal arterial pressure.

Reninism —The condition produced by overproduction of renin.

Renin substrate —Hypertensinogen.

Renipelvic —Concerning the pelvis of the kidney.

Reniportal —Pertaining to the renal portal system.

Renipuncture —Surgical puncture of the capsule of the kidney.

Renitis —Inflammation of the kidney.

Rennet —A fluid containing the milk coagulating enzyme rennin.

Rennin —Chymosin. Milk-curdling enzyme. An enzyme which coagulates milk into curd, found in gastric juice of the infants.

Renninogen —Prorennin. From which rennin is formed.

Reno-, Ren- —Prefixes meaning kidney.

Renocutaneous —Pertaining to the kidneys and skin.

Renogastric —Pertaining to the kidney and stomach.

Renogenic —Originating in or from the kidney.

Renogram —Record of rate of removal from the blood by kidneys of a dose of radioactive iodine (^{131}I) injected intravenously.

Renography —Radiography of the kidney.

Renointestinal —Pertaining to the kidney and the intestine.

Renomegaly —Enlargement of the kidney.

Renopathy —Nephropathy.

Renoprival —Pertaining to or caused by lack of kidney function.

Renopulmonary —Pertaining to the kidneys and the lungs.

Renotrophic —Capable of producing hypertrophy of the kidney.

Renotrophin —Renotropin. An agent affecting the growth or nutrition of the kidney.

Renotropic —Having special affinity for the kidney tissue.

Renotropin —Renotrophin.

Renovascular —Pertaining to the blood vessels of the kidney.

Renule —An area of the kidney supplied by a branch of renal artery.

Renunculus —Reniculus.

Rep. —Repetatur in Latin. Let it be repeated.

Repair —To mend.

Repellent—An agent that repels the injurious insects.

Repercolation —Repeated percolation.

Repercussion —1. An action causing subsidence of a swelling, tumor or eruption. 2. Ballottement.

Repercussive —1. Causing repercussion. 2. Repellent.

Replacement —The act of replacing.

Replantation —Surgical reimplantation of the part of the body, which has been removed as that of the hand or leg etc.

Repletion —Condition of being full or satisfied.

Replicate —To repeat.

Replication —1. A turning back of a part of the body. 2. In medical examinations, repetition of an experiment to confirm the result of the previous experiment.

Replicon —A segment of a chromosome or of the DNA of a chromosome that can replicate.

Repolarization —The process whereby the membrance, cell or fiber, after depolarization, is polarized again, with positive charges on the outer and negative charges on the inner surface.

Reportable disease —A disease that must be reported to the health officer by the doctor.

Repositio —Reposition.

Reposition —Returning of an organ or tissue to the normal position.

Repositioning —The placement of a part or organ of the body in its original place.

Repositor —An instrument used for returning the displaced organ or tissue to the normal position, *e.g.*, the instrument for replacing the inverted uterus.

Repressed —Suppressed.

Repression —Restrain, inhibition or suppression.

Repressor —That which restrains, inhibits or suppresses.

Reproduce —To give rise to offspring.

Reproducibility —Ability to cause to exist again or to present again.

Reproduction —1. Process by which animals and plants produce offspring. 2. The creation of a similar structure or situation.

Asexual reproduction —Reproduction without fusion of the sexual cells, as by fission or budding.

Sexual reproduction —Reproduction by means of sexual or germ cells in which a male germ cell (spermatozoon) fuses with a female germ cell (ovum or egg).

Somatic reproduction —Asexual reproduction.

Reproductive —Pertaining to reproduction or having the power to reproduce.

Repullulation —Production of a new growth by budding or sprouting.

Repulsion —1. Opposite to attraction. 2. The act of driving back. 3. The force exerted by somebody on another tu cause separation.

Research —A critical investigation.

Resect —To cut out a part of an organ or a structure.

Resectable —Removable completely by excision, as said of a malignant growth.

Resection —Excision of a part of an organ or structure.

Gastric resection —Surgical resection of a part of the stomach.

Transurethral resection —Surgical removal of the prostate by means of an instrument passed through the urethra.

Wedge resection —Surgical removal of a wedge-shaped or triangular piece of a tissue, as from the ovary.

Resectoscope —An instrument with a wide-angle telescope and electrically activated wire loop for removal of the prostate gland or a piece of it for biopsy, through urethra.

Resectoscopy —Resection, or to obtain a piece of the prostate gland for biopsy through urethra, by means of the resectoscope.

Reserve —1. To hold or which is held back for future use, as alkali reserve of the body available for neutralization of acid. 2. An extra supply utilized in emergency, *e.g.*, ability of the heart to perform extra work in emergency. 3. Self-control of one's feelings and thoughts.

Reserve air —Additional quantity of air that can be expelled from the lungs over the normal quantity, which is from 1200 to 1600 c.c.

Reservoir —1. A place or cavity for storage of fluids. 2. An alternate or passive carrier of a disease-producing organism.

Residency —A period of 1 year and often 3 to 4 years for medical graduates or post graduates to be trained in medical job, in a hospital.

Resident —A medical graduate and licensed physician obtaining further training in medicine in a hospital.

Residua —Plural of residuum.

Residual —1. Pertaining to a residue. 2. Any aftereffect of the experience influencing the later behavior.

Residual air —Air remaining in the lungs after the fullest-expiration which is about 1500 c.c. in an adult.

Residual function —The functional capacity remaining after an illness or injury.

Residual urine —Urine left in the urinary bladder after urination which occurs in case of enlarged prostate.

Residue —The remainder of something after a part is removed.

Residue-free diet —Diet without cellulose or roughage (fiber).

Residuum —Residue or the remainder.

Resilience —Elasticity.

Resilient —Elastic.

Resin —A gum-like organic substance secreted by certain plants or produced synthetically, which is insoluble in water but soluble in alcohol.

Resina —Resin.

Resinoid —Resembling a resin.

Resinous —Of the nature of, or pertaining to, resin.

Resistance —1. Opposition, or counteracting force such as the force of a liquid or air to retard that which is passing through it or opposition of the body or a conductor to the passage of an electric current. 2. The natural ability of a normal organism to remain unaffected by injurious organisms in its environment, or the capability of the body to check the growth of pathogenic organisms, or damage by their toxic products. Immunity is resistance associated with the presence of antibodies which have a specific action on infectious microorganisms. 3. In psychoanalysis, opposition to the coming into consciousness of the repressed matter.

Drug resistance —The ability of a microorganism of not being affected by a durg.

Peripheral resistance —The resistance to the blood flow through small blood vessels, especially the arterioles and capillaries.

Resistant —One who or that which resists.

Resistivity —A measure of a material's resistance to the passage of electrical current.

Resistor —An element included in an electric circuit to provide resistance to the flow of current.

Resolution —1. Subsidence of a disease, or of inflammation without suppuration, or the return to the normal. 2. Decomposition.

Resolve —1. To subside or to return to normal. 2. To decompose.

Resolvent —Promoting disappearance of inflammation.

Resonance —1. The quality of sound heard on percussion of a hollow part of the body such as chest or abdomen. Decrease of resonance is called dullness and its increase, flatness. 2. A vocal sound heard on auscultation.

Amphoric resonance —Sound resembling that produced by blowing over the mouth of an empty bottle.

Bandbox resonance —Pulmonary resonance heard on percussing the chest of patients with emphysema.

Cracked-pot resonance —A pulmonary resonance similar to the sound produced by a cracked pot heard on percussion of chest in advanced cases of tuberculosis when cavities are present.

Skodiac resonance —Increased percussion resonance over the upper part of the lung when there is pleural effusion in the lower part.

Tympanitic resonance —Resonance heard by percussing a hollow structure such as the stomach or colon, distended with air.

Vesicular resonance —Normal pulmonary resonance.

Vocal resonance —Sound of speech heard through the chest-wall on auscultation.

Resonant —Producing a vibrating sound on percussion.

Resonating —Vibrating sympathetically with a source of sound.

Resonating cavities —The resonator of the voice including upper part of the larynx, pharynx, nasal cavity, paranasal sinuses and mouth cavity.

Resonator —An instrument used to intensify the sounds.

Resorb —1. To absorb again. 2. To undergo resorption.

Resorbent —Promoting the absorption of abnormal matter, as blood clots.

Resorption —1. Act of removal by absorption, as of the pus. 2. Lysis and assimilation of a bone or enamel of a tooth. 3. Reabsorption.

Resorptive —Capable of reabsorbing.

Respirable —Capable for respiration.

Respiration —The exchange of oxygen and carbon dioxide between atmosphere and the body cells, including inspiration and expiration. Oxygen is taken up during inspiration which reaches the pulmonary alveoli and there by diffusion oxygen mixes up with the blood and is transported to the body cells and carbon dioxide from body cells is carried by blood to the alveoli from where it is given off during expiration.

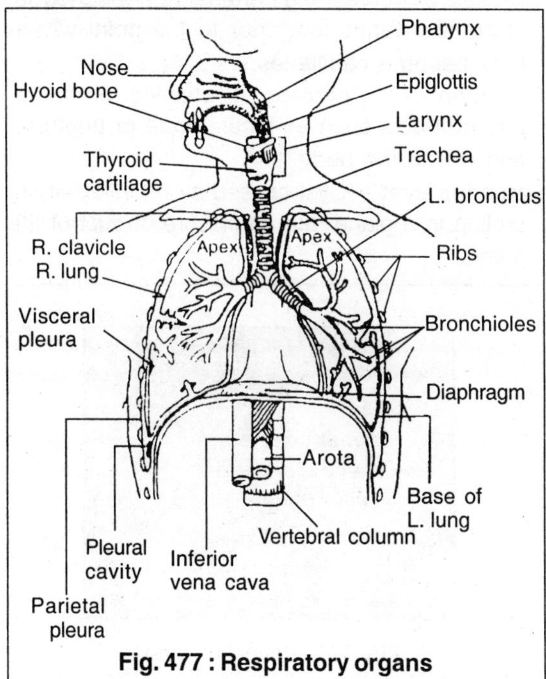

Fig. 477 : Respiratory organs

Abdominal respiration —Respiration occurring by abdominal muscles and diaphragm while the chest does not move, as seen in lobar pneumonia.

Accelerated respiration —Respiration occurring at above normal rate i.e. exceeding 25 per minute in an adult. It results from physical exertion or mental disturbances and may occur in diseases such as pneumonia and asthma etc.

Aerobic respiration —Respiration in which air or free oxygen is utilized.

Amphoric respiration —A form of respiration in which the sound heard on auscultation in case of a large pulmonary cavity or pneumothorax, is like that made by blowing across the mouth of a bottle.

Anaerobic respiration —Respiration in which free oxygen does not take part, it is obtained from chemical reactions.

Artificial respiration —Respiration artificially given to the patient with suspended breathing.

Cell respiration —Internal respiration.

Cheyne-stokes respiration —See under this heading of letter 'C'.

Decreased respiration —Respiration in which respiratory rate is less than normal rate for the individual's age, as occurs in uremia, diabetic coma, hysteria and shock etc.

External respiration —The exchange of oxygen and carbon dioxide between the air in lungs and blood within capillaries in the walls of the alveoli.

Fetal respiration —Placental respiration. Exchange of gases in the placenta between blood of the fetus and that of the mother.

Forced respiration —To increase the rate and depth of respiration voluntarily.

Internal respiration —The exchange of gases between body cells and the blood.

Interrupted respiration —Respiration in which inspiratory and expiratory sounds are not continuous.

Intrauterine respiration —Respiration by the fetus in the uterus before birth.

Kussmaul's respiration —Deep, gasping respiration, which is a characteristic of air hunger or diabetic coma.

Labored respiration —Dyspnea or difficult breathing.

Slow respiration —Respirations occurring at the rate of below 12 per minute.

Thoracic respiration —Respiration occurring by chest movements only and the abdominal wall does not take part.

Respirator —An apparatus for giving artificial respiration.

Respiratory —Pertaining to respiration.

Respiratory anemometer —A form of respirometer used in investigating pulmonary function.

Respiratory quotient —The result of dividing the amount of carbon dioxide in expired air by the amount of oxygen inhaled, which is normally 0.9.

Respiratory system —The organs used in the exchange of gases, including nose, pharynx, larynx, trachea, bronchi and lungs.

Respire —1. To breath. 2. To consume oxygen and release carbon dioxide.

Respirometer —An instrument for determining the nature of respiration.

Respite —Short-term, intermittent care for the patients with chronic or debilitating diseases.

Response —A reaction resulting from a stimulus, such as contraction of a muscle or secretion of a gland or the result of a treatment which may be favorable or unfavorable.

Rest —1. Repose after exertion. 2. Freedom of mind or body from activity. 3. Remainder. 4. A remnant of embryonic tissue that persists in the adult.

Restenosis —Recurrent stenosis as of a cardiac valve or vessel.

Restiform —Rope-shaped.

Resting —Taking rest; inactive.

Resting cell —1. A cell which is not dividing. 2. A cell that is not performing its normal function.

Restitutio ad integrum —Complete restoration to health.

Restitution —1. A return to a former state. 2. The act of correcting. 3. The spontaneous realignment of the head of the fetus with the fetal body after the head has completely emerged through the vagina.

Restless —Uneasy.

Restlessness —Uneasiness.

Restoration —1. To return to a previous state, as a return to health or replacement of a part to its normal position. 2. In dentistry, the material or device which replaces a tooth or teeth and the adjacent tissues.

Restorative —1. Pertaining to restoration. 2. A remedy which is helpful in regaining health and strength.

Restraint —Forcible control, confinement, restriction or device or method used to save a patient from injuring himself.

Resuscitate —To perform resuscitation.

Resuscitation —Anabiosis. Restoration to life after apparent death.

Resuscitator —An apparatus used for initiating respiration in the persons in whom breathing has stopped.

Retained —Kept from departure or escape.

Retainer —1. Any apparatus for keeping something in place. 2. In dentistry, an apparatus for keeping a tooth or partial denture in proper position.

Retardate —A mentally retarded person.

Retardation —Delay; hindrance; delayed mental or physical development.

Retarder —A substance used in dentistry to slow the chemical hardening of a material such as gypsum etc.

Retch —Involuntary attempt to vomit.

Retching —Involuntarily attempting to vomit.

Rete —A network or neshwork. A plexus of blood vessels or nerves, *e.g.*, arterial rete—a network of small arteries just prior to the point where they become capillaries.

Retention —The process of retaining the excretory products such as feces, urine or perspiration etc. in the body.

Retention cyst —Cyst caused by retention of secretion in a gland, due to closure of duct of the gland.

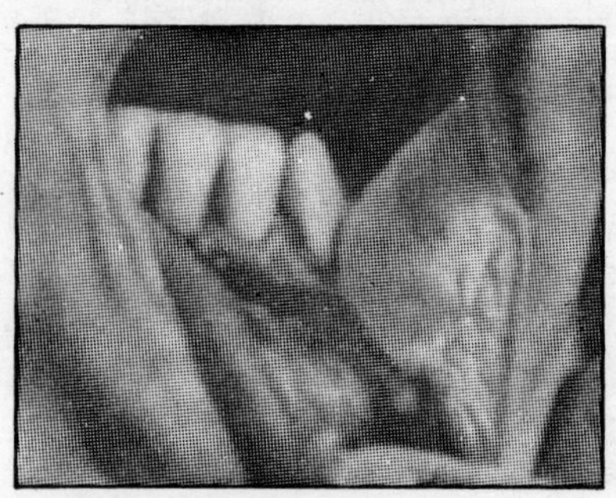

Fig. 478 : Retention cyst

Retention defect —Inability to remember the objects shortly after they are seen.

Retention enema —Enema to be retained to provide nourishment, medicate the mucous membrane or to produce anesthesia.

Retention with overflow —Spasm of the sphincter, causing failure to empty the bladder at urination, resulting in retention of urine in the bladder with only overflow dribbling away.

Retentive —Having the power of retaining.

Retentivity —Remanence.

Retia —Plural of rete.

Retial —Pertaining to a rete.

Reticula —Plural of reticulum.

Reticular —Resembling a net.

Reticular cells —1. The cells of reticular connective tissue. 2. Phagocytic cells present in the lymphatic and myeloid tissues.

Reticular layer —Layer of the connective tissue

forming deeper portion of the dermis under which lies papillary layers.

Reticular tissue —Connective tissue consisting of reticular fibers and cells found principally in the bone marrow and lymph nodes.

Reticulate —Of the nature of a network.

Reticulated —1. Pertaining to a reticulum. 2. Net-like.

Reticulation —The formation or presence of a network.

Reticulo- —A prefix meaning network.

Reticulocyte —An immature red blood cell containing a network of granules or filaments.

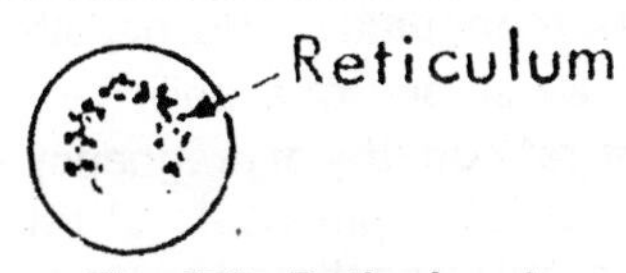

Fig. 479 : Reticulocyte

Reticulocytopenia —Deficiency of reticulocytes in the blood.

Reticulocytosis —An excess of reticulocytes in the circulating blood.

Reticuloendothelial —Pertaining to the reticuloendothelium or reticuloendothelial system.

Reticuloendothelial cell —Histiocyte; macrophage. A phagocytic cell of the reticuloendothelial system.

Reticuloendothelioma —A malignant tumor composed of reticuloendothelial tissue.

Reticuloendotheliosis —Hyperplasia of reticuloendothelium.

Reticuloendothelium —Tissue of the reticuloendothelial system.

Reticulohistiocytoma —A granulomacytosis of the histiocytes and multinucleated giant cells involving the skin, mucous membrane and synovial membranes of the long bones.

Reticulohistiocytosis —Reticuloendotheliosis.

Reticuloid —Resembling reticulosis.

Reticuloma —A tumor composed of reticuloendothelial cells.

Reticulopenia —Deficiency in number of reticulocytes in the blood.

Reticulosarcoma —A malignant tumor composed of large monocytic cells originating in the reticuloendothelium of the lymph and other glands.

Reticulosis —Reticulocytosis.

Reticulospinal —Pertaining to the reticulum and spinal column.

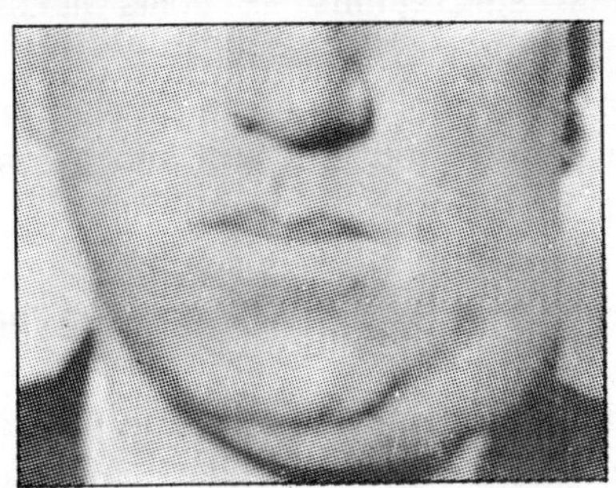

Fig. 480 : Reticulosarcoma

Reticulum —1. A small net-work, especially a protoplasmic network in a cell. 2. Reticular tissue.

Retiform —Reticular. Resembling a network.

Retina —The innermost or the third layer of the eyeball on which image of an object is formed.

Retinaculum —1. A structure holding an organ or part in its place. 2. An instrument for retracting the tissues during operation.

Retinal —Pertaining to the retina.

Retinal break —A break in the continuity of the retina, usually caused by an injury to the eye.

Retinectomy —Excision of a portion of the retina by surgery.

Retinene —Xanthopsia. An orange-yellow colored pigment formed in the retina by the action of light on rhodopsin; an aldehyde of vit. A.

Retinitis —Inflammation of the retina.

Actinic retinitis —Retinitis due to exposure to intense light or other forms of radiant energy.

Albuminuric retinitis —Inflammation of the retina occurring in chronic kidney disease and malignant hypertension.

Circinate retinitis —Retinitis associated with a circle of white spots about the macula.

Diabetic retinitis —Inflammation of the retina occurring in diabetes of long duration.

Disciform retinitis —Retinitis accompanied by degeneration of the retina in the region of macula.

Exogenous purulent retinitis —Retinitis occurring by infectious organisms entering the eye from outside as a result of perforation of a wound.

Exudative retinitis —Chronic retinitis with elevations around the optic disk.

Hemorrhagic retinitis —Retinitis with profuse hemorrhage into the retina.

Metastatic retinitis —Acute purulent retinitis resulting from lodgement of infective emboli in the retinal vessels.

Punctate retinitis —Retinitis characterized by numerous white or yellow spots in the fundus of eye.

Retinitis pigmentosa —A chronic progressive disease starting in childhood characterized by degeneration with wide spread pigmentation of the retina but without inflammation. Night vision becomes defective followed by contraction of the visual field.

Retinitis proliferans —Retinitis in which vascularized masses of connective tissue project from retina into the vitreous, resulting from recurrent hemorrhage.

Solar retinitis —Retinitis occurring due to exposure of the retina to sun rays.

Suppurative retinitis —Retinitis with suppuration due to pyogenic organisms.

Syphilitic retinitis —Retinitis resulting from syphilis.

Retinoblastoma —A malignant tumor of the retina, occurring in children.

Retinochoroid —Pertaining to the retina and choroid of the eye.

Retinochoroiditis —Inflammation of the retina and choroid.

Retinocystoma —Glioma of the retina.

Retinodialysis —Disinsertion. Detachment of the retina at its periphery.

Retinoid —Resembling the retina.

Retinol —Vitamin A_1, a form of vitamin A found in mammals.

Retinomalacia —Softening of the retina.

Retinopapillitis —Papilloretinitis. Inflammation of the retina and optic papilla.

Retinopathy —Any disease of the retina.

Arteriosclerotic retinopathy —Retinopathy associated with arteriosclerosis and hypertension.

Circinate retinopathy —A disease of the retina in which a circle of white spots is formed in the retina around the macula.

Diabetic retinopathy —Retinopathy occurring in diabetes mellitus.

Hypertensive retinopathy —Retinopathy associated with essential or malignant hypertension.

Leukemic retinopathy —Retinopathy occurring in all types of leukemia characterized by engorgement and tortuosity of the retinal veins, scattered hemorrhages, and edema of the retina and optic disk.

Solar retinopathy —Pathological changes occurring in the retina after looking directly at the sun as are usually seen following a solar eclipse.

Syphilitic retinopathy —Retinopathy occurring in the later stages of syphilis.

Toxemic retinopathy of pregnancy —Sudden occurrence of angiospasm of retinal arterioles followed by scattered hemorrhages, star-figure edema at the macula and papilledema in pregnancy as occurs in hypertension.

Toxic retinopathy —Changes in retina occurring due to prolonged administration of various drugs.

Retinopexy—In case of retinal detachment, fixation of the detached portion of the retina to the underlying tissue.

Retinoschisis —Splitting of the retina into two layers with the cyst formation between the layers.

Retinoscope —An instrument used for performing retinoscopy.

Retinoscopy —Skiascopy. Projection of light into eyes and determination of the errors of refraction by movement of the reflected light rays, by means of retinoscope.

Retinosis —Any degenerative condition of the retina without inflammation.

Retinotomy —To incise the retina.

Retire —To go to bed.

Retisolution —Dissolution of the Golgi structures.

Retispersion —Transference of the Golgi structures to the periphery of the cell.

Retoperithelium —Epithelium covering a reticulum.

Retort —A flask-shaped vessel with long neck used in distillation.

Retothelium —Reticuloendothelium.

Retract —To draw back.

Retractibility —Capability of being drawn back.

Retractile —Capable of being drawn back.

Retraction —The act of drawing back.

Retractor —1. An instrument for holding open the margins of a wound. 2. A muscle that draws back an organ or part of the body.

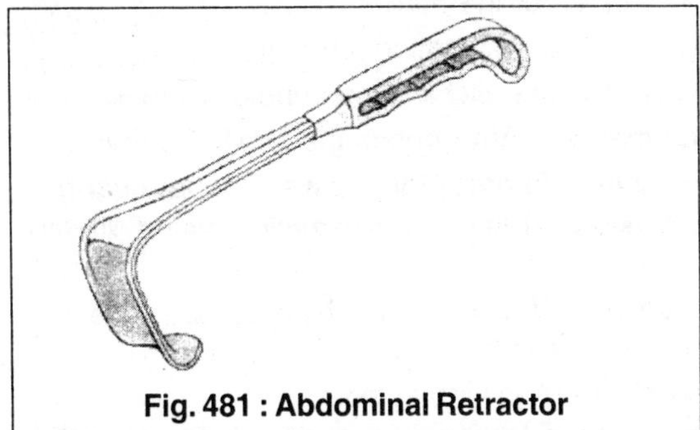

Fig. 481 : Abdominal Retractor

Retrad —Toward the posterior part of the body.

Retrain —To train again.

Retreat —Act of withdrawing from difficult life situations.

Retrenchment —The process of removing excess of tissue by plastic surgery.

Retrieval —In psychology, the process of bringing the remembered information back to the consciousness.

Retro- —A prefix meaning backward.

Retroaction —Action in a reversed direction.

Retroauricular —Behind the auricle of the ear.

Retrobuccal —Pertaining to the back part of the mouth.

Retrobulbar —Behind the eyeball or the medulla oblongata.

Retrocalcaneobursitis —Achillobursitis.

Retrocecal —Behind the cecum.

Retrocedent —Going backward or returning.

Retrocervical —Behind the cervix of the uterus.

Retrocession —1. A going backward. 2. A relapse. 3. Backward displacement as of the uterus.

Retroclusion —Stopping of arterial bleeding by compressing the artery with a needle.

Retrocolic —Behind the colon.

Retrocollic —Pertaining to the back of the neck.

Retrocollic spasm —Wryneck with spasm of posterior muscles of the neck causing the head drawing backward.

Retrocollis —Retrocollic spasm.

Retrocursive —Stepping or turning backward.

Retrodeviation —Backward displacement.

Retrodisplacement —Backward or posterior displacement.

Retroduction —Retrograde.

Retroduodenal —Behind the duodenum.

Retroesophageal —Behind the esophagus.

Retrofilling —The placement of a filling material into a dental root through an opening made in the apex of the tooth.

Retroflected —Retroflexed.

Retroflection —Retroflexon.

Retroflexed —Bent backward.

Retroflexion —The bending of an organ backward as that of the uterus.

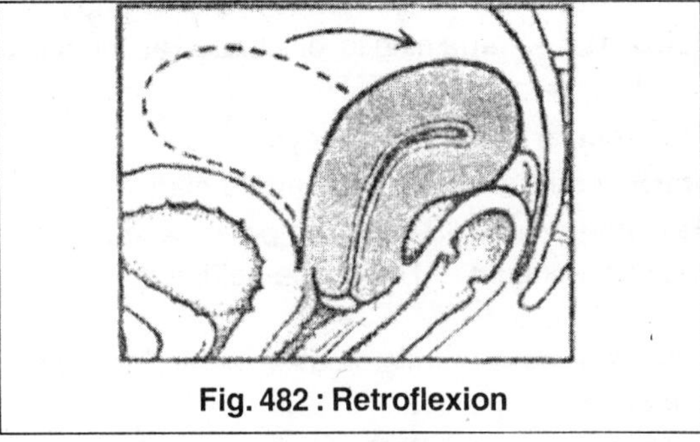

Fig. 482 : Retroflexion

Retrognathia —Backward location of the mandible.

Retrognathic —Pertaining to the retrognathia.

Retrognathism —Retrognathia.

Retrograde —1. Going backward. 2. Becoming worse from better.

Retrograde amnesia —To forget the recent events but to remember the past ones.

Retrograde flow —Flow of a fluid against the normal direction.

Retrograde pyelography —Pyelography performed by injecting a radiopaque dye from below, through the ureter.

Retrography —Mirror writing which is a symptom of some brain diseases.

Retrogression —A going backward or returning to its earlier stage, involution, degeneration or atrophy of a tissue or structure.

Retrogressive —Marked by retrogression.

Retroinfection —Infection transmitted by the fetus in uterus to the mother.

Retroinhibition —Feedback inhibition.

Retroinsular —Behind the insula.

Retroiridian —Behind the iris.

Retrojection —The washing out of a cavity by injecting a fluid.

Retrojector —A syringe with a long tube attached to its nozzle, used in retrojection.

Retrolabyrinthine —Situated behind the labyrinth of the ear.

Retrolental —Behind the lens of the eye.

Retrolenticular —Retrolental.

Retrolingual —Behind the tongue.

Retromammary —Behind the mammary gland.

Retromandibular —Behind the mandible or lower jaw.

Retromastoid —Behind the mastoid process.

Retromolar —Posterior to the last molar teeth.

Retromorphosis —Retrograde metamorphosis.

Retronasal —Pertaining to, or situated at, the back part of the nose.

Retro-ocular —Behind the eye.

Retroparotid —Behind the parotid gland.

Retroperitoneal —Behind the peritoneum.

Retroperitoneum —The space behind the peritoneum.

Retroperitonitis —Inflammation behind the peritoneum.

Retropharyngeal —Behind the pharynx.

Retropharyngitis —Inflammation of the back portion of the pharynx.

Retropharynx —Back portion of the pharynx.

Retroplacental —Behind the placenta.

Retroplasia —Degeneration of a cell or tissue into a more primitive form.

Retroposed —Displaced backward.

Retroposition —Backward displacement.

Retropubic —Behind the pubic bone.

Retropulsion —1. A pushing back of a part, as of the fetal head in labor. 2. Tendency of walking backward seen in some nervous disorders.

Retrorunning —Habit of running backward which causes pain in the muscles and joints.

Retrospection —The process of surveying and reviewing the past.

Retrospective —Pertaining to retrospection.

Retrospondylolisthesis —Posterior displacement of a vertebra.

Retrosternal —Behind the sternum.

Retrosternal pulse —A venous pulse felt over the suprasternal notch.

Retrotarsal —Behind the tarsus of the eye.

Retrouterine —Behind the uterus.

Retroversioflexion —Retroversion and retroflexion of the uterus.

Retroversion —A turning backward of an entire organ, as of the uterus.

Retroverted —Denoting retroversion.

Retrovesical —Behind the urinary bladder.

Retrovirus —Any virus of the family Retroviridae.

Retrude —To apply force inward or backward.

Retrusion —The process of forcing inward or backward.

Reunient —1. Connecting the tissues. 2. The ductus reuniens.

Reunion —A joining again.

Revaccination —Vaccination for a second time.

Revascularization —Restoration of blood flow to a part of the body by the development of new blood vessels again.

Revellent —Producing revulsion.

Reverberation —The repeated echoing of a sound.

Reversal —1. Turning in the opposite direction. 2. A change in an instinct to its opposite, as from love to hate.

Reversible —Able to be reversed.

Reversion —1. A returning to a previous condition, or regression. 2. Inheritance of a character from some remote ancestor, which has not appeared for several generations.

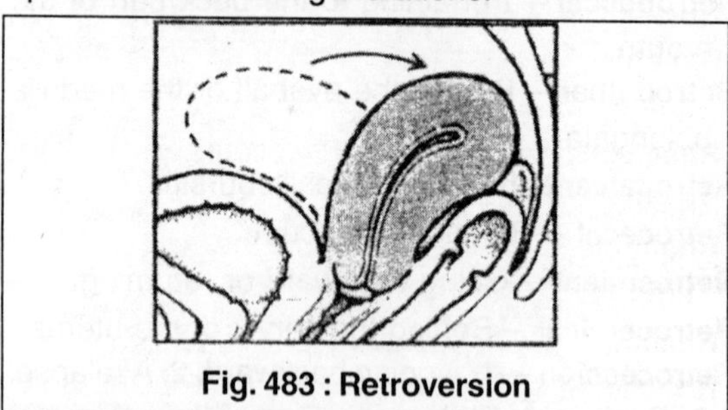

Fig. 483 : Retroversion

Revivescence —Revivification.

Revivification —Restoration to life.

Revulsant —Revulsive.

Revulsion —1. The act of transferring a disease from one part of the body to another by quick withdrawal of blood from that part. 2. Counterirritation.

Revulsive —1. Causing transfer of a disease from one part of the body to another. 2. A counterirritant.

Reye's syndrome —A syndrome marked by acute encephalopathy and fatty infiltration of the liver and possibly of the pancreas, heart, kidney, spleen and lymph nodes, seen in children under the age of 15 years following acute viral infection.

R. F. A. —Right fronto-anterior fetal position.

R. F. P. —Right fronto-posterior fetal position.

R. F. T. —Right fronto-transverse fetal position.

R. H. —Releasing hormone.

Rh —Rhesus, a monkey (Macaca rhesus) in which the Rh factor was first identified.

Rhabdo- —A prefix which means rod.

Rhabdocyte —Metamyelocyte.

Rhabdoid —Resembling a rod.

Rhabdomyoblastoma —Rhabdomyosarcoma.

Rhabdomyolysis —Destruction of skeletal muscle with excretion of myoglobin in the urine.

Rhabdomyoma —A tumor containing striated muscle fibers.

Rhabdomyosarcoma —An extremely malignant tumor of the skeletal muscle.

Rhabdophobia —Morbid fear of being beaten with a rod or stick.

Rhabdosarcoma —Rhabdomyosarcoma.

Rhabdovirus —Any of a group of rod-shaped RNA viruses of which rabies virus is transmitted to man from the infected animal and causes rabies.

Rhachialgia —Pain occurring in the vertebral column.

Rhachiocampsis —Curvature of the spinal column.

Rhachioplegia —Spinal paralysis.

Rhachioscoliosis —Curvature of the spinal column laterally.

Rhachis —Spinal column.

Rhachischisis —A congenital cleft in the spinal column.

Rhachitis —Rickets.

Rhacoma —Ragged,irregular abrasion.

Rhacous —Wrinkled, lacerated.

Rhagades —Linear fissures on the skin, especially at the corners of the mouth or anus causing pain or fine linear scars.

Rhagadiform —Fissured or cracked.

-rhage, -rhagia —Suffixes which mean bleeding or profuse discharge.

Rhagma —A fracture, rupture or laceration.

Rh antiserum —Human serum containing Rh antibodies.

Rhaphe —Raphe.

-rhaphy —A suffix which means suturation.

Rh blood group —Landsteiner and Wiener in 1940 discovered antigens on the surface of red blood cells of the rhesus monkey, which they called Rh factor. It is present in the blood of many people. When Rh factor is present in an individual's blood, the blood is called Rh^+ (Rh positive), when Rh factor is absent, it is called Rh^- (Rh negative). If an individual with Rh^- blood receives a transfusion of Rh^+ blood, it causes the formation of anti-Rh agglutinin (an antibody) which on subsequent transfusions of Rh^+ blood attaches to the antigen on the red blood cells, causing them to agglutinate and hemolysis of red blood cells.

-rhea —A suffix meaning to flow.

Rhegma —Rhagma.

Rhegmatogenous —Arising from or due to a rhegma.

Rhembasmus —Wandering of mind.

Rheo- —A prefix indicating electric current, or stream or flow of the liquids.

Rheobase —The minimal electric current required to produce stimulation.

Rheobasic —Pertaining to rheobase.

Rheoencephalography —The technique of measuring blood flow of the brain.

Rheologist —A specialist in rheology.

Rheology —Study of the deformation and flow of fluids as that of blood through the heart and blood vessels.

Rheometer —1. Galvanometer. 2. An apparatus for measuring the rapidity of blood stream.

Rheometry —Measurement of electric current or blood flow.

Rheostat —An apparatus maintaining resistance for controlling the amount of electric current entering a circuit.

Rheostosis —Occurrence of hyperostosis marked by the presence of streaks in the long bones.

Rheotaxis —The moving of an organism with its long axis parallel with the direction of flow in the stream of a liquid.

Rheotropism —Rheotaxis.

Rhestocythemia —The occurrence of broken-down erythrocytes in the blood.

Rheum, Rheuma —Any watery or mucous discharge.

Rheumarthritis —Rheumatoid arthritis.

Rheumatalgia —Chronic rheumatic pain.

Rheumatic —Pertaining to the rheumatism.

Rheumatic fever —An acute disease characterized by fever, joint pains frequently followed by carditis.

Rheumatid —Any skin lesion caused by rheumatic disease.

Rheumatism —Any disease characterized by inflammation, degeneration, pain and stiffness in the joints, muscles and other associated structures. It includes arthritis (infectious, rheumatoid, gouty, relapsing and psychogenic), arthritis due to rheumatic fever or trauma, myositis, bursitis and fibromyositis etc.

Rheumatismal —Pertaining to rheumatism.

Rheumatoid —Of the nature of, or resembling rheumatism.

Rheumatoid arthritis —Inflammation of the joints with stiffness and pain and hypertrophy of the cartilages causing crippling deformity of the joints.

Rheumatoid factor —An immunoglobulin present in blood serum of the adult patients of rheumatoid arthritis which is helpful in diagnosing the disease.

Rheumatologist —Specialist in rheumatic diseases.

Rheumatology —The branch of medical science dealing with the rheumatic diseases.

Rhexis —The rupture of an organ or of a blood vessel.

Rh. factor —See blood group.

Rhicnosis —Wrinkling of the skin due to atrophy of the subcutaneous tissue, especially elastic fibers.

Rhigosis —Shivering. Perception of cold.

Rhigotic —Pertaining to rhigosis.

Rhin —The nose.

Rhin-, Rhino- —Prefixes meaning nose.

Rhinal —Nasal. Pertaining to the nose.

Rhinalgia —Pain in the nose.

Rhinarium —The nasal region.

Rhinedema —Edema of the nose.

Rhinencephalic —Pertaining to rhinencephalon.

Rhinencephalon —The olfactory lobe of the brain.

Rhinencephalus —Rhinocephalus.

Rhinenchysis —A nasal douche or washing out the nasal cavities.

Rhinesthesia —The sense of smell.

Rhineurynter —An elastic bag for dilating the nostrils.

Rhinion —The lower end of the suture between the nasal bones.

Rhinism —Rhinolalia. To speak in the nasal voice.

Rhinitis —Inflammation of the nasal mucous membrance.

Acute rhinitis —Coryza.

Allergic rhinitis —Hay fever. Vasomotor rhinitis. Rhinitis due to sensitivity of the nasal mucous membrane to an allergen.

Atrophic rhinitis —Chronic inflammation with atrophy of the nasal mucous membrane and formation of dry crusts and there is absence of sense of smell.

Caseous rhinitis —Rhinitis with the accumulation of offensive cheeselike material in the nose and seropurulent discharge.

Chronic rhinits —Chronic inflammation of the nasal mucous membrane with hypertrophy of the mucous membrane or formation of polypi.

Fibrinous rhinitis —Rhinitis with the formation of false membrane in the nasal cavities.

Hypertrophic rhinitis —Rhinitis with thickening and swelling of the mucous membrane.

Purulent rhinitis —Chronic rhinitis with pus formation.

Vasomotor rhinitis —Rhinitis due to transient changes in the tone and permeability of the blood vessels (as occurs in allergic rhinitis) brought on by such stimuli as chilling, fatigue, anger, and anxiety and accompanied by watery discharge from the nose.

Rhino- —A prefix meaning nose.

Rhinoanemometer —An apparatus for determining the presence of nasal obstruction by measuring the rate of flow of air through the nasal passages.

Rhinoantritis —Inflammation of the nasal cavity and maxillary antrum.

Rhinobyon —A tampon or plug for the nose.

Rhinocanthectomy —Rhinommectomy.

Rhinocele —The ventricle of the olfactory lobe of the brain.

Rhinocephalia —Rhinocephaly.

Rhinocephalus —A fetus with partially or completely fused eyes and the nose as proboscis above the eyes.

Rhinocephaly —A congenital deformity in which the eyes are partially or completely fused into one and the nose present as proboscis above the eyes.

Rhinocheiloplasty —Plastic surgery of the nose and upper lip.

Rhinocleisis —Rhinostenosis. Nasal obstruction.

Rhinodacryolith —A lacrimal calculus in the nasal duct.

Rhinodymia —Presence of double nose on a normal face.

Rhinodynia —Rhinalgia.

Rhinogenous —Arising from the nose.

Rhinokyphosis —A deformity of the nose bridge.

Rhinolalia —Rhinism.

Rhinolaryngitis —Inflammation of the nasal mucous membrane and the larynx at a time.

Rhinolith —A nasal calculus.

Rhinolithiasis —The formation of nasal calculus.

Rhinologic —Pertaining to rhinology.

Rhinologist —A specialist in nasal diseases.

Rhinology —The branch of medical science which deals with the diseases of the nose.

Rhinomanometer —An apparatus used for measuring the amount of nasal obstruction.

Rhinomanometry —To measure the air flow and air pressure within the nose during respiration, and the nasal obstruction can be calculated from the figures obtained.

Rhinometer —An instrument for measuring the nose or its cavities.

Rhinomiosis —Surgical reduction in size of the nose.

Rhinommectomy —Rhinocanthectomy. Surgical excision of the inner canthus of the eye.

Rhinomycosis —Fungus infection of the mucous membranes and secretions of the nose.

Rhinonecrosis —Necrosis of the nasal bones.

Rhinopathy —Any disease of the nose

Rhinopharyngeal —Pertaining to the nasopharynx.

Rhinopharyngitis —Inflammation of the nasopharynx.

Rhinopharyngocele —A tumor of the nasopharynx.

Rhinopharyngolith —A calculus in the nasopharynx.

Rhinopharynx —Nasopharynx. Upper part of the pharynx continuous with the nasal passages.

Rhinophonia —A nasal tone in speaking.

Rhinophore —A nasal cannula to facilitate breathing.

Rhinophycomycosis —Fungus infection of the nasal and paranasal sinuses which may spread to the brain.

Rhinophyma —Acne rosacea. Nodular swelling with congestion and redness of the skin of the nose.

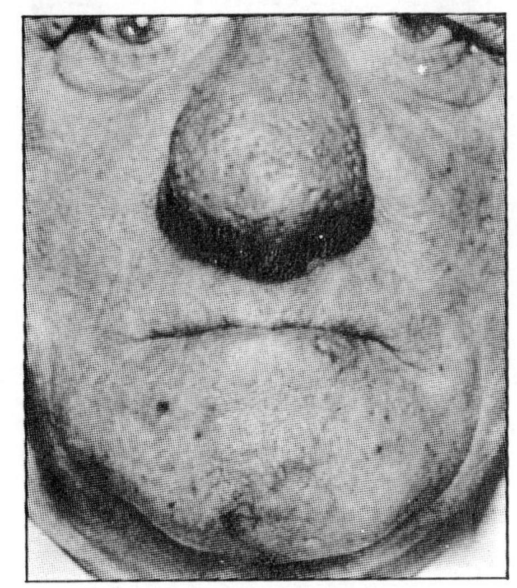

Fig. 484 : Rhinophyma

Rhinoplasty —Plastic surgery of the nose.

Rhinopneumonitis —Inflammation of the mucous membranes of the nose and the lungs.

Rhinopolypus —A polypus of the nose.

Rhinorrhagia —Epistaxis; nose bleed.

Rhinorrhea —Thin watery discharge from the nose.

Rhinosalpingitis —Inflammation of the mucous membrane of the nose, and eustachian tube.

Rhinoscleroma —A chronic infectious disease of the nose and nasopharynx with the development of stony hard growths in the form of patches or nodules.

Rhinoscope —An instrument for examination of the nose.

Rhinoscopic —Pertaining to a rhinoscope or rhinoscopy.

Rhinoscopy —Examination of the nose with the rhinoscope, either through anterior nares (anterior rhinoscopy) or through posterior nares with a small mirror in the nasopharynx (posterior rhinoscopy).

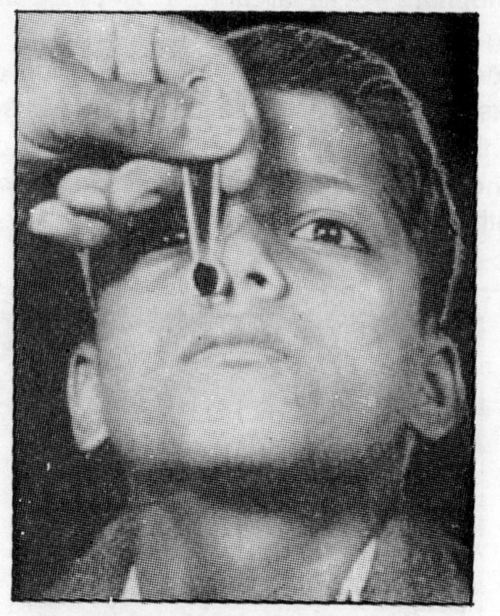

Fig. 485-A Anterior rhinoscopy

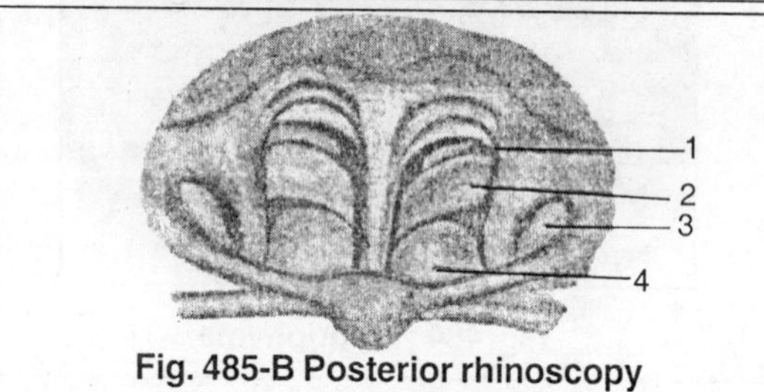

Fig. 485-B Posterior rhinoscopy

1. Superior turbinate, 2. Middle turbinate
3. Eustachian orifice, 4. Inferior turbinate

Rhinosinusitis —Inflammation of the mucous membrane of the nose and paranasal sinuses.

Rhinosporidiosis —A fungal disease caused by the fungus Rhinosporidium seeberi characterized by the development of pedunculated polyps on mucous membrane of the nose, larynx, eyes and sometimes the penis and vagina.

Rhinostenosis —Rhinocleisis. Obstruction of the nasal passages.

Rhinotomy —To make an incision into the nose.

Rhinotracheitis —Inflammation of the nasal mucous membranes and trachea.

Rhinovaccination —To apply a vaccine on the mucous membrane of the nose.

Rhinovirus —A genus of viruses belonging to the family Picornaviridae that causes common cold.

Rhitidectomy —Rhytidectomy.

Rhitidosis —Rhytidosis.

Rhizo- —A prefix meaning root.

Rhizodontropy —The process of attaching an artificial crown onto the root of a tooth.

Rhizodontrypy —To puncture a root of a tooth.

Rhizoid —Rootlike.

Rhizome —A rootlike stem growing under the ground.

Rhizomelia —A disorder involving the shoulder and hip joint.

Rhizomelic —Concerning the hip joint and shoulder joint.

Rhizomeningomyelitis —Radiculomeningomyelitis

Rhizomucor —A genus of the fungi belonging to the family Mucoraceae that causes mucormycosis.

Rhizoneure —A nerve cell forming a nerve root.

Rhizotomy —Division or transection of a nerve root.

Rhodamine —A red fluorescent dye.

Rhodo- —A prefix which means red.

Rhodogenesis —Regeneration of a visual purple after it has been bleached by light.

Rhodophylactic —Pertaining to rhodophylaxis.

Rhodophylaxis —Ability of the retinal epithelium to regenerate the visual purple that has been bleached by light.

Rhodopsin —Visual purple, a purple-red, photosensitive pigment in the retinal rods which is bleached by light to yellow stimulating the retinal sensory nerve endings.

Rhombencephalon —Hindbrain.

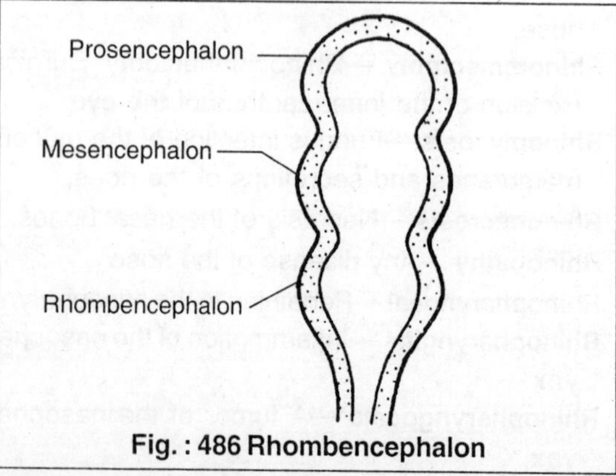

Fig. : 486 Rhombencephalon

Rhombic —Rhomboid. Pertaining to the rhombencephalon.

Rhombocele —The cavity of the hindbrain.

Rhomboid —Shaped like an oblique rectangle with oblique angles.

Rhomboidal —Rhomboid.

Rhomboid fossa —The 4th ventricle of the brain.

Rhombomere —Neuromere.

Rhoncal, Rhonchial —Pertaining to or produced by a rattle in the throat.

Rhonchi —Plural of rhonchus.

Rhonchus —A rattling in the throat or a rale in the bronchi.

Rhopheocytosis —Formation of vacuoles at the surface of a cell by which the cell aspirates surrounding material.

Rhotacism —Too much or improper use of the letter 'r' sound.

Rhyparia —Sordes. Foul substance collected in the mouth in some fevers.

Rhypophagy —Scatophagy. Coprophagy.

Rhypophobia —Mysophobia. Morbid fear of defecation, feces or dirt.

Rhythm —1. A measured movement; the recurrence of an action or function at regular intervals. 2. In electroencephalography, the regular occurrence of an impulse.

Alpha rhythm —Electroencephalographic waves with the frequency of 8-12 per second of a normal person in quiet resting state.

Atrioventricular rhythm —Nodal rhythm. Rhythmic origin of cardiac impulses from atrioventricular (A-V) node when sinoatrial (S-A) node becomes inactive.

Beta rhythm —Electroencephalographic waves with the frequency of 18 to 30 per second occurring during intense activity of the nervous system.

Biological rhythm —Occurrence of certain phenomena in living organisms regularly.

Cantering rhythm —Gallop rhythm.

Circadian rhythm —The regular recurrence of certain biological activities approximately at every 24 hours, regardless of darkness of night or day light.

Coupled rhythm —Heart beats occurring in pairs in which every alternate beat is weak and it does not produce pulse at the wrist.

Delta rhythm —Electroencephalographic waves having the frequency below 4 per second which occur in deep sleep, in infancy or in brain tumor or brain hemorrhage.

Ectopic rhythm —A cardiac rhythm originating outside the sinoatrial node.

Gallop rhythm —Abnormal heart rhythm with three sounds in each cycle.

Gamma rhythm —Electroencephalographic waves with the frequency of 50 per second.

Nodal rhythm —Atrioventricular rhythm.

Pendulum rhythm —Rhythm with two similar cardiac sounds, resembling the sound of a ticking clock.

Sinus rhythm —Normal cardiac rhythm originating in the sinoatrial node.

Theta rhythm—Electroencephalographic waves having the frequency of 4 to 7 per second, occurring mainly in children but in adults also in emotional stress.

Ventricular rhythm —Ventricular contractions occurring in complete heart block.

Rhythmic —Pertaining to rhythm.

Rhythmical —Rhythmic.

Rhythmicity —Ability to beat.

Rhytidectomy —Excision of the skin for removal of the wrinkles.

Rhytidoplasty —Elimination of the skin wrinkles by plastic surgery.

Rhytidosis —Wrinkling of the cornea usually before death.

Rib —Any one of the 12 narrow and curved bones

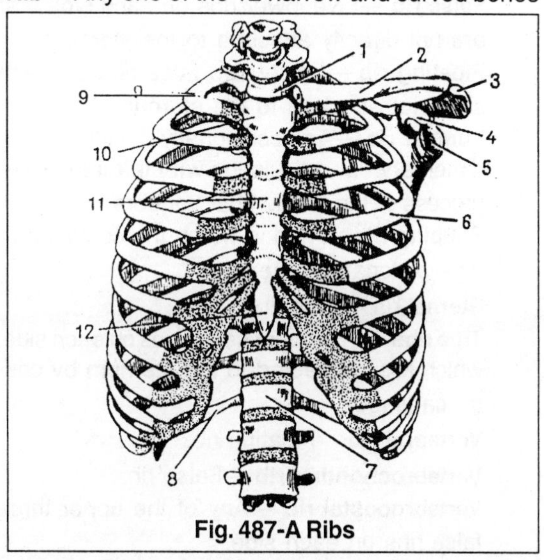

Fig. 487-A Ribs

1. First thoracic vertebra, 2. Clavicle, 3. Acromial process of scapula, 4. Coracoid process of scapula, 5. Glenoid cavity of scapula, 6. Ribs, 7. 12th thoracic vertebra, 8. 12th rib, 9. 1st rib, 10. Manubrium, 11. Body of sternum 12. Xiphoid process of sternum

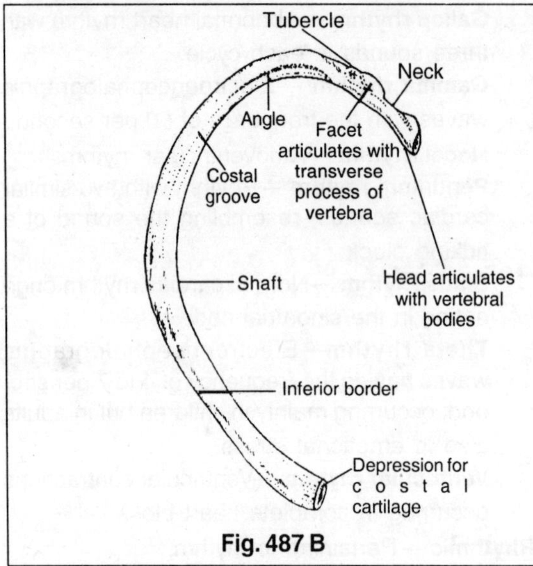

Fig. 487 B

on each side, extending laterally and anteriorly from the sides of the thoracic vertebrae, forming the major portion of the thoracic skeleton.

Abdominal rib —False rib.

Asternal rib —False ribs.

Bifid rib —A rib which bifurcates.

Cervical rib —A supernumerary rib arising from a cervical vertebra, usually the lowest.

False rib —Five lower ribs on each side that are not directly attached to the sternum.

Floating rib —Lower two false ribs on each side, not attached to the sternum.

Lumbar rib —An occasionally developing rudimentary rib, articulating with the transverse process of the first lumbar vertebra.

Slipping rib —A rib in which the costal cartilage dislocates repeatedly.

Sternal rib —True rib.

True ribs —The upper seven ribs on each side, which are connected to the sternum by costal cartilages.

Vertebral rib —Floating rib.

Vertebrochondral rib —False rib.

Vertebrocostal rib —Any of the upper three false ribs on each side.

Vertebrosternal rib —True rib.

Ribbon —A long, thin, band-shaped structure.

Riboflavin —Vitamin B_2, a water-soluble vitamin of the B-complex group.

Ribosomes —These are the structures much smaller than mitochondria found in the cytoplasm of the cell, which exist singly, or in clusters called polyribosomes or polysomes. Ribosomes contain ribonucleoprotein and form protein.

Rickets —A disease of the infants and children

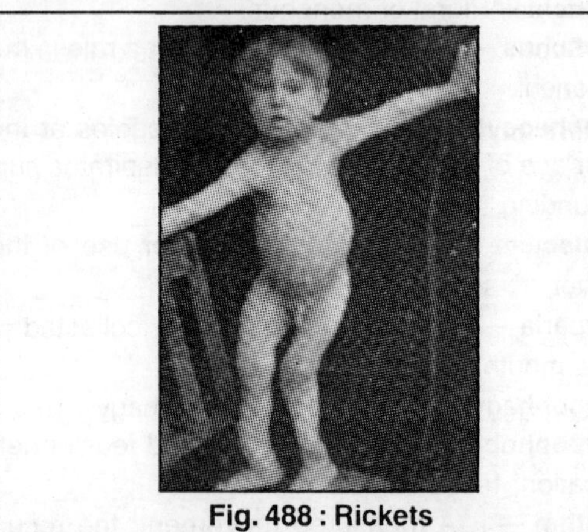
Fig. 488 : Rickets

due to vitamin D and calcium deficiency, marked by delay in walking, dentition and closure of the fontanelles, bending and distortion of the bones, muscular pain and sweating of the head at night.

Renal rickets —A form of rickets occurring in childhood due to severe chronic renal insufficiency.

Rickettsia —A genus of microorganisms of the family Rickettsiaceae, order Rickettsiales, occupying a position between viruses and bacteria. They are transmitted to man by lice, fleas, ticks and mites and cause various diseases.

Rickettsial —Pertaining to or caused by rickettsiae.

Rickettsicidal —Destructive to rickettsiae.

Rickettsiosis —Infection with rickettsiae.

Rickettsiostatic—Preventing or slowing the growth of rickettsiae.

Rickety —Affected with rickets.

Rider's bone —Bony formation in the adductor muscle of the leg of the person who rides horse extensively.

Ridge —An elongated projecting structure or crest (rough margin of a thing).

Alveolar ridge —The bony process of the maxilla or mandible that contains the tooth sockets.

Dental ridge —Cuspidate margin of a tooth.

Dermal ridges —The ridges on the surface of the fingers which make up the fingerprints.

Epicondylic ridge —One of the two ridges for muscular attachments on the humerus bone.

Gluteal ridge —A ridge extending obliquely from the greater trochanter of the femur bone for the attachment of the gluteus maximus muscle.

Supraorbital ridge —A curved ridge of the frontal bone over the orbital opening.

Riedel's lobe —Tongue-shaped process of the liver.

Right-eyed —Dextrocular.

Right-footed —Dextropedal.

Right-handed —Writing or working with the right hand.

Rigid —Stiff or hard or unflexible.

Rigidity —Stiffness, hardness or unflexibility.

Rigor —1. Chill. 2. Rigidity.

Rigor mortis —The stiffness of a dead body.

Rim —A border or edge.

Rima —A fissure, cleft or slit, *e.g.*, an elongated slit between the eyelids, lips of mouth and between the vocal cords.

Rimae —Plural of rima.

Rimose —Fissured or cracked.

Rimula —A minute fissure, as of the spinal cord or brain.

Rind —A thick outer coating of an organ.

Ring —1. A circular opening. 2. Any circular organ or area.

Deep inguinal ring —The opening of the inguinal canal situated deeply inside the abdominal wall, between the anterior superior iliac spine and the pubic tubercle, through which spermatic cord in the male and round ligament in the female enter the inguinal canal.

Superficial inguinal ring —The opening of the inguinal canal situated superficially in the abdominal wall through which spermatic cord in the male and round ligament in the female emerges from the inguinal canal. Inguinal hernia may also appear through this ring.

Ringworm —Tinea. Fungus infection of the skin, hairs and nails.

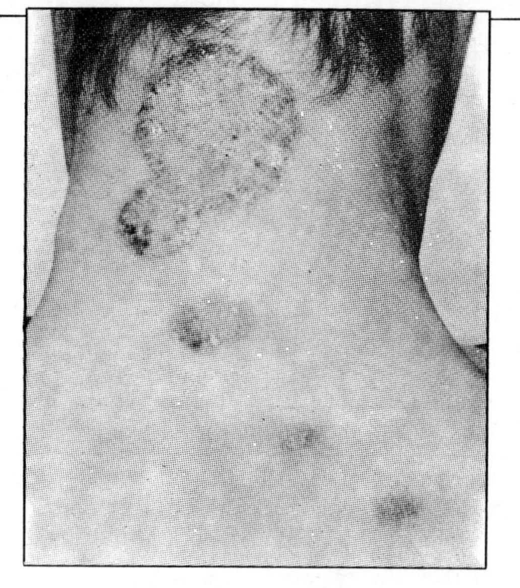

Diag. 489 : Ringworm

Rinne's test —A test for comparing the hearing through bone conduction with that through air conduction. For this, a vibrating tunning fork is held by its stem on the mastoid process of the ear until it is no longer heard by the patient. Then it is held close to the external auditory meatus. If the patient still hears the vibrations, it is positive Rinne's test, i.e., the hearing through air conduction is greater than that through bone conduction. If the tunning fork is not heard through the ear, the test is repeated. At this time the vibrating tunning fork is at first held close to the external auditory meatus until the sound is no longer heard, then the fork is placed on the mastoid process of the ear. If the sound is still heard, it is called negative Rinne's test.

Rinse —1. To wash lightly. 2. A solution or water used to rinse.

Ripaults' sign —A change in the shape of the pupil produced by unilateral pressure on the eyeball.

Ripening —1. Softening and dilatation of the cervix of uterus during labor. 2. Maturation of a cataract.

Risk —The probability that some harmful event will occur.

Risus —Laughter, laugh.

Risus sardonicus —A laughing expression in tetanus, caused by spasm of the facial muscles.

Ritgen's maneuver —Delivery of a child's head by

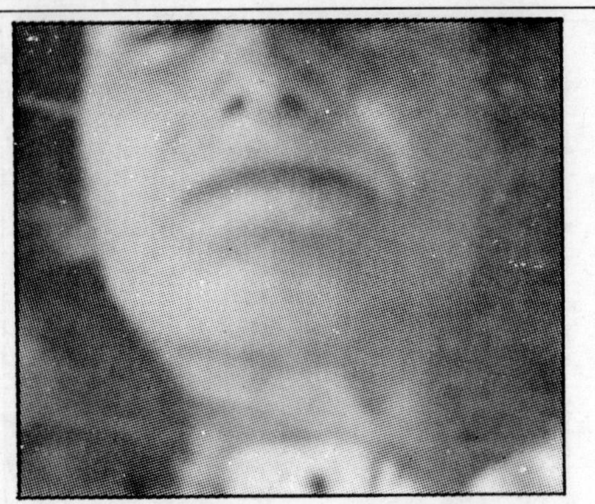
Fig. 490 : Risus sardonicus

applying pressure on the perineum of the mother and also to apply pressure on the head of the child with other hand, to control the speed of the delivery.

Ritter's disease —Generalized impetigo of the newborn.

Ritual —Essential routine.

Rivalry —Competition.

Rivalry sibling —The competition between children for attentiton and affection of others, especially of their parents.

Rivalry strife —Alternate perception of two different images when the fields of vision of two eyes cannot combine in one visual image.

Rivinus' canals —Ducts of the sublingual glands.

Rivinus' glands —Sublingual glands.

Rivus lacrimalis —Lacrimal pathway. The passage through which tears travel from the lacrimal glands to the outlet of the lacrimal canaliculus.

R. L. E. —Right lower extremity.

R. L. L. —Right lower lobe of the lung.

R. L. Q. —Right lower quadrant (of abdomen)

R. M. A. —Registered Medical Assistant; right mentoanterior presentation (of the fetal face).

R. M. L. —Right middle lobe (of lung).

R. M. P. —1. Registered medical practitioner. 2. Right mentoposterior presentation (of the fetal face).

R. M. V. —Respiratory minute volume.

R. N. —Registered Nurse.

RNA —Ribonucleic acid.

R. N. C. —Registered Nurse Certified.

R. O. A. —Right occipitoanterior position of the fetus.

Roar —To make a loud sound or to talk very loudly.

Roaring —A loud cry.

Robertson's pupil —Argyll Robertson pupil.

Robert's pelvis —Transversely contracted pelvis due to osteoarthritis of the sacroiliac joints.

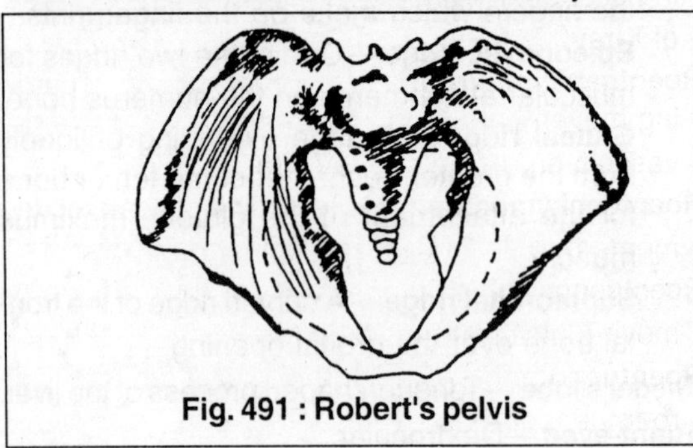
Fig. 491 : Robert's pelvis

Robust —Of strong constitution.

Rod —1. A slender, straight bar. 2. One of the bar-shaped light sensitive bodies along with cones in the retina.

Rodent —An animal of the class mammalia and of the order Rodentia such as rat, squirrel and guinea pig etc. that takes food by gnawing.

Rodenticide —Killing rodents.

Rodent ulcer —Basal-cell carcinoma. A cancerous ulcer of basal cells of the skin developing usually on the upper two-third portion of the face with raised (but not everted as in epithelioma) margin and granular floor, destroying slowly the adjacent soft tissues and bones.

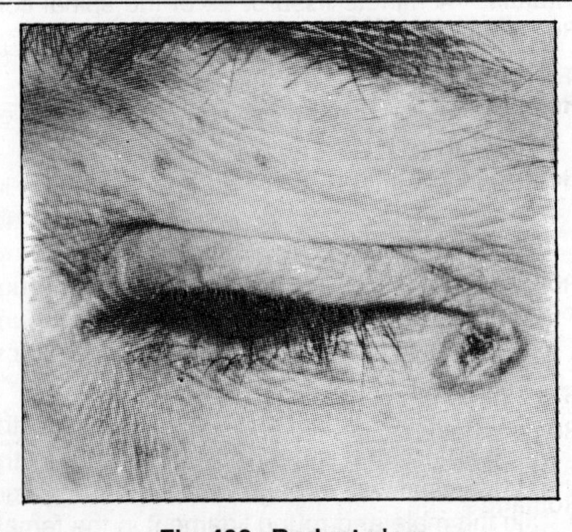
Fig. 492 : Rodent ulcer

Rodonalgia —Erythromelalgia. A vasomotor disease characterized by neuralgia in the limbs with swelling, redness and fever.

Roentgen —The international unit of exposure dose for X-rays or gamma rays.

Roentgenism —The disease caused by misuse of X-ray.

Roentgenkymogram —A record in the form of tracing of heart's movements, as determined by use of X-ray.

Roentgenkymograph —An apparatus for recording movements of the heart and attached large vessels on a single X-ray film.

Roentgenkymography —Recording of heart movements by use of roentgenkymograph.

Roentgenocinematography —X-ray examination by moving picture photography.

Roentgenogram —Radiogram. A film produced by roentgenography.

Roentgenograph —Radiograph.

Roentgenography —Radiography. The taking of pictures (roentgenogram or radiogram) of the internal organs of the body by X-ray.

Roentgenologist —Radiologist.

Roentgenology —Radiology.

Roentgenometer —Radiometer.

Roentgenometry —Measurement of the intensity of X-ray.

Roentgenoscope —A fluoroscope.

Roentgenotherapy, Roentgentherapy —Radiotherapy. Treatment of the diseases by X-ray.

Roentgen ray —X-ray.

Roger's disease —Ventricular septal defect.

Rolando's area —Motor area in the cerebral cortex.

Rolando's fissure—Sulcus entralis. Fissure between the parietal and frontal lobes.

Roll —1. A thing formed into a cylinder. 2. To move in the same direction over and over again; to go round; to revolve on its axis.

Roller —A strip of a cloth or gauze rolled up in cylinder form for surgeon's use or a rolled bandage.

R.O.M. —Range of motion.

Romanopexy —Sigmoidopexy. Fixation of the sigmoid flexure for prolapse of the rectum.

Romanoscope —An instrument of examining the sigmoid flexure.

Rombergism —Romberg's sign.

Romberg's sign —Inability to maintain the body balance and tendency to fall down while standing with the eyes closed and the feet close together.

Rongeur —An instrument for removing small pieces of bone.

Rooming-in —Placing of infants in the same hospital room in which their mothers are present, just after delivery.

Root —1. Underground part of a plant. 2. Proximal end of a nerve. 3. Portion of an organ burried in the tissues. 4. The part of a tooth embedded in the socket (alveolus) of the jaw bones.

Root arteries —Arteries accompanying nerve roots into the spinal cord.

Root canal —Pulp cavity of root of a tooth.

Rootlet —A small root.

Root pick —Apical elevator. A dental instrument used to recover the fragments of the dental root resulting from tooth extraction.

Root planing —In dentistry, abrading of the rough surfaces of a dental root to achieve a smooth surface.

R.O.P. —Right occipitoposterior (fetal presentation).

Rosa —Rose.

Rosacea —A chronic disease of the skin of the nose, forehead and cheeks characterized by flushing of the face followed by redness due to dilatation of the blood capillaries with the appearance of papules and pustules.

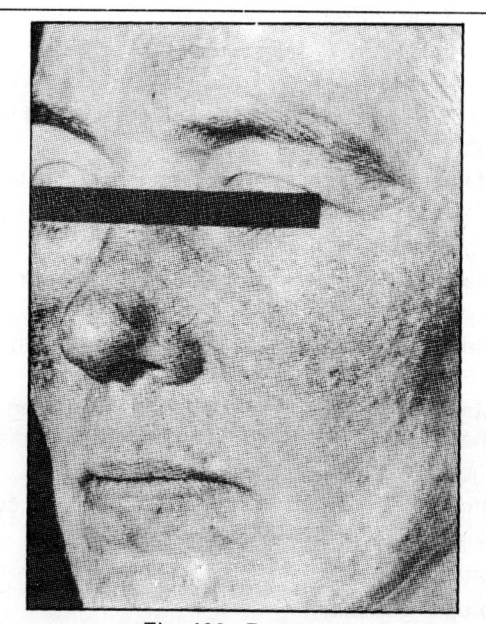

Fig. 493 : Rosacea

Rosaniline —A basic dye used in preparing other dyes.

Rosary —A structure resembling a string of beads.

Rachitic rosary —Bead-like prominences occurring in succession, along the costal cartilages in rickets.

Rosenbach's sign —Occurrence of fine rapid tremors of the closed eyelids in hyperthyroidism.

Rosenbach's test —A test for determination of bile in the urine.

Roseola —1. Any rose-colored skin rash. 2. Exanthema subitum.

Roseolous —Resembling or pertaining to roseola.

Rose's position —A position in which the patient lies fully extended on the operation table with the head hanging down over the end of the table to prevent aspiration of blood during operation on the mouth and lips.

Rosette —1. Resembling a rose. 2. Malarial parasite Plasmodium malariae in its mature phase.

Rostellum —A fleshy beak of the scolex of a tapeworm bearing hooks.

Rostra —Plural of rostrum.

Rostrad —Toward a rostrum, or cephalad.

Rostral —1. Resembling a beak. 2. Toward the head.

Rostralis —Rostral.

Rostrate —Beaked; having a beak.

Rostriform —Beak-shaped.

Rostrum —Any beaked structure.

Rot —Decay.

R. O. T. —Right occipitotransverse position of the fetus.

Rotameter —An apparatus for measuring the flow of gas or a liquid.

Rotate —To turn, to twist or to revolve.

Rotation —The process of turning, twisting or revolving.

Rotator —A muscle which rotates an organ on its axis.

Rotavirus —A group of RNA viruses belonging to the family Reoviridae that causes mostly diarrhea in infants and small children.

Rototome —A rotating instrument used for cutting tissues in arthroscopic surgery.

Rotula —Kneecap. Patella bone.

Rotular —Patellar.

Rough —Not smooth or of uneven surface.

Roughage —Indigestible material in the diet such as fibers of fruits and vegetables and cereals which stimulate peristaltic movements of the intestine and cause evacuation of the bowels.

Rouleau —A group of red blood cells arranged in cylinder form.

Roundworm —A round earthworm-shaped intestinal worm belonging to the class Nematoda.

R P F —Renal plasma flow.

R. Ph. —Registered Pharmacist.

R P O —1. Radiation protection officer. 2. Right posterior oblique.

R. Q. —Respiratory quotient.

-rrhagia —A suffix meaning excessive discharge or hemorrhage.

-rrhaphy —A suffix meaning surgical suturing.

-rrhea —A suffix meaning excessive flow.

-rrhexis, -rhexis —Suffixes which mean rupture.

Rub —Friction sound produced by one surface moving over another surface, as produced by both layers of the pleura in pleurisy, heard on auscultation.

Rubber-dam —A thin rubber sheet used by dentists to seal off the tooth from saliva in the mouth during dental treatment.

Rubedo —Temporary redness of the skin.

Rubefacient —Causing redness of the skin by dilating the blood vessels and producing local congestion.

Rubefaction —Redness of the skin caused by the application of an irritant-material.

Rubella —German measles. An acute viral infection resembling measles, characterized by slight fever, sore throat and pink macular rash appearing on 1st or 2nd day, beginning on the face and spreading over the whole body and enlargement of the superficial cervical and post auricular glands.

Rubeola —1. Measles. 2. Rubella.

Rubeosis —Redness. Formation of new blood vessels.

Rubeosis iridis —Formation of new blood vessels on the anterior surface of the iris.

Ruber —Red.

Rubescent —Growing red; flushing.

Rubiginous —Rusty.

Rubigo —Rust.

Rubin's test —A test for patency of the fallopian tubes.

Rubner's test —1. A test for glucose or lactose in the urine. 2. A test for carbon monoxide in the blood.

Rubor —Redness, one of the cardinal signs of inflammation.

Rubriblast —Pronormoblast.

Rubric —Red or pertaining to red nucleus.

Rubricyte —Polychromatic normoblast.

Rubrospinal —Pertaining to the red nucleus and the spinal cord.

Rubrothalamic —Pertaining to the red nucleus of the brain and thalamus.

Rubrum —Red.

Rubulavirus —Mumpvirus. A genus of viruses belonging to the family Paramyxoviridae that causes mumps.

Ructus —Eructation; belching.

Rudiment—A small incompletely developed structure which has been more fully developed in the embryo.

Rudimentary —Of the nature of a rudiment.

Rudimentum —Rudiment.

Ruff —A collar or ruffle.

Rufous —Ruddy. Reddish.

Ruga —A crease, wrinkle or fold.

Rugae —Plural of ruga.

Rugine —1. Elevator of periosteum. 2. A raspatory.

Rugitus —A rumbling sound in the intestines.

Rugose, Rugous —Having many creases or wrinkles.

Rugosity —1. The condition of being rugose. 2. A crease, wrinkle or fold.

Rugous —Rugose.

R. U. L. —Right upper lobe of the lung.

Ruler —Scale.

Rum —Spirit distilled from sugarcane.

Rumblossom —Rhinophyma.

Rum fits —Occurrence of epileptiform convulsions following withdrawal of chronic use of alcohol.

Ruminant —An animal that regurgitates food to chew it again.

Rumination —Regurgitation with rechewing of the previously swallowed food.

Ruminative —One who is characterized by preoccupation with certain thoughts and ideas.

Rump —Buttock or gluteal region.

Run —To exude pus or mucus.

Runaround, Runround —Whitlow. Superficial infection around the fingernail.

Rundown —Weak; debilited.

Running —Exudation of pus or mucus.

Rupia —Thick, dark, lamellated crusts adhered to the skin occurring in tertiary syphilis.

Rupioid —Resembling rupia.

Rupophobia —Rhypophobia.

Rupture —The tearing or breaking of an organ or tissue.

R U Q —Right upper quadrant (of abdomen).

Rush —Strong peristaltic movement.

Russell body —A small hyaline body found in cancerous and simple inflammatory growths.

Russian bath —Hot vapor bath followed by friction and sinking in cold water.

Rust's disease —Tuberculosis of the cervical vertebrae and their joints.

Rusty —Rubiginous.

Rut-formation —Lack of interest in the environment, fixing the mind upon a single object.

Rutidosis —Rhytidosis. Rytidosis.

Rutilizm —The condition of having red or golden brown hair.

R. V. —Residual volume.

Ryle's tube —A rubber tube used for withdrawing the contents of the stomach.

Rytidosis —Rhytidosis. Rutidosis.

S —Chemical symbol for sulfur.

S. —Semis (half); sinister (left).

S–A, SA, S.A. —Sinoatrial.

Sabulous —Sandy or gritty.

Saburra —Sordes. Foulness of the mouth or stomach due to decayed food.

Saburral —1. Pertaining to foulness of mouth or stomach due to decayed food. 2. Sandy or gritty.

Sac —A baglike organ or structure.

- **Air sacs** —Alveoli of the lungs.
- **Amniotic sac** —Amnion. A thin membrane, containing amniotic fluid, enclosing the fetus.
- **Conjunctival sac** —The cavity formed by the conjunctiva, lying between the eyelids and anterior surface of the eyeball.
- **Hernial sac** —A saclike protrusion of the peritoneum containing an organ.

Saccades —Involuntary jerky movements of both eyes occurring simultaneously on changing them from viewing one object to another.

Saccadic —Pertaining to the intermittent involuntary jerky movements of the eyes.

Saccate —1. Pertaining to, or shaped like a sac. 2. Encysted. Enclosed in a sac.

Saccharated —Containing sugar.

Saccharephidrosis —Presence of sugar in sweat.

Sacchari- —Saccharo-

Saccharic —Pertaining to sugar.

Saccharide —One of a series of carbohydrates, including the sugars.

Sacchariferous —Producing or containing sugar.

Saccharification —Conversion into sugar.

Saccharify —To convert starch or cellulose into sugar.

Saccharimeter —An instrument for determining the amount of sugar in a solution.

Saccharin —A synthetic product, 300 to 500 times as sweet as sugar, used as artificial sweetner.

Saccharine —Sweet. Of the nature of, or having the quality of, sugar.

Saccharo- —A prefix which means sugar.

Saccharogalactorrhea —Excessive secretion of sugar in the milk.

Saccharolytic —Capable of splitting up sugar.

Saccharometabolic —Pertaining to the metabolism of sugar.

Saccharometabolism —Metabolism of sugar.

Saccharometer —Saccharimeter.

Saccharomyces —Yeasts. A genus of fungi, reproducing by budding.

Saccharomycetic —Pertaining to or caused by yeast fungi.

Saccharomycosis —Any disease caused by yeasts.

Saccharorrhea —Presence of sugar in the body fluids, as in urine or perspiration.

Saccharose —Sucrose. Cane sugar.

Saccharosuria —Presence of saccharose in the urine.

Saccharum —Sugar.

Saccharuria —Presence of sugar in the urine.

Sacciform —Saccate.

Saccular —Shaped like a sac.

Sacculated —Consisting of small sacs or saccules.

Sacculation —Formation of a sac or sacs.

Saccule —A small sac.

Sacculocochlear —Pertaining to the saccule and cochlea of the ear.

Sacculus —Saccule.

Saccus —A sac.

Sacrad —Toward the sacrum.

Sacral —Pertaining to the sacrum.

Sacral flexure —Rectal curve in front of the sacrum.

Sacralgia —Pain in the sacrum.

Sacral index —Sacral breadth multiplied by 100 and divided by sacral length.

Sacralization —Fusion of the 5th lumbar vertebra with the sacrum.

Sacral plexus —Network of sacral nerves from which sciatic nerve originates.

Sacrectomy —Excision of a part of a sacrum.

Sacro- —A prefix indicating relationship to the sacrum.

Sacroanterior —Position of the fetus in the uterus in which sacrum of the fetus lies anteriorly.

Sacrococcygeal —Pertaining to the sacrum and coccyx.

Sacrocoxalgia —Pain in the sacrococcygeal joint.

Sacrocoxitis —Inflammation of the sacrococcygeal joint.

Sacrodynia —Sacralgia.

Sacroiliac —Pertaining to the sacrum and ilium.

Sacroiliac joint —The joint between the hip bone and sacrum.

Sacroiliitis —Inflammation of the sacroiliac joint.

Sacrolisthesis —A deformity in which the sacrum is in front of the last lumbar vertebra.

Sacrolumbar —Of, or pertaining to the sacrum and lumbar vertebra.

Sacroposterior —Position of the fetus in the uterus in which sacrum of the fetus lies posteriorly.

Sacrosciatic —Pertaining to the sacrum and ischium.

Sacrospinal —Pertaining to sacrum and the spinal column.

Sacrotomy —To make an incision into the lower portion of the sacrum.

Sacrouterine —Pertaining to the sacrum and uterus.

Sacrovertebral —Pertaining to the sacrum and vertebral column.

Sacrum —A triangular bone made up of five fused vertebrae just above the coccyx, which is the base of the vertebral column and with the coccyx, forms the posterior boundary of the true pelvis.

Sactosalpinx —Dilated fallopian tube due to retention of secretions.

Saddle —The structure resembling a seat used to ride a horse, *e.g.* the base of an artificial denture.

Saddle area —The portion of the buttocks, perineum and thighs that come in contact with the seat of the saddle.

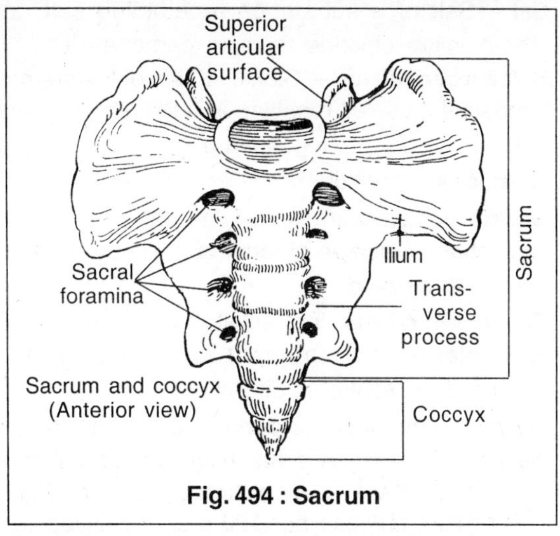

Fig. 494 : Sacrum

Saddle back —Lordosis. Excessively curved lower back.

Saddle joint —A concavoconvex articulation.

Saddle nose —A nose with a depressed bridge which is a sign of congenital syphilis.

Sadism —The derivation of sexual pleasure from inflicting mental or physical pain on others.

Sadist —One who practices sadism.

Sadistic —Pertaining to or characterized by sadism.

Sadness —Sorrowfulness.

Sadomasochism —Sexual pleasure related to both sadism and masochism.

Sadomasochist —The person who is both sadist and masochist.

Saemisch's ulcer —Infectious serpiginous ulcer of the cornea.

Sag —To bulge in a downward direction.

Sage —Saliva.

Sagging —Bulging in a downward direction.

Sagitta —Otoliths.

Sagittal —1. Arrow-shaped. 2. Situated in the direction of sagittal suture or anteroposterior plane.

Sagittalis —Sagittal.

Sagittal plane —See under plane.

Sagittal sulcus —A groove on the inner surface of the parietal bones, forming a channel for the superior sagittal sinus.

Sago —A starchy substance prepared from various palms.

Saint vitus' dance —Sydenham's chorea.

Sal —Salt or a substance resembling salt, as ammonium chloride, sodium carbonate etc.

Salaam convulsion —Clonic spasm of the sterno-mastoid muscles resulting in such a movement as one is performing salaam.

Salacious —Lustful.

Salient —Projection.

Salifiable —Capable of forming a salt by combining with an acid.

Salify —To convert into a salt.

Salimeter —An instrument for measuring the strength of saline solutions.

Saline —Containing or pertaining to salt; salty.

Saline solution —A solution of sodium chloride and distilled water. A solution containing .9 gm. of sodium chloride per 100 c.c. of distilled water is isotonic to the body and hence it is known as normal saline and used in transfusion in dehydration.

Salinometer —An instrument for determining the quantity of salt in a solution.

Saliva —The enzyme-containing secretion of the salivary glands, which moistens food, aids mastication and deglutition and begins digestion of food.

Salivant —Stimulating the flow of saliva.

Salivary —Pertaining to, producing or formed from saliva.

Salivary glands —The glands of the mouth which secrete saliva. There are three types of salivary glands – parotid, submandibular and sublingual salivary glands, each in pair.

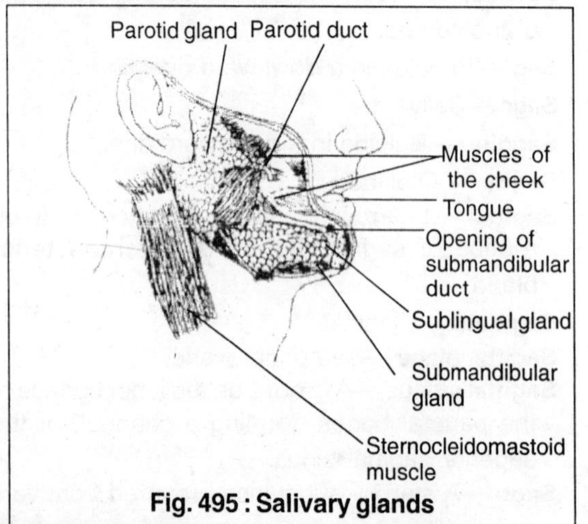

Fig. 495 : Salivary glands

Salivate —To expel an excess of saliva.

Salivation —1. The secretion of saliva. 2. Ptyalism.

Salivator —Increasing the flow of saliva.

Salivatory —Causing salivation.

Salivolithiasis —Sialolithiasis.

Salk vaccine —A vaccine containing killed poliomyelitis viruses, used to produce immunity against poliomyelitis.

Sallow —Yellowish color of the skin.

Salmonella —A genus of aerobic (facultative anaerobic bacteria) belonging to the family Enterobacteriaceae, which includes mainly Salmonella typhi that causes typhoid fever and Salmonella paratyphi causing paratyphoid fever in humans.

Salmonellosis —Infection with bacteria of genus Salmonella.

Salpingectomy —Surgical removal of the fallopian tube.

Salpingemphraxis —Obstruction of the eustachian tube.

Salpinges—Plural of salpinx.

Salpingian —Pertaining to the eustachian tube or fallopian tube.

Salpingioma —Any tumor of the fallopian tube.

Salpingitic —Pertaining to salpingitis.

Salpingitis —Inflammation of the fallopian or auditory tube.

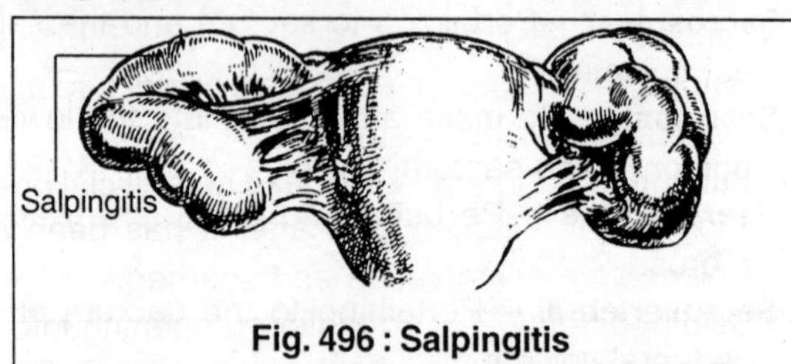

Fig. 496 : Salpingitis

Salpingo- —A prefix indicating fallopian or eustachian tube.

Salpingocele —Hernia of the fallopian tube.

Salpingocyesis —Tubal pregnancy, a form of ectopic pregnancy in which the embryo develops in the fallopian tube.

Salpingogram —X-ray film of the fallopian tube.

Salpingography —X-ray examination of the fallopian tubes after injection of a radiopaque substance.

Salpingolithiasis —Presence of calculi in the fallopian tube.

Salpingolysis —Surgical separation of the adhesions in the fallopian tube.

Salpingoneostomy —To reopen the fallopian tube closed by fimbrial adhesions, by surgery.

Salpingo-oophorectomy —Salpingo-ovariectomy. Excision of a fallopian tube and ovary.

Salpingo-oophoritis —Inflammation of a fallopian tube and ovary.

Salpingo-oophorocele —Hernia containing a fallopian tube and ovary.

Salpingo-oothecitis —Salpingo-oophoritis.

Salpingo-oothecocele —Salpingo-oophorocele.

Salpingo-ovariectomy —Salpingo-oophorectomy.

Salpingoperitonitis —Inflammation of the peritoneum covering the fallopian tubes.

Salpingopexy —Fixation of a fallopian tube.

Salpingopharyngeal —Pertaining to the auditory canal and pharynx.

Salpingoplasty —Tuboplasty. Repair of the fallopian tube by plastic surgery.

Salpingorrhagia —Hemorrhage from a fallopian tube.

Salpingorrhaphy —Suture of a fallopian tube.

Salpingosalpingostomy —Surgical attachment of one fallopian tube to the other.

Salpingoscope —An instrument for examining the nasopharynx and eustachian tube.

Salpingoscopy —Endoscopy of the fallopian tubes.

Salpingostenochoria —Stenosis or stricture of the eustachian tube.

Salpingostomatomy —To make an artificial opening into a fallopian tube after it has been occluded by inflammation and scarring.

Salpingostomy —1. To make an opening into an occluded fallopian tube for drainage. 2. Surgical restoration of the patency of a fallopian tube.

Salpingotomy —To make an incision into a fallopian tube.

Salpingo-ureterostomy —Surgical connection of a fallopian tube with the ureter.

Salpingysterocyesis —A form of ectopic pregnancy in which the embryo is located at the entrance of fallopian tube into the uterus.

Salpinx —The fallopian or eustachian tube.

Salt —1. Sodium chloride or common salt. Salt containing 1 part of sodium or potassium iodide to 10,000 parts of sodium chloride, is called iodized salt, which is an important source of iodine in the diet, which prevents the goiter to develop. 2. A chemical compound resulting from interaction of a base and an acid, e.g., aromatized ammonium chloride (smelling salt) and bile salts (the salt of glycocholic and taurocholic acid present in bile) 3. Saline purgative, as Epsom salt (magnesium sulfate) etc.

Saltation —1. The act of leaping or dancing, as in Chorea. 2. Mutation.

Saltatory —Marked by leaping or dancing.

Salting in —The increase in solubility, as observed for some proteins, by adding dilute salt solutions.

Salting out —The separation of a protein from its solution by precipitation, by adding a salt such as ammonium sulfate, sodium chloride or magnesium sulfate.

Salt solution, physiological —Normal saline.

Salubrious —Promoting health or wholesome.

Saluresis —Excretion of sodium chloride in the urine.

Saluretic —Pertaining to, or promoting the excretion of sodium chloride in the urine.

Salutarium —Sanitarium. Sanatorium.

Salutary —Salubrious.

Salve —An ointment for wounds.

Sample —A specimen, pattern.

Sampling —The selection of a portion to represent the whole.

Sanation —The process of healing.

Sanative —Of the nature of healing, healing or curative.

Sanatorium —Sanitarium. An institution for the preservation of health or for the treatment of sick persons, especially the patients with chronic diseases such as tuberculosis etc. or mental disorders.

Sanatory —Conductive to health.

Sand —Matter occurring in minute particles.

Sandfly —Two-winged fly of the genus Phlebotomus, which transmits sandfly fever and various types of leishmaniasis.

Sane —Of sound mind.

Sangui-, Sanguin-, Sanguino- —Prefixes meaning blood or bloody.

Sanguicolous —Living in the blood, as a parasite.

Sanguifacient —Making blood.

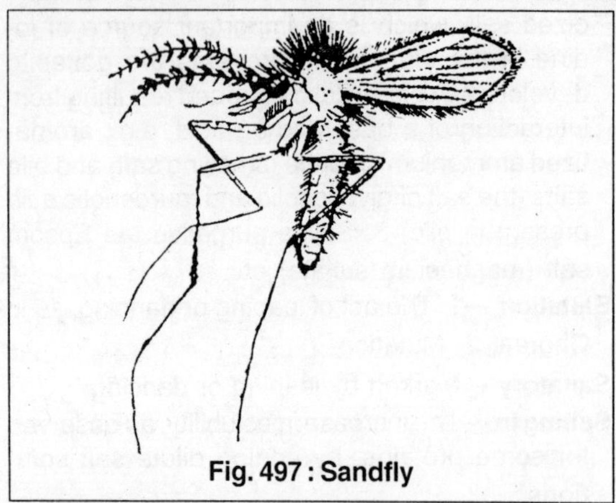
Fig. 497 : Sandfly

Sanguiferous —Conducting or containing blood, as the circulatory organs.

Sanguification —Hematopoiesis. Conversion into, or production of blood.

Sanguifluxus —Hemorrhage.

Sanguimotor, Sanguimotory —Pertaining to blood circulation.

Sanguine —1. Pertaining to, or consisting of, blood. 2. Bloody. 3. Cheerful.

Sanguineous —1. Bloody; pertaining to blood 2. Plethoric. Full of blood.

Sanguinolent —Containing, or tinged with blood.

Sanguinopoietic —Sanguifacient.

Sanguinopurulent —Pertaining to, or containing blood and pus.

Sanguinous —Sanguineous.

Sanguirenal —Pertaining to the blood supply of the kidneys.

Sanguis —Blood.

Sanguisuga —A leech or blood sucker.

Sanguivorous —Subsisting on blood.

Sanies —A thin, fetid, greenish discharge from a wound containing serum, pus and blood.

Saniopurulent —Partly sanious and partly purulent.

Sanioserous —Partly sanious and partly serous.

Sanious —A wound marked by thin, fetid, greenish discharge containing serum, pus and blood.

Sanitarian —The person skilled in sanitation and public health science.

Sanitarium —Sanatorium.

Sanitary —1. Promoting or pertaining to health. 2. Clean.

Sanitary napkin —Sanitary pad used for absorbing menstrual blood.

Sanitation —1. The establishment of conditions favorable to health. 2. Cleanliness.

Sanitization —The act of making sanitary.

Sanitize —To make sanitary.

Sanitizer —That which makes clean.

Sanity —Soundness of mind.

Sap —Natural juice of an organism essential for vitality.

Cell sap —Hyaloplasm. The fluid portion of the protoplasm.

Nuclear sap —Karyolymph. Fluid portion of a cell nucleus.

Saphena —The name given to small saphenous vein or the large saphenous vein of the leg.

Saphenectomy —Surgical removal of the saphenous vein.

Saphenous —Pertaining to, or associated with a saphenous vein or nerve in the leg.

Saphenous nerve —A branch of femoral nerve supplying the medial side of the leg, ankle and foot.

Saphenous veins —Two superficial, small and great saphenous veins of the leg.

Sapid —Tasty.

Sapo —Soap.

Saponaceous —Soapy.

Saponatus —Mixed with soap.

Saponification —Conversion of an oil or fat into a soap.

Saponify —To convert into a soap.

Sapor —Taste.

Saporific —Imparting a taste or flavor.

Sapphism —Lesbianism. Female homosexuality.

Sapremia —Septicemia.

Sapro- —A prefix which means decay or decayed matter.

Saprobe —An organism such as a bacterium or fungus that lives on dead organic matter.

Saprobic —Pertaining to a saprobe.

Saprodontia —Dental caries.

Saprogen —Any microorganism causing or produced by putrefaction.

Saprogenic —Causing putrefaction or resulting from it.

Saprogenous—Saprogenic.

Saprophilous —Saprophytic.

Saprophyte —Any organism living upon decaying or dead organic matter.

Saprophytic —Pertaining to a saprophyte.

Saprostomous —Having a foul breath.

Saprozoic —An animal living on decaying or dead organic matter.

Saprozoonosis —A disease transmitted by animals to humans in which the causative organism requires both, an animal host and a nonanimal (food, soil, plant) reservoir for completion of its life cycle.

Sarapus —The person having flat feet.

Sarcitis —Myositis.

Sarco- —A prefix meaning flesh.

Sarcoadenoma —Adenosarcoma. A fleshy tumor of a gland.

Sarcobiont —A microorganism living on flesh.

Sarcoblast —Myoblast.

Sarcocarcinoma —A malignant tumor of sarcomatous and carcinomatous nature.

Sarcocele —Fleshy swelling or tumor of the testis.

Sarcogenic —Producing flesh or muscle.

Sarcoid —1. Resembling flesh. 2. Tuberculoid lesion of sarcoidosis.

Sarcoidosis —A disease of unknown cause characterized by granulomatous lesions that may affect any organ or tissue of the body.

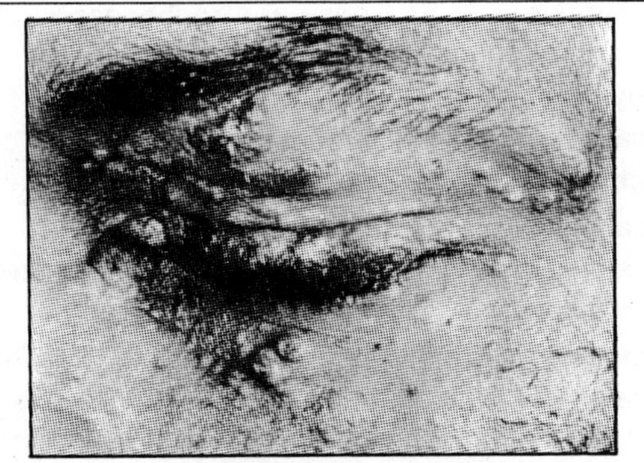

Fig. 498 : Sarcoidosis

Sarcolemma —A membrane covering each striated muscle fiber.

Sarcolemmal, Sarcolemmic, Sarcolemmous —Pertaining to the sarcolemma.

Sarcology —A branch of medical science dealing with the study of soft tissues of the body.

Sarcolysis —Decomposition of the soft tissues or flesh of the body.

Sarcolytic —Decomposing flesh.

Sarcoma —A malignant tumor or cancer of the connective tissue such as muscle or bone, which may affect the bones, bladder, kidneys, liver, spleen and lungs etc.

Sarcomatoid —Resembling a sarcoma.

Sarcomatosis —Development of many sarcomas at various sites.

Sarcomatous —Of the nature of, or like a sarcoma.

Sarcomphalocele —Fleshy tumor of the umbilicus.

Sarcophagy —Habit of eating flesh.

Sarcoplasm —The cytoplasm of the muscle cells.

Sarcoplasmic —Pertaining to sarcoplasm.

Sarcoplast —An interstitial cell of muscle, capable of being transformed into muscle.

Sarcopoietic —Forming flesh or muscle.

Sarcoptes —A genus of mites, including Sarcoptes scabiei, which causes scabies in man.

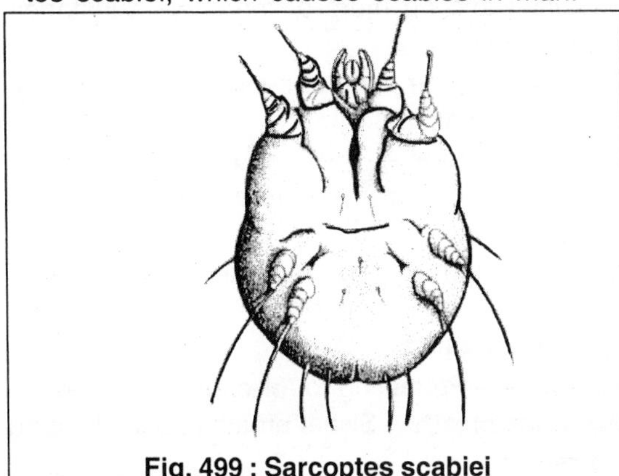

Fig. 499 : Sarcoptes scabiei

Sarcoptic —Of, pertaining to, or caused by mites of the genus sarcoptes.

Sarcosis —1. An abnormal increase of flesh. 2. The development of numerous fleshy tumors.

Sarcostosis —Ossification of fleshy or muscular tissue.

Sarcotic —Forming or pertaining to the formation of flesh.

Sarcous —Pertaining to the flesh or muscle.

Sarmassation —Erotic squeezing or kneading of the female organs.

Sartorius —The longest muscle in the body which is ribbon-shaped and found in the leg.

Sashmi —The general term used for a food made of raw fish that may be a source of infection of human tissues.

Sat. —Saturated.

Satellite —A small structure attached to a large one.

Satellite cells —Neuroglial cells enclosing the bodies of neurons in spinal ganglia.

Satellitism —The growing of certain bacterial species more vigorously than colonies of bacteria of unrelated species of the neighborhood.

Satellitosis —The accumulation of neuroglial cells about neurons of the central nervous system, seen in some degenerative and inflammatory diseases.

Satiation —The state of being fulfilled.

Satiety —Full satisfaction, especially with food.

Saturate —1. To dissolve a substance in a solution upto that extent beyond which no more of the substance can be dissolved. 2. To impregnate to the greatest possible extent.

Saturated —Holding all that can be dissolved in a solution and no more of the given substance can be dissolved.

Saturation —The state of being saturated or the act of saturating.

Saturation index —The amount of hemoglobin present in a known volume of blood compared to the normal.

Saturation time —Time required for the arterial blood of a person inhaling pure oxygen, to become saturated.

Saturnine —Pertaining to, or caused by lead.

Saturnine breath —Sweet breath caused by lead poisoning.

Saturnism —Plumbism. Lead poisoning.

Satyriasis —Excessive sexual desire in the male.

Satyrism —Satyriasis.

Satyromania —Satyriasis.

Saucerization —Surgical formation or formation by trauma of a depression in a tissue.

Sauriasis —Ichthyosis.

Savory —Having pleasant taste or odor.

Saw —A cutting instrument with one edge of sharp toothlike projections.

Saxifragant —Dissolving or breaking the calculi, especially in the bladder.

S. b. —Chemical symbol for antimony.

S. c. —Subcutaneously.

Scab —1. Crust of a cutaneous or superficial wound formed by drying up of the discharge. 2. To become covered with a crust.

Scabicidal —Destructive to scabies mite.

Scabicide —Killing the mite Sarcoptes scabiei, causing scabies.

Scabies —A highly contagious skin disease caused by the itch mite, Sarcoptes scabiei. The female itch mite bores into the skin forming burrows, most commonly on the hands between the fingers, attended by intense itching and eczema caused by scratching.

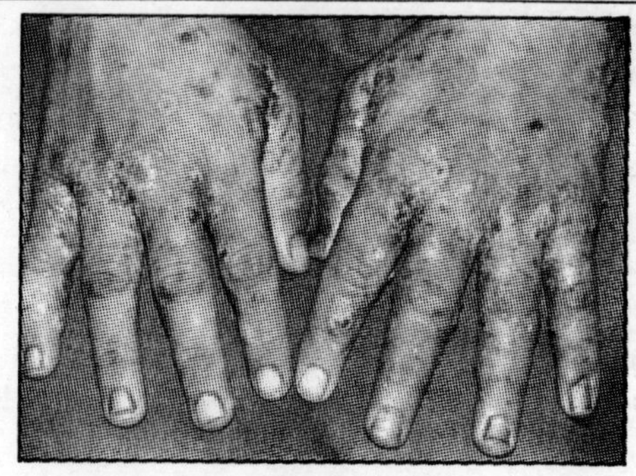

Fig. 500 : Scabies

Scabietic —Pertaining to scabies.

Scabieticide —Scabicide.

Scabiphobia —Morbid fear of acquiring scabies.

Scabrities —1. Scaliness and roughness of the skin. 2. Roughness of the inner surface of the eyelids.

Scala —Any of the three spiral ducts of the cochlea.

Scalae —Plural of scala.

Scald —To burn with hot liquid or vapor or a burnt in this way.

Scalding —A burning pain on urinating.

Scale —1. A small, thin crust covering the skin. 2. An instrument for the measurement of some property as temperature, weight, length and breadth and hardness etc. 3. Layer of tartar on the teeth. 4. To remove the layer of tartar from the teeth.

Scaled —Having scales or crusted.

Scalene —Having unequal sides and angles, said of a triangle.

Scalenectomy —Resection of a scalenus muscle.

Scalenotomy —To make an incision in a scalenus muscle.

Scaler —A dental instrument for removal of calculus from the teeth.

Scaling —Removal of tartar or calculus from the teeth.

Scall —Dermatitis of the scalp producing eruption with crust formation from drying up of the discharge.

Scalloping —A series of indentations on a normally smooth margin of a structure.

Scalp —Covering of the cranium, which includes skin with hair and subcutaneous tissue etc.

Scalpel —A small, straight surgical knife with a convex edge.

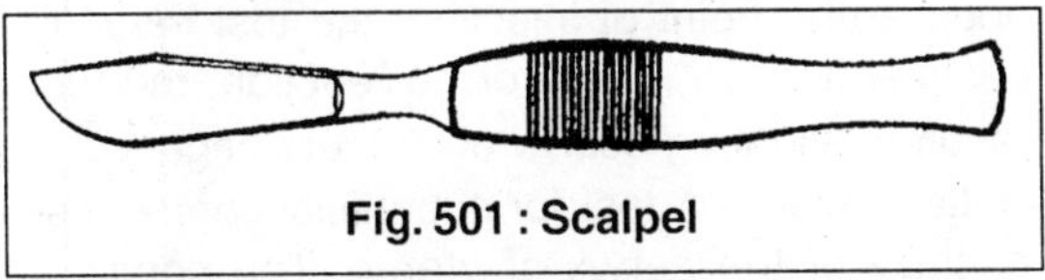

Fig. 501 : Scalpel

Scalpriform —Shaped like a chisel.

Scalprum —A toothed instrument for removing the bone pieces.

Scaly —Resembling or characterized by scales.

Scan —1. Short form of scintiscan, identified by the name of the organ examined, *e.g.*, brain scan, thyroid scan, liver scan etc. 2. An image, record or data obtained by scanning, usually identified by the technology or device employed, *e.g.*, computed tomography scan, (CT scan), ultrasound scan etc.

Scanner —An apparatus used for scanning.

Scanning —Recording on a photographic plate the emission of radioactive waves, from a specific substance injected into the body, which is concentrated in a specific tissue such as the thyroid gland, brain or liver.

Scanty —Too much less or insufficient.

Scapha —Scaphoid fossa. Elongated depression of the ear between the helix and antihelix.

Scapho- —A prefix which means boat.

Scaphocephalic —Having boat-shaped head.

Scaphocephalism —The condition of having a boat-shaped head.

Scaphocephalous —Scaphocephalic.

Scaphocephaly —Scaphocephalism.

Scaphohydrocephalous —Scaphohydrocephaly.

Scaphohydrocephaly —Hydrocephaly and scaphocephaly combined.

Scaphoid —1. Boat-shaped. 2. A proximal boat-shaped bone of the carpus or tarsus.

Scaphoid fossa —Scapha.

Scaphoiditis —Inflammation of the scaphoid bone.

Scapi —Plural of scapus.

Scapula —Shoulder blade. The large, flat, triangular bone forming the posterior part of the shoulder, which articulates with clavicle and humerus bones.

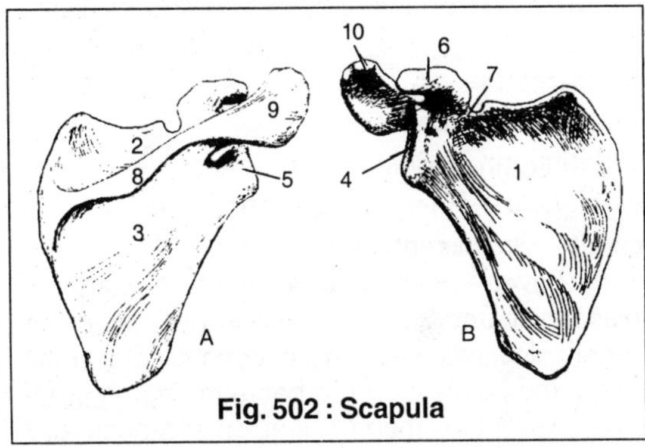

Fig. 502 : Scapula

A- Posterior aspect, B- Anterior aspect
1. Subscapular fossa
2. Supraspinous fossa
3. Infraspinous fossa
4. Glenoid cavity
5. Neck of scapula
6. Coracoid process
7. Notch
8. Spine
9. and 10. Acromial process

Scapulalgia —Pain occurring in the region of the scapula bone.

Scapular —Of, or pertaining to, the scapula bone.

Scapulary —A shoulder bandage.

Scapulectomy —Surgical excision or resection of the scapula bone.

Scapulo- —Combining form which means shoulder.

Scapuloclavicular —Pertaining to the scapula and clavicle bone.

Scapulodynia —Pain occurring in the shoulder.

Scapulohumeral —Pertaining to the scapula and humerus bone.

Scapulopexy —Fixation of the scapula bone to the ribs.

Scapulothoracic —Pertaining to the scapula bone and the thorax.

Scapus —Shaft.

Scar —Cicatrix. A mark left after healing of a wound or injury.

Scarification —The making of numerous superficial incisions or scratches in the skin.

Scarificator —Scarifier. An instrument for making small incisions in the skin.

Scarifier —Scarificator.

Scarify —To produce scarification.

Scarlatina —Scarlet fever.

Scarlatinal —Pertaining to or caused by scarlatina.

Scarlatinella —A mild disease resembling measles and scarlet fever.

Scarlatiniform —Resembling scarlatina.

Scarlatinoid —Resembling scarlet fever.

Scarlet —Bright red color.

Scarlet fever—Scarlatina. An acute contagious disease characterized by sore throat, fever with rapid pulse, followed by rash consisting of small bright red points on a red base, fading on pressure. The rash appears first on the neck and chest, rapidly extends over the body and finally involves the extremities with subsequent desquamation. With the appearance of rash the tongue becomes coated with white fur and papillae are enlarged.

Scatacratia —Fecal incontinence.

Scatemia —Toxemia caused by absorption of toxin from the intestine.

Scato- —A prefix denoting relationship to dung or feces.

Scatologic —Concerning fecal matter.

Scatology —Coprology.

Scatoma —Fecaloma. Stercoroma.

Scatophagy —Coprophagy. Rhypophagy.

Scatoscopy —Examination of the feces for diagnostic purposes.

Scatter —Diffusion of X-rays, produced by a medium through which the rays pass. When the X-rays are reflected by striking an object, they scatter backwards, and thus are known as back scatter.

Scattergram —A display of data on a chart so that each value is indicated by a symbol.

Scatula —A square pillbox.

Scavenger cell —The phagocytic cell which by process of phagocytosis removes the waste matter and thus acts as scavenger, *e.g.*, macrophage or a neutrophil leukocyte.

Scavenging —The act of cleaning.

Scelalgia —Pain in the leg.

Schema —A plan, shape, outline or diagram.

Schemata —Plural of schema.

Schematic —Pertaining to a plan, shape, outline or diagram.

Schematograph —An instrument for making a tracing in reduced size of the outline of the body.

Scheme —Plan.

Scheroma —Xerophthalmia. The disease caused by the deficiency of lacrimal fluid.

Schick test —A test for determining the degree of immunity to diphtheria, by giving an intradermal injection of 0.1 ml. of dilute diphtheria toxin. If after 3 to 4 days a red inflamed area is developed at the point of injection, the test result is postive. If there is little or no reaction, the test result is slightly positive or entirety negative.

Schiller's test —A test for superficial cancer, especially of the cervix of uterus. The cervix is painted with iodine solution. Cancer cells due to absence of glycogen do not stain with iodine solution, by which their presence can be detected.

Schilling's classification —Classification of the polymorphonuclear neutrophils into 4 categories according to the number and arrangement of their nuclei.

Schindylesis —A form of joint in which one bone is fitted into a groove of another.

Schisto- —A prefix meaning split or cleft.

Schistocelia —Congenital fissure of the abdomen.

Schistocephalus —A fetus with a cleft head.

Schistocormia —A fetus with a cleft trunk.

Schistocystis —Fissure of the bladder.

Schistocyte —A fragment of a red blood cell seen in the blood in hemolytic anemia.

Schistocytosis —Presence of schistocytes in the blood.

Schistoglossia —A cleft tongue.

Schistomelia —Congenital cleft of a limb.

Schistomelus —A fetus with a cleft limb.

Schistoprosopia —Congenital fissure of the face.

Schistoprosopus —A fetus with a fissured face.

Schistorrhachis —Spina bifida. Protrusion of the membranes through a congenital fissure in the lower portion of the vertebral column.

Schistosoma —A genus of blood flukes belonging to the family Schistosomatidae, class trematoda.

Schistosome —Common name for a member of genus Schistosoma.

Schistosomia —A deformed fetus with a fissure in abdomen with the rudimentary limbs, if they are present.

Schistosomiasis —A parasitic disease caused by blood fluke Schistosoma.

Schistosomicide —Destroying schistosomes.

Schistosomus —Schistosomia.

Schistosternia —Schistothorax.

Schistothorax —Fissure of the thorax.

Schistotrachelus —A fetus with a cleft in the neck.

Schizaxon —An axon dividing into two nearly equal branches.

Schizencephaly —A deformd fetus with a longitudinal cleft in the skull.

Schizo- —Combining form indicating division.

Schizoblepharia —Fissure of an eyelid.

Schizocyte —Schistocyte.

Schizocytosis —Schistocytosis.

Schizogenesis—Reproduction by fission.

Schizogony —The asexual reproduction of a sporozoite by multiple fission within the body of the host, giving rise to merozoites, especially in the life cycle of malarial parasite.

Schizogyria —A cleft in the cerebral convolutions.

Schizoid —Resembling or affected with schizophrenia.

Schizoidism —The condition of being affected with schizophrenia.

Schizomycete —Any organism belonging to the class Schizomycetes.

Schizomycetes —A class of plant microorganisms including bacteria that multiply by fission.

Schizomycetic —Pertaining to or caused by a schizomycete.

Schizont —1. A stage appearing in the life cycle of a sporozoite resulting from multiple fission. 2. A stage in asexual phase of life cycle of malarial parasite in red blood cells.

Schizonticide —Destroying schizonts.

Schizonychia —Splitting of the nails.

Schizophasia —Disordered speech.

Schizophrenia —A mental disorder characterized by deterioration of mental activity. The patient has delusions, hallucinations, ambivalence, incoherence of speech, and of the daily works with thoughts, loss of emotion, loss of interest, withdrawal from the real world to imaginary world and regressive behavior.

Acute schizophrenia —Schizophrenia in which the symptoms occur abruptly, which may subside or become chronic over time.

Ambulatory schizophrenia —A mild form of schizophrenia in which the patient is not required to be admitted in the hospital.

Catatonic schizophrenia —A form of schizophrenia in which the patient remains quite inactive or becomes very excited, sometimes even violent.

Paranoid schizophrenia —Schizophrenia characterized by delusions of grandeur or persecution.

Reactive schizophrenia —Schizophrenia caused by environmental conditions.

Undifferentiated schizophrenia —A form of schizophrenia which cannot be classified under other forms of schizophrenia and characterized by delusions, incoherence, or grossly disorganized behavior.

Schizophrenic —Pertaining to, or affected with schizophrenia.

Schizoprosopia —Fissure of the face.

Schizotonia —Uneven tone of the muscle groups.

Schizotrichia —Splitting of hair at the ends.

Schizozoite —Merozoite.

Schneiderian membrane —Mucous membrane of the nose.

Schonlein's disease —Purpura, idiopathic thrombocytopenic. An allergic purpura occurring with drug sensitivities, serum sickness, and other allergic disorders, usually accompanied by pain in the joints and abdomen.

Schuffner's dots —Granules present in the red blood cells when they are infected by malarial parasite, Plasmodium vivax.

Schwalbe's ring —The peripheral margin of Descemet's membrane of the eye.

Schwann cell —A cell of the peripheral nervous system that form the myelin sheath and neurilemma of the peripheral nerve fibers.

Schwannoma —A benign tumor of the neurilemma.

Schwannosis —Hypertrophy of the sheath of Schwann of a nerve or neurilemma.

Schwann's sheath —Neurilemma.

Sciage —A sawing movement of the hand in massage.

Sciatic —1. Pertaining to the sciatic nerve or ischium. 2. Pertaining to, caused by, or afflicted with sciatica.

Sciatica —Pain in the leg along the course of sciatic nerve felt at the back of thigh running down the inside of the leg. It is caused by inflammation, injury or compression of the sciatic nerve.

Sciatic nerve —Largest nerve in the body, which arises from the sacral plexus on each side, passes from the pelvis through greater sciatic foramen, down the back of the thigh where it divides into tibial and peroneal nerves.

Science —Systematic knowledge.

Scientific —Pertaining to science.

Scientist —One learned in science.

Scieropia —Defective vision in which the things appear to be in a shadow.

Scintigram —An image produced by scintiphotography.

Scintigraphy —Scintiphotography.

Scintillascope —An apparatus for viewing the effect of ionizing radiation, alpha particles, on a fluorescent screen.

Scintillation —A spark emitting from the body produced by radioactive substances.

Scintiphotograph —The image obtained by scintiphotography.

Scintiphotography —Scintigraphy. To take the photographs of the sparks emitted by radioactive substances injected into body. It is performed to determine the out line and function of organs and tissues in which the radioactive substance is collected.

Scintiscan —To produce a map of sparks produced by a radioactive substance injected into the body, by using scintiphotography. The intensity of the map indicates the differential accumulation of a substance in the various parts of the body.

Scintiscanner —The apparatus used in doing scintiscan.

Scintography —Scintiphotography.

Scirrhoid —Pertaining to, or resembling a hard carcinoma.

Scirrhoma —A hard carcinoma or scirrhus.

Scirrhosarca —Hardening of the flesh, especially of the newborn infant.

Scirrhous —Hard or hardened.

Scirrhus —Hard cancerous tumor due to overgrowth of fibrous tissue.

Scission —Dividing, cutting or splitting.

Scissiparity —Schizogenesis.

Scissor gait —See gait.

Scissura —A cleft or fissure.

Scissurae —Plural of scissura.

Scler- —A prefix which means hardness or relationship to sclera.

Sclera —A tough white fibrous tissue, covering approximately the posterior five-sixths surface of the eyeball, which is continuous anteriorly with the cornea and posteriorly with the external sheath of optic nerve.

Scleradenitis —Inflammation and induration of a gland.

Sclerae —Plural of sclera.

Scleral —Pertaining to the sclera.

Scleratogenous —Sclerogenous.

Sclerectasia —Protrusion of the sclera.

Sclerectoiridectomy —Partial excision of the sclera and of the iris.

Sclerectoiridodialysis —Sclerectomy and iridodialysis.

Sclerectomy —1. Excision of a part of the sclera. 2. Removal of adhesions after otitis media.

Scleredema —Chronic progressive thickening and hardness of the skin occurring mostly in children and women, and beginning from the head and neck spreads downwards to the body.

Sclerema —Scleroderma. Hardening of the skin.

Sclerencephalia —Sclerosis of the brain.

Sclerencephaly —Sclerencephalia.

Scleriasis —Hardening of the skin or of the eyelid.

Scleriritomy —To make an incision into the sclera and iris.

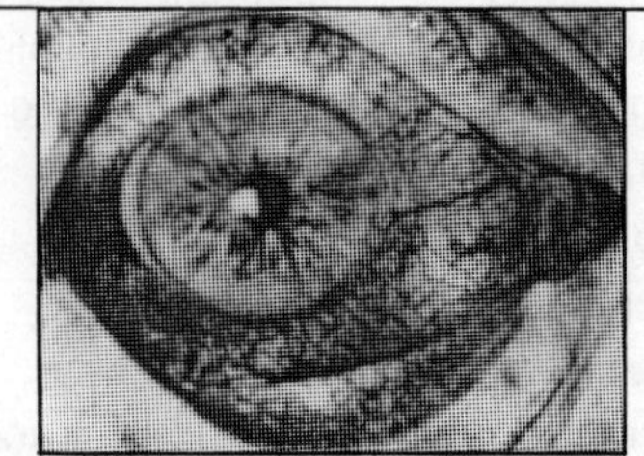

Fig. 503 : Scleritis

Scleritis —Sclerotitis.

Scleroatrophy —Sclerotylosis.

Scleroblastema —The embryonic tissue from which bone is formed.

Scleroblastemic —Pertaining to or derived from scleroblastema.

Sclerocataracta —A hard cataract.

Sclerochoroidal —Pertaining to both the sclera and the choroid.

Sclerochoroiditis —Inflammation of the sclera and choroid.

Scleroconjunctival —Pertaining to the sclera and conjunctiva.

Scleroconjunctivitis —Inflammation of the sclera and conjunctiva.

Sclerocornea —The sclera and cornea both combined as one coat.

Sclerodactylia —Acroscleroderma.

Sclerodactyly —Sclerodactylia.

Scleroderma —Chronic hardening and shrinkage of the skin and any part of the body including heart, lungs, kidneys and gastrointestinal tract.

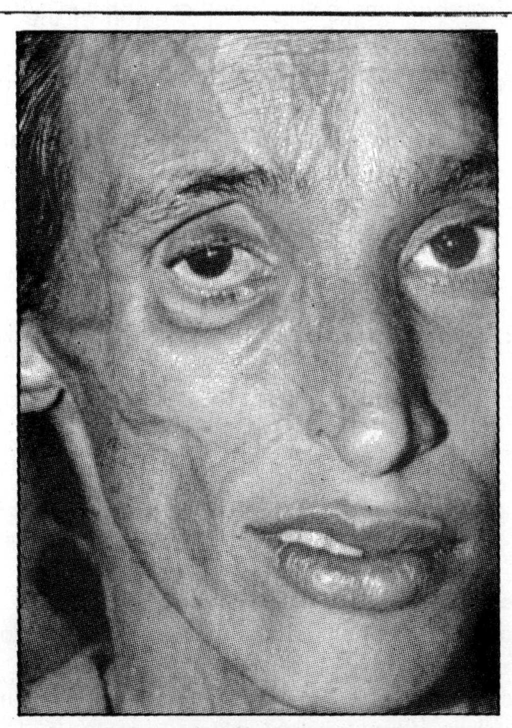

Fig. 504 : Scleroderma

Sclerodermatitis —Inflammation of the skin with thickening and hardening.

Sclerodermatous —Pertaining to scleroderma.

Sclerogenic —Sclerogenous.

Sclerogenous —Producing sclerosis or hardening of the tissue.

Scleroid —Having hard texture.

Scleroiritis —Inflammation of both the sclera and iris.

Sclerokeratitis—Inflammation of the sclera and cornea.

Sclerokeratoiritis —Inflammation of the sclera, cornea and iris.

Sclerokeratosis —Sclerokeratitis.

Scleroma —A circumscribed, indurated area of granulation tissue in the mucous membrane or skin.

Scleromalacia —Softening of the sclera.

Scleromere —1. Any segment or metamere of the skeleton. 2. The caudal half of a sclerotome.

Sclerometer —An instrument for determining the density or hardness of a substance.

Scleromyxedema —A form of lichen myxedematosus characterized by generalized eruption of the nodule and diffuse thickening of the skin.

Scleronychia —Hardening and thickening of the nails.

Scleronyxis—Surgical puncture of the sclera.

Sclero-oophoritis —Sclerosis and inflammation of the ovary.

Sclerophthalmia —Congenital advancement of sclera upon the cornea leaving only the central part clear.

Scleroplasty —Plastic surgery of the sclera.

Scleroprotein —A simple protein insoluble in chemicals and fibrous in structure, found in bones, cartilages, hair and nails, which support or protect the body.

Sclerosal —Sclerous.

Sclerosant —Causing sclerosis.

Sclerose —To become, or cause to become, hardened or sclerotic.

Sclerosed —1. Affected with sclerosis. 2. Hardened.

Sclerosing —Causing sclerosis.

Scleroses —Plural of sclerosis.

Sclerosis—A hardening or induration of an organ or tissue, due to inflammation, degeneration or fibrous tissue formation.

Amyotrophic lateral sclerosis—Progressive muscular atrophy resulting from degeneration of the anterior horn cells and pyramidal tract. It rapidly progresses and usually ends in bulbar paralysis.

Arterial sclerosis —Arteriosclerosis. Hardening of the coats of the arteries.

Arteriolar sclerosis —Arteriolosclerosis. Hardening of the coats of the arterioles.

Diffuse sclerosis —Hardening of the large areas of the brain and spinal cord.

Disseminated sclerosis —Multiple sclerosis.

Scleroskeleton —Bones formed as a result of ossification of the fibrous structures, such as ligaments, fasciae and tendons.

Sclerostenosis —Hardening combined with contraction of the tissues.

Sclerostomy —To make an incision into the sclera.

Sclerotherapy —Treatment of piles by using sclerosing agents.

Sclerothrix —Brittleness of the hair.

Sclerotic —1. Pertaining to or affected with sclerosis. 2. Pertaining to sclera.

Sclerotica —Sclera.

Scleroticectomy —Sclerectomy.

Scleroticochoroiditis —Sclerochoroiditis.

Scleroticonyxis —Scleronyxis.

Scleroticopuncture —Scleronyxis. Scleroticonyxis.

Scleroticotomy —Sclerotomy.

Sclerotitis —Scleritis. Inflammation of the sclera

Sclerotome —1. A knife used in the incision of sclera. 2. One of the segments of mesenchymal tissue lying on each side of the notochord, which develop into vertebrae and ribs.

Sclerotomy —Scleroticotomy. To make an incision into the sclera.

Sclerotrichia —Hardness and brittleness of the hair.

Sclerous —Hard or indurated.

Scobinate —Having a rough, uneven or nodular surface.

Scoleces —Plural of scolex.

Scoleciform —Like a scolex.

Scolecoid —Resembling a worm.

Scolecology —Helminthology.

Scolex —The head of the tapeworm containing hooks or suckers by which it attaches itself to the wall of the intestine.

Scoliokyphosis —Scoliosis and kyphosis combined.

Scolioma —Curvature of the vertebral column.

Scoliometer —An apparatus for measuring the curvatures, especially the lateral curvatures of the vertebral column.

Scoliorachitic —Pertaining to, or afflicted with curvature of the spinal column caused by rickets.

Scoliosiometry —Scoliosometry. Measurement of the curvatures of the vertebral column.

Scoliosis —Lateral curvature of the vertebral column.

Congenital scoliosis —Scoliosis present since birth.

Coxitic scoliosis —Scoliosis occurring in the lumbar region caused by tilting of the pelvis in hip disease.

Empyematic scoliosis —Scoliosis following empyema and retraction of one side of the chest.

Functional scoliosis —Scoliosis that is actually not caused by a deformity in the vertebral column but by another condition such as unequal length of the legs.

Habit scoliosis —Scoliosis due to habitually assumed improper posture or position.

Idiopathic scoliosis —Scoliosis due to unknown causes.

Inflammatory scoliosis —Scoliosis due to inflammatory disease of the vertebrae.

Ischiatic scoliosis —Scoliosis due to a hip disease.

Myopathic scoliosis —Scoliosis due to weakness of the spinal muscles.

Osteopathic scoliosis —Scoliosis caused by bony deformity of the vertebral column.

Rachitic scoliosis —Scoliosis due to rickets.

Sciatic scoliosis —Scoliosis due to sciatica.

Static scoliosis —Scoliosis due to unequal length of the legs.

Scoliosometry —Scoliosiometry.

Scoliotic —Pertaining to, or afflicted with, scoliosis.

Scoliotone —An apparatus for correcting the curvature of the vertebral column in scoliosis.

Scoop —Spoon-shaped surgical instrument.

-scope —A suffix meaning an instrument for viewing or examining.

Scopometer —An instrument for measuring the density of a suspension.

Scopophilia —Voyeurism.

Scopophobia —Morbid fear of being seen.

Scopophobiac —The person who is afraid of being seen.

-scopy —A suffix meaning examination or inspection.

Scoracratia —Scatacratia. Inability to retain feces.

Scorbutic —Pertaining to or affected with scurvy.

Scorbutigenic —Causing scurvy.

Scorbutus —Scurvy.

Scordinema —Yawning and stretching with fatigue and heaviness of the head, a prodromal symptom of some infectious disease.

Score —Reckoning as compared to a standard one.

Apgar score —A numerical expression of an infant's condition, usually determined one minute after birth. The heart rate, respiration, muscle tone, response to stimuli and color, each graded 0, 1 or 2. The maximum total score is 10. Those with low scores require immediate attention if they are to survice.

Scoretemia —Scatemia.

Scoto- —A prefix indicating relationship to darkness.

Scotochromogen —Any microorganism that produces a pigment (chromogen) when grown in light or darkness.

Scotodinia —Vertigo with black spots before the eyes and faintness of vision.

Scotogram, Scotograph —A record of the effect of a radiation made on a photographic plate in the dark.

Scotograph —Scotogram.

Scotoma —An area of depressed vision in the visual field, surrounded by an aea of less depressed or normal vision.

Scotomagraph —An apparatus for recording scotomata.

Scotomata —Plural of scotoma.

Scotomatous —Pertaining to, of the nature of, or afflicted with scotoma.

Scotometer —An instrument for detecting and measuring scotoma in the visual field.

Scotometry —The detection and measurement of scotomata.

Scotomization —The development of scotomata, especially mental scotomata wherein the patient denies the existence of everything, that conflicts his or her ego.

Scotophilia —Nyctophilia. Attraction for darkness or night.

Scotophobia —Nyctophobia. Morbid fear of darkness or night.

Scotopia —Night vision. Adjustment of the eyes for the vision in dark or night.

Scotopic —Pertaining to scotopia.

Scotopsin —The protein portion of the rods of the retina of the eye.

Scotoscopy —Skiascopy. Examination of the internal organs by fluoroscope.

Scraping —An abrading.

Scratch —1. A mark or superficial wound made by scraping with the nails or with a sharp instrument. 2. To rub the skin, especially with the fingernails, to relieve itching.

Scratching —Abrading.

Scratch test —To place a few drops on a scratched area of the skin, of appropriately diluted solution of the test material, suspected of being an allergen. If the material is an allergen, a wheal will be developed within 15 minutes.

Screatus —A neurosis characterized by sudden periodic attacks of hawking or snoring.

Screen —1. A flat area upon which moving pictures or slides are viewed or X-ray pictures are visualized. 2. To make a fluoroscopic examination. 3. A structure or substance resembling a curtain used to protect from a damaging effect as that of X-rays or sun rays, or as a shield 4. General examination of the body to determine the presence of a disease or symptoms. 5. Selection of the employees.

Screening —1. An examination of a large number of people to determine the presence of a particular disease, *e.g.*, chest X-ray for tuberculosis. 2. Fluoroscopy.

Screw-worm —Spiral worm.

Scribe —To write, trace or mark by making a line with a pointed instrument.

Scrobiculate —Pitted.

Scrobiculus cordis —Epigastric fossa.

Scrofula —Tuberculous cervical lymphadenitis.

Scrofulide —Scrofuloderma.

Scrofuloderma —Tuberculous infection of the skin, usually secondary to tuberculous cervical lymphadenitis, marked by ulcers resulting usually from a tuberculous sinus.

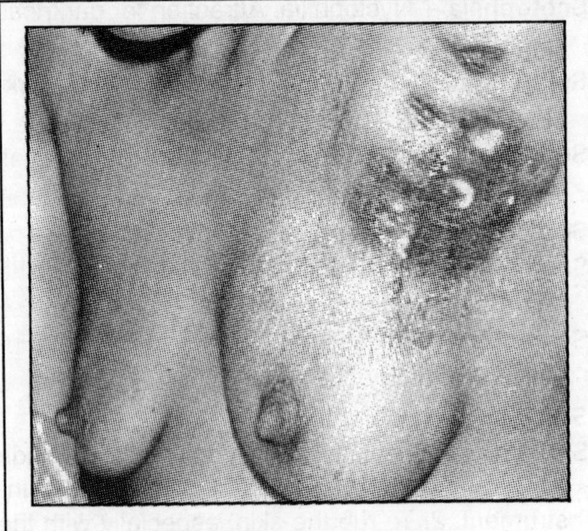

Fig. 505 : Scrofuloderma

Scrofulosis —Scrofula.

Scrofulous —Pertaining to, or afflicted with scrofula or scrofuloderma.

Scrotal —Pertaining to the scrotum.

Scrotectomy —Excision of a part of the scrotum.

Scrotiform —Scrotum-shaped.

Scrotitis —Inflammation of the scrotum.

Scrotocele —Scrotal hernia.

Scrotoplasty —Plastic surgery on the scrotum.

Scrotum —A pouch in the male containing testis with epididymis and part of the spermatic cord.

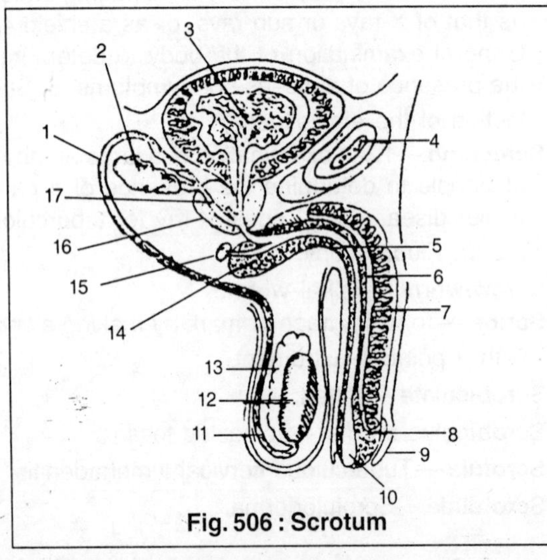

Fig. 506 : Scrotum

1. Vas deferens, 2. Seminal vesicle, 3. Urinary bladder, 4. Symphysis pubis, 5. Urethra, 6. Corpus spongiosum, 7. Corpus cavernosum, 8. Glans penis, 9. Prepuce, 10. Urethral dilatation 11. Scrotum, 12. Testis 13. Epididymis, 14. Dilatation of the corpus spongiosum, 15. Cowper's gland, 16. Prostate gland, 17. Ejaculatory duct

Scrubbing—Cleaning by rubbing hardly.

Scruple —20 grains or 1.296 gms.

Scum —A small thin layer of bacteria or impurities floating on the surface of a culture.

Scurf —Dandruff.

Scurvy —A disease due to deficiency of ascorbic acid (vitamin C) characterized by anemia, spongy gums with a tendency of bleeding, subcutaneous hemorrhage and hemorrhage from the mucous membrane, loosening of the teeth, pain in the limbs and joints and great weakness.

Scuta —Plural of scutum.

Scutate —Scutiform.

Scute —A thin plate, especially the bony plate separating the upper tympanic cavity and mastoid cells.

Scutiform —Shield-shaped.

Scutula —Plural of scutulum.

Scutular —Having small indented crusts of the skin.

Scutulum —A yellow cup-shaped crust due to fungus infection over the hair follicle on the scalp, accompanied by itching.

Scutum —Scute.

Scybala—Plural of scybalum.

Scybalous —Of the nature of, or composed of hard fecal matter.

Scybalum —A hard mass of fecal matter in the intestine.

Scyphiform —Scyphoid.

Scypho- —A prefix meaning cup.

Scyphoid —Cup-shaped.

S. D. —1. Skin dose 2. Standard deviation.

SDA —Specific dynamic action.

S.E. —Standard error.

Seal —1. To close firmly. 2. The material such as an adhesive or wax used to close airtight. 3. An impression of a stamp made on a paper.

Sealant —A material used as an airtight closure.

Searcher —Sound. An instrument for detecting the stones in the bladder.

Seasickness—Motion sickness caused by travelling in the ship.

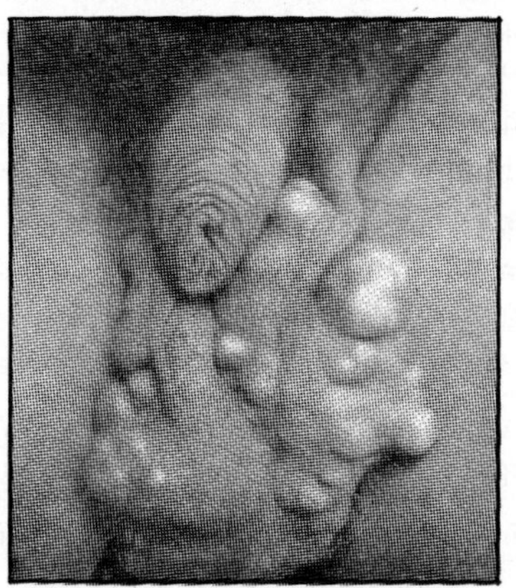

Fig. 507 : Multiple sebaceous cysts in the scrotum

Seat —The structure upon which another structure rests or is supported.

Seatworm —Pinworm.

Seb- —A prefix which means sebum.

Sebaceous —Pertaining to, containing or secreting sebum.

Sebaceous cyst —A cyst filled with sebum.

Sebaceous glands —The glands of the skin secreting sebum, which open into the hair follicles.

Sebastomania —Theomania. Religious madness.

Sebiagogic —Sebiferous.

Sebiferous —Sebiparous.

Sebiparous —Sebiferous. Producing sebum or fatty matter.

Sebolite, Sebolith —Calculus in a sebaceous gland.

Seborrhagia —Seborrhea.

Seborrhea —Excessive secretion of the sebaceous glands.

Seborrheic —Afflicted with or like seborrhea.

Seborrheid —Seborrheic dermatitis.

Seborrhoic —Seborrheic.

Sebotropic —Stimulating the secretion of sebum from the sebaceous glands.

Sebum —The oily secretion of the sebaceous glands of the skin.

Sec. —Abbreviation for second.

Secernent —Secreting.

Seclusion of pupil —Synechia, annular.

Secodont —Having molar teeth with cutting edges on the cusps.

Secondaries —1. Secondary metastasis. 2. Lesions of secondary syphilis.

Secondary —1. Next to or second in order 2. Produced by a parimary cause.

Secondary areola —Pigmentation around the nipples during pregnancy.

Secondary hemorrhage —Hemorrhage appearing more than 24 hours after an injury or operation or from the uterus after delivery, that is due to sepsis.

Secondary radiation —X-rays produced by the interaction between primary radiation and the substance being radiated.

Second intention —Healing by adhesion of two granulated surfaces.

Second sight—Alteration in refractive powers of lens of the eye so that reading is possible again without glasses, in incipient cataract.

Secreta —The products of secretion.

Secretagogue —Secretogogue. Stimulating or causing secretion.

Secrete —To form a secretion.

Secretin —A hormone secreted by the mucous membrane of duodenum and jejunum when acid chyme enters the intestine. It stimulates the secretion of pancreatic juice and bile and intestinal secretion.

Secretinase —An enzyme of the serum that inactivates secretin.

Secretion —1. The process by which a glandular organ produces a substance. 2. The substance produced by a glandular organ. If the substance flows out through a duct, *e.g.*, saliva, it is called an external secretion, if it is returned to the blood or lymph, *e.g.*, insulin, it is called an internal secretion.

Secretogogue —Secretagogue.

Secretoinhibitory —Inhibiting secretion.

Secretomotor —That, especially a nerve which stimulates secretion.

Secretor —One who secretes the substances of blood group ABO into the mucous secretions such as saliva or gastric juice.

Secretory —Pertaining to or promoting secretion.

Sectarian —A medical practitioner who adopts unscientific methods of treatment such as sorcery or religious acts etc.

Sectile —Capable of being cut.

Sectio —Section.

Section —1. Process of cutting, *e.g.*, sesarean section—to incise the abdominal wall and uterus for delivery of the infant. 2. A segment or division of an organ or part of the body. 3. A surface made by cutting.

Sectioning —The cutting of very thin sections of tissues for examination under the microscope.

Sectioning ultrathin —The cutting of extra-ordinary thin (less than 1 micron in thickness) sections, especially for examination under electron microscope.

Sector —The area of a circle between two radii and an arc.

Sectoranopia —Loss of vision in a sector of the visual field.

Sectorial —Cutting.

Secunda —Secondary.

Secundigravida —The woman who is pregnant for the second time.

Secundina —Secondary. That which follows.

Secundines —Afterbirth. Placenta, umbilical cord and the membranes that are expelled during the third stage of labor, *i.e.*, after birth of a child.

Secundipara —A woman who has produced two infants at separate times, each weighing 500 grams or more, whether they are viable or not.

Secundiparity —The condition of being secundipara.

Secundis Horis —Every two hours.

Secundum artem —According to the rule.

Sedate —To calm.

Sedation —1. The allaying of excitement, especially by the administration of a sedative. 2. The state of being calmed.

Sedative —Soothing. Calming. Allaying excitement. Sedative may be local, general, nervous or cardiac.

Sedentary —1. Sitting habitually or of the habit of not doing physical work. 2. Pertaining to an occupation requiring minimal physical exercise.

Sedigitate —Sexdigitate. Having six digits on, one or both hands or feet.

Sediment —Precipitate. The substance that settles down at the bottom of a liquid.

Sedimentate —To cause the formation of a sediment.

Sedimentation —Precipitation. Formation of sediment.

Sedimentation rate —Erythrocyte sedimentation rate (ESR). The rate at which red blood cells in the blood in a long, narrow tube settle down, which is the distance the red blood cells fall in one hour. It is normally less than 10 mm per hour in males and slightly higher in females.

Sedimentator —A centrifugal machine.

Sedimentometer —An apparatus for recording the sedimentation rate of the blood.

Seed —1. The mature ovule of a plant. 2. Semen. 3. A capsule containing radium used in radium therapy for the treatment of cancer. 4. To introduce the microorganisms into a culture medium.

Segment —A part or section of an organ or body, lobe, a small piece.

Segmenta —Plural of segmentum.

Segmental —Pertaining to, resembling, or composed of segments.

Segmentation —Cleavage. Division into similar parts.

Segmentectomy —Removal of an anatomic segment of any organ or gland by surgery.

Segmented —Divided into segments.

Segmenter —A stage in the development of the malarial parasite plasmodium in the red blood cell in which the parasite undergoes schizogony.

Segmentum —Segment.

Segregation —Separation.

Segregator —An instrument consisting of two ureteral catheters for obtaining urine from each kidney separately.

Seguin's signal symptom —Involuntary contractions of the muscles occurring just before an attack of epilepsy.

Seisesthesia —Perception of concussion.

Seismesthesia —Perception of vibrations.

Seismotherapy —Sismotherapy.

Seizure —A sudden attack of pain, or of a disease such as epilepsy.

- **Clonic seizure** —See convulsion.
- **Convulsive seizure** —An attack of epilepsy.
- **Febrile seizure** —See convulsion.
- **Grand mal seizure** —See epilepsy.
- **Jacksonian seizure** —See epilepsy.
- **Myoclonic seizure** —See epilepsy.
- **Petit mal seizure** —See epilepsy.

Selection —The process of choosing or selecting.

Selective —Capable to be selected.

Selene unguium —A small semilunar structure of the nail.

Self —In immunology, an individual's own antigenic make-up.

Self-abuse —Masturbation.

Self-analysis —Autoanalysis.

Self-concept —An individual's perception of self in relation to others and the environment.

Self-conscious —Conscious of one's self.

Self-consciousness —Self-conscious state.

Self-defence —Defence of one's self.

Self-differentiation—The differentiation of a structure or tissue resulting from the action of intrinsic causes.

Self-digestion —Autodigestion.

Self-efficacy —Personal judgement of own's ability to succeed in reaching a specific goal.

Self-esteem —Self-concept.

Self-hypnosis —Hypnotizing one self.

Self-infection —Autoinfection.

Self-limited —Denoting a disease that without treatment tends to cease after a definite period, *e.g.*, influenza.

Self-registering —Automatically registering.

Self-tolerance —Tolerance to self-antigens.

Sella —Saddle.

Sellar —Concerning the sella turcica.

Sella turcica —A depression on the upper surface of the sphenoid bone, in which the pituitary gland is situated.

Semantics —Study of the meanings of words and the rules of their use.

Semeiography —A description of the signs and symptoms of a disease.

Semeiology —Symptomatology.

Semeiosis —Study of the disease by symptoms.

Semeiotic —Symptomatic. Of, or pertaining to symptoms.

Semeiotics —Symptomatology.

Semelincident —Occurring only once in a person.

Semen —A thick, opalescent, viscid secretion discharged at ejaculation from urethra of the male. It consists of the secretions of various glands associated with urogenital tract (prostate etc.) and contains spermatozoa which have been produced in the testes and stored in the seminal vesicles.

Semenarche —The beginning of the production of the semen during puberty.

Semenuria —Seminuria. Spermaturia.

Semi- —A prefix meaning half.

Semicanal —A canal which opens at one side.

Semicartilaginous —Partially cartilaginous.

Semicircular —In the form of a half circle.

Semicircular canals —Superior, posterior and inferior canals of the inner ear.

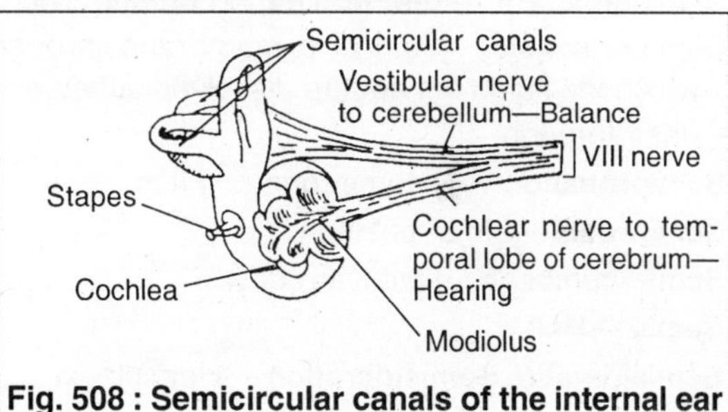

Fig. 508 : Semicircular canals of the internal ear

Semicoma —Partial impairment of the consciousness from which the patient may be aroused.

Semicomatose —One who is in semicoma state.

Semiconscious —Semicomatose.

Semicrista —A small or rudimentary crest.

Semidecussation —Incomplete crossing of the nerve fibers.

Semierection —An incomplete erection.

Semiflexion —Position of a limb midway between flexion and extension.

Semilunar —Shaped like a crescent or half-moon.

Semilunar cusp —One of the three segments of the aorta, or of the pulmonary valve between the right ventricle and the pulmonary artery.

Semilunare —The lunate bone of the wrist.

Semilunar lobe —A lobe on the upper surface of the cerebellum.

Semiluxation —Subluxation.

Semimembranous —Composed partly of a membrane.

Seminal —Pertaining to semen.

Seminal duct —Spermatic duct.

Seminal emission —Discharge of semen.

Seminal filament —Spermatozoon.

Seminal fluid —Semen.

Seminal vesicle —See vesicle, seminal.

Semination —Insemination.

Seminiferous —Producing or carrying semen.

Seminoma —A malignant tumor of the testis.

Seminomatous —Pertaining to a seminoma

Seminormal —Half of the normal.

Seminuria —Semenuria. Spermaturia.

Semiology —Semeiology. Symptomatology.

Semiorbicular —Semicircular.

Semiotic —Semeiotic. Symptomatic.

Semiotics —Semeiotics. Symptomatology.

Semipenniform —Feather shaped on one side.

Semipermeable —Said of a membrane through which the fluids but not the dissolved substance pass through.

Semipronation —A semiprone position.

Semiprone —Sims' position.

Semirecumbent —Half lying down.

Semis —Half.

Semisideratio, Semisideration —Hemiplegia.

Semisolid —Partly solid.

Semisopor —Semicoma.

Semispinal —Denoting the muscles attached partially to the spinous processes of the vertebrae.

Semisulcus —A small sulcus joining with another small sulcus form a complete sulcus.

Semisupination —A position midway between supination and pronation.

Semisupine —Not completely supine.

Semisynthetic —Produced by chemical alteration of a naturally occurring substance.

Semitendinous —Being partially tendon.

Semitertian —Malarial fever which is partly tertian ann partly quotidian.

Senescence —The process of growing old.

Senile —Pertaining to old age.

Senilism —Premature old age.

Senility —The physical and mental weakness associated with the old age.

Senium —Old age.

Senopia —Gerontopia. Second sight. Improvement of the near vision of a old person, a sign of incipient cataract.

Sensate —Able to perceive touch and other sensations.

Sensation —The effect produced by impulses conveyed by a stimulated afferent nerve to the sensorium.

Cutaneous sensation —A sensation arising from the receptors of the skin.

Delayed sensation —Sensation not experienced immediately after a stimulus.

External sensation —Sensation produced by the stimuli present outside the body.

Girdle sensation —Zonesthesia.

Gnostic sensation —Sensation pertaining to knowledge, as recognizing the things by seeing or touching.

Internal sensation —Subjective sensation.

Palmesthetic sensation —Sensation felt in the skin from vibration.

Primary sensation —Sensation resulting from direct stimulus.

Referred sensation —Reflex sensation. Sensation which seems to arise from the source other than the actual one.

Subjective sensation —Internal sensation. The sensation which does not result from the stimulus outside the body but results from the stimulus present within the body itself.

Tactile sensation —A sensation produced through sense of touch.

Sense —1. The faculty by which the conditions or properties of the things outside or inside the body are perceived. 2. Power of understanding.

Color sense —The faculty by which colors are perceived and distinguished.

Kinesthetic sense —Muscular sense.

Light sense —The sense by which the degrees of intensity of light are distinguished.

Muscular sense —The sense by which muscular movements are perceived.

Position sense —Posture sense.

Posture sense —The ability through muscular sense to perceive the position or attitude of the body or its parts.

Pressure sense —The sense by which the pressure upon the surface of the body is perceived.

Sixth sense —Cenesthesia. The sense of normal functioning of the body organs.

Space sense —The sense by which the things in the space, their relationship and dimensions are recognized.

Special senses —The five senses of sight, hearing, smell, touch and taste.

Static sense —The sense that makes it possible to maintain equilibrium.

Stereognostic sense —The sense by which shape and consistency of the things held in fingers are perceived.

Tactile sense —Sense of touch.

Temperature sense —The sense by which the differences of temperature is detected.

Time sense —The sense by which differences in time intervals is detected.

Sensibility —Ability to feel, perceive or to respond to stimuli.

Deep sensibility —1. The sensibility existing after an area of the skin is made anesthetic. 2. The sensibility of deep tissue (muscle, tendon, etc.) to pressure, pain and movement.

Epicritic sensibility —Superficial sensibility. Sensibility to light touch and temperature.

Splanchnesthetic sensibility —Sensibility of the internal organs.

Sensibilization —Sensitization.

Sensible —Perceptible to the senses.

Sensiferous —Causing or transmitting sensations.

Sensigenous —Causing or starting a sensory impulse.

Sensimeter —An apparatus for recording the degree of sensitiveness of various areas of the body.

Sensitinogen —The antigens which sensitize the body.

Sensitive —Able to respond to stimuli or abnormally susceptible to a substance, as a drug or foregin protein.

Sensitivity —The condition or quality of being sensitive.

Sensitization —The process of making sensitive to a specific substance (antigen) such as a protein or pollen.

Sensitize —To make sensitive.

Sensitized —Made sensitive to a specific substance.

Sensitizer—The substance which makes the susceptible person react to the same or other irritants.

Sensitometer —An apparatus for determining the penetrating power of light.

Sensitometery —In radiology, the procedure of measuring film response to radiation by observing its density.

Sensomobile —Capable of moving in response to a stimulus.

Sensomobility —Ability for movement in response to a stimulus.

Sensomotor —Sensorimotor.

Sensor —1. A sense organ. 2. An apparatus sensitive to physical stimuli such as temperature, light, sound, radiation, magnetism or movement and equipped to record the phenomena being detected and to sound an alarm if the value falls below or rises above a certain level.

Sensorial —Pertaining to the sensorium, the area of sensation in the brain.

Sensoriglandular —Pertaining to glandular excretion in response to stimulation of a nerve.

Sensorimetabolism —Occurrence of metabolic activity in response to sensory nerve stimulation.

Sensorimotor —Sensomotor. Both sensory and motor.

Sensorimuscular —Muscular activity in response to a sensory nerve stimulation.

Sensorineural —Of or pertaining to a sensory nerve.

Sensorium —The portion of the cerebral cortex that acts as a center of sensations.

Sensorivascular —Sensorivasomotor.

Sensorivasomotor —Vascular changes occurring due to stimulation of a sensory nerve.

Sensory —1. Pertaining to the sensation. 2. Afferent.

Sensory amusia —Inability to distinguish the musical sounds.

Sensory aphasia —Inability to understand written or spoken words.

Sensory area —Any area of the cerebral cortex in which sensations are perceived.

Sensory nerve —A nerve composed of sensory fibers, or an afferent nerve conveying sensory impulses to the sensorium.

Sensory registration —Registration of a sensation in the brain.

Sensory unit —A single sensory nerve fiber with all its branches and their terminals.

Sensual —The person whose actions are dominated by emotions.

Sensualism — The condition in which one's actions are dominated by emotions.

Sensuality —Sensualism.

Sensulato —In a broad sense.

Sensuous —Pertaining to or affecting the senses.

Sensustricto —In a strict sense.

Sentient —Sensitive.

Sentiment —Emotion. Feeling.

Sentimental —Emotional.

Separation —Disuniting.

Separative —Pertaining to separation.

Separator —That which separates.

Separatorium —An instrument for separating the pericranium from the skull.

Sepsis —The presence in the blood of disease-producing microorganisms or their toxins, or the condition produced by their presence, *e.g.*, puerperal sepsis, *i.e.* infection of the genital tract following childbirth.

Septa —Plural of septum.

Septal —Pertaining to a septum.

Septan —Recurring every seventh day.

Septate —Divided by a septum.

Septectomy —Excision of a septum, esp. the nasal septum or part of it.

Septemia —Septicemia.

Septi- —A prefix meaning seven.

Septic —1. Pertaining to sepsis. 2. Pertaining to pathogenic organisms or their toxins.

Septicemia —Blood poisoning. Bacteremia. Presence of pathogenic bacteria in the blood. The condition is characterized by chills, fever, peteche and abscess formation.

Septicemic —Pertaining to, due to, or of the nature of septicemia.

Septic fever —Fever due to septicemia.

Septicophlebitis—Septic inflammation of a vein.

Septicopyemia —Septicemia and pyemia combined.

Septicopyemic —Pertaining to septicopyemia.

Septigravida —A woman pregnant for the seventh time.

Septimetritis —Inflammation of uterus due to sepsis.

Septipara —The woman who has given birth to seven children, alive or dead, each weighing 500 gms. or more.

Septivalent —Having a valency (combining power) of seven.

Septomarginal —Pertaining to the margin of a septum.

Septometer —1. An instrument for measuring the width of nasal septum. 2. An apparatus for determining bacterial contamination of the air.

Septonasal —Pertaining to the nasal septum.

Septoplasty —Plastic surgery of the nasal septum.

Septorhinoplasty —Plastic repair of the defects or deformities of both the nasal septum and the external nose.

Septostomy —Surgical formation of an opening in a septum.

Septotome —An instrument for cutting or removing a section of the nasal septum.

Septotomy —To incise a septum, especially the nasal septum.

Septula —Plural of septulum.

Septulum —A small separating wall or septum.

Septum —A wall dividing into two cavities, *e.g.*, atrial septum—a wall between atria of the heart; nasal septum—a wall dividing the nasal cavity into two portions.

Septuplet —One of seven children born from the same pregnancy.

Sequel —Sequela.

Sequela —A morbid condition following or resulting from a disease.

Sequence —Succession.

Sequential —Occurring in sequence.

Sequester —1. To separate a small portion from the whole body. 2. Sequestrum.

Sequestra —Plural of sequestrum.

Sequestral —Pertaining to a sequestrum.

Sequestrant —A sequestering agent.

Sequestration —1. The formation of sequestrum. 2. Isolation of a patient.

Sequestrectomy —Excision of a sequestrum.

Sequestrotomy —Sequestrectomy.

Sequestrum —A piece of necrosed bone separated from the surrounding tissue.

Sera —Plural of serum.

Seralbumin —Albumin of the blood.

Serendipity —An unexpected finding or result obtained during investigation on some other subject.

Serial —In numerical order, in continuity.

Sericeps —Silk sac used in making traction on the head of the fetus.

Series —Arrangement of similar things in succession or forming a kind of chain.

Seriflux —Serous discharge.

Serious—Grave.

Seriscission —The division of the pedicle of a tumor or other tissue by tying a silk ligature around it.

Sero- —A prefix meaning pertaining to serum.

Seroalbuminuria —Presence of serum albumin in the urine.

Serocolitis —Pericolitis. Inflammation of serous coat of the colon.

Seroconversion —Development of the specific antibodies in the serum in response to an infectious disease or immunization.

Seroculture —A bacterial culture on blood serum.

Serocystic —Composed of cysts containing serous fluid.

Serodermatosis —Skin disease with serous effusion into the epidermis.

Serodiagnosis —Diagnosis of disease made by observing the reactions of blood serum.

Seroenteritis —Inflammation of the serous coat of the intestine.

Seroepidemiology—Epidemiologic study of a disease based on the detection of infection by serum examination.

Serofast —Serum-fast.

Serofibrinous —Composed of serum and fibrin.

Serofibrous —Pertaining to serous and fibrous surface.

Seroflocculation —Flocculation produced in serum by an antigen.

Serogroup —A group of bacteria containing a common antigen.

Serohepatitis —Inflammation of peritoneal covering of the liver.

Seroimmunity —Immunity produced by the administration of an antiserum.

Serolipase —Lipase found in blood serum.

Serologic, Serological—Pertaining to or the study of sera.

Serologist —Specialist in serology.

Serology —The scientific study of serum.

Serolysin —A bactericidal substance or lysin found in the blood serum.

Seroma —A collection of serum in the tissues resembling a tumor.

Seromembranous —1. Both serous and membranous. 2. Pertaining to or composed of serous membrane.

Seromucoid —Resembling the serum and mucus.

Seromucous —Pertaining to or composed of both serum and mucus.

Seromuscular —Pertaining to the serous and muscular coats of the intestine.

Seromyotomy—To incise the wall of a hollow viscus involving the serous membrane and the muscular layer but not the mucosa.

Seronegative —Producing a negative reaction to serological tests.

Seroperitoneum —Hydroperitoneum. Fluid in the peritoneum.

Seropositive —Producing a positive reaction to serological tests.

Seroprevention —Seroprophylaxis.

Seroprognosis —Prognosis of a disease determined by seroreactions.

Seroprophylaxis—Seroprevention. Prevention of a disease by the administration of serum.

Seropurulent —Composed of serum and pus, as an exudate.

Seropus —A collection of serum and pus.

Seroreaction —1. A reaction occurring in serum or by the action of a serum. 2. Reaction to an injection of serum marked by rash, fever, pain etc.

Seroresistance —Failure of a serum reaction to be negative.

Seroresistant —Pertaining to seroresistance.

Seroreversion —A loss in serological reactivity which may be spontaneous or in response to therapy.

Serosa —Any serous membrane such as peritoneum, pleura, and pericardium etc.

Serosamucin —Mucoid material found in serous fluids as synovial fluid.

Serosanguineous —Composed of or of the nature of serum and blood.

Seroserous —Pertaining to two or more serous surfaces.

Serositis —Inflammation of a serous membrane.

Serosity —The quality of being serous.

Serosynovial —Pertaining to serous and synovial material.

Serosynovitis —Synovitis with effusion of serum.

Serotaxis —Edema of the skin caused by the application of a strong, cutaneous irritant.

Serotherapy —Orotherapy. Treatment of disease with human or animal blood serum containing antibodies.

Serothorax —Hydrothorax.

Serotonergic —Pertaining to the action of serotonin.

Serotonin —A hormone 5-hydroxytryptamine (**5-HT**), present in blood platelets, gastrointestinal mucosa, pineal body, mast cells and central nervous system, which inhibits gastric secretion, stimulates the smooth muscles, and causes constriction of the blood vessels. It transmits the nerve impulses.

Serotoninergic —Pertaining to the neurons that release serotonin hormone.

Serotype —The type of a microorganism determined by its constituent antigens.

Serous —1. Pertaining to or resembling serum. 2. Producing or containing serum.

Serous gland —A gland secreting a watery fluid containing albumin, as the parotid gland.

Serous inflammation —Inflammation with serous exudate or inflammation of a serous membrane.

Serovaccination —A process in which an injection of a serum is given to produce immediate passive immunity combined with bacterial vaccination to produce subsequent active immunity.

Serovar —Serotype.

Serozyme —Prothrombin.

Serozymogenic —Pertaining to a serous fluid and enzymes.

Serpiginous —Creeping.

Serpigo —Any creeping skin eruption *e.g.*, ring worm or herpes etc.

Serrate—Dentate. Toothed.

Serrated —Having a sawlike margin.

Serration —1. The state of being serrated. 2. Formation of a serrated structure. 3. A single tooth of serrated margin.

Serrefine —A type of forceps for compressing bleeding vessels.

Serrenoeud —An apparatus for tightening ligatures.

Serrulate —Finely toothed.

Serrulated —Serrulate.

Serum —1. After clotting, the watery portion of blood is called as serum which is plasma excluding fibrinogen. 2. Blood serum from an animal rendered immune against a pathogenic organism, to be injected into a patient with the disease resulting from the same organism, to produce immunity in him. 3. Any serous fluid moistening the surfaces of serous membranes.

Serumal —Pertaining to or derived from serum.

Serum-fast —Not being destructed by the serum.

Serum rash —Rash first seen at the site of an injection of serum.

Serum sickness —A hypersensitivity reaction occurring several days after administration of an antiserum or certain drug therapy characterized by skin rash, enlarged lymph nodes, fever and pain in the joints.

Servation —The use or function of an organ.

Servomechanism —A process which is believed to be a self-regulatory device, *e.g.*, the reaction of the pupil to light.

Sesamoid —Denoting a sesamoid bone.

Sesamoid bone —A small nodular bone embedded in a tendon or joint capsule.

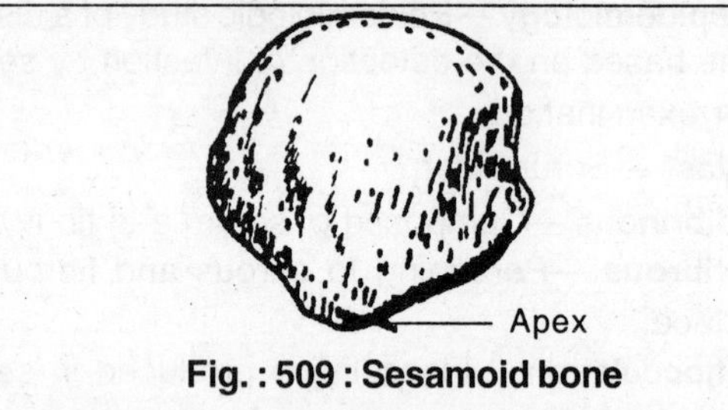

Fig. : 509 : Sesamoid bone

Sesamoiditis —Inflammation of a sesamoid bone.

Sesquihora —Every one and half hour.

Sessile —Without peduncle.

Set —1. To fix firmly in place, as to set a bone in reduction of a fracture. 2. To allow an amalgam or plaster to harden.

Seta —Plural of set.

Setaceous —1. Bristle-like 2. Having bristle.

Setiferous —Having bristles.

Setigerous —Setiferous.

Seton —A wisp of threads, a strip of gauze or a wire used to pass through the subcutaneous tissues or a cyst to form a sinus or fistula.

Setting —Hardening, as of amalgam.

Set-up —To fix.

Severe —Acute.

Sewage —Matter carried through sewers.

Sewer —The channel for carrying off waste and filth.

Sex —1. A distinctive character that differentiate males and females in most animals and plants. It is based on the type of gametes produced by the gonads, ova (macrogametes) being of the female, and sperm (microgametes) of the male. 2. The category in which the individual is placed on such basis.

Sex chromosomal —Sex as determined by the presence of female X X or male X Y genotype in somatic cells.

Sex gonadal —The sex as determined on the basis of gonadal tissue present (ovarian or testicular).

Sex morphological —The sex as determined by the form of the external genital organs.

Sex psychological —The individual's self thinking of his or her sex, and emotions accordingly.

Sex chromatin —Sex chromatin is the mass seen within nuclei of the normal female somatic cells. One of the two X chromosomes in each somatic cell of the female is genetically inactivated. The sex chromatin represents the inactivated X chromosome.

Sex chromosomes —Chromosomes concerned with the determination of sex, which in humans are X (female) and Y (male). The normal female has two X chromosomes and the normal male has one X and one Y chromosome.

Sex-conditioned —Sex-influenced.

Sexdigital —Having six fingers and toes.

Sexdigitate —Sexdigital. Sedigitate.

Sex drive —Motivation for sexual pleasure.

Sexduction —The process of transfer of bacterial genes from donor (male) bacterium to the recipient (female) by being attached to sex factor.

Sexivalent —Capable of combining with six atoms of hydrogen.

Sex-limited —Occurring only in one sex.

Sex-linked —Controlled by a gene located on the sex chromosome.

Sexology —Scientific study of the sexuality.

Sex surrogate —In sex therapy, the use of a substituted sex partner.

Sextan —Occurring every sixth day.

Sextigravida —A woman pregnant for the sixth time.

Sextipara —The woman who had produced 6 infants at separate pregnancy, each infant weighing 500 gms. or more, whether alive or dead.

Sextis Horis —Every six hours.

Sextuplet —One of six children born of a single pregnancy.

Sexual —Pertaining to or having sex.

Sexual abuse —Sexual molestation or rape.

Sexual intercourse —Coitus. Copulation.

Sexuality —1. The condition of having sex. 2. The characteristics that differentiate between male and the female. 3. Constitution and life of an individual as related to sex.

Sexualization —The act of acquiring sexual power.

Sexual reflex —Erection of the penis and ejaculation resulting from direct stimulation of the genital organs or indirectly from emotion during sleeping or awaking.

Shadow —The shade cast by an object.

Shadow-casting —A technique to increase the visibility of the material to be examined under the ultramicroscope, by spraying it with metal such as gold and chromium etc.

Shadowgram, Shadowgraph —A print on a photographic plate exposed to X-ray.

Shaft —The middle main long part of a cylindrical body, as that of a long bone between its wider ends.

Shakes —1. Shivering caused by a chill. 2. Tremulousness of chronic alcoholics.

Shaking palsy —Parkinson's disease. Paralysis agitans.

Shallow —Having little depth.

Shaman —The person who treats the diseases by magic as well as by medicines.

Shank —Shin.

Shape —1. External form of a thing, appearance. 2. To mold to a particular form.

Sharkskin —A condition seen in pellagra in which openings of sebaceous glands become plugged with a dry yellowish material.

Shear —The distortion of the body caused by two opposite parallel forces.

Sheath —A covering structure, usually of an elongated part.

Lamellar sheath —Nerve sheath. Connective tissue sheath covering a bundle of nerve fibers.

Muscle sheath —A membrane covering a muscle.

Myelin sheath —A sheath composed of lipids and protein around the axons of certain nerves.

Synovial sheath —A double-layered sheath, consisting of an inner visceral layer lying upon and adhering to a tendon and an outer parietal layer. The space between the two is filled with synovial fluid. These are found especially in the hands and feet.

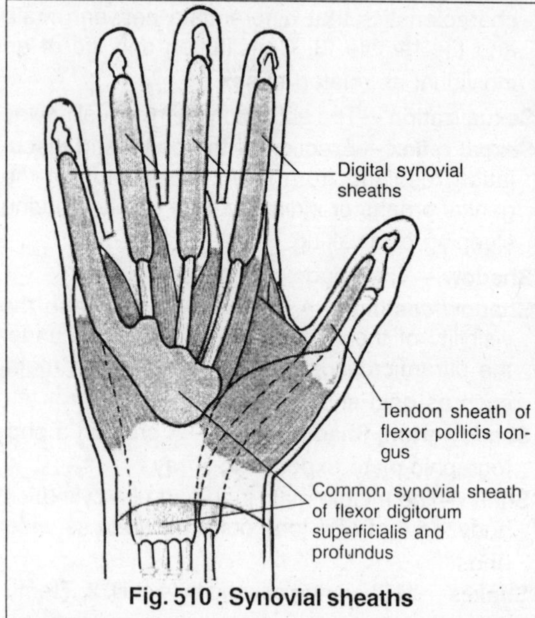

Fig. 510 : Synovial sheaths

Shedding —1. Falling off of the milk teeth. 2. Casting off of the outer layer of the epidermis. 3. Loss of bacteria from the skin.

Sheet —A rectangular piece of cotton or cloth for bed covering.

Shelf —A slab of stone projecting from the wall for keeping things.

Shelf-time —1. The time a food may be kept safely to eat, on a shelf. 2. The period a substance or medicine can be kept safely without its disintegration.

Shell —A hard covering as that of an egg.

Shield —Any protective structure or device as nipple shield.

Shift—A change in position or direction.

Shiga's bacillus —Shigella dysenteriae. The bacillus causing a form of dysentery.

Shigella —A genus of nonmotile, gram-negative, rod-shaped bacteria, belonging to the family Enterobacteriaceae which causes digestive trouble ranging from mild diarrhea to severe and fatal dysentery.

Shigellosis —Infection with Shigella causing bacillary dysentery.

Shin —Shank. The anterior edge of the tibia or the portion of leg from knee to the ankle.

Shingles —Herpes zoster.

Shiver —1. A slight tremor, as from cold or fear. 2. To tremble or shake.

Shivering —Trembling from cold or fear.

Shock —Insufficient return of blood to the heart for normal function, due to severe peripheral circulatory failure caused by hemorrhage, dehydration, drug reaction, trauma, infection, poisoning and myocardial infarction etc. It is characterized by low temperature and low blood pressure, rapid and thready pulse and paleness of the skin.

Allergic shock —Anaphylactic shock.

Anaphylactic shock —Shock resulting from an injection of protein substance or serum to which the patient is sensitive.

Anesthesia shock —Shock caused by an overdose of anesthesia.

Cardiogenic shock —Shock resulting from inadequate blood supply to the circulatory system and tissues due to inadequate cardiac output.

Deferred shock —Secondary shock. Shock occurring late (3 to 30 hours) following an injury or burn.

Delayed shock —Deferred shock.

Electric shock —Shock resulting from the passage of electric current through any part of the body.

Hemorrhagic shock —Shock resulting from acute hemorrhage.

Hypovolemic shock —Shock caused by a reduction in volume of blood, resulting from dehydration or hemorrhage.

Insulin shock —Shock resulting from an overdosage of insulin which causes too reduction of blood sugar.

Irreversible shock —Shock of such severity that is not treatable and death can not be prevented.

Protein shock—Shock occurring after administration of an injection of a protein.

Psychic shock —Mental shock. Shock due to excessive fear, joy, anger, grief.

Secondary shock —Defferred shock.

Septic shock —Shock caused by the presence of gram-negative bacteria within the body.

Serum shock —Shock occurring as an allergic reaction to an injection of a serum.

Surgical shock —Shock occurring following an operation.

Traumatic shock —Shock occurring due to an injury or surgery.

Shock therapy —Treatment of some mental diseases, chiefly of depression by inducing convulsions by passing electric current through the brain.

Shooting —Acute or severe.

Shortsightedness —Myopia. Nearsightedness.

Shot —A hypodermic injection.

Shotgun prescription —Prescription containing many drugs given with the hope that one of the drugs may prove effective.

Shotty —Like shot.

Shoulder—The junction of the clavicle and scapula where the arm joins the trunk.

Shoulder blade —The scapula bone.

Shoulder girdle—The portion of the upper extremities consisting of two scapulae and two clavicles, which attach the bones of the upper extremities to the vertebral column.

Show —Appearance of blood through vagina just prior to labor or menstruation.

Shreds —Fine threadlike structures of mucus seen in recently excreted urine, that indicates the inflammation of urinary tract or associated organs.

Shrill —Piercing or sharp sound.

Shudder —To tremble with fear.

Shunt —1. A physiological passage between two natural channels, especially between blood vessels. 2. To turn to one side or to bypass. 3. A surgically created passage to divert flow from one main route to another, also the operation of performing the shunt.

Arteriovenous shunt —The diversion of blood from an artery directly to a vein through the capillaries.

Cardiovascular shunt —Diversion of blood through an opening from the right side of heart to the left side or from the pulmonary to the systemic circulation (right-to-left shunt), or from the left side of heart to the right side or from the systemic to the pulmonary circulation (left-to-right shunt).

Dialysis shunt —Arteriovenous shunt.

Left-to-right shunt —A diversion of blood from the left side of the heart to right (as through a septal defect) or from the systemic circulation to the pulmonary circulation (as through a patent ductus arteriosus).

Portacaval shunt —Postcaval shunt. Surgical creation of a connection between the portal vein and the vena cava.

Right-to-left shunt —The passage of blood from the right side of the heart into the left (as through a septal defect), or from the pulmonary artery into the aorta (as through a patent ductus arteriosus).

SI —Systeme International. International System of measurement.

SIADH —Syndrome of inappropriate antidiuretic hormone.

Siagonantritis —Inflammation of the maxillary sinus.

Sial- —A prefix which means saliva or salivary glands.

Sialaden —Salivary gland.

Sialadenitis —Inflammation of a salivary gland.

Sialadenoncus —A tumor of the salivary gland.

Sialadenosis —Noninflammatory swelling of the salivary glands.

Sialadenotropic —Affecting salivary glands.

Sialagogue —Sialogogue. Increasing flow of saliva.

Sialaporia —Deficiency in the secretion of saliva.

Sialectasia, Sialectasis —Dilatation of a salivary gland.

Sialemesia —Sialemesis.

Sialemesis —Vomiting of saliva or vomiting caused by excessive secretion of saliva.

Sialic —Salivary. Pertaining to or resembling saliva.

Sialine —Pertaining to the saliva.

Sialism, Sialismus —Ptyalism.

Sialitis —Inflammation of a salivary gland.

Sialo- —Sial-

Sialoadenectomy —Excision of a salivary gland.

Sialoadenitis —Sialadenitis.

Sialoadenotomy —Incision of a salivary gland.

Sialoaerophagia —The swallowing of saliva and air.

Sialoaerophagy —Sialoaerophagia.

Sialoangiectasis —Dilatation of salivary gland duct.

Sialoangiitis —Sialoangitis.

Sialoangiography —Sialography.

Sialoangitis —Inflammation of a salivary duct.

Sialocele —A cyst of a salivary gland.

Sialodochitis —Sialoangitis.

Sialodochoplasty —Repair of a salivary gland by plastic surgery.

Sialoductitis —Sialoangitis.

Sialogen —An agent that induces salivation.

Sialogenous —Forming saliva.

Sialogogic —Producing or increasing the secretion of saliva.

Sialogogue —Sialagogue. Sialogogic.

Sialogram —X-ray film of the salivary glands and their ducts.

Sialography —Sialoangiography. X-ray examination of the salivary glands and their ducts.

Sialoid —Pertaining to or resembling saliva.

Sialolith —A salivary calculus.

Sialolithiasis —The formation of calculi in the salivary glands.

Sialolithotomy —Removal of a calculus from a salivary gland or duct.

Sialometaplasia —Metaplasia of the salivary glands.

Sialometry —A measurement of the secretion of saliva.

Sialoncus —A tumor under the tongue produced by obstruction of a salivary gland or duct.

Sialoporia —Deficient secretion of the saliva.

Sialorrhea —Sialism. Ptyalism.

Sialoschesis —Suppression of secretion of saliva.

Sialosemeiology —Study of the saliva for diagnosis.

Sialosis —The flow of saliva.

Sialostenosis —Narrowing of a salivary duct.

Sialosyrinx —1. Fistula into the salivary gland. 2. A syringe for washing out the salivary ducts. 3. Drainage tube for the salivary ducts.

Sialotic —Pertaining to the flow of saliva.

Sib —1. Sibling. A brother or sister. 2. A blood relative.

Sibilant —Whistling or hissing.

Sibilation —The act of producing hissing sound.

Sibilismus —A hissing sound.

Sibilus —A hissing rale.

Sibling —A brother or sister.

Sibship —Relationship between individuals born of the same parents.

Sicca —Dry.

Siccant —Drying.

Siccative —Drying or that which dries.

Sicchasia —Nausea.

Siccolabile —Altered or destroyed by drying.

Siccostable —Resistant to drying.

Siccus —Dry.

Sick —Patient. Suffereing from a disease

Sickle cell —Meniscocyte.

Sicklemia —Sickle cell anemia. Presence of sickle cells in the blood.

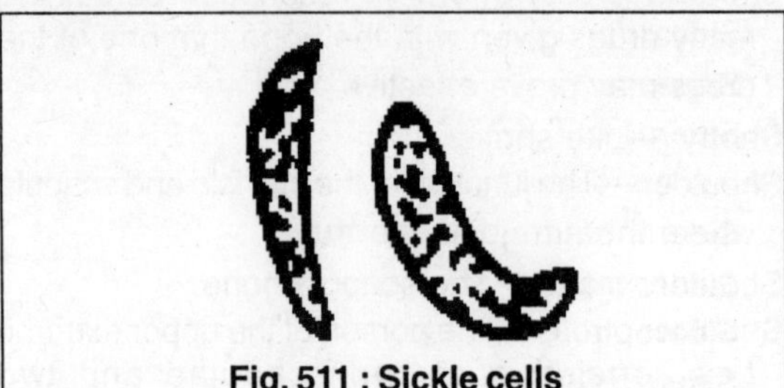

Fig. 511 : Sickle cells

Sickling —Development of red blood cells into sickle cells in the blood.

Sickness —Illness. Disease. State of being unwell.

- **Altitude sickness** —Mountain sickness.
- **Decompression sickness** —See under 'D' (decompression illness).
- **Morning sickness** —See under 'M'.
- **Motion sickness** —See under 'M'.
- **Mountain sickness** —Altitude sickness.
- **Radiation sickness** —A sickness caused by irradiation characterized by anorexia, nausea, vomiting, leukopenia, and thrombocytopenia causing hemorrhage.

Sea sickness —Motion sickness, occurring in boat travellers.

Serum sickness —Sickness occurring after administration of an injection of serum.

Side —One of the outer surfaces of an object.

Side-effect —The effect of a drug other than desired.

Side position —The position in which the patient lies on one side with the thighs flexed and the under arm behind the back.

Sideration —1. A sudden attack of a disease. 2. Application of electric sparks for the treatment of disease.

Siderism, Siderismus —Metallotherapy.

Sidero- —A prefix meaning iron or steel.

Sideroblast —A nucleated red blood cell containing iron granules in its cytoplasm.

Siderocyte —A red blood cell containing non-hemoglobin iron.

Sideroderma —Bronze coloration of the skin from disordered disintegration of hemoglobin.

Siderodromophobia —Morbid fear of railway travel.

Siderofibrosis —Fibrosis associated with deposits of iron, as in spleen.

Siderogenous —Producing or forming iron.

Sideropenia —Deficiency of iron in the blood.

Sideropenic —Characterized by deficiency of iron in the blood.

Siderophage —Siderophore.

Siderophil —A cell having affinity for iron.

Siderophile —Siderophil.

Siderophilin —Transferrin.

Siderophilous —Having a tendency to absorb iron, as the red blood cells.

Siderophore —A macrophage containing hemosiderin.

Sideroscope —An instrument for finding iron particles in the eye.

Siderosilicosis —Silicosiderosis.

Siderosis —1. A form of pneumoconiosis due to inhalation of iron particles. 2. Excess of iron in the blood. 3. The deposit of iron in the tissues.

Siderosis hepatic —The deposit of an abnormal amount of iron in the liver.

Siderosis urinary —The presence of hemosiderin granules in the urine.

Siderosome —A reticulocyte containing iron granules.

Siderotic —Pertaining to siderosis.

SIDS —Sudden Infant death syndrome.

Siemens —The SI unit of electrical conductivity, the symbol for which is mho.

Siemens' syndrome —Ichthyosis congenita.

Sieve —An apparatus consisting of a mesh with holes of uniform size, used for separating the particles above a certain size from the solutions or powders.

Sievert —A unit of absorbed radiation energy derived from SI units. One sievert is equal to 1 J/kg or 100 rem.

Sig. —An abbreviation for the Latin word signa which means, in prescription writing to label it.

Sigault's operation —Symphysiotomy. Division of the pubic symphysis to enlarge the pelvic outlet to facilitate the delivery.

Sigh —A deep inspiration followed by expiration during which a slow sound is heard.

Sight —1. Vision. Power of seeing. 2. A thing seen.

Day sight —Nyctalopia. Night blindness.

Far sight —Hyperopia, hypermetropia.

Near sight —Myopia.

Night sight —Hemeralopia. Day blindness.

Old sight —Presbyopia.

Second sight —Senopia.

Sigmatism —Excessive or defective use of "S" sound in speech.

Sigmoid —Pertaining to the sigmoid flexure of the colon.

Sigmoid colon — The 'S' shaped and about 15 inches long portion of the large intestine, extending from the descending colon to the rectum, situated in the left iliac region of the pelvis.

Sigmoidectomy —Excision of all or part of the sigmoid colon.

Sigmoiditis —Inflammation of the sigmoid colon.

Sigmoidopexy —Fixation of the sigmoid colon to the abdominal wall for prolapse of rectum.

Sigmoidoproctostomy —Surgical anastomosis of the sigmoid colon to the rectum.

Sigmoidorectostomy —Sigmoidoproctostomy.

Sigmoidoscope —An endoscope for visual examination of the sigmoid colon.

Sigmoidoscopy —Inspection of the sigmoid colon by use of sigmoidoscope.

Sigmoidosigmoidostomy —Surgical creation of a connection between two segments of the sigmoid colon.

Sigmoidostomy —Surgical creation of an artificial opening from the sigmoid colon to the body surface.

Sigmoidotomy —To make an incision into the sigmoid colon.

Sigmoidovesical —Pertaining to the sigmoid colon and urinary bladder or to an opening between them.

Sign —1. An indication of the existence of something. 2. Any objective evidence of a disease, *i.e.*, the evidence perceptible to the examining doctor, as opposed to the subjective evidences (symptoms) which are perceptible to the patient. 3. A symbol or abbreviation used in pharmacy.

Signa —Signetur (Sig.)

Signal —Samething that causes an action.

Signature —The part of a prescription containing the directions to the patient.

Significant —Important.

Silent —Free from noise; mute (not speaking anything.)

Silent disease —A disease that does not produce obvious symptoms or signs.

Silicatosis —Pneumoconiosis due to inhalation of silicate dust.

Siliceous, Silicious —Containing silica.

Silicic —Pertaining to silica or silicon.

Silicoanthracosis —Silicosis combined with pneumoconiosis, in workers of coal mines.

Silicosiderosis —A type of pneumoconiosis in which inhaled dust contains silicate and iron particles.

Silicosis —A type of pneumoconiosis due to inhalation of the dust of silica, characterized by the formation of small discrete nodules.

Silicotic —Pertaining to or affected with silicosis.

Silicotuberculosis —Silicosis associated with pulmonary tuberculosis.

Siliqua olivae —Fibers appearing to encircle the olive of the brain.

Siliquose —Pertaining to or resembling a pod or husk.

Siliquose cataract —Cataract with a dry and wrinkled lens capsule.

Siliquose desquamation —Shedding off the dried vesicles from the skin.

Silt —Sediment.

Silver fork deformity —A deformity in the colles' fracture of the wrist and hand resembling the curvature of the back of a table fork.

Simesthesia —Sensibility felt in a bone.

Simian crease —A crease on the palm of the hand.

Similia similibus curantur —The homeopathic principle that a drug producing pathological symptoms in healthy person will cure such symptoms in a diseased person.

Similimum —A medicine that causes a symptom quite similar to that produced by the disease, as a homeopathic medicine.

Simmond's disease —The condition in which complete atrophy of the pituitary gland causes loss of function of the thyroid gland, adrenal glands and gonads (ovaries and testes) with atrophy of the genital organs and loss of secondary sex characteristics, premature senility and emaciation.

Simon's position —The position in which patient lies on back, legs flexed on thighs, thighs on abdomen, hips are somewhat elevated and thighs are strongly abducted. It is employed in operations on the vagina.

Simple —1. That is not complex 2. That is not compound.

Simple fracture —Fracture in which skin is not ruptured.

Simple inflammation —Inflammation without formation of pus.

Sims' position —See under position.

Simul —At once or at the same time, usually written in prescription.

Simulation —1. Pretense of having a disease. 2. Imitation of symptoms of one disease by another.

Simulator —An apparatus which creates a condition similar to the desired one.

Simultanagnosia —The failure to perceive simultaneously all the elements of a scene.

Sinapized —Containing mustard.

Sincipital —Pertaining to the sinciput.

Sinciput —The upper and front part of the head.

Sinew —A tendon.

Sing. —Of each.

Singer's node —Chorditis nodosa. Small whitish nodes formed on one or both vocal cords in the persons who misuse their voice.

Singleton —A single fetus developing.

Singulation — Hicupping.

Singulis Horis —Every hour.

Singultous —Pertaining to hiccup.

Singultus —Hiccup.

Sinister —Left; on the left side.

Sinistrad —Toward the left.

Sinistral —1. Pertaining to the left side. 2. A left-handed person.

Sinistrality —Left-handedness.

Sinistraural —Hearing better with the left ear.

Sinistro- —A prefix which means left or toward the left.

Sinistrocardia —Displacement of heart to the left of the medial line.

Sinistrocerebral —Pertaining to or located in the left cerebral hemisphere.

Sinistrocular —Seeing better with the left eye.

Sinistrocularity —Condition of seeing better with the left eye.

Sinistroflexion —A bending toward the left.

Sinistrogyration—A turning to the left.

Sinistromanual —Left-handed.

Sinistropedal —Walking on left foot in preference to the right.

Sinistrorotation —Sinistrotorsion.

Sinistrorse —Turned to the left.

Sinistrotorsion —A twisting or turning toward the left, as of the eye.

Sinistrous —Awkard, unskilled.

Sinoatrial —Sinoauricular. Pertaining to the sinus venosus and atrium of the heart.

Sinoatrial node —See under node.

Sinoauricular —Sinoatrial.

Sinobronchitis —Chronic paranasal sinusitis with recurrent bronchitis.

Sinogram —X-ray film of a sinus after injecting a radiopaque substance into it

Sinography —Radiography of the sinuses.

Sinopulmonary —Pertaining to or affecting the paranasal sinuses and the lungs.

Sinuitis —Sinusitis.

Sinuotomy —Sinusotomy.

Sinuous —Twisted.

Sinus —1. A cavity within a bone, *e.g.*, paranasal sinuses which are air containing cavities in the bones of the skull continuous with the nasal cavities. 2. Dilatation of a blood vessel, *e.g.*, carotid sinus, which is the dilatation of the common carotid artery at its bifurcation. 3. A passage or fistula through which pus is discharged, *e.g.*, pilonidal sinus.

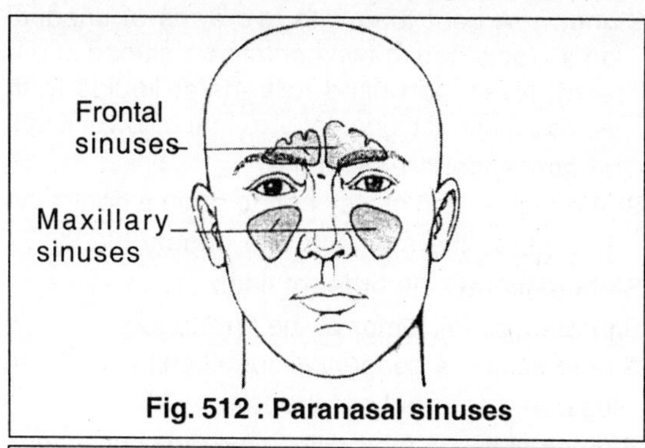

Fig. 512 : Paranasal sinuses

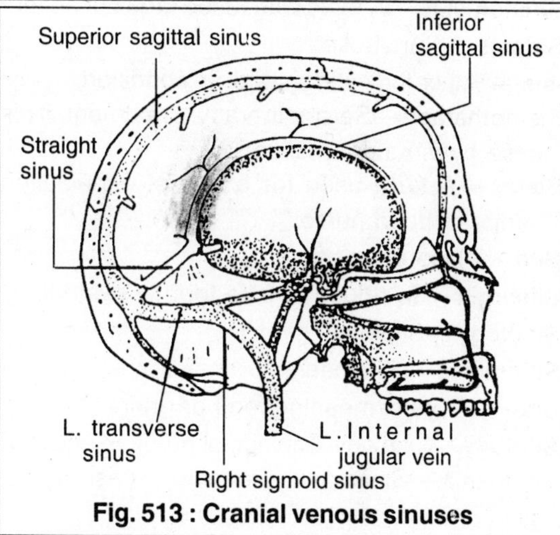

Fig. 513 : Cranial venous sinuses

Sinus arrhythmia —An increase in heart rate during inspiration and decrease on expiration.

Sinus bradycardia —Heart rate of 50 beats or less per minute.

Sinusitis —Inflammation of a sinus, especially a paranasal sinus.

Sinusoid —1. Resembling a sinus. 2. A minute blood vessel slightly larger than a capillary and has a lining of reticuloendothelium, found in such organs as the liver, spleen, adrenal glands and bone marrow.

Sinusoidal —Pertaining to a sinusoid.

Sinusotomy —To make an incision into a sinus.

Sinus rhythm —The normal cardiac rhythm commencing at the sinoatrial node.

Sinus tachycardia —A heart rate of 90 beats or more per minute.

Siphon —A bent tube with two arms of unequal length, attached to two containers placed at different levels and used to transfer liquids from the container of higher level to that of lower level, by atmospheric pressure.

Siphonage —Use of a siphon to drain a body cavity such as the stomach and urinary bladder.

Siphonaptera —An order of fleas.

Siphonoma —A tumor of the fine tubes.

Sirenomelia —A congenital condition in which the legs are fused but not the feet.

Sirenomelus —A fetus with fused legs but no feet.

Siriasis —Sunstroke.

-sis —Suffix indicating state or condition.

Sismotherapy —Seismotherapy. Treatment of disease by vibratory massage.

Sister —A term used for a nurse, especially a senior or head nurse.

Site —Place or position.

Sitieirgia —To refuse to take food in hysteria.

Sitiology —Sitology.

Sitiomania —Sitomania.

Sito- —A prefix meaning food or grain.

Sitology —Sitiology. Science of nutrition and food.

Sitomania —Sitiomania. Periodic excessive hunger.

Sitophobia —Morbid fear of food.

Sitotaxis —Sitotropism.

Sitotherapy—Treatment of disease by food.

Sitotoxin —Any poison developed in food.

Sitotoxism —Poisoning by food.

Sitotropism —Response of living cells to the presence of food elements.

Situation —Position, circumstance, condition, location.

Situs —A position or site.

Situs inversus viscerum —An abnormal displacement of the viscera of thorax and abdomen to the opposite side of the body.

Situs perversus —Malposition of any internal structure.

Sitz bath —See under bath.

SI units —International system of units of measurment.

Skateboard —An apparatus used for rehabilitation of the upper extremity.

Skatole —A malodorous, crystalline substance betamethyl indole found in the feces, formed by protein decomposition in the intestine.

Skatoxyl —Oxidation product of skatole found in the urine in certain diseases of the large intestine.

Skein —The coiled threads of chromatin seen in the prophase of mitosis.

Skeneitis —Skenitis.

Skelalgia —Pain in the leg.

Skeletal —Pertaining to the skeleton.

Skeletal muscle —Striated muscle. Voluntary muscle. A muscle attached to the skeleton.

Skeletization —1. Extreme emaciation. 2. Removal of soft parts from the body leaving only the skeleton.

Skeleto- —Combining form meaning skeleton.

Skeletogenous —Forming skeleton.

Skeletogeny —The formation of the skeleton.

Skeletology —Te branch of anatomy dealing with the study of skeleton.

Skeleton —The bony framework of the body consisting of 206 bones, 80 of the trunk and 126 of the limbs.

Skene's glands —Paraurethral glands. Two small glands, one by its duct opening on each side of the floor of posterior portion of urethra in female.

Skenitis —Inflammation of the Skene's glands.

Skeocytosis —1. Presence of immature white blood cells in the peripheral blood. 2. Deviation to the left.

Sketch —An outline.

Skew —1. Turned to one side. 2. Asymmetrical.

Skew deviation —The turning of one eye upward and outward and of the other downward and inward.

Skia- —A prefix indicating a relation with shadows.

Skiagram —X-ray picture.

Skiameter —An instrument for measuring the intensity of X-ray.

Skiascopy —1. Retinoscopy. 2. Fluoroscopy.

Skill —Expertness.

Skin —The outer protective covering of the body consisting of the corium or dermis and epidermis.

Alligator skin —Ichthyosis.

Bronzed skin —The dark skin in Addison disease.

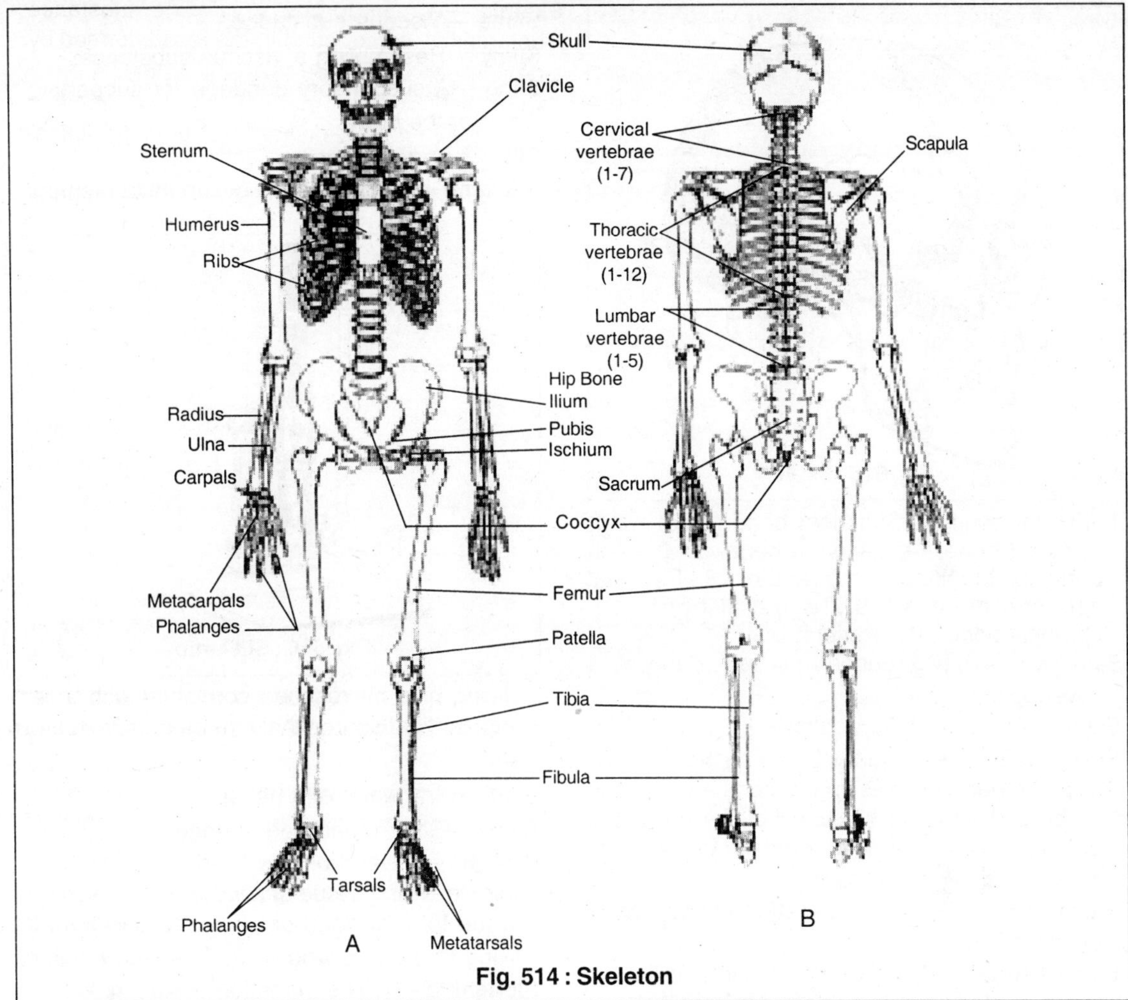

Fig. 514 : Skeleton

Deciduous skin —Keratolysis. Shedding of the epidermis.

Elastic skin —Skin with the property of great elasticity.

False skin —Epidermis.

Farmer's skin —Dry, wrinkled skin.

Glabrous skin —Smooth skin without hair.

Glossy skin —Smooth and shining skin.

Hidebound skin —Scleroderma.

Loose skin —Hypertrophy of the skin.

Marble skin —Cutis marmorata. Temporary purplish discoloration of the skin on exposure to cold.

Parchment skin —Atrophy of the skin with stretching.

Photodamaged skin —Damaged skin due to chronic sun exposure.

Piebald skin —Vitiligo. Leukoderma.

Thick skin —Skin of the palms and soles.

Thin skin —Skin of the body other than that of the palms and soles.

Toad skin —Phrynoderma.

True skin —Corium (dermis) or the inner layer of the skin.

Skin writing —Dermatographia.

Skip —To leap, to jump, to omit, to disappear, to shift from one subject to another.

Skoda's rales —Bronchial rales heard through consolidated lungs in pneumonia.

Skoda's resonance —Resonance heard above the line of fluid in pleurisy with effusion or above consolidation in pneumonia.

Skull —The bony framework of the head, composed of 8 cranial and 14 facial bones and the teeth.

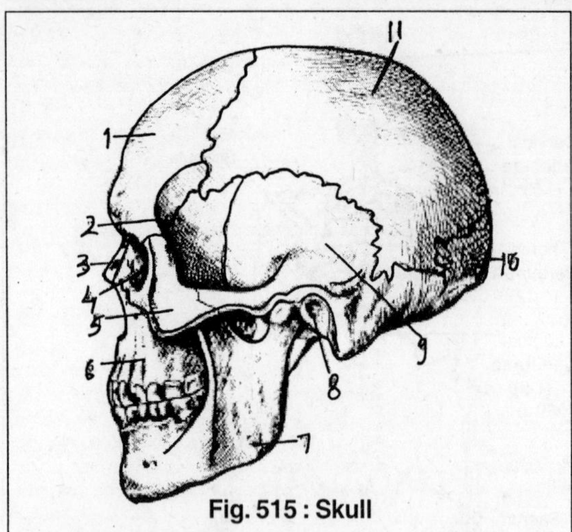

Fig. 515 : Skull

1. Frontal bone, 2. Sphenoid bone (great wing) 3. Nasal bone, 4. Lacrimal bone, 5. Zygoma bone, 6. Maxilla, 7. Mandible, 8. External acoustic meatus, 9. Temporal bone, 10. Occipital bone, 11. Parietal bone

Skull cap —Upper rounded portion of the skull covering the brain.

Slant —To slope, to turn obliquely.

Slaughter-house —A place for killing the animals.

Sleep —A period of rest for the body and mind in which physiological functions of the body and consciousness are diminished and voluntary body functions are absent.

Sleep apnea —Periodic cessation of respiration during sleep.

Sleep disorder —Any condition that interferes with sleep, excluding environmental factors such as noise, excess of heat or cold, movements (as by travelling in a train, bus or other vehicle) or change in altitude.

Sleep drunkenness —Somnolentia.

Sleep epilepsy —Narcolepsy.

Sleeping sickness —Trypanosomiasis.

Sleeplessness —Absence of sleep.

Sleep terror disorder —Repeated sudden awakening from sleep with crying due to terror, as seen mostly in children.

Sleep walker —Somnambulist. Walker in sleep.

Sleep walking —Somnambulism. Habit of walking in the sleep.

Slide —1. A thin plate of glass or other transparent substance on which the material to be examined under the microscope is placed. 2. A photograph prepared to be used in a film slide projector to be shown on the screen.

Slime —Viscous substance.

Slimy —Resembling a viscous substance.

Sling —A suspensory bandage for supporting a part of the body.

Slit —A narrow opening.

Slit lamp —In ophthalmology, an instrument consisting of a microscope combined with a rectangular light source that can be narrowed into a slit.

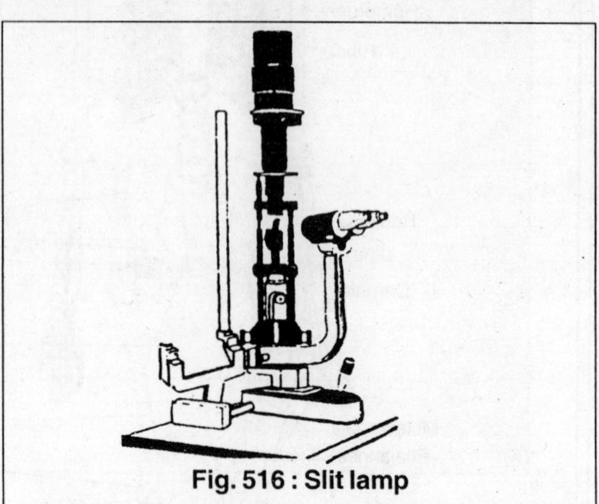
Fig. 516 : Slit lamp

Slop —Dirty water of a house.

Slope —Slant or inclined surface.

Slough —1. Dead or necrosed tissue separated from the living tissue or a wound. 2. To separate in the form of dead or necrosed part from the living tissue or a wound. 3. To shed or cast off.

Sloughing —1. The formation of slough. 2. Separation of dead or necrosed tissue from the living tissue.

Slow —1. Dull minded. 2. Of retarded speed, as the pulse. 3. A disease or a fever which is not progressive.

Sludge —Waste material of the city, industries and commercial areas.

Sluggish —Slow moving, inactive.

Sluice —Waterfall.

Sluice way —Spillway.

Slumber —Light sleep; cat-nap.

Slur —To pronounce indistinctly, to conceal, to decrease.

Slurry —A thin watery mixture.

Small intestine —See intestine.

Smallpox —Variola. An acute contagious, systemic, viral disease characterized by high fever

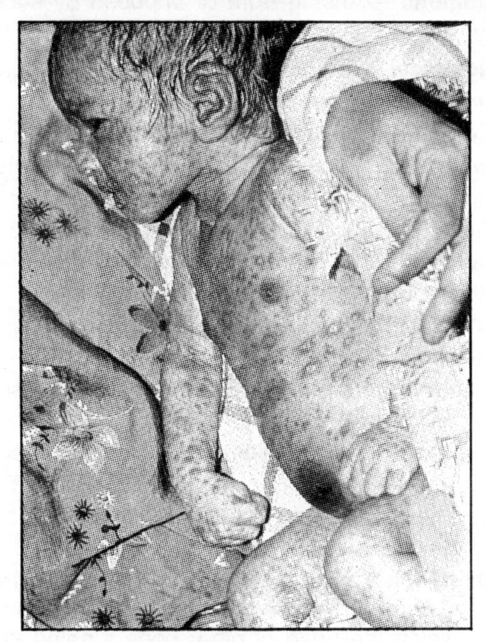

Fig. 517 : Small pox

and the appearance of macules, papules, vesicles, pustules successively and the formation of crusts which shed off leaving small pits.

Smear —1. A specimen for microscopic examination prepared by spreading the material across the slide. 2. Material obtained from infected area of the body to be spread on the slide for microscopic examination or to be spread over solid culture medium.

Blood smear —A thin film of blood on a glass slide, prepared for staining and microscopic examination.

Pap smear —Papanicolaou smear. A smear of the vagina or cervix obtained for the study of cells for early detection of cancer.

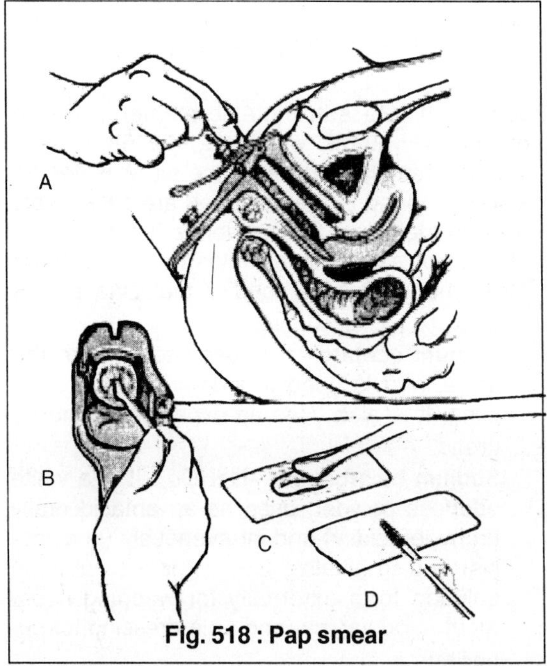

Fig. 518 : Pap smear

Smegma —Thick cheesy secretion of the sebaceous glands emitting foul smell, found under labia minora about the clitoris in female and under the prepuce of penis in male.

Smegmalith —Smegmolith.

Smegmatic —Pertaining to or composed of smegma.

Smegmolith —A calculus in the smegma.

Smell—1. The perception of odor by nose. 2. Odor, pleasant or offensive (bad) 3. To emit an odor.

Smell-brain —Rhinencephalon.

Smelling salt—Ammonium carbonate.

Smith-Petersen nail —A special nail possessing 3 flanges, for stabilizing fractures of the neck of femur bone.

Smith's fracture —Colles fracture.

Smog —Fog and smoke combined.

Smudging —A speech defect in which difficult consonants are not spoken.

Snap —A short, sharp sound, *e.g.*, opening sound—a short, sharp sound heard in early systole, associated with opening of the mitral valve in mitral stenosis.

Snapping finger—A sharp, cracking sound produced by bending the finger.

Snare —An instrument with a wire loop for removing polyps or tumors by tightening the wire loops around them at the base.

Sneeze —To expel air forcibly through the nose and mouth by spasmodic contraction of muscles of expiration, due to irritation of the nasal mucous membrane.

Snellen's chart —Reading chart for testing visual acuity, on which black letters gradually increasing in size from smallest on the bottom to largest on the top are printed.

Snellen's test—Test for visual acuity in which the patient reads letters on snellen's chart at a certain distance with one eye, then with the other eye and then with both the eyes.

Snip —To cut with the scissors.

Snore —1. Rough noisy breathing during sleep, due to vibration of the uvula and soft palate. 2. To produce snore during sleep.

Snoring rale —Low snoring rale that continues during inspiration.

Snout —Long projecting nose of a beast.

Snow blindness —See under blindness.

Snuff —A medicinal powder inhaled through the nose.

Snuffles —Obstructed nasal breathing with mucous discharge from the nasal mucous membrane in infants, chiefly in congenital syphilis.

SOAP —SOAP is the collective form of the headings to be written on the patient's chart. S indicates the subjective data obtained from the patient and others close to him. O indicates the objective data obtained by observations, physical examination and investigations etc. A refers to assessment of the patient's status through analysis of the problem. P designates the plan for further care of the patient. If the patient is suffering from many diseases, a SOAP entry is made for each disease on the chart.

Soap —A cleansing chemical compound formed by an alkali acting on a fatty acid, such as sodium stearate.

Soap liniment—A solution of soap and camphor in alcohol and water, used as a stimulant and rubefacient.

S.O.B.—Short of breath.

Sob—1. Convulsive drawing of breath in weeping or to weep with convulsive drawing of breath. 2. Loud weeping.

Socia—An ectopic, supernumerary or accessory portion of an organ.

Social—Pertaing to a society.

Socialization—The process of adapting an individual to social customs and teaching to behave properly in the society.

Social phobia—Fear of being social.

Socia parotidis—Accessory parotid gland.

Socio- —A prefix meaning social or society.

Socioacusis—Effects of environmental noise on the intensity of hearing.

Sociobiology —The branch of biology in which the effects of biological and genetic factors on social behavior are studied.

Sociogenic —Arising from or imposed by society.

Sociological —Pertaining to sociology.

Sociologist —A specialist in sociology.

Sociology—The study of human social behavior, laws and customs and functions of the society.

Sociomedical—Pertaining to sociology and medicine.

Sociometry—The branch of sociology concerned with the measurement of social behavior.

Sociopath—Psychopath. A person with antisocial personality.

Sociopathic personality—See personality, antisocial.

Sociopathy—The condition of being antisocial (sociopathic).

Sociotherapy—Treatment of disease by socioenvironmental factors.

Socket—A hollow in the body into which a corresponding organ is fitted, *e.g.*,a socket in a bone into which the head of other bone forming the joint is fitted.

Eye socket—Orbit.

Tooth socket—A dental alveolus or cavity which contains the root of the tooth.

Soda—Term applied to baking soda (sodium bicarbonate) and caustic soda (sodium hydroxide) etc.

Sodic—Pertaining to or containing soda or sodium.

Sodio- —Combining form denoting a compound containing sodium.

Sodium—It is a soft metallic element, atomic number 11, atomic weight 22.989768, symbol Na. It is readily oxidized in the air or water. Its salts are found in the body and are extensively used in medicine. Sodium ion is the chief constituent of extracellular fluids in the body. Its most important salts used in medicine are as follows.

Sodium acetate—It is used to alkalize the urine, and is used in kidney dialysis solutions. It is also used as expectorant and diuretic.

Sodium bicarbonate—$NaHCo_3$. It is a white odorless powder, used as an antacid orally (in hyperacidity) and intravenously (in acidosis) and to alkalize urine. It is also used in solution form externally for washing nose, mouth and vagina, and as a dressing for minor burns.

Sodium carbonate—Na_2Co_2. It is a white crystalline powder which is also known as washing soda. It is used as a lotion or alkaline bath in the treatment of skin diseases.

Sodium chloride—NaCl. It is common salt which is generally added to food to make it tasty. It is white crystalline compound and is the chief constituent of blood and other body fluids. The sodium and chlorine ions are important in maintaining the proper electrolyte balance in body fluids. It is used in the preparation of normal saline solution (.9% aqueous solution) which is isotonic and physiological solution, and is used intravenously or by transfusion in the treatment of dehydration. It is also used as an emetic.

Sodium citrate—It is a white granular powder which is used as an anticoagulant for blood.

Sodium fluoride—It is a white crystalline powder which is added to drinking water and used as a 2% solution for application on the teeth for prevention of dental caries.

Sodium iodide—A colorless crystalline solid which is used as an expectorant.

Sodomist, Sodomite—A person who practices sodomy.

Sodomy—Anal intercourse, usually between males.

Soemmering's ring—Annular swelling of the periphery of the lens capsule.

Soemmering's spot—Macula lutea retinae, a yellow spot in the center of retina.

Soft—Not hard or solid.

Soft diet—A diet consisting of semisolid or liquid food materials.

Softening—Malacia. The process of becoming soft.

Soft palate—Velum palatinum. The posterior musculomembranous part of the roof of mouth partly separating the mouth and the pharynx.

Soft sore—See chancroid.

Soil—The earth, the ground, the stain with feces.

Sol—A liquid colloidal solution.

Sol.—Solution.

Solac—An object or a person that gives relief in pain or mental disturbances.

Solar—1. Pertaining to the sun or its rays. 2. The solar plexus.

Solarium—A room specially designed for heliotherapy or phototherapy.

Solar plexus—The celiac plexus, behind the stomach and between the adrenal glands and consisting of two, celiac and superior mesenteric ganglia, from which sympathetic fibers pass to the internal organs.

Solar reflex—Plantar reflex.

Solar therapy—Heliotheraphy.

Solation—The liquefaction of a gel into a solution.

Solder—A fusible alloy used for joining metals.

Soldering—To make one tissue adhere to another by a laser technique.

Sole —Planta. The bottom of the foot.

Soleus—A flat, broad muscle of the calf of the leg.

Solid—Not liquid, gaseous or hollow.

Solidification —The act of solidifying.

Solidify—To make or become solid.

Solidity—Compactness.

Solipsism—The belief that the world consists only of the individual himself and his own experiences.

Solitary—Single or existing separately.

Solitude—A lonely place; seclusion from society.

Solubility—The quality of being dissolved.

Soluble —Capable of being dissolved.

Solum—Bottom or the lowest part.

Solum tympani—The floor of the tympanic cavity.

Solute—The substance disssolved in a solvent to form a solution.

Solutio—Solution.

Solution—1. Liquid containing dissolved substances. 2. The process of mixing a solid substance homogeneously with a liquid so that the dissolved substance can not be distinguished from the solvent liquid.

Aqueous solution—A solution containing water as the solvent.

Buffer solution—A solution of which the acidity or alkalinity is not changed upon adding a small amount of acid or alkali.

Colloidal solution—A solution in which the solute is suspended and not dissolved such as albumin etc.

Contrast solution —A solution containing a radiopaque substance, which is used to facilitate x-ray examination of the body cavities.

Hyperbaric solution—A solution with a specific gravity greater than that of the solution to which it is being compared.

Hypertonic solution—A solution having a greater osmotic pressure than that of the cells or body fluids, so it draws water out of the cells shrinking their cytoplasm.

Hypotonic solution—A solution having a lesser osmotic pressure than that of the cells or body fluids, so it causes water to enter the cells and thus inducing swelling and possibly rupture of red blood cells.

Isobaric solution—A solution with a specific gravity equal to that of the solution with which it is being compared.

Isosmotic solution—A solution with the same osmotic pressure as that of the solution with which it is being compared.

Isotonic solution—A solution that has the same osmotic pressure as that of the cells or body fluids.

Normal solution —A solution containing 1 gram equivalent weight of reagent in 1 L (1000 ml.) of solution, which is expressed by 1N.

Oral rehydration solution —A solution containing 3.5 grams of sodium chloride, 2.9 gms. potassium chloride, 2.9 gms. trisodium citrate and 1.5 gms. glucose dissolved in one liter of drinking water, used for drinking in dehydration.

Saturated solution—A solution that contains all the solute that can be dissolved by the solvent.

Seminormal solution—A solution containing ½ gm. equivalent weight of reagent in 1 L (1000 ml.) of solution, which is expressed by N/2.

Solv—Dissolve.

Solvate—A compound formed by reaction between solvent and solute.

Solvent—Dissolving or forming a solution.

Soma—1. The body as distinguished from the mind. 2. All of the body cells except the germ cells. 3. The cell body.

Somal—Somatic.

Somasthenia—Somatasthenia. Chronic bodily weakness.

Somat-, Somato—Prefixes indicating relationship to the body.

Somatalgia—Bodily pain.

Somatasthenia—Somasthenia.

Somatesthesia—The consciousness or awareness of the body.

Somatesthetic—Pertaining to somatesthesia.

Somatic—1. Pertaining to the body. 2. Characteristic of the body. 3. Pertaining to the body wall in contrast to the viscera.

Somaticosplanchnic—Somaticovisceral.

Somaticovisceral —Pertaining to the body and the viscera.

Somatist—The person who believes that mental disorders are originated from the body.

Somatization—The conversion of mental disorders into bodily symptoms.

Somatochrome—A nerve cell in which the nucleus is completely surrounded by the cytoplasm.

Somatogenic—Originating in the body.

Somatology—The study of the structure and functions of the human body.

Somatome—1. An instrument for cutting the body of a fetus. 2. Somite.

Somatomedin—A substance synthesized in the liver that regulates growth by its action on the effect of growth hormone on cartilage and bone.

Somatomegaly—Abnormally large size of the body.

Somatometry—Measurement of the body.

Somatopagus—Two fetuses fused together at the trunk.

Somatopathic—Suffering from bodily disease and not from mental one.

Somatopathy—Any disease of the body exclusive of mental one.

Somatoplasm —The protoplasm of all the body cells except that of the germ cells.

Somatopleural—Pertaining to somatopleure.

Somatopleure—The body wall of an embryo formed by the outer ectoderm and a layer of somatic mesoderm underlying it.

Somatoprosthetics—The art and science of replacement of the external missing or deformed parts of the body prosthetically.

Somatopsychic—Pertaining to both body and mind.

Somatopsychosis—Any mental disease that is a symptom of a bodily disease.

Somatoschisis—A fetus with a cleft in the trunk.

Somatoscopy—Examination of body.

Somatosensory—Sensation pertaining to the body's superficial and deep parts.

Somatosexual—Pertaining to the body and sexual characteristics.

Somatostatin—A hormone of hypothalamus that inhibits the release of somatotropin hormone and the secretion of insulin and gastrin.

Somatostatinoma—A somatostatin secreting tumor of the islets of Langerhans of the pancreas.

Somatotherapy —Treatment of the diseased body.

Somatotonia—The personality in which there is predominance of the physical activity.

Somatotopagnosis—Inability to identify any part of the body.

Somatotrope—Any of the cells of the anterior pituitary gland that secrete somatostatin (growth hormone).

Somatotroph—A cell of the anterior pituitary gland that produces somatotropin (growth-stimulating hormone).

Somatotrophic—1. Affecting the body cells. 2. Stimulating growth.

Somatotrophin—Somatotropin.

Somatotropic—Affecting the body or body cells.

Somatotropin—Growth-stimulating hormone of the anterior pituitary gland.

Somatotype—A particular type of body build.

Somatotypology—The study of somatotypes.

Somesthesia—Somatesthesia.

Somesthetic—Pertaining to the sensations and sensory structures of the body.

Somite—One of the paired, blocklike masses of mesoderm, arranged in the from of segments alongside the neural tube of the embryo. Each somite gives rise to a muscle supplied by a spinal nerve and a pair gives rise to a vertebra.

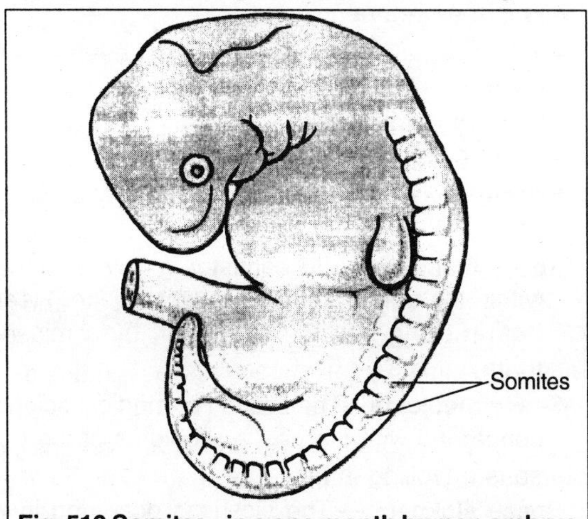

Fig. 519 Somites : in a one month human embryo

Somnambulance—Somnambulism.

Somnambule—The person who walks while asleep.

Somnambulism—Sleep-walking.

Somnambulist—Somnambule.

Somnifacient—Hypnotic. Producing sleep.

Somniferous—Producing sleep or pertaining to that which produces sleep.

Somnific—Producing sleep.

Somniloquence—Somniloquism.

Somniloquism—Talking in one's sleep.

Somniloquist—The person who talkes in sleep.

Somniloquy—The act of talking during sleep.

Somnipathist—The person affected wtih any sleep disorder or who is under the influence of hypnosis.

Somnipathy—1. Any sleep disorder. 2. Hypnotism.

Somnocinematograph—An apparatus for recording motions of the sleeping persons.

Somnolence—1. Sleepiness. 2. Drowsiness.

Somnolency—Somnolence.

Somnolent—1. Sleepy. 2. Drowsy.

Somnolentia—1. Somnolence or drowsiness. 2. Disturbed sleep of a drunkard with excitement or violent behavior.

Somnolescent—Inclined to sleep, drowsy.

Somnolism—Condition of being in hypnotic state.

Sone—A unit of sound.

Sonic—Of, pertaining to, or determined by sound.

Sonicate—To expose to sound waves.

Sonication—Exposure to sound waves.

Sonification—The production of sound, or of sound waves.

Sonifier—An instrument producing sound waves.

Sonify—To produce sound.

Sonitus—Tinnitus aurium.

Sonochemistry—The branch of chemistry concerned with chemical changes caused by sound, particularly ultrasound.

Sonogram—Ultrasonogram. The record obtained by ultrasonography.

Sonograph—Ultrasonograph.

Sonographer—Ultrasonographer.

Sonography—Ultrasonography.

Sonolucent—In ultrasonography, not reflecting the ultrasound waves back to their source, *i.e.* not producing the echoes.

Sonometer—An instrument which causes sound to produce anesthesia, used by dentists.

Sonomotor—Pertaining to the movements caused by sound.

Sonorous—Resonant; making noise.

Sophisticate—To adulterate.

Sophistication—In medicine, adulteration of any substance.

Sophomania—Ove r confidence on one's own wisdom.

Sopor—An unnaturally deep sleep.

Soporiferous—Promoting sleep.

Soporific—Producing deep sleep, or narcotic.

Soporose, Soporous—Marked by deep sleep or coma.

Sorb—To attract and retain the substances by absorption or adsorption.

Sorbefacient—Causing or promoting absorption.

Sorbent—That which absorbs.

Sordes—Foul brown crusts on the teeth and about the lips, usually found in low grade pyrexia.

Sore—1. Tender or painful. 2. Painful Ulcer.

Soreness—Pain or ache.

Sore throat—Pharyngitis, laryngitis or tonsillitis.

Soroche—Mountain sickness.

Sororiation—Growth of the breasts at puberty.

Sorption—The condition of being absorbed.

S. O. S.—When necessary.

Souffle—A soft blowing sound heard in auscultation, or auscultatory murmur; a bruit.

Cardiac souffle—Heart murmur.

Fetal souffle—Fetal murmur. The murmur heard over the uterus in late pregnancy due to compression of the umbilical cord of the fetus.

Funic souffle —Fetal souffle.

Placental souffle —See Under 'P'.

Splenic souffle—Sound heard over spleen in malaria.

Uterine souffle—A sound produced by blood entering dilated arteries of the uterus in the last months of pregnancy, occurring simultaneously with the pulse of the mother.

Sound—1. Sensation produced in the ear by vibrations of the air or other medium. 2. The energy of vibrations that gives rise to sensations in the ear. 3. A noise. 4. An instrument for introduction into a cavity or canal to detect a foreign body or to dilate a stricture. 5. Healthy, not diseased.

Blowing sound—A whistling sound produced by expulsion of air through a small aperture with moderate force.

Bottle sound—Sound as of a fluid in a bottle.

Breath sounds—Respiratory sounds heard on auscultation.

Cardiac sounds—Heart sounds.

Cracked-pot sound— Sound as produced on striking a cracked pot heard over the pulmonary cavities.

Ejection sound—High-pitched clicking sound heard just after the first heart sound.

Fetal heart sound—Sound produced by the heart of the fetus.

Friction sound—Sound produced by rubbing together two inflamed mucous surfaces.

Heart sound—The two sounds "lubb" and "dupp" of the heart heard over the cardiac region.

Percussion sound —Any sound made by percussion.

Respiratory sound—The sound heard over the lungs.

Succussion sound—A splashing sound heard over a cavity filled with a fluid.

Urethral sound—An instrument used for detecting the location of a calculus or stricture in the urethra.

Soup—A liquid food prepared from vegetables or meat.

Sour—Of acid taste.

Sp—1. Spirit 2. Species.

Space—1. An area or cavity in the body. 2. Heaven.

Space maintainer—In dentistry, a device placed within the dental arch to prevent adjacent teeth from moving into the space left by a missing tooth.

Space medicine—The branch of medical science concerned with the health problems of the persons travelling in air.

Space sickness —The sickness occurring in air travellers characterized by vertigo which occurs when the head is actively moved in a weightless environment, general malaise, nausea and vomting.

Spall—1. A fragment. 2. To break up into fragments.

Spallation—1. The process of breaking into very small parts. 2. The release of inert particles into the blood stream.

Span—Full extent as the full extent of life.

Spanogyny—More males than females or decrease in births of female children.

Sparer—A substance destroyed by catabolism but even then it lessens catabolic action upon other substance.

Sparganoma—A mass containing spargana, the larvae of a tapeworm of the genus Diphyllobothrium.

Sparganosis—Infection with the larvae (spargana) of any tapeworm, especially those of the genus Diphyllobothrium, which invade the subcutaneous tissue causing inflammation and fibrosis.

Sparganum—A larva of a tapeworm especially of the genus Diphyllobothrium. Plural is spargana.

Sparge—To introduce air or gas into a liquid.

Spargosis—1. Distention of the female breasts with milk. 2. Elephantiasis. Thickening of the skin.

Spasm—A sudden involuntary contraction of the muscles.

Bronchial spasm—Spasm of the muscular coats of smaller bronchi causing asthma.

Carpopedal spasm—Involuntary muscular contraction of the hands and feet.

Choreiform spasm—Spasmodic movements resembling chorea.

Clonic spasm—Alternate contraction and relaxation of the muscles.

Habit spasm—Tic. Spasm due to habit.

Myopathic spasm—The spasm accompanying disease of the muscles.

Nodding spasm—Clonic spasm of the sternomastoid muscles causing nodding of the head.

Tetanic spasm—1. Muscular spasm occurring in tetanus. 2. Tonic spasm.

Tonic spasm—Involuntary muscular contractions continued for a long time.

Toxic spasm—Spasm caused by a toxin.

Spasmatic—Spasmodic.

Spasmo- —A prefix meaning spasm.

Spasmodic—Pertaining to, resembling or marked with spasm.

Spasmogen—Causing spasm.

Spasmogenic—Causing spasms.

Spasmology—The study of spasms.

Spasmolygmus—Hiccough or sobbing due to spasmodic closure of the glottis.

Spasmolysin—That which abolishes the spasms.

Spasmolysis—Abolition of the spasm.

Spasmolytic—Antispasmodic.

Spasmophemia—Stuttering.

Spasmophilia—Abnormal tendency to spasm or convulsions.

Spasmophilic—Pertaining to spasmophilia.

Spasmous—Of the nature of spasm.

Spasmus—Spasm.

Spastic—1. Resembling spasms, or of the nature of spasm. 2. Produced by spasm. 3. The person afflicted wtih spasms.

Spastic gait—A stiff movement of the legs while walking.

Spasticity—A condition of increased tone or contractions of muscles causing stiffness and awkard movements.

Spatia—Plural of spatium.

Spatial—Pertaining to space.

Spatium—Space.

Spatula—A flat, thin, somewhat flexible knife-shaped instrument, used for spreading or mixing semisolid materials on a smooth surface.

Spatulate—To mix something by spatula.

Spatulated— Mixed with spatula.

Spatulation—The process of mixing materials homogeneously by spatula on a smooth surface.

SPCA—Serum prothrombin conversion accelerator (blood coagulation Factor VII).

Specialist—One who has special knowledge in some branch of medical science.

Specialization—The act of gaining special knowledge in some branch of medical science.

Specialize—To become specialist.

Specialty—The branch of medical science in which a specialist practices.

Speciation—The formation of new species of organisms by evolutionary process.

Species—In biology, a category of classification of living organisms, just below genus.

Species-specific—The characteristics of a species.

Specific—1. Peculiar, particular, special. 2. A medicine that is curative for a particular disease or symptom. 3. A disease always produced by the same type of organism. 4. Restricted in use, effect etc., to a particular organ, function etc. 5. Pertaining to a species.

Specific dynamic action—The increase in metabolic rate resulting from absorption of food.

Specific gravity—The weight of a substance compared with that of water of equal volume.

Specificity—The state of being specific.

Specilla—Plural of specillum.

Specillum—1. Lens. 2. Button-shaped probe.

Specimen—Sample. A part of a thing to show kind and quality of the whole, as a specimen of urine.

Speck—A small spot.

Spectacles—See glasses.

Spectra—Plural of spectrum.

Spectral—Pertaining to a spectrum.

Spectro- —A prefix which means spectrum.

Spectrochemistry—The study of chemical substances and their identification by means of spectroscopy.

Spectrocolorimeter—An apparatus for detecting color blindness by isolating a single color of the spectrum.

Spectrofluorometer—An instrument for measuring the degree of fluorescence.

Spectrogram—A graph of a spectrum.

Spectrograph—An instrument made to photograph the spectra on a sensitive photographic plate.

Spectrography—The procedure of photographing or tracing a spectrum.

Spectrometer—An instrument used for determining the wavelength of light produced by a spectroscope.

Spectrometry—The process of determining the wavelength of light rays by using spectrometer.

Spectrophobia—Morbid fear of mirrors or of one's mirrored image.

Spectrophotofluorimetry—Measurement of the intensity and quality of a fluorescence by means of a spectrophotometer.

Spectrophotometer—An apparatus for determining the quantity of color in a solution by comparing the transmitted light with the spectrum.

Spectrophotometry—Determination of the quantity of color in a solution by the use of a spectrophotometer.

Spectroscope—An instrument for separating the light into its component colors by means of a prism through which light passes to form a spectrum for inspection.

Spectroscopic—Concerning a spectroscope.

Spectroscopy—The use of spectroscope.

Spectrum—A band of seven colors formed by passage of the white light through a glass prism. These colors are of different wavelengths ranging from 7700 Angstrom units (A.U.) to 3900 A.U. and are in order from the shortest wavelength to longest as violet, indigo, blue, green, yellow, orange and red which appear as rainbow.

Absorption spectrum—The spectrum formed after light rays have passed through a substance that absorbs some of the colors into it. The spectrum is specific for various chemicals.

Broad spectrum—A term used for antibiotics effective against various microorganisms.

Chromatic spectrum—Visible spectrum.

Invisible spectrum—The spectrum above the red (7700 A.U. wavelength) or below the violet (3900 A.U. wavelength) is invisible to the eye.

Visible spectrum—Chromatic spectrum. The spectrum of the colors from violet to red with the wavelenths of 3900 to 7700 A.U. is visible to the eye.

Speculum —An instrument for opening or distending an orifice, canal or cavity of the body for visual examination, *e.g.*, ear speculum which is a short funnel-shaped tube for examination of the ear.

Ear speculum—A short funnel-shaped tube for examination of the ear.

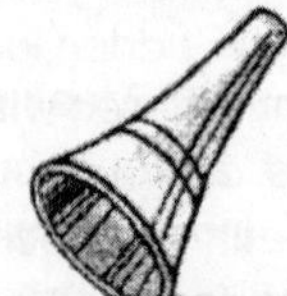

Fig. 520 A : Ear speculum

Eye speculum—An instrument for keeping the eyelids apart during inspection or operation on the eye.

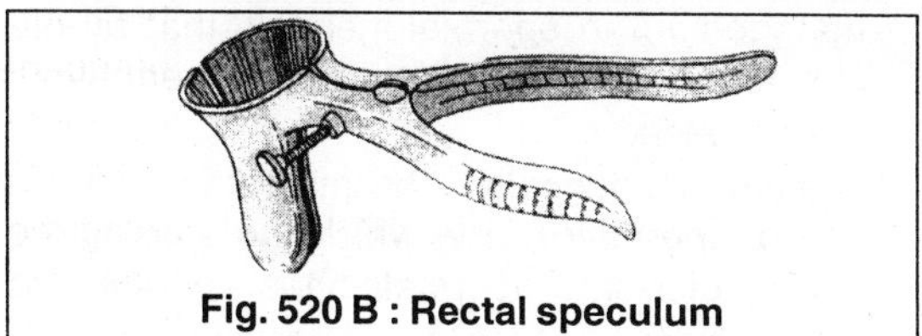
Fig. 520 B : Rectal speculum

Rectal speculum—A tubular speculum with obturator for rectal examination.

Vaginal speculum—A speculum with two opposing broad and flattened blades which after being inserted into the vagina, are pushed apart, used for inspection of the vagina and cervix.

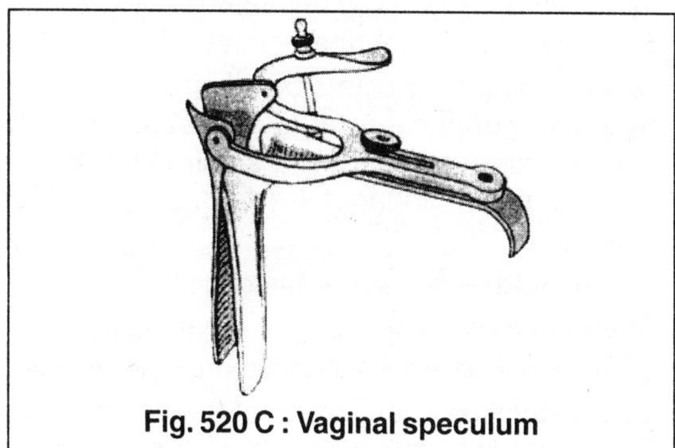
Fig. 520 C : Vaginal speculum

Speech—1. Expression of thoughts by vocal sounds. 2. Utterance of the words. 3. Spoken words.

Aphonic speech—Whispering.

Ataxic speech—Defective speech resulting from muscular incoordination, usually the result of a disorder of cerebellum.

Cued speech—A language for the deaf persons that combines lip reading, and gestures provided by the hands.

Echo speech—Echolalia.

Esophageal speech—Speech produced by vibration of air in the esophagus, in the person who has got excised his/her larynx.

Explosive speech—Sudden loud speech produced in the person afflicted with organic brain disease or mental disorder.

Interjectional speech—Speech characterized by inarticulate sounds.

Mirror speech—A speech defect in which the letters of a word are spoken reversely.

Pressed speech—Rapid and incoherent speech which may not be understandable to the listener.

Scamping speech—Clipped speech. Speech in which words difficult to pronounce are omitted.

Scanning speech—Speech in which syllables of words are separated by long pauses.

Slurring speech—Indistinct pronunciation.

Staccato speech—Slow and laborious speech with each syllable pronounced separately.

Stammering speech—Stuttering speech. Hesitant or faltering speech.

Spell—A paroxysm.

Sperm—1. Semen. 2. Spermatozoa.

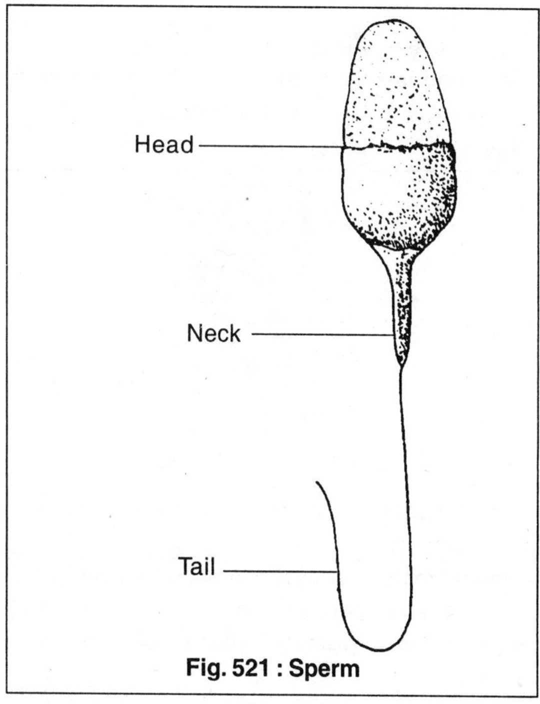

Fig. 521 : Sperm

Sperma-, Spermato-, Spermo- —Prefixes meaning semen, spermatozoa.

Sperma—1. Semen. 2. Male germ cell.

Spermacrasia—Aspermia. Lack of spermatozoa in the semen.

Spermagglutination—Agglutination of the spermatozoa.

Spermatemphraxis—Obstruction in the ejection of semen.

Spermatic—Pertaining to semen or sperm.

Spermatic cord—See under cord.

Spermatic duct—Seminal duct. Any duct that conveys semen, especially the ductus deferens and the ejaculatory duct.

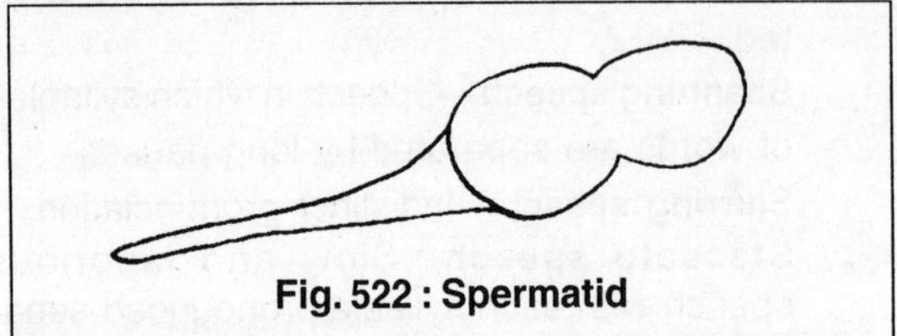

Fig. 522 : Spermatid

Spermaticidal—Destructive to or killing spermatozoa.

Spermaticide—Spermaticidal. Spermicide.

Spermatid—Spermatoblast.

Spermatin—A mucilaginous substance in the semen.

Spermatism—Ejaculation of semen.

Spermatitis—Deferentitis. Inflammation of the spermatic cord or of the ductus deferens.

Spermato- —A prefix meaning sperm.

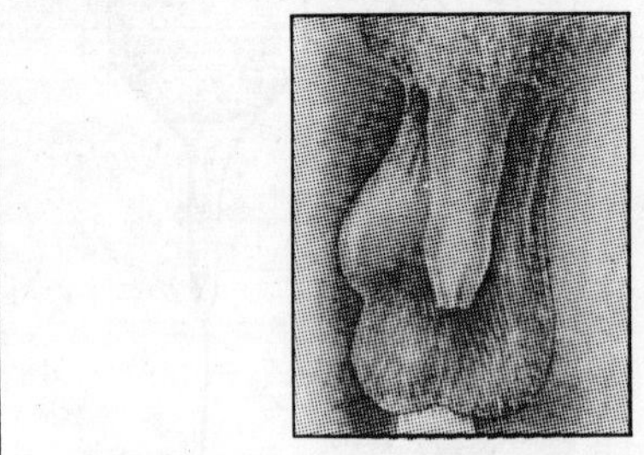

Fig. 523 : Spermatocele

Spermatoblast—Spermatid. A rudimentary spermatozoon.

Spermatocele—A cystic tumor of the epididymis containing spermatozoa.

Spermatocelectomy—Excision of a spermatocele.

Spermatocidal—Spermaticidal.

Spermatocide—Spermatocidal. Spermicide.

Spermatocyst—1. A seminal vesicle. 2. Spermatocele.

Spermatocystectomy—Excision of a seminal vesicle.

Spermatocystitis—Seminal vesiculitis. Inflammation of a seminal vesicle.

Spermatocystotomy—To make an incision into a seminal vesicle.

Spermatocytal—Pertaining to the spermatocytes.

Spermatocyte—A cell originating from a spermatogonium in spermatogenesis that by division forms spermatids from which spermatozoa are produced.

Spermatocytogenesis—The initial stage of formation of spermatozoa in which the spermatogonia develop into spermatocytes and then into spermatids.

Spermatogenesis—The process of formation of the spermatozoa.

Spermatogenetic—Spermatogenic.

Spermatogenic—Producing spermatozoa.

Spermatogenous—Spermatogenic.

Spermatogeny—Spermatogenesis.

Spermatogone—Spermatogonium.

Spermatogonium—A large unspecialized male germ cell originating in a seminal tubule and that in spermatogenesis gives rise to spermatocytes.

Spermatoid—Like a spermatozoon.

Spermatology—The study of the semen.

Spermatolysin—A lysin destroying spermatozoa.

Spermatolysis—Destruction of the spermatozoa.

Spermatolytic—Destroying spermatozoa.

Spermatopathia—Any disease of the semen.

Spermatopathy—Spermatopathia.

Spermatophobia—Morbid fear of spermatorrhea.

Spermatopoietic—Forming the semen.

Spermatorrhea—Frequent involuntary escape of the semen without sexual excitement.

Spermatoschesis—Suppression of the semen.

Spermatospore—Spermatogonium.

Spermatotoxin—Spermatoxin.

Spermatovum—An impregnated ovum.

Spermatoxin—A toxin that destroys the spermatozoa.

Spermatozoa—Plural of spermatozoon.

Spermatozoal—Pertaining to the spermatozoa.

Spermatozoan—Spermatozoal.

Spermatozoicide—Spermicide.

Spermatozoon—A mature male germ cell formed within the seminiferous tubules of the testes from spermatids. It is about 51 microns in length and divided into 3 parts, 1st is a broad oval, flattened head with a nucleus and a flagellum, 2nd is protoplasmic neck in the middle and 3rd is the tail. It fertilizes the ovum by piercing it with its head.

Spermaturia—Seminuria. Presence of semen in the urine.

Spermectomy—Excision of a part of the spermatic cord.

Spermia—Plural of spermium.

Spermic—Pertaining to spermatozoa.

Spermicidal—Spermicide.

Spermicide—Killing spermatozoa.

Spermiduct—The ejaculatory duct and vas deferens considered as one.

Spermiogenesis—The second stage in the formation of spermatozoa, in which the spermatids transform into spermatozoa.

Spermiogram—Record of examination of the spermatozoa in semen.

Spermium—Mature male germ cell or spermatozoon.

Spermo- —Sperma.

Spermoblast—Spermatid. Spermatoblast.

Spermolith—A calculus in the seminal vesicle or spermatic duct.

Spermolysin—Spermatolysin.

Spermolysis—Spermatolysis.

Spermolytic—Spermatolytic.

Spermoneuralgia —Neuralgic pain in the spermatic cord.

Spermophlebectasia—Varicosity of the spermatic veins.

Spermoplasm—The protoplasm of the spermatozoon.

Spermosphere—A mass of spermatoblasts derived from spermatogonia.

Spermospore—Spermatogonium.

Spermotoxin —Spermatoxin.

Sp. gr.—Specific gravity.

Sph.—Spherical.

Sphacelate—To become gangrenous or necrotic.

Sphacelation—1. The process of becoming gangrenous or necrotic. 2. Gangrene or necrosis.

Sphacelism—1. Sphacelation or necrosis. 2. Sloughing.

Sphaceloderma —Gangrene of the skin.

Sphacelous —Gangrenous; necrosed; sloughing.

Sphacelus—A slough or a mass of gangrenous tissue.

Sphagiasmus—Spasm of the muscles of neck occurring in convulsion of epilepsy.

Sphagitis—Inflammation of the throat.

Sphenethmoid—Sphenoethmoid.

Sphenion—The tip of the sphenoidal angle of the parietal bone.

Spheno- —A prefix meaning wedge-shaped or sphenoid bone.

Sphenobasilar —Pertaining to the sphenoid bone and the basilar portion of the occipital bone.

Sphenoccipital—Concerning the sphenoid and occipital bones.

Sphenocephalus—A fetus with wedge-shaped head.

Sphenocephaly—The condition of having a wedge-shaped head.

Sphenoethmoid —Pertaining to the sphenoid and ethmoid bones.

Sphenoethmoidectomy —To remove diseased portion of sphenoid and ethmoid bones, by surgery.

Sphenofrontal —Pertaining to the sphenoid and frontal bones.

Sphenoid—Wedge-shaped.

Sphenoidal—Concerning the sphenoid bone.

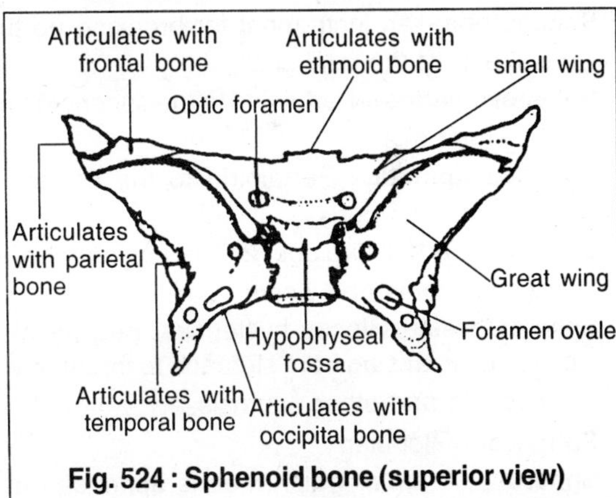

Fig. 524 : Sphenoid bone (superior view)

Sphenoid bone —The large bone at the base of the skull between the occipital and ethmoid bones in front, and the parietal and temporal bones at the side.

Sphenoid fissure —Fissure in sphenoid and frontal bones for nerves and blood vessels.

Sphenoiditis—Inflammation of the sphenoidal sinus or necrosis of the sphenoid bone.

Sphenoidostomy—To make an opening into a spenoid sinus.

Sphenoidotomy —To make an incision into the sphenoid bone.

Sphenomalar—Concerning the sphenoid and malar bones.

Sphenomaxillary —Pertaining to the sphenoid bone and maxilla.

Spheno-occipital —Pertaining to the shenoid and occipital bones.

Sphenopalatine —Pertaining to the sphenoid and palatine bones.

Sphenoparietal —Pertaining to the sphenoid and parietal bones.

Sphenopetrosal —Pertaining to the sphenoid bone and the petrous portion of the temporal bone.

Sphenorbital —Pertaining to the sphenoid bone and the orbits.

Sphenosis—A condition in which fetus becomes wedge-shaped in the pelvis of the mother.

Sphenosquamosal—Squamosphenoid.

Sphenotemporal —Pertaining to the sphenoid and temporal bones.

Sphenotic—A fetal bone that becomes part of the sphenoid bone.

Sphenotresia—Perforation of base of the skull of a fetus in craniotomy.

Sphenotribe—An instrument for breaking up the basal part of the fetal skull.

Sphenovomerine—Pertaining to the sphenoid and the vomer bone.

Sphenozygomatic—Pertaining to the sphenoid and zygomatic bones.

Sphere—1. A ball or globe. 2. The environment in which one lives and works.

Spheresthesia—Globus hystericus. Feeling of a ball or lump arising from stomach to throat, seen in hysteria and other neurosis.

Spherical—Globular.

Sphero- —A prefix which means spherical or a sphere.

Spherocylinder—A lens with a spherical and a cylindrical surface.

Spherocyte—A spherical red blood cell.

Fig. 525 : Spherocyte

Spherocytosis—Presence of spherocytes in the blood.

Spheroid —Sphere-like body.

Spheroidal—Resembling a sphere.

Spherolith—A very small stone in the kidney of the newborn.

Spheroma—A spherical tumor.

Spherometer—An apparatus to determine the curvature of a surface.

Spheroplast—A bacterium from which the rigid cell wall has been incompletely removed.

Spherospermia—Round spermatozoa without tails.

Spherule —A very small sphere.

Sphincter—A circular muscle closing a natural orifice or passage, *e.g.*, anal sphincter which closes the anus, the external one being of striated muscle and the internal one of plain muscle.

Sphincteral—Pertaining to a sphincter.

Sphincteralgia—Pain in a sphincter muscle.

Sphincterectomy—Excision of a sphincter muscle.

Sphincterial, Sphincteric—Sphincteral.

Sphincteric—Sphincteral.

Sphincterismus—Spasm of anal sphincter muscles.

Sphincteritis—Inflammation of a sphincter muscle.

Sphincteroid—Resembling a sphincter.

Sphincterolysis—Separation of iris from the cornea in anterior synechia.

Sphincteroplasty—Plastic surgery upon a sphincter muscle.

Sphincteroscope —An instrument for inspection of the anal sphincter.

Sphincteroscopy—Inspection of the internal anal sphincter with sphincteroscope.

Sphincterotome—An instrument for cutting a sphincter.

Sphincterotomy—To incise a sphincter muscle.

Sphygmic—Pertaining to the pulse.

Sphygmo- —A prefix indicating pulse.

Sphygmobolometer—An apparatus for measuring force of the pulse.

Sphygmocardiogram —A tracing of the heart beat and radial pulse.

Sphygmocardiograph—An apparatus for recording the radial pulse and the heart beat simultaneously.

Sphygmocardioscope —Sphygmocardiograph.

Sphygmochronograph —A sphygmograph for recording time between the heart beat and the pulse.

Sphygmodynamometer—Sphygmobolometer.

Sphygmogram—A tracing of the pulse made by using the sphygmograph.

Sphygmograph—Polygraph.

Sphygmographic—Pertaining to or made by a sphygmograph.

Sphygmography—To record the arterial pulse by using a sphygmograph.

Sphygmoid—Resembling the pulse.

Sphygmology—Scientific study of the pulse.

Sphygmomanometer—An instrument for measuring the arterial blood pressure (Blood pressure instrument). It is of two types, aneroid and mercury.

Sphygmomanometry—Measurement of the blood pressure by means of a sphygmomanometer.

Sphygmometer —Sphygmograph. An instrument for measuring the pulse.

Sphygmometroscope—An instrument used for auscultation of the pulse.

Sphygmo-oscillometer—An instrument resembling an aneroid sphygmomanometer used for measuring systolic and diastolic blood pressure.

Sphygmopalpation—Palpation of the pulse.

Sphygmophone—An instrument for hearing the pulse beat.

Sphygmoscope —An instrument for showing the heart's movements and pulse beats.

Sphygmosystole—The segment of the sphygmogram that corresponds to the heart's systole.

Sphygmotonograph—An instrument for recording graphically both the pulse and the blood pressure simultaneously.

Sphygmotonometer—An instrument for measuring elasticity of the arterial walls.

Sphygmoviscosimetry—Measurement of the pressure and viscosity of the blood.

Sphygmus—A pulse or pulsation.

Sphyrectomy—Excision of the malleus.

Sphyrotomy—To incise the malleus.

Spica—A figure-of-8 bandage, with turns crossing each other.

Spicae—Plural of spica.

Spicular—Pertaining to or resembling a spicule.

Spicule—A small, sharp needle-shaped structure.

Spiculum—Spicule.

Spider-burst—The area on the leg in which dilated capillaries radiate from a central point.

Spider cells—Branching cells in neuroglia.

Spider fingers—Arachnodactyly. Abnormally long, slender and curved fingers.

Spider nevus—Nevus araneus. A growth of the skin in which dilated capillaries radiate from a central red point resembling a spider.

Spigelian line—Linea semilunaris. A line on the abdomen lying parallel to the median line and marking the edge of the rectus abdominis muscle.

Spigelian lobe—A small lobe behind the right lobe of liver.

Spike—A sharp upward deflection in a tracing, as on the encephalogram.

Spill —An overflow.

Spillway —The contour of the teeth through which food escapes from the cusps during mastication.

Spiloma, Spilus—Nevus. A mole or discoloration of the skin.

Spiloplaxia—A red spot appearing in leprosy.

Spilus—A flat form of nevus pigmentosus.

Spina—1. The spine. 2. A thornlike process or projection.

Spina bifida—A congenital defect in which the laminae of the vertebrae in vertebral column do not fuse together through which meninges usually protrude.

Spinae—Plural of spina.

Spinal—Pertaining to a spine, vertebral column or spinal cord.

Spinal anesthesia —Narcosis. Anesthesia produced by an anesthetic injected into the spinal canal.

Spinal canal —Canal of the vertebral column containing the spinal cord.

Spinal column—The vertebral column enclosing the spinal cord and consisting of 33 bones : 7 cervical, 12 dorsal or thoracic, 5 lumbar, 5 sacral fused to from 1 bone, and 4 in the coccyx fused to from 1 bone.

Spinal cord—See under cord.

Spinal fluid—Cerebrospinal fluid.

Spinal ganglion—Knotlike enlargement on the dorsal or posterior root of a spinal nerve consisting of nerve cell bodies.

Spinalgia—Pain in the region of the vertebral column.

Spinalis—Spinal.

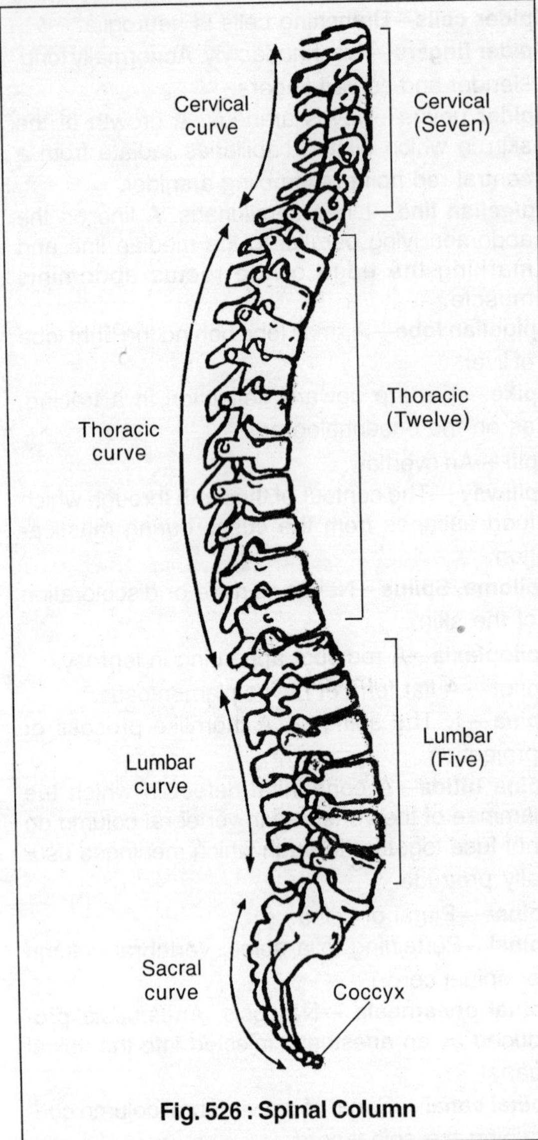

Fig. 526 : Spinal Column

Spinal nerves—31 pairs of nerves arising from the spinal cord consisting of 8 cervical, 12 thoracic, 5 lumbar, 5 sacral and 1 coccygeal, corresponding with the spinal vertebrae.

Spinal puncture—See lumbar puncture.

Spinal stenosis—Narrowing of the spinal canal.

Spinate—Having thorns or thorn-shaped.

Spindle—A fusiform or tapering on both ends.

Spindle-shaped—Fusiform.

Spine—1. A sharp thorn-like process of bone. 2. Spinal column, vertebral column or back bone.

Spinifugal—Moving away from the spinal cord.

Spinipetal—Moving toward the spinal cord.

Spinnbarkeit—The elasticity of cervical mucus, by which the day of ovulation can be detected. The cervical mucus is placed on a glass slide and then drawn up with a forceps. It can be drawn to the maximum i.e. it is of the maximum elasticity on the day of ovulation, after which the elasticity diminishes.

Spinobulbar—Pertaining to the spinal cord and medulla oblongata.

Spinocellular—Pertaining to or like prickle cells.

Spinocerebellar—Concerning spinal cord and cerebellum.

Spinocollicular—Spinotectal.

Spinocortical—Corticospinal. Pertaining to the spinal cord and cerebral cortex.

Spinoglenoid—Pertaining to the spine and the glenoid cavity of the scapula.

Spinomuscular—Pertaining to the spinal cord and the muscles supplied by the spinal nerves.

Spinoneural—Pertaining to the spinal cord and the nerves given off from it.

Spinose—Spinous.

Spinotectal —Pertaining to the spinal cord and the tectum, the dorsal portion of the midbrain.

Spinothalamic—Pertaining to the spinal cord and thalamus.

Spinous—Pertaining to or like a spine.

Spinous process—A pointed outgrowth at the posterior part of each vertebra.

Spinthariscope—Scintillation counter. An instrument used for the detection of radioactivity.

Spintherism—Sensation of sparks before the eyes.

Spintheropia—Spintherism in fishes etc.

Spiracle—Breathing hole in fishes etc.

Spiradenoma—Benign tumor of the sweat glands.

Spiral—Coiled, twisted, winding like a screw.

Spirilla—Plural of spirillum.

Spirillar—S-shaped.

Spirillicidal—Destroying spirilla or spirochetes.

Spirillicide—Spirillicidal.

Spirillolysis—The destruction of spirilla.

Spirillosis—A disease caused by the presence of spirilla in the blood.

Spirillotropic—Being attracted toward spirilla.

Spirillotropism—The ability to attract spirilla.

Spirillum—A spiral-shaped bacterium.

Spirit—1. Strong alcoholic liquid or liquor. 2. Any distilled or volatile liquid. 3. A solution of volatile or essential liquid such as spirit chloroform. 4. Essence. 5. Soul. 6. Courage.

Spiritual therapy—Treatment of the diseases by applying spiritual knowledge.

Spirituous—1. Pertaining to alcohol. 2. Alcoholic.

Spiritus—Spirit. Alcoholic solution of a volatile substance.

Spiro-, Spir- —Prefixes which mean 1. Coil or coil-shaped.

Fig. 527 Spirochaeta Treponema pallidum

Spirochaeta pallidum —Treponema pallidum. A slender, spiral, motile bacterium of the family Spirochaetaceae and order Spirochaetales which causes syphilis.

Spirochetal—Pertaining to spirochetes.

Spirochetalytic—Spirocheticidal.

Spirochete—Any microorganism of the order Spirochaetales.

Spirochetemia—Presence of spirochetes in the blood.

Spirocheticidal —Destructive to spirochetes.

Spirocheticide—Spirocheticidal.

Spirochetolysis —The destruction of spirochetes by lysis.

Spirochetosis —Any infection with spirochetes.

Spirochetotic—Pertaining to or afflicted with spirochetosis.

Spirocheturia —Presence of spirochetes in the urine.

Spirogram—A record made by a spirograph of the respiratory movements.

Spirograph—An instrument for recording the respiration.

Spiroid—Resembling a spiral.

Spirokinesis—To move in spiral direction.

Spiroma—Spiradenoma.

Spirometer—Pneometer. An apparatus for measuring the air capacity of the lungs.

Spirometry—The measurement of the air capacity of the lungs.

Spiroscope—An apparatus for measuring the air capacity of the lungs.

Spissated—Inspissated.

Spissitude—Thickness of a liquid caused by evaporation.

Spit—1. Saliva. 2. To expectorate saliva.

Spiteful—Jealous.

Spitter—One who spits.

Spitting—The expelling of saliva from the mouth.

Spittle—Saliva.

Splanchna—The intestines or the viscera.

Splanchnapophysis—A skeletal element, such as the lower jaw involved in the function of the digestive tract.

Splanchnectopia—Displacement of a viscus or the the viscera.

Splanchnemphraxis—Obstruction occurring in any internal organ, especially in the intestine.

Splanchnesthesia—Sensation of the internal organs.

Splanchnesthetic—Pertaining to the sensation of the internal organs.

Splanchni-, Splanchno- —Prefixes which mean viscera.

Splanchnic—Pertaining to the viscera or internal organs.

Splanchnicectomy—Excision of part of the splanchnic nerve.

Splanchnic nerves—Three nerves from the thoracic sympathetic ganglia supplying the viscera.

Splanchnicotomy—Transection of a splanchnic nerve.

Splanchnoblast—A rudiment of a viscus.

Splanchnocele—Hernia of a viscus.

Splanchnocoele—The rudimentary cavity of the embryo (coelom) from which visceral cavities are formed.

Splanchnocranium—Viscerocranium.

Splanchnodiastasis—Displacement or separation of any viscus.

Splanchnodynia—Pain occurring in the abdominal region.

Splanchnography—Anatomical description of the viscera.

Splanchnolith—A calculus in the intestine.

Splanchnologia—Splanchnology.

Splanchnology—The study of the viscera.

Splanchnomegaly—Visceromegaly. Enlargement of a viscus.

Splanchnomicria—The condition of having small viscera.

Splanchnopathia—Splanchnopathy.

Splanchnopathy—Any disease of the viscera.

Splanchnopleural—Pertaining to splanchnopleure.

Splanchnopleure—A layer of the embryo formed by the union of visceral layer of mesoderm with entoderm from which the muscles and connective tissue of the digestive tract develop.

Splanchnopleuric—Splanchnopleural.

Splanchnoptosia, Splanchnoptosis—Prolapse of the viscera.

Splanchnosclerosis—Hardening of the viscera.

Splanchnoscopy—X-ray or transillumination examination of the viscera.

Splanchnoskeletal—Pertaining to splanchnoskeleton.

Splanchnoskeleton—Skeletal structures connected with the viscera.

Splanchnosomatic—Viscerosomatic.

Splanchnotomy—Dissection of the viscera.

Splanchnotribe—An instrument for crushing the intestine to close its lumen temporarily.

Splash—To be scattered in drops.

Splashing—Spattering.

Splay—To open the end of a tubular structure by making a longitudinal incision, to increase its diameter.

Splayfoot—Talipes valgus. Flat foot.

Spleen—A large, dark red and spongy gland situated in the upper left part of the abdominal cavity lateral to the cardiac end of the stomach. It is enclosed by a dense capsule, and on one side of it is the hilum through which the splenic vessels and nerves enter and exit. Its function is the formation of all types of blood cells in the embryo and newborn, but only lymphocytes and monocytes in adults, serving as a blood storage, the disintegration of red blood cells and the setting free of hemoglobin, which the liver converts into bilirubin, acts as a filter for blood by removing the bacteria and the disintegrated or useless red blood cells etc., from the circulation.

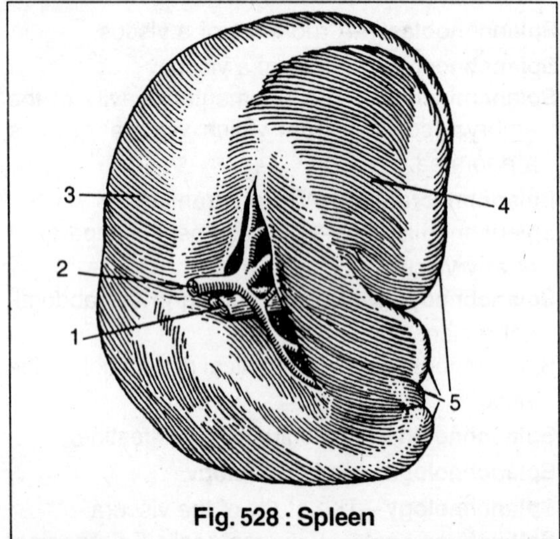

Fig. 528 : Spleen

1. Splenic vein, 2. Splenic artery, 3. Site of contact with left kidney, 4. Site of contact with stomach, 5. Anterior border of spleen.

Accessory spleen—A nodule of the splenic tissue connected with the spleen.

Floating spleen—Spleen that is not fixed.

Lardaceous spleen—Enlarged spleen due to deposition of fat.

Movable spleen—Floating spleen.

Sago spleen—Spleen appearing as the grains of sago.

Wandering spleen—Floating spleen.

Waxy spleen—Spleen affected with amyloid degeneration.

Splenadenoma—Tumor of the spleen caused by hyperplasia of its pulp.

Splenalgia —Splenodynia. Pain in the spleen.

Splenceratosis—The hardening of the spleen.

Splenectasia, Splenectasis—Splenomegaly.

Splenectomy—Excision of the spleen.

Splenectopia, Splenectopy—Spleen, floating. Displacement or mobility of the spleen.

Splenelcosis—Ulcer or abscess formation in the spleen.

Splenemia—Congestion of the spleen with blood.

Splenemphraxis—Congestion of the spleen.

Spleneolus—Accessory spleen.

Splenetic—Splenic. Pertaining to or suffering from disease of the spleen.

Splenetic flexure—The bend made by the union of transverse and descending colon on the left side near the spleen.

Splenial—Pertaining to the splenium.

Splenic—Splenetic.

Splenicterus—Inflammation of the spleen associated with jaundice.

Spleniculus—Accessory spleen.

Splenification—Splenization.
Spleniform—Resembling the spleen.
Splenitis—Inflammation of the spleen.
Splenium—1. A bandage or compress. 2. A bandlike structure.
Splenization—Splenification. The change in a tissue, as of the lung, into the tissue resembling that of the spleen.
Spleno- —A prefix meaning spleen.
Splenocele—Hernia of the spleen.
Splenoceratosis—Splenceratosis.
Splenocleisis—Inducing the formation of fibrous tissue on the surface of the spleen by friction or application of gauze.
Splenocolic—Pertaining to the spleen and colon.
Splenocyte —A monocyte or lymphocyte of the spleen.
Splenodynia—Splenalgia.
Splenogenic, Splenogenous—Originating in the spleen.
Splenogram—X-ray film of the spleen.
Splenography—1. X-ray examination of the spleen. 2. A description of the spleen.
Splenohemia—Splenemia.
Splenohepatomegaly—Enlargement of the spleen and liver.
Splenoid—Like spleen.
Splenokeratosis—Hardness of the spleen.
Splenolaparotomy—To make an incision into the spleen through the abdominal wall.
Splenology—Study of the functions and diseases of the spleen.
Splenolymphatic—Pertaining to the spleen and lymph nodes.
Splenolysin—A lysin which destroys the splenic tissue.
Splenolysis—Destruction of the splenic tissue by lysin.
Splenoma—A tumor of the spleen.
Splenomalacia—Softening of the spleen.
Splenomedullary —Pertaining to or originating in the spleen and bone marrow.
Splenomegalia, Splenomegaly —Enlargement of the spleen.
Splenometry —Measurement of the spleen.
Splenomyelogenous—Produced in the spleen and bone marrow.
Splenomyelomalacia—Softening of the spleen and bone marrow.
Splenoncus—Splenoma.
Splenonephric—Lienorenal. Pertaining to the spleen and kidney.
Splenonephroptosis—Downward displacement of the spleen and kidney.
Splenopancreatic—Pertaining to the spleen and pancreas.
Splenopathy—Any disease of the spleen.
Splenopexia—Splenopexy.
Splenopexy —Fixation of the spleen.
Splenophrenic—Concerning the spleen and diaphragm.
Splenopneumonia—Pneumonia with splenization of the lung.
Splenoportogram —X-ray picture of the spleen and portal vein taken after an injection of a radiopaque substance.
Splenoportography—X-ray examination of the speen and portal vein after an injection of a radiopaque substance into the spleen.
Splenoptosia—Splenoptosis.
Splenoptosis—Downward displacement of the spleen.
Splenorenal—Splenonephric.
Splenorenal shunt—Anastomosis of the splenic vein to the renal vein to enable the blood from the portal system to enter the general venous circulation, which is performed in cases of portal hypertension.
Splenorrhagia—Hemorrhage from the spleen.
Splenorrhaphy —Suture of wound of the spleen.
Splenosis—Implantation and subsequent growth of splenic tissue within the abdomen resulting from disruption of the spleen.
Splenotomy—To make an incision into the spleen.
Splenotoxin —A toxin produced by or acting on the splenic cells.
Splenule—Accessory spleen.
Splenulus—A rudimentary or accessory spleen.
Splenunculus—Accessory spleen.
Splint —An appliance made of wood or metal used for the fixation or protection of displaced, movable or injured parts of the body.
Splinter—1. A fragment from a fractured bone. 2. A small pointed piece of a material piercing or embedded in the skin.
Splinting—Fixation of a dislocation or fracture with a splint.

Split—1. A longitudinal fissure. 2. Affected with split.

Split foot—Cleft foot.

Split hand—Cleft hand.

Split pelvis—Congenital failure of pubic bones to form a union at the symphysis.

Splitter—One who or that which splits.

Splitting—The act of dividing lengthwise.

Split tongue—Cleft or bifid tongue.

Spodogenous—Caused by accumulation of waste material in an organ.

Spodophagous—Destroying the waste matters in the body, said of scavenger cells.

Spodophorous—Removing or carrying off waste materials from the body.

Spondyl- —A prefix meaning vertebra.

Spondylalgia—Pain in the vertebrae.

Spondylarthritis—Arthritis of the vertebral column.

Spondylarthrocace—Tuberculosis of the vertebrae.

Spondylexarthrosis—Dislocation of a vertebra.

Spondylitic—1. Pertaining to spondylitis. 2. The person affected with spondylitis.

Spondylitis—1. Inflammation of one or more vertebrae. 2. Tuberculosis of the vertebrae.

Spondylizema—Downward displacement of a vertebra due to destruction or softening of the vertebra below it.

Spondylo- —A prefix meaning a vertebra.

Spondyloarthropathy—Disease of the joints of the vertebral column.

Spondylocace—Spondylarthrocace.

Spondylodymus—Twin fetuses united at the vertebrae.

Spondylodynia—Spondylalgia.

Spondylolisthesis—Forward displacement of a lower lumbar vertebra over the sacrum.

Spondylolisthetic—Concerning spondylolisthesis.

Spondylolysis—The breaking down of a vertebra.

Spondylomalacia—Softening of the vertebrae.

Spondylopathy—Any disease of the vertebrae.

Spondyloptosis—Spondylolisthesis.

Spondylopyosis—Pus formation in a vertebra.

Spondyloschisis—Congenital fissure of one or more of the vertebral arches.

Spondylosis—Vertebral ankylosis.

Spondylosyndesis—Surgical formation of an ankylosis between vertebrae.

Spondylotherapy—1. Treatment of disease of the spine. 2. Manipulation of the spinal column in the treatment of disease.

Spondylothoracic—Pertaining to vertebra and the thorax.

Spondylotomy—Surgical cutting of the vertebral column to correct a deformity or to facilitate the delivery of a child.

Spondylous—Pertaining to a vertebra.

Sponge—1. A porous, absorbent mass, as a pad of gauze or cotton surrounded by gauze, or the elastic fibrous skeleton of certain marine animals. 2. Short term for sponge bath. 3. To moisten or to clean.

Sponge graft—A sponge placed in an ulcer to cause granulation.

Spongia—Sponge.

Spongiform—Like sponge.

Sponging—Sponge bath. To moisten the body with sponge.

Spongio- —A prefix meaning sponge.

Spongioblast —Any of the embryonic epithelial cells developing about the neural tube, some of which develop into neuroglial and some into ependymal cells.

Spongioblastoma—A tumor of the brain composed of spongioblasts.

Spongiocyte—A neuroglial cell.

Spongioid—Spongiform.

Spongioplasm —Fibrillar network supporting the fluid of protoplasm.

Spongiose—Resembling a sponge.

Spongiosis—Intercellular edema of the spongy layer of the skin.

Spongiositis—Inflammation of the corpus spongiosum of urethra.

Spongiosum—Spong-like, porous.

Spongy—Resembling a sponge.

Spontaneous—Occurring without apparent cause; voluntary.

Spontaneous fracture—Fracture of a demineralized bone as in osteoporosis, which is painless.

Spoon—An instrument with a handle and a cup-shaped structure at the end.

Sporadic—1. Occurring occasionally. 2. Occurring singly. 3. Scattered widely.

Sporangiophore—A supporting stalk for a spore sac of certain fungi.

Sporangium—A sac containing spores, as in certain fungi.

Spore—1. An oval body produced within some bacteria, which is not destroyed by environmental change. 2. A sexual or asexual reproductive cell of the lower animals, such as protozoa, fungi and algae etc.

Sporicidal—Destructive to the spores.

Sporicide—Sporicidal.

Sporidium—A protozoan spore.

Sporiferous—Producing spores.

Spork—A utensil for the persons who are unable to do work properly with the upper limbs.

Sporo- —A prefix meaning spore.

Sporoblast—A body in the oocyst of malarial parasite in the mosquito from which later on the sporozoite develops.

Sporocyst—1. A sac containing spores or reproductive cells. 2. A sac around a sporoblast secreted by certain protozoa prior to spore production. 3. The stage in the life-cycle of trematode worm in which a saclike organism develops from a miracidium in the snail host, containing germ cells which gives rise to daughter sporocysts.

Sporogenesis—The production or formation of spores.

Sporogenic—Producing or forming spores.

Sporogenous—Concerning sporogenesis.

Sporogeny—Sporogenesis.

Sporogony—The sexual life-cycle of sporozoa, especially that of the malarial parasite in the mosquito.

Sporont—A mature protozoon in its sexual life-cycle.

Sporophore—The spore-bearing portion of an organism.

Sporophyte —The spore-bearing stage of a plant.

Sporoplasm—The protoplasm of a spore.

Sporotrichosis—Chronic fungal disease of the skin and superficial lymph nodes, caused by the fungus Sporotrichum, characterized by the formation of abscesses, nodes and ulcers.

Sporozoa — Plural of sporozoon. A large class of parasitic protozoa(phylum Apicomplexa) with simple spores and lack of locomotor organs as flagella and cilia etc. in adult stages.

Sporozoan—1. Pertaining to sporozoa. 2. A sporozoon.

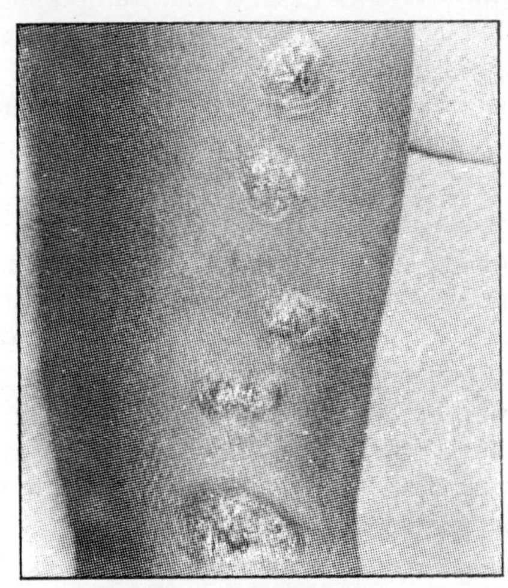

Fig. 529 : Sporotrichosis

Sporozoite—An elongated sickle-shaped cell developing from the sporoblast within the oocyst in the life-cycle of malarial parasite.

Sporozoon—Sporozoan.Singular of sporozoa.

Sport—Mutation.

Sporular—Pertaining to a spore.

Sporulation—Production of spores.

Sporule—A small spore.

Spot —Loculus. Macula. Papule. Pustule. A small area on the surface appearing different from the surrounding area, *e.g.*, blind spot *i.e.*, the optic disk where the optic nerve enters the retina.

Spotted —Marked with spots.

Spotting—Appearance of bloodtinged discharge from the vagina, usually between menstrual periods or at the onset of labor.

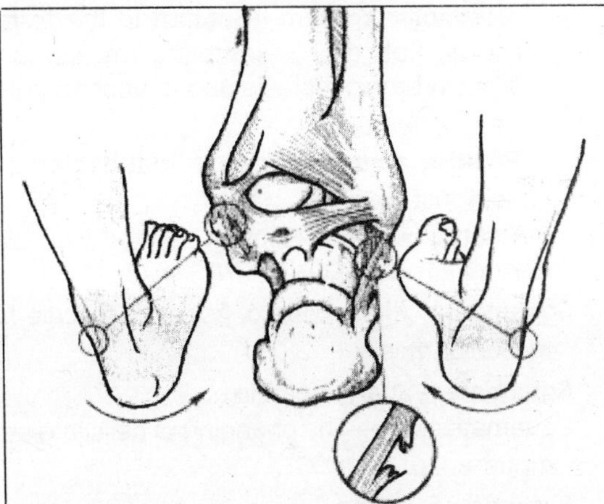

Fig. 530 : Sprain involving the ankle ligaments

Sprain—Wrenching of a joint with partial rupture of its ligaments, which generally occurs in foot or ankle joint.

Spray—1. A medicated liquid converted into minute flying particles. 2. Atomizer. 3. To discharge a liquid in the form of minute flying particles.

Sprayer—One who or that which sprays.

Spreader—1. An instrument used to distribute a substance over a surface or area. 2. A device for making space between structures.

Spring—1. The season of the year that comes after winter and before summer. 2. A returning back of a part of a machine or body to its original position through its elasticity.

Spring finger—Trigger finger.

Sprout—To germinate; to grow.

Sprouting—Germinating; growing.

Sprue—A chronic disease occurring in both tropical and nontropical regions due to impaired absorption of glucose, fats and vitamins, characterized by weakness, loss of weight, dyspepsia and steatorrhea.

Spud—A small spadelike blade to dislodge a foreign substance.

Spur—A sharp, pointed, outgrowth, as from the bone, *e.g.*, calcaneal spur.

Spurious—False; not genuine; adulterated.

Sputum—Matter expelled from the mouth by coughing which comes from the lungs.

Bloody sputum—Sputum containing blood, as occurs in pulmonary tuberculosis.

Negative sputum—Sputum not containing the acid-fast bacillus.

Nummular sputum—Sputum in the form of round, flat, disk resembling the coins, as seen in bronchiectasis and advanced pulmonary tuberculosis.

Positive sputum—Sputum that contains the acid-fast bacillus.

Rusty sputum —Sputum stained with blood or blood pigments.

Squama—1. A thin plate of bone. 2. A scale from the epidermis.

Squamate—Scaly; scalelike.

Squamatization—The changing of cells into squamous cells.

Squame—Squama.

Squamocellular—Pertaining to or having squamous cells.

Squamomastoid—Pertaining to the squamous and mastoid portions of the temporal bone.

Squamo-occipital —Pertaining to the squamous portion of the occipital bone.

Squamoparietal—Pertaining to the squamous portion of the temporal bone, and the parietal bone.

Squamopetrosal—Petrosquamosal. Pertaining to the petrous and the squamous portions of the temporal bone.

Squamosa—The squamous part of temporal bone.

Squamosae—Plural of squamosa.

Squamosal—Squamous.

Squamosphenoid—Pertaining to the squamous portion of the temporal bone, and the sphenoid bone.

Squamous—Scalelike or thin platelike structure.

Squamous bone—Upper anterior portion of temporal bone.

Squamous cells—Flat, scaly cells of the epithelium.

Squamous epithelium—The epithelium consisting of flat cells.

Squamous suture—A suture between temporal and parietal bones.

Squamozygomatic—Pertaining to the squamous portion and the zygomatic portion of the temporal bone.

Squarrose, Squarrous—Scurfy or scaly.

Squatting—A position with the hips and knees flexed and the buttocks resting on the heels.

Squint—Strabismus.

S. R. —Sedimentation rate.

Stab—1. To pierce or a wound produced by piercing with a knife or pointed instrument. 2. Bacterial culture.

Stab culture—Bacterial culture in which bacteria are introduced into a solid gelatin medium with a wire or needle.

Stabile—Stable. Not movable. Not being changed.

Stability—The quality of being stable.

Stabilization—To make something such as a structure or chemical reaction stable.

Stabilizer—A device for obtaining stability.

Stable—Firm; fixed.

Staccato—Intermittent.

Stactometer—An instrument for measuring fluid in drops.

Stadia—Plural of stadium.

Stadiometer—An instrument for measuring standing or sitting height.

Stadium—Stage.

Staff—1. A group of doctors, nurses and compounders etc. associated with a hospital. 2. A grooved instrument used as a guide for the surgical knife to be introduced into the urethra and bladder. 3. A wooden rod or rodlike structure.

Stage—1. Stadium. A period in the course of a disease or in the life history of an organism. 2. The platform of a microscope on which the slide with the object to be studied is placed.

Acme stage—The climax or the critical stage of a disease.

Amphibolic stage—The period between acme and decline of a disease.

Cold stage—Period of chillness at the onset of malarial fever.

Decrement stage—Period of decrease of fever or other symptoms.

End stage—The fully developed stage of a disease.

Eruptive stage—Period in which exanthema appear.

First stage of labor—Period from the onset of regular uterine contractions till the full dilatation of the cervix.

Hot stage—Stage of fever in malaria.

Increment stage—Period of increase of fever or other symptoms.

Invasive stage—Period in which the pathogenic organism is present in the body prior to the onset of disease.

Second stage of labor—The period from the full dilatation of the cervix to the expulsion of the child from the uterus.

Sweating stage —The third or terminal stage of malaria during which sweating occurs.

Third stage of labor—Period of labor during which placenta and fetal membranes are expelled from the uterus.

Stagger—To walk unsteadily.

Staggers—A form of vertigo occurring in decompression illness.

Staging—1. The determination of different stages in the course of a disease or the life history of an organism. 2. The classification of tumors, especially the malignant tumors according to their structures, extension, response to the treatment and to the patient's prognosis.

Stagnant—Not flowing.

Stagnate—To cease to flow.

Stagnation—Cessation of flow of any fluid in the body.

Stain—1. Spot. An area of discoloration of the skin. 2. A dye or pigment used in coloring the tissues or cells, to be identified and studied under the microscope. 3. To apply a dye or pigment to a tissue or object to be studied under the microscope.

Acid-fast stain—See under 'A'.

Albert's stain—A stain used for examination of diphtheria bacilli, which contains toluidine blue, methyl green, glacial acetic acid, 95% alcohol and water.

Differential stain—Contrast stain. A stain used to color one part of a tissue, unaffected when another part is stained by another color.

Field stain—It is used in staining for thick blood films of malarial parasites, which contains methylene blue, Azur I dye, anhydrous disodium hydrogen phosphate, anhydrous potassium dihydrogen phosphate and distilled water.

Giemsa stain—A stain containing powdered Giemsa stain, methanol and glycerol, used in staining tissues, blood cells, Negri bodies, chromosomes, spirochetes and protozoa.

Gram stain—A stain used to differentiate bacteria for which a smear is fixed by flaming, stained in a solution of crystal violet, treated with iodine solution and then with alcohol-acetone, rinsed, decolorized and then counterstained with safranin O. Bacteria staining purple-black are gram-positive and those staining pink are gram-negative.

Leishman stain—It is used for staining the thin blood films.

Staining—The process of coloring a substance, especially a tissue with a dye or pigment for its examination and identification its different parts under the microscope.

Staircase phenomenon—Treppe.

Stalagmometer—An instrument for determining the number of drops in a given amount of fluid.

Stalk—An elongated anatomical structure resembling a plant stalk, attached to an organ or structure.

Stamina—Strength. Patience.

Stammer—To speak with hesitation and repetition.

Stammering—1. A speech defect in which one speaks with hesitation and repetition. 2. Hesitating or faltering in speech.

Stanch—To stop the flow of blood.

Standard—That which has been established by custom or authority as a measure or model with which other similar things are compared.

Standardization—The act of standardizing, as standardization of drugs by testing their effects upon animals.

Standardized—That which has been made standard.

Standstill—Cessation of activity, as of the heart or lungs.

Stannic—Resembling or containing tin.

Stannous—Stannic.

Stannum—Tin.

Stapedectomy—Excision of the stapes bone in the ear in order to improve hearing.

Stapedial—Pertaining to the stapes bone of the ear.

Stapedii—Plural of stapedius.

Stapediotenotomy—To incise the tendon of the stapedius muscle.

Stapediovestibular —Pertaining to the stapes bone and vestibule of the ear.

Stapedius—A small muscle of the middle ear inserted in the stapes bone.

Stapedotomy—An operation for the improvement of hearing in otosclerosis.

Stapes—An ossicle (small bone) in the middle ear that articulates with the incus.

Staphylagra—An instrument for holding the uvula.

Staphyle—Uvula.

Staphylectomy—Uvulectomy.

Staphyledema—Edema of the uvula.

Staphyline—1. Uvular. Pertaining to the uvula. 2. Botryoid. Resembling a bunch of grapes.

Staphylion—The midpoint of the posterior edge of the hard palate.

Staphylitis—Inflammation of the uvula.

Staphylium—Nipple.

Staphylo- —A prefix which means uvula, resembling or pertaining to bunch of grapes or pertaining to Staphylococcus.

Staphyloangina—Sore throat due to Staphylococcus.

Staphylococcal—Pertaining to or caused by staphylococcus.

Staphylococcemia—Presence of staphylococcus in the blood.

Staphylococci—Plural of staphylococcus.

Staphylococcic—Staphylococcal.

Staphylococcolysis—Destruction of Staphylococci.

Staphylococcosis—Infection by Staphylococcus.

Staphylococcus—A gram-positive bacterium of the genus Staphylococcus present on the skin and in the upper respiratory tract, which causes abscess formation and upper respiratory infection.

Staphylococcus aureus—A gram-positive bacterium found commonly on the skin (hair follicles) and mucous membrane, especially those of the nose and mouth. Its toxin causes furunculosis, formation of boils, abscess, carbuncle, etc., and stomatitis, pulpitis, pharyngitis, bronchopneumonia, endocarditis, meningitis, osteomyelitis, suppurative arthritis, infection of the urinary tract and food poisoning etc.

Staphylococcus epidermidis —A species of bacteria found generally on the skin but does not cause any disease.

Staphylococcus saprophyticus—It can cause urinary tract infections.

Staphyloderma —Skin infection with staphylococci.

Staphylodermatitis—Dermatitis caused by staphylococci.

Staphylodialysis—Relaxation and elongation of the uvula.

Staphylohemia—Staphylococcemia. Presence of staphylococci in the blood.

Staphylolysin—1. A hemolysin produced by a staphylococcus. 2. An antibody causing lysis of staphylococci.

Staphyloma—Protrusion of the cornea or sclera of the eye.

Staphylomatous—Pertaining to or resembling a staphyloma.

Staphyloncus—Enlargement or a tumor of the uvula.

Staphylopharyngorrhaphy—Repair of the defects in the uvula or soft palate and the pharynx, by operation.

Staphyloplasty—Plastic surgery of the uvula or soft palate.

Staphyloptosia, Staphyloptosis —Elongation of the uvula.

Staphylorrhaphy—Suture of a fissured palate.

Staphyloschisis—Cleft palate. Fissure of the uvula and soft palate.

Staphylotome—An instrument for cutting the uvula.

Staphylotomy—1. Incision of the uvula. 2. Excision of a Staphyloma.

Staphylotoxin—The toxin produced by a species of Staphylococcus.

Stapling—In surgery, the process of uniting two tissues together, such as the two ends of the intestine, by using special staples compatible with the tissues.

Star—Any star-like structure, *e.g.*, stellate veins of the kidney.

Starch—The chief storage of carbohydrates in plants.

Stare—To look with fixed eyes.

Startling—To move suddenly from surprise, sudden feelings or emotions.

Starvation —The condition of being without food for a long period of time.

Starve—To deprive of food or to die of hunger.

Stases—Plural of stasis.

Stasibasiphobia—Delusion on one's inability to stand erect or to walk, or fear to make the attempt.

Stasimorphia, Stasimorphy—Deformity occurring due to failure in growth.

Stasiphobia—Stasibasiphobia.

Stasis—Stoppage of flow of fluids, as of the blood and urine etc.

Intestinal stasis—Stoppage of the normal passage of intestinal food due to obstruction or impairment of the peristaltic movements.

Venous stasis—Stoppage of blood flow due to venous congestion.

Stat—Immediately; at once.

State—Condition or situation.

Static—At rest; not in motion; in equilibrium.

Static balance—Static equilibrium.

Static electricity—Electricity produced by friction.

Static equilibrium—The ability to maintain a steady position of the head and body in relation to gravity.

Statics—The science of matter at rest.

Static splint—A splint used for positioning, stability, protection or support.

Statim—Stat.

Station—1. The position assumed on standing. 2. A stopping place.

Stationary—Remaining in a fixed condition.

Statistical—Pertaining to statistics.

Statistics —The science dealing with the systematic collection and analysis of numberical data pertaining to any subject.

Morbidity statistics—Statistics pertaining to the diseases.

Vital statistics—Statistics dealing with births, deaths and marriages.

Statoacoustic—Pertaining to balance and hearing.

Statoconia—Otoliths.

Statoconium—Singular of statoconia.

Statokinetic—Pertaining to reactions of the body caused by movement.

Statokinetics—Adjustment of the moving body to maintain static equilibrium.

Statokinetic reflexes—Reactions resulting from body movements.

Statolith—A minute calciferous granule within the gelatinous membrane.

Statometer—An instrument for measuring the degree of exophthalmos.

Statosphere—Centrosome.

Stature—The height or tallness of a person in standing position

Status—Condition or state, *e.g.*, status asthmaticus, a sudden intense and continuous attack of asthma, not curable by usual treatment.

Staunch—To stop the flow of blood from a wound.

Stauroplegia—Alternate hemiplegia. Paralysis of one side of the face, and of trunk and extremities of the opposite side.

Staxis—Hemorrhage.

S.T.D. —1. Skin test dose. 2. Sexually transmitted disease.

Steal—The deviation of blood flow from its normal passage.

Steam—Vapor of boiling water.

Steam tent—A device that permits the inhalation of vapors.

Steapsin—Lipase. The fat-splitting enzyme of the pancreatic juice.

Stear- —A prefix meaning fat.

Steariform—Resembling fat.

Stearodermia—Disease of the sebaceous glands of the skin.

Stearrhea—Seborrhea oleosa. Excessive secretion of the sebum or fat.

Steatadenoma—Tumor of the sebaceous glands.

Steatitis—Inflammation of the adipose tissue.

Steato- —A prefix which means fatty.

Steatocele—Fatty tumor within the scrotum.

Steatocryptosis—Any disease of the sebaceous glands.

Steatocystoma—A sebaceous cyst.

Steatocystoma multiplex—Formation of numerous sebaceous cysts.

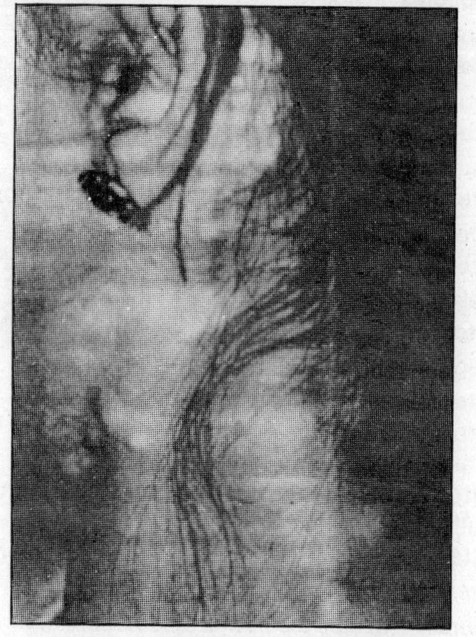

Fig. 531 : Steatocystoma multiplex : Numerous subcutaneous cysts.

Steatogenous—Lipogenic.

Steatolysis—Lipolysis.

Steatolytic—Lipolytic.

Steatoma—1. Lipoma. 2. Sebaceous cyst.

Steatomatosis—Steatocystomamultiplex.

Steatomatous—Marked with numerous sebaceous cysts.

Steatonecrosis—Necrosis of the fatty tissue, in small patches

Steatopathy—Any disease of the sebaceous glands.

Steatopyga —Steatopygia.

Steatopygia—Abnormal deposition of fat in the buttocks, seen mostly in women.

Steatopygous—Pertaining to or having steatopygia.

Steatorrhea—1. Presence of excess of fat in the feces. 2. Seborrhea.

Steatosis—1. Fatty degeneration. 2. Disease of the sebaceous glands.

Stegnosis—1. Stenosis; closing of a passage. 2. Checking of a secretion. 3. Constipation.

Stegnotic—Astringent. Constipating.

Stellae—Plural of stella.

Stellate—Star-shaped; arranged in such a way that the parts radiate from a center.

Stellate cell—Star-shaped cell.

Stellate fracture—Fracture in which numerous fissures radiate from the central point of injury.

Stellate veins—Star-shaped masses of veins on the surface of the kidney.

Stellectomy—Excision of the stellate ganglion.

Stellula —A small star-shaped mass or figure.

Stem —Any stalklike supporting structure.

Stenion —The terminations of the shortest transverse diameter of the skull in the temporal region.

Steno- —A prefix meaning narrow or short.

Stenobregmatic—Denoting a skull with narrowing of the upper and frontal portions.

Stenocardia—Angina pectoris.

Stenocephalia—Stenocephaly.

Stenocephalic—Pertaining to, or characterized by, stenocephaly.

Stenocephalous—Stenocephalic.

Stenocephaly—Narrowness of the cranium or head.

Stenochoria—Stenosis. Partial constriction of the lacrimal duct.

Stenocompressor—An instrument for compressing Stensen's duct to stop the flow of saliva.

Stenocoriasis—Contraction of the pupil.

Stenocrotaphia—Narrowness of the skull in the temporal region.

Stenocrotaphy—Stenocrotaphia.

Stenopaic, Stenopeic—Having a narrow opening or slit.

Stenopeic—Stenopaic.

Stenosal—Stenotic.

Stenosed—Constricted; narrowed.

Stenosis—Stricture. Constriction or narrowing of an opening or passage of the body.

Aortic stenosis—Narrowing of the orifice of the aortic valve.

Bronchial stenosis—Bronchiostenosis.

Mitral stenosis—Stenosis of the mitral valve or the left atrioventricular orifice, which is usually the result of rheumatic heart disease.

Pyloric stenosis—Narrowing of the pyloric sphincter.

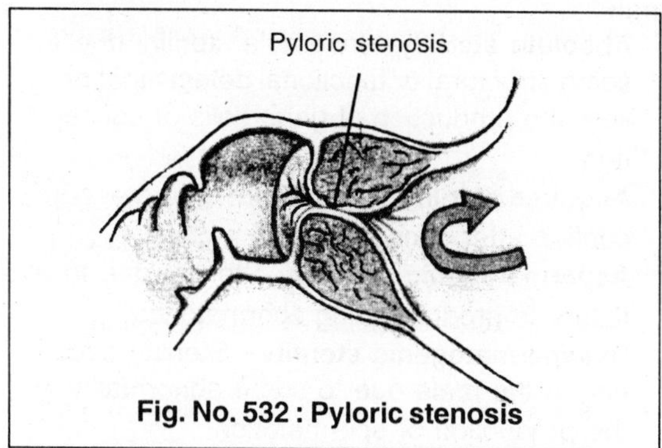

Fig. No. 532 : Pyloric stenosis

Stenostenosis—Stricture of the parotid duct.

Stenostomia—Narrowing of the mouth.

Stenothermal, Stenothermic—Living only within a little variation of temperature, said of bacteria.

Stenothorax—An abnormally narrow thorax.

Stenotic—Produced by or characterized by stenosis.

Stensen's duct—The excretory duct of the parotid gland.

Stent—A device or mold of a suitable substance used to hold a tissue in place or to support a skin graft or the tubular structures that are being anastomosed.

Stentorophonic—Speaking loudly or producing loud sound.

Stephanial—Pertaining to stephanion.

Stephanion—The point at the intersection of the superior temporal ridge and coronal suture.

Steppage gait—See under gait.

Sterco- —A prefix indicating relationship to feces.

Stercobilin—A brown pigment derived from bile which gives the characteristic color to feces.

Stercobilinogen—A colorless substance derived from urobilinogen, present in the feces which turns brown on oxidation.

Stercolith—A fecal calculus.

Stercoraceous—Pertaining to or consisting of feces.

Stercoral—Pertaining to feces.

Stercorolith—Stercolith.

Stercoroma—A tumor-like mass of fecal matter in the rectum.

Stercorous—Resembling feces.

Stercus—Excreta. Feces or dung.

Stere-, Stereo- —Prefixes meaning solid, solidity or having three dimensions.

Stere —One cubic meter.

Stereo- —A prefix which means solid, three dimensional or firmly established.

Stereoagnosis —Astereognosis.

Stereoanesthesia—Inability to recognize the things by feeling their form.

Stereoarthrolysis—Surgical formation of a movable new joint in bony ankylosis.

Stereoauscultation—Auscultation with two stethoscopes on different parts of the chest.

Stereocampimeter—An instrument for measuring the visual field of both eyes simultaneously.

Stereocilia—Plural of stereocilium.

Stereocilium—A nonmotile long microvillus (protoplasmic projection from the surface of the cells).

Stereocolpogram—Picture of the vagina and cervix taken with the stereocolposcope.

Stereocolposcope—An instrument used for inspection of the vagina and cervix in three dimensions (length, breadth and height).

Stereoencephalotome —A guiding instrument used in stereoencephalotomy.

Stereoencephalotomy—Surgical incision of the brain after locating the specific area, with the guidance of stereoencephalotome.

Stereognosis—Ability to recognize form of the solid things by touch.

Stereogram—Stereoscopic X-ray film.

Stereograph—A stereoscopic x-ray apparatus.

Stereography—Stereoradiography.

Stereoisomer—A compound showing stereoisomerism.

Stereoisomeric—Pertaining to stereoisomerism.

Stereoisomerism—The condition in which two or more substances have the same empirical formula but different structural formula.

Stereology—Study of three-dimensional aspects of objects.

Stereometer—An instrument for measuring a solid with three-dimensional aspects.

Stereometry—The measurement of three dimensions (lengh, breadth and height) of a solid substance.

Stereo-ophthalmoscope —An ophthalmoscope by which the fundus of eye of the patient is seen simultaneously by both eyes of the examiner.

Stereo-orthopter—A mirror-reflecting apparatus for correcting strabismus.

Stereophorometer—A prism-refracting device used for correcting the defective vision.

Stereophotography—Photography that produces effect of solidity or depth in the picture.

Stereophotomicrograph—The picture showing solidity or depth of a microscopic object.

Stereopsis—Stereoscopic vision.

Stereoradiography —Taking of X-ray films of an object from two slightly different angles so that on seeing that through a stereoscope, the effect of solidity or depth of that object may be produced.

Stereoroentgenography—Stereoradiography.

Stereoscope—An instrument showing the solidity or depth of an object seen by combining images of two pictures.

Stereoscopic, Stereoscopical—1. Pertaining to the stereoscope or its use. 2. Having the effect of a stereoscope.

Stereoscopy—The technique by which two images of the same object are blended into one, giving a three-dimensional appearance to the single image.

Stereospecific—Specific for only one of the possible receptors on a cell.

Stereotactic—Stereotaxic.

Stereotaxic—Pertaining to stereotaxis.

Stereotaxis—1. A method of precisely locating areas in the brain which is essential to be performed in certain neurological operations. 2. Taxis in response to contact with a solid substance.

Stereotaxy—Stereotaxis.

Stereotropic—Pertaining to stereotropism.

Stereotropism—A turning of an object toward (positive stereotropism) or away from (negative stereotropism) a solid substance.

Stereotypy—Persistent repetition of senseless words or acts.

Steric—Pertaining to the arrangement of atoms in a chemical compound.

Sterilant—An agent destroying microorganisms.

Sterile—1. Aseptic or free from living microorganisms. 2. Not fertile i.e., not producing child.

Sterility —1. Condition of being free from living microorganisms. 2. Inability of a female to become pregnant or a male to impregnate a female.

Absolute sterility—Incurable sterility due to some structural or functional defects that prevent the production of germ cells or conception.

Acquired sterility—The failure of further conception after once produced a child.

Aspermatogenic sterility—Sterility due to a failure to produce living spermatozoa.

Dysspermatogenic sterility—Sterility occurring in the male due to some abnormality in the production of spermatozoa.

Female sterility—Inability of a woman to conceive.

Male sterility—Inability of a male to produce spermatozoa, or viable spermatozoa.

Primary sterility—Sterility due to failure of the testis or ovary to produce functional germ cells.

Relative sterility—Sterility due to causes other than defect of sex organs.

Sterilization—1. Process of completely removing or destroying all microorganisms on a substance by heat, by exposure to gas such as formaldehyde or ethylene oxide, exposure to ionizing radiation, or by filtering gases or liquids through a porous material which removes the microorganisms. 2. Process by which an individual is made unable for reproduction such as surgical removal of testes or ovaries (castration) or inactivation by irradiation, or by tying off or removal of a part of reproductive ducts (vas deferens or fallopian tubes).

Sterilize—1. To make free from microorganisms 2. To make unable for reproduction.

Sterilizer—An apparatus for destroying microoganisms as an autoclave.

Sterna—Plural of sternum.

Sternad—Toward the sternum.

Sternal—Pertaining to the sternum.

Sternalgia—Sternodynia.

Sternal puncture—To pierce the sternum with a large-bore needle to obtain a specimen of bone marrow from the sternum.

Sternebra—Any of the segments of the sternum in early life which later on fuse to form the body of sternum.

Sternebrae—Plural of sternebra.

Sternen—Pertaining to the sternum but not to other structures.

Sterno- —Combining form meaning sternum.

Sternoclavicular—Pertaining to the sternum and clavicle bone.

Sternocleidal—Sternoclavicular.

Sternocleidomastoid —Pertaining to the sternum, clavicle and mastoid process.

Sternocostal—Pertaining to the sternum and ribs.

Sternodymia—Condition in which deformed twin fetuses are joined at the sternum.

Sternodymus—Twin fetuses joined at the sternum.

Sternodynia—Sternalgia. Pain in the sternum.

Sternohyoid—Pertaining to the sternum and hyoid bone.

Sternoid—Resembling the sternum or breast bone.

Sternomastoid—Pertaining to sternum and mastoid process of temporal bone.

Sternopagia—Sternodymia.

Sternopagus—Sternodymus.

Sternopericardial—Pertaining to the sternum and pericardium.

Sternoschisis—Congenital fissure of the sternum.

Sternothyroid—Pertaining to the sternum and thyroid cartilage or gland.

Sternotomy—To incise the sternum.

Sternotracheal—Pertaining to the sternum and trachea.

Sternotrypesis —Surgical perforation of the sternum.

Sternovertebral—Pertaining to the sternum and the vertebrae.

Sternum—An elongated flat bone in the median line of the thorax in front, consisting of 3 segments—manubrium (topmost segment), body (middle segment) composed of 4 separate segments joined by cartilage in youth, and xiphoid process (lower segment).

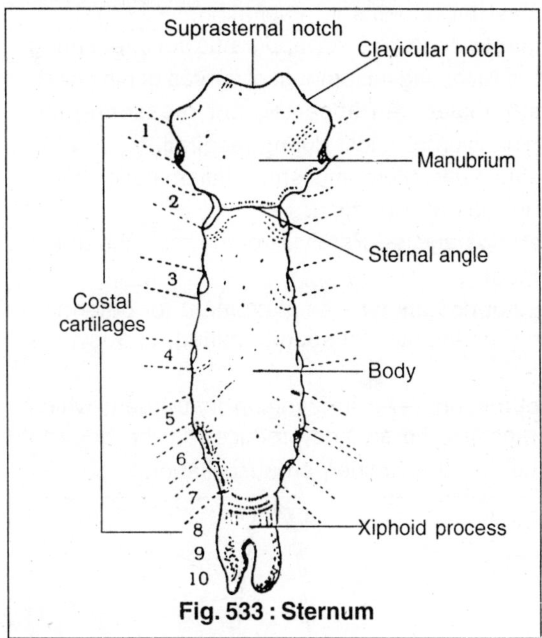

Fig. 533 : Sternum

Sternutament—Sternutatory.

Sternutatio—Sneezing.

Sternutation—Act of sneezing.

Sternutator—An agent inducing sneezing.

Sternutatory—Causing sneezing.

Steroid —Any of a group of compounds, which includes sex hormones and hormones of the adrenal cortex (corticosteroids), precursor of the D vitamins, sterols, bile acids, saponins, glucosides of digitalis and certain carcinogenic substances.

Steroidal—Pertaining to the steroid.

Steroidogenesis—Production of steroids, as by the adrenal glands.

Sterol—A steriod with one OH (alcohol) group, e.g., cholesterol, ergosterol.

Stertor—The act of snoring or snorous breathing.

Stertorous—Pertaining to or characterized by stertor or snoring.

Stethalgia —Pain in the chest.

Stetharteritis—Inflammation of the aorta or other arteries in the chest.

Stetho- —A prefix indicating chest.

Stethocyrtograph—Stethokyrtograph.

Stethogoniometer—An apparatus for measuring the curvature of the chest.

Stethogram—Phonocardiogram.

Stethograph—An apparatus for recording the chest movements in respiration.

Stethokyrtograph—An apparatus for measuring and recording the amount of curves of the chest.

Stethometer—An apparatus for measuring the expansion of chest during respiration.

Stethomyitis, Stethomyositis—Inflammation of the muscles of the chest.

Stethoparalysis—Paralysis of the muscles of the chest.

Stethophonometer—An instrument for determining the intensity of sound emitted, in auscultation.

Stethoscope—An intervening instrument which transmits the sounds produced in the body to the ear of examiner, on auscultation.

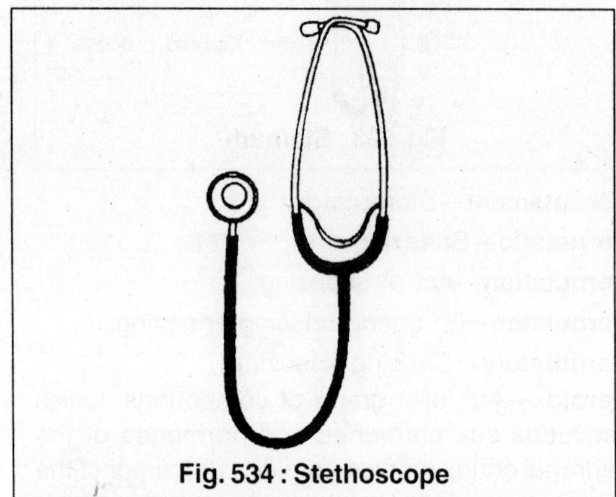

Fig. 534 : Stethoscope

Binaural stethoscope—A stethoscope in which there are two ear pieces for use with both the ears.

Bowless type stethoscope—A stethoscope in which the chest piece is a shallow metal cup about 4.5 cm. in diameter, the mouth of which is covered with a rubber diaphragm.

Differential stethoscope—A stethoscope having two chest pieces so that two sounds in different parts of the chest may be heard simultaneously and compared.

Electronic stethoscope—A stethoscope used to intensify the sounds heard from the body on auscultation.

Single stethoscope—A rigid or flexible stethoscope designed for one ear only.

Stethoscopic—Pertaining to stethoscope.

Stethoscopy—Examination with the stethoscope.

Stethospasm—Spasm of chest muscles.

Sthenia —A condition of unusual strength.

Sthenic—Active; strong.

Stheno- —A prefix meaning strength, power or force.

Sthenometer—An apparatus for measuring the muscular strength.

Sthenometry—Measurement of bodily strength.

Stiff—Rigid, firm, inflexible.

Stiff-neck fever—1. Dengue. 2. Cerebrospinal meningitis.

Stiffness—Rigidity; firmness.

Stigma —1. Any mental or physical mark or peculiarity that aids in diagnosis of a disease. 2. Hemorrhagic lesions occurring on the hands and feet, resembling cruciform (x) wounds.

Stigmata—Plural of stigma.

Stigmatic—Pertaining to or marked with a stigma.

Stigmatism—1. The possessing of stigmata. 2. The condition in which light rays are accurately focused on the retina.

Stigmatization—The formation of stigmata.

Stigmatometer—Astigmatometer. An instrument for testing eye refraction.

Stilet, Stilette—A small sharp-pointed probe.

Stillbirth—Birth of a dead child.

Stillborn—Born dead.

Stillicidium—A dribbling or flowing drop by drop.

Still's disease— Juvenile rheumatoid arthritis.

Stilus—Stylus.

Stimulant—An agent which increases the functional activity of the body.

Stimulate—To increase the functional activity of an organ or structure.

Stimulating—That which stimulates.

Stimulation—The process of stimulating.

Stimulator—Stimulating.

Stimuli—Plural of stimulus.

Stimulus—Any agent (chemical substance etc.), factor, act, energy (electrical energy etc.), influence of environmental change, physical change as contact with objects or change in pressure, etc., that increases functional activity of an organ or part of the body or causes excitement or irritation.

Sting—1. The dart of a poisonous insect. 2. To pierce dart.

Stinger—Burner.

Stippling—Spotted appearance, as of the retina in certain ocular diseases.

Stirrup—Stapes.

Stitch—1. A sudden, transient, cutting or spasmodic local pain. 2. Suture. 3. To unite the skin or flesh with suture.

Stockinet—Tubular woven material of uniform size open at both ends, used to hold bandages in place or apply uniform pressure on a leg or arm or a finger.

Stocking—An elastic covering for the foot and leg protecting them from the effect of weather and applying uniform pressure upon them.

Stoichiology—The study of cell physiology.

Stoichiometric—Pertaining to stoichiometry.

Stoichiometry—Chemical calculations.

Stoke—A unit of viscosity of a fluid equal to .0001 square meter per second.

Stokes-Adams syndrome—Unconsciousness with convulsions caused by interference in blood flow of the brain.

Stoke's disease—Exophthalmic goiter. Hyperthyroidism.

Stoke's lens—An apparatus to diagnose astigmatism.

Stom- —A prefix meaning stomach.

Stoma —A mouth, opening or pore.

Stomach —The musculomembranous dilated saclike portion of the alimentary canal between the esophagus and duodenum, below the diaphragm to right of spleen, partly under the liver. It is composed of fundus or upper round part, a body or middle part, and pylorus or the small distal portion. It secretes gastric juice which when mixed with food forms chyme, a semisolid substance suitable for further digestion by the intestines.

Stomachal—1. Pertaining to the stomach. 2. Stomachic.

Stomachalgia—Pain occurring in the stomach.

Stomachic—1. Concerning the stomach. 2. A medicine that increases the functional activity of the stomach.

Stomach intubation—To pass a tube into the stomach to obtain the gastric contents.

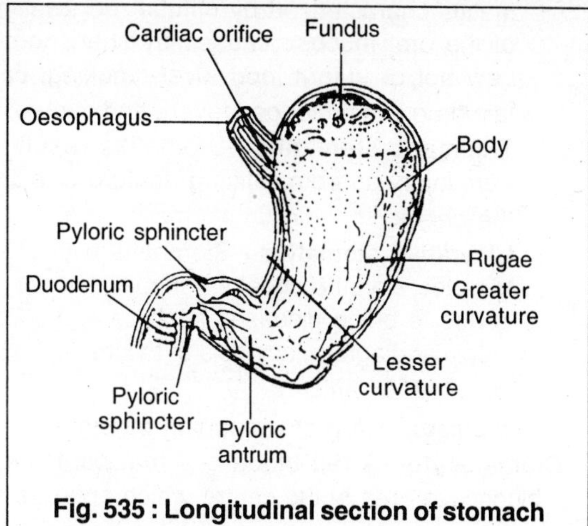

Fig. 535 : Longitudinal section of stomach

Stomachoscopy—Gastroscopy.

Stomach pump—An apparatus for removing stomach contents through a tube inserted into the stomach, through the mouth or nose.

Stomach tube—A tube used to wash out or to introduce food or liquids into the stomach.

Stomal—Pertaining to stoma.

Stomata—Plural of stoma.

Stomatal—Pertaining to stomata.

Stomatalgia—Pain in the mouth.

Stomatic—Pertaining to the mouth.

Stomatitis—Inflammation of the oral mucosa.

Angular stomatitis—Perleche.

Aphthous stomatitis—Stomatitis characterized by small, round white vesicles on the cheeks, lips and tongue which break leaving shallow ulcers surrounded by a red border. It is caused by injury, debility, gastro-intestinal disturbances, nutritional deficiencies or local infection with streptococci or staphylococci.

Catarrhal stomatitis—Simple stomatitis.

Corrosive stomatitis —Stomatitis occurring as a result of exposure to corrosive substance.

Membranous stomatitis—Stomatitis with the formation of a false membrane.

Parasitic stomatitis—Thrush. It is caused by yeastlike fungus Candida albicans, especially in infants and young children, characterized by the formation of white patches on oral mucosa, gums and tongue.

Simple stomatitis—Catarrhal stomatitis. Stomatitis characterized by diffuse red swelling of the oral mucosa caused by sharp tooth, very hot or irritant food, over-smoking, certain drugs, in prolonged fevers and cachexia.

Traumatic stomatitis—Stomatitis resulting from injury as from ill-fitting denture or biting the cheek.

Ulcerative stomatitis—Stomatitis with shallow ulcers on the cheeks, tongue, and lips. It is due to blood diseases such as acute leukemia and agranulocytosis or to infection with vincent's organisms.

Stomato- —A prefix meaning mouth.

Stomatocyte—A red blood cell that contains a biconcave area in the centre which appears as a slit.

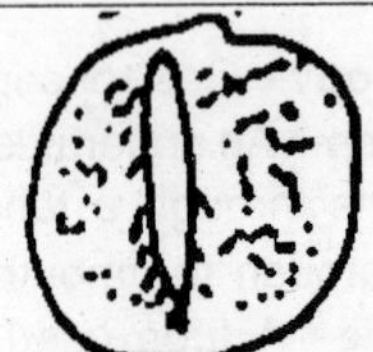

Fig. 536 : Stomatocyte

Stomatocytosis—A hereditary disorder of the red blood cells in which red blood cells are swollen due to entry of excess of sodium ions and water into them through their defective membranes.

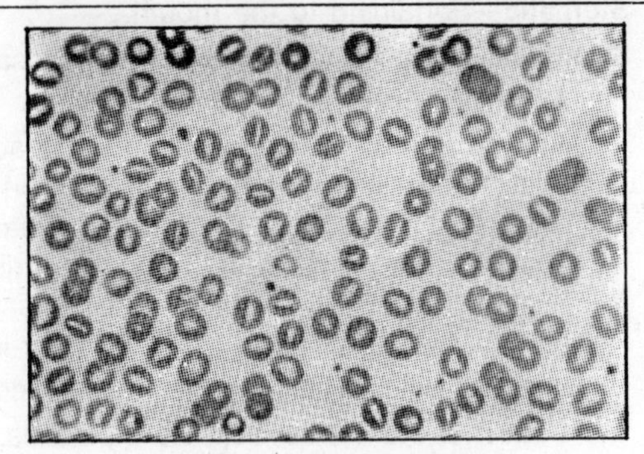

Fig.537 : Stomatocytosis

Stomatodeum—Stomodeum.

Stomatodynia—Stomatalgia.

Stomatodysodia—Halitosis.

Stomatogastric—Pertaining to the mouth and stomach.

Stomatognathic—Denoting the mouth and jaws together.

Stomatologic—Pertaining to stomatology.

Stomatologist—Specialist in mouth diseases.

Stomatology—Branch of medical science dealing with the mouth and its diseases.

Stomatomalacia—Abnormal softening of any structure of the mouth.

Stomatomenia—Bleeding from the mouth at the time of menstruation.

Stomatomy—Surgical cutting of the edges of mouth of the uterus to facilitate delivery.

Stomatomycosis—Any fungal disease of the mouth.

Stomatonecrosis—Cancrum oris. Noma. Gangrenous ulcerative stomatitis.

Stomatonoma—Cancrum oris.

Stomatopathy—Any disease of the mouth.

Stomatoplasty—Repair of the mouth by plastic surgery.

Stomatorrhagia—Bleeding from the mouth.

Stomatoscope—An instrument for examining the mouth.

Stomatosis—Stomatopathy.

Stomatotomy—Stomatomy.

Stomion—The median point of the oral slit when the lips are closed.

Stomocephalus—A fetus with very small jaws and mouth.

Stomodeal—Pertaining to the stomodeum.

Stomodeum—The ectodermal depression at the head end of the embryo, which forms the anterior portion of the oral cavity.

-stomy—A suffix meaning artificial or surgical opening.

Stone —Calculus.

Stool—Feces. Waste matter discharged from the bowels.

Bilious stool—Yellowish or yellowish-brown stool containing bile.

Fatty stool—Stool containing fat, as occurs in pancreatic disease.

Lienteric stool—Stool containing undigested food.

Rice water stool—White watery stool of cholera, which resembles rice water.

Stooping—The bending of the head downward.

Stop needle—A needle with an eye at the tip and a disk on the shaft to prevent more penetration of the needle, than desired.

Storm—1. A sudden and temporary exacerbation of the symptoms of a disease. 2. Great excitement. 3. Violent attack.

Stout—1. Strong 2. Corpulent. Having a bulky body.

Strabismal—Strabismic.

Strabismic—Pertaining to or afflicted with strabismus.

Strabismologist—Specialist in strabismology.

Strabismology—Study of strabismus.

Strabismometer—An instrument for measuring strabismus.

Strabismus—A visual defect in which visual axes of both eyes are not directed toward an object simultaneously. Squint.

Accommodative strabismus—Bilateral strabismus. Strabismus due to disorder of occular accommodation.

Alternating strabismus—Strabismus affecting either eye alternately.

Bilateral strabismus—Accommodative strabismus.

Convergent strabismus—Esotropia. Strabismus in which deviating eye turns inward.

Deorsum vergens strabismus—Hypotropia. Strabismus in which the deviating eye turns downward.

Divergent strabismus —Exotropia. Strabismus in which the deviating eye turns outward.

Intermittent strabismus—Strabismus recurring at intervals.

Mechanical strabismus—Strabismus occurring due to restriction of action of the ocular muscle within the orbit.

Monocular strabismus—Strabismus in which the same eye habitually deviates.

Paralytic strabismus—Strabismus that is due to paralysis of an ocular muscle.

Spastic strabismus—Strabismus due to contraction of an ocular muscle.

Vertical strabismus—Hypertropia. Strabismus in which deviating eye turns upward.

Strabometer—Strabismometer.

Strabotome—A knife used in the operation of strabismus.

Strabotomy—Operation for strabismus.

Strain—1. Overexertion of some part of the body. 2. To injure by excessive effort or by excessive use. 3. To make a great effort as in defecation. 4. To filter. 5. A group of organisms within a species or variety characterized by some particular quality. 6. Tension. 7. Pressure.

Strainer—Filter.

Strait—A constricted or narrow passage.

Stramonium—The dried leaves of Datura stramonium.

Strand—A single thread or fiber.

Strangalesthesia—Zonesthesia.

Strangle—To suffocate or be suffocated from compression of the trachea.

Strangulated—Too much constricted so as to cause the air or blood supply to be cut off, as a strangulated hernia.

Strangulation—Compression or constriction of a part so that its blood supply is obstructed.

Strangury —Painful drop by drop urination.

Strap—1. A band, as of adhesive plaster, used to hold dressings in place or to attach the surfaces of a wound. 2. To bind with strips of adhesive plaster.

Strapping—To apply strips of adhesive plaster on a part for its support or to compress it.

Stratification—Arrangement in layers.

Stratified—Arranged in layers.

Stratified epithelium—Epithelium consisting of more than one layer of cells, each layer with differently shaped cells.

Stratiform—Stratified.

Stratigraphy—Tomography.

Stratum—A layer, *e.g.*, stratum corneum, the outermost layer of the epidermis.

Streak—Stria. A line or stripe, as primitive streak.

Stream—A steady flow of a fluid.

Streaming movement—Ameboid movement. (See under movement)

Streblodactyly—Camptodactyly.

Strength—Vigour; power.

Strengthening—Increasing power.

Strephosymbolia—1. The condition in which the objects are seen reversed as in a mirror. 2. Difficulty in distinguishing between similar but oppositely facing letter, *e.g.*, p-q, b-d.

Strepitus—A sound heard on auscultation.

Strepticemia—Streptococcemia.

Strepto- —A prefix meaning twisted.

Streptoangina—A sore throat with membrane formation caused by streptococci.

Streptococcal—Caused by or pertaining to streptococci.

Streptococcemia—Strepticemia. Presence of streptococci in the blood.

Streptococci—Plural of streptococcus.

Streptococcic—Pertaining to, caused by or resembling streptococci.

Streptocccicosis—Any infection with streptococcus.

Streptococcolysin—A lysin produced by streptococcus.

Streptococcus—A gram-positive bacterium of the genus Streptococcus belonging to the family Streptococcaceae.

Streptococcus equisimilis—It is found in the upper respiratory tract and causes erysipelas, puerperal sepsis, pneumonia, osteomyelitis and endocarditis etc.

Streptococcus faecalis—Enterococcus faecalis. It is found in the human intestine and feces as a part of the normal flora and it may cause urinary tract infection.

Streptococcus mutans—A species of streptococci that causes dental caries and endocarditis.

Streptococcus pneumoniae—A species of Gram-positive, oval or spherical and diplococci bacteria that causes pneumonia, especially lobar pneumonia, meningitis, conjunctivitis, endocarditis, septic arthritis, osteomyelitis and otitis media etc.

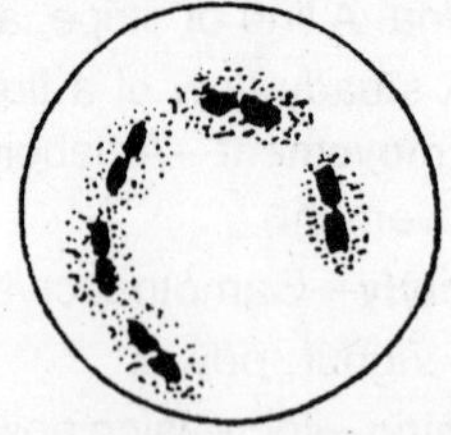

Fig. 538 : Streptococcus pneumoniae

Streptococcus pyogenes—This type of streptococcus is found in the mouth, throat and respiratory tract and causes pus formation and suppurative diseases.

Streptocolysin —Streptococcolysin.

Streptodermatitis—Inflammation of the skin caused by streptococci.

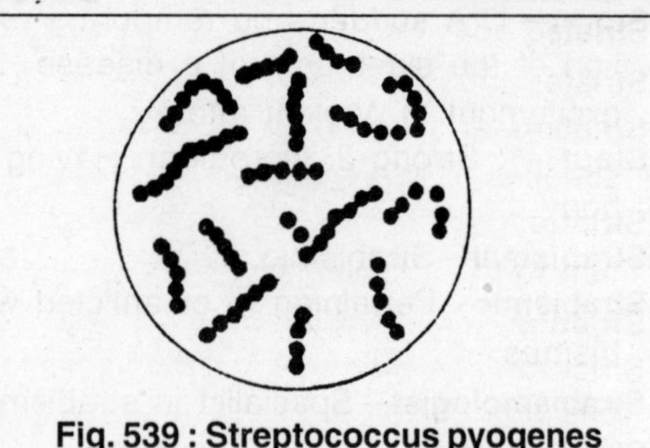

Fig. 539 : Streptococcus pyogenes

Streptoleukocidin—A toxin produced by streptococcus, which is destructive to white blood cells.

Streptolysin—Streptococcolysin.

Streptomycetaceae—A family of aerobic Gram-positve bacteria.

Streptosepticemia—Septicemia due to streptococci.

Stress—1. Emphasis. 2. Effort. 3. Physical stress—pressure, mechanical force, pathogenic organisms and injury. 4. Psychological stress—fear, anxiety, crisis and gladness etc. 5. Stress which is required by the biological organisms to maintain their lives, when it exceeds it produces pathological changes in the organism.

Stress breaker—A device incorporated into a fixed or removable partial denture, to relieve abutting teeth from excessive stress during chewing.

Stress incontinence—See under incontinence.

Stressor—An agent or condition which produces stress.

Stretch—To extend.

Stretcher—A litter for carrying the sick, injured or dead person.

Stretch mark—Stria atrophica.

Stretch receptor—A proprioceptor located in a muscle or tendon that is stimulated by a stretch.

Stria—Streak. A line or band elevated or depressed below the surrounding tissue, or differing in color and structure.

Stria atrophica—Stretch mark. A fine pinkish-white or gray line seen in parts of the body where skin has been stretched, as seen on the abdomen during pregnancy.

Striae—Plural of stria.

Striatal—Pertaining to the corpus striatum.

Striate, Striated—Stripped; having striae or streaks.

Striated body—Corpus striatum.

Striated muscle—See muscle.

Striation—1. The condition of being stripped or streaked. 2. Stria or a series of streaks.

Striatonigral—Projecting from the corpus striatum to the substantia nigra.

Striatum—Corpus striatum.

Stricture—An abnormal narrowing of a tube, duct, passage or hollow organ, such as ureter, urethra or esophagus.

Stricturotome—An instrument for cutting the strictures.

Stricturotomy—Operation of cutting strictures of the urethra.

Strident—Stridulous.

Stridor—A harsh, high-pitched respiratory sound.

Congenital laryngeal stridor —Stridor heard at birth or during first 3 weeks of life, due to laryngeal obstruction.

Stridulous—Strident. Producing a sharp, grating sound.

String—A slender cord or cordlike structure.

Striocerebellar—Pertaining to, or affecting the corpus striatum and the cerebellum.

Strip—1. To remove all the contents from a canal such as the urethra or a blood vessel by pressing it with the finger running along it. 2. To remove the bark.

Stripe—1. In anatomy, a line, band, streak or stria. 2. In radiography, a linear opacity which is different in density from the adjacent parts of the image.

Stripper—One who strips.

Stripping—1. Removal, as of a covering 2. Stripper.

Strobila—The body of an adult tapeworm.

Strobilae—Plural of strobila.

Strobiloid—Resembling a chain of segments of a tapeworm.

Stroboscope—An instrument that produces intermittent light flashes which are shown on moving or vibrating objects. This makes the object appear to be stationary.

Stroke—1. A sharp blow. 2. A sudden attack. 3. Sudden loss of consciousness followed by paralysis caused by hemorrhage into the brain, formation of an embolus or thrombus which occludes an artery. 4. Sudden occurrence of hyperpyrexia due to exposure to heat (heat stroke or sunstroke). 5. To pass the hand gently in one direction.

Stroker—One who strokes.

Stroke volume—The amount of blood ejected by the left ventricle at each beat, which varies with the age, sex and exercise.

Stroma—The supporting tissue or matrix of an organ.

Stromal, Stromatic—Pertaining to, or resembling the stroma of an organ.

Stromata—Plural of stroma.

Stromatolysis—Destruction of the stroma of a cell.

Stromatosis—Presence of the stromata throughout the endometrium of the uterus.

Stromic—Stromal.

Stromuhr—Rheometer. An instrument for measuring the rapidity of blood flow through a blood vessel.

Strongyloides—A genus of roundworms that infect man and present in the human intestine.

Strongyloidiasis — Strongyloidosis.

Strongyloidosis—Infestation with strongyloides.

Strongylosis—Disease caused by infection with a parasitic worm Strongylus stercoralis.

Strophocephaly—Congenital distortion of the head and face.

Strophulus—Papular urticaria.

Structural—Pertaining to the structure.

Structure—The manner in which anything is constructed.

Struma—Goiter.

Strumectomy—Surgical removal of a goiter.

Strumiform—Resembling a goiter.

Strumiprivous—Pertaining to or caused by removal of the thyroid gland.

Strumitis —Thyroiditis. Inflammation of a thyroid gland.

Strumous—1. Scrofulous. Affected with scrofula. 2. Affected with goiter.

Strumpell-Marie disease—Rheumatoid spondylitis.

Strumpell's sign —Dorsiflexion of the foot when the thigh is flexed on the abdomen, which is a sign of spastic paralysis of the leg.

Strychnine—A poisonous alkaloid obtained from the plant Strychnous nux-vomica. It stimulates all the parts of the central nervous system, and has been used as a stomachic, antidote for depressant poisons and in the treatment of myocarditis.

Strychninism—Chronic strychnine poisoning.

Strychnism—Strychninism.

STS—Serological test for syphilis.

STU—Skin test unit.

Stuart factor—Thrombokinase.

Stump—The distal end of a limb left after amputation.

Stump hallucination—Phantom limb. Feeling of still possessing a limb after its amputation.

Stun—To make unconscious by a blow or injury.

Stunned—One who became unconscious by blow or injury.

Stunt—To retard the growth; to make dwarf.

Stunting—Retarding growth.

Stupe—A cloth or sponge made wet with hot water containing a medicine, used for fomentation, *e.g.*, turpentine stupe which is prepared by adding a little amount of turpentine to hot water.

Stupefacient—Narcotic. Soporific.

Stupefactive—Producing narcosis or stupor.

Stupefying—Stupefactive.

Stupor—1. Unconsciousness, numbness, inactivity or drowsiness with suppression of feelings. 2. A condition of reduced responsiveness.

Stuporous—Affected with stupor.

Stupration—Rape.

Stutter—To hesitate and repeat in speech.

Stuttering—A speech defect in which there is spasmodic repetition of the same syllable and hesitation.

Sty, Stye—Hordeolum. Inflammation of a sebaceous gland of the eyelid.

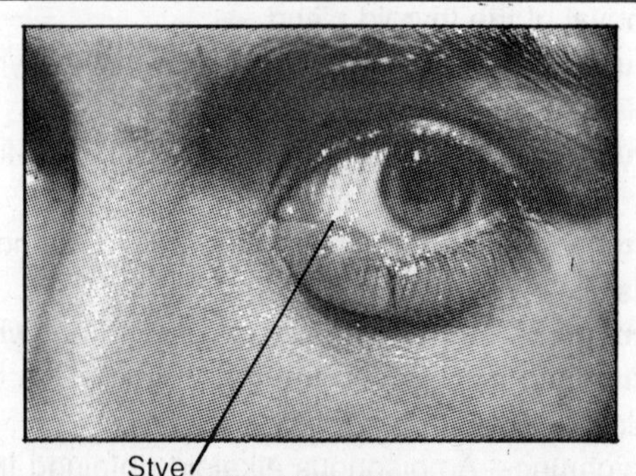

Fig. 540 : Stye

Style, Stylet—1. A metal wire to be introduced into a rubber catheter or cannula to stiffen it or to remove the debris from its lumen. 2. A thin probe.

Stylet—Style.

Styliform—Long and pointed.

Stylo- —A prefix meaning styloid process.

Stylohyal—Stylohyoid.

Stylohyoid—Pertaining to the styloid process and hyoid bone.

Styloid—Long and pointed.

Styloiditis—Inflammation of a styloid process.

Styloid process—A pointed process of the temporal bone projecting downwards.

Stylomandibular—Pertaining to the styloid process of temporal bone and the mandible.

Stylomastoid—Pertaining to the styloid and mastoid processes of the temporal bone.

Stylomaxillary—Pertaining to the styloid process of temporal bone and the maxilla.

Stylostaphyline—Concerning the styloid process of temporal bone and the uvula.

Stylosteophyte—A peg-shaped outgrowth from a bone.

Stylus—1. Stylet. 2. Pencil-like pointed medicinal preparation for external application.

Stype—A tampon or pledget of cotton or other material.

Stypsis—The use of an astringent.

Styptic—Astringent.

Sub- —A prefix which means below, beneath or under, inside, in small quantity, less than normal, and moderately.

Subabdominal—Below the abdomen.

Subabdominoperitoneal —Subperitoneoabdominal. Beneath the abdominal peritoneum.

Subacid—Moderately acid.

Subacidity —Deficient acidity.

Subacromial—Below the acromion.

Subacute—Some what acute or between acute and chronic, said of a disease.

Subalimentation—Insufficient nourishment.

Subanal—Below the anus.

Subanconeus—Below the elbow.

Subaortic—Below the aorta.

Subapical—Below the apex.

Subaponeurotic—Below an aponeurosis.

Subarachnoid—Between arachnoid and pia mater.

Subarachnoid cisternae—Large subarachnoid spaces in the form of cavities at the base of the brain.

Subarachnoid space —Space between arachnoid and pia mater containing cerebrospinal fluid.

Subarcuate—Slightly arched.

Subareolar—Below the areola.

Subastragalar—Beneath the astragalus.

Subastringent—Mildly astringent.

Subatomic—Of or pertaining to the constituents of an atom.

Subaural—Below the ear.

Subauricular—Below the auricle of the ear.

Subaxial—Below an axis.

Subaxillary—Below the axilla.

Subbasal—Beneath any base or basal membrane.

Sub-brachycephalic—Having slightly short head with the index of about 80.

Subcalosal—Below the corpus callosum.

Subcapsular—Below a capsule, especially the capsule of the brain.

Subcartilaginous—1. Beneath a cartilage 2. Partly cartilaginous.

Subcecal—Below the cecum.

Subchondral—Below or under a cartilage.

Subchorionic—Beneath the chorion.

Subchoroidal—Beneath the choroid coat of the eye.

Subchronic—The condition of between subacute and. chronic.

Subclass—In animal classification between a class and an order.

Subclavian—Subclavicular.

Subclavicular—Subclavian. Below the clavicle bone.

Subclinical—Pertaining to the stage of a disease before appearance of its typical symptoms.

Subconjunctival—Beneath the conjunctiva.

Subconscious— Partially conscious.

Subconsciousness—The state of being partially conscious.

Subcoracoid—Beneath the coracoid process.

Subcortex—White substance of the brain underlying the cortex.

Subcortical—Pertaining to the area beneath the cerebral cortex.

Subcostal—Beneath the ribs.

Subcostalgia—Pain in the region over the subcostal nerve.

Subcostosternal—Below or beneath the ribs and sternum.

Subcranial—Below the cranium.

Subcrepitant—Partially crepitant, said of a rale.

Subcrepitation —Presence of subcrepitant rales.

Subculture —To make a culture of bacteria with material derived from another culture.

Subcurative—A dose of a medicine which is partially curative.

Subcutaneous—Hypodermic. Beneath the skin.

Subcuticular—Subepidermal.

Subcutis—The layer of connective tissue beneath the skin.

Subdelirium—Mild delirium.

Subdeltoid—Beneath the deltoid muscle.

Subdental—Beneath the teeth or a tooth.

Subdermal—Below the skin.

Subdiaphragmatic—Subphrenic. Below the diaphragm.

Subdorsal—Below the dorsal area.

Subduct—To draw down.

Subdural—Between the dura mater and the arachnoid mater.

Subendocardial—Below the endocardium.

Subendothelial—Below the endothelium.

Subendothelium—Subendothelial.

Subendymal—Beneath the endyma.

Subependymal—Subendymal.

Subepidermal—Subcuticular. Beneath the epidermis.

Subepidermic—Subepidermal.

Subepithelial —Beneath the epithelium.

Subepithelium—Subepithelial.

Subfamily—A division between family and genus.

Subfascial—Beneath a fascia.

Subfebrile —Mild fever.

Subfertility—Less than normal capacity for reproduction.

Subflavous—Yellowish.

Subfrontal—Below the frontal lobe of the brain.

Subgenus—In animal classification, between a genus and species.

Subgingival—Beneath the gingiva.

Subglenoid—Below the glenoid fossa.

Subglossal—Sublingual. Hypoglossal. Beneath the tongue.

Subglossitis—Inflammation of the under surface or tissues of the tongue.

Subglottic—Beneath the glottis.

Subgranular—Not completely granular.

Subgrondation, Subgrundation —Depression of one fragment of a broken bone beneath the other, as of the cranium.

Subgrundation —Subgrondation.

Subhepatic—Below the liver.

Subhyoid—Below the hyoid bone.

Subicteric—Mildly jaundiced.

Subiliac—Below the ilium.

Subilium—The lowest part of the ilium.

Subinfection—Mild infection with very few sings or symptoms.

Subinflammation—Mild inflammation.

Subinflammatory—Mild inflammatory.

Subintimal—Beneath the intima.

Subintrant—Having paroxysms or cycles occurring so rapidly that they intermingle.

Subinvolution—Incomplete involution.

Subjacent—Located beneath.

Subject—1. A patient undergoing treatment, observation or investigation. 2. A dead body used for dissection.

Subjective —Perceived only by patient and not by examiner, as perception of the symptoms.

Subjugal—Below the zygomatic bone.

Subkingdom—In classification of the animal kingdom, a division between kingdom and phylum.

Sublatio—Elevation, removal or detachment of a part of the body.

Sublatio retinae—Detachment of the retina.

Sublation—Sublatio.

Sublesional—Beneath a lesion.

Sublethal—Insufficient to cause death; almost fatal.

Sublimate—1. A substance obtained or prepared by sublimation. 2. To perform sublimation.

Sublimation—The conversion of a solid directly into a gaseous state without being changed into liquid.

Sublime—To evaporate a solid substance directly into a gaseous state and condense it again.

Subliminal—1. Below the threshold of sensation, *i.e.*, too weak to arouse sensation or to cause muscular contraction. 2. Below the normal consciousness.

Sublimis—Near the surface.

Sublingual—Beneath the tongue.

Sublinguitis—Inflammation of the sublingual gland.

Sublobular—Beneath a lobule.

Sublumbar region—Below the lumbar region.

Subluxate—To dislocate partially.

Subluxation—Partial dislocation.

Submammary—Below the mammary gland.

Submandibular—Below the mandible.

Submandibularitis—Inflammation of the submandibular gland.

Submarginal—Near to or next to a margin or border of a part.

Submaxilla—The mandible.

Submaxillary—Below the maxilla.

Submedial, Submedian—Below or close to the middle.

Submembranous—Containing partly membranous material.

Submental—Below the chin.

Submerge—To place in water.

Submerged tooth—A tooth that is below the plane of occlusion.

Submicron—A measure of less than 1 micron.

Submicronic—Smaller than 1 micron in size, which is visible with ultramicroscope only.

Submicroscopic—Too small to be seen through a microscope.

Submorphous—Neither completely amorphous nor crystalline, as some calculi.

Submucosa—The layer of areolar connective tissue beneath a mucous membrane.

Submucous—Beneath a mucous membrane.

Submuscular—Below the muscle.

Subnarcotic—Mild narcotic.

Subnasal—Under the nose.

Subnasion—The point of the angle between the nasal septum and the surface of the upper lip.

Subneural—Beneath a nerve.

Subnormal—Below normal.

Subnormality—The condition of being subnormal.

Subnotochordal—Lying beneath the notochord.

Subnucleus—A secondary nucleus into which a nucleus of the central nervous system may be divided.

Suboccipital—Below the occiput.

Suboptimal—Less than optimum.

Suborbital—Below the orbit.

Suborder—In animal classification, between an order and a family.

Subordination—To work under control of another.

Suboxidation—Deficient oxidation.

Subpapular—Very slightly papular.

Subparietal—Below the parietal bone or lobe.

Subpatellar—Beneath the patella.

Subpectoral —Beneath the pectoral muscle.

Subpelviperitoneal —Beneath the pelvic peritoneum.

Subpericardial—Beneath the pericardium.

Subperiosteal—Beneath the periosteum.

Subperitoneal—Beneath the peritoneum.

Subperitoneoabdominal—Subabdominoperitoneal

Subperitoneopelvic—Subperitoneal.

Subpharyngeal—Beneath the pharynx.

Subphrenic—Subdiaphragmatic.

Subphylum—In animal kingdom, a category between a phylum and a class.

Subpial—Beneath the pia mater.

Subplacenta—Decidua parietalis. The endometrium during pregnancy lining the entire uterine cavity, except at the site of implantation of the blastocyst.

Subplacental—Beneath the placenta.

Subpleural—Beneath the pleurae.

Subplexal—Below or beneath any plexus.

Subpontine—Below the pons.

Subpreputial—Under the prepuce.

Subpubic—Beneath the pubic bone.

Subpulmonary—Below the lung.

Subpyramidal—Beneath a pyramid of the kidney.

Subretinal—Beneath the retina.

Subscapular—Below the scapula bone.

Subscleral—Beneath the sclera of the eye.

Subsclerotic—1. Subscleral. 2. Not completely sclerosed.

Subscription—That part of a prescription in which direction for compounding the ingredients is given.

Subserosal—Subserous.

Subserous—Beneath a serous membrane.

Subside—To disappear.

Subsidence—Gradual disappearance of a disease.

Subsidiary—Supplementary.

Subsistence—The minimum amount of something essential for life as that of food.

Subspecies—Inferior to a species.

Subspinous—Below a spinous process or the spinal column.

Substage—An attachment to a microscope, below the stage, supporting the condenser.

Substance—Material of which any organ or tissue is composed.

Colloid substance—Jelly-like substance in colloid degeneration.

Gray substance—Gray matter of the brain and spinal cord.

Ground substance —The matrix or intercellular substance.

Ketogenic substance—A substance that in its metabolism gives rise to ketone bodies.

Pressor substance—A substance that elevates the arterial blood pressure.

Transmitter substance—Neurotransmitter.

White substance—White matter of the brain and spinal cord.

Substandard—Below standard.

Substantia—Substance.

Substantiae —Plural of substantia.

Substernal—Beneath the sternum.

Substernomastoid—Beneath the sternomastoid muscle.

Substitute—Anything or medicine which may be used in place of another.

Substitution—Replacement of one thing by another.

Substrate, Substratum—1. An underlying layer or base or foundation. 2. A substance upon which an enzyme acts.

Substructure —The underlying or supporting portion of an organ.

Subsultus—Any tremor or twitching.

Subsylvian—Situated below the Sylvian fissure.

Subtarsal—Below the tarsus.

Subtendinous—Below a tendon.

Subtentorial—Beneath the tentorium of the cerebellum.

Subterminal —Close to the end of an extremity.

Subtetanic—Suffering from mild tetanus.

Subthalamic—1. Pertaining to the subthalamus. 2. Located below the thalamus.

Subthalamus—Portion of the diencephalon lying below thalamus and above the hypothalamus.

Subthreshold—Below the threshold.

Subtile, Subtle—1. Mentally acute. 2. Very fine.

Subtotal —Less than the whole.

Subtraction—The process by which undesired overlying structures can be removed from a x-ray picture.

Subtribe—In animal classification, a category between a tribe and genus.

Subtrochanteric—Below a trochanter.

Subtrochlear—Below the trochlea.

Subtuberal—Lying below any tuber.

Subtympanic—Below the tympanum.

Subumbilical —Below the umbilicus.

Subungual, Subunguial—Beneath a nail.

Suburethral—Beneath the urethra.

Subvaginal—Inside a tubular sheath, or below the vagina.

Subvalvar—Below a valve.

Subvalvular—Subvalvar.

Subvertebral—On the ventral side of the vertebral column or of a vertebra.

Subvirile—With deficient virility.

Subvitrinal—Beneath the vitreous body.

Subvolution—The operation of turning over a flap to prevent adhesions.

Subwaking—Between waking and sleeping.

Subzonal—Beneath a zone.

Subzygomatic—Beneath the zygomatic bone.

Succagogue—The substance which stimulates glandular secretion.

Succedaneous—Pertaining to a substitute.

Succedaneum—A substitute, *i.e.*, a drug or other thing that can be used in place of another.

Succenturiate—Acting as a substitute.

Succession—A series of things following one another.

Succi —Plural of succus.

Succorrhea—Excessive secretion of any juice, especially of the digestive juice.

Succubus—A bad horrible dream.

Succus—Any fluid or juice secreted by the living tissues as gastric juice which is the secretion of stomach walls.

Succussion—Shaking of the body to detect the presence of fluid and air in the body cavity, especially in the thorax, by listening the splashing sound.

Suck—To draw a fluid into the mouth as milk from the breast.

Sucker—A person or thing that sucks.

Sucking pad—Mass of fat in the cheeks of infant which aids the infant in sucking.

Suckle—To feed at the breast.

Suckling—A young child nursed at the breast.

Sucrase—An enzyme in the intestinal juice which splits sucrose into glucose and fructose.

Sucrose—Can-sugar.

Sucrosemia—Presence of sucrose in the blood.

Sucrosuria—Presence of sucrose in the urine.

Suction—Withdrawal of a fluid or gas by reduction of air pressure over it, with an aspirator.

Suctorial—1. Concerning sucking. 2. Equipped for sucking.

Sudamen—A whitish vesicle produced by retention of sweat in the horny layer of the skin, appearing after excessive sweating or in some febrile diseases.

Sudamina—Plural of sudamen.

Sudaminal —Concerning the sudamina.

Sudanophilia —Affinity for Sudan dye.

Sudanophilic—Staining readily with sudan dyes.

Sudanophobic—Not staining with sudan dyes.

Sudation —The process of sweating.

Sudatoria—Hyperhidrosis. Excessive sweating.

Sudatorium—1. A hot air bath. 2. A room used for the administration of hot air bath.

Sudokeratosis—Horny outgrowths of the skin that obstruct the ducts of the sweat glands.

Sudomotor—Stimulating the secretion of sweat gland.

Sudor —Sweat; perspiration.

Sudoral—Pertaining to, caused by or affected with sweating.

Sudoresis—Diaphoresis.

Sudoriferous—Producing or conveying sweat.

Sudorific—Diaphoretic. Producting or stimulating the secretion of sweat.

Sudoriparous—Sudoriferous.

Sudorometer—An instrument for measuring the amount of perspiration.

Sudorrhea—Hyperhidrosis.

Suffocate—To impair respiration.

Suffocating—Impairing respiration.

Suffocation—Impairment of respiration.

Suffusion—1. Extravasation. Spreading of a body fluid into the surrounding tissues. 2. The moistening of the body as the treatment.

Sugar—A sweet carbohydrate, the two principal groups of which are disaccharides and monosaccharides.

Suggestibility—Sympathism. Susceptibility to suggestions of others.

Suggestible—Susceptible to suggestions of others.

Suggestion—Presentation of an idea to the mind.

Suggestive—Pertaining to suggestion or able to be suggested.

Suggillation—Ecchymosis.

Suicide—The taking of one's own life.

Suicidology—Science of suicide.

Sulcal—Pertaining to a sulcus.

Sulcate, Sulcated—Furrowed or grooved.

Sulciform—Like a sulcus.

Sulculus—A small sulcus.

Sulcus—A furrow, groove or slight depression, especially on the surface of the brain.

Cerebellar sulci—Fissures between the folia in the cerebellum.

Cerebral sulci—Fissures between the gyri or convolutions in the cerebrum.

Coronary sulcus—A groove on the outer surface of the heart making the division between the atria and the ventricles.

Sagittal sulcus—Groove for superior sagittal sinus.

Skin sulci—The numerous grooves of variable depth on the surface of the skin.

Sulcus centralis—A fissure dividing the frontal and parietal lobes of each cerebral hemisphere.

Sulfhemoglobin—Sulfmethemoglobin. A substance formed by the action of hydrogen sulfide on blood.

Sulfhemoglobinemia—Presence of sulfhemoglobin in the blood.

Sulfurated—Combined or charged with sulfur.

Sullage—Filth.

Sumendum—To take.

Summation—Cumulative effect of the stimuli applied to a muscle or nerve.

Sunburn—Dermatitis due to excessive exposure to sunlight.

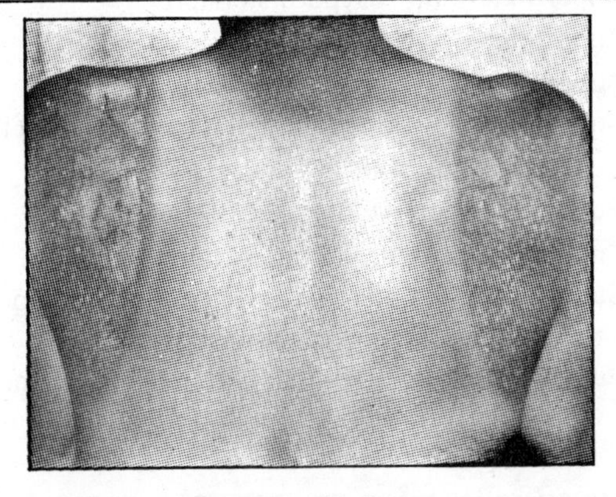

Fig. 541 : Sunburn

Sunglasses—Eyeglasses that protect the eyes from exposure to sun.

Sunscreen—Any substance in the form of an ointment or cream, used to protect the skin from sun rays.

Sunstroke —Heatstroke. An acute condition caused by excessive exposure to sun, characterized by hyperpyrexia (temperature being above 105^{0}°F), delirium or convulsions and coma.

Suntan—Darkening of the skin caused by exposure to the sun.

Super- —A prefix which means above, superior, beyond or excessive or extreme.

Superabduction—To draw away extremely.

Superacidity—Excess of acidity.

Superacromial —Supra-acromial.

Superactivity—Hyperactivity.

Superacute—Very acute.

Superalimentation—Hyperalimentation. To feed more food than required by the body or for appetite in the treatment of wasting diseases.

Superalkalinity —Excessive alkalinity.

Superanal—Supra-anal.

Superantigen—An antigen that simultaneously activates large numbers of T cells.

Supercilia—Plural of supercilium.

Superciliary—Pertaining to or situated in the region of an eye brow.

Supercilium—1. An eyebrow. 2. A hair of the eyebrow.

Superclass—In animal classification, a category between a phylum and a class.

Superdicrotic—Hyperdicrotic.

Superdistention—Hyperdistention.

Superduct—To elevate.

Super ego—Overgrowth of ego.

Supereruption—Movement of a tooth beyond the normal plane of occlusion.

Superexcitation—Excessive excitement.

Superextension—Extreme extension.

Superfamily—In animal classification, a category between an order and a family.

Superfecundation—Fertilization of two or more ova during the same menstrual cycle, by two separate sexual intercourse.

Superfetation—The presence of two fetuses of different ages in the uterus, due to fertilization of two ova at different menstrual periods.

Superficial—Situated on or near the surface.

Superficialis—Superficial.

Superficial reflex —Reflex induced by very light stimulus, such as touching the skin with cotton.

Superficies—An outer surface.

Superflexion—Excessive flexion.

Supergenual —Above the knee.

Superheated—Too much hot.

Superimpregnation—Fertilization occurring during pregnancy.

Superinduce —To bring on in addition to an already existing condition.

Superinfection—A new infection caused by an organism different from that which caused the initial infection, and which is not affected by the treatment given to the initial infection.

Superinvolution—Hyperinvolution.

Superior—1. Comparatively higher or situated above something else. 2. Better than.

Superiority complex—An overexhibition of one's own superiority in order to compensate for one's feeling of inferiority.

Superjacent—Located just above.

Superlactation—Hyperlactation. Excessive secretion of milk or continuous secretion of milk beyond the normal time.

Superlethal—A dose of a drug, or an injury, greater than that required to cause death.

Supermedial—Above the middle.

Supermotility—Hyperkinesia. Excessive motility.

Supernatant—1. Floating on the surface of a liquid, as oil on water. 2. The clear liquid lying above a layer of precipitated insoluble material.

Supernumerary —More than the normal number.

Supernutrition—More than the normal nutrition.

Superolateral—Above and to the side.

Superovulation—Occurrence of ovulation frequently or production of a large number of ova at one time.

Superparasite—A parasite that is parasitic on another parasite.

Superparasitism —The condition in which the host is infested or infected with a large number of parasites.

Superpetrosal—Above or at the upper part of the petrous portion of the temporal bone.

Supersaturate—To add more of a substance to a solution that can be held in the form of solution permanently.

Superscription—The heading of a prescription containing the symbol **Rx**, signifying (Latin) recipe which means "take".

Supersecretion—An excess of any secretion.

Supersensitive—Hypersensitive.

Supersensitiveness—Hypersensitiveness.

Supersoft—Extremely soft.

Supersonic—1. Ultrasonic. 2. Travelling at the speed greater than that of the sound.

Superstructure—The visible portion of a structure.

Supertension—Extremely increased tension.

Supervascularization—Increase in vascularity.

Supervenosity—Abnormally decreased oxygen in the venous blood.

Supervention—The development of a new disease as a complication to the existing disease.

Supervirulent —More virulent than usual.

Supervitaminosis—Hypervitaminosis. Excess of accumulation of vitamins in the body due to an excessive amount of vitamins in the diet or due to their administration in excess, as medicines.

Supervoltage —A term applied to an X-ray produced at the voltage between 500 to 1000 kilovolts.

Supinate—To turn the palm upward or to raise the medial margin of the foot or to lie straight upon the back.

Supination—The act of supinating.

Supinator—A muscle which causes supination of the forearm.

Supine —1. Lying on the back with the face upward. 2. Position of the hand or foot with the palm or foot facing upward.

Supplemental —Supplementary. Additional.

Supplemental air —Reserve air.

Supplementary—Supplemental.

Supplementary air—Reserve air.

Supply—To provide what is required.

Support—To uphold, to sustain, to nourish.

Supporter—Upholding, sustaining, nourishing.

Suppository—A medicated cylindrical or conical mass to be introduced into a body orifice, as the rectum, vagina or urethra where it dissolves and its medicine is absorbed.

Suppress—To put down, to stop.

Suppressant —One who suppresses or an agent that stops secretion, excretion or normal discharge of the body.

Suppression—Stoppage of a natural production of a secretion, or excretion or normal discharge of the body.

Suppurant—Suppurative. Causing or promoting suppuration.

Suppurate —To form pus.

Suppuration—Pyogenesis. Formation of pus.

Suppurative—Causing or promoting pus formation.

Supra- —A prefix which means above.

Supra-acromial —Above the acromion.

Supra-anal—Above the anus.

Supra-auricular —Above the auricle of the ear.

Supra-axillary —Above the axilla.

Suprabuccal—Above the cheek.

Suprabulge—The part of a dental crown that converges toward the occlusal surface of that tooth.

Supracerebellar—Above the upper surface of the cerebellum.

Supracerebral—On or above the surface of the cerebrum.

Suprachoroid —Situated above the choroid layer of the eyeball.

Suprachoroidea—Suprachoroid lamina. The outermost layer of the choroid.

Suprachoroid lamina—Suprachoroidea.

Supraciliary —Superciliary.

Supraclavicular—Above the clavicle.

Supracolic—Above the colon.

Supracondylar—Above a condyle.

Supracostal —Above the ribs.

Supracotyloid—Above the acetabulum.

Supracranial—Above the cranium.

Supracristal—Above a crest or ridge.

Supradiaphragmatic —Above the diaphragm.

Supraduction—Sursumduction.

Supraepicondylar —Above an epicondyle.

Supragingival—Above the gingiva.

Supraglenoid —Above the glenoid cavity.

Supraglottic—Above the glottis.

Supraglottitis—Inflammation of the epiglottis.

Suprahepatic—Above the liver.

Suprahyoid—Above the hyoid bone.

Suprainguinal—Above the groin.

Supraintestinal—Lying over the intestine.

Supraliminal —Above the threshold of sensation; conscious.

Supralumbar—Above the lumbar region.

Supramalleolar—Above a malleolus.

Supramammary—Above a breast.

Supramandibular—Above the mandible.

Supramarginal—Above a margin.

Supramastoid—Above the mastoid process of the temporal bone.

Supramastoid crest—Temporal line. A ridge on the superior edge of the posterior root of the zygomatic bone.

Supramaxilla —Maxilla. The upper jaw-bone.

Supramaxillary —1. Pertaining to the upper jaw. 2. Located above the upper jaw.

Suprameatal —Above a meatus, especially the external auditory meatus.

Supramedial—Above the medial line.

Supramental—The most posterior midline point, above the chin, on the mandible.

Supranasal—Above the nose.

Supraneural—Above a nerve.

Supranuclear—Located above a nucleus in the brain.

Supraoccipital—Above the occiput.

Supraocclusion—Projection of a tooth beyond the normal occlusal plane.

Supraocular—Above an eye-ball.

Supraorbital —Above an orbit.

Suprapatellar—Above the patella.

Suprapelvic—Above the pelvis.

Supraphrenic—Above the diaphragm.

Suprapontine—Above the pons.

Suprapubic—Above the pubic region.

Suprapubic cystotomy—Surgical opening of the urinary bladder from just above the pubic symphysis.

Suprarenal—1. Above a kidney. 2. Adrenal or suprarenal gland.

Suprarenalectomy—Adrenal-ectomy.

Suprarenal gland—Adrenal gland.

Suprarenalism—Adrenalism.

Suprarenalopathy—Any disease caused by abnormal functioning of the adrenal glands.

Suprascapular—Above the scapula.

Suprascleral —On the outer surface of the sclera.

Suprasegmental—Above the segmented portion.

Suprasegmental brain—It includes cerebrum, midbrain and cerebellum of the brain.

Suprasellar—Above the sella turcica.

Suprasonic, Supersonic—Musical sound with frequencies of vibration above 20,000 cycels per sec.

Supraspinal—Above the spine.

Supraspinous—Above any spinous process.

Suprastapedial—Above the stapes ossicle of the inner ear.

Suprasternal—Episternal. Above the sternum.

Suprasymphysary—Above the pubic symphysis.

Supratemporal—Above the temporal bone.

Supratentorial—Above the tentorium of the cerebellum.

Suprathoracic—Above the thorax.

Supratonsillar—Above tonsil.

Supratrochlear —Above a trochlea, especially that of the humerus.

Supraturbinal —Supreme nasal concha.

Supratympanic—Above the tympanic membrane of the ear.

Supravaginal—Above the vagina or any sheath.

Supravalvar—Above the valves, either pulmonary or aortic.

Supravalvular—Supravalvar.

Supraventricular—Above a ventricle, especially that of the heart.

Supravergence—Sursumvergence. Upward movement of one eye.

Supraversion—1. A turning upward. 2. The coming out of a tooth from the line of occlusion.

Supravesical —Above the urinary bladder.

Sura—Calf of the leg.

Sural—Pertaining to the calf of the leg.

Suralimentation—Hyperalimentation. Superalimentation. Treatment by overfeeding.

Surditas—Deafness.

Surdity—Deafness.

Surdomute—Deaf and dumb.

Surefooted—Being able to walk without stumbling or falling.

Surface—1. The exterior boundary of an object. 2. The external or internal exposed parts of a hollow structure.

Surfactant —That which lowers the surface tension, *e.g.*, oils.

Surgeon—A specialist in surgery.

Dental surgeon—Specialist in dental surgery.

Surgery—1. The branch of medical science which deals with the correction of defects and deformities, repair of injuries and diagnosis and treatment of certain diseases, by operations or by manual procedures. 2. Operation room. 3. The work performed by the surgeon.

Ablative surgery—An operation in which a part is removed.

Ambulatory surgery—An operation performed on a patient who is admitted to and discharged from the hospital on the same day.

Aural surgery—Surgery of the ear.

Closed surgery—An operation performed with out incision into the skin, *e.g.*, reduction of a fracture or dislocation.

Conservative surgery —Surgery in which as much as possible of a diseased structure, organ or part is retained.

Cosmetic surgery—An operation performed to improve the appearance.

Dental surgery—Operations performed on the teeth.

Exploratory surgery—An operation performed for diagnostic purposes.

Major surgery—Major and serious operations, usually performed under general anesthesia, in which there is risk of life.

Minor surgery—Minor operations performed for minor conditions and injuries in which there is no risk of life.

Open heart surgery—An operation performed on the heart in which it is opened.

Oral surgery—Surgery performed on the mouth and associated structures.

Orthopedic surgery—Surgery performed for the correction of deformities, and treatment of bone and joint diseases.

Plastic surgery—Surgery concerned with the repair or restoration or improvement in the shape and appearance of defective, damaged or missing structures, which is usually performed by transferring a tissue from a part or person to another part or person.

Radical surgery—Surgery in which whole of the diseased portion of the body including adjacent area of lymphatic drainage is removed.

Reconstructive surgery—An operation performed to repair a defect or to reconstruct a loss part.

Subtotal surgery—An operation in which only a part of an organ is removed, as subtotal hysterectomy in which uterus is removed leaving the cervix in place.

Surgical—Pertaining to surgery.

Surgical fever—Fever following an operation or injury.

Surgical neck—Constrictive part of the shaft of humerus bone below the tuberosities where fracture commonly occurs.

Surrenal—Suprarenal. Above a kidney.

Surrogate—A substitute; a thing or person that replaces another.

Sursanure—A superficially healed ulcer with pus inside.

Sursumduction—The turning upward of a part, as of an eye without the other one.

Sursumvergence—An upward movement, especially of an eye, the other eye not moving.

Sursumversion—The turning upward of both the eyes simultaneously.

Surveillance —The controlling of something.

Survey—To take a general view.

Survival—To remain alive.

Susceptibility—The state of being susceptible.

Susceptible—Readily affected or acted upon.

Suscitate—To stimulate to greater activity.

Suscitation—Excitation. The act of stimulating to greater activity.

Suspended—1. Hanging. 2. Temporarily inactive.

Suspension—1. Temporary cessation, as of pain or of any vital process. 2. Treatment, chiefly of diseases of vertebral column, by suspending the patient by chin and shoulders. 3. A medical preparation in which solid particles are mixed but not dissolved in a fluid.

Suspensoid—Colloid suspension.

Suspensory—1. A structure of the body as a ligament, muscle or bone which supports a part or an organ. 2. A sling or bandage for supporting a part, especially the scrotum.

Suspiration—The act of sighing.

Suspirious—Sighing.

Sustentacular—Supporting.

Sustentaculum —A support or supporting structure.

Susurrus —A murmur.

Sutura—1. Synarthrosis. 2. Suture.

Suturae—Plural of sutura.

Sutural —Pertaining to a suture.

Suturation—Application of sutures, or stitching.

Suture—1. Synarthrosis. 2. Line of union of bones in an immovable joint, as those between the skull bones. 3. To unite the margins of a wound

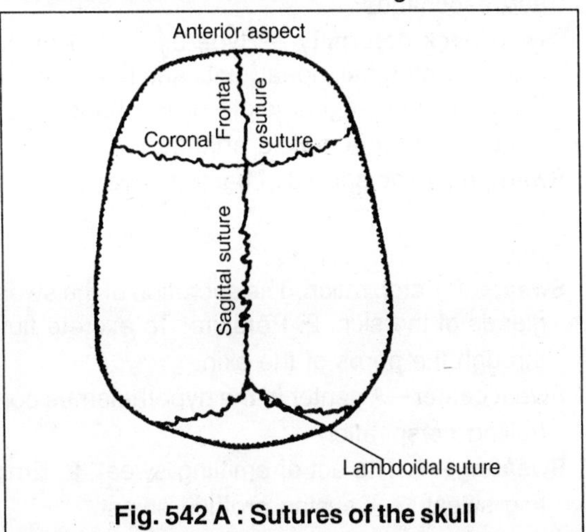

Fig. 542 A : Sutures of the skull

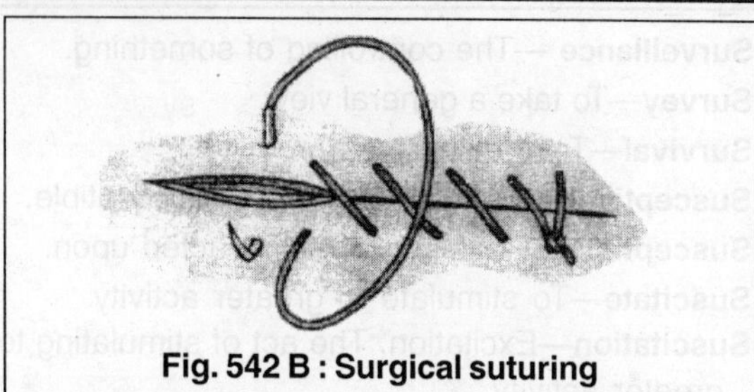

Fig. 542 B : Surgical suturing

by stitching. 4. The thread, wire or other material used in stitching. 5. The line of union formed by stitching a wound.

Suturectomy —Removal of cranial suture by surgery.

Sutured —Stitched.

Swab —1. A pad of cotton or gauze or other absorbable material attached to the end of a wire or stick, used for cleansing the cavities, applying medicines or for obtaining a piece of tissue or secretion for bacteriological examination. 2. To wipe with tha swab.

Swaddling—To keep an infant by wrapping with clothes tightly.

Swage—1. To shape metal by hammering or by moulding in a cast. 2. To fuse a suture thread to a needle.

Swager—A dental device used to shape silver amalgam or gold by applying pressure from different directions simultaneously.

Swallow—Deglutition. To cause something to pass from mouth into the stomach through throat and esophagus.

Swallowing—The process of passing something form mouth into the stomach, through the throat and esophagus.

Swan neck deformity —Hyperextension of the proximal interphalangeal joints and flexion of the distal interphalangeal joints of the hand, seen frequently in rheumatoid arthritis.

Swarming—The spread of bacteria over a culture medium.

Sway-back—Lordosis.

Sweat—1. Perspiration. The secretion of the sweat glands of the skin. 2. Perspire. To excrete fluid through the pores of the skin.

Sweat center—A center in the hypothalamus controlling perspiration.

Sweating—1. The act of emitting sweat. 2. Emitting sweat. 3. Causing profuse sweat.

Swelling—An abnormal transient enlargement of an organ or part of the body.

Swift's disease—Acrodynia.

Swine—A pig.

Switch—An apparatus used to break or open an electrical circuit or to divert the electric current from one conductor to another.

Swoon—1. A fainting 2. To faint.

Sycoma—Condyloma. A large soft wart.

Sycophant—Flatterer.

Sycosiform—Resembling sycosis.

Sycosis—Chronic inflammation of the hair follicles, especially of the beard (sycosis barbae).

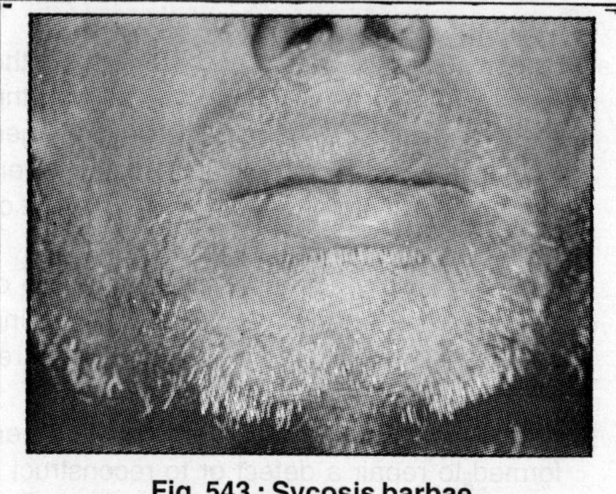

Fig. 543 : Sycosis barbae

Sycotic—Pertaining to or affected with sycosis.

Sydenham's chorea—See under chorea.

Syllabic utterance—Scanning speech.

Syllable stumbling —Dyssyllabia.

Syllabus—An outline of a course of study.

Syllepsis—Conception or fertilization.

Sylvian aqueduct—A narrow canal from 3rd to 4th ventricle of the brain.

Sylvian fissure—The fissure separating the temporal lobe from the frontal and parietal lobes.

Sym- —Combing form meaning with, along, beside.

Symballophone—A special stethoscope with two chest pieces, used for locating a lesion in the chest by comparing the different sounds detected by two chest pieces.

Symbion—Symbiont.

Symbiont—Commensal. An organism living with another in a state of symbiosis.

Symbiosis—The living together in close association of two dissimilar organisms. If neither organism is harmed, the association is termed as commensalism, if both organisms are benefitted from each other, the association is mutualism and if one organism is harmed and the other is benefitted, the association is known as parasitism.

Symbiote —Symbion. Symbiont.

Symbiotic—Concerning symbiosis.

Symblepharon—Adhesion of the conjunctiva of eyelid to the eyeball.

Symblepharopterygium—Abnormal adhesion of the conjunctiva to the eyeball resembling a pterygium.

Symbol—Sign.

Symbolia—Ability to recognize an object by the sense of touch.

Symbolism—1. A mental condition in which every thing that occurs is supposed as a symbol of the patient's own thoughts. 2. An expression of the sexual thoughts embedded in the mind, unconsciously in terms recognized by the observer.

Symbolization—A mental process by which an object, idea or quality of another comes to represent in the patient's subconscious mind.

Symbolophobia—Morbid fear of expressing one's self in words or action.

Symbrachydactyly—Webbing of the fingers that are abnormally short.

Syme's operation—1. Amputation of the foot at the ankle joint with removal of the malleoli. 2. Surgical removal of the tongue. 3. External urethrotomy.

Symmelia—Fusion of legs.

Symmelus, Symelus —A fetus with fused legs.

Symmetrical—Exhibiting symmetry.

Symmetromania—Mania for making symmetrical movements such as moving both arms.

Symmetry—Correspondence in size, shape and arrangement of parts of opposite sides of a body.

Sympath-, Sympatho- —Prefixes meaning the sympathetic part of the autonomic nervous system.

Sympathectomize—To perform sympathectomy.

Sympathectomy —Transection, resection or excision of a part of the sympathetic division of the autonomic nervous system.

Sympatheoneuritis—Inflammation of sympathetic nerve.

Sympathetectomy —Sympathectomy.

Sympathetic—1. Pertaining to the sympathetic nervous system. 2. Pertaining to or caused by sympathy.

Sympatheticalgia —Pain in the cervical sympathetic ganglion.

Sympathetic irritation —Irritation of a structure in sympathy of another associated structure which has been irritated.

Sympathetic nervous system—A large part of the autonomic nervous system which consists of ganglia, nerves, and nerve plexuses that supply the involuntary muscles.

Sympatheticoparalytic —Occurring due to paralysis of the sympathetic nervous system.

Sympatheticopathy —Any disease resulting from disorder of the sympathetic nervous system.

Sympathetic ophthalmia—Inflammation of one eye caused by a similar inflammation in the other eye.

Sympatheticotonia —Sympathicotonia.

Sympatheticotonic—Characterized by increased vasoconstriction and hence by high blood pressure due to overactivity of the sympathetic nervous system.

Sympatheticotripsy —Sympathicotripsy.

Sympathetic plexus—A plexus formed by the sympathetic nerves and ganglia.

Sympathetoblast—Sympathicoblast.

Sympathic—Sympathetic.

Sympathicectomy —Sympathectomy.

Sympathicoblast —A primitive sympathetic nerve cell.

Sympathicoblastoma —A malignant tumor consisting of sympathicoblasts.

Sympathicolytic—Sympatholytic.

Sympathicomimetic—Sympathomimetic.

Sympathiconeuritis—Inflammation of the sympathetic nerves.

Sympathicopathy—Sympatheticopathy.

Sympathicotonia—Sympatheticotonia. Increased tone of the sympathetic nervous system with a tendency to vascular spasm and high blood pressure.

Sympathicotonic—Pertaining to or characterized by sympathicotonia.

Sympathicotripsy—Sympatheticotripsy. Crushing of a sympathetic ganglion, nerve or nerve plexus.

Sympathicotropic —Having affinity for the sympathetic nervous system.

Sympathicus—The sympathetic nervous system.

Sympathism —Suggestibility. A condition in which a person accepts and responds readily to suggestions or opinions of another.

Sympathist —The person who accepts and responds readily to suggestions or opinions of another.

Sympathizer —1. An eye affected with sympathetic ophthalmia. 2. One who exhibits sympathy.

Sympathoadrenal —Pertaining to or affecting the sympathetic nervous system and the adrenal amedulla.

Sympathoblast —Sympathicoblast.

Sympathoblastoma—Sympathicoblastoma. A tumor consisting chiefly of sympathoblasts with scattered neuroblasts and spongioblasts.

Sympathoglioblastoma—A tumor made up of sympathoblasts with scattered neuroblasts and spongioblasts.

Sympathogonia—Embryonic cells which develop into sympathetic cells.

Sympathogonioma—A tumor consisting of sympathogonia.

Sympatholytic —Antiadrenergic. Inhibiting or destroying the impulses from the sympathetic nervous system.

Sympathomimetic —Adrenergic. Producing effects resembling those produced from stimulation of the sympathetic nervous system, as the effects resulting from injection of epinephrine.

Sympathy—1. Relationship between two organs or parts of the body through which one unaffected organ or part is affected from disease of other organ or part, without actual transmission of the causative organism. 2. To feel pity for another's grief. 3. The feeling as another feels, as weeping on weeping of other person.

Symperitoneal—Pertaining to the surgical adhesion between two portions of the peritoneum.

Sympexion—A small stone in the prostate gland or seminal vesicles.

Sympexis—Arrangement of red blood cells due to the effect of surface tension.

Symphalangia—Congenital ankylosis of the proximal phalangeal joints.

Symphalangism—1. Ankylosis of the joints of fingers or toes. 2. The condition of webbed fingers or webbed toes.

Symphalangy—Symphalangism.

Symphyogenetic—Pertaining to the combined effect of heredity and environment upon the development and function of an organism.

Symphyseal—Symphysial. Pertaining to a symphysis.

Symphyseotomy —The cutting of pubic symphysis to enlarge the pelvis during delivery.

Symphysic—Symphysial.

Symphysiectomy —Symphyseotomy.

Symphysion—The most anterior point of the alveolar process of the mandible.

Symphysiorrhaphy—Suture of a divided symphysis.

Symphysiotome —An instrument for dividing a symphysis.

Symphysiotomy —To divide the pubic symphysis to facilitate delivery, by enlarging the pelvic outlet.

Symphysis —1. The line of fusion of two bones, *e.g.*, the junction of pubic bones on midline in front. 2. An immovable joint in which the opposite bony surfaces are firmly united by a disk of fibrocartilage, as a vertebral joint.

Symphysodactyly—Syndactylism.

Symplasmatic —Pertaining to the union of protoplasm as in giant cell formation.

Symplast—A multinucleated cell that has formed by fusion of separate cells.

Sympodia—Fusion of the lower extremities.

Symport—The mechanism for carrying two different molecules or ions in the same direction through a membrane.

Symptom—Any change in the body or its function recognized by the person, that indicates the presence of a disease in the body.

- **Accessory symptom**—A minor symptom.
- **Accidental symptom**—A symptom occurring incidentally during the course of a disease, but not related to the disease.
- **Cardinal symptom**—Main symptom in making the diagnosis of a disease.
- **Concomitant symptom**—Accessory symptom.
- **Constitutional symptom**—General symptom.

Delayed symptom—Symptom appearing late.

Equivocal symptom—Symptom that may occur in may diseases.

Induced symptom—Symptoms produced artificially by a drug or other means, generally for diagnostic purposes.

Local symptom—Symptom occurring locally.

Objective symptom—Sign. Symptom apparent to the observer.

Presenting symptom—Symptom that compels the patient to go under treatment.

Prodromal symptom—Prodrome. Symptoms indicating an approaching disease.

Rational symptom —Subjective symptom.

Signal symptom —A premonitory symptom of a dangerous condition as the aura of an epileptic seizure.

Static symptom—A symptom pertaining to the disease of a single organ or structure.

Subjective symptom—Symptom that is perceptible only to the patient.

Sympathetic symptom —A symptom occurring at a site remote from that of occurrence of a disease.

Withdrawal symptom—Symptoms occurring following sudden withdrawal of a substance or drug to which a person is addicted.

Symptomatic—Pertaining to or of the nature of a symptom.

Symptomatology—1. The study of the symptoms. 2. The combined symptoms of a disease.

Symptomatolytic —Causing the disappearance of symptoms.

Symptom complex—Syndrome. A group of symptoms occurring together.

Symptomolytic—Symptomatolytic.

Symptosis—Wasting of an organ or body gradually.

Sympus—A fetus with fused legs.

Syn- —A prefix which means joined or together.

Synache—Inflammation of the throat that causes obstruction in the air passage.

Synactosis—Malformation resulting from abnormal fusion of parts of the body.

Synadelphus—A deformed fetus possessing eight limbs.

Synalgia—Referred pain. See under pain.

Synalgic—Pertaining to or characterized by referred pain.

Synanastomosis—An anastomosis between several blood vessels.

Synandrogenic—Enhancing the effects of androgens.

Synaphoceptors—Receptors stimulated by direct contact.

Synapse—The junction between the processes of two neurons or between a neuron and an effector organ where neural impulses are transmitted.

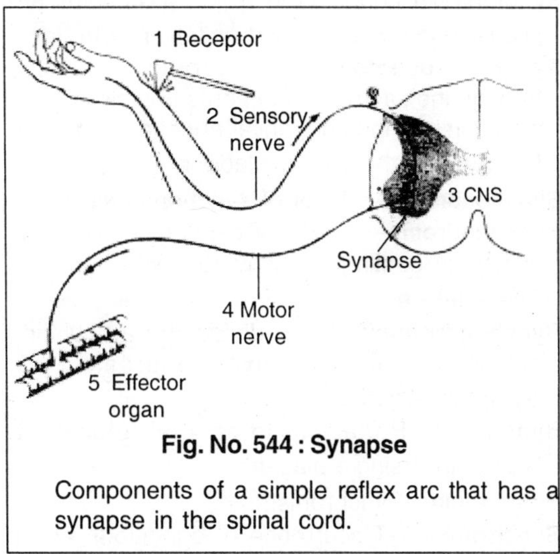

Fig. No. 544 : Synapse

Components of a simple reflex arc that has a synapse in the spinal cord.

Axodendritic synapse—Connection between an axon of one neuron and the dendrites of another.

Axodendrosomatic synapse—Connection between an axon of one neuron and the dendrites and body of another.

Axosomatic synapse—Connection between an axon of one neuron and the body of another.

Synapsis—1. Synapse. 2. In gametogenesis, the process of 1st maturation division in which there is conjugation of pairs of homologous chromosomes forming double chromosomes.

Synaptic—Pertaining to a synapse or synapsis.

Synaptolemma—The membrane at a synapse separating two neurons.

Synaptology—Study of the synapse.

Synarthrodia—Synarthrosis.

Synarthrodial—Pertaining to a synarthrosis.

Synarthrophysis—Progressive ankylosis in the joint.

Synarthrosis—Immovable joint.

Syncanthus —Adhesion of the eyeball to the structures of the orbit.

Syncaryon—Synkaryon.

Syncephalus—A deformed fetus with one head, one face but four ears.

Syncephaly—The condition of being syncephalus.

Syncheilia—Synchilia.

Syncheiria—Synchiria.

Synchilia—Congenital adhesion of the lips.

Synchiria—A condition in which a stimulus applied to one side of the body is felt on both sides.

Synchondroseotomy—An operation of cutting through the sacroiliac ligaments and closing the pubic arch in the congenital absence of the anterior wall of the urinary bladder.

Synchondroses—Plural of synchondrosis.

Synchondrosis—A type of cartilaginous joint in which the cartilage is converted into bone before adult life.

Synchondrotomy—1. To divide the articulating cartilage of a synchondrosis. 2. Symphyseotomy.

Synchorial—Pertaining to several fetuses attached to a single placenta.

Synchronia—Synchronism.

Synchronism—Occurrence of conditions at the same time.

Synchronous —Occurring at the same time.

Synchrony—Occurrence of two separate events simultaneously.

Synchysis—Fluid condition of the vitreous body of the eye.

Syncinesis—Synkinesis.

Synciput—Sinciput. Anterior and upper half portion of the cranium.

Synclinal—Leaning in the same direction toward a point.

Synclitic—Pertaining to synclitism.

Synclitism—Parallelism between the planes of fetal head and those of the maternal pelvis.

Synclonus—1. Clonic contraction of various muscles together. 2. A disease characterized by muscular tremors.

Syncopal —Pertaining to or marked by syncope.

Syncope—1. A faint; temporary loss of consciousness due to insufficient blood flow to the brain, which results from low blood pressure, and may occur in conditions of angina pectoris, and hysteria etc.

Syncopic—Syncopal.

Syncretio—Adhesions between opposing inflamed surfaces.

Syncytial—Of or pertaining to a syncytium.

Syncytioma—Chorioma. A tumor of the chorion which may be benign (mole) or malignant (choriocarcinoma).

Syncytiotrophoblast—Syntrophoblast.

Syncytium—1. A multinucleated mass of protoplasm produced by dissolution of the cell walls, *e.g.*, a striated muscle fiber. 2. Coenocyte. A group of cells in which the protoplasm of one cell mixes up with the protoplasm of the adjacent cells, such as the mesenchyme cells of the embryo.

Syndactyl, Syndactyle—Syndactylous.

Syndactylia—Syndactyly.

Syndactylism—Fusion of two or more fingers.

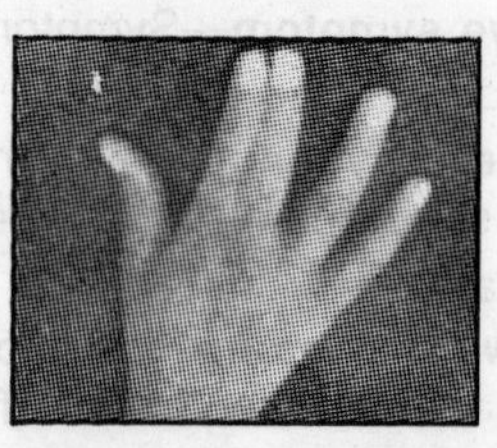

Fig. 545 : Syndactylism

Syndactylous—Pertaining to syndactylism.

Syndactyly—Syndactylism.

Syndectomy —Peridectomy. Peritectomy.

Syndesis—1. Surgical immobilization or ankylosis of a joint. 2. Condition of being bound together.

Syndesmectomy—Excision of a portion of a ligament.

Syndesmectopia—Abnormal position of a ligament.

Syndesmitis—1. Inflammation of the ligament. 2. Conjunctivitis.

Syndesmodial—Syndesmotic.

Syndesmography—A description of the ligaments.

Syndesmologia— Concerning with the articulations of joints and their ligaments.

Syndesmology—Study of the ligaments, joints, their movements, and their diseases.

Syndesmoma—A tumor of the connective tissue.

Syndesmopexy—Joining of two ligaments or fixation of a ligament at a new place.

Syndesmophyte—1. A bony outgrowth from a ligament. 2. A bony bridge formed between vertebrae.

Syndesmoplasty—Repair of a ligament by plastic surgery.

Syndesmorrhaphy—To stitch a ligament.

Syndesmosis—A joint in which the bones are bounded by ligaments.

Syndesmotic—Syndesmodial. Pertaining to syndesmosis.

Syndesmotomy—To incise a ligament.

Syndrome—A group of signs and symptoms that collectively indicate a particular disease, *e.g.*, burning feet syndrome, nephrotic syndrome, Plummer-vinson syndrome, and Stokes-Adams syndrome etc.

Hurler syndrome—A mucopolysaccharidosis due to deficiency of the enzyme α-L-iduronidase, characterized by gargoyle-like face, dwarfism, kyphosis, deformity of the limbs, limitation of the joint movement, spade-like hands, severe mental retardation, cloudy corneas, deafness, hepatosplenomegaly.

Locked-in syndrome—An infarct in the basilar part of the pons resulting in tetraplegia, dysphagia, facial diplegia with preserved consciousness.

Turner's syndrome—In this syndrome there are usually 45 chromosomes in the patient, second chromosome is usually absent. It is a form of gonadal dysgenesis and marked by dwarfism, webbing of the neck, low posterior hair line, increased angle of the elbow, cubitus valgus, sexual under development, pigeon chest and cardiac defects. In male, urinary frequency is increased and there may be dysuria and low back pain. In female, primary amenorrhea and under development of the breasts are the usual complaints.

Syndromic—Pertaining to or occurring as a syndrome.

Synechia—Adhesion of parts of the body, especially adhesion of iris to the cornea or lens.

Synechiae—Plural of synechia.

Synechiotomy—Synechotomy.

Synechotome—An instrument for breaking up the adhesions.

Synechotomy —The breaking up of an adhesion.

Synecology—The study of the organisms in relationship to their environment in group form.

Synectenterotomy—The breaking of the intestinal adhesions.

Synencephalocele —Encephalocele with adhesion to adjacent structures.

Syneresis—Contraction of a gel resulting in its separation from the liquid, as shrinkage of fibrin on blood clotting.

Synergetic—Synergic.

Synergia—Synergy.

Synergic—Synergetic. Exhibiting cooperation, as certain muscles working together.

Synergism—Combined action of two or more agents such as drugs producing an effect that is greater than the total effects produced by each drug separately.

Synergist—1. Adjuvant. A drug which acts to enhance the action of another. 2. A muscle or organ which acts in cooperation with another.

Synergistic—1. Pertaining to synergy. 2. Acting together.

Synergy—Correlated action or cooperation of two or more structures or drugs.

Synesthesia—1. To feel a sensation in one place due to a stimulation applied to another place. 2. The feeling of a sensation of a different sense than the one being stimulated, *e.g.*, hearing a sound produces a sensation of smell or color.

Synesthesialgia—A pain felt by the patient is of different character.

Synezesis—Closure of the pupil.

Syngamy—1. Sexual reproduction. 2. The union of two gametes to form a zygote in fertilization.

Syngeneic—Isologous.

Syngenesious—Derived from an individual of the same species, said of a tissue transplants.

Syngenesis—1. Arising from the germ cells derived from both parents and not from either one alone. 2. The state of having descended from a common ancestor.

Syngenetic—Pertaining to syngenesis.

Syngenic—Syngeneic.

Syngnathia—Congenital adhesions between the jaws.

Syngraft —A tissue or organ transplanted between genetically identical individuals.

Synhidrosis—Excessive sweating associated with another condition.

Synidrosis—Synhidrosis.

Synizesis—1. Occlusion. 2. Clumping of nuclear chromatin occurring during prophase of mitosis.

Synkaryon —A nucleus formed by the fusion of two pronuclei.

Synkinesis—An involuntary movement accompanying a voluntary movement.

Synkinetic—Pertaining to or marked by synkinesis.

Synnecrosis—The relationship between groups or individuals that causes mutual death.

Synonychia—Fusion of two or more nails of the digits, as in syndactylism.

Synonym—A word having the same meaning as another.

Synophrys —Growing together of both the eyebrows.

Synophthalmia —Cyclopia.

Synophthalmus—Cyclops.

Synopsia—Congenital fusion of the eyes.

Synopsis —A general view; summary; abstract.

Synoptophore—An instrument for diagnosing and treating strabismus.

Synoptoscope—Synoptophore.

Synorchidism—Synorchism.

Synorchism—Congenital fusion of the testes into one mass.

Synoscheos —Adhesion between penis and the scrotum.

Synosteography—A description of the joints.

Synosteology—Study of the joints.

Synosteosis—Synostosis.

Synosteotomy —Dissection of the joint.

Synostosis —Union of adjacent bones forming joint or of separate bones or parts of a single bone, by osseous tissue.

Synostotic—Pertaining to synostosis.

Synotia—The union of, or approximation of, the ears occurring in an embryo due to absence or incomplete development of the mandible.

Synotus—A fetus whose ears are united or approximated.

Synovectomy —Excision of a synovial membrane.

Synovia —Synovial fluid. A colorless, transparent, viscid fluid found in the joint cavities, bursae and tendon sheaths, secreted by the synovial membrane.

Synovial—Pertaining to synovia.

Synovial bursa—Bursa.

Synovial crypt —Diverticulum of a synovial membrane of a joint.

Synovial cyst—A cyst of the synovial membrane containing synovial fluid.

Synovial fluid—Synovia.

Synovialis—Synovial.

Synovial membrane —Membrane lining the capsule of a joint.

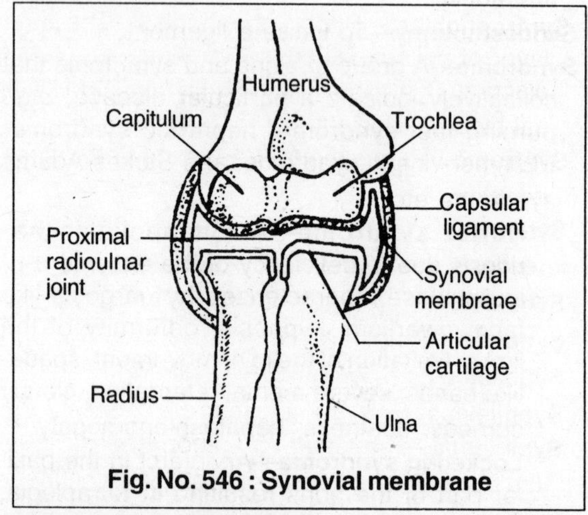

Fig. No. 546 : Synovial membrane

Synovialoma—Synovioma.

Synovioma—A tumor arising from a synovial membrane.

Synoviparous —Forming synovial fluid.

Synovitis—Inflammation of a synovial membrane, which may be dry (with little or no effusion), purulent (with pus formation within the synovial cavity) or serous (with nonpurulent effusion).

Synovium —A synovial membrane.

Synpolydactyly—Polydactyly and syndactyly combined.

Syntactic—Pertaining to or affecting a joint.

Syntasis—To stretch.

Syntaxis—Articulation.

Syntectic —Pertaining to wasting or cachexia.

Syntexis—Wasting or cachexia.

Synthermal—Having the same temperature.

Syntheses—Plural of synthesis.

Synthesis—1. Production of a compound artificially or naturally, by union of elements composing it. 2. The process of forming a complex substance from simpler elements or compounds, as the synthesis of protein from amino acids.

Synthesize—To produce by synthesis.

Synthetic—Made by synthesis.

Synthorax—Thoracopagus.

Syntone—One who adjusts oneself according to the environment, life situation and society.

Syntonic—Pertaining to the personality characterized by adjustment according to the environment, life situations and society.

Syntripsis—A comminuted fracture or act causing it.

Syntrophoblast—Syncytiotrophoblast. The outer layer of cells covering the chorionic villi of the placenta, which are in contact with the maternal blood or decidua.

Syntropic—Pertaining to the turning in the same direction.

Syntropy— A turning or pointing in the same direction.

Synulosis —Formation of scar tissue.

Synulotic—Promoting scar tissue formation.

Syphilelcosis—Formation of ulcers in syphilis.

Syphilelcus—A syphilitic ulcer or chancre.

Syphilemia—Presence of Treponema pallidum, the causative bacterium of syphilis, in the blood.

Syphilid, Syphilide—A skin lesion of the secondary syphilis.

Syphilimetry—A test for determining the intensity of syphilitic infection.

Syphiliphobia—Syphilophobia. Morbid fear of syphilis.

Syphilis—An infectious, chronic, venereal disease caused by a spirochete Treponema pallidum producing many skin lesions but any organ or tissue of the body may be involved. It is transmitted by direct sexual contact, transfusion of infected blood or plasma, contact with infected material or in the uterus by passage of the organisms from mother to the fetus. The organism may enter through any broken place in the skin or mucous membrane. The disease is divided into three stages—

Primary stage—In primary stage 2 to 4 weeks after infection a lesion changing from a small red papule to a small ulcer and then to a hard chancre, which is infectious and painless, appears usually on the penis or vulva but may appear at any place on the skin or mucous membrane. Lymph nodes become hard and enlarged about two weeks after the appearance of the lesion.

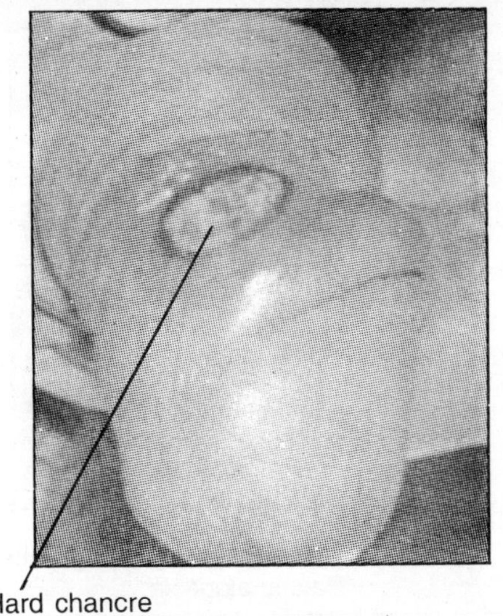

Fig.547 : Primary syphilis

Secondary stage—About 6 weeks after the appearance of hard chancre multiform skin eruptions (syphilids) appear on the trunk and extremities. Condyloma may be formed at the anal margin, vulva or under the breasts. Brownish pigmentation with areas of leucoderma may develop on the neck. Alopecia of general or patchy type may occur. Enlargement and induration of regional lymph nodes may occur. Headache, fever, malaise and sore

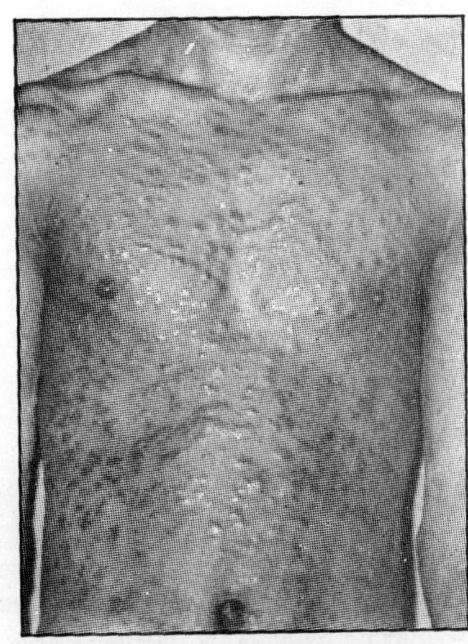

Fig. 548 A : Secondary syphilis : Multiple skin eruptions (syphilides)

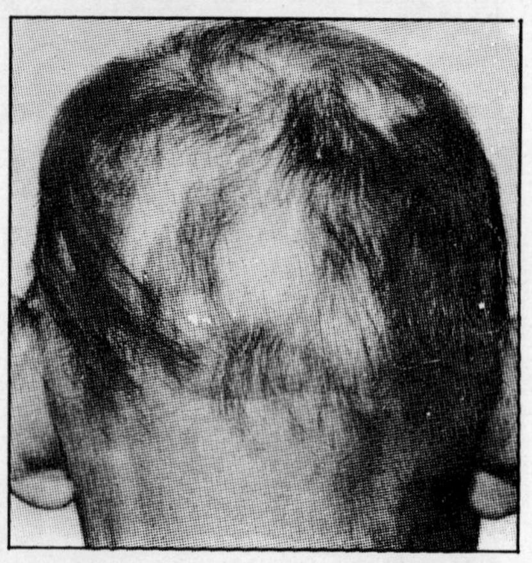

Fig. 548 B : Secondary stage of syphilis
Patchy alopecia

throat are common. There may be severe pain in the joints and periosteum.

Tertiary stage—Some years after the secondary stage it begins. It is characterized by the formation of gumma which may occur in every part of the body. It ulcerates leaving punched out ulcer. Heart and blood vessels (cardiovascular syphilis), and the central nervous system (neurosyphilis), are frequently involved. Tabes dorsalis, paresis (general paralysis of the insane) may result.

Cardiovascular syphilis—Syphilis of the heart and great blood vessels, especially the aorta.

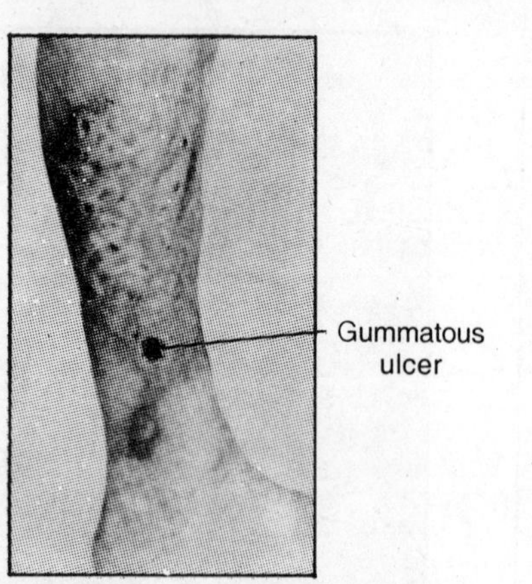

Fig. 549 : Tertiary stage of syphilis

Congenital syphilis —Prenatal syphilis. Syphilis transmitted from mother to the fetus in uterus.

Extragenital syphilis—Syphilis in which the primary chancre is located elsewhere than on the genital organs.

Innocentium syphilis—Syphilis not caused by sexual intercourse.

Latent syphilis—Phase of syphilis in which symptoms are absent, and the disease is diagnosed by serological tests.

Neurosyphilis—Syphilis of the central nervous system (brain and spinal cord).

Visceral syphilis—Syphilis of the internal organs.

Syphilitic—Pertaining to, caused by or affected with syphilis.

Syphiloderm, Syphiloderma—A skin disease caused by syphilis.

Syphilogenesis, Syphilogeny—The development of syphilis.

Syphilography—A description of syphilis.

Syphiloid—Like syphilis.

Syphilologist—A specialist in syphilis.

Syphilology—The scientific study of syphilis.

Syphiloma—A tumor originated from syphilis, or gumma.

Syphilomania—Syphilophobia.

Syphilopathy—Any syphilitic disorder.

Syphilophobia—Morbid fear of syphilis.

Syphilophobic—Pertaining to or affected with syphilophobia.

Syphilophyma—Any growth or excrescence due to syphilis.

Syphilosis—Generalized syphilitic disease.

Syphilotherapy—Treatment of syphilis.

Syphilotropic—Especially susceptible to syphilis.

Syphilous—Syphilitic.

Syphionthus—Copper-colored patches of the skin seen in syphilis.

Syr.—Syrup.

Syrigmophonia—A whistling sound in pronunciation of "S" due to a denture peculiarity.

Syrigmus—A hissing or ringing sound heard in the ears.

Syringadenoma—Tumor of a sweat gland.

Syringadenosus—Pertaining to the sweat glands.

Syringe—1. An instrument for injecting a fluid into the body, cavity or blood vessel, or for withdrawing a fluid from a cavity or blood vessel. 2. To wash out a cavity or to introduce a fluid with a syringe.

Syringeal—Pertaining to a syrinx.

Syringectomy—Fistulectomy.

Syringitis—Inflammation of the eustachian tube.

Syringoadenoma—Syringocystadenoma.

Syringobulbia—The presence of cavities in the medulla oblongata.

Syringocarcinoma—Cancer of a sweat gland.

Syringocele —The central canal of the spinal cord.

Syringocystadenoma—Adenoma of the sweat glands.

Syringocystoma—Cystic tumor of a sweat gland.

Syringoencephalomyelia —The presence of cavities in the brain and spinal cord.

Syringoid—Resembling a tube.

Syringoma—Tumor of the sweat glands.

Syringomeningocele—Meningocele resembling syringomyelocele.

Syringomyelia—Presence of fluid-filled cavities in the substance of spinal cord.

Syringomyelitis—Inflammation of the spinal cord with dilatation of the central canal.

Syringomyelocele—A hernia of the spinal cord through a bony defect in the spina bifida, the cavity of which is connected with the central canal of the spinal cord.

Syringomyelus—Abnormal dilatation of the central canal of the spinal cord.

Syringopontia —Presence of cavities in the pons.

Syringosystrophy—Twisting of the fallopian tube.

Syringotome—Fistulatome.

Syringotomy—Fistulectomy.

Syrinx—1. Fistula. 2. A tube. 3. Eustachian tube.

Syrup—A concentrated solution of sugar in water to which some medicine is added, usually used as a tasty vehicle for drugs.

Syrupus—Syrup.

Syrupy—1. Pertaining to syrup. 2. Of the consistency of the syrup.

Syssarcosic—Syssarcotic.

Syssarcosis—The union of bones by muscles.

Syssarcotic—Syssarcosic. Pertaining to syssarcosis.

Systaltic—Pulsating. Contracting and dilating alternately.

System—A group of interconnected structures or organs that act together for a common purpose or to produce the result which is not possible by action of one alone; *e.g.*, digestive system, respiratory system and cardiovascular system etc.

Systema—System.

Systematic—1. Pertaining to a system. 2. Methodical.

Systematization—The process of organizing according to a plan.

Systematized—Arranged methodically.

Systemic—General. Pertaining to or affecting the body as a whole.

Systemic circulation—Circulation through the whole body except lungs.

Systemic remedy —A remedy that acts on the body as a whole.

Systemoid—1. Resembling a system. 2. Pertaining to tumors made up of several types of tissues.

Systole —The part of the cardiac cycle in which the heart is in contraction which occurs in the interval between first and second heart sound.

- **Aborted systole**—A premature systole not associated with the pulsation of a peripheral artery.
- **Atrial systole**—The contraction of the atria by which blood is propelled from them into the ventricle.
- **Extra systole**—See extrasystole.
- **Premature systole**—Extrasystole.
- **Ventricular systole**—Contraction of the ventricles.

Systolic—Pertaining to the systole.

Systolic discharge—The amount of blood propelled by the heart at each systole.

Systolic murmur—A murmur heard during systole of the heart.

Systolometer—1. An apparatus for determining the force of the cardiac contraction. 2. An instrument for analyzing the heart sounds.

Systremma—Cramp in the calf muscles of the leg, the muscles forming a hard knot.

Syzygial—Pertaining to syzygium.

Syzygiology—The study of interrelationship or interdependence of the whole, as opposed to the study of separate parts or isolated functions.

Syzygium—Fusion of two stru ctures, organs or parts of the body without loss of their identity.

Syzygy—Syzygium.

T—Temperature; time; intraocular tension.

Tabacism—Tabacosis. Chronic tobacco poisoning.

Tabacosis—Tabacism.

Tabacum —Tobacco.

Tabagism —Nicotinism. Poisoning from excessive use of tobacco or nicotine.

Tabefaction —Wasting of the body by disease.

Tabella —A mass of medicated material formed into a small disk.

Tabellae —Plural of tabella.

Tabes —A progressive wasting of the body or part of it due to a chronic disease.

Tabes dorsalis —A condition of tertiary syphilis in which there is degeneration of the posterior columns of the spinal cord and sensory nerve trunks, about 10–25 years after infection with spirochete, Treponema pallidum. It is characterized by paroxysms of lightning pains in the limbs, progressive difficulty in walking or unsteadiness, abnormality in micturition, visceral disturbances and numbness or tingling felt in the legs or trunk.

Tabes mesenterica —Emaciation due to tuberculosis of the mesenteric glands in children.

Tabescense —The condition of wasting away gradually.

Tabescent —Wasting away gradually.

Tabetic —Pertaining to or afflicted with tabes.

Tabetic crisis —Acute abdominal pain occurring due to syphilis.

Tabetic foot —Twisted foot in locomotor ataxia.

Tabetiform —Resembling tabes.

Tabic —Tabetic.

Tabid —Tabetic.

Tablature —Separation of the chief cranial bones into inner and outer layers by cancellous bony tissue.

Table —A flat layer or surface or a thin flat plate as of bone.

Tablespoon —A household unit of capacity containing about 4 drachms or 15 mls. of a liquid.

Tablet —A small, disklike mass of medicinal powder.

Buccal tablet —Tablet which is placed in mouth between the cheek and gums until it is dissolved and absorbed through the oral mucosa.

Enteric-coated tablet —Tablet coated with a material which is not dissolved by the gastric juice.

Sublingual tablet —Tablet which dissolves when placed beneath the tongue to permit direct absorption of the active ingredients by the oral mucosa.

Vaginal tablet —Tablet to be placed within the vagina for local action as in leucorrhea.

Taboo, Tabu —Restricted or prohibited or set apart for religious purposes.

Taboparalysis —Taboparesis.

Taboparesis —Taboparalysis. General paralysis of the insane accompanying the tabes dorsalis.

Tabophobia —Morbid fear of being afflicted with tabes.

Tabular —1. Having the form of a table. 2. Arranged in tables.

Tabule —Tablet.

Tac —Influenza.

Tache —A colored spot or macule.

Tachetic —Marked by taches.

Tachistoscope —An apparatus for determining the speed of visual perception.

Tachogram —The graphic record of the rate of flow of blood.

Tachograph —A tachometer used to record the speed continuously.

Tachography —The recording of the rate of flow of blood graphically.

Tachometer —An instrument for measuring movements.

Tachometric —Pertaining to tachometer.

Tachy- —A prefix which means swift or rapid.

Tachyarrhythmia —Rapid heart rate associated with an irregularity in the normal heart rhythm.

Tachyauxesis —Growing of a part of an organism more rapidly than the whole body.

Tachycardia —Abnormal rapidity of the heart rate.

Atrial tachycardia —Rapid heart rate, usually 161-190 beats per minute, arising from an atrial focus.

Ectopic tachycardia —Rapid heart beats due to impulses arising from outside the sinoatrial node.

Essential tachycardia —Persistent techycardia due to functional disorder of the heart.

Fetal tachycardia —Heart rate of 160 or more per minute of the fetus.

Junctional tachycardia —Tachycardia due to impulses arising in the atrioventricular junction i.e. atrioventricular node.

Nodal tachycardia —Junctional tachycardia.

Orthostatic tachycardia —Tachycardia occurring on standing.

Paroxysmal tachycardia —Tachycardia that starts and stops suddenly, due to impulses arising in the atrium (paroxysmal atrial tachycardia), in the atrioventricular node (paroxysmal nodal tachycardia) or in the ventricle (paroxysmal ventricular tachycardia).

Reflex tachycardia —Tachycardia resulting from stimuli out side the heart that reflexly increases the heart rate.

Sinus tachycardia —Simple tachycardia due to impulses arising in the sinoatrial node in which the heart rate is more than 100 per minute. It occurs due to exercise, in starvation, fever, infection, anemia, hemorrhage, thyrotoxicosis, cardiac failure and other many conditions and by certain drugs such as epinephrine and atropine etc.

Supraventricular tachycardia —Combination of nodal tachycardia and atrial tachycardia.

Ventricular tachycardia —Tachycardia due to impulses arising from a focus in the ventricles in which the heart rate is 150-200 per minute.

Tachycardiac —Pertaining to or afflicted with tachycardia.

Tachycardic —Pertaining to rapid heart rate.

Tachycrotic —Pertaining to, causing, or characterized by a rapid pulse.

Tachygastria —Increased rate of contractions of the stomach.

Tachylalia —Rapidity of speech.

Tachymeter —An instrument for estimating the speed of anybody in motion.

Tachyphagia —Rapid eating.

Tachyphasia —Tachyphrasia.

Tachyphemia —Tachyphrasia.

Tachyphrasia —Tachyphasia. Excessive speech or rapid speech.

Tachyphrenia —Mental hyperactivity.

Tachyphylaxis —Rapid immunization against the effect of toxic dose of a substance by previously injecting the small doses of the same substance.

Tachypnea —Very rapid respiration.

Tachyrhythmia —Tachycardia. Rapid heart beat.

Tachysystole —Abnormally rapid systole.

Tachytrophism —Increased metabolism.

Taciturn —Not talkative.

Tacky —Slightly adhesive.

Tactile —1. Pertaining to touch. 2. Perceptible to touch.

Tactile disk —Tiny expanded end of a sensory nerve fiber found in the epidermis and in epithelial root sheath of a hair.

Taction —1. Sense of touch. 2. Touching.

Tactometer —An instrument for measuring sensibility of touch.

Tactor —Any tactile organ.

Tactual —Tactile. Pertaining to touch

Tactus —Touch.

Taedium vitae —Weariness of the life developing suicidal tendency.

Taenia —Tapeworm. A genus of the parasitic flat, bandlike worms belonging to the class Cestoda, phylum Platyhelminthes, of which Taenia saginata and Taenia solium are important, that in adult life live in the intestine of man.

taenia —1. Tapeworm. 2. Any bandlike structure.

Taeniacide —Killing the tapeworms.

Taeniafuge —Anything that expels the tapeworms.

Taeniasis —Infestation with tapeworms.

Taeniform —Resembling a tapeworm in structure.

Taenifuge —Taeniafuge.

Taeniophobia —Morbid fear of becoming infested with tapeworms.

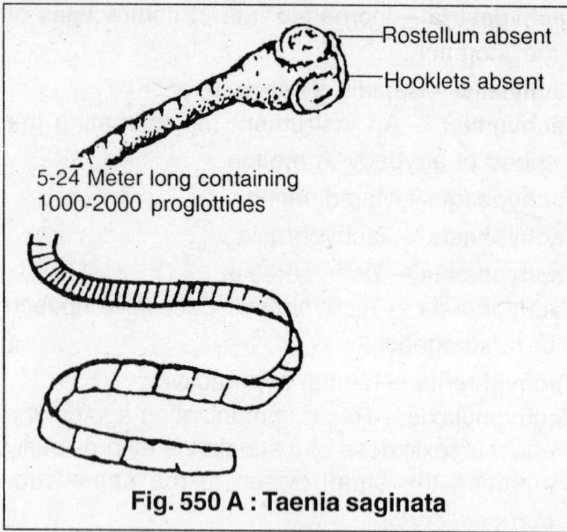

Fig. 550 A : Taenia saginata

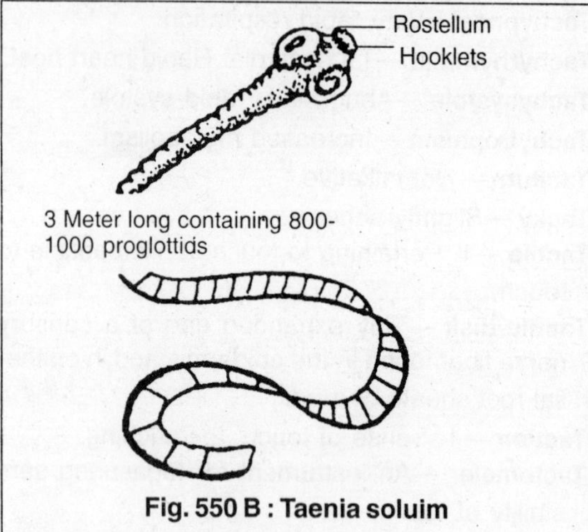

Fig. 550 B : Taenia soluim

Tag —1. A small polyp or growth. 2. A small thread with pointed metal pieces for binding pieces of paper.

Tail —Posterior most, long, flexible portion of an animal or the terminal portion of the spinal cord.

Tailor's cramp —Spasm of the muscles of the arms and hands occurring in a tailor.

Taint —Spot; to cause putrefaction; blemish on reputation.

Takayasu's arteritis —Inflammation of the aorta with one or more of the large branches of the aortic arch.

Talalgia —Pain in the heel or ankle.

Talar —Pertaining to the talus bone, the ankle.

Talc. —A soft, soapy powder.

Talcosis —Disease caused by inhalation of talcum powder.

Talcum —Talc.

Talectomy —Surgical removal of the heel-bone.

Tali —Plural of talus.

Talipedic —Clubfooted.

Talipes —Clubfoot, a congenital deformity of the foot in which the foot is deviated out of its normal position.

Talipes calcaneous —Talipes in which foot is flexed and the heel alone touches the ground, so that the patient walks on the inner side of heel.

Talipes calcaneovalgus —Talipes calcaneous and talipes valgus combined.

Talipes calcaneovarus —Talipes calcaneous and talipes varus combined.

Talipes cavus —Talipes in which there is excessive plantar curvature.

Talipes equinovalgus —Talipes equinus and talipes valgus combined.

Talipes equinovarus —Talipes equinus and talipes varus combined.

Talipes equinus —Talipes in which the foot is extended and the patient walks on the toes.

Talipes valgus —Talipes in which the heel and foot are turned outward so that the patient walks on inner side of the foot.

Talipes varus —Talipes in which the heel is turned inward so that the patient walks on outer side of the foot.

Talipomanus —Clubhand, a congenital deformity of the hand in which it is deviated from its normal position.

Talo- —A prefix which means talus.

Talocalcaneal —Pertaining to the talus and calcaneus bones.

Talocalcanean —Talocalcaneal.

Talocrural —Pertaining to the talus and leg bones.

Talocrural articulation —The ankle joint.

Talofibular —Pertaining to the talus and fibula bones.

Talonavicular —Pertaining to the talus and navicular bones.

Talonid —The posterior part of a lower molar tooth.

Taloscaphoid —Talonavicular.

Talotibial —Pertaining to the talus and tibia bones.

Talus —The ankle bone (astragalus) articulating with the tibia, fibula, calcaneus, and navicular bone.

Tambour —A drum-shaped apparatus used in

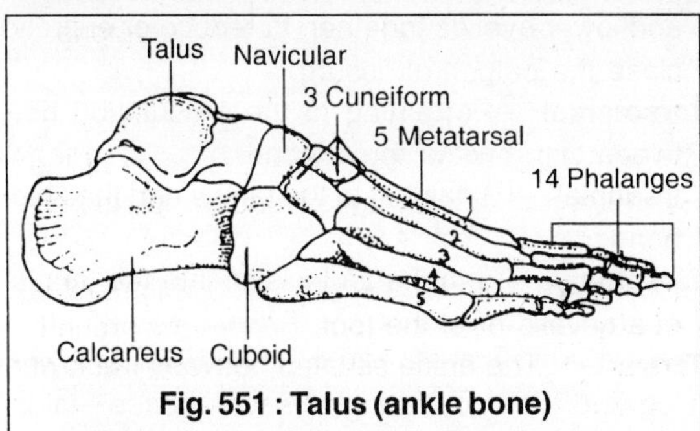

Fig. 551 : Talus (ankle bone)

transmitting and registering arterial pulsations, blood pressure and respiratory movements.

Tampon —A pad or plug made of cotton, sponge or other material used to arrest hemorrhage or for the absorption of secretions, as used in menstrual period for the absorption of menstrual fluid in the vagina or in plugging the nostrils to stop bleeding from the nose, etc.

Tamponade —1. Tamponage. To use or make use of a tampon. 2. Pathologic compression of a part.

Tamponage —Tamponade.

Tamponing, Tamponment —Tamponade (1)

Tang —1. A strong taste or flavor. 2. The sharp point of a knife.

Tangentiality —Disturbance in a conversation in which one tends to digress readily from one topic in conversation to another.

Tank —A reservoir.

Tannate —Any of the salts of tannic acid, all of which are astringent.

Tanner —One who converts raw hide into leather.

Tannery —A factory where raw hide is converted into leather.

Tannin —Tannic acid.

Tantrum —To display great anger with or without violent action.

Tanyoz's sign —1. In ascites, the downward displacement of the umbilicus. 2. In pregnancy, the upward displacement of the umbilicus.

Tanyphonia —A fine, weak voice resulting from tension of the muscles of the vocal cords.

Tap —1. To drain off fluid from a cavity by paracentesis. 2. A light blow.

Tape —1. A long, narrow, flexible strip of cotton, cloth, paper, plastic or other material, e.g., adhesive tape. 2. To wrap a part of the body with a long bandage.

Tapeinocephalic —Pertaining to or having flattened head.

Tapeinocephaly —The condition of having flattened head.

Tapeta —Plural of tapetum.

Tapetum —A thin sheet of fibers from the corpus callosum forming the roof and lateral walls of the inferior and posterior horns of the lateral ventricles of the brain. The fibers pass to the temporal and occipital lobes.

Tapeworm —A long, flattened, tape-shaped intestinal parasite belonging to the class Cestoda, phylum Platyhelminthes, which consists of a scolex with hooks and suckers for attachement to the intestinal wall, and a series of segments.

Taphophilia —Abnormal attraction for graves.

Taphophobia —Abnormal fear of being buried alive.

Tapia syndrome —Paralysis of the pharynx and larynx on one side and atrophy of the tongue on the opposite side, caused by a lesion affecting the 10th (Vagus) and 12th (hypoglossal) cranial nerves on the side in which the pharynx is affected.

Tapinocephalic —Pertaining to flatness of the top of skull.

Tapinocephaly —Flatness of top of the skull.

Tapotement —Tapping in massage.

Tapping —See 1. Paracentesis. 2. Tapotement.

Tar —A dark-brown or black, viscid liquid obtained from distillation of wood, coal and organic matter, etc.

Tarantism —A dancing mania.

Tardive —Progressing slowly, as a disease; late.

Tare —The weight of the vessel into which a substance is placed and weighed.

Tared —A vessel of known weight.

Tarentism —Tarantism.

Target —A structure or organ toward which something is directed or which is affected by a particular agent, e.g., a hormone or drug.

Target cell —A red blood cell with a rounded dense central area surrounded by a light ring.

Tarsadenitis—Inflammation of the tarsus of eyelid and the meibomian glands.

Tarsal —Pertaining to the tarsus of eyelid or to the ankle.

Tarsal bones —Seven bones of the ankle.

Tarsale —A tarsal bone.

Tarsalgia —Pain in the ankle or tarsus.

Tarsal glands —Meibomian glands. Sebaceous glands embedded in the tarsus of eyelid and opening on its margin.

Tarsalia —Plural of tarsale.

Tarsalis —One of the tarsal muscles.

Tarsectomy —1. Excision of one or more of the tarsal bones. 2. Excision of the tarsus of an eyelid.

Tarsectopia —Dislocation of the tarsus.

Tarsectopy —Tarsectopia.

Tarsen —Within the tarsus.

Tarsi —Plural of tarsus.

Tarsitis —1. Inflammation of the tarsus of eyelid; blepharitis. 2. Inflammation of the tarsus of foot.

Tarso- —A prefix which means flat of the foot or margin of the eyelid.

Tarsocheiloplasty —Repair of margin of an eyelid by plastic surgery.

Tarsoclasia —Surgical fracture of the tarsus of foot for correcting clubfoot.

Tarsoclasis —Tarsoclasia.

Tarsomalacia —Softening of the tarsus of an eyelid.

Tarsomegaly —Enlargement of a heel bone or calcaneus.

Tarsometatarsal —Pertaining to the tarsus and the metatarsus.

Tarso-orbital —Pertaining to the tarsus of eyelid and the orbit.

Tarsophalangeal —Pertaining to the tarsus of foot and phalanges of the toes.

Tarsophyma —Any tumor of the tarsus of an eyelid.

Tarsoplasia —Tarsoplasty.

Tarsoplasty —Blepharoplasty. Plastic surgery of the tarsus of eyelid.

Tarsoptosis —Flatfoot.

Tarsorrhaphy —Suture of the margins of upper and lower eyelids together, to reduce or entirely close the palpebral fissure.

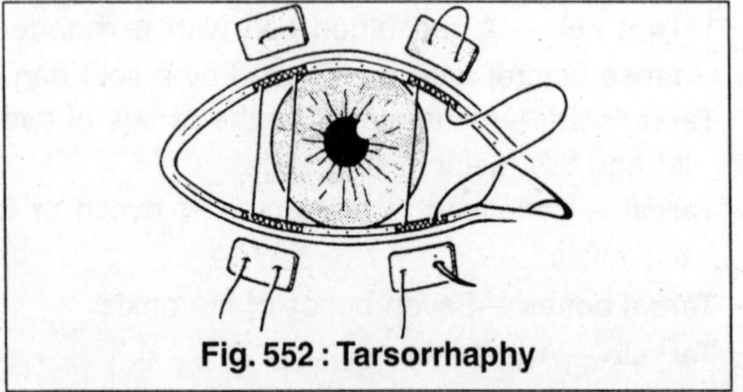
Fig. 552 : Tarsorrhaphy

Tarsotarsal —Pertaining to the articulation between two rows of tarsal bones.

Tarsotibial —Pertaining to the tarsus and the tibia bone.

Tarsotomy —To make an incision into the tarsus of an eyelid or of the foot.

Tarsus—1. The ankle situated between the lower leg and foot, consisting of seven bones—talus (astragalus), calcaneus, navicular, medial, intermediate and lateral cuneiform, and cuboid. 2. The curved plate of dense fibrous tissue forming the supporting structure of the eyelids.

Tartar —Calcareous matter deposited upon the teeth.

Tartaric —Pertaining to tartar.

Tartrate —A salt of tartaric acid.

Tartrated —Combined with or containing tartar or tartaric acid.

Tastant —Any substance stimulating the sense of taste.

Taste —The peculiar sensation caused by contact of substances with the tongue.

After taste —Taste remaining persistent after removal of the stimulus.

Taste buds —Oval structures situated on the surface of the tongue, soft palate, epiglottis, and some portion of the pharynx, containing sensory and taste cells. On stimulation they give rise to sense of taste.

Taster —The person capable of detecting a particular substance by taking its taste.

Tattooing —Production of permanent marks on the skin by piercing it and introducing colors.

Taurocholemia —Presence of taurocholic acid in the blood.

Taurodontism —A condition in which the teeth have abnormally large and deepened pulp chambers so that the pulp chambers enchroach on the roots of the teeth.

Tauto- —A prefix meaning the same.

Tautomenial —Concerning the same menstrual period.

Tautomer —A chemical substance capable of tautomerism.

Tautomeral —Pertaining to the same part.

Tautomeric —Exhibiting or capable of exhibiting, tautomerism.

Tautomerism —Stereoisomerism in which two formulae exit in dynamic equilibrium so that as the amount of one substance is changed, the other is changed into the other form to maintain the equilibrium.

Taxa —Plural of taxon.

Taxis —1. The response of an organism to a stimulus, moving toward (positive) or away from (negative) the stimulus. 2. Exertion of force in manual replacement of an organ, or reduction of a hernia or dislocation.

Taxon —A category of taxonomy, e.g., species, genus, family, order, class or phylum.

Taxonomic —Pertaining to taxonomy.

Taxonomy —The branch of science dealing with the classification of organisms.

T. b. —Tuberculosis.

TBSA —Total body surface area.

T-cell receptor —TCR—A molecule present on the surface of T-cells which is for receiving a particular antigen.

T cells —Lymphocytes which mature in the thymus gland are called T cells. When they enter the blood circulation, they produce delayed immunity by enhancing the production of antibody forming cells.

T. D. S. —Three times a day.

Tear —To separate or pull by force.

Tearing —Separating or pulling by force.

Tears —The watery, lightly alkaline and saline liquid secreted by the lacrimal glands which moistens the conjunctiva.

Tease —To separate a tissue into minute parts with a fine needle to prepare it for microscopic examination.

Teaspoon —A household unit of volume which is equal to approximately 5 milliliters.

Teat —Nipple of the mammary gland or any protuberance resembling a nipple.

Teatulation —The development of a nipple like elevation.

Technic —Technique.

Technical —Requiring technique or special skill.

Technician —The person skilled in the performance of technical procedures, who is diploma or degree holder to perform them.

Technique —1. The method of performing a task. 2. The skill applied in performing a task or operation.

Techno- —A prefix which means art or skill.

Technocausis— Electrocautery.

Technologist —A person skilled in performing a specific technical procedure, who has degree for that.

Technology —The science of techniques.

Technotonia —Child-murder.

Tecta —Plural of tectum.

Tectal —Pertaining to tectum.

Tectiform — Root-shaped.

Tectocephalic —1. Pertaining to possession of a boat-shaped cranium. 2. Having a boat-shaped cranium.

Tectocephaly —Scaphocephalism. Possession of a boat-shaped cranium.

Tectology —Structural morphology.

Tectonic —Pertaining to the changes in the structure of the eye, especially the cornea.

Tectorial —Tegmental. Of the nature of, or pertaining to a covering.

Tectorium —1. Tegmentum. Tectum. Any rooflike structure. 2. Corti's membrane.

Tectospinal —Extending from tectum of the midbrain to the spinal cord.

Tectum —1. Any rooflike structure. 2. The dorsal portion of the midbrain.

Tedious —Difficult; tiresome.

Teenage —Adolescent. Pertaining to the person who is 13 to 19 years of age.

Teeth —Organs of mastication projecting from each jaw. They are of two types I. Deciduous or milk teeth—They are 20 in number and include 2 incisors, 1 canine and 2 molars in each half of both the jaws. They begin to erupt at about the 6th month of age, and all are being erupted by the end of second year or soon after. II. Permanent teeth—They are 32 in number and include 2 incisors, 1 canine, 2 premolars and 3 molars in each half of both the jaws. Incisors are in front on each side of the midline in each jaw. They are meant for biting. Canine is the third tooth on each side of the midline in each jaw. It is for holding and tearing. The two premolar teeth are on each side in each jaw between the canine and molar teeth. Molars are the posterior teeth on either side in each jaw. They are for grinding and chewing.

Hutchinson's teeth —A sign of congenital syphilis in which lateral incisors of the upper jaw are extended downward, and central incisors of the same jaw are notched at the cutting edge, seen only on permanent teeth. **Wisdom teeth** —The third permanent molar teeth which erupt in the last.

Teething —Dentition. Eruption of the teeth.

Teetotal —Pertaining to abstinence from all intoxicating substances.

Teetotalism —Total abstinence from intoxicating substances.

Teetotallar —The person who never uses intoxicating substances.

Tegmen —A structure that covers a part of the body, or roof.

Tegmenta —Plural of tegmentum.

Tegmental —Tentorial. Pertaining to a tegment.

Tegmentum —1. Tegument. A roof or covering. 2. Tectum. Dorsal portion of the midbrain.

Tegument —1. Integument. The skin or the covering of the body. 2. Any covering structure.

Tegumental, Tegumentary —Pertaining to the skin; covering.

Teichopsia —Scintillating scotoma. An irregular outline around a luminous patch in the visual field occuring following mental or physical labor or eye strain etc.

Teinodynia —Tenodynia. Tenalgia.

Tel-, Tele-, Telo- —A prefix which means end, other end or distant.

Tela —Any weblike tissue or structure.

Telae —Plural of tela.

Telalgia —Referred pain.

Telangiectases —Plural of telangiectasis.

Telangiectasia, Telangiectasis —Dilatation of a group of blood capillaries or small blood vessels.

Telangiectasis —Telangiectasia.

Telangiectatic —Pertaining to telangiectasis.

Telangiectodes —Tumors containing telangiectasia.

Telangiitis —Inflammation of the capillaries.

Telangioma —A tumor made up of dilated capillaries or arterioles.

Telangion —A capillary or terminal arteriole.

Telangiosis —Any disease of the capillaries.

Tele-, Tel- —Prefixes which mean the end or far away.

Telecanthus —Abnormally increased distance between the medial canthi of the eyelids.

Telecardiogram —Telelectrocardiogram.

Telecardiography —Process of taking telecardiogram.

Telecardiophone —A stethoscope for making the heart sounds audible at a distance from the patient.

Teleceptive —Pertaining to teleceptor.

Teleceptor —Teloceptor. A sense organ such as the eye, ear and nose that responds to a stimulus arising at some distance from the body.

Telecinesia —Telekinesis.

Telecurietherapy —To apply radiation therapy from a source distant from the patient.

Teledendrite, Teledendron —Telodendron. A terminal process of an axon.

Telediagnosis —To make the diagnosis of a disease at a place distant from the patient, on the basis of data transmitted electronically to the physician.

Telediastolic —Concerning the last phase of the diastole.

Telefluoroscopy —Transmission of fluoroscopic images to television for study at a distant place.

Telegamic —Attracting female from a distance.

Telegenesis —Artificial fertilization.

Telekinesis —To move an object according to the will without touching.

Telelectrocardiogram —Telecardiogram. An electrocardiogram taken at a distance from the patient with the galvanometer attached to him by a long wire from the instrument.

Telemedicine —To provide consultation or to prescribe medicines by a physician at a remote place from the patient, by observing the patient's condition on the television screen.

Telemeter —An electronic instrument for making the measurements of a distant object and transmitting the data electronically.

Telemetry —The making of measurements of a distant object, the data being transmitted electronically.

Telemnemonic —Becoming aware of the memory of another person.

Telencephalic —Pertaining to the endbrain.

Telencephalization— Corticalization. Encephalization. Transference of function from subcortical centres to the cortex of the brain.

Telencephalon —The embryonic endbrain.

Teleneurite —The branching end of an axon.

Teleneuron —A nerve ending.

Teleo- —A prefix meaning perfect, complete.

Teleological —Concerning teleology. Serving an ultimate purpose in development.

Teleology —The theory that every thing is directed toward some final purpose.

Teleomitosis —Completed mitosis.

Teleonomic —Pertaining to teleonomy.

Teleonomy —The concept that the existence of a structure or function in an organism indicates that it had a evolutionary survival value.

Teleoperator —A machine operated by a person at a distance.

Teleopsia —A visual defect in which objects appear to be farther away than they actually are.

Teleorganic —Vital. Necessary to life.

Teleotherapeutics —The treatment of disease by hypnotic suggestion.

Telepathist —The person who claims the ability of reading the mind of others.

Telepathy —Telesthesia. The transmission of thoughts of one person to the mind of another person at a distance, without use of sensory organs or physical agents.

Teleradiogram —An X-ray picture obtained by teleradiography.

Teleradiography —Teleroentgenography.

Teleradiology —The transmission of an X-ray picture to a distant place where it is interpreted by a radiologist.

Teleradium —The radium source distant from the area being treated.

Telereceptor —An organ such as the eye, that can receive the sense stimuli from a distance.

Telergy —1. Automatism. 2. Imaginary action of one's thoughts upon the brain of another person at a distance, by transmission of some unknown energy.

Teleroentgenogram —An X-ray picture obtained by teleroentgenography.

Teleroentgenography —Teleradiography. Radiography in which the X-ray tube is 6½–7 feet away from the body, done to minimize distortion of the picture by securing parallelism of the rays.

Teleroentgentherapy —Teletherapy.

Telescope —An optical instrument for viewing distant objects.

Telesthesia —Telepathy. Perception at a distance.

Telesystolic —Pertaining to the termination of the cardiac systole.

Teletactor —An apparatus used by the deaf person to receive sound through the skin.

Teletherapy —Treatment of disease by the therapeutic agent, *e.g.*, radiation kept at a distance from the body.

Teletypewriter —A typewriter connected to a telephone used by deaf persons to communicate by sending and receiving typewritten messages.

Telluric —Pertaining to or originating from the earth.

Tellurism —The concept that emanations from the earth cause disease.

Teloceptor —Teleceptor.

Telodendron —Teledendrite.

Telogen —Resting phase of hair growth cycle.

Teloglia —Accumulation of neurolemmal cells at the end of a motor nerve fiber near the neuromuscular junction.

Telognosis —Diagnosis based on the defects found in X-ray film, transmitted electronically to the physician.

Telokinesia —Telophase.

Telolemma —The covering of a motor endplote.

Telomere —The end of an extremity of a chromosome.

Telophase —The last phase of mitosis.

Telotism —The entire performance of a function as that of a sense organ.

Temper —State of one's mood.

Temperament —Nature, disposition or mental state.

Temperance —Moderation in one's thoughts and actions, especially with respect to use of alcohol etc.

Temperate —Moderate (not excessive); self restrained; calm.

Temperature —Degree of hotness.

Absolute temperature —Temperature measured from absolute zero, which is – 273.15°C and – 459.67°F.

Ambient temperature —Temperature of the environment or of a place.

Axillary temperature —Temperature taken by placing thermometer in the axilla, which is usually .5 to 1.0° F (0.28° to .56° C) lower than oral temperature.

Critical temperature —Temperature below which a gas may be converted to liquid form by pressure.

Inverse temperature —Body temperature which is higher in the morning than in the eveing.

Maximum temperature —Temperature above which bacterial growth does not take place.

Mean temperature —The average temperature for stated period in a given locality.

Minimum temperature —The temperature below which bacterial growth does not take place.

Normal temperature —Temperature of the body of a healthy person taken orally which is 98.6° F (37° C).

Optimum temperature —Most suitable temperature for the performance of a function, for bacterial growth or for the action of an enzyme.

Oral temperature —Temperature taken by placing thermometer in the mouth under the tongue with lips closed, for at least 3 minutes.

Rectal temperature —Temperature taken by inserting a thermometer into the anal canal.

Subnormal temperature —Temperature below the normal of 98.6°F (37°C).

Template —A model or mold which is used as a guide in making a duplicate.

Temple —The region of the head on each side in front of the ear and over the zygomatic arch.

Tempolabile —Becoming changed spontaneously within a definite time.

Tempora —The temples.

Temporal —1. Pertaining to the temple. 2. Pertaining to time or limited in time.

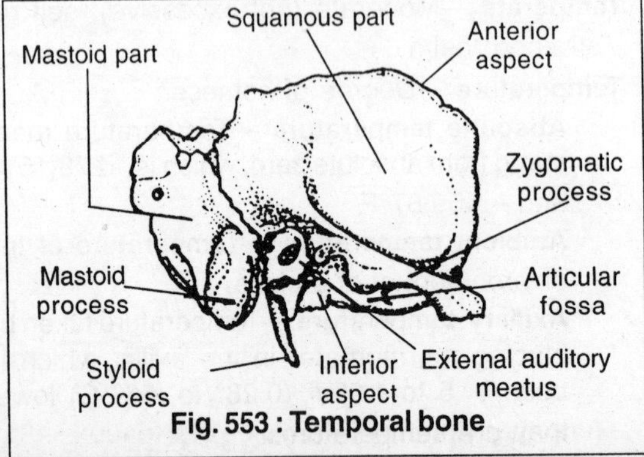

Fig. 553 : Temporal bone

Temporalis —Muscle in temporal fossa that elevates the mandible.

Temporis —Singular of tempora.

Temporo- —A prefix which means temple of the head.

Temporoauricular —Pertaining to the temporal and auricular areas.

Temporohyoid —Pertaining to the temporal and hyoid bones.

Temporomalar —Temporozygomatic.

Temporomandibular —Pertaining to the temporal bone and the mandible.

Temporomaxillary —Pertaining to the temporal and maxillary bones.

Temporo-occipital —Pertaining to the temporal and occipital bones.

Temporoparietal —Pertaining to the temporal and the parietal bones.

Temporopontine —Pertaining to, or situated between temporal lobe of the brain and the pons.

Temporosphenoid —Pertaining to the temporal and sphenoid bones.

Temporozygomatic —Pertaining to the temporal and zygomatic bones.

Tempostabile —Not being changed with the time.

Tempostable —Tempostabile.

Temulence —Drunkenness.

Tenacious —Adhesive.

Tenacity —Adhesiveness.

Tenacula —Plural of tenaculum.

Tenaculum —Hooklike, pointed surgical instrument for grasping and holding a part, as an artery.

Tenalgia—Tenodynia.

Tendency —Inclination.

Tender —Sensitive to touch or pressure.

Tenderness —Sensitiveness to touch or pressure.

Tendinitis —Tenonitis. Tenontitis. Tendonitis.

Tendinoplasty —Tendoplasty. Tenoplasty.

Tendinosis —1. Degeneration of a tendon from repetitive injury. 2. Tendinitis without inflammation.

Tendinosuture —Tenorrhaphy.

Tendinous —Pertaining to, composed of, or resembling tendon.

Tendinous synovitis —An inflammation of a tendon's synovial sheath.

Tendo —A tendon.

Tendolysis —To separate a tendon from adhesions.

Tendomucin —A form of mucin found in the tendon.

Tendon —A cord of fibrous connective tissue continuous with the muscle and attaching it to a bone or other parts, *e.g.*, Achilles or calcaneal tendon which is thickest and strongest tendon at lower end of the gastrocnemius muscle at the back of the heel, attaching it to the calcaneus bone.

Tendonitis —Inflammation of a tendon.

Tendon reflex —Contraction of a muscle on percussion of its tendon.

Tendon spindle —A fusiform nerve ending in a tendon.

Tendoplasty —Tendinoplasty.

Tendosynovitis —Tendovaginitis. Tenosynovitis.

Tendotome —A knife for cutting tendon.

Tendotomy —Tenotomy

Tendovaginal —Pertaining to a tendon and its sheath.

Tendovaginitis —Tenosynovitis. Inflammation of a tendon and its sheath.

Tenectomy —Excision of a lesion of a tendon or of a tendon sheath.

Tenesmic —Pertaining to or like tenesmus.

Tenesmus —Spasmodic contraction of anal or vesical sphincter with pain and ineffectual straining at defecation or urination.

Tenia —1. A flat band or strip of soft tissue. 2. A tapeworm of the genus Taenia.

Teniae —Plural of tenia.

Tenial —Pertaining to a tapeworm or to a flat hand or strip of soft tissue.

Teniasis —Presence of tapeworms in the body.

Tenicide —Taeniacide.

Teniform —Tenioid.

Tenifugal —Having the power to expel tapeworms.

Tenifuge —That which expels tapeworms.

Tenioid —Ribbon-shaped or resembling a tapeworm.

Teniola —A slender tapeworm or a band-like structure.

Tennis elbow —A condition usually caused by strain in playing tennis, characterized by pain over lateral epicondyle of the humerus bone radiating to outer side of the arm and forearm and aggravated by dorsiflexion and supination of the wrist. There is weakness of the wrist and difficulty in grasping objects.

Teno- —A prefix meaning tendon.

Tenodesis —Surgical fixation of a tendon to a bone.

Tenodynia —Tenalgia. Pain in a tendon.

Tenofibril —Tonofibril.

Tenolysis —Tendolysis.

Tenomyoplasty —Repair of a tendon and muscle by plastic surgery.

Tenomyositis —Inflammation of the muscle with its tendon.

Tenomyotomy —Excision of a portion of a tendon and muscle.

Tenonectomy —Excision of a part of a tendon.

Tenonitis —1. Tendinitis. Tenontitis. 2. Inflammation of a Tenon's capsule.

Tenonometer —An apparatus for measuring the intraocular pressure.

Tenon's capsule —A thin connective tissue covering of the eyeball behind the conjunctiva.

Tenontitis —Tendonitis. Tendinitis.

Tenontodynia —Tenalgia.

Tenontography —Description of tendons.

Tenontolemmitis —Tenosynovitis.

Tenontology —Study of tendons.

Tenontomyoplasty —Tenomyoplasty.

Tenontomyotomy —Cutting of a tendon of a muscle with excision of the muscle as a whole or of its part.

Tenontoplastic —Pertaining to tenontoplasty.

Tenontoplasty —Tenoplasty.

Tenontothecitis —Tendovaginitis.

Tenophyte —A cartilaginous or osseous growth on a tendon.

Tenoplasty —Tendinoplasty. Tendoplasty. Tenontoplasty. Repair of tendons by plastic surgery.

Tenoreceptor —Proprioceptive nerve ending in a tendon.

Tenorrhaphy —Suture of a tendon.

Tenositis —Tenontitis. Tendonitis.

Tenostosis —Conversion of a tendon into bone.

Tenosuspension —In surgery, use of a tendon in supporting a structure.

Tenosuture —Tenorrhaphy.

Tenosynovectomy —Excision of a tendon sheath.

Tenosynovitis—Inflammation of a tendon sheath.

Tenotome —An instrument for making a cross section of a tendon.

Tenotomist —Specialist in tenotomy.

Tenotomy —Surgical section of a tendon.

Tenovaginitis —Tenosynovitis.

Tense —Stretched, rigid, tight, with mental stress.

Tensiometer —An apparatus for determining the surface tension of a liquid.

Tension —1. The act of stretching or the condition of being stretched. 2. Pressure as arterial blood pressure. 3. Mental stress.

Tension suture —A suture applied to reduce the pull on the edges of a wound.

Tensometer —An apparatus for testing the tensible strength of materials.

Tensor —Any muscle that makes a part tense.

Tensores —Plural of tensor.

Tent —1. A plug of soft material. 2. A mask, *e.g.*, oxygen mask.

Tentacle —A slender process in invertebrates for feeding, prehension or locomotion.

Tentoria —Plural of tentorium.

Tentorial —Pertaining to a tentorium.

Tentorium —A part of the body resembling a tent.

Tentorium cerebelli —The process of dura mater between the cerebrum and cerebellum, supporting the occipital lobes.

Tephromalacia —Softening of the gray substance of brain or spinal cord.

Tephromyelitis —Inflammation cf the gray matter of the spinal cord.

Tephrosis —Incineration; cremation.

Tephrylometer —An apparatus for measuring thickness of the cerebral cortex.

Tepid —Slightly warm; lukewarm.

Tepidarium —A place for warm bath.

Tepor —Moderate heat.

Ter- —A prefix which means three times.

Teracurie —A unit of radioactivity, 10^{12} curies.

Teramorphous —Similar to a congenitally deformed fetus.

Teras —Deformed fetus, a monster.

Teratic —Pertaining to a deformed fetus.

Teratism —Congenital or acquired physical deformity.

Atresic teratism —Teratism in which normal openings of the body such as the mouth, anus or vagina etc. fail to form.

Ceasmic teratism —Teratism in which there is failure of the lateral halves of a part to unite, as in cleft palate.

Ectogenic teratism —Teratism in which some parts of the body are absent or defective.

Ectopic teratism —Teratism in which some organs or parts of the body are displaced.

Hypergenic teratism —Teratism in which there is redundancy of a part of the body, e.g., polydactylism.

Symphysic teratism —Teratism in which normally separated parts are fused.

Terato- —A prefix indicating deformed fetus.

Teratoblastoma —A tumor containing embryonic material that does not represent all three germinal layers.

Teratocarcinoma —A carcinoma developing from the epithelial cells of a teratoma.

Teratogen —Anything that causes teratogenesis.

Teratogenesis —The development of abnormal structures in an embryo, resulting in a monster.

Teratogenetic —Concerning teratogenesis.

Teratogenic —Teratogenetic.

Teratogenicity —The property or capability of producing malformation.

Teratogenous —Developing from deformed fetal parts.

Teratogeny —Teratogenesis.

Teratoid —Like a monster.

Teratoid tumor —Teratoma.

Teratologic —Pertaining to teratology.

Teratology —The branch of medical science dealing with the study of congenitally deformed fetuses.

Teratoma —Dermoid cyst. A congenital cystic

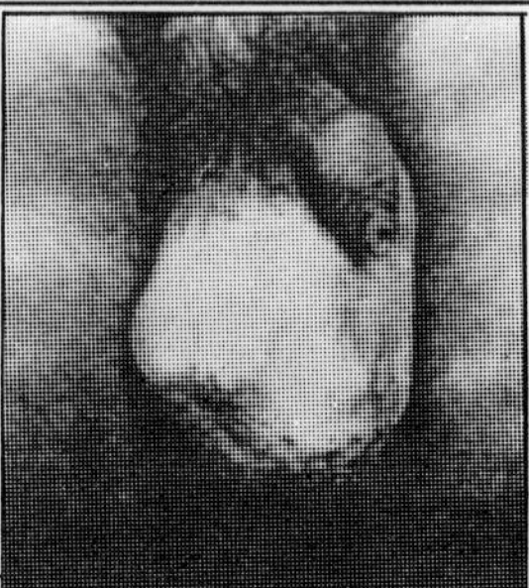

Fig. 554 : Teratoma of the testis

tumor usually found in the ovary or testis, containing embryonic all three germ layers.

Teratomatous —Pertaining to or resembling a teratoma.

Teratophobia —Morbid fear of giving birth to a malformed child.

Teratosis —The condition of being a deformed fetus.

Teratospermia —Presence of deformed spermatozoa in the semen.

Teratozoospermia —Teratospermia.

Terebrant —Piercing.

Terebrating —Terebrant.

Terebration —1. The act of boring. 2. A boring pain.

Teres —Round and long, said of certain muscles or ligaments.

Tergal —Pertaining to the back or dorsal surface.

Tergum —The back.

Ter in die —Three times a day.

Term —A definite period of time, especially that of pregnancy.

Terminad —Toward the terminus.

Terminal —1. Pertaining to an end. 2. Placed at the end. 3. The end.

Terminal cancer —Advanced cancer.

Terminal illness —An illness which causes the patient to die.

Terminal infection —Infection appearing in the late stage of another disease, which is often fatal.

Terminatio —The termination or ending.

Termination —1. The cessation of a function. 2. The distal end of a part.

Termini —Plural of terminus.

Terminology —Nomenclature.

Terminus —An ending.

Terms —Menses.

Ternary —1. Third; triple; threefold. 2. Chemical substance made up of three chemical elements.

Terra —Earth or soil.

Terrace —To suture in several rows, in closing a wound through thickness of tissues.

Terrific —Dreadful; causing terror.

Territoriality —The tendency of individuals to defend a particular domain or influence.

Terror —Extreme fear.

Tertian —Occurring every third day, usually said of malaria fever.

Tertiarism —A collective term for all the symptoms of the tertiary stage of syphilis.

Tertiarismus —Tertiarism.

Tertiary —Third in order or stage as tertiary syphilis.

Tertigravida —A woman pregnant for the third time.

Tertipara —A woman who has been pregnant for three times and produced three viable infants.

Tessellated —Made up of little squares.

Test —1. An examination. 2. A chemical reaction.

Testa —A shell.

Testalgia —Pain in the testis.

Testectomy —Orchectomy. Orchidectomy.

Testes —Plural of testis.

Testicle —A testis.

Testicond —The condition of having undescended testes.

Testicular —Pertaining to a testicle.

Testiculus —Testis.

Testis —One of the two reproductive glands of male contained in the scrotum that produces semen and male sex hormone—testosterone.

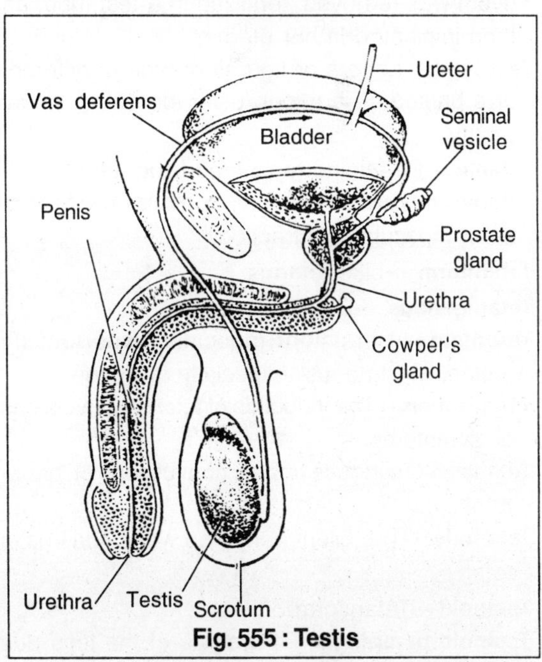

Fig. 555 : Testis

Abdominal testis —Undescended testis.

Cryptorchid testis —Undescended testis.

Displaced testis —A testis located abnormally within the inguinal canal or pelvis.

Ectopic testis —A testis located at abnormal place as in the perineum outside the scrotum.

Inverted testis —A reversed testis in the scrotum so that epididymis attaches to the anterior instead of the posterior part of the testis.

Movable testis —Retractile testis.

Retractile testis —A testis which ascends to the upper part of the scrotum or into the inguinal canal.

Undescended testis —A testis which has failed to descend into the scrotum and remains in the inguinal canal or abdominal cavity.

Testitis —Orchitis.

Test meal —A small meal of definite quantity and composition, given to the patient for chemical analysis of the stomach contents or X-ray diagnosis of the stomach diseases.

Testoid —Resembling a testis.

Testopathy —Any disease of the testes.

Testosterone —A male sex hormone produced by the testes.

Test tube baby —A baby born to a mother whose ovum was removed, fertilized in a test tube, an then implanted in her uterus.

Test type —Letters or figures of type of different size printed on a paper, used for testing visual acuity.

Tetanic —Pertaining to or producing tetanus.

Tetanic convulsion —A tonic convulsion with constant muscular contraction.

Tetaniform —Like tetanus.

Tetanigenous —Causing tetanus.

Tetanism —Persistent muscular hypertonicity resembling tetanus, especially in infants.

Tetanization —The induction of tetanic convulsions or symptoms.

Tetanize —To induce tetanic convulsions or symptoms.

Tetanode —The silent period between spasms in tetany.

Tetanoid —Tetaniform.

Tetanoid paraplegia —Paralysis of the legs due to lateral sclerosis of the spinal cord.

Tetanolysin —The hemolytic component of the toxin produced by Clostridium tetani, the bacillus causing tetanus.

Tetanometer —An instrument for measuring the force of tonic muscular spasms.

Tetanomotor —An instrument which causes tonic spasms in the muscles, by stimulating their nerves mechanically.

Tetanophil, Tetanophilic —Possessing an affinity for tetanus toxin.

Tetanospasmin —The neurotoxic component of the toxin produced by Clostridium tetani, the causative bacillus of tetanus, which causes convulsions in tetanus.

Tetanotoxin —Tetanus toxin.

Tetanus —An acute infectious disease, often fatal caused by neurotoxin (tetanospasmin) of tetanus bacillus Clostridium tetani, entering the body through a wound. It is characterized by lock jaw, general muscular spasm, opisthotonus, seizures, respiratory spasms and paralysis.

Acoustic tetanus —Experimental tetanus, induced by a faradic current.

Anticus tetanus —Tetanus in which the body is bent backward. (Emprosthotonos)

Artificial tetanus —Tetanus produced by a drug such as strychnine.

Ascending tetanus —Tetanus in which muscle spasms occur first in the lower part of the body and then ascend upward, finally in the muscles of the head and neck.

Cephalic tetanus —A form of tetanus occurring due to a wound on the head or face, especially one near the eyebrow, after a brief incubation (1-2 days) period. It is marked by trismus, facial paralysis on one side and dysphagia.

Chronic tetanus —Tetanus in which symptoms occur after a long period of an injury and they are not so severe.

Cryptogenic tetanus —Tetanus in which the site of entry of the organism is not known.

Descending tetanus —Tetanus in which muscle spasms occur first in the head and neck and then in other muscles of the body.

Dorsalis tetanus —Tetanus in which the body is bent backward.

Idiopathic tetanus —Tetanus in which the site of entery (wound) of organisms is not visible.

Infantile tetanus —Neonatorum tetanus.

Lateralis tetanus —A form of tetanus in which the body is bent sideways.

Local tetanus —Tetanus characterized by spasm of certain muscles near the wound.

Neonatorum tetanus —Tetanus occurring in very young infants, usually due to infection of the umbilicus.

Postoperative tetanus —Tetanus occurring following an operation.

Puerperal tetanus —Tetanus occurring following childbirth.

Tetanus dorsalis —Tetanus in which the body is bent forward. (Opisthotonos)

Tetanus lateralis —Tetanus in which the body is bent sideway.(Pleurothotonos)

Toxic tetanus —Tetanus caused by overdose of nux vomica or strychnine.

Traumatic tetanus —Tetanus following an injury infected with Clostridium tetani.

Tetanus antitoxin —1. An antibody that develops in the blood as a result of infection by the tetanus bacillus, Clostridium tetani or inoculation with tetanus toxin or toxoid. 2. An antitoxin derived from the blood of horse that was immunized against tetanus toxin. It is used as a prophylactic or in the treatment of tetanus by producing passive immunity in man. Its prophylactic dose is 1500 units injected subcutaneously and for the treatment 5000 to 20,000 units injected subcutaneously or intravenously.

Tetanus immune globulin —Immune globulin from human blood, for use in persons not previouly immunized against tetanus, which produces fewer side effects than tetanus antitoxin developed in the horse serum.

Tetanus toxoid —It is tetanus toxin which is modified so that its toxicity is greatly reduced but its capacity to produce active immunity is not changed.

Tetany —A condition caused by deficiency of calcium in the blood, deficiency of vitamin D causing deficient absorption of calcium, parathyroid deficiency, alkalosis, occurring frequently in children, and during lactation period and pregnancy in women due to excessive demands of calcium. It is characterized by intermittent numbness and tingling of the limbs, hyperflexion of the wrist and ankle joints (carpopedal spasm), muscular twitching, cramps and convulsions.

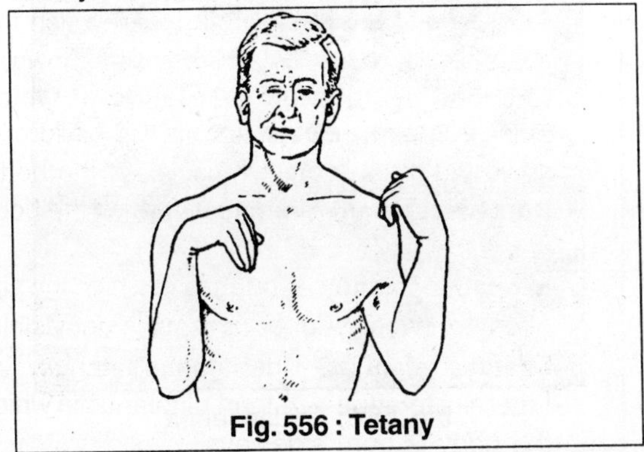

Fig. 556 : Tetany

Gastric tetany —Severe tetany due to stomach diseases accompanied by difficult respiration and tonic, painful spasms of the limbs.

Hyperventilation tetany —Tetany caused by continued forced inspiration and expiration.

Hypocalcemic tetany —Tetany caused by low serum calcium or vitamin D.

Latent tetany —Tetany produced by mechanical or electrical stimulation of the nerves.

Parathyroid tetany, Parathyroprival tetany —Tetany caused by hypofunction or removal of parathyroid glands.

Rachitic tetany —Tetany occurring in rickets.

Tetany of alkalosis —Tetany due to a loss of acid from the body or an increase in alkali.

Tetartanopia, Tetartanopsia —Symmetrical blindness in the same quadrant of each visual field.

Tetra-, Tetr- —Prefixes meaning four.

Tetra-amelia —Absence of upper and lower limbs.

Tetrabasic —Having four replaceable hydrogen atoms, said of an acid or acid salt.

Tetrablastic —Having four germinal layers—the ectoderm, endoderm and two mesoderms.

Tetrabrachius —A deformed fetus having four arms.

Tetrachirus —A deformed fetus with four hands.

Tetracrotic —A pulse tracing with four upward elevations in the descending limb of the wave.

Tetracuspid —Quadricuspid. Having four cusps.

Tetrad —A group of four similar or related things, as an element having a valence, or combining power, of four; or a group of four cells produced by division into two planes of certain cocci.

Tetradactyl —Having only four fingers or toes on a hand or foot.

Tetradactyly —The presence of four digits on a hand or foot.

Tetradic —Pertaining to tetrad.

Tetragenous —Pertaining to the organisms, especially bacteria, that divide into groups of four.

Tetragon —Tetragonum.

Tetragonum —A four-sided figure.

Tetralogy —The combination of four symptoms or elements.

Tetramastia, Tetramazia —The presence of four breasts.

Tetramastigote —Having four flagella.

Tetramastous —Having four breasts.

Tetramelus —Conjoined twins having four arms or four legs.

Tetrameric, Tetramerous —Having four parts.

Tetranopsia —Quadrantanopia.

Tetraotus —Tetrotus.

Tetraparesis —Muscular weakness of all the four extremities.

Tetraperomelia —Congenital malformations of all the four limbs.

Tetraphocomelia —Congenital absence of the proximal portion of all the four limbs, the hands and feet being attached directly to the trunk by a small irregularly shaped bone.

Tetraplegia —Quadriplegia.

Tetraplegic —Quadriplegic. Suffering from paralysis of all the four limbs.

Tetraploid —Having four sets of chromosomes.

Tetraploidy —The condition of having four sets of chromosomes.

Tetrapod —Having for feet.

Tetrapus —A deformed fetus with four feet.

Tetrascelus —A deformed fetus with four legs.

Tetrasomic —Having four chromosomes instead of two of a pair in a diploid cell.

Tetrasomy —The presence of four chromosomes instead of two of a pair in a diploid cell.

Tetrastichiasis —A deformed fetus having four rows of eyelashes.

Tetratomic —Having four atoms.

Tetravalent —Quadrivalent. Having the valence of four.

Tetrotus —A deformed fetus having two faces, four eyes and four ears.

Tetroxide —A chemical compound containing four atoms of oxygen.

Tetter —A term used for various vascular skin diseases such as herpes, ringworm or eczema.

Texis —To give birth.

Textiform —Formed like a network.

Textoblastic —Forming adult tissue or regenerative, said of cells.

Textural —Concerning the structure or constitution of a tissue.

Texture —The structure or constitution of a tissue.

Textus —Tissue.

T fracture —A fracture in which bone splits both longitudinally and transversely.

Thalamectomy —Excision of the thalamus.

Thalamencephalic —Pertaining to the thalamencephalon.

Thalamencephalon —Diencephalon. The part of the diencephalon that includes the thalamus, metathalamus and epithalamus.

Thalami —Plural of thalamus.

Thalamic —Pertaining to thalamus.

Thalamo- —A prefix meaning thalamus.

Thalamocele, Thalamocoele —The third ventricle of the brain.

Thalamocortical —Pertaining to the thalamus and cerebral cortex.

Thalamolenticular —Pertaining to the thalamus and lenticular nucleus.

Thalamotomy —Surgical destruction of a portion of thalamus.

Thalamus —Largest part of diencephalon, lying between hypothalamus and epithalamus, forming a portion of the lateral wall of 3rd ventricle of the brain. All sensory impulses except of olfactory, visual and auditory impulses, are received by the thalamus and relayed to the cerebral cortex.

Thalassemia —A hereditary hemolytic anemia. It is of two types. I. Thalassemia major (homozygous form)–It occurs in childhood. It is very se-

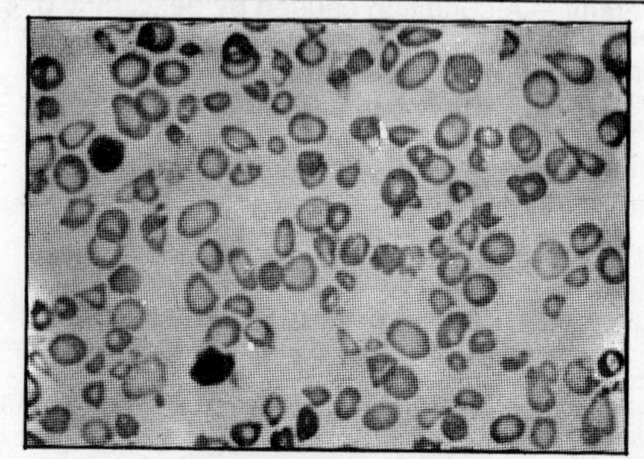

Fig. 557 : Thalassemia

rious hemolytic, hypochromic and microcytic anemia, incompatible with long life, and characterized by enlargement of the heart and spleen and thickening of the cranial bones and skeletal deformities due to increased bone marrow activity. II. Thalassemia minor (heterozygous form)–It is mild hemolytic anemia with hemoglobin levels of 6 to 10 gm. per 100 ml. of blood. The red blood cells are microcytic and hypochromic and may number more than 6,000,000 per cu. mm. of blood. It is usually asymptomatic. Prognosis is good.

Thalassophobia —Morbid fear of the sea.

Thalassoposia —Drinking of sea water.

Thalassotherapy —Treatment of the diseases by sea-water.

Thallus —A simple plant devoid of roots, stem and leaves, like a fungus.

Thamuria —Abnormal frequent urination.

Thanato- —A prefix which means death.

Thanatobiological —Pertaining to the processes of life and death.

Thanatognomonic —Indicating the approach of death.

Thanatography —To write one's symptoms and thoughts while dying.

Thanatoid —Resembling death.

Thanatology —The science of death.

Thanatomania —Mania for suicide.

Thanatometer —An instrument for determining the occurrence of death by taking internal temperature.

Thanatophidia —Poisonous snakes.

Thanatophobia —Necrophobia. Morbid fear of death.

Thanatophoric —Fatal, lethal.

Thanatophoric dwarfism —See dwarf, micromelic.

Thaumatropy —The transformation of one form of tissue into another.

Thaumaturgic —To work miracles or magic.

Thea —Tea.

Theaism —Chronic poisoning from excessive drinking of tea.

Theatre —A room for performance, as operation theatre.

Thebaic —Pertaining to or derived from opium.

Thebaine —An alkaloid obtained from opium.

Theca —A sheath or case, as pericardium covering the heart.

Thecae —Plural of theca.

Thecal —Pertaining to a sheath.

Thecitis —Inflammation of the sheath of a tendon.

Thecodont —Having teeth that are inserted in sockets.

Thecoma —A tumor of the ovary.

Thecomatosis —Increased connective tissue in the ovary.

Thecostegnosia, Thecostegnosis —Contraction of a tendon sheath.

Theinism, Theism —Chronic poisoning from excessive tea drinking, marked by palpitation, insomnia, nervousness, headache and dyspepsia.

Thelalgia —Pain in the nipples.

Thelarche —The beginning of development of breasts at puberty.

Thelasis —The act of sucking.

Thele —Nipple.

Theleplasty —Mammilliplasty.

Thelerethism —Erection of the nipple.

Thelia —Plural of thelium.

Thelitis —Acromastitis. Inflammation of the nipples.

Thelium —1. A papilla. 2. A nipple.

Theloncus —A tumor of a nipple.

Thelophlebostemma —A dark circle of veins about a nipple.

Thelorrhagia —Hemorrhage from the nipple.

Thelygenic —Producing only female offspring.

Thenad —Toward the palm or thenar eminence.

Thenal —Pertaining to the palm or thenar eminence.

Thenal eminence —Ball of the thumb.

Thenar —1. Palm of the hand or sole of the foot. 2. Pertaining to the palm. 3. The fleshy part of hand at the base of thumb.

Thenar eminence —The palmar eminence at the base of thumb.

Thenen —Pertaining to the pain, especially of the palm.

Theomania —Religious mania.

Theophobia —Morbid fear of anger of god.

Theoretical —Based on theory.

Theory —A supposition or assumption which becomes principle when generally accepted.

Theotherapy —Treatment of the diseases by spiritual therapy and religious methods.

Theque —A round or oval collection or nest of melanin-containing nevus cells in the epidermis.

Therapeusis —Therapeutics.

Therapeutic —1. Pertaining to or for the treatment of disease. 2. Curative.

Therapeutics —The branch of medical science concerned with the application of remedies and treatment of diseases.

Therapeutist —Therapist.

Therapia —1. Therapy. 2. Therapeutics.

Therapist —A person skilled in the treatment of diseases in a specific field of health care, as physiotherapist.

Therapy —Treatment of a disease or pathological condition.

Anticoagulant therapy —Treatment by anticoagulant drugs to decrease the tendency of blood to coagulate and cause thrombosis.

Behavior therapy —Treatment of a mental disorder by changing the behavior of the patient.

Collapse therapy —Treatment of pulmonary tuberculosis by producing a pneumothorax on the affected side, which causes the lung on that side to be at rest.

Diathermic therapy —Treatment of diseases by diathermy.

Electroconvulsive therapy —See under letter 'E'.

Fever therapy —Treatment of some diseases by causing fever artificially.

Insulin shock therapy —See under letter 'I'.

Occupational therapy —Treatment of some diseases, and to prevent disability the patient is made to be engaged in some work or to play some game.

Physical therapy —See under 'P'

Radiation therapy —Radiotherapy.

Replacement therapy —Treatment to replace the absent or diminished natural substance in the body, *e.g.*, insulin or thyroid hormone etc.

Serum therapy —Serotherapy.

Shock therapy —See under 'S'

Spiritual therapy —See under 'S'

Substitution therapy —Administration of a substance which the body normally produces, such as hormone.

Vaccine therapy —Treatment of a disease by producing active immunization against it by injection of bacteria or their products.

Therm —A heat unit.

Thermacogenesis —An increase of body temperature by drug therapy.

Thermaerotherapy —Treatment of the diseases by application of hot air.

Thermal —Pertaining to heat.

Thermalgesia —Pain caused by heat.

Thermalgia —Causalgia.

Thermal radiation —Heat radiation.

Thermal sense —Thermesthesia.

Thermanalgesia —Inability to feel pain by heat due to a cerebral lesion.

Thermanesthesia —Thermoanesthesia.

Thermatology —The study of heat in the treatment of disease.

Thermelometer —An electric thermometer for measuring small temperature variations.

Thermesthesia —Thermoesthesia.

Thermesthesiometer —An apparatus for measuring the sensibility to heat.

Thermhyperesthesia —Excessive sensibility to heat.

Thermhypesthesia —Thermohypesthesia.

Thermic —Pertaining to heat.

Thermistor —A thermometer for quickly measuring very small changes in temperature.

Thermo- —A prefix meaning hot or heat.

Thermoalgesia —Thermalgesia.

Thermoanalgesia —Thermanalgesia.

Thermoanesthesia —Thermanesthesia. Inability to recognize heat and cold.

Thermobiosis —Ability to exist at high temperature.

Thermobiotic —Able to exist at high temperature.

Thermocauterectomy —Excision of an organ or part of the body by thermocautery.

Thermocautery —Cauterization by a heated wire.

Thermochemistry —The branch of chemistry dealing with temperature changes accompanying chemical reactions.

Thermochroic —A substance that transmits a portion of heat and absorbs the rest of it.

Thermochroism —Property of a substance to transmit a portion of heat and to absorb the rest of it.

Thermochrose —The property of heat rays of reflection, refraction and absorption, similar to that of light rays.

Thermochrosis —Thermochroism.

Thermochrosy —Thermochrose.

Thermocoagulation —To coagulate a tissue to destroy it by high-frequency currents.

Thermocouple —Thermopile.

Thermocurrent —An electric current produced by thermoelectric means.

Thermode —An apparatus for heating or cooling a part of the body.

Thermodiffusion —Increased diffusion of a substance due to increased heat.

Thermodilution —Reduction in temperature in a liquid that occurs when it is introduced into a colder liquid.

Thermoduric —Able to live in high temperatures.

Thermodynamics —The branch of physics dealing with the heat and energy, their interconversion and their problems.

Thermoelectric —Pertaining to thermoelectricity.

Thermoelectricity —Electricity generated by heat.

Thermoesthesia —Thermesthesia. Ability to recognize temperature differences.

Thermoexcitory —Stimulating production of heat in the body.

Thermogenesis —The production of heat, especially in the body.

Thermogenetic —Thermogenic.

Thermogenic —Producing heat.

Thermogenics —The science of heat.

Thermogenous —Thermogenic.

Thermogram —A graphic record of temperature variations.

Thermograph —An apparatus for recording variations of heat.

Thermography —The graphic recording of temperature variations of the body by thermograph.

Thermohyperalgesia —Intense pain by heat.

Thermohyperesthesia —Extreme sensitiveness to heat.

Thermohypesthesia —Diminished sensitivenss to heat.

Thermohypoesthesia —Thermohypesthesia.

Thermoinhibitory —Arresting the generation of heat in the body.

Thermojunction —Thermopile.

Thermolabile —Changed or destroyed easily by heat.

Thermolamp —Lamp used to provide heat.

Thermology —The science of heat.

Thermolysis —1. Chemical decomposition by heat. 2. Loss of heat from the body by evaporation, radiation etc.

Thermolytic —Pertaining to, or promoting thermolysis.

Thermomassage —Massage with heat.

Thermometer —Temperature scale. An instrument for determining the temperature.

Alcohol thermometer —A thermometer containing alcohol.

Celsius thermometer —Centigrade thermometer. It is scientific thermometer on which boiling point of water is 100°C and freezing point is 0°C, thus divided into 100 degrees.

Centigrade thermometer —Celsius thermometer.

Clinical thermometer —Thermometer by which body temperature is measured. It contains mercury which remains stationary at the measured point until shaken down. It is marked by signs of 94° to 110°F. Normal body temperature is 98.4°F.

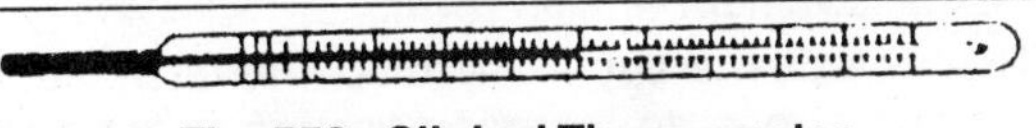

Fig. 558 : Clinical Thermometer

Fahrenheit thermometer —Thermometer on which boiling point of water is 212°F and freezing point is 32°F.

Gas thermometer —Thermometer filled with gas, such as air, helium, or oxygen.

Mercury thermometer —A thermometer containing mercury for measurement of temperature.

Recording thermometer —Thermometer that continuously measures and records temperature.

Rectal thermometer —Thermometer that is inserted into the rectum for measuring the body temperature.

Spirit thermometer —Thermometer filled with spirit or alcohol instead of mercury, for measuring low temperatures.

Surface thermometer —Thermometer for measuring temperature of the body's surface.

Thermometric —Pertaining to measurment of heat or a thermometer.

Thermometry —Measurement of temperatures.

Thermoneurosis —Rise of temperature in hysteria and other nervous disorders.

Thermopenetration —Thermoradiotherapy.

Thermophagy —Eating of extremely hot food.

Thermophile —Thermophil.

Thermophilic —Growing best at high temperatures, said of bacteria.

Thermophils —Organisms that grow best at elevated temperature, *i.e.*, at 40° to 70° C.

Thermophobia —Morbid fear of heat.

Thermophore —1. An apparatus for retaining heat. 2. An instrument for estimating sensibility to heat.

Thermophylic —Resistant to destruction by heat, characteristic of certain bacteria.

Thermopile —Thermocouple. An apparatus for measuring slight temperature changes.

Thermoplacentography —Use of thermography for determining the site of placental attachment.

Thermoplastic —That which becomes softened or malleable by heat.

Thermoplegia —Heatstroke or sunstroke.

Thermopolypnea —Quickened breathing due to excessive heat or high fever.

Thermoradiotherapy —Thermopenetration. Application of heat to the deep tissues of the body by diathermy.

Thermoreceptor —A nerve ending stimulated by a rise of body temperature.

Thermoregulation —Heat regulation.

Thermoregulator —Thermostat.

Thermoregulatory —Pertaining to heat regulation.

Thermoresistant —Thermophylic.

Thermoscope —An instrument for indicating slight differences of temperature, without recording them.

Thermostabile —Not affected by heat.

Thermostable —Thermostabile.

Thermostasis —The maintenance of body temperature.

Thermostat —An apparatus regulating the temperature automatically.

Thermosteresis —Loss of heat.

Thermosterilization —Sterilization by heat.

Thermosystaltic —Contracting under the stimulus of heat, as a muscle.

Thermosystaltism —Contraction, as of the muscles, under the stimulus of heat.

Thermotactic, Thermotaxic —Pertaining to regulation of body temperature.

Thermotaxis —1. Regulation of bodily temperature. 2. Thermotropism. The movement of certain organisms or cells toward (positive thermotaxis) or away from (negative thermotaxis) heat.

Thermotherapeutics —Thermotherapy. Treatment of the diseases by use of heat.

Thermotherapy —Thermotherapeutics.

Thermotic —Pertaining to heat.

Thermotics —The science of heat.

Thermotolerant —Able to live normally in high temperature.

Thermotonometer —An instrument for measuring the muscular contraction caused by heat.

Thermotoxin —A poison formed in the tissues due to excessive heat.

Thermotropism —Thermotaxis.

Theroid —Having animal instincts and characteristics.

Therology —The study of mammals.

Thesaurismosis —Accumulation of substances in excess in certain cells, usually due to a metabolic disease.

Thesaurismotic —A substance that accumulates in excess in certain cells, usually due to a metabolic disease.

Thesaurosis —Accumulation of foreign or normal substances in the body.

Theta —The 8th letter in the Greek alphabet, θ.

Thiersch's graft —A method of skin grafting in which the epidermis and a portion of dermis is used.

Thigh —The portion of leg between hip joint and the knee.

Thigh-friction —A form of masturbation.

Thigmesthesia —Sensitivity to touch.

Thigmotaxis —The movement of certain motile cells on touching.

Thigmotropism —Thigmotaxis.

Thinking —To consider.

Thinning —A decreasing in the thickness of a liquid, by adding a solvent to it.

Third intention —Healing of a wound by filling with granulations.

Thirst —A desire for drink.

Thixolabile —That which is changed by shaking.

Thixotropic—A gelatinous substance that becomes fluid on shaking and becomes gelatinous again on standing.

Thixotropism —Thixotropy.

Thixotropy —The property of a gelatinous substance to become fluid on shaking and then to become gelatinous again on standing.

Thlipsencephalus —A deformed fetus with a defective or absent skull.

Thomas splint —A splint extending from a ring at the hip to beyond the foot, allowing traction on a fractured leg, in its long axis.

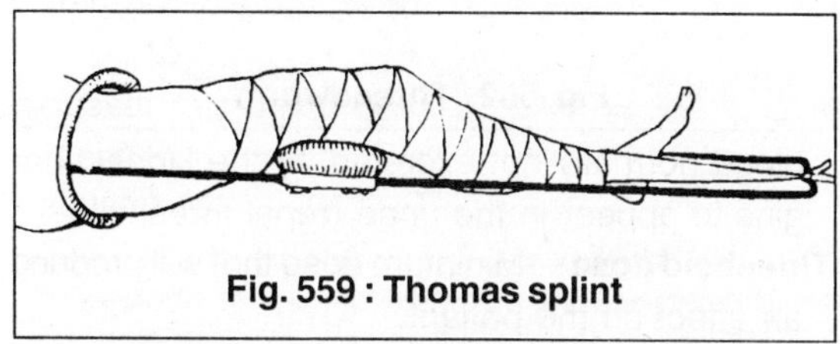

Fig. 559 : Thomas splint

Thoracalgia —Pleurodynia. Pain in the chest wall.

Thoracectomy —To incise the chest wall.

Thoracentesis —Pleurocentesis. Thoracocentesis.

Thoraces —Plural of thorax.

Thoracic —Pertaining to the chest.

Thoracic cage —The bony structure surrounding the thorax.

Thoracic limbs —Upper extremities.

Thoracicoabdominal —Pertaining to the thorax and abdomen.

Thoracicohumeral —Pertaining to the thorax and humerus.

Thoraco- —A prefix meaning chest or chest wall.

Thoracoabdominal —Thoracicoabdominal.

Thoracoacromial —Pertaining to the thorax and acromion.

Thoracocautery —The use of cautery in breaking up pulmonary adhesions to collapse a lung.

Thoracoceloschisis —Congenital fissure of the thorax and abdomen.

Thoracocentesis —Thoracentesis. Surgical puncture of the chest wall for aspiration of fluid from the thoracic cavity, by using a needle.

Thoracocyllosis —Deformity of the thorax.

Thoracocyrtosis —Excessive curvature of the chest wall.

Thoracodelphus —A deformed fetus with a single head and thorax but four legs.

Thoracodidymus —Two conjoined twins united at the thorax.

Thoracodorsal—Pertaining to the external posterior chest wall.

Thoracodynia —Pain in the chest.

Thoracoepigastric —Pertaining to the thorax and epigastrium.

Thoracogastroschisis —Thoracoceloschisis.

Thoracolaparotomy —Thoracotomy and laparotomy performed at a time.

Thoracolumbar —Pertaining to the thorax and the lumbar vertebrae.

Thoracolysis —Separation of a lung that is adhered to the chest wall.

Thoracomelus —A deformed fetus with an extra leg attached to the chest.

Thoracometer —An instrument for measuring the expansion of the chest.

Thoracometry —The measurement of the thorax.

Thoracomyodynia —Pain in the muscles of the chest.

Thoracopagus —Conjoined twins united at the thorax.

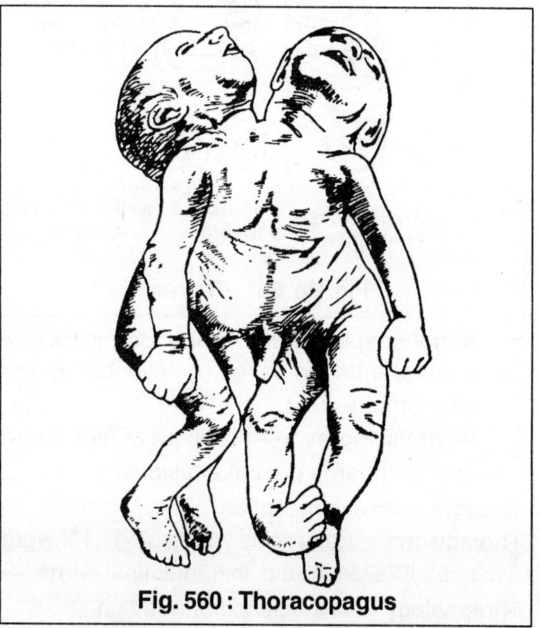

Fig. 560 : Thoracopagus

Thoracoparacephalus —Unequal conjoined twins in which the head of the parasitic (smaller) twin is attached to the thorax of the autosite (larger) twin.

Thoracopathy —Any disease of the thorax, its organs or tissues.

Thoracoplasty —Surgical removal of portions of the ribs, so that the chest wall may collapse a diseased lung.

Thoracopneumoplasty —Plastic surgery of both the chest and the lung.

Thoracoschisis —Congenital fissure of the chest wall.

Thoracoscope —An endoscope for inspection of the thoracic cavity through an intercostal space.

Thoracoscopy —Inspection of the pleural cavity with a thoracoscope.

Thoracostenosis —Narrowness of the thorax.

Thoracostomy—To make an incision in the chest wall, with maintenance of the opening for drainage.

Thoracotomy —Surgical incision of the chest wall.

Thorax —Chest. The part of the body between base of the neck and the diaphragm, surrounded by ribs.

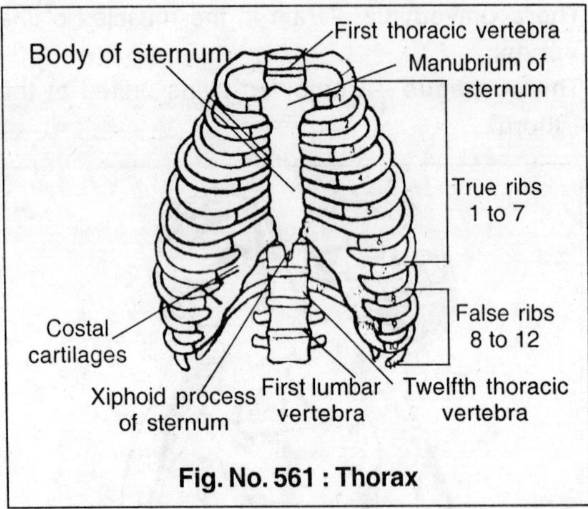

Fig. No. 561 : Thorax

Barrel-shaped thorax —Rounded thorax like a barrel found in cases of advanced pulmonary emphysema.

Peyrot's thorax —An obliquely oval thorax seen with large pleural effusions.

Thought —Idea, conception.

Threadworm —Enterobius vermicularis. Pinworm. A threadlike, long and thin intestinal worm.

Threpsology —The science of nutrition.

Threshold —The point at which an effect begins to be produced, *e.g.*, the lowest intensity of a stimulus which just produces a sensation, or the concentration at which a substance in the blood normally not excreted by the kidney, begins to appear in the urine (renal threshold).

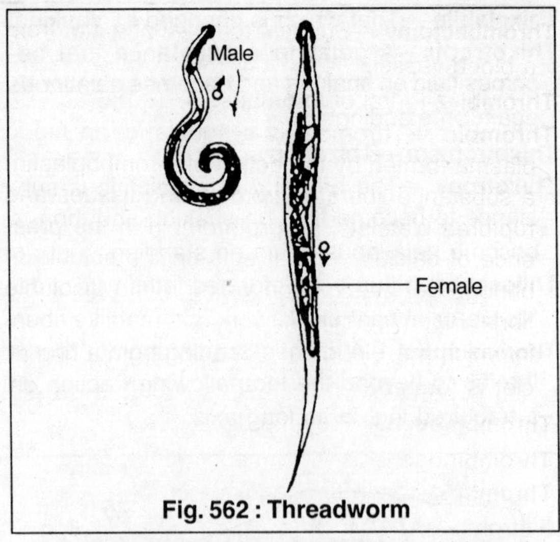

Fig. 562 : Threadworm

Threshold dose —Minimum dose that will produce an effect on the patient.

Thrill —1. Fremitus. A vibration felt on palpation. 2. A shivering from excitement as from horror.

Aneurysmal thrill —Thrill felt on palpation of an aneurysm.

Aortic thrill —Thrill heard over aortic aperture in valvular defects.

Arterial thrill —Thrill heard over an artery.

Diastolic thrill —Thrill felt over the precordium during diastole in aortic insufficiency.

Hydatid thrill —Thrill felt on palpation of a hydatid cyst.

Presystolic thrill —Thrill sometimes felt over the apex of the heart just before the contraction of the ventricles.

Systolic thrill —Thrill felt over the precordium during systole in aortic or pulmonary stenosis or ventricular septal defect.

Thrix —Hair.

-thrix —A suffix which means hair.

Throat —1. The pharynx and the fauces. 2. The anterior part of the neck.

Throb —1. Pulsation 2. To pulsate

Throbbing —Pulsating or beating.

Thromb- —A prefix which means blood coagulation or blood clot.

Thrombapheresis —Thrombocytapheresis.

Thrombase —Thrombin.

Thrombasthenia —Thromboasthenia.

Thrombectomy —Surgical removal of a clot from a blood vessel.

Thrombi —Plural of thrombus.

Thrombin —Thrombin is a substance in blood plasma formed by the action of thromboplastin, a substance liberated from injured tissues and ruptured platelets, on prothrombin in the presence of calcium ions. It acts on the soluble fibrinogen of plasma converting it into insoluble fibrin. Fibrin forms a network of threadlike fibers in which the blood cells are entangled, thus a clot is formed.

Thrombinogen —Prothrombin.

Thrombinogenesis —Formation of thrombin.

Thrombo- —A prefix meaning clot of blood or a thrombus.

Thromboangiitis —Inflammation of the inner coat of a blood vessel with the formation of blood clot.

Thromboangiitis obliterans —Buerger's disease.

Thromboarteritis —Thrombosis associated with the inflammation of an artery.

Thromboasthenia —Thrombasthenia. A platelet abnormality characterized by defective clot retraction and lack of aggregation of platelets, manifested by bruising, excessive bleeding following an injury and epistaxis etc.

Thromboblast —Megakaryocyte.

Thromboclasis —Thrombolysis.

Thromboclastic —Thrombolytic.

Thrombocyst —Thrombocystis. A membranous sac formed around a thrombus.

Thrombocystis —Thrombocyst.

Thrombocytapheresis —Removal of platelets from the withdrawn blood and retransfusion of the remainder of blood into the donor.

Thrombocytasthenia —A group of hemorrhagic diseases occurring due to morphological abnormality in the platelets and not due to decrease in their number.

Thrombocyte —A blood platelet.

Thrombocythemia —An increase in number of platelets in the blood.

Thrombocytin —Serotonin.

Thrombocytocrit —An apparatus for measuring the platelet volume in a given quantity of blood.

Thrombocytolysis —Destruction of platelets.

Thrombocytopathy —Any abnormality or defect of the blood platelets.

Thrombocytopenia —Thrombopenia.

Thrombocytopoiesis —The formation of blood platelets.

Thrombocytosis —Increase in the number of platelets in the blood.

Thromboelastogram —Registration of the coagulation process of blood by a thromboelastograph.

Thromboelastograph —An apparatus for registering the coagulation process of blood.

Thromboembolectomy —Excision of an embolic thrombus.

Thromboembolic —Pertaining to thromboembolism.

Thromboembolism —The blocking of a blood vessel by a thrombus that has been detached from the site of its formation and carried by blood to this blood vessel.

Thromboendarterectomy —Surgical removal of an obstructing thrombus together with a portion of the inner coat of the obstructed artery.

Thromboendarteritis —Inflammation of the inner coat of an artery with thrombus formation.

Thromboendocarditis —Formation of a clot on inflamed heart valve.

Thrombogen —Prothrombin.

Thrombogene —Blood coagulation factor V.

Thrombogenesis —The formation of a blood clot.

Thrombogenic —Forming a clot.

Thromboid —Resembling a thrombus or clot.

Thrombokinase —Blood coagulation factor X.

Thrombokinesis —Coagulation of the blood.

Thrombolic —Pertaining to a thrombolus.

Thrombolus —An embolus composed mainly of agglutinated platelets.

Thrombolymphangitis —Inflammation of a lymphatic vessel due to obstruction by thrombus formation.

Thrombolysis—Thromboclasis. The breaking up of a thrombus.

Thrombolytic —Pertaining to or breaking up a thrombus.

Thrombon —The part of the hematopoietic system concerned with platelet formation.

Thrombonecrosis —Necrosis of the walls of a blood vessel, with thrombosis in its lumen.

Thrombopathy —Thrombocytopathy.

Thrombopenia —Thrombocytopenia. Decrease in number of platelets in blood.

Thrombophilia —A tendency to the occurrence of thrombosis.

Thrombophlebitis —Inflammation of a vein associated with thrombus formation.

Thromboplastic —Pertaining to or promoting clot formation in the blood.

Thromboplastid —A blood platelet.

Thromboplastin —The third blood coagulation factor, a substance in the blood and tissues which in the presence of calcium ions, aids in the conversion of prothrombin to thrombin.

Thromboplastinogen —Blood coagulation factor VIII. See coagulation factors.

Thrombopoiesis —Thrombocytopoiesis.

Thrombopoietin —A chemical substance that acts on the bone marrow to stimulate platelet formation.

Thrombosed —Coagulated or affected with thrombosis.

Thromboses —Plural of thrombosis.

Thrombosin —Thrombin.

Thrombosinusitis —Inflammation of a sinus, especially of a paranasal sinus with thrombus formation in it.

Thrombosis —The formation or presence of a blood clot within a blood vessel.

Atrophic thrombosis —Marasmic thrombosis. Thrombosis due to feebleness of blood circulation, as in marasmus.

Cerebral thrombosis —Clot formation within a cerebral blood vessel which may cause cerebral infarction.

Coagulation thrombosis —Thrombosis due to coagulation of fibrin in a blood vessel.

Compression thrombosis —Thrombosis due to arrest of blood circulation in a vessel by compression, as from a tumor.

Coronary thrombosis —Thrombosis of a coronary artery which commonly causes myocardial infarction.

Embolic thrombosis —Thrombosis caused by an embolus which obstructs a blood vessel.

Infective thrombosis —Thrombosis in which there is bacterial infection.

Plate thrombosis —Thrombosis due to accumulation of blood platelets.

Puerperal thrombosis —Blood clot formation in a vein following delivery.

Traumatic thrombosis —Thrombosis occurring following an injury.

Venous thrombosis —Thrombosis occurring in a vein.

Thrombostasis —Stasis of blood in a part of the body, causing or caused by formation of blood clot.

Thrombosthenin —A protein present in the platelets that causes retraction of blood clot.

Thrombotic —Pertaining to, caused by, or of the nature of, a thrombus.

Thrombus —A blood clot formed within the heart or a blood vessel from constituents of the blood, obstructing the heart cavity or blood vessel.

Agonal thrombus —A thrombus formed in the heart just at the time of death.

Antemortem thrombus —A thrombus formed in the heart or large blood vessels before death.

Mural thrombus —Parietal thrombus. A thrombus attached to the wall of the endocardium.

Occluding thrombus —A thrombus completely closing a blood vessel.

Parietal thrombus —A thrombus attached to the wall of a vessel.

Postmortem thrombus —A thrombus formed in the heart or a large blood vessel after death.

Through illumination —Transillumination.

Thrush —Fungus infection of the mouth or throat, caused by Candida albicans, especially in infants and young children characterized by the formation of white patches and ulcers.

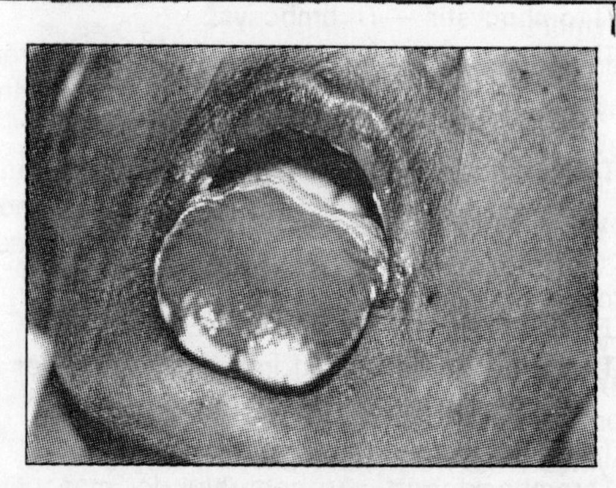

Fig. 563 : Thrush

Thrust —To move forward suddenly and forcibly.

Thrypsis —Comminuted fracture. A fracture in which the bone is broken into pieces.

Thumb —Pollex. The first, short and thick digit on the radial side of the hand, having 2 phalanges.

Thylacitis —Inflammation of the sebaceous glands of the skin.

Thymectomize —To excise the thymus gland.

Thymectomy —Excision of the thymus gland.

Thymelcosis —Ulceration of the thymus gland.

-thymia —A suffix indicating a state of the mind.

Thymic —Pertaining to the thymus gland.

Thymicolymphatic —Pertaining to the thymus and lymph glands.

Thymin —A hormone-like substance secreted by the thymus gland which interferes with the post synaptic neuromuscular transmission.

Thymion —A wart.

Thymitis —Inflammation of the thymus gland.

Thymo- —A prefix denoting relationship to the thymus gland.

Thymocyte —A lymphocyte derived from the thymus gland.

Thymogenic —Originating from the mind.

Thymokesis —Abnormal enlargement of the thymus gland.

Thymokinetic —Stimulating the thymus gland.

Thymoleptic —Any drug which changes the mood in serious mental disorder such as depression or mania.

Thymolysis —Destruction of the thymus gland tissue.

Thymolytic —Destructive to thymus gland tissue.

Thymoma —A tumor arising from epithelial tissues of the thymus gland.

Thymopathy —Any disease of the thymus gland.

Thymopexy —Fixation of an enlarged thymus gland in a new position.

Thymopoietin —A hormone-like substance secreted by the thymus gland, which induces differentiation of thymocytes.

Thymoprival —Thymoprivic.

Thymoprivic —Pertaining to or caused by removal or atrophy of the thymus gland.

Thymoprivous —Thymoprivic.

Thymosin —A hormone-like substance secreted by the thymus gland, which promotes the maturation of T-lymphocytes.

Thymotoxic—Poisonous to the thymus gland.

Thymus —A lymphoid gland situated in the mediastinal cavity anterior to and above the heart, which reaches its maximum weight at about puberty and then undergoes involution. Its important function is to develop immunity in the newborn infant. Thymic lymphocytes develop

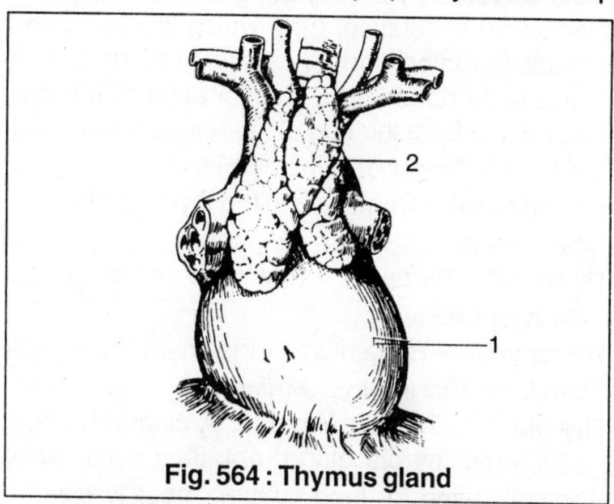

Fig. 564 : Thymus gland

1. Pericardium 2. Thymus.

into T cells and begin to maturate. When they enter the blood circulation, they produce immunity by enhancing the production of antibody forming cells. Thymus gland also secretes hormone-like substances thymin, thymopoietin, and thymosin.

Thymusectomy —Surgical excision of the thymus gland.

Thyreo-, Thyro- —Prefixes meaning thyroid.

Thyreoplasia —Defective development of the thyroid gland with abnormal functioning.

Thyroadenitis—Inflammation of the thyroid gland.

Thyroaplasia —Imperfect development of thyroid gland.

Thyroarytenoid —Pertaining to the thyroid gland and arytenoid cartilages.

Thyrocalcitonin —Calcitonin.

Thyrocardiac —Pertaining to the thyroid gland and heart.

Thyrocele —Goiter.

Thyrocervical —Pertaining to the thyroid gland and cervix.

Thyrochondrotomy —Surgical incision of the thyroid cartilage.

Thyrocolloid —A colloid substance in the thyroid gland.

Thyrocricotomy —To divide the cricothyroid membrane.

Thyroepiglottic —Pertaining to the thyroid gland and epiglottis.

Thyrofissure —Laryngofissure

Thyrogenic, Thyrogenous —Originating in the thyroid gland.

Thyroglobulin —1. An iodine-containing glycoprotein secreted by the thyroid gland and stored in its colloid substance, from which thyroxine and triiodothyronine hormones are produced. 2. A substance obtained by fractionation of the thyroid gland form the hog. It is administered orally in the treatment of hypothyroidism.

Thyroglossal —Pertaining to the thyroid gland and the tongue.

Thyrohyal —Pertaining to the thyroid cartilage and the hyoid bone.

Thyrohyoid —Pertaining to the thyroid gland or cartilage and the hyoid bone.

Thyroid —1. Thyroid gland. 2. A cleaned, dried, powdered thyroid gland, obtained from those animals used for food by man, usually pigs.

Thyroid crisis —Thyroid storm.

Thyroidea accessoria —Accessory thyroid gland.

Thyroidectomize —To excise the thyroid gland.

Thyroidectomized One whose thyroid gland has been removed.

Thyroidectomy —Excision of the thyroid gland.

Thyroid gland —An endocrine gland situated at base of the neck, on both sides of lower part of the larynx and upper part of the trachea. It consists of two lateral lobes joined together by an

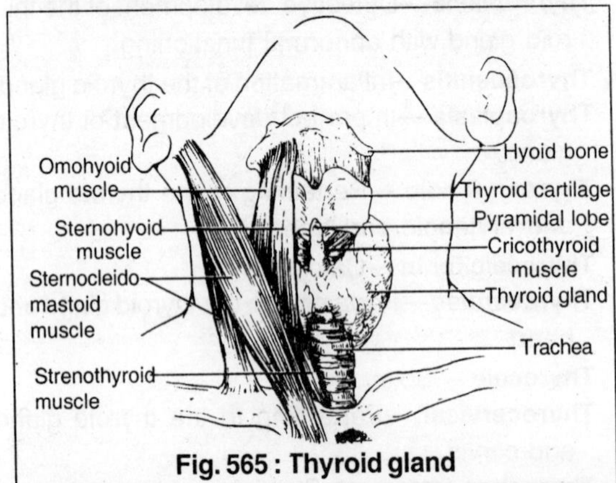

Fig. 565 : Thyroid gland

isthmus. It secretes two active hormones thyroxine and tri-iodothyronine, which are mainly concerned wtih the metabolism.

Thyroidism —Hyperthyroidism. Disease caused by hyperactivity of the thyroid gland.

Thyroiditis —Inflammation of the thyroid gland.

Thyroidology —The study of the thyroid gland.

Thyroidomania —Mania associated with hyperthyroidism.

Thyroidotomy —Incision of the thyroid gland.

Thyroid-stimulating hormone —A hormone secreted by the anterior pituitary gland that stimulates the thyroid to secrete its two hormones—thyroxine and triiodothyronine.

Thyroid storm —A complication of thyrotoxicosis in which there is sudden onset of fever, sweating, tachycardia, pulmonary edema or congestive heart failure, tremulousness and restlessness.

Thyrointoxication —Hyperthyroidism.

Thyrolaryngeal —Pertaining to the thyroid gland and the larynx.

Thyrolingual —Thyroglossal.

Thyrolysin —That which destroys the thyroid tissue.

Thyrolytic —Destructive to the thyroid gland.

Thyromegaly —Enlargement of the thyroid gland.

Thyromimetic—Producing effects similar to those produced by thyroid hormones or by thyroid gland.

Thyroparathyroidectomy—Surgical removal of the thyroid and parathyroid glands.

Thyropathy —Any disease of the thyroid gland.

Thyropharyngeal —Pertaining to the thyroid gland and the pharynx.

Thyroplasty —The changing of the appearance of the thyroid cartilage adjacent to the vocal cords, by plastic surgery.

Thyroprival —Pertaining to, affected with or caused by loss of function or removal of the thyroid gland.

Thyroprivia —Hypothyroidism.

Thyroprivic —Thyroprival.

Thyroprivous —Thyroprivic.

Thyroprotein —Thyroglobulin.

Thyroptosis —Downward displacement of the thyroid gland into the thorax.

Thyrosis —Any disease caused by abnormal function of the thyroid gland.

Thyrotherapy —Treatment of the diseases with preparations of the thyroid gland.

Thyrotome —A knife for cutting thyroid cartilage.

Thyrotomy —1. Cutting of the thyroid cartilage. 2. The operation of cutting the thyroid gland.

Thyrotoxic —Pertaining to, or affected, with toxic activity of the thyroid gland.

Thyrotoxicosis —Goiter, exophthalmic; Grave's disease. A toxic condition due to overactivity of the thyroid gland, characterized by enlargement of the thyroid gland, bulging of the eyes, tremors of the fingers and tachycardia.

Thyrotoxin —A toxin produced in the thyroid gland.

Thyrotrophic —Thyrotropic.

Thyrotrophin —Thyrotropin.

Thyrotropic —Having affinity for, or stimulating the thyroid gland.

Thyrotropin —Thyroid-stimulating hormone. A hormone of the anterior pituitary gland which stimulates the thyroid gland.

Thyrotropism —Affinity for the rhyroid gland.

Thyroxine —An iodine-containing hormone of the thyroid gland, which increases the rate of cell metabolism. It is used in the treatment of hypothyroidism.

Tibia —The inner and larger bone of the leg between knee and ankle, articulating with the femure bone above and with the talus below.

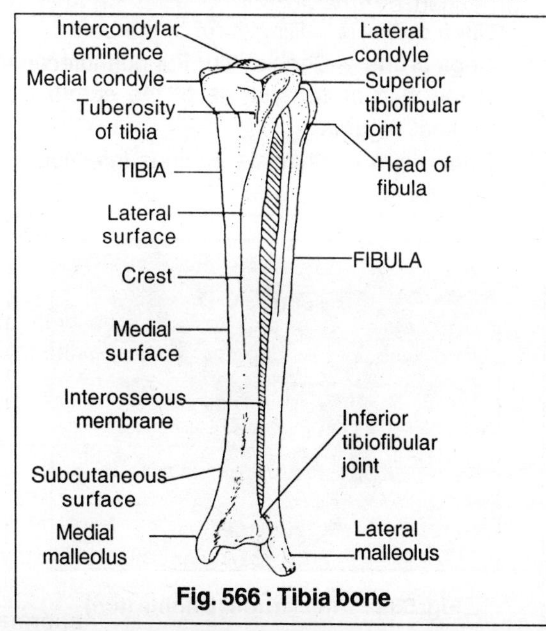

Fig. 566 : Tibia bone

Tibiad —Toward the tibia bone.

Tibiae —Plural of tibia.

Tibial —Pertaining to the tibia bone.

Tibialgia —Pain in the tibia bone.

Tibialis —Tibial.

Tibio- —A prefix which means tibia bone.

Tibiocalcanean —Pertaining to the tibia and calcaneus bones.

Tibiofemoral —Pertaining to the tibia and femur bones.

Tibiofibular—Pertaining to the tibia and fibula bones.

Tibionavicular —Pertaining to the tibia and navicular bones.

Tibioperoneal —Tibiofibular.

Tibioscaphoid —Tibionavicular.

Tibiotarsal —Pertaining to the tibia bone and tarsus.

Tic —A spasmodic, involuntary, repetitive muscular contraction most commonly affecting the face, neck or shoulder muscles.

Tick —A blood sucking parasite.

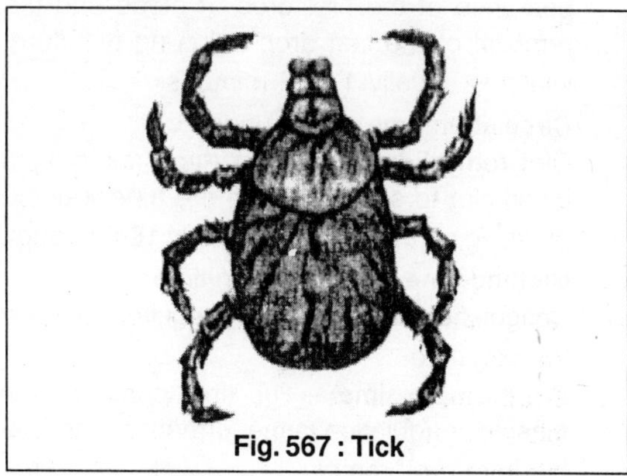

Fig. 567 : Tick

Tickle —1. A peculiar sensation caused by touching slightly, especially in certain areas, resulting in reflex muscular movements or laughter. 2. To arouse such sensation by touching slightly.

Tickling —The act of titillation.

T. I. D. —Three times a day.

Tidal —Periodically rising and falling or increasing and decreasing.

Tidal air —Volume of air inhaled and exhaled with each normal respiration, which is about 500 c.c. for an adult.

Tide —Periodical rise and fall or increase and decrease, e.g., a temporary increase in the acidity of urine after fasting (acid tide) or temporary increase in alkalinity of urine following awakening and after meals (alkaline tide) or increase of fat in the lymph and blood after a fatty meal.

Tigroid —Stripped or spotted or marked like a tiger.

Tigroid bodies —Nissl bodies.

Tigrolysis —Chromatolysis.

Tilmus —Carphology.

Tilt —A sloping position, inclination.

Tiltometer —An apparatus for measuring the degree of tilt of a bed or operation table.

Timbre —Musical quality of a sound by which it is distinguished.

Time —That relation of events which is expressed in terms of past, present and future, and measured by units such as minutes, hours, days, months, or years.

Bleeding time —The time consumed in bleeding from a small wound, which is usually tested by puncturing the ear lobe or the finger. It is the time interval between the appearance of the first drop of blood and the removal of the last drop following puncture, which is usually 1 to 3 minutes.

Circulation time —See under 'c'.

Clot retraction time —The time taken by a blood clot to separate from the tube wall expressing serum, which is usually 18-24 hours.

Clotting time —Coagulation time.

Coagulation time —The time required for blood to coagulate.

Prothrombin time —The time consumed in plasma coagulation in the formation of thrombin from prothrombin.

Reaction time —The period between application of a stimulus and its response.

Setting time —The time taken by a material to become hard as dental amalgam, plaster, cement etc.

Timer —An apparatus for measuring or regulating time.

Tinct. —Tincture.

Tinctable —Stainable.

Tinction —1. The process of staining 2. A stain.

Tinctorial —Pertaining to staining or color.

Tinctura —Tincture.

Tincturation —The making of a tincture from an appropriate drug.

Tincture —An alcoholic solution prepared from an animal or vegetable drug or a chemical substance, *e.g.*, tincture of iodine.

Tine —A sharp, pointed prong.

Tinea —Rigworm. A fungus infection of the skin caused by various species of fungi belonging to the genera Trichophyton, Epidermophyton and Microsporum, occurring on various parts of the body. According to the part affected, it is of the following types.

Tinea barbae —Barber's itch. Fungus infection of the beard.

Tinea capitis —Fungus infection of the scalp.

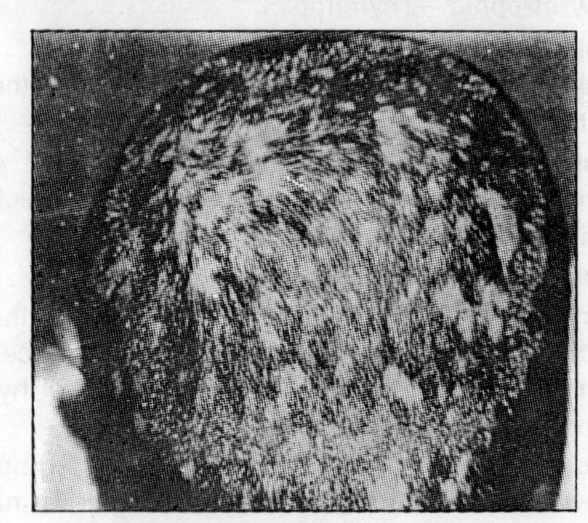

Fig. 568 : Tinea capitis

Tinea corporis —Ringworm of the body.

Tinea cruris —Dhobie itch. Fungus infection of the skin of contact, as of the scrotal or inguinal regions.

Tinea nigra —Pityriasis. Fungus infection of the skin of the palm.

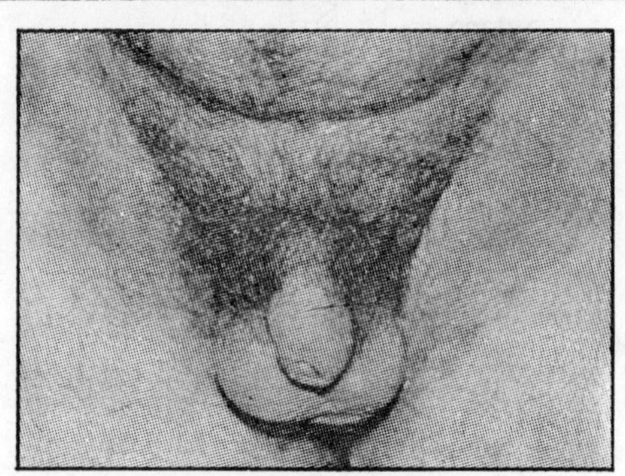

Fig. 569 : Tinea cruris (Dhobie itch)

Tinea pedis —Athlete's foot. Chronic fungus infection of skin of the foot.

Tinea unguium —Onychomycosis. Fungus disease of the nails.

Tingibility —The property of being stainable.

Tingible —Stainable.

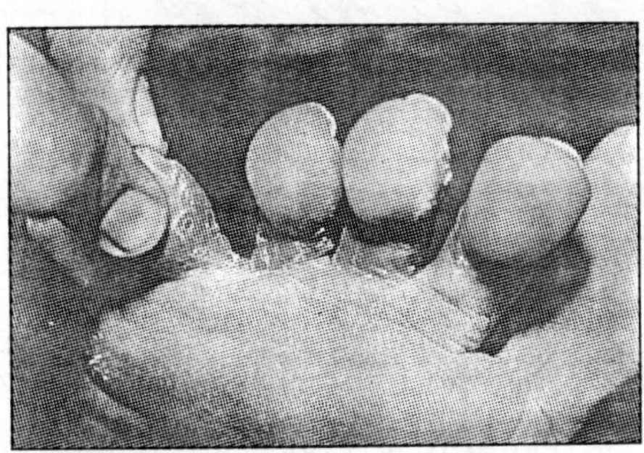
Fig. 570A : Tinea pedis (Athlete's foot)

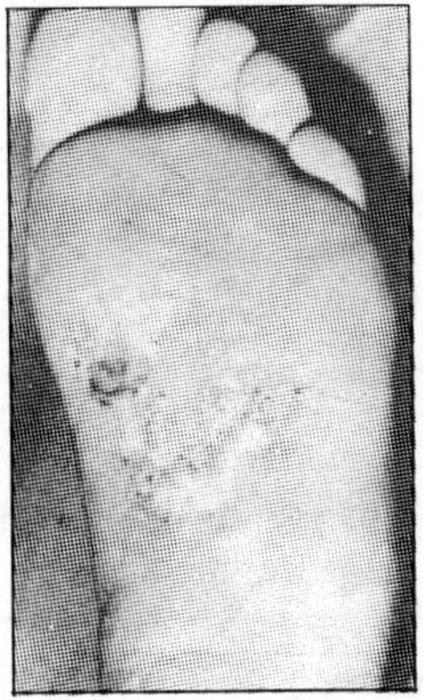
Fig. 570B : Tinea pedis involving sole

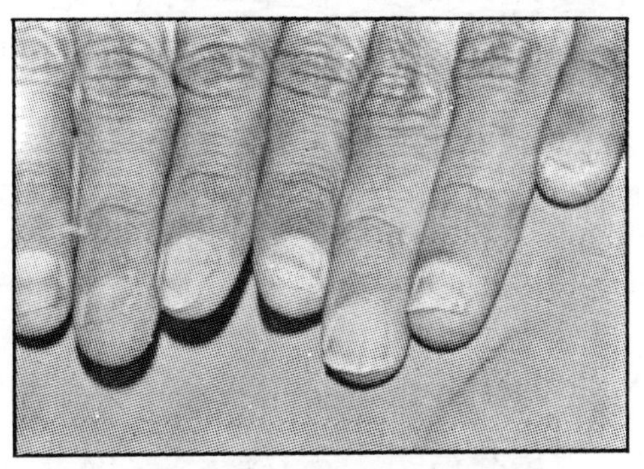
Fig. 571 : Tinea unguium

Tingle —A prickling or stinging sensation.

Tingling —Feeling of a prickling or stinging sensation.

Tinnitus —Ringing, buzzing or other sounds heard in the ear by the patient.

Tint —Light color.

Tintometer —A scale of different colors with which the color of blood or other fluid is compared to determine its intensity.

Tintometric —Pertaining to the determination of colors by comparison with a scale of colors.

Tintometry —Determination of color by comparison with a scale of colors.

Tip —An end or apex of a part.

Tipped uterus —Malposition of the uterus.

Tipping —Angulation of a tooth about its long axis.

Tiqueur —The person afflicted with a tic.

Tire —To become fatigued.

Tirefond —An instrument like a corkscrew for raising the depressed portions of bone or for removing the foreign body.

Tires —The condition characterized by constipation, vomiting, muscular tremors and pain.

Tiring —Wiring about the fragments of a bone.

Tissue —A group of similar cells which together perform a particular function.

Adenoid tissue —Lymphoid tissue.

Adipose tissue —Fatty tissue.

Areolar tissue —Loose connective tissue made up of interlacing fibers.

Bony tissue —Bone.

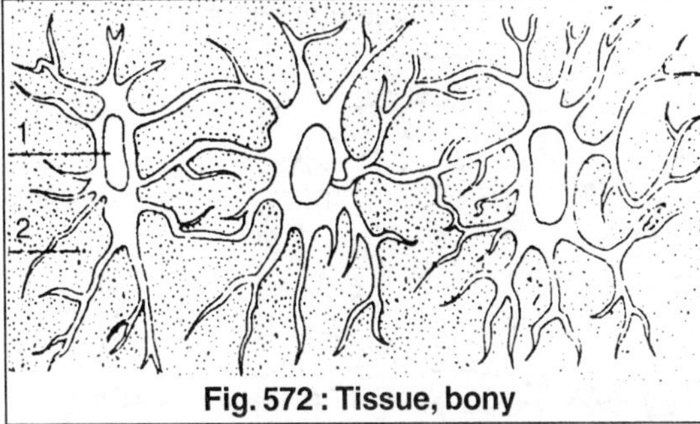

Fig. 572 : Tissue, bony

1. Bone cells or osteocytes. 2. Intercellular substance

Cancellous tissue —Spongy tissue of bone.

Cartilaginous tissue —The substance of cartilage.

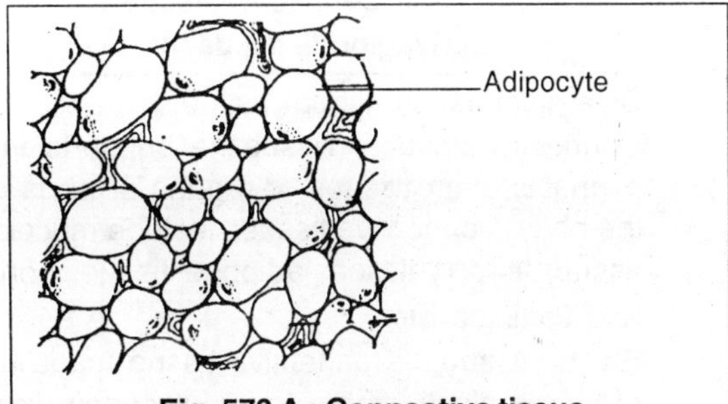

Fig. 573 A : Connective tissue Adipose tissue

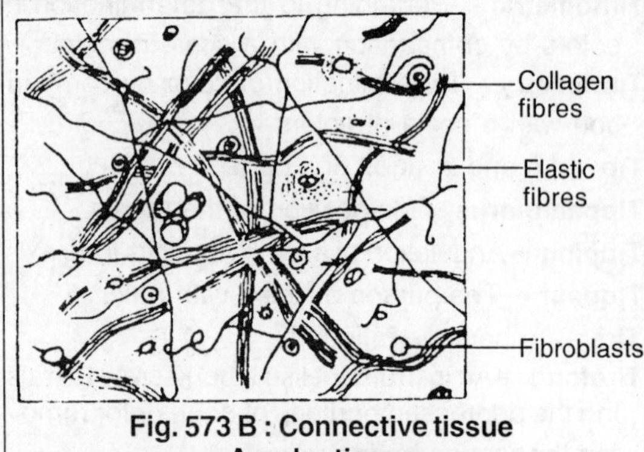

Fig. 573 B : Connective tissue Areolar tissue

Elastic fibres
Cells

Fig. 573 C I : Connective tissue Cartilaginous tissue

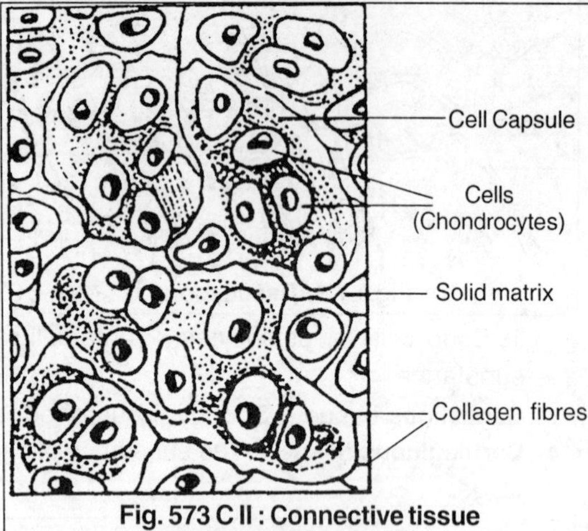

Fig. 573 C II : Connective tissue Cartilaginous tissue

Cicatricial tissue —Scar tissue.

Connective tissue —Tissue that supports and connects other tissues or organs or parts of the body. Connective tissues include mucous tissue, fibrous tissue, adipose tissue, bone and cartilage etc.

Elastic tissue —Connective tissue made up of yellow elastic fibers found in certain ligaments etc.

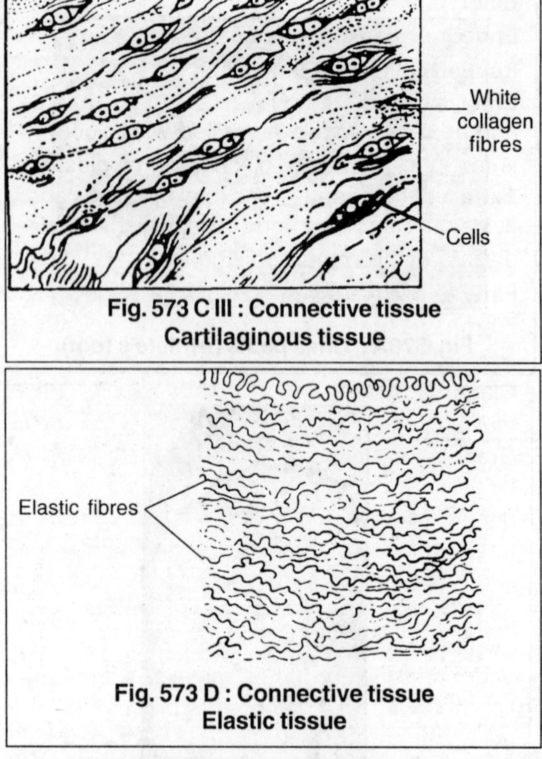

Fig. 573 C III : Connective tissue Cartilaginous tissue

Fig. 573 D : Connective tissue Elastic tissue

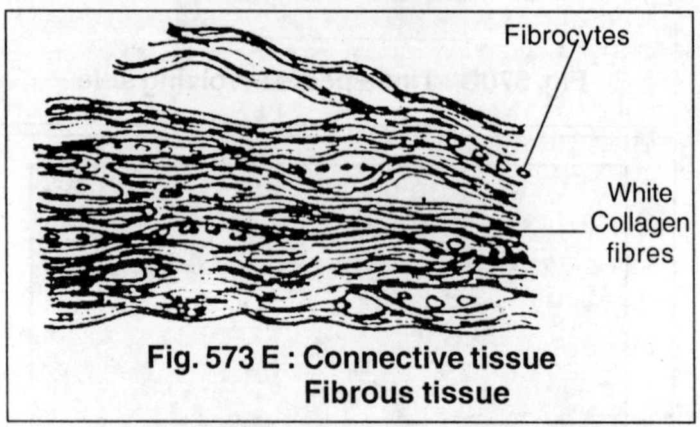

Fig. 573 E : Connective tissue Fibrous tissue

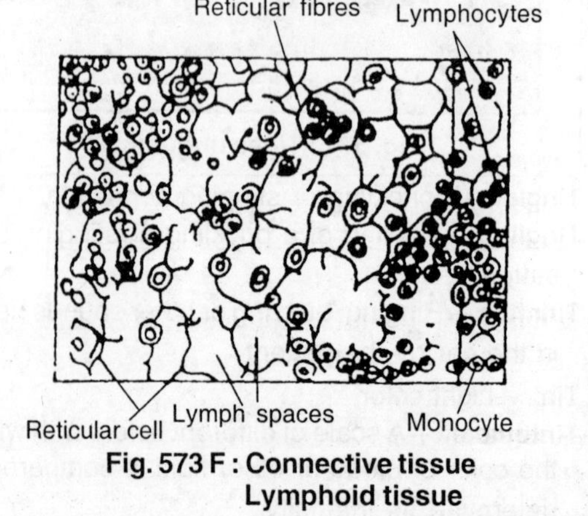

Fig. 573 F : Connective tissue Lymphoid tissue

Embryonic tissue —Mucous tissue.

Endothelial tissue —Endothelium.

Epithelial tissue —Epithelium.

Erectile tissue —Spongy tissue that expands and becomes hard when filled with blood. It is found in the penis, clitoris and nipples.

Extracellular tissue —The total of tissues and fluids outside of the body cells, which include plasma, lymph and cartilage etc.

Fatty tissue —Tissue consisting of body fat.

Fibrous tissue —The common connective tissue of the body, composed mainly of fibers.

Glandular tissue —A group of epithelial cells that produces secretions.

Granulation tissue —A newly formed vascular tissue produced in healing of wounds and becoming cicatricial tissue.

Interstitial tissue —Network of connective tissue between the cellular elements of an organ.

Lymphoid tissue —A collection of developing and mature lymphocytes mingled with a lattice of connective tissue. It is present in the adenoids and tonsils etc.

Mucous tissue —Embryonic tissue. A jelly-like connective tissue, as occurs in the umbilical cord.

Muscular tissue —The substance of the muscle.

Nerve tissue, Nervous tissue —All of the tissue of the central and peripheral nervous system.

Osseous tissue —The specialized tissue forming the bone.

Reticular tissue —Connective tissue consisting of reticular cells and fibers.

Scar tissue —Cicatricial tissue. A thick fibrous tissue formed on a healed wound.

Sclerous tissue —Firm connective tissue such as bone and cartilage.

Skeletal tissue —Bones and cartilages.

Subcutaneous tissue —The layer of areolar tissue lying under the skin.

Tissue factor —Coagulation factor III.

Tissue-trimming —The molding of tissue border.

Tissular —Pertaining to living tissues.

Titer —The quantity of a substance required to react with or to correspond to a given amount of another substance.

Titillation —A pleasant feeling.

Titrant —In chemistry, a solution which is added in titration.

Titrate —To determine by titration.

Titration —Determination of a given component in solution by adding a liquid reagent of known strength until the component has been consumed by reaction with the reagent, which is indicated by change in color of the solution.

Titre —Titer.

Titrimetric —Pertaining to titrimetry.

Titrimetry —Analysis by titration.

Titubation —A staggering gait, seen in diseases of the cerebellum.

Toadskin —A condition characterized by excessive dryness, wrinkling and scaling of the skin.

Tobaccoism —Nicotinism. Tobacco poisoning.

Toco- —A prefix indicating relationship to the childbirth.

Tocodynagraph —An apparatus for measuring the intensity of uterine contractions.

Tocodynamography—The recording of the intensity of uterine contractions.

Tocodynamometer —Tocometer.

Tocograph —Tocodynagraph.

Tocography —Tocodynamography.

Tocology —Obstetrics.

Tocolysis —Inhibition of uterine contractions.

Tocolytic —Inhibitor of uterine contractions.

Tocometer —Tocodynamometer. An instrument for measuring and recording the force of contractions of the uterus during labor.

Tocopheral —Vitamin E.

Tocophobia —Morbid fear of childbirth.

Tocus —Parturition. Childbirth.

Toe —A digit of the foot.

Toe clonus —Contraction of the big toe caused by sudden extension of the first phalanx.

Toe drop —Inability to lift the toes.

Toenail —Unguis.

Toe reflex —A condition in which strong flexion of the great toe flexes all the muscles below the knee.

Toilet —1. The cleansing and dressing of a wound. 2. A receptacle for use during defecation and urination to collect and dispose of these waste products.

Toilet training —To train the child to control urination and defecation until she is placed on a toilet.

Toko- —Toco-

Tokodynagraph —Tocodynagraph.

Tolerance —The ability to endure without any adverse effect, *e.g.*, glucose tolerance, *i.e.* the ability of the body to absorb and utilize glucose, or exercise tolerance, *i.e.* the amount of physical exercise that can be done without tiredness.

Tolerant —Capable of enduring drugs without experiencing ill effects.

Tolerize —To induce tolerance.

Tolerogen —That which causes the body unable to react to an antigen, by forming an antibody.

Tolerogenesis —Production of immunologic tolerance.

Tolerogenic —Producing immunological tolerance.

Tollwut —Rabies.

-tome —A suffix which means cutting or cutting instrument.

Tomo- —A prefix denoting a section or layer.

Tomogram —An X-ray picture of a tissue section by tomography.

Tomograph —A special X-ray apparatus by which the X-ray picture of a particular depth of an organ is taken.

Tomography —Obtaining of the X-ray picture by tomograph of a tissue section or of particular depth of a tissue or of an organ.

Tomomania —Mania of a surgeon for performing unnecessary operations.

-tomy —A suffix which means a cutting or an incision.

Tonaphasia —Inability to remember a tune due to cerebral lesion.

Tone —1. The tension or resistance of a muscle or vessel against an elongation or stretch. 2. The healthy state of the body or any of its organs or parts. 3. Musical or vocal sound.

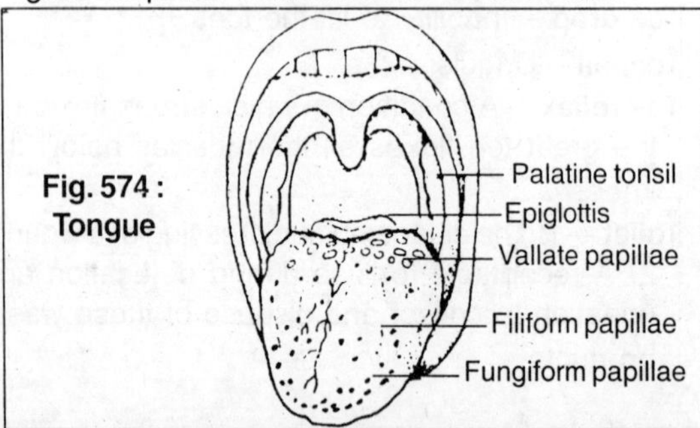

Fig. 574 : Tongue

Tone deafness —Amusia.

Toner —A solution used in toning.

Tongue —The freely movable muscular organ on the floor of mouth, which is the chief organ of taste and aids in mastication and swallowing of food, and in speech.

Bifid tongue —Tongue with lengthwise cleft at its anterior end.

Black hairy tongue —The presence of a brown furlike patch on the dorsum of tongue.

Burning tongue —Glossodynia.

Cleft tongue —Bifid tongue.

Coated tongue —The tongue covered with a whitish or yellowish layer consisting of desquamated epithelium, food debris, bacteria or fungi etc.

Deviation of tongue —Turning of the tongue from the midline when protruded.

Dotted tongue —Stippled tongue.

Dry tongue —Dry and shriveled tongue, usually indicative of dehydration.

Fissured tongue —Tongue with numerous deep furrows or grooves on its dorsal surface.

Furred tongue —Tongue coated with white fur as seen in fevers.

Furrowed tongue —Fissured tongue.

Geographical tongue —The tongue possessing white raised patches surrounding a red area, resembling a geographical map.

Hairy tongue —Tongue with the papillae elongated and hairlike.

Magenta tongue —Magenta-colored tongue seen in riboflavin deficiency.

Scrotal tongue —Fissured tongue resembling the skin of scrotum.

Smoker's tongue —Leukoplakia.

Smooth tongue —Condition of tongue resulting from atrophy of papillae, found in anemia and malnutrition.

Stippled tongue —Dotted tongue.

Tremulous tongue —Tremulousness of the tongue occurring in hyperthyroidism.

Trifid tongue —A tongue in which the anterior end is divided into three parts.

Trombone tongue —Rapid involuntary protrusion and retraction of the tongue.

Tongue-swallowing —The slipping back of the relaxed tongue into the pharynx, in an unconscious person lying on the back.

Tongue-tie —Ankyloglossia.

Tonic —1. Pertaining to or characterized by tension, especially muscular tension. 2. Restoring normal tone. 3. A medicine that increases strength and tone.

Tonicity —1. Property of possessing tone, especially muscular tone. 2. The state of tissue tone or tension.

Tonicoclonic —Tonoclonic.

Tonic spasm —A persistent, involuntary muscular firm contraction.

Tonitrophobia —Brontophobia.

Tono- —A prefix which means tone or tension.

Tonoclonic —Both tonic and clonic, said of muscular spasms.

Tonofibril —Tenofibril. A bundle of fine filaments (tonofilaments) present in the cytoplasm of certain cells, especially epithelial cells.

Tonofilament —A filament of a tonofibril.

Tonogram —The record produced by tonography.

Tonograph —A recording tonometer.

Tonography —The recording of changes in intraocular pressure.

Tonometer —An instrument for measuring tension or pressure, especially intraocular pressure.

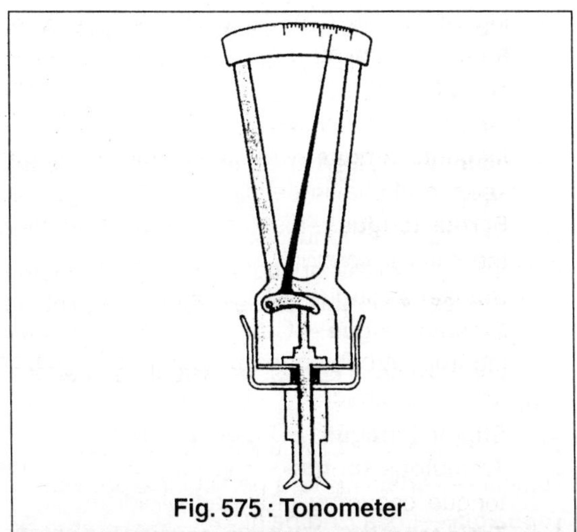

Fig. 575 : Tonometer

Tonometry —The measurement of tension or pressure of a part, as intraocular pressure.

Tonophant —An instrument for visualizing sound waves.

Tonoplast —The membrane surrounding an intracellular vacuole.

Tonoscillograph —An instrument producing graphic records of arterial and capillary pressures.

Tonoscope —1. An apparatus for examining the brain by means of sound. 2. An apparatus for producing sound visible by registering the vibrations on a screen.

Tonotropic —Denoting the shortening of the resting length of a muscle.

Tonsil —A mass of lymphoid tissue.

Cerebellar tonsil —A rounded mass of lymphoid tissue on the inferior surface of the cerebellum.

Faucial tonsil —Palatine tonsil.

Lingual tonsil —A mass of lymphoid tissue situated at the root of the tongue.

Luschka's tonsil —Pharyngeal tonsil.

Nasal tonsil —A mass of lymphoid tissue on the nasal septum.

Palatine tonsil —A mass of lymphoid tissue situated between the pillars of fauces (tonsillar fossa) on either side of the pharynx.

Pharyngeal tonsil —The diffused lymphoid tissue on the roof of the posterior wall of the pharynx.

Tonsilla —Tonsil.

Tonsillae —Plural of tonsil.

Tonsillar —Pertaining to a tonsil.

Tonsillar crypt —A deep indentation into the pharyngeal surface of a tonsil.

Tonsillary —Pertaining to a tonsil.

Tonsillectomy —Surgical removal of a tonsil.

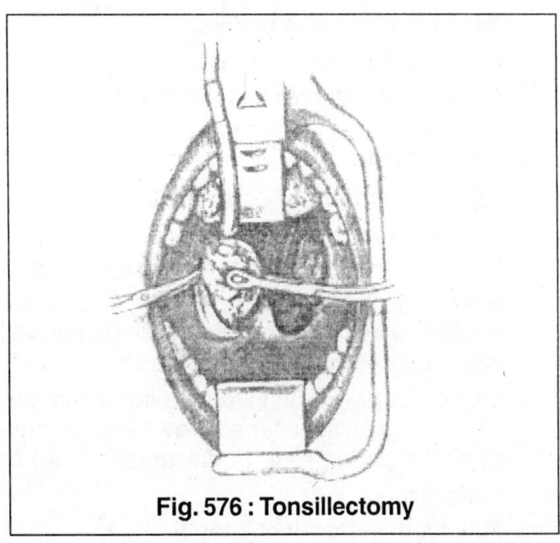

Fig. 576 : Tonsillectomy

Tonsillith —Tonsillolith.

Tonsillitis —Inflammation of a tonsil, especially the palatine tonsil.

Tonsilloadenoidectomy —Excision of the tonsils and adenoids of the pharynx.

Tonsillolith —A calculus in a tonsil.

Tonsillopathy —Any disease of the tonsil.

Tonsilloscopy —Inspection of the tonsils.

Tonsillotome —An instrument used for excision of a tonsil.

Tonsillotomy —Incision of a tonsil.

Tonus —Tone or tonicity.

Tooth —One of the small, bonelike structures for biting and mastication of food, projecting from each jaw.

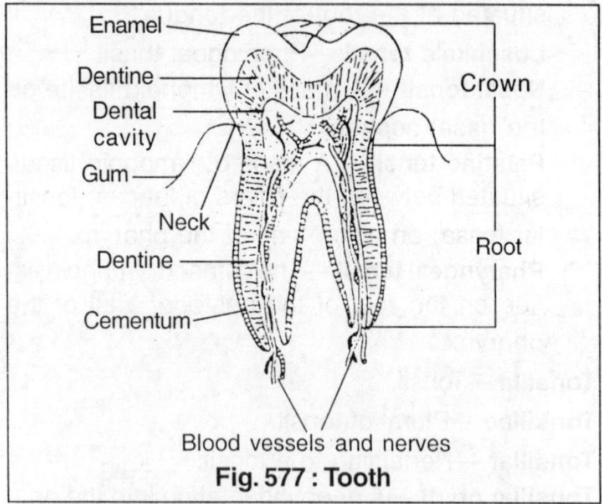

Fig. 577 : Tooth

Accessional tooth —The third molar tooth.

Anatomic tooth —Artificial tooth which is duplicate of a natural tooth.

Bicuspid tooth —Premolar tooth.

Canine tooth —See under 'c'.

Cheek tooth —Molar tooth.

Cuspid tooth, Cuspidate tooth —Canine tooth.

Cutting tooth —The maxillary and mandibular anterior teeth.

Deciduous tooth —See under 'D'.

Hutchinson's tooth —See under 'H'.

Impacted tooth —A tooth which is unable to erupt.

Implanted tooth —An artificial tooth implanted permanently into the jaw.

Incisor tooth —Cutting tooth. One of the four teeth with a chisel-shaped crown and a single conical tapering root, in the anterior part of each jaw.

Milk tooth —Deciduous tooth.

Molar tooth —Grinding teeth. There are six molar teeth in each jaw, three on either side behind the premolar teeth in permanent dentition but four molar teeth in deciduous dentition, two on either side behind the canine teeth. Each molar tooth having a somewhat quadrangular crown with four or five cusps on the grinding surface. The root is bifid in the lower jaw but trifid in the upper jaw.

Permanent tooth —One of 32 teeth which begin to erupt from fifth to seventh year and completed till the 17th to 23rd year, the last of the 3rd molars appears in the last.

Premolar tooth —There are four premolar teeth with two cuspid crowns, two on either side between the canine and molar teeth, in permanent dentition only.

Primary tooth —Deciduous tooth.

Temporary tooth —Deciduous tooth.

Tricuspid tooth —A tooth having a crown with three cusps.

Toothache —Odontalgia, odontodynia. Pain in a tooth.

Top-, Topo- —Prefixes which mean place.

Topagnosis —Inability to localize the site of sensation of touch.

Topalgia —Localized pain.

Topectomy —Excision of a small and specific area of the frontal cortex of brain in the treatment of certain mental diseases.

Topesthesia —Topognosia, Topognosis.

Tophaceous —1. Pertaining to a tophus. 2. Sandy or gritty.

Tophi —Plural of tophus.

Tophus —A deposit of sodium urate in the cartilage of ear or in the tissues about the joints in gout.

Tophyperidrosis —Excessive sweating in a local area.

Topica —Remedies for local external use.

Topical —Pertaining to a particular area; local.

Topoalgia —Localized pain.

Topoanesthesia —Inability to recognize the location of the sensation of touch.

Topochemistry —The chemical composition at specific sites of a structure as at the surface membrane of a cell.

Topognosia, Topognosis —Topesthesia. Ability to recognize the location of sensation of touch.

Topographic —Pertaining to description of special regions.

Topography —Description of a part of the body.

Topology —1. The study of all the structures and their relationships in a given region. 2. In obstetrics, the relationship of the presenting part of the fetus to the outlet of the pelvis.

Toponarcosis —Local anesthesia.

Toponeurosis —Neurosis of a localized area.

Toponym —The name of a region.

Toponymy —Nomenclature of the regions of the body.

Topophobia —Morbid fear of a particular region of the body.

Topothermesthesiometer —An apparatus for measuring local temperature sense.

Torcular herophili —The union of the sinuses.

Toric —Pertaining to a torus.

Tormina —Severe gripping pains in the bowels.

Torminal —Affected with tormina.

Torminous —Torminal.

Torose, Torous —Knobby or bulging.

Torpent —Inactive; dormant.

Torpid —Inactive; sluggish.

Torpidity —Inactivity; sluggishness.

Torpor —Abnormal inactivity; dormancy; numbness; apathy.

Torque —A force causing rotatory motion.

Torr —A pressure of 1 mm. of mercury under normal atmospheric temperature and pressure.

Torrefaction —Roasting or parching, especially a drug to dry it.

Torrefy —To roast or to parch.

Torsiometer —An instrument for measuring the rotation of eyeball around the visual axis, *i.e.* its anteroposterior axis.

Torsion —Act of twisting or the condition of being twisted at its axis.

Torsionometer —An apparatus for measuring the rotation of vertebral column around the long axis.

Torsive—Twisted.

Torsiversion —Rotation of a tooth around its long axis.

Torso —The trunk of the body.

Torsoclusion —1. Acupressure with twisting of a blood vessel to stop bleeding. 2. Malocclusion characterized by rotation of a tooth on its long axis.

Tort —A wrongful act or injury committed by one person against another person or his/her property, which may be intentional or unintentional.

Torticollar —Pertaining to torticollis.

Torticollis —Wryneck. Stiff neck with torsion caused by spasmodic contraction of the neck muscles.

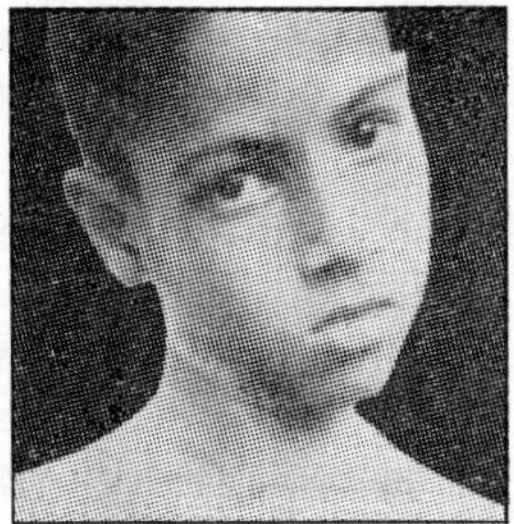

Fig. 578 : Torticollis

Congenital torticollis —Torticollis present at birth.

Dermatogenic torticollis —Torticollis with pain occurring due to skin lesions in the neck.

Hysterical torticollis—Torticollis due to hysteria.

Ocular torticollis —Torticollis from inequality in sight of the two eyes.

Rheumatic torticollis —Stiffness of the neck in rheumatism.

Tortipelvis —Muscular spasms distorting the vertebral column and hip.

Tortuous —Twisted. Having many twists or turns.

Torture —To inflict mental or physical trouble.

Toruli —Plural of torulus.

Toruloid —Beaded.

Toruloma —A nodule of cryptococcosis.

Torulosis —Cryptococcosis.

Torulus —Papilla.

Torus —A bulging or elevation or swelling.

Totality —Completeness.

Totipotence —Totipotency.

Totipotency —The ability of a cell to develop into a large number of different tissues.

Totipotent —A cell capable of developing into a large number of different tissues, as a fertilized ovum.

Totipotential —Totipotent.

Touch —1. The sense by which contact of an object with the skin is recognized. 2. Palpation with the hand.

After touch —Persistence of the sensation of touch after the contact with stimulus has ceased.

Double touch —Vaginal and rectal examination made at the same time.

Tourniquet —A band to be bound tightly around a limb to arrest the circulation temporarily in distal area, to stop bleeding or to facilitate the intravenous injection or venipuncture.

Towelette —A small towel used in surgery or obstetrics.

Tox-, Toxi-, Toxo- —Prefixes meaning toxin or poison.

Toxanemia —Anemia due to a hemolytic toxin.

Toxemia —1. The condition caused by the spread of bacterial toxins throughout the body, by bloodstream. 2. A condition resulting from metabolic disturbances, *e.g.*, toxemia of pregancy.

Toxemic —Causing blood poisoning (toxemia).

Toxenzyme —A poisonous enzyme.

Toxic —Poisonous. Pertaining to or caused by poison.

Toxicant—1. Any poison. 2. Poisonous.

Toxicemic —Toxemic.

Toxicide —Destructive to toxins.

Toxicity —The quality or degree of being poisonous.

Toxico- —A prefix which means poisonous.

Toxicoderma —Any skin disease resulting from a poison.

Toxicodermatitis —Inflammation of the skin due to a poison.

Toxicodermatosis —Toxicoderma.

Toxicogenic —Caused by, or producing, a poison.

Toxicoid —Like a poison.

Toxicologic —Pertaining to toxicology.

Toxicologist —A specialist in toxicology.

Toxicology —The science of poisons.

Toxicomania—Intense desire for poisons or narcotics.

Toxicopathic —Pertaining to any disease caused by a poison.

Toxicopathy —Any disease caused by a poison.

Toxicopexis —The fixation or neutralization of a poison in the body.

Toxicopexy —Toxicopexis.

Toxicophidia —Thanatophidia.

Toxicophobia —Morbid fear of being poisoned.

Toxicosis —Any diseased condition resulting from poisoning.

Endogenic toxicosis —Autointoxication. Disease caused by a poison produced within the body.

Exogenic toxicosis —Disease caused by a poison not produced in the body.

Retention toxicosis —Any toxic condition caused by substances formed in the body that normally are excreted.

Toxidermitis —Toxicoderma.

Toxiferous —Containing, producing or conveying a poison.

Toxigenic —Producing toxins or poisons.

Toxigenicity —The property of producing toxins.

Toxigenous —Toxigenic.

Toxignomic —Having the toxic action peculiar to a poison.

Toxin —A poisonous substance which is a form of protein, produced by some plants, animals, and pathogenic bacteria.

Bacterial toxins —Toxins produced by bacteria including exotoxins, endotoxins and toxic enzymes.

Botulinal toxin, Botulinum toxin —Toxin produced by Clostridium botulinum, the causative organism for botulism.

Dermonecrotic toxin —Toxin that causes necrosis of the skin.

Dick toxin —Any erythrogenic toxin produced by some streptococci.

Diphtheria toxin —The specific toxin produced by Corynebacterium diphtheriae.

Erythrogenic toxin —Dick toxin.

Extracellular toxin —Exotoxin.

Fatigue toxin —A toxin present in the body due to muscular fatigue.

Intracellular toxin —Endotoxin.

Plant toxin —Phytotoxin.

Tetanus toxin —An exotoxin produced by Clostridium tetani.

Toxin-antitoxin —A nearly neutral mixture of diphtheria toxin with its antitoxin, which is used for immunization against diphtheria.

Toxinic —Pertaining to a toxin.

Toxinicide —Destructive to the toxins.

Toxinogenic —Toxigenic.

Toxinogenicity —Toxigenicity.

Toxinology —The branch of science concerned with the toxins.

Toxinosis —Any disease caused by a toxin.

Toxipathic —Concerning toxicosis.

Toxipathy —Toxicosis. Any disease caused by a toxin.

Toxiphobia —Toxicophobia.

Toxisterol —A toxic substance formed by excessive irradiation of ergosterol or calciferol.

Toxitabellae —Poisonous tablets.

Toxitherapy —Treatment of diseases by use of toxins.

Toxituberculid —A skin lesion resulting from the action of a toxin produced by Mycobacterium tuberculosis.

Toxoalexin —An alexin that counteracts bacterial toxins.

Toxoid —Anatoxin. A toxin of which toxicity has been destroyed by use of heat or a chemical agent but its ability of inducing formation of antibodies on injection is not destroyed, *e.g.*, diphtheria toxoid or tetanus toxoid, etc.

Toxolysin —Toxicide. Antitoxin.

Toxonosis —Toxicosis.

Toxophil, Toxophile —Specially attracted toward toxins.

Toxophilic —Concerning a toxophile. Easily susceptible to a toxin.

Toxophore —A portion of a toxin which produces the toxic effect.

Toxophorous —Pertaining to a toxophore.

Toxophylaxin —A substance that neutralizes bacterial toxins.

t. p. r. —Temperature, pulse, respiration.

Trabecula —A fibrous band of connective tissue extending from the wall or capsule of an organ into its subtance.

Trabeculae —Plural of trabecula.

Trabeculae carneae cordis —Thick muscular bands attached to the inner walls of the ventricles of heart.

Trabecular —Pertaining to a trabecula.

Trabecularism —Condition of having a trabecula.

Trabeculate —Having trabeculae.

Trabeculation —1. The occurrence of trabeculae in the walls of an organ. 2. The process of forming trabeculae.

Trabeculectomy —The creation of a fistula between the anterior chamber of the eye and the subconjunctival space, through excision of some trabeculae under the sclera, in the treatment of glaucoma.

Trabeculoplasty —Photocoagulation of the trabeculae of the eye by using laser, to allow the escape of aqueous humor in the treatment of glaucoma.

Trabs —A supporting band, *e.g.*, corpus callosum which is the arched band of white fibers connecting the cerebral hemispheres.

Trace —1. A very small quantity. 2. A visible mark.

Tracer —1. One who traces. 2. An instrument for tracing. 3. An apparatus for recording graphically the outline or movements of an object. 4. A substance by which the progress of a compound through the body may be observed.

Trachea —Windpipe. The cartilaginous tube linned with mucous membrane descending from the larynx at the level of 6th cervical vertebra and dividing into two main branches, right and left bronchus at the level of 5th dorsal vertebra.

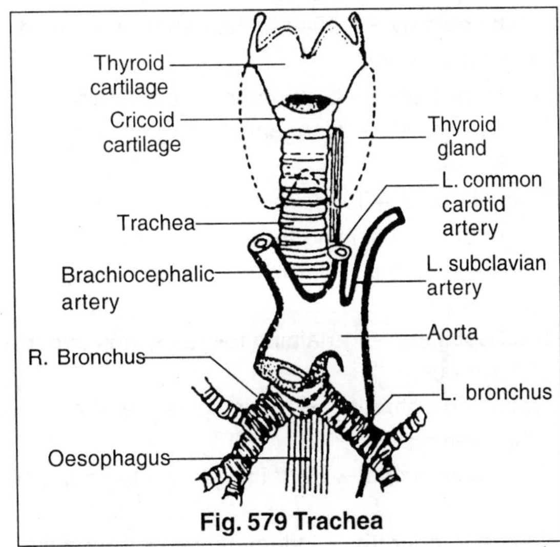

Fig. 579 Trachea

Tracheaectasy —Dilatation of the trachea.

Tracheal —Pertaining to the trachea.

Trachealgia —Pain in the trachea.

Tracheitis —Inflammation of the trachea.

Trachelagra —Rheumatism of muscles of the neck resulting in torticollis.

Trachelectomy —Cervicectomy. Excision of the cervix of uterus.

Trachelematoma —A hematoma located on the neck.

Trachelism, Trachelismus —Backward spasm of the neck.

Trachelitis —Cervicitis.

Trachelo- —A prefix which means neck.

Trachelocele —Tracheocele.

Trachelocyrtosis —Trachelokyphosis.

Trachelocystitis —Inflammation of the neck of the bladder.

Trachelodynia —Pain in the neck.

Trachelokyphosis —Excessive anterior curvature of the cervical portion of the vertebral column.

Trachelology —Scientific study of the neck and its diseases.

Trachelomastoid —A muscle of the neck.

Trachelomyitis —Inflammation of muscles of the neck.

Trachelopanus —1. Swelling of the lymphatic vessels of the neck. 2. Engorgement of the lymphatic vessels of the cervix of the uterus.

Trachelopexia —Trachelopexy.

Trachelopexy —Fixation of the cervix of uterus to the adjacent structures.

Tracheloplasty —Repair of the cervix of uterus by plastic surgery.

Trachelorrhaphy —Suturing of a torn cervix uteri.

Tracheloschisis —Congenital opening or fissure in the neck.

Trachelotomy —To incise the uterine cervix.

Tracheo- —Combining form meaning trachea.

Tracheoaerocele —Hernia or cyst of trachea containing air.

Tracheobiliary —Pertaining to the trachea and the biliary duct.

Trachelobregmatic —Pertaining to the neck and the bregma.

Tracheobronchial —Pertaining to the trachea and bronchi.

Tracheobronchitis —Inflammation of the trachea and bronchi.

Tracheobronchomegaly —Widening of the trachea and main bronchi, usually congenitally.

Tracheobronchoscopy —Inspection of the interior of the trachea and bronchi through a bronchoscope.

Tracheocele —Herniation of the mucous membrane of the trachea.

Tracheoesophageal —Pertaining to the trachea and esophagus.

Tracheolaryngeal —Pertaining to the trachea and larynx.

Tracheolaryngotomy —To make an incision into the larynx and trachea.

Tracheomalacia —Softening of the cartilages of trachea.

Tracheomegaly —An abnormally dilated trachea.

Tracheopathia, Tracheopathy —Any disease of the trachea.

Tracheopharyngeal —Pertaining to the trachea and pharynx.

Tracheophonesis —Auscultation of the heart sounds at the sternal notch.

Tracheophony —Sound heard in auscultation over the trachea.

Tracheoplasty —Repair of the trachea by plastic surgery.

Tracheopyosis —Tracheitis with pus formation.

Tracheorrhagia —Hemorrhage from the trachea.

Tracheoschisis —Fissure of the trachea.

Tracheoscope —An instrument used in tracheoscopy.

Tracheoscopic —Pertaining to tracheoscopy.

Tracheoscopy —Inspection of the interior of trachea.

Tracheostenosis —Narrowing of the trachea.

Tracheostoma —Opening into the trachea, through the neck.

Tracheostomize —To perform a tracheostomy.

Tracheostomy —To make an opening into the trachea through the neck.

Tracheotome —An instrument used for incising the trachea.

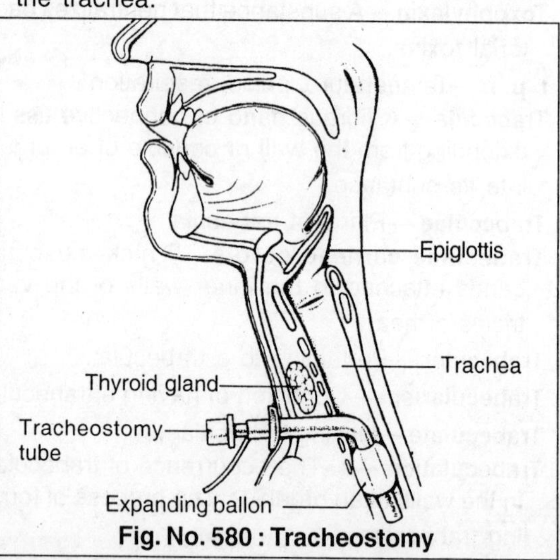

Fig. No. 580 : Tracheostomy

Tracheotomy —Incision of the trachea through the skin and muscles of the neck overlying it.

Trachitis —Tracheitis.

Trachoma —A form of chronic contagious conjunctivitis, caused by a strain of Chlamydia trachomatis, with the formation of follicles on the eyelid conjunctiva. The condition is characterized by photophobia, pain and lacrimation etc.

Trachomatous —Pertaining to or having trachoma.

Trachychromatic —Pertaining to a nucleus with very deeply staining chromatin.

Trachyonychia —Rough-surfaced nails.

Trachyphonia —Roughness or hoarseness of the voice.

Tracing —A graphic record of some activity such as respiratory movements, heart beat or electrical activity of the brain.

Tract —1. A pathway. 2. A longitudinal assemblage of tissues or organs having the same function.

Afferent tract —White fibers in the spinal cord carrying nerve impulses toward the brain.

Alimentary tract —Digestive tract. The canal from the mouth to the anus.

Efferent tract —Fibers in the spinal cord that carry nerve impulses from the brain.

Respiratory tract —The respiratory organs in continuity form the nose to the pulmonary alveoli.

Urinary tract —The passage from kidney to the outside of the body, which includes the pelvis of the kidney, ureter, bladder and urethra.

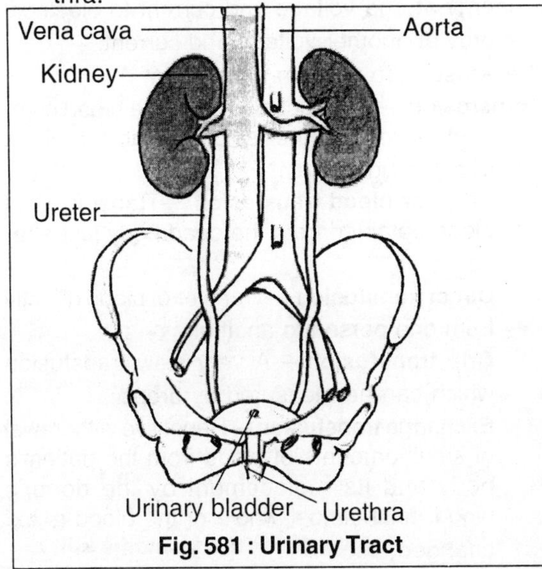

Fig. 581 : Urinary Tract

Tractella —Plural of tractellum.

Tractellum —An anterior locomotor flagellum of a protozoon.

Traction —The act of drawing or pulling.

Axis traction —Traction in line with the long axis, as of the pelvis through which a fetus is to be drawn.

Bryant traction —Traction applied upon the lower limbs placed vertically, in fractures of the femur in children.

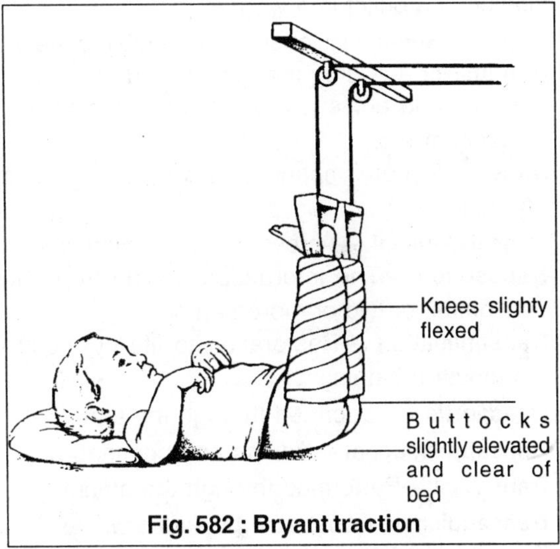

Fig. 582 : Bryant traction

Cervical traction —Traction applied to the cervical spine by applying a force to lift the head.

Elastic traction —Traction exerted by elastic agents such as rubber bands.

External traction —Traction applied to any fracture.

Intermittent traction —Traction applied intermittently.

Skeletal traction —Traction exerted directly upon the long bones by means of wires, etc.

Weight traction —Traction exerted by means of weight.

Tractor —An apparatus for applying traction.

Tractotomy —Surgical section of a nerve tract in the central nervous system.

Tractus —A tract.

Tragal —Pertaining to the tragus.

Tragi —Plural of tragus.

Tragion —A point at the upper margin of the tragus of the ear.

Tragomaschalia —Odorous sweating from the axilla.

Tragophonia, Tragophony —Egophony.

Tragopodia —Knock-knee.

Tragus —Antilobium. Cartilaginous projection in front of the external opening of the ear.

Trainable —A mentally retarded person who is capable to be trained.

Trait —Any characteristic peculiar to an individual.

Trajector —An instrument for determining the location of a bullet in a wound.

Trance —Semiconsciousness resembling sleep.

Tranquilizer —A drug that acts to reduce mental tension and anxiety, *e.g.*, chlorpromazine and diazepam etc.

Trans- —A prefix meaning across, beyond and through.

Transabdominal —Across the abdominal wall.

Transaction —The interaction arising from the encounter of two or more persons.

Transanimation —Restoration to life by mouth-to-mouth breathing.

Transaortic —Performed through the aorta.

Transappendageal —Across an appendage.

Transatrial —Performed through the atrium.

Transaudient —Penetrable by sound waves.

Transaxial —Across the long axis of a structure or part.

Transbasal —Through the base of the skull.

Transbronchial —Across the bronchi.

Transcalent —Diathermal. Penetrable by heat rays.

Transcapillary —Across the endothelial wall of a capillary.

Transcatheter —Performed through the lumen of a catheter.

Transcervical —Performed through the mouth of the cervix uteri.

Transcondylar —Across the condyles.

Transcortical —Joining two parts of the cerebral cortex.

Transcutaneous —Percutaneous.

Transdermic —Percutaneous.

Transduce —To convert one form of energy to another.

Transducer —An apparatus for converting one form of energy to another as pressure or temperature to an electrical impulse.

Transductant —A cell that acquired a new character by means of transduction.

Transduction —The transfer of a genetic fragment from one bacterium to another by bacteriophage.

Transdural —Through or across the dura mater.

Transection —1. The cutting across a long axis. 2. A cross section.

Transepithelial —Occurring across or through an epithelium.

Transethmoidal —Across or through the ethmoid bone.

Transfer, Transference—The passage of a symptom from one part of the body to another.

Transferrin —A globulin in the blood serum that binds and transports iron.

Transfix —To pierce across with a sharp instrument.

Transfixation —The act of piercing across with a sharp instrument.

Transfixion —A cutting across from within outward as in amputation.

Transforation —Perforation of the fetal skull at the base.

Transforator —An instrument for perforating the fetal skull.

Transformant —A bacterium that has received genetic material from another bacterium by means of transformation.

Transformation —Metamorphosis. Change of form or structure.

Transformer —An apparatus to change electrical energy at one voltage and current to electrical energy at another voltage and current.

Transfuse —To perform transfusion.

Transfusion —Introduction of blood, a blood component, saline or other solution, into the blood stream through a vein.

Cadaver blood transfusion —Transfusion of blood obtained from the dead body just after death.

Direct transfusion —Transfer of blood directly from one person to another.

Drip transfusion —A very slow transfusion which can be measured by drops.

Exchange transfusion —Repetitive withdrawal of small amounts of blood from the patient's body and its replacement by the donor's blood, until almost whole of the blood is exchanged.

Indirect transfusion —In this method of transfusion blood from a donor is stored in a suitable container and then it is transfused to the patient.

Transgene —A newly introduced gene.

Transgenic —An organism into which genetic material from another organism has been introduced.

Transglottic —Vertical crossing of the glottis.

Transhiatal —By way of a hiatus.

Transient —Of short duration.

Transiliac —Extending between the two ilia.

Transilient —Jumping across or passing over.

Transillumination —Inspection of a cavity or organ by passing strong light through its wall from the opposite side.

Transilluminator —An instrument used in transillumination.

Transinsular —Across the insula of the brain.

Transischiac —Extending from one ischium to the other.

Transisthmian —Across an isthmus.

Transition —Passage from one condition or position to another, or from one part to another part.

Transitional —Pertaining to or marked by transition.

Translation —To convert into another form.

Translocation —The alteration of a chromosome either by transfer of a portion of it to another chromosome or by transfer to another portion of the same chromosome.

Translucent —Semi-transparent.

Translucid —Translucent.

Transmembrane —Through or across a membrane.

Transmigration —The wandering across or through, especially the passage of white blood cells through the walls of capillaries into the tissues.

Transmissible —Capable of being transferred, as an infectious disease.

Transmission —The transfer, as of a disease, from one person to another.

Transmitter —One who transmits.

Transmural —Spreading or involving the entire thickness of the wall of an organ or cavity.

Transmutation —1. Evolutionary change of one species into another. 2. The change of one chemical element into another.

Transnasal —Through the nose.

Transocular —Across the eye.

Transonance —Transmission of sounds through an organ, as of heart sounds through the lungs and chest wall.

Transorbital —Passing through the orbit.

Transparent —Transmitting light rays so that things at the back of the substance are visible.

Transparietal —Through the wall.

Transperitoneal —Across or through the peritoneum.

Transpirable —Capable to excrete through the skin or membranes, as perspiration.

Transpiration —The emission of water, gas or vapor through the skin or a membrane.

Transpire —To emit the vapor from the skin or respiratory tract.

Transplacental —Through the placenta.

Transplant —1. To transfer tissue or an organ from one part of the body to another as done in grafting and plastic surgery. 2. A tissue or organ used in transplantation.

Transplantar —Across the sole of the foot.

Transplantation —The grafting of living tissue or organ taken from one part of the body to another part, or to another person.

Allogeneic transplantation —Transplantation of a material from a donor to another person.

Autologous transplantation —Transplantation of a material from one place in the body to another place.

Autoplastic transplantation —Homoplastic transplantation. Transplantation of a tissue from one part to another part of the same body.

Bone marrow transplantation —See under 'B'

Corneal transplantation —Keratoplasty.

Heart-lung transplantation —Simultaneous transplantation of the heart and both the lungs.

Heterotopic transplantation —Transplantation in which the transplant is placed in a different place in the recipient than it had been in the donor.

Homoplastic transplantation —Autoplastic transplantation.

Homotopic transplantation —Transplantation in which the transplant is placed in the same place in the recipient as it had been in the donor.

Renal transplantation —Transplantation of a kidney from a donor to restore kidney function in a recipient suffering from renal failure.

Tooth transplantation —The transfer of a tooth from one alveolus to another.

Transpleural —Through the pleurae.

Transport —Movements of substances, especially of electrolytes, nutrients and liquids across the cell walls.

Transpose —To transfer one tissue or organ to another place.

Transposition —1. Exchange of position. 2. Displacement of a viscus to the opposite side. 3. Transplantation of flap of a tissue, without separating it completely from its original position until it is united at its new location.

Transpubic —Performed through the pubic bone.

Transsection —Transection.

Transsegmental —Extending across a segment.

Transseptal —Across a septum.

Transsexual —1. The person possessing intense desire to be of the opposite sex. 2. The person whose external sex has been changed to resemble that of the opposite sex.

Transsexualism —Intense desire to be of the opposite sex by getting changed one's external sex organs.

Transsphenoidal —Through or across the sphenoid bone.

Transsynaptic —The nerve impulses transmitting across a synapse.

Transtemporal —Crossing the temporal lobe of the cerebrum.

Transthalamic —Across the thalamus.

Transthermia —Production of heat in the deep tissues by electric current.

Transthoracic —Across the thorax.

Transthoracotomy —To make an incision across the thorax.

Transtympanic —Across the tympanic membrane or tympanic cavity.

Transubstantiation —The replacement of one tissue by another.

Transudate —A fluid substance that has passed through a membrane, especially through the capillary walls.

Transudation —Oozing of a fluid through a membrane, especially of the serum from capillary walls.

Transude —To ooze or to pass a liquid gradually through a membrane.

Transureteroureterostomy —Section of one ureter and joining its both ends to the opposite ureter.

Transurethral —Performed through the urethra.

Transvaginal —Through the vagina.

Transvector —An animal that transmits a toxin that it does not produce and by which it itself is not affected.

Transvenous —Through a vein.

Transversalis —A structure occurring at right angles to the long axis of the body.

Transverse —Situated at right angles to the long axis of the body.

Transversectomy —Excision of a transverse process of a vertebra.

Transversion —The eruption of a tooth at the site of another tooth.

Transversocostal —Costotransverse.

Transversus —Transverse. Lying across the long axis of a part or organ.

Transvesical —Through the bladder.

Transvestism, Transvestitism —To derive sexual pleasure from dressing in clothes of the opposite sex.

Transvestite —The person who derives sexual pleasure from dressing in clothes of the opposite sex.

Trapezial —Pertaining to the trapezium.

Trapeziform —Trapezoid-shaped.

Trapeziometacarpal —Concerning or connecting the trapezium and metacarpal bone of the thumb.

Trapezium —1. A four-sided figure in which none of the sides are parallel. 2. The first bone on radial side of the distal row of bones of the wrist, which articulates with the metacarpal bone of the thumb.

Trapezius —A flat, triangular muscle of the neck and shoulder.

Trapezoid —A four-sided figure in which only two sides are parallel.

Trap, food —A space in or between teeth where particles of food may become lodged.

Trauma —Physical or psychological injury.

Traumata —Plural of trauma.

Traumatic —Caused by or pertaining to an injury.

Traumatism —Morbid condition resulting from an injury or wound.

Traumatize —To cause trauma.

Traumato- —A prefix indicating a relationship to trauma.

Traumatology —The branch of surgery dealing with the injuries and wounds.

Traumatonesis —Repair of a wound by suturing.

Traumatopathy —Disease resulting from trauma.

Traumatophilia —To feel pleasure from trauma.

Traumatopnea —Passage of air in and out of a wound in the chest wall.

Traumatopyra —Fever resulting from a trauma.

Traumatosepsis —Occurrence of septicemia following a wound.

Traumatotherapy —Treatment of injury.

Travail —Childbirth.

Tray —A flattened vessel.

Treadmill —A drum-like apparatus on which the patient of heart disease walks on foot, used in the determination of cardiac insufficiency.

Treatise —An essay or a book.

Treat —To cure a disease by medicines, surgery or other measures.

Treatment —The combating of a disease or disorder.

Active treatment —Treatment directed specifically toward cure of a disease or injury.

Causal treatment —Treatment directed toward removal of the cause of disease.

Conservative treatment —The withholding of administration of medicines or performance of an operation until these are indicated.

Dental treatment —Treatment of the dental diseases.

Dietetic treatment —Treatment of the diseases by regulation of diet.

Electric shock treatment —Electroshock therapy.

Empiric treatment —Treatment of the diseases based on observation and experiences and not on a scientific basis.

Expectant treatment —Treatment for relief of symptoms as they arise, leaving cure of the disease to nature.

Light treatment —Phototherapy.

Medical treatment —Treatment of diseases by use of medicines.

Palliative treatment —Treatment for relief of symptoms rather than curing the disease.

Preventive treatment, Prophylactic treatment —Treatment directed for the prevention or prophylaxis of the disease.

Radiation treatment —Treatment of diseases by x-rays or ultraviolet rays etc.

Rational treatment —Treatment employed on scientific basis.

Shock treatment —Shock therapy.

Solar treatment —Treatment of diseases by exposure to sunlight.

Specific treatment —Treatment adapted specifically for removal of the disease.

Starvation treatment —Treatment of the diseases by fasting.

Supportive treatment —Treatment employed to supplement specific therapy.

Surgical treatment —Treatment of the disease by operation.

Symptomatic treatment —Expectant treatment.

Tree —A structure with branches resembling a tree, *e.g.,* bronchial tree (bronchi and their branches).

Trema —1. Foramen. 2. Vulva.

Trematoda —A class of the phylum Platyhelminthes (the flatworms).

Trematode —A parasitic flatworm of the class Trematoda.

Trematodiasis —Disease caused by a flatworm.

Trematoid —Trematode.

Tremble —To shiver.

Trembles —Milk sickness.

Trembling —Shivering.

Tremelloid, Tremellose —Jelly-like.

Tremogram —A graphic record of tremors made by a tremograph.

Tremograph —An apparatus for recording tremors.

Tremolabile —Easily destroyed or inactivated by shaking, said of a ferment.

Tremophobia —Morbid fear of trembling.

Tremor —An involuntary trembling.

Action tremor —Tremor of the hand while working as when writing or lifting a cup.

Alcoholic tremor —Tremor occurring in alcoholics.

Coarse tremor —Slow tremor.

Continuous tremor —Tremor occurring continuously.

Essential tremor —Tremor of the head and upper limbs, that usually begins in early adult life.

Familial tremor —Inherited tremor occurring in several members of a family.

Fibrillary tremor —Tremor caused by contractions of separate muscular fibrillae, rather than a muscle or muscles.

Fine tremor —A rapid tremor.

Flapping tremor —Asterixis.

Forced tremor —A tremor continuing after voluntary motion has ceased.

Head tremor —Head-nodding.

Hunt's tremor —A tremor occurring with every voluntary movement, present in cerebellar lesions.

Hysterical tremor —Fine tremor occurring in hysteria intermittently in one limb.

Intention tremor —Tremor occurring on attempting voluntary movement.

Persistent tremor —Continuous tremor. A tremor that is constant whether an individual is at rest or moving.

Physiological tremor —A tremor occurring in normal individuals which may be transient and associated with excessive physical exertion, excitement, hunger, fatigue or other causes.

Postural tremor —Tremor that occurs when the limbs or trunk are kept in certain positions.

Psychogenic tremor —Hysterical tremor.

Rest tremor —Tremor occurring when the involved part is at rest but diminished or absent when it becomes active, as in parkinsonism.

Senile tremor —A tremor occurring in old age.

Volitional tremor —Trembling of the limbs or body when doing some physical work, seen in multiple sclerosis and other nervous diseases.

Tremorgram —Tremogram.

Tremostable —That which is not altered or destroyed on shaking.

Tremulor —An apparatus for applying vibratory massage.

Tremulous —Trembling or shaking.

Tremulousness —The state of being tremulous.

Trench —A long narrow cut, a ditch.

Trench foot —A condition resembling frostbite involving the feet of soldiers who stand in cold water for long periods of time.

Trench mouth —Acute necrotizing ulcerative gingivitis.

Trend —The inclination.

Trendelenburg position —The position in which the patient's head is low and the body and legs are elevated.

Trepan —1. To perforate the skull. 2. Trephine. A saw for cutting the skull.

Trepanation —Trephination.

Trephination —Trephining def. (1)

Trephine —1. To perforate with a trephine. 2. Trepan. A cylindrical saw for removing circular piece of bone from the skull. 3. An instrument for removing a circular area of cornea.

Trephining —1. The process of cutting bone with a trephine. 2. The removal of a circular piece of cornea with a trephine.

Trephocyte —Trophocyte.

Trepidant —Trembling.

Trepidatio —Trepidation.

Trepidatio cordis —Palpitation.

Trepidation —1. A trembling. 2. Fear, anxiety.

Treponema —A genus of spirochetes, parasitic in man that belong to the family Treponemataceae. Treponema pallidum is the causative organism of syphilis.

Treponematosis —Infection with Treponema.

Treponeme —Any organism of the genus Treponema.

Treponemiasis —Infestation with Treponema.

Treponemicidal —Destroying Treponemas.

Trepopnea —Respiration with more comfort in a definite position.

Treppe —Staircase phenomenon. The gradual increase in muscular contraction, when the heart or a muscle is stimulated rapidly at regular intervals.

Tresis —Perforation.

T R H —Thyrotropin releasing hormone.

Tri- —A prefix meaning three.

Triad —1. A group of three associated things. 2. Trivalent.

Triage —The sorting out and classification of the

sick or injured persons during war or other disaster to determine priority of need of treatment.

Triakaidekaphobia —Triskaidekaphobia. Superstition about the number 13.

Triamelia —Absence of three limbs.

Triangularis —Triangular muscle of the chin.

Triangulum —Triangle.

Triatomic —Containing three atoms.

Tribade —Lesbian.

Tribadism —An attempt by the women to imitate heterosexual intercourse with each other.

Tribasic —Composed of three replaceable hydrogen atoms.

Tribasilar —Having three bases.

Tribasilar synostosis —Condition resulting from premature fusion of three bones—occipital, sphenoid and temporal, of the skull, which results in arrested cerebral development and mental deficiency.

Tribe —In animal classification a category below a family or subfamily and superior to a genus.

Tribology —The study of friction and its effects on the body, especially the articulating surfaces of bones in the joints.

Triboluminescence —Luminescence or sparks produced by mechanical energy as by grinding, rubbing or breaking of certain crystals.

Tribrachia —Condition of having three arms.

Tribrachius —A fetus with three arms.

Tributaries —Small branches which flow into the big ones.

Tricellular —Three-celled.

Tricephalus —A deformed fetus with three heads.

Triceps —Three-headed, as a triceps muscle.

Trichalgia —Trichodynia. Pain produced by touching or moving the hair.

Trichangia —The blood capillaries.

Trichangiectasia, Trichangiectasis —Telangiectasia. Dilatation of the capillaries.

Trichangion —Telangion.

Trichatrophia —Brittleness of the hair resulting from atrophy of the root.

Trichauxe, Trichauxis —Hypertrichosis.

Trichi-, Tricho- —Prefixes meaning hair.

-trichia —A suffix which means a condition or type of hair.

Trichiasis —1. Ingrowing of the eyelashes so that they rub against the cornea, causing irritation. 2. Appearance of hair-like filaments in the urine.

Trichilemmal —Pertaining to the outer root sheath of a hair.

Trichilemmoma —A benign tumor of the lower outer root sheath of the hair.

Trichion —The midpoint of the hair line at the top of the forehead.

Trichite —Trichocyst.

Trichitis —Inflammation of the hair bulbs.

Tricho- —A prefix indicating relationship to hair.

Trichoanesthesia —Loss of hair sensibility.

Trichobacteria —Bacteria possessing flagella or filaments.

Trichobezoar —A hair ball in the stomach or intestine.

Trichocardia —Inflammation of the pericardium with elevations resembling hair.

Trichoclasia, Trichoclasis—Trichorrhexis. Brittleness of the hair.

Trichocryptosis —Any disease of the hair follicles.

Trichocyst —A minute elongated cyst arranged around the periphery of a protozoon, containing a fluid which when discharged serves for offence or defence, found in ciliates.

Trichodynia —Trichalgia.

Trichodystrophy —Defective nutrition or growth of hair, often resulting in alopecia.

Trichoepithelioma —A benign tumor of the skin arising from the hair follicles.

Trichoesthesia —Sensation felt on touching hair.

Trichogen —An agent stimulating the growth of hair.

Trichogenous —Stimulating hair growth.

Trichoglossia —Hairy condition of the tongue.

Trichoid —Hairlike.

Trichokryptomania —Trichorrhexomania.

Tricholemmoma —Trichilemmoma.

Tricholeukocyte —A cell of the hair.

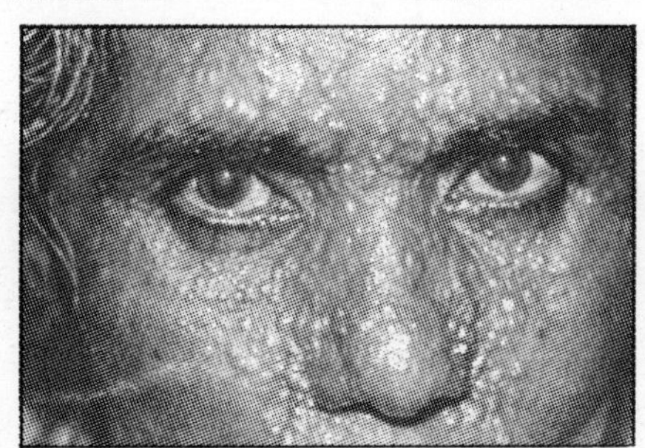

Fig. 583 : Trichoepithelioma

Tricholith —A hair ball in the intestine that has been calcified.

Trichologia —Trichotillomania.

Trichology —Study of the hair, its diseases and treatment.

Trichoma —1. Entropion.Inversion of one or more eyelashes. 2. Entangled matted hair in which crusts and small insects are embedded.

Trichomadesis —The falling out of the scalp hair.

Trichomatosis —Entangled matted hair due to fungus disease of the scalp and lack of cleanliness.

Trichomatous —Of the nature of or affected with trichoma.

Trichome —A hairlike structure.

Trichomegaly —Excessive growth of the eyelashes and brow hair.

Trichomonacide —Destructive to trichomonads.

Trichomonad —A parasite of the genus Trichomonas.

Trichomonal —Pertaining to Trichomonas.

Trichomonas —A genus of flagellate parasitic protozoa of which species Trichomonas vaginalis is found in the vagina that causes leucorrhea in women.

Trichomoniasis —Infestation with the organisms of genus Trichomonas.

Trichomycetosis —Trichomycosis.

Trichomycosis —Any disease of the hair caused by a fungus.

Trichonodosis —The formation of nodules on the hair shafts due to a fungus.

Trichonosis, Trichonosus —Any diseased condition of the hair.

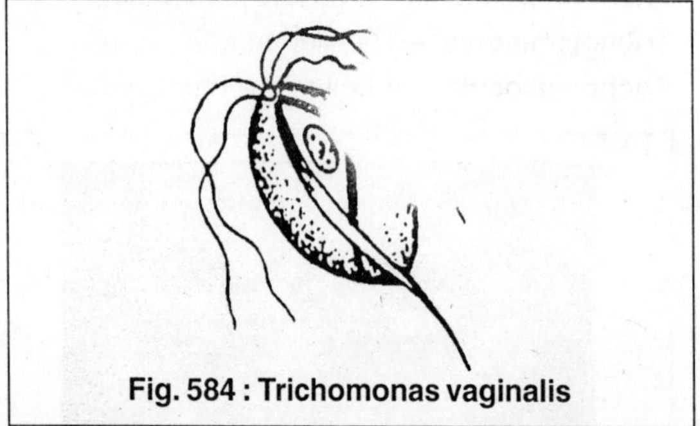

Fig. 584 : Trichomonas vaginalis

Trichopathic —Pertaining to disease of the hair.

Trichopathophobia —Morbid fear of growing hair, especially on the face experienced by women.

Trichopathy —Any disease of the hair.

Trichophagia, Trichophagy —The habit of eating hair.

Trichophobia —Morbid fear of the hair or of touching it.

Trichophytic —1. Pertaining to Trichophyton. 2. Promoting hair growth.

Trichophytid —A secondary skin eruption which is an allergic reaction to a fungus of the genus Trichophyton that occurs in the area remote from the site of infection.

Trichophytin —An extract from cultures of the fungi of the genus Trichophyton, used as an antigen for skin tests for trichophytosis.

Trichophytobezoar —A hair ball found in the stomach or intestine.

Trichophyton —A genus of parasitic fungi that live in the skin, hair and nails and cause various dermatomycosis and ringworm infections.

Trichophytosis —Infection with fungi of the genus Trichophyton.

Trichopoliosis —Poliosis.

Trichoptilosis —Splitting of the hairs at the ends.

Trichorrhea —Rapid loss of hair.

Trichorrhexis —Trichoschisis. Condition in which the hairs split and become feather-like.

Trichorrhexomania —Mania for breaking off the hair with fingernails.

Trichoschisis —Trichoptilosis. Splitting of the hairs.

Trichoscopy —Inspection of the hair.

Trichosis —Any disease or abnormal growth of the hair.

Trichosis decolor —Canities. Any abnormal coloring or lack of coloring of the hair.

Trichosis setosa —Coarse hair.

Trichosomatous —A protozoon having flagella with a small body.

Trichosporon —A genus of fungi that are normal flora of the respiratory and digestive tracts that may infect the hair.

Trichosporosis —Infection of the hair with Trichosporon.

Trichostasis spinulosa —A congenital disease in which hair follicle is plugged with a dark horny mass consisting of many fine lanugo hairs.

Trichotillomania —Mania for pulling out hair.

Trichotomous —Divided into three.

Trichotomy —Division into three parts.

Trichotoxin —An antibody or cytotoxin that destroys the ciliated epithelium.

Trichotrophy —Nutrition of the hair.

Trichroic —Exhibiting three different colors on viewing in three different aspects.

Trichroism —The exhibition of three different colors on viewing in three different aspects.

Trichromat —A person who sees three primary colors.

Trichromatic —Trichromic.

Trichromatism —Trichroism.

Trichromatopsia —Normal color vision for all three primary colors.

Trichromic —Trichromatic. 1. Pertaining to or exhibiting three colors. 2. Able to distinguish only three primary colors.

Trichterbrust —Funnel-shaped chest.

Trichuriasis —Presence of worms of genus Trichuris in the intestine.

Trichuricide —Destructive to Trichuris.

Trichuris —A genus of intestinal nematode parasites including species Trichuris trichiura (whipworm) that mainly infects man.

Tricipital —1. Three-headed. 2. Pertaining to the triceps muscle.

Tricorn —1. One of the lateral ventricles of the brain. 2. Tricornute.

Tricornic —Tricornute.

Tricornute —Having three horns.

Tricrotic —Having three notches on a sphygmograph tracing from one beat of the pulse.

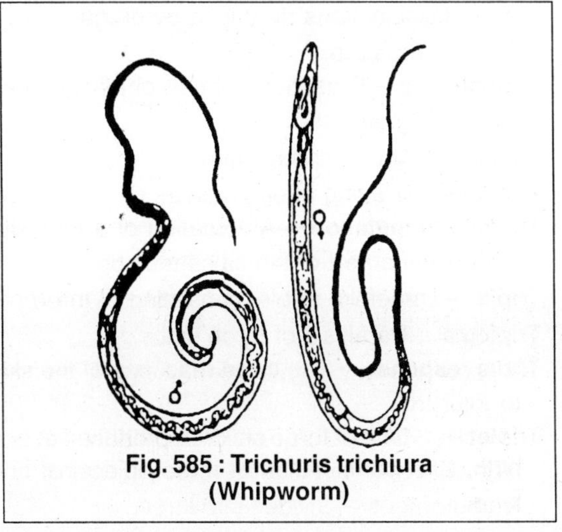

Fig. 585 : Trichuris trichiura (Whipworm)

Tricrotism —The condition of having three notches on a sphygmograph tracing from one beat of the pulse.

Tricrotous —Tricrotic.

Tricuspid —Having three points or cusps, as a valve of the heart.

Tricuspidal —Tricuspid.

Tricuspidate —Tricuspid.

Tricuspid atresia —Stenosis of the tricuspid valve.

Tricuspid murmur —A murmur caused by stenosis of the tricuspid valve or by its incompetency.

Tricuspid orifice —Right atrioventricular aperture.

Tricuspid tooth —Tooth with a crown that has three cusps.

Tricuspid valve —Right atrioventricular valve.

Tridactylism —Presence of only three digits on a hand or foot.

Tridactylous —Tridigitate. Having three fingers or toes.

Trident, Tridentate —Having three pongs.

Tridermic —Developed from ectoderm, endoderm and mesoderm.

Tridermoma —A teratoid growth containing all three germ layers.

Tridigitate —Tridactylous.

Tridymus —Triplet.

Trielcon —An instrument with three branches for removing bullets or other foreign substances from wounds.

Triencephalus —A deformed fetus without eyes, ears and nose.

Trifacial —Trigeminal. Pertaining to the fifth cranial nerve.

Trifacial neuralgia —Trigeminal neuralgia.

Trifid —Split into three parts.

Trifocal —Having three foci.

Trifurcation —Division into three branches.

Trigastric —Having three bellies, as certain muscles.

Trigeminal —Pertaining to trigeminus or fifth cranial nerve.

Trigeminal nerve —Fifth cranial nerve.

Trigeminal neuralgia —Facial neuralgia, sharp pain along the course of trigeminal nerve.

Trigeminus —Trigeminal nerve. Fifth cranial nerve.

Trigeminy —The occurrence in threes, especially the occurrence of three pulse beats in rapid succession.

Trigger —1. Stimulus. 2. To start suddenly.

Trigger action —A physiological action or a pathological change initiated by a sudden stimulus.

Trigger finger —The condition in which flexion or extension of a digit is arrested temporarily but the digit returns to its normal position with a jerk.

Trigger substance —A chemical substance that initiates a process.

Triglycerides —Combination of glycerol wtih three of five different fatty acids in the blood. Lipids (fatty substances) in the blood are triglycerides which are insoluble in water and hence are transported in combination with protein, as lipoproteins.

Trigocephalus —A deformed fetus with triangular face.

Trigona —Plural of trigonum.

Trigonal —1. Triangular. 2. Pertaining to a trigone.

Trigone —Trigonum. A triangular area, especially at the base of the urinary bladder, between the two openings of the ureters, and the urethra.

Trigonectomy —Excision of the trigone of the urinary bladder.

Trigonid —The first three cusps of a lower molar tooth.

Trigonitis —Inflammation of the trigone of the bladder.

Trigonocephalic —Having a triangular head.

Trigonocephalus —Trigonocephalic.

Trigonocephaly —The condition of having triangular head.

Trigonum —Trigone.

Trihybrid —The offspring of parents differing in three inherited characters.

Tri-iniodymus —A deformed fetus with a single body and three heads joined at the occiput.

Tri-iodothyronine —A hormone of the thyroid gland.

Trilabe —Lithotrite. A three-pronged forceps for removing foreign substances from the urinary bladder.

Trilaminar —Three-layered.

Trilateral —Pertaining to, or having three sides.

Trill —A tremulous sound.

Trilobate —Having three lobes.

Trilobed —Trilobate.

Trilocular —Having three spaces or cavities.

Trilogy —A group or series of three events.

Trimanual —Performed with three hands.

Trimastigote—Having three flagella.

Trimensual —Occurring every three months.

Trimester —A period of three months.

First trimester —First three months of pregnancy.

Second trimester —Second and middle three months of pregnancy.

Third trimester —The third and last three months of pregnancy.

Trimmer —An instrument used to snape something by cutting off the material along its margin.

Trimorphic —Trimorphous.

Trimorphism —The condition of living in three different forms.

Trimorphous —Living in three different forms as certain insects live in larva, pupa and adult forms.

Triocephalus —A deformed fetus with rudimentary head without eyes, nose and ears.

Triolism —Sexual activity involving three persons of both sexes.

Triophthalmos—A deformed fetus with three eyes.

Triopodymus —A deformed fetus with three fused heads and three faces.

Triorchid, Triorchis —A person with three testes.

Triorchidism —The presence of three testes.

Triotus —A person with a third ear.

Trioxide —A molecule containing three atoms of oxgen.

Trip —Hallucinations produced by drugs.

Tripara —Tertipara.

Triphalangia —Presence of three phalanges in a thumb or great toe.

Triphalangism —Triphalangia.

Triphasic —Having three phases.

Tripier's amputation —Amputation of a foot with removal of a part of the calcaneus bone.

Triple —Threefold; treble; consisting of three.

Triplegia —Paralysis of three limbs.

Triple response —The three reactions of the skin to injury.

Triplet —1. One of three children produced at one birth. 2. A combination of three objects of one kind.

Triplex —Triple or threefold.

Triploblastic —Consisting of three germ layers—ectoderm, endoderm and mesoderm.

Triploid —Having triple the haploid number of chromosomes.

Triploidy —The presence of triple the haploid number of chromosomes.

Triplokoria —The presence of three pupils in one eye.

Triplopia —Condition in which three images of the same object are seen.

Tripod —Having three feet.

Tripodia —The presence of three feet.

Tripoding —Use of three bases for support, *e.g.*, two legs and a cane.

Triprosopus —A deformed fetus with three faces.

Tripsis —1. The process of trituration. 2. Massage.

-tripsy —A suffix which means intentional crushing of something.

Tripus —The conjoined twin having three feet.

Triquetral —Triangular.

Triquetrous —Triangular.

Triquetrum —Three-cornered.

Triradial, Triradiate —Having three rays; radiating in three directions.

Triradius —The figure at the base of each finger in the palm, produced by dermal ridges running in three directions forming a triangle.

Trisaccharide —The carbohydrate that upon hydrolysis yields three molecules of simple sugars.

Triskaidekaphobia —Triakaidekaphobia.

Trismic —Pertaining to trismus.

Trismoid —Trismus-like.

Trismus —Spasm of the muscles of mastication resulting in lockjaw.

Trisomic —An individual possessing an additional (3rd) chromosome of one type in a diploid cell (2n+1).

Trisomy —The presence of an additional (3rd) chromosome of one type in a diploid cell.

Trisplanchnic —Pertaining to the three great body cavities, *i.e.*, skull, thorax and abdomen.

Trist —Sad; unhappy.

Tristichia —The presence of three rows of eyelashes.

Tristimania —Melancholia.

Trisulcate —Having three furrows.

Tritanomalopia —Tritanopia.

Tritanope —The person affected with blue blindness.

Tritanopia —Blue blindness.

Triticeous —Shaped like a grain of wheat.

Triturable —Capable to be powdered.

Triturate —1. To make powder by rubbing. 2. A powder made by rubbing.

Trituration —1. The process of making powder by rubbing or grinding. 2. A finely powdered substance.

Triturator —An apparatus for rubbing the substances continuously.

Trivalence —Condition of being trivalent.

Trivalency —Trivalence.

Trivalent —Having a valence of three.

Trivalve —Having three valves.

Trizonal —Having three zones or layers.

Trocar —A sharp-pointed instrument contained in a metal cannula, used to puncture a cavity wall and withdraw fluid.

Troch —Troche.

Trochanter —Either of the two bony processes below the neck of the femur bone. The larger one is greater trochanter and the smaller is lesser trochanter.

Trochanterian, Trochanteric —Pertaining to a trochanter.

Trochanterplasty —Repair of the neck of the femur by plastic surgery.

Trochantin —Lesser trochanter.

Trochantinian —Pertaining to the lesser trochanter of the femur bone.

Troche —Lozenge.

Trochisci —Plural of trochiscus.

Trochiscus —A medicated tablet or lozenge.

Trochlea —1. A structure having the function of a pulley. 2. The articular smooth surface of a bone upon which an another bone glides.

Trochleae —Plural of trochlea.

Trochlear —1. Pertaining to a trochlea. 2. Of the nature of a pulley.

Trochleariform —Pulley-shaped.

Trochlearis —1. Trochlear. 2. Trochleiform.

Trochleiform —Trochleariform.

Trochocardia —Rotatory displacement of the heart on its axis.

Trochocephalia, Trochocephaly—Roundedness of the head due to premature fusion of the frontal and parietal bones.

Trochoid —Pulley-shaped.

Trochoides —A rotatory joint.

Tromomania —Delirium tremens.

Troph-, Tropho- —Prefixes which mean nourishment.

Trophectoderm —Trophoblast.

Trophedema —Chronic permanent edema of the feet or legs.

Trophesy —Defective nutrition due to disorder of the trophic nerves.

Trophic —1. Pertaining to or dependent upon nutrition. 2. Resulting from interruption of nerve supply.

-trophic —A suffix meaning nutrition.

Trophicity —Nutritional influence.

Trophism —Nutrition.

Tropho- —Troph-

Trophoblast —The outermost layer of the blastocyst, which attaches the fertilized ovum to the uterine wall and becomes placenta.

Trophoblastic —Concerning trophoblast.

Trophoblastoma —Chorioepithelioma.

Trophocyte —A cell of the testis that provides nutrition to the developing spermatozoa.

Trophoderm—Trophoblast together with mesoderm underlying it.

Trophodermatoneurosis —Acrodynia.

Trophodynamics —Study of the forces and factors concerned with nutrition.

Trophology —The science of nutrition.

Trophoneurosis —Any trophic disorder of a part of the body due to deficiency of its nerve supply.

Trophoneurotic —Pertaining to trophoneurosis.

Trophonosis—Trophopathia.

Trophonucleus —A nucleus in a protozoon concerned with the vegetative metabolic functions and not reproduction.

Trophopathia—1. Any disorder of nutrition. 2. A trophic disease.

Trophopathy—Trophopathia.

Trophoplast —A granular protoplasmic body.

Trophotaxis —Trophotropism.

Trophotherapy —Treatment of the diseases by diet.

Trophotropic— Pertaining to trophotropism.

Trophotropism —Trophotaxis. The movement of cells away from or toward nutritive substances.

Trophozoite —A sporozoan parasite receiving nourishment from its host during its growing stage.

-trophy —A suffix meaning food or nutrition.

Tropia —Strabismus.

-tropic —A suffix meaning a turning toward or having affinity for.

Tropical —Pertaining to the tropics.

Tropical lichen —Prickly heat.

-tropin —A suffix indicating the stimulating effect of a substance, especially a hormone, on its target organ.

Tropism —Involuntary movement of an organism toward (positive tropism) or away from (negative tropism) an external stimulus such as light, darkness, heat or cold etc.

Tropoelastin —The precursor of elastin.

Tropometer —1. An instrument for measuring the rotation of the eyeballs. 2. An instrument for measuring the torsion in long bones.

Trough —A groove or channel.

Trousseau's sign —A sign of advanced tetany in which muscular spasm occurs as a result of pressure applied to nerves and vessels of the upper arm.

Trousseau's spots —Formation of the streak on the skin with fingernail seen in meningitis and other cerebral diseases.

True pelvis —Portion of the pelvis below iliopectineal line.

True ribs —Seven uppper ribs.

Truncal —Pertaining to the trunk.

Truncate —1. To amputate or to deprive of limbs. 2. Having the end cut off squarely.

Trunci —Plural of truncus.

Truncus —Trunk.

Trunk —The part of the body excluding head and limbs or a large structure, *e.g.*, blood vessel, nerve or lymphatic vessel from which smaller branches arise, or which is formed by the union of these branches.

Trusion —Malposition of a tooth or teeth.

Truss —A belt used for hernia.

Try-in —The preliminary insertion of a denture (trial denture) to determine its fitness.

Trypanocide, Trypanocidal —Destructive to trypanosomes.

Trypanolysis —The destruction of trypanosomes.

Trypanolytic—Destructive to trypanosomes.

Trypanosoma—A genus of parasitic, flagellate protozoa found in the blood, of which species T. rhodesiense is transmitted by the tsetse fly and causes sleeping sickness in East Africa.

Trypanosomal —Pertaining to trypanosoma.

Trypanosome —Any protozoon of the genus Trypanosoma.

Trypanosomiasis —Disease caused by trypanosomes as African sleeping sickness.

Trypanosomic —Pertaining to trypanosomes.

Trypanosomicide —Trypanocide.

Trypanosomid —A skin eruption caused by trypanosome.

Trypsin —A proteolytic enzyme formed in the intestine by the action of enterokinase on trypsinogen, secreted by the pancreas.

Trypsinogen —The inactive form of trypsin found in pancreatic juice, becomes activated when mixed with enterokinase in the intestine.

Trypsogen —Trypsinogen.

Tryptic —Pertaining to trypsin.

Tryptolysis —The hydrolysis of proteins by trypsin.

Tryptone —A peptide produced by the action of trypsin on a protein.

Tryptophan —An essential amino acid for human metabolism present in protein.

Tryptophanuria —Presence of tryptophan in the urine.

Tsetse fly —An African fly that causes sleeping sickness.

T S H —Thyroid-stimulating hormone.

T S H–R F —Thyroid-stimulating hormone releasing factor.

Tsp —Teaspoon.

Tub —A receptacle for bathing.

Tuba —Tube.

Tubae —Plural of tuba.

Tubage —Introduction of a tube into a canal.

Tubal —Pertaining to a tube, especially the fallopian tube.

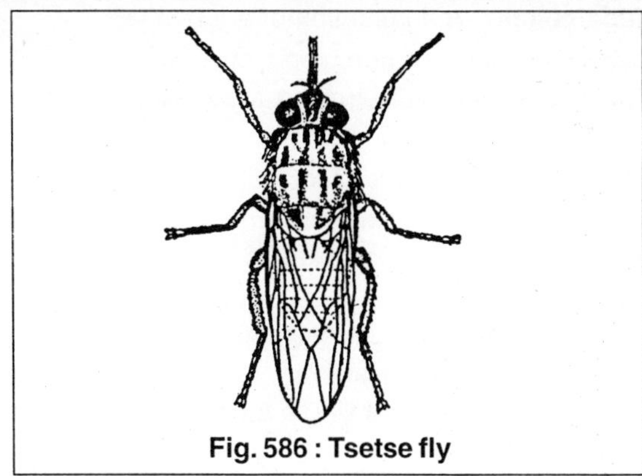

Fig. 586 : Tsetse fly

Tubal nephritis —Inflammation of the kidney tubules.

Tubal pregnancy —Pregnancy in one of the fallopian tubes.

Tubatorsion —The twisting of a fallopian tube.

Tubba, Tubboe —Yaws that attacks the palms and soles.

Tube —A long, hollow, cylindrical organ or instrument.

Tubectomy —Surgical removal of all or part of a tube, especially the fallopian tube.

Tuber —A swelling or protuberance.

Tubera —Plural of tuber.

Tubercle —1. A small, rounded mass produced by infection with Mycobacterium tuberculosis. 2. A small nodule or eminence on a bone for attachment of a tendon, or on the skin or mucous membrane.

Tubercula —Plural of tuberculum.

Tubercular —Pertaining to or marked by nodules.

Tuberculate, Tuberculated —Covered with nodules.

Tuberculation —The formation of tubercles.

Tuberculid —Tuberculoderma. A papular skin eruption caused by toxins of tuberculosis.

Tuberculide —Tuberculid.

Tuberculigenous —Causing tuberculosis.

Tuberculin —A liquid extracted from tubercle bacillus, used in the diagnosis of tuberculosis.

Tuberculin test —A test to determine the presence of a tuberculous infection, based on a skin reaction to tuberculin. Tuberculin may be applied on the skin by intradermal injection or by rubbing on scarified skin. A local inflammation is observed in infected person after 48 to 96 hours.

Tuberculitis —Inflammation of a tubercle.

Tuberculocele —Tuberculosis of a testis.

Tuberculocidal —Destroying Mycobacterium tuberculosis.

Tuberculocide —Tuberculocidal.

Tuberculoderma —Tuberculid.

Tuberculofibroid —Denoting fibroid degeneration of tubercles.

Tuberculofibrosis —Chronic pneumonia with formation of fibrous tissue.

Tuberculoid —Resembling a tubercle or tuberculosis.

Tuberculoma —A tuberculous tumor or abscess.

Tuberculomania —An abnormal belief that one is affected with tuberculosis.

Tuberculophobia —Morbid fear of being affected with tuberculosis.

Tuberculoprotein —A protein derived from tubercle bacilli.

Tuberculosilicosis—Silicosis complicated by pulmonary tuberculosis.

Tuberculosis —The disease caused by the bacillus Mycobacterium tuberculosis which most commonly affects the lungs, but other parts of the body such as gastrointestinal tract, bones, joints, nervous system, skin and lymph nodes etc., are also involved. It is characterized by the formation of tubercles, caseation, necrosis, abscess, fibrosis and calcification. Infection is acquired from contact with an infected person or an infected cow or through drinking contaminated milk.

Aerogenic tuberculosis —Tuberculosis occurring through air, by inhaling infected droplets.

Avian tuberculosis —Tuberculosis of the birds due to Mycobacterium avium.

Bovine tuberculosis —Tuberculosis of the cattle due to Mycobacterium bovis, transmitted to man.

Cutaneous tuberculosis —Occurrence of skin lesions due to infection with Mycobacterium tuberculosis.

Disseminated tuberculosis —Miliary tuberculosis.

Endogenous tuberculosis —Tuberculosis arising from a tubercle in another site of the body.

Enteric tuberculosis —Tuberculosis of the digestive tract occurring as a complication of pulmonary tuberculosis, resulting from expectoration and swallowing of the bacteria Mycobacterium tuberculosis. It can also be caused by ingestion of Mycobacterium bovis in infected milk.

Exogenous tuberculosis —Tuberculosis arising from a source outside of the body.

Hematogenous tuberculosis —The spread of tuberculosis from a primary site to another site through the blood stream.

Miliary tuberculosis, Acute tuberculosis —Acute tuberculosis in which minute tubercles are formed in various organs of the body, due to spread of the bacilli through the body via blood stream.

Open tuberculosis —Tuberculosis in which there are lesions from which tubercle bacilli are being discharged out of the body.

Primary tuberculosis —It generally occurs in children but also occurs in adults and characterized by the formation of primary complex in the lung.

Pulmonary tuberculosis —Tuberculosis of the lungs.

Secondary tuberculosis —Tuberculosis generally found in adults and characterized by the formation of cavity in the lung.

Verrucosa tuberculosis, Warty tuberculosis —Tuberculosis of the skin caused by infection from outside of the body, characterized by the formation of warts.

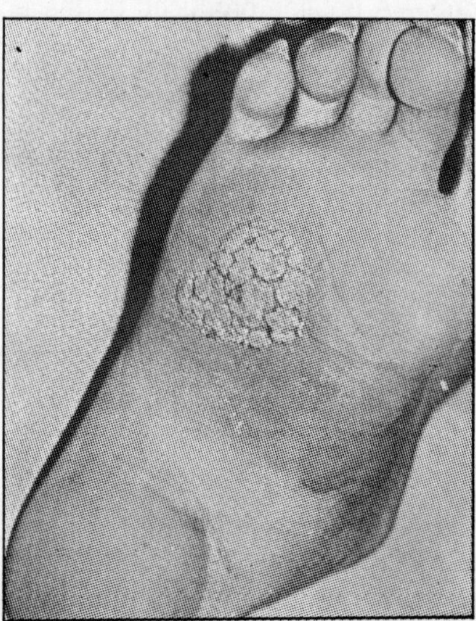

Fig. No. 587 : Verrucosa tuberculosis, Warty tuberculosis, wart formation on the sole

Tuberculostate —An antitubercular agent.

Tuberculostatic —Arresting the growth of Mycobacterium tuberculosis.

Tuberculotherapeutic —Pertaining to the treatment of tuberculosis by tuberculocidal drugs.

Tuberculotic —Pertaining to or suffering from tuberculosis.

Tuberculous —Tuberculotic.

Tuberculum —Tubercle.

Tuberiferous —Tuberous.

Tuberose —Tuberous.

Tuberosis —The condition characterized by the presence of nodules.

Tuberositas —Tuberosity.

Tuberosity —1. An elevation on a bone to which a muscle is attached. 2. A tubercle, nodule or prominence.

Tuberous —Pertaining to tubers.

Tubi —Plural of tubus.

Tubo- —A prefix meaning tube.

Tuboabdominal —Pertaining to the fallopian tube and the abdomen.

Tuboligamentous —Pertaining to the fallopian tube and broad ligament of the uterus.

Tubo-ovarian —Pertaining to the fallopian tube and the ovary.

Tubo-ovariotomy —To incise the fallopian tubes and the ovaries.

Tubo-ovaritis —Inflammation of the fallopian tube and ovary.

Tuboperitoneal —Pertaining to the fallopian tube and peritoneum.

Tuboplasty —Salpingoplasty.

Tuborrhea —Discharge from the eustachian tube.

Tubotorsion —The act of twisting a tube.

Tubotympanal —Pertaining to the tympanum and the eustachian tube.

Tubotympanic —Pertaining to the auditory tube and the tympanic cavity of the ear.

Tubotympanum —The auditory tube and tympanic cavity considered together.

Tubouterine —Pertaining to the fallopian tube and uterus.

Tubovaginal —Pertaining to the fallopian tube and the vagina.

Tubular —Pertaining to or having the form of a tube or tubule.

Tubulature —The short neck of a retort.

Tubule —A small tube or canal, *e.g.*, renal tubules and seminiferous tubules etc.

Tubuli —Plural of tubulus.

Tubuliform —Tubular.

Tubulization —The repairing of severed nerves in which the nerve ends are placed in a tube of absorbable material.

Tubuloalveolar —Consisting of tubules and alveoli.

Tubulocyst —A cyst formed by the dilation of a duct or canal.

Tubulodermoid —A dermoid cyst caused by a persistent embryonal tubular structure.

Tubuloneogenesis —Formation of new tubules.

Tubuloracemose —Denoting a gland that has tubular and racemose structure.

Tubulorrhexis —Rupture of the renal tubules.

Tubulose —Tubulous.

Tubulous —Containing tubules.

Tubulus —Tubule.

Tubus —Tube.

Tuft —A small clump, cluster or coiled mass.

Tug —Tugging.

Tugging —A pulling sensation, as occurs in trachea (tracheal tugging) due to aneurysm of the arch of the aorta.

Tularemia —An acute plague-like infectious disease caused by Francisella tularensis (Pasteurella tularensis), which is transmitted to man by the bite of an infected tick or other blood sucking insect, or by direct contact with the infected animals.

Tumefacient —Producing swelling.

Tumefaction —1. A swelling. 2. The act of swelling or the state of being swollen.

Tumefy —To swell or to produce swelling.

Tumentia —Swelling.

Tumescence —1. The condition of being swollen or tumid. 2. A swelling.

Tumescent —Turgescent.

Tumid —Swollen.

Tumor —1. A spontaneous growth of tissue. 2. Swelling, one of the four cardinal signs of inflammation. 3. Swelling or enlargement.

Adenoid tumor —Adenoma.

Adipose tumor —Lipoma.

Amyloid tumor —Nodular amyloidosis. Accumulation of amyloid as hard masses or nodules beneath the skin or mucous membrane.

Benign tumor —It is not progressive, not recurring after removal and not giving rise to metastasis and usually surrounded by a fibrous capsule.

Blood tumor —Hematoma.

Dermoid tumor —Dermoid cyst.

Fibroid tumor —A benign tumor of the myometrium composed of fibrous tissue.

Malignant tumor —It grows rapidly, recurring after removal, giving rise to metastasis and not curable by treatment and threatens life.

Mixed tumor —A tumor composed of two or more types of tissue.

Tumoraffin —Oncotropic. Specially attracted toward tumor cells.

Tumoricidal —Destructive to tumor cells.

Tumorigenesis —Production of tumors.

Tumorigenic —Producing tumors.

Tumorous —Tumor-like.

Tumultus —Excessive activity or motility.

Tumultus cordis —Palpitation and irregular action of the heart.

Tunic —A covering or coat.

Tunica —A membrane or other structure covering or lining a body part or organ.

Tunica adventitia —Outer coat of an artery or any tubular structure.

Tunica albuginea —The white fibrous coat enclosing an organ as testis or ovary.

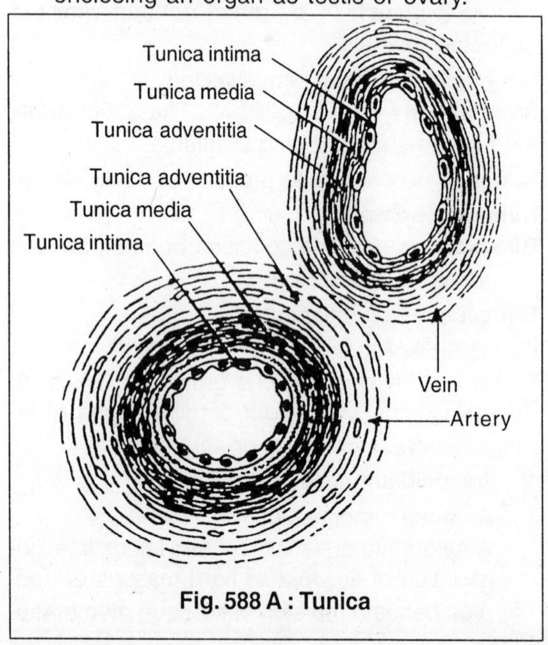

Fig. 588 A : Tunica

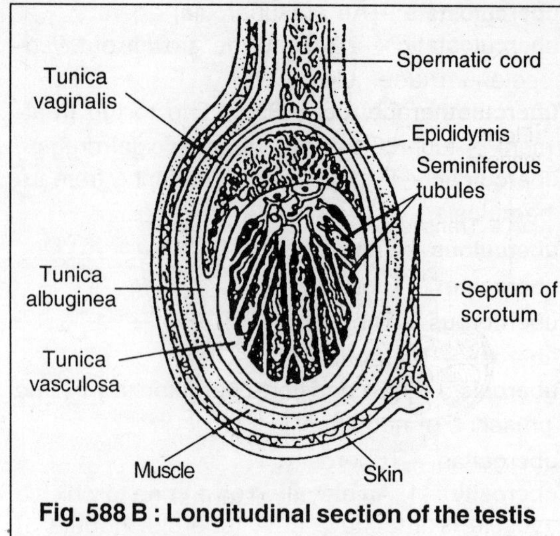

Fig. 588 B : Longitudinal section of the testis

Tunica externa —Outer coat of an artery.

Tunica interna —Tunica intima.

Tunica intima —Inner coat of an artery.

Tunica media —Middle muscular coat of an artery.

Tunica mucosa —Mucous membrane lining various structures.

Tunica vaginalis —The serous membrane covering the front and sides of the testis.

Tunicae —Plural of tunica.

Tuning fork —See fork.

Tunnel —A narrow passageway through a solid body, completely enclosed except at the ends for entrance and exit, *e.g.*, carpal tunnel which is a canal in the wrist enclosed by osteofibrous material through which the median nerve and the flexor tendons pass.

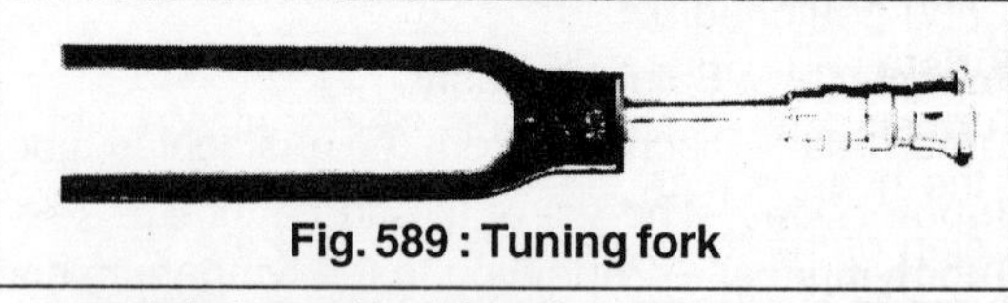

Fig. 589 : Tuning fork

Turbid —Muddy; not clear.

Turbidimeter —An apparatus for measuring the turbidity of a fluid.

Turbidimetric —Pertaining to the measurement of turbidity.

Turbidimetry —The measurement of turbidity of a fluid.

Turbidity —Muddiness; cloudiness.

Turbinal, Turbinate —Shaped like an inverted cone.

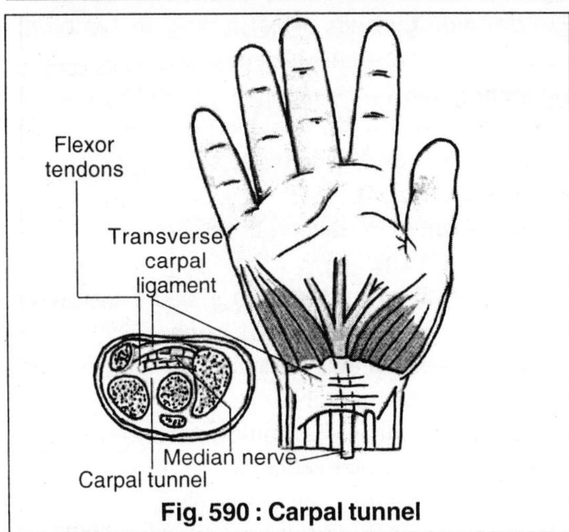

Fig. 590 : Carpal tunnel

Turbinated —Top-shaped.

Turbinectomy —Excision of a turbinate bone (nasal concha).

Turbinotome —An instrument for excision of a turbinate bone.

Turbinotomy —Incision of a turbinate bone.

Turbulence —Violence.

Turgescence —Distention or enlargement of a part of the body.

Turgescent —Becoming distended.

Turgid —Distended or swollen.

Turgidity —The state of being swollen.

Turgometer —An apparatus for measuring turgidity.

Turgor —1. Distention or swelling. 2. Normal tension in a cell.

Turista —Traveller's diarrhea.

Turmschadel —A congenital deformity in which the head is high and rounded due to early fusion of the three major sutures of the skull.

Turner's syndrome —Dysgenesis, gonadal.

Turning —Variation.

Turn of life —The menopause.

Turn-over —Invert.

Turricephaly —Oxycephalia, oxycephaly.

Turunda —A drain, or tampon or suppository.

Turundae —Plural of turunda.

Tusk —A very large tooth projecting beyond the lips.

Tussal —Tussive.

Tussicular —Tussive.

Tussiculation —A short, dry cough.

Tussigenic —Producing cough.

Tussis —A cough.

Tussive —Tussal. Tussicular. Pertaining to a cough.

Tutamen —A protecting covering or structure, as eyelids and eyelashes for the eyes.

Tutamina —Plural of tutamen.

Twang —Nasal quality of voice.

T wave —Portion of the electrocardiogram that is because of repolarization of the ventricles, which may be positive or negative depending upon the lead used in taking ECG.

Tweezers —An instrument with pincers that are squeezed together to grasp or extract fine structures.

Twig —The final branch of a blood vessel or nerve.

Twin —One of the two children born at one birth.

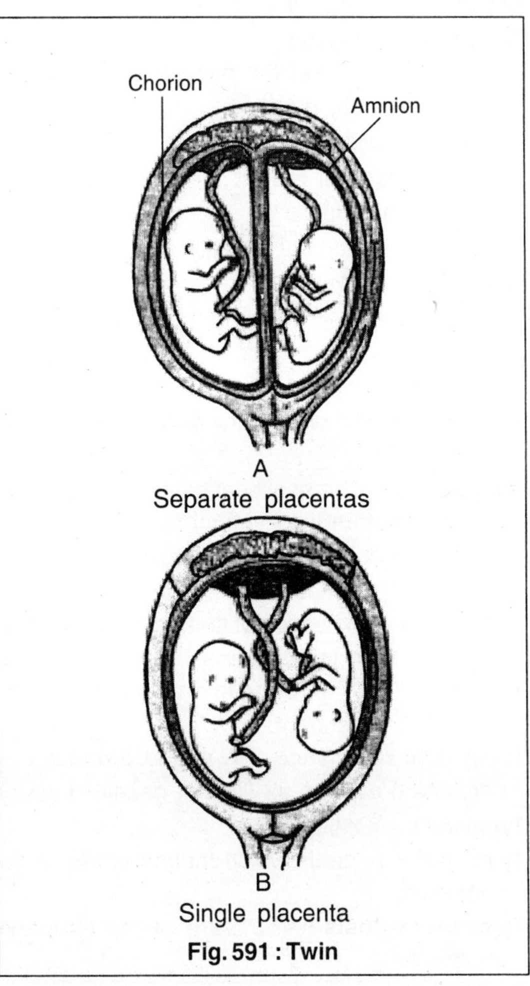

Fig. 591 : Twin

Allantoidoangiopagous twins —Twins united by the umbilical vessels only.

Conjoined twins —Monozygotic twins whose bodies are joined.

Dizygotic twins —Twins developed from two separate ova fertilized at the same time.

Impacted twins —Twins that are so impacted in the uterus as to prevent normal delivery.

Monozygotic twins —Twins that develop from one fertilized ovum.

Parasitic twins —The smaller of the unequal conjoined twins.

Twinge —A sudden sharp pain.

Twinning —The production of twins.

Twitch —1. A quick spasmodic contraction of a muscle. 2. Jerk.

Twitching —Repeated spasmodic contractions of portion of a muscle.

Tylectomy —Lumpectomy.

Tylia —Plural of tylion.

Tylion —The point at the middle of the anterior edge of the optic groove.

Tyloma —A callus or callosity.

Tyloses —Plural of tylosis.

Twilight —Faint light.

Tylosis —Formation of a callus.

Tympanal —Tympanic.

Tympanectomy —Excision of the tympanic membrane.

Tympania —Tympanites.

Tympanic —1. Of or pertaining to the tympanum. 2. Resonant.

Tympanicity —The quality of being resonant.

Tympanic membrane —Membrane forming the lateral wall of the cavity of middle ear.

Tympanism —Tympanites.

Tympanites —Distention of abdomen due to presence of gas in the intestines.

Tympanitic —1. Pertaining to or affected with tympanites. 2. Resonant.

Tympanitic resonance —A sound produced by percussion over an air-filled or gas-filled cavity.

Tympanitis —Otitis media.

Tympano- —A prefix which means cavity of the middle ear.

Tympanocentesis —Puncture of the tympanic membrane.

Tympanoeustachian —Pertaining to tympanic cavity and the eustachian tube.

Tympanogenic —Arising from the middle ear.

Tympanography —X-ray examination of the eustachian tube and middle ear after introducing a contrast medium.

Tympanohyal —Pertaining to the tympanic cavity and hyoid bone.

Tympanomalleal —Pertaining to the tympanic membrane and the malleus bone.

Tympanomandibular —Pertaining to the tympanic cavity and the mandible.

Tympanomastoid —Pertaining to the tympanic cavity and mastoid process.

Tympanomastoidectomy —Removal of the mastoid process including a portion of auditory canal and tympanic membrane.

Tympanomastoiditis —Inflammation of the middle ear and mastoid cells.

Tympanometry —Measurement of the mobility of the tympanic membrane.

Tympanophonia, Tympanophony —Autophony.

Tympanoplasty —Plastic surgery of the tympanic membrane.

Tympanosclerosis—Presence of hard fibrous tissues around the ossicles of the middle ear.

Tympanosis —Tympanites.

Tympanosquamosal —Squamotympanic. Pertaining to the tympanic and squamous parts of the temporal bone.

Tympanostapedial —Pertaining to the tympanic cavity and stapes.

Tympanostomy —Myringotomy.

Tympanotemporal —Pertaining to the tympanic cavity and temporal bone.

Tympanotomy —Myringotomy.

Tympanous —Afflicted with tympanites.

Tympanum —Eardrum. Cavity of the middle ear.

Tympany —1. Tympanites. 2. Resonance.

Type —The general character of a person, disease or substance etc.

Typhinia —Relapsing fever. See under fever.

Typhlectasis —Distention of the cecum.

Typhlectomy —Cecectomy.

Typhlenteritis —Typhlitis.

Typhlitis —Inflammation of the cecum.

Typhlo- —A prefix indicating relationship to the cecum or to the blindness.

Typhlodicliditis —Inflammation of the ileocecal valve.

Typhloempyema —Presence of an abdominal abscess following typhlitis.

Typhloenteritis —Typhlitis.

Typhlolexia —Alexia.

Typhlolithiasis —Formation of calculus in the cecum.

Typhlology —Study of blindness.

Typhlomegaly —An abnormal enlargement of the cecum.

Typhlon —The cecum.

Typhlopexia —Typhlopexy.

Typhlopexy —Suturing of the movable cecum to the abdominal wall.

Typhlorrhaphy —Repairing of the cecum by suturing.

Typhlosis —Blindness.

Typhlospasm —Spasm of the cecum.

Typhlostenosis —Narrowing of the cecum.

Typhlostomy —To establish a permanent cecal fistula.

Typhlotomy —Cecotomy.

Typhloureterostomy —Implantation of a ureter in the cecum.

Typho- —A prefix which means pertaining to fever or to typhoid.

Typhobacillosis —Poisoning due to toxins produced by the typhoid bacillus.

Typhoid —1. Resembling typhus. 2. Typhoid fever.

Typhoidal —Resembling typhoid.

Typhoid carrier —An individual who has recovered from typhoid fever but who harbors the bacteria of typhoid, usually in the gallbladder which are excreted in the urine and feces.

Typhoid fever —Enteric fever. An acute infectious disease characterized by continued fever, caused by Salmonella typhi, a gram-negative, motile bacillus that is transmitted by infected water, milk, food, by inhalation of bacilli, by flies, patient and carriers. The bacilli localize in Peyer's patches of the small intestine causing ulcers which heal or may bleed or perforate. The disease runs the course of three weeks. The signs and symptoms of the disease are as follows—

First week—The patient complains of general weakness, frontal headache, aching in the limbs, loss of appetite, constipation, insomnia and fever. The temperature gradually rises (step-ladder fashion) which drops 1/2 to 1 degree each morning and by the end of week may reach 102° F to 103° F. The pulse is slow in comparison to the rise of temperature and is dicrotic. It is usually 90 to 100 per minute. The tongue is coated with white fur with the edges and tip clean. Typhoid spots (rose spots) may appear about the seventh day on the trunk and abdomen, fading on pressure. Spleen becomes palpable. There is leucopenia, 4000 to 5000 white blood cells per c.mm.

Second week—The patient is more prostrated and headache is less marked. Insomnia may be troublesome and delirium may occur. The temperature remains sustained at about 101° F to 103° F. It often rises abruptly very high, 104° F to 105° F. Abdomen is distended and there is great tendency to diarrhea.

Third week—In the third week toxemia increases and the patient may pass into coma and may die but there is usually improvement toward the end of this week and the temperature begins to fall. There is however risk of hemorrhage and perforation of ulcers of the small intestine. The patient becomes very weak.

Convalescence period—After the third week the temperature gradually falls to normal, tongue becomes clear, spleen is not palpable. There is anemia, loss of hair and desquamation. General condition improves. Sometimes relapse may occur.

Typholysin —A lysin destructive to typhoid bacilli.

Typhomalarial —Suffering from typhoid with malaria.

Typhomania —Muttering delirium characteristic of typhoid fever and typhus.

Typhopneumonia —Pneumonia occurring with typhoid fever.

Typhosepsis —Typhoid septicemia.

Typhous —Pertaining to typhus fever.

Typhus —Any of a group of acute infectious diseases characterized by high fever, maculopapular eruption appearing from the third to seventh day, severe headache, great prostration and nervous symptoms.

Epidemic typhus —An infectious disease caused by Rickettsia prowazekii and transmitted from man to man by body louse.

Murine typhus —An infectious disease caused by Rickettsia typhi, transmitted from rat to man by rat flea and rat louse.

Recrudescent typhus —Brill's disease. Relapsing epidemic typhus.

Typical —Having the characteristics of, pertaining to, or conforming to, a type.

Typing —Identification of type, *e.g.*, determination of the blood group of an individual.

Typology —The science of classifying, as of bacteria according to type.

Typoscope —An apparatus aiding in reading for the patients of amblyopia or cataract.

Typus —Type.

Tyrannism —Sadism.

Tyremesis —Tyrosis. Vomiting of curdy material by infants.

Tyriasis —Elephantiasis.

Tyrogenous —Produced by cheese.

Tyroid —Cheesy.

Tyroma —A tumor containing cheesy material.

Tyromatosis —Caseation.

Tyrosinemia —A hereditary disease marked by excess of tyrosine in the blood, and it passes in the urine, resulting in cirrhosis of the liver, renal tubular involvement and hypoglycemia.

Tyrosinosis —A condition resulting from defective metabolism of tyrosine, whereby its oxidation products appear in the urine.

Tyrosinuria —Presence of tyrosine in the urine.

Tyrosis —1. Caseation. 2. Vomiting of cheesy material by infants. 3. Curdling of milk.

Tyrosyluria —Increased products of tyrosine in the urine.

Tyrotoxism —Poisoning caused by a toxin present in milk or cheese.

Tysonitis —Inflammation of the preputial glands.

Tyson's glands —Preputial glands.

U —1. Unit. 2. Chemical symbol for uranium.

Uberous —Fertile; fruitful.

Uberty —Fertility; fruitfulness.

Uffelmann's test —A test for the determination of lactic acid in gastric juice.

Uhthoff's sign —Occurrence of nystagmus in multiple disseminated sclerosis.

Ulaganactesis —Irritation in or about the gums.

Ulalgia —Pain in the gums.

Ulatrophia —Shrinking of the gums.

Ulcer —A break in the continuity of the skin or mucous membrane caused by sloughing of necrotic inflammatory tissue.

Aphthous ulcer —A small oral ulcer caused by aphthous stomatitis.

Callous ulcer —A chronic ulcer with indurated, elevated edges and no granulations, which does not heal.

Carcinomatous ulcer —A cancerous ulcer with raised and everted edges, resembling a cauliflower.

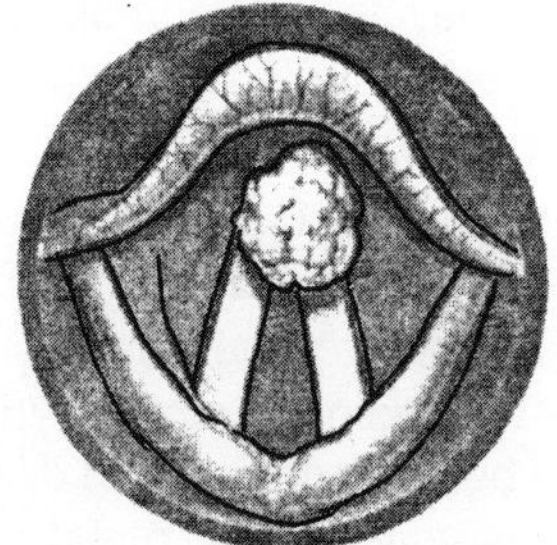

Fig. 592 : Carcinomatous ulcer of the vocal cords

Chronic ulcer —A long standing ulcer with fibrous scar tissue in its floor.

Decubitus ulcer —Bedsore. For decubitus ulcer see under 'D'.

Dental ulcer —An ulcer formed on the oral mucosa due to trauma inflicted by teeth.

Duodenal ulcer —A peptic ulcer situated in the duodenum.

Fungus ulcer —An ulcer caused by fungus infection in which the granulations protrude above the edges of the wound and bleed easily.

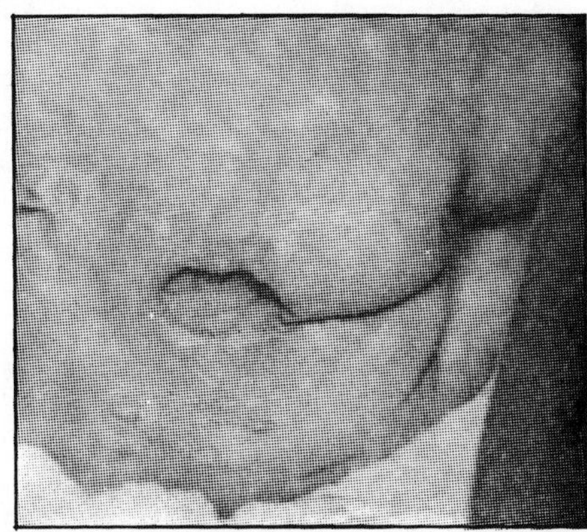

Fig. 593 : Decubitus ulcer or Bedsore

Gastric ulcer —A peptic ulcer situated in the stomach.

Healing ulcer —Ulcer with red granulation tissue in the floor, without inflammation of the edges and with slight serous discharge.

Indolent ulcer —A chronic, nearly painless ulcer usually found on the leg, characterized by hard and elevated edges and few or no granulations, and showing no tendency to heal.

Peptic ulcer —An ulcer of the mucous membrane of stomach or duodenum, due to action of the acid of gastric juice.

Perforating ulcer —An ulcer involving the entire thickness of an organ or of the wall of an organ, creating an opening on both surfaces, as the intestine.

Phagedenic ulcer —An ulcer that spreads rapidly and disintegrates the tissues, producing a slough and discharge.

Rodent ulcer —A malignant ulcer of the skin with raised edges, commonly found on the upper part of the face, which slowly destroys the bones and tissues.

Serpiginous ulcer —A creeping ulcer of which one part heals and the other part extends further.

Simple ulcer —A local ulcer with no severe inflammation or pain.

Specific ulcer —An ulcer caused by specific disease such as tuberculosis or syphilis etc.

Stercoraceous ulcer, Stercoral ulcer —1. An ulcer caused by pressure of impacted feces. 2. A fistulous ulcer through which feces escapes.Stercoral ulcer-Stercoraceousulcer

Stercoral ulcer — Stercoraceous ulcer

Stress ulcer —A peptic ulcer caused by acute or chronic physical or mental stress.

Traumatic ulcer —An ulcer caused by an injury.

Trophic ulcer —An ulcer caused by lack of nutrition of a part of the body.

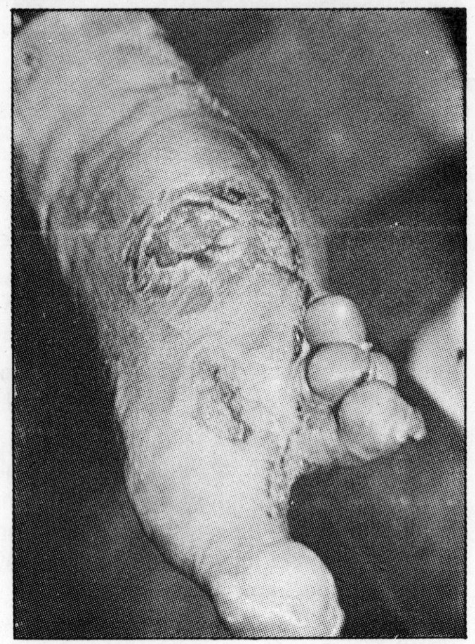

Fig. 594 : Trophic ulcer of the foot

Tropical ulcer —A chronic, sloughing ulcer on the lower limbs, occurring in tropical regions.

Varicose ulcer —An ulcer, especially of the lower limbs, occurring due to varicose veins.

Venereal ulcer —An ulcer produced by a venereal disease, as syphilis etc.

Ulcera —Plural of ulcus.

Ulcerate —To produce or become affected with an ulcer.

Ulcerated —Of the nature of or affected with an ulcer.

Ulceration —The formation of an ulcer.

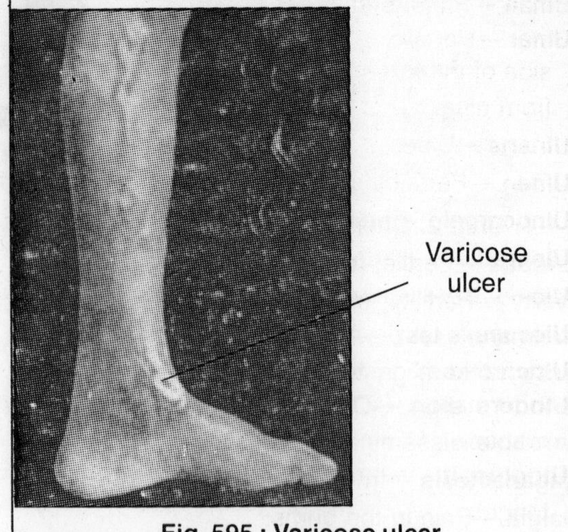

Fig. 595 : Varicose ulcer

Ulcerative —Pertaining to or causing ulceration.

Ulcerative colitis —See under colitis.

Ulcerogangrenous —Characterized by the formation of both, ulcer and gangrene.

Ulcerogenic —Producing ulcer.

Ulceroglandular —Formation of an ulcer at the site of infection followed by enlargement of the regional or general lymph nodes.

Ulceromembranous —Characterized by the formation of ulcer and a fibrous pseudomembrane.

Ulceromembranous tonsillitis —Tonsillitis that ulcerates and develops a membrane.

Ulcerous —Pertaining to, of the nature of, or affected with an ulcer.

Ulcus —Ulcer.

Ulectomy —1. Excision of scar tissue. 2. Gingivectomy. Excision of the gums.

Ulegyria —A condition in which gyri of the cerebral cortex become narrow and distorted, which may be congenital or the result of scar tissue formation from injury.

Ulemorrhagia —Bleeding from the gums.

Ulerythema —An erythematous disease of the skin with formation of scar tissue and atrophy.

Uletic —Pertaining to the gums.

Uletomy —Cicatricotomy.

Uliginous —Muddy.

Ulitis —Gingivitis.

Ulna —The inner and larger bone of the forearm, which is on the side opposite that of the thumb.

Ulnad —Toward the ulna bone.

Ulnae —Plural of ulna.

Ulnar —Pertaining to the ulna bone, to the medial side of the forearm or to nerve or artery named from ulna.

Ulnaris —Ulnar.

Ulnen —Pertaining to ulna.

Ulnocarpal —Pertaining to the ulna and carpus.

Ulnoradial —Pertaining to the ulna and radius.

Ulo- —A prefix meaning scar or scarring.

Ulocace —Ulceration of the gums.

Ulocarcinoma —Cancer of the gums.

Ulodermatitis —Dermatitis with scar tissue formation.

Uloglossitis —Inflammation of the gums and tongue.

Uloid —Scarlike.

Uloncus —Swelling or tumor of the gums.

Ulorrhagia —Bleeding from the gums.

Ulorrhea —Discharge from the gums.

Ulosis —Cicatrization. Formation of scar tissue.

Ulotic —Cicatricial. Forming scar tissue.

Ulotomy —1. Incision of the scar tissue. 2. Incision of the gums.

Ulotrichous —Having short woolly hair.

Ulotripsis —Stimulation of the gums by massage.

Ultimate —Final or last.

Ultra- —Prefix meaning beyond, excess.

Ultrabrachycephalic —Having a very short skull with an index of 90 or more.

Ultracentrifugation —To cause separation and sedimentation of molecules of a substance by exceedingly high centrifugal force, by placing the substance in an ultracentrifuge machine which is rotated at very high speed.

Ultracentrifuge —A very high-speed centrifuge machine used in ultracentrifugation.

Ultradian —Pertaining to the phenomena occurring in living organisms, which repeat within every 24 hours.

Ultradolichocephalic —Having a very long skull with an index of less than 65.

Ultrafilter —The filter used in ultrafiltration.

Ultrafiltration —Filtration through a filter which removes ultramicroscopic (very minute) particles.

Ultraligation —Ligation of a blood vessel beyond the origin of a branch.

Ultramicrobe —A microorganism that is not visible by the ordinary microscope.

Ultramicroscope —Microscope by which objects invisible through an ordinary microscope, may be seen.

Ultramicroscopic —Submicroscopic.

Ultramicroscopy —To see the objects by ultramicroscope.

Ultramicrotome —A microtome that makes extremely thin slices of a tissue.

Ultramicrotomy —To cut extremely thin sections of an object by using ultramicrotome, for ultramicroscopic examination.

Ultrasonic —Pertaining to the sound of frequency above 20,000 cycles per second, which is not audible.

Ultrasonics —The science dealing with the study of inaudible sounds with frequencies of more than 20,000 cycles par second.

Ultrasonogram —The image produced by use of ultrasonography.

Ultrasonograph —Sonograph. Computerized instrument used to create an image using ultrasound.

Ultrasonographer —Songrapher, Echographer. A person who performs and/or interprets ultrasonographic examinations.

Ultrasonography —To obtain image or photograph of an organ or tissue by using ultrasound. Ultrasound waves strike the tissues of different densities and produce the echoes of different intensities which are recorded, that give the image of the tissues.

Ultrasonosurgery —To perform an operation, particularly in the central nervous system by use of ultrasound.

Ultrasound —Inaudible sound with the frequency of 20,000 to 10,000,000,000 cycles per second.

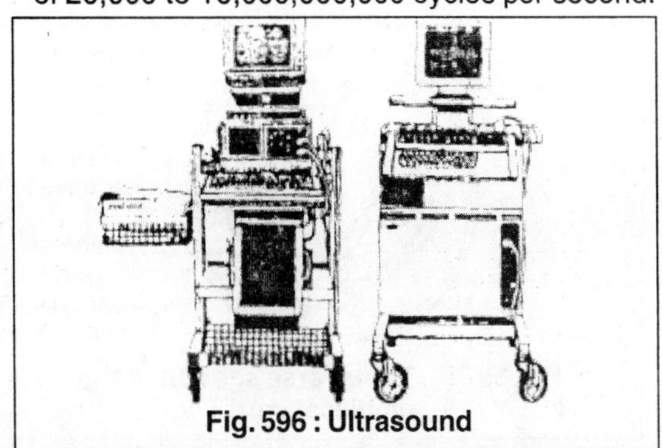

Fig. 596 : Ultrasound

Ultrastructure —A very minute structure visible only under the ultramicroscope.

Ultratherm —A short-wave diathermy machine.

Ultraviolet —Beyond the visible spectrum at its violet end.

Ultraviolet radiation —The emitting of ultraviolet rays from the sun or an artificial source.

Ultraviolet rays —Invisible rays of the spectrum which are beyond the visible violet end, with the wavelength between 3900 to 1800 Angstrom units.

Ultraviolet therapy —Treatment of diseases as rickets with ultraviolet radiation.

Ultromotivity —Power of spontaneous movement.

Ululation —The loud crying, of mentally ill persons.

Umbilical —Pertaining to the umbilicus.

Umbilical cord —A cord connecting the fetus with the placenta, which contains two arteries and one vein surrounded by a gelatinous substance known as Wharton's jelly.

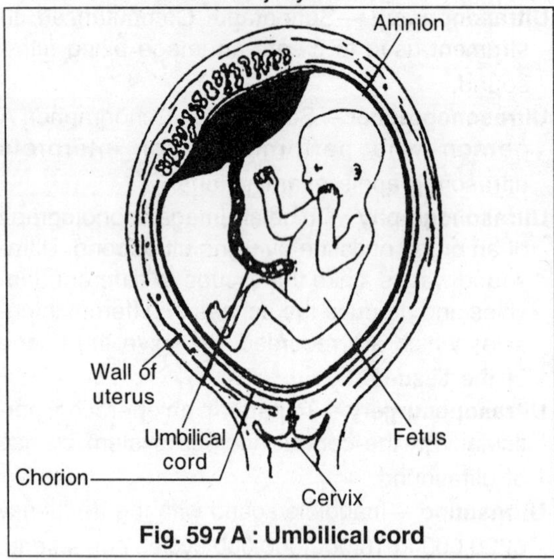

Fig. 597 A : Umbilical cord

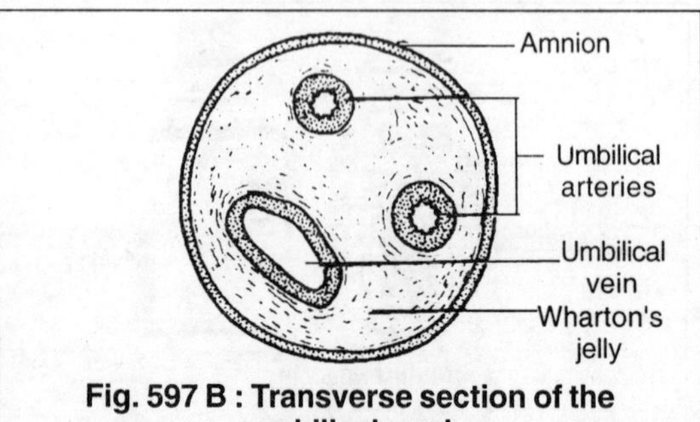

Fig. 597 B : Transverse section of the umbilical cord

Umbilical hernia —A hernia in the region of the umbilicus.

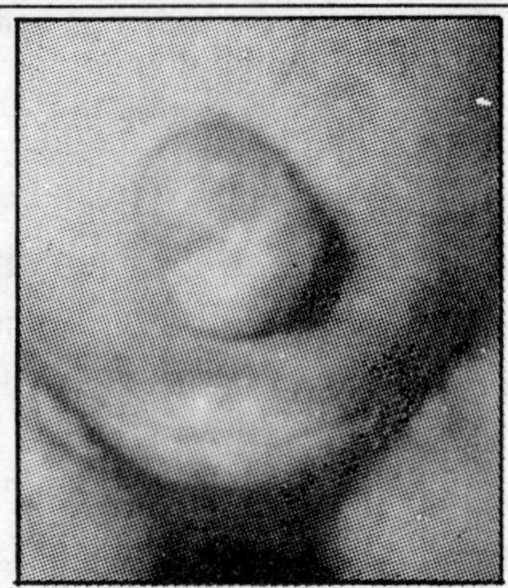
Fig. 598 : Umbilical hernia

Umbilical souffle —A hissing sound arising from the umbilical cord.

Umbilicate —Pertaining to or shaped like the umbilicus.

Umbilicated —Having depression resembling the umbilicus.

Umbilication —1. A depression resembling the umbilicus. 2. Formation of a depression on the top of an abscess or vesicle.

Umbilicus —Navel. 1. A depression in the middle of the abdomen. 2. The scar marking the site of attachment of the umbilical cord in the fetus.

Umbo —Projecting center of a round surface.

Umbra —The edge of an x-ray picture.

Umbrella filter —A filter placed in a blood vessel to prevent embolus from passing that point.

Un- —A prefix meaning back, reversal and not.

Uncal —Pertaining to the uncus of the brain.

Uncarthrosis —Bone disease involving the uncinate processes of vertebrae.

Unci —Plural of uncus.

Uncia —An ounce.

Unciform —Hook-shaped.

Unciforme —Unciform.

Uncinaria —Hook-worm.

Uncinariasis —Hook-worm disease.

Uncinate —Hook-shaped; hooked.

Uncinate convolution —Uncinate gyrus.

Uncinatum —Hooked.

Uncipressure —Pressure applied with a hook to stop the bleeding.

Uncomplemented —Not united or associated with complement and thus inactive.

Unconditioned reflex —A natural or inborn reflex action, not acquired.

Unconscious —Insensible or not responding to sensory stimuli.

Unconsciousness —Insensibility or the condition of not responding to sensory stimuli.

Unco-ossified —Not ossified into one bone.

Uncovertebral —Pertaining to the uncinate process of a vertebra.

Unction —1. An ointment. 2. Inunction. Application of an ointment.

Unctuous —Oily or greasy.

Uncture —Ointment.

Uncus —1. Any hook-shaped structure 2. Hooked anterior end of hippocampal gyrus.

Underachiever —A person whose achievements are less than that which is predicted to be possible.

Underbite —A condition in which the lower incisors pass in front of the upper incisors when the mouth in closed.

Undernutrition —Inadequate nutrition from any cause.

Understain —To stain less deeply than usual.

Undertoe —Displacement of the great toe underneath the others.

Underventilation —Hypoventilation.

Underweight —A condition in which the body weight of a person is at least 10% less than what is normal for that person.

Undescended —That which has not descended as an undescended testis which remains in the inguinal canal or abdominal cavity at birth and does not descend into the scrotum.

Undifferentiated —Not differentiated; primitive.

Undifferentiation —Anaplasia.

Undine —A small glass flask for washing eyes.

Undinism —Awakening of sexual desire by urination or at sight of urine.

Undulant —Moving like waves.

Undulate —Wavy or having a wavy border.

Undulation —A wavelike motion or pulsation.

Ung. —Unguentum. Ointment.

Ungual —Pertaining to or resembling the nails.

Ungual phalanx —Terminal phalanx of each finger and toe.

Unguent —Ointment.

Unguentum —Ointment.

Ungues —Plural of unguis.

Unguiculate —Clawlike; having claws or nails.

Unguinal —Ungual.

Unguis —Nail.

Ungula —An instrument for removing dead fetus from the uterus.

Uni- —A prefix meaning one.

Uniarticular —Pertaining to a single joint.

Uniaxial —Having only one axis.

Unibasal —Having only one base.

Unicameral —Monolocular. Having only one cavity or chamber.

Unicamerate —Unicameral.

Unicellular —Having only one cell.

Unicentral —Having only one center.

Uniceps —Having a single head or origin, as a muscle.

Unicorn —Having a single cornu or horn.

Unicornous —Unicorn.

Unicuspid —Having a single cusp.

Unicuspidate —Unicuspid.

Unifamilial —Pertaining to or occurring in a single family as a disease.

Uniflagellate —Having a single flagellum.

Uniforate —Having only one opening.

Uniform —Having only one shape.

Unigerminal —Pertaining to a single ovum or germ.

Uniglandular —Pertaining to or affecting a single gland.

Unigravida —A woman who is pregnant for the first time.

Unilaminar —Having a single layer.

Unilaminate —Unilaminar.

Unilateral —Pertaining to, affecting or occurring on only one side.

Unilobar —Having a single lobe.

Unilocular —Having a single cavity.

Unimolecular —Monomolecular.

Uninuclear —Having only one nucleus.

Uninucleated —Uninuclear.

Uniocular —Pertaining to or having only one eye.

Union —The act of joining two or more things into one or the state of being so joined, as of the ends of a broken bone or edges of a wound.

Unioval —Uniovular. Monozygotic.

Uniovular —Unioval. Pertaining to or formed from a single ovum.

Unipara —Primipara.

Uniparous —Primiparous.

Unipolar —1. Having or pertaining to a single pole. 2. Having a single process as a nerve cell.

Unipotent, Unipotential —Having only one power, as producing cells of one order only.

Uniseptate —Having only one septum.

Unisex —1. Lack of differentiation between male and female, especially with respect to hair style or clothing. 2. Suitable for use by either sex.

Unisexual —Having the sex organs of one sex only.

Unit —1. A single of many similar things; one segment of a whole thing that is made up of such similar segments. 2. A determined amount of anything adopted as a standard of measurement.

Angstrom unit —An international unit of wavelength which is 1/10,000,000 of a millimeter or 1/254,000,000 of an inch.

Coronary care unit —A department of a hospital specially designed and equipped for care and emergency treatment of patients with severe heart disease.

Intensive care unit —A department of a hospital with special equipments and specialists for the care of seriously ill patients.

International unit —A unit defined by the International conference for unification of Formulae. International conference for unification of Formulae

Kienbock's unit —A unit of X-ray exposure equal to 0.1 erythema; symbol is X.

Light unit —The amount of light one fit from a standard candle.

SI unit —Any of the units of the International System of Units adopted at the eleventh International Conference of Weights and Measures in 1960. SI Units include meter (length), kilogram (weight), second (time) and ampere (electric current), etc.

Unit of heat —1. Calorie (gram calorie, Kilocalorie) 2. Joule.

Unit of wavelength —Angstrom unit. Nanometer.

Unitarian —Composed of a single unit.

Unitary —Pertaining to a single unit.

Uniterminal —Having only one terminal.

Univalence —The condition of having only one valence.

Univalency —Univalence.

Univalent —Monovalent. Having a valence of one.

Universal —General.

Universal antidote —An antidote used in poisoning where the specific antidote is unknown or not available.

Universal donor —A person of blood group O whose blood may be transfused to a person of the other A B O blood groups, without danger.

Universal recipient —A person of blood group AB who may receive blood of the person of any blood group, without danger.

Unmedullated —Unmyelinated.

Unmyelinated —Without a myelin sheath.

Unphysiological —Contrary to physiological principles.

Unrest —Disquiet, instability.

Unsanitary —Insanitary.

Unsaturated —1. Capable of dissolving or absorbing more. 2. Denoting compounds in which two or more atoms are united by double or triple bonds.

Unsaturated compound —An organic compound having double or triple bonds between the carbon atoms.

Unsex —To deprive of the sex glands (testes or ovaries) or the sexual character.

Unsound —Unhealthy.

Unsoundedness —Unhealthiness.

Unstriated —Unstriped. Without striations, as smooth muscle.

Unstriped —Unstriated.

Unwell —Sick; ill.

Unwholesome —Not favourable to health.

Upper —Higher in place.

Upsiloid —Shaped like the letter U or V.

Uptake —Absorption by tissues or an entire organism.

Urachal —Pertaining to urachus.

Urachus —A fibrous cord extending from the apex of the bladder to the umbilicus.

Uracrasia —1. Disordered state of the urine. 2. Inability to retain the urine.

Uracratia —Inability to retain urine.

Uragogue —Diuretic.

Uraniscochasm —Uranoschisis.

Uranisconitis —Inflammation of the palate.

Uraniscoplasty —Uranoplasty.

Uraniscorrhaphy —Uranoplasty. Suturing of a cleft palate.

Uraniscus —Palate.

Uranoplasty —Repair of the cleft palate by plastic surgery.

Uranoplegia —Paralysis of the muscles of soft palate.

Uranorrhaphy —Uraniscorrhaphy.

Uranoschisis —Cleft palate.

Uranostaphyloplasty —Correction of the defect of soft and hard palates by plastic surgery.

Uranostaphylorrhaphy —Correction of the defect of soft and hard palates by suturing.

Uranostaphyloschisis —Cleft or fissure of the soft and hard palates.

Uranoveloschisis —Uranostaphyloschisis.

Urapostema —An abscess filled with urine.

Uraroma —Sweet odor of the urine.

Urarthritis —Arthritis due to gout.

Urate —A salt of uric acid, normally present in the urine.

Uratemia —Presence of urates, especially sodium urate in the blood.

Uratic —Pertaining to urates or gout.

Uratolysis —The decomposition of urates.

Uratolytic —Causing the decomposition of urates.

Uratoma —A concretion of urates found in the joint in gout; tophus.

Uratosis —The deposit of urates in the tissues.

Uraturia —Lithuria. Excess of urates in the urine.

Urceiform —Pitcher-shaped.

Urceolate —Urceiform.

Ur-defense —A belief such as religious or scientific belief that is essential to maintain the mental health of the individual.

Urea —The chief nitrogenous constituent of urine and the chief nitrogenous end-product of protein metabolism, which is formed in the liver from amino acids and from ammonia compounds. Its excess in urine indicates the condition uremia.

Urea frost —White flaky deposits of urea seen on the skin of patients with advanced uremia.

Ureagenesis —Ureapoiesis.

Ureagenetic —Pertaining to or producing urea.

Ureal —Pertaining to or containing urea.

Ureameter —Ureometer. An apparatus for determining the amount of urea in urine.

Ureametry —To determine the amount of urea in urine.

Ureapoiesis —Production of urea.

Urease —An enzyme that accelerates the hydrolysis of urea into carbon dioxide and ammonia.

Urecchysis —Effusion of urine into the tissues.

Uredema —Swelling due to presence of urine in the subcutaneous tissues.

Ureic —Ureal.

Urelcosis —Ulceration of the urinary tract.

Uremia —The toxic condition associated with renal failure, produced by retention of end-products of protein metabolism (urea etc.), which are normally excreted by the kidneys. It is characterized by persistent dull headache, nausea, vomiting, vertigo, convulsions and coma.

Uremic —Pertaining to or caused by uremia.

Uremigenic —Caused by or causing uremia.

Ureogenesis —Formation of urea.

Ureometer —Ureameter.

Ureometry —Ureametry.

Uresiesthesia, Uresiesthesis —Normal tendency of urination.

Uresis —Urination.

Ureter —A tube which originates in the pelvis of the kidney and terminates in the base of the bladder through which urine passes from the kidney to the bladder.

Ureteral —Concerning the ureter.

Ureteralgia —Pain in the ureter.

Uretercystoscope —A cystoscope combined with a ureteral catheter.

Ureterectasia —Ureterectasis.

Ureterectasis —Dilatation of the ureter.

Ureterectomy —Excision of a ureter.

Ureteric —Ureteral.

Ureteritis —Inflammation of the ureter.

Uretero- —A prefix meaning ureter.

Ureterocele —Cystlike dilatation of the ureter near its opening into the bladder.

Ureterocelectomy —Excision of a ureterocele.

Ureterocervical —Pertaining to the ureter and the cervix uteri.

Ureterocolic —Pertaining to the ureter and the colon.

Ureterocolostomy —The implantation of ureter into the colon.

Ureterocystanastomosis —Ureteroneocystostomy.

Ureterocystoneostomy —Ureteroneocystostomy.

Ureterocystoplasty —Repair of the ureter and urinary bladder by plastic surgery.

Ureterocystoscope —Uretercystoscope.

Ureterocystostomy —Ureteroneocystostomy.

Ureterodialysis —Rupture of a ureter.

Ureteroenteric —Pertaining to a ureter and the intestine.

Ureteroenterostomy —Formation of a passage between a ureter and the intestine.

Ureterography —X-ray examination of the ureter, after injection of a radiopaque substance.

Ureteroheminephrectomy —In case of reduplication of the kidney and ureter on one side, surgical removal of the reduplicated portion.

Ureterohydronephrosis —Dilatation of the ureter and pelvis of kidney due to collection of urine resulting from obstruction in its out flow.

Ureteroileoneocystostomy —Anastomosis of the upper segment of a partially destroyed ureter to a segment of ileum, the lower end of which is then implanted into the urinary bladder, to restore the continuity of the urinary tract.

Ureteroileostomy —Anastomosis of a ureter to an isolated segment of the ileum, which is connected to an opening in the abdominal wall so that urine passes through this opening.

Ureterolith —A calculus in the ureter.

Ureterolithiasis —Formation of a calculus in the ureter.

Ureterolithotomy —Incision of ureter for removal of calculus.

Ureterolysis —1. Rupture of the ureter. 2. Paralysis of the ureter. 3. Surgical freeing the ureter from adhesions.

Ureteroneocystostomy —Ureterocystoneostomy. Ureterocystostomy. Surgical formation of a new passage between a ureter and the bladder.

Ureteroneopyelostomy —Ureteropyeloneostomy. Surgical formation of a new passage between a ureter and the renal pelvis.

Ureteronephrectomy —Surgical excision of a kidney with its ureter.

Ureteropathy —Any disease of the ureter.

Ureteropelvioplasty —Repair of the junction of the ureter and the renal pelvis by plastic surgery.

Ureterophlegma —Accumulation of mucus in the ureter.

Ureteroplasty —Plastic surgery of the ureter.

Ureteroproctostomy —Surgical formation of a passage from the ureter to the lower portion of rectum.

Ureteropyelitis —Inflammation of the pelvis of kidney and a ureter.

Ureteropyelography —X-ray examination of the ureter and renal pelvis.

Ureteropyeloneostomy —Ureteroneopyelostomy.

Ureteropyelonephritis —Inflammation of the ureter, renal pelvis and kidney.

Ureteropyeloplasty —Repair of a ureter and renal pelvis by plastic surgery.

Ureteropyelostomy —Ureteropyeloneostomy.

Ureteropyosis —Suppurative inflammation of a ureter.

Ureterorectostomy —Ureteroproctostomy.

Ureterorenoscope —A fiberoptic endoscope used in ureterorenoscopy.

Ureterorenoscopy —Inspection of the interior of the ureter and kidney by using a ureterorenoscope.

Ureterorrhagia —Hemorrhage from the ureter.

Ureterorrhaphy —Suture of the ureter.

Ureteroscope —An instrument which is passed through the urinary bladder up into the ureter to inspect its lumen and collecting system of the kidney.

Ureterosigmoid —Pertaining to the ureter and the sigmoid colon.

Ureterosigmoidostomy —Implantation of the ureter into the sigmoid flexure.

Ureterostegnosis —Ureterostenosis.

Ureterostenosis —Stricture of a ureter.

Ureterostoma —An opening through which ureter enters the bladder.

Ureterostomy —To make a permanent opening into the ureter.

Ureterotomy —Incision of the ureter.

Ureterotrigonoenterostomy —Surgical excision of the trigone of the bladder with one or both of the ureteral openings and implanting it into the intestine.

Ureteroureteral —Pertaining to two parts of the same ureter or the union of one ureter with the other.

Ureteroureterostomy —To form a passage from one ureter to another.

Ureterouterine —Pertaining to the ureter and uterus.

Ureterovaginal —Pertaining to a ureter and the vagina.

Ureterovesical —Pertaining to a ureter and urinary bladder.

Ureterovesicostomy —Reimplantation of a ureter into the bladder.

Urethra —A canal through which urine passes from bladder to the outside of the body.

Prostatic urethra —The prostatic part of male urethra which is about 2.5 cm. in length.

Urethra muliebris —The female urethra.

Urethra virilis —The male urethra.

Urethral —Pertaining to the urethra.

Urethralgia —Pain in the urethra.

Urethrascope —Urethroscope.

Urethratresia —Imperforation or occlusion of the urethra.

Urethrectomy —Excision of the urethra or part of it.

Urethremorrhagia —Urethrorrhagia.

Urethremphraxis —Urethrophraxis.

Urethreurynter —Urethral dilator.

Urethrism, Urethrismus —Irritability or chronic spasm of the urethra.

Urethritis —Inflammation of the urethra.

Gonococcal urethritis, Specific urethritis — Urethritis caused by gonococcus.

Nongonococcal urethritis, Nonspecific urethritis, Simple urethritis —Urethritis not due to gonococcal infection.

Urethro- —A prefix which means urethra.

Urethrobulbar —Pertaining to urethra and the bulb of the penis.

Urethrocele —Prolapse of urethra in the female.

Urethrocystitis —Inflammation of the urethra and bladder.

Urethrocystometrography —Urethrocystometry.

Urethrocystometry —To measure pressure in the urinary bladder and urethra simultaneously.

Urethrocystopexy —Plastic surgery of the urethra bladder junction to relieve stress incontinence of urine.

Urethrodynia —Urethralgia.

Urethrograph —An instrument for measuring the caliber of urethra.

Urethrography —X-ray examination of the urethra after the injection of a radiopaque substance into it.

Urethrometer —An instrument for measuring the diameter of urethra.

Urethrometry —Measurement of diameter of the urethra.

Urethropenile —Pertaining to the urethra and penis.

Urethroperineal —Pertaining to the urethra and perineum.

Urethroperineoscrotal —Pertaining to the urethra, perineum and scrotum.

Urethropexy —Surgical fixation of the urethra.

Urethrophraxis —Urethremphraxis. Obstruction of the urethra.

Urethrophyma —A tumor of the urethra.

Urethroplasty —Plastic surgery of the urethra.

Urethroprostatic —Pertaining to the urethra and prostate gland.

Urethrorectal —Pertaining to the urethra and the rectum.

Urethrorrhagia —Bleeding from the urethra.

Urethrorrhaphy —Suture of a urethral fistula.

Urethrorrhea —Abnormal discharge from the urethra.

Urethroscope —An instrument for visual examination of the interior of the urethra.

Urethroscopic —Pertaining to urethroscope or urethroscopy.

Urethroscopy —Visual examination of the interior of the urethra with a urethroscope.

Urethrospasm —Spasm of the urethra causing its constriction.

Urethrostaxis —Oozing of blood from the urethra.

Urethrostenosis —Narrowing of the urethra.

Urethrostomy —Surgical formation of a permanent opening of the urethra at the perineal surface.

Urethrotome —An instrument for cutting a urethral stricture.

Urethrotomy —The cutting of the urethral stricture.

Urethrotrigonitis —Inflammation of the urethra and the trigone of the bladder.

Urethrovaginal —Pertaining to the urethra and vagina.

Urethrovesical —Pertaining to the urethra and bladder.

Urethrovesicopexy —Surgical suspension of the urethra and the base of the urinary bladder from the posterior surface of the pubic symphysis or anterior abdominal wall for correction of stress incontinence of urine.

-uretic —A suffix which means urine.

Uretic —Diuretic. Increasing the excretion of urine.

Urgency —Earnest necessity to urinate.

Urhydrosis —The presence of urea in the sweat.

U R I —Upper respiratory infection.

Uric —Of or pertaining to urine.

Uricacidemia —Excess of uric acid in the blood.

Uricaciduria —Excess of uric acid in the urine.

Uricemia —Uricacidemia.

Uricocholia —Presence of uric acid in the bile.

Uricolysis —The decomposition of uric acid.

Uricolytic —Decomposing the uric acid.

Uricometer —An apparatus for determining the amount of uric acid in the urine.

Uricopoiesis —Production of uric acid.

Uricosuria —Excretion of uric acid in the urine.

Uricosuric —Pertaining to or affected with uricosuria or increasing the excretion of uric acid in the urine.

Uridrosis —Urhydrosis.

Uriesthesia —Uresiesthesia.

Uriesthesis —Uresiesthesis.

Urina —Urine.

Urinal —A receptacle for urine.

Urinalysis —Analysis of the urine.

Urinary —Pertaining to, secreting, or containing urine.

Urinary bladder —A container in the body receiving urine excreted by the kidneys.

Urinary calculus —A calculus formed in the urinary tract.

Urinary casts —Casts of kidney tubules passed in the urine.

Urinary diversion —The surgical redirection of urine flow.

Urinary incontinence —See incontinence.

Urinary reflex —Desire to urinate resulting from accumulation of urine in the bladder.

Urinary stammering —Temporary hindrances during micturition.

Urinate —Micturate. To pass urine from the bladder.

Urination —The act of passing urine from the bladder.

Urine —The fluid filtered from the blood by kidneys, which is excreted from the kidneys and stored in the bladder and discharged normally voluntarily through the urethra.

Urinemia —Uremia.

Uriniferous —Carrying urine.

Urinific —Uriniparous.

Uriniparous —Forming urine.

Urinogenital —Urogenital.

Urinogenous —Urogenous.

Urinology —Urology.

Urinoma —A cyst containing urine.

Urinometer —An apparatus for determining the specific gravity of urine.

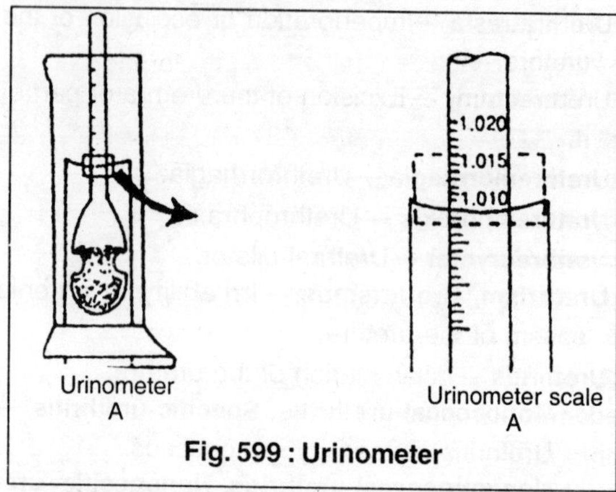

Fig. 599 : Urinometer

Urinometry —Determination of specific gravity of the urine.

Urinophil —Growing in the urine, as some bacteria.

Urinoscopy —Uroscopy.

Urinose, Urinous —Pertaining to or of the nature of or containing urine.

Urinosexual —Urogenital.

Urinous —Pertaining to or of the nature of urine.

Uriposia —The drinking of urine.

Uro- —A prefix meaning pertaining to urine.

Uroammoniac —Containing urine and ammonia.

Urobilin —A brown pigment formed by oxidation of urobilinogen.

Urobilinemia —Presence of urobilin pigments in the blood.

Urobilinicterus —Jaundice due to urobilinemia.

Urobilinogen —A colorless compound formed in the intestine by the action of intestinal bacteria on bilirubin.

Urobilinogenemia —Presense of urobilinogen in the blood.

Urobilinuria —Excess of urobilin in the urine.

Urocele —Distension of the scrotum caused by accumulation of urine.

Urocheras —Calcareous sediment in the urine.

Urochesia —The discharge of urine in the feces.

Urochrome —A pigment derived from urobilin, found in the urine that gives the urine its characteristic color.

Uroclepsia —Involuntary discharge of urine.

Urocrisia —Diagnosis by examining the urine.

Urocrisis —Urocrisia.

Urocyanogen —A blue pigment in the urine, especially in patients with cholera.

Urocyanosis —Indicanuria. Blue discoloration of the urine.

Urocyst —The urinary bladder.

Urocystic —Pertaining to the urinary bladder.

Urocystis —The urinary bladder.

Urocystitis —Inflammation of the urinary bladder.

Urodynamics —The dynamics of flow of urine in the urinary tract.

Urodynia —Pain during urination.

Uroedema —Uredema.

Uroenterone —Urogastrone.

Uroerythrin —Purpurin. A red pigment sometimes present in the urine.

Uroflowmeter —An apparatus that measures urine flow rates during micturition.

Urofuscin —A red-brown pigment sometimes found in urine, especially in cases of porphyrinuria.

Urofuscohematin —A reddish brown pigment present in the urine in some diseases.

Urogastrone —A polypeptide present in the urine which is a potent inhibitor of gastric secretion.

Urogenital —Urinogenital. Pertaining to the urinary and reproductive organs.

Urogenous —1. Producing urine. 2. Urinogenous. Originating in the urine.

Urogram —An X-ray film of a part of the urinary tract.

Urography —X-ray examination of any part of the urinary tract after introducing a radiopaque substance.

Ascending urography, Cystoscopic urography —Retrograde urography. Urography after injection of a contrast medium into the bladder through the urethra.

Descending urography, Excretion urography, Excretory urography, Intravenous urography —Urography after intravenous injection of a radiopaque substance which is excreted by the kidney and studied by X-ray during excretion.

Retrograde urography —Ascending urography, cystoscopic urography.

Urogravimeter —Urinometer.

Urohematin —Urobilin.

Urohematonephrosis —Distension of the renal pelvis with blood and urine.

Urohematoporphyrin —Urobilin.

Uroheparin —An inactive form of heparin excreted in the urine.

Urohypertensin —A pressure substance derived from the urine.

Urokinase —An enzyme obtained from human urine that is used as thrombolytic agent and administered intravenously.

Urokinetic —Resulting reflexly from stimulation of the urinary organs.

Urolagnia —Sexual excitement associated with urine or urination.

Urolith —A calculus in the urine or the urinary tract.

Urolithiasis —The formation of urinary calculi or the illness associated with urinary calculi.

Urolithic —Pertaining to urinary calculi.

Urolithology —The study of urinary calculi.

Urologic —Pertaining to urology.

Urological —Urologic.

Urologist —Specialist in urology.

Urology —Uronology. The branch of medical science concerned with the urinary tract in both sexes and genital tract in the male.

Urolutein —A yellow pigment seen in the urine.

Uromancy —Use of urinalysis for diagnosis of disease.

Uromelanin —Melanin, a black pigment occasionally found in the urine.

Uromelus —Sirenomelus. A congenitally deformed fetus with lower limbs fused.

Urometer —Urinometer.

Urometry —Urinometry.

Uroncus —A swelling or cyst containing urine.

Uronephrosis —Hydronephrosis. Nephrohydrosis.

Uronology —Urology.

Uronophil —Growing best in urine, as some microorganisms.

Uronophile —A microorganism that grows best in a culture containing urine.

Uronoscopy —Uroscopy.

Uropathogen —A microorganism causing disease of the urinary system.

Uropathy —Any disease of the urinary system.

Uropenia —Deficient secretion of urine.

Uropepsin —The end product of pepsin metabolism, excreted in the urine.

Urophanic —Appearing in the urine.

Urophein, Urophaein —Gray pigment sometimes found in the urine.

Urophosphometer —An instrument for determining the amount of phosphorus in the urine.

Uroplania —Discharge of urine from the organs other than the urinary tract.

Uropoiesis —The formation of urine.

Uropoietic —Pertaining to the formation of, or forming urine.

Uroporphyria —Porphyria in which excess of uroporphyrin is excreted in the urine.

Uroporphyrin —A reddish pigment present in the urine and feces in cases of porphyria.

Uroporphyrinogen —A precursor of uroporphyrin.

Uropsammus —Gravel of urine.

Uropurpurin —A purple pigment sometimes found in the urine.

Uropyonephrosis —Presence of urine and pus in the renal pelvis.

Uropyoureter —Accumulation of urine and pus in the ureter.

Uroradiology —Radiology of the urinary tract.

Urorectal —Pertaining to the urinary tract and the rectum.

Urorosein —Urorrhodin.

Urorrhagia —Polyuria.

Urorrhea —Enuresis.

Urorrhodin —Urorosein. A rose-colored pigment seen in the urine in certain infectious diseases such as typhoid fever and tuberculosis.

Urorubin —A red pigment found in the urine.

Urorubrohematin —A reddish pigment occasionally found in the urine in various chronic diseases.

Uroscheocele —Urocele.

Uroschesis —Suppression or retention of urine.

Uroscopic —Pertaining to uroscopy.

Uroscopy —Examination of the urine for diagnosis of the disease.

Urosemiology —The study of urine as an aid to diagnosis.

Urosepsis —Septic poisoning from retention and absorption of urinary substances in the tissues.

Urosis —Any disease of the urinary organs.

Urostealith —A urinary calculus containing fatty substances.

Urothelium —The epithelium of the urinary bladder.

Urothorax —The presence of urine in the thoracic cavity.

Urotoxia —Toxicity of the urine.

Urotoxicity —Urotoxia.

Urotoxin —Toxic substances in the urine.

Uroureter —Distension of the ureter with urine.

Urous —Of the nature of urine.

Uroxanthin —A yellow pigment found in the urine.

Urtica —A blister or wheal.

Urticant —Producing urticaria.

Urticaria —Hives. Nettle rash. A vascular reac-

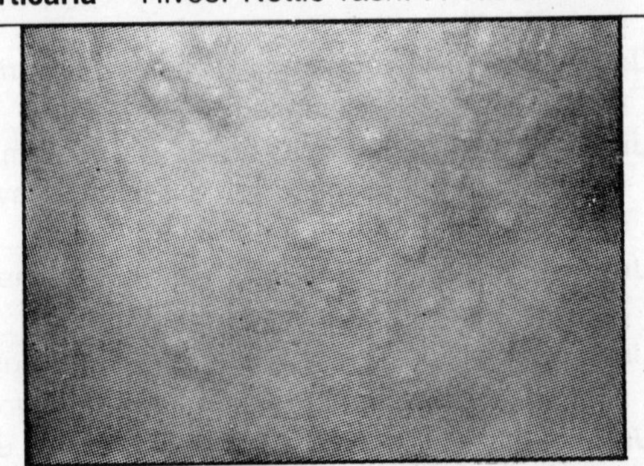

Fig. 600 : Urticaria

tion of the skin characterized by transient appearance of wheals attended by itching, caused by certain foods, drugs, infection or emotional stress.

Urticarial —Pertaining to urticaria.

Urticate —1. To produce urticaria. 2. Afflicted with urticaria.

Urtication —1. The development of urticaria. 2. A burning sensation as of stinging with nettles.

Ustion —Cauterization.

Ustulation —Drying or parching of a moist drug.

Ustus —Burned.

Ut dict. —Ut dictum. As directed.

Utend —Utendus. To be used.

Uter-, Utero- —Prefixes indicating relationship to the uterus.

Uteralgia —Pain in the uterus.

Uterectomy —Hysterectomy. Surgical removal of the uterus.

Uteri —Plural of uterus.

Uterine —Pertaining to the uterus.

Uterine souffle —A vascular sound heard in the pregnant uterus by stethoscope.

Uterine subinvolution —See subinvolution.

Uterine tube —Fallopian tube.

Uteroabdominal —Pertaining to the uterus and abdomen.

Uterocele —Hernia containing the uterus.

Uterocervical —Pertaining to the uterus and the cervix uteri.

Uterocystostomy —To form a passage between cervix of the uterus and the bladder.

Uterofixation —Hysteropexy. Fixation of a displaced uterus.

Uterogenic —Produced in the uterus.

Uterogestation —Pregnancy in the uterus; normal pregnancy.

Uterography —X-ray examination of the uterus.

Uterolith —Hysterolith.

Uterometer —Hysterometer.

Uteroovarian —Pertaining to the uterus and ovary.

Uteroparietal —Pertaining to the uterus and the abdominal wall.

Uteropexia, Uteropexy —Hysteropexy.

Uteropexy —Hysteropexy.

Uteroplacental —Pertaining to the uterus and placenta.

Uteroplasty —Repair of the uterus by plastic surgery.

Uterorectal —Pertaining to the uterus and rectum.

Uterosacral —Pertaining to the uterus and sacrum.

Uterosalpingography —Hysterosalpingography.

Uterosclerosis —Sclerosis of the uterus.

Uteroscope —Hysteroscope.

Uteroscopy —Hysteroscopy.

Uterotome —Hysterotome.

Uterotomy —Hysterotomy.

Uterotonic —Increasing the tone of uterine muscle.

Uterotractor —An instrument for applying traction to the uterine cervix.

Uterotrophic —Causing an effect on the uterus.

Uterotubal —Pertaining to the uterus and fallopian tubes.

Uterotubography —Hysterosalpingography.

Uterovaginal —Pertaining to the uterus and vagina.

Uteroventral —Uteroabdominal.

Uterovesical —Pertaining to the uterus and bladder.

Uterus —Womb. The hollow muscular organ of the female reproductive system in which the fertilized ovum is implanted and developing embryo and fetus is nourished. Its cavity opens into the vagina below and into a fallopian tube on each side.

Infantile uterus —An undeveloped uterus.

Uterus acolis —Uterus without cervix.

Uterus arcuatus —A uterus with a depressed arched fundus.

Uterus bicornis —Uterus with two cornua.

Uterus biforis —A uterus in which the external os is divided into two parts by a septum.

Uterus bilocularis —Uterus divided into two parts by a septum.

Uterus bipartite —Uterus septate.

Uterus cordiformis —Heart-shaped uterus.

Uterus duplex —Double uterus.

Uterus fetal —Uterus that is retarded in development.

Uterus gravid —Pregnant uterus.

Uterus septate —Bipartite uterus. A uterus divided into two cavities by an anteroposterior septum.

Uterus unicornis —Uterus with a single cornu.

Utricle —1. The larger of two sacs of the mem-

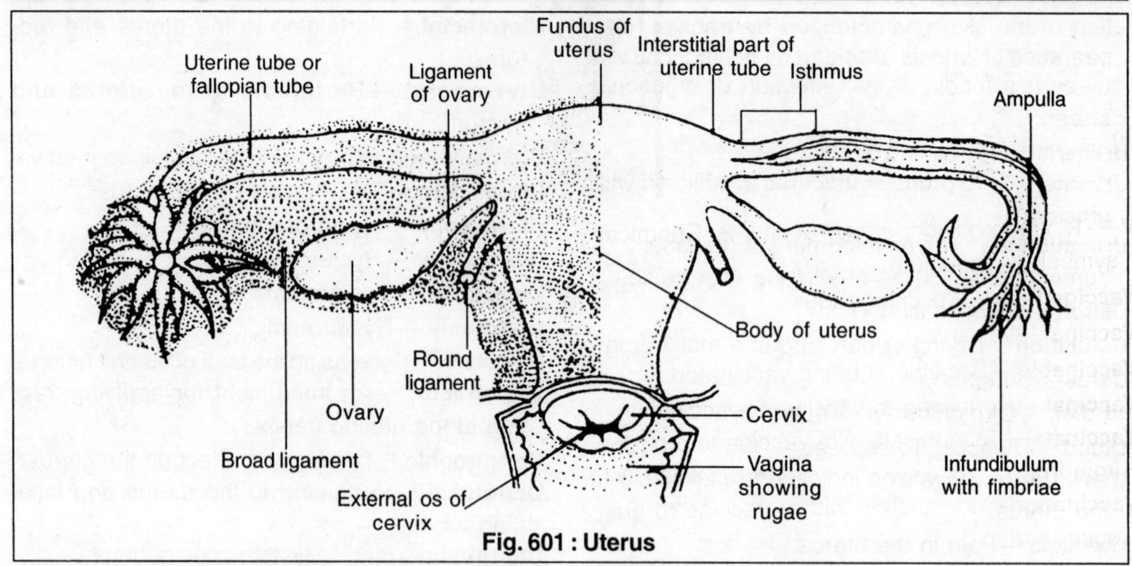

Fig. 601 : Uterus

branous labyrinth of the internal ear. 2. Any small sac.

Prostatic utricle, Urethral utricle —A small blind pouch in the substance of the prostate.

Utricular —1. Pertaining to the utricle. 2. Like a bladder.

Utriculi —Plural of utriculus.

Utriculitis —Inflammation of the utricle.

Utriculoplasty —Reduction of the size of the uterus by excising a longitudinal wedge-shaped section of it.

Utriculosaccular —Pertaining to the utricle and saccule of the labyrinth.

Utriculus —A utricle.

Utriform —Bottle-shaped.

Uvaeformis —Vascular lamina of the choroid.

Uvea —The middle pigmented layer of the eye consisting of the iris, ciliary body and choroid.

Uveal —Pertaining to the uvea.

Uveitic —Suffering from or pertaining to uveitis.

Uveitides —Plural of uveitis.

Uveitis —Inflammation of the uvea.

Uveoencephalitis —Harada syndrome characterized by bilateral retinal edema, uveitis, choroiditis and detachment of the retina with temporary or permanent deafness, graying of hair and alopecia.

Uveoneuraxitis —Uveitis with optic neuritis.

Uveoparotitis —Inflammation of the parotid gland and uveitis.

Uveoplasty —Repair of the uvea by plastic surgery.

Uveoscleritis —Scleritis due to extension of uveitis.

Uviform—Shaped like a grape.

Uviofast —Unaffected by ultraviolet radiation.

Uviol —A special kind of glass which is unusually transparent to ultraviolet rays.

Uviolize —To use ultraviolet rays in the treatment of diseases.

Uviometer —An instrument for measuring the intensity of ultraviolet light.

Uvioresistant —Uviofast.

Uviosensitive —Sensitive to the effects of ultraviolet rays.

Uvula —A hanging small fleshy mass, especially the palatine uvula.

Uvulaptosis —Uvuloptosis.

Uvular —Pertaining to the uvula.

Uvularis —Muscle of the uvula.

Uvulatome —Uvulotome.

Uvulatomy —To incise the uvula.

Uvulectomy —Excision of the uvula.

Uvuli —Plural of uvula.

Uvulitis —Inflammation of the uvula.

Uvulopalatopharyngoplasty —Palatopharyngoplasty. Excision of the extra palatal and oropharyngeal tissue in cases of snoring, with or without sleep apnea.

Uvulopalatoplasty —Palatoplasty.

Uvuloptosis —Relaxation and hanging of the uvula.

Uvulotome —Uvulatome. An instrument for removal of the uvula.

Uvulotomy —Uvulatomy.

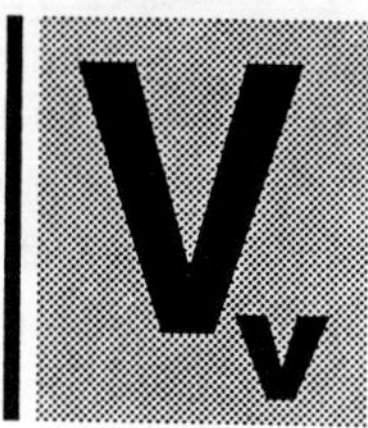

V —1. Vibrio; vision; visual acuity. 2. Chemical symbol for vanadium.

Vaccigenous —Vaccinogenous.

Vaccina —Vaccinia.

Vaccinable —Capable of being vaccinated.

Vaccinal —Pertaining to vaccine or vaccination.

Vaccinate —To inoculate with vaccine to produce immunity.

Vaccination —Inoculation with a vaccine to produce immunity.

Vaccinator —The person who vaccinates.

Vaccine —A suspension of live attenuated or killed microorganisms (bacteria, viruses etc.), of their toxins, or of substances extracted from them, to be introduced into the body for the prevention or treatment of infectious diseases.

Attenuated vaccine —Vaccine prepared from the live bacteria or viruses of which virulence is destroyed but their power to produce immunity is retained.

Autogenous vaccine —Homologous vaccine. Bacterial vaccine prepared from cultures of the material obtained from a lesion of the patient to be treated.

Bacterial vaccine —A suspension of bacteria killed or attenuated, in saline solution, used for injection into the body to develop active immunity against the same bacterium.

B C G vaccine —Vaccine prepared from Mycobacterium tuberculosis, used to produce active immunity against tuberculosis.

Cholera vaccine —Vaccine prepared from killed Vibrio cholerae; used to produce immunity against cholera.

DTP vaccine —A mixture of diphtheria and tetanus toxoids and vaccine prepared from killed Bordetella pertussis, used to produce active immunity against diphtheria, tetanus and whooping cough. It is administered intramuscularly.

Hepatitis B vaccine —Vaccine prepared from the surface antigen (HBs Ag) of the hepatitis B virus, used for immunization against Hepatitis B.

Heterologous vaccine —Vaccine prepared from the organisms obtained from a source other than the patient to be treated.

Homologous vaccine —Autogenous vaccine.

Influenza vaccine —Vaccine prepared from inactivated influenza virus, used to produce immunity against influenza.

Measles virus, inactivated vaccine —Vaccine prepared from inactivated measles virus. It is used only when there is contraindication to the use of live attenuated measles vaccine.

Measles virus, live attenuated vaccine —Vaccine prepared from live attenuated virus of measles, which is preferred to use.

Mixed vaccine —A vaccine prepared from more than one type of bacteria or viruses.

Mumps vaccine —Vaccine prepared from killed or live attenuated mumps virus, used to produce active immunity against mumps.

Pertussis vaccine —A vaccine made from killed pertussis bacilli, used to immunize against whooping cough.

Poliomyelitis vaccine —Vaccine prepared from killed polioviruses, injected subcutaneously, used to produce immunity against poliomyelitis.

Rabies vaccine —Vaccine prepared from killed, fixed virus of rabies, used to prevent rabies in a person following bite by a rabid animal.

Smallpox vaccine —Vaccine prepared from vaccinia virus, used to produce immunity against smallpox.

Triple vaccine —Vaccine made from cultures of three types of microorganisms.

Tuberculosis vaccine —BCG vaccine.

Typhoid vaccine —Vaccine prepared from killed organism Salmonella typhosa to immunize against typhoid.

Vaccinia —Cowpox, a contagious viral disease of

cows which is produced in humans by inoculation with cowpox virus, used to produce immunity by forming antibodies against smallpox. It is also transmitted by contact with a vaccinated person or an infected cow.

Vaccinial —Resembling vaccinia.

Vacciniform —Of the nature of or resembling vaccinia or cowpox.

Vaccinin —The inoculable principle of cowpox.

Vacciniola —Secondary general eruption occurring after local eruption from vaccine.

Vaccinist —Vaccinator.

Vaccinization —Vaccination repeated at short intervals until it is stopped.

Vaccinogen —A source of vaccine.

Vaccinogenous —Producing vaccine.

Vaccinoid —Resembling vaccinia.

Vaccinostyle —A pointed stylus used in vaccination.

Vaccinotherapeutics —Treatment of diseases by injection of bacterial vaccines.

Vaccinum —Vaccine.

Vacuolar —Pertaining to, of the nature of, or containing vacuoles.

Vacuolar degeneration —Swelling of cells with an increase in the number and size of vacuoles.

Vacuolate —Vacuolated.

Vacuolated —Containing vacuoles.

Vacuolation —1. Formation of vacuoles. 2. The condition of being vacuolated.

Vacuole —A space or cavity in the protoplasm of a cell filled with air or fluid.

Autophagic vacuole —A vacuole that contains pieces of ribosomes or mitochondria.

Contractile vacuole —A cavity filled with fluid in the protoplasm of certain protozoa. It gradually increases in size and is then emptied by sudden contraction.

Heterophagous vacuole —A vacuole that contains substances which come from outside the cell.

Vacuolization —Formation of vacuoles.

Vacuum —A space devoid of air.

Vacuum aspiration —Removal of the uterine contents by creating vacuum in the uterus by a suction apparatus attached to a catheter.

Vacuum extractor —A suction cup attached to the fetal head for applying traction to the fetus during delivery.

Vade mecum —A useful thing which a person keeps with him at all times, *e.g.*, a dictonary or a hand book.

Vagal —Pertaining to the vagus nerve.

Vagectomy —Excision of a segment of a vagal nerve.

Vagi —Plural of vagus.

Vagina —1. A canal in the female, from the vulva to the cervix uteri. 2. A sheath or sheathlike structure.

Vaginae —Plural of vagina.

Vaginal —Pertaining to the vagina, to the tunica vaginalis, or to any sheath.

Vaginalectomy —Vaginectomy. Excision of the tunica vaginalis.

Vaginal hysterectomy —Surgical removal of the uterus through vagina.

Vaginalitis —Inflammation of the tunica vaginalis testis.

Vaginapexy —Colpopexy. Vaginofixation.

Vaginate —Forming or enclosed in sheath.

Vaginectomy —1. Excision of the vagina or a part of it. 2. Resection of the tunica vaginalis testis.

Vaginism —Vaginismus.

Vaginismus —Painful spasm of the vagina.

Vaginitis —1. Colpitis. Inflammation of the vagina. 2. Inflammation of a sheath. 3. Inflammation of the tunica vaginalis of the testis.

Adhesive vaginitis —Inflammation of the vagina producing adhesions between its walls.

Amebic vaginitis —Vaginitis caused by Entamoeba histolytica.

Atrophic vaginitis —Postmenopausal vaginitis. Senile vaginitis. Vaginitis occurring following menopause, which is associated with estrogen deficiency. It is characterized by atrophy of the vagina with intense itching around it and lack of vaginal secretion.

Candidal vaginitis —Vaginitis caused by infection with the fungus Candida albicans.

Emphysematous vaginitis —Vaginitis with the formation of gas bubbles in the connective tissues.

Postmenopausal vaginitis —Atrophic vaginitis.

Senile vaginitis —Atrophic vaginitis.

Trichomonas vaginalis vaginitis —Vaginitis caused by infection with Trichomonas vaginalis, a flagellate protozoon.

Vagino- —A prefix which means vagina.

Vaginoabdominal —Pertaining to the vagina and abdomen.

Vaginocele —Colpocele.

Vaginodynia —Colpodynia. Pain in the vagina.

Vaginofixation —Colpopexy.

Vaginogenic —Originating in the vagina.

Vaginogram —X-ray picture of the vagina.

Vaginography —X-ray examination of the vagina.

Vaginohysterectomy —Vaginal hysterectomy.

Vaginolabial —Pertaining to the vagina and labia.

Vaginometer —An instrument for measuring the length and expansion of the vagina.

Vaginomycosis —A fungus disease of the vagina.

Vaginopathy —Any disease of the vagina.

Vaginoperineal —Pertaining to the vagina and perineum.

Vaginoperineoplasty —Colpoperineoplasty.

Vaginoperineorrhaphy —Colpoperineorrhaphy. The sewing of the tear involving both the vagina and perineum.

Vaginoperineotomy —To make an incision into the vagina and perineum.

Vaginoperitoneal —Pertaining to the vagina and peritoneum.

Vaginopexy —Colpopexy.

Vaginoplasty —Colpoplasty.

Vaginoscope —Colposcope.

Vaginosis —Disease of the vagina.

Vaginotome —An instrument for making an incision in the vaginal walls.

Vaginotomy —Colpotomy.

Vaginovesical —Pertaining to the vagina and bladder

Vaginovulvar —Pertaining to the vagina and vulva.

Vagitis —Inflammation of the vagus nerve.

Vagitus —The cry of an infant.

Vagitus uterinus —The cry of an infant in the uterus before birth.

Vago- —A prefix which means vagus nerve.

Vagoglossopharyngeal —Pertaining to the vagus and glossopharyngeal nerves.

Vagolysis —Surgical destruction of the vagus nerve.

Vagolytic —1. Pertaining to vagolysis. 2. An agent having the effect similar to that produced by interruption of impulses transmitted by the vagus nerve.

Vagomimetic —An agent having the effect similar to that produced by stimulation of the vagus nerve.

Vagopressure —Pressure exerted on the vagus nerve.

Vagosympathetic —The cervical sympathetic and vagus nerves considered together.

Vagotomy —Surgical transection of the vagus nerve.

Vagotonia —Irritability of the vagus nerve.

Vagotonic —Pertaining to the irritability of the vagus nerve.

Vagotonin —A hormonal preparation from the pancreas which increases vagal tone.

Vagotropic —Affecting the vagus nerve.

Vagotropism —Affinity for the vagus nerve, as of a drug.

Vagovagal —Reflex action occurring entirely through the vagus nerve, *i.e.*, through afferent and efferent impulses transmitted through the vagus nerve.

Vagrant —Wandering from one place to another without a fixed home.

Vagus —Pneumogastric or 10th cranial nerve, the vagus nerve which on stimulation slows the heart rate.

Vagus pulse —Pulse with slow rate due to stimulation of the vagus nerve.

Valence, Valency —Degree of combining power or replacing power of an atom or group of atoms, hydrogen atom being the unit of comparison.

Valent —Possessing valence.

Valetudinarian —A chronic patient.

Valgoid —Pertaining to valgus or suffering from talipes valgus.

Valgus —The part of the body bent outward, away from the midline of the body, as talipes valgus.

Valid —Effective, correct, producing the desired result, legal.

Validate —To ensure the validity and correctness of a thing.

Validity —1. The degree to which data or results of a study are correct. 2. Soundness. 3. Lawfulness.

Valine —A naturally occurring amino acid, essential for normal growth in infants and nitrogen metabolism in adults.

Valinemia —Presence of excess of valine in the blood.

Valla —Plural of vallum.

Vallate —Having an edge around a depression.

Vallate papilla —See circumvallate papillae.

Vallecula —A depression or furrow.

Vallecula cerebelli —A longitudinal deep fissure on the inferior surface of cerebellum in which medulla oblongata is situated.

Vallecula ovata —A depression in the liver in which gallbladder is situated.

Valleculae —Plural of vallecula.

Valley —Vallecula.

Vallis —Vallecula cerebelli.

Vallum —Any raised, more or less circular edge.

Vallum unguis —Fold of skin overlaping the nail.

Valoid —Fluid-extract of the same strength, as the original drug.

Value —Worth, price, importance, to estimate the worth of.

Valva —Valve.

Valvae —Plural of valva.

Valval —Pertaining to a valve.

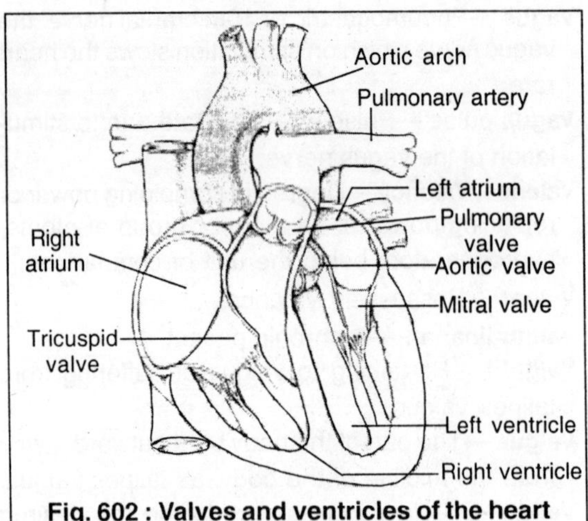

Fig. 602 : Valves and ventricles of the heart

Valvar —Valval.

Valvate —Valvular.

Valve —A membranous structure in a hollow organ or passage that temporarily closes and prevents backward flow of fluid through it.

Aortic valve —Valve between the left ventricle of the heart and the aorta.

Artificial valve —A man-made cardiac valve.

Atrioventricular valves —The valves between the right atrium and right ventricle (tricuspid valve) and the left atrium and left ventricle (bicuspid valve or mitral valve).

Bicuspid valve —Mitral valve. Left atrioventricular valve. The valve closing the orifice between the left atrium and the left ventricle of the heart.

Cardiac valve —One of the four (right atrioventricular or tricuspid, pulmonary, left atrioventricular or bicuspid or mitral and aortic valves) valves of the heart that control the blood flow in the heart.

Ileocecal valve —Valve situated between the ileum and large intestine.

Mitral valve —Bicuspid valve.

Pulmonary valve —The valve between right ventricle and the opening into the pulmonary artery.

Pyloric valve —A prominent circular fold of mucous membrane at the pyloric orific of the stomach.

Right atrioventricular valve —Tricuspid valve.

Semilunar valve —The half moon-shaped aortic and pulmonary valves of the heart.

Tricuspid valve —The valve between the right atrium and right ventricle of the heart.

Valvectomy —Excision of a valve, especially a heart valve.

Valviform —Valve-shaped.

Valvoplasty —Plastic surgery of a valve.

Valvotomy —To make an incision into a valve.

Valvula —A small valve.

Valvulae —Plural of valvula.

Valvular —Valvate. Pertaining to, affecting, or having a valve.

Valvule —Valvula.

Valvulitis —Inflammation of a valve, especially of a heart valve.

Valvuloplasty —Repair of a valve, especially a heart valve by plastic surgery.

Valvulotome —An instrument for incising a valve.

Valvulotomy —Valvotomy.

Van den Bergh's test —A test to detect the presence of bilirubin in blood serum or plasma.

Vapor —1. Steam. 2. Gas. 3. Exhalation. 4. Medicinal substance for inhalation.

Vaporium —An apparatus for applying hot, cold, or medicated vapor.

Vaporization —1. The conversion of a solid or liquid into a vapor; distillation. 2. Vapotherapy.

Vaporize —To convert a substance into a vapor.

Vaporizer —An apparatus for converting a liquid into a vapor spray.

Vaporous —Consisting of, pertaining to, or producing vapor.

Vaporthorax —Presence of multiple bubbles of water vapor in the pleural space in between the lungs and the chest wall in a person exposed to high altitude.

Vapotherapy —Treatment of the diseases by vapor.

Variability —The state of being variable.

Variable —Changeable.

Variance —The state of being variable or changeable or deviate.

Variant —1. That which, or one who, is variable. 2. Having the tendency to change.

Variate —Variable.

Variation —Difference.

Varication —1. The formation of a varix. 2. A varicosity.

Variceal —Of or pertaining to a varix or varices.

Variced —Pertaining to a varix.

Varicella —Chickenpox.

Varicellation —Inoculation with the virus of chickenpox to protect against that disease.

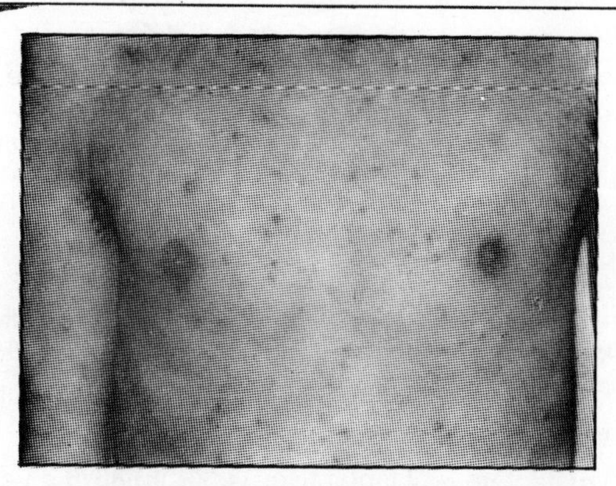

Fig. 603 : Varicella (Chickenpox)

Varicelliform —Resembling varicella.

Varicelloid —Varicelliform.

Varicellovirus —Varicella-zoster virus.

Varices —Plural of varix.

Variciform —Varicose. Resembling a varix.

Varicoblepharon —A varicose swelling of the eyelids.

Varicocele —Enlargement of veins of the spermatic cord (pampiniform plexus) forming a scrotal swelling usually on the left side in adolescent males, which feels like a bag of worms.

Varicocelectomy —Excision of a varicocele.

Varicography —X-ray examination of the varicose veins.

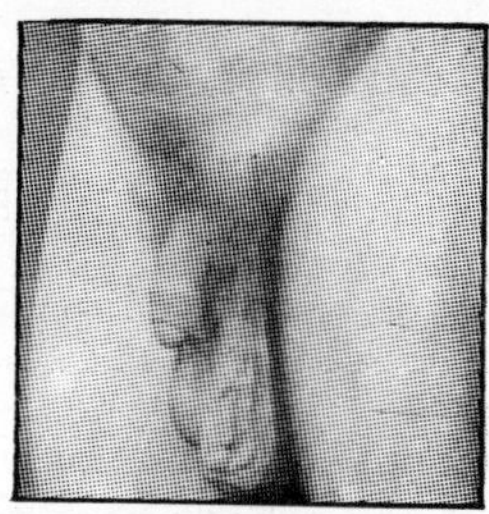

Fig. 604 : Varicocele with left inguinal hernia

Varicoid —Like a varix.

Varicole —Varicocele.

Varicomphalus —A varicose tumor of the umbilicus.

Varicophlebitis —Varicose veins with inflammation.

Varicose —Variciform. Of the nature of, or pertaining to a varix; distended, swollen or knotted, said of veins.

Varicoses —Plural of varicosis.

Varicose ulcer —An ulcer that forms as a result of varicose veins, most commonly on medial side of the lower half of the leg.

Varicose veins —Enlarged, twisted superficial veins, most commonly seen in the lower limbs.

Varicosis —Varicose condition of the veins.

Varicosity —1. The condition of being varicose. 2. Varix. A varicose vein.

Varicotomy —Excision of a varicose vein.

Varicula —Varix of the conjunctiva.

Varicule —A small varicose vein usually seen in the skin.

Variety —In animal classification, a subcategory of a species.

Variola —Smallpox.

Variolar —Pertaining to smallpox.

Variolate —1. To vaccinate with smallpox virus. 2. Having the lesions appearing like those of smallpox.

Variolation, Variolization —Inoculation with smallpox virus.

Variolic —Variolar.

Varioliform —Resembling smallpox.

Variolization —Variolation.

Varioloid —Varioliform.

Variolous —Variolar.

Varix —An enlarged, twisted vein, artery or lymphatic vessel.

Varnish —A solution of gums and resins in a solvent. When these are applied to a surface the solvent evaporates leaving a hard, more or less flexible layer. In dentistry, a varnish is used to protect sensitive area of the tooth such as the pulp.

Varolian —Pertaining to the pons varolii.

Varus —A part of the body bent inward, *i.e.*, toward the midline of the body, as talipes varus.

Vas —A vessel or duct, *e.g.*, a blood vessel, or vas deferens which is the excretory duct of the testis. It transports the sperm from each testis to the prostatic urethra.

Vasa —Plural of vas.

Vasal—Pertaining to a vas or vessel.

Vasalgia —Pain in a vessel.

Vascular —Pertaining to or composed of blood vessels.

Vascularity —The condition of being vascular.

Vascularization —The formation of new blood vessels in tissues.

Vascularize —To become vascular by the formation of new blood vessels.

Vascularized —Rendered vascular by the formation of new blood vessels.

Vascular ring —An arterial ring encircling the trachea and esophagus congenitally.

Vascular system —The system which includes arteries, arterioles, capillaries, venules and veins.

Vascular tuft —Chorionic villi.

Vascular tumor —Angioma. Telangioma. Hemangioma. Tumor containing dilated blood vessels.

Vasculature —1. The arrangement of blood vessels in the body or any part of it. 2. The supply of blood vessels to a specific region.

Vasculitis —Angiitis.

Vasculocardiac —Cardiovascular.

Vasculogenesis —Development of the vascular system.

Vasculogenic —Inducing vas-cularization.

Vasculomotor —Vasomotor.

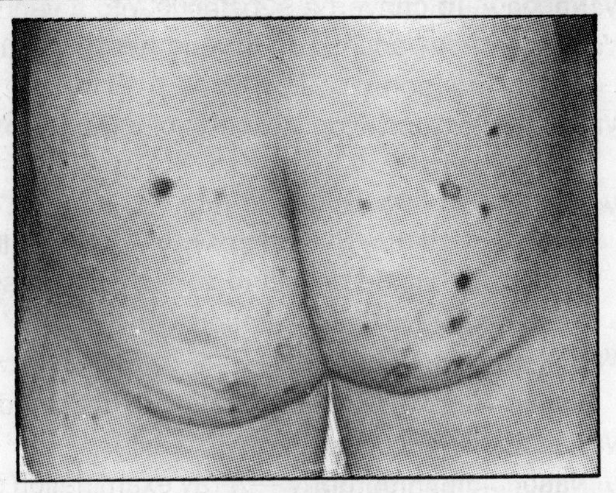

Fig. 605 : Cutaneous vasculitis : Punched out necrotic ulcers

Vasculopathy —An disease of the blood vessels.

Vasculum —A tiny vessel.

Vasectomy —Excision of the vas deferens or part of it, usually done on both sides to produce sterility in the male.

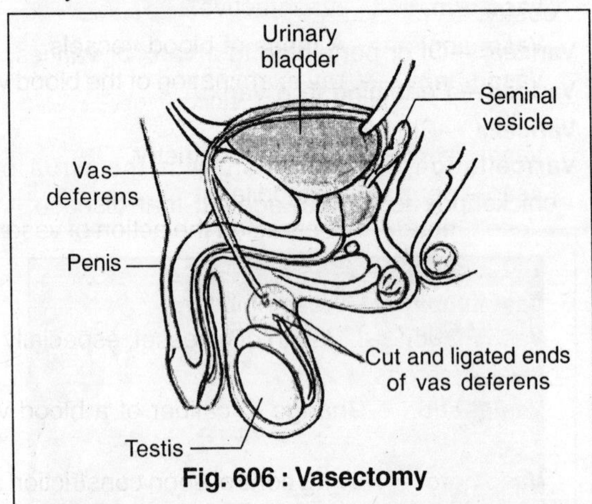

Fig. 606 : Vasectomy

Vasectomy reversal —Rejoining of the previously severed vas deferens, by surgery.

Vasifaction —Angiopoiesis.

Vasifactive —Vasofactive. Vasoformative.

Vasiform —Resembling a vessel.

Vasitis —Inflammation of the vas deferens.

Vaso- —A prefix which means a vessel, as a blood vessel.

Vasoactive —Exerting an effect on blood vessels.

Vasoconstriction —Decrease in the caliber of blood vessels.

Vasoconstrictive—Causing constriction of the blood vessels.

Vasoconstrictor —Vasoconstrictive.

Vasodepression —Decrease in the resistance of blood vessels with low blood pressure.

Vasodepressor —1. Lowering blood pressure by causing dilatation of blood vessels. 2. Decreasing blood circulation.

Vasodilatation —Dilatation of, or increase in the caliber of blood vessels.

Vasodilation —Vasodilatation.

Vasodilative —Vasodilator.

Vasodilator —Causing dilatation of the blood vessels.

Vasoepididymography —X-ray examination of the vas deferens and epididymis after injection of a contrast medium.

Vasoepididymostomy —Formation of a passage between the vas deferens and the epididymis.

Vasofactive —Vasifactive. Vasoformative. Forming new blood vessels.

Vasoformation —Angiopoiesis.

Vasoformative —Vasofactive.

Vasoganglion —A mass of blood vessels.

Vasography —X-ray examination of the blood vessels.

Vasohypertonic —Vasoconstrictor.

Vasohypotonic —Vasodilator.

Vasoinhibitor —Decreasing the action of vasomotor nerves.

Vasoinhibitory —Vasoinhibitor.

Vasoligation —Ligation of a vessel, especially the vas deferens.

Vasomotion —Change in caliber of a blood vessel.

Vasomotor —Having control upon constriction and dilatation of the blood vessels.

Vasomotor epilepsy —Epilepsy with vasomotor changes in the skin.

Vasomotor reflex —Constriction of the cutaneous blood vessels in response to a stimulus to the skin.

Vasomotor spasm —Spasm of the smaller arteries.

Vasomotory —Vasomotor.

Vasoneuropathy —A disease caused by combined vascular and neurologic defect.

Vasoneurosis —Angioneurosis.

Vaso-orchidostomy —To connect the epididymis to the severed end of the vas deferens.

Vasoparalysis —Angiohypotonia. Angioparalysis. Paralysis, atonia or hypotonia of the blood vessels.

Vasoparesis —Partial paralysis of the vasomotor nerves.

Vasopermeability —Permeability of a blood vessel.

Vasopressin —A hormone secreted by cells of the nuclei of hypothalamus from where it is transported to posterior lobe of the pituitary gland and stored there for release, as necessary. It is an antidiuretic hormone and constricts blood vessels raising the blood pressure, and increases peristalsis.

Vasopressor —Causing constriction of blood vessels and raising blood pressure.

Vasopressure —Pressure exerted on a blood vessel.

Vasopuncture —Puncture of the vas deferens.

Vasoreflex —A reflex action that changes the caliber of blood vessels.

Vasorelaxation —Decrease of vascular pressure.

Vasorrhaphy —Suture of the vas deferens.

Vasosection —The cutting of a vessel or vessels, especially of the vas deferens.

Vasosensory —Pertaining to sensation in the blood vessels.

Vasospasm —Angiospasm. Spasm of a blood vessel.

Vasospastic —Pertaining to or characterized by vasospasm.

Vasostimulant —Stimulating vasomotor action.

Vasostomy —The formation of an opening into the vas deferens.

Vasothrombin —Thrombin derived from the lining cells of the blood vessels.

Vasotomy —To make an incision into the vas deferens.

Vasotonia—The tone or tension of blood vessels.

Vasotonic —1. Pertaining to the tone of a vessel. 2. Increasing tone of a vessel.

Vasotribe —Angiotribe.

Vasotripsy —Angiotripsy.

Vasotrophic —Concerning with the nutrition of blood vessels.

Vasotropic —Affecting blood vessels.

Vasovagal —Pertaining to the action of stimuli from the vagus nerve on blood vessels.

Vasovagal syncope —Sudden faint due to hypotension, occurring on stimulation of vagus nerve in mental stress, pain or trauma.

Vasovasostomy —Rejoining of the previously cut ends of vas deferens.

Vasovesiculectomy —Excision of the vas deferens and seminal vesicle.

Vasovesiculitis —Inflammation of the vas deferens and seminal vesicle.

Vastomy —Section of the vas deferens, usually with ligation.

Vastus —Great, said of muscles.

Vater's corpuscles —Ovoid end organs of nerves supplying the skin.

Vater's papilla —Papilla of vater. Ampulla of vater.

Vault —Dome-shaped structure.

VC —Vital capacity.

V. D. —Venereal disease.

V. D. H. —Valvular disease of the heart.

VDRL —Venereal Disease Research Laboratory.

Vection —The carrying of disease-producing microorganisms from an infected person to a healthy person.

Vectis —A curved lever for making traction on presenting part of the fetus in labor.

Vector —1. A carrier, usually an arthropod or insect, of disease-producing organisms, that transmits them from infected to a noninfected person. 2. A quantity comprising magnitude, direction and sense represented by a straight line of appropriate length and direction.

Biological vector —An arthropod vector wherein the disease-producing organism develops or multiplies before becoming infective for a noninfected person.

Mechanical vector —An arthropod vector in which disease-producing organism does not develop or multiplies.

Vectorcardiogram —A graphic record of the direction and magnitude of electrical forces of the heart's action by means of a continuous series of vector loops.

Vectorcardiography —To record graphically the direction and magnitude of electrical forces of the heart's action by means of a continuous series of vector loops.

Vectorial —Pertaining to a vector.

Vectorscope —An instrument for viewing vectorcardiogram.

Vegan —A purely vegetarian person who excludes all protein of animal origin from the diet.

Veganism —Strict attachment to a vegetable diet, with exclusion of all animal products including milk or cheese, etc.

Vegetable —1. Pertaining to or derived from plants. 2. A herbaceous plant cultivated for food. 3. The edible portion of the plants used as food, including seeds, root, stem, leaves, flowers and fruits.

Vegetal —1. Pertaining to a plant or plants or vegetation. 2. Vegetative.

Vegetarian —One who eats only vegetable food.

Vegetarianism —Strictness for substances originating from plants in one's diet.

Vegetate —To grow as plants.

Vegetation —Any plantlike fungoid growth.

Vegetative —1. Having the power to grow, as plants. 2. Of, pertaining to, or characteristic of plants. 3. Of or pertaining to asexual reproduction, as by budding or fission. 4. Functioning involuntarily or unconsciously. 5. Quiescent, passive.

Vegetoanimal —Pertaining to plants and animals.

Vehemence, Vehemency —Violence.

Vehement —Violent.

Vehicle —Excipient.

Veil —1. A covering structure. 2. Caul. A piece of amniotic sac occasionally covering the face of a newborn infant. 3. Slight huskiness of the voice.

Vein —A vessel in which dark red blood (the blood that has given up most of its oxygen to the tissues) flows toward the heart, except pulmonary vein which carries pure (oxygenated) blood from the lungs.

Veined —Marked by veins or lines resembling veins on the surface.

Veinlet —Venule.

Vela —Plural of velum.

Velamen —Any covering membrane.

Velamenta —Plural of velamentum.

Velamentous —Like a veil.

Velamentum —A membranous covering.

Velamina —Plural of velamen.

Velar —Pertaining to a velum or veil.

Veliform —Velamentous.

Vellication —Spasmodic twitching of muscular fibers.

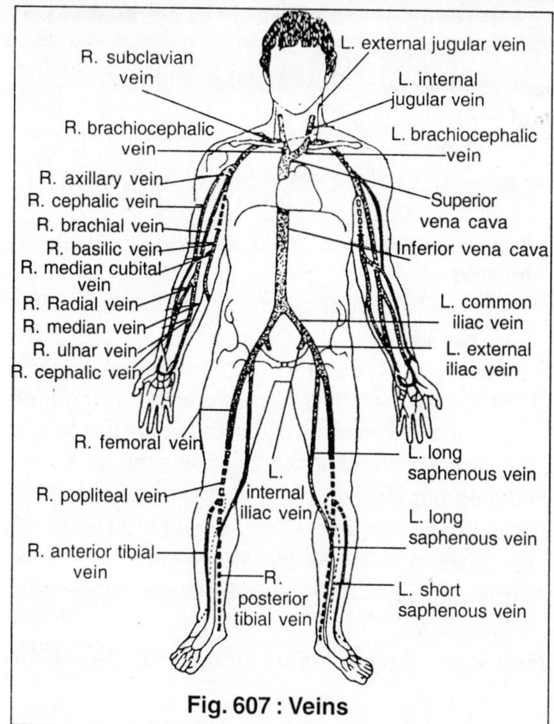

Fig. 607 : Veins

Vellus —Fine hair present on the body after lanugo of the newborn infant is gone.

Velocity —Speed of movement.

Velopharyngeal —Pertaining to the soft palate and the pharynx.

Velosynthesis —Staphylorrhaphy.

Velpeau's bandage —See under 'Bandage'.

Velpeau's deformity —A deformity seen in colle's fracture, in which the lower fragment of the radius bone is displaced backward.

Velum —A veil-like structure.

Vena —A vein.

Inferior vena cava —The principal vein draining blood from the lower portion of the body, which is formed by the union of two common iliac veins and opens into the right atrium of the heart.

Superior vena cava —The principal vein draining blood from the upper portion of the body, which is formed by the union of right and left brachiocephalic veins and opens into the right atrium of the heart.

Venacavography —X-ray examination of the vena cava.

Venae —Plural of vena.

Venae comitantes —Two or more veins accompanying an artery.

Venation —The distribution of veins to an organ or structure.

Venectasia —Phlebectasia.

Venectomy —Phlebectomy.

Veneer —A man-made material such as an acrylic resin, that can be attached to the surface of a tooth.

Venenation —1. Poisoning. 2. The condition of being poisoned.

Venene —A mixture of venoms from poisonous snakes.

Veneniferous —Carrying poison.

Venenific —Producing poison.

Venenosalivary —Venomosalivary.

Venenosity —The condition of being poisonous.

Venenous —Poisonous.

Venepuncture —Venipuncture.

Venereal —Pertaining to or occurring due to sexual intercourse.

Venereal bubo —Enlarged lymph node in the inguinal region resulting from a venereal disease.

Venereal disease —A disease acquired through sexual intercourse with a person afflicted with the disease, *e.g.*, syphilis, gonorrhea, etc.

Venereal sore —Chancroid.

Venereal urethritis —Inflammation of the urethra occurring in gonorrhea.

Venereal wart —Condyloma; verruca acuminata.

Venereologist —A specialist in venereal diseases.

Venereology —The study and treatment of venereal diseases.

Venereophobia —Cypridophobia. Morbid fear of venereal disease.

Venery —Coitus.

Venesection —Phlebotomy. Venisection.

Venin —Toxic substance in a snake venom.

Venin-antivenin —A vaccine to counteract snake poison.

Veniplex —A plexus of veins.

Venipuncture —Surgical puncture of a vein.

Venisection —Phlebotomy. Venesection.

Venisuture —Phleborrhaphy.

Veno- —A prefix meaning vein.

Venoatrial —Venoauricular. Pertaining to the vena cava and the atrium.

Venoauricular —Venoatrial.

Venoclysis —Phleboclysis.

Venoconstrictor —An agent that constricts a vein.

Venofibrosis —Phlebosclerosis.

Venogram —Phlebogram. 1. X-ray picture of veins. 2. A tracing of the venous pulse.

Venography —Phlebography 1. X-ray examination of the veins. 2. The making of a tracing of the venous pulse.

Venom —A poison excreted by some insects, spiders or snakes, etc. and transmitted to man by bites or stings.

Venomization —To mix snake venom with a material.

Venomosalivary —Secreting saliva with venom in it.

Venomotor —Pertaining to, or controlling constriction or dilatation of veins.

Venomous —1. Poisonous. 2. Secreting poison.

Veno-occlusive —Pertaining to or characterized by obstructon of the veins.

Venoperitoneostomy —To insert the cut end of saphenous vein into the peritoneal cavity to drain ascitic fluid.

Venopressor —Pertaining to venous blood pressure.

Venosclerosis —Phlebosclerosis.

Venose —Having veins.

Venosinal —Pertaining to the vena cava and the right atrium of the heart.

Venosity —An excess of venous blood or supply of a large number of veins in a part of the body.

Venospasm —Contraction of a vein.

Venostasis —Phlebostasia. Phlebostasis.

Venostat —An apparatus for performing compression upon the veins.

Venostomy, Venous cutdown—cutdown

Venothrombotic —Inducing the formation of thrombi in veins.

Venotomy —Phlebotomy. To make an incision into a vein.

Venous —Pertaining to the veins or the blood passing through them.

Venous blood —The dark blood in the veins.

Venous hum —Murmur heard on auscultation over the large veins of the neck.

Venous hyperemia —Venosity.

Venous return —The amount of blood returning to the atria of the heart.

Venovenostomy —Phlebophlebostomy.

Vent —An opening or outlet in a cavity for excretion, or anus.

Venter —1. A belly-shaped part of the body; central fleshy portion or belly of a muscle. 2. Abdomen or stomach. 3. Hollowed part or cavity of the body.

Ventilate —To oxygenate the blood in the pulmonary capillaries.

Ventilation —1. The process of supplying a room continuously with fresh air and withdrawing foul air. 2. The exchange of air between the lungs and the surrounding air. 3. The amount of air inhaled per day.

Ventilation coefficient —The amount of air respired for absorption of one liter of oxygen.

Ventilaton rate —The amount of air respired in one minute.

Ventilator —An apparatus for artificial respiration of the lungs.

Ventouse —A glass or glass-shaped vessel used in cupping.

Ventrad —Toward the ventral side.

Ventral —Pertaining to the belly or abdomen, anterior portion or the front side of the body.

Ventralis —Ventral.

Ventricle —A small cavity or chamber, as in the heart or brain.

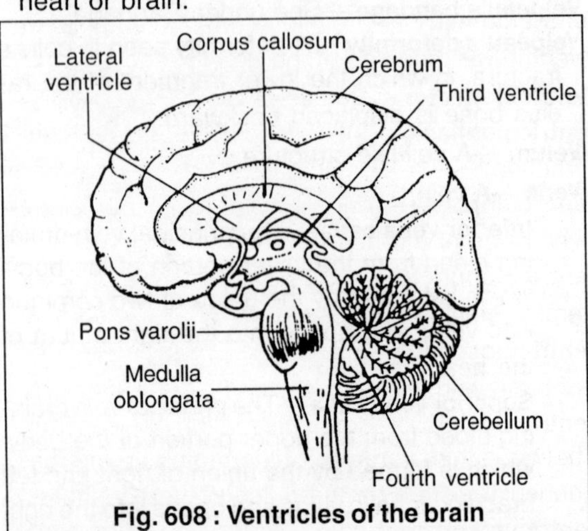

Fig. 608 : Ventricles of the brain

Ventricornu —The anterior horn of gray matter of the spinal cord.

Ventricose —1. Inflated or distended. 2. Corpulent.

Ventricular —Pertaining to a ventricle.

Ventricularis —Ventricular.

Ventriculectomy —Reduction of the volume of a dilated left ventricle by partial resection of the myocardium.

Ventriculi —Plural of ventriculus.

Ventriculitis —Inflammation of a ventricle.

Ventriculo- —A prefix which means ventricle.

Ventriculoatrial —Pertaining to both ventricles and atria.

Ventriculoatriostomy —To introduce a catheter with a valve opening in one side only, into a cerebral ventricle to drain cerebrospinal fluid from there to the right atrium of the heart via jugular vein, for relief of hydrocephalus.

Ventriculocisternostomy —Surgical creation of an opening between the ventricles of the brain and cisterna magna, for drainage of cerebrospinal fluid.

Ventriculogram —X-ray film of the cerebral ventricles.

Ventriculography —1. X-ray examination of the ventricles of the brain after introduction of air or other contrast medium. 2. X-ray examination of the ventricles of the heart after injection of a contrast medium.

Ventriculomastoidostomy —To establish a communication between the lateral cerebral ventricle and the mastoid antrum by means of a polythene tube for the relief of hydrocephalus.

Ventriculometry —The measurement of the intraventricular pressure of the brain.

Ventriculonector —Bundle of His.

Ventriculophasic —Influenced by ventricular contraction.

Ventriculoplasty —Repair of a defect of one of the ventricles of the heart by plastic surgery.

Ventriculopuncture —Surgical puncture of a lateral ventricle of the brain.

Ventriculoscopy —Examination of the ventricles of brain with an endoscope.

Ventriculostomy —Surgical creation of a passage between third ventricle of the brain and interpeduncular cistern for the relief in hydrocephalus.

Ventriculosubarachnoid —Pertaining to the cerebral ventricles and subarachnoid space.

Ventriculotomy —To make an incision into a ventricle.

Ventriculovenous —Pertaining to or communicating with a cerebral ventricle and vein.

Ventriculus —1. A ventricle. 2. The stomach.

Ventricumbent —Prone. Lying on abdomen.

Ventriduct —To bring toward the abdomen.

Ventriduction —The bringing or pulling toward the abdomen.

Ventrimeson —The median line on the ventral surface of the body.

Ventro- —A prefix meaning abdomen or ventral (anterior) surface of the body.

Ventrocystorrhaphy —To sew a cyst or the bladder to the abdominal wall.

Ventrodorsal —From the front to the back.

Ventrofixation —Fixation of a viscus by suturing, *e.g.*, the uterus, to the abdominal wall.

Ventrohysteropexy —Ventrofixation of the uterus.

Ventroinguinal —Pertaining to the ventral and inguinal regions.

Ventrolateral —Both ventral and lateral.

Ventromedian —Both ventral and median.

Ventroptosia, Ventroptosis —Gastroptosis.

Ventroptosis —Ventroptosia.

Ventroscopy —Celioscopy. Examination of the abdominal cavity by illumination.

Ventrose —Having a belly-like swelling.

Ventrosity —The condition of having an enlarged abdomen; obesity.

Ventrosuspension —Ventrohysteropexy.

Ventrotomy —Celiotomy. Laparotomy.

Ventrovesicofixation —To fix the uterus to the abdominal wall and bladder.

Venturimeter —An instrument for measuring the flow of fluids through vessels.

Venula —Venule

Venulae —Plural of venula.

Venular —Venulous. Pertaining to venule.

Venule —A terminal smallest vein which is continuous with a capillary.

Venulous —Venular.

Venus's collar —Pigmentation around the neck in syphilis.

Verbigeration —Abnormal repetition of meaningless words and phrases.

Verbomania —Mania for excessive talking.

Verge —A circumference or ring, *e.g.*, anal opening on the surface of the body.

Vergence —Movement of the eyes in opposite drections in adjusting to near or far vision.

Verification —The act of confirming.

Vermes —Plural of vermis.

Vermi- —A prefix which means worm or wormlike.

Vermicidal —Killing the intestinal worms.

Vermicide —Vermicidal.

Vermicular —Wormlike.

Vermicular pulse —Small rapid pulse giving wormlike feeling in the fingers.

Vermiculation —A wormlike movement as peristaltic movement of the intestine.

Vermicule —1. A small worm. 2. Having a wormlike shape.

Vermiculose —Vermiculous.

Vermiculous —1. Wormlike. 2. Infested with worms.

Vermiculus —A small worm or wormlike structure.

Vermiform —Worm-shaped.

Vermiform appendix —A 2.5 to 20 cm. long, narrow, worm-shaped tube, closed at the distal end, connected with the cecum. Its inflammation is called appendicitis.

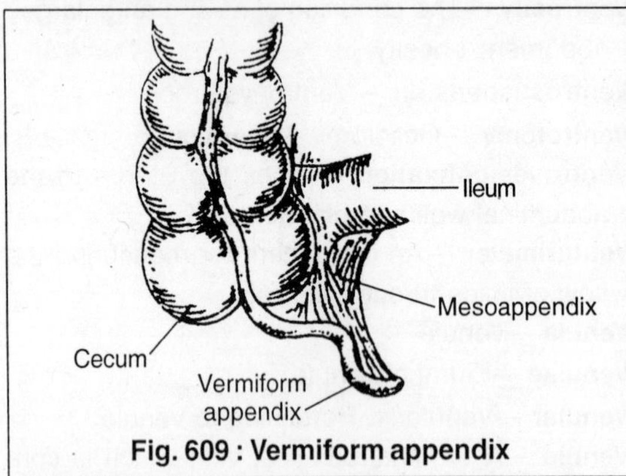

Fig. 609 : Vermiform appendix

Vermifugal —Expelling worms from the intestine.

Vermifuge —Anthelmintic. Vermicide.

Vermilion border —The junction of the pinkish red area of the lips with the surrounding skin.

Vermilionectomy —Surgical removal of the vermilion border of the lip.

Vermin —Small animals and insects such as mice, lice or bedbugs, etc., causing disease.

Verminal —Pertaining to or caused by worms.

Vermination —Infestation with worms or vermin.

Verminosis —Infestation with vermin.

Verminous —Pertaining to or infested with worms or vermin.

Vermiphobia —Morbid fear of being infested with worms.

Vermis —1. A worm. 2. V. cerebelli, which is the median part of the cerebellum between its two lobes.

Vermix —Appendix.

Vernacular —Belonging to one's own country.

Vernal —Pertaining to or occurring in the spring.

Vernix —Varnish, *e.g.*, vernix caseosa, which is protective covering of the fetus during intrauterine life, composed of sebum, desquamated epithelial cells and lanugo.

Verruca —Wart or wartlike structure.

- **Verruca acuminata** —A pointed, reddish venereal wart about the genital organs and the anus caused by a virus.
- **Verruca digitata** —Wart seen on the face and scalp from which a cutaneous horn develops.
- **Verruca filiformis** —Small threadlike warts seen on the neck and eyelids.
- **Verruca necrogenica** —Tuberculosis verruca.
- **Verruca plana** —A small, smooth, slightly raised wart seen mostly in children.
- **Verruca plantaris** —Plantar wart occurring on the sole of the foot.
- **Verruca vulgaris** —Common warts occurring anywhere on the skin.

Verrucae —Plural of verruca.

Verruciform —Wartlike.

Verrucose, Verrucous —Wartlike; warty.

Verrucosis —The development of multiple warts.

Verrucous —Verrucose.

Verruga —Verruca.

Versicolar —Having, or changeable in many colors.

Version —1. The change of position, especially that of the fetus in uterus, which may occur naturally or may be done manually by the doctor to facilitate delivery of the fetus. 2. The deviation of an organ such as uterus from its normal position.

- **Bimanual version** —Bipolar version.
- **Bipolar version** —Changing of the position of

the fetus in uterus by acting upon both poles of the fetus, either by external or combined (external and internal) manipulation.

Cephalic version —Turning of the fetus so that the head presents.

Combined version —Changing of the position of the fetus in uterus by combined internal and external manipulation.

External version —Turning of the fetus in uterus by external manipulation.

Internal version —Turning of the fetus in uterus by internal manipulation with one hand or fingers inserted through the vagina.

Pelvic version —Turning of the fetus with manipulation so that pelvis presents.

Podalic version —Turning of the fetus so that breech presents.

Postural version —Version obtained by changing the position of the mother.

Spontaneous version —Turning of the fetus occuring spontaneously by uterine muscular contractions.

Vert —To turn.

Vertebra —[Plural is vertebrae] It is one of the 33 bones of the vertebral (spinal) column comprising 7 cervical, 12 thoracic, 5 lumbar, 5 sacral and 4 rudimentary coccygeal vertebrae. In adults, the five sacral vertebrae fuse to form a single bone called sacrum, and 4 coccygeal vertebrae fuse to form a single bone called coccyx.

Basilar vertebra —The lowest lumbar vertebra.

Caudate vertebrae —Vertebrae of the tail.

Cervical vertebrae —7 vertebrae of the cervix.

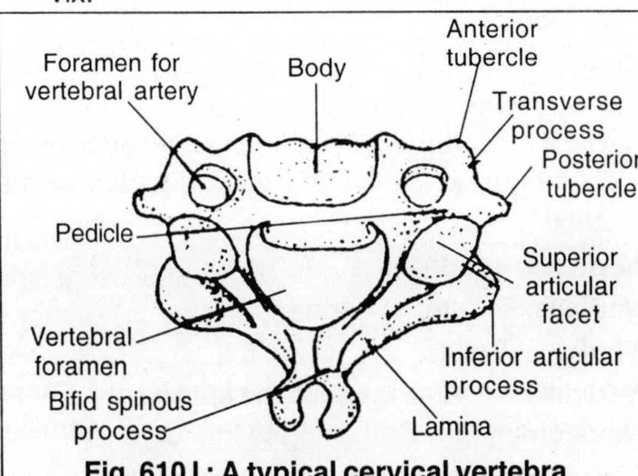

Fig. 610 I : A typical cervical vertebra (3rd to 6th cervical vertebra)

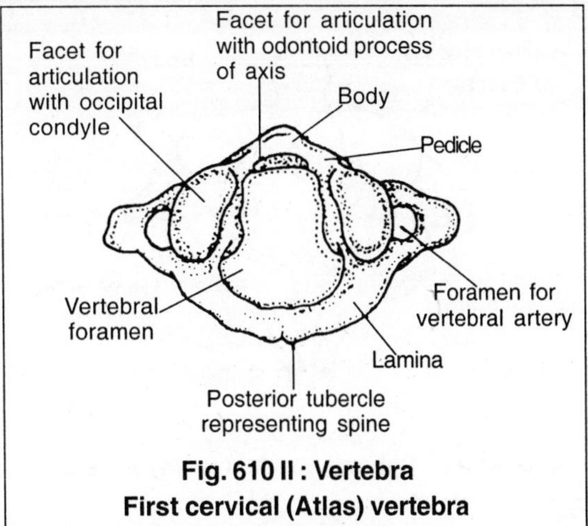

Fig. 610 II : Vertebra First cervical (Atlas) vertebra

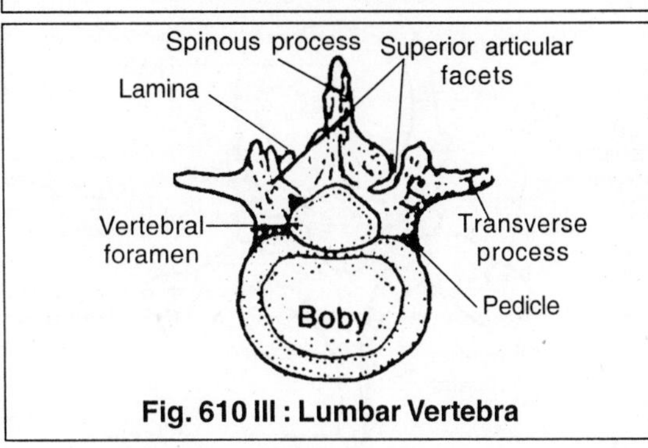

Fig. 610 III : Lumbar Vertebra

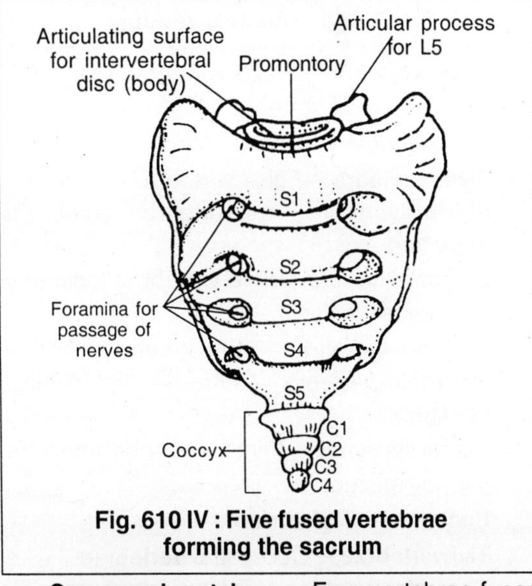

Fig. 610 IV : Five fused vertebrae forming the sacrum

Coccygeal vertebrae —Four vertebrae fused together forming the coccyx.

Dentata vertebra —Axis. The second cervical vertebra.

Dorsal vertebrae —Thoracic vertebrae.

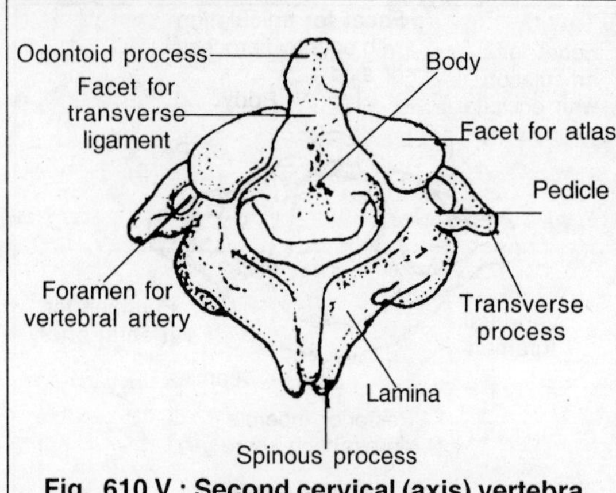

Fig. 610 V : Second cervical (axis) vertebra

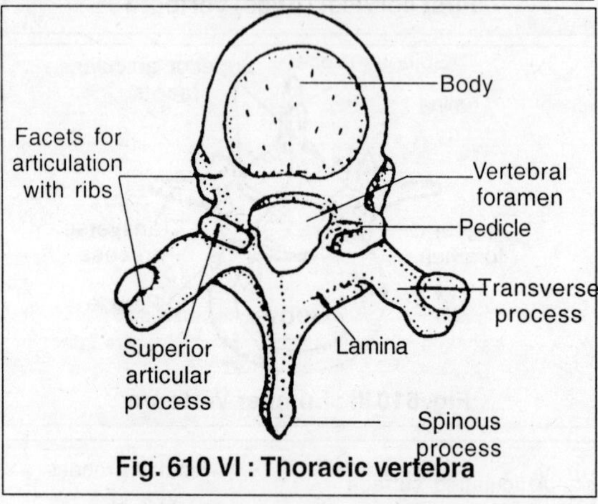

Fig. 610 VI : Thoracic vertebra

False vertebra —Fixed vertebra. The sacral and coccygeal vertebrae that fuse.

First cervical vertebra —Atlas.

Fixed vertebra —False vertebra.

Flexion vertebra —All vertebrae except the atlas and axis.

Lumbar vertebra —Five vertebrae located in the lumbar region.

Magnum vertebra —The sacrum.

Odontoid vertebra —Axis. Second cervical vertebra.

Sacral vertebrae —Five fused vertebrae forming the sacrum.

Second cervical vertebra —Axis.

Tail vertebrae —Coccygeal vertebrae.

Thoracic vertebrae —Twelve vertebrae in the thoracic region which articulate with the ribs.

True vertebrae —The vertebrae that remain unfused throughout life; the cervical, thoracic and lumbar vertebrae.

Vertebral —Pertaining to a vertebra or the vertebral column.

Vertebral canal —Spinal canal. The long, hollow space formed by the union of vertebral foramina, which contains the spinal cord.

Vertebral column —Spinal column.

Vertebral ribs —The lowest two or floating ribs.

Vertebrarium —The vertebral column.

Vertebrata —A subphylum of the phylum Chordata which includes all the animals that have a vertebral column.

Vertebrate —Having a vertebral column.

Vertebrated —Composed of jointed segments.

Vertebrectomy —Excision of a vertebra or of its part.

Vertebro- —A prefix indicating vertebra.

Vertebroarterial —Pertaining to the vertebral artery.

Vertebrobasilar —Pertaining to the vertebral and basilar arteries.

Vertebrochondral —Pertaining to a vertebra and a costal cartilage.

Vertebrocostal —Costovertebral. Pertaining to a vertebra and a rib.

Vertebrofemoral —Pertaining to vertebrae and the femur bone.

Vertebrogenic —Arising in a vertebra or in the vertebral column.

Vertebroiliac —Pertaining to the vertebrae and the ilium bone.

Vertebromammary —Pertaining to the vertebral and mammary areas.

Vertebrosacral —Pertaining to the vertebrae and the sacrum.

Vertebrosternal —Pertaining to a vertebra and the sternum.

Vertex —The top, especially the top of the head.

Vertex cordis —Apex of the heart.

Vertical —1. Perpendicular to the horizontal plane or upright. 2. Pertaining to or situated at the apex.

Verticalis —Vertical.

Vertices —Plural of vertex.

Verticil —Vortex.

Verticillate —Arranged like the spokes of a wheel.

Verticomental —Pertaining to the top of the head and the chin.

Vertiginous —Pertaining to or afflicted with vertigo.

Vertigo —A sensation of movement of one's self (subjective vertigo) or of the objects of one's surroundings (objective vertigo).

Auditory vertigo —Vertigo due to disease of the ear.

Central vertigo —Vertigo caused by the disease of the central nervous system.

Cerebral vertigo —Vertigo due to brain disease.

Epidemic vertigo —Vertigo occurring in epidemic form which is due to vestibular neuronitis.

Epileptic vertigo —Vertigo occurring with an epileptic attack or following it.

Essential vertigo —Vertigo occurring from an unknown cause.

Gastric vertigo —Vertigo associated with gastric disturbances.

Horizontal vertigo —Vertigo occurring on lying horizontally.

Hysterical vertigo —Vertigo accompanying hysteria.

Labyrinthine vertigo —Vertigo due to disease of labyrinth of the ear.

Laryngeal vertigo —Vertigo due to laryngeal spasm.

Nocturnal vertigo —Vertigo occurring when going to sleep.

Objective vertigo —Vertigo in which fixed objects appear to be moving.

Ocular vertigo —Vertigo caused by the disease of the eye.

Organic vertigo —Vertigo due to injury of the brain.

Positional vertigo, Postural vertigo—Vertigo that occurs when the head is in a specific position.

Toxic vertigo —Vertigo due to presence of a toxin in the body.

Vertical vertigo —Vertigo occurring on standing upright.

Vertometer Lensometer. Focimeter.

Verumontanitis —Inflammation of the colliculus seminalis.

Verumontanum —Colliculus seminalis. An elevation on the floor of prostatic portion of urethra where the seminal ducts enter.

Very low density lipoproteins—See lipoproteins.

Vesania —Unsoundness of the mind.

Vesica –[Plural vesicae]—A bladder, *e.g.*, urinary bladder and gallbladder, etc.

Vesical —Pertaining to the urinary bladder.

Vesical calculus —Stone in the urinary bladder.

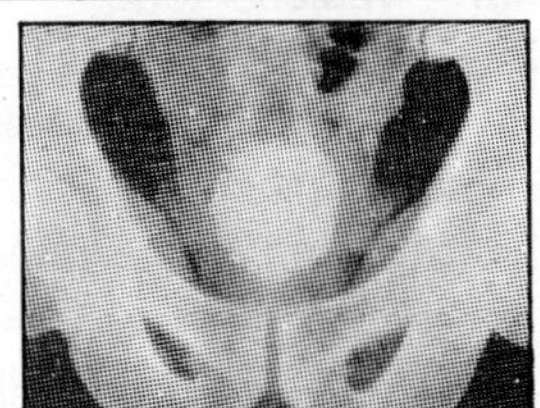

Fig. 611 : Vesical calculus

Vesical reflex —The inclination to urinate caused by moderately distended urinary bladder with urine.

Vesicant —Blistering. Producing blisters.

Vesicate —To form a vesicle.

Vesication —1. The process of producing blisters. 2. A blister.

Vesicatory —Pertaining to, or causing blisters.

Vesicle —1. A small bladder or sac containing fluid. 2. A small blister.

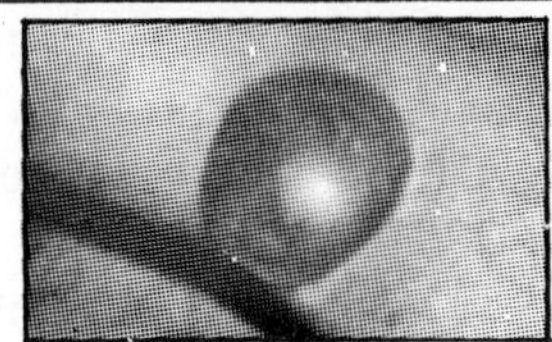

Fig. 612 : Vesicle

Vesicle seminal —One of the two membranous saclike structures in the male, lying behind the bladder close to the prostate gland. The duct from it joins the vas deferens on each side to form the ejaculatory duct. It serves as a reservoir for the semen and also secretes a thick viscous fluid that forms a part of the semen.

Vesico- —Prefix meaning bladder.

Vesicoabdominal —Pertaining to the urinary bladder and the abdomen.

Vesicobullous —Eruption of many vesicles of different sizes.

Vesicocele —Cystocele.

Vesicocervical —Pertaining to the urinary bladder and the cervix of the uterus.

Vesicoclysis —Introduction of fluid into the bladder.

Vesicoenteric —Pertaining to the urinary bladder and the intestine.

Vesicofixation —Attachment of the urinary bladder to the abdominal wall.

Vesicointestinal —Vesicoenteric.

Vesicolithiasis —Cystolithiasis.

Vesicoprostatic —Pertaining to the urinary bladder and the prostate gland.

Vesicopubic —Pertaining to the urinary bladder and the pubis.

Vesicopustular —Pertaining to a vesicopustule.

Vesicopustule —A vesicle in which pus is developing.

Vesicorectal —Pertaining to the urinary bladder and the rectum.

Vesicorectostomy —To anastomose the posterior wall of the urinary bladder to the rectum, by surgery.

Vesicosigmoid —Pertaining to the urinary bladder and the sigmoid colon.

Vesicosigmoidostomy —To form a passage between the urinary bladder and the sigmoid colon.

Vesicospinal —Pertaining to the urinary bladder and the vertebral column.

Vesicostomy —The formation of an opening into the bladder.

Vesicotomy —To make an incision into the bladder.

Vesicoumbilical —Pertaining to the urinary bladder and the umbilicus.

Vesicoureteral —Pertaining to the urinary bladder and a ureter.

Vesicourethral —Pertaining to the urinary bladder and the urethra.

Vesicouterine —Pertaining to the urinary bladder and the uterus.

Vesicouterovaginal —Pertaining to the urinary bladder, the uterus and the vagina.

Vesicovaginal —Pertaining to the urinary bladder and the vagina.

Vesicovaginorectal —Pertain-ing to the urinary bladder, the vagina and the rectum.

Vesicovisceral —Pertaining to the urinary bladder and a viscus.

Vesicula —[Plural vesiculae]—A vesicle.

Vesicular —Pertaining to or composed of vesicles or small blisters on the skin.

Vesicular eczema —Eczema accompanied by the formation of vesicles.

Vesicular murmur —Vesicular breathing. The normal respiratory sound heard on auscultation.

Vesicular rale —A crepitant rale, a crackling sound at the end of inspiration, usually at the base of lungs.

Vesicular resonance —Percussion sound heard over the normal lung.

Vesiculase —An enzyme in prostatic fluid that coagulates semen.

Vesiculate —Vesicular.

Vesiculated —Having vesicles.

Vesiculation —Formation of vesicles.

Vesiculectomy —Partial or complete excision of a vesicle, especially a seminal vesicle.

Vesiculiferous —Producing vesicles.

Vesiculiform —Shaped like a vesicle.

Vesiculitis —Inflammation of a vesicle, especially seminal vesicle.

Vesiculo- —A prefix meaning vesicle.

Vesiculobronchial —Pertaining to vesicles and the bronchi.

Vesiculocavernous —Both vesicular and cavernous.

Vesiculogram —An X-ray picture of the seminal vesicle.

Vesiculography —X-ray examination of the seminal vesicles.

Vesiculopapular —Pertaining to or composed of vesicles and papules.

Vesiculoprostatitis —Inflammation of the urinary bladder and the prostate gland.

Vesiculopustular —Having both vesicles and pustules.

Vesiculotomy —To make an incision into a vesicle, especially a seminal vesicle.

Vesiculotubular —Having both vesicular and tubular qualities.

Vesiculotympanic —Having both vesicular and tympanic qualities.

Vesp, Vespar —An evening.

Vessel —A canal, tube or duct for carrying a fluid in the body, *e.g.*, a blood vessel carrying blood and lymphatic vessel carrying lymph, etc.

Vestibula —Plural of vestibulum.

Vestibular —Pertaining to a vestibule.

Vestibularis —Vestibular.

Vestibulate —Possessing a vestibule.

Vestibule —A small space or cavity at the entrance of a canal, *e.g.*, vestibule of the ear which is the middle part of the inner ear, behind the cochlea and in front of the semicircular canals, and vestibule of the vagina, which is the space between the labia minora in which the urethra and vagina open.

Vestibulocochlear —1. Pertaining to the vestibulum and cochlea of the ear. 2. Statoacoustic.

Vestibulocochlear nerve —8th cranial nerve.

Vestibulogenic —Arising in a vestibule, as that of the ear.

Vestibulo-ocular —Pertaining to the vestibular and oculomotor nerves.

Vestibulopathy —Any disease of the vestibule.

Vestibuloplasty —Plastic surgery of the vestibule of the mouth.

Vestibulospinal —Pertaining to the vestibule and the spinal cord.

Vestibulotomy —To make an incision into the vestibule of the inner ear.

Vestibulourethral —Pertaining to the vestibule of the vagina and the urethra.

Vestibulum —Vestibule.

Vestige —The remnant of a structure that has been more fully developed and functioned in a previous stage of development of the individual or species.

Vestigial —Rudimentary. Pertaining to the vestige.

Vestigium —[Plural vestigia]—Vestige.

Veterinarian —A doctor of veterinary medicine.

Veterinary —1. Pertaining to the domestic animals, their diseases and treatment. 2. Veterinarian.

Veterinary medicine —The branch of medical science that deals with the diseases of animals and their treatment.

V. F. —Vocal fremitus.

V. H. —Viral hepatitis.

Via —Any passage in the body such as intestinal, nasal and vaginal, etc.

Viability —Ability to live after birth.

Viable —Able to live after birth.

Viae —Plural of via.

Vial —A small glass bottle for medicines.

Vibex—A narrow, linear mark or streak formed due to subcutaneous effusion of blood.

Vibices —Plural of vibex.

Vibrapuncture —To introduce the medicine into the skin by tatto technique.

Vibratile —Moving to and fro.

Vibration —1. A to-and-fro rapid movement. 2. Shaking of the body as the treatment of a disease, a form of massage.

Vibrative —Vibratory.

Vibrator —An apparatus for producing artificial vibration of the body or its parts.

Vibratory —Vibrating or causing vibration.

Vibrio —A genus of curved, motile, gram-negative bacteria. Vibrio cholerae is comma-haped, causes cholera in man.

Vibriocidal —Destructive to bacillus vibrio, especially Vibrio cholerae.

Vibrion —A vibrio.

Vibrioses —Plural of vibriosis.

Vibriosis —Condition of being infected with vibrio.

Vibrissae —[Singular vibrissa] Stiff hairs growing in the nostrils.

Vibrissal —Pertaining to the vibrissae.

Vibromassage —Massage given by a mechanical vibrator.

Vibromasseur —An instrument for producing vibratory massage of the ear.

Vibrometer —An apparatus for measuring the vibratory sensation threshold.

Vibrotherapeutics —Use of vibration in the treatment of diseases.

Vicarious —Acting as a substitute; occurring in an abnormal situation.

Vicarious menstruation —Bleeding during menstruation from the site other than vagina, as from the nose, breasts, etc.

Vicarious respiration —Increased respiration in one lung when it is lessened or abolished in other lung.

Videoendoscope —An endoscope fitted with a video camera.

Videoendoscopy —Endoscopy performed with an endoscope fitted with a video camera.

Videognosis —Diagnosis of a disease made by data and X-ray pictures transmitted to the television.

Videokeratoscope —A keratoscope fitted with a video camera.

View —Sight.

View box —In radiology, a uniform light source to view a radiograph.

Vigil —Sleeplessness. Wakefulness.

Vigilambulism —Automatism occurring while the person is awake that resembles somnambulism.

Vigilance —Alertness or watchfullness for whatever may occur.

Viginti —Twenty.

Vigintinormal —Consisting of a twentieth of a normal, as a solution.

Vigor —Physical or mental power.

Villi —Plural of villus.

Villiferous —Having villi.

Villitis —Villositis.

Villoma —A villous tumor.

Villose, Villous —Pertaining to, or possessing villi or fine hairlike processes.

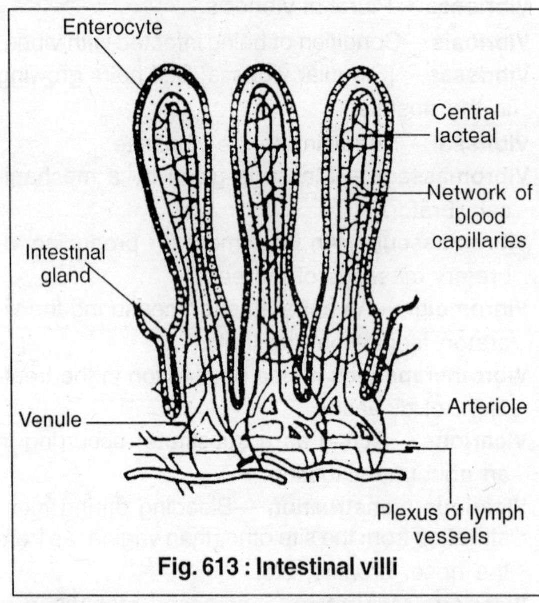

Fig. 613 : Intestinal villi

Villositis —Inflammation of the villi of placenta.

Villosity —1. Condition of being covered with villi. 2. A villus.

Villous —Villose.

Villus —[Plural Villi]—A small filamentous process found on free surface of certain membranes, *e.g.*, chorionic villus, which is one of the tiny vascular projections from the chorion which help to form the placenta, and intestinal villus, which is one of the minute projections of the intestinal mucosa into the lumen of the small intestines. They absorb fluid and nutrients.

Villusectomy —Synovectomy.

Vincent's angina —See under angina.

Vincula —Plural of vinculum.

Vinculum —Ligament. Frenulum. Frenum. A uniting band.

Vinegar —1. A weak and impure solution of acetic acid. 2. A medicinal preparation of dilute acetic acid.

Vinic —Concerning wine.

Vinous —Containing or of the nature of wine.

Vinum —Wine.

Violaceous —Having a purple discoloration, especially of the skin.

Violate —To injure a person, especially to rape a female.

Violence —1. Injury or physical discomfort. 2. Rape.

Violet —The color produced by a mixture of red and blue.

Viraginity —Feeling of a female of being a male though she is aware that her body is female.

Viral —Pertaining to or caused by a virus.

Viremia —Presence of viruses in the blood.

Vires —Plural of vis.

Virga —Penis.

Virgin —A woman who has not had sexual intercourse.

Virginal —Pertaining to a virgin or to virginity.

Virginal membrane —Hymen.

Virginity —The state of being virgin.

Viricidal —Virucidal.

Viricide —Virucide.

Virile —Masculine.

Virile reflex —The sudden downward movement of a completely relaxed penis when the prepuce is pulled upward.

Virilescence —The development of male secondary sex characters in the female.

Virilia —The male sexual organs.

Virilism —The presence or development of male secondary sex characters in a woman.

Virility —1. The condition of possessing male sex characters. 2. Sexual power in the male.

Virilization —Development of male secondary sex characters in a female such as change of voice and development of beard and moustaches etc.

Virilizing —Causing virilism.

Virion —A complete viral particle; a unit of genetic material surrounded by a protective coat that acts as a vehicle for its transmission from one cell to another.

Viripotent —1. Sexually mature, as applied to a male. 2. Marriageable, as applied to a female.

Viroids —Small, naked, infectious molecules of RNA.

Virolactia —Secretion of viruses in the milk.

Virologist —Specialist in virology.

Virology —The study of viruses and the diseases caused by them.

Viropexis —The fixation of a virus particle to a cell.

Virose, Virous —Poisonous.

Virucidal —Viricidal. Destructive to a virus.

Virucide —Viricide. An agent that destroys or inactivates a virus.

Virucopria —Presence of virus in feces.

Virulence —1. The degree of pathogenicity of a microorganism to produce disease. 2. The property of being virulent.

Virulent —1. Extremely poisonous or injurious. 2. Infectious.

Viruliferous —Producing or carrying a virus.

Viruria —Presence of viruses in the urine.

Virus —A minute infectious organism not visible by ordinary microscope but visible by ultramicroscope, living within a cell as a parasite for its nutrition, and for metabolism and reproduction.

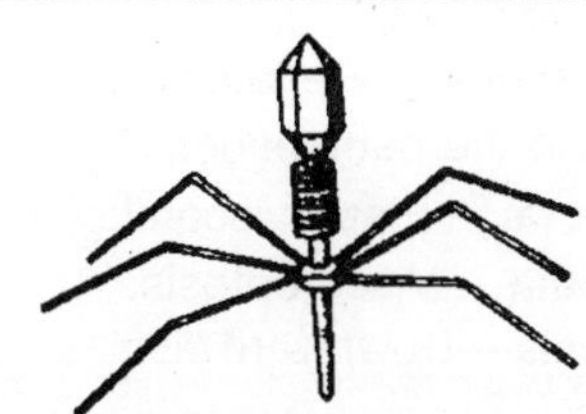

1. Bacterial virus or bacteriophage

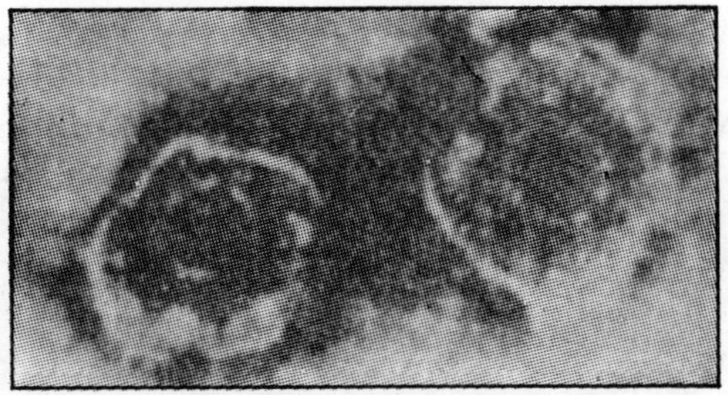

2. Chickenpox virus

3. Hepatitis B virus

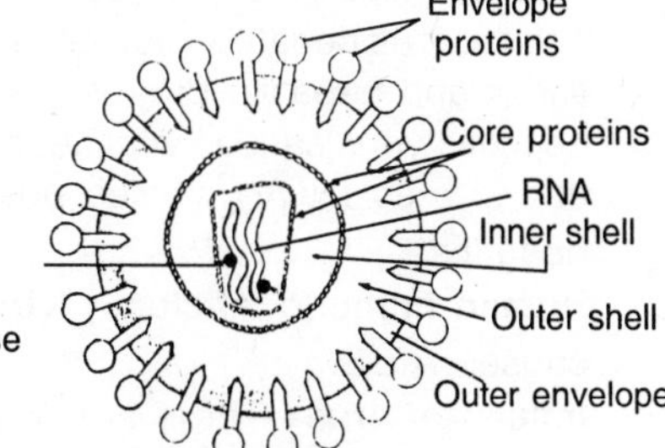

4. AIDS virus (HIV)

5. Influenza virus

6. Poliomyelitis virus

7. Rabies virus

Fig. 614 : Viruses

Attenuated virus —A virus so modified as to excite the production of protective antibodies, but not producing the specific disease.

Bacterial virus —A bacteriophage.

Chicken pox virus —Varicella zoster virus. A virus causing chicken pox.

Common cold virus —A virus causing common cold or coryza.

Dengue virus —A virus that causes dengue.

DNA virus —A group of viruses containing

Deoxyribonucleic acid (DNA). It includes adenoviruses, herpesviruses, poxviruses, parvoviruses, papovaviruses.

Enteric viruses —Viruses of the genus Enterovirus.

Hepatitis viruses —There are 5 types of hepatitis viruses, *i.e.*, A, B, C, D & E hepatitis viruses that cause hepatitis. Hepatitis A virus (HAV) and hepatitis B virus (HBV) are the chief hepatitis viruses. Hepatitis A virus (HAV) or infectious hepatitis virus causes viral hepatitis A and hepatitis B virus (HBV) or serum hepatitis virus causes viral hepatitis B. Hepatitis C virus (HCV) causes post-transfusion hepatitis.

Human immunodeficiency virus (HIV) —It causes AIDS.

Influenza virus—There are 3 types, *i.e.*, A, B, C of influenza virus that cause influenza.

Latent virus —A virus that causes a disease in the infected individual after a long period of the infection.

Lytic virus —Any virus that after infecting a cell, lyses it.

Measles virus —A virus that causes measles, usually in children.

Mumps virus —It causes parotitis or mumps, sometimes with complications of orchitis, oophoritis and pancreatitis etc.

Neurotropic virus —A virus that reproduces in the nerve tissue.

Oncogenic virus —A virus causing cancer.

Poliomyelitis virus —A virus that causes poliomyelitis.

Rabies virus —A virus that causes rabies.

Smallpox virus —Variola virus.

Varicella zoster virus —It causes herpes and chickenpox.

Virusemia —Viremia.

Virus shedding —The release of a virus from the host.

Virustatic —Stopping the growth of viruses.

Vis —[Plural is vires]. Force or energy.

Vis afronte —Force that attracts.

Vis formativa —Energy resulting in the development of new tissue.

Vis medicatrix naturae —Natural healing power of the body.

Viscera —[Singular is viscus]—Internal organs enclosed within a cavity, especially the abdominal organs.

Viscerad —Toward the viscera.

Visceral —Pertaining to a viscus or viscera.

Visceral cavity —Body cavity containing the viscera.

Visceralgia —Pain in any viscus.

Visceral pleura —See under pleura.

Visceral skeleton —The pelvis, ribs, and sternum enclosing the viscera.

Viscerimotor —Visceromotor.

Viscero- —A prefix which means pertaining to the viscera.

Viscerocranium —The part of the skull derived from the embryonic pharyngeal arches.

Viscerogenic —Originating in a viscus.

Viscerograph —An instrument for recording the mechanical activity of the viscera.

Visceroinhibitory —Inhibiting the action of a viscus.

Visceromegaly —Splanchnomegaly. Enlargement of the abdominal viscera.

Visceromotor —1. Conveying motor impulses to the viscera. 2. Pertaining to the essential movements of the viscera.

Visceromotor reflex —An increase in the tonicity of the abdominal muscles resulting from painful stimuli originating in a viscus.

Visceroparietal —Pertaining to the viscera and the abdominal wall.

Visceroperitoneal —Pertaining to the abdominal viscera and the peritoneum.

Visceropleural —Pleurovisceral.

Visceroptosia —Visceroptosis.

Visceroptosis —Downward displacement of a viscus.

Viscerosensory —Pertaining to the sensation in the viscera.

Visceroskeletal —Pertaining to the visceral skeleton.

Visceroskeleton —Splanchnoskeleton. The bony framework protecting the viscera, such as the ribs and sternum or pelvic bones etc.

Viscerosomatic —Pertaining to the viscera and the body.

Viscerotome —An instrument used at postmortem examination for obtaining a piece of liver for microscopic examination.

Viscerotomy —To make an incision into a viscus.

Viscerotonia —Personality traits characterized by general relaxation and love for comfort, sociability and conviviality.

Viscerotrophic —Pertaining to trophic conditions associated with viscera.

Viscerotropic —Primarily acting on the viscera.

Viscid —Adhering. Sticky.

Viscidity —Stickiness.

Viscidosis —Cystic fibrosis.

Viscoelasticity —The property of being viscous and elastic.

Viscometer —Viscosimeter.

Viscosimeter —An apparatus for measuring viscosity of a substance.

Viscosimetry —Measurement of the viscosity of a substance.

Viscosity —Stickiness.

Viscous —Sticky, gummy, having high viscosity.

Viscus —[Plural is viscera]—See viscera.

Visibility —The quality of being visible.

Visible —Capable of being seen.

Visile —1. Pertaining to vision. 2. Readily remembering the objects seen.

Vision —Sight. Act of viewing external objects.

- **Achromatic vision** —Complete color blindness.
- **Binocular vision** —Normal vision. Viewing an object with both eyes, of which two images, one from each eye, are fused to appear as one.
- **Colored vision** —Chromatopsia.
- **Day vision** —The seeing better during the day than at night.
- **Dichromatic vision** —Perception of only two primary colors, either blue and yellow or red and green.
- **Double vision** —Diplopia.
- **Field of vision** —The maximum area upto which an eye can see.
- **Half vision** —Hemianopia.
- **Low vision** —Loss of vision that cannot be corrected by medicines, surgery or with eyeglasses.
- **Monocular vision** —Vision with one eye.
- **Multiple vision** —Polyopia.
- **Night vision** —Viewing an object in the darkness of night or in reduced light.
- **Oscillating vision** —Oscillopsia.
- **Peripheral vision** —Vision resulting from rays falling on the retina outside of the macula lutea.
- **Phantom vision** —Experience of vision in the eye surgically removed.
- **Phototopic vision** —Day vision.
- **Triple vision** —Triplopia. A visual defect in which three images of the same object are seen.
- **Tunnel vision** —A condition in which there is concentric reduction in the visual field, as though one is looking through a long tube.
- **Yellow vision** —Xanthopsia.

Visit —To go to see a patient.

Visitor —One who visits.

Visual —Pertaining to the vision.

Visual acuity —Acuteness or sharpness of vision.

Visual angle —The angle between the line of sight and the ends of the object seen.

Visual axis —The line of vision from the object seen through the center of the pupil to macula lutea.

Visual field —The space within which objects can be seen when the eye is fixed.

Visualization —1. The process of making visible. 2. To see an object in imagination.

Visualize —1. To make visible. 2. To see an object in imagination.

Visual plane —The plane in which visual axes of both eyes lie.

Visual point —Center of vision

Visual-purple —Rhodopsin.

Visual yellow —A pigment formed in the retina by the action of light on visual purple.

Visuoauditory —Pertaining to seeing and hearing.

Visuognosis —The recognition and interpretation of what is seen.

Visuomotor —Denoting the ability to synchronize visual information with physical movement, *e.g.*, driving a car.

Visuopsychic —Both visual and psychic.

Visuosensory —Pertaining to the recognition of visual impressions.

Visuospatial —Pertaining to visual perception of spatial relationships.

Vita —Life.

Vita glass —Windo glass containing quarta for transmitting the ultraviolet rays of sunlight.

Vital —1. Pertaining to life. 2. Essential for life.

Vital capacity —Volume of air that can be expelled after full inspiration.

Vital center —Respiratory center in the medulla.

Vital force —The natural strength that keeps one alive.

Vitalism —The theory that existence of life is not due to a chemical or mechanical force.

Vitalist —One who believes in vitalism.

Vitalistic —Pertaining to vitalism.

Vitality —1. Strength of life. 2. The state of being alive.

Vitalize —To give life to.

Vitalometer —An instrument used to measure the response of a nerve in a tooth pulp to an electrical stimulus.

Vitals —The organs essential for life.

Vital signs —The signs of life, *i.e.*, heart beat, respiration, body temperature and blood pressure.

Vital statistics —Statistics of birth rate (natality), death rate (mortality) and morbidity rate.

Vitamer —A substance or compound which has vitamin activity.

Vitamin —Any of a group of organic substances found in many foods, which are essential in minute quantities for normal metabolism, growth and development of the body. They may be fat or water soluble. Vitamins are of 6 types—A, B, C, D, E, and K.

Vitamin A —A fat soluble vitamin found in fish liver oils, egg yolk, liver, butter, cheese, and green leafy and yellow vegetables in most of which it exists as its precursor—carotene. It is essential for normal growth and development, and the integrity and normal function of the epithelial tissues. Its deficiency in the diet causes impaired growth and development in children, lessened resistance to infection, keratomalacia, xerophthalmia and night blindness.

Vitamin B —A group of water-soluble vitamins which are destroyed by excessive heating for 2 to 4 hours. It includes the following factors.

Vitamin B_1 or Thiamine hydrochloride —It is found in whole grains, yeast, legumes, nuts, egg yolk, fruits and vegetables. Its daily requirement for an adult is about 2 mg. It affects growth, mental stability and carbohydrate metabolism. Its deficiency causes neuritis, mental instability, loss of weight and beriberi.

Vit. B_2 or Riboflavine —It is found in milk, egg, meat, fish, poultry, yeast, liver and green vegetables. Its daily requirement for an adult is about 1 mg. It is essential for growth and associated with tissue repair. Its deficiency causes impairment of growth, fissures developing on the skin, especially on the corners of mouth (angular stomatitis), and glossitis.

Vit. B_6 or Pyridoxine hydrochloride —It is found in rice, bran, pulses, yeast, liver, egg, fish and cabbage, etc. Its daily requirement for an adult is about 1 mg. Its deficiency causes peripheral neuropathy, vomiting in pregnancy, convulsions in children and depression in adults.

Vit. B_{12} or Cyanocobalamin —It is found in milk, cheese, meat, fish, egg and liver. Its daily requirement for an adult is about 5 µg. (5 microgram). Its deficiency causes pernicious anemia and subacute combined degeneration of the spinal cord.

Nicotinic acid or Niacin —It is found in milk, grains, liver, meat and green vegetables, etc. Its daily requirement for an adult is about 10 mg. Its deficiency causes pellagra, so it is also known as pellagra preventing factor and is used in the treatment of pellagra. It is also used in the treatment of cerebral thrombosis, angina pectoris and thromboangiitis obliterans (Buerger's disease), due to its vasodilator action.

Folic acid —It is found mostly in spinach, green leaves and milk, etc. Its daily requirement for an adult is upto 1 mgm. It is concerned with the formation of red blood cells and its deficiency causes macrocytic anemia.

Pantothenic acid —It is found in wheat flour, milk, egg yolk, meat, etc., and commercially available as calcium pantothenate. It is important for growth. Its deficiency is rare. However burning feet syndrome, alopecia and sterility may occur.

Choline —It is mostly found in yeast, milk and egg yolk, etc. It is a lipotropic factor and its deficiency causes enlargement of the liver due to fatty degeneration. Fatty liver and alcoholic cirrhosis liver improves with choline.

Inositol —It is found mostly in orange and lemon, etc. Its deficiency in man is rare.

Biotin —It is found in all common diets, especially in meat and yeast. Its deficiency in man is rare.

Para-aminobenzoic acid

Vitamin C or Ascorbic acid —A water-soluble vitamin found in lemon, orange, amla, tomato, green vegetables, apples, peas, germinating cereals and especially in mother's milk. Its requirement for an infant is 15 to 50 mg., for an adult 50-100 mg., for pregnant woman and lactating mother 100-150 mg. per day. It is destroyed by heating in the presence of oxygen. It is necessary for the formation of intercellular substance of connective tissue and maintaining the integrity of intercellular cement in many tissues, especially capillary walls. Its deficiency causes scurvy.

Vitamin D or Antirachitic vitamin —The vitamin D group includes D_2 (calciferol), D_3 (irradiated 7-dehydrocholesterol), D_4 (irradiated 22-dihydroergosterol) and D_5 (irradiated dehydrositosterol). It is a fat-soluble vitamin and is found in cod liver oil, milk, butter, cheese, egg yolk and is produced in the skin as vit D_2 (calciferol) on exposure to sunlight, by the action of ultraviolet rays of sunlight on ergosterol present in the skin, or may be produced artificially by the action of ultraviolet rays on ergosterol. Its daily requirement for an adult is about 1000 I.U. It is necessary for calcium and phosphorus absorption and hence it is required for normal development of bones and teeth. Its deficiency causes rickets in children and osteomalacia in adults, and dental caries.

Vitamin E or antisterility vitamin —It is also called Alpha tocopherol. It is a fat-soluble vitamin which is found in wheat germ oil, cereals, egg yolk, green vegetables, milk, etc., and produced artificially. It is not destroyed on heating. Its daily requirement is 5 to 15 mg. It is necessary for normal reproduction and normal muscular development and has vasodilator action. Its deficiency causes sterility and abortion or death of fetus in uterus, and diseases of the muscles. It is used in the treatment of sterility, abortion and muscular diseases. Due to its vasodilator action it is used in angina pectoris, intermittent claudication and Raynaud's disease.

Vitamin K or Anti-hemorrhagic factor —It is a fat-soluble vitamin and found in spinach, soyabean, cauliflower, cabbage, milk, egg, fish, meat, etc., as vit. K_1. It is also synthesized in the colon by bacterial action as vit. K_2. It helps in coagulation of blood, being associated with the formation of prothrombin in the liver. Its deficiency prolongs blood-clotting time and causes hemorrhage. It is used in case of hemorrhage.

Vitaminoid —Of the nature of vitamin.

Vitaminology —Study of vitamins.

Vitellary —Vitelline.

Vitelliform —Pertaining to or resembling the yolk of egg.

Vitellin —A protein of egg yolk containing lecithin.

Vitelline —Pertaining to the yolk of an egg or the ovum.

Vitellogenesis —Production of yolk.

Vitellointestinal —Pertaining to the embryonic yolk sac and the intestinal tract.

Vitellus —The yolk of an ovum, especially the yolk of a hen's egg.

Vitiate —To render impure or to destroy.

Vitiation —The act of impuring, as of the blood.

Vitiligines —Depigmented areas of the skin.

Vitiliginous —Pertaining to vitiligo.

Vitiligo —An acquired leucoderma.

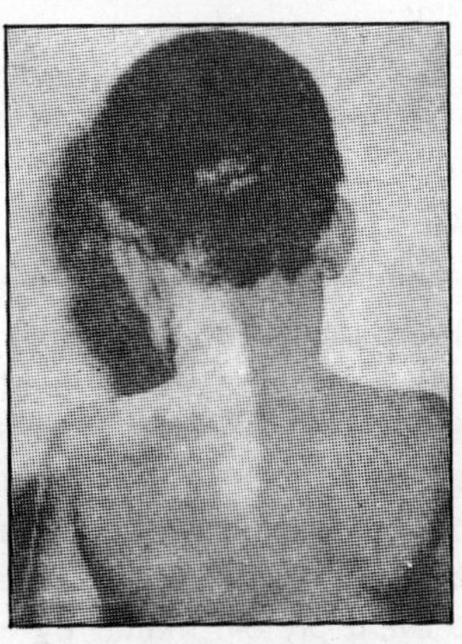

Fig. 615 : Vitiligo

Vitiligoidea —Xanthoma.

Vitium —A fault or defect.

Vitrectomy —Surgical removal of the substances of the vitreous chamber, and their replacement by a sterile physiological solution.

Vitreitis —Hyalitis.

Vitreocapsulitis —Hyalitis.

Vitreodentin—An abnormally hard and glasslike dentine.

Vitreoretinal —Pertaining to the vitreous and the retina.

Vitreoretinopathy—Any disease of the retina with complications in the vitreous body.

Vitreous—1. Glasslike or hyaline. 2. Vitreous body.

Vitreous body—A transparent jellylike mass filling the cavity of the eyeball.

Vitreous chamber—The portion of the cavity of eyeball behind the lens.

Vitreous humor—The clear watery fluid filling the vitreous body.

Vitreous membrane —Inner membrane of the choroid.

Vitrescence—Becoming hard and transparent like glass.

Vitreum—The vitreous body of the eye.

Vitrification—The process of converting dental porcelain into a smooth, viscous substance by heat.

Vitriol —Any crystalline sulfate.

Vitronectin—A plasma glycoprotein involved in inflammatory and repair reactions at the site of tissue damage.

Vitrum—Glass.

Vivaria—Plural of vivarium.

Vivarium—A place for keeping living animals, particularly animals used in medical research.

Vives—Enlarged glands.

Vivi- —Combining form meaning alive.

Vividialysis—Dialysis through a living membrane.

Vividiffusion —Circulation of blood through a closed apparatus in which it is passed through a membrane for removal of substances which are ordinarily removed by the kidneys.

Vivification—1. Conversion of lifeless protein of food into living protein matter by assimilation. 2. Trimming of the surface of a wound to aid union of tissues.

Viviparity—The ability to produce living young rather than laying an egg which hatch and produce living young.

Viviparous—Giving birth to a living young which develops within the body of the mother.

Vivisect—To dissect a living animal for experimental purposes.

Vivisection—Dissection of a living animal for physiological or pathological investigations.

Vivisectionist—One who practices or believes in vivisection.

Vivisector—One who practices vivisection.

Vivisepulture—To bury an individual alive.

VLDL—Very low density lipoprotein.

Vocal—Pertaining to voice.

Vocal cords—Two thin, reedlike folds of tissue within the larynx which vibrate as the air passes between them, producing sound.

Vocal folds—Vocal cords.

Vocal fremitus—Vibration of chest-wall felt on palpation while the patient is speaking.

Vocalization—The pronouncing of words.

Vocal ligament—A strong band of elastic tissue lying within the vocal fold.

Vocal resonance—Sound heard in auscultation of lung while the patient is speaking.

Voces—Plural of vox.

Voice—Sound produced by vibration of the vocal cords and uttered by the mouth.

Voice-box—Larynx.

Void—1. To cast out as waste matter, especially the urine. 2. To evacuate the bowels or bladder.

Vol.—Volume.

Vola, Volar—Pertaining to the palm or the sole.

Vola manus—Palm.

Vola pedis—Sole of the foot.

Volaris—Volar.

Volatile—Evaporating easily.

Volatilization—Conversion of a solid or liquid into a vapor.

Volatilize—To vaporize a liquid or solid.

Volition—The act or power of willing.

Volitional—Performed by will power.

Volkmann's ischemic contracture—Flexion of all the phalanges with flexion of the wrist due to fibrosis of the flexor muscles of the forearm, which feel hard and inelastic. It is commonly

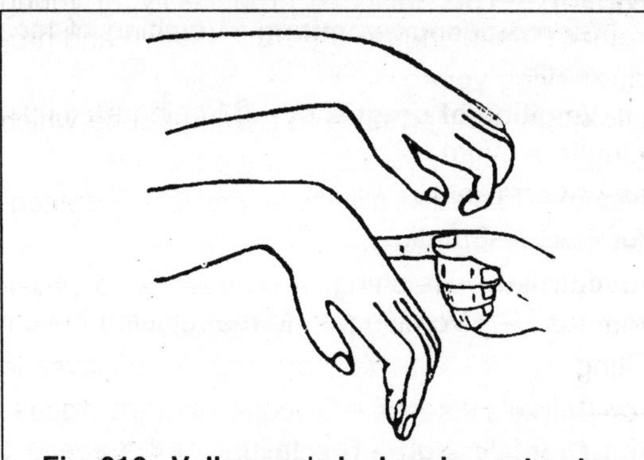
Fig. 616 : Volkmann's ischemic contracture

found in children as a complication of supracondylar fracture of the humerus bone or fracture of the bones of forearm.

Volley—Simultaneous discharge of a number of impulses from a center within the brain or spinal cord.

Volsella—Vulsella.

Volt—An electrical unit which is electromotive force required to produce one ampere of current through a resistance of one ohm.

Voltage—Electromotive force measured in volts.

Voltaic—Concerning electricity produced by a battery.

Voltaism—Galvanism.

Voltammeter—An apparatus for measuring both volts and amperes.

Voltampere—A unit of electrical power which is obtained by multiplying 1 volt by 1 ampere which is equivalent to 1 watt or $^{1}/_{1000}$ kw.

Voltmeter—An apparatus for measuring the voltage.

Volubility—Excessive speech.

Volume—The space occupied by a substance or a three-dimensional region, or capacity of a container, expressed in cubic unit.

Expiratory reserve volume —The maximal amount of air that can be expired from the lungs after a normal expiration.

Inspiratory reserve volume—The maximal amount of air that can be inspired after the end of a normal inspiration.

Mean corpuscular volume—M.C.V. See under letter 'M'.

Minute volume —The volume of air expelled from the lungs per minute.

Packed cell volume—Hematocrit.

Residual volume—The volume of air remaining in the lungs at the end of maximal expiration.

Stroke volume—The volume of blood ejected from a ventricle in one heart beat.

Tidal volume—The volume of air inspired and expired during one respiratory cycle.

Volumenometer—Volumometer.

Volumetric—Pertaining to measurement of volume.

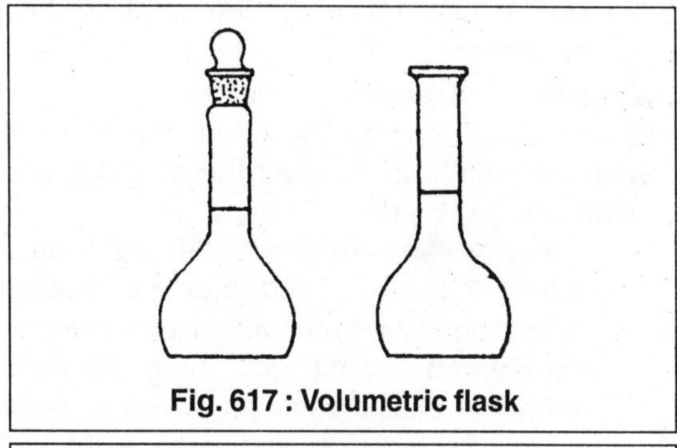
Fig. 617 : Volumetric flask

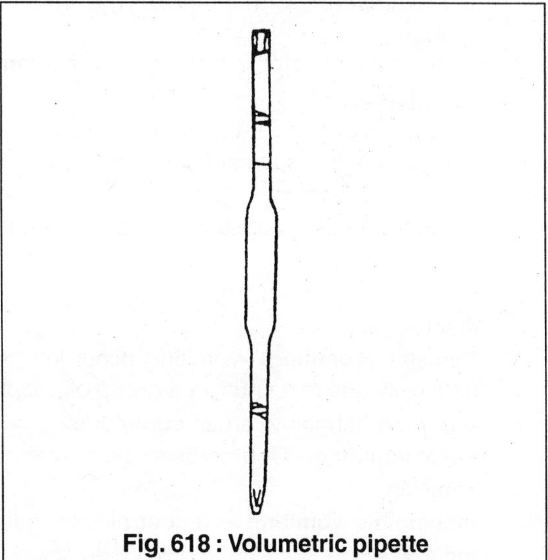
Fig. 618 : Volumetric pipette

Volumometer—An apparatus for measuring volume.

Voluntary—Pertaining to or accomplished according to, the will.

Voluntary muscle—A muscle controlled by the will, as skeletal muscles.

Voluptuous—Sensual.

Volupty—Sexual pleasure.

Volute—Convoluted.

Volvulus—A torsion of a loop of the intestine, causing obstruction.

Vomer—Thin bone forming the posterior and posterior inferior part of the nasal septum.

Vomerine—Pertaining to vomer bone.

Vomerobasilar—Pertaining to the vomer bone and base of the skull.

Vomeronasal—Pertaining to the vomer and nasal bones.

Vomica—1. Sudden and profuse expectoration of pus and putrescent matter. 2. A cavity in a lung, caused by suppuration and the breaking down of the tissue.

Vomicose—1. Ulcerous. 2. Purulent.

Vomit —1. Matter expelled from the stomach through mouth. 2. To eject the stomach contents through mouth.

Bilious vomit—Vomit containing a large amount of bile which indicates the intestinal obstruction distal to the ampulla of vater.

Black vomit—Vomit containing the blood mixed with gastric contents, which is generally associated with hemorrhage into the stomach.

Vomiting —Forcible ejection of stomach contents through the mouth.

Cerebral vomiting—Vomiting due to some brain disease, especially the elevated cerebrospinal pressure.

Cyclic vomiting—Vomiting that recurs periodically.

Dry vomiting—Vomiting in which only gas is ejected.

Epidemic vomiting—Vomiting occurring epidemically due to a virus, in a group of people, *e.g.*, in a school or small community.

Fecal vomiting—Copremesis, stercoraceous vomiting.

Incoercible vomiting—Uncontrollable vomiting.

Induced vomiting —Vomiting produced artificially by administering certain medicines or stimulating the posterior pharynx manually.

Morning vomiting—Morning sickness.

Pernicious vomiting—Severe vomiting of pregnancy which may threaten life.

Projectile vomiting—Vomiting in which the stomach contents are ejected with great force.

Psychogenic vomiting—Vomiting associated with emotional stress and anxiety.

Stercoraceous vomiting—Vomiting of fecal matter.

Vomiting of pregnancy —Morning sickness.

Vomition—Vomiting.

Vomitive—Emetic.

Vomitory —Emetic.

Vomiturition—Retching.

Vomitus —1. Vomiting. 2. Matter ejected in vomiting.

Von Gierke's disease—Glycogen storage disease.

Von Graefe's sign—The failure of the eyelid to move downward promptly with the eyeball, a sign of exophthalmic goiter.

Voorhee's bag—An inflatable rubber bag for dilating the cervix uteri to induce labor.

Voracious—Having an insatiable appetite.

Vortex—A structure having a spiral appearance, as the hairs of the skin.

Vortices—Plural of vortex.

Vorticose—Whorled.

V.R.—Right vision; ventilation rate; vocal resonance.

Vox—Voice.

Voyeur—One who derives sexual pleasure from looking at sexual acts of others.

Voyeurism—The derivation of sexual pleasure from looking at sexual acts of others.

Vuerometer—An apparatus for measuring the distance between the eyes.

Vulgaris—Ordinary; common.

Vulnerable—Capable to be injured easily.

Vulnerant—Inflicting injury.

Vulnerary—1. Pertaining to wounds or the healing of wounds. 2. An agent that promotes healing of wounds.

Vulnus—A wound or injury.

Vulsella, Vulsellum—Volsella. A forceps with a sharp, pointed hook at the end of each blade.

Vulva—Female external genital organs, including mons pubis, labia majora and labia minora, clitoris, vestibule of the vagina and vaginal opening.

Vulvae —Plural of vulva.

Vulval, Vulvar—Pertaining to the vulva.

Vulvectomy—Excision of the vulva.

Vulvismus—Vaginismus.

Vulvitis—Inflammation of the vulva.

Atrophic vulvitis—Inflammation of the atrophic vulva, with severe itching.

Follicular vulvitis—Inflammation of the hair follicles of the vulva.

Leukoplakic vulvitis —Kraurosis vulvae. A chronic atrophic vulvitis.

Mycotic vulvitis—Vulvitis caused by various fungi, most commonly candida albicans.

Vulvo- —A prefix meaning a covering or vulva.

Vulvocrural—Pertaining to the vulva and thigh.

Vulvodynia—Pain occurring in the valval area.

Vulvopathy—Any disease of the vulva.

Vulvouterine—Pertaining to the vulva and the uterus.

Vulvovaginal—Pertaining to the vulva and vagina.

Vulvovaginal glands—Bartholin's glands.

Vulvovaginitis—Inflammation of the vulva and vagina.

Vulvovaginoplasty—Repair of the vulva and vagina by plastic surgery.

VV—Veins.

V/V —Volume of solute per volume of solvent.

V/W—Volume of a substance per unit of weight of another substance.

W—1. Chemical symbol for tungsten. 2. Watt (a unit of electric energy)

Wadding—Carded cotton or wool in sheets, used for surgical dressings.

Waddle—Waddling gait.

Wafer—A thin sheet of flour paste used to enclose a dose of a medicine in powder form. 2. A flat vaginal suppository.

Waist—The part of the trunk between the thorax and hips.

Wakeful—Unable to sleep; sleepless.

Wakefulness—Sleeplessness.

Walcher's position—The position in which hips of the patient are at the edge of the bed and legs are hanging down.

Walk—1. To move on foot. 2. The manner of moving on foot, gait.

Walker—Crutch, a mobile device used to assist a person in walking.

Walking cast—A cast making the patient able to walk.

Walking typhoid —Mild typhoid fever in which the patient is able to walk.

Wall—A surrounding or limiting structure of a cell, vessel, organ or cavity such as an artery, vein, stomach or chest, etc.

Wallerian degeneration—The degeneration of a nerve fiber (axon) that has been severed from its cell body.

Walleye—1. White opacity of the cornea. 2. Turning of the eyes outward.

Wandering—Moving about; not fixed.

Wandering abscess—The abscess that burrows into the surface and appear on it at a point distant from its origin.

Wandering kidney—Dislocated floating kidney.

Wandering mind—Fluctuated mind.

Wandering spleen—Dislocated floating spleen.

Wane—Decrease or decline, fade.

Wangensteen's method—A method for relieving postoperative abdominal distention by removing gas and fluid from the intestine by using intranasal catheter, attached to an electric suction pump. By reducing atmospheric pressure, continuous suction is affected by this apparatus.

Wangensteen tube —A tube used as an intranasal catheter in combination with a suction siphonage apparatus, for the relief of postoperative abdominal distention.

Warburg apparatus—A capillary manometer used for determining oxygen consumption and carbon dioxide prouction of small pieces of tissues.

Ward—A large room in a hospital for the care of several patients, usually more than the four.

Wardrop's disease—Onychia maligna. Acute inflammation of the nail bed with fetid ulceration and loss of the nail, in debilitated persons.

Wardrop's operation—Ligation of an artery for an aneurysm at a distance beyond the aneurysmal sac.

Warehousemen's itch—Eczema of the hands from touching irritating substances.

War gases—Gases used to produce poisonous or irritant effects in the war.

Warm blooded—The animals including man, whose blood temperature remains constant and does not change with the variation in the atmospheric temperature.

Wart—Verruca. A localized overgrowth of the epidermis and papillae, which is caused by a virus or it may be a benign tumor.

Common wart—Verruca vulgaris.

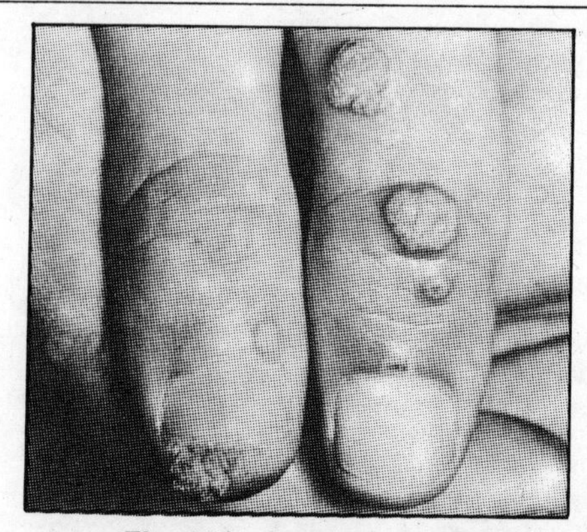

Fig. 619 : Common warts

Fig wart—Venereal wart. Condyloma acuminatum. A figlike growth occurring on the genital organs.

Genital wart—A wart occurring on the genital organs, caused by human papillomavirus (HPV). In women, these warts may be associated with cancer of the cervix.

Moist wart—Condyloma latum. A broad, flat, mucous patch coated with gray exudate, occurring on the folds of moist skin, especially about the vulva or anus, in syphilis.

Plantar wart—See verruca plantaris.

Postmortem wart—Warts seen on the hands of the persons performing postmortem examinations.

Seborrheic wart—A patch of horny hypertrophy occurring on the face of the aged person.

Senile wart —Seborrheic wart.

Tuberculous wart —Tuberculosis verrucosa. Wart occurring on the skin or mucous membrane caused by tuberculous infection.

Venereal wart—Condyloma acuminatum. An ordinary pointed wart upon the skin, especially on the mucocutaneous junction of the genital organs and anus, caused by a virus.

Verruca filiformis—See under verruca.

Verruca vulgaris—See under verruca.

Wartpox—Occurrence of papules which persist for a time like warts.

Warty—Resembling or of the nature of warts.

Wash—1. The act of cleaning a part or all of the body. 2. A solution used for washing a part of the body, as eye lotion for washing the eyes.

Washerwoman's itch—Eczema of the hands of laundry workers.

Wassermann-fast—Showing positive reaction to Wassermann test even after antisyphilitic treatment.

Wassermann reaction—Serum complement fixation test for the diagnosis of syphilis.

Wastage—Loss by waste.

Waste—1. Diminution of bulk or strength of the body or of its part. 2. Useless material for further use within the organism. 3. To spend in vain.

Waste products—Feces, urine, dead skin, hair, nails and carbon dioxide etc.

Wasting—Emaciating. Causing loss of size or strength of the body or of its part.

Wasting palsy—Progressive muscular atrophy.

Water—1. A clear, colorless, odorless, tasteless liquid, H_2O. 2. A solution of a medicine in water.

Alkaline water —A water that contains calcium or sodium bicarbonates in large amount.

Distilled water—Water purified by distillation.

Hard water—Water that contains salts of magnesium and calcium dissolved in it.

Heavy water—Water of which freezing and boiling point is higher and which is not capable for the life.

Lime water—Alkaline solution of calcium hydroxide, $Ca(OH)_2$, in water.

Mineral water—A water that contains appreciable amounts of minerals, which is generally used therapeutically.

Potable water—A water free from contamination and fit for drinking.

Purified water—Mineral free water obtained by distillation or by removing ions from it.

Pyrogen-free water—A water free from fever-producing organisms.

Saline water—A water containing sodium chloride (Common salt) in sufficient quantity.

Soft water—Water that contains very little dissolved salts of magnesium or calcium.

Water bed—A rubber mattress partially filled with warm water (100° F or 37.8° C), used in preventing and treating bed sores.

Water borne—Transmitted by drinking water.

Water cure—Hydrotherapy.

Water for injection—Distilled and sterilized water stored in ampules for use by injection.

Water-hammer pulse—See under pulse.

Waterhouse-Friderichsen syndrome—A condition occurring mainly in children under 10 years of age, due to acute adrenal insufficiency occurring as a result of hemorrhage into adrenal gland, caused by meningitis. It is characterized by vom-

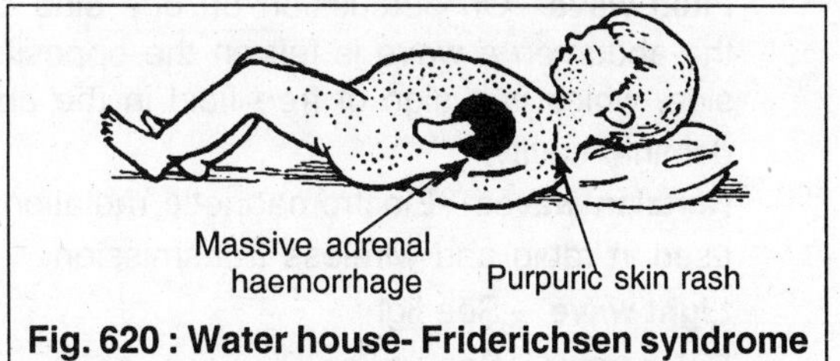

Fig. 620 : Water house- Friderichsen syndrome

iting, diarrhea, extensive purpura, cyanosis, convulsions and collapse.

Water intoxication—Excess of water in the body characterized by the symptoms of throbbing headache, hypertension, dizziness, abdominal cramp, hallucination and convulsion.

Water on brain—Hydrocephalus.

Waters—Popular name for amniotic fluid.

Water syringe—A syringe used in dentistry for spraying water to a localized area of the denture.

Watt—A unit of electric power, being the work done at the rate of 1 joule per second. One watt is the power produced by one ampere of current flowing with a force, of one volt.

Wattage—The electrical energy produced or consumed by an electrical apparatus, expressed in watts.

Wattmeter—An instrument for measuring wattage.

Wave —1. A temporary elevation of the surface of a liquid, which propagates forwards. 2. A vibrating movement. 3. An oscillation seen in the recording of an electrocardiogram, encephalogram or other graphic record of physiological activity.

Alpha wave—Rhythm, alpha.

Beta wave—Rhythm, beta.

Brain wave—Rhythmic fluctuation of the electrical impulses, produced by the brain.

Delta wave—Rhythm, delta.

Dicrotic wave —Second wave in a dicrotic pulse.

Electrocardiographic waves —Waves seen in an electrocardiogram showing the electric activity of the heart muscle.

Excitation wave—The excitatory impulse that originates in the sinoatrial node of the heart and reaches the atrioventricular node through muscle of the atria and then continues to the ventricles, causing contractions of the cardiac chambers.

Fluid wave—On percussion on one side of the abdomen a wave is felt on the opposite side, which is a sign of free fluid in the abdominal cavity.

Hertzian waves—Electromagnetic radiations used in radio and wireless transmission.

Light wave —See light.

Pulse wave—See under 'P'

Radio waves—Electromagnetic waves between the frequencies of 10^{11} and 10^{14} hertz.

Sound waves—Vibrations of a vibrating medium that, on stimulating sensory receptors of the cochlea in the inner ear give rise to sensations of sound.

Ultrasonic waves—Sound waves of very high frequency, i.e., of the frequency greater than 20 kilo hertz, which do not produce sound audible to the human ear.

Wavelength—The distance from the top of one wave to the top of the next one.

Wax—1. Beeswax, a plastic substance deposited by honey-bees, used in medicine in pure form in making ointments. 2. Earwax or cerumen.

Waxing—In dentistry, moulding of the wax around the outline of a denture.

Waxy—Pertaining to or resembling wax.

Waxy cast—Dense highly refractile urinary cast, occurring in severe chronic renal disease.

Waxy degeneration—Amyloid degeneration seen in wasting diseases.

W. B. C.—White blood cells.

Weak—1. Lacking energy. 2. Dilute, as a solution.

Weaken—To reduce strength.

Weakness—Loss of physical strength.

Weal—Happiness: welfare.

Wean—To deprive of a child from breast feeding by substituting other nutrient substances.

Weanling—An infant recently changed from breast feeding to other forms of nourishment.

Weanling diarrhea—Diarrhea occurring in an infant who has been deprived of the breast milk.

Wear—Wasting or deterioration caused by friction.

Web—A tissue or membrane connecting the adjacent structures.

Webbed—Having a web, as the toes of a duck's feet.

Webbing—The joining of adjacent structures congenitally, by a tissue or membrane not normally present there.

Weber's gland—One of the mucous glands of the tongue.

Weber's paralysis—Paralysis of the oculomotor nerve on one side and spastic hemiplegia on the other side.

Weber's test—A test for unilateral deafness. In this test the base of a vibrating tunning fork is placed against the middle of the forehead. If both the ears are healthy, the sound will be heard equally by them. In unilateral nerve-type deafness, the sound will be heard by healthy ear, whereas in a conductive type deafness, sound will be heard by the deaf ear.

Wechsler intelligence scale for children —An intelligence test for pre school (5 to 8 years of age) children.

Wedge—1. A piece of metal or wood, thick at one end and sloping at the other. 2. A solid of five sides.

Wedge-shaped—Having one end thick and the other sloping.

Weed—Grass or wild plants.

Weeping—1. Shedding tears. 2. That from which water cozes. 3. Moist.

Weeping eczema—See under eczema.

Weeping sinew—A circumscribed cystic swelling of a tendon sheath.

Weidel's reaction—Test for the presence of xanthine bodies and uric acid.

Weigert's law—A law stating that loss or destruction of tissue results in the formation of an excess of new tissue during repair.

Weight—The measure of heaviness.

Atomic weight—The weight of an atom of a chemical element as compared with the weight of an atom of carbon-12, which is taken as 12000. Its abbreviation is at. wt.

Avoirdupois weight—A system of weight in which the units are the dram (27.344 grains), ounce (16 drams), and pound (16 ounces).

Birth weight—It is the first weight of an infant obtained within less than 60 minutes after birth. Normal birth weight is 2500 grams or more, low birth weight is less than 2500 grams, very low birth weight is less than 1500 grams and extremely low birth weight is less than 1000 gms.

Dry weight—The weight of a material remaining after removing the water, *e.g.*, after heating above 100° C.

Equivalent weight—The weight in grams of an element that combines with or replaces 1 gram of hydrogen.

Molecular weight—The weight of a molecule attained by totaling the weight of its atoms.

Weight in volume —The amount by weight of a solid substance dissolved in a measured quantity of liquid which is expressed as w/v in which w is the number of grams of solid substance and v is 100 mls of solution.

Weight in weight —The amount by weight of a solid substance dissolved in a known amount by weight of liquid which is expressed as w/w in which w/ is the number of grams of the solid substance and /w 100 grams of solution.

Weismannism —A theory that acquired characteristics are not inherited.

Welch's bacillus—Clostridium perfringens, the bacillus causing gas gangrene.

Welt—An elevation on the skin caused by a lash, blow or allergy in which the skin is not broken.

Wen—1. Sebaceous cyst. 2. Steatoma.

Wernicke's encephalopathy—Encephalopathy caused by vitamin B_1 (thiamine hydrochloride) deficiency occurring in chronic alcoholism, gastric carcinoma or hyperemesis gravidarum.

Wernicke syndrome—A condition of chronic alcoholics, largely due to vitamin B_1 deficiency characterized by nystagmus and ataxia with tremor.

Wet brain —Increased amount of cerebrospinal fluid with edema of the meninges, due to alcoholism.

Wet dream —Nocturnal seminal emission.

Wet nurse—A woman who breastfeeds another's child.

Wet nurse phenomenon —The production of milk in response to repeated stimulation of the nipples in a nonpregnant woman who has previously been pregnant.

Wet pack—A form of bath given to reduce fever in which the patient is wrapped in cold wet sheets, covered by a blanket.

Wharton's duct—Duct of the submandibular salivary gland opening into the mouth at the side of the frenum.

Wharton's jelly —Gelatinous substance of the umbilical cord.

Wheal—A circumscribed elevation on the skin disappearing quickly, and accompanied by itching. It is seen in urticaria, allergy and insect bites etc.

Wheel —An instrument in the form of a wheel.

Wheel chair—A special chair with large wheels for transporting the patients, who are unable to walk.

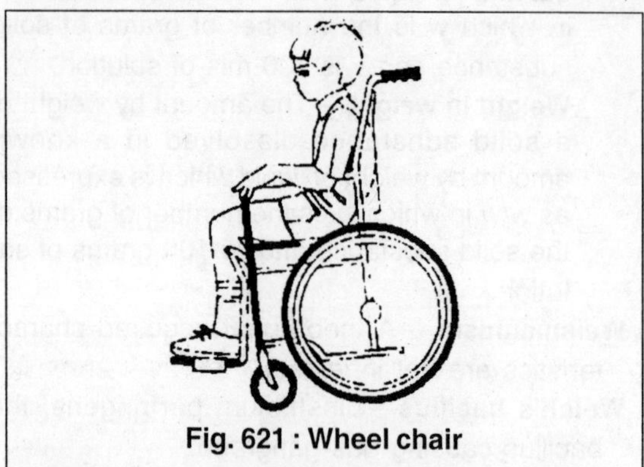

Fig. 621 : Wheel chair

Wheeze—A whistling sound heard during respiration.

Wheezing—Occurrence of whistling sounds during difficult breathing such as in asthma or other respiratory disorders.

Whelk—1. A wheal. 2. A nodule or tubercle on the face.

Whey —The watery part of milk separated from the curd in coagulation.

Whiff—1. A puff of air. 2. A slight inhalation or exhalation, as of tobacco smoke.

Whinolalia—To speak excessively through the nose with distortion of speech.

Whiplash—A popular term for cervical sprain caused by sudden jerky movement.

Whipple's disease—Lipodystrophy, intestinal.

Whipworm—Trichuris trichiura. Round worm.

Whirl—1. To revolve rapidly. 2. Dizziness.

Whirlbone—1. Knee cap or patella. 2. The head of the femur.

Whisky—A liquor prepared from barley.

Whisper—To speak with a low, soft voice.

Whistle—1. A sound produced by pressing lips and ejecting air forcibly through mouth. 2. An instrument through which a shrill sound can be produced by blowing air into it. 3. Shrill sound of wind.

White ant —Termite.

White cell—The leukocyte.

White gangrene—Gangrene caused by local anemia.

Whitehead —Milium.

White leg—Phlegmasia alba dolens. Inflammation of the femoral vein marked by white swelling of the leg.

White line—Linea alba.

White of egg —The albumin of egg.

White of eye—Sclera.

Whitepox—Variola minor. Mild form of smallpox.

Whites—Leucorrhea.

White softening —Softening of any part of the body that has become white and anemic.

Whitlow—Felon. Paronychia. Abscess of the end of a finger or toe.

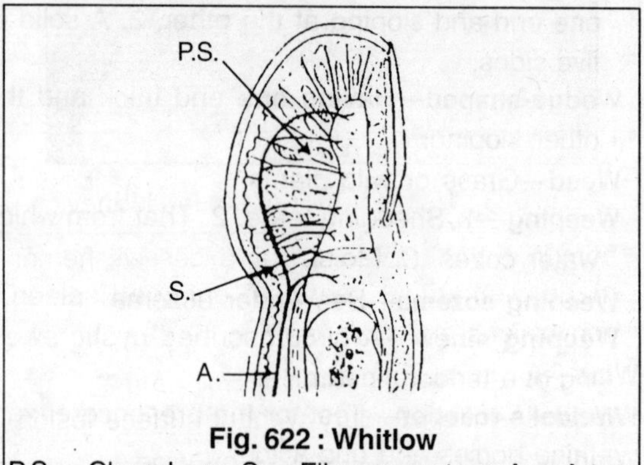

Fig. 622 : Whitlow
P.S. = Closed sac, S. = Fibrous septum, A. = Artery

W. H. O.—World health organization.

Whole body counter—An instrument that detects the radiation present in the entire body.

Wholism—Holism.

Whoop—The sonorous and convulsive inspiration of whooping cough.

Whooping cough—Pertussis. An infectious disease caused by the bacillus Bordetella pertussis, characterized by catarrh of the respiratory tract, followed by peculiar paroxysms of cough, ending in a prolonged whooping respiration.

Whorl—Vortex. A spiral arrangement.

Whorled—Arranged in whorls.

Widal's reaction or test —An agglutination test for typhoid fever.

Will—1. Mental faculty for choosing or deciding upon an act or thought; desire. 2. Power of controlling one's actions. 3. A written document for the ownership of the property after death of an ancestor.

Wilms tumor—A rapidly developing tumor of the kidney occurring in children.

Wilson's disease—Hepatolenticular degeneration.

Winckel's disease—A fatal disease of the new-

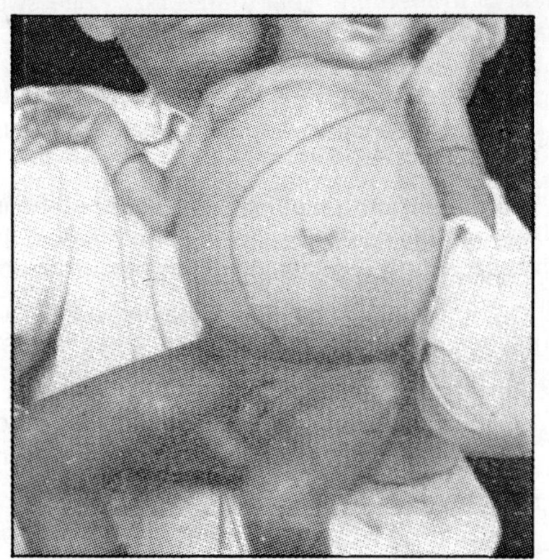

Fig. 623 : Wilm's tumor of the left kidney.

born infant characterized by excessive hemorrhage, hematuria, jaundice, enlarged spleen, convulsions and collapse.

Wind—Air in motion; gas.

Windage—Internal injury without surface lesion.

Windburn—Erythema caused by wind.

Windchill—The cooling effect of the wind on the exposed human skin.

Windchill factor—Loss of heat from exposure of skin to wind, which is proportional to the speed of the wind.

Winding sheet—Shroud. A sheet used for wrapping a dead body.

Window—See fenestra.

Windowing—To make a hole in anything, especially a plaster cast, to relieve pressure on the skin or bony area.

Windpipe—Trachea.

Wine—1. Fermented juice of any fruit, usually of grapes which contains 10–15% alcohol. 2. Vinum. Solution of a medicinal substance in wine.

Wine glass—A glass vessel of measure of approximately 2 fluid ounces (60 mls.) for wine.

Wing—A winglike structure of the body, especially the great and small wings of the sphenoid bone.

Wink—To close and open the eyelids quickly.

Winker—One who winks.

Winking—The act of closing and opening the eyelids quickly.

Jaw winking—Involuntary simultaneous closing of the eyelids as the jaw is moved.

Wire (वायर)—1. A slender, elongated, flexible structure of metal. 2. To join the fragments of a fractured bone together by a wire. 3. In dentistry, to apply wire around the dental arch to correct the irregularities of position of the teeth.

Wiring—Fastening bone fragments by wire.

Wirsung, duct of —Pancreatic excretory duct.

Wiry—Resembling a wire, or feeling of a wire as occurs in a variety of pulse.

Wisdom tooth—The last molar tooth on each side of each jaw. These four teeth erupt latest by 25 th year of age or may never erupt.

Witches milk—Milk secreted by the newly born infant.

Withdrawal —Abstention from drugs, alcohol or narcotics to which a person is addicted.

Withdrawal syndrome—Abstinence syndrome.

Withering —Shrivelling.

Witzelsucht—A mental condition produced by frontal lobe lesions characterized by self-amusement from making poor jokes and puns and telling the pointless stories.

Wolffian body—Mesonephros. An embryonic organ on each side of the vertebral column.

Wolffian cyst— A cyst lying in one of the broad ligaments of the uterus.

Wolffian duct —Mesonephric duct. Embryonic duct leading from the mesonephros to cloaca from which develop ductus epididymis, vas deferens, seminal vesicle, ejaculatory duct, ureter and pelvis of the kidney.

Wolffian tubules—Mesonephric tubules. 30 to 34 embryonic tubules developing within the mesonephros and opening into the mesonephric duct.

Wolman's disease —Enlargement of the liver and spleen, calcification of adrenal glands and development of foam cells in the bone marrow and other tissues in infants, due to an inherited metabolic disorder.

Womb—Uterus.

Wood alcohol—Methyl alcohol.

Wood lamp—Ultraviolet lamp.

Wood light—Ultraviolet light.

Wood rays—Ultraviolet rays.

Wood wool—Specially prepared wood fibers for surgical dressings.

Woolsorter's disease —Anthrax, pulmonary.

Wordblindness—Inability to understand the written or printed words.

Word-deafness—Inability to understand the spoken words, although the sound is heard.

Word salad —The speaking of meaningless words.

Workaholic —A person who is compelled to do some work by investing all his/her energy.

Work out —To solve.

Work-up—The procedures done in making a diagnosis, including history taking, physical examination, pathological tests, X-ray and electrocardiogram, etc.

World Health Organization—WHO.

Worm—1. Any small, limbless, creeping animal. 2. Median portion of the cerebellum. 3. Any wormlike structure.

Wormian bone—One of the small, irregular bones of the cranial sutures.

Worried well—The persons who are actually well but due to their anxiety or imagined illness, they frequently undergo treatment and want to be assured about their health.

Wound—Break in the normal continuity of the skin or a body structure caused by injury.

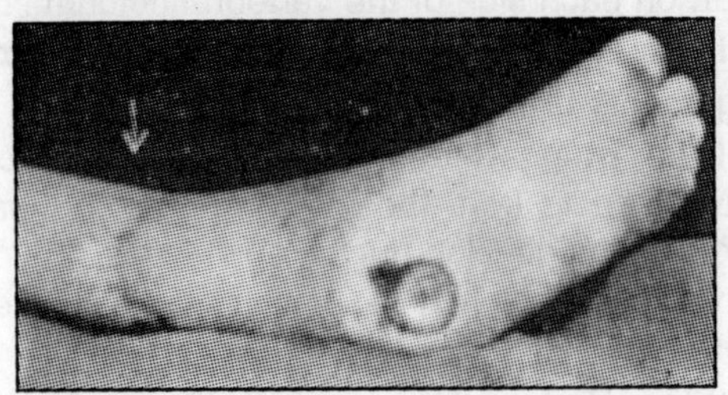

Fig. 624 : Perforating wound on the sole

Abraded wound—Abrasion.

Avulsed wound—A wound resulting from avulsion.

Bullet wound—A puncture wound made by a bullet in which the point of entrance of bullet is small and that of exit is larger.

Contused wound—A bruise caused by a blunt object, in which the skin is not broken, but the tissues under the skin are ruptured leaving the skin unbroken. The blood vessels ruptured under the skin cause blue discoloration.

Crushing wound—Wound formed by a crush of a part of the body.

Gunshot wound—A wound made by a bullet.

Incised wound—A clean wound caused by a sharp cutting instrument.

Lacerated wound—A torn wound with ragged edges (not a clean wound) caused by a blunt object or stick.

Nonpenetrating wound—Wound of some internal organ in which there is no break in the continuity of the surface of the skin.

Open wound—The wound having a free outward opening.

Penetrating wound, Puncture wound —Wound caused by a sharp object which passes through the skin into the underlying tissues.

Perforating wound—Wound in which the object causing the wound enters the body and emerges out, such as a bullet.

Puncture wound —Penetrating wound.

Septic wound—Infected wound.

Stab wound—A wound formed by stabbing of a knife.

Subcutaneous wound —A wound extending below the skin into the subcutaneous tissue, but not affecting the underlying bones or other organs.

Tunnel wound —Wound which has the opening of entrance and exit of equal diameter.

W-plasty —Plastic surgery to prevent the contracture of a straight line scar in which the edges of the wound are cut in the form of a series of w, and are sutured together in a Zig-Zag manner.

W. R.—Wassermann reaction.

Wrap—A cover or to cover by winding something.

Wrench—A sprain.

Wrinkle—1. Unevenness or fold of the skin. 2. To cause unevenness or make folds in the skin.

Wrist—The carpus. The region of the arm lying between the forearm and hand.

Wrist drop—A condition in which hand is flexed at the wrist and cannot be extended, due to injury of the radial nerve or paralysis of the extensor muscles of the hand and fingers.

Writer's cramp—A cramp affecting the muscles of the thumb and two adjacent fingers afer prolonged writing.

Writing hand—Position of the hand seen in paralysis agitans in which fingers assume the po-

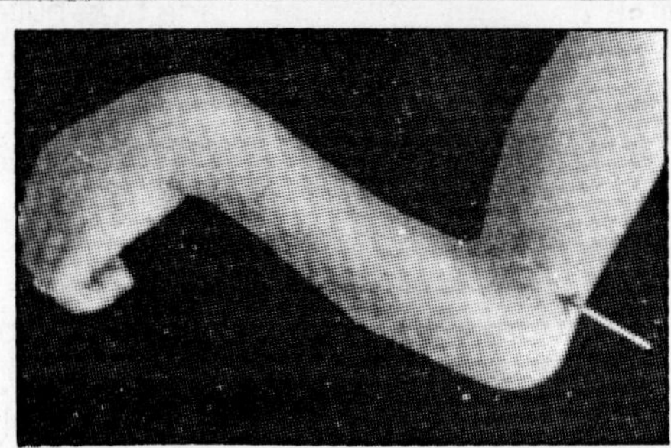

Fig. 625 : Wrist drop due to injury to the radial nerve.

sition as holding a pen in writing due, to contraction of muscle of the hand.

Wryneck—Torticollis.

W. S.—Water-soluble.

Wt.—Weight.

Wuchereria —A genus of filarial worms of the class Nematoda, found in warm regions of the world.

Wuchereria bancrofti —Filaria bancrofti. Filarial worm that causes elephantiasis, lymphangitis and chyluria.

Wuchereriasis—Filariasis. Elephantiasis.

W/V.—Weight in volume.

W/W.—Weight in weight.

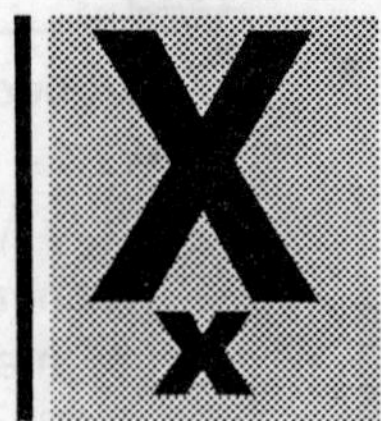

X—Symbol for xanthine.

Xanchromatic—Xanthochromic.

Xanth-, Xantho-—Prefixes meaning yellow.

Xanthelasma—Xanthoma.

Xanthelasmoidea—Chronic skin disease of the childhood characterized by the formation of wheals, followed by brownish-yellow patches.

Xanthemia—Carotenemia. Presence of yellow pigment carotene in the blood.

Xanthene—A chemical compound from which various dyes are formed.

Xanthic—1. Yellow. 2. Pertaining to xanthine.

Xanthic calculus—A urinary calculus containing xanthine.

Xanthine—It is a metabolic product of purine bases adenine and guanine and a precursor of uric acid, found in muscular tissue, liver, spleen, pancreas and other organs and in the urine.

Xanthinuria—Excretion of large amounts of xanthine in the urine.

Xanthism—Rufous albinism of the hair, skin and eyes etc.

Xanthiuria—Xanthinuria.

Xanthochroia—Yellowish discoloration of the skin.

Xanthochromatic—Xanthochromic.

Xanthochromia—Yellow discoloration, as of the skin or cerebrospinal fluid.

Xanthochromic—1. Pertaining to any yellow thing or to xanthochromia. 2. Yellow colored.

Xanthochroous—Having a yellow complexion.

Xanthocyanopia, Xanthocyanopsia —Xanthokyanopy. A type of color blindness in which only blue and yellow colors are visible but not red and green.

Xanthocyte—A cell containing yellow pigment.

Xanthoderma —Yellowness of the skin.

Xanthodont—Having yellow teeth.

Xanthogranuloma—A tumor having characteristics of both granuloma and xanthoma.

Juvenile xanthogranuloma—A skin disease in which yellow, yellow-brown, pink or brown papules develop on the scalp, face, upper trunk and on the extensor surface of the extremities, in infancy or eary childhood, which usually disappear within two to three years spontaneously.

Necrobiotic xanthogranuloma—Necrosed large xanthogranulomas.

Xanthogranulomatous—Pertaining to, of the nature of, or affected by xanthogranuloma.

Xanthokyanopy—Xanthocyanopia.

Xanthoma—Slightly elevated, flat, soft papule, nodule or a plaque occurring in the skin due to deposition of lipid.

Diabetic xanthoma—Xanthoma associated with diabetes mellitus.

Disseminatum xanthoma—Xanthomas occurring all over the body.

Eruptive xanthoma—Xanthomas developing suddenly in crops.

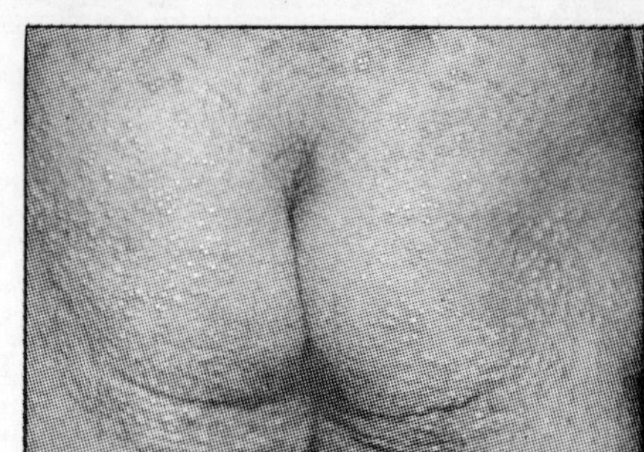

Fig. 626 : Eruptive Xanthoma

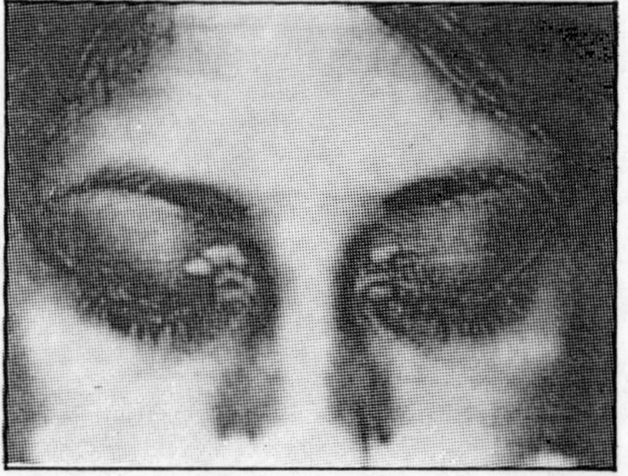

Fig. 627 : Palpebarum Xanthoma

Multiplex xanthoma—Disseminatum xanthoma.

Palpebrarum xanthoma—Xanthoma developing in the eyelid.

Tuberous xanthoma—A hereditary xanthoma occurring on the neck, shoulders, trunk and on the skin of the joints, especially the elbows and knees, consisting of small elastic and yellowish nodules.

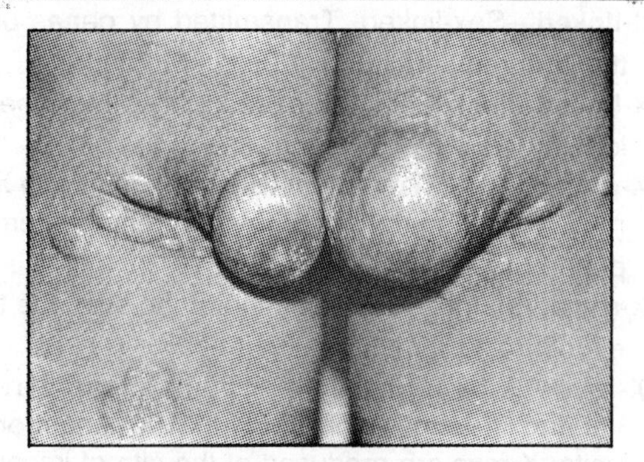

Fig. 628 : Tuberous xanthoma

Xanthomatosis—Formation of multiple xanthomas.

Xanthomatous—Pertaining to xanthoma.

Xanthophose—Visual sensation of yellow color.

Xanthophyll—A yellow pigment derived from carotene, present in some plants and egg yolk.

Xanthoproteic—Derived from or pertaining to xanthoprotein.

Xanthoprotein—Yellowish substance produced by heating proteins with nitric acid.

Xanthopsia—A condition in which objects are seen yellow.

Xanthopsin —The visual purple produced by light acting on rhodopsin.

Xanthopsis—Yellow pigmentation.

Xanthorrhea—Yellow purulent discharge from the vagina.

Xanthosis—The yellowing of the skin resulting from ingestion of excessive amount of carrots, etc., containing the pigment carotene.

Xanthous—Yellow.

Xanthuria —Xanthinuria.

Xanthylic—Pertaining to xanthine.

X chromosome —The chromosome that determines female characteristics. In the normal female there are two X chromosomes and in the male one X chromosome and one Y chromosome.

Xeno- —A prefix meaning strange or foreign material.

Xenobiotic—An antibiotic foreign to an organism, *i.e.*, not produced in that organism.

Xenogeneic—Tissue used for transplantation that is obtained from a species other than that of the recipient.

Xenogenesis—Heterogenesis.

Xenogenous—Caused by a foreign body, or originating outside the organism.

Xenograft—Heterograft.

Xenology —The study of parasites and their relationships to one another, and their hosts.

Xenomenia—Vicarious menstruation.

Xenoparasite—An ectoparasite that due to weakness of its host lives on another host.

Xenophobia—Morbid fear of strangers.

Xenophonia—Alteration in the quality of the voice.

Xenophthalmia —Inflammation of the eye caused by a foreign body.

Xenorexia—An abnormality of appetite in which a person persistently eats foreign substances.

Xenotransplantation—Transplantation of animal tissues or organs into human body.

Xeransis—A gradual loss of moisture in the tissues.

Xerantic —Causing dryness.

Xerasia—Abnormal dryness, brittleness and finally loss of hair.

Xero- —A prefix meaning dry.

Xerocheilia—Dryness of the lips.

Xerocyte—A red blood cell that is dehydrated and seems half dark and half light.

Xerocytosis—Presence of a large number of xerocytes or dehydrated red blood cells in the blood.

Xeroderma—Excessive dryness and roughness of the skin; milk ichthyosis.

Xerogram—Xeroradiograph.

Xerography —Xeroradiography.

Xeroma—Xerophthalmia.

Xeromammography—Xeroradiography of the breast.

Xeromenia —The appearance of the symptoms of menstruation without bleeding.

Xeromycteria—Dryness of the nasal passages.

Xeronosus—Dryness of the skin.

Xerophagia—The eating of dry food.

Xerophagy—Xerophagia.

Xerophthalmia—Abnormal dryness and thickening of the conjunctiva and cornea, due to some disease of the eye or to vitamin A deficiency.

Xerophthalmus—Xerophthalmia.

Xeroradiograph—Xerogram.The permanent record made by xeroradiography.

Xeroradiography—The reproduction of X-ray picture by using a dry process in which a plate covered with a powdered substance, such as selenium, electrically and evenly charged, is held between the metal plates. The X-rays alter the charge or the substance to varying degrees depending upon the tissues they have traversed. This produces the image.

Xerosialography—Examination of the salivary glands and their ducts by xeroradiography.

Xerosis—Abnormal dryness as of the conjunctiva, skin, mucous membrane and mouth etc.

Xerostomia—Dryness of the mouth due to lack of saliva.

Xerotes—Dryness.

Xerotic—Dry.

Xerotocia—Dry labor due to diminished amount of amniotic fluid.

Xerotripsis—Dry friction.

Xiphi-, Xipho-—Prefixes meaning xiphoid process.

Xiphisternal—Pertaining to the xiphoid process.

Xiphisternum—Xiphoid process.

Xiphocostal—Pertaining to the xiphoid process and the ribs.

Xiphodynia—Pain in the xiphoid process.

Xiphoid—Sword-shaped.

Xiphoidalgia—Xiphodynia.

Xiphoiditis—Inflammation of the xiphoid process.

Xiphoid process—Ensiform. The lowest sword-shaped portion of the sternum.

Xiphopagotomy—Surgical separation of twins joined at the xiphoid process.

Xiphopagus—Symmetrical twins joined at the xiphoid process.

X-linked—Sex-linked. Transmitted by genes on the X chromosome.

X-linked disorder—A disease caused by genes located on the X chromosome.

X-radiation —1. Treatment with or exposure to X-rays. 2. Electromagnetic waves or energy composed of X-rays.

X-ray dermatitis—Inflammation of the skin due to exposure to x-rays.

X-rays—A high-energy electromagnetic wave varying in length from 0.05 to 100 Angstrom units. X-rays are produced at the site of impact of high-velocity electrons on the target (a plate of heavy metal such as tungsten) in a vacuum tube, which are invisible to the eye. Electrons are produced from a hot filament by applying a difference of potential between their source and a siutable target. X-rays penetrate most of the opaque substances to some extent, so are used for taking photographs of the internal organs, and parts of the body for diagnostic and therapeutic purposes.

Xyrospasm —An occupational spasm of the fingers and arms as seen in barbers.

Xysma—Fragments of tissue sometimes seen in stools of diarrhea.

Xyster—Raspatory.

Yard —A measure of 3 feet or 36 inches, which is equal to 0.9144 meter.

Yaw—A lesion of yaws.

Mother yaw—A large granulomatous lesion, most commonly present on the hand, leg or foot.

Yawn—To open the mouth widely and take deep inspiration, sometimes with stretching of the hands.

Yawning—One who opens the mouth widely and takes deep inspiration.

Yaws—Frambesia. A nonvenereal, systemic infectious disease, occurring most commonly in children in the tropical region caused by spirochete, Treponema pertenue and characterized by formation of a granuloma which ulcerates and later on heals leaving a scar.

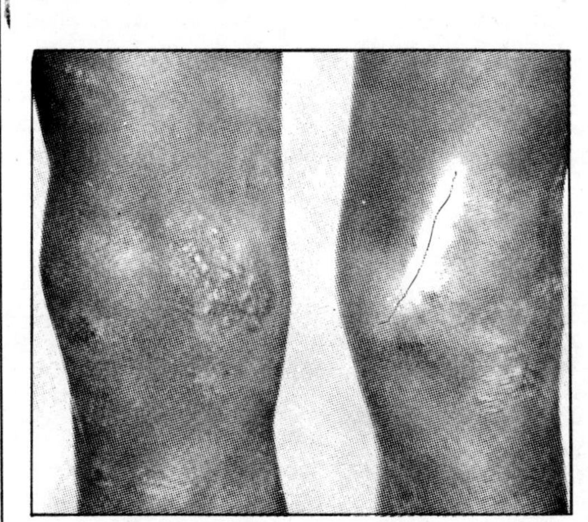

Fig. 629 : Early yaws

Y cartilage—The cartilage that connects the pubis, ilium and ischium and extends into the acetabulum.

Y chromosome—A chromosome that determines the male sex. Normal males possess one Y chromosome and one X chromosome. Normal females possess two X chromosomes.

Yeast—A fungus found in fruits, vegetables, soil and animal feces etc. and is capable of fermenting carbohydrates.

Brewer's yeast—Yeast used in making liquors, and baking bread.

Dried yeast—Dried yeast used as a source of proteins and vitamin B complex.

Yellow body—The corpus luteum.

Yellow fever—An acute infectious disease characterized by fever, jaundice, albuminuria and hematemesis, caused by a virus that occurs in South America and West Africa.

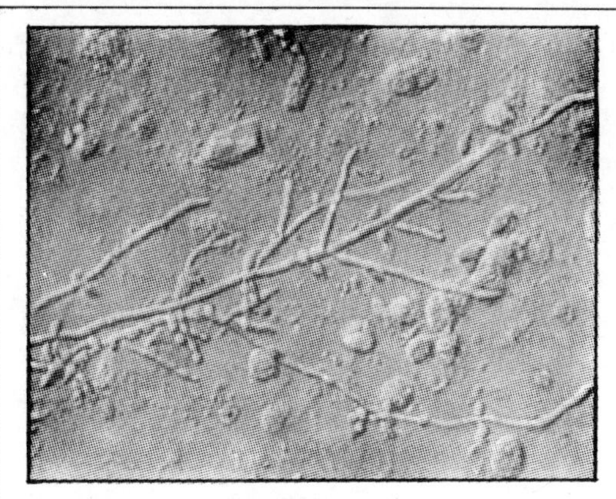

Fig. 630 : Yeast

Yellow spot—1. Macula flava laryngis. A small, yellow nodule at the anterior end of each vocal cord. 2. Macula lutea retinae. A yellow spot in the center of retina.

Yellow vision—Xanthopsia.

Yerba—A Herb.

Yersinia—A genus of gram-negative bacteria.

Yersiniosis—Infection with yersinia.

Yersin's serum—An antitoxic serum for the plague.

Yield—To produce.

Y ligament—A Y-shaped ligament covering the upper and anterior parts of the hip joint.

Y-linkage—The state of a gene being borne on the Y chromosome.

Yoga—This term is associated with physical postures and regulation of breathing.

Yogurt, Yoghurt—A milk curdled by the action of Lactobacillus bulgaricus.

Yoke—A tissue connecting two structures.

Yolk—The nutrient stored in the ovum.

Young—Not old.

Young's rule—A method for calculating the dose of medicine for a child. Divide the age of the child by her age plus 12. The result represents the fraction of the adult dose to be administered, *e.g.*, a child of 3 years of age requires the following fraction of the adult dose. 3/3+12 = 3/15 = 1/5.

Youth—Period between childhood and maturity.

Ypsiliform—Y-shaped.

Z—Zero. Zone.

Z—Symbol for atomic number.

Zavanelli maneuver—The returning of the head of the fetus taking birth with difficulty in intractable shoulder presentation, by hands.

Zea—Maize.

Zeaxanthin—A carotine (precursor of vit. A) found in cereals, fruits, seeds and egg yolk etc.

Zeaxanthol—Zeaxanthin.

Zeis' glands—Sebaceous glands of the eyelid close to its free edge. Each gland is associated with an eyelash.

Zeitgeist—The courage or the conception of the people at a particular time.

Zelophobia—Morbid fear of jealousy.

Zelotypia—Insanity in jealousy.

Zenkerism—Zenker's degeneration.

Zenker's degeneration—Zenkerism. A glassy or waxy hyaline degeneration of skeletal muscles in acute infectious diseases, especially in typhoid fever.

Zenker's diverticulum—Herniation of the mucous membrane of the esophagus through a defect in the esophageal wall.

Zenker's fluid—A tissue fixative consisting of mercuric chloride, potassium dichromate, glacial acetic acid and water. It is used to examine cells, particularly nuclei in detail.

Zeoscope—An apparatus for determining the amount of alcohol in a liquid.

Zero—1. Nothing. 2. The lowest point on the centigrade thermometer (0° C) which is the temperature of melting ice, from which graduation starts. It is equivalent to 32° on the fahrenheit thermometer.

Absolute zero—The lowest temperature at which all gases liquefy, which is—273.15° C or —459.67° F.

Zestocausis—Cauterization with a tube containing heated steam.

Ziehl-Neelsen method—Method for staining Mycobacterium tuberculosis.

Zieve's syndrome—Transient jaundice, hemolytic anemia, hyperlipemia and abdominal pain following the intake of a large amount of alcohol.

Zig-zag—Having sharp turns.

Zinc—A metallic element.

Zinciferous—Containing zinc.

Zincoid—Resembling or pertaining to zinc.

Zincum—Zinc.

Zingiber—A genus of plants of ginger.

Zn.—Chemical symbol for zinc.

Zoacanthosis—Dermatitis caused by penetration into the skin of hairs, bristles or stingers of lower animals.

Zoanthropic—Pertaining to or marked by zoanthropy.

Zoanthropy—Delusion of being an animal.

Zoe—Life.

Zoetic—Vital. Pertaining to life.

Zoic—Pertaining to animal life.

Zoite—Sporozoite.

Zollinger-Ellison syndrome—A codition caused by non-insulin secreting tumor of the pancreas, which secretes the gastrin hormone excessively. This stimulates the stomach to secrete a large amount of hydrochloric acid and pepsin, which is turn causes the formation of peptic ulcer of the stomach and intestine.

Zona—1. A zone; band; girdle. 2. Herpes zoster.

Zona ciliaris—Ciliary processes combined.

Zona facialis—Herpes zoster of the face.

Zona fasciculata—The thick middle layer of the adrenal gland.

Zona glomerulosa—The outermost layer of the adrenal cortex just inside the capsule.

Zona ophthalmica—Herpes zoster of the area supplied by the ophthalmic nerve.

Zona pellucida—Inner thick membranous layer of the ovum.

Zona reticularis—The innermost layer of the adrenal cortex.

Zonae—Plural of zona.

Zonal—Pertaining to zona.

Zonary—Pertaining to or shaped like a zone.

Zonary placenta—A placenta arranged in the form of a broad ring around the chorion.

Zonate—Ringed or having concentric layers of different types.

Zondek-Aschheim test —A test for pregnancy in which urine of the patient is injected subcutaneously into an immature female mouse. It the mouse is dead, pregnancy is indicated.

Zone—An encircling area or boundary.

- **Abdominal zone**—Abdominal region.
- **Ciliary zone**—The peripheral part of anterior surface of the iris of the eye.
- **Epileptogenic zone**—An area of the brain that when stimulated produces an epileptic seizure.
- **Erogenous zone** —An area of the body that on stimulation produces sexual excitement, such as breasts, lips, genital organs and buttocks and anal region etc.

Zonesthesia —A sensation, as a cord is constricting the body.

Zonifugal—Passing outward from within a zone.

Zoning—The occurrence of a stronger reaction in a lesser amount of the serum, in serologic test, in case of syphilis.

Zonipetal—Passing from without into a zone.

Zonography—A form of tomography with a relatively thick plane of focus, that is especially used in renal radiography.

Zonoskeleton—Proximal bones to which limbs are attached, such as the hip bone, scapula and clavicle.

Zonula—Zonule. A small zone.

- **Ciliary zonula**—Suspensory ligament of the lens of the eye.

Zonulae—Plural of zonula.

Zonular—Pertaining to zonula.

Zonular cataract—A cataract in which opacity is limited to certain layers of the lens.

Zonular space—The space between the fibers of the ligaments of the lens.

Zonule—Zonula.

Zonulitis—Inflammation of the ciliary zonule.

Zonulolysis—To dissolve the ciliary zonule by use of enzymes, to allow surgical removal of the lens.

Zonulotomy—To make an incision into the ciliary zonule.

Zonulysis—Zonulolysis.

Zoo- —A prefix meaning animal.

Zoobiology—The biology of animals.

Zooblast—An animal cell, especially an immature cell.

Zoochemistry—Biochemistry of animals.

Zoochrome —A naturally occurring pigment in animals or humans.

Zoodermic—Performed with the skin of an animal, as in skin grafting.

Zoodynamics—Physiology of animals.

Zooerastia —Zoophilia.

Zooerasty —Bestiality.

Zoofulvin—A yellow pigment obtained from the feathers of certain birds.

Zoogenesis—Zoogeny.

Zoogenous—Acquired from animals.

Zoogeny—The development and evolution of animals.

Zoogeography—The scientific study of the distribution of animals on earth.

Zoogonous—Viviparous.

Zoogony—Viviparity.

Zoograft —A graft of tissue obtained from an animal.

Zoografting—The grafting of an animal tissue on a human body.

Zooid—Animal-like.

Zoolagnia—Sexual desire for animals.

Zoologist—Specialist in zoology.

Zoology—The science of animals.

Zoomania—Mania for obtaining the animals.

Zoom lens—A type of eye lens that can be adjusted to focus on near or distant objects.

Zoonoses—Diseases of animals transmissible to man.

Zoonosis—Singular of zoonoses.

Zoonotic—Pertaining to zoonoses.

Zooparasite—An animal parasite.

Zoopathology—Pathology of the animal diseases.

Zoophagous—Carnivorous. Living upon animal food.

Zoophile—Fond of animals.

Zoophilia—Fondness of animals.

Zoophilic—Zoophile. One who likes animals.

Zoophilism—Zoophilia.

Zoophobia—Morbid fear of animals.

Zoophyte—A plantlike animal.

Zooplankton—Small animal present in natural water.

Zooplasty —Zoografting.

Zoopsia—Hallucination with vision of animals.

Zoopsychology—Psychology of the animals.

Zoosadism—Sexual pleasure from distressing the animals.

Zooscopy—Scientific observation of animals.

Zoosmosis—The process of osmosis in the living tissues.

Zoospermia—Presence of the living spermatozoa in the ejaculated semen.

Zoospore—A motile, asexual, flagellated spore moving by one or more flagella, as produced by certain algae and fungi.

Zoosterol—Any sterol derived from animals.

Zootechnics—The technique of breeding of domestic animals and caring for them.

Zootherapeutics—Treatment of the animals.

Zootic—Concerning animals.

Zootomy—Dissection of the animals.

Zootoxin—Any toxin produced by an animal, as snake venom, etc.

Zootrophic—Concerning the animal nutrition.

Zoster—Herpes zoster.

Zosteriform—Zosteroid.

Zosteroid—Resembling herpes zoster.

Z-plasty—A technique of plastic surgery in which a defect of the skin is repaired by transposition of two triangular flaps which are made by a Z-shaped incision, for the relaxation of scar contractures.

Zr.—Chemical symbol for zirconium.

Zwitterions—Ions that have both positive and negative regions of charge.

Zyg- —A prefix meaning a tissue connecting two structures; joined and junction.

Zygal—Pertaining to a tissue connecting two structures.

Zygapophyseal—Pertaining to zygapophysis.

Zygapophyses—Plural of zygapophysis.

Zygapophysial—Zygapophyseal.

Zygapophysis—The articular process of a vertebra.

Zygion—The most lateral point on the zygomatic arch.

Zygocyte—Zygote.

Zygodactyly—Syndactylism.

Zygoma—1. The zygomatic process of the temporal bone. 2. Zygomatic arch. 3. Zygomatic or malar bone.

Zygomatic—Pertaining to zygoma.

Zygomatic arch—The arch formed by articulation of the zygomatic process of each zygomatic bone with the zygomatic process of the temporal bone, on each side of the cheeks.

Zygomatic bone—Malar bone. Cheek bone. Bone on either side of the face below the eye.

Zygomaticoauricular—Pertaining to the zygomatic bone and the auricle.

Zygomaticofacial—Pertaining to the zygoma and the face.

Zygomaticofrontal —Pertaining to the zygoma and the frontal bone.

Zygomaticomaxillary—Pertaining to the zygoma and the maxilla.

Zygomatico-orbital—Pertaining to the zygoma and the orbit.

Zygomaticosphenoid —Concerning the zygoma and the sphenoid bone.

Zygomaticotemporal—Pertaining to the zygoma and temporal bone.

Zygomatic process—A thin downward projection of squamous portion of the temporal bone, and a portion of the zygomatic bone forming zygomatic arch.

Zygomatic reflex—The movement of the lower jaw toward the percussed side when the zygoma is percussed.

Zygomaticum—The zygomatic bone.

Zygomaxillary—Pertaining to the cheek bone and upper jaw.

Zygomycetes—Phycomycetes. A class of fungi that causes mucormycosis and entamophthoramycosis.

Zygomycosis—Fungus infection of the zygomatic bone.

Zygon—The band connecting the two parallel limbs of a cerebral fissure.

Zygopodium—The intermediate portion of the limb skeleton, *i.e.*, radius and ulna bones of the upper limb, and tibia and fibula bones of the lower limb.

Zygosis—Sexual union of two unicellular animals.

Zygosity—Pertaining to the sexual union of two unicellular animals.

Zygosperm—Zygospore.

Zygospore—A spore formed by fusion of two morphologically identical structures.

Zygosyndactyly—Complete or incomplete webbing of the fingers or toes.

Zygote—The cell formed by the union of a male and female gamete; the fertilized ovum.

Zygotic—Pertaining to a zygote.

Zygotoblast—Sporozoite.

Zygotomere—Sporoblast.

Zymase—Fermenting enzyme.

Zyme- —A prefix which means enzymes or fermentation.

Zyme—An enzyme or ferment.

Zymic—Pertaining to enzymes.

Zymogen—Proenzyme. A substance that develops into an enzyme.

Zymogene—Microorganism causing fermentation.

Zymogenesis—Transformation of a proenzyme (zymogen) into an active enzyme.

Zymogenic—1. Causing fermentation. 2. Pertaining to or producing a zymogen.

Zymogenous—Zymogenic.

Zymogram—Strips of paper in which the locations of enzymes separated electrophoretically are demonstrated.

Zymohydrolysis—Zymosis. Decomposition brought about by a ferment.

Zymoid—Resembling an enzyme.

Zymologic—Pertaining to zymology.

Zymologist—Specialist in zymology.

Zymology—The science of fermentation.

Zymolysis—Fermentation. Zymosis.

Zymolyte—Substrate. Substance upon which a ferment acts.

Zymolytic—Causing fermentation; fermentative.

Zymometer—An apparatus for measuring fermentation.

Zymonema—A genus of fungi.

Zymonematosis—Condition caused by zymonema.

Zymophoric, Zymophorous—Having fermentative properties.

Zymophyte—A microorganism causing fermentation.

Zymoplastic—Producing ferment.

Zymoprotein—Any protein that also acts as an enzyme.

Zymose—Invertin or invertase.

Zymosis—1. Fermentation. 2. The process by which an infectious disease develops. 3. An infectious disease.

Zymosterol—A steroid obtained from yeast.

Zymosthenic—Increasing the strength and activity of an enzyme.

Zymotic—Pertaining to or produced by fermentation.

Weight and Measurements

Units of Weight

Teragram=1,000,000,000,000, grams

Gigagram=1,000,000,000 grams

Megagram=1,000,000 grams

Kilogram=1,000 grams=15,432.35 grains = 35.274, avoirdupois ounces=32.151 apothecaries or troy ounces=2.2046 avoirdupois pounds.

Hectogram=100 grams=1,543.23 grains.

Decagram=10 grams=154.323 grains.

Gram (unit)=1gm.=15.432 grains=0.25720 apothecaries' dram=0.03527 avoirdupois ounce=0.03215 apothecaries' or troy ounce=0.002205 avoirdupois pound.

Decigram=0.1 gm.=1.5432 grains

Centigram=0.01 gm.=0.15432 grain.

Milligram=0.001 gm. =0.015432 grain.

Microgram=.000001 gm. =.000015432 grain.

Nanogram=0.000000001 gm. =.000000015432 grain. Picogram=.000000000001 gm. =.000000000015432 grain

1 Grain=64.7989 milligrams=0.0648 gram= 0.00208 apothecaries' ounce= 0.0001429 avoirdupois pound=.000065 kilogram.

1 Ounce=480.0 grains=31.1 grams=1 apothecaries' ounce=0.06855 avoirdupois pound=0.0311 kilogram.

1Lb (Pound)=7000.0 grains=453.5924 grams=14.583 apothecaries' ounces=1.0 avoirdupois pound=0.45354 kilogram

1 Dram (apothecaries')=3.8879 grams.

Apothecaries' weight

20 grains=1 scruple 3 scruples=1 dram

8 drams=1 ounce 12 ounces=1 pound

Avoirdupois weight

27.343 grains=1 dram

16 drams=1 ounce

16 ounces=1 pound

100 pounds=1 hundredweight

2000 pounds=1 short ton

2240 pounds=1 long ton

1 oz. troy=480 grains

1 oz avoirdupois=437.5 grains.

1 lb. troy=5760 grains

1 lb. avoirdupois=7000 grains.

Troy Weight

24 grains=1 penny weight, 20 penny weight=1 ounce, 12 ounces=1 Pound

Units of Length

1μ =1 micrometer=0.001 millimeter. 1 millimeter =1000 micrometer.

1 millimeter=0.1 centimeter=0.03937 inch =0.00328 foot=0.0011 yard=0.001 meter

1 centimeter=10 millimeter=0.3937 inch =0.03281 foot=0.0109 yard=0.01 meter.

1 inch=25.4mm.=2.54 cm.=0.0833 foot =0.0278 yard=0.0254m.

12 inches=1 foot.

1 ft.=304.8 mm.=30.48 cm.=12.0 inch=0.333 yard=0.3048 meter, 3 feet=1 yard, 1 yard.=914.40 mm.=91.44 cm.=36.0 inch=3 feet=0.9144 m.

1 meter=1000 mm.=100 cm.=39.37 inch =3.2808 feet=1.0936 yard.

Kilometer=1000 meters=0.6215 mile.

1 mile=5280 feet=1.609 kilometers.

Cubic Measure

1 cubic centimeter=0.06102 cubic inch.

1 cubic inch=16.3872 cubic centimeters, 1728 cubic inches=1 cubic foot.

1 cubic foot=0.02832 cubic meter, 27 cubic feet=1 cubic yard

1 cubic meter=1.3079 cubic yard=35.314 cubic feet.

Units of Volume

1 milliliter=16.23 minims=0.2705 fluid dram=0.0338 fluid ounce=0.061 cubic inch=0.001 liter=0.00106 quart.

1 fluid dram=3.697 milliliters=0.125 fluid ounce=0.226 cubic inch=0.00369 liter =0.00391 quart

1 cubic inch=16.3866 milliliters=4.4329 fluid drams=0.5541 fluid ounce=0.01639 liter=0.0173 quart.

1 fluid ounce=29.573 milliliters=8 fluid drams=1.8047 cubic inches=0.02957 liter =0.03125 quart.

1 pint=473.166 milliliters=16 ounces=½ quart.

1 quart=946.332 milliliters=256.0 fluid drams=32.0 fluid ounces=57.75 cubic inches=.9463 liter.

1 liter=1000 milliliters=270.52 fluid drams=33.815

fluid ounces=61.025 cubic inches=1.0567 quarts

1 gallon=4 quarts=8 pints=3.785 liters.

Household weights

Approximately 60 drops=5mls.=1 dram=1/8 ounce=1 teaspoonful

1 teaspoonful=1/8 fl. oz=1 dram.

3 teaspoonful=1 tablespoonful

1 tablespoonful=½ fl. oz.=4 drams.

16 tablespoonful (liquid) = 1 cup.

12 tablespoonful (dry)=1 cup.

1 cup=8 fl. oz.

1 tumbler or glass=8 fl. oz.=½ pint.

Units of time

1 millisecond=one thousandth of a second.

1 second=1/60 of a minute.

1 minute=1/60 of an hour.

1 hour=1/24 of a day.

Symbols and their Meanings

♏ Minim.

ʒ Dram

fʒ Fluid dram.

℥ Ounce.

f℥ Fluid ounce.

O pint.

lb Pound.

℞ Recipe; take.

$\overline{a\,a}$ of each

A, A U Angstrom unit.

C' Complement.

$\overline{C}$ With.

$\overline{P}$ After

Δ Change, heat.

Eo Electroaffinity. Capability of the ions to retain their electric charge.

mμ Millimicron or micromillimeter.

↓ Decrease.

μg Microgram.

mEq Milliequivalent. The concentration of electrolytes in a certain volume of solution.

mg. Milligram

mg% Milligrams percent; milligrams per 100 mls.

↑ Increase.

QO_2 Oxygen consumption.

PO_2 Partial pressure of oxygen.

PCO_2 Partial pressure of carbon dioxide.

$\overline{s}$ Without.

$\overline{ss}$, ss one-half.

μm Micrometer.

μ Micron.

μμ Micromicron.

$+$ Plus; excess; acid reaction; positive.

$-$ Minus; deficiency; alkaline reaction; negative.

$\pm$ Either positive or negative; indefinite.

Number; following a number; pounds.

$\div$ Divided by.

$\times$ Multiplied by; magnification.

$=$ Equal.

$\cong$ Approximately equal.

$>$ Greater than.

$<$ Lesser than.

$\nless$ Not less than.

$\ngtr$ Not greater than.

$\leqq$ Equal to or less than.

$\geqq$ Equal to or greater than.

$\neq$ Not equal to.

$\sqrt{}$ Root; square root.

$\sqrt[2]{}$ Square root.

$\sqrt[3]{}$ Cube root.

∞ Infinity.

: Ratio; "is to."

:: Equality between ratios, "as."

$\therefore$ Therefore.

° Degree.

% Percent.

π —3.1416—ratio of circumference of a circle to its diameter.

, ♂ Male.

○, ♀ Female.

$\rightleftharpoons$ Denoting a reversible reaction.

Abbreviations and their Meanings

ABBR—abbreviation.

ABG—arterial blood gas.

abs. feb.—without fever.

a.c.—before eating.

ad—to; upto.

adhib—to be administered.

ad lib—as desired.

ADM—administration.

admov.—apply.

ad part. dolent—to the painful parts.

ad sat.—to saturation.

adst. feb.—when fever is present.

ad us. ext—For external use.

aeq.—Equal.

AF—atrial fibrillation.

ag. feb.—when fever increases.

agit.—Shake; stir.

agit. ante sum—Shake before taking.

A I—aortic incompetence.

alb.—white.

alt. dieb.—every other day.

alt. hor—every other hour.

alt. noc.—every other night.

AM—morning.

ant.—anterior.

A-P—anterior-posterior.

ap—before dinner.

app.—approximately.

Aq.—water. जल,

aq. dest.—distilled water.

aq. frig.—cold water.

at. wt.—atomic weight.

bal.—bath.

bene.—well.

bib.—drink.

b.i.d.—twice daily.

b.i.n.—twice a night.

bis in 7d.—twice a week.

BM—bowl movement.

BP—blood pressure.

B.P.—British Pharmacopeia.

C—Calorie (Kilocalorie)

c—calorie (small calorie)

ca—about or approximately.

cal.—calorie.

cap.—capsule.

cat.—cataplasma. Poultice.

CBC—Complete blood count.

CC—chief complaint

cc—cubic centimeter.

cito disp.—let it be dispensed quickly.

c.m.—tomorrow morning.

cm.—centimeter.

c.m.s.—to be taken tomorrow morning.

c.n.—tomorrow night.

CNS—Central nervous system.

coch. mag.—a tablespoonful

coch. parv.—a teaspoonful.

collyr.—An eyewash.

comp.—composition; compound.

contra.—against.

cont. rem.—let the medicines be continued.

CSF—cerebrospinal fluid.

cv—cardiovascular.

cyath.—glassful.

D—dose.

d.—give.

d—density.

/d—per day.

D & C—dilatation and currettage.

dB—decibel.

dc—discontinue.

d.d. in d.—from day to day.

dec.—Pour off.

def.—defecation.

dent. tal. dos.—give of such doses.

det—let it be given.

dieb. alt.—every other day.

dieb. tert.—every third day.

dil.—dilute, diluted.

dim.—one-half.

div.—divide.

DOA—dead on arrival.

DPT—diphtheria- pertussis-tetanus (vaccine)

dr.—dram.
ECG—electrocardiogram.
ECT—electroconvulsive therapy.
ED—Emergency Department.
EDC—estimated date of confinement.
EEG—electroencephalogram.
e.g.—for example.
EMG—electromyogram.
emp.—Plaster.
EMS—emergency medical service.
emuls.—an emulsion.
ENT—ear, nose and throat.
ER—Emergency Room.
ESR—erythrocyte sedimentation rate.
en., enem.—enema.
esp.—especially.
et—and.
Ex.—example.
exhib.—let it be given.
ext.—spread.
F.—Fahrenheit.
f—female.
F.A.—first aid.
FEV—forced expiratory volume.
fl. dr.—fluid dram.
fl. oz.—fluid ounce.
FSH—follicle-stimulating hormone.
g, gm.—gram.
garg.—a gargle.
GI—Gastrointestinal.
gr.—grain.
grad.—by degrees.
Gtt, gtt—drops.
guttat—drop by drop.
GYN—gynecology.
h, hr—hour.
haust.—a draught.
Hg.—mercury.
h.s.—tonight.
hor. decub—bed time.
hr—hour.
h.s.—bed time.
idem—the same.
i.e.—that is.
im—intramuscular.
in d.—daily.
inf.—infusion.
inhal.—inhalation.
inj.—injection.
instill.—instillation.
int.—Thoroughly.
iop—intraocular pressure.
IQ—intelligence quotient.
IU—international unit.
IUCD—intrauterine contraceptive device.
IUD—intrauterine device.
IUFD—intrauterine fetal death.
IV—intravenous.
IVP—intravenous pyelogram.
J—joule.
kcal.—kilocalorie.
Kg.—Kilogram.
KUB—kidney, ureter, and bladder.
L—liter.
lab.—laboratory.
lb—pound.
LD_{50}—lethal dose, medium.
LH—luteinizing hormone.
lin.—a liniment.
liq.—liquid; fluid.
lmp—last menstrual period.
lot.—lotion.
LTD—lowest tolerated dose.
M.—mix.
M—molar, muscle.
mac.—macerate.
man. prim.—first thing in the morning.
MED—minimum effective dose.
med.—a medicine.
m. et n.—morning and night.
mEq.—milliequivalent.
mist.—mixture.
mitt.—send.
mm—millimeter.
m.mol—millimole.
mod.—moderate sized.
mod. praesc.—as prescribed.
moll.—soft.
mol. wt.—molecular weight.
mor. sol.—in the usual manner.

μEq.—microequivalent.
mv—millivolt.
NF.—National Formulary.
no—number.
noct. maneq.—night and morning.
NPN—nonprotein nitrogen.
n.p.o.—nothing by mouth.
nunc.—now.
O.—Pint.
OB.—Obstetrics.
OC—oral contraceptive.
O.D.—right eye.
O.L.—left eye.
om. mane vel. noc.—every morning or night.
omn. bid.—every 2 days.
omn. bih.—every 2nd hour.
omn. hor.—every hour.
omn. noct.—every night.
om. ¼h.—every 15 minutes.
oz—ounce.
p.a.a.—let it be applied to the affected area.
paren.—parenterally.
part. aeq.—equal parts.
part. vic.—individual doses.
PBI.—Protein-bound iodine.
p.c.—After meal.
per—through or by.
pert.—pertaining.
ph—Hydrogen ion concentration.
PI—Present illness; previous illness.
pil.—pill.
pl.—plural.
PM—afternoon, evening.
p.o.—by mouth.
P.p.—melting point.
p.p.a.—the bottle being first shaked.
ppm.—parts per million.
post.—posterior.
p.r.—through the rectum.
p.r.n.—as needed.
pro. rat. aet.—according to patient's age.
pt.—pint.
pulv.—powder.
p.v.—through the vagina.
q.h.—every hour.
q.2h.—every two hours.
q 3h—every 3 hours.
q.1.D.—four times a day.
q.l.—as much as wanted.
q.p.—at will.
q.s.—sufficient quantity.
qt—quart.
quotid.—daily.
q.v.—which see.
rad—radiation absorbed dose.
RBC—red blood cells.
red. in pulv.—reduced to powder.
rel.—relating, related.
REM—rapid eye movements.
repetat., rep.—to be repeated.
RNA—ribonucleic acid.
RPM—revolutions per minute.
RQ—Respiratory quotient.
RS.—related subjects.
rub.—red.
s.—singular.
S.—mark.
SA—sinoatrial.
s. a. or sec. a.—by skill.
sc—subcutaneous.
semih.—half an hour.
sig.—write.
sing.—of each.
SOB—Shortness of breath.
sol.—solution.
solv.—dissolve.
s.o.s.—if necessary.
S/p—no change after.
sp. gr.—specific gravity.
spt.—spirit.
ss.—a half.
st.—let it (them) stand.
STD—Sexually transmitted diseases.
subind.—frequently.
sum.—let him take, to be taken.
sum. tal.—take 1 such.
suppos—a suppository.
SYM.—symptoms.
SYMB.—symbol.
SYN.—synonym.

syr.—syrup.
T.—temperature.
tab.—tablet.
tere—rub.
t.i.d.—Three times a day.
tere bene.—rub well.
t.i.n.—three times a night.
tinct.—tincture.
top.—topically.
tr.—tincture.
TSD—time since death.
TSH—thyroid-stimulating hormone.
ung.—ointment.
ur.—urine.
USP—United States Pharmacopeia.
UTI—urinary tract infection.
UV—ultraviolet.
Vin—wine.
Vitel.—yolk of an egg.
Vol.—Volume.
Vol.%—Volume percent.
WBC—White blood cells.
w.s.—water soluble.
wt.—weight.
w/v.—weight by volume.